The New International Dictionary of New Testament Theology

The New International Dictionary of

Volume 2: G-Pre

New Testament Theology

Colin Brown
GENERAL EDITOR

Translated, with additions and revisions, from the German

THEOLOGISCHES BEGRIFFSLEXIKON
ZUM NEUEN TESTAMENT

Edited by Lothar Coenen, Erich Beyreuther *and* Hans Bietenhard

GRAND RAPIDS, MICHIGAN 49530

ZONDERVAN™

The New International Dictionary of New Testament Theology

Originally published in German under the title:
THEOLOGISHES BEGRIFFSLEXICON ZUM NEUEN TESTAMENT

© 1967, 1969, 1971 by Theologisher Verlag Rolf Brockhaus, Wuppertal. English Language edition volume 1 copyright © 1975, 1986, Zondervan, Grand Rapids, Michigan, U.S.A., and The Paternoster Press, Ltd. Exeter, Devon, U.K.

Requests for information should be addressed to:
Zondervan, *Grand Rapids, Michigan 49530*

Library of Congress Cataloging-in-Publication Data

Main entry under the title:
    The new international dictionary of New Testament theology

        "Translated, with additions and revisions, from the German *Theologishes Begriffs-lexicon zum Neuen Testament,* edited by Lothar Coenen, Erich Beyreuther and Hans Bietenhard."
        "Companion volume: The new international dictionary of the Christian Church."
        Includes bibliographical references and indexes.
        ISBN 0-310-33210-9 (vol. 2)
        ISBN 0-310-33238-9 (4 volume set)
        1. Bible.   N.T.—Theology—Dictionaries.   2. Bible.   N.T.—Dictionaries.
    I. Brown, Colin.
    BS2397.N48
    230'.03   75-38895

Printed in the United States of America

07 08 / DC/ 20 19 18 17

Contents

Preface

Omnis recta Dei cognitio ab obedientia nascitur – "All right knowledge of God is born of obedience." This was the testimony of Calvin in his *Institutes of the Christian Religion*, 1, 6, 2. It could be said that church history is the story of how the people of God have learned this truth the hard way. The relevance of Calvin's observation does not stop there. What applies to institutions applies equally to individual lives. Yet the Christian religion is not one of relentless dour demands and gritted determination to do better next time. As Calvin went on to say, "Surely in this respect God has, by his singular providence, taken thought for mortals through all ages."

The Bible is not only the primary historical source for our knowledge of ancient Israel and the beginnings of the Christian church; it is the record of God's gracious dealings with his people in times past and the Word of God for them today. The obedience to which God calls is not blind submission but a considered response to himself as he has revealed himself in the past – and as he continues to reveal himself in the present in the light of the past.

The Reformers distinguished three aspects of faith: cognition, assent and trust. Without the element of trust theology is a mere intellectual exercise which becomes increasingly irrelevant in the modern world. But unless our trust has a basis in fact – and can be shown to have a basis in fact – then faith is at the mercy of the crank and the fanatic. Clearly, studying a work like *The New International Dictionary of New Testament Theology* is no substitute for the obedience of which Calvin spoke. Knowledge of God comes about in the whole range of life through response to the God who reveals himself and illuminates our way in his Word. But in order to be obeyed the Word must first be understood. It is with the understanding of the Word, as it is expressed in the words of the New Testament, that this dictionary is concerned.

The present volume contains 106 main articles on New Testament concepts, comprising 256 studies arranged under key Greek words or themes. The entries under the key Greek words are normally divided into three parts as follows:

CL Discussion of the word in secular Greek. Uses of the word are illustrated by reference not only to classical literature but also to inscriptions and papyri. But in view of the expressly theological interest of the dictionary discussion here is kept to a minimum.

OT Discussion of the word and related terms in the OT. The language of the church in the NT era was Greek, and the Old Testament Scriptures used by the church were largely the Greek translation of the Hebrew known as the Septuagint (LXX). The discussion is therefore based on the terms as they occur

7

in the LXX, but comparing the LXX throughout with the corresponding Hebrew Masoretic text. This section also takes account of terms as used by Philo, Josephus, the Dead Sea Scrolls and rabbinic writers.

NT Discussion of the word and related terms in the NT, noting statistical occurrences, the use in relation to the background, and specific emphases of individual writers and writings.

For further discussion of the layout and scope of the dictionary the reader is referred to the Introduction to Volume I.

The New International Dictionary of New Testament Theology is based upon the *Theologisches Begriffslexikon zum Neuen Testament* which was first published in German in 1965. In preparing this work for English readers the opportunity has been taken to make revisions and to incorporate extensive new material. This second volume contains 22 completely new articles and a total of 71 new entries on key Greek words and related themes. However, in addition much new material has been incorporated into the revision of the existing articles. The bibliographies have been completely revised. As in Volume I, they have been divided into two sections: (a) works in English, and (b) works in other languages. The purpose is to offer readers a conspectus of literature as a guide to the immense amount of work that has been carried out in biblical studies in recent years. The separation of the two sections will enable them to see at a glance which works are relevant to their particular needs. Most English readers will naturally wish to consult the works in the first section. On the other hand, it was decided to include titles not available in English in order to meet the needs of the more specialist student.

In his review of the first volume of this Dictionary Dr. I. H. Marshall suggested that "It is probably best taken as a reference work to the words used in any particular NT text, by means of which the reader may be guided to the ideas expressed by those words and thus have a better understanding of the text" (*EQ* 48, 1976, 106). The Editor finds himself in basic agreement with this view, if it be stressed that to understand the words of the text one has also to penetrate the thought-world of their background. In preparing this English edition the overriding aim has been to present a concise and yet balanced guide to the theological vocabulary of the NT in the light of international contemporary scholarship. Like all other academic disciplines, theological study has experienced a knowledge-explosion in the last half-century. It is essential to the purpose of *The New International Dictionary of New Testament Theology* to enable the reader to explore for himself the new avenues of discovery that have been opened up and to weigh for himself the views of scholars who have contributed to the modern study of the Bible.

The draft translation of the German original was prepared by a team of scholars which included Professor G. H. Boobyer, the Rev. Dr. Colin Brown, Mr. H. L. Ellison, the Rev. M. C. Freeman, the late Rev. Dr. George Ogg, Mr. John D. Manton, the Rev. Philip J. Seddon, the Rev. David Sharp and the Rev. Dr. A. J. M. Wedderburn. A particular debt of gratitude is owed to Professor F. F. Bruce, Rylands Professor of Biblical Criticism and Exegesis in the University of Manchester. In addition to the contributions which appear over his name, Professor Bruce has read the entire work in galley and page proof. He has been unstinting in the advice and expert help that he has given from first to last. Thanks are also due to the Rev. A. C. Thiselton of the University of Sheffield for reading the typescript of the bibliographies and for making many helpful suggestions. Once again the Rev. Michael Sadgrove has shouldered the heavy burden of proof-reading in the course of his doctoral studies at Oxford. The magnificent indexes are entirely the work of the Rev. Norman Hillyer whose sharp and fresh eye has also contributed to the correction of the page proofs. On numerous points of detail the Editor has benefited from the advice and comments of many friends and colleagues in addition to those already named. Among them are Dr. Cleon Rogers, Principal of the Freie Theologische Akademie, Seeheim, Bergstrasse, the Rev. J. A. Motyer, the Rev. G. T. D. Angel, the Rev. P. J. Budd, Miss J. G. Baldwin, Miss E. M. Embry and Miss M. Langley of Trinity College, Bristol, Mr. Alan Millard of the University of Liverpool, Dr. D. W. Burdick of the Conservative Baptist Theological Seminary, Denver, Colorado, Dr. Janice Allister and Dr. M. G. Barker.

The article on Prayer contains the Eighteen Benedictions used in daily Jewish prayer, in the translation of the Rev. R. A. Stewart which first appeared in his book *Rabbinic Theology: An Introductory Study*, published by Oliver and Boyd, 1961. They are reproduced here by kind permission. Scripture quotations in this Dictionary from the Revised Standard Version of the Bible are used by permission of the owners of the copyright, the Department of Christian Education of the National Council of the Churches of Christ in the United States of America.

Finally, the Editor would like to record once more his appreciation of the happy co-operation at all stages of the work with the Editor of the German edition, Dr. Lothar Coenen, and the German publishers, the Theologischer Verlag Rolf Brockhaus of Wuppertal, and to thank them for their kind agreement to the features incorporated in the English edition. He also wishes to pay tribute to the skill and craftsmanship of the staff of Redwood Burn in producing such a handsome book from a typescript which was often well-nigh illegible.

A full list of abbreviations and a key to the transliteration of Hebrew, Greek and Arabic words will be found in Volume 1, pp. 31–47. Volume 1, pp. 49–72, also contains a Glossary of Technical Terms which defines many of the terms currently used in theological discussion.

For this new printing of the Dictionary, the opportunity has been taken to make a number of minor corrections and alterations, and the bibliographies have been updated in the Addenda.

C. Brown, 1981.

Table of Articles in Volume II

11

15

Contributors

Editors and Advisors

Editor of the English edition . . . . **Colin Brown**

General Editor of the German edition **Lothar Coenen**

Greek philology, philosophy and
classical background . . . . . **Gerhard Fries**

Old Testament and Septuagint . . . **Horst Seebass**

Qumran . . . . **Reinhard Deichgräber**

Rabbinics . . . . **Hans Bietenhard**

New Testament philology and theology **Hans Bietenhard**

Church history and historical
theology . . . . **Erich Beyreuther**

Bibliographical consultant to the
German edition . . . . **Werner Georg Kümmel**

Indexes . . . . **Norman Hillyer**

Contributors to Volume 2

In the following list the author's work is denoted by the Greek words or sub-title which follow the title.

Sverre Aalen, Dr. theol., Professor, Oslo
Glory, Honour, *doxa, timē*

Gervais T. D. Angel, M.A., M.Ed., Dean of Studies, Trinity College, Bristol
Leaven, *zymē*; Prayer, Ask, Kneel, Beg, Worship, Knock, *erōtaō, krouō*

Gleason L. Archer, Jr., B.A., LL.B., A.M., Ph.D., B.D., Professor, Trinity Evangelical Divinity School, Deerfield, Illinois
Possessions, Treasure, Mammon, Wealth, Money, *Coins in the Bible and Theological Issues*

Joyce G. Baldwin, B.A., B.D., Dean of Women, Trinity College, Bristol
Gold, Silver, Bronze, Iron, *chrysos, argyrion, chalkos, sidēros*

Karl-Heinz Bartels, Dr. theol., Niderbieber
One, Once, Only, *hapax, heis, monos*

Wolfgang Bauder, Cologne
Goal, Near, Last, End, Complete, *engys* (part); Grow, *pleonazō* (part); Humility, Meekness, *praÿs*; Hunger, Thirst, Food, Taste, Eat, Drink, *peinaō*

Hartmut Beck, Karlsruhe
Judgment, Judge, Deliver, Judgment Seat, *paradidōmi*; Peace, *eirēnē* (part)

Oswald Becker, Bonn
Gift, Pledge, Corban, *arrabōn*

Ulrich Becker, Dr. theol., Professor, Hanover
Gospel, *euangelion*

Ulrich Becker, Osterwald über Wunstorf
Hard, Hardened, *sklēros*; Lie, Hypocrite, *pseudomai* (part)

Otto Betz, Dr. theol., Professor, Tübingen
Might, Authority, Throne, *dynamis*, *exousia*

Erich Beyreuther, Dr. theol., Feldkirchen, Munich
Good, Beautiful, Kind, *agathos*, *kalos*, *chrēstos*; Joy, Rejoice, *agalliaomai*, *euphrainō*, *chairō* (part); Like, Equal, *isos*, *homoios* (part); Possessions, Treasure, Mammon, Wealth, Money, *peripoieomai*

Hans Bietenhard, Dr. theol., Professor, Steffisburg
Greek, *Hellēn*; Heaven, Ascend, Above, *anō*, *ouranos*; Hell, Abyss, Hades, Gehenna, Lower Regions, *abyssos*, *hadēs*, *gehenna*, *katōteros*; Lord, Master, *despotēs*, *kyrios*; Name, *onoma* (part); Paradise, *paradeisos* (part); People, Nation, Gentiles, Crowd, City, *dēmos*, *ethnos*, *laos*, *ochlos*, *polis*; Please, *areskō*, *eudokeō*

Christian Blendinger, Nuremberg
Hand, Right Hand, Left Hand, Laying on of Hands, *dexia*; Might, Authority, Throne, *thronos*

Jürgen Blunck, Solingen
Height, Depth, Exalt, *bathos*, *hypsos*

Georg Braumann, Dr. theol., Billerbeck
Hunger, Thirst, Food, Taste, Eat, Drink, *esthiō*, *pinō*; I Am, *egō eimi* (part); Present, Day, Maranatha, Parousia, *hēmera* (part), *parousia*

Colin Brown, M.A., B.D., Ph.D., Professor, Fuller Theological Seminary, Pasadena, CA
Generation, *genea* (part); Gift, Pledge, Corban, *korban*; God, Gods, Emmanuel, *theos* (part), *Emmanouēl* (part); Guard, Keep, Watch, *phylassō* (part), *grēgoreō*, *agrypneō*; Guilt, Cause, Convict, Blame, *aitia* (part); Hand, Right Hand, Left Hand, Laying on of Hands, *aristeros*, *euōnymos*, *cheir* (part); Head, *kephalē* (part); Heaven, Ascend, Above, *anabainō* (part); Holy, Consecrate, Sanctify, Saints, Devout, *hagios* (part); Incense, Myrrh, *smyrna*; Light, Shine, Lamp, *phōs* (part); Love, *phileō* (part); Magic, Sorcery, Magi, *mageia* (part); Man, *anēr* (part), *arsēn*; Marriage, Adultery, Bride, Bridegroom, *gameō* (part), *hyerakmos*; Miracle, Wonder, Sign, *sēmeion* (part); Moses, *Mōÿsēs* (part); Necessity, Must, Obligation, *prepō* (part); New, *kainos* (part); Nineveh, *Nineuē* (part); Number, *chilias*; Open, Close, Key, *anoigō* (part), *kleis* (part); Other, *allos*, *heteros* (part); Parable, Allegory, Proverb, *parabolē* (part); Paradise, *paradeisos* (part); Patience, Steadfastness, Endurance, *anechomai* (part), *makrothymia* (part), *hypomenō* (part); Peace, *eirēnē* (part); Poor, *ptōchos* (part); Possessions, Treasure, Mammon, Wealth, Money, *thēsauros* (part), *mamōnas*; Prayer, Ask, Kneel, Beg, Worship, Knock, *proseuchomai* (part), *proskyneō* (part), *entynchanō*; Present, Day, Maranatha, Parousia, *hēmera* (part), *maranatha* (part), *The Parousia and Eschatology in the NT*

Frederick Fyvie Bruce, M.A., D.D., F.B.A., Emeritus Professor, University of Manchester
Image, Idol, Imprint, Example, *hypogrammos*; Myth, *mythos*; Name, *onoma* (part); Noah, *Nōe*

Lothar Coenen, Dr. theol., Wuppertal
Poor, *penēs*
Bruce A. Demarest, M.A., Ph.D., Associate Professor, Conservative Baptist Theological
Seminary, Denver, Colorado
Melchizedek, Salem, *Melchisedek, Salēm*
James D. G. Dunn, M.A., B.D., Ph.D., Lecturer, University of Nottingham
Pentecost, Feast of, *pentēkostē*
Günther Ebel, Speyer
Persecution, Affliction, Tribulation, *diōkō*
Johannes Eichler, Frankfurt am Main
Inheritance, Lot, Portion, *klēros*; Possessions, Treasure, Mammon, Wealth, Money,
thēsauros
Henry Leopold Ellison, B.A., B.D., Dawlish, Devon
Levite, *Leuitēs*
E. Margaret Embry, B.A., B.D., Lecturer, Trinity College, Bristol
Laugh, *gelaō*
Hans-Helmut Esser, Dr. theol., Professor, Horstmar bei Münster
Grace, Spiritual Gifts, *charis*; Humility, Meekness, *tapeinos*; Law, Custom, Elements,
ethos, nomos, stoicheia; Mercy, Compassion, *eleos, oiktirmos, splanchna*; Poor,
ptōchos (part)
Ulrich Falkenroth, Dr. theol., Braunschweig
Patience, Steadfastness, Endurance, *anechomai* (part), *makrothymia* (part), *hypomenō*
(part)
Michael Farmery, B.D., Bristol
Like, Equal, *homoios* (part)
Günter Finkenrath, Burscheid-Hilgen
Joy, Rejoice, *chairō* (part); Like, Equal, *homoios* (part)
Otto Flender, Villigst
Image, Idol, Imprint, Example, *eikōn*; Layman, *idiōtēs*
Richard Thomas France, M.A., B.D., Ph.D., Senior Lecturer in New Testament, London
Bible College, Northwood, Middlesex
Oil, Olive, Gethsemane, *elaion*; Pour, *ekcheō*
Johannes Gess, Kassel
Image, Idol, Imprint, Example, *charaktēr*; Lamb, Sheep, *amnos*
Jürgen Goetzmann, Essen
House, Build, Manage, Steward, *oikos, oikodomeō, oikonomia*; Mind, *phronēsis*
Friedrich Graber, Riehen, Basel
Heal, *therapeuō* (part), *iaomai* (part)
Walther Günther, Dr. theol., Stuttgart
Godliness, Piety, *sebomai*; Grow, *auxanō*; Lead Astray, Deceive, *planaō*; Lie,
Hypocrite, *hypokrinō*; Love, *agapaō* (part), *phileō* (part); Marriage, Adultery, Bride,
Bridegroom, *gameō* (part), *nymphē*
Joachim Guhrt, Bentheim
Offence, Scandal, Stumbling Block, *proskomma, skandalon*
Hermann Haarbeck, Schwelm
Lament, Sorrow, Weep, Groan, *klaiō, koptō, lypeō* (part); New, *kainos* (part), *neos*;
Old, *palai*
Hans-Christoph Hahn, Bad Boll
Light, Shine, Lamp, *lampō, lychnos, phainō, phōs* (part); Openness, Frankness,
Boldness, *parrhēsia*
Günther Harder, Dr. theol., Dr. jur., Professor, Berlin
Nature, *physis*

Murray, J. Harris, M.A., Ph.D., Professor, Bible College of New Zealand, Auckland, New Zealand
Number, *dekatē*
Roland K. Harrison, B.D., M.Th., Ph.D., D.D., Professor, Wycliffe College, Toronto
Lame, Crippled, *kyllos, chōlos*; Leprosy, *lepros, lepra*
Colin J. Hemer, M.A., Ph.D., Librarian, Tyndale Hall, Cambridge
Nicolaitan, *Nikolaitēs*; Number, *arithmos* (part), *dyo, treis, tritos, eniautous treis kai mēnas hex, pente, oktō, deka, tesserakonta, hebdomēkonta*
David Hill, B.D., S.T.M., Ph.D., Senior Lecturer, University of Sheffield
Gate, Door, *pylē, pylōn, thyra*
Norman Hillyer, B.D., S.Th., formerly Librarian of Tyndale House, Cambridge
Herb, Plant, Grass, *lachanon*; Incense, Myrrh, *libanos*
Ernst Hoffmann, Vevey
Hope, Expectation, *elpis, apokaradokia*
Otfried Hofius, Dr. theol., Professor, Paderborn
Miracle, Wonder, Sign, *sēmeion* (part), *teras*
Bertold Klappert, Dr. theol., Göttingen
King, Kingdom, *basileia*; Lord's Supper, *deipnon*
Hans Kropatschek, Lic. theol., Göttingen
Hunger, Thirst, Food, Taste, Eat, Drink, *brōma*
Fritz Laubach, Dr. theol., Hamburg
Hand, Right Hand, Left Hand, Laying on of Hands, *cheir* (part)
Hans-Georg Link, Dr. theol., Cologne
Goal, Near, Last, End, Complete, *engys* (part), *eschatos*; Guilt, Cause, Convict, Blame, *elenchō*; I Am, *egō eimi* (part); Lament, Sorrow, Weep, Groan, *lypeō* (part); Lie, Hypocrite, *pseudomai* (part); Life, *bios, zōē*; Love, *agapaō* (part); Necessity, Must, Obligation, *dei* (part); *opheilō* (part); New, *kainos* (part)
Thomas McComiskey, B.A., B.D., Ph.D., Professor, Trinity Evangelical Divinity School, Deerfield, Illinois
Guilt, Cause, Convict, Blame, *amemptos*; Israel, Jew, Hebrew, Jacob, Judah, *Iakōb, Iouda*; Judgment, Judge, Deliver, Judgment Seat, *bēma, katadikazō*; Lament, Sorrow, Weep, Groan, *brychō, pentheō, stenazō*; Light, Shine, Lamp, *emphainizō*; Marriage, Adultery, Bride, Bridegroom, *koitē*; Nineveh, *Nineuē* (part)
Ralph P. Martin, M.A., Ph.D., Professor, Fuller Theological Seminary, Pasadena, California
Image, Idol, Imprint, Example, *apaugasma, hypodeigma, paradeigmatizō*; Mark, Brand, *stigma, charagma, kaustēriazō*
Reinhold Mayer, Dr. theol., Wiss. Rat, Tübingen
Israel, Jew, Hebrew, Jacob, Judah, *Israēl*
Robert Morgenthaler, Dr. theol., Professor, Muri bei Bern
Generation, *genea* (part); Necessity, Must, Obligation, *anankē*
Leon L. Morris, B.Sc., Ph.D., formerly Principal of Ridley College, Melbourne
Gall, Poison, Wormwood, *cholē, ios, apsinthos*
John Alexander Motyer, M.A., B.D., Principal of Trinity College, Bristol
Jonah, *Iōnas*
Dietrich Müller, Marburg
Grow, *pleonazō* (part); Heal, *therapeuō* (part), *iaomai* (part), *hygiēs*; Height, Depth, Exalt, *hypsoō*; Open, Close, Key, *kleis* (part); Pharisee, *Pharisaios*
Wilhelm Mundle, Lic. theol., Professor, Marburg
Godliness, Piety, *eulabeia*; Hear, Obey, *akouō, hypakouō*; Hide, Conceal, *katalyptō, kryptō*; Image, Idol, Imprint, Example, *eidōlon*; Inheritance, Lot, Portion, *meros*;

Miracle, Wonder, Sign, *thauma*; Patience, Steadfastness, Endurance, *kartereō*; Present, Day, Maranatha, Parousia, *maranatha* (part)

Karlfried Munzer, Gauting
Head, *kephalē* (part)

Carl Heinz Peisker, Dr. theol., Mülheim, Ruhr
Hinder, Prevent, Forbid, *enkoptō, kōlyō*; Open, Close, Key, *anoigō* (part); Parable, Allegory, Proverb, *parabolē* (part), *paroimia*

John Pridmore, M.A., Witley
Orphan, *orphanos*

Horst Reisser, Ilten
Marriage, Adultery, Bride, Bridegroom, *moicheuō*

Karl Heinrich Rengstorf, D. theol., Dr. theol., D.D., Professor, Münster
Jesus Christ, Nazarene, Christian, *Iēsous, Nazarēnos, Christos, Christianos*

Reinier Schippers, Dr. theol., Professor, Amsterdam
Goal, Near, Last, End, Complete, *telos*; Persecution, Tribulation, Affliction, *thlipsis*

Ernst Dieter Schmitz, Wuppertal
Knowledge, Experience, Ignorance, *ginōskō*; Number, *arithmos* (part), *tessares, hepta, dōdeka*

Johannes Schneider, D. theol., Dr. theol., Professor, Berlin
God, Gods, Emmanuel, *theos* (part)

Walter Schneider, Hanover
Judgment, Judge, Deliver, Judgment Seat, *krima*

Hans Schönweiss, Dr. theol., Stuttgart
Prayer, Ask, Kneel, Beg, Worship, Knock, *aiteō, gonypeteō, deomai, proseuchomai* (part), *proskyneō* (part)

Eduard Schütz, Dr. theol., Hamburg
Knowledge, Experience, Ignorance, *aisthēsis, agnoeō*

Hans-Georg Schütz, Dr. theol., Dortmund
Guard, Keep, Watch, *tēreō, phylassō* (part); Hand, Right Hand, Left Hand, Laying on of Hands, *epitithēmi*

Helmut Schultz, Marburg
Jerusalem, *Ierousalēm*

Horst Seebass, Dr. theol., Münster
Holy, Consecrate, Sanctify, Saints, Devout, *hagios* (part), *hieros, hosios*; Join, Cleave to, *kollaomai*; Moses, *Mōÿsēs* (part)

Friedel Selter, Rheinkamp-Repelen
Other, *allos, heteros* (part); Possessions, Treasure, Mammon, Wealth, Money, *ploutos, chrēma*

Burghard Siede, Coburg
Heaven, Ascend, Above, *anabainō* (part)

Theo Sorg, Stuttgart
Heart, *kardia*

Friedrich Thiele, Kassel
Guilt, Cause, Convict, Blame, *aitia* (part), *enochos*; Large, Small, *megas, mikros*

Erich Tiedtke, Frankfurt am Main
Hunger, Thirst, Food, Taste, Eat, Drink, *geuomai*; Necessity, Must, Obligation, *dei* (part), *opheilō* (part)

Allison A. Trites, M.A., Ph.D., Acadia Divinity College, Acadia University, Wolfville, Nova Scotia
Gather, Scatter, *synagō, skorpizō*

Rudolf Tuente, Bremerhaven
Lamb, Sheep, *probaton*

Herwart Vorländer, Dr. phil., Professor, Ludwigsburg
Gift, Pledge, Corban, *dōron*, Man, *anēr* (part), *anthrōpos* (part)
J. Stafford Wright, M.A., formerly Principal of Tyndale Hall, Bristol
God, Gods, Emmanuel, *theos* (part), *Emmanouēl* (part); Magic, Sorcery, Magi, *mageia* (part); Man, *anthrōpos* (part)

G

Gall, Poison, Wormwood

These words are linked by the common association of bitterness and harmfulness. The notions of bitterness and poison seem to have been closely connected in the thought of antiquity. The terms vary in the extent of the destructiveness that they signify, but there is nothing attractive about any of them. This leads to a common usage in a metaphorical sense, and all three are employed to convey thoughts of bitterness and the like.

χολή, ἰός, ἄψινθος

χολή (cholē), gall, bile; ἰός (ios), poison; ἄψινθος (apsinthos), wormwood.

CL & OT *cholē* appears to be cognate with the Lat. (*h*)*olus*, perhaps also with the Gk. *chloē* (green shoot, grass), and to refer in the first instance to the colour of bile, from which it comes to be used of gall or bile itself. But the impressive thing was clearly its bitter taste. Arndt (891) cites the tragedian Philocles: *epekaleito Cholē dia to pikron* (who "was called *Cholē* because of his bitterness"). In the LXX the word translates a variety of Heb. words and all three meanings, "gall", "poison" and "wormwood" are found: (1) *merōrâh*, gall (Job 20:14); (2) *rō'š*, poison (Deut. 32:32; Ps. 69:21 [68:22]; cf. Matt. 27:34); (3) *la'anâh*, wormwood (Prov. 5:4; Lam. 3:15). On occasion the word refers to a plant (e.g. Deut. 29:18; 32:32), but it remains uncertain which plant is meant.

There is dispute over the derivation of *ios*, and whether it means "arrow" as well as "poison", or whether this is another word. O. Michel is emphatic that the two should be distinguished and connects the word for poison with the Sanskrit *viṣa* and the Lat. *virus* (*TDNT* III 334; cf. Liddell-Scott, 832). In secular Gk. the term is used of a variety of poisons, especially of the poison of snakes (Liddell-Scott note its use also for the venom of a mad dog). It is used for the rust on iron and also of other deposits, such as verdigris and the patina on bronze statues. In the LXX *ios* is used for *ḥel'âh*, rust (Ezek. 24:6, 11 f.), and *ḥēmâh*, poison (Ps. 140[139]:3). It also occurs in the LXX of Ps. 14 [13]:3; the Epistle of Jeremy 12, 24; Prov. 23:32; and Lam. 3:13, where it means an arrow.

apsinthos occurs in several secular Gk. forms. Most usual is the neut. *apsinthion*, but the fem. *apsinthia* is also found as well as the form *apsinthos* which is usually designated fem., but which is masc. in Rev. 8:11 (perhaps because it is the name of a star, *astēr*, which is masc.). This last form is not found in the LXX or in classical authors. All the forms noted refer to some variety of the plant group *Artemisia*, of which several varieties occur in Palestine. All of them have a very bitter taste. *apsinthion* occurs in Aquila's translation of Prov. 5:4; Jer. 9:15(14); 23:15.

NT Two of the terms are used in the NT in the literal sense. *cholē* is used of the wine mixed with "gall" which was offered to Jesus as the soldiers prepared to crucify him (Matt. 27:34). In view of the parallel in Mk. 15:23, it seems that the word here refers to myrrh. ([Ed.] "According to the Talmud (San. 43a, cf. Prov. 31.6–7) a man about to be executed could beg a 'grain of incense' (a narcotic) in wine in order to dull his senses and alleviate pain. Jesus refuses the sedative and heroically endures his sufferings to the end" [D. Hill, *The Gospel of Matthew*, 1972, 353]. Matt. 27:48; Mk. 15:36; Lk. 23:36; and Jn. 19:29 f. relate how a soldier subsequently gave Jesus *oxos*, sour wine or wine vinegar, which relieved the thirst more effectively than water and was popular in the lower strata of society because it was cheaper than ordinary wine [Arndt, 577 f.]. Like Matt. 27:34, this may also have been seen as a fulfilment of Ps. 69:21[68:22]. Gos. Pet. 5:15 f. gives the impression that the *cholē* was actually poison [cf. the MT of Ps. 69:21] which was mixed with wine and given to Jesus to hasten his death before nightfall. Jesus' death ensued not long afterwards.) *apsinthos* likewise appears to be understood literally in Rev. 8:11: "The name of the star is Wormwood. A third of the waters became wormwood, and many men died of the water, because it was made bitter." It is part of a vision of judgment on the ungodly world (see further discussion below).

But all the terms are also used metaphorically and this is the more important usage for an understanding of the NT. Outside the NT *cholē* is used for "bitter anger", "wrath" (Liddell-Scott, 1997), but this does not appear to be the case in the NT. The thought is always that of bitterness. Thus Simon Peter charged Simon Magus with being "in the gall [*cholē*] of bitterness" (Acts 8:23), when he had offered the apostle money for the gift of conferring the Holy Spirit by the laying on of hands. The thought is that to have such a complete misunderstanding of Christianity is not simply to be pleasantly mistaken. It is to find oneself in a situation which must be described in terms of bitterness. Simon had had an inkling of what Christianity was all about. He had welcomed the gospel and accepted baptism. It is not clear whether he himself received the laying on of hands (→ Hand), but he was certainly numbered among the band of converts. It was an exceedingly bitter thing when a man of whom so much might well have been expected proved to be so completely out of harmony with the gospel. He was caught in a bitter bondage to sin.

So it is with *ios*. In Romans 3 Paul is concerned with the universality of sin and with the way sin finds expression in what men say. "The poison of asps" is under the lips of sinners (Rom. 3:13), a quotation Paul takes from Ps. 140:3 (LXX 139:4). In his catena of quotations Paul lays emphasis on what words can do, referring to the throat, the tongue, the lips and the mouth ("feet" and "eyes" are mentioned once each, vv. 15, 18, but no other part of the body). The deadliness of wicked speech is stressed. James likewise finds "poison" an apt word for the untamed tongue. He thinks that such a tongue is capable of all sorts of evil and brings out the harm it causes by referring to it as "full of deadly poison" (Jas. 3:8). It is apparently the same word when James castigates the rich for their "rusted" gold and silver and sees the "rust" as evidence against them and as something that will in due course eat them up (Jas. 5:3). There is a problem in that → gold and silver do not rust, but James is speaking metaphorically and expressing forcefully the view that the treasures of the rich are tarnished and tainted and tainting.

There is a problem in the use of *apsinthos* in Rev. 8:11. It is used as the name of a star and then it describes the water into which the star fell. Obviously the water became bitter and the name of the star is connected with this bitterness. The problem is that in Revelation the water causes death, whereas wormwood, at least as we understand the term, is bitter but not poisonous. The author may have in mind a substance other than the wormwood we know and which was genuinely poisonous. Or he may be employing a way of speech we have already noted in antiquity whereby bitterness and poison were connected. He may be reasoning from the bitterness of the taste to the bitterness of the results. This fits in also with the fact that in the OT wormwood is used of God's punishment of the wicked, e.g. "Thus says the Lord of hosts, the God of Israel: Behold, I will feed this people with wormwood, and give them poisonous water to drink" (Jer. 9:15 RSV; cf. 23:15; Lam. 3:15, 19; the LXX does not use *apsinthos*, but the meaning is the same).

L. Morris

→ Bitter, → Dragon, Serpent, Scorpion, Sting, → Wine

Arndt, 128 f., 379, 891; Liddell-Scott, 229, 832, 1997; O. Michel, *ios*, *TDNT* III 334 ff.

Gate, Door

πύλη, πυλών

πύλη (*pylē*), gate, door; πυλών (*pylōn*), gate, gateway, entrance.

CL In classical Greek *pylē* is used, mostly in the plural, to mean the gates of a town, although it appears in the tragedians with the meaning house-door (→ *thyra*). It can be employed in a general sense to designate any entrance or opening (e.g. a geographical pass or straits). The gates of Hades is a fairly common periphrasis for the nether world, the realm of the dead (cf. Homer, *Il.* 5, 646; 9, 312; *Od.* 14, 156; Aesch., *Ag.* 1291). *pylōn* means a gateway or gate-house.

OT In the LXX *pylē* translates chiefly *ša'ar* which is used to refer to: (a) the gate of a city, building, farm or village; (b) the area immediately inside a city-gate; and (c) the gate(s) of death (Job 38:17; Ps. 107:18), of Sheol (Isa. 38:10) and of heaven (Gen. 28:17). *pylōn* usually translates *ša'ar* or *petaḥ*: the latter denotes an entrance, gate or doorway.

NT 1. *Literal Meaning.* In the NT *pylē* denotes: (a) a city-gate (Lk. 7:12; Acts 9:24; 16:13): that Jesus suffered outside the gate (Heb. 13:12; cf. Lev. 16:17) emphasizes that his suffering represents the true offering of the Day of Atonement and that, in his death, he is classified with law-breakers who were stoned outside the camp (Lev. 24:14; Num. 15:35); (b) a gate of the temple (Acts 3:10; cf. Acts 3:2 which uses *thyra*); (c) a prison gate (Acts 12:10) → *thyra*.

2. *Figurative Use.* (a) *pylē* is used of the narrow gate (cf. Lk. 13:24 which, in a rather different context, uses *thyra*) through which one must pass to enter into life (Matt. 7:13 f.). This image was familiar in the ancient world and here indicates an entrance that is difficult to find and hence ignored by many. The Matthean instruction on the two gates and two ways – and these are synonymous metaphors – is not

so clearly eschatological in character as the corresponding verse in Lk. In the context of the well-known catechetical schema the words form an appeal to decision to follow Christ and face all the consequences that obedience entails.

(b) *pylē* is used of the gates of Hades in Matt. 16:18. The image expresses the commonly-held ancient idea that the underworld was secured by strong gates which prevented escape and barred access to invaders. In pre-Christian Jewish usage the expression functions as a *pars pro toto* term for Hades (→ Hell), i.e. the realm of the dead, even death itself (Isa. 38:10; Wis. 16:13; 3 Macc. 5:51; Ps. Sol. 16:2). It is improbable that the gates of Hades in Matt. 16 denotes the ungodly powers of the underworld which assail the rock (cf. *TDNT* VI 927), for Hades is not regarded as the abode of evil powers, whence they emerge to attack men. In the light of the Jewish background, the image is best understood as affirming that death, in spite of its hitherto unconquerable power, will not win control over the rock or, more probably, over the *ekklēsia* erected on the rock: death will not vanquish the messiah who builds the church, nor the members of the messianic community.

pylōn denotes: (a) the gateway or porch of a house (Matt. 26:71; Lk. 16:20; Acts 10:17; 12:13; in Acts 12:14 it appears to mean the actual gate to be opened); (b) the gate of a city (Acts 14:13, perhaps temple-portals) and, in particular, the gates of the New Jerusalem (Rev. 21:12 f., 21, 25; 22:14).   *D. Hill*

| θύρα | θύρα (*thyra*), door, entrance. |

CL In classical Greek *thyra* denotes a house-door and occasionally the house itself, expressing the whole by the part. The phrase "at the door(s)" may be used to indicate nearness of place or time: to be "at the door" of a king or other influential person means to be paying court to, or seeking benefit from him. The noun can also be used, in a general sense, for any entrance, literal or metaphorical.

OT In the LXX *thyra* often translates: (a) *peṭaḥ* which denotes an opening, doorway or gate; and (b) *deleṭ* which denotes a house-door, a gate, and figuratively, any aperture (e.g. an animal's jaws, human lips).

NT 1. *Literal Meaning*. In the NT *thyra* is used to mean: (a) the door of a house or room (Matt. 6:6; 25:10; Mk. 1:33; 2:2; 11:4; Lk. 11:7; Jn. 18:16; 20:19; Acts 5:9; 12:13); (b) the door of the temple (Acts 3:2; 21:30); (c) prison doors (Acts 5:19, 23; 12:6; 16:26 f.) which miraculously open to liberate apostles: the motif – which may reflect the developing use of the theme in the biographies of heroic figures in antiquity – affirms that the progress of the gospel cannot be hindered by imprisonment or bonds; (d) the entrance to a cave-tomb (Matt. 27:60; Mk. 16:3); (e) the opening in a stone enclosure (Jn. 10:1 f.).

2. *Figurative Use*. (a) The phrase "before" or "at the door(s)" indicates nearness in time or place (Matt. 24:33; Mk. 13:29; Acts 5:9; Jas. 5:9).

(b) The image of the open door denotes the provision of opportunity. This usage, which has parallels only in Rabbinic literature (cf. SB III 631; and *TDNT* III 174), is found in missionary contexts. God opens a door for the missionary (for the Word, in Col. 4:3) by giving him a field in which to work (1 Cor. 16:9; 2 Cor. 2:12; Rev.

3:8 (?)) and he opens a door of faith to Gentiles by giving them the possibility of believing in Christ (Acts 14:27).

(c) The opposite figure, the closed door (Matt. 25:10; Lk. 13:25; Rev. 3:7) carries the sense of judgment. The narrow door in Lk. 13:24 (cf. Matt. 7:13 f. where *pylē* is used in a different context) denotes the entrance into the eschatological → kingdom of God, and the shutting of that door indicates irrevocable loss of an opportunity. According to Rev. 3:8, the exalted Christ alone has the authority to grant access to the eschatological realm. Rev. 3:20 is best understood in an eschatological setting: the returning Saviour seeks fellowship with the disciple in a festal meal; the door is opened by obedience and faith. The NT only once expressly refers to the door of heaven (Rev. 4:1), though the figure – reflecting an ancient oriental view of the world – probably underlies other passages which speak of the opening and closing of heaven (Lk. 4:25; Rev. 11:6).

(d) The "I am the door" sayings in Jn. 10:7, 9. If, as seems probable, the more difficult reading "door" (and not "shepherd", so p⁷⁵ and Sah.) is the correct one in v. 7, and if that image is interpreted in terms of vv. 1–3, then the sense is that Jesus is the gate *to* the sheep, the door whereby the genuine shepherd approaches the flock. In v. 9 the image is that of the gate through which the sheep go in and out, i.e. that Jesus is the gate *for* the sheep to go into the fold, the gate leading to salvation and life (cf. Jn. 14:6), an idea which may be indebted to a messianic interpretation of Ps. 118:20. The image of Jesus as the gate to salvation appears early in patristic exegesis (Ign., *Phil.* 9:1; Hermas, *Sim.* 9, 12, 3 f.). It is not likely that v. 9 gives expression to a Johannine revelation-formula: it is rather a pointer to the interpretation of the figure in the opening verses. We need not suppose that v. 7 and v. 9 are drawn from different sources or that one is supplemental to the other. They are two explanations of Jesus as the gate. The only unity in the discourse of Jn. 10 is christological: Jesus draws to himself every image which the picture of sheep, shepherd and sheepfold suggests. (For other "I am" sayings → I Am.; → also Open). *D. Hill*

(a). Arndt, 366, 736; E. F. F. Bishop, "The Door of the Sheep – Jn. x. 7–9", *ExpT* 71, 1959–60, 307 ff.; R. E. Brown, *The Gospel according to John, I–XII*, 1966, 385 f.; O. Cullmann, *Peter: Disciple, Apostle, Martyr*, 1962²; J. Jeremias, *thyra, TDNT* III 173–80; and *pylē, TDNT* VI 921–28; P. W. Meyer, "A Note on John 10:1–18", *JBL* 75, 1956, 232–35; J. A. Robinson, "The Parable of the Good Shepherd (John 10:1–5)", *ZNW* 46, 1955, 233–40 (reprinted in *Twelve New Testament Studies*, 1962, 67–75).

(b). E. Fascher, "Ich bin die Tür: eine Studie zu Joh. 10, 1–18", *Deutsche Theologie* 9, 1942, 34–57, 118–35.

Gather, Scatter

συνάγω

συνάγω (*synagō*), gather; ἐπισυνάγω (*episynagō*), gather together; συλλέγω (*syllegō*), gather up; τρυγάω (*trygaō*), gather in; συστρέφω (*systrephō*), gather together; ἀθροίζω (*athroizō*), gather together; συναθροίζω (*synathroizō*), gather together; ἐπισυναγωγή (*episynagōgē*), gathering together; ἐπαθροίζομαι (*epathroizomai*), be gathered even more.

CL In secular Greek *synagō* is used of bringing together, collecting or convening (Homer, Herodotus). It appears in a hostile sense of joining battle (*Iliad*). It can refer to uniting in marriage (Aeschylus), or to concluding from premises (Aristotle). Sometimes it speaks of gathering together stores or crops (Xenophon).

OT In the LXX *synagō* is employed about 350 times, and stands chiefly for the Heb. *'āsap*. It is used of collecting things, especially fruits (Exod. 23:10; Lev. 25:3, 20; Isa. 17:5), but also ears of grain (Ruth 2:7), quails (Num. 11:32), money (2 Ki. 22:4; 2 Chr. 24:11), and the ashes of a red heifer (Num. 19:9). More importantly, the verb may refer to the gathering together of persons such as men, people, nations, armies (Exod. 3:16; 4:29; Num. 11:16; 21:16, 23; 2 Sam. 10:17; 12:29). It is also used of being gathered to one's people in Sheol (2 Ki. 22:20; 2 Chr. 34:29[28]). Other passages speak of the gathering of the dead slain in battle for the purpose of burial (Jer. 9:22[21]; Ezek. 29:5).

The verb *qāḇaṣ* also means to gather, and is used of collecting grain (Gen. 41:35, 48), booty (Deut. 13:16[17]), money (2 Chr. 24:5), birds (Isa. 34:15,[16]) and beasts (Ezek. 39:17). In the passive it frequently refers to the assembling of persons (Gen. 49:2; Isa. 45:20; 48:14; 49:18; 60:4; 2 Chr. 20:4). In the intensive form it is used of gathering grapes (Isa. 62:9), and of assembling people (Deut. 30:3, 4; Jer. 31[38]:10), particularly of God recalling and assembling the exiles (Isa. 40:11; 43:5; 56:8). Reference is made to gathering the nations for judgment (Mic. 4:12; Isa. 66:18), and to Yahweh's gathering his dispersed people, sometimes under the figure of a flock (Mic. 2:12[11]; 4:6).

NT In the NT *synagō* appears 59 times (24 in Matt., 5 in Mk., 6 in Lk., 7 in Jn., 11 in Acts, 5 in Rev. and once in Paul). In Matt. gathering refers to people (crowds, 13:2; wedding guests, 22:10), or things (birds, 6:26; fish, 13:47; vultures, 24:28). It is contrasted with → *skorpizō* (scatter) in connection with the mission of the church (12:30; 25:24, 26). There are frequent references to the assembling of the religious leaders (2:4; 22:34, 41; 26:3, 57; 27:17; 27:62; 28:12), and one reference to the whole Roman cohort gathering in the Praetorium at the crucifixion (27:27). The nations will be gathered together at the last judgment (25:32), and the messiah will gather the wheat into his barn (3:12; cf. 13:30, where the reapers are the angels who are sent by the Son of man). Wherever several believers gather in Christ's name, he will be in the midst (18:20). In 25:35, 38, 43 *synagō* means invite in, receive as a guest.

Lk. notes the gathering of the chief priests and scribes to condemn Jesus (22:66), the selfish collecting of material things (12:17, 18), and the prodigal's reckless selling of his goods (15:13). On the other hand, he recognizes that the messiah will gather the elect (3:17), and cites Jesus' principle that "he who does not gather with me scatters" (11:23).

In Jn. the fragments from the feeding of the five thousand are gathered up (6:12, 13). Christian workers gather fruit unto life eternal (4:36), and Christ's mission is to gather into one the children of God scattered abroad (11:52). Fruitless branches, however, are gathered and burned (15:6). Jesus often gathers his disciples to Gethsemane (18:2), and the chief priests and Pharisees gather or convene a council (11:47).

In Acts there are references to the church gathering for prayer (4:31), instruction (11:26), information (14:27; 15:30), consultation (15:6) and the breaking of bread (20:7, 8). The Jewish religious leaders assemble (4:5); so do Herod and Pilate

(4:26, 27). In Pisidian Antioch practically the whole city gathers to hear the word of God (13:44).

The only instance of *synagō* in Paul occurs in 1 Cor. 5:4 where believers assemble to deal with a case of incest requiring excommunication (→ Destroy, art. *olethros* NT 3).

In Rev. we read of gathering for the great eschatological battle (16:14, 16; 19:19; 20:8) and for the great supper of God (19:17).

episynagō is used in Jesus' lament over Jerusalem (Matt. 23:37; Lk. 13:34), in eschatological passages speaking of the gathering of the elect (Mk. 13:27; Matt. 24:31), and in connection with crowds gathering about Jesus (Mk. 1:33; Lk. 12:1). In Lk. 17:37 *episynagō* is used in a warning: "As surely as vultures find the carcass, so surely will divine judgement come; therefore always be ready!" (*Oxford Annotated Bible*, 1271; → Bird NT).

The verb *syllegō* is utilized for collecting grapes (Matt. 7:16; Lk. 6:44), good fish (Matt. 13:48), and of gathering up the tares for destruction (Matt. 13:28, 29, 30, 40, 41).

trygaō appears as a stylistic variation for *syllegō* in Lk. 6:44. In Rev. 14:18, 19 it speaks of gathering the clusters of the vine where the wine press of God's wrath is in view.

Several other words refer to gathering together (cf. Latin *congregare*), but are used sparingly: (1) *systrephō* in Acts 28:3, of Paul's gathering a bundle of sticks; (2) *athroizō* in Lk. 24:33, of the eleven apostles and others gathered together in Jerusalem; (3) *synathroizō* in Acts 12:12, of the believers assembled in the home of John Mark's mother; (4) *epathroizomai* in Lk. 11:29 of crowds gathered.

The noun *episynagōgē* in 2 Thess. 2:1 refers to the "gathering together" of believers to Christ at the Parousia (cf. Latin *congregatio*).　　　　*A. A. Trites*

| σκορπίζω |

σκορπίζω (*skorpizō*), scatter, disperse, distribute; διασκορπίζω (*diaskorpizō*), scatter, disperse, waste; διαλύω (*dialyō*), break up, dissolve, disperse; διασπείρω (*diaspeirō*), scatter; διασπορά (*diaspora*), dispersion.

CL The verb *skorpizō* is probably adopted from the Macedonian dialect about the time of Alexander. It means scatter, disperse. Examples tend to be late: Hecataeus in *Phrynichus* (p. 218); Strabo 4, 4, 6; Pseudo-Lucian, *Asinus* 32; Aelianus, *Varia Historia* 13, 45; Josephus, *Ant.* 16, 10. *diaskorpizō* also means scatter, disperse. It appears in Aelianus, *Varia Historia* 13, 46; Polybius 1, 47, 4; 27, 2, 10; and Josephus, *Ant.* 8, 404. *diaspeirō* speaks of scattering (e.g., Sophocles and Herodotus). In the Christian era it is sometimes used in the passive of churches (cf. Lucian, *Toxaris* 33; Iamblichus, *De vita Pythagorica* 35, 253; Josephus, *Ant.* 7, 244; 12, 278). *dialyō*, which generally means break up, dissolve, can be used of the dispersing of a crowd (Herodotus 8, 11; Josephus, *Ant.* 20, 124).

OT In the LXX *diaspeirō* appears approximately 60 times, *diaskorpizō* around 50, *skorpizō* about 14 and *dialyō* about a dozen times. These represent quite a number of Hebrew verbs, the chief of which are *pûṣ*, *nāp̄aṣ* and *zārâh*. The first of these verbs is used generally intransitively of those who disperse themselves and are

33

scattered; e.g., a people (Gen. 11:4; Num. 10:35; 1 Sam. 11:11; 14:34; Ps. 68:1 [2]; Ezek. 46:18) or a flock (Ezek. 34:5; Zech. 13:7). Similarly, *nāp̄aṣ* is used reflexively of a people dispersing themselves and being scattered (1 Sam. 13:11; Isa. 33:3; cf. Gen. 9:19) as well as transitively of dashing or shattering a people (Jer. 13:14; 51[28]:23).

The verb *zārâh* means to scatter, cast loosely about, spread (e.g., Exod. 32:20; Num. 17:2[16:37]; Mal. 2:3). It can mean to winnow, that is, disperse by casting up and scattering in the wind (Isa. 30:24; Jer. 4:11; Ruth 3:2). At times it speaks of the routing of enemies (Jer. 15:7; Isa. 41:16; Ezek. 5:2), or the dispersing of the nations (Lev. 26:33; Ezek. 5:10; 6:5; 30:26).

NT *skorpizō* occurs only 5 times in the NT, once in connection with the persecution of Christians (Jn. 16:32) and once in the pastoral allegory of Jn. 10, where the "wolf snatches the sheep and scatters them" (Jn. 10:12). Both Matt. and Lk. draw attention to the missionary principle enunciated by Jesus: "He who is not with me is against me, and he who does not gather with me scatters" (Matt. 12:30 = Lk. 11:23). Jesus here takes the theme of gathering and scattering which is applied in the OT to the people of God (Isa. 40:11; 49:6; Ezek. 34:13, 16) and applies it to his own significance in the end-time. The comparable inverted form of the saying, "he that is not against us is for us" (Mk. 9:40; Lk. 9:50) occurs in the context of casting out demons. "But they are not contradictory, if the one was spoken to the indifferent about themselves, and the other to the disciples about someone else" (A. H. McNeile, *The Gospel according to St. Matthew*, 1915, 177; cf. D. Hill, *The Gospel of Matthew*, 1972, 217). Paul uses the verb once in a quotation from Ps. 112:9 when he is advocating charity and benevolence (2 Cor. 9:9).

diaskorpizō (9 times in NT) refers on occasion to the squandering of resources, either one's own or those entrusted to him by another (Lk. 15:13; 16:1). The verb also highlights the persecution and dispersion of the messianic community, for the "shepherd" will be smitten and the "sheep" scattered (Mk. 14:27; Matt. 26:31; cf. Zech. 13:7). Luke uses it in the *Magnificat* to express Mary's confidence in God's ability to turn tables on the lofty (Lk. 1:51). A striking instance of the scattering of the proud appears in the case of Judas the Galilean, whose followers are dispersed when he is discredited as a messianic pretender (Acts 5:37). Matthew twice contrasts "scattering" and "gathering" in an *argumentum ad hominem* involving sowing and reaping (Matt. 25:24, 26). John sees the mission of Jesus embracing Gentiles as well as Jews, in order that he might "gather into one the children of God who were scattered abroad" (Jn. 11:52).

The verb *dialyō* appears only once in the NT when Gamaliel draws attention to the futility of the revolt led by Theudas and the subsequent dispersal of his followers (Acts 5:36).

The verb *diaspeirō* is used 3 times of the dispersion of the early Christians through persecution (Acts 8:1; 11:19). The beneficent result of such circumstances was the proclamation of the Christian message in new areas; the persecution paved the way for missionary advance. It is not surprising, then, to find an epistle directed to "God's elect, strangers in the world, scattered throughout Pontus, Galatia, Cappadocia, Asia and Bithynia" (1 Pet. 1:1). The word *diaspora* also appears in Jas. 1:1 of "the Twelve Tribes dispersed throughout the world", while the customary usage of the LXX is maintained in Jn. 7:35, where it is a technical term for the "dispersion of the Jews among the Gentiles" (cf. Deut. 30:4; Ps. 146[147]:2).

A. A. Trites

→ Foreign, → Seed, Harvest

(a). Arndt, 187, 789 f.; S. W. Baron, *A Social and Religious History of the Jews*, I–XV, 1952–73²; BDB, 62 f., 867 f.; J. Bright, *A History of Israel*, 1972²; M. Grant, *The Jews in the Roman World*, 1973; T. Nicol, "Dispersion", *International Standard Bible Encyclopaedia*, ed. J. Orr, II 855–59; K. L. Schmidt, *diaspora*, *TDNT* II 98–104; W. L. Walker, "Gather", *International Standard Bible Encyclopaedia*, III 1177 f. On the dispersion of the Jews generally see W. Förster, *Palestinian Judaism in New Testament Times*, 1964; F. C. Grant, *Ancient Judaism and the New Testament*, 1960; M. Hengel, *Judaism and Hellenism*, I–II, 1975; Moore, *Judaism*, I–III; T. Reinach, "Diaspora", *JE* IV 559–74; S. Safrai, M. Stern, D. Flusser and W. C. van Unnik, eds., *The Jewish People in the First Century*, I, 1974; J. A. Sanders, "Dispersion", *IDB* I 854 ff.; Schürer, I–II; F. Zweig, "Israel and the Diaspora", *Judaism* 7, 1958, 147–50.
(b). A. Causse, *Les Dispersés d'Israël*, 1929; J. Juster, *Les Juifs dans l'Empire romain*, 1914; K. G. Kuhn, "Die inneren Gründe der jüdischen Ausbreitung", *Deutsche Theologie* 2, 1935, 9–17; K. Müller, ed., *Die Aktion Jesu und die Reaktion der Kirche*, 1972.

Generation

γενεά

γενεά (*genea*), generation, family, clan, race, age; γενεαλογία (*genealogia*), genealogy, family tree; γενεαλογέω (*genealogeō*), trace descent; ἀγενεαλόγητος (*agenealogētos*), without genealogy.

CL & OT *genea*, derived from the root *gen-*, means birth, also (noble) descent, then descendants, family, race (i.e., those bound together by a common origin). Those born at the same time constitute a generation ("three generations of men are a hundred years", Hdt. 2, 142). Associated with this is the meaning: the body of one's contemporaries, an age. In the LXX *genea* is almost always the translation of *dôr* and means generation, in which case the whole history of Israel is often regarded as a work of God extending through many generations ("from generation to generation", "from all generations").

The noun *genos*, formed from the same stem and related to the verb *ginomai* (→ Birth), is frequently translated by race (except where it corresponds to the Hebrew *mîn* = "kind" in Gen. 1). Both in the LXX and in the NT its prime meaning is nation, people or tribe, and therefore is discussed under → people.

NT *genea* occurs 43 times in the NT, mainly in the Gospels and Acts; on the other hand its compounds are found only rarely: *genealogeomai* occurs once, *genealogia* twice, *agenealogētos* once.

1. The meaning of the word in the NT comes from the idea of historical sequence referred to above. It occurs 4 times in Matt. 1:17, in the context of Christ's genealogy. The remote past is denoted – as in OT and late Jewish usage – by the phrase *apo geneōn*, from (all) generations (Col. 1:26; Acts 15:21). Similarly the unending future is expressed by *eis geneas kai geneas*, "to all generations" (lit. "to generations and generations") (Lk. 1:50; 1:48; Eph. 3:21). Acts 13:36 refers to David's generation, and Acts 14:16; Eph. 3:5 to earlier generations. *genealogia*

35

occurs in the NT only in 1 Tim. 1:4 and Titus 3:9, and alludes specifically to the practice of searching back through one's family tree in order to establish ancestry. On any straightforward exegesis, those doing this can only have been Jews who, starting out from OT and other genealogies, were propagating all kinds of "Jewish myths", quite probably pre-Christian gnostic speculations. But it is also possible that the Ebionites were using similar arguments to attack the doctrine of the miraculous birth of Jesus which was circulating in the Christian church (cf. the genealogies in Matt. 1 and Lk. 3). (On the genealogies of Jesus → Son.)

In Gen. 14 → Melchizedek is introduced without any such statement as is usual elsewhere in the OT regarding a person's ancestry ("son of . . ."). For that reason he is described in Heb. 7:3 as *agenealogētos*, and in 7:6 as *mē genealogoumenos*, i.e. he can have had no natural ancestry like others. The author of Heb. is certainly not attempting to call in question indirectly the true humanity of Jesus. For him this is bound up with his true divinity.

2. Almost all the remaining NT *genea*-passages speak of "this generation" (*hē genea hautē*). This construction in Greek, with the demonstrative regularly following its noun, is clearly the equivalent of *haddōr hazzeh*. It is interesting that the OT does not know this stereotyped phrase in its NT sense, though Ps. 12:7 comes very close to it (cf. Gen. 7:1; Exod. 1:6; Deut. 1:35). In these passages the demonstrative has a pejorative character, i.e. the reference is to a class of people who in this world stand over against the children of light and are further described as faithless (Mk. 9:19), faithless and perverse (Matt. 17:17), adulterous (Mk. 8:38), evil and adulterous (Matt. 12:39), evil (Lk. 11:29), crooked (Acts 2:40), crooked and perverse (Phil. 2:15). The Song of Moses in Deut. 32 (vv. 5 and 20) seems here to have had a certain influence on the wording. In these passages the temporal, "genealogical" element is completely absent. The emphasis lies entirely on the sinfulness of this class, this type of people.

3. In Jesus' discourse about the future the phrase clearly bears this second meaning: Mk. 13:30; Matt. 24:34; Lk. 21:32. Indeed, in every other NT passage where *hautē* forms part of this phrase, it has the same pejorative character. But since the discourse refers to this *genea* "passing away", the temporal, genealogical element is also present, though of secondary importance. By using this phrase, Jesus appears to set a time limit for certain events, and the question then is: Which events are they? There are various conflicting views.

(a) Only a comprehensive analysis of Mk. 13 and its parallels can clarify the situation, but the following brief observations may be made. Mk. 13:1–36 with its 600 words is the most extensive complete section within the basic synoptic tradition ("triplex traditio marciana", de Solages). Like Mk. 4, it is an important piece of early Christian *didachē* (teaching); indeed the Gospel of Mk. as a whole bears the marks not of *kērygma* (proclamation) but of *didachē*. (Note the use in Mk. of the word-group *didaskein; didachē; didaskalos;* → teaching, and in particular Mk. 1:22, 27; 4:1, 2; 11:18; 12:38.) In Mk. 13:1–4 a purely didactic situation is outlined as the *Sitz im Leben*. Attempts have been made, on the basis of literary criticism, to exclude a greater or lesser portion of Mk. 13:1–36 as being of non-Marcan origin. Such attempts have failed, however, since both in terms of word-frequency and of grammar the whole passage is thoroughly Marcan in character. It is very significant that a succession of recent investigators have made their incisions at totally different places. To call the whole chapter (or part of it) "apocalyptic" can only be misleading, for there is a complete absence of apocalyptic features: history written as prophecy, descriptions of heaven, astronomical speculations, symbolism based on animals or colours or numbers, visions, heavenly messages brought by angels, pseudonymity, precise expressions of time, portrayal of conditions in heaven or hell. Moreover, where isolated ideas or phrases are borrowed from apocalyptic, these are re-moulded in typically non-apocalyptic, indeed anti-apocalyptic fashion. The imperatives which dominate the whole chapter are essentially non-apocalyptic. Many modern form-critics see the passage as a hortatory discourse of early Christian *didachē* which originated as separate elements but was put together in its present form by the author and by the church tradition available to him. In the context of the whole gospel it is clearly presented as a farewell discourse. This type of address occurs frequently in the literature of pre-Christian times and of late Judaism, as well as in the rest of the NT. Its essential and recurring features are warnings of future apostasy and persecution, the promise of coming redemption and the exhortation to watchfulness.

(b) It is precisely these features that are present in Mk. 13 and its parallels, coupled with a tradition according to which Jesus announces the coming destruction of → Jerusalem (1–4; 14–20). The Lucan parallel to Mk. 13:14–20 (Lk. 21:20–24) shows clearly enough how Lk. understood Mk.'s cryptic language, but as Dodd, Michaelis and others have shown, this by no means implies that Lk. was prophesying after the event. Such a conclusion is suggested only by a theological interpretation, which sees Jerusalem as the embodiment of the people of Israel, whose hearts God had hardened in judgment, whilst the "times of the Gentiles" (*kairoi ethnōn*), in the sense of the "times when salvation comes to the Gentiles", had already begun (cf. Acts 28:24–28; Rom. 11:25, 26). These times cannot be calculated in advance (Lk. 17:20 f.). But they will soon come to an end with the coming of the → kingdom of God, the → Son of man, and the → Day of the Lord. (Lk. 18:8 and 21:34–36 suggest that Lk. expected that the end may come at any moment within his own lifetime.) Whilst in Lk. the "end" of Jerusalem and the "end of the world" are clearly separated from one another, Matt. has closely linked the two together. The sentence pronounced upon Jerusalem was available both to him and to Lk. in the logia source (Matt. 23:37–39 = Lk. 13:34, 35) and in the special material (Matt. 22:7; Lk. 19:41–44; 23:28–32). This close association in Matt. is shown by the form of the question in 24:3, and with particular clarity by the expression "immediately" in 24:29 (*eutheōs*), and in general by the entirely new version of the discourse which he gives. The expression *synteleisthai* in Mk. 13:4 is not by any means a technical term of apocalyptic as has been asserted (Acts 21:27 being quoted in support!), and the adverbial phrase of time in Mk. 13:24 ("but in those days after that tribulation") is linguistically semitic and ambiguous, telling us very little. Mk. occupies, so to speak, a middle position, as indeed he does in textual matters throughout. (Cf. de Solages' conclusive arguments; see bibliography below.)

Only by such considerations can the word in Mk. 13:30 and its parallels be explained. In Matt. it has the sense of *this generation*, and according to the first evangelist, Jesus expected the end of this age (→ Time, art. *aiōn*) to occur in connection with the judgment on Jerusalem at the end of that first generation (see

Mk. 9:1 and Matt. 16:18). But in view of the happenings of A.D. 70 and their theological relation to the preaching of Paul, Lk. understood *genea* as a *class of people*, perhaps even as *Israel*. Since the special material and the logia source do not link the judgment on Jerusalem and the end of the world, and since the text of Mk. 13 in general (especially vv. 13 and 24) has an indefinite and open ring, we must conclude that in this regard Jesus expressed himself in an ambiguous manner. The evangelists, however, were not copyists, but witnesses who, led by the Spirit, testified to the word they had heard and brought it to bear upon their own times.

Acts 8:33 is a literal rendering of Isa. 53:8. The passage is interpreted christo-logically, but the precise interpretation presents difficulties. It is fairly certain that "generation" is used in its genealogical sense. However, E. Haenchen thinks that it may be understood as referring to "spiritual descendants". The sentence would then mean: "The number of his disciples will grow incalculably, because he has become the Exalted" (*The Acts of the Apostles*, 1971, 312).   *R. Morgenthaler*

4. The events referred to in Mk. 13:30 par. Matt. 24:34 and Lk. 21:32 have generally been taken to refer to cosmic events associated with the second coming of Christ. (For the survey of views see G. R. Beasley-Murray, *Jesus and the Future: An Examination of the Criticism of the Eschatological Discourse, Mark 13, with Special Reference to the Little Apocalypse Theory*, 1954; cf. the same author's *A Commentary on Mark Thirteen*, 1957.) But if these events were expected within the first generation of Christians (and "generation" is the most probable transla-tion of *genea*), either Jesus or the evangelists were mistaken. The failure of events to materialize has been put down to a postponement of the catastrophe and to a telescoping of events, comparable with seeing a mountain range at a distance. The perspective makes the mountains appear to stand close together, and indeed rela-tively speaking they do stand close together. However, there is an alternative inter-pretation of the passage which points out that insufficient attention has been paid to the prophetic language of the passage as a whole.

The imagery of cosmic phenomena is used in the OT to describe *this-worldly* events and, in particular, historical acts of judgment. The following passages are significant, not least because of their affinities with the present context: Isa. 13:10 (predicting doom on Babylon); Isa. 34:4 (referring to "all the nations", but especially to Edom); Ezek. 32:7 (concerning Egypt); Amos 8:9 (the Northern Kingdom of Israel); Joel 2:10 (Judah). The cosmic imagery draws attention to the divine dimension of the event in which the judgment of God is enacted. The use of Joel 2:28-32 in Acts 2:15-21 provides an instance of the way in which such pro-phetic cosmic imagery is applied to historical events in the present (cf. also Lk. 10:18; Jn. 12:31; 1 Thess. 4:16; 2 Pet. 3:10 ff.; Rev. 6:12-17; 18:1). Other OT passages relevant to the interpretation of the present context are Isa. 19:1; 27:13; Dn. 7:13; Deut. 30:4; Zech. 2:6; 12:10-14; Mal. 3:1. In view of this, Mk. 13:24-30 may be interpreted as a prophecy of judgment on Israel in which the → Son of man will be vindicated. Such a judgment took place with the destruction of Jeru-salem, the desecration of the → Temple and the scattering of Israel – all of which happened within the lifetime of "this generation." The disintegration of Israel as the people of God coincides with the inauguration of the → kingdom of the Son of man. Such an interpretation fits the preceding discourse and the introductory remarks of the disciples (Mk. 13:1 ff. par.). It would not, however, pre-empt the → judgment of mankind in general. (See further J. Marcellus Kik, *Matthew XXIV: An Exposition*, 1948; R. T. France, *Jesus and the Old Testament*, 1971, 227–39.) → Present: The Parousia and Eschatology in the NT   *C. Brown*

(a). E. L. Abel, "The Genealogies of Jesus HO CHRISTOS", *NTS* 20, 1973–74, 203–10; G. R. Beasley-Murray, *Jesus and the Future: An Examination of the Criticism of the Eschatological Discourse, Mark 13, with Special Reference to the Little Apocalypse Theory*, 1954; and *A Commentary on Mark Thirteen*, 1957; F. Büchsel, *genea* etc., *TDNT* I 662–65; C. H. Dodd, "The Fall of Jerusalem and the 'Abomination of Desolation' ", *Journal of Roman Studies*, 1947, reprinted in *More New Testament Studies*, 1968, 69–83; L. Gaston, *No Stone on Another: Studies in the Significance of the Fall of Jerusalem in the Synoptic Gospels*, 1970; T. F. Glasson, *His Appearing and His Kingdom: The Christian Hope in the Light of its History*, 1953; M. D. Johnson, *The Purpose of the Biblical Genealogies: With Special Reference to the Setting of Genealogies of Jesus*, Society for New Testament Studies Monograph Series 8, 1969; W. Kelber, *The Kingdom in Mark: A New Place and a New Time*, 1974; J. M. Kik, *Matthew XXIV: An Exposition*, 1948, reissued in *An Eschatology of Victory*, 1971; W. G. Kümmel, *Promise and Fulfilment: The Eschatological Message of Jesus*, 1961²; A. L. Moore, *The Parousia in the New Testament*, 1966; G. Neville, *The Advent Hope: A Study of the Content of Mark XIII*, 1961; B. de Solages, *A Greek Synopsis of the Gospels*, 1959; W. Strawson, *Jesus and the Future Life: A Study in the Synoptic Gospels*, 1959; R. R. Wilson, "The Old Testament Genealogies in Recent Research", *JBL* 94, 1975, 169–89.

(b). G. Bolsinger, "Die Ahnenreihe Christi nach Matthäus und Lukas", *BuK* 12, 1957, 112 ff.; F. Busch, *Zum Verständnis der synoptischen Eschatologie, Mk. 13 neu untersucht*, 1938; J. Conrad, *Die junge Generation im Alten Testament*, *AzTh* 1/40, 1970; E. Grässer, *Das Problem der Parusieverzögerung in den synoptischen Evangelien und in der Apostelgeschichte*, 1957; G. Harder, "Das eschatologische Geschichtsbild der sogenannten kleine Apokalypse Mk. 13", *ThV*, 1952, 71 ff.; M. Meinertz, " 'Dieses Geschlecht' im Neuen Testament", *BZ* 1, 1957, 283 ff.; A. Pfleiderer, "Über die Komposition der eschatologischen Rede Mt. 24:4 ff.", *Jahrbuch für Deutsche Theologie*, 1868; A. Piganiol, *Observation sur la Date de l'Apocalypse synoptique*, 1924; E. des Places, "*Ipsius enim genus sumus* (Act. 17, 28)", *Biblica* 43, 1962, 388 ff.; G. C. B. Pünjer, "Die Wiederkunftsreden Jesu", *ZWT* 2, 1878, 153–208; A. Schlatter, *Der Evangelist Matthäus*, 1929, 554; E. F. Strömer, *Die grosse Zukunftsrede des Herrn nach Matthäus*, 24, 1922.

Gift, Pledge, Corban

A gift (*dōron* and related words) is qualified by the reason for which it is given and the end which it is intended to serve. Its characteristic feature is not the act of giving (*didōmi*), but the intention behind it. This can be to fulfil an obligation or cancel a debt. But a gift may also be a present given without ulterior motive. When man gives something to God, his gift has the character of an offering (→ Sacrifice). But in the NT the theological emphasis lies, significantly, on the idea of gift as a present from God to man, In this connection → Jesus Christ and his redeeming work appear as the one great fundamental gift of God. There is also the gift of the Holy → Spirit with his various *charismata* (→ Grace). The former gives man union and → fellowship with Christ; the latter equips him for service arising from this fellowship. The *arrabōn*, first instalment, earnest, is a more specific idea, denoting the pledge which guarantees fulfilment (→ Fullness) of the → promise.

ἀρραβών	ἀρραβών (*arrabōn*), first instalment, down payment, deposit, pledge, earnest.

CL & OT The Gk. word *arrabōn* (borrowed from the Semitic, cf. Heb. 'ērābōn) is a legal concept from the language of business and trade. It is found only rarely

(Isaeus, Aristotle and later grammarians such as Suidas) and means: (1) an instalment, with which a man secures a legal claim upon a thing as yet unpaid for; (2) an earnest, an advance payment, by which a contract becomes valid in law; (3) in one passage (Gen. 38:17 ff.) a pledge. In each case it is a matter of payment by which the person concerned undertakes to give further payment to the recipient (Arndt, 109). A metaphorical use is also possible (e.g. skilfulness as an *arrabōn* of life, Antiphon, *Frag.* 123, 6).

NT In all three passages where the word occurs in the NT the Holy → Spirit is referred to.

1. Eph. 1:14 interprets the other two passages: the Spirit as the present earnest of our future → inheritance guarantees our complete, final salvation, i.e. eternal communion with God. This statement, as also 2 Cor. 1:22, is probably associated with → baptism (→ Seal). In the sealing of the believer, the Holy Spirit is given to the human → heart (*kardia*) as an earnest. The future reality represented by the earnest of the Spirit appears in 2 Cor. 5:5 as the "house" expected from heaven, which will one day replace the present "tent", our earthly body. Thus in Paul the Spirit is not the earnest of a soul freed from its earthly body, but of a new existence in an immortal body (heavenly garment; → Clothe).

2. Similarly Rom. 8:23 speaks of "the first fruits [*aparchē*] of the Spirit". Here the genitive "of the Spirit" explains the meaning of *aparchē* (gift of firstfruits; → Sacrifice; cf. 2 Cor. 1:22; 5:5). E. Schweizer holds that *aparchē*, like *arrabōn*, does not mean a preliminary participation in the Spirit. The present reality of the Spirit is a sign and pledge of that which is to come (*TDNT* VI 422). In Polycarp 8:1 Jesus Christ is referred to as *arrabōn*. But the NT avoids this and speaks of him only as *engyos* (surety; → Covenant).

In all three NT passages, however, the *arrabōn* should not be understood to imply that, in giving the earnest of the Spirit, God is legally our debtor. Even the instalment of the Spirit remains a free, undeserved gift of God to men.

O. Becker

δῶρον

δῶρον (*dōron*), gift, present; δωρεά (*dōrea*), gift; δωρεάν (*dōrean*), as a present, gratis; δωρέομαι (*dōreomai*), give, present; δώρημα (*dōrēma*), present; δίδωμι (*didōmi*), give, grant; δόμα (*doma*), gift; προσφορά (*prosphora*), presentation, offering, gift.

CL *dōron* (found already in Mycenean Greek) is from the same root as *didōmi*.

metadidōmi means to give a share in; *dosis* and *doma*, gift, are infrequent. The derivative vb. *dōreomai*, present, is used in the mid. (originally also in the act.). Corresponding to it are the Attic noun *dōrēma* present, and *dōrea*, present, gift, bestowal. The acc. of the latter, *dōrean*, is used adverbially in the sense of gratis, undeservedly, as a present.

In extra-Biblical use, *dōron* (similarly *dōrea*) denotes especially a complimentary gift. As a gift from the gods (e.g. in Homer), it can also mean dispensation. Brought by men to the gods, *dōron* denotes a consecrated gift. It can also mean tax, tribute, or bribe.

OT 1. The LXX uses *dōron* to render several Hebrew words with the following principal meanings: (a) generally, a present such as men give to one another (Gen. 24:53; 32:13, 18 f. and passim); (b) tribute (Jdg. 3:15, 17 f. and passim; Jdg. 5:19 = booty); (c) bribe (Exod. 23:7 f.; Deut. 16:19; 27:25; Ps. 15:5 and passim; Deut. 10:17 and passim; negatively when the reference is to God; (d) most frequent is the cultic meaning offering, Heb. *qorbān*, especially in Lev. and Num. (Lev. 1:2 f., 10, 14; 2:1, 4 ff. etc.; Num. 5:15; 6:14, 21 etc.; also for *minḥâh* in Gen. 4:4; for *nēḏer* in Deut. 12:11 and passim), often with the vb. *prospherō*, to bring, to offer (*prosphora*, offering; the act of offering); (e) a gift brought to God in recognition of his greatness and power (by kings, Pss. 68:30; 72:10; by peoples, Isa. 18:7, cf. Ps. 68:32 etc.); (f) a gift from God (Gen. 30:20).

dōron rarely appears in late Jewish literature. *dōrēma* appears in the LXX only once, in the Apocrypha (Sir. 31[34]:18).

2. *dōreomai*, rare in the LXX, stands for 3 Hebrew verbs having the sense of "giving": (a) by men to one another (*nāṭan*, Est. 8:1; also Prov. 4:2); (b) by man to God (*qorbān*, Lev. 7:15 [LXX v. 5]); (c) by God to men (*zāḇaḏ*, Gen. 30:20). Much more frequent is *didōmi*, which as a rule renders the Hebrew *nāṭan*, to give (likewise used in this threefold way), but also a large number of other verbs.

3. *dōrea* occurs frequently in late Jewish literature, but in the canonical books always in the adverbial acc. form *dōrean*. It corresponds in meaning to the Heb. term *ḥinnām*: (a) for nothing (without payment, Exod. 21:2, 11; Num. 11:5; 2 Sam. 24:24 and passim; without recompense, Gen. 29:15; Jer. 22:13 and passim); (b) without cause (1 Sam. 19:5; 25:31; Ps. 35:7 and passim); (c) in vain (Ezek. 6:10; Mal. 1:10).

NT 1. (a) In the NT *dōron* (19 times) stands once for the human gift (Rev. 11:10; cf. Matt. 7:11 par. Lk. 11:13 *doma*) and once for the divine gift (Eph. 2:8). For the latter *dōrea* is found more often (e.g. Jn. 4:10; Acts 2:38; Rom. 5:15, 17; 2 Cor. 9:15; Eph. 4:7; Heb. 6:4). In Rom. 5:16 and Jas. 1:17 *dōrēma* is used (in the latter passage together with *dosis*). For the rest *dōron* is the offering (e.g. Matt. 5:23 f.; 23:18 f.; Mk. 7:11; Lk. 21:1–4; Heb. 5:1; 8:3 f.; 9:9; 11:4; while in Matt. 2:11 it is the gift of adoration). The occasional combination with *prospherō* to bring, offer, underlines the connection with the OT sacrifice system. In this sense *dōron* is parallel to *thysia*, offering (→ Sacrifice), and *prosphora*, offering.

(b) *didōmi* (416 times in the NT) is found in all the nuances of presenting, giving, bestowing, granting, etc., both (i) among men (Matt. 7:11a; Acts 20:35 and passim; also *dōreomai* Mk. 15:45; and *metadidōmi* Lk. 3:11; Rom. 1:11; 12:8; Eph. 4:28; 1 Thess. 2:8); and (ii) by God (Matt. 7:11b; 1 Jn. 4:13; Rev. 2:7, 17; cf. also 3:21 and passim; *dōreomai* 2 Pet. 1:3). The meaning to offer also occurs (Lk. 2:24), while a metaphorical meaning is found in Mk. 10:37; Acts 13:20 and passim.

(c) *dōrean* (8 times in the NT) has the threefold meaning common in the OT: (i) gratis, gratuitously, for nothing (Matt. 10:8; Rom. 3:24; 2 Cor. 11:7; 2 Thess. 3:8; Rev. 21:6; 22:17); (ii) without cause (Jn. 15:25, OT quotation from Pss. 35:19; 69:4); (iii) in vain (Gal. 2:21).

2. *dōron* and *didōmi* as cultic terms (→ Sacrifice) are found in contexts where the subject-matter is the regular offering (Matt. 5:23 f.; 8:4; Lk. 2:24; in Lk. 21:1, 4

with the meaning money-offering). There are also other passages (Mk. 7:11; Matt. 15:5) which emphasize, in line with OT prophecy, that offerings (even in a metaphorical sense) are no substitute for obedience to God's will (cf. Isa. 1:10–17; Mic. 6:6–8; also Deut. 10:12 f.). The problem of the sacrificial cult is squarely faced in the Epistle to the Hebrews (5:1 ff.; 8:3 f. and passim), where a contrast is drawn between the merely temporary OT system with its offerings (*dōron* and *thysia*) made by men, and the final, once-for-all offering of Christ (*prosphora* and *thysia*) (7:26–28; 9:25 ff.; 10:10 ff. and passim; cf. also Eph. 5:2).

3. This opens up the NT teaching that God is a God who gives, and that his giving is seen supremely in the redeeming work of Christ (→ Redemption).

(a) There are general statements to the effect that God "gave" his → Son (Jn. 3:16) and passages where Jesus as such is referred to as "the gift of God" (*dōrea*, Jn. 4:10). The statement that Christ has "given" himself for us, for our sins, appears as a credal formula in Gal. 1:4; 1 Tim. 2:6 (for literature on NT credal formulae → Confess).

(b) In addition there are references which point particularly to Jesus' death on the cross: Jesus gave his life as a ransom for many (Mk. 10:45 par.; cf. Jn. 10:15b). Likewise Lk.'s account of the Last Supper (22:19) speaks of Christ's body "given for you."

(c) This gives to Christians the assurance of belonging for ever to the → church of Christ. Jn. in particular sees the basis for this assurance in the fact that the church has been given to Christ by God (10:28 f.; cf. 17:6 ff.). Moreover, to belong to this church means to share in the gift of eternal → life (10:28; cf. 3:15 ff.; 11:25 f.; 17:3).

(d) In Paul the gift-motif is incorporated into his preaching of the free and unmerited grace of God (N.B. *dōrean*, Rom. 3:24) which declares the sinner justified "without works" (→ Righteousness; → Grace; → Reconciliation). *dōrea* or *dōrēma* (Rom. 5:15–17; 2 Cor. 9:15), taken together with *charisma*, sums up the whole of God's saving work of pardon, justification and reconciliation (cf. also Eph. 2:8).

(e) God is praised as the giver of all good gifts in general (Jas. 1:17; cf. Matt. 7:11b etc.). All who call upon him for his gifts can do so with the utmost confidence (Matt. 7:7). Yet the one great gift which he gives to his church is his → Spirit (2 Cor. 1:22; 5:5; 1 Thess. 4:8; Lk. 11:13; cf. Acts 2:38; 8:17; 10:47; 19:6; also the OT quotations in Acts 2:17 f. [Joel 2:28 ff.] and Heb. 8:10 [Jer. 31:33]). In the church, all other "gifts" (usually *charisma*, → Grace) are the results of this one gift (Rom. 12:3 ff.; 1 Cor. 12:1 ff.; cf. also 2 Pet. 1:3). In the letters of Rev. 2 and 3 the gift of eternal life is promised to him who "overcomes" trial and temptation.

(f) *doma*, gift, occurs only at Matt. 7:11 (cf. Lk. 4:6); Eph. 4:8 (on the interpretation of this verse → Heaven, art. *anabainō*); and Phil. 4:17.

4. The man who has received Christ as a free gift, responds to the twofold → commandment (Matt. 22:37–40) by a twofold giving:

(a) He gives himself to God (cf. 2 Cor. 8:5 and similar passages). According to the NT, this is the only legitimate "offering" which can and should be brought by men to God (Rom. 12:1 and passim). It includes the "sacrifices" of word and deed (Heb. 13:15 f.; 1 Pet. 2:5), and may mean even the laying down of one's life for Christ (Phil. 2:17).

(b) He gives himself to other men, as required by the "new commandment" (Jn. 13:34). This shows itself in the first instance within the church, where the giving should be a reflection of God's giving. To give simply and without ulterior motives (Rom. 12:8) is the way in which God gives (Jas. 1:5). See also 2 Cor. 9:7 on God's love for the cheerful giver (*dotēs*, found only here in the NT); Mk. 12:41–44 = Lk. 21:1–4 (Jesus' verdict on the poor widow's gift); and the precepts of the Sermon on the Mount (Matt. 5:42; cf. Lk. 6:38). But the Christian, having first received the gift of the gospel, is concerned to pass this gift on to others. This is giving in its profoundest sense (Rom. 1:11; 1 Thess. 2:8; cf. Matt. 10:8b).

H. Vorländer

κορβᾶν

κορβᾶν (*korban*), corban, gift; κορβανᾶς (*korbanas*), temple treasury.

OT The Gk. word *korban* is transliterated from the Heb. *qorbān* and denotes a gift consecrated to God (Lev. 1:2; 22:27; 23:14; Num. 7:25; Ezek. 20:28; 40:43). Many scholars think that these passages reflect the outlook of post-exilic Judaism. The offerings mentioned include both sacrifices and gifts.

Later Judaism used the word in a more technical sense. Josephus mentions those who "dedicate themselves to God, as a corban, which denotes what the Greeks call a *gift*" (*Ant.* 4, 73; cf. *Ap.* 1, 167). Release from the vow could be obtained by payment of an appropriate sum. Rab. practice was formulated in the Mishnah in the tractate on Nedarim (Vows), see especially sections 1, 3, 8, 9, 11 and the developments in the Babylonian Talmud (Ned. 1:4; 2:2; and 3:2). The rabbis appear to be divided over the extent to which a gift vowed as corban (also later termed *kōnām*) was binding. The Mishnah indicates that most of them held that duty to one's parents constituted grounds for release from a gift vowed to God. (Ned. 9:1). The Babylonian Talmud attributed this view to the school of Shammai, whereas that of Hillel took the more rigorist view. "If anyone expressly lays such a corban on his relatives, then they are bound by it and cannot receive anything from him that is covered by the corban" (Ned. 3:2). The context of these pronouncements show that the question was not so much the handing over of certain things to God but their withdrawal from use by specified persons.

NT The rigorist position which permitted a man to neglect the care of parents on the grounds that the gift is dedicated to God as corban was denounced by Jesus according to Mk. 7:11 (The par. in Matt. 15:5 uses *dōron*, gift, offering, instead of the technical term *korban*.) The act is condemned as an act of hypocrisy in the words of Isa. 29:13 (cf. Mk. 7:6 f.; Matt. 15:7). The Pharisaic teaching on this point is characterized as "tradition" which makes void the → "word of God" (Mk. 7:13). The scribes might have claimed the support of Deut. 23:21 ff. and Num. 30:1 ff. in teaching that vows could not be broken. But they had allowed obligation to something that was relatively trivial to take precedence over a fundamental, humanitarian → command (in this case the Fifth Commandment [Exod. 20:12, par. Deut. 5:16]).

korbanas (Matt. 27:6; cf. Josephus, *War* 2, 175) denotes the temple treasury in which everything offered as *korban* (or the price of its redemption) was collected.

The chief priests declined to put into it Judas' thirty pieces of silver on the grounds that they were "blood money." C. Brown

→ First, → Fruit, → Grace, Spiritual Gifts

(a). B. Ahern, "The Indwelling Spirit, Pledge of our Inheritance", *CBQ* 9, 1947, 179–89; J. Behm, *arrabōn*, *TDNT* I 475; M. Black, *An Aramaic Approach to the Gospels and Acts*, 1967³, 139; F. Büchsel, *didōmi*, *TDNT* II 166–73; J. D. M. Derrett, "KORBAN, HO ESTIN DŌRON", *NTS* 16, 1969–70, 364–68; N. Q. Hamilton, *The Holy Spirit and Eschatology in St. Paul*, 1957, 17–40; J. H. A. Hart, "Corban", *JQR* 19, 1907, 615–50; C. C. Oke, "A Suggestion with Regard to Rom. 8:23", *Interpretation*, 2, 1957, 455–60; K. H. Rengstorf, *korban*, *TDNT* III 860–66; S. S. Smalley, "Spiritual Gifts and I Corinthians 12–16", *JBL* 87, 1968, 427–33.
(b). SB I 711.

Glory, Honour

Two different Gk. word-groups are represented by the Eng. words glory and honour. From classical Gk. onwards *timē* denoted recognition of another's work by giving him the position and honours he merited. It is always something given to God or one's fellow-man (though not necessarily one's social superior). *doxa* is often used as a synonym, but in the Bible it is a quality belonging to God and is recognized by man only in response to him. It is more often translated *glory*. It suggests something which radiates from the one who has it, leaving an impression behind. As such, it is in applicable to relationships between men.

δόξα

δόξα (*doxa*), radiance, glory, repute; *δοξάζω* (*doxazō*), praise, glorify; *ἔνδοξος* (*endoxos*), honoured, glorious; *ἐνδοξάζω* (*endoxazō*), honour, glorify; *συνδοξάζω* (*syndoxazō*), glorify together; *κενόδοξος* (*kenodoxos*), desirous of praise, conceited, boastful; *κενοδοξία* (*kenodoxia*), desire for praise, conceit, vanity, illusion.

CL This word-group affords one of the clearest examples of change in meaning of a Gk. word, when it came under the influence of the Bible. The basic meaning of *doxa* in secular Gk. is opinion, conjecture. This ranges from the opinion about a person or thing that I am prepared to defend to the valuation placed on me by others, i.e. repute, praise.

Accordingly, the noun *doxa* in secular Gk. means expectation, view, opinion, conjecture, repute, praise, fame. The vb. *doxazō* means: think, imagine, suppose, magnify, praise, extol (→ Think, art. *dokeō* NT).

OT 1. The concepts of *doxa* and *doxazō* were transformed in the LXX. This is shown, for example, by the fact that the original meaning "opinion" is not found. The meanings praise and honour are shared with secular Gk. But whereas *doxa* is seldom used for the honour shown to a man (for this *timē* is employed), it is frequently used for the honour brought or given to God (cf. e.g. Ps. 29:1; Isa. 42:12). This usage meant losing contact with secular Gk. The meaning of pomp, power, earthly majesty is based on OT (Isa. 17:4; 35:2; Hag. 2:3). But above all, *doxa* expresses God's glory and power (Pss. 24:7 ff.; 29:3; Isa. 42:8). In spite of the new reference of the words, the general structure of their meaning remains

44

unchanged, for in LXX also they are used for appearance, i.e. for the manifestation of a person, with special stress on the impression this creates on others. This aspect is essential for our understanding of the concept.

2. Behind this new meaning lies the Heb. OT concept of *kāḇôḏ*, glory, honour. The LXX represents this by *doxa* and gives it essentially the same meaning. When it is used of God, it does not mean God in his essential nature, but the luminous manifestation of his person, his glorious revelation of himself. Characteristically, *kāḇôḏ* is linked with verbs of seeing (Exod. 16:7; 33:18; Isa. 40:5), and appearing (Exod. 16:10; Deut. 5:24; Isa. 60:1). We may recognize this *kāḇôḏ* in creation (Ps. 19:1 [MT 19:2]; Isa. 6:3), but it expresses itself above all in salvation history, i.e. in God's great acts (Exod. 14:17 f.; Ps. 96:3), and especially in God's presence in the sanctuary (Exod. 40:34 f.; 1 Ki. 8:10 f.; Ps. 26:8), which can be conceived as fire (Lev. 9:23 f.; Ezek. 43:2; Exod. 24:17). In 1 Sam. 4:21 f. the loss of the ark of God to the Philistines meant that "The glory has departed from Israel". The event was reflected in the name Ichabod (*'íkāḇôḏ*, where is the glory?). The ark symbolized the divine presence which could not be borne (1 Sam. 5 f.; cf. Exod. 33:17–23). In the last days a full manifestation of the *kāḇôḏ* was expected. Its purpose was to bring salvation to Israel (Isa. 60:1 f.; Ezek. 39:21 f.), but also to convert the nations (Ps. 96:3–9; Zech. 2:5–11 [MT 2:9–15]). This glory is normally found only in God, though in Ezek. 8:2; 1:7, 13 and Dan. 10:5 f. angelic beings show some of its characteristics.

3. The inter-testamental period showed a strong interest in the heavenly world. The concept of glory is not confined, as in the OT, to God's self-revelation. It is also applied to the realities of heaven; God, his throne, and the angels. In such cases glory may be used with a watered-down meaning, as an epithet which may be applied in the language of liturgy and hymns to almost any concept which is linked with God. Of importance is the notion that → Adam in paradise possessed glory but lost it through the Fall (cf. G. Kittel, *TDNT* II 246; SB IV 940 ff., 1138). This led to the idea that men too could share in the glory (but cf. Exod. 33:17–23; 34:29–36).

In Qumran it was expected that the elect would "inherit all the glory of Adam" (1QH 17:15; cf. CD 3:20). Apocalyptic writings also specially stressed the sharing of the saved in glory, while the rabbis described salvation rather as the vision of the glory of God. More nationalistic concepts understood the eschatological revelation of glory one-sidedly as a glorification of Jerusalem and Israel. Isa. 60:1 ff. was used as a proof-text (cf. SB IV 894, 960). The nations would be drawn by the visible manifestation of glory, would stream to Jerusalem and would accept the faith of Israel.

NT A. 1. *doxa* is found 165 times in NT, 77 cases being in the Pauline epistles (including Rom. 16 times; 1 Cor. 12 times; 2 Cor. 19 times), it also figures prominently in the Petrine letters (1 Pet. 10 times; 2 Pet. 5 times), the Johannine writings (Jn. 18 times; Rev. 17 times), and Lk. (13 times), though the word-group is completely lacking in 1, 2 and 3 Jn. John (23 times) is the chief user of *doxazō*, found more than 60 times in all. For other forms see A.3.

2. The meaning of *doxa* and *doxazō* is a continuation of the LXX usage and the underlying Heb. (cf. OT 1, 2 above). As a result, the ideas of opinion and conjecture

are not found. We can separate the various shades of meaning as follows. The references given are representative instances.

(a) The meanings honour, fame, repute and in the case of the vb. to honour, praise, and the special uses to seek honour (Jn. 7:18; 8:50; 5:44; 1 Thess. 2:6) and to receive honour (Jn. 5:41, 44) belong to general Gk. usage. The specifically biblical connotation may be seen in expressions like "to give God glory" (Lk. 17:18 AV, RV; Acts 12:23; Rom. 4:20; Rev. 4:9; 11:13), "to the glory of God" (Rom. 15:7; 1 Cor. 10:31), in the so-called doxologies (Lk. 2:14; 19:38; Rom. 11:36; Gal. 1:5; Phil. 4:20; Eph. 3:21; 1 Tim. 1:17), and in application to Christ (Rom. 16:27; 2 Tim. 4:18; Heb. 13:21; 1 Pet. 4:11; 2 Pet. 3:18; Jude 25).

(b) When applied to men or earthly powers with the meaning of splendour, radiance, glory, *doxa* reflects OT usage: e.g. "all the kingdoms of the world and the glory of them" (Matt. 4:8 par. Lk. 4:6; Matt. 6:29; 1 Pet. 1:24).

(c) *doxa* in the sense of God's glory, majesty and power is pre-eminently the inheritance of the OT. The attempt to link it with Hel. usage (cf. Arndt. 202 f.) is untenable, for the magical texts quoted have themselves been influenced by Jewish thought. God is "the God of glory" (Acts 7:2), "the Father of glory" (Eph. 1:17), "the majestic glory" (2 Pet. 1:17). The expression "the glory of God" is frequent (e.g. Matt. 16:27; Acts 7:55; Rom. 1:23; 6:4; Eph. 3:16; 1 Tim. 1:11; Rev. 15:8). The → power of God can be mentioned along with his glory (Matt. 5:13 [many MSS]; Col. 1:11; 2 Thess. 1:9; Rev. 19:1). The concept is also applied to Christ: to his earthly life (Lk. 9:32; Jn. 1:14; 2:11; 1 Cor. 2:8), his exalted existence (Lk. 24:26; Jn. 17:5; Rom. 8:17; Phil. 3:21; 2 Thess. 2:14; 1 Tim. 3:16), his return (Matt. 16:27 par. Mk. 8:38, Lk. 9:26; Matt. 24:30 par. Mk. 13:26, Lk. 21:27; Tit. 2:13; 1 Pet. 4:13; Jude 24 [but this latter probably refers to the Father]), to his pre-existence (Jn. 12:41; 17:5) and also as an all-embracing epithet (Jn. 17:22, 24; 2 Cor. 3:18; 4:4, 6; 2 Thess. 2:14; cf. 1 Cor. 2:8).

The vb. also is used in a corresponding sense, especially in Jn. Its meaning oscillates between transfigure, cause to share in God's glory (Jn. 7:39; 12:16) and make the glory of God or of the Son effective (Jn. 11:4; 13:31 f.; 17:1, 4 f.).

(d) The NT also contains evidence of the concept which had been widespread since Ezekiel, that angels and other heavenly beings are endowed with glory (cf. OT 2, 3 above). This is found in manifestations from heaven, where stress is laid on the visible light, a concept taken from the concept of *kābôḏ* (Lk. 2:9; 9:31; Acts 22:11; Rev. 18:1). It is carried a step further when angelic powers are called *doxai* in Jude 8 and 2 Pet. 2:10 (cf. E.M.B. Green, *2 Peter and Jude*, 1968, 104 f., 168 f.). Paul is using Jewish language when he speaks of the *doxa* of the stars (1 Cor. 15:40 f.).

(e) When Paul speaks of the glory of the first man (1 Cor. 11:7; perhaps also Rom. 3:23) and explains the shining of Moses' face as the shining of the glory (2 Cor. 3:7, 13, 18; cf. Exod. 34:30) he is also using Jewish concepts (cf. C. K. Barrett, *The First Epistle to the Corinthians*, 1968, 252; *The Second Epistle to the Corinthians*, 1973, 115–126).

(f) Equally of Jewish origin is the important conception (cf. OT 3, above) that believers share in the glory (Jn. 17:22; 2 Cor. 3:18; Rom. 8:30 vb.) or will do so (Rom. 8:17; vb. 8:18, 21; 1 Cor. 2:7; 2 Cor. 4:17; Phil. 3:21; 1 Thess. 2:12; Heb.

2:10; 1 Pet. 5:1, 4, 10). The Christian hope is "the hope of glory" (Col. 1:27; cf. Eph. 1:18; 2 Thess. 2:14; 2 Tim. 2:10).

3. The other forms of the word-group need only brief mention. *syndoxazomai* (only Rom. 8:17), be glorified together with someone, has essentially the same meaning as 2 (f) above. *endoxazomai* (only 2 Thess. 1:10, 12) is synonymous with *doxazomai* in meaning to be recognized as glorious (cf. 2 (c)). The adj. *endoxos* (4 times) means glorious; in 1 Cor. 4:10 it is to be linked with 2 (a), in Lk. 7:25 with 2 (b), in Eph. 5:27 with 2 (f). Lk. 13:17 looks back to the OT concept that glory is revealed in the mighty acts of God (cf. OT 2). *kenodoxos* (only Gal. 5:26) and *konodoxia* (only Phil. 2:3) express the vain desire for honour. This meaning is not unknown in secular Gk., but it is in Christian literature that those words first find wider usage.

B. 1. For the Greeks fame and glory were among the most important values in life. The rabbis also had a high esteem for a man's honour. In Matt. 6:2 Jesus censured a piety which looks for honour from men. In Jn. 5:44 he stated that this attitude is incompatible with faith. Paul, following the example of Jesus (Jn. 5:41; 8:50; cf. Heb. 5:4 f.; 2 Pet. 1:17), did not seek glory from men (1 Thess. 2:6). He voluntarily accepted dishonour (2 Cor. 6:8; 4:10), strove to carry out his service to the honour of the Lord (2 Cor. 8:19 ff.), and looked to the honour and praise which Christ would give him as reward on his day (1 Thess. 2:19 f.; Phil. 2:16). Paul's statement that in the final judgment the righteous will receive "glory and honour and immortality" refers to eternal life itself (Rom. 2:7, 10; 5:2).

2. The glory of this world is depreciated in the light of eschatology (cf. NT A. 2 (b) above). Jesus, however, could also see the glory of the creation (Matt. 6:29; par. Lk. 12:27).

3. The highest duty of man is to glorify and praise God in worship, word and act (Matt. 5:16; Rom. 1:21; 1 Cor. 6:20; 10:31). In the doxologies (cf. NT A. 2 (a) above) there is no clear indication as to whether we should add the ind. or subj. of the vb. to be. 1 Pet. 5:11 suggests the former.

4. In the contexts mentioned under 1 and 3 *doxa* can in general be rendered honour. In such cases *timē* may be used as a synonym. Occasionally the two words are used together. We can, however, always hear the overtone of glory when honour is given to God and in similar settings (cf. NT A. 2 (a) above), for it must include the recognition of God's glory.

(a) The NT concept of glory shows an important expansion of the OT concept of *kāḇôḏ* in certain directions. This is due to the NT eschatological outlook. In the NT glory means the divine-eschatological reality or manner of existence. Salvation lies in man and nature having a share in this manner of existence.

(b) This concept does not, however, cancel the link with the OT *kāḇôḏ*. For glory manifests itself in the NT, just as in the OT, in the operation of God's power and salvation in "salvation history". It appears above all in Christ and his work of salvation (Matt. 17:2–5 par. Mk. 9:2–7, Lk. 9:29–35; Jn. 1:14; 2:11; 2 Cor. 4:4, 6), in believers (Jn. 17:22; 2 Cor. 3:18; Eph. 1:18; 3:16; Col. 1:11), and indeed already in the old covenant (2 Cor. 3:7–11). Just as in the OT, glory is partly linked with God's action (Rom. 6:4) and is partly an attribute of his being (cf. NT A. 2 (c)). The presence of this "personal" *doxa* of God in Christ means the presence of salvation (Jn. 1:14; 17:22; 2 Cor. 4:4, 6).

(c) The expectation of a revelation of glory at the end of time (cf. OT, 2 above) is also derived from the OT. The thought in both Judaism and the NT that the eschatological glory will take the believers and the whole creation up into itself by a new creation or transfiguration is, however, new (Rom. 8:18, 21; 1 Cor. 15:43; 2 Cor. 3:18; 4:17; Phil. 3:21; Col. 3:4; 1 Pet. 5:1). Nevertheless, the concept had been anticipated by Isa. 66:19, 22.

(d) The way in which heaven is included in this concept is important for the understanding of the NT idea of glory. Heaven in the NT is not, as was later generally believed, the permanent and final scene for the revelation of glory. Glory reveals itself from heaven, but its goal is the transfiguration of the created world and mankind. It takes place in the transformed creation. Significantly the eschatological glory appears in a revelation from heaven (Matt. 24:30; Phil. 3:20 f.; Col. 3:4; Rev. 21:10 f.).

(e) Glory with its transforming power is operative even now among believers (2 Cor. 3:18; Rom. 8:30; cf. (b) and NT A. 2 (f) above) through the resurrection of Christ and our fellowship with him, who is "the first fruits of those who have fallen asleep" (1 Cor. 15:20).

5. It is a matter of debate whether Jn. shares this outlook. But here too glory is to be understood as a revelation of God, or as the intervention of his power in history (Jn. 1:14; 2:11; 11:4; 12:41). We can hardly interpret the relatively strong diminution of interest in eschatology in this gospel as meaning that heaven has replaced the eschatological completion as the goal of all that exists. The glorification of Jesus is not accomplished merely by his entry into heaven; it becomes a reality by his sufferings, death, resurrection (Jn. 12:23–28), and finally by the witness of the Spirit (Jn. 14:16). In other words it is a parallel concept to the "righteousness" of Jesus (Jn. 16:8–11; cf. 1 Tim. 3:16).

6. The transfiguration of Jesus (Matt. 17:1–8 par. Mk. 9:2–8, Lk. 9:28–36) corresponds in the Synoptics to the continuing possession of *doxa* in Jn., though only in Lk. 9:32 does the narrative use this word. The transfiguration is a parallel on a higher plane to Moses' meeting with God on Mount Sinai (Exod. 24:15 ff.; 33:18–34:35). However, it is not to be understood, as in the case of Moses, as merely a reflection caused by temporary contact with the heavenly world, but rather as a revelation of the glory which Jesus possessed continually but not openly. We can deduce this from the fact that the transfiguration preceded the voice from heaven. At his parousia Jesus will be revealed in his glory and power (Matt. 19:28 par. Lk. 22:30; 24:30). *S. Aalen*

| τιμή |

τιμή (*timē*), price, value, honour, respect; τιμάω (*timaō*), set a price on, honour; ἀτιμία (*atimia*), shame, dishonour, disgrace; ἄτιμος (*atimos*), despised, dishonoured; ἀτιμάζω (*atimazō*), dishonour, treat shamefully; ἔντιμος (*entimos*), respected, honoured, valuable, precious.

CL 1. The word *timē* (from the *Iliad* on) is used in secular Gk. with the following main meanings: (a) worship, esteem, honour (used of people); (b) worth, value, price (of things); (c) compensation, satisfaction, penalty.

2. In Gk. thought *timē* is the proper recognition which a man enjoys in the community because of his office, position, wealth etc., and then the position itself,

the office with its dignity and privileges. The *timē* of a person, state, or deity must be distinguished from that of another. It is a personal possession. Slaves had no *timē*.

3. Every deity was shown honour because of the sphere of influence he controlled. This was done by sacrifice and hymns of praise. The gods on their part "honoured" men by giving them their earthly positions of honour and good fortune.

4. Shame and dishonour (*atimia*) put a person outside the community. *atimia* was the technical term for the deprivation of a citizen's rights.

5. The Stoics (cf. Epictetus) tried to rise above insult and disgrace by pretending that they did not touch the true self but only the body and visible possessions. Honour derived from position, such as that of a king, was regarded as a matter of indifference. They found fault, however, with the disgraceful treatment of slaves.

OT 1. (a) In contrast to its use of *doxa*, the LXX seldom uses *timē* for God's honour. Normally it applies *timē* to human honour, although both words usually render Heb. *kābōd*. Man has a position of honour in the creation (Ps. 8:3–8 [4–9]). Honour and position of office belong together (cf. *timaō* beside *archē* in Ps. 139:17 [LXX 138:17]). Honour should be shown to parents (Exod. 20:12; Sir. 3:3–16), the old (Lev. 19:32), to kings and the mighty (Dan. 2:37; Job 34:19 LXX). The rabbis stressed the honour due to a teacher of the law, and also one's neighbour including the poor (cf. also Prov. 14:21, 31 [LXX]; Sir. 10:23) and Jewish slaves, but not to Canaanite ones. There was a difference of opinion about the honour to be shown to a non-Israelite.

(b) A man marked out by honour might expect a corresponding position, wealth (Gen. 31:1 LXX; Isa. 16:14 LXX), and influence (Job 29:20; 30:4, 8, LXX – sometimes *doxa* is used in such passages). A worthy appearance (2 Sam. 10:5 LXX; Isa. 53:3), fitting speech (Sir. 5:13; cf. Job 29:21–25), and generosity (Prov. 22:9, LXX) also went with it.

2. (a) The godless experience *atimia* (Isa. 10:16 LXX; Jer. 23:40; cf. Dan. 12:2). The people did not grasp where the deepest dishonour lay, i.e. in faithlessness to God (Jer. 6:15), and this had to be recognized (Ezek. 16:63).

(b) For the godly in the OT there was the problem of how dishonour could come to them (Job 10:15; 30:1–12). Only the → Servant of the Lord bears shame patiently (Isa. 53:3) and leaves his cause in God's hand. Judaism ascribed an atoning value to the death of the martyrs and regarded it as honourable (4 Macc. 1:10;17:20; Josephus, *War* 2, 151). The pious rejected the scorn of the godless as something derived from a false outlook. The true basis of honour is not earthly prosperity but virtue and wisdom (Wis. 3:14–5:5). Mankind should be honoured provided that the fear of the Lord is there (Sir. 10:19). A sublimation and restriction of the concept of honour may be detected here. Apart from Isa. 53, no positive value was given to shame.

NT 1. The word-group is not strongly represented in the NT. *Timē* is found 41 times, *timaō* 21 times, the other forms more rarely. Only Paul uses *atimia*.

2. (a) Only the positive forms are used in the sense of price, sum of money: e.g. *timē* (price) in 1 Cor. 6:20; *timaō* (to set a price on) in Matt. 27:9 ("the price of him on whom a price had been set by some of the sons of Israel"); and *entimos* (precious) in 1 Pet. 2:4, 6.

(b) The meaning of *timaō* in the sense of show honour is rare (e.g. Acts 28:10 (RSVmg)). It is not clear whether *timē* should be rendered honour or honorarium, i.e. remuneration in 1 Tim. 5:17 (cf. Sir. 38:1; so J. N. D. Kelly, *The Pastoral Epistles*, 1963, 125).

(c) Generally *timē* represents the recognition of the dignity of an office or position in society. Examples are the authorities (Rom. 13:7; 1 Pet. 2:17), owners of slaves (1 Tim. 6:1), a wife (1 Pet. 3:7), the sexes in general (1 Thess. 4:4), service in the church (cf. 4 (c) below). In Heb. 5:4 *timē* means the honour of a position or the position itself (cf. 1 Pet. 1:17). The honouring of God is uppermost in the doxologies, where both *doxa* and *timē* occur (1 Tim. 1:17; 6:16; Rev. 4:11). For the vb. cf. also Jn. 5:23, 8:49. Honour should be shown to all men (1 Pet. 2:17).

(d) *timē* is used for exaltation in the ultimate eschatological salvation (Rom. 2:7, 10; 1 Pet. 1:7; 2:7; Jn. 12:26).

3. (a) In the case of *atimos* the negative aspect sometimes receives less stress. It can mean without honour, unhonoured, less honourable (1 Cor. 12:23). In 1 Cor. 4:10 it is stronger, and means despised.

(b) *atimazō* means to handle shamefully, with or without physical maltreatment: e.g. the tenants of the vineyard (Mk. 12:4 par. Lk. 20:11), the treatment of the apostles by the Sanhedrin (Acts 5:41), the poor (Jas. 2:6).

(c) *atimia* is generally translated in the NT by dishonour, e.g. of a man's long hair (1 Cor. 11:14; RSV "is degrading"), of the dead body (1 Cor. 15:43), of the apostles "in honour and dishonour" (2 Cor. 6:8). RSV renders *atimia* by "ignoble" in 2 Tim. 2:20 which speaks of various kinds of vessels.

(d) None of the uses deviates from secular Gk. A deepening ethical sense can be found in Rom. 1:26, where under the OT influence *atimia* means "shameful" (NEB, cf. v. 24 where *atimazomai* is rendered "degradation"). In secular Gk. *aischros* (cf. Lat. *turpis*) could be used in such contexts.

4. (a) As in Gk. society and the OT, *timē* is also used in the context of the social order decreed by God. *timē* is respect for the standing and task of a person who has his place in this order. When it is applied to things, it means the recognition of the value something has according to recognized norms. It may be summarized by saying that *timē* is high valuation based on position in an organized whole. This whole is God's world of men, animals and things. The distinctive distribution of honour among things of varying worth is important. The resultant order and grades of honour must be respected not only by the one placed lower, but also by the one placed higher. While the wife is placed below her husband, but she is to receive full honour from her husband (1 Pet. 3:1, 7).

(b) Things and animals have no honour. In the ancient world this was true also of slaves (though both the Stoics and the NT judge otherwise), because they had no right to direct their lives; they were looked on as things which had *timē* in the sense only of value or worth. Even this was not inherent, but was placed on them by their owner.

(c) The Biblical teaching about natural relationships, e.g. man and wife, parents and children, the authorities (see above NT 2(c), OT 1(a)), was developed from this. The same principle was applied to church life. Honour was to be shown the elders (1 Tim. 5:17, but see above 2(b)), widows (1 Tim. 5:3), and the responsible leaders of the congregation in general (Phil. 2:29). It is noteworthy, however, that this hierarchical line is crossed by one offering honour to those on a lower level. Those who carry out the lowest services should be shown particular honour (1 Cor. 12:23 f.; cf. the admonition to show mutual honour, Rom. 12:10). Those who carry out their service in purity are all vessels for honour (2 Tim. 2:20).

(d) Man's intrinsic honour is based on his position of dominion in creation (Ps. 8:5–8 [MT 8:6–9]). To that extent it is conferred by his status in the structure. However, it is also derived from man's being formed in the → image of God which determines his essential nature. All men should be honoured (1 Pet. 2:17; cf. Rom. 12:10; this was also the teaching of the Stoics, though they did not base it on the *imago Dei*). Hence slaves were members of the church (1 Cor. 12:13; 7:22 f.; Eph. 6:9), just as much as non-Israelites. In the church the restoration of the image of God has once more become universally possible (Col. 3:10 f.).

(e) This does not lead, as it did with the Stoics, to the reduction in principle of all to the same level and to the refusal of special honour to those holding office. The uniqueness of the NT concept of honour lies in the universal claim to honour because of the *imago Dei*. At the same time honour is given to office in its various expressions. The honour of man and the honour of office are not mutually exclusive any more than are the honour of man and the honour of God. True enough, preference for one side or the other must sometimes be shown in definite cases, e.g. in the relationship between husband and wife (1 Cor. 11:2 ff.) where Paul seems to see a special aspect of the image of God in the man (vv. 7,14), i.e. presumably the gift of leadership. (Elsewhere the subjection of the wife is counter-balanced by the love of the husband which becomes a reciprocal subjection [Eph. 6:21–33; Col. 3:18 ff.].)

(f) According to the NT, therefore, the Christian must not despise any class of man. He must, however, be willing to bear personal dishonour. This is not because it was not real suffering as the Stoics thought. The NT agrees with the Stoic and Jewish Wisdom Literature, in contrast with the early Israelite, that material possessions and wealth no longer constitute a basis for honour. Hence to lose them is in itself nothing to be ashamed of. On the other hand, the NT does not reduce the ground for honour, as did the Stoics, to an inner quality, such as virtue or wisdom. Dishonour, through being despised or suffering physical violence, must be borne for the sake of love after the pattern shown by Christ (Isa. 53:3–8; 1 Pet. 2:23 f.; Heb. 12:2; 1 Cor. 4:10). It is to be endured by the power of God (2 Cor. 6:7 f.), and is made less bitter by the hope of eternal life and glory (1 Pet.1:7; Heb. 12:2; 1 Cor. 15:43; 2 Cor. 4:17, cf. 4:8). All this presupposes that it is as a righteous person that one suffers shame (1 Pet. 3:13, 17).

(g) The dishonour caused by sin, disgrace and degradation is something quite different (Rom. 1:24, 26). Sin of this kind is not regarded simply as a moral lapse. The shame lies essentially in the fact that the man has fallen from the honour given him by God in creation and has misused his body. Honour is also lost not only by perversions but by false asceticism (Col. 2:23).   *S. Aalen*

On *doxa*:
(a). I. Abrahams, *The Glory of God*, 1925; G. R. Berry, "The Glory of Jahweh and the Temple", *JBL* 56, 1937, 115–17"; L. H. Brockington, "The Presence of God, a Study of the Use of the Term 'Glory of Yahweh'", *ExpT* 57, 1945, 21–25; and "The Septuagintal Background to the New

Testament use of *doxa*" in D. E. Nineham, ed., *Studies in the Gospels: Essays in Memory of R. H. Lightfoot*, 1955, 1–8; G. B. Caird, "The Glory of God in the Fourth Gospel: An Exercise in Biblical Semantics", *NTS* 15, 1968–69, 265–77; G. H. Davies, "Glory", *IDB* II 410 ff.; C. H. Dodd, *The Interpretation of the Fourth Gospel*, 1953, 201–13; A. H. Forster, "The Meaning of *doxa* in the Greek Bible", *Anglican Theological Review*, 12, 1929–30, 311–16; D. M. Hay, *Glory at the Right Hand: Psalm 110 in Early Christianity*, 1974; D. Hill, "The Request of Zebedee's Sons and the Johannine DOXA-Theme", *NTS* 13, 1966–7, 281–5; E. Jacob, *Theology of the Old Testament*, 1958, 79–82; G. Kittel and G. von Rad, *dokeō, doxa* etc., *TDNT* II 232–55; H. G. May, "The Departure of the Glory of Yahweh", *JBL* 56, 1937, 309–21; J. Morgenstern, "Biblical Theophanies", *Zeitschrift für Assyriologie und verwandte Gebiete* 25, 1911; 139–93; A. M. Ramsey, *The Glory of God and the Transfiguration of Christ*, 1949; A. Richardson, *An Introduction to the Theology of the New Testament*, 1958, 64–67, 182 ff.; C. Ryder Smith, *The Bible Doctrine of Man*, 1951, 116–23 and 223–29.

(b). S. Aalen, *Die Begriffe "Licht" und "Finsternis" im Alten Testament, im Spätjudentum und im Rabbinismus*, Skrifter utg. av Det Norske Vitenskaps-Akad. i Oslo, Hist.-filos. Kl. 1, 1951; H. Baltensweiler, *Die Verklärung Jesu*, 1959; H. Bietenhard, *Die himmlische Welt im Urchristentum und Spätjudentum*, 1951; W. Caspari, *Die Bedeutungen der Wortsippe kbd im Hebräischen*, 1908; H. J. Duplacy, "L'espérance de la gloire de Dieu dans l'Ancien Testament", *Bible et Vie Chrétienne* 8, 1954; A. von Gall, *Die Herrlichkeit Gottes*, 1900; F. Hesse and E. Fascher, "Herrlichkeit Gottes", *RGG³* III 273 ff.; H. Kittel, *Die Herrlichkeit Gottes*, 1934; E. Larsson, *Christus als Vorbild*, 1962, 275 ff.; A. Laurentin, *Doxa:* I *Problèmes de Christologie: Études des Commentaires de Jean 17.5 depuis des Origines jusqu' à Thomas d'Aquin;* II *Dossier des Commentaires de Jean 17.5*, 1972; J. Schneider, *Doxa, Neutestamentliche Forschungen* III/3, 1932; B. Stein, *Der Begriff kᵉḇôḏ Jahwe und seine Bedeutung für die alttestamentliche Gotteserkenntnis*, 1939; M. Steinheimer, *Die "Doxa tou Theou" in der römischen Liturgie*, 1951; C. Westermann, *kbd, THAT* I 794–812.

On *timē*:
(a). Arndt, 825; G. W. Harrelson, "Honor", *IDB* II 639 f.; J. Pedersen, *Israel, its Life and Culture*, I–II, 1926, 213–44; R. Schnackenburg, *The Moral Teaching of the New Testament*, 1965 (see index); J. Schneider, *timē, TDNT* VIII 169–80.

(b). M. Greindl, *Kleos, Kydos, Euchos, Timē, Phatis, Doxa*, Dissertation, Munich, 1938; K. Keyssner, *Gottesauffassung und Lebensauffassung im griechischen Hymnus, Würzburger Studien zur Altertumswissenschaft* 2, 1932; B. Reicke, "Zum sprachlichen Verständnis von Kol. 2, 23", *StTh* 6, 1952, 39–53 (especially 47–51); R. Reitzenstein, *Die hellenistischen Mysterienreligionen*, 1927³, 252 ff.; G. Steinkopf, *Untersuchungen zur Geschichte des Ruhmes bei den Griechen*, Dissertation, Halle, 1937.

Goal, Near, Last, End, Complete

Gk. and Buddhist thought has a cyclical understanding of the world in terms of eternal, circular movement. By contrast, Christianity developed a fundamentally historical understanding of the world in which existence began with → creation and will reach its consummation at the end of the world. Beginning and end, primal time and final time are not poles in a continuous process divorced from → time, separated only by interludes of human activity. According to the Christian understanding of the → beginning, the path of history which began with creation will lead to a final consummation. This is the goal and destiny of creation which will contain more than was given at the beginning. These ideas find expression in the NT statements about the *telos*, the goal and end of the divine purposes. Paul uses the the noun *skopos* (goal) which is attested only in Phil. 3:14. The adverbs *engys* (near) and *makran* (far) and the adj. *eschatos* (last) are basically designations of place. They have acquired a temporal sense particularly in the LXX and the NT.

In biblical language *engys* frequently denotes temporal proximity, whereas *eschatos* is applied chiefly to the final times and the last day.

ἐγγύς

ἐγγύς (*engys*), near; ἐγγίζω (*engizō*), approach, come near; μακράν (*makran*), far.

CL 1. In secular Gk. the adv. *engys* (used from Homer onwards as the opposite of *makran* and *porrō*, far) means: (a) near (in space), near by (e.g. Thuc, 3, 55, 1); (b) near in the sense of temporally imminent (e.g. Epict., *Dissertationes* 3, 26, 6); (c) with numbers, nearly (e.g. Xen., *Hell.* 2, 4, 32); (d) related or similar (e.g. Plato, *Phd.* 55a; *Rep.* 3, 319e); (e) in the figurative sense of intellectual proximity (e.g. Epict., *Dissertationes* 1, 2, 14).

2. The later vb. *engizō* (Aristot. onwards), trans. to bring near, occurs mostly intrans. meaning to approach, to come near (e.g. Polyb. 4, 62, 5), occasionally with the addition "(to) the gods" (e.g. Epict., *Dissertationes* 4, 11, 3).

OT In the LXX *engys* mostly translates the Heb. *qārōḇ*. *engizō* translates forms of *qārab*, draw near, approach, and *nāḡaš*, draw near, approach. The words are often found alongside the opposites *makran*, far, and *makrothen*, from afar, which render formations from the stem *rāḥaq*, to withdraw.

1. (a) In the spatial sense *engizō* is frequently found in phrases which describe approach to cultic centres (e.g. Exod. 3:5). Only the priests who conform to the requirements of the cultic prescriptions can draw near Yahweh's sanctuary (Lev. 21:21, 23; Ezek. 40:46; cf. Ezek. 44:13). *engizō* can also denote more generally participation in worship (Isa. 29:13; Ecc. 4:17) and even a devout attitude of nearness to God (Ps. 119:169; Hos. 12:7 [EVV v. 6]).

(b) Like *makran* (distant, far), *engys* (near) can also characterize the approval of Yahweh. It is one of the distinctive characteristics of the God of Israel, who can also work from afar (Ps. 136:8; 139:2), to draw near to his people. "What great nation is there that has a god so near to it as the Lord our God is to us, whenever we call upon him?" (Deut. 4:7; cf. also Ps. 34:19; Jer. 23:23 LXX). The nearness of God is not understood as a static condition, but as the free divine act of approaching (*theos engizōn*). It is experienced above all in Israelite worship (cf. Ps. 145:18).

(c) The pair of words "the near and the far" (Deut. 13:7; Isa. 33:13; 57:19; Ezek. 6:12) is a description of totality, meaning and embracing all. Later on in Judaism *engys*, near, marks out the Israelite as distinct from non-Israelites, and within Israel the righteous as distinct from the godless. For the meaning next of kin, one's relative, cf. Lev. 21:2 f.; Job 6:15; Est. 1:14 (→ Brother).

2. As an indication of time, the word-group expresses the imminent approach of the Day of Yahweh. In opposition to the way of thinking that saw that day in the far distance (cf. the quotations in Isa. 5:19; Ezek. 12:22, 27; Amos 6:3), the prophets proclaimed its nearness. This day always brings with it the impending judgment (Isa. 13:6; cf. also Ezek. 7:7; 30:3; Joel 1:15; 2:1; Zeph. 1:7, 14) which occasions darkness and terror. Only the later chapters of Isa. announce the approach of a new age of salvation which will bring forth salvation and righteousness (Isa. 46:13; 50:8; 51:5; 56:1).

3. The priestly language of the OT lived on, albeit transformed in meaning, in the Qumran literature. The community viewed itself in a priestly light. One who

comes to the community may thus draw near to God. The words "come near" and "send away" (in the case of refusal) became technical terms for entrance into the community (cf. 1 QS 6:16, 19, 22). In a similar way, "to come near" is a technical expression in Rab. Judaism for the recruiting of a proselyte.

NT The vb. *engizō*, to approach, to come near, is chiefly used in the NT by the Synoptics and Acts with its original meaning. Paul and Heb. use it more rarely, and in John it is not found at all. The adv. *engys*, near, also occurs most frequently in the Synoptics. There are a number of instances in John, but Paul scarcely uses it at all.

1. (a) In the *spatial* sense *engys*, near, is used a greater number of times than *engizō*, to come near. In Acts and Jn. the adv. *engys* has almost exclusively a local meaning (e.g. Acts 1:12, "which is near to Jerusalem"; Jn. 19:20, "was near to the city"). Occasionally the vb. serves to indicate both place and motion (e.g. Mk. 11:1 [cf. Matt. 21:1; Lk. 19:29], "when they drew near to Jerusalem").

(b) The terms are more frequently used with a temporal meaning: the hour of the passion has drawn near (Matt. 26:45), the end of all things has come near (1 Pet. 4:7), summer is near (Matt. 24:32), the Passover was near (Jn. 2:13).

2. (a) The theological interpretation of the vb. *engizō*, to come near, in the Synoptics is linked with Isa.'s proclamation of salvation: *ēngiken hē basileia tōn ouranōn*, the → kingdom of heaven has drawn near (Matt. 4:17 par. Mk. 1:15; Matt. 3:2; 10:7; Lk. 10:9, 11; cf. above OT 2). Behind the formulation *ēngiken*, it has drawn near, stands the thought of the divine → promise and preparation. The perf. *ēngiken* (the most frequently used tense of *engizō*) thus expresses the end of the time of preparation. God's kingdom *has* drawn near, i.e. in the proclamation and work of Jesus it *is* already in the present time. "Thus Mk. also sees Jesus' proclamation not as the first step of a coming kingdom, but as the consummation which has now made its appearance and become real here" (E. Lohmeyer, *Das Evangelium des Markus*, 1967 [17], KEK I, 2, 30). Corresponding to *ēngiken*, has drawn near, is the negative formulation *ou makran*, not far, which expresses the overcoming of the separation between God and man (e.g. Mk. 12:34).

(b) *engys* and *engizō* are also used in the context of the awaited apocalyptic end-time and the return of the → Son of man. Lk. in particular awaits the future of the all-embracing → kingdom of God. The desolation of Judaea and cosmic catastrophes will announce the dawn of the end of the world (Lk. 21:20 ff.). "So with you when you see these things happening, know that the kingdom of God is near" (Lk. 21:31; cf. v. 28 "when these things begin to take place . . . your redemption is drawing near"). The connection between the dawn of the kingdom of God in the coming of Jesus and the awaited coming of the Son of Man in the establishment of the reign of God is brought out by Matt. and Mk. Apart from this, both use *engizō* only in connection with the fate of Jesus (Matt. 21:1 par. Mk. 11:1, Lk. 19:29; Matt. 26:46 par. Mk. 14:42). (On the time and character of these events → Generation; → Present, art. *parousia*.)

3. (a) Whereas in the Synoptics the vb. is used in both perf. and fut., expressing the consequent tension, Paul relates these terms exclusively to the future. In Rom. 13:12 and Phil. 4:5 the prospect of the approaching day and the coming Lord provide the basis for the admonitions to the Christians to live a life full of hope.

"If the deliverance is near, then it is the hour to wake up from sleep" (A. Schlatter, *Gottes Gerechtigkeit*, [1935] 1952, 359).

(b) The word-group in the Catholic Epistles and Heb. similarly refers to the near return of Christ and the imminent end of all things (Jas. 5:8; 1 Pet. 4:7; Heb. 10:25). Thus *engizō* in the NT designates almost exclusively the drawing near of God and of his salvation to men. Only Heb. 7:19 and Jas. 4:8 speak of a responsive drawing near of man to God. *W. Bauder, H.-G. Link*

ἔσχατος

ἔσχατος (*eschatos*), extreme, last, least; ἔσχατον (*eschaton*) (noun), end, (adv.) finally; ἐσχάτως (*eschatōs*), finally.

CL 1. (a) The adj. *eschatos*, attested from Hom. onwards, is a superlative form derived from the prep. *ek/ex*, out of, away from, and originally designated the person or thing that was furthest outside (*ex*). Spatially it meant the place furthest away (e.g. Hesiod, *Theog.* 731, the utmost ends of the earth), temporally the last events of a series (e.g. Hdt., 7, 107), materially the extreme, rarely the highest (e.g. Libanius, *Orationes* 59, 88, greatest wisdom), mostly the lowest place in order of rank (e.g. Plato, *Tht.* 209b; Diod. Sic. 8, 18, 31, the most miserable of men).

(b) Substantively *to eschaton* means the end in spatial and temporal respects (e.g. Hdt. 7, 140; 8, 52). Without the art. *eschaton* can be used just like *eschatōs* as an adv., both meaning "finally" (e.g. Xen., *Anab.* 2, 6, 1; *P.Oxy.* 886, 21).

2. The Gk. language uses the term *eschatos* to designate the end-point of a continuously conceived succession of circumstances. It corresponds with naturalistic Gk. thinking that the "extreme" is initially represented as the "ends of the earth" (Dem. *Ep.* 4, 7; Xen., *Vect.* 1, 6; Theocritus, 15, 8). In qualitative respects *eschatos* designates an extreme positive or negative intensification (Pindar, *Ol.* 1, 113, the highest reaches its peak with kings; Plato, *Rep.* 361a, greatest injustice; *Gorgias* 511d, extreme danger). In Aristotle the term denotes the conclusion of a logical path of thought and thus contributes to the systematization of the thought-processes (*An.* 3, 10, 433a, 16). As the expression of order of rank among men, *eschatos* means the opposite of *prōtos* (→ first): the lowest and most miserable of men (Dio Cass., 42, 5, 5; Dio Chrys., 21, [38] 37; Appian, *Bell.Civ.* 2, 77, §322). The temporal dimension is expressed in occasional prospects of the end (e.g. Diod. Sic., 19, 59, 6, the last, i.e. the concluding and final decision) and in the comprehensive designation of God as "the first and the last" (*prōtos kai eschatos*) e.g. Ps. Arist., *Mund.* 401a, 28). But this is the least developed sense. Gk. thought has no developed eschatological understanding of time, i.e. one directed towards a future goal or end of the historical process.

OT The very different historical understanding of existence in the OT writing is immediately apparent in a preliminary survey. *eschatos* occurs some 150 times in the LXX. It has local significance only in isolated cases (e.g. Deut. 28:49; Isa. 48:20; 49:6; Jer. 6:22, *ap'* or *heōs eschatou tēs gēs*, from or to the ends of the earth). It is not found at all in a disqualificatory sense. Its use is predominantly in the temporal sense to translate formations from the root of *'aḥar* (after, behind) and meaning last, finally, outcome, end. In the historical books the term plays no real

55

role, apart from the characteristic and stereotyped phrase "from beginning to end" (cf. 2 Chr. 16:11; 20:34; 25:26). On the other hand, *eschatos* features particularly in prophetic and apocalyptic expectations of the future.

1. A number of prophets use the formula "at the end of the days" (*be'aḥᵃrît hayyāmîm*, LXX *ep' eschatou tōn hēmerōn*, e.g. Hos. 3:5; Isa. 2:2; 41:23; Mic. 4:1; Jer. 23:20; 30:24; 49:39; Ezek. 38:16). This indicates the future-directed thinking of the prophets which pointed Israel's self-understanding – till then largely orientated around past events – in a totally new direction. Moreover, the context in which this formulation is found reveals that the prophets do not think of "the end of the days" in mythical or non-historical terms. It was a renewed historical time-span, the final or end-time. Finally, it is noteworthy that the formula is mostly encountered in announcements of salvation or prefacing them. Eschatological time will be stamped by Yahweh's saving activity. Yahweh will make it possible for his people to turn back (Hos. 3:5). He will destroy his enemies (Jer. 23:20; 30:24). The nations will come to Jerusalem and receive instruction from Israel (Isa. 2:2 ff.; Mic. 4:1 ff.). Salvation will penetrate "to the end of the earth" (Isa. 48:20; 49:6). Here the local significance has a universal eschatological function. In all this Yahweh will reveal himself as holy (Ezek. 38:16, 23). However much the individual pictures of salvation presented by the various prophets differ, the expectation of a comprehensive age of salvation "at the end of the days" brought in by Yahweh himself is common to them all.

2. Apocalyptic literature contains numerous allusions to the end of the days (e.g. Dan. 2:28, 45; 10:14; 2 Esd. 6:34; Syr. Bar. 6, 8). They are distinguished from the prophetic expectation by the progression from the more simple pictures of the future into the realm of the visionary, allegorical, and other-worldly. A certain element of calculation concerning the final times is discernible (Dan. 8:19 ff.; 10:14; 12:5 ff.; 2 Esd. 14:5). According to the apocalyptic outlook, dramatic battles will take place between various world-powers. There will be cosmic catastrophes in the final times, before Yahweh establishes his transcendent imperishable → kingdom (cf. especially Dan. 2:3 ff.; 7:17 ff.). The end of this world signifies the simultaneous beginning of the coming one (2 Esd. 6:7; 7:113).

In Rabbinic Judaism the calculation of the end (*qēṣ*) is concentrated on the arrival of the messiah (2 Esd. 12:32; cf. SB III 671; IV 1003, 1006).

The formula "the end of the days" (*'aḥᵃrît hayyāmîm*) is also found in the Dead Sea Scrolls (e.g. 1QpHab 2:5 f.; 9:9; CD 4:4; 6:11). The calculating tendency of apocalyptic has here hardened into a rigid deterministic understanding of the final time. It is the fixed and predetermined time of divine visitation (1QS 3:18, 23; CD 8:2 f.), when the godless and wickedness will be annihilated, but the righteous and truth will live for ever (1QS 4:18 ff.; 1QH 6:30 f.). It is not the saving character of the final times that stands in the foreground – as it does in the prophets – but the day of disaster, judgment and vengeance (1QS 10:18 ff.; CD 19:5–16). Only a small community of elect (4Qflor 1:19), "the poor of the flock" (CD 19:9), will be saved. By contrast with the expectations of Rab. Judaism, the members of the Qumran sect understand themselves as already the eschatological community of the saved in Israel (1QSa 1:1). It is they who obediently fulfil the divine regulations (CD 20:27 f.), and will be demonstrated to be the true Israel at the end of days (CD 20:33 f.).

NT As in the LXX, the spatial aspect of *eschatos* in the NT fades into the background. In Acts (1:8; 13:47) as in Isa. (see above OT 1) the spatial formula "to the end of the earth" (*heōs eschatou tēs gēs*) has a universal eschatological significance. More important are the material overtones of the least and lowest (e.g. Lk. 14:9), frequently in the antithesis of *prōtos* and *eschatos* (e.g. Mk. 9:35). But in the NT, the chief stress again falls on the temporal dimension of *eschatos*. On the one hand, it distinguishes the time characterized by the coming of Jesus from the past (e.g. Heb. 1:2). On the other hand, it contrasts the final future of God with the present (e.g. Jn. 11:24). *eschatos* is a concept which features in the Gospels (Matt. 10 times; Jn. 7 times). It also plays a particular role in Paul (6 times) and Rev.

1. The Synoptic Gospels record 4 times a maxim from the proclamation of Jesus about the first and the last (Mk. 10:31; Matt. 19:30; 20:16; Lk. 13:30). "Many who are first will be last, and the last first [*esontai prōtoi eschatoi kai eschatoi prōtoi*]." This maxim, formulated with inversion in antithetical parallelism, possibly meant originally something like: "How quickly man's fortunes change overnight" (cf. J. Schniewind on Mk. 10:31, *Das Evangelium nach Markus*, [1931] 1968, 136). In the mouth of Jesus this aphorism undergoes an eschatological radicalization as the conclusion of a discussion concerning the rewards of discipleship (Mk. 10:28–31 par.). The antithesis of first and last indicates a succession of rank customary amongst men (see above CL 2). The first are the nobles in society, kings and rulers; the last are the lowest, slaves and outcasts. The point of this *logion* of Jesus lies in the fact that in the coming age this order of precedence will be reversed. In the kingdom of God earthly power structures are stood on their head. God stands on the side of those who are the last and lowest on earth. To them, like the poor followers of Jesus, the kingdom of God is promised, whereas those who regard themselves as its first candidates, the noble, the rich and the pious, are excluded from it (Lk. 13:28 ff.; Matt. 8:11 f.). Jesus' followers are given the commission of anticipating and realizing now in the present this eschatological reversal of all values. It is in this sense that Jesus answers the disciples' disputes about seniority with the reminder: "If anyone wants to be first, let him be last of all and servant of all" (Mk. 9:35).

2. (a) Both the way of life and the proclamation of Paul are in accord with this instruction of Jesus. He counters the Corinthian enthusiasts by saying that God has paraded the apostles as the lowest of men, like those condemned to death, a spectacle and the scum of the world – not for ever but "to this day" (1 Cor. 4:9–13; → Dirt, art. *peripsēma, perikatharma*). This may be compared with 1 Cor. 15:8, where with the thought of negative quality is linked the significance of the chronological conclusion of the list of witnesses ("last of all") (cf. G. Kittel, *TDNT* II 697; → Birth, art. *ektrōma*).

(b) Within the framework of his Adam–Christ typology (cf. Rom. 5:12–21; 1 Cor. 15:21 f.) Paul contrasts in 1 Cor. 15:45 the first man → Adam (NT 3(e)) with Christ "the last Adam" (*eschatos Adam*). Adam and Christ are not here thought of as individual persons, but each as representatives of a whole humanity. The "last Adam" therefore does not mean the last man either numerically or chronologically, but – as the allusion to the gnostic primal man myth in v. 47 shows – Christ as the new, the second representative of a new humanity created in his image, by contrast with the first humanity summarised in Adam (cf. C. Colpe, *TDNT* VIII 474 ff.). Paul therefore understands the risen Christ, the creator of life, as the eschatological prototype of God's new humanity. With the resurrection of Jesus the final time has already begun.

(c) The letters of other authors confirm that this is not only a Pauline idea, but one belonging to early Christian eschatology generally. In Heb. 1:2 the prophetic expectation of the final times expressed in the formula *ep' eschatou tōn hēmerōn* ("in the last days", cf. above OT 1) is related to the present time of the early Christians by the addition of the demonstrative *toutōn* ("these", i.e. "in these last days"). This has come about through the fact that "God has spoken *to us* by a Son". With the enthronement of Jesus as → Son and as → Lord of → Creation the turning-point of the ages has come. Hebrews understands the early Christian present as the beginning of the final time. 1 Pet. also speaks of Christ "revealed at the end of the times" (1:20; cf. also Mk. 12:6), and 1 Jn. makes the recipients of his letter emphatically aware that they are living in the "last hour" (2:18). To the NT writers, the characteristics of the final time, now dawned, include the outpouring of the → Spirit (Acts 2:17; cf. Joel 2:28–32), the growth of moral corruption (2 Tim. 3:1 ff.), and the appearance of scoffers (2 Pet. 3:3; Jude 18) and → antichrists (1 Jn. 2:18).

(d) The term *eschatos* does not, however, serve merely to denote the new time which has begun with the coming of Jesus. It also refers to the final, consummative action of God that is still to come. In 1 Cor. 15:23 ff. Paul makes use of apocalyptic ideas (see above OT 2) in order to express the chronological sequence of the future events of the final times. In this scheme death is chronologically the last and physically the hardest enemy to be destroyed before the final goal (→ *telos*) of God is reached (v. 26 ff.).

3. Only in John's Gospel is explicit allusion found to the "last day" (*eschatē hēmera*, e.g. 6:39 f., 44, 54; 11:24; 12:48). It is absent from the synoptics. The expression takes up and continues the prophetic exposition of the "day of Yahweh" (on this see G. von Rad, *Old Testament Theology*, II, 1965, 119–125). R. Bultmann contends that these passages have been redacted by the early church (cf. his treatment of 6:27–59 in *The Gospel of John*, 1971, 218–34). But in view of the context (cf. 6:39 f.), and of the existential bent of his interpretation (e.g. on 11:24 f.), this must remain a hypothesis on the level of conjecture. The decisive mark of the "last day", according to the Johannine witness, is the resurrection of the dead. The judgment of unbelievers (12:48) represents the negative side of this. Thus in the expectation of the end in John's Gospel, as in the eschatological proclamation of the prophets (see above OT 1), it is not the thought of judgment, but the all-embracing salvation that stands in the foreground.

4. (a) The deterministic thinking about judgment in the Dead Sea Scrolls (see above OT 3) did not find acceptance in the NT. The only reminder of the conceptions of vengeance of the Qumran sect is the vision in Revelation of the seven last plagues, through which the divine wrath is discharged (15:1 ff.; 21:9; → Anger, Wrath). But the climax of this vision is not in the annihilation of enemies, but in the song of praise to the → Lamb (15:3; 19:7 ff.; 21:22).

(b) The formula "the first and the last" (*ho prōtos kai ho eschatos*) is only found as a self-designation of the exalted Christ (1:17; 2:8; 22:13). This goes back to the

Heb. wording of the divine predicates in Isa. 41:4; 44:6; 48:12. In the Gk. translation of this expression the LXX has avoided the divine title of *eschatos* and uses a paraphrase instead, perhaps because of negative undertones. The formula belongs essentially to the synonymous phrases "the Alpha and the Omega" (Rev. 1:8; 21:6; 22:13; Alpha being the first, and Omega the last letter of the Gk. alphabet), and "the beginning and the end" (22:13). The application of these divine predicates to the exalted Christ means the ascription to him of a rank equal with God's with the attribution of the functions of Creator and Perfecter. *H.-G. Link*

| τέλος |

τέλος (*telos*), end, conclusion, close, goal; τελέω (*teleō*), bring to an end, finish, complete, carry out, accomplish; τελειόω (*teleioō*), bring to completion, complete, accomplish, finish, fulfil, make perfect; τέλειος (*teleios*), complete, perfect; τελειότης (*teleiotēs*), perfection, maturity; τελείωσις (*teleiōsis*), perfection, fulfilment; τελειωτής (*teleiōtēs*), perfecter; συντέλεια (*synteleia*), completion, close, consummation; συντελέω (*synteleō*), bring to an end, complete, carry out, fulfil, accomplish; τελευτάω (*teleutaō*), come to an end, in the sense of die; τελευτή (*teleutē*), end, euphemism for death.

CL 1. (a) The noun *telos* is derived from a root *tel-*, which means to turn round (*telos* = tax; Dem., *Or.* 20, 19). Originally it meant the turning point, hinge, the culminating point at which one stage ends and another begins; later the goal, the end. Marriage is in this sense a *telos* (Artemidorus, *Onirocriticus* 2, 49; the spouse is *teleios*, complete, Pausanias 8, 22, 2), as also is death (Xen., *Institutio Cyri* 8, 7, 6; Plato, *Leg.* 4, 717e). *telos* can mean the completion of intellectual development (Plato, *Menexenus* 249a) and physical (Plato, *Leg.* 8, 834c) development, as the use of the term *teleios* also makes clear (Hdt. 1,183,2). *telos* can have dynamic character, and is used, for example, of the ratification of a law (Aristot., *Pol.* 6, 8p, 1322b, 13; cf. *teleō*, to bring to a *telos*, to complete, e.g. to make his word come true [Hom. *Il.* 14, 44]).

This dynamic character is also clear in the religious sphere, where sacrifices and religious rites are called *telē*; their intention is to bring men nearer to God (Soph., *Ant.* 143). Also of significance is the religious description of God as the *archē kai telos*, the beginning and end of all things (cf. K. Preisendanz, *Papyri Graecae Magicae*, IV, 2836 f.). He alone embraces beginning and end (Scythinos; cf. Diels I, 189, 32 f.). The function of the formula is thus to make a statement which embraces totality.

(b) Anything that has reached its *telos* is *teleios*, complete, perfect (e.g. unblemished sacrifical animals, Hom., *Il.* 1, 66). Both a doctor and a thief can be perfect (Aristot. *Metaph.* 4, 16p, 1021b, 15 ff.). One brings something to completion, to perfection (*teleioō*, e.g. Aristot., *Eth. Nic.* 3p, 1174a, 15 f.). The pass. of *teleioō*, to be made perfect, i.e. to reach perfection, is used equally of human adulthood (Plato, *Symp.* 192a) and of fully-grown plants (Aristot., *Gen. An.*, 776a, 31). The noun *teleiotēs* occurs only rarely. It denotes a state of completeness or perfection (e.g. Aristot., *Phys.*, 8, 7p, 261a, 36). *teleiōsis* is the carrying out of the *teleioun*, the realization, execution, conclusion (e.g. of some work [cf. W. Dittenberger, *Sylloge*

*Inscriptionum Graecarum*³ II, 799, 1, 29]). A *teleiōtēs* is one who effects the *teleioun*, the perfecter. This word is hitherto only once attested in Christian literature (Heb. 12:2).

2. In Gk. philosophy *telos* has the primary meaning of goal. For the pre-Socratics the goal of life was delight in the beautiful (Leucippus), contentment (*euthymia*, Democritus; cf. F. Copleston, *A History of Philosophy*, I, 1946, 125 f.), and contemplation (*theōria*, Anaxagoras, *Frag.* 29; cf. Diels II, 13,11). In Plato and Aristotle the *telos* to which one aspires is an ethical goal (Plato, *Rep.* 2 introduction; Aristot., *Eth. Nic.* introduction), and ultimately happiness and bliss (*eudaimonia*). In the realm of ethics, therefore, Plato can equate the concept of the perfect (*teleios*) with that of the good (*agathos*) (*Phlb.* 61a).

In gnosticism "perfection" is a technical term in the myth of the "redeemed Redeemer." He is the "perfect man" (cf. Hippol., *Haer.* 5, 7, 37). Anyone who is saved by him through true knowledge is the "perfect" gnostic (cf. Hippol., *Haer.* 5, 8, 30). Whether *teleios* was a technical term for initiates in the Hel. mystery religions is disputed (cf. the literature referred to by Arndt, 817).

οτ 1. (a) *telos* occurs more than 150 times in the LXX, chiefly in adverbial combinations. Thus *eis to telos*, for ever, is the puzzling and erroneous translation of the Heb. phrase *lamᵉnaṣṣēaḥ* in the heading of 55 Pss. and Hab. 3:19. It should probably be translated by "for the choirmaster" or "for musical performance" (cf. H.-J. Kraus, *Psalmen*, I, 5; cf. A. A. Anderson, *The Book of Psalms*, I, 1972, 48). *eis telos* is found more than 15 times as translation of *lāneṣaḥ*, for ever (e.g. Job 20:7; Ps. 9:7; Hab. 1:4). Starting from the basic meaning "to the finish," *eis telos* can mean utterly (e.g. 2 Chr. 12:12), or, when understood temporally, for ever (e.g. Job 23:7). Sometimes *eis telos* is used where there is no MT equivalent (e.g. Gen. 46:4; Ezek. 15:4). It is also of importance that *telos* occurs repeatedly as a translation of *qēṣ*, *qāṣeh* or *qᵉṣāṯ*, end, border, boundary. In such cases it means conclusion, end (cf. 2 Sam. 15:7; 2 Ki. 8:3). *qēṣ* in the eschatological sense is translated in the LXX not by *telos*, but by *synteleia*, completion (see below, 2(a)).

(b) *teleō* is found some 30 times for 8 Heb. equivalents: most frequently (7 times) for the vb. *kālâh* (qal and piel) meaning to bring to an end, to fulfil (e.g. Ruth 2:21; Ezra 9:1). It occurs in the pass. as a religious term: to consecrate oneself (e.g. to the service of Baal Peor, cf. Num. 25:3, 5; Ps. 105:28; Hos. 4:14).

(c) *teleios* is attested 20 times in the LXX: 7 times as equivalent of the Heb. root *šālēm*, to be sound, and 7 times for *tām(îm)*, complete, sound. The stress lies on being whole, perfect, intact. It is used of the heart which is wholly turned towards God (1 Ki. 8:61; 11:4), and of the man who has bound himself wholly to God (Gen. 6:9; cf. Deut. 18:13). The thought of totality is also shown in the mention of a total depopulation (Jer. 13:19), and in the fact that whole-offerings can be called *teleiai* (Jdg. 20:26; 21:4).

(d) *teleioō* (25 instances) has likewise the semantic content of being perfect and whole: to show oneself perfect, i.e. blameless (2 Sam. 22:26, hith. of *tāmam*; cf. Sir. 31:10); to make beauty perfect (Ezek. 27:11). It is used 9 times in the Pentateuch as a religious term (apart from Lev. 4:5) to translate the Heb. phrase *millē'* (*yāḏ*), to fill (the hand), i.e. to consecrate for the cult (e.g. Exod. 29:9, 29). But *teleioō* also means to bring to its conclusion (2 Chr. 8:16; Neh. 6:16).

(e) *teleiotēs* (occurring only 5 times) can also be an equivalent for formations from the root *tām* signifying perfection or integrity (Jdg. 9:16, 19; Prov. 11:3). Wis. 6:15 speaks of perfection of understanding.

(f) *teleiōsis* (16 times in the LXX) occurs mainly in connection with cultic usage. On 10 occasions it translates *millû'îm* (e.g. Exod. 29:22, 26; cf. (d)) and means consecration. It occurs chiefly in connection with the consecration of priests.

2. (a) In the apocalyptic literature of the OT the Heb. *qēṣ* is understood eschatologically (see above 1 (a)). The LXX translates it chiefly by *synteleia*, end, completion (e.g. Dan. 8:19; 11:27). In this eschatological sense *qēṣ* in Rab. literature refers chiefly to the days of the messiah's coming which were ordained before the end of the world (cf. SB I 671; III 416). The end of the world can also be spoken of idiomatically in the sense of going on for ever (e.g. Yeb. 1:1; Nazir. 1:3).

(b) In Qumran the use of *qēṣ* as an eschatological technical term is not attested. The final times are called *haqqēṣ hā'aḥᵃrôn*, the last time (1 QpHab 7:7, 12; cf. also the expression *gᵉmar haqqēṣ*, the consummation of time, 1QpHab 7:2). Otherwise *qēṣ* means time, period, in general.

In Qumran the term "perfect" is coloured by the OT. Those who are perfect (*tāmîm*) are those who keep God's law wholly and so walk perfectly in his ways (1QS 1:8; 2:2). In a narrower sense the members of the community are called "the perfect" (1QS 8:20; cf. 8:4 ff.).

(c) Philo has a double *telos* in the life of man: → wisdom (*sophia*), i.e. the perfect and direct understanding of God which comes about by learning, and → virtue (*aretē*) which is attained by practice (cf. W. Völker, *Fortschritt und Vollendung bei Philo von Alexandrien*, 1938, 176 f., 203 ff.). He has three stages on the way to perfection: beginners, advanced and perfect (*Leg. All.* 3, 159). To Philo repentance holds second place to perfection (*teleiotēs*) and the "unbroken perfection of virtues stands nearest to divine power" (*Abr.* 26). Both Philo (*Plant.* 93) and Josephus (*Ant.* 8, 280) have the comprehensive description of God as *archē kai telos*, beginning and end (see above, CL 1 (a)).

NT In the NT the words of this group occur fairly often: *telos* 41 times, *teleō* 28 times, *teleios* 20 times, *teleioō* 23 times, *teleiotēs* twice, *teleiōtēs* once (Heb. 12:2) and *teleiōsis* twice. A striking point is that *telos* occurs relatively frequently in the Synoptics and Paul, *teleō* particularly in the Synoptics and in Rev., whereas *teleios* and its derivatives are more common in Heb. than in any other NT writing.

1. *The Letters of Paul.* (a) Paul uses *telos* to mean end-result, ultimate fate (cf. G. Delling, *telos*, *TDNT* VIII 55). Rom. 6:21 f. speaks of the alternatives which face man as a result of his conduct: death (v. 21) or life (v. 22; cf. Ps. 73:17). According to Phil. 3:19, the enemies of the cross of Christ find their ultimate fate in eternal destruction (cf. also 2 Cor. 11:15). *telos* occurs 3 times after a preposition: "who will sustain you to the end [*heōs telous*]" (1 Cor. 1:8); "understand fully [*heōs telous*]" (2 Cor. 1:13); "at last [*eis telos*]" (1 Thess. 2:16 RSV, cf. mg. "completely", "for ever"). *telos* means end in the sense of cessation in Rom. 10:4 (in Christ the law has ceased to be the way of salvation), and also 2 Cor. 3:13 (the end of the brightness on the face of Moses concealed by the veil). ([Ed.] M. Black, however, argues that *telos* in Rom. 10:4 involves more than the simple idea of cessation. As in 1 Pet. 1:9, the idea conforms more closely to classical Gk.: "the logical end

of a process or action – its issue, consummation, perfection – and thus in philosophical writings its chief good." The idea is similar to that of 1 Tim. 1:5: "the end of the commandment is love." Black concludes that Christ is the end of the law in the sense of "the climactic development (practically 'perfection', 'perfecting')" which in turn implies the cessation of the validity of the "old law" (*Romans*, New Century Bible, 1973, 138; cf. E. E. Schneider, "Finis Legis Christus," *ThZ* 20, 1964, 410–22; R. Bultmann, "Christ the End of the Law," *Essays Philosophical and Theological*, 1955, 36–66; F. Flückiger, "Christus, des Gesetzes Telos," *ThZ* 11, 1955, 153–7; R. Bring in *StTh* 20, 1966, 1–36.)

1 Cor. 10:11 deals with the ends of the times which "have come over us" (H. Conzelmann, *Der erste Korintherbrief*, 1969[11], KEK 5; cf. C. K. Barrett, *The First Epistle to the Corinthians*, 1968, 227 f.): the old time will soon be past; we are living at the close of time (cf. 1 Cor. 7:29, 31: 16:21). In 1 Cor. 15:24 *telos* means the conclusion of the eschatological events (cf. Mk. 13:7 par. Matt. 24:6, Lk. 21:9), the point of time when Christ hands over the → kingdom to his → Father. *telos* as goal is found in 1 Tim. 1:5. Finally, in Rom. 13:7 *telos* means tax (cf. v. 6 [*telein*], to pay taxes).

(b) *teleō* twice means to achieve one's object: of the power of Christ in the weakness of the apostle (2 Cor. 12:9); of the desires of the flesh (Gal. 5:16). In two other places it means to bring to an end: of fulfilling the Law (Rom. 2:27); and of completing one's course (2 Tim. 4:7). Acts 20:24 uses *teleioō* in this sense (cf. 13:25). In Rom. 13:6 *teleō* means to pay (cf. above (a)).

(c) *teleios* occurs 5 times meaning mature, adult: 1 Cor. 2:6; 14:20; Phil. 3:15 (Paul's statement in v. 12 that he has "not yet become perfect [*ouch hoti ēdē teteleiōmai*]" means that he has not yet attained the final thing, the victor's prize of the heavenly calling in Christ Jesus [v. 14]); Eph. 4:13 (the church is figuratively called a "grown man"); and Col. 1:28 (the grown man as the goal of the apostle's instructions).

Twice *teleios* is that which is wholly in accord with God's will (Rom. 12:2, cf. Gen. 6:9; and Col. 4:12). In 1 Cor. 13:10 "the perfect" means the future world, in which everything imperfect (v. 9) which distinguishes our present world, is overcome. In Col. 3:14 love is called "the bond of perfectness [*syndesmos tēs teleiotētos*]" (AV; cf. RSV "which binds everything together in perfect harmony"). For by it the gifts given to the → church (v. 12 f.) are fitted together into a whole.

2. *The Synoptic Gospels*. (a) In the eschatological discourses of Jesus *telos* is used as a technical term for the end of the → world (Matt. 24:6 par. Mk. 13:7; Matt. 24:14; Lk. 21:9; cf. the expression *synteleia* [*tou*] *aiōnos*, the consummation of the age, Matt. 13:39 f., 49; 24:3; 28:20). It also occurs several times in the prepositional combination *eis telos* (cf. NT 1 (a)). This probably refers to the end of the world (Matt. 10:22; 24:13 = Mk. 13:13), since this is mentioned in the context (Matt. 24:6, 14; Mk. 13:7). In Lk. 18:5 *eis telos* means finally.

The phrase *telos echein*, to have an end, occurs twice. In Mk. 3:26 a kingdom in which division dominates is said to have an end, i.e. ceases to stand (cf. on this Lk. 1:33: the reign of Christ has no end). Lk. 22:37 attributes to Jesus the statement that "what has been written about me has an end [RSV 'fulfilment']," for the words of Scripture (Isa. 53:12) are being fulfilled in him. *telos* as outcome is found in Matt. 26:58, and as tax in Matt. 17:25 (cf. v. 24 where *telein* means to pay).

(b) Typical for Matt. is his use of *teleō* in redactional passages. His formula "when Jesus had ended" concludes the five great instructional discourses (7:28; 19:1; 26:1; 11:1; 13:53). Matt. 10:23 (the disciples will not have come to the end of the towns of Israel before the parousia breaks upon them) and Lk. 12:50 (Jesus is in great distress until his baptism, i.e. his suffering [cf. Mk. 10:38], has been completed) also have the sense of "carrying through to the end." Lk., however, uses the vb. twice in the pass. for the fulfilment of Scripture (Lk. 18:31; 22:37; cf. also Acts 13:29) and once in the act. for the fulfilling of the → law (Lk. 2:39).

(c) The adj. *teleios* occurs only in Matt. In 5:48 there is the summons to be perfect, as the heavenly → Father is perfect. In the light of the context, this is a command to be compassionate, to love friend and foe (cf. Lk. 16:36). To serve God with an undivided heart (cf. OT 1 (c)) can also mean: sell your possessions and give them to the poor (19:21).

(d) The vb. *teleioō* is used only in Lk. When the days of the Passover feast were ended the boy Jesus stayed behind at Jerusalem (Lk. 2:43). Jesus told the Pharisees to tell Herod that, "the third day I shall be completed" (Lk. 13:32). Despite Herod Antipas' threats of murder he intended to continue his work for the salvation of men "today" and "tomorrow". What his completion on the third day signifies is not entirely clear. Does it mean that God will put an end to his work on the third day? Or does Jesus mean: Whatever violence men inflict on me I shall go on working, for "on the third day" I shall be completed notwithstanding, i.e. rise from the dead (cf. 9:22; 18:33; 24:7, 46)? (→ Number, art. *tritos*.)

Finally *teleiōsis* also occurs in Lk. 1:45 meaning "fulfilment."

3. *James and 1 Peter*. In Jas. the stress lies on *teleios* (which occurs 5 times), in 1 Pet. on *telos* (which 4 times).

(a) *teleios* has also the basic meaning of "whole" in James. One is perfect, i.e. not lagging behind in any point (1:4), when one is patient and forbearing. Jas. calls the law of → freedom, by which he means the commandment to love one's neighbour (2:8), perfect (1:25), because this alone makes men really free (cf. Jn. 8:31 f.; Gal. 5:13). That God's gifts can be called perfect (1:17) goes without saying. According to Jas., the man who does not offend in his words is whole and without fault (3:2). *teleioō* accordingly means to become whole: only through works is faith brought to wholeness (2:22, cf. vv. 17, 20). Elsewhere Jas. also uses *telos* as outcome (5:11; cf. Matt. 26:58) and *teleō* as to fulfil (a law 2:8; cf. Lk. 2:39).

(b) 1 Pet. uses *telos* as goal (1:9), as an eschatological term (4:7; cf. Matt. 24:6), as ultimate fate (4:17; cf. Rom. 6:21 f.), and as meaning finally (3:8). *teleiōs*, used adverbially, occurs in 1:13, meaning entirely.

4. *Hebrews*. In Heb. this word-group occurs with the greatest frequency, relatively speaking (18 times); only the vb. *teleō* is lacking.

(a) By contrast with its use in the rest of the NT, *teleioō* is here attested 9 times, nearly always with cultic overtones (cf. OT 1 (d)). It means to make perfect, in the sense of consecrate, sanctify, so that – like the OT priests – one can come before God. Heb. uses the vb. to elucidate the distinction between Christ, the high → priest perfected through suffering (2:10) and eternally perfect (7:28), who was thus able to be the source of eternal salvation for his people (5:9), and the priests of the old → covenant who were men subject to weakness (7:28), and whose → sacrifices could not perfect their consciences (9:9; cf. also 10:1). Christ alone was able to perfect his people by a single sacrifice (10:14). The → law (7:19), i.e. the Levitical priesthood, has utterly failed to bring about sanctification (*teleiōsis*, 7:11). Therefore, Heb. calls Christ's heavenly sanctuary the "more perfect" (9:11) by contrast with the earthly one.

teleioō is twice used without cultic reference. Heb. 11:40 means that the witnesses to faith under the old covenant (v. 39) did not reach perfection, for this was alone given by Christ (cf. 10:14). Now, however, they too have come to share in the perfection (12:23).

(b) *teleios*, meaning adult, occurs in 5:14. *teleiotēs*, "maturity" (RSV, 6:1), correspondingly means that part of Christian doctrine which is intended for adults It is the opposite of *archē*, → beginning (5:12; 6:1).

teleiōtēs stands alongside *archēgos* in 12:2 (cf. the formula *archē kai telos*, see CL 1 (a)): Jesus is the beginner and perfecter of faith. He has not only maintained faith right to the end (5:7 f.; 12:3); he has also laid the foundation of faith (cf. 1:3).

(c) *telos* occurs in 2 prepositional combinations: *mechri telous*, to the end (3:14, this same phrase in v. 6 probably derives from v. 14); and *achri telous*, until the end (6:11). *telos* means outcome in 6:8 and end in 7:3.

5. *The Johannine Writings. teleioō* occurs (a) 5 times in Jn. and *teleō* twice; (b) 4 times in 1 Jn.; (c) *teleō* twice in Jn. Rev. has *teleō* 8 times and *telos* 8 times.

(a) In Jn. 4:34; 5:36; 17:4, *teleioō* is used where Jesus speaks of the works of the → Father which he has to accomplish. On the → cross he can say that they are accomplished (*tetelestai*, it is finished, 19:30, cf. v. 28). In the High Priestly Prayer Jesus prays that his own may be perfected in unity (17:23), so that the world may recognize the sending of Christ (cf. v. 21). In Jn. 19:28 *teleioō* is used of the Scriptures being fulfilled (cf. Ps. 22:18). *telos* occurs once, in the prepositional combination *eis telos* (13:1): Jesus loved his own to the end, i.e. perfectly, wholly.

(b) In 1 Jn. the pass. of *teleioō* is used 4 times with reference to → love. Love of God reaches its wholeness, when men keep his word (2:5) and love their neighbours (4:12). This love attains its goal in that they are liberated from fear on the day of judgment (4:17; cf. 2:28). One who knows fear is not perfectly determined by this love, for perfect love drives out fear (4:18).

(c) Revelation has *teleō* 6 times meaning to finish, or (pass.) to be finished. Rev. 11:7 refers to the completion of a testimony. Rev. 15:1 announces the seven last plagues upon the world in which God's wrath is brought to completion (cf. v. 8). Rev. 20 speaks 3 times of the end of the thousand-year reign (vv. 3, 5, 7; → Chiliasm in *Glossary of Technical Terms*). Rev. 10:7 and 17:17 deal with the mystery of God or the words of God being fulfilled. What God has previously determined is fulfilled (cf. Lk. 18:31; 22:37).

The formula "beginning and end" (cf. Isa. 41:4; 44:6; 48:12) expresses the power of God (21:6) and Christ (22:13) which embraces time and creation. Just as God is the beginning and end (cf. 1:8), the creator and perfecter of all things, so also is the exalted Christ (cf. 1:17; 2:8). Rev. has *telos* once in the prepositional combination *achri telous*, until the end (2:26). It occurs in a summons to hold fast continually the works of Christ.

6. In summing up the theological function of the word-group in the NT, a distinction can be drawn between an eschatological and an anthropological aspect. The

two are bound up with the general areas of meaning associated with *telos* on the one hand and *teleios* on the other.

(a) First and foremost is the eschatological function of *telos*. The dynamic, goal-directed character of the noun is further underlined by the frequent use of the vb. *teleō*. This aspect stands out with particular clarity in those passages which are concerned with the future consummation both in the Synoptics (cf. the so-called Little Apocalypse, Mk. 13 par.), the Pauline letters (e.g. Phil. 3:19) and Rev. (e.g. 20:1 ff.). The important point here is that the end is not understood simply as the mechanical cessation of movement. It is the consummating conclusion of a dynamic process, the goal of which manifests the realization of its meaning and its intentions. Since *telos* is a term with heavy apocalyptic overtones, the historically conditioned apocalyptic images and computations linked with it cannot be taken over wholesale without more ado by contemporary eschatological thought about the future promised in Christ. Rather, the universal, cosmic themes and implications inherent in them must be restated within the framework of Christian eschatology.

(b) Connected with the idea of the end as the completion and realization of a goal is the sense of *teleios* as that which has reached its goal, and is thus completed and perfected. To the extent that the whole is achieved only at the end, *teleios* may be applied in its fullest sense only to God (e.g. Matt. 5:48) and Christ (e.g. Heb. 7:28). In the context of individual human development *teleios* applies to the man who has reached maturity, the grown man who has come of age (especially in Paul). The NT does not speak of an ideal of ethical perfection which is to be realized by degrees (cf. G. Delling, *TDNT* VIII 77). Rather, when viewed against the background of the OT concepts of *tāmîm* and *šālēm* and applied to people's actions, *teleios* signifies the undivided wholeness of a person in his behaviour. It is in this sense that the later writings of the NT, especially Matt. (e.g. 19:21) and James (e.g. 1:4), frequently use the word. When applied to man and ethics, therefore, *teleios* denotes not the qualitative end-point of human endeavour, but the anticipation in time of eschatological wholeness in actual present-day living. Christian life in the NT is not projected idealistically as a struggle for perfection, but eschatologically as the wholeness which a person is given and promised.

R. Schippers

→ Abomination of Desolation, → Beginning, → Present, → Time

(a). R. Bultmann, "Christ the End of the Law", *Essays Philosophical and Theological*, 1955, 36–66; A. Deissler and F. Mussner, "Perfection", *EBT* II 658–67; G. Delling, *telos* etc., *TDNT* VIII 49–87; E. E. Ellis, "Present and Future Eschatology in Luke", *NTS* 12, 1965–66, 27–41; R. N. Flew, *The Idea of Perfection in Christian Theology*, 1934; E. Fuchs, *skopos*, etc. *TDNT* VII 413–17; E. Käsemann, "An Apologia for Primitive Christian Eschatology", in *Essays on New Testament Themes*, 1964, 169–95; G. Kittel, *eschatos*, *TDNT* II 697 f.; W. G. Kümmel, *Promise and Fulfilment*, 1957; J. Moltmann, *Theology of Hope*, 1967; C. F. D. Moule, "Obligation in the Ethic of Paul", in W. R. Farmer, C. F. D. Moule and R. R. Niebuhr, eds., *Christian History and Interpretation* (John Knox Festschrift), 1967, 401 ff. (on *telos* in Rom. 10:4); R. Niebuhr, *The Nature and Destiny of Man*, II *Human Destiny*, 1943; M. Noth, "The Understanding of History in Old Testament Apocalyptic", in *The Laws in the Pentateuch and Other Studies*, 1966, 194–214; H. P. Owen, "The 'Stages of Ascent' in Heb. v. 11–vi. 3", *NTS* 3, 1956–57, 243–53; J. du Plessis, *Teleios: The Idea of Perfection in the New Testament*, 1959; H. Preisker, *engys* etc., *TDNT* II 330–33; A. Wikgren, "Patterns of Perfection in the Epistle to the Hebrews", *NTS* 6, 1959–60, 159–67; R. Schnackenburg, "Christian Adulthood according to the Apostle Paul", *CBQ* 25, 1963, 254–370.

(b). J. Blinzler, "Vollkommenheit", *LTK* X 863 f.; R. Bring, *StTh* 20, 1966, 1–36; G. Delling, "Zur Paulinischen Teleologie", *TLZ* 75, 1950, 12 ff.; J. Dupont, " 'Soyez parfaits' (Mt. 5:48), 'Soyez miséricordieux' (Lc. 6:36)", *Sacra Pagina* 1959, 150–62; C. M. Edsman, A. Jepsen, R. Meyer, H. Conzelmann, H. Kraft, and P. Althaus, "Eschatologie", *RGG*³ II 650 ff.; F. Flückiger, "Christus, des Gesetzes Telos", *ThZ* 11, 1955, 153–7; P. Hoffmann, "*Die Toten in Christus*". *Eine religionsgeschichtliche und exegetische Untersuchung zur Paulinischen Eschatologie, NTAbh* Neue Folge 2, 1966; K. Karner, "Gegenwart und Endgeschichte in der Offenbarung des Johannes", *TLZ* 93, 1968, 641 ff.; B. Klappert, *Die Eschatologie des Hebräerbriefes, ThEH* 156, 1969; J. Kögel, "Der Begriff *teleioun* im Hebräerbrief", in *Theologische Studien für Martin Kähler*, 1905, 35–68; H. Kosmala, *Hebräer-Essener-Christen*, 1959, 208–39; H. Kremers and R. Prenter, "Eschatologie", *EKL* I 1152 ff.; H. W. Kuhn, *Enderwartung und gegenwärtiges Heil*, StUNT 4, 1966; W. G. Kümmel, "Die Eschatologie der Evangelien", *ThBl* 15, 1936, 225 ff., reprinted in *Heilsgeschehen und Geschichte*, 1965, 48 ff.; W. Lohff, "Telos", *RGG*³ VI 678 ff.; U. Luck, *Die Vollkommenheitsforderung der Bergpredigt, ThEH* 150, 1968; R. Mach, *Der Zaddik in Talmud und Midrasch*, 1957; R. Mehl, "Vollkommenheit", *RGG*³ VI 1486 ff.; N. Messel, *Die Einheitlichkeit der jüdischen Eschatologie, BZAW* 30, 1915; O. Michel, "Die Lehre von der christlichen Vollkommenheit nach der Anschauung des Hebräerbriefs", *ThStKr* Neue Folge 1, 1934–35, 333–55; H. P. Müller, "Zur Frage nach dem Ursprung der biblischen Eschatologie", *Vetus Testamentum* 14, 1964, 276 ff.; F. Nötscher, *Gotteswege und Menschenwege in der Bibel und in Qumran*, 1958; and "Heiligkeit in den Qumranschriften", *Revue de Qumran* 2, 1959–60, 163–81 and 315–44; O. Plöger, *Theokratie und Eschatologie, WMANT* 2, 1959; K. Prümm, "Das neutestamentliche Sprach- und Begriffsproblem der Vollkommenheit", *Biblica* 44, 1963, 76 ff.; B. Rigaux, "Révélation des mystères et perfection à Qumran et dans le Nouveau Testament", *NTS* 4, 1957–58, 237–62; SB IV 799–1015; F. J. Schierse, *Verheissung und Heilsvollendung. Zur theologischen Grundfrage des Hebräerbriefes*, 1955; H. Schlier, *Christus und die Kirche im Epheserbrief*, 1930; R. Schnackenburg, "Die Vollkommenheit des Christen nach den Evangelien", *Geist und Leben* 32, 1959, 420–33; E. E. Schneider, "Finis Legis Christus", *ThZ* 20, 1964, 410–22; J. Schreiner, "Das Ende der Tage, Die Botschaft von der Endzeit in den alttestamentlichen Schriften", *BuL* 5, 1964, 180 ff.; C. Spicq, "La perfection chrétienne d'après l'Epître aux Hébreux", *Mémorial J. Chaine*, 1950, 337–52; G. Stählin, "Fortschritt und Wachstum. Zur Herkunft und Wandlung neutestamentlicher Ausdrucksformen", *Festgabe J. Lortz*, II, 1958, 13–25; W. Thüsing, *Erhöhungsvorstellung und Parusieerwartung in der ältesten Christologie*, 1970; W. Völker, *Fortschritt und Vollendung bei Philo von Alexandrien, TU* 49/1, 1938.

God, Gods, Emmanuel

θεός

θεός (*theos*), God; *θεῖος* (*theios*), divine; *θειότης* (*theiotēs*), deity; *θεότης* (*theotēs*), deity, divinity.

CL The etymology of the Gk. word has not yet been clarified; the only thing that is certain is that it was originally a title.

1. Gk. religion was polytheistic. The gods were represented in anthropomorphic form as personal beings who exercised a determining influence on the world and fate of men, but who themselves were dependent on a superior fate. As they were not creator-gods, they were not thought of as outside the universe and transcendent. The cosmos included both gods and men. The influence of the gods was not universal, but was limited by their natures and attributes. They were not → righteous in the OT sense. The Gk. gods had form. Consequently, the statement "God is spirit" (Jn. 4:24) could not be applied to them. From Aeschylus onwards the different gods came increasingly to be identified. Their convergence into one divine being was prepared by the pre-Socratic thinkers and the ideas of classical tragedy.

2. The Gk. philosophical understanding of god was non-personal. Philosophers sought the origin of all things and the principle that shaped the world. In the process

of rationalizing and moralizing, brought about by philosophical criticism and reflection, an important transformation of the Gk. concept of god took place. The divine forms were spiritualized and finally replaced by general concepts like "world reason," "the divine," and "being," which influenced and formed the world as powers giving it meaning and creating order. In Hellenistic syncretism the various Gk. and non-Gk. divinities were assimilated and even equated as a result of the recognition that behind the diverse names stood the same entities. This is particularly clear in the Isis cult. Not infrequently these tendencies lead to the honouring of one godhead as the divine All. The development reached its height in Neo-Platonism, where the divine is the universal One which has no objective existence or personality. It is being itself which is manifested through a series of hypostases and emanations in the world, since it is the ground and force behind everything that is.

OT The religion of the OT and Judaism is monotheistic and personal.

1. In the OT the words *'ēl*, *'elôah* and *'elōhîm*, from related roots, are generic designations of God. Alongside and alternating with them stands the individual, personal name *Yahweh* (cf. G. Quell, *theos*, *TDNT* III 79 ff.). The cult names formed with *'ēl* are as a rule connected with local shrines.

'ēl is a word common to all Semitic languages. It occurs as a common noun (the god, god) and also as the proper name for a particular god. This is clearly demonstrated in the texts from Ugarit in North Syria (14th century B.C.). It is true also of the Canaanites in the first and second millennia B.C. and the patriarchs, for whom *'ēl* is clearly not the highest god in a pantheon, but the only God, whom they honoured on the basis of his revelation. He appears as *'ēl 'elyôn*, "God Most High" (Gen. 14:18–22, RSV who was blessed by → Melchizedek); *'ēl rō'î*, "God of Seeing" (Gen. 16:13 RSV); *'ēl 'ōlām* "the Everlasting God" (Gen. 21:33 RSV, so called by Abraham); *'ēl bêṭ'ēl*, "God of Bethel" (Gen. 31:13; 35:7, so called by Jacob; Bethel meaning lit. "house of God"); *'ēl 'elōhê yiśrā'ēl*, "God, the god of Israel" (Gen. 33:20); and *'ēl šadday*, "God Almighty" (Gen. 17:1; 28:3; 35:11; 48:3; 49:25; Exod. 6:3). (On these titles see A. Alt, "The God of the Fathers", in *Essays on Old Testament History and Religion*, 1966, 3–66, especially 8 ff.) God is most frequently referred to as *šaddai*, Almighty, in Job where it is used along with El, Elohim, Eloah and Yahweh (cf. E. Dhorme, *Job*, 1967, lxv ff.). The shrine of Shechem seems to have been the first central shrine of the twelve united tribes (Jos. 24).

'elōhîm, though plur. in form, is seldom used in the OT as such (i.e. gods). Even a single heathen god can be designated with the plur. *'elōhîm* (e.g. Jdg. 11:24; 1 Ki. 11:5; 2 Ki. 1:2). In Israel the plur. is understood as the plural of fullness; God is the God who really, and in the fullest sense of the word, is God.

J. Schneider

2. The origin and meaning of the divine name Yahweh has been the subject of considerable discussion. Some scholars derive it from a primitive form Yah which they regard as an interjection associated with the moon cult (cf. G. R. Driver, *ZAW*, 46, 1928, 24). It is suggested that it derives from *Ya-huwa*, meaning "O he" (cf. M. Buber, *Moses*, (1946) 1958, 49 f.; S. Mowinckel, "The Name of the God of Moses," *Hebrew Union College Annual* 32, 1961, 121–33). But this has been rejected

on the grounds that to regard the name as an interjection makes it difficult to account for the religious content which faith has always found in the name and the revelatory value which is attached to it (cf. E. Jacob, *Theology of the Old Testament*, 1964[3], 48). It is more likely that the name is connected with the verbal root *hwy* or *hwh*, meaning to be (cf. R. de Vaux, "The Revelation of the Divine Name YHWH" in J. I. Durham and J. R. Porter, eds., *Proclamation and Presence: Old Testament Essays in Honour of Gwynne Henton Davies*, 1970, 59 ff.; E. Jacob, op. cit., 50 f.; J. P. Hyatt, *Exodus*, 1971, 79; T. C. Vriezen, "'Ehje 'ᵃšer 'ehje", in W. Baumgartner *et al., Festschrift Alfred Bertholet*, 1950, 498–512).

The only interpretation of the name Yahweh given in the OT is at the theophany of the burning bush (Exod. 3:13 ff. attributed to the E source or tradition). "Then Moses said to God, 'If I come to the people of Israel and say to them, "The God of your fathers has sent me to you," and they ask me, "What is his name?" what shall I say to them?' God said to Moses, 'I AM WHO I AM [MT: *'ehyeh 'ᵃšer 'ehyeh*]'. And he said, 'Say to this people of Israel, 'I AM [*'ehyeh*] has sent me to you.' " God also said to Moses, 'Say this to the people of Israel, "The LORD [MT: YHWH], the God of your fathers, the God of Abraham, the God of Isaac, and the God of Jacob, has sent me to you"; this is my name for ever, and thus I am to be remembered throughout all generations' " (RSV).

There has been considered debate as to the translation and meaning of the words *'ehyeh 'ᵃšer 'ehyeh*. This is partially reflected in the RSV mg alternative translations: "I AM WHAT I AM" and "I WILL BE WHAT I WILL BE." J. P. Hyatt lists five lines of interpretation (op. cit., 75 ff.). (i) That the reply is intentionally evasive, because it is God's nature to remain hidden, or because to know God's name might give man power over him. But against this is the fact that the name is revealed to Moses in v. 15. (ii) God is the eternally existent one. (iii) "I am because I am." This suggests that there is no cause for God's existence outside himself. (iv) "I will be what I will be," or "I will be what I intend to be." (v) "I am he who is," or "I am the one who is." He is the God who alone has real existence. For discussion of the syntax involved in this translation see E. Schild, *Vetus Testamentum* 4, 1954, 296–302; J. Lindblom, *Annual of the Swedish Theological Institute*, III 1964, 4–15; B. Albrektson "On the Syntax of *'hyh 'šr 'hyh* in Exodus 3:14," in P. R. Ackroyd, and B. Lindars, eds., *Words and Meanings: Essays Presented to David Winton Thomas*, 1968, 15–28.

R. de Vaux holds that the best rendering of the formula is "I am He who Exists" (op. cit., 71). Yahweh is the God whom Israel must recognize as really existing. This is not presented as part of a metaphysic of being (cf. Thomas Aquinas, *Summa Theologiae* I, Q. 2 art. 3). In the context of Exodus the revelation of the divine name is a proclamation to Israel of the one with whom they have to do. God is calling his people out of → Egypt and promises to be with Moses for that purpose (Exod. 3:10 ff.; 4:12; 15, 22 f.; 6:2 f.; cf. J. A. Motyer, *The Revelation of the Divine Name*, 1959). The proclamation of the Decalogue begins with the words: "I am Yahweh" (Exod. 20:2; cf. Deut. 6:5). The first commandment requires exclusive worship and service (Exod. 20:3, cf. 5). When Moses sought God's presence, he was not permitted to see God's → face but nevertheless received the reply: "I will make all my goodness pass before you, and will proclaim before you my name Yahweh; and I will be gracious to whom I will be gracious, and will show mercy on whom I will show mercy" (Exod. 33:19). The God who thus reveals himself to Moses and to Israel is distinct from the deities of Egypt and Canaan with their fertility rites concerned with the cycle of nature. He remains a mystery, and yet he is graciously active in the history of his people.

It is possible that the name of Yahweh existed outside Israel prior to Moses, but there is no conclusive proof (for a review of evidence see R. de Vaux, op. cit., 49–56; E. Jacob, op. cit., 48 ff.). Nevertheless, Exod. 3 does not appear to give a new name for the first time but the explanation of a name known already but now identified as that of the saving God of Israel. Although Israel did not work out a metaphysical doctrine of → time, the idea of God as "He who Is" is paralleled by numerous other statements about God in the OT (Pss. 90:1; 102:27 f.; Hab. 1:2; Exod. 30:8; Isa. 41:4; 48:12). But the thought of time is also bound up with that of Yahweh's ongoing presence (Gen. 20:28; Jos. 3:7; Jdg. 6:12; Isa. 49:6, 26; cf. E. Jacob, op. cit., 52).

The Heb. name *YHWH ṣᵉbāʾôṯ*, Lord of hosts, occurs some 279 times. It is absent from the Pentateuch, Jos. and Jdg., but is frequent in the prophets (especially Isa. 1–39 [54 times]; Jer. [77 times]; and Zech. 1–8 [44 times]). The hosts in question have been variously interpreted as the earthly armies of Israel, the armies of the stars, and the celestial armies of spirits and angels. E. Jacob relates the title to the ark of the → covenant accompanied by the armies of Israel in battle (1 Sam. 17:45; 2 Sam. 6:2, 18; 7:2, 8, 26 f.; 1 Chr. 17:7; cf. op. cit., 55). He notes that it is found most frequently among the prophets for whom Yahweh was above all a warrior God. It is not simply a case of the prophets transferring the hosts from the terrestrial to the celestial plane. The term refers to the totality of forces over which Yahweh rules. But possibly the term also had polemical overtones, directed against the cult of the stars and spirits, claiming by its use that Yahweh also controlled them. In the LXX the term is translated by *kyrios pantokratōr*, → Lord Almighty (2 Sam. [2 Ki.] 5:10; 7:8, 25 ff.; cf. Jer. 3:19; Hos. 12:6; Amos 3:18; 4:13; 5:14; Zeph. 2:10; 2 Macc. 8:18; 3 Macc. 6:2; Arndt, 613 f.) and *basileus tōn dynameōn*, → king of powers (Ps. 67:13 LXX). The term *pantokratōr* is taken up by 2 Cor. 6:18; Rev. 1:8; 4:8; 11:17; 15:3; 16:7, 14; 19:15; 21:22. The Gk. transcription *sabaōth* (which occurs some 65 times in the LXX and other versions) is twice used in the NT (Rom. 9:29 = Isa. 1:9; Jas. 5:4; cf. Arndt, 746).

The name of Yahweh was combined with various Heb. verbs to form proper names: e.g. Jehoiachin (Yahweh establishes, from Yahweh and *kûn*), Jonathan (Yahweh gives, from Yahweh and *nāṯan*), and Joshua (Yahweh is salvation, from Yahweh and *šûaʿ* or *yēšûaʿ*). The latter is the oldest name containing Yahweh (Koehler-Baumgartner, 370). M. H. Segal sees in its early existence evidence that the name Yahweh was known prior to the revelation to Moses (*The Pentateuch*, 1967, 4). Joshua is the Heb. form which underlies the name of → Jesus.

The form *Jehovah* arose out of a misunderstanding which in turn arose out of the reluctance of pious Jews to pronounce the divine name (c. 300 B.C.). Instead they uttered the word *ʾᵃdōnāy*, my Lord. In the MT the divine name was written with the consonants of *YHWH* and the vowels of *ʾᵃdōnāy*, as a reminder to say the latter whenever the word was read. The divine name appears as *yᵉhōwâh* in the MT. The LXX reflects the Jewish reluctance to pronounce the divine name and puts the word *kyrios*, → Lord, in its place. The RSV and other Eng. versions also reflect the practice by giving the word LORD in capital letters whenever the name *YHWH* stands in the text. The Lat. likewise gives the word *Dominus*, Lord, for *YHWH*. The form *Jehovah* is thus a malformation giving what is virtually a transliteration of a word which is found in the text of the Heb. OT, but which was never actually used as a word. It became current in the sixteenth century and is attested in the Lat. of P. Galatinus in the form *Iehoua* (*De Arcanis Cath. Veritatis*, 1516, II, 1 f., xlviii). In 1530 Tyndale used *Iehouah* in his translation of Exod. 6:3 (Wycliffe had *Adonay*). Subsequently Jehovah became the standard spelling. But → also Lord, art. *kyrios* OT 2.   *C. Brown*

It was only in the course of history that the belief in the superiority of Israel's God over all other gods led to the development of absolute monotheism. Jeremiah was probably the first to support the proposition that the gods of the heathen are no gods (Jer. 2:11). This knowledge was first given full expression in Isa. 40:55. The God of Israel is the Lord of all, whose sovereign power fills all the earth (Isa. 6:3). There are no gods apart from the One (Isa. 41:4; 42:8; 43:10 ff.; 45:3, 6; 48:11). (See further H. H. Rowley, *The Re-Discovery of the Old Testament*, 1945, 77–93; G. E. Wright, *The Old Testament against its Environment*, 1950, 9–41; C. F. Whitley, *The Prophetic Achievement*, 1963, 93–128.)

3. The LXX is characterized by the Hellenizing of Israelite–Jewish monotheism and by the reduction of the designations of God. Thus the Heb. words *'ēl, 'ᵉlōah* and *'ᵉlōhîm* are as a rule rendered by *theos*, "God", and in exceptional cases by *kyrios*, "Lord", or other expressions. Apart from *theos* and *kyrios*, *'ēl* is translated about 20 times by *ischyros*, "Mighty One", "Powerful One", otherwise by *dynamis* "Might", "Power" (Neh. 5:5), or *dynastēs* "Prince", "Ruler", "Potentate" (Sir. 46:5, 6). The name Yahweh or Yah, which is mostly translated by *kyrios*, is replaced by *theos* only about 330 times (G. Quell, *TDNT* II 79).

4. The OT contains no all-embracing definition of the concept of God. On the other hand, it makes an extensive range of statements which testify to the being of God and have their basis in the divine revelation. Nor is there in the OT any theogony; it does not go beyond the assertion that God is. He is the first and the last (Isa. 41:4; 44:6; 48:12), the eternal, the almighty and the living one (Ps. 36:10), the creator of heaven and earth (Gen. 1:1; 2.4, etc.); the Lord, who guides the destinies of the nations, but who has made → Israel a people for his own possession (Exod. 19:5 f.). Israel stands, therefore, under his special protection. Yahweh not only leads, guides and gives Israel his promises; he also imposes his judgments when he goes his own way. God is the commanding and demanding God who makes his will known and demands obedience. The history of Israel is the history of God with this → people. Thus Israel's belief in God is founded on a theology of history.

It expresses a conception of God as personal, that God is capable of all the emotions that a person can have: → love, → anger, → repentance and other emotions. But even if human characteristics can be attributed to him, he cannot be compared with any human being (Hos. 11:9). The transcendent God who dwells in light, where no one can approach, is exalted above time and space and is therefore unique in his Godhead, not to be portrayed or localized (cf. Exod. 20:4). He is the eternal → king (Isa. 52:7) who rules over all the → kingdoms of the world (Isa. 37:16).

The most fundamental feature of God's being is expressed by the word → "holy". In the OT this has become the characteristic attribute of God. He is the

Holy One (Isa. 40:25; Hab. 3:3; Hos 11:9). But the holy, transcendent God steps out of his concealment through his word and his acts of revelation, and repeatedly communicates with his people in demonstrations of power and glory.

The holy God is just in all that he does (cf. Ps. 7:11). He is the → judge who condemns unrighteousness and to whom man has to answer. But the OT also testifies to his → grace and → mercy (e.g. Exod. 34:6; Ps. 103:8). He comforts the pious (Job 15:11), → blesses him and helps him in his need (Pss. 45:7; 90:1; 94:22). Through the personal relationship between God and his people there is created an I-Thou relation between God and the individual believer who can turn to him in → prayer in all his needs.

God in the OT is also called → Father; he is the father of the people of → Israel (Exod. 4:22 f.; Deut. 32:6; Isa. 63:16; Jer. 31:9; Hos. 11:1). However, a full knowledge of the divine grace and love which embraces the whole world is only arrived at through the revelation of the new → covenant. Nevertheless, the OT testifies to the fact that God forgives transgressions and → sins (Exod. 34:6 f.). He has mercy on his people in everlasting grace (Isa. 54:8), and in particular takes up the cause of the poor and needy, and widows and orphans (Isa. 49:13; Ps. 146:9). Therefore, even in the OT God is not just a dreaded → enemy of man in his unholiness; he also makes it possible for him both to trust and love, because he himself loves his chosen people.

5. Judaism confessed the one God in unswerving loyalty and fought passionately against pagan polytheism. But it saw the one God working in a multitude of mediatorial and → angelic beings. Dualistic concepts were taken up in apocalyptic writings. It was this, E. Stauffer argues, that gave the fundamental monotheistic conviction of the OT the character of a "dynamic monotheism" (*TDNT* III 96).

The rabbis laid great stress on avoiding the name of God; in its place they put a whole system of substitute terms: e.g. → Heaven (*ha-šāmayim* or *šāmayim*), the → Lord (*'adōnāy*) and later the → Name (*ha-šēm*) (cf. K. G. Kuhn, *TDNT* III 92 ff.). In addition there were abstract terms like Glory, Power and the Abode (of God).

6. The Essenes of the Qumran community took over a cosmological dualism which was probably influenced by Zoroastrianism: e.g. God and Belial, →light and darkness, → Spirit of truth and Spirit of falsehood. To this corresponds the anthropological opposition of → flesh and spirit, the pious and the godless, sons of light and sons of darkness. However, the dualism of the two spirits that rule the world is subordinated to the fundamental OT, Jewish idea of God as the creator of all things. For he created the spirits of light and of darkness which lie at the basis of his working (1QS 3:25; cf. 3:19–26).

The Qumran texts give a series of designations of God. God is not only the creator of the world and of men, but also in a special way the "God of Israel" (1QM 1:9 f.; 14:4; 18:6), the "Father of the sons of truth" (1QH 9:35). His majesty and glory are expressed in his being called the "Prince of gods," the "King of majesties," the "Ruler of all creatures" (1QH 10:8), the "Highest" or the "Highest of all" (1QS 4:22; 1QGen Ap 2:4; 20:12), the "God of gods" (1QM 14:16), the "King of kings" (*ibid.*), the "Ruler over all the kings of the earth" (1QGenAp 20:13). He is the "God of knowledge" (1QS 3:15; 1QH 1:26), full of deep and unfathomable secrets (1QS 11:5; 1QH 10:3; 12:13), who hides all wisdom within himself

(1QH 12:10) and thus is the foundation of knowledge (1QS 10:12). The eternal God (1QH 13:13) is wise (1QH 9:17), just (1QH 11:7, 18; 14:15), all his deeds are just (1QH 13:19), the True (1QH 15:25) and Holy (1QM 19:1), but also the God who is full of grace, favour, goodness and mercy (1QH 4:32, 37; 7:30 f.; 9:34; 10:14, 16; 11:29), who forgives sins and by his righteousness cleanses men from their guilt and from the "terrors of falsehood" (1QH 4:37; cf. 1QS 11:14; 1QHFr 2:13). He is the source of judgments (1QS 10:18) and acts of grace (1QS 10:16) found in history and the life of individuals.

All this is experienced by the pious who belong to the sons of light. Through the grace and goodness of God they receive → justification and atonement (1QS 11: 13 f.). But above all they have received through revelation and instruction, the → mysteries of God and of his mighty acts which are otherwise hidden from men (1QH 11:9f., 17).

The Qumran doctrine of God stands out as being rigidly deterministic. God's actions are determined by a fixed plan (1QS 3:15; 11:11; 1QH 18:22). Nothing happens apart from his will (1QS 3:15; 11:17, 19; 1QH 1:20; 10:9), for all authority is in his power.

This is especially true for the personal life of the individual. The pious poet acknowledges, "Thou hast not cast my lot in the congregation of vanity, nor hast thou placed my portion in the council of the cunning" (1QH 7:34). "Thou hast known me from [the time of] my father [and hast chosen me] from the womb" (1QH 9:30). His hand leads him at all times and his just rebuke accompanies all his perversity (1QH 9:32 f.). He can only speak because God opens his mouth (1QH 11:33). All his thinking and planning is determined by God (1QH 10:5 f.).

The eschatological statements of Qumran are also strongly characterized by determinism. God created the righteous for eternal salvation and lasting peace, but the "perverse" for the time of his wrath (1QH 14:15 ff.); from their mother's womb they were "dedicated to the Day of Massacre" (ibid., 15:17). The "lot" of Belial will bring judgment to eternal destruction (1QM 1:5); all "men of lies" will be destroyed (1QH 4:20).

The influence of the Qumran texts on the NT has been greatly overestimated. In the case of the doctrine of God, at any rate, no real connections are to be found. Primitive Christianity is much more independent in the expression of its theological thought than is often accepted. (This is true also of the cases when it has borrowed Jewish apocalyptic and gnostic concepts as vehicles for primitive Christian theology and preaching.)

7. Philo's concept of God has been affected by his attempt to link the OT idea of Yahweh with the Platonic-Stoic idea of God. When he speaks of the God of Israel, he distinguishes between *ho theos* and *ho kyrios*. *ho theos* is the good God, the Creator; *ho kyrios* the kingly Lord of the world. By omitting the definite article and speaking of *theos* he indicates the "second God," the Word. Philo also makes extensive use of the philosophical concept of *to theion*, the divine. For Philo God is fully transcendent and also the active power in everything. He produces out of himself the original, typical ideas, and forms them into the visible world. The Word is his mediator for creation and revelation. (See further H. A. Wolfson, *Religious Philosophy*, 1961; and *Philo: Foundations of Religious Philosophy in Judaism, Christianity and Islam*, I–II, 1962³.)

NT The NT rests firmly on the foundation of the OT, when it speaks about God, but its emphases are new. He is the God who is near, the Father of Jesus Christ who justifies freely by his grace (cf. the Pauline concept of the → righteousness of God). His action in election bursts all claims to exclusiveness. But it is the same God who reveals himself here as in the OT, and whose plan of salvation, there promised, comes to fulfilment here.

1. *The one God*. (a) *theos* is the most frequent designation of God in the NT. Belief in the one, only and unique God (Matt. 23:9; Rom. 3:30; 1 Cor. 8:4, 6; Gal. 3:20; 1 Tim. 2:5; Jas. 2:19) is an established part of primitive Christian tradition. Jesus himself made the fundamental confession of Judaism his own and expressly quoted the Shema (Deut. 6:4 f.; Mk. 12:29 f.; cf. Matt. 22:37; Lk. 10:27). This guaranteed continuity between the old and the new → covenant. For the God whom Christians worship is the God of the fathers (Acts 3:13; 5:30; 22:14), the God of → Abraham, of → Isaac and of → Jacob (Acts 3:13; 7:32; cf. Matt. 22:32; Mk. 12:26; Lk. 20:37), the God of Israel (Matt. 15:31; Lk. 1:68; Acts 13:17; cf. 2 Cor. 6:16; Heb. 11:16), and the God of → Jesus Christ (2 Cor. 1:3; Eph. 1:3; 1 Pet. 1:3). Just as God once made → Israel his → people, so now he has chosen those who believe in Christ as an elect race and a holy people for his possession (Acts 15:14; 20:28; 1 Pet. 2:9; Heb. 11:25). → Faith is in him (Rom. 4:3; Gal. 3:6; Tit. 3:8; Jas. 2:23; Heb. 6:1; 1 Pet. 1:21), → hope is on him (Acts 24:15; Rom. 4:18; 2 Cor. 3:4; 1 Pet. 3:5), and → prayer is to him. The community of Jesus may have no false gods beside him, whether Mammon (Matt. 6:24), the → "belly" (Phil. 3:19) or the cosmic powers (Gal. 4:8 ff.). It must serve him alone, do his will and remain faithful to him.

(b) Confession of the one God appears in Eph. 4:6 in an expanded form ("one God and Father of us all, who is above all and through and in all"), which glorifies, no doubt under Jewish-Hel. influence, the omnipresence of the rule of God. Similar formulae, referring now to God, now to Christ, occur in Rom. 11:36 and 1 Cor. 8:6. (See further J. N. D. Kelly, *Early Christian Creeds*, 1972³, 1–29; O. Cullmann, *The Earliest Christian Confessions*, 1949; V. H. Neufeld, *The Earliest Christian Confessions*, 1963; E. Stauffer, *New Testament Theology*, 1955, 244 ff.)

(c) The one God is the living and only true God (Rom. 3:30; Gal. 3:20; 1 Thess. 1:9; 1 Tim. 1:17; 2:5; Jude 25; cf. Jn. 17:3). He is the God whom the heathen do not know (1 Thess. 4:5). It is true that Paul reckons with the existence of "so-called" gods, who have authority as demonic powers over the heathen, but for the Christians there is only the one God (1 Cor. 8:5 f.). Even if the honour and power of gods does not belong to the *stoicheia* (→ Law, article *stoicheia*) which the Galatians previously worshipped, they can still intrude divisively between the young congregation and their God (Gal. 4:8 f.).

This one God is called "our God" (Acts 2:39; 2 Pet. 1:1; Rev. 4:11; 7:12; 19:5). The individual believer, above all Paul, can speak quite personally of him as *his* God (Rom. 1:8; 1 Cor. 1:4; 2 Cor. 12:21; Phil. 1:3; 4:19; Phlm. 4). Belief in the one God involves turning away from all heathen ways. Therefore in missionary preaching testimony to God is linked with the struggle against the worship of false gods (Acts 14:15; 17:24 f.; 19:26).

(d) The Epistles and especially Acts give a partial picture of the excesses of the NT world and their local expression. According to Acts, Paul was painfully impressed in Athens by the many figures of gods and shrines which he saw as he went through the city (Acts 17:16, 23). Just how strongly the cult of Artemis dominated the religious life of Ephesus is clear from the impressive account in Acts 19:23–41. (On the background to this see E. Haenchen, *The Acts of the Apostles*, 1971, 571 ff.) Here things came to a head through a violent clash with the silversmiths who derived great profit from making little models of the temple of Artemis and felt their economic existence threatened by Paul's preaching. 1 Cor. 8:1–7 indicates the significance of sacrificial meals in the heathen cultus at Corinth. → Magic played an important part in Hel. times; in Acts it is mentioned in 8:9 (Samaria), 13:6 (Cyprus) and 19:13 ff. (Ephesus). In Ephesus, as a result of the powerful testimony borne to the Christian message of salvation, the books of magic were publicly burned (Acts 19:19). (See further below, section 9.)

Conversion to the true and living God was experienced by those who had become believers as a gift of grace; for they had been freed from bondage to false gods (1 Thess. 1:9). But for many Christians the fascinating power of the heathen cults had not entirely lost its force. Therefore Paul explained to the Corinthians, "I do not want you to be partners with demons" (1 Cor. 10:20), for the heathen presented their sacrifices to demonic beings and not to God (see further C. K. Barrett, *The First Epistle to the Corinthians*, 1968, 236 ff.).

2. *The transcendent God.* (a) God is the creator, sustainer and Lord of the world (Acts 17:24; Rev. 10:6), the master-builder of all things (Heb. 3:4). He exercises his lordship from → heaven, for heaven is his throne and the earth his footstool (Matt. 5:34; 23:22; Acts 7:49). He is the Almighty with whom nothing is impossible (Mk. 10:27). No one can hinder, let alone destroy, his work (Acts 5:39; cf. 2 Tim. 2:9). He is the highest (Mk. 5:7; Lk. 1:32; Acts 7:48; 16:17; Heb. 7:1), the great → king (Matt. 5:35), the king of the nations (Rev. 15:3).

(b) Prayer is a powerful witness to belief in the transcendent God, for → prayer is directed to God who is in heaven (Matt. 6:9; cf. Jn. 17:1), but who hears the suppliant here. At present the → Satanic and demonic powers still stand opposed to God's rule on earth. Therefore the congregation of Jesus prays for the full revelation of his *basileia* (→ kingdom), for the full accomplishment of his will ("on earth as it is in heaven," Matt. 6:10), and for the hallowing of his → name (Matt. 6:9). In Jesus the kingdom of God has already broken in; it has been demonstrated by his powerful and wonderful acts. He has broken into Satan's realm and driven out demons by the "finger of God" (Lk. 11:20); but only the age to come will bring the full establishment of the kingdom of God. Then Christ will conquer the powers opposed to God (1 Cor. 15:24; 2 Thess. 2:8; Rev. 21:8, 27). When he has completed this his last task, God will be all in all (1 Cor. 15:28).

3. *The personal character of God.* When speaking about the personal character of God, it is illegitimate to transfer to God the concept of the human personality. God must not be imagined to possess a limiting → form. On the other hand, we are only capable of speaking of him in concepts which belong to our categories of thought. Moreover, if the personal character of God is ignored or restricted, the meaning of revelation is drastically changed. A depersonalized God is not the God of the NT.

The God to whom the NT testifies is the God who speaks and acts; he reveals himself through word and deed. He works in sovereign, absolute power (Jn. 5:17).

He makes his will known in → command and demand, and brings everything to the → goal that he has → determined. After he had spoken in the old → covenant in many ways to the fathers in the prophets, he has spoken in these last days "to us" through the Son, who reflects his → glory and bears the very stamp of his nature (Heb. 1:1 ff.). In the preaching of the word he addresses every man personally and receives into his → fellowship all who believe on Jesus. There are countless illustrations of this I-Thou relationship in the NT; it is the distinguishing mark of genuine biblical piety. Without it Christian belief in God would lack its ultimate depth.

(b) It belongs to the personal character of God that he is → Spirit (Jn. 4:24). Activities of the Spirit and of power proceed from him. The Spirit of God descended on Jesus at his → baptism (Matt. 3:16; cf. 12:18). Filled by this Spirit, he worked as the messiah sent by God. Matt. 12:28 states explicitly that he cast out the evil spirits through the Spirit of God. Christians are characterized by having, not the spirit of the world, but the Spirit who is from God (1 Cor. 2:12), for the natural man does not understand anything that comes from the Spirit of God (1 Cor. 2:14 f.). Only the spiritual man is capable of knowing God (1 Cor. 2:11) and of penetrating the depths of God. God has revealed his secret wisdom to believers through his Spirit (1 Cor. 2:10). He dwells in them and thus becomes the formative power of their being (1 Cor. 2:11).

In this age limits are imposed on the believer's knowledge. In God's rule over salvation history there are "times and seasons" of true revelation which he has reserved for himself (Mk. 13:32; Acts 1:7; 1 Thess. 5:2), "judgments" which are incomprehensible and "ways" which are unsearchable (Rom. 11:33). Nevertheless, → mysteries, which have been hidden in God from the beginning of time until now, have been made known through the proclamation of the message of salvation. The apostolic ministry, given by grace, testifies to the world of the unfathomable riches of Christ. Through the Christian community the knowledge about God's manifold wisdom has penetrated even as far as the cosmic powers (Eph. 3:8–10). Paul saw himself as the custodian of the mysteries of God (1 Cor. 4:1).

In 1 Cor. 6:11 the apostle explains that the Spirit of God (in conjunction with the name of the Lord Jesus Christ) has washed, sanctified and justified Christians. Through the divine Spirit working in them they are no longer in the realm of the → flesh but in that of the Spirit. Hence they live according to the Spirit (Rom. 8:4–14).

True confession of Christ is brought about by the Spirit of God (Rom. 10:9; 1 Cor. 12:3; cf. Matt. 16:17). In situations of suffering he gives the word that is necessary for the defence of and witness to the gospel (Matt. 10:20). He rests on those who are abused on account of the name of Christ (1 Pet. 4:14).

(c) The personal character of God finds special expression in the confession of God as → Father. Jesus' relationship to God is essentially determined by his Father–Son relationship. As the "only-begotten" Son, he is bound to God in a special way, as Jn.'s use of the *monogenēs* is intended to show (cf. Jn. 1:14, 18; 3:16, 18; 1 Jn. 4:9). ([Ed.] Lit. the Gk. means "of a single [*monos*] kind [*genos*]." While *genos* is distantly related to *gennan*, beget → Birth, there is little linguistic justification for translating *monogenēs* as "only begotten." The latter practice originated with Jerome who translated it by the Lat. *unigenitus* to emphasize Jesus' divine

75

origin in answer to Arianism. The word *monogenēs* reflects the Heb. *yāḥiḏ*, only, precious [Gen. 22:2, 12, 16, of Isaac], and is used in Heb. 11:17 of Isaac who was unique in the sense of being the sole son of promise, but who was not the only son whom Abraham begat. Perhaps the word may best be translated as "unique". Jn. clearly intends to distinguish Jesus' unique relationship with the Father from that of others who become children of God through him [cf. Jn. 1:14 with v. 13]. For further discussion see Arndt, 528; D. Moody, *JBL* 72, 1953, 213–19; R. E. Brown, *The Gospel According to John*, I, 1966, 13 f.)

In → prayer Jesus called God "Abba, Father" (Mk. 14:36) or → "Father" (Matt. 11:25 f.; Lk. 23:24; Jn. 11:41; 17:1; 5, 11). At other times he spoke of him as his heavenly Father (e.g. Matt. 10:33; 16:17). Jn. emphasizes the Father-Son relationship between God and Jesus (about 80 times) more strongly than the Synoptics (but see the fuller version of Peter's confession of Christ in Matt. 16:16 ff. par. Mk. 8:29, Lk. 9:20; cf. Jn. 6:68 f.). Jesus also gave his disciples the right to approach God with the invocation "our Father" (Matt. 6:9; Lk. 11:2). In the quiet room at home the individual may pray personally to his Father (Matt. 6:4, 6, 18). The name "Father" is applied to God in illustrations and parables (e.g. Lk. 15:11 ff.). As Father, God is the God who is near to whom man can turn in believing trust with all his petitions. Moreover, God is the sustainer of the creatures he has made. He receives them with fatherly goodness and surrounds them with his care (Matt. 6:26–32; 10:29–31).

The NT epistles use the solemn, confessional formula "the God and Father of our Lord Jesus Christ" (Rom. 15:6; 2 Cor. 1:3; Eph. 1:3; Col. 1:3; 1 Pet 1:3). In Christ believers are related to God as children. His Spirit testifies to them that they are God's children (Rom. 8:16). Therefore, in prayer they too may cry "Abba, Father" (Gal. 4:6; Rom. 8:15). This is a gift of grace procured through the Spirit of the Son of God.

The idea of the children of God takes on a special colouring in 1 John. Here the statements are no longer determined, as in Paul, by the concept of adoption, of being received into the place of a child, but by that of begetting (→ Birth, art. *gennaō*). Christians are God's children because they have been begotten by God (1 Jn. 3:9; cf. 2:29; 4:7). This means that the origin of their new being is to be found solely in God (1 Jn. 4:4). With this are linked statements of a mystical nature. John knew not only a Christ-mysticism but also a God-mysticism. There is true fellowship with God only when Christians abide in God and when God abides in them (1 Jn. 4:16). But as God is love, this means abiding in love. Out of this deep, inner relationship with God arises a completely new, concrete, ethical obligation: love of the brethren which must lead to practical aid (1 Jn. 3:16 f.).

4. *The attributes of God.* (a) In the NT there is no fixed, systematically ordered doctrine of the attributes of God. But there is a wealth of allusions, especially in expressions of prayer and faith and in descriptions of divine acts. More rare than in the OT but nevertheless present are allusions to the → holiness of God (Jn. 17:11; 1 Pet. 1:15; Rev. 3:7; 4:8; 15:4), his (present and future) wrath (→ Anger) (Rom. 1:18; 2:5; 9:22; Eph. 5:6; 1 Thess. 1:10; Rev. 6:17; 11:18; 14:10), and his glory (Acts 7:2; Rom. 1:23; 6:4; Eph. 3:16; 1 Thess. 2:12; Tit. 2:13; Rev. 15:8; 21:11, 23). It is otherwise in the case of the kingly rule of God (→ Kingdom), which in the Synoptic Gospels forms the centre of Jesus' preaching, but which in the

proclamation of the apostles withdraws into the background in favour of the message of Christ. Only once is God called *teleios*, in the sense of moral perfection (Matt. 5:48, → Goal). The → will of God is spoken of more often (as commanding, demanding and gracious); his mysterious counsel (Acts 20:27) and plan of salvation (Eph. 1:3-11) are also spoken of. Paul strongly emphasizes the faithfulness of God (Rom. 3:3; 1 Cor. 1:9; 10:13; cf. 2 Cor. 1:18). God abides by his → promises and fulfils them (Rom. 9:6 ff.; → Fullness, art. *plēroō*). For Israel this means that God's gifts of grace and their election by God are irrevocable (Rom. 11:29). God does not lie (Heb. 6:18; cf. Tit. 1:2); he is utterly true and his testimony is absolutely valid (Jn. 3:33).

(b) God is the eternal (Rom. 16:26) and only wise God (Rom. 16:27). Beside these expressions stand others which are to be found in contemporary philosophical language. Thus God is described as the invisible (Rom. 1:20; Col. 1:15 f.; 1 Tim. 1:17; Heb. 11:27) and the immortal (Rom. 1:23; 1 Tim. 1:17). In 1 Tim. 1:11 and 6:15 he is called by an attribute taken over from Hellenistic Judaism, the "blessed" God. The doxology in 1 Tim. 6:15 f. is reminiscent of the prayers of the Hellenistic synagogue (for a review of background ideas see C. Spicq, *Les Épîtres Pastorales*, 1947, 200 f.). It confesses God in solemn words as the only Sovereign, the King of kings, the Lord of lords, who alone is immortal, who dwells in unapproachable light and whom no man has ever seen nor can see.

Paul's description of God in the Areopagus speech (Acts 17:24) also betrays Hellenistic influence. It uses Isa. 42:5 freely and has affinities with Seneca, *Ep.* 41, 3 (cf. E. Haenchen, *The Acts of the Apostles*, 1971, 522; cf. also 2 Ki. 19:18; Dan. 5:4 LXX; Wis. 13:10). God created the world and everything that is in the world. The Lord of heaven and earth does not dwell in temples made by human hands. Nor is he served by human hands, as though he needed anything, since he himself gives to all beings life and breath and everything else. Though some of these expressions may sound strange today, Paul was concerned to testify to the true and living God in terms that were relevant to his day. This is the God whom the heathen of Athens worshipped, more unconsciously than consciously, and to whom they had erected an altar with the inscription "To an unknown god [*agnōstō theō*]" (Acts 17:23). (E. Norden interpreted this as a reference to the unknown God of Gnosis in *Agnostos Theos*, 1913, 57 ff., but this is generally recognized as incorrect [cf. E. Haenchen, op. cit., 521, and also Arndt, 12]). The apostle could even press into service for his missionary task the words of a Greek poet which carry the stamp of pantheistic mysticism, "In him [God] we live and move and have our being" (Epimenides); "We are his offspring" (Aratus, *Phaenomena* 5; cf. Acts 17:28; see also below, section 9). ([Ed.] For Paul, man had a natural awareness of God which was consonant with the revelation of God in the OT and Christian experience. This knowledge is sufficient to show the error of identifying God with any finite thing or creature. Paul does not argue that man may arrive at such a conclusion as the result of a metaphysical proof. Man has this awareness already, and reflection on the finite character of the natural order should be sufficient to tell him that God is not to be identified with anything or anyone within that order [Acts 14:17; Rom. 1:19 ff., 32; and possibly Rom. 2:12-16, though this last passage may well refer to Gentile believers who have responded to the gospel without having had the law and who thus fulfil the promise of the new covenant of

77

Jer. 31:31 ff.]. For further discussion see N. B. Stonehouse, *Paul before the Areopagus and Other New Testament Studies*, 1957, 1–40; H. P. Owen, "The Scope of Natural Revelation in Rom. 1 and Acts 17," *NTS* 5, 1958–9, 133–43; C. Brown, *Karl Barth and the Christian Message*, 1967, 94–98; and the literature listed by E. Haenchen, op. cit., 516.)

(c) A central concept in Paul's theology is the → righteousness of God (Rom. 1:17, 21 f.; 9:30; 10:3; 2 Cor. 5:21; Phil. 3:9). It is a judging but also a saving righteousness. God is just when he condemns sinful mankind. But he is equally just when he bestows his forgiving grace on those who have believed in Christ and in the salvation procured through him. For Christ's sake, in whom God himself offered the atoning sacrifice for the → guilt of mankind, he does not count their sins against them but pronounces them righteous. Thus the *dikaiosynē theou* forms the foundation of Paul's doctrine of → justification (cf. L. Morris, *The Apostolic Preaching of the Cross*, 1963[3], 273 ff.; D. Hill, *Greek Words and Hebrew Meanings*, 1967, 82–162).

(d) Because God is the initiator of salvation, both he and Christ are called *sōtēr*, saviour (1 Tim. 1:1; 2:3; 4:10; Tit. 1:3; 2:13; 3:4). God sent his Son into the world (Gal. 4:4) and delivered him to death for us (Jn. 3:16; 1 Jn. 4:10; cf. Rom. 8:32). The saving act of God is proclaimed through the word of the cross which is understood by believers as God's power and God's wisdom (1 Cor. 1:18, 24). For Christ has been made by God our → wisdom, righteousness, sanctification (→ Holy) and → redemption (1 Cor. 1:30).

Paul can call the whole message of salvation, declared to the world, the → "gospel of God" (Rom. 15:16; 1 Thess. 2:2; 1 Tim. 1:11; cf. also 1 Pet. 4:17). It brings salvation to everyone who believes (Rom. 1:16; cf. 1 Cor. 2:5). At the same time the offer of salvation, which comes through the proclamation, is universal. God desires that all men should be saved and come to the knowledge of the truth (1 Tim. 2:4), for his saving grace has appeared to all men (Tit. 2:11).

The power of God (→ Might) is not only at work in the gospel; it has demonstrated itself to be powerful from the beginning. Every man can recognize the invisible being of God in the works of creation (Rom. 1:20). It is also the power of God which raised Christ from the dead (Acts 2:24, 32; Rom. 8:11; 10:9) and thereby ushered in the new creation of mankind and of the universe. Believers even now experience the transcendent → fullness of God's power (2 Cor. 4:7), his mighty strength (Eph. 1:19; 3:20). Hence the apostle prays that they may be continually built up through the Spirit, according to the riches of his glory, with power in the inner man (Eph. 3:16). But the ultimate aim of faith, knowledge and love is to be filled with all the fullness of God (Eph. 3:19).

John has the expression which does not occur elsewhere in the NT, "to have God" (1 Jn. 2:23; 2 Jn. 9). Having God, which includes having the Son (1 Jn. 5:12), is bound up with a firm, true confession of Christ, free from every false doctrine (1 Jn. 5:11; → Fellowship, art. *echō*).

(e) The saving power of the divine being is expressed in a series of genitives which are connected with the noun God. God is the God of → peace (Rom. 15:33; 16:20; 1 Thess. 5:23; Phil. 4:9; 1 Cor. 14:33; cf. Heb. 13:20), the God of → mercy (Lk. 1:78), the Father of mercies and the God of all → comfort (2 Cor. 1:3; cf. Rom. 12:1), the God of all grace (1 Pet. 5:10, 12), who has blessed us in

Christ with the fullness and the riches of his grace (Eph. 1:7), the God of → love (2 Cor. 13:11).

(f) The full depth of God's being, is expressed in the statement: God is love (1 Jn. 4:8). His → love embraces the lost world which has turned away from him. It is the decisive reason for his saving and redeeming activity. He has proved his love by giving up his Son to death in order that all who believe on him may have eternal life (Jn. 3:16). Above all his love is for the individual believer; God loved us (1 Jn. 4:10); we are the beloved of God (Col. 3:12).

All real love has its origin in God (1 Jn. 4:7). Whoever does not love has not known God (1 Jn. 4:8). The love of God is poured out in our hearts through the Holy Spirit (Rom. 5:5). It is the highest spiritual → gift, without which all the other *charismata* are meaningless (1 Cor. 13).

As God of love, God is rich in → goodness, forbearance and patience (Rom. 2:4). Tit. 3:4 speaks of the goodness and kindness of God towards men, using Hel. language associated with the solemn courtly style for the Hel. ruler and frequently discussed by philosophers (cf. C. Spicq, *Les Épîtres Pastorales*, 1947, 275 f.).

5. *God and Christ.* The uniqueness of → Jesus Christ as the → Son of God is most fully developed in Jn. and the epistles. He was "descended from → David according to the → flesh" (Rom. 1:3; cf. Matt. 1:1–17; Lk. 3:23–38; Acts 2:30; 2 Tim. 2:8; and cf. Mk. 12:35 f. par. Matt. 22:21, Lk. 20:41). And he was "designated Son of God in power according to the Spirit of holiness by his resurrection from the dead, Jesus Christ our Lord" (Rom. 1:4). Perhaps the correct meaning here is: "whom God decreed Son of God with power . . . through resurrection . . ." (cf. M. Black, *Romans*, 1973, 36). The allusion is to the divine decree of Ps. 2:6 ff. (cf. L. C. Allen, "The Old Testament Background of *prohorizein* in the New Testament," *NTS* 17, 1970–71, 104 ff.; see also on this passage M. E. Boismard, "Constitué Fils de Dieu," *RB* 40, 1953, 5–17; E. Schweizer, "Röm. 1:3 f. und der Gegensatz von Fleisch und Geist vor und bei Paulus," *EvTh* 15, 1955, 563–71; E. Linnemann, "Tradition und Interpretation in Röm. 1:3 ff.," *EvTh* 31, 1971, 264–75; and for patristic interpretations M. F. Wiles, *The Divine Apostle: The Interpretation of St Paul's Epistles in the Early Church*, 1967, 80 f.). According to the developed christology of Jn. 1:1, he existed already before his earthly existence as the divine → Word (*logos*) with God. Thus he comes from God (Jn. 3:2; 13:3; 16:27 f.). It was God himself who sent him into the world at the time that he had determined to carry out his saving purposes among men (Gal. 4:4 f.). Therefore he comes with divine authority; God is with him (Jn. 3:2). He is the image of the invisible God (Col. 1:15); in him the fullness of the Godhead dwells bodily (Col. 2:9). Because he has come from God, he alone is capable of bringing an authentic message from God (Jn. 1:18). Thus he is the only true and trustworthy revealer. He and the Father are one (Jn. 10:30; 14:10; 17:11, 21). Therefore, whoever sees him sees God (Jn. 12:45; 14:9).

(b) There is not only a oneness of being shown by God and Jesus Christ, but also a complete harmony in speech and action. The words which Jesus speaks are words he has heard from the Father (Jn. 14:10); the works he performs are the works of God (Jn. 9:4). They serve to reveal the divine glory and therefore to glorify God (Jn. 17:4). This is expressed particularly in Jesus' words of self-disclosure in statements using divine → "I am" formulae (*egō eimi*) which in the

OT are self-revelations of God himself. He is the → light (Jn. 8:12; cf. 1:4, 8 f.; 9:5; 12:35), → life (Jn. 14:6; cf. 31:5 f.; 10:10 ff.; 28; 17:2 f.; 20:31), → truth (14:6; cf. 1:14, 17; 4:23 f.; 8:32), the living → bread (Jn. 6:48; cf. vv. 51 ff., 63), → water (Jn. 4:13 ff.; cf. 6:35; 7:38), and the only way to God (Jn. 14:6; cf. 10:9). (On the background and significance of these terms see C. H. Dodd, *The Interpretation of the Fourth Gospel*, 1953; and the commentaries on *John* by R. Schnackenburg, I, 1968; R. E. Brown, I, 1966, II, 1971; B. Lindars, 1972; and L. Morris, 1972.) In Rev., too, there occur divine I-am formulae like, "I am the first and the last," which come now from the mouth of God and now from that of the eternal Christ (Rev. 1:8, 17; 21:6; 22:13). It is clear that in the NT belief in God is most closely bound up with belief in Christ. The fate of men before God is decided by their position in relation to Christ.

(c) But Jesus Christ does not usurp the place of God. His oneness with the Father does not mean absolute identity of being. Although the Son of God in his pre-existent being was in the → form of God, he resisted the temptation to be equal with God (Phil. 2:6). In his earthly existence he was obedient to God, even unto death on the cross (Phil. 2:8). He is the mediator, but not the originator, of salvation (2 Cor. 5:19; Col. 1:20; Heb. 9:15), the → lamb of God who bears the sins of the world (Jn. 1:36). After the completion of his work on earth he has indeed been raised to the right → hand of God (Eph. 1:20; 1 Pet. 3:22) and invested with the honour of the heavenly *Kyrios*, → Lord (Phil. 2:9 f.). But he is still not made equal to God. Although completely co-ordinated with God, he remains subordinate to him (cf. 1 Cor. 15:28). This is true also of his position as eternal high → priest in the heavenly sanctuary according to Heb. (Heb. 9:24; 10:12 f.; cf. Ps. 110:1). He represents us before God (cf. also Rom. 8:34). If in Rev. 1:13 ff. the appearance of the heavenly son of man is described with features from the picture of the "Ancient of Days" (God) of Dan. 7, this is not to say that Christ is equal with God. In Rev. a distinction is always made between God and the "Lamb" (cf. Rev. 5:6 ff.; → Like).

6. *Christ as God.* A few NT texts raise the question whether the Son of God is also called God.

(a) Rom. 9:5 is disputed. After Paul has expounded the position of Israel in salvation history and has emphasized as an especial advantage the fact that Christ, according to the flesh, stems from this people, he adds a relative clause, which runs lit. "who is over all God blessed for ever. Amen." It would be easy, and linguistically perfectly possible to refer the expression to Christ. The verse would then read, "Christ who is God over all, blessed for ever. Amen." Even so, Christ would not be equated absolutely with God, but only described as a being of divine nature, for the word *theos* has no article. But this ascription of majesty does not occur anywhere else in Paul. The much more probable explanation is that the statement is a doxology directed to God, stemming from Jewish tradition and adopted by Paul. Overwhelmed by God's dealings with Israel, Paul concludes with an ascription of praise to God. The translation would then read, "The one who is God over all be blessed for ever. Amen." or alternatively, "God who is over all be blessed for ever. Amen." ([Ed.] See further M. Black, *Romans*, 1973, 130; B. M. Metzger, "The Punctuation of Rom. 9:5", in B. Lindars and S. S. Smalley, eds., *Christ and Spirit in the New Testament. In Honour of Charles Francis Digby Moule*, 1973, 95–112;

W. L. Lorimer, *NTS* 13, 1966–67, 385 f.; H.-W. Bartsch, "Röm. 9:5 und 1 Clem. 32:4: eine notwendige Konjektur im Römerbrief," *ThZ* 21, 1965, 401–9; H. M. Faccio, *De Divinitate Christi iuxta S. Paulum: Röm. 9:5*, 1945; for patristic interpretations M. F. Wiles, *The Divine Apostle: The Interpretation of St Paul's Epistles in the Early Church*, 1967, 83 ff.; and J. Murray, *The Epistle to the Romans*, II, 1965, 245–8. Murray claims that the passage cannot be treated as a doxology to God the Father, since it does not follow the form of doxologies elsewhere in the LXX and the NT. The application of *theos* to Christ suits the context and could be regarded as the culmination of a sequence of privileges given to Israel which Paul is enumerating. Moreover, comparable assertions of divinity may be found in 2 Thess. 1:12; Tit. 2:13; Phil. 2:6; Col. 2:9; and 2 Cor. 3:17. The assertion of Christ's Lordship is in accord with Paul's teaching elsewhere [cf. Rom. 1:4; 14:9; Eph. 1:20, 23; Phil. 2:9–11; Col. 1:18 f.; cf. also Matt. 28:18; Jn. 3:35; Acts 2:36; Heb. 1:2 ff.; 8:1; 1 Pet. 3:22]. Hence, Murray argues that "God blessed for evermore" stands in apposition to Christ.)

(b) Several passages in Jn. contain ascriptions of divinity. Jn. 1:1 (RSV) declares: "In the beginning was the Word, and the Word was with God, and the Word was God [*kai theos ēn ho logos*]." ([Ed.] The fact that there is no definite article before *theos* here has been taken to imply that the Word may be understood as being some kind of divine being but not in the fullest sense of the term. Such views have been put forward from Origen [*Commentary on Jn.* 2, 2], whose views were taken up by the Arians in the fourth century, to the Jehovah's Witnesses today. The passage is rendered by the *NEB*: "what God was, the Word was." J. A. T. Robinson appealed to it in support of his plea for a restatement of orthodox christology [*Honest to God*, 1963, 71; cf. *The Human Face of God*, 1973, 182; and the discussion by E. D. Freed, "Honest to John," *ExpT* 75, 1963–64, 61 ff.]. R. E. Brown considers the *NEB* rendering more accurate than saying simply that the Word was "divine" [*The Gospel according to John*, I, 1966, 5]. In any case, the adj. for "divine" is *theios*, whereas it is the noun *theos* that is used here. R. E. Brown points out that there are instances of nouns with the definite article after the vb. "to be" in Jn. (e.g. 11:25; 14:6), implying that we might expect the article here if Jn. had meant to say that "the word was God." On the other hand, the passage conforms to the pattern that in the NT definite nouns which *precede* the vb. regularly lack the article [cf. E. C. Colwell, *JBL* 52, 1933, 12–21; Funk, 143, §273; Moule, 116]. Hence, the RSV translation would be the correct one. For further discussion see B. M. Metzger, *ExpT* 63, 1951–52, 125 f.; J. G. Griffiths, *ExpT* 62, 1950–51, 314 ff.; N. Turner, *Insights*, 17; E. M. Sidebottom, *The Christ of the Fourth Gospel*, 1961, 48 f.; L. Morris, op. cit., 77. On the patristic interpretation of Jn. generally see M. F. Wiles, *The Spiritual Gospel: The Interpretation of the Fourth Gospel in the Early Church*, 1960; and F.-M. Braun, *Jean le Théologien*, I–III, 1959–66.)

On *monogenēs* see above 3 (c). In Jn. 1:18 a number of very good MSS read *monogenēs theos* ("the only God" RSVmg) instead of *ho monogenēs hyios* ("the only Son" RSV). The unusualness of such a reading is regarded by some as grounds for accepting its authenticity (cf. L. Morris, op. cit., 113 f.). If so, it would be a further affirmation of the deity of the Word.

Jn. 20:28 contains the unique affirmation of Thomas addressing the Risen Christ as God: "My Lord and my God [*ho kyrios mou kai ho theos mou*]." The statement marks the climax of the Gospel. God has become visible for Thomas in the form of Jesus. The climax of Johannine teaching occurs in the confessional formula of 1 Jn. 5:20 which asserts the full identity of essence of Christ and God: "And we know that the Son of God has come and has given us understanding, to know him who is true; and we are in him who is true, in his Son Jesus Christ. This is the true God and eternal life" (RSV). This gives a lit. reproduction of the Gk. words. An alternative translation is: "This [Christ] is the true one, God and eternal life."

(c) This is the nearest that the NT comes to asserting the full identity of Christ with God. Tit. 2:13 speaks of "awaiting our blessed hope, the appearing of the glory of our great God and Saviour Jesus Christ" (RSV, cf. RSV mg. "of the great God and our Saviour"). Hesitation has been expressed about appealing to this text as such an instance. "The application of the formula "great God" to Jesus which was a title for God firmly rooted in late Judaism would be completely unique in the New Testament" (J. Jeremias, *NTD* 9, 58). Paul's teaching in Phil. 2:6 speaks against complete equation, when it draws a distinction in the words, "though he was in the form of God, did not count equality with God a thing to be grasped." E. Stauffer is doubtless correct when he writes: "The Christology of the NT is carried to its logical conclusion with the thorough-going designation of Christ as *theos*" (*TDNT* III 106). *J. Schneider*

(d) Jesus' cry of desolation is recorded in Matt. 27:46 and Mk. 15:34. Both give a version of Jesus' words in the original language and add their own translation: "*ēli ēli lema sabachtani*? that is 'My God, my God, why hast thou forsaken me?' " (Matt.); "*elōi elōi lama sabachthani* which means, 'My God, my God, why hast thou forsaken me?' " (Mk.). The cry corresponds to the opening words of Ps. 22 which in the MT reads '*ēlî* '*ēlî lāmâh* '*ᵃzabtānî*. Mk. appears to have written the Aram. '*elōi*. The bystanders evidently took it to be a call to → Elijah who was taken up to heaven (2 Ki. 2:9–12) and was believed to rescue the righteous in distress (SB IV, 2, 76 ff.).

From the earliest times the cry has been felt to raise problems for christology. These are reflected in the MSS variants and the version of Gos. Pet 5:19: "My power, O power, thou hast forsaken me!" (cf. K. Stendahl, *The School of St. Matthew*, 1967², 83–7; Henn.-Schn., I, 184). It is felt that the words imply an abandonment by God which is incompatible with belief in his divinity, and a lack of trust on Jesus' part. Nevertheless, Matt. and Mk. did not shirk to record it. The cry expresses a sense of utter desolation, such as Jesus had not even experienced on occasions of temptation, rejection and in Gethsamene. His faithfulness to God's will had led him to the point where that will had to be done without the conscious awareness of God's presence. This was the experience of the Psalmist. And in recording the cry the evangelists may well have seen in it further fulfilment of Ps. 22 (cf. Matt. 27:35; Mk. 15:24; Lk. 23:34; Jn. 19:25 with Ps. 22:18; and Matt. 27:39, 43; Mk. 15:29; Lk. 23:35 with Ps. 22:7 f.; cf. also Heb. 2:12 with Ps. 22:22; see further B. Lindars, *New Testament Apologetic*, 1961, 89–93; H. Gese, "Psalm 22 und das Neue Testament", *ZTK* 65, 1968, 1–22). The poignancy of the parallels and the solemnity of the narrative may have been too great for the evangelists to pause to speak of → fulfilment. Jesus' cry is all the more poignant in view of the taunt (also made to the Psalmist): he trusts in God, let God deliver him. The suggestion that the cry was an interpretation put into the mouth of Jesus' perhaps in the light of the Ps. (cf. R. Bultmann, *The History of the Synoptic Tradition*, 1963, 313) raises more problems than it solves, for it is incredible that the church would have invented an utterance which appears to go back on all that Jesus had taught. The cry reveals the anguish felt by Jesus in being utterly rejected by friend and foe alike and in dying the most excruciating death. At the same time we may say with C. E. B. Cranfield that the cry is to be understood in the light of Mk. 14:36 (and par. Matt. 26:39; Lk. 22:42; Jn. 12:27) and the Pauline interpretation of Jesus' death in 2 Cor. 5:21 and Gal. 3:13. "The burden of the world's sin, his complete self-identification with sinners, involved not merely a felt, but a real, abandonment by his Father" (*The Gospel According to Saint Mark*, 1963, 458).

The parallels with Ps. 22 may, however, be pursued even further. G. Dalman has suggested that for the Jews the opening words were recognized as an effective prayer for help in the light of the latter part of the Ps. (*Jesus-Jeshua*, 1929, 206). The Psalmist survives his immediate desolation to praise God in the congregation (v. 22; cf. Heb. 2:12). All the ends of the earth shall remember and turn to the Lord (v. 27). Dominion belongs to the Lord and he rules over the nations. (v. 28). Posterity shall serve him and proclaim his deliverance to a people yet unborn (vv. 30 f.). If the earlier part of the Ps. may be seen as being fulfilled in Jesus' death, the latter may be said to find fulfilment in the revelation of the risen Christ in the great commission to evangelize (Matt. 28:16–20).   *C. Brown*

7. *God and the Church.* The community of believers is called the *ekklēsia tou theou* (Acts 20:28; 2 Cor. 1:2; 10:32; 11:16, 22; 15:9; 2 Cor. 1:1; Gal. 1:13; 1 Thess. 2:14; 2 Thess. 1:4; 1 Tim. 3:5, 15; → Church). It consists of those chosen by God and called to be saints (Rom. 1:7; cf. the opening address of most of Paul's epistles) and who have received all the gifts of salvation and grace. They have peace with God (Rom. 5:1), for they have been reconciled through Christ (2 Cor. 5:18). As the beginning of God's new creation (2 Cor. 5:17) they are his workmanship, created in Christ Jesus for good works (Eph. 2:10). God works in them both to will and to accomplish (Phil. 2:13), and gives them assurance of the completion of their salvation (Rom. 5:2, Phil. 3:21). At the return of Christ he will give life to their mortal bodies (Rom. 8:11) and a share in his glory and in eternal life.

(b) The church is the → temple of God (1 Cor. 3:16; 2 Cor. 6:16; Eph. 2:21); God's holy building into which all believers are placed as living stones (1 Pet. 2:4); the dwelling of God in the Spirit in which Christians are members of God's household (Eph. 2:19, 21). It is the new people of God (1 Pet. 2:9) which forms the → body of Christ in which believers have a share in the *plērōma*, the fullness of the being of God and Christ (Col. 2:10; Eph. 1:23; → Fullness, art. *plēroō*). The community stands under God's protection. It is hidden in him, for God is on its side (Rom. 8:31). Therefore no power, whatever it may be called, is capable of separating it from God's love.

Paul emphasized strongly that the *ekklēsia* of God consists of Jews and Gentiles. This is because Christ has reconciled Jews and Gentiles to God in one body through the → cross. Whoever receives the word of reconciliation (2 Cor. 5:19) and believes in Christ has free access to the Father (Eph. 2:18). In God's people of the new → covenant racial and national differences are removed.

8. *The Trinity*. The NT does not contain the developed doctrine of the Trinity. "The Bible lacks the express declaration that the Father, the Son, and the Holy Spirit are of equal essence and therefore in an equal sense God himself. And the other express declaration is also lacking, that God is God thus and only thus, i.e. as the Father, the Son, and the Holy Spirit. ·These two express declarations, which go beyond the witness of the Bible, are the twofold content of the Church doctrine of the Trinity" (Karl Barth, *CD*, I, 1, 437). It also lacks such terms as *trinity* (Lat. *trinitas* which was coined by Tertullian, *Against Praxeas*, 3; 11; 12 etc.) and *homoousios* which featured in the Creed of Nicea (325) to denote that Christ was of the same substance as the Father (cf. J. N. D. Kelly, *Early Christian Doctrines*, 1968[4], 113, 233–7). But the NT does contain the fixed, three-part formula of 2 Cor. 13:13 (EVV 14) in which God, the Lord Jesus Christ and the Spirit are mentioned together (cf. 1 Cor. 12:4 ff.). The Trinity of Father, Son and Holy Spirit occurs only in the baptismal formula in Matt. 28:19. The later addition, 1 Jn. 5:8 (in Lat. texts from the 6th cent.), contains the triad, the Father, the Word and the Holy Spirit (cf. E. Stauffer, *TDNT* III 108 f.). An extension of the triadic form in which, however, the important element is "the one God," "the one Lord" and "the one Spirit," appears in Eph. 4:4 ff. Gal. 4:4 ff. does not, strictly speaking, present a formula. It sets out the action of God in salvation history, placing God, Christ and the Holy Spirit in their right relationship: God first sends the Son and then the Spirit of his Son to continue the work of Jesus on earth.

On the other hand, God and Christ especially are closely connected in two-part formulae: "one God, the Father . . . and one Lord, Jesus Christ" (1 Cor. 8:6). "one God . . . and one mediator between God and men" (1 Tim. 2:5). In this connection Matt. 23:8–10 must also be mentioned, where Jesus draws the disciples' attention to the fact that they have one master (himself) and one God in heaven. In all these statements the two facts, that God and Christ belong together and that they are distinct, are equally stressed, with the precedence in every case due to God, the Father, who stands above Christ. (On the formulae see E. Stauffer, *New Testament Theology*, 1955, 235–57, J. N. D. Kelly, *Early Christian Creeds*, 1972[3], 6–29; V. F. Neufeld, *The Earliest Christian Confessions*, 1963.)

A close relationship exists also between Christ and the Holy → Spirit. Thus Paul can say outright that the Lord is the Spirit (2 Cor. 3:17). In John's Gospel the Holy Spirit (the Paraclete, → Advocate) appears with "certain independence" (E. Stauffer, *TDNT* III 107). But in his work he is bound to the exalted Christ (Jn. 16:14; "He will take what is mine"). Christ and the Holy Spirit are in an interchangeable relationship. But even here there is no strict, dogmatic assertion. Although the Spirit is distinguished from Christ and subordinated to him, it can be said in 1 Jn. 2:1 that Christ is the Paraclete with the Father. All this underlines the point that primitive Christianity did not have an explicit doctrine of the Trinity such as was subsequently elaborated in the creeds of the early church. (For discussions of the Trinity in the NT see L. Hodgson, *The Doctrine of the Trinity*, 1943, 38–84; A. E. J. Rawlinson, ed., *Essays on the Trinity and the Incarnation*, 1933; Karl Barth, *CD*, I, 1, 339–560; G. A. F. Knight, *A Biblical Approach to the Doctrine of the Trinity*, 1953; A. W. Wainwright, *The Trinity in the New Testament*, 1962.)

J. Schneider

9. *Pagan Deities*. It is unlikely that the average Greek and Roman took the old gods and goddesses seriously, but tradition and superstition led people to altars, shrines and images. The multiplicity of altars at Athens moved Paul to describe the Athenians as *deisidaimonesterous* (Acts 17:22), a comparative form compounded from *deidō* (fear) and *daimōn* (a deity or demon). The adj. *deisidaimōn* often means superstitious. But Paul evidently intended it in a more positive sense, i.e. "quite religious" (cf. the noun *deisidaimonia* which can mean superstition, fear or reverence for the divinity in a good sense, and religion [cf. Arndt. 172]).

The main Gk. pantheon, with the Roman equivalents given in brackets, was: Zeus (Jupiter), Hera (Juno), Apollo (Apollo or Phoebus), Ares (Mars), Poseidon (Neptune), Aphrodite (Venus), Hermes (Mercury), Athene (Minerva), Artemis (Diana), Hades or Pluto (Pluto or Orcus).

In 1 Cor. 10:20 Paul equated pagan deities with demons, but in addressing the intelligent Athenians, he quoted with approval Epimenides, Aratus, *Phaenomena* 5, and Cleanthes, *Hymn to Zeus* 4 (cf. F. F. Bruce, *The Acts of the Apostles*, 1951, 338 f.; see also above, section 4 (b)). "Yet he is not far from each one of us, for 'In him we live and move and have our being'; as even some of your poets have said, 'For we are indeed his offspring'" (Acts 17:27 f.). The poets are actually praising Zeus, but Paul makes it clear that he treats the quotations as referring to their highest conception of the supreme God, or rather their non-conception, the Unknown God, of whom he proceeded to speak.

The following Greek deities are named in the NT. (i) *Zeus* and *Hermes*. At Lystra, after an outstanding miracle of healing, Barnabas and Paul were treated as heavenly visitants, the dignified Barnabas as Zeus and Paul, the talker, as Hermes (Acts 14:8-18). (ii) *Ares*. At Athens Paul was taken to the Areopagus, or Hill of Ares, where speakers were allowed to hold forth, as at Hyde Park Corner in London, and where the Athenian Council met (Acts 17:19). (iii) *Artemis*. Her temple at Ephesus was one of the wonders of the world, and Paul's successful preaching roused the makers of shrine souvenirs (Acts 19:21-41). The Ephesian Artemis was only loosely identified with Artemis the huntress. Statues and descriptions show that she was the great Mother Goddess. (iv) *Hades*. In classical Gk. the god's name came to stand for his kingdom of the underworld, although it was quite common to use the expression *en Hadou* (gen. instead of dat.), meaning "in the house of Hades." In the NT the word is used of the place or state only (e.g. [*en tō Hadē*] Lk. 16:23; → Hell, art. *hadēs*).

Two Canaanite gods appear in quotations from the OT: Baal (Rom. 11:4; 1 Ki. 19:18) and Moloch (Acts 7:43; Amos 5:26). *J. Stafford Wright*

10. There are several compound words in the NT which indicate an actual or potential link with God. (i) *theosebeia* (1 Tim. 2:10) means reverence for God, piety, religion. *theosebēs* (Jn. 9:31) means God-fearing, devout, a worshipper of God. The vb. *theosebeō*, to worship God, does not occur in the NT but is found in Ep. Diog. 3:1 in early Christian literature. In all these forms the root is from the vb. *sebō*, worship or reverence, plus *theos*, God (→ Godliness, art. *sebomai*). Proselytes were sometimes referred to as *sebomenoi* [*ton theon*] (e.g. Acts 13:43; 18:7). These God-fearers were Gentiles who accepted the Jewish way of life in general, but did

not bind themselves to keep all the ritual details of the → law, in particular → circumcision (→ Conversion, art. *prosēlytos*). (ii) *theostygēs* (Rom. 1:30) is a compound from *stygeō*, to hate, plus *theos*. In cl. Gk. it means God-hated or God forsaken. But in its sole NT occurrence an active meaning appears necessary, i.e. God-hating, haters of God (RSV). (iii) *Theophilos*, Theophilus, is derived from *phileō*, to love. Its meaning is either "dear to God", as generally in cl. Gk., or "lover of God." In the NT it occurs only in Lk. 1:3 and Acts 1:1 as the name of the person for whom Luke writes. It is almost certainly a proper name, perhaps a pseudonym for some well-known person, but it could stand for any Christian reader (for discussion and literature see F. F. Bruce, *The Acts of the Apostles*, 1951, 65 f.; E. Haenchen, *The Acts of the Apostles*, 1971, 136 f.). (iv) *theios* occurs 3 times in the NT. With the art., *to theion* means the Deity (Acts 17:29). As an adj., it means divine and is used with power and nature in 2 Pet. 1:3 f. (v) *theiotēs* (Rom. 1:20) means deity: God's "invisible nature, namely, his eternal power and deity has been clearly perceived in the things that have been made" (see above, 4 (b)). *theotēs*, deity, divinity (Col. 2:9), is a stronger word and is used as an abstract noun for *theos* in connection with the incarnation: "For in him the whole fulness of deity dwells bodily." By contrast the weaker words *to theion* (Acts 17:29) and *theiotēs* (Rom. 1:20) speak of the Gentile awareness of the deity. (See further H. S. Nash, *theiotēs-theotēs*, *JBL* 18, 1899, 1–34; Moulton-Milligan, 286 ff.; and Arndt, 354, 357 ff. for the terms discussed above.)   *J. Stafford Wright*

| 'Εμμανουήλ | 'Εμμανουήλ (*Emmanouēl*), Emmanuel. |

OT The name Emmanuel which occurs in Isa. 7:14 and 8:8 means lit. "God [is] with us" (Heb. *'immānû 'ēl*). In the context of the times of Isaiah and King Ahaz the name is given to a child as yet not conceived with the promise that the danger now threatening Israel from Syria and Samaria will pass "before the child knows how to refuse evil and choose the good." Thus, the child and its name is a sign of God's gracious, saving presence among his people. The name can have either a minimum or a maximum significance. It could be a general statement that the birth and naming of the special child will indicate that the good hand of God is upon us. Or it could be a divine name meaning that God's presence with us is to be found in the child. In justification of the latter interpretation is the name of the one whom we may fairly regard as the same child in Isa. 9:6. One of his names here is *'ēl gibbôr* which, in the light of its application to Yahweh himself in 10:21, means Mighty God. (See further E. J. Young, *The Book of Isaiah*, I, 1965, 283–94, 306 f., 335 ff.; O. Kaiser, *Isaiah 1–12*, 1972, 96–106; J. Lindblom, *A Study on the Immanuel Section of Isaiah*, 1958 reprint; J. A. Motyer, "Context and Content in the Interpretation of Isaiah 7:14," *TB* 21, 1970, 118–25.)

NT Matt. 1:23 sees the angel's promise to Joseph of the son conceived in Mary by the Holy Spirit, who is to be called "Jesus, for he will save his people from their sins," as a fulfilment of Isa. 7:14. The quotation corresponds largely with the LXX, though the LXX does not give a translation of the name to indicate its significance. It does not necessarily mean that a virgin birth was prophesied, for *parthenos* could be used of others than virgins (e.g. Gen. 34:3), and similarly the Heb. *'almâh* could mean a young woman married or single (Gen. 24:43; Exod. 2:8; Pss. 68:25; Prov. 30:19; Cant. 1:3; 6:8). On the question of the virgin birth see J. Orr, *The Virgin Birth of Christ*, 1907; J. G. Machen, *The Virgin Birth of Christ*, [1930] 1958; T. Boslooper, *The Virgin Birth*, 1962; R. E. Brown, *The Virginal Conception & Bodily Resurrection of Jesus*, 1973. This question rests on the interpretation of verses other than Matt. 1:23. The name Emmanuel is not applied to Jesus elsewhere in the NT. The point of the present passage is to see in the birth of Jesus a saving act of God, comparable with the birth of the first Emmanuel. Both births signify God's presence with his people through a child. But whereas the earlier event in Isaiah's day was regarded at the time as having decisive significance, in the light of the coming of Jesus it proves to be merely the anticipation of the really decisive saving act and presence of God. For Matt.'s concept of fulfilment → Fullness, art. *plēroō*, NT 1 (c). See also on this passage W. C. van Unnik, "Dominus Vobiscum", in A. J. B. Higgins, ed, *New Testament Essays: Studies in Memory of T. W. Manson*, 1959, 270–305.

One may link Matt.'s quotation, written in the light of the disciples' experience of Jesus Christ, with Lk. 1:35, where the unique act of the Holy Spirit means that the child will be "the Son of God." Thus "God with us" is to be taken in a similar way. The child will be God come to earth. The conception by the Holy Spirit draws attention to the role of God in the birth and life of Jesus.

J. Stafford Wright, C. Brown

On God in the OT and in the ancient world:

(a). W. F. Albright, *Archaeology and the Religion of Israel*, 1956; *From Stone Age to Christianity*, 1957; and *Yahweh and the Gods of Canaan*, 1968; A. Alt, "The God of the Fathers", in *Essays on Old Testament History and Religion*, 1966, 1–77; L. R. Bailey, "Israelite *'ēl šadday* and Amorite *bêl šadê*", *JBL* 87, 1968, 434–38; T. Boman, *Hebrew Thought Compared with Greek*, 1960; but see also the discussion of Boman's metholodogy in J. Barr, *The Semantics of Biblical Language*, 1961; M. Buber, *The Prophetic Faith*, 1960; J. S. Chesnut, *The Old Testament Understanding of God*, 1968; R. E. Clements, *God and Temple*, 1965; A. Deissler, "God", *EBT* I 298–309; R. C. Dentan, *The Knowledge of God in Ancient Israel* 1968; W. Eichrodt, *Theology of the Old Testament*, I–II, 1961–67; O. Eissfeldt, " 'My God' in the Old Testament", *EQ* 19, 1947, 7 ff.; M. Eliade, *From Primitives to Zen*, 1967; J. Ferguson, *The Religion of the Roman Empire*, 1974²; J. Goldingay, " 'That You May Know that Yahweh is God': A Study in the Relationship between Theology and Historical Truth in the Old Testament", *TB* 23, 1972, 58–93; W. L. Holladay, " 'Yahweh, Maker of Heaven and Earth': A Study in Tradition Criticism", *JBL* 91, 1972, 321–37; J. P. Hyatt, "Was Yahweh Originally a Creator Deity?", *JBL* 86, 1967, 369 ff.; B. van Iersel, *The Bible on the Living God*, 1965; E. Jacob, *Theology of the Old Testament*, 1964³; E. O. James, *The Ancient Gods*, 1960; N. B. Johnson, *Prayer in the Apocrypha and Pseudepigrapha: A Study in the Jewish Conception of God*, 1948; A. Jukes, *The Names of God in Holy Scripture*, (1888) 1967; G. A. F. Knight, *A Christian Theology of the Old Testament*, 1959; C. J. Labuschagne, *The Incomparability of Yahweh in the Old Testament*, Pretoria Oriental Series 5, 1966; T. Ling, *A History of Religion East and West*, 1968; G. van der Leeuw, *Religion in Essence and Manifestation: A Study in Phenomenology*, 1964²; H. Miskotte, *When the Gods are Silent*, 1967; J. A. Motyer, *The Revelation of the Divine Name*, 1959; and "Context and Contents in the Interpretation of Isaiah 7:14", *TB* 21, 1970, 118–25; A. Marmorstein, *The Old Rabbinic Doctrine of God*, (1927) 1937; M. Noth, "God, King and Nation", in *The Laws the Pentateuch and Other Studies*, 1966, 145–78; J. Barton Payne, *The Theology of the Older Testament*, 1962, 120–76; J. Plastras, *The God of Exodus*, 1966; G. von Rad, *Old Testament Theology*, I, 1962, 203–19; H. Ringgren and A. V. Ström, *Religions of Mankind: Yesterday and Today*, 1967; H. H. Rowley, "The Nature of God", in *The Faith of Israel: Aspects of Old Testament Thought*, 1956, 48–75; and *The Religion of Israel*, 1956; H. J. Schoeps, *The Jewish-Christian Argument: A History of Theologies in Conflict*, 1963; N. Smart, *The Religious Experience of Mankind*, 1969; R. A. Stewart, *Rabbinic Theology*, 1961, 18–46; R. de Vaux, "The Revelation of the Divine Name YHWH", in J. I. Durham and J. R. Porter, eds., *Proclamation and Presence: Old Testament Essays in Honour of Gwynne Henton Davies*, 1970, 48–75; Th. C. Vriezen, *An Outline Theology of the Old Testament*, 1958, 128–98; H. J. Wicks, *The Doctrine of God in the Jewish Apocrypha and Apocalyptic Literature*, 1915; H. M. Wolf, "A Solution to the Immanuel Prophecy in Isaiah 7:14–8:22", *JBL* 91, 1972, 449–56; R. C. Zaehner, *The Dawn and Twilight of Zoroastrianism*, 1961.

(b). K. L. Bellon, "Der Sinn der Frage nach dem Ursprung der Gottesidee", *Zeitschrift für Missionswissenschaft* 38, 1954, 318 ff.; H. A. Brongers, "Die Wendung *bᵉšēm jhwh* im Alten Testament", *ZAW* 77, 1965, 1ff.; M. Buber, "Die Götter der Völker und Gott", *Festschrift* for O. Michel, 1963, 44–57; E. L. Dietrich, "Die rabbinische Kritik an Gott", *ZRGG* 7, 1955, 193 ff.; O. Eissfeldt, *Vom Werden der biblischen Gottesanschauung*, 1926²; and "Jahwe, der Gott der Väter", *TLZ* 88, 1963, 481–90; A. Gelin, "Le monothéisme d'Israel", *Lumière et Vie* 29, 1956, 9–26; V. Hamp, "Monotheismus im Alten Testament", *Sacra Pagina* 1, 1959, 44–56; J. Hempel, *Gott und Mensch im Alten Testament*, *BWANT* III, 2, 1936²; W. Jaeger, *Die Theologie der frühen griechischen Denker*, 1953; J. Jeremias, *Theophanie. Die Geschichte einer alttestamentlicher Gattung*, *Wissenschaftliche Monographien* 10, 1965; R. Knieriem, "Das erste Gebot", *ZAW* 77, 1965, 20 ff.; H.-J. Kraus, "Der lebendige Gott", *Biblisch-theologische Autsätze*, 1972, 1–36; W. F. Otto, *Die altgriechische Gottesidee*, 1926; and *Die Götter Griechenlands*, 1934²; H. D. Preuss, *Jahweglaube und Zukunftserwartung*, *BWANT* 87, 1968; G. von Rad, *Gottes Wirken in Israel: Vorträge zum Alten Testament*, 1974; B. Renaud, *Je suis un Dieu jaloux*, 1963; R. Rendtorff, "El, Baal und Jahwe. Erwägungen zum Verhältnis von kanaanitischer und israelitischer Religion". *ZAW* 78 Neue Folge 37, 227 ff.; H. Schrade, *Das verborgene Gottesbild und Gottesvorstellung in Israel und im Alten Orient*, 1949; H. Seebass, *Der Erzvater Israel und die Einführung der Jahweverehrung in Kanaan*, 1966; N. Söderblom, *Das Werden des Gottesglaubens*, 1926²; C. Steuernagel, "Jahwe und die Vätergötter" in *Festschrift* for G. Beer, 1935; U. von Wilamowitz-Moellendorff, *Der Glaube der Hellenen*, I, 1955²; H. Wildberger, "Das Abbild Gottes, Gen. 1, 26–30", *ThZ* 21, 1965, 481 ff.

On God in the NT:

(a). A. W. Argyle, *God in the New Testament*, 1965; R. M. Grant, *The Early Christian Doctrine of God*, 1966; R. G. Crawford, "Is the Doctrine of the Trinity Scriptural?", *SJT* 20, 1967, 282–94; D. A. Hagner, "The Vision of God in Philo and John: A Comparative Study", *Journal of the Evangelical Theological Society*, 142, 1971, 81–93; H. Kleinknecht, G. Quell, E. Stauffer and K. G. Kuhn, *theos*, *TDNT* III 65–123; G. A. F. Knight, *A Biblical Approach to the Doctrine of the Trinity* (*SJT* Occasional Papers No. 1), 1953; J. Jeremias, *The Prayers of Jesus*, 1967; T. W. Manson, *The Teaching of Jesus*, 1935², 89–170; H. W. Montefiore, "God as Father in the Synoptic Gospels", *NTS* 3, 1956–7, 1–11; K. Rahner, "Theos in the New Testament", *Theological Investigations*, I, 1965², 79–148; J. A. Sanders, "Dissenting Deities and Philippians 2:1–11", *JBL* 88, 1969, 279–90; R. Schnackenburg, "God", *EBT* I 309–16; E. Schweizer, "What is Meant by 'God'?", *Interpretation* 21, 1967, 421–34; H. F. D. Sparks, "The Doctrine of Divine Fatherhood in the Gospels", in D. E. Nineham, ed., *Studies in the Gospels: Essays in Memory of R. H. Lightfoot*, 1955, 241–62; W. C. van Unnik, "Dominus Vobiscum", in A. J. B. Higgins, ed., *New Testament Essays: Studies in Memory of T. W. Manson*, 1959, 270–305; A. W. Wainwright, "The Confession 'Jesus is God' in the New Testament", *SJT* 10, 1957, 274–99; and *The Trinity in the New Testament*, 1962.

(b). H. Braun, *Gesammelte Studien zum Neuen Testament und seiner Umwelt*, 1967²; G. Delling, "Partizipiale Gottesprädikationen in den Briefen des Neuen Testaments", *StTh* 17, 1963, 1–59; J. Feiner and M. Löhrer, eds., *Mysterium Salutis*, II, 1967; W. G. Kümmel, "Die Gottesverkündigung Jesu und der Gottesgedanke des Spätjudentums", *Judaica* 1, 1945, 40–68, reprinted in *Heilsgeschehen und Geschichte*, 1965, 107–25; J. Leipoldt, *Das Gotteserlebnis Jesu im Lichte der vergleichenden Religionsgeschichte*, 1927; W. Marchel, *Abba, Vater!*, 1963; C. Müller, *Gottes Gerechtigkeit und Gottes Volk. Eine Untersuchung zu Röm. 9–11*, *FRLANT* 86, 1964; T. Müller, *Gottesbild und Gottesbeziehung im Neuen Testament*, 1966; E. Pax, "Die Epiphanie Gottes im Neuen Testament", *BuK* 19, 1964, 106 ff.; E. Rohde, "Gottesglaube und Kyriosglaube bei Paulus", *ZNW* 22, 1923, 43 ff.

God in Systematic Theology:

(a). J. Baillie, *Our Knowledge of God*, 1939; K. Barth, *CD*, I, 1–2, *The Doctrine of the Word of God*; *CD* II, 1–3, *The Doctrine of God*; H. Bavinck, *The Doctrine of God*, 1951; L. Berkhof,

Systematic Theology, 1938; 19–178; E. Brunner, *Dogmatics*, I, *The Christian Doctrine of God*, 1949; J. Daniélou, *God and Us*, 1967; E. Farley, *The Transcendence of God*, 1962; E. J. Fortman, *The Triune God: A Historical Study of the Doctrine of the Trinity*, 1972; R. T. France, *The Living God*, 1970; R. S. Franks, *The Doctrine of the Trinity*, 1953; H. Gollwitzer, *The Existence of God as Confessed by Faith*, 1965; R. P. C. Hanson, *The Attractiveness of God: Essays in Christian Doctrine*, 1973; C. F. H. Henry, "God", *ZPEB* II 742–58; E. Hill, "Our Knowledge of the Trinity", *SJT* 27, 1974, 1–11; C. Hodge, *Systematic Theology*, I, reprint 1960, 191–482; L. Hodgson, *The Doctrine of the Trinity*, 1943; J. R. Illingworth, *Personality: Human and Divine*, 1894; *The Doctrine of the Trinity Apologetically Considered*, 1907; and *Divine Transcendence*, 1911; E. Jüngel, *The Doctrine of the Trinity*, 1976; J. N. D. Kelly, *Early Christian Creeds*, 1972[2]; *Early Christian Doctrines*, 1968[4]; and *The Athanasian Creed*, 1964; J. K. Mozley, *The Impassibility of God: A Survey of Christian Thought*, 1926; and *The Doctrine of God*, 1928; J. I. Packer, *Knowing God*, 1973; W. Pannenberg, *Basic Questions in Theology*, I-III, 1970–73; L. G. Patterson, *God and History in Early Christian Thought*, 1968; G. L. Prestige, *God in Patristic Thought*, 1936; K. Rahner, *The Trinity*, 1970; "Remarks on the Dogmatic Treatise 'De Trinitate' ", *Theological Investigations*, IV, 1966, 77–102; A. E. J. Rawlinson, ed., *Essays on the Trinity and the Incarnation*, 1928; C. C. Richardson, *The Doctrine of the Trinity*, 1958; N. H. G. Robinson, "God", in A. Richardson, ed., *A Dictionary of Christian Theology*, 1969, 137–46; and "Trinitarianism and Post-Barthian Theology", *JTS* N. S. 20, 1969, 186–201; E. Schillebeeckx, *God and Man*, 1969; D. Sölle, *Christ the Representative: An Essay in Theology after the "Death of God"*, 1967; H. E. W. Turner, "Trinity", in A. Richardson, op. cit., 345–51; B. B. Warfield, "The Biblical Doctrine of the Trinity" and "The God of our Fathers and the Lord Jesus Christ", in *Biblical and Theological Studies*, 1952, 29–59 and 60–78; A. C. Welch, *The Trinity in Contemporary Theology*, 1952; H. Zahrnt, *The Question of God*, 1966; and *What Kind of God? A Question of Faith*, 1971.

(b). G. Aulén, *Das christliche Gottesbild in Vergangenheit und Gegenwart*, 1930; K. H. Bernhardt, "Fremde Götter", *BHHW* I 589 ff.; K. Goldammer *et al.*, "Gott", *RGG*[3] II 1701 ff.; H. Gollwitzer, "Das Wort "Gott" in christlicher Theologie", *TLZ* 92, 1967, 161 ff.; J. Haeckel *et al.*, "Gott", *LTK* IV 1070 ff.; H.-J. Iwand, *Glauben und Wissen. Nachgelassene Werke*, 1961, 27 ff.; E. Jacob and W. Schmauch, "Gott", *BHHW* I 585 ff.; W. Knevels, *Die Wirklichkeit Gottes*, 1964; W. Künneth, *Von Gott Reden?*, 1965; B. Lonergan, *De Deo Trino*, 1961; and *Divinarum Personarum Conceptionem Analogicam*, 1957; F. Mildenberger, "Überlegungen zum Gottesbegriff", *ZTK* 62, 1965, 458 ff.; O. Plöger, W. Kasch and W. Wiesner, "Gott, Gottesglaube", *EKL* I 1639 ff.; H. H. Schrey, "Zwischen Orthodoxie und Häresie. Die doppelte Verantwortung unseres Redens von Gott", *Evangelische Kommentare*, 1968, 250 ff.

On God in philosophy and philosophical theology:
J. Adam, *The Religious Teachers of Greece*, 1908; T. J. J. Altizer and W. Hamilton, *Radical Theology and the Death of God*, 1968; J. Barnes, *The Ontological Argument*, 1972; P. A. Bertocci, *The Person God Is*, 1970; J. Bowker, *The Sense of God*, 1973; C. Brown, *Philosophy and the Christian Faith*, 1971[2]; S. C. Brown, *Do Religious Claims Make Sense?* 1969; M. Buber, *Eclipse of God*, 1952; R. Bultmann, "What Does it Mean to Speak of God?" and "The Problem of 'Natural Theology' " in *Faith and Understanding: Collected Essays*, 1969, 53–65 and 313–331; D. R. Burrell, *The Cosmological Arguments*, 1967; J. Collins, *God in Modern Philosophy*, 1960; M. Durrant, *The Logical Status of God"*, 1973; and *Theology and Intelligibility*, 1973; H. H. Farmer, *The World and God*, 1935; A. M. Farrer, *Finite and Infinite*, 1943; F. Ferré, "Is Language about God Fraudulent?", *SJT* 12, 1959, 337–60; and *Language, Logic and God*, 1962; and *Basic Modern Philosophy of Religion*, 1965; A. G. N. Flew, *God and Philosophy*, 1966; A. G. N. Flew and A. MacIntyre, eds., *New Essays in Philosophical Theology*, 1955; E. Boyce Gibson, *Theism and Empiricism*, 1970; K. Hamilton, *God is Dead: The Anatomy of a Slogan*, 1966; R. W. Hepburn, *Christianity and Paradox*, 1958; J. Hick, *Philosophy of Religion*, 1963; *Evil and the God of Love*, 1966; *Arguments for the Existence of God*, 1970; *God and the Universe of Faiths*, 1973; J. Hick, ed., *The Existence of God*, 1964; J. Hick and A. McGill, eds., *The Many-Faced Argument*, 1968; W. Hordern, *Speaking of God: The Nature and Purpose of Theological Language*, 1965; W. D. Hudson, *A Philosophical Approach to Religion*, 1974; F. von Hügel, *The Reality of God and Religion and Agnosticism*, 1931; E. O. James, *The Concept of Deity*, 1950; D. Jenkins, *Guide to the Debate about God*, 1966; A. Kenny, *The Five Ways*, 1969; R. H. King, *The Meaning of God*, 1974; H. D. Lewis, *Our Experience of God*, 1959; B. Lonergan, *Insight*, 1957; *Collection*, 1967; *Philosophy of God and Theology*, 1974; and *A Second Collection*, 1975; J. Macquarrie,

Principles of Christian Theology, 1966; *God-Talk*, 1967; *Thinking about God*, 1975; T. McPherson, *The Argument from Design*, 1972; and *Philosophy and Religious Belief*, 1974; E. L. Mascall, *He Who Is*, 1943; *Existence and Analogy*, 1949; *The Secularisation of Christianity*, 1965; and *The Openness of Being*, 1971; W. I. Matson, *The Existence of God*, 1965; W. R. Matthews, *God in Christian Thought and Experience*, 1930; H. Meynell, *God and the World*, 1971; B. Mitchell, *The Justification of Religious Belief*, 1973; B. Mitchell, ed., *Faith and Logic*, 1957; R. C. Neville, *God the Creator: On the Transcendence and Presence of God*, 1968; S. M. Ogden, *The Reality of God*, 1967; T. W. Ogletree, *The "Death of God" Controversy*, 1968; J. Oman, *The Natural and the Supernatural*, 1931; R. Otto, *The Idea of the Holy*, 1925; H. P. Owen, *The Moral Argument for Christian Theism*, 1965; *The Christian Knowledge of God*, 1969; *Concepts of Deity*, 1971; and "God, Concepts of" in P. Edwards, ed., *The Encyclopedia of Philosophy*, III 344–48; N. Pike, *God and Timelessness*, 1970; N. Pittenger, *God in Process*, 1967; A. Plantinga, *God and Other Minds: A Study of the Rational Justification for Belief in God*, 1967; and A. Plantinga, ed., *The Ontological Argument*, 1968; A. S. Pringle-Pattison, *The Idea of God in the Light of Recent Philosophy*, 1920; I. T. Ramsey, *Religious Language: An Empirical Placing of Theological Phrases*, 1957; *Christian Empiricism*, 1974; I. T. Ramsey, ed., *Words about God*, 1971; J. A. T. Robinson, *Honest to God*, 1963 (cf. D. L. Edwards, ed., *The Honest to God Debate*, 1963); and *Exploration into God*, 1967; N. H. G. Robinson, "The logical placing of the name 'God' ", *SJT* 24, 1971, 129–48; F. Schaeffer, *Escape from Reason*, 1968; *The God Who is There*, 1968; and *He is There and He is Not Silent*, 1972; F. Sontag, *Divine Perfection*, 1962; G. F. Stout, *God and Nature*, 1952; A. E. Taylor, "Theism", *ERE* XII 261–87; W. Temple, *Nature, Man and God*, 1934; F. R. Tennant, *Philosophical Theology*, II, *The World, the Soul and God*, 1937; P. Tillich, *Systematic Theology*, I, 1953; T. F. Torrance, *God and Rationality*, 1971; I. Trethowan, *The Basis of Belief*, 1960; and *Absolute Value: A Study in Christian Theism*, 1970; B. Tyrrell, *Bernard Lonergan's Philosophy of God*, 1974; G. N. A. Vesey et al., *Talk of God: Royal Institute of Philosophy Lectures 1967–1968*, 1969; K. Ward, *The Concept of God*, 1974; C. C. J. Webb, *Religion and Theism*, 1934; V. White, *God and the Unconscious*, 1952; and *God the Unknown, and Other Essays*, 1956. A. N. Whitehead, *Religion in the Making*, 1926; and *Process and Reality* 1929.

Godliness, Piety

When faced with that which is awe-inspiring, sublime, or holy, man always keeps a respectful distance and sometimes is seized with fear. The idea of distance is basic to the *sebomai* group of words. They denote the appropriate attitude to that which merits reverence, ranging from respect for one's fellow-men and the rules of society to reverence in public worship. On the other hand, the *eulabēs* group of words has more the character of caution and circumspection, and with this background came to be used for the normal religious attitude. The adj. *sebomenos*, which became the regular term for non-Jews who attached themselves to the synagogue, is discussed separately under → Conversion (art. *prosēlytos*).

εὐλάβεια	εὐλάβεια (*eulabeia*), fear, awe, piety; εὐλαβής (*eulabēs*), devout; εὐλαβέομαι (*eulabeomai*), to reverence, to be afraid.

CL The *eulabeia* word-group is found in profane Greek from the 3rd or 4th cent. B.C. Originally it denoted caution, circumspection, discretion, and then in later Gk. reverence (cf. R. Bultmann, *TDNT* II 751; Liddell-Scott, 720). The meanings discretion, fear and reverence are found in early Christian literature (Lampe, 567). From the basic meaning of *eulabeia* there evolved the additional idea of fear, dread, anxiety.

OT In the LXX the vb. in particular occurs frequently. The original meaning of *eulabeomai*, to take care, is clearly recognizable in Deut. 2:4; Sir. 18:27; 26:5.

For that reason the word is not used for numinous terror (→ Miracle). The meaning to → fear predominates in the LXX: Exod. 3:6; 1 Sam. 18:15, 29 (chiefly for the Heb. *yārē'* or *gûr*). It is frequently found in combination with *phobeisthai* from which it cannot be sharply distinguished (e.g. in Jer. 5:22; Mal. 3:16). But *eulabeomai* can also stand for the Heb. *ḥāsâh*; the appropriate translation is then to trust, to seek or take refuge, or to honour (Nah. 1:7; Zeph. 3:12 and passim). *eulabeomai* thus approaches the idea of devoutness. The adj. *eulabēs*, devout, godly, is found with the *v.l.* *eusebēs* in Mic. 7:2; Sir. 11:17; Acts 22:12. The noun *eulabeia* is found in Jos. 22:24 and Wis. 17:8 with the meaning fear; in Prov. 28:14 it means circumspection.

NT 1. *eulabēs* occurs 4 times in the NT and means as in the LXX devout, God-fearing. Thus in Lk. 2:25 Simeon is described as *dikaios kai eulabēs*, righteous and devout. In Acts 2:5 the witnesses from the Jewish diaspora on the day of → Pentecost are described as "devout men", likewise in Acts 8:2 the men who buried Stephen. In Acts 22:12 Ananias who was sent by the Lord to Saul is said to have been *anēr eulabēs* according to the law, i.e. his Jewish piety revealed itself in his keeping of the law.

2. *eulabeia* occurs in the NT only in Heb. 5:7 and 12:28. In Heb. 5:7 the old translations differ in their understanding of the words *eisakoustheis apo tēs eulabeias*. The Old Latin translates *a metu*, i.e. heard (set free) from his fear. The Vulgate rendering, however, is more likely: *pro sua reverentia*, Jesus was heard for his devoutness, i.e. his obedience (v. 8). The raising of Jesus from the dead was God's answer to his Son's supplication in the days of his flesh (cf. Phil. 2:8 ff.). In Heb. 12:28 the understanding of *eulabeia* as fear is suggested by v. 29 (cf. Phil. 2:12, "fear and trembling"); but the rendering "devoutness" is equally possible. The vb. *eulabeisthai* is found in the NT only in Acts 23:10 (*eulabētheis* as an alternative to *phobētheis*, which has the same meaning but is better attested in the MSS; → fear), and in Heb. 11:7, where *eulabētheis* denotes the attitude of → Noah while building the ark; the translation "in the fear of God" would seem to be correct.

W. Mundle

| σέβομαι |

σέβομαι (*sebomai*), to reverence, shrink back in fear, worship; σεβάζομαι (*sebazomai*), show religious reverence, worship; σέβασμα (*sebasma*), object of religious reverence, holy thing, sanctuary; εὐσεβέω (*eusebeō*), reverence, be devout; εὐσέβεια (*eusebeia*), devoutness, piety, fear of God, religion; εὐσεβής (*eusebēs*), God-fearing, devout, pious; θεοσέβεια (*theosebeia*), fear of God, reverence for God, devoutness; θεοσεβής (*theosebēs*), devout, God-fearing; ἀσέβεια (*asebeia*), impiety, godlessness; ἀσεβής (*asebēs*), godless, impious; σεμνός (*semnos*), honourable, worthy of reverence, venerable, holy; σεμνότης (*semnotēs*), honourableness, dignity, holiness.

CL 1. The root *seb-* meant originally to step back from someone or something, to maintain a distance. From this spatial meaning, as contexts often gave the reason for maintaining a distance, there developed the metaphorical idea of trepidation ranging from shame, through wonder, to something approaching fear.

This attitude is evoked by that which is sublime and majestic, or by the risk of failure.

The act. *sebō* (post-Homeric) is rare; as a rule the mid. forms *sebomai* or *sebazomai* (from *sebas*) are used. The combination with *eu* (well, which in compounds was used to imply abundance) rarely occurs in the case of the vb. (*eusebeō*); on the other hand the noun *eusebeia* and the adj. *eusebēs* are frequently found. The word *theosebeia*, which in form conveys the more restricted idea of one's attitude towards deities, does not in fact differ essentially either in use or meaning from *eusebeia*. *sebasma* is an object of religious reverence, an idol; in the plur. it often means the cult.

The negative, *asebēs*, *asebeia*, is used to denote an outrage against someone, whereby established laws and ordinances are broken.

semnos and *semnotēs* denote that which is sublime, majestic, holy, evoking reverence. The difference between these words and *sebō* is that they contain a stronger aesthetic element: thus a royal throne, an ornament, or sublime music can be so described. The adj. and the noun often denote the majesty of deity, but sometimes also the solemnity, serious purpose and grandeur of a man.

2. Words deriving from the stem *seb-* are very frequent in Gk., and convey the idea of devoutness and religiousness so characteristic of the Greeks. This devoutness does not consist – as in the Bible – in a committed obedience to a single, personally-conceived God; but rather in a holy trepidation, wonder, or admiration called forth by a majesty in things, men or deities. Accordingly religious homage can be paid to very different objects: one's country, a landscape, dreams, parents, heroes, the dead, etc. Later this basic idea fades, and *sebomai* can assume the meaning to bless or congratulate.

For the Greeks those who are worthy of reverence are above all the members of one's own family (including one's ancestors), the gods and the laws ordained by them. In religious usage there is an easy transition from respect or honour to the reverence of the cult. *eusebeia* is one of the virtues of the man who is righteous and acceptable to the gods.

The negative form *asebeia* likewise has an ethical and religious content. Because of the close connection between the ordinances of the Gk. city state (→ People, art. *polis* CL) and the worship of the gods, the *asebēs* is often named side by side with the *adikos* (→ sin); want of reverence for the gods and neglect of cultic obligations were considered anti-social. In the case of a man who was a misfit in the community, *adikia* was that aspect of his behaviour which was against the ordinances, while *asebeia* described that aspect which was against the gods. *asebeia* refers specifically to the cult of the state in Athenian trials for "impiety" (especially the one against Socrates). In Greece the worship of the gods declined more and more in favour of a philosophical ideal and an ethico-moral attitude. A philosopher could be an atheist (*atheotēs*), and Christians also were described in this way because they did not reverence the old gods (cf. Lampe, 44 f.). Being accused of denying the old gods, however, did not mean they were accused of *asebeia*; for the term *asebēs* was reserved exclusively for the man with no religion and no morals (Liddell-Scott, 255).

OT These ideas rarely appear in the LXX because the basis of OT piety is quite different from that of Hellenism. God the creator lays claim to man's service in thought, word and deed; he requires active obedience, not devout trepidation

92

to which lip-service is paid just on fixed occasions in cultic homage, or in the sphere of intellectual rhetoric. This active obedience, together with worship, is the characteristic feature of the fear of God (*phobos theou*, → Fear), which is essentially the OT (as opposed to the Gk.) idea of piety. Thus, in the few cases where *eusebeia* and its cognates are used, it usually renders words from the root *yārē'*, to fear. But often they are without Heb. equivalent. For *eusebeia* see Prov. 1:7; 13:11; Isa. 11:2; 33:6; Wis. 10:12; Sir. 49:3; 4 Macc. 5:18, 24, 31, 38; 6:2, 22 etc.; *eusebeō* Dan. LXX Su. 64; 4 Macc. 9:6; 11:5, 8, 23; 18:2; *eusebēs* Jud. 8:31; Job 32:3; Prov. 12:12; 13:19; Eccl. 3:16; Sir. 11:17, 22; 12:2, 4; Isa. 24:16; 26:7; 32:8; 4 Macc. 1:1, 7; 6:31; 7:16; 10:15 etc.; *eusebōs* 4 Macc. 7:21.

Only in the Wisdom literature, in Job and the Apocrypha (esp. 4 Macc.), do *eusebeia* and its related words occur more frequently – an indication of Hel. influence. The same is true of the *semnos* word-group (of which the noun and adv. appear once each, and the vb. not at all): out of 12 occurrences, 3 are in Prov., one is a *v.l.*, and all the rest are in Macc. This adj. describes that which is sublime, holy and thus worthy of God; in contrast with *hagios* (→ holy), therefore, it is the aesthetic element which predominates. For *semnos* see Jdg. 11:35; Prov. 6:8; 8:6; 15:26; 2 Macc. 6:11, 28; 8:15; 4 Macc. 5:36; 7:15; 17:5; for *semnotēs* 2 Macc. 3:12; *semnōs* 4 Macc. 1:17.

In the LXX the negative compound *asebēs* is used synonymously with *adikos*, unrighteous, unjust, and describes both an individual action and the general attitude of men, in departing from God. An injustice among men, particularly in Israel, is at the same time an offence against God and his commandments (cf. CL above). Thus *asebeia* and *adikia* stand very close to *hamartia*, → sin: social order and social justice are inseparable from worship. *asebēs* renders some 16 Heb. expressions and is particularly frequent in Job (e.g. 3:17; 6:19; 8:13, 19f., 22; 40:7[12]); Pss. (e.g. 1:1, 4 ff.; 9:23, 34 [10:2, 13]; 50[51]:13); and especially Prov. (e.g. 1:7, 10, 22, 32; 2:22; 3:25, 33, 35). For *asebeia* see, e.g., Deut. 9:4 f.; 18:22; Ps. 5:10; Prov. 1:19, 31; 11:5 f. The vb. *asebeō* is rather less common than the adj. and the noun (e.g. Deut. 17:13; 18:20; Job 9:20 f.; 10:2 f., 7, 15; 34:8, 10).

NT 1. In the NT this word-group is rarely found. Apart from the OT quotation in Mk. 7:7 par. Matt. 15:9 (= Isa. 29:13 LXX), *sebomai* occurs only in Acts, usually in its adjectival form as a technical term to denote the Gk. adherents of Jud. (→ Conversion, art. *prosēlytos*). In Acts 17:23 and 2 Thess. 2:4 *sebasma* is the heathen object of worship. *sebazomai* appears only in Rom. 1:25, where it means to show religious reverence. The vb. *eusebeō* (only twice), the adj. *eusebēs* (3 times), the adv. *eusebōs* (twice) and the noun *eusebeia* (15 times) are, apart from 4 instances in Acts, confined to the Pastoral Epistles and 2 Pet. In Acts 25:21, 25 *sebastos* is simply the Greek translation of Augustus – the exalted one; in Acts 27:1 it is used adjectivally to describe a cohort as "imperial", a common designation of certain auxiliary cohorts.

Like *hosios* (→ holy) which frequently stands alongside *dikaios* (→ righteousness), *eusebēs* and *eusebeia* denote a moral attitude in the Gk.-speaking world. Both ideas occur frequently in Hel. Jud. They are almost entirely lacking in the earlier NT literature, though very much in evidence in the Pastoral Epistles. This fact is best explained by supposing that early Christianity used these words at first for non-Christian piety and that only later did the Pastoral Epistles and 2 Pet. give them Christian content. Exceptions are the negative forms *asebeia*, godlessness (in thought and attitude) and the adj. *asebēs*, which are already found in Paul (Rom.).

2. Whilst *latreuō* (→ serve) is a neutral word for cultic worship, *sebomai* retains the anthropological emphasis of typical Gk. piety, i.e. deference to that which is sublime and exalted. It is very difficult to use such language in relation to God and Christ, because the Christian is in personal union with them, a union in obedience and trust.

In Rom. 1:18 Paul describes pre-Christian man as enslaved by *asebeia* and *adikia* "ungodliness and wickedness" (RSV; → sin), and states that the wrath of God rests upon him for giving divine honours to the creature rather than the creator (Rom. 1:25). He thus pronounces judgment upon all contemporary religious activity, for being wise in its own eyes, it fails to make any contact with the one true God and with his holy purpose either in the realm of worship or in that of interpersonal relationships. Here, as in the LXX, there is no longer a sharp distinction between *asebeia* and *adikia* (but cf. CL), because in the light of Christ's revelation, both are *hamartia* (→ sin). This important term gained ascendancy over *asebeia*, as indeed over all other terms which denote the outworkings of the power of evil.

As in the OT, *hamartōlos* and *asebēs* can stand side by side in Paul to describe the sinner whom Christ makes righteous (cf. Rom. 5:6 with 5:8; Rom. 4:5). The Pastoral Epistles take over this association (1 Tim. 1:9; cf. 1 Pet. 4:18). But here *asebeia* is in particular the antithesis of the much used *eusebeia*. According to Tit. 2:12, → grace leads us to turn away from an irreligious existence in order to live *sōphronōs kai dikaiōs kai eusebōs*, soberly, uprightly and godly. In 2 Tim. 2:16 the false teachers' alienation from God is described as *asebeia*.

3. The word *theosebēs*, which has the ring of Gk. piety about it, is used in Jn. 9:31. The additional thought that piety consists in doing the will of God shows, however, that this statement is firmly rooted in OT-Jewish tradition. In Acts the fear of God is described by the combination of *eusebēs* and *phoboumenos* (10:2): God is revered in that man fears him, i.e. offers him veneration, worship and sacrifice. At the same time the appropriate distance is maintained, because man is a sinner. This also explains the technical term *sebomenos* used in Acts. It denotes those Gentiles who worshipped the God of the Jews without wholly belonging to his people, i.e. without circumcision and minute observance of the law (Acts 13:43, 50; 16:14; 18:7; → Conversion, art. *prosēlytos*). This group of words is naturally used also for Gentile veneration of the gods (cf. Acts 17:23; 19:27).

4. The Pastoral Epistles use the relevant Gk. vocabulary more freely than the other NT writings, the probable reason being that → faith (*pistis*) is here more of a virtue than in Paul's other epistles and now means primarily a Christian attitude to life. Only on that account can the OT phrase *phobos theou* (fear of God) be rendered so consistently by the Hel. *eusebeia*, though to be sure the attitude of the believer – *zēn eusebōs en Christō Iēsou*, "live godly in Christ Jesus" (2 Tim. 3:12; cf. 1 Clem. 1:2) – is based on faith in Christ (1 Tim. 3:16; cf. 6:3), and its secret is the revelation of God in the flesh. The NT devout person now understands himself as a follower of Jesus Christ. Consequently devoutness becomes one in a series of Christian virtues (1 Tim. 6:11; Tit. 1:1; 2:12). Thus *pistis*, faith, here takes on a

special colouring as compared with its use elsewhere in the NT. Good works are definitely included in it (1 Tim. 2:10; 5:4) – not however in the sense of justification by works which was precisely the error for which the false teachers are attacked (1 Tim. 4:7 f.; 6:5 f.; 2 Tim. 3:5). Faith is now seen as something ethical and relating to this world; only once is it defined in relation to its ultimate goal, the coming → kingdom of God (1 Tim. 4:8).

5. The use of the *semnotēs* group (noun 3 times, adj. 4 times) also fits into this framework. In Paul it is used only once (Phil. 4:8), where directions are being given to Christians for the conduct of their everyday lives. Otherwise it occurs almost exclusively in the Pastoral Epistles. *semnotēs* differs from *eusebeia* in that it indicates, without direct reference to God, an ethical and aesthetic outlook resulting in decency and orderliness. Seriousness both of doctrine and of life is expected of the leaders of the church. By ruling their own families well and setting a good example, they are to bring up their children to be obedient and to lead honourable lives (1 Tim. 2:2; 3:4, 8; Tit. 2:2, 7).

6. In Jude and 2 Pet. Christians are described as the righteous who live, like Noah and Lot, in the midst of *asebeis*, ungodly men (Jude 4, 15, 18; 2 Pet. 2:5 f.; 3:7). Here *eusebeia* is seen as the Christian manner of life, which keeps Christ's return constantly in view (2 Pet. 3:11 f.). The Christian who lives in this expectation attains to knowledge and is preserved from temptation (2 Pet. 1:3–8; 2:9).

W. Günther

(a). R. Bultmann, *eulabēs* etc., *TDNT* II 751–4; W. Foerster, *sebomai* etc., *TDNT* VII 168–96.
(b). W. Foerster, "*eusebeia* in den Pastoralbriefen", *NTS* 5, 1958–9, 213 ff.; J. Jeremias, "Hebr. 5, 7–10", *ZNW* 44, 1952–53, 107 ff.; E. M. Kredel and A. Auer, "Frömmigkeit", *LTK* IV 398 ff.; H. J. Schultz, *Frömmigkeit in einer weltlichen Welt*, 1959; A. Strobel, "Die Psalmengrundlage der Gethsemane-Parallele Hebr. 5, 7 ff.", *ZNW* 45, 1954, 252 ff.

Gold, Silver, Bronze, Iron

χρυσός

χρυσός (*chrysos*), gold; χρυσίον (*chrysion*), a piece of gold, gold coin; χρυσόω (*chrysoō*), adorn with gold; χρυσοῦς (*chrysous*), golden.

CL The Gk. word is a borrowing from the Near East, Heb. *ḥārûṣ*, Assyr. *ḥurāšu*. This may reflect the fact that gold was rare in Greece before Alexander the Great captured Persia's stores of gold, but in Egypt, W. Arabia, in the mountains of Armenia and Persia gold was widely used and the goldsmith's art perfected from the third millennium B.C. Hesiod in *Works and Days* wrote of a golden age and a golden race of men who reflected the glory of the immortals.

OT In the LXX *chrysos* and *chrysion*, which became interchangeable terms, translate six different Heb. words for gold, of which the most common is *zāhāb*. These probably indicated differing degrees of purity in the gold which was often mixed with varying percentages of silver (cf. Gen. 2:11 f.). There were three ways of working gold. It could be melted and cast into moulds to form solid figures (Exod. 32:4), beaten into sheets with which objects could be covered (Exod. 25:11), or beaten into a particular shape (Exod. 25:31). Besides the cultic associations of

95

gold in both the Tabernacle and the → Temple, in countries round about it was made into idols (Exod. 20:23). It was frequently used for jewellery (Gen. 41:42; Jdg. 8:26) and at a comparatively early date it was used for currency (2 Ki. 18:14; 23:33). Since royalty throughout the ages made use of gold for crowns and thrones, cups and drinking bowls (1 Ki. 10:18, 21; Est. 1:7), gold became an appropriate gift for a king (Ps. 72:15). In Daniel's interpretation of Nebuchadrezzar's → dream the Babylonian king is the head of gold (Dan. 2:38). Because gold is indestructible it becomes a symbol for great value and enduring worth (Prov. 8:18 f.).

NT In the NT the danger of covetousness and the association of idolatry colour the thinking of several writers (Acts 17:29; 20:33; 1 Tim. 2:9; Jas. 5:3; 1 Pet. 1:18; Rev. 9:20). On the other hand, gold is presented to the infant Jesus (Matt. 2:11; → Gift; → Incense), and symbolizes lasting value (1 Cor. 3:12) and heaven's perfection (Rev. 21:18, 21).   *J. G. Baldwin*

| ἀργύριον |

ἀργύριον (argyrion), silver; ἄργυρος (argyros), [less frequent] silver; ἀργυροῦς (argyrous), made of silver.

CL The Gk. word derives from the adj. *argos*, shining, white, and occurs first in Homer. While the word denotes anything silver, it often has the significance of money. In Hesiod the silver age followed the golden and was inferior to it.

OT In LXX *argyrion* translates the Heb. *kesep̄*, which occurs frequently in the OT, often in connection with gold. Silver had been known as early as gold, but it was less plentiful in ancient Babylon and Egypt. It is first mentioned in the Bible as a medium of exchange (Gen. 23:15) and this use predominates in the OT. But it was also used for jewellery (Exod. 3:22; Cant. 1:11) and was sometimes fashioned into an idol (Jdg. 17:3). Mining for silver is mentioned in Job 28:1, and because it was rarely found in pure form, but was most frequently mixed with other metals, it regularly needed refining and so became symbolic of God's refining process in men's hearts (Isa. 1:25; Zech. 13:9; Mal. 3:3).

NT As in the case of gold, silver in the NT is associated with idolatry (Acts 17:29; 19:24; Rev. 9:20). It is corruptible and a potential source of corruption (Matt. 26:15); it is therefore an unworthy goal for living (Jas. 5:3; 1 Pet. 1:18). Indeed the follower of Jesus may be called upon to do without it altogether (Matt. 10:9).
                          J. G. Baldwin

| χαλκός |

χαλκός (chalkos), copper, bronze (not brass, AV, RV), a copper coin; χαλκίον (chalkion), a copper vessel or implement; χαλκεύς (chalkeus), coppersmith.

CL Since copper was the first metal to be worked in Greece, *chalkos* became the word for metal in general and applied at first also to iron. Later it also included bronze, copper to which a small amount of tin had been added.

OT In the LXX copper (Heb. *n^eḥōšet*) is first mentioned, together with iron, in connection with Tubal-Cain, who made cutting instruments (Gen. 4:22). This draws attention to an important development in the history of mankind. Copper weapons, mace heads, helmets, axe blades, were developed in the Early Bronze period, and a cache of 450 copper objects, including a socketed axehead of *c.* 3100 found at Nahal Mishmar in the Judean desert in 1961, has pushed back into the fourth millennium the achievement of high technical standards. Bronze probably made its appearance *c.* 2000 B.C., but copper remained in use for objects which did not need to be cast, and both metals became much more common from this time on. A hard cutting edge was achieved on this soft metal by hammering.

The altar of sacrifice in the tabernacle was bronze covered (Exod. 38:2), whereas its carrying rings were cast (38:5), and Solomon imported Hiram from Tyre to oversee the lavish bronze and copper work connected with the Temple (1 Ki. 7:13–47). Copper smelting was carried out as early as 4000 B.C. at Timnah, a mining site about 15 miles north of Elath. It was here that N. Glueck thought (in 1940) he had found King Solomon's mines, but B. Rothenberg has now proved that Egyptians operated these mines in the 14th–12th centuries B.C. In 1974 a network of underground mines and shafts, penetrating for hundreds of yards in all directions and at several levels, was excavated. These mines are at least a thousand years older than the earliest previously explored underground mines. The deepest workings are several hundred feet below the surface and are supplied with ventilation by air channels, roughly the diameter of a thumb, yet very few technical errors were noted. The description of mining in Job 28:1–11 will be illuminated by the new evidence now available.

([F. F. Bruce] In Ezek. 1:4, 27; 8:2 *ḥašmal*, which LXX renders *ēlektron*, electrum, silver-gold alloy, may mean brass [like Accad. *elmešu*]; the imagery of Ezekiel's inaugural vision "will have been suggested to him ... by ... the work of a Babylonian brass-founder" [G. R. Driver, "Ezekiel's Inaugural Vision", *VT* 1, 1951, 60–62].)

NT The word occurs only 6 times in the NT meaning copper coin (Matt. 10:9; Mk. 6:8; 12:41), the material from which an idol is made (Rev. 9:20), a commodity of merchandise (Rev. 18:12) and a clanging gong (1 Cor. 13:1), such as was used in various cults and here symbolizing the emptiness of speaking in tongues when devoid of understanding and love. The compound *chalkolibanon* (Rev. 1:15) describes an alloy, the exact nature of which is not known.

J. G. Baldwin

σίδηρος

σίδηρος (*sidēros*), iron; σιδηροῦς (*siderous*), made of iron.

CL The Gk. word meant not only iron but also anything made of iron and a place for selling iron. In Homer's time iron was highly valued and pieces were given as prizes. Hesiod considered the Iron Age in which he lived to be the epitome of human evil. The word is used symbolically by Homer to mean hard, stubborn, merciless.

OT In the LXX the word occurs frequently, translating Heb. *barzel* (Aram. *parzel*). Anatolian armourers were experimenting as early as the third millennium B.C.

with iron blades for swords, and one example from Dorak is dated 2500 B.C. The metallurgy of iron is believed to have been developed by the Hittites during the second millennium B.C. Deuteronomy mentions "the iron furnace" (Deut. 4:20), and it will be interesting to see how old smelting crucibles in the Sinai and Negev regions prove to be. Hittite iron was brought to Palestine by merchants from Tyre and later by the Philistines, who monopolized the blacksmith's art (1 Sam. 13:19, 20). The Canaanites had chariots of iron (i.e. with iron fittings) in the Judges period (Jos. 17:16; Jdg. 1:19; 4:3). By the time of David iron was used for nails (1 Chr. 22:3), though bronze was still being used in large quantities. The OT uses iron as a symbol of strength (Ps. 2:9; Jer. 1:18), endurance and hardness (Job 19:24; Mic. 4:13), and cruelty (Dan. 7:7, 19; Amos 1:3). In Nebuchadrezzar's image (Dan 2) iron with clay represented the last human kingdom before God's kingdom filled the earth.

NT In the NT the word is used in a symbolic sense (Rev. 2:27; 9:9; 12:5; 19:15), and once as an item of merchandise (Rev. 18:12). Rev. 2:27; 12:5; and 19:15 interpret Ps. 2:9 christologically as a picture of Christ reigning in → judgment. The iron sceptre may have been a short-handled battle mace (A. A. Anderson, *The Book of Psalms*, I, 1972, 69). *J. G. Baldwin*

D. R. Bowes, "Bronze", *ZPEB* I 655 f.; "Gold", *ZPEB* II 771 f.; "Iron", *ZPEB* III 307 ff.; "Silver", *ZPEB* V 437 f.; N. Glueck, "Ezion-geber", *BA* 88, 1965, 70–87 (this article revises some of the author's earlier opinions); A. Negev, ed., *Archaeological Encyclopedia of the Holy Land*, 1972, 208–11; B. Rothenberg, *PEQ* 104, 1962, 5–71; S. M. Paul and W. G. Dever, eds., *Biblical Archaeology*, 1973, 193–204; C. Singer, E. J. Holmyard, A. R. Hall and T. I. Williams, eds., *A History of Technology*, I, 1954, 582–88.

Good, Beautiful, Kind

Just as the concept → evil can have different, distinct shades of meaning, the ideas contained in the concept good are expressed in NT Gk. by three word-groups, each with its own separate emphasis. *agathos* is used generally for what is good and useful, especially moral goodness in relation to God who is perfect. *kalos* can be used as a synonym, but in comparison with the ethical and religious emphasis of *agathos*, it stresses more the aesthetic aspect, and stands for beautiful, fine, free from defects. When applied to acts, it means noble, praiseworthy. For Plato the *kalon* is the realization of the *agathon* in the sphere of objects. *chrēstos* expresses the material usefulness of things with regard to their goodness, pleasantness and softness.

| ἀγαθός | ἀγαθός (agathos), good; ἀγαθοεργέω (agathoergeō), do good; ἀγαθοποιέω (agathopoieō), do good; |

ἀγαθοποιός (agathopoios), doing good, one who does good; ἀγαθοποιΐα (agathopoiia), doing good; ἀγαθωσύνη (agathōsynē), goodness, uprightness, generosity.

CL As an adj. in secular Gk. *agathos* means serviceable and good; used in conjunction with a noun it denotes the excellence of the object described. Used as a noun, *to agathon* and the plur. *ta agatha* mean the good or good things which evoke a state of well-being. They may be material, intellectual, moral or religious, depending on one's ideal for life. It is only *agathos* itself which is used with this wide range of meaning from the time of Homer to Koine Gk. All the other derivatives listed above do not occur until the LXX or the NT. Cl. Gk. used *euergeteō* and other terms in their place.

1. In Gk. philosophy the concept of the good plays a major rôle. For Plato the idea of the good is the all-embracing, highest, and indeed dominant idea or form. For the good is the power which preserves and supports in contrast to evil which spoils and destroys (*Rep.* 608 e). In Plato the idea of the good has a religious colouring (*Rep.* 517 b 7–c 4), but Aristotle applies it as a formal concept to the totality of human relations. In his *Ethics* he defines the goal of all action as the attainment of some form of good (*Eth. Nic.* 1, 1; cf. F. Copleston, *A History of Philosophy*, I, 1946, 160 ff., 177 ff., 332–50; W. Grundmann, *agathos, TDNT* I 11 f.).

2. In Hel. thought the ancient humanistic attitude to life was shattered (→ Foreign, art. *xenos*) and the predominant meaning of the concept of good is once again religious. According to the Hermetic writings, the salvation brought about by the deity, i.e. deification, is the good (*Corp. Herm.* 1, 26). Thus the predicate good was reserved for the deity who brings salvation (*to agathon ho theos*, God is the good; 2, 16; cf. 1, 7; 6, 3 f.; 11, 17), for he alone is free from attachment to the material (cf. W. Grundmann, *TDNT* I 12 f.).

As an expounder of Hel. Jud., Philo names *enkrateia* (moderation, *Spec. Leg.* 1, 149), *eusebeia* (fear of God, *Spec. Leg.* 4, 147) and *sophia* (wisdom, *Rer. Div. Her.* 98) as the highest possessions by means of which the soul finds the way to God, the highest good (W. Grundmann, *TDNT* I 13).

OT 1. In the OT the concept of the good is indissolubly linked with personal faith in God. An idea of the good, freed from the concept of God as personal – comparable with the ideas in Gk. and Hel. thought – is inconceivable. The good is always a gift from God and as such is outside the control of man in his own strength (Gen. 3:5). It is presupposed throughout that God is the One who is good, and not just "the good." This realization is further developed within the OT in the course of a deepening of the relationship of the people and of individuals to God (e.g. Pss. 34:10 [MT 34:11]; 84:11 [MT 84:12]; 23:6).

Thus *ṭôḇ* became the regular designation of the goodness of God's character or actions. The LXX translates *ṭôḇ* in this connection almost exclusively by *to agathon*, and thus approaches the Graeco-Hellenistic outlook. It only rarely employs the nearly synonymous → *kalos* (e.g. Gen. 1:18). Thus God, according to the usage of the LXX, becomes man's highest good, and man finally becomes the lord of this good in the sense that he acquires a right to "good" treatment, as long as he regards God as his highest good.

2. That → God is the One who is good is made clear in the OT through his saving dealings with his chosen people, in the giving of the → law (Deut. 30:15; Prov. 28:10), in the historical events of the Exodus from → Egypt and the conquest of Canaan (Exod. 18:9; Num. 10:29 ff.). The Israelite found renewed reason for praising God as the One who is good in the knowledge that everything that comes from him is good, whether it be his work in creation (Gen. 1:18; *ṭôḇ* here also

embraces the aesthetic moment of beauty), his → word (Isa. 39:8), his → spirit (Ps. 143:10), even when appearances seem to say the opposite (Gen. 50:20).

The constant tension between God's → promises and their incomplete → fulfilment was bearable for Israel, because they recognized that God's promises in all their temporal fulfilments always look beyond themselves towards a final, eschatological fulfilment. The good which God has promised to his people will come to its real fulfilment in messianic, eschatological salvation. It is in this sense that texts like Isa. 52:7 and Jer. 32:41 have been interpreted messianically by Israel.

Recognition of the goodness of God could not be taken away from the → remnant even by hard, shattering, historical events like the exile. Nevertheless, Yahweh's goodness, his benevolent action in history, had been temporarily withdrawn from Israel and was deeply concealed. In the Wisdom literature, for example, striking expression is given to the way in which man saw his own limitations without illusion in the presence of the incomprehensible God. He recognizes the uncertainty of all life's values and the vanity of existence (Eccl. 3:12; 5:17), and sees clearly man's inability to achieve good (Eccl. 7:20). But in the last analysis even this scepticism, in which God is withdrawn and man stands alone, could not destroy the knowledge of the goodness of God, of his benevolent activity.

Post-exilic Judaism and Rab. theology also held firmly to the fact that God is good. For Rab. Judaism God's goodness brings salvation. It is revealed in the Law which is good and can be carried out. In carrying out God's law, man can now himself do good and be good (SB III 92 f.; IV 466 ff., 536 ff.). Nevertheless, essential goodness can only be realized in a man's personal relationships with God and with his fellow-men (Mic. 6:8).

3. The Qumran sect by the Dead Sea radicalized this unshaken confidence that good could be achieved into a strict asceticism, and linked it with the command to hate for ever the sons of wickedness. But here too – as consistently throughout the OT – it is the newly emerging songs of praise which are the genuine expressions of the sect's piety. They begin and end with the praise of God and his benevolent actions even in the midst of need and oppression. What stands out is what has been asserted in every period of Israel's history and expressed most completely in the Psalms (e.g. Pss. 16:2; 118:1; cf. 1 Chr. 16:34, 2 Chr. 5:13), namely that God himself is the One who is really and exclusively good. In the language of the LXX, he is the highest good.

NT *agathos* occurs very frequently (107 times) in all the NT writings except Rev. (where *kalos* does not occur either). The compounds formed with *poieō* are rare, and are found almost exclusively in 1 Pet. (apart from 3 occurrences of *agathopoieō* in Lk.). *agathoergeō* occurs only once (1 Tim. 6:18), and *agathōsynē* in 4 places in the Pauline writings.

1. According to the Synoptics, the OT statement about God's essential goodness is radicalized in Jesus' preaching: *oudeis agathos ei mē heis ho theos*, no one is good save God alone (Mk. 10:17 f.; Lk. 18:18 f.; Matt. 19:17). However, this does not prevent a natural application of the predicate "good" to the moral differences between men, who do good as well as evil (Matt. 12:35; 25:21; and par. Lk. 6:45; 19:17), an application which includes within it the goodness of God (Matt. 5:45; 22:10 and often).

But this admission of normal differences and the demand for works of love (Matt. 5:16; 25:31–45, where → *kalos* is used instead of *agathos*) must not be separated from Jesus' preaching as a whole. Jesus calls sinners to repentance. In this connection it is impossible to ignore the call, "Unless your righteousness exceeds that of the scribes and Pharisees, you will never enter the kingdom of heaven" (Matt. 5:20). "You therefore must be perfect, as your heavenly Father is perfect" (Matt. 5:48).

2. Jn. 5:29 proclaims judgment according to works. But this statement too has to be seen within the context of the whole message (cf. Jn. 10:27–29; 15:5 ff.). It is only in Jesus Christ that man is given a new opportunity of existence. In so far as he receives a share in God's goodness he also can pass on good to others by doing good. According to Jn. 10:11 and 14, Jesus is the good (→ *kalos*) → shepherd who lays down his life and makes available here and now the eternal good of redemption. In these passages *kalos* is used as a synonym for *agathos*. In Jn. 1:46 (in the form of a proverb?) the sceptical question is posed, "Can anything good (*agathon*, i.e. salvation) come out of Nazareth?" ([Ed.] L. Morris points out that the question does not reflect any known opinion of Nazareth; it is most likely to be understood as the utterance of a man who could not conceive of the messiah coming from such an insignificant place. The difference between *agathos* and *kalos* in Jn. appears to be grammatical: *agathos* is used predicatively at 1:46 and 7:12, as a noun at 5:29, while *kalos* is always attributive (*The Gospel according to John*, 1972, 165; cf. G. D. Kilpatrick, *The Bible Translator* 11, 1960, 173 f.).)

3. Paul takes up the message of the Synoptic Gospels. He too acknowledges the relative difference between good and evil men. Within God's sustaining order of things, the civil authorities receive their dignity and task to maintain law and order and punish evildoers (Rom. 13:1–4). The concept *agathopoios*, used only in 1 Pet. 2:14, also belongs in this context: the man who does right will receive praise from the authorities.

But the distinction which is justified among human institutions breaks down before God. The natural man is irretrievably in bondage to the powers of → sin and → death, and has no right to claim the attribute "good" for himself. Even if he is a fanatical observer of the law, which is good, it only works death for him (Rom. 7:18 ff.; cf. 3:20; 6:23; Gal. 3:10 ff.). But through the redemption which has taken place in Christ goodness overflows the believer. "We know that in everything God works for good with those who love him, who are called according to his purpose" (Rom. 8:28 RSV, cf. *v.l.* in RSV mg "in everything he works for good", or "everything works for good"; see M. Black, "The Interpretation of Romans viii 28" in *Neotestamentica et Patristica, Supplements to NovT* 6, Festschrift for O. Cullmann, 1962, 166–72; and *Romans*, 1973, 124; cf. also Rom. 11:32–36).

In Christ the believer is created for good works (Eph. 2:10), and receives a good → conscience (cf. Acts 23:1; 1 Tim. 1:5, 19). This also underlies the urgent exhortations to bear → fruit in good works (Col. 1:10), to seek to do good (1 Thess. 5:15) and to do it to everyone (Rom. 15:2; 16:19; Gal. 6:6, 10). Likewise, in Rom. 15:14 (cf. 2 Thess. 1:11) believers are exhorted to *agathōsynē*, good and fitting behaviour. *agathos* is essentially a quality which a man has (*TDNT* I 16 f., 18).

All honour is due to the one who does good (Rom. 2:7). Paul also maintains the concept of judgment according to works (2 Cor. 5:10; Gal. 3:10). But comparison with Rom. 8:31–39 is not intended. The gift and the task of the new life are kept in tension, with both aspects fully emphasized. Just as *kalos* can stand for *agathos*, Paul employs *kalopoieō* (2 Thess. 3:13) and *agathoergeō* once (1 Tim. 6:18), as synonymous expressions meaning to do good. *agathoergeō* also occurs once in Acts 14:17, where it refers to God who does good. A striking fact is the marked preference for → *kalos* as opposed to *agathos* in the Pastorals.

4. In the remaining NT writings *agathapoieō*, to do good, is used only in 1 Pet. 2:15, 20; 3:6, 17; 3 Jn. 11; and Lk. 6:9, 33, 35. *agathopoiia*, doing good, is employed only in 1 Pet. 4:19. Such right action is the visible proof that a man has really and gratefully grasped the new opportunity for existence as his own. 1 Pet. 3:16, 21 indicate the good conscience which the believer ought to demonstrate to the pagan.

In contrast, Heb. 9:11 and 10:1 lay their emphasis upon future, eschatological gifts (cf. 1 Pet. 4:19). In this age there is a permanent tension between God, who is good and who gives good gifts, and reality, characterized by sin and death, in which the Christian's life is caught up. It is in this perspective that the promise of Phil. 1:6 stands and has meaning: "He who began a good work in you will bring it to completion at the day of Jesus Christ." Therefore the warning of Gal. 6:9 also holds good: "Let us not grow weary in well-doing, for in due season we shall reap, if we do not lose heart."   *E. Beyreuther*

| καλός |

καλός (*kalos*), good, beautiful, noble; καλοποιέω (*kalopoieō*), do good.

CL 1. *kalos* (cf. Sanskrit *kalya*, healthy, strong, excellent) has as its basic meaning: organically fit, suitable, useful, sound, e.g. a suitable harbour (Homer); a healthy body (Plato); pure, genuine gold (Theognis); an unblemished sacrifice (Xenophon). Aesthetic judgments were very early attached to the concept of the fit and organically sound. *kalos* then also came to mean the aesthetically beautiful. Finally the concept was broadened again and gained the additional sense of morally good (Sophocles, Pindar and others). Thus, in the course of the history of Greek thought, the concept *kalos* achieved an inclusive meaning, linked with *taxis* (order) and *symmetria* (symmetry). In this context *kalos* came to mean "the total state of soundness, health, wholeness and order, whether in external appearance or internal disposition. For the Gk., then, the term applies particularly to the world of the divine" (W. Grundmann, *kalos TDNT* III 537).

2. A Greek ideal for life and education was expressed by the phrase *kalos kai agathos* which showed the aristocracy how it should live. An education based on the arts and exemplary behaviour moulded the nobleman in the ethics of his class. In Homer it is an expression of ancient European aristocratic pride among the leading tribes of Greece. For them inherited position had to be earned afresh by meeting high and inexorable demands. It had to be embraced along with a heroic bearing, self-discipline, and the will to be fair in all dealings between noble and commoner. Thus *kalos* and *agathos* were united in the single concept *kalos kagathos* (cf. W. Grundmann, *TDNT* III 538 f.).

Socrates and Plato raised this chivalrous class-ethic to the position of the general goal of all Gk. educational principles. In their writings the *kalos kagathos* is a man who is respectful and fair, thoughtful and discreet, moderate and capable in the way he conducts his life, a man for whom everything is in order (*Grg.* 470e, 518a–c; *Rep.* 3, 425d).

3. Finally Plato raised the concept *kalos* in the sphere of philosophy and religion to the status of an eternal idea by linking it with the experience of *erōs* (→ love). The unremitting longing and striving of the soul is directed towards the *kalon*. *erōs* is the force which drives men to seek and to recognize the *kalon* in this world (*Symp.* 204, 211 ff.; cf. *Phdr.* 249 ff.). That which links the divine and earthly realms and which gives life meaning and an eternal dimension is the *kalon*. Earthly beauty partakes of the eternal archetype of the beautiful. This religious significance which Plato's doctrine of ideas imparted to the concept *kalos* was retained throughout the development of Hellenistic Christian thought. For Plotinus the *kalon* was what flowed forth, the equivalent of the idea (*Enneads*, 1, 6; cf. 6; 7). Ecstasy, as a glimpse of the eternal beauty, is the highest experience. It is granted only to beautiful souls who grow to maturity on earth through the virtues of self-discipline, fearlessness and freedom from attachment.

For Augustine, too, and for Thomas Aquinas true beauty is at one with the eternally true and good, and is only found with God; everything on earth is merely a reflection of the divine beauty (cf. Augustine, *De Civ.* 19, 3; 22, 19; *De Pulchro*; Aquinas, *Summa Theologiae*, 1 Q. 5, 4; 1ᵃ 2ᵃᵉ Q. 27, 1).

OT The meaning which the Greeks gave to *kalos*, which became decisive for Christian antiquity and via Christendom for the development of thought throughout the western world, scarcely penetrated the world of the OT or the NT. In the LXX *kalos* is used as the translation of *yāpeh* (e.g. Gen. 12:14; 29:17; 39:6; 41:2) and denotes a beautiful external appearance. But *kalos* occurs most frequently beside → *agathos* and → *chrēstos* as a translation of *ṭôb*. It means good, not so much in the sense of an ethical evaluation as in that of pleasant, enjoyable, beneficial. *kalos*, as opposed to *agathos*, is what is pleasing to Yahweh, what he likes or what gives him joy, whereas *agathos* suggests more the application of an ethical standard. But it is impossible to draw any clear-cut lines of demarcation for the basic meaning of the Heb. *ṭôb*, for it contains both aspects. Only in one place does the use of *kala* give rise to what is probably the expression of an aesthetic judgment (Gen. 1:31). Perhaps one should translate even here *kai idou kala lian* as "and behold [it was] completely successful" (cf. MT: "and behold it was very good"). It means fair or beautiful in, e.g., Gen. 6:6; 12:14; 2 Sam. 11:2; 13:1. Otherwise it is striking that there is no room in the OT for the Greek ideal of beauty as a motive for living and for education. Everything is directed towards the will of God which is expressed in the law. Any ideal of self-perfection is thus excluded. Hence *kalos* is frequently used as a synonym for → *agathos* (cf. Mal 2:17; Mic. 6:8; Isa. 1:17; and also Num. 24:1; Deut. 6:18; 12:28; 2 Chr. 14:2 [MT 14:1]; and later Prov. 3:4). In the story of the fall *kalos* is used in the description of the tree of the knowledge of good and evil (Gen. 2:17; cf. v. 18; 3:5 f., 22). The LXX translates the Heb. *ṭôb wārā'* by *kalon kai ponēron*, "good and evil" (→ Adam; → Evil; → Knowledge; → Sin).

NT It is striking that in the NT *kalos* is used almost as frequently as *agathos* to denote good, and this happens consistently throughout the NT writings (*agathos* 104 times; *kalos* 99).

1. In the Synoptic Gospels, John the Baptist demanded from those who would enter the fellowship of the → kingdom good → fruit (*karpon kalon*, Matt. 3:10 par. Lk. 3:9). Jesus made the same demand (Matt. 7:17 ff.; 12:33; cf. Lk. 6:43 ff.). The parables speak of good seed (*kalon sperma*), good men (*kaloi*) who are caught in the net (Matt. 13:24, 27, 37, 38), and good ground (*kalē gē*) in which the word flourishes (Matt. 13:23 par. Mk. 4:20 Lk. 8:15). It is in this sense that Jesus calls men to good → works (*kala erga*, Matt. 5:16). Once again *kalos* is used almost synonymously with *agathos*. The fine or good works which Jesus expects are summed up in the maxim of Matt. 25:40, "As you did it to one of the least of these my brethren, you did it to me." They remain connected with the works of love which served as directives for the practice of mercy in Judaism (cf. Isa. 58:6–7, where they are already listed). At the same time the *kala erga* are removed from all thought of striving after reward (cf. Lk. 10:30 ff., the parable of the Good Samaritan; → Reward).

In the story of the anointing at Bethany (Mk. 14:6) Jesus, aware of his imminent passion, placed the deed of love which had been done to him higher than the almsgiving of his disciples. The opportunity for this act – the anticipatory anointing of his body and thus the affirmation by his disciples of his path of suffering – only offered itself in this historical moment.

2. In Jn. Jesus is the good → shepherd (*ho poimēn ho kalos*). Here *kalos* is used to bring into focus his office as shepherd in all its uniqueness, in contrast to contemporary false claims to the office of shepherd and to the shepherd-gods of antiquity (Jn. 10:11, 14). He is the good, the lawful shepherd, because he opposes the wolf at the risk and at the cost of his life. ([Ed.] This may be seen against the OT background of Yahweh as shepherd [Gen. 49:24; Pss. 23; 78:52 f.]. The patriarchs were shepherds. Ungodly kings were denounced as wicked shepherds [1 Ki. 22:17; Jer. 10:21; 23:1 f.]. Ezek. 34:5 f. pictures Israel as a flock without a shepherd and Yahweh as the true shepherd [vv. 11–16]. Cf. C. K. Barrett, *JTS* 48, 1947, 163 f.; R. E. Brown, *The Gospel according to John*, I, 1966, 397 f.)

Jn. 10:31 speaks of Jesus' many good works (*polla erga kala*) in the context of a controversy with the Jews. It is not the works that are in dispute, but his messianic claim, the evidence for which is in these very works.

3. Paul employs *kalos* as a synonym for → *agathos*; it does not convey anything which could not be expressed by *agathos* (cf. Rom. 7:18, 21; 2 Cor. 13:7; Gal. 6:9; 1 Cor. 7:1, 8, 26).

4. On the other hand, the preference for *kalos* in the Pastorals is striking (cf. 1 Tim. 5:10, 25; 6:18; Tit. 2:7, 14; 3:8, 14; 1 Tim. 3:1). Military imagery, in particular, is linked with the concept *kalos* (cf. 1 Tim. 6:12; 2 Tim. 2:3; 1 Tim. 1:18; 2 Tim. 4:7). But in other contexts *kalos* is used remarkably often instead of *agathos* (cf. 1 Tim. 1:8; 3:7; 3:13; 4:6; 6:19; 2 Tim. 1:14; 1 Tim. 4:4). The reason for this usage here is clear. The word was a favourite in popular Hellenistic speech and it expressed a Hellenistic sense of values. It is used here in order to express the more clearly for the second generation of Christians what characterizes discipleship of Christ. In any case, both OT and NT right on into the Catholic Epistles

(Jas. 2:7; 3:13; 4:17; 1 Pet. 2:12; 4:10) demonstrate a use of the term *kalos* which, without undergoing any change of meaning, is freely employed to express Biblical ideas in the context of Gk. language and thought.   *E. Beyreuther*

χρηστός

χρηστός (*chrēstos*), mild, pleasant, kind, good; χρηστότης (*chrēstotēs*), goodness, kindness, friendliness; χρηστεύομαι (*chrēsteuomai*), show kindness.

CL *chrēstos* originally denoted usefulness, and hence what appeared useful, good, suitable and proper (e.g. mild wine). This was very soon followed by the broadening of the concept to include moral excellence and perfection, in which inner greatness was linked with genuine goodness of heart. So *chrēstos* meant morally good and honourable, the capacity to show kindness to everyone. Used as a noun, *to chrēston* meant a friendly nature, kindness; in the plur. *ta chrēsta*, kind actions (Herodotus). In the same way the noun, *hē chrēstotēs*, from Euripides on, acquired the meaning of friendliness, kindness, mildness, and was used in inscriptions as a title of honour for rulers and important public figures.

OT 1. In the LXX the Hebrew word *ṭôḇ* in its many shades of meaning is translated by *chrēstos* along with → *agathos* and → *kalos*. There is little contemplation in the OT of the goodness of God in and of itself. On the other hand, his benevolent activity is constantly sung and recognized in hymns of praise. *chrēstos* and *chrēstotēs* are favourite, although not the only, words for expressing the abundance of good which God in his → covenant faithfulness displays to his people and to all men as his creatures. This constant mercy and readiness to help on the part of God is one of the essential themes of the Pss. (e.g. 25:7 f.; 31:19 [MT 31:20]; 65:11 [MT 65:12]). But *chrēstos* also occurs in prophetic texts, especially in Jeremiah (e.g. 40[33]:11; cf. 24:2 f., 5). This picture of the kindness of God grows deeper in the face of the bewildering recognition of the enduring nature of sin. Yet he still remains kind! Nor could the fate of the nation after the exile, with its conviction that God's dealings are incomprehensible, suppress the acknowledgment that Yahweh is kind (cf. 2 Macc. 1:24).

2. The Qumran documents continue the same train of thought. Just as the OT expected the pious, for his part, to show kindness which should reflect the kindness he had received from God, the sect also expected its members to show gracious kindness to one another. The often recurring phrase used to denote this is *'ahaḇat ḥeseḏ*, gracious love (e.g. 1QS 2:24; 5:4, 25; 8:2). Beside mercy (*raḥamîm*) and patience the Spirit of Light shows "eternal kindness" (*ṭôḇ 'ôlāmîm*, cf. 1QS 4:3). But in unexpected juxtaposition to the demand for gracious kindness towards one another stands the command for "eternal hatred" of the sons of wickedness (1QS 4:17). Here we can see, as it was radicalized in later Judaism, the limitation of the OT command to love or show kindness which was not taken to include unconditional love of one's enemies.

NT In the NT *chrēstos* occurs 7 times; *hē chrēstotēs* 10 times; the former 3 times, the latter exclusively in Paul.

1. *chrēstos* is used of things, as in secular Gk., to denote their goodness (Lk. 5:39, good wine).

105

2. The concept is used in Lk. to break down the limitation of the OT commandment to love (Lk. 6:35). God's kindness embraces even the ungrateful, and the wicked (obstinate sinners); because it is without limit, it calls for unconditional love for their enemies on the part of Jesus' disciples. Jesus invited those who had become exhausted by legalistic piety to take upon themselves his easy yoke (*ho gar zygos mou chrēstos*, Matt. 11:30). In experiencing his kindness, men are to be like him in showing kindness towards others (v. 29).

3. While *chrēstos* only appears 3 times in the Synoptic Gospels, the Johannine writings and the Catholic epistles do not employ the word at all. But Paul makes striking use of it together with the noun *chrēstotēs* which he prefers.

In his attack on self-righteous Jewish piety he shows that the goodness of God is no cheap grace which is there to be made a convenience of. It should lead to a horror of one's unwillingness to repent so that God's aim of converting men to himself may be achieved (Rom. 2:4).

Especially in his use of the noun *hē chrēstotēs* the apostle makes repeated use of the idea of the incomprehensible kindness of God. He does not desire the death of the sinner but his salvation (Rom. 11:22; Eph. 2:7; Tit. 3:4). His purpose is to show the meaning of kindness in the life of the man whom Christ has grasped. Kindness and gentleness belong to the visible gifts of the Spirit (Gal. 5:22). Love (→ art. *agapē*) shows itself as kindness (1 Cor. 13:4, expressed here by the vb. *chrēsteuetai hē agapē*). For kindness is an unmistakable and essential characteristic of love. Because kindness is one of the chief gifts of the Spirit, it becomes the subject of the exhortation of Col. 3:12: "Put on then, as God's chosen ones, compassion, kindness." As a direct out-working of *agapē*, it is always alive and active, breaking out spontaneously in the life of the man who is led by Christ. This completes the circle from the original kindness of God who created the world and men, separated a people for himself, and remains kind despite sin and wickedness, to the revelation of his incomprehensible kindness in Jesus Christ in the fullness of → time. Here God's saving activity reaches its → goal. In Jesus Christ God's fatherly kindness can be seen as in a mirror. Moreover, the members of the Christian community, the church, have to choose as their path in the world the way of kindness which they must show to all men. At the same time they have to choose it in a world which often betrays little sign of it.

E. Beyreuther

(a). W. Barclay, *Flesh and Spirit*, 1962, 97–102; M. Buber, *Good and Evil: Two Interpretations*, 1953; G. W. Buchanan, "The Old Testament Meaning of the Knowledge of Good and Evil", *JBL* 75, 1956, 114–20; W. M. Clark, "A Legal Background to the Yahwist's Use of 'Good and Evil' in Genesis 2–3", *JBL* 88, 1969, 266–78; I. Engnell, " 'Knowledge' and 'Life' in the Creation Story", *Supplements to Vetus Testamentum* 3, 1955, 103–19; R. Gordis, "The Knowledge of Good and Evil in the Old Testament and the Qumran Scrolls", *JBL* 76, 1957, 123–38; W. Grundmann, *agathos* etc., *TDNT* I 10–18; W. Grundmann and G. Bertram, *kalos*, *TDNT* II 536–56; R. Koch, "Good and evil", *EBT* I 317–21; L. J. Kuyper, "To Know Good and Evil", *Interpretation* 1, 1947, 490 ff.; H. D. A. Major, "The Tree of the Knowledge of Good and Evil", *ExpT* 20, 1908–9, 427 ff.; A. Millard, "For He is Good", *TB* 17, 1966, 115 ff.; C. L. Mitton, "Motives for Goodness in the New Testament", *ExpT* 63, 1951–52, 73 ff.; C. J. Orlebeke and L. B. Smedes, *God and the Good*, 1975; G. von Rad, *Old Testament Theology*, I, 1962, 154–60; B. Reicke, "The Knowledge Hidden in the Tree of Paradise", *JSS* 1, 1956, 193–201; C. Spicq, *Agape in the New Testament*, I–II, 1963–65; F. L. R. Stachowiak, "Goodness", *EBT* I 321–8; H. S. Stern, "The Knowledge of Good and Evil", *Vetus Testamentum* 8, 1958, 407 ff.; K. Weiss, *chrēstos* etc. *TDNT* IX 472–81; J. W.

Wenham, *The Goodness of God*, 1974; F. Wisse, "The Righteous Man and the Good Man in Romans v. 7", *NTS* 19, 1972–73, 91 ff.
The following works deal with ethical aspects of the question of "good": W. W. Bartley, *Morality and Religion*, 1971; R. M. Hare, *The Language of Morals*, 1952; T. W. Manson, *Ethics and the Gospel*, 1960; I. T. Ramsey, ed., *Christian Ethics in Contemporary Philosophy*, 1973, reprint; S. S. Smalley, "Good, Goodness", in C. F. H. Henry, ed., *Baker's Dictionary of Christian Ethics*, 1973, 267 f.; C. L. Stevenson, *Ethics and Language*, 1944; J. O. Urmson, *The Emotive Theory of Ethics*, 1968; G. H. von Wright, *The Varieties of Goodness*, 1963.
(b). J. Begrich, "Die Paradieserzählung", *ZAW* 50, 1932, 93 ff.; J. Chatillon, "Dulcedo", *Dictionnaire de la Spiritualité* III 1777–95 (Volume XXIV); J. Coppens, "La Connaissance du Bien et du Mal et le Péché du Paradis", *Analecta Lovaniensia Biblica et Orientalia*, 1948; J. de Fraine, "Jeux de mots dans le récit de la chute", *Mélanges Bibliques A. Robert*, 1957, 47–59; P. Humbert, *Études sur le Recit du Paradis et de la Chute dans la Genèse*, 1940, 82–116; H. Junker, *Die biblische Urgeschichte*, 1932; A. I. Mennessier, "Douceur", *Dictionnaire de la Spiritualité* III 1674–85 (Volume XXIV); H. Renckens, *Urgeschichte und Heilsgeschichte: Israels Schau in die Vergangenheit nach Gen. 1–3*, 1961²; H. Schmidt, *Die Erzählung von Paradies und Sündenfall*, 1931; S. H. Siedl, *Qumran – eine Mönchsgemeinde im Alten Bund*, 1963, 195–209; C. Spicq, "Bénignité, mansuétude, douceur, clémence", *RB* 54, 1947, 321–9; F. L. R. Stachowiak, *chrēstotēs, ihre biblisch-theologische Entwicklung und Eigenart*, 1957; A. Vögtle, *Die Tugend – und Laster-Kataloge im Neuen Testament*, *NTAbh* 16, 4/5, 1936; S. Wibbing, *Die Tugend- und Lasterketaloge im Neuen Testament und ihre Traditionsgeschichte unter besonderer Berücksichtigung der Qumran-Texte*, *BZNW* 25, 1959; K. Winkler, "Clementia", *RAC* III 106–31; J. Ziegler, *Dulcedo Dei, Alttestamentliche Abhandlungen* 13/2, 1937.

Gospel, Evangelize, Evangelist

εὐαγγέλιον

εὐαγγέλιον (*euangelion*), good news, gospel; εὐαγγελίζω (*euangelizō*), bring or announce good news, proclaim, preach; mid. εὐαγγελίζομαι (*euangelizomai*), bring good news, proclaim glad tidings, proclaim, preach; εὐαγγελιστής (*euangelistēs*), proclaimer of glad tidings or of the gospel, evangelist.

CL 1. The mid. vb. *euangelizomai* (Aristophanes), *euangelizō*, a form not encountered until later Gk., together with the adjectival noun *euangelion* (Homer) and the noun *euangelos* (Aesch.), are all derived from *angelos*, messenger (probably an Iranian loan-word originally), or the vb. *angellō* (announce; → Angel). *euangelos*, messenger, is one who brings a message of victory or other political or personal news that causes joy. In the Hel. period the word can also mean one who announces oracles. Similarly the vb. *euangelizomai* means to speak as a messenger of gladness, to proclaim good news; and where it is used in a religious sense, to promise. *euangelizomai* also gains a religious meaning when it is used in connection with the appearance of a "divine man", whose approach is announced with joy (e.g. of Apollonius of Tyana in Philostratus, *VA* 1, 28, 3rd cent. A.D.). On the other hand, the vb. is often found with its original sense weakened to make it synonymous with *angellō*, to bear a message, announce.

2. The noun *euangelion* means: (a) the reward received by the messenger of victory (his good news brings relief to the recipients; therefore he is rewarded); (b) the message itself, chiefly a technical term for the message of victory, but also used of political and private messages bringing joy. Such messages are seen as a gift of the gods. When the message has been received, sacrifices are offered to them

out of gratitude but also in order to hold the gods to their gift (cf. the phrase *euangelia thyein*, to celebrate good news by sacrifice, first found in Isocrates). "Behind such sacrifices lies the animist's distrust of his own religious cult: hurry to thank the gods for the message, or else you may miss the good fortune of which it tells" (J. Schniewind, *Euangelion*, 1931, 182).

(c) It is chiefly in connection with oracles (i.e. the promise of some future event) and in the imperial cult that *euangelion* acquires a religious meaning. In the latter sphere news of the divine ruler's birth, coming of age, or enthronement, and also his speeches, decrees and acts are glad tidings which bring long hoped-for fulfilment to the longings of the world for happiness and peace. An instance of this is the decree of the Greeks of the province of Asia *c.* 9 B.C. marking the birthday of Augustus (23 September) the beginning of the civil year: "It is a day which we may justly count as equivalent to the beginning of everything – if not in itself and in its own nature, at any rate in the benefits it brings – inasmuch as it has restored the shape of everything that was failing and turning into misfortune, and has given a new look to the Universe at a time when it would gladly have welcomed destruction if Caesar had not been born to be the common blessing of all men. . . . Whereas the Providence (*pronoia*) which has ordered the whole of our life, showing concern and zeal, has ordained the most perfect consummation for human life by giving to it Augustus, by filling him with virtue for doing the work of a benefactor among men, and by sending in him, as it were, a saviour for us and those who come after us, to make war to cease, to create order everywhere . . . and whereas the birthday of the God [Augustus] was the beginning for the world of the glad tidings [in the Greek the 'Evangel'] that have come to men through him . . . Paulus Fabius Maximus, the proconsul of the province . . . has devised a way of honouring Augustus hitherto unknown to the Greeks, which is, that the reckoning of time for the course of human life should begin with *his* birth" (quoted from E. Barker, *From Alexander to Constantine: Passages and Documents Illustrating the History of Social and Political Ideas 336* B.C.–A.D. *337*, (1956) 1959, 211 f.; cf. W. Dittenberger, *Orientis Graeci Inscriptiones*, II, No. 458; for other data on background see G. Friedrich, *TDNT* II 721–5). The proclamation of this *euangelion* does not merely herald a new era: it actually brings it about. The proclamation is itself the *euangelion*, since the salvation it proclaims is already present in it.

3. It is not difficult to trace the connection between this religious use of the word *euangelion* in the Hel. world, especially in the imperial cult, and its use in the NT. The latter takes up a term widely used in the Hel. world and loaded with religious concepts, when it speaks of its own *euangelion* or gospel. At the same time the OT roots of the NT concept of *euangelion* must not be ignored.

OT 1. In the Gk. translation of the OT *euangelion* never appears in the sing. form.
The plur., used to render the Heb. *bᵉśôrâh*, means reward for good news (2 Sam. 4:10). Occasionally *euangelia*, a form unknown in the NT, also appears for the Heb. *bᵉśôrâh* in the sense of glad tidings (e.g. 2 Sam. 18:20, 22). On the whole, however, the substantival forms are not of particular importance. Of greater significance for the further development of the concept is the fact that the vb. *euangelizomai* – which is likewise not found frequently elsewhere and is limited to a few writings – comes to stand for the Heb. *biśśar*, to announce, tell, publish (e.g.

1 Ki. 1:42; Jer. 20:15). This verb is the term used in the Pss. 40:9[10]; 68:11[12]; 96:2 ff. and Isa. 41:27 and 52:7 to herald Yahweh's universal victory over the world and his kingly rule. With his enthronement (cf. the enthronement psalms, especially Ps. 96) and with his return to Zion (in Isa.) a new era begins. The messenger of good tidings (*meḇaśśēr*, substantival part., translated by *euangelizomenos* in the LXX) announces this new era of world history and inaugurates it by his mighty word. Peace and salvation have now come; Yahweh has become king (Isa. 52:7; cf. also 40:9); his reign extends over the whole world (Ps. 96:2 ff.). This "'gospel' is effective speech, a powerful saying, a word which brings its own fulfilment. In the mouth of his messengers God himself speaks: he speaks and it is accomplished; he commands and it is done (Ps. 33:6)" (G. Gloege in *Theologie für Nichttheologen*, I, 1963, 100). The act of proclamation is itself the dawn of the new era. Hence it is easy to understand the special significance that attaches to the messenger of the good news. With his arrival on the scene and the delivery of his message, salvation, redemption and peace become a reality. (Cf. on this Isa. 61:1, where the connection between message and mission is particularly prominent; → Apostle.)

2. When the LXX was translated, this concept of the messenger of glad tidings and his powerful, effective word was no longer understood, and the meaning was weakened. The proclamation of the message was separated from the action originally associated directly with it (cf. e.g. Isa. 52:7, where LXX translates: "Your God will be king"). Neither Philo nor Josephus takes up the concept of the messenger of glad tidings as found in Isa. in their use of *euangelion* and *euangelizomai*. They use the words in the normal Hel. sense (cf. *War*, 2, 420; 4, 656; cf. *TDNT* II 725 f.). They do not therefore contribute anything further to our understanding of the NT use of these terms. The same cannot however be said of Rab. Judaism.

3. Rab. Judaism kept alive the concept of the messenger of good tidings. He was variously expected: as an unknown figure, the forerunner of the Messiah, or as the Messiah himself (→ Jesus Christ). The content of his message was already familiar from Isa., and was therefore no longer of primary interest. The important thing about him was rather that the *meḇaśśēr* is coming, and by his proclamation he will usher in the era of salvation. Everything depends on his appearance and on his act of proclamation (cf. Pes. R. 36 [162a] SB III 9ff.; cf. also 1QM 18:14, where the messenger's self-designation as "messenger of good news" is a clear echo of Isa. 61). Here the same observation may be made that was made concerning OT usage. The eschatological event finds expression in the vb. (*biśśar* means to preach the eschatological message of joy) and in particular the participial noun (*meḇaśśēr*, the eschatological messenger of joy), but not in the noun. *beśôrâh*, good news. This fact suggests that the NT term *euangelion* is derived from Gk. usage rather than the Heb., or more precisely from the language of the imperial cult. The question cannot be decided with certainty, especially since "The imperial cult and the Bible share the view that accession to the throne, which introduces a new era and brings peace to the world, is a gospel for men" (*TDNT* II 725). The only difference, in fact, is in the content of the *euangelion*.

NT 1. Although the vb. *euangelizomai* and the noun *euangelion* are such important NT terms, the two words are found with varying degrees of frequency in the various writings of the NT. *euangelizomai* is found only once in Matt. (11:5). In Lk.-Acts, on the other hand, it occurs 25 times, in Paul 21 times (including twice in Eph.), twice in Heb., and 3 times in 1 Pet. In addition *euangelizō* is found twice in Rev. Although the vb. is not found in Mk., the noun occurs there 7 times, and 4 times in Matt. Luke, however, shows a distinctive predilection for the verbal form *euangelizomai*; he uses the noun only twice (Acts 15:7 and 20:24). The noun *euangelion* occurs particularly often in Paul (60 times, including 4 times in Eph., and 4 times in the Pastoral Epistles), and once each in 1 Pet. and Rev. The fact that the Johannine writings (gospel and epistles) know neither the vb. nor the noun is most remarkable. It may perhaps be explained by the characteristic theology underlying them, their so-called present eschatology. It would be a mistake, however, to assume that because certain NT writings do not use the vb. or the noun, the thought expressed by them is therefore completely lacking. In the Johannine writings, for instance, the concept is expressed by terms like *martyreō*, to witness, and *martyria*, → witness.

2. It has been questioned whether Jesus himself used the term *euangelion* (or, to be more precise, its Heb. or Aram. equivalent) as a broad description of his message. Nevertheless, the term is attributed to him in Mk. 1:15; 8:35; 10:29; 13:10; 14:9; [16:15]; Matt. 4:23; 9:35; 24:14; 26:13; cf. also Mk. 1:1, 14). It is possible that Jesus indicated that the words of messianic expectation in Isa. 35 and 61 are fulfilled in his words and actions (cf. Matt. 11:5 f. = Lk. 7:22, Q: *ptōchoi euangelizontai*, the glad tidings go out to the poor; also Lk. 4:18, where Jesus refers to Isa. 61:1). But if so, they are fulfilled in a way which will disappoint (Matt. 11:6) the expectations popularly attached to the messenger of glad tidings in Isa. (i.e. political liberation and the destruction of Israel's enemies). Certainly the answer to the Baptist's question in Matt. 11:5 f. means that the glad tidings awaited since Isa. are now being proclaimed and are already effective.

The really decisive question is not whether Jesus himself used the word *euangelion* but whether it is a word appropriate to the substance of his message. There is no doubt that Jesus saw his message of the coming → kingdom of God (Mk. 1:14) which is already present in his word and action as good news. "Blessed are your eyes, for they see, and your ears, for they hear" (Matt. 13:16). This message of joy is no longer to be separated from the messenger who brings it, and this messenger is Jesus himself (cf. Lk. 11:20; Matt. 5:1 f.; cf. *TDNT* II 728 f.). Moreover, he appears not only as the messenger and author of the message, but at the same time as its subject, the one of whom the message tells. It is therefore quite consistent for the early Christian church to take up the term *euangelion* to describe the message of salvation connected with the coming of Jesus.

3. There is good reason to believe that it was Paul who established the term *euangelion* in the vocabulary of the NT. That is not to say that he was the first to use this word without further qualification for the total content of the message, and to make it synonymous with the name of → Jesus Christ. On the contrary, Paul's frequent use of the word *euangelion* absolutely (at least 23 times without further qualification to describe the content of the message) suggests that he was taking over phraseology already familiar to his readers. The latter knew what the content of the gospel was. It is thus reasonable to suppose that in the early churches this terminology had developed by analogy out of that associated with the "gospel"

of the imperial cult, though also in conscious opposition to the latter. In the sphere of missionary outreach in particular, the message of salvation through Jesus Christ came into conflict with the political, messianic message by reason of its universal claims. It was inevitable that very soon OT statements and ideas, especially from the prophecy of Isa., would become linked with this Hel. terminology, "This could readily happen, not least because the connection between the Hellenistic-Oriental concepts of the redeemer and the ideology of the saviour-king that stands behind deutero-Isaiah was suggested by the subject matter itself" (W. Schnee-melcher in Henn. Schn., I, 72).

In Paul *euangelion* has become a central concept of his theology. It means the familiar good news: that God has acted for the salvation (→ redemption) of the world in the incarnation, death and resurrection of Jesus (cf. the development of these ideas in confessional formulae in Rom. 1:1 ff.; 1 Cor. 15:1 ff.). In so far as this event is already promised in the OT, the OT belongs to the gospel. (*epangelia*, → promise, is closely related both linguistically and conceptually to *euangelion*, and it is significant that the conflict of law and gospel appears in Paul's writings in connection with this term.) However, *euangelion*, as used by Paul, does not mean only the content of what is preached, but also the act, process and execution of the proclamation. Content and process of preaching are one. They are not separated in thought (Rom. 1:1), apart from when they are set close alongside each other (1 Cor. 9:14, 18). For in the very act of proclamation its content becomes reality, and brings about the salvation which it contains. "The gospel does not merely bear witness to salvation history; it is itself salvation history" (G. Friedrich, *TDNT* II 731). The action of → proclamation is denoted not only by the vb. *euangelizomai* (as e.g. in 1 Cor. 1:17), but also by *euangelion* used as a noun of action. Thus in 2 Cor. 8:18 *euangelion* means preaching of the gospel. Similarly the gen. in the phrases "gospel of God", or "gospel of Christ", and "of the Son of God" (e.g. Rom. 1:1; 15:16; 1 Cor. 9:12; 2 Cor. 2:12) should be taken as both objective and subjective: Christ or God is both the content and author of the gospel. It is difficult to make a clear distinction here, since Paul sometimes stresses the one aspect and sometimes the other. Wherever it is proclaimed (*euangelizesthai* in 2 Cor. 11:7; Gal. 1:11; *kēryssein* in Gal. 2:2; 1 Thess. 2:9; *katangellein* in 1 Cor. 9:14; *lalein* in 1 Thess. 2:2), this gospel is charged with power. It creates → faith (Rom. 1:16 f.; Phil. 1:27), brings salvation, life (Rom. 1:16; 1 Cor. 15:2) and also → judgment (Rom. 2:16). It reveals God's → righteousness (Rom. 1:17), brings the fulfilment of → hope (Col. 1:5, 23), intervenes in the lives of men, and creates churches. Since this gospel is no invention of man (Gal. 1:11), but rather God or Christ himself speaking through his messengers, the → apostles, the gospel is closely associated with the apostolate (2 Cor. 10–13). (See also Gal. 2:7 f., where *euangelion* in the sense of the proclamation of the message is clearly set out as the purpose and content of the *apostolē* or apostolic mission of both Paul and Peter, to the Gentiles as well as to the Jews.) Just as in Isa. 40:9; 52:7; and Nah. 1:15 the heralds and watchmen on the walls proclaim the coming of God, so the messengers proclaim the gospel (Rom. 10:15). Paul was conscious of having been called to bring the gospel to the Gentiles especially (Rom. 1:1; Gal. 1:16), and so to carry the eschatological event beyond the borders of Israel (Rom. 15:9). His whole activity was *euangelizesthai* (1 Cor. 1:17). As the "partner of the gospel"

111

(1 Cor. 9:23), therefore, he could speak of "his gospel" (e.g. Rom. 16:25; 2 Cor. 4:3). By this he meant the one gospel which was preached in Jerusalem (Gal. 1:6–9; 2 Cor. 10:13–16) and which has only now broken out of the bounds of the Jewish law, and become the gospel for the Gentiles, freed from the law (Gal. 1:16; 2:7, 8; Rom. 1:15). Paul's opponents, on the other hand, have "another gospel" (Gal. 1:6–10; 2 Cor. 11:4). They make attacks upon Paul. But since apostleship and the preaching of the gospel belong together, every attack on Paul and his apostleship is an attack on the gospel, and vice versa. To preach the gospel is not to commend oneself, but – as if compelled (1 Cor. 9:16) – to commend the Lord (2 Cor. 10:18; 4:5; Gal. 1:10).

4. In the Synoptic Gospels likewise, *euangelion* is the name given to the good news of the saving event in Jesus Christ, as preached in the church. The separate evangelists do, however, have different emphases when it comes to detail. These are conditioned by their respective theological outlooks:

(a) Mark stands very close to the Pauline use of *euangelion*, always using it absolutely except at 1:1 and 1:14. Since it is evident that he uses it in redactional passages, scholars have assumed that he was the one who introduced this word (taking it over perhaps from Paul) into the synoptic tradition. Matt. and Lk. are dependent on him, but modify his ideas. Mk., like Paul, sees Jesus Christ as both content and author of the gospel. Where it is proclaimed, he is present and at work – present to such a degree that what is done for the gospel's sake is done for Jesus' sake as well (Mk. 8:35; 10:29). The content of this gospel is the history of Jesus with its individual events (cf. Mk. 14:5). Mk. does not record them merely out of historical interest, but rather uses the narrative about Jesus in order to express what the gospel is. It is not information about a glorious divine redeemer, but the message of salvation through the suffering Son of man whose hidden glory as → Son of God did not become apparent except to his followers (→ disciple) on the way of the cross. Mk. therefore sets *euangelion* as a kind of title over his whole book (1:1, "The beginning of the gospel of Jesus Christ, the Son of God"); this means that these stories are not merely reports about Jesus, but an address. They are the good news in which Jesus is proclaimed as the living Lord and in which he himself addresses the readers of the Gospel of Mark, bringing about and strengthening faith (Mk. 1:15).

(b) In contrast with this use of *euangelion* in Mk., Matt. never uses the word without further qualifying it as "the gospel of the kingdom" (4:23; 9:35) or "this gospel" (26:13; cf. also 24:14). In so doing he has shifted the emphasis. In the foreground now is the idea of Jesus as the bringer and proclaimer of the gospel. The content of the gospel is now to be seen chiefly in the → teaching in which Jesus instructs his disciples (4:23; 9:35; 24:14; but in 26:13 "gospel" refers to the passion narrative). But in so far as the church passes on this gospel, Jesus himself is also its content (cf. especially Matt. 24:14; 26:13).

(c) In Luke-Acts the term *euangelion* is found only at Acts 15:7 and 20:24. Possibly this has to do with his particular scheme, according to which the era of Jesus must be distinguished from the era of the church, and so too the preaching of Jesus from that of the apostles. Thus he can describe as *euangelion* the apostolic preaching (Acts 15:7; 20:24), but not the preaching of Jesus. Particularly instructive in this context is the alteration of *euangelion* in Mk. 10:29 to *basileia* in Lk.

18:29. This suggestion is not upset by the fact that Lk. evidently has a special predilection for the vb. *euangelizesthai*. It no longer has the pregnant meaning which it has for Paul, who uses it to embrace the whole work of Jesus, but has almost become a technical term for proclamation. Further evidence in this direction is provided by the fact that it is used interchangeably with other verbs of → proclamation like *kēryssein* (cf. here the Markan version behind Lk. 4:43; 9:6; and also Lk. 4:18), *katangellein* (Acts 13:5, 38; 15:36; 16:17; 17:23; 26:23), *didaskein* (Lk. 20:1, → teach). Moreover, Lk. generally qualifies this oral proclamation by a phrase like "kingdom of God" (4:43; 8:1) or "Jesus" (Acts 5:42; 8:25; 11:20). Thus Lk. can also describe the Baptist's activity as *euangelizesthai* (3:18), although he explicitly stresses that the kingdom of God was not proclaimed until after the Baptist (16:16). *euangelizesthai* thus practically regains here its broader, more general Hel. meaning of proclaiming good news, and is no longer a term with christological overtones.

5. The other NT writings which use *euangelion* or *euangelizomai* on the whole follow the above outline of Paul. They tend to bring out certain aspects of this powerful gospel which is not a human word but the word of God (1 Pet. 1:12). It was entrusted to Paul as a preacher, apostle and teacher (2 Tim. 1:11). Its message of Jesus Christ, risen from the dead, and descended from David (2 Tim. 2:8) is not limited to a single, past event, but is experienced as a word charged with power in the present so that it cannot be fettered by human chains (2 Tim. 2:9). This gospel produces rebirth and new life (1 Pet. 23–25). It brings peace (Eph. 2:17; 6:15), and draws together the near and the far off, the Gentiles and the Jews (Eph. 3:1–9). It gives salvation (Eph. 1:13), and has "brought life and immortality to light" (2 Tim. 1:10).

6. However varied may be the emphasis and development of the term *euangelion* in the NT, the reference is always to the oral proclamation of the message of salvation and never to something fixed in writing, such as a → book or a letter. This is shown not least by the synonyms of *euangelion* and *euangelizomai*: *kēryssein*, *katangellein*, *lalein*, *logos*, etc. This oral message is one, even if Paul speaks of "his" gospel (*euangelion mou*, Rom. 2:16). The NT knows only the gospel; the plur. "the gospels" is a contradiction of its nature (G. Bornkamm, *RGG*[3] II 749).

Nevertheless, from the 2nd cent. onwards reference is made to gospels, meaning the written gospels (cf. Iren., *Haer.* 3, 11, 8; cf. 3, 1, 1; Clem. Alex., *Strom*, 1, 136, 1; cf. Lampe, 555 ff.). This is the outcome of a development which can be traced in its origin back to Mk. Mk. associated the gospel with the stories about Jesus which he had written down, but he did not identify the two. The introductory phrase "The beginning of the gospel of Jesus Christ" (1:1) clearly does not mean that in what follows he is writing a biography of Jesus (see above 4 (a)). This identification did, however, take place at a later stage as a result of an historicizing tendency which may already be seen in Matt. and Lk. Hence, "gospel" came to be used as a description of a book, and consequently the plural form *ta euangelia* became possible as a collective term for these "reports". This was not yet true in the case of Lk. For in his prologue (1:1–4) he did not employ the term "gospels" for the narratives about Jesus which were evidently in bountiful supply in his day. Instead he used *diēgēsis*, narrative. In the course of the 2nd cent., however, this use of the term for a type of literature without parallel in the NT world became established. At the same time the NT insight was retained. For the four gospels "testify to the one gospel, to the proclamation of salvation in Jesus Christ" (W. Schneemelcher, Henn. Schn., I, 75). Similarly Luther declared: "The gospel . . . is not in truth that which is written in books and set down in letters, but rather a spoken message and living word, and a voice which sounds out into the world and is publicly proclaimed, that it may be heard everywhere" (*Weimarer Ausgabe* XII, 259).

7. *euangelistēs* is a term for one who proclaims the *euangelion*. This word, which is very rare in non-Christian literature, but common enough in early Christian writings, is found in the NT only at Acts 21:8 (of Philip who had been one of the Seven, Acts 6:5; cf. also 8:5 ff.), Eph. 4:11 (along with apostles, prophets, pastors and teachers), and in 2 Tim. 4:5 (of Timothy). In these three passages the evangelist is distinguished from the apostle. This is especially obvious in the case of the evangelist Philip, whose activity has to be ratified by the apostles Peter and John (Acts 8:14 f.). The term *euangelistēs* is thus clearly intended to refer to people who carry on the work of the apostles who have been directly called by the risen Christ. But it is difficult to decide whether the reference is to an office, or simply to an activity. These evangelists may have been engaged in missionary work (Acts 21:8), or church leadership (2 Tim. 4:5). As a term for the author of a gospel, *euangelistēs* is not found before the time when *euangelion* is used to describe a book and "gospels" are spoken of (cf. Lampe, 559). *U. Becker*

→ Confess, → Law, → Proclaim, → Scripture, → Teach, → Word

(a). R. S. Barbour, *Traditio-Historical Criticism of the Gospels: Some Comments on Current Methods*, 1972; K. Barth, *God, Grace and Gospel*, 1959; J. W. Bowman, "The term *Gospel* and its Cognates in the Palestinian Syriac", in A. J. B. Higgins, ed., *New Testament Essays: Studies in Memory of Thomas Walter Manson*, 1959, 54–67; F. F. Bruce, "Galatian Problems 3: The 'Other' Gospel", *BJRL* 53, 1971, 253–71; *Jesus and Christian Origins outside the New Testament*,1974; and "The Speeches in Acts – Thirty Years After", in R. Banks, ed., *Reconciliation and Hope*, 1974, 53–68; R. Bultmann, *Theology of the New Testament*, I, 1952, 87 ff.; *The History of the Synoptic Tradition*, 1968²; M. Burrows, "The Origin of the Term Gospel", *JBL* 44, 1925, 21–33; H. Conzelmann, *The Theology of St. Luke*, 1960; M. Dibelius, *From Tradition to Gospel*, reprinted 1971; C. H. Dodd, *The Apostolic Preaching and its Developments*, 1936; and *Gospel and Law*, 1951; C. F. Evans, "The Kerygma", *JTS* 7, 1956, 25–41; G. Friedrich, *euangelizomai, euangelion, TDNT* II 707–37; K. Grayston, "'Not Ashamed of the Gospel'", *StudEv* 11 1964, 569–73; F. W. Grosheide, "The Pauline Epistles as Kerygma", in *Studia Paulina in Honorem J. de Zwaan*, 1953, 139–43; R. H. Gundry, "Recent Investigations into the Literary Genre 'Gospel'", in R. N. Longenecker and M. C. Tenney, eds., *New Dimensions in New Testament Study*, 1974, 97–114; D. Guthrie, *New Testament Introduction*, I, 1965, *The Gospels and Acts;* W. H. P. Hatch, "The Primitive Christian Message", *JBL* 58, 1939, 1–39; S. Johnson, *The Theology of the Gospels*, 1966; W. G. Kümmel, *Introduction to the New Testament*, 1975²; X. Léon-Dufour, *The Gospels and the Jesus of History* 1968; W. Marxsen, *Mark the Evangelist*, 1969; C. F. D. Moule, *The Birth of the New Testament*, 1962; and "The Intention of the Evangelists", in A. J. B. Higgins, ed., op. cit., 165–79; H. Palmer, *The Logic of Gospel Criticism*, 1968; J. Rohde, *Rediscovering the Teaching of the Evangelists*, 1968; B. Reicke, "A Synopsis of Early Christian Preaching", in A. Fridrichsen, ed., *The Root of the Vine*, 1953, 128–60; J. Schmid, "Gospel", *EBT* I 328–32; W. Schneemelcher, "Gospels: Non-Biblical Material about Jesus", in Henn.-Schn., I, 69–84; R. H. Strachan, "The Gospel in the New Testament", *IB* VII 3–31; B. H. Streeter, *The Four Gospels*, 1924; V. Taylor, *The Formation of the Gospel Tradition*, 1933; H. G. Wood, "Didache, Kerygma and Evangelion", in A. J. B. Higgins, op. cit., 306–14.
(b). M. Albertz, *Die Botschaft des Neuen Testaments*, I/1, 1947; R. Asting, *Die Verkündigung des Wortes im Urchristentum*, 1939; P. Bläser, "Evangelium", *Handbuch theologischer Grundbegriffe*, I, 1962, 355 ff.; G. Gloege, "Evangelium", *Theologie für Nichttheologen*, I, 1963, 97 ff.; E. Haenchen, *Der Weg Jesu. Eine Erklärung des Markus-Evangeliums und der kanonischen Parallelen*, 1966; A. Harnack, *Entstehung und Entwicklung der Kirchenverfassung in den zwei ersten Jahrhunderten*,

1910, 234 ff.; P. Hoffmann, ed., *Orientierung an Jesus. Zur Theologie der Synoptiker. Für Josef Schmid*, 1973 (see especially the article by R. Schnackenburg.); O. Michel, "Evangelium", *RAC* VI, 1965, 1107 ff.; E. Molland, *Das paulinische Evangelium. Das Wort und die Sache*, 1934; H. Ristow and K. Matthiae, *Der historische Jesus und der Kerygmatische Christus*, 1961[2]; W. Schmauch, "Evangelium", *EKL* I 1213 ff.; K. L. Schmidt, "Die Stellung der Evangelien in der allgemeinen Literaturgeschichte", *Eucharisterion*, II (dedicated to H. Gunkel), 1925, 50–134; J. Schniewind, *Euangelion. Ursprung und erste Gestalt des Begriffs Evangelium*, (1927–31) 1937–41; E. Schweizer, "Die theologische Leistung des Markus", *EvTh* 24, 1964, 337 ff.; G. Strecker, *Der Weg der Gerechtigkeit. Untersuchung zur Theologie des Matthäus*, 1966[2]; and "Literarische Überlegungen zum *euangelion*-Begriff im Markusevangelium", in H. Baltensweiler and B. Reicke, eds., *Neues Testament und Geschichte. O. Cullmann zum 70. Geburtstag*, 1972, 91–104.

Grace, Spiritual Gifts

χάρις

χάρις (*charis*), grace, gracefulness, graciousness, favour, thanks, gratitude; χάρισμα (*charisma*), gift given out of goodwill; χαρίζομαι (*charizomai*), show favour or kindness, give as a favour, to be gracious to someone, to pardon; χαριτόω (*charitoō*), endue with grace.

CL 1. Words formed from the Gk. root *char* indicate things which produce wellbeing. They belong to the Indo-European family of words which includes Old High German *ger* (greed); New High German *Geier* (vulture; cf. Eng. *gerfalcon*); Lat. *caritas*; Eng. greedy; cf. *chara* (→ Joy). *charis* (from Homer on) which is not always clearly distinguished in literature from *chara* (from Sappho on) means that which brings wellbeing among men (cf. *charma*), while *chara* (→ Joy) is the individual experience or expression of this wellbeing. From this basic meaning of the noun the individual meanings of *charis* are derived: grace, favour, beauty, thankfulness, gratitude, delight, kindness; expression of favour, good turn, benefit; in the plur. debt of gratitude, gratitude, recompense, thanks (these meanings from Euripides on). The acc. sing. with *echein* means to be grateful; with the addition of *pros tina* it means to have someone's goodwill. Linked with *apodounai*, or *ōphelein*, the acc. sing. means to return thanks or to owe thanks. Indicative of the characteristic use of the noun are: (a) the combinations (without the article) with *eis*, for someone's good, as a favour; *en*, for the benefit of; *pros*, to oblige someone, in kindness, as desired; *syn*, to the satisfaction of; (b) the adverbial use *charin tinos* to someone's advantage, for someone's sake, on account of.

charis designates not only the attitude of the gods but also that of men (e.g. the emperor's dispensations). Like *charma* (cf. Lat. *carmen*, spell, whence charm, French *charme*), *charis* can also designate the physical causes of the benevolent gift, charm, attraction, and in the plur. it can mean amiable characteristics. In mythology personifications of *charis* occur: Charis is the exceedingly beautiful wife of Hephaestus; *hai Charitēs*, the Graces, are the creators and bestowers of charm.

2. The derived noun *charisma*, gracious gift, donation (only from God to men) is found in pre-Christian literature only in one LXX version of Sir. 7:33; 38:30; Ps. 30:20 (Theod.); Philo. *Leg.All.* 3, 78; Sib. 2, 54. In post-Christian secular literature it occurs in Alciphron 3, 17, 4 (2nd cent. A. D.) meaning a benevolently dispensed gift (cf. Arndt, 887).

115

3. The vb. *charizomai* (common from Homer onwards) does not occur with God as its subject until Aelius Aristides (2nd cent. A.D.), when it means to give graciously. When applied to men's dealing with one another, it means to do something pleasant for someone, to be kind, gracious, or obliging, to oblige or gratify someone (from Diodorus Siculus, 1st cent. B.C.). With the construction *tini pros ti*, it is used in the sense of courting a god's favour by sacrifice; and in the case of a woman, to grant favours, to indulge her passions. *charisamenos* used absolutely means as a favour. In the context of ethics and law it means to grant, remit, forgive, or pardon, with the dat. of the person and the acc. of the thing (since Dionysius of Halicarnassos, 1st cent. B.C.). It is used particularly in the sense of granting someone's life (to a third party), i.e. to set him free to please someone (cf. NT below on Acts 3:14; 25:11, 16; 27:24; Phlm. 22). In the perf. and plupf. pass. the vb. means to be pleasant, agreeable, or desired. The perf. part. has the sense of a noun, pleasantness, agreeableness (cf. the formula *hōs kecharismenoi*, as those who have received a gift).

4. The vb. *charitoō* occurs only in a few LXX and extra-canonical passages (Sir. 18:17; Ps. 17:26 [Sym.]; Aristeas 225 and Test. Jos. 1:6), always with reference to divine blessing. Otherwise it is confined to the NT and late post-Christian secular literature (Libanius, 4th cent.).

OT 1. The LXX uses the word *charis* about 190 times of which only about 75 have a Heb. equivalent. Among the equivalents the noun *ḥēn* (61 times) is the most frequent, mostly in the sense favour, inclination. It rarely means attractiveness, beauty, charm (e.g. Ps. 45:2 [MT 45:3; LXX 44:3]). Occasionally it is used as an adj. (Prov. 1:9; 4:9; 5:19). Other equivalents are *rāṣôn*, what is acceptable (between men, Prov. 10:32), favour which one seeks from God (Prov. 11:27), favour which one obtains from God (Prov. 12:2); *ḥeseḏ* (twice), favour (Est. 2:9, 17, here parallel to *ḥēn*); *raḥam* (twice, plur.; → Mercy, arts. *oiktirmos* and *splanchna*), brotherly feeling (Dan. 1:9), compassion (Gen. 43:14) once each; *ṭôḇ*, a good thing (Prov. 18:22); *gᵉḏûlâh*, sign of honour (Est. 6:3); as a conjunction or preposition *bammeh*, why (2 Chr. 7:21); *biḡlal*, on account of (variant of 1 Ki. 14:16); *ḥālāq* (Ezek. 12:24), accommodating with smooth flattery (W. Zimmerli, *Ezechiel*, *BKAT* ad loc.).

2. (a) The use of the word *ḥēn* clarifies the meaning of "grace" in history and actions. It denotes the stronger coming to the help of the weaker who stands in need of help by reason of his circumstances or natural weakness. He acts by a voluntary decision, though he is moved by the dependence or the request of the weaker party. A typical expression used to describe such an event from the standpoint of the weak is the formula to find favour in someone's eyes, i.e. to acquire his favour, liking, benevolence, condescension, and understanding. The action itself is what makes the weaker party acceptable: e.g. Jacob to Esau (Gen. 32:5, MT 32:6); Joseph to Potiphar and Pharaoh's men (Gen. 3:4 and 50:4); the Egyptians to Joseph (Gen. 47:25); Ruth to Boaz (Ruth 2:2, 10, 13); a young wife to her husband (here in the negative, Deut. 24:1); Hannah to Eli (1 Sam. 1:18); David to Saul and Jonathan (1 Sam. 16:22; 20:3); Joab to David (2 Sam. 14:22); Esther to the king (Est. 8:5 etc.). This acceptance is desired (Zech. 4:7) or experienced (Eccl. 9:11) as fortune or salvation. Often it can only be understood as the result

116

of the special intervention of God who supplies grace to the weak (Gen. 39:21; Exod. 3:21; 11:3; 12:36).

(b) *ḥēn* denotes relatively seldom the activity of God. It is used mostly in the sense of his undeserved gift in election. Noah (Gen. 6:8) is singled out of mankind sentenced to destruction (cf. below on Gen. 8:21 f.). The choice of this one individual allows us to recognize mercy in the midst of judgment. Moses, the chosen mediator, was permitted to remind Yahweh of his electing gift (Exod. 33:12, 13a) and therefore request a renewed gift of Yahweh (Exod. 33:13b, 16; cf. Num. 11:1), recognizable as Yahweh's care in history for the → covenant people and renewed on account of the mediator's intercession (Exod. 33:17). David also surrendered himself in moments of crisis to the providence of God (2 Sam. 15:25). Bowing before God, → humility and petition appear here not as necessary preconditions of the merciful gift of God, but as the way open to man. Wisdom literature recognized, in the relationship between man's humility and divine grace, something of the character of a law (Prov. 3:34, taken up in 1 Pet. 5:5). The translation of Zech. 12:10 is disputed: AV "spirit of grace", RSV "spirit of compassion." The passages refer to the eschatological outpouring of the spirit upon men (cf. Joel 2:28 [MT 3:1]) which is described as "a spirit of compassion and supplication" (RSV). The meaning lies somewhere between "sympathy", "commiseration" (Koehler-Baumgartner, 314) and being touched (K. Elliger, *Kleine Propheten*, *ATD* 25, 1967[6] ad loc.). It is followed by *taḥᵃnûnîm* also from the root *ḥnn* (RSV "supplication"). (See further J. G. Baldwin, *Haggai, Zechariah, Malachi*, 1972, 190 ff.)

(c) Even the postponement in history of punishment is a gracious act of God (2 Ki. 13:23, *ḥnn*). Where the concept is not found, the idea frequently is (e.g. 1 Ki. 21:29; 2 Ki. 10:30; 14:26). Various writers on OT theology rightly point out that, over and above the occurrences of the concept of grace, the OT teaches that "every creature lives by the grace of God" (L. Koehler, *Old Testament Theology*, 1957, 124) and that Yahweh's grace "produces everything that furthers life" (G. von Rad, *Old Testament Theology*, I, 1962, 229). The theological ideas of the Yahwist in which the increase of sin is followed by the greater increase of grace must be considered here: deluge followed by the Noahic covenant (esp. Gen. 8:21 f.); the tower of → Babel followed by the Abrahamic covenant for the blessing of all peoples (Gen. 11–12). In Ps. 63:3 (MT 63:4) the OT is already advancing to the "discovery of the spiritual as a reality beyond the frailty of the corporeal" (von Rad, op. cit., I, 403): "Thy steadfast love [Gk. *eleos* → mercy] is better than life."

3. In addition to the established OT concepts, the apocryphal Wisdom Literature speaks of grace as a reward for good works which include benevolence (Sir. 12:1; 17:22; 35:2; 40:17; the pass. is used as a substitute for the divine name), renunciation and self-denial, especially that of the martyr (Wis. 3:14 *tēs pisteōs charis*, the gracious reward of faith for "the eunuch whose hands have done no lawless deeds"; cf. Isa. 56:3 ff.). On the grace of martyrdom, see 4 Macc. 11:12 where the tyrant is said to bestow great favour through enabling the martyr in his suffering to demonstrate his loyalty to the law.

4. In the Qumran texts a distinctive theology of grace is found. It is linked particularly with the concept *ḥesed* and also with *rāṣôn*. *ḥēn* is not mentioned. It is a theology which, within the bounds of covenant grace (1QM 12, 3 etc.; → Mercy,

art. *eleos* OT), expresses in confession and prayer hope for the gift of God reserved for the individual (1QS 11:12 f. ["through his showing favour comes my justification"]; 1QH 2:23, 25; 4:37; 7:27, 35; 9:10 ["I chose judgment upon myself . . . for I wait for your mercy"]; 9:14 ["hope . . . through your mercy"]; 11:31; 16:12). Although the Qumran and Pauline documents stand close to each other in their deep recognition of human sin and the consequent knowledge that God can justify and pardon, a fundamental difference exists. Radical liberation from the → law has not yet taken place (cf. H. Braun, see bibliography; H. Conzelmann, *An Outline Theology of the New Testament*, 1969, 223 ff.). The divine pleasure (*rāṣôn*) works as providence and foreknowledge which make possible knowledge and a change for the good (1QS 11:18; 10:6; 14:13 etc.). Through obedience and sacrifice this good pleasure can be influenced (1QS 9:4 f.; 1QM 2:5).

5. Rab. literature contains more than a one-sided doctrine of justification by works. On the one hand, grace can be procured by human behaviour (cf. SB I 767 f.; II 152). Grace may come about only where works are lacking, for rewards are given only for deeds (2 Esd. 8:31–33, 36; cf. SB III 201 on Rom. 4:4; 268 on Rom. 9:15 = Exod. 33:19; further IV 21 ff. Excursus on the Sermon on the Mount). On the other hand, there is the belief that grace is necessary for every action. Grace initiates and completes even the actions of the elect (Aristeas 195; cf. SB III 618 f.). The divine reward is a reward of grace (cf. SB IV 486 ff. on Matt. 20:1–16). According to SB IV 490, the early synagogue did not hold fast the idea of reward by grace. It even denied that one could recognize election by success in the world. The successful man may be suspected of having already forfeited his future reward.

NT The NT employs the term *charis* 155 times, mostly in the Pauline letters (100 times) especially in 1 and 2 Cor. (10 and 18 times), Rom. (24 times) and Eph. (12 times). In the Catholic Epistles it is found most frequently in 1 Pet. (10 times); it occurs in Heb. (8 times). Acts uses *charis* 17 times, Lk. 8 and Jn. 4; the word is lacking in Matt. and Mk. With the exception of one text in 1 Pet., *charisma* is an exclusively Pauline concept (16 times). *charizesthai* occurs only in Paul (16 times) and Luke (Lk. 3 times; Acts 4 times), likewise *charitoun* (once each).

1. In Jesus' teaching the concept of grace in the sense of the undeserved gift of God evidently did not occur. But the theme of his teaching and his acts as a whole centred on God's condescension to the weak, poor, hopeless, lost (Matt. 11:5, 28 ff.; Mk. 10:26 ff.; Lk. 15). Immeasurable remission of debt (Matt. 18:21–34), gracious reward in the kingdom of God (Matt. 20:1–16), and pardon leading to a new life (Lk. 13:6–8; 7:36–50; 19:9 f.) are central themes in his ministry.

2. (a) In the few places where Lk. introduces the concept of grace into Jesus' words it means reward in the last day, payment for something taken as a matter of course (Lk. 6:32–34; cf. Matt. 5:46; Lk. 17:9), and means almost the opposite to its basic meaning. In Lk. 4:22 the expression "words of grace" seems to include both the astonishing rhetorical force of Jesus' words, his authority (see v. 22c "Is not this Joseph's son?"; cf. Eph. 4:29; Col. 4:6), the boldness of his claims (cf. v. 21 with vv. 18 f.), and also the content of his teaching (Matt. 11:5; cf. above 1 (a)).

Otherwise Lk. uses *charis* in its OT sense to express the favour and the acceptability of Mary or the child Jesus before God (1:30; 2:40) and men (2:52; quoting

1 Sam. 2:26). In the history of doctrine a special significance attaches to the angel's greeting to Mary, "Favoured one!" (*kecharitōmenē* Lk. 1:28; AV, "highly favoured"). This does not exalt Mary in her essential being over the rest of mankind. (The same is true of Stephen, for example, who is full of grace, Acts 6:8.) But Mary is promised as a special favour of God a unique role in the history of God's saving purposes, of being the handmaid of the Lord, and this came about (*genoito*, Lk. 1:38).

(b) In Acts grace is that power which flows from God or from the exalted Christ, and accompanies the activity of the apostles giving success to their mission (Acts 6:8; 11:23; 14:26; 15:40; 18:27). It appears in "the word of grace" which is identical with the → gospel (13:43; 20:24). The Lord himself confirms it (14:3). It is that which enables men to believe (18:27). The word of grace is that which builds up believers (20:32). Even where the sense "favour with men" is present God's initiative is the decisive factor (2:47; 4:33). It occurs exclusively in the sense of human favour only in 24:27; 25:3, 9. The Pauline contrast of law and grace (cf. 4 (a)) is echoed in the Peter's speech which contrasted the unnecessary "yoke" (*zygos*, see Matt. 11:28 ff.) of → circumcision with "the grace of the Lord Jesus" (15:10 f.).

charizesthai is employed in Acts 4 times in the sense of granting someone's life to a third party (3:14; 27:24) and handing over someone (25:11, 16).

3. In Jn. *charis* occurs 4 times in the prologue only, where it is perhaps influenced by Pauline thought. It plays no further part in the Gospel. The antithesis of law and grace (1:17) is typically Pauline (cf. 4 (a)). The evangelist has here, as in 1:14 (cf. Exod. 34:6, "abounding in steadfast love [*ḥeseḏ*] and faithfulness [*ᵉmeṯ*]), linked *charis* with one of his favourite concepts, → truth. As in Paul, the event of Christ (here in particular in his earthly life) is identified with grace. As in Eph., Col., and the Pastorals (see below 5 and 6), grace is seen as the essence of his → glory (*doxa*, v. 14); it is poured out in overflowing → fullness (*charin anti charitos*, "grace upon grace," v. 17; cf. v. 14). In the teaching of Jn. as a whole, the gift which the Revealer brings such as "life" and "light" are identified with Jesus Christ himself, and can only be understood as gifts of his grace (→ "I am" sayings).

4. For Paul *charis* is the essence of God's decisive saving act in Jesus Christ, which took place in his sacrificial death, and also of all its consequences in the present and future (Rom. 3:24 ff.). Therefore, the use of *charis* at the beginning and end of the Pauline letters is much more than a mere polite cliché. "Grace" is not just a good wish for salvation; it is qualified as the grace of Christ (cf. 2 Cor. 13:13 [EVV v. 14], where it is linked with the name of Jesus).

(a) The apostle unfolds the reality and power of *charis* in a stubborn conflict with Rab. ideas of justification by works and synergism (see above OT 5; → Law NT 2). This leads him to set up in contrast two antithetical, mutually exclusive series of ideas: grace, gift, the righteousness of God, superabundance, faith, gospel, calling, in grace and hope on the one side; and law, reward, sin, works, accomplishment owed, one's own righteousness, honour, worldly wisdom, futility on the other side. The person and work of the Son made it possible for justice in the judge's pardon not to conflict with grace (Rom. 3:21 ff.; 8:32; Gal. 2:20 f.; Phil. 2:8 ff.). In Christ, therefore, God's grace is given as a precious gift (1 Cor. 1:4). Apart from him there can be no talk of grace (cf. 1 Cor. 1:30 f.; see also Jn. 1:14,

16 f.). But this also means that grace can never become a quality which an individual may possess in his own right, nor may it ever be placed at his disposal.

(b) In the following extracts from his letters Paul uses the series of ideas mentioned above, or aspects of them. *charis* occurs in a central position, or at the climax of the argument. Most often it is defined by means of a contrast.

(i) Rom. 3:21-31: Men are justified by his (God's) grace as a gift (*dōrean*; → Gift, art. *dōron*) through the redemption which is in Christ Jesus (v. 24). Here grace is pardon by the divine judge who reckons to the sinner the → righteousness of Christ.

(ii) Rom. 4:2, 25: The ideas "of grace [*kata charin*]" and "as debt [*kata opheilēma*]", i.e. a reward for work accomplished, are mutually exclusive (v. 4). "That is why it depends on faith, in order that the promises may rest on grace and be guaranteed to all his [Abraham's] descendants – not only to the adherents of the law but also to those who share the faith of Abraham, for he is the father of us all" (v. 16). Only the free gift of God ensures the extension of the saving → promise to all men.

(iii) Rom. 5:15-21 and 6:1: Rom. 5:15 declares that "the free gift [*charisma*] is not like the trespass [*paraptōma*]." Here *charisma* is used in the sense of *charis*. *charisma* is the gift of life, which as "the grace of God and the free gift in the grace of that one man Jesus Christ abounded for many" (v. 15, cf. by contrast v. 20b). But grace is not given to let men go on in → sin (6:1). It does not owe its origin to sin, nor can it be manipulated by men. It is a new reality, a dominion established once and for all by Jesus Christ. Like a mighty lord, it exercises kingly rule (*basileuein*). Its ground is the new → righteousness of Christ, and its → goal is eternal → life (5:21).

(iv) Rom. 6:12-23 carries this thought further. Vv. 14 f. argue that the man who has died with Christ and lives in him (cf. v. 11) no longer lives under the dominion of sin (*hamartia*), but under that of grace. V. 15 takes up the formula and guards against its misunderstanding (as above in 6:1 f.). God's gracious gift (*charisma*) of eternal life has made the power of death as the wages of sin something that belongs to the past which is now done away with (v. 21 ff.).

(v) Rom. 11:5 f.: "God's gracious choice" (*eklogē charitos*) and the life based on → "works" (*ex ergōn*) have nothing in common. Otherwise grace would no longer be pure grace. It would be compromised by the Rab. principle of accomplishment and achievement (see above OT 5).

(vi) 2 Cor. 1:12. To the Jewish desire for control of one's fate through works of law (see (i), (ii), (v)) corresponds the Greek striving for autonomy by means of earthly → wisdom (*sophia sarkikē*). Grace opposes the pride of both as the sole source of power for the apostolic mission (see below) and for the Christian's life (cf. 1 Cor. 1:30 f.).

(vii) In Gal. 2:21 Paul formulates the climax of his theology of grace: "I do not nullify the grace of God; for if justification were through the law [*dia nomou*], then Christ died to no purpose" (here *dōrean* in its negative sense).

(viii) Gal. 5:1-6. Paul accuses the Galatian churches in v. 4 of doing what he repudiated for himself in 2:21, i.e. of wanting by implication to be justified through the law. By doing this he says that they are "severed from Christ" and "fallen

120

away from grace." They have plunged into the abyss of their own righteousness and thus of bondage.

(c) Apart from the antithetic use of *charis* and law, Paul employs the concept of grace in various other connections. (i) With the exclamation "but thanks be to God" (*charis de tō theō* or *tō de theō charis;* Rom. 6:17; 7:25; 1 Cor. 15:57; 2 Cor. 2:14; 8:16; 9:15) at crucial points in his letters Paul praises the gracious acts of God (Rom. 7:25; cf. 1 Tim. 1:12; 2 Tim. 1:3; and in Heb. 12:28 the phrase *echōmen charin*, "let us be grateful" [RSV]). (ii) When one partakes in that which is by nature good without a load on the conscience, one does it "with thankfulness" (*chariti*) (1 Cor. 10:30). (iii) The spiritual song is understood as thankfulness to God (Col. 3:16). (iv) In 1 Cor. 16:3 and 2 Cor. 8:6, 7, 19, *charis* is the technical term for the gift of gratitude and love (RSV, NEB, "gift") for the collection for the Jerusalem community.

(d) Arising out of the basic act of pardon and legal acquittal (Rom. 8:31 ff.), Paul understands the whole movement of the Christian life from beginning to end as grace (2 Cor. 6:1–9; Rom. 5:2; cf. also Jn. 1:16). It is guaranteed by being anchored in the purpose of God (*prothesis*) (Rom. 8:28). Human weakness, not self-determination, is its sphere of activity (2 Cor. 12:9). The grace of God makes the new man what he is (1 Cor. 15:10). (It might even be said that he remains as dependent on it as the released prisoner is upon the connections, help and tasks offered by the after-care service which make life in freedom possible for him.) This is as true of the apostolic mission in particular (Rom. 1:5; 12:3; 15:5; 1 Cor. 3:10; Gal. 2:9; Phil. 1:7) as it is of the Christian life in general (Rom. 12:3, 6; 1 Cor. 1:4 ff.; 2 Cor. 4:15; 6:1; 8:1; 9:8, 14; Phil. 1:7, grace as the bond of fellowship). The relationship with Christ is frequently expressed by *dia*, through. When grace is said to be "given", or to "overflow" etc., the intention is to acknowledge its reality in human life, and not to imply that it is a thing or an object.

(e) The manifold outworking of the one grace in individual Christians through the one → Spirit is called by Paul *charisma*, a personal endowment with grace. This is the specialized use of *charisma* as distinct from the general (see above on Rom. 5:15 f.; 6:23). In Rom. 12 and 1 Cor. 12 Paul develops the meaning of this special, spiritual endowment for service for the life of the community. It has both inward and outward-looking aspects: prophecy as a gift of proclamation, service, teaching (*didaskalia*), spiritual exhortation (*paraklēsis*), leadership in the congregation, and also beneficence and compassion (→ Mercy; cf. Rom. 12:6–8). In addition Paul has already listed in 1 Cor. 12:9 ff. and 28 ff. → faith, the gift of healing, special authority to distinguish between spirits, speaking in tongues, the interpretation of tongues and, as first in the order of functions, the service of the → apostle (v. 28). It is inconceivable to Paul that there should be any Christian without some gift of grace. At the same time, a single individual may be characterized by more than one gift of grace. Paul himself had, beside his apostleship (2 Cor. 1:11), the gift of celibacy (1 Cor. 7:7) which did not belong of necessity to the apostolate (1 Cor. 9:5). He also had the gift of tongues (1 Cor. 14:18), and no doubt also prophecy, teaching and administration. Capacity for spiritual service is determined by one's present *charisma*. It must not be overstepped through ambition (1 Cor. 12:11–27; Rom. 12:3–5; cf. also 1 Pet. 4:10). On the other hand, Paul encouraged desire (*zēloute*) for the best gifts (1 Cor. 12:31), which can be attained not through achievements, but only through → prayer and obedience (→ Faith, art. *peithomai*). Rom. 11:29 designates as *charismata* the abiding privileges of Israel in salvation history (cf. 9:4 f.).

(f) The vb. *charizomai*, like the noun, is used chiefly in connection with the decisive, gracious gift of God. Rom. 8:32 speaks of the all-embracing gift of God in the giving of his Son (cf. Jn. 3:16). The Spirit of God leads to the knowledge of what God has bestowed (1 Cor. 2:12). Already in the old → covenant the free gift of God is linked only with the → promise (*epangelia*, Gal. 3:18), and not with the → law. Readiness to suffer for Christ's sake is, like faith, given to the church by grace for Christ's sake. It is expressed in the pass. in Phil. 1:29, to avoid use of the divine → name. By the prayer of the household of Philemon the imprisoned Paul hoped that he would be granted to that church as a guest (pass. as above, Phlm. 22).

The second meaning of the vb. is to forgive (e.g. 2 Cor. 2:7, 10; cf. also Eph. 4:32; Col. 3:13; 2:13). Christians are to forgive each other, since God in Christ (or the Lord) has forgiven them. In 2 Cor. 12:13 the vb. is used almost ironically to mean excuse.

5. In the letter to the Ephesians *charis* occurs in only two places. It is used as indicated above under 4(b) in an antithetical connection: "dead through our trespasses, made alive together with Christ, by grace [*chariti*] you have been saved" (2:5): "by grace . . . through faith . . . the gift of God" in opposition to "not your own doing . . . not because of works, lest any man should boast" (2:8 f.). In contrast to the earlier epistles, however, *charis* is connected in both places not with *dikaioō*, justify (which does not occur in Eph. and Col.), but with *sōzō*, save. The emphasis is thus shifted from forensic justification to effective salvation (cf. R. Bultmann, *Theology of the New Testament*, 1955, II 176), i.e. from pardon to blessing (Eph. 1:6). Hence grace is connected with *charitoō*, to favour, bless. It looks forward to exaltation (Eph. 1:6 f.; 2:7), though it is still related to "redemption through his blood" (1:7; cf. 2:15; 4:9).

The cognitive aspect of grace which comes to men in the gospel is stressed in Col. 1:6. Grace and → truth belong together (Col. 1:5b; cf. Jn. 1:14). In Eph. 4:7 *charis* is used in the sense of *charisma*: "grace [*charis*] was given to each one of us according to the measure of the gift [*dōrea*] of Christ."

6. In the Pastorals 1 Tim. 1:12 ff. alludes autobiographically to Rom. 5:20b. 2 Tim. 1:9 takes up the connection of the purpose of God and the grace of Christ (cf. Rom. 8:28 with 32), and gives with Tit. 2:11 a doxology of joy over the present → revelation (*phaneroō* or *epiphainō*) of grace. As in Eph., grace and salvation are connected in Tit. 2:11 (*sōtērios*, saving); grace works to train us (*paideuousa*) away from the world and towards eschatological hope. In Tit. 3:7 grace has a double connection. On the one hand, it refers back to the Saviour Jesus Christ who pours out the renewing Holy Spirit (cf. vv. 5 f.). On the other, it is related to justification in the truly Pauline sense (*dikaiōthentes tē ekeinou chariti*, "justified by his grace"). Christ's grace brings about – likewise forensically – the appointment of heirs to future life. Otherwise the Pastorals say nothing more about individual gifts of grace, but only speak of grace for office (so *charis*, 2 Tim. 2:1). *charisma* is passed on through the → laying on of hands (1 Tim. 4:14; 2 Tim. 1:6).

7. Of the remaining NT epistles 1 Pet. and Heb. come nearest to the Pauline understanding of grace.

(a) Like Eph. and Col., 1 Pet. does not specifically link grace and justification. It speaks of the grace of God which is given through Christ (1:10, announced by the prophets), the future revelation of which determines conduct and hope (1:13), and as stewards of which, in its manifold forms (4:10; 5:10), Christians should live. Grace also permits the endurance of undeserved suffering to be understood as approved by God (2:19 f.; cf. also 5:10). In the concluding message the standing of the addressees in grace is confirmed as true (5:12).

(b) Heb. 2:9 understands grace as God's care in salvation history which is made effective in Jesus' substitutionary death. Therefore the throne on which Christ sits to rule is "a throne of grace." Here forgiveness (= grace and compassion, *eleos*; → Mercy) can be received from the one who can sympathize with the weak, for he has identified himself with them as high → priest.

(c) The remaining texts in Heb. are concerned with the problem of cheap grace. In this they may be compared with similar texts in the Catholic Epistles. To abuse the spiritual gift by one's way of life is worse than transgressing the Mosaic law (10:29); grace once abandoned is not to be regained (12:15 ff.). But firmness of heart remains, in spite of all exhortations, a gift of God and not the result of keeping special regulations (13:9). The danger of falling away occurs in Jas. 4:6; the Spirit's offer of gifts outweighs his yearning demands (there follows a quotation from Prov. 3:34; cf. 1 Pet. 5:5, above OT 2). 2 Pet. 3:18 can even paradoxically exhort us to grow in grace, in contrast to falling from our own firm position (cf. Gal. 5:4 with 1 Cor. 12:31). Jude 4 warns against the misuse (*metatithēmi*) of grace to satisfy our passions, a danger which Paul had already repulsed in Rom. 6:1 (cf. above 4 (b) (ii), (iii)).

8. In general the Apostolic Fathers hardened the development in the understanding of grace which can be seen in the later Pauline and Catholic Epistles. Grace is institutionalized as grace for the community and for office. It is an aid for the preservation of correct → teaching and of the ethics of the new law (→ command, cf. R. Bultmann, op. cit., II, 210 f., 216; T. F. Torrance, *The Doctrine of Grace in the Apostolic Fathers*, 1948). *H.-H. Esser*

→ Gift, → Mercy, → Spirit

(a). D. R. Ap-Thomas, "Some Aspects of the Root *ḥnn* in the Old Testament", *JSS* 2, 1957, 128–48; F. Büchsel and J. Herrmann, *hileōs*, *TDNT* III 300–23; G. C. Berkouwer, *The Triumph of Grace in the Theology of Karl Barth*, 1956; R. Bultmann, *Theology of the New Testament*, I, 1952 (see index); D. Doughty, "The Priority of *CHARIS*", *NTS* 19, 1972–3, 163–80; W. Eichrodt, *Theology of the Old Testament*, I, 1961, II, 1967; O. Eissfeldt, "The Promise of Grace to David in Isaiah 55:1–5", in B. W. Anderson and W. Harrelson, eds., *Israel's Prophetic Heritage*, 1962, 196–207; E. E. Ellis, "Spiritual Gifts in the Pauline Community", *NTS* 20, 1973–4, 128–44; G. Farr, "The Concept of Grace in the Book of Hosea", *ZAW* 70, 1958, 98–107; N. Glueck, *Ḥeseḏ in the Bible*, 1967; E. Jauncey, *The Doctrine of Grace*, 1925; H.-J. Kraus, *Worship in Israel*, 1966; W. F. Lofthouse, "*ḥēn* and *ḥeseḏ* in the Old Testament", *ZAW* 51, 1933, 29–35; H. D. McDonald, "Grace", *ZPEB* II 799–804; J. Moffatt, *Grace in the New Testament*, 1931; R. S. Moxon, *The Doctrine of Sin*, 1925; T. Y. Mullins, "Greeting as a New Testament Form", *JBL* 87, 1968, 418–26; A. Nygren, *Agape and Eros*, 1953²; W. L. Reed, "Some Implications of *ḥēn* for Old Testament Religion", *JBL* 73, 1954, 36–41; J. Schildenberger and G. Trenkler, "Grace", *EBT* I 337–44; C. Ryder Smith, *The Bible Doctrine of Grace*, 1956; N. H. Snaith, *The Distinctive Ideas of the Old Testament*, 1944, 94–130; O. J. Thomas, "Irresistible Grace", *Vox Evangelica* 4, 1965, 55–64; T. F. Torrance, *The Doctrine of Grace in the Apostolic Fathers*, 1948; N. P. Williams, *The Grace of God*, 1930.

(b). H. Braun, "Das Erbarmen Gottes über den Gerechten. Zur Theologie der Psalmen Salomos", *ZNW* 43, 1950–51, 1 ff. (reprinted *Gesammelte Studien zum Neuen Testament*, 1967², 8 ff.); and "Röm. 7, 7–25 und das Selbstverständnis des Qumran-Frommen", *ZTK* 56, 1959, 1 ff. (reprinted op. cit., 100 ff.); U. Brockhaus, *Charisma und Amt: Die paulinische Charismenlehre auf dem Hintergrund der frühchristlichen Gemeindefunktionen*, 1972; N. Glueck, *Das Wort ḥeseḏ im alttestamentlichen Sprachgebrauch, BZAW* 47, (1927) 1961²; A. von Harnack, *Sanftmut, Huld und Demut*, 1920; J. Haspecker, "Gnade", *LTK* IV 977–80; J. Hempel, *Gott und Mensch im Alten Testament*, 1936²; M. Hengel, *Nachfolge und Charisma, BZNW* 34, 1968; N. J. Hein, E. Würthwein, G. Stählin, E. Kähler, and W. Joest, "Gnade", *RGG³* II 1630 ff.; A. Jepsen, "Gnade und Barmherzigkeit im Alten Testament", *KuD* 7, 1961, 261–71; J. Köberle, *Sünde und Gnade im religiösen Leben des Volkes Israel*, 1905; O. Loew, *Charis*, 1908; E. Lohse, *Märtyrer und Gottesknecht*, 1963²; H. Niederstrasser, *Kerygma und Paideia. Zum Problem der erziehenden Gnade*, 1967; O. Perels, "*charisma* im Neuen Testament", *Fuldaer Hefte*, 15, 1964, 39 ff.; J. Schreiner, *Sion – Jerusalem. Jahwes Königssitz*, 1963; H. J. Stoebe, "Die Bedeutung des Wortes ḥāsād im Alten Testament", *Vetus Testamentum* 7, 1961, 261–71; H. J. Stoebe, W. Kasch and W. Pannenberg, "Gnade", *EKL* I 1604 f.; G. P. Wetter, *Charis*, 1913; R. Winkler, "Die Gnade im Neuen Testament", *ZSTh* 10, 1933, 642–80; J. Wobbe, *Der Charisgedanke bei Paulus*, 1932; J. Ziegler, *Die Liebe Gottes bei den Propheten, Alttestamentliche Abhandlungen* 11, 3, 1930.

Greek

| "Ελλην |

"Ελλην (*Hellēn*), a Greek; 'Ελλάς (*Hellas*), Greece; 'Ελληνικός (*Hellēnikos*), Greek; 'Ελληνίς (*Hellēnis*), a Greek woman; 'Ελληνιστής (*Hellēnistēs*), a Hellenist; 'Ελληνιστί (*Hellēnisti*), adv. Greek, in the Greek language.

CL *Hellēn* means a Greek, as opposed to a Barbarian. In Homer the word denotes a Thessalian tribe in the region of Pharsalos. In Herodotus it has become the name for all Greeks. In between are the mythological genealogies which invented a hero, Hellen, son of Deucalion (there is also a tradition that he is a son of Zeus), father of the Doric and Aeolian tribal heroes (as early as Hesiod).

The opposition between Greek and non-Greek was one of culture and not religion. In the period after Alexander the Great, especially in the east, all who had adopted Greek language, culture and way of life were counted as "Greeks", even though they were of a different ethnic origin.

OT 1. In the LXX *Hellēn* is sometimes used for Heb. *yāwān* or *yᵉwānîm* (actually the Ionians; Dan. 8:21; 10:20). The experiences of the Jews under Antiochus IV Epiphanes resulted in the word Greek taking on the additional shade of meaning "hostile to the Jews", as in 2 Macc. 4:36; 11:2; cf. *Hellēnikos* in 4:10, 15; 6:9; 11:24; 13:2. It thus had the overtone of pagan (→ People, art. *ethnos*). In this way *Hellēn*, originally a term of respect, was surrendered to the language of religious contempt, because the Jew began from his belief in the one God, whereas the Greek, in his contempt for the Jews, began from his philosophical culture.

Elsewhere in the LXX *Hellas* occurs in Isa. 66:19; Ezek. 27:13 (in both cases for Heb. *yāwān*; RSV Javan); 1 Macc. 1:1; 8:9; Dan. 11:2 *v.l.*; *Hellēn* for *yāwān* in Joel 3(4):6; Zech. 9:13; Dan. 11:2; for *pᵉlištîm* (Philistines) in Isa. 9:12 (11); and without Heb. equivalent in Joel 2:25 *v.l.*; Dan. 7:6 *v.l.*; 1 Macc. 1:10; 6:2 *v.l.*; 8:18; 3 Macc. 3:8; 4 Macc. 18:20; *Hellēnikos* in Jer. 26 (46):16; 27 (50):16 (in both cases the Heb. is different); 4 Macc. 8:8; Ezek. 4:8 *v.l.*; *Hellēnis* in 2 Macc. 6:8 *v.l.*

124

2. The world into which Christianity entered was characterized by the pervading influence of Gk. culture, above all in the eastern part of the Roman empire. The conquests of Alexander the Great and his policy of Hellenization, which was continued by his successors, caused the Gk. language and Gk. ways to become the decisive cultural factor. Gk. cities arose everywhere, including Syria and Palestine, bursting the old tribal groupings of the native peoples (which was their professed intention). The upper strata in these cities spoke Gk. which became the language of trade in the eastern part of the Roman empire and which was also widely understood in Palestine. Just how far the process of Hellenization had gone can be seen, for example, in the case of the Jews of Alexandria in Egypt, for whom a Greek translation of the Bible, the LXX (Septuagint → Glossary of Technical Terms) had to be made in the third century B.C. For many of the people no longer understood or spoke their ancestral Hebrew (Aramaic) tongue. The LXX was far from being the only translation. It became the best known, because it was adopted by the Greek-speaking Christians. This in turn led to new translations of the MT into Gk. in opposition to the LXX. (See further S. Jellicoe, *The Septuagint and Modern Study*, 1968, which contains an extensive bibliography.)

Philo of Alexandria (*c.* 20 B.C.–*c.* A.D. 50) was a Hellenistic philosopher and writer who sought to restate Jewish belief in terms of Gk. philosophy. (For his major writings which were written in Gk see the table of abbreviations.) He developed an allegorical method of interpreting the OT which saw Gk. philosophical ideas embodied in the history and institutions of Israel. In his system he accorded a central place to the Logos (→ Word) as the creative power which orders the world and the intermediary which enables men to know God. (On Philo see H. A. Wolfson, "Philo Judaeus", in *The Encyclopedia of Philosophy*, ed. P. Edwards, IV, 1967, 151–5; and *Philo: Foundations of Religious Philosophy in Judaism, Christianity and Islam*, I–II, 1962³.) Besides Philo there were numerous other Jewish authors who used Gk. language and thought forms to proclaim and spread as missionaries Jewish belief in God and the → law. Flavius Josephus (*c.* A.D. 37–*c.* 100) wrote his celebrated history of the *Jewish War* (*c.* 77, probably originally in Aramaic) and his *Antiquities of the Jews* (*c.* 94) with a view to gaining Roman sympathies. (See further H. Montefiore, *Josephus and the New Testament*, 1960.)

1 Macc. gives an account of the heavy inroads the Gk. spirit and the Gk. attitude to life had made into the Jerusalem priesthood. There was even a risk of losing fundamental religious tenets, and many were prepared to apostatize from their fathers' faith in God and turn from the → law. This and the violent and clumsy attempts at Hellenization made by Antiochus Epiphanes (d. 163 B.C.) provoked a reaction in the circles loyal to the law, which issued in the Maccabean movement (cf. 2 Macc. 6:1 ff.). Relatively soon, however, the Maccabees themselves became Hellenized. Thus the ranks of pious Jews, loyal to the law, were penetrated by Gk. thought, teaching and myths (including the idea of tradition, the immortality of the soul, and myths of the beyond). Even the Rabbis understood Gk. and were acquainted with Homer. The very numerous Gk. loan-words in the Talmud and Midrash are evidence of the cultural supremacy of Greece, even in the realm of Judaism. A reaction which, however, could not make much headway, showed itself at the beginning of the second cent. A.D., when the learning of Gk. was prohibited. The prohibition was soon afterwards watered down to one against

the learning of Gk. "wisdom" (*Sot.* 9:14; cf. *Sot.* 49b). The Jewish Karaite sect in the ninth cent. A.D. also arose in opposition to Gk. philosophy. In calling Jews back to a study of the Scriptures alone, it was opposing Gk. influences in the Talmud and other bodies of writing.

NT In the NT *Hellas*, Greece, occurs only in Acts 20:2. Of the 26 occurrences of *Hellēn* in the NT, 10 are in Acts and 13 in Paul's letters; it does not appear in the Synoptics. *Hellēnis* is found in Acts 17:12 and Mk. 7:26. It is used to describe the Syrophoenician woman, but it is not absolutely clear what is meant by the double description. It is certain that the woman who probably spoke Gk. was a pagan whom Jesus helped on account of her faith. ([Ed.] W. L. Lane suggests that, "She was a member of the Hellenized citizen class in the Phoenician republic of Tyre, a Gentile by birth and culture. She is designated a Syrophoenician because Phoenica belonged administratively to the province of Syria and was distinguished from Libophoenicia with its centre at Carthage in North Africa" [*The Gospel of Mark*, *NLC* 1974, 260; cf. Did. Sic. 19,93; Polyb. 3,33; Strabo, 17,3,9].) *Hellēnikos*, Greek (adj.), occurs only in Rev. 9:11. The name of the angel of the abyss is *en tē Hellēnikē* (supply *glōssē*), i.e. "in the Greek language", Apollyon (→ Destroy, art. *apōleia* NT 4). *Hellēnisti* means in Greek; the title on Jesus' cross was written in Hebrew, Latin and Greek (Jn. 19:20). The officer who rescued Paul from the mob was surprised to discover that Paul understood Gk. (Acts 21:37).

Hellēnistēs (a new formation from the verb *Hellēnizein*) means a man who speaks Gk. and lives as a Gk. (Acts 6:1; 9:29). In Acts 9:29 the word refers to Jews who sought to kill Paul, and in Acts 6:1 it refers to Gk.-speaking Jewish Christians who were strictly orthodox Jewish Christians and not Greeks at all. Paul's later struggle for a gospel free from the law would otherwise be incomprehensible (cf. also Acts 10 f. and 15), and uncircumcised pagans were certainly not accepted into synagogue congregations.

1. In Jn. 7:35 the Jews suggest that Jesus intends going to the Gk. dispersion, to the Jews who lived among the Greeks, and from this base to teach them. In Jn. 12:20 ff. *Hellēnes* refers to Gk.-speaking proselytes (→ Conversion, art. *prosēlytos*) and not pagans, for they wanted to worship in the → Temple. They wanted to see Jesus. This gives rise to a prospect of the mission to the Gentiles for which Jesus' death is a prerequisite. It was Gk.-speaking Jewish Christians who first preached the gospel to the Greeks (Acts 11:20). This was done above all by Paul and his companions (Acts 17:4; 19:10; etc.). Whenever the Jews refused the message, Paul turned to the Greeks. Jews and Greeks lived everywhere side by side, with the result that mixed marriages took place. From one of these came Timothy (Acts 16:1). Paul was accused of taking Greeks into the Temple and thus of defiling it (Acts 21:28). Sometimes the word *Hellēn* can also mean a proselyte (Acts 14:1; 17:4; → Conversion, art. *prosēlytos*).

2. The expression "Jews and Greeks" which occurs especially in Paul's writings can stand for the whole of humanity (1 Cor. 1:24; 10:32; 12:13; Gal. 3:28; Col. 3:11). The Jews are mentioned first as an expression of their privileged place in salvation history. But God is just as much God of the Greeks as of the Jews (Rom. 10:12). Paul was set aside in a special way to exercise his apostolic ministry among the Greeks (Rom. 1:14; Gal. 1:16; 2:9; cf. Eph. 3:6 f.; 1 Tim. 2:7). Not all pagans

were *Hellēnes*, for alongside them Paul refers also to barbarians and Scythians (Rom. 1:14; Col. 3:11). The *Hellēnes* were characterized by their seeking → wisdom (art. *sophia*), which made the cross of Christ seem folly to them (1 Cor. 1:22 f.).

The picture painted by Paul in Rom. 1:18–32 of the Greeks (v. 16) or the heathen (→ People, art. *ethnos*) is a gloomy one. Nevertheless, God directs his message as much to them as to the Jews (Rom. 1:16; 2:9, 3:9). If the Greek does good and fulfils what the law requires, he will receive honour like the Jew (Rom. 2:9 f., 14–16; cf. Jer. 31:33 f.). (On revelation to the Gentiles → God, art. *theos*, NT 4 (b), 9.) As the Greeks were all pagans from the beginning, the concepts pagan and Greek are interchangeable when contrasted with that of the Jew (cf. Rom. 3:29 f. with 1 Cor. 1:22–24). The Greeks figure here as the foremost representatives of the pagan world. The church in Corinth was given the warning not to offend the Jews, the Greeks or the church of God (1 Cor. 10:32). The non-Christian population of Corinth fell into the two first-mentioned groups, alongside which the church now stood as a new people (→ People, art. *laos*).

In this new people of God, the → church, differences of origin are removed. God who in reality had always been the God of the Greeks (Rom. 10:12), though they did not recognize him, has now become consciously and in fact their God, in that they have believed in Jesus Christ and through the Holy Spirit they have been → baptized into one → body (1 Cor. 12:13).

Whoever has been baptized into Jesus Christ is God's child and has put on Christ, whether he is Jew or Greek, and so the man who was born a *Hellēn* now belongs to the offspring of → Abraham (Gal. 3:26–29). Being a Greek or a Jew belongs to the old man, which has to be put away along with all its evil characteristics (Col. 3:11; cf. v. 5–10, 12 f.). *H. Bietenhard*
→ Israel, → People

(a). A. W. Argyle, "The Greek of Luke and Acts", *NTS* 20, 1973–74, 441–45; R. Bultmann, *Primitive Christianity in its contemporary Setting*, 1956; G. Dix, *Jew and Greek: A Study in the Primitive Church*, 1953; C. H. Dodd, *The Bible and the Greeks*, 1935; E. von Dobschütz, "Hellenism", *DAC* I 547 ff.; F. C. Grant, *Roman Hellenism and the New Testament*, 1962; R. H. Gundry "The Language Milieu of First-Century Palestine", *JBL* 83, 1964, 404 f.; W. K. C. Guthrie, *The Greeks and their Gods*, 1954²; E. Haenchen, *The Acts of the Apostles*, 1971; N. G. L. Hammond, *History of Greece*, 1967²; M. Hengel, *Judaism and Hellenism*, I–II, 1974; G. H. C. MacGregor and A. C. Purdy, *Jew and Greek: Tutors unto Christ. The Jewish and Hellenistic Background of the New Testament*, 1959²; I. H. Marshall, "Palestinian and Hellenistic Christianity: Some Critical Comments", *NTS* 19, 1972–73, 271–287; C. F. D. Moule, "Once More, Who were the Hellenists?" *ExpT* 70, 1958–59, 100 ff.; S. Safrai, M. Stern, D. Flusser and W. C. van Unnik, eds., *The Jewish People in the First Century: Historical Geography, Political History, Social, Cultural and Religious Life and Institutions*, I, 1974; Schürer (see index); J. N. Sevenster, *Do You Know Greek? How Much Greek Would the First Jewish Christians have Known? Supplements to NovT* 19, 1968; J. B. Skemp, *The Greeks and the Gospel*, 1964; N. Turner, "The Literary Character of New Testament Greek", *NTS* 20, 1973–74, 107–14; S. G. Wilson, *The Gentiles and the Gentile Mission in Luke–Acts*, 1973; H. Windisch, *Hellēn* etc., *TDNT* II 504–16.

(b). A. Bauer, *Vom Griechentum zum Christentum*, 1910; J. Jüthner, *Hellenen und Barbaren*, 1923; J. Kaerst, *Geschichte des Hellenismus*,² I, 1917, II, 1926; W. Nestle, *Griechische Religiosität*, III, 1934, 5 ff.; F. R. Walton, "Griechische Religion", *RGG*³, III 1860 ff.; U. von Wilamowitz-Moellendorff, *Der Glaube der Hellenen*, I–II, (1931–32) 1955².

Grow

auxanō and *pleonazō* both denote increase in quantity or quality. *auxanō* is a word to do with plant-life and originally denoted the natural process of growth into fruition. It is only used in a positive sense in the NT. *pleonazō* is a quantitative word which originally meant to overflow, and thus to exceed. In figurative NT usage the differences are still clearly discernible.

αὐξάνω

αὔξω and αὐξάνω (*auxō, auxanō*), grow, cause to grow, increase; αὔξησις (*auxēsis*), growth, increase; ὑπεραυξάνω (*hyperauxanō*), grow abundantly; προκοπή (*prokopē*), progress, advancement, furtherance; προκόπτω (*prokoptō*), go forward, advance, make progress, prosper.

CL The vb. is attested since Pindar, both in the short form *auxō* and in the strengthened form *auxanō*, and means to cause to grow, to cause to increase. Trans. it is used equally for natural growth, such as that of fruits, and for increase and advancement in respect and power. The mid.-pass. can also mean to be exalted, glorified, or praised. The noun *auxēsis* is used from the Pre-Socratics and Hdt. onwards, and means growth; in the phrase *auxēsin poieisthai*, to cause to grow, to grow. *hyperauxanō* is used from Andocides onwards, meaning to grow abundantly, plentifully, or extravagantly. The Lat. *augere* (increase, grow), *augustus* (august, venerable) are cognates. Probably deriving from the same root is Lat. *auxilium* (help).

Our word is particularly used of natural growth. On the same lines is the use of the word for the waxing of the moon and and the sun (Kalendarium of Antiochus [c. A.D. 200] on 25 Dec.; cf. E. Norden, *Die Geburt des Kindes*, 1924, 99 ff.; Arndt, 121). No specific philosophical or religious significance stand out in the Gk. world, by contrast with *prokoptō* and *prokopē* which both in Stoic philosophy and in Philo denote ethical advance.

OT In the LXX *auxanō* stands for *pārâh* 11 times in the qal, meaning to be fruitful, plentiful; 8 times in the act. hiph. meaning to make fruitful or plentiful. God is mainly the subject of the process of causing growth (thus Gen. 17:20 of Ishmael; and Gen. 35:11 in the blessing to Jacob who is to become a great nation; cf. Jer. 3:16; 23:3). It is frequently linked with *plēthynō*, to fill, to multiply, and occurs in the original creation ordinance to humanity and subsequently renewed to the Jewish people to be fruitful and multiply (Gen. 1:22, 28; 9:1, 7 to Noah; 17:6 to Abraham). In the parabolic promise of Isa. 61:11 the process of growth is not viewed as something automatic and inevitable. The point of the comparison is the difference between the first state and the last. The surprising thing is that the beginning and and end stages are two completely different states. Where previously there was nothing, God's creative will becomes effective: he creates righteousness and praise. Sir. 43:8 speaks of the waxing of the new moon. Here, too, God is the originator of the growth.

NT 1. In the NT *auxanō* is found 22 times, including 4 times in 1 and 2 Cor., twice in Eph., 3 times in Col., and 7 times in Lk. The noun *auxēsis* occurs only in Eph. 4:16 and Col. 2:19 in connection with the vb.

2. Natural growth is alluded to directly only in Lk. 1:80 and 2:40, where the child Jesus is said to grow in physique (→ Age) and in the → Spirit.

3. (a) *auxanō* features in Mk.'s version of the parable of the sower (Mk. 4:8), the parable of the mustard seed (Matt. 13:32; Lk. 13:19), and the saying about the lilies of the field (Matt. 6:28). According to the synoptic account of Jesus' preaching, the picture of plant-like growth illustrates the coming of the kingdom through the word in the face of all opposition. God is the one who causes to grow that which he himself sows through Jesus, or plants through his servants (cf. also 1 Cor. 3:6 f.; 2 Cor. 9:10).

(b) In the teaching of Paul *auxanō* is significantly lacking in Rom. and Gal. It is not part of the doctrine of justification, but belongs to paraenesis. Only God can cause the church to grow (1 Cor. 3:5–11). Only by remembering its origin which is given in Jesus Christ (1 Cor. 3:11) can the church truly grow (→ Firm, art. *themelios* NT 1). The thought here is not solely of numerical increase, but also of maturity and the consolidation of the community in Christ from which good works naturally grow (2 Cor. 9:6–11).

(c) Eph. 2:20 ff. does not contradict the picture of 1 Cor. 3:11, where the apostles and prophets are said to be the foundation on which the building grows (→ House, art. *oikos, oikodomeō*). For Jesus Christ is described as "the chief cornerstone" (cf. Pss. 118:22; Matt. 21:42; Mk. 12:10 f.; Lk. 20:7; Acts 4:11; 1 Pet. 2:7; → Rock, Stone, Cornerstone, art. *gōnia*). Moreover, the church was by this time uniquely dependent on the witness of the apostles and prophets for the preaching of Christ. Therefore the growth of the community in Eph. derives ultimately from Jesus Christ who at the same time holds the building together (cf. 2:20 f. with 1:5 ff., 10; 2:10; 4:15 f.). Growth does not mean that the gospel calls men into some kind of extra-historical existence. Because Christians are placed in the fellowship of the people of God, they are thereby placed in a historical process which is determined by the promise of the world-wide rule of Christ. The existence together of Jews and Gentiles as children in the presence of the Lord of the church opens up a new dimension for the church as it grows into a single structure. "The growth of the church in personal holiness in Christ is a continuous process. The present tense of *auxein* makes this clear. *auxein* is the mode of the church's being. The church exists as it grows. It is only ever holy in so far as being holy, it becomes holy, and both 'in Christ' " (H. Schlier, *Der Brief an die Epheser*, 1965⁵, 144).

(d) The conception of building corresponds with that of the growing → body (Eph. 4:15 f.; Col. 2:19). Some scholars think that both ideas are taken from gnosticism. Eph. 4:15 f. shows the way that this growth is to take place. When truth is spoken in love, and love takes effect, the church grows into Christ, the one → head. According to Col. 1:6, all growth springs from the gospel. As men are moved by the gospel, they grow in knowledge of God (Col. 1:10 f.) and in grace (cf. 2 Pet. 3:18).

4. The NT can also speak of growth in → faith (2 Cor. 10:15; 2 Thess. 1:3; 2 Pet. 3:18 *v.l.*). Faith is conditioned by one's personal circumstances as well as by God's saving acts in history. It is brought about and renewed by the → Word, the living Christ himself. But it undergoes transformation in the life of the Christian. The believer always has his own particular history in relation to his Lord. He lives between the "no longer" and the "not yet" (cf. Phil. 3:12–15; R. Bultmann,

Theology of the New Testament, I, 1952, 322). The decision which leads to → baptism is admittedly taken only once, but faith needs to be constantly renewed (cf. Rom. 14:1; 1 Thess. 3:10). Faith grows out of the obedience of the believer in the fellowship of the Christian community (2 Thess. 1:3; cf. Phil. 1:25 f.). It leads to a more effective → witness in the world (2 Cor. 10:15 f.). Quantitative and qualitative growth are closely connected. The final goal of growth in faith is the day of Christ (Phil. 1:6). Growing faith always works outwards, bringing → fruit and bearing witness (2 Thess. 1:3; 2 Cor. 10:15). A summons to growth in faith can even be given in the imperative (2 Pet. 3:18 *v.l.*).

5. In Acts growth is an important word for the missionary activity of the community (6:7; 12:24; 19:20). Acts 7:17 ("the people grew and multiplied in Egypt") provides a clear reminder of OT salvation history. The promise to Israel (Exod. 1:7) is eschatologically applied to the Christian community (Acts 12:24; cf. also Did. 16:3; 1 Clem. 33:6).

6. The derivation of the expression "He must increase, but I must decrease" is disputed. R. Bultmann traces it back to an astral picture (*The Gospel of John*, 1971, 174). G. Delling rejects this in favour of the ancient linguistic usage of increasing or decreasing in esteem or importance (*TDNT* VIII 519). The emphasis surely lies here on increase in influence and importance. The Baptist points to his Lord and withdraws his own light so that the One to whom he points may be seen.

auxanō is distinguished from the noun *prokopē* (Phil. 1:25; 1 Tim. 4:15) and the vb. *prokoptō* (Lk. 2:52; Rom. 13:12; Gal. 1:14; 2 Tim. 2:16; 3:9, 13) meaning advance, progress, in that in the NT it occurs exclusively in a positive sense. It has thus more positive theological associations. For not every "advance" is also "growth". W. Günther

---

πλεονάζω

πλεονάζω (*pleonazō*), to be or become more or great, to grow, to increase; ὑπερπλεονάζω (*hyperpleonazō*), to be present in great abundance.

CL *pleonazō*, used from Thuc. onwards, is formed from *pleon* (more), the comparative of *polys* (much, many), with the ending -*azein*, and means to be or become (too) much or many. The augmented form *hyperpleonazō*, to be present in excessive quantity, is rare. The developed basic meaning of *pleonazō* appears intrans. as to be or become (too) great, to exceed the correct amount, and thus fig. to be overweening or to become presumptuous. It also means to overflow (of a sea or a river), to augment, to become (too) numerous (e.g. the Jews in Rome), to be present in plentiful abundance (e.g. joys), to be rich in something, to have more than is necessary, to abound in, and, as a commercial term, to have a balance (of cash). Trans. *pleonazō* occurs as to make rich, to increase or multiply, to cause to grow. In ethical contexts (as in Thuc., Dem., Aristot., Stoics) *pleonazō* denotes in a censorious way that which violates the ideal of moderation, reason and natural wholeness.

OT The LXX has *pleonazō* 28 times; of these, 18 render Heb. equivalents, generally '*āḏap* to be surplus, and *rāḇâh* to be or become many: e.g. of good (Exod. 16:18,

23), people (1 Chr. 4:27; 5:23; Jer. 30:19), money etc. (2 Chr. 24:11; 31:5; Sir. 35:1), sins (Sir. 23:3).

NT In the NT *pleonazō* occurs 9 times (intrans. 7 times in Paul and 2 Pet. 1:8; trans. in 2 Thess. 1:3); *hyperpleonazō* only in 1 Tim. 1:4. It always expresses in the NT a process of growing, multiplying or increasing. It stands in contrast with *perisseuō* which expresses in an eschatological sense the element of the abundance which far exceeds all measurement and of the fullness which overflows all previously fixed boundaries (→ Fullness, art. *perisseuō*). *pleonazō* renders more the idea of development, the growth process of something: "that grace may abound" (Rom. 6:1); "your faith is growing" (2 Thess. 1:3); "if these things [godliness, love etc.] abound" (2 Pet. 1:8). *perisseuō* exceeds *pleonazō* in expressing superabundant quantity. This emerges in a number of passages, in which both terms stand in the same context.

1. In Rom. 5:20 Paul is formulating the relationship between → law and → grace. Through the → law (art. *nomos*) sin increases (*pleonazō*) to its full extent and exposes the hopelessness of humanity in the face of death. But grace has abounded all the more (*hypereperisseusen*) in the new age. The more hopelessly man entangles himself in increasing sin, the greater is God's liberating act in giving pardon. This view of the relationship between sin and grace obviously led to a misunderstanding in Judaism, which Paul goes into in Rom. 6:1 ff.

It is interesting that Paul here (6:1) now uses *pleonazō* with reference to grace and not, as one might have supposed, *perisseuō*. In this context Paul is concerned with the process of grace becoming greater. It cannot be stimulated by a conscious persistence in sin.

2. 2 Cor. 4:15 also links *charis*, grace, with *pleonazō*. As grace extends (*pleonasasa*) to more and more people, thanksgiving overflows (*perisseusē*) to the glory of God. "Grace makes its way on earth" (G. Klein).

3. In Phil. 4:17 Paul links *pleonazō* with various business terms (*eis logon doseōs kai lēmpseōs*, in settlement of giving and receiving [of a mutual account], v. 15; cf. Arndt, 479; *eis logon hymōn*, credited to your account, v. 17; cf. Arndt, 479). *pleonazō* is also to be understood from this context. With reference to the contribution of the Philippians Paul says: "It is not the gift that I value; what is valuable to me is the interest that is mounting up [*pleonazonta*] in your account" (JB). The use of *perisseuō* in v. 18 ("I have more than enough") shows again the particular thrust of *pleonazō*.

4. Paul prayed that the Lord might grant the Thessalonians to grow (*pleonasai*) and overflow (*perisseusai*) in → love for one another (1 Thess. 3:12). *pleonazein* is thus intensified by *perisseuein*.

5. *pleonazō* occurs in the sense of *perisseuō* in the OT quotation (Exod. 16:18) in 2 Cor. 8:15: "He who gathered much had nothing over", i.e. had no more than was necessary.   *W. Bauder, D. Müller*

→ Fruit, → Seed

G. Delling, *pleonazō* etc., *TDNT* VI 263–74; G. Stählin, *prokopē* etc., *TDNT* VI 703–19; and "Fortschritt und Wachstum. Zur Herkunft und Wandlung neutestamentlicher Ausdrucksformen", *Festgabe für J. Lortz*, II, 1957, 13–25.

Guard, Keep, Watch

People only guard things which they think are valuable, whether they are people, prisoners or things. To guard something is to make oneself dependent on what one guards, because it can only be done by sacrificing time and freedom to it. *tēreō* and *phylassō* are verbs which express this watching over and guarding. Both were originally used in the former sense, but were then applied figuratively to preserving the law, commandments and traditions. Anyone who keeps such ordinances thereby allows his life and actions to be determined by them.

τηρέω

τηρέω (*tēreō*), preserve, keep; τήρησις (*tērēsis*), observance; παρατηρέω (*paratēreō*), watch (closely), observe; παρατήρησις (*paratērēsis*), observation.

CL *tēreō* means: (a) have in view, perceive, observe; then (act.) wait for (the right time or opportunity), lie in wait for (a person); (mid) be on the watch, be on one's guard; (b) guard, watch over, preserve (things, persons, and also ethical values, e.g. loyalty, faith, chastity); (c) pay attention to, obey, comply with (teachings, customs, legal demands). The derivative noun *tērēsis* (Thuc. onwards) consequently means: (a) guard, custody, detention; (b) prison; (c) (fig.) observance, obeying, fulfilling (of commands, laws). The compound *paratēreō* (Dem. onwards) is identical with the simple vb. in act. and mid., but the noun *paratērēsis* (first in Polyb.) is used only for the observance of legal demands.

OT 1. In the LXX → *phylassō* is much commoner than *tēreō*, which is found only 38 times – in addition variations in Symm., Theod., Alexandrinus add 6 more cases – of which a good two-thirds come in the translation of the Heb. canonical books, and the remainder in the Apoc. A majority of the passages are in the Wisdom Literature (Prov. has 15), then come the historical books. There is only one example in the prophetic books (Jer. 20:10), interestingly enough in the lit. sense of lying in wait for a person. Like *phylassō*, though not in the same proportion, *tēreō* mainly represents the Heb. *šāmar*, the nuances of which (according to Koehler-Baumgartner, 993 f.) are very much the same as those in the secular meanings of *phylassō* and *tēreō*, and also *nāṣar*. The predominant meaning of *tēreō* in the LXX is that of religious observance with either God's commands (1 Sam. 15:11; Prov. 19:16) or those of Wisdom (Prov. 3:1) as the object. There is an interesting parallelism between *phylassō* and *tēreō* in Prov. 13:3; 16:17; 19:16: he who guards his mouth, his way, keeps the commandment (in each case *phylassō*) preserves or keeps his life (*tēreō*). For Dan. 9:4, where God's covenant loyalty – *tēreō* with *diathēkē* – is made dependent on the obedience of the community → *phylassō*. *tēreō* is also used a few times of the guarding of persons or things, and in Gen. 3:15 of the woman's seed and the serpent.

2. *tērēsis* is found in the LXX only in apocryphal books. In Wis. 6:18, Sir. 32:23 it is used for the result of the love of wisdom or of the commandments. Otherwise it is used for the guarding of persons, or of the city. *paratēreō* is found only 6 times in the LXX, generally with the force of waylay, lie in wait for. *paratērēsis* is found only as a variant reading in Exod. 12:42.

NT 1. There are only 31 instances of *phylassō* in the NT as against the more than 400 in the LXX, but *tēreō* is found 70 times to the LXX's 38. Thus the NT prefers the word less used in the LXX. This is particularly noticeable in John (Gospel, 18 times; Letters, 7 times) and Acts (11 times). It cannot be said with certainty whether this is due to this word's being particularly suited to convey a spiritual meaning.

In the NT it means: (a) guard, keep watch (e.g. Acts 16:23; Matt. 27:36); (b) keep (e.g. Jn. 2:10; 12:7; 2 Pet. 2:4); (c) keep blameless, uninjured (e.g. 1 Thess. 5:23; 1 Cor. 7:37; 1 Tim. 5:22); (d) protect (e.g. Jn. 17:15); (e) hold fast (e.g. Rev. 16:15; Eph. 4:3); (f) hold, follow, e.g. the law (Jas. 2:10), the → sabbath (Jn. 9:16), traditions (Mk. 7:9), the commands of Jesus (Jn. 14:15, 21; 15:10, etc.).

2. Of the 70 occurrences in the NT barely a half are found with the last-mentioned meaning, which is also approximately the case with *phylassō*. It is noteworthy, however, that in contrast to *phylassō*, with few exceptions (e.g. Mk. 7:9; Jn. 9:16; Jas. 2:10), *tēreō* does not have the force of keeping Jewish or Judaizing (Acts 15:5) tradition rejected by the Christians (cf. the polemical use of *paratēreō* in Gal. 4:10 applied to Jewish customs), but that of keeping a new Christian tradition.

This is set out clearly in Christ's final command (Matt. 28:20), where the exalted Christ commands the → church to keep the new righteousness which he had taught, e.g. in the Sermon on the Mount. It is possible that in Matt. 19:17, in his conversation with the rich young man and in contrast to his legalistic righteousness (cf. *phylassō*), and in Matt. 23:3, where he contrasts the Pharisees' teaching and practice, Jesus in demanding the keeping of the commandments meant the better righteousness (Matt. 5:20) and hence the true understanding of the Mosaic Law. If that is so, Matthew consciously uses *tēreō* in contrast to its apparent synonym *phylassō*. The same usage is found in 1 Cor. 7:19, where the keeping (*tērēsis*) of the commandments of God is to be understood in terms of Christian ethics. In the Pastorals (1 Tim. 6:14; 2 Tim. 4:7), however, *tēreō* is used like → *phylassō* of the keeping of the tradition.

In Rev., linked with *logos* (word), *entolē* (command), and *pistis* (faith), *tēreō* has the force of keeping fast a confession, both in facing false doctrine and in meeting a martyr's death (2:26; 3:3, 8, 10; 12:17; 14:12). All the Johannine passages, whether they are concerned with the keeping of the word or commandments by the church or the individual (e.g. Jn. 8:51; 15:10; 1 Jn. 2:3; 3:22), or with God's or Christ's keeping of the church (Jn. 17:11, 15; 1 Jn. 5:18), have to do with remaining in the church or in Christ. There is a special shade of meaning in Jn. 14:15, 21, 23 f. Here in the setting of Christ's farewell discourse love to him, the revealer, is described as personal and immediate relationship to him. Bultmann points out that "keeping his commandments" or his "word" has here an anti-mystical point (*The Gospel of John*, 1971, 613 f.).

The reference of *paratērēsis* (observation) in Lk. 17:20 cannot be established with certainty. Probably the word is used of the observation of apocalyptic signs. There is, however, just the possibility that the keeping of the law is intended.

paratēreō, apart from Gal. 4:10 (see above), is found only with the meaning of lie in wait for (Mk. 3:2 par. Lk. 6:7; 14:1; 20:20; Acts 9:24 – Eng. versions "watch").   *H.-G. Schütz*

| φυλάσσω | φυλάσσω (*phylassō*), guard, preserve, keep; φυλακή (*phylakē*), watch, guard, prison; φρουρέω (*phroureō*), guard, keep in custody, preserve. |

CL 1. The etymology of *phylassō* has not been established. In the act. it means, intrans.: (a) be sleepless, watch, keep guard, e.g. *nykta phylassō* (Homer), to watch all night; (b) serve as garrison (for or in a city). This leads to the trans. use: guard, provide with a guard, hold in prison; (c) guard, preserve – originally of things, property, persons and then fig. of love, loyalty, respect; (d) watch over, store (in safe keeping); (f) hold in honour (e.g. friendship), obey (an order, oath, law), attend to. In the mid. it has the same force as act. (a), (b), and also means guard for oneself, store, be careful, be on one's guard. In the LXX it has also the force of act. (f).

2. The vb. *phroureō*, compounded of *pro* and *hora-*, to pay attention to something (→ See, art. *horaō*), when used trans. has the same meaning as *phylassō*.

OT In the LXX *phroureō* is found only 4 times, all in apocryphal books, and thus it does not represent any original Heb. word in the text. *phylassō*, on the other hand, is found well over 400 times, and in a number of the Pseudepigrapha, viz. Eth. Enoch, Aristeas, Test. XII, Sib., and in Philo. No distinction in meaning is made between act. and mid. 378 times it translates *šāmar*, guard, watch, keep; 10 times *nāṣar*, follow, obey; and in isolated cases 9 other Heb. verbs. While *phylassō* is found in almost all the books of the LXX, it is found most commonly in the Pent., apart from Gen., and especially in Deut., in 1–2 Ki. (LXX 3 Ki., 4 Ki.), 1–2 Chr., Pss., Prov., Wis., Sir., Ezek. Its commonest use is for the obedience to and keeping of the law, cultic regulations, the word of God in general or of the covenant. The subject of the vb. can be the whole people of Israel, groups within it, or individuals (Exod. 12:24; Lev. 18:4; Deut. 5:1; Ps. 78[77]:10; Prov. 19:16; Ezek. 11:20). It is easy to trace the development of the concept in the OT from the original thought of fulfilling the covenant obligations (positive or negative) to the inter-testamental idea of keeping the law as the way to salvation (cf. Dan. 9:4 and various passages in 1 and 4 Macc., e.g. 1 Macc. 2:53; 8:26, 28; 4 Macc. 5:29; 6:18; 15:10; 18:7). Hence at the end of this development of meaning the covenant loyalty of God is regarded as dependent on the keeping of the law by the community. ([Tr.] This is undoubtedly the general impression created, but does not do justice to all the evidence. Much in the Jewish prayer-book, or a Midrashic saying like, "It was not for their works that the Israelites were delivered from Egypt, or for their father's works, and not by their works that the Red Sea was cloven in sunder, but to make God a name" [C. G. Montefiore and H. Loewe, eds., *A Rabbinic Anthology*, 1938, 92] shows that apparently positive remarks about Israel's keeping of the law have to be interpreted in a wider framework.) The use of *šāmar* in the Qumran literature, above all in the Manual of Discipline and the Damascus Document, shows this tendency predominantly (1 QS 5:2, 9; 8:3; CD 2:18, 21; 3:2 f.; 6:14, 18; 10:14, 16; 16:7; 19:1 f., 9. 28; 20:17, 22; on legalism at Qumran see M. Black, *The Scrolls and Christian Origins*, 1961, 118–24, 169 ff.). The other meanings of *phylassō* enumerated under CL are also found in the LXX but much more rarely. To be stressed is the usage found especially in the Pss., of God's protecting actions for his people or the pious (cf. Ps. 12:7[8]; 17:8; 145:20).

NT 1. In the NT *phylassō* means: (a) keep watch (Lk. 2:8); (b) guard (e.g. Acts 12:4; 23:35); (c) protect, guard (of God or Christ: Jn. 17:12; 2 Thess. 3:3; 2 Tim. 1:12; 2 Pet. 2:5; Jude 24; or of men: Jn. 12:25); in the mid. or with a reflex. pron., beware of, abstain from (Lk. 12:15; Acts 21:25; 2 Tim. 4:15; 2 Pet. 3:17; 1 Jn. 5:21); (d) observe, hold, e.g. the law (Gal. 6:13), the commandments (Mk. 10:20 par. Matt. 19:20, Lk. 18:21), the words of Jesus (Jn. 12:47), the decisions of the apostles (Acts 16:4).

2. Obey, hold: in each of the first two Gospels the word is used once only: Matt. 19:20; Mk. 10:20. In each case it has the contemporary religious sense of keeping the law (see above OT). Although both here and in Lk. 18:21 there is no direct criticism of Jewish observance of the law, the radical demand made by Jesus on the rich young ruler is indirectly a complete rejection of it.

Paul uses it only in the Jewish sense, but the context can give it a particular nuance. In Rom. 2:26 it is anti-legal; in Gal. 6:13 anti-Judaistic.

The same connotation of keeping the law is found in Acts 7:53, where Stephen in his defence denies that the Jews had ever kept the law, i.e. their conception of how the law should be kept was rejected from the standpoint of primitive Christianity. Acts 21:24 approves of the Jewish observance, because the Jewish Christian also did so. Luke shows Paul in agreement with the Jewish Christian standpoint.

The Jewish legacy to primitive Christianity is found in a much more important form when *phylassō* is used with tradition, the handing on of the Christian message and teaching. In Acts 16:4 Paul and Timothy delivered to the churches of Asia Minor the *dogmata*, decisions (→ Command), of the original apostles, who represented the one, true church. There is a similar concept in the Pastorals (1 Tim. 5:21; 6:20; 2 Tim. 1:14). The future of the church depends on the disciples of the apostles guarding, working out, making real the inheritance from the apostles. Note 2 Tim. 1:12 where the Lord himself guards it. While Protestants are apt to see here elements leading to Catholicism, it is highly probable that in the position portrayed by Luke and the Pastorals this step of stressing tradition was necessary and unavoidable. *phylassō* is found frequently in Luke (2:8; 11:21; 12:15) and Acts (12: 4; 23:35) in its lit. meaning. It also has a lit. sense in 2 Tim. 4:15; Jn. 12:25; 2 Pet. 2:5.

In Jn. 12:47 the expression "[not to] keep my words" means quite simply not to believe in me, Jesus, as the Revealer sent by God. Belief and keeping Jesus' words are defined in terms of each other.)

3. Protect, guard: 2 Thess. 3:3 deals with preserving the church's faith: God is the One who guards the church from the evil one (NEB). The basic thought of the passage is eschatological; the concrete background is the threat of a rising false doctrine within the church. The position is similar in Jude 24 and Phil. 4:7 (where *phroureō*, guard [cf. 2 Cor. 11:32], is used as also in 1 Pet. 1:5). The church is commended to the protection of God in its fight against false doctrine. In Jn. 15:21 the church is exhorted to be itself on guard against idols. Jn. 17:11 f. is concerned with the maintenance of the unity of the church and its exclusive relationship to Christ. Here *phylassō* and *tēreō* are used together as synonyms; God, or Christ, is the subject. *phroureō* is used in Gal. 3:23 in a special sense for the role of the law in the history of salvation: "Now before faith came, we were confined [*ephrouroumetha*] under the law, kept under restraint until faith should be revealed" (RSV).

H.-G. Schütz

4. The noun *phylakē* means: (a) guard or watch (of the shepherds over their flocks in Lk. 2:8); (b) the place of guarding or prison; Matt. 5:25 par. Lk. 12:58 as a picture of the place of judgment; Matt. 14:3, 10 par. Mk. 6:17, 27, Lk. 3:20 of John the Baptist; Matt. 18:30 again as a picture of judgment in the parable of the unforgiving servant; Lk. 21:12 in the context of warnings about what will happen to Christ's disciples; Lk. 22:33 of Peter's professed willingness to go to prison; Lk. 23:19, 25 of Barabbas; Acts 5:19, 22, 25 of the imprisonment of Peter; Acts 8:3; 22:4; 26:10 of Saul's (Paul's) erstwhile persecution of believers; Acts 12:4 f., 10 of Peter's escape from prison; Acts 16:23, 24, 27, 37, 40 in the accounts of Paul and Silas at Philippi; 2 Cor. 6:5; 11:23 in Paul's account of how Christ has enabled him to triumph over weakness and calamity; Heb. 11:36 in the list of trials that have been overcome by faith; 1 Pet. 3:19 of "the spirits in prison" identified by B. Reicke as the underworld or place of punishment in → hell (cf. *The Disobedient Spirits and Christian Baptism*, 1946, 116 f.), → also Death, art. *thanatos* NT 2 (b); Rev. 2:10 of the fate of some of the believers at Smyrna who are exhorted to remain faithful unto death so that they may receive the crown of life; Rev. 18:2 of the fallen city of → Babylon which has become the "haunt" (Arndt, 875; RSV) of every unclean spirit and bird; Rev. 20:7 of the place in which → Satan is cast for a period of a thousand years prior to the final tribulation and his ultimate subjection (→ Chiliasm in the *Glossary of Technical Terms*); (c) guard, sentinel (Acts 12:10); (d) watch of the night reflecting the Roman practice of dividing the time between 6 p.m. and 6 a.m. into four periods (Matt. 14:25; Mk. 6:48; cf. Josephus, *Ant.* 18, 356), though Matt. 24:43 and Lk. 12:38 may reflect the Heb. and Gk. practice of having only three watches (Arndt, 875; cf. Josephus, *War*, 5, 510). Mk. 13:35 uses the common designations *opse* (late, in the evening), *mesonyktion* (at midnight), *alektorophōnia* (at cock-crow), *prōi* (early, early in the morning), all in the context of the exhortation to watch, "for you do not know when the master of the house will come."

Related words which occur in the NT are: *phylakizō*, imprison (Acts 22:19); *phylaktērion*, lit. a safeguard, means of protection, especially an amulet or phylactery (Matt. 23:5, a small box containing scripture texts bound on the forehead and arm during prayer, cf. Exod. 13:9, 16; Deut. 6:8; 11:18; they were regarded as a mark of devotion to the law and also as a protection against demonic influence [Arndt, 876; but see also D. Hill, *The Gospel of Matthew*, 1972, 310; and J. Bowman, *Stud.Ev.*, I, 1959, 523 ff., who thinks that prayer-bands were not so-called in the time of Jesus and that the reference is a warning against ostentatious wearing of amulets or charms]; they are mentioned in the context of warnings against Pharisaic concern for merely external righteousness); *phylax*, guard, sentinel (Matt. 27:65D; Acts 5:23; 12:6, 19). *C. Brown*

| γρηγορέω | γρηγορέω (*grēgoreō*), watch, be on the alert, be watchful.

OT *grēgoreō* is a late pres. found in Hel. Gk. and is formed from the perf. *egrēgora* of *egeirō* (rouse, stir). In the LXX it stands for '*āmaḏ* (stand) in Neh. 7:3, and for *šāqaḏ* (watch) in Jer. 5:6; 38(31):28; Lam. 1:14; Dan. 9:14 (Theod.). It has no Heb. equivalent in Bar. 2:9; 1 Macc. 12:27; Test. Ben. 10:1; cf. Josephus, *Ant.* 11, 47.

NT Followers of Christ are exhorted to be watchful and alert either to dangers or for opportunities in Matt. 24:42; 25:13; 26:41; Mk. 13:35, 37; 14:38; Acts 20:31; 1 Cor. 16:13; Col. 4:2; 1 Thess. 5:6, 10; 1 Pet. 5:8; Rev. 3:2 f.; 16:15. On *nēphō* (be sober) → Drunken, Sober.   *C. Brown*

| ἀγρυπνέω |

ἀγρυπνέω (*agrypneō*), keep oneself awake, be awake, keep watch, guard, care; ἀγρυπνία (*agrypnia*), wakefulness.

CL & OT *agrypneō* is found from Theognis onwards, in papyri, Philo and the LXX where it occurs 11 times (chiefly for *šaqad*, watch), e.g. Job 21:32; Pss. 101(102): 7; 126(127):1. The noun *agrypnia* occurs in the LXX only in the Apoc. (10 times), e.g. Sir. 34(31):1 f., 20.

NT Jesus charged his disciples to be on the alert (Mk. 13:33; Lk. 21:36). A similar charge is repeated in Eph. 6:18 at the climax of the discourse on the Christian's armour. In Heb. 13:17 obedience to leaders is urged "for they are keeping watch over your souls, as men who will have to give account." The noun occurs only in the plur. in 2 Cor. 6:5 and 11:27 of Paul's "watching" or "sleepless nights" endured for the sake of the church.   *C. Brown*
→ Command, → Law, → Teach

(a). Arndt, 13 f., 166, 822 f., 875 f.; G. Bertram, *phylassō* etc., *TDNT* IX 236–44; H. Riesenfeld, *tēreō* etc., *TDNT* VIII 140–51.
(b). G. Eichholz, "Bewahren und Bewähren des Evangeliums", in H. Gollwitzer and T. Traub, eds., *Hören und Handeln. Festschrift für Ernst Wolf zu seinem 60. Geburtstag*, 1962.

Guilt, Cause, Convict, Blame

Whereas → sin is a general word for doing wrong in the sight of God, guilt is a legal and judicial term which implies criminal responsibility in the eyes of a court of law, whether that court is human or divine. This is illustrated by the adj. *enochos*, a legal term used to indicate that a person accused before a court is guilty. *aitia* denotes the ground of the charge. On the other hand, the meaning of the group of words connected with *elenchō* extends well beyond the legal sphere. In the OT and the NT the concept of guilt is personalized and radicalized through its association with Yahweh or the Father of Jesus Christ. → Righteousness; → Forgiveness; → Reconciliation.

| αἰτία |

αἰτία (*aitia*), ground, cause, reason, charge; αἴτιος (*aitios*), responsible, guilty; αἰτίωμα (*aitiōma*), charge; ἀναπολόγητος (*anapologētos*), inexcusable; ἀναίτιος (*anaitios*), innocent; ἄμεμπτος (*amemptos*), blameless; ἀνέγκλητος (*anenklētos*), blameless, irreproachable.

CL *aitia* means the ground or motive of a thought or action; in a causal sense the origin, occasion, of a thing, event or phenomenon. In Gk. philosophy the word occurs for the first time in accounts of the thought of Anaximander (middle of the

6th century B.C.). From the 5th century onwards (e.g. Aristotle) it becomes the established term for the origin, cause, of natural phenomena (cf. Aristot., *Phys.* 194 b 16; *Met.* 983 a 26; F. Copleston, *A History of Philosophy*, II, 1946, 311–9).

Nevertheless, *aitia* is only seldom used in a good or neutral sense (cf. Liddell-Scott, 44). Usually the word carries the sense of charge, accusation, blame (as in Aesch., Plato), indicating the responsibility and guilt which attaches to an act. Likewise *aitiōma*, a word not found before Acts, but occurring in classical Gk. from Aesch. in the form *aitiama*, means a charge against a wrongdoer. *aitios* means culpable, responsible. The compound adj. *anapologētos* is used in the same context to indicate the hopelessness of a case for the defence at law; it is found in the 2nd century B.C. (e.g. Polyb.), and means without excuse.

OT 1. The LXX uses *aitia* consistently. The word occurs 21 times in addition to 3 translations in secondary MSS. Of these 18 are in the Apocrypha without Heb. equivalent (except for Wis. 17:13); 1–4 Macc. account for 13 instances. Apart from 4 Macc. 1:16, where the philosophical concept of causation dominates, every example of *aitia* in the LXX has to do with some event which belongs to the darker side of life: fighting (2 Macc. 4:42), idolatry (Wis. 14:27), death (Wis. 18:18; 1 Macc. 9:10), sensual pleasure (Susanna 14, Theod.). As in classical Gk., the term is hardly ever used in a good sense, but rather as a technical term in irregular situations or in trials.

2. The other OT examples confirm this. In Gen. 4:13 the Yahwist uses the term '*āwōn*, iniquity, in the cry of Cain: "My punishment [LXX *aitia*] is too great." The culpable act and the punishment as its inevitable consequence are for him causally related (cf. G. von Rad, *Old Testament Theology*, I, 1962, 266). Job 18:14 contains an aphorism on the inescapable destiny of the wicked to be smitten by a fatal disease. Here the LXX translation differs from the Heb. text, using *aitia* in its description of death as a kind of majestic stroke of fate. Finally, Prov. 28:17 concludes that "for reason of [Heb. '*āšûq*] blood-guilt", i.e. murder, a person must go to the grave, wandering in insecurity.

3. *aitios* is found only at 1 Sam. 22:22 (apart from 6 examples in the Apocrypha, where it means having become guilty). Here David declares that he "has occasioned the death" of certain priests. *anapologētos* and *aitiōma* do not occur in the LXX.

NT In the NT this group of words is not frequent: *aitios* and *aitiōma* occur only once each (in Heb. and Acts), *aitia* 20 times (only in the Gospels, Acts and Heb.).

1. Some texts use *aitia* in a purely causal sense (for this reason, therefore), stating the reason why something happens. Thus the woman with an issue of blood gave Jesus the reason why she had touched him (Lk. 8:47). Peter inquired the reason for the visit (Acts 10:21). Timothy's mother and grandmother are a ground for a special reminder (2 Tim. 1:6). Similar uses are found in 2 Tim. 1:12; Tit. 1:4; Heb. 2:11. The noun *aitios* is used in Heb. 5:9 in a positive sense of Christ as the "source" (RSV) of eternal salvation for all who obey him.

2. In a second group of passages *aitia* is found in connection with legal charges and accusations brought against someone. At Matt. 19:3 the Pharisees asked whether → divorce is lawful "for every cause" as though it were the inevitable consequence of such causes, whereas Jesus' answer makes possible a new beginning

for the disordered marriage. In v. 10, however, *aitia* means a case. Possibly there is an allusion here to a concurrent discussion on the connection between marriage and discipleship which presented a choice between a wife and the Lord. Acts 22:24; 23:28; 25:18, 27 refer to the trials of Paul. In each case the passage is concerned to bring to light the ground of the charges brought against Paul, or to show that they cannot be established. Acts 26:7 uses for such unprovable allegations the noun *aitiōma*, charge (here only in the NT). *aition* is used in a similar sense in the story of the disturbance led by Demetrius (Acts 19:40): there is danger that a charge will be laid because of this disorder for which no satisfactory explanation or reason can be given.

3. A third group has to do with the occasion for a death sentence.

(a) The inscription on the cross specified the charge on which Jesus was condemned to death, the "cause" of death (Matt. 27:37; Mk. 15:26). This indicated to the onlooker that the execution was inevitable because of Jesus' claim to kingship. The Gospels, however, testify to a deeper necessity than the immediate human factors, for it sprang from the purpose of God (→ Necessity, art. *dei*). In Acts 13:28 this "cause" of death is mentioned again in a speech of Paul, and described as unjustified in terms of human justice.

(b) In the report of the trial before Pilate into which are interwoven many legal ideas Pilate pronounces his repeated conclusion that he can find no guilt in Jesus deserving death (in Jn. 18:38; 19:4, 6, *aitia;* in Lk. 23:4, 14, 22, *aition*). Hence in the Gospel accounts the demand of the crowd for the death of the innocent one is all the more culpable (→ Cross, art. *stauros*, NT 1). In a similar sense, cf. the use of → *enochos*, guilty. (On the trial of Jesus see E. Bammel, ed., *The Trial of Jesus*, 1970; J. Blinzler, *The Trial of Jesus*, 1959; D. R. Catchpole, *The Trial of Jesus*, 1971.)

(c) Acts 28:18 mentions the charge made against Paul of committing a capital crime. Since, however, there was insufficient ground (*aitia*) for the accusation, the Romans wished to save him from unjust condemnation to death.

4. The words of this group are used in the OT and NT to indicate the responsibility of a man for his action, together with the resultant consequences. The same applies to *anapologētos* which occurs twice in Paul's letter to the Romans and means the state of being without excuse in a legal sense. In the light of eschatology, the ungodly have no possibility of being excused. They stand under God's destroying wrath (→ Anger; Rom. 1:20). No man is able, under any circumstances, to make an excuse to God (Rom. 2:1). Everyone, whether Jew or Gentile, is deservingly subject to death, and therefore, as the argument of Rom. 2 continues, man is totally dependent on God's free → grace and goodness in Jesus Christ. He took our sentence of death on himself and by this means has truly "excused" us. The theological emphasis given to the theme that Christ "must" suffer in this way is a logical counterpart to the ideas associated with this group of words.   *F. Thiele*

5. The adj. *anaitios*, innocent, occurs in Acts 16:37 and Matt. 12:5, 7. *amemptos* means blameless, of the Mosaic covenant (Heb. 8:7) and the heart (1 Thess. 3:13), otherwise only of persons (Phil. 3:6 [cf. Gen. 17:1]; 2:15 [cf. Job 1:1]; Lk. 1:7). The adv. *amemptōs* occurs at 1 Thess. 2:10; 3:13 *v.l.*; 5:23. Both adj. and adv. are connected with *memphomai*, find fault with, blame (Mk. 7:2 *v.l.*; Rom. 9:19; Heb. 8:8; cf. Arndt, 44, 503). *anenklētos* means blameless, irreproachable, of Christians

who will be presented blameless by Christ on the day of the Lord (1 Cor. 1:8; cf. Col. 1:22). A blameless life is also required of Christian leaders in the present (1 Tim. 3:10; Tit. 1:6 f.).   *C. Brown*

| ἐλέγχω |

ἐλέγχω (*elenchō*), bring to light, expose, set forth, convict, convince, punish, discipline; ἔλεγχος (*elenchos*), proof, evidence, conviction, reproof, correction; ἐλεγμός (*elegmos*), conviction, reproof, punishment; ἔλεγξις (*elenxis*), conviction, rebuke, reproof.

CL 1. *elenchō* is found from Homer onwards (e.g. *Il.* 9, 552; *Od.* 21, 424), probably originally (like the noun *elenchos*, reproach) in the sense of blame, insult; then in the sense of test, examine, enquire into a matter (cf. *TDNT* II, 473 n. 2). In Plato (*Soph.* 242b; *Grg.* 470c; *Phdr.* 273b, etc.) and Aristotle (*Soph.El.* 170ª 24; *Eth.Nic.* 1146ª 23), *elenchō* is used of the logical exposition of the facts of a matter for the purpose of refuting the (usually sophistical) argument of an opponent. Thus the word developed its principal meaning of convince, refute (e.g. Democ., *Frag.* 60, 222; Zeno, *Frag.* 41). In Stoicism the concept was transferred from the intellectual argument to the application of philosophical ethics. Epictetus is concerned with correcting the practical principles of living (*Dissertationes* 1, 26, 17; 2, 1, 32; 2, 14, 20; 2, 26, 4; 3, 9, 13; 3, 23, 33 and often). Philo (*Spec. Leg.* 3, 54; 4, 6, 40 and often) and Josephus (*War* 7, 330, 447 and often) spoke of the correction which men receive from their own consciences, the Logos, the truth, or from God. The idea of correction finally appears again in Hellenistic and Jewish literature in contexts which produce the meaning, to accuse, convict (Appian, *Bella Civilia* 5, 28; Diod. Sic. 13, 90, 4); and *elenchō* acquired a sense which brought it near to *paideuō*, or *paideia*, the basic concept of Gk. education and learning (→ Teach, art. *paideuō*).

2. The noun *elenchos*, current from Pindar onwards, has a similar variety of meanings. It means: (a) proof (Demosthenes 4, 15; Plato, *Grg.* 471e; especially Aristot., *Soph.El.* 1, 165ª 2); (b) conviction *BGU* 1138, 13; *Epigrammata Graeca ex lapidibus conlecta*, 1878, 814; (c) correction, reproof, censure (Philo, *Rev. Div. Her.* 76). The nouns *elegmos* and *elenxis*, common in the LXX and the NT, are found chiefly in the Hellenistic period, and consequently have as a rule the meaning of conviction or correction.

OT In the LXX *elenchō* is used in the great majority of cases to render the hiph. of
yākaḥ: to bring to account, to correct. *elenchos* generally represents the corresponding noun *tôkaḥat*, rebuke, correction. It is worthy of note that the words of this group are found in this sense mainly in the later books of the OT (Job, Pss., Prov.), and in the Apocrypha (Wis., Sir.). *elegmos* is used in Isa. 37:3 and 50:2 with the meaning of rebuke, reproach, disgrace. At Num. 5:18 f., 23 f., 27 the LXX translates the "water of bitterness" used in the ordeal by the difficult phrase *hydōr tou elegmou*, water of conviction. *elenxis* occurs only at Job 21:4; 23:2, where it renders the Heb. *śiaḥ*, concern, complaint.

1. The historical books occasionally use *elenchō* in secular contexts: because of a dispute about a well, Abraham complained to Abimelech, king of Gerar (Gen. 21:25); in the quarrel between Jacob and Laban, the kinsmen were to judge (Gen.

31:37) etc. In these cases *elenchō* refers to the clarification of a practical point at dispute, not an intellectual question (see above, CL 1).

2. In prophetic proclamation the vb. has a legal character, as is shown from its use alongside the terms righteousness and judgment. The task of the priests to pronounce judgment and give advice is clearly presupposed (Hos. 4:4; Ezek. 3:26; cf. Amos 5:10; Isa. 29:21; Mal. 2:7). In a negative sense, the prophetic message of judgment spoke of reproof (Jer. 2:19) and the day of punishment (Hos. 5:9) which Yahweh will bring upon his rebellious people. Positively, it proclaimed salvation in terms of justice for the poor (Isa. 11:3 f.) and the helpful healing instruction which Yahweh will give to the nations (Isa. 2:4; Mic. 4:3).

3. This group of words comes into its own in the Wisdom Literature, chiefly in the sense of correction and punishment. On the one hand, the Psalmist prays for preservation from divine punishment (Ps. 6:1); on the other the correction which comes from Yahweh, or from just men, is regarded as a help and benefit (Ps. 141:5; Job 5:17). This thought is developed particularly in proverbial wisdom. While the ungodly neither accepts nor deserves correction, the wise man is grateful for it, for he recognizes in it the love of Yahweh (Prov. 9:7 f.; 3:11 f.; 29:15). As may be seen from the repeated parallel use of *elenchō* and *paideuō* (in Prov. 3:12, Aquila and Symmachus replace *elenchei* with *paideuei;* 15:12; Sir. 18:13), or *elenchos* and *paideia* (Prov. 6:23), the use of the words of this group in the Wisdom Literature comes close to the Stoic ideal of education and character training (cf. on this G. von Rad, *Old Testament Theology*, I, 1962, 418–59). The godly man is trained by correction and discipline to follow the right path in life (Prov. 6:23; 5:12 f.; 19:25; Sir. 18:13).

4. On grounds of the exhortation in Lev. 19:17, "You shall reason with your neighbour", correction played an important part in Judaism both as a commandment to love one's neighbour, and as a task which earns merit (Sifra Lev. 19:17; Sanh. 21b; Pes. K. 25, 163 b; cf. SB I 787 ff.). It has a special importance in the Qumran texts. He who observes his brother transgressing the law, must censure him, at first before witnesses (CD 7:2). If this correction achieves nothing, the case must be brought before the whole community which then proceeds to punish the sinner (1QS 3:6).

NT The words of this group are found in the NT in the gospels (especially Jn.), and also in the later epistles (especially the Pastorals). The majority of examples occur in the later writings. Mk. does not use these words and the early example in Paul is at 1 Cor. 14:24.

1. In the Gospel of John, *elenchō* means, as in the prophetic warnings of judgment, to reveal and convict of sin. It is the negative, reverse side of God's saving work of revelation (Jn. 3:20; 16:8; cf. also Eph. 5:13; Jude 15). The thing revealed is expressed by means of *peri* with the gen. (Jn. 8:46, sin; 16:8 ff., sin, righteousness and judgment; cf. Lk. 3:19, an illegitimate marriage; Jude 15, deeds of ungodliness).

2. *elenchō* is found particularly frequently in hortatory passages (e.g. Eph. 5:13). The Pastoral Epistles assign to the leader of the community the task of rebuking church members (1 Tim. 5:20; 2 Tim. 4:2; Tit. 2:15) and of convicting opponents of their error (Tit. 1:9, 13). The corresponding activity is called *elegmos* in 2 Tim.

3:16, and *elenxis* in 2 Pet. 2:16. In this connection mention should also be made of the instructions about church order in Matt. 18:15 ff., where it is said that erring church members should first be told privately of their fault, then in the presence of several witnesses and, if this be fruitless, the matter should be laid before the whole church (cf. the corresponding procedure at Qumran, see above OT, 4).

3. It may be seen from the citation of Prov. 3:11 f. at Heb. 12:5 and Rev. 3:19, that the Hellenistic concept of education (see above CL, 1; OT, 3) has also found its way into the NT. In both cases *elenchō* and *paideuō* are used in parallel.

4. The interpretation of *elenchos* in Heb. 11:1 presents difficulties. Its meaning here can be deduced only from its context in the definition of faith given in this chapter. The sentence falls into two parts. The second half is a parallelism, to be compared with the first part: *elenchos* strengthens *hypostasis*, and *pragmata ou blepomena*, things not seen, explains *elpizomena*, things hoped for. The concepts are unmistakably Hellenistic in character. The purpose of the statement is not so much to encourage subjective assurance of faith, as if faith could give the status of reality to what lies in the future. It is rather to secure a "firm link with objectivity" (O. Michel, *Der Brief an die Hebräer*, KEK 13, 1966[12], 373). Accordingly, *elenchos* should be interpreted neither subjectively, as if it denoted absence of doubt, nor in a hortatory sense, as if it meant correction, nor yet in an intellectual sense, meaning evidence. Rather it should be understood in its context in the theology of Heb. in a strictly theological sense, as referring to conviction, about the power of the future world promised by God which is here described in the language of secular Gk. as "things not seen" (on the whole subject see O. Michel, op. cit., 372 ff.; → Faith, art. *pistis* NT 4; → Form, art. *hypostasis* NT 2). Heb. 11:1 would then mean: "But faith is the pledge of things hoped for, the conviction of things we cannot see."

H.-G. Link

ἔνοχος

ἔνοχος (*enochos*), guilty, subject to, liable to, or deserving a thing or penalty; ἐνέχω (*enechō*), hold fast, be subject to.

CL Gk. literature has the adj. *enochos*, derived from *enechō* (Pindar), meaning to hold fast; pass., to be held fast, be subject to (Plato, Xenophon, Isocrates). It is frequently used as a technical legal term: a person is made liable, or subject to a certain penalty under the law. The forum (lawcourt, laws, men or gods) before which he is guilty or liable is usually referred to in the dative (e.g. Xen., *Memorabilia* 1, 2, 64). Frequently *enochos* is also used with the gen. of the crime (Plato, *Laws* 2, 914e) or of the punishment.

OT The LXX has *enochos* 21 times in the same sense as secular Gk. The term is used in the LXX chiefly to refer to a person who is condemned to → death because of an action incurring blood-guilt. *enochos* serves to translate Heb. formulae expressing the death penalty (e.g. Gen. 26:11; Exod. 22:2; Lev. 20:9–27, in cases of sodomy, incest, homosexuality, soothsaying, etc. "their blood be upon them"; Num. 35:27; Deut. 19:10; Jos. 2:19, the blood-oath taken by the spies before Rahab). In Isa. 54:17 (LXX) *enochos* is used of those who incur guilt by engaging in a legal dispute with Israel.

NT The 10 NT examples of *enochos* follow the same pattern.

1. Matt. 5:21 f. Here, in a threefold progression, the respective courts before which a lawbreaker is arraigned are referred to in the dative: *krisis*, local court; *synedrion*, supreme national court; *gehenna*, → hell (the place of punishment is named at once in the acc. instead of the supreme judge). The lesser or greater degree of guilt is reflected in the nature of the court and the severity of the punishment involved (cf. A. Schlatter, *Der Evangelist Matthäus*, 1963[6], 165–71; and also W. D. Davies, *The Setting of the Sermon on the Mount*, 1964, 236 ff.; D. Hill, *The Gospel of Matthew*, 1972, 120 ff.; → Curse, art. *rhaka*; → Wisdom, Folly, art. *mōria*).

2. Jas. 2:10 uses *enochos* of the lawbreaker. Every single sin, however insignificant it may appear to be, makes the doer "totally guilty", and therefore liable to → judgment.

3. It is in accordance with OT usages when, in the Matthean and Marcan accounts of the trial of Jesus, the death sentence is pronounced using the term *enochos*. The high priest regards the evidence of blasphemy (→ Revile) as conclusive in Jesus' case, and declares him "guilty of death" (*enochos thanatou estin*, Matt. 26:66; cf. Mk. 14:64). The two other occurrences of *enochos* likewise have a legal character.

(a) Heb. 2:15 explains the significance of the death of Jesus, which frees those who were "condemned" to be slaves (i.e. of the devil and of death).

(b) 1 Cor. 11:27 concludes that he who takes the bread and wine unworthily becomes "guilty" of the body and blood of the Lord present in them. The Lord gave himself up to death for the sake of the brethren; the opposite action, loveless behaviour towards one's neighbour (cf. Matt. 5:21 f.), results in guilt. Here too the term *enochos* is used of a matter of life and death.

4. Similarly Mk. 3:29 uses *enochos* with a gen. of the penalty; he who blasphemes against the → Holy Spirit will be guilty of an "eternal sin" (→ Revile, art. *blasphēmeō*).

F. Thiele

ἄμεμπτος

ἄμεμπτος (*amemptos*), blameless; ἀμέμπτως (*amemptōs*), blamelessly; μέμφομαι (*memphomai*), find fault; μεμψίμοιρος (*mempsimoiros*), fault-finding; μέμψις (*mempsis*), reason for complaint.

CL The word *amemptos* is used most frequently in secular Gk. in the sense of blameless, without reproach. It may be used of persons (Euripides, Demosthenes) and things (Xenophon, Plutarch), in the latter case suggesting perfection. On occasion *amemptos* was used with the connotation "content", in the sense that one is not characterized by blaming (Xenophon, Cyril). The word occurs in Wis. 10:5, 15; 18:21 in the sense of moral purity.

The vb. *memphomai* means to blame, to find fault with. With the dat. and acc. of the person it may connote the idea of regarding someone as blameworthy (Herodotus).

The adj. *mempsimoiros* is used in secular Gk. to characterize one who was apt to find fault (Isocrates, Lucian), while *mempsis* indicates the ground of, or reason for, complaint or blame (Aeschylus). It is used in Wis. 13:6 of those who failed to see God behind his created works. "For these men there is but small blame."

OT In the LXX *amemptos* occurs as the translation of several Heb. words meaning clean, pure (*bar, zākâh, zākak, ḥaṗ*), perfect, complete (*tām, tāmîm, ṭāhēr, nāqî*), to be righteous (*ṣāḍaq*), and possibly straight, upright (*yāšār*). The adj. *amemptos* occurs in parallelism with *katharos* in Job 11:4 to describe the blamelessness of Job's character. In this instance it stands for the Heb. *bar* (pure). The vb. *zākâh* is translated by *amemptos* in Job 15:14 in the LXX. In this verse *amemptos* occurs in parallelism with *dikaios* (righteous). In Job 33:9 the Heb. *ḥaṗ* is translated by *amemptos* and qualified by the phrase "I have not transgressed." In Job 2:3 it is difficult to ascertain whether *amemptos* stands for *yāšār* or *tām*. In Job 1:8 the Heb. *tām* is translated by *amemptos* in a verse describing Job's blamelessness, and in Job 22:3 it stands for the Heb. *ṣāḍaq* (be righteous). In most instances the word *amemptos* connotes moral purity. It was applied also, however, to the heavenly bodies (Job 15:15; 25:5) and Job's doctrine (Job 11:4). The adv. *amemptōs* occurs in Est. 3:13 in the sense of honourable or well intentioned, with regard to Artaxerxes' efforts to unify his empire.

In Job 33:10 *mempsis* occurs as the translation of the Heb. *tᵉnû'âh* (opposition, or occasion for opposition). It is used in parallelism with the phrase "he counts me as his enemy." The sense is that of reason for complaint. In Job 39:7 the word *mempsis* occurs as the translation of *tᵉšû'âh* (shout). Since it describes the shouts of a driver to the wild donkey, it may connote the idea of scolding, hence censure. In Job 15:15(A); 33:23; and Wis. 13:6 the word connotes the concept of fault or blame.

NT The word *amemptos* occurs in the NT in the sense of moral purity in Lk. 1:6, where it is used in the sense of blamelessness with regard to the commandments of the Lord. In Phil. 3:6 Paul uses the word to describe his standing with regard to the law. The connotation of the word in these instances is that the individual is not guilty of disobedience to the laws of God, hence there is no blameworthiness nor susceptibility to charge as far as the law is concerned.

The word is used in a somewhat similar sense in Phil. 2:15 to describe the moral purity of those believers who do not grumble or question. They are further described as without blemish (*amōmos*). In 1 Thess. 3:13 Paul expresses the desire that the Thessalonian Christians may be "blameless in holiness" at the *parousia* (cf. Matt. 25:34–40; → Present, art. *parousia*). This blamelessness is the result of their abounding in love one for another (v. 12).

The adv. *amemptōs* occurs in 1 Thess. 2:10 and 5:23. In the former verse it describes the activity of Paul among the Thessalonians in regard to there being no cause for censure or blame on his part. In the latter verse Paul uses the word of the effect of the total work of sanctification at the *parousia*.

The verb *memphomai* is attested in Rom. 9:19 and Heb. 8:8 as well as the TR of Mark 7:2. In each instance the basic connotation of blame or find fault obtains.

In the TR of Mark 7:2 the word is used of the reaction of the Pharisees to some of Jesus' disciples who were eating with unwashed hands. The implication is that the Pharisees found the disciples open to blame, because they were guilty of violating the Jewish tradition. (→ Baptism, art. *niptō*; → Hand, art. *cheir*.)

In Rom. 9:19 the word is used by Paul in a rhetorical question that occurs in an exposition of the sovereignty of God: "Why does he yet find fault?" In the light of God's sovereign inexorable purposes one may raise the question of human responsibility. The word *memphomai* clearly connotes "guilt" or blameworthiness in this context for Paul's argument is that God's sovereignty does not free sinful men of fault or guilt before God.

The word *amemptos* is applied to the first covenant in Heb. 8:7 in a negative sense. If the first covenant had been faultless there would have been no need for another.

In Heb. 8:8 *memphomai* occurs with the dative of the person in a sense similar to the above but in contrast to *amemptos* (v. 7). The Sinaitic covenant has been described as not being faultless (*amemptos*). A fault of the old covenant is found in the people to whom it was given (vv. 8, 9) who did not keep it, for "he finds fault [*memphomenos*] with them" (v. 8). The context does not seem to indicate that the intrinsic nature of the commandments was changed, but rather the mode of reception of the covenant (vv. 8–12, quoting Jer. 31:31–34).

The word *memphomai* then connotes the act of blaming or finding fault, i.e. to regard an individual or object as having fault or blame.

The word *mempsimoiros* (lit. finding fault with one's lot [*moira*]) occurs only once in the NT in Jude 16 in the sense of grumbler, malcontent.   *T. McComiskey*
→ Cross, → Judgement, → Punishment, → Redemption, → Sin

(a). F. Büchsel, *elenchō* etc., *TDNT* II 473–76; W. Grundmann, *memphomai* etc., *TDNT* IV 571–4; H. Hanse, *echō* etc., *TDNT* II 828 (on *enechō*); R. S. Moxon, *The Doctrine of Sin*, 1922; C. Ryder Smith, *The Bible Doctrine of Sin*, 1953; F. R. Tennant, *The Concept of Sin*, 1912; H. Thielicke, *Theological Ethics*, I, 1968, II, 1969 (see indexes); N. P. Williams, *The Ideas of the Fall and Original Sin*, 1929. On the psychological and pastoral aspects of guilt see D. Belgum, *Guilt: Where Religion and Psychology Meet*, 1963; H. McKeating, *Living with Guilt*, 1970; J. G. McKenzie, *Guilt: Its Meaning and Significance*, 1962; K. Rahner, "Guilt and its Remission: The Borderland between Theology and Psychotherapy", *Theological Investigations*, II, 1963, 265–82; and "Does Traditional Theology Represent Guilt as Innocuous as a Factor in Human Life?", *Theological Investigations*, XIII, 1975, 133–51; P. Tournier, *Guilt and Grace: A Psychological Study*, 1962; A. Uleyn, *The Recognition of Guilt: A Study in Pastoral Psychology*, 1969.
(b). G. Bally, "Schuld und Existenz", *Wege zum Menschen*, 9, 1960, 305 ff.; M. Boss, *Lebensangst, Schuldgefühle und psychotherapeutische Befreiung*, 1965²; M. Buber, "Schuld und Schuldgefühle", in A. Sborowitz, ed., *Der leidende Mensch*, 1960, 106 ff.; G. Condrau, "Angst und Schuld im menschlichen Dasein", *Wege zum Menschen* 3, 1966, 65 ff.; H. Dombois, ed., *Die weltliche Strafe in der evangelischen Theologie*, 1959; P. Guilluy, ed., *La Culpabilité Fondamentale: Péché Originel et Anthropologie Moderne*, 1975; H. Harsch, *Das Schuldproblem in Theologie und Tiefenpsychologie*, 1964; A. Köberle, "Das Schuldproblem in theologischer und tiefenpsychologischer Sicht", in W. Bitter, ed., *Psychotherapie und Seelsorge*, 1952, 154 ff.; K. Koch, "Sünde und Schuld", *RGG³* VI 476 ff.; F. Leist, "Die Grenzen zwischen Tiefenpsychologie und Seelsorge", in W. Bitter, op. cit., 163 ff.; H. Lindinger, "Die Erfahrung von Schuld und Tod beim heutigen Menschen", *Wege zum Menschen* 4, 1967, 121 ff.; R. Pfisterer, "Die Schuld – Schande oder Chance?", *Wege zum Menschen* 7/8, 1962, 240 ff.; R. Schneider, *Der Mensch vor dem Gericht der Geschichte*, 1946; E. Schweizer, "Schuld und Tod in biblischer Sicht", *ZNW* 27, 1956, 728 ff.; G. Suttinger, "Der schuldiger Täter als psychologisches Problem", *Wege zum Menschen* 7/8, 1962, 225 ff.

H

Hand, Right Hand, Left Hand, Laying on of Hands

The uses of the word *cheir*, hand, are many and various. It can mean fig. side, power, handwriting or army. In Biblical usage particular importance is attached to the use of *cheir* as part for the whole, as a substitute for a person and his activity and dealings. Thus the hand of God stands for his majesty and supreme power in the affairs of men. On the other hand, Jesus and his disciples were delivered into the hands of men. The thought here is of surrender to the power and mercy of their enemies (→ Judgment, art. *paradidōmi*). Related to this use of *cheir* is the notion of the right hand, *dexia* (*cheir*). This expresses a person's power and authority. To sit at the right hand (*en dexia*) signifies the possession of equal → power and dignity (→ Glory, art. *doxa*). Finally, the laying on of hands plays a special part in the NT in commissioning and empowering. This is dealt with in the art. on *epitithēmi tas cheiras*.

δεξιά

δεξιός (*dexios*), right; δεξιά (*dexia*), right hand.

CL *dexios* which is related to Latin *dexter* means right. It is possible that there is a connection with *dechomai*, to receive; *dexios* would then mean acceptable. Attested from Homer on, it means: (a) right (opposite to left); *hē dexia cheir*, the right hand, then the right side in general; (b) skilful (opposite to clumsy); (c) lucky. The plur. *dexiai* can mean contract, because of the handshake which sealed it. The right hand symbolizes power, success, good fortune, loyalty.

This also holds true in the NT. For the right hand in agreement see Gal. 2:9. The angel in the tomb was sitting on the right side (Mk. 16:5; cf. also Jn. 21:6). In the final judgment those who are chosen are summoned to the right hand of the Son of man (Matt. 25:31 ff.).

OT The Heb. *yāmîn* is the only OT equivalent of *dexios*. God's right hand is often spoken of symbolically, especially in the Pss. It provides support (Ps. 18:35, MT 18:36) and victory (Ps. 118:15). It even expresses the omnipresence of God which embraces men everywhere (Ps. 139:10). Benjamin, lit. son of the right hand, is interpreted as son of good fortune (Gen. 35:18). The place at a man's right hand is important as a place of honour (1 Ki. 2:19; Ps. 45:9, MT 45:10; Zech. 3:1).

Ps. 110:1 is particularly significant in the light of its use in the NT. The king of Israel, placed by Yahweh at his right hand, perhaps at his accession to the throne, is honoured as God's co-regent, who by war and victory will overthrow the enemies of Israel, and thus of God. (For discussion of background see A. Weiser, *The Psalms*, 1952, 692–7; A. A. Anderson, *The Book of Psalms*, II, 1972, 768–72.)

146

NT In the NT Ps. 110:1 plays an important role in connection with statements about the messiah. The verse is quoted or referred to indirectly 19 times, of which 7 are in the Synoptics, 3 in Acts, 3 in Paul, 5 in Heb. and 1 in Pet. It is only here that *dexios* has any theological significance. (It occurs altogether 54 times, most frequently in Matt.)

1. Ps. 110:1 was probably interpreted messianically already in pre-NT times. At all events, Jesus expounded it in this sense in Mk. 12:35 ff. par. Matt. 22:41–6, Lk. 20:41–4. For Rab. Judaism the messiah was God's eschatological, political co-regent who would establish a visible kingdom of God on earth. Jesus clearly rejected the political aspects of messiahship and was guarded in his attitude to the title of Son of David (→ Son). But in the final days of his ministry he alluded to him as if to a third person. ([Ed.] The context in Matt. and Mk. is particularly significant, for Jesus' question to the Pharisees about the Christ immediately follows the lawyer's question to Jesus as to which is the great commandment. The reply that Jesus gave was: "You shall love the Lord your God with all your heart, and with all your soul, and with all your mind" [Matt. 22:37]. He then added the second great commandment and went on to ask, referring to Ps. 110:1: "How is it then that David, inspired by the Spirit, calls him Lord?" [Matt. 22:37]. The implication is that as well as the → Lord whom men are commanded to serve and worship with their whole being there is another Lord who has the same title and sits at the Lord's right hand. The question is put hypothetically, but it also has bearing on who Jesus is and what is his divinely appointed rôle. The hearers were unable to give an answer. In the verses that follow Jesus went on to pronounce judgment on the scribes and Pharisees whose teaching and practice had caused them to miss the significance of what God is saying and doing.)

At his trial (Mk. 14:62 par. Matt. 26:64, Lk. 22:69), although unarmed and ridiculed, Jesus solemnly declared that he was "the Son of man" who will sit "at the right hand of Power" (Dan. 7:13 combined with Ps. 110:1). With this unheard-of claim he demanded recognition that God exercises his power in a way differing radically from that of the world. God works under and indeed by means of conditions of the greatest human powerlessness. The one who will come in judgment at the right hand of God's throne (→ Power, art. *thronos*) is the → Lamb who was slain (Rev. 5:6).

2. This is the only sense in which the primitive church could speak of Jesus being seated at God's right hand. This is pictured in various ways. Rom. 8:34 lays more emphasis upon the priestly function of the heavenly intercessor. Col. 3:1 stresses the fact that Christ is now hidden in the divine world above. On the other hand, Eph. 1:20 and 1 Pet. 3:22 underline the original meaning of his co-regency. For Heb. especially Jesus' session at God's right hand ("the point in what we are saying" [8:1]) is not the exercise of worldly power but the reign of the One who has offered himself as a sacrifice and has therefore been exalted above all angels (1:3, 13). This sacrifice of himself which has led to his exaltation is the unchangeable source of all the blessings of salvation towards which the tired Christian community must hasten (12:2). However, his session at God's right hand does not yet mean the immediate defeat of all his enemies. This is reserved for the eschatological consummation (10:12; cf. 1 Cor. 15:25).

3. A polemical motive is added in Acts. The proclamation of Jesus' session at

God's right hand (2:34) and his exaltation to that position (2:33; 5:31) becomes a word of judgment upon the Jews and their pride in the Law. The one they killed is the messiah! Stephen saw him standing at God's right hand (7:55 f.), "as if to meet Stephen" (J. A. Bengel, *Gnomon of the New Testament*, 1873, II, 583). That Jesus is standing at God's right hand indicates that he has the role of witness for the defence; he appears before God as a witness on behalf of his own witnesses on earth. The witness stands, the judge sits! *C. Blendinger*

ἀριστερός, εὐώνυμος

ἀριστερός (*aristeros*), left; εὐώνυμος (*euōnymos*), left.

OT The Heb. *śᵉmō'l* (e.g. Gen. 15:15; 24:9) is normally translated by *aristeros*. But *euōnymos* is also used. Significance is attached to which hand Jacob used in blessing in Gen. 48:14. Both the right and left hands are mentioned in Jdg. 16:29 but without any theological significance. But the left is a symbol for folly and ill fortune in Eccles. 10:2.

NT Paul speaks of having "weapons of righteousness for the right hand and the left" (2 Cor. 6:7) in his defence of his ministry. The expression *ex aristerōn* is used by James and John who wanted the chief places for themselves on the right and left hands of Jesus (Mk. 10:37). By contrast Lk. 23:33 mentions the two malefactors crucified on the right and left hand of Jesus. In all these instances *aristeros* has a good or at least neutral sense. *euōnymos* is used in the same contexts in Mk. 10:40 and 15:27; cf. Matt. 20:21, 23; 27:38. It has a neutral sense in Acts 21:3 and Rev. 10:2. But it has a pejorative sense in Matt. 25:33, 41 in the parable of the sheep and the goats which is in keeping with its lit. meaning. For *euōnymos* means lit. of good name or omen, well-named, thus avoiding the ill-omen attaching to the left. It thus became a euphemism for the left (cf. the secular background in Liddell-Scott, 740, 240). *C. Brown*

χείρ

χείρ (*cheir*), hand; πυγμή (*pygmē*), fist; δάκτυλος (*daktylos*), finger.

CL *cheir* is found from Mycenaean Greek (Linear B) on. The hand, the member of the human → body that a man puts to the most active use, serves him both in his work and in defence of himself. His strength and energy are made effective through his hands. Therefore the hand is particularly important.

In secular Gk. the plur. *cheires* and *dynameis* (power(s)) can be used synonymously. But the hand does not stand simply as a symbol of power. When it is linked with a personal name, it stands as a substitute for the person himself in action. *cheir* means handwriting in Hyperides (4th cent. B.C.) and Philodemus (1st cent. B.C.), cf. the related usage in the formula *tē eme cheiri*, with my own hand (1 Cor. 16:21; Gal. 6:11).

OT 1. The OT speaks of a person's activity as the work of his hand. The hand (Heb. *yāḏ*) is a symbol of human → power. Thus, to fall into someone's hand means to come into their power (Gen. 32:11, MT 32:12; Jdg. 2:14; Jer. 27:6 f.). In

2 Sam. 18:18 *cheir* (corresponding to the Heb. *yāḏ*) means a mark or monument (cf. Isa. 56:5). *cheir* is likewise a symbol for divine omnipotence (2 Chr. 20:6; Ps. 89:21 [MT 89:22]). God's hand created heaven and earth and with his hand he controls them (Isa. 48:13). For Israel God's hand means salvation and release; but for their enemies, destruction and ruin (Exod. 7:4; 9:3; 1 Sam. 7:13). The hand of the Lord is used in the same way to express God's righteous punishment (1 Sam. 5:6, 11), but also his loving care (Ezr. 7:6; Job 5:18; Ps. 145:16; Isa. 49:16) and his divine protection (Isa. 51:16).

2. Both in figurative language about God and with reference to men the two hands do not have equal status. By comparison with the left hand a higher value is placed upon the right, because it is the one that is active (Exod. 15:6, 12; Ps. 118:15 f.; Isa. 41:13; cf. Matt. 5:30). There is an extraordinary richness about the use of the hand in sign and figurative language. It serves to express displeasure, passionate excitement (Num. 24:10), but also to express humble supplication (2 Chr. 6:12 f.; Ps. 28:2), joy (Ps. 47:1 [47:2]) and sorrow (Jer. 2:37), scornful malicious joy (Ezek. 6:11), solemn oath (Gen. 14:22; 24:2, 9; 47:29; Ezr. 10:19) and loyal citizenship (Prov. 6:1 ff.; 22:26). The sign on the hand (Exod. 13:9, 16; Deut. 6:8; 11:18) is a permanent and picturesque way of expressing constant remembrance of God's saving acts and of his commandments for his people. To fill someone's hand means to install him to priestly office (Num. 3:3). Washing the hands serves not only to fulfil the commandments concerning purification (Exod. 30:18 ff.), but also to signify an affirmation of innocence and a clear conscience (Deut. 21:6; Ps. 26:6; cf. Job 17:9; Ps. 24:4; Matt. 27:24). This richness of meaning which belongs to the concept hand in the OT lives on into Rab. Judaism and continues in the NT.

NT The word *cheir* occurs 176 times in the NT with a few additional occurrences in variant readings. It appears most frequently in Luke's writings (Lk. 26 times; Acts 45), no doubt because of his preference for OT turns of phrase (especially in Acts).

1. *cheir* is often found, used literally, in the combination *podes kai cheires*, feet and hands (Matt. 18:8; 22:13; Lk. 24:39; Jn. 11:44; Acts 21:11). The phrase *dia cheiros tinos* (also plural), through someone, by someone (e.g. Mk. 6:2; Acts 5:12; 7:25; 11:30) is a Semitism representing the Heb. *bᵉyāḏ*, by, with. Similarly, *eis cheiras* translates Heb. *lîḏê*, to, for. The hands can stand for a person (Acts 17:25). *cheir* is used 25 times in connection with the laying on of hands (→ *epithesis tōn cheirōn*).

2. As in the OT, the hand of the Lord means the embodiment of divine power. It is also applied to Christ in Jn. 3:35; 10:28; 13:3. It works in creation (Acts 7:50; Heb. 1:10) and in God's plan of salvation (Acts 4:28; *cheir* in combination with *boulē*). It expresses his righteous punishment (Acts 13:11; Heb. 10:31), and also the special care (Lk. 1:66), security and protection (Lk. 23:46; Jn. 10:29) which God grants to all those who trust him. God's hand indicates his wonder-working power with which he accompanies the apostolic proclamation of the gospel (Acts 4:30; 11:21) and is represented as operating "by the hand of an → angel" (Acts 7:35). It also indicates God's hidden wisdom with which he leads his people on earth through suffering (1 Pet. 5:6). Hand, finally, can be a periphrasis

149

for a hostile power, into whose control a man is delivered (esp. Matt. 17:22 par.
Mk. 9:31, Lk. 9:44, Matt. 26:45 par. Mk. 14:41; Acts 21:11), but from whose
hand he can also be set free (Acts 12:11; 2 Cor. 11:33).

3. *cheir* is frequently used in connection with the verb *ekteinō*, to stretch out.
Jesus commanded a sick man to stretch out his hand (Matt. 12:13 par. Mk. 3:5,
Lk. 6:10). He stretched out his hand to → heal (Matt. 8:3 par. Mk. 1:41, Lk. 5:13;
cf. Acts 4:30). Stretching out the hand can be an orator's gesture (Acts 26:1) and
a sign indicating the bystanders (Matt. 12:49). It can happen with hostile intent
(Lk. 22:53) or refer indirectly to a disciple's death by crucifixion (Jn. 21:18).

F. Laubach

The Jewish (though not OT) practice of ceremonially washing the hands before
meals (Mk. 7:1–4) was condemned by Jesus as an instance of scrupulous observance of an outward ordinance of man, practised at the expense of neglecting the
word of God (vv. 6 ff.; cf. Matt. 15:8 ff.; Isa. 29:13) and failure to realize that
evil comes from the heart (Mk. 7:14–23; cf. Matt. 15:10–20). Mk. 7:3 contains the
word *pygmē* which the RSV deliberately omits on account of the uncertainty of its
meaning. Although there are variant readings in some MSS, it is supported by the
majority of early MSS. C. E. B. Cranfield suggests that the explanation is to be
sought in the Jewish custom of different sorts of ritual washing. Dipping up to the
wrist was less serious than plunging up to the wrist. *pygmē* is a dat. form of the
noun meaning "fist". The expression in Mk. *pygmē nipsōntai* may refer to the former act, or perhaps to washing with a fistful of water. (Cf. *The Gospel according to
Saint Mark*, 1959, 233; and for further suggestions P. R. Weis, "A Note on *pygmē*,"
NTS 3, 1956–7, 233 ff.; → Baptism, Wash, art. *niptō*.) Pilate's act of washing his
hands before the crowd (Matt. 27:24) was a public gesture disclaiming responsibility.
Although the crowds accepted responsibility for Jesus' blood, the gesture was
equally empty, for moral responsibility cannot be disposed of by outward gestures.

The finger (*daktylos* [in the LXX chiefly for *'eṣba'*]) is mentioned in Matt. 23:4;
Mk. 7:33; Lk. 11:46; 16:24; Jn. 8:6, 8; 20:25, 27. The expression "finger of
God" (Lk. 11:20; cf. Exod. 8:19) is paralleled in Matt. 12:28 by → "Spirit of
God." "In all likelihood it is Jesus' own phrase by which he defines his mission in
terms of the Exodus . . . as he does elsewhere. See on 6:17–49; 9:10–17). The escha-
tological presence of the Spirit is the presence of the kingdom. See on 10:1–20"
(E. E. Ellis, *The Gospel of Luke*, 1966, 165).

cheirotoneō means to choose (originally elect by raising hands) (2 Cor. 8:19),
and appoint (Acts 14:23). *cheiropoiētos*, made by human hands, underlines the
distinction between God's action and man's (Mk. 14:58; Acts 7:78; 17:24; Eph.
2:11; Heb. 9:11, 24).   *C. Brown*

ἐπιτίθημι

ἐπιτίθημι τὰς χεῖρας (*epitithēmi tas cheiras*), to lay
hands on; ἐπίθεσις τῶν χειρῶν (*epithesis tōn cheirōn*),
laying on of hands.

CL *epithesis* (from Plato on) means: (a) laying on, application (of things); (b)
setting upon, attack (only in the LXX, Aristeas, Philo and Josephus). The
phrase *epithesis tōn cheirōn*, the laying on of hands, occurs only in Philo and the
NT. On the other hand *epitithēmi tēn cheira* or *tas cheiras*, to lay the hand or hands
on someone or something, also occurs in Gk. inscriptions and in the LXX.

Miraculous healings, performed by means of the laying on of hands, are attributed in Hel. literature to Asclepius, Zeus and to other gods and wise men (→ Heal, art. *iaomai; TDNT* III, 196 ff.).

OT 1. Even though the substantival combination *epithesis tōn cheirōn* does not occur in the LXX, it probably goes back to the corresponding verbal expression, *epitithēmi tas cheiras* (Heb. *sāmak yāḏayim*) in the LXX which has two basic associations in the LXX. Numerically speaking, by far the more important usage of this verbal expression in the LXX is the one which describes how the sacrificer laid his hand on the head of the sacrificial animal. The meaning of this action is seen most clearly in the ritual for the great Day of Atonement (Lev. 16), where the laying on of hands is not an act of blessing but is believed to be a real transference of guilt to the scapegoat. To drive out the goat meant to drive out sin itself. But in the case of the other forms of sacrifice which from the point of view of the history of religions are less primitive, it is to be observed that sacrifice and laying on of hands coincide (so in almost every chapter in Lev.). For to deny that foreign divinities have any power over the people of Israel meant that they now have to commit to Yahweh their evil and allow him to destroy it.

2. Alongside this, though more rare, is the laying on of hands as an act of blessing (Genesis 48:18). It is no doubt closely related to the ritual of laying on of hands on the occasion of a man's installation in an office (Num. 27:18, 23, and frequently in the Pent.). The laying on of hands means, therefore, if one compares the two very different acts of removal of sin and blessing, that there passes to the one on whom hands are laid the particular quality of the one who performs the act. He passes on his special blessing or burdens the scapegoat with the burden which he himself had carried.

3. The two passages which took on the greatest significance for Rab. Judaism were those which dealt with Moses' appointment of Joshua to be his successor (Num. 27:15 ff.; Deut. 34:9). In the former passage, by means of the laying on of hands Moses invested Joshua with his authority. In the latter he invested him with his spirit of wisdom. Rab. Judaism saw here the obligatory model and the origin of its own ordination practice, which was understood as the handing on of the spirit of Moses from the present teacher to the pupil (*cf. TDNT* VI 962; IX 429; SB I 807; SB II 648–55).

NT In the majority of passages in which it occurs in the NT (altogether 40 times) *epitithēmi* is connected with the laying on of hands. *epithesis tōn cheirōn* only appears 4 times.

1. The verbal expression *epitithēmi tas cheiras* is used predominantly in the NT in connection with miracles of healing (Matt. 9:18; Mk. 5:23; 6:5; 7:32; 8:23; Lk. 13:13; Acts 28:8), performed by Jesus and the apostles as signs that the messianic age had already dawned. The expression also appears in Matt. 19:13, 15 to denote a gesture of blessing the children who were brought to Jesus. As the par. in Mk. 10:16 shows, there is no thought of a magical means of blessing. The gesture of blessing symbolizes, rather, the gracious offer of a share in the kingdom of God made to those who are not of age, i.e. to such as approach God with the attitude of children. (→ Child, art. *pais* NT 2.)

Acts 8:17 ff.; 9:17; 19:6 belong in the context of the → baptism. The Holy → Spirit is given to those who are baptized and have the apostles' hands laid on them. This may be the idea behind 1 Tim. 5:22. But equally the laying on of hands here could be a gesture accompanying the readmission to fellowship of a penitent sinner or heretic. The possibility of "ordination" also cannot be excluded. Two passages take us directly into the sphere of Jewish ordination: Acts 6:6 where the seven Hellenists were appointed to serve in the daily distribution to their section of the community, and Acts 13:3 where Paul and Barnabas are sent out. Here the thought of authorizing and commissioning to a specific work predominates.

2. The substantival expression occurs once in connection with baptism (Acts 8:17 ff.). On another occasion it denotes one of the elementary doctrines of Christ (Heb. 6:2). Twice (1 Tim. 4:14; 2 Tim. 1:6) it denotes the rite by which Timothy was ordained. According to these two passages, Timothy had conferred upon him through the laying on of hands by the elders or Paul the gift of grace for leading the congregation, preaching the word and teaching or refuting false teachers. It is surmised by those who on literary grounds deny the Pauline authorship of the Pastoral Epistles that the church here, which dates from the beginning of the 2nd cent., is using a historical fiction. Its aim was to give apostolic justification to its understanding of ordination (the conferment of grace for office), which has departed from the Pauline understanding of the free working of the Spirit.

3. It is striking that in every passage, where the laying on of hands appears in connection with ordination or sending out for a particular service, it is always carried out by people who at that moment possess different gifts. In Acts 6:6 the laying on of hands is performed by the apostles; in Acts 13:3 by prophets and teachers; in 1 Tim. 4:14 by the elders; and in 2 Tim. 1:6 by Paul. This suggests that the NT does not yet recognize the power of ordination as being restricted to a particular office, e.g. that of the apostles.

Reference must also be made to the close connection between the laying on of hands and intercessory prayer. This indicates that there is no thought of the transfer of a particular quality, necessary for office, from one office-bearer to another involving the idea of succession. The idea that the gifts of grace are at men's disposal is sharply contradicted by Peter's clash with Simon Magus (Acts 8:18 ff.). It is God himself who equips his servants with his gifts and sends them out. This happens through the prayer of the church. The laying on of hands bears witness to the church's conviction that their prayers which are founded on God's promises have been heard. *H.-G. Schütz*

→ Apostle, → Bishop, → Serve

(a). Arndt, 106, 169, 736, 888; H. von Campenhausen, *Ecclesiastical Authority and Spiritual Power in the Church of the First Three Centuries*, 1969; J. G. Davies, *He Ascended into Heaven* (Bampton Lectures, 1958), 1958; D. Daube, "The Laying on of Hands" in *The New Testament and Rabbinic Judaism*, 1956; B. S. Easton, "Jewish and Early Christian Ordination", *Anglican Theological Review*, 5, 1922–23, 308–19; 6, 1923–24, 285–95; abridged in *Early Christianity: The Purpose of Acts and Other Papers*, 1955, 135–43; A. Ehrhardt, "Jewish and Christian Ordination", *Journal of Ecclesiastical History* 5, 1954, 125–38; reprinted in *The Framework of the New Testament Stories*, 1964, 132–50; E. Ferguson, "Laying on of Hands: Its Significance in Ordination" *JTS* New Series 26, 1975, 1–12; K. Grayston, "The Significance of the Word Hand in the New Testament", in *Festschrift B. Rigaux*, 1970, 479–87; W. Grundmann, *dexios, TDNT* II 37–40; D. M. Hay, *Glory at the Right Hand: Psalm 110 in Early Christianity*, 1973; F. Hahn, *The*

Titles of Jesus in Christology, 1969, especially 129 ff.; J. N. D. Kelly, *Early Christian Creeds*, 1972³;
G. W. H. Lampe, *The Seal of the Spirit*, 1951, 223–31; E. Lohse, *cheir* etc., *TDNT* IX 424–38;
S. New, "The Name, Baptism, and the Laying on of Hands", in F. J. Foakes-Jackson and K. Lake,
The Beginnings of Christianity, V, 1933, 121–40; W. D. McHardy, "Mark 7³ – A Reference to the
Old Testament?", *ExpT* 87, 1975–76, 119; J. Newman, *Semikhah*, 1950; J. K. Parratt, "The
Laying on of Hands in the New Testament", *ExpT* 80, 1968–69, 210–14; J. J. M. Roberts, "The
Hand of Yahweh", *VT* 21, 1971, 244–51; H. Schlier, *daktylos*, *TDNT* II 20 f.; K. L. Schmidt,
pygmē, *TDNT* III 915 ff.; M. H. Shepherd, Jr., "Hands, Laying on of", *IDB* II 521 f.; H. P. Smith,
"The Laying on of Hands", *American Journal of Theology* 17, 1913, 47–62; C. H. Turner, *cheirotonia, cheirothesia, epithesis cheirōn*, *JTS* 24, 1923, 496–504; P. R. Weis, "A Note on *pygmē*",
NTS 3, 1956–57, 233–36; J. Ysebaert, *Greek Baptismal Terminology*, 1962.
(b). N. Adler, *Taufe und Handauflegung*, 1951; and "Die Handauflegung im Neuen Testament
bereits ein Bussritus? Zur Auslegung von 1 Tim. 5, 22", *Neutestamentliche Aufsätze*, Festschrift
J. Schmid, 1963, 1 ff.; J. Behm, *Die Handauflegung im Urchristentum*, 1911; J. Coppens,
L'imposition des mains et les rites connexes dans le Nouveau Testament et dans l'Église ancienne,
1925; J. Daniélou, "La Session à la droite du Père," in *The Gospels Reconsidered: A Selection of
Papers read at the International Congress on the Four Gospels in 1957*, 1960, 68–77; J. Galtier,
"Imposition des mains", *Dictionnaire de Théologie Catholique*, VII, 1972, 1302–1425; E. Lohse,
Die Ordination im Spätjudentum und im Neuen Testament, 1951; U. Luck, *Hand und Hand Gottes.
Ein Beitrag zur Grundlage und Geschichte des biblischen Gottesverständnisses* (dissertation,
Münster), 1959; R. Mayer and N. Adler, "Handauflegung", *LTK* IV 1343 ff.; S. Morenz, H. D.
Wendland and W. Jannasch, "Handauflegung", *RGG³* III 52 ff.; G. Révész, *Die menschliche Hand*,
1944; O. Weinreich, *Antike Heilungswunder*, 1909; A. S. van der Woude, *yāḏ*, *THAT* I 667–74.

Hard, Hardened

> σκληρός

σκληρός (*sklēros*, hard, rough; σκληρότης (*sklērotēs*),
hardness; σκληρύνω (*sklērynō*), to be, become, hard;
σκληροτράχηλος (*sklērotrachēlos*), stiff-necked, obstinate; σκληροκαρδία (*sklērokardia*), hard-heartedness; πωρόω (*pōroō*), harden, become hard; πώρωσις
(*pōrōsis*), hardness; παχύνω (*pachynō*), thicken, make insensitive.

The concepts of being or making hard, firm, rigid and thick are expressed in the
NT by the word groups *sklēros*, *pōros* (*pēros*) and *pachys*. The meanings converge
with the result that substitutions take place in the course of the transmission of the
NT text.

CL 1. *sklēros* (in secular Gk. from Hesiod on) means dry, hard, rough. From it is
formed the noun *sklērotēs*, hardness. The vb. *sklērynō* was originally a medical
term (first attested in Hippocrates). In the active it means to harden; in the passive,
to grow hard. *sklērotrachēlos* (attested in Aesop and the LXX) means stiff-necked,
stubborn, obdurate.

2. *pōroō* (from Hippocrates on) is derived from *pōros*, tufa or tuff (porous stone),
and means to harden, to form a callus (when broken bones heal), and thus to
petrify, to become hard. The word is only used figuratively in the NT. The same is
true of the verbal noun *pōrōsis*, hardening. In almost every NT passage where
pōroō and *pōrōsis* occur, *pēroō* and *pērōsis* appear as variants. *pēroō* means
to make lame, to maim; and when used of the eyes, to blind. Correspondingly
pērōsis means maiming, and then shortsightedness, blindness. This root is also
used figuratively and in this sense means virtually the same as *pōroō*. As *pēroō*

153

occurs more frequently in literature, the substitution of the words in the process of copying is easily explained. *pōroō* doubtless represents the original form of the text.

3. *pachynō* is derived from *pachys*, thick, fat (in secular Gk. from Aeschylus on). It originally meant to thicken, to fatten; then by extension to make impervious (to water). Hence figuratively it came to mean to make insensitive, and in the passive, to be insensitive.

OT The most frequent Heb. equivalent for *sklēros* and its derivatives is *qāšâh*.

ḥāzaq and other vbs. are also used, but these word groups are rare. Hardening, according to the OT understanding, results from the fact that men persist in shutting themselves to God's call and command. A state then arises in which a man is no longer able to hear and in which he is irretrievably enslaved. Alternatively, God makes the hardening final, so that the people affected by it cannot escape from it.

1. In the oldest OT narratives it is always non-Israelites who are hardened. The most important narrative is that of the hardening of Pharaoh (Exod. 4 ff.). After every appeal by Moses and every plague we read, "Still Pharaoh's heart was hardened" (Exod. 7:13, 22; 8:15, etc.). It is God who hardens Pharaoh's heart (in passages attributed to the Elohistic strand). Whole peoples too are hardened by God, e.g. the Canaanites: "For it was the Lord's doing to harden their hearts that they should come against Israel in battle, in order that they should be utterly destroyed, and should receive no mercy" (Jos. 11:20). Non-Israelites were hardened, therefore, only when they came into contact with Israel, for the hardening of the peoples was one of the means God used to fulfil his purpose for Israel.

2. Not until the great prophets is → Israel also seen as a hardened people. This is expressed most strongly in Isa. God's word had come to the priests and prophets in Jerusalem, but they did not want to listen. Hence, God's word became a word of judgment against them, "that they may go, and fall backward, and be broken" (Isa. 28:12 f.). On the occasion of his call Isaiah received the command, "Make the heart of this people fat, and their ears heavy, and shut their eyes; lest they see with their eyes and hear with their ears, and understand with their hearts, and turn and be healed" (Isa. 6:10). God's judgment on his people is not that he no longer speaks to them. Rather his word is still proclaimed with utter clarity. But because the people hitherto have not wanted to listen, from now on they will be unable to. The vineyard which did not want to bear fruit (Isa. 5:1–7) is now unable to, because God has forbidden the clouds to rain on it. God's judgment encompasses the destruction of the people (Isa. 6:11).

3. This contention that it is God himself who mercilessly hardens Israel is an extreme statement. The later prophets do not speak with the same severity. Jeremiah spoke of hardening, but he no longer named God as its cause. For Jeremiah the cause is the obstinacy of the people who give heed to the false prophets, whereas for Isaiah the prophet himself is carrying out God's commission. It is interesting that the LXX softens Isa. 6 by transmitting the command to Isaiah in the indicative: "for the heart of this people is stupefied; and their ears are dull of hearing; and they have shut their eyes, that for a while they may not see with their eyes; and hear with their ears; and understand with their hearts; and return that I may heal them."

The decisive new element is the promise in the later period of God's new →
covenant. Then Israel will hear and recognize the Lord (Jer. 31:33 f.), and men
will receive a new, no longer a hard, heart and a new spirit (Ezek. 36:26 f.).

4. In the Wisdom Literature the righteous and the godless are constantly
contrasted. The latter are characterized in many passages as hardened (Prov. 28:14;
29:1). Here attention is directed more to the guilt occasioned by hardness. Hardening is the continually mounting refusal on the part of man to listen to God's
command. It is not, however, inevitable. There is room, therefore, for the appeal,
"O that today you would hearken to his voice! Harden not your hearts" (Ps. 95:8).
For God's judgment takes place as a result of hardness. No longer is hardness
itself a judgment from God as in Isa.

NT All these words are comparatively rare in the NT. They occur throughout the
Synoptics (11 out of a total of 26 occurrences), a few times in Acts, in Paul
(*pōroō* and its derivatives, and *sklērotēs*), in Heb. (*sklērynō* 4 times) and in Jude and
Jas. (*sklēros* once in each).

1. (a) *sklēros* is used in its metaphorical sense of things: *anemōn sklērōn*, strong
rough winds (Jas. 3:4); of Jesus' words, *sklēros estin ho logos houtos*, "this is a hard
[unacceptable] saying" (Jn. 6:60). God will punish the ungodly because of all the
hard things (some MSS add, words) which they have spoken against him (Jude 15
quoting Eth. Enoch. 1:9). It is also used of people: the *kyrios*, the master in the
parable of the talents, is described in Matt. 25:24 as *sklēros anthrōpos*, a hard, i.e.,
hard-hearted man. *sklēros* is used absolutely in Acts 26:14: "It is hard for you
[i.e. difficult; *sklēron soi*] to kick against the goad." A few ancient MSS and versions also include this phrase in Acts 9:4.

(b) *sklērotēs* occurs in Rom. 2:5 and describes a human characteristic. By their
hard and impenitent hearts the Jews are storing up for themselves the wrath of the
coming judgment, on account of their self-righteousness and impenitence.

(c) *sklērynō* is used transitively with a human subject: "Do not harden your
hearts" (Heb. 3:8, 15; 4:7). The appeal of Ps. 95:8 is repeated three times; the
community must not forfeit God's promise. With "God" as subject the word
occurs in Rom. 9:18: "He hardens the heart of whomever he wills." Exod. 4:21
(the hardening of Pharaoh) is doubtless in the background here. God punishes by
abandoning people to their sin (cf. Rom. 1:24, 26, 28).

Heb. 3:13 takes up the appeal of v. 8 in the passive, "that none of you may be
hardened by the deceitfulness of sin." In Acts 19:9 it is said of the Jews in Ephesus
that some of them were "hardened" at Paul's preaching in the synagogue and
openly abused his teaching.

(d) *sklērotrachēlos* occurs only in Acts 7:51. In his speech Stephen calls the Jews
"stiff-necked and uncircumcised in heart and ears," like their fathers always
resisting the Holy Spirit, unwilling to listen to God and killing his prophets.

2. (a) *pōroō* is used metaphorically in all five passages where it occurs. In Mk.
6:52 the word is used of the hardening of Jesus' disciples. "Their hearts were
hardened," so that they still did not understand who the Lord was (cf. 8:17). In
Jn. 12:40 it refers to the Jews again at whose hand Jesus met with rejection. The
word occurs in a proof-text (Isa. 6:9 f.; while it does not follow the LXX, it uses

155

the indicative as in the LXX). The two Pauline passages also refer to the Jews: "the rest [i.e. the non-elect] were hardened" (Rom. 11:7); and "their minds were hardened" (2 Cor. 3:14).

(b) Two passages also apply the verbal noun *pōrōsis* to the Jews. Jesus is grieved at their "hardness of heart" (Mk. 3:5; cf. Mk. 10:5 par. Matt. 19:8, *sklērokardia*). Paul states in Rom. 11:25, "a hardening has come upon Israel." In Eph. 4:18 it is said of the Gentiles, "they are darkened in their understanding, alienated from the life of God because of their hardness of heart."

3. Both passages where *pachynō* occurs (Matt. 13:15; Acts 28:27) quote from Isa. 6:9 f. (here the quotation is used as in the LXX).

4. All these words, including the adj. *sklēros*, are used in an exclusively metaphorical and theological sense and denote the same idea: the reluctance of men to respond to God. In the NT men who do not open themselves to the gospel are described as hardened. The same can be said of Jews and Gentiles, and also of Jesus' disciples who did not understand the → cross to which they were to become witnesses. The prophetic idea that God hardens men is taken over from the OT (e.g. Rom. 11) without for a moment losing sight of man's personal responsibility (Rom. 2:5). Thus in the NT hardening also describes the inability to hear which renders a man liable to judgment. This applies also to the appeals in Heb. These are meaningful only because hardness is broken down with the promise of forgiveness and a new beginning (cf. 8:9 f.). With the gospel God also gives the ability to understand it (cf. however Heb. 6:4 ff.).

God has "given up" men to their sin (Rom. 1:24). But in Christ he gives a new opportunity of hearing through his Spirit; he fulfils the promises of the OT. Over against hardening, the inability to receive the word of God, stands → faith, the obedient reception of the word. The question whether, despite Christ's coming, the Jews will remain hardened, is grappled with by Paul in his exposition of God's plan of salvation in Rom. 9–11.   *U. Becker*

→ Determine, → Elect, → Heart, → Lead Astray, → Sin

(a). G. L. Archer, *A Survey of Old Testament Introduction*, 1964, 116; G. C. Berkouwer, *Faith and Perseverance*, 1958; and *Sin*, 1971; B. S. Childs, "The Hardening of Pharaoh", *Exodus*, 1974, 170–75; L. J. Kuyper, "The Hardness of Heart according to Biblical Perspectives", *SJT* 27, 1974, 459–74; I. H. Marshall, *Kept by the Power of God: A Study of Perseverance and Falling Away*, 1969; G. von Rad, *Old Testament Theology*, II, 1965; H. Räisänen, *The Idea of Divine Hardening. A Comparative Study of the Notion of Divine Hardening, Leading Astray, and Inciting to Evil in the Bible and the Qur'an*, Publications of the Finnish Exegetical Society 25, 1972; K. L. Schmidt and M. A. Schmidt, *sklēros* etc., *TDNT* V 1028–31; E. J. Young, *The Book of Isaiah*, 1965, 253–65.
(b). J. Gnilka, *Das Problem der Verstockung Israels nach den synoptischen Evangelien und der Apostelgeschichte*, 1961; F. Hesse, *Das Verstockungsproblem im Alten Testament. Eine frömmigkeitsgeschichtliche Untersuchung*, *BZAW* 74, 1955; F. Hesse, R. Gyllenberg, J. Moltmann, "Verstockung", *RGG³* VI 1383 ff.; E. Jenni, "Jesajas Berufung in der neueren Forschung", *ThZ* 15, 1959, 321 ff.; K. L. Schmidt, "Die Verstockung des Menschen durch Gott: Eine lexikologische und biblisch-theologische Studie", *ThZ* 1, 1945, 1–17.

Head

| κεφαλή |

κεφαλή (*kephalē*), head; ἀνακεφαλαιόομαι (*anakephalaioomai*), sum up, recapitulate.

CL *kephalē*, head, attested from Homer on, is related to the Gothic word *gibla* (Eng. gable) but also to Eng. head. Derivatives from it include *kephalaion*, main point (Heb. 8:1), sum of money (Acts 22:28); *kephalaioō*, sum up, late Gk. strike on the head (Mk. 12:4); late Gk. *kephalis*, little head (Heb. 10:7 "roll" of a book) and *anakephalaioomai* (see below). In secular Gk. *kephalē* means:

1. The head of man or beast, the coping of a wall, the capital of a column etc., the source or mouth of a river, the beginning or end of a month, etc. In Plato the "head of a speech" is its conclusion (→ Goal, art. *telos*).

2. What is decisive, superior. In Gk. anthropology the head takes precedence over all other members; it is, or in it lies, the authoritative principle, the reason (*hēgemonikon*). If the emphasis is upon the idea of origin, *kephalē* takes on some of the meanings of *archē* (→ Beginning). But the head of a community is never referred to as a *kephalē* (*TDNT* III 673).

3. *kephalē* also stands for the life of an individual. As early as Homer it was used in a similar way to *psychē* (→ Soul). Thus, curses which name the head are directed against the whole person and his life.

OT 1. In the LXX *kephalē* most frequently translates the Heb. *rô'š*. Beside *kephalē* numerous other equivalents for *rô'š* are to be found: e.g. frequently *archē* (→ beginning: Ps. 137[136]:6; Isa. 41:4); *prōtotokos* (→ first; 1 Chr. 5:12), *kephalē* has the primary meanings we know from cl. Gk.: the head of a man (Gen. 28:11), of a beast (Gen. 3:16), the top of a mountain (Gen. 8:5) or of a tower (Gen. 11:4) etc.

2. The head is particularly important in the language of gesture. It was shaven in times of grief (Ezek. 7:18). The man who was under a vow did not shave it (Num. 6:5; cf. Acts 18:18). It was covered (2 Sam. 15:30) or strewn with ashes (2 Sam. 13:19) as a sign of penitence.

([Ed.] Prov. 25:21 f. states: "If your enemy is hungry, give him bread to eat; and if he is thirsty, given him water to drink; for you will heap coals of fire on his head, and the LORD will reward you" (RSV). The thought is taken up in Rom. 12:20. After urging believers not to avenge themselves, for "Vengeance is mine, I will repay, says the Lord" (Rom. 12:19; cf. Deut. 32:35; Lev. 19:18), Paul declares: "No, if your enemy is hungry, feed him, if he is thirsty give him drink; for by doing so you will heap burning coals upon his head. Do not be overcome by evil, but overcome evil with good." The imagery behind this thought is debated. It has been suggested that it derives from an Egyptian penitential ritual in which live coals were endured as an act of contrition (S. Morenz, "Feurige Kohlen auf dem Haupt," *TLZ* 78, 1953, 187–92; cf. W. Klassen, "Coals of Fire: Sign of Repentance or Revenge?", *NTS* 9, 1962–3, 337–50). Morenz suggests that while the rite was probably confined to Egypt, the metaphor was more widely used (cf. W. McKane, *Proverbs*, 1970, 592). R. B. Y. Scott also suggests "A form of torture; but to return good for evil will be more effective in overcoming enmity, and so the enemy" (*Proverbs*, 1965, 156). Scott notes similar thoughts in Exod. 23:4 f.; Prov. 20:22; 24:17 f. D. Kidner comments: "The *coals of fire* represent the pangs which are far better felt now as shame than later as punishment (Ps. 140:10). Cf. *Amenemope*, chapter 2:19 ff." (*Proverbs*, 1964, 160, cf. 23). He sees the saying as representing the climax of ideas in Prov. 24:11 f., 17 f., 29. In his use of the text Paul omits the thought of personal reward for the Christian. His concern is that the life of the believer should be free from all thought of revenge, that the enemy might be convicted (though not necessarily converted – for that is God's work) by kindness, and that the way to overcome evil is not to repay in kind (which only leads to bondage to it) but to repay it with good. The repetition of Deut. 32:35 at Heb. 10:30 suggests that it may have had a firm place in early catechetical teaching (cf. M. J. Dahood, *CBQ* 17, 1955, 19–24). The juxtaposition with Prov. 12:25 represents Paul's gloss on it, and provides an introduction to Paul's teaching on how both Jewish and Gentile believers should regard the governing authorities (13:1).)

3. Via expressions like "per head" (Exod. 16:16, RSV "apiece") and "head by head" (Num. 1:2), the use of *kephalē* in the LXX was extended to cover the life of the individual. The OT sees man in action as a unity, but in each case it singles out that part of him which is significant. In this case it is the head as source of the life-stream. The head can be used as the equivalent of the person and his whole existence (e.g. 2 Ki. 25:27; Ps. 3:3; Ezek. 9:10; 33:4; 1 Sam. 25:39; cf. Acts 18:6; Matt. 27:25). In Isa. 43:4 *kephalē* stands for *nepeš* and denotes the → life of each individual within the people.

4. By comparison with the other nations Israel will be "the head and not the tail" (Deut. 28:13; cf. Isa. 9:14). Thus *kephalē* in the LXX can denote also the head, i.e. the one who occupies a position of superiority in the community (cf. Jdg. 10:18; 1 Ki. 21:12, Codex A). But "this use does not have the further thought that those ruled by the *kephalē* are in the relation to it of a *sōma*" (H. Schlier, *TDNT* III 675). The head of the statue (Dan. 2:31 f.) only represented one kingdom in and of itself, and does not carry any implications about its relation to the body.

5. In Jewish literature *rô'š* is used like *kephalē* in the LXX sometimes in connection with Deut. 28:13 (e.g. Jub. 1:16). The usage does not extend beyond the meanings already mentioned. The head, which the members obey, is a metaphor for unity (Test. Zeb. 9). The word was also used to refer to Adam as the head of created beings (Sl. Enoch 2:22), to the head of those who worship idols (Heb. Enoch 5:6), to the head of the synagogue (the president, Sot. 7:7 f.). This use of *rô'š* is continued without further development in the Qumran texts.

6. Philo's use of *kephalē* was seminal. The *logos* (→ word) is the head of the universe which God has created, its source of life, overlord, ruler. "He stamps the world like a seal, separates species and genera like one who cuts . . . and by means of the heavenly *eikōn* [→ Image] gives them a part in God" (C. Colpe, *RGG³* V 343; → Knowledge, art. *ginōskō*).

7. In contrast to near-eastern and Orphic mythology which saw the whole cosmos encompassed in the head and body of the highest god (→ Time, art. *aiōn*), Philo represented belief in God as the creator of the cosmos. In certain forms of gnosticism (→ Knowledge), however, the former belief returned and Aion, whose body is the cosmos and from whom as primal man all men take their form, receives the characteristics of the redeemer (*sōtēr*; → Redemption, art. *sōzō*). He has this role in gnostic mythological speculation on the basis of his cosmological rank and not on that of any saving work in history. The gnostic use of *kephalē* very much resembles that of *archē*. Above all *kephalē* serves to denote not only the unity of the

158

body, but also the controlling influence over it. The post-Christian Odes of Solomon speak of the head concept of the first man in a manner comparable with that in which the NT speaks of Christ. "For they have become my members and I their head. Praise be to You, our Head, Jesus Christ!" (Od. Sol. 17). (On Hellenistic and gnostic evidence see H. Schlier, *TDNT* III 676 ff.)

NT 1. In the NT, where *kephalē* appears 75 times, the word occurs primarily in its basic meaning of the head of a man (Matt. 14:8), of an animal, or of demons (Rev. 17:3). *kephalē* occurs by far the most frequently in Rev. (19 times) where it refers to those human and animal forms who are characterized by the shape or the ornament of their heads. The head bears the tokens of honour and dignity (Rev. 4:4; 19:12; etc.), but also those of shame (Rev. 13:1). In the passion narrative Jesus' head is frequently mentioned (Matt. 27:29 f., 37; Mk. 15:19, 29; Jn. 19:2, 30). The smiting of Jesus' head stands in marked contrast with the anointing of it (Matt. 26:7; Mk. 14:3; Lk. 7:46) and the promise to faithful disciples that not a hair of their head shall perish (Matt. 10:30; Lk. 21:18; cf. 12:7). The head of Jesus is also mentioned in the resurrection narratives (Jn. 20:7, 12). The head of John the Baptist is mentioned in Matt. 14:8, 11 and Mk. 6:24–28. On the phrase *kephalē gōnias*, head of the corner Matt. 21:42 par. Mk. 12:10, Lk. 20:17; cf. Acts 4:11; 1 Pet. 2:7; quoting Ps. 118:22, → Rock.

2. The head is mentioned in the NT also in connection with the customs of fasting and penitence (Matt. 6:17; Acts 18:18; Rev. 18:19). As we know from the LXX the shaking of the head signifies that a claim and its consequences have been rejected (Matt. 27:39). With the phrase, "Your blood be upon your heads!" the departing apostle placed upon the Corinthian Jews the responsibility for the rejection of the messiah (Acts 18:6; cf. on this point Matt. 27:25 which is also evidence that *kephalē* stands for the individual as a whole). The numbering of the hairs of the head (Matt. 10:30) and the saying that "not a hair of your head will perish" (Lk. 21:18) speak of God's promise to preserve those who commit themselves into his hands. In wanting to have his head washed (Jn. 13:9), Peter wanted his whole life to be cleansed. Jesus prohibited swearing by one's head. "Whoever risks his head for something in an oath speaks as if he had power over his own life" (T. Zahn on Matt. 5:36). The rabbis refused to allow anyone to retract an oath by the life of the head (San. 3:2). *K. Munzer*

3. 1 Cor. 11:2–15 contains a discussion of reasons why women should be required to veil the head during public worship. In Judaism women were always veiled in public (cf. J. Jeremias, *Jerusalem in the Time of Jesus*, 1969, 358 ff.). E. Käsemann claims that Paul is here trying to introduce into the Corinthian church a custom which was foreign to Greek women (*New Testament Questions of Today*, 1969, 210; cf. also SB III 427–34). The customs seem to have varied from place to place (cf. W. Ramsay, *The Cities of Paul*, 1907, 202 ff.; A. Jaubert, "La voile des femmes (I Cor. xi. 2–16)" *NTS* 18, 1971–2, 424 ff.). But Paul's teaching here may have been influenced by the presence of Jews in Corinth who maintained Jewish practices in their synagogue worship and who may well have looked with a critical eye on what was going on in the church. Immediately before the present passage Paul has urged that no offence be given to Jews, the Greeks or to the church (1 Cor. 10:32), and that the church

should follow him in trying to please all men and in being imitators of Christ (1 Cor. 10:33–11:1). The underlying problem was one of freedom in the light of the new and equal standing of the sexes before God. "The Corinthian watch-word 'freedom', which, considered both in itself and in connection with the specific case at issue, seems to be more enlightened than the Pauline reaction to it, suffers from the basic defect of enthusiastic piety; it takes account of freedom exclusively as freedom from burdensome compulsion. The apostle, on the other hand, is concerned here, as always, with the freedom which knows itself to be called to serve and it is just this freedom which he sees threatened where enthusiasm is rattling at the doors of the existing order and proclaiming its allegedly just claims in the name of the Spirit" (E. Käsemann, op. cit., 211). Paul is concerned not only with freedom but with order in society. For him the rôle and relationships of the sexes which are determined by creation are not abolished by salvation. This must be reflected in public worship (cf. A. Jaubert, op. cit., 419 f.). He advances the following arguments for the subordinate role of women and for the veiling of the woman's head which results from it.

(a) The hierarchy of the order: God-Christ-man-woman in which each of the first three members is the head of the following (v. 3). Here head is probably to be understood not as "chief" or "ruler" but as "source" or "origin" (F. F. Bruce, *1 and 2 Corinthians*, 1971, 103; cf. S. Bedale, "The Meaning of *kephalē* in the Pauline Epistles", *JTS* New Series 5, 1954, 211 ff.). The creation narrative of Gen. 2:21 ff. assigns a priority to man (cf. also Eph. 5:22 ff.; Col. 3:18 f.; 1 Tim. 2:11 ff.). But the Christian knows that Christ has a greater priority as the archetypal man (cf. 8:6; 15:46–49; Col. 1:16), and the head of Christ is God (cf. 3:23; 8:6). F. F. Bruce points out that there is a transition from the sense of head in v. 3 to its literal sense in vv. 4–6 and from now on there is an oscillation between the two senses. He also notes that what Paul has in mind here when he speaks of covering the head is a veil which conceals the whole head including the hair. (The present-day Jewish practice of men wearing a hat in the synagogue appears to reverse the practice here.) Paul argues that for a man to pray with his head covered is to dishonour his head (v. 4, cf. v. 7), because it implies that he is abdicating the sovereignty and dignity given to him by the Creator. But for a woman to pray or prophesy with her head unveiled dishonours her head (v. 5), for this is tantamount to a denial of her relation to man in the ordinances of creation. It is just as dishonourable as if her head were shaven which was a commonly accepted sign of dishonour (cf. the case of Bernice in Josephus, *War* 2, 313 f.; M. D. Hooker, "Authority on her head: an examination of 1 Cor. xi. 10", *NTS* 10, 1963–64, 410). Paul's argument at this point has two premises. The one is the propriety of covering the head in the presence of a superior; the other is the constitutional relationship of man and woman which gives a certain priority to the man. Given these two premises the propriety of veiling the woman in worship (which of all times is the most solemn occasion for recognizing the divine ordering of things) logically follows. However, in a situation where the former premise is neither recognized nor understood, the validity of the conclusion no longer has the same weight as it did in Paul's day.

(b) The priority of man in the order of creation in relation to the glory of God (vv. 7–9, 12). The argument is now developed in relation to the concept of → glory. Gen. 1:26 f. states that → man (Heb. *'āḏām*; Gk. *anthrōpos*) was made in the

→ image of God, i.e. male and female together. Here Paul speaks only of the male (Gk. *anēr*). Perhaps he is reading Gen. 2:18 ff. in the light of Gen. 1:26 f. On the other hand, he also couples together here the concepts of image and glory in a way which goes beyond the Gen. narratives. "For a man ought not to cover his head, since he is the image and the glory of God; but woman is the glory of man" (v. 7). Elsewhere Paul argues that man has fallen short of the glory of God (Rom. 3:23; cf. 1:21), and that the glory of God is revealed in the gospel in the face of Christ (2 Cor. 4:4 ff.) who restores the image of God in man (Col. 3:10). In addition to the priority of man in the created order and the significance of veiling, Paul here has two further premises which are implied in his conclusion. On the one hand, the glory of God should not be veiled in the presence of God, for this would be a contradiction in terms. Hence, the man should not be veiled. On the other hand, woman is the glory of man (for woman was made for man, cf. v. 9). Hence, the glory of man should be veiled in the presence of God (cf. F. F. Bruce, op. cit., 105 f.). Again it may be said that the practical application drawn from these premises depends upon how far they are understood and recognized in a community.

(c) The reference to the angels (v. 10). Here the Gk. texts says: "That is why the woman ought to have authority [*exousia*] over the head because of the angels." The substitution of "veil" (RSV) is an interpretative gloss which obscures the point. The veil is a sign of the woman's authority. In Christ she has an equal status with men before God. M. D. Hooker (op. cit.) argues that the veil was a sign of this new authority which was denied her in the synagogue. As a woman she may pray or prophesy (v. 5), but she must maintain due regard for her place in the created order. Whereas the man shows his authority by not being veiled, the woman shows hers by wearing a veil. The wearing of the veil manifests both the liberty and the restraint that belongs to the woman in Christ. The liberty (as in all things) derives from freedom in Christ; the restraint (as elsewhere) derives from the ordering of society which has divine sanction.

It seems unlikely that → angels are mentioned here because of possible sexual attraction (cf. Jude 6 and a possible interpretation of Gen. 6:2; Tertullian, *On the Veiling of Virgins* 7). F. F. Bruce sees the appeal to angels as an argument for propriety in gatherings of the people of God because angels are guardians of the created order (op. cit., 106; cf. G. B. Caird, *Principalities and Powers*, 1956, 17–22). In the Qumran texts angels were said to be present at meetings of the congregation (1QSa 2:8 f.; cf. 1 QM 7:6). A. Jaubert, however, claims that there is no support for regarding angels as guardians of order in meetings. She stresses the context of worship here and the rôle of angels in worship elsewhere. For angels are charged with the task of transmitting prayers to God (Rev. 8:3). They are the sign of the divine presence (Ps. 131 LXX). Angels enter communion with the congregation (1 QM 12:8; 1 QH 3:19–23). Therefore no offence should be given them (1QSa 2:5–9; 1 QM 7:6; CD 15:15 ff.; cf. A. Jaubert, op. cit., 427). The major premise of the argument is that one should not give offence, and in this particular case to the angels. The minor premise which is implied is that the veil is a sign of a woman's status and authority in the Christian community. Therefore women should be veiled in worship. Again it may be said that, whilst the guiding principles for Paul's recommendation hold good, the continued application of it depends upon the continued acceptance of all the premises of the argument. In a culture where the significance of veiling is no longer understood in the same way, the argument no longer has the same force.

(d) The appeal to custom grounded in the natural order (vv. 13–15). Paul shares the view that it is natural for men to have their hair short, though it may be grown longer on occasion in connection with a vow (Acts 18:18; cf. also Epictetus, 1, 16, 9–14 quoted by C. K. Barrett, *The First Epistle to the Corinthians*, 1968, 256 f.). The statement that the long hair of the woman is "her pride", "given to her for a covering" (v. 15) does not imply that if she has sufficient hair, she does not need to be veiled. Rather, the veiling of the woman in worship is seen as consonant with nature. The argument cannot be taken to imply scriptural sanction for insisting that man today must have closely cropped hair. What might be regarded as long hair in a male in twentieth-century western society might have passed for short hair in first-century middle-eastern society. On the other hand, unkempt inordinately long hair in a male is generally regarded as degrading (cf. v. 14). Paul's view of the woman's hair as "her pride" may also take up the thought that, just as in the presence of God the glory of man must be veiled (see above (b)), so too must the "pride" of the woman. In each case Paul uses the same word *doxa*. V. 16 concludes the argument by stating that this is the practice recognized by Paul and the other churches. The passage has been cited in support of the contention that women must wear hats in worship today. If this application were valid, the argument would support not the wearing of hats but veiling in the eastern sense. However, the above discussion has shown that its force depends upon the common understanding of certain premises which were valid in the context of Paul's culture. Where these no longer obtain, the conclusions also no longer obtain, even though the motivating principle of maintaining the liberty of the spirit with due regard to the order of nature and society still holds.   *C. Brown*

4. In Eph. 4 the head is contrasted with the → body (art. *sōma*): Christ is the head of his body (v. 15). The body is supplied from the head and grows because of it (v. 16). To describe the relationship of the Lord to his people, the → church, Eph. makes use of the concept of the primal man: the church is to grow *eis andra teleion*, into the perfect or complete man (v. 13). In this picture, Christ is the head, and as head he sustains the whole body. Thus, in v. 15 the head determines the relationship of love and truth in the body of Christ, i.e. the fellowship of those who practise truth and through love grow up into him. The relationship of *kephalē* to *sōma* expresses the authority of Christ (cf. Col. 2:10) and the corresponding subordination of the church. It expresses participation and dependence of the body on the head for the gift of life. It also contains "the element of an eschatological orientation of the Church" (H. Schlier, *TDNT* III 680). The head is always the heavenly goal of the body which cannot be attained except in a body sustained by faith and revelation. Eph. 1:21 f. declares that all powers are now subject to Christ who is "the head of all things for the church." The *archē*, the principality which previously was so important, is now one of the many subject to Christ. The application to Christ of *archē* (RSV "beginning") in Col. 1:18 (where he is also said to be "the head of the body, the church") does not contradict this, for here the word stands in polemic juxtaposition to the *archai* (v. 16). (→ Beginning, art. *archē*.)

K. Munzer

5. The rare vb. *anakephalaioomai*, which is found in Aristotle but is more common in late Gk. literature, means to bring something to a *kephalaion*, to sum up, recapitulate. It is found in the OT only in Theod. and the Quinta to Ps. 71:20. It is used in Rom. 13:9 of the individual commandments which are "summed up in this word, 'You shall love your neighbour as yourself.' " In Eph. 1:10 it occurs in the statement of God's "plan for the fullness of time to recapitulate [*anakephalaiōsasthai*] all things in Christ, the things in the heavens and the things upon the earth." The RSV translation "unite" stresses the unity implied in the vb. as does J. B. Lightfoot's comment that it implies "the entire harmony of the universe, which shall no longer contain alien and discordant elements, but of which all the parts shall find their centre and bond of union in Christ" (*Notes on the Epistles of St. Paul*, 1895, 322). The thought of unity has affinity with the use of the vb. in Rom. and is one of the great themes of Eph. (cf. 2:14–22; 4:3 f.). But there may also be the overtone of renewal which is in fact a condition of unity. Christ and his people, both Jew and Gentile, comprise the "one new man" (2:15; cf. 4:13). Moreover, this affects the whole created order. In his body which represents the *plērōma* (→ Fullness), the heavenly domain of his presence, Christ draws all things to himself, and fills all in all (2:22; cf. 1:10). The church is "the centre, the mid-point from which Christ exercises his invisible lordship over the whole whole" (O. Cullmann, *The Christology of the New Testament*, 1963[2], 229). The concept of recapitulation (Lat. *recapitulatio;* Gk. *anakephalaiōsis*) features in the thought of Irenaeus (*Haer.* 5, 29, 2) and other church fathers (cf. H. Schlier, *TDNT* III 681 f.; Lampe, 106).   *C. Brown*

→ Body, → Church, → Flesh, → Fullness, → Hand

(a). N. Adler, "Head", *EBT* I 355–60; S. Bedale, "The Meaning of *kephalē* in the Pauline Epistles", *JTS* New Series 5, 1954, 211–15; and "The Theology of the Church", in F. L. Cross, ed., *Studies in Ephesians*, 1956, 64–75; R. W. Crabb, *The kephalē Concept in the Pauline Tradition with Special Emphasis on Colossians*, Dissertation, San Francisco Theological Seminary, 1966 (microfilm); O. Cullmann, *The Christology of the New Testament*, 1959; R. H. Fuller, *The Foundations of New Testament Christology*, 1965; M. D. Hooker, "Authority on her head: an examination of 1 Cor. xi. 10", *NTS* 10, 1963–64, 410 ff.; G. Howard, "The Head/Body Metaphors of Ephesians", *NTS* 20, 1973–74, 350–6; E. Käsemann, "A Primitive Christian Baptismal Liturgy", in *Essays on New Testament Themes*, 1964, 149–68; *New Testament Questions of Today*, 1969, 410–2; E. Lohse, *Colossians and Philemon*, 1971, 52 ff.; J. A. T. Robinson, *The Body: A Study in Pauline Theology*, 1952; H. Schlier, *kephalē, anakephalaioomai, TDNT* III 673–82; W. O. Walker, Jr., " 1 Corinthians 11:2–16 and Paul's View Regarding Women", *JBL* 94, 1975, 94–110.
(b). P. Benoit, "Corps, tête et plérôme dans les épîtres de la captivité", *RB* 63, 1956, 5–44; P. Brunner, "Das Hirtenamt und die Frau", *Lutherische Rundschau* 8, 1959; H.-J. Gabathuler, *Jesus Christus, Haupt der Kirche – Haupt der Welt: Der Christushymnus Kolosser 1, 15–20 in der theologischen Forschung der letzten 130 Jahre, ATHAnt* 45, 1965; A. Jaubert, "La voile des femmes (I Cor. xi. 2–16)", *NTS* 18, 1971–72, 419–30; H. Lietzmann, *An die Korinther I/II*, revised by W. G. Kümmel, *HNT* 9, 1969[5]; E. Lohmeyer, *Die Briefe an die Kolosser und an Philemon, KEK* 9, with supplement by W. Schmauch, 1968[14]; H. Schlier, *Christus und die Kirche im Epheserbrief*, 1930.

Heal

When human well-being and good health are impaired, God is actively involved in the work of restoration, and Christians have the responsibility of sharing in this ministry. The idea of bringing about recovery from bodily or mental sickness is expressed most frequently by *therapeuō* (cf. Eng. "therapy"), and sometimes by *iaomai*. *therapeuō* originally carried the idea of attendance upon superiors, or of cultic service (like *thrēskō*, which has a related root). But significantly this idea is very rare in the NT, where the whole direction and purpose of such service is changed. Anyone or anything healed, i.e. freed from infirmity and sickness, is spoken of as *hygiēs*. *hygiainō*, the related vb., is used for bodily healing only in Lk., where it is synonymous with *therapeuō* and *iaomai*. It appears principally in the Pastoral Epistles in connection with sound → teaching.

θεραπεύω	θεραπεύω (*therapeuō*), heal, cure; θεράπων (*therapōn*), servant; θεραπεία (*therapeia*), service, treatment.

CL & OT In profane Greek *therapeuō* has the meaning to serve, to be in service to
 (a superior); thus also to serve, in the sense of venerating the gods, i.e. in cultic worship, to care for (e.g. as a doctor), whence finally to cure, usually by medical means.

The LXX frequently uses *therapōn* for the Heb. *'ebeḏ*, attendant, servant. The use of the vb. seems rather imprecise, even haphazard: twice for *yāšaḇ*, to sit (Est. 2:19; 6:10); once for *'āḇaḏ* (Isa. 54:17); once for *ḥālâh* (piel), to appease (Prov. 19:6); once for *bāqaš* (piel), to seek (Prov. 29:26).

NT With regard to the incidence of *therapeuō* in the NT, it is significant (a) that
 out of 43 occurrences, no less than 40 are found in the Synoptics and the Acts; (b) that, except in one place (Acts 17:25), *therapeuō* has exclusively the meaning to heal. This means that in the NT *therapeuō* is never used in its profane sense to serve (cf. *therapeia* Lk. 12:42, "household servants"; or *therapōn* Heb. 3:5, "servant"). The cultic usage for the worship of God is found only in Acts 17:25, where Paul concludes from Isa. 42:5 (cf. Acts 17:24 f.) that God as the Creator of the world and the Lord of heaven and earth does not dwell in temples made by man and therefore cannot be "worshipped" in the sacrificial cult (cf. Acts 7:42 f.). ([F.F.B.] The emphasis of Acts 17:25 is better brought out in the NEB rendering: "It is not because he lacks anything that he accepts service [*therapeuetai*] at men's hands.")

1. Only in Lk. 4:23 in the proverb "Physician, heal yourself" and in 8:43 (the woman with the issue of blood "could not be healed by anyone") does *therapeuō* denote healing by ordinary medical means. In the rest of the passages *therapeuō* is used to describe the miraculous healings wrought by Jesus and his disciples.

(a) In the Gospels the work of Jesus is presented in terms of teaching and working → miracles (Matt. 4:23 f.; 9:35; Lk. 6:18 and passim). Healing plays an essential part in Christ's miraculous work, but the latter must be seen in the context of his teaching if it is to be understood aright. This is especially clear in the composition of the Gospel of Matt., where the two great collections of Jesus' → teaching (chs. 5–7) and of his → miracles (chs. 8–9) are enclosed between the two almost identical verses Matt. 4:23 and 9:35 (Jesus "taught in their synagogues and preached the gospel of the kingdom, and healed all manner of sickness and all manner of disease among the people", *therapeuō* being used in both places). This emphasizes Christ's twofold office of teaching and healing (cf. H. J. Held in G. Bornkamm, G. Barth and H. J. Held, *Tradition and Interpretation in Matthew*, 1963, 246).

While Jesus again and again heals the sick (Matt. 4:24; 12:15; 14:14; 15:30 and passim), this does not put him into the category of the Hel. *theioi anthrōpoi* (divine men), who in their miraculous acts of healing demonstrated their divine abilities. Rather, the Servant of the Lord is → fulfilling the OT prophecies by his healing miracles (Matt. 8:16, 17; cf. Isa. 53:4). The healings do not prove Jesus to be the Christ, but viewed against their OT background they are seen to be Christ's act of obedience and thus a necessary element in his messianic work. This conviction lies behind the many summaries (Matt. 4:24; Mk. 1:34; 3:10 and passim) which emphasize that all who turn to Jesus find healing – a further echo of the OT (cf. Isa. 53). This is why he has power to heal on the → Sabbath (Matt. 12:10; Mk. 3:2; Lk. 6:7; 13:14). In taking up the cause of the helpless Jesus proves himself to be the → Servant of God (Matt. 8:7; 19:2).

(b) In Mk. 6:5, 6 there is the remarkable statement that in Nazareth Jesus could do no mighty work. It is quite clear from most of the detailed accounts of healing that → faith on the part of those concerned is already present before they are healed by Jesus (cf. Matt. 8:8–10, 13; 9:27 ff.; 15:21 ff.; Lk. 8:43 ff.; cf. Mk. 5:34 and passim). Thus after the disciples' failure to heal the lunatic boy (Matt. 17:16), the father confidently turned to Jesus for help, and his faith was vindicated, for the lad was healed (v. 18). Healing is faith's reward, because faith is confident that even when men have done their utmost and failed, the power of God in Christ is inexhaustible. Thus healing does not initiate faith but assumes it (cf. Mk. 6:5 f.). It is not that faith is the power which effects the miracle; it is rather preparedness for the miracle.

(c) Christ healed men not only of bodily infirmities but also of demon possession (Matt. 8:16; Mk. 1:34; 3:10 f.; Lk. 4:40 f. and passim), here too revealing his messianic claims. Satanic powers are subject to his power and word, and by exercising power over the demons through his word, he is utterly different from the ordinary exorcists of his time. As he casts out → demons, we glimpse the splendour of Christ the King.

(d) Jesus also gave his disciples a share in his healing power (Matt. 10:1, 8; Mk. 6:13; Lk. 9:1, 6). They entered into his work not only in the sense of teaching his doctrine, but in the sense of being empowered for the same messianic works which he himself performed. For this, implicit faith is required (Matt. 17:16 ff.), the faith by which the early church experienced the enabling Christ in its midst (cf. Acts 5:16; 8:7 and passim). In the healings wrought by the disciples the church was given a token of the active presence of its exalted Lord.

2. To summarize: In the NT the stories of healing are not told in order to "prove" the messiahship of Jesus by demonstrating his power over natural laws. "The miracle does not consist in the breaking of the causal nexus of natural law. This does not come within the purview of the NT. The real miracle is victory in the conflict with forces which struggle for mastery over this cosmos. The NT thus looks into the depths of world occurrence" (H. W. Beyer, *TDNT* III 131). Although the healing miracles, in common with all the miracles in the Gospels, are repeatedly given prominence as outworkings of the Lord's power (cf. Matt. 14:14; 19:2, where *therapeuein* replaces *didaskein*), nevertheless they are not regarded as having any importance in their own right.

F. Graber, D. Müller

$\overset{\cdot}{\iota}\acute{a}o\mu a\iota$	$\overset{\cdot}{\iota}\acute{a}o\mu a\iota$ (*iaomai*), to cure, to restore; $\overset{\cdot}{\iota}a\sigma\iota\varsigma$ (*iasis*), healing; $\overset{\cdot}{\iota}a\mu a$ (*iama*), healing; $\overset{\cdot}{\iota}a\tau\rho\acute{o}\varsigma$ (*iatros*), physician.

CL *iaomai* (from Homer onwards), to cure, restore, is used in the literal sense as a medical term, and also metaphorically and figuratively: to free from an evil, e.g. ignorance (Sallust) or some intellectual shortcoming; to heal psychological illnesses etc. Likewise the nouns *iasis* and *iama*, healing, and *iatros*, physician, are used both literally and metaphorically.

1. The various types of medical treatment throughout human history can be properly understood only when one is acquainted with the ideas which have been held regarding the different causes of sickness (→ weakness), i.e. what has to be fought against in healing. Apart from external injuries, where the cause is obvious, sicknesses are for primitive man not simply physiological phenomena, the causes and nature of which can be investigated, and which can therefore possibly be cured. Originally sicknesses were ascribed to attacks by external forces (by gods, demons, → sin, → guilt, → magical powers such as a → curse, the ban etc.). To bring about a cure a number of methods were employed: exorcisms (to cast out demons); various magical practices (the earliest beginnings of medicine); influences based on suggestion; or prayers and offerings, in an attempt to appease the deity. Both the sickness and its cure, therefore, were believed to arise from the intervention of a superior will, though this is not to say that the origins of rational medical treatment are to be found only in magic and enchantment. As early as the 3rd cent. B.C. the science of medicine reached its first flowering among the ancient Egyptians. But the honour of having set medical science upon an empirical and rational basis belongs above all to the Greeks (cf. F. Büchsel, *TDNT* III 195). Already from Homer we learn of the high esteem enjoyed by physicians in general (cf. *Il.* 2, 514), especially those of Egypt (cf. *Od.* 4, 220–233), though admittedly he had not reached the point of distinguishing clearly between medicine and magic. The oath of Hippocrates (born 460 B.C.) is a remarkable testimony to the fact that, as medicine in Greece came into its own, there gradually arose a specific code of ethics among physicians (for text and literature see F. Büchsel, *TDNT* III 196; C. F. H. Henry, ed., *Baker's Dictionary of Christian Ethics*, 1973, 291).

2. It remains true, however, that in the ancient world no clear line of demarcation can be drawn between rational and magical ideas of reality. In his attempts to cope with life, the man of antiquity came face to face with an immense variety of powers, so complex as to be generally beyond the grasp of our minds, which think exclusively in scientific terms. It follows that the relationship between the origins of medicine as a rational science, and "supernatural" healings attributed to superior powers, is inextricably involved. Thus we constantly find that among different peoples special healing deities were worshipped (in earlier Gk. times e.g. Apollo, later Asclepius; in Egypt e.g. Imhotep; in the Assyrian–Babylonian world Tammuz). Temple-like edifices were built to them and used as healing centres (e.g. the celebrated Asclepieion of Cos or the temple of Epidauros), where priests acted as physicians and ran what can only be described as a healing business. All kinds of offerings were presented, not merely in order to obtain a cure but also as thanksgiving for miraculous cures already obtained. In the ancient world there were numerous accounts of miraculous healing, often embellished to the point of being

grotesque. Anything was possible. We even read of tricks being played on the deity in order to obtain a cure, whereupon the deity would avenge himself with a punitive miracle.

Kings were originally chief priests as well, and as such had the gift of healing (cf. the royal customs which still obtained in the Middle Ages, e.g. Shakespeare's *Macbeth* IV, 3, or Philip the Fair of France: "The King touches you, God heals you"). It is therefore no surprise to read, e.g., that the Emperor Vespasian healed the blind and lame by his touch and with the use of spittle (*TDNT* III 198).

F. Büchsel sums up the situation when he says that "the gods are doctors and saviours both in a cosmic and universal sense and also in an inward sense. The typically Greek thought form of analogy leads here to a particular conception of divine rule in the world. The gods become mediators between Zeus and men, and as such they dispense healing" (*ibid.*).

OT 1. In the LXX *iaomai* stands frequently for the Heb. *rāpā'*, to heal, cure. It is characteristic of faith in Yahweh that he alone is the source of all healing ("I, Yahweh, am your healer", Exod. 15:26; cf. 2 Ki. 5:7). To turn to a physician (let alone another deity) for healing could on occasion be unbelief, distrust of Yahweh, and an offence against the First Commandment (2 Ki. 1; and 2 Chr. 16:12). As sicknesses come from Yahweh himself, he is the only one who can bind up and heal (Job 5:18). For the same reason the OT knows little of the distinction between external ills with an obvious cause (injuries sustained through accident, in war, from animals' bites, etc.), and other ills arising from within (cf. CL above, 1). In every aspect of his life man is dependent on Yahweh alone. This does not mean that demons and other powers have nothing to do with sickness. Rather they are thought of as being in God's service (cf. Exod. 12:23; Hab. 3:5 and passim).

This view of sickness and healing as marks of Yahweh's visitation or of his renewed favour often brings a man – particularly the devout man – into grievous inward conflict (cf. the Book of Job and the Psalms, e.g. Pss. 38; 51; and especially 88). This can lead to rebellion against Yahweh, when the malady is felt to be undeserved (Ps. 73:21; Job 9:17 ff.). And yet the devout man turns in prayer, lamentation and thanks to God alone as the only one who can grant him healing (Ps. 30:3; 103:3; cf. Wis. 16:12).

In spite of this radical attitude to sickness and healing, there are some passages which indicate the use of medical treatment (e.g. 1 Ki. 17:21; 2 Ki. 4:34; 5:13 ff.; 20:7), though the means used here by the prophets are seldom "medical" as we understand the word. These are miraculous cures, carried out in reliance upon the healing power of Yahweh.

In the OT the → priest is not regarded as a healer. His function was restricted to that of a medical officer of health who ascertained that healing had taken place (Lev. 13 f.). The earlier books contain very few references to physicians (cf. Gen. 50:2; Isa. 3:7; Jer. 8:22). These probably go back to Egyptian or later to Greek influences. This situation changed at a much later period (cf. especially Sir. 38). But here too, even though the work of a physician is regarded in a positive light, he is God's servant in the strictest sense. It is God who appoints him and through prayer grants him wisdom for his work (vv. 1 f.; 9-14). An important element in the OT understanding of sickness and healing is the idea that bodily sickness is very closely connected with sin and is therefore a manifestation of God's wrath against specific transgressions (Ps. 32:1 ff.; 38:3 ff.; 39 f. and passim). Here healing becomes a picture of forgiveness, of God's mercy, of his nearness (Isa. 6:10; Ps. 30:3; 41:5; 103:3 and passim).

2. In Judaism, too, medicine was generally held in considerable suspicion, although we do read of rabbis who were also physicians. Judaism shared the ideas which were widespread in relation to miraculous healings. Incantations, invocations and other practices (e.g. the use of spittle in healing) still play a large part (cf. SB I 627; II 15, 17; IV 527 ff.). With few exceptions, the rabbis themselves do not appear in tradition as miraculous healers. "Most closely related historically to the NT tradition" are perhaps "the old biblical materials (Abraham as a miracle-worker in the apocryphal Genesis 20:21 ff.) and the Rab. miracles stories of the Tannaitic period (e.g. R. Hanina ben Dosa according to Ber. 34b)" (O. Michel *BHHW* II 679; cf. Moore, *Judaism*, I, 177 f.; II, 235 f.).

NT In the NT *iaomai* occurs 26 times, of which 20 are in the Synoptic Gospels and Acts; *iasis* 3 times, all in Lk.; *iatros* 6 times, all in the Synoptic Gospels, except Col. 4:14 [" Luke the beloved physician"]; *iama* 3 times, all in 1 Cor. 12. It is clear from these figures that, apart from *iama*, this word-group occurs chiefly in the Synoptic Gospels and esp. in Lk. (20 times out of a total 38).

1. The use of *iaomai* corresponds in the Gospels and in Acts to that of → *therapeuō*. Hence, the remarks made under *therapeuō* on the theological assessment of healing miracles apply here also. The cures wrought by Jesus and then by his disciples are signs of the incoming → kingdom of God (Lk. 9:2, 11, 42; Acts 10:38 and passim) and are thus the fulfilment of OT prophecy (cf. Isa. 35:3–6; 61:1 f. etc.). "For the Evangelist Jesus is the one upon whom God's Spirit rests, and who brings in the eschatological time of salvation; in his liberating and redeeming work he fulfils God's will, which has already been declared by the prophets . . . in Scripture. A general amnesty for debtors and prisoners, as in the year of release, becomes a picture of the ministry of Jesus" (O. Michel, *BHHW* II 679 f.).

This is not to deny that the NT shares the view of sickness which was common at that time (cf. Lk. 13:11; Acts 12:23 and passim). As we saw under CL and OT, the miraculous cures wrought by Jesus are not without parallels in the extra-biblical world. In the opinion of many scholars the deeds reported of Jesus and his disciples are not always free from embellishments and accretions of later miraculous detail (cf. Mk. 5:1 ff.; Lk. 22:51; Acts 12:23; 5:15 f. and passim; or the heightened account in Mk. 5:21–43 par. Matt. 9:18–26, Lk. 8:40–56; Lk. 7:11 ff.; Jn. 11:1 ff.). But even though the NT records of healing show all the familiar features (e.g. the helplessness of physicians, Mk. 5:26 ff.; the instantaneous nature of the miracle, Lk. 8:47; the patient's ability to carry his own mattress home, Jn. 5:8 ff., etc.), a comparison with the romantically embellished stories found e.g. in the Gospel of Thomas or in the apocryphal Acts of the Apostles reveals a striking fact. The NT accounts are simple and straightforward. They do not aim to glorify some miracle-worker of the ancient world, or even miracles as such. In most cases, the original account of what took place is still very much in mind, and such events are viewed in the light of Christ's message. Farce, magic and sensationalism are absent. The healings wrought by Jesus are determined by his → word and → faith (Matt. 8:8, 13;

15:28; Lk. 7:7 and passim). They are therefore (for all their similarities) fundamentally different from the healings in the rest of the ancient world. Jesus also breaks through the narrow Jewish doctrine of retribution (i.e. that every sickness must be the result of a certain → sin; cf. Jn. 9:2 ff.), without thereby denying the basic connection between sin and sickness (e.g. Jn. 5:13 f.; cf. Jas. 5:16). The focal point of all the healings is not the miracle but the healer himself, whose authoritative preaching has brought in the dawn of the new age (cf. the repeated statement in Lk. that Jesus healed all: Lk. 6:19; Acts 10:38). "In all the Gospels the power of Jesus is described as an obvious fact, self-evident both to his disciples and to his opponents. What then is meant by the express statement that a special power came forth from him (Mk. 5:30 ff.; Lk. 6:19)? This idea, which has close Hellenistic associations, is meant realistically and is clearly connected with a certain view of the Spirit" (O. Michel, op. cit., 680 f.).

Even though our rational thinking finds certain difficulties in regard to healing miracles, we should beware of resting content with merely psychological explanations. With our modern historical approach we are in danger of missing the real force of the language and of the claims which it makes. For as a rule the real point of a miracle is not the miracle itself but what it reveals of Jesus. "In spite of every analogy, the miraculous healings of Jesus thus occupy a unique position in religious history. They are inseparably connected with the uniqueness of Jesus and with His unparalleled sense of mission" (A. Oepke, *TDNT* III 213).

2. In 1 Cor. 12 the word *iama*, healing, occurs 3 times as Paul enumerates the various spiritual gifts. All the apostles were given gifts of healing as well as being commissioned to preach the gospel (*therapeuō* is used in Matt. 10:18; Mk. 6:13; Lk. 9:1; *iaomai* in Lk. 9:2; see also Acts, e.g. 2:43). But Paul here makes it clear that healing can also be carried out by individuals whom God has expressly endowed with a spiritual gift for this purpose. The gift of healing is one function among others, all of which are co-ordinated with one another in the church as the body of Christ.   *F. Graber, D. Müller*

| ὑγιής | ὑγιής (*hygiēs*), healthy, well; ὑγιαίνω (*hygiainō*), make well again, cure. |

CL *hygiēs* (from Homer onwards) means: (a) lit. healthy (in body), strong, active, sound; (b) metaphorically of good understanding, sensible, shrewd, sober, of good judgment. Likewise *hygiainō* means to be healthy, to be of sound mind, to be shrewd or sensible. From Aristotle onwards *hygiaine* was often used in the sense of "farewell!"

In Gk. literature (as early as Homer and especially later in Gk. popular philosophy) *hygiēs* or *hygiainō* (frequently in conjunction with *logos*) is commonly used to describe an idea or opinion as judicious, sensible, i.e. "healthy" as opposed to being false or "sick" (cf. e.g. Plato, *Phdr.* 242c; Epictetus 1, 11, 28; 3, 9, 5; Philo, *Abr.* 223; 275).

OT In the LXX *hygiēs* and *hygiainō* (about 50 times) are used only in a direct sense (e.g. Gen. 37:14; Isa. 38:21; cf. Lev. 13:10 ff. for *miḥyâh*, growth of new flesh. Generally *hygiaine* stands for the Heb. *šālôm*, used as in later profane Gk. as a greeting in the sense, "Peace be to you" (1 Sam. 25:6; 2 Sam. 18:28; 20:9; also Gen. 29:6; 43:27 f.; Exod. 4:18; cf. 2 Macc. 9:19 and passim).

NT Of the 23 passages in which *hygiēs* or *hygiainō* are found in the NT, no less than 12 are in the Gospels and 9 in the Pastoral Epistles. Otherwise the word group is found in the rest of the NT only in Acts 4:10 and 3 Jn. 2.

1. In the Gospels and Acts *hygiēs* and *hygiainō* are used without exception in the literal sense of healthy, well.

(a) Generally the well-being is the result of a healing miracle (→ miracle; cf. *therapeuō* and *iaomai*) wrought by Jesus (Matt. 15:31; 12:13; Lk. 7:10; Jn. 5:9 ff.) or the disciples (Acts 4:10). → Faith occasions the saving act and so the healing. According to Mk. 5:25 ff., this faith was not always free from magical elements, but the word of Jesus, "Go in peace, and be healed [*hygiēs*] of your disease", confirms even this unusual miracle.

In all these passages, however, *hygiēs* and *hygiainō* do not denote merely a physically healthy condition. Anyone healed through meeting Jesus is a person healed in his entire being by the word of the messiah (Jn. 7:23), i.e. also saved from his sin (cf. Lk. 5:21 ff.). In the healing of the lame, the blind and the deaf (Matt. 15:21; cf. Mk. 7:37; 8:23) the promise of God's coming (Isa. 35:4 ff.) was fulfilled. In these passages, therefore, good health is not the result of medical treatment but indicates a more profound healing, i.e. it is a sign that the age of salvation has dawned.

(b) As in the above passages, *hygiainonta* in Lk. 15:27 does not mean merely physical well-being (cf. 15:24). Having returned from this period of alienation and come home to his father's house, the prodigal is re-instated to his original status as son, i.e. he has now become well. In Jesus and his healing word man encounters the Father running to meet him and is restored to full health. Thus when faced with those who object to his mingling with the outcasts of society, Jesus justifies his mission with the aphorism: "Those who are well [*hygiainontes*] have no need of a physician, but those who are sick" (Lk. 5:31). It is quite possible that Jesus is here adopting a popular saying in order to justify his behaviour and to show that he was acting as the messiah (cf. Mk. 2:17, where the word used is *ischyontes*, the strong). When Jesus called the Pharisees and scribes "those who are well", he may not have intended it to be taken ironically. In this case he was not disputing their "good health", though it must now prove itself in a right attitude to the work of God in Christ (cf. Lk. 15:28–32), lest it degenerate into self-righteousness and is destroyed. ([Ed.] On the other hand an ironical meaning is a natural one in view of what is said about the religious leaders elsewhere in Lk. [5:17, 21, 30, 33; 6:2, 7; 7:30, 36; 10:25–29; 11:37–54; 12:1; 13:33; 14:1 ff.; 15:2; 16:14; 17:20 f.; 19:39].)

2. The metaphorical meaning is found in the Pastoral Epistles, where *hygiainō* and *hygiēs* are characteristic terms for "(to be) sound". Thus *hygiainein (en) tē pistei*, to be sound in the faith (Tit. 1:13; 2:2); *hygiainousa didaskalia*, sound doctrine (1 Tim. 1:10; 2 Tim. 4:3; Tit. 1:9; 2:1); *hygiainontes logoi*, the sound words of Jesus Christ (1 Tim. 6:3; 2 Tim. 1:13; cf. *logos hygiēs*, Tit. 2:8). In this usage the influence of Greek popular philosophy upon the Pastoral Epistles is felt (see above CL). Such a usage is completely absent from the LXX. In the Pastoral

Epistles, however, *hygiainō*, which is nowhere used in the rest of the NT in association with "word" or "doctrine", should not be taken to imply that the message of Christ simply has to be made acceptable to the intellect. Rather, problems such as heresy are to be solved by an appeal to the fixed norms of Pauline doctrine (1 Tim. 1:6 ff.; 6:3; 2 Tim. 4:3 f. and passim; cf. 1 Tim. 1:1 ff.; Tit. 1:1–3 etc.). "The church uses doctrine as such to combat the 'enthusiasm' of the gnostics, and sound doctrine, handed down in its purity, to combat their false doctrine" (W. Schmithals, *RGG³* V 145). This approach, however, reveals the change which has taken place in the way the message is understood. Whereas in the earlier Pauline epistles the gospel is viewed as something dynamic (cf. his dialectic of wisdom and foolishness), the Pastoral Epistles see it as a fixed body of received doctrine which can be used as a clear-cut standard to counter heresy. ([Ed.] This must not, however, be overstated, for in the same letter which made use of this dialectic Paul could also claim to be handing on the tradition which he received as the basis of faith [1 Cor. 15:8 ff.; cf. 1:18 ff.].) In the Pastoral Epistles false doctrine is opposed not by detailed specific refutation, but with the simple assertion that it does not conform to the doctrinal tradition and so is not "healthy" or "sound". Hence, to be "sound in faith" (Tit. 2:2) means to hold the received apostolic doctrine as normative and binding.

The important place occupied by *hygiainō* and *hygiēs* in the Pastoral Epistles has often figured largely in the debate as to the authorship of these epistles (cf. the excursus on 1 Tim. 1:10 in M. Dibelius and H. Conzelmann, *The Pastoral Epistles* [*Hermeneia*] 1974; and the survey by W. Kasch in *EKL* III, 79 f. On the question of authorship see further C. Spicq, *Les Épîtres Pastorales*, 1947, xxi–ccviii; D. Guthrie, *The Pastoral Epistles*, 1957, 11–53; J. N. D. Kelly, *The Pastoral Epistles*, 1963, 1–36.)
D. Müller

→ Blind, → Body, → Deaf, Dumb, → Flesh, → Lame, → Leprosy, → Miracle, → Weakness, Sickness, → Work

(a). P. E. Adolph, "Healing, Health", *ZPEB* III 54–58; H. J. Blair, "Spiritual Healing. An Enquiry", *EQ* 30, 1958, 147–51; C. J. Brim, *Medicine in the Bible*, 1936; E. Andrews, "Healing, Gifts of", *IDB* II 548 f.; J. P. Baker, *Salvation and Wholeness*, 1973; H. W. Beyer, *therapeia* etc., *TDNT* III 128–32; T. W. Crafer, *The Healing Miracles in the Book of Acts*, 1939; F. N. Davey, "Healing in the New Testament", in *The Miracles and the Resurrection*, SPCK Theological Collections 3, 1964, 50–63; V. Edmunds and G. C. Scorer, *Some Thoughts on Faith Healing*, 1956; H. W. Frost, *Miraculous Healing*, 1951; E. M. B. Green, *The Meaning of Salvation*, 1965, 218–25; J. A. Hardon, "The Miracle Narratives in the Acts of the Apostles", *CBQ* 16, 1954, 303–18; R. K. Harrison, "Medicines of the Bible", *Canadian Association of Medical Students and Internes Journal*, 10, 1, 1951, 17–20; and "Healing, Health", *IDB* II 541–48; K. Heim, *Jesus the Lord*, 1959; H. J. Held, "Matthew as Interpreter of the Miracle Stories", in G. Bornkamm, G. Barth and H. J. Held, *Tradition and Interpretation in Matthew*, 1960, 165–299; W. K. Hobart, *The Medical Language of St. Luke*, 1882 (but on this subject see also A. Harnack, *Luke the Physician*, 1907; and H. J. Cadbury, *Style and Literary Method of Luke*, 1920); D. Johnson, *In the Service of Medicine*, 1968; R. A. Lambourne, *Community, Church and Healing*, 1963; M. J. Langford, "The Problem of the Meaning of 'Miracle' ", *Religious Studies* 7, 1971, 43–52; H. van der Loos, *The Miracles of Jesus*, NovT Supplements 9, 1965; J. S. McEwen, "The Ministry of Healing", *SJT* 7, 1954, 133–52; H. N. and A. L. Moldenke, *Plants of the Bible*, 1952; F. Mussner, *The Miracles of Jesus: An Introduction*, 1970; H. P. Newsholme, *Health, Disease and Integration*, 1929; G. von Rad, *Old Testament Theology*, I, 272–79; A. Oepke, *TDNT* III 194–215; A. Richardson, *The Miracle Stories of the Gospels*, 1941; A. Schlemmer, *Faith and Medicine*, 1957; A. R. Short, *The Bible and Modern Medicine*, 1953; C. R. Smith, *A Physician Examines the*

Bible, 1950; R. Swinburne, *The Concept of Miracle*, 1970; M. F. Unger, "Divine Healing", *Bibliotheca Sacra* 128, 1971, 234–44; A. Vögtle, "The Miracles of Jesus against their Background", in U. J. Schultz, ed., *Jesus in His Time*, 1971, 96–105; L. D. Weatherhead, *Psychology, Religion and Healing*, revised ed. 1954; J. Wilkinson, "A Study of Healing in the Gospel according to John", *SJT* 20, 1967, 442–61; "Healing in the Epistle of James", *SJT* 24, 1971, 326–45; and "The Mission Charge to the Twelve and Modern Medical, Missions" *SJT* 27, 1974, 313–28. H. W. Wolff, *Anthropology of the Old Testament*, 1974, 143–48.

(b). K. Beth, "Heilung", *RGG³* III 194 ff.; W. Beyer, *Gibt es Heilungen von körperlicher Krankheit durch Geisteskraft?*, 1921; H. Doebert, *Das Charisma der Krankenheilung*, 1960; A. Dupont-Sommer, "Exorcisme et guérisons dans les écrits de Qoumrân", *Vetus Testament Supplements 7, Congress Volume*, 1959, 246 ff.; F. Fenner, *Die Krankheit im Neuen Testament*, 1930; H. Greeven, *Krankheit und Heilung*, 1948; H. Haag, ed., *Bibel-Lexikon*, 1956, 963 f., 1724 ff.; A. Harnack, "Medizinisches in der ältesten Kirchengeschichte", *TU* 8, 4, 1892; J. Hempel, " 'Ich bin der Herr dein Arzt' (Exod. 15, 26)", *TLZ* 82, 1957, 809–26; "Heilung als Symbol und Wirklichkeit im biblischen Schrifttum", *Nachrichten von der Gesellschaft der Wissenschaften zu Göttingen* Philosophisch-historische Klasse, 1958, 3, 237–314; J. Hempel and O. Michel, "Heilen", *BHHW* II 678 ff.; P. Humbert, "Maladie et médecine dans l'Ancien Testament", *Revue d'Histoire et de Philosophie Religieuses*, 41, 1964, 1–29; W. Kasch, "Pastoralbriefe", *EKL* III 79 ff.; J. Leipoldt, *Von Epidauros bis Lourdes*, 1957; J. Ott, "Die Bezeichnung Christi als *iatros* in der urchristlichen Literatur", *Der Katholik* 90, 1910, 454 ff.; J. Scharbert, *Der Schmerz im Alten Testament*, 1955; F. J. Schierse, "Hat Krankheit einen Sinn?", *Stimmen der Zeit* 84, 1959, 241–55; W. Schmithals, "Pastoralbriefe", *RGG³* V, 145.

Hear, Obey

The word hear embraces both physical hearing and the apprehension of something with the mind. Similarly, the Gk. vb. *akouō* and the noun *akoē*, as used in the NT, can have both meanings, though originally these words denoted only the former. Various compounds are used to denote apprehension with the mind. *eisakouō* and *epakouō* stress attentive listening, while the emphatic forms *hypakouō* and *hypakoē* (lit. hear beneath) mean to obey and obedience. The linguistic and conceptual relationship between *akouō* and *hypakouō* recurs in Old and Middle Eng. in the use of the same word for both hear and obey. It can still be traced in some modern languages, e.g. Ger. *hören* and *gehorchen*. The former includes the latter, and in some contexts can be substituted for it. Conversely, *parakouō* and *parakoē* (lit. hear beside) denote inattentive hearing, missing, not hearing, and thus disobedience.

ἀκούω

ἀκούω (*akouō*), hear, listen, attend, perceive by hearing; ἀκοή (*akoē*), hearing, the ear, a thing heard, message, teaching, report, rumour; ἀκροατής (*akroatēs*), hearer; εἰσακούω (*eisakouō*), obey, pass. to be heard; ἐπακούω (*epakouō*), listen to, hearken to; ἐπακροάομαι (*epakroaomai*), listen attentively; παρακούω (*parakouō*), fail to hear, take no heed; παρακοή (*parakoē*), disobedience; ἐνωτίζω (*enōtizō*), pay attention to, hear.

CL 1. *akouō* (Homer on) means to hear and refers primarily to the perception of sounds by the sense of hearing. The person or thing heard is in the acc.; the person from whom something is heard is in the gen. or else is indicated by the preps. *apo, para* or *ek*. An impersonal obj. can also be in the gen. Hearing, however, covers not only sense perception but also the apprehension and acceptance by the mind of the content of what is heard. This led to differences of linguistic usage which are discussed below in connection with Heb. *šāma'* and which also occur in secular Gk.

The related noun *akoē* (attested from Homer on) means: (a) hearing, the sense of hearing; (b) the act of hearing; (c) the organ of hearing, the ear; (d) the content of hearing, the message.

2. Hearing plays a part in every religion. The general tendency of the Gk. and Hel. world, however, was to stress the seeing of the divinity (cf. W. Michaelis, *horaō, TDNT* V 320 f.). It is seldom that one meets in the apocalyptic literature of Hel. mysticism (Apuleius, *Corpus Hermeticum*, 2nd or 3rd cents. A.D.) hearing as a means through which revelation has been received. On the other hand, the idea that the gods hear and listen is not foreign to paganism. We read of the ears of the gods, and the adj. *epēkoos*, listening, answering, is applied to the divinity on many Hel. inscriptions.

ot 1. In the LXX *akouō* or *akoē* stands consistently for Heb. *šāmaʿ*. It shares the shades of meaning of the Heb. vb. Here too the primary meaning is that of sense perception (e.g. the hearing of a trumpet, 2 Sam. 15:10). However, apprehension is immediately involved as soon as one receives a statement, piece of news or message (Gen. 14:14). Apprehension demands acceptance, listening (Gen. 4:23; 23:11), understanding (Gen. 11:7; 42:3), and attention to the thing heard ("Listen to . . ." Gen. 3:17; 23:16; Exod. 24:7). Hence, *šāmaʿ* acquired the meaning of obey. *šāmaʿ* in this sense is often rendered in the LXX by the emphatic compounds *eisakouō*, listen, obey (e.g. Gen. 42:21 f.; Exod. 6:12, 30), *epakouō*, listen (and answer), obey (Jdg. 2:17; cf. 1 Macc. 10:38), and → *hypakouō*, obey. The noun *akoē* (Heb. *šᵉmûʿâh* or *šēmaʿ*) denotes the act of hearing (Ps. 17[18]:44), but mostly the content of a message (cf. Exod. 23:1; 1 Sam. 2:24; Isa. 53:1; Jer. 10:22). On God's hearing see 3 below.

2. (a) In biblical revelation hearing has a much greater significance than in the Gk. or Hel. worlds. For God meets man in his word, and man therefore is charged with hearing God's word. This does not exclude God's revelation in the visible sphere; the mental process is not to be separated from the sense perception. Two examples help to clarify this. God revealed himself to Moses in the burning thorn bush (Exod. 3:1 ff.), and in the vision which constituted his call Isaiah saw Yahweh in the temple surrounded by the seraphim singing their praises (Isa. 6:1 ff.). But here, as in other cases of the visible revelation of God's commission, it is connected with the prophetic mission. It takes place through the word, and must be heard and followed. Likewise, the visions which are frequently described in the prophetic writings (e.g. Amos 7–9; Jer. 1:11 ff.) require interpretation. Here too seeing and hearing are a unity. The prominence of hearing in the OT is demonstrated by the frequency of the phrases, *nᵉʾum YHWH* (thus says the Lord) and *wayᵉhî dᵉḇar YHWH* (the word of the Lord came). Readiness to hear on the part of those who receive the revelation is expressed in 1 Sam. 3:10: "Speak, for thy servant hears" (cf. O. Procksch, *legō, TDNT* IV 91–100).

(b) Moses, "with whom the Lord used to speak face to face" (Exod. 33:11), lived in the memory of his people as the model bearer of the divine, verbal revelation. The Decalogue (→ Command) was given to Moses according to Exod. 20:1 ff. and Deut. 5:6 ff. Deut. 5:1 is introduced by the solemn "Hear, O Israel". This *šᵉmaʿ yiśrāʾēl* also stands as an urgent warning before the command to love God (Deut. 6:4 ff.). Alongside the warning however, we frequently find the complaint

173

that Israel has not heard, but has rebelled. God has not given to Israel "a mind to understand, or eyes to see, or ears to hear" (Deut. 29:4).

The prophetic revelation presupposed that the content of God's will was already known (Mic. 6:8). As bearers of the divine revelation, the prophets warned the people, the nations and even heaven and earth to hear God's word which was coming through themselves (Isa. 1:2, 10; Jer. 2:4; 7:2; 9:20 [MT 9:19]; Mic. 1:2). But equally we hear them complaining that Israel had not heard the voice of its God, nor was willing to do so (Hos. 9:17; Jer. 7:13; Ezek. 3:7). Thus the pre-exilic prophets, in particular, became preachers of → judgment. God lets his judgment fall on a people that will not hear; nor is he any longer willing to hear this people (Isa. 1:15; cf. Ezek. 8:18). Part of this judgment was the hardening that Isaiah was to bring upon the people. They were to be unreceptive to God's revelation: "Hear and hear, but do not understand; see and see, but do not perceive" (Isa. 6:9 ff.). In the catastrophes which overtook Israel, culminating in the destruction of Jerusalem and the Babylonian captivity, the post-exilic prophets saw God's judgment on the people for their unwillingness to hear (Zech. 7:8–14). The prayers of confession of the returning exiles (Ezr. 9; Neh. 9) show that a wide circle of the people shared this view.

Thus Israel became the people of the → law who wished to render the obedience they owed to God by the painstaking fulfilment of his will down to the last detail. For this reason the most important part of the tradition was the Torah, the Law, contained in the Five Books of Moses. Here the strongest emphasis is given to the relation between hearing and doing (Exod. 19:5, 8; Deut. 28:1; 30:11–14). As the divinely commissioned bearers of revelation, the prophets stood beside the law at the centre of religious faith. "The law and the prophets" is in the NT a comprehensive description of the OT writings. To hear them is the task of the pious Israelite (cf. Matt. 22:40; Lk. 16:29). The prophetic writings particularly served to feed the messianic hope. In later Judaism, especially in the apocalyptic literature connected with the book of Daniel (2 Esd., Ad. Dan. etc.), the era of messianic salvation was depicted in increasingly glorious colours (→ Jesus Christ). The Qumran texts also illustrate the strength of this hope.

(c) The tendency to listen to the law was strengthened in later Judaism by the rise of the synagogues (→ Church, Synagogue), with their regular → Sabbath worship alongside the sacrificial worship offered in the Jerusalem Temple. The synagogue became the focal point of the Jewish communities beyond the borders of Palestine. The recitation of the Shema (consisting of the extracts Deut. 6:4–9; 11:13–21; Num. 15:37–41) had a fixed place in their worship. In addition the daily recitation of the Shema was for the pious Jew an obligation of faith and witness. In principle any suitably qualified member of the community was entitled to expound the law in the synagogue services. Nevertheless, the formation of the class of scribes (→ Rabbis) is understandable. Their expositions of scripture were originally handed down orally but later from the 2nd cent. A.D. they were fixed in writing in the Mishnah and the Talmud (→ Glossary of Technical Terms). Thus hearing acquired even greater significance in Judaism, especially since in the rabbinic view the time of revelation was over. Only one echo of revelation remained, the *baṭ qôl* (daughter of the voice), which God made use of from time to time, but which possessed no binding doctrinal authority for the rabbis (SB I 125 ff.).

3. Just as men hear God, God hears men. It is in this way that the living God differs from idols which have ears but do not hear (Ps. 115; 135:17 etc.). Later Judaism continued this judgment (Wis. 15:15). So the Psalmists pray, "Incline thy ear to me, hear my words" (Ps. 17:6; cf. 31:2; 86:1 etc.). And in the figurative sense the OT often speaks of the ears of God who hears what men say (Num. 12:2) – the cry for help and also the grumbling of his people (Exod. 3:7; Num. 14:27). Alongside *akouō* the LXX often uses the emphatic *eisakouō* (e.g. Exod. 16:7, 8, 9, 12).

Not only does God hear prayer, he also answers it. This too can be expressed by *šāma'* and *akouō* (Ps. 29:10 LXX). But in these cases we more often find the LXX using the compounds *eisakouō* and *epakouō*. The latter is particularly frequent in the language of prayer and also as a rendering of Heb. *'ānâh*, to answer, grant a request (cf. *eisakouein* for Heb. *'ānâh* [e.g. Ps. 3:4; 19:1, 6, 9 LXX; Isa. 49:8].

enōtizomai, pay attention to, hear, is derived from *ous*, ear. It is a biblical word-formation on the basis of Heb. *he'ezîn* (e.g. Ps. 5:1[2]; 38:12[39:13]), give ear to, from the root *'zn* in the hiph. Thus the OT contains a whole range of statements in which the pious Israelite expressed his certainty that God hears and answers prayer. It is put particularly beautifully in Ps. 94:9: "He who planted the ear, does he not hear?" On the other hand, man's guilt can step between God and man and make God's ear → deaf, so that he does not hear (Isa. 59:1 f.).

NT 1. The NT usage of *akouō* follows essentially that of secular Gk. and the LXX. We find it with the acc. in Matt. 7:24 (hear the word); with gen. in Matt. 2:9 and Mk. 14:64 (hear the king, hear blasphemy); with *apo* in 1 Jn. 1:5; with *ek* in 2 Cor. 12:6 (hear from him or me); with *para* in Jn. 8:40 (hear from God as Creator).

The noun *akoē* denotes: (a) the sense of hearing (1 Cor. 12:17); (b) the act of hearing (2 Pet. 2:8; also Rom. 10:17; Gal. 3:2, 5, *ex akoēs pisteōs*, as the result of hearing in faith, so T. Zahn, J. A. Bengel and A. Schlatter); (c) the ear, especially in the plur. (e.g. Mk. 7:35; Acts 17:20); (d) in Matt. 4:24; 14:1 etc. *akoē* denotes the news (about Jesus). The *logos akoēs* (1 Thess. 2:13; Heb. 4:2) is the word of proclamation, the message. In the quotation from Isa. 53:1 LXX reproduced in Rom. 10:16 *akoē* also means message. Hence the *akoē pisteōs* (Rom. 10:17; Gal. 3:2, 5) is the apostolic message which has faith as its content and is spoken and received as God's word (1 Thess. 2:13). The intensive in the quotation from Isa. 6:9 in Matt. 13:14 is a Hebraism: *akoē akousete*, by hearing you will hear.

Of the compounds, *eisakouō* is used of hearing (obeying) by men, 1 Cor. 14:21 (in dependence on Isa. 28:11; Deut. 1:43; on God's hearing see below, 5). *parakouō* (in secular Gk. from the 5th cent. B.C., rare in the LXX) means in Matt. 5:36 to fail to hear, leave unheeded (cf. Isa. 65:11 LXX). In Matt. 18:17 it means to refuse to hear, to be disobedient. The noun *parakoē*, disobedience, occurs once in Plato, never in the LXX, and otherwise only in post-Christian usage. It refers in Rom. 5:19 to Adam's disobedience to God; in 2 Cor. 10:6 to the Corinthians' disobedience to Paul, and in Heb. 2:2 to human disobedience to the word of God spoken through angels. *enōtizomai* has a similar meaning (cf. above OT 3), and occurs in Acts 2:14 of human hearing (cf. RSV "give ear to"). The rare word *epakroaomai* (from Plato on, not in the LXX) means to listen to (Acts 16:25). The related noun *akroatēs*, listener (from the 5th cent. B.C.; also Isa. 3:3; Sir. 3:29 LXX) occurs in

Rom. 2:13 and Jas. 1:22, 23, 25, where the hearer of the law (or of the word) is contrasted with the doer.

2. (a) The many shades of meaning of *akouō* become apparent when we ask the theological question *how* man hears the NT message. The content of this message is → Jesus Christ, the messiah promised under the old → covenant. To those who believe in him are given the fullness of salvation and a new revelation which surpasses that of the OT. This revelation which has been manifested in him is perceived not just through hearing but with all the senses (Jn. 1:14; 1 Jn. 1:1). Essentially, it is a question of hearing and seeing (→ See, art. *horaō*). Jesus pronounced a blessing on the eyes and ears of those who had become witnesses of the salvation longed for by the pious of former generations (Matt. 13:16 f.; Lk. 10:23 f.). To the disciples sent to him by the imprisoned Baptist Jesus said: "Go and tell John what you hear and see" (Matt. 11:4 par. Lk. 7:22). Alongside his words stand Jesus' mighty acts. On the mount of transfiguration Jesus' disciples saw his hidden glory and heard the voice saying to them: "Listen to him" (Matt. 17:5 par. Mk. 9:7, Lk. 9:35). The shepherds' song of praise in the Christmas story, as well as the confession of the apostles before the Sanhedrin, referred to what they had heard and seen (Lk. 2:20; Acts 4:20).

(b) Not only Jesus' earthly appearance but also the events of Easter and → Pentecost are perceived by hearing and seeing. Paul's crucial vision of Christ (1 Cor. 15:9) is amplified by Acts 22:14, 15. Paul was to be a witness of what he had seen and heard. The gospels tell the same about the other disciples: seeing the risen Christ is bound up with hearing the apostolic commission which Jesus gave to his disciples (Matt. 28:18 ff.; Mk. 16:15; Lk. 24:46 ff.; Jn. 20:21; Acts 1:8). The events of Pentecost whose far-reaching effects in the Christian community we see in 1 Cor. 12–14 were perceived originally through seeing and hearing (Acts 2:33). Paul's revelations and visions, mentioned in 2 Cor. 12:1 ff., are also related to this event. In a trance the apostle heard "things that cannot be told, which man may not utter" (v. 4). Hearing also plays an important part in the visions of Rev. (Rev. 1:10; 5:11, 13 etc.). On the other hand, the mystery of our salvation is unfathomable; what God has prepared for those who love him no eye has seen and no ear heard nor any human heart conceived (1 Cor. 2:9).

(c) The message of Christ is grounded in a crucial revelatory event. The connection with OT revelation is preserved: the gospel has been proclaimed in advance through the prophets in holy scripture (Rom. 1:2). For the receipt of the Christian message faith is required. But faith presupposes hearing, and this in turn rests on preaching (Rom. 10:14 ff.; cf. Ps. 19:4; Deut. 32:21; Isa. 65:1 f.). On the other hand, as Jn. 20:29 implies, seeing is not a necessary condition for faith.

(d) The NT does not distinguish between Jesus' word and that of the → apostles in the sense that "he who hears you hears me" (Lk. 10:16; cf. Matt. 10:40; Jn. 13:20; Gal. 4:14; and also Mk. 9:37.; Matt. 18:5; Lk. 9:48). The apostles are fully authorized witnesses of Jesus. The word which Jesus spoke has been reliably handed on by those who heard it (Heb. 2:3). To hear the message is to hear Christ and to hear the word of truth (Eph. 1:13; 4:20 f.) or the word of God (Acts 13:7, 44 etc.). Where this hearing leads to faith, → baptism is the natural consequence (Acts 16:32 f.; 18:8; 19:5).

3. We also find in the NT the OT connection of hearing with doing. In the

Sermon on the Mount Jesus appears as the expounder of the will of God revealed in the law. His word is more than the word which was spoken to the men of old (Matt. 5:21). In his teaching the authority given to him is expressed. It is an authority which marks his essential difference from the scribes (Matt. 7:28 ff.; Mk. 1:22). Therefore, in the parable which concludes the Sermon on the Mount the Lord compares the man who hears and does his word with a man who builds his house on rock (Matt. 7:24 ff.). In Lk. 11:28 Jesus pronounces a blessing on those who hear and keep (*phylassein*, → Guard) his word. Jn. 10:16, 27 refer to the sheep who hear Jesus' voice and follow it. In Rom. 2:13 Paul contrasts the doers of the law with the hearers (*akroatai*). The mere hearers are unbelieving Jews, who do not let the law point them to Christ; the doers, according to the context, are believing pagans who demonstrate that the works of the law are written in their hearts (2:14 f.; cf. Jer. 31:33). Similarly in Jas. 1:22 f. the doers of the word are contrasted with the hearers. For the NT understands → faith not merely as hearing but as obeying (→ *hypakouō, hypakoē*). Doing the will of God, therefore, can only come about from this fundamental attitude of obedience.

([Ed.] In Mk. 12:29 f. Jesus cites the *Shema* (Heb. *š̌ema'*, "Hear") or creed of Israel recited daily by the pious Jew which consisted of Deut. 6:4–9; 11:13–21; Num. 15:37–41. The passages themselves declare that the Israelite was to be in daily, constant remembrance of his obligation to love God with his whole being. The words quoted by Jesus are: "Hear, O Israel: the Lord our God, the Lord is one; and you shall love the Lord your God with all your heart, and with all your soul, and with all your mind, and with all your strength." The quotation largely follows the LXX, though *ischys* (strength) is substituted for *dynamis* (power) and the Heb. text has *lēḇāḇ* (heart) which is paraphrased in Mk. by two nouns *kardia* (heart) and *dianoia* (mind). Jesus quoted the Shema in response to a question by a scribe: "Which commandment is the first of all?" (Mk. 12:28). Matt. 12:24–37 gives a parallel account of the same incident, though omitting Deut. 6:4. Moreover, in both accounts Jesus immediately added of his own accord a second commandment which was not in the Shema but drawn from Lev. 19:18: "The second is this, 'You shall love your neighbour as yourself.' There is no other commandment greater than these" (Mk. 12:31; cf. Matt. 22:39 which adds "On these two commandments depend all the law and the prophets" [v. 40]). Lk. 10:25–40 also contains a discussion of the two great commandments which also brings together Deut. 6:5 and Lev. 19:18. But there are certain significant differences: the occasion is different; in Matt. and Mk. it is Jesus who brings the two OT passages together in response to the scribes' question, whereas in Lk. it is a lawyer in response to Jesus' question; in Matt. and Mk. the centre of interest is the summary of the law, whereas in Lk. it is the practical outworking of the law expressed in the parable of the Good Samaritan that is the centre of interest. Such considerations have led T. W. Manson, *The Sayings of Jesus*, 1949, 259 f., and C. E. B. Cranfield, *The Gospel according to Saint Mark*, 1959, 376, to conclude that the two accounts are not parallel or doublets but refer to different occasions. On the debate about the great commandment → Command, art. *entolē;* → Large, art. *megas;* → Love.)

4. (a) Hearing the word does not always lead to faith, i.e. to the acceptance of the word of God (Mk. 4:16; Lk. 8:13). Understanding must be added to hearing if the sown seed of the word is to bear fruit (Matt. 13:23; 15:10). The contrary attitude

which does not understand the word heard and will not accept it results eventually in hardening (→ Hard). Therefore we find repeatedly in the NT, especially with respect to the Jewish nation, references to the sentence of hardening pronounced in Isa. 6:9 ff. (cf. Matt. 13:13 ff. par. Mk. 4:12, Lk. 8:10; Jn. 12:40; Acts 28:27; Rom. 11:8). In Jn. the Jews are plainly told that such hearing is in reality no hearing (Jn. 5:37; 8:43). This is what Stephen meant when he described the judges at his trial as "uncircumcised in heart and ears", and their subsequent behaviour bore out the accusation (Acts 7:51, 57). Even Jesus' disciples were not protected against failure to understand and hear (Mk. 8:17 f.). Similarly in Heb. believers are urgently warned, with reference to Ps. 95:8, against becoming hardened (Heb. 3:7-11; 4:3-11).

A contrast to this hardening is presented by the receptivity of those whose ears God has opened (Isa. 50:5) and who keep the word in a pure and good heart (Lk. 8:15). It is only to this kind of hearing that the mystery of the kingdom of God is revealed (Matt. 13:11 par. Mk. 4:11, Lk. 8:10). But although such hearing and understanding are God's gift, human activity is by no means excluded. We see this in the numerous and varied calls for attention: "He who has ears to hear, let him hear" (Matt. 11:15; 13:9 par. Mk. 4:9, Lk. 8:8); "Hear and understand" (Matt. 15:10); "Take heed what you hear" (Mk. 4:24); "He who has an ear, let him hear what the Spirit says to the churches" (Rev. 2:7, 11, 17, 29; 3:6, 13, 22).

(b) Jn. 5:25, 28 deals with hearing at the time of consummation; the dead in their graves will hear the voice of the Son of God, awakening some to the resurrection of life and others to judgment. The raising of Lazarus, whom Jesus called out of his grave with a loud voice (Jn. 11:43), is the anticipation of this final event.

5. Less is said in the NT about God's hearing than in the OT. The ears of God are mentioned twice in references to OT passages: Jas. 5:4, cf. Isa. 5:9; and 1 Pet. 3:12, cf. Ps. 34:16. Rev. 9:20 takes the statement that idols do not hear from the OT. But God hears those who are pious and do his will (Jn. 9:31). Believers may be confident that God hears their prayers when they are in accordance with his will (1 Jn. 5:14). Stephen's speech (Acts 7:34 quoting Exod. 3:7) refers to Israel's being heard in Egypt. *epakouō* occurs in the NT only in the quotation from the LXX of Isa. 49:8 (2 Cor. 6:2). *eisakouō* is used in the NT in the sense of to hear and answer only in the pass. In Lk. 1:13 and Acts 10:31 it refers to the hearing of the prayers of Zechariah and Cornelius. In Matt. 6:7 Jesus criticizes those who like the Gentiles hope to succeed in making their prayers heard by the multiplication of words. Heb. 5:7 deals with the hearing of Jesus' prayers. On several occasions Jesus expressed the certainty that God hears prayer (Matt. 7:7-12; Lk. 11:5-13; Jn. 16:23 f.). Heb. 5:7 f. speaks of the prayers Jesus offered "in the days of his flesh . . . with loud cries and tears" (referring to Gethsemane, cf. Matt. 26:36-46 par. Mk. 14:32-42, Lk. 22:40-46), adding that Jesus "was heard for his godly fear". Heb. sees the answer to these prayers in Jesus' exaltation as "the source of salvation to all who obey him" as high priest after the order of → Melchizedek (vv. 9 f.). This confirms the assurance, expressed in the story of Lazarus, that God always heard and answered Jesus (Jn. 11:41). Correspondingly, Jesus always heard God as his Father, and as mediator passed on the revelation which he had heard from his Father (Jn. 8:26, 40; 15:15). Christ's relationship with his Father has its deepest roots in this mutual hearing. *W. Mundle*

178

ὑπακούω	ὑπακούω (hypakouō), listen, obey; ὑπακοή (hypakoē), obedience; ὑπήκοος (hypēkoos), obedient.

CL & OT The vb. *hypakouō*, to listen to, answer, obey (which is derived from *akouō*) was used in secular Gk. from Homer on with the dat. of the person or thing, and also (as in the LXX) with the gen. of the person. The specialized meaning to open (to answer a request for entrance) occurs in Xenophon, Plato and other writers. The noun *hypakoē*, obedience, is rare and appeared late in secular Gk. (6th cent. A.D.). The adj. *hypēkoos*, obedient, is attested from the 5th cent. B.C. The LXX uses *hypakouō* mostly to render Heb. *šāma'*. Obedience is shown to men (Gen. 16:2; 22:18), to wisdom (Sir. 4:15; 24:22), and to God (e.g. Jer. 3:13, 25). In Isa. 50:2; 66:4 *hypakouō* translates Heb. *'ānâh*, answer. In Isa. 65:24 (with the *v.l. ek-*) it denotes God's answer to human crying. The noun *hypakoē* also means an answer (2 Sam. 22:36, the only instance in the LXX). The adj. *hypēkoos*, obedient is used in Deut. 20:11 of subject peoples, and in Prov. 4:3; 13:1 of a son's obedience to his father.

NT 1. In Acts 12:13 *hypakouō* means to open in the sense of "answering the door".

Elsewhere the word group (vb. 21 times, noun 15, most frequently in Paul) denotes obedience. The pattern of this obedience is Jesus Christ of whom it is said that he was obedient unto death on the cross (Phil. 2:5, 8). Through his obedience, which stands in contrast to Adam's disobedience, "the many" have been made righteous (Rom. 5:19). Heb. has a similar thought. Through his suffering Jesus learned obedience; thus he has become the source of eternal salvation to those who obey him (5:8 f.). His obedience to his Father does not exclude his being the Lord whom the demonic powers and the forces of nature obey (Mk. 1:27; 4:41 par. Matt. 8:27, Lk. 8:25).

The apostle Paul, on the other hand, sought to bring every thought captive in obedience to Christ; Christ is the highest authority over human reason (2 Cor. 10:5). The obedience we render to Christ is the obedience of faith. As an apostle to whom has been committed the preaching of the glad good news Paul made it his aim to establish this obedience among the nations (Rom. 1:5; 16:26). He has this obedience in view in Rom. 15:18 and 16:19. It includes submission to the apostle through whom Christ speaks (2 Cor. 7:5; 13:3; 10:5 f.; Phlm. 15). It is obedience to the preaching which brings righteousness (Rom. 6:16 f.), and to the truth (1 Pet. 1:22). 1 Pet. 1:2 and 14 also refer to this obedience: Christians are "children of obedience", because this obedience must embrace their whole lives.

2. The use of the noun corresponds to that of the vb. Apart from Phil. 2:8, where it refers to Christ, the adj. *hypēkoos* also occurs in 2 Cor. 2:9 and Acts 7:39. Paul found in the Philippians (Phil. 2:12) the obedient attitude which he had expected from the Corinthians (2 Cor. 2:9). He had to warn the Thessalonians to have nothing to do with those who would not obey the apostolic instructions (2 Thess. 3:14). Besides those who obey the message of faith (Acts 6:7) there are those who refuse to obey the gospel (Rom. 10:16; 2 Thess. 1:8). Beneath all this lies the understanding of faith as an act of obedience. Moreover, obedience to Christ cannot be separated from obedience to his messengers and to the message they proclaim. Such obedience must work itself out in the life of the Christian. Christians are hindered by obeying the sinful passions of the body (Rom. 6:12). From

179

obedience to the Lord it follows that one must submit willingly to earthly authorities, parents and masters; and these too must of course acknowledge the Lord Christ as the highest authority (Eph. 6:1–9; Col. 3:18–20). As an example and a warning from the OT, Acts 7:39 mentions the Israelites who refused obedience to Moses (Num. 14:3 f.). In contrast, Heb. 11:8 names Abraham as an example of believing obedience (cf. Gen. 12:1–8). *W. Mundle*

→ Command, → Disciple, → Faith, → Law, → See, → Word

(a). D. Bonhoeffer, *The Cost of Discipleship*, 1959⁶; R. Bultmann, *Jesus and the Word*, 1934, 53–75; *Theology of the New Testament*, I, 1952, 314 ff.; D. Daube, *Civil Disobedience in Antiquity*, 1972; C. H. Dodd, *Gospel and Law*, 1951; J. Horst, *ous, TDNT* V 543–59; G. Kittel, *akouō, TDNT* I 216–25; R. N. Longenecker, "The Obedience of Christ in the Theology of the Early Church", in R. Banks, ed., *Reconciliation and Hope* (Leon Morris *Festschrift*), 1974, 142–52; W. Michaelis, *horaō TDNT*V 315–82; P. S. Minear, *The Obedience of Faith, SBT* Second Series 19, 1971; H. R. Moehring, "The Verb *akouein* in Acts 9, 7 and 12, 9", *NovT*3, 1959, 80 ff.; C. F. D. Moule, "Obligation in the Ethic of Paul", in W. R. Farmer, C. F. D. Moule and R. R. Niebuhr, eds., *Christian History and Interpretation: Studies Presented to John Knox*, 1967, 389–406; O. Procksch, *legō, TDNT* IV 91 ff.; R. Schnakenburg, *The Moral Teaching of the New Testament*, 1965; A. Stöger, "Obedience", *EBT* II 616–20.
(b). H. von Campenhausen, "Recht und Gehorsam in der ältesten Kirche", *ThBl* 20, 1941, 279 ff.; R. Deichgräber, "Gehorsam und Gehorchen in der Verkündigung Jesu", *ZNW* 52, 1961, 119 ff.; E. von Dobschütz, "Die fünf Sinne im Neuen Testament", *JBL* 48, 1929, 378 ff.; J. Gnilka, "Zur Theologie des Hörens nach den Aussagen des Neuen Testaments", *Bibel und Leben* 2, 1961, 71 ff.; S. Gross, "Der Gehorsam Christi", *Geist und Leben* 29, 1956, 2–11; R. Gyllenberg, "Glaube und Gehorsam", *ZSTh* 4, 1937, 547 ff.; E. Kamlah, "*hypotassesthai* in den neutestamentlichen 'Haustafeln' ", in O. Böcher and K. Haacker, eds., *Verborum Veritas. Festschrift für Gustav Stählin*, 1970, 237–44; J. Kaufmann, *Der Begriff des Hörens im Johannesevangelium*, Dissertation, Gregorian University, Rome, 1969–70; O. Kuss, "Der Begriff des Glaubens im Neuen Testament", *ThG* 27, 1935, 695 ff.; K. Lammerts, *Hören, Sehen und Glauben im Neuen Testament*, 1966; W. Mundle, *Der Glaubensbegriff des Paulus*, 1932, 29 ff.; K. H. Schelkle, *Die Passion Jesu in der Verkündigung des Neuen Testaments*, 1949; A. Schlatter, *Der Glaube im Neuen Testament*, 1927⁴, 611 f.; *Gottes Gerechtigkeit*, 1935, 316 f.

Heart

κaρδία

καρδία (*kardia*), heart; *καρδιογνώστης* (*kardiognōstēs*), knower of hearts; *σκληροκαρδία* (*sklērokardia*), hardness of heart.

CL *kardia* was used in secular Gk. in literal and metaphorical senses. On the one hand, it denoted the heart as an organ of the body and the centre of physical life (particularly in Aristotle). On the other hand, it was regarded as the seat of the emotions and the source of spiritual life in general. Used in specific senses with reference to nature, it meant the pith of wood and the seed of plants. *kardia* also had the general sense of centre, the innermost part (of men, animals or plants).

Especially in Homer and the tragedians, *kardia* received a considerably extended range of meaning. It not longer indicated merely the centre of the body but also the intellectual and spiritual centre of man as a whole.

(a) *kardia*, the seat of the emotions and feelings, of the instincts and passions. In this context the Greek thought of emotions like joy and sadness, courage and cowardice, strength and fear, love, hatred and anger (Homer, *Il.* 21, 547).

(b) Homer, in particular, brought together the heart and reason without clearly separating thought and feeling. (*Il.* 21, 441). From this point it is only a short step to seeing the heart as the centre of man's will and as the seat of his power of decision (*Il.* 10, 244).

OT The OT uses *lēḇ* and *lēḇāḇ* for heart. *lēḇ* occurs in the older strata and *lēḇāḇ* does not appear until Isa. The OT also uses heart in the two meanings, lit. and metaphorical. The LXX renders *lēḇ* predominantly by *kardia*, more rarely by *dianoia* (mind) and *psychē* (soul). The nuances of the concept are as clearly recognizable here as in the OT. *kardia* occurs predominantly in a general sense, referring to the whole man.

1. Viewed as a bodily organ, the heart is the seat of strength and of physical life (Ps. 38:10[11]; Isa. 1:5). When the heart is strengthened by food the whole man is revived (Gen. 18:5; Jdg. 19:5; 1 Ki. 21:7).

2. In the metaphorical sense *lēḇ* is the seat of man's spiritual and intellectual life, the inner nature of man. Here the close connection between spiritual and intellectual processes and the functional reactions of the heart's activity is particularly clearly seen. This explains the close contact between the concepts *lēḇ* and *nepeš* (→ Soul) which can even be used interchangeably (cf. Jos. 22:5; 1 Sam. 2:35; Deut. 6:5). In the OT *lēḇ* is also the seat of man's feeling, thinking and willing:

(a) The heart is the seat of the emotions, whether of joy (Deut. 28:47) or pain (Jer. 4:19), of tranquillity (Prov. 14:30) or excitement (Deut. 19:6), etc.

(b) The heart is the seat of the understanding and of knowledge, of rational forces and powers (1 Ki. 3:12; 4:29[MT 5:9]), as well as fantasies and visions (Jer. 14:14). But folly (Prov. 10:20 f.) and evil thoughts also operate in the heart.

(c) The will originates in the heart, also the carefully weighed intention (1 Ki. 8:17) and the decision which is ready to be put into effect (Exod. 36:2).

lēḇ, however, means less an isolated function than the man with all his urges, in short, the person in its totality (Ps. 22:26[27]; 73:26; 84:2[3]). It is "a comprehensive term for the personality as a whole, its inner life, its character. It is the conscious and deliberate spiritual activity of the self-contained human ego" (W. Eichrodt, *Theology of the Old Testament*, II, 1967, 143). Here OT usage contrasts with that of secular Gk., for there the heart, with all its differentiations of meaning, has only one function within the system of spiritual and intellectual processes.

3. Since the idea of responsibility is particularly related to the heart, "that which comes out of the heart is quite distinctively the property of the whole inner man, and therefore makes him, as a consciously acting ego, responsible for it" (W. Eichrodt, op. cit., 144). Since, in the OT, the only corrective to this responsibility of man is to be found in Yahweh, the heart is also the organ through which man, either as godly or as disobedient, meets God's word and acts. It is the seat of awe and worship (1 Sam. 12:24; Jer. 32:40); the heart of the godly inclines in faithfulness to the law of God (Isa. 51:7), that of the ungodly is hardened and far from God (Isa. 29:13). It is in the heart that conversion to God takes place (Ps. 51:10, 17[12, 19]; Joel 2:12).

4. The kidneys (Heb. *keláyôṯ*; Gk. *nephros*, only in plur.; in the NT only Rev. 2:23, citing Jer. 11:20) are frequently mentioned in close connection with the heart. They are – in the metaphorical sense – the seat of the deepest spiritual emotions and motives (Ps. 7:9[10]; 26:2; Jer. 17:10; 20:12; cf. 1 Sam. 24:5[6];

25:31; *lēḇ*, → conscience), so secret that men cannot fathom them. Only God is able to search and test them.

5. (a) Philo and Josephus use "heart" exclusively as a bodily organ, the central part of physical life, without clearly defining the seat of the inner life. Philo leaves open the question of whether the *hēgemonikon*, the controlling reason, is to be found in the heart or in the brain, though he shows many echoes of OT usage. The metaphorical sense, which predominates in the OT, drops very much into the background, especially in Josephus.

(b) On the other hand, Rab. Judaism – like the OT – can speak of the heart as the centre of life, even of life before God, of the good and evil thoughts that dwell in the heart, but also of the worship of God which the heart offers (prayer; cf. e.g. Sifre Deut. 41). (On Philo, Josephus and Rab. Jud. see J. Behm, *kardia*, *TDNT*, III 609 ff.)

NT The NT use of *kardia* coincides with the OT understanding of the term, just as much as it differs from the Gk. The meaning of heart as the inner life, the centre of the personality and as the place in which God reveals himself to men is even more clearly expressed in the NT than in the OT. In passages where OT would have used heart in the sense of person, NT often uses the personal pronoun (e.g. Matt. 9:3; 16:7; 21:25, 38; 2 Cor. 2:1). Nevertheless *kardia* occurs in 148 passages in the NT: in Paul 52 times; the Synoptics 47; Acts 17; Catholic Epistles 13; Heb. 10; Jn. 6 and Rev. 3 times.

1. (a) *kardia* as the centre of physical life and man's psychological make up. *kardia* occurs relatively seldom in the sense of the bodily organ, the seat of natural life (Lk. 21:34; Acts 14:17; Jas. 5:5). By contrast, it more frequently denotes the seat of intellectual and spiritual life, the inner life in opposition to external appearance (2 Cor. 5:12; 1 Thess. 2:17; cf. 1 Sam. 16:7). The powers of the → spirit, → reason, and → will have their seat in the heart in the same way as the movements of the → soul, the feelings, the passions and the instincts. The heart stands for man's ego. It is simply the person ("the hidden person of the heart", 1 Pet. 3:4).

(b) *kardia* as the centre of spiritual life. The most significant instances of *kardia* in the NT occur in those passages which speak of man's standing before God. The heart is that in man which is addressed by God. It is the seat of doubt and hardness as well as of faith and obedience.

A striking feature of the NT is the essential closeness of *kardia* to the concept *nous*, mind. *nous* can also have the meaning of person, a man's ego. Heart and mind (*noēmata*, lit. thoughts) can be used in parallel (2 Cor. 3:14 f.) or synonymously (Phil. 4:7). In such cases the element of knowledge is more heavily emphasized with *nous* than with *kardia*, where the stress lies more on the emotions and the will (R. Bultmann, *Theology of the NT*, I, 1952, 222). Thus it is the person, the thinking, feeling, willing ego of man, with particular regard to his responsibility to God, that the NT denotes by the use of *kardia*.

2. Sin marks, dominates and spoils not only the physical aspects of natural man, not only his thinking and willing, feeling and striving as individual elements, but also their source, man's innermost being, his heart. But if the heart has been enslaved by sin, the whole man is in bondage. Evil thoughts come from the heart (Mk. 7:21 pár. Matt. 15:19). Shameful desires dwell in the heart (Rom. 1:24).

The heart is disobedient and impenitent (Rom. 2:5; 2 Cor. 3:14 f.), hard and faithless (Heb. 3:12), dull and darkened (Rom. 1:21; Eph. 4:18). Referring to his opponents, Jesus quoted the prophet Isaiah, "Your heart is far from me" (Mk. 7:6; par. Matt. 15:8). Equally he rebuked his disciples for their lack of faith and their hardness of heart (Mk. 16:14; cf. Lk. 24:25, 32). Neither can the Gentiles excuse themselves before God, for they carry in their hearts the knowledge of what is good and right in God's sight (Rom. 2:15; → Covenant, art. *diathēkē;* → God, art. *theos* NT 4(b)).

"The heart is deceitful above all things, and desperately corrupt; who can understand it?" Jeremiah's complaint (17:9) voices the view of the NT also. No man can understand his heart, let alone change it. Man without God lives under the power of sin, which has taken up its abode in his heart and from this vantage point enslaves the whole man.

3. God alone can reveal the things hidden in the heart of man (1 Cor. 4:5), examine them (Rom. 8:27) and test them (1 Thess. 2:4). Because corruption stems from the heart it is there that God begins his work of renewal. *kardia* is "the place where God deals with man . . . that part of a man . . . where, in the first instance, the question for or against God is decided" (Gutbrod). Just as the heart is the seat of faithlessness, it is also the seat of faith (Rom. 10:6–10). In Rom. 2:5 the human heart is described as *ametanoētos,* impenitent. Hence "it is apparent that penitence (*metanoia,* change of mind) is a matter of the "heart" (*kardia*) (Bultmann, op. cit., I, 221). Conversion takes place in the heart and is thus a matter of the whole man. God's word does not simply capture the understanding or the emotions, but it pierces the heart (Acts 2:37; 5:33; 7:54).

This conversion of the heart to → faith is not achieved through the will or desire of the human heart (1 Cor. 2:9), but solely because God opens a man's heart (Acts 16:14) and lets his light illumine the heart (2 Cor. 4:6). God bears his witness to man by sending into his heart the Spirit of his Son (2 Cor. 1:22). When this Spirit takes up his dwelling in the heart, man is no longer a slave to sin, but a son and heir of God (Gal 4:6 f.). God pours his love into his heart (Rom. 5:5). Through faith Christ can take up residence in the heart (Eph. 3:17).

4. The heart of man, however, is the place not only where God arouses and creates faith. Here faith proves its reality in obedience and patience (Rom. 6:17; 2 Thess. 3:5). Here the word of God is kept (Lk. 8:15). Here the peace of Christ begins its rule (Col. 3:15). God's grace strengthens and establishes the heart (Heb. 13:9). The NT describes a heart directed unreservedly to God as a "pure heart" (Matt. 5:8; 1 Tim. 1:5). This purity of heart is based solely on the fact that the blood of Christ cleanses it (Heb. 10:22; cf. 1 Jn. 1:7), and Christ dwells in it by faith (Eph. 3:17).

5. Two further related words which occur in the NT must be mentioned here.

(a) *kardiognōstēs* is unknown to secular Gk. and to the LXX, and occurs in the NT only in Acts 1:24 and 15:8 and later in patristic writings. It describes God as the knower of hearts. The fact that God sees, tests and searches the hidden depths of the human heart is commonly stated in both the OT and the NT (1 Sam. 16:7; Jer. 11:20; 17:9 f.; Lk. 16:15; Rom. 8:27; 1 Thess. 2:4, Rev. 2:23, cf. above OT, 3). This belief in the omniscience of God is expressed succinctly by the adj. *kardiognōstēs.*

183

(b) *sklērokardia*, unknown in secular Gk., occurs in the LXX in Deut. 10:16; Sir. 16:10; Jer. 4:4 (Heb. equivalent *'orlāṯ lēḇāḇ*). Otherwise it is found only in the NT (Mk. 10:5 par. Matt. 10:8; Mk. 16:14; similarly Rom. 2:5) and in patristic writers. Hardness of heart is the closedness of the self-centred man to God, his offer and demands, and also to his fellowmen. The natural man has a stony heart, turned against God and his neighbour, until God's intervention gives him a new, obedient heart (cf. Ezek. 36:26 f.). *T. Sorg*

→ Body, → Hard, → Head, → Man

(a). J. B. Bauer, "Heart", *EBT* I 360–63; C. A. Briggs, "A Study of the Use of *lēḇ* and *lēḇāḇ* in the Old Testament", in *Semitic Studies in Memory of A. Kohut*, 1897, 94–105; R. Bultmann, *Theology of the New Testament*, I, 1952, 220–27; F. Baumgärtel and J. Behm, *kardia* etc., *TDNT* III 605–14; R. C. Dentan, "Heart", *IDB* II 549 f.; R. Jewett, *Paul's Anthropological Terms*, 1971; A. R. Johnson, *The Vitality of the Individual in the Thought of Ancient Israel*, 1949; L. J. Kuyper, "The Hardness of Heart according to Biblical Perspective", *SJT* 27, 1974, 459–74; J. Pedersen, *Israel*, I–II, 1926, 99 ff.; K. Rahner, *Theological Investigations*, III, 1967, 321–52; D. M. Stanley, " 'From his heart will flow rivers of living water' (Jn. 7:38)", *Cor Jesu*, I, 1959, 507–42; H. W. Wolff, *Anthropology of the Old Testament*, 1974, 40–58.

(b). J. M. Bover, "Das heilige Herz Jesu im Neuen Testament", *Zeitschrift für Askese und Mystik* 13, 1938, 285–301; G. E. Closen, "Das Herz des Erlösers in den heiligen Schriften des Alten Bundes", *Zeitschrift für Askese und Mystik* 18, 1943, 17–30; J. Doresse, "Le Coeur", *Études Carmélitaines* 29, 1950, 82–97; B. de Gerardon, "Le coeur, la bouche, les mains. Essai sur un schème biblique", *Bible et Vie Chrétienne* 1, 4, 1953, 7–24; A. Guillaumont, "Les sens du noms du coeur dans l'antiquité", *Le Coeur: Études Carmélitaines* 29, 1950, 41–81; P. Joüon, "Locutions hébraïques avec la préposition *'al* devant *lēḇ*, *lēḇāḇ*", *Biblica* 5, 1924, 49–53; M. Koehler, *Le Coeur et les Mains*, 1962; F. H. von Meyenfeldt, *Het Hart (lēḇ, lēḇāḇ) in Het Oude Testament*, 1950; F. Nötscher, *Gotteswege und Menschenwege in der Bibel und in Qumran*, Bonner Biblische Beiträge 15, 1958; G. Pidoux, *L'Homme dans l'Ancien Testament*, 1953; H. Rahner, *Cor Salvatoris*, 1954, 19–45; H. Rusche, "Das menschliche Herz nach biblischem Verständnis", *Bibel und Leben* 3, 1962, 201 ff.; N. Schmidt, "Anthropologische Begriffe im Alten Testament", *EvTh* 24, 1964, 374–88; F. Stolz, *lēḇ*, *THAT* I 861–67.

Heaven, Ascend, Above

Man has always contrasted heaven with his earthly environment (→ Earth). To the physical relationship there has also corresponded a metaphysical one. As well as being a spatial term, heaven became a general expression for everything that has power over man, the domain of gods and spirits. The Gk. word *ouranos* includes both aspects, the firmament and the abode of God (cf. the difference between sky and heaven in Eng.). Sometimes it is replaced by the purely formal *anō*, above (in opposition to *katō*, below; → Hell). The vb. *anabainō* is used in a purely technical sense, especially of the ascent to the temple mountain, to the sanctuary, and also of Jesus' exaltation and ascension (→ Height).

ἀναβαίνω	ἀναβαίνω (*anabainō*), go up, mount up; καταβαίνω (*katabainō*), descend; μεταβαίνω (*metabainō*), pass over.

CL *anabainō* is found from Homer on. The root-word, *bainō*, which is absent from the NT, means to go, walk (the NT substitutes *erchomai*; → Come). The compound *anabainō* indicates movement towards a destination: to go up, mount up, ascend, grow up. The spatial meaning predominates; one climbs a mountain, mounts a platform, goes upstairs. If the destination is a holy place, the going up involves performance of some cultic act. A man goes up to the temple (situated on a higher level) to pray; the mystic is promised ascent to the world of the gods, heaven or Olympus (*Mithraic Liturgy* 10, 22).

ot In the LXX *anabainō* most frequently renders ʿā*lâh* (go up, ascend, climb) and
is used particularly of going up to the mountain of God, the sanctuary and Jerusalem (Exod. 34:4; 1 Sam. 1:3; 2 Ki. 19:14). In Gen. 28:12 Jacob's dream pictured a "ladder", or more precisely a ramp or stair-like pavement, which, in accordance with the ancient concept of the world, led up to the gate of heaven. This was the place where intercourse between the earth and the upper divine world took place. God's messengers were going up and down, "fulfilling divine commands or supervising the earth" (G. von Rad, *Genesis*, 1961, 279; → Babylon). In Jon. 2:7 descent into the underworld signifies condemnation and death, and ascent signifies pardon and life.

nt 1. The NT retains the basic spatial sense: to climb a mountain, or go up to
Jerusalem for the Passover (Lk. 2:4; 18:10; Jn. 7:8 ff.; Acts 3:1; Gal. 2:1). *anabainō* occasionally denotes the growth of plants (Matt. 13:7; so also occasionally in the LXX, cf. Gen. 41:5), and metaphorically the rise of ideas (Lk. 24:38; 1 Cor. 2:9) and the ascent of prayers to God (Acts 10:4).

2. The specific cultic connotation fades in the Synoptics behind a more general spiritual meaning. When Jesus came up out of the water of the Jordan or climbed a mountain, his ascent was the prelude to some action on the part of God. Thus Jesus received the → Spirit after his baptism, cf. also instances of prayer, teaching, healing and calling (Matt. 3:16 par. Mk. 1:10; Matt. 5:1; 14:23; 15:29; Mk. 3:13; Lk. 9:28).

3. Jn. uses *anabainō* as a fixed expression for the ascent of the Son of man (similarly Acts 2:34; Rom. 10:6 f.; Eph. 4:8). In this sense the vb. is complemented by *katabainō*, descend. Both concepts describe a movement which originates from heaven and is directed towards the earth, and vice versa. The stress is not on some kind of journey to heaven; the decisive element is Jesus' going from and to God. This is naturally expressed in the spatial categories of the ancient world concept. Christ, as the pre-existent Logos (→ Word), bridges the gulf between heaven and earth and becomes man (Jn. 3:13; cf. Prov. 30:4; Jn. 6:33, 38, 41 f.). With his elevation on the cross he ascends "where he was before" (Jn. 6:62). His descent reveals the Father's love; his ascent God's sovereign power. In his descent Jesus is the revealer; in his ascent the perfecter through whom his people receive the fatherhood of God and the brotherhood of the Son (Jn. 20:17). In his descent and ascent he bridges the gulf between God and the world, between light and darkness. Some scholars see in this a background of gnostic ideas, but if so they are ignored in the presentation of Jesus as the Word become flesh (Jn. 1:14; → Height, art. *hypsoō*). (On this cf. L. Morris, *The Gospel according to John*, 1971, 222 ff. with R. Bultmann, *The Gospel of John*, 1971, ad loc., and *Theology of the New Testament*, I, 1952, 37, 166 ff.)

The → Son stands in a permanent relationship to the → Father, which is described with the help of the vision of the ascending and descending angels (Jn.

185

1:51; cf. Gen. 28:12). Thus in the earthly presence of the Son of man descent and ascent are repeated, in that his thoughts are derived from the Father and his acts are directed to the Father.

4. (a) *metabainō* (pass over) is used in Jn. to describe the passage from death to life. As Jesus crossed the frontier in his elevation on the cross, so man does in the obedience of faith. The believer passes over into the risen Christ's sphere of life (Jn. 5:24; 13:1; 1 Jn. 3:14).

(b) *katabainō* also denotes the eschatological arrival of the *kyrios* (→ Lord) and the heavenly → Jerusalem (1 Thess. 4:16; Rev. 3:12; 21:2, 10). But already God's good and life-giving gifts are coming down to us, above all his trustworthy word that we should be a kind of first fruits of his creatures (Jas. 1:17 f.). Similarly Jesus is the living bread which has already come to us from God himself and been made a present reality (Jn. 6:50, 58).   *B. Siede*

5. The ascent and descent of Christ is referred to in Eph. 4:8 ff. in connection with a discussion of unity and gifts in the church. V. 8 alludes to Ps. 68:18 [LXX 67:19; MT 68:19]: "Therefore it is said, 'When he ascended on high he led a host of captives, and he gave gifts to men' " (RSV). There are, however, certain obvious differences from the Ps. The latter is in the 2nd per. sing. and refers to receiving and not giving gifts: "Thou didst ascend the high mount leading captives in thy train, and receiving gifts among men, even among the rebellious, that the LORD God may dwell there" (RSV). The verse "alludes to the homage before God when, returning from a war, he has occupied his throne to receive the voluntary or enforced gifts of homage rendered to him" (A. Weiser, *The Psalms*, 1962, 488). E. K. Simpson relates it specifically to David's capture of the Jebusite fortress (2 Sam. 5:6 f.) which became his capital, → Jerusalem, and the ascent of the ark there (cf. 2 Sam. 6:15 f.; also Ps. 24). The idea of giving rather than receiving gifts is supported by the Syriac version of the OT (the Peshitta) and the Targum or Aramaic paraphrase of the Pss., where the passage is interpreted of Moses' ascent of Sinai to receive the law. (This may have been influenced by the reference to Sinai in the preceding verse. In later Judaism Pentecost was regarded as the anniversary of the giving of the law.) Eph. 4:8 is probably best regarded not as a direct quotation from the OT as a prophecy of the bestowal of gifts, but as an interpretative gloss on the Ps. explaining what God is doing *now* in contrast with the situation described in the Ps. The introductory words "Therefore it is said" render the Gk. *dio legei*, lit. "therefore ... says", with the subject understood. The same expression occurs again in Eph. 5:14 introducing a quotation which is not to be found in scripture (cf. also Rom. 15:10; 2 Cor. 6:2; Gal. 3:16). It is possible that "scripture" should be supplied as subject as in Rom. 10:11. But as neither Eph. 4:8 nor Eph. 5:14 are verbatim quotations it seems more likely that "God" (or the Spirit) is to be understood as the subject and what follows is what God is now saying to the church. In other words, the Ps. has now to be read in the light of the descent and ascension of Christ which has brought about a reversal of the situation in which the victors received gifts from the vanquished.

The argument goes on to state that the words "he ascended" imply that "he had also descended into the lower parts of the earth" (v. 9). The latter may be taken as either (i) Hades (→ Hell; cf. Acts 2:25–35; cf. Ps. 16:10); (ii) the tomb

($\rightarrow$ Bury); or (iii) the earth, the gen. being a gen. of definition. The ascent is fulfilled in the resurrection and ascension (cf. Phil. 2:8), the ultimate purpose of which is "that he might fill all things" (v. 10; cf. 1:23; Col. 2:9; $\rightarrow$ Fullness). The gifts that are then enumerated as the result of the ascension might at first sight appear as an anticlimax. They are seen in terms of the gift to the church of apostles, prophets, evangelists, pastors and teachers (v. 11). But in the context of the argument God's ultimate purpose for mankind is growth in personal maturity in Christ (vv. 12–16, cf. 1 ff.). These gifts are directly related to that growth, for they carry on the ministry of Christ to the church (cf. v. 7).

For further discussion of this passage see F. F. Bruce, *The Epistle to the Ephesians*, 1961, 81 ff.; E. K. Simpson and F. F. Bruce, *The Epistles to the Ephesians and the Colossians*, 1957, 91 f.; B. Lindars, *New Testament Apologetic*, 1961, 52 ff., who sees Eph. 4:8 as an instance of *midrash pesher* deliberately modifying the text; cf. also E. E. Ellis, *Paul's Use of the Old Testament*, 1957, 144.　　　　*C. Brown*

ἄνω

ἄνω (*anō*), above, upwards, up; ἄνωθεν (*anōthen*), from above; κάτω (*katō*), below, downwards, down.

CL *anō*, lit. above, upwards, earlier in time. It can describe land or mountains in contrast to the sea, or the sky and heaven in comparison with the earth, or even the earth in contrast to the underworld (F. Büchsel, *anō*, TDNT I 376; Liddell-Scott, 169).

OT Judaism emphasized strongly the contrast between above and below, i.e. between heaven as God's sphere and the earth as man's. On the other hand, there is a parallelism between what exists above and what exists and happens on earth. Thus, as heaven cannot exist without the twelve constellations, earth cannot exist without the twelve tribes. Similarly God studies the Torah in heaven as men do on earth (SB II 116). In this case, that which is above is prior in time.

Stimulated by Hel. ideas, Philo worked out an extensive speculation on above and below (cf. *Rev. Div. Her.* 70; *Gig.* 22; *Som.* 1, 139). But this did not prove significant either for Jud. or the NT. Philo saw the upper and lower worlds as divided into levels. The lowest level is the material, and on the highest God stands. The sky forms as it were a spiritual material, the transitional level between the upper and lower worlds. (For examples of gnostic cosmology see W. Foerster, *Gnosis: A selection of Gnostic Texts*, I, 1972; II, 1974.)

NT In the NT there are no cosmological speculations which set God and the world in radical opposition, attributing the latter to some other deity. God is the Creator and Lord of the whole world. Nevertheless, there is a contrast in so far as a distinction is drawn between the holy God and the sinful world.

Jesus lifted up his eyes, i.e. towards heaven, where God dwells according to the ancient world concept (Jn. 11:41; cf. Acts 2:19). In contrast to his enemies who are "from below [*katō*]", from this sinful $\rightarrow$ world, he is "from above [*anō*]" i.e. from God, to whom he will return (Jn. 8:23; cf. 13; cf. L. Morris, *The Gospel according to John*, 1971, 446 f.).

In Gal. 4:25 f. there is a reference to → "Jerusalem above," which is free and is the mother of Christians, in contrast to the present Jerusalem, which, with her children subject to the law, is in slavery.

The "upward call" which Paul presses towards is the call of God in Jesus Christ (Phil. 3:14). Correspondingly Paul encourages his readers to "seek the things that are above". This is more narrowly defined by a reference to the fact that Jesus Christ is seated at the right hand of God (Col. 3:1 f.; → Hand, art. *dexios*). On *anōthen* → Birth, art. *gennaō*. *H. Bietenhard*

οὐρανός

οὐρανός (*ouranos*), heaven; οὐράνιος (*ouranios*), heavenly; ἐπουράνιος (*epouranios*), heavenly; οὐρανόθεν (*ouranothen*), from heaven.

CL *ouranos*, heaven, possibly related to an Indo-European root meaning water, rain, means that which moistens or fructifies. The related adj. *ouranios* means what is in heaven, comes from heaven, or appears in the heavens, i.e. heavenly. But it can also mean what is appropriate to a god, i.e. divine, and can even stand for god or the deity. On the other hand, it can mean simply that which belongs to the firmament or sky. *epouranios* means in heaven, belonging to the divine heaven.

1. *ouranos* is found in Gk. from Homer on meaning the vault of heaven, the firmament. Viewed as that which embraces everything, *ouranos* is divine. In pre-Homeric religious myth Uranus (in its Latinized form) derived from the → earth, Ge, which he impregnated in a holy marriage. According to the myth, Uranus was castrated and deposed as a god by Cronus the son of Uranus and Ge. But the image of the god Uranus remained alive until imperial times. In Orphic mythology heaven derived from the upper half of the cosmic egg. According to Homer, the (brazen, iron) heaven rests on pillars which Atlas carries. In heaven dwell the → gods, the immortal *ouranioi* or *epouranioi*, above all Zeus. One also finds in Gk. writing the idea of a heavenly garment.

In the Gk. enlightenment the old mythological concepts dissolved; *ouranos* became simply the firmament, and *ouranios* was applied to phenomena appearing in this firmament. In Plato heaven can be equated with the → all, the cosmos (→ Earth). The starry heavens viewed as the dwelling place of the gods became the starting point for the investigation of existence and absolute knowledge. Hence Plato used *ouranios* to denote what really is and what is truly coming to be. The Stoics understood heaven as the outermost layer of the ether, and then also as the directing world principle. In Gk. the expression "earth and heaven" can denote the whole world. (See further H. Traub, *TDNT* V 498 ff.)

2. In gnostic systems the *ouranioi*, the heavenly ones, have a body and are transitional beings of a supernatural nature. (See further *TDNT* V 501; W. Foerster, op. cit., see indexes.)

OT 1. *The OT concepts of heaven*. (a) In the OT concepts of heaven there are many links with ancient oriental ideas. The underworld (→ Hell, art. *hadēs*), → earth (art. *gē*) and heaven together form the cosmic building. The scant references suggest the picture of the flat disc of the earth, surrounded by the ocean, above which heaven or the firmament forms a vault like an upturned bowl or a hollow

188

sphere. Above this there is the heavenly ocean (Gen. 1:8; Ps. 148:4–6). According to the ancient oriental view, there are many other heavenly spheres beyond the firmament which is visible from the earth. Such concepts are echoed in the expression "the heaven of heavens" (Deut. 10:14; 1 Ki. 8:27; Ps. 148:4). The OT, however, lacks a single, definitive and comprehensive cosmogony (→ Creation; and cf. A. Heidel, *The Babylonian Genesis*, 1963²).

The OT understanding of the world is throughout sober and rational, even if there are occasional echoes in poetical language of ancient mythological ideas. Thus heaven is said to have windows (Gen. 7:11; 2 Ki. 7:2) through which the waters restrained by the firmament can pour. Heaven rests on pillars (Job 26:11) or on foundations (2 Sam. 22:8). It is like a pitched → tent (Isa. 40:22; 44:24; Ps. 104:2). It is an unrolled scroll (Isa. 34:4; → Book, art. *biblos*) and can be torn (Isa. 64:1 [MT 63:19]). Together with the earth and the water under it, the heavens make up the universe (cf. Exod. 20:4; Ps. 115:15–17). But there is no word for universe in Heb. It is compared to a → house in which the heavens are like a loft (Ps. 104:3; Amos 9:6). In addition to the firmament, the air above the earth can also be called the heavens (e.g. Gen. 1:26; 6:7; → Demon, Air, art. *aēr*).

(b) Above the firmament there are the storehouses of snow, hail (Job 38:22), wind (Jer. 49:36; Job 37:9; Ps. 135:7), and likewise the waters (Ps. 33:7; Job 38:37) which return to heaven when it has rained (Job 36:27; Isa. 55:10).

(c) In the sense of horizontal expanse it is possible to speak of the four ends of heaven (Jer. 49:36; Zech. 2:6[10]; 6:5; Dan. 7:2). Man cannot ascend to heaven (Deut. 30:12; Prov. 30:4). The attempt to build a tower whose top will reach to heaven is arrogant folly which is punished (Gen. 11:4 ff.; → Babylon).

(d) Heaven is the embodiment of permanence (Deut. 11:21; Ps. 89:29[30]). On the other hand, prophetic preaching also refers to judgment on the heavens (Jer. 4:23–26; Isa. 13:13; 34:4; 50:3; 51:6); God's judgment is a cosmic catastrophe. Isaiah speaks of the creation of a new heaven (Isa. 65:17; 66:22).

(e) The "host of heaven" means the stars (Gen. 2:1; Deut. 4:19; Jdg. 5:20), or supernatural spiritual beings (1 Ki. 22:19; Job 1:6 ff.; → Spirit). This host is under a commander (Jos. 5:14); it has fiery horses (2 Ki. 2:11; 6:17). Under Assyrian influence the host of heaven became the object of worship, a practice against which the prophets protested (e.g. 2 Ki. 17:16; 21:3). In Deut. 4:19 the host of heaven is assigned to the peoples of the world for worship (cf. NEB).

(f) In the OT, however, heaven is never accorded any ruling function. This is shown, for example, in the fact that the stars in the firmament are merely lights which serve to divide up the calendar (Gen. 1:14). They are not, therefore, considered to be gods, or the manifestations or vehicles of gods. The ancient oriental viewpoint has, in this respect, been radically demythologized. Astrological ideas which elsewhere were richly developed in the East appear only on the periphery (Deut. 18:9 ff.; Isa. 47:13; Jer. 10:2).

(g) Ancient oriental concepts also lie behind the correspondence between the heavenly and the earthly, especially in the case of things which have a sacral value. Thus, in the priestly view, the Tabernacle was built following a heavenly model (Exod. 25:9, 40). Ezekiel speaks of a scroll which already pre-existed in heaven (Ezek. 2:9 ff.; cf. Isa. 34:5 on God's sword). The future, i.e. the whole eschatological order of salvation, is prefigured and already exists or has happened in heaven,

189

so that it precedes the earthly event (Zech. 2 f.). The → "Son of man," as the personification of the eschatological people of God, is already present in heaven (Dan. 7:13 ff.).

2. *Yahweh and heaven.* (a) More important for faith than these cosmological concepts is the statement that Yahweh created the heavens and the earth, i.e. the whole universe (Gen. 1:1; cf. Isa. 42:5; Ps. 33:6). Like the whole creation, the firmament and the heavens praise Yahweh (Ps. 19:1[2]). The heavenly beings praise Yahweh because of his acts, for everything that happens on earth reveals God's glory (Ps. 29:9; → Glory, art. *doxa*).

(b) Many interpret passages like Jdg. 5:4 f., Deut. 33:2 and Hab. 3:3, to mean that in an earlier period Yahweh was conceived as dwelling on Sinai from which he came and intervened in history, while later people believed that Yahweh dwelt on Zion (Amos 1:2; Isa. 8:18). But religious interest did not centre on Yahweh's dwelling, but on the God who deals with Israel and the nations. So apparently contradictory statements can stand side by side. In 1 Ki. 8:12–13 Yahweh is said to dwell in the darkness of the Holy of Holies, i.e. in the → Temple. 1 Ki. 8:27, on the other hand, says that the whole of heaven could not contain him.

(c) As Israel entered into deeper contact with Canaanite religion, it took from the cult of Baal an important expression which it assimilated to its own faith in Yahweh. Yahweh was now described as the God or king of heaven, and this title became in fact very popular (Ezr. 5:11 f.; 6:9 f.; 7:12, 21, 23; Dan. 2:18 f., 28, 37, 44; cf. Gen. 11:5; 24:3; Ps. 29:10). It could now be said that Yahweh, like the Canaanite gods, rides on the clouds (Deut. 33:26; Ps. 68:4[5]; cf. 18:10[11]; Isa. 19:1). As king of heaven, Yahweh had built his palace upon the heavenly ocean (Ps. 104:3). Like the Ugaritic father god, El, Yahweh was imagined as enthroned in heaven, surrounded by heavenly beings and taking → counsel with them (1 Ki. 22:19 ff.; Isa. 6:3 ff.; Job 1:6 ff.; Ps. 82:1; Dan. 7:9 ff.). It is remarkable how forcefully and how freely such originally foreign views could be accepted in Israel and transferred to Yahweh. The gods of the Canaanite pantheon had become Yahweh's servants. So Yahweh is the only God in heaven above and on earth below (Deut. 4:39; 10:14).

(d) This view of Yahweh as enthroned in heaven eventually obliterated completely the old view of the God of Sinai: Yahweh came down from his dwelling above the firmament (Exod. 24:9 ff.) to Sinai (Exod. 19:18). Above all according to the theology of Deut., Yahweh dwells in heaven and speaks from there (Deut. 4:36; 12:5, 11, 21; 26:15; etc.). Only his "Name" (*šēm;*→ Name) dwells on earth, according to this view, and that only in the → Temple in → Jerusalem. Further reflection still is revealed in the statement that all heaven cannot contain Yahweh (1 Ki. 8:27; Ps. 113:5 f.). Neither the visible nor the invisible world could enclose Yahweh, for they were after all both created by him. But in any case he is superior to them and does not allow himself to be confined in any way in them.

(e) Just as Yahweh is in heaven, his → Word which remains eternally has its place in heaven (Ps. 89:2[3]; 119:89). The godly man, praying in his need, complains that Yahweh is hidden (Lam. 3:4), and asks him to rend the heavens and come down (Isa. 64:1 [MT 63:19]). Yahweh who dwells in heaven is invoked in prayer (Deut. 26:15; 1 Ki. 8:30), while the suppliants raise their hands to heaven (Exod. 9:29, 33). The same thing happens at the taking of an oath (Deut. 32:40).

(f) It is possible for Yahweh to take chosen people to himself in heaven (Gen. 5:24; 2 Ki. 2:11; cf. Ps. 73:24). This is a particular favour and honour, for on the OT view heaven is not otherwise the place where the dead or the soul go (cf. → Hell, art. *hadēs*).

3. *The LXX and late Judaism.* (a) With few exceptions, *ouranos* in the LXX (667 times) always occurs as the rendering of *šāmayim*. It is in the plur., 51 times, a usage introduced through the LXX but unknown in secular Gk. It may be explained as translation Gk. (for the Heb. *šāmayim* is plur.) and as a plur. of completeness (above all in the Pss.). In later writings the frequency of the plur. increases considerably, indicating that the ancient oriental conception of several heavens had begun to have an effect (2 Macc. 15:23; 3 Macc. 2:2; Wis. 9:10; Tob. 8:5, etc.).

In Judaism the tendency to avoid the use of God's name became increasingly stronger (cf. Exod. 20:7). In its place substitutes were used, among them "heaven" (1 Macc. 3:18 f.; 4:10 f.; 12:15; Pirke Aboth 1:3, 11). Later even heaven was replaced (e.g. by *māqôm*, place). *ouranios* only occurs 9 times in the LXX, for the God of Israel (1 Esd. 6:15; → Lord, art. *kyrios*), his power (Dan. 4:23; → Might, art. *exousia*), the angels as a heavenly army (4 Macc. 4:11; cf. Lk. 2:13), and the children of God (2 Macc. 7:34). *epouranios* only occurs 7 times in the LXX.

(b) Contact with the intellectual climate of the ancient East resulted in a variety of cosmological speculations in pseudepigraphic and Rab. writings. In them apocalyptists and Rabbis undertake journeys to heaven and give revelations about things on the other side, but no generally binding doctrines about these things were ever arrived at. Some apocalyptic writings know only of one heaven (Eth. Enoch, 4 Esd., Syr. Bar.). Others speak of three heavens (Test. Lev. 2 f., according to the original text), of five heavens (Gr. Bar.). Sl. Enoch, Test. Abr., and Rab. tradition speak of seven heavens. A further result of eastern influence is the doctrine that everything corresponds to an archetype and pattern in heaven, and that all earthly existence and events are prefigured in heaven (→ *anō*). Astronomical instruction is given allegedly as revelations from the → angels (Eth. Enoch 72–82; Jub.). But also we are shown all meteorological phenomena (rain, sun, etc.) coming from heaven, where they are kept in store-houses. Angels are set over both as controllers and supervisors.

(c) In certain writings → Paradise is located in heaven, either in the third (Sl. Enoch 8:1–8; Ass. Mos. 37), or especially in Rab. tradition in the seventh. Even → hell (art. *gehenna*) can be located in heaven. After death the righteous go to heavenly dwelling-places.

There are many traditions about the heavenly Jerusalem. Speculation was particularly concerned with God's throne in heaven (in connection with Ezek. 1 f.; Exod. 24:9–11; 1 Ki. 22:19 ff.; Isa. 6:1 ff.; Dan. 7:9 f.) and with the → angels in heaven, their names, classes and functions. It was believed that God was worshipped in a heavenly cultus, the archangel Michael sacrificed on a heavenly altar, and the heavenly beings sang songs of praise.

Finally, → Satan is also to be found in heaven. In connection with OT traditions he is viewed as the → accuser of men before God (cf. Job 1 f.), and also as an evil power opposed to God. Jewish traditions about the heavenly treasure-houses are important (→ Possessions, art. *thēsauros*). In them are kept, e.g., the good works

191

of men, and also the heavenly → books and tablets on which are written the fate of earthly beings. Also recorded are the → rewards and punishments that await the last → judgment.

(d) Philo combined Gk. and OT ideas. The *ouranos noētos*, the immaterial heaven of conceptual thinking present only in idea (*Spec. Leg.*, 1, 302; *Op. Mund.* 29; *Decal.* 102), must be distinguished from the *ouranos aisthētos*, the tangible heaven which must not be deified (*Op. Mund.*, 117). The visible heaven depends on both spiritual and earthly things. Heaven actualizes the unity of the whole cosmos. Philo speaks of the heavenly man as *ouranios*, a copy of God (*Op.Mund.*, 82). In so far as every man is a part of him, every man is also an inhabitant of heaven. Correspondingly Philo can talk about heavenly and earthly virtues. (See further H. Traub, *TDNT* V 502 f.)

NT In the NT *ouranos* occurs 272 times; most frequently in Matt. (82 times) especially in the phrase *basileia tōn ouranōn*, the → kingdom of heaven. *ouranos* occurs 34 times in the writings of Luke (of which 26 are in Acts); 18 times each in Mk. and Jn.; 21 times in Paul and 52 in Rev. Apart from Matt., it occurs mostly in the sing. *ouranios* occurs only 9 times, of which 7 are in Matt. in the phrases "your heavenly Father" (5:48; 6:14, 26, 32; 23:9) and "my heavenly Father" (15:13; 18:35). Behind this there lies an Aram. phrase which is translated in other passages (e.g. 18:19) by "my [your] Father in heaven." *epouranios* is found 18 times in the NT, of which 11 are in Paul, 6 in Heb. and one in Jn. In contrast to the very limited use of *ouranios*, *epouranios* is the adj. which was clearly preferred and which later prevailed.

1. *Conceptions of the world.* (a) The NT also presupposes ancient eastern world views. Rev. makes the most statements about heavenly beings and objects, but the interest is not cosmological but theological and soteriological. There is clearly no attempt to give definitive instruction about the geography of heaven as in certain Rab. writings (cf. above OT 3). In this context it is striking that there is never any mention of several heavens but only of one. The only passage in the NT which, in agreement with Rab. teaching, speaks of three heavens is 2 Cor. 12:2–4, but we are not given any more precise information (cf. P. E. Hughes, *Paul's Second Epistle to the Corinthians*, 1962, 432 ff.). As in the OT, the expression "heaven and earth" means the universe (Matt. 5:18, 34 f.; 11:25; 24:35; Lk. 12:56, etc.). Occasionally a reference to the sea is added, giving rise to a tripartite formula (Acts 4:24; 14:15; Rev. 14:7). Since, according to this world picture, heaven is "above" (→ *anō*), people raise their hands or their eyes towards it (Mk. 6:41 par. Matt. 14:18, Lk. 9:16; Mk. 7:34; Lk. 18:13; Jn. 17:1; Acts 1:11; 7:55; Rev. 10:5). The air can also be called heaven (Matt. 6:26; 16:2; 8:20; Mk. 4:32; Lk. 8:5; Acts 10:12; 11:6). In heaven, i.e. the firmament, are set the stars (→ Sun, Moon, Stars) which in eschatological discourse about the parousia fall to the earth (Mk. 13:25 par. Matt. 24:29; Lk. 21:25; Rev. 6:13; 8:10; 9:1; 12:4 → Present, art. *parousia*). Portents are seen in heaven (Rev. 12:1, 3; 15:1; → Miracle, art. *sēmeion*). Jesus refused to perform a miracle from heaven (Mk. 8:11 f. par. Matt. 16:1). On the other hand, the beast (→ Animal), as → Antichrist, performs such miracles (Rev. 13:13).

(b) There are → angels in heaven as messengers and servants of God (Matt. 18:10; Mk. 12:25; 13:32 par. Matt. 24:36; Eph. 3:15; Rev. 12:7; 19:1). They come from and return to heaven (Matt. 28:2; Lk. 2:15; 22:43; Gal. 1:8). They appear in the visions of John (Rev. 10:1; 18:1 etc.). → Satan is thrown out of heaven so that he may no longer → accuse Jesus' disciples (Lk. 10:18; Jn. 12:31; Rev. 12:12; cf. Isa. 49:13 LXX). At this, heaven and the martyrs in heaven rejoice (Rev. 18:20; 11:12; 7:14). It is at this point that a development begins in cosmological thinking which leads eventually to a fundamental difference between the late Jewish apocalyptic and the Christian views of heaven. Since Satan has been banished from heaven as the consequence of Jesus Christ's saving work, everything dark and evil vanishes from heaven, with the result that it becomes a world of pure light (thus in the post-NT writings which deal with the heavenly realm, e.g. Asc. Isa.). Where evil powers in heaven are mentioned, the reference is primarily to the air or to the firmament (Eph. 2:2; 3:10; 6:12; Acts 7:42). Their sphere of influence, therefore, is entirely this side of God's realm of light.

(c) In agreement with the OT it is stated that God created heaven and earth (Acts 4:24; 14:15; 17:24; Rev. 10:6; 14:7), and that he will re-create them (2 Pet. 3:13; Rev. 21:1). The present heaven is passing away like the earth (Mk. 13:31 par. Matt. 24:35, Lk. 21:32; Heb. 12:26; 2 Pet. 3:7, 10, 12; Rev. 20:11), but Jesus' words remain (Mk. 13:31 par. Matt. 24:35, Lk. 21:33). God is Lord of heaven and earth (Matt. 11:25; Acts 17:24; Matt. 5:34; Acts 7:49; cf. Isa. 66:1).

(d) God is said to dwell "in heaven", but there is never any evidence of reflection on the difficulties inherent in this statement. Occasionally God is referred to by the OT expression "God of heaven" (Rev. 11:13; 16:11). Heaven itself is God's throne (Matt. 5:34), and God's throne is said to be in heaven (Acts 7:49; Heb. 8:1; Rev. 4 f.). It follows from this (in correspondence with Rab. terminology, see above OT 3 (c)) that heaven can be used as a substitute for → God (Matt. 5:10; 6:20; Mk. 11:30; Lk. 10:20; 15:18, 21; Jn. 3:27), especially in Matt. in the expression "the kingdom of heaven" (3:2, 4:17; etc.; → Kingdom).

It is more important theologically that God is called → "Father in heaven" (Matt. 5:16, 45; 6:1, 9; 7:11, 21; 10:32 f.; 12:50): in Christ God turns towards man. Because God is in heaven his revelation takes place from heaven (Matt. 11:27). At Jesus' baptism and at other crises in his earthly ministry God's voice was heard from heaven (Mk. 1:11 par. Matt. 3:17, Lk. 3:22; Jn. 12:28; cf. Heb. 12:25). The seer heard voices from heaven (Rev. 10:4, 8; 11:12; 14:13; 18:4; 21:3), and the Holy → Spirit came down from heaven (Mk. 1:10 par. Matt. 3:16, Lk. 3:21; Acts 2:2; 1 Pet. 1:12). But in the same way God's wrath goes forth from heaven: in the form of the fire of judgment (Lk. 17:29; cf. 9:54; Rev. 20:9), and in general upon all the ungodliness and unrighteousness of men (Rom. 1:18).

(e) According to Acts 14:17, God gives rain and fruitful seasons ouranothen, from heaven, implying both the physical and spiritual source. The only other occurrence of the word is in Acts 26:13, where it is used as an alternative to ek tou ouranou, from heaven (cf. Acts 9:3; 22:6). In period of drought heaven is considered to have been shut up at God's command (Lk. 4:25; Jas. 5:17 f.; Rev. 11:6).

(f) The NT also speaks of treasures of salvation in heaven. → Rewards (art. misthos) are in heaven (Matt. 5:12 par. Lk. 5:23). There is treasure in heaven (Matt. 6:20). The → names of the disciples are recorded in heaven (Lk. 10:20; cf. Heb. 12:23). Their → inheritance is there also (1 Pet. 1:4). Christians have a building (2 Cor. 5:1 f. oikodomē; cf. → House) and their citizenship or their home

(Phil. 3:20) in heaven. There is mention of a heavenly → Jerusalem which is the Christians' true home (Gal. 4:26; Heb. 12:22; Rev. 3:12; 21:2; 10), and even of a → temple in heaven (Rev. 11:19; but cf. 21:22).

2. *Christological statements.* (a) The statements about heaven are particularly important when they stand in relation to → Jesus Christ. At his baptism the heavens opened, the Holy → Spirit descended upon him and God the Father acknowledged him (Matt. 3:16 f.; cf. above 1 (d)): the eschatological events began in Jesus and in him God was near. Heaven was open above him because he himself was now the door of heaven and of God's house (Bethel) on earth (Jn. 1:51; cf. Gen. 28:12). Jesus taught his disciples to pray that God's will would be done on earth as in heaven (Matt. 6:10; → Prayer, art. *proseuchomai*). When Jesus gave authority to Peter or to the disciples, their actions were valid in heaven, i.e. with God (Matt. 16:19; 18:19; → Bind; → Open).

Because their guardian angels behold God's face, Jesus taught that little ones come under his special protection (Matt. 18:10; → Large, art. *mikros*). The Dead Sea Scrolls witness to belief in angels sharing in the community's worship (1QSa 2:9 f.) and in their rôle as guardians of the meek and needy (1QH 5:20 ff.; cf. D. Hill, *The Gospel of Matthew*, 1972, 275). The Jesus of Nazareth who stood before the Sanhedrin will sit at God's right hand (→ Hand, art. *dexios*) and come with the clouds of heaven (Mk. 14:62 par. Matt. 26:64, Lk. 22:69; cf. Ps. 110:1; Dan. 7:13). At the parousia the sign of the Son of man will appear in heaven (Matt. 24:30; → Son, art. *hyios tou anthrōpou*). The Son of man will gather his → elect from one end of heaven to the other (Mk. 13:27 par. Matt. 24:31; cf. Deut. 4:32; Zech. 2:6[10]). All power in heaven and on earth has been given to the Risen One (Matt. 28:18). He is the → Lord (art. *kyrios*) who has been raised to God's throne and to whom everything on earth and in heaven will pay homage (Phil. 2:10). He bestows the Holy Spirit from heaven and displays wonders and signs in heaven (Acts 2:17 f., 32–36). The Christian community is waiting for him to come to judge and to save (Phil. 3:20; 1 Thess. 1:10; 4:16; 2 Thess. 1:7). The disciple's task is to wait for the coming of the Lord, not to look up into heaven (Acts 1:10 f.). Heaven must receive Christ until the parousia (Acts 3:21). As the → Lamb (art. *amnos*) who has been exalted to God's throne, Christ has the power to open the sealed book and thus to set in motion the final phase of the world's history (Rev. 5:3, 5 f.). Therefore the whole of creation praises him (Rev. 5:11 ff.). This means, moreover, that Christ does not belong to the realm of the world, but to the realm of God. As the One who has come from heaven and returned there, Jesus Christ reveals himself as the true → bread (art. *artos*) from heaven, by means of which God bestows eternal life (Jn. 6:31 f., 38, 41 f., 50 f.; cf. Exod. 16:4, 13–15).

(b) As in the OT (Exod. 25:9), the earthly sanctuary in Heb. is a copy of the heavenly one. But as such it is only a shadow and the heavenly sanctuary is the only true and real one. This heavenly sanctuary is still, eschatologically speaking, to come (Heb. 8:5; 9:23 f.). Since Christ has entered the heavenly sanctuary, he has shown himself to be the true High → Priest (8:5). The Christian's calling to → faith is also *epouranios* (3:1; cf. Phil. 3:14). So too are the gifts, the eschatological salvation which Christians have tasted (6:4; 9:28). The homeland of the pilgrim people of God (11:16) and their Jerusalem, viewed as an eschatological → goal, are likewise *epouranios*, heavenly (12:22).

According to Heb., Jesus' exaltation (1:3; 8:1; → Height) signifies the fulfilment of his high priestly office. He has passed through the heavens and has been raised higher than they (4:14; 7:26; 9:11, 23 f.), since he has reached the very throne of God. There he has performed his real, true priestly service (8:1 f.), at the same time fulfilling and surpassing that of the OT. One cannot say in detail what cosmological perspectives underlie this statement. However, it seems clear that God is thought of here as not dwelling in heaven, i.e. not within his creation to which heaven of course belongs, but above or beyond the heavens. This idea is the outcome of reflection, although even here God's transcendence over his creation is still expressed in spatial terms.

(c) Certain special emphases are to be found in Eph. and Col. Christ is not only the agent of → creation (cf. 1 Cor. 8:6): primitive Christianity had no special belief in creation apart from belief in Christ. Christ was before anything created came to be, and he himself was not created (Col. 1:16). Christ is the instrument, the agent and the goal of creation; without him nothing can exist. Special emphasis is laid on the fact that everything, including the heavenly powers, was created "in Christ" and has been reconciled through him (Col. 1:15–23). The very heavenly powers were created solely for Christ (Col. 1:16; cf. 1 Cor. 15:24: Christ will destroy the heavenly powers). Christ is → head over all principalities and powers (cf. Col. 2:20). (On the background ideas see R. P. Martin, *Colossians: The Church's Lord and the Christian's Liberty*, 1972, 4–20.)

It is the exalted Christ who has penetrated all the heavenly spheres and come down to earth. He has broken through the barrier erected by the evil powers which isolated men from God (Eph. 1:10; 4:9; cf. Pss. 67:18[LXX]; 68:18[MT]; Rom. 9:5). Similarly Eph. 1:23 and 4:10 apply to Christ the OT statement that Yahweh fills heaven and earth. This is a consequence of the thought of Eph. 1:10 (cf. Col. 1:16, 20) that every created thing has its goal in Christ and has no independent existence apart from him. → Creation is strictly related to the redeemer and to → redemption. Creation and redemption, therefore, cannot be sundered in the gnostic fashion. Admittedly there are echoes of gnostic thought in the statement that heaven is filled with demonic powers which enslave men (Eph. 1:10–23; Col. 1:16 f.). The passages quoted, however, show equally that everything is understood as referring strictly to Christ (Col. 1:20), and creation is envisaged from the standpoint of redemptive history (Col. 1:16 f.).

Christ's exaltation (Phil. 2:9 f.) is expressed in Eph. 1:10 by means of the image of the primal man with → body and → head. Everything is bound together under Christ as head, whether on earth or in heaven (i.e. all the members of the body, the complete → "all"). There is no other realm but that of Christ. Eph. 3:15 puts it somewhat differently: heaven and earth are realms in which there are races or tribes (cf. Eth. Enoch 69:4; 71:1; 106:5; cf. the Rab. expression "higher families" for the angelic world) whose Father is God.

3. (a) In Jn. the word *ouranos*, heaven, only occurs in the sing. This is an indication that both gnostic and Jewish speculations about the heaven are absent. God's will to save and the salvation effected by Jesus Christ determine the statements about heaven. Jesus comes from heaven and returns there. In principle the Son of man who has come down from heaven has much to say about heaven (*epourania*) and the plans of God concealed there. But such statements would call forth an

even smaller response of faith than those he makes about God's present activity on earth (Jn. 3:12 f., 31 f.).

(b) 1 Cor. 15:40 refers to the bodily form of heavenly beings – whether stars or angelic powers. Christ, the pre-existent, risen and coming One, is the heavenly → man, whose image, i.e. whose bodily form, Christians will receive at the parousia (1 Cor. 15:48 f.). All beings, even the heavenly ones, will bow the knee before the risen and exalted Jesus Christ (Phil. 2:10 f.). God has raised Jesus to his right hand, *en tois epouraniois* (from *ta epourania*, a circumlocution for heaven), i.e. in heaven, and thus blessed Christians with spiritual blessing (Eph. 1:3, 20). For spiritually they have already risen with Christ and been exalted to heaven (Eph. 2:6; cf. Ps. 110:1). The manifold wisdom of God will be made known to the principalities and powers in heaven (Eph. 3:10; the same phrase as above): the saving work of Christ has cosmic significance. According to 2 Tim. 4:18, Christ's kingdom is *epouranios*, i.e. it possesses heavenly authority and glory, and it is therefore superior to every temptation and persecution which the apostle has to suffer. *H. Bietenhard*

→ Angel, → Demon, → Hand, → Height, → Hell, → Kingdom, → Myth, → Satan

(a). K. Barth, *CD* III 3, 369–531; J. S. Bonnell, *Heaven and Hell*, 1956; P. G. Bretscher, "Exodus 4:22–23 and the Voice from Heaven", *JBL* 87, 1968, 301–11; R. Bultmann, *The Gospel of John*, 1971; J. G. Davies, *He Ascended into Heaven: A Study in the History of Doctrine* (Bampton Lectures, 1958), 1958; W. Eichrodt, *Theology of the Old Testament*, I, 1967, 186–209; T. H. Gaster, "Heaven", *IDB* II 551 f.; D. K. Innes, "Heaven and Sky in the Old Testament", *EQ* 43, 1971, 144–48; J. N. D. Kelly, *Early Christian Creeds*, 1951; R. Koch, "Ascension", *EBT* I 37–42; K. Lake, "The Ascension" and "The Mount of Olives and Bethany" in F. J. Foakes Jackson and K. Lake, eds., *The Beginnings of Christianity*, V, 1923, 16–22, 475 f.; A. T. Lincoln, "A Re-Examination of 'the Heavenlies' in Ephesians", *NTS* 19, 1972–73, 468–83; W. A. Meeks, "The Man from Heaven in Johannine Sectarianism", *JBL* 91, 1972, 44–72; J. Michl, "Heaven", *EBT* I 363–69; W. Milligan, *The Ascension and Heavenly Priesthood of our Lord*, 1898; H. Odeberg, *The View of the Universe in the Epistle to the Ephesians, Lunds Universitets Årsskrift* N. F. Avd. 1, Band 29, Nr. 6, 1934; G. von Rad and H. Traub, *ouranos, TDNT* V 497–543; J. Schneider, *bainō, TDNT* I 518–23; C. Schoonhoven, *The Wrath of Heaven*, 1966; U. Simon, *Heaven in the Christian Tradition*, 1958; W. M. Smith, *The Biblical Doctrine of Heaven*, 1968; and "Heaven", *ZPEB* III 60–64; L. I. J. Stadelmann, *The Hebrew Conception of the World*, 1970, 37–125; H. B. Swete, *The Ascended Christ: A Study in the Earliest Christian Teaching*, 1910; G. Widengren, *The Ascension of the Apostle and the Heavenly Book*, 1950.

(b). G. Bertram, "Die Himmelfahrt Jesu vom Kreuz", *Festgabe für A. Deissmann*, 1927, 187–217; H. Bietenhard, *Die himmlische Welt im Urchristentum und Spätjudentum, WUNT* 2, 1951; H. Diels, "Himmels- und Höllenfahrten von Homer bis Dante", *Neue Jahrbücher des klassischen Altertums*, 50, 1922, 239–52; R. Eisler, *Weltman telund Himmelszelt*, 1910; T. Flügge, *Die Vorstellung über den Himmel im Alten Testament* 1937; G. K. Frank, *Himmelund Hölle*, 1970; H. Gebhardt, "Der Himmel im Neuen Testament", *Zeitschrift für kirchliche Wissenschaft und kirchliches Leben* 7, 1886, 555–75; H. Grass, *Ostergeschehen und Osterberichte*, 1970⁴; J. Haecke, J. Schmid, J. Ratzinger, *LTK* V 352–58; J. Heller, "Himmelund Möllenfahrt nach Römer 10, 6–7", *EuTh* 5, 1972, 478 ff.; R. Holland, "Zür Typik der Himmelfahrt", *ARW* 23, 1925, 207–220; F. H. Kettler, "Enderwartung und himmlischer Stufenbau im Kirchenbegriff des nachapostolischen Zeitalters", *TLZ* 79, 1954, 358 ff.; A. Klawek, "Der Himmel als Wohnung der Seligen im neutestamentlichen Zeitalter", *Collectanea Theologica*, 13, 1932, 111–24; G. Lohfink, "Der historische Ansatz der Himmelfahrt Christi", *Catholica*, 17, 1963, 44 ff.; E. Lohmeyer, *Das Evangelium nach Matthäus, KEK* Sonderband, 1962³, 75 ff.; W. Michaelis, "Zur Uberlieferung der Himmelfahrtgeschichte", *ThBl* 4, 1925, 101–109; A. Oepke, "Unser Glaube an die Himmelfahrt Christi", *Luthertum*, 5, 1938, 161–86; G. Schille, "Die Himmelfahrt", *ZNW* 57, 1966, 183 ff.; H. Schlier, *Christus und die Kirche im Epherbrief, BHTh* 6, 1930; H. Westphal, "Jahves Wohnstätten", *ZAW* Beiheft 25, 1908, 251–73.

Height, Depth, Exalt

βάθος

βάθος (*bathos*), depth; βαθύς (*bathys*), deep.

CL 1. *bathos* is related linguistically to *bēssa* (Doric *bassa*), valley floor, cleft. There is also a close connection with *abyssos*, bottomless (lit. unfathomable; → Hell).

2. *bathos* expresses distance from the speaker, but not only downwards. It can be horizontal or even upwards. *bathos*, therefore, denotes the extension of a thing in any spatial dimension (cf. *bathos trichōn*, length of hair). In military usage *bathos* indicates the number of men standing behind one another. It is frequently used in conjunction with → *hypsos* to denote the full extent of an object in every dimension. Figuratively, *bathos* expresses: (a) the completeness, intensity, fullness or greatness of an object (especially in conjunction with *hypsos*), or of a human quality (wisdom, understanding, soul); and (b) inscrutability and hiddenness.

The derived adj. *bathys* has the same shades of meaning as the noun. The neut. form used as a noun, *to bathy*, means that which is deep-seated, that which comes from the bottom of the heart.

3. Hel. and especially gnostic religion took up the figurative meaning in speaking of the depth of deity and of → God as depth (Tert., *Adv. Val.* 1; Iren., *Haer.* 1, 21, 2; Hippol., *Haer.* 5, 6, 4; cf. H. Schlier, *TDNT* I 517). This last expression indicates that God was thought of primarily as a-personal and not as "Thou" or "He", as something static and inscrutable and not as the Living One, the Self-Revealing.

OT 1. In the OT (LXX) *bathos* is used chiefly as equivalent of Heb. *mᵉṣûlâh*. In its lit. meaning *bathos* is used only of the depth of the sea (Exod. 15:5; Neh. 9:11; Zech. 10:11). In its fig. sense *bathos* always denotes that which is separated from God. *bathos*, therefore, stands for the inner need of the man troubled by guilt and → sin (Ps. 130[129]:1) and for the external need of pressing circumstances (Ps. 69:2,14[68:3,15]). *bathos* expresses the most extreme separation from God (the depths of the sea, Jon. 2:4; Mic. 7:19) in passages where the frontier between literal and figurative meanings is fluid. In Ezek. *bathos* stands for *taḥtî* and thus for the underworld (cf. 26:20; 31:14, 18; 32:18 f., 24). Here, too, *bathos* expresses separation from God. Heb. *maᵃᵃmaqqîm*, depths, is also rendered in the LXX *bathos* (Isa. 51:10 etc.), while the adj. *bathys* is used for the words in the '*āmōq* group (cf. Job 11:8; 12:22; Ps. 63[64]:6; Prov. 18:4).

2. It is significant that Heb. *tᵉhôm* is not rendered *bathos* but *abyssos* (→ Hell). English versions nevertheless translate it by deep (cf. Gen. 1:2; Job 28:14). While *bathos* always contains the idea of separation from God, *abyssos* suggests a final, primeval, terrible and mysterious depth.

3. The Qumran texts speak of the depth of the mysteries of God (1QS 11:19; 1QM 10:11).

NT *bathos* appears 8 times in the NT; the adj. *bathys* 4. The literal sense occurs only in the Synoptics: depth of soil (Matt. 13:5 par. Mk. 4:5), the depth of the sea (Lk. 5:4). *bathys* is used figuratively in 2 Cor. 8:2 (deep poverty) to underline the extremity of the poverty. Elsewhere we find a figurative meaning related, not to the OT, but to Hel. and Rab. usage.

1. Rom. 11:33 and 1 Cor. 2:10 speak of the depth of God or the depth of the knowledge of God. This refers to the unfathomable nature of the ways and judgments of God, as opposed to the mere superficiality of human insight. But it also suggests the richness of the ways and means available to God in the pursuit of his plan of salvation. It is important that God is not reduced here to an impersonal "It". God is not described as the ultimate ground of all being, but as the One who has revealed himself in Jesus Christ in whom are hidden the ultimate mysteries. *bathos* reflects, therefore, the paradox of unveiling and veiling which is Christian → revelation.

2. Similarly, in Eph. 3:18 *bathos* occurs in conjunction with other spatial terms in order to express the comprehensiveness of God's grace and of salvation in Christ. Christian faith should not be satisfied with the fragmentary or the superficial.

3. On the other hand, in Rom. 8:39 *bathos* is linked with *hypsōma* (cf. Isa. 7:11), and clearly describes some kind of power which oppresses mankind. In astrology *bathos* is the part of heaven below the horizon from which the stars rise. Powers emanating from the stars are perhaps intended here. What is theologically decisive, however, is the statement that even the powers (of the stars) of the deep have been defeated by the power of the love of God in Jesus Christ – a statement of great relevance even today.

4. Of the four occurrences of the adj. *bathys* in the NT, only Rev. 2:24 is of theological significance (cf. Lk. 24:1; Jn. 4:11; Acts 20:9). Here the deep things of Satan are referred to, in parallel with the deep things of God. This takes up a slogan from a gnosticizing movement. What is meant is participation in all the ungodliness of this world (in order to "prove" the more effectively the power of grace and of salvation in Christ). To plunge into such depths, however, does not mean control over these powers but surrender to them and the consequent loss of salvation.

J. Blunck

ὕψος

ὕψος (*hypsos*), high; ὑψηλός (*hypsēlos*), high, exalted, proud; ὕψωμα (*hypsōma*), height, the exalted; ὕψιστος (*hypsistos*), highest, most exalted.

CL 1. *hypsos*, attested from Aeschylus on, denotes primarily extension upwards in space, height (only of things, not of people); figuratively (a) the superiority and exaltation of a thing or person over another; (b) unattainability. In the case of people *hypsos* could take the negative sense of → pride. In conjunction with → *bathos*, it denotes the complete dimensions and aspects of an object.

2. The adj. *hypsēlos*, attested from Homer on, was also originally spatial in meaning: high (buildings, plants, position), and was used figuratively in both a positive (sublime) and a negative sense (pompous, high-sounding). Secular Gk. had many compounds of *hypsēlos*, but none came into the NT. Instead, there is a new formation, *hypsēlophroneō*, to think highly (of oneself), to be proud (only 1 Tim. 6:17).

3. *hypsōma* is first attested in late Gk. after the translation of the LXX, meaning height, exaltation, what is exalted. It was always used in figurative senses, e.g. in Plutarch as an astrological term for the closest approach of a star to the zenith (opposite, *tapeinōma*) (Arndt, 858).

OT In the LXX *hypsos* stands for a variety of Heb. words (*qōmâh, mārôm, gāḇah*).
1. (a) It is used literally to denote the height of an object (the dark, Gen. 6:15 [LXX 6:16]; a mountain, 2 Ki. 19:23; Ps. 95 [LXX 94]:4; the Temple, Ezr. 6:3; a tree, Ezek. 31:14).

(b) Used absolutely, *hypsos* often denotes the heavenly realm (→ Heaven), the realm of God, that which is closely related to God (Heb. *mārôm*: Pss. 68:19 [LXX 67:18]; 102:20 [LXX 101:19]; 144[LXX 143]:7; Isa. 40:26; cf. Isa. 7:11; also frequently in the Qumran texts). It is thus the opposite of → *bathos* (that which is separated from God). Thus both *hypsos* and *hypsistos* (e.g. Gen. 14:18 f.; Ps. 17 [18]:13) can be simply a substitute for → God himself. (On *hypsistos* see Arndt, 858.)

(c) In relation to men, *hypsos* in Isa. 2:17 stands for human pride. In 1 Macc. 10:24 it has the sense of encouragement.

2. (a) The adj. *hypsēlos* occurs in the LXX in as great a variety of meanings as in secular Gk. (60 times for Heb. *bāmâh*; 43 times for derivatives of the root *gāḇah*; 31 times for *rûm*; 19 for *nāṭâh*). Used as a noun, it acquired special significance. More emphatic than *hypsos*, it denotes the realm of God (Ps. 93[LXX 92]:4; Lam. 1:13), the place where God dwells (Isa. 33:5, 16; 57:15). The Spirit from on high (Isa. 32:15) is the Spirit of God.

(b) However, in a remarkable reversal of this usage, the word is also used to translate Heb. *bāmôt*, the Canaanite shrines and pagan high places (Jer. 19:5; 2 Chr. 14:2; 17:6; Ezek. 6:3).

NT 1. *hypsos* in the spatial sense occurs only in Rev. 21:16 in the description of the measurements of the new Jerusalem. Similarly *hypsēlos* is used literally in Matt. 4:8; 17:1; Mk. 9:2 and Rev. 21:10, 12 of mountains and walls. In these contexts the dimensional aspect is uppermost, but there are symbolic overtones.

2. (a) In accord with OT usage, both words serve to denote the realm of God or his dwelling (Lk. 1:78) to which Jesus is exalted (Eph. 4:8 citing Ps. 68:19, → Heaven, art. *anabainō*; Heb. 1:3; cf. Ps. 110:1) to sit at God's right → hand interceding for men (cf. Heb. 9:24). Even in the figurative meaning the spatial concept – in accordance with the ancient view of the world – still remains in the background (→ Heaven). But it is not primary, for it has been transcended by the non-spatial. This is seen most clearly in Heb. 7:26. *hypsēlos* here acquires the meaning of the wholly other in contrast to what man and the cosmos can conceive.

In gnostic systems the thought is of the place, the sanctuary of God, beyond the heavenly spheres, which are filled with → angels and powers. This may be compared with the Epistle to the Hebrews where the exaltation of Christ is pictured in terms of the Day of Atonement ritual (cf. chs. 9–10 with Lev. 16). Having penetrated these heights, the high-priest Jesus Christ has been installed to exercise his sovereignty. In this exaltation he experiences fulfilment because of his obedience in suffering, which reached its climax in Jesus' sacrifice of himself on the cross (→ *hypsoō*). "But, above all, the doctrine of the sanctifying sacrifice on the cross is fitted into a scheme of thought in which the going up to heaven is the really important event. In the Epistle to the Hebrews this going up to heaven corresponds to the High Priest's going into the Sanctuary. This however cannot be done without a sacrifice. Thus the sacrifice on the cross opens to the new High Priest the way to heaven" (E. Schweizer, *Lordship and Discipleship*, 1960, 72).

(b) Lk. 24:49 speaks of power from on high. Here likewise *hypsos* is a periphrasis for → God and stands on the same footing as Rab. formulae for avoiding the Divine Name. The same is true of *hypsistos*, the Highest (e.g. Lk. 1:32, 35, 76; Acts 7:48). Acts 13:17 also reflects OT ideas (cf. Exod. 6:6). The arm is an expression of the might and power of God. Describing this arm as *hypsēlos*, raised, stretched out, is a vivid way of expressing the idea that God's power is not in repose but in action.

3. (a) In Jas. 1:9 *hypsos* appears in contrast with *tapeinōsis* (→ Humility, art. *tapeinos*), and is therefore best rendered "exaltation" (RSV; cf. "high position", Arndt, 858). The passage refers to the salvation already given and yet still to come in Christ which paradoxically reverses all human relationships and in the faith exalts those who are lowly. The poor man (which in Jas. is a religious term virtually synonymous with Christian) is to hold fast here and now to this eschatological exaltation by faith.

(b) On the other hand, since this exaltation is not something the Christian earns for himself for a quality which he possesses in himself but is Christ's gift to him, he can be commanded not to think of himself as *hypsēlos* (Rom. 11:20) but to associate with the lowly (Rom. 12:16). Since exaltation is the work of God, every personal desire for exaltation is an abomination to him (Lk. 16:15).

4. The NT use of *hypsōma* probably reflects astrological ideas (see CL 3), and hence denotes cosmic powers. Rom. 8:39 and 2 Cor. 10:5 are both concerned with powers directed against God, seeking to intervene between God and man. They are possibly related to the *stoicheia tou kosmou*, the elemental powers of this world, (cf. Col. 2:8, 20). However high and mighty they may seem, they are to be strenuously resisted (2 Cor. 10:5) in the knowledge that not even they can separate the Christian from Christ (Rom. 8:39).   *J. Blunck*

| ὑψόω |

ὑψόω (*hypsoō*), exalt, raise; ὑπερυψόω (*hyperhypsoō*), raise above all heights.

CL For etymology → *hypsos*. The idea of exaltation played an important role in the myths which were a part of the religious background of the OT. This is illustrated by the concept of exaltation in the Babylonian creation epic, Enûma Elish (*c.* 1000 B.C.; cf. A. Heidel, *The Babylonian Genesis*, 1963²; *ANET*, 60–72) which begins "When above the heaven had not (yet) been named". The mythological introduction to the work describes the struggle of the Babylonian god Marduk with the gods of chaos (the sea-dragon, Tiamat, and the primal usurper of divine sovereignty, Kingu). The victorious Marduk created the material world out of the divided halves of Tiamat and men out of the blood of Kingu. He is therefore raised in the assembly of the gods to the position of sovereignty over the world. He then correspondingly raises his earthly representative, Hammurabi, and installs him as ruler over men.

A text from the Egyptian king myth (14th cent. B.C.) which belongs to the coronation liturgy of the god-king, also related how pharaoh Thut-mose III was raised by the sun god Rê himself to the realm of light, and there crowned and installed as the god's son (cf. *ANET*, 373 ff.).

The significance of exaltation is different in the Babylonian myths of Adapa (A. Heidel, op. cit., 147–53; *ANET*, 101 ff.) and Etana (*ANET*, 114 ff.). Adapa was the man who worked his way up to heaven and could not obtain the food of life there. The enterprise foundered on the punitive justice of the gods, who reduce man to the confines appointed to him. In the myth of Etana, Etana tried in vain to reach Ishtar's throne in heaven on the back of an eagle which was under an obligation to him. His aim was to achieve immortality without dying. Both myths involve an attempt at exaltation through man's own efforts, whereas in the Babylonian creation myth and the Egyptian king myth the exaltation is the work of the gods.

ot *hypsoō* occurs 150 times in the LXX, standing 94 times for the Heb. *rûm* and its derivatives, 19 for *gābah* and its derivatives (9 out of 13 in Ezek.), 12 each for *gādal* and *nāśā'*. *hyperhypsoō* occurs about 50 times, and has a Heb. equivalent in only 4. The basic meaning is exalt (Pss. 18 [LXX 17]:46; 27 [LXX 26]:5, 6; 30 [LXX 29]:1; 34 [LXX 33]:3; 57 [LXX 56]:5, 11; 108 [LXX 107]:5; Exod. 15:2; Ezek. 28:2), be high (Pss. 89 [LXX 88]:13; 61 [LXX 60]:2); then by extension to stretch out (mostly of the hand, Isa. 23:4), to be loud (to raise the voice, Isa. 37:23; 52:8), to grow (Ezek. 31:4, 10), to bring up (Isa. 14:26), to be beautiful (Isa. 4:2; Ps. 89 [LXX 88]:16; EVV exalt, extol), to praise (Pss. 107 [LXX 106]:32; 118 [LXX 117]:28; EVV to exalt, extol). In the OT God alone has the right to exalt (and also to bring low, 1 Sam. 2:7). Man always runs the risk, therefore, of overreaching himself by self-exaltation. Thus in a few passages *hypsoō* acquires the meaning to be proud, haughty, presumptuous, arrogant (Pss. 37 [LXX 36]:20; 131 [LXX 130]:1, 2; Ezek. 28:5).

For the LXX, exaltation no longer has the same meaning as in the Babylonian and Egyptian myths. Nor does it have the same meaning as in the dualistic redemption teaching of Hel. syncretism, where in a mystical and mythological system the concept of exaltation achieved decisive importance (cf. especially the excellent essay by G. Bertram referred to in the bibliography). The following LXX usages are theologically significant.

(a) The exaltation of the righteous, i.e. of all those who in their extreme need through poverty, oppression, or deprivation of rights (→ Humility, art. *praÿs*) seek help from Yahweh alone (cf. Pss. 37 [LXX 36:34]; 89 [LXX 88:17]; 112 [LXX 111:9]). "In so far as it speaks of the exaltation of men, the LXX is concerned with a sociological question which as such is drawn into the light of revelation" (G. Bertram, op. cit., 71). The righteous man who encounters God experiences exaltation in his every-day circumstances lifting his life to a new plane. Thus the righteous man is promised a positive transformation of his present situation through Yahweh's intervention.

(b) The exaltation of God by the individual worshipper or the congregation. Behind this in the background is the liturgy for the festival of the god's enthronement in the Egyptian king myth which is important for the origin of the concept, but is no longer of any real significance. In the LXX the exaltation of God has already become a liturgical formula by which worshippers pay homage to God (e.g. Ps. 99 [LXX 98]:5, 9), and in which they acknowledge their loyalty to Yahweh as cosmic Lord above all other gods (cf. Ps. 97 [LXX 96]:9). Personal piety, however, also expresses itself by means of this liturgical formula: "magnify the Lord and let us exalt his name" (Ps. 34 [LXX 33]:3). In the OT the exaltation of Yahweh includes the exaltation of his people. The instalment of the earthly ruler in the enthronement Psalm corresponds to it (cf. Bertram, 50; cf. Ps. 148:14).

(c) Self-exaltation, i.e. the exaltation that man seeks to bring about in independence of the God who claims his obedience and provides for his needs (cf. Ps. 75 [LXX 74]:4, 5). By exalting himself and in self-gratification relying on his own strength, man places himself in opposition to God and calls forth Yahweh's humbling intervention (Ps. 75 [LXX 74]:7; Isa. 2:11, 17).

To sum up, the LXX, in so far as it relies on the MT, has taken over the concept of exaltation from the latter's religious environment, but has consistently demythologized it. Exaltation is a means of expressing God's saving activity in the realm of earthly affairs and of testifying to man's gratitude in worship and praise. Negatively it expresses man's disobedient self-assertion.

2. The apocalyptic writings of post-canonical Jewish literature were much more receptive to mythological ideas. Recalling Moses' ascent to the mountain of God, temporary exaltation, understood realistically or ecstatically, became in the apocryphal tradition the vehicle of divine revelations (cf. Eth.Enoch 39:3; 52:1; 89:52; 90:31; 2 Esd. 14:9, 49; Gr.Bar. 2 ff.).

The righteous are promised a place in → heaven at a final exaltation (Dan. 7:22; Syr.Bar. 13:3). Enoch's translation in the books associated with his name, during which he received his revelations close to God, plays a special role in this context. As son of man he is exalted to the highest heaven to the lord of spirits (Eth. Enoch 70 ff.).

The way of the righteous as it is described in Wis. 2: 10–20; 3: 7–10; 4:10 and 5: 1–5 is also particularly worth mentioning. The ungodly do violence to the righteous man because he boasts of knowing God. He is ill-treated and killed so that God may demonstrate whether he is his son. God exalts him, and men do not understand. At the final judgment the righteous will oppose his adversaries to their terror, and will receive the kingdom of glory. "The way of the righteous one depicted here is even in many details the way which Jesus has actually gone" (E. Schweizer, *Lordship and Discipleship*, 1969, 30).

3. Exaltation was understood differently in the mystery religions. Through the mysteries the way to exaltation was revealed to the soul, a way which the redeemer had trodden already. This way lead to a personal exaltation with the rebirth of the devotee. Here too exaltation received soteriological significance: it was the path to redemption which could be anticipated in ecstatic experience (→ Knowledge, art. *ginōskō* CL 2; on this subject see G. Wagner, *Pauline Baptism and the Mystery Religions*, 1967).

NT *hypsoō* occurs 20 times in the NT. It means to make great, as in Paul's speech in Acts 13:17 (the God, who made the people of Israel great in Egypt); to exalt (12 times as a contrast to bring low). The theologically important passages are those in which *hypsoō* denotes the exaltation of Jesus (6 times: Jn. 3:14; 8:28; 12:32, 34; Acts 2:33; 5:31).

1. Behind the sayings on self-abasement and self-exaltation (Matt. 23:12; Lk. 14:11; 18:14) lies the basic form of the two-part OT Jewish *māšāl* (cf. Job 22:29;

Prov. 29:23; Sir. 3:18; and also OT 1 (a)). The righteous, lowly, humble and suffering man is promised exaltation as a → reward. This teaching acquired a new significance in the context of the message of Jesus. Jesus put the whole of human life once more on the basis of obedience towards God (→ Hear). In so far as the Pharisees ascribed respect and honour to themselves, they were denying God the obedience of service. The true disciple must be ready to follow Jesus along the path of humility to suffering (cf. Lk. 14:27), in order selflessly to serve the despised, his neighbour. He is promised exaltation at the resurrection (Lk. 14:13 f.) and the fulfilment at the eschatological judgment of the promises made in the beatitudes (Matt. 5:1–12). This still future exaltation means justification before God in the final judgment on the ground of discipleship. However, the immediate present already takes on a new form for the disciple in anticipation. The man who exalts himself is the man who, having attempted to secure his life, will lose it in God's eschatological judgment (cf. Lk. 17:33; cf. also Lk. 1:52; 10:12, 15 par. Matt. 10:15). In their exhortations, therefore, 1 Pet. 5:6 and Jas. 4:10 warn Christians to submit to God (or to his → hand), in order to share in exaltation in the future → glory.

2. (a) The first christological statements, following the description of the way of the righteous in Israel, clearly see the resurrection and the exaltation of Jesus together. This is particularly plain in Acts 2:33 and 5:31 which describe as exaltation Jesus' resurrection and his installation as Lord (cf. 2:36). As these passages suggest a different emphasis to the Lucan theology of the ascension in Acts 1, we must be dealing here with earlier tradition. According to this tradition, the Easter event was *the* decisive event for salvation, because in it the crucified One was installed as Lord and Christ, i.e. exalted (Acts 2:36). Jesus' exaltation signifies the completion of God's action in his → anointed and at the same time the beginning, continuance and the expected fulfilment of Christ's Lordship over church and world.

(b) The concept of exaltation also occurs in the hymn quoted by Paul in Phil. 2:5–11 (2:9 *hyperhypsōsen*). Jesus' humiliation (vv. 6–8) is contrasted with his exaltation (vv. 9–11). His exaltation is the consequence of his obedience in suffering and consists in his designation as sovereign, not only over the community of believers but over the whole universe. In granting to Jesus the new name of → Lord (*Kyrios*), believers acknowledge in his exaltation Christ's victory, i.e. a transfer of authority over the universe (cf. Col. 1:19, 20). (On Phil. 2:5–11 → Empty, art. *kenos*; → Form, arts. *morphē* and *schēma*.) Similar statements expressed in different language occur frequently in the NT: e.g. Rom. 1:4 "designated [*horisthentos*] Son of God" (→ Determine, art. *horizō*); 1 Tim. 3:16 "taken up [*anelēmphthē*] in glory". In this exaltation (1 Tim. 3:16) "Jesus is 'vindicated'. This is also the oldest comment in which the Easter events constitute the justification of the way of Jesus. They demonstrate that Jesus was 'the Righteous One' " (E. Schweizer, op. cit., 65). Justification resulted in the victorious return to the Father and in the enthronement of the Saviour. "Here even more than in Phil. 2:9–11 it is emphasized that his dominion is so all-embracing that it has welded heaven and earth together again" (E. Schweizer, op. cit., 66).

(c) The concept of exaltation plays an important part in the christology of Jn., where it is used, as frequently in the OT, in parallel with glorification, *doxazō*

(→ Glory, art. *doxa*; e.g. Jn. 17:5 see above OT 1). The idea of exaltation plays a similar part in the christology of Heb., although the word *hypsoō* itself is not used (cf. 2:7 "crowned"; 1:9 "anointed"; 1:13; 10:12; 12:2 "seated at the right hand of God"; 5:5). Jn. takes over the idea of the exaltation of the righteous, as it had already appeared in the LXX but where it had been understood historically in terms of this world, or psychologically. But more particularly Jn. takes over the form of the idea present in Jewish apocryphal writing (Eth.Enoch, 2 Esd., Jub., Syr. Bar). and in Rab. literature, and corrects it. The object of this correction is to show that there is only *one* exaltation, the exaltation of Christ (3:14; 8:28; 12:32, 34). Like *anabainō* (→ Heaven), *hypsoō* is a periphrasis for the return of the revealer from the world to his heavenly home (cf. R. Bultmann, *The Gospel of John*, 1971, 152 f.). If, with E. Schweizer, we accept that Jesus saw himself as the → Son of man, in order in this one term to embrace the double nature of his activity as of this world in humiliation and suffering and as exalted in full authority and glory (op. cit., 41), then Jn. uses this idea consistently and already describes the crucifixion as the exaltation of Jesus (Jn. 3:14; 8:28; cf. 12:34). In a unique ambiguity the concept of exaltation is applied both to the physical act of being lifted up on the cross and to the exaltation to new glory, power and honour. This can only be understood on the basis of Jn.'s view of Jesus' death as the ultimate consequence and goal of his obedience. This means that in the eyes of the world, his goal is nothing more than the lifting up on the cross. "Yet they do not suspect that by 'lifting him up' they themselves make him their judge. The double-meaning of 'lifting up' is obvious. They lift Jesus up by crucifying him; but it is precisely through his crucifixion that he is lifted up to his heavenly glory as the Son of Man. At the very moment when they think that they are passing judgment on him he becomes their judge" (Bultmann, op. cit., 350). By contrast, the believer recognizes in Jesus' obedience unto death his complete oneness with the Father, and thus knows that the crucifixion is the return of the Son to glory, and redemption for the believer (Jn. 12:32). The lifting up on the cross, therefore, is the beginning of exaltation into the glory of the Father. The Johannine teaching on exaltation is Jn.'s counterpart to the realistic presentations of the ascension in the synoptics.

(d) The statements about the humiliation of God in Jesus Christ and his exaltation have affinities with views from the OT, from extra-canonical and Rab. Jewish writings and from gnostic thought. In the NT as in the OT exaltation is, however, understood not in terms of myth but of history. Despite the great variety of christological statements and developments in the NT, there is one essential concern which is contained in the concept of the exaltation of Jesus and is preserved in all the NT writings. It is that the crucified is the One whom God has called to life to be Lord of the dead and of the living (Rom. 14:9), who has conquered every power and dominion including sin and death, so that under his Lordship the company of believers may go on its way comforted. *D. Müller*

→ Heaven, → Hand, → Hell

(a). K. Barth, "The Exaltation of the Son of Man", *CD* IV 2, 3–377; G. Bertram, *hypsos* etc. *TDNT* 602–20; O. Cullmann, *The Christology of the New Testament*, 1959; E. Lohse, *Colossians and Philemon, Hermeneia*, 1971; G. H. C. Macgregor, "Principalities and Powers: the Cosmic Background to Paul's Thought", *NTS* 1, 1954-55, 17–28; K. H. Schelkle, "Exaltation", *EBT* I 242 f.; H. Schlier, *bathos, TDNT* I 517 f.; E. Schweizer, *Lordship and Discipleship*, 1960; P. H.

Vaughan, *The Meaning of 'bāmâ' in the Old Testament: A Study of Etymological Textual and Archaeological Evidence, Society for Old Testament Study Monograph Series 3*, 1974. On passages in the Psalms see the commentaries by A. A. Anderson, I–II (*New Century Bible*, 1972) and A. Weiser (*Old Testament Library*, 1962).

(b). G. Bertram, "Der religionsgeschichtliche Hintergrund der Erhöhung in der LXX", *ZAW* 68, 1956, 57 ff.; H. Bleienstein, "Der erhöhte Christus", *Geist und Leben* 27, 1954, 84–90; J. Daniélou, "La session à la droite du Père", in *The Gospels Reconsidered: A Selection of Papers read at the International Congress on the Four Gospels in 1957*, 1960, 68–77; W. Thüsing, *Die Erhöhung und Verherrlichung Jesu im Johannesevangelium, Neutestamentliche Abhandlungen* 21, 1, 1960; A. Vergote, "L'exaltation du Christ en croix selon le quatrième évangile", *Ephemerides Theologicae Lovanienses* 28, 1952, 5–23.

Hell, Abyss, Hades, Gehenna, Lower Regions

In speaking about the ultimate fate of the dead the Bible makes use of a variety of concepts. In some cases they are simply taken over under outside religious influence, but in others there has been a subsequent characteristic transformation. There is no unified picture of an unambiguously formulated doctrine, and the power of → death must also be seen in the light of the victory of the → cross. *hadēs* is the temporary abode of the dead, to which they are banished. It is not clear whether the rare term *katōteros* stands for the depths of the human world, threatened by death, or the depths of the realm of the dead itself. Judaism is the source of the two terms *abyssos* and *gehenna*. *abyssos* means a particular place of terror which constitutes a refuge for demons; *gehenna* is the eschatological fiery hell to which the ungodly will be eternally condemned at the last → judgment. → Heaven; → Life; → Paradise; → Time.

| ἄβυσσος |

ἄβυσσος (*abyssos*), abyss, pit, underworld.

CL & OT *abyssos* is really an adj., meaning bottomless, unfathomable. Used by itself with the noun *gē* (earth) understood, it means a bottomless place, hence abyss. In late Gk. the word stood for the primal deep, the primal ocean, the realm of the dead, the underworld.

It occurs about 25 times in the LXX, mostly to translate Heb. *tᵉhôm*, the primal ocean (Gen. 1:2), deep waters (Ps. 42:7 [LXX 41:7]), the realm of the dead (Ps. 71:20 [LXX 70:20]). Rab. Judaism also maintained the meaning primal flood for *tᵉhôm*. However, the word also stands for the interior of the earth, where bodies are found which cause uncleanness. The abyss also came to stand for the prison of fallen spirits (Eth.Enoch 10:4 ff.; 18:11 ff.; Jub. 5:6 ff.).

NT In the NT *abyssos* is the prison for → demons (Lk. 8:31; Rev. 9:1 f.). It is closed, but the smoke of subterranean fires rises from it (Rev. 9:1 f.). It is ruled by a prince – not → Satan (Rev. 9:11). Weird creatures emerge from it (Rev. 9:3 ff.), as does the beast (→ Animal; → Antichrist, Rev. 11:7; 17:8). Satan is bound in it for the thousand years' reign (Rev. 20:1, 3).

Rom. 10:7 f., following the LXX of Ps. 106:26 (MT 107:26), uses the word to describe the realm of the dead. It is impossible for a living man to descend into the *abyssos*.
H. Bietenhard

205

ᾅδης	ᾅδης (*hadēs*), Hades, the underworld, the realm of the dead.

CL The etymology of the word *hadēs* is uncertain. It either comes from *idein* (to see) with the negative prefix, *a-*, and so would mean the invisible; or it is connected with *aianēs*, and would have meant originally gloomy, gruesome.

hadēs occurs in Homer (in the form of *Aïdēs*) as the proper name of the god of the underworld (*Il.*, 15, 188), while in the rest of Gk. literature it stands for the underworld as the abode of the dead who lead a shadowy existence in it (cf. Hesiod, *Theog.* 455; Homer, *Od.* 4, 834). After Homer it can mean the grave, death. Only gradually did the Gks. also attach to the concept the ideas of → reward and → punishment. The good and the righteous were rewarded in *hadēs*, the wicked and the godless received a variety of punishments there. In cl. Gk. it is also spelled *Aïdēs* (Ionic), *Aïdas* (Doric).

OT 1. In the LXX *hadēs* occurs more than 100 times, in the majority of instances to translate Heb. *šeʾôl*, the underworld which receives all the dead. It is a land of darkness, in which God is not remembered (Job 10:21 f.; 26:5; Ps. 6:5; 30:9 [LXX 29:9]; 115:17 [LXX 113:25]; Prov. 1:12; 27:20; Isa. 5:14). These concepts cannot be squared exactly with that of the grave of the ancestors, the family burial place, where the dead are to be found. What is decisive is the theological statement that Yahweh does not remember the dead, that they are cut off from him and outside his activity in history (Ps. 88:5, 11[LXX 87:5, 11]). They also stand outside the cult and its influence. In death there is no proclamation or praise (Ps. 88:11 [LXX 87:11]; Isa. 38:18). The dead are unclean and therefore, in sharp contrast with surrounding religions, Israel's dead enjoyed no sacral worship. There was no cult of the dead, and necromancy was expressly forbidden (Deut. 18:11). The exceptional case of 1 Sam. 28:7 ff. and the mention of the raising of a dead boy (2 Ki. 4:32 ff.) suggest that there was no rigid divide between dead and living. But no one in Israel could comfort himself with the hope of one day being reunited with the departed. The shades themselves suffer under their decay (Job 14:21 f.).

On the other hand, *šeʾôl* not only lies on the border of life in the beyond. It also penetrates the circle of the living on every side, through illness, weakness, imprisonment, oppression by enemies and by death. Thus the psalmist in his prayers can say that he has already in a sense been in *šeʾôl*, but has been rescued by Yahweh. It was possible also for Israel to equate with *šeʾôl* the → wilderness, or at least to attribute the qualities of death to it (Jer. 2:6, 31). Wherever the voice of Yahweh is not heard or he abandons a man, there the reality of → death and *šeʾôl* begins (Job 12:24 ff.). Dying, therefore, is not a bio-physical process; it is the disintegration or ending of the life-relationship with Yahweh. Nevertheless, Yahweh's power does not cease at the frontier of the realm of the dead (Amos 9:2; Ps. 139:8 [LXX 138:8]), although he is not concerned about the realm of the dead. "The realm of the dead remained an indefinable third party between Yahweh and his creation" (G. von Rad, *Old Testament Theology*, II, 1965, 350). Only exceptionally did faith (Job 14:13–22) or the poetic imagination (Isa. 14:9 ff.; Ezek. 32:20 ff.) concern themselves with the realm of the dead. There are only isolated hints at hope beyond death (Job 19:25–27; Ps. 49 [LXX 48]; 73:23 ff. [LXX 72:23 ff.]). So at the frontiers of the OT there appears the hope of → resurrection (→ Death, OT 2; cf. H. H. Rowley, *The Faith of Israel*, 1956, 150–76).

2. In Rab. Judaism, under Persian and Hel. influence, the doctrine of the immortality of the → soul appeared, and this altered the concept of *hadēs*. The earliest attestation of this doctrine is Eth.Enoch 22. This chapter is closely related to Lk. 16:22 ff. (cf. also Eth.Enoch 51:1; 102:5; 103:7; 2 Macc. 6:24): reward and punishment begin, after death, in *hadēs*. According to Josephus (*Ant.* 18, 14; cf. *War* 2, 163; 3, 375; SB IV 1166, 1182 ff.), this was the position of the → Pharisees and the Essenes, in contrast to that of the → Sadducees. A later view states that the souls of the righteous, after death, enter heavenly blessedness, while the souls of the ungodly are punished in *hadēs*. *hadēs* thus lost its role as the resting place of all souls and became a place of punishment for the souls of the ungodly (cf. Eth.Enoch 63:10; Pss.Sol. 14:6 f.; 15:11; Gr. Bar. 4).

Under the influence of the doctrine of the → resurrection *hadēs* lost its role as the eternal resting place of souls and became a preparatory, temporary resting place for souls until the resurrection (cf. Eth.Enoch 51:1; Test.Ben. 10; Sib. 4:178–190; 2 Esd. 5:45). 2 Esd. 7:78–100 attempts to establish a compromise between the doctrines of immortality and of the resurrection. According to this, the souls of the righteous enjoy for a time in the beyond a foretaste of the blessedness which will be theirs after the resurrection. The ungodly, on the other hand, receive a foretaste of the punishment that awaits them after the last judgment. This compromise did not prevail in Judaism.

NT In the NT *hadēs* occurs 10 times, and that only in Matt., Lk., Acts and Rev. In the other writings other terms occur (→ *abyssos;* → *gehenna*).

1. Hades lies within the earth, so that one has to go down to it (Matt. 11:23; Lk. 10:15; cf. Matt. 12:40 *kardia tēs gēs*, the heart of the earth). It is a prison (*phylakē*, 1 Pet. 3:19; Rev. 20:7). Like a city or town it has → gates (Matt. 16:18), and is locked with a key which Christ holds in his hand (Rev. 1:18). The gates "will not close to imprison (in death) those who belong to the messianic community" (D. Hill, *The Gospel of Matthew*, 1972, 261). On the other hand, Rev. 20:14 seems to indicate that Hades, like → death, may be thought of as a person. At the resurrection Hades must give up its dead again (Rev. 20:13). So it is not an eternal but only a temporary place or state. According to Acts 2:27, 31 and Lk. 16:23, 26, all the dead are in Hades. According to other passages, only the spirits of the ungodly are in Hades (1 Pet. 3:19; Rev. 20:13 f.). According to Rev. 20:4, the martyrs will rise and reign with Christ for a thousand years (→ Number; → Glossary of Technical Terms, art. *Chiliasm*).

2. A NT innovation, by comparison with Judaism, is the fact that Jesus has risen to an eternal life (Heb. 7:16). He has taken the power of death and the devil from them (Heb. 2:14), and is Lord of the dead and of the living (Rom. 14:9). Through faith in Christ ideas are transformed: Hades cannot affect the church (Matt. 16:18 f.; 1 Pet. 3:19 ff.; 4:6; Rev. 1:18). Anyone who dies is united with Christ (Phil. 1:23; 2 Cor. 5:8) – even though naked, i.e. without a body (2 Cor. 5:2 f.) – or is in the heavenly Jerusalem (Heb. 12:22), or under the heavenly altar (Rev. 6:9) like the martyrs, or before God's throne (Rev. 7:9; 14:3). Christ has

preached to the spirits in prison (1 Pet. 3:19 ff.; 4:6). The saving work of Jesus Christ embraces the dead, and nothing is beyond the grace of Christ.

3. The fact that in the NT there is no description of ideas about the beyond must be connected with this emphasis on the all-embracing dominion and grace of Christ. There is no doctrine of the beyond or any geography of the beyond. This is in sharp contrast to certain Rab. Jewish and also Christian writings down to Dante's *Divine Comedy*. Perhaps, however, it was the very silence of the NT about the details of the beyond and of the temporary state which excited the curiosity of the pseudo-pious and led to dissatisfaction with placing one's hope in Christ alone. The idea that the statements of scripture have to be enlarged upon by human imagination indicates a lack of faith. A contributory factor here is the substitution of the Gk. doctrine of the immortality of the soul in place of the NT doctrine of the resurrection of the dead (1 Cor. 15). This comes about in unreflective Christianity which fails to ask whether the belief is grounded in the NT or in pagan Gk. thought.

H. Bietenhard

γέεννα

γέεννα (*gehenna*), Gehenna, hell.

OT The word *gehenna* does not appear in the LXX or Gk. literature. It is the Gk. form of the Aram. *gēhinnām*, which in turn goes back to the Heb. *gē hinnōm*. This originally denoted a valley lying to the south of Jerusalem (today, *Wadi er-Rabâbi*), the valley of the son (or sons) of Hinnom (Jos. 15:8; 18:16; Isa. 31:9; 66:24; Jer. 32:35; 2 Chr. 33:6). (See L. H. Grollenberg, *Atlas of the Bible*, 1957, 96, 114 f., 152.) Child sacrifices were offered in this valley (2 Ki. 16:3; 21:6). Josiah had it desecrated (2 Ki. 23:10). According to Jer. 7:32; 19:6 f., it will be the place of God's judgment.

Jewish apocalyptic assumed that this valley would become, after the final judgment, the hell of fire (Eth.Enoch 90:26 f.; 27:1 ff.; 54:1 ff.; 56:3 f.). Hence the name *gehenna* came to be applied to the eschatological hell of fire in general, even when it was no longer localized at Jerusalem (e.g. 2 Esd. 7:36; Syr.Bar. 59:10; 85:13, Sib. 1:103). In time *gehenna* became simply the place of punishment and so attracted the corresponding ideas about Hades (→ *hadēs*). *gehenna* thus became a temporary place of punishment (until the final judgment). At about the end of the 1st cent. A.D. or the beginning of the 2nd the doctrine of a fiery purgatory arose among the Rabbis. All those in whose cases merit and guilt are equally balanced go to *gehenna*. There they are purified and, if they do penance, inherit paradise. Alongside this we find the concept of an eschatological Gehinnom judgment, limited in time, after the last judgment (SB IV 1022–1118).

NT For the NT *gehenna* was a pre-existent entity (Matt. 25:41), a fiery abyss (Matt. 13:42, 50). It was the place of eschatological punishment after the last judgment, punishment of eternal duration (Matt. 25:41, 46; 23:15, 33). Body and soul are judged in it (Mk. 9:43, 45, 47 f.; Matt. 10:28). It was also to be distinguished from Hades which houses the souls of the dead *before* the last judgment. The same punishment will overtake → Satan and the → demons, the beast (→ Animal) from the abyss, the false → prophet, → death and Hades (Matt. 25:41; 8:29; Rev.

19:20; 20:10, 14f.). In contrast with later Christian writings and ideas, the torments of hell are not described in the NT, "If they are mentioned, it is only to rouse consciences to fear of the wrath of the heavenly Judge" (J. Jeremias, *TDNT* I 658; cf. Matt. 10:28; Lk. 12:5). Neither does the NT contain the idea that Satan is the prince of *gehenna*, to whom sinners are handed over for punishment.

H. Bietenhard

κατώτερος

κατώτερος (*katōteros*), lower.

CL & OT *katōteros* is the comparative of *katō*, under. In the LXX it stands for *tahtôn* and occurs mostly in the Pss. to denote any area in which life is threatened, or the realm of the dead itself (Pss. 62[63]:9; 85[86]:13; 87[88]:6; 138[139]:15).

NT In the NT the word occurs only in Eph. 4:9 (Christ descended) *eis ta katōtera merē tēs gēs*, "into the lower parts of the earth".

The following questions arise: Is the comparative *katōteros* here used in the sense of the superlative (into the lowest regions of the earth) or of the positive (into the regions of the earth, which lie below; so Radermacher, see bibliography)? Is *gēs* a gen. of apposition? In that case the expression would mean, the lowest parts, namely the earth. If *gēs* is a partitive gen. the expression would mean the lowest parts of the earth. Funk § 167, following F. Büchsel, *TDNT* III 641, takes it to mean the regions under the earth. Does *katōteros* correspond to the expression which occurs in the OT, the lowest (regions) of the earth, which can refer to the earth itself (Ps. 139:15 [LXX 138:15]) and also to Hades, lying under the earth (Ps. 63:9 [LXX 62:9]; Tob. 13:2)? According to a Rab. tradition (attested around A.D. 250 in R. Jehoshua b. Levi), one of the names for Gehinnom (→ *geenna*) was lowest land, lowest earth (Heb. *'ereṣ hattahtît*, cf. Erub. 19a; SB IV 1023 f.). Hence the phrase, the lower parts of the earth, could be a rendering of this Heb. expression.

It is possible that Eph. was dependent on an older Jewish exposition of Ps. 68:18 [LXX 67:18]. Moses ascended into heaven to receive the Torah and to transmit it to men (SB III 596). This exposition was then applied to Christ. The ascent of which the Ps. speaks is to be referred to the same person (Christ) who previously descended (→ Heaven, art. *anabainō* for alternative exegesis of Eph. 4:8). Then the question arises whether "he descended" and "the lower parts of the earth" must not refer to the death of Jesus. Jesus' death belongs to his full manhood. Anyone who dies, according to the Jewish view, goes into the realm of the dead; and this realm of the dead lies under the earth (→ *hadēs*). So this passage would not imply an actual battle with Hades which the redeemer had to fight, but only the entering of the dead Jesus into the realm of the dead (F. Büchsel, *TDNT* III 641; → Flesh, NT 2 (a)).

If the view is correct, that Jesus became man in such a way that he took man's final destiny upon himself and had to descend into the realm of the dead, light is thrown on the statement of Eph. 1:20-23. The "all in all" which he fills means the highest → heights and the lowest depth (the realm of the dead). It also means that he has thus received power over all beings, in particular over the spirits.

Other passages in Eph. which deal with Jesus' death speak only of an event on earth (Eph. 5:2, 25). In any case, even if it is the death of Jesus and his related entering into Hades that the passage has in mind, this latter idea is emphasized. Moreover, no weight at all is attached to the spatial concept. Ultimately it matters little whether the earth itself or regions lying beneath its surface are meant here. What is important is the fact that Christ is the exalted One and conqueror of all powers and dominions, and that as such he gives → gifts to his church. In modern exposition the reference of this passage to the *descensus ad inferos* ("he descended into hell" in the Apostles' Creed) is almost without exception rejected (cf. J. N. D. Kelly, *Early Christian Creeds*, 1972³, 378–88 for the historical background of the idea). *H. Bietenhard*

→ Death, → Demon, → Fire, → Gate, → Heaven, → Judgment, → Satan

(a). J. S. Bonnell, *Heaven and Hell: A Present-Day Christian Interpretation*, 1956; S. G. F. Brandon, *The Judgment of the Dead: An Historical and Comparative Study of the Idea of a Post-Mortem Judgment in the Major Religions*, 1967; and *Man and his Destiny in the Great Religions*, 1962; H. Buis, *The Doctrine of Eternal Punishment*, 1957; and "Hell", *ZPEB* III 114 ff.; F. Büchsel, *katō* etc , *TDNT* III 640 ff.; R. Bultmann, "Polis and Hades in Sophocles' Antigone", *Essays Philosophical and Theological*, 1953, 22–35; W. Eichrodt, "The Underworld", *Theology of the Old Testament*, II, 1967, 210–28; T. H. Gaster, *Thespis*, 1950; and "Dead, Abode of the", *IDB* I 787 f.; J. Jeremias, *abyssos*, *TDNT* I 9 f.; *geenna*, *TDNT* I 657 f.; *hadēs*, *TDNT* I 146–49; J. N. D. Kelly, *Early Christian Creeds*, 1972³, 378–88; J. Kürzinger, "Descent into Hell", *EBT* I 202–6; F. Loofs, "Descent to Hades (Christ's)", *ERE* IV 654–63; J. A. MacCulloch, "Descent to Hades (Ethnic)", *ERE* IV 648–54; and *The Harrowing of Hell*, 1930; J. Michl, "Hell", *EBT* I 369 ff.; B. Reicke, *The Disobedient Spirits and Christian Baptism*, 1946; S. S. Smalley, "The Eschatology of Ephesians", *EQ* 28, 1956, 152–7; L. I. J. Stadelmann, *The Hebrew Conception of the World*, 1970; H. Vorgrimler. "Christ's Descent into Hell: Is it Important?", *Concilium*, I 2, 1966, 75–81.
(b). C. Barth, *Die Errettung vom Tode in den individuellen Klage- und Dankliedern des Alten Testaments*, 1947; G. Beer, "Der Biblische Hades", in *Theologische Abhandlungen zu Ehren H. J. Holtzmanns*, 1902; A. Bertholet, *Die israelitischen Vorstellungen vom Zustande nach dem Tode*, 1899; and "Zu den babylonischen und israelitischen Unterweltvorstellungen", *Festschrift Paul Haupt*, 1926, 8–18; H. Bietenhard, *Die himmlische Welt im Urchristentum und Spätjudentum*, 1951; and "Kennt das Neue Testament die Vorstellung vom Fegefeuer?", *ThZ* 3, 1947, 101 ff.; P. Dhorme, "Le séjour des morts chez les Babyloniens et les Hébreux", *RB* 4, 1908, 59–78; E. Ebeling *Tod und Leben nach den Vorstellungen der Babylonier*, I, 1931; J. Felten, *Neutestamentliche Zeitgeschichte*, II, 1925³, 227–42, 258–63; J. Gnilka and J. Ratzinger, *LTK* V 445–49; G. K. Frank, *Himmel und Hölle*, 1970; F. C. Grant, W. von Soden, H.-J. Kraus, B. Reicke, "Hölle", *RGG³* III 400 ff.; A. Grillmeier, "Der Gottessohn im Totenreich", *ZTK* 71, 1949, 1–53, 184–203; and in *LTK* V 450–55; J. Kroll, *Gott und Hölle*, 1932; A. Lods, *La Croyance à la Vie Future et le Culte des Morts dans l'Antiquité Israélite*, 1906; G. Quell, *Die Auffassung des Todes in Israel*, 1925; T. Sartory and G. Sartory-Reidick, *In der Hölle brennt kein Feuer*, 1968; SB III 596 f.; IV 2, 1016 ff.; K. Schilder, *Wat is de Hel?*, 1930; F. Schwally, *Das Leben nach dem Tode*, 1892; C. Spicq, "La révelation de l'enfer dans la Sainte Écriture", in G. Bardy *et al.*, *L'Enfer*, 1950, 91–143; K. Tallquist, *Sumerisch-akkadische Namen der Totenwelt* 1934; P. Volz, *Die Eschatologie der jüdischen Gemeinde im neutestamentlichen Zeitalter*, 1934, 256–72, 309–32.

Herb, Plant, Grass

λάχανον

λάχανον (*lachanon*), herb, vegetable; βοτάνη (*botanē*), plant; ἄνηθον (*anēthon*), dill; ἡδύοσμον (*hēdyosmon*), mint; κύμινον (*kyminon*), cummin; πήγανον (*pēganon*), rue; χόρτος (*chortos*), grass, hay.

CL In secular Gk. *lachanon*, related to *lachainō* (dig), denotes garden herbs and vegetables, as opposed to wild plants (Epicrates, Plato). *botanē*, from *boskō* (graze), is used of pasture, herbs, weeds. *anēthon* means dill, the plant *Anethum graveolens*, employed in seasoning. *hēdyosmon* is mint (*Mentha viridis, M. longifolia*) derived from *hēdys*, sweet, pleasant, and *osmaomai*, smell. *kyminon*, cummin, is the aromatic seed of *Cuminum cyminum*, grown for flavouring dishes; used proverbially of a skinflint prepared to saw the tiny seed in half (Sophron). *pēganon* is rue, the culinary and medicinal herb *Ruta graveolens*. *chortos* means an enclosed feeding space; by extension, pasturage; and so fodder, grass, hay.

oT Four of the above terms appear in the LXX, but with one exception only in the literal sense. (a) *lachanon* as in secular Gk. stands for edible herbs and vegetables. (b) *botanē* translates *deše'* (grass), from a Heb. verb meaning to sprout abundantly (Gen. 1:11; Jer. 14:5); *'ēśeḇ* (cultivated plants) in Exodus (e.g. 9:22); and *ḥāṣîr* (herbage in general, Job 8:12). (c) *kyminon* transliterates the Heb. *kammōn*, cummin (Isa. 28:25, 27). (d) *chortos* nearly 50 times renders the Heb. *'ēśeḇ*, seed-bearing annuals springing up after rain: grass, weeds, vegetables, cereals. The character of *chortos* inspires metaphors and similes. Defeated enemies are like down-trodden grass (4 Ki. 19:26); men flourish like sprouting grass (Ps. 71:16) and as suddenly wilt (Ps. 101:4, 11), for human life is transient (Isa. 40:6).

NT 1. *Primary Meanings.* In the NT *lachanon* is consistently used for herbs (Lk. 11:42) and *chortos* for grass (Matt. 14:19) or the early grasslike blades of crops (Matt. 13:26). Jesus deplores the Pharisees' concern for tithing insignificant herbs (*lachanon*) like mint (*hēdyosmon*), rue (*pēganon*), dill (*anēthon*), and cummin (*kyminon*), to the neglect of weightier matters (Matt. 23:23; Lk. 11:42), and in excess of the law's requirements (Deut. 14:22–23).

2. *Extended Meanings.* (a) In Rom 14:2 Paul refers to certain converts from Judaism eating only vegetables (*lachanon*) because their feeble grasp of Christian liberty keeps them from disregarding either Jewish dietary laws or the possibility that shop-meat has been associated with pagan sacrifices. (b) In Heb. 6:7 responsive believers are likened to fertile land heavy with crops (*botanē*). (c) Human life is transitory like *chortos* (grass) (Jas. 1:10, 11; 1 Pet. 1:24, quoting Isa. 40:6, 7). *chortos* (hay), possible but poor building material, illustrates unsatisfactory Christian service (1 Cor. 3:12). God's care over short-lived grass guarantees his far greater concern for human needs (Matt. 6:30). → Fullness, art. *chortazō*.

N. Hillyer

G. Bornkamm, *lachanon*, *TDNT* IV 65 ff.; H. N. and A. L. Moldenke, *Plants of the Bible*, 1952; A. E. Rüthy, *Die Pflanze und ihre Teile*, 1942; W. Walker, *All the Plants of the Bible*, 1957.

Hide, Conceal

Both vbs. dealt with here have the same primary meaning, to hide. But whereas *kalyptō* is used more in the sense of to cover or conceal, the more frequently used vb. *kryptō* means to hide away, make secret. However, the meaning cannot always be precisely distinguished. In theological use they occur in contexts chiefly concerned with man's ability to see and experience, on the one hand, and the will and activity of God, on the other. Often they are used in passages asserting that God will make himself, or what is hidden, open to human experience or sight.

| καλύπτω | καλύπτω (*kalyptō*), cover, hide, conceal; ἀνακαλύπτω (*anakalyptō*), uncover, unveil; κατακαλύπτω (*kataka-lyptō*), cover up, veil; κάλυμμα (*kalymma*), veil, covering.

CL & OT *kalypto*, to conceal, cover (attested from Homer in classical Gk., but rare in Attic prose), is found in later Gk. in both lit. and fig. senses. In the LXX it stands for the Heb. *kissâh* (piel), and is used of the cloud which covered Sinai and of the darkness which covers the earth (Exod. 24:15; Isa. 60:2). In Ps. 32:5 the word is used of concealing; in Ps. 85:2 of God's covering of sin in forgiveness. The word is frequent in Pss. (e.g. 31:5; 43:15; 84:2) and Ezek. (e.g. 7:18; 16:8; 24:7 f.).

anakalyptō, used for Heb. *gālâh*, to disclose, uncover, reveal, is related in meaning to *apokalyptō* (→ Revelation). It is attested in cl. Gk. from the 5th cent. B.C. In the LXX it is used in Job 12:22 of the uncovering of hidden depths shrouded in darkness; in 33:16 of the uncovering of the mind (*nous*) of men. In Isa. 47:3 Babylon, addressed figuratively as a virgin, is threatened with the uncovering of her nakedness (*aischynē*) as a divine punishment, while in Jer. 13:22 Judah is similarly threatened with the lifting of her skirts (a symbol of humiliation).

katakalyptō, to hide, cover up, attested in cl. Gk. from Homer, is found in Exod. 26:34 and Num. 4:5 of the covering of the ark with a curtain. In Isa. 6:2 the seraphim cover their faces and their feet with their wings. In the mid. meaning, to cover oneself, Tamar is said in Gen. 38:15 to have veiled her face, i.e. like a prostitute. The rare verbal adj. *akatakalyptos*, unveiled (Lev. 13:45), occurs in the NT only in 1 Cor. 11:5, 13 (→ Head).

kalymma, veil, covering, attested in cl. Gk. from Homer, is used in Exod. 34:34–35 of the veil worn by Moses to cover his face. In Num. 4:6, 8, 12 etc. the word (along with *katakalymma*) is used of the cloths with which the holy objects like the ark of the covenant, the altar, the altar vessels etc. were kept from being touched or seen. To look at them or touch them could mean death (Num. 4:15, 20).

NT 1. The words of this group are relatively rare in the NT and are found only in Matt., Lk., 1 and 2 Cor. 1 Pet and Jas. (a) In the lit. sense *kalyptō* is found at Matt. 8:24 (the ship is covered by the waves); Lk. 8:16 (no one covers a lamp with a vessel); and Lk. 23:30 (people will say to the hills, "Cover us!").

(b) A fig. use is found in the general statement, "There is nothing covered that will not be revealed" (Matt. 10:26 = Lk. 12:2). Lk.'s version has here the intensified form *synkekalymmenon*, while the parallel tradition in Mk. 4:22 = Lk. 8:17 has → *krypton*. The statement allows of various applications; but in the context it refers here to the commission given by Jesus to his → disciples. The word told to them in secret is to be proclaimed publicly from the rooftops (Matt. 10:27).

2. In 1 Cor. 11:1–6 Paul deals with the question of women's veils. This is the only place in the NT where the mid. *katakalyptesthai* to veil oneself (twice, in vv. 6–7), and the adj. *akatakalyptos*, unveiled (vv. 5, 13), are found. Paul demands that a → woman wear a veil when praying or prophesying in church (vv. 4–5; cf. the women "who prophesied" in Acts 21:9). This requirement is in keeping with the strict Jewish and Oriental sense of what is fitting, according to which it would be unthinkable for a woman to appear in public without a veil (v. 13). The Gk. custom was probably not uniform, but the church in the international city of Corinth was scarcely a purely Greek church. Paul wishes this custom to be observed not only

in Corinth but also in the other churches (v. 16). Because, however, of the variety of circumstances, this was not by any means the case (A. Oepke, *TDNT* III 563). The puzzling thing is the ground for this ruling given in v. 10 (over and above the reference in v. 13 to what is fitting): the women are to have an "authority" on their head. The authority (*exousia*) refers to the head-covering, the veil (Old Latin texts translate it *velamen*); but the odd expression *exousia* is not adequately explained (cf. W. Foerster, *exousia*, *TDNT* II 570 f.). Just as difficult are the words "because of the angels". Are the angels the guardians of the natural order (vv. 8, 9; cf. Gen. 2:21 ff.)? Or is the veil a protection against fallen angels who might wish to lead the women astray? Attempts have been made to find a background for such an interpretation in Gen. 6:1 ff., where it is recorded that the "sons of God" (the reference is to angelic powers) took to wife the daughters of men. Jewish literature of the NT period expanded this story further (Eth.Enoch 6; Syr.Bar. 56; Test.Reub. 5). The brevity of Paul's reference makes it difficult to be certain of the correct interpretation. (For further discussion of this whole passage → Head, NT 3.)

3. (a) The word *kalymma*, covering, is found 4 times in the NT, all in 2 Cor. 3:13–16. Here Paul makes reference to Exod. 34:33–35, where it is recorded that Moses put a veil over his face, because the Israelites feared the divine radiance which came from it (Exod. 34:30; cf. Num. 4:15, 20). Paul disregards the fear motive. He interprets the passage to mean that Moses put on the veil in order that the Israelites might not see the end of the temporary radiance. The passing → glory (*doxa*) of the old covenant is contrasted with the eternal glory of the new (v. 11). This veil remains unlifted, we read in vv. 14 f., up to the present day when the "old covenant" is read. It lies over the minds of the Jews who cannot grasp the true meaning of the old covenant as a pointer to Christ. Just as Moses removed the veil when he went in to God (Exod. 34:34), so will the veil be removed from Israel when they are converted to the Lord, i.e. when they allow themselves to be ruled by the → Spirit (v. 16; cf. v. 17, *ho de kyrios to pneuma estin*, the Lord is the Spirit). (On this whole passage see P. E. Hughes, *Commentary on the Second Epistle to the Corinthians*, 1962, 107–34; W. C. van Unnik, "With Unveiled Face", *Nov T* 6, 1963, 153ff.)

(b) The same context contains in vv. 14 and 18 the only NT instances of the vb. *anakalyptō*. There is no question as to the meaning to unveil, uncover. But the exegesis of v. 14, which says that the veil remains over the reading of the "old covenant", is difficult. The AV translates, "until this day remaineth the same vail untaken away"; the RSV, "it remains unlifted, because only through Christ is it taken away" (reading a comma after *menei*, "remains"). P. Bachmann interprets the words *mē anakalyptomenon* as an acc. absolute and translates: "without it being revealed that (*hoti*) it (i.e. the "old covenant" as a way of salvation) has been done away in Christ" (*Der Zweite Brief des Paulus an die Korinther*, 1922³, 168). In any case the thought which Paul wishes to convey is that for Christians the veils have been removed which would prevent them from seeing "the light of the gospel of the glory of Christ" (4:4, 6). This is clear from v.18, where he goes on to give expression to the assurance of Christian faith: "We all, with unveiled [*anakekalymmenō*] face, beholding the glory of the Lord" (cf. H. D. Wendland, *Die Briefe an die Korinther*, *NTD* 7, 1963, 157 ff.). The effect of this beholding is that the beholders

213

are changed by the Lord, who is the Spirit (v. 17), into the likeness of the one whom they behold (→ See).

In contradiction to the statement of 2 Cor. 3:18 stands the verdict which, according to 2 Cor. 4:3, opponents pass upon the Pauline gospel: the Pauline gospel is "veiled" (*kekalymmenon*). In other words, it is obscure or contradictory. Paul throws back the criticism in his opponents' teeth by saying that it is veiled for those who are perishing, for those who are unable to see the light of the gospel, because they have been blinded by Satan (2 Cor. 4:4). This judgment agrees with the remarks about the unbelieving Jews which have been made in 2 Cor. 3:13.

4. In 1 Pet. 4:8 the readers are exhorted to love on the ground that love covers (*kalyptei*) a multitude of → sins. In Jas. 5:20 the same grounds are given in an exhortation to bring back a sinner from the error of his way (cf. also 1 Clem. 49:5; 2 Clem. 16:4). Probably what we have here is a catch-phrase which had its origin in Prov. 10:12 (Heb. text). The epistles of Clement interpret it in the sense of "justification by works": love wins for him who practises it the forgiveness of his sins. Another interpretation is possible, and more in keeping with the language used. → Love covers up, by means of the → forgiveness which it instils, a multitude of sins in others. *W. Mundle*

κρύπτω

κρύπτω (*kryptō*), hide, conceal; ἀποκρύπτω (*apokryptō*), hide; κρυπτός (*kryptos*), hidden, secret; ἀπόκρυφος (*apokryphos*), hidden; κρυφαῖος (*kryphaios*), and κρύφιος (*kryphios*), hidden.

CL 1. *kryptō*, to hide, conceal, fig. to keep secret, is attested in cl. Gk. from Homer.

From the Hel. aorist *ekrybēn* (common in the LXX, e.g. Gen. 3:8) is derived the vb. *krybō*, which has the same meaning (found in the NT only in the form *periekryben*, she kept herself hidden [Lk. 1:24]). The derivative *apokryptō* (Homer) has the same meaning. It is not possible to draw an absolute distinction between its range of meaning and that of the similar vb. → *kalyptō*, to hide. The same may be said of the adjectives *kryptos* and *apokryphos*, hidden (Homer and 5th cent. B.C. respectively). The group also includes the adv. *kryphē*, secretly (in the NT at Eph. 5:12 only), and the adj. *kryphaios*, hidden, which is found only in biblical usage (Jer. 23:24; Lam. 3:10; in the NT only at Matt. 6:18, par. to *en tō kryptō*, in secret, vv. 4, 6). The noun *kryptē*, vault, cellar, hidden corner (attested from 3rd cent. B.C.), is found in the NT only at Lk. 11:33.

2. The hiddenness of the deity is not emphasized greatly in Gk. and Hel. religion. Although the Hymn to Isis from Andros (1st cent. B.C.) speaks of the secret (*apokrypha*) symbols of Hermes, and Iamblichus (3rd cent A.D.) mentions *ta krypta*, the hidden things, of the goddess Isis (cf. Arndt, 93, 455; A. Oepke, *kryptō*, *TDNT* III 961–6), the Hel. mystery religions are no exception. The most one can say is that the word *apokryphos*, hidden, plays a great part in books of magic and astrological texts. The biblical doctrine of God, with its awareness of his transcendence and its emphasis on the unapproachability and hiddenness of God, is largely foreign to Gk. and Hel. religion.

OT 1. In the LXX *kryptō* is found in the lit. sense of to hide (e.g. Gen. 3:8, 10) as well as in the fig. sense of to keep secret (e.g. Gen. 18:17; 1 Sam. 3:17, 18). It represents various Heb. roots with the same basic meaning, e.g. *ḥāḇā'*, to hide,

conceal (Gen. 3:8, 10; 1 Sam. 14:11), *khd* (piel), to hide, conceal (1 Sam. 3:17; cf.
A. Oepke, *TDNT* III 967). *apokryptō*, to hide, usually has the fig. meaning (Isa.
40:27; Wis. 6:22). The adj. *kryptos* is used in both the lit. and the fig. senses (2
Macc. 1:16; Deut. 29:29). *apokryphos*, hidden, is used in Isa. 45:3, 1 Macc. 1:23
and Dan. 11:43 of secret treasures. The expression *en apokryphō*, in secret, is also
found (e.g. Deut. 27:15; Ps. 10:8).

2. (a) The hiddenness and unapproachability of God is depicted impressively in
the OT in the story of the call of → Moses. Moses is not allowed to approach the
God who has revealed himself to him in the burning bush, but turns his face away
(LXX *apestrepsen*); he is afraid of God's face (Exod. 3:6; → God, OT 2). Similarly
the people do not dare to approach God at Sinai; Moses alone dares to go forward
into the darkness (Exod. 20:21).

The same basic concept is found in later writings. In the secret place of thunder
God hears his people's cry of distress (Ps. 81:7). At the consecration of the temple
Solomon declared that God wishes to dwell in darkness (1 Ki. 8:12). This also
applies in the fig. sense to God's hidden guidance: the painful misfortunes of Israel
are regarded as judgments of God in which his comfort remains hidden (Hos.
13:14). The God of Israel is a hidden God, and yet he remains the saviour. He
hides his face in wrath, but he returns to his people with everlasting → grace (Isa.
45:15; 54:8). Though Israel's way may be hidden from God, it is not cut off from
the comfort of the Lord who gives power and strength to the weary (Isa. 40:27, 29).

(b) God hides himself from men, but man cannot hide from God. God is the
Lord who fills heaven and earth (Jer. 23:24). Everywhere man is surrounded by
God's presence; God's eye sees even in the darkness, nothing is hid from Him
(Ps. 139:7–12, 15; Sir. 39:19). To flee from God, as the case of Jonah shows (Jon.
1:3), is therefore a hopeless quest. Above all, human sin is not hidden from God
(Jer. 16:17). There is no gloom or darkness where evildoers can hide themselves
(Job 34:22; Sir. 17:15, 20). Sinful man is therefore threatened by God on every
side. Before this terrible God he must creep into the earth's recesses (Isa. 2:10). To
him God is like a bear lying in wait or a lion in hiding (Lam. 3:10). And so Job
complains that God hides his face from him like an enemy (Job 13:24). Similarly
the psalmists complain that God hides his face from them and is far from them
(Pss. 10:1; 44:24); but man's sin is not hidden from God (Ps. 69:5). The awareness
of personal guilt and distance from God finds strong expression in the Pss. All the
more urgent, therefore, is the plea made to God by the righteous: "Hide not thy
ear from my cry" (Lam. 3:56). Finally, the sighing of the righteous cannot remain
hidden from God (Ps. 38:9). He therefore must stand before God with his sin and
confess it; if he does not hide it, he can obtain God's forgiveness (Ps. 32:5). He
asks this forgiveness also for hidden faults (Ps. 19:12). The psalmists know of the
gracious God in whose goodness they may find refuge (Ps. 27:5; 31:19–20). One
of the effects of this attitude of faith and trust is the desire to hide God's commandments in one's heart, i.e. to be their guardian (Ps. 119:11, 19).

(c) Thus in the OT expression is given in a variety of ways to the tension between
the hiddenness of God and his → revelation. As the hidden God, he reveals what
is hidden, the hidden things which concern the future (Dan. 2:22; Sir. 42:19; 48:25).
This opens up the way which leads to Jewish apocalyptic which has its beginning
in the book of Daniel. God is revealed also in his judgments, as the righteous →

judge who brings to light what is hidden (Eccl. 12:14; 2 Macc. 12:41). Thus he reveals to Abraham the coming judgment on Sodom. Here it is hinted, but not explicitly said, that he is the gracious God whose wrath does not continue for ever (Gen. 18:23–33).

3. In Judaism of the NT period, the apocalyptic literature which continues the tradition of the book of Daniel concerns itself a great deal with the hidden things, especially in so far as they have to do with the future. In the Book of Enoch the "Son of Man" (→ Son, art. *hyios tou anthrōpou*), the "chosen one", will reveal all the treasures of what is hidden, and all secrets of wisdom will proceed from the thoughts of his mouth (Eth.Enoch 46:3; 51:3). The Qumran texts speak of a secret knowledge of the will of God which remains hidden to outsiders and is attainable only by the sect-community by way of the law and the prophets (1QS 4:6; 9:17; 11:6; 1QH 5:25; 8:10 f.). Even in Rab. Judaism the awareness of the hiddenness of God and his mysteries does not totally disappear (SB I 578 f., 659 f.), but it is balanced by the conviction of the pious Jew that the full and valid → revelation of God has been given him in the → law. The Jew, as characterized by Paul, possesses in the law "the embodiment of knowledge and truth" (Rom. 2:20); this fits him to be a guide to the blind and a light to those who are in darkness (cf. Rom. 2:17–20).

NT 1. In the NT *kryptō* occurs 19 times, and *apokryptō* 4 times. In the parallel passages, Matt. 11:25 = Lk. 10:21, Matt. uses *kryptō* and Lk. *apokryptō*. Of the adjectives, *kryptos* occurs 17 times; *apokryphos* 3 times (Mk. 4:22; Lk. 8:17; Col. 2:3); *kryphaios* twice (Matt. 6:18, *v.l. en tō kryptō*). The sayings in Matt. 10:26 and Lk. 12:2 (8:17) are variations of the one in Mk. 4:22, "There is nothing hidden that shall not be made manifest." The parallelism of the sayings indicates that no clear line of distinction can be drawn between the meanings of the words above mentioned, nor indeed between them and the related → *kalyptō* (cf. Lk. 23:30 with Rev. 6:16). The words are often used in their lit. sense: Matt. 13:44 mentions the treasure hidden in a field, while in the parable of the talents the unfaithful servant hides his money in the earth (25:18, 25). Similarly the woman hides the leaven in the flour (Matt. 13:33 *enekrypsen*; cf. Lk. 13:21). In a reference to Exod. 2, Heb. 11:23 records the hiding of the child Moses after his birth.

2. Of theological significance are the sayings which deal with the hiddenness of revelation and of the revelatory work of God. The → revelation which God gives through Jesus to babes remains hidden from the wise and prudent (Matt. 11:25 par. Lk. 10:21). The hiddenness of revelation corresponds to the hiddenness of the → kingdom of heaven. This is the message of the parables of the leaven and of the hidden treasure (Matt. 13:33, 44). Just as the kingdom is hidden, so must the disciples' almsgiving, prayers and fasting, be done in secret; the Father who sees in secret will → reward them. Jesus emphasized this in the face of a type of piety which sought to make a display of itself (Matt. 6:4, 6, 18). The passion predictions of Jesus indicate that for the disciples the divine plan remains for the present hidden; it is not revealed to them until after the resurrection (Lk. 18:34; cf. Mk. 9:32; Lk. 9:45). Similarly it is Jerusalem that failed to recognize the salvation which Jesus desired to bring her: the things that made for her peace remained hidden from her eyes (Lk. 19:42).

The saying in Matt. 10:26 gives rise in v. 27 to the commission to the disciples to spread the message: this is the way in which what has been hidden is to be made known. This is the interpretation that Matthew gives to the purpose of parables: they are intended to express what has been hidden since the foundation of the world (Matt. 13:35, quoting Ps. 78:2). The message is not to be spread by word alone, but also by the works of the disciples. The city set on a hill cannot be hid, and a light is not placed under a bushel or in a hidden corner, but on the lampstand, so that all may see it (Matt. 5:14 ff.; Lk. 11:33).

The Gospel of John says that Joseph of Arimathea was a secret (*kekrymmenos*) disciple (19:38) for fear of the Jews. In contrast to this, Jesus confessed at his trial before the high priest: "I have said nothing secretly" (Jn. 18:20). His task has been to manifest the Father's → name before men (Jn. 17:6). In apparent contradiction to this attitude, Jn. 7:8–10 records that Jesus did not go up to Jerusalem, although his brothers who did not believe in him urged him to do so. It was at the time of the Feast of Tabernacles (7:2 ff.). He did not go to this festival, because his time was not yet fulfilled. He went, but not until later and then secretly (vv. 8, 10). According to Jn. 8:59 he hid from the Jews and left the temple when they tried to stone him. When the Jews decided to put him to death, he no longer went about openly among them, but went into hiding (11:54, *apēlthen*, he went away). The reason for this is given in Jn. 10:17, 18. Men cannot and must not be allowed to take his life from him at their volition; Jesus gave it up on his own resolve, when his hour had come, (Jn. 7:8; 13:1; 17:1). His action was determined by the relationship of love with his heavenly Father with whom he is one (Jn. 10:17, 30). The hiddenness of Jesus serves to expose his lack of dependence upon man, and his majesty and union with God. It does not mean that the revelation of Christ is intended to remain hidden to all, for Jesus is the → light of the world (Jn. 8:12). But it is given only to the disciples (Jn. 17); unbelievers are subject to the judgment of total blindness (9:39).

3. (a) Paul declares that the apostolic message is the hidden wisdom of God which God has ordained from all eternity for our glory (1 Cor. 2:7, *apokekrymmenēn*). It has its origin in divine → revelation (Rom. 16:25; 1 Cor. 2:10; Gal. 1:12). Its content is Christ whom God has made → wisdom for us (1 Cor. 1:30); the Spirit-inspired message brings us knowledge of God (1 Cor. 2:10 f.).

(b) Ephesians and Colossians carry these ideas still further. The message is the secret hidden since the beginning of the world to former generations, but now revealed to the saints (Col. 1:25 ff.), and the holy apostles and prophets (Eph. 3:5 ff.). It proclaims to us the Christ present in Christians and his unsearchable riches (Col. 1:27; Eph. 3:8). In this Christ are hidden all the treasures of wisdom; thus OT language about hidden treasures (see above OT 1) is interpreted as referring to Christ (Col. 2:3). Not only, however, does Christ bestow knowledge; he is also the hidden life of the Christian. Christians are buried with him in → baptism, and raised by faith to a new life. This life is hid with Christ in God (Col. 2:12; 3:3). Therefore they can take no part in the "hidden things of shame" (2 Cor. 4:2), in the works of darkness which take place in secret and yet cannot remain hidden (Eph. 5:12; cf. 1 Tim. 5:25).

(c) In 1 Peter Christian women are called to a life with Christ: their holiness of life is to be evident from the fact that they do not adorn themselves with costly outward finery, but that their adornment is the "hidden person of the heart with the imperishable jewel of a gentle and quiet spirit" (1 Pet. 3:4). The mark of this hidden person who conducts his or her life with Christ is a life of hope, submission and fear of God (vv. 2, 5, 6).

4. (a) Paul describes the believing Christian in Rom. 2:29 as a "Jew inwardly [*en tō kryptō*]." Through the → Spirit who has been given to Christians in faith and guarantees their status as children of God (Rom. 8:15 ff.; Gal. 4:6), they have received a circumcision of the → heart. This circumcision "made without hands" (Col. 2:11 f.) means that in → baptism they share in Christ's burial and resurrection (cf. Rom. 6:3 ff.). Thus they become members of the true people of God. "For we are the true circumcision, who worship God in spirit, and glory in Christ Jesus, and put no confidence in the flesh", Paul writes to the Philippians (Phil. 3:3). The Jew who is one outwardly (*en tō phanerō*, Rom. 2:28) only relies on the circumcision of the flesh. This circumcision proves that he is a member of the Jewish people, → Israel "according to the flesh" (1 Cor. 10:18). In contrast to this is the "Israel of God" (Gal. 6:16), the church of Christ, to which the Christian may belong as a member of the true people of God, as "a Jew inwardly", even without belonging outwardly to the Jewish people.

(b) Rev. 2:17 speaks of the "hidden manna", the gift of the heavenly world. Manna was the secret food provided by God which Israel received from heaven on her journey through the wilderness (Exod. 16:4; → Bread, art. *manna*). In Jewish expectation (Syr.Bar. 29:8) it was to be given to Israel anew at the end of the ages. This gift will be received by "him who conquers", who retains through all trials his loyalty to God. Ultimately this gift is Christ himself: he is the → bread of God which comes down from heaven (Jn. 6:33 ff.).

(c) From all this it is clear that language about the hiddenness of God and of divine things is connected with the NT's forward look into the future. God is the judge who will bring into judgment the secrets of men (Rom. 2:16), and will bring to light the hidden things of darkness and reveal the purposes of the heart (1 Cor. 4:5), just as the Spirit of God already at work in Christians discloses the secrets of the heart (1 Cor. 14:25).

(d) Revelation takes up OT prophecies (Isa. 2:10 f.; Jer. 4:29; Hos. 10:8) and describes how on the day of judgment the kings and great men of the earth will have to hide in caves and clefts of the rocks: they will cry out to the mountains and rocks, "Fall on us and hide us from the face of God and from the wrath of the Lamb" (Rev. 6:15; cf. Lk. 23:30).

5. The idea of judgment is only one side of NT expectation concerning the future. First and foremost the NT looks forward to the coming Lord: when Christ, the hidden life of Christians, shall appear, then they will appear with him in glory (Col. 3:3 f.). Then that knowledge which is here enjoyed only in part and which cannot lift the veil of God's hiddenness will no longer be obscure. It will no longer be a matter of seeing "in a mirror dimly" (1 Cor. 13:12), but will be turned into sight, face to face. To see the → face of God is here no longer a ground for fear, but the fulfilment of the Christian's joyful hope.

6. (a) The word "apocryphal" has passed into common usage because of the so-called apocryphal literature (→ Glossary of Technical Terms). This consists of secret, hidden writings, which were not read out in church. The way was paved for the appearance of this literature by the fact that in the NT period the authority

of → Scripture, or the Scriptures, was already established, while the question of which writings belonged to the authoritative, "canonical" Scriptures was not yet fully resolved. In 1 Cor. 2:9, for instance, Paul cites a passage which is not to be found in our biblical texts, though it bears some resemblance to Isa. 64:4 (cf. also 65:17). According to some of the early Fathers (Origen on Matt. 27:4; Ambrosiaster on 1 Cor. 2:9; and Jerome on Isa. 64:4), it was in the *Apocalypse of Elijah* which has not come down to us except in a fragment which does not contain the words. It was frequently quoted especially by gnostic writers and was ascribed to Jesus by Act.Pet. 39 and Gos.Thom. 17. In Jude 14 the prophecy of Enoch is mentioned, and a passage is cited from the apocryphal Apocalypse of Enoch (Eth.Enoch 1:9). The mention of Jannes and Jambres, the magicians who opposed Moses (2 Tim. 3:8) likewise presupposes the use of an apocryphal tradition (*TDNT* III 990). In the canonical tradition their names are not mentioned (cf. Exod. 7:10 ff.). Later, from Jerome onwards (c. 380 A.D.), the title "Apocrypha" was limited to those books included in the LXX and the Latin Vulgate which was based on it which do not appear in the Heb. canon of the OT. The designation of these books as apocryphal did not however settle finally the question of their canonicity. At the Council of Trent (Session IV, 1546) the Roman Catholic Church pronounced them canonical (cf. H. Denzinger, *Enchiridion Symbolorum*, 1957^{31}, §§ 783 f.). Luther declared them to be "good and useful to read", and with some reservation included them in his translation of the Bible. The Church of England recognized that the Church reads them "for example and instruction of manners; but yet doth it not apply them to establish any doctrine" (Article VI). In the Reformed Churches of the Calvinistic tradition they were generally rejected; but the attitudes of the various churches were not uniform. (See further *The Cambridge History of the Bible*, I–III, 1963–70 [see indexes]; B. M. Metzger, *An Introduction to the Apocrypha* 1969^3; R. H. Charles, ed., *The Apocrypha and Pseudepigrapha of the Old Testament*, I–II, [1913] 1963.)

It is important to note the distinction between the apocryphal literature and apocalyptic writings, the subject of which is revelations about the events of the last days (→ Glossary of Technical Terms, art. *Apocalyptic*; → Revelation).

(b) In addition to the OT Apocrypha there is a body of NT Apocrypha, consisting of those writings which are related to the NT either by literary form or by date of origin. These include Apocryphal gospels and books of Acts, like the Gospel according to the Hebrews, the Gospel according to the Egyptians, the Gospel of Thomas, the Acts of Peter, Paul, John and Thomas, spurious Epistles like that of Paul to the Laodiceans, books of revelation like the Apocalypse of Peter. (For critical edition see E. Hennecke and W. Schneemelcher, eds., *New Testament Apocrypha*, I–II, 1963–65.) Recent discoveries at Nag Hammadi in Upper Egypt in 1946 have enriched our knowledge of this literature. These writings which arose particularly in gnostic circles and which are fictional and wildly imaginative in content, were sometimes rejected from the outset by the church, and sometimes after a period of vacillation. (For texts see R. M. Grant, *Gnosticism: An Anthology*, 1961; and W. Foerster, *Gnosis: A Selection of Gnostic Texts*, I, 1972; II, 1974.) To the NT Apocrypha are sometimes (but mistakenly) reckoned the Apostolic Fathers (1 and 2 Clement, the *Shepherd* of Hermas, the *Didache* and other writings [cf. J. B. Lightfoot, *The Apostolic Fathers*, I–V, 1889–90, one-volume ed., 1891

revised; C. C. Richardson, ed., *Early Christian Fathers*, 1953]). These books are close to the NT in time, and to some extent in content. The fact that some of them are to be found in ancient MSS of the Bible indicates that for a time there was uncertainty as to whether they belonged to the NT. *W. Mundle*
→ Knowledge, → Revelation

(a). B. Altaner, *Patrology*, 1960, 47–96; S. Barabas, "Apocrypha, Modern", *ZPEB* I 213 ff.; R. Bultmann, "Adam, where art Thou?", in *Essays Philosophical and Theological*, 1955, 119–32; and "Concerning the Hidden and Revealed God", in *Existence and Faith*, 1964, 25–38; *The Cambridge History of the Bible*, I, ed. P. R. Ackroyd and C. F. Evans, 1970; II, ed. G. W. H. Lampe, 1969; III, ed. S. L. Greenslade, 1963; R. H. Charles, *Religious Developments between the Old and New Testaments*, 1914; R. H. Charles, ed., *The Apocrypha and Pseudepigrapha of the Old Testament*, I–II, (1913) 1963; O. Eissfeldt, *The Old Testament: An Introduction*, 1965, 560–668; M. S. Enslin, "Apocrypha, NT", *IDB* I 166–69; C. T. Fritsch, "Apocrypha", *IDB* I 161–66; E. J. Goodspeed, *Modern Apocrypha*, 1956; R. K. Harrison, *Introduction to the Old Testament*, 1970; and "Apocrypha", *ZPEB* I 205–10; E. Hennecke and W. Schneemelcher, eds., *New Testament Apocrypha*, I–II, 1963–65; M. R. James, *The Apocryphal New Testament*, 1924 and reprints; R. McL. Wilson, "Apocryphal New Testament", *ZPEB* I 210–13; B. M. Metzger, *An Introduction to the Apocrypha*, 1969³; A. Oepke, *kalyptō*, *TDNT* III 556–92; A. Oepke and R. Meyer, *kryptō*, *TDNT* III 957–1000; R. H. Pfeiffer, *History of New Testament Times with an Introduction to the Apocrypha*, 1957; D. S. Russell, *The Method and Message of Jewish Apocalyptic 200 B.C.–A.D. 100*, 1964; D. M. Scholer, *Nag Hammadi Bibliography*, 1949, 1969, 1971; C. C. Torrey, *The Apocryphal Literature*, 1945; W. C. van Unnik, "With Unveiled Face", *NovT* 6, 1963, 153 ff.
(b). A. Böhlig and P. Labib, *Koptisch-gnostische Apokalypsen aus Kodex V von Nag Hammadi*, 1963; J. Göttsberger, "Die Hülle des Mose nach Ex. 34 und 2 Kor. 3", *BZ* 16, 1924, 1 ff.; SB III 427 ff.
For works on gnosticism → bibliography under Knowledge.

Hinder, Prevent, Forbid

Hindrances may take a variety of forms. They may be solid and physical (like rocks) or psychological (like lack of insight). We may meet them suddenly all at once or as a continuing impediment. They may affect a particular plan or our whole being. The Gk. vbs. *enkoptō* and *kōlyō* correspond to this variety of meanings. *enkoptō* denotes a temporary (originally military) obstacle. *kōlyō*, on the other hand, generally signifies a human obstacle which frequently affects the whole person, and in the NT specifically the relationship of the individual to God.

ἐγκόπτω

ἐγκόπτω (*enkoptō*), hinder, thwart; ἐγκοπή (*enkopē*), hindering, hindrance; ἐγκοπὴν διδόναι τινί (*enkopēn didonai tini*), hinder something.

CL & OT The vb. *enkoptō*, composed of *en-* (in) and *koptō* (to strike), originally meant to knock in or cut into. The meaning hinder arose out of its military use. During a retreat the road might be cut into (i.e. broken up), in order to delay the pursuing enemy. The noun *enkopē* therefore denoted originally merely a temporary hindrance (cf. *proskomma*, → Offence), and only very late (1st cent. B.C.) a permanent impediment. The vb. is followed by the dat. (in the NT by the acc., by analogy with *kōlyō*). A following infin. is frequently in the gen. (to be translated in the NT almost as a consecutive by "so that"; Funk § 400, 4; cf. Rom. 15:22). The following infin. is frequently accompanied by *mē* or *mē ou*, according to whether the expression is used positively, negatively or interrogatively, a usage which seems to us pleonastic (Funk § 429; cf. Gal. 5:7). Neither vb. nor noun occurs in the LXX. The vbs. of hindering in the OT do not have the special nuances of *enkoptō*.

NT The noun occurs once, and the vb. 5 times (3 times in Paul and once each in Acts and 1 Pet.). In the NT these words indicate an occurrence which hinders progress in the realm of → faith or in the Christian life, bringing it to a standstill, if not permanently at least for the moment. Such a hindrance is always of a kind that can be overcome.

The → proclamation of the → gospel could thus have been hindered, if Paul had allowed himself to receive money from the churches which came into being as the result of his preaching (1 Cor. 9:12). This hindrance was not of permanent consequence, but in particular cases was nontheless considerable. Therefore, Paul waived his rights (*exousia*) which in themselves could not be contested. Again, Paul's mission in Rome was only delayed by the fact that he had to complete projects which he had begun in other places (Rom. 15:22). Paul wanted to go to Thessalonica, but the visit was repeatedly hindered by → Satan (1 Thess. 2:18). It is no longer possible to determine what hindrances Paul classified as Satan's work. It might have been an illness (2 Cor. 12:7; cf. on this point Phil. 2:25–30) or the machinations of the Jews (1 Thess. 2:15 f.).

In Gal. 5:7 the Christian life is compared to a race, the running of which is hindered by false teachers. The true way of faith has been endangered by sectarian, legalistic, gnostically inclined Jewish Christians (so W. Schmithals and K. Wegenast; see bibliography), because they have perverted the gospel (1:7) and threaten to destroy the unity of the church (4:17).

Insufficient → knowledge (art. *ginōskō*; cf. B. Reicke, see bibliography) can also act as a hindrance to men's prayers (1 Pet. 3:7). The trouble here is that, under the influence of prevailing pagan custom, men have tended to despise their wives instead of recognizing them as partners. The passage has nothing to do with the common prayers of married couples, nor with marriage as a hindrance to prayer. Similar concepts of hindering occur in 1 Cor. 13:1 and 11:20–29 (where the vb. is not used). In the former it is a lack of love which hinders effective preaching, and in the latter a selfish lack of brotherly consideration which prevents the proper celebration of the → Lord's Supper.

The Aram. and Syriac versions and also the misleading ref. to Job 19:2 and Isa. 43:23 (which have *enkopon* and not *enkopēn poiein*) have resulted in the erroneous translation of *enkoptō* as "weary" in Acts 24:4 (KJV, Moffatt). However, the basic meaning of *enkoptō* makes good sense: "In order not to hinder you any further [i.e. by this long speech from carrying out of your administrative duties]" (cf. F. F. Bruce, *The Acts of the Apostles*, 1952², 421; E. Haenchen, *The Acts of the Apostles*, 1971, 653). Burden, delay or detain are also possible translations (G. Stählin, *TDNT* III 855; Arndt, 215).   *C. H. Peisker*

| κωλύω | κωλύω (*kōlyō*), hamper, hinder, prevent, restrain, forbid. |

CL The vb. *kōlyō* is attested from Pindar on. Although its etymology is obscure (possibly from *kolos*, stunted), it originally meant to cut short, and then to hinder, etc. It is used with a separative gen.: *kōlyō tina tinos*, hinder someone in something (cf. Acts 27:43). In the NT the gen. is frequently replaced by *apo* (Funk §180, 1; cf. Lk. 6:29). As in the case of *enkoptō*, a following infin. is often in the gen., in the NT always without *mē* (Funk § 429). There are familiar idioms such as *ti kōlyei*, why not? and *ouden kōlyei*, proceeʝ by all means (so far as I am concerned).

OT The vb. occurs approximately 33 times in the LXX. In 20 of these instances there is no Heb. equivalent, as the passages occur in the Apocrypha. It also occurs in a few Jewish Pseudepigrapha (Gr.Enoch, Aristeas, Test.XII) and in Philo and Josephus. The LXX employs *kōlyō* most frequently to translate Heb. *kālā'* (8 times); it stands also for *māna'* (3 times), and once each for *šûḇ* (hiph.) and *'āzar*. The basic meaning is to hinder (cf. Ezek. 31:15; Job 12:15). It is used mostly in the sense of to restrain, withold. The objects of this action can be people (Gen. 23:6; Num. 11:28; Ps. 119:101) and things (wind, water, Eccl. 8:8; Ezek. 31:15; Job 12:15). The subject may be God (1 Sam. 25:26; Ezek. 31:15) or men (Moses, Num. 11:28; the writer, Pss. 40:10; 119:101).

kōlyō can denote holding back in secular contexts, where a man is the subject and things are prevented, refused, denied or withheld (Gen. 23:6; Test. Sim. 2:12). But it can be used in a religious sense, both with regard to its cause and effect. In this case it is God, one of his servants or the righteous man who does the witholding. Here *kōlyō* refers especially to the relationship of the people or of an individual to God.

NT *kōlyō* occurs 23 times in the NT of which 12 are in Lk. and Acts. Luke's use of the word is significant. Besides a purely secular use in connection with tax evasion (Lk. 23:2), he has also a theological use. In Acts 16:6 Paul is prevented by the Holy Spirit from preaching the gospel in the Roman province of Asia. By this comment Luke intends to demonstrate God's leading along the road towards Europe. Here *kōlyō* is used as a synonym for *enkoptō*.

1. (a) From the point of view of the object, the hindering relates mostly to people: soldiers are prevented from killing Paul (Acts 27:43); children are prevented from coming to Jesus (Mk. 10:14 par. Matt. 19:14, Lk. 18:16); Paul was prevented from going to Rome (Rom. 1:13) and from continuing his mission (1 Thess. 2:16). 1 Cor. 14:39 seems to be an exception, as it refers to speaking in tongues. Even so, people are directly involved.

(b) Such hindrances can stem directly from a person: a Roman centurion (Acts 24:23; 27:43); disciples or a baptizing church (Mk. 10:14 par.); circumstances (Rom. 1:13); or death (Heb. 7:23).

(c) The answer to the question, "What is hindered?" indicates clearly the dominant theological use of the vb. Most frequently it is the preaching of the gospel that is hindered (Acts 16:6; Rom. 1:13; 1 Thess. 2:16; in the widest sense, 1 Cor. 14:39). Since service is also a form of proclamation, Lk. 6:29 (cf. Mk. 14:39; Matt. 26:42) belongs to this context. Comparison of Lk. 11:52 with Matt. 23:13 reveals how the two evangelists interpreted Jesus' condemnation of the experts in the law: "But woe to you, scribes and Pharisees, hypocrites! because you shut the kingdom of heaven against men; for you neither enter yourselves, nor allow those who would enter to go in" (Matt.); "Woe to you lawyers! for you have taken away the key of knowledge; you did not enter yourselves, and you hindered those who were entering" (Lk.). Writing for Gentile readers, Lk. omits the words "kingdom of heaven", and interprets the denunciation in terms of witholding → knowledge.

2. It is striking that both Paul (e.g. Rom. 1:13) and Luke (cf. Acts 16:6) see the ultimate origin of hindrances affecting Christians not in the actions of the people concerned but in God himself (or the → Spirit of God, or Jesus). However, a disciple's own decisions and actions (whether in his dealings with his fellow men, or more particularly in his marriage relationship) clearly affect whether his faith is able to grow and develop, or whether it is constricted and hindered (cf. 1 Cor. 9:4, 7 ff.; 1 Pet. 3:7). The same applies to the church as a whole.

This leads to the question of witholding → baptism. As early as the 1st cent., when enquiries were made whether there were any obstacles in the way of a candidate for baptism, *kōlyō* became the technical term for the refusal of baptism (O. Cullmann, *Baptism in the New Testament*, 1950, 75), and Mk. 10:14 par. Matt. 10:13 ff., Lk. 18:15 ff. were used in argument against scruples over infant baptism (Cullmann, op. cit., 76 ff.; cf. Tertullian, *De baptismo*, 18). This may be due to the use of *kōlyō* in connection with baptism in the NT (Acts 8:36; 10:47; 11:17) and in early Christian baptismal texts (Gos.Eb.; Epiph., *Haer.* 30, 13, 8; Pseudo-Clement, *Homilies* 13, 4, 1; 13, 11, 2).   *C. H. Peisker*

(a). K. Aland, *Did the Early Church Baptize Infants?*, 1963; O. Cullmann, *Baptism in the New Testament*, 1950; J. Jeremias, *Infant Baptism in the First Four Centuries*, 1960; and *The Origins of Infant Baptism: A Further Study in Reply to Kurt Aland*, 1963; G. Stählin, *kopetos* etc., *TDNT* III 830–60.
(b). J. Jeremias, "Mc. 10.13–16 Parr. und die Übung der Kindertaufe in der Urkirche", *ZNW* 40, 1941, 243 ff.; B. Rehm, *Die griechisch-christlichen Schriftsteller der ersten vier Jahrhunderte*, 1953; B. Reicke, *Die Gnosis der Männer nach 1 Petrus 3, 7, BNZW* 21, 1957², 296 ff.; W. Schmithals, "Die Häretiker in Galatien", *ZNW* 47, 1956, 25 ff.; K. Wegenast, *Das Verständnis der Tradition bei Paulus und in den Deuteropaulinen, WMANT* 8, 1962, 36 ff.

Holy, Consecrate, Sanctify, Saints, Devout

The expressions "holy" and "the holy" denoted at the beginning of the history of religion power (*mana*), taboo, and then, generally the sphere of divine power which man felt to be superior and threatening. The opposite of the holy was the profane, the sphere of human life outside the realm of the holy. The roots of religion lie in the efforts to separate the holy by means of cultic and ritual processes from the desecration and contamination caused by the profane. The Greeks used three different word-groups to denote the holy. *hieros*, with its numerous derivatives, denotes the essentially holy, the taboo, the divine power, or what was consecrated to it, e.g. sanctuary, sacrifice, priest. In contrast, *hagios* – the most frequent word-group in the NT – contains an ethical element. The emphasis falls on duty to worship the holy. *hosios* also points in this direction. On the one hand, it indicates divine commandment and providence; on the other, human obligation and morality.

223

ἅγιος

ἅγιος (hagios), holy, sacred; ἁγιάζω (hagiazō), make holy, consecrate, sanctify; ἁγιασμός (hagiasmos), holiness, consecration, sanctification; ἁγιότης (hagiotēs), holiness; ἁγιωσύνη (hagiōsynē), holiness; ἁγίασμα (hagiasma), sanctuary; ἁγιαστήριον (hagiastērion), sanctuary.

CL There is no certain etymology for *hagios*. It is related to *hazomai* (from *hagiomai*) which is not found in the LXX or the NT, meaning to stand in awe of the gods or one's parents, e.g. Apollo (Homer, *Il.* 1, 21), and also to respect, e.g. of Zeus who respects those who stand under the protection of Pallas (Aesch., *Eumenides* 1002). Used metaphorically, it occurs in the expression: "it does not fill me with dread of death" (Eur., *Orestes* 1116). Negatively, it means to be filled with holy anger (Eur., *Frag.* 348). Accordingly, the adj. *hagios* would suggest less the taboo than the holy which was worthy of worship. *hagios* is not found in Homer, Hesiod or the tragedians who use the related *hagnos* (→ Pure) in a sense which corresponds very closely with the OT *qādôš*. Its connection with *hagios* is uncertain and perhaps improbable (cf. *TDNT* I 88).

hagios is found from Hdt. on, e.g. the shrine (*hiron*) of Aphrodite is holy (2, 41); an oath is also holy (Aristot., *Mirabilia* 834b 11). People, too, can be described as holy (Aristoph., *Birds* 522; despite *TDNT* I 88). Hellenism used the word as an epithet describing oriental gods (Isis, Serapis, Baal; *TDNT* I 89), whence it was also transferred to Gk. gods.

Beside *hagios* we find *hagizō*, consecrate, from which by extension *hagiazō* is formed. The latter, with its derivatives *hagiasma*, sanctuary, holiness, *hagiasmos*, holiness, *hagiastērion*, sanctuary, occurs chiefly in the LXX. The late nouns *hagiotēs* and *hagiōsynē*, holiness (also chiefly in the LXX), are derived from *hagios. hagios* was not particularly frequent in Gk. apart from the LXX. It was doubtless used as the equivalent of Heb. *qādôš*, because it expressed, in contrast to → *hieros*, not the holy in and of itself, but the challenge to worship which issues from the holy.

OT In the LXX only *hagiazō*, *hagiasma*, and *hagios* play any part. *hagiasmos* (without a clear Heb. equivalent), *hagiastērion* (4 times [3 times for Heb. *miqdāš*]), *hagiotēs* (only 2 Macc. 15:2) and *hagiōsynē* (5 times) are also found. The word-group serves predominantly to translate Heb. *qādôš* and its derivatives. In addition there are the (rare) occurrences of *nāzîr*, Nazirite, to be considered.

The decisive element in the OT concept of the holy, in contrast to the profane (*ḥōl*; cf. *ḥillēl*, defile), is not so much the awesome divine power. Rather, through certain places, objects or occasions men enter into relatively direct contact with the divine power which can be awesome, if men treat it in a profane way (1 Sam. 6:20). The basic idea is not that of separation (though this is favoured by some scholars, cf. N. H. Snaith, *The Distinctive Ideas of the Old Testament*, 1944, 24 ff.), but the positive thought of encounter which inevitably demands certain modes of response. Although Heb. worship was particularly concerned with this encounter, the sphere of the holy was wider than the cult. The holy is therefore a pre-ethical term. On the other hand, it is a concept which posits ethical values. This ethic is not the first stage of human morality, but the expression of the holiness of Yahweh in a world of both similar and different sacred practices. For example, sexual intercourse is in no way immoral. But compared with sacred practices, it is a profane act which therefore makes one impure for coming into contact with the holy (1 Sam. 21:4 ff. [MT 5 ff.]; Exod. 19:15).

1. (a) The word group does not occur frequently in the oldest sources. Yahweh is once called "this holy God" by the Philistines, because they were exposed to great disaster when they did not show proper respect for the ark of the → covenant (1 Sam. 6:19 f.). Although the OT mentions many cultic centres, only twice are places described as holy (Gilgal-Jericho, Jos. 5:15) or as holy ground (Exod. 3:5, the call of Moses; → God, OT 2). 2 Ki. 4:9 takes us out of the sphere of the cultus. The Shunammitess recognized Elisha, the man of God, as holy, i.e. like Samson full of sacred power (Jdg. 13:7; 16:17).

(b) The use of the vb. to make holy, or sanctify, is more uniform in the context of its setting than the noun and the adj. A man sanctified himself, when he had been temporarily excluded from the life of the community by uncleanness (2 Sam. 11:4), or when he came into contact with God (theophany, Exod. 19:10 ff.; holy war, 1 Sam. 21:5 ff.; family sacrifice at which Yahweh was the highest-ranking relative, 1 Sam. 16:5). One could also sanctify people (1 Sam. 7:1, to the priesthood) or things (Jos. 6:19, Jdg. 17:3 etc., silver; 1 Ki. 8:64, the temple forecourt) and thus place them at God's disposal. It is important also to mention that the LXX translates the expression "a Nazirite to God" (Samson, Jdg. 13:7; 15:17) by "a holy one of God." As Num. 6:1 ff. shows, the case of the Nazirite is a special form of consecration.

(c) One can only surmise that the rise of the great royal sanctuaries (Jerusalem, Bethel) occasioned in turn an extension of the use of the word holy. Little is known of this process. 1 Sam. 21:4 mentions holy bread; Jer. 11:15 holy sacrificial flesh. Part of the piety of the Pss. probably belongs here. The Psalmist speaks of Yahweh's holy → temple (Ps. 5:7 [MT 8] and often), of the holy hill (3:4 [MT 5]; 15:1), of holy Zion (2:6), of the holy court (29:2 LXX, RSV "array"), and also of holy heaven (20:6 [MT 7]), or the holy height from which Yahweh hears (102:19 [MT 20]), and correspondingly of his holy throne (47:8 [MT 9]). Yahweh is terrible and holy (99:3). None of the gods is holy as he is, for none casts down the exalted and raises the humble as he does (1 Sam. 2:2).

2. Prophetic polemic was scarcely directed against objects and practices which are described as holy. This is possibly connected with the wider application of the term holy. This is illustrated by the thought expressed in Ps. 24:3 f.: "Who shall stand in his holy place? He who has clean hands and a pure heart, who does not lift up his soul to what is false, and does not swear deceitfully." This suggests that, from the outset, self-consecration in the cult and the holy were never purely ritualistic matters but were concerned with one's way of life.

(a) This is clearly the case in Amos. 2:7 and 4:2. Hos. 11:9 has perhaps a similar message. Yahweh, the Holy One in the midst of his people, is nonetheless not a destroyer or demon, even when the people had been guilty of great profanity. The Holy One intends purification through a devastating catastrophe. His purpose is not destruction, but a new future for Israel. The use of the term is vividly illustrated in Isa. After the thrice-repeated "holy" of the heavenly attendants Isaiah acknowledged himself to be a man of unclean lips, whereupon his guilt was taken away and his sin covered (6:3–7). The passage contains the special Isaianic expression "the Holy One of Israel" which is used particularly in two contexts. (i) Instead of leaning on the Holy One of Israel, the people have relied on horses and chariots (31:1; cf. 30:15; 10:20). But as the Holy One, Yahweh himself intends to obtain justice in war for his people. (ii) The sinful people, laden with guilt, has despised the Holy One of Israel (1:4; cf. 30:12 f.) and will therefore be smitten by him.

(b) Another aspect of holiness occurs in the Deuteronomic formula "the holy people." In so far as the people are holy to Yahweh, their God (Deut. 7:6; 14:2, 21; 26:19), the formula explains their separation from the practices and cult objects of foreign religions (e.g. 14:21, not eating what dies of itself; 7:5, destroying altars, Asherim, graven images, etc.). As, in the last analysis, it is the whole Torah that distinguishes Israel from the foreign nations, Deut. 26:18 f. declares that through keeping the whole Torah Israel will become a people holy to Yahweh. The underlying thought here finds particularly fine expression in the "Law of Holiness" (Lev. 17–26). Lev. 19 which probably combines groups of laws of different kinds is headed, "You shall be holy for I am holy" (v. 2; cf. also 20:7).

(c) Jeremiah made very little use of the word group. However, Jer. 1:5 is important: Yahweh consecrated Jeremiah from his mother's womb to be a prophet to the nations. The words occur much more frequently in Ezek. Special mention may be made of the phrase to show oneself holy before someone. With the exception of Ezek. 28:22 (judgment on Sidon), it always refers to the house of → Israel (i.e. Judah). The clearest example is Ezek. 36:23. Yahweh's → name has been profaned through the scattering of the people, and the exiles have contributed to its further profanation. But when Yahweh gathers his people from the four corners of the earth, he will manifest himself in them before all the nations as the Holy One, and the nations will acknowledge that he is Yahweh. This means that they will recognize Yahweh as God, even if he were not their own God.

(d) If the manifestation of holiness here means the salvation of Judah, the same idea is plainly expressed in Isa. 40–55 especially in the title "the Holy One of Israel." The Holy One, the Creator of Israel (45:11; cf. 43:15), who will redeem Israel out of slavery like a kinsman (43:14), is at the same time the Creator of the world and the Lord of the nations (40:25). As such he is sufficiently removed from his people to punish them without bias, but he is also sufficiently powerful, after the punishment, to create something utterly new. Therefore nations will run to the Holy One of Israel, because he will glorify Israel (55:5).

3. By far the most extensive occurrences of the word group are to be found in the cultic, ritual texts which many scholars trace back to the exilic and post-exilic periods (Exod. 25–Num. 10; Ezek. 40–48; and parts of 1 and 2 Chr.).

(a) Everything which belongs to the realm of the cultus is holy. There are numerous holy occasions (e.g. the great → feasts, new moons, → sabbaths, year of jubilee). All the objects which serve the cultus are also holy (e.g. → temple, tent and ark, altars and their equipment, → first fruits, anointing oil, → incense). In the ritual of the oath, holy → water is used (Num. 5:17). The temple has holy → money (Exod. 28:2 ff.); the priests have holy garments (Exod. 28:2 ff.); the high priest a breast plate with the inscription "Holy to Yahweh". Sometimes holiness can be thought of almost physically: it is transferred by contact (Exod. 29:37; 30:29) and improper contact can be fatal (Num. 4:15, 20). Similarly uncleanness is also transferable (Hag. 2:11 ff.). As purity is the proper characteristic of everything that is

226

holy (→ Pure), it is the duty of everyone who takes part in the cultus to be pure (to sanctify oneself). Whoever is unclean must quickly take steps to purify himself. There are also holy people (→ priests, → Levites, Nazirites) and the holy anointing of the Davidic kings (Ps. 89:20 [MT 21]; cf. 1 Sam. 24:6 [MT 7]). A distinction can be drawn between the holy and the holiest. The sense of this distinction, however, is less a gradation of the holiness which derives from God than a gradation of human dealings with the Holy One.

(b) An important factor for understanding this strictly ordered cultic holiness, which for the most part must have been priestly knowledge, is that it received its significance, not from itself, but from a changed awareness in the post-exilic period. This awareness was stamped, on the one hand, by a passionate determination to be obedient, and, on the other, by the experience of catastrophic guilt which demanded the most meticulous care in dealings with the Holy One. This care does not contradict Hos. 6:6 ("I desire steadfast love and not sacrifice"), but is the ancient cultic means of letting the → fear of Yahweh be the beginning of all wisdom.

(c) Three additional details should be noted. (i) Occasionally the term *hagioi*, holy ones, saints, stands for heavenly companions of God (e.g. Dan. 7:21 ff.; in a different sense 7:18). (ii) Only rarely are the members of the holy nation called saints or holy. In a late wisdom Ps. saints are mentioned in parallel to those who fear Yahweh (34:9 [MT 10] → Convert; cf. 16:3, where the context is unfortunately corrupt). In Dan. 7:18 they are those who stand by their God in the war between Yahweh and the world powers, and receive the kingdom. (iii) On only three occasions is Yahweh's → Spirit called holy (Ps. 51:11 [MT 13]; Isa. 63:10 f.). In Isa. 63:10 f. the Spirit referred to is the Spirit whom God put among his people in the exodus but whom Israel has grieved through rebellion.

4. (a) Inter-Testamental Judaism introduced no real innovations into this scheme of holiness, apart from the fact that the Scriptures were now also called holy (1 Macc. 12:9; → Writing). Insignificant as this change might appear, it was nevertheless revolutionary. For from now on the Scriptures were to form the new pivotal point for the system of holiness in Judaism, thereby replacing the → temple. This process was, admittedly, only completed in the Rab. writings with their theory of the Holy Spirit as the Spirit who speaks in the Scriptures (*TDNT* VI 382 f., 385 f.). Hence, the pupils of the scribes (the holy → People) and those who obeyed the Torah were in particular regarded as holy (SB II 691 ff.). Meanwhile, as it was not the system of temple holiness that played the decisive role in every-day life but the exposition of the Torah in terms of wisdom determined by the scribes, holiness focussed more and more upon daily life. Nevertheless, temple holiness which was commanded in the Scriptures and which became a kind of religious rule was not neglected.

(b) An important feature was the slow development of the term "the saints" for the members of the Jerusalem cultic community. 1 Macc. 1:46 is significant: Antiochus' men wanted to profane the sanctuary and the saints, i.e. those who were true to the law and had by their suffering demonstrated that they steadfastly belonged to Yahweh. The same situation of suffering no doubt lies behind Tob. 12:15: the holy ones (angels) present to God the prayers of the saints.

(c) The book of Enoch and the Qumran corpus indicate a further extension of the term. Eth.Enoch 48:8 f. pronounces judgment on the mighty ones of the earth who will be delivered into the hands of the elect. "As straw in the fire so shall they burn before the face of the holy: As lead in the water shall they sink before the face of the righteous, And no trace of them shall any more be found." The context shows that it is suffering that qualifies the righteous as holy who will be vindicated in due course (cf. v. 7).

(d) In Qumran the community saw itself as the eschatological, priestly community of the saved in which the ordinances of purification which were originally obligatory only for the priests were made binding for all the members. The concept of holiness plays a big part in the Qumran texts especially in expressions of self-designation. The community described itself as "the saints of his people" (e.g. 1QM 6:6), God's "holy people" (1QM 14:12), "men of holiness" (1QS 8:13 etc.), and the "remnant of holiness" (1QS 8:21). It is the eschatological temple, "a House of Holiness for Israel, an Assembly of Supreme Holiness for Aaron" (1QS 8:5 ff.). Its members formed a unity with the heavenly community of → angels who were likewise called "Holy Ones" (cf. 1QS 11:8, 1QH 11:12). Thus there prevailed at Qumran a priestly concept of holiness in which the temple cult was replaced by special ways of obedience to the Torah such as washing, cultic meals, and especially observance of the calendar (1QS 9:3 ff.).

NT When we leave the realm of the OT and enter that of the NT, two facts stand out. First, God is only seldom described as holy (Jn. 17:11; 1 Pet. 1:15 f.; Rev. 4:8; 6:10), and Christ is only once called holy in the same sense as God (Rev. 3:7; cf. 1 Jn. 2:20). The concept of holiness in the NT is determined rather by the Holy → Spirit, the gift of the new age.

Secondly and following from this, the proper sphere of the holy in the NT is not the cultus but the prophetic. The sacred no longer belongs to things, places or rites, but to the manifestations of life produced by the Spirit. But since prophecy did not readily lend itself to the building up of a corporate consciousness, as time went on use was made of the holy priesthood (→ Priest) and the royal priesthood of all the saints. Hence cultic, sacral conceptions of holiness were again extensively taken up in the early church.

1. (a) A number of passages remain entirely within the framework of OT tradition: God's → name is called holy (Lk. 1:49), also his → covenant (Lk. 1:72; cf. 1 Macc. 1:15, 63), his → angels (Mk. 8:38; Lk. 9:26; Acts 10:22; Jude 14; Rev. 14:10), his attendants (Eph. 2:19; Col. 1:12; 1 Thess. 3:13; Rev. 18:20), the → Prophets (Lk. 1:70), and the → Scriptures (Rom. 1:2), especially the → law (Rom. 7:12). Matt. 23:17, 19; 24:15; 27:53 and Lk. 2:23 are concerned entirely with the Jewish cultus.

(b) The synoptic tradition introduces the specifically NT emphasis. Jesus was addressed by the demons as "the Holy One of God" (Mk. 1:24; Lk. 4:34). In the LXX this title occurs only in Jdg. 13:7 and 16:17 and means that the bearer has been filled by the holy. This expression indicates that Jesus was endowed at his → baptism with the Holy → Spirit and was driven into the wilderness for forty days by the Spirit, like one of the ancient prophets or a Nazirite, before he performed his first miracle (Mk. 1:21 ff.). We find probably the same concept in Lk. 1:35: "the child to be born will be called holy, the Son of God." As Samson was a holy one of God from his mother's womb (Jdg. 13:7), Jesus was holy from his conception, i.e. filled by the Holy Spirit (cf. Mk. 6:20 of John the Baptist).

A somewhat different, but analogous, idea can be recognized in Acts 4:27 (cf. 3:14), where Jesus is called God's "holy servant" (→ Son of God, art. *pais theou*). The inhabitants of Jerusalem have rejected him, as they had always denied and killed the prophets in the past (7:51 f.). In all these cases holy means belonging to God and authorized by God. Hence, resistance to Jesus is equivalent to resistance to God. *H. Seebass*

(c) The first petition of the Lord's Prayer contains the words: "Hallowed be thy name [*hagiasthētō to onoma sou*]" (Matt. 6:9; Lk. 11:2). The vb. appears only here and at Matt. 23:17, 19 in the Synoptic Gospels. "To 'hallow' the name (i.e. the nature of God as known through his self-revelation in history) means, not only to reverence and honour God, but also to glorify him by obedience to his commands, and thus prepare the coming of the Kingdom" (D. Hill, *The Gospel of Matthew*, 1972, 136). J. Jeremias links the petition with the Kaddish, an ancient Aramaic prayer which formed the conclusion of the synagogue service and which he believes Jesus knew from childhood. Jeremias reconstructs the prayer as follows: "Exalted and hallowed be his great name in the world which he created according to his will. May he let his kingdom rule in your lifetime and in your days and in the lifetime of the whole house of Israel, speedily and so on. And to this say: amen" (*The Prayers of Jesus*, 1967, 98). According to Jeremias, the first two petitions of the Lord's Prayer make entreaty for the revelation of God's eschatological kingdom. "Every accession to power by an earthly ruler is accompanied by homage in words and gestures. So it will be when God enters upon his rule" (ibid.; cf. Rev. 4:8; 11:17; 22:20; cf. 1 Cor. 16:22; Ezek. 36:23). The petitions are a cry from the depths of distress. From a world enslaved by evil, death and Satan, the disciples are to lift their eyes to the Father and cry out for the revelation of his glory, knowing in faith that he will grant it. According to Ernst Lohmeyer, the sanctification prayed for is both positive and negative. "First, it means the abolition of everything in the sensory realm contradictory to God's holiness – for the only one who is holy in his being and his actions is the one who, like the angels in the service of God, matches his actions with his being and his being with his actions. So, secondly, it means the elevation and therefore the consummation of all human and historical being in the holiness of God: 'You must be perfect as your heavenly Father is perfect.' This process of sanctification also leads beyond itself, for its ultimate end is not the sanctification of the world through God, but the sanctification of God through the world. Even the world and mankind are only elements in the process of sanctification in which God sanctifies himself" (*The Lord's Prayer*, 1965, 73; cf. Matt. 5:48; Hab. 2:14; Num. 14:21; Isa. 11:9). *C. Brown*

2. (a) In the Pauline epistles those who name Jesus as their Lord are called *hoi hagioi*, the saints. This was primarily not an ethical expression but a parallel to concepts like "called" (Rom. 1:7; 1 Cor. 1:2; 2 Cor. 1:1), "elect" (Rom. 8:33; Col. 3:12) and "faithful" (Col 1:2). It implies association with the Holy Spirit. Christ is their sanctification as well as their righteousness and redemption (1 Cor. 1:30), and thus the One in whom they become holy to the true God. "You were

washed, you were sanctified, you were justified in the name of the Lord Jesus Christ and in the Spirit of our God" (1 Cor. 6:11; cf. 2 Thess. 2:13; 1 Pet. 1:1 f.). From the resurrection on, Jesus is the Christ in the power which operates according to the Spirit of holiness (Rom. 1:4). Holiness is a condition of acceptance at the parousia and of entering upon the inheritance of God's people (Col. 1:12; Acts 20:32; 26:18). In all these cases holiness implies a relationship with God which is expressed not primarily through the cultus but through the fact that believers are "led" by the Holy Spirit (Rom. 8:14). As in the OT, holiness is a pre-ethical term. At the same time, as in the OT, it demands behaviour which rightly responds to the Holy Spirit.

(b) Sanctification is like the growth of fruit which results in eternal life (Rom. 6:19–22; cf. 1 Thess. 4:3–7). Spiritual, rational worship is the offering of oneself as a living, holy sacrifice, acceptable to God (Rom. 12:1). The saints are not simply "nice" and worthy people. They are those who are called, and an essential aspect of sanctification is love for all the saints (Eph. 1:15), standing by them in need (Rom. 12:13), and not profaning the sacred by bringing disputes with fellow-believers before secular authorities, but allowing the saints to judge them (1 Cor. 6:1 f.). In Paul's judgment, a non-Christian marriage partner does not profane the Christian. On the contrary, the non-Christian partner is sanctified by the Christian, just as the children of the marriage are also sanctified (1 Cor. 7:14). Because it is God himself who sanctifies (1 Thess. 5:23), bearing fruit unto sanctification is all the more important (Rom. 6:22; cf. Phil. 2:12–16).

3. (a) Heb. presents a highly specialized aspect of holiness. Christ, as the high priest, is the one who sanctifies his people (13:12; 2:11), and officiates in a sanctuary not made with hands (9:24; 8:2). The division of Israel's earthly sanctuary (*ta hagia*) into Holy Place and Holy of Holies (9:2 f.) shows that ultimate access to the sanctuary has not yet been achieved. But Christ has entered the sanctuary once for all with the gift of his blood and has achieved eternal redemption (9:12; 10:14). His self-offering makes absolute the animal sacrifices of the temple. By the will of God "we have been sanctified through the offering of the body of Jesus Christ once for all" (10:10). But Heb. warns us, "since we have confidence to enter the sanctuary" (10:19), not to defile the blood of the covenant, through which each one has been sanctified; "for we know him who said, 'Vengeance is mine, I will repay.' And again, 'The Lord will judge his people' " (10:29 f.; cf. Deut. 32:35 f.). Therefore we are to strive for peace with all men and the holiness without which no one can see God (12:14). Conversely, the holy brethren (3:1) are to recognize the discipline which God applies as a help, for God disciplines in order that we may win a share in his holiness (*hagiotēs*, 12:10; cf. Prov. 3:11 f.).

(b) 1 Pet. is particularly significant in the further development of the concept. To the idea of sanctification by the Spirit (1:2) there is added the blunt warning, "As obedient children, do not be conformed to the passions of your former ignorance, but as he who has called you is holy, be holy yourselves in all your conduct" (1:14 f.; cf. Lev. 19:2). This is continued in 2:5: "and like living stones be yourselves built into a spiritual house, to be a holy priesthood, to offer spiritual sacrifices acceptable to God through Jesus Christ." Thus the dynamic of the outpouring of the Spirit is here restated in terms of the holy functions of the priesthood.

H. Seebass

(c) Believers are again seen as → priests in Rev. 1:6, 5:10 and 20:6. But Rev. also depicts the future abode of Christians as the holy city, the new → Jerusalem (21:2, 10; 22:19). The most significant feature of Jerusalem was the fact that it contained the → temple, the focal point of meeting between God and man. But in the new Jerusalem there is no temple, "for its temple is the Lord God the Almighty and the Lamb" (21:22). These pictures present both a continuity with the divinely appointed institutions of Israel and a radical break with the historic Israel. It has been argued that to see the church in such institutional terms represents an institutionalizing of the dynamic, charismatic character of the primitive Christian community. In so doing the church was guarding itself against the type of excesses which befell the church at Corinth. But the use of this imagery has a more significant function. On the one hand, its application to the church means that the historic institutions in Israel are now obsolete. On the other hand, the use of the concepts of priest, temple and holy city in this dynamic and spiritual way affords a perspective to the suffering, persecuted church which enables it to see its situation and role in terms of God's purposes.

(d) In the Fourth Gospel the adj. *hagios* is used only of the → Father (Jn. 17:11 in the high priestly prayer of Jesus in the address "Holy Father"), the → Spirit ("this is he who baptizes with the Holy Spirit", 1:33; the → "advocate" or "paraclete", 14:26; "He breathed on them, and said to them, 'Receive the Holy Spirit' ", 20:22), and the → Son (6:69). This latter passage occurs in Jn.'s account of Peter's confession. In Jn. Jesus is not confessed as the Christ (cf. Matt. 16:16; Mk. 8:29; Lk. 9:20) with all its Jewish overtones, but as the "Holy One of God [*ho hagios tou theou*]" (cf. L. Morris, *The Gospel According to John*, 1971, 388 ff.). The expression is rare. It occurs in the NT only in the address of the demoniac at Capernaum (Mk. 1:24; Lk. 4:24; cf. Pss. 16:10; 106:16). Although Jn. was thoroughly aware of Jewish christology (1:39 ff., 49 ff.; 4:25; 10:36; 12:13; 20:31; cf. C. H. Dodd, *The Interpretation of the Fourth Gospel*, 1953, 228 ff.; E. M. Sidebottom, *The Christ of the Fourth Gospel*, 1961, 70 f.), he apparently refrains from giving an accepted christological title here. Nevertheless, the fact that he uses the epithet "holy" elsewhere only of the Father and the Spirit sets Jesus with God and not man. The expression "the Holy One" strikingly occurs in the only instance of *hagios* in the Johannine epistles: "But you have been anointed by the Holy One, and you all know" (1 Jn. 2:20). The reference is evidently to the Holy Spirit, but the context closely links this with the Father and the Son (cf. vv. 22 ff.).

The vb. *hagiazō* occurs 4 times in Jn. and is absent from the Johannine epistles. In the first instance it denotes the special consecration of Jesus to do the will and work of the Father, but its goal is that men might also be consecrated to do God's will. As such, it extends the use of the adj. In reply to the Jews who were about to stone him for blasphemy ("because you, being a man, make yourself God", 10:33; cf. Lev. 24:16), Jesus pointed to the extension of the word "God" to men in the OT (10:34; cf. Ps. 82:6) but carefully avoided the title "God" for himself. Instead, he asked: "Do you say of him whom the Father consecrated [*hēgiasen*] and sent into the world, 'You are blaspheming,' because I said, 'I am the Son of God'?" (10:36), and went on to claim to be doing the work of the Father. In the high priestly prayer Jesus prayed: "Sanctify [*hagiason*] them in the truth; thy word is truth. . . . And for their sake I consecrate [*hagiazō*] myself, that they also may be consecrated

231

[*hēgiasmenoi*] in truth" (17:17, 19). Leon Morris draws attention to the use of *hagiazō* in the LXX for the sanctifying of priests (e.g. Exod. 28:41; 29:1, 21) and sacrifices (e.g. Exod. 28:38; Num. 18:9). "He set Himself apart for the doing of the Father's will, and in this context this must surely mean death. It points us to Calvary and all that Calvary means. This is connected with the disciples in two ways. It is 'for their sakes.' He dies for them, to do for them that which they could not do for themselves. And further it is 'that they themselves also may be sanctified in truth.' He dies with a view to the disciples being sanctified, being set apart for God" (op. cit., 731 f.; cf. also E. C. Hoskyns, *The Fourth Gospel*, ed. F. N. Davey, 1947², 502 ff.). On → truth see Jn. 1:17 and 3:21; cf. L. Morris, op. cit., 293 ff. Doing the will of God is also doing the truth (cf. Ps. 119:142 LXX). To do this, men need to be consecrated, as the context of all these pronouncements in Jn. make clear.

C. Brown

| ἱερός |

ἱερός (*hieros*), holy; ἱερατεία (*hierateia*), priestly office or service; ἱερατεύω (*hierateuō*), hold or perform the office of a priest; ἱερουργέω (*hierourgeō*), perform holy service, act as a priest; ἱεράτευμα (*hierateuma*), priesthood; ἱεροπρεπής (*hieroprepēs*), befitting a holy person or thing; ἱεροσυλέω (*hierosyleō*), rob temples; ἱερόθυτος (*hierothytos*), devoted, sacrificed to a divinity; ἱερεύς (*hiereus*), priest; ἀρχιερεύς (*archiereus*), high priest; τὰ ἱερά (*ta hiera*), sacrifice; ἱερωσύνη (*hierōsynē*), priestly office, priesthood; τὸ ἱερόν (*to hieron*), sanctuary, temple.

The words derived from *hieros* not only form a common group philologically, but are also related internally in their meaning. They are therefore treated all together in the CL section. In the OT and NT sections, the reader is referred to the article on Priest for words connected with priesthood.

CL *hieros* is that which is determined, filled or consecrated by divine power. In contrast to → *hagios*, holy, → *hosios*, devout, pious, and *semnos*, revered, august (→ Godliness, art. *sebomai*), all of which contain an ethical element, *hieros* denotes what is holy in and of itself, quite apart from any ethical judgment. It is not used of the gods themselves, but of their activities. The expression *hieron genos athanatōn*, holy race of immortals (Hesiod, *Theog.* 21), reflects the idea that the race of the immortals represents in the universe the realm of the absolutely holy. Thus *hieros* means: (a) what belongs to the sphere of the gods; (b) what has been sanctified by the gods; (c) what has been consecrated to the gods.

1. (a) Among objects described as holy are the head of Zeus (Homer, *Il.* 15, 39) and his bed (Hesiod, *Theog.* 57), the abode of the gods (the snowy regions of Olympus, Aristoph., *Nubes* 270), the scales of Kronos (Homer, *Il.*, 16, 658), the bow of Hercules (Soph., *Phil.* 943), and the chariot of Achilles to whom the son of Kronos had granted divine horses (Homer, *Il.* 17, 464).

(b) The gods sanctified, e.g., the light (Hesiod, *Works* 337), the air, night and day (Homer, *Il.* 8, 66; 11, 194), the earth (Soph., *Phil.* 706), fruitful ground (Aristoph., *Nubes* 282), the rivers and streams poured out by Zeus (Homer, *Od.* 10,

351), the threshing-floor, because it is sacred to Demeter (Homer, *Il*. 5, 499), the fish consecrated to Poseidon (Homer, *Il*. 16, 407), and also cities like Ilium, Pergamum, Thebes, Athens, islands like Euboea and even the Hellespont. Similarly, people are said to be *hieroi*, because they possess a trait which comes from the gods. This is illustrated by phrases like *hieron menos Alkinooio* or *hierē is Tēlemachoio* (Homer, *Od*. 7, 167; 2, 409); Alcinous received his power from Zeus and Telemachus his might from Athene. In Pindar, *Pyth*. 5, 97, kings are called *hieroi*, because they received their sovereignty from the gods. But Democritus said of the poet that he writes through divine afflatus and sacred inspiration, *met' enthousiasmou kai hierou pneumatos* (*Frag*. 18). From the time of Augustus (63 B.C.–A.D. 14) the Roman emperor was addressed by the title *hieros*. Not only his person but everything connected with him came to be counted as *hieros*, because it had been sanctified by the gods, e.g. the *hiera grammata*, the imperial decrees (cf. G. Schrenk, *TDNT* III 225).

2. (a) The thought of consecration to the gods leads into the realm of the cultus which was the decisive general factor in determining the meaning of *hieros*, as a glance at its compounds demonstrates. Even if everything which is called *hieros* does not belong directly to the cultus, it nevertheless remains associated with it. This remains true, when the choruses in the theatre are called *hieroi*, for they convey a divine message (Aristoph., *Ranae* 674, 686), when non-cultic songs consecrated to the gods are *hieroi*, and the circle in which justice is administered is called *hieros* (Homer, *Il*. 18, 504). Again, *hieros* can similarly be used of people, especially of those who have been initiated into the mysteries (cf. Aristoph., *Ranae* 652, *anthrōpos hieros*).

(b) *ta hiera*, lit. the holy things (rarer in the sing.), denotes above all the sacrifice (e.g. Homer, *Il*. 1, 147), and occasionally the sacrificial animal (Homer, *Il*. 2, 420). In post-Homeric times it frequently denoted the omens which accompanied the sacrifice. *ta hiera* was more commonly used for cultic objects (images, vestments, sacred utensils etc.), cultic actions, and for the cultus in general (e.g. Hdt., 1, 172; cf. 3 Macc. 3:21).

(c) *to hieron* has predominantly the meaning of sanctuary, cultic centre. In contrast to *naos*, temple building, and to *temenos*, sacred area (→ Temple), it is a more general term which can denote the temple building, the sacred area, and also the sacred grove as the local cultic centre.

(d) *hierōsynē* is not particularly frequent and means priesthood, in the sense of office, service and living. In contrast, *hierateia* means priestly activity, the office, but this too is not very frequent. The related vb. *hierateuō*, perform the office of a priest, was not used until a later period. The vb. *hierasthai*, to be a priest, is more ancient and both words are derived from it. The related adj. *hieratikos* occurs frequently and generally denotes anything priestly. *hierateuma* is found only in the LXX (→ Priest).

3. *hierourgeō*, perform sacred rites, *hieroprepēs*, befitting the sacred, *hierosyleō*, rob a temple or commit sacrilege, and their derivatives need no further explanation. But further comment is necessary on *hierothytos* and especially *hiereus* and *archiereus*.

(a) *hierothytos* means devoted, offered to a god, sacrificed, and is a specifically cultic term. The plur. *ta hierothyta* means the sacrifice or sacrificial flesh. In a metaphorical sense it occurs in Pindar, *Frag.* 78, of human sacrificial death as an offering to the gods.

(b) *hiereus* means priest, sacrificer, diviner. In Homer it occurs in par. to *mantis* (*Il.* 1, 62; 62, 221). In so far as the priest is skilled in dealing with the sacred he is also a soothsayer who can give information on things to do with the gods.

A → sacrifice did not necessarily have to be offered by a priest. The head of the family could carry out the family sacrifice, the chief of the tribe the tribal sacrifice, and the magistrate the sacrifice for the city. Isoc. laid down the ideal, *tēn basileian hōsper hierōsynēn pantos andros einai nomizousin,* "they believe that kingship, like priesthood, belongs to every man" (2, 6). But the great and important cultic centres required continuous care and therefore an official priesthood which lived in accordance with temple rather than family tradition. Even if the work of the priests included dealing with many sacred objects, their most obvious and appropriate activity was nevertheless the slaughter of the sacrifices. Hence, *hiereuō,* to sacrifice, has also the meaning of slay and kill (*Il.* 2, 34; Procopius Gazaeus 2, 25).

(c) *archiereus* as a title occurs first in references to non-Gk. high priests (Hdt. 2, 142, of Egyptian high priests of high rank after the king; cf. the Greek titles *hierapolos,* chief priest, *hierarchēs,* president of sacred rites, high priest). Plato used it in connection with his ideal state (*Laws* 12, 947a); the *archiereus* was to stand annually at the head of all the officiating priests.

In the Hel. period under the Seleucids there were official *archiereis* for the satrapies of the day. The chief priests of the great sanctuaries carried the same title. Even under the Ptolemaic kings *archiereis* are sometimes mentioned. Under the Romans the system of the Seleucids was continued. The provincial high priest of the imperial cult was called *archiereus tou Sebastou (tōn Sebastōn).* At the head stood the emperor himself as *pontifex maximus.* From Polyb. (3rd–2nd cents. B.C.) on, *archiereus* was translated by the Lat. *pontifex.* Over and above these, the title *archiereus* was also granted to local high priests and to the heads of religious communities, in so far as these were centred on a sanctuary.

OT In the LXX the following words form a unified group, for they all go back to the Heb. *kōhēn,* in form the participle of *kāhan,* to be a priest, serve as priest (its etymology is uncertain and does not add anything to our understanding of the word): *hierateia, hierateuō, hierateuma, hieratikos* (without Heb. equivalent), *hiereus, hierourgeō* (without Heb. equivalent), *hierourgia* (without Heb. equivalent), *hierōma* (without Heb. equivalent), *hierōsynē, archierasthai* (without Heb. equivalent), *archierateuō* (without Heb. equivalent), *archiereus, archierōsynē* (without Heb. equivalent). If one ignores completely peripheral words (e.g. *hierosyleō* and its derivatives in 1 and 2 Macc.; *hierodoulos* in 1 Esd.), these form the overwhelming majority of instances, the only exceptions being *hieros* (6 times for Heb. equivalents) and *hiereia* (2 Ki. 10:20 for Heb. *ʿaṣārâh,* a solemn assembly for Baal).

hieros did not fit the Jewish concept of holiness prevailing at the time of the translation of the LXX, because it meant what is holy in and of itself apart from any ethical element, whereas since the exile only what conformed to the Torah could to the Jewish mind be holy. Even the temple in Jerusalem was not generally called *to hieron* until the strongly Hel. writings of the LXX (also Philo and Josephus; exceptions are 1 Chr. 29:4; cf. 1 Chr. 9:27; 2 Chr. 6:13). The word-group could, however, be used for the priest and his activities, for this was essentially a matter of the cultus for which, according to the law, no one else could be qualified. For *hiereus*, *hierateia* and *hierateuma* see the discussion under → Priest.

NT 1. In the NT most of the words in the group occur only rarely.

(a) *hierothyton* (only 1 Cor. 10:28) is the meat (→ Flesh) which had been slaughtered in the pagan cult. The fact that some Christians continued to eat it, knowing its origin, caused questions of → conscience at Corinth which Paul sought to resolve by directing the church to the glory of God and concern for others (1 Cor. 10:31 ff.).

(b) *hieroprepēs*, befitting a holy person or thing, worthy of reverence (only Tit. 2:3) corresponds with the "preference for solemn and cultic style" in the Pastorals (*TDNT* III 254). The context suggests that the nearest parallel usage would be one like Plut., *On the Education of Children* 14p. 11c, where it is *hieroprepestaton* to accustom boys to the truth. Thus in Tit. 2:3 the older women in the congregation should be conformed to propriety in their behaviour.

(c) *hieros*, sacred, holy, occurs in 2 Tim. 3:15 in a similarly solemn context of the "sacred writings." Similar formulae are frequent in Philo and Josephus (cf. *TDNT* III 227). Although the word was otherwise not popular, it could perhaps be used more easily of the Scriptures because they possessed a sacred quality all their own. In a comparison (1 Cor. 9:13) Paul uses *ta hiera* in its usual sense of sacred actions.

(d) *hierosylos*, temple robber, one who commits sacrilege. In Acts 19:37 Paul and his companions were defended by the town clerk of Ephesus against the charge of being sacrilegious and blasphemers against pagan temples. Paul was accused of teaching that "gods made with hands are not gods" and thus of undermining both trade and the temple of Artemis (Acts 19:26 f.). The related vb., *hierosyleō*, rob temples (Rom. 2:22), apparently alludes to a problem frequently aired in Rab. discussion. To what extent was it permissible to do business in pagan-temple utensils and property, although they were ritually unclean? Under certain circumstances such dealings were allowed, if they contributed to the damaging of the pagan cult. Paul seems to be rejecting such devious practices (cf. O. Michel, *Der Brief an die Römer*, 1955[10] ad loc.). ([Ed.] The verse may also allude to the practice of some Jews of removing gold and silver idols from shrines for private profit (cf. Josephus, *Ant.* 4, 8, 10.)

(e) *hierourgeō*, perform holy service, act as a priest with regard to something. In Rom. 15:16 Paul makes metaphorical use of the language of the cultus; the Gentiles must now offer sacrifice to the true God. A sacrifice can only be acceptable, if it fulfils all the conditions for acceptance. The only true offering is the gospel. Paul has been ordained, therefore, not as priest but as *hierourgōn* of the gospel, in order to give correct instruction in offering sacrifice.

2. *to hieron* and *hiereus/archiereus* occur more frequently. *to hieron* is, almost without exception, a technical term for Herod's temple (exceptions: any sanctuary, 1 Cor. 9:13; the temple of Artemis, Acts 19:27). The most important difference between it and *naos* (→ Temple) is that *to hieron* is never spiritualized. It always means the structure with its walls, gates, porticos, courts and buildings. The pinnacle (Matt. 4:5; Lk. 4:9) of the *hieron*, which never denoted the temple itself, was perhaps the South-East corner of the outer wall, below which the ground fell

235

away steeply into the Kidron valley. Lk. 3:37 and Mk. 12:4 ff. refer to the court of the women; Acts 3:8 to the court of the men; Mk. 11:15 perhaps to the outermost court, that of the Gentiles. Jn. 10:23 mentions Solomon's portico, one of the great colonnades which surrounded the court of the Gentiles and in which teaching took place (Mk. 11:27–13:1; Matt. 21:23–24:1; Lk. 20:1–21:38; Jn. 5:14; 7:14, 29; 8:20; Acts 3:11; 5:12, 21, 25, 42), and also prayer (Acts 2:46; Lk. 18:10). Three points are of theological importance.

(a) The Gospels make it clear that Jesus was frequently in the temple and that he did not condemn the form of piety which made use of it. According to Mk. 13:1 ff. and par. Matt. 24:1, Lk. 21:5, he announced the destruction of the temple with sorrow. When he drove the money-changers and dealers in animals out of the the court of the Gentiles and forbade anyone to carry merchandise through it (Matt. 22:12 ff.; Mk. 11:15 ff.; Lk. 19:45 ff.), he justified his action by saying that the temple was God's house set apart for prayer but men have made it a den of robbers (cf. Isa. 56:7; Jer. 7:11). It has become a house of trade (Jn. 2:16). Jesus did not seek to free himself from the obligations of the religion of his fathers which was held together by the temple. Nevertheless, he did not hesitate to purify it with the authority of the one who, when the material temple was destroyed, would in three days build the true *naos* (Jn. 2:19; cf. Mk. 14:58; Acts 6:14). The idea of a special holy place is now superfluous.

(b) The earliest Jewish Christians followed Jesus by using the temple for their prayers (Lk. 24:53; Acts 2:46).

(c) The evangelist Luke shows a particular interest in Jesus' devotion to the temple (2:46), and in that of the early Christians and even in that of Paul, the apostle of the Gentiles (Acts 21:26 ff.; 22:17; 24:12, 18, 25:8). He does this to prove that the Christians are the true people of God and have been unjustly accused by the Jews.

3. For *hiereus* and *archiereus* which belong to the same group → Priest.

H. Seebass

ὅσιος	ὅσιος (hosios), holy, devout, pious; ὁσιότης (hosiotēs), holiness, devoutness, piety; ἀνόσιος (anosios), unholy.

CL In Gk. literature the earliest form of word of this group is *hosiē*. It stood for what was in accordance with divine direction and providence. "It is not in accord with divine appointment to contrive evil one against another" (Homer, *Od.* 16, 423). *hosiēs pleon eipein* (Emp. 4, 7) means to say more than is required of one. More particularly *hosios* can mean the obligations laid on men in ritual and ceremonies, e.g. burial rites. The adj. *hosios* (found, like *hosiotēs*, from Plato on) therefore has the general sense of sanctioned or allowed by divine or natural law. *hosios* is seen in perspective when it is compared, on the one hand, with *dikaios* (→ Righteousness). Thus *ta hosia kai dikaia* (Plato, *Politics* 301d) means what is established by human agreement and divine ordinance. On the other hand, it may be compared with → *hieros* which, as a cultic ritual taboo or as what has been sanctified through the sanctuary, stands in contrast with the profane even when it has been consecrated to a god. Thus *kosmein tēn polin kai tois hierois kai tois hosiois* (Isoc., 153b) means to adorn the city with sacred and profane buildings.

Used of people, *hosios* means pious, religious; of actions, pure, clean (Emp., 4, 2, the mouth; Aesch., *Cho.* 378, the hands; cf. 1 Tim. 2:8). To describe the gods, it is used late and very rarely along with *dikaios* (*CIG* 3830).

OT *hosios* is used predominantly to translate Heb. *ḥāsîd* (a poetical word, occuring chiefly in the Pss.). *ḥāsîd* denotes the man who readily accepts the obligations which arise from the people's relationship to God, "the loyal, the pious one" (Koehler-Baumgartner, 319). It is related to *ḥesed* which denotes the loyal, loving-kindness of Yahweh for Israel within his → covenant (cf. W. Eichrodt, *Theology of the Old Testament*, I, 1961, 232–9). The earliest occurrence (Deut. 33:8) in the blessing of Levi describes the fellowship of the Levites as "thy *ḥāsîd*", because Levi has proved loyal when tested by God. But *ḥāsîd* occurs most frequently in the plur. and means the congregation gathered for worship (e.g. Ps. 85:8[9]) serving God (Ps. 79:2). "Gather to me my faithful ones [*ḥᵃsîday*], who made a covenant with me by sacrifice!" (Ps. 50:5). The gentile nations are not *ḥāsîd*, and within the people of God the *ḥᵃsîdîm* are contrasted in the liturgical Ps. 15 with those declared guilty. Even in the context of strict observance of the → law, *ḥāsîd* can have the sense of trusting. Because Yahweh forgives sins, everyone who is *ḥāsîd* towards him prays to him (Ps. 32:6; cf. 52:9 f.[10]). It can also mean that whoever trusts in his integrity (LXX *hosiotēs*) is righteous (Prov. 14:32).

ḥᵃsîdîm as the name of a particular group within Jud. does not occur until the time of the Maccabees (1 Macc. 2:42; 7:13; 2 Macc. 14:6). This group seems to have lived in accordance with apocalyptic tradition and therefore to have observed the law particularly strictly. The absence of the word in the Qumran documents is, however, striking. Clearly it was not a self-designation of the community but a name attached to it by those outside. ([Tr.] There are grounds for thinking that the term dropped out of use, when this group split into two or more parties.)

God is twice described as *hosios*. In Deut. 32:4 it translates *yāšār*, upright; God observes the decrees which he himself has made. In Ps. 145:17 it stands for *ḥāsîd*. God supports the fallen, satisfies the hungry and is near to those who pray to him (cf. also Wis. 5:19). God takes *hosiotēs* as an invincible shield (see below on Rev. 15:4). *ta hosia* (Deut. 29:19[18], *šālôm*), are correspondingly, the kindnesses which one expects from God, and in Isa. 55:3 (plur. of *ḥesed*) the successes which David could expect from God (David as a witness to the power of God among the nations).

NT 1. In the NT *hosios* is a rare word (8 occurrences, of which 5 are in quotations; *hosiotēs* twice; *anosios* twice). The most important OT use (*hosioi*, the congregation) does not appear. The members of the Christian community are not *ḥᵃsîdîm*, but chosen ones (*eklektoi*; → Election, art. *eklegomai*) and saints (→ *hagios*). Only in the more strongly Hel. writings is there occasional use of *hosios* (e.g. Lk. 1:75, of Jewish piety) and the negative *anosios* (1 Tim. 1:9, where the law is said to have been laid down for the unholy; cf. 2 Tim. 3:2). Eph. 4:24 mentions *hosiotēs* as one of the qualities of the new man.

2. God is twice called *hosios* in quotations. The hymn of Rev. 15:3, 4 goes back to Ps. 145:17 and its context (God alone is *hosios*). Rev. 16:5 recalls Deut. 32:4; God is equally *dikaios* (just in judgment) and *hosios* (holy in judgment), when he condemns evildoers.

3. The use of *hosios* in Heb. 7:26 is unique. Here the word is used absolutely in the way in which elsewhere it can be used only of God. As high priest (*archiereus*), Christ is completely *hosios*, utterly without sin and utterly pure, so that his offering is sufficient once for all. Acts 2:27 and 13:35 (quoting Ps. 16:10) make a different point. God's promise, not to let his Holy One (*hosios*; cf. Heb. *ḥāsîḏ*) see destruction, was not fulfilled in David. It has only now been fulfilled in Christ. By virtue of the → resurrection Jesus is the true *ḥāsîḏ*, although he was condemned by the religious authorities as a religious criminal. Hence, he is also heir to the kindnesses which David was to expect from God (Acts 13:34, quoting Isa. 55:3), and has been given authority to judge all nations (Acts 17:31).   *H. Seebass*

→ Lord, → Priest, → Sacrifice, → Serve, Deacon, Worship, → Temple

(a). E. H. Askwith, *The Christian Conception of Holiness*, 1900; J. G. Davies, "The Concept of Holiness", *London Quarterly Review* 185, 1960, 36–44; W. Eichrodt, *Theology of the Old Testament*, I, 1961; II, 1967 (see index); J. H. Elliott, *The Elect and the Holy*, Supplements to NovT 12, 1966; G. Fohrer, *History of Israelite Religion*, 1973; F. Hauck, *hosios*, *TDNT* V 489–93; O. R. Jones, *The Concept of Holiness*, 1961; L. E. Keck, "The Poor and the Saints in Jewish Christianity and Qumran", *ZNW* 57, 1966, 54 ff.; J. Muilenburg, "Holiness", *IDB* II 616–25; S. Neill, *Christian Holiness*, 1960; M. Noth, "The Holy Ones of the Most High", *The Laws in the Pentateuch and Other Studies*, 1966, 215–28; R. Otto, *The Idea of the Holy*, 1923; E. Pax, "Holy", *EBT* I 372–75; O. Procksch and K. G. Kuhn, *hagios* etc., *TDNT* I 88–115; G. von Rad, *Old Testament Theology*, I, 1962, 203–7 and 271–79; H. Ringgren, *The Prophetical Conception of Holiness*, 1948; and *Israelite Religion*, 1966; J. C. Ryle, *Holiness*, (1879) 1952; D. S. Shapiro, "The Meaning of Holiness in Judaism", *Tradition* 7, 1, 1965, 46–80; G. Schrenk, *hieros* etc., *TDNT* III 221–32; N. H. Snaith, *The Distinctive Ideas of the Old Testament*, 1944, 21–50; N. Walker, "The Origin of the 'Thrice-Holy' ", *NTS* 5, 1958–59, 132 f.; A. S. Wood, "Holiness", *ZPEB* III 173–83.
(b). R. Asting, *Die Heiligkeit im Urchristentum*, 1930; W. W. von Baudissin, *Studien zur semitischen Religionsgeschichte*, II, 1878; H. Bardtke, "Heilig und Profan", *EKL* II 52 ff.; J. Dillersberger, *Das Heilige im Neuen Testament*, 1926; J. Hänel, *Die Religion der Heiligkeit*, 1931; B. Häring, *Das Heilige und das Gute*, 1950; E. Issel, *Der Begriff der Heiligkeit im Neuen Testament*, 1881; K. Koch, "Die Eigenart der priesterschriftlichen Sinaigesetzgebung", *ZTK* 55, 1958, 36 ff.; G. Lanczkowski *et al.*, "Heilig", *RGG³* III 146 ff.; F. J. Leenhardt, *La Notion de Sainteté dans l'Ancien Testament*, 1929; O. Schilling, *Das Heilige und das Gute im Alten Testament*, 1956.

Hope, Expectation

Of the various terms which express hope or expectancy, the most frequently used and the richest in meaning in NT Gk. are the noun *elpis*, the vb. *elpizō* and their derivatives. Both words denote, on the one hand, the act of hoping, but both include also the idea of the object hoped for. Thus *ta elpizomena* means the good things hoped for, and *elpis* the object of good hope as well as the act of hope. The other words, which are dealt with in a second article, form a group because of their common derivation from the stem *dok-* or *dek-*, to receive, accept, and have an essentially narrower range of meaning. The noun *apokaradokia* denotes a longing, almost impatient expectancy. *prosdokaō* and *prosdokia* imply fearful anticipation of something (catastrophe, war). *prosdechomai*, beside its frequent meaning, to take up, accept, can also mean wait for, expect, and is therefore also treated here.

ἐλπίς

ἐλπίς (*elpis*), expectation, hope; ἐλπίζω (*elpizō*), expect, hope; ἀπελπίζω (*apelpizō*), expect back; προελπίζω (*proelpizō*), hope in advance.

CL *elp-*, the stem of *elpis, elpizō*, was formed from the root *vel (cf. Lat. *velle*, to wish) by extension with *p* (also retained in Lat. *voluptas*, desire). In secular Gk. *elpis* does not correspond with our word hope, since it is a general word for the anticipation of future events of all kinds, of good (hope) or evil (fear). A synonym of *prosdokia*, expectation, it can be used to denote hope by the addition of adjs. like *agathē, glykeia, hilara* (good, bright, joyful). The vb. *elpizō* means not only hope, but also expect, suppose, think.

Living hope as a fundamental religious attitude was unknown in Gk. culture. Admittedly Theognis said, "As long as you live by honouring the gods, hold on to hope!" and Horace called *fides* (faith, loyalty) the companion of *spes* (hope). But in the final analysis men had to stand without hope before the hostile forces of guilt and death. Sophocles' chorus lamented, "The highest remains, never to be brought to life." Seneca called hope the definition of "an uncertain good". But deification and immortality promised by the mystery religions were human pipe dreams. (For further examples see R. Bultmann, *elpis, TDNT* II 518 ff.)

OT 1. *Hope in the Heb. OT.* (a) Heb. has four main vbs. meaning to hope: (i) *qāwâh* (connected with *qāw*, stretched out, plumbline), to be stretched out towards, to long after, wait for (with God as obj. 26 times); (ii) *yāḥal*, to wait, long (for God, 27 times); (iii) *ḥāḵâh*, to wait (for God, 7 times); (iv) *śāḇar*, to wait, hope (for God, 4 times). The four corresponding nouns are not much in evidence (they are used in 9 passages of hope in God). The most common is *tiqwâh* (17 times). Various forms of *beṭaḥ* which has more the meaning of trust and security are also translated by *elpis* in the LXX (see 2 below). Hoping as an act stands in the foreground and occurs in promises and exhortations, but most of all as a confession of assurance, especially in the Pss. The Heb. vbs. of hoping are closely connected with those of trust (→ Faith, art. *pistis*).

(b) Of 146 passages in which vbs. or nouns describe hoping, half do so in a secular sense. In these it is an expectation combined with certainty and tension, directed towards some definite desired object or event still lying in the future. Whether the certainty supporting such an expectation is valid and has an objective basis, or whether it is grounded in a subjective and erroneous assessment is an open question. What characterizes the judgment of this secular hope is the fact that in many passages, despite its personal intensity, it is described as futile. Prov. in particular emphasizes that the fool's hope (i.e. that of the godless) will come to nothing (11:7).

(c) The testimony of the OT to hope in God. This hope is often the subject of the OT even where the terms do not occur. In formal structure it resembles secular hope (see above), but is essentially different in content, basis and effects. In the 73 passages in which the hope of the faithful of Israel is expressed through the vb. or noun Yahweh is named as the object of hope. "To hope in Yahweh", "to wait for Yahweh" are expressions created by the OT writers. Those Babylonians whose prayers have come down to us never called their gods their "Hope". But an Israelite could pray, "Thou, O Lord, art my hope" (Ps. 71:5). Jeremiah spoke of "Thou hope of Israel" (14:8; 17:13). Thus Yahweh was the object, embodiment and guarantor of his people's hope. People wait for his name (Ps. 52:9 RSV mg.), for his word of forgiveness (Ps. 130:5), his arm (Isa. 51:5), his salvation (Gen. 49:18).

In eschatological passages the content of the hope is not expressed in abstract terms but in the form of a vision. For this reason the words of hope seldom occur there (but see Isa. 25:9; 42:4; 51:5; Hab. 2:3). The horizon of hope in the OT stretches far beyond what the majority of witnesses could see in terms of personal hope for their individual lives. It embraces Yahweh's coming in glory, his reign over a new → earth, the → conversion of Israel and the nations, and the new → covenant, based on the → forgiveness of sins. An important element in the maintenance of a pure hope was the struggle of the classical → prophets against false prophets, with their false hope and dreams of salvation. A glance at the prophetic writings and the Pss. shows that Israel, throughout a history so frequently marked by judgment in the shape of different calamities, repeatedly looked to God for the continuation of his gracious dealings with them (cf. Hos. 12:7; Jer. 31:17; Isa. 40:31; Ps. 40:1). Such hope, therefore, was a gift of God (Ps. 62:5, "my hope is from him"; Jer. 29:11, "to give you a future and a hope"). Wherever, humanly speaking, the future seemed a dead end, prophets of judgment like Hosea, Jeremiah and Ezekiel opened up the divine perspective of a new beginning (cf. Hos. 2; Jer. 29:1 ff.; 31:31–34; Ezek. 36;37). In the Pss., where in a lament fearful pleading is followed by statements of joyous hope, form critics explain the latter as "priestly oracles of salvation", promises of salvation from God mediated to the worshipper by a priest.

(d) (i) As a subjective attitude, the hope of faith, like secular hope, is a concrete personal expectation. Despite the "not yet" of the realization of salvation, it looks forward confidently though not without tension. However, Yahweh, for whom it waits, is not like us men. Since he knows, promises and brings to pass what the future holds for his people, hope attains unparalleled assurance in the realm of revelation. Despite everything which at present runs counter to the promise, the one who hopes trusts God for his faithfulness' sake not to disappoint the hope he has awakened through his word (Isa. 8:17; Mic. 7:7; Ps. 42:5).

(ii) Hand in hand with confident anticipation of God's gracious dealing goes submission to the sovereign rule of the Almighty. The time and manner of fulfilment are left to him. Therefore hope and the → fear of God are parallel in many Pss. (e.g. 33:18; 147:11; cf. Prov. 23:17, 18). To the one who fears the Lord a future and hope are promised.

(iii) Through confidence and humility hope becomes a patient, persevering waiting which can endure anxiety.

(iv) Waiting for God does indeed make men "still" but not inactive. It demonstrates the new strength (Isa. 40:31) they have received by the overcoming of temptation and by actions directed towards the hoped for future. During the siege Jeremiah bought a field to bear witness to the word of the Lord that "houses and fields and vineyards shall again be bought in this land" (32:6 ff.).

2. *LXX and Rab. Judaism.* (a) The LXX uses *elpizō* primarily to translate vbs. of trusting: (a) 46 times for *bāṭaḥ*, to feel safe, to rely; (b) 20 times for *ḥāsâh*, to take refuge, to hide; (c) 16 times for *yāḥal*, to wait; (d) only twice for *qāwâh*, to wait anxiously. This last is translated a further 26 times by *hypomenō* (→ Patience), which means to hold out rather than expect. This marked rapprochement with the vbs. of trusting distinguishes LXX usage from that of secular Gk. and prepares the way for the NT understanding of *elpizō*.

(b) The whole of post-OT Judaism is characterized by a variety of eschatological expectations, directed in the first place towards the coming of the messiah and the restoration of the kingdom of Israel. These hopes were often disappointed. Men rose with messianic claims and set the enthusiasm of the people ablaze. But sooner or later all these movements collapsed. This explains the pessimistic streak which accompanied the eschatological expectations of the Rabbis. God's kingdom could only come when Israel was completely obedient to the law. But this gave rise to an element of uncertainty: who could really say what complete obedience was? This made the individual's personal hope uncertain too: who could say that God was really pleased with him? The Pss. Sol., on the other hand, contain the messianic hope, and in the books of the Maccabees the resurrection of the body is attested as a hope. (See further R. Bultmann and K. H. Rengstorf, *TDNT* II 523-30; S. Mowinckel, *He That Cometh*, 1959, 261-450; → Jesus Christ.)

(c) In contrast to this pessimistic view the community of Qumran continued to affirm that there was hope for men and that this hope was founded in God's saving actions. Nevertheless, this hope was only valid for the → elect of God.

(d) In Hel. Judaism the messianic hope retreated behind the idea of the immortality of the → soul (see especially Philo who hoped only for the moral consummation of the individual soul).

NT 1. *Occurrence.* It is a remarkable fact of NT usage that *elpizō* and *elpis* play no great role in the Gospels. Only the vb. appears, once each in Matt. (quotation from the OT, Matt. 12:21 = Isa. 42:4) and Jn. (5:45), and three times in Lk. (6:34; 23:8; 24:21), in the sense of subjective expectation. The main emphasis on hope is found in the Pauline writings (19 out of 31 occurrences of the vb.; 36 out of 51 of the noun), and of these particularly in Rom. (4 and 13 occurrences respectively). Also prominent are the occurrences in the literature indebted to the Pauline tradition: 1 Pet. (2 and 3 times) and Heb. (1 and 5 times). In Acts both vb. and noun (2 and 8 times) are used particularly of the "hope of Israel" which is interpreted as hope in the resurrection.

apelpizō: the suffix *ap-* (*apo*) negatives the meaning of the simple vb., hence *apelpizō* means to cease to hope, to give up hope, to doubt. In the NT it occurs only in Lk. 6:35. Here, however, we have a departure from the meaning that can be demonstrated elsewhere, and the word means, to hope in return: lend, expecting nothing in return (cf. Vulg. *nihil inde sperantes*).

proelpizō: to hope before, only in Eph. 1:12. The "before" means either, if "we" embraces the Jewish Christians: we hoped in Christ before Gentile Christians received faith and hope; or it denotes the messianic hope which the Jews had before Christ's coming.

2. *Meaning.* In the NT the words never indicate a vague or a fearful anticipation, but always the expectation of something good (cf. *prosdokia agathou*). Where the vb. is followed by a prep. (*eis tina, epi* and *en tini*), the latter refers to the object on which the hope is set. In many passages *elpis* denotes not the personal attitude but the objective benefit of salvation towards which hope is directed (thus Gal. 5:5; Col. 1:5; Tit. 2:13). Where vb. or noun are used absolutely without further qualification the reference is usually to the eschatological fulfilment (thus Rom. 8:24; 12:12; 15:13; Eph. 2:12 etc.; → Goal, art. *eschatos*).

3. *The revelation of Christ as a new situation.* All the NT witnesses are agreed that through the coming of the promised Christ the situation described in terms of hope in the OT has been fundamentally altered. In the Redeemer the world's day of salvation has broken in as God's great "today". What was previously future has now in him become present for faith: → justification, personal relationship to God as his → child, the indwelling of the Holy → Spirit, the new → people of God comprising believers from → Israel and the nations. The presence of salvation is most strongly emphasized in the realized eschatology of Jn. Therefore the word *elpis* does not occur there. Its absence from Rev. is for a different reason. The thoroughly visionary picture of the end and of the foreground of the parousia replaces the abstract. Because of the new situation the hope of the NT is reshaped as regards both content and basis. However, since the "today" of salvation is only apparent to faith, it acquires a double aspect: to the "now" one has to add "not yet" (1 Jn. 3:2), to the "having" (→ Fellowship, art. *echō*) and "being in Christ" one has to add hope in him and looking for him.

4. *Hope, faith and love.* Hope is such a fundamental part of the Christian position that this can be described as rebirth to a "living hope" (1 Pet. 1:3). In paganism there were, of course, ideas of a metaphysical future, but no hope providing comfort and freedom from the fear of death (Eph. 2:12; 1 Thess. 4:13). The significance of *elpis* is further clarified by the fact that, along with *pistis* (→ Faith) and *agapē* (→ Love), it forms part of the primitive Christian triad (the three fundamental elements of the Christian life, e.g. 1 Thess. 1:3; 1 Cor. 13:13). None of them can exist without the others. There can be no hope without faith in Christ, for hope is rooted in him alone. Faith without hope would, by itself, be empty and futile (1 Cor. 15:14, 17).

5. *The essential features of NT hope are given decisive shape by three factors.*

(a) *Its content.* It is never ego-centric, but always centred on Christ and on God. Its heart is not the blessing of the individual but the universal kingly rule of God, in which he will be "all in all" (1 Cor. 15:28). Resurrection does not mean the resumption of a life *en sarki*, in the → flesh, nor even *kata sarka*, according to the flesh, but the fulfilment of the life received through the new → birth, *en pneumati*, in the → Spirit, *kata pneuma*, according to the Spirit (cf. Rom. 8). For "the last Adam became a life-giving spirit" (1 Cor. 15:45). In the realm of the word *elpis*, its content is defined as: → salvation (1 Thess. 5:8), → righteousness (Gal. 5:5), → resurrection in an incorruptible body (1 Cor. 15:52 ff.; Acts 23:6; 24:15), eternal → life (Tit. 1:2; 3:7), seeing God and being conformed to his likeness (1 Jn. 3:2 f.; → Image), the → glory of God (Rom. 5:2) or simply *doxa* (Col. 1:27; cf. 2 Cor. 3:12, the abiding *doxa* of NT service).

(b) *Its basis.* This does not rest on good works (→ law) but on the gracious work of God in Jesus Christ. He is therefore called "our hope" (1 Tim. 1:1; Col. 1:27, "Christ in you, the hope of glory"). This Christ is no stranger to the community of hope but the One whom they recognize in the gospel as the crucified and risen Lord and whose presence they know through the Spirit. Thus their hope is in the "future of the One who has come" (Kreck). With the gift of his own Son for all God gives the certainty that he will give us everything with him through our transfer into the Christian community (Rom. 8:32). Because Christ has risen as the → "first fruits", we shall also all rise (1 Cor. 15:20 ff.). The Coming One is the Exalted One, whom

God has already set over all things and given to the church as its head (Eph. 1:22).

(c) *Its nature as a gift.* As *elpis agathē* (good hope), hope is a gift of the Father's grace (2 Thess. 2:16) like faith, and is therefore aroused through the message of salvation (Col. 1:23) in which we receive our call. In this *klēsis* (→ Call, art. *kaleō*) the goal of hope in all its riches gives enlightenment (Eph. 1:18), and hope unites those who have been called (Eph. 4:4). Through the power of the Holy Spirit we receive a superabundance of hope (Rom. 15:13), for he is given us as the → first fruits (Rom. 8:23). His indwelling in believers is the guarantee of their resurrection (Rom. 8:11).

6. *The characteristics of hope as a subjective attitude.* One cannot separate hope as a personal attitude from the objective content of hope, since hope is not a theoretical knowledge about a promised future salvation but a function of a living faith.

(a) It is always a confident, sure expectation of divine saving actions. Without shutting its eyes to the needs and judgments in the foreground of the parousia, hope looks at the coming city of God. *pistis* and *elpis* are most closely connected (see NT above, 4). Faith gives "substance" to our hope (Heb. 11:1 NEB) or is the "assurance of things hoped for" (on this verse → Form, art. *hypostasis*). In Rom. 4:18 → Abraham's faith is presented as faith *par' elpida ep' elpidi*, "in hope against hope", i.e. against what human judgment of the future declared to be impossible he set the hope given him through God's promise. Faith and hope have in common the fact that their object is still invisible and unprovable (cf. Rom. 8:24 ff. *ho ou blepomen, elpizomen*, "we hope for what we do not see"). But, like faith, NT hope carries unconditional certainty within itself (see 5(a)-(c)). Therefore, confessions of hope can be introduced by *pisteuomen*, "we believe" (Rom. 6:8), *pepeismai*, "I am sure" (Rom. 8:38), *pepoithōs*, (I am) "certain" (Phil. 1:6). Certain that God's promises of salvation will be realized, the Christian glories in his hope, i.e. he gratefully praises God's grace (Rom. 5:2, *kauchōmetha ep' elpidi*, "we rejoice on the basis of our hope"; cf. Heb. 3:6, *to kauchēma tēs elpidos*, "pride in our hope").

(b) *elpis* and *agapē*. Like faith and hope, *agapē* (→ Love) and hope are also essentially related in the NT. If 1 Cor. 13:7 states that love "hopes all things", Col. 1:4, 5 speaks of "the love which you have for all the saints, because of the hope...." Paul calls the Christians in Thessalonica his "hope and joy" (1 Thess. 2:19), and says in 2 Cor. 1:7, "our hope for you is unshaken". NT hope extends both heart and vision. The church, as it waits for the redemption of the body, even feels solidarity with the whole *ktisis* (→ Creation) as it lies in travail, and hopes for it (Rom. 8:20-23; on this passage see M. Black, *Romans*, 1973, 121 ff.).

(c) NT hope is a patient, disciplined, confident waiting for and expectation of the Lord as our Saviour. To hope is to be set in motion by the goal ahead, awaiting in this movement towards the goal. It demonstrates its living character by the steadfastness with which it waits, by *hypomonē* (→ Patience, art. *hypomenō*), by the patient bearing of the tension between the now, as we walk (for the moment) *dia pisteōs*, by → faith (2 Cor. 5:7), and our future manner of life (cf. Rom. 8:25; 1 Thess. 1:3). This waiting is something active, for it involves overcoming. Although the waiting may be painful, this too is reckoned positively as "travail" which

243

announces "rebirth" (Matt. 24:8). Therefore those who hope are comforted and confident (2 Cor. 5:8; 2 Thess. 2:16; 1 Thess. 4:18). Hoping is disciplined waiting. Therefore, in 1 Pet. 1:13 the warning, "set your hope fully upon the grace . . .", is preceded by "gird up your minds", i.e. be ready for the onslaught. To this context belongs the fundamental renunciation of all calculations of the future, the humble recognition of the limits set to our knowledge, the submission of our wishes to the demands of the battle for life to which we have been appointed. The goal of our hope calls us to "watch and pray". The man who competes for an earthly → crown makes the necessary sacrifices (1 Cor. 9:25). Hope becomes the motive for personal purity (1 Jn. 3:3), spurs us on to strive for holiness (Heb. 12:14) without which no man can see God. Filled with the longing to return home to his Lord, the apostle seeks his glory in pleasing him (2 Cor. 5:8 f.). Hope requires us to hold fast our confession of it without wavering (Heb. 10:23) and to be ready to give an answer to anyone who asks us to give an account of our hope (1 Pet. 3:15). Finally, however, NT hope is a joyful waiting (Rom. 12:12; → Patience, art. *hypomenō*). It gives courage and strength. It protects the inner man as a helmet protects the head (1 Thess. 5:8). As a ship is safe when at anchor, our life is secured by hope which binds us to Christ, our great High Priest who has entered the sanctuary (Heb. 6:18 f.). *E. Hoffmann*

ἀποκαραδοκία

ἀποκαραδοκία (*apokaradokia*), eager expectation; ἐκδέχομαι (*ekdechomai*), expect, wait for; ἐκδοχή (*ekdochē*), expectation; ἀπεκδέχομαι (*apekdechomai*), wait, wait eagerly; προσδέχομαι (*prosdechomai*), receive, welcome; προσδοκάω (*prosdokaō*), wait for, look for, expect; προσδοκία (*prosdokia*), expectation.

CL & OT While *ekdochē* (Heb. 10:27 f.) and *prosdokia* (Lk. 21:26; Acts 12:11 f.) are only used of fearful anticipation, *apokaradokia* appears twice in Paul in confessions of hope. The word does not occur in pre-Christian Gk., but the use of the simple vb. *karadokeō* (wait for) is widespread in Hel. Gk. It is formed from the noun *to kara*, the head, and *dechomai*, accept. In *apokaradokeō* the prefix *apo-* (according to Bertram) strengthens a negative element. This would make the meaning: to anticipate something longingly but anxiously (cf. the negative effect of *apo-* in *apelpizō*, to doubt; *apoginōskō*, to give up; *apeipon* – aor. of *apolegō*, to forbid, renounce). The compounds of *dechomai* formed with *ek-*, *apo-* and *pros-*, and *prosdokaō*, mostly denote patient waiting for a future goal.

NT 1. In the NT *apokaradokia* only occurs in Rom. 8:19 and Phil. 1:20. Luther translated Rom. 8:19 as "anxious waiting". The Gk. fathers, however, interpreted the noun without any negative tinge as "intense anticipation", "strong and excited expectation". At all events, the emotional force of eschatological expectancy is strongly emphasized here. NEB therefore translates Phil. 1:20 as "I passionately hope". Rom. 8:19 ascribed to the *ktisis*, → creation, a longing for the revelation of the children of God. It is they alone who know that the creation has been subjected to decay *ep' elpidi*, "in hope". Hope, → *elpis*, does not remove the tension from *apokaradokia*, but frees it from fear and uncertainty. So the two words can stand together (Phil. 1:20) and bear witness to the fact that the power of expectation does not lie in strength of feeling but in the certainty which God has given and which is peculiar to hope.

2. *ekdechomai, apekdechomai, prosdechomai*. The words formed from the stem *men-* are rare in the NT, occurring once each (*perimenō* Acts 1:4, object: the promise of the Father, i.e. the Holy Spirit) and *anamenō* (1 Thess. 1:10, object: the Son). *hypomenō* means to await only in the LXX, but not in the NT (but cf. *hypomonē* in Rev. 3:10, "the word of patient endurance"; → Patience). The words formed with the roots *dek-* and *dok-*, however, occur frequently in this sense.

(a) *ekdechomai* means await, wait for. In this sense it occurs 6 times, of which three are in secular contexts (Acts 17:16; 1 Cor. 11:33; 16:11), one in a comparison (Jas. 5:7 of the farmer who waits for the fruit of the fields) and two refer to waiting for the *eschata*, the last things (Heb. 10:13; 11:10). Christ, seated at the right → hand of the Father, is waiting for the moment when his enemies will be made his footstool (cf. Ps. 110:1). And → Abraham was waiting for the city with sure foundations (a picture of heaven as a world of blessedness and perfect communion with God).

(b) *apekdechomai* (8 times, of which 6 are in Paul and 1 in Heb. and 1 in 1 Pet.). The word does not occur in the LXX. The prefix *ap/apo* emphasizes the distance between the state of waiting and the time of fulfilment of what is hoped for. Through it the one who is waiting is compelled to persevere. NEB renders the word in Gal. 5:5 "eagerly wait". But generally it is only the context which implies the manner of waiting. In terms of content the expectation is directed towards the returning Lord (Phil. 3:20), who will prove himself to be our "Saviour" as he transforms our bodies, towards our entry into the full riches of sonship through the resurrection of the body (Rom. 8:23), and therefore towards *dikaiosynē*, → righteousness, in the last judgment (Gal. 5:5). Since the human and the non-human creation share equally in the effects of the fall and in salvation, creation's anticipation of freedom from the curse of death is directed ultimately towards the entrance into glory of the children of God (Rom. 8:19). The children of God, aware of the nature of hope (Rom. 8:24), are waiting *di' hypomonēs* (v. 25), in patient endurance of the suffering of the present age.

(c) *prosdechomai* means I accept, but mostly I wait (14 times, of which 7 are in secular contexts). Where it is used of the expectations of faith it denotes (i) the messianic expectation of Israel (Lk. 2:25, 38: Simeon was waiting for the consolation of Israel; Anna spoke to those who were waiting for the salvation of Jerusalem), and (ii) the eschatological goal of salvation (resurrection, Acts 24:15; mercy in the judgment, Jude 21; the incomparable glory that will come with the epiphany, Tit. 2:13).

3. *prosdokaō*, I wait, wait for, look for someone or something, expect, occurs 16 times, of which 5 are in sayings, 2 in 2 Pet. In Matt. 11:3 par. Lk. 7:9 f. it appears in the Baptist's question about the expected messiah. In Matt. 24:50 it is used of Jesus' parousia, which comes unexpectedly. 2 Pet. 3:13 identifies the goal of expectation as "new heavens and a new earth in which righteousness dwells", and v. 12 as the inbreaking of the day of God. Those who wait are at one and the same time the *speudontes*, which some interpret as those who strive (thus C. Maurer

245

TDNT VI 726) and are zealous (Arndt, 771) some as those who hasten the day
through their holy conduct.   *E. Hoffmann*
→ Fullness, → Present, → Promise

(a). Advisory Commission, World Council of Churches, *Christ the Hope of the World*, 1954; A. Barr, " 'Hope' (*elpis, elpizō*) in the New Testament", *SJT* 3, 1950, 68–77; J. B. Bauer, "Hope", *EBT* I 376–79; E. Brunner, *Our Eternal Hope*, 1954; R. Bultmann, *Theology of the New Testament*, I, 1952, 319–23, 344–47; R. Bultmann and K. H. Rengstorf, *elpis*, *TDNT* II 517–35; G. B. Caird, W. Pannenberg, I. T. Ramsey, J. Klugmann, N. Smart, and W. A. Whitehouse, *The Christian Hope*, SPCK Theological Collections 13, 1970; H. Conzelmann, *Outline Theology of the New Testament*, 1969, 184–91; E. H. Cousins, ed., *Hope and the Future of Man*, 1973; W. M. Cunningham, "The Theology of Hope: An English Language Bibliography", *Canadian Journal of Theology*, 15, 1969, 131–37; W. J. Dalton, " 'So that Your Faith May Also Be Your Hope in God' (1 Peter 1:21)", in R. J. Banks, ed., *Reconciliation and Hope* (Leon Morris Festschrift), 1974, 262–74; F. J. Denbeaux, "Biblical Hope", *Interpretation* 5, 1951, 285–303; J. E. Fison, *Christian Hope*, 1954; T. F. Glasson, *His Appearing and his Kingdom: The Christian Hope in the Light of its History*, 1953; K. Hanhart, "Paul's Hope in the Face of Death", *JBL* 88, 1969, 445–57; B. C. Hanson, *Hope and Participation in Christ: A Study in the Theology of Barth and Pannenberg*, Dissertation, Princeton Theological Seminary, 1971; F. Kierstiens, "The Theology of Hope in Germany Today", *Concilium* 6, 9, 1970, 101–11; W. G. Kümmel, *Promise and Fulfilment*, 1961; and "Eschatological Expectation in the Proclamation of Jesus", in J. M. Robinson, ed., *The Future of Our Religious Past: Essays in Honour of Rudolf Bultmann*, 1971, 29–48; M. D. Meeks, *Origins of the Theology of Hope*, 1974; P. S. Minear, *Christian Hope and the Second Coming*, 1954; "Time of Hope in the New Testament", *SJT* 6, 1953, 337–61; and "Hope" *IDB* II 640–43; C. Maurer, *prosdokaō*, *TDNT* VI 725 ff.; J. Moltmann, *Theology of Hope*, 1967; *Hope and Planning*, 1971; *Theology and Joy*, 1973; and *The Experiment Hope*, 1975; P. H. Monsma, "Hope", *ZPEB* III 198 ff.; C. F. D. Moule, *The Meaning of Hope*, 1963; G. O'Collins, "The Principle and Theology of Hope", *SJT* 21, 1968, 129–44; J. A. T. Robinson, *Jesus and his Coming*, 1957; and *In the End, God*, 1968²; H. Sasse, "Some Thoughts on Christian Hope", *Reformed Theological Review*, 26, 1967, 41–54; H. Schlier, "On Hope", *The Relevance of the New Testament*, 1968, 142–55; H. C. Snape, "Man's Future on Earth and Beyond; The Christian Hope Today", *The Modern Churchman*, 7, 1963, 84–92; D. Stewart, "In Quest of Hope: Paul Ricoeur and J. Moltmann", *Restoration Quarterly* 13, 1970, 31–52; G. Vos, "Eschatology in the Psalter", *Princeton Theological Review* 18, 1920, 1–43; D. E. H. Whiteley, *The Theology of St Paul*, 1964, 233 ff.; D. D. Williams, "Tragedy and the Christian Eschatology", *Encounter* 24, 1963, 61–73; W. Zimmerli, *Man and His Hope in the Old Testament*, 1971.

(b). H. Bardkte, H. Conzelmann, E. Schlink, "Hoffnung", *RGG*³ III 415 ff.; G. Bertram, *apokaradokia*, *ZNW* 49, 1958, 264 ff.; P. A. H. de Boer, "Études sur le sens de la racine *qwh*", *Oudtestamentische Studien*, 10, 1954, 225–46; J. van der Ploeg, "L'espérance dans l'Ancien Testament", *RB* 61, 1954, 481–507; W. Grossouw, "L'espérance dans le Nouveau Testament", *RB* 61, 1954, 508–32; W. Grundmann, "Überlieferung und Eigenaussage im eschatologischen Denken des Apostels Paulus", *NTS* 8, 1961–62, 12–26; C. H. Hunzinger, "Die Hoffnung angesichts des Todes in Wandel der paulinischen Aussagen", in *Leben angesichts des Todes. Helmut Thielicke zum 60. Geburtstag*, 1968; W. D. Marsch, ed., *Diskussion über die "Theologie der Hoffnung"*, 1967; E. Neuhäusler and P. Engelhardt, "Hoffnung", *LTK* V 416 ff.; J.-H. Nicolas, "Valeur de l'espérance enseignée par l'Écriture", *Dictionnaire de la Spiritualité*, 1960, 1209–16; P. Otzen, " 'Gute Hoffnung' bei Paulus", *ZNW* 40, 1958, 283 ff.; A. Pott, *Das Hoffen im Neuen Testament*, 1915; G. Sauter, *Zukunft und Verheissung*, 1965, and "Erwägungen zum Begriff and Verständnis der Hoffnung heute", *EvTh* 8/9, 1967, 406 ff.; J. Schreiner, "Die Hoffnung der Zukunftsschau Israels", in F. Hoffmann *et al.*, eds., *Sapienter Ordinare. Festschrift für E. Kleineidam*, 1969, 29 ff.; H. Schwantes, *Schöpfung der Endzeit*, 1963; E. Schweizer, "Gegenwart des Geistes und eschatologische Hoffnung bei Zarathustra, Spätjüdischen Gruppen und den Zeugen des Neuen Testaments", in W. D. Davies and D. Daube eds., *The Background of the New Testament and its Eschatology, In Honour of Charles Harold Dodd*, 1956, 482–508 (reprinted) in *Neotestamentica*, 1964, 153 ff.); T. C. Vriezen, "Die Hoffnung im Alten Testament", *TLZ* 78, 1953, 577 ff.; C. Westermann, *Theologia Viatorum* 4, 1952, 19 ff.; and "Das Hoffen im Alten Testament", in *Forschung am Alten Testament*, *ThB* 24, 1964, 219 ff.

House, Build, Manage, Steward

| οἶκος |

οἶκος (oikos), house, dwelling-place; οἰκία (oikia), dwelling, house; οἰκέω (oikeō), dwell, inhabit; κατοικέω (katoikeō), inhabit; κατοικητήριον (katoikētērion), dwelling place, habitation; κατοικίζω (katoikizō), settle; ἐνοικέω (enoikeō), live in, dwell in; οἰκεῖος (oikeios), belonging to the house, member of the household.

CL *oikos* is attested as early as Mycenaean Gk. and has been handed down from Homer on. It means both the dwelling place and the structure. *oikia*, from Herodotus on, denotes the dwelling, the house. Originally the two words were differentiated in meaning, in that *oikia* denoted the dwelling place, and *oikos* the whole house, the premises, the family property, and even the inhabitants of the house. This original distinction was maintained in Attic law, where *oikos* meant the inheritance and *oikia* the house itself. Later, particularly after the LXX, the distinctions were not maintained and the words were used synonymously.

In popular speech *oikos* meant any kind of house, but frequently also a particular house and even a temple. In such cases the divine name attached to *oikos* indicated the god to whom the temple was dedicated. But the word was also used in the metaphorical sense. It denoted the family, the property and other similar concepts connected with the house itself.

The vb. *oikeō*, which belongs to *oikos* and *oikia*, occurs frequently in Gk. from Homer on, and also in the LXX. Used intrans. it means to have one's dwelling, dwell; trans. to inhabit, occupy.

OT 1. *oikos* and *oikia* appear very frequently in the LXX chiefly to translate the Heb. *bayiṯ*. Both words denote the building (the house, and also palace or temple). But because Heb., like Gk., has no word for the small social unit which we call the family, *bayiṯ* (and hence LXX *oikos*) acquired, in addition to its original meaning of dwelling place, that of household (those bound together by sharing the same dwelling place), in a broader sense that of family and clan, and even that of the still bigger tribal unit (e.g. the house of Judah). When Ps. 127:1 says that God must build the house if it is to endure, it refers both to the communal lot of those who dwell under one roof, and also to their heirs and descendants (2 Sam. 7:11 f., 16, 18 f., 25–29) who are obliged to give one another unconditional protection (the father's house).

2. Used with God's name, *oikos*, as in secular Gk., means the temple, the sanctuary: *oikos theou* (house of God) or *oikos kyriou* (house of the Lord). Both expressions are common. Beside criticism of the idea that anyone could build God a house (2 Sam. 7:5 f.; 1 Ki. 8:27; Isa. 66:1) we find sincere expressions of joy at the privilege of being able to be in the house of the Lord, especially in the Pss. (e.g. 23:6; 26:8; 27:4; 52:8[10]); 84:4, 10[5, 11]; 92:13[14]; 122:1). To this feeling corresponds the longing for God's house on the part of those who are prevented from being there (cf. Ps. 42:4[5]).

3. It is questionable whether, in the OT, the idea of the "house of God" is transferred from the → temple to the congregation worshipping there, in the same way that a transference of meaning has taken place from "house" (dwelling place) to "family" (community). All the statements about the house of God remain firmly

247

attached to the earthly sanctuary. The only verse which expressly lies behind the NT understanding of the congregation as the "house of God" (Num. 12:7 = Heb. 3:2, 5) does not refer directly to the temple but to the land in which Yahweh (through his people) has settled and therefore reigns. It is more conceivable that an extended use of "house of David" for the people of God prepared the way for the idea that the community was "God's house" and "God's building" (cf. the promise to rebuild "the booth of David that is fallen" [Amos 9:11; Acts 15:16]).

4. Going beyond the OT we find that in various phrases in the Qumran documents "house" denotes the Qumran community which understood itself as a temple or sanctuary (1QS 5:6; 8:5, 9; 9:6; CD 3:19). On the whole subject → Temple; → Holy; cf. B. Gärtner, *The Temple and the Community in Qumran and the New Testament, Society for New Testament Studies Monograph Series* 1, 1965.

NT In the NT, *oikos* and *oikia*, which are virtually used as synonyms, have the same range of meaning as in secular Gk. and in the LXX. Nevertheless, they occur in a number of characteristic phrases peculiar to the NT (see below 4 (b)–(f) and 5). In these *oikos* appears far more frequently.

1. The most frequent use of both *oikos* and *oikia* is in the lit. sense of house (e.g. Matt. 2:11; 7:27–7; 9:7; Mk. 7:30) and in the simple metaphorical sense of family, household (e.g. Matt. 13:57; Mk. 6:4; Jn. 4:53; 1 Cor. 1:16; 16:15; 2 Tim. 1:16; 4:19) (cf. Arndt, 559 f., 562 f.).

2. Passages which use *oikos theou* for the → temple are self-explanatory (Mk. 2:26 par. Matt. 12:4, Lk. 6:4; Matt. 21:13 par. Mk. 11:17, Lk. 19:46 = Isa. 56:7; Jn. 2:16 f.; Lk. 11:51). The only question which one has to ask about Acts 7:46–50 is whether there is here a criticism of Solomon's building of a house (v. 47) in its contrast with David's request to be allowed to make God a tent dwelling (*skēnōma* v. 46; → Tent). The statement, illustrated by the quotation from Isa. 66:1, that "the Most High does not dwell in houses made with hands" (v. 48) has been thought to support such an interpretation, according to which Solomon's building of the temple was a deviation from the true worship of God. (Cf. E. Haenchen, *The Acts of the Apostles*, 1971, 285 ff. who points out that Judaism did not represent Yahweh as dwelling in the temple but only his name. Nevertheless, Stephen's words would have had a blasphemous ring for Jews.)

3. The passages which speak of "the house of Israel," "the house of Jacob," or "the house of Judah" (Matt. 10:6; 15:24; Acts 2:36; Heb. 8:8, 10 citing Jer. 31:31 ff.; Lk. 1:33; Acts 7:42–43 citing Amos 5:25–27) are linked with the metaphorical sense of house, family, race (cf. also "house of David" Lk. 1:27, 69; 2:4) which they extend in the direction of the people of God. In this they are following the example of the OT, as the frequent references to the OT in these illustrations show.

4. (a) The NT designation of the Christian community as the house of God which is "an integral part of the primitive Christian *kērygma*" (O. Michel, *TDNT* V 126), goes beyond the OT model. This meaning of house may have had several roots. There are the OT concepts of God's proprietary rights over his people (expressed there, admittedly, more through the images of the vine, the vineyard and the plantation, Hos. 10:1; Isa. 5:7; Jer. 2:21; Ps. 80:8 ff.[9 ff.]; cf. 1 Cor. 3:6 ff.), but which apply equally in the case of the house (→ People; → Generation). Gnostic

248

ideas of a "heavenly building", identical with the heavenly body of the primal man and redeemer may also have exercised an influence if they were earlier than the NT (→ Body; → Head; cf. also O. Michel, *TDNT* V 122 f.). Further, one must take into consideration the fact that the Qumran documents also see the community as a holy house, built on the foundation of truth (1QH 7:8 f.).

(b) In its exposition of Num. 12:7, Heb. 3:1–6 is linked to the OT in its terminology. But it extends the thought. Moses and Christ are contrasted: Moses as "faithful in all God's house as a servant", Christ as the "son" and the "builder" of the house and, as such, superior. Whatever sense "house" may have had in Num. 12:7 (all Israel as God's people or God's "royal household"; so T. J., cf. O. Michel, *Der Brief an die Hebräer*, KEK 13, 1966¹², 96), for the writer of Heb. it meant that the Christian community (→ Church) is "God's house," as 3:6b demonstrates. "We are his house, if we hold our confidence and pride in our hope firm to the end" (RSV mg.).

(c) What is important in this connection is not only that God or Christ is regarded as the builder of the house. In contrast to Philo, it is not the individual, the "pure soul" that is seen as God's house, but the Christian community as a whole which is designated as such (cf. O. Michel, *TDNT* V 123–30). Moreover, the passages in which Paul speaks of the body as the temple of the Holy Spirit (1 Cor. 3:16; 6:19) and which are undoubtedly connected with the idea of the house of God, are not to be understood purely individualistically. They deal objectively with the Christian community and the problems which arise from the fellowship.

(d) Eph. 2:19–22 shows that the ideas contained in the terms "house of God" and "temple of God" naturally run into one another. Here, no less than six different derivatives of *oikos* (nevertheless, not *oikos* itself) are used to describe the spiritual reality of the community under the metaphor of the temple and of the building. They are *paroikos* (v. 19, stranger, → Foreign), *oikeios* (v. 19, members of the household; cf. Gal. 6:10), *epoikodomeō* (v. 20, build on; cf. 1 Cor. 3:10, 12, 14; 1 Pet. 2:5 *v.l.*; Acts 20:32 t.r.; Col. 2:7; Jude 20), *oikodomē* (v. 21, building, structure; cf. 4:12, 16, 29; → *oikodomeō* below), *synoikodomeō* (v. 22, build together), and *katoikētērion* (v. 22, dwelling-place; cf. Jer. 9:10; Rev. 18:2). In 1 Pet. 2:4 f. the images again overlap. Christians are exhorted to allow themselves to be built up as spiritual stones into a spiritual house (→ *oikodomeō*), in order to present spiritual sacrifices to God as (and here the picture changes) a spiritual priesthood. When 1 Pet. 4:17 reckons that the judgment will begin with the house of God, the natural assumption is that the Christian community is the house of God. Similarly, 1 Tim. 3:15 expressly identifies "the house of God" with "the church of the living God, the pillar and bulwark of the truth".

(e) Given the figurative use of the terms, it was inevitable that many related concepts and images would be introduced to elucidate the truth concerning the Christian community which is expressed in the phrase "the house of God". There is the idea of the foundation (1 Cor. 3:10–12; Eph. 2:20; 2 Tim. 2:19; → Firm, art. *themelios*), of Christ as the corner stone (Acts 4:11; Eph. 2:20; 1 Pet. 2:4) and Christians as living stones (1 Pet. 2:5; → Rock), of the pillars (1 Tim. 3:15) and above all of the temple (1 Cor. 3:16 f.; 6:19; 2 Cor. 6:16; Eph. 2:21; → Temple). All these passages and concepts, as well as all the derivatives of *oikos*, must be taken into account in one's interpretation.

(f) It is strange, however, that the concept of the house of God remains confined to the idea of a spiritual building and is not extended in the sense of the family, the other metaphorical meaning of *oikos*, which could have been used in the sense of the family of God. Probably the phrase "the house of God" was, through OT thought, too closely linked to the sanctuary for such an extension to be possible.

5. (a) What could be conveyed by the idea of the family of God had, in fact, already come into being in the primitive Christian community through the house churches. The household as a community (the family included the slaves, according to the ancient concept of it) formed the smallest unit and basis of the congregation. The house churches mentioned in the NT (Acts 11:14; 16:15, 31, 34; 18:8; 1 Cor. 1:16; Phlm. 2; 2 Tim. 1:16; 4:19) no doubt came into being through the use of the homes as meeting places. The gospel was preached in them (Acts 5:42; 20:20), and the Lord's supper was celebrated in them (Acts 2:46). The conversion of the head of the house brought the whole family into the congregation and – however it is to be understood – into the faith (Acts 16:31, 34; 18:8; cf. Jn. 4:53 where, as an exception to the rule in this connection, we find *oikia* and not *oikos*).

The NT also speaks of the → baptism of whole households in the same way (1 Cor. 1:16; Acts 16:15; cf. Acts 16:33; perhaps also Acts 18:8). The question whether one may conclude from these indications that the primitive church practised infant baptism is discussed in the articles on Baptism.

(b) The formation of the house churches, which can be explained on the basis of the missionary situation, was of the greatest significance for the spreading of the gospel. With them the early church took over the natural order of life, without falling into idealization of the house churches. The way in which the Gospels take up Micah's prophecy of the end-time (Mic. 7:6 = Matt. 10:35 f. par. Lk. 12:53) indicates that the primitive community had to reckon with the disruption of the family for the sake of the gospel. Those who take this upon themselves are promised "now in this time" new "houses and brothers and sisters and mothers and children" (Mk. 10:29 f. par. Matt. 19:29, Lk. 18:29 f.). The place of the disrupted family is taken by the family of God, the Christian community.

6. In Jesus' word of revelation in Jn. 14:2 the disciples are promised that many dwelling places are ready in the Father's house, into which the disciples will be received when the Lord returns. Rab. and gnostic parallels (cf. also Eth.Enoch 45:3), which suggest the idea of the right to a heavenly dwelling, help to explain the expression *oikia tou patros mou*, "my Father's house". Two factors ought, however, to warn us against an over-hasty mythological localization of the concept: (a) the linking of the promise of a dwelling to the return, and thereby to the fulfilment of the kingdom of God, and (b) the similarity of the expression to the idea of the house of God (*oikos theou* and *naos theou*) and the related thought of the right of sanctuary (cf. A. Schlatter, *Der Evangelist Johannes*, 1930, 292).

7. (a) The vb. *oikeō* occurs in the NT both in the lit. and in the metaphorical sense. 1 Cor. 7:12 f., which deals with the living together of the Christian and non-Christian partners in mixed marriages, belongs to the former category. 1 Tim. 6:16 stands on the borderline between lit. and metaphorical meanings: God "dwells in unapproachable light". Jewish and Hel. ideas (see the whole verse) are combined in this statement of the unutterable beauty of God. In the metaphorical sense *oikeō* is used in describing the inner processes in man (5 passages out of 8): the

phrase "sin . . . dwells in me" (Rom. 7:20; cf. 7:18) depicts the old man, while the truth about the new man is testified to in the sentence, repeated like a confession of faith, "the Spirit of God dwells in you" (Rom. 8:9, 11; 1 Cor. 3:16). *katoikizō* occurs in the same sense in Jas. 4:5.

(b) The compound *katoikeō* occurs more frequently in the NT than *oikeō*. Intrans. it means dwell; trans. inhabit. Beside the widespread use of the word in its lit. meaning, it also is used for the possession of a man by God, by Christ or by ungodly powers. Demons "dwell" in a man (Matt. 12:45 par. Lk. 11:26); but to believers God's purpose is "that Christ may dwell in your hearts through faith" (Eph. 3:17). Col. 2:9 can say of Christ that "in him the whole fullness of deity dwells bodily" (cf. Col. 1:19) and thus express in language which has affinities with gnosticism the complete union between Christ and God (but → Fullness, art. *plēroō*, NT 5 (b)).

The noun *katoikētērion*, dwelling place, home, which has its origins in the LXX, occurs in connection with the great picture of the Christian community as the spiritual building and temple (Eph. 2:19–22).

(c) A further compound, *enoikeō*, dwell in, indwell, is only used in the metaphorical sense in the NT, in fact similarly to *katoikeō*. God himself will dwell among men (2 Cor. 6:16 citing Lev. 26:11 f.), and the Holy Spirit dwells in believers (Rom. 8:11; 2 Tim. 1:14). But the word of Christ (Col. 3:16) and faith (2 Tim. 1:5) may also be said to dwell in men. On the other hand, the same may be said of sin (Rom. 7:17).

(d) The adj. *oikeios* occurs from Hesiod on and means "belonging to the house". In the NT it is only used as a noun meaning member of the household. The lit. meaning appears in 1 Tim. 5:8. In the other two passages it is determined by the understanding of the congregation as the house of God (see above 4). Eph. 2:19 assures the Gentiles that they are no longer strangers (*paroikoi*; → Foreign) but members of the household (*oikeioi* – note the play on words!), accepted into the full fellowship of the house of God, i.e. the Christian community. Gal. 6:10 reminds the Christian of his duty to do good to all, but has him begin specifically with "those who are of the household of faith," the members of the family of God.

J. Goetzmann

οἰκοδομέω

οἰκοδομέω (*oikodomeō*), build, build up; οἰκοδομή (*oikodomē*), the process of building, a building; ἐποικοδομέω (*epoikodomeō*), build on something, build further; συνοικοδομέω (*synoikodomeō*), build together with.

CL The vb. *oikodomeō*, attested from Hdt. on, means to build, build up, and is used in many ways in the lit. sense, but also in the fig. The noun *oikodomē*, building up, building, occurs frequently in Koine Gk.; it meant originally the process of building.

OT In the LXX *oikodomeō* stands for Heb. *bānâh* and occurs frequently (almost 350 times). It is used in most cases in the lit. sense for the erection of a building. *oikodomē*, on the other hand, occurs very rarely and almost entirely in later writings (17 passages; for Heb. words only 4 times in Chr. and Ezr.).

The metaphorical use of *oikodomeō*, which occurs particularly in Jer., is interesting. To "plant" and to "build" go together; they are God's work and have their opposites in God's → judgment to "break down" and "pluck up" (Jer. 1:10; 24:6). It is God himself who will rebuild Israel (Jer. 31:4; 33:7). He does his work by putting his words in the mouths of the prophets (Jer. 1:9 f.). He leads the peoples into the fellowship of the people of Israel and thus "builds them up" (Jer. 12:14 ff.). This OT use of the concept particularly influenced Paul's usage. A further element in the OT, which became effective in the NT, is the recognition that men cannot build a house for God (Isa. 66:1; → *oikos*).

NT 1. The apocalyptic-messianic use of *oikodomeō* in the gospels (only one passage in Jn.) is linked to this recognition. At the same time it also takes over from the OT the traditional opposition of build and → destroy (*katalyein*). Such usage occurs in Mk. 14:58, and par. Matt. 26:61; Jn. 2:19 ff.; and also Matt. 16:18. Jesus' enigmatic saying, which was used to prove the accusation against him at his trial, speaks of destroying the temple that is made with hands and in three days building another, not made with hands (Mk. 14:58). Jn. 2:19 ff. interprets this in terms of the → resurrection and even alters *oikodomēsō* ("I will build"), which was probably the original word, to the ambiguous *egerō* ("I will raise", v. 19). Since that time Mk. 14:58 has stood in the shadow of this interpretation, although this passage – independent of Jn. 2:19 ff. – can be understood perfectly well as a prophecy of the erection of the new temple, the eschatological community. Moreover the promise to Peter in Matt. 16:18 agrees with such an understanding. Even if the question has to remain open, whether the fut. *oikodomēsō* refers in both passages to the parousia of the Son of Man (cf. Mk. 13:26 f.; → Present) or to the power of Christ's resurrection and of Pentecost to build up the community, there is an ultimate reference to the community (→ Church) as the eschatological "building of God".

2. The usage of Acts is also to be seen against its OT background. Acts 15:16 refers to Amos 9:11 and perhaps to Jer. 12:15 ff. and promises the eschatological restoration of the people of Israel. Acts 9:31 and 20:32 have "a typically ecclesiastical ring" (O. Michel, *TDNT* V 139) without any reference to the action of the messiah.

3. The most important passages for the understanding of the concept occur in Paul's letters, where, moreover, almost all the occurrences of the noun are to be found. However, the verbal use is more important. *oikodomē* has the meaning of a building only in 1 Cor. 3:9 and 2 Cor. 5:1 (see below, 5); otherwise it denotes the process of building and has the same meaning as the vb.

(a) The term describes the apostolic activity (2 Cor. 10:8; 13:10; 12:19) against the background of OT models (cf. Jer. 1:10; 24:6; especially the opposition of "destroy" and "build up"). 1 Cor. 3:5–17 also belongs here. In this passage Paul combines two images, that of planting and that of building, in order to illustrate the process of building the "temple of God" (the Christian community; v. 16) in one great allegory.

(b) Apart from the activity of the apostle, *oikodomeō* is used to describe the growth (→ Grow) and expansion of the community through the Spirit. "*oikodomē* denotes the goal of knowledge, yet also the inner growth of the community and the content and purpose of its liturgical life and its meetings" (O. Michel, *TDNT* V 141). Therefore, there is one rule which applies to everything which happens within the community: it must serve to build up the community (1 Cor. 14:12, 17, 26; Rom. 14:19; 15:2; 1 Thess. 5:11; Eph. 4:29). Thus the → gifts of → grace and offices are judged according to what they contribute to the building up of the community (1 Cor. 14:3–5; Eph. 4:12). Paul scolds the Corinthians: "Knowledge puffs up, but love builds up" (1 Cor. 8:1). The enthusiasts in Corinth probably had a slogan, "Knowledge builds up," which Paul is here correcting. Similarly in 1 Cor. 10:23 Paul corrects the Corinthian slogan, *panta exestin*, "All things are lawful", by urging people to ask themselves whether their actions are conducive to building up the community.

(c) It is striking that the positive use of the word always refers to the community. Paul uses sharp words (cf. 1 Cor. 14:19) to criticize the man who speaks in a tongue on his own to "edify [*oikodomei*] himself" (1 Cor. 14:4). Edification which is not aimed at serving others is self-centred and pointless.

4. While 1 Cor. 3 mixes the images of planting and building, a further image appears alongside that of building in Eph. 4:12, 16, the image of the → body of Christ. This hints at gnostic ideas and leads to the thought that the building grows (like an organism). The same idea of the building "growing" (the corner stone of which, Jesus Christ has indeed already been put in position; → Rock) appears in Eph. 2:19 ff. (cf. also Ps. 118:22 f.; Matt. 21:42; Mk. 12:10 f.; Lk. 20:17; Acts 4:7; 1 Pet. 2:7). To be built into this growing building, on which God himself is building, means to be put in as a "living stone" (1 Pet. 2:5). All these passages are concerned with the unity and holiness of the temple of God, the Christian community.

5. 2 Cor. 5:1 is the only passage where *oikodomē* is used as an anthropological term in a sense which, at least at first sight, is individualistic. The transient tent of the earthly body is here contrasted with an eternal *oikodomē*, prepared by God, not made with hands.

6. The compounds *synoikodomeō* (build together; pass. be built into [Eph. 2:22]) and *epoikodomeō* (build on something, build further) underline once again by the prepositions used the idea of fellowship which is contained in the concept of "building up". Believers are rooted and grounded in Christ (Col. 2:7). The Christian community is built up together in the co-operation of all the participants (1 Cor. 3:10–4), and in unity with apostles and prophets (Eph. 2:20), to become the one holy community of the Lord.

J. Goetzmann

| οἰκονομία |

οἰκονομία (*oikonomia*), management, office; οἰκονόμος (*oikonomos*), steward; οἰκονομέω (*oikonomeō*), manage, administer, plan.

CL *oikonomia*, attested from Xen. and Plato on, denoted primarily the management of a household, but was soon extended to the administration of the state (the title of one of Xen.'s books), and finally was used for every kind of activity which results from the holding of an office.

oikonomos (from Aesch. on) was used of people, and has a more concrete meaning. It denotes the house-steward, and then by extension the managers of individual departments within the household, e.g. the porter, the estate manager, the head cook, the accountant, all domestic officials who were mostly recruited from among the slaves. Similarly, *oikonomeō* means to manage as a house-steward, order, regulate.

OT The occurrence of the words in the LXX does not give much help towards understanding the NT concept. *oikonomia* only occurs in Isa. 22:19, 21, and then in the original meaning of administration, office. *oikonomos* appears somewhat more frequently and is likewise used in the technical sense of the word for a court official, chiefly the royal palace governor (*'al habbayiṭ*, e.g. Eliakim in 2 Ki. 18:18, 37; 19:2; Isa. 36:3, 22; 37:2; cf. also 1 Ki. 4:6; 16:9; 18:3; Est. 1:8; 8:9).

NT In the NT, too, the word-group does not appear at all frequently: *oikonomia* occurs 9 times, *oikonomos* 10 times and *oikonomeō* only once (Lk. 16:2). Nevertheless, something like a specific NT usage has been established which has two main different aspects.

1. (a) The words are used in their technical sense to denote the occupation of household and estate managers and their tasks (Lk. 12:42; 16:1 ff.; cf. the use as a title with the name in Rom. 16:23, "Erastus the city treasurer" [cf. H. J. Cadbury, "Erastus of Corinth", *JBL* 50, 1931, 42–58]). Gal. 4:2 also belongs in this category. Here *oikonomos* is used to describe man's age of minority before the sending of Christ, but it also serves within the metaphor as the designation of an occupation, in order to clarify a legal concept: "But he is under guardians [*epitropous*] and trustees [*oikonomous*] until the date set by the father" (RSV). In Lk., the only gospel in which *oikonomos* and *oikonomia* appear, *oikonomos* is used alternately with *doulos*, slave (Lk. 12:42 ff.; cf. par. Matt. 24:45 ff.). Admittedly all the passages in Lk. occur in parables, so one can on this ground speak in a certain sense of a metaphorical use of the words.

([Ed.] Interesting light on the parable in Lk. 16:1–17 has been shed by J. D. M. Derrett, "The Parable of the Unjust Steward", *NTS* 7, 1961, 198–219, reprinted in *Law in the New Testament*, 1970, 48–77. Making extensive use of Jewish laws and customs in the light of later sources, Derrett puts forward a rationale of the parable. The Mosaic Law forbade the taking of interest on loans from fellow Jews [Exod. 22:25; Lev. 25:36; Deut. 23:19 f.]. The Pharisees who had considerable business concerns found ways of evading the intention of the law without transgressing the letter. They argued that the law was concerned with protecting the destitute and not with business enterprises for mutual profit. So long as a man had some of the commodity which he wished to borrow he was not destitute. The bills in the parable preserve the letter of the law by not mentioning interest but only the amount to be repaid in terms of commodities. The steward who was legally entitled to act in his master's name saw an opportunity to make provision for his future needs by ingratiating himself with his master's debtors. He simply cancelled the interest and got the debtors to sign new notes stating the original amount of principal to be repaid. The master was quick to appreciate the shrewdness of the move. For it not only helped to feather the unjust steward's nest, but it also put the master right in the eyes of the law. By forfeiting the illegal exorbitant interest he was at least

254

conforming to the requirements of the law. In its context the parable is a reminder to the disciples to exercise stewardship of this world's goods [→ Possessions, art. *mamōnas*], so that when mammon fails "they" [i.e. the poor, or possibly even God] may receive them "in the eternal habitations" [v. 9]. The following verses emphasize the point that while wealth is not to be sought for its own sake, wise and diligent stewardship of it in the master's service is important. Faithful stewardship in this determines whether God will entrust to the disciple true riches [vv. 10 f.].)

(b) The position is similar in the rest of the NT. In 1 Cor. 4:1 Paul uses *oikonomos* metaphorically to describe the apostolic task and, just as in the gospels, alongside *doulos*. Also as in the gospels (Lk. 12:42; 16:10 f.; Matt. 25:21 ff.; cf. Lk. 19:17 ff.), 1 Cor. 4:2 names faithfulness as the essential requirement in a steward. In the same way Tit. 1:7 requires that "a bishop, as God's steward, must be blameless." In 1 Pet. 4:10 all the members of the community, as recipients of the gifts of grace, are called "stewards of God's varied grace."

(c) To understand the concepts of *oikonomia* and *oikonomos* one must refer to their roots in the concept of the house, as it is in the NT (→ *oikos*). God's people, God's community, is his house, which he builds up through the work of those he has called to the task, to whom he entrusts the stewardship of the house. They are not to look upon these household affairs as their own; they are merely stewards of the gifts entrusted to them and have to give an account of their stewardship (Lk. 16:2; cf. the parable of the pounds, Lk. 19:11 ff., cf. Matt. 25:14 ff., which must be taken into account in the explanation of the concept, even though *oikonomos* does not appear in them). In addition to the gifts of the Spirit (1 Pet. 4:10) it is above all the → gospel which is thought of as something entrusted to stewards. Thus in 1 Cor. 4:1 Paul introduces himself and his fellow-workers as "servants of Christ and stewards of the mysteries of God." Likewise in 1 Cor. 9:17 Paul calls the preaching of the gospel a "commission" (*oikonomia*) from which he cannot withdraw. Col. 1:25 and Eph. 3:2 perhaps also belong in this category. In these passages the divine office committed to the apostle is under discussion. Admittedly there could be some doubt in both cases whether the meaning here is not "plan of salvation" (see below, 2).

2. The use of the word *oikonomia* moves in a second direction in the sense of God's plan of salvation. This meaning, related to salvation history, could have arisen on the basis of the breadth of meaning of the Gk. word (see above, 1), which can denote the plans and arrangements of the authorities as well as measures through which the help of heavenly powers can be obtained (e.g. in the magical papyri referred to by O. Michel, *TDNT* V 152). In Eph. it is used for God's plan of salvation, which was hidden from eternity in God (Eph. 3:9), and now, in the fullness of time, has been realized in Christ (Eph. 1:10). The soteriological sense of the concept figured alongside other uses in the later patristic literature (e.g. Justin, *Dial.* 30, 3; 45, 4; Irenaeus, *Haer.* 1, 10, 3; 4, 33, 7; see Lampe, 940–3).

3. The first and second meanings of the term are nevertheless not completely independent. Because God allows his plan of salvation to be proclaimed through men (1 Cor. 4:1; cf. the use of *mystērion*, → secret, here and in Eph. 3:9), the work of the *oikonomos* is rooted in the divine *oikonomia*. Just as → time has its function in God's plan, a definite period of time is given to the steward, even though he may not himself know how long it is (Lk. 12:46). At the end of it he must render his

255

remains meek in the face of insults, the judge who is lenient in judgment, and the king who is kind in his rule. Hence they appear often in pictures of the ideal ruler and in eulogies on men in high positions.

In Gk. and Hel. philosophy both concepts express social virtues and ideals of high value. Aristot. considered that they were the happy mean between passion and lack of feeling (*TDNT* VI 646).

OT 1. *epieikeia* is found 10 times in the LXX and *epieikēs*, including the adv., 6 times, without any real Heb. equivalent. They are used to describe God's gracious gentleness in his rule (1 Sam. 12:22; Ps. 86:5; Wis. 12:18), and also the actions of a king (2 Macc. 9:27), of a prophet (2 Ki. 6:3), and of the pious (Wis. 2:19).

2. *praÿs*, found 19 times in the LXX, translates 'ānî (3 times), poor, afflicted, humble; and more generally its later variant 'ānāw, poor, humble, meek. The fact that the LXX can translate 'ānāw (21 times in the OT) and 'ānî (65 times in the OT) also by *penēs* and *ptōchos* (→ Poor) and → *tapeinos* shows that the Heb. terms had a much wider connotation which is not satisfied by any of the LXX renderings. The poor were those in Israel who were without landed property. They were wrongfully restricted, disinherited, and deprived of the fullness which God willed (→ Poor, art. *penēs*, OT 3). Hence they were often the victims of unscrupulous exploitation (Isa. 32:7; Ps. 37:14; Job 24:4). In a general sense 'ānî denotes the defenceless, those without rights, the oppressed, those who are cheated, exploited and cursed (cf. Pss. 9 and 10).

Yahweh, however, takes the part of the 'ānî (Exod. 22:21–24; Deut. 24:14 f.), as do the prophets (Isa. 3:14 f.; Amos 2:7; 8:4; Zech. 7:10) and the wisdom literature (Prov. 14:21; 22:22; 31:9, 20). Since Yahweh is the God of those without rights (Pss. 25:9; 149:4; 34:2[3]), he hears and comforts those who find no mercy among their fellow-men (Isa. 29:19; Job 36:15) and will finally reverse all that is not now in their favour (Isa. 26:6; Pss. 37:11; 147:6). Hence 'ānî and particularly 'ānāw change their meaning from those who are materially poor, and become the self-chosen religious title of those who in deep need and difficulty humbly seek help from Yahweh alone, or have found it there (e.g. Pss. 40:17[18]; 102[102:1], title; Zeph. 2:3; 3:12; Isa. 41:17; 49:13; 66:2). In the Qumran texts they are used generally of the community members (→ Poor, art. *ptōchos*, OT 5). Hence the word is sometimes used with the meaning meek, humble, modest (Num. 12:3; Eccl. 6:8).

In the messianic passages of the OT God's king is depicted as the helper of all who have been deprived of their rights and of all the needy (Pss. 45:4[5]; 72; Isa. 11:4; 61:1). The term 'ānî is never applied to God, but in Zech. 9:9 (cf. Num. 12:3; Sir. 45:4) it is a title of honour given to the messiah. As he rides the animal used by the socially insignificant, his way leads to the poor and those deprived of their rights. ([Ed.] Although rulers of Israel had ridden asses at an earlier period in history [Jdg. 5:10; 10:4; 12:14; 2 Sam. 16:2] the horse was the appropriate mount for the mighty [but note the scorn of the war-horse in v. 10; cf. Isa. 2:7; 31:1]. The ass was the appropriate mount for one who comes on a mission of peace [cf. J. G. Baldwin, *Haggai, Zechariah, Malachi*, 1972, 165 f.].)

The sense of 'ānî is transformed in a number of passages, including Zech. 9:9, which the LXX renders by *praÿs* and thus substitutes for the more passive Heb.

concept a Hel. act. and ethical meaning. A positive lack is transformed into the praiseworthy virtue of "gentleness" or "humility". This is the dominant concept in Sir. 1:27; 4:8; 10:28 etc., and Josephus *Ant.* 19, 7, 3; 3, 6, 7; 5, 2, 12; 6, 1, 2; 7, 6, 1. ([Tr.] However, since the 2nd and 3rd of the Sir. passages are found in the Heb. original with this meaning, it shows that the Hel. concept had influenced Palestinian Heb. by the early 2nd cent. B.C.)

NT The words are found in the NT in Paul, Jas., 1 Pet., Acts (once *epieikeia*) and
   Matt. (3 times *praÿs*). Clear OT influence is found only in Matt. For the rest, Hel. concepts are dominant. How far NT thought is based on the LXX and its OT background is not clear. Attention may be drawn to two points.

1. Both *praÿtēs* and *epieikeia* are marks of Christ's rule. In contrast to the representatives of a political messianism Jesus repudiated the use of force to bring about the rule of God. His activity on earth is that of the OT king who brings salvation without using force or war (Matt. 11:29; 21:5 = Zech. 9:9). Since, however, Matt. 11:29 has Sem. thinking behind it (cf. Isa. 42:2 f.; 53:1 ff.; Zech. 9:9; cf. *TDNT* V 993, n. 289), *praÿs* here suggests '*ānî*, in the Heb. sense, and so stresses the human humility of the messiah. Luther saw him as a "Beggar-king" who had no means of enforcing his rights and who ultimately had to suffer all manner of injustice. In 2 Cor. 10:1 Paul mentions *praÿtēs* and *epieikeia* as characteristics of Jesus' attitude to men during his life on earth, and holds them out as an example to the church.

2. The words now express an attitude demanded of the Christian, though they are applied also to non-Christians (Acts 24:4, where *epieikeia* is used by the Jewish spokesman Tertullus in addressing the procurator Felix; 1 Pet. 2:18, of masters of slaves). They stand in the lists of virtues as concrete expressions of Christian love (Gal. 5:23; 1 Tim. 6:11; 1 Pet. 3:4) and of "the wisdom from above" (Jas. 3:17). They state the rule for the way in which Christians and non-Christians should live together (Phil. 4:5; Tit. 3:2). They also apply in dealing with Christians who have committed sins (1 Cor. 4:21; Gal. 6:1; 2 Tim. 2:25), and in the midst of enmity and persecution (1 Pet. 3:16). Christians should set an example of this (Jas. 3:13), especially → bishops (1 Tim. 3:3).

([Ed.] *praÿs* occurs in the third Beatitude: "Blessed are the meek, for they shall inherit the earth" (Matt. 5:5). David Hill suggests that they are the same as the poor (v. 3) and that since the vb. *klēronomeō* appears in Deut. 4:1, 16:20, and Ps. 68:36 (LXX) with reference to possessing the land of Israel, the thought here is of possessing or inheriting the new promised land (*The Gospel of Matthew*, 1972, 111). Just as obedience and righteousness are, for the Deuteronomist, the conditions of entrance into the promised land, so humble obedience to the teaching contained in the Beatitudes is the condition of entering the new land of God's kingdom. The verse takes up the theme of Ps. 37:11. Hill notes that the Ps., the themes of which are close to the whole series of the Beatitudes, was taken by the Qumran sect as a prophecy in process of fulfilment through the establishment of their messianic community (4QpPs37; cf. op. cit., 112). The Beatitude promises that those who are now oppressed and despised and have nothing to call their own (like Israel prior to the conquest of Canaan) will enter the → inheritance of God's rule upon earth. At the same time it is a veiled statement about Jesus himself.)

When the NT advocates *praÿtēs*, it does not imply an attitude dependent solely on the human will. It is a sign of salvation: of "calling" (Eph. 4:2), election (Col. 3:12), and the work of the Holy Spirit (Gal. 5:23). It is not a virtue in the Hel. sense, but a possibility of life and action given by God. It is not an aspect of human temperament. It comes about when men are linked with Christ and are conformed to his → image. *W. Bauder*

ταπεινός

ταπεινός (*tapeinos*), lowly, humble; ταπεινόω (*tapeinoō*), make low, humble; ταπείνωσις (*tapeinōsis*), abasement, humiliation; ταπεινόφρων (*tapeinophrōn*), humble-minded; ταπεινοφροσύνη (*tapeinophrosynē*), lowliness of mind, humility.

CL *tapeinos* was originally used (from Pindar in the 5th cent. B.C. on) with the sense of low-lying. Metaphorical uses were soon developed: (a) low socially, poor, of little social position and influence (Hdt., 5th cent. B.C. onwards), powerless, unimportant; (b) as a result of one's social standing, with slavish outlook, a synonym of not free; (c) despondent, downcast (Thuc., 5th cent. B.C. onwards; cf. Eng. "I'm feeling down"); (d) in Socratic and post-Socratic ethical teaching the word was separated from its social links, but retained a depreciatory connotation. Men should avoid the two extremes of arrogance, provocation and pride (*hybris*), and of grovelling, servile behaviour and base flattery. (e) Occasionally the word is used with a good connotation in individual, social, ethical and religious contexts. Where this is so, it does not mean humble, but unassuming (in Xen.), obedient, conforming one's behaviour to the righteous laws of the gods (Aesch., Plato). In all these uses there remains the memory of the original physical meaning of below, low, in comparison with that which is above or higher.

The vb. *tapeinoō* (from Hippocrates, 5th cent. B.C. onwards) represents in all its varieties of meaning the various shades of meaning of the adj.: to level, humble (socially, politically, economically), harm, make small, make humble, discourage (with fate or life as subject), make one obedient, or self-effacing, make a person obey a regulation (of the reason) (and also the appropriate pass. forms). The reflex. form with *heauton* and the mid. (from Diod.Sic., 1st cent. B.C. onwards used also for mental states) meaning humble oneself, demean oneself, are used normally only in a derogatory sense. Yet Philodemus of Gadara (1st cent. B.C.) demands that those who humbled themselves, should be comforted and lifted up (*TDNT* VIII 4) and Plut. (1st cent. A.D.) mentions the custom of humbling oneself before the gods by covering the head during sacrifice and prayer (*TDNT* VIII 5).

tapeinotēs (Thuc., 5th cent. B.C. onwards) is found only in secular contexts apart from Sir. 13:20. It generally conveys the experience of humiliation, lowliness, and powerlessness, while *tapeinōsis* (from Plato, 5th–4th cents. B.C. onwards) suggests rather the process of humiliation, etc.

The compounds with *phronein*, think, judge, be disposed, are the vb. *tapeinophronein*, the adj. *tapeinophrōn*, and the noun *tapeinophrosynē*. They first occur in secular literature in the 1st and 2nd cents. A.D. (Josephus, Plutarch, Epictetus), always with a depreciatory connotation: e.g. to think poorly, ill; to be ill-disposed, faint-hearted, or weakly; to have a servile mind. The LXX, however, which does not use the noun, has the vb. (which means be humble, modest) once in Ps. 131(130):2 for the MT quieten the mind, and the adj. once in Prov. 29:23, meaning lowly in spirit in a good sense. The opposite in both passages and in Sir. 13:20 (see above) is → pride, insolence and arrogance.

OT The fundamental difference between the Gk. and the biblical use of these words has already been indicated. In the Gk. world, with its anthropocentric view of man, lowliness is looked on as shameful, to be avoided and overcome by act and thought. In the NT, with its theocentric view of man, the words are used to describe those events that bring a man into a right relationship with God and his fellow-man (cf. *TDNT* VIII 11 f.).

1. *tapeinos* and its cognates are found about 270 times in the LXX, the adj. 66 times, the vb. c. 160 times, and *tapeinōsis* 40 times. For the compounds see above. They represent 7 Heb. roots: by far the most common is *'ānâh* (86 times), to oppress, afflict, humble (→ *praÿs*); *šāpal* (42 times), to become low, be abased; *kāna'* (15 times), be subdued, humbled; *dākā'*, *dākâh* (13 times), crush, humiliate; *dal*, *dālal* (7 times), low, insignificant, helpless, downcast; *šāḥaḥ* (6 times), bow down, crouch; *yiggâh* (5 times), vex, grieve. *'ªnāwâh* (derived from *'ānâh*), humility, the attitude of the mind of the one who bends down, occurs only 4 times (Prov. 15:33; 18:12; 22:4; Zeph. 2:3).

2. In its translation of these Heb. concepts the LXX uses the full range of meaning of this word-group and adds a few variants of its own; e.g. to humble a woman in a sexual sense (2 Sam. 13:12; Deut. 21:14; Ezek. 22:10 f.); to rape (Gen. 34:2, etc.); to bow one's soul, i.e. fast (e.g. Lev. 16:29; Isa. 58:3). But above all the words occur in expression of belief in what Yahweh has done. It is God himself by his acts in history who brings down the proud and arrogant, and chooses and rescues the humiliated. This recognition is expressed in a number of ways.

(a) The prophets expressed it in warnings of judgment (cf. Amos 2:6b, 7 with 2:6a, 13 ff.; 8:6 with 8:7 f.; Isa. 2:9, 11, 17; 5:15; 10:33 f.; 14:32, against the Philistines; Zeph. 2:3, Ezek. 21:26[31]) and in promises (Zeph. 3:12; Ezek. 17:24; Isa. 49:13; 53:8 ["In his humiliation his judgment was taken away", LXX]; Isa. 54:11; 66:2b; 26:6).

(b) The historical books see it in events. This is shown in their general theological attitudes and in their corresponding choice of language (Jdg. 4:23; 6:15 ff., choice of Gideon; 1 Sam. 1:11, 16, Hannah's prayer, and 2:7 ff., her song of praise; 7:13; 18:23 ff.; 2 Sam. 22:28, in David's thanksgiving for victory; 1 Chr. 17:10, in the promise given to David, 1 Ki. 8:35 par. 2 Chr. 6:26; cf. Ps. 18:27 ([MT 28; LXX 17:28]). These speeches, prayers and songs have a common characteristic theme.

(c) The Pss. and Lam. repeat it in their certainty expressed in their prayers (e.g. Pss. 10:17 f. [LXX 9:38 f.]; 25:18 [LXX 24:18]; 31:7 [MT 31:8; LXX 30:8]; 34:18 [MT 34:19; LXX 33:19]; 38:8, 22 [MT 38:9, 23; LXX 37:9, 23]; 44:19, 25 f. [MT 44:20, 26 f.; LXX 43:20, 26 f.]; 51:17 [MT 51:19]; 74:21 [LXX 73:21]). There is the frequent parallelism with → poor. In Ps. 82 [LXX 81] the relationship of v. 3 with vv. 5ff. shows that the gods are incapable of giving justice to the lowly, and so God himself must judge (v. 8). Other examples are Pss. 90:3 [LXX 89:3], where *dakkā*', meaning crushed matter, dust, is translated by *tapeinōsis*; 102:15–20 [MT 102:16–21; LXX 101:16–21], especially v. 17; 113:5–9 [LXX 112:5–9], a song of praise; 116:10 [LXX 115:1], cf. with v. 1 [LXX 114:1 f.], a hymn of thanks; 119 [LXX 118]; 50, 67, 71, 75, 92, the law of God comforts in lowliness; 107 [LXX 106]; 131:2 [LXX 130:2], 136:23 [LXX 135:23], a hymn of thanks; 138:6 [LXX 137:6], cf. 113:5–9; 142:6 [MT 142:7; LXX 141:7]; Lam. 1:5b, 8b, 12c, 20; 2:5c, 18, 20; 3:32–34 (cf. with vv. 31, 37 f.); Isa. 25:1–5.

(d) Proverbs in the wisdom literature speak of humility as the fruit of experience and as a rule for life: e.g. cf. Job 5:11 with 8:12, 21 (LXX and Vulg. only, not MT); Prov. 3:34 (the LXX is more explicit than the MT); 11:2, cf. v. 1; 15:33 (MT "humility"), par. to "the fear of the Lord" (the LXX has *tapeinos* only in some MSS, but cf. 16:2 where it is lacking in the MT); in 16:19 *tapeinōsis* is par. to *praÿthymos*, gentleness; 18:22; 2:4, the LXX translates humility [MT] by wisdom; cf. also 25:7; 29:23; Eccles. 10:6; Sir. 7:11; 10:15 ff.; 11:12 f.

3. The members of the Qumran sect called themselves the → poor, and in the Community Rule virtuous humility is mentioned along with loving kindness (the opposites of anger and grumbling), truth, right thinking, faithfulness, unity and patience as the great virtue of the community (1QS 2:24; 4:3; 5:3, 25). But this attitude stands alongside a hatred for the ruling sons of darkness (1QS 9:22; 11:1). Humility is the proper attitude before God: "his iniquity shall be expiated by the spirit of uprightness and humility" (1QS 3:8) and man's humility submits to God's chastisement (1QH 17:22); "his flesh . . . is made clean by the humble submission of his soul to all the precepts of God" (1QS 3:8).

4. Apocalyptic literature sees in humility the eschatological attitude to which the promise of the reward and the help of God are addressed (Test.Gad. 5:3; 2 Esd. 8:47–54).

5. For the rabbis, humility also had a high place in the scale of virtues that men should attempt to attain (cf. SB I 191–194). A humble spirit was regarded as the characteristic sign of the Jew (cf. especially the polemic against the pride of the Gentiles, Pirke Aboth 5:21). Jesus' teaching indicates the discrepancy between this high theoretical claim and arrogant Rab. and Pharisaic practice (Matt. 23:1 ff.; Lk. 18:9–14). They were humble among themselves, but they considered ignorance of the → law as due either to sin or to God's disfavour. They equated human effort with God's grace, and so had a faulty concept of God and of themselves.

NT Members of the word-group are found 34 times in the NT: *tapeinos* 8 times, *tapeinoō* 14 times, *tapeinōsis* 4 times, the compound *tapeinophrōn* once, and the noun *tapeinophrosynē* 7 times (only in Acts and the epistles). Their distribution is: Matt. 4 times, Lk. 7 times, Acts twice, Rom. once, 2 Cor. 4 times, Eph. once, Phil., 4 times, Col. 3 times, Jas. 4 times, 1 Pet. 4 times. Thus no members of the word-group are found in Mk., the Johannine writings or epistles other than those mentioned above.

1. In Matt. and Lk. the words are closely linked with the proclamation of the eschatological breaking-in of the kingly rule of God. This is the new element in the frequent use of OT and Jewish texts. Lk. introduces the theme already in the introductory chs. of his Gospel. The mother of Jesus in the *Magnificat* praised the grandeur of God in OT phrases (1 Sam. 1:11; cf. Ps. 113:5–9), "for he has regarded

the low estate of his handmaiden" (Lk. 1:48), where handmaiden, i.e. slave, inter-prets low estate (cf. v. 38). "He has . . . exalted those of low degree" (Lk. 1:52; cf. 1 Sam. 2:7; Job 5:11; Ps. 75:7[8]; Ezek. 21:26[MT 21:31]). The work of John the Baptist (Lk. 3:1 ff.) is then presented as preparing for the coming of God, and in accordance with the prophecy of Isa. 40:3 ff.: "every mountain and hill shall be brought low" (Lk. 3:5).

He who thus came went the way of humility (Matt. 11:29, see below). He could, therefore, (a) in his warning against desire for status (Lk. 14:11; cf. Mk. 10:15; Matt. 18:4; 1 Pet. 5:5; Prov. 3:34; 25:7), (b) in his controversy with the Pharisees (Lk. 18:14), and (c) in his attack on them and the scribes (Matt. 23:12), promise that he who humbles himself (*tapeinoun heauton*) will be exalted at the last by God. (The passive is used to avoid the mention of God's name.) At the same time he threat-ened the proud with the last judgment, each time using the same proverb (cf. 1 Sam. 2:7; 2 Sam. 22:28; Ezek. 21:26[31]; Sir. 7:11) but giving it in the eschato-logical situation a quite new meaning (A. Dihle, *RAC* III 748).

The foundation of this promise, admonition and warning is found in Jesus' own way of life, as he interpreted it in his invitation in Matt. 11:28 ff. He is "meek" (*praÿs*) and "lowly in heart" (*tapeinos tē kardia*). The two thoughts stand in parallel and show that Jesus was submissive before God, completely dependent on him, and devoted to him, and at the same time humble before men whose servant and helper he had become (Lk. 22:27; Mk. 10:45; Matt. 20:28; cf. W. Grund-mann, *TDNT* VIII 20). That is why he can call those who labour and are heavy laden to himself and offer them eschatological rest as they follow him; contrast Sir. 51:23–30 with its call to follow simply the ethical example set by the teacher of the law (cf. A. Schlatter, *Der Evangelist Matthäus*, 1963[6], 386 ff.). "The highest dignity of Jesus and his willingness to accept the cross . . . are one" (J. Schniewind, *Das Evangelium nach Matthäus*, *NTD* 8, 1960[9], ad loc.). See also Phil. 2:6 ff. below.

Matt. 18:1–5 with its teaching on humility shows that Jesus' call to discipleship should not be confused with ethical attainment. The demand to humble oneself like the child placed among the disciples does not mean that one should make oneself lower than one actually is. Rather, one should know, like the child, how lowly one really is. Humility is to know how lowly we really are before God. At the same time the use of the word "child" is a reminder of the → Father in → heaven. This kind of humility and lowliness are joy and bliss (J. Schniewind, ad loc.; cf. J. Jeremias, *The Parables of Jesus*, 1963[2], 190 f.), for they permit one to share in the royal rule of heaven.

2. (a) The central position of the Saviour's invitation in Matt. corresponds to that of the hymn to Christ in Phil. 2:6–11 in Paul's letters. In the description of Jesus Christ's work from his self-emptying (v. 7 → Empty, art. *kenos*), through his self-humbling (v. 8c gives Paul's decisive addition to the hymn he had taken over), to his exaltation by God, all the main lines of the OT proclamation of God's sovereign control of history come into focus as they find their fulfilment. Here God stands by his word. At the same time the self-humiliation of Jesus Christ inaugur-ates the new life under his rule (vv. 10 f.). It is the basis of *tapeinophrosynē*, humility (v. 3), willingness to serve, conforming to his example; cf. also v. 5, "have this mind among yourselves . . . ." The meaning of self-humiliation is doubly defined in Jesus Christ. On the one hand, he became obedient unto death, even the uttermost shame

of the cross. On the other hand, he had no other support than the incredible promise of the faithfulness of God (cf. Pss. 22; 25:18; 31:17 [MT 31:8]; 90:3; 119:50, 92, 150; and especially Isa. 53:7-12, cf. H. W. Wolff, *Jesaja 53 im Urchristentum*, 1952³, 98 f.).

(b) Acts 8:35 expounds Isa. 53:7 f., quoted from the LXX, as referring to the humiliation and exaltation of Jesus Christ (cf. H. W. Wolff, op. cit., 90 ff.).

(c) Paul understood his apostolic service to be one of following the Lord, who gave him strength through his own exaltation won through self-humiliation (Phil. 4:12 f.). Hence Paul knew "how to be abased" (*tapeinousthai*). This probably refers to being hungry and in need, suffering want and affliction (cf. 2 Cor. 11:23–29; 12:7-10). It may also include the physical work which, his enemies insinuated, was a penance for some hidden sin, but which Paul defended on the grounds that it enabled him to proclaim the gospel without charge (2 Cor. 11:7) and build up the church by his teaching. (For use of the vb. in the sense of "confess one's guilt" cf. A. Schlatter, op. cit., 545.) Acts faithfully conveys Paul's understanding of his apostolic service in the statement, "serving the Lord with all humility and with tears and with trials" (Acts 20:19). Paul recognized God's action both in humbling him through the failures (2 Cor. 12:21) which were manifest in the continuing strife (v. 20) and immorality (v. 21c) of the Corinthians, and in comforting those who were humbled by strife and inner fears (2 Cor. 7:5 f.; cf. Isa. 49:13). In the midst of the difficulties of his service Paul was supported by the → hope that the coming Lord would transform our body of humiliation (*to sōma tēs tapeinōseōs hēmōn*, Phil. 3:21; "our lowly body" RSV), i.e. our mortal body and make it like his glorious body.

(d) In three passages in Paul's letters words from this group are used with their original derogatory sense, in each case ironically in a polemical context. In 2 Cor. 10:1 Paul quotes the taunt of his opponents that he was so "feeble" (*tapeinos*), when he was "face to face" with them (NEB), but was bold when far away. In Col. 2:18, 23 he warns against the opponents who take pleasure in self-abasement, worship of angels and asceticism, each time using *tapeinophrosynē*.

(e) Paul's exhortation to humility is also rooted in the effective reality of Christ. Rom. 12:16 (cf. v. 1) warns against haughtiness and recommends, "give your-selves to humble tasks" (RSV mg.) or "associate with the lowly" (RSV tx., NEB) – depending on whether *tois tapeinois* is taken as neut. or masc. Similarly Eph. 4:2 (cf. v.1) and Col. 3:12 (cf. v.1) enjoin willingness to serve (in each case *tapeinophrosynē;* RSV; "meekness"; NEB "gentleness") which unites the church and holds it together (see above OT 3, on the community Rule at Qumran). Both passages use *tapeinophrosynē* parallel to *praÿtēs* (→ *praÿs* NT), and the latter speaks of putting on willingness to serve like a garment (cf. below on 1 Pet. 5:5).

3. The exhortations in Jas. and 1 Pet. do not add anything new to the OT and Pauline calls to humility. Jas. 1:9 f. speaks of the socially low, the poor, in contrast to the rich. Those who belonged to them could boast of their exaltation, while the rich, paradoxically, should boast that they were subject to death (*tapeinōsis*, cf. v. 10c). Both statements were made in the light "of the coming transformation of the world" (M. Dibelius, *Der Brief des Jakobus*, KEK 15, 1956⁸, ad loc.). Jas. 4:6b, par. 1 Pet. 5:5c, is a quotation from Prov. 3:34 (LXX), which promises God's favour to the humble. Both draw the conclusion (Jas. 4:10 par. 1 Pet. 5:6): "Humble

yourselves before the Lord and he will exalt you" (cf. Gen. 16:9; Sir. 2:17). Since no literary dependence between the two letters can be demonstrated, the similarity points to "a common Christian exhortation" (*TDNT* VIII 19; cf. M. Dibelius, op. cit., 30). 1 Pet. 5:5 contains the metaphor of putting on clothing: "Clothe yourselves, all of you, with humility [*tapeinophrosynē*]" (cf. Jn. 13:4).

4. Gradually the concept of "humility" in the church was reduced from an eschatological expectation and a manner of life consistent with it to a term describing an inclination to penance and fasting, and their practical expression, especially in 1 Clem. and Hermas (cf. *TDNT* VIII 25 f.).   *H.-H. Esser*

→ Empty, → Grace, → Love, → Patience, → Poor, → Pride

(a). A. A. Anderson, *The Book of Psalms*, I–II, 1972; G. Bornkamm, "On Understanding the Christ-hymn (Philippians 2:6–11)", *Early Christian Experience*, 1969, 112–22; W. Grundmann, *tapeinos*, *TDNT* VIII 1–26; B. Häring, *The Law of Christ*, I, 1961; II, 1963; F. Hauck, *penēs*, *TDNT* VI 37–40; F. Hauck and E. Bammel, *ptōchos*, *TDNT* VI 865–82; F. Hauck and S. Schulz, *praÿs*, *TDNT* VI 645–51; D. Kidner, *Psalms 1–72*, 1973; and *Psalms 73–150*, *TC*, 1975; R. Leivestad, " 'The Meekness and Gentleness of Christ' II Cor. x. 1", *NTS* 12, 1965–66, 156–64; M. Maher, " 'Take my yoke upon you' (Matt. xi. 29)", *NTS* 22, 1975–76, 97–103; W. Michaelis, *praÿpatheia*, *TDNT* V 939; C. F. D. Moule, "The Manhood of Christ", in S. W. Sykes and J. P. Clayton, eds., *Christ, Faith and History*, 1972, 95–110; H. Preisker, *epieikeia*, *TDNT* II 588 ff.; A. Stöger, "Humility", *EBT* II 385–90; A. Weiser, *The Psalms*, 1962.

(b). A. Dihle, "Demut", *RAC* III 735 ff.; R. A. Gauthier, *Magnanimité, l'Ideal de la Grandeur dans Philosophie païenne et dans la Théologie chrétienne*, 1951; A. Gelin, *Les Pauvres de Jahvé*, 1953; L. Gilen, "Die Demut des Christen nach dem Neuen Testament", *Zeitschrift für Askese und Mystik* 13, 1938, 266 ff.; A. von Harnack, "Sanftmut, Huld und Demut in der alten Kirche", in *Festschrift* for J. Kaftan, 1920, 113–29; E. Kamlah, *Die Form der katalogischen Paränese im Neuen Testament*, *WUNT* 7, 1964; E. Käsemann, *Die Legitimität des Apostels*, 1956; E. Kutsch, "*ᵃnāwâh* (Dissertation, Mainz), 1960; H.-J. Kraus, *Die Psalmen*, I–II, *BKAT* 15, 1972⁴; E. Larsson, *Christus als Vorbild*, 1967; J. Leipoldt, "Vom Kinde in der alten Welt", in *Reich Gottes und Wirklichkeit*, *Festschrift* for E. Sommerlath, 1961, 343 ff.; R. Mehl, "Sanftmut", *RGG*³ V 1363 f.; G. Mensching, E. Kutsch, A. Benoit, R. Mehl, "Demut", *RGG*³ I 76–82; R. North, " 'Humilis corde' in luce Psalmorum", *Verbum Domini* 28, 1950, 153–61; S. Rehrl, *Die Wortgruppe zu griechisch tapeinos und das Problem der Demut in der profan-griechischen Literatur im Vergleich zu Septuaginta and Neuen Testament*, 1961; and *Das Problem der Demut in der profanischen Literatur im Vergleich zu LXX und Neuen Testament*, 1961; H. Rosman, "In omni humilitate", *Verbum Domini* 21, 1941, 272–80; O. Schaffner, *Christliche Demut*, 1959; A. Schlatter, *Jesu Dienst*, 1904; F. Sinner, *Die christliche Demut*, 1925; G. Strecker, *Der Weg der Gerechtigkeit*, *FRLANT* 82, 1962, 173 f.; K. Thieme, *Die christliche Demut*, 1906; W. C. van Unnik, "Zur Bedeutung von *tapeinoun tēn psychēn* bei den apostolischen Vätern", *ZNW* 44, 1952–53, 250 ff.; S. Wibbing, *Die Tugend- und Lasterkataloge im Neuen Testament*, *BZNW* 25, 1959; and "Demut", *EKL* I 862 ff.; H. W. Wolff, *Jesaja 53 im Urchristentum*, 1952³.

Hunger, Thirst, Food, Taste, Eat, Drink

Eating and drinking are basic to human life. In the world of the ancient east, which suffered frequently from famines and droughts, they assume a particular importance. Five different groups of words are examined here. Man's need of sustenance is denoted by the vbs. *peinaō*, to hunger (cf. *limos*, hunger), and *dipsaō*, to thirst. Satisfaction of hunger is denoted by *esthiō*, to eat, and in a specialized sense by *geuomai*, to taste, enjoy. The thing eaten is *brōma*, food. *pinō*, with its numerous derivatives, denotes drinking. As time went on all these words acquired metaphorical significance and were used to express spiritual nourishment or the lack of it.

| πεινάω | πεινάω (*peinaō*), hunger; διψάω (*dipsaō*), to thirst; δίψος (*dipsos*), thirst; λιμός (*limos*), hunger, famine. |

CL 1. *peinaō* means to hunger; *dipsaō*, to thirst; the corresponding nouns are *limos*, famine and its effect, hunger, and *dipsos*, thirst. The range of meaning of these words is not limited to physical want, but extends to the intellectual and spiritual life (from Plato and Xenophon). They express a passionate longing for something without which one cannot live, e.g. freedom, honour, fame, wealth, praise, enlightenment. This desire is often emphasized by bracketing hunger and thirst together.

2. The ancients attributed famine to the wrath of the gods. Vegetation gods and cults were therefore supposed to guarantee the provision of food (cf. the Canaanite Baals). In the later mystery religions these old fertility gods satisfied men's hunger for enduring eternal → life.

It was the task of rulers (e.g. the pharaohs of Egypt) to protect their subjects against hunger. But every case of hunger and thirst presented an obligation to help whoever was in need.

3. Gk. philosophers generally attempted to educate their adherents to free themselves from enslavement to the needs of the body. Thus the Stoics sought to make themselves independent of all the vicissitudes of life by the practice of asceticism, and the gnostics to free themselves from a sensual attachment to the world through the denial of the body (which belongs to material world, alienated from God), in order to attain to the realm of the spirit.

OT 1. In the LXX *peinaō* mostly translated the Heb. *rā'ēḇ*, to be hungry, but also *'āyēp̄*, to be weary, faint or exhausted, and *yā'ēp̄*, to be weary or faint. *limos* stands consistently for *rā'āḇ*, hunger; *dipsaō* and *dipsos* mostly for formations from the root *ṣāmē'* thirst(y), but also for *ṣiyyāh*, to be dry, and *'āyēp̄*, weary, faint. While *peinaō* and *dipsaō* or *dipsos* each occurs about 50 times in the LXX, *limos* is attested over 100 times. *limos* denotes acute lack of food, famine; *peinaō* stresses long drawn-out hungering.

2. Hunger and thirst are reckoned as the worst forms of lack, and of the two thirst is even more distressing than hunger in the sun-drenched east. Among the causes is failure of the rains with consequent failure of the harvest (1 Ki. 17:1), so that one can even speak of the thirst of the land. Hunger and thirst are also connected with war, wanderings in the desert (Ps. 107:5), idleness (Prov. 19:15), and particularly godlessness (Ps. 34:10; Isa. 65:13; Sir. 40:9). God sends hunger and thirst as a → judgment and as a salutary means of → humbling the godless attitudes of men (Deut. 32:24; 2 Sam. 24:13; Ezek. 5:15 f.; as a punishment in → hell they are not mentioned before 2 Esd. 8:59). In times of famine Israel sought help in more fertile → Egypt (Gen. 12:10; 41:53 ff.; 42:1 ff.). But it was in times of need (e.g. during the wandering in the wilderness, and in the land of Canaan) that Israel learned that God was her real Saviour from need (Exod. 16:3 ff.; 17:3 ff.; cf. 1 Ki. 8:37 ff.). Yahweh takes up the cause of the hungry who belong to the dispossessed → poor (1 Sam. 2:5). While judgment is pronounced on those who are filled, there is the promise of salvation for the hungry (Ps. 107:36 ff.; 146:7; Isa. 65:13). God demands from the devout a corresponding attitude to the poor (Isa.

265

58:7, 10; Ezek. 18:7, 16), among whom even their enemies must not be overlooked (Prov. 25:21).

3. This word group is occasionally used metaphorically of thirst for God (Ps. 42:2; 63:1; 143:6) and of striving after wisdom (Sir. 51:24). Amos 8:11–13 speaks of a hungering after the word of God alongside an actual famine: God can in the end withhold everything as a punishment. Several passages directed to the Jewish people during the Babylonian exile have particular significance. Though at present discouraged (Isa. 40:27–31) and poor (41:17 f.; 49:9 f.; 55:1), they will be allowed by God to return home. He will transform the arduous route through the desert into an oasis journey (Isa. 41:19; 43:20; 48:21, as at the exodus), and their wasted homeland itself into a "garden of salvation" (Ezek. 34:29; cf. Isa. 35:1, 6 f.). This material well-being includes the idea of spiritual salvation (Isa. 44:3; Jer. 31:12).

4. (a) In Philo Gk. and Jewish elements are mingled together. On the one hand, he encourages moderation and the discipline of the body in order to concentrate on the more important matter of satisfying the soul (*Spec.Leg.* 2, 201). On the other hand, he calls hunger the "most insupportable of all evils" (*Spec.Leg.* 2, 201; cf. *TDNT* VI 14).

(b) In Rab. Judaism hunger and thirst no longer come within the sphere of God's promises, but merely serve as inducements to better keeping of the law (e.g. Pss. Sol. 5:1–12; 10:1–6; 13:7–10). The Rabbis still only understood times of need as punishing or at best purifying, misfortunes which one attempted to counter by good works (cf. SB II 643 f.; IV 536–558).

NT Of the terms discussed *peinaō* occurs most frequently in the NT (about 25 times), chiefly in the synoptics and especially in Matt. Of the 16 occurrences of *dipsaō* in the NT, 9 are in the Johannine writings (Jn. and Rev.). *limos* is used by a variety of authors, but only 12 times in all.

OT and NT take man's physical need very seriously. But it is not only the stomach (→ Belly) but the whole man that needs to be satisfied. External well-being and inner salvation are most closely related. This explains the fact that many NT statements about hunger and thirst show a peculiar ambiguity, making it scarcely possible to distinguish the literal from the metaphorical.

1. The NT also speaks of famines (Lk. 4:25; Acts 7:11). They are among the terrors of the end time (Matt. 24:7 par. Mk. 13:8, Lk. 21:10; Rev. 6:8; 18:8; cf. Syr.Bar. 27:6), and the occasion of special measures of assistance (Acts 11:28). Hunger can move a man to → conversion, where questions about food raise questions about faith (Lk. 15:14, 17).

2. (a) Lk., in particular, depicts Jesus as the advocate of the poor and hungry (Lk. 1:53 = Ps. 107:9; Lk. 6:21), understanding hunger in the broadest sense. Believers should not fear hunger, as if there were no God to help them. The present order of things is questionable. In the future order God will act on behalf of the needy. Therefore, Jesus calls them → blessed already in view of the coming day of God, when he will bestow the → gifts of the time of salvation. For those who can expect nothing from this world, and direct all their hope towards God, there will be no more hunger (Lk. 6:21). There is no promise, however, for those who are

satisfied in this world. On the contrary, they are threatened with the prospect of mourning and weeping (Lk. 6:25). Thus the Lucan Beatitudes and Woes (Lk. 6:21, 25) contrast the present hunger and deprivation of the poor, for whom is the promise of divine help and future salvation, with the future hunger of those who are at present satisfied and rich, for whom there will be condemnation without promise (cf. Lk. 16:19–31, the rich man and poor Lazarus; on this see J. D. M. Derrett, "Dives and Lazarus and the Preceding Sayings", *Law in the New Testament*, 1970, 78–99).

(b) The Beatitude of Matt. 5:6 understands hunger as "hunger and thirst for righteousness." In contrast to the self-righteousness of Jewish legalism "hunger for righteousness" means the felt need and consequent longing for divine righteousness (cf. Matt. 6:10, third petition of the Lord's Prayer, "Thy will be done . . ."). According to Matt., those who hunger are the same as those who believe and long for the kingdom of God (6:33). Their promised filling begins with the coming of Jesus and continues until everything else is theirs as well.

(c) Hunger and thirst in the Johannine writings have a double meaning. Natural thirst (Jn. 4:13) and physical hunger (6:1 ff.) convey the longing for life in general. Jesus seizes upon this longing in order to show that it is only through contact with himself, the life-giver, that it is satisfied (4:14 f.; 6:35, "I am the bread of life"; alluding to Exod. 16:3 ff., 7:37). But what is promised in all the sayings about the satisfaction of hunger and thirst is only fully received in God's new world. Then all the physical and spiritual needs of earth will be ended (Rev. 7:16; 21:6; 22:17 = Isa. 49:10; 55:1; cf. Lk. 1:53; 6:21 par. Matt. 5:6).

3. The description in the gospels of Jesus himself having to suffer hunger and thirst serves to show the Son of God in his humanity. After 40 days of fasting hunger became for Jesus a temptation from the devil to use his authority as Son of God to satisfy his own need through a miracle (Matt. 4:2; Lk. 4:2; cf. Mk. 1:12 f.). Only in obedience to God's word was he able to stand firm, for "Man shall not live by bread alone, but by every word that proceeds from the mouth of God" (Matt. 4:4; cf. Lk. 4:4; Deut. 8:3). He cursed the fig-tree which did not satisfy his hunger for fruit (Matt. 21:18 f. par. Mk. 11:12 ff.; → Fruit, art. *sykē*) and thereby demonstrated in parabolic fashion how a curse will fall upon all who do not bear the fruit of → righteousness. On the cross he thirsted though he offered himself as the living water to satisfy all thirst (Jn. 19:28; cf. Ps. 69:21; → Gall).

4. For the sake of their calling the disciples shared Jesus' poverty. Jesus defended their action of plucking ears of corn on the → sabbath (Matt. 12:1–8 par. Mk. 2:23–28, Lk. 6:1–5). Hunger and thirst were also among the deprivations that Paul had to undergo for the crucified Christ, in contrast to the enthusiasts in Corinth who fallaciously believed that they already enjoyed full possession of all the good things of the coming world (1 Cor. 4:8; 2 Cor. 11:27). When they assembled for worship, the latter pitilessly took no notice of the hungry among them (1 Cor. 11:21, 34). Hunger and thirst are not necessarily signs of God's disfavour. They may afflict, but they cannot separate from the love of God (Rom. 8:35). If Paul nevertheless was able to overcome them, he did so not on the basis of asceticism or superior knowledge, but through Christ alone (Phil. 4:12).

5. Hunger and thirst are occasions for the exercise of love. Their satisfaction is reckoned among the works of mercy which are set up as a standard at the judgment

of the world (Matt. 25:35, 37, 42) and which should include one's enemy (Rom. 12:20 = Prov. 25:21 f.; → Head). We have to remember also that in those who hunger and thirst Jesus Christ himself meets us incognito (Matt. 25:37, 42), "disguised in the uniform of misery" (Matthias Claudius; cf. Acts 11:28 ff.).

W. Bauder

βρῶμα

βρῶμα (brōma), food; βρῶσις (brōsis), eating, consuming, food; βρώσιμος (brōsimos), eatable; γάλα (gala), milk.

CL brōma (from Hippocrates on) and brōsis (from Homer on) both mean: (a) what is eaten, food; (b) eating (as a process); rarely, in the metaphorical sense, the food of immortality.

OT In the LXX both words translate almost exclusively the Heb. word group connected with the vb. 'ākal, to eat. They mostly mean food, and only rarely eating as a process (e.g. Jer. 15:3). eis brōsin is a frequent phrase meaning "for food" (of men: Gen. 1:29; 2:9; 3:7; 9:3; etc.; of animals: Gen. 1:30; Jer. 7:33; 19:7; etc.).

God, who has assigned food to both men and beasts (Gen. 1:29 f.; 2:16; 9:3), also looks after his people's food throughout their history (cf. Ps. 78:18, 30; Gen. 41:35 ff.). The food, which God gives, is an expression of the righteousness which he has also given (Jon. 2:23 LXX).

This group of concepts does not occur in the LXX in the metaphorical sense for spiritual or supernatural food (nevertheless Deut. 8:3 points in this direction; → Bread, art. manna).

NT brōma occurs in the NT 17 times, of which 10 are in Paul: (a) in its literal sense, food (e.g. Matt. 14:15; Mk. 7:19; Rom. 14:15, 20; 1 Cor. 8:8, 13); (b) in the metaphorical sense (e.g. Jn. 4:34; 1 Cor. 3:2; 10:3). brōsis (11 times) is used (a) for the act of eating (e.g. Rom. 14:17; 1 Cor. 8:4; 2 Cor. 9:10; Col. 2:16); (b) as the synonym of brōma both literally (Heb. 12:16) and metaphorically (Jn. 4:32; 66:27, 55); (c) exceptionally of an insect that consumes (Matt. 6:19).

1. The literal use. In the NT, as in the OT, food is seen as God's gift which should be asked for daily ("give us this day our daily bread"; → Bread, art. epiousios) and received thankfully (1 Tim. 4:4). Ascetic and ritual tendencies, which classed certain foods as taboo, are rejected by the NT as false teaching (Col. 2:16 f.; 1 Tim. 4:3 ff.; Heb. 13:9; cf. Heb. 9:10). No food is unclean as such (Mk. 7:18 f.; cf. Acts 10:14 f.), and no food therefore possesses any special significance for our relationship to God (1 God. 8:8; cf. 1 Cor. 6:13). It is not the observance of particular commands or prohibitions concerning food which decides our participation in God's salvation; the → kingdom of God is realized in righteousness and peace and joy in the Holy Spirit (Rom. 14:17).

Christians can be commanded to avoid a particular food (meat offered to idols), however, if a brother by eating will be plunged into a conflict of → conscience, because his conscience is still prisoner of the idea that the use of this food is something prohibited and offensive to God (Rom. 14:15, 20; 1 Cor. 8:13). Out of

268

love for the tempted brother for whom Christ died the Christian who is "strong" in → knowledge must be able to forego a particular food. The possibility of sinning, however, does not lie in the food offered to the idol (1 Cor. 8:4) but in the man himself (cf. 1 Cor. 10:27).

2. *brōma* is used figuratively in contrast to *gala*, milk, in 1 Cor. 3:2. True proclamation of the word is always attuned to the receptivity of the hearer. But since faith involves a process of maturing, the "babe" in the faith cannot yet "digest" the deepest truths of divine wisdom. It is too strong meat for him.

The heavenly food mentioned in 1 Cor. 10:3 is the manna which in a miraculous way kept the people of Israel alive when earthly food was lacking. This food is interpreted typologically with reference to the Lord's Supper (→ art. *pinō* NT 4 (a) below; → Bread, art. *manna*; → Lord's Supper).

Food is also referred to metaphorically in Jn. 4:32. Jesus startlingly described the work that he did in fulfilment of his → Father's commission as the food (*brōsis*; *v.l. brōma*) on which he lived. Jesus' actions, indeed his whole life, constitute a revelation which does not have its origin in himself but which he receives from his Father. His work is none other than the living out of this revelation. Jesus' description of his work (vv. 32, 34) as his food means that he has come "not only *for* this service, but indeed *through* this service" (R. Bultmann, *The Gospel of John*, 1971, 195).

brōsis is mentioned three more times in Jn. in connection with feeding on Christ. "Do not labour for the food which perishes, but for the food which endures to eternal life, which the Son of man will give to you; for on him has God the Father set his seal" (Jn. 6:27). "For my flesh is food indeed, and my blood is drink indeed" (Jn. 6:55). Christ himself is now the food. "Jesus *gives* the bread of life in that he *is* the bread of life" (R. Bultmann, op. cit., 227). The man Jesus becomes, as Christ, "the bread which came down from heaven" (Jn. 6:41). To eat this bread is another way of describing what it is to believe in Jesus, "for he who comes to me shall not hunger, and he who believes in me shall never thirst" (Jn. 6:35). H. Kropatschek

---

| γεύομαι | γεύομαι (*geuomai*), taste, partake of, enjoy, experience. |

CL & OT *geuomai* (root *geus, gys;* cf. Lat. *gustare*, Ger. *kosten*, to taste) means to taste, and hence figuratively to partake of, enjoy, and experience. In the OT the word occurs in the figurative sense only in Ps. 34:8 ("Taste and see that the Lord is good"); Job 20:18; and Prov. 31:18. Otherwise it is always used literally (cf. Gen. 25:30; 1 Sam. 14:24 ff.; Jon. 3:7). In the OT the figurative meaning expresses the element of experience. It translates the Heb. *ṭā'am*, taste, perceive.

NT In the NT *geuomai* occurs 15 times (of which 10 are in the Gospels and Acts) and is used as in secular Gk. and in the LXX.

1. Taste is used in a literal sense in (e.g.) Matt. 27:34; Jn. 2:9; Acts 10:10; and Col. 2:21. The Colossian church was distracted by a "philosophy" (Col. 2:8) which "made use of terms which stemmed from Jewish tradition, but which had been transformed in the crucible of syncretism to be subject to the service of 'the

269

elements of the universe.' It is this service which they are now supposed to express. Since the angelic powers are in charge of the order of the cosmos and the course of the stars, their sacred seasons and times must be observed and the regulations, codified in a list of taboos, must be followed" (E. Lohse, *Colossians and Philemon, Hermeneia*, 1971, 116). By setting apart areas of life as controlled by demonic powers, this group at Colossae was in effect calling in question the victory of Christ over the whole world. Col. counters this by asking: "If with Christ you died to the elemental spirits of the universe, why do you live as if you still belonged to the world? Why do you submit to regulations? 'Do not handle, Do not taste, Do not touch' (referring to things which all perish as they are used), according to human precepts and doctrines? These have indeed an appearance of wisdom in promoting rigour of devotion and self-abasement and severity to the body, but they are of no value in checking the indulgence of the flesh" (Col. 2:20–23).

The parable of the great banquet concludes with the pronouncement: "For I tell you, none of those men who were invited shall taste my banquet" (Lk. 14:24). Here Jesus himself is speaking through the master in the parable pronouncing the rejection of those who rejected the invitation to the messianic banquet on account of worldly concerns. The literal sense of "taste" symbolizes participation in the → kingdom of God.

2. The figurative sense. 1 Pet. 2:3 takes up the words of Ps. 34:8, when it says, "For you have tasted the kindness of the Lord." The readers are urged to put away malice, guile, insincerity and slander (2:1) and grow up in a way appropriate to those who have been "born anew" (1:23). "Like newborn babes, long for the pure spiritual milk, that by it you may grow up to salvation" (2:2; → Birth; → Conversion). In view of the connection of the passage with Ps. 34, E. G. Selwyn suggests that its force is best brought out if it is rendered: "if you have responded to the Psalmist's words, 'taste and see that the Lord is good', i.e. if you have taken the initial step of adherence to Christ" (*The First Epistle of St. Peter*, 1946, 157). The word "if [*ei*]" is to be understood in the sense of "seeing that" (RSV "for"; cf. 1:17; Funk §§ 371 f.). Selwyn also suggests that Ps. 34 lies behind the thought of 1 Pet. at numerous points (cf. v. 10 with 1:15 ff.; v. 5 with 1:17 and 2:4; vv. 13–17 quoted verbatim in 3:10 ff.; v. 23 with 1:18, 13; and v. 20 with the epistle passim). He conjectures its use in the church of Asia Minor as part of a catechetical document, a persecution document or a baptismal hymn.

Ps. 34:8 may also be reflected in Heb. 6:4 ff.: "For it is impossible to restore again to repentance those who have once been enlightened, who have tasted the heavenly gift, and have become partakers of the Holy Spirit, and have tasted the goodness of the word of God and the powers of the age to come, if they then commit apostasy, since they crucify the Son of God on their own account and hold him up to contempt." It is not clear whether the author is thinking specifically of the forgiveness of sins, the gift of salvation, the Holy Spirit, or Christ himself. I. H. Marshall thinks it unlikely that the Holy Spirit is meant in view of the following reference to him, and that it is most probable that salvation is in mind (*Kept by the Power of God*, 1969, 137). He suggests that the emphasis in tasting is not that of taking a sip, as Calvin thought. (In Heb. 2:9 Christ tasted death in the sense that he experienced its bitter taste to the full.) The amount consumed is not the point, but the fact of experiencing what is eaten. The Christians to whom this is addressed have already experienced something of the future age, the world that is to come. If in this experience believers thus receive a foretaste, the passage is an instance of the characteristic tension between the "already" and the "not yet" in the life of the Christian.

On the expression "to taste death" (already present in ancient Jewish literature, cf. SB I 751 ff. on Matt. 16:28) compare 1 Sam. 15:32; Sir. 41:1 (the bitterness of death). The promise of Mk. 9:1 and Lk. 9:27 that some would see the coming of the kingdom (or the Son of man coming in his kingdom, Matt. 16:28) without tasting death, i.e. without dying, is to be explained by the expected nearness of the event. It was an expectation which (Adolf Schlatter suggested) itself experienced "by God's ruling not only fulfilment but also expansion and modification." ([Ed.] However, the passage has also been understood to refer to the transfiguration which in fact took place shortly after, the resurrection, and also to the coming of the Son of man in judgment on Jerusalem [on Matt. 24:34 par. → Generation].)

The statement of Heb. 2:9 that Jesus "tasted death for every one" sees his death as an act of salvation. His condemnation as a sinner does not spare man from physical death, but takes away his fear of death, because through it death's power of eternal destruction was broken (cf. vv. 14 f.). Similarly, Jn. 8:52 contains the promise: "Truly, truly, I say to you, if any one keeps my word, he will never taste death."

E. Tiedtke

ἐσθίω

ἐσθίω (esthiō), eat.

CL Along with drinking, eating is necessary for the maintenance of physical life (cf. Homer, *Od.*, 2, 305; cf. Lk. 24:41). Eating is pleasant, but indulgence is a vice (cf. Xen., *Mem.* 2, 1, 24 ff.: "You should always be concerned about the pleasure you find in eating and drinking. . . . My friends, she said, call me Eudaimonia [prosperity, good fortune, happiness, personified as a divinity], but those who hate me . . . Kakia [badness, personified]"). Those who seek their pleasure in eating and drinking (cf. *Xen.*, *Mem.* 2, 1, 9), should understand that the gods do not give what is really good and beautiful without effort and diligence (*Xen.*, *Mem.* 2, 1, 28: "If you wish the earth to bear you a rich harvest, you must do the earth service"; cf. Lk. 17:7 f.). Over and above the physical, men have sought to commune with the deity through sacramental meals and foods, and so obtain a share in the divine and immortal powers of life or even in the deity itself. The early Christian writer, Ignatius of Antioch, spoke of "breaking one bread, which is the medicine of immortality and the antidote that we should not die but live for ever in Jesus Christ" (Eph. 20). For this use of food in non-Christian religions see R. Bultmann, *The Gospel of John*, 1971, 223 f. On the purely physical level the two extremes are gluttony (cf. Homer, *Od.* 21, 69) and asceticism (cf. Apuleius, *Metamorphoses* 11, 23).

OT All food in the OT is understood as the gift of God, whether it is the produce of man or whether it grows naturally (Deut. 14:4). This places man under obligation to God and under his direction (Gen. 3:2 f.). Thus, abstinence from or consumption of certain foods (Lev. 7:23 ff.; cf. the fruit of "the tree of the knowledge of good and evil", Gen. 2:17) are tests of man's obedience to God. Disobedience (Gen. 3:6) can bring punishment (Gen. 3:17). But in general, the satisfaction of man's need of food is traced to God (Ps. 22:26); not having enough to eat or being unable to eat (Ps. 102:4, 9 f.; cf. Acts 9:9) is seen as a sign of God's anger and punishment (cf. Hos. 4:10). The righteous and the devout do not need to worry about their food (Ps. 127:2; Isa. 3:10; cf. Matt. 6:25), for their relationship with God is in order (Eccl. 9:7). After the meal God should be praised (Deut. 8:10), and not forgotten (Deut. 6:11 f.). Since eating is not something the man should do in isolation but is an expression of relationship with God, one must share one's bread with the hungry (Isa. 58:7; cf. Lk. 16:19 f.). One can eat and drink to God's glory (Exod. 24:11; cf. 1 Cor. 10:31) and make ritual sacrifices of food to him (Lev. 2:3, 6, 9 ff.). In later apocalyptic thought one can eat and drink with God and so be in fellowship with him (cf. Joseph and Aseneth 8:5; 15:4). At the consummation of time those who have been hungry will eat their fill, and manna in abundance will once again fall from above (Syr.Bar. 29:6 ff.). On vegetarian asceticism see Test.Jud. 15:4, where Judah is said not to have tasted wine or meat even in his old age (cf. Rom. 14:21). Isa. 22:13 describes the irresponsible behaviour of those who care for nothing but eating and drinking (cf. Matt. 24:38; Lk. 12:19; 1 Cor. 15:32; Livy 26, 13; Hdt. 2, 193; Diod.Sic. 2, 23; *The Gilgamesh Epic, ANET*, 90; the Egyptian proverb, *ANET*, 415; *A Song of the Harper, ANET*, 467; see E. J. Young, *A Commentary on Isaiah*, I, 1969, 103).

NT 1. The various traditions about John the Baptist (Mk. 2:18; Matt. 11:18; Mk. 1:6) recount that he fasted and lived abstemiously. Despite Matt. 11:19, it is no longer possible to determine whether the historical Jesus in fact differed from the Baptist on this point, even though the gospels recount how Jesus cultivated table fellowship with others as well as with his disciples (Mk. 14:18). This is seen as an expression of fellowship (Lk. 13:26), and in Luke's theology as an expression of genuine eye-witness testimony (Acts 10:41). He ate with the Pharisees (Lk. 7:36) and with sinners (Mk. 2:16).

The mode of life of the primitive Christian church, however, was by no means ascetic (Mk. 2:19). A feature was the joyful common meals (Acts 2:46; cf. Lk. 15:23; but cf. also 1 Cor. 11:20 ff.). Ritual prohibitions were rejected (Gal. 2:12; Mk. 7:1 ff.). The mistaken conclusion that table fellowship with Jesus guaranteed acceptance in the kingdom of God is countered in Lk. 13:26 ff.; cf. Matt. 7:21 ff.; 25:41; Lk. 6:46. The complaint that Jesus was eating with tax collectors and sinners is met in Mk. 2:16 f. by the statement that Jesus had not come to call the righteous, but sinners (see below under *pinō*, 3 (a)). Table fellowship symbolizes fellowship in general. Even Luke's account of the distant parousia retains the significance of table fellowship in the kingdom of God (Lk. 14:15; 22:30). The stories of the feedings in Mk. 6:34 ff. and 8:1 ff. are part of the → miracle stories which glorify Jesus' power and greatness (par. Matt. 14:13–21, Lk. 9:10–17, Jn. 6:1–13, and Matt. 15:32–39).

2. Eating is discussed in the context of mission in so far as the missionary is entitled to support (1 Cor. 9:14; Matt. 10:10; Lk. 10:7). The command to work belongs among the exhortations to the church; for whoever will not work should not eat (2 Thess. 3:10).

3. Eating and drinking became a particular problem in Corinth. Certain groups there sought to prove their "strength" and "freedom" by deliberate participation in sacrifices to idols (1 Cor. 10:14 ff.). Paul had to point out to them that one can have communion either with God or with idols and demons, but not with both. They are mutually exclusive (1 Cor. 10:20 ff.). There was also the further question whether it was permissible to buy and eat meat that had been sacrificed to idols and was now offered for sale in the market. Paul answered this question in the affirmative (v. 25), but with the proviso that one has to take into account the "weak" (1 Cor. 8:9 ff.; 10:32; cf. Rom. 14 f.). Even the → Lord's Supper gave rise to a crisis in Corinth. For in the absence of the apostle certain irregularities, the precise nature of which are no longer clearly recognizable, endangered the common meal. W. Schmithals suggests that there was an attempt to replace by a secular meal the sacramental meal that had been handed down to them, since a meal which had the Crucified One as its content was considered shocking and, in the light of their new-found strength, nonsense (*Gnosticism in Corinth*, 1971). This resulted in Paul reasserting the death of the Lord in the centre of the feast (1 Cor. 11:26). G. Bornkamm suggests that the Corinthians in no sense wanted to do away with the Lord's Supper, but on the contrary saw it as so highly important that the preceding meal became a matter which one could conduct according to one's own pleasure and for one's own enjoyment (*Early Christian Experience*, 1969, 146 ff.). The abuses in Corinth may also be interpreted as a failure of the church to understand itself at the Lord's Supper as the → body of Christ (cf. 1 Cor. 6:15; 10:16; 11:29; 12:27), because the meal was being profaned as in the description in 1 Cor. 11:21 (cf. 1 Cor. 5:11). In practice it was threatened with replacement by a straightforward meal to satisfy hunger. The expression *to idion deipnon*, "his own meal", denotes a meal utterly separated from Christ – not only from the crucified Christ (cf. *to idion sōma*, "his own body" [1 Cor. 6:18; 7:4]). Perhaps *idion*, own, belonging to the individual, for oneself, belonged to the Corinthians' terminology and referred to the falsely understood strength and freedom (cf. 1 Cor. 7:7). At all events it is not, as is frequently assumed, a question of a private meal of individuals which Paul contrasted with the common celebration of the Lord's Supper, in which all the members of the church, both rich and poor, ought to take part.

4. (a) Another question is raised by Jn. The true → bread (Jn. 6:32) is Jesus himself (vv. 35, 48). Coming to him, i.e. faith in him, ensures eternal life (v. 27), whereas ordinary food has no lasting effect (vv. 49 f.). Verses 51 ff. go beyond what has been said before in that they further define eating, which previously meant faith as eating Jesus' *sarx*, flesh (→ the Lord's Supper).

(b) The eating of the Book of the Revelation (Rev. 10:9; cf. Ezek. 3:1 ff.) means the real appropriation of the revelation, the content of which (cf. ch. 12 ff.) is described as "sweet" (denoting victory) and "bitter" (symbolizing struggle).

(c) In Heb. 13:10 it is not clear whether the altar refers to the Lord's Supper, Jesus' cross, an unrealistic doctrine of the Lord's Supper (cf. O. Michel, *Der Brief an die Hebräer*, KEK 13, 1966[13]), or simply means that every non-Christian sacrificial meal is to be rejected. F. F. Bruce suggests that "altar" here means "sacrifice". It is a case of metonymy, as when we say that someone keeps a "good table", meaning thereby "good food" (*The Epistle to the Hebrews*, 1964, 399 f.).

G. Braumann

| πίνω | πίνω (pinō), drink; ποτίζω (potizō), water, give to drink; ποτήριον (potērion), cup; πόμα (poma), a drink; πόσις |

(*posis*), drinking, a drink; πότος (*potos*), drinking, i.e. revelry.

CL 1. *pinō* (Homer onwards) means to drink; the compound *katapinō* (Hesiod, Hdt. on) strengthens the meaning of the simple vb.: to drink up, swallow (e.g. of the earth soaking up water, Plato, *Crit.* 111 D). The related vb. *potizō* (Hippocrates on) has the trans. meaning: to enable someone to drink; to allow to drink, to give to drink, to water (of animals). The noun *hē posis* (Homer on) denotes (a) the act of drinking (Hdt. 1, 172); (b) what is drunk, the drink (Jn. 6:55). *to poma* (Pindar) and *to poton* (Homer on, not in the NT) have the same meaning, drink, while *ho potos* (Xenophon) means drinking together, revelry (in the NT only 1 Pet. 4:3). *potērion* (Alcaeus, Sappho on), finally, is the drinking vessel, the cup or goblet, and plays an important role in the NT texts on the Lord's Supper.

2. Drinking satisfies thirst and refreshes (Nestor to Machaon after they have survived a battle: "Now drink..." [Homer, *Il.* 14, 5]). In popular opinion it was considered a pleasure (but he asked him whether he knew the good in order to show him, should he say something about these, that is food and drink, that they can sometimes be evil [Xen., *Mem.* 3, 8, 2]). It can become a passion (Ought one not first to investigate who controls gluttony and the desire for drink? [Xen., *Mem.* 3, 6, 1]). In philosophical discussions a similar view of life runs up against criticism (Will not those who have given themselves up to gluttony and the desire for drink probably enter the species of the ass and similar beasts? [Plato, *Phd.* 81, 2]). But the Greeks were not only familiar with drinking as a means of satisfying a physical thirst or providing a physical pleasure. Over and above this, it had a special place in the mystery religions especially in sacral meals (cf. *TDNT* VI 137 f.). Drinking, above all of water, supplies real, supernatural powers and life-giving knowledge (Eth.Enoch. 22:9; Od.Sol. 6:18: for all recognized one another in the Lord and were redeemed through the eternal immortal water; *Corp.Herm.* 1, 29: and they were fed from the immortal water). *kai doiē soi ho Osiris to psychron hydōr*, "and may Osiris give you the cold water" is a wish often repeated on funerary inscriptions (see E. Rohde, *Psyche*, [1907] II, 391; cf. also R. Bultmann, *The Gospel of John*, 1971, 178–87, 302–6; Arndt, 664).

OT In the vast majority of cases (215 times) the LXX translates the qal of *šātâh*, to drink, by *pinō*, while *potizō* renders the hiph. of *šāqâh*, to give to drink, water.

1. In view of frequently occurring shortages of → water, thirst (Exod. 17:1 ff. → art. *peinaō*) and drinking (1 Ki. 17:3 f.) are of particular significance in the OT world. The Lord proclaimed his sovereignty and mystery in asking Job: "Who has cleft a channel for the torrents of rain, and a way for the thunderbolt, to bring rain on a land where no man is, on the desert in which there is no man; to satisfy the waste and desolate land, and to make the ground put forth grass?" (Job 38:25 ff.). Rain transforms eastern lands into a "watered garden" (cf. Isa. 55:10), while the lack of it causes almost all vegetation to wither and results in catastrophic famines (1 Ki. 18:2 ff.). Closely connected with the shortage of water is the presence of bad and undrinkable water (Exod. 15:23).

2. The ability to satisfy thirst is attributed to God. "Thou visitest the earth and waterest it, thou greatly enrichest it; the river of God is full of water; thou providest

their grain, for so thou has prepared it" (Ps. 65:9). Drink was not understood as a → gift of creation put at man's disposal once and for all at the creation, but as a gift which is continually received anew from God and is the cause of thanksgiving (Exod. 15:22 ff.; Jdg. 15:18). Correspondingly, thirst which cannot be quenched was understood as God's anger and punishment (Isa. 5:13). When the quenching of thirst is taken for granted, God has been forgotten (Jer. 2:6). In responsibility to him Israel had to handle water carefully (Ezek. 34:18 ff.), and not only because it was felt to be a particular blessing of the cultivated land.

3. Used figuratively, drinking can stand for the way God's gifts and judgments come to men. According to whether it is the cup of his wrath (cf. Jer. 25:15 ff.; Isa. 51:17; Ps. 60:3; 75:8) or his gracious gift (Ps. 116:13; cf. also Isa. 55:1), the drink leads to destruction or to salvation. Equally figuratively, Amos 8:11 speaks of thirst for the word of God which can be quenched only if God wills.

NT The NT speaks of drinking and eating in a variety of connections. Five groups of ideas can be distinguished: 1. practical piety; 2. the attitude of John the Baptist and Jesus; 3. table fellowship; 4. the Lord's Supper; 5. the Johannine water of life.

1. (a) Like eating, drinking is referred to literally. The interesting thing about the use of the word to drink is the way the relationship between a man and his neighbour and a man and God is presented. Eating and drinking, like dress, are relativized (Matt. 6:25 ff., 31 par. Lk. 12:29); life itself is more important. God can be relied on to take care of these matters. Seeking the kingdom of God and his righteousness (Matt. 6:33; cf. Lk. 12:31) should hold a man's interest, and then these questions of daily living, to which eating and drinking belong, settle themselves. There is no eschatological element here, and the argument remains on the level of popular wisdom (cf. SB I 436). One can rest all one's cares on God.

(b) Observance of the distinction between clean and unclean foods belongs to the old → covenant (Acts 10:14; → Animal; → Bird). Peter's vision in which this distinction was abolished symbolizes the abolition of Jewish exclusiveness and the inclusion of the Gentiles in the → people of God.

(c) The materialistic attitude is rejected which looks no further than this life (1 Cor. 15:32; cf. Lk. 12:19; → esthiō OT). Those who are given to eating and drinking and fail to recognize this situation and responsibility towards God (Matt. 24:48 ff.; Lk. 12:19), will nevertheless be called to account (Matt. 24:38 ff.; cf. Lk. 17:27 ff.).

2. (a) This underlines the fact that eating and drinking are not to be seen as ends in themselves, or as pleasures for the self-indulgent, but in the light of responsibility to God and men. Paul saw the problem in terms of the church. Although the Christian has complete freedom to eat and drink what he likes (1 Cor. 9:4), he is bound to take account of his neighbour (Rom. 14:21). The question is seen christologically in Matt.: in the poor to whom a drink is given (potizō) Christ himself is encountered (Matt. 25:37, 42). Lk. 10:7 gives a practical directive for mission.

(b) The problem is understood eschatologically by John the Baptist. The seriousness of imminent events cast its shadow over the present age (Mk. 1:5 f.). Therefore

John neither ate nor drank (Matt. 11:18 f. par. Lk. 7:34; on John see C. H. H. Scobie, *John the Baptist*, 1964).

(c) The behaviour of the "Son of man" is depicted as a direct contrast to this for he both ate and drank (ibid.). A number of stories refer to the eating and drinking of Jesus and the disciples. Jesus also ate and drank with sinners (Mk. 2:16; cf. Lk. 5:30, 33). A clear eschatological motivation is lacking ([Ed.] unless we see in Jesus' actions his reinterpretation of the messianic banquet). Perhaps Jesus, in contrast to John the Baptist, waited for the imminent events with joy rather than with pessimistic seriousness and for this reason put himself on the side of the sinners.

3. (a) Drinking takes on a deeper significance when, along with eating, it expresses the unity which exists among those who share in a meal. Thus there will be those who will call upon the fact that they have eaten and drunk with Jesus in order to claim a place at his side in eternity (Lk. 13:26). But Jesus will reply that he never knew them (v. 27; cf. Matt. 7:21 ff.; 25:41; Lk. 6:46). For the relationship was merely formal. On the other hand, the disciples are promised that they will eat and drink at Jesus' table (Lk. 22:30). This deeper meaning also lies behind Lk. 5:30: by eating with sinners the disciples, like Jesus, stand on their side. Lk. brings an important qualification by inserting the words "to repentance" (Lk. 5:32; cf. Mk. 2:16 f.). Jesus did not come "to call the righteous, but sinners to repentance."

(b) The request of the sons of Zebedee to sit at Jesus' side in eternity has an apocalyptic-eschatological character (Matt. 20:20; Mk. 10:35–37; cf. Lk. 22:24 ff.), but it is striking that Jesus' answer is in no way apocalyptic or eschatological. It points rather to his death: the cup is understood as the cup of suffering, the → baptism as the baptism of death (Matt. 20:22; Mk. 10:38). The "cup" of suffering is mentioned again in Matt. 26:39; Mk. 14:36; Lk. 22:42; cf. Jn. 18:11. Jesus requested his Father to let the cup of suffering (*potērion*) pass from him. In the OT the cup is a symbol of judgment and retribution (cf. Ps. 75:9; Isa. 51:17 f.; Jer. 25:15 ff.).

4. (a) Drinking is referred to figuratively in 1 Cor. 10:4 (cf. Exod. 17:6; Num. 20:11). Some think that Paul may be alluding in v. 3 f. to the → Lord's Supper as a saving event which is already anticipated pneumatically in the time of Moses (cf. the twice used word *pneumatikos* in v. 4 [lit. "spiritual", "pertaining to the spirit"; → Spirit]). Thus the allusion would be not figurative or parabolic but real and actual. This means therefore that there is a real identity between the ancient and the new saving events and not merely an analogy (E. Käsemann, "The Pauline View of the Lord's Supper", in *Essays on New Testament Themes*, 1964, 113 f.; but cf. R. Bultmann, *Theology of the New Testament*, I, 1952, 36). However it is not certain how this drinking from Christ is to be understood. W. Heitmüller saw in it an affinity with the mystery cults: "The food and drink are Jesus Christ" (*RGG*[1] I, 40). H. von Soden understood it as the drink which comes from Christ as its source, that is, the drink that Christ gives: "Christ gives the drink, not Christ is the drink" (*Sakrament und Ethik bei Paulus*, 1931, 264).

([Ed.] This division of opinion is reflected among English-speaking scholars. E. E. Ellis writes: "The Old Covenant like the New, had a food and drink in which Christ was [typically] present" [*Paul's Use of the Old Testament*, 1957, 131]. He takes *pneumatikos* in v. 4 to mean "in its typical or prophetic significance", and links this up with the use of *typoi*, v. 6 ["examples", "types"] and *typikōs*, v. 11 ["typologically", "as an example or warning", Arndt, 837; → Image, art. *typos*]. But A. T. and R. P. C. Hanson both reject the idea of typology in the sense of a similar situation prefiguring Christ in some kind of allegorical way, and say that the rock really was Christ present with his people [A. T. Hanson, *Jesus Christ in the Old Testament*, 1965, 21; R. P. C. Hanson, *Allegory and Event*, 1959, 79 f.].)

(b) The same uncertainty occurs with respect to 1 Cor. 10:16 f. V. 16 is no doubt a tradition taken over by Paul (Käsemann, op. cit., 109 ff.), which explained the cup (*potērion*) as a sharing (not fellowship) in the body and blood of Christ. V. 17 is no doubt an expansion of the tradition by Paul. While Käsemann claims that, "In Christ one is at the same time the body of Christ" (*Leib und Leib Christi*, 1933, 168), H. Schlier maintains that "Paul is only saying that this body of the church belongs to Christ, is his possession" (*Christus und die Kirche im Epheserbrief*, 1930, 41).

(c) The same question arises in the words which interpret the Lord's Supper tradition in Paul's account (1 Cor. 11:23–26). Is the eating and drinking of bread and wine identical with sharing in the exalted Christ or only a pointer to the earthly Christ, in so far as his death is the ground of our salvation?

The synoptics connect the Lord's Supper with the Passover meal (Matt. 26:17; Mk. 14:12; Lk. 22:7, 15). This raises the critical question of the original meaning of the Lord's Supper. Is it to be understood against a Hellenistic background and therefore not as a means of realizing the presence of Jesus, instituted by Jesus himself? Or is it to be understood as an interpretation of the death of Jesus in its significance for the salvation of the church? → Lord's Supper; → Feast, art. *pascha*.

5. Jn. 4:10 ff. raises the question of the → water of life (v. 11). Ordinary water quenches the thirst only for the time being (v. 13). (The kingdom of God and eating and drinking are two different things [Rom. 14:17; cf. Col. 2:16].) But the water which Jesus gives bestows eternal life (v. 14). One must therefore come to Jesus (Jn. 7:37; cf. Isa. 55:1), i.e. have faith in him (on the imperative form cf. R. Bultmann, *Theology of the New Testament*, II, 1955, 23). While the gift here is Jesus himself (cf. also Jn. 6:51 ff.), in Jn. 7:36 it is related to the Spirit as the Spirit of Christ.   *G. Braumann*

→ Bread, → Fast, → Feast, → Lord's Supper, → Wine

(a). J. Behm, *brōma*, *TDNT* I 642–45; *geuomai*, *TDNT* I 675 ff.; *esthiō*, *TDNT* II 689–95; J. Behm and G. Bertram, *dipsaō* etc., *TDNT* II 226–29; A. C. Bouquet, *Everyday Life in New Testament Times*, 1954, 69–79; R. Bultmann, *The Gospel of John*, 1971; L. Goppelt, *peinaō*, *TDNT* VI 12–22; and *pinō*, *TDNT* VI 135–60; D. R. Hall, "St. Paul and Famine Relief: A Study in Galatians 2:10", *ExpT* 82, 1970–71, 309 ff.; E. W. Heaton, *Every Day Life in Old Testament Times*, 1956, 81–115; N. Hillyer, " 'Spiritual Milk . . . Spiritual House' ", *TB* 20, 1969, 126; J. C. Hurd, Jr., *The Origin of 1 Corinthians*, 1965; J. Jeremias, *The Eucharistic Words of Jesus*, 1966²; J. P. Lewis, "Food", *ZPEB* II 581–87; J. F. Ross, "Food", *IDB* II 304–8; and "Drink", *IDB* I 871 f.; H. Schlier, *gala*, *TDNT* I 645 ff.; W. Schmithals, *Gnosticism in Corinth*, 1971.

(b). E. Bammel and F. Schmidt-Clausing, "Fasten", *RGG*³ II 881 ff.; O. Böcher, "Ass Johannes der Täufer kein Brot (Luk. vii. 33)?", *NTS* 18, 1971–72, 90 ff.; W. Nauck, "Speisevorschriften", *EKL* III 1080 f.; E. Siglmayr and R. Rendtorff, "Speiseverbote", *RGG*³ VI 230 ff.; G. Strecker, *Der Weg der Gerechtigkeit*, 1962.

I

I Am

| $\dot{\epsilon}\gamma\grave{\omega}$ $\epsilon\dot{\iota}\mu\acute{\iota}$ | $\dot{\epsilon}\gamma\grave{\omega}$ $\epsilon\dot{\iota}\mu\acute{\iota}$ (egō eimi), I am; $\dot{\epsilon}\gamma\acute{\omega}$ (egō), I. |

CL The *ego eimi* formula does not occur in classical literature, and there are scarcely any relevant parallels in later periods. But the wider context, particularly of the Near East, demands special attention, not because of any direct influence on the NT, but because of similarities of content and form. An emphatic "I"-style can be demonstrated in ancient India: I was Manu and I Sūrya, I am Kaksivat . . . I compel Kutsa, the son of Arjuna; I am Kavi Usanas, look at me! (cf. E. Schweizer, *Egō eimi*, 1965², 16). The Mandaean analogies are particularly interesting: I am the life, that was from of old . . . I am the glory, I am the light (Ginza 207, 34 ff.); I am the first glory (Ginza 592, 26; cf. Schweizer, op. cit., 37, and C. K. Barrett, *The Gospel According to St. John*, 1955, 242). However, the history of the traditions in the Mandaean texts is disputed and Christian influence cannot be excluded. Probably the "I-am" sayings belong to the older strata and not to later interpretation. In terms of content, some scholars hold that the "I-am" statements are not intended to be mere metaphors: vine, light and water are not images or figures of speech, but actual substances understood mythologically (cf. Schweizer, op. cit., 12 ff.).

OT 1. In the OT the Heb. words for "I", *'anî* and *'ānōkî*, are very common. But statistics are of little consequence in the LXX, since it translates the Heb. equivalents mechanically by *ego*, "regardless of whether it is emphatic or un-emphatic, necessary or superfluous in Greek, or used of God or men" (Schweizer, op. cit., 23). As a result, *ego eimi* in the LXX is not an exclusively religious formula.

2. Nevertheless, certain "I"-formulae are noteworthy. The so-called self-presentations are important in this connection, in which Yahweh makes himself known as the promised saving God of the fathers (Gen. 15:7; 17:1; 28:13; 35:11; cf. also the opening of the Decalogue, "I am the Lord your God, who . . ." [Exod. 20:2]; and *ego eimi ho ōn* "I am the existing One" [Exod. 3:14 LXX]). This self-presentation was necessary in the polytheistic world of the ancient orient; it sought to secure the trust of the recipient of the revelation in this one God alone. In terms of content, God is the one who acts in history. In the passages in Ezek. where God is speaking the Heb. phrase recurs: *'anî* YHWH ("I [am] Yahweh"; cf. Ezek. 33:29; 36:36; 37:6, 13; 39:28). In Deut. God's action in history is demonstrated in the dialectic of judgment and salvation, and on this basis obedience and honour are

278

due to God as the only God (Deut. 32:39 ff.). According to D. Daube, the expression *'ᵃnî hû'* ("I [am] he"; cf. Deut. 32:39; Isa. 40:10, 13 etc.) "can hardly signify 'I am this or that', referring back to some previous attribute. In the Old Testament it appears in the sense of 'I am the Absolute' or the like, and this application certainly prepared the ground for the *egō eimi* of the Messianic Presence" (*The New Testament and Rabbinic Judaism*, 1956, 327). The most universal and clearest expression of this power of Yahweh over nature and history is to be found in the passages in Isa., where Yahweh declares: "I am the Lord, who made all things, who stretched out the heavens alone, who spread out the earth" (44:24); "I am the first and the last; besides me there is no god" (44:6; cf. 43:11; 45:5, 22). A similar "I"-style, when God is speaking, occurs in Jewish and Christian apocalyptic literature (Eth.Enoch 108:12; Apoc.Abr. 9:3; Jub. 24:22).

3. *egō*, uttered by men, occurs in the first-person speeches of the prophets (e.g. in the Servant Songs, Isa. 48:12; 49:1 ff.; cf. 50:4 ff.; 61:1) and in the wisdom literature (Prov. 8). Later the apocalyptic writers were fond of using the "I"-style, and frequently did so to convey secret revelations (cf. Dan. 7:15, 28; Sl.Enoch 39:2). The Damascus Rule from Qumran also speaks in the style of wisdom: "Hear now, my sons, and I will uncover your eyes that you may see and understand the works of God" (CD 2:14).

NT In the NT *egō* and *egō eimi* differ in significance in Jn., the synoptic tradition, Rev. and Paul.

1. *The "I am" Sayings in Jn. egō eimi* occurs as a fixed formula in the pronouncements in Jn. These "I am" sayings are to be distinguished from those in which Jesus uses the emphatic "I" (cf. Jn. 7:29; 9:39).

(a) The Johannine usage is typified by its formal structure: first there is the "I am" which is followed by a visual picture which can be further qualified by an adj. or a participle. The sentence structure raises the question whether the "I" is the subject or the predicate. If the "I" is the subject, we have to ask what it is that the predicate answers. R. Bultmann distinguishes the following types of "I am" pronouncements (*The Gospel of John*, 1971, 225 f.). (i) The *presentation formula* replies to the question, "Who are you?" (cf. Gen. 17:1; Aristophanes, *Plutus* 78: "I am in fact Plutus"). (ii) The *qualificatory formula* answers the question, "What are you?" (cf. Epictetus, *Dissertationes* 4, 8, 15 f.; Ezek. 28:2, 9). The reply to such a question is "I am such and such . . ." or "I am the sort of man who. . . ." (iii) In the *identification formula* the speaker identifies himself with another person, power or object. Thus the Egyptian god Rê identifies himself with Chepre: "I am he who arose as Chepre" (*Altorientalische Texte*, 1; cf. Jn. 11:25; 14:6). (iv) The *recognition formula* differs from the others in that the "I" is the predicate. It answers the question, "Who is so and so?" with the answer "I am". Bultmann submits that "In the *egō-eimi* statements Jn. 6:35, 41, 48, 51; 8:12; 10:7, 9, 11, 14; 15:1, 5 we clearly have recognition formulae, even if in the source they were perhaps intended as presentation or qualificatory formulae" (op. cit., 226).

(b) A further question is the meaning of the visual picture in the pronouncement. One view is that we are dealing with similes, parables, metaphors or allegories, when Jesus says, "I am the bread of life"; "I am the light of the world"; "I am the good shepherd" etc. Thus Jesus is compared with a shepherd and his followers with sheep. Another view is that Jesus is in reality the embodiment of the shepherd and his followers the sheep (cf. the Johannine *alēthinos*, true, genuine, real, in Jn. 1:9; 4:23, 37; 6:32; 7:28; 8:16; 15:1; 17:3; 19:35; 1 Jn. 2:8; 5:20). Some exegetes favour this interpretation on the grounds of the religious background material (see above CL), context and detailed exegesis, although parabolic and allegorical elements cannot be excluded. Thus, Jesus would not only be compared with a shepherd; he *is* the shepherd in the fullest sense of the term. He is not only compared with a vine. The vine cannot show who and what Jesus is; rather the true vine is Jesus and no other (Jn. 15:1). Jesus is not only like a door. He is the door; this reality, this divine truth, applies to no one but him.

(c) This interpretation suggests a polemical situation which prompts the question: Against whom are these pronouncements directed? Some scholars think that the Johannine pronouncements arose out of a situation in which various people other than Jesus were designated as the vine, the shepherd etc. These have been identified with gnostic redeemer figures (cf. R. Bultmann, op. cit., 367–70 on the shepherd, and 530 ff. on the vine which he identifies with the mythical tree of life). Thus the Johannine pronouncements would repudiate their claims and declare that the → bread of life, the → light of the world, the door → (Gate), the → shepherd etc. are Jesus alone. ([Ed.] However, the idea of a gnostic background for these pronouncements has been rejected by numerous authorities on Johannine thought. Thus, B. Lindars maintains that the categories of thought in Jn. 15 are moral and not gnostic [*The Gospel of John*, 1972, 487]. R. E. Brown holds that the OT and Judaism supplied the raw material for the teaching about the door, the shepherd and the vine [*The Gospel According to John*, I, 1966, 397 f.; II, 1971, 669–72]. See also L. Morris, *The Gospel According to John*, 1972, ad loc.; and R. Schnackenburg, *The Gospel According to St. John*, I, 1968, 543–57, Excursus VI on "The Gnostic Myth of the Redeemer and the Johannine Christology".)

(d) The sources and traditions behind the "I am" sayings are disputed, and can be further determined only by closer exegesis of the individual passages. For further discussion see C. H. Dodd, *The Interpretation of the Fourth Gospel*, 1953; and *Historical Tradition in the Fourth Gospel*, 1963; the works listed above and the numerous journal articles that they refer to.

(e) Jesus is the → bread of life, in that he is what he gives (Jn. 6:35, 41, 48, 51). This bread of life, i.e. Jesus himself, provides eternal → life (6:47). It comes from → heaven (v. 51), and access to it is through → faith (v. 47). Jesus is the → light of the world (→ Earth, art. *kosmos*), and in following him one has the light of life (the light is defined by means of the gen., Jn. 8:12). The bread of life is identical with the light of life. In contrast to all others Jesus is the door (→ Gate, art. *thyra*); for Jesus gives access to salvation (10:7, 9). The saying about the "good" → shepherd has the same meaning: this real, unique shepherd is Jesus who gives his life for the sheep (→ Lamb, Sheep) and saves them (10:11). He knows his sheep and they know him. This is not in the weakened sense of being aware of, or having a theoretical knowledge of, but in the sense of being intimately related to (vv. 8, 14). Anyone who has questions about the → resurrection should turn to Jesus. For there is no resurrection outside his person; it is personified in him (11:25). Anyone who asks where, what or who is the way, the truth and the life will not only find an explanation in Jesus' teaching; Jesus himself is that which these terms refer to

(14:6). Jesus is the true, heavenly vine; between him and ourselves there exists a real union (15:1, 5).

(f) In the judgment of the present writer, the "I am" sayings are not to be regarded as parabolic pictures designed to illustrate the significance of Jesus, so that one could grasp the intended reality on the basis of the picture. It is rather the reverse. It is Jesus himself who determines the meaning of the picture.

G. Braumann

2. *egō and* egō eimi *in the Remaining NT Writings.* (a) *The Synoptic Gospels.* (i) The account of Jesus' walking on the water (Matt. 14:22–23; Mk. 6:45–52; cf. Jn. 6:15–21) suggests a theophany containing OT and Hel. motifs. The phrase "and he meant to pass by them" (Mk. 6:48c) is reminiscent of Yahweh's passing before Moses on Sinai (Exod. 33:18 ff.) or before Elijah on Horeb (1 Ki. 19:11 ff.). It expresses the "strange sublimity" of God's appearance (E. Lohmeyer, *Das Evangelium des Markus, KEK* 1/2, 1967[17], ad loc.). Meanwhile the disciples in the boat are in a state of panic-stricken fear and think that the suddenly appearing figure is a ghost (Mk. 6:49), a frequent motif in Hel. stories of the sea. Mk. impressively contrasts the disciples' opinion, "It is a ghost", with Jesus' revealing reply, "Take heart, it is I [*egō eimi*]; have no fear" (Mk. 6:50). Only this self-revelation of Jesus convinces them of the reality of the appearance; the unrecognized figure makes himself known as the disciples' trusted helper and master (cf. Lohmeyer, ad loc.).

(ii) Each of the six antitheses of the Sermon on the Mount (Matt. 5:21–48) distinguishes Jesus' message from what was said to the men of old by the provocative formula *egō de legō hymin*, "but I say to you." This formula, which has no parallel in Rab. teaching (G. Eichholz, *Auslegung der Bergpredigt, BSt* 46, 1965, 70), is not intended to replace OT law by a new law. Rather the "I say to you" marks Jesus as the lawful and true expositor of the Torah. In contrast to the scribes with their abbreviations and casuistic distortions, Jesus goes back to the original meaning of the Torah, to the will of God. By so doing he brings the Torah's demands to bear once more (cf. G. Strecker, *Der Weg der Gerechtigkeit*, 1962, 146). The *egō de legō hymin* is directed in the name of God against contemporary Judaism's misrepresentations of his will. To this extent Matt. understands the antitheses not as a contradiction but as the fulfilment of the original intention of the Torah (Matt. 5:17).

(iii) Similarly, the emphatic *egō* of Jesus in his appeal to the weary and burdened to come to him (Matt. 11:28–30) is directed against the unlawful claims of the rabbinic teachers of the law who burdened men with their innumerable prohibitions. Jesus calls those who labour under the burden of the Pharisaic law to come under his "yoke" which offers rest and refreshment. "Because Christ's law, in contrast to the rules of the Pharisees, leads to rest, it can be called *chrēstos*, good, useful, although according to its content it is harder; and in so far as Jesus' load already gives *anapausis*, rest, it can be called light, although its demands are weightier" (G. Strecker, op. cit., 174; cf. M. Maher, " 'Take my yoke upon you' (Matt. xi. 29)", *NTS* 22, 1975–76, 97–103; → Burden).

(iv) In the synoptic apocalypse Jesus warns against people who will arise in his name and lead many astray by the use of the words *egō eimi* (Matt. 24:5; Mk. 13:6; Lk. 21:8), the "technical formula for the self-revelation of Christ" (*TDNT*

II 353). Here the early Christian church separated itself from those who unlawfully and for dishonest ends claimed the authority of Jesus. On the other hand, at his examination before the Sanhedrin, Jesus answered the High Priest's question, "Are you the Christ?" with the words *egō eimi* (Mk. 14:61 f.). In the early Christian church there was clearly discussion about the identity of the messiah (cf. Jn. 1:20) and Jesus. Jesus answered the question about his messiahship in the affirmative and, according to Mk.'s account (14:64), was promptly condemned to death for blasphemy by the Jewish authorities. (See further D. R. Catchpole, *The Trial of Jesus: A Study in the Gospels and Jewish Historiography from 1770 to the Present Day*, 1971.)

(v) Finally, the risen Christ led his disciples to recognize his identity with the crucified Jesus through the use of the *egō eimi* formula (Lk. 24:39). Seeing his hands and feet and touching him was proof of the reality of the resurrection which overcame the disciples' doubts (vv. 38, 41). In the closing scene of Matt. (28:16–20) the risen Christ announced the power he had received from God ("All authority in heaven and on earth has been given to me", v. 18) and, by means of the "I-am" formula, promised his presence with the disciples until the end of the age.

(b) *Revelation.* In Rev. the *egō* of Christ's sayings and the *egō* of the pronouncements of God occur side by side. The reason for this lies in the almost identical positions that the writer attributes to Christ and God vis-à-vis the world, so that sometimes the same *egō*-sayings can appear on the lips of both Christ and God. In Rev. 1:8 God is the subject of the sentence, "I am the Alpha and the Omega, who is and who was and who is to come", while in Rev. 1:17 f. the Son of man speaks, "I am the first and the last, and the living one." Both verses are derived from Isa. 44:6. The first and the last corresponds to the Alpha and the Omega. The most complete identification of Christ and God is expressed at the end of Rev. The subject of the sentence in Rev. 21:6, "I am the Alpha and the Omega, the beginning and the end," is God; in Rev. 22:13 it is Jesus. (In the latter case the words "the first and the last" are inserted after Alpha and Omega, the first and last letters of the Gk. alphabet.)

(c) *Paul.* Alongside of Paul's autobiographical use of "I" (e.g. Gal. 1:13 ff.) is the *egō* of Rom. 7:7 ff. which raises special problems. Three interpretations may be mentioned. (i) Some scholars see a tension here with the description that Paul gives in Phil. 3:6 of his life under the law as a Jew which he describes as "blameless". The description in Rom. 7 is marked by conflict, strife and failure to keep the law. Hence, they claim that the *egō* here is not autobiographical ([Ed.] although it may be pointed out that the description of Paul's former life as "blameless" in Phil. 3:6 implies no more than what passed for "blameless" among the Jews). (ii) The best known exegesis of Rom. 7 is that of the Reformers which applied the *egō* generally to the life of every Christian and the dialectic of *simul justus et peccator* (i.e. that believer was justified and a sinner at one and the same time). But some think that this overlooks the development of thought from ch. 7 to ch. 8, where Paul makes unambiguously positive statements about the Christian's present life in the Spirit (cf. the *nyni* or *nyn* in Rom. 3:21 and 8:1). ([Ed.] Nevertheless, it may be noted that the conflict described in Rom. 7:21–25 between "the law of God" which the *egō* delights in and serves with the mind and "the law of sin" which the *egō* serves with the flesh is presented in the present tense. Moreover, it may be asked whether the unbeliever does actually delight in "the law of God" in this way.) (iii) An alternative view is represented by a number of modern exegetes, including G. Bornkamm, H. Conzelmann and W. G. Kümmel. This sees Paul in Rom. 7 as looking back from the Christian's standpoint over the human existence under the law which Christ went through and overcame. In ch. 8 he describes what is now intended for the Christian through the Spirit. It is only to Paul as a believer that the hopeless inner strife and wretchedness of man under the law becomes apparent. Thus, the *egō* of Rom. 7 embraces Paul's own judgment, the standpoint of Judaism under the law and the conflict of the man who wishes to assert himself. ([Ed.] For further discussion see M. Black, *Romans*, 1973, 100–108; G. Bornkamm, "Sin, Law and Death (Romans 7)", *Early Christian Experience*, 1969, 87–104; H. Braun, *Röm. 7, 7–25 und das Selbstverständnis der Qumran Frommen*, 1963; R. Bultmann, "Romans 7 and the Anthropology of Paul", *Existence and Faith*, 1960, 147–57; C. E. B. Cranfield, *Romans*, I, *ICC*, 1975, 340–370; E. Fuchs, "Existentiale Interpretation von Röm. 7, 7–12 und 21–23", *Glaube und Erfahrung*, 1965; H. Jonas, "Philosophical Meditation on the Seventh Chapter of Paul's Epistle to the Romans", in J. M. Robinson, ed., *The Future of Our Religious Past: Essays in Honour of Rudolf Bultmann*, 1971, 333–50; E. Käsemann, *An die Römer*, HNT 8a, 1974³, 190–204; K. Kertelge, *ZNW* 62, 1971, 105–14; W. G. Kümmel, "Röm. vii und die Bekehrung des Paulus", *Untersuchungen zum Neuen Testament* 17, 1929; O. Kuss, *Der Römerbrief*, I, 1963, 462–85; C. L. Mitton, "Romans vii reconsidered" *ExpT* 65, 1953–54, 78 ff., 99 ff., 132 ff.; J. I. Packer, "The Wretched Man in Romans VII", *StudEv* II, 1964, 621–27; O. J. F. Seitz, "Two Spirits in Man: An Essay in Biblical Exegesis", *NTS* 6, 1959–60, 82–95; E. W. Smith, "The Form and Background of Romans 7, 24–25a", *NovT* 13, 1971, 127–35).

H.-G. Link

(a). W. J. P. Boyd, " 'I am Alpha and Omega' (Rev. 1:8; 21:6; 22:13)", *StudEv*, II, 1961, 326 ff.; R. E. Brown "EGŌ EIMI – 'I AM' ", *The Gospel According to John*, I 1966, 532–38; R. Bultmann, *The Gospel of John*, 1971, 225 ff.; H. Conzelmann, *An Outline Theology of the New Testament*, 1969, 349–52; D. Daube, "The 'I am' of the Messianic Presence", *The New Testament and Rabbinic Judaism*, 1956, 325–29; W. D. Davies, "Matthew 5:17, 18", *Christian Origins and Judaism*, 1962, 31–66; P. B. Horner, *The "I am" of the Fourth Gospel*, 1971; W. Manson, "The EGŌ EIMI of the Messianic Presence in the New Testament", in *Jesus and the Christian*, 1967, 174–83; D. M. Stanley, " 'I Am the Genuine Vine' (John 15:1)", *The Bible Today*, 8, 1963; 484–91; E. Stauffer, *egō*, *TDNT* II 343–62.

(b). H. Becker, *Die Reden des Johannesevangeliums und der Stil der gnostischen Offenbarungsrede*, *FRLANT* 68, 1956; R. Borig, *Der wahre Weinstock*, 1967; C. Colpe, "Traditionsüberschreitende Argumentation zu Aussagen Jesu über sich selbst", in G. Jeremias *et al.*, eds., *Tradition und Glaube, Festgabe K. G. Kuhn*, 1971; G. Eichholz, *Auslegung der Bergpredigt*, BSt Neue Folge 46, 1965, 70 f.; A. Feuillet, "Les *egō eimi* christologiques du Quatrième Évangile", *Recherches de Science Religieuse*, 54, 1966, 5 ff., 213 ff.; A. Hajduk, "*Egō eimi* bei Jesus und seine Messianität", *Communio Viatorum* 6, 1963, 55 ff.; A. Jaubert, "L'Image de la Vigne (Jean 15)", in *Oikonomia* (O. Cullmann Festschrift), 1967, 93–99; E. Norden, *Agnostos Theos*, 1926²; K. Rudolf, *Die Mandäer*, 1960; S. Schulz, *Komposition und Herkunft der Johanneischen Reden*, 1960, 70–131; B. Schwank, " 'Ich bin der Wahre Weinstock' (Joh. 15, 1–17)", *Sein und Sendung* 28, 1963, 244–58; E. Schweizer, *Egō eimi. Die religionsgeschichtliche Herkunft und theologische Bedeutung der johanneischen Bildreden, zugleich ein Beitrag zur Quellenfrage des vierten Evangeliums*, *FRLANT* 56, (1939) 1965²; G. Strecker, *Der Weg der Gerechtigkeit*, 1962; W. Zimmerli, "Ich bin Jahwe", *Gottes Offenbarung*, ThB 19, 1963; H. Zimmermann, "Das absolute *egō eimi* als die neutestamentliche Offenbarungsformel", *BZ* 4, 1960, 54–69, 266–76.

Image, Idol, Imprint, Example

The word image suggests a visual or mental representation. It may refer to the object that is seen or to the mental representation of it that the observer forms in his mind. Since the concept is a complex one, it is not surprising that various words are used in Gk. and that these tend to merge and overlap. The terms used are: *charaktēr*, image, mark or stamp, formed by impressing a pattern; *idea*, appearance, in Plato's philosophy the archetypal forms which underly the entities in our material world, in logic the class or kind (the term is important in Gk. philosophy, but is not found in the NT); *eikōn*, replica, likeness, image; *eidōlon*, image, outline, a form which generally lacks substance and does not possess the same degree of reality as *eikōn;* in biblical Gk. it signifies an image of a god, an idol. Other related concepts are *typos*, visible impression, copy, image, form, figure, type (→ Type, Pattern); and *homoiōma*, likeness, image, appearance (→ Like). *apaugasma*, effulgence, radiance, reflection; *hypodeigma*, proof, example, model; and *paradeigmatizō*, expose to public disgrace, make an example of, are also discussed in this article.

εἴδωλον

εἴδωλον (*eidōlon*), image, idol; εἰδωλόθυτον (*eidōlothyton*), meat offered to idols; εἰδωλεῖον (*eidōleion*), temple of an idol; κατείδωλος (*kateidōlos*), full of idols; εἰδωλολάτρης (*eidōlolatrēs*), idolater, worshipper of idols; εἰδωλολατρία (*eidōlolatria*), idolatry, worship of idols.

CL *eidōlon* is used by Homer for the phantoms and shades in Hades (*Il.* 5, 451; *Od.* 4, 796). It can also mean any unsubstantial form, an image reflected in a mirror or water, an image or idea in the mind. Apart from Polybius 31, 3, 13–15, it was not generally used for the images of the gods in cl. Gk. (→ *eikōn*).

OT Although *eidōlon* is used to render some 15 Heb. terms in the LXX, it refers without exception to the images of the heathen gods and the deities represented by them. They include *gillûlîm*, idols (always in a disdainful sense, e.g. Lev. 26:30; Deut. 29:16 [17]; Ezek. 6:4 ff., 13; 36:17 f., 25; 37:23); and *terāpîm*, idols (again used disdainfully, perhaps connected with the idea of perishing, Gen. 31:19; 34 f; → Israel, art. *Iakōb*, OT). To express the image of God in man, even where the Heb. word is also applied to an idol, the term → *eikōn* is used. This Hel.-Jewish usage reflects Jewish contempt for heathen polytheism. *eidōleion* and *eidōlion* are also Hel.-Jewish terms and are contemptuous expressions for the temples of heathen idols (Ezr. 1:7 [LXX 1 Esd. 2:10]; Bel 9; 1 Macc. 10:83; 1 Cor. 8:10). Similarly *eidōlothyton* means meat offered to idols (4 Macc. 5:2; cf. 1 Cor. 8:1, 4, 7, 10; 10:19, 28 t.r.; Acts 15:29; 21:25; Rev. 2:14, 20; Did. 6:3).

The prohibition against serving other gods and the prohibition against making *eidōla* are linked already in the Decalogue (Exod. 20:3 f.; Deut. 5:7 f.). The depreciation of images based on this prohibition leaves its traces everywhere in the OT. This does not imply, however, that there is no reality behind the heathen idolatrous worship. Idols are *bdelygmata*, abominations, behind which stand *daimonia* (→ Demon), demonic powers, with which one cannot come into contact without moving God to wrath (Deut. 32:16 f., 21). In 2 Chr. 24:18 the worship of idols is equated with that of the Asherim, i.e. of the powers behind the idols.

Israel often succumbed to the temptation to open the doors to these powers, especially when the rise of the Assyrian and Babylonian empires gave the impression that their gods were more powerful than the God of Israel (Isa. 36:19 f.). Jer. 44:15–19 and Ezek. 8 give graphic and terrible pictures of how widely heathen idol worship had spread in Israel in their day. The prophetic message to Israel was that the misfortune which had overtaken the people was God's punishment for falling away from Yahweh and compromising with the heathen cultus (Isa. 10:11; Jer. 9:13–16; Ezek. 8:17 f.). The call to repentance combined a demand for right behaviour towards one's neighbour (Amos 5:14 f.; Hos. 4:1 ff.; Isa. 1:15 ff.) with the demand to turn away from false gods (Hos. 14:8[9]). The prophets never grew tired of stressing to the people how impotent and vain (*mataios*, → Empty) were the idols (Ezek. 8:10; 1 Chr. 16:26; 2 Chr. 25:15). For they are merely the creation of men's hands which cannot hear or see, or do anything (Hos. 8:4 f.; 13:2; Jer. 14:22; Hab. 2:18 f.; cf. Ezek. 8:10; 2 Chr. 11:15). The sharpest polemic against the cult images in an exilic setting occurs in Isa. 40:18 ff.; 44:9–20; 46:1 f. The making of the idols is described in language that renders them ludicrous; and the power of Yahweh who moulds history is contrasted with them (Isa. 45–48). He will destroy the false gods (Jer. 10:10–15; Ezek. 6:4 ff., 13; Mic. 1:7), and men will throw away their idols on the day of God's judgment (Isa. 2:18 ff.).

This thought also appears in the polemic of late Judaism against idols and polytheism (e.g. Wis. 14:15; the letter of Jeremiah in Bar. 6; and the story of Bel, Ad. Dan. 14). Even though the gods of the heathen are looked on as nonentities, contact with them is regarded as defiling (Ezek. 37:23). Houses defiled by the presence of idols had to be ritually cleansed (1 Macc. 13:47). The thought that demonic powers stand behind heathen idolatry lived in Rab. Judaism (SB III 48–60). Hence the pious Jew was strictly forbidden to eat meat offered to idols (SB III 54, 377 f.).

In the Qumran texts "idol" is used metaphorically for the sins which, as "idols of the heart" (cf. Ezek. 14:4), hinder men in their service of God (Heb. *gillûlîm* in 1QS 2:11, 17; 4:5; 1QM 4:15, 19; 1Q22 1:7; 4Qflor 1:17; CD 20:9; cf. A. R. C. Leaney, *The Rule of Qumran and its Meaning*, 1966, 134 f.).

NT The NT continues the usage of the LXX. A sign of this is that *hierothyton*, meat offered in sacrifice, found in secular Gk., occurs only in 1 Cor. 10:28 (on the lips of one who may be a pagan), while elsewhere we have *eidōlothyton* (Acts 15:29; 21:25; 1 Cor. 8:1, 4, 7, 10; 10:19; Rev. 2:14, 20). But there are also new word formations not found in the LXX. In Acts 17:16 it is said that Athens was *kateidōlos*. On the analogy of *katadendros*, rich in trees, it is best to translate it "full of idols." Linked with *latreia*, service or worship of God (cf. Rom. 9:4; → Serve) we find the compounds *eidōlolatrēs*, idolater (4 times) and *eidōlolatria*, idolatry (7 times). From the NT these words passed into early Christian literature.

1. The NT continues not merely the vocabulary of the OT but also its condemnation of the worship of false gods. The fact that this word-group is not found in the Gospels indicates that in Palestine the controversy had ceased to be of importance. As soon as the apostolic preaching moved into the non-Jewish, Hellenistic world it immediately revived. Turning to the "living and true God" (1 Thess.

1:9) was impossible without a turning away from idols and pagan worship. Their retention was a sign of lack of repentance (Rev. 9:20).

Paul's arguments in Rom. 1:18–32 are particularly concerned with this controversy. He showed himself a Jew in his stress on the nothingness of the idols, but he recognized the demonic powers behind them to which a man subjects himself when he participates in the heathen cultus. That is why *eidōlolatria* is one of the serious sins against which Christians have repeatedly to be warned (1 Cor. 5:10 f.; 10:7, 14). In the lists of sins it is frequently mentioned, and stands linked with *pharmakeia*, sorcery (→ Magic), and *pleonexia*, → covetousness (cf. Gal. 5:19 ff.; Eph. 5:5; Col. 3:5; Rev. 9:20 f.; 21:8; 22:15). According to Jesus, mammon (→ Possessions) is also a false god (Matt. 6:24).

2. From this basic attitude to idols it followed that Christians were debarred from eating the meat of animals that had been offered in heathen → sacrifice. The NT texts are consistent in this matter. According to Acts, the apostles were unanimous that Gentile Christians should refrain from sacrificial meat, called in this context *alisgēmata*, pollutions (Acts 15:20, 29; 21:25). This prohibition adopted at the apostolic council was justified by a reference to Jewish practice (15:21), as we find also in Paul (1 Cor. 10:32). It presupposes that in this matter Jews and Christians were basically in agreement.

In 1 Cor. 8 and 10 the practical problems that sprang from this basic attitude are examined in detail. In ch. 8 Paul argues with those in Corinth who maintained that the eating of such meat was harmless for they realized that the false gods had no real existence (1 Cor. 8:1–6). Some scholars identify this group with gnostics (cf. W. Schmithals, *Gnosticism in Corinth*, 1971). Presumably the teachers of false doctrine combatted in Rev. argued in the same way (Rev. 2:14, 20). Paul agreed that idols had no real existence (1 Cor. 8:4), but expected that those who realize this would out of love show consideration to those who did not; they must not cause these to eat such meat (1 Cor. 8:9–13).

Paul gives the underlying reasons for his attitude in ch. 10. Basing himself on Deut. 32:17, he explains that demons stand behind the idols. → Fellowship with Christ, which Christians enjoy in the Lord's Supper, excludes communion with these powers. Christians should not challenge the Lord. If they do, they will bring down his judgment on them (1 Cor. 10:7–10, 14–22). Christians were under no obligation to enquire fearfully whether the meat bought in the market (generally near the temple) or served at a meal came from a sacrifice. If, however, it was pointed out that it was sacrificial meat, then, out of regard for the → conscience of the one who pointed it out, Christians ought not to eat it, even if their own → conscience (perhaps on the strength of Ps. 24:1) permitted it (1 Cor. 10:25–30). The OT roots of the NT faith are particularly clearly visible in this consistent condemnation of pagan worship and this attitude to sacrificial meat.

W. Mundle

| εἰκών | εἰκών (*eikōn*), image, likeness, form, appearance. |

CL *eikōn*, derived from *eoika*, which has a present force, meaning to be similar, like (from the rare *eike*, attested by Homer, meaning it seemed good, it appeared) means image, copy: (a) a painting, statue, figure on a coin, figure of a god; (b) comparison, simile; (c) image, likeness, semblance, representation. In Gk. thought an image shares in the reality of what it represents. The essence of the thing appears in the image, e.g. the god is himself present and operative in his image (cf. magic and miracles performed through images).

OT *eikōn* is used for 5 different Heb. words including *pesel* (Isa. 40:19 f.), *t^eḇûnâh*
(Hos. 13:2), *d^emûṭ* (Gen. 5:1), and *semel* and *sēmel* (Deut. 4:16; 2 Chr. 33:7), but it occurs chiefly for *ṣelem* (Gen. 1:26 f.; 5:1, 3; 9:6; 1 Sam. 6:11; 2 Ki. 11:18; Pss. 39 [38]:6; 73 [72]:20; Ezek. 7:20; 16:17; 23:14; Dan. 2:31) and *ṣ^elēm* (Dan. 2:31, 34 f.; 3:1-18). It has no Heb. equivalent in Wis. 2:23; 7:26; 13:13, 16; 14:15, 17; 15:5; 17:21; Sir. 17:3.

Already in the early period of belief in Yahweh associated with Moses images were strictly prohibited (Exod. 20:4; Deut. 27:15). For the image was not the full reality and would only confuse Israel's relationship with the true God (Deut. 4:16; 2 Ki. 11:18). Among Israel's neighbours the image of a god served as a means of controlling the god. It was a source of power in the priest's hand in his dealings with the deity (cf. K. H. Bernhardt, *Gott und Bild*, 1956). In the Babylonian exile Israel learnt to mock the making of idols (Isa. 40:19 f.) but also to be terrified by them (Ezek. 7:20; 8:5; 16:17; 23:14). Both lines of thought can be traced in Dan. 2 and 3.

In contrast, Israel's relationship with God is based on his → covenant and → word. Religious images can reveal nothing of his nature (→ *eidōlon*). Only man can be called the image (*ṣelem*) of God (Gen. 1:26 f.; 5:1 ff.; 9:6). The goal and purpose of the image of God in man is dominion over the world. "God set man in the world as a sign of his own authority, in order that man should uphold his – God's – claims as Lord" (G. von Rad, *Old Testament Theology*, I, 1962, 146; cf. Ps. 8:5 f.; Sir. 17:3 f.). The OT knows nothing of man losing this image through the fall. ([Ed.] This question was debated by Karl Barth and Emil Brunner in *Natural Theology*, 1946, where Brunner accused Barth of maintaining that the image was obliterated by sin. Brunner held that the *material* aspect of the image which was bound up with man's original righteousness was in fact lost. But the *formal* aspect, man's rational nature, his capacity for culture, and his humanity, remain, and this provides a basis for natural theology. To this Barth replied that Brunner's argument was irrelevant to establishing a natural theology, for the knowledge of God can only come from God himself and this has nothing to do with man's formal capacities. Subsequently Barth modified his teaching on the divine image, without, however, taking Brunner's point. Referring to the plural subject in Gen. 1:26 ["Let us make man in our image, after our likeness"], Barth observes: "The relationship between the summoning I in God's being and the summoned divine Thou is reflected both in the relationship of God to the man whom he has created, and also in the relationship between the I and the Thou, between male and female, in human existence itself" [*CD* III, 1, 196]. Barth understands the image in terms of the mutual relations between man and woman which in turn reflects the relationship of Yahweh to Israel and Christ to the church [cf. *CD* III 1, 183 ff., 201 ff., 322].)

The idea of the fall marring the image of God is implied in Wis. 2:23 (cf. Wis. 13-15). Rabbinic Judaism did not question the *imago Dei* (image of God) in principle. But the possibility was considered that through an individual's sin it might be diminished or even lost (cf. G. Kittel, *TDNT* II 392 ff.).

NT In Matt. 22:20; Mk. 12:16; Lk. 20:24, *eikōn* is used of the emperor's image on the denarius. These coins were hated by pious Jews, both because of their implied breach of the second commandment and because it was an image of a foreign ruler. (On this passage see J. D. M. Derrett, "Render unto Caesar . . ." in *Law in the New Testament*, 1970, 313–38; F. F. Bruce, "Render to Caesar", in *The Zealots and Jesus*, ed. C. F. D. Moule and E. Bammel [forthcoming]; → Caesar.)

In Rev. the image of the beast (13:14; → Animal; → Number) is a cultic image (perhaps that of the emperor, or Nero *redivivus* [cf. R. H. Charles, *The Revelation of St. John*, *ICC*, I, 1920, 360]). Worship of it means apostasy. The classical world knew of images of the gods which spoke and moved (Rev. 13:15); cf. Charles, op. cit., 361).

In Heb. 10:1 *eikōn* signifies the true form of the good things to come which has appeared in Christ, in contrast to the law which is a mere shadow of these things. In 2 Cor. 4:4 and Col. 1:15 Christ is said to be the image or likeness of God. There is no difference here between the image and the essence of the invisible God. In Christ we see God (cf. Jn. 14:9). By participating in Christ man has once more gained the image of God (Rom. 8:29) which man was intended to be (1 Cor. 11:7). Christ realized man's destiny to be God's image which was marred through sin. In communion with Christ we are transformed into his image. Paul can speak of this transformation as a present happening (2 Cor. 3:18; Col. 3:10), and also as a yet future, eschatological event (1 Cor. 15:49; Phil. 3:21). "Like all the gifts in which Christians share, the *eikōn* is an *aparchē* [first fruits, → Sacrifice] . . . This means that it now is, and yet that it is still to be" (G. Kittel, *TDNT* II 397).

O. Flender

| χαρακτήρ | χαρακτήρ (*charaktēr*), impress, stamp, reproduction, representation, outward appearance, form. |

CL & OT *charaktēr* (Aeschylus onwards) is a noun derived from *charassō*, notch, indent, and means one who sharpens, scratches, and later one who writes in stone, wood or metal. Thence it came to mean an embosser and a stamp for making coins, and from this, looking to the result, the embossed stamp made on the coin, character in writing, style. Finally, it came to mean the basic bodily and psychological structure with which one is born, which is unique to the person and which cannot be changed by education or development, though it may be hidden or effaced. Hence, it also means individuality, personal characteristics. In Philo the human soul is called the *charaktēr* of divine power and the Logos is entitled the *charaktēr* of God (cf. *Leg. All.* 3, 95–104; *Ebr.* 133, 137; *Rer. Div. Her.* 38; *Plant.* 18; *Det. Pot. Ins.* 83).

This concept cannot really be found in the OT, though it reminds us slightly of the passages about the *imago Dei*. The word is found in the LXX (e.g. Lev. 13:28), but without a specific theological meaning (for Heb. *ṣārebet*, scar).

NT *charaktēr* is found only once in the NT. Christ is the *charaktēr tēs hypostaseōs autou*, "the very stamp of his [God's] nature" (Heb. 1:3 RSV), i.e. the One on whom God has stamped or imprinted his being. This means that the NT use is entirely different from our modern concept of character which develops itself by a will that seeks to conform to principles. Similarly, when Heb. 5:8 declares that Jesus learnt obedience through what he suffered, there is no thought of our concept of character-formation. It is probably linked with the Son's obedience to the Father tested in temptation (O. Michel, *Der Brief an die Hebräer*, KEK 13, 1966[12] ad loc.). The Son possesses the stamp of God's nature just as he is the → *apaugasma tēs doxēs tou theou*, "the effulgence of God's splendour" (NEB). He who sees and recognizes him, sees and knows the Father (Jn. 14:7 ff.); cf. also → *eikōn tou theou*, the image of God.

The context of Heb. 1 makes it clear that the writer's purpose was to stress the glory of the Son who had entered history and the uniqueness of the revelation of God in the unique One. In v. 3 we have probably an early hymn, as in Phil. 2:6 ff. and 1 Tim. 3:16. The Son who controls the beginning and the end (v. 2) stands in a unique relationship (a) to God whose effulgence (→ *apaugasma*) and stamp (*charaktēr*) he is; (b) to the universe which he upholds; and (c) to the church which he has purified from sins. The Epistle is equally concerned with the pre-existent, the historical and the glorified Christ in whom we have our true High → Priest. Commenting on the word *charaktēr*, F. F. Bruce writes: "Just as the image and superscription on a coin exactly correspond to the device on the die, so the Son of God 'bears the very stamp of his nature' (RSV). The Greek word *charaktēr*, occurring only here in the New Testament, expresses this truth even more emphatically than *eikōn*, which is used elsewhere to denote Christ as the 'image' of God (II Cor. 4:4; Col. 1:15). Just as the glory is really in the effulgence, so the substance (Gk. *hypostasis*) of God is really in Christ, who is its impress, its exact representation and embodiment. What God essentially is, is made manifest in Christ. To see Christ is to see what the Father is like" (*Commentary on the Epistle to the Hebrews*, NLC, 1964, 6).   *J. Gess*

| ἀπαύγασμα |

ἀπαύγασμα (*apaugasma*), radiance, effulgence, reflection.

apaugasma may be translated either as effulgence, radiance (in the act. sense) or reflection (in the pass. sense). It derives from *augazō*, to shine forth, or to illuminate (2 Cor. 4:4). *diaugazō* is found in 2 Pet. 1:19 in the first meaning. The cognate noun *augē*, radiance, is rendered at Acts. 20:11 by dawn, or daybreak, i.e. when the sun shines forth.

CL *apaugasma* is found only in Hellenistic writers who use the noun with the meanings noted above. It is not attested before the Wisdom of Solomon, but a Stoic influence on Philo's use of the term has been suspected. Philo says that what God breathed into Adam was "an effulgence" [*apaugasma*] of his blessed, thrice-blessed nature" (*Spec.Leg.* 4, 123; cf. Philo in *Op. Mund.* 146). In *Plant.* 50 (cf. *Mut. Nom.* 181; *Som.* 1, 71, 115, *Migr.Abr.* 71) Philo uses *apaugasma* as a synonym of → *eikōn* and *mimēma* meaning "reflection". The same sense is attested in Plutarch, *Mor.* 83d, 934d. Of special interest for the NT background is the use of cognate terms in the Isis aretalogies, found at Cyme. Isis confesses: *egō en tais tou hēliou augais eimi,* "I am in the beams of the sun". Isis is also praised as enlightener of the world and an emanation of God.

OT The most significant text is Wis. 7:25 f., where divine wisdom is hailed as "a breath of the power of God, and a pure emanation of the glory of the Almighty . . . she is a reflection of eternal light [*apaugasma . . . estin phōtos aidiou*], a spotless mirror of the working of God, and an image of his goodness [*eikōn tēs agathotētos autou*]." In this setting wisdom is hypostatized as a source of light whose shining forth (*apaugasma*) is understood as "effulgence" or "reflection" (RSV). The former meaning finds support in the view that, since wisdom is praised for her active role in uniting man and God, the sense of "radiance" is better. But most scholars prefer "reflection", though with hesitation.

NT The single text to be considered is Heb. 1:3: *hos ōn apaugasma tēs doxēs kai charaktēr tēs hypostaseōs autou,* where there are several echoes of the Wis. tribute. In Heb. the verse stands in a doxological, possibly hymnic tribute to the cosmic Christ who is described as either the radiance of the divine *doxa* as the sunlight conveys the brightness and intensity of the sun (Kittel: we may compare for this sense, Philo, *Som.* 1, 239), or God's reflection in a way comparable with the thought of Christ as the *eikōn,* "image" or mirror (Wis. 7:26) or the *morphē* (RSV "form") of God (→ Form, arts. *morphē* and *hypostasis*). Either way, the verse is a piece of wisdom christology that interprets Christ as the supreme and final revelation of the Father. On balance, the act. sense of "radiance" is to be chosen in preference to "reflection".   *R. P. Martin*

| ὑπόδειγμα | ὑπόδειγμα (*hypodeigma*), proof, example, model. |

CL The classical form is *paradeigma* (much preferred to *hypodeigma* by Phrynichus, *Eclogae* 4). In Hellenistic Greek *hypodeigma* means an example (with *paradeigma* as a synonym, Plutarch, *Agesilaus*, 15, 4) with a transferred sense of demonstration, sample, pattern or model (→ *typos* is a synonym), in either the good sense of a model to copy or as a warning example of what to avoid.

The main occurrences of the noun are in Polybius, used of examples seen in soldiers (3, 17, 8), in Hannibal's speeches (3, 111, 6) or a rhetorical "proof" in a speech (6, 54, 6). Liddell-Scott (1878) cite inscriptions that have *pros hypodeigma aretēs* ("for example of virtue"), a usage paralleled in Plutarch, *De Marcello*, 20, 1 ("examples of civic virtues").

Philo has an important discussion of the Levitical tabernacle as a model of the divine plan (*Leg.All.* 3, 102) which Moses glimpsed and Bezalel constructed (*Som.* 1, 206; *Vit.Mos.* 2, 76; "the shape of the model" (*ho typos tou paradeigmatos*; see too *Leg.All.* 3, 108).

OT The occurrences of the noun are in Ezek. 42:15 (RSV "temple area", where LXX has the "ground-plan of the house")); Sir. 44:16, Enoch was "an example of repentance": 2 Macc. 6:28, 31, the Maccabean martyrs are a "noble example", as in 4 Macc. 17:23.

NT The usage divides between the two meanings given in the LXX: (a) a "figure" or "copy", a meaning restricted to Heb. 8:5; 9:23. The Levitical furnishings and service function as a "copy" (RSV) of their heavenly counterparts which, for the author, alone have substantial reality; (b) "example" in the twofold way of either issuing a call to imitation, as in Jn. 13:15 and Jas. 5:10; or in the bad sense serving as a warning, as in Heb. 4:11 and 2 Pet. 2:6. *R. P. Martin*

| ὑπογραμμός |

ὑπογραμμός (*hypogrammos*), lit. under-writing, outline, copy, example.

The word is late. Philo uses it in the sense of outline, as a near-synonym of *skia*, shadow (frag. 7). The commonest use of the noun (cf. the vb. *hypographō*) is for the faint outlines of letters which were traced over by pupils learning to write, then also of the sets of letters written at the top of a page or other piece of writing material to be copied repeatedly by the learner on the rest of the page (cf. Clem. Alex., *Strom.* 5, 8, 49, 48). It is this sense which is applied metaphorically in 1 Pet. 2:21 to the example left by Christ for his disciples to follow, especially in his patient endurance of undeserved suffering. (→ Scripture, Writing NT 1 (b) (end).)

F. F. Bruce

| παραδειγματίζω |

παραδειγματίζω (*paradeigmatizō*), expose to public disgrace, make an example of.

The compound verb is more frequently found than the simple *deigmatizō* to expose, exhibit, make public (Matt. 1:19 *v.l.;* Col. 2:15). The prefix *para-* has an intensive force, so the vb. comes to mean to expose to public disgrace.

CL The vb. is late Gk. In Polybius the chief meanings are to make a public example of someone, such as Aristomachus the tyrant (2, 60, 7), the people of Rhodes (29, 19, 5), or the revolt of the Aravacae (35, 2, 10). See too Plutarch, *Mor.* 520b, in the sense of to make oneself infamous or "a sorry spectacle". In the meaning of example in the good sense, there are several illustrations in the papyri (e.g. *P.Oxy.* II, 237, "following a most illustrious example").

OT The vb. is understood as to "hang publicly" (Num. 25:4 LXX) as a method of execution which involves public exposure. The same meaning is seen in Ezek. 28:17 and Dan. 2:5; and also in 3 Macc. 7:14 (of the apostate Jews who deserve to be put to a shameful death) and in Mordecai's prayer in the Gk. additions to Esther (following 4:17).

NT The only texts to use the verb are Matt. 1:19 (*v.l.* where the stronger verb *paradeigmatizō* is weakly attested) and Heb. 6:6. Rejection of Christ by apostasy means that he is crucified anew and put to open disgrace. Apostates and *lapsi* expose him to public shame in that act of denial. The association of the vb. with *anastauroō* (crucify again) may be a reminiscence of the fate of the leaders of the Jewish apostasy at Baal-peor who were "hung up" before Yahweh (Num. 25:4, see above). *R. P. Martin*

→ Follow, → Form, → Like, Equal, → Mark, Brand, → Type, Pattern

On *eidōlon* and cognates:
Arndt, 220; F. Büchsel, *eidōlon* etc., *TDNT* II 375–80; J. C. Hurd, Jr., *The Origin of I Corinthians*, 1965; Liddell-Scott, 384 f.

On *eikōn*:
(a). K. Barth, *CD* III 1, 182–206; G. C. Berkouwer, *Man: The Image of God*, 1962; D. Cairns, *The Image of God in Man*, 1953; H. von Campenhausen, "The Theological Problem of Images in the Early Church", *Tradition and Life in the Church*, 1968, 171–200; W. Dürig, "Image", *EBT* II 392 ff.; D. J. A. Clines, "The Image of God in Man", Tyndale Old Testament Lecture, 1967, *TB* 19, 1968, 53–103 (contains extensive review of other writers on the subject); W. Eichrodt, *Theology of the Old Testament*, II, 1967, 122–31; F. Horst, "Face to Face. The Biblical Doctrine of the Image of God", *Interpretation* 4, 1950, 259–70; P. K. Jewett, *Man as Male and Female: A Study in Sexual Relationships from a Theological Point of View*, 1975; G. Kittel, G. von Rad, H. Kleinnecht, *eikōn*, *TDNT* II 381–97; A. R. C. Leaney, "Conformed to the Image of His Son" *NTS* 10, 1963–64, 470–79; J. M. Miller, "In the 'Image' and 'Likeness' of God", *JBL* 91, 1972, 289–304; T. W. Overholt, "The Falsehood of Idolatry", *JTS* New Series 16, 1965, 1–12; R. H. Pfeiffer, "Images of Yahweh", *JBL* 45, 1926, 211–22; N. W. Porteous, "Image of God", *IDB* II 682–85; R. Prins, "The Image of God in Adam and the Restoration of Man in Jesus Christ", *SJT* 25, 1972, 32–44; G. von Rad, *Old Testament Theology*, I, 1962, 212–19; J. F. A. Sawyer, "The Meaning of *b*ᵉ*ṣelem* *'*ᵉ*lōhîm* ('In the Image of God') in Genesis I–II", *JTS* New Series 25, 1974, 418–26; S. G. Wilson, "Image of God", *ExpT* 85, 1973–74, 356–61; H. W. Wolff, *Anthropology of the Old Testament*, 1974, 159–66.

On the role of images and symbolism in revelation and religious knowledge see E. R. Bevan, *Symbolism and Belief*, 1938; G. Cope, *Symbolism in the Bible and in the Church*, 1959; F. W. Dillistone, ed., *Myth and Symbol*, SPCK Theological Collections 7, 1966 (includes papers by P. Tillich, M. Eliade, I. T. Ramsey and others); T. Fawcett, *The Symbolic Language of Religion*, 1970; S. Hook, ed., *Religious Experience and Truth: A Symposium*, 1962; E. L. Mascall, *Words and Images*, 1957; and *Theology and Images*, 1963.

(b). K. H. Bernhardt, *Gott und Bild*, 1956; E. Brunner, "Der Ersterschaffene als Gottes Ebenbild", *EvTh* 11, 1951–52, 298 ff.; W. Dürig, *Imago*, 1952; F. Eltester, *Eikōn im Neuen Testament*, *BZNW* 23, 1958; J. B. Frey, "La Question des Images chez les Juifs à la Lumière des Récentes Découvertes", *Biblica* 15, 1934, 265 ff.; H. Gross, "Die Gottebenbildlichkeit des Menschen", in *Lex Tua Veritas. Festschrift für Hubert Junker*, ed. H. Gross *et al.*, 1961, 89–100; J. Hempel, *Das Bild in Bibel und Gottesdienst*, 157; P. Humbert, " 'L'Imago Dei' dans l'Ancien Testament", *Études sur le Récit du Paradis et de la Chute dans la Genèse*, 1940, 153–75; J. Jervell, *Imago Dei. Gen. 1:26 f. im Spätjudentum, in der Gnosis und in den paulinischen Briefen*, *FRLANT* 28, 1960; L. Koehler, "Die Grundstelle der Imago-Dei-Lehre, Gen. 1:26", *ThZ* 4, 1948, 16 ff.; J. Konrad, *Abbild und Ziel der Schöpfung. Untersuchungen zur Exegese von Genesis 1 und 2 in Barths Kirchlicher Dogmatik III, 1*, 1962; E. Larsson, *Christus als Vorbild*, 1962; E. Lohse, "Imago Dei bei Paulus", in *Libertas Christiana* (Festschrift F. Delikat), *Beiträge zu Evangelischer Theologie* 26, 1957; K. L. Schmidt, "*Homo Imago Dei* im Alten Testament und Neuen Testament", *Eranos-Jahrbuch* 15, 1947–48, 154 ff.; H. Schrade, *Der verborgene Gott*, 1949; G. Söhngen, "Die biblische Lehre von der Gottebenbildlichkeit des Menschen", *Münchener Theologische Zeitschrift* 2, 1951, 42 ff.; J. J. Stamm, "Die Imago-Lehre von Karl Barth und die alttestamentliche Wissenschaft", in *Antwort. Festschrift für Karl Barth*, ed. E. Wolf *et al.*, 1956, 84–98; and *Die Gottebenbildlichkeit des Menschen im Alten Testament*, 1959; C. Stange, "Das Ebenbild Gottes", *TLZ* 949, 79 ff.; W. Vischer, "Du sollst dir kein Bildnis machen", in *Antwort*, 764–72; T. C. Vriezen, "La Création de l'Homme d'après l'Image de Dieu", *Oudtestamentische Studiën* 2, 1943, 87–103; C. Westermann, "Bild", *BHHW* I 249 ff.; H. Wildberger, "Das Abbild Gottes", *ThZ* 21, 1965, 245–59, 481–501.

On *charaktēr*:
(a). Arndt, 884; J. Geffcken, "Character", *ExpT* 21, 1909–10, 426 f.; Liddell-Scott, 1977; U. Wilckens and G. Kelber, *charaktēr*, *TDNT* IX 418–23; R. Williamson, *Philo and the Epistle to the Hebrews*, Arbeiten zur Literatur und Geschichte des hellenistischen Judentums, 4, 1970, 74–80.
(b). F. J. Dölger, *Sphragis, Studien zur Geschichte und Kultur des Altertums* 5, 3/4, 1911; F. W. Eltester, *Eikōn im Neuen Testament*, *BZNW* 23, 1958, 52 ff.; A. Körte, "*CHARAKTĒR*", *Hermes* 64, 1929, 69–86.

On *apaugasma:*
(a). G. Kittel, *augazō, apaugasma, TDNT* I 507 f.; G. von Rad, *Wisdom in Israel*, 1972; J. M. Reese, *Hellenistic Influences on the Book of Wisdom*, 1970. Commentaries on *Hebrews* by F. F. Bruce (*NLC*, 1964); H. W. Montefiore (*BNTC*, 1964); J. Héring (1970).
(b). R. Deichgräber, *Gotteshymnus und Christushymnus in der frühen Christenheit*, 1967; F. W. Eltester, *Eikōn im Neuen Testament*, 1958; A. J. Festugière, "L'arétalogie d'Isis de la Korè Kosmu", *Revue Archéologique* 6, 1949, 376–81; J. Jervell, *Imago Dei*, 1960 (on the theological aspects); C. Larcher, *Études sur le Livre de la Sagesse*, 1969; B. L. Mack, *Logos und Sophia. Untersuchungen zur Weisheitstheologie im hellenistischen Judentum*, 1973; P. Roussel, "Un nouvel hymne à Isis", *Revue des Études Grecques* 42, 1929, 137–68; A. Salač, "Hymne isiaque de Kume", *Bulletin de Correspondance Hellénique* 51, 1927, 378–83; W. Schencke, *Die Chokma (Sophia) in der jüdischen Hypostasenspekulation*, 1913; C. Spicq, *L'Épître aux Hébreux*, I–II, 1952–53; K. Wengst, *Christologische Formeln und Lieder des Urchristentums*, 1972.

On *hypodeigma*:
Arndt, 851; E. K. Lee, "Words Denoting 'Patterns' in the New Testament", *NTS* 8, 1961–62, 166–73; Liddell-Scott, 1878; H. Schlier, *hypodeigma, TDNT* II 32 f. Commentaries on *Hebrews* by F. F. Bruce (*NLC*, 1964); H. W. Montefiore (*BNTC*, 1964); C. Spicq, I–II (1952–53).

On *paradeigmatizō*:
Arndt, 619; Moulton-Milligan, 481 f.; H. Schlier, *paradeigmatizō, TDNT* II 32. Commentaries on *Hebrews* by F. F. Bruce (*NLC*, 1964); C. Spicq, I–II (1952–53); A. T. Hanson, *Studies in Paul's Technique and Theology*, 1974, 4 ff.; G. E. Mendenhall, *The Tenth Generation*, 1973, 105–121.

Incense, Myrrh

λίβανος

λίβανος (*libanos*), λιβανωτός (*libanōtos*), frankincense; θυμίαμα (*thymiama*), incense; θυμιάω (*thymiaō*), burn incense; θυμιατήριον (*thymiatērion*), censer.

CL (a) In secular Gk. *libanos* is the frankincense-tree, *Boswellia carterii*, of India, Arabia, and Somalia; and, by extension, the tree's aromatic gum frankincense, for which the derivative *libanōtos* is also used (Herodotus).

(b) *thymiama* (incense) is the general term for fragrant substances (i) burned with sacrifices or for fumigation purposes, or (ii) used in embalming. The vb. *thymiaō* (from *thyō*, offer in sacrifice) means to burn so as to produce smoke, and more particularly to burn incense or to fumigate. The related noun *thymiatērion* is the censer.

OT (a) Apart from one instance of *libanōtos* (1 Chr. 9:29), the LXX always uses *libanos* for the Heb. *lᵉḇōnâh* (white, the colour of the gum when first solidified). Brittle, glittering, and bitter to the taste, frankincense produced a gratifying if expensive fragrance when burned (Cant. 3:6; 4:6, 14). Besides being an ingredient of the special incense constantly used in OT worship, pure frankincense was burned with showbread (Lev. 24:7) and cereal-offering (Lev. 2:2), but not sin-offerings Lev. 5:11).

(b) *thymiama* (incense) and its verb *thymiaō* occur frequently for the Heb. *qᵉṭōreṭ* (sweet smoke) and *qiṭṭēr* or *hiqṭîr* (make sacrifices smoke). *thymiatērion* in the LXX always means censer (2 Chr. 26:19; Ezek. 8:11; 4 Macc. 7:11). The holy incense was a special compound reserved for the divine service (Exod. 30:34–35) and used to strict instructions (Lev. 16:12–13; cf. Lev. 10:1–11). Morning and evening the high priest burned incense before the veil of the holy of holies (Exod.

30:7, 8). On the Day of Atonement he entered the holy of holies carrying burning incense, the fumes of which provided an atonement (Heb. *kpr*, cover) for him as he approached the mercy-seat (Lev. 16:12–13; cf. Num. 16:46). Rising incense smoke symbolized praise (Isa. 60:6) and prayer (Ps. 141:2), worship fragrant to God. In the messianic age converted Gentiles will gladly bring abundant incense to the Temple (Isa. 60:6), indicative of their newly begun worship of God.

NT 1. *Primary Meanings.* (a) The frequent part played by incense in Jewish worship is reflected in the many OT references. In the NT, however, *libanos* occurs only twice (Matt. 2:11; Rev. 18:13) and has its literal meaning of frankincense. In Rev. 8:3, 5 *libanōtos* unusually means not frankincense but censer, the vessel for carrying incense.

(b) *thymiaō* (burn incense) occurs only in Lk. 1:9–11, together with the noun *thymiama*. In the second Temple the daily offering of incense devolved upon ordinary priests. One "new to the incense", i.e. one without the privilege before, was chosen by lot (Mishnah *Yoma* 2.4). Zechariah was carrying out this duty for the only time in his life when he had his vision. *thymiatērion* appears once (Heb. 9:4) and is translated not as censer (so always in the LXX) but as altar of incense.

2. *Extended Meanings.* (a) *libanos* (frankincense), brought to the infant Jesus (Matt. 2:11), symbolizes both his divinity and his priestly office of intercession (Heb. 7:25). The bringing of frankincense by Gentiles to the messiah was a Jewish expectation (Isa. 60:6). In Rev. 8:3, 5 the association of one and the same censer (*libanōtos*) with intercession and judgment shows the potency of Christian prayer in fulfilling God's purposes.

(b) Apart from Lk. 1:10, 11 *thymiama* occurs only in Rev. 5:8; 8:3, 4, where incense in the heavenly temple represents the prayers of the saints.

N. Hillyer

σμύρνα

σμύρνα (*smyrna*), myrrh; μύρον (*myron*), ointment, perfume.

OT Myrrh is a gum which comes from the *Commiphora myrrha* which grows in Somaliland, Ethiopia and Arabia and which exudes from the trunk and branches giving a pleasant fragrance. The LXX uses *smyrna* to translate the Heb. *mōr* or *môr*. In Exod. 30:23 it is an important ingredient in the anointing oil used in the consecration of the tabernacle and the priests. In Ps. 45(44):8 its fragrance is mentioned in connection with the oil of gladness with which God anoints his chosen king. It is also mentioned in Cant. 3:6; 4:6, 14; 5:1, 5, 13; Sir. 24:15; cf. Est. 2:12.

The word translated as myrrh in Gen. 37:25; 43:11 is the Heb. *lōṭ* (Gk. *staktē*), probably meaning laudanum, as at the time myrrh may not have been introduced. It was an item of trade and was regarded as a worthy gift.

NT *smyrna* was among the gifts brought to the infant Jesus brought by the Gentile Magi (Matt. 2:11). Here and elsewhere outside the Bible it is mentioned together with incense (cf. *TDNT* IV 264; VII 458). The gifts might have been interpreted as a fulfilment of Ps. 72(71):10 f. (cf. SB I 83 f. for rabbinic messianic interpretation of this passage and also Ps. 68:31 f.).

At the burial of Jesus Nicodemus brought a mixture of myrrh and aloes weighing a hundred pounds (Jn. 19:39). The large amount was probably an expression of honour. Jn. 19:40 indicates that the practice was followed of laying the spices (*arōmata*) between the clothes in which the body was wrapped (cf. also Mk. 16:1; Lk. 23:56; 24:1). This attempt to preserve the body of Jesus suggests that none of those involved expected an immediate resurrection.

The passive participle of the vb. *smyrnizō* occurs in Mk. 15:23 in the reference to the "wine mingled with myrrh" which was offered to Jesus by the soldiers prior to the crucifixion. This is often taken to be an anodyne given to condemned prisoners to blunt their consciousness (cf. San. 43a). However, W. Michaelis thinks that this was just a drink given by the soldiers to the exhausted (*TDNT* VII 459). But → Gall, Poison, Wormwood.

The word *myron* is probably best translated as ointment or perfume (cf. Matt. 26:7, 12; Mk. 14:3 ff.; Lk. 7:37 f., 46; 28:56; Jn. 11:2; 12:3, 5; Rev. 18:13).

C. Brown

(a). Arndt, 531, 766; H. F. Beck, "Incense", *IDB* II 697 f.; G. W. van Beek, "Frankincense and Myrrh", *BA* 23, 1960, 70–95; K. Galling, "Incense Altar", *IDB* II 699 f.; M. Haran, "The Use of Incense", *Vetus Testamentum* 10, 1960, 113–29; W. Michaelis, *libanos, libanōtos*, *TDNT* IV 263 f.; and *smyrna* etc., *TDNT* VII 459 ff.; H. N. and A. L. Moldenke, *Plants of the Bible*, 1952; W. E. Shewell-Cooper, "Myrrh", *ZPEB* IV 326; J. A. Thompson, "Incense", *ZPEB* III 274 ff.; L. E. Toombs, "Incense, Dish for", *IDB* II 698 f.; J. C. Trever, "Myrrh", *IDB* III 478 f.

(b). F. Blome, *Die Opfermaterie in Babylonien und Israel*, 1934; M. Löhr, *Das Räucheropfer im Alten Testament*, 1927; I. Löw, *Die Flora der Juden*, I–IV, 1926–34 (see index); A. Schmidt, *Drogen und Drogenhandel im Altertum*, 1924.

Inheritance, Lot, Portion

The idea of inheritance in the Bible is a reminder that God has not intended man to lead an autonomous, isolated, self-sufficient existence. Man's life has an allotted place in the great movement of history. God has given him both gifts and responsibilities to be exercised with regard to others. The Gk. word *klēros*, inheritance, and other words related to it are used to express that which is received from the past. But they also look forward to the future. In its deepest, theological sense the believer's inheritance is something which comes from God himself. In the OT it has a physical dimension in the shape of the promised land. In the NT it is a spiritual inheritance which comes through the → kingdom of God and the promise of eternal → life. Like the → covenant, the concept of inheritance expresses a fundamental relationship between God and man. It depicts God's desire to give his people a secure abode. On the other hand, this group of words by itself does not convey how men may enter into this inheritance. The word *meros*, part, is also included here, because it involves the idea of sharing.

κλῆρος

κλῆρος (*klēros*), inheritance, lot; κληρόω (*klēroō*), cast lots, determine by lot; κληρονομέω (*klēronomeō*), inherit; κληρονομία (*klēronomia*), inheritance; κληρονόμος (*klēronomos*), inheritor, heir; συγκληρονόμος (*synklēronomos*), fellow heir.

CL *klēros* is derived from *klaō*, break. In the first instance it means a lot. Used from Homer on it meant originally the fragment of stone or piece of wood which was used as a lot. Lots were drawn to discover the will of the gods. Since land was divided by lot, probably in the framework of common use of the fields, *klēros* came to mean a share, land received by lot, plot of land, and finally inheritance. The vb. belonging to this is *klēroō*, to draw lots, apportion by lot. *klēronomia* compounded from *klēros* and *nemō*, allot, is first the activity of dividing by lot, then the portion so divided, the inheritance. The *klēronomos* is one who has been given a *klēros*, the inheritor. *synklēronomos* is a fellow heir, and *klēronomeō* means be an heir, inherit.

OT 1. Lots (Heb. *gôrāl*) were drawn in the OT also to discover God's will. The high priest wore the lots, Urim and Thummim, in the breastplate of judgment attached to the ephod (Exod. 28:30; Lev. 8:8). He discovered the will of God by their means (Num. 27:21; Ezr. 2:63; Neh. 7:65). According to the Blessing of Moses (Deut. 33), the discovery of God's will and the teaching of his law (*tôrâh*) belong together (vv. 8, 10). A linguistic link between *tôrâh* and the vb. *yārâh*, to throw, i.e. cast lots to ascertain God's will, has been suggested, but many authorities question this and numerous derivations have been put forward (cf. Koehler-Baumgartner, 403). All heathen and magical oracles and oracular methods were an abomination to Yahweh and were denied to Israel by divine decree (Deut. 18:9–14). Guidance by lots was permitted only when carried out in obedience to God. But even there God could refuse to give an answer (1 Sam. 14:37; 28:6), or forbid the casting of lots (according to some interpretations of Ezek. 24:6; but cf. RV, RSV, NEB). On the other hand, God could reveal himself to the heathen through the casting of lots and other means of divination (Jon. 1:7; Ezek. 21:21 [MT 21:26]). (On the Urim and Thummim see H. L. Ellison, "Urim and Thummim", *ZPEB* V 850 ff.; J. Lindblom, "Lot-Casting in the Old Testament", *Vetus Testamentum* 12, 1962, 164 ff.; I. Mendelsohn, "Urim and Thummim", *IDB* IV 739 ff.; E. Robertson, "The Urim and Thummim; What were they?", *Vetus Testamentum* 14, 1964, 67 ff.; R. de Vaux, *Ancient Israel*, 1961, 350 ff.)

There are numerous examples of the casting of lots in Israel. In Jos. 7:14 and 1 Sam. 14:41 lots were used to discover the one under the ban. Saul was chosen as king by lot (1 Sam. 10:20 f.). In Chr. and Neh. lots were cast for priestly office and to choose who was to live in Jerusalem (cf. 1 Chr. 24:5 f.). In NT times priestly functions in the Temple were fixed by lot and lots continued to be cast over the goats (Lev. 16:8) on the Day of Atonement (SB II 596 f.). Lots could be used in legal actions (Prov. 18:18). Captives and booty could be divided by lot among the victors (Joel 3:3 [MT 4:3]; Obad. 11; Nah. 3:10; Ps. 22:18 [MT 22:19]). Even in a later, more sophisticated period it was recognized that God controlled the lot (Prov. 16:33).

2. Of special significance is the relationship of casting lots and the settlement of the land. Two different conceptions emerge in the OT.

(a) The one is clearly derived from cultic circles. It maintains that the land is Yahweh's inheritance (e.g. 1 Sam. 26:19; Jer. 2:7; Ezek. 38:16; Joel 1:6; Pss. 68:9 [MT 68:10]; 79:1) in which he lives and should be worshipped (Jos. 22:19; Exod. 15:17). The idea that the land is God's property is found generally in the cultic systems of Israel's neighbours and appears in the Baal cultus. It is, however, very difficult to derive the OT concept from its Canaanite background. "The notion that Yahweh is the true owner of the land can be traced to the very oldest commandments of Yahweh, and was evidently current at a time when syncretism with the features of Canaanite religion had not even begun to appear" (G. von Rad, *The Problem of the Hexateuch and Other Essays*, 1966, 88). In the OT the landowner is no mythical deity like Baal linked with the soil, but the God who acts in history, who brought his people out of → Egypt, and chose them from among the other peoples (Deut. 32:8 f.; 1 Ki. 8:51, 53). Hence, we frequently find the statement that not merely the land but also Israel itself is God's heritage (e.g. Deut. 9:26–29; 2 Ki. 21:14; Isa. 19:25; 47:6; Jer. 10:16 = 51:19; Mic. 7:18; Joel 2:17 f.; Pss. 33:12; 74:2). It is also expressed by saying that Israel is God's property (s²gullāh, Exod. 19:5; Deut. 7:6; 14:2; 26:18). Sometimes it is not clear whether Israel or the land is meant, for land and people belong so closely together by God's appointment (cf. 2 Sam. 14:16, cf. Joel 3:2 [MT 4:2]).

(b) However, the other, more historical idea is the predominant conception in the OT. The land is Israel's heritage which had been promised by God already to → Abraham and the patriarchs and was given to Israel through conquest. Under Joshua, Israel took possession of the land from God, conquering it and dividing it by lot (e.g. Num. 26:52–56; Jos. 13:19). The → Levites also had their cities apportioned to them by lot (1 Chr. 6:54–81 [MT 6:39–65]). The conclusion to the division of the land is given by Jos. 21:43 ff. Since the land is God's, God's regulations should control it. Israel is called to keep God's → commandments, in order to live and remain in the land (Deut. 30:15–20; Jos. 22:1–5; cf. Jer. 7:1–7).

The recurring statement that the priests and Levites have "no portion or inheritance with their brothers; the Lord is their inheritance" (Deut. 10:9; 18:1 f.; 12:12; Num. 18:20; Jos. 13:14, cf. Ezek. 44:28) calls for special attention in this context. In the first instance it states a regulation for the Levites' livelihood, giving them a share in the offerings and cultic gifts. Yet through the example of the Levites Israel is to learn that God's people must not seek safety and security through the land but only in the Lord and giver of the land, Yahweh.

The affirmations of faith in the Pss. that God is the comfort and portion of the one who prays contain the same thought (73:25 f.; 142:5 [MT 142:6]; Lam. 3:24). "The Lord is my chosen portion and my cup; thou holdest my lot. The lines have fallen for me in pleasant places; yea, I have a goodly heritage" (Ps. 16:5 f.). In the last analysis, such affirmations of faith go back to the promise to → Abraham to whom God promised not merely descendants and land, but also that he himself would be his shield and exceeding great reward (Gen. 15:1 RV). This promise was fulfilled in the conquest, but was not exhausted by it.

The message of the post-exilic prophets links these two groups of statements, showing that God stands by his promises. Even though the people have been exiled the land and its mountains remain theirs. The Lord will give it anew to his people (Ezek. 36 f.). Once again it will be divided by lot (Ezek. 45:1; 47:13 f.; 48:29; Isa. 49:8). Aliens also will receive their portion (Ezek. 47:22 f.).

The OT statements may have many strata and may frequently interlock, but there is always a link between the conquest and the lot. Moreover, it always testifies to Yahweh's action in history among his people whom he chose and to whom he gave the land by lot. According to Jos. 13–19, it was divided by lot among the tribes after Israel had conquered it at God's command. After the death of Joshua the allotted land had to be claimed by conquest from the Canaanites (Jdg. 1:3). The land was always seen as a possession and heritage given by God. This explains also the regulations for the sabbatical year and the year of jubilee (Lev. 25) providing for the restoration of property and slaves, for the land is Yahweh's property and is therefore subject to his claims and regulations.

3. The terms used in the OT to express these ideas are *gôrāl*, lot; *yāraš*, to possess; and especially *naḥᵃlâh*, possession, inheritance, heritage. The LXX renders *gôrāl* almost always by *klēros*. For *naḥᵃlâh* it uses mainly *klēros*, lot, portion, and *klēronomia*, inheritance. *yāraš* and its derivatives are represented by *klēronomeō* inherit, acquire, obtain, come into possession of, *klēros* and *klēronomia*.

For the other Heb. concepts (e.g. *ḥēleq*, portion, share; *sᵉgullâh*, property; *ḥebel*, portion of ground), the LXX uses also *meris*, share, *periousios*, one's own, chosen, especial, *schoinisma*, piece of land measured by a measuring-line, an allotted piece of land. Clearly the concept *naḥᵃlâh*, inheritance, best represents the relationship of Israel to the land given it by God, because it gives expression to the element of having received a present, to the inalienable vocation, and above all to the plan and the action in history behind it.

4. What is the difference between *klēros* and *klēronomia*? Sometimes both terms are used interchangeably for *naḥᵃlâh* (e.g. Num. 18:23 f.; 32:18 f.; Jos. 17:4; cf. Jdg. 2:9). However, *klēros*, which meant originally lot, stresses more the individual piece of land allotted by lot, whereas *klēronomia* points more to the fact of inheritance with all its connotations already mentioned. *klēros* may be used in the plural, but *klēronomia* is never so used. *klēronomia* has the richer associations in the context of salvation history.

5. In late Judaism *gôrāl* came to be used for the individual's fate in the last day (cf. already Isa. 57:6; Dan. 12:13), more or less in the sense of the heritage of the righteous. The rabbis spoke of inheriting the land (cf. Ps. 37:9, 22, 29), the coming age, future reward, the garden of Eden, and also Gehenna (→ Hell). Here we meet the thought of rewards (SB I 829, 981; IV, 2 1116).

6. In the Qumran writings *gôrāl*, lot, assumes a central position. Here it denotes the fate predestinated by God (1QS 2:17; 1QM 13:9), signifying either that one belongs to God, the sons of light, the spirits of knowledge, etc., or to Belial, the sons of darkness and its spirits. Hence it has the meaning of adherents, party (1QS 2:2, 5; 1QH 3:22, 24 f.; 1QM 1:1, 5, 11; 4:2; 13:2–5). From this comes almost the meaning class, rank (1QS 1:10; 2:23; CD 13:12). "To cast the lot" often means to determine a person's fate or even to judge (1QS 4:26; 1QH 3:22). When the term *naḥᵃlâh* is used, it has overtones of double predestination and the eschatological outlook of the Qumran community (1QS 4:15 ff.; 1QH 14:19; 17:15), though sometimes it bears the OT meaning (1QM 10:15; 19:4).

An important concept for the NT background is the belief that the community shared in the lot of the holy ones, i.e. → angels (1QS 11:7 f., 1 QH 3:21 f.; 11:11 f.; 1QSb 4:25 f.). Angels were believed to be present in the camp of the community (1QM 7:6; 12:1 f.; 1QSa 2:8 f.). But the elect on earth could also be called holy ones (e.g. 1QSb 4:23) and similarly the community "the people of the saints of the covenant, instructed in the laws and learned in wisdom ... who have heard the voice of Majesty and have seen the Angels of Holiness" (1QM 10:10 f.; cf. Vermes, *Scrolls*, 136 f.). Behind this lies the idea that the earthly community is incorporated into the community of the angels, and has thus obtained the spiritual riches belonging to the angels.

The reception of novices was made dependent on "the decision [lot] of the Council of the Congregation" (1QS 6:16, cf. 18, 21). Though the word "lot" is used, it is doubtful whether casting of lots is really meant, though this is found in CD 13:4 and 1QS 5:3 (cf. A. R. C. Leaney, *The Rule of Qumran and its Meaning*, 1966, 166 f.). Nor is it clear whether the testing of the novices was believed to reveal how God had determined their lot in heaven. For that could be recognized by a man's behaviour on earth (CD 20:3 f.).

NT *klēros* occurs in 10 passages in the NT.

1. *klēros* in the lit. sense of lot. All four Gospels state that the soldiers cast lots for Jesus' garments at the crucifixion (Matt. 27:35; Mk. 15:24; Lk. 23:34; Jn. 19:24; cf. also Barn. 6:6). Jn. sees it explicitly as a fulfilment of Ps. 22:18 [21:19] ("they divide my garments among them, and for my raiment they cast lots"). It represents the ultimate degradation of a human being. The Psalm is an expression of desolation (on its significance in connection with Jesus' passion → God, art. *theos* NT 6 (d)). But in it the Psalmist recognizes that it is God who is in control and who alone can give help: "But thou, O Lord, be not far off! O thou my help, hasten to my aid" (Ps. 22:19). The Gospel accounts of the passion see God himself behind the events and Jesus as the one who fulfils the descriptions of the Psalmist.

Acts 1:26 records that the final decision as to which of the two candidates, Joseph called Barsabbas, who was surnamed Justus, or Matthias, should fill Judas' place among the twelve → apostles, was determined by lot. Both candidates met the necessary qualifications of being a member of the company who had followed Jesus throughout his earthly ministry and of being a witness of Jesus' resurrection (Acts 1:21 f.). The lots were cast following the prayer: "Lord, who knowest the hearts of all men, show which one of these two thou hast chosen to take the place in this ministry [*diakonia*] and apostleship [*apostolē*] from which Judas turned aside to go to his own place" (Acts 1:24 f.). Earlier Judas is referred to as having been "numbered among us, and was allotted his share [*klēros*] in this ministry [*diakonia*]" (v. 17). Here *klēros* is used in its other main sense. There is a profound sense of divine overruling throughout. The vb. used in Acts 1:26, *edōkan* (lit. "they gave" lots) rather than the expected *ebalon* ("they cast"), has given rise to the suggestion that the matter was put to a vote (cf. F. J. Foakes Jackson and K. Lake, eds., *The Beginnings of Christianity*, I IV, 1933, 15). This seems to be the interpretation of the Western text of Acts. But "to give a lot" is a Heb. idiom (F. F. Bruce, *The Acts of the Apostles*, 1952², 80). E. Haenchen points out that in this procedure "The human factor is excluded: it is God who is choosing" (*The Acts of the Apostles*, 1971, 162). On the procedure cf. 1 Sam. 14:41 LXX; 1 Chron. 26:14; Prov. 16:33; SB II 596.

klēroō occurs once in the NT. Lit. it means to appoint by lot. It occurs in Eph. 1:11 in the clause *en hō eklērōthēmen* (lit. "in whom our lot is cast", cf. Arndt, 436). The RV, however, takes the vb. in the sense of 2 below: "in whom we were made a heritage, having been foreordained, according to the purpose of him who worketh all things after the counsel of his will". *proskleroō* means allot, assign, and in the pass. to be attached to, join. It is in this latter sense that it is used in Acts 17:4, where it has lost its etymological overtones.

2. *klēros* and *klēronomia* as inheritance. With the meaning share, inheritance, *klēros* is found 4 times in the NT. *klēronomia* is found 14 times; *klēronomos*, heir, 15; *synklēronomos*, fellow heir, 4; *klēronomeō*, inherit, 18 times; and *kataklēronomeō*, give as an inheritance, once. The words occur in the Synoptic Gospels, the Pauline Epistles, 1 Pet., frequently in Heb., and once in Rev. Apart from *klēros* in the sense of lot, the whole group is absent from the Johannine writings. In Lk. 12:13 *klēronomia* has the basic secular sense of inheritance. Elsewhere (and perhaps even here) it has theological overtones influenced by the OT. *kataklēronomeō* occurs in Paul's review at Pisidian Antioch of salvation history in his reference to the seven Canaanite nations whose land God gave Israel as an inheritance (Acts 13:19; cf. Deut. 7:1; Jos. 14:1).

(a) The concept of inheritance has soteriological and eschatological dimensions. It is linked with God's historical saving acts. The idea of possession of the promised land passes beyond its first fulfilment in history to its later historical fulfilment in Christ and beyond that to the future final fulfilment at the end of time. It is in this way that the eschatological tendency found already in the OT is worked out. The essential thought is that of inheriting the promise to which believers are called. According to various different strata of NT witness, the object of this promise, the *naḥᵃlâh* in the OT, is the kingdom of God (1 Cor. 6:9; 15:50a; Gal. 5:21; Eph. 5:5; Matt. 25:34; Jas. 2:5). In the Beatitudes, Jesus puts side by side the promise of the kingdom of heaven and that of inheriting the → earth (*gē*; Matt. 5:5; cf. 5:10). By this he indicated that the promised land of the OT is replaced by the all-embracing concept of the → kingdom of God. This kingdom embraces all those promises the fulfilment of which is yet future. This is shown when we look at the other things promised as an inheritance in the NT: eternal life (Matt. 19:29; Lk. 18:18; Tit. 3:7); salvation (Heb. 1:14); the imperishable (order) (1 Cor. 15:50b); an inheritance, imperishable, undefiled, unfading, kept in heaven (1 Pet. 1:4); the → blessing (Heb. 12:17; 1 Pet. 3:9); the → promises (Heb. 6:12; 10:36); or as in Rev. 21:7 "these things" (RV, NEB "all this"). In these statements OT thought is retained and at the same time transformed (Rom. 4:13 ff.; Heb. 6:17; cf. Acts 7:5; 13:19).

(b) This inheritance, however, is not merely future. It can be recognized already now in faith (Eph. 1:18). According to Heb. 11:7, → Noah inherited the righteousness which comes by faith. In Eph. 1:11–14 we are told that "we have been given our share in the heritage" (NEB v. 11; cf. section 1 above) and have the guarantee of this inheritance in the Holy Spirit whom we have received. The first at least of the Beatitudes suggests that the poor in spirit already possess the kingdom of heaven even though its full realization, like that of the remaining Beatitudes, lies in the future (Matt. 5:3; cf. Lk. 6:20; → Poor).

(c) The fact that salvation is future and yet present comes from our being inheritors through Jesus Christ (Eph. 1:11 f.) and his death (Heb. 9:15). He who has come and will come again, has brought us the inheritance. Indeed, he is the inheritance and the kingdom (cf. the OT statements about the heritage of the Levites and the expressions of faith in Pss.). Through him we are fellow-heirs (Rom. 8:17).

300

The parable of the tenants of the vineyard (Matt. 21:33-41 par. Mk. 12:1-12, Lk. 20:9-19; cf. Isa. 5:1-7) shows Jesus as the heir, and introduces the OT concept of the → remnant. Yahweh has chosen Israel as his people. It is his vineyard and inheritance. He gave it the land, but it had been disobedient. Now there was only a remnant. This remnant, repeatedly referred to by the prophets, is ultimately a single individual, Jesus, the Son. But through him the remnant grows into a great multitude of believers who are fellow-heirs. Thus the rich young ruler should have become an heir with him of eternal life (Matt. 19:16-30, par. Mk. 10:17-31; Lk. 18:18-30).

Alongside the witness of the Synoptics is that of Paul who gives special prominence to the connection between the promise to → Abraham and the church as the heir in Christ. In Rom. 4:13 Paul declares that "through the righteousness of faith" the promise to Abraham that he should inherit the world becomes ours. In the faith that we share in Christ we become heirs. If this depended on the → law and not on Christ, "faith is made void [*kekenōtai*]" (Rom. 4:14 RV). He who is Christ's is Abraham's offspring and so his heir (Gal. 3:29; cf. 4:1, 7; Tit. 3:7).

Heb. develops this testimony. By an oath to Abraham God promised salvation "to the heirs of the promise" (6:17; → Swear). They already have the future inheritance, but only in hope (6:18). They inherit it as did Abraham "through faith and patience" (6:12). The one who has opened the way to this promise is Jesus (6:20). He is the son and heir (1:2, 4). The stress in Heb. is rather different from that in Paul. The future nature of the heritage and the need to hold fast to the promise are more strongly emphasized, but the basic concept is the same. In Heb. 11:7, just as in Paul, faith is seen as believing and acting on the word of God. It is by this that Noah became "an heir of the righteousness which comes by faith" (cf. Rom. 4:3; Gal. 3:6; Gen. 15:6).

Jas. 2:5 echoes the teaching of the Synoptics. It treats the question of the heirs of the kingdom, even though the relationship to Jesus, through whom we become heirs, is not expressed. "Has not God chosen those who are poor in the world to be rich in faith and heirs of the kingdom which he has promised to those who love him?" There is a firm link between → election, → promise and inheritance throughout the NT.

(d) Since Jesus is the heir and also the one who has given himself for us, we cannot have this inheritance except in relation to him. This involves practical obedience (Heb. 11:8), and demands patient endurance (Heb. 6:12). Without it we shall not inherit the kingdom of God (Gal. 5:21; 1 Cor. 15:50a). In his parable of the final judgment (Matt. 25:31-46) Jesus shows how this relationship to him involves love in our dealings with others through whom he comes to us (cf. the parable of the Good Samaritan [Lk. 10:25-37]). Jesus' conversation with the rich young ruler also shows that eternal life can be inherited only in the obedience of faith, by those who follow Jesus (Matt. 19:29; Mk. 10:29; cf. Lk. 18:29).

Because Jesus has appointed us as heirs, we are not merely fellow-heirs with him but also joint heirs with each other (1 Pet. 3:7). This involves our relationship with others (1 Pet. 3:9), as is shown in the two parables mentioned in the previous paragraph and also in the one of the unforgiving servant (Matt. 18:23-35; cf. 6:15). This obedience in faith is neither work to acquire merit (as with the rabbis) nor a burden (as the rich young ruler imagined). It is the concomitant of faith

301

which is required to possess the salvation of God and his Son (1 Jn. 5:12; 2:23; 2 Jn. 9; → Possessions). Jesus' call to follow him is in itself a gift of eternal life, the kingdom of God and fellowship with him. Col. 3:24 speaks of receiving "the inheritance as your reward." But the passage makes it clear that this is not earned as of right but a gift of God which is still to be appropriated. As Paul puts it in Gal. 3:18: "God gave it to Abraham by a promise."

(e) Finally, the NT makes it clear that the inheritance of the promise is not only for God's chosen people → Israel. Through Christ the Gentiles have become fellow-heirs with them. Paul stresses again and again that in Christ all believers without distinction are children of God and inheritors of the promise (Gal. 3:23–29; cf. 4:30; Rom. 4:13 f.). This sharing in the inheritance by the Gentiles is clearly expressed in Eph., Col. and Acts. In Eph. 3:6 the Gentiles are fellow-heirs in Christ through the gospel. Eph. 1:3–14 contains an exposition of how the church received its inheritance in Christ. He is the ground and instrument of the whole of God's plan of salvation [oikonomia, v. 10]. The election of all believers before the foundation of the world is based on him (v. 4). In him they have redemption through his blood (v. 7), standing as sons, and hence a share in the inheritance, to the praise of his grace. The Gentiles share in it; cf. the change of "we" (v. 11 f.) to "you" (v. 13) and the stressed "also", suggesting Paul's identification of himself with the Jewish people and the inclusion of Gentile believers alongside of Jewish believers in the Ephesian church (cf. also Eph. 2:1–3:6).

According to Acts 26:15–18, Paul was commissioned by the risen Lord to open the eyes of the Gentiles, that they may turn from darkness to light that they may receive forgiveness of sins and an inheritance (RSV "place", klēros not klēronomia) among those who are sanctified by faith in Christ. The language perhaps recalls that of the Qumran community with its idea of the community of the last days sharing with the holy ones (→ angels) in light (cf. Acts 20:32; Eph. 1:18). The "holy ones" in the Qumran texts can, however, also mean the community of the last days, and the term "holy ones" or "saints" (hagioi) was applied to the early church (→ Holy). However we understand this, the passage contains the revolutionary thought that the Gentiles obtain a share in this "lot" through faith in Jesus Christ. Col. 1:12 also perhaps contains another reminder of Qumran concepts. The Gentile church in Colossae has a "share in the inheritance [merida tou klērou] of the holy ones in light" (cf. 1QS 11:7, 8; but the expression is found already in the LXX, e.g. Deut. 10:9; Num. 18:20; Ps. 15:5, where, however, klēronomia stands instead of klēros). For the walk in light see Ps. 56:13 (MT 56:14); Isa. 2:5; 60:1 ff. See further E. Lohse, Colossians and Philemon, 1951, 35 ff. On meris → meros.

OT and Qumran phraseology is found also in Acts 8:21, when John and Peter have to deny Simon Magus "part or lot in this word" i.e. the gospel. The expression is here a formula of excommunication (E. Haenchen, op. cit., 305, who notes formal resemblance with Deut. 12:12; 14:27; Ps. 77:37 LXX). In Acts 17:4 the term prosklēroō has become so weakened that we may accept RSV rendering, "Some of them . . . joined Paul and Silas"; yet behind this watered down linguistic usage there is the thought that a great many of the devout Greeks and some leading women in Thessalonica had through God obtained a share in the promised heritage and had been placed in it. In 1 Pet. 5:3 the plur. klēroi (RSV "your charge") probably means the local church in its several parts or districts (fixed by lot?).

E. G. Selwyn takes it to refer to "spheres of pastoral care" and notes a possible allusion to Deut. 9:29 (*The First Epistle of Peter*, 1947², 231).

(f) We can probably best explain John's omission to use the concept of inheritance by the stress of his witness on the present nature and universality of salvation in Christ rather than on the eschatological fulfilment of salvation history. Since he is battling against the unbelief of the Jews, it is more important for him to stress what the church possesses in Christ than what it is to inherit. Perhaps Rev. 21 summarizes best what the NT has to say about the inheritance: the kingdom of God, the eternal glory without death, suffering and sin, God himself the Father and ourselves his sons through faith in Christ – that is the inheritance, not merely for the individual, but also for the whole church.   *J. Eichler*

| μέρος | μέρος (*meros*), part, share, portion, lot; μερίς (*meris*), part, portion. |

CL From 5th cent. B.C. *meros* is found in secular Gk. with many shades of meaning.
It could be said to supersede *moira*, lot, portion, part, share, which though very frequently found from Homer on, came to be confined to the power of the deities to determine fate. Moira was, in fact, the goddess of fate. *meros* means a part, e.g. of the body, a landscape, a territory, especially, in the plur., a locality, or party. Metaphorically it means a share, a concern, a social class; in Koine Gk. also business. It often stands in adverbial phrases with prepositions: *ana meros*, *apo merous*, *ek merous*, *kata meros* (cf. *meros ti*), the meanings of which can no longer be sharply separated with absolute certainty. We find examples of "one after another", "partly", "specially", and "partially" for each of them.

OT In the LXX *meros* represents a number of Heb. words, especially *qāṣeh* and its cognates. Here too it means a part (*ḥᵃmîšît*, Gen. 47:24). Its commonest use is to express locality: e.g. border (Exod. 16:35; Jos. 18:19 f.), area of land (Jos. 2:18; 1 Sam. 30:14), end, edge (Jos. 13:27; 15:2). When things are being described, *meros* means side (e.g. Exod. 26:26 f.; 32:15). In Prov. 17:2 it is a share in an inheritance, and in 2 Macc. 15:20 a place.
meris also stands for several Heb. nouns, especially *ḥēleq* (e.g. Gen. 14:24; 31:14; Deut. 10:9; 12:12; 18:1, 8; 32:9; Jos. 14:4; 15:13; Pos. 50[49]:18; 73[72]:26; 119[118]:57; 142[141]:5), *ḥelqâh* (e.g. Gen. 33:19; 2 Sam. 2:16; 14:30), *mānâh* (e.g. Exod. 29:26; Lev. 7:33[23]), and *mᵉnāṭ* (e.g. Neh. 12:44, 47; 13:10).

NT In the NT *meros* means a part of the body, an estate, or dress (Lk. 11:36; 15:12; Jn. 19:23), the side of a boat (Jn. 21:6), a party, e.g. of Pharisees or Sadducees (Acts 23:6, 9). Often it denotes a district or place (Matt. 2:22; 15:21). The meaning of "the lower [or lowest] parts of the earth" (Eph. 4:9) is uncertain. It could mean Jesus' descent among the dead in death (F. Büchsel, *TDNT* III 641), or his coming down to the earth (M. Dibelius, *An die Epheser*, *HNT* 12, 1953³ ad loc.). In spite of Büchsel's impressive argument an element of uncertainty remains.
meros means occupation or trade in Acts 19:27, and case or matter in 2 Cor. 3:10; 9:3. In the story of the feet washing, Jesus says to Peter: "If I do not wash

303

you, you have no part in me" (NEB, better: "you are not in fellowship with me", Jn. 13:8). This sharing is enjoyed by the Christian, if he is a living member of the body, the church (1 Cor. 12:27; Eph. 4:16; → Body; → Fellowship). One can also have one's share or place with the hypocrites and godless (Matt. 24:51; Lk. 12:46). It depends on which group one is a member of whether one has a share in the first resurrection and the tree of life (Rev. 20:6; 22:19) or in the lake that burns with → fire, the second → death (Rev. 21:8).

   meros is used adverbially in the expression *apo merous* (Rom. 11:25) of the "partial hardening" (NEB) that has come upon Israel. This rendering preserves the Gk. better than the RSV: "a hardening has come upon part of Israel" (→ Hard; cf. also O. Glombitza, "Apostolische Sorge. Welche Sorge treibt den Apostel Paulus zu den Sätzen Rom. 11, 25 ff. ?", *NovT* 7, 1965, 312–18). *apo merous* means "on some points" (Rom. 15:15), "in part" (2 Cor. 1:14) and "for a while" and "to some degree" (2 Cor. 2:5) (cf. Arndt, 507). The precise shade of meaning is determined by context. *ana meros* means "one after the other" (1 Cor. 14:27). *ek merous* means "individually" (1 Cor. 12:27), and "in part" (1 Cor. 13:9 f., 12), where Paul is stressing the incomplete, fragmentary and transitory character of → knowledge in contrast with → love. When the perfect comes, the imperfect will pass away (1 Cor. 13:10). *en merei* means "with regard to" (Col. 2:16), and *kata meros* (Heb. 9:5) "point by point".

   meris means part, in the sense of a district (Acts 16:12) and share or portion in Lk. 10:42; Acts 8:21 (cf. Deut. 12:12); 2 Cor. 6:15 ("What accord has Christ with Belial? Or what has a believer in common with an unbeliever?"); and Col. 1:12 (→ *klēros*, NT 2 (e)).   W. Mundle
→ Covenant, → Earth, Land, World, → Israel, → Levite

(a). Arndt, 435 f., 506 f.; O. J. Baab, "Inheritance", *IDB* II 701 ff.; E. M. Blaiklock, "Inheritance" *ZPEB* III 277 ff.; A. M. Brown, *The Concept of Inheritance in the Old Testament* (Dissertation, Columbia, New York) 1965; F. Büchsel, *katō*, *TDNT* III 640 ff.; W. D. Davies, *The Gospel and the Land: Early Christianity and Jewish Territorial Doctrine*, 1974; J. Herrmann and W. Foerster, *klēros*, *TDNT* III 758–85; J. D. Hester, "The 'Heir' and *Heilsgeschichte*: A Study of Gal. 4, 1 ff.", in *Oikonomia. Festschrift O. Cullmann*, 1967, 118–25; and *Paul's Concept of Inheritance*, *SJT* Occasional Papers, 9, 1968; M. Noth, *The Laws of the Pentateuch and Other Studies*, 1966; W. Pesch, "Inheritance", *EBT* II 394–98; G. von Rad, *Theology of the Old Testament*, I, 1962, 296–305; and "The Promised Land and Yahweh's Land", in *The Problem of the Hexateuch and Other Essays*, 1966, 79–93; J. Schneider, *meros*, *TDNT* III 594–98.

(b). J. Benzinger, *Hebräische Archäologie*, 1927³, 392 ff.; P. Diepold, *Israels Land* BWANT 95, 1972; F. Dreyfus, "Le thème de l'héritage dans l'Ancien Testament", *Revue des Sciences Philosophiques et Théologiques* 42, 1958, 3–49; G. Hölscher, *Geschichte der israelitischen und jüdischen Religion*, 1922; G. Lanczkowski, "Los", *RGG*³ IV 451; F. Nötscher, *Biblische Altertumskunde*, 1940, 133 ff.; SB I 829; II 596; III 625; H. H. Schmid, *yāraš*, *THAT* I 778–81.

Israel, Jew, Hebrew, Jacob, Judah

| 'Ισραήλ | 'Ισραήλ (*Israēl*), Israel; 'Ισραηλίτης (*Israēlitēs*), Israelite; 'Ιουδαῖος (*Ioudaios*), Jew; 'Ιουδαϊκῶς (*Ioudaikōs*), Jewish; 'Εβραῖος (*Hebraios*), Hebrew (noun); 'Εβραΐς (*Hebraïs*), Hebrew (fem. adj.). |

ot 1. *Etymology and First Occurrence*. The name Israel (Heb. *yiśrā'ēl*) is formed from the noun *'ēl* (God) and a verbal predicate. An explanation of it is given in

Gen. 32:28 in the context of the story of Jacob (→ *Iakōb*) wrestling with God: "Your name shall no more be called Jacob, but Israel, for you have striven with God and with men, and have prevailed" (cf. Hos. 12:4). Hence, the name has been interpreted to mean *He who strives with God*, the vb. being *šārar*, to rule, or *šārâh*, contend, fight. This interpretation seems to be supported by the story. However, elsewhere *'ēl* is never the object in proper names, but is always the subject. Hence, the interpretation *God strives* has also been put forward. *'ēl* is a generic name for → God in Heb., as contrasted with the proper name Yahweh. (For further discussion of suggested explanations see G. A. Danell, *Studies in the Name Israel in the Old Testament*, 1946, 22–28.)

For the personal history of Israel → *Iakōb*. Israel was used as a personal name (e.g. Gen. 50:2; Exod. 1:1; 1 Chron. 1:34). But it was also used as a tribal and national name: "the sons of Israel" (Lev. 1:2; Jdg. 2:4); "the → house of Israel" (Exod. 40:38; 1 Sam. 7:2; Isa. 46:3), a term specifically applied to the northern kingdom (1 Ki. 12:21; Hos. 5:1; Amos 5:1; Mic. 1:5), but which was also used as a title of honour for the southern kingdom (Isa. 5:7; Jer. 10:1) (cf. Koehler-Baumgartner, 407 f.). The earliest external reference to the Israelites outside the OT occurs in an inscription on a pillar set up by Merneptah, king of Egypt, c. 1220 B.C., to celebrate his victories. In it he boasts: "Israel lies desolate; its seed is no more" (cf. D. Winton Thomas, ed., *Documents from Old Testament Times*, 1958, 139, see also plate 8; text also in *ANET*, 376 ff.). In the opinion of C. Virolleaud, Israel occurs as a personal name at Ugarit (*Le Palais Royal d'Ugarit*, V, 1965, 69, 3).

Judah (Heb. *yᵉhûdâh*) occurs as a geographical term to denote the mountainous desert region south of Jerusalem (Jos. 20:7; 21:11; Jdg. 1:16; Ps. 63:1). The tribe which settled there bore the name of Judah, the son of Jacob and Leah (Gen. 29:35). The precise etymology is uncertain, though Gen. 29:35 suggests a link with *yādâh*, praise, in Leah's remark on the birth of her son, "'This time I will praise the Lord'; therefore she called his name Judah." The three first root letters (*yhw*) could contain the divine name. The Heb. words *yᵉhûdî* and *yᵉhûdît* (fem.), Judaean, and the Gk. *Ioudaios*, Jewish, Jew and *Ioudaia*, Judea refer particularly to the place of origin.

Hebrew (Heb. *'ibrî*; Gk. *Hebraios*) is an old word of uncertain meaning. The Hebrews no doubt belong linguistically and in reality to the Habiru people who are frequently mentioned in Babylonian, Ugaritic and Egyptian texts of the mid 2nd cent. Like the Accadian *Khabiru* and the Egyptian root *'pr*, the biblical word is a legal term. It denoted people of equal social standing without regard to their ethnic origins (their personal names derive from a variety of linguistic areas), who, not having a permanent home or possessions, entered the service of the settled population on a contractual basis (servants in Egypt, 1 Sam. 14:21). In closely knit groups, forerunners of the tribes, these nomadic shepherds penetrated the arable land. The native Canaanites perhaps called them the *'ēber* people, the "outlanders" (e.g. Gen. 14:13), because they had come from *'ēber*, from the (land) beyond, i.e. from the eastern and southern steppes. Hence, the word Hebrew was used by other peoples in the old stories sometimes in a derogatory manner, sometimes by Israel in dealings with foreigners in a self-deprecating manner (Gen. 40:15; 43:32; Exod. 1:15–19; 2:11–13; 3:18, God of the Hebrews; 1 Sam. 4:6, 9; 13:3,

305

19; 29:3). Certain passages are sometimes taken to imply that the term Hebrew was used for a dependent, economically weak people, a group contrasting with those in Israel who were free (Exod. 21:2; Deut. 15:12; Jer. 34:9, 14).

2. *Israel and Judah in the Course of History.* (a) Early history. After the occupation of the land by the house of Joseph the small band of tribes (the sons of Leah?) expanded into a league of twelve tribes (→ People, art. *phylē*), a cultic, non-political community of those whom the God of Israel had chosen (Jos. 24). Under the pressure exerted by the Philistines, the defence forces of the individual tribes were no longer sufficient. Saul, having been elected king (1 Sam. 9–12), demanded military service, united the tribes politically (at least in the north), and thereby founded a state to which was transferred the name of the sacral twelve tribe league, Israel. This double basis in religion and politics set up at the very outset a tension which was to run through and determine Israel's history.

Israel, the northern state, exercised autonomy in religion and politics for a good 200 years after David's united kingdom was split following the death of Solomon. The God of Israel was worshipped at the sanctuaries of Bethel and Dan. In 733 and 722 Assyria defeated Israel (cf. 2 Ki. 15–17). (Israel was also called Ephraim by the contemporary prophets, e.g. Isa. 7:1–9, after the central region associated with the name of the younger of the two sons of Joseph [Gen. 40:50 ff.]. Ephraim and Manasseh were counted as tribes equal with the tribes descended from the sons of Jacob.) As the result of deportations and the mingling of the remainder of the inhabitants with newly settled people (which had the express intention of producing a cultural and religious syncretism) there arose the Assyrian province of Samaria (→ Samaritan).

Judah, the kingdom which David had created from the southern tribes, survived the northern kingdom by about one and a half centuries, partly no doubt on account of its dynastic basis and its more skilful politics. Under Babylonian overlordship things went much better for Judah than formerly for the northern kingdom under Assyria. Thus under the Persians the division of Judah could be reversed.

The southern kingdom received important theological support. Isaiah, continuing the line of earlier court prophets, glorified the → Davidic dynasty in Zion. By taking over the name Israel for the southern kingdom after the fall of the northern kingdom, he defined theological hopes in accordance with actual political circumstances. The sphere of salvation was narrowed down to the remnant, Judah. At the same time, the state of Judah acquired a new worth through the old name with its traditional associations (cf. Isa. 24–28).

By contrast with this Zionism with its accent on Judah's present, Jeremiah presented a theology of dispersion which was open to God's future. He retained the name Israel for the northern kingdom which had already been destroyed a century ago. Without prejudice to Josiah's attempt to restore the state of Israel (2 Ki. 23), Jeremiah proclaimed that the old Israel was finished. Nevertheless, God would one day recreate from it his people. They would be a community which, as in olden times so now in the end-time, would once again be stateless (cf. 3:11 ff.; 31; 37:7 ff.). On the pattern of the time of → Moses, God would draw up a new → covenant with them, this time writing the commandments in their hearts (Jer. 31:31–34). These hopes for Israel meant, however, that Jeremiah had to announce judgment and destruction for the state of Judah which he loved and for which he pleaded before God (Jer. 14 ff.). The human and political defences had to fall to make room for God's new creation.

(b) Israel before God in prophetic theology. God's relationship to Israel is expressed in a variety of metaphors: God is → father, → king, saviour (→ Redemption), guardian, refuge, comforter, dew. Correspondingly, Israel is a → son, bride, wife (→ Woman), → possession, vineyard, and → vine. These mostly personal terms indicate a relationship of partnership. God lets his beloved son know both what he does for him and what he requires of him (Deut. 10:12; also Mic. 6:8). Through such instruction, which is a wider concept than either → commandment or → law, Israel became the people that dwelt alone (Num. 23:9). It was distinguished and separated from all other peoples (Deut. 4:5–10). In the holy land of Israel this holy people was to live for the holy God in holiness (Lev. 11:44 f.; 19:2; 20:26; → Holy). Israel's → election was at the same time a commission. Although the least significant of the peoples (Deut. 7:7), Israel still had to be for them a prince and a light, a witness to God by his very existence (Isa. 43:8 ff.). Election meant loneliness, difference, renunciation, readiness to → suffer (Isa. 52:13–53:12), and a heavy → burden.

Israel continually ran the risk of falling back into Canaanite cults, succumbing to the temptations of her environment, and of wanting to be like the other peoples. This meant that the relationship of trust could be damaged from the human side, but not destroyed. For the covenant with Israel remained irrevocable for God's sake. To make this fact certain beyond all doubt, use was made of concepts taken from the realm of law: God will not abandon his legal claim on Israel (Amos 9:1 ff.); nor will he publish a bill of → divorce (Isa. 50:1). Lest his name be blasphemed among the heathen for faithlessness, God remained true to the oath which he swore to the fathers (Ezek. 20:9, 14, 22; Deut. 7:8). Even → judgment is a sign of his faithfulness. Through God's servants the → prophets of Israel (Ezek. 38:17) who intercede to the point of self-immolation (Exod. 32:32; Jer. 30 f.), Israel is warned, and threatened and comforted. But in all this we have only different forms of the same invitation to repentance. God's own faithfulness to the covenant makes it possible for Israel to be purified and the covenant relationship renewed. The hope of the restoration of the whole of Israel does not rest on Israel's righteousness but on God's love to the fathers (Exod. 32:11–14; Deut. 9:5), and his freedom which chose Israel contrary to all expectations (Ezek. 16:59–63).

(c) The struggle for Israel in the post-exilic period. Shortly after the return of the exiles from Babylon the prophets announced a turning point in the coming of salvation (cf. Hag. 2:20–23; Zech. 6:9–15). But three generations later Ezra and Nehemiah saw in these semi-political dreams a danger to Israel's continued existence. The latter left to the Persians the management of political relations and concentrated on the internal building up of the covenant community in Jeremiah's sense on the basis of Holy Scripture. What had hitherto been the privilege of the priests now became a common possession (cf. Neh. 8).

From the time of Alexander the Great (356–323 B.C.) onwards Judaism lived under the influence of the pervading Hel. culture. However, as soon as adaptation to the environment threatened to lead to the abandonment of their particularity, resistance movements arose, principally on religious grounds. The successful Maccabean rebellion which broke out in 168 B.C. led once again, under the

Hasmoneans, to a compromise between self-consciousness and openness to the environment. This is shown by the coins with their bilingual inscriptions.

In the following period, after Pompey had captured Jerusalem and reduced the area (63 B.C.) the half-Jew Herod (37–4 B.C.; cf. Josephus, *Ant.* 14, 9, 2), reigned as king by favour of Rome, and procurators exploited and provoked the Jews. The distinction between the Jews and the surrounding nations became progressively sharper, until under the leadership of the Zealots there occurred a series of bloody conflicts with the Romans and the friends of Rome. This is illustrated by the inscriptions on the coins of the period: the revolutionary coinage of the years 66–70 and 132–135, partly overstampings of Roman coins, are inscribed in the old Heb. script as an indication of the return of Israel's original times in the present end-times. The inscriptions are more programmes than descriptions of reality: "Shekel of Israel", "Salvation of Zion", "For the freedom of Jerusalem", "First year of the salvation of Israel", "Second year of the freedom of Israel". The Roman inscription, however, runs: "Judaea capta" ("Conquered Judah"). (On the coins of the period see G. L. Archer, "Coins", *ZPEB* I 901–11; A. Reifenberg, *Ancient Jewish Coins*, 1947²; and *Israel's History in Coins from the Maccabees to the Roman Conquest*, 1953; L. Kadman *et al.*, *The Dating and Meaning of Ancient Jewish Coins*, 1958; E. Stauffer, *Christ and the Caesars*, 1955; → Possessions: Coins in the Bible and Theological Issues.)

After the exterminations of Jews of the dispersion under Trajan (A.D. 98–117) and the failure of the messiah Simon Bar Kokhba ("son of a star", cf. Num. 24:17) in A.D. 132, at the peak of the conflict, not only were those who remained faithful to the instruction to be exterminated, but the name of the people was to be obliterated. Hadrian decreed that Jerusalem should be a Roman colony to be known as *Aelia Capitolina* (after himself and Jupiter) and the land *Syria Palaestina* (Land of the Philistines).

Nevertheless, even under the most difficult conditions, remnant Jewish communities repeatedly migrated back. At first they even managed to maintain a certain cultural standing, as the Palestinian Talmud and the ruins of synagogues bear witness. Their overlords changed: Romans, Arabs, Crusaders, Turks and British came and went. In 1948, under the pressure of the terrible situation of the Jews and with the approval of world public opinion, there arose once again a state with the ancient name of Israel.

NT The inter-Testamental period and the NT era witnessed an intense struggle over the identity of the true Israel in the face of foreign rule, the competing groups within Judaism and the emergence of the church.

1. *Israel and its Environment.* Despite the many strata within it, Judaism was a relatively unified whole compared with the other peoples. As bearers of revelation in the struggle against the heathen even the early Jesus-groups recognized themselves as naturally on the side of Israel, or rather as belonging to Israel. Hence, the rise of the Christian church must be seen against the background of the competing groups within Judaism which were concerned with the identity and destiny of Israel.

(a) Israel's Hel. environment, with its striving for cultural unity, exercised on Judaism, especially in the dispersion, a powerful attraction. In good times it was possible to take over not only the language but also many Hel. manners, so long as they were not connected with a pagan cult and therefore incompatible with Jewish principles. This openness and recognition of the nations was expressed theologically in the acceptance of the first stages of a messianic humanity among them, "sons of → Noah" (who kept the principal commandments of Gen. 9:4; cf. Acts 15:28 ff.; Sanh. 56a–b) and the pious among the nations (Hullin 92a; Baba Kamma 38a). Through mission which had its theological roots in the universal claim of the one God who desires the salvation of all the nations (cf. the Songs of the Servant of Yahweh in Isa. 41 f. and 49), the tension between Israel and the nations was removed by the anticipation of the reunion expected in the end-time (Pesahim 87b; cf. 1 Cor. 12:13; Gal. 3:28).

Thus post-exilic Judaism became a missionary religion, ready to accept anyone who confessed the one God of Israel (→ One, art. *heis*). Success was great, especially among women who were not → circumcised but only baptized. About one in ten of the inhabitants of the Hel. Mediterranean world was a Jew, not by birth but by belief (cf. Sib. 3, 271; 1 Macc. 15:22 f.; Philo, *Flacc.* 45 f.; *Leg.Gai.* 281–283; Josephus, *War* 2, 19, 2; *Ant.* 14, 7, 2; Acts 2:9–11).

But this very openness, which was what the best among the nations found attractive about Judaism, also gave rise to hatred and persecutions. In times of crisis the position of Jews before the law worsened and enmity led to pogroms (like the persecutions under Trajan, A.D. 115–117). Jews were faced with the choice either of giving up their Jewishness and adopting the pagan gods and the cult of the emperor, or of renouncing the privilege of cultural and political equality. The result was that those who remained faithful to their community withdrew into a kind of ghetto existence, involving a separation that was neither national nor racial but completely religious in character. In order not to further the worship of idols, dealings with pagans were limited or, as in the 18 regulations which were introduced by the Shammaites before the rebellion of A.D. 66 (Shabbath 17a–b), almost completely prevented. As the theology of the Talmud shows, Pharisaism, based on the OT, made the whole of Israel immune to the damaging influences of Hel. anti-Jewish culture and gave it a self-consciousness which supplied the power to survive as a community for thousands of years amid the hatred and persecution of a hostile environment.

(b) The use of the terms relating to the Jews was determined by these conflicts. The word Hebrew (noun and adj.) has the most neutral meaning. It denotes in particular the language and the script, and then also the people who use them. In worship the Bible was read sentence by sentence in the Heb. original and then translated into current Aram. in the form of the Targums. Where it is used without any special significance, Hebrew frequently means the current Aramaic (Josephus *Ant.* 2, 13, 1; cf. also *Hebraïs* the Hebrew [language], Acts 21:40; 22:2; 26:14; *Hebraïsti*, in Hebrew, Jn. 5:2; 19:13, 17, 20; 20:16; Rev. 9:11; 16:16). In place of the ancient Heb. characters square characters were employed (even among the copyists of sacred texts), which developed out of the Aram. state script. The ancient Heb. script, used for the inscriptions on revolutionary coinage, was expressly rejected by Pharisaic teachers. Especially when used by foreigners the word Hebrew can serve to denote the land (Tacitus, *Histories* 5, 5) and its people (Test. Jos. 12:2 f.; 13:3; Jub. 47:5 f.). Since language, education and the structure of theology are largely determined by the fact of belonging to a particular cultural sphere, the word

309

of differentiation (cf. Acts 6:1) could sometimes in the conflict acquire an apologetic or a polemical tone. Paul emphasized in 2 Cor. 11:22 and Phil. 3:5 his Heb.-speaking origins and affiliations as something positive. In the sayings about Hebrews in the gnostic Gospel of Philip (especially 1 and 46) everything Hebrew is devalued as an obsolete preliminary to true faith.

Judah, Jew, Jewish and Judaism are more terms with a political and sociological colouring. They denote in the first instance membership of the nation (Tacitus, *Histories*, 5, 5), but then also people who turn to Judaism (Dio Cass., 37, 17) and live according to Jewish customs (cf. *Ioudaïkos*, Jewish in Tit. 1:14, of myths; with the adv. *Ioudaïkōs* and vb. *ioudaïzō*, live as a Jew, Gal. 2:14). To this context belongs the noun first coined by the LXX, *Ioudaïsmos*, Judaism, as a way of life and faith (Gal. 1:13 f.; cf. 2 Macc. 2:21; 8:1; 14:38; 4 Macc. 4:26; Arndt, 380). This usage was taken over by the Jews themselves, especially in dealings with foreigners (Elephantine Papyri; 1 Macc. 3:34; 8:23 ff.; Tob. 1:18). But Jew also occurs as a self-designation on the coins of the Hasmonean period, in Philo and Josephus. In the NT it is used of individuals and in the plur. of groups, occurring some 194 times with almost every shade of meaning, of which 79 instances are in Acts, especially from ch. 13 on, 71 in Jn., 24 in Paul, but only 11 in the Synoptic Gospels (see 2 (e) below). Occasionally, especially in exegetical contexts, the word has a respectful sense (Megillah 12b–13a; Midrash Est. 2:5[93a]; Sib. 5, 249). But the word Jew was often used by Gentiles as a contemptuous term of abuse (Midrash Lam. 1:11[55a]). The Gentile world did not understand the peculiarity and necessary separation of the Jewish people (Ad.Est. 13:12 ff. [LXX after 4:17]). Because they could not take part in the Gentile cults and social life, they were regarded as godless, haters of foreigners, and even as haters of men in general (3 Macc. 3:4 ff.; Josephus, *Ap.* 2, 121–124, 145–150; Megillah 13b; Midrash Est. 3:8[95b], a warning against Jews; *BGU* 1079). Alexandrian writers, in particular, spread horrific tales about the history and worship of the Jews which were readily believed and copied (Manetho, Chairemon, Lysimachus, Apion; cf. Josephus, *Ap.* 1, 219–2, 150; Tacitus, *Histories*, 3–5; *Ann.* 2, 85). Contempt for Judaism (Cicero, *Pro Flacco*, 28; Pliny, *Nat.Hist.* 13, 4; Juvenal, *Satires* 14, 96–106) also resulted in hatred which worked itself out in bloody persecution (Philo, *Flacc.* 41–96; *Leg.Gai.* 120–139).

Intensified by such anti-Jewish attitudes on the part of others, Judaism's consciousness of itself as Israel developed. This is the most pregnant of the theological concepts consistently used within the community. It occurs frequently in the NT (68 times), most often in Paul (17 times, of which 11 are in Rom.), then 12 in Matt., 12 in Lk. and 15 in Acts, rarely in Mk. and Jn. (twice and 4 times respectively). *Israēlitēs* occurs 5 times in Acts (always as a form of address; cf. 2:22; 3:12; 5:35; 13:16; 21:28), 3 times in Paul (Rom. 9:4; 11:1; 2 Cor. 11:22) and once in Jn. (1.47). Each time it refers to Jews as members of the people of God. The world was created for Israel's sake (2 Esd. 7:11; Gen. R. 12[8d]). Israel is God's possession (Aboth 6:10) and the first-born (Pss.Sol. 18:4). It owes its special character solely to the gift of instruction (Exod. R. 30[89d]). Even if Israel is despised in this world (Lev. R. 32[122a]), suffering is itself a sign of the love of God (Pss.Sol. 18:4; Midrash Cant. 1:5[87b]) who is with them even in dispersion (Megillah 29a). God stands by his promises (Makkoth 24a–b). He will gather all those who have been scattered (Eth.Enoch 90:33; Test. Jos. 19 f.; Eighteen Benedictions, especially the 10th request; for text → Prayer, art. *proseuchomai* OT 5). They will possess the land (Matt. 5:5; → Inheritance), and all Israel has a share in the world to come (Sanhedrin 11:1).

2. *The Struggle over Israel within Judaism.* (a) Israel in the Hel. period. Post-exilic Judaism was divided geographically between the homeland and the dispersion. Parallel with this was the cultural division between Hebrews and Hellenists. But there were also Jews of the dispersion who emphasized their connection with the Heb. (or Aram.) language and culture and separated themselves from Jews who were more open towards Hel. culture. There were synagogues of the Hebrews in Rome and Corinth (cf. also Trypho in Justin, *Dial.* 1, 3). On the other hand, there were in Jerusalem Jewish groups who in language and perhaps also in customs were Hellenists (2 Macc. 4:13; Acts 6:1; 9:29).

Those who lived in Israel retained close links with those who lived in the dispersion. Jerusalem was supported materially by the latter in the form of the temple tax (cf. the alms for Jerusalem in 2 Cor. 8 f.), while remaining itself a religious focal point with its pilgrim festivals and regular embassies sent out to Jewish communities. However, there was no common political action, either during the rebellions in Israel or the persecutions in the dispersion.

From the sociological point of view Israel was divided into several classes: priests, Levites, Israelites, proselytes (mostly of equal standing with the Israelites [cf. CD 14:3–6]), subordinate temple slaves and the offspring of illegitimate marriages (Ezr. 8:20; TJ Horayoth 3:5; Yebamoth 8:5). However, because the question of how Israel could continue to exist before God in this period was interpreted in a variety of ways, there arose groups which all maintained that they were the true community (e.g. Sadducees, baptists, apocalyptists, Pharisees, and Zealots). Membership of these groups no longer depended on origin but on the decision of the individual to accept a particular doctrinal opinion. The boundaries of the parties were fluid, and it was possible to transfer from one to another. Thus Josephus tried different groups (*Life* 10 ff.), and disciples of John transferred their allegiance to the Jesus group (Jn. 1:38–40).

These groups were themselves further divided into sub-groups. Thus, within the Pharisees there was a Zealot wing, hostile to foreigners, and a missionary wing friendly towards Rome (the parties of Shammai and Hillel; cf. Shabbath 31a). Similar splits arose also among the followers of Jesus (Gal. 1 f.; 1 Cor. 1:12; 3:4; 2 Cor. 11).

The idea of election, the continued existence of Israel and the formulation of instruction in purity were hammered out in continuous debate over points of doctrine and constant conflict. The passion with which the struggle for Israel's reality was fought is a sign of the vitality of the prophetic spirit in this period.

(b) Polemic. The course of this conflict was bitter. It was of the kind that could only come about among brothers disputing a common heritage. The fight had been going on for a long time according to rules handed down in the different schools before the Jesus movement arose and entered the debate.

The methods of polemic were various. Opponents were denounced in forthright language, as can be seen by the use in the NT of terms like hypocrite (Matt. 23:13; cf. Ass.Mos. 7) and generation of vipers (1QH 3:12–18; Matt. 3:7). Wholesale

311

appeal was made to history, as when Paul saw the behaviour of the Jews, "who killed . . . the Lord Jesus", as typical of their treatment of the prophets (1 Thess. 2:14 f.). An opponent's positive points could be assertively transformed into negatives (cf. the sons of darkness, 1QS 1:10; 1QM 1:1; the law in Paul, Gal 3:10–13; Rom. 4:13 ff.; the devil and lies instead of God and truth, 1QS 2:4 f.; 1QM 1:1; CD 6:1; 1QH 5:26 f.; 7:12; 1QpHab 10:9 f.; Jn. 8:41–44; Rev. 3:9). Cf. also Paul's interpretation of current Jewish attitudes in the light of the Scriptures in 2 Cor. 3:4–18 and Gal. 4:21–31. Such polemic had the air of prophetic denunciation: Israel is stubborn (CD 1:14 quoting Hos. 4:16) and godless (Test.Lev. 14:4). God has hidden his face from Israel (CD 1:3). In the process Judah, in particular, became a negative concept (CD 4:3; 4:11; 8:3, the princes of Judah have become like those who remove the bounds, quoting Hos. 5:10). This exegesis was also applied to disloyal members of the community (CD 19:26 f.), so that the speakers sound almost like Gentile opponents of Judaism. In line with this, Paul, the missionary to the Gentiles, took up the arguments of the Gentile-Jewish polemic (1 Thess. 2:14–16). We meet the sharpest form of the polemic in the Johannine writings, which in their generalizing usage seem to separate themselves entirely from the Jews.

Jewish writing remains so polemically involved that dangerous misunderstandings are unavoidable, where the different sides are considered in isolation. After the destruction of the temple feelings were so intense that opposing positions were treated as non-existent. Thus the Talmud is almost completely silent about its opponents. The last step is legal separation through the introduction of the petition on heretics into the Eighteen Benedictions: "May the Nazarenes and heretics disappear in a moment; they shall be erased from the book of life and not be written with the faithful" (cf. Berakoth 28b–29a). This legal act of formal exclusion is presupposed in Jn. 9:22 and 12:42.

(c) The remnant and Israel as a whole. The positive side of such polemic was an apologetic presentation of one's own position. Each individual group relied on the fact that it was the separated → remnant of Israel which would lead to the eschatological community of the saved. A sign of this is the frequent use in these contexts of the prep. "out of" (Heb. *min*, "from", in the sense of separation from something; e.g. a plant root to spring from Israel, CD 1:7; raised from Aaron, from Israel, CD 6:2 f.; those few who have departed, CD 8:16, 40). The self-consciousness arising from this separation expresses itself in such self-designations as "the house of truth", "house of holiness", "house of steadfastness" (1QS 5:5 f.; 8:5–9; 9:5; CD 3:19).

It is striking, however, that everyone refrains from simply identifying his group with the eschatological total-Israel. Thus 1 Cor. 10:18 lacks a corresponding "Israel according to the spirit". The nearest approach to this is the "community of the new covenant" (1QpHab 2:3; CD 6:19; 8:21; cf. 1 Cor. 11:25; 2 Cor. 3:6; Lk. 22:20). Even if primarily one's own group is intended, an open attitude towards a future gathered Israel is retained (1QSa 2:12). Separation *from* Israel is election *for* Israel (1QS 5:5 f.; 8:5; 9:5; Test. 8:2). The community of the remnant realizes its commission to call the entire people to repentance. The natural way of belonging to Israel by descent (the child of a Jewish mother is a Jew) enters into tension with being a Jew through obedience (which particularly in the case of men demands a

312

decision to learn and to fulfil the commandments). This was never devalued but remained a basic tenet. The goal was an eschatological community in a renewed form, as it was already foreshadowed in the present in the groups and as the community at Sinai represented all future communities which are already included in it (Deut. 29:15; cf. Pesahim 10:5). The community of the remnant is a → light for the whole community (Test.Lev. 14:3; cf. Matt. 5:14). For their sakes the whole of Israel will be saved in the end (Test.Sim. 6:2, 5; 7:2; Test.Ben. 10:11; cf. Rom. 11:26; Sanhedrin 11:1). The clearest expression of hope for the whole of Israel occurs in prayers which frequently conclude with a reference to the whole of Israel (Gal. 6:16; Eighteen Benedictions; Berakoth 60b; Shabbath 12b; the *Ahabah* spoken before the *Shema*; and often in the canticle *Yigdal*). The remnant of the elect in the NT also hoped for the salvation and the re-establishment of Israel as one people (Mk. 13:27; Lk. 24:21; Acts 1:6). The expected judgment will be carried out through the twelve disciples, whose → number indicates the totality of Israel (Matt. 19:28; Lk. 22:30).

Out of this belonging together in the hope of Israel on the basis of common Scriptures there resulted a mutual sense of responsibility in every conflict, just as the prophet was the accuser and intercessor at one and the same time and took his people's sufferings on himself. Internal Jewish polemic followed directly from the affirmation of Israel; it sought the realization of the complete Israel.

(d) The Messiah and Israel. All the groups were united in the belief that Israel's hope would be realized in individual figures who would usher in the eschatological salvation. It was in the time of most extreme need that people hoped that God would make himself known to them, and lead them out of their obscurity and ambiguity. All these many attempts at messianic realization found people ready to believe in them, and all ended in apparent catastrophe: from the Teacher of Righteousness at Qumran (Num. 24:17; the star from Jacob applied to the Teacher, CD 7:18 f.), from John and Jesus via the messianic pretenders reported by Josephus (*War* 2, 4, 1–3), to the Zealot leaders (Josephus, *War* 5, 1, 1–2) and Bar Kokhba. Only two groups survived the catastrophe: the → Pharisees, from whose tradition Rabbi Johanan ben Zakkai excluded all messianic or Zealot tendencies at Jamnia (A.D. 70); and the Jewish believers in Jesus who stressed their eschatological, messianic beliefs over against the Pharisees. The messianic belief of the earliest stratum of NT tradition can, therefore, be considered representative of a thoroughly Jewish outlook at the time of the second temple.

Each group took and applied key statements from the Jewish scripture to the person who for them represented Israel. This representative is the elect one among the community of the elect, the righteous one among the righteous, the son among the sons, the servant among the servants (Isa. 53), who takes Israel's suffering on himself. The Son of man, the figure of judgment representing the people of Israel in Dan. 7:13 (→ Son of God) was now referred to the messiah. As God constantly speaks to Israel, he also speaks to the Christ. As Israel is enabled in a unique way to hear and to obey, the Christ is also (Jn. 5:19, 36; Matt. 5:17; 11:27). Terms can therefore also be applied to him which in the Heb. Scriptures denoted Israel; e.g. the vineyard, the vine (Jer. 2:21; Ps. 80:8 f.; 2 Esd. 5:23; Jn. 15:1–8), the corner stone (Matt. 21:42; Mk. 12:10 f.; Lk. 20:17; Acts 4:11; Eph. 2:20; 1 Pet. 2:6–8; cf. Ps. 118:22 ff.; → Rock); the dove, metaphor for Israel (Ps. 68:13;

2 Esd. 5:26; → Bird), descends on Jesus at his baptism (Matt. 3:16; Mk. 1:10; Lk. 3:22).

In all the groups history was polemically interpreted. Past history and especially contemporary events were adapted in the manner of a pesher (cf. CD, 1QS, 1QM, and the passion narrative in the NT). The connection of Israel and the messiah runs through the entire NT which is a consistent, urgent, infinitely varied pesher seeking to prove that to be consistent with itself Judaism must recognize Jesus as the messiah (cf. especially Lk. 2:30–32, 38; 24:21, 24, 44; → Jesus Christ). According to Luke, faith in Jesus is nothing but the legitimate extension of Pharisaic belief (Acts 1–5; 28:20, 23). In every apparent antithesis the messiah stands in continuity with Israel as its fulfilment (Matt. 5:17). According to Jn. 1:47, no one is a "true son of Israel" until he has recognized Jesus as Israel's messiah, the fulfilment of ancient promises and the renewal of the old covenant which has never been revoked. In Rev. the conversion of the Jews is presented as the high point of the eschatological victory (7:1–8).

The messiah and Israel stand inseparably together. Whoever does not decide for this elect One opposes him. Whoever refuses to trust him (cf. faith in the Teacher, 1QpHab 8:1–3, with faith in Jesus throughout the NT) has thereby decided against Israel. He has lost his descent from Abraham (Jn. 8:49) and belongs to the synagogue of Satan (Rev. 3:9). He is a son of darkness, a member of the community of Belial (CD 4:13, 16; 8:2; 1QH 4:10–16). Nevertheless, both the one who evinces such trust (even though it should be proved false) and the one who refuses it stand within Judaism.

Israel and its Scriptures are the critical principle by which every messianic pretender must be judged: the messiahs of Qumran were expected from Aaron and Israel (CD 6:2 f.; 1QSa 2:11–21); the messiah Jesus from the patriarchs (Rom. 1:3; 9:5; Matt. 1:1–17 par. Lk. 3:23–38; Matt. 11:2–6; Jn. 5:39; cf. Sanhedrin 93b, 98b; Shabbath 63a). This was the only way in which Israel could protect herself against excess in spirit and prophecy, against the majority of messianic pretenders and against overhasty solutions of the problems of her existence. The witnesses of the NT also knew that the reality of Israel is the touchstone of christology. Therefore they clung passionately to Israel as the basic foundation of the Christ event. Therefore, there emerges from the NT itself the sharpest opposition to any abandonment of Israel (Rom. 9–11; Jn. 4:22). Only in living union with Israel is → Jesus the Christ. Without this historical reality he dissolves into an idea, a gnostic myth, and a docetic speculation. Hence in the case of the messiah Jesus, → baptism and → Lord's Supper are the feasts of Israel. The → cross he bore was a sharing in the suffering of Israel. Although Jewish Christians engaged in the dialogue within Judaism found themselves cut off because of him from their Jewish brethren, the NT demonstrates that Jesus, the Jew and Hebrew, represents Israel completely in his person. He is bound up with Israel from first to last.

(e) Mission. This identification of the bringer of salvation with Israel entails consequent missionary activity among Jews. As Jesus turned exclusively to the lost sheep of the house of Israel, his messengers were to go only into the towns of Israel (Matt. 10:5 f.; 15:24). Paul, the Jewish missionary (1 Cor. 9:20), also demonstrated the priority of Judaism in salvation history (Rom. 1:16) by always going first of all to the Jews (Acts 13:14; 41:1), and always acknowledging that he was a

Jew (2 Cor. 11:22; Phil. 3:5; Acts 22:3). Despite the failures of his Jewish mission he held fast to Israel, his people (cf. Acts 28:20). On the basis of the Jewish Scriptures Paul demonstrates in Rom. 9–11 in a kind of commentary-cum-anthology of OT teaching that it is just Israel's present hardening which is causing the message of Christ to come to the Gentiles who thus acquire a share in Israel's salvation. In the end-time which is imminent the whole of Israel will be saved by God himself (Rom. 11:26). An anticipatory sign of this undiminished faithfulness of God is Jewish Christianity, the faithful remnant of Judaism, represented by Paul himself. The question may be asked whether Paul's removal of the barrier between Israel and the Gentiles did not hasten the division of Israel, even though this was not his intention.

The position of the various NT writers vis-à-vis Judaism is revealed in their use of terms. Thus in Paul Jew is used 24 times, very often in opposition to → Greek, Gentile, and mostly in a positive sense. Israel (17 times) stands for either the historic people or the eschatological whole Israel but significantly not for Paul's own community. In the Synoptics as a whole, Israel stands for the people and also the land (e.g. Matt. 20:1, 21:1). It is used in preference to Jew. Matt. contains the expression "house of Israel" (Matt. 10:6; 15:24 f.; cf. Acts 7:47; Heb. 8:8; 10:2). Jew is used particularly in the phrase "King of the Jews" (Matt. 27:11, 29, 37; cf. 42; Mk. 15:2, 9, 12, 18, 26; Lk. 23:3, 37 f.; Jn. 18:33, 39; 19:3, 19, 21) and almost without exception on the lips of Gentiles with somewhat deprecating overtones (Matt. 2:2; 28:15; Mk. 7:3; Lk. 7:3; 23:51). The use of the word Israel in general clearly maintains the connection with the reality and hope of Israel. In Acts Israel is used more frequently in the account of the Palestinian church (11 out of 15 passages; cf. 28:20 with 1:6; 2:36), while Jew is used more frequently in the narrative of Paul's missionary journeys (68 out of 79 passages). This corresponds to Hel. usage. In Jn. it is clear from the few but fundamental passages where Israel is used (1:49 and 12:13 of Jesus as king; 1:31 as the one to be revealed through John), that the writer is still within the sphere of the whole of Israel, even though his polemic is extremely sharp. This is expressed in the Johannine use of Jew (70 times), which can indeed be used neutrally of the people or the religious community (e.g. 4:9; 18:35) and as in the Synoptics (King of the Jews, 18:33; 19:19 ff.). But mostly it has the effect of expressing aloofness or, especially where it denotes the ruling classes (e.g. 1:19; 7:11; 18:12), sharp rejection. While the Synoptics, especially Matt., distinguish Jesus' opponents according to the groups they belong to, Jn. speaks in a general way of the Jews. In Rev. Jew has a positive sense. But it is not applied to the community which does not believe in Jesus (2:9; 3:9). Israel is the true eschatological people of God (2:14; 7:4; 21:12).

3. *From the Gentile Mission to the Gentile Christian Church.* Only when those to whom the Jewish mission was originally addressed overwhelmingly rejected the offer did the mission to the Gentiles arise (Acts 13:46). The tradition therefore had to be restated to meet the demands of missionary practice among Gentiles. The history of Israel which had been so prominent in addressing the Jews (cf. Acts 2:17–36; 3:22–26; 7:2–53) was dropped from the instruction given, because the people did not have the preparation necessary to understand it. (The revelation on Sinai is not mentioned in any confession of faith.) But despite this reduction, God's encounter with the Gentiles remained rooted in the historical experience of

315

Israel in the teaching of the Jewish missionaries to the Gentiles. The Jesus-covenant is the extension of the Sinai covenant (cf. Rom. 9–11; 1 Cor. 11:25; 2 Cor. 3:6 ff.; Gal. 4:24 ff.; Heb. 8:8 ff.; 10:16 ff.). In terms of world history the Christ-event became the inclusion of the nations in the Sinai event.

Because of mounting internal tensions and disappointment over the attitude of the dispersion, the position of Jewish Christians in the land of Israel became continually more difficult. Step by step they were transformed from a competing group to the independent opponents of the Pharisees who now represented orthodox Judaism. From A.D. 70 onwards Jewish Christians saw their own way of faith as something distinct from that of the synagogue in the Jewish community. Legal separation from the synagogue (above 2 (b)) meant exclusion from every area of communal life (Tosefta Hullin 2:21 ff.).

The path of Gentile Christianity turned from Judaism and led into Gentile anti-Semitism, which was on the increase after the catastrophe. The prophets' criticism of Israel was misunderstood as anti-Jewish and repeated irresponsibly. Even when the words were kept their meaning was distorted to imply the opposite, and this served to sharpen Gentile hatred of Jews. In place of living and healthy dialogue between the groups there arose what was more like a dogmatizing monologue.

In Clement of Rome (perhaps a Jewish Christian, shortly before A.D. 100) one can still trace a nearness to the world of the Heb. Bible and to Judaism (cf. 1 Clem. 4:13; 8:3; 29:2 f.; 31:2–4; 43; 55:6). But Ignatius of Antioch, a Gentile Christian, writing c. A.D. 115, at the time of the persecutions under Trajan, expressed the opinion that a Christian must necessarily be an opponent of Jews (*Mag.* 8; 10:3). Barnabas and Justin, both Gentile Christians, wrote during and after the war against Bar Kokhba. Barnabas uses the word Israel mostly in connection with his exegesis of the Bible against Israel (sometimes historical, often typological, 4:15; 6:7; 8:1–3; 11:1; 12:2, 5; 16:5), but he does not yet dare to take over this word for the → church. Justin, on the other hand, asserts boldly: "We are . . . the true spiritual Israel" (*Dial.* 11, 5; cf. 100, 4; 123, 9). Their own Bible remains obscure to the Jewish people, because they do not listen to the voice of the Lord. Only the church possesses true insight (Barn. 8:7; 10:12; Just., *Dial.* 9, 1; 33, 1 f.). Israel has a greatness beyond time, which has never belonged to the Jews but always to Christians (the contesting of the covenant, Barn. 4:6). The way of Barnabas and Justin became the way of the church. After the council of Nicaea (A.D. 325) it was finally stated that church and synagogue have nothing in common (cf. Eusebius, *Vita Constantini* 3, 18).

R. Mayer

’Ιακώβ

’Ιακώβ (*Iakōb*), Jacob; ’Ιάκωβος (*Iakōbos*), James; ’Ιουδαία (*Ioudaia*), Judea; ’Ιούδας (*Ioudas*), Judah, Judas, Jude.

OT Jacob was the second son of Isaac and Rebekah and grandson of the patriarch Abraham. He was favoured by his mother, while Isaac was partial to his other son Esau. Early in his life Jacob obtained the birthright due his brother Esau by giving him "a mess of pottage" in return for the birthright. This transfer of birthright is illustrated in the Nuzi material where the rights of primogeniture allowed for transferal of privilege to another (cf. *ANET*, 219 f.). According to the Deuteronomic legislation, the right of the first-born included a double portion of the paternal estate (Deut. 21:17), and most probably involved leadership of the clan as well (Gen. 27:29).

The subterfuge by which Jacob obtained the blessing of Isaac was initiated and encouraged by Rebekah (Gen. 27:5–17). The blessing (Gen. 27:27–29) apparently was regarded as having the validity that a last will and testament has in contemporary practice. This too is illustrated in the Nuzi material where the last words of a dying father were upheld in litigation before witnesses (*ANET*, 220).

The deception led to Jacob's flight to the home of his uncle Laban. As he stopped for the night at Luz, Jacob had a dream of a ladder reaching to heaven (Gen. 28:10–17). In the → dream the Lord spoke to Jacob reiterating the promise given earlier to Abraham (Gen. 12:7; 13:15, 16; 15:17–21; 17:1–8; 24:7). Not only did the reiteration of the promise include the affirmation that the land would belong to the descendants of the patriarchs (Gen. 28:13), but that they and their descendants would be the vehicle by which God's favour would extend to the Gentiles (28:14).

Jacob's dramatic encounter with the Lord led to his calling the site Bethel (i.e. "house of God") and that site continued to be known as Bethel throughout the OT tradition. Jacob was hired by Laban and in return for seven years of labour he was to receive Laban's daughter Rachel as his wife. Laban however deceived Jacob into marrying his other daughter Leah and Jacob continued to work for seven more years that he might marry Rachel.

Leah became the mother of Jacob's sons Reuben, Simeon, Levi, Judah, Issachar and Zebulun.

Rachel, however, did not bear children immediately and, in keeping with the prevailing custom frequently cited in the Nuzi material (*ANET*, 220), gave a concubine, Bilhah, to her husband. Bilhah became the mother of Dan and Naphtali. At length Rachel gave birth to two sons, Joseph and Benjamin. Jacob also had two sons, Gad and Asher, by Zilpah, Leah's maid.

Relations between Jacob and Laban and his family became strained due in part to Jacob's increase in wealth (Gen. 31:1, 2), and a separation was effected by Jacob. On hearing of Jacob's departure Laban pursued him. When he reached Jacob he berated him for several things including the alleged theft of the family gods (Gen. 31:30), which, in reality, Rachel had taken and secreted in the camel's saddle. The possession of the family gods (*tᵉrāpîm*), according to the Nuzi material, designated the one who had the right to the paternal estate. After a mutual agreement that they would not again interfere with one another Jacob resumed his journey. (On the background of this period see E. A. Speiser, "New Kirkuk Documents Relating to Family Laws", *Annual of American Schools of Oriental Research* 13, 1930, 1–73; C. H. Gordon, "Biblical Customs and the Nuzu Tablets", *BA* 3, 1940, 1–12; and "The Patriarchal Narratives", *JNES* 13, 1954, 56–59.)

In a dramatic event at the river Jabbok Jacob wrestled with a man whom he identified as God (Gen. 32:30). It was during this experience that Jacob's name was changed to Israel (→ *Israēl*). The site of the encounter was named Peniel ("face of God") by Jacob.

As the homeward journey continued, Jacob encountered Esau (Gen. 33:1–4) whose approach he had heard of earlier (Gen. 32:6). A reconciliation was effected by the two brothers which seems to have been an enduring one.

After an unfortunate experience with the clan of Shechem (Gen. 34), Jacob removed to Bethel but not before he had all the images of foreign deities removed from his household. After the images were buried under an oak at Shechem the Lord appeared to Jacob and the terms of the Abrahamic covenant were again affirmed.

On the journey from Bethel Jacob suffered the loss of his wife Rachel, who died while giving birth to Benjamin. This tragedy was soon followed by the death of his father Isaac (Gen. 35:29) and the banishment of his son Joseph to Egypt (Gen. 37).

Joseph rose to power in Egypt and his wisdom and foresight led to his overseeing the storage of food in Egypt. This propitious act enabled the Egyptians to have provisions while many in the surrounding areas were ravaged by famine. The famine struck Canaan and Jacob sent his sons to Egypt to obtain food. He kept his youngest son Benjamin with him, however. Alleging that they were spies, Joseph required them to bring Benjamin to Egypt to prove their word and, hence, their innocence. After bringing Benjamin to Egypt, Joseph identified himself as their brother and arranged to have Jacob brought to Egypt as well. Jacob lived in Egypt for 17 years. When he was near death he exacted from Joseph the promise that he would bury him in Canaan. He adopted Joseph's sons, Ephraim and Manasseh (Gen. 48:1–6) and pronounced a → blessing on them as well as his own sons (Gen. 48:8–49:27). Jacob died at the age of 147 years and was buried with his ancestors in the cave of Machpelah (Gen. 50:1–13).

The name Jacob became an eponym for Israel and occurs frequently with that connotation in the OT (Num. 23:7, 10, 23; Psa. 14:7; Isa. 48:20; Amos 3:13 etc.).

The patriarch Jacob is frequently cited in the OT in connection with the acts of God on his behalf. God is frequently described as the God of Abraham, Isaac and Jacob (Exod. 3:6, 15) and the covenant given to the patriarchs is cited in the same connection (2 Ki. 13:23). Malachi assured the people that the love shown by God to Jacob had not been withheld from them with the words, "I have loved Jacob but I have hated Esau" (Mal. 1:2, 3). Typical of the way in which the intertestamental literature maintains the covenantal aspects of the name Jacob is the citation in 2 Macc. 1:2 where it is affirmed that God will remember his covenant with the patriarchs.

Iakōbos (James) is the Hellenized form of *Iakōb*. This form is used frequently by Josephus for the name of the patriarch Jacob.

NT In the NT *Iakōb* denotes both the patriarch Jacob and the father of Joseph (Matt. 1:15, 16). Aside from the citation of the name Jacob in the genealogies of Matt. and Lk. (Matt. 1:2, 15 f.; Lk. 3:34), several allusions are made to events in Jacob's life by the NT writers. In Jn. 4:5, 6, 12 reference is made to a plot of ground that Jacob gave to Joseph which was the site of Jacob's well (Gen. 33:19; 48:22). Stephen in Acts 7 refers to several events in the life of Jacob (vv. 8, 12, 14) and the writer of Hebrews cites Jacob in Heb. 11, specifically in his relationship to the → promise given to → Abraham (v. 9) and as an example of → faith (v. 21). The transfer of the birthright is cited by the writer of Hebrews (12:16, 17) who uses Esau's selling of his birthright as a warning to his readers not to put off repentance.

In Rom. 9:6–13 Paul cites the events surrounding the birth of Jacob and Esau in a passage explicating the fact that God's work of election is not based on works (v. 11). Paul in this passage refers to the purposes expressed in the words spoken by God before the births of Jacob and Esau, "the elder shall serve the younger" (Gen. 25:23). He quotes Mal. 1:2, 3 in this connection as well. Allusion is made to Jacob's dream at Bethel in John 1:51 where Christ transfers the image of the ladder to himself.

"The God of Abraham, Isaac and Jacob" is an expression that occurs in the NT as well as the more singular expression, "The God of Jacob". In his defence of his teaching on the resurrection Jesus used the formula "The God of Abraham, Isaac and Jacob" to illustrate that God was the God of the living (Matt. 22:32; Mark 12:26; Luke 20:37). The same expression was used by Peter (Acts 3:13) in its specific connection with the patriarchs, "the God of our fathers" in speaking to Jews. The appellation "God of Jacob" in Acts 7:46 is used as an appellation for God and seems to reflect the language of Ps. 132:5.

Jacob is mentioned along with the patriarchs Abraham and Isaac in Matt. 8:11 where their fellowship in heaven is the reward of the people of faith. Jacob is used as an eponym of the Jewish nation in Luke 1:33 and Rom. 11:26 (the latter being a free quotation from Isa. 59:20).   *T. McComiskey*

| 'Ιούδα | 'Ιούδα (*Iouda*), Judah; 'Ιούδας (*Ioudas*), Judah, Judas. |

OT The word *Iouda* in the NT, LXX and secular Gk. represents the Heb. word *yᵉhûdâh* (Judah). The meaning of the word is uncertain but probably means "praised" (Gen. 29:35; → *Israēl*, OT 1).

In the OT Judah was the fourth son of Jacob. His mother was Leah. He seems to have held great influence among his brothers as evinced by their acquiescence to his wish that Joseph be sent to Egypt (Gen. 37:26, 27) and by his acting as spokesman for them in Egypt (Gen. 43:3–10; 44:16–34). Judah figures prominently in the blessing of Jacob where he was promised a position of honour among his brothers, as well as the prospect of sovereignty and dominion realized in a future king (Gen. 49:10 RSV).

Several others in the OT also bore the name Judah (Ezr. 3:9; 10:23; Neh. 11:9; 12:8, 36). The name Judah continued to be born by the tribe of which Jacob's son was the progenitor. The tribe does not seem to have distinguished itself greatly in the history of Israel, although it did comprise a vanguard in a strategic encounter with the Canaanites (Jdg. 1:1–7).

The territory occupied by the tribe of Judah consisted mainly of highland country in the area of Canaan westward from the Dead Sea. The territory extended to the Mediterranean Sea and was bounded on the north by the tribal territories of Benjamin and Dan. The Negev formed the southern boundary.

The rôle of the tribe of Judah in the period of the united monarchy seems to have been no different from that of any other tribe. However, when the division of the monarchy occurred the southern kingdom became known as the kingdom of Judah, although elements in the tribe of Benjamin remained loyal to the house of David as well.

319

The history of the kingdom of Judah was threatened by internal and external difficulties. Not all her kings were wise, but several made positive contributions to her welfare. During the reign of Uzziah (767–739 B.C.) the fortunes of Judah as well as of Israel were greatly enhanced by the quiescence of Assyria on the world scene. This period of affluence, however, was characterized by an internal sickness, for the → covenant stipulations were being violated leading to societal wrongs that the eighth century prophets warned would lead to her downfall. Under Hezekiah (716–686 B.C.) a serious Assyrian incursion came to an end with the withdrawal of the Assyrian forces. While Hezekiah's foreign policy was, at times, unwise (Isa. 30:15) his contribution to the kingdom of Judah was generally commendable.

Following Hezekiah's reign the fortunes of Judah began to suffer again. The burgeoning Assyrian influence in Syro-Palestine ultimately led to the defeat of Judah. Nebuchadnezzar extracted tribute from Judah some time after his rise to power in 605 B.C., but successive attacks ultimately led to the end of Judah as a kingdom in 587 B.C.

NT In Matt. 2:6 *Iouda* occurs in the sense of the territory of Judah in a quotation from Micah 5:2. The reference is to Bethlehem of Judea (Matt. 2:5) which was located in the territory of Judah. In Luke 1:39 *Iouda* occurs in the expression *eis polin Iouda*. Since Luke invariably uses *Ioudaia* for the province it seems more likely that *Iouda* here is a town now unknown.

In Heb. 7:14 reference is made to the descent of Christ from the tribe of Judah, a tribe which had no priestly prerogatives. The point is made that the Levitical priesthood was unable to achieve perfection for its adherents, hence the need for another priest. This represents a change in the law (v. 12), for Christ did not descend from the tribe of Levi which, according to the law, was the tribe from which the priests were to be chosen.

In Heb. 8:8 the house of Judah is cited along with the house of Israel to represent the whole nation. The reference here is to the two kingdoms of the divided monarchy and occurs in a quotation from Jer. 31:31–34 where the new covenant is predicted.

The tribe of Judah is cited in Rev. 5:5; 7:5 as well. In the former, Christ's descent from the tribe of Judah is reflected in the appellation "Lion of the tribe of Judah" (→ Animal). In Rev. 7:5, the tribe of Judah is cited along with other tribes with whom the group numbering "a hundred and forty-four thousand" is associated (→ Number, art. *chilias* NT 4).

Ioudas occurs as the name of several individuals in the NT. (1) The fourth son of Jacob (Matt. 1:2, 3; Luke 3:33, 34). (2) An ancestor of Christ (Luke 3:26). The spelling here however is *Ioda* (Joda RSV). He is the son of Joanan. (3) An ancestor of Christ (Luke 3:30) who was the son of Joseph. (4) Judas, surnamed the Galilean, who participated in an insurrection during a tax census under Quirinius (Acts 5:37). See also Josephus (*Ant.* 18). (5) Judas of Damascus (Acts 9:11) who gave Saul of Tarsus (Paul) lodging after Saul's vision on the road to Damascus. It was there that Ananias was to go to find Saul. (6) Judas, a brother of Jesus (Matt. 13:55; Mark 6:3). This Judas is considered by some to be the same as Jude, the author of the NT epistle. (7) Judas, the son of James, one of the twelve apostles (Luke 6:16; Acts 1:13). He was one of the group who engaged in prayer in an upper room after

320

the ascension of Christ. (8) Judas Iscariot, the son of Simon, who betrayed Jesus. The meaning of Iscariot is not clear. It may have been a Hellenization of the Heb. "man of Qerioth". He is cited first in the accounts of the choosing of the twelve (Matt. 10:4; Mark. 3:19; Luke 6:16). His betrayal of Jesus (John 13:26-30) was decisively carried out after Jesus said to him, "What you are going to do, do quickly" (RSV). After an unsuccessful effort to atone for his wrong by returning the money paid him for his treachery Matthew records that Judas hanged himself (27:5; → Akeldama; cf. B. Gärtner, *Iscariot, Facet Books*, 1971). (9) Judas Barsabbas was one of the two chosen to accompany Paul and Barnabas to Antioch (Acts 15:22). Judas Barsabbas was chosen along with Silas by the Jerusalem Council to substantiate the council's decision. *T. McComiskey*

→ Abraham, → Babylon, → Egypt, → Election, → Greek, → Jerusalem, → Jesus Christ, → Levite, → People, → Pharisee, → Priest, → Prophet, → Sadducee, → Samaritan, → Temple

(a). Y. Aharoni, *The Land of the Bible: A Historical Geography*, 1967; W. F. Albright, *From the Stone Age to Christianity*, 1957²; *Yahweh and the Gods of Canaan*, 1968; *Archaeology and the Religion of Israel*, 1953³; *The Biblical Period from Abraham to Ezra*, 1963; and *The Archaeology of Palestine*, revised ed. 1960; A. Alt, *Essays on Old Testament History and Religion*, 1966; B. W. Anderson, *Understanding the Old Testament*, 1957; G. L. Archer, "Hebrew Language", *ZPEB* III 66–76; M. Avi-Yonah, *Encyclopedia of Archaeological Excavation in the Holy Land*, I–IV, 1976–; L. Baeck, *The Pharisees*, 1957; S. W. Baron, *A Social and Religious History of the Jews*, I–XV, 1952–73²; J. Bright, *A History of Israel*, revised ed. 1972; and "Hebrew Religion", *IDB* II 560–70; F. F. Bruce, *Israel and the Nations*, 1963; M. Buber, *Two Types of Faith*, 1951; and *The Prophetic Faith*, 1960; D. R. Catchpole, *The Trial of Jesus: A Study in the Gospels and Jewish Historiography from 1770 to the Present Day*, 1971; H. Cazelles, "The Hebrews", in D. J. Wiseman, ed., *Peoples of Old Testament Times*, 1973, 1–28; G. A. Danell, *Studies in the Name Israel in the Old Testament*, 1946 (see also the review by I. Engnell in *Symbolae Biblicae Upsalienses* 7, 1946); W. D. Davies, *The Gospel and the Land: Early Christianity and Jewish Territorial Doctrine*, 1974; J. D. M. Derrett, "Cursing Jesus (I Cor. xii. 3): The Jews as Religious 'Persecutors' ", *NTS* 21, 1974–75, 544–54; S. Dubnov, *History of the Jews*, I–IV, revised by M. Spiegel, 1967–71; W. Eichrodt, *Theology of the Old Testament*, I, 1961, II, 1967; O. Eissfeldt, *The Old Testament: An Introduction*, 1965; I. Epstein, *Judaism*, 1945; and *The Jewish Way of Life*, 1946; L. Finkelstein, ed., *The Jews: Their History, Culture and Religion*, I–IV, 1949; G. Fohrer, *History of Israelite Religion*, 1973; W. Förster, *Palestinian Judaism in New Testament Times*, 1964; E. R. Goodenough, *Jewish Symbols in the Graeco-Roman Period*, I–XIII, 1953–65; J. van Goudoever, "The Place of Israel in Luke's Gospel", *NovT* 11, 1966, 111 ff.; L. Goppelt, *Jesus, Paul and Judaism*, 1964; F. C. Grant, *Ancient Judaism and the New Testament*, 1960; and *Roman Hellenism and the New Testament*, 1962; M. Grant, *Herod the Great*, 1971; 1962 L. H. Grollenberg, *Atlas of the Bible*, 1956; A. Haldar, "Israel, Names and Associations of", *IDB* II 765 f.; A. T. Hanson, *Studies in Paul's Technique and Theology*, 1974; R. K. Harrison, *A History of Old Testament Times*, 1957; and *Introduction to the Old Testament*, 1970; M. Hengel, *Judaism and Hellenism*, I–II, 1974; S. Herrmann, *A History of Israel in Old Testament Times*, 1975; H. W. Hoehner, *Herod Antipas*, 1972; E. Jacob, *Theology of the Old Testament*, 1959; A. Jeffrey, "Hebrew Language", *IDB* II 553–60; J. Jervell, *Luke and the People of God: A New Look at Luke-Acts*, 1972; J. Jocz, *The Jewish People and Jesus Christ*, 1949; E. Käsemann, "Paul and Israel", *New Testament Questions of Today*, 1969, 183–87; Y. Kaufmann, *The Religion of Israel*, 1961; H.-J. Kraus, *Worship in Ancient Israel*, 1966; G. Lindeskog, "Israel in the New Testament", *Svensk Exegetisk Årsbok* 26, 1961, 57 ff.; J. McKay, *Religion in Judah under the Assyrians, 732–609 B.C.*, *SBT Second Series* 26, 1973; I. H. Marshall, "Palestinian and Hellenistic Christianity: Some Critical Comments", *NTS* 19, 1972–73, 271–87; A. D. H. Mayes, *Israel in the Period of the Judges*, *SBT Second Series* 29, 1974; G. F. Moore, *Judaism in the First Centuries of the Christian Era*, I–III, 1927–30; J. Morgenstern, "Israel, Social and Economic Development of", *IDB* II 766–70; S. Mowinckel, *He That Cometh*, 1956; J. Munck, "Israel and the Gentiles", *Paul and the Salvation of Mankind*, 1959, 247–81; and *Christ and Israel*

1967; M. Pearlman, *The Maccabees*, 1973; J. H. Negenman, *New Atlas of the Bible*, ed. H. H. Rowley, 1969; M. Noth, *The History of Israel*, 1960²; and *The Laws of the Pentateuch and Other Studies*, 1966; S. Pancaro, "The Relationship of the Church to Israel in the Gospel of St. John", *NTS* 21, 1974–75, 396–405; J. Pedersen, *Israel, Its Life and Culture*, I–II, 1926, III–IV, 1940; J. B. Pritchard, *Ancient Near Eastern Texts Relating to the Old Testament*, 1955²; G. von Rad, *Old Testament Theology*, I, 1962, II, 1965; G. von Rad, K. G. Kuhn, W. Gutbrod, *Israël* etc., *TDNT* III 357–91; O. S. Rankin, *Jewish Religious Polemic in Narrative, Poetry, Letters and Debate*, (1956) 1969; P. Richardson, *Israel in the Apostolic Church*, 1969; H. Ringgren, *Israelite Religion*, 1966; C. Roth and G. Wigoder, eds., *Encyclopaedia Judaica*, I–XVI, 1971–72; L. Roth, *Judaism: A Portrait*, 1960; H. H. Rowley, "Israel, History of", *IDB* II 750–65; *The Missionary Message of the Old Testament*, 1945; *From Joseph to Joshua*, 1951; *The Faith of Israel*, 1956; *From Moses to Qumran*, 1963; *Men of God: Studies in Old Testament History and Prophecy*, 1963; *The Servant of the Lord and Other Essays*, 1965²; and *Worship in Ancient Israel*, 1967; S. Safrai, M. Stern *et al.*, *The Jewish People in the First Century: Historical Geography, Political History, Social, Cultural and Religious Life and Institutions*, I, 1974; S. Sandmel, *We Jews and Jesus*, 1965; S. Sandmel, ed., *Old Testament Issues*, 1969; E. Schürer, *A History of the Jewish People in the Time of Jesus Christ*, I, 1–2, II, 1–3, 1885–90; Vol. I revised by G. Vermes, F. Millar and M. Black, 1973; C. H. H. Scobie, "North and South: Tension and Reconciliation in Biblical History", in J. R. McKay and J. F. Miller, eds., *Biblical Studies: Essays in Honour of William Barclay*, 1976, 87–98; M. H. Shepherd, Jr., "The Jews in the Gospel of John. Another Level of Meaning", *Anglican Theological Review*, Suppl. Series 3, 1974, 95–112; I. Singer, ed., *The Jewish Encyclopedia*, I–XII, 1901–6; J. N. Sevenster, *The Roots of Pagan Anti-Semitism in the Ancient World*, 1975; A. N. Sherwin-White, *Roman Society and Roman Law in the New Testament*, 1963; R. A. Stewart, *Rabbinic Theology*, 1961; W. B. Tatum, "The Epoch of Israel: Luke i–ii and the Theological Plan of Luke-Acts", *NTS* 13, 1966–67, 184–95; H. St. J. Thackeray, *Josephus: The Man and the Historian*, 1967; D. W. Thomas, ed., *Documents from Old Testament Times*, 1958; J. A. Thompson, "Israel, Religion of", *ZPEB* III 354–72; S. van Tilborg, *The Jewish Leaders in Matthew*, 1972; V. A. Tscherikover, *Hellenistic Civilization and the Jews*, 1959; R. de Vaux, *Ancient Israel: Its Life and Institutions*, 1961; G. Vermes, *Jesus the Jew*, 1973; C. Vriezen, *An Outline of Old Testament Theology*, 1958; and *The Religion of Ancient Israel*, 1967; M. Weipert, *The Settlement of the Israelite Tribes In Palestine*, 1971; A. L. Williams, *Adversus Judaeos: A Bird's Eye View of Christian Apologiae until the Renaissance*, 1935; D. J. Wiseman, *Illustrations from Biblical Archaeology*, 1958; H. W. Wolff, *Old Testament Anthropology*, 1974; G. E. Wright, *The Old Testament against its Environment*, 1950; *God Who Acts*, 1952; *Biblical Archaeology*, 1962²; and *The Old Testament and Theology*, 1969; G. E. Wright ed., *The Bible and the Near East, Essays in Honour of William Foxwell Albright*, 1961; S. Zeitlin, *The Rise and Fall of the Judean State*, I–II, 1967–69.

(b). M. Avi-Yonah, *Geschichte der Juden im Zeitalter des Talmud in den Tagen von Rom und Byzanz*, 1962; O. Bächli, *Israel und die Völker*, *AThANT* 41, 1962; K. Bernhardt, *Schalom. Studien zur Glaube und Geschichte Israels. A. Jepsen zum 70. Geburtstag*, *AzTh* Reihe 1, 46, 1971; H. Bietenhard, "Kirche und Synagoge in den ersten Jahrhunderten", *ThZ* 4, 1948, 174 ff.; E. Bickermann, *Der Gott der Makkabäer*, 1937; N. A. Dahl, *Das Volk Gottes*, 1941; N. A. Dahl and G. Schrenk, "Der Name Israel", *Judaica* 6, 1950, 161 ff.; P. Diepold, *Israels Land*, *BWANT* 95, 1972; E. Dinkler, "Prädestination bei Paulus", in W. Schneemelcher, ed., *Festschrift für Günther Dehn*, 1957, 81–82; W. Eckert, N. P. Levinson and M. Stöhr, eds., *Antijudaismus im Neuen Testament? Abhandlungen zum christlich-jüdischen Dialog*, 2, 1967; W. Eichrodt, *Israel in der Weissagung des Alten Testaments*, 1951; W. Förster, *Die jüdische Frage*, 1959; J. B. Frey, *Corpus Inscriptionum Judaicarum*, 1958; V. Fritz, *Israel in der Wüste*, Marburger theologische Studien 7, 1970; L. Fuchs, *Die Juden Ägyptens*, 1924; K. Galling, *Die Erwählungstradition Israels*, 1928; A. George, "Israël dans l'oeuvre de Luc", *RB* 75, 1968, 481–525; G. Gerlemann, *yisrā'ēl*, *THAT* I 782–85; N. N. Glatzer, *Geschichte der talmudischen Zeit*, 1937; E. Grässer, "Die antijüdische Polemik im Johannesevangelium", *NTS* 10, 1964–65, 74–90; J. H. Grolle, *Gesprek met Israël*, 1949; M. Hengel, *Die Zeloten*, 1961; *Israel und die Kirche. Eine Studie im Auftrag der General-Synode der Niederländischen Reformierten Kirche*, 1961; and "Die Begegnung von Judentum und Hellenismus im Palästina der vorchristlichen Zeit", in O. Böcher and K. Haacker, eds., *Verborum Veritas. Festschrift für Gustav Stählin*, 1970, 329–48; J. Janssen, *Juda in der Exilzeit*, *FRLANT* 69, 1956; J. Juster, *Les Juifs dans l'Empire Romain*, 1914; H.-J. Kraus and R. R. Geis, eds., *Versuche des Verstehens. Dokumente jüdisch-christlicher Begegnung aus den 1918–1933*, 1966; H. Kremers, *Das Verhältnis der Kirche zu Israel*, 1964; M. Krupp, *Vergesse ich dein Jerusalem*, 1962; J. Leipoldt, *Antisemitismus in der alten Welt*, 1933; G. Lindeskog, *Die Jesusfrage im neuzeitlichen Judentum*, 1938; F. W. Marquardt, *Die Juden im Römerbrief*, TheolStud 107, 1971; W. D. Marsch and K. Thieme, *Christen und Juden*, 1961; W. Maurer, *Kirche und Synagoge*, 1953; O. Michel, "Spätjüdisches Prophetentum", in *Neutestamentliche Studien für Rudolf Bultmann*, 1954, 60 ff.; "Polemik und Scheidung", in *Festschrift für W. Freytag*, 1959, 185 ff.; "Das Judentum Jesu", *Deutsches Pfarrerblatt* 60, 1960, 465 ff.; *Der Brief an die Römer*, KEK 13, 1966[12]; and "Jesus der Jude", in H. Ristow and K. Matthiae, eds., *Der historische Jesus und der kerygmatische Christus*, 1962[2], 310–16; C. Müller, *Gottes Gerechtigkeit und Gottes Volk. Eine Untersuchung zu Römer 9–11*, FRLANT 86, 1964; M. Noth, *Die israelitischen Personennamen im Rahmen der gemeinsemitischen Namengebung*, 1928; and *Das System der zwölf Stämme Israels*, 1930; A. Oepke, *Das neue Gottesvolk*, 1950; G. von Rad, *Das Gottesvolk im Deuteronomium*, 1929; L. Ragaz, *Israel, Judentum, Christentum*, 1943[2]; G. Rosen, *Juden und Phönizer*, 1929; L. Rost, *Israel bei den Propheten*, 1937; and *Die Vorstufen von Kirche und Synagoge im Alten Testament*, 1938; H. H. Schaeder, *Esra der Schreiber*, 1930; A. Schlatter, *Synagoge und Kirche bis zum Barkochba-Aufstand*, 1966; R. Smend, "Zur Frage der altisraelitischen Amphiktyonie", *EvTh* 31, 1971, 623 ff.; G. Schrenk, *Der göttliche Sinn in Israels Geschick*, 1943; and "Was bedeutet 'Israel Gottes'?", *Judaica* 5, 1949, 81 ff.; M. Simon, *Verus Israel, Étude sur les Relations entre Chrétiens et Juifs dans l'Empire Romain*, 1948; V. Solovjov, *Das Judentum und die christliche Frage*, 1884; J. J. Stamm, *Der Staat Israel und die Landverheissungen in der Bibel* 1961[2]; P. Tillich, *Die Judenfrage, ein christliches und ein deutsches Problem*, 1953; W. Trilling, *Das wahre Israel. Studien zur Theologie des Matthäus-Evangeliums*, 1964[3]; T. C. Vriezen, *Die Erwählung Israels nach dem Alten Testament*, 1953; W. Zimmerli, *Israel und die Christen*, 1964.

J

Jerusalem

'Ιερουσαλήμ

'Ιερουσαλήμ (*Ierousalēm*), and 'Ιεροσόλυμα (*Hieroso-lyma*), Jerusalem; Σιών (*Siōn*), Zion.

CL *Ierousalēm* and *Siōn* are proper nouns, unknown in early secular Gk. The form
Hierosolyma was used for the city in the Roman province of Judea and *Hieroso-lymitēs* for an inhabitant of Jerusalem by Strabo, Dio Cassius and Jewish Hel. writers like Philo and Josephus. Hel. Judaism of the dispersion took advantage of this rendering of the Heb. name to liken it to Gk. *hieros*, holy, in order to distinguish the city as the *hiera polis* of Judaism.

OT 1. The Israelites found Jerusalem as the name of the original Canaanite city-state (cf. Jos. 10:1) and took it over. The etymology has only recently been explained. This Canaanite name means something like "Foundation of Salem", i.e. of a god who, according to Ugaritic texts, embodied the twilight. His sanctuary was in this settlement, which originally was situated on the hill Zion. In later history Jerusalem remained the name of the whole of the expanding settlement. Even after David had seized it, the city retained its name. But it was also called City of David, a term which was later used only of the old city, however. Sometimes, therefore, Zion, Jerusalem and the City of David are synonymous (cf. 2 Sam. 5:6 ff.; 1 Ki. 8:1; 1 Chr. 11:4 ff.; 2 Chr. 5:2).

2. The etymology of the name Zion (Heb. *ṣiyyôn*) cannot be explained with certainty. Some think, on the basis of related Syr. and Arab. roots, that it is possible to discover the meaning barren mountain. A different etymological derivation might give the meaning mountain fortress, stronghold. All that is certain is that it derives from Canaan's pre-Israelite period and represents a description of the terrain, a geographical name. From the earliest times Zion was the name of the south-east hill, site of the original Jebusite fortress and of the ancient Canaanite settlement of Jerusalem (Jos. 10 and the historical reminiscence of Ezek. 16:2 ff.), which are referred to synonymously as early as the second millennium B.C. The name of the city in Jdg. 19:10 f. and 1 Chr. 11:4 is Jebus, derived from the proper noun Jebusite, the name also given to the inhabitants by the Amarna letters (1400–1350 B.C.). But the city never made this name its own, and it did not prevail.

3. (a) In the OT writings *yerûšālayim* occurs as the name of the city far more frequently than *ṣiyyôn* (660 times and 154 respectively). In the canonical texts the LXX transcribes the Heb. original as *Ierousalēm* (fem.) and in the Apocrypha occasionally as *Hierosolyma* (neut. plur.). While in the canonical texts, in accordance with the Heb. original, the inhabitants are described as *enoikountes Ierousalēm* (Isa. 5:3; Zech. 12:10), as *hyioi Ierousalēm*, sons of Jerusalem (Joel 3:6; cf. Zech.

324

9:9, *thygater Ierousalēm*, daughter of Jerusalem), we meet in the Apocrypha the new term *Hierosolymitēs* (e.g. Sir. 50:27; 4 Macc. 4:22; 18:25; cf. Mk. 1:5; Jn. 7:25).

(b) As a neutral city, belonging neither to Judah nor Israel and yet lying exactly between the two territories, Jerusalem was an ideal capital for King → David. Since he captured it with an army of mercenaries it remained independent, at the same time King David's private possession (cf. 2 Sam. 5:6–10).

M. Noth, however, sees the bringing of the ark of Yahweh into the temple in Jerusalem (2 Sam. 6) as the decisive act for the further significance of the city (M. Noth, *The Laws in the Pentateuch and Other Studies*, 1966, 29 ff., 132–44, 250–54). This act gave to the Jerusalem → temple the role of the old amphictyonic central sanctuary, which was to achieve very great importance in Israel's hopes for the future. Only the original transfer of the ark to the Jerusalem temple could explain why Jerusalem, a Canaanite city, with its peculiar independent position as seat of the Davidic dynasty, should become *the* cultic centre of → Israel. Even after the northern kingdom's break with the south, Jerusalem retained its central theological significance for both kingdoms (1 Ki. 12:27, 28). "Even though the sanctuary in Jerusalem became a cultic centre for the tribes on account of the presence of the Ark, this shrine itself became more and more a central holy place, gaining as such an importance of its own" (Noth, op. cit., 142). Yahweh of hosts, who once was enthroned above the ark (2 Sam. 6:2), is now the one "who dwells on Mount Zion" (Isa. 8:18), on the "mountain of the house of the Lord" (Isa. 2:2 f.; Mic. 4:1 f.).

G. Fohrer, on the other hand, disputes the continued influence of amphictyonic ideas (*TDNT* VII 302 ff.). After its transfer the ark no longer played an essential rôle and the recognition of Jerusalem by the Israelites (1 Ki. 12:26 ff.) was a Deuteronomistic construction or to be attributed to the annexation of Israel by Josiah (cf. Jer. 41:5).

Whatever the truth may be, in the early history of Israel Jerusalem, as the royal capital, was the centre of the political kingdom and honoured as such. As temple city of the centralized cult, the city was still a spiritual and religious centre, much visited even after the dissolution of the political unity. The holy city (Isa. 48:2; 52:1) became more and more the focus of theocratic hopes. Historical experiences, but also theological reflection, strengthened and extended the idea of the inviolability and indestructibility of the temple city (cf. Isa. 36 ff.; 2 Ki. 18 ff.; 2 Chr. 32; Jer. 7:4). During the exile, in particular, it was the embodiment of every longing (Ps. 137). From here it was only a short step to join the name of the city with eschatological expectations (Jer. 31:38 ff.). It was expected that Jerusalem would become the focus for the whole world, to which all the Gentiles would stream (Jer. 3:17), and which would then be called "a house of prayer for all peoples" (Isa. 56:7). In all this complex of ideas Jerusalem and Zion are frequently used together.

(c) When the prophets came to speak about the conditions which they themselves could observe in Jerusalem, however, a different picture was revealed. Jerusalem had fallen away from God and become a prostitute. The worship of idols and disregard of God's commandments were rife in the city. The kings and the citizens along with them were going their own political ways, unconcerned about the will of God (cf. the relevant passages in Isa., Jer., Mic., Ezek.). Hence, the prophets announced to the city the → judgment of God (cf. e.g. Jer. 6:22 ff.; Isa. 32:9 ff.), judgment which could not be prevented because the corrupt people would not turn and repent (Jer. 4:3 f.). Foreign peoples and kings would carry out the judgment, which would result in a cleansed and purified Jerusalem (Isa. 40). It was Yahweh's intention to do good to Jerusalem once again (Zech. 8:15), and at the end of the age the city "shall be holy and strangers shall never again pass through it" (Joel 3:17 [4:17 MT]). The eschatological Jerusalem was always thought of, however, only as an improved, renewed earthly city; never as supernatural and heavenly. Therefore the nations could go on pilgrimage to it and accept a new way of life (Isa. 2:2 ff.), and turn to Yahweh (Jer. 3:17). From Jerusalem streams of blessing would pour out into the world (Ezek. 47:1 ff.). From this sanctified city Yahweh would reign over the whole world (Isa. 24:23). Here would be his throne (Jer. 3:17).

4. (a) The name *Siōn* was at first not used by the Israelites. Only later did prophets and poets take up the name again. In so doing they extended or shifted its meaning. On the one hand, Zion together with Jerusalem could be applied to the whole expanded city, and Zion could be equated with Judah (e.g. Jer. 14:19; Ps. 69:35) and occasionally even with Israel (Isa. 46:13; Ps. 149:2). On the other hand, Zion was no longer reckoned as the south-east hill but included the north-east hill with the temple buildings on it (cf. Ps. 2:6; 20:2). Yahweh is God on Zion (Ps. 99:2; 135:21) and (according to Jer. 8:19) the Lord of hosts dwells on Mount Zion. The inhabitants of Zion (like the inhabitants of other cities) were called sons or daughters of Zion (e.g. 2 Ki. 19:21; Pss. 9:4; 149:2; Isa. 1:8; 3:16 f.; Zech. 9:9).

(b) If one examines the use of this loan-word one finds it particularly frequently where the emphasis is on the cultic location as a sacral focus where the presence of Yahweh is felt. "Going up to Zion" is the same thing as "going to the Lord" (Jer. 31:6). It is in Zion that Yahweh dwells (Ps. 9:11).

5. (a) The use of the names in early Judaism does not differ from that of the OT. Jerusalem/Zion was the beloved city, towards which one turned one's face, in whatever part of the world, during the daily times of prayer. One went there on pilgrimage, whenever possible at the great festivals, and wished to die and be buried there. Huge sums of money flowed to Jerusalem from the dispersion in the form of temple tax, with the help of which the sacrificial ritual was maintained.

(b) Eschatological ideas developed. Alongside the concept that the earthly city would be the scene of Yahweh's victory (2 Esd. 13:25 ff.; Sib. 3:663 ff.) there developed in the apocalyptic literature a belief in the heavenly, pre-existent Jerusalem (Syr.Bar. 4:2 ff.), descending to earth at the end of the age (2 Esd. 10:27, 54; 13:36). According to another conception, it remains in heaven as the place in which the righteous will eventually dwell (Sl.Enoch 55:2). The new Zion/Jerusalem will be of unimaginable beauty (Tob. 13:16 ff.), inhabited by vast multitudes (Sib. 5:251 f.), ruled over by God himself (Sib. 3:787); the focus of this gigantic city is the new temple, to which → gifts are brought (Tob. 13:10 f.).

NT 1. (a) In the NT the name Jerusalem occurs 139 times. As in the LXX we meet in the NT the two forms *Ierousalēm* (76 times) and *Hierosolyma* (63 times). While Matt., Luke (in Lk. and Acts) and Paul in Gal. use both forms, Mk. and Jn. use only the Hel. form, and Paul, on the contrary (in Rom. and 1 Cor.), Heb. and

Rev. use only the transcribed Semitic form. The name is completely absent from the Pastoral and Catholic Epistles.

(b) The name Zion occurs only 7 times in the NT: Rom. 9:33 and 1 Pet. 2.6 (citing Isa. 28:16); Rom. 11:26 (citing Isa. 59:20; cf. Ps. 14:7). In Matt. 21:5 and Jn. 12:15, likewise citing the OT (cf. Zech. 9:9; Isa. 40:9; 62:11), we are dealing with the inhabitants who are addressed as the daughter of Zion. Only Heb. 12:22 and Rev. 14:1 use the name independently.

2. (a) In the Synoptics and Acts Jerusalem frequently denotes simply the place, in order to locate an event (Lk. 13:4), to name the starting point or destination of a journey (Lk. 10:30), or to emphasize the importance of an event because even the inhabitants of the capital have become aware of it (Mk. 1:5; Matt. 4:25; Lk. 6:17).

(b) However, a theologically significant idea is often linked with the use of the geographical name. To the theocratically minded Jew Jerusalem is God's choice as focus of the world. This theocratic conception means that it is not men but Yahweh alone who rules. He exercises his sovereignty through two institutions: the priesthood, or the Zadokite high priest, and the scribes, the Rabbis. Thus, according to Ps. 48:2, Jerusalem is "the city of the great King" (Matt. 5:35), where the temple stands in which the true and only valid sacrificial service can be maintained. Therefore, people go to Jerusalem (Lk. 2:22 ff.), to "the holy city" (Matt. 4:5; 27:53), because it is there that the house of God is situated (cf. Lk. 2:46, 49), which is indissolubly linked to the theocratic institution of the priesthood.

The other theocratic institution, the spiritual authority which knows and expounds the scriptures and therefore the will of God, is also situated in Jerusalem. The priests who supervise the correct performance of the ritual and the scribes who are responsible for the proper observance of the → law, are the representatives of these two establishments. Therefore "scribes from Jerusalem" appear in different parts of Palestine in the fulfilment of their duties (Mk. 3:22; 7:1).

(c) Because Jerusalem has this theocratic significance, it plays a decisive role in the events of the passion. Jesus had to go to Jerusalem in order to fulfil his mission there at the centre of the world of OT Jewish faith (Matt. 16:21; Lk. 9:31). There he confronted the two theocratic institutions: the priests as functionaries of the cult (cf. Lk. 19:45 ff.) and the scribes as keepers of the Mosaic tradition (Matt. 23). Therefore, it was not a matter of no significance where Jesus suffered, died, was buried and rose again. His sacrifice only made sense and was only effective in Jerusalem (Mk. 10:33 f.). But the paradox consists in the fact that the sacrifice was rejected by the theocratic institutions while accepted by God, as the accounts of the resurrection testify (cf. also Mk. 8:31). Hence, Jerusalem is once described as the home of the opponents of Jesus, who are seeking to kill him (Mk. 11:18). From the theological point of view, however, Jerusalem is the setting in which the institutions of the Jewish faith, the cult and the law, are taken up in Jesus' actions (Mk. 11:15–17) and teaching (Mk. 11:18) and are judged by God himself in the crucifixion. "As a place of prayer the temple should reflect the attitude that a man has nothing to achieve or offer to God; consequently it should be open to all men. In this way the whole principle of legalism is fully overcome" (E. Schweizer, *The Good News according to Mark*, 1971, 233).

3. Jerusalem is particularly important in the theology of Luke. "At the beginning (1:5–25) and at the end (24:53) [of Luke's Gospel] there are references to events

which took place in the temple. The promise given to the ancient people of God is fulfilled in the history of Jesus and His Church. The true Israel assembles in the holy place" (E. Lohse, *TDNT* VII 331). Acts goes further in this direction, in that Jerusalem is the place which "links the history of Jesus with the beginning of that of the community, cf. Ac. 10:39; 13:27, 31" (E. Lohse, *TDNT* VII 335). Hence, Jesus' disciples, to whom he had appeared after his resurrection, remained at his express command in Jerusalem (Lk. 24:49, 52), to wait for the outpouring of the Holy Spirit (Acts 1:4; 2:1 ff.). In accordance with their commission they proclaimed the divine events to all peoples beginning from Jerusalem (Lk. 24:47; Acts 5:20 f.). They took over the functions both of the scribes and of the servants of the temple (Lk. 24:53; Acts 2:46; 3:1 ff.; 5:25, 42), by offering praise to God in the temple as the true daily sacrifice. The city remains the focus of the world and the city of God's people. The so-called apostolic council gathered within its walls (Acts 15:1 ff.; 21:18). Emissaries went out from Jerusalem (Acts 8:14; 11:22, 27) and returned there (19:21; 21:15).

4. One must mention, however, another train of thought in the Synoptics which corresponds to the OT prophetic message (see above OT 3 (c)) that Jerusalem is the evil city. It kills the messengers of God (Matt. 23:37 ff. par. Lk. 13:34 ff.). A prophet is nowhere more in danger than in Jerusalem (Lk. 13:33). The city does not recognize what belongs to its peace (Lk. 19:42). Its inhabitants have not wanted to be gathered (Matt. 23:37). Therefore, it comes under judgment (Lk. 19:43 f.) which will be carried out by means of foreign peoples (Lk. 21:20). Jerusalem will be destroyed (Matt. 23:38; Lk. 21:24). Therefore the discerning should weep (Lk. 23:28 ff.). The judgment of Jerusalem begins when the veil in the temple is torn in two (Matt. 27:51 par. Mk. 15:38) and the graves outside the city open (Matt. 27:52 f.). But something new arises from the ruins. Jesus will return to the destroyed city and be greeted with the cry which welcomes the messiah (Matt. 23:39, citing Ps. 118:26).

5. (a) In Jn. Jerusalem is not only the scene of the passion but also the place where Jesus reveals his → glory. Many deeds and miracles take place in the city. Jn. alone records that Jesus quite frequently came from Galilee to Jerusalem (2:13 ff.; 5:1 ff.; 7:10 ff.; 12:12 ff.). Finally, for Jn. Jerusalem is also the place where the change from the old to the new → covenant took place.

(b) Paul was born at Tarsus (Acts 21:39; 22:3), but revisited it after his conversion (Acts 9:30; 11:25). W. C. Van Unnik holds that Jerusalem was the scene of his boyhood and upbringing (*Tarsus or Jerusalem: The City of Paul's Youth*, 1962). For Paul too Jerusalem is the centre of Christendom but in a different sense from the Synoptics and Acts. The gospel went out from Jerusalem (Rom. 15:19), and has brought into being a new unity between Gentiles and Jews, the *ekklēsia* (cf. Eph. 2:14; → Church). Paul emphasizes his agreement with the apostolic council in Jerusalem (Gal. 2:1 ff.). But he does not view this as the highest authority. If he seeks out the apostles (cf. Gal. 1:18–20), it is out of brotherly love and respect; for they preceded him chronologically (Gal. 1:17 f.). But he received his commission and instructions like the others from the Lord himself (Gal. 1:1; 2:2). Because the Gentile Christians have received a share in the spiritual blessings of the original church in Jerusalem, it is natural for Paul that the Jerusalem church should be rendered "service in material blessings" in the form of financial help (Rom. 15:27).

The objection that this "service for Jerusalem" (v. 31) was a kind of tax corresponding to the Jewish temple tax is weakened by the fact that Paul expects only freewill gifts as each individual sees fit (1 Cor. 16:2; 2 Cor. 8:7 f.; 9:7). We must, rather, view this as, on the one hand, the legitimation of the Gentile Christian churches towards Jerusalem and, on the other hand, the external documentation of the interdependence of Gentile Christianity and the original Jerusalem church (cf. also 2 Cor. 8:14 f.; 9:12; → Poor, art. *ptōchos* NT 4(a)). On the place of Jerusalem in Paul's apostolic strategy and eschatological thinking see F. F. Bruce, "Paul and Jerusalem", *TB* 19, 1968, 3–25. Commenting on Rom. 11:26 (cf. Isa. 59:20 f.), "the Deliverer shall come *out of Zion*, and shall turn away ungodliness from Jacob", Bruce writes: "Not only did the gospel first go out into all the world from Jerusalem; Jerusalem (if this reading of Paul's language is correct) would be the scene of its glorious consummation" (op. cit., 25).

(c) In Rev. Jerusalem is described (albeit without mention of the name) as the historical scene of the passion (11:8) and as involved in the events of the end. As the wicked city ("which is allegorically called Sodom and Egypt") it will be "trampled over", while the temple and those who worship in it will be saved (11:1 ff.; cf. Lk. 21:24). In 14:1 the OT name for the temple hill, Mount Zion, is used and it is stated that at the end of the age the prophecy of Joel 2:32 (3:5 MT) will be fulfilled on Mount Zion.

6. Apart from the topographical uses of the name indicated so far, there also occurs in the NT the idea of the heavenly Jerusalem.

(a) In Gal. 4:26 Paul speaks of Jerusalem above (*hē anō Ierousalēm*) which, according to an allegorical interpretation, is the free woman who has given birth to believers (→ Abraham, arts. *Sarra, Hagar* and *Isaak*). In Jewish apocalyptic tradition heavenly Jerusalem was the pre-existent place where God's glory was always present. For Paul it was also the place of freedom from the law. This "Jerusalem above" forms a sharp contrast to "present Jerusalem" (*hē nyn Ierousalēm*), the earthly city which, equally on the basis of an allegory, is called the mother of unbelievers (v. 25; → Parable, art. *parabolē* NT 9).

(b) Heb. 12:22 speaks of *Ierousalēm epouranios*, heavenly Jerusalem, within which Mount Zion is situated. "But this place is not just the goal of the pilgrimage of the people of God which has no abiding city on earth (13:14). The community has already come to Zion, the heavenly Jerusalem. The new Jerusalem is the city in which the new *diathēkē* has been made through the blood of Jesus" (E. Lohse, *TDNT* VII 337; → Covenant).

(c) In Rev. 3:12; 21:2 "new Jerusalem" is described as a heavenly city. At the end of the age it will descend from heaven as the bride of the exalted Christ, and receive as its citizens all those who have been marked as conquerors (3:12). This beautiful city (21:2, 10 f.) which has descended to earth is of vast extent (v. 12 f.). But one thing is absent from it: the temple, "for its temple is the Lord God the Almighty and the Lamb" (v. 22). This view forms a contrast with Jewish expectation in which it is the temple which marks the focal point of heavenly Jerusalem.

→ David, → Israel, → Temple, → Solomon   *H. Schultz*

(a). Y. Aharoni, *The Land of the Bible: A Historical Geography*, 1967; M. Avi-Yonah, *Jerusalem*, 1960; E. Bevan, *Jerusalem under the High Priests*, 1924; F. F. Bruce, "Paul and Jerusalem", *TB* 19,

1968, 3–25; M. Burrows, "Jerusalem", *IDB* II 843–66; G. Dalman, *Sacred Sites and Ways: Studies in the Topography of the Gospels*, 1935; L. Gaston, *No Stone on Another: Studies in the Significance of the Fall of Jerusalem in the Synoptic Gospels*, 1970; G. Fohrer and E. Lohse, *Siōn, Ierousalēm* etc. *TDNT* VII 292–338; R. Furneaux, *The Roman Siege of Jerusalem*, 1973; J. Jeremias, *Jerusalem in the Time of Jesus*, 1969; K. Kenyon, "Excavating Jerusalem", *BA* 27, 1964, 34–52; *Jerusalem: Excavating 3000 Years of History*, 1967; and *Digging up Jerusalem*, 1974; C. Kopp, *The Holy Places of the Gospels*, 1963, 249–417; J. Munck, "Paul and Jerusalem", *Paul and the Salvation of Mankind*, 1959, 182–308; A. Negev, ed., *Archaeological Encyclopedia of the Holy Land*, 1972; M. Noth, "Jerusalem and the Israelite Tradition", *The Laws in the Pentateuch and Other Studies*, 1966, 132–44; A. Parrot, *The Temple of Jerusalem*, 1957; J. B. Payne, "Jerusalem", *ZPEB* III 459–95; N. W. Porteous, "Jerusalem-Zion: the Growth of a Symbol", *Living the Mystery*, 1967, 93–111; J. M. Roberts, "The Davidic Origin of the Zion Tradition", *JBL* 92, 1973, 329 ff.; J. Simons, *Jerusalem in the Old Testament*, 1952; G. A. Smith, *Jerusalem: The Topography, Economics and History from the Earliest Times to* A.D. 70, I–II, 1908; A. Stöger, "Jerusalem", *EBT* II 409–19; W. C. van Unnik, *Tarsus or Jerusalem: The City of Paul's Youth*, 1962.
(b). A. Alt, "Jerusalems Aufsteig", *ZDMG* 1925, 1 ff.; R. Bach and W. Schmauch, "Jerusalem", *EKL* II 257 ff.; H. Bardtke, "Der Tempel von Jerusalem", *TLZ* 11, 1972, 801 ff.; E. Fascher, "Jerusalems Untergang in der urchristlichen und altkirchlichen Überlieferung", *TLZ* 89, 1964, 81 ff.; H. Gese, *Vom Sinai zum Zion*, 1974; H. Guthe, "Jerusalem", *RE* VIII 666–93; and *Die griechisch-romischen Städte des Ostjordanlandes*, 1918; J. Jeremias, "Lade und Zion", in H. W. Wolff, ed., *Probleme biblischer Theologie. G. von Rad zum 70. Geburtstag*, 1971; M. Join-Lambert, *Jérusalem Isaraélite, Chrétienne, Musalmane*, 1958; H. Kosmala, "Jerusalem", *BHHW* II 820 ff.; M. Krupp, *Vergesse ich dein Jerusalem*, 1962; E. Lohmeyer, *Galiläa und Jerusalem*, *FRLANT* 52, 1936; F. Maas and J. Weigelt, "Jerusalem", *RGG*³ III 593 ff.; T. Maertens, *Jérusalem cité de Dieu*, 1954; W. Schmauch, *Orte der Offenbarung und der Offenbarungsort im Neuen Testament*, 1956, 81–121; K. L. Schmidt, "Jerusalem als Urbild und Abbild", *Eranos Jahrbuch* 18, 1950, 207–48; J. Schreiner, *Sion-Jerusalem, Jahwes Königssitz. Theologie der heiligen Stadt im Alten Testament*, 1963; E. Stauffer, *Jerusalem und Rom im Zeitalter Jesu Christi*, 1957; O. H. Steck, *Friedenvorstellungen im Alten Jerusalem, Psalmen, Jesaja, Deuterojesaja*, 1972; L.-H. Vincent, "Les noms de Jérusalem", *Memnon* 6, 1913, 88–124; L.-H. Vincent and F.-M. Abel, *Jérusalem Recherches de Topographie, d'archéologie et d'histoire*, I *Jérusalem antique*, 1912; II *Jérusalem nouvelle*, 1914–24; L.-H. Vincent and A.-M. Stève, *Jérusalem de l'Ancien Testament*, I, *Archéologie de la Ville*, 1954; II–III *Archéologie du Temple. Évolution historique et monumentale de la Ville*, 1956.

Jesus Christ, Nazarene, Christian

The name Jesus Christ actually consists of a proper name, Jesus, and title, Christ, which are linked in a new and unique way. It is thus a formula which expresses the faith of the earliest Christians in Jesus of Nazareth as their Master and Lord, Saviour-King and the universal Redeemer promised by God to his people Israel. This formula achieved a permanent central significance for all subsequent generations of Christians as an appropriate statement of the object of their faith. In view of this, it is necessary to deal first with the name Jesus and the related historical and theological questions. We shall then turn to the title, Christ, ascribed to Jesus of Nazareth by his disciples, and finally focus on Jesus of Nazareth as the Christ.

| Ἰησοῦς | Ἰησοῦς (*Iēsous*), Jesus.

OT *Iēsous* is the Gk. form of the OT Jewish name *Yēšuaʿ*, arrived at by transcribing the Heb. and adding an -*s* to the nom. to facilitate declension. *Yēšuaʿ* (Joshua) seems to have come into general use about the time of the Babylonian exile in place of the older *Yᵉhôšûaʿ*. The LXX rendered both the ancient and more recent forms

330

of the name uniformly as *Iēsous*. Joshua the son of Nun, who according to the tradition was Moses' successor and completed his work in the occupation of the promised land by the tribes of Israel, appears under this name (cf. Exod. 17:8–16; 24:13; 32:17; 33:11; Num. 11:27 ff.; 13:8; 14:6–9, 30–38; 27:18; 21 ff.; Deut. 31:3, 7, 8, 14 f., 23; 34:9; and the Book of Joshua. It is the oldest name containing the divine name Yahweh, and means "Yahweh is help" or "Yahweh is salvation" (cf. the vb. *yāša'*, help, save). Joshua also appears in one post-exilic passage in the Heb. OT (Neh. 8:17) as *Yēšua'* the son of Nun, and not as in the older texts, *Yᵉhôšûa'*.

Among Palestinian Jews and also among the Jews of the dispersion the name Jesus was fairly widely distributed in the pre-Christian period and in the early part of the Christian era. According to Aristeas 48 f. (2nd cent. B.C.; more exact dating disputed), it was borne by two of the Palestinian scholars who were engaged on the translation of the Heb. Pentateuch into Gk. in Alexandria. We are probably led further back still, chronologically, by Jesus ben Sirach, the author of the Book of Sirach (Ecclesiasticus) in the Apocrypha (cf. Sir. 50:27). The Jewish historian Flavius Josephus, who lived in the 1st cent. A.D. and came from a Palestinian priestly family, names no fewer than 19 bearers of the name Jesus in his voluminous writings in Gk. These come both from the ancient and the recent history of his people and about half were contemporaries of "Jesus the so-called Christ" whom he also mentions (*Ant.* 20, 9, 1). The name also occurs about this time, however, in numerous non-literary Jewish texts, among them inscriptions on graves (at Leontopolis or Tell el-Yehudieh north east of Cairo, *ZNW* 22, 1923, 283) and on ossuaries from the neighbourhood of Jerusalem. Some of these are written in Heb. or Aram., others in Gk. One Aram. example bears the name *Yēšua' bar Yᵉhôsēp*, Joshua son of Joseph (E. L. Sukenik, *Jüdische Gräber Jerusalems um Christi Geburt*, 1931, 19 f., see also the illustrations).

NT 1. The NT readily fits into this picture which shows the name Jesus widely spread among the Jews at the time of Jesus of Nazareth and his disciples. Thus in Luke's genealogy of Jesus (3:29) it is borne by one of his ancestors, without the fact being noted as anything extraordinary. Col. 4:11 mentions a Jewish Christian Jesus, who according to the custom of the time and perhaps also as a Roman citizen bore a second non-Semitic name, Justus. In the light of what has already been said it is natural that Joshua should also appear in the NT as "Jesus" (Acts 7:45; Heb. 4:8). There are fairly clear indications that even Barabbas, the Zealot between whom and Jesus Pilate asked the people to choose, had Jesus as his first name. The textual tradition of Matt. 27:16 f. makes clear that the connection of the name with this man was felt at a relatively early period to be a difficulty; at least it is suppressed by the majority of MSS, including some ancient and valuable ones. Examples of similar interference with the original text can be seen, or are probable, in a whole range of other NT passages, among them those where the combined tradition no longer shows the name Jesus (cf. alongside Lk. 3:29; Acts 7:45; 13:6; Col. 4:11 especially Mk. 15:7; Phlm. 23 f.; cf. A. Deissmann, in G. K. A. Bell and A. Deissmann, eds., *Mysterium Christi*, 1930, 18 ff.). The motive here is clearly deep reverence for the name Jesus; it is felt that it can be permitted to no one other than Jesus as "the pioneer and perfecter of our faith" (Heb. 12:2). Reverence for the name Jesus had as its logical outcome – and that very rapidly – the almost general renunciation on the part of Christians of its further secular use. But it is no less significant that by the end of the 1st cent. the name Jesus had become uncommon as a personal name among the Jews too. In its place the OT name $Y^ehôšûa^c$ reappeared with a wide distribution, accompanied by *Iasōn* as the Gk. equivalent among the Jews of the dispersion among whom, in the course of assimilation, the name had already been taken up for a long time (cf. Aristeas 49; Josephus *Ant.* 12, 10, 6). In the same context belongs the fact that Talmudic Judaism soon accustomed itself, when it was obliged to name Jesus of Nazareth, to referring to him as *Yešû* and not as *Yešua^c*. Although the reason for this may lie in the purely external fact that the Christians referred to their Lord as *Yešû* (giving up the *a^c* of the basic Heb. form), it is also an expression, not only of Jewish antipathy, but also of how far this name, among all names, had become unique to the Christians.

2. According to Matt. 1:21 and Lk. 1:31, Jesus' name was determined by heavenly instruction to the father (Matt.) or the mother (Lk.). Matt. in this context also gives an interpretation of the name Jesus. In passing, it describes the future task of Mary's son as to "save his people from their sins." This interpretation is certainly connected with the meaning of the name $Y^ehôšûa^c$ (formed from the divine name and *šua^c*, from the root *yš^c*) which, as we have shown, has a continuing life in the Gk. *Iēsous*: "Yahweh is our help" or "Yahweh is our helper" (see M. Noth, *Die israelitischen Personennamen im Rahmen der gemeinsemitischer Namengebung*, 1928, 154). That the meaning of the name was thoroughly well known at this period is attested by the Alexandrian Jewish exegete and philosopher of religion, Philo, when he interprets Joshua's name as follows: *Iēsous sōtēria kyriou*, Jesus means salvation through the Lord (*Mut.Nom.* 121). Although OT passages like Ps. 31 (30 LXX):8; 130(129 LXX):8 may therefore have influenced the form of Matt.'s words in the narrowing of salvation to the forgiving of the people's sins, their originality is obvious: they attribute to Jesus what was formerly reserved for God. The same understanding of the name Jesus and a corresponding testimony probably lies behind Lk. 2:11, where the → angel of the Lord on the night of Jesus' birth announced him to the shepherds as *sōtēr*, saviour. In this regard one must not overlook the fact that it is particularly in Lk. that witness is borne to Jesus as the saviour of sinners (cf. Lk. 15) and that the angel's message (2:11) no doubt looks back to Lk. 1:76. In both places, each completely independent of the other, we have before us a very early christology, with a similar theological approach to Phil. 2:9. It is clear that as far as they are concerned the name Jesus already contains, in the form of a promise, what is later fulfilled in the title Lord applied to the risen and glorified Jesus of Nazareth for the salvation of all mankind. This is clearly something quite different from Barn. 12:8 ff. with its typological interpretation of certain traits in the biblical picture of Joshua with reference to Jesus of Nazareth, even though it is on the ground that both have the same name in Gk. In the former case we are in the presence of early kerygmatic tradition; in the latter of theological and apologetical reflection. *K. H. Rengstorf*

| $Na\zeta\alpha\rho\eta\nu\acute{o}\varsigma$ | $Na\zeta\alpha\rho\eta\nu\acute{o}\varsigma$ (*Nazarēnos*), $Na\zeta\omega\rho\alpha\tilde{i}o\varsigma$ (*Nazōraios*), Nazarene, from Nazareth. |

1. Since there were many bearers of the name Jesus it was necessary to distinguish between them by means of some additional name. It is therefore quite within the bounds of the ordinary that Jesus is sometimes denoted in the gospels as the son of Joseph (Lk. 3:23; 4:22; Jn. 1:45; 6:42) or even as the son of Mary (Mk. 6:3). The latter is evidently after the death of Joseph. This form of distinction nevertheless may carry more local colouring. Alongside it and beyond it the designation of Jesus as *Nazarēnos* or *Nazōraios* achieved importance and lasting significance. In the textual tradition the two designations are sometimes mixed. This compels the conclusion that for the writers there was no difference in meaning between them. Nevertheless their juxtaposition requires a few comments.

2. Mk. consistently used *Nazarēnos* (1:24; 10:47 *v.l. Nazōraios*; 14:67; 16:6). Lk. 4:34 no doubt depends on Mk. 1:24 and the Gospel contains *Nazarēnos* at one other point in the material peculiar to itself (24:19 with *v.l.*). Otherwise, especially in Acts, Luke consistently uses *Nazōraios* (Lk. 18:37; Acts 2:22; 3:6; 4:10; 6:14; 22:8; 26:9) and by this procedure expresses the fact that for him the two words mean the same. Matt. (2:23; 26:71) and Jn. (18:5, 7; 19:19, i.e. only in the passion narrative) only have the second form. Apart from the Gospels and Acts, neither word occurs in the NT. As far as their sense is concerned, for Matt. (cf. 2:23 with 21:11), Luke (Acts 10:38) and Jn. (1:45) they clearly mean that the Jesus thus referred to came from Nazareth in Galilee. The geographical connection of the two words with Galilee is supported in different ways by Matt. 26:69; 26:71; and Acts 24:5; 1:11. As a term to denote Christians in Gk. areas (Acts 24:5), *Nazōraios* seems to have disappeared quite early in favour of *Christianos* (Acts 11:26), while it was retained in this sense in Jewish areas and survives today in Heb. *noṣrî* as a designation for one who believes in Jesus. There have been similar sounding terms for Christian elsewhere in the Near East from ancient times on. Nevertheless, they do not necessarily rest on the direct influence of Jewish Christian or even of Jewish tradition, but result from the fact that the Syrian church took over *Nazōraios* from NT Gk. as a loanword into its own language and passed it on to its non-Christian environment.

3. The linguistic connection of both words with the place name *Nazaret*, Nazareth or Nazara (Matt. 4:12; Lk. 4:16) in Matt., Lk. and Jn. has been frequently and strongly contested from M. Lidzbarski on. It is now clear that the thesis that Nazareth the place is a pure invention because a place name was necessary to correspond to *Nazōraios* in the Jesus tradition can no longer be entertained. The name has appeared as *nṣrt* initially in a Jewish inscription, probably from a synagogue, in Caesarea, dated from the period after Hadrian, so that there is at last a piece of early Jewish evidence for the existence of the place as a Jewish settlement (M. Avi-Yonah, "A List of Priestly Courses from Caesarea", *Israel Exploration Journal* 12, 1962, 137 ff.). But the philological derivation of *Nazōraios* from Nazareth by H. H. Schaeder, now also supported by Ruth Stiehl, still fails to find unanimous agreement. Recently a new root has been found for the use of *Nazōraios* in a piece of Haggadic theologizing, conceptually thoroughly refined, and connected on the one hand with Isa. 42:6 ff.; 49:6 ff. and on the other with Isa. 11:1. It is thought, to do justice to the facts, that on the one hand the word refers to Christians (they are those who are kept) and on the other to Jesus (he is the *nēṣer*, the "shoot from the stump" of Isa. 11 with all its implications for the future) (B. Gärtner).

333

Nevertheless, it should be regarded as methodologically questionable to wish to explain *Nazōraios* without reference to *Nazarēnos*. The most likely solution is that we have in both words the same assertion in the form of a derivation from *nṣrt*, the only difference being that in *Nazarēnos* we have a pure Gk. formation, whereas in *Nazōraios* an additional Aram. element is used which expresses belonging (cf. Ruth Stiehl).

But however the problem of the relationship of the two designations to the place name may or may not be resolved, the contexts almost unanimously reveal that both words in the NT have essential undertones of dissociation and at the same time contempt. The best commentary one can refer to is Nathaniel's rhetorical question to Philip, "Can anything good come out of Nazareth?" (Jn. 1:46). At all events, for all the witnesses, Jesus' origins in Nazareth are a sign of his lowliness. Nobody understood this as well or emphasized it as unmistakably as Jn., when in his account the description of Jesus as *Nazōraios* found its place in the inscription for his cross on the initiative of the Roman procurator (19:19). Here finally, so to speak, the reader's attention is once again drawn to the fact that Jesus' origins in a place without status or prestige in the surrounding world formed a glaring contrast to the claim with which he had appeared before them.   *K. H. Rengstorf*

Χριστός

Χριστός (*Christos*), Christ; *χρίω* (*chriō*), spread, (in biblical Gk.) anoint; *Μεσσίας* (*Messias*), Messiah.

Christ is derived via the Lat. *Christus* from the Gk. *Christos*, which in the LXX and the NT is the Gk. equivalent of the Aram. *mᵉšîḥā'*. This in turn corresponds to the Heb. *māšîaḥ* and denotes someone who has been ceremonially anointed for an office (→ Anoint). The Gk. transliteration of *mᵉšîḥā'* is *Messias*, which like *Iēsous* is made declinable by the added -*s*. The word messiah, however, occurs only twice in the Gk. NT, only in Jn. 1:41; 4:25. On both occasions it is translated, no doubt by the evangelist himself, as *Christos*. On both occasions it refers to Jesus of Nazareth. The LXX does not use the foreign word but, like the NT (with the exception of the passages mentioned), consistently employs the corresponding Gk. word. The word, therefore, was not first coined by the Christians. In using it the NT authors and their sources were clearly taking over a word and concept which were already available and current in the pre-Christian period. This state of affairs is borne out by, among other things, the OT apocryphal and pseudepigraphal writings.

CL The Gk. word comes from *chriein*, to rub lightly, spread (over something) and requires, apart from its use in the NT, more precise information about what is used. It can be done with oil, as for example with a human body after bathing (as early as Homer), but also with poison, as in the preparation of arrows for battle (also Homer), paint, whitewash (cf. also however Jer. 22:14), or even cosmetics. Basically the word describes a thoroughly secular, everyday process, and has no sacral undertones at all. Naturally this is true for Gk. ears also of the verbal adj. *christos* derived from it. It characterizes an object or a person as rubbed or smeared with whitewash, cosmetics, paint etc., and in given cases anointed. It is anything but an expression of honour. Where it refers to people, it even tends towards the disrespectful. This is certainly the reason why, on the one hand, in non-Christian circles *Christos*, in its reference to Jesus, was soon confused with the Gk. name *Chrēstos* (pronounced *Christos* with long *i*), and why, on the other hand, the Jewish translator of the Bible, Aquila, thought it right in his Gk. version of the OT to render *māšîaḥ* or *m^ešîḥā'*, not by *christos* but by *ēleimmenos* from *aleiphein* which, unlike *chriein*, always means to → anoint. In any case, the meaning of the root is an essential condition for *christos*, as used of Jesus of Nazareth, to have been able so disproportionately quickly and so completely to acquire the character of a proper name. Nevertheless, one must not overlook in this connection the fact that the Heb. vb. *māšaḥ*, for which *chriein* is the LXX equivalent, seems to be fundamentally connected with fat or oil in the sense of to grease (with oil) (E. Kutsch, *Salbung als Rechtsakt im Alten Testament und im alten Orient*, BZAW 87, 1963, 9 f.).

OT 1. In the OT two office bearers are expressly described as *māšîaḥ* i.e. as anointed (with oil): the high priest as the one responsible for the official cult (→ Priest) and the → king. The reason for this pairing lies in the fact that in both cases the anointing, corresponding to its character as a legal act, is as essential for the conferring of the authority connected with the office as it is for the resulting responsibility before God as the God of Israel. However, only the figure of the king has to be reckoned as messianic in the sense of specific messianic expectation. This is not altered by the fact that in the documents from Qumran (on the basis of Zech. 4:1 ff., 11 ff.) there is once again talk of the coming of two men anointed of the Lord (see further below) and that in the NT picture of Jesus as messiah alongside the kingly features expressly priestly features are not lacking (→ Priest).

2. The expectation is ultimately related to the idea of the kingship and the sovereign kingly rule of God on the basis of the OT revealed faith. The varying judgments on the monarchy in 1 Sam. 8–11 notwithstanding, it is difficult not to come to the conclusion that the institution of the monarchy, when it came to it, binds on the king for the time being a special responsibility for the things of God. This is clear from the censures which the pious historians of the OT passed on individual kings of Israel or Judah, according to whether or not they had ruled and lived consistently with faith in God as the one true God. The crucial factor is no doubt the element of responsibility in the affairs of God on the basis of transferred power. This must be so if, after the Davidic kings to whom must be ascribed considerable significance for the development of the messianic expectation, like Saul before them, a foreigner such as the Persian king Cyrus (Isa. 45:1) can be described as God's anointed, i.e. *māšîaḥ*. He, like them, is one of God's chosen instruments in the pursuit of God's universal aim of the salvation of all people through the people he has made his own possession. Recognition of the divine freedom implied here is all the more essential, as the expectation of a messianic, kingly saviour figure was clearly associated from an early date with the tribe of Judah (Gen. 49:8 ff.).

A far-reaching influence on the development of the idea of the messiah as a historical figure of increasingly supernatural dimensions was the increasingly vivid memory of the magnificent and successful period of → David's rule, the first king from Judah (cf. Isa. 9:2–7 [MT 1–6]; 11:1 ff.; Mic. 5:2–6 [MT 1–5]). Whether and how far we have also to reckon with influence on the expectation from the pre-Davidic priest-kings of → Jerusalem, which David captured and made his capital (2 Sam.

5:6 ff.; 6:1 ff.), cannot be decided with certainty. Nevertheless, it may be acknowledged that there are certain "sacral" elements in the OT picture of the messiah, as in that of later Judaism, which would be best explained on this basis. However this may be, it cannot seriously be doubted that the dominant motif in the idea of the messiah is the kingly one, and that all other motifs are secondary to it.

3. It is all the more important to emphasize this because, with respect to the practice of anointing in Israel in the early period, it is necessary to make careful historical and terminological distinctions. According to recent investigations (especially those of E. Kutsch), although the anointing of the king and the anointing of the high priest (or originally of all the priests?) are similar in form, their life-setting was entirely different. The background of both was ancient oriental custom. Nevertheless, the anointing of the Judaic kings seems to have been (even and precisely when it was performed by representatives of the people; cf. 2 Sam. 2:4 ff.; 5:3) essentially associated with the gift and with the solemn ritual transfer of authority, power and honour (Heb. $k\bar{a}\underline{b}\hat{o}\underline{d}$; Gk.; *doxa*; → Glory). The anointing gave the one anointed a position of power and the right to exercise it. It also brought him corresponding respect, together with honour and on occasion also wealth. On the other hand, there is much to support the idea that the anointing of the priests was first and foremost a cultic purification with the object of enabling the priests to conduct valid worship.

4. In this context it is worthwhile considering further the description of the Persian king Cyrus as the anointed of God (Isa. 45:1), even though he had clearly not been anointed as king in accordance with (Israelite) Judaic custom. We see here a sublimation of the concept which makes it independent of the external act by transferring the entire weight on to God's appointment of the one designated by the anointing. In this case the anointed one is no more and no less than the one chosen in a special way by God and placed under his command. God's anointed is thus dependent on God as well as integrated into his plan in obedience to his will. This helps to explain why the Judaic kings (contrary to the pattern of ancient sacral monarchies elsewhere) together with the OT Jewish messiah never themselves acquired divine features even in the so-called Enthronement Psalms, such as Pss. 2 and 110. As the Lord's anointed, they remained in their kingship as dependent on God as they were utterly responsible to him (cf. on Saul, 1 Sam. 12:3, 5; 24:6–11; cf. also 9:1 ff. with 15:10 ff.; on David, 2 Sam. 19:22; 23:1; cf. also 1 Sam. 16:1 ff. with 2 Sam. 11–12; on Zedekiah, Lam. 4:20; on Cyrus, see above). On the other hand, it follows from this that at any given moment the king, i.e. the actual reigning monarch of Judah from the house of David, can be introduced in the Pss. as God's anointed without further special explanation (Pss. 18:50; 20:6; 28:8; 84:9; 89:38, 51; 132:10, 17; cf. also 1 Sam. 2:10; Hab. 3:13). However, in this context also belongs the fact that → David (cf. 2 Sam. 3:18; 7:5), and his successors (→ Solomon, 1 Ki. 3:7 ff.; 8:28 ff.; later kings not mentioned by name Ps. 89:39; cf. Pss. 86:2, 4, 16; 143:2), and even a post-exilic claimant like Zerubbabel (Hag. 2:23; cf. Zech. 3:8) are called the → servants of God. This is thoroughly consistent with what has already been said. Son (Ps. 2:7; 89:26 f.) and servant, in so far as they serve to describe the relationship of the anointed one to God, are not mutually exclusive. From God's point of view they belong inseparably together. However, it must be stressed that, because in the text before us it is impossible to

recognize kingly features, it is very difficult to give a precise answer to the question whether or not the Servant Songs (Isa. 43:1 ff.; 49:1 ff.; 50:4 ff.; 52:13 ff.) refer to a kingly figure as messiah. Hence, scholars are less and less inclined to allow an essential connection with the expectation of a future saviour king. They tend to explain them, as far as their original intention is concerned, in other ways (cf. → Son of God, art. *pais theou*). On the other hand, there is a basis for it in the idea of responsibility under the claims of God among his people if even a prophet like Elisha (1 Ki. 19:16; cf. however also Isa. 61:1) can appear in the ranks of the anointed, and if this idea as such persisted until the Christian era (1QM 11:7; CD 2:12 f.).

5. It has been rightly pointed out that the OT exhibits no clear developments of the messianic expectation. All that can be demonstrated is the presence of the expectation as such in the passages already referred to and in others extending via Jer. 23:5 ff. and Ezek. 34:23 f.; 37:24 f. (cf. 17:22 f.) to Haggai and Zechariah. Until this point they exhibit a strange uniformity. (The "branch of David" introduces a kind of golden age, but does it in the latter days, to a certain extent in the form of the establishing of the kingly rule of God.) It is not until the Hel. period that this is overtaken by a sharp materialization of the concept in the direction of the expectation of an eschatological Jewish national ideal ruler figure who would nonetheless transcend national frontiers. It seems that the colours at least in part were taken from the picture of the Maccabees and Hasmoneans and introduced into the older expectation orientated towards the memory of David. We see this most clearly in Pss. Sol. 17:21 ff.; 18:5 ff. Here the specific concept of the messiah also appears in fixed form. Significantly its association with the Davidic tradition did not have the result that the messiah could only be imagined as coming from the line of David. A notorious example of one who was no descendant of David is Simeon ben Kosebah, whom no less a person than the leading Rabbi Akiba greeted as Bar Kokhba, the "star out of Jacob" promised in Num. 24:17 and thus identified him as messiah (*c.* A.D. 132; T. J. Taanith 4:8:68d; 48 ff.; Euseb., *H.E.* 4, 6, 2; on Bar Kokhba see S. Abramsky in *Encyclopaedia Judaica* IV 227–39). His collapse, which severely shook messianism, may nevertheless have contributed to the fact that in Judaism's liturgical texts the hope of a messiah from the line of David has persisted to this day, even if the expectation as such has undergone drastic transformations. The latter, however, lie outside the scope of the present study.

6. However, the expectation of a Davidic messiah represents only one type of messianism in the period between the exile and A.D. 135. Altogether it took a variety of forms. It was influenced not only by → Moses (cf. Deut. 18:15 ff.) and → Elijah (Sir. 48:10; cf. K. H. Rengstorf, *Das Evangelium nach Lukas*, NTD 3[15], 1972, on Lk. 9:51 ff.) but also in apocalyptic texts and traditions (Eth.Enoch, 2 Esd.) by the idea of a son of man (cf. Dan. 7:13 ff.; → Son of God etc., art. *hyios tou anthrōpou*) as a bringer of salvation who is sometimes also thought of as pre-existent. Even the expectation of a messianic high priest is not lacking. The brightness of this hope is reflected very impressively in the texts that have been found by the Dead Sea. It is they which leave no doubt that the messianic hope with which Jesus and the primitive church were faced was anything but unified and unambiguous. This is a fact of great significance for judging correctly what is represented in the NT as messianism.

NT 1. *Christos* in the NT (→ art. *Iēsous*). The decisive feature of the NT against the background of contemporary messianic expectation is summed up in the thesis that the combined NT witness to Jesus of Nazareth, however varied in details, is consciously christological. Wherever the NT is concerned with Jesus, it is concerned with him as Christ, i.e. as Messiah. This includes the fact that, for the whole of the NT, messianism no longer stands under the sign of expectation but under that of fulfilment. Everywhere the Christ event is spoken of in the perfect or past tense. The writings do indeed look into the future as well, sometimes very intensively. But the One who is awaited comes as the One who has already come. He is not someone unknown; he is as well known to those who await him as they are to him (cf. Jn. 10:14).

2. It is significant that the essential unity of the proclamation of Christ with the title messiah is established, objectively as well as subjectively, with the least ambiguity in the witness of John which, however, comes relatively late in the NT. It is attested particularly in Jn. 1:41 and 4:25. In both passages messiah and Christ are expressly equated (cf. OT 2 above). Both passages lead to the conclusion that we must ascribe to Palestinian Jews the fact that in the messiah the central concept in Jewish messianic expectation has become the possession of the developing Hel. church. It has found its way into the language of their worship and preaching, and has established itself there. No doubt the transmission of this faith came about through the transmission of confessional and catechetical summaries of the message about Jesus. These were originally formulated in Aram. or Heb. on the territory of the primitive church. Subsequently they were translated into Gk. as the mission to the Gk. churches extended beyond the boundaries of Palestinian Jewry. The best illustration of the process lies in 1 Cor. 15:1 ff. Here we have the text of the gospel which Paul had transmitted to the Corinthians and which he himself had previously received. Along with everything else we find *Christos* without the article. Despite many hesitations, this reference to the messiah without the def. art. must stem from the usage of contemporary Palestinian Jews (see further 1 Cor. 15:12 ff., 16 f., 20, 23; cf. Gal. 2:20 f.; 3:16; 5:1; 1 Cor. 5:7; Rom. 5:6, 8; 6:4, 9; 8:10, 34; and also 1 Pet. 2:21; 3:18; cf. K. H. Rengstorf, *Die Auferstehung Jesu*, 1967[5], 129 ff.). The influence of the LXX can be eliminated, for almost all that occurs there is the phrase *christos kyriou*, the Lord's, i.e. God's, anointed. Consequently, the Christian faith in Jesus, so far as it is expressed as faith in Christ, has to be traced back to the earliest Palestinian Christianity. In the Gk. churches, therefore, the word *christos*, when linked with Jesus, completed relatively quickly the transition from an adj., which it is essentially, to a proper name. And in the process it retained its traditional reference to Jesus' status. Therefore, wherever it appears, even as part of the name it refers to the majesty of Jesus.

3. The occurrence of *Christos* (without any art.) in the fragment of earlier kerygma taken up by Paul in 1 Cor. 15:3–5 gives us a glimpse of a unique fact. The tradition of the primitive church which may be seen here, certainly one of the oldest fragments of tradition in the whole of the NT, finds no contradiction between Jesus' violent death on the → cross (cf. 1:18 "For the word of the cross . . .") and the name of Christ ascribed to him. This is all the more remarkable, because it seemed natural to the contemporaries of the early Christians that the collapse of a messianic pretender was the decisive proof of the spuriousness of his own claims

338

and of the hopes centred on him by his followers (cf. Acts 5:36 f. with Mk. 15:29 par. Matt. 27:17 and the later judgment of the "son of the star", Simeon ben Kosebah, as the "son of lies"). We find the same situation as in the fragment quoted in other pre-Pauline passages incorporated by the apostle into his own proclamation, e.g. Rom. 4:25 (where *paredothē* certainly refers to the death of Jesus and not to Judas' betrayal), or Rom. 3:25 (with its reference to Jesus' blood as a sin offering). To mention nothing else, the same line is followed by all four NT evangelists when they take over as part of the kerygma (most clearly in Jn. 18:36 f.; 19:19 ff.) the inscription on the cross (cf. Matt. 27:37; Mk. 15:26; Lk. 23:36). This was intended to expose Jesus as pseudo-king of the Jews, i.e. as pseudo-messiah, but the evangelists make it an involuntary proclamation of Jesus as messiah by his enemies, because that was what God willed. This is expressed in the kerygma with the help of the idea that Jesus, just because he was messiah/Christ, and not despite the fact, had to suffer and die. Thus God expressly determined things in this way with regard to Jesus' messiahship. This is attested by the primitive formula of Lk. 24:26, the predictions of suffering in the synoptic gospels (→ Suffer), the Johannine sayings of Jesus like Jn. 3:14; 12:34, and not least by Jesus' farewell discourse in Jn. (Jn. 14–16; see further below). The clear impression we receive from all these passages is that, when it represented itself as the community of Jesus, the primitive church intended to represent itself simply as the messianic community. For in its preaching of Jesus as messiah it was at the same time interpreting itself messianically in relation to its life, its historical origins and its aims. If at a relatively early date Christians began to consider themselves as the → Israel of God (Gal. 6:16), i.e. the true Israel, as distinct from Israel according to the → flesh (1 Cor. 10:18), the rational and spiritual roots for this lie in the messianism that has just been outlined. The messianism which was already to hand and which was linked with Jesus was, therefore, neither spiritualized nor re-interpreted. Rather, it was taken up and set out on a large scale. Paul attests the same for the Gk. churches when in 1 Cor. 15:25 he leaves the last event before the end in the form of the kingly rule of the Christ/messiah. Naturally further passages in the Synoptic Gospels which in any case were not intended for Jewish readers, form comparisons with Jesus as → king. Examples are the parable of the royal wedding (Matt. 22:1 ff.), the parable of the judgment of the world (Matt. 25:31 ff.: the Son of man is king, vv. 31, 34, 40), and also a saying like Lk. 22:25 f. which explains the particular nature of Jesus' kingship in terms of his disciples' self-sacrifice in the service of others.

The most surprising fact is the part played by Jesus' messiahship in the latest of the four Gospels, Jn. The crucial question throughout the whole book is always that of a correct understanding of Jesus' kingship, beginning with the conversation between Jesus and Nathanael (Jn. 1:47 ff.; but cf. before that 1:19 f., 41, 45) via 6:1 ff. and 12:12 ff. (to mention but two passages) to the dialogue between Pilate and Jesus (18:33 ff.) and that between Pilate and the chief priests (19:21 f.). In the discussion with the Samaritan woman Jesus discloses his messiahship (4:25 f.). One will not be mistaken if one recognizes in the solemn *Iēsous Christos* the confessional formula of John's own church (17:3; cf. 1:17; 20:31; cf. further 1 Jn. 2:22; 4:2; 5:1; 2 Jn. 7). In this formula the second word has lost nothing of its predicative character, and therefore ought really to be written with a small initial letter. Here the primitive christological inheritance is preserved in all its splendour and without any contraction. Jn. clearly lacks all the traditional illustrative material which characterizes the picture of Christ in Rev. (the lion of the tribe of Judah, 5:5; the shoot of David, 22:16; etc.). But that does not alter the fact that here too at the turn of the century full continuity in christology is maintained with the primitive Palestinian church. This was decisive for the impending attempts at conceptual formulations of the catholic faith in Christ.

4. Naturally the messianic element in the NT faith in Christ and in the NT confession of Christ is inseparable from that event which, in the witness of the NT, is called the → resurrection of Jesus from the dead. Jesus' resurrection is reckoned as his resurrection as Christ/messiah (cf. Acts 2:31 with 1 Cor. 15:4, and also Rom. 1:4). It appears everywhere as something done by God to the crucified and buried Jesus (cf. Acts 2:36) and moreover as his vindication by God himself (cf. Rom. 6:7 ff.; 1 Tim. 3:16). It is fully consistent, therefore, that in Jesus' statements about his suffering, the announcement of his death is always accompanied by that of his resurrection. This is not so much intended to discredit the opponents who refused to believe him and delivered him up to death on the cross as to secure his messiahship, which seemed to be disproved by his death on the cross (cf. Lk. 24:26 with 24:19 ff.). One should not, therefore, underestimate the fact that the resurrection event, however it may be interpreted historically, has its proper place in Jesus' messiahship. The fact that the passage of the gospel into a non-Jewish environment made no difference to this is so significant, because it not only illustrates how a Christian church consisting of former Jews and former Gentiles understood itself, but in general it sheds a great deal of light on that church's relationship to history. In a formal way the church's consciousness of the special nature of its own origins in a historically unique event is here bound into a confession. This involves, however, not only the so-called Jesus of history in his unchangeable historical form. It also expresses a permanent affirmation of the spiritual heritage common to all Christians in "Old Testament" history and revelation, and at the same time decisively renounces all unhistorical religiosity and preaching. What Paul writes in Rom. 9–11 about the relation of the Christian church to Judaism presupposes a confident reliance upon the messiahship of Jesus which God has legitimated just as much as does the expectation of a new heaven and a new earth in Rev. (cf. especially 5:1 ff.; 22:16). This is linked to the risen and exalted Jesus (cf. Rev. 1:5, 18), or the certainty that the coming of the → kingdom of God is linked with Jesus as the Christ (Acts 28:31; Lk. 17:20 f.). To this extent the whole of Christian preaching, which is conceived in principle in the NT as a unity but carried out in detail in a variety of forms, has its source and its centre everywhere in the messiahship of Jesus which God has confirmed.

5. Finally, the formula *Iēsous Christos* leads to the question whether the linking of Jesus' name with the title of messianic dignity and honour was the work of his church, in which it expressed its eschatological faith, or whether in any way Jesus himself was responsible for it. This poses the problem of Jesus' messianic consciousness. Since it cannot be dealt with here in the necessary breadth, some few reflections may all the same lead to the indispensable minimum of conclusions which are demanded.

(a) Since historical criticism began to occupy itself with the NT Gospels and the tradition handled by the evangelists, it has always been maintained that the sources are not sufficient to confirm the statement that Jesus himself had a messianic consciousness. To support this view scholars today point not only to the kerygmatic character of even the accounts of Jesus' examination before the Sanhedrin with his confession of messiahship, but also to the fact that one of the two main synoptic sources, the so-called sayings source Q contains nothing that attributes messiahship to Jesus, With respect to both reasons, however, one must now recommend caution. On the one hand, even today Q still rests on a working hypothesis. On the other hand, there is still the need to explain how the kerygma by itself arrived at the idea of having Jesus represent himself to the Sanhedrin as the messiah if he and his disciples did not regard him as the messiah during his lifetime. All the same one should reckon with the possibility, on the evidence of the tradition that is available to us, that Jesus himself neither developed a specific messianic programme nor, and this is of the greatest importance, referred to himself in any form as messiah. According to the narrative tradition, he simply permitted people to attribute to him messianic titles like "Son of David" (Mk. 10:47 f. etc.; → Son), without adopting an attitude of agreement or of denial towards them. Furthermore, the picture of Jesus which is reflected in the tradition when critically analysed, leads us to suppose that he conformed to none of the traditional messianic descriptions. Thus he called in question by his person the attachment to himself of the current messianic expectation of a political saviour-king, by his own followers. This appears to extend to the correctness of all contemporary messianic expectations. Even an event like Peter's so-called confession at Caesarea Philippi (Matt. 16:13–23; Mk. 8:27–33; Lk. 9:18–22), accepting its historical reliability, does not take us fundamentally beyond this conclusion. It boils down to the fact that the events connected with his passion and Easter would have been bound to appear quite differently in the tradition, if at any point in time Jesus had given precise information about himself, where his messiahship was concerned. Finally one must add to the picture that has already been drawn the fact that the tradition does not allow Jesus to triumph over death and the grave as the man he was, but, in the case of his resurrection, makes him the object of a mysterious direct action on the part of God. Moreover, the tradition is never in the position to reveal this mystery, nor is it ever inclined to. The result, without abandoning oneself to an exaggerated scepticism with regard to the sources, is a fairly unanimous picture. It is described, very imperfectly and in an unbalanced fashion, by the ambiguous phrase, the messianic secret. Nevertheless, the phrase still points in a direction in which the answer to the question posed at the outset is to be found.

(b) The problem can only be properly understood, i.e. as it was in the tradition and by Jesus himself, when account is taken of the fact that Jesus' whole ministry was deliberately concentrated on his immediate surroundings and within this especially on his disciples. This means that one cannot talk of him apart from them, and in particular that one cannot ask questions about his self-consciousness, whatever form it took, without reference to them. This is all the more necessary in view of the rôle of his disciples in the things "concerning Jesus of Nazareth" (Lk. 24:19), which may not have been a very significant episode but which all the same was an episode. As the quoted passage itself suggests, the category of prophet which has recently been invoked again though with strong qualifications to help define Jesus' self-consciousness (cf. E. Käsemann, "The Problem of the Historical

341

Jesus", *Essays on New Testament Themes*, 1964, 15–47), would never have sufficed to divest the history of Jesus of its episodic character, if it had stopped at his death. It cannot be mere coincidence that the tradition contains no suggestion that he himself used this category or the idea of his inspiration in connection with his own person, or that he passed it on to his followers. In the mouth of the disciples on the Emmaus road it is just as much the writer's own attempt to understand Jesus as are the other attempts in the tradition (cf. Mk. 6:14 ff. par. Matt. 14:1 f.; Lk. 9:7 f.). For its part, the tradition makes clear that as far as it is concerned the only proper attitude towards Jesus is that which the whole NT calls *pistis*, → faith which involves simple trust. What is really remarkable about Jesus' dealings with his disciples is that he sought right from the beginning and continually thereafter to bring them into this attitude which, because it leads of necessity to a particular kind of behaviour, contradicts any mere theory about him and indeed radically excludes it. The disciples themselves did not finally achieve this attitude or behaviour until after the Easter events. Nevertheless, it must be the person of Jesus and the impression that the disciples received from him which were responsible for the association of this attitude with the use of the category of messiah. But then we can only deal with impressions which they received from the Jesus of history during his lifetime (cf. Lk. 24:32). This must be reckoned to exclude the possibility that the situation created by Easter was appropriate for laying down the foundation of a messianic theory about Jesus. The new situation did not encourage the development of ideas but final personal decisions and corresponding actions. This could only come about if the picture of the risen Jesus and that of the earthly Jesus were not contradictory but mutually interpretative on the ground of their connection with him.

(c) The result, therefore, is that the remaining questions about Jesus' self-consciousness or self-understanding in relation to the category of messiahship must be shown from the tradition itself to be wrongly posed. The only question to ask would be about the traits in the person of Jesus which predisposed his disciples after Easter to see no alternative to formulating their faith in him in the way they did, in the context of the messianic hope of their people as it was expressed in the scriptures and the traditions. The question is all the more important as the preaching of the messiah by its reference to the office of the king of salvation, contained particular elements predisposing it to become the crystallizing point of christology. Nevertheless, this touches on a range of problems which cannot be dealt with here. Enough has been said to show that it was the mystery of the person of Jesus which was responsible for the disciples feeling themselves confronted by the question of the messiah in the earthly Jesus. On the basis of their encounters with the risen Jesus, the disciples finally answered it by the confession that he was the messiah and that in him God has fulfilled his → promise to the house of → David and to → Israel of salvation for the whole of mankind in a manner that is nevertheless only accessible to faith.

(d) Naturally the name Jesus Christ means more to Christianity than the messianic status of a certain Jesus of Nazareth, in whom God fulfilled his promises to the fathers. Every aspect of the salvation which God has intended for and bestowed upon the world is, for the whole of the NT, bound up in Jesus, in so far as he is the Christ. In Jesus as the one who is the Christ "the whole fullness of deity dwells bodily" (Col. 2:9; → Fullness) for the salvation of all those who put their trust in him and appropriate to themselves the fruit of his death and resurrection (Rom. 4:24 f.). To express this a single title like Messiah or Christ is just not sufficient. Therefore, when the NT kerygma expounds the salvation bound up in Christ, it makes use of other titles of honour which are appropriate to the particular reference. These emphasize in turn the side of his person or of his work on which the particular title depends, like → Son of God, → Lord or also our Lord, Saviour (→ Redemption, art. *sōzō*), mediator (→ Covenant, art. *mesitēs*). Nevertheless, if Christ has been transformed from a title of honour to a part of Jesus' name, this corresponds to the essential feature in his historical appearance which at the same time must be reckoned as the condition of his whole work as mediator of salvation: his obedient submission to God's will as manifested in the process of God's self-revelation in the history of the people of Israel. To this extent Jesus' affirmation of his messiahship, whether or not it was explicitly announced, is for the whole kerygma the presupposition of his path to the cross. It is equally the presupposition of his resurrection and exaltation on God's part. This element in Jesus' messiahship, central for christology, is represented nowhere in the NT as clearly and at the same time as comprehensively as in the christological hymn which Paul introduced into his letter to the Philippians (Phil. 2:5 ff.; → Empty, art. *kenos*). Here he describes Jesus' path via the incarnation, the life of obedience and the death of obedience on the cross to the resurrection and to exaltation at God's side as the path of Christ Jesus, i.e. of that messiah who is identical with Jesus of Nazareth.

K. H. Rengstorf

| Χριστιανός | Χριστιανός (*Christianos*), Christian. |

The identification of the messiah with Jesus of Nazareth brought the disciples the name *Christianoi*. Compared with other names for the followers of Jesus, like disciple or believer, the word is quite rare in the NT. By its whole formation it is a word which defines the one to whom it is applied as belonging to the party of a certain *Christos*, very much as *Hērōdianos* is a technical term for the followers of Herod (Mk. 3:6; 12:13; Matt. 22:16). Its use also presupposes that for the Gk. environment of developing Christianity *christos* had taken on the meaning of a proper name, a process which would have been facilitated by the resemblance to the name *Chrēstos*, pronounced *Christos*. According to Acts 11:26, *Christianos* was first used for Christians in Syrian Antioch. This passage, like the two others in which the word occurs in the NT (Acts 26:28; 1 Pet. 4:16), leads us to suppose that, being applied to Christians by outsiders, it contained an element of ridicule and that in this it did not differ from the description *Nazarēnos* or *Nazōraios* (see above). Like it and like many other names formed in the same way, it soon clearly became a name which those called by it felt honoured to bear. *K. H. Rengstorf*

→ Anoint, → Birth, → Confess, → God, → Present, → Proclamation, → Resurrection, → Son, → Spirit, → War, Revolution

On Jesus and the Quest of the Historical Jesus:
(a). P. Althaus, *The So-Called Kerygma and the Historical Jesus*, 1959; C. C. Anderson, *Critical Quests of Jesus*, 1969; and *The Historical Jesus: A Continuing Quest*, 1972; H. Anderson, *Jesus*

and Christian Origins, 1964; C. K. Barrett, *Jesus and the Gospel Tradition*, 1967; H.-W. Bartsch, ed., *Kerygma and Myth: A Theological Debate, Volumes I and II combined with enlarged Bibliography*, 1972; F. W. Beare, *The Earliest Records of Jesus*, 1962; G. K. A. Bell, and A. Deissmann, eds., *Mysterium Christi: Christological Studies by British and German Theologians*, 1930, see especially Deissmann's essay on "The Name 'Jesus' ", 3–30; E. Best, *The Temptation and the Passion: The Markan Soteriology, Society for New Testament Studies Monograph Series 2*, 1965; G. Bornkamm, *Jesus of Nazareth*, 1960; J. Bowker, *Jesus and the Pharisees*, 1973; C. E. Braaten and R. A. Harrisville, eds., *The Historical Jesus and the Kerygmatic Christ: Essays on the New Quest of the Historical Jesus*, 1964; S. G. F. Brandon, *Jesus and the Zealots*, 1967; C. Brown, *Jesus in European Protestant Theology 1778–1860: A Study of Trends in Theological Method*, (Dissertation, Bristol) 1969; R. E. Brown, "The Problem of the Virginal Conception of Jesus", *Theological Studies*, 33, 1972, 3–34 (reprinted in *The Virginal Conception & Bodily Resurrection of Jesus*, 1973); F. F. Bruce, "History and the Gospel", *Faith and Thought* 93, 1964, 121–45; *New Testament History*, 1969; *Jesus and Christian Origins outside the New Testament*, 1974; and "Myth and History", in C. Brown, ed., *History, Criticism and Faith: Four Exploratory Studies*, 1976, 79–100; R. Bultmann, *Jesus and the Word*, 1934; and *Jesus Christ and Mythology*, 1958; H. J. Cadbury, *The Peril of Modernizing Jesus*, 1937; E. C. Colwell, *Jesus and the Gospel*, 1963; H. Conzelmann, *Jesus: The classic article from RGG³ expanded and updated*, 1973; O. Cullmann, *Jesus and the Revolutionaries*, 1970; G. Dalman, *Jesus-Jeshua*, 1929; and *The Words of Jesus, Considered in the Light of Post-Biblical Jewish Writings and the Aramaic Language*, 1902; H. Daniel-Rops, *Jesus in his Time*, 1955; M. Dibelius, *Jesus*, 1949; C. H. Dodd, *History and the Gospel*, 1938; *The Founder of Christianity*, 1970; and "The Portrait of Jesus in John and the Synoptics", in W. R. Farmer, C. F. D. Moule, and R. R. Niebuhr, eds., *Christian History and Interpretation: Studies Presented to John Knox*, 1967, 183–98; F. G. Downing, *The Church and Jesus: A Study in History, Philosophy and Theology*, 1968; J. D. G. Dunn, "Jesus – Flesh and Spirit: An Exposition of Romans I. 3–4", *JTS* New Series 24, 1973, 40–68; "The Messianic Secret in Mark", *TB* 21, 1970, 92–117; and *Jesus and the Spirit*, 1975; G. Ebeling, "Jesus and Faith" and "The Question of the Historical Jesus and the Problem of Christology", *Word and Faith*, 1963, 201–46 and 288–304; A. Edersheim, *The Life and Times of Jesus the Messiah*, I–II, 1881; W. R. Farmer, *The Synoptic Problem: A Critical Analysis*, 1964; and "An Historical Essay on the Humanity of Jesus Christ", in W. R. Farmer, C. F. D. Moule and R. R. Niebuhr, eds., op. cit. 101–26; W. Foerster, *Iēsous, TDNT* III 284–93; R. T. France, "The Authenticity of the Sayings of Jesus", in C. Brown, ed., op. cit.; and *Jesus and the Old Testament*, 1971; J. W. Fraser, *Jesus and Paul: Paul as Interpreter of Jesus from Harnack to Kümmel* 1974; E. Fuchs, *Studies of the Historical Jesus*, 1964; R. H. Fuller, *The Mission and Achievement of Jesus*, 1954; E. J. Goodspeed, *A Life of Jesus*, 1967; L. Goppelt, *Jesus, Paul and Judaism: An Introduction to New Testament Theology*, 1964; R. M. Grant, *The Earliest Lives of Jesus*, 1961; J. J. Gunther, "The Family of Jesus", *EQ* 46, 1974, 25–41; D. Guthrie, *Jesus the Messiah*, 1972; and "Jesus Christ", *ZPEB* III 497–583; C. Gore, *Jesus of Nazareth*, 1929; B. Gustafsson, "The Oldest Graffiti in the History of the Church?" *NTS* 3, 1956–57, 65–69; F. Hahn, *Mission in the New Testament*, 1963; A. C. Headlam, *The Life and Teaching of Jesus the Christ*, 1923; C. F. H. Henry, ed., *Jesus of Nazareth: Saviour and Lord*, 1966; A. J. B. Higgins, *Jesus and the Son of Man*, 1964; and *The Tradition about Jesus*, 1969; M. D. Hooker, "Christology and Methodology", *NTS* 17, 1970–71, 480–87; A. M. Hunter, *Interpreting the New Testament, 1900–1950*, 1951; and *The Work and Words of Jesus*, 1954; J. Jeremias, *The Unknown Sayings of Jesus*, 1957; and *New Testament Theology*, I, *The Proclamation of Jesus*, 1971; J. Jocz, *The Jewish People and Jesus Christ*, 1951²; M. Kähler, *The So-called Historical Jesus and the Historic Biblical Christ*, 1964; E. Käsemann, "The Problem of the Historical Jesus", *Essays on New Testament Themes*, 1964, 15–47; L. E. Keck, *A Future for the Historical Jesus*, 1972; J. N. D. Kelly, *Early Christian Creeds*, 1972³; and *Early Christian Doctrines*, 1968⁴; J. Klausner, *Jesus of Nazareth*, 1929; W. G. Kümmel, *The New Testament: The History of the Investigation of its Problems*, 1973; G. E. Ladd, *A Theology of the New Testament*, 1975, 13–309; X. Léon-Dufour, *The Gospels and the Jesus of History*, 1968; H. K. McArthur, ed., *In Search of the Historical Jesus*, 1970; H. Z. Maccoby, "Jesus and Barabbas", *NTS* 16, 1969–70, 55–60; C. C. McCown, *The Search for the Real Jesus, A Century of Historical Study*, 1940; H. D. A. Major, T. W. Manson and C. J. Wright, *The Mission and Message of Jesus: An Exposition of the Gospels in the Light of Modern Research*, 1937; T. W. Manson, *The Teaching of Jesus*, 1935²; *The Sayings of Jesus*, 1950; *The Servant-Messiah*, 1953; "Materials for a Life of Jesus", *Studies in the Gospels and Epistles*, edited by M. Black, 1962, 3–145; and "The Life of Jesus; some tendencies in present-day research", in W. D. Davies and D. Daube eds., *The Background of the New Testament and its Eschatology. In Honour of Charles Harold Dodd*, 1956, 211–21; C. F. D. Moule, "Jesus in New Testament Kerygma", in O. Böcher and K. Haacker, eds., *Verborum Veritas: Festschrift für Gustav Stählin*, 1970, 15–26; F. Mussner, *The Historical Jesus in the Gospel of St. John*, 1967; S. Neill, *The Interpretation of the New Testament, 1861–1961*, 1964; R. C. Nevius, "The Use of the Definite Article with 'Jesus' in the Fourth Gospel", *NTS* 12, 1965–66, 81–5; G. Ogg, *The Chronology of the Public Ministry of Jesus*, 1940; G. Parrinder, *Jesus in the Qur'an*, 1965; N. Perrin, *Rediscovering the Teaching of Jesus*, 1967; J. Peter, *Finding the Historical Jesus*, 1965; J. Reumann, *Jesus in the Church's Gospels: Modern Scholarship and the Earliest Sources*, 1970; N. H. Ridderbos, *Paul and Jesus*, 1958; H. Riesenfeld, "The Gospel Tradition and its Beginnings", in *The Gospels Reconsidered. A Selection of Papers read at the International Congress on the Four Gospels in 1957*, 1960, 131–53 (reprinted in *The Gospel Tradition*, 1971); J. M. Robinson, *The Problem of History in Mark*, 1957; and *The New Quest of the Historical Jesus*, 1959; J. Rohde, *Rediscovering the Teaching of the Evangelists*, 1968; W. Sanday, *Outlines of the Life of Christ*, 1905; and *The Life of Christ in Recent Research*, 1907; F. Schleiermacher, *The Life of Jesus*, (1832) 1975; U. J. Schultz, ed., *Jesus in His Time*, 1971; A. Schweitzer, *The Quest of the Historical Jesus: A Critical Study of its Progress from Reimarus to Wrede*, 1954[3]; and *The Psychiatric Study of Jesus*, 1968; E. Schweizer, "Mark's Contribution to the Quest of the Historical Jesus", *NTS* 10, 1963–64, 421–32; and *Jesus*, 1971; G. N. Stanton, *Jesus of Nazareth in New Testament Preaching*, 1974; E. Stauffer, *Jesus and his Story*, 1960; N. B. Stonehouse, *Origins of the Synoptic Gospels: Some Basic Questions*, 1964; D. F. Strauss, *The Life of Jesus Critically Examined* (ET 1846), ed., P. C. Hodgson, 1973; E. L. Sukenik, "The Earliest Records of Christianity", *American Journal of Archaeology*, 51, 1947, 351–65; cf. with J. P. Kane, "By No means 'The Earliest Records of Christianity'", *Palestine Exploration Quarterly*, 103, 1971, 103–8; E. F. Sutcliffe, *A Two Year Public Ministry*, 1938; E. Trocmé, *Jesus and his Contemporaries*, 1973; F. T. Trotter, ed., *Jesus and the Historian. Written in Honour of Ernst Cadman Colwell*, 1968; V. Taylor, *The Names of Jesus*, 1953; *The Life and Ministry of Jesus*, 1954; and "Does the New Testament Call Jesus 'God'?", *New Testament Essays*, 1970, 83–89; H. E. W. Turner, *Jesus Master and Lord*, 1953; and *Jesus the Christ*, 1976; G. Vermes, *Jesus the Jew*, 1973; A. Vögtle, "Jesus Christ", *EBT* II 419–37; A. W. Wainwright, "The Confession 'Jesus is God' in the New Testament", *SJT* 10, 1957, 274–99; H. G. Wood, *Jesus in the Twentieth Century*, 1960; W. Wrede, *The Messianic Secret*, ET 1971; H. Zahrnt, *The Historical Jesus*, 1963.

(b). H.-W. Bartsch, "Theologie und Geschichte in der Überlieferung vom Leben Jesu" *EvTh* 32, 128 ff.; W. Beilner, *Christus und die Pharisäer* 1959; P. Biehl, "Zur Frage nach dem historischen Jesus", *ThR* Neue Folge 24, 1956–57, 54 ff.; J. Blank, *Jesus von Nazareth*, 1972; F.-M. Braun, *Jesus Christus in Geschichte und Kritik*, 1950; H. Braun, *Jesus, Themen der Theologie* 1, 1970; F. Büchsel, *Jesus*, 1947; M. Craveri, *Das Leben des Jesus von Nazareth*, 1970; N. A. Dahl, "Der historische Jesus als geschichtswissenschaftliches und theologisches Problem", *KuD* 1, 1955, 104 ff., E. Fuchs, *Jesus. Wort und Tat*, 1970; J. R. Geiselmann, "Der Glaube an Jesus Christus: Mythos oder Geschichte", *ThR* 126, 1946, 257–77 and 418–39, H. Gollwitzer, "Zur Frage der 'Sündlosigkeit Jesu' ", *EvTh* 31, 1971, 496 ff.; E. Grässer, A. Strobel, R. C. Tannehill, W. Eltester, *Jesus in Nazareth*, *BZNW* 40, 1972; W. Grundmann, *Die Geschichte Jesu Christi*, 1957; E. Haenchen, "Vom Wandel des Jesusbildes in der frühen Gemeinde" in O. Böcher and K. Haacker, eds., op. cit., 3–14; E. Jüngel, *Paulus und Jesus, Hermeneutische Untersuchungen zur Theologie* 2, 1962; K. Kertelge, *Rückfrage nach Jesus: Zur Methodik und Bedeutung der Frage nach dem historischen Jesus*, 1974; H. W. Kuhn, "Der irdische Jesus bei Paulus als traditionsgeschichtliches und theologisches Problem", *ZTK* 67, 1970, 295 ff.; W. G. Kümmel, "Jesusforschung seit 1950", *ThR* Neue Folge 31, 1966, 15 ff. and 289 ff.; O. Kuss, " 'Bruder Jesus'. Zur 'Heimholung' des Jesus von Nazareth in das Judentum", *Münchener theologische Zeitschrift* 23, 1972, 284 ff.; F. Lentzen-Deis, "Der Glaube Jesu", *Trierer Theologische Zeitschrift* 80, 1971, 141 ff.; E. Lohse, "Die Frage nach dem historischen Jesus in der gegenwärtigen neutestamentlichen Forschung", *TLZ* 87, 1962, 162–74; and *Die Geschichte des Leidens und Sterbens Jesus Christi*, 1964; T. Lorenzmeier, "Wider das Dogma von der Sündlosigkeit Jesu", *EvTh* 31, 1971, 452 ff.; M. Machoveč, *Jesus für Atheisten*, 1972; W. Marxsen, "Zur Frage nach dem historischen Jesus", *TLZ* 87, 1962, 575–80; K. Niederwimmer, *Jesus*, 1968; B. Rigaux, "L'Historicité de Jésus devant l'exégèse récente", *RB* 65, 1958, 481–522; J. Roloff, *Das Kerygma und der irdische Jesus*, 1970; and "Auf der Suche nach einem neuen Jesusbild", *TLZ* 98, 1973, 561 ff.; F. J. Schierse, ed., *Jesus von Nazareth*, 1972; R. Schippers, *Jezus Christus in het historisch Onderzoek*, 1969; G. Schneider, *Die Frage nach Jesus*, 1971; J. Schneider, "Der Beitrag der Urgemeinde zur Jesus-Überlieferung im Lichte der neuesten Forschung", *TLZ* 87, 1962, 401 ff.; F. Schnider, *Jesus der Prophet*, 1975; H. Schürmann, *Das Geheimnis Jesus*, 1972; E. Sjöberg, *Der verborgene Menschensohn in den Evangelien*, 1955; A. Schweitzer, *Geschichte der Leben-Jesu-Forschung*, 1951[6] (fuller than ET *The Quest of the Historical Jesus*); W. Trilling, *Fragen zur Geschichtlichkeit Jesu*, 1967[2]; A. Vögtle, "Jesus Christus", *LTK* V 619–53; and "Exegetische Erwägungen zum Wissen und Selbstbewusstsein Jesu", *Gott in Welt*, II, 1964, 608–66.

On Nazarene and Nazareth:
(a). W. F. Albright, "The Names 'Nazareth' and 'Nazoraean' ", *JBL* 45, 1946, 397 ff.; M. Black, *An Aramaic Aproach to the Gospels and Acts*, 1967[3], 197 ff.; *The Scrolls and Christian Origins: Studies in the Jewish Background of the New Testament*, 1961, 70 ff.; F. F. Bruce, *Commentary on the Book of Acts*, NLC 1954, 69 f., 465; E. Grässer, "Jesus in Nazareth (Mark VI. 1–6a): Notes on the Redaction and Theology of St Mark", *NTS* 16, 1969–70, 1–23; R. H. Gundry, *The Use of the Old Testament in St Matthew's Gospel*, 1967, 97–104; D. Hill, *The Gospel of Matthew*, 1972, 86 ff.; C. Kopp, *The Holy Places of the Gospels*, 1963, 49–86; B. Lindars, *New Testament Apologetic*, 1961, 195 f.; G. F. Moore, "Nazarene and Nazareth", in F. J. Foakes Jackson and K. Lake, eds., *The Beginnings of Christianity*, I, 1920, 426–32; W. O. E. Oesterley, "Nazarene and Nazareth", *ExpT* 52, 1940–41, 410 ff.; H. H. Schaeder, *Nazarēnos, Nazōraios, TDNT* IV 874–79; K. Stendahl, *The School of St. Matthew and its Use of the Old Testament*, 1969[2], 103 f., 198 ff.
(b). P. Benoit, *L'Évangile selon Saint Matthieu*, 1961, 46; P. Bonnard, *L'Évangile selon Saint Matthieu*, 1963, 30; B. Gärtner, *Die rätselhaften Termini Nazoräer und Iskariot*, 1957; E. Lohmeyer, *Galiläa und Jerusalem*, FRLANT 52, 1936; E. Schweizer, "Er wird Nazoräer heissen", *Neotestamentica: Deutsche und englische Aufsätze 1951–63*, 1963, 51–55; R. Stiehl, "Aramäisch als Weltsprache" in *Beiträge zur Geschichte der Alten Welt*, I 1964, 74.

On Christ:
(a). J. A. Allan, "The 'In Christ' Formula in Ephesians", *NTS* 5, 1958–59, 54–62; A. W. Argyle, *The Christ of the New Testament*, 1952; D. E. Aune, "A Note on Jesus' Messianic Consciousness and 11Q Melchizedek", *EQ* 45, 1973, 161–65; D. M. Baillie, *God was in Christ: An Essay on Incarnation and Atonement*, 1961[2]; H. Berkhof, *Christ the Meaning of History*, 1966; G. C. Berkouwer, *The Person of Christ*, 1954; M. Black, "The Christological Use of the Old Testament in the New Testament", *NTS* 18, 1971–72, 1–14; and *A Survey of Christological Thought, 1872–1972*, The Croall Centenary Lecture, 1972; H. Boers, "Jesus and the Christian Faith: New Testament Christology since Bousset's *Kyrios Christos*", *JBL* 89, 1971, 451–56; D. Bonhoeffer, *Christology*, 1966; W. Bousset, *Kyrios Christos: A History of the Belief in Christ from the Beginnings of Christianity to Irenaeus*, 1970; W. H. Brownlee, "Messianic Motifs of Qumran and the New Testament", *NTS* 3, 1955–56, 12–30; and *The Meaning of the Qumran Scrolls for the Bible*, 1964; E. Brunner, *The Mediator: A Study of the Central Doctrine of the Christian Faith*, 1934; R. Bultmann, *Theology of the New Testament*, I, 1952, II, 1955; "Christ the End of the Law" and "The Christological Confession of the World Council of Churches", in *Essays*, 1955, 36–66 and 273–90; "On the Question of Christology", "The Significance of the Historical Jesus for the Theology of Paul", and "The Christology of the New Testament", in *Faith and Understanding*, 1969, 116–44, 220–46 and 262–85; R. E. Brown, *Jesus God and Man: Modern Biblical Reflections*, 1968; R. P. Casey, "The Earliest Christologies", *JTS* New Series 9, 1958, 253–77; S. Cave, *The Doctrine of the Person of Christ*, 1925; L. Cerfaux, *Christ in the Theology of St. Paul*, 1959; *Concilium* I, 2, 1966 (whole issue devoted to Catholic reappraisal of aspects of christology); R. G. Crawford, "Is Christ inferior to God?", *EQ* 1971, 43, 203–9; J. M. Creed, *The Divinity of Jesus Christ: A Study in the History of Christian Doctrine since Kant*, 1938; O. Cullmann, *Christ and Time: The Primitive Christian Conception of Time and History*, 1951; *The Christology of the New Testament*, 1963[2]; and *Salvation in History*, 1967; D. Cupitt, *Christ and the Hiddenness of God*, 1971; N. A. Dahl, "Christ, Creation and the Church", in W. D. Davies and D. Daube, eds., op. cit., 422–43; E. Dinkler, "Peter's Confession and the 'Satan' Saying: The Problem of Jesus' Messiahship", in J. M. Robinson, ed., *The Future of Our Religious Past: Essays in Honour of Rudolf Bultmann*, 1971, 169–202; R. Eisler, *The Messiah Jesus and John the Baptist according to Flavius Josephus' Recently*

Discovered 'Capture of Jerusalem' and the Other Jewish and Christian Sources, 1931; F. V. Filson, Jesus Christ the Risen Lord, 1956; P. T. Forsyth, The Person and Place of Jesus Christ, 1909; R. T. Fortna, "Christology in the Fourth Gospel: Redaction Critical Perspectives", NTS 21, 1974–75, 489–504; H. W. Frei, The Identity of Jesus Christ: The Hermeneutical Bases of Dogmatic Theology, 1975; R. H. Fuller, The Foundations of New Testament Christology, 1965; L. Gaston, "The Messiah of Israel as Teacher of the Gentiles", Interpretation 29, 1975, 24–40; T. F. Glasson, "The Uniqueness of Christ: The New Testament Witness", EQ 43, 1971, 25–35; F. Gogarten, Christ the Crisis, 1970; A. Grillmeier, Christ in Christian Tradition, 1975²; W. Grundmann, F. Hesse, M. de Jonge, A. S. van der Woude, chriō etc., TDNT IX 493–581; F. Hahn, The Titles of Jesus in Christology, 1969; A. T. Hanson, Jesus Christ in the Old Testament, 1965; "The Reproach and Vindication of the Messiah" and "Christ the First Fruits, Christ the Tree", in Studies in Paul's Technique and Theology, 1974, 13–51 and 104–25; and Grace and Truth: A Study in the Doctrine of the Incarnation, 1975; K. Heim, Jesus the Lord: The Sovereign Authority of Jesus and Gods' Revelation in Christ, 1959; G. S. Hendry, The Gospel of the Incarnation, 1959; M. Hengel, The Son of God: The Origin of Christology and the History of Jewish-Hellenistic Religion, 1976; J. Hick, "The Christology of D. M. Baillie", SJT 11, 1958, 1–12; A. J. B. Higgins, "The Priestly Messiah", NTS 13, 1966–67, 211–39; and Jesus and the Son of Man, 1965; J. W. Jack, The Historic Christ, 1933; E. G. Jay, Son of Man, Son of God, 1965; S. Katz, "Christology – A Jewish View", SJT 24, 1971, 184–200; L. E. Keck, "Mark 3 7–12 and Mark's Christology", JBL 84, 1965, 341 ff.; J. D. Kingsbury, Matthew: Structure, Christology, and Kingdom, 1975; J. Klausner, From Jesus to Paul, 1944; and The Messianic Idea in Israel, 1956; J. Knox, The Humanity and Divinity of Christ: A Study of Pattern in Christology, 1967; W. Kramer, Christ, Lord, Son of God, 1966; W. G. Kümmel, Promise and Fulfilment: The Eschatological Message of Jesus, 1961²; E. D. La Touche, The Person of Christ in Modern Thought, 1912; B. Lindars and S. S. Smalley, Christ and Spirit in the New Testament. In Honour of Charles Francis Digby Moule, 1973; R. N. Longenecker, The Christology of Early Jewish Christianity, 1970; H. R. Mackintosh, The Doctrine of the Person of Christ, 1912; J. McIntyre, The Shape of Christology, 1966; T. W. Manson, The Servant-Messiah, 1953; W. Manson, Jesus the Messiah. The Synoptic Tradition of the Revelation of God in Christ: With Special Reference to Form-Criticism, 1943; I. H. Marshall, "The Development of Christology in the Early Church", TB 18, 1967, 77–93; and The Origins of New Testament Christology, 1976; B. A. Mastin, "A Neglected Feature of the Christology of the Fourth Gospel", NTS 22, 1975–76, 32–51; S. Mowinckel, He That Cometh, 1956; J. Obersteiner, "Messianism", EBT II 575–82; R. L. Ottley, The Doctrine of the Incarnation, 1929⁷; W. Pannenberg, Jesus – God and Man, 1968; T. H. L. Parker, ed., Essays in Christology for Karl Barth, 1956; N. Perrin, A Modern Pilgrimage in New Testament Christology, 1974; N. Pittenger, Christology Reconsidered, 1970; N. Pittenger, ed., Christ for Us Today, 1967; T. E. Pollard, Johannine Christology and the Early Church, 1970; A. E. J. Rawlinson, The New Testament Doctrine of Christ, 1926; A. E. J. Rawlinson, ed., Essays on the Trinity and Incarnation, 1928; H. M. Relton, A Study in Christology, 1917; H. Riesenfeld, "The Mythological Background of New Testament Christology", in W. D. Davies and D. Daube, eds., op. cit., 81–95; J. A. T. Robinson, Jesus and his Coming: the Emergence of a Doctrine, 1957; "The Most Primitive Christology of All?", Twelve New Testament Studies, 1962, 139–53; and The Human Face of God, 1973; L. Sabourin, The Names and Titles of Jesus: Themes of Biblical Theology, 1967; R. Schnackenburg, "The Gnostic Myth of the Redeemer and the Johannine Christology", in The Gospel according to St. John, I, 1968, 543–57; H. J. Schoeps, The Jewish-Christian Argument: A History of Theologies in Conflict, 1965; G. Scholem, The Messianic Idea in Judaism, 1971; E. Schweizer, Lordship and Discipleship, 1960; E. M. Sidebottom, The Christ of the Fourth Gospel in the Light of First-Century Thought, 1961; C. Simonson, The Christology of the Faith and Order Movement, 1972; L. B. Smedes, The Incarnation: Trends in Modern Anglican Thought, 1953; D. Sölle, Christ the Representative: An Essay in Theology after the 'Death of God', 1967; S. W. Sykes and J. P. Clayton, eds., Christ, Faith and History, 1972; V. Taylor, The Person of Christ in the New Testament Teaching, 1958; H. E. Tödt, The Son of Man in the Synoptic Tradition, 1965; W. C. van Unnik, "Jesus the Christ", NTS 8, 1961–62, 101–16; A. R. Vine, An Approach to Christology, 1948; W. Vischer, The Witness of The Old Testament to Christ, 1949; B. B. Warfield, The Lord of Glory, 1907; and The Person and Work of Christ, 1950.

(b) H. R. Balz, Methodische Probleme der neutestamentlichen Christologie, WMANT 25, 1967; H.-W. Bartsch, "Wie redete die frühe Christenheit von Jesus Christus?", KidZ 19, 1964, 58 ff.; J. Becker, "Wunder und Christologie", NTS 16, 1969–70, 130–48; K. Berger, "Zum traditionsgeschichtlichen Hintergrund christologischer Hoheitstitel", *NTS* 17, 1970–71, 391–425; "Die königlichen Messiastraditionen des Neuen Testaments", *NTS* 20, 1973–74, 1–44; and "Zum Problem der Messianität Jesu", *ZTK* 71, 1974, 1 ff.; O. Betz, "Die Frage nach dem messianischen Bewusstsein Jesu", *NovT* 6, 1963, 20 ff.; J. Blank, *Krisis. Untersuchungen zur johanneischen Christologie und Eschatologie*, 1964; O. Böcher, *Christus Exorcista: Dämonismus und Taufe im Neuen Testament*, 1972; T. Boman, *Die Jesus-Überlieferung im Lichte der neuren Volkskunde*, 1967; C. Burger, *Jesus als Davidsohn*, *FRLANT* 98, 1970; H. Dembowski, "Jesus Christus – Herr der Götter," *EvTh* 29, 1969, 572 ff.; O. Eissfeldt, "Christus", *RAC* II 1250 ff.; E. Fascher, "Christologie oder Theologie? Bemerkungen zu O. Cullmanns *Christologie des Neuen Testaments*", *TLZ* 87, 1962, 882–910; G. Friedrich, "Jesus Christus", *BHHW* II 859 ff.; J. Gnilka, "War Jesus Revolutionär?", *BuL* 12, 1971, 67 ff.; A. Grillmeier and H. Bacht, eds., *Das Konzil von Chalkedon*, I–III, 1951; E. Güttgemanns, "*Christos* in 1. Kor. 15, 3b – Titel oder Eigenname?", *EvTh* 28, 1968, 533 ff.; U. Hedinger, "Christus und die Götter Griechenlands", *EvTh* 30, 1970, 97 ff.; E. Haenchen, "Die frühe Christologie", *ZTK* 63, 1966, 145 ff.; I. Herrmann, *Kyrios und Pneuma*, 1961; B. van Iersel, "*Der Sohn*" *in den synoptischen Jesusworten*, Supplements to *NovT* 3, 1964[2]; J. Jeremias, "Artikelloses *Christos*. Zur Ursprache von 1. Kor. 15, 3b–5", *ZNW* 57, 1966, 211 ff.; H. Karpp, "Christennamen", *RAC* II 1114 ff., U. Kellermann, *Messias und Gesetz*, *BSt* 61, 1972; H. Kessler, *Die theologische Bedeutung des Todes Jesus*, 1971[2]; E. Kränkl, *Jesus der Knecht Gottes*, 1972; W. G. Kümmel *et al.*, *Jesus Christus: Das Christusverständnis im Wandel der Zeiten, Eine Ringvorlesung der Theologischen Fakultät der Universität Marburg, Marburger theologische Studien* 1, 1963; E. Larsson, *Christus als Vorbild*, 1962; F. M. T. de Liagre Böhl *et al.*, "Messias", *RGG*[3] IV 900 ff.; G Lindeskog, "Christuskerygma und Jesustradition", *NovT* 5, 1962, 144–56; E. Lohmeyer, *Gottesknecht und Davidssohn*, *FRLANT* 61, 1953[2]; R. Maddox, "Methodenfragen in der Menschensohnforschung", *EvTh* 32, 1972, 143 ff.; H. J. Margull, "Tod Jesu und Schmerz Gottes", in *Leben angesichts des Todes. H. Thielicke zum 60. Geburtstag*, 1968; W. Marxsen, *Anfangsprobleme der Christologie*, 1960; C. Maurer, "Das Messiasgeheimnis des Markusevangeliums", *NTS* 14, 1967–68; 515–26; U. B. Müller, *Messias und Menschensohn in jüdischen Apokalypsen und in der Offenbarung Johannes, Studien zum Neuen Testament* 6, 1972; F. Neugebauer, "Das Paulinische 'in Christo' ", *NTS* 4, 1957–58, 124–38; and, *Jesus der Menschensohn*, *AzTh* 50, 1972; R. Pesch, *Jesu ureigene Taten? Ein Beitrag zur Wunderfrage, Quaestiones Disputatae* 52, 1970; E. Peterson, "Christianus", in *Frühkirche, Judentum und Gnosis*, 1959, 64 ff.; P. Pokorny, "Jesus, Glaube, Christologie", *ThZ* 18, 1962, 268–82; K. H. Rengstorf, *Die Auferstehung Jesu*, 1967[5], 129 ff.; K. H. Rengstorf and S. von Kortzfleisch, *Kirche und Synagoge*, I, 1968, 23 ff.; M. Rese, *Alttestamentliche Motive in der Christologie des Lukas*, (Dissertation, Bonn) 1965; H. Ristow and K. Matthiae, eds., *Der historische Jesus und der kerygmatische Christus*, 1960; L. Ruppert, *Jesus als der leidende Gerechte?*, 1972; K. L. Schmidt, *Jesus Christus im Zeugnis der Heiligen Schrift und der Kirche*, 1936; W. Schmithals, *Jesus in der Verkündigung der Kirche*, 1972; N. Scholl, *Jesus – nur ein Mensch?* 1971; D. F. Strauss, *Der Christus des Glaubens und Jesus der Geschichte*, (1865) *Texte zur Kirchen– und Theologiegeschichte* 14, 1971; G. Strecker, "Die historische und theologische Problematik der Jesusfrage", *EvTh* 29, 1969, 453 ff.; K. Schubart, *Der historische Jesus und der Christus unseres Glaubens*, 1962; G. Sevenster, W. Pannenberg and P. Althaus, "Christologie", *RGG* I 1745–89; W. Thüsing, *Die Erhöhung und Verherrlichkeit Jesu im Johannes-Evangelium*, 1960; and *Per Christum in Deum*, *NTAbh* 1, 1968[2]; P. Vielhauer, "Zur Frage der christologischen Hoheitstitel", *TLZ* 8, 1965, 569 ff.; and "Ein Weg zur neutestamentlichen Christologie?", *EvTh* 25, 1965, 24 ff. (reprinted in *Aufsätze zum Neuen Testament*, 1965, 141 ff.); and "Erwägungen zur Christologie des Markusevangeliums" (in *Aufsätze Zum Neuen Testament*, 199 ff.); A. Vögtle, *Messias und Gottessohn, Theologische Perspektiven*, 1971; P. G. Wacker, "Christus ohne Kirche?" *ThG* 64, 1974, 1 ff.

Join, Cleave to

| κολλάομαι | κολλάομαι (*kollaomai*), join, cleave to, stick to; προσκολλάομαι (*proskollaomai*), cleave to, stick to. |

CL *kollaomai*, found from Pindar onwards, is a cognate of *kolla*, glue (Hdt. onwards) and means to glue in contrast to nailing, to join together tightly.

Literal examples are gluing a broken pot, to glue inlay work of gold and ivory, to steep barley in water, to close a wound (Galen). It is also used of the penetration of poison into a body (Hippocrates). Metaphorically it occurs in the phrase *kekollētai genos pros ata*, the uniting of humanity in a delusion (Aesch., *Agamemnon* 1566). The compound *proskollaomai* means to stick to.

OT 1. The LXX uses both words predominantly to render Heb. *dābaq*, cling, cleave to, and once each for *nāga'* (hiph.), *nāgaš*, *nāsar*, and *rābas*. The basic meaning can be found in Pss. 22:15 (MT 22:16); 137:6; Job 29:10; Lam. 4:4, where the tongue cleaves to the gums for thirst. Similarly it can be said that → leprosy, pestilence or diseases cleave to a person (2 Ki. 5:27; Deut. 28:21, 60).

2. It frequently means to join someone, to cleave to him (e.g. Ruth. 2:8, 21; 2 Sam. 20:2; Pss. 101:3[MT 101:4]; 119:31; Job 41:15; 41:9; 1 Macc. 3:2; 6:21).

3. It also is used of the permanent relationship of man and woman (Gen. 2:24). As is shown by 1 Esd. 4:20 ("A man leaves his own father, who brought him up, and his own country, and cleaves to his wife"), it refers to more than the sexual union of man and wife and extends to the whole relationship. Because Solomon "clung" to foreign wives (1 Ki. 11:2) he came under their religious influence. "The man who consorts [*kollōmenos*] with harlots" (Sir. 19:2) comes under an influence inconsistent with wisdom.

4. The contrast is union with God. "You shall fear the Lord your God; you shall serve him and cleave to him" (Deut. 10:20; cf. 6:13; 2 Ki. 18:6; Sir. 2:3; Jer. 13:11). The stress here is on inner union with God in contrast to the cultic and legal one of the context.

NT *kollaomai* is found in the NT only in the pass. or mid., and follows the usage of the LXX.

1. The basic meaning is found in Lk. 10:11, "The dust . . . that clings [*kollēthenta*] to our feet"; cf. also Rev. 18:5 lit. "her sins cleaved to her [*ekollēthēsan*] high up to heaven" (cf. Jer. 51:9 [LXX 28:9]; contrast *TDNT* III 822).

2. The commonest usage is to join someone, to be near: the prodigal son joined himself to foreign citizens (Lk. 15:15); Philip joined the chariot of the Ethiopian (Acts 8:29); Paul tried to join the church (Acts 9:26); some who had joined Paul came to faith (Acts 17:34); though the people of Jerusalem held the Christians in high honour, no non-Christian ventured to join them (Acts 5:13); it was reprehensible for a Jew to "associate with" (*kollasthai*) anyone of another nation (*allophylos*), i.e. heathens (Acts 10:28), because they did not have the → law.

3. Matt. 19:5 and Eph. 5:31 both quote Gen. 2:24 (→ Marriage; → Divorce).

(a) Matt. 19:5: marriage is indissoluble, because in it two persons become one living being. This refers to the relationship of the partners and not merely the sexual union (contrast *TDNT* III 822).

(b) Eph. 5:31: Christ left his Father to be completely with his bride, the *ekklēsia* (→ Church) and to begin a new life with her (*sarka mian*, one → flesh). Just as in Ezek. 16, the husband here comes as *sōtēr*, saviour (Eph. 5:23). His wife – the new → people of God – is decked with imperishable riches (Eph. 5:26 f.; cf. Ezek. 16:10–13). The marriage relationship is a "great mystery" which reflects the relationship of Christ and the church (Eph. 5:32).

4. The believer's union with God necessitates that he must detest the evil and "hold fast to what is good" (Rom. 12:9). Since with his body he is a member of the → body of Christ, he cannot become one body, a human unity, with a harlot. For "he who is united with the Lord becomes one spirit with him" (1 Cor. 6:17). He should also live in this Spirit, and perfectly imitate the actions and revelation of his Lord. But if he unites himself with a harlot, he will become like her (1 Cor. 6:16). The one who has sexual relations with a harlot is not committing a purely physical act which does not touch the spirit. The whole man reveals himself in all that he does. He who unites himself to a harlot has a common existence with her. There is no purely sexual sin. The spirit of the brothel and the Spirit of Christ mutually exclude one another. *H. Seebass*

→ Disciple, → Discipline, → Divorce, → Marriage

E. Best, *One Body in Christ*, 1955; A. Isaksson, *Marriage and Ministry in the New Temple*, 1965, 18 ff. and *passim*; J. A. T. Robinson, *The Body: A Study in Pauline Theology*, SBT 5, 1952; J. P. Sampley, '*And the Two Shall Become One Flesh*': *A Study of Traditions in Ephesians 5:21–33*, Society for New Testament Studies Monograph Series 16, 1971; K. L. Schmidt, *kollaō*, *proskollaō*, *TDNT* III 822 f.

Jonah

| ᾽Ιωνᾶς | ᾽Ιωνᾶς (*Iōnas*), Heb. *yônâh*, Jonah.

The NT references to Jonah are exhausted by those passages in which Jesus alludes to him in the course of certain controversial exchanges with the Pharisees (Matt. 12:38–41; 16:4; Lk. 11:29–32). These references are both general to the career of Jonah, and particular, in that they refer to him as a → sign.

OT The Gk. *sēmeion* is occasionally used in LXX as equivalent to *môpēṭ* (Exod. 11:9, 10), i.e. that which by its remarkable nature excites wonder and attracts attention; occasionally also it translates *nēs*, a banner, i.e. that which catches the eye. But for the most part it translates '*ôṭ*, a sign. It is thus involved in two distinct meanings. On the one hand, a sign (e.g. Deut. 13:1) is something performed in order to persuade people to an immediate response; on the other hand, a sign can be offered (e.g. Exod. 3:12) as a future confirmation of the truth of some present fact. This background is clearly present in the sign element in Jesus' references to Jonah.

Four matters call for brief enquiry in the story of Jonah. First, what was the motive for his flight (Jon. 1:3 ff.)? The majority view is that he was a religious particularist and fled from the possibility of seeing Israel's privileges being shared with the heathen. It ought to be noted, however, that Jewish opinion, as reflected in the Babylonian Talmud which appoints the Book of Jonah to be read in its entirety on the Day of Atonement, thus stressed the repentance of the Ninevites as an example which the people of God were called to follow (Meg. 31a; cf. M. D. Goulder, *Midrash and Lection in Matthew*, 1974, 187, 334). This was the very point which Jesus sought to make. Rather than thus expose his people, Jonah risked his own life, willing to die on their behalf. It is not unworthy of note that, in quoting Exod. 34:6, 7 (Jon. 4:2), he omitted the reference to divine strictness of judgment.

Secondly, the book of Jonah records his own comment on his remarkable experience. In his prayer, the fish's belly becomes "the belly of Sheol" (Jon. 2:2; → Hell). While recognizing that Sheol is frequently metaphorical for that which is dark, threatening and likely to end in death, the use of the metaphor here, coupled with the reference to the "pit" (v. 6) must form part of the OT background to Jesus' use of the incident.

Thirdly, we must ask in what terms Jonah preached to Nineveh. All that is recorded (Jon. 3:4) is a proclamation of coming judgment. It was the force of this word, and the recognition of the divine authorization which lay behind it which implemented the response of repentance. As far as is noted, Jonah made no reference to his experience in the fish.

Fourthly, the call to repentance was heeded and God expressed his total satisfaction with this (Jon. 3:10 ff.) It was what he wanted and therefore effectively produced remission.

NT In speaking of the people of his day as "evil and adulterous" (Matt. 12:39; Lk. 11:29 agrees with *ponēra* [evil] but does not add *moichalis* [adulterous]), Jesus undoubtedly intended to set up a parallelism between them and Nineveh (Jon. 1:2): "wicked" in heart and life and "adulterous" physically and spiritually. Their spiritual vacuity is sharply underlined by the Lord in his refusal of the sign which they sought. Matt. 16:1 notes that they wished a "sign from heaven", presumably something unequivocally from God, something which would authenticate Jesus mainly because he himself had no involvement in its performance – a sign of the sort offered in Isa. 7:10. To Jesus (cf. Matt. 11:4) this was rank blindness in the face of his constant performance of his own works before their eyes. In this context he set up a threefold comparison. First, he made an open comparison between himself and Jonah (Matt. 16:4; Lk. 11:30). Especially in the former of these references he left his hearers to their own interpretative devices. In the latter, there is a significant change of tense: "as Jonah became [*egeneto*] . . . the Son of man shall be [*estai*]. . . ." That is to say, reviewing the story of Jonah, they can well see that he was a divinely sent persuader (a sign of the first category above), a watershed, a heaven-sent opportunity which came once and did not return. Even so, there will be that about the Son of man (a sign of the second category) which will, at some later point, make them aware that he too was sent from God and that in him too they reached, for good or ill, a point of no return.

Secondly, Jesus compared Jonah's experience of a three-day sojourn in the fish to his own coming sojourn "in the heart of the earth" (Matt. 12:40). This is largely rejected by commentators (*IDB*, McNeile, Plummer) as a typical Matthaean embellishment, pursuant to his supposed penchant for snatching Bible-fulfilments out of the air. McNeile's criticism that Jesus was not in fact three days in the tomb is more indicative of a weak case than of critical acumen. In the light of our own discussion immediately above, the question is rather to what Jesus was looking forward when he predicted a coming event in the light of which his own status as a Jonah-type sign would be clear. His resurrection from an unequivocal experience of death would be the very "sign from heaven" which once they had faithlessly sought and would not, even when it happened, be able to recognize – as Jesus full well foresaw (cf. Lk. 16:31). Matthew's record of the comparison between Jonah in a Sheol-like situation and Jesus actually "in the heart of the earth" is distinctly apt.

The third element in the sign-comparison which Jesus made is between Jonah's preaching and its result and his own preaching and its result (Matt. 12:41; Lk. 11:32). The comparison here is *a fortiori*. The ensuing judgment on impenitence will be greater because the one who calls to repentance is greater. In the light of the OT testimony to the status of the prophet, Jesus can here be seen as claiming the honour due to his deity, exactly as in Matt. 23:34. *J. A. Motyer*

→ Fish, → Miracle, → Nineveh, → Number

(a). G. Ch. Aalders, *The Problem of the Book of Jonah*, 1948; L. C. Allen, *The Books of Joel, Obadiah, Jonah and Micah, New International Commentary on the Old Testament*, 1976; R. A. Edwards, *The Sign of Jonah in the Theology of the Evangelists and Q, SBT* Second Series 18, 1971; and *A Theology of Q: Eschatology, Prophecy and Wisdom*, 1975; M. D. Goulder, *Midrash and Lection in Matthew*, 1974; D. Hill, *The Gospel of Matthew*, 1972; J. Howton, "The Sign of Jonah", *SJT* 15, 1962, 288–304; J. Jeremias, *Iōnas, TDNT* 406–10; A. Helmbold, "Jonah, Book of", *ZPEB* III 675–79; A. R. Johnson, "Jonah II 3–10: A Study in Cultic Phantasy", in H. H. Rowley, ed., *Studies in Old Testament Prophecy Presented to Professor Theodore H. Robinson*, 1950, 82–102; O. Linton, "The Demand for a Sign from Heaven (Mark. 8.11–12 and par.)", *StTh* 19, 1965, 112–29; A. H. McNeile, *The Gospel According to St. Matthew*, 1915; C. Moxon, *to sēmeion Iōna, ExpT* 22, 190–11, 566 ff.; W. Neil, "Jonah, Book of", *IDB* II 964–67; A. Plummer, *An Exegetical Commentary on the Gospel according to St. Matthew*, 1909; R. B. Y. Scott, "The Sign of Jonah: An Interpretation", *Interpretation* 24, 1970, 16–25; R. V. G. Tasker, *The Gospel according to St. Matthew*, 1961.
(b). O. Glombitza, "Das Zeichen des Jona (Zum Verständnis von Matthäus 12. 38–42)", *NTS* 8, 1961–62, 359–66.

Joy, Rejoice

There are three main groups of words in the NT which denote human joy and happiness and express its special character. In the case of *chairō* physical comfort and well-being are the basis of joy. Hence the use of the vb. in the good wishes which people express on greeting one another and on parting. They refer to the benefits of health and happiness which, in fact, people wish for themselves. On the other hand, *euphrainō* indicates the subjective feeling of joy, and *agalliaomai* the outward demonstration of joy and pride and the exultation experienced in public worship.

ἀγαλλιάομαι

ἀγαλλιάομαι (*agalliaomai*), exult, rejoice greatly, be overjoyed; ἀγαλλίασις (*agalliasis*), exultation, great joy.

CL *agalliaomai*, exult, shout for joy, rejoice greatly, and the corresponding noun *agalliasis*, exultation, are found only in the LXX, the NT and in Jewish and Christian writers dependent on them. They are later formations from the profane Greek *agallō* and *agallomai* (from Homer onwards) which occur with the following meanings: (a) to adorn, honour, glorify, revere (in Plato and Aristotle); (b) to make a show, boast of something (Herodotus); (c) to enjoy, experience pleasure in something (Homer); (d) to be in raptures (Herodotus). This is the basic human emotion of joy which takes possession of the whole man.

OT 1. In the LXX *agalliaomai* and *agalliasis* occur most frequently as the translation of *gîl* (rejoice, rejoicing) and *rānan* (cry in joy). They indicate the cultic
festive joy, which expresses itself publicly over God's acts of salvation in the past
and present (e.g. Ps. 32:11), but is not orgiastic as in the Canaanitish cults. The
significance of these words soon extended beyond the sphere of public worship.
agalliaomai came to express both corporate and individual attitudes of thankful
joy before God (cf. Pss. 9:14; 16:9; 21:1; 31:7; 35:27; 92:4). This rejoicing not
only testifies to past experiences of God's salvation; it also exults in his faithful
dealings which are still future (cf. Hab. 3:18) and which the believer sees ensured
by Yahweh. The keynote of public worship remains, but the rejoicing embraces
even the created universe, the silent witnesses to God's mighty acts such as the
heavens, the earth, the mountains, the islands, which all join in the jubilation or are
called upon to do so (Pss. 19:5; 89:12; 96:11; and 97 passim). Even God himself
joins in (Isa. 65:19). Under the prophets both during and after the exile, Israel's
rejoicing in his God, even in wretched situations, broadened out to include anticipatory gratitude for final salvation and messianic joy (Isa. 61). It was in this
eschatological direction that the Heb. attitude of thanks and praise reached its
profoundest expression (cf. Pss. 96:11 ff.; 97:8; 126:2, 5; Isa. 25:9).

2. Loud, exultant rejoicing over God's acts of salvation in the past, present and
the eschatological future continued to be characteristic of Rab. theology and the
piety of Rab. Judaism (SB IV 2, 851 f.). The whole aim of the Jew's life was to
glorify God. Jubilation thus accompanied "the dramatic history of the Jewish
people like the strains of some heavenly choir, and in the liturgy became the dominant element in their religious life" (E. Stauffer, *Jerusalem und Rom*, 1957, 102).

3. In contrast with Rab. Judaism, the Qumran community held that the day of
salvation had already begun. In praise and prayer (especially in the Hodayot [1QH]
and in the concluding part of the Community Rule [1QS 10:11]) they rejoiced in
God who in his mercy had granted them salvation and given them insight into his
→ secrets.

NT 1. In the NT *agalliaomai* occurs 11 times and *agalliasis* only 5 times (cf. *chairein*
which occurs 74 times). The words are used as in the LXX, but with this difference. In the OT exultant rejoicing arises from gratitude and unshakeable trust in the
God who has constantly helped and still is helping his people Israel. He will do
away with all want and distress in his final act of deliverance at the coming of
messiah. In the NT the rejoicing turns to the God who now in Jesus Christ has
already inaugurated the eschatological age of salvation and will gloriously complete
it on Christ's return.

(a) In the Gospels there is jubilation even before the coming of Jesus. Zechariah
sang for joy when the forerunner of the Lord was born (Lk. 1:14), and even the
child in Elizabeth's womb shared in the rejoicing (Lk. 1:44). Jesus spoke of devout
Israelites who for a short time rejoiced in the light of John the Baptist (Jn. 5:35).
In her song of praise Mary rejoiced that she had been granted a place in God's
saving purpose (Lk. 1:47), while Jesus himself as the bringer of salvation not only
called upon men to rejoice but joined in himself. The Beatitudes conclude with
the exhortation: "Rejoice and be glad, for your reward is great in heaven" (Matt.
5:12; cf. Lk. 6:23). Jesus rejoiced in spirit because the time of salvation was at hand.

353

It was revealed to babes but at the same time, since it also involves judgment, it was hidden from the wise (Lk. 10:21; cf. Matt. 11:25). Even → Abraham (one of "the just men made perfect", Heb. 12:23) rejoiced that he had a part in the day of salvation (Jn. 8:56). The early → church regarded itself as the → elect of the last days because of God's saving work in Jesus Christ. It made Christ's cross, resurrection and future return the basis of its rejoicing, and thus interpreted David's joy christologically (Acts 2:26, where Peter quotes Ps. 16:10). The Philippian jailer rejoiced (ēgalliasato) with his whole family because he had come to faith and had been incorporated into the saved community of the last days through → faith and → baptism (Acts 16:34). At the cultic meal of the breaking of bread the early church sang with joy as they anticipated the parousia of the risen Christ. They observed the → Lord's Supper "in exultation [en agalliasei]" (Acts 2:47; cf. J. Jeremias, *The Eucharistic Words of Jesus*, 1966², 254).

(b) Paul does not use the word, but is no stranger to the idea. He expresses it partly through the vb. *kauchasthai*, to → boast.

(c) In the rest of the NT (with the exception of Mk. and Jas.) the word appears sporadically. In Heb. 1:9 God himself is represented as addressing Christ. He → anoints his son with the → oil of gladness [*agalliasis*], i.e. with consecrated oil as used at joyous feasts (cf. Ps. 45:7). In Jude 24 the church bows in praise before him "who is able to keep you from falling and present you without blemish before the presence of his glory with rejoicing [en agalliasei]" (cf. Acts 2:46). In 1 Pet. the church is called upon to look away from its sufferings in the last days, for they are insignificant in comparison with the rejoicing which will break forth at the end of time (1 Pet. 1:6, 8; 4:13). In Rev. believers are summoned by a voice at the end of time crying, "Let us rejoice and exult [chairōmen kai agalliōmen] and give him the glory (Rev. 19:7). In Matt. 5:12; Lk. 1:14; 1 Pet. 1:8; and 4:13 chairō and agalliaomai are also used together.

2. *agalliasis*, the festive joy which takes in the past and points to the future, thus becomes the characteristic attitude of the NT church and of the individual Christians in it. Its public worship is full of joy, as at the eschatological banquet (cf. Rev. 19:7–9). Joy is experienced through the salvation achieved by Jesus Christ in the past, personally experienced in the present, and confidently expected in the future. Looked at in this way, the → sufferings of this present time are alleviated. For even while they weigh heavily upon us we have paradoxically good reason to rejoice. Such rejoicing is grounded entirely in the person of Christ. The Lord himself, risen, present and returning, is the basis for all our joy.

E. Beyreuther

εὐφραίνω

εὐφραίνω (*euphrainō*), gladden, cheer (up); εὐφροσύνη (*euphrosynē*), joy, gladness, cheerfulness.

CL The vb. *euphrainō* is found in colloquial Greek from Homer onwards, and means in the active to cheer, to gladden a person; in the middle and passive to make merry. The noun *euphrosynē* (from Homer onwards) means merriment, joy, good cheer. Such joy stems largely from those events and situations which give rise to communal rejoicing, such as a banquet. Nevertheless, philosophers also use the word for introspective and spiritual joy.

OT In the LXX the word is used far more frequently than → *chairō* and is not sharply distinguished from → *agalliaō*. It chiefly renders words from the stem *śāmaḥ* (rejoice, gladden); and in Isa. more frequently words from *rānan* (cry in joy) and *śîś* (rejoice). Its use is concentrated in certain books of the OT such as Deut., the Deuteronomistic historical works, and particularly the Pss., Lam., Eccl., and Isa. (especially passages attributed to Deutero- and Trito-Isaiah). In addition it is used with remarkable frequency in Sir. The distribution is similar in the case of the noun. The word is clearly the appropriate expression for the united joy expressed at the cultic celebrations or sacrificial feasts. But the OT concept of God (→ God OT) prevents the type of ecstatic orgy, so common in heathenism, where the distinction between human and divine became blurred.

Joy can also be that of the heart of an individual, especially in response to God's help in situations of need (e.g. Ps. 13:5). Finally, *euphrainō* is used alongside *agalliaō* to express the eschatological joy in which even the heavens and the earth participate (Pss. 96:11; 97:1), God also rejoicing with them (Isa. 65:19). Joy is a feature of God's eternal world. At this point it may be observed that festive joy at the great communal feasts – the human enjoyment of eating, drinking and bodily refreshment – becomes a vivid picture of eschatological joy.

For the rest a wide diversity of usage can be found, a fact indicated by numerous Hebrew equivalents: joy as an emotion (e.g. Ps. 16:11); joy in someone or something (2 Sam. 1:26; Eccl. 11:9); joy in God (Neh. 8:10; Ps. 33:21); joy in God's word (Jer. 15:16; Ps. 119:14); joy in the keeping of the commandments (Ps. 119:162); joy in the time of salvation (Isa. 35:10; 52:12).

In the piety of Rab. Judaism joy is still of great importance. Joy in God's law now occupies a large place (cf. Pss. 19, 119). The festivals, especially Passover and the Feast of Tabernacles, are joyous occasions (→ Feast).

Joy characterizes the expected time of salvation. In Qumran, salvation is seen as already present, and there is rejoicing over God's redemptive gifts (cf. 1QM 12:13; 13:12 ff.; 17:7 f.; 1QH 11:23, 30; 18:15; CD 20:33).

Philo's piety is especially marked by *euphrosynē*. Taking festive joy as his starting point, he finds joy merely in seeking God (e.g. *Spec.Leg.* 36). God himself radiates joy by means of the Logos, especially upon all who by their virtues prove themselves worthy. Everything that belongs to God has this same characteristic: wisdom (*sophia*) is full of delight (*chara*), joy (*euphrosynē*) and other good things (*Rer. Div. Her.* 315; cf. R. Bultmann, *TDNT* II 773 f.).

NT In the NT the word *chairō* is clearly preferred as the term for joy (by contrast with its relative infrequency in the LXX). *euphrainō* occurs 14 times, of which no less than 8 are in the Lucan writings (cf. Luke's liking for OT phrases), 3 in Paul and 3 in Rev. *euphrosynē* is found twice only, in Acts. Five out of the total are OT quotations.

1. The words are clearly connected with the rejoicing to be found at a festive banquet, and this indicates the OT origins of their usage. *euphrainō* thus denotes in the NT the joy of the festive company, not the subjective emotion of an individual. In Lk. 12:19; 16:19 it refers to eating, drinking and enjoying oneself – in the latter

instance doubtless in revelry among convivial friends. This is what man without God sees as supremely worthwhile and what material possessions are for. On the other hand, emphasis on the joy wrought by God is a peculiar feature of the Lucan writings (→ *chairō* NT 3). Luke's Gospel is irradiated by joy. Thus in Lk. 15:23, 32 there is an invitation to make merry over the return of the lost son, while according to Lk. 15:29 the elder son enviously desires a similar joyous feast for himself.

Acts 14:17 speaks of joy in the gifts of nature as being God's gifts in creation. Acts 2:26, 28, applying Ps. 16:8–11 to the resurrection, speaks of joy in the presence of God. On the other hand, Acts 7:41 refers to the shameless rejoicing of Israel when worshipping before the golden calf (cf. Exod. 32:4, 6).

2. Paul normally uses the vb. *chairō* (even in the context of 2 Cor. 2:2), but in Rom. 15:10 and Gal. 4:27 he is influenced by OT quotations. In Rom. 15:10 he sees the fulfilment of Deut. 32:43: the reason for rejoicing is that the message of Christ has now come to the Gentiles. Similarly in Gal. 4:27 the call to rejoice is applied to the → Jerusalem that is above, the church of the new → covenant composed of Jews and Gentiles.

3. Likewise in Rev. 12:12 and 18:20 which are based on OT quotations (cf. Isa. 44:23; 49:13; Jer. 51:48; Rev. 11:10 is not so based), it is eschatological rejoicing which is expressed by *euphrainō*. The fact that eschatological joy often appears in the NT under the figure of a joyous feast, and that Jesus himself, when on earth, does not scorn to join in the festivities of the common meal, indicates that the word *euphrainō* is in complete accord with the joyous message of the gospel.

E. Beyreuther

| χαίρω | *χαίρω* (*chairō*), be glad, rejoice; *χαρά* (*chara*), joy. |

CL *chairō*, to be glad, rejoice (related to the Sanskrit *haryati*, to take pleasure in, and the Old High German *geron*, to desire), and *chara*, joy, are attested from Homer onwards. *chairein epi* (also *dia, en, peri*) means to rejoice over someone or something. The reason for the joy is introduced with *hoti* (that) or appears in a participial form. The pres. imperative frequently occurs in the greeting *chaire* (sing.), *chairete* (plur.), "Hail!" At the opening of a letter in the infin. *chairein*, is often used in which case the vb. *legei* has to be supplied (cf. Funk § 480): "[... says] greetings!" The same formula is used in drinking a toast, "Good health!", and at parting, "Farewell!" The phrases *chairein charan megalēn* (be filled with intense joy) and *chara chairein* (rejoice greatly), which occur in the NT, doubtless go back to OT influence (Matt. 2:10; cf. Jon. 4:6; Jn. 3:29; cf. Isa. 66:10). *chara* denotes both the state and the object of the joy.

Also to be noted is the etymological connection with *charis* (grace) which has not always been clearly distinguished in meaning from *chara*.

OT In the LXX *chara* appears only in the later writings (principally Wis. and 1–4 Macc.) and is chiefly a translation of the Hebrew words *śimḥâh*, joy, gladness, and *śāśōn*, joy. It is distinguished from *charis*, which most frequently translates *ḥēn*, grace, favour. For the most part words from the stem *śāmaḥ*, to be glad, also *gîl*, rejoice and *śîś*, to be glad, are rendered by *chairō*.

There is no clear distinction between the usage of *chairō* and that of *euphrainō*, the Heb. equivalent of which is also predominantly *šāmaḥ*. The two words are often synonymous (Lam. 4:21; Prov. 29:6; Est. 8:17; 9:27 and passim), though Sir. 30:16 does permit a certain differentiation. Basically, *euphrainō* is nearer to → *agalliaomai*, as it also translated in words such as *šîr*, to sing. *chairō* covers both the subjective feeling and the objective cause of joy. Of all the words in this group it thus comes closest to the Heb. *šālôm*, → peace, salvation, and in fact is used to translate this in Isa. 48:22; 57:21 (cf. Tob. 13:14[15] *charēsontai epi tē eirēnē sou* "shall rejoice over thy peace"). The vb. and the noun do not often appear in the context of joy in worship (Ps. 30:11); *agalliaomai* and *euphrainō* are used almost exclusively in such passages.

1. A non-specific use as a greeting occurs particularly in 1–4 Macc. The general meaning to be glad, to be pleased, is found in e.g. Gen. 45:16; Isa. 39:2; cf. 2 Ki. 20:13.

In the OT there is no apology for joy in the good things of life, such as health (Sir. 30:16), wise children (Prov. 23:25), eating and drinking (1 Ki. 3:1; cf. Ps. 104:14 f.), peace in the land (1 Macc. 14:11; → *euphrainō*). But the author of Prov. also warns that joy is transitory and is threatened by the vicissitudes of life: after laughter comes weeping (Prov. 14:13).

2. God is the giver of all joy and of all → blessings (1 Ki. 8:66). He gives his gracious word (1 Ki. 8:56) which far outweighs all transitory blessings. This word comforts and strengthens in times of temptation and distress (Jer. 15:16). It enables men to endure until such time as God turns mourning into joy (Ps. 126:5). The fear of the Lord is thus a source of joy (Sir. 1:12). Consequently *chairō* serves also to describe eschatological joy, rejoicing over ultimate salvation and peace (Joel 2:21, 23; Isa. 66:10, 14; Zech. 10:7; Tob. 13:25 in conjunction with → *agalliaomai*).

3. In Rab. Judaism joy in the → law is emphasized. Reading the Pentateuch is described as the joy of the law (cf. SB IV 154; *TDNT* II 773 f.), or "fullness of joy" (cf. SB II 566 on Jn. 16:24). In Philo divine → wisdom is a source of joy (*Rer. Div. Her.* 315). God alone has pure joy; it is other-worldly, but comes to man in mystic union with him (*Abr.* 201–207; *Spec. Leg.* 2, 54 f.).

4. In Qumran joy (*śimḥâh*) also springs from knowledge of the truth (1QH 11:30), but here it is the knowledge of God's → election and of his → mercy towards his elect. There is a decisive contrast between present sadness in affliction and chastisement (1QH 9:24) and the joy of final victory (1QM 13:12 f.; 14:4; 18:8 and often). A banner in the final battle bears the inscription "Joy of God" (1QM 4:14), and after the victory the sons of light will be translated to glory and everlasting joy (1QH 13:6).

NT In the NT the vb. and noun occur chiefly in the Gospels and Pauline Epistles (the vb. 74 times; the noun 59 times). The writings with the most instances of *chairō* and *chara* are found as follows: 20 times in Lk.; 11 in Acts; 18 in Jn.; 12 in Matt.; 14 in Phil.; 13 in 2 Cor.; 7 in Rom.; and 6 in 1 Thess. It is no accident that the words appear particularly where there is express mention of the eschatological fulfilment in Christ, of being in him, and of hope in him. But it ought not to be overlooked that the whole NT message as the proclamation of God's saving work in Christ is a message of joy (→ Gospel).

357

1. The general use as a greeting needs only brief mention. *chairein* is used at the beginning of a letter in Acts 15:23; 23:26; Jas. 1:1 (→ Book). In 2 Jn. 10 those addressed are warned to refuse hospitality to teachers of heretical doctrine, so as to avoid all involvement in their evil deeds. In Matt. 28:9 the risen Christ makes himself known to his disciples using the familiar, everyday *chairete*. When in Matt. 26:49; 27:29 par. Mk. 15:18, Jn. 19:3, Jesus is saluted in derision as rabbi or King of the Jews (→ Israel) there is a concealed irony since he is quite unwittingly given the salutation which is his due. In Lk. 1:28, Mary is startled not so much by the *chaire* itself, as by the message which follows it.

2. According to the Synoptic Gospels, the coming of Jesus brings in a time of joy: "Can the wedding guests mourn as long as the bridegroom is with them?" (Matt. 9:15 par. Mk. 2:19, Lk. 5:34; → Fast). The fact that he brings in the eschatological salvation distinguishes him plainly from John the Baptist and the OT prophets: the blind see and the lame walk, lepers are cleansed and the deaf hear, the dead are raised and the poor have the gospel preached to them (Matt. 11:5 par. Lk. 7:22). The effect of his work and preaching is to bring joy (Lk. 19:6). Even when he became an offence and the way of those who tread in his footsteps leads to suffering and persecution, the joyful assurance of salvation should not be lost: "Rejoice and be glad, for your reward is great in heaven!" (Matt. 5:12). Jesus is the coming judge of the whole world. Hence he who remains faithful to Christ's commission and receives the word with no mere ephemeral joy (Matt. 13:20 par. Mk. 4:16, Lk. 8:13), will hear one day the welcoming summons to the joyous banquet of his Lord. On *chara* in the sense of banquet, festive dinner, and its possible use in this sense in Matt. 25:21, 23 see Arndt, 884; SB I 879, 972. On the parable of the great supper see J. Jeremias, *The Parables of Jesus*, 1963², 63–69 (cf. Matt. 22:2 f.; Rev. 19:7, 9). When the disciples met the risen Christ, they were seized not only with → fear but also with great joy (Matt. 28:8; cf. Mk. 16:8; Lk. 24:9).

3. (a) Lk.'s Gospel has joy as one of its basic themes. Already in the birth narrative the note is clearly heard. Zechariah is promised joy and gladness; many will rejoice at the birth of John (Lk. 1:14) because of what God is now about to do on behalf of his people (cf. 2:15). When Elizabeth meets the mother of the Saviour (cf. 2:11) the child leaps for joy in her womb (*en agalliasei*, "for joy", 1:44). Jubilant praise of God, in the majestic language of the OT Psalms, is expressed in the *Magnificat* of Mary (*ēgalliasen*, "rejoiced", 1:47) and in the hymn of Zechariah (1:68 ff.). The basis and content of this great joy is the Christmas message that in Jesus God has visited and redeemed his people (1:68), that he has taken care of lost mankind, as he had promised to the fathers (1:55) and to the prophets (1:70), and that he has good will (*eudokia*, 2:14) towards men.

Joy is an important consequence of Jesus' → miracles (13:17). The seventy disciples may share in his power over evil spirits and be filled with joy and pride (10:17), but joy in God's electing love counts for still more: "But rejoice that your names are written in heaven" (10:20; cf. Matt. 7:22 f.). God deals mercifully with the lost; everything depends upon that. There is joy in heaven over one sinner who repents (Lk. 15:7, 10, 23). Indeed, the whole of Lk. 15 with its parables of the lost sheep, the lost coin and the lost son presents Jesus calling upon men to rejoice with him over the lost returning to the Father (15:6, 9, 32).

358

In contrast with the note of fear and awe which concludes the authentic text of Mk. (16:8), the conclusion of Lk. is remarkable for its amazement and over-flowing joy (Lk. 24:11, 41, 52). V. 46 might be regarded as a resumé of Lk.'s entire Gospel. Following upon the age of Jesus comes the age of the church (v. 47), when repentance will be preached in his name. (Here too there is the implication that repentance brings joy!) This is the message which will be carried beyond the boundaries of Israel and preached to all nations.

(b) This process is recorded in the Acts, where there are repeated expressions of joy over the irresistible worldwide expansion of the church. There is first of all the joy of the → apostles in suffering shame and persecution for Christ's sake (5:41; cf. Matt. 5:11 f.). Men experience such joy through the enabling of the Holy → Spirit (13:52; cf. 7:55). Persecution cannot halt the victorious course of the gospel (20:24 *v.l. meta charas* "with joy"). There is joy over the ingathering of the Gentiles (11:23; 13:48; 15:3). When the gospel is preached to the Gentiles and they are baptized, the persons concerned are filled with joy (8:8, 39; 15:31).

4. In the Gospel of John the eschatological term *chara peplēromenē*, perfect joy, fullness of joy (likewise in 1 Jn. 1:4; 2 Jn. 12), is an important feature. It occurs as early as 3:27, where John the Baptist's joy is now full on account of the "bridegroom", the promised revealer of heavenly truth (cf. Matt. 9:14 f. par. Mk. 2:18 f., Lk. 5:33 f.). The eschatological hour has now arrived, in which con-tinuous sowing exists side by side with the harvest time (4:35 f.), and in which Jesus is already accomplishing the work he was given to do (4:34). Abraham in heaven joins in the rejoicing over this day when the harvest begins to be gathered (8:56). The perfect joy which Jesus has, because he is in full communion with the Father (14:20) and does his will (4:34), is to be granted to the disciples also (15:11). This he asks from the Father (17:13), and therefore exhorts his own to abide in him (15:4) and in his love (15:9). His work of love is completed as he lays down his life for his "friends" (15:13); it will only be fully revealed, however, when he goes away from them (16:10). But he does not leave them behind as → orphans (14:18). He prays the Father to send the *paraklētos* (14:16, 26; → Advocate), manifests himself to them as the risen one (14:19; 20:20 "the disciples rejoiced [*echarēsan*]"), and promises them that prayer in his name will be heard (15:7, 16).

The world cannot take away this joy and consolation any more than it can take away the → peace which he gives (14:27; 16:33), for they are grounded in → revelation and do not belong to this world. This is the reason why his disciples are to be separate from the world and are to expect the world's hatred and persecu-tion (15:19; 16:2). But fear is banished because Jesus has overcome the world (16:33; cf. 1 Jn. 1:4). Present sadness will be turned into joy (16:22). This escha-tological joy "is not described as a psychic condition of rapture but is defined as the situation in which believers no longer need to ask for anything" (R. Bultmann, *The Gospel of John*, 1971, 583).

5. The Pauline Epistles testify to the paradox that Christian joy is to be found only in the midst of sadness, affliction and care. Indeed, this is precisely where it gives proof of its power.

(a) This joy has its source beyond mere earthly, human joy. It is joy *en kyriō*, in the Lord, and therefore outside ourselves. This is why Paul constantly reminds his readers of its existence and exhorts them to manifest it (Phil. 3:1; 4:4, 10; Rom.

12:12; 2 Cor. 6:10). It is the "joy of faith" (Phil. 1:25; Rom. 15:13). It has its basis in the → hope and confidence of → faith, which despite all fightings and fears (2 Cor. 7:5) is certain of justification through Christ (Rom. 8:31 f.) and looks forward to his return as the risen Lord. As the joy of faith, it is also a → fruit of the → Spirit (Gal. 5:22), and is spoken of as joy in the Holy Spirit (Rom. 14:17; 1 Thess. 1:6). It is thus a spiritual gift, and in this respect approximates to the idea of *charis*, → grace. Because faith and its consequent joy do not come from ourselves, Paul can be confident and rejoice even when Christ is preached with base motives. The important thing is that God should do his gracious work and that as many men as possible should share in the gospel (Phil. 1:5 f., 15–18).

(b) In 2 Cor. Paul places joy in direct contrast to *thlipsis*, affliction (→ Persecution, Tribulation), by which he means not only the distress caused by outward trials, but also the sorrow aroused by his apostolic rebukes. He protests to the Corinthians that "we work with you [*synergoi esmen*] for your joy" (2 Cor. 1:24). He wrote as he did not to cause *thlipsis* (2:4) but that his joy, which is joy *en kyriō*, "in the Lord" (13:11; cf. Phil 3:1), might be shared by all (2:3). The lives of the Corinthians are to be ruled not by passive resignation or the worldly grief (*lypē*) which produces death (7:10), but by the joy of a purified faith. Having sharply rebuked them earlier, Paul has regained his confidence in them (7:13), for his admonition has had a salutary effect. Indeed, he almost implies that he has been too severe (7:11). Since his anxiety has been removed by Titus' report (7:16), he now has even stronger grounds for rejoicing.

(c) Paul wrote the Epistle to the Philippians from prison (possibly in Ephesus) and at the time was still uncertain of the outcome of his trial. There is evidence that he felt lonely (2:20 f.), and that faithful preaching of the gospel was in jeopardy (1:15 ff.; 2:21). Once again there was *thlipsis* (4:14; cf. Col. 1:24), occasion for anxiety. Yet there were also grounds for thankfulness and unmitigated joy: thankfulness for the participation of the Philippians in the gospel (1:5), and joy over the continuing proclamation of Christ (1:18). Constrained by the gospel and by Christ himself, Paul exhorts his readers to rejoice together with him (2:17 f.), to cast care behind them (4:16), and to be of one mind in the fellowship of the Spirit (2:1 f.). What if there is occasion for anxiety; what if Paul is soon to meet his death, so long as Christ is magnified in his body (1:20)!

In Phil. joy is thus a continuous "defiant 'Nevertheless' " (K. Barth, *The Epistle to the Philippians*, 1962, 120; cf. Phil. 2:17; 4:4). This "nevertheless" draws its strength not from itself but from untiring prayer which lays every need before God (4:6; cf. 1 Thess. 5:16; Col. 1:11). It takes heart at the spread of the gospel throughout the world (1:5 f.; 1 Thess. 3:9; Col. 2:5) and at the flourishing growth of missionary churches (Phil. 4:10; cf. 1 Thess. 2:20: "For you are our glory and joy"). But above all it is joy in the Lord (Phil. 4:4).

(d) The present period of trial and distress is limited. The Lord is at hand! (Phil. 4:5; cf. 1 Thess. 5:2 f.; 3:3). Hence joy is based primarily on the → hope that after suffering together we shall be glorified together (Rom. 8:17). This joyous and confident waiting for the day of Christ puts our present experience into true perspective. *Gaudium in domino parit veram aequitatem*: "Joy in the Lord brings forth true peace of mind" (J. A. Bengel, quoted by Barth, op. cit., 121). On the one hand, this "gentleness" (Phil. 4:5 RV mg.) gives us leisure from ourselves so that we can sympathize with others (Rom. 12:15). On the other hand, it reminds us that our present joys and sorrows belong to this life only and are not our final lot (1 Cor. 7:30; 2 Cor. 6:10).

6. This Pauline teaching about joy in affliction and temptation proved its value when the later NT epistles were being written. By this time, the persecution of Christians was already so severe as to threaten the very existence of the church (1 Pet. 4:13; cf. Rom. 8:17). But being robbed of their material goods could not deprive them of their joy (Heb. 10:34). This is well illustrated by the last lines of Luther's hymn *Ein' feste Burg*, inspired by Ps. 46:

> And, though they take our life,
> Goods, honour, children, wife,
> Yet is their profit small;
> These things shall vanish all:
> The city of God remaineth (Carlyle's translation).

For all that, persecution still brought very real distress (Heb. 12:11). Hence believers are urged to exercise patience (Heb. 10:36) and to continue obediently in sound doctrine (Heb. 12:17). Christ has voluntarily given up his own joy and taken upon himself the shame of the cross. Only looking to him can we obtain patience and endurance in temptation (Heb. 12:2; cf. 1 Pet. 1:8 f.).

Jas. 1:2 comes close to teaching Christians to rejoice in martyrdom (cf. Acts 5:41). In the course of the church's history, however, this has often degenerated into virtually seeking martyrdom for its own sake. Jas. 4:9 f. is not to be taken legalistically, as if this were the saving faith of the NT. Such a view is precluded by obedience to the risen Lord. For it would deny the ultimate, once-for-all value of his work on the cross. *E. Beyreuther, G. Finkenrath*

→ Cry, → Lament, → Laugh, → Suffer

(a). W. Beilner, "Joy", *EBT* II 438–42; R. Bultmann, *agalliaomai* etc., *TDNT* I 19 ff.; *euphrainō* etc., *TDNT* II 772–75; and *The Gospel of John*, 1971, 505 ff.; H. Conzelmann and W. Zimmerli, *chairō* etc., *TDNT* IX 359–415; D. W. Harvey, "Rejoice Not, O Israel!" in B. W. Anderson and W. Harrelson, eds., *Israel's Prophetic Heritage*, 1962, 116–27; J. Moltmann, *Theology and Joy*, 1973.
(b). M. Ammermann, *Die religiöse Freude in den Schriften des Alten Bundes*, 1942; E. G. Gulin, *Die Freude im Neuen Testament*, I–II, 1932–36; U. Holtzmeister, " 'Gaudete in Domino semper' et 'Beati qui lugent' ", *Verbum Domini* 22, 1942, 257–62; P. Humbert, "*Laetari et exsultare* dans le vocabulaire religieux de l'Ancien Testament", *Revue d'Histoire et de Philosophie Religieuses* 22, 1942, 185–214; and *Opuscules d'un Hébraisant*, 1958, 119–45; R. Laurentin, *Structure et Théologie de Luc I–II*, 1964; W. Nauck, "Freude im Leiden", *ZNW* 46, 1955, 68–80; J. Perrier, *La Joie dans l'Évangile de Jésus*, 1962; B. Reicke, *Diakonie, Festfreude und Zelos in Verbindung mit der altchristlichen Agapenfeier*, 1951; H. Rusche, "Die Freude: Ein biblischer Grundbegriff", *BuK* 5, 1964, 141 ff.; E. Schick and A. Auer, "Freude", *LTK* IV 361 ff.; A. B. du Toit, *Der Aspekt der Freude im urchristlichen Abendmahl*, 1965; R. Voeltzel, *Das Lachen des Herrn*, 1961.

Judgment, Judge, Deliver, Judgment Seat

It is sometimes necessary to examine whether human behaviour conforms to certain standards. Such examination, together with the ultimate assessment and, if necessary, condemnation, is expressed in the NT by the extensive word-group connected with *krinō*, to judge. Since *paradidōmi* can mean "to hand over" (for judgment or punishment) it is also discussed here together with *bēma*, judgment seat, and *katadikazō*, condemn. However, in view of its basic meaning "to transmit" this word-group is further dealt with under → Teach.

| κρίμα |

κρίμα (*krima*), dispute, decision, verdict, judgment; κρίνω (*krinō*), separate, judge, consider, decide; ἀνακρίνω (*anakrinō*), investigate, examine; κρίσις (*krisis*), decision, crisis; κριτής (*kritēs*), a judge; συγκρίνω (*synkrinō*), compare, interpret; κατάκριμα (*katakrima*), punishment, condemnation; κατακρίνω (*katakrinō*), condemn; κατάκρισις (*katakrisis*), condemnation; καταγινώσκω (*kataginōskō*), condemn.

CL *krima*, judgment, is found once in Aeschylus but does not acquire a clear meaning until quite late (from the LXX onwards). It is formed from *krinō*, to judge, which in its numerous compounds (both nouns and vbs.) had come to occupy a major place in legal terminology. *krinō* did not originate as a legal term, however, nor are its meanings restricted to the legal sphere.

1. (a) From its basic meaning to separate, sift (so in Homer), the word acquired in Gk. literature its own shades of meaning in connection with human value-judgments: to discriminate, divide, distinguish, select, acknowledge, approve, estimate, prefer. At the same time the "assessment" aspect became prominent, so that *krinō* means to judge, pronounce judgment, decide, and also to be of the opinion, to purpose. In the mid. and pass. it means to dispute, debate, or fight.

(b) The compound *synkrinō* reveals a similar process in its meanings to compare, judge, measure. It also means (like *krinō* used in the mid.) to explain, expound, and interpret (dreams).

(c) *anakrinō*, found from Thucydides onwards, expresses the questioning process which leads to a judgment: to examine, cross-examine, interrogate, inquire, and investigate.

(d) The noun *krima*, like the vb., embraces a variety of meanings: decision, verdict, and also controversy, dispute.

(e) In this meaning *krima* is parallel to its derivative *krisis*, which means decision (of a referee), crisis (in battle, sickness, etc.), and also separation, selection, dissension, dispute.

(f) The person making the decision or selection is called *kritēs*: critic, judge, referee (the word is very rare in secular Gk., and in Attic and Ion. Gk. is never used for a lawcourt judge). Derived from this is the substantival adj. *kritikos* (found from Plato onwards), a competent, experienced judge.

2. (a) *krinō* as a technical legal term means to judge, to bring to judgment, or condemn. The judgment, *krima*, can be divine or human, and the judges, *kritai*, authorized office-bearers or unauthorized persons. Divine judicial authority is such that generally judgment and its effect are seen as one, so that *krima* means not only judgment but also condemnation, damnation and punishment.

(b) The compound *katakrinō* has a similar meaning: to condemn. The rare noun *katakrisis* means condemnation. The noun *katakrima*, is first found in the 1st cent. B.C. with the meaning punishment, damnation. Its meaning in the *Corpus Papyrorum Raineri* (ed. 1895) is noteworthy: legal liability in respect of a piece of land.

(c) The word *autokatakritos* is found in Philo and occurs sporadically elsewhere. Formed from the adj. and the prefix *auto*, self, it has no longer a strictly legal but rather a moral character and means self-condemned. Another rare compound is *prokrima* (not found until the 2nd cent. A.D.), a technical legal term for the interim judgment reached en route to the final verdict; then also, morally, prejudice, preconceived idea (which stands in the way of a judicial decision). A moral assessment is also expressed by *kataginōskō*, found from Aeschylus and Herodotus onwards, meaning to condemn, literally to observe something (bad) in someone, to catch in the act, to recognize as guilty, to despise.

OT 1. In the LXX *krinō* is used mainly as a translation of the Heb. words *šāpaṭ*, *dîn* and *rîḇ*. Thus *krinō*, to judge, acquired a meaning which went beyond its general Gk. usage, for *dîn* means not only to judge, but also to punish, wrangle, vindicate, and obtain justice for a person (Gen. 15:14; 2 Sam. 19:9; Gen. 30:6; Deut. 32:36; Ps. 54:3; Jer. 5:28). *rîḇ* means to quarrel, to litigate, to carry on a lawsuit (Gen. 26:21; Jdg. 8:1; 21:22; 1 Sam. 24:16). *šāpaṭ*, which occurs the most frequently, adds still further shades of meaning, so that to judge comes to mean "to rule" (Exod. 2:14; 1 Sam. 8:20; 2 Sam. 15:4, 6). He who judges brings salvation, peace and deliverance, especially to the persecuted and oppressed (cf. Deut. 10:18). "Give the king thy justice, O God, and thy righteousness unto the royal son! May he judge thy people with righteousness, and thy poor with justice" (Ps. 72:1 f.). The judges (LXX *kritai*) who in Jdg. are called "great" are the deliverers, helpers or saviours, raised up by God. They obtain justice for the tribes of Israel in the face of their enemies, annihilate or drive out their oppressors, and so bring salvation, rest and peace to the land (Jdg. 3:9, 15). *krima* can also mean statute (Lev. 18:5; 20:22), and in Jer. 51:10 the Heb. *ṣᵉḏāqâh*, righteousness, is translated by *krima*.

2. In Israel justice was originally dispensed not according to absolute moral standards but with a view to restoring peace within the community concerned, whether the family, the tribe, or the nation. In difficult cases it meant removing the offending member. After the conquest justice was dispensed partly in the context of family and tribe by the heads of families and tribal elders, and partly in the context of the local community by the elders sitting in the gate of a town or village, all full citizens having right to speak (Ruth 4:1 ff.). In Jerusalem officials (called commanders in Deut. 1:15 RSV; princes e.g. Isa. 1:23; Jer. 26) were appointed as judges. Certain officials whose function is not quite clear were called "judges of Israel". According to M. Noth, a list of these is seen in the enumeration of the so-called "minor judges" in Jdg. 10:1–5; 12:7–15 (*The History of Israel*, 1958, 101).

3. In Israel all justice is ascribed to God: Yahweh is Lord and judge (Deut. 1:17). As judge he helps his people (Jdg. 11:27; 2 Sam. 18:31). He never deviates from justice (Ps. 7:12), and will not suffer his honour to be brought into disrepute. Heaven and earth or the peoples of the earth are often called upon to act as a tribunal (Isa. 1:2; Jer. 2:12; Mic. 6:1; Ps. 50:1–6). He judges the nations (Gen. 11:1 ff.; Ps. 67:5; Amos 1:2; Joel 4:2; Mal. 3:2 ff.), especially on the "day of Yahweh", when he will destroy all ungodliness (Isa. 2:12–18; 13:9; Jer. 46:10; Ezek. 30:3 ff.; Zeph. 1:7–18; → Present, art. *hēmera*). He comes to the aid of anyone suffering violence and injustice (Gen. 4:9 ff.). One must submit to his inscrutable judgment (Job). His judgments are just, i.e. they are in harmony with

363

his faithfulness, whereby he espouses the cause of his chosen people, guides them and ensures their safety. Thus God's judgment is motivated by love, grace and mercy, and its outcome is salvation (Isa. 30:18; Ps. 25:6–9; 33:5; 103:6 ff.; 146:7). "He will vindicate his people and have compassion on his servants" (Deut. 32:36 RSV).

4. In the judgment discourses of the prophets it is God's judgment upon Israel which receives most attention (Amos 5:18; 8 and 9; Hos. 4:1; Mic. 1; Jer. 2:4–9; Isa. 41:1 ff.; 48:1 ff.; 50:1 ff.). Since Israel is the elect nation, it will be judged (Amos 3:1 ff.; Ezek. 20:33–38). Moreover, Yahweh the judge is → king of the universe and uses nations and powers as instruments of his judgment. The key to the message of the major prophets "lies in the light of the fact that, as far as saving history is concerned they see an entirely new day dawning for Israel; they see a new action of God approaching her, which will bring with it heavy punishments but also mysterious acts of preservation. In view of this – so the prophets are convinced – it will no longer be enough to appeal to the old saving appointments, for this new divine saving activity, and it alone, is to decide the question of the existence or non-existence of Israel" (G. von Rad, *Old Testament Theology*, II, 1965, 395; cf. Isa. 5:1 ff.; Hos. 13:5–9; Jer. 31:31 ff.).

5. In the post-exilic period the description of God's judgment acquired certain apocalyptic features. Its character as punishment is emphasized: God's enemies, whether men or supernatural powers, will be dashed to pieces (a host on high, Eth.Enoch 10:6; God and Magog, Sib. 3). The "congregation of wickedness" will be annihilated, while the "sons of light" will attain salvation (cf. 1QS 3 and 4; 1QM 3:9–19 of the Qumran community). The doctrine of retribution led men to regard any calamity as God's judgment upon them for some offence; this in turn had an adverse effect upon their social life, and shook their faith in divine justice. Belief in a further judgment after death (Ps.Sol. 3:1 ff.; Eth.Enoch) offered a way out of this mental anguish, since it meant that the process of exact retribution could be lengthened. Judgment would still fall, even though men might not live to see it. God or the Son of man is the judge of the world at the "last day" (2 Esd. 7; Eth.Enoch).

NT 1. In addition to the metaphors of harvest (→ seed), sifting, and separation (cf. Matt. 13:30 f., 40 f., 49; 24:31, 40 f.; 25:31 ff.) the NT contains a great deal of legal and semi-legal language where *krima*, *krinō* and their derivatives are used with the same complex meanings as are found in Gk. literature and in the LXX.

(a) *krinō* has the following meanings: to distinguish, give preference, approve (Rom. 14:5a to esteem one day as better than another; Rom. 14:5b to approve each day, i.e. esteem all days alike). In addition it means to consider, regard as (Acts 13:46; 16:15; 26:8); to speak or think ill of, to decide, to judge (Matt. 7:1 f; Lk. 7:43; Acts 4:19; 15:19; Rom. 14:3 ff.; 1 Cor. 4:5; 10:15; 29; 2 Cor. 5:14; Col. 2:16). *prokrima* is similarly used ("without prejudice", 1 Tim. 5:21). *krinō* also means to decide, resolve (Acts 3:13 and *passim*; Rom. 14:13; 1 Cor. 2:2; 5:3; 7:37; Tit. 3:12). *synkrinō* means to interpret (1 Cor. 2:13, "interpreting spiritual truths to those who possess the Spirit"), and to compare (2 Cor. 10:12). *anakrinō* occurs with the meaning to inquire (Acts 17:11; 1 Cor. 10:25, 27; 14:24), to examine,

364

interrogate (Lk. 23:14; Acts 4:9; 12:19; 24:8; 28:18; 1 Cor. 4:3; 9:3), to judge of, to form an estimate of (1 Cor. 2:14).

(b) *krinō* and *krima* are very frequently used in the NT in a strictly judicial sense, *krinō* meaning to judge; in the pass. to bring to trial, condemn, punish; in the mid. to dispute.

Men judge according to the → law (Jn. 18:31; Acts 23:3; 24:6). The apostles and the church judge (1 Cor. 5:12; 1 Cor. 6:2 f.; the world and angels). Paul is put on trial (Acts 23:6). The people cannot come to a right judgment (Lk. 12:57). The wicked servant is punished on the basis of his own statements (Lk. 19:22; → Punishment). People go to law to settle disputes (Matt. 5:40; 1 Cor. 6:6). The noun *krima* is used similarly: the disciples of Jesus should not judge, and with the judgment that a man pronounces on others he himself will be judged (Matt. 7:1 ff.). The Christians in Corinth have disputes (lawsuits) with one another (1 Cor. 6:7). *krisis* is similarly used: judgment by the authorities (Matt. 5:21); judgment passed by one man upon another (Jn. 7:24), or by the angels upon the devil (2 Pet. 2:11; Jude 9). *kritēs* means the authorized (Matt. 5:25; Lk. 12:14, 58; 18:2) and the unauthorized (Jas. 2:4; 4:11) judge, also anyone who brings injustice to light (Matt. 12:27). *autokatakritos* (only in Tit. 3:11) is the man who is self-condemned. *kataginōskō* (1 Jn. 3:20 f.; Gal. 2:11) means to be recognized as guilty and condemned by one's own heart or conduct. Condemnation by men is also expressed by *katakrinō*: the people of → Nineveh will appear at the last judgment with this generation and will condemn it (Matt. 12:41; cf. Heb. 11:7). "Has no one condemned you?" (Jn. 8:10, cf. 11). "In passing judgment upon another you condemn yourself" (Rom. 2:1). "Who is to condemn?" (Rom. 8:34). Jesus is condemned to death (Matt. 20:18; 27:3; Mk. 14:64). The noun *katakrisis* occurs twice: "dispensation of condemnation" (2 Cor. 3:9) and "not to your condemnation" (2 Cor. 7:3). When combined with the genitive, *krima tēs pornēs* means the judgment of the harlot (Rev. 17:1), and *krima thanatou* capital punishment (Lk. 24:20).

LXX influence appears when *krima* means rule: authority to rule is given to the disciples and martyrs (Lk. 22:30; Rev. 20:4); the twelve apostles rule over the twelve tribes (Matt. 19:28); likewise when *krisis* means justice (Matt. 12:18; 23:23; Acts 8:33).

God and Jesus judge (Jn. 5:22, 29 f. and often; Acts 6:10). They are called *kritēs*, judge (2 Tim. 4:8; Heb. 12:23; Jas. 4:12; 5:9; Acts 10:42), and God's word is called *kritikos*, a discerner (Heb. 4:12). When the passive form is used, the reference is similarly to the activity of the divine judge (Rev. 11:8). Christ judges the living and the dead (2 Tim. 4:1; 1 Pet. 4:5 f.), the secrets of men (Rom. 2:16), the world (Acts 17:31), every man according to his works (1 Pet. 1:17; Rev. 20:12 f. cf. 2 Cor. 5:10). The noun *krima* is used in the same way: Jesus has come to bring judgment (Jn. 9:39); God's judgments are unsearchable (Rom. 11:33); his activity as a judge begins with the church (1 Pet. 4:17); future and eternal judgment is in his hands (Acts 24:25; Heb. 6:2). Divine judgment often includes → punishment (Jn. 3:17 f.; Rom. 2:12; 3:6; 1 Cor. 11:13 f.; 2 Thess. 2:12; Heb. 10:30; 13:4; Jas. 5:9). God's condemnation is just (Rom. 2:2 f.; 3:8) and swift (2 Pet. 2:3). The prince of this world is condemned (Jn. 16:11). Divine condemnation, issuing, as the word implies, in damnation, is expressed by *katakrima* (Rom. 5:16, 18; 8:1). Damnation is also expressed by the verb *katakrinō*, which can have God, as well

365

as men, for its subject: God condemned sin in the flesh (Rom. 8:3). He has turned Sodom and Gomorrah to ashes and condemned them (2 Pet. 2:6). When we are judged, we are chastened so that we may not be condemned along with the world (1 Cor. 11:32); cf. also the passive in Mk. 16:16 and Rom. 14:23. *krisis* is frequently used synonymously with *krima*, judgment: the judgment of God or of Christ (Jn. 5:30; 2 Thess. 1:5); the day (hour) of judgment (Matt. 10:15 and often; 2 Pet. 2:9; 3:7; 1 Jn. 4:17; Jude 6; Rev. 14:7; 1 Tim. 5:24; Heb. 9:27). Divine judgment brings separation (Jn. 3:19) and destruction (Heb. 10:27). He who hears Jesus' word and believes him does not come into judgment (Jn. 5:24). The dead who have done evil will arise to judgment (Jn. 5:29).

2. Just as in the OT all judgment is ascribed to God, so also in the NT all human judgment and punishment stands within the wider context of God's sovereign judgment, a principle expressed with the utmost clarity in Matt. 7:1: "Judge not, that you be not judged". The church of Christ has been entrusted with the task of judging in matters which affect its members (1 Cor. 5:12; 6:2). Human relationships are to be regulated by love, even extending to love of one's enemies, but measured by the standard of God's perfect righteousness, no man remains righteous in God's sight. All men fall under his wrath, and are without excuse (Rom. 1–3). This is the reason why ultimately no man has a right to judge another. Dire warnings are addressed to the unmerciful and the arrogant who are blind to their own lost condition, who are not ready to forgive and to pray for their enemies (Matt. 5:23 ff., 43 ff.; 7:1–5; Lk. 18:9 ff.).

The unsearchableness of God's judgments (Rom. 11:33) means that the doctrine of retribution can no longer be rigidly upheld. The human principle of "tit for tat" has no place in the divine judge's dealings with men (Lk. 6:32; 13:1–5; Jn. 9:2 f.). That God *is* judge, however, is basic to the NT, not merely as regards the frequency with which it is mentioned but also from the point of view of content. It is a doctrine which impinges upon many other major aspects of the NT message (→ Glory; → Righteousness; → Grace; → Lord; → Love; → Reward; → Guilt; → Punishment; → Sin; → Forgiveness; → Reconciliation; → Anger, Wrath). On the other hand, words like "judgment", "to judge", etc., are associated with human legal concepts, and as such are incapable of expressing the unsearchableness of God, particularly when his unsearchable decrees reveal his love. This is the other side of God's character, displayed throughout the NT, but in such a way as to show the unmistakable influence of the OT and of Jewish apocalyptic.

Jesus, like John the Baptist, preached by word and deed the nearness of divine judgment, which stirs men up both to hope and to repentance (Lk. 13:6 ff.) and brings woe upon the unrepentant (Matt. 11:20 ff.; 12:41 f.). The fact of coming judgment means that all men are advancing towards God's final verdict on themselves and their works. Before God nothing is forgotten, whether deed or word. The judgment of God is the great reality of man's life (Matt. 10:28), and the only way of escaping condemnation is to be forgiven.

For Paul and the early church, Jesus is the judge of all the world, as God the Father is. Divine patience still gives men time to repent and believe in Christ who for us has been made "to be sin, who knew no sin, so that in him we might become the righteousness of God" (2 Cor. 5:21; cf. Rom. 3:23 ff.; Gal. 3:13; Col. 2:13 ff.). The judge is the Saviour. Judgment already rests upon unbelievers because they refuse the Saviour, while believers escape condemnation (Jn. 3:16 ff.; 11:25 f.). They have confidence as they anticipate the day of judgment, and this confidence issues in ethical results here and now. The eschatological tension in the statements about judgment is broken neither by the emphasis in Jn. upon its being present, nor by the emphasis in Rev. upon its being future, though the apocalyptic elements figure differently.

The principles of judgment in the NT are a development of those found in OT prophecy. It is the elect one who is judged, for divine judgment falls upon Christ crucified. Yet this is God's saving work, for in judging Christ, he remains faithful to his elect people and honour, and bound to uphold his covenant. The wrath of God is fully revealed only by the gospel (Rom. 1–3), as the "word of the cross" is preached. Christ "is set for the fall and rising of many" (Lk. 2:34).

W. Schneider

| παραδίδωμι | παραδίδωμι (*paradidōmi*), deliver up, give up, hand over.

CL *paradidōmi*, from Pindar onwards, has a wide range of uses and denotes all aspects of deliberate giving or giving over: to deliver up, to give away, to offer, to give up, to hand over, to betray. As a legal term, it means to bring before a court, to deliver up a prisoner (*eis* with the acc. expressing destination and purpose). The person concerned is delivered up e.g. to the dark chaos of doom (magic papyri), to death (papyri) or to discipline (Demetrius of Phaleron). It can cover the handing over of a captive (where this has a minimal effect on the situation of the person concerned), right through to the reprehensible act of betrayal, whereby a free man of good repute, who may well be innocent, is ruined.

In its connection with *paradosis*, tradition, the transmission of doctrine, the vb. is dealt with under → Teach, art. *paradidōmi*.

OT The LXX uses *paradidōmi* about 200 times. Although in the Heb. text 26 different words underlie the Gk. vb., *paradidōmi* stands chiefly (about 150 times) for the Hebrew *nāṭan*, which primarily means to give, but secondarily (with a preposition) to hand over, to deliver. The formula *paradounai eis cheiras tinos*, to deliver into someone's hands, is not found in secular Gk., but in the LXX it is very frequent and is carried over from there into the NT. The formula stems ultimately from the wars of Yahweh. Before a battle began, a priest or a prophet would be asked to consult the oracle, and if all was well, the answer would be: "I (Yahweh) deliver them into your hand, O Israel." If Israel was disobedient, then Yahweh would deliver them into the hands of strange peoples (Jdg. 2:14, plunderers; 6:13, Midianites; Isa. 65:12, the sword; Jer. 32:4, the king of Babylon). In the language of the Deuteronomist the old formula came to mean the total annihilation of all the earlier inhabitants of the land (e.g. Deut. 1:8). From then on it became even more widely used. Its origin accounts for the fact that the subject of the vb. is almost always God, and that in practically every case it implies handing over to ruin, to defeat, to annihilation, to death. In Isa. 43:3 it is said that Yahweh has given Egypt, Ethiopia and Seba as a ransom for Israel, i.e. he has inflicted defeat upon them that he may obtain Israel for himself. An analogy is found in

367

Isa. 53:5 where Yahweh's Servant is said to have been delivered over to death "for our transgressions" for the deliverance of many. This doubtless means that his own people were guilty of betraying Yahweh's Servant, but his death awoke them out of their sin of rejecting him. (For fuller discussion → Son, art. *pais theou*.)

NT 1. In the NT *paradidōmi* occurs in all 120 times; of these 84 are in the Gospels, 13 in Acts, only 19 altogether in the Pauline Epistles (6 in Rom., 7 in 1 Cor., 3 in Eph., 1 each in 2 Cor., Gal., 1 Tim.), 3 in 1 and 2 Pet., 1 in Jude. It does not occur at all in Heb., Rev., and the Epistles of Jn.

In the NT *paradosis* never occurs in the sense of handing over or betrayal, but only in the sense of the transmission of doctrine (→ Teach, art. *paradosis*).

2. The basic meaning of the vb. in the NT is to deliver up to judgment and death. The statement that John the Baptist was delivered up (*paredothē*, Matt. 4:12) signifies his imprisonment leading to his execution. The adversary delivers to the judge (Matt. 5:25), and the judge to the officer (Lk. 12:58). Jesus' followers will be delivered to the council (Matt. 10:17) and to synagogues (Lk. 21:12), and will be exposed to persecution and oppression (Matt. 24:9). Brother is delivered up by brother to death (Mk. 13:12), cf. also Acts 8:3 and 22:4 (Saul in his persecution of Christians) and Acts 12:4 (the arrest of Peter).

3. Most of the passages in which *paradidōmi* occurs refer, however, to Jesus' announcement of his suffering and to the passion itself (→ Suffer). He is delivered into the hands of men (Matt. 17:22 par. Mk. 9:31, Lk. 9:44), to the high priests and scribes (Matt. 20:18), to the Gentiles (Matt. 20:19 par. Mk. 10:33, Lk. 18:22), to Pilate (Matt. 27:2), to the death sentence (Lk. 24:20) and to crucifixion (Matt. 26:2). Judas, the person who delivers him up, is the betrayer. The frequent use of *paradidōmi* in the NT, particularly in the passion narratives, reflects the fact that it is a technical term used in law and in martyrology. The words of institution of the → Last Supper contain *paradidōmi* only once (1 Cor. 11:23), with reference to Christ's atoning death: *en tē nykti hē paredideto*, "on the night in which he was betrayed [or delivered up]"; cf. the *hyper hymōn* "for you" in v. 24.

4. The vb. is occasionally used for deliverance to something other than a human court of justice: to shameful lusts (Rom. 1:24); the Gentiles give themselves up to unchastity and this in itself is a judgment (Eph. 4:19); Israel was given over to worshipping the host of heaven (Acts 7:42). In 1 Cor. 5:5 and 1 Tim. 1:20 Paul delivers men to Satan (→ Destroy, art. *olethros*). According to Jewish tradition, → Satan was the executor of the divine judgment.

5. Finally *paradidōmi* is found in the context of dying, i.e. of giving up one's life: to give up one's spirit, i.e. to expire (Jn. 19:30); to give up one's life, i.e. to risk one's life (Acts 15:26); the Son of God who gave up himself (Gal. 2:20; cf. Eph. 5:25 and Rom. 8:32).

6. Only in a few passages does *paradidōmi* occur in a context other than that of judgment and death. Thus the fact that divine power is delivered to Jesus is an evidence of his messianic sovereignty (Matt. 11:27; Lk. 10:22; Matt. 28:18; cf. 1 Cor. 15:24). But the devil also asserts that he can grant power to whomsoever he will, since it has been placed at his absolute disposal (Lk. 4:6). In Acts 14:26 Paul and Barnabas in Antioch are commended or committed to the grace of God, i.e. placed under its protective power.   *H. Beck*

| $\beta\tilde{\eta}\mu\alpha$ | $\beta\tilde{\eta}\mu\alpha$ (bēma), judgment seat. |

CL In secular Gk. bēma is used in the sense of step or stride, as in walking (Pindar, Aeschylus). It has also the associative connotation of a pace as a unit of measure. The word is also used as a platform for a public speaker and, in legal contexts, it denotes the place where litigants stood for trial (Demosthenes, Aeschines).

OT In the LXX bēma stands for two Heb. words miḏrāḵ and miḡdāl. The word miḏrāḵ, from the root dāraḵ (tread), denotes the area covered by placing down the foot, hence a footbreadth. It occurs only in Deut. 2:5 where it is used in the sense of a unit of measure. In this context the Lord affirmed to Moses that he would not allow the people of Israel to take any of the territory belonging to the descendants of Esau, "not so much as for the sole of the foot to tread on." A somewhat similar expression utilizes the word māqôm (place) rather than miḏrāḵ (Deut. 11:24; Jos. 1:3). In this latter expression the emphasis is more geographical and the concept of space or area is minimized. The word miḡdāl, from the root gāḏal (grow up, become great) chiefly denotes a tower, but is used in Neh. 8:4 of a wooden platform on which Ezra stood to read from the book of the law. The word is used in the same sense in the parallel passage in 1 Esd. 9:42. In Sir. 19:30 bēma occurs in the plur. (but in the v.l. S² bēma podos in the sing.) in the sense of the steps of a man, i.e. his manner of walking which reveals his character. Eth.Enoch 62:3, 5 depicts the Son of man judging the mighty on his throne.

NT In the NT bēma occurs once in the sense of step as a unit of measure (Acts 7:5). It is found in the expression bēma podos ("a foot's length" RSV), i.e. a small area. The usage is similar to the Heb. expression in Deut. 2:5.

The word is used most frequently in the NT of the platform or dais on which was placed a seat for an official. The bēma was the platform from which orations were made (Acts 12:21) as well as the place where civil officials held session to hear certain legal cases and render judgment in such cases (Matt. 27:19; Jn. 19:13; Acts 18:12, 16 f.; 25:6, 10, 17). Thus Jesus was brought before the bēma of Pilate (cf. A. N. Sherwin-White, Roman Society and Roman Law in the New Testament, 1965², 24 ff.), and the Jews at Corinth accused Paul before the tribunal of the Proconsul Gallio who drove them out, but ignored the beating of Sosthenes. The remains of a public rostrum still stand among the ruins of Corinth (cf. O. Broneer, "Corinth: Center of Paul's Missionary Work in Greece", BA 14, 1951, 91 f.). Later Paul appeared before the bēma of Festus at Caesarea.

The word was twice used by Paul in his letters of the judgment seat. Rom. 14:10 speaks of "the judgment seat of God," and the following verse cites Isa. 45:23 as confirmation that all men will appear before it (cf. also Phil. 2:10 f.). 2 Cor. 5:10 speaks of "the judgment seat of Christ", drawing attention to the fact that Christ will be the judge of all men (cf. Matt. 16:27; 25:31–46). In Rom. 14:10 ff. the emphasis is on the rôle of the litigant before the bēma: "So each of us shall give account of himself to God." In 2 Cor. 5:10 the emphasis falls on the judgment rendered: "So that each one may receive good or evil, according to what he has done in the body." Both passages draw attention to the reversal of rôles: Jesus who (like his apostle) appeared before the judgment seat of men and suffered unjust

369

judgment will one day sit in righteous judgment over unjust men. But Paul reminds his readers that believers are not exempt from this scrutiny and judgment. Even though reconciled (cf. 2 Cor. 5:20 f.) and justified (Rom. 5:1; 8:1), they still have to give account and have their work tested (cf. 1 Cor. 3:13 ff.).

T. McComiskey

| καταδικάζω |

καταδικάζω (*katadikazō*), condemn; καταδίκη (*katadikē*), condemnation.

CL The vb. *katadikazō* means to condemn, render judgment against, in secular Gk. (Herodotus, Lucian). The noun *katadikē* denotes a legal sentence or judgment brought against someone.

OT *katadikazō* occurs in the LXX as the translation of the vb. *rāša'* and its adj. *rāšā'* as well as the vbs. *'āwaṭ* and *ḥûḇ*.

The vb. *rāša'* (be wicked) has the meaning to condemn as guilty in the hiphil and it is this sense of the word that is reflected in *katadikazō* (Job 34:29; Pss. 36[37]:33; 93[94]:21). The adjectival form *rāšā'* (guilty) occurs in Ps. 108(109):7.

The vb. *'āwaṭ* in the piel has the meaning bend or make crooked and hence, by extension, means to pervert, subvert or falsify. It is used by Amos (8:5) of the falsification of weights in dispensing food. In the LXX this word is translated by *katadikazō* in Lam. 3:36 in the sense of subverting one in a cause.

katadikazō is used to translate the piel form of *ḥûḇ* (qal, be guilty; piel, make guilty) in Dan. 1:10. In this context the word is used with "head" in the sense of to make one's head guilty, i.e. to inculpate one and hence endanger his life.

In the Wisdom of Solomon *katadikazō* occurs 4 times always in the sense of formal condemnation (Wis. 2:20; 11:10; 12:15; 17:11). The noun *katadikē* occurs in Wis. 12:27 of the condemnation that was pronounced on those who do not heed God.

NT *katadikazō* is always used in the NT in the sense of condemn, pass judgment against, find guilty (Matt. 12:7, 37; Lk. 6:37; Jas. 5:6). This is particularly clear in Matt. 12:37 where the word is contrasted with *dikaioō* (justify). In Lk. 6:37 *katadikazō* is used in connection with *krinō* (judge) in which case it seems to connote the formal act of passing judgment rather than the cognitive process by which that judgment is reached (*krinō*). The same concept is evident in the metaphorical usage of the term by James in Jas. 5:6 where the use of the word condemn represents the formal pronouncement of judgment before the execution of the sentence: "You have condemned, you have killed the righteous man." The noun *katadikē* occurs only once in the NT (Acts 25:15) in the sense of a sentence of guilt.

T. McComiskey

→ Death, → Hell, → Life, → Present, → Punishment, → Resurrection, → Reward, → Righteousness, → Satan, → Son of God

(a). A. Alt, "The Origins of Israelite Law", *Essays on Old Testament History and Religion*, 1966, 79–132; J. A. Baird, *The Justice of God in the Teaching of Jesus*, 1963; K. Barth, "The Command as the Judgment of God", *CD*, II, 2, 733–81; "The Judge Judged in our Place", and "The Judgment of God", *CD*, IV, 1, 211–83, 528–68; D. Bonhoeffer, *Ethics*, 1964²; G. Bornkamm,

"The Revelation of God's Wrath (Romans 1–3)", and "Sin, Law and Death (Romans 7)", *Early Christian Experience*, 1969, 47–70; 87–104; S. G. F. Brandon, *The Judgment of the Dead: An Historical and Comparative Study of the Idea of a Post-Mortem Judgment in the Major Religions*, 1967; F. Büchsel and V. Hentrich, *krinō* etc., *TDNT* III 921–54; R. Bultmann, *Theology of the New Testament*, I, 1952, 65–92; II, 33–69; and *The Gospel of John*, 1971, 257 ff., 278 ff.; R. H. Charles, *A Critical History of the Doctrine of a Future Life in Israel, in Judaism, and in Christianity, or Hebrew, Jewish and Christian Eschatology*, 1913²; C. E. B. Cranfield, "The Parable of the Unjust Judge and the Eschatology of Luke-Acts", *SJT* 16, 1963, 297–301; H. Cunliffe-Jones, "God's Judgment of the Individual after Death", *London Quarterly Holborn Review* 35, 1967, 116–28; J. D. M. Derrett, *Law in the New Testament*, 1970; W. Eichrodt, *Theology of the Old Testament*, I, 1961, 371–87; II, see index; A. M. Fairhurst, "The Problems Posed by the Severe Sayings Attributed to Jesus in the Synoptic Gospels", *SJT* 23, 1970, 77–91; L. Gaston, *No Stone on Another: Studies in the Significance of the Fall of Jerusalem in the Synoptic Gospels*, Supplements to *NovT* 23, 1970; H. E. Guillebaud, *The Righteous Judge: A Study of the Biblical Doctrine of Everlasting Punishment*, 1964; E. Käsemann, "Sentences of Holy Law in the New Testament", *New Testament Questions of Today*, 1969, 66–81; L. Koehler, *Hebrew Man*, 1956; J. P. Martin, *The Last Judgment in Protestant Theology from Orthodoxy to Ritschl*, 1963; A. L. Moore, *The Parousia in the New Testament*, Supplements to *NovT* 13, 1966; L. Morris, *The Biblical Doctrine of Judgment*, 1960; C. F. D. Moule, "The Judgment Theme in the Sacraments", in W. D. Davies and D. Daube, *The Background of the New Testament and its Eschatology, In Honour of Charles Harold Dodd*, 1956, 464–81; S. Mowinckel, *He That Cometh*, 1956; M. Noth, *The History of Israel*, 1958, 97–108; W. Pesch, "Judgement", *EBT* II 442–49; G. von Rad, *Old Testament Theology*, I, 1962; II, 1965, see indexes; W. Robinson, "The Judgment of God", *SJT* 4, 1951, 136–47; C. Roetzel, *Judgment in the Community*, 1972; and "The Judgment Form in Paul's Letters", *JBL* 88, 1969, 305–12; R. de Vaux, *Ancient Israel*, 1961, 143–63, 353 ff.; G. Vos, *The Pauline Eschatology*, 1952.

(b). P. Althaus, *Die letzten Dinge*, 1956⁶; J. Blank, *Krisis. Untersuchungen zur johanneischen Christologie und Eschatologie*, 1964; G. Bornkamm, "Der Lohngedanke im Neuen Testament", *Theologie und Verkündigung*, 1947, 7 ff.; and "Das Gottesgericht in der Geschichte", *Studien zur Antike und Christentum*, 1959, 47 ff.; H. Braun, *Gerichtsgedanke und Rechtfertigung bei Paulus*, 1930; E. Dinkler, "Rechtsnahme und Rechtsverzicht. Zum Problem der Ethik bei Paulus", *ZTK* 49, 1951, 167 ff., reprinted in *Signum Crucis*, 1967, 204 ff.; F. Horst, "Recht und Religion im Bereich des Alten Testaments", *EvTh* 16, 1956, 49 ff.; L. Mattern, *Das Verständnis des Gerichtes bei Paulus*, 1966; F. Nötscher, *Zur theologischen Terminologie der Qumran-Texte*, 1956; and *Gotteswege und Menschenwege in der Bibel und in Qumran*, 1958; W. Richter, "Zu den 'Richtern Israels'", *ZAW* 77, 1965, 40 ff.; SB IV, 2, 1119–1212; H. Schuster, "Rechtfertigung und Gericht bei Paulus", *Stat Crux Dum Volvitur Orbis*, 1959, 57 ff.; P. Volz, *Eschatologie der jüdischen Gemeinde*, 1934², 89–97; R. Walker, "Die Heiden und das Gericht. Zur Auslegung von Röm. 2, 12–16", *EvTh* 20, 1960, 302 ff.; O. Weber, *Grundlagen der Dogmatik*, II, 1962, 718 ff.

King, Kingdom

| βασιλεία |

βασιλεύς (*basileus*), ruler, king; βασιλεία (*basileia*), kingship, kingly rule, kingdom; βασιλεύω (*basileuō*), to be king, rule; συμβασιλεύω (*symbasileuō*), share the rule; βασίλειος (*basileios*), royal; βασιλικός (*basilikos*), royal, kingly; βασίλισσα (*basilissa*), queen.

CL 1. The noun *basileus* occurs as early as Linear B, and is originally a general term for a ruler; later more specifically a king.

(a) In Mycenaean Gk. *basileus* does not mean sovereign of a state, but a subordinate prince or leader; the king is here the *anax*, i.e. divine ruler. The title *anax* and the ideas that went with it disappeared with time, and *basileus* took on the meaning of king in this sense (cf. T. B. L. Webster, *From Mycenae to Homer*, 1958).

(b) In Homer *basileus* is used of an hereditary, legitimate ruler, whether his sphere of influence be great or small. Thus Odysseus can be described as a *basileus* in Ithaca. The power of the king, from Homer onwards, is traced back to Zeus, and the king described as "nourished by Zeus [*diotrephēs*]" (cf. Homer, *Il.* 2, 196). Hesiod extols the king's wisdom and competence to judge, and makes him inspired by the Muses (*Theogonia* 886).

(c) After monarchy had given place to the rule of an aristocracy, and then in various Greek cities one of the nobles set himself up as monarch, a new term came into being for those who ruled in this fashion, *tyrannos*, one who has gained the rule by illegitimate means. Nothing derogatory is implied by this term about the way the rule is exercised. Not until the "slaying of the tyrants" (514 B.C. in Athens), and the subsequent glorification of those responsible, Harmodios and Aristogeiton, does the word *tyrannos* take on a negative meaning, and the term *basileus*, which has no longer any more than a marginal place in Greek political life, re-emerge as the title of a just and legal ruler. Plato in particular took this view, with his strong condemnation of the tyrant and his moral upgrading of the *basileus* by the requirement that kings should be philosophers and philosophers kings (*Republic* 5, 473d; *Politicus* 292e; cf. Aristotle, *Politics* 3, 1284a, 13).

(d) The Hellenistic concept of divine kingship is not derived from Plato. The development is adequately explained by the political traditions of the Macedonian monarchy and of the divine kingship of the Achaemenidae, and the overshadowing of both by the personality of Alexander the Great (356–323 B.C.). The special names of the Diadochoi, e.g. "benefactor", *euergetēs*, serve in the process of eliminating rivals, and are to be understood as divine attributes. One of the Diadochoi, Antiochus IV Epiphanes of Syria (*c.* 215–163 B.C.), became as a result of his attempt to force Hellenization on the Jews a symbol of man's opposition to

God (on the erection of an altar to Zeus in the temple at Jerusalem [Mk. 13:14]
→ Abomination of Desolation).

(e) The Hellenistic idea of divine kingship originating with Alexander the Great
was revived again in the Roman emperor cult. It was only by taking over the
Hellenistic concept of the incarnation of divinity in the emperor that Augustus
(63 B.C.–A.D. 14) was able to comprehend in his own person the imperium as a
single whole, a unification for which there was neither national nor cultural
precedent. The effect of the confession *kyrios Iēsous*, used by the Christians in
proclaiming Jesus as the Lord, was to destroy this vital ideology of the Roman
imperium, and the reaction it called forth was the persecution of Christians during
the first three centuries (→ Confess). (On ruler worship in the Roman Empire see
H. Lietzmann, *The Beginnings of the Christian Church*, 1949[2], 163 ff.)

2. The abstract noun *basileia* is of later origin than *basileus*, and is attested first
in Hdt. 1, 11 (in the Ionic form *basilēiē*).

(a) The original meaning of the term *basileia* is the fact of being king, the position
or power of the king, and it is best translated office of king, kingly rule (e.g.
Aristotle, *Politics* 3, 1285b, 20).

(b) Besides this meaning there is a second meaning which emphasizes the geographical aspect of *basileia*; for the status of a king is shown by the area over which
he reigns. *basileia* assumes therefore the meaning kingdom, signifying the state or
area over which a king reigns (*P.Oxy* 1257, 7).

3. The vb. *basileuō* (Homer) means: (a) to be king, to reign (e.g. Homer, *Il.* 2,
203; *Od.* 2, 47); (b) inceptive: to become king, to begin to reign (Hdt. 2, 2). The vb.
symbasileuō expresses the idea of ruling with (cf. Polyb., 30, 2, 4). The adjectives
basileios and *basilikos* (Hdt., Aesch.) both express that which appertains to a king:
royal. Finally the fem. term for king must be mentioned, *basilissa*, queen. This
superseded the Attic forms *basilis* and *basileia*, and is found in the comic poet
Alcaeus and in Xenophon, *Oeconomicus* 9, 15, and frequently in later writers (e.g.
Philo and Josephus).

OT In the LXX the words of this root are very frequent, mostly as translations of
Heb. derivatives of the root *mālak*, to be king, to reign. In contrast to the NT
(see below NT introductory paragraph), the term *basileus*, which appears frequently
in almost all the books and especially in the historical writings, is far and away the
most common. *basileia* occurs comparatively rarely (400 times) and not until
Daniel does it begin to have a meaning of its own beside *basileus*. It is also important to observe that the words are used first and foremost for earthly kings and
their secular government, and only secondarily of Yahweh's kingship. This means
that the concept of Yahweh's kingly rule can only be presented in connection with
the Israelite monarchy.

1. (a) From the conquest onwards, all the peoples with whom Israel came in
contact had kings. Israel herself did not adopt monarchy as an institution until
relatively late. This is all the more surprising in view of the fact that the Edomites,
Moabites and Ammonites, who conquered their own territories during the same
period as Israel, went over to government by a national monarchy soon after their
settlement. The Israelites, on the other hand, continued for two centuries after the
conquest of Canaan to function as a sacred confederation of tribes with a central

sanctuary. Israel's initial hesitation to adopt the institution of monarchy is bound up with the concept of the holy war, which Yahweh himself conducts on Israel's behalf (Exod. 14:14; Jos. 23:10; Jdg. 7:22; cf. G. von Rad, *Der heilige Krieg im alten Israel*, 1965⁴, 6 ff., 14 ff.). Yahweh himself is seen as commander-in-chief of the Israelite army, and as the one to whom the land unconditionally belongs.

(b) Israel's constant harassment by the occasional subjection to the Philistines was the surface reason for the introduction of the monarchy. According to the older tradition (1 Sam. 9:1–10:16; 11:1–11, 14 f.), Yahweh himself took the initiative in view of the political extremity of his people, and had Saul the Benjaminite anointed king by Samuel (1 Sam. 9:16). Alongside this positive assessment of the monarchy, there was from the very beginning a rejection of it on the grounds of the theocratic lordship of Yahweh. This view flourished particularly in the northern kingdom. Thus there is a line stretching from Gideon of Manasseh ("I will not rule over you . . . Yahweh will rule over you" [Jdg. 8:23]), through Hosea the last prophet of the northern kingdom with his anti-monarchical tendency (Hos. 3:4; 7:3; 13:10 f.), to the Deuteronomistic account of the setting up of the monarchy in Israel (1 Sam. 8:1–22a; 10:17–27). Here the demand of the people, "Appoint for us a king to govern us like all the nations," received the answer from Yahweh, "They have rejected me from being king over them" (1 Sam. 8:5–7). The juxtaposition of the two accounts, one positive and the other critical, of the introduction of the monarchy (1 Sam. 8–12), makes clear the problem which beset the Israelite monarchy from the outset. On the one hand, it was seen as Yahweh's gift; on the other, as his rival.

(c) Of decisive significance for the Judean monarchy was the religious ratification it received through Nathan's prophetic promise to → David (2 Sam. 7:1–11b, 16). The house of David is here promised everlasting duration (verse 16). Because of this Davidic → covenant, the right of David's hereditary successors to the kingdom of Judah was never called in question. The dynasty was assured of continuance despite all the ups and downs which the throne underwent. By contrast the monarchy of the northern kingdom, after the non-renewal under Jeroboam I of the union with Judah (1 Ki. 12:1 ff.), never achieved the stability of the Davidic dynasty. Here the old ideal of charismatic leadership, as it had been known in Israel's formative period, lived on. According to it, only Yahweh's call fitted anyone for the office of ruler.

Another feature of the theology of kingship in Judah, in contrast to the Egyptian concept of a king who is divine by nature, is the adoption of the ruler as the son of Yahweh. This was celebrated at the festival of enthronement and hymned in the royal Psalms (e.g. Ps. 2:7; 45:7; 110:1). However, the less the kings of Judah in their historical reality measured up to the standards set forth in the theology of kingship, the more strongly did the expectation of an eschatological messianic king develop, who would finally fulfil the prophecy of Nathan and the associated concepts of kingship (Amos 9:11–15; but cf. Gen. 49:8–12). Isaiah in particular, a prophet who had close associations with the theology of kingship, prophesied of a branch of David that would bring in a new era of righteousness and peace (Isa. 11:1–9; 9:2–7; cf. also the messianic prophecies of Mic. 5:2 ff.; Jer. 23:5 f.; Ezek. 17:22 ff.; → Jesus Christ, art. *Christos* OT; → Son of God, art. *hyios Dauid*).

2. The kingship of Yahweh is an aspect of faith found neither in the wisdom

literature, the oral teaching of many of the prophets, nor in a considerable number of historical narratives. It is frequent, on the other hand, in the hymns of the Psalter (the so-called enthronement-Psalms), later prophetic writings including the prophecies to the nations in Jeremiah (e.g. Jer. 46:18; 48:15; 51:57), and in the narrative parts of the book of Daniel. Thus it tends to feature in the later parts of the OT. This suggests that the concept of Yahweh's kingship was not a constitutive element in the original faith of Israel (cf. A. Alt, *Kleine Schriften zur Geschichte des Volkes Israel*, I, 1968[4], 348). This is not to say that Israel did not from the first place herself under the rule of Yahweh. On the contrary, faith in the absolute lordship of Yahweh within the tribal confederacy goes back to the days before the formation of a political state (see above 1 (a)).

(a) The earliest example of the title king being used of Yahweh is in the 8th century "My eyes have seen the King, the Lord of hosts" (Isaiah 6:5). It is no coincidence that the title of king for Yahweh appears in the course of a vision which came to Isaiah in the central sanctuary at → Jerusalem. Texts discovered at Ugarit (in Syria) have revealed that in the Syro-Canaanite world there existed the idea of the "God most high" (cf. Gen. 14:18 f.) who bore the title of king (*melek*). The use of *melek* as a title for Yahweh has as its background the Syro-Canaanite world of ideas, and was probably originally drawn from the sacral traditions of the Jebusite city of Jerusalem and transferred to Yahweh there (Isa. 6:5). There is evidence of the existence of the *mōlek* cult (AV Molech, Moloch) among the original inhabitants of pre-Israelite Jerusalem (Lev. 18:21; 2 Ki. 23:10). Yahweh therefore would not have been described as *melek* before the time of the monarchy.

The divine title *melek* brought with it even in the Syro-Canaanite setting, a claim to universal authority which found expression particularly in lordship over the pantheon of gods. This universal claim is also reflected in the OT passages which talk about Yahweh the *melek*. Yahweh's kingship has a cosmic dimension: he is the creator of the world (cf. Pss. 24:1; 93:1; 95:3 ff.); "his kingdom rules over all the earth" (Ps. 47:2); he is the king of the nations (cf. Jer. 10:7; Ps. 47:3; 99:2).

(b) In addition to this concept of Yahweh being king, we find the dynamic concept of Yahweh becoming king. This finds expression especially in the enthronement-Psalms in the cry "Yahweh has become King!" (Pss. 47:8; 93:1; 96:10; 97:1; 99:1). (Note: Eng. versions have "The Lord reigns" for this Heb. perfect.)

The inseparability of the two concepts "Yahweh is king" and "Yahweh has become king" becomes especially evident in the later chapters of Isa. Yahweh is "King of Jacob" or "King of Israel" (Isa. 41:21; 44:6). Put in context of announcing the new exodus, a herald now brings to the city of Jerusalem the message: "Your God reigns" (Isa. 52:7). The enthronement-Psalms do not primarily announce an eschatological event, but a present reality experienced in the cultic ceremony. The proclamation of the reign of Yahweh as an eschatological event is now associated with the historical act of the new exodus. It is not nature and the cycle of the seasons (as in Babylonia), but the historical actions of Yahweh which form the basis of his "enthronement". (On the much-debated theory of an enthronement festival of Yahweh in Israel, cf. H.-J. Kraus, *Psalmen*, BKAT 15, I, § 6 XLIII f.; Excursus on Ps. 24, pp. 201 ff.; → Might, art. *thronos* OT 4).

(c) In the Judaean messianic theology of kingship the lordship of Yahweh is combined with the hoped-for lordship of the messiah. Thus it is the same prophet,

Isaiah of Jerusalem, who was the first to use the royal title for Yahweh and who almost always related it to the currently reigning son of David. Even the messianic prince of the future is for Isaiah no autocrat, but one who is appointed (*śar*, official, vizier) and receives his office from God (Isa. 9:7; 11:1 f.). The rule of the future, messianic son of David is accordingly a delegated exercise of authority, representing the kingly rule of Yahweh.

The anti-monarchical bias of the northern kingdom (1 Sam. 8:7) stands in contrast to this, with a non-messianic eschatology (Hosea). This is also represented by Deutero-Isaiah who proclaimed from exile the kingship of Yahweh (Isa. 41:21; 44:6) and his eschatological enthronement (Isa. 52:7). Finally, in Ezekiel we find side by side the titles of king (Ezek. 37:24) and prince (Ezek. 37:24) for the messianic servant David.

3. The noun *mal*ᵉ*kût* is an early Heb. abstract noun with the meaning kingdom, reign. The reference is to power rather than to locality.

(a) The term *mal*ᵉ*kût* in the OT usually refers in a purely secular sense to political kingdoms (cf. 1 Sam. 20:31; 1 Ki. 2:12; 1 Chr. 12:23; 2 Chr. 11:17; Jer. 49:34; Dan. 9:1).

(b) Although the secular meaning of *mal*ᵉ*kût* is the most common one, there are occasional references to God's rule as his *mal*ᵉ*kût*, kingship, which he is presently exercising (Ps. 103:19; 145:11–13; Dan. 4:3). This is analogous to the use of *melek*, king, as an epithet of Yahweh.

(c) In later texts Yahweh's kingship is interpreted in an eschatological sense. The recognition begins to emerge of a kingdom of Yahweh at the end of time which breaks through all national barriers. One day Yahweh will rule over the whole earth. His throne will be in Jerusalem, and all nations will make their pilgrimage to Zion to worship him there (Isa. 24:23; Zech. 14:9; Obad. 21). A characteristic of the eschatological expectation of the later prophets is that Yahweh's *mal*ᵉ*kût* is always presented as immanent (cf. G. von Rad, *TDNT* I 568 ff.).

(d) Finally, in Dan. 7, this immanent eschatology is elevated to a transcendent level, in the concept of the kingdom of the "son of man" (v. 13 f.) and the kingdom of "the saints of the Most High" (v. 27). The son of man (→ Son of God, art. *hyios tou anthrōpou*) is an individual (v. 14) who represents the Most High (v. 27), as the king of Judah represented the people. In other words, when power is committed to the son of man, it is at the same time being given to the saints of the Most High. By these are meant the heavenly beings who surround God (M. Noth *The Laws in the Pentateuch and Other Studies*, 1966, 215–28; cf. Ps. 89:5–7; Job 15:15; Deut. 33:2; Zech. 14:5). The transfer of power to the son of man, representing the saints of the Most High, takes place within the heavenly realm (v. 12: "with the clouds of heaven there came one like a son of man"), so that the earthly empires symbolized by the four beasts are replaced by the transcendent rule of the saints of the Most High represented by the son of man. In the idea that God has a definite plan for the world (the four empires in succession), and in the dualism of the four world empires seen as the era of the evil one as over against the kingdom of God seen as transcendent, we have already the most important elements of apocalyptic.

4. (a) The expression kingdom of heaven (*mal*ᵉ*kût šāmayim*; Gk. *basileia tōn ouranōn*) owes its origin to the endeavour of Rab. Judaism to find an alternative for the divine name in the phrase *mal*ᵉ*kût YHWH* (kingdom of Yahweh) by using

either *šekînâh*, glory (Gk. *doxa*) or *šāmayim*, heaven (Gk. *ouranos*). Kingdom of heaven is therefore a term which implies the essential idea that "God rules as King". It is a Jewish expression which is purely theological in its reference.

Since the kingdom of heaven is not evident in this world, it is necessary to decide for or against it by a decision of will. The expression "to take upon oneself the yoke of the kingdom of Yahweh" means to confess allegiance to the one God as King (cf. SB I 173 ff.). The opportunity to accept or reject the kingdom will, however, come to an end when Yahweh reveals himself at the end of time. In the theology of Rab. Judaism the kingdom of God is a purely eschatological concept (K. G. Kuhn *TDNT* I 574).

(b) As happened earlier with the OT eschatology of the northern kingdom (see above 2 (c)), there is a tension in Judaism between the expectation of the messiah, as a nationalistic, Israelite king at the end of time, and the hope of the eschatological revelation of the kingdom of God. In the last days the messiah will come, ascend the throne of Israel, and subject to himself all the nations of the earth (cf. SB IV 968 f.). Not until then will the hitherto hidden kingdom of heaven emerge from the transcendent realm. But there is in Judaism no inner connection between the coming of the national messianic king and the coming of the rule of God. This is further confirmed by the fact that the people of Israel as such receives no mention in statements concerning the kingdom of God. Membership of the nation can no longer be a determining factor, when it is a personal decision before God that is required. Thus proselytes can also take upon themselves the "yoke of the kingdom of God" (SB I 176). It should be noted further that in Rab. literature the term kingdom of heaven is comparatively rare and that it does not carry the same theological significance that it does in the preaching of Jesus. This helps to explain why those Jews who thought along nationalistic lines in terms of a nationalistic kingly messiah were bewildered by Jesus, while in the apocalyptic circles the expectation of the kingdom of God continued to live on. In the Qumran writings there are occasional references to the kingdom of God, but the Essenes had no expectation of its coming.

(c) The Apocryphal writings of the LXX in general follow the OT pattern of thought about the kingdom of God. In some places, however, where there is no Heb. equivalent, we may detect Hellenistic influence. Thus the LXX can identify the *basileia* with the four cardinal virtues (4 Macc. 2:23), and in Wis. 6:20 we read, "The desire for wisdom leads to a kingdom." This shift to an ethical meaning, in keeping with popular philosophy, is completed by Philo (cf. *Migr.Abr.* 97; *Abr.* 261; *Sacr.* 49; *Som.* 2, 244). The actual content of the *basileia* is the rule of the sage, seen as the true king (see above CL 1 (c)). The result of this shift of meaning was that the eschatological character of the term as used in the OT was inevitably lost. "The *basileia* constitutes a chapter in his moral doctrine. The true king is the wise man" (K. L. Schmidt, *TDNT* I 576). Josephus does not speak of *basileus* and *basileia*, but of *hēgemōn*, governor, and *hēgemonia*, direction, administration (cf. A. Schlatter, *Wie sprach Josephus von Gott?*, 1910, 11 f.; for these terms in the NT → Caesar, art. *hēgemōn*).

NT In the NT *basileia* is used more frequently than *basileus* and *basileuō* (cf. above OT introductory paragraph). Taking the words from this root together, we find

377

that they belong chiefly to the vocabulary of the Synoptic Gospels. In Matt. and Lk.-Acts *basileus*, and to an even greater extent *basileia*, play a positively decisive rôle. The two nouns are used only occasionally in Jn., the Pauline corpus, and the other NT epistles, but they come to the fore again in Rev. The vb. *basileuō*, on the other hand, appears only occasionally in the Synoptic Gospels, though more often in Rev. It has its maximum theological significance in Paul (Rom., 1 Cor.).

1. *basileus in the NT.* The NT follows closely the precedent set by the OT and Judaism in giving to God and Christ alone the full right to the title king. Human kings, by contrast, are generally regarded as of limited importance.

(a) The earthly kings referred to are frequently those who set themselves against God and his Christ: Pharaoh (Acts 7:10; Heb. 11:23, 27); Herod the Great (Matt. 2:1 ff.; Lk. 1:5); Herod Antipas (Matt. 14:8); Herod Agrippa I (Acts 12:1, 20); Herod Agrippa II (Acts 25:13 f. etc.); Aretas (2 Cor. 11:32); and the Roman emperor (1 Tim. 2:2; 1 Pet. 2:13; Rev. 17:9 ff.). These rulers are called "kings of the earth" (Matt. 17:25; Acts 4:26; Rev. 1:5; 6:15); "kings of the Gentiles (Lk. 22:25); or "kings of the whole world" (Rev. 16:14; cf. Ps. 2:2 and 89:27; cf. *TDNT* I 576 f.).

Just as the OT is at variance with oriental views of divine kingship, so the NT is opposed to Hellenistic and Roman ideas of this kind: the earthly king is not an incarnation of the deity, since no one but God or the messiah can occupy such a position. Thus in Rev., in sharp contrast to the presumptuous claims to divinity of Domitian, only God is recognized as king of the nations *basileus tōn ethnōn* (Rev. 15:3 *v.l.*), and only Christ as the king of kings, *basileus basileōn* (Rev. 19:16; 17:14). The OT attitude to the great kings is found again in the NT with regard to the "kings of the east" (Rev. 16:12): the supremacy of God is asserted by making them a rod in his hand, only to destroy them at the last day if they do not submit to him in obedience (Rev. 17:2 ff.; 18:3 ff.; 19:18 ff.; 21:24).

(b) Only → David and → Melchizedek receive a positive assessment, by contrast with the earthly kings mentioned otherwise in the NT: David, because as the king chosen by God (2 Sam. 7) he is the forefather of Jesus Christ (cf. Matt. 1:6; Acts 13:22); Melchizedek, because as the priest-king of Salem (Gen. 14:18) he is the OT type of the high priesthood of Christ (Heb. 7:1 ff.).

(c) Jesus "who was descended from David according to the flesh" (Rom. 1:3; Matt. 1:6) is described in the NT as the messianic King of the Jews (*basileus tōn Ioudaiōn*) or King of Israel (*basileus Israēl*) (→ Israel, art. *Israēl* NT). Son of David, King of the Jews, King of Israel are messianic titles (→ Son of God).

(i) The first thing we notice here is that these titles are used principally in the section of the Gospels portraying the trial before Pilate (Mk. 15; Matt. 27; Lk. 23; Jn. 18 f.), and here exclusively on the lips of the Jewish opponents of Jesus, or of Pilate and his soldiers. *basileus tōn Ioudaiōn* does not appear as a self-designation of Jesus. Thus Jesus was accused by the throng of saying that he was "Christ a king" (Lk. 23:2). Jesus was asked by Pilate, "Are you the king of the Jews?" (Mk. 15:2 par. Matt. 27:11, Lk. 23:3). The people were confronted by Pilate with a decision: "Do you want me to release for you the King of the Jews?" (Mk. 15:9 par. Matt. 27:17; cf. Lk. 23:17). And after the condemnation of Jesus, the soldiers mocked him in the praetorium with the words, "Hail, King of the Jews!" (Mk. 15:18 par. Matt. 27:29). On the cross the inscription of the charge read "The

King of the Jews" (Mk. 15:26 par. Matt. 27:37, Lk. 23:38, Jn. 19:19). Like the soldiers on guard (Lk. 23:37), the rulers of the people mocked as they passed by, "Let the Christ, the King of Israel, come down now from the cross, that we may see and believe" (Mk. 15:32 par. Matt. 27:42, Lk. 23:35).

(ii) If it is true, as the Roman inscription on the cross makes probable, that Jesus was condemned on a charge of claiming to be the messianic king of Israel, and if this claim is never found on the lips of Jesus, we may suppose that the basis of the charge is to be seen and found largely in the way Jesus behaved. (O. Cullmann regards the inscription as "almost irrefutable proof that Jesus in some way made himself the subject of his preaching on the Kingdom of God soon to come" [*Salvation in History*, 1967, 109; cf. *The State in the New Testament*, 1957, 8–49].) At any rate it is unlikely that the Jewish leaders acted out of pure malice in accusing Jesus of being a pretender to the throne, or that Pilate had no other intention in ordering the inscription on the cross than to make mock of Jewish messianism. (On the crucifixion of Jesus → Cross, art. *stauros* NT 1; on the trial of Jesus see D. R. Catchpole, *The Trial of Jesus: A Study in the Gospels and Jewish Historiography from 1770 to the Present Day*, 1971.) Rather we should note that Jesus himself saw his miracles of healing, his casting out of demons, and his preaching of the gospel to the poor as the fulfilment of Isaianic prophecies (Isa. 29:18 f.; 35:5 f.; 61:1 f.), and accordingly as messianic events (Matt. 11:2–6; Lk. 4:16–27). Moreover, his two principal actions during the last days at Jerusalem—the entry into Jerusalem (Matt. 21:1–9; Mk. 11:1–10; Lk. 19:28–38; Jn. 12:12–19) and the cleansing of the temple (Matt. 21:12 f.; Mk. 11:15–19; Lk. 19:47 f.)—make it clear that Jesus knew himself to be the fulfiller of messianic prophecies (cf. Isa. 62:11; Zech. 9:9; 2 Ki. 9:13; Ps. 118:26; and Exod. 30:13; Lev. 1:14; Isa. 56:7; Jer. 7:11 for OT allusions in these narratives).

(iii) It is also demonstrable that Jesus was confronted during his ministry with the question whether he was the messiah, when for instance in connection with the feeding of the five thousand the people wanted "to make him king" (Jn. 6:15). Similarly, in the "old reliable tradition" (W. G. Kümmel, *Promise and Fulfilment*, 1961[2], 111) John the Baptist's question (Matt. 11:3 par. Lk. 7:19 f.) used a term for the messiah which was not at all common among the Jews, "the coming one [*ho erchomenos*]" (→ Come, art. *erchomai* NT 3), in asking whether Jesus was he. Jesus' answer here is characteristic, in that he did not respond to the question directly with an open declaration of his messiahship. Instead he pointed to the fulfilment of Isaianic prophecies in veiled language that challenged the hearer to make up his mind (Matt. 11:5 par. Lk. 7:22). In view of the lowliness of Jesus the messiah, it is the visible messianic actions which retain more significance for the outsider. The fact that Jesus saw himself to be the king of the Jews and messiah of his people, and yet concealed it in this way, is his "messianic secret" (on the question of Jesus' messianic consciousness → Jesus Christ, art. *Christos* NT 5 and the literature under both *Iēsous* and *Christos*; → also Secret).

The same point is brought out by the short answer of Jesus, recorded by all the evangelists, to Pilate's question, whether he is the King of the Jews: "You say so [*sy legeis*]" (Matt. 27:2; Mk. 15:2; Lk. 23:3). Only once did Jesus openly reveal this messianic secret, and that is in the trial before the Sanhedrin (Matt. 26:57–75; Mk. 14:53–72; Lk. 22:54–71). To the question of the high priest, "Are you the

Christ?" he replied unequivocally with the statement, "I am; and you will see the Son of man sitting at the right hand of Power, and coming with the clouds of heaven" (Mk. 14:62; cf. Matt. 26:64; Lk. 22:69; on the Son of man, → Son of God, art. *hyios tou anthrōpou* NT).

(iv) In the earliest Christian writings outside the Synoptic tradition and John's Gospel, i.e. in Acts and the writings of Paul, there is no mention of "King of Israel" or "King of the Jews". Nevertheless, it can be seen from a passage like Acts 17:7 that Christians in Thessalonica were being denounced by the Jews for confessing allegiance to Jesus as another king (*basilea heteron*). There is a certain irony in the way the Jews accused Christians of opposing the quasi-divine claims of the Roman emperor. However, it is basically true to say that with the application of the messianic title Christ to Jesus, the proclamation of Jesus as king of Israel faded eventually into the background, giving way to a christological, soteriological kerygma which focussed on the → Cross and → resurrection of Jesus (cf. Rom. 4:25; 1 Cor. 15:3 f.). (On the formation of the kerygma see C. H. Dodd, *The Apostolic Preaching and its Developments*, 1936; "The Framework of the Gospel Narrative", *New Testament Studies*, 1953, 1–11; cf. the not altogether convincing critique by D. E. Nineham, "The Order of Events in St. Mark's Gospel – an Examination of Dr. Dodd's Hypothesis" in D. E. Nineham, ed., *Studies in the Gospels: Essays in Memory of R. H. Lightfoot*, 1955, 223–40; → Proclamation.).

(d) In his *Institutes of the Christian Religion* 2, 15 Calvin expounded the three offices of Christ as → prophet, → priest and king, showing how these offices were anticipated by the corresponding figures in the OT and how they are appropriated by believers. The thought of the people of God sharing in kingship goes back to the OT. Exod. 19:6 contains the promise based on the → covenant: "And you shall be to me a kingdom of priests [*basileia hierateuma*] and a holy nation" (cf. Isa. 61:6). This thought is applied to Christian believers in Rev. 1:6 and 5:10 (where *basileia* is used in both cases). In the former passage it refers to believers in the present time; in the latter it is part of the "new song" of the saints before the → lamb.

The same thought occurs in 1 Pet. 2:9: "But you are a chosen race, a royal priesthood [*basileion hierateuma*], a holy nation, God's own people, that you may declare the wonderful deeds of him who called you out of darkness into his marvellous light" (RSV). The word translated here as "royal", *basileion*, can be taken either as a neut. adj. agreeing with *hierateuma* (as in RSV) or as a noun, i.e. group of kings (cf. E. Best, *I Peter*, 1971, 107 f.). Although there is no actual occurrence of the word in this sense, Best holds that its form indicates that such a meaning is possible. Moreover, it accords with the Targumic interpretation of Exod. 19:6 and the Christian tradition of Rev. 5:10, where the glorified saints "shall reign [*basileusousin*] on earth" (cf. Rev. 1:6).

The vb. *basileuō*, reign, is used of the reign of believers in Rom. 5:17 (where it is contrasted with the reign of death, cf. 5:14, 17, 21; cf. also the reign of sin, Rom. 6:12); 1 Cor. 4:8 (here ironically of the lordly behaviour of the Corinthians which, in fact, falls short of true reigning); and Rev. 20:4, 6; 20:5 (of the reign of the saints on earth and in glory). For the idea of reigning expressed in other terms see Eph. 2:6; 2 Tim. 2:12; Jas. 2:5 (cf. the third Beatitude "Blessed are the meek, for they shall inherit the earth, Matt. 5:5; → Inheritance, art. *klēroō*). For other instances of *basileuō* see Matt. 2:22; Lk. 1:33; 9:14; 1 Cor. 15:25; 1 Tim. 6:15; Rev. 11:15, 17; 19:6. See further J. H. Elliott, *The Elect and the Holy, Supplements to NovT* 12, 1966; and E. Best, "I Peter 2:4–10, A Reconsideration", *NovT* 11, 1969, 270–93.

(e) *basilissa*, queen, occurs only 4 times in the NT. Matt. and Lk. both record the saying about the queen of the South in the context of the sign of → Jonah. "The queen of the South will arise at the judgment with this generation and condemn it; for she came from the ends of the earth to hear the wisdom of Solomon, and behold, something greater than Solomon is here" (Matt. 12:42 par. Lk. 11:31; cf. 1 Ki. 10:1–10; 2 Chron. 9:1–12; → Solomon). Although Sheba is today identified with Arabia, Josephus connected the Queen of Sheba with Ethiopia (*Ant.* 2, 10, 2; 8, 6, 5 f.). Later Arabic legend made her Solomon's wife, and the Ethiopian royal line claims descent from Solomon and the Queen of Sheba. In the NT she is an example to the Jews of the lengths to which a non-Jew might go in seeking wisdom. All the more reason have the Jews themselves cause to leave their ways, for paradoxically there is in Jesus the Galilean preacher "something greater than Solomon." Acts 8:27 might be regarded as an illustration of a similar response of a non-Jew. The Ethiopian → eunuch is described there as "a minister of Candace the queen of the Ethiopians, in charge of all her treasure, [who] had come to Jerusalem to worship." He too was a seeker. The episode is all the more pointed in the light of the persecution by the Jews which has just scattered the Jerusalem church (Acts 8:1), the eunuch's study of scripture (Isa. 53:7 f.; Acts 8:32 f.), and the fact that he was a eunuch. By contrast Babylon who plays the queen is judged (Rev. 18:7).

2. *The use of basileia in the NT.* (a) General. For the earthly, human king there is a corresponding earthly, human kingdom. In this sense *basileia* means, according to context, the office of king (e.g. Lk. 19:12, 15; Rev. 17:12) and also the area governed, domain (e.g. Matt. 4:8 par. Lk. 4:5; Mk. 6:23; Rev. 16:10). In almost all these passages the earthly kingdoms stand in contrast – though this is often unexpressed – to the *basileia tou theou*, kingdom of God, since they are subject to "the god of this world", the *diabolos*, devil, → Satan (Matt. 4:8). In Matt. 12:26 there is even explicit mention of the *basileia* of the devil. This is particularly true with regard to the Roman Empire, described in Rev. expressly as the beast (Rev. 13:1; → Animal, art. *thērion*).

(b) Kingdom of God. *hē basileia tou theou* is a term of central importance only within the Synoptic tradition. The form of the expression varies: Mk. and Lk. speak of the kingdom of God, while Matt. has kingdom of heaven and kingdom of the Father. Evidence that Mk. and Lk. preserve in *basileia tou theou* the older form used by Jesus himself is provided by two observations. First, both the sayings-source and Mk. have this formula in the places where Matt. speaks of the *basileia tōn ouranōn*, kingdom of heaven (Mk. 1:15; Matt. 4:17; Lk. 6:20 par. Matt. 5:3). Secondly and more important, Matt. itself contains four instances of the older term kingdom of God (12:28; 19:34; 21:31; 21:43). Jesus probably, therefore, spoke exclusively of the *basileia tou theou*. This is not to say that he never used a circumlocution for the divine name. It is exemplified by Matt. 5:4, where the passive *paraklēthēsontai*, "they shall be comforted", means that God will comfort them; and Lk. 16:9, where the plur. "they" i.e. the angels, will receive you into the eternal habitations means that God will receive you (cf. also Lk. 12:20; 23:31). ([Ed.] The "they" in Lk. 16:9 might, however, also be taken to refer to those benefited by the use of mammon.) Where *basileia* is used alone, without the addition of *tou theou*, it is qualified by its context: *tēn hetoimasmenēn hymin basileian*, "the kingdom prepared for you" (Matt. 25:34; cf. 6:10); God will throw the sons of the kingdom into the outer darkness (Matt. 8:12; cf. Lk. 12:32; 22:29).

(c) The Kingdom of God to come in the future. In order to understand Jesus' proclamation of the Kingdom of God, it is best, in accordance with the apocalyptic, eschatological character of that proclamation, to start with those passages which deal with the coming of the Kingdom of God in the near future. Mk. 1:15 records the theme of Jesus' preaching in a pregnant sentence: "The kingdom of God has come near [*ēngiken hē basileia tou theou*]" (cf. Matt. 3:2; 5:17). The same theme is found in other places: "The kingdom of God is near [*engys estin*]" (Lk. 21:31; → Goal, art. *engys*); it "is coming [*erchetai*]" (Lk. 17:20; → Come, art. *erchomai*, NT 3). Thus Jesus did not preach that there was a kingdom of God to which one must confess allegiance (cf. Rab. Judaism, see above OT 4 (a)), but that the rule of God is coming.

Just as when the fig-tree puts out leaves summer is known to be near, so the events of the present guarantee that God's rule will soon break in on the world (Matt. 24:32 f.; Mk. 13:28 f.; Lk. 21:29 ff.; → Fruit, art. *sykē*). It is to this sudden, unexpected irruption of the kingdom of God that Jesus' parables of the Parousia point: the sudden coming of the flood (Matt. 24:37 ff.; Lk. 17:26 ff.; → Noah), the unexpected entrance of the burglar (Matt. 24:43 f.; Lk. 12:39 f.), the surprise of the doorkeeper and the servant at the homecoming of their master (Matt. 24:45 ff.; cf. Lk. 12:42–6), the sudden arrival of the bridegroom (Matt. 25:1–13). All these are pictures of the sudden irruption of the catastrophe, of the eschatological crisis which is impending a short time ahead: "Truly, there are some standing here who will not taste death before they see the kingdom of God come with power" (Mk. 9:1; cf. Matt. 16:28; Lk. 9:27).

For Jesus the advent of the kingdom was so imminent that he vowed not to "drink of the fruit of the vine until the kingdom of God comes" (Lk. 22:18; cf. Mk. 14:25). The Parousia (→ Present) of the Son of man will take place even before the disciples have finished proclaiming the kingdom of God in Israel (Matt. 10:23). From these references it may be concluded that Jesus proclaimed the imminent advent of the kingdom of God within the lifetime of his hearers' generation (Mk. 9:1; 13:30). (On the interpretation of this → Generation, art. *genea* NT.; → Present).

(d) The Kingdom of God in the present. Although for Jesus the realization of God's rule is still in the future, its urgent proximity already casts its shadow over the present: "If it is by the Spirit of God that I cast out demons, then the kingdom of God has come upon you" (Matt. 12:28; cf. Lk. 11:20). The casting out of → demons reveals that the devil has been bound by one stronger than he (Matt. 12:29; Mk. 3:27; Lk. 11:21). The disarming of → Satan, an event which the Jews expected in the end-time (SB I 167 f.), has taken place (Lk. 10:18); in the works of Jesus the kingdom of God is already a present reality.

To the Pharisees' question, "When is the kingdom of God coming?", Jesus can therefore answer, "The kingdom of God is in the midst of you" (Lk. 17:20 f.; not as AV "is within you"). (On the prep. *entos* used here see Arndt, 268 f. and the literature there referred to.) Because the kingdom is already present, the friends of the bridegroom cannot fast (Mk. 2:19; cf. Matt. 9:15; Lk. 5:34); and it is the Father's good pleasure, *eudokēsen* (aorist), to give Jesus' disciples (the "little flock") the kingdom (Lk. 12:32). With the appearance of John the Baptist, according to an early logion, the era of the old revelation of God came to an end, and at the same time the new era began. The kingdom of God, already present, is "violently assaulted [*biazetai*]" (Matt. 11:12 f.; cf. Lk. 16:16). "The allusion may be to the opposition of Satan and evil spirits to the Kingdom, or to the violence of Herod Antipas to John; but a more likely explanation is that the reference is either to Zealots who try to bring in the Kingdom by employing force against the Romans or to Jewish antagonists of Jesus who continue to persecute Christians" (D. Hill, *The Gospel of Matthew*, 1972, 200).

(e) The Kingdom of God and the person of Jesus: an eschatology in process of realization. In comparing the eschatology of Jesus with that of Judaism, it is not sufficient to characterize the former as the ultimate extreme of imminent expectation. Of far more importance is Jesus' claim that the verdict to be passed on men in the final judgment is already determined by the attitude they adopt to himself in the present age. "Every one who acknowledges me before men, I also will acknowledge before my Father who is in heaven" (Matt. 10:32; cf. Lk. 12:8). He who hears the words of Jesus and does them will survive the eschatological crisis. The unrepentant cities, on the other hand, will be condemned, because in spite of the "mighty works" done in them by Jesus (Matt. 11:21 ff.; cf. Lk. 10:13 ff.), they have not repented. Jesus himself will appear as the eschatological judge (Matt. 25:31). He will disown those who merely say "Lord, Lord" (Matt. 7:23; cf. Lk. 13:27), and plead before the Father the cause of those who have confessed him (Matt. 10:32; cf. Lk. 12:8). A man's final destiny is decided by the attitude he adopts to Jesus' word and action (Matt. 7:24–27; cf. Lk. 6:47 ff.), in other words by his attitude to Jesus himself. For this present age, marked as it is by the activity and preaching of Jesus, bears a special relation to the coming day of → judgment. The new and distinctive factor, compared with the Rab. view of the kingdom of God, is not simply that it is coming, but that it is inextricably bound up with the person of Jesus. As W. G. Kümmel puts it, "It is the person of Jesus whose activities provoke the presence of the eschatological consummation and who therefore stands at the centre of his eschatological message" (op. cit., 108). The future rule of God has already in the person of Jesus become a reality in word and deed. The coming, imminent kingdom of God is already present in him. The interpretation of this teaching has led to radically divergent theses in the course of theological discussion. (For a more detailed survey of eschatological interpretation → Present: The Parousia and Eschatology in the NT.)

The school of Ritschl regarded the kingdom of God in the present as an ethical attitude which produces a moral society. Ritschl discarded apocalyptic, eschatological expectation as an outdated relic of Judaism. Johannes Weiss and Albert Schweitzer took the opposing view known as "consistent eschatology" or "thoroughgoing eschatology". They rightly pointed out that Jesus himself linked his message with Jewish apocalyptic by making its central theme the announcement that the end of the world was impending (A. Schweitzer, *The Quest of the Historical Jesus*,

(1910) 1954³, see especially ch. 19 on "Thoroughgoing Scepticism and Thoroughgoing Eschatology", 328–95). According to Schweitzer, the distinctively new element in the preaching of Jesus, as compared with apocalyptic, is the nearness of the world catastrophe.

In contrast to this solution offered by "consistent eschatology", a large proportion of scholars in the English-speaking world have, under the influence of C. H. Dodd, completely eliminated "futurist eschatology" from the proclamation, seeing it as a product of re-Judaizing within the Christian community, and speak of a "realized eschatology" in Jesus' preaching. In view of the presumed Aramaic original Dodd translates Mk. 1:15 as "The kingdom of God has come" (*The Parables of the Kingdom*, 1935, 44). He has thus reinstated an important element in Jesus' proclamation of the kingdom of God, as against the views of A. Schweitzer, though he too has over-emphasized one side. Dodd subsequently modified his way of describing his understanding of NT eschatology. He came to speak of "an eschatology that is in process of realization", a view which comes close to that of J. Jeremias (*The Parables of Jesus*, 1963², 230; cf. C. H. Dodd, *The Interpretation of the Fourth Gospel*, 1953, 447).

Rudolf Bultmann is in basic agreement with Schweitzer's "consistent eschatology". "There can be no doubt that Jesus like his contemporaries expected a tremendous eschatological drama" (*Jesus and the Word*, 1935, 38). However, Bultmann attempts by means of his existential interpretation to distill from the mythical, apocalyptic future hope of Jesus the real meaning in existential terms. For him the expectation of the end of the world as a future event in time is an expression of the conviction that it is in the present moment that man is faced with a decision. Thus "every hour is the last hour" (op. cit., 52; cf. *History and Eschatology*, [1957] 1962, 154 f.). The true meaning of the eschatological preaching of Jesus concerning the impending kingdom of God lies, according to Bultmann, in the assertion that man is faced with a decision. "The future Kingdom of God, then, is not something which is to come in the course of time, so that to advance its coming one can do something in particular, perhaps through penitential prayers and good works, which become superfluous in the moment of its coming. Rather, the Kingdom of God is a power *which, although it is entirely future, wholly determines the present*" (op. cit., 51).

Against this view it must be maintained that it is not the purpose of Jesus' proclamation of the kingdom of God simply to call men to repentance and face them with a decision. At the centre of Jesus' message is the proclamation of the urgent proximity of God's kingdom, the announcement that God is about to inaugurate his world-wide reign. Repentance and decision are consequences, but not the actual theme of Jesus' proclamation of the impending kingdom (cf. Matt. 3:2; 4:17). The fact that Jesus averted a question which sought an apocalyptic timetable (Lk. 17:20 f.) must not be interpreted as an indication that the announcement of the kingdom of God is concentrated in the existential meaning.

Jesus, therefore, preached the kingdom of God neither solely as a present reality nor exclusively as a future event. Rather, he was aware that the future rule of God was present in his actions and in his person. He spoke, therefore, of the future kingdom, which would suddenly dawn, as already realizing itself in the present. Thus the nature of Jesus' eschatology is probably best described by the expression "an eschatology in process of realization" (E. Haenchen quoted by J. Jeremias, op. cit., 230). For the connection between the proclamation of the kingdom of God and the Son of man sayings, → Son of God, art. *hyios tou anthrōpou*.

3. *The Kingdom of God in the preaching of Jesus.* (a) As depicted in the preaching of Jesus, the kingdom of God may be characterized as being "opposed to everything present and earthly, to everything here and now. It is thus absolutely miraculous" (K. L. Schmidt, *TDNT* I 584). Man can, therefore, neither hasten the coming of the kingdom of God by doing battle with God's enemies (as the Zealots hoped), nor force it to appear by scrupulous observation of the law (as the Pharisees hoped). He can only await its coming in patience and confidence, as in the parables of the mustard seed (Matt. 13:31 f.; Mk. 4:30 ff.), the leaven (Matt. 13:33), and the seed growing secretly (Mk. 4:26–29).

(b) This kingdom is coming in the form of a cosmic catastrophe (Lk. 17:26; Mk. 13:26; 14:62), ushered in by the appearance of the → Son of man. Jesus thus aligned himself, not with the concept of an earthly, nationalistic messiah, but with the apocalyptic tradition in Judaism with its expectation of the Son of man. At the same time he avoided describing events in detail, although he clearly used apocalyptic imagery (e.g. the heavenly feast in the kingdom of God, Mk. 14:25; Matt. 8:11). Also connected with this toning down of apocalyptic ideas is Jesus' rejection of all attempts to discern signs of the end: "The kingdom of God is not coming with signs to be observed" (Lk. 17:20).

(c) Although Jesus shared with apocalyptic writers a cosmic, universal type of eschatology, in contrast to the political and nationalistic concept of the messiah, he nonetheless upheld the OT doctrine of election (Matt. 10:6) with the associated belief that it is the will of Yahweh to reach the whole world through the nation of → Israel. This is not to say that Israel has a special claim on God's favour. Indeed, Israel is in danger of being put to shame by the heathen on the day of judgment (Matt. 12:42 par. Lk. 11:31). The kingdom will be taken from Israel and given to the Gentiles (Matt. 21:43). God will cast the sons of the kingdom (Israel) into outer darkness (Matt. 8:12; cf. Lk. 13:28). But Jesus promised the Twelve (→ Apostle), as the representatives of the eschatological people of God, the office of judges and rulers in the future kingdom of God (Matt. 19:28; Lk. 22:28 ff.; cf. Mk. 10:35–45).

(d) The facts that the kingdom is the gift of God (Lk. 12:32) and that it is appointed to men (*diatithēmi*) by → covenant (Lk. 22:29) have their counterparts in the teaching that a person can only receive it like a child (Mk. 10:15 par. Lk. 18:17; cf. Matt. 18:3; Jn. 3:3) and that it is something for which one must wait (Mk. 15:43 par. Lk. 23:51). Particularly frequent is the metaphor of entering (*eiserchesthai*) the kingdom of God (Matt. 5:20; 7:21; 18:3; 19:23 f.; 23:13; Jn. 3:5). Entry into the kingdom in the fullest sense lies in the future (Matt. 25:34; Mk. 9:43 ff.). But the presence of the kingdom of God in the person of Jesus faces the individual with a clear-cut decision. The Yes or No nature of this situation is illustrated by the hyperbole of Jesus: "If your right hand causes you to sin, cut it off and throw it away; it is better to lose one of your members than let your whole body go into hell" (Matt. 5:30; cf. 18:8 f.; Mk. 9:43–48). Some have even made themselves → eunuchs for the kingdom's sake (Matt. 19:12). "No one who puts his hand to the plough and looks back is fit for the kingdom of God" (Lk. 9:62). The decision is

385

not a result of mere enthusiasm; it is to be made after careful previous consideration (Lk. 14:28–32) and in obedience to Jesus' word (Matt. 7:24–27). But when it is made, it involves a readiness for sacrifice which may mean self-denial to the point of being hated by one's own family (Matt. 10:17 ff., 37). Yet the decision is not born of a rigid fanaticism, but against a background of overwhelming joy at the greatness of God's gift (cf. the parables of the hidden treasure and the pearl of great price, Matt. 13:44–46).

(e) The kingdom of God is utterly transcendent and supernatural: it comes from above, from God alone. When God's kingdom comes, the hungry will be filled and the sad will be comforted (cf. the Beatitudes, Matt. 5:3–10; Lk. 6:20 ff.). It demands that men should love their enemies (Matt. 5:38–42; Lk. 6:27 f., 32–36), and they will be as free from care as the birds of the air and the lilies of the field (Matt. 6:25–33; Lk. 12:22–31). Here again it is Jesus himself, in whom alone the future kingdom of God is present, in whose words and deeds that kingdom has already appeared. It has come already, in that Jesus seeks out the company of tax-collectors and sinners, offering them fellowship at table and so promising them forgiveness of their sins. As the king invites to his feast the beggars and homeless (Matt. 22:1–10), as the father's love receives back again the prodigal son (Lk. 15:11–32), as the shepherd goes out after the lost sheep (Lk. 15:4–7), as the woman searches for the lost coin (Lk. 15:8–10), as the master out of the goodness of his heart pays the labourers hired at the last hour the full day's pay (Matt. 20:1–15), so Jesus goes to the poor to give them the promise of forgiveness, "for theirs is the kingdom of heaven" (Matt. 5:3). Only sinners, who know what it is like to have a great burden of → guilt (Lk. 7:41–43), can appreciate the remission of sins through the goodness of God. For "those who are well have no need of a physician, but those who are sick" (Mk. 2:17; cf. Matt. 9:12; Lk. 5:31).

The distinctive feature of Jesus' proclamation of the kingdom of God is not therefore that he brought a new doctrine of the kingdom, or that he revolutionized people's apocalyptic and eschatological expectations, but that he made the kingdom of God inseparable from his own person. The new thing about Jesus's preaching of the kingdom is "He himself, simply his person" (J. Schniewind).

4. *The Kingdom of God and the Kingdom of Christ outside the preaching of Jesus.* (a) The Kingdom of Christ. Jesus himself spoke only of the *basileia tou theou*, the kingdom of God, which he tied up inextricably with his own person. Only in this sense did he declare it to be already present. After the resurrection the church, convinced that he had been exalted to the status of → Lord (*kyrios*, Phil. 2:9–11; Acts 2:36), maintained Jesus' christological emphasis in the preaching of the kingdom, and accordingly went on to speak of the *basileia* of Christ. They thus preserved the christological interpretation which Jesus had given to the kingdom of God, i.e. the inseparable connection between Jesus and the kingdom: only in himself is the kingdom of God present.

Where we read of the *basileia* of Christ we are dealing with the language of the early church. This is shown not only by the fact that the "conception of the Kingdom of Christ is foreign to the oldest stratum of tradition" (J. Jeremias, op. cit., 82), but also by the observation that the majority of texts which speak of the *basileia* of Christ may be recognized as redactional adaptations of an older original. Mk. 9:1 is older than Matt. 16:28; and Mk. 10:37 is older than Matt. 20:21.

basileia tou hyiou tou anthrōpou in Matt. 13:41 is an expression peculiar to Matt. and is found otherwise only at Matt. 16:28. The subordinate clause "that you may eat and drink in my kingdom" in Lk. 22:30 is lacking in the Matthaean parallel, Matt. 19:28.

This redaction of older versions is a legitimate development. Thus according to Jn. 18:36, Jesus says: "My kingdom is not of this world." Likewise 2 Tim. 4:18 speaks of the confidence of being delivered from every kind of evil and of being "saved for his heavenly kingdom [*eis tēn basileian autou epouranion*]" (cf. 2 Tim. 4:1; 2 Pet. 1:11). The inseparable connection between the person of Jesus and the presence of God's kingdom is expressed most clearly of all when Jesus Christ himself becomes an equivalent for "kingdom of God", as is shown by the following comparisons. Whereas Joseph of Arimathea was waiting for "the kingdom of God" (Mk. 15:43), believers are awaiting "their Lord" (Phil. 3:20). Whereas Jesus' message may be summed up as "The kingdom of God is at hand [*ēngiken hē basileia tou theou*]" (Mk. 1:15), James says, "The coming of the Lord is at hand [*hē parousia tou kyriou ēngiken*]" (Jas. 5:8). The disciple forsakes his family for Jesus' sake (*heneken emou*, Mk. 10:29) or for the sake of the kingdom of God (*heneken tēs basileias tou theou*, Lk. 18:29). This present → generation is to see the coming of "the kingdom of God" (Mk. 9:1), or of "the Son of man coming in his kingdom" (Matt. 16:28; cf. also Lk. 21:31 and Mk. 13:29). In Samaria Philip preached "good news about the kingdom of God and the name of Jesus Christ" (Acts 8:12; cf. 28:31).

The phrase "*basileia* of Christ" and the equation of "kingdom of God" with Jesus Christ are thus seen to be the result of the change-over from an implicit to an explicit christology. They make it clear that Jesus' proclamation of the kingdom of God was in no way displaced in the early church by the proclamation of Jesus Christ. The post-resurrection christology, in which Jesus Christ is the centre of the kerygma, is rather the outcome of the realization that the kingdom of God is present only in the person of Jesus Christ, so that one can only properly speak of the kingdom of God by speaking of Jesus Christ. Since the kingdom is bound up with the person of Jesus, the good news which Jesus preached of the dawning of God's kingdom becomes, after Easter, the → gospel of Jesus Christ and the proclamation of his kingdom.

(b) *Jesus' proclamation of the kingdom of God and the kerygma outside the synoptic tradition.* The kingdom of God, which is the central concept in the preaching of Jesus, has only a peripheral place outside the Synoptic Gospels. In its place we find the christological kerygma of the → cross and → resurrection of Jesus, the expectation of the Parousia and the general resurrection of the dead, and the use of terms such as → life (*zōē*, in Jn.) and → righteousness (*dikaiosynē*, in Paul). Is there a logical sequence from Jesus' preaching of the kingdom to the christological kerygma and the Pauline doctrine of justification?

At this point a survey of the synonyms used in the synoptic tradition for the term *basileia tou theou* is illuminating. Matt. 6:33 says that men are to seek the *basileia* of God and his *dikaiosynē*; in the par. Mk. 9:42–48 we find instead next to one another the expressions *eiselthein eis tēn zōēn*, to enter life (Mk. 9:43, 46; cf. Matt. 7:13) and *eiselthein eis tēn basileian tou theou*, to enter the kingdom of God (Mk. 9:47). Following the question of the rich young man, "What must I do

387

to inherit eternal life [*zōēn aiōnion*]?" (Mk. 10:17), Jesus remarks in conversation with his disciples "How hard it will be for those who have riches to enter the kingdom of God [*tēn basileian tou theou*]!" The phrase "to inherit eternal life" (Mk. 10:17) has a counterpart in "to inherit the kingdom prepared for you [by God]" (Matt. 25:34). Paul says at Rom. 15:17: "the kingdom of God ... is righteousness and peace and joy in the Holy Spirit [*dikaiosynē kai eirēnē kai chara en pneumati hagiō*]." Likewise in Rev. 12:10 we find *hē sōtēria* (salvation), *hē dynamis* (power) and *hē basileia tou theou* linked together. In place of the request for seats "in your glory [*en tē doxē sou*]" (Mk. 10:37) the par. Matt. 20:21 has a request for seats "in your kingdom [*en tē basileia sou*]". Lk. 21:31 refers to the nearness of God's kingdom, whereas a few verses earlier Jesus declares, "Raise your heads, because your redemption [*apolytrōsis*] is drawing near" (Lk. 21:28).

The Beatitudes (Matt. 5:3–10; cf. Lk. 6:20 ff.) which promise God's salvation to the poor, the parables of the Kingdom which testify to God's mercy towards sinners (Matt. 22:1–10; Lk. 15:11–32; 15:4–7, 8–10), and finally the synonyms for kingdom of God to be found within the synoptic tradition itself (→ Righteousness, → Life, → Redemption, → Glory), all go to demonstrate that the future kingdom of God, already present in the person of Jesus, is God's saving activity towards the individual. This saving activity of God, which is tied to Jesus and mediated by him alone, is likewise at the centre of the kerygma outside the synoptic tradition. Thus John speaks of eternal life (*zōē aiōnios*, Jn. 3:15, 36 etc.), referring to the goal of salvation, while Paul speaks of the righteousness, life or redemption which is given in Christ. In the writings of Paul and John these terms are to be understood with strict reference to christology (cf. "I am the resurrection and the life" [Jn. 11:25; cf. 3:15]; and the Pauline "in Christ", especially in Rom. 6). When in Rom. 4:5 Paul declares that the righteousness of God consists in "justifying the ungodly", he is taking up the central concern of Jesus' preaching of the kingdom, namely the promise of salvation to the poor and the sinners. The futurist eschatology in the preaching of Jesus is likewise retained in the expectation of his Parousia and the general resurrection of the dead. Pauline theology which is a development of christology contains, like the preaching of Jesus, both a present and a future element, since the crucified and risen one is also the one who is to come. By tying salvation to the person of Jesus and by developing christology along the lines of soteriology, pneumatology and eschatology, Paul has maintained a consistent and legitimate extension of Jesus' preaching of the kingdom of God, although he has adapted this to the post-resurrection situation as regards the cross and resurrection.

(c) Kingdom of God and Kingdom of Christ. Evidence that the kingdom of Jesus Christ is in the NT view the same as the kingdom of God is also to be seen in the fact that in parts of the NT outside the synoptic tradition both expressions are found together, sometimes God being named first, and sometimes Christ. Thus it is equally acceptable to speak of "the kingdom of Christ and of God" (Eph. 5:5) and of the world dominion "of our Lord and of his Christ" (Rev. 11:15). The rule of Christ and the rule of God are in other words identical. When the rule of Christ has become established, it is taken up into the rule of God (Rev. 5:10; 2:4, 6; 22:5); at the end of time Christ hands back to the Father the kingdom he has received from him (1 Cor. 15:24–28).

John's prophecy of the saints reigning a thousand years (Rev. 20:1-7) is, from the point of view of historical criticism (*Traditionsgeschichte*), an interpretation of the apocalyptic motif of a messianic kingdom as a period preceding the final realization of the kingdom of God. The doctrine of the millennium represents a coming together of the two parallel kinds of eschatology current in 1st century Judaism: the nationalistic, messianic eschatology, and the cosmic, universal view. The length of this messianic reign as a period preceding the kingdom of God is variously given in Jewish apocalyptic writings. The rule of Christ and the rule of God are not, however, two kingdoms following one another in succession, but one kingdom of Christ which issues finally in the kingdom of God. (On the interpretations of pre-millenarianism, post-millenarianism and amillenarianism → Chiliasm in the *Glossary of Technical Terms*, and → Number, art. *chilias*.)   *B. Klappert*
→ Caesar, → Parable, → Present

(a). S. Aalen, " 'Reign' and 'House' in the Kingdom of God in the Gospels", *NTS* 8, 1961–62, 215–40; A. Alt, "The Monarchy in Israel and Judah", *Essays on Old Testament History and Religion*, 1966, 239–59; K. Barth, "The Royal Man", *CD* IV, 2, 154–264; A. Bentzen, *King and Messiah*, 1955; L. Berkhof, *The Kingdom of God: The Development of the Idea of the Kingdom, especially since the Eighteenth Century*, 1951; J. Bright, *The Kingdom of God*, 1953; S. Brown, " 'The Secret of the Kingdom of God' (Mark 4:11)", *JBL* 92, 1973, 60–74; M. Buber, *Kingship of God*, 1967³; M. Burrows, "Thy Kingdom Come", *JBL* 74, 1955, 1–8; L. Cerfaux, *Christ in the Theology of St. Paul*, 1959, 92–106; D. J. A. Clines, "The Evidence for an Autumnal New Year in Pre-Exilic Israel and Judah Reconsidered", *JBL* 93, 1974, 22–40; and "The Psalms and the King", *Theological Students Fellowship Bulletin*, 71, 1975, 1–6; O. Cullmann, "The Kingship of Christ and the Church in the New Testament", *The Early Church*, 1956, 105–40; N. A. Dahl, "Parables of Growth", *StTh* 5, 1952, 132–66; G. Dalman, *The Words of Jesus*, 1902; D. Daube, "Violence to the Kingdom", *The New Testament and Rabbinic Judaism*, 1956, 285–300; C. H. Dodd, *The Parables of the Kingdom*, 1935; J. H. Eaton, *Kingship and the Psalms*, SBT 1976; I. Engnell, *Studies in Divine Kingship in the Ancient Near East*, (1943) 1967; J. de Fraine, "Kingship", *EBT* II 470 ff.; H. Frankfort, *Kingship and the Gods*, 1948; R. H. Fuller, *The Mission and Achievement of Jesus*, 1954; A. Gelston, "A Note on *YHWH mlk*", *Vetus Testamentum* 16, 1966, 507–12; T. F. Glasson, *His Appearing and His Kingdom: The Christian Hope in the Light of its History*, 1953; J. Gray, "The Kingship of God in the Prophets and Psalms", *Vetus Testamentum* 11, 1961, 1–26; F. Hahn, *The Titles of Jesus in Christology: Their History in Early Christianity*, 1969; R. H. Hiers, *The Kingdom of God in the Synoptic Tradition*, 1970; S. H. Hooke, ed., *Myth, Ritual and Kingship*, 1958; M. Hopkins, *God's Kingdom in the Old Testament*, 1963; J. Jeremias, *The Parables of Jesus*, 1963²; A. R. Johnson, *Sacral Kingship in Ancient Israel*, 1955; S. E. Johnson, "King Parables in the Synoptic Gospels", *JBL* 74, 1955, 37 ff.; W. Kelber, *The Kingdom in Mark: A New Place and a New Time*, 1974; J. D. Kingsbury, *Matthew: Structure, Christology, and Kingdom*, 1975; H. Kleinknecht, G. von Rad, K. G. Kuhn, and K. L. Schmidt, *basileus* etc., *TDNT* I 564–93; W. G. Kümmel, *Promise and Fulfilment: The Eschatological Message of Jesus*, 1961²; and "Eschatological Espectation in the Proclamation of Jesus", in J. M. Robinson, ed., *The Future of our Religious Past, Essays in Honour of Rudolf Bultmann*, 1971, 29–48; G. E. Ladd, *Crucial Questions about the Kingdom of God*, 1952; "The Kingdom of God: Reign or Realm?" *JBL* 81, 1962, 230–38; "The Life-Setting of the Parables of the Kingdom", *JBL* 82, 1963, 193–99; *The Gospel of the Kingdom: Scriptural Studies in the Kingdom of God*, 1959; and *Jesus and the Kingdom: The Eschatology of Biblical Realism*, 1966 (rev. ed., *The Presence of the Future*, 1974); R. Leivestad, *Christ the Conqueror*, 1954; G. Lundström, *The Kingdom of God in the Teaching of Jesus*, 1963; V. Maag, "*malkut YHWH*", *Congress Volume, Vetus Testamentum Supplements* 7, 1960, 129–53; S. Mowinckel, *He That Cometh*, 1956; *The Psalms in Israel's Worship*, I–II, 1962; and "General, Oriental and Specific Israelite Elements in the Israelite conception of the Sacral Kingdom", in *La Regalità Sacra. The Sacral Kingship, Studies in the History of Religions* 4, 1959, 283–93; M. Noth, "God, King and Nation in the Old Testament" and "The Holy Ones of the Most High", *The Laws in the Pentateuch and Other Studies*, 1966, 145–79, 215–28; R. Otto, *The Kingdom of God and the Son of Man: A Study in the History of Religion*, 1938; N. Perrin, *The*

Kingdom of God in the Teaching of Jesus, 1963; and *Jesus and the Language of the Kingdom: Symbol and Metaphor in New Testament Interpretation,* 1976; H. Ridderbos, *The Coming of the Kingdom,* 1962; A. Robertson, *Regnum Dei: Eight Lectures on the Kingdom of God in the History of Christian Thought* (Bampton Lectures, 1901), 1901; J. A. T. Robinson, *Jesus and his Coming,* 1951; R. Schnackenburg, "Kingdom of God", *EBT* II 455–70; and *God's Rule and God's Kingdom,* 1963; A. Schweitzer, *The Kingdom of God and Primitive Christianity,* 1968; H. E. Tödt, *The Son of Man in the Synoptic Tradition,* 1965; R. de Vaux, "The King of Israel, Vassal of Yahweh", in *The Bible and the Ancient Near East,* 1972, 152–66; G. Vos, *The Teaching of Jesus Concerning the Kingdom of God and the Church,* 1951; T. B. L. Webster, *From Mycenae to Homer,* 1958; R. N. Whybray, "Some Historical limitations of Hebrew Kingship", *Church Quarterly Review,* 163, 1962, 136–50; and *The Succession Narrative,* 1968; G. Widengren, "King and Covenant", *JSS* 2 1957, 1–32.

(b). A. Alt, *Kleine Schriften zur Geschichte des Volkes Israel,* I–III, 1956–64; K. H. Bernhardt, *Das Problem der altorientalischen Königsideologie im Alten Testament, Supplements to Vetus Testamentum* 8, 1961; H. Bietenhard, *Das tausendjährige Reich,* 1955; J. Bonsirven, *Le Règne de Dieu,* 1957; H. Conzelmann, "Gegenwart und Zukunft in der synoptischen Tradition", *ZTK* 54, 1957, 277 ff.; N. A. Dahl, "Der gekreuzigte Messias", in H. Ristow and K. Matthiae, eds., *Der historische Jesus und der kerygmatische Christus,* 1960, 149 ff.; E. Fascher, "Gottes Königtum im Urchristentum" *Numen* 4, 1957, 85 ff.; J. de Fraine, "L'aspect religieux de la royauté Israélite", *Analecta Biblica* 3, 1954; K. Galling, H. Conzelmann, E. Wolff, G. Gloege, "Reich Gottes", *RGG*[3] V 912 ff.; H. Gross, *Weltherrschaft als religiöse Idee im Alten Testament und Judentum,* 1953; and *Die Idee des ewigen und allgemeinen Weltfriedens im alten Orient und im Alten Testament,* 1956; G. Harder, "Das Gleichnis von der selbstwachsenden Saat", *ThV* 1948–49, 51 ff.; J. Héring, *La Royaume de Dieu et sa Venue,* (1937) 1959[2]; E. Jüngel, "Die Gottesherrschaft als die Jesu Verkündigung autorisierende Macht", *Paulus und Jesus,* (1962) 1967[3], 174 ff.; H.-J. Kraus, *Die Königsherrschaft Gottes im Alten Testament,* BHTh 13, 1951; W. G. Kümmel, "Futurische and präsentische Eschatologie im ältesten Christentum", *NTS* 4, 1959–60, 113–26 (reprinted in *Heilsgeschen und Geschichte,* 1965, 351 ff.); J. Lebram, "Die Weltreiche in der jüdischen Apokalyptik", *ZNW* 55, 1964, 143 ff.; E. Lohse, "Die Gottesherrschaft in den Gleichnissen Jesu", *EvTh* 18, 1958, 145 ff.; W. Michaelis, "Reich Gottes und Äonenwende in der Verkündigung Jesu", in *Neutestamentliche Aufsätze. Festschrift für J. Schmid,* 1963, 161 ff.; R. Morgenthaler, *Kommendes Reich,* 1952; S. Mowinckel, *Zum israelitischen Neujahrsfest und zur Deutung der Thronbesteigung-Psalmen,* 1952; F. Mussner, "Die Bedeutung von Mk. 1, 14 f. für die Reich-Gottes-Verkündigung Jesu", *Trierer Theologische Zeitschrift* 68, 1957; 257 ff. (reprinted in *Praesentia Salutis. Gesammelte Studien zu Fragen und Themen des Neuen Testament,* 1967, 81 ff.); G. von Rad, *Der heilige Krieg im alten Israel,* (1951) 1965[4], 6 ff., 14 ff.; L. Rost, "Königsherrschaft Jahwes in vorköniglicher Zeit?", *TLZ* 85, 1960, 721 ff.; A. Rüstow, "*entos hymōn estin.* Zur Deutung von Lk. 17, 20–21", *ZNW* 51, 1960, 197 ff.; W. Schmidt, *Königtum Gottes in Ugarit und Israel,* 1961; R. Schnackenburg, "Das 'Reich Gottes' im Neuen Testament", *BuL* 1, 1960, 143 ff.; J. A. Soggin, *melek, THAT* 1 908–20; E. Staehelin, *Die Verkündigung des Reiches Gottes in der Kirche Jesu Christi. Zeugnisse aus allen Jahrhunderten und allen Konfessionen,* I–VII, 1951–65; A. Strobel, *Kerygma und Apokalyptik,* 1967; P. Vielhauer, "Gottesreich und Menschensohn in der Verkündigung Jesu", in *Festschrift für G. Dehn,* 1957, 51 ff. (reprinted in *Aufsätze zum Neuen Testament,* 1965, 55 ff.); G. Widengren, *Sakrales Königtum im Alten Testament und Judentum,* 1955; H. A. Wilcke, *Das Problem eines messianischen Zwischenreiches bei Paulus, AThANT* 51, 1967.

Knowledge, Experience, Ignorance

One of the most important marks of man as a rational being is his capacity to order and clarify his impressions of the world that surrounds him and to articulate standards of behaviour. Cognition, practical knowledge and theoretical understanding are attained when the mind reflects on and judges sense experience. Originally both *aisthanomai* and *ginōskō* referred to experiencing an object through the senses. But whereas *aisthēsis* and its cognates expressed physical apprehension through the senses apart from the intellectual act of interpretation, *ginōskō* and its cognates included from the very first the idea of grasping and understanding the object perceived by the mind. Owing largely though not exclusively to the usage of the LXX, *aisthanomai* came to be confined to perception by the senses. The words of the *ginōskō* group, however, embrace the whole gamut of knowledge from knowing things to knowing persons. When this process results in an item or body of knowledge which may serve as a basis for further thought and action, *oida* (infin. *eidenai*), to know, is used parallel to the perf. of *ginōskō*. Both contain the implication of certainty based on experience. Examples of the use of *oida* are given under *ginōskō*.

The present article is concerned mainly with the activity of knowing. It therefore does not include a comprehensive study of the complexities of gnosticism. On points where the latter touches on theology and Christian conduct see the appropriate key term (e.g. → Lord's Supper, → Heaven, → Body, → Soul).

The article on *agnoeō*, not to know, be ignorant of, deals with the opposite of knowledge, and illustrates the extent to which experience, knowledge, and obedience are linked in biblical thought.

αἴσθησις

αἴσθησις (*aisthēsis*), experience; αἰσθητήριον (*aisthē-tērion*), organ of sense, faculty.

CL *aisthēsis* means perception by the senses (in contrast to knowledge through rational deduction), experience, sensation; in an ethical context it means judgment, e.g. on the worthlessness of desire (Epict., *Dissertationes* 2, 18, 8). *aisthētērion* is the organ of sense.

OT In the LXX *aisthēsis* is used predominantly in the wisdom literature, especially as a rendering of *da'at*, knowledge, wisdom, with the meaning of true insight. It can frequently include ethical discrimination and decision. *aisthētērion* is the organ where this discrimination is made (cf. Jer. 4:19). This insight stands in contrast to inexperience (Prov. 1:4), lack of → discipline (Prov. 12:1) and folly (Prov. 15:7). The father urges his son "to cry out for insight" (Prov. 2:3) for such → wisdom brings true knowledge of God (Prov. 2:4 ff.). The two are so identified that the opposite can be said, "The fear of the Lord is the beginning of knowledge" (Prov. 1:7). Experience of God and experience of the world belong inseparably together.

NT In the NT *aisthēsis* and *aisthētērion* are each used only once.

1. In Phil. 1:9 Paul places discernment (*aisthēsis*) and knowledge (*gnōsis*) side by side as two of love's expressions and functions. Knowledge is directed primarily to God; true discernment is necessary for human relationships, where it must distinguish between good and evil and judge accordingly (cf. especially v. 10).

2. Heb. 5:14 says of "the mature" that they "have their faculties [*aisthētēria*] trained by practice to distinguish good from evil." The concrete organ of sense has here become virtually a habitual ability which must, however, be developed and which enables believers to distinguish between the spirits. It is a spiritual gift which must be developed in practice.   *E. Schütz*

391

| γινώσκω |

γινώσκω (ginōskō), know, come to know, understand, comprehend, perceive, recognize; γνῶσις (gnōsis), knowledge; ἐπιγινώσκω (epiginōskō), know, understand, recognize; ἐπίγνωσις (epignōsis), knowledge, recognition.

CL The original form gignōskō is found from Homer on; the shortened form ginōskō was Aeolic and Ionic, but appears in common Gk. from Aristotle (384–322 B.C.). They are formed from the root gno-, found in Lat. (g)noscere, ignorare, and Eng. can and know. The nouns gnōsis and gnōmē, means of knowing, thought, judgment, opinion, are from the same root.

1. In secular Gk. the vb. is used with the following range of meanings.

(a) Basically it means to notice, perceive, or recognize a thing, person, or situation through the senses, particularly the sight. (Seeing and ginōskō are linked in Homer, Od. 15, 532 and 24, 217.) This leads to an intelligent ordering in the mind of what has been so perceived in the world of experience. Thus the vb. also means experience, learn, get to know: what has been experienced becomes known to the one who has experienced it. This leads to the difference in meaning (which becomes clear in the later linguistic usage) between ginōskō and aisthanomai, perceive (without necessarily understanding). The noun gnōsis (from Heraclitus on) also originally expressed the act of knowing through experience.

(b) Occasionally ginōskō means to distinguish, for experience or recognition of a phenomenon among similar or different ones may lead to this (cf. Homer, Il. 5, 128, 182).

(c) Familiarity leads to personal acquaintance. Hence ginōskō also means to know in a personal way (Heracl., Frag. 97), to understand (already in Homer Od. 16, 136), to know (Democ., Frag. 198; used par. with oida), to be acquainted with, to be expert (gnōstos, an expert, Plato, Rep. 1, 347d), and to judge (Dem. 658, 23). Similarly gnōsis is repeatedly found with the meaning knowledge, insight (in Plato and Sophocles), and gnōmē with that of insight (Herodotus, Thucydides), reflection (Xen., Cyr. 1, 3, 10), will, disposition, and finally judgment, opinion, verdict.

(d) ginōskō may be used to express a relationship of trust between persons, i.e. to recognize as friend, love as a friend (Xen., Cyr. 1, 4, 27; cf. gnōstos, familiar with, from Aesch., Cho. 691). It is questionable whether the Hellenistic usage, to know (carnally) i.e. to have sexual relations with, is derived from this. It is possible that the borrowing of a non-Gk. usage lies behind it. It has, however, been pointed out that its root is related to Lat. gignere, beget (cf. H. Leisegang, Die Gnosis, 1955[4], 32; → Birth, art. ginomai).

(e) Knowledge of situations can be reached by reflecting, judging and investigating, i.e. by logical thought-processes. The inscription at Delphi, gnōthi sauton, "Know thyself", is a summons to reflection and self-examination.

(f) Since verdicts in criminal and civil courts were based on a weighing of given facts, they could be expressed by ginōskō in the passive, with the meaning to be judged.

(g) The object of knowledge may be a concrete object or an idea in the mind of the thinking subject. Especially in philosophy speculative cognition in this latter sense plays a great part. But even here knowing was regarded in great measure as seeing, "the seeing of the soul [omma tēs psychēs]" (cf. Plato Rep. 533). This may be seen from the concrete character of the expressions used for speculation: e.g. *theōreō* look at, observe, contemplate; *skopeō* look into, examine, inspect; and by calling the knowledge so obtained *eidos*, idea (Democritus, Plato; → Image). The goal of philosophical knowledge was seeing – not the seeing of transient and changeable earthly phenomena, but of the lasting and real, which could be seen only by the eyes of the soul. Accordingly in such contexts one should render *ginōskō* by gain insight, perceive (intuitively). The objects of such insight may ultimately belong to the religious sphere (Herach., *Frag.* 5).

With *ginōskō* there is always the implication of grasping the full reality and nature of the object under consideration. It is thus distinguished from mere opinion (*dokeō*; → Think), which may grasp the object half-correctly, inadequately or even falsely. This finds expression in the late phrase attributed, perhaps wrongly, to Apollonius of Tyana *gnōsis theōn, ou doxa*, "Knowledge of the gods, not opinion" (*Epistula* 52).

2. The above indicated uses of *ginōskō* and its derivatives are also found in Hel. Gk. In addition, however, we find a growing use of the terms, based on a fairly loose link with the language of Gk. philosophy. They appear in the widely different systems of thought and conceptual schemes influenced by syncretism which from an early period have been bracketed together under the title of gnosticism (Gk. *gnōsis*). However, the terms gnosis and gnostic were used by only some of these groups to describe themselves (cf. Iren., *Haer.* 1, 11, 1; 1, 26, 3; Pauly-Wissowa, VII 2, 1004 ff.; H. Jonas, *The Gnostic Religion*, 1963[2], 32 ff.). It lies beyond the scope of the present article to attempt a comprehensive survey of gnostic thought, but certain features of gnosticism may be mentioned.

(a) In Hellenistic culture men adopted a new attitude to the world which involved an *a priori* doubt about the possibility of arriving at the truth about the world and reality along rational lines. Man experiences the world and history more or less as an impenetrable fate which he cannot influence and to which he is handed over like a powerless slave without his consent. He finds the world more a prison than a home. His existence on earth and in history is lived out in a strange land and in misery. Hence, he looks for freedom and escape from the compulsion imposed on him in an alien world. He finds one way of escape in *gnōsis*. In this context it does not mean the mental penetration of things by logical thought as was the case in Gk. philosophy, for it was now widely held that the answer of the universe to rational questions was either silence or lies. The answer of the gnostic was not from within this world, but from the non-cosmic, from outside the universe, from a divine source, diametrically opposed to the cosmic. It came through revelation given in grace to men (cf. Od.Sol. 7:3, 6). The cosmic presupposition of gnosticism was dualism which made an absolute separation between God and the world. The ways and means by which one could acquire knowledge of this other reality were varied, and included sacramentalism, magic, mysticism, semi-philosophical speculation.

(b) By the nature of things *gnōsis* was primarily man's knowledge of himself, of his true nature, which would explain to him his inharmonious relationship with his manner of existence on earth and in history. It would thus show him the way back to → salvation. It was a knowledge of past, present and future. It is the knowledge "who were we? what have we become? where were we? into what have we been cast? whither are we hastening? from what are we delivered? what is birth? what is rebirth?" (Clement of Alexandria, *Excerpta ex Theodoto*, 1, 78, 2; cf. W. Foerster, *Gnosis*, I, 1972, 230). *gnōsis* included cosmology, cosmogony and theological knowledge only in so far as they might teach man what he is; "man stands in the centre of the gnostics' interest" (G. Quispel, *Gnosis als Weltreligion*, 1951, 29).

(c) The gnostic myth of "the tragic history of the soul" (*TDNT* I 695) which appears in many different forms, attempts to give the answer to the gnostic's question about his own nature. This myth tells of the divine origin of the → soul, which as the result of a primeval fall was exiled and fettered to matter, which is hostile to God, i.e. to the → body. "Man by nature does not belong in any way to this world; his original home is beyond the spheres of the visible universe" (G. Quispel, ibid.). That is why man cannot feel at home in the cosmos, for this cosmos and the God of the soul have nothing in common. Hence, man is plagued by a vague, hopeless longing to leave the world. The less he has been lost to the cosmos, the stronger is the longing. If he has surrendered completely to the cosmos there is no hope of salvation left for him. He perishes along with matter, since there is no "soul-substance" left in him, for this alone is capable of salvation. The process of salvation begins when the hopeless and vague longing is replaced by instruction about the unknown God out there (*agnōstos propatōr* or *patēr*, Epiph., *Haer*. 1, 23, 1; *agnōstos theos*, Iren., *Haer*. 4, 20, 2), the original divinity of the soul, its "fall", the cosmos and its matter which is anti-God, and about the way the soul takes to its divine home. All this is an illumination which comes to man as an external "call" and divine → revelation. If the call is heard by those that belong to it, there is no obstacle to prevent the divine soul from returning to the divinity and being deified (*Corp. Herm*. 1, 26a; 13, 4). Salvation is here and now. The return can be anticipated in the ecstatic state (cf. Iren., *Haer*., 3, 15, 2). "He who has achieved *gnōsis* is good, and pious, even already divine" (*Corp. Herm*. 10, 9). Though *gnōsis* gives the appearance of being a way to salvation through grace, it is in fact a grandiose attempt at self-salvation, for all that is redeemed and glorified is the soul which is in any case essentially divine. The gnostic is a *physei sōzomenos*, someone saved by nature (Clem.Alex., *Strom*. 2, 3; cf. 4, 13).

(d) All this led to a characteristic gnostic attitude to life which was itself termed *gnōsis* (Iren., *Haer*. 1, 33, 3). It expressed itself in a feeling of superiority over all non-gnostics – in Christian gnosticism, over all mere believers. This may be seen both in their extreme claims, e.g. to be *theon egnōkenai monoi*, the only ones to know God (Clem.Alex., *Strom*. 3, 4, 31), and in their negative ethics, ascetic or antinomian, which were motivated by the gnostic's assurance that his true self was not part of the cosmos. Hence there was no reason why he should obey the claims he attributed to the cosmos. Moral rules were either demands of purely cosmic powers intended to reduce men to slavery (Iren., *Haer*. 1, 23, 3) or purely human values (Iren., *Haer*. 1, 25, 4). Whether by asceticism or libertinism, the gnostic sought to demonstrate his scorn of them and his freedom from all worldly ties.

Gnosticism is, therefore, a general term denoting a manner of life which sprang from a denial of the validity of human existence in history and the cosmos. It found expression for its beliefs in a syncretistic mythology, and expressed itself in the negation of ethics.

394

OT In the OT, as with the common Gk. attitude, knowledge is derived through the senses; the thing to be known must present itself to the senses and so let itself be known. Hence we find vbs. of hearing (→ Hear) and seeing (→ See) parallel to vbs. of knowing (e.g. Exod. 16:6 f.; Deut. 33:9; 1 Sam. 14:38; Isa. 41:20). It is easy to understand why the LXX rendered *rāʾâh*, see (Jdg. 2:7), *ḥāzâh*, see (Isa. 26:11), and *šāmaʿ*, hear (Neh. 4:15[MT 4:9]), by *ginōskō*. The concepts of knowing in Gk. and Heb. thought largely coincide, and for both experience through the senses is fundamental.

1. In the LXX the *ginōskō* word-group is used mainly to render words formed from the Heb. root *yāḏaʿ* which has a very wide range of meaning. If one starts with the basic meaning (a) to notice, experience, observe (e.g. Gen. 3:7; 41:31; Jdg. 16:20; Eccl. 8:5; Isa. 47:8; Hos. 5:3), then the observing of things like good and bad (2 Sam. 19:35 [MT 19:36]) or right and left (Jon. 4:11) leads to distinguishing between them. Hence, *ginōskō* means (b) to distinguish between. Knowledge passed on by a third party gives the meaning (c) of know by learning (Prov. 30:3). (d) Experience becomes a reality in a relationship based on familiarity with the person or thing known. The use of *yāḏaʿ* in the wisdom literature is an example of this. It speaks of a knowledge which is empirical and living, obtained by observation of the world and life as the work of God, which in turn leads to an upright life before God (Prov. 2:6; Eccles. 8:17). (e) Knowledge, i.e. familiarity with a thing or situation, can result in technical ability, i.e. to know how to do something (1 Ki. 7:14 [LXX 7:2]; cf. Gen. 25:27; 1 Sam. 16:16, 18; Isa. 47:11). (f) In certain circumstances observation and resultant action (or failure to act) become closely linked. Hence, *ginōskō* also means to concern oneself with, care for, trouble oneself with, or their negatives (e.g. Prov. 27:23; Pss. 1:6, 37:18 [LXX 36:18]; 119:79 [LXX 118:79], and to want to have to do with (or its negative) (e.g. Deut. 33:9). Frequently in theological contexts it is a question of knowledge not properly obtained, leading to lack of interest (e.g. Jer. 8:7; Ps. 95:10[LXX 94:10]; Isa. 1:3). (g) To know can also mean to have sexual relations with (Gen. 4:1; 19:8; cf. 2:23; → Join). (h) To know another person "face to face" means to have a personal and confidential relationship with another person (e.g. Deut. 34:10). The expression has no sexual connotations. When God knows a person (Jer. 1:5) or a people (Amos 3:2) he chooses or → elects him (cf. Num. 16:5 LXX). This knowledge, understood as election, is gracious and loving (see above (f)), but it demands a personal response. (i) The distinctiveness of the OT concept of knowledge is clearly seen in passages which speak of man's knowledge of God, i.e. of his grateful and obedient recognition (see 2 below). "If one asks . . . for the central concept which makes comprehensible the varied uses of the one root, it is to be found in the concept of cognition. All the activities listed are merely variations on this" (H. W. Wolff, "Erkenntnis Gottes im Alten Testament", *EvTh* 15, 1955, 426 f.).

2. Knowledge of God is always linked with God's acts of self-revelation. This is illustrated in the formula, "And you [or they] shall know that I am Yahweh." This is found 54 times in Ezek., and occurs also elsewhere in the OT. It is always linked with the proclamation of some specific act by Yahweh: e.g. Ezek. 6:7, 13, 14; 7:4; 11:10, 11 f.; 12:14 f., 16 (after pronouncement of judgment on Israel); 25:5 (after pronouncement of judgment on Ammon); 28:26; 37:6 (after a promise of salvation); cf. also Exod. 6:7; 7:5, 17; 14:4, 18; 16:6, 12; 29:46; 1 Ki. 20:13,

28; Isa. 45:3, 6 f.; 49:23, 26. In 2 Ki. 5:15 Naaman the Syrian comes to a knowledge of the God of Israel through the healing of his → leprosy. In Sir. 36:4 f. God is asked to reveal himself to the nations, that they too may recognize that there is no other God beside Yahweh (cf. the 4th benediction in the Eighteen Benedictions; for text → Prayer, art. *proseuchomai* OT 5).

It is not only the uniqueness of Yahweh's acts in the past or future that leads to a knowledge of God. The testimony to God's past actions, by which the past is repeatedly made present (Exod. 10:1 f.; 18:8–11), and signs grounded in salvation history (including the → sabbath) are capable of bringing about knowledge of Yahweh (Exod. 31:13; Ezek. 20:12–20). Hence, knowledge of God arises uniquely from the revealing acts of God and the testimony to them. In fact, knowledge of God and knowledge of his acts coincide (Mic. 6:5). Knowledge of God in the OT is not concerned with the speculative question of the being of God, but in the God who, working in → grace and → judgment, has turned to men. To know him means to enter into the personal relationship which he himself makes possible.

Israel's intimate relationship with God required that the nation's conduct should correspond to God's actions. The command "Be still, and know that I am God" (Ps. 46:10[MT 46:11; LXX 45:11]) does not in the first instance mean that the nations attacking Yahweh's city should undergo a purely religious conversion to Yahweh. Rather, they should abandon their rebellion in recognition of Yahweh's rule in history. In the rhetorical questions of Jer. 22:15 f., knowledge of God is clearly interpreted as doing justice and righteousness, particularly to the poor and needy. In Jdg. 2:10 f. not knowing Yahweh and his work done for Israel results in doing evil in the sight of Yahweh. Similarly in Hos. 4:1 f. knowledge of Yahweh is directly related to specific behaviour; lack of faithfulness and disloyalty to the → covenant are bound up with lack of knowledge of God. The result is a breakdown of human relationships. For Hosea too knowledge of God means knowledge of God's saving acts for Israel (13:4, cf. also 4:6; 5:4; 6:6; 8:2). (On Hosea see H. W. Wolff, " 'Wissen um Gott' bei Hosea als Urform von Theologie", *EvTh* 12, 1952–53, 533 ff.; and *Hosea, Hermeneia*, 1974.) In the wisdom literature fear of Yahweh and knowledge of God are interchangeable terms (→ Fear, art. *phobos*).

3. Summary. While the Gks. were concerned with detached knowledge and a speculative interest in the metaphysical nature of things, the OT regards knowledge as something which continually arises from personal encounter. When the OT makes statements about → God and → creation, we should not regard them as ontological deductions, but as declarations of faith in response to God's → revelation. For knowledge of God is related to the revelation of God in the historic past and the promised future, in the earthly sphere in which God's creatures have their being. As Israel continually inquired into God's revelation in the past, present and future, he discerned the purposes and demands of God in worship and in conduct.

4. (a) The confrontation between Hellenistic Judaism and polytheism led to the development of a semi-dogmatic concept of the knowledge of God. The knowledge of God meant above all knowing that there was one God, and combatting the claims of heathen deities to be gods (cf. Jud. 2:20; Ep.Jer. passim; cf. Sib. 3:429 f.). The question of the possibility of knowing God was also raised and answered as the Stoics did by stressing the possibility of knowing him through his creation (e.g. Wis. 13:1–9; Syr.Bar 54:17 f.; Philo, *Virt.* 215 f.; Syr.Bar. 54:17 f.). Judaism was

obviously also involved in controversy with the gnostics. Hagigah 2:1 (Mishnah and Tosefta) warns against speculations about what was before the creation, and what will be when the earth passes away (cf. H. Jonas, *Gnosis und spätantiker Geist*, II, 1, 1954, 206; H. Bietenhard, *Die himmlische Welt im Urchristentum und Spätjudentum*, 1951, 53 ff.; SB I 191; III 33, 378). This does not exclude the possibility that a gnostic answer may have been given to the question of the knowability of God, as may be inferred from the expression *phōs gnōseōs*, light of knowledge, occurring a number of times in Test.XII (e.g. Test.Lev. 4:3; 18:3; Test.Ben. 11:2; cf. Philo, *Migr.Abr.* 34 f.; *Som.* 2, 226).

(b) There appear to be some contacts between the OT and the Hel.-gnostic concepts of knowledge because in both knowledge of God comes by revelation. In the latter, however, the place of history is consistently denied, whereas in the former the knowledge of God is inseparably bound up with God's revelation in time and space.

(c) In the inter-testamental period the Qumran texts, in which *yāḍaʿ* and *daʿat* are central ideas, show a remarkable development of the OT concept of knowledge. In a number of passages knowledge stands by itself. It is one of the most important fruits of salvation enjoyed by pious members of the Qumran sect (cf. 1QHab. 11:1; 1QS 10:9, 12; 11:6, 15; 1QH 2:18; 11:24; CD 2:4). God himself is the "God of knowledge" (cf. 1QS 3:15), i.e. the God who possesses all knowledge and from whom alone man can acquire knowledge. An act of predestination is involved (cf. 1QS 4:25; 1QH 1:7; → Foreknowledge). Hence, God's knowledge is not purely intellectual. There are many objects of human knowledge. Of these "the secrets" or "the hidden things" are frequently mentioned (e.g. 1QH 12:13; 1QS 5:11), by which the sect meant the revealed secrets of creation, history and the last days. In this we see the affinity of Qumran teaching with later apocalyptic. God's loyalty is also to be known (cf. 1QH 9:9), as is God's goodness (1QH 14:17), wisdom (1QH 15:12), glory (1QH 15:20) and even God himself (1QH 1:31). Hence, the community could call itself "the knowing ones" (1QH 11:14; 14:15). Alongside this the knowledge of the will of God as revealed in the Torah plays an important part. Upon it depended a man's reception and place in the community (1QS 2:22; cf. 1QS 5:21 ff.). Similar usage occurs in the parallel concepts, *śāḵal*, the root of which means to have insight, and *bîn*, to distinguish, hiph. to understand, and the corresponding nouns. It has been argued that the Qumran texts with their stress on the concept of knowledge betray the influence of gnostic thought on Palestinian Judaism. However, the fundamental differences in cosmology, anthropology, soteriology and ethics must not be overlooked.

NT 1. *Survey of use and meaning in the NT. ginōskō* is found 221 times, of which 82 are in the Johannine literature, 50 in Paul (including the Pastoral Epistles), and 44 in Lk.-Acts; and *epiginōskō* 44 times, of which 12 instances are in Paul (including the Pastorals), and 20 in Lk.-Acts. *gnōsis* and *epignōsis* occur 29 times and 20 times respectively, no less than 38 of them being in Paul (*gnōsis* 23 times; *epignōsis* 15 times). John does not use them at all, possibly deliberately. The verbal adj. *gnōstos* is found 15 times (almost only in Jn. and Lk.); *gnōmē* (predominantly in Paul and Rev.) 9 times.

In a large number of cases we have the general and popular use of the words.

Since Gk. and OT usage are so close, we cannot normally determine the background. A few examples must suffice: to hear of (Mk. 5:43; Jn. 4:1; Phil. 1:12); notice (Matt. 16:8; Mk. 6:33 *epiginōskō*; 13:28 f.); feel (Mk. 5:29 f.); recognize (Matt. 7:16 *epiginōskō*; Lk. 24:16; Jas. 2:20, learn); know (Lk. 12:46 ff.; Jn. 1:48; 21:17 together with *oida*; Rom. 7:15 RSV "understand"); understand (Mk. 5:13 together with *oida*; Lk. 18:34 together with *synienai*; Jn. 13:7 together with *oida*); find out (Jn. 13:35; 15:18; 19:4; 1 Jn. 2:3, 5); distinguish (1 Cor. 14:7), know how to (Matt. 16:3).

The noun *gnōmē* is found almost only in the usual meaning of opinion, judgment. Thus in 1 Cor. 7:25 the opinion of the apostle is clearly distinguished from the "command of the Lord", but it is still authoritative (cf. v. 40). In Rev. 17:13 it occurs in the phrase "of one mind" (cf. 1 Cor. 1:10; Rev. 17:17). In Acts 20:3 Paul *egeneto gnōmēs*, came to the opinion, i.e. decided to return through Macedonia.

2. *The influence of OT usage.* The universal use of the LXX in the primitive church, as in Diaspora Judaism, ensured a linguistic continuity between the OT and the NT documents, or rather between the terms available and their use in the NT *kērygma*. But the standpoint of the NT writers who were in part Gentile Christians speaking to members of the pagan world and the subject matter of their message, the revelation of God in Jesus Christ, modified and gave a new stress to the OT concept of knowledge. Where it expresses a personal relationship between the one who knows and the one known, the NT concept of knowledge is clearly taken from the OT. This applies to sexual relations (Matt. 1:25; Lk. 1:34) and also to where *ginōskō* means have to do with as in Matt. 7:23, "I never knew you", i.e. I never had anything to do with you (cf. Mk. 14:71, where Peter denies his relationship to Jesus, though he uses *oida*). The statement in 2 Cor. 5:21 that Christ "knew no sin" does not mean that he had no intellectual knowledge of sin, but rather that Jesus had no personal truck with sin. It is this that brings out the enormity and irony of the pronouncement: "For our sake he made him to be sin" (→ Sin). Similarly Rom. 7:7 should be paraphrased: "The human I would have had no intimate dealings with sin had it not been for the law" (cf. Rom. 3:20: "since through the law comes knowledge of sin").

ginōskō has also the sense of have to do with, have dealings with, know personally, in 2 Cor. 5:16. The meaning of this verse is the subject of much controversy. *oidamen* ("we know") occurs in the first half and *ginōskō* is used twice in its second half in the forms *egnōkamen* ("we knew") and *ginōskomen* ("we know"). In 2 Cor. 5:11–21 Paul is involved in controversy with opponents who attacked him personally and his claim to be an → apostle. They maintained that he was lacking in visible spiritual qualities which would authenticate his claim to be an apostle, e.g. ecstatic phenomena (v. 13). They probably charged him with being a braggart who commended only himself. Paul is probably referring to this in v. 11 ("we persuade men") and in v. 12 ("we are not commending ourselves"). Part of Paul's defence is the reference to Christ's death "for all", through which "all have died" (vv. 14 f.), including the man with supposed, visible, spiritual qualities. So, says Paul, from now on – ever since the events linked with Christ, which mean a transformation of all values, the turning point of the ages – "we know no one after the flesh", according to his visible demonstration of the Spirit and power.

We must understand this as the consequence of all dying with Christ (v. 14). In order to show how obvious this is, he inserts the statement which should be clear to all, in v. 16 b: "Even though we may have had acquaintance with Christ according to the flesh", i.e. with the visible Christ as he was on earth, "we do not know him as such", i.e. have to do with him as such, but only with the invisible, risen Christ in whose service we stand. Because Christ had died and been raised for all he is the invisible Lord of all, and his lordship is externally inescapable. Hence both the apostle and his claims to apostleship, in common with all else that has died with Christ, are not subject to judgment by external and the normal visible standards. "In Christ" only the new creation is of value. The old, including judgment by outward appearances (*en prosōpō*, v. 12), has passed away and "a new order has already begun" (v. 17 NEB). In the light of this argument, it is clear that Paul in 2 Cor. 5:16 is neither affirming nor denying that he knew the earthly Jesus personally. Equally it has no bearing on the meaning of the historic Jesus for Paul.

(a) We find the influence of the OT most clearly in those contexts where the vb. means to give recognition to. In 1 Cor. 16:18 Paul urges, "Give recognition to [*epiginōskete*] such men", i.e. to colleagues who have shown their devoted service. In 1 Cor. 4:19 Paul tells the Corinthians that, when he comes he will not recognize, i.e. give weight to, the words of the arrogant ("self-important" NEB) or their power. In Matt. 17:12 Jesus speaks of the scribes' failure to recognize John the Baptist as → Elijah come again, which in effect meant that "they did with him whatever they pleased." In the letter to the church in Philadelphia the exalted Jesus promised that Jews would come to the (Gentile?) Christian church and recognize that the Risen One loved them (Rev. 3:9; cf. Rev. 2:23). In so doing he reversed Jewish eschatological hope (cf. E. Lohmeyer, *Die Offenbarung des Johannes*, HNT 16, 1970[3] ad loc.).

Phrases such as "know God's decree" (Romans 1:32), "know the law" (Rom. 7:1), "know his will" (Rom. 2:18; Acts 22:14), do not imply a merely theoretical knowledge, but the recognition that it applies to the person individually and demands his obedience. (When Paul in Rom. 2:20 calls the law "the embodiment of knowledge and truth" in his description of the Jew, he implies a clear distinction between existential knowledge and theoretical truth.) The Pharisees' remark that "the crowd who do not know the law are accursed" (Jn. 7:49) reflects a well-attested scorn of rabbinic scholars for the common people (cf. SB II 494–521). It contains the implication that the common people would not have gone after Jesus if they had really known and obeyed the law. But in recording it Jn. sees an unconscious irony in the Pharisees' own failure to see where the law was pointing them (cf. 7:42, 51 with 5:39 f.; 11:49 ff.). 2 Cor. 10:5 contains the juxtaposition of "the knowledge of God" and "to obey Christ." Even where Paul clearly borrows the concept of knowledge held by the (Jewish) Hellenistic popular philosophy, he recasts it. In Rom. 1:28 "The knowledge of God as a question and accessible possibility does not concern him. What concerns him, rather, is the question whether this knowledge is personal (1:28), whether the truth of God remains truth and its power is acknowledged (1:18, 25)" (G. Bornkamm, *Early Christian Experience*, 1969, 56). If such acknowledgment which manifests itself in living obedience is refused, the judgment of God is inevitable. The statement in Rom. 1:21 that those who had known God had become futile in their thinking must have appeared as a contradiction in terms to Hellenistic thought (→ Empty, art. *mataios*). Their futility is a result of not knowing God (cf. Wis. 13:1; → *agnoeō*). Paul, however, considered that the knowledge of God necessarily included proper glorification and gratitude. Hence, the heathen who rejected God reduced this knowledge to mere intellectual activity, and what they considered wisdom was in fact nothing but folly (Rom. 1:22 f.). The very fact that, though the heathen undoubtedly knew God, they refused him due recognition, is the measure of their lack of excuse (Rom. 1:19 f.; cf. also Jn. 1:10; 1 Cor. 1:21; Gal. 4:8 f.; see further the whole argument of Bornkamm's essay on "The Revelation of God's Wrath (Romans 1–3)" in op. cit., 47–70). Such recognition of God, where it is found, is a → gift of God and not something natural. It is based on his → revelation and therefore remains dependent on revelation (1 Cor. 13:8; 14:6; cf. 2 Cor. 8:7; 2 Pet. 1:5). Other passages are Phil. 1:9; Col. 1:9 f. (which contains a prayer for a growth in love with knowledge or in knowledge of the will of God; cf. Eph. 1:17); 2 Pet. 1:2 (in the prayer for blessing in the introduction); 1 Cor. 1:5; Col. 3:10 (note the pass. vb.); 1 Cor. 2:11, 14. Consequently, this knowledge of God which comes about through the acceptance of salvation in the → forgiveness of sins alone can be nothing other than the gift of God (cf. Lk. 1:7).

Nevertheless, in apparent contradiction to its gift-like charismatic character, knowledge in the NT involves the ready will of the man who receives it. Through disobedience, ingratitude and prevarication he can fail to appropriate it. Hence, the imperatives and exhortations in the NT are calls to grasp the gift and use it aright in the changing circumstances of life (e.g. 1 Cor. 14:27; Eph. 5:5; Jas. 1:3; 5:20; cf. Lk. 10:11; Acts 2:36, where the "house of Israel" is called upon to recognize the crucified Jesus as the messiah in the light of the events of → Pentecost; cf. also the imperative in the parable in Matt. 24:43). 2 Cor. 8:9 ff. involves the outworking of knowledge in practical behaviour. Here the knowledge "of the grace of our Lord Jesus Christ, that though he was rich, yet for your sake he became poor, so that by his poverty you might become rich" finds expression in the collection for Jerusalem, which Paul was urging. One should not interpret it, as does Lietzmann, to mean simply that Christ is an example of generosity (H. Lietzmann, *An die Korinther, HNT* 9, 1969[5] ad loc.). We may also doubt that in 1 Pet 3:7 it is correct to render the appeal to husbands to live with their wives *kata gnōsin* by "considerately" (RSV) or "with understanding" (NEB). It is rather a call to the practical demonstration of the knowledge (of God or of Christ) in the marriage relationship (cf. *TDNT* I 708). Knowledge in the sense of recognition is thus always linked with the practical behaviour of the one who knows and has to do with his way of life (Col. 1:9 f.) which should bring credit to the One known.

(b) We also find typical OT usage in the NT in the case of God's knowledge. This refers to God's loving, electing knowledge of men (cf. 2 Tim. 2:19 quoting Num. 16:5; the passives in 1 Cor. 8:3 [see below]; 1 Cor. 13:12; and Gal. 4:9). Rom. 11:33 should be mentioned in this connection. God's knowledge here includes the whole activity of God, which takes in Gentiles and Jews alike. It is eternally valid for his creatures and triumphs over guilt and disobedience. Rom. 10:2 is a sort of counterpart. Here Paul acknowledges the Jews' zeal for God, but it is not *kata epignōsin*, "in accordance with [real] knowledge" (cf. Arndt, 291). "This does not mean that the Jews lack a deeper insight into the being of God. The knowledge they lack is the knowledge and recognition of God's ways" (E. Gaugler, *Der Brief an die Römer*, 1959² ad loc.).

(c) There are, however, passages where *ginōskō* implies theological and theoretical knowledge. This overtone cannot be immediately derived from OT usage (see 4 below). Matt. 13:11 and Lk. 9:10 (cf. Mk. 4:11) speak of a hidden knowledge granted only to the → disciples, concerning "the mysteries of the → kingdom of God". This knowledge made them authoritative interpreters of the → parables, which otherwise are hidden from men (→ Explain; → Hide; → Secret). Col. 2:2 contains the phrase *epignōsin tou mystēriou tou theou Christou*. The uncertainty of how the text should be taken is reflected by the *v.l.* which has *theou kai patros kai tou Christou* ("God and Father and of Christ") and by several other variants (cf. E. Lohse, *Colossians and Philemon*, 1971, 82). But the RSV seems to give the most likely rendering: "the knowledge of God's mystery, of Christ". At any rate, it has a certain esoteric colouring. Essentially it involves a knowledge of God, but this knowledge is described as a mystery which is not open to all, but only to the saints to whom God has proclaimed his secret (Col. 1:26).

But even the knowledge of theological truths, e.g. of a particular teaching about baptism, has as its object obedience which expresses itself in life (Rom. 6:6). The express purpose of such knowledge mentioned is that "we might no longer be enslaved to sin."

3. *The use of the word-group in the NT controversy with Gnosticism.* A number of contemporary scholars see evidence of a conflict with gnosticism in a variety of NT passages. ([Ed.] The bibliography at the end of this article gives details of works by Bultmann, Jonas, Schmithals and others who adopt this view, together with works by R. McL. Wilson and E. M. Yamauchi and others who take a more cautious view. In assessing what influence, if any, gnosticism had on the NT several facts need to be borne in mind. The extant sources of gnosticism, like the known leading gnostic teachers, are substantially later than the NT. Certain gnostic ideas appear to be indebted to the NT itself. Moreover, the extant gnostic texts display a wide variety of beliefs which make it impossible to treat gnosticism as if it were a homogeneous belief-system. It would be uncritically simplistic to label someone a "gnostic" simply because he lays claim to *gnōsis* [knowledge] and to attribute to him without further evidence the belief-systems of Valentinus or Basilides. On the other hand, there were those in NT times who vaunted their superior knowledge [1 Cor. 1:18–2:16; 8:1; 13:12 f.; cf. Col. 2:8; 1 Tim. 4:7; 6:20]. It may be that in such passages we should see incipient tendencies which later flowered into gnosticism as we know it. But it would be anachronistic to read into these references ideas for which we have evidence only in the 2nd and 3rd centuries.)

The NT writers frequently found themselves in conflict with travelling preachers who had their own version of the apostolic *kērygma*. Timothy was expressly warned against the "godless chatter" and the "contradictions" of knowledge (*gnōsis*) falsely so called (1 Tim. 6:20). In Rev. 2:24 opponents are mentioned who claimed to have learned "the deep things of Satan". It may well be that the writer has sarcastically and with true critical judgment turned round their claim to have learned "the deep things of God" (E. Lohmeyer, op. cit., 29; E. Lohse, *Die Offenbarung des Johannes*, NTD 11, 1966², 29). There is much in Paul's letters (especially 1 and 2 Cor.; Phil. 3:2 ff.; Col., especially 2:4–23, and perhaps Gal.), and in the

401

whole Johannine literature and Jude that might be understood against the background of anti-gnostic controversy. Our purpose here is to investigate whether the understanding of knowledge in these NT writers has been influenced by their gnostic opponents, and if so in what measure.

(a) Paul. In his discussion of the use of food offered to idols Paul quoted the claim: "We know that all of us possess knowledge [*gnōsis*]" (1 Cor. 8:1). *gnōsis* is here thought to be used in typically gnostic fashion without the article. Hence, it cannot refer merely to knowledge about such food. The important thing is the possession of *gnōsis*. The deduction was drawn that one may eat food offered to idols without any scruples. The one who has *gnōsis* is the one who knows the true being of God and his own originally divine being (cf. 2 Cor. 13:5, where Paul ironically is aiming his shafts at gnostic self-knowledge). He thus recognizes the non-reality of the universe, its earthly, historical relationships and regulations, and finds no problem in eating food offered to idols (cf. Phil. 3:19a; Rev. 2:20) or in immorality (1 Cor. 6:12–20; Phil. 3:19b.; cf. Rev. 2:20). He considers the question of resurrection irrelevant (1 Cor. 15:12; cf. Phil. 3:10–16). For such a man even the historical, earthly Jesus has no relevance (cf. "Jesus be anathema" [1 Cor. 12:3; → Curse]; "enemies of the cross of Christ" [Phil. 3:18]). Christian gnosticism applied the dualism of spirit and matter to its christology which was, therefore, always docetic. Paul measured this gnostic knowledge with the yard-stick of love: "Knowledge puffs up, but love builds up" (1 Cor. 8:2b.). The gnostic with his knowledge was interested only in himself and his claim to a superior freedom loosed from all earthly ties. Love, on the other hand, is concerned with the building up of the church, i.e. with the salvation of others in the fellowship of Jesus Christ, including the weak (1 Cor. 8:9) who do not possess this knowledge (1 Cor. 8:7), and surely also the outsiders and unbelievers (1 Cor. 14:23).

The knowledge claimed by the Corinthians was thus unacceptable to Paul. "If any one imagines that he knows something, he does not yet know as he ought to know" (1 Cor. 8:2). This may be compared with 1 Cor. 15:34, where Paul says that some people have an *agnōsian . . . theou*, "ignorance of God". In view of this, Paul was compelled to explain what he understood by knowledge. He found it possible to express knowledge only passively, as a being known (cf. Gal. 4:9, where he corrects the thought of an active human knowledge of God by adding "or rather to be known by God"). This being known is not the counterpart of some previous active comprehension of God by man, but rather of loving God (cf. 1 Cor. 8:3). Full and real knowledge of God is rather part of the eschatological → promise and expectation (1 Cor. 13:12). Paul totally rejected the fantastic gnostic anticipation of the *eschaton* (→ Goal, art. *eschatos*), in which being known by God and the perfect knowledge of God by man come together by simply disregarding existence on earth and in the body (cf. 2 Tim. 2:18b). For Paul the whole stress lay on God's having known us before time. Thus the *gnōsthēnai*, being known by God, involves election (cf. G. Bornkamm, op. cit., 186). If there is any human knowledge of God, it is the mediated knowledge of God as he revealed himself in the life and work of Christ. It is the Spirit-given "knowledge of God in the face of Jesus Christ" (2 Cor. 4:6). Before the *eschaton* we can know God only as we know Jesus Christ (Phil. 3:10; cf. Col. 2:2 f.). But Christ is not to be known through theological speculation, but rather as one is met by him and as one

402

acknowledges him as the Lord (Phil. 3:8). Such acknowledgement is the counterpart to having been known by God. Where it does not exist, it is useless to speak of knowledge; "if any one does not recognize this, he is not recognized" (1 Cor. 14:38). Hence → love for God is the counterpart of having been known by God (1 Cor. 8:3). Love for God, however, takes shape in new obedience to the Lord Jesus Christ and freedom from the lordship of sin (cf. "in growing conformity with his death" [Phil. 3:10 NEB] with Rom. 6:3–3), in fellowship with Christ's sufferings, and in strenuous service in the resurrection power of Christ, while one presses on to the promised resurrection from the dead (Phil. 3;10). True knowledge is the knowledge which God revealed everywhere through the apostolic witness (2 Cor. 2:14). It is not the final fulfilment. At present it is only fragmentary (1 Cor. 13:12), but it looks to fulfilment. As Paul said in Philem. 6, knowledge is *epignōsis pantos agathou, tou en hēmin eis Christon*, "knowledge of all the good that is ours in Christ." The Corinthian gnostics in their pride did not want to know anything of this knowledge. Hence, Paul ironically demanded of them to "acknowledge that what I am writing to you is a command of the Lord" (1 Cor. 14:37). In the light of all this it is clear that Paul's polemics remain essentially within the limits of the OT concept of knowledge. At the same time he amplifies and works out this concept christologically.

(b) John. The terminology of the Johannine statements about knowledge is influenced by the gnostic outlook as is the Johannine vocabulary and thought-world generally. What this means for the theological statements in Jn. will be discussed later. The gnostic influence on the concept of knowledge may be seen, if the statements involving *ginōskō* are detached from their contexts and examined on their own. The very fact that knowledge can represent a mutual and inner fellowship between Jesus and his own, and between Jesus (the Son) and God (the Father) in Jn. 10:14 f., points to a gnostic background. J. Jeremias (*TDNT* VI 496, note 106), argues, however, that this reflects a Semitism and not Hellenistic mysticism, as R. Bultmann maintains in *The Gospel of John*, 1971, 380 ff. The possibility of describing knowledge as → fellowship is based on the personal equality of the one who knows, the messenger of God who mediates the knowledge, and the God who is to be known who is utterly transcendent. A gnostic and dualistic contrast between God and the world is indicated by the statement that the world cannot receive "the Spirit of truth because it neither sees him nor knows him" (Jn. 14:17). The hatred experienced by Jesus and his disciples (Jn. 15:18; cf. 16:2 f.) is to be understood as a result of the irremovable distinction between the divine and the earthly. Similarly the voice of revelation cannot be recognized as such by those who have the devil and not God as → father (Jn. 8:42–47). Conversely the knowledge of God includes knowledge of the One he has sent and becomes co-terminous with eternal life (Jn. 17:3), as with the gnostics. This knowledge which brings salvation is possible only through the call from outside, the coming of the → Son of God who has given understanding (*dianoia*), i.e. the ability to know him who is true (1 Jn. 5:20).

The dependence of Johannine language and the Johannine view of knowledge on the terminology of gnosticism is understandable if one realizes that the recipients of the Christian message and its opponents influenced the form in which it was expressed. John's purpose is to speak to gnostics and therefore he uses their language. He faces the gnostic on his own ground and combats him with his own weapons. This does not make the gospel a myth or John a gnostic. We should, however, investigate what this may mean for our concept of knowledge.

One might say that John has given the gnostic myth an entirely new orientation. The gnostic understood knowledge as self-knowledge, through which man came to realize that he was a stranger in the universe and also that he was divine. He thus experienced deliverance from the world and history alike. For John, knowledge is of a personal reality that stands over against man. This Other is God mediated by revelation. Since "no one has ever seen God" (Jn. 1:18), there can be no immediate knowledge of God or direct fellowship with God. But God may be known in the One he has sent, his Son (cf. the synoptic parallels Matt. 11:27 and Lk. 10:22). The Son is not, like the saviour in gnosticism, a mythological figure. He bears the historical name Jesus which unambiguously locates him in time and space. He is the Logos (→ Word) who has become → flesh (Jn. 1:14; 1 Jn. 1:1–4). He who sees Jesus sees the Father (Jn. 14:9; 12:45). He who has known him will know the Father also, for he has already known him and seen him (Jn. 14:7). Hence, fellowship with God can come only through fellowship with Jesus, for this fellowship corresponds to Jesus' fellowship with God (Jn. 10:14 f.). On both levels it is expressed by ginōskō.

The fellowship between Jesus and those that are his, made effective by mutual knowledge, does not imply, as in gnosticism, the deification of man and his complete removal from the world and history. In Jn., knowledge gains its form from the one God and his revelation in history through historical channels. By sending his Son, God revealed his love to his own (Jn. 17:23; 1 Jn. 4:9 f.) and to the world (Jn. 3:16). The Son loved his own according to the measure of his Father's love to him (Jn. 15:9; 17:26). Therefore, knowledge by the one loved by God and Jesus finds expression in the sphere of history in love: "He who does not love does not know God; for God is love" (1 Jn. 4:8). Just as the Son demonstrated his love for the Father by obedience to God's → command (Jn. 14:31), so he who knows demonstrates his knowledge by keeping God's command (1 Jn. 2:3 ff.), above all that of loving his → brother (1 Jn. 4:7 f.; cf. 2:7–11), and by not sinning (1 Jn. 3:6). Thus ginōskō has a double application: it means knowing the love of God shown in the sending of his Son (Jn. 17:8; 1 Jn. 3:16), and the obedience of love based on it which is also described as obedience to the message proclaimed (1 Jn. 4:6). Such knowledge is already eternal → life here and now (Jn. 17:3), because it is a life in history derived from God's historical revelation. In view of all this, John's concept stands out as deliberately and diametrically opposed to that of gnosticism.

The striking equation of → faith and knowledge in the relationship of man to God is also part of the polemic against gnosticism which at the very least depreciated faith in contrast to knowledge. While Jn. 17:3 attributes eternal life to knowledge, Jn. 3:36 attributes it to faith. In the Johannine version of Peter's confession (Jn. 5:69) one might be tempted to see faith as the first step subordinate to knowledge, but in 1 Jn. 4:16 the order is "know and believe."

Gnostic self-satisfaction which is concerned only with one's own salvation is opposed by emphasis on the existence of the church in brotherly love (Jn. 13:35) and unity (Jn. 17:21 ff.). Moreover, the ultimate goal behind this will be reached only when the world comes to believe that the Son has been sent, and when this revelation becomes known throughout the universe. Such an affirmation is possible only if John does not share the gnostic dualism of cosmos (creation) and salvation. For the gnostic this dualism was insurmountable, because it was decreed by a pre-cosmic fall. According to the gnostic view, the universe was completely and fatally incapable of knowing God and of being redeemed. For John the world remains God's creation (Jn. 1:1 ff.; cf. 1 Jn. 2:14). Not to know, which showed itself in hatred against Jesus and his disciples, is a result of refusing to believe the revelation given (Jn. 8:42 f.) which in turn incurs guilt (cf. E. Käsemann, *Ver-kündigung und Forschung*, 1946², 192 f.). "If the 'Jews' are unable to understand, it is because they are unable truly to hear. They are prepared to hear only what they already know, even though of course they are interested in deepening and enriching this knowledge; but they are not prepared to hear anything new, and so to surrender all that they knew before, and with it the condition of such knowledge, their own understanding of themselves. They *cannot* hear in this way! To raise the question why they cannot hear would only be to show a lack of understanding that in this sphere being able to do something and willing to do something are one and the same" (R. Bultmann, op. cit., 317). The summons to knowledge and faith thus remains even for the world; God's love for the world in sending his Son which is now presented as something real has opened up a new dimension of reality.

Although Jn.'s vocabulary has clear affinities with gnosticism, his subject matter equally clearly stands much nearer to the concept of knowledge in the OT tradition than the mythical speculations of gnosticism.

4. *Later developments.* (a) In the Pastorals, and to some extent in 2 Pet., *epignōsis* has received a special stamp through the controversy with gnosticism which deviates from the OT usage. In the earlier Pauline Epistles and the Johannine writings church doctrine was still in the course of development in the controversy with gnosticism. In the Pastorals, however, a definite doctrinal tradition is evident, and all entanglement with "godless and silly myths" (1 Tim. 4:7) is forbidden. Hence, gnostic terminology has been in great measure eliminated and replaced by other terms. *gnōsis* is regarded as a technical term for the gnostic heresy (cf. 1 Tim. 6:20) and *epignōsis* takes its place, when it refers to Christian knowledge (1 Tim. 2:4; 2 Tim. 2:25; 2:7; Tit. 1:1). It has, however, quite clearly an intellectual, semi-dogmatic stress. The knowledge of God's truth is of equal importance with experi-ential profession of the Lord, and finally pushes it into the background. Hence, conversion to the Christian faith can be described almost technically as coming to a knowledge (*epignōsis*) of the truth (1 Tim. 2:4; 2 Tim. 3:7; cf. Heb. 10:26; 1 Tim. 5:3; 2 Tim. 2:25; Tit. 1:1; 2 Pet. 2:21). Examples of this concept of truth may be found in Eth.Enoch 105:2 and Sib. 1:20.

In 2 Pet. *epignōsis* is used in a similar theoretical, technical way in connection with God's call. Knowledge is here of the orthodox tradition, of the catholic doctrinal teaching (2 Pet. 1:2, 3, 8; 2:20) which, as in the Pastorals, must become effective in a corresponding manner of life. It is interesting that *gnōsis* has a good sense in 2 Pet. (cf. 1:5 f.; 3:18). This does not apply to ch. 2, where an anti-gnostic writing (Jude) has been incorporated which uses only *epignōsis* (2:20) and *epiginōskō* (2:21).

(b) The controversies of early Christianity with gnosticism had a decisive

405

effect on many aspects of the church's teaching and concepts. They partly explain the development of the office of teacher (→ Bishop) by which correct exegesis of Scripture was to be guaranteed, and the fixing of the canon of Scripture so as to exclude heretical writings from the church's use. The drawing up of various creeds finds its place here also. Gnostic influences continued for a long time to show their influence on Church theology (for evidence of gnosticism in the early church see W. Foerster, *Gnosis: A Selection of Gnostic Texts*, I, *Patristic Evidence*, 1972).

E. D. Schmitz

ἀγνοέω

ἀγνοέω (*agnoeō*), not know, be ignorant; ἀγνόημα (*agnoēma*), error; ἄγνοια (*agnoia*), ignorance; ἀγνωσία (*agnōsia*), lack of knowledge; ἄγνωστος (*agnōstos*), unknown.

CL & OT *agnoeō* means not to know and is used against the full background of the Gk. concept of knowledge (→ *ginōskō*). It does not refer merely to something not grasped by the mind, but can also mean make a mistake or be in error. In Dan. 9:15 it is used beside *hamartanō*, to sin. Similarly *agnoēma* (in the NT only in Heb. 9:7) is used not merely for error but also for an offence done in ignorance. *agnoia* similarly refers not only to the fact of not knowing, but can be used in a general sense for ignorance or lack of education. The positive opposites are *gnōsis* (→ *ginōskō*) and *sophia* (→ Wisdom). The Stoics considered ignorance to be the root of all evil, and sometimes identified the two. In the Hellenistic terminology of gnostic dualism *agnōsia* was "lack of the knowledge essential to the salvation of the soul, i.e., the knowledge about God, of the fate of the soul and of true direction for life" (R. Bultmann, *TDNT* I 118). If a man was living without knowledge, it was either because he had not received the revelation or had refused it. Had he received it, it would have freed him from his ignorance of his origin.

In legal settings *agnoia* means ignorance of the law; *kat' agnoian* means unwittingly (e.g. Lev. 22:14). The LXX uses *agnoia* (mostly for Heb. *'āšām*) concretely in the sense of *agnoēma*, also meaning (unintentional) → guilt, offence, error, generally (e.g. Lev. 5:18). *agnōstos*, meaning both unknowable and unknown, is found in the LXX, without Heb. equivalent, and Acts 17:23 (only here in the NT) only in the latter sense.

NT *agnoeō* is found 21 times in NT (15 times in Paul), but *agnoia* only 4 times, *agnōsia* twice, *agnoēma* and *agnōstos* each twice.

1. *agnoeō* occurs in the following senses:

(a) Not to understand in the sense of not being able to grasp (Mk. 9:32 and Lk. 9:45, in each case of a passion prediction by Jesus).

(b) Not to know, not be informed (e.g. 2 Pet. 2:12, where the godless revile in matters they do not know, about which they have not been informed); especially in the phrase *ou thelō hymas agnoein*, "I do not want you to be ignorant", i.e. uninformed (RSV sometimes "I want you to know") (Rom. 1:13; 11:25; 1 Cor. 10:1; 12:1; 2 Cor. 1:8; 1 Thess. 4:13), always with the address "brethren". The implicit double negative is used by Paul to stress that he wishes to end his readers' lack of knowledge by making them share in his knowledge. *agnoeō* is used also in the formula *ē agnoeite*, "or do you not know?" (Rom. 6:3; 7:1, "or" omitted by RSV) with the force of not knowing, or perhaps rather of failing to realize. In both passages a present knowledge is presupposed which implies a need to respond to the gospel. Almost all the passages cited above deal with a partial recognition of faith in Christ, as the object of *agnoeō*. It never means merely a lack of intellectual knowledge which can be removed by a neutral statement of facts. It is used in the OT sense. This lack of knowledge can be removed only by knowledge intimately linked with an existential recognition and acceptance (cf. *ginōskō* CL and OT).

(c) An ignorance that leads astray. In 1 Tim. 1:13 Paul, looking back on his past, says, "I received mercy because I had acted ignorantly in unbelief." Ignorance is here the trait that marked out his life that had gone astray until his → conversion to the Christian faith which always includes knowledge. The same shade of meaning is found in Heb. 5:2, "ignorant and wayward". OT language is here used, contrasting unknowing, unintentional → sins with deliberate ones. In the context, the meaning of *agnoeō* is expanded from unknowing to undesired, so that it comes to denote the sins for which there is atonement in contrast to those for which there is none.

(d) A failure to know in the sense of a disobedient closing of the mind to the revealing word of God (Acts 13:27; Rom. 10:3). This is not simply a lack of knowledge, but "a false understanding, a false path in knowing and thinking" (O. Michel *Der Brief an die Römer*, KEK 4, 1966[13], on Rom. 10:3). Ignorance and disobedience are here used as parallels; ignorance is the guilty turning away from the revelation of God in Jesus Christ. The guilty ignorance of the Jews cannot be conquered by introspection or some kind of self-reformation. It can only be dealt with by God himself as he forgives and reveals himself in the gospel. This is not merely an erring ignorance (see above (c)). It reflects the OT link between knowledge and right conduct (and correspondingly between wilful rejection of knowledge and judgment). (On the consequent hardening of Israel → Hard.)

1 Cor. 14:38 should probably be included in this connection: "If anyone does not recognize [*agnoei*], he is not recognized [*agnoeitai*]." The second half of the verse speaks of God's recognition. For Paul is claiming to speak by "a command of the Lord" (v. 37). Hence, to reject the command is to reject God with the implied corollary that this involves non-recognition by not only Paul but by God himself.

(e) To be unknown. In 2 Cor. 6:9 Paul says that he is "unknown", i.e. to the world, for he is not included among its great ones. On the other hand, he was well known to God and the church. See also Gal. 1:22.

2. (a) In Acts 3:17 *agnoia* is used in the juridical sense of the LXX. The guilt of the Jews is, from the viewpoint of the subject, a sin arising from ignorance. On the other hand, the Stoic-Jewish sense is found in the other cases of its use, among them being some which betray gnostic usage (→ *ginōsko*). Acts 17:30 refers to past heathenism as ignorance (cf. Acts 14:16; Rom. 3:25). The history of mankind is from the point of view of salvation divided into two periods; before and after Christ. The period before the decisive and basic revelation of God in Christ is characterized by the ignorance which prevailed. "The times of ignorance God overlooked, but now he commands all men everywhere to repent."

(b) *agnōstos* in Acts 17:23 means simply unknown in the inscription "To an unknown God" on an altar at Athens. Paul addressed the Athenians as those who had until then honoured the unknown God without knowledge, but whom he was now proclaiming as the revealed One. The unknown God among the gods is in fact the true and only One. He is the God of the OT and of salvation-history. The mention of ignorance was not intended to justify and excuse men; it was to introduce them to God's saving purposes and to lead them to the joy of repentance. (On the inscription see F. F. Bruce, *The Acts of the Apostles*, 1952², 335 f.; and E. Haenchen, *The Acts of the Apostles*, 1971, 516, 520 ff.; → God, art. *theos* NT 1 (d), 4 (b)).

E. Schütz

→ God, → Light, → Myth, → Reason, → Revelation, → Secret, → Truth, → Wisdom

On knowledge and experience in general:

(a). G. Bornkamm, "The Revelation of God's Wrath (Romans 1–3)", in *Early Christian Experience*, 1969, 47–70; E. Brunner, *Truth as Encounter: A New Edition, Much Enlarged, of The Divine-Human Encounter*, 1964; R. Bultmann, *agnoeō* etc., *TDNT* I 115–21; and *ginōskō* etc., *TDNT* I 689–719; W. D. Davies, " 'Knowledge' in the Dead Sea Scrolls and Matthew 11:25–30", *HTR* 46, 1953, 113–39, reprinted in *Christian Origins and Judaism*, 1962, 119–44; C. H. Dodd, "Knowledge of God", in *The Interpretation of the Fourth Gospel*, 1953, 151–69; G. Delling, *aisthanomai* etc., *TDNT* I 187 f.; E. E. Ellis, " 'Wisdom' and 'Knowledge' in I Corinthians", *TB* 25, 1974, 82–98; B. Gärtner, *The Areopagus Speech and Natural Revelation*, 1955; J. B. Lightfoot, *The Epistles of Paul to the Colossians and to Philemon*, 1879, 137 f.; J. A. Robinson, *St. Paul's Epistle to the Ephesians*, 1904, 249 ff.; cf. the comments on Lightfoot and Robinson by R. E. Picirilli, "The Meaning of 'Epignosis' ", *EQ* 47, 1975, 88 ff.; B. Reicke, "Da'at and Gnosis in Intertestamental Literature", in E. E. Ellis and M. Wilcox, eds., *Neotestamentica et Semitica: Studies in Honour of Matthew Black*, 1969, 245–55; N. B. Stonehouse, *Paul before the Areopagus and Other New Testament Studies*, 1957; H. Zimmermann, "Knowledge of God", *EBT* II 472–78.

(b). E. Baumann, "*yāḏaʿ* und seine Derivate", *ZAW* 28, 1908, 22 ff., 110 ff.; and " 'Wissen um Gott' bei Hosea als Urform der Theologie?", *EvTh* 15, 1955, 416 ff.; G. J. Botterweck, "*Gott erkennen*" *im Sprachgebrauch des Alten Testaments*, *Bonner Biblische Beiträge* 2, 1951; A. Fridrichsen, "Gnosis: Et Bidrag til Belysning ave den Paulinske Terminologi og Erkjennelsesteori", *Festschrift E. Lahmann*, 1927, 85–109; F. Hesse, *Das Verstockungsproblem im Alten Testament*, *BZAW* 74, 1955; K. Niederwimmer, *Der Begriff der Freiheit im Neuen Testament*, 1966; E. Norden, *Agnostos Theos*, (1913) 1971⁵; F. Nötscher, *Zur theologischen Terminologie der Qumran-Texte*, 1956, 15–79; R. Prenter, *Connaître Christ*, 1966; E. Prucker, *Gnōsis Theou. Untersuchungen zur Bedeutung eines religiösen Begriffs beim Apostel und bei seiner Umwelt*, 1937; H. Schlier, "Gnosis", in *Handbuch theologischer Grundbegriffe*, I, 1962, 562 ff.; W. Schottroff, *yāḏaʿ*, *THAT* I 682–701; *Die Ausdrücke für den Begriff des Wissens in der vorplatonischen Philosophie*, *Philologische Untersuchungen*, 29, 1924; and *Platon, Mit den Augen des Geistes*, 1955; H. W. Wolff, " 'Wissen um Gott' bei Hosea als Urform von Theologie", *EvTh* 12, 1952–53, 533 ff.; and "Erkenntnis Gottes im Alten Testament", *EvTh* 15, 1955, 426 ff.; W. Zimmerli, *Erkenntnis Gottes nach dem Buch Ezechiel*, *AThANT* 27, 1954.

Works on gnosticism and its bearing on the NT:

(a). A complete critical edition of the Nag Hammadi codices and Codex Berolinensis 8502 is under preparation in *The Coptic Gnostic Library*, published under the auspices of The Institute for Antiquity and Christianity. Other editions of texts and discussions include: C. K. Barrett, "The Theological Vocabulary of the Fourth Gospel and the Gospel of Truth", in W. Klassen and G. F. Snyder, eds., *Current Issues in New Testament Interpretation: Essays in Honor of Otto A. Piper*, 1962, 210–23; W. Bauer, *Orthodoxy and Heresy in Earliest Christianity*, 1971; F. H. Borsch, *The Christian and Gnostic Son of Man* ,1970; R. Bultmann, *Primitive Christianity in its Contemporary Setting*, 1956; and *The Gospel of John*, 1971; F. C. Burkitt, *Church and Gnosis*, 1932; R. P. Casey, "Gnosis, Gnosticism and the New Testament", in W. D. Davies and D. Daube, eds., *The Background of the New Testament and its Eschatology. In Honour of Charles Harold Dodd*, 1956, 52–80; H. Chadwick, "Gnosticism", *OCD*, 470 f.; F. L. Cross, ed., *The Jung Codex: A Newly Recovered Gnostic Papyrus*, 1955; J. Doresse, *The Secret Books of the Egyptian Gnostics: An Introduction to the Gnostic Coptic Manuscripts discovered at Chenoboskion; With an English Translation and Critical Evaluation of the Gospel according to Thomas*, 1960; J. W. Drane, "Gnosticism and the New Testament 1", *Theological Students Fellowship Bulletin* 68, 1974, 6–13; "Gnosticism and the

New Testament 2", ibid. 69, 1974, 1–7; E. S. Drower, "A Mandaean Bibliography", *Journal of the Royal Asiatic Society*, 1953, 34–39; W. Foerster, *Gnosis: A Selection of Gnostic Texts*, I, *Patristic Evidence*, 1972; II, *Coptic and Mandaic Sources*, 1974; B. Gärtner, *The Theology of the Gospel of Thomas*, 1961; R. M. Grant, *Gnosticism: An Anthology*, 1961; and *Gnosticism and Early Christianity*, 1966²; R. M. Grant and D. N. Freedman, *The Secret Sayings of Jesus, With an English Translation of the Gospel of Thomas*, 1960; K. Grobel, *The Gospel of Truth: A Valentinian Meditation on the Gospel*, 1960; R. Haardt, *Gnosis: Character and Testimony*, 1971; E. Hennecke and W. Schneemelcher, eds., *New Testament Apocrypha*, I–II 1963–65; R. A. Johnson, *The Origins of Demythologizing: Philosophy and Historiography in the Theology of Rudolf Bultmann*, *Supplements to Numen* 28, 1974; H. Jonas, *The Gnostic Religion: The Message of the Alien God and the Beginnings of Christianity*, 1963²; R. Macuch, *Handbook of Classical and Modern Mandaic*, 1965; H. Montefiore and H. E. W. Turner, *Thomas and the Evangelists*, 1962; J. Munck, "The New Testament and Gnosticism", in W. Klassen and G. F. Snyder, eds., op. cit., 224–38; A. D. Nock, "Gnosticism", *HTR* 57, 1964, 255–79 (reprinted in *Essays on Religion and the Ancient World*, II, 1972, 940 ff.); E. H. Pagels, *The Gnostic Paul: Gnostic Exegesis of the Pauline Letters*, 1975; M. L. Peel, *The Epistle to Rheginos: A Valentinian Letter on the Resurrection*, 1969; H. C. Puech, "Gnosis and Time", *Papers from Eranos Yearbooks, Man and Time*, 1958; G. Quispel, "Gnosis", *Vox Theologica*, 39, 1969, 27–35; and "Gnosticism and the New Testament", in J. P. Hyatt, ed., *The Bible in Modern Scholarship*, 1965, 252–71; with responses by R. Mc. L. Wilson and H. Jonas, op. cit., 272–93; B. Reicke, "Traces of Gnosticism in the Dead Sea Scrolls?" *NTS* 1, 1954–55, 137–41; A. Richardson, "Gnosis and Revelation in the Bible and in Contemporary Thought", *SJT* 9, 1956, 31–45; W. Schmithals, *Paul and James*, SBT 46, 1963; *Gnosticism in Corinth*, 1971; and *Paul and the Gnostics*, 1972; R. Schnackenburg, "The Gnostic Myth of the Redeemer and the Johannine Christology", *The Gospel according to St. John*, I, 1968, 543–57; W. C. van Unnik, *Newly Discovered Gnostic Writings: A Preliminary Survey of the Nag Hammadi Find*, 1960; E. Voegelin, "History and Gnosis", in B. W. Anderson, ed., *The Old Testament and Christian Faith*, 1964, 64–89; R. McL. Wilson, *The Gnostic Problem*, 1958; *Studies in the Gospel of Thomas*, 1960; *The Gospel of Philip*, 1962; "Gnostics – in Galatia?", *StudEv*, IV 1, 1968, 358–67; *Gnosis and the New Testament*, 1968; E. M. Yamauchi, *Mandaic Incantation Texts*, 1967; "The Present Status of Mandaean Studies", *JNES* 25, 1966, 88–96; *Gnostic Ethics and Mandaean Origins*, 1970; and *Pre-Christian Gnosticism: A Survey of the Proposed Evidences*, 1973.
(b). U. Bianchi, ed., *Le Origini dello Gnosticismo, Colloquio di Messina 13–18 Aprile 1966, Studies in the History of Religions* (Supplements to *Numen*) 12, 1967; A. Böhlig, *Mysterion und Wahrheit. Gesammelte Beiträge zur spätantiken Religionsgeschichte*, 1968; W. Bousset, "Gnosis", Pauly-Wissowa VII 1502 ff.; and "Gnostiker", ibid., 1534 ff.; L. Cerfaux, "De Saint Paul a l'Évangile de la Verité", *NTS* 5, 1958–59, 103–12; J. Dupont, *Gnosis: La Connaissance Religieuse dans les Épîtres de Saint Paul*, 1949; W. Eltester, ed., *Christentum und Gnosis*, BZNW 37, 1969; E. de Faye, *Gnostiques et Gnosticisme*, 1925²; A.-J. Festugière, *La Révélation d'Hermès Trismégiste*, I–IV, 1949–54; D. Georgi, *Die Gegner des Paulus im 2. Korintherbrief*, 1964; H. Jonas, *Gnosis und spätantiker Geist*, I, *Die mythologische Gnosis* (1934) 1964³, II, *Von der Mythologie zur mystischen Philosophie*, 1954; J. Krull, *Die Lehre des Hermes Trismegistos, Beiträge zur Geschichte der Philosophie des Mittelalters*, 12, 1914; H. Leisegang, *Die Gnosis*, 1955⁴; G. Quispel, *Gnosis als Weltreligion*, 1951; R. Reitzenstein, *Das mandäische Buch des Herrn der Grösse und die Evangelienüberlieferung*, 1919; *Poimandres* (1904) 1966; *Die hellenistischen Mysterienreligionen* 1927; and *Die Vorgeschichte der christlichen Taufe* (1929) 1967; K. Rudolf, *Die Mandäer*, I–II, 1960–61; K. Rudolf, ed., *Gnosis und Gnostizismus*, 1975; K.-W. Tröger, ed., *Gnosis und Neues Testament. Studien aus Religionswissenschaft und Theologie*, 1973.

L

Lamb, Sheep

In the ancient world sheep together with other small livestock were kept in herds, and for that reason are usually referred to in the plural. The word *probaton*, which is relatively frequent in the NT, was originally a generic term for all four-legged animals, especially tame domestic animals, only later was it restricted to sheep. *amnos* denoted from the outset a young sheep, frequently a one-year-old lamb, especially as used for sacrifice on numerous cultic occasions. In non-sacrificial contexts, the lamb as an animal for slaughter was called *arēn*. The diminutive form *arnion* originally meant lambkin, but later simply a lamb. In a figurative theological context (especially in Matt. and Jn.) Israel and the Christian church are often referred to as sheep (*probata*), and occasionally (in Jn. and 1 Pet.) Jesus is likened to a lamb, *amnos* (in Jn.), *arnion* (in Rev.).

> ἀμνός

ἀμνός (*amnos*), lamb; ἀρήν (*arēn*), lamb; ἀρνίον (*arnion*), lamb.

CL *amnos*, found infrequently from Sophocles and Aristophanes onwards, denotes a lamb as distinct from → *probaton*, sheep. In the LXX both *amnos* and *arēn* are used, while *arnion* is no longer felt to be a diminutive, either in the LXX or in the NT.

OT In the OT *amnos* (Hebrew *kebeś*) is used chiefly in passages classed among the Priestly writings and in Ezek., i.e. in writings of a cultic and sacrificial character. The lamb plays an important role as a sacrificial animal in Israel's public worship. Lambs are presented as burnt offerings and sacrifices (Lev. 9:3, Num. 15:5) to atone for and to cleanse the people as a whole or individual persons (e.g. → lepers, Lev. 14:10) at the sanctuary. According to Exod. 12:5, at the yearly Passover → feast each family consumed a lamb that was without blemish, a male a year old, in memory of the exodus from Egypt. (At the exodus itself the blood of the lamb was smeared upon the door-posts and lintels of Jewish houses [Exod. 12:7, 13, 23].) In his prophecy of the new temple Ezek. mentions lambs as gifts for the → Sabbath-offering and the feast-offering (46:4, 11). Isa. 53:7 is particularly illuminating: the patiently suffering → Servant of the Lord is compared with a lamb being led to the slaughter and remaining dumb before its shearers. Here for the first time a person is spoken of as fulfilling the function of a sacrificial animal. Acts 8:32 cites Isa. 53:7, and sees in the passage a reference to the "good news of Jesus" (Acts 8:35).

NT 1. In the NT Jesus is described 4 times as *amnos* (Jn. 1:29, 36; Acts 8:32; 1 Pet. 1:19). In Jn. 1:29, 36 John the Baptist describes Jesus, whom he has baptized, as *ho amnos tou theou*, "the lamb of God". This is not merely a comparison in which Jesus is said to be *like* a lamb; rather he *is* the lamb of God. Both Acts 8:32 and 1 Pet. 1:19 contain *hōs* (as), but this is not true of Jn. 1:29, 36. J. Jeremias (*TDNT* I 339) suggests that this phrase may have been borrowed from Isa. 53, and also from the Passover lamb idea. He points out that the Aramaic word *ṭalyā'* means both lamb and boy, servant, and says that the meaning "servant" makes the genitive intelligible: Jesus, the servant of God. Then this led eventually to the possible (but most likely not the original) translation *amnos tou theou*.

Interesting and thought-provoking as this is, it is preferable to understand this unusual genitive construction in the light of the relative clause *ho airōn tēn hamartian tou kosmou* ("that takes away the sin of the world") and to link this with Isa. 53: the lamb (of God) bears the sin of the world. (For interpretation of the Servant see H. H. Rowley, *The Servant of the Lord and Other Essays*, 1965².)

If "lamb" stands for "offering", then the Baptist's statement becomes clear. No offerings brought by men can take away the sin of the world. But God himself provides an offering, which does indeed take it away. He gave his only Son and did not spare him (cf. Rom. 8:31–32, probably an echo of Gen. 22). There is a considerable contrast between the Baptist's words in Jn. 1:29 and those in the Synoptic Gospels, where messiah is said to be coming with his fan in his hand, sweeping his threshing floor (Matt. 3:12; Lk. 3:17). Jn. 1:29, however, is to be seen against the background of Jesus' baptism (1:32–34), when he publicly identified himself with sinners and their lot. Once God has delivered up his Son to death the eschatological time of salvation can be said to have begun.

In the NT Jesus is described as a lamb in three different respects: (a) Acts 8:32 stresses his patient suffering; (b) 1 Pet. 1:19 emphasizes the sinlessness and perfection of his sacrifice by the phrase "without blemish and without spot"; (c) Jn. 1:29, 36 describe the atoning power of his death: he bears, i.e. wipes out, the sin of the world (cf. J. Jeremias, *TDNT* I 340).

2. *arēn* occurs once in the NT in Lk. 10:3, where it is said that the disciples will be as defenceless as sheep among wolves (→ Animal).

3. *arnion*. In Jn. 21:15 Christ exhorts Peter: "Feed my lambs [*boske ta arnia mou*]". "The church belongs to Christ, and needs faithful pastoral oversight by his disciple (cf. Augustine: "Feed my sheep as mine and not as yours [*oves meas pasce sicut meas, non sicut tuas*]" (*Tractatus in Ioannis Evangelium* 123). Apart from Jn. 21:15, *arnion* is found exclusively in Rev. (27 times). It is important to note the observation by J. Jeremias (*TDNT* I 340) that by the NT period this word was no longer thought of as a diminutive. There is therefore no biblical basis for referring to Christ as a "lambkin", however endearing the idea may be. The thought is rather that the judge of all the earth is he who died for us, and even as sovereign Lord he still bears the marks of his passion (Rev. 5:6).

arnion occurs 4 times in Rev. 5 (vv. 6, 8, 12 f.), where Christ is seen in this twofold aspect. On the one hand, he is the Lord, the one who opens the seals and who is to be worshipped. On the other hand, he is *esphagmenon arnion* ("a lamb that was slain") having redeemed men of all races to God by his → blood, and made them → kings and → priests (Rev. 5:9, 10). He is both *arnion* and *leōn*, a lion (→

411

Animal). The eschatological wrath from which kings, rulers, freemen and slaves all wish to hide is *orgē tou arniou*, "the wrath of the Lamb" (Rev. 6:16). In ch. 7 it is said that the blood of the Lamb has cleansing power. The robes of the martyrs were cleansed not by their martyrdom, severe as it was, but solely by the blood of the Lamb. The Lamb is worshipped at the same time as God (7:10). Rev. 19:7, 9 speaks of the marriage of the Lamb, the church being the bride. The 12 apostles are called apostles of the Lamb. God and the Lamb illumine the city of God (21:14, 23).

4. In summary it can be said that *amnos tou theou* denotes God's offering, Christ, whom he destined to bear the sin of the world, while *arnion* emphasizes the fact that he who is eternal Lord is also Christ crucified for us.   *J. Gess*

| πρόβατον | πρόβατον (*probaton*), sheep.

CL In Gk. antiquity the word *probaton* in its widest sense denoted all four-footed animals (especially tame, domestic ones) as opposed to swimming and creeping animals. It is possible that the word derives from the vb. *pro-bainō*, to go before. In mixed herds it was the small livestock (especially the sheep) which, being weaker than the other animals, went ahead of them. At first the word was used only in the plur. (i.e. of a flock or herd), but later the sing. use appeared, meaning specifically a sheep. Aristophanes (*Nubes*, 1203) uses it metaphorically as a term of abuse: anything inferior or stupid (e.g. a simpleton) is likened to a sheep. It can also have a positive sense, however, being used as a metaphor for a person who needs to be guided by someone else (Epictetus, *Dissertationes*, 3, 22, 35).

OT As a translation of Heb. *ṣō'n* (small livestock) *probaton* in the OT means primarily the sheep as a useful and gregarious animal (Gen. 30:38, Isa. 7:21; Amos 7:15), and less as a sacrifice (Lev. 1:2; for this the more frequent word is → *amnos*, Heb. *keḇeś*, the lamb available for sacrifice). *probaton* (almost exclusively in the plur. *probata*) is used metaphorically for "the people" (under the king as *poimēn*, → shepherd; 2 Sam. 24:17), especially God's people (Ps. 74:1, the congregation; 77:20; 78:52). The essential point here is the sheep's need of protection. Without the shepherd's guidance the flock is scattered (Ezek. 34:5, 6); each sheep goes its own way (Isa. 53:6); the sheep wander about and fall victims to the dangers of the wilderness (Ezek. 34:5 f.); they must be guided by a skilful shepherd to the right pastures if they are to survive (Ps. 23). Hence, the people of Israel in the wilderness, and without a leader, are like "sheep which have no shepherd" (Num. 27:17). The individual also, without God's guidance, "goes astray like a lost sheep" (Ps. 119:176). Yahweh himself provides for his scattered flock by appointing shepherds such as the messianic king (Jer. 23:1 ff.; Ezek. 34:23), or → Moses (Ps. 77:20; Isa. 63:11), or by himself acting as the shepherd of his people (Ps. 78:52 f.; 80:1; Isa. 40:11). By repeatedly calling themselves God's sheep, therefore, the people of Israel were acknowledging first that, left to themselves, they were defenceless, and secondly that they were trusting in the guidance of their own good shepherd, Yahweh himself (Ps. 23; 95:7; 100:3).

NT In the NT *probaton* is remarkably frequent in Matt. (11 times) and in Jn (17 times), compared with the other books.

1. From the use which Jesus makes of sheep in his parables and teaching, it is clear that his contemporaries understood very well how utterly lost a sheep was if left to itself without a shepherd's care (Lk. 15:4). They knew that a sheep's great need was loving, unselfish protection (Matt. 12:11; Lk. 15:4), and this basic fact lies behind Christ's use of the metaphor. A sheep without a shepherd is "harassed and helpless" (Matt. 9:36), it "strays" (1 Pet. 2:25) and is "lost" (Matt. 10:6; 15:24). In following OT usage and likening his people to a flock of sheep without a shepherd (Mk. 6:34; cf. Num. 27:17; 1 Ki. 22:17), Jesus draws attention to the fact that they are heading for certain destruction, unless deliverance is forthcoming. In the same way Christians in 1 Pet. are reminded that before their conversion they were "straying like sheep" (1 Pet. 2:25), i.e. hopelessly lost and at the mercy of false shepherds (cf. Ezek. 34:5). But Jesus is "the great shepherd of the sheep" (Heb. 13:20), who is sent first of all to "the lost sheep of the house of Israel" (Matt. 15:24).

2. On the other hand, the term "sheep" is applied in Matt. to the exclusive band of disciples gathered by Jesus. In sending them forth to preach (10:16; cf. *arnas*, lambs, Lk. 10:3), Jesus likens them to defenceless sheep sent by the shepherd into the midst of ferocious wolves, i.e. the church of the last days is under the constant threat of dispersal by its enemies (Matt. 26:31 par. Mk. 14:27). This quotation applies to Jesus and the disciples the prophecy of Zech. 13:7 which reads in the MT: "Strike the shepherd and the flock [*ṣō'n*] will be scattered," and in the LXX "Strike the shepherd and scatter the sheep [*probata*]." It is interpreted christologically in the Gospels, with the implication that Jesus' followers are the true Israel and that it is God who will smite Jesus. The context of Zech. suggests that it is a judgment on the shepherd. The "sheep" who consciously or unconsciously have done the will of God will not be finally separated from the goats until the shepherd himself separates them at the great day of judgment (Matt. 25:32 f.).

3. Whereas in Matt. the thought is more of the flock being gathered from among the lost sheep of the people of Israel (10:6; 15:24), in Jn. *probaton* denotes Christ's elect people, "his own" (10:14). The sheep know the → voice of their shepherd, hear his call and follow him. As the good shepherd, Jesus knows his sheep, calls them, guards them from the wolf and lays down his life for them (Jn. 10:1-11). Whereas in Matt. the relation between shepherd and flock is that of king to the people of God, in Jn. the shepherd is the Son who comes forth from God in order to reveal him, while the flock is the church listening to his voice. When there is "one flock and one shepherd" (Jn. 10:16; cf. 17:20 f.), i.e. when at last Jews and Gentiles are gathered into one church under one Lord, then the purpose of Christ's saving work is achieved.

4. As in the OT, *probaton* hardly ever means a sacrificial animal (only in Jn. 2:14; Acts 8:32; Rom. 8:36), this idea being expressed in the NT mainly by the words → *amnos* and *arnion*, especially as metaphors for Christ in his vicarious suffering and sovereign power. *R. Tuente*

→ Animal, → Servant, → Shepherd

(a). C. K. Barrett, "The Lamb of God", *NTS* 1, 1955–56, 210 ff.; J. B. Bauer, "Lamb of God", *EBT* II 478 f.; J. Blenkinsopp, "The Lamb of God", *Clergy Review*, 50, 1965, 868–72; G. S.

Cansdale, *Animals of Bible Lands*, 1970; C. H. Dodd, *The Interpretation of the Fourth Gospel*, 1953, 230–38; J. D'Souza, *The Lamb of God in Johannine Writings*, 1968; G. Florovsky, "The Lamb of God", *SJT* 4, 1951, 13–28; A. T. Hanson, *The Wrath of the Lamb*, 1957; N. Hillyer, " 'The Lamb' in the Apocalypse", *EQ* 39, 1967, 228–36; J. Jeremias, *amnos* etc., *TDNT* I 338–41; E. E. May, *Ecce Agnus Dei: A Philological and Exegetical Approach to John 1:29–36*, 1947; L. Morris, *The Gospel According to John*, 1971, 143 ff.; H. Preisker and S. Schulz, *probaton* etc., *TDNT* VI 689–92; E. M. Sidebottom, *The Christ of the Fourth Gospel in the Light of First Century Thought*, 1961; J. G. S. S. Thomson, "The Shepherd-Ruler Concept in the OT and its Application in the NT", *SJT* 8, 1955, 406–18; W. Tooley, "The Shepherd and the Sheep Image in the Teaching of Jesus", *NovT* 7, 1964–65, 15 ff.; S. Virgulin, "Recent Discussion on the 'Lamb of God' ", *Scripture* 13, 1961, 74–80.

(b.) C. Burchard, "Das Lamm in der Waagschale", *ZNW* 57, 1966, 219 ff.; F. Gryglewicz, "Das Lamm Gottes", *NTS* 13, 1966–67, 133–46; T. Holtz, *Die Christologie der Apokalypse des Johannes*, *TU* 85, 1962; J. Jeremias, "Das Lamm, das aus der Jungfrau hervorging (Test.Jos. 19, 8)", *ZNW* 57, 1966, 216 ff.; K. Koch, "Das Lamm, das Ägypten vernichtet. Ein Fragment aus Jannes und Jambres und sein geschichtlicher Hintergrund", *ZNW* 57, 1966, 79 ff.

Lame, Crippled

These two words are closely related functionally in popular usage. A cripple is generally understood to be someone deprived of the use of a limb or a member of the body, or one who is partially disabled and thus lacks the natural functions of a limb. While a lame person is also disabled, the particular area affected is thought of in terms of the legs. Hence one who is lame moves about with some difficulty, perhaps walking with a limp, and may well experience pain in the process.

κυλλός

κυλλός (*kyllos*), crooked, crippled, maimed.

CL In Greek medical authors *kyllos* was used of crooked or disabled legs, feet and ears, though properly of legs bent outwards by diseases such as rickets or disabled through badly reduced fractures or other forms of surgical accident. This contrasted with the condition described in Hippocrates and some non-medical authors as *blaisos*, in which the legs bent in at the knees (*genu varum*) and the feet splayed out somewhat. The background of *kyllos* was predominantly medical, but occasionally the term was used metaphorically.

OT Being of a rather rare and technical nature, the word *kyllos* did not occur in the LXX or other Gk. versions of the OT or Apocrypha. Similarly there is no single Heb. word for cripple, the closest being the late Heb. adj. *'iṭṭēr*, hampered, impeded (which in biblical Heb. is followed by *yaḏ yᵉmînô*, "his right hand", and means impeded on the right side, and so "left-handed", Jdg. 3:15; 20:16), and *nāḵeh*, smitten, afflicted, without further specification as to the nature of the disability (2 Sam. 4:4; 9:3; and fig. in Isa. 66:2).

NT *kyllos* is a comparatively rare word in NT usage, occurring 4 times only. In Matt. 15:30 f. the RSV reads "maimed" (NEB "crippled"), following the AV, RV, as also in Matt. 18:8 and Mk. 9:43. The NEB has "maimed" in the latter two references. The Matthean passages do not indicate the type of disability, suggesting that the persons involved may have included the congenitally afflicted as well as those who had sustained crippling accidents. In Matt. 18:8 and Mk. 9:43 the reference is more specific, describing the voluntary amputation of a hand as a means of forestalling sin from a source which was already jeopardising entry to eternal life. The severing of the hand at the wrist was an ancient oriental method of punishing thieves, and is still practised today in parts of the east. The use of *kyllos* to describe a maimed or crippled hand is a comparatively late development in both the classical and medical authors. *R. K. Harrison*

| χωλός | χωλός (*chōlos*), lame, halt, maimed; παραλυτικός (*paralytikos*), paralytic. |

CL The classical writers from Homer onwards employed *chōlos* to describe a lame condition in the legs or feet which produced a halting or limping gait. At a later period the word came to be used, like *kyllos*, to designate a deformed or impaired condition of the hand, as in Hippocrates and others. In the Greek papyri it was used in both the literal and metaphorical sense of lameness.

OT The word *chōlos* occurred in the LXX as the equivalent of the Heb. *pissēaḥ*, lame with respect to the feet (as in 2 Sam. 9:13; 19:27). Whether congenital or acquired, this condition disqualified a man from holding office as a → priest in → Israel (Lev. 21:18). This prohibition formed part of the concept of → holiness for the nation, and was especially important for those participating in the sanctuary rituals, of whom a high standard was required. The basic postulate was that whatever approached, or was offered up to, God must be perfect, so that priests had to be free from both ceremonial impurity and physical defects (Lev. 21:1 ff.; Deut. 15:21). In the same way sacrifices must be without blemish (Lev. 22:19 ff.), to symbolize the offering of the very best of human productivity to God. Otherwise punishment would result (cf. Mal. 1:7 ff.). The term *pissēaḥ* is comparatively rare in the OT, occurring only about a dozen times. In Isa. 33:23 and 35:6 the lame are mentioned in connection with the promised future. See also 2 Sam. 5:6, 8 f.; 9:13; 19:27(26); Job 29:15.

NT With the meaning of lame or maimed, *chōlos* occurs 14 times in the NT. In Matt. 11:5; 15:30 f.; 18:8; Mk. 9:45; Lk. 7:22; Acts 3:2; 14:8; Heb. 12:13, the reference is either implicitly or explicitly to impairment of the legs and feet, Acts 3:7 mentioning specifically the feet (*baseis*) and ankles (*sphyra*), two terms which do not occur elsewhere in the NT. Of a more indeterminate nature is the use of *chōlos* in Matt. 21:14; Lk. 14:13, 21; Jn. 5:3 and Acts 8:7. In the NT the lame, maimed or crippled were invariably regarded as among the underprivileged members of society, and therefore as objects of charity, whether of a secular (cf. Lk. 14:13) or Christian (cf. Acts 3:2 ff.) nature.

The adj. used as a noun, *paralytikos*, lame person, paralytic, occurs in Matt. 4:24; 8:6; 9:2, 6; Mk. 2:3–5, 9 f.; Lk. 5:24 *v.l.*; Jn. 5:3 *v.l.* The synonym *paralytos* is found only at Mk. 2:9 *v.l.* *R. K. Harrison*

→ Blind, → Body, → Deaf, → Heal, → Leper, → Weakness

Arndt, 458, 625, 897; Liddell-Scott, 1008 f., 1317, 2014; and bibliography under → Heal.

415

Lament, Sorrow, Weep, Groan

Laughter and tears, and → joy and sorrow belong together as elements of human emotion. Sorrow may manifest itself in weeping, or other outward demonstrations of grief or remain concealed as inner anguish. In Gk. several verbs are used to express this range of emotions. *klaiō*, weep, cry out, expresses man's immediate and outward reaction to suffering. *koptō* stresses the aspect of public grief, which can manifest itself in various customs such as smiting the breast, cutting oneself, wailing or singing set funeral dirges (cf. also *thrēneō*, wail, sing a lament or dirge; *pentheō*, mourn, lament). *lypeō* covers the widest range from physical pain to inward grief; in general it means in the active to give pain, and in the passive to be grieved. Also examined here are *brychō*, gnash; *pentheō*, mourn; and *stenazō*, groan.

| κλαίω | κλαίω (*klaiō*), weep; κλαυθμός (*klauthmos*), weeping. |

CL 1. *klaiō*, found from Homer onwards, means intrans. to cry aloud, weep; trans. bewail. In secular Gk. *klaiō* does not express remorse or sorrow, but physical or mental pain which is outwardly visible.

OT In the LXX *klaiō* is used mostly as the translation of *bākâh*, weep, cry aloud.
It expresses profound grief (1 Sam. 1:7; Lam. 1:16), and also deep sorrow in mourning for the dead (Gen. 50:1). But it may equally express supreme joy, as at the meeting of Jacob and Joseph (Gen. 46:29). The whole personality is involved, as it is in the case of a crying child (Gen. 21:16; Exod. 2:6). A Greek might bewail his personal fate or that of his people, but in the OT the thought is rather that of expressing dependence on God, by addressing one's cries or complaints to him in prayer (e.g. Samson in Jdg. 15:18; 16:28; cf. Isa. 30:19). A further OT feature is the cultic lamentation of the whole people before Yahweh, usually accompanied by a general fast (Jdg. 20:23, 26), such occasions providing the *Sitz im Leben* for such songs of national lamentation as Pss. 74; 79; 80.
The noun *klauthmos* stands most frequently for the Heb. *bᵉkî*, the nominal form of *bākâh* (weep). *bᵉkî* is the most common word in Heb. for weeping (e.g. Gen. 45:2; Deut. 34:8; Jdg. 2:2; Isa. 15:2 f.). It stands for the participial form of *bākâh* in Job 30:31; Isa. 30:19 and Jer. 22:10. In Mic. 7:4 *klauthmos* represents the Heb. *mᵉbukâh* from the root *bôk* which basically means to confuse. It is possible that the translators of the LXX understood the word as a derivation of *bākâh*.

NT 1. *klaiō* is similarly used in the NT, i.e. to express violent emotion, e.g. at parting (Acts 21:13), when thinking of the enemies of Christ (Phil. 3:18), when facing dying and death (Mk. 5:38; Lk. 7:13, 32; Jn. 11:31, 33; Acts 9:39), or generally when face to face with affliction (Rom. 12:15; 1 Cor. 7:30). On the other hand, tears of joy are not mentioned in the NT.
2. In the third Beatitude of Lk. *hoi klaiontes nyn*, "those that weep now" (6:21), are contrasted with those who are rich and full, who laugh now and of whom all men speak well (6:25 f.). The latter are self-righteous, pharisaical persons, "who need no repentance" (15:7), who think highly of themselves, going through life full of self-assurance and with no sense of guilt. "Those that weep now", on the

other hand, live humbly in complete dependence upon God, since they are conscious of their guilt (Matt. 26:75; Lk. 7:38) and therefore acknowledge that God's assessment of them is just, as did the tax collector in the temple. Christ's promise to them is: "You shall laugh." His disciples' weeping over their guilt and the sufferings of this present time will give way, at the end of time, to the laughter of the children of the kingdom.

3. By contrast, those who laugh now are warned: *penthēsete kai klausete*, "you shall mourn and weep" (Lk. 6:25). Where *klaiō* has a future reference in the NT, it is connected with warnings of disaster: those who now are godless and scornful will be put to shame in the final judgment. To intensify the severity of these statements *klaiō* is sometimes combined with another vb. of mourning: *penthēsete kai klausete* ("you shall mourn and weep", Lk. 6:25; cf. Jas. 4:9); *klausete kai thrēnēsete hymeis* ("you will weep and lament", Jn. 16:20); *klausousin kai kopsontai* ("[they] will weep and wail", Rev. 18:9).

4. In order to avoid lamentation in the future which will be too late, James exhorts his readers to weep now. "Be wretched and mourn and weep. Let your laughter be turned to mourning and your joy to dejection. Humble yourselves before the Lord and he will exalt you" (Jas. 4:9 f.). Perhaps James is recalling the words of Jesus in Lk. 6:25 (cf. C. L. Mitton, *The Epistle of James*, 1966, 162).

5. The noun *klauthmos*, weeping, occurs frequently in the NT in the expression "weeping and gnashing of teeth" (→ *brychō* below). In this instance the word describes the remorse associated with the → judgment, particularly among the Jews who had rejected their opportunity. In Matt. 2:18 *klauthmos* (*v.l. thrēnos*, dirge) is associated with *odyrmos polys* ("loud lamentation") in the quotation from Jer. 31:15 which is seen as being fulfilled in the slaughter of the innocents at Bethlehem (→ Fulfil, art. *plēroō*).　　　　　　　　　　　　　　　*H. Haarbeck*

κόπτω

κόπτω (koptō), strike; κόπτομαι (koptomai), beat the breast; κοπετός (kopetos), mourning, lamentation.

CL The word is found in this sense from Homer's *Iliad* onwards. It has a derivative: *kopetos*, lamentation for the dead. *thrēnos* is used similarly in Ion. and Att. in the sense of a lament or dirge, the vb. *thrēneō*, to wail, bewail, being derived from it. There is widespread evidence from antiquity for public mourning and lamentation for the dead. Smiting on the breast and cheeks, loud wailing or dirge-singing were originally intended to drive away the spirits of the dead or to honour the dead. Various mourning customs, some of them violent, extend into the Hellenistic period. Originally carried out on behalf of the dead, they later became increasingly a general expression of grief at death.

OT 1. In the OT there are numerous parallels to the burial customs of the surrounding world. The LXX translates Heb. *sāp̄aḏ*, make lamentation, by *koptomai* (e.g. Gen. 23:2; 1 Ki. 25:1; 28:3; Jer. 16:5 f.).

The Israelites had a variety of customs associated with mourning for the dead (Gen. 23:1–2; 37:34–35; 2 Sam. 3:31–34): cutting oneself, shaving off one's hair, eating mourning bread, drinking from the cup of consolation (Jer. 16:5–7);

417

calling in mourning women (Jer. 9:16–21); putting on sackcloth (Isa. 15:2–3); removing one's beard (Isa. 7:20); beating one's breast (Nah. 2:7; cf. Jer. 31:19). But the most prominent and abiding feature of mourning was wailing (Isa. 15:2; Jer. 22:18; 34:5; Amos 5:16) and the set funeral dirge (2 Sam. 1:17–27; 3:33 ff.).

2. Mourning for the dead held a special place in the preaching of the prophets. Whilst Lam. bewails and interprets the divine judgment which has already befallen Judah and → Jerusalem, the prophets announced – in the "prophetic perfect" and indeed often in the form of a lament for the dead – a catastrophe which still lies in the future (Mic. 1:8; Jer. 9:10; Amos 5:1–2; 16–17; Ezek. 32:1–16). By doing this they aimed to arouse the people and call them to repentance (Jer. 9:18; Ezek. 19; 27:30–34). But it is characteristic of Israel's faith that again and again even as the message of destruction rings in their ears, it changes into hope in God who will deliver them and turn "mourning into dancing" (Ps. 30:11).

3. In Judaism, heathen mourning practices were forbidden (Lev. 19:28; Deut. 14:1), but it was customary before or at a burial to wail and lament for the dead, to beat the breast and so to fulfil one's loving obligations toward the dead person. On the other hand, it was believed that the dead person could still hear the lamentation and the praise until the stone was rolled before the grave, and that he was comforted by the vehement expressions of sorrow.

4. In the Hellenistic period, attempts were made by the state (with the support of enlightened philosophy) to check the extravagances which had crept into mourning customs. These attempts, however, met with little success. A marked feature of this period was the funeral song, used by men and women, relatives and professional mourners as a cultic lamentation for the dead.

NT In the NT *koptō* occurs only 8 times and then exclusively in the Synoptic Gospels and Rev. *kopetos* is used only once (Acts 8:2). *apokoptō* is found 6 times in different books, while *enkoptō* and *enkopē* are Pauline words (6 times in all; → Hinder). The verbs *thrēneo* and → *pentheō*, which are closely related to *koptō* in meaning, occur 4 times (Matt. 11:17; Lk. 7:32; 23:37; Jn. 16:20) and 10 times respectively, and mainly in the Gospels.

1. Evidence of the existence of Jewish mourning customs in the time of Jesus is given by Jesus' parable of the children lamenting the dead when playing at funerals (Matt. 11:17; Lk. 7:32). The story of Jairus's daughter (Matt. 9:23; Mk. 5:38; Lk. 8:52) shows that following immediately upon a person's death, the lamentation was begun by a great crowd of relatives, neighbours and mourning women. After the death of Lazarus (Jn. 11:17, 30) and four days after the burial, i.e. at the culmination of a seven-day period of mourning, there gathered in Bethany a great crowd of neighbours and acquaintances from Jerusalem, weeping (v. 33) and seeking to console Mary and Martha (vv. 19, 31). Mourning women met Jesus on the way to Golgotha (Lk. 23:27), and in the early Christian church "devout men" came together after the death of Stephen to make "great lamentation" over him (Acts 8:2).

2. What significance attaches to the fact that Jesus wept on the way to the grave of Lazarus (Jn. 11:35)? Do not his tears express his compassion for men, subject as they are to death and all its woe? Does he not "groan in spirit" (vv. 33, 38 AV) because of the faithless and hopeless lamentation for the dead with which he finds

himself surrounded? He has come to take upon himself man's suffering and distress, his abandonment and death, so becoming the conqueror of death. His saving, life-giving work puts an end to lamentation for the dead (Lk. 7:13). How can the Pharisees expect wailing and lamentation of him who is life and who brings life? The cross and resurrection of Jesus manifest his victory over death. There is no place for hopeless lamentation in his presence; to indulge in it is nothing other than doubt and unbelief. Sorrow over death for the Christian does not mean being left to his own resources, but in his very natural grief he is sustained by the hope of the resurrection of the dead.

3. Thus the characteristic of the Christian church is not lamentation for the dead, but the hope of life in Christ Jesus (Rom. 6:23). Since God's gift in Jesus is eternal life, lamentation for the dead belongs to those who are far from God, who are themselves under the sentence of death and who have no hope. The new world of eternal life which we hope for because of Jesus' death and resurrection knows no tears and lamentation, for "death shall be no more, neither shall there be mourning nor crying nor pain any more, for the former things have passed away" (Rev. 21:4). All natural mourning for those who have fallen asleep is now irradiated by the living hope of the resurrection (Rom. 8:17, 18). By faith in the conqueror of death we enter into the truth of Christ's promise: "Your sorrow will turn into joy" (Jn. 16:20).   *H. Haarbeck*

| λυπέω |

λυπέω (*lypeō*), inflict pain; λυπέομαι (*lypeomai*), feel pain, be sad; λύπη (*lypē*), sorrow, pain.

CL In Hellenism *lypē* denotes physical pain and emotional suffering. Joy and sorrow are part and parcel of human life, and already in Gk. tragedy, sorrow (*pathos*) had been recognized as one of life's basic components. Aeschylus saw it as an educative factor (*pathei mathos*, learning from suffering, *Ag.* 177), which is the basis of all Gk. tragedy. Hellenistic philosophy understood sorrow as the antithesis to the joy that is worth striving for (*hēdonē*, pleasure [→ Desire]; *euphrosynē*, cheerfulness, → joy; *eudaimonia*, happiness). The Stoics saw it as man's task to overcome sorrow by means of frugality and impassiveness. Only at a later period, particularly in gnosticism, was a more positive understanding of sorrow attained: through accident, sickness and pain man is refined and brought to salutary repentance.

OT The LXX translates 13 different Hebrew verbs by *lypeō* (some 50 times) to denote physical hardship, pain, sorrow, grief, mourning, fear, displeasure and anger. There is, however, no clear distinction between this word-group and such concepts as *odynē*, pain; *thymoō*, make (become) angry; *orgizō*, to be angry; or such roots as *kako-* (bad) and *ponēro-* (evil). The different Heb. words reveal the amazing ability of oriental man to differentiate between feelings, especially in the case of such basic emotions as sorrow and joy. The emotions concerned are always those of everyday life, and are not subjected to any kind of theoretical analysis.

It is interesting to note that *lypeō* and *lypē* are used principally in the later writings of the OT and in the Apocrypha (especially Dan., Prov., Sir., and 4 Macc.). The only explanation of sorrow and pain given in Gen. 3 is that *lypē* is sent by

God as a result of the fall of man (vv. 16 ff.). This basic interpretation of human life as *en lypē* ("in sorrow") does not stand alone. The wisdom literature speaks of the *lypē* that is present even in joy (Prov. 14:13) and has to be overcome (Sir. 30:21 ff.). When Isaiah (1:5) says that the whole heart of the people is turned *eis lypēn* ("to sorrow"), he means that they are in the worst state imaginable. On the other hand, eschatological salvation is promised as a time without sorrow and sighing (Isa. 35:10; 51:11); the age to come will know nothing but joy and glory (2 Esd. 7:13).

Judaism did not advance beyond a generalized conception of *lypē*, closely tied to morality.

NT In the NT (as in the LXX) there are fewer references to mourning than to the opposite concept of → joy. *lypeō* occurs 21 times, and *lypē* only 14 times, whereas → *chairō* and → *chara* are found 69 and 60 times respectively. The ratio of these words associated with sorrow to those associated with rejoicing is thus roughly 1:4. While Matt. prefers the vb. *lypeō* and Jn. the noun *lypē*, both vb. and noun are used most frequently in 2 Cor., a fact which indicates Paul's profound personal understanding of "godly sorrow".

1. In general in the NT *lypē* denotes physical as well as emotional pain. Jesus experienced fear and dread before his death (Matt. 26:37, 38), and the disciples sorrow in Gethsemane (Lk. 22:45). Paul was "grieved" (perhaps even ill-treated) by a member of the Corinthian church (2 Cor. 2:5). Both in the OT and the NT, the sufferings of this present time are seen as contrary to the purpose of creation; hence the longing to be free of them. In 2 Cor. 2:1 ff. Paul hopes that the Corinthians will cause him no further grief. The OT expectation of salvation is taken over by the NT, future consolation being promised to those who are now sorrowing (Matt. 5:4 has *pentheō*, whereas Lk. has *lypeō*). Rev. looks forward to a new heaven and a new earth from which pain and sorrow will be banished (7:17; 21:4).

2. Paul portrays *lypē* as an essential mark of the Christian life. In 2 Cor. 7:8–11 he contrasts the *kata theon lypē*, godly sorrow, with the *lypē tou kosmou*, the sorrow of the world. While worldly sorrow laments personal disappointment and the transitoriness of life, godly sorrow brings one to see one's own guilt and leads to penitence. "For godly grief produces a repentance that leads to salvation and brings no regret, but worldly grief produces death" (v. 10). Within the framework of his theology of the cross Paul speaks of himself as taking up the → cross of Christ (Gal. 6:14). This lays upon his shoulders the cross of this world's sorrow and pain; hence the catalogues of his sufferings, found in 2 Cor. 4:8 ff. and 11:23 ff. While the non-Christian fears the loss of his own life, the Christian finds new life (2 Cor. 4:11; Phil. 3:10 f.) in being crucified with Christ (Rom. 6:6). This leads to paradox in the experience of the believer. All the normal values relating to life and suffering are reversed (cf. the antitheses of 2 Cor. 6:3–10, especially v. 10: *hōs lypoumenoi, aei de chairontes*, "as sorrowful, yet always rejoicing").

3. That which Paul describes as a present paradox in Christian experience is set out in Jn. 16:20–22 as a temporal sequence. The church at the present time is sad, because of Christ's departure and apparent absence, though for the "world" this is a cause for rejoicing. Jn. shows that the present lot of the church is to endure loneliness and the world's hatred; these, together with the fact that Jesus is no

longer visibly present with her, are some of the reasons for her *lypē*. At the same time, however, the departing Christ promises his church joy at his return; this joy no one will take from her (v. 22).   *H. Haarbeck, H.-G. Link*

βρύχω

βρύχω (*brychō*), gnash; βρυγμός (*brygmos*), gnashing.

CL The vb. *brychō* is used in secular Greek of the act of eating noisily or greedily, as well as the act of gnashing the teeth. It was also used metaphorically in the sense of gnawing or eating away as in the case of a disease (Sophocles). The noun *brygmos* connotes a biting (Nicander) and a gnashing of the teeth (Eupolis). It is used in Sir. 51:3, apparently in the sense of biting, for the writer gives thanks for deliverance from "the gnashings of teeth about to devour me."

OT In the LXX *brychō* occurs in the sense of gnashing the teeth at someone. In each instance it stands for the Heb. *ḥāraq*. This word is used only in the OT poetic literature, where it connotes the act of gnashing the teeth. In every instance the gnashing of the teeth is in demonstration of anger (Job 16:9; Pss. 35:16; 37:12; 112:10), with the possible exception of Lam. 2:16 where it may convey the idea of mocking.

The noun *brygmos* occurs in Prov. 19:12 to translate Heb. *naham*, where it denotes the wrath of a king. *naham* is used of the growling of a lion (Prov. 28:15; Isa. 5:29, 30), and figuratively of groaning (Prov. 5:11; Ezek. 24:23). In Isa. 5:29, 30 the word seems to imply the growl of a lion as it devours its prey. The fem. form of the noun is used figuratively of the roaring of the sea (Isa. 5:30) and the groaning of the heart (Ps. 38:9).

NT In the NT *brychō* is used only once (Acts 7:54) and occurs in an expression describing the angry reaction of those who listened to Stephen's speech. Their reaction was one of rage and "grinding the teeth." The act of grinding the teeth here is clearly expressive of anger.

The noun *brygmos* always occurs in the set expression *ekei estai ho klauthmos kai ho brygmos tōn odontōn* ("there shall be weeping and gnashing of teeth"). The expression occurs in Matt. 8:12; 13:42, 50; 22:13; 24:51; 25:30; Luke 13:28, and always describes the condition of the wicked in the future life. The precise meaning of this expression can be derived only from its usage in each context, for there are no precise parallels in secular Gk. and Jewish literature (K. H. Rengstorf, *TDNT* I 642). While it is true that in many instances the usage of *brychō* in the expression "to gnash the teeth" connotes anger, the association of the word with *klauthmos* (weeping), and the figure of torment that accompanies the term in Matt. 13:42, 50 seems to indicate that the gnashing of the teeth is not an indication of rage but of extreme suffering and remorse.   *T. McComiskey*

πενθέω

πενθέω (*pentheō*), be sad, grieve, mourn; πένθος (*penthos*) grief, sadness, mourning.

CL The vb. *pentheō* means to lament or mourn, frequently with the connotation of mourning for someone (Herodotus, Aeschylus). The noun *penthos* is used in secular Greek in the sense of "mourning" or "sorrow". It is used especially of the external signs of mourning, as when mourning for the dead.

OT In the LXX *pentheō* stands chiefly for the vb. *'ābal* which means to mourn, and in the majority of cases connotes the act of mourning over realized or impending misfortune. It is frequently used figuratively of inanimate objects such as the earth, the land, or parts of the structure of cities upon which catastrophe has come or is yet to come (cf. Isa. 3:26; 24:4; 33:9; Jer. 4:28; 23:10; Lam. 2:8; Hos. 4:3). A sense of loss frequently pervades the description of catastrophe. It is also used of mourning over the death of an individual (2 Ki. 14:2; 1 Chron. 7:22), of remorse in general (Neh. 8:9), and of the sorrow experienced during the absence of a loved one 2 Ki. 13:27; 19:1).

The vb. *pentheō* also stands for the Hebrew *'āmal* (to be weak, to languish) in Isa. 16:8; 19:8; 24:4, 7; 33:9. The frequent use of *'āmal* in contexts of mourning may indicate that it was used occasionally to describe the psychological and physical effects of mourning. In Gen. 23:2 and 50:3 *pentheō* stands for the Heb. *bākâh* (weep), and in Ps. 78(77):63 it is used somewhat dubiously to translate *hālal* (praise).

In Jer. 23:10 *pentheō* occurs as the translation of *nûḏ* (to flutter or quiver, hence also to show the emotion of grief), and in Ezek. 31:15 it occurs as the translation of *qāḏar* (to darken oneself, i.e., mourn). The vb. thus connotes various aspects of sorrow including the outward demonstration of remorse.

The noun *penthos* represents the Heb. *'ēḇel*, the specific meaning of which is akin to the verbal form *'āḇal*, mourning (e.g. Gen. 27:1; 50:10 f.; Amos 5:16; 8:10; Isa. 60:20).

NT The vb. *pentheō* occurs in Matt. 9:15 in the sense of sorrow over the absence of a loved one, and in Mark 16:10 it is used of those who mourned the death of Christ. Paul uses it of the sorrow he may have to experience when he learns that some have not repented of their sins (2 Cor. 12:21).

In the Lucan account of the Beatitudes the word occurs as the antithesis of → laugh (6:25) describing the eventual mourning of those who laugh now. The reference here is to those who are not contrite now and who will later experience the results of their lack of contrition. In the Matthean account of the Beatitudes (5:4) the word *pentheō* is used of sorrow in a general sense.

In Rev. 18:11, 15, 19, the judgment on → Babylon is mourned by those who trafficked with her. The deep sense of loss at the destruction of their source of wealth pervades the description of their reaction.

The term is used by Paul and James in a sense closely paralleling the concept of godly sorrow or repentance. In 1 Cor. 5:2 Paul uses *pentheō* to describe the attitude that should characterize the Corinthian Christians relative to the immorality among them. He describes their present attitude as "arrogant" (*pephysiomenoi*, lit. "puffed up") and indicates that they should rather "mourn" (*epenthēsate*) over the situation. James exhorts sinners to "mourn and weep" as an aspect of their humbling themselves before God. This attitude of mind will lead to God's exalting them (4:8–10).

The noun *penthos* is used by James in a sense similar to his use of the vb., i.e., in the sense of godly sorrow. In Jas. 4:8, 9 he calls on sinners to draw near to God, cleanse their hands, purify their hearts, be wretched (*talaipōrēsate*), mourn (*penthēsate*) and weep. The section is concluded by the exhortation to humble themselves before the Lord and he will exalt them (→ Humility, → Height, art. *hypsoō*).

In Rev. 18:7 f. *penthos* is used in the sense of sorrow due to catastrophe and loss. In this context it describes the sorrow and mourning to come on → Babylon at her fall. By contrast in Rev. 21:4 it is used in the sense of sorrow in general, the removal of which will lead to the → joy to be experienced by men when the future state is realized in the new → Jerusalem. *T. McComiskey*

στενάζω

στενάζω (*stenazō*), to sigh, groan; στεναγμός (*stenagmos*), sigh, groan, groaning.

CL The vb. *stenazō* is used in secular Greek of sighing or moaning. It occurs transitively in the sense of sighing over or bemoaning. The noun *stenagmos* connotes a sighing or groaning.

OT In the LXX *stenazō* stands for several Hebrew words. It represents the verb *'ābal* in Isa. 19:8 and is used again for *'ānâh* in the same verse. Both Heb. words connote the general concept of mourning. On several occasions it stands for the niphal of *'ānaḥ* which means chiefly to sigh or groan, connoting the sighing of grief due to physical suffering, loss or distress (Isa. 24:7; Lam. 1:8, 21; Ezek. 21:6 f. [11 f.]).

In Ezek. 26:15 it stands for *'ānaq*, a word which denotes the groaning of the wounded in its two occurrences in the qal (Ezek. 26:15; Jer. 51:52) and which in the niphal connotes sighing as an expression of grief (Ezek. 9:4; 24:17).

Once (Isa. 59:11) *stenazō* represents *hāmâh* (growl, murmur) where it describes the roaring of a bear. It stands for *zā'aq* (cry out) in Job 31:38 where it is used metaphorically to describe the crying out of the land. In Nah. 3:7 it represents *nûd* (flutter, show grief) in a context asking who will bemoan → Nineveh. In Job 24:12 *stenazō* represents *'āgam* (to be grieved) and in Job 30:25 it stands for *šāwa'* (cry out for help).

The noun *stenagmos* represents noun forms of several of the previously cited Hebrew verbs, most frequently *'ᵃnāqâh*. On one occasion, however, it stands for *hērôn* (Gen. 3:17) which means pregnancy. The LXX rendering seems to be a metaphorical use of *stenagmos*. It also represents *nᵉ'āqâh* from *nā'aq* (groan) in Exod. 2:24; 6:5; Jdg. 2:18 where it is used of groaning as a result of physical affliction and distress.

It stands for *nāham* (growl, groan) in Ps. 37:8, where it describes the groaning of the Psalmist in his distress, and for *ṣārâh* (distress) in Jer. 4:31 where it describes the anguish of a woman in travail.

NT The vb. *stenazō* is used in Mark 7:34 in the general sense of sighing as the expression of inward emotion. Paul uses the term exclusively of sighing in the sense of longing for something (Rom. 8:23; 2 Cor. 5:2, 4). In Heb. 13:17, however, *stenazō* stands as the antithesis of "joyfully" (*meta charas*) and hence is a surrogate for "sorrow" in this context.

James uses the vb. with the phrase *kat' allēlōn* to connote the concept of grumbling or complaining "against one another" (5:9).

The noun *stenagmos* is used in two instances in the NT. In Acts 7:34 it is used to describe the groaning of the Israelites in their slavery in → Egypt. In this usage it is reminiscent of the use of *nᵉ'āqâh* in the OT which is used on three of four occasions to describe the groanings of the Israelites while under oppression.

In Rom. 8:26 the word is used in the expression *stenagmois alalētois*, "with sighs too deep for words" (RSV), to refer to the intercession of the Holy → Spirit. There is a progression in the context where Paul moves from the groaning of the creation (v. 22) to the groaning of the Christian. The clear element of a sympathetic relationship of the Holy Spirit to the spirit of the believer (vv. 9, 16) and the reference to the groaning of the believer in the immediately preceding context (v. 23) seem to warrant the view that the groaning is shared by the Holy Spirit and the believer. The groanings of the heart are observed by the one who "searches the hearts of men" (v. 27) but are not expressed audibly. These deep groanings are not lost to the Spirit but utilized in his intercession for the believer. The deep emotive elements in *stenagmos* are to be retained here. It is the groaning of distress or deep emotion. (For further discussion of this passage → Prayer, art. *entynchanō*.)

T. McComiskey

→ Bury, → Cry, → Joy, → Laugh

(a). R. Bultmann, *lypē* etc., *TDNT* IV 313–24; and *penthos* etc., *TDNT* VI 40–43; T. Collins, "The Physiology of Tears in the Old Testament", *CBQ* 33, 1971, 18–38, 185–97; N. K. Gottwald, *Studies in the Book of Lamentations*, SBT 14, 1954; F. F. Hvidberg, *Weeping and Laughter in the Old Testament*, 1962; K. H. Rengstorf, *brychō* etc., *TDNT* I 641 ff.; and *klaiō* etc., *TDNT* III 722–26; J. F. Ross, "Job 33:14–30: The Phenomenology of Lament", *JBL* 94, 1975, 38–46; J. Schneider, *stenazō* etc., *TDNT* VII 600–3; G. Stählin, *thrēneō* etc., *TDNT* III 148–55; and *kopetos* etc. *TDNT* III 830–52.
(b). C. Westermann, "Struktur und Geschichte der Klage im Alten Testament", *ZAW* 66, 1954, 44 ff.

Large, Small

The twin concepts, large and small, in Gk. *megas* and *mikros*, are put together here because the two words are always being related to each other, whether in quantitative mathematical comparisons or in qualitative value judgments. The words take on a particular importance in the NT through being used to express qualification or disqualification in the sight of God. The nouns formed from *megas* are also used to express attributes of God.

| μέγας | μέγας, μεγάλη, μέγα (*megas, megalē, mega*), large, great; |

μεγαλύνω (*megalynō*), make large, great, magnify; μεγαλειότης (*megaleiotēs*), grandeur; μεγαλωσύνη (*megalōsynē*), majesty; μεγαλεῖα (*megaleia*), mighty deeds.

CL 1. *megas*, great, is the antonym of → *mikros*, small, and occurs from Mycenaean Greek (Linear B) onwards in literature, the papyri and inscriptions. Its use ranges from the measurement of physical shapes and spaces, via qualities, to designations of rank (e.g. in Homer, Aeschylus, Pindar). Used as an epithet of honour, *megas* occurs frequently in the formula of acclamation, *megas theos*, great god, and in connection with the names of gods. While the superlative, *megistos*, is also attested as early as the *Iliad*, the comparative, *meizōn*, does not occur until Heraclitus. According to the context, the emphasis of *megas* varies in translation: fully grown, important, magnificent, powerful.

2. The derived vb. *megalynō* occurs first in Thucydides. Used transitively it means to make great, and is chosen for figurative use in the sense of to praise, glorify. The two nouns *megaleiotēs*, grandeur, splendour, and *megalōsynē*, majesty, splendour, are not attested in pre-Christian literature. *megaleia*, good and mighty deeds, is the neut. plur. of *megaleios* used as a noun; this adj. is first used by Xenophon and Menander.

ot 1. The LXX employs all five words to translate several Heb. words by far the most numerous of which are those formed from the root *gdl* (great). It is impossible to establish a specific connotation for *megas* (which occurs about 820 times) in different OT writings. The same is true of *megalynō* (93 times), which had just begun to emerge in secular Gk. at the time of the composition of the earliest LXX writings.

2. (a) The fact that *megas* was chosen to translate several Heb. words suggests that at that time the translators were not making great efforts always to find the exactly corresponding Gk. term, but were generalizing. On the other hand, *megas* was not always chosen where *gādōl* occurs in the Heb. text (e.g. Gen. 15:14; Isa. 12:6).

(b) In contrast to the wide-ranging use of the adj. the derived nouns have a clear denotation. In addition to two verses in the Apocrypha (1 Esd. 1:5; 4:40), *megaleiotēs* is used in Jer. 33:9 (LXX 40:9) and Dan. 7:27 (where, however, Theodotion has *megalōsynē*) in connection with the fact that God's activity in Israel will extend also to every people of the earth in power and glory. *megalōsynē* occurs in 32 places, of which 11 are in the Apocrypha and 7 in Dan. It is used predominantly in expressions of God's surpassing greatness and power (e.g. 2 Sam. 7:23). God redeemed → Israel for himself (→ Redemption, art. *lytron*), and created a place especially for his people to live in. Similarly in 1 Chr. 17:19 and Ps. 150:2 the thought is of God's creative will and of his lordship over history, and in particular his glorious deeds. There is, therefore, a twofold usage: (a) to describe God's greatness; and (b) to summon men to see and praise God's greatness, i.e. to glorify him (→ Glory).

megaleia has the same almost exclusive reference to Yahweh's mighty acts (e.g. Deut. 11:2; Ps. 106:21 [LXX 105:21]). At times the OT presents Yahweh as greater than all gods (cf. Exod. 18:11; Ps. 77:13 [LXX 76:13]).

nt 1. The *megas* word-group is attested 258 times in the NT. The adj. occurs particularly frequently in Lk. (194 times, and the comparative *meizōn* a further 48 times) and in Acts (64 times), but also 30 times in Matt.; it is also particularly prominent in the later letters (Pastorals, Eph., 2 Pet., Jude, and Heb.), while the group rarely appears in the earlier Pauline writings (e.g. Rom. 9:2; 1 Cor. 12:31; 13:13; 2 Cor. 10:15). Jn. is characterized by the use (13 times) of the comparative *meizōn*, against 5 times for *megas*. But it is in Rev. that the greatest number of occurrences (80) are to be found. The combination small and great, meaning all without distinction, which is typical of Acts but which also occurs in Rev. (e.g.

Acts 8:10; 26:22; Rev. 11:18; 20:12), rests on LXX usage (cf. Gen. 19:11; 1 Sam. 30:2).

(a) *megas* is theologically important in various synoptic sayings of Jesus. These reveal his rejection of the Rab. Jewish striving after piety, as it was then practised in a world strictly divided into great and small, i.e. into people of higher and lower standing. The sayings concern rewards and true greatness in the kingdom of heaven. They cut across the Pharisaic attitude to commandments (Matt. 5:19 f.), warn about the enmity of man (Lk. 6:23), and call for love of one's enemies (Lk. 6:35). Jesus' own attitude is further illustrated by his teaching on the → sabbath which leads to the declaration that "something greater than the temple is here" (Matt. 12:6), namely the order of the → kingdom of God, which is already present.in the actions and person of Jesus himself.

(b) The reasons for the 80 instances of *megas* in Rev. are bound up with the literary form in which apocalyptic thought is expressed. *megas* also occurs in the apocalyptic discourses in the Gospels (Matt. 24:21, 24, 31; Mk. 13:2; Lk. 21:11, 23). It is used in the larger-than-life symbolism which characterizes the eschatological dimension of events, e.g. the day (Rev. 6:17), the earthquake (16:18), and the city (18:2, 10, 16, 18 f., 21). Particularly striking is the occurrence (21 times) of *phōnē megalē*, "with a great [i.e. loud] voice". The expression indicates especially the sovereignty of God which drowns all other sounds in the voices of his messengers (e.g. Rev. 1:10; 5:2; 7:2; 10:3; 11:15; 16:1; 21:3; → Angel). The note of divine sovereignty is also heard in the loud voice of the multitude praising him (e.g. Rev. 5:12; 6:10; 7:10; 19:1). The phrase is found also with a similar meaning in the Gospels, where it is used, moreover, both of the cry of Jesus on the cross (Matt. 27:50; Mk. 15:37; Lk. 23:46) and also of the demons' cry of terror (Lk. 4:33; → Word, art. *phōnē*).

2. As a result of the normative usage of the LXX and of inter-Testamental tradition in a Hellenistic environment, all three nouns have a similar meaning. *megaleiotēs* is reserved in the NT for God's majesty, supremacy and splendour (Lk. 9:43; 2 Pet. 1:16; cf. Acts 19:27 where on heathen lips it refers to the great goddess Artemis). *megalōsynē*, which is a synonym for it, occurs in Heb. 1:3; 8:1; Jude 25, as a surrogate and periphrasis for God, expressing his sublime majesty. Apart from the *v.l.* in Lk. 1:49, *megaleia* occurs only in Acts 2:11, where the Jews of the Dispersion visiting Jerusalem express amazement at hearing the followers of Jesus "telling in our own tongues the mighty works of God" (→ Pentecost).

3. In Jn. the comparative *meizōn* appears only in the discourses. It brings into prominence Jesus' claims and the unique effectiveness of his work. In authority he is "greater" than Jacob (→ Israel), → Abraham or other men, for he brings → life (4:12; 8:53; 5:20, 36). His works have been given him by the Father who, however, despite the unity and equality which exist between the two, is "greater" than Jesus himself (10:29; 14:28). The commission with which the Father sends the Son is balanced by the Son's obedience in carrying out his work of love.

4. *megas* takes on special significance in a number of passages which have particular theological importance in that they have no exact parallels in pre- and non-Christian literature. Jesus' teaching thus presents something quite new.

(a) In Matt. 22:36, 38 Jesus is asked a controversial question about the *entolē megalē*, the great commandment (cf. Mk. 12:28 which has "first commandment of all"). The use of the positive instead of the superlative, i.e. "great" instead of "greatest", is a Semitism (cf. Moulton, *Grammar*, III, 31). Jesus replied by referring to the double commandment to love God and one's neighbour. He thus made an essential organic connection between Deut. 6:5 and Lev. 19:18, which was not commonly made in Jewish legal thought (but cf. Lk. 10:25 ff. and Test. Iss. 5:2, the date of which is disputed; → Command, art. *entolē*). ([Ed.] Some rabbinic teaching tended to emphasize the equal importance of all commandments [Mekilta Exod. 6; Sifre Deut. 12:28; 13:19; 19:11; cf. D. Hill, *The Gospel of Matthew*, 1972, 306], but there were also tendencies in Judaism to seek a single principle [cf. D. Daube, *The New Testament and Rabbinic Judaism*, 1956, 247–73].) Similarly, the works that Jesus does and the "greater works" that the disciples will do are to be understood as combining this love for God and love for man. Jesus utterly rejected the casuistical comparison of commandments, and focused his radical demand on love in the form of service which must underlie all works (→ Serve, art. *diakoneō*; → Love, art. *agapē*; → Hear, art. *akouō*).

(b) In the case of the corresponding pericope in Lk., which meets us in a different setting, Jesus' answer is linked directly with the parable of the Good Samaritan (10:25 ff.). This makes clear how, in Jesus' understanding of love, a special standard for reckoning greatness and smallness applies. His own story is the standard example for those who would obey the two-fold "greatest" commandment, who would turn to God in love and, by so doing, also towards their neighbour. (On the parable see W. Monselewski, *Der barmherzige Samariter*, *Eine auslegungsgeschichtliche Untersuchung zu Lukas* 10, 25–37, 1967; J. D. M. Derrett, "The Parable of the Good Samaritan", *Law in the New Testament*, 1970, 208–27.)

(c) Thus, as regards function, the "greatest commandment" goes hand in hand with the definition of greatness and smallness in the kingdom of heaven, as it appears in the passage where the disciples argue about precedence (Matt. 18:1–5; Mk. 9:33–37; Lk. 9:46 ff.). Jesus demonstrated by his action the supremely valid guideline for his disciples. He put a child in their midst and declared, "Whoever receives one such child in my name" (Matt. expands in v. 4: "Whoever humbles himself like this child," i.e. acknowledges his own smallness), whoever in this way offers service to the small, is *ho meizōn*, the greatest in the kingdom of heaven.

(d) In this devaluation and revaluation of worldly orders of precedence the structure of the Christian community, determined by the model of Christ, emerges as one based on service to others. It is essentially a fellowship characterized by service (cf. Lk. 22:26 f., where the greatest is used as a parallel to, indeed as a synonym of the one who serves: also Matt. 20:26; 23:11; Mk. 10:43 f.). The discussions about the greatness or smallness of John the Baptist are to be understood in just the same way (Matt. 11:11; Lk. 7:28). His status, because of what happened in the era of Jesus, is revalued in so far as Jesus, with the ushering-in of the → kingdom of God, performs the greatest work, while the Baptist still belongs to the previous era of expectation (cf. W. Grundmann, *TDNT* IV 534 f.).

F. Thiele

| μικρός | μικρός (*mikros*), small, little; ἐλάσσων (*elassōn*), smaller, younger; ἐλάχιστος (*elachistos*), very small, the least; |

ὀλίγος (*oligos*), little, small, few.

CL The adj. *mikros*, small, is found in Gk. literature from Homer on as the antonym of → *megas*, great. In evaluations and comparisons the two words express a quantitative or qualitative difference which can refer to things, living beings and periods of time. *elassōn* (smaller, younger) is the comparative of *mikros* and *elachistos* (very small, the least) the superlative. A comparative, not found until later, was formed from this, i.e. *elachistoteros*, the very least. *oligos* also occurs in Gk. literature from Homer on. It designates a small quantity, a small number, also a few people or a few days.

OT 1. The LXX uses *mikros*, together with its comparative and superlative, about 190 times to translate a variety of concepts, of which *qāṭān*, *qāṭōn* (small, young) and *mᵉʿaṭ* (a few) are the most frequent. They are as widely used as in Hel. Greek, e.g. little houses (Amos 6:11), a small light (Gen. 1:16), something almost (lit. by a little) happened (Ps. 73:2 [LXX 72:2]), a younger son, a small boy (1 Sam. 16:11; Isa. 11:6). Sometimes there is the combination "small and great" in the sense of → all (e.g. Deut. 1:17; Ps. 115:13 [LXX 113:21]).

The LXX uses also *oligos* (103 times, of which 51 are in the Apocrypha) as does secular Gk., e.g. a few days (Gen. 29:20), a small number of Israelites (Deut. 4:27), man's short span of life, indicating God's punishment (Job 10:20; Ps. 109:8, LXX 108:8). *oligos* is most frequently used in the LXX to translate the Hebrew *mᵉʿaṭ*, few, a little.

2. In addition, OT writers use *mikros* and its derivatives to denote humility towards God. Gideon called himself the least in his family, from the weakest clan (Jdg. 6:15). The language of Solomon's prayer after succession to the throne uses the courtly style of ancient oriental kingly formulae: "I am but a little child [*paidarion mikron*]; I do not know how to go out or come in" (1 Ki. 3:7; cf. *RGG³* III 1711). Self-effacement before God on the part of God's elect enjoys his favour (cf. Isa. 60:22).

3. The OT clearly emphasizes that Yahweh is frequently on the side of the very people who have little in the way of possessions (e.g. Ps. 37:16 f. [LXX 36:16 f.]). He often helps by means of small things, e.g. "It is an easy thing for the LORD to help through a few" (1 Sam. 14:6). Such thoughts "express the transvaluation of all values before God and His Kingdom" (H. Seesemann, *TDNT* V 171).

4. The Rabbis often referred to young disciples as "little ones". But they also called them "immature pupils" which carried derogatory undertones in comparison with *megas*, great (cf. SB I 591 f.).

NT 1. In the NT the lines laid down by the OT are continued. Thus *mikros* is used in such expressions as small of stature (Lk. 19:3), of little value (Jn. 2:10), younger in age (Rom. 9:12; 1 Tim. 5:9). The juxtaposition of small and great as a periphrasis in Semitic style for "all" also occurs quite often (e.g. Acts 8:10; Heb. 8:11; Rev. 13:16; 19:5, 18).

oligos (40 times, of which 26 are in the Synoptic and Acts) is similarly used. The reversal of values mentioned above is theologically significant (e.g. Matt. 25:21, 23; Lk. 19:17). God will not treat man's faithfulness in matters of little importance with contempt, but reward it.

2. The Pauline writings contain the word-group relatively rarely. 1 Cor. 5:6 and Gal. 5:9 mention the proverb about the far-reaching effects of a little → leaven.

The adv. *mikron* and the superlative *elachistos* occur in contexts in which Paul speaks of himself, passing judgment or by way of example, in the same self-effacing manner which we have seen in the OT (e.g. 1 Cor. 15:9; 2 Cor. 11:1, 16; Eph. 3:8 with the special form *elachistoteros*, he is "the very least" of all the saints). 1 Tim. 4:8 declares that bodily training is of a little (*oligon*) value.

3. (a) With one exception Jn. uses *mikros* only in a temporal sense, i.e. a little, a little while (13:33; 14:19). The almost pleonastic heaping up of the word in 16:16–19 denotes first of all the time between Jesus' discourse and his coming arrest in Gethsemane "in a little while" and then the short interval until his disciples meet him after his resurrection. The passage focuses on the eschatological tension of the short interval. At the same time an element of → comfort is implied.

(b) Jn. 7:33 and 12:35 are also to be understood in a temporal sense, as is Heb. 10:37 with its reference to a "very, very short time [*mikron hoson hoson*]" (cf. Isa. 26:20 LXX).

4. The Synoptics use *mikros* in one way which differs from the usage of Hellenistic and Jewish literature. Despite their enthusiasm over the innocence of children (→ Child), the latter nevertheless undervalued the "little ones" and "children" (cf. O. Michel, *TDNT* IV 651 f.). Jesus, on the other hand, was specially concerned for their protection. He sharply warned anyone who caused the least of those who believe in him to stumble (Mk. 9:42; Lk. 17:2; → Offence, art. *skandalon*). Conversely, those who do good to the least of these are promised eschatological reward (Matt. 10:42; 25:40, 45).

The implications for the Christian community in Matt. 18:1–6, 10, 14 (cf. Mk. 9:33–34, 37, 42; Lk. 9:46 ff.; 17:1 f.) clearly correspond to the character and ways of God. The kingdom of God is not attained by quarrels over precedence and lust for greatness but by being least, by self-effacing service (→ Humility; → Serve), and poverty (→ Poor) which relies entirely on the sufficiency of God's help.

The sayings about the little grain of mustard seed (Matt. 13:31 f.; Mk. 4:30 ff.; Lk. 13:18 f.), which becomes a great tree, about the little flock (Lk. 12:32) and about John the Baptist being less than the "least in the kingdom of God" (Lk. 7:28) are also to be interpreted from this standpoint. In the Christian community, and therefore before God, the only thing that counts is the renunciation of all the greatness that one has striven after. *F. Thiele*

→ Age, Stature, → Child, → Command, → Disciple, → Poor, → Possessions

a). Arndt, 298 f., 523; W. Grundmann, *megas* etc., *TDNT* IV 529–44; W. G. Kümmel, *Promise and Fulfilment: The Eschatological Message of Jesus*, SBT 23, 1961², 92 ff.; O. Michel, *mikros* etc., *TDNT* IV 64859.
(b). O. Bächli, "Die Erwählung des Geringen im Alten Testament", *ThZ* 22, 1966, 285 ff.; O. Michel, " 'Diese Kleinen' – eine Jüngerbezeichnung Jesu", *ThStKr* 108, 1937–38, 401 ff.

Laugh

γελάω | γελάω (*gelaō*), laugh; καταγελάω (*katagelaō*), laugh at, mock; γέλως (*gelōs*), laughter.

CL 1. The word group as a whole was in use in Greek literature from the time of Homer onwards and covered a whole range of meanings from free and joyous laughter to ridicule and scorn. The compound *katagelaō* is an intensification,

429

meaning either laugh loudly or sneer. The words were not only applied to men but also to the gods. K. H. Rengstorf (*TDNT* I 661) notes that for the Romans and the Greeks merry laughter was a divine characteristic which featured in the theophanies (cf. Virgil, *Eclogues* 4, 60 ff. where laughter following the birth of a child denoted its divine character). "*gelōs* is a mark of deity which also spreads *gelōs* in the world around" (K. H. Rengstorf, ibid.).

2. Three categories of humour and irony in the secular Gk. world are of interest by comparison and contrast with the biblical presentation.

(a) Gk. comedy. The production of a combination of satyric plays and tragedies in connection with the festival of Dionysus continued well into the NT era, and the practice had spread throughout the Gk. world. The plots of the comedies include fantasy and burlesque. The satirical element was very strong. Prominent men in contemporary society were parodied and even mythology and theology are treated with great irreverence. It has been argued, however, that, although the gods were made to appear foolish and cowardly, the reality of their power was consistently assumed. J. Jónsson, using Friedländer's example of Diogenes Laertius, "who says that the Stoic Cleanthes did not care when he was made fun of in a comedy, because the gods themselves, like Dionysus and Hercules, had been able to take a good joke," concludes that the religious humour is to be understood not as laughing at the gods, but rather as taking part in their own joy (*Humour and Irony in the New Testament*, 1965, 35 f.; cf. Diog. Laert. 7, 173; P. Friedländer, "Lachende Götter," *Die Antike* 10, 3, 1934, 223). He also cites Carl Schneider who holds that "at the beginning of the Christian era the optimistic and joyful attitude to life was so common and so deeply rooted in the religious feeling of the people that humour was a natural expression of religion" (op. cit., 35; cf. C. Schneider, *Geschichte des antiken Christentums*, I, 1954, 162 f.).

(b) The dramatic irony of the tragedies. The themes of classical tragedy most often concerned the relation of man to the powers controlling the universe and how these powers determined his destiny. Frequently the audience is given a glimpse behind the scenes and is enabled to foresee the course of events.

(c) Socratic irony. Socrates, as portrayed by Plato, is a teacher of philosophy who employed humour to great effect as a means of education. He played the part of an *eirōn*, one who says less than he thinks (Aristot., *Eth.Nic.* 2, 7, 12) confessing his own ignorance and by means of relentless ironical questions forcing his disciples to abandon their self-confident opinions.

Many scholars have pointed to the connection between Socratic irony and the comedy characteristic of a ridiculous and boastful pretender (*alazōn*, Aristot., *Eth.Nic.* 2, 7, 12) who is humiliated by an *eirōn* in the form of a god, fate, or the facts of life (cf. J. Jónsson, op. cit., 37 f.; P. Friedländer, op. cit., 214; J. Kruuse, *Humorister*, 1945, 53 ff.). One is reminded of the characterization of the "fool" in the Bible (cf. Prov. 12:15; Pss. 14:1; 53:1; Lk. 12:20). D. O. Via points to a similar motif in the early Christian kerygma (cf. 1 Cor. 1:18–31, where the → "wisdom" of the world is brought to nothing by the "foolishness" of God [*Kerygma and Comedy in the New Testament*, 1975, 45 ff.]).

ot 1. The vb. is used in the LXX to translate *śāḥaq* (Job 29:24; Ps. 51[52]:6; Lam. 1:7), *ṣāḥaq* (Gen. 1:17; 18:12 f.; 15), *śāmaḥ* (Job 22:19), and is without

Heb. equivalent in 1 Esd. 4:31; Ezra. 4:17; Job 19:7; Jer. 20:8; Dan. LXX Bel. 18; Dan. Theodotion Bel 7, 19; 4 Macc. 5:28. The noun *gelōs* occurs mostly for the Heb. *śeḥōq* and is found in Gen. 21:6; Job 8:21; 17:6; Prov. 10:23; Eccl. 2:2; 7:4(3), 7(6); 10:19; Wis. 5:3; Sir. 19:30; 21:20; 27:13; Amos 7:9; Mic. 1:10; Jer. 20:7; 31(48):26, 39; Lam. 3:14; Ezr. 23:32; 4 Macc. 5:28. K. H. Rengstorf claims that the words are used exclusively for the true or supposed superiority towards another expressed in scorn or laughter (Ps. 80:6; Prov. 1:26; 2 Chron. 30:10; Job 12:4; Eccl. 7:6; cf. *TDNT* I 659). They are never used for righteous or religious → joy. In Gen. 17:17; 18:12; 13:15 the contrast is between laughter and belief. In Prov. 10:23 *gelōs* is the mark of a fool, contrasted with wise conduct. Rengstorf further points out that laughter is rarely attributed to God (Pss. 2:4; 37:13; 59:8; Prov. 1:26) and it only expresses his absolute superiority over the ungodly who will not accept him as God even though they are nothing beside him (*TDNT* I 661).

Certain possible exceptions, however, should be noted. (a) In Gen. 21:6 the laughter here appears to refer to two different things: a God-given joy for Sarah, "God has made laughter for me", and man's scornful scepticism, "everyone who hears will laugh over me." The LXX gives the whole clause a positive meaning by substituting *synchairō* in the second clause. *gelōs* had to be retained in the first half since Sarah is commenting on the aptness of the name Isaac (*yiṣḥāq*) which is a self-reproachful reminder of their unbelief (Gen. 21:3; → Abraham, arts. *Sarra* and *Isaak*). (b) In Job 29:24 the positive meaning of the Heb. – a smile which encourages – is interpreted by the LXX to refer to ridicule. (c) In Ps. 126:2 laughter is associated with the joy of the time of salvation. Rengstorf argues that this again refers to the laughter of triumph over opponents (*TDNT* I 661 f.). But the context does not make this explicit and again the LXX prefers *chara* (→ Joy) to *gelōs*.

It may be concluded therefore that in the OT *śāḥaq* and *ṣāḥaq* are not in general the marks of righteous joy either for God or man and *gelōs* is even less so.

2. Humour and irony in the OT. The above conclusions should not, however, be taken to indicate that the OT is humourless. Scholars have been divided on this question, some regarding humour, i.e. playfulness, as inappropriate to the seriousness of the subjects treated. It must be conceded that the assessment of humour is a highly subjective process. If for example Nebuchadnezzar's madness in Dan. 4 is regarded by some as humorous (W. F. Stinespring, *IDB* II 662), the dividing line between tragedy and comedy is a very narrow one. Jónsson maintains that humour may change according to the state of mind of the person, his attitude towards the object, and his philosophy of life (op. cit., 23).

There is, however, a general consensus of opinion about certain types of humour to be found in the OT.

(a) Lighthearted portrayal of people and situations feature in the narrative passages: e.g. the characterization of Jacob and Esau (Gen. 25:27–34); Jacob meets his match in Laban (Gen. 29:15–30); the early life of Joseph (Gen. 37:1–11), the story of Balaam (Num. 22); Abimelech's death at the hands of a woman (Jdg. 9:50–54); David dressed in armour (1 Sam. 17:38).

(b) Very extensive use of word play. Names are regularly seen to be significant. In Gen. 25:26 "Jacob" suggests "following at the heel" in order to supplant (*'āqab*); hence Gen. 27:36 and Jer. 9:4 (on Jacob → Israel, art. *Iakōb*). The

431

prophets' words include many bitter puns. "The Lord God showed me . . . a basket of summer fruit [*qayiṣ*] . . . Then the Lord said to me, 'The end [*qēṣ*] has come upon my people Israel' " (Amos 8:1 f.; cf. also e.g. Hos. 8:7; 12:11; Isa. 5:7; Jer. 1:11–12).

(c) Quiet educational humour. This is best illustrated by the book of Proverbs, where the teacher gently teases his disciples and makes the sinner look ridiculous (e.g. 6:9–10; 19:24; 27:15). It is possible to understand Ecclesiastes in this way too (cf. 3:16–22).

(d) Dramatic irony. This is used to good effect in the story of Joseph (Gen. 42:6–45:4), and it is present throughout the book of Job. In so far as the reader is admitted beforehand into the knowledge of God's activity it might even be called divine irony (see below NT 2 (b) on John's Gospel).

(e) Prophetic irony of varying degrees, from mild sarcasm to bitter satire. This is used on the one hand with the intent of recalling God's people to a true awareness of their rebellion against him. It is found in: Samuel's descriptions of kingship (1 Sam. 8:10–18); the ironic words of God himself (Job 40:6 ff.); numerous passages in the latter prophets (e.g. Isa. 1:2–3; 28:9–10; 30:10). On the other hand, ironical scorn and ridicule is hurled at other nations and their gods, who have dared to challenge the God of Israel: Elijah's taunts at the prophets of Baal (1 Ki. 18:27); Isaiah's mockery of idols and those who make them (Isa. 44:9–20); the comical picture of the arrival of the king of Babylon in Sheol (Isa. 14:3–21). When this reaches the point of simple exultation over the weakness and downfall of one's enemies, as in Nahum, there does not appear to be much humour in it, though Rengstorf's conclusions above imply that the verb *gelaō* was primarily used in this context.

3. Rabbinic literature. It was the concern of the Rabbis at all times to maintain the majesty of God. According to Rengstorf, the Rabbis seldom spoke of laughter. *ṣāḥaq* is used for the attitude which is the exact opposite of serious application to Torah. "*ṣāḥaq* is contrasted with a pious sense of dependence on God which is well pleasing to Him. In *ṣāḥaq* there is a rejection of God as the reality which determines all things and an affirmation of man as an autonomous being" (*TDNT* I 659). The four verses noted above where God is said to laugh were assembled by the Rabbis as a surprising phenomenon and there was an attempt by them to show that the vb. in Ps. 2:4 could be taken as a piel: God will make his enemies the objects of mutual derision (Midrash Ps. 2:6).

Again, however, we discover that this has no bearing on the Rabbinic attitude to humour. Jónsson collects together evidence to show how the Talmudic literature makes a wide use of humour (op. cit. 51–89). Humour is employed when dealing with personal relationships, nature, the after life and even the Scriptures. There are humorous pictures of God, and Satan is shown in a ridiculous light. It is not permissible, however, to scoff at or parody Scripture disrespectfully, or use it to express improper ideas. The main characteristics of Rabbinic humour are self-irony and educative humour, but never humour for its own sake. Humour never becomes brutal except where serious heresies are attacked. Jónsson suggests that a knowledge of types of Rabbinic humour can supply us with a guide for recognizing humour in the teachings of Jesus (op. cit., 51 ff.).

NT 1. The incidence of the *gelaō* word-group follows the usage found in the OT rather than secular Gk. usage. In the account of Jairus's daughter *katagelaō* is the scornful, superior laughter of those who ridiculed Jesus, believing that he could do nothing about someone already dead (*kai kategelōn autou*, "and they laughed at him", Matt. 9:24; Mk. 5:40; Lk. 8:53). The story itself illustrates the power of God in Jesus over man's ultimate enemy, → death, and at the same time the emptiness of unbelief which is heightened by the use of this vb. Jesus' act shows him to be in the succession of → Elijah (1 Ki. 17:17–24) and Elisha (2 Ki. 4:17–37). Peter also performed a similar act (Acts 9:36–42). In Jas. 4:9 *gelōs* denotes activity which is inappropriate: "Be wretched and mourn and weep. Let your laughter be turned to mourning and your joy to dejection." For the thought cf. Eccl. 2:2; 7:2–6; Tob. 2:6; Sir. 21:20; 27:13. Above all it seems to reflect that of the Sermon on the Plain: "Blessed are you that weep now, for you shall laugh [*gelasete*]. . . . Woe to you that laugh now [*gelōntes*], for you shall mourn and weep" (Lk. 6:21b, 25b). Here laughter is associated with salvation joy with no thought of triumph over enemies. The parallelism between laugh and mourn is not recorded in the Sermon on the Mount (Matt. 5:6) where the saying refers to mourning (→ Lament). The thought in Lk. may be influenced by Ps. 126:1 f.: "When the Lord restored the fortunes of Zion, we were like those who dream. Then our mouth was filled with laughter [Heb. *śᵉḥôq*; LXX, however, *chara*, joy], and our tongue with shouts of joy; then they said among the nations, 'The Lord has done great things for them.' " The coming age of salvation was to be a time of joy for Israel (Test.Jud. 25); but rabbinic ethics rejected laughter in relation to it, as this was something which only God could give (Midrash Ps. 126:2; Ber. 31a; cf. SB IV, 2, 965 f.; *TDNT* I 662).

2. Humour in the NT. Again it is possible to isolate various categories of humour.

(a) The humour of Jesus in the Synoptics. Jónsson maintains that Jesus combines the rabbinic educational humour with the prophetic irony. "It may depend on our mood whether we hear the stern and threatening voice of the prophet with his sharp irony or the mild traditional humour of the Rabbi" (op. cit., 198). Jesus had a sense of comical features in the situations of daily life: a man who rushes out of the temple leaving his offering behind (Matt. 5:23–24); Matt. 5:40 is comical when it is realized that the traditional way of describing a fully dressed man was to speak of his coat, cloak and shoes! Matt. 24:43 alludes to the idiotic attitude of a man who does not prepare against robbery unless he knows the thief is coming, as a picture of men's lack of readiness for the coming of the Son of man. Matt. 4:19 is perhaps a playful picture. Lk. 7:31 notes the comical inconsistencies of people. Jesus used word play (*aphanizousin . . . phanōsin*, "disfigure . . . may be seen", Matt. 6:16; *Petros . . . petra* "Peter . . . rock", Matt. 16:18; → Rock), exaggeration (the speck and the log, Matt. 7:3; the three measures of meal, Matt. 13:33), and paradox ("who would save his life will lose it, Mk. 8:35; cf. Matt. 16:25; Lk. 9:24; Jn. 12:25 f.). He probably employed contemporary proverbs and humorous rabbinic parables (e.g. the humorous side to the picture of the rich man in Hades, still wishing to use Lazarus as a lackey (Lk. 16:23–37; cf. Talmudic humorous stories about the after-life). The use of the word *apechousin* in Matt. 6:2, 5, 16 virtually amounts to: they have had their salary and been given the receipt (A. Deissmann, *Light from the Ancient East*, 1911, 112; cf. the traditional comic stories about rewards in ML). Jónsson follows H. Clavier in his attempt to classify

433

the irony of Jesus (op. cit., 177; cf. H. Clavier, "La méthode ironique dans l'enseignement de Jésus" *Études Théologiques et Religieuses*, 1929–30, 61–5), but it is probably not possible to do this in a way which makes any clear distinctions. Jesus' response to the Canaanite woman (Mk. 7:27 par. Matt. 15:26) could have been an ironical quotation of a Jewish saying. Many of the questions Jesus directed at his opponents have an ironical ring (Matt. 9:5 par. Mk. 2:9; Lk. 5:23; Matt. 12:12 par. Mk. 3:4; Lk. 6:9; Matt. 21:25, par. Mk. 11:30, Lk. 20:4). There is irony in the way he takes well known concepts and gives them a different meaning, e.g. Mk. 2:17 where "righteous" means "self-righteous". Clavier suggests that the words of Mk. 4:11–12 are ironical, considering the blindness of the disciples (cf. Mk. 8:17–18; op. cit. 74 ff.). The language of Matt. 23 is comparable with much of the biting irony of the OT prophets.

(b) Divine irony. Jónsson points out that it would be inappropriate to speak of the humorous, i.e. comical, in John's Gospel. However, John's christology which presents so markedly a human Jesus and an eternal Christ in the same person introduces into the Gospel a sort of dualism and hence a special kind of irony. Words and ideas carry two senses at the same time (cf. 1:36; 2:19–22; 4:32; 6:20; 11:50; 12:7); and this enigma is highlighted in the Gospel by the questions which reveal lack of understanding of Jesus' words and deeds (cf. 2:18; 2:20; 3:4; 4:11). Whatever men say or do simply serves the purpose of the divine will. To a certain extent all the evangelists make use of this motif, especially in the Passion narratives (cf. the widespread use the title → king in questions, accusations, taunts and the inscription over the cross). It was probably part of the primitive passion tradition.

(c) Lighthearted portrayal of people and situations in narrative passages (as in OT and Jesus' teaching). This is found both in the Gospels and the book of Acts (cf. the gently humorous description of Zacchaeus in Lk. 19:1–6; Peter's reactions in Jn. 13; the escape from prison, Acts 5:17–32; the unclean food from heaven offered to Peter in Acts 10:9–16; Peter left knocking at the door, Acts 12:12–16; the tribune's misunderstanding, Acts 21:37–40).

(d) The humour of Paul. Paul, the Pharisee, enjoyed scholarly argumentation and there is considerable humour and irony in the tussles he had with his opponents. He posed paradoxical questions (Gal. 2:17; Rom. 3:29; Rom. 6:1; 7:7). He employed humorous illustrations, e.g. the vessel and the potter which also figured in classical and rabbinic literature as well as in the OT (Rom. 9:20–23; cf. Isa. 29:16; 45:9; Jónsson, op. cit., 225); the protest of the different parts of the body (1 Cor. 12:14–26); the instruments out of tune (1 Cor. 14:7 f.). He used word play: *mēden ergazomenous ... periergazomenous*, "not doing work ... busybodies" (2 Thess. 3:11; → Busybody). In speaking of the runaway slave Onesimus (whose name *onēsimos* means useful or beneficial), Paul remarks: "Formerly he was useless [*achrēston*] to you, but now he is indeed useful [*euchrēston*] to you and to me" (Phlm. 11; cf. also *onaimēn*, benefit, v. 20). Finally Paul was prepared to speak of himself in humorous terms. He was a nervous and unimpressive speaker: "And I was with you in weakness and in much fear and trembling" (1 Cor. 2:3). He was a laughing-stock in the arena: "For I think that God has exhibited us apostles as last of all, like men sentenced to death; because we have become a spectacle to the world to angels and to men" (1 Cor. 4:9). His boasting turns out to be a list of his sufferings and → weaknesses, or things for which he can claim no credit such as the

gospel and the commission given to him (1 Cor. 9:15–18; 2 Cor. 10:1–13:4; →
Boast). Paul's attitude to boasting may be compared with what he says about the
alazōn, boaster, braggart (Rom. 1:30; 2 Tim. 3:2; cf. Hab. 2:5; Prov. 21:24; see
also above CL 2 (c) and G. Delling, *TDNT* I 226 f.).

(e) Several flashes of humour in the other NT books. James' humorous similes:
the double-minded man (1:6 ff.); the rudder and the → fire (3:1–6); the idiotic
statement, "be warmed and filled" (2:16). In 1 Jn. there is some word play;
antichristos . . . hymeis chrisma echete, "Antichrist . . . you have an anointing"
(1 Jn. 2:18).

3. It would be wrong to give the impression that humour and irony are dominant
characteristics of the Bible, but it has been suggested that they are more theologically significant than scholars have usually allowed. At the simplest level the
Bible consists of much teaching and exhortation and every good teacher knows
that his words must be spiced with humour and irony if they are to rivet attention,
especially of those who are reluctant to listen. Irony may be understood as a
special branch of humour, and true humour is one aspect of → joy. Jónsson refers
to E. F. Carritt's theories that failure provides the food for humour, but only where
failure is not a sign of fatal disaster and where there is a sense of inner superiority
(op. cit., 17 ff.; cf. E. F. Carritt, *Theory of Beauty*, 1949, 333). This superiority,
says H. Höffding, following a similar line of thought (*Den Store Humor*, 1916,
52 ff.), in true humour is not the self-security of arrogance, but the consciousness
of being master of the situation, not indifferent to the seriousness of the battle, but
assured that nothing of true value can ever be destroyed (Jónsson, op. cit., 16 ff.).
If such reasoning is correct, humour is the natural expression of the religious joy
represented in the Bible. Jónsson approves with reservations R. Voeltzel's description of the irony of the OT which results from the fact that God, while condemning the mocking which is a sign of rebellion against himself, cannot help
seeing the ridiculous and comical in the revolt and fighting of the helpless creatures
who intend to frustrate his purposes (op. cit., 13, 48 f.; cf. R. Voeltzel, *Le Rire du
Seigneur*, 1955, 103). Similarly Barth, taking a different interpretation of Gen.
17:17 and 18:12, argues that laughter is man's humble reaction to the amazing
and ridiculous fact of man being a recipient of God's honour (K. Barth, *CD* III,
4, 665). Jesus came with a joyful message, and though he took the opposition
seriously he was profoundly conscious that the victory lay with God. Hence his
light-hearted humour (Jónsson, op. cit., 195 f.). Similarly it should be accepted as
natural "that humour was a fairly strong sentiment among the first Christians,
not in spite of the 'eschatological' situation, but because of it . . . just where we
might expect the sense of the tragic humour breaks forth, triumphing, because
failure will not be allowed to hinder the work of God" (Jónsson, op. cit., 255).

Certainly irony is written into the basic facts of redemption: God promised a
childless man who was "as good as dead" (Heb. 11:12) that he would be father
of a nation; he chose not a great and powerful nation to serve his purposes, but a
small one which was despised and often at the mercy of its powerful neighbours;
the climax of the world's rejection of God – the cross – was in fact the means he
used to redeem the world (1 Cor. 2:6–8); hence the Christian knows that he is
strongest when most aware of his weakness (2 Cor. 12:10). Biblical theology has
irony in its very essence.

Finally, however, we must notice from the above discussions that for the OT and NT *gelaō* is not the appropriate expression of joy or true humour. As with *paizō*, play, make sport, or *empaizō*, ridicule, make fun of, mock, trick, it is associated too closely with idolatry, licentiousness and irreverence. Joy is expressed in such words as *chairō*, rejoice; *agalliaō*, exult, be overjoyed; *euphrainō*, make glad; *orcheomai*, dance; *auleō*, play the flute; *adō*, sing; *psallō*, sing praise (with an instrument). The humour of the Bible is dancing and singing through the spoken and written word.   *E. M. Embry*
→ Joy, → Lament, → Pride

(a). G. Bertram, *paizō* etc., *TDNT* I 625–36; M. D. Goldman, "Humour in the Hebrew Bible", *Australian Biblical Review* 2, 1952, nos. 1–2; R. K. Harrison, "Humor", *ZPEB* III 224 ff.; F. F. Hvidberg, *Weeping and Laughter in the Old Testament*, 1962; J. Jónsson, *Humour and Irony in the New Testament, Illuminated by Parallels in Talmud and Midrash*, 1965; K. H. Rengstorf, *gelaō* etc., *TDNT* I 658–62; F. Rosenthal, *Humour in Early Islam*, 1956; J. Reumann, "St. Paul's Use of Irony", *Lutheran Quarterly* 7, 1955, 140–45; W. F. Stinespring, "Humor", *IDB* II 660 ff.; D. O. Via, *Kerygma and Comedy in the New Testament*, 1975 (concerned with comparing the structure of Gk. comedy with that of the kerygma of Paul and Mark than with humour as such); G. Webster, *Laughter in the Bible*, 1960; D. Zuver, *Salvation by Laughter*, 1933.
(b). H. von Campenhausen, "Ein Witz des Apostels Paulus und die Anfänge des christlichen Humors", in *Neutestamentliche Studien für Rudolf Bultmann*, BZNW 21, (1954) 1957², 189–93; "Christentum und Humor", *ThR* 27, 1961, 65–82; H. Clavier, "La méthode ironique dans l'enseignement de Jesus", *Études Théologiques et Religieuses*, 1929–30; "L'ironie dans l'enseignement de Jésus", *NovT* 1, 1956, 3–20; "L'ironie dans le quatrième Évangile", *Studia Evangelica*, 1959, ed. K. Aland, F. L. Cross, J. Daniélou, H. Riesenfeld, W. C. van Unnik, *TU* 73 261–76; and "Les sens multiples dans le Nouveau Testament", *NovT* 2, 1958, 185–98; P. Friedländer, "Lachende Götter", *Die Antike* 10, 3, 1934; J. Kruuse, *Humorister*, 1945; R. Voeltzel, *Le Rire du Seigneur*, 1955.

Law, Custom, Elements

The social life of man requires structure and commonly recognized rules of conduct. Within this context, the Gk. word with the widest range of meaning is *nomos*, which originally denoted a system for distributing property, based upon collective agreement. Then it acquired the more general sense of a commonly agreed public order, or, in the plur., the laws that regulate life. However, *nomos* or the plur. *nomoi* has a religious basis, being anchored in transcendence and therefore claiming absolute validity, either as authoritative divine commands or as cosmic principles. *ethos*, on the other hand, is usage or custom (unwritten but not therefore any less plain or valid), i.e. that which is normally done. In the NT it also means the custom of the priesthood. *stoicheion* denoted originally the line or rank in which one stands, hence the basic order to which one has to conform. The *stoicheia* are therefore the elements, the basic constituents of the cosmic and the human order.

ἔθος

ἔθος (*ethos*), usage, custom; ἦθος (*ēthos*), custom, way of life.

CL 1. *ethos*, found from Aeschylus onwards, stems from the root *sweth* (cf. Lat. *suetus*, accustomed, customary; Ger. *Sitte*, custom and means tradition, wont, usage, custom. With the prepositions *ex, kata, dia, en* or the instrumental dative it means "according to [these] principles" or "in the usual way".

2. The related word *ēthos*, since Homer, is a rather more abstract term, not easily distinguishable in English, however, from *ethos*.

OT In the canonical text of the OT neither word has any real Heb. equivalents; nevertheless, in the LXX *ēthos* occurs 7 times and *ethos* 8 times.

1. The Heb. form *kᵉmišpāṭ* is translated by *ethos* in a few places, including Jdg. 18:7 *v.l.*; 1 Ki. 18:28 *v.l.*: "according to the [popular, Gentile] custom", "after the manner of...." *ethos* is used thus in the sense of popular custom and particularly in connection with → feasts. In the extra-canonical writings the word always refers to a custom traditional within a given class or nation: e.g., giving presents to members of the royal family (1 Macc. 10:89); the custom of the ancestors (2 Macc. 11:25; 4 Macc. 18:5) or of the priests (Dan. Bel. 15 *v.l.*); customs relating to execution (2 Macc. 13:4), or to public worship. Even when a custom is reversed, the resulting custom can come to be ethically and legally binding (4 Macc. 18:5; Wis. 14:16, *hōs nomos*, as a law; → *nomos*).

2. In the LXX *ēthos* ordinarily conveys the idea of basic human motives or attitudes (4 Macc. 1:29; 2:7; 2:21; 5:24), a frame of mind (4 Macc. 13:27); also a manner of life resulting from certain ethical or psychological impulses, e.g., directly from the law (Sir. Prol. 27, *v.l. ennomos*; → *nomos* NT) or from virtue (4 Macc. 13:27 see above); or, negatively, from a general attitude of deceit (Sir. 20:26).

NT In the NT the two words are found 13 times altogether (*ēthos* only once, i.e. 1 Cor. 15:33; *ethos* 3 times in Lk., 7 times in Acts, once in Jn., once in Heb.). The range of meaning extends from religious custom (frequently indistinguishable from popular *mores*) to personal habit, although no hard and fast distinctions can be drawn. Some passages merely give objective information on customs or traditions, while others reflect the clash of early Christian teaching and practice with the way of life found in traditional Judaism and late antiquity. It is helpful to consider these groups separately.

In the narrative sections of the Gospels *ethos* is variously qualified as the custom of the priesthood (Lk. 1:9); the custom relating to the Passover and to the education of sons (Lk. 2:42; when the son reaches puberty at the age of 12, the father has the duty of introducing him to the requirements of God's law by taking him to the three great → feasts); Jewish burial custom (Jn. 19:40); or Christ's personal custom, e.g. of visiting the synagogue (Lk. 4:16, *kata to eiōthos autō*, "as his custom was"; cf. Acts 17:2) or, as a festival pilgrim, of teaching daily in the temple and spending the following night near the Mount of Olives outside the city (Lk. 22:39), a custom with a long tradition behind it, making it easy for Judas and the temple officers to locate him.

The following passages introduce us to early Christian polemic: Acts 15:1, the confrontation between Jewish and Gentile Christians over the necessity of circumcision (note the appeal is to the custom of → Moses [cf. Lev. 12:3], not to that of → Abraham [cf. Gen. 17:10]); previously Stephen (Acts 6:14) and subsequently Paul (Acts 26:3; 28:17) were accused of altering the customs delivered by Moses or the fathers; cf. the charge against Jesus that he wished to annul the law (Mk. 2:23 ff.; 3:2 ff.; 7:14 f.; Matt. 5:18, 21). Paul's opponents accused him of being the enemy both of the → people and of the law (cf. *nomos* NT) and of endangering both by his sectarian activities (Acts 21:28; 24:5). Paul himself appealed to Roman legal custom (Acts 25:16; cf. A. N. Sherwin-White, "Paul before Felix and Festus", *Roman Society and Roman Law in the New Testament*, 1963, 48–70). An appeal to Roman political and religious law was also made by the Roman slave-owners at Philippi (Acts 16:21) against what they conceived to be Jewish customs and religious propaganda. For Romans were forbidden to become proselytes of the Jewish religion which was a *religio licita*, legally recognized religion, and Philippi was a Roman *colonia* (cf. E. Haenchen, *The Acts of the Apostles*, 1971, 496; A. N. Sherwin-White, op. cit., 78 f., 177).

Finally, the use of *ēthos* and *ethos* shows something of the internal dangers facing the early Christian church: the church is doomed if it allows itself to be infected by the immoral habits of the surrounding world (*ēthos*, 1 Cor. 15:33). Here Paul cites the saying from the 4th cent. comedy *Thais* by Menander, "Bad company ruins good morals." Heb. 10:25 states that for some people non-attendance at public worship had already become a habit (*ethos*), an attitude of indifference which the church must seek to overcome by spiritual exhortation, pointing out the imminence of the day of judgment. *H.-H. Esser*

νόμος

νόμος (*nomos*), law, norm; νομικός (*nomikos*), pertaining to the law, learned in the law, hence legal expert, jurist, lawyer; νομίμως (*nomimōs*), conforming to the law, according to rule; νομοδιδάσκαλος (*nomodidaskalos*), teacher of the law; νομοθεσία (*nomothesia*), lawgiving, legislation; νομοθετέω (*nomotheteō*), make laws, legislate, ordain, enact; νομοθέτης (*nomothetēs*), lawgiver; ἀνομία (*anomia*), lawlessness; ἄνομος (*anomos*), lawless, unlawful; ἔννομος (*ennomos*), under law, orderly; παρανομέω (*paranomeō*), break the law, act contrary to the law.

CL 1. (a) The noun *nomos* is formed from the vb. *nemo*, distribute, deal out, assign, grant, especially in the sense of assigning property, apportioning pasture or agricultural land (cf. *nomē*, pasture). In other words, the reference is to those processes which are essential whenever men live together in a community, whether small or great. Relationships to earthly possessions have to be determined in a legally binding fashion, so that private and communal ownership may become a reality. Thus the basic vb. covers all shades of meaning from merely handing something over for a given period of time, right through to transferring something, once and for all, to the ownership of another person. By means of appropriate prepositions, personal or non-personal objects, and other qualifying phrases, ethical value-judgment can be expressed: to grant equally, exercise fairness, be impartial, also to favour, pass over, reject. The same vb. can also indicate the result of distributing property: to appropriate, own or possess, occupy, utilize; pass. to belong to. The communal aspect can still be seen in the mid.: to distribute (e.g. an inheritance) between one another.

(b) The fig. sense covers the idea of guarding what has been entrusted: to watch over, protect; and also the way the recipient is regarded by the person who distributes: to esteem, regard as, take for, respect.

2. In the same way, the word *nomos* (found in literature from the time of Hesiod, 7th cent. B.C.) originally referred to distributing and what follows from it. It meant that which has been laid down, ordered or assigned; but more particularly the results of this, namely arrangements which become regularized and attain the status of tradition. The word therefore denotes custom, usage, statute, law, especially in the context of distribution of goods, and of law and order.

The legal, ethical and religious meanings of *nomos* are inseparable in antiquity, for all goods were believed to come from the gods, who upheld order in the universe and in relations between men. Hence, the universal conviction, found throughout history, that law is linked to the divine – an idea which has persisted subconsciously even in periods when the purely human aspects of law have been emphasized (see below). The close interrelationship between the worship of the gods, the customs of the time and one's duty to the state was expressed in the charge levelled at Socrates, namely that he failed to reverence the gods officially worshipped (*nomizein*) by the city, or at least that he did not worship them as everyone else did (Plato, *Apol.* 24b; → Godliness, art. *sebomai*).

3. Used in a political context, *nomos* was regarded as the most essential feature of the *polis* or city-state, i.e. the judicial norm, legal custom, the "law of the land." From about the 5th cent. B.C. onwards, the *nomos* was written down as *nomoi* (plur. laws), thereby acquiring the specific meaning of written law, the constitution (of the *polis*), the coercive law of the state, which had to be obeyed upon pain of punishment. This purely political view of *nomos* led to relativization and an increasingly man-centred approach to law. Many Gk. tragedies rest on the fact that one law stands over against another, both claiming validity but mutually incompatible. Hence, men are caught in the toils of such conflict, as in Sophocles' *Antigone*. Indeed, *nomos* is sometimes even disparaged as a human exaggeration, compared with *physis* (→ Nature) or universal law.

4. Philosophy (even that of the Sophists), kept alive the awareness that, since human laws are so fallible, man cannot exist unless he conforms to cosmic, universal law. Only when a man is inwardly in harmony with the universe does he have peace of mind amid the vicissitudes of life (as the Stoics). Whereas the Sophists criticized the idea of absolute validity attaching to *nomos*, Plato and Aristotle each in his own way connected it with the *nous*, the human spirit, and thereby once again with the divine (cf. H. Kleinknecht, *TDNT* IV 1032). The period of late antiquity in the time of the NT suffered from no longer having a *nomos* of binding force throughout the known world. Most of the gnostic systems sought to project earthly law into the higher sphere of the ground of all being. This represented a wistful attempt to regain, by religious means, the lost unity of law itself and of life lived under the law.

OT 1. In the LXX *nomos* occurs about 430 times, of which about 200 are without Heb. equivalents; for the rest, the commonest equivalent is *tôrâh*, with *dāṭ* occurring 16 times and *ḥōq*, *ḥuqqâh* 12 times. In the canonical OT, *nomos* is concentrated most heavily in the Pentateuchal books other than Gen., occurring about 60 times, of which 25 are in Deut. and 20 in Lev. Next come Ezra and Nehemiah, if one counts the apocryphal 1 Esd. (53 times), then the Pss. (40 times, of which 27 are in Ps. 119 (LXX 118). Among the prophets Jer. uses the word most frequently (15 times). The frequent use of the word in the extra-canonical books (it occurs about 100 times in the Books of the Maccabees and 30 times in Sir.) indicates the importance of law in the Judaistic thought of the last two centuries B.C. Of the derivatives (see NT below) only *anomia* (lawlessness; about 150 times) and *anomos* (lawless; about 50 times) are numerically significant in the LXX.

2. This paragraph deals with those passages in the LXX where *tôrâh* is translated by *nomos*. It is important to note that *tôrâh* frequently does *not* mean "law" in the modern sense of the term. At a time when the Jews saw "law" as the transcript of an eternal norm, and the Greeks likewise thought of *nomos* as having definite content, the predominant use of the latter word must have produced a striking translation.

(a) Originally *tôrâh* (mostly used in the sing.) meant an instruction from God, a command for a given situation. The plur. which also occurs indicates the concreteness and variability of such instructions (cf. Exod. 16:28; 18:16, 20, translated, significantly enough, by *ton nomon*, "the law", in all three places). Instruction for given situations was also given by the prophets (Isa. 1:10; 5:24 and passim; Mic. 4:2; Jer. 6:19), by the priests (Hos. 4:6; Jer. 2:8; Deut. 17:9, 11; Ezek. 7:26) or by a judge (Deut. 17:9, 11 f.). The prophets threatened judgment on those priests and prophets who issued their own instruction without having received it from Yahweh (Jer. 2:8; 8:8; Zeph. 3:4; Ezek. 22:26).

(b) Human counsel given by a teacher of wisdom (Prov. 13:14; 28:4, 7, 9) can also be called *tôrâh* and *nomos*.

(c) Nearer the concept of law are the specific instructions for the different kinds of offering (Lev. 6 and passim); or for a definite priestly procedure (Num. 5:29, when adultery is suspected); or with regard to the Nazirites (Num. 6:13, 21).

(d) Only after the Deuteronomic reform did phrases such as "the law of Yahweh" become widespread, epitomizing the laws in general, and without any further qualification or any enumeration of the individual laws involved (2 Ki. 10:31; Exod. 13:9; Amos 2:4, a Deuteronomic expansion of a Yahwistic basic text; Jer. 8:8 and passim); similarly "the law of God" (Jos. 24:26 and passim), delivered by Moses (Jos. 8:31 [LXX 9:2]; 2 Ki. 23:25 and passim). Deut. is itself called "the book of this law" (Deut. 28:61; cf. 29:20; 30:10; 31:26; cf. G. von Rad, *Old Testament Theology*, I, 1962, 221; Jos. 1:8; 2 Ki. 22:8, 11), and after the Exile the whole Pentateuch is so called (Neh. 8:3). Corresponding to this is the formula "written in the law", found in the post-exilic literature (Neh. 8:14; 10:35 [LXX 34], 37 [LXX 36]; Dan. 9:11; 2 Chr. 23:18 and passim), where the law is seen as a written norm.

(e) The verbs used in connection with *tôrâh* indicate whether the latter is conceived of as oral instruction or as written law. Oral instruction is presupposed by such formulae as: to teach instruction (Exod. 18:20); to hear it (Isa. 42:24); to forget it (Hos. 4:6); to despise it (Isa. 5:24); to violate it (Hos. 8:1). On the other hand, the following phrases indicate written law: to observe, to keep the law (Ps. 119 [LXX 118]:34, 44; Prov. 28:4 and passim); to → walk in the law, i.e. to order one's life by the law (Exod. 16:14; Ps. 78 [LXX 77]:10; 119 [LXX 118]:1; 2 Chr. 6:16 and passim).

3. *ḥōq* denotes: (a) Yahweh's sacrificial requirement, his right to receive sacrifice (Lev. 6:15 [LXX 22]); or (b) the legal system proclaimed in the cult, to which

Israel is bound (Jos. 24:25; cf. A. Alt, *Essays on Old Testament History and Religion*, 1966, 126; G. von Rad, op. cit., I, 30). The fem. *ḥuqqâh* (in the plur. *ḥuqqôt*) has the meaning: (a) creation ordinances, laws of nature (Jer. 31[LXX 38]: 36); (b) the ordinance of the passover (Exod. 12:43; Num. 9:3, 14 and passim; [→ Feast, art. *pascha*]); (c) statutes regulating everyday life (Lev. 19:19, 37); (d) sacrificial ordinances (Jer. 44 [LXX 51]:23).

4. The equivalent *dāṭ* occurs only in the late OT writings, always denoting a written law: either (a) the law of God (Ezr. [LXX 2 Esd.] 7:12, 14, 21, 25, 26; Dan. 6:6 [LXX 6:5]; here identical with religion, worship of God); 7:25; Est. 3:8 (plur. interpreted as the laws of the people); or (b) the law or decree of the king (Ezr. 7:26; Est. 1:8, 13, 15, 19, 3:8; 4:16).

5. This survey is sufficient to show that we cannot speak simply of "the law in the OT" as if it expressed a uniform concept, much less of the OT itself as law. Even in the Pentateuch the later generic term *tôrâh* or law is an example of the part standing for the whole (see above 2 (d)). There are essentially three types of "law" to be distinguished:

(a) *Casuistic law*, which was pre-Israelite in origin, and was largely taken over after the conquest from Canaanite legal custom. It has its setting "in the gate", where the law was administered. Large sections of the Book of the Covenant (Exod. 21:1–23:19) contain such lists of laws, each with the characteristic form: "if . . . then. . . ."

(b) *Apodeictic law*, which is of genuine Israelite origin, stemming from the period when the tribes were still mobile, and set out in thematic series of ten or twelve for ease of memorizing: "he that . . . shall surely be put to death" (Exod. 21:12. 15 ff. and passim); or "I am Yahweh . . . thou shalt not . . ." (as in the Decalogue, Exod. 20:2 ff.; → Command). Here the setting is the worshipping community, especially at the feast of the covenant and the feast of the renewal of the covenant; such law "watches over man in his humanity" (G. von Rad, op. cit., I, 195). In the OT, incidentally, the Ten Commandments were never called "law" (ibid.).

(c) *Purely cultic regulations*, to be carried out and expounded by the → priests (see above 2 (c); cf. also Hag. 2:11 [LXX 12]).

The law inherent in such passages is part and parcel of the → covenant. It is the rule of life for those who have been redeemed (see the First Commandment, which is the basis of the other nine). It sets out "the obedience of men who have come of age" (von Rad, op. cit., I, 198; cf. Deut. 30:14). The commandments "were not a law, but an event, with which Jahweh specifically confronted every generation in its own *hic et nunc* [here and now], and to which it had to take up its position" (op. cit., 199). The law thus had a prophetic character. This original view of law changed in the post-exilic period, when the community was considered to be actually *constituted* by the law (Neh. 8). The law came to be viewed as a set of rigid rules, instead of serving the community as an ordinance of salvation. (On the whole subject see G. von Rad, op. cit., I, 187–279 and the various works listed in the bibliography below.)

6. For the Qumran sect's view of law → Command, art. *entolē*, OT 3.

7. (a) In the Judaism of the last two centuries B.C. and at the time of Jesus *nomos* was used in an absolute sense: the law was an absolute in itself and was independent of the covenant. It is fulfilment of the law that determines one's membership of the

people of God. Israel no longer saw her special status as due to Yahweh's living self-revelation in the course of her history, but considered this status to rest upon the obedience of those who were righteous in terms of the law (→ Pharisees). Visible observance of the law was what distinguished the true Israel both from non-Jews and from the godless Jewish masses. In other words, the law had assumed a dominant role as mediator between God and man, and had become personified as an intermediary with a hypostasis of its own. The whole of life could be regulated, and was regulated by the law. In Hellenistic Judaism especially, the law came to stand alongside → wisdom, which had likewise come to be seen as having a hypostasis. In this respect the law had become separated from its original setting, namely the → covenant as given by God. Moreover, it could now be presented as universal law, i.e. as universally valid. This was important in the Hellenistic world, where any system of thought had to be able to compete apologetically with existing philosophies. Furthermore, its universality was extended backwards in time. The patriarchs, it was claimed, already knew it, in fact it antedated the whole of creation. By universalizing the law in this way and detaching it from the covenant, Hellenized Jews were able to give it a rational basis and proclaim it as a superior philosophy (→ Command, art. *dogma* OT). The method they adopted was to allegorize it, which involved cutting it loose from its historical roots.

(b) Similarly, Rabbinic Judaism no longer saw God's self-revelation as tied to the covenant, but rather to the Torah as a covenant ordinance. Thus the Torah came to occupy the place of a "canon within the canon", even before the latter was finally determined; i.e. the Torah became normative over against the other two sections of the OT, namely the Prophets and the Writings. These were held merely to develop what was already germinally present in the Torah. Israel believed that the Torah (identical with the Pentateuch) had been delivered ready-made by God to Moses. God had committed himself to it, but not only so, he is eternally committed to it. Man's life and death hung upon fulfilling its commands, and with it his religious pride and shame (see Lk. 18:9–14). The Torah was regarded as capable of fulfilment. As an aid towards this goal, use was made both of casuistry and of summaries of the law in the form of a few commandments or of one basic commandment. Rabbi Hillel (*c.* 20 B.C.) instructed a proselyte: "What you do not like, do not do to your neighbour. That is the whole Torah, everything else is merely interpretation; go and study it" (Shab. 31a; cf. SB I 460). The dictum states the negative counterpart of the Golden Rule in Matt. 7:12. Rabbi Hillel also claimed that Amos (5:4) and Hab. (2:4) reduced the Torah to one commandment (Mak. 23b–24a; cf. W. Gutbrod, *TDNT* IV 1058 f.). In the Judaism of the time of Christ, the study and fulfilment of the Torah were considered to be the way to righteousness and the way to → life (cf. Lk. 10:28).

NT In the NT the noun *nomos* (191 times) occurs most frequently in Paul: 119 times, predominantly in Rom. (72 times), Gal. (32), 1 Cor. (9). Non-Pauline books where the word occurs fairly frequently are Acts (17 times), Jn. and Heb. (14 each), Jas. (10), Lk. (9), Matt. (8). *nomos* does not occur in Mk., in the Catholic Epistles apart from Jas., or in Rev. Its infrequent appearance in the Synoptic Gospels should not blind us to the fact that Jesus dealt intensively with the whole problem of the law (cf. Mk. 2:23–28; 10:1–12 and passim).

442

1. The summaries of Christ's work as given in Jn. 1:17 and Eph. 2:14–18 also apply to his own preaching. In all that he said and did, he removed the law from its mediatorial position and opened up immediate access to God (cf. especially the group of parables in Lk. 15; also 18:9–27; Matt. 11:28–30 and many other synoptic passages).

(a) His testimony to the significance of John the Baptist (Matt. 11:7–19) is enhanced to become an indirect testimony to himself (vv. 11–15): the Baptist is → Elijah come again (v. 14), who brings one divine dispensation to an end, and proclaims the arrival of a new one where the kingdom of God comes directly among men (cf. Mal. 4:5; Matt. 17:10–13; Jn. 1:21; Lk. 1:17). Thus the preaching and teaching of the prophets and of the law reaches its → goal (v. 13) and comes to an end. "The prophets and the law" here are regarded to some extent formally as constituent parts of the OT scriptures, but the main reference is to their content as salvation history. The wording here draws attention not only to the precedence accorded to the prophets over the law, but also to the dynamic view of both: they proclaim, preach, prophesy (*propheteuein*; → Prophecy). The parallel passage in Lk. 16:16 makes a point of inserting these words of Jesus into the whole scheme of salvation history: "law and prophets until John" (note the absence of a vb.). From that point onwards the → kingdom of God is proclaimed directly, like the news of great victory (*euangelizetai*; → Gospel).

Similarly, in the antitheses of the Sermon on the Mount (Matt. 5:21–48) Jesus put an end to all self-satisfaction at having kept individual commandments of the law (vv. 20, 46). He dealt with them radically by pointing out that at root they require absolute conformity to the requirements of the divine majesty in thought as well as in deed (vv. 20, 48). Thus he made the unprecedented claim that what was said in the law to the men of old (vv. 21, 27, 31, 33, 38, 43) is now made out of date once and for all by himself: "But I say unto you . . . ." (v. 22, 28, 32, 34, 39, 44). In the eyes of those who did not acknowledge him as bringing in God's kingdom or recognize his teaching as being the rule of life for the church of the last days, this claim must have made his condemnation for seeking to abolish the law (v. 17) a foregone conclusion.

(b) Jesus makes it clear at this point, however, that his claim was not levelled against the law (Matt. 5:17–19), but against man's self-righteous attitude to the law (vv. 19–20; cf. Paul in Rom. 7:12). He set himself to fulfil in detail the law's demand for a life of utter obedience to God (v. 17; cf. 3:15), as he had done already from his circumcision onwards, and continued to do until his death on the cross. Even his condemnation was in accordance with established Jewish law (cf. Jn. 19:7). The inviolability of the law (Matt. 5:18; cf. Lk. 16:17) likewise determined Christ's attitude in conversation with the teachers of the law (*nomikoi*), who were specialists in the ethical interpretation of the law, and the theological leaders of the → Pharisees. Jesus shared the view that the law could be summed up in two great commandments (Matt. 22:34–39; cf. Lk. 10:25–28), but he rejected the Pharisees' gradations within the double commandment. (On the two great commandments → Command, art. *entole*; → Hear, art. *akouo*; → Large, Small, art. *megas*.) Moreover, in his repeated cries of "Woe to you!" (Matt. 23:13–16, 23, 25, 27, 29; cf. Lk. 11:42 ff. 46 f., 52) he condemned their failure to recognize the basic intention of the law, namely → justice, → mercy and → faith (Matt. 23:23).

(c) In the words of Jesus and in the usage of Matt. and Lk. the reference is generally to the whole law as a part of Scripture, without any further delineation of content. (This does not apply, of course, to verbatim quotations from the Torah.) Thus: "the law" (Matt. 5:18; 12:5; Lk. 2:27; 10:26; 16:17); "the law and the prophets" (Matt. 5:17; see above 1 (a)); "the law of the Lord" (Lk. 2:23, 24, 39); "the law of Moses" (Lk. 2:22; cf. also Acts 28:23 "... and the prophets"); "Moses and the prophets" (Lk. 24:27). The threefold formula "Moses and the prophets and the psalms" also occurs (Lk. 24:44).

2. Paul, confronted as he was by his own Pharisaic past and by his Jewish and Jewish Christian opponents, developed a theology of the law that is connected historically with the promise and on a personal level with Christ. In doing so, however, he is far from regarding himself as a second teacher of Christianity either in addition to, or in place of Jesus. His teaching remains within the limits previously laid down by Jesus; he merely brings out the basic significance of Christ's work, now completed in the → cross and → resurrection. As Lk. 10:25–37 shows, it is possible to keep the law fully (v. 37) only by being in fellowship with him, listening to his loving voice, and → following him. In the same way, after his resurrection, it is only the man who is "in Christ" who can keep the law, not with any thought of works-righteousness, but rather out of gratitude and in the liberty of one set free to love and obey. Paul also follows Jesus (see above 1 (a)) in denying the absoluteness of the law and the idea that it alone was the way to salvation (see below (a)–(d)). He took this position, however, not because of any emotional complexes arising from his being a converted Pharisee (cf. Phil. 3:5–11), but because he saw the uniqueness and newness of Christ. As the → Apostle to the Gentiles, he has the prophetic insight to realize that without a comprehensive theology of law as a background, the universal claims of the → gospel would lack all justification and credibility (see Rom. and Gal.).

Paul used *nomos* for the Pentateuch (Rom. 3:21b; Gal. 4:21) and for the whole of Scripture (Rom. 3:19, a generic term for the quotations of vv. 10–18, taken from all three parts of Scripture: 1 Cor. 14:21 citing Isa. 28:11 f. and Deut. 28:49), but especially for the Mosaic law, and the Decalogue in particular (Rom. 2:14a; 2:17; 3:28; 7:12; Gal. 5:3) in its demand for unconditional obedience from the Jews. Rom. 2:14b is to be translated "The Gentiles are law to themselves" (RSV), because the implication is that God has given them the law in another way (cf. v. 15). ([Ed.] Karl Barth has argued, however, that this passage refers to Gentile converts who, in fulfilment of the prophecy of the new covenant in Jer. 31:33, have the law "written on their hearts" [cf. *CD* I, 2, 304; II, 2, 242, 604; IV, I, 33, 369, 395; J. B. Souček, "Zur Exegese von Röm. 2:14 ff." in *Antwort. Karl Barth zum siebzigsten Geburtstag*, ed. E. Wolf, C. von Kirschbaum, R. Frey, 1956, 99–113].) Paul also uses *nomos* to indicate a part of the law (e.g. marriage law, as it affects the woman, Rom. 7:2b), and in the metaphorical sense, mostly defined by a genitive (e.g. Rom. 3:28, divine commands in the widest sense; Rom. 7:23c, 25b; 8:2; Gal. 6:2, genitive of authorship; Rom. 7:23 a and b, regular principle). Paul often personifies the law: it speaks (Rom. 3:19); it says (Rom. 7:7; 1 Cor. 9:8); it works (Rom. 4:15); it rules (Rom. 7:1). In doing this, he is not subscribing to the idea of law as a hypostasis (see above OT 7), but he means that the law is the mouthpiece of the living God.

Paul views the law against the background of the → cross of Christ. (a) In his death on the cross Jesus upheld the law's condemnation of all men. He became a curse (Gal. 3:13; cf. Deut. 21:23). He was made sin, yet only as the representative for the sins of others (2 Cor. 5:21; cf.: "he was reckoned with the transgressors", *meta anomōn*, Lk. 22:37; Mk. 15:28; both quoting Isa. 53:12). These statements indicate a deliberate, vicarious act by Jesus on our behalf.

(b) At the same time he fulfils all the obedience required by the law (Phil. 2:8). Paul's addition of the words "even death on a cross" in v. 8b to what was probably an already existing hymn stresses Christ's complete oneness with those enslaved under the law. (On this hymn see R. P. Martin, *Carmen Christi: Phil. ii. 5–11 in Recent Interpretation and in the Setting of Early Christian Worship*, 1967; → Empty, art. *kenos*.) Now that he has fulfilled the law, salvation rests not on our meeting certain conditions, but upon the simple fact that the law has now been fulfilled (Rom. 3:31).

(c) Having → faith, the Christian is no longer under the law (1 Cor. 9:20b). He is free to be "as one outside the law [*anomos*] to those outside the law [*anomois*]" (note the play on words in the four-fold use of this adj., v. 21). He is also free to fulfil the law in → love (Rom. 13:10b; Gal. 5:14, 22), to be as one under the law (1 Cor. 9:20) to those under the law, i.e. the Jews. The author and inspirer of such love is the Holy → Spirit of God and of Christ, who translates the Christian from the realm of the law and the → flesh with its resulting → sin and → death (Rom. 8:4; Gal. 5:18, 22).

(d) Since Christ is the end and → goal (*telos*) of the law for believers (Rom. 10:4), Paul can look back from his vantage-point, as it were, and describe the law, both as having no more part to play in salvation, and at the same time as having a valid function apart from Christ (Rom. 5:20 f.; Gal. 3:19–29). The law, which is holy and good (Rom. 7:12), was one of God's gifts to Israel (Rom. 9:4, here *nomothesia* means the giving of the law). It came in (Rom. 5:20), being introduced by God into the history of sinful man (Gal. 3:19) in order to "increase the trespass" (Rom. 5:20; cf. 7:8–13; 1 Cor. 15:56b; → Command, art. *entolē* NT 2 (a)), and in order to "confine" men under law and sin, with no prospect of escape until Christ should come (Gal. 3:22 f.) – a dreadful thought, were it not for God's superabundant grace (Rom. 5:20b) and his gift of sonship (Gal. 3:25 ff.)!

(e) The individual who stands before God "under the law" (*en nomō*, Rom. 2:12b) has to reckon with the following consequences: the law demands entire obedience (Gal. 3:10, quoting Deut. 27:26); only he who *does* the law will live and be justified (Gal. 3:12b, quoting Lev. 18:5; Rom. 2:13b), while he who does not is condemned (Gal. 3:10; Rom. 2:12b). No one is justified before God merely by hearing or knowing the law (Rom. 2:12, 13a). To be justified one needs to be made alive, which is precisely where the law fails (Gal. 3:21; Rom. 7:9 f.); only those who have faith in Christ are made alive (Gal. 3:26 f.). Thus law is linked with → sin, and → faith with → promise. However, the law is not contrary to the promise (Gal. 3:17), rather it has an educational part to play, both within redemptive history and in individual experience, driving men to Christ and to faith in him. The law is a *paidagōgos*, "custodian" (Gal. 3:24, 25; RSV). The word means lit. "boy-leader". The *paidagōgos* was usually a slave whose duty it was to take the pupil to school and supervise his conduct generally (Arndt, 608; → Teach, art.

paideuō). The law produces the startling realization of sin which does not save (Rom. 3:20; 7:7); but it calls forth a cry for help in one's lost condition (Rom. 7:24), a cry which can be answered effectively only by Jesus Christ (Rom. 7:25).

(f) Even the man who sins "without the law", i.e. one before Christ came, or outside the bounds of Christianity, does not conform to the will of God (Rom. 3:23; note the twofold use in Rom. 2:12a of the adv. *anomōs*, found only here in the NT). Outside the law men are judged by God according to whether they have done right (Rom. 2:6 f.), for the Gentiles can know what is good, the work of the law being written in their hearts (v. 15; cf. 1:32). Thus a Jew who does the law is in the same position as a Gentile who does good works (vv. 13, 7), while a Jew who sins under the law is in the same position as all men, whether Jew or Gentile, who do evil (vv. 12b, 9). Whether they live within the Jewish law, or outside, it both groups will meet with the same → judgment, without respect of persons (vv. 11 f., 16), according to their works. Destruction and death await all men (Rom. 3:23, 27; 7:10, 11c, 13), for no one has put into practice his knowledge of what is good (3:23; 7:18 f., 21). All men, therefore, depend for salvation upon the work of Christ which has to be appropriated by faith (Rom. 3:25 f., 29 f.), without the works of the law (v. 28), and also without the participation (*chōris*) of the law (v. 21). The words "But now" introduce a totally new situation.

(g) This indicates the fundamental weakness of the law, namely that its only answer to sin is to forbid it and condemn it. Law cannot overcome sin, because it depends on the co-operation of the → flesh, which is weak (Rom. 8:3). Here "the flesh" means would-be autonomous human nature, incapable of obedience. The law is part of the fabric of this world (→ *stoicheia*), and therefore cannot lead us beyond it. What the law demands can be wrought only by the Spirit on the basis of the work of Christ (v. 4; see above (e)). The law is essentially a letter that kills, while the life of the new covenant is the → Spirit who makes alive (Rom. 7:6; 2 Cor. 3:6).

(h) The commandment to love, which can be fulfilled in the Spirit (see above (c) and (g)), can now be called the "law of Christ" (Gal. 6:2; cf. 1 Cor. 9:21: to be *ennomos* of Christ, to be *under the law* of Christ). It is the Torah of the Lord, which he himself has lived out. Now, on raising men to spiritual life, he can require of them its fulfilment.

(i) Occasionally the law is invoked as a secondary authority, in order to provide scriptural support for Paul's injunctions to the Christian church. In 1 Cor. 9:8 ff. he makes allegorical use of Deut. 25:4 to back up his claim that, as an apostle, he had the right to be materially supported by the church. In 1 Cor. 14:21 he combines quotations from Deut. 28:49 and Isa. 28:11 f. in order to regulate speaking with tongues, and in 1 Cor. 14:34 he refers to Gen. 3:16 to support his command that women be silent in the church, a command which is probably not meant to apply generally, but specifically to speaking with tongues: women are not to push in themselves forward in this matter. Basically, however, the life of the church is controlled not by the principle: "Anything contrary to the law is sin", but rather by "Whatever does not proceed from faith is sin" (Rom. 14:23).

3. In Eph. (which some scholars count as deutero-Pauline) and the Pastoral Epistles there are statements which are in complete accord with Paul's theology of the law, but also some others which show that controversy had now arisen over

the law's function and which *prima facie* uphold the law as a regulative principle.

(a) Eph. 2:15 is fully in line with Paul's doctrine of the law (see above 2 (b) and especially → Command art. *dogma* NT).

(b) In the struggle against (gnostic?) libertinism and asceticism 1 Tim. 1:8 repeats the assertion of Rom. 7:12 that the law is good. But whereas Rom. develops the rôle of the law in provoking and convicting of sin, 1 Tim. 1:9 f. enumerates various categories of sin condemned by the law. Christ has appeared "to deliver us from all lawlessness [*anomia*]" (Tit. 2:14, quoting Ps. 130:8). The law is "a rule of life which is self-evident to the respectable man; the others [the *anomoi*, the lawless] experience it rightly as compulsion" (M. Dibelius, *Die Pastoralbriefe*, ed. H. Conzelmann, *HNT* 13, 1966⁴ on 1 Tim. 1:9). The "just" in this verse no longer appears to be a man justified by → faith (cf. Rom. 1:17; Gal. 3:11). In Rom. Paul did not say that the law is good when it is used lawfully (*nomimōs*); for his position regarding the law's absolute holiness, and also regarding the use of the law, see Rom. 7:12 ff. The false teachers of the law (*nomodidaskaloi*, 1 Tim. 1:7) are those who preach antinomianism (as here) and also those who lead the church astray with their ascetic demands (1 Tim. 4:1–3). This passage is thoroughly Pauline in its exhortation to receive God's good gifts of creation in a spirit of faith and thanksgiving, and not to stand aloof from them in the interests of certain ascetic regulations. Like 1 Tim., Tit. 3:9 recommends the avoidance of quarrels about the law (*machas nomikas*). The Gk. background is apparent in the use of *nomikos*, lawyer (Tit. 3:13) and of *nomimōs*, according to the rules of the contest (2 Tim. 2:5). In the apocalyptic section 2 Thess. 2:1–12 the fact that Christ's return has not yet occurred is explained in Jewish apocalyptic fashion as follows: the man of lawlessness (*anthrōpos tēs anomias*, v. 3) or the lawless one (*anomos*, v. 8) must first appear, and the mystery of lawlessness, although already at work, is not yet revealed (v. 7; cf. Matt. 24:12; see A. Oepke, *Die Briefe an die Thessalonicher*, *NTD* 8, 1965¹⁰ ad loc.; L. Morris, *The Epistles of Paul to the Thessalonians*, *NLC*, 1959, 217–32; → Antichrist; → Present: The Parousia Eschatology in the NT).

4. In his logical development of Pauline thought the writer of Heb. sees the law, especially the sacrificial law, as a manifestation of the old → covenant, inferior to and now superseded by the new covenant (8:13; 10:9b). There are extensive passages proving the superiority of the single, once-for-all → sacrifice of Christ, the great High Priest, over the offerings of the OT priests, a sacrifice, moreover, in which he himself is both the offering and the offerer (4:14–5:10; 7:1–10, 18; cf. also the Moses-Christ typology of 3:1–6).

Thus in working out his teaching on inferiority and superiority, the writer puts *nomos* in the negative part of his comparisons: cf. 7:5 with 7:6–8 (→ Melchizedek as a type of Christ, and the contrast "those descendants of Levi who receive the priestly office ... but this man ..."); 7:12 with 7:13 ff.; 7:16a with 7:15, 16b, "not according to a legal requirement concerning bodily descent"; 7:19a with 19b, "the law made nothing perfect ... on the other hand, a better hope"; 7:28a with 7:28b, "the law men appointed in their weakness ... but the word of the oath ... appoints a Son"; 8:4 f. with 8:5b and 6, "priests who offer gifts according to the law ... serve as a copy and shadow. ... a more excellent ministry ... a better covenant ... better promises"; 9:19 ff. with 9:24 ff., the repeated sacrifice of the high priest with the "once for all" sacrifice of Christ; 10:1 with 10:2b, "offered year after year . . . once cleansed"; 10:8 with 10:9a, 10, offerings made according to the law but not desired . . . the readiness of Christ to do the will of God.

The vb. *nomotheteō*, to give laws (pass., to receive laws) is similarly used to present the same antithesis: the people of the old covenant received the law under the Levitical priesthood (7:11), while Christ is the mediator of a better covenant, legally instituted on the basis of better promises (8:6).

As in Paul, the overcoming of lawlessness (*anomia*) by Christ is the ground on which the new covenant is based: the Son has hated lawlessness (1:9, quoting Ps. 45:7), and the Holy Spirit, speaking through the prophets, promised that one day it would be finally forgiven; that day has now come (10:17, quoting Jer. 31:34). Since the new covenant is now a reality, the writer can state that the law never made anything perfect (7:19; 10:1c), and that the OT sacrifices are finished: "where there is forgiveness, there is no longer any offering for sin" (10:18).

5. In the Gospel of Jn. Christ and the Jews clash vehemently over the question of the law. For Jesus claims personally to reveal God, whereas they represent the rebellious "world". They measure him by the law (7:23, 52; 8:5; 12:34, where passages from the Pss. [110:4] and the Prophets [Isa. 9:7; Ezek. 37:25; Dan. 7:14] are treated as law; 19:7), and he in return measures them by the law. He has an absolute knowledge of it, expounds it and uses it to expose their hypocrisy (7:19; 8:17; 10:34; 15:25; in both of the last named passages Ps. 82:6 and 35:19 are called "law"). These disputes are thought by Bultmann and others to reflect the controversy with Jewish gnosticism on the part of the author and the churches he represents (cf. R. Bultmann, *The Gospel of John*, 1971, ad loc.; but → Knowledge, art. *ginōskō*).

The Gospel of Jn. develops the basic thesis (1:17) that, as compared with the law given by → Moses, the → knowledge and → truth revealed in Jesus Christ bring the full revelation of God. (Bultmann, op. cit., 79, points out the similarity here to Pauline thought.) Christ's repeated use of "your law" (8:17; 10:34) and "their law" shows that the Son is not subject to the law. He charged the Jews with appealing to Moses merely in self-justification; not one of them kept the law (7:19; cf. Rom. 2:17–24). When it comes to healing and forgiveness, he cut through the pedantry and complacency with which they treated the law (7:23; 8:5 ff.). The passage about the woman taken in adultery (7:53–8:11), which is a later insertion in the Gospel of Jn. and is missing from the best manuscripts, clearly reveals the tension between Jesus and his opponents who were zealous for the law. He used the law or the "writings" of the OT to support his testimony to himself (8:17; cf. Deut. 19:15; 10:34; cf. Ps. 82:6). The Jews, on the other hand, were prevented from recognizing God's present revelation in Christ, the → scripture being to them nothing but the letter, i.e. rules and regulations (5:39; 12:34; cf. Ps. 110:4; Isa. 9:7; Ezek. 37:25; Dan. 7:14).

The extent to which the handling of the law had become a matter for the specialists and therefore something to be exploited, is shown by the debate in the Sanhedrin after an abortive attempt to arrest Jesus. "The people do not know the law" (7:49), say the Pharisees, while one of their number, Nicodemus, has to point out their own disregard of the law (v. 51). (On the well-attested scorn of rabbinic scholars for the common people of the land see SB II 494–521; → People, art. *ochlos*.)

The last legal debate (before Pilate) over the fate of Jesus demonstrates the utter paradox of his opponents' enslavement to the law. As an occupied people, the Jews were not permitted to carry out the death penalty laid down in Lev. 24:16; and Exod. 20:7 (cf. Jn. 5:18). By demanding that Christ's accusers should judge him according to their own law, Pilate adroitly extracts from them admission of their hatred and also of their impotence (18:31). Only by appealing to their own law, the law of Moses (19:7) can the Jews get their prisoner put to death, albeit by a method which treats their law with contempt. By thus rejecting the revelation of Christ, however, they merely make his willing sacrifice a reality. At the same time the judgment of the law falls not only upon him, but upon them (15:2 ff.), as Jesus has warned them it would (cf. Ps. 69:5; on the condemnation of Jesus as "King of the Jews" → King, art. *basileus*, NT 1 (c)).

6. In 1 Jn. 3 and 4 the equation of sin with lawlessness or transgression of the law (*anomia*) occurs twice. This does not imply some new legal ethic, but combats what many scholars regard as the gnostic heresy of sinlessness (see 1:8, 10; cf. 2 Pet. 2:1 f., 8, a polemic against the type of life characterized by "lawless deeds [*anomois ergois*]"). 1 Jn. distinguishes between "sin unto death" (5:16b) which is apostasy from true faith in Jesus, the Son of God (5:1–12), and "sin not unto death" (5:16a and 17), which can be confessed and forgiven (1:9). He who remains in the true faith acknowledges that he needs forgiveness for his transgressions against the law (*anomia*), and that such forgiveness is available to him. For him everything depends on abiding in Christ (2:1b; 3:6), he then keeps the → commandments and does what is well-pleasing to God (3:22 ff.; cf. W. Marxsen, *Introduction to the New Testament*, 1968, 262 ff.).

7. James uses twice the apparently contradictory phrase "the law of liberty [*nomos eleutherias*]" (1:25; 2:12), both times in connection with his peculiar emphasis on not merely hearing but doing the word (1:22). The addition of the adj. *teleios* (perfect) in 1:25 shows a background of Jewish thought (cf. Ps. 19:7), while the combination "law of liberty" in Gk. has a mainly Stoic origin. The phrase probably comes from the Jewish-Christian diaspora and refers chiefly to those collections of Christ's sayings, such as the Sermon on the Mount (Matt. 5–7) and the Discourse on the Plain (Lk. 6:20 ff.), which were regarded as the rule of life. Any man putting them into practice was thereby set free from a literal observance of the OT law (see M. Dibelius, *Der Brief des Jakobus*, KEK 15, 1964[11], 110–113, 138). On both occasions the reward of blessedness is promised to him who obeys the law of liberty. The preceding context and 2:13 make it clear that deeds of → mercy (art. *eleos* NT 5 (b)) are the chief element in the law of liberty. Jas. also calls this law the "royal law [*nomos basilikos*]" (2:8), which can be summarized in the command to love one's neighbour. ("Royal" need not necessarily refer to Jesus the King; it may equally refer simply to the grandeur of this commandment; see M. Dibelius, op. cit., 32 ff.) He who keeps this commandment is free from the fear of having to keep the whole of the Jewish law by a minute observance of every single commandment (2:10 f.; cf. Gal. 3:10). It is still true, however, that he who rides roughshod over this royal law by showing partiality will finally fall under "judgment without mercy", exactly as if he had not kept the OT law (2:13a). The prohibition of slander and judging (4:11 f.) has its origins both in the OT (Lev. 19:16) and in the NT (Matt. 7:1–5; cf. Rom. 2:2), like many of James' sayings. The

meaning of "law" will then depend on how it is taken, being either an injunction in the OT sense, or alternatively "the law of liberty", a summary of Christ's injunctions (see above). The import remains the same, however. To speak ill of a brother (a fellow church-member) is to speak ill of the law and to sit in judgment upon it. Again, man is meant to be a doer of the law (see above) but the lawgiver (*nomothetēs*) and judge are one, and a man who judges another has ultimately to do with him whose judgment is final (4:12; cf. Rom. 14:4). The twofold use of "one" for the divine name (common in Judaism) with the predicate *ho dynamenos* ("who is able . . .") enables the reader to identify the "lawgiver" as both the Father and the Son. (On the attitude of James and Paul to justification, faith and works → Faith, art. *pistis* NT 4.)

8. Acts gives a vivid picture of the controversies over the law which arose in the early church. On the one hand, there were the Jews and Jewish Christians who remained true to the law, and on the other, Hellenistic Christians who thought in universal terms (see above 3; also E. Haenchen, *The Acts of the Apostles*, 1971, 100–3, 112 f., 267 f., 362 f., 440–72). With the exception of 15:5 and 23:29 all references to the law are found in discourses which, while not having the nature of purely independent evidence, accord well with the author's historical approach and bring both persons and situations into sharp relief. There is a striking parallel between the accusations and prosecution which the Hellenistic Christian leaders had to face, and the treatment meted out to Jesus. To that extent the disciples are indeed not above their master (Matt. 10:23 ff.).

The charges levelled against them were as follows: speaking against the → temple and the law (6:13, against Stephen, see also v. 11); persuading people to worship God in a way that is "contrary to the law [*para ton nomon*]" (18:13, against Paul in Corinth); teaching "all men everywhere" against the people, the temple and the law (21:28, against Paul in Jerusalem; cf. also 21:21). For similar charges concerning the temple see Matt. 26:61 par. Mk. 14:58; 24:2 par. Mk. 13:2; Jn. 2:19–21; and concerning the law: Matt. 5:17 f.; Rom. 3:31. In the course of his defence, Stephen asserted that the temple is not God's dwelling place (7:48 f.) and went so far as to charge the Jews with not keeping the law (7:53; cf. Rom. 3:19 f.; Jn. 7:19). This so provoked the Jews that he was immediately lynched, being stoned to death before his trial was properly over (7:57 ff.). Paul, on the other hand, when defending himself against his Jewish accusers before Festus, opened his speech with the assertion that he had committed no offence either against the law of the Jews or against the temple (25:8).

This is in line with the policy he had adopted ever since his recent arrival in Jerusalem. Having welcomed him to the city with joy, the Jewish Christians pointed out that they had remained zealous for the law (21:20), and referred to the unfavourable reports about him which were in circulation, the essence of which was that he taught the Jews to forsake → Moses, → circumcision and Jewish custom (→ *ethos* NT). Since his life was in danger, they advised him to show the Jews and Jewish Christians that he was true to the law (*phylassōn ton nomon*, v. 24) by undertaking the discharge of four destitute Nazirites, an act of charity considered particularly pious among the Jews. This advice to Paul, and the fact that they insisted once again that Gentile Christians should observe the so-called apostolic decree (cf. 15:28 f.), show the efforts made by the Jerusalem church leadership to maintain the utmost loyalty to the Jews and at the same time not to lose contact with Gentile Christianity as promoted by Paul (on 21:15–26 see Haenchen, op. cit., 606–18).

Paul complied with the request of the Jerusalem church and behaved as a devout Jew (21:26), but being recognized again by Jews from Asia Minor, who protested publicly (21:27 f.) against his missionary activities, he was very nearly lynched. Claudius Lysias, the tribune of the occupying forces, permitted him to address the people after his arrest, whereupon Paul emphasized his upbringing in the law (22:3) and also Ananias' loyalty to the law (22:12; cf. his speeches when defending himself before Felix and Agrippa, 24:14; 26:5). The high priest who had him struck on the mouth during interrogation was accused by Paul of violating the law (*paranomein*; see Lev. 19:15a; cf. Jn. 18:22 f.) while administering the law (23:3).

This positive attitude of Paul to the law is explained by his freedom from the law, as set out in 1 Cor. 9:19 ff. (see above 2 (c)). He knew that he was in the service of the gospel, and saw no inconsistency between his present attitude and his insistence, when writing from Corinth to Rome, that in God's purposes of salvation the law has now come to an end (Rom. 10:4; cf. Rom. 11:13 f.). The picture of Paul which emerges from the Acts is of an apostle who, on the one hand, opposed the Jewish Christians in their demand that Gentile converts be obliged to practise circumcision and to keep the law (15:18), but who, on the other hand, delivered the terms of the apostolic decree to the churches (16:4; cf. 15:28 f.), and even had his (half-Jewish, half-Greek) assistant Timothy circumcised out of regard for the Jews (16:3). When preaching in the synagogue at Pisidian Antioch, Paul appeared to present Christ as merely completing the justification left unfinished by the law (13:38). Alternatively, we may see it as Lk.'s intention to delineate in broad terms Paul's preaching of justification as distinguished from the law of Moses (cf. E. Haenchen, op. cit., 412).

It is noteworthy that the Roman authorities tended to reject the charge of total illegality levelled against the preaching of the early Christians and to treat such matters as mere controversies over Jewish law: Gallio (18:15); Claudius Lysias (23:29); cf. Pilate (Jn. 18:31).

9. For the view of Christian faith as a "new law" in the post-apostolic period, see → Commandment, art. *entolē*, NT 4, 5.   *H.-H. Esser*

| $\sigma\tau o\iota\chi\epsilon\tilde{\iota}\alpha$ | $\sigma\tau o\iota\chi\epsilon\tilde{\iota}\alpha$ (stoicheia), elements, rudiments; $\sigma\tau o\iota\chi\epsilon\omega$ (stoicheō), be in line with, hold to; $\sigma\upsilon\sigma\tau o\iota\chi\epsilon\omega$ (sy-stoicheō), stand in the same line, correspond to, conform to. |

CL The root *stichos* or *stoichos* means row, rank, line, especially battle line (since Herodotus, 5th cent. B.C.), but also line of verse (cf. the words distich, acrostic). From this root came the vbs. *stichaomai*, dep. mid., and *stoicheō*, to be in a row or line, to belong to a row, to remain in a line, to march in rank and file (found in literature from the beginning of the 4th cent.); or (metaphorically), to step into line (by giving an undertaking); also the noun *to stoicheion*: especially the gnomon on a sundial, or the shadow on a sundial, the length of the shadow, or metaphorically,

451

a part of a word (i.e. letter, syllable), component part of the universe (i.e. element), hence original component (i.e. beginning, foundation, etc.). All these meanings are in evidence by the beginning of the 4th cent. B.C. The derivative *systoicheō* (from the 2nd half of the 4th cent.) has an intensive meaning: to be in the same line, to keep in line.

OT In the LXX the noun occurs only in the Apocrypha, and then only 3 times (always plur.). In two places (Wis. 7:17; 19:18) the meaning is "elements of the universe", "matter", and in the other (4 Macc. 12:13) "the substance of human life". The vb. *stoicheō* is found only in Eccl. 11:6, in the sense to succeed, to prosper; the Heb. equivalent *kāšēr* has the further meaning to be fitting (cf. Est. 8:5; see above CL).

NT 1. In the NT the vb. occurs only 5 times (once in Acts and 4 times in Paul). Acts 21:24c gives the clearest sense: "will see that you too are in the ranks as one who keeps the law [*stoicheis kai autos phylassōn ton nomon*]" (G. Delling, *TDNT* VII 668; → *nomos* NT 8). In other words, the reference is to leading a closely regulated life, living according to definite rules. This is also shown by Phil. 3:16: "Only let us hold true to what we have attained [*stoichein*]." This is the earliest and shortest reading; the other readings elaborate on the common standard by which our lives are to be lived, or the need for a common outlook. In Gal. 6:16 Paul uses the word "canon" to describe the rule just given in v. 15, and links it with the vb.: "keep to this rule of life" (RSV: "walk by this rule"). Gal. 5:25b should accordingly be paraphrased: "conduct our lives in conformity with the Spirit" (cf. H. Schlier, "order our lives according to the Spirit," *Der Brief an die Galater*, KEK 7, 1951[11], ad loc.). In Rom. 4:12 the idea of constancy in a given direction is provided by the context: "follow in the footsteps of the faith of our father Abraham" (cf. Arndt, 777). The compound *systoicheō* (Gal. 4:25) concludes one of the two lines of descent from → Abraham in vv. 22 ff., that namely of slavery: Hagar belongs to the same line (*systoichei*) as the present → Jerusalem. Sinai, the mountain on which the law was given, is here linked with *stoicheō* just as "law" is in Acts 21:24.

2. The noun is used exclusively in the epistles of the NT (7 times, always in the plur.; 4 times in Paul, once in Heb. and twice in 2 Pet.). The two apocalyptic passages, 2 Pet. 3:10, 12, are the simplest to interpret: the reference to "the elements" (v. 10) means earth, water and air, of which only the first is named explicitly, the last being understood as "the heavens". When the world is consumed these elements will be dissolved or will melt (vv. 10, 12) in the primeval element, fire. The meaning of Heb. 5:12 is also clear, because of the presence of *archē*, → beginning. The linking of these two words in *ta stoicheia tēs archēs*, "first principles" or "rudimentary elements" has a derogatory ring which is further emphasized by the reminder that the readers need milk and not solid food. The recipients of Heb. are not familiar with even the first principles of the faith. The elementary doctrines are further defined in 6:1 ff.

In the case of Gal. 4:3, 9 and Col. 2:8, 20 it is a disputed question whether or not the *stoicheia tou kosmou*, the "elements of the world", are angels, demons, gods, i.e. personified forces as taught by a certain gnostic heresy. Most commentators hold this to be the case (cf. G. Delling, *TDNT* VII 684 ff., footnotes 95–108). But Delling himself takes the passage in Gal. 4 to refer to the Torah with its statutes and the world of false gods which the readers once served. In Col. the expression refers to religion before and outside Christ. However, the question is relatively unimportant, since the hierarchy of beings taught by gnosticism, while partly syncretistic from the viewpoint of the history of religion, was in fact the product of a philosophico-religious view of the world and of existence (cf. H. Jonas, *The Gnostic Religion*, 1963²; → Knowledge).

The important point is that in Gal. 4:1–11 Paul has nothing positive to say about "the elements of the world"; he knows they have been overcome by Christ the Redeemer. Compared with him they are weak and beggarly (v. 9; → poor, art. *ptōchos* NT 3 (b)) and not the gods (v. 8) the Gentiles believed them to be before conversion. Even the law is reckoned as among the elements of the world (cf. the 1st person plur., vv. 3, 5) and hence is declared null and void. Thus "the elements of the world" cover all the things in which man places his trust apart from the living God revealed in Christ; they become his gods, and he becomes their slave (cf. Luther's exposition of the First Commandment in the *Large Catechism*).

In Col. 2:8, human tradition and "the elements of the world" both come under the heading of "philosophy" which seeks to prey upon men (*sylagōgein*). Such "philosophy", however, has long since been defeated by Christ and has appeared as a captive in his triumphal procession (vv. 10–15; on the Col. heresy cf. G. Bornkamm, *Gesammelte Aufsätze*, I, 1958², 139–86; M. D. Hooker, "Were there false teachers in Colossae?" in B. Lindars and S. S. Smalley, eds., *Christ and Spirit in the New Testament. Studies in honour of C. F. D. Moule*, 1973, 315–31). Just as in Gal. 4:3, 5 "the elements of the world" and the law are combined, so in Col. 2:20 "the elements of the world" are disapprovingly linked with "regulations" by the word *dogmatizein* (→ Command, art. *dogma* NT 1 (b) and 3). He who has died with Christ (v. 20) has nothing further to do with them and so is freed from the burdens they would impose on his day-to-day life (vv. 21 ff.; on the new life in Christ, see 3:1). "The worship of the elements of the world is based on the assumption that the problem of life is both ultimate and insoluble. The early Christians, however, believed that they had the answer, and that it lay in the character and work of God" (E. Lohmeyer, Excursus "Elemente der Welt", *Die Briefe an die Philipper, an die Kolosser und an Philemon*, KEK 9, 1956¹¹, 103 f.).

H.-H. Esser

→ Command, → Covenant ,→ Fullness, → Goal, → Gospel, → Israel, → Moses, → Promise, → Prophet, → Righteousness, → Teach, → Work

On law in the OT and in the ancient world:
(a). A. Alt, "The Origins of Israelite Law", *Essays on Old Testament History and Religion*, 1966, 79–132; H. Cazelles, "Law in the Old Testament", *EBT* II 480, 84; D. Daube, *Studies in Biblical Law*, 1947; W. D. Davies, *Torah in the Messianic Age and for the Age to Come*, 1952; O. Eissfeldt, *The Old Testament: An Introduction*, 1965, 155–241; I. Engell, "The Pentateuch", *Critical Essays on the Old Testament*, 1970, 50–67; Z. W. Falk and H. J. Wolff, "Private Law", in S. Safrai, M. Stern, D. Flusser and W. C. van Unnik, eds., *The Jewish People in the First Century*, 1974, 504–60; R. K. Harrison, *Introduction to the Old Testament*, 1970, 493–662; M. Jastrow, *Dictionary of the Talmud*, 1930; H. Kleinknecht and W. Gutbrod, *nomos* etc., *TDNT* IV 1022–59; H. Jonas, *The Gnostic Religion*, 1963²; L. Koehler, *Old Testament Theology*, 1957, 107–10; B. Lindars, "Torah in Deuteronomy", in P. R. Ackroyd and B. Lindars, eds., *Words and Meanings: Essays Presented to David Winton Thomas*, 1968, 117–36; H. Miskotte, *When the Gods are Silent*, 1967; E. Nielsen, *The Ten Commandments in New Perspective*, SBT Second Series 7, 1968; M. Noth, *The Laws in the Pentateuch and Other Studies*, 1966; G. Oestborn, *Tora in the Old Testament*, 1945; A. Phillips,

Ancient Israel's Criminal Law: A New Approach to the Decalogue, 1970; G. von Rad, Old Testament Theology, I, 1962, 187–279; II, 1965, 388–409; and The Problem of the Hexateuch and Other Essays, 1966; J. J. Stamm and M. E. Andrew, The Ten Commandments in Recent Research, SBT Second Series 2, 1967; R. de Vaux, Ancient Israel: Its Life and Institutions, 1961, 143–63; J. Weingreen, "The Deuteronomic Legislator – A Proto-Rabbinic Type", in J. I. Durham and J. R. Porter, eds., Proclamation and Presence: Old Testament Essays in Honour of Gwynne Henton Davies, 1970, 102–32; revised in From Bible to Mishna, 1976; W. Zimmerli, The Law and the Prophets: A Study of the Meaning of the Old Testament, 1965.

(b). J. Begrich, Thorah, BZAW 66, 1936; G. Bertram, "Zur Bedeutung der Religion der Septuaginta in der hellenistischen Welt", TLZ 92, 1967, 245 ff.; H. Cazelles, Études sur le Code de l'Alliance, 1946; A. Dünner, Gerechtigkeit nach dem Alten Testament, 1963; O. Eissfeldt, "Das Gesetz ist zwischeneingekommen", TLZ 91, 1966, 1 ff.; C. Feucht, Untersuchungen zum Heiligkeitsgesetz, 1963; R. Hentschke, "Gesetz und Eschatologie in der Verkündigung der Propheten", Zeitschrift für evangelische Ethik 4, 1960, 46 ff.; F. Horst, Gottes Recht. Gesammelte Studien zum Recht im Alten Testament, 1961; H. Jonas, Gnosis und spätantiker Geist, I, 1964³; II, 1, 1954; B. Reicke, Die zehn Worte in Geschichte und Gegenwart. Zählung und Bedeutung der Gebote in den verschiedenen Konfessionen, Beiträge zur Geschichte der biblischen Exegese 13, 1973; R. Rendtorff, Die Gesetze in der Priesterschrift, 1963²; H. Graf Reventlow, Das Heiligkeitsgesetz, 1961; D. Rössler, Gesetz und Geschichte. Untersuchungen zur Theologie der jüdischen Apokalyptik und der pharisäischen Orthodoxie, 1962²; J. Schreiner, Die zehn Gebote im Leben des Gottesvolkes. Dekalogforschung und Verkündigung, 1966; E. Würthwein, "Der Sinn des Gesetzes im Alten Testament", ZTK 55, 1958, 255 ff.; W. Zimmerli, "Das Gesetz im Alten Testament", TLZ 85, 1960, 481 ff.

On law in the NT:

(a). L. Baeck "The Faith of Paul", Journal of Jewish Studies 3, 1952, 93–110; R. Banks, "Matthew's Understanding of the Law: Authenticity and Interpretation in Matthew 5:17–20", JBL 93, 1974, 226–42; Jesus and the Law in the Synoptic Tradition, Society for New Testament Studies Monograph Series 28, 1976; and "The Eschatological Role of Law in Pre- and Post-Christian Jewish Thought", in R. Banks, ed., Reconciliation and Hope: New Testament Essays on Atonement and Eschatology Presented to L. L. Morris on his 60th Birthday, 1964, 173–85; R. S. Barbour, "Loyalty and Law in New Testament Times", SJT 11, 1958, 337–51; G. Barth, "Matthew's Understanding of the Law", in G. Bornkamm, G. Barth and H. J. Held, Tradition and Interpretation in Matthew, 1963, 58–164; P. Bläser, "Law in the New Testament", EBT II 185–95; G. Bornkamm, Early Christian Experience, 1969; and Paul, 1971; B. H. Branscomb, Jesus and the Law of Moses, 1930; F. F. Bruce, "Paul and the Law of Moses", BJRL 57, 1974–5, 259–279; R. Bultmann, "Christ the End of the Law", Essays Philosophical and Theological, 1955, 36–66; and The Gospel of John, 1971; C. E. B. Cranfield, "St. Paul and the Law", SJT 17, 1964, 43–68; and The Epistle to the Romans, ICC, I, 1975; W. D. Davies, Law in the Messianic Age, 1952; Paul and Rabbinic Judaism, 1955²; "Matthew 5:17, 18", Christian Origins and Judaism, 1962, 31–66; The Setting of the Sermon on the Mount, 1964; and The Sermon on the Mount, 1966; G. Delling, stoicheō etc., TDNT VII 666–87; J. D. M. Derrett, "Law in the New Testament", ZNW 56, 1965, 184 ff.; and Law in the New Testament, 1970; C. H. Dodd, "Natural Law in the Bible", Theology 49, 1946, 130–33, 161–67 (reprinted in New Testament Studies, 1953, 129–43); "ennomos Christou", More New Testament Studies, 1968; 134–48 (first published in Studia Paulina, in honorem Johannis de Zwaan, 1953); and Gospel and Law: The Relation of Faith and Ethics in Early Christianity (Bampton Lectures in America, 1950), 1951; J. W. Drane, Paul - Libertine or Legalist? A Study in the Theology of the Major Pauline Epistles, 1975; A. Ehrhardt, "Christian Baptism and Roman Law", The Framework of the New Testament Stories, 1964, 234–55; E. E. Ellis, Paul's Use of the Old Testament, 1957; H. L. Ellison, "Paul and the Law – 'All Things to All Men' ", in W. W. Gasque and R. P. Martin, eds., Apostolic History and the Gospel: Biblical and Historical Essays presented to F. F. Bruce on his 60th Birthday, 1970, 195–202; R. T. France, Jesus and the Old Testament, 1971; W. Gutbrod, nomos etc., TDNT IV 1059–91; E. Haenchen, The Acts of the Apostles, 1971; G. E. Howard, "Christ the End of the Law: The Meaning of Romans 10:4 ff.", JBL 88, 1969, 331–37; J. Jervell, "The Law in Luke-Acts", HTR 64, 1971, 21–36; E. Käsemann, "Sentences of Holy Law in the New Testament", in New Testament Questions of Today, 1969, 66–81; G. E. Ladd, A Theology of the New Testament, 1975, 495–510; R. Longenecker, Biblical Exegesis in the Apostolic Period, 1975; F. Lyall, "Roman Law in the Writings of Paul – Aliens and citizens", EQ 48, 1976, 3–14; M. Maher, " 'Take my yoke upon you' (Matt. xi. 29)", NTS 22, 1975–76, 97–103; J. M. Meyers,

Grace and Torah, 1975; H. Preisker, *ethos*, *TDNT* II 372 f.; H. Schlier, *Principalities and Powers in the New Testament*, 1961; R. Schnackenburg, *God's Rule and Kingdom*, 1963; H. J. Schoeps, *Paul: The Theology of the Apostle in the Light of Jewish Religious History*, 1961, 168–218, 280–93; E. Schweizer, "Observance of the Law and Charismatic Activity in Matthew", *NTS* 16, 1969–70, 213–30; A. N. Sherwin-White, *Roman Society and Roman Law in the New Testament*, 1963; J. G. Strelan, "Burden-Bearing and the Law of Christ: A Re-examination of Gal. 6.2", *JBL* 94, 1975, 266–76; M. J. Suggs, *Wisdom, Christology and Law in Matthew's Gospel*, 1970; J. B. Tyson, "'Works of Law' in Galatians", *JBL* 92, 1973, 423–31; D. E. H. Whiteley, *The Theology of St. Paul*, 1964, 76–86; R. McL. Wilson, "Nomos: The Biblical Significance of Law", *SJT* 5, 1952, 36–48.

(b). W. Andersen, *Ihr Seid zur Freiheit berufen: Gesetz und Evangelium nach biblischem Zeugisn*, Biblische Studien 41, 1964; K. Berger, *Die Gesetzauslegung Jesu*, I, *WMANT* 40, 1972; L. Baeck, *Paulus, die Pharisäer und das Neue Testament*, 1961; P. Bläser *Das Gesetz bei Paulus*, 1941; "Glaube undSittlichkeit bei Paulus", in *Vom Wort des Lebens* (Festschrift M. Meinertz), 1951, 114–21; and "Gesetz und Evangelium", *Catholica* 14, 1960, 1–23; G. Bornkamm, *Das Ende des Gesetzes. Paulusstudien. Gesammelte Aufsätze*, I, 1966[5]; M. Dibelius, "Die Bergpredigt", *Botschaft und Geschichte*, I, 1953, 79 ff.; *Der Brief des Jakobus*, *KEK* 15, 1964[11]; *An die Kolosser, an die Epheser, an Philemon*, *HNT* 12, ed. H. Greeven, 1953[3]; and *Die Pastoralbriefe*, *HNT* 13, ed. H. Conzelmann, 1970[3]; C. Dietzfelbinger, *Paulus und das Alte Testament*, *ThEH* 95, 1961; K. Galley, *Altes und neues Heilsgeschehen bei Paulus*, 1965; C. Haufe, "Die Stellung des Paulus zum Gesetz", *TLZ* 91, 1966, 171 ff.; J. Jeremias, "Paulus als Hillelit", in E. E. Ellis and M. Wilcox, eds. *Neotestamentica et Semitica: Studies in Honour of Matthew Black*, 1969, 88–94; E. Jüngel, "Das Gesetzzwische n Adam nud Christus", *ZTK* 60, 1963, 42 ff.; and *Paulus und Jesus. Eine Untersuchung zur Präzisierung der Frage nach dem Ursprung der Christologie*, 1967[3]; W. G. Kümmel, "Paulus und die jüdische Traditionsgedanke", *ZNW* 33, 1934, 105 ff. (reprinted in *Heilsgeschehen und Geschichte*, 1965, 15 ff.); and "'Das Gesetz und die Propheten gehen bis Johannes' – Lukas 16, 6 im Zusammenhang der heilsgeschichtlichen Theologie der Lukasschriften", in O. Böcher and K. Haacker, eds., *Verborum Veritas. Festschrift für Gustav Stählin zum 70. Geburtstag*, 1970, 89–102; O. Kuss, "*nomos* bei Paulus", *Münchener Theologische Zeitschrift* 17, 1966, 173–227; H. Ljungman, *Das Gesetz erfüllen. Mt. 5, 17 ff. und 3, 15 untersucht*, 1954; E. Lohmeyer, *Die Briefe an die Philipper, an die Kolosser und an Philemon*, *KEK* 9, 1956[11]; E. Lohse, *Christologie und Ethik im Kolosserbrief*, *BZNW* 30, 1964; S. Lyonnet, *Liberté chrétienne et Loi nouvelle*, 1953; C. Maurer, *Die Gesetzlehre des Paulus*, 1941; O. Michel, *Der Brief an die Römer*, *KEK* 4, 1966[13]; F. Neugebauer, *In Christus. Eine Untersuchung zum paulinischen Glaubensverständnis*, 1961; K. Niederwimmer, *Der Begriff der Freiheit im Neuen Testament*, 1966; A. Oepke, *Die Briefe an die Thessalonicher*, *NTD* 8, 1965[10]; K. H. Schelkle, *Paulus – Lehrer der Väter. Die altkirchliche Auslegung von Röm. 1–11*, 1959; H. Schlier, *Der Brief an die Galater*, *KEK* 7, 1951[11]; E. E. Schneider, "Finis legis Christus, Röm. 10, 4", *ThZ* 20, 1964, 410 ff.; H. J. Schoeps, "Jesus und das jüdische Gesetz", *Studien zur unbekannten Religions- und Geistesgeschichte*, 1963, 41 ff.; A. Schulz, *Unter dem Anspruch Gottes. Das neutestamentliche Zeugnis von der Nachahmung*, 1967; H. Schürmann, "Wer daher eines dieser geringsten Gebote auflöst . . .", *BZ* 4, 1960, 238–50; E. Schweizer, "Die 'Elemente der Welt' Gal. 4, 3. 9; Kol. 2, 8.20", in O. Böcher and K. Haacker, eds., op. cit., 245–59; G. Söhngen, *Gesetz und Evangelium*, 1957; P. Stuhlmacher, *Gottes Gerechtigkeit bei Paulus*, 1965; W. Trilling, *Das wahre Israel. Studien zur Theologie des Matthäus-Evangelium*, 1959; P. G. Verwejs, *Evangelium und neues Gesetz in der ältesten Christenheit bis auf Marcion*, 1960; R. Walker, "Allein aus Werken", *ZTK* 61, 1964, 155 ff.

On the law generally in theology:

(a). K. Barth, *CD*, I, 2; II, 2; III, 3; III, 4; IV, 1; IV, 2; IV, 3 (see indexes); and "Gospel and Law", in *God, Grace and Gospel*, *SJT Occasional Papers No. 8*, 1959, 3–27; C. Brown, *Karl Barth and the Christian Message*, 1967 (see index); E. Brunner, *The Divine Imperative: A Study in Christian Ethics*, 1937; J. H. Deibert, "Law-Gospel or Gospel-Law?", *SJT* 15, 1962, 225–34; G. Ebeling, "On the Doctrine of the *Triplex Usus Legis* in the Theology of the Reformation", and "Reflections on the Doctrine of the Law", *Word and Faith*, 1963, 62–78, 247–81; J. Ellul, *The Theological Foundation of Law*, 1961; E. F. Kevan, *The Grace of Law: A Study in Puritan Theology*, 1964; W. Lillie, *The Law of Christ: The Christian Ethic and Modern Problems*, 1956; J. Murray, *Principles of Conduct: Aspects of Biblical Ethics*, 1957; I. T. Ramsey, ed., *Christian Ethics and Contemporary Philosophy*, 1966; H. Thielicke, *Theological Ethics*, I, *Foundations*, 1968; II, *Politics*, 1969 (see indexes); G. Wingren, *Creation and Law*, 1961.

(b). P. Althaus, *Gebot und Gesetz*, 1952; W. Andersen, *Der Gesetzbegriff in der gegenwärtigen theologischen Diskussion*, *ThEH* 108, 1963; H. Beintker, "Zur Vollmacht der ethischen Forderung des Gehorsams", *TLZ* 91, 1966, 241 ff.; H. Berkhof, "Gesetz und Evangelium", in *Vom Herrengeheimnis der Wahrheit. Festschrift H. Vogel*, 1962, 127 ff.; G. Bornkamm, "Gesetz und Natur", *Studien zu Antike und Christentum. Gesammelte Aufsätze*, II, 1959, 93 ff.; R. Bring, "Die Erfüllung des Gesetzes", *Kerygma und Dogma* 5, 1959, 1 ff.; O. Bückmann *et al.*, "Gesetz", *EKL* 1 1551 ff.; K. Frör, "Die theologische Lehre von Gesetz und Evangelium und ihre Bedeutung für Pädagogik", in *Glauben und Erziehen. Festgabe G. Bohne*, 1962, 127 ff.; H. Gerdes, "Die Frage von Gesetz und Evangelium in der gegenwärtigen theologischen Diskussion", in *Wahrheit und Glaube, Festschrift E. Hirsch*, 1963, 100 ff.; H. von Glasenapp *et al.*, "Gesetz", *RGG*³ II 1511–33; H. Gollwitzer, "Zum Verhältnis von Gesetz und Evangelium", *Theologia Viatorum* 8, 1960–61, 30 ff.; and "Zur Einheit von Gesetz und Evangelium", in E. Wolf, C. von Kirschbaum, R. Frey, eds., *Antwort. Karl Barth zum siebzigsten Geburtstag*, 1956, 287–309; H.-J. Iwand, *Gesetz und Evangelium Nachgelassene Werke*, IV, ed. W. Kreck, 1964; W. Joest, *Gesetz und Freiheit*, 1960³; K. H. Kandler, "Evangelium nihil aliud quam expositio legis", *Neue Zeitschrift für sytematische Theologie*, 4, 1962, 127 ff.; W. Kreck, "Schöpfung und Gesetz", *Kirche in der Zeit* 15, 1960, 369 ff.; E. Lange, *Die zehn grossen Freiheiten*, 1965; A. T. van Leeuwen, *Christentum in der Weltgeschichte*, 1966; W. Matthias, "Der anthropologische Sinn der Formel Gesetz und Evangelium", *EvTh* 22, 1962, 410 ff.; R. C. Schultz, *Gesetz und Evangelium in der lutherischen Theologie des 19. Jahrhunderts, Arbeiten zur Geschichte und Theologie des Luthertums*, 4, 1955; G. Wingren, "Adam, wir und Christus", *Kerygma und Dogma* 7, 1961, 54 ff.; E. Wolf, "Christum habere omnia Mosis, Bemerkungen zum Problem Gesetz und Evangelium", *Für Kirche und Recht. Festschrift für J. Keckel*, 1959, 287 ff.; W. Zimmerli, "Das Gesetz und die Freiheit", *Juden, Christen, Deutsche*, 1961, 294 ff.

Layman

ἰδιώτης

ἰδιώτης (*idiōtēs*), layman, unlettered, uneducated, unskilled.

CL *idiōtēs* (from *idios*, own, personal, private), found in Gk. from Herodotus onwards, means: (a) a private person as opposed to an occupant of a public office (e.g. a ruler), or an individual citizen as opposed to the state or the totality of citizens; (b) a layman as opposed to an expert (e.g., a priest, judge, or philosopher); generally, an unlettered person as opposed to one who has knowledge; (c) an outsider as opposed to one who "belongs".

OT *idiōtēs* occurs in the LXX only in Prov. 6:8b, without a Heb. equivalent. The rabbis borrowed the word from the Gk., in the form of *heḏyôṭ*, and used it similarly for (a) a private person as opposed to the king; (b) a layman as opposed to an expert, particularly an expert in the law, and virtually an equivalent for *'am hā'āreṣ*, the people of the land or common people (cf. T. Taan. 4:12) because of their lack of learning; (c) man as opposed to God.

NT In the NT *idiōtēs*, which occurs only 5 times, is used as in CL (b) and (c) above, but not as in CL (a).

In Acts 4:13 the word is used in the sense of unlettered, uneducated: "When they ... perceived that they were uneducated [*anthrōpoi agrammatoi*], common men [*idiōtai*], they wondered" (RSV). Likewise 2 Cor. 11:6: "Even if I [Paul] am unskilled in speaking [*idiōtēs tō logō*], I am not in knowledge" (RSV).

The *idiōtai* in 1 Cor. 14:16 are all those who do not possess the gift of tongues and who therefore, not understanding what is said when this gift is exercised, cannot join in the → Amen to the church's thanksgiving. Similarly, in 1 Cor. 14:23,

24, the same word refers to those who are "uninitiated" into speaking in tongues. They are unbelievers (*apistoi*), i.e. non-Christians, who attend Christian meetings from time to time. For their sakes, Paul urges that public worship should be intelligible. The context lends no support to the view (e.g. of Arndt, 371) that these *idiōtai* are those not in full church membership, i.e. proselytes or catechumens.

If *idiōtēs* is translated by "layman", it is important to note that the NT word is not used to distinguish church members from priests or clergy, for such a distinction was not drawn in the NT church. Rather, the word denotes outsiders as distinct from Christians. A distinction between church members and clergy was first made in A.D. 95 by Clement of Rome, who applied to believers the word *laïkos* (from *laos*, people; 1 Clem. 40:5). The original emphasis was simply that all belonged to the *laos*, the → people (cf. H. H. Walz, *RGG*³, IV 204; Lampe, 790, 792). *O. Flender*

Arndt, 371; H. Schlier, *idiōtēs*, *TDNT* III 215 ff.; Lampe, 668; Moulton-Milligan, 299.

Lead Astray, Deceive

πλανάω

πλανάω (*planaō*), lead astray, cause to wander, mislead; πλάνη (*planē*), wandering, delusion, error; πλάνος (*planos*), leading astray, deceitful, deceiver, imposter; ἀποπλανάομαι (*apoplanaomai*), go astray, wander away; (ἐξ-)ἀπατάω ((*ex-*)*apataō*), trick, deceive; ἀπάτη (*apatē*), deception, trickery, deceitfulness; παραλογίζομαι (*paralogizomai*), cheat, deceive, delude.

CL The Gk. root *plan-* has its origin in the Indo-Germanic root **pela-* to spread out. Also related are the French *flâner*, to saunter around (cf. also German *flanieren*), and the Norwegian *flana*, to drive around. The original meaning of *planaō* (Homer) implies movement in space: in the act., to lead astray; in the mid. and pass., to go astray, be led astray. *planē* or *planos* (first found in the tragic poets) means going astray, roaming; *planētēs* is a wanderer.

1. (a) The active form of the vbs. *planaō* and *apoplanaō* is seldom used in its lit. sense. But in a transferred sense the vb. means to lead astray, deceive, by one's behaviour or one's words. This can refer to a person's judgment or to actions in the realm of morals. (*apo-*)*planaomai* means lit., to wander from or roam about. It can be used of men, powers, beasts, rumours, dreams, and even of blood or breath pulsing through the body. It is by no means to be assumed that it always has a negative undertone. In a transferred sense the vb. comes to mean to wander off course, miss the mark, in thought, speech or action. Here again the word carries no implication of guilt. The most that can be said is that it contains a summons to right judgment (cf. → Sin, art. *hamartia* CL).

(b) In classical tragedy man's mistakes are seen as a fate laid upon him by the gods (as in the cases of Oedipus and Prometheus). In Plato the way to right insight leads through error. The gnostics and the mystery cults used the word almost as a technical term for man's entanglement in the world from which he must be released.

(c) Similar meanings characterize the other derivatives of this group of words. *planos* as an adj. (Menander) means inconstant, unsteady, deceiving; as a noun it means deviation wandering about, or imposter. *planē* has the same meaning as

457

the vb.: vacillation and error are characteristics of human life which are at first stated as facts without further qualification. Thus in Plato *planē* can be used to express digression of thought. The change to a negative sense can only be said to have occurred when *planē* is used of disorder of the parts of the soul which leads to *adikia*, injustice, and *kakia*, evil.

2. (*ex*)*apataō* and *apatē* are sometimes synonymous in meaning with words from the root *plan-*. The emphasis is, however, somewhat different. The basis for deceit and trickery is here not to be sought in *agnoia*, ignorance, so much as in an *epithymia*, desire. *apatē* accordingly comes to mean pleasure, enjoyment, that which is diverting, the pleasant illusion of the theatre. The noun can be personified and occurs as a woman's name. A negative sense is not at first attached to it, though this develops later.

3. *paralogizomai*, attested from Isocrates, is a negative form of *logizomai*, to calculate, reckon, consider. It connotes deception, cheating by false reasoning.

OT 1. There is no direct Heb. equivalent to the group of words derived from *plan-*.
planaō most frequently stands for *tā'âh* (qal, to wander about; hiph., to lead astray). The classical meaning of the Gk. word is taken over in the LXX. The spatial sense of the vb. is found where mention is made of leading the → blind astray (Deut. 27:18), and is also the basic concept behind the description of people staggering as a result of drinking wine (cf. Isa. 19:13 f.; 28:7; → Drunken, Sober). The frequent use of the term in combination with *hodos*, way, has its origin in the spatial sense of the term (cf. Isa. 35:8). It corresponds to Israel's way of life, when wandering sheep are used as an illustration of man's existence (cf. Deut. 22:1; Isa. 13:14; 53:6; Ps. 119:176). The fate of the people in the wilderness wanderings is seen in Num. 14:29, 33 as a punishment of God for their disobedience (cf. also Deut. 2:14). The people go astray by ignoring God's commandment and practising idolatry (cf. Deut. 13:6). Those who lead them astray are idols (Amos 2:4), false prophets (Jer. 23:32), and unfaithful kings (2 Chron. 33:9). Even God himself appears in the role of one who leads astray (Job 12:33; Ezek. 14:9; Isa. 63:17). Because Israel's path every now and again leads her astray, turning and salvation are necessary. This basic relationship to God is aptly expressed by the picture of sheep who cannot exist without a → shepherd (→ Lamb, Sheep, art. *probaton*).

2. *apataō* is chiefly used for verbal forms of *pātâh*, which in the qal and niphal means to be deceived, be simple; in the piel to deceive, seduce; and in the pual to be led astray. The deception can be used as a human strategem to dupe others (e.g., Samson's in Jdg. 14:15; 16:5). Gen. 3:13 speaks of the serpent's deception in enticing the woman to eat the forbidden fruit. In a vision of Micaiah ben Imlah the personified spirit offers, in Yahweh's royal council, to become a lying spirit and to entice King Ahab and his prophets (1 Ki. 22:21 ff.). On the other hand, there is the Psalmist's testimony: "I sought God . . . and I was not deceived" (Ps. 76:3 LXX).

3. In the inter-Testamental period some important elements are added to the concept of being led astray. The agents are often spirits or powers, especially, for example, the sons of God (Gen. 6:1 ff.) and the *diabolos* (→ Satan; SB I 136 ff.). Apocalyptic literature predicts the *planē* as a precursor of the end of the world, the day of the messiah (SB IV 977 ff.).

4. The Qumran texts speak, on the one hand, of a wandering astray of the children of light which is brought about by evil spirits and impulses (1QS 3:21; CD 2:17; 3:4, 14), and, on the other hand, of men who have appeared as deceivers of the community (CD 20:11; 1QH 2:14, 19; 4:7, 12; 16:20).

NT The active vb. (*apo-*)*planaō* is used in the NT almost exclusively in an apocalyptic sense (Matt. 24:4 f., 11, 24; Mk. 13:5 f.; Lk. 21:8; Rev. 2:20; 12:9; 13:14; 18:23; 19:20; 20:3, 8, 10) and of false teachers (2 Tim. 3:13; 1 Jn. 1:8; 2:66; 3:7). The nouns also often appear in this context (e.g. 2 Thess. 2:11; 2 Pet. 2:18; 3:17; Jude 11, 13; 1 Jn. 4:6; 2 Jn. 7). The primary, spatial sense is seen most clearly where the picture of sheep is expressly introduced (Matt. 18:12 f.; 1 Pet. 2:25), or in combination with *hodos*, way (2 Pet. 2:15; cf. also Heb. 11:38). It is never, however, spatial and nothing more: there is always a theological meaning associated with its use. The mid. (*apo-*)*planaomai* is used in the sense of to be wrong, to be led astray, to err (Tit. 3:3; Heb. 3:10 = Ps. 95:10; Heb. 5:2; Jas. 5:19; Matt. 22:29; Mk. 12:24; 1 Tim. 6:10). Similarly the formula, often used by the Stoics (cf. *TDNT* VI 244), *mē planasthe*, means "Do not be deceived", make no mistake" (Gal. 6:7; 1 Cor. 6:9; 15:33; Jas. 1:16). The pure passive sense, to be deceived, is to be found e.g., at Matt. 18:12; Jn. 7:47; 2 Tim. 3:13. The noun *planē* refers to a specific mistake (Matt. 27:64; 2 Pet. 3:17; Jude 11), or to more general confusion, error, lack of discipline and restraint (Rom. 1:27; Eph. 4:14; 1 Jn. 4:6). The nouns *planētēs* and *planēs* occur only in variant readings of Jude 13 in the sense of a wandering star or planet, with which Jude compares the false teachers. The point of the comparison is the apparently irregular movement of the planets which seemed to violate the order of the heavens and which was attributed to the disobedience of the angels controlling them. As punishment the latter were imprisoned for ever in the abyss (Eth.Enoch 18:13–16; 21:1–10; cf. J. N. D. Kelly, *The Epistles of Peter and Jude*, BNTC 1969, 274). *planos* is used both as an adj. (of deceitful spirits, 1 Tim. 4:1); and as a noun, deceiver, imposter (of Jesus in Matt. 27:63; of those who deny that Jesus Christ has come in the flesh, 2 Jn. 7; of Paul and his colleagues, 2 Cor. 6:8).

(*ex-*)*apataō* and *apatē* occur in 2 Cor. 11:3 and 1 Tim. 2:14 with reference to Gen. 3; in 2 Thess. 2:3; Eph. 5:6; Col. 2:8 in connection with false teachers; and in Matt. 13:22 par. Mk. 4:19; Rom. 7:11; 2 Thess. 2:10; Heb. 3:13; 2 Pet. 2:13 in the ethical sense of enticement by → sin or to sin.

paralogizomai occurs only at Col. 2:4 and Jas. 1:22, meaning to delude (with beguiling speech) and to deceive oneself (by being merely a hearer and not a doer of the word).

The terms we have considered can be used synonymously as far as their theological meaning is concerned. The differences of meaning in NT usage correspond to the various shades of meaning mentioned in OT above.

1. The picture of sheep that get lost and perish, having no shepherd, is widely used in the OT (cf. Num. 27:17; 1 Ki. 22:17; Ps. 119:176; Isa. 53:6; Ezek. 34; Zech. 13:7). In the NT it is taken up again in various contexts (Matt. 10:6; 12:11 f.; 14:14 par. Mk. 6:34 [= Num. 27:17; 1 Ki. 22:17] Lk. 9:11; Matt. 18:12; Matt. 26:31 par. Mk. 14:27 [= Zech. 13:7]; Lk. 15:4; Jn. 10; 1 Pet. 2:25). *planaō* and its cognates are part of the framework of this picture. Nearly all the

459

places where these words are used may be interpreted in terms of this background, even when it is not expressly mentioned. Jesus is the → way (*hodos*) and the → truth (*alētheia*) (Jn. 14:6). To be removed from him, the shepherd, means to wander about without guidance or protection and so be in danger of getting lost. The vbs. *planaō* and *apollyō* (→ destroy) are interchangeable in this context (cf. Matt. 18:12 with Lk. 15:4 ff.). Where we read of nations going astray (Rev. 18:23), of those who have wandered from the right way (2 Pet. 2:15; Jas. 5:20), or the people of God going astray (Heb. 3:10 [= Ps. 95:10]; 5:2), there is this underlying image coupled sometimes with the wilderness wanderings of Israel. It is also implicit in the passages where mention is made of false teachers who lead astray (e.g. Matt. 24:4 ff.; Jn. 7:12; 1 Jn. 3:7; Rev. 20:8–10).

2. Life prior to becoming a Christian is described as *planē*, error (Rom. 1:27; Eph. 4:14; Tit. 3:3; 1 Pet. 2:25). This is a time of being without the guidance and support of a Lord and shepherd. It is a time of unbelief and of sin, even though the wandering itself occurred apart from the → law of Moses (cf. Rom. 1:18 ff.).

For the man who is under the law, to go astray is sin (*hamartia*, Rom. 7:11). To wander away from the faith (1 Tim. 6:10) or from the truth (Jas. 5:19 f.), the deception of the heart (Rom. 16:18; Heb. 3:10,13; Jas. 1:26) is both sinful and incurs guilt (cf. also 2 Thess. 2:10).

The story of the → fall is the archetype of deception and disobedience as a result of appetite and desire (2 Cor. 11:3, 1 Tim. 2:14). Here the *apataō* group of words come into their own. Riches are seductive (Matt. 13:22 par. Mk. 4:19; 1 Tim. 6:10), and there are other desires lying in wait to deceive the believer (Rom. 16:18; Eph. 4:22; 2 Pet. 2:13).

In the background are dark powers, such as the spirit of deception (1 Tim. 4:1; 1 Jn. 4:6), the → Antichrist (2 Jn. 7), and ultimately → Satan himself who causes error and confusion (Rev. 12:9; 20:10).

3. The danger for the Christian is of deceiving himself (1 Cor. 3:18; 1 Jn. 1:8) which can lead to falling away from right doctrine. Hence the need for the oft-repeated warning *mē planasthe*, "Do not be deceived" (1 Cor. 6:9; 15:33; Gal. 6:7; Jas. 1:16; cf. also 2 Thess. 2:3). He who is not firmly grounded in the faith is in danger of missing the true → knowledge (→ *ginōskō*), since numerous false teachers threaten the church (1 Thess. 2:3; 2 Thess. 2:3; Eph. 4:14; Col. 2:8; 1 Jn. 2:26; 3:7; 4:6; 2 Tim. 3:13; 2 Pet. 2:18; 3:17). To be led astray by false teaching, in the form of philosophy or empty words, and to be led astray into definite acts of sin, are processes that go hand in hand. On the opposite side is the → truth (Jas. 5:19 f.) which must be held firmly by faith in him who is himself the truth.

4. Jesus is hated and persecuted by the Jews because they see in him the one who leads the people astray (Matt. 27:63; Jn. 7:12, 47). In the eyes of those who do not believe the apostles are imposters (2 Cor. 6:8), although they are servants of the truth. In this struggle to uphold the truth the church is pointed to him who himself experienced the weakness of a man (Heb. 5:2), and who can therefore provide support. Faith in him is the yardstick of truth and error. Seen in this light, the church's opponents turn out to be deceivers who themselves have been deceived, and the → Pharisees are those who really lead the people astray (Matt. 22:29; Mk. 12:24, 27; cf. 2 Tim. 3:13). For the Christian there is no other criterion of truth than Jesus Christ.

5. The final demonstration of the truth lies in the future, in the final revelation of Jesus Christ at his second coming. The era of the church is the era of fighting for the truth. The apostles' testimony is proclaimed to all nations (Matt. 28:18 ff.), but at the same time the powers increasingly bring in confusion and error (Matt. 24:4 f., 11, 24; Mk. 13:5 f.; Lk. 21:8; cf. Rev. 18:23; 20:3, 8). It is against the background of this final climax of the struggle that most of the texts containing the terms we have been considering are to be understood. The end event consists of the coming of the Lord to take home the lost and those who have gone astray, and to make an end of all *planē*, deception (2 Pet. 3; 2 Thess. 2; Rev. 12:9; 13:14).

W. Günther

→ Animal, → Antichrist, → Knowledge, → Lamb, Sheep, → Present, → Prophet, → Shepherd, → Teach, → Tempt, → Walk

(a). W. Bauer, *Orthodoxy and Heresy in Earliest Christianity*, 1972; G. R. Beasley-Murray, *A Commentary on Mark Thirteen*, 1957; H. Braun, *planaō* etc., *TDNT* VI 228–53; R. Bultmann, *Theology of the New Testament*, II, 1955, 127–42, 203–18; M. D. Hooker, "Were there false teachers at Colossae?", in B. Lindars and S. S. Smalley, eds., *Christ and Spirit in the New Testament. In Honour of Charles Francis Digby Moule*, 1973, 315–32; Liddell-Scott, 181, 1316 f., 1411; A. L. Moore, *The Parousia in the New Testament, Supplements to NovT* 13, 1966; A. Oepke, *apataō* etc. 384 f.; H. Räisänen, *The Idea of Divine Hardening. A Comparative Study of the Notion of Divine Hardening, Leading Astray, and Inciting to Evil, in the Bible and the Qur'an*, Publications of the Finnish Exegetical Society 25, 1972.
(b). G. Quell, *Wahre und falsche Propheten*, 1952.

Leaven

ζύμη

ζύμη (*zymē*), leaven; ζυμόω (*zymoō*), ferment; ἄζυμος (*azymos*), unleavened.

CL *zymē* appears in secular Gk. from Aristotle (4th cent. B.C.) to the Tebtunis Papyri (2nd cent. A.D.). *zymoō* first appears in Hippocrates (5th cent. B.C.). Leaven, in fermenting grain, is *not* yeast, but old, sour dough, stored and stimulated as a fermentation agent by adding juices, which was "hidden" (Matt. 13:33 par. Lk. 13:21) in the new dough in order to permeate it and give it lightness. In the Roman state cult the Flamen Dialis was not permitted to come into contact with leaven, because, claimed Plutarch (*Quaestiones Romanae* 109), it weakens, sours and corrupts.

OT 1. *zymē* is used lit. in the LXX and in Josephus in cultic contexts concerned with regulations for feasts and sacrifices (e.g. Exod. 12:15, 19; Deut. 16:3; Josephus, *Ant.* 3, 252 f.). It was not necessarily taboo in Jewish ritual. Leaven was used in the peace and wave offerings (Lev. 7:13), but was forbidden in the cereal offerings consumed by fire (Lev. 2:11; 6:17). In the ritual of the Passover and the Feast of Unleavened Bread all leaven was cleaned out from every Jewish home annually for the 14 Nisan, and only unleavened bread was eaten from that evening and the seven days following (Exod. 12:14–20), commemorating the hurried flight from Egypt (Exod. 12:34, 39). While this spring-clean was a cult ordinance, it served the hygienic purpose of breaking any chain of infection established by successive use of sour leaven (C. L. Mitton, "Leaven", *ExpT* 84, 1972–73, 339 f.).

461

2. Figuratively leaven was given different meanings in rabbinic tradition. Rabbi Alexander used it as a metaphor for human restraints on obeying God (I. Abrahams, *Studies in Pharisaism and the Gospels*, I, 1917, 52 ff.), whereas Rabbi Chiyya bar Abba described as leaven the Torah with its power to lead Israelites who observe it back to God (SB I 728). Philo also gave it divergent transferred meanings. On the one hand, it symbolized swelling arrogance, indulgence and pretension (*Quaest. in Exod.* 1, 15; 2, 14). On the other hand, it suggested complete (spiritual) nourishment and blissful joy (*Spec.Leg.* 2, 185).

NT 1. *zymē* and *zymoō* appear in the Synoptic Gospels and in Paul. Each instance is in a literary figure: parable, metaphor, proverb and type. The point of the various uses varies from context to context, despite the frequent claim among scholars that in the NT "leaven is used symbolically to symbolize an evil influence which spreads like an infection" (C. L. Mitton, op. cit., 342).

(a) *Parable*. In Matt. 13:33 par. Lk. 13:21 the hidden but persistent expansion of the → kingdom of God – seen in the words and works of Jesus – is compared to leaven hidden in dough until it permeates the whole. H. Odeberg interprets the parable as a warning against evil (*Herren kommer*, 1962, 199–201), and C. L. Mitton as a comparison with the influential power of evil (op. cit., 341). However, the point of the preceding parable of the mustard seed is expansion by something minute (cf. the proverb in 1 Cor. 5:6). The Gospel of Thomas stresses the expansive property of leaven in its use of the parable (B. Gärtner, *The Theology of the Gospels of Thomas*, 1961, 230 f.). The point in Matt. and Lk. appears to be expansion by secret, hidden permeation, not evil influence (B. Gerhardsson, "The Seven Parables in Matthew 13", *NTS* 19, 1972–73, 22 f.). No indication is given of the significance of the dough, whether it is meant to refer to the culture of society or to the territorial *orbis terrarum*.

(b) *Metaphor*. In Mk. 8:15 leaven is an attribute of the Pharisees and of Herod (*v.l.* of the Herodians), of which the disciples are to beware. Matt. 16:11 f., in a warning against Pharisees and Sadducees, interprets the metaphor as "teaching", and Lk. 12:1, in a warning against Pharisees alone, as "hypocrisy". Several scholars (e.g. V. Taylor, *The Gospel According to St. Mark*, 1953, 365) believe that the warning suggests that leaven indicates something evil, but this is not necessarily so (H. Windisch, *TDNT* II 906). If the Pharisees were making a similar claim for the Torah as that made later by Rabbi Chiyya bar Abba (see OT 2, above), then the warning which is not explained in the Marcan version would have been understood without explanation. Further, in this case, Matt. rightly interpreted the metaphor, as did Lk., when writing to a Christian public, since Pharisaic observance of the Torah in the view of Jesus (cf. Matt. 6:2 ff.; 23:13) was no longer a vital faith but a mask.

(c) *Proverb*. In 1 Cor. 5:6 and Gal. 5:9 Paul uses the words, "A little leaven leavens the whole lump." Proverbial in form, but not found outside Paul as a proverb, these words might have been associated in the Christian church with the parable of the leaven. Windisch suggests that Jesus elaborated the point of the proverb in the parable (op. cit., 905). But since the parable is not evidenced prior to the formation of the Gospel tradition outside Paul, it is possible that the parable gave rise to the proverb in the church. For synoptic tradition elsewhere seems to have influenced material in NT epistles (cf. H. Riesenfeld, *The Gospel Tradition and its Beginnings*, 1957, 15). In 1 Cor. the proverb symbolizes the notion that the continuing presence of a transgressor in the community renders the community guilty of the transgression (v. 1) and in Gal. the imagery refers to the influence of false teachers on the understanding of the congregation.

(d) *Type*. In 1 Cor. 5:7 Paul exhorts the community to "clean out the old leaven." This might be an injunction to expel the offender (v. 13) or to divest themselves of the "boast" of association with the transgression. The grounds for the command are that Christ the Passover (→ lamb) has been sacrificed, that the Christians are "unleavened", and that the festival is to be kept by expelling leaven (malice and evil) and by partaking of unleavened bread (sincerity and truth). This type (*not* allegory, A. T. Hanson, *Studies in Paul's Technique and Theology*, 1974, 112 ff.) recalls the Passover ritual and the Christian identification of Christ with the Passover → lamb (Jn. 19:14, 31; 1 Pet. 1:19). The Jews cast out the leaven before eating the Passover; the believer is to cast out leaven, because the Passover sacrifice has already taken place, whereby he is accepted and made new by God (1 Cor. 6:11). This is a classic example of Pauline ethical teaching in which the acts of God in Christ on behalf of the Christian – expressed in the indicative mood – are the grounds for exhortation to Christ-like living – expressed in the imperative mood – both by renouncing evil and pursuing good as God works within the believer. Other examples are found in Rom. 6; 1 Cor. 6:19 f.; Col. 2:20–4:1.

2. *azymos*, unleavened. Apart from the uses in 1 Cor. 5:7 f. (see above 1 (d)), this word is found elsewhere in the NT in the plur. form *ta azyma*, meaning the Feast of Unleavened Bread. This was originally a harvest festival (Exod. 23:14–17), celebrated in the month Abib. It became part of the Passover ritual, set for 15–21 Nisan, but also dated to begin on 14 Nisan (Josephus, *Ant.* 2, 15, 1; 14, 2, 1), as we find in Mk. 14:12. The Jews regularly equated the Passover with the Feast of Unleavened Bread (Ezek. 45:21; Josephus, *War*, 2, 10), as Lk. 22:1 does.

G. T. D. Angel

→ Bread, → Feast, → Hunger, → Sacrifice

O. T. Allis, "The Parable of the Leaven", *EQ* 19, 1947, 254 ff.; Arndt, 340; J. P. Lewis, "Leaven", *ZPEB* III 901 ff.; Liddell-Scott, 757; C. L. Mitton, "Leaven", *ExpT* 84, 1972–73, 339–42; H. Windisch, *zymē* etc., *TDNT* III 902–6.

Leprosy

Leprosy is an ancient designation of a fairly extensive class of diseases, the principal symptoms of which were of a cutaneous nature. Leprosy appears to have been endemic in various parts of the ancient orient, being described as far back as the third millennium B.C. It was held in abhorrence by the Hebrews partly because of the pathology itself, and partly because it was accompanied by ceremonial defilement which rendered the sufferer unclean. For these reasons the leper, once his condition was properly diagnosed, was banished from society.

| λεπρός | λεπρός (*lepros*), leprous, but chiefly used as a noun describing a leper. |

463

CL Classical writers employed the adjective *lepros* to describe anything rough, scabby or scaly. Among ancient Greek leather workers the best straps and reins were supposedly those prepared from roughly textured (*ek leprōn*) skins or hides. In Hippocrates and Dioscorides the adj. was used to describe a leprous person, i.e., someone with a scaly skin affliction such as psoriasis.

OT *lepros* occurs in the LXX in Lev. 13:45; 14:2 f.; 22:4; Num. 5:2 etc. as the equivalent of *ṣārûa'* and *m^eṣōrā'*, participial forms of *ṣāra'*, to become diseased in the skin. If the Heb. is equivalent to the Akkadian *ṣinnītu*, it would describe any kind of skin eruption, of which clinical leprosy (Hansen's disease) would be one form. It should be observed that the instructions given in Lev. 13 to the priests to enable them to detect leprosy also suggested that skin afflictions other than clinical leprosy might be present in individuals, thus furnishing the possibility of differential diagnosis. Perhaps for this and other reasons the term *lepros* was sufficiently flexible in nature to include such common dermatological conditions as *impetigo*, *psoriasis*, *eczema*, *acne vulgaris* and the like, as well as leprosy itself. Specific diagnoses will be considered below in the section on *lepra*.

NT NT writers employed *lepros* as a noun, leper, and in this sense it occurs 9 times only. The cleansing of a leper is referred to in Matt. 11:5; Mk. 1:41 f.; Lk. 7:22; 17:12, as part of the healing ministry of Christ. Lk. 4:27 cited an OT miracle whereby Elisha healed the leprosy of Naaman (2 Kings 5:1 ff.). *lepros* was also used of Simon, formerly a leper, in Matt. 26:6; Mk. 14:3. The word was employed in as broad a sense as its OT counterpart, and the fact that some clinical manifestations called for cleansing, or a priestly declaration of cleanness, implies that the conditions described by *lepros* varied in severity, and doubtless included specific instances of Hansen's disease.   *R. K. Harrison*

| λέπρα |

λέπρα (*lepra*), leprosy.

CL In Herodotus and the medical authors, *lepra* was employed as a description of a cutaneous disease which gave a scaly or uneven texture to the skin. It was associated by Herodotus (1, 138) and Hippocrates with *leukē*, a whitish affliction of the skin, and seems to have been acquired *leucodermia* (*vitiligo*). This is a condition of the skin in which there is an absence of pigment, the result being the presence of irregular pale or white patches. The Greek medical authors also employed another term, *elephas*, or *elephantiasis*, to describe a different and much more serious chronic disorder (*elephantiasis Graecorum*), which was found frequently in Egypt, the symptoms of which corresponded largely to those now associated with clinical leprosy. Curiously enough, only one case of this latter disease has been discovered among Egyptian mummies to date, despite the common association by classical writers of leprosy with Egypt.

OT *lepra* occurs in the LXX as the Gk. equivalent of the Heb. *ṣāra'at*, traditionally rendered by leprosy in the EVV, but by "malignant skin-disease" in NEB. The term *ṣāra'at* described a kind of eruptive condition which could be exhibited by leather (Lev. 14:55), clothing (Lev. 13:47, 59), and the walls of houses (Lev. 14:44), as well as by human beings. The various forms in which ṣāra'aṭ could be manifested were described in detail in Lev. 13 using ancient Heb. technical terms which unfortunately are very difficult for the modern student to comprehend. The situation is not made any easier by such translations of ṣāra'aṭ as the NEB "malignant skin-disease". This generalized designation unfortunately leaves no room for the specific diagnosis of clinical leprosy, which Lev. 13 clearly allows.

Preliminary symptoms included a swelling indicative of possible morbid changes (š^e'ēṭ; LXX oulē), a localized tissue-crust on the epidermis (sappaḥaṭ; LXX sēmasia), and a whitish-red swollen spot (bahereṭ; LXX tēlaugēma). Since any or all of these could presage clinical leprosy, the sufferer presented himself to the priest for examination. If subcutaneous penetration was exhibited along with a whitening of the small local cuticular hairs, a malignant state was suspected and the patient was declared unclean. But if the skin tissue, while swollen, was not actually inflamed (13:4) and did not indicate subcutaneous changes of a morbid nature or discolouration of local hair, the patient was quarantined for seven days. If on reexamination the swollen area of the whitish spot had not increased in size, a further seven days' quarantine could be followed by a priestly diagnosis of a benign skin condition. But if there was a spreading of the eruption in the skin subsequently, it was diagnosed as leprosy (13:8). A chronic state of leprosy was indicated by depigmented hairs and ulcerated tissue in an area of swollen white skin, this also rendering the sufferer unclean. But if the whole body was covered with patches of depigmented skin (probably acquired leucodermia), the individual who manifested this condition was pronounced clean (13:13). The mild type of ulceration found in many cutaneous diseases was also kept under observation, and degenerative changes resulted in a diagnosis of leprosy. Differential diagnosis turned upon the degree of cutaneous penetration of the disease. If the dermis and local cutaneous hairs exhibited pathological changes, leprosy was diagnosed. Otherwise the sufferer could be regarded as being afflicted with eczema, vitiligo, acne, psoriasis, or some analogous skin disease. A condition which may have been a keloid, marked by indurated patches of a whitish colour on a larger pinkish or purplish area of skin, was described in Lev. 13:18 ff. Once again, the degree of localization and skin penetration determined the nature of the affliction, which at best is rather obscure. Scalp disease was treated in the same manner as other forms of skin eruptions, so that an itchy condition (NEB "scurf") such as ringworm could be differentiated from more serious cutaneous diseases. Alopecia (baldness) did not involve ritual defilement (13:40 f.) unless the pathology characteristic of leprosy was also present. The term ṣāra'aṭ was also applied to material damaged by molds or fungi (13:47 ff.), and to the mineral efflorescence on the walls of houses (14:34 ff.).

What was diagnosed as ṣāra'aṭ undoubtedly included genuine cases of clinical leprosy, the cause of which was identified by Hansen in 1871 as a minute fungus, Mycobacterium leprae, but which is now identified as a bacillus. The developed disease, if allowed to run its full course, may exhibit three forms. The nodular (lepromatous) type produces lumps in the facial tissues and a form of cutaneous induration which results in a characteristic leonine appearance. Degenerative changes also occur in nose and throat membranes. An anaesthetic (tuberculoid) variety attacks the nerves of the skin, producing depigmented areas in which there

465

is no feeling. The local hair often undergoes morbid changes, blisters and perforating ulcers frequently form on these patches and elsewhere, and it is common for the extremities of the arms and legs to be affected. In such cases necrosis occurs and the diseased part will then be rejected by the body, leaving a well-healed stump (*lepra mutilans*). A third form of leprosy combines the symptoms of the first two kinds in varying degrees, and like them is chronic in nature.

NT In the NT *lepra* occurred 4 times only in passages apparently describing the same incident (Matt. 8:3; Mk. 1:42; Lk. 5:12 f.). Luke noted the advanced nature of the condition (RSV "full of leprosy"; NEB, "covered with leprosy"), but apart from this it is not easy to determine the true nature of the complaint. It may have been acquired *leucodermia*, since the sufferer seems to have been moving in society to some extent, although the possibility of an advanced case of clinical leprosy should not be discounted. In Lk. 17:12 ff. Jesus cures ten lepers (*leproi andres*).

([Ed.] In the parable of the rich man and Lazarus the latter is said to have been "full of sores [*heilkōmenos*]" (Lk. 16:20; cf. Arndt, 251). On this parable see the article by J. D. M. Derrett listed in the bibliography below.)

→ Heal, → Miracle   *R. K. Harrison*

S. G. Browne, "Leprosy", *Medicine*, 1972–74, 1549–57; *Leprosy in the Bible*, 1974²; and S. G. Browne, ed., *Leprosy Review*; R. G. Cochrane, *Biblical Leprosy: A Suggested Interpretation*, 1963²; J. D. M. Derrett, "Dives and Lazarus and the Preceding Sayings", *Law in the New Testament*, 1970, 78–99; R. K. Harrison, "Leprosy", *IDB* III 111 ff.; W. Michaelis, *lepra* etc., *TDNT* I 233 f.; J. N. Sanders, "Those whom Jesus Loved", *NTS* 1, 1954–55, 29 ff.

Levite

Λευίτης

Λευί(ς) (*Leui[s]*), Levi; *Λευίτης* (*Leuitēs*), Levite; *Λευιτικός* (*Leueitikos*), Levitical.

OT A Levite was any descendant of Jacob's third son, Levi (Heb. *lēwî*; Gen. 29:34), but the term is relatively seldom so used in OT. Normally it refers to the male descendants of Levi apart from the priests, the descendants of Aaron, i.e. to those entitled to serve in the sanctuary in a subordinate role. Where the expression "the priests the Levites" (RSV, NEB, "the Levitical priests") is used, its meaning is probably that of genuine priests in contrast to those from other tribes who might arrogate the position to themselves. Deut. 18:1 is not likely to mean, as is so often held, that all Levites were priests, even though a Levite was obviously welcomed when an Aaronic priest was not available (Jdg. 17:13).

In the course of time the Levites diminished in importance, largely for economic reasons. Num. 18:21, 24 gave the whole tithe to the Levites, who were expected to give a tithe of it to the priests (Num. 18:26 ff.). It seems clear, however, that as the priestly clans multiplied, the Levites were increasingly squeezed out of the more important sanctuaries, except from menial posts, especially after Josiah's reformation, and in practice it is improbable that they continued to receive their share of the tithe. As a result comparatively few Levites returned from Babylonia with Zerubbabel and Joshua (cf. Ezr. 2:40 with 2:36–39), and Ezra had great difficulty in persuading any to accompany him (Ezr. 8:15–20).

Nehemiah restored the tithe position (Neh. 10:37 f.), but at an unspecified period the tithes were taken from the Levites in favour of the priests, as is implied by Josephus' language (*Life* 15; *Ant.* 20, 8, 8). This is confirmed by Rab. sources (Hullin 131; Yeb. 86). Their importance was further diminished by their teaching functions being largely taken over by the scribes. In addition, the lower ranks of temple servants, many of them descendants of slaves, gradually obtained the right to call themselves Levites. This helps to explain the rarity of their mention in the NT.

NT 1. Levi is found as a proper name 8 times in NT; viz. the son of Jacob 3 times (Heb. 7:5, 9, Rev. 7:7); two ancestors of Jesus (Lk. 3:24, 29); a son of Alphaeus, presumably Matthew, three times (Mk. 2:14; Lk. 5:27, 29). Since in Jesus' genealogy Levi is presumably a purely personal name with no suggestion of Levitical origin, there are no adequate grounds for supposing that Levi (Matthew) was of the tribe of Levi.

2. Levites are referred to 3 times in NT.

(a) The leading Pharisees in Jerusalem ("the Jews") sent priests and Levites to question John the Baptist (Jn. 1:19). The choice was probably motivated by the fact that the tribe of Levi generally had the divinely given privilege of teaching (Deut. 33:10).

(b) A priest and a Levite are linked in the parable of the Good Samaritan (Lk. 10:31 f.). The suggestion of greater interest or humanity on the Levite's part conveyed by AV in contrast to RV and later translations is due to its use of an inferior text.

(c) Barnabas, a native of Cyprus, was a Levite (Acts 4:36). It is impossible to establish whether he functioned in the Jerusalem temple. The mention of Cyprus may be a preparation for Acts 13:4–12; 15:39, in which case he may have moved to Jerusalem as a young man; he had relations there (cf. Col. 4:10). If, on the other hand, he had been won for Christ on a visit, and his home and property were in Cyprus, then he would probably not have functioned in the temple.

3. Heb. 7:11 uses the term "the Levitical priesthood" as a variant to "the Aaronic priesthood". It stresses that the priests were of the tribe of Levi, unlike the priest for ever after the order of Melchizedek, who was of the tribe of Judah.

→ Melchizedek, → Priest, → Temple, → Tent   *H. L. Ellison*

R. Abba, "Priests and Levites", *IDB* III 876–89; R. Brinker, *The Influence of the Sanctuaries in Early Israel*, 1946; A. Edersheim, *The Temple, Its Ministry and Services, as they were at the Time of Jesus Christ*, 1874; A. K. Helmbold, "Levite", *ZPEB* III 912; D. A. Hubbard, "Priests and Levites", *NBD* 1028–34; J. Jeremias, *Jerusalem in the Time of Jesus*, 1969; Y. Kaufmann, *The Religion of Israel*, 1960, 193–200; H. H. Rowley, "Early Levite History and the Question of the Exodus", *JNES* 3, 1944, 73–78; H. Strathmann, *Leu(e)i* etc., *TDNT* IV 234–39; R. de Vaux, *Ancient Israel*, 1961, 358–71 (see also bibliography 544 f.); G. E. Wright, "The Levites in Deuteronomy", *Vetus Testamentum* 4, 1954, 325–30.

Lie, Hypocrite

In Gk. two different groups of words are used for lying, the antithesis of telling the → truth. *hypokrinō* stems originally from the world of the theatre. In a positive sense, it refers to the "answering" of the dialogue, and to the exposition and interpretation in the play. In the negative, it is used of an actor who has not identified himself with his rôle. Hence, the meanings of play-acting, disguise, and then hypocrisy (cf. the corresponding nouns *hypokrisis*, hypocrisy and *hypokritēs*, a hypocrite).

pseudomai, to lie, and *pseudos*, a lie, express the opposite of *alētheia*, truth, even more clearly. The great number of compound words derived from the root *pseud-* indicates the extent and the importance of the use of this idea in ancient and in Christian literature.

ὑποκρίνω

ὑποκρίνω (*hypokrino*), answer, pretend, dissimulate; ὑπόκρισις (*hypokrisis*), pretence, hypocrisy; ὑποκριτής (*hypokritēs*), pretender, hypocrite, a godless man; ἀνυπόκριτος (*anhypokritos*), unfeigned, genuine.

CL *hypokrinō* is a compound verb based on *krinō*, judge (→ Judgment). The mid.
form *hypokrinomai* is the one generally used. Its original meaning was to give final judgment on a question; but it also came to mean to reply, expound, interpret (e.g. dreams).

In secular Gk. these words have primary reference in the world of the theatre. By *hypokritēs* one should understand either the "answerer" who appeared on stage and turned the self-contained speeches of the chorus into dialogue form; or the "interpreter" (Homer used the word in this sense) who explained the situation to the audience. *hypokrisis* has various shades of meaning: reply, interpretation, play-acting, and then also (via "rôle-playing") appearance, hypocrisy, dissimulation. *anhypokritos* is rarely used in secular literature, and indicates someone who is inexperienced as an actor; and in a metaphorical sense unfeigned, genuine, simple.

OT 1. The LXX translates Heb. *'ānâh* by *hypokrinomai*, reply, in Job 39:32 [40:2].
The vb. occurs only rarely and then in late writings (Sir. 1:29; 35[32]:15; 36[33]:2; 2 Macc. 5:25; 6:21, 24; 4 Macc. 6:15, 17). *hypokritēs* renders Heb. *ḥānēp*, someone estranged from God. This word, too, occurs only in Job 34:30; 36:13. *ḥānēp* is also translated by *anomos*, lawless, and *asebēs*, godless, in the LXX (→ Law; → Godliness).

The term denotes what elsewhere is graphically described as the man with a "double heart" and "false lips" (Ps. 12:3 f.); he always has God on his lips, but keeps him far from his → heart (Jer. 12:2). Job 36:13 describes the *hypokritēs* as an angry and taciturn man who is too proud to call for help when he needs it. Such a man should not be in a position of authority, because he directs all his efforts to the oppression of his subjects (Job 34:30).

2. There was a rabbinic saying that 90 per cent of all the hypocrisy in the world was to be found in Jerusalem (SB I 718; cf. Jer. 23:15). Hypocrisy was one of the chief sins denounced in Judaism. The → Pharisees were especially condemned, because of their frequent hypocrisy (SB I 388 f., 921 ff.; IV 336 f.).

NT The NT uses these words exclusively in the metaphorical sense of hypocrisy; they occur mainly in the Synoptic Gospels, especially in Matt. The vb. is only found in Lk. 20:20, of the spies sent by the chief priests to trap Jesus; and in Gal. 2:13 in the compound form *synhypokrinomai* ("And with him the rest of the Jews acted insincerely [*synhypekrithēsan*], so that even Barnabas was carried away by their insincerity [*hypokrisei*]"). The noun *hypokrisis* is used in a variety of contexts; *hypokritēs* is the regular expression for wicked and godless people – the scribes and Pharisees are particularly so described by Jesus. *anhypokritos* is chiefly linked with *agapē* (→ love) and *pistis* (→ faith).

1. The use of the vb. in Lk. 20:20 is close to the meaning to play a rôle, act as if, pretend: they made out that they were honest men (Vulg. *simulare*). Gal. 2:13 has a similar reference: Peter did not remain true to his commission; he was playing a double game, trimming his sails to the wind. Clear knowledge of the right course of action is assumed; but it is the actual situation that gives the decisive judgment on his behaviour, and thus Peter became a hypocrite.

2. Jesus called the attempts of his opponents to catch him out with their crafty questions hypocrisy (*hypokrisis*; cf. Matt. 22:18; Mk. 12:15). It involves a quite deliberate pretence, similar to that of a stage performance. (In passing, it may be noted that the attitude of the early Church to the theatre was overwhelmingly negative.)

Exhortations in the Epistles, in such passages as 1 Tim. 4:2 and 1 Pet. 2:1, put *hypokrisis* alongside lying (→ *pseudomai*) and slander. It is the kind of behaviour that attempts to cover up sin by putting oneself in a favourable light at the expense of truth.

3. The noun *hypokritēs* is found in the Gospels, exclusively on the lips of Jesus. Matt. 15:7 ff. quotes Isa. 29:13 as prophetic of the Pharisees and scribes of Jesus' day: "You hypocrites! Well did Isaiah prophesy of you, when he said: 'This people honours me with their lips, but their heart is far from me; in vain do they worship me, teaching as doctrines the precepts of men' " (cf. Mk. 7:6 f.).

The Pharisees were by no means the only ones to be so addressed. The epithet applies to anyone who rejects the truth about God in Jesus (→ Lead Astray, art. *planaō*). Through his teaching and actions Jesus revealed to men the unhappy state of their delusion and sought to open their eyes to their true situation before God. Hypocrisy is not simply a conscious act of dissimulation, but a perverse → blindness. It is illustrated by the question in the Sermon on the Mount as to how anyone can remove a speck from someone else's eye when he has a log in his own eye (Matt. 7:3 ff.; cf. Lk. 6:41 f.; SB I 446). Anyone who prays in public is doing his religious duty, but Jesus warned against the hypocrisy of praying to be seen by men. They should rather pray in secret and likewise give alms in secret (Matt. 6:5 ff.; cf. 6:2 ff.). Jesus did not condemn the Pharisees because of their serious and pious attitude towards the → law as such. Rather, it was their understanding of righteousness and their ways of evading its demands that he condemned (→ Gift, art. *korban*). Moreover, the fact that the pious Jews did not recognize Jesus as the fulfiller of the law showed how far they were from God (Matt. 15:2 ff. par. Mk. 7:5 ff.).

Pharisees and scribes (→ Writing) were the prime examples of unbelief, being unable to see beyond their own traditionalism and to interpret the signs of the time (Lk. 12:56) because of their reliance on their own piety. Thus they remained outside the coming → kingdom (Matt. 23:1–25:46; Mk. 12:37–40; Lk. 12:41–48;

20:45 ff.). Their characteristic feature is their "objective self-contradiction" (J. Schniewind), or rather their self-deluding blindness (Matt. 23:16 ff.). Outwardly they appeared to be men of God, but in reality they were sinners who were guilty in God's sight because they did everything possible to repel and ward off the salvation which comes in Jesus. That is why Jesus characterized them as *hypokritai* in the series of woes he pronounced on them which are scarcely without parallel in severity (Matt. 23:13 ff.; cf. Lk. 11:42–52).

4. *anhypokritos* is an adj. only found in the Epistles. In 3 of the 6 instances it is used to qualify love, *agapē* (Rom. 12:9; 2 Cor. 6:6), and brotherly love, *philadelphia* (1 Pet. 1:22). Such → love comes from an open and genuine heart without ulterior motives. It does not deliberately put on show. The same is said of faith in two places (1 Tim. 1:5; 2 Tim. 1:5). This adj. expresses the fact that → faith is not affected by considerations of expediency. It grows spontaneously out of the union of the Christian with the living Christ, and, rooted in the heart, it finds its expression in a transparent life. This is also true of the → wisdom that comes from above (Jas. 3:17). *W. Günther*

ψεύδομαι

ψεύδομαι (*pseudomai*), lie, deceive by lying; ψευδής (*pseudēs*), deceitful, mendacious, a liar; ψεῦδος (*pseudos*), a lie; ψεύστης (*pseustēs*), a liar; ἀψευδής (*apseudēs*), guileless, truthful.

CL Though these words occur in Gk. from the time of Homer, the etymology is not clear. The noun *pseudos* means a lie, the antithesis of the → truth, *alētheia* (cf. Plato, *Hippias Minor* 370e). The only part of the vb. used in the NT is the mid. *pseudomai*, lie, or deceive by lying (12 instances). The following derivatives also occur in the NT: (a) *pseudēs*, untruthful, deceitful; and as a noun, liar (3 times); (b) *pseudos*, lie (11 times); (c) *ho pseustēs*, liar (11 times); (d) *apseudēs*, candid (once). Apart from compound words, such as *pseudomartyreō*, give false witness, which also occur in the Synoptics, there are a number of words beginning with *pseud-* (false-) which are found mainly in Pauline and Johannine writings.

OT In the LXX *pseudomai* is primarily used to translate Heb. *kāḥaš*, deny, disclaim, act secretively, deceive, lie. *pseudos* is the equivalent of Heb. *šeqer*, fraud, deception, falsehood.

1. The OT proclaims that God is truthful. He and his word can be trusted (→ Faith, art. *peithomai*; → Truth). When salvation or calamity is prophesied, it is also fulfilled. "God is not a man that he should lie. . . . Has he said and will he not do it? Or has he spoken, and will he not fulfil it?" (Num. 23:19; cf. 1 Sam. 15:29). The God-ness of God is proved by the truth of his word and his faithfulness in → fulfilling it.

2. Man, however, has fallen prey to a lie; he has dissociated himself from God, and does not let him be the Lord who, in truth, he is. The → prophets make the accusation that God's people have fallen prey to a lie. Instead of trusting their Lord, they rely on their own strength and on political alliances. They listen to false prophets (Jer. 5:31; Ezek. 13:19 and after), who flatter them and give them false prophecies of salvation, who preach about "drinking and strong drink" (Mic. 2:11), and who use whitewash over their sins (Ezek. 22:28; → Black, White). Hosea proclaimed

the charge from God, "You have ploughed iniquity, you have reaped injustice, you have eaten the fruit of lies" (10:13). The most serious accusation was that the people have put their faith in idols instead of in God (→ Image, art. *eidōlon*) which the prophets call lies. "Their lies have led them astray" (Amos 2:4). Lies have become their refuge (Isa. 28:15), and they have renounced their God (Isa. 59:13; Jer. 5:12). Lying, in the eyes of the prophets, is not so much an ethical offence as a basic moral attitude, which turns its back on the true God. It therefore falls prey to the delusion of the lie, as it does to the "nothingness" of existence (→ Empty). To put one's trust in a delusory lie instead of in the true God is called by Isaiah a "covenant with death" (28:15). God's judgment falls on all who deny him and preach lies: "Because you have uttered delusions and have seen lies, therefore behold, I am against you, says the LORD GOD" (Ezek. 13:8; cf. Isa. 28:17). Only a remnant will survive God's judgment – those "who do no wrong and who speak no lies" (Zeph. 3:13).

3. As in the prophets, so also in the Pss. those who turn from God are described as liars. "The wicked go astray from the womb, they err from their birth, speaking of lies" (Ps. 58:3). "I said in my alarm, All men are liars" (Ps. 116:11 RV mg.). But the devout man holds firm to God: "Blessed is the man who makes the Lord his trust, and does not turn to the proud, to those who go astray after false gods! [MT *kāzāb*, lie; LXX *manias pseudeis*, lying fooleries]" (Ps. 40:4; MT 40:5; LXX 39:5). God makes an end of all liars (Ps. 5:6).

4. In the laws of the OT there is no explicit, general prohibition against lying, but it can plainly be deduced from a whole collection of individual examples where lying is specifically forbidden. Most notably, there is the command not to bear false witness (Exod. 20:16; cf. Prov. 21:28). Such a thing would be particularly reprehensible, because, according to OT law, judgment can be given solely on the basis of the evidence of two → witnesses (cf. Num. 35:30; Deut. 17:6 f.; 19:15 ff.). There are further prohibitions: against perjury (Lev. 19:12; → Deny) and against embezzlement of stolen or lost property (Lev. 6:2 f. [MT 5:21 f.]). Lev. 19:11 relates them: "You shall not steal, nor deal falsely, nor lie to one another."

5. Rabbinic texts likewise declare that God has nothing to do with lies. He "created everything in the world, except for lies, which he did not create . . . men concieved those in their own hearts" (Pes.R. 24 (125b)). In San. 103a four groups of men are named who will not see God: scoffers, hypocrites, liars and slanderers. False evidence given against a neighbour is reckoned by God "as if you were to declare that I had not created the world in six days" (Pes.R. 21 107b). To bear false witness against a neighbour is to bear false witness against God.

6. What could be observed in the OT and in Rab. writings is stated even more emphatically in the Qumran writings. Lies belong on the side of God's adversary and to the powers of darkness. The "ways of the spirit of falsehood" include "wickedness and lies" (1QS 4:9). Lies are the mark of those who belong to the godless just as the members of God's community are always called "sons of truth". Belial (→ Satan) uses lies to lead the godly astray from God; hence several times in CD and 1QpHab a historical opponent of the sect who is mentioned is referred to as the "Liar" or the "Spouter of Lies". But God saves the godly from the "jealousy of the teachers of lies" who "scheme against him a devilish scheme" (1QH 4:10). In the → judgment all lies will be destroyed along with the powers of darkness, and men will

be cleansed from all their terrible delusions: for God will "sprinkle them with the Spirit of Truth as one sprinkles water for purification." But the godly man already confesses: "I will not keep Belial within my heart, and in my mouth shall be heard no folly or deceitful lie" (1QS 10:22).

NT In the NT 15 different words contain the root *pseud-* (false). These are found in nearly all the NT writings, but whereas the Synoptic Gospels make only very sparing use of them, they play an important role in Johannine and Pauline writings. Besides the simple use of vb., noun and adj. (*pseudomai*, lie; *pseudos*, lie; *pseustēs*, liar; *pseudēs*, deceitful), which comprise the major part of the NT instances, there are numerous compound words. These include: *pseudadelphos*, false brother (2 Cor. 11:26; Gal. 2:4; → Brother); *pseudapostolos*, false apostle (2 Cor. 11:13; → Apostle); *pseudodidaskalos*, false teacher (2 Pet. 2:1; → Teach); *pseudologos*, speaking lies (1 Tim. 4:2); *pseudomartyria*, false witness (Matt. 15:19; 26:59); *pseudomartys*, one who gives false witness (Matt. 26:60; 1 Cor. 15:15; → Witness); *pseudoprophētēs*, false prophet (Matt. 7:15; 24:11, 24; Mk. 13:22; Lk. 6:26; Acts 13:6; 2 Pet. 2:1; 1 Jn. 4:1; Rev. 16:13; 19:20; 20:10; → Prophet); and *pseudochristos*, false Christ (Matt. 24:24; Mk. 13:22).

1. (a) The NT takes up the OT witness to the truthfulness and truth of God. Tit. 1:2 speaks of God as the *apseudēs theos*, God who does not lie. God's → truth does not come to light in the unveiling of being in the way that the Greeks understood *alētheia*. Rather, God's truth is to be seen as truthfulness in the way that he keeps faith with his → promises in history. This was the way that Israelites stressed the unchangeable nature of God's decrees. God added the guarantee of an oath to his promise, "so that through two unchangeable things [i.e. the promise and the oath] in which it is impossible that God should prove false, we who have fled for refuge might have strong encouragement to seize the hope set before us" (Heb. 6:18). Since the God who raised Jesus from the dead is the source of truth, Paul could defend himself by claiming in the last resort that God knows that he is not lying (2 Cor. 11:31; Gal. 1:20).

(b) The revelation of God's truth in Jesus Christ lets the other side of the picture come to light – the lies of men. For men have "exchanged the truth about God for a lie and worshipped and served the creature rather than the Creator" (Rom. 1:25). (On this see further G. Bornkamm, "The Revelation of God's Wrath (Romans 1–3)", *Early Christian Experience*, 1969, 47–70.) The revelation of God's wrath against human wickedness (Rom. 1:18–3:20) leads in Rom. 3:4 to the confession: "Let God be true though every man be false, as it is written, 'That thou mayest be justified in thy words, and prevail when thou art judged'" (cf. Ps. 116:1 LXX; Zeph. 3; Ps. 51:4 ff.). "Paul, following the Psalmist, pictures a scene in court, where God and men plead against each other; when this happens God is sure to leave the court in the right" (C. K. Barrett, *A Commentary on the Epistle to the Romans*, 1957, 63).

2. (a) John's Gospel presents a radical dualism of God and the devil in terms of truth and lie, in a manner similar to that of the Qumran texts, which in their way sharpened the OT outlook. Jn. 8:44 describes the devil as a murderer and a liar. Lying and death stand opposed to the truth and life of the Revealer. Lying, here, does not simply mean telling untruths; it connotes the will which is directed against

God, the hatred of disbelief, and the resulting futility. Bultmann interprets this in existentialist terms. "It is because of this nothingness that the *pseudos* kills, because it robs the man who imagines it is real of his own authenticity" (R. Bultmann, *The Gospel of John*, 1971, 321). See also Jn. 8:41–47, where Jesus accuses his opponents of lying. In Jn. *pseudos* is not primarily a moral offence; it connotes the hatred which disbelief feels for the truth of the Revealer. Such lying can quite easily think of itself as the height of piety, and it is this that makes it so terrible. It happens everywhere, where men seek their own glory and put up barriers to resist Christ's revelation.

(b) This thought is expanded in 1 Jn. The lie here is that men "make God a liar", when they maintain that they have not sinned (1:10; cf. 5:10). 1 Jn. is also directed against false teachers who preach lies (cf. Rev. 2:2), denying Jesus as the Christ (1 Jn. 2:22). In the Johannine literature "lie" is used in the widest sense to mean hatred of Christ, and in consequence man's life without God, characterized by delusion and death.

3. (a) The antithesis of truth and lie is not only the determining factor which distinguishes between Jesus' disciples and his enemies. It also operates within the church of Christ in the responses of obedience and disobedience (→ Hear) to the word of truth. As an ethical problem, lying is not on the same level as quarrelsomeness or unchastity. These belong to the imperfect state of man on earth and as such stand in continual need of sanctification (→ Holy). But lying, like loving, is the expression of one of the basic aspects of the human condition which is determined either by the power of lies or by the power of love. "Why has Satan filled your heart to lie to the Holy Spirit?" (Acts 5:3). The sin of Ananias was not that he had witheld his property, for he was entitled to dispose of it as he pleased, but that he had lied to God in professing to have given it all to the church whilst retaining something for himself (Acts 5:4).

(b) In 1 Jn., men's false evaluation of themselves in relation to God (see above 2 (a)) means that any contradiction between the confession of faith (→ Confess) and the life of the members of a congregation involves them in lies. To profess fellowship with Christ is incompatible with a continued → walk in darkness (1:6). To profess knowledge of Christ is incompatible with simultaneous disobedience to his commands (2:4). To profess to love God is incompatible with continuing to hate one's brother (4:20). In such cases both the claims and the life of a Christian become a lie, excluding him from the truth of God. Here, too, it is apparent that for 1 Jn. lying is not only a moral offence, but also the manifestation of existence without God.

(c) The admonitions in Eph. and Col. have individual faults in mind, when their readers are told to throw off falsehood and to speak the truth to each other (Eph. 4:25; Col. 3:9). This command can be made, because the Christian has put off "the old man [*ton palaion anthrōpon*]" (Eph. 4:22; Col. 3:9) and may put on "the new man" [*ton kainon anthropon*]" (Eph. 4:24; cf. Col. 3:10), and is therefore in the position to stop lying. Rev. also understands lying in specific terms: no liar (*pseudēs*) or perpetrator of horrible deeds will enter the new → Jerusalem (21:8; cf. 21:27; 22:15). Those who belong to the Lamb stand opposed to liars: "No lie was found on their lips" (14:5). ([Ed.] But as in Jn. and 1 Jn. there is the overtone that lying and falsehood stand in fundamental opposition to God. Thus the Jews at

Philadelphia are described as "the synogogue of Satan", who claim to be Jews but lie [3:9]. See also the references to the false prophet [*pseudoprophētēs*; 16:13; 19:20; 20:10] who leads men to oppose God and the church and who likewise has no part in the new Jerusalem.)

4. In conclusion, we can say that God is the truthful One who is faithful in history and who fulfills his word and his promises. When he reveals himself in Christ, man's godlessness is unmasked and seen to be the lie that it is. A lie is not simply a single act: it is an attitude of existence which determines the whole of life. Because it resists the one who gives life, it is the deceitful accomplice of → death. Such an existence in the "lie" manifests itself in individual lies which reveal who is in control of men. Man without God is trapped in lies, unable to see through the deception and destined for death. Only where the lie is exposed by the truth of Christ and man comes under the Lordship of Christ and becomes a new man can the counterfeit existence based on deceit and untruth be overcome. This is the basis of the Christian ethical demand to stop telling lies.

→ Lead Astray, → Pharisee, → Truth   *U. Becker, H.-G. Link*

(a). W. Beilner, "Hypocrite", *EBT* II 390 ff.; H. Conzelmann, *pseudos* etc., *TDNT* IX 594–603; D. Hill, *The Gospel of Matthew*, 1972; M. D. Hooker, "Were there false teachers at Colossae?" in B. Lindars and S. S. Smalley, eds., *Christ and Spirit in the New Testament. In Honour of Charles Francis Digby Moule*, 1973, 315–32; T. Overholt, *The Threat of Falsehood: A Study in the Theology of the Book of Jeremiah*, 1970; S. van Tilborg, *The Jewish Leaders in Matthew*, 1972; U. Wilckens, *hypokrinomai* etc., *TDNT* VIII 559–71.

(b). W. Beilner, *Christus und die Pharisäer*, 1959, 227–35; H. D. Betz, *Der Apostel Paulus und die sokratische Tradition. Eine exegetische Untersuchung zu seiner "Apologie" 2 Korinther 10–13*, *BHTh* 45, 1972; G. Bornkamm, "Heuchelei", *RGG³* III 305 f.; G. F. Else, *Wiener Studien* 72, 1959, 75–107; P. Joüon, "*hypokritēs* dans l'évangile et hébreu hanaf", *Recherches de Science Religieuse* 20, 1930, 312–17; J. Klein, E. Fuchs, G. Gawlick, "Wahrhaftigkeit, Wahrheit", *RGG³* VI 1511 ff.; M. A. Klopfenstein, *Die Lüge nach dem Alten Testament*, 1964; and *kāḥaš*, *THAT* I 825–28; W. G. Kümmel, "Die Weherufe über die Schriftgelehrten und Pharisäer (Mt. 23, 13–26), Antijudaismus im Neuen Testament?", *Abhandlungen zum christlich-jüdischen Dialog*, II, 1967, 141 f.; L. Lemme, "Heuchelei", *RE* III 21 ff.; A. Lesky, "Hypokrites", *Festschrift U. E. Paoli*, 1964, 469–76; J. Maier, "Weitere Stücke aus dem Nahumkommentar aus der Höhle 4 von Qumran", *Judaica* 18, 1962, 2-5–50; J. Schniewind, *Das Evangelium nach Matthäus*, *NTD* 2, 1968¹²; N. H. Søe, "Wahrhaftigkeit", *EKL* III 1716 ff.

Life

The term life denotes the organic functioning of plants, animals and men. Life and → death are the opposite categories basic to all living things; both categories relate to and interpret the other. Human life is unique. It is not merely instinctive but is capable of self-realization and open to formative influences. In Gk. a distinction is made between *zōē* which tends to mean life as a vital, natural force, and *bios* which has a stronger ethical content and means manner of life. It is instructive that the NT takes over the first of these two words to denote that fellowship with God which men enjoy as a specific gift from God himself. For further information on the Gk. and the biblical views → Death.

βίος

βίος (*bios*), life; βιόω (*bioō*), live; βιωτικός (*biōtikos*), pertaining to life.

CL The noun *bios* (since Homer; derived from the corresponding vb. *bioō* and related to Lat. *vivere*, live, and Eng. "quick") denotes life in its concrete outward manifestations. It is used generally for "lifetime" or "duration of life" (Plato, *Symp.* 181d, 203d; *Leg.* 6, 770a; 7, 802a), and specifically for an individual's way of life, which, however, is seen not as a once-for-all historical event but as a "type" of supertemporal behaviour existing alongside other possible "types" (Plato, *Leg.* 2, 663b; *Rep.* 617d ff.). The Greeks' ethical view of life is expressed with great clarity by Aristotle, who distinguishes between the following ways of life: pleasure-loving (*apolaustikos*); active (*praktikos*) or political (*politikos*); and contemplative (*theōrētikos*) (*Eth.Nic.* 1, 3p 1095b, 14 ff.). Later *bios* acquired the concrete meanings livelihood, trade, wealth (cf. *biōtikos*, pertaining to life, everyday, Polybius 4, 73, 8; Diogenes Laertius 7, 22; Epictetus, *Dissertationes* 1, 26, 3, 7).

OT In the LXX *bios* usually translates *yāmîm*, days, the plural of *yôm*, day, when it renders a Heb. equivalent. Following OT historical thought, the LXX adopts mainly the temporal meaning of *bios*, i.e. the duration of life (cf. the Heb. expression "a man's days"). The word does not occur at all in the Pentateuch or the Prophets, while in Cant. 8:7 it means wealth, and in Prov. 31:14 food.

The meaning of the word is clearest in Job, where it occurs 13 times. Man's life, in all its wretchedness, is likened to forced labour (7:1), a shadow (8:9), vanity (7:16), sorrow (15:20). By contrast, Wisdom promises the godly man length of life (Prov. 3:2), a gift which she holds in her right hand (Prov. 3:16), while the godless are punished with a short fleeting life (Wis. 2:1, 4, 5).

In 4 Macc., Hel. influence replaces the temporal meaning of *bios* with an ethical meaning. Just as Aristotle had applied a variety of adjs. to the noun (see above CL), so 4 Macc. describes it as a way of life which is true to the law (*nomimos*, 5:36; 7:15); upright (*orthos*, 1:15); pleasant (*hēdys*, 8:23); even divine (*theios*, 7:7).

NT Unlike *zōē*, *bios* is surprisingly rare in the NT, occurring only 11 times (*bioō* only once, 1 Pet. 4:2). All three meanings normal in profane Gk. are to be found, but with characteristic shifts of emphasis.

1. *bios* has a clearly temporal meaning (duration of life) only in the Koine version of 1 Pet. 4:3; likewise *bioō* in the previous verse. In 1 Tim. 2:2 and 2 Tim. 2:4 it has the more general sense of (everyday) life, a meaning shared on occasion with *zōē*.

2. The NT uses *bios* mostly (6 times) in the concrete, somewhat external sense which it had acquired in late antiquity: that of wealth, fortune. Mk. 12:44 and Lk. 21:4 speak of the poor widow putting "her whole living" into the treasury, while Lk. 15:12, 30 tells of the prodigal son wasting his living on harlots. Similarly, according to 1 Jn. 3:17, real love shows itself in the concrete act of sharing this world's goods with a brother in need.

3. The specifically Gk. use of *bios* to mean "manner of life" (see above CL) is only hinted at in the NT. "The pride of life" in 1 Jn. 2:16 refers to ostentatious living, and in Lk. 8:14 there is an allusion to "the cares, riches and pleasures of life". In other words, the NT attitude here is purely negative. The reason why this specifically Gk. conception of *bios* is not adopted by the NT is that according to the latter, man does not live his life for himself or to develop his own virtues, but is answerable to God for living in the service of others.   *H.-G. Link*

| $\zeta\omega\acute{\eta}$ | $\zeta\omega\acute{\eta}$ (zōē), life; $\zeta\acute{\alpha}\omega$ (zaō), live; $\zeta\tilde{\omega}ov$ (zōon), living creature; $\zeta\omega o\gamma ov\acute{\epsilon}\omega$ (zōogoneō), procreate, give life to, keep alive; $\zeta\omega o\pi oi\acute{\epsilon}\omega$ (zōopoieō), make alive, give life to.

CL zaō, contracted to zō, and its corresponding noun zōē, are both found from Homer onwards. Somewhat later, during the period of Herodotus and the precursors of Socrates, the noun zōon appears, covering men (logika zōa, rational creatures) and animals (aloga zōa, irrational creatures) as distinct from inanimate objects. Apart from its use in Heb. 13:11 and 2 Pet. 2:12, zōon in the NT is confined to Rev. and refers to the four living creatures by the heavenly throne (→ Cherub). The two compound vbs. zōogoneō and zōopoieō stem from a still later period, that of Aristotle and Theophrastus. Both vbs. refer to the life-processes of nature, usually the procreation of animals and the growth of plants. This is particularly true of zōogoneō, which therefore occurs sporadically and only incidentally in the NT. zōopoieō, on the other hand, is a more technical word occasionally used in soteriological contexts where there is no reference to natural history.

1. In classical Gk., life refers in the first place to that living quality of → nature which is shared alike by men, animals and plants (for what follows cf. R. Bultmann, *TDNT* II 832–43). For the Greeks, therefore, life belongs to the category of natural science, being characterized by the power of self-movement as distinct from mechanical movement (Plato, *Leg.* 10, 895c ff; *Phaedr.* 245c ff.; Aristotle, *An.* 2, 2 p 412b, 16 f.; p 413a, 22 ff.). The cause of life is considered to be the psychē (→ soul), which Diogenes of Apollonia imagined as an ètherial substance (aēr), while Xenophanes thought of it as a fluttering breath (pneuma) (H. Diels, *Die Fragmente der Vorsokratiker*, I, 425, 42). Just as psychē and zōē belong very closely together in Gk. thought, so do psychē and sōma (→ body) (Plato, *Phaedr.* 105c ff.; Aristotle, *An.* 2, 1p 412b, 7 ff.); natural life is made up of the components soul and body.

Not only each single individual but also the whole universe is thought of as a living organism (zōon empsychon, Plato, *Tim.* 30b) or as a world with a soul (kosmos empsychos). Even the gods are imagined largely as living creatures (zōa) having bipartite natures analogous to the human body and soul (Aristotle, *Metaph.* 11, 7 p 1072b, 28 ff.). Thus Plato distinguishes between living creatures which are thnēta (mortal, i.e. men), and athanata (immortal, i.e. gods) (*Tim.* 38c ff.).

The Greeks considered a third component to be specific to human life, namely, the → reason, mind, or understanding (nous). While the sōma and to some extent the psychē go to make up natural life, the nous is a divine element which enters human life from outside, enhancing it beyond the natural life e.g. of animals and producing a type of existence capable of various alternatives (→ bios). This idea is expressed not merely by the variety of dative constructions which can be found with zaō (e.g. patridi for the fatherland, Demosthenes, *Orationes* 7:17; patri, for one's father, Dionysius of Halicarnassus, 3, 17, 7), but also by the adjs., advs. and preps. which can be added and which qualify "life" as being good (agathē), orderly (kosmiōs), reasonable (kata logon) or bad (aischra) (Plato, *Rep.* 521a; *Leg.* 7, 806e; 3, 944c).

2. Among the Stoics the slogan kata physin zēn, to live according to nature, assumed great importance. This phrase, however, does not imply instinctive

existence, but rather life which is virtuous (*kat' aretēn*) or lived according to reason (*kata logon*), and which enables the man who is otherwise "dead" to fulfil the purpose of his existence (*eu zēn*, to live well; cf. Epictetus, *Dissertationes*, 1, 9, 19; 2, 9, 7 f.; 3, 1, 25 f.; 4, 11, 3). The phrase → *bios kata physin*, life according to nature, is also found, in this same sense. Whereas the Greeks of the classical period saw their ideal as active involvement in the public affairs of the *polis*, in the Hellenistic period the Stoics idealized complete withdrawal from the outward bustle of the world, and the cultivation of one's own inner life.

3. While the Stoics distinguished between outward and inward life, neo-Platonism differentiated between life in this world and life beyond this world. According to Plotinus, man indeed possesses natural life, but the life which is perfect (*teleia*) and true (*alēthinē*) is to be found only in the one divine realm of the One (*hen*). The way to this true life leads via abnegation of the body, and cleansing (*katharsis*) from all earthly things, to the moment of sight or vision (*thea*), when man attains the true life and becomes one with it (cf. Plotinus, *Enneads* 1, 4, 3; 6, 7, 31; and often). In other words, life is seen as an upward ascent.

4. Gnosticism, by contrast, saw life as a descent. *zōē*, often associated with *phōs*, light (e.g. *Corp.Herm.* 1, 12), is something essentially divine, a tangible fluid in the divine world, definitely a physical entity, but at the same time something indestructible and possessed of lifegiving power; in a word immortality (*athanasia*; *Corp.Herm.* 1, 28). In the human world this pure divine life is intermingled with matter, being imprisoned in the body. It is not present in its fullness but only in the form of tiny, scattered sparks of life. Hence, one must break free from the prison-house of the body in order to enjoy, at least temporarily, the ecstatic vision (*gnōsis*, → knowledge), i.e. to attain to the unity which exists between the inner sparks of life and the supernatural life of the divine world (*Corp.Herm.* 1, 6). This true life is attained on earth only in fleeting moments of → ecstasy. Its full enjoyment must be reserved for the future, when all the particles of life and light presently scattered within matter reunite in the divine world (*Corp.Herm.* 12, 15:14, 10; and passim).

Thus in the history of Gk. philosophy two trends are visible within this area of thought: first, true life is progressively divorced from concrete, everyday events and transferred to a supernatural, divine world; and secondly, life is increasingly seen as something tangible, "scientific", so that *true* human life manifests itself not so much in the continuum of historical events as in discontinuous moments of ecstatic vision, totally divorced from history.

OT 1. The relevant Heb. vocabulary is as follows: noun, *ḥayyîm*; vb., *ḥāyâh*; adj., *ḥay*. The Israelites in the OT viewed life as something thoroughly natural, vital and pertaining to this world. The Gk. division of life into body, soul and reason was a completely alien concept to them. It is true that in Heb. *nepeš*, soul (e.g. Jos. 10:28), or *bāśār*, flesh, (e.g. Gen. 6:13) can be used in place of *ḥayyîm*. But when this occurs it is an example not of analytical Gk. thought but of the synthetic oriental approach, where the part represents the whole, and where the whole of human life is included but viewed from a given standpoint. In those passages where the life is said to be the → blood (Lev. 17:14 LXX: *hē . . . psychē pasēs sarkos haima autou estin*; cf. Lev. 17:11; Gen. 9:4; Deut. 12:23), this is to be understood not as a scientific statement, but rather as an assumption made against the background of

477

early oriental ritual (cf. the rite of the Passover in Exod. 12). The aim is to draw attention not so much to a life at man's disposal but rather to the fact that life is not man's to dispose of. The Israelites thought of life not as a natural or scientific phenomenon, but primarily as duration, the days of a man's life which are granted him by Yahweh, the Lord of life (Gen. 25:7; 47:28; Deut. 32:39; → *bios* OT). Long life was considered to be special evidence of the divine → blessing promised to the obedient (Gen. 15:15; 25:8; Deut. 5:16; 30:19; Prov. 3:1 f.; cf. 2 Ki. 20:1 ff.). The power of death, on the other hand, invades human life in the form of sickness, hatred or loneliness (Ps. 18:5 f.; 33:19; 56:13; 116:8; → Death OT). In common with orientals generally, the Israelites were strangers to the Gk. ideal of a life which is aloof and contemplative (*theōrētikos*; cf. *bios* CL). Rather, their ideal was a life of active involvement, a life expressed, e.g. by → hunger and thirst (e.g. Jdg. 15:18 f.), → hatred and → love (e.g. Gen. 24:27), → desires and lusts (e.g. 1 Sam. 1; 2 Sam. 13). To the Israelites, as to orientals in general, the sheer vitality, concreteness and diversity of life were a source of the utmost delight (1 Ki. 3:11 ff.; Prov. 3:16; Job 2:4); life synonymous with health, well-being and success (Mal. 2:5; Prov. 2:19; Ps. 56:13; Eccl. 9:9). An essential feature of life, however, was attendance at the sanctuary. Here the worshipper joined in fellowship with the living in praising Yahweh, the Creator of life, and was even granted the occasional privilege of gazing upon him albeit indirectly (Exod. 33:18 ff.; Ps. 27:4; 65:5; 84:5; 142:7; see below OT, 5). Only in extreme despair was there any thought of death which would put an end to a life that had become intolerable (Jer. 20:14 ff.; Job 3:11 f.; Tob. 3:10).

2. While the Israelites were unanimous in their conviction that Yahweh is to be praised as the author of life (Jer. 17:13; Ps. 36:9; 139:13 ff.), the Yahwist's reflections on the origin of life produce some idiosyncratic statements on related issues not otherwise touched on in the OT. According to Gen. 2:7, Yahweh formed man from the dust of the ground and breathed divine breath into the lifeless body so that he became a living being (*nepeš ḥayyâh*). Here the distinction is not, as the LXX translation *psychē zōsa* (living soul) suggests, between the body and the soul, but rather between the → body and the life. The whole physical, emotional and intellectual life of man stems from God. If he withdraws his breath of life, then man crumbles to dust (Ps. 104:29 f.; Job 34:14 f.; cf. G. von Rad, *Old Testament Theology*, I, 1962, 149; and *Genesis*, 1963[2], 71–83).

The trials and tribulations common to man – toil and failure, shame and fear, the pains of childbirth – are said by the Yahwist to have been caused by man's primeval fall into sin (Gen. 3). That which the Yahwist sees as divine punishment is not so much death (which before the Exile was accepted as one of the given factors of the human situation; cf. Gen. 2:17; 3:19); rather it is the shortening of the life span (Gen. 6:3), and in particular the various trials of life. These are the discords which mar all human existence, the original harmony of life having been broken (cf. von Rad, *Genesis*, 83–99).

3. The specifically Israelite view of life is expressed most clearly in Deut. At the → feast commemorating the renewal of the → covenant, the worshipping community is confronted by the word of Yahweh with a choice between life and death (Deut. 30:1–20). The obedient are promised blessing, prosperity and life, while the disobedient can expect nothing but curse, adversity and death (Deut. 30:15, 19).

The living power of God's word extends even to man's physical existence: "Man does not live by bread alone, but . . . by everything that proceeds out of the mouth of Yahweh" (Deut. 8:3). Deut. is most insistent that true life comes not from magical rites and ceremonies but from keeping the word of Yahweh. For this word "is no trifle, but it is your life" (Deut. 32:47; cf. Lev. 18:5).

4. In the same way the prophets call Israel back to Yahweh; this is Israel's only chance of life, threatened as he is with imminent disaster (Amos 5:4, 14). Isaiah laments over the scoffers among the people who have entered into a covenant with death (Isa. 28:15). Jeremiah sets the way of life and of death (Jer. 21:8) once more before a faithless Israel, that has forsaken the source of life (Jer. 2:13; 17:13). Ezekiel stresses repeatedly that the righteous man shall live, while the godless man must die (Ezek. 3:18 ff.; 14:20; 18:4, 9, 13, 17, 20 ff.; 33:11; 37:5). Here the gift of natural life becomes an integral part of the → covenant, obedience to which means prosperity and blessing, while the transgressor forfeits his right to live. The accounts of Ezek.'s visions occasionally contain the phrase *rûaḥ haḥayyâh* (LXX *pneuma zōēs*), which is a paraphrase for the creative, life-giving power of God (Ezek. 1:20 f.; 10:17; 37:5, 10).

Jeremiah's distinction between the two ways is taken up in the wisdom literature, where → Wisdom offers to guide men along the pathway to life, while the ways of → folly lead to death (Prov. 2:18 f.; 3:2, 18; 4:4, 10, 22; 5:6; 6:23; 8:35; 9:11, 18 and passim).

5. In the Psalms Yahweh is portrayed as he who gives life and delivers from → death (Ps. 16:11; 27:1; 31:4 f. and passim). With the passage of time, however, godly men increasingly found that their expectations of long life and prosperity were utterly contradicted by their day-to-day experiences. Hence in later Pss. the traditional view of life becomes relative, and true life is seen as arising from fellowship with Yahweh. "Thy loving kindness is better than life" (Ps. 63:3). Life is now viewed metaphorically in terms of spirituality and life-mysticism (G. von Rad, *The Problem of the Hexateuch and Other Essays*, 1966, 258 f.) which seeks refuge and finds satisfaction in living fellowship with Yahweh (Ps. 16:5, 9 ff.; 23; 36:8 ff.). Ps. 73 goes a step further. The assurance of Yahweh's nearness, and the sense of security which this brings, give the worshipper a hope beyond death: "My flesh and my heart may fail, but God is . . . my portion for ever" (Ps. 73:26). Faced with the necessity of justifying the ways of God to men, and persuaded of Yahweh's faithfulness to his covenant promises, the OT believer finds himself being led to hope for better things beyond the grave, i.e. his view of life becomes eschatological. "Wholly apart from magic and mythology there grew up a confidence based simply and solely upon the certainty of an irrefragable relationship with God" (G. von Rad, op. cit., 264; cf. Ps. 49:16; Job 19:25 ff.; → Death, art. *thanatos*, OT 2 (e)).

In apocalyptic the hope of a future life, hitherto held by individual psalmists, has become an expectation of future resurrection now held by the whole nation (Isa. 26:19; Dan. 12:2; cf. SB I, 885 f.; D. S. Russell, *The Method and Message of Jewish Apocalyptic 200 B.C.–A.D. 100*, 1964, 353–90).

6. The LXX frequently reinterprets the OT view of life in terms of the Gk. *zōē* (cf. LXX Deut. 32:39; Ps. 55:14 [56:13]; 118 [119]; Prov. 16:15; Job 19:25; 33:30).

To a large extent, late Judaism adopted the OT view of life (Meg. 27b; Taan.

20b; Ber. 55a; cf. SB IV 267, 275, 629), but under Hellenistic influence true life was increasingly seen as the gift of eternal life (*zōē aiōnios*), life without end (4 Macc. 7:19; 15:3; 16:25; 17:12; 18:19; and often). Hence, as in the NT, eternal life could be referred to simply as *zōē* (Test.Jud. 25:1) or *zēn* (Pss.Sol. 15:15). From the Maccabean period onwards belief in a hereafter, → resurrection and eternal life was widespread among Jewish theologians (cf. SB III 481 ff.). As in gnosticism, so also in late Judaism *zōē* is frequently found in association with *phōs*, light, and *gnōsis*, knowledge (cf. Hos. 10:12 LXX).

In Hellenistic Judaism belief in the → resurrection of the dead was largely replaced by the doctrine of the immortality of the → soul (Wis. 8:19 f.; Josephus, *War* 7, 8, 7). Earthly life lost significance (Wis. 4:8 f.), or was even regarded as the prison-house of the soul (Philo, *Leg.All.* 2, 57; 3, 21, 151); the act of dying gained ever-increasing significance (4 Macc. 15:12; 2 Macc. 8:21; Josephus, *War* 7, 8, 7), and true life, i.e. life which is *athanatos*, immortal, was transferred to the world beyond (4 Macc. 15:3; Pss.Sol. 3:16; Philo, *Op.Mund.* 155 f.).

On the other hand, the usage found in the Qumran texts is strikingly similar to that of the OT, the only new feature being the rather formal association of life with the blessings of salvation (1QS 3:7; 4:7; 1 QH 2:20, 31; 9:66; 1QM 1:9; 12:3; CD 3:20).

NT References to the important matter of life occur, as one might expect, in all the books of the NT. It is in the theology of Paul and of John that the doctrine of life is most clearly expressed, and it is evident that the NT teaching contains elements which are of OT, late Jewish and also Gk. origin.

1. (a) The OT view of life is recalled most strongly in the Synoptic Gospels. Natural life is regarded as a priceless possession (Mk. 8:37). Jesus is frequently called upon to exercise his power in order that sick or dying men might live (Mk. 5:23, aorist *zēsē*, that she may live; cf. Jn. 4:47 ff.) or even to restore to earthly life those who are already dead (Mk. 5:35 ff.; Lk. 7:11 f.; Jn. 11:1 ff.). As in the OT, temporal categories are used for life (Lk. 1:75; cf. Heb. 7:3; Rom. 7:1 ff.), which is regarded as something dynamic, but at the same time bounded and transient (Acts 17:28; Jas. 4:14). It is no merely natural occurrence, but an event which can succeed or fail (Lk. 15:13, *asōtōs zēn*, to live dissolutely; 2 Tim. 3:12, *eusebōs zēn*, to live a god-fearing life). True life depends on the word of God (Matt. 4:4, quoting Deut. 8:3), while to live away from God is described as being dead (Lk. 15:24, 32). The basic necessities of life, such as food and clothing, are by no means despised; rather they are gratefully received as gifts of the Creator (Matt. 6:25 ff.; Lk. 12:15). God, who can kill and make alive (Matt. 10:28; Rom. 4:17), is the undisputed Creator (Acts 17:25), the Lord (Lk. 12:20; Acts 10:42; Jas. 4:15) and the embodiment of life; he is the living God (Matt. 16:16; 26:63) and the God of the living (Matt. 22:32; Mk. 12:27; Lk. 20:38).

(b) Over against the present life there stands the life to come (Mk. 10:30; 1 Tim. 4:8; "Godliness is of value in every way, as it holds promise for the present life and also for the life to come [*zōēs tēs nyn kai tēs mellousēs*]"). It is described as "eternal life" (*zōē aiōnios*; Matt. 19:16; par. Mk. 10:17, Lk. 18:18; Matt. 25:46; cf. 2 Tim. 1:10, *zōē kai aphtharsia*, life and immortality). One attains this not by reason of the immortality of the soul – this Gk. idea is completely foreign to the

NT – but as a gift from God who raises the dead (Matt. 22:31 f. par. Mk. 12:26 f., Lk. 20:36 f.). The fact that the future life is occasionally referred to by the use of *zōē* alone, i.e. without any qualifying phrase (see above OT 6), indicates that such life is regarded as real and true, the very life of God himself (Matt. 18:18; Mk. 9:43, 45). There is no implication here, however, of the devaluation of earthly life found in later Hellenism. On the contrary, man's relationship to God's will in this present life determines his destiny in the life to come (Matt. 19:16 par. Mk. 10:17, Lk. 18:18; Lk. 10:25). Matt. 7:13 f. (cf. Lk. 13:23 f.) takes up the idea of the two ways found in Deut. 30:19; Jer. 21:8, Wisdom and inter-Testamental literature, Qumran and later Christian writings (cf. Prov. 8:20; 9:6; 12:15; 16:25; 2 Esd. 7:7 ff.; Test.Ash. 1:3, 5; Pirke Aboth 2:12 f.; 1QS 3:20; Did. 1:1; Barn. 18:1; → Walk, art. *hodos*; see also above OT 4). This close relationship between the present and the future life is put most impressively in the parable of the last → judgment (Matt. 25:31 ff.): the disobedient will suffer eternal punishment, while the righteous will enter into eternal life (Matt. 25:46).

2. (a) Paul's view of life is deeply affected by the → resurrection of Christ from the dead (1 Cor. 15:4), which, being an accomplished fact, has proved the power of divine life over death (Rom. 14:9). The apostle sees Christ as the very embodiment of God's living power, conquering death and raising the dead (2 Cor. 13:4). Life means Christ's everlasting life, life from the dead and beyond the grave.

Through his resurrection Christ, the Last → Adam, has become the author of a new life for mankind (Rom. 5:12 ff.; 1 Cor. 15:20 ff.). The life of Christians is not their own life but the life of Christ: Christ lives in them (Gal. 2:20; Phil. 1:21), they live the life of Christ (2 Cor. 4:10). Their life is justified by Christ (Rom. 5:18), and by his life they will be saved (Rom. 5:10). The life of Christ is mediated to Christians neither as a power (as with the gnostics), nor through mystic union, but by the → word of life (Phil. 2:16; cf. 2 Tim. 1:10; Tit. 1:2 f.) and by the creative power of the quickening → Spirit (Rom. 8:2, 6, 10 f.; 1 Cor. 15:45).

(b) The new Spirit-wrought life of believers (Rom. 6:4) does not try to escape from everyday life into Stoic or gnostic indifference and asceticism. Rather, as Paul sees it, the Christian is to serve his fellow-men responsibly, in whatever historical situation he finds himself. Since he no longer lives for himself (Rom. 14:7; 2 Cor. 5:15), but for God (Rom. 6:10 f.) and Christ (Rom. 14:8; 2 Cor. 5:15), his life shows positive, tangible results (Gal. 5:25, 26) as he follows in the footsteps of Christ and takes up Christ's → cross (2 Cor. 4:9 f.). Hence, Paul can make the paradoxical statement: "We are treated . . . as dying, and behold we live" (2 Cor. 6:8 f.), since life comes from and through death. Not living for oneself means having an attitude of love for others (Rom. 13:8–10; 14:11 ff.). It is important to notice the datives and *syn*-constructions which Paul uses with *zaō*, in order to teach that "living for . . ." and "living with . . ." belong to the very structure of life.

(c) In the believer's new life there is a tension between present and future, indicative and imperative (Gal. 5:25). His new life exists already but has not yet been fully manifested (Col. 3:3, 4). Christ's → resurrection is the pledge of our own future resurrection to an eternal life where death and all the imperfections of the present creation will be things of the past (Rom. 8:18 ff.). "For as in Adam all die, so also in Christ shall all be made alive" (*zōopoiēthēsontai*, 1 Cor. 15:22; → Adam).

The new life is not confined to historical time, but points forward to eternal life when the last enemy, death, is vanquished (1 Cor. 15:26, 28; Rom. 6:22; Gal. 6:8). Paul depicts the transition from temporal to eternal life in terms of cosmic drama, miraculous transformation and rapture (1 Thess. 4:13–17; 1 Cor. 15:20 ff., 35 ff., 51 ff.). In this he is following apocalyptic tradition, using apocalyptic imagery and symbolism. He does not engage, however, in the speculations of late Judaism, but confines himself to figurative hints concerning the form which the future life will take. It will be a bodily life (1 Cor. 15:35 ff.; 2 Cor. 5:1 ff.; note that the Jews could not conceive of life in a disembodied state; → Body). It will involve seeing → face to face (1 Cor. 13:12; cf. 2 Cor. 5:7), entering into the fullness of → righteousness, → peace and → joy (Rom. 14:17), → glory (*doxa*, 2 Cor. 3:8 f.) or glorification (Rom. 8:17), but above all being with Christ forever (1 Thess. 4:17; 2 Cor. 5:8; Phil. 1:23).

3. (a) Jn. presents the Word as being eternal life even before his incarnation. He has lived eternally with God and for the benefit of men (Jn. 1:4; 1 Jn. 1:1 f.), i.e. he is the source of divine life and power both in the old and in the new creation. In his incarnation he is the revelation of God, but he not only brings eternal life by his word (Jn. 6:68; 10:28; 12:50; 17:2); he himself *is* the true life (1 Jn. 5:20), as his various → "I am" sayings indicate: "I am the bread of life" (Jn. 6:35, 48), "the light of the world (Jn. 8:12), "the resurrection and the life" (Jn. 11:25), "the way, the truth and the life" (Jn. 14:6). The pre-existent Son of the eternal Father is sent into the world to give life to men both by his word and in his own person (Jn. 6:33; 10:10; 1 Jn. 4:9).

(b) The life of God is received by → faith. He who believes in the Son has life (1 Jn. 5:12), eternal life (Jn. 6:40, 47); he has already passed from death to life (Jn. 5:24; 1 Jn. 3:14). The eternal life which is granted to believers expresses itself in love (Jn. 15:9–17) and in joy (Jn. 16:20–24). According to 1 Jn. 3:14, brotherly love is the criterion of true life: "He who does not love remains in death. We know that we have passed out of death into life, because we love the brethren."

(c) Although at many points Jn.'s view of life corresponds to that of the gnostics, he moves in the opposite direction, for whereas the gnostics transferred eternal life to an almost inaccessible world beyond time and space, Jn. brings it right into the present and anchors it firmly to the word, the commandment and the person of Christ (Jn. 17:3). Possessing this eternal life here and now, believers find death and judgment no longer factors to be reckoned with (Jn. 5:24; 11:25), for such life has the seeds of eternity within it (Jn. 4:14; 6:27; 12:25). All that remains for Christ's disciples is to see the divine glory (*theōrōsin tēn doxan*, Jn. 17:24); and their salvation will be complete (cf. R. Bultmann, *TDNT* II 870 f.).

4. Rev. combines the → Son of man tradition with the figure of a slain → lamb: "I am the first and the last, and the living one; I died, and behold I am alive for evermore, and I have the keys of Death and Hades" (Rev. 1:17 f.; cf. 1:13 ff.; 4:9 f.). Whereas the Gospel of Jn., with its Hellenistic background, concentrates wholly on the present life, Rev. goes back to Jewish traditions and concerns itself exclusively with the life to come. In the vision of the new → Jerusalem, the mythical, early oriental pictures of the tree of life and the water of life, familiar from the story of the Garden of Eden (Gen. 2:9–17), reappear as symbols of the fulness of life in the new city of God (Rev. 22:2–14, 19; 21:6; 22:1, 17). The vision of the new

→ heaven and the new earth is the most wide-ranging in its promises: the last enemy, death, will be vanquished (cf. Paul, 1 Cor. 15:26) and our eternal life with God will be utter perfection: "God himself will be with them; he will wipe away every tear from their eyes and death shall be no more, neither shall there be mourning nor crying nor pain any more, for the former things have passed away" (Rev. 21:3 f.).   H.-G. Link

→ Adam, → Animal, → Birth, → Creation, → Judgment, → Man, → Death, → Resurrection, → Righteousness, → Sin, → Soul, → Time

(a). K. Barth, *CD* III 2, "The Creature"; and *CD* III, 4 "Freedom for Life", 324–64; G. R. Beasley-Murray, "The Contribution of the Book of Revelation to the Christian Belief in Immortality", *SJT* 27, 1974, 76–93; G. Bornkamm, "Baptism and New Life in Paul (Romans 6)", *Early Christian Experience*, 1969, 71–86; S. G. F. Brandon, "Life after Death IV. The After-Life in Ancient Egyptian Faith and Practice", *ExpT* 76, 1964–65, 217–220; F. F. Bruce, "Paul on Immortality", *SJT* 24, 1971, 457–72; R. Bultmann, *Theology of the New Testament*, I, 1952, 203–10, 345–52; *Primitive Christianity in its Historical Setting*, 1956; *The Gospel of John*, 1971; J. C. Coetzee, "Life in John's Writings and the Qumran Scrolls", *Neotestamentica* 6, 1972, 48–66; C. H. Dodd, *The Interpretation of the Fourth Gospel*, 1953, 144–50; W. Eichrodt, *Theology of the Old Testament*, II, 1967, 496–529; A. J. Feldman, *The Concept of Immortality in Judaism Historically Considered*, 1964; D. H. Gard, "The Concept of the Future Life according to the Greek Translator of the Book of Job", *JBL* 73, 1954 137–43; D. Hill, "The Background and Biblical Usage of *zōē* and *zōē aiōnios*", *Greek Words and Hebrew Meanings: Studies in the Semantics of Soteriological Terms*, 1967, 82–201; L. Hodgson, "Life after Death II. The Philosophers: Plato and Kant", *ExpT* 76, 1964–65, 107 ff.; S. H. Hooke, "Life after Death V. Israel and the After-Life", *ExpT* 76, 1964–65, 236–39; and "Life after Death VI. The Extra-Canonical Literature", ibid., 273–76; G. E. Ladd, *A Theology of the New Testament*, 1975, 254–69; W. B. J. Martin, "Life after Death III. The Poets – Victorian and Modern", *ExpT* 76, 1964–65, 140–43; H. Miskotte, *When the Gods are Silent*, 1967; C. L. Mitton, "Life after Death VII. The After-Life in the New Testament", *ExpT* 76, 1964–65, 332–37; S. Mowinckel, *He That Cometh*, 1956; J. Pedersen, *Israel: Its Life and Culture*, I–II, 1926, 99–181 (on the soul), 453–96 (on the world of life and death); G. von Rad, *Old Testament Theology*, I, 1962; II, 1965 (see indexes); *Genesis*, 1963²; and " 'Righteousness' and 'Life' in the Cultic Language of the Psalms", *The Problem of the Hexateuch and Other Essays*, 1966, 243–66; H. H. Rowley, "The Good Life" and "Death and Beyond", *The Faith of Israel*, 1956, 124–49, 150–76; G. von Rad, G. Bertram, R. Bultmann, *zaō* etc., *TDNT* II 832–75; D. S. Russell, *The Method and Message of Jewish Apocalyptic 200 B.C. – A.D. 100*, 1964, 353–90; E. Schmitt, "Life", *EBT* II 499–503; R. Taylor, "The Eschatological Meaning of Life and Death in the Book of Wisdom I–V", *Ephemerides Theologicae Lovanienses* 42, 1966, 72–137; V. Taylor, "Life after Death I. The Modern Situation", *ExpT* 76, 1964–65, 76–79; R. W. Thomas, "The Meaning of the Terms 'Life' and 'Death' in the Fourth Gospel and in Paul", *SJT* 21, 1968, 199–212; G. Widengren, "Life after Death VIII. Eschatological Ideas in Indian and Iranian Religion", *ExpT* 76, 1964–65, 364–67; H. W. Wolff, *Anthropology of the Old Testament*, 1974.
(b). C. Barth, "Leben und Tod", *EKL* II 1040 ff.; G. Dautzenberg, *Sein Leben bewahren. Psyche in den Herrenworten der Evangelien, Studien zum Alten und Neuen Testament* 14, 1966; F. Delekat, "Tod, Auferstehung, ewiges Leben", *EvTh* 21, 1961, 1 ff.; L. Dürr, *Die Wertung des Lebens im Alten Testament und antiken Orient*, 1926; E. Ebeling, *Tod und Leben nach den Vorstellungen der Babylonier*, 1931; G. Gerleman, *ḥāyâh*, *THAT* I 549–57; M. L. Henry et al., *Leben angesichts des Todes, Beiträge zum theologischen Problem des Todes. Helmut Thielicke zum 60. Geburtstag*, 1968; A. Hultkranz, "Leben", *RGG³* IV 248 f.; P. Kleinert, "Zur Idee des Lebens im Alten Testament", *ThStKr* 68, 1895, 693–732; H.-J. Kraus, "Der lebendige Gott", *EvTh* 27, 1967, 169–200; J. Lindblom, *Das ewige Leben*, 1914; O. Michel, "Der Mensch zwischen Tod und Gericht", *Deutsche Theologie* 8, 1941, 10 ff.; F. Mussner, *Zōē. Die Anschauung vom "Leben" im vierten Evangelium unter Berücksichtigung der Johannesbriefe*, 1952; H. Pribnow, *Die johanneische Anschauung vom "Leben"*, 1934; O. Procksch, "Der Lebensgedanke im Alten Testament", *Christentum und Wissenschaft* 4, 1928, 145 ff.; G. Quell, *Die Auffassungen des Todes in Israel*, 1925; G. von Rad, "Alttestamentliche Glaubensaussagen von Leben und Tod", *Allgemeine evangelisch-lutherische Kirchenzeitung* 71, 1938, 826 f.; E. Schmitt, *Leben in den Weisheitsbüchern Job, Sprüche und Jesus Sirach*,

1954; J. N. Sevenster, *Leven en Dood in de Evangelien*, 1952; B. Steffen, "Ewiges Leben", *EKL* I 1217 ff.; H. Thielicke, *Tod und Leben*, 1946; T. C. Vriezen, E. Lohse, D. Georgi, H. Conzelmann, P. Althaus, "Ewiges Leben", *RGG*³ II 799 ff.; W. Zimmerli, "'Leben' und 'Tod' im Buche des Propheten Ezechiel", *ThZ* 13, 1957, 494–508.

Light, Shine, Lamp

Light always involves the removal of → darkness, a contrast common to all the word-groups dealt with in this article. *phōs* denotes brightness, light itself, or that which radiates light, e.g. a lamp or torch. But since light is essential to all life, light and → life are closely linked, as are → darkness and → death. *phōs*, therefore, has a wide range of associations in figurative language, from the light of life and the soul to salvation or happiness. The vb. *lampō* and its compounds describe the function or effect of the light coming from an object (or, metaphorically, from men, etc.). *phainō* is largely synonymous with *lampō*, but it lays greater stress on the object itself. It therefore means in cl. Gk. to bring to light; in the pass. to become visible, appear; and in the mid. (as most often in the NT) *phainomai* means to let oneself be seen, to appear as something, to have the appearance of. *lychnos* originally meant the same as *lychnia*, i.e. a lampstand for diffusing the beam of the lamp (*lampas*) placed upon it. Later, however, *lychnos* came to be used for the lamp itself, and figuratively for the eye. Like *phōs*, *phengos* means light, but occurs only three times in the NT: twice with reference to the light of the moon (Matt. 24:29; Mk. 13:24; both quoting Isa. 13:10), and once (Lk. 11:33) referring to the light of a lamp.

λάμπω

λάμπω (*lampō*), shine; λαμπάς (*lampas*), torch, lamp; λαμπρός (*lampros*), beaming, bright, shining, radiant, gleaming, beautiful; λαμπρότης (*lamprotēs*), brilliance, splendour, large-heartedness; λαμπρῶς (*lamprōs*), brilliantly, splendidly, sumptuously; ἐκλάμπω (*eklampō*), shine forth; περιλάμπω (*perilampō*), surround with light.

CL 1. *lampō*, found since Homer, especially in Gk. poetry, is generally intrans. and means to shine (rarely trans., to illuminate). In its lit. sense it refers to sources of light such as the sun, lightning, a torch or a lamp, but it is frequently used fig. in reference to men, e.g. eyes flashing with anger, shining faces, radiant beauty. The compound *perilampō* is used trans. in the sense of to surround with light, while *eklampō* (since Aeschylus) is intrans. and means to shine forth, e.g. of the sun. The noun *lampas* (since Aeschylus) means a torch (made of resinous pine-wood) or a lamp (i.e. an oil-vessel with a wick). *lamprotēs*, on the other hand, is abstract, meaning brilliance, or fig. large-heartedness, and is found from Herodotus onwards. Finally, the adj. *lampros* (since Homer) means beaming, gleaming, shining white (cf. *leukos*, white, gleaming), and the adv. *lamprōs* (since Aeschylus) means brilliantly, splendidly, sumptuously.

2. While in its primary sense *lampō* describes the function of light (→ *phōs*), in illuminating → darkness (*skotos*), used metaphorically it can refer to a shining hero striking fear into men's hearts (e.g. Homer, *Il.* 20, 46). Justice and certain virtues are also said to shine forth.

The flaming torch is associated with the Eleusinian deities and with Artemis and

Hecate, i.e. it is a symbol of purification and serves to drive away demonic powers. A further connection with deity is seen when, e.g., a grove is said to light up at the appearance of a god (cf. Hesiod, *Scutum Herculis* 71). Such passages, however, are rare, for on the whole the Gk. concept "does not specifically associate that which shines with the divine" (A. Oepke, *TDNT* IV 18). Only later, under Egyptian and particularly under oriental influence, does a "religion of light" properly so-called, arise within the Hel. world, reaching its full development in gnosticism (→ *phōs*).

OT In the LXX *lampō* and *eklampō* stand for the Heb. equivalents *ṣāḥaḥ* (to shine), *zāhar* (hiph. trans. to illumine, to teach; intrans. to shine) and *nāḡah* (to shine, to light; hiph. to cause to shine).

([T. McComiskey] In the LXX *lampas* represents the Heb. *lappîḏ* which means torch and is so used in Gen. 15:17; Jdg. 7:16, 20; 15:4, 5. It was used frequently in the OT to describe something of brilliant or dazzling appearance. In Ezek. 1:13 the word describes the undulating light in the midst of the four creatures [cf. Dan. 10:6]. In Nahum 2:4[5] the word describes the gleaming of chariots and in Job 41:10[11] the exhalations of Leviathan. In Isa. 62:1 the word describes the visible manifestation of Israel's deliverance among the nations. And in Zech. 12:6 the clans of Judah are likened to a flaming torch that ignites sheaves. The word *lampas* also represents the Aramaic *nebraštā'* [lampstand] in Dan. 5:5. In the LXX *lamprotēs* stands for the Heb. *nō'am* in Psa. 90[89]:17. The word *nō'am* means pleasantness or favour with no intrinsic concept of brightness.)

These words are important theologically since, in certain contexts, they indicate that God manifests himself as light and hence as a source of illumination, though Yahweh himself is rarely found as the subject of one of these vbs. (see 2 Sam. 22:29: "my God lightens my darkness"; cf. Ps. 18:28, where, however, the vb. is *phōtizein*). As a rule his *kāḇōḏ*, the radiance of his glory (→ Glory, art. *doxa*) is represented in terms of man-made or natural luminaries.

Thus flaming torches (*lampades pyros*) indicate the presence of God (Gen. 15:17; Ezek. 1:13); cf. Exod. 19:18; 24:17, where Yahweh is associated with the smoke and → fire on Mount Sinai, and similarly in the Sinai narrative his presence as lawgiver is made known by flashes of lightning (Exod. 20:18). In Zech. 4:1 ff. there is the vision of the seven-branched candlestick with lamps symbolizing the eyes of the Lord which survey the whole earth. Presumably "the ever-burning lamp in the temple is a representation of the *kāḇōḏ*" (S. Aalen, *Die Begriffe "Licht" und "Finsternis" im Alten Testament, im Spätjudentum und im Rabbinismus*, 1951, 75). Certainly the seven-branched lampstand (Exod. 25:31 ff.) is "a symbol of life and light" just as the lamp is "a symbol of happiness and prosperity" (cf. Jer. 25:10; Prov. 31:18; 13:9; Job 29:3), and therefore, to the godly man, they point back to God as the "Lord and source of all these blessings" (S. Aalen, op. cit., 66). Even Job 41:10 ff. fits this context of ideas, for Leviathan pictured as a crocodile spitting out sparks of fire (v. 19) is an impressive illustration of the power and greatness of the Creator.

Hence in the OT lightning, flaming torches and lamps frequently indicate a theophany or otherwise draw attention to the glory of Yahweh. Furthermore, there is often a close connection between flaming torches and divine → judgment (cf. Num. 16:35), an association vividly portrayed in Zech. 12:6, where the princes of Israel, as instruments of divine justice, are likened to flaming torches ready to consume Israel's enemies (cf. Nah. 2:4). Occasionally the radiance of the divine glory can also be reflected by men acting on behalf of Yahweh. There is no suggestion anywhere, however, of "a passing of the divine substance of light into man" (A. Oepke, *TDNT* IV 22). Nevertheless, the future of the → covenant people is radiant with light and life (cf. Ps. 36:9; Dan. 12:3 Theodotion's Gk. text), while that of the godless is dark (Prov. 4:18, 19). These latter ideas in particular are developed in late Judaism (2 Esd. 7:97; Eth.Enoch 51:5; cf. A. Oepke, *TDNT* IV 23 f.).

NT In the NT *lampō* occurs 7 times, *perilampō* twice, *eklampō* once, *lampas* and *lampros* 9 times each, and *lamprotēs* and *lamprōs* once each. Out of 30 occurrences in all, 9 are in Matt., and 7 in Rev.

1. The words are used in their lit. sense to denote the shining of the sun (Acts 26:13; cf. 2 Cor. 4:6, where as in the OT stress is laid on the creative act of God in causing light to break forth); similarly of lightning (Lk. 17:24; cf. Rev. 8:10) and of a light upon a lampstand (Matt. 5:15 f. par. Lk. 11:33 f.).

Equally lit. is the use of *lampades* (plur. of *lampas*) both for torches (Jn. 18:3 in the account of Jesus' arrest; cf. Rev. 4:5; 8:10) and for (oil-) lamps (Matt. 25:1, 3 f., 7 f.; Acts 20:8).

2. The adj. *lampros* can denote the magnificence of a garment, indicating affluence or luxury (Jas. 2:2 f.; cf. Lk. 23:11; Rev. 19:8). Used without immediate reference to clothing, it pictures the faded splendour of the "harlot of Babylon" (Rev. 18:14), or, adverbially, the luxurious living of the rich man in Lk. 16:19. In these passages the words begin to have metaphorical significance, for true splendour comes only from heaven. Thus Paul, on his way to Damascus, is suddenly surrounded by a light "brighter than the sun" (Acts 26:13: *ouranothen hyper tēn lamprotēta tou hēliou perilampsan me phōs*), and similarly, in Lk. 2:9, the shepherds are surrounded with the radiance of the → angels, who, in the NT generally, appear as shining figures in a blaze of light (Acts 10:30; 12:7; Rev. 15:6; cf. Matt. 28:2 f.; Rev. 18:1).

3. But supremely it was → Jesus Christ himself who was so "transfigured" by divine radiance that his face shone (*elampsen*) like the sun and his garments became white as light (Matt. 17:2; cf. Mk. 9:2 f.; Lk. 9:29). In John's vision of the future he appears as the bright morning star (Rev. 22:16). This and related word-groups are particularly important in John's vision (→ *lychnos*; → *phōs*); cf. the reference to the river of the water of life, "bright as crystal", flowing from the throne of God (Rev. 22:1). As the lightning illuminates the whole sky, so (according to Lk. 17:24) will it be at Christ's parousia. "Then the righteous will shine like the sun in the kingdom of their Father" (Matt. 13:43, quoting Dan. 12:3).

Until that time Christ's disciples have the task of shining like lights on a lampstand (Matt. 5:15 f. → *lychnos*; cf. Rev. 1:12, 20; 2:1), which is made possible only by sharing with Paul in the experience of 2 Cor. 4:6.　　　　*H.-C. Hahn*

| λύχνος | *λύχνος* (*lychnos*), lamp, light; *λυχνία* (*lychnia*), candlestick, lampstand. |

CL & OT Already in Homer *lychnos* (root *leuk;* cf. Latin *lux*, light) means light, lamp (cf. Homer, *Od.* 19, 34). At a later period this was almost invariably some form of oil-lamp (*lampas*). The latter was often placed upon a lampstand or candlestick (*lychnia*, since Plutarch) in order to diffuse the beam.

In the Gk. world and among the Israelites, lamp and lampstand were important both as everyday objects (cf. 2 Ki. 4:10), and for the part they played in public worship (cf. especially the seven-branched candlestick in the tabernacle and the temple, e.g. Exod. 25:13 ff.; Heb. 9:2).

NT In the NT *lychnos* occurs 14 times (of which 6 are in the writings of Lk. and 3 in Rev.), and *lychnia* 11 times (of which 7 are in Rev.). The importance of lights and lamps (e.g. for the household, Lk. 15:8) explains why Jesus used them to illustrate his disciples' function in the world: as the lamp on the candlestick lights up the surrounding darkness, so the disciples are to have an illuminating effect upon their environment (Matt. 5:15 ff.; Mk. 4:21; Lk. 8:16; 11:33). The eye is called "the light [*lychnos*] of the body" (Matt. 6:22; Lk. 11:33). "On its health depends whether the blessings of light come to man" (W. Michaelis, *TDNT* IV 326). The ensuing reference to the eye being *haplous*, single or sound, is taken by D. Hill to reflect the Heb. *tām* (Aram. *š^elīm*) meaning singleness of purpose, undivided loyalty (*The Gospel of Matthew*, 1972, 142). Hill endorses the gloss of F. V. Filson: " If a man divides his interest and tries to focus on both God and possessions, he has no clear vision, and will live without clear orientation and direction" (*A Commentary on the Gospel according to St. Matthew*, 1960, 100).

While Jesus described himself as light (→ *phōs*), his forerunner John the Baptist is likened to a burning and shining lamp (*ho lychnos ho kaiomenos kai phainōn*, Jn. 5:35). Similarly, two witnesses are compared to two lampstands (Rev. 11:4, cf. Zech. 4:3, 11–14), and the seven churches are symbolized by seven golden lampstands (Rev. 1:12 f., 20; 2:1). The source of the witnesses' and the churches' light is indicated by 2 Pet. 1:19, where the word of prophecy is called "light" in that it looks forward to the glory of Christ. It is clear from Rev. 2:5 that the light of Christian witness can become dull and even go out, and that it can be renewed only by repentance (cf. Heb. 6:4 ff., concerning the apostasy of those who have been enlightened).

Babylon is warned that when she sinks in ruin, "The light of the lamp shall shine in thee no more" (Rev. 18:23; → Babylon). The heavenly → Jerusalem, on the other hand, will be illuminated by the glory of God (Rev. 21:23), which makes all lamps superfluous (Rev. 22:5) for God himself will be the sole light. Until that day, the Christian may be said to live in eschatological tension; he is therefore called to be watchful, as in the vivid metaphors of Lk. 12:35: "Let your loins be girded and your lamps burning".   *H.-C. Hahn*

| φαίνω |

φαίνω (*phainō*), shine; φαίνομαι (*phainomai*), mid. shine, appear, become manifest, come into view.

CL & OT Both active and passive forms are found from Homer onwards. The active *phainō* (intrans. only) means to shine (e.g. of the sun, the moon, or a lamp); similarly the passive *phainomai*, which, however, more frequently means to appear, come into view. In the LXX the mid. occurs almost exclusively, but without any clear Heb. equivalent; usually it translates '*ôr* (hiph.), to let shine and *rā'âh* (niph.), to be seen, appear.

NT 1. In the NT *phainō* occurs 9 times, of which 7 are in the Johannine writings.

It generally refers to the light of natural luminaries such as celestial bodies (Phil. 2:15), the sun (Rev. 1:16; 21:23; cf. 8:12) and the moon (Rev. 21:23) (→ Sun, Moon, Stars), but may also refer to the light of a lamp (→ *lychnos*) (Jn. 5:35; 2 Pet. 1:19; Rev. 18:23). In all these passages, however, the light concerned is contrasted with a stronger source of light, e.g. the sun and the moon will be superfluous when the glory of God illumines the heavenly Jerusalem (Rev. 21:23). Only in two places does *phainō* refer to the "true" light itself, i.e. Christ (Jn. 1:5; 1 Jn. 2:8).

2. *phainomai* which occurs 22 times in the NT, of which 17 are in the Synoptic Gospels, is used for the appearing of a star (Matt. 2:7), and also for the appearing of tares among the wheat (Matt. 13:26). It occurs similarly in the birth narratives where → angels appear in → dreams (Matt. 1:20; 21:3, 19), and in other narratives such as those of → Elijah's rumoured appearance (Lk. 9:8) and the appearances of the risen Christ (Mk. 16:9). Similarly, the appearance of certain phenomena will accompany his return (Matt. 24:27, 30). The idea of becoming visible is present in Matt. 9:33 (of Christ's deeds); Jas. 4:14 (of a mist, to which man's brief life is compared); and 1 Pet. 4:18 (of the ungodly at the last → judgment). Matt. 6:5, 16, 18 and 23:27 f. take what men are or do in secret, and contrast this, either positively or negatively, with outward appearances. Paul tells the Corinthians that his primary concern is their well-being, not his own good "showing" before God (2 Cor. 13:7). Mk. 14:64 and Lk. 24:11 refer to the way something "appears" to a person (similarly Rom. 7:13: the true nature of sin being revealed to a person through the law).

Heb. 11:3 is theologically significant. Here the prime cause of "things which are seen" (*blepomena*; → See) is said to be God's creative word. In this way the doctrine of *ex nihilo* → creation is safeguarded against the error of materialism, which would teach that the "aeons" have evolved spontaneously from "things which appear" (*phainomena*). (→ Faith, art. *pistis*; → Form art. *hypostasis*.)

H.-C. Hahn

ἐμφανίζω

ἐμφανίζω (*emphanizō*), reveal, make known; ἐμφανής (*emphanēs*), visible.

CL In secular Gk. *emphanizō* is used basically in the sense of to manifest, exhibit, and passively to become visible. The word also connotes the ideas of making plain (Plato, Sophocles), declaring or explaining (Aristotle). The adj. *emphanēs* connotes the idea of visible, open, manifest.

OT In the LXX *emphanizō* stands once for the Heb. '*āmar* (Est. 2:22). The vb. '*āmar* means to say or tell. Thus, in this context *emphanizō* is used in the sense of declare. The word also stands for the hiphil of *yāḏa'* (know) in Exod. 33:13, where → Moses prays that he may "have made known" to him the ways of God.

The sense here is that of making known or revealing the ways of God. In Isa. 3:9 *emphanizō* occurs as the translation of the negative clause *lō' kihēdû* ("they do not hide it"). The context indicates that it is their sin that they fail to hide; the LXX presents the act positively, i.e. they "manifest" or "display" their sin. In Exod. 33:18 *emphanizō* represents the Heb. *rā'âh* (hiph.). The Heb. *rā'âh* is the common word for see, and in the hiphil means to show or exhibit.

emphanes (neut.) represents the niphal of the Heb. *kûn* (establish) in Isa. 2:2 and Mic. 4:1 which describes the exalted position of the mountain of the → house of the Lord over the mountains. *emphanes* here is probably used in the sense of conspicuous or manifest. This connotation is not inherent in the Heb. *kûn* which is used only in the sense of to be firm, establish (cf. Ass. *kânu*, be firm). The LXX seems to be expansive in its translation at this point.

In Isa. 65:1 *emphanēs* represents the niphal of the Heb. *dāraš* (seek). In this context the Lord indicates that he was sought by those who did not ask for him. The LXX understands *dāraš* in the sense of to manifest, perhaps understanding the niphal in its reflexive sense, i.e. "I permitted myself to be known," hence "I manifested myself."

In Exod. 2:14 *emphanēs* stands for the niphal of *yāda'* (know). In this context Moses becomes aware of the fact that his murder of the Egyptian has become known.

NT In the NT the vb. *emphanizō* occurs in the sense of declare, inform on 5 occasions. In Acts 23:15 the word occurs with the dative *tō chiliarchō*, the military tribune, the commander of a cohort in charge of Paul (cf. Arndt, 890). In Acts 24:1 the word is used in conjunction with the clause *kata tou Paulou* in a legal context referring to the act of informing against or presenting a case against Paul. The word is used in a similar sense in Acts 25:2, 15 with *peri* as the preposition in v. 15. In Acts 23:22 the word is used of the act of imparting information. It describes the act of a young informant who disclosed information to the tribune mentioned above.

In Heb. 11:14 the word *emphanizō* is used in the sense of show or manifest. Those who acknowledge their transience on the earth show or demonstrate by this acknowledgment the fact that they are seeking a homeland.

emphanizō occurs several times in the sense of appear. In Matt. 27:53 it is used of the saints who appeared in Jerusalem at the → resurrection of Christ. In Jn. 14:21 f. it is used of the spiritual presence of Christ with the one who keeps Christ's → commandments. It thus connotes here a manifestation to the spiritual faculties rather than to the senses. In Heb. 9:24 the verb is used of Christ's appearance in the presence of God.

The adj. *emphanēs* is used in the NT on two occasions. In Acts 10:40 it occurs in the sense of manifest in the phrase *edōken auton emphanē genesthai*, "made him manifest" (RSV). The context refers to the post-resurrection appearance of Christ to certain witnesses.

In Rom. 10:20 the word occurs in a quotation from Isa. 65:1: "I have been found by those who did not seek me; I have shown myself [*emphanēs egenomēn*] to those who did not ask for me." As in the LXX rendering of this verse noted above, *emphanēs* represents the niphal of *dāraš*. The quotation, like the preceding one

489

from Deut. 32:21, illustrates the fulfilment of OT prophecy and the consistency of God in receiving the Gentiles, whereas → Israel, as ever, has remained disobedient, (Rom. 10:21; cf. Isa. 65:2).   *T. McComiskey*

φῶς

φῶς (*phōs*), light, brilliance, brightness; φωτίζω (*phō-tizō*), light up, illumine, bring to light; φωτισμός (*phōtismos*), illumination, enlightenment; φωτεινός (*phōteinos*), shining, bright, radiant; φωστήρ (*phōstēr*), luminary, brightness; φωσφόρος (*phōsphoros*), bearing light, morning star.

CL 1. In Homer there is frequent use of the noun *to phaos*, later abbreviated, e.g. by the tragedians, to its Att. form *phōs*. Its basic meaning of light, brightness, also covers the following nuances among others: sunlight, daylight, torch, fire (-light), eyesight. Figuratively *phōs* means the light of life, i.e. life itself, which is highly valued as something bright, and as being comparable with salvation, happiness or military triumph. The bringer of such salvation can also be referred to as *phōs*.

The vb. *phōtizō* (since Aristotle), formed from the same stem, is almost always trans., meaning to light up, illumine, bring to light, make visible. Its corresponding noun *phōtismos* denotes brilliance, radiance, or bringing to light, making manifest, revelation. There is also the adj. *phōteinos* (since Xenophon), shining, bright.

A further derivative from *phōs* is *phōstēr* (since Heliodorus), luminary or brightness, and from Euripides onwards the morning star is termed *phōsphoros*.

2. Relatively early in Gk. usage *phōs* (in contrast with *skotos*, → darkness, or *nyx*, night) came to mean the sphere of ethical good, whereas misdeeds are said to take place in darkness. Hence it is the task, e.g., of a judge, to bring hidden things "to light".

Plato's comparison of the idea of the good with sunlight (*Rep.* 507e–509b) is deeply significant for the history of ideas. By entering the sphere of epistemology (→ knowledge), *phōs* became greatly enriched in its range of connotation. A context such as this can stress its illuminating qualities, while another can emphasize its function as a healer, for even in the Gk. world there was a connection between "the notion of sin and the image of darkness, and the notion of a redemption and salvation from evil and the image of the light" (J. Stenzel, *Die Antike*, I, 1925, 256; cf. R. Bultmann, *The Gospel of John*, 1971, 42). Light possesses powers essential to true life. Hence "to be in the light" comes to mean simply "to live", whereas to be in Hades (→ Hell) is to be in darkness.

3. In the Gk. as in other religions the metaphor of light has a certain importance. The gods are said to live in a world of brightness, the world from which Prometheus stole → fire. "He kindled the light of fire for mortal men" (K. Kerenyi, *Prometheus*, 72). Torch-races were held as part of the cultic veneration of the gods, and in certain mystery cults the cleansing and refining effect of fire (like that of water) played no small part. But Gk. religion never became a religion of light in the strict sense of the term (cf. A. Oepke, *TDNT* IV 19). Such a religion came into being only in later Hellenism.

Gnosticism (→ Knowledge, art. *ginōskō*) marked the climax of this process. It saw a basic, essential difference between light and darkness which stood over against each other as hostile powers, each being sovereign within its own sphere. Man, who by nature is in darkness, needs to liberate the elements of light within his own soul, and free them from earthly matter so that they may be re-united with the supernatural world to which they really belong and so attain to true life. Light and → life are inseparably connected; similarly, "in gnosticism light and spirit are considered to be essentially one" (H. Leisegang, *Die Gnosis*, 1955⁴, 27). "Light is the matter of the other world which flows on him who is willing to receive it and imports divine powers. Light, life, and later knowledge are interchangeable concepts" (A. Oepke, *TDNT* 20 IV). This gnostic religion of light was carried still further in Manichaeism and Mandaeism.

ot 1. In the OT there are frequent references to light and its effects. Having quoted B. Jacob and A. Dillmann, who respectively describe light as "the sublimest element" and "the finest of all elementary forces", G. von Rad adds his own epithet: "the first-born of creation" (*Genesis*, 1963², 49; cf. Gen. 1:3 ff.). He points out that this primeval light has pride of place over all other lights: even the stars are "in no way creators of light, but only mediating bearers of a light that was there without them and before them" (op. cit., 54). The sun, being the brightest star, is assigned to the day (Gen. 1:14 ff.; Sir. 43:2 ff.), and each new day begins with the ushering in of morning light (2 Sam. 23:4). The moon and stars seek to penetrate the darkness of the night at least to some degree (Gen. 1:16; Sir. 43:6 ff.). Surrounded as they were by "a cultural and religious atmosphere that was saturated with all kinds of astrological false belief" (von Rad, ibid.; cf. Wisd. 13:1 f.), the Israelites laid great stress on light having been created, in order to render abortive any attempt to deify it. There is only the one God Yahweh. He creates light and darkness (Gen. 1:3 ff.; Isa. 45:7; Jer. 31:35; Sir. 43:1 ff.), and since he is → Lord also of the darkness, he is able to turn even darkness into light (Ps. 139:11 f.).

(a) In the OT there are frequent references to light as a kind of attribute of God: light is his garment (Ps. 104:2). His nearness and presence are indicated by light (cf. Exod. 13:21 f.; Neh. 9:12; Dan. 2:22, "the light dwells with him"; Hab. 3:4, "his brightness was like the light"; Isa. 60:19 f. in an eschatological context). In particular his countenance is said to be the origin of the light proceeding from him (Ps. 4:6; 44:3; 89:15). S. Aalen comments: "It is probably true to say that throughout the OT light is a feature of God's self-manifestation rather than of his heavenly being" (*RGG*³ IV 358).

For man the light of Yahweh means salvation, an idea clearly expressed in Ps. 27:1: "The Lord is my light and my salvation; whom shall I fear?" (cf. Job 22:28). The light which comes from God sets the bounds of every man's life, and arises upon all men (cf. Job 25:3; Sir. 42:16). Each man, however, must still turn to the light; in fact, he must look beyond it to its source, and consciously acknowledge the might of the Creator.

The light of the ungodly is worthless. It goes out (Job 18:5 f.), or is taken from them (Job 38:15). They grope in darkness (cf. Job 12:25; Prov. 4:19), and even after death darkness will still surround them (Ps. 49:19), while God will redeem the soul of the righteous "from the power of Sheol" (Ps. 49:15; → Hell).

(b) Even during his earthly life, however, the godly man enjoys the light of the

491

living (Ps. 112:4, "Light rises in the darkness for the upright"; cf. Job 33:30; Ps. 56:13; Prov. 4:18; 13:9). He enters into an experience of God's saving power when he opens his heart to the light of God's word (Ps. 119:105; cf. Prov. 6:23 and Wis. 7:10, 26, where the → law and → wisdom respectively are referred to as light). Only in the light of God does man see light (Ps. 36:9). Only when enlightened by God does the nature of reality dawn upon him, and that not by any mystical illumination. Rather, having turned to God, he receives, along with the gift of salvation, practical "orientation for his life" (cf. S. Aalen, *Die Begriffe "Licht" und "Finsternis" im Alten Testament, in Spätjudentum und im Rabbinismus*, 1951, 65). His life must be lived in the light, i.e. in concrete obedience to God's → commandments. Just as the "pillar of fire" marked Israel's route at the time of their exodus from Egypt (Exod. 13:21 f.), so the law shows how a man is to walk in the light, i.e. how a godly Israelite ought to live (cf. the exhortation of Isa. 2:5). The prophets in particular lay great stress on the importance of walking in holiness and righteousness. He who walks in the light himself can also become a light for others, i.e. a mediator of the covenant on behalf of all mankind (said of the Servant of the Lord, Isa. 42:6; 49:6; cf. 58:10, acts of mercy are like beams of light). This missionary outlook is marked by a world-wide hope, even in the OT, for the truth of Yahweh will go forth as "a light to the nations" (Isa. 51:4), and they will flock to the light of God (Isa. 60:3).

2. An antithesis found particularly in the OT Wisdom Literature, that of light and darkness as the respective spheres of the God-fearing and the ungodly (e.g. Prov. 4:18 f.), receives radical treatment in the Qumran texts. Within the religious community on the North-West shores of the Dead Sea there developed a dualism of light and darkness, probably under the influence of the Persian religion of light. On earth the "sons of the light" – in this case identified with the members of the Qumran community – are locked in conflict with the "sons of darkness" (1QS 1:9, 18, 24; 2:5, 16, 19; 3:13 and often; cf. the title of 1QM, "War of the Sons of of Light against the Sons of Darkness"; on this see the edition of Y. Yadin, *The Scroll of the War of the Sons of Light against the Sons of Darkness*, 1962).

This confrontation within history corresponds to a similar one in the metaphysical world of spirits. The Prince of Light (1QS 3:20; CD 5:18; 1QM 13:10) is opposed as lord of the world by an Angel of Darkness (1QS 3:20, 21). But there is a causal, indeed almost a predestinarian link between the respective sides in this conflict and the two opposing camps into which mankind is divided: "Those born of the truth spring from a fountain of light, but those born of falsehood spring from a source of darkness. All the children of righteousness are ruled by the Prince of Light and walk in the ways of light; but all the children of falsehood are ruled by the Angel of Darkness and walk in the ways of darkness" (1QS 3:19 ff.; cf. Vermes, *Scrolls*, 76). Nevertheless, the sons of light are still subject to attacks from the Angel of Darkness and his spirits (ibid.) and their situation would be desperate apart from the help of the "God of Israel". He represents the limit of the power of darkness, for in Qumran, just as in the OT, he is regarded as the creator both of the spirits of light and also of those of darkness (1QS 3:26). Dualism extends, therefore, into the transcendent realm of spirits, but it is not carried further to include God himself. Darkness is not his equal, as it is in Mazdaism, for he remains ultimately the Lord and as such the guarantor that the eschatological hopes of the sons of light will be realized. The latter, of course, must live as those who have been enlightened (cf. 1QS 11:5), continually walking in the ways of light, i.e. in conformity to the Torah and to the rules of their order (cf. 1QS 1:16–2:18; 3:3). Then their way will be bathed in the light of glory yet to come, while all that awaits the ungodly is darkness (cf. 1QS 2:7 f.; 4:6 ff., 12 f., and often; for the antithesis of the way of light and the way of darkness see 1QS 3:20 f.; cf. Sl.Enoch 30:15 A). The dualism between light and darkness is conceived of not so much in material terms as in gnosticism, but rather in ethico-historical terms.

3. Philo used *phōs* particularly with reference to questions of → knowledge. Hence *sophia*, → wisdom, and *epistēmē*, knowledge, are called *phōs dianoias*, the light of knowledge (*Spec.Leg.* 1, 288; *Migr.Abr.* 39 f.), i.e. they cast true light upon the whole question of existence. Under Plato's influence, Philo saw the noetic as playing an important part in a man's appropriation of salvation. But since, like others in the history of religion, he viewed salvation in terms of light, it is easy to see why he used the metaphor of light for epistemological concepts.

The *logos* is light (*Leg.All.* 3, 171 ff.; → Word), similarly the human *nous* or understanding (*Post.C.* 57 f.; → Reason). By describing → conscience as *phōs* (*Deus Imm.* 135; *Jos.* 68), he indicates the connection between knowledge and ethical behaviour, a connection already assumed as self-evident by Plato. Pride of place among the virtues, however, is held not by the philosophical concept of *erōs* (→ Love), but by piety and love towards God. He is the one and only God, dwelling, according to Philo, in a heaven of brightness and light (*Jos.* 145). But God himself is regarded as "the first light", and "the archetype of every other light" (*Som.* 1, 75) – yet another indication of Philo's attempt to combine Hellenistic philosophy with the faith of Israel.

NT In the NT *phōs* occurs 72 times, of which 33 are in the Johannine writings, 14 in the Synoptic Gospels, 13 in Paul and 10 in Acts; *phōtizō* occurs 11 times; *phōtismos* twice (2 Cor. 4:4, 6); *phōteinos* 4 times; *phōstēr* twice (Phil. 2:15; Rev. 21:11); and *phōsphoros* only once (2 Pet. 1:19).

1. (a) The original, literal meaning is found in reference to the light of the sun (Rev. 22:5), which is absent at night (Jn. 11:10), the light of lamps (Lk. 8:16; 11:33; 15:8; Acts 16:29; Rev. 18:23; 22:5) and the warm glow of a fire (Mk. 14:54; Lk. 22:56).

(b) The bright cloud used by God in the transfiguration of his Son (Matt. 17:5) points beyond itself to God, whose appearing is inevitably accompanied by effulgence. The Son, too, is surrounded by radiance: "His face shone like the sun, and his garments became white as light" (Matt. 17:2). Here light is a manifestation of the presence of God; in some other places it indicates the appearing of the exalted Christ (Acts 9:3; 22:6, 9, 11; 26:13), and in yet others the coming of angels as messengers from God himself (Acts 12:7; cf. Matt. 28:2 f.).

The disciples are also described as light or light-bearers (Matt. 5:14, 16; Lk. 12:35; cf. Eph. 5:8; Phil. 2:15), since it is their task to pass on the divine light which they have received. That which they heard from Jesus in secret (i.e. in the intimacy of his closed circle of friends) they are to proclaim fearlessly "in the light" (a stock phrase meaning "in public") (Matt. 10:27; cf. Lk. 12:3). As missionaries of Christ, they are to shine out into the world, not with their own light but with the very light of heaven itself, for in the NT light is associated with God's dwelling-place (1 Tim. 6:16), or even with God himself (1 Jn. 1:5), whence it streams forth into this world.

2. It is John in particular who portrays Jesus Christ as light breaking in upon the → darkness of the world (→ Earth, art. *kosmos*). Already in the prologue to his Gospel, light and life are linked together, i.e. Christ is the only remedy for men who by nature are in darkness (Jn. 1:4; cf. 8:12). John the Baptist is called a witness to the light, though the difference between him and the light itself is made very clear (Jn. 1:6 ff.; 5:35 f.). "The true light that enlightens every man" came into the world in the person of Jesus Christ (Jn. 1:9). R. Bultmann comments: "He is the *proper, authentic* light, who alone can fulfil the claim to give existence the proper understanding of itself.... The exclusiveness of the revelation which occurred in Jesus is further brought out by the relative clause *ho phōtizei*: he and only he is the Revealer for all men" (*The Gospel of John*, 1971, 53; cf. Jn. 3:19; Lk. 2:32, quoting Isa. 42:6; 49:6). The same note of exclusiveness is sounded very clearly in one of Christ's celebrated → "I am" sayings, where he also indicates the consequences for men: "I am the light of the world; he who follows me will not walk in darkness, but will have the light of life" (Jn. 8:12; cf. 9:5; 12:46; → See). " 'The light' designates the nature of Jesus directly. He is not like a light; he *is* 'the light' " (H. Conzelmann, *An Outline Theology of the New Testament*, 1969, 351). R. Bultmann expounds the significance of this light as follows: "By making the world bright, it makes it possible for men to see. But sight is not only significant in that it enables man to orientate himself in respect to objects; sight is at the same time the means whereby man understands himself in his world, the reason he does not 'grope in the dark', but sees his 'way' " (op. cit., 40). Recognizing the way is not sufficient, however. We have to → walk in it, for he who is the light and the way does not want mere admirers, but believing followers. Hence the injunction: "Believe in the light, that you may become sons of light" (Jn. 12:36).

An admonition such as this is necessary because the natural man loves darkness rather than light (Jn. 3:19). This may be compared with 2 Cor. 4:4, where Paul speaks of men blinded by the god of this world "to keep them from seeing the light of the gospel of the glory of Christ who is the likeness of God". This can only be changed by a creative act of God parallel to the original creation of light. "For it is God who said, 'Let light shine out of darkness,' who has shone in our hearts to give the light of the knowledge of the glory of God in the face of Christ" (2 Cor. 4:6; cf. Gen. 1:3). And even though it is certainly true that since the coming of Jesus Christ "darkness is passing away" (1 Jn. 2:8), the Christian coming to the light still needs to be urged to keep the commandment of brotherly love (1 Jn. 2:8 ff.). For only "he who loves his brother abides in the light" (1 Jn. 2:10). The prerequisite for doing the → truth – here as elsewhere closely associated with the idea of light – is communion with him who is the light of the world, Jesus Christ. In order to abide in him, the Christian must walk in the light, live for his brethren and constantly seek forgiveness through the power of the → blood of Christ (1 Jn. 1:6 f.).

3. Although using these words less frequently than John, Paul gives them a similar theological content. Light and darkness are as incompatible as → righteousness and lawlessness (→ sin; cf. 2 Cor. 6:14), ideas influenced possibly by Qumran.

494

The content of light or illumination, however, can only be christological: God has shone in our hearts "to give the light of the knowledge of the glory of God in the face of Christ" (2 Cor. 4:4, 6 [see above 2]; cf. 2 Tim. 1:10). Through him we share "in the inheritance of the saints in light" (Col. 1:12).

In turn those who once were darkness have become, as believers, "children of light", and are now "light in the Lord" (Eph. 5:8; cf. 1 Thess. 5:5; Lk. 16:8). Such sonship, however, makes ethical demands upon its recipients: "The fruit of light is found in all that is good and right and true" (Eph. 5:9). Thus it is necessary to walk according to the light, and all the more so since Christians bear a missionary responsibility for the world about them, a responsibility which they can only meet by living "as lights in a dark world" (Phil. 2:15; cf. Acts 13:47, quoting Isa. 49:6), even though this may perhaps involve them in conflict (Heb. 10:32).

In this world the Christian lives his life, so to speak, between God and → Satan. The latter can even disguise himself as "an angel of light" (2 Cor. 11:14). Hence Christians must put on "the armour of light" (Rom. 13:12; → Weapon). Only he who has fought a good fight in this armour has no need to fear the day when "the Father of lights" (Jas. 1:17) will bring to light what is hidden (1 Cor. 4:5).

H.-C. Hahn

4. Like the OT and late Judaism, the NT describes the future of the ungodly in terms of eschatological → darkness which symbolizes perdition. Believers, on the other hand, have a → hope which enables them to see the end of time differently. This too can be depicted in terms of light. In the new → Jerusalem there will no longer be sun, moon or created light, "for the glory of God is its light [lit. illuminated it, *ephōtisen autēn*] and its lamp [*lychnos*] is the Lamb. By its light shall the nations walk; and the kings of the earth shall bring their glory to it" (Rev. 21:23 f.; cf. 22:5 which adds that there will be no more night). While the ungodly are excluded (Rev. 21:8, 27; 22:3, 11, 18 f.), there is an echo here of the universal coming to the light by the Gentiles alongside Israel which featured in the eschatological proclamation of Isa. 2:2-5; 24:23; 60:1, 19. Here too the light of Yahweh supersedes created light.

2 Pet. 1:19 contains the admonition: "You would do well to pay attention to this as to a lamp shining in a dark place, until the day dawns and the morning star [*phōsphoros*] rises in your hearts." There are no lexical grounds for interpreting *phōsphoros* (lit. light-bringer) of the → sun. The term was used in cl. Gk. of the morning star, the planet Venus (Liddell-Scott, 1968), which precedes the dawn. For stars as messianic symbols see Num. 24:17: "There shall come a star out of Jacob" (which was applied to Bar Kokhba whose name means "Son of a Star"; → Jesus Christ, art. *Christos*; → Israel; cf. also Test.Lev. 18:3; Test.Jud. 24:1-5; 1QM 11:6 f.; Lk. 1:78; Rev. 22:16). The term *heōsphoros*, bringer of morn, morning star, is likewise attested in cl. Gk. (Liddell-Scott, 752). It occurs in the LXX in a lit. sense in 1 Sam. (Ki.) 30:17; Job 3:9; 11:17; 38:12; 41:9(10); Ps. 110(109):3. But in Isa. 14:12 it is a title applied to the king of → Babylon whose fall Isaiah proclaims. The Heb. here is *hêlēl*, shining star, "Day Star" (RSV). O. Kaiser conjectures a background of Ugaritic mythology (*Isaiah 13-39; A Commentary*, 1974, 38 ff.) which may have had its origin in the fact that as it rises, the morning star grows feebler because of the rays of the sun. The thought of Christ as the morning star in

2 Pet. 1:19 presents a marked contrast with this. The verse gives "a pictorial description of the way in which, at His Coming, Christ will dissipate the doubt and uncertainty by which their hearts are meanwhile beclouded and will fill them with a marvellous illumination" (J. N. D. Kelly, *A Commentary on the Epistles of Peter and of Jude*, 1969, 323, who notes similar expressions in Philo, *Ebr.* 44; *Decal.* 49).

C. Brown

→ Black, White, Red, → Creation, → Darkness, Night, → Present, Day, → See, → Sun, Moon, Stars

(a). K. Barth, "The Light of Life", *CD*, IV, 3, 1, 38–165; R. Bultmann, *The Gospel of John*, 1971 (see index); R. Bultmann and D. Lührmann, *phainō* etc., *TDNT* IX 1–10; J. H. Charlesworth, "A Critical Comparison of the Dualism in 1QS 3:13–426 and the 'Dualism' Contained in the Gospel of John", in J. H. Charlesworth, ed., *John and Qumran*, 1972, 76–106; H. Conzelmann, *phōs* etc., *TDNT* IX 310–58; C. H. Dodd, *The Bible and the Greeks*, 1935; and *The Interpretation of the Fourth Gospel*, 1953, 201–12; E. R. Goodenough, *By Light Light: The Mystic Gospel of Hellenistic Judaism*, 1935; H. G. May, "The Creation of Light in Gn. 1:3–5", *JBL* 58, 1939, 203–10; W. Michaelis, *lychnos* etc., *TDNT* IV 324–27; A. Oepke, *lampō* etc., *TDNT* IV 16–28; R. Schnackenburg, "Light", *EBT* II 503–9; and *The Gospel according to St John*, I, 1968; D. Tarrant, "Greek Metaphors of Light", *The Classical Quarterly*, 54, 1960, 181–7; D. O. Via, "Darkness, Christ, and the Church in the Fourth Gospel", *SJT* 14, 1961, 172 ff.; Y. Yadin, *The Scroll of the War of the Sons of Light against the Sons of Darkness*, 1962.
(b). S. Aalen, *Die Begriffe "Licht" und "Finsternis" im Alten Testament, im Spätjudentum und im Rabbinismus*, 1951; and "Licht und Finsternis", *RGG³* IV 357 ff.; H. Bardtke, *Die Handschriftenfunde am Toten Meer*, 1953, 97 ff.; G. Baumbach, *Qumran und das Johannesevangelium*, 1958, 46 ff.; J. C. Bott, "De notione lucis in scriptis s. Ioannis Ap.", *Verbum Domini* 19, 1939, 81–91; R. Bultmann, "Zur Geschichte der Lichtsymbolik im Altertum, *Philologus* 97, 1948, 1 ff. (reprinted in *Exegetica*, 1967, 323 ff.); and "Weihnachten", *Glauben und Verstehen*, III, 1960, 76 ff.; B. Bussmann, *Der Begriff des Lichtes beim heiligen Johannes*, 1967; C. Colpe, "Lichtsymbolik im alten Iran und antiken Judentum", *Studium Generale*, 18, 1965, 116–33; M. Dibelius, "Die Vorstellung vom göttlichen Licht", *Deutsche Literaturzeitung*, 1915, 1496 ff.; J. Dupont, "Jésus-Christ. Lumière du Monde", *Essais sur la christologie de S. Jean*, 1951, 61–105; C. Edlund, *Das Auge der Einfalt*, 1952; K. Galling, "Lampe", *Biblisches Reallexikon*, 1937, 347 ff.; F. Heiler, *Erscheinungsformen und Wesen der Religion*, 1961, 43 ff.; J. Hempel, "Die Lichtsymbolik im Alten Testament", *Studium Generale* 13, 1960, 352–68; P. Humbert, "La Thème Véterotestamentaire de la lumière", *Revue de Théologie et de Philosophie* 99, 1966, 1–6; F. N. Klein, *Die Lichtterminologie bei Philon von Alexandrien und in den hermetischen Schriften*, 1962; G. Molin, *Die Söhne des Lichts. Zeit und Stellung der Handschriften vom Toten Meer*, 1954; F. Nötscher, *Zur Terminologie der Qumran-Texte*, 1956, 76 ff.; E. Percy, *Untersuchungen über den Ursprung der johanneischen Theologie*, 1939, 23–79; H. Preisker, "Jüdische Apokalyptik und hellenistischer Symbolismus im Johannes-Evangelium, dargelegt am Begriff 'Licht' ", *TLZ* 77, 1952, 673–78; M. Saeb, *'ôr*, *THAT* I 84–90; H. Schär, *Erlösungsvorstellungen und ihre psychologischen Aspekte*, 1950; R. Schnackenburg, *Die Johannesbriefe*, 1963²; G. Stählin, "Jesus Christus, das Licht der Welt", *Universitas* (Festschrift A. Stohr), I, 1960, 58–78; H. Sedlmayr, *Der Tod des Lichtes*, 1964, 9 ff.; W. von Soden, "Licht und Finsternis in der sumerischen und babylonisch-assyrischen Religion", *Studium Generale* 13, 1960, 647–53; L. R. Stachowiak, "Die Antithese Licht-Finsternis: ein Thema der paulinischen Paränese", *ThQ* 143, 1963, 385–421; R. von Ungern-Sternberg, "Die Bezeichnungen 'Licht' und 'Finsternis' im Alten Testament", *Deutsches Pfarrerblatt* 65, 1965, 642 ff.; G. P. Wetter, *Phos*, 1915.
For works relating to gnosticism → the bibliography under Knowledge.

Like, Equal

Although it is impossible to make a clear and universally applicable differentiation between the two word-groups, as they are often interchangeable, in general the *isos* group indicates more strongly an external, objectively measurable and established likeness and correspondence, while the words connected with *homoios* express more substantial, essential likeness, hence correspondence in particular characteristics, specific or generic likeness. Although the term does not appear in the NT, a note on *homoousios* has been appended to the article on *homoios* in view of the crucial importance of the term in the debates on the person of Christ in the early church. It was opposed by the Arians but included in the Creed of Nicea (325) asserting that Christ was "of the same substance as the Father", and as such passed into the Nicene Creed.

| ἴσος |

ἴσος (*isos*), equal, corresponding to; ἰσότης (*isotēs*), equality, fairness; ἰσότιμος (*isotimos*), of equal value; ἰσόψυχος (*isopsychos*), of like soul or mind.

CL 1. Already in frequent use in Homer, *isos* and *isotēs* in their earliest stage express a fundamental rule in the sharing of the booty of war. Care had to be taken to ensure not only the equality of quantity but also the equality of value of the objects which were divided up. Hence, *isos* and *isotēs* indicate:

(a) *Numerical and physical equality*, e.g., of number, value (equal interest rates, number of votes, sums of money, dimensions in space or time; water and wine mixed in equal parts, etc.).

(b) By extension, *substantial equality*, e.g., of the copy with its original, of the assertions of witnesses, of the chances in war.

(c) *Political and legal equality*. The concept received a spiritual meaning in Gk. literary and legal life. Gk. democracy in the city states rested on the principle that all citizens possessed equal standing in society and enjoyed equal rights. *isos* and *homoios* were used as standing expressions for these political equalities. Judicial impartiality also rested upon the application of the principle of equality to all parties. Hence, *isos* became the expression for impartial, and came close to meaning the same as *dikaios*, just (→ Righteousness), so that the two concepts could be interchanged. Beyond impartiality in the legal sphere the application of the principle of equality meant particularly that which must be conceded to every citizen, that which is right and fair.

2. The relationship between justice and fairness was differently defined in the individual philosophical schools. In Stoic teaching on virtue, rectitude and fairness stem from the will for justice. In Philo (*Spec.Leg.* 4, 231) it is the other way round: *isotēs mētēr dikaiosynēs*, "fairness is the mother of justice." Finally, the two concepts can become an interchangeable pair: *ison ē dikaion*, "fair or right."

3. (a) Behind the idea of legal equality and fairness lay fundamental philosophical convictions about the essential equality of all men, convictions not yet thought out when we meet them in Homer, but philosophically established in Plato and Aristotle. In the originally rigoristic Stoic ethic the thought of the homogeneity of mankind even led to the levelling out of the natural differences in good or evil thoughts and deeds, with the result that graduations were looked upon as of only little significance and no longer as decisive. Good is good and evil is without distinction evil.

497

(b) As a principle of order *isotēs* means cosmic harmony, the balancing of all forces. This cosmic principle is reflected in human striving for equality.

(c) This sense of equality, so strongly developed in Gk. intellectual life, led eventually in Hellenism via the veneration of heroes to the doctrine of deification through the application of philosophical ideas to the concept of salvation. Already in Homer's epic, as later in tragedy, the heroes who were believed to possess divine power were spoken of as *daimoni isos, isotheos, isodaimōn,* godlike, like the gods. Plato showed in philosophy the ideal way: *homoiousthai tō theō kata to dynaton,* "become as far as possible like god" (*Theaet.* 176). Correspondingly, the ideal "divine man" was also to a certain extent equal to god, *isotheos* (cf. Homer, *Il.* 2, 565; *Od.* 1, 324; Plato, *Phdr.* 255a).

OT 1. In the LXX *isos* and *isotēs* are not very frequent. *isos* for the most part translates the comparative particle *kᵉ* (thus predominantly, in Job, e.g. 5:14; 10:10) or *'eḥaḏ* in comparative juxtapositions (thus in Ezek. 40:5–9). Of the many compounds formed with *isos,* only *isopsychos* has a Heb. counterpart: *kᵉ'erkî,* my equal (Ps. 55:13 [MT 55:14]; cf. Deut. 13:6). No others appear until writings of the Hellenistic period and express more strongly Hellenistic ideas, which are connected above all with the political principle of equality: e.g., *isēgoreomai,* to speak with the same freedom (Sir. 13:11); *isomoiros,* having an equal share (2 Macc. 8:30); *isonomeō,* to have equal rights (4 Macc. 5:24); *isopolitēs,* a full citizen with equal rights (3 Macc. 2:30).

2. In the language of wisdom and religion, on the other hand, one can establish characteristic differences from Gk. usage which stand out even more clearly in the case of → *homoios* and its derivatives. The natural, essential equality of all men is seen above all in their transitoriness and frailty, in the suffering of birth and death (Wis. 7:3 6). In contrast to Gk. veneration of heroes and the thought of a deification of man, the fundamental distance between God and his mortal creatures is stressed: no mortal may dare wish to be God's equal (*isotheos,* 2 Macc. 9:12), not even the heavenly beings may be likened to him (*isoō,* Ps. 89:7). "The OT echoes with majestic monotony the question 'Who is like God?' " (G. Stählin, *TDNT* III 352; cf. Isa. 44:7, *tis hōsper egō,* "Who is like me?"; similarly Jer. 10:6; 49:19). For this reason the Satanic suggestion, "You shall be as God!" (Gen. 3:5, LXX *theoi,* "gods") is the fundamental temptation of man and his succumbing to it stands at the beginning of a human history full of suffering (on Gen. 1:26 → *homoios* OT).

3. In Rabbinic Judaism, with all its delight in the law and striving after faithfulness to it, there was the idea that, despite the different standards of fulfilment of the law in this life, in eternity all believers in the messiah would receive equal rewards as a gift of grace (SB I 832 f.). For the messiah will so lead his people that every member, in the presence of his grace, will be equal to all the others (Ps. Sol. 17:41–46).

NT In the NT we find the adj. *isos* 8 times (in all four Gospels, also in Acts, Phil., and Rev.) – this includes the neut. plur. *isa* used as an adv. in Phil. 2:6; *isotēs* 3 times (2 Cor. and Col.); *isotimos* only in 2 Pet. 1:1; *isopsychos* only in Phil. 2:20.

1. In a few passages the use of *isos* remains within the framework of secular Gk., as it is reflected partly in the LXX: it marks equality of size (Lk. 6:34; Rev. 21:16) and conversely at the trial of Jesus the lack of unanimity in the evidence of the

witnesses (Mk. 14:56, 59). In Phil. 2:20 Paul recommends Timothy to the congregation as a fully like-minded (*isopsychos*) and reliable colleague.

2. (a) The equality among Christians, which transcends all national and religious frontiers, with regard to their participation in salvation (→ Fellowship) is experienced as a supernatural act, through one and the same experience of the Spirit, which removes all barriers between Jewish Christians and Gentiles (Acts 11:17; cf. 2 Pet. 1:1, *isotimos*, "of the same kind", lit. "equal in value"). This removal of differences is continued by Jesus' statement on the eschatological equality of Christians. They will receive the same → reward (*misthos*) in heaven as a gift of grace, whether they entered the work in the vineyard early or late (Matt. 20:12).

(b) The existing social inequalities of the members of the congregation, however, are not denied or simply removed. But the fellowship of poor and rich, of masters and slaves, receives new rules and standards, and this through → love as a new regulating principle of life between Christians. Thus masters are exhorted to treat their slaves justly and with fairness (*isotēs*; Col. 4:1). They are no longer a possession subject to their master's caprice, but → brothers in Christ. Brotherly love always cares for the needy as, for example, in the original community in Jerusalem (Acts 2:44 f.; 4:36 f.), so that the differences also between wealthy and poor do not become a cause of distress (→ Fellowship, art. *koinos*).

With these assumptions Paul can appeal to the Corinthians on the ground of their experience of equality as Greeks when he exhorts them as something self-evident to give of their own surplus to meet the lack of the community in Jerusalem, so that there might be an equality (*isotēs*; 2 Cor. 8:13, 14).

This new attitude of brotherly love means being free to love one's → enemy. It surpasses the law of give in order to get, which even sinners practise when they help one another in order "to receive as much again" (Lk. 6:34).

(c) External inequality is not called into question, neither are internal differences within the community. The → gifts (*charismata*) of → grace are various and are variously divided (Matt. 25:14 f.; 1 Cor. 12:28 ff.; Rom. 12:6 ff.; Eph. 4:16; Mk. 4:24; Rom. 12:3). But from the picture of the → body and its members Paul demonstrates their coordination and their equality of value in Christ (1 Cor. 12:12 ff.). The uniting force is love (1 Cor. 13).

The idea of → reward (*misthos*), undergoes a limitation in the NT. It is not the "axle of piety" as it was, so often, in Judaism (cf. Sir. 44:21). If it is still retained, it is chiefly in relation to the last → judgment, which will not leave unbelief and its deeds unpunished. But grace cannot be earned. It is a gift, of which all who receive it are equally unworthy (Rom. 11:32).

The secular forms of equality, "which are determined by earthly law and righteousness, are confronted in the NT by another kind of equality which is established by the love of Christians and by the divine gifts of grace" (G. Stählin, *TDNT* III 348).

3. Two passages speak of Jesus' equality with God.

(a) In Jn. 5:17 Jesus says, "My Father is working still, and I am working." Previously he had broken the → Sabbath commandment, whereupon the Jews taxed him with making himself equal with God. In certain respects they were right to do so, for on their assumptions they could only understand his assertion of equality as a flagrant presumption of independence from God (R. Bultmann, *The*

Gospel of John, 1971, 245; SB II 462 ff.), whereas for Jesus it signified exactly the reverse. As the obedient Son, he revealed the Father, without the greatness of the Father (Jn. 14:28) which was working through him being thereby damaged. The Son is thus equal to the Father in the harmony of their working (5:19 ff.). One can therefore conceive the equality of Jesus with God expressed in Jn. 5:18 as "equality of dignity, will and nature" (*TDNT* III 353).

(b) The hymn to Christ in Phil. 2:6–11 contains the assertion that Jesus "did not count equality with God a thing to be grasped [*ouch harpagmon hēgēsato to einai isa theō*], but emptied himself taking the form of a servant, being born in the likeness [*homoiōmati*] of men" (vv. 6 f.). The numerous complex problems of this passage can only be barely indicated here. First may be noted the contention of E. Käsemann that this statement comes in a "sequence of occurrences in a single event" and therefore does not present "a definition of essence in the manner of a patristic christology" (*Exegetische Versuche und Besinnungen*, I, 1960, 75). Thus it does not permit us to treat it in isolation as a statement of the kind of equality with God possessed by the pre-existent Jesus. The decisive point is the assertion of pre-existence and the consequent existence in the sphere of God. The striking thing, therefore, in the statement of Phil. 2:6 f. is that the Pre-existent One entered without reserve the sphere of man, death and historical existence in all its ambiguity. It is not just a question of exemplary obedience (v. 8), or "model humility" (E. Lohmeyer, *Kyrios Jesus*, [1928] 1941, 42), but objectively of incarnation. The revelation involves renouncing the glory of divine status and living under the conditions of a fully human existence. For discussion of kenotic christology and the interpretation of Phil. 2 → Empty, art. *kenoō*; → Form, arts. *morphē* and *schēma*.

E. Beyreuther

| ὅμοιος |

ὅμοιος (*homoios*), like, of the same nature, similar; ὁμοίως (*homoiōs*), likewise, so, similarly, in the same way; ὁμοιόω (*homoioō*), make like, compare; ὁμοιότης (*homoiotēs*), likeness, similarity, agreement; ὁμοίωμα (*homoiōma*), likeness, image, copy, appearance; ὁμοίωσις (*homoiōsis*), likeness, resemblance; ὁμοιοπαθής (*homoiopathēs*), with the same nature; παρόμοιος (*paromoios*), like, similar; παρομοιάζω (*paromoiazo*), be like; ἀφομοιόω (*aphomoioō*), make like, similar.

CL 1. The adj. *homoios* is derived from the root, *homos*, which is connected with *hama*, at the same time, together (cf. Lat. *simul*, at the same time, together; *similis*, like), and has been in general use since Homer. Four meanings are to be distinguished:

(a) Of the same kind, like, of the same condition, referring to persons and things. As a mark of such a state of affairs, *homoios* more frequently occurs linked with *isos*, to emphasize expressly similarity of kind. On the other hand, *homoios* and *isos* can even on occasion be interchanged.

(b) Of the same character, hence of the same value, endowed with the same rights (fellow-member of a party, like-minded companion). Thus *hoi homoioi*, the peers, in Sparta and similarly constituted Gk. city states, were the citizens who possessed the same right of access to all offices (Xenophon, *Hellenica* 3, 3, 5).

(c) What is divided equally to all, the *common*, e.g. in possessions or fate (*homoiē moira*, Homer, *Il.* 18, 20).

(d) In geometry *homoios* signifies similar figures in the sense of equal (cf. *TDNT* V 187).

2. The vb. *homoioō* remains within this range which the adj. occupies. From Homer on it is used in this sense trans. to make someone like a person or thing, then to hold in similar regard, to compare; pass. to be like, to resemble.

3. The nouns *homoiotēs*, *homoiōsis* and *homoiōma* are at times virtually synonymous meaning likeness, resemblance.

(a) *homoiotēs* (from the pre-Socratic philosophers onwards) and the rarer *homoiōsis* are very close in meaning. With *homoiotēs* the stress falls on similarity of kind, likeness, correspondence, which, perhaps, has only just been produced or discovered and has not existed from the beginning. *homoiōsis*, making or being like or similar, occurs among the grammarians in the sense of comparison, analogy. It is also used of species (Aristotle, *De Plantis* 2, 6, p. 826b, 32 f.).

(b) *homoiōma* seldom occurs in secular Gk., and means what is like-shaped, likeness, image. The stress here also lies on a correspondence and similarity, in this case with reference to the concrete, individual form. *homoiōma* is moving, therefore, in the direction of *eikōn* (→ Image). But even if Plato sometimes used the two concepts synonymously, there remains a possible distinction in so far as *eikōn* is considered more as an entity in itself, whereas *homoiōma* stresses more the element of comparison. It means what is similar or like, a copy (cf. *TDNT* V 191).

4. *homoiopathēs* means literally suffering the same, then generally of similar disposition. The rare *paromoios* means similar in the sense of almost the same, and therefore presupposes a certain lack of correspondence with the thing copied or compared. *paromoiazō*, to be similar, is only found in the NT (Matt. 23:27). Similarly, *aphomoioō* means to make like, to copy; in the pass. to be or become like.

ᴏᴛ In the LXX *homoios* has predominantly two Heb. equivalents which belong to the realm of simple comparison and, taken by themselves, have no particular significance: $k^e mô$, the extension of the comparative particle k^e, as; and *mîn*, kind, sort, in expressions like of the same kind, the like, e.g. similar types of animal in Lev. 11:14 ff. In contrast the vb. *homoioō* occurs chiefly for *dāmâh*, to be like and the nouns *homoiōsis* and to a lesser extent *homoiōma* for $d^e mût$, pattern, shape, likeness. One can recognize here an extensive correspondence with Gk. usage. *homoioō* occurs frequently in the introduction to illustrations and → parables (e.g. Ps. 144:4; Cant. 2:17; 7:8; Sir. 13:1; *dāmâh* in each case). It also features in statements about the incomparability of Yahweh; e.g. "To whom will you compare me?" (Isa. 46:5). In Gen. 34:15, 22 f. *'ôt*, consent to, seems to have been wrongly translated by *homooiō*.

Of the nouns *homoiōma* occurs most frequently (some 40 times including non-canonical LXX writings); more rarely *homoiōsis* (5 times for $d^e mût$, 9 times all told), *homoiotēs* only 5 times (once for *mîn*). *homoiōma* stands for *tabnît*, image (Deut. 4:16 ff.), and $t^e mûnâh$, image in connection with the Second Commandment (Exod. 20:4). In Ezek. 1:4 (*'ayin*) and Ezek. 1:5, 16, 22, 26; 2:1 (1:28); 8:2; 10:1,

10, 21 f., 23:15 (*d^emût*) *homoiōma* denotes the mysterious forms that the prophet saw. For Isa. 40:18 *tini homoiōmati hōmoiōsate auton* the best translation is perhaps: "What kind of copy will you make of him?" *homoiotēs* in Gen. 1:11 f. is to be translated kind and in Wis. 4:19 and 4 Macc. 15:4 similarity. In just the same way *pasa homoiōsis* in Ezek. 8:10 (*taḇnît*) means kinds or images (of creeping and four-footed beasts) and in Ezek. 10 similarity. Dan. 10:16 (Theodotion) *hōs homoiōsis hyiou anthrōpou* is best rendered "like the form of a man" (Heb. *ben 'āḏām*, lit. son of man, means man).

In contrast to the incomparability of Yahweh, otherwise so strongly stressed (see also *isos* OT), Gen. 1:26 states that God created man *kat' eikona hēmeteran kai kath' homoiōsin* "in our image and likeness". *eikōn* translates the Heb. *ṣelem* and *homoiōsis* the Heb. *d^emût*. Admittedly man is here accorded a special creaturely worth and even has a special *kāḇôḏ*, glory (Ps. 8:9). But the statement on the image of God has its real point rather "in the purpose for which the image is given to man" (G. von Rad, *Old Testament Theology*, I, 1962, 144). There is no direct explanation of the likeness. The plur. may even be understood as a concealment. The *hēmeteran* (our) may mean nothing more than that man was created "'*^elōhîm*-like" (cf. Ps. 8:5 [MT 8:6] *m^e'aṭ mē^e'lōhîm*, "little less than God"; cf. LXX *brachy ti par' angelous*, "a little less than angels"). In other words, man is God's authorized agent and has his worth only as such (von Rad, op. cit., 146; → Image, art. *eikōn* for other interpretations).

NT The majority of NT occurrences appear, in the case of the adj., adv. and vb., in the Gospels (21 out of 45 occurrences of *homoios*, 19 out of 31 of *homoiōs*, 12 out of 15 of *homoioō*). However, *homoios* occurs 21 times in Rev. On the other hand, the majority of instances of the nouns are in the Pauline writings and Heb. (*homoiōma* 4 times in Rom. and once in Phil. out of a total of 6; *homoiotēs* only twice in Heb.; *homoiōsis* once in Jas.). *homoioō* and *aphomoioō* each occur only once in Heb. (the only occurrence of the latter); and *homoiopathēs* once each in Acts and Jas.

1. Where adj. and vb. (also the single instance of *paromoiazō*, be like, Matt. 23:27) occur in the Gospels, they are found predominantly in the introductory formula to Jesus' → parables, especially in Matt. Lk. prefers the form of the parable without introduction (e.g. Lk. 7:41; 10:30; 12:16). Only Matt. uses (10 times) the formulae: *homoia estin hē basileia tōn ouranōn*, "the kingdom of heaven is like" (13:31, 33, 44, 45, 47; 20:1); *hōmoiōthē hē basileia tōn ouranōn*, "the kingdom of heaven may be compared to" (Matt. 13:24; 18:23; 22:2); and *homoiō-thēsetai hē basileia tōn ouranōn* "the kingdom of heaven shall be compared" (Matt. 25:1). Mk. 13:34 (cf. 4:31) simply has *hōs*, as; and Matt. 25:14 *hōsper*, as. The Aramaic underlying these formulations is a terse construction in the dative case using *l^e*. J. Jeremias holds that this should be rendered: "It is the case with . . . as with. . . ." (*The Parables of Jesus*, 1963², 101). The point of comparison, e.g., in Matt. 13:45 is not the merchant but the pearl; in Matt. 22:2 it is not the king but the wedding feast, etc. The construction corresponding to the developed dative beginning occurs, e.g., in Lk. 13:20 f., "To what shall I compare the kingdom of God? Where it is concerned it is as . . .", or more broadly Mk. 4:30 f. (On the whole question see J. Jeremias, op. cit., 100–3; → Parable, art. *parabolē*).

2. In other passages *homoios* is found in very varied connections.

(a) In Matt. 22:39, in the double commandment, love for one's neighbour is placed beside love for God as its necessary counterpart and illustration (*homoia*; → Brother, art. *plēsion*; → Command; → Law; → Love). According to Jn. 8:55, Jesus would be a liar, a denier of the revealing and sending God like his opponents (*homoios hymin pseustēs*, "a liar like you"), if he were to be silent and avoid giving offence (cf. R. Bultmann, *The Gospel of John*, 1971, 300 f.).

(b) *homoios* also occurs in connection with the polemic against the worship of false gods in Acts 17:29. The idea that God cannot be depicted struck a chord among educated Gks.; but it was to just such that the speech before the Areopagus sought to present an apology for Christianity as the model of the only true worship of the "unknown god" (v. 23; → God, art. *theos* NT 4 (b)). Rom. 1:23 also belongs to the polemic against the worship of false gods. Through their images the heathen have "exchanged the glory of the immortal God for images resembling [*en homoiō-mati eikonos*] mortal man or birds or animals or reptiles" (cf. O. Michel, *Der Brief an die Römer*, KEK 4, 1966[13], 60; N. Hyldahl, "A Reminiscence of the Old Testament in Romans i. 23", *NTS* 2, 1955–56, 285–88; G. Bornkamm, "The Revelation of God's Wrath (Romans 1–3)", *Early Christian Experience*, 1969, 47–70; C. E. B. Cranfield, *The Epistle to the Romans*, ICC, I, 1975, 119 f.). Thereby the revelation of the true God was negated, the God to whom, according to vv. 19 f., the heathen also had access (→ God, art. *theos* NT 4 (b)).

Acts 14:11 is also concerned with a naive, heathen belief in false gods. Here the crowd thought that their gods, Zeus and Hermes, had taken on human form (*homoiōthentes*) in Barnabas and Paul. The apostles protested, indicating that they too were ordinary men (*homoiopathēs*, of like nature) and mere messengers of the living God (v. 15). *homoiopathēs* occurs otherwise only in Jas. 5:17 → Elijah was like us a mortal man.

(c) 1 Jn. 3:2 expresses the expectation that we shall be like Jesus (*homoioi autō esometha*) at his parousia, and see him as he is (→ Present, art. *parousia*). For the present we are instructed to seek the true knowledge of Christ in his word and this word only allows us a token knowledge of his true being (cf. 1 Cor. 13:12). At the parousia, on the other hand, an unimpaired relationship will be possible, on "the same level of being" (F. Hauck, *NTD* 10, 129 f.). However, the writer does not intend this isolated remark to be a speculative description of future likeness to God. He prefaces it with the observation: "we are God's children now; it does not yet appear what we shall be." And he follows it with an exhortation to purity.

In Rev. 1:13 and 14:14 the "one like a son of man" is to be interpreted within the framework of Son of man christology (→ Son of God, art. *hyios tou anthrōpou*). The "son of man" of Dan. 7:13, the divinely appointed, kingly judge of the world, is the exalted Christ, the coming messiah. On the grammatical construction see Funk §182(4).

(d) *homoios* occurs elsewhere in comparisons, without having any particular stress of its own: in Gal. 5:21 in the phrase "and the like [*kai ta homoia*]"; similarly in Mk. 7:13 "and many such things [*kai paromoia toiauta polla*]"; cf. also, e.g., Rev. 2:18; 4:3, 6, 7 in symbolic comparisons. The same applies in Rev. 9:7 for *homoiōma* which RSV and Arndt (570) render "appearance".

3. *homoiōma* plays an important rôle in the christological statements of Rom.

and Phil. in expressing both the divinity of the Pre-existent One and the humanity of the Incarnate One.

(a) Rom. 5:14 asserts that mankind as a whole, like → Adam, has been subjected to the rule of death, even if it has not sinned in exactly the same way as he (*epi tō homoiōmati*). Adam is the → type of Christ, the Last Adam (cf. 1 Cor. 15:45). What Christ brings about by grace surpasses by far the equivalent effect of the fall of the first man (*pollō mallon*, v. 15; → Fullness, art. *perisseuō*).

(b) Rom. 6:5 presents certain difficulties of exegesis: "For if we have been united [*symphytoi gegonamen*] with him in a death like his [*tō homoiōmati tou thanatou autou*], we shall certainly be united in a resurrection like his [*alla kai tēs anastaseōs esometha*]" (RSV). The interpretation depends on whether one understands *homoiōma* in this verse concretely as a picture, the symbolic representation of something else, or as the actual realization of an event by means of a symbolic representation. If one prefers the second rarer, but here very appropriate alternative, the text would mean: "In the act of baptism the death of Jesus Christ is present, although in a different form from that on Golgotha," and we are "received into the same saving event" (*symphytoi* means lit. "grown together"; O. Michel, op. cit., 154; cf. J. Schneider also *TDNT* V 192–95).

(c) Rom. 8:3 also presents difficulties. "For God has done what the law, weakened by the flesh, could not do: sending his own Son in the likeness of sinful flesh [*en homoiōmati sarkos hamartias*] and for sin [*kai peri hamartias*] he condemned sin in the flesh" (RSV). The difficulties have their origin in the theological problem of grasping conceptually the incarnation, i.e. the paradox of how Christ can be fully God and fully man, and applying it to the justification of the sinner. "Paul wants to emphasize that the power of sin is a cosmic unity, but that it is broken into at one absolutely specific point" (O. Michel, op. cit., 190). By remaining obedient under the form of our bodily existence and bearing its burden Jesus "became in a unique sense a sign of the righteousness of God" (O. Michel, ibid.).

(d) Similarly in Phil. 2:7 the Incarnate One is described as "being born in the likeness of men [*en homoiōmati anthrōpōn genomenos*]" (RSV). He took on human form, and became like man. There are still those who try to interpret this likeness as not real, but merely apparent. J. Schneider, for example, appears to come near to this, when he says that "even as man He remained at the core of His being, what He had been before" (*TDNT* V 197). All interpretations which tend in this direction can hardly avoid the danger of some form of docetism, even when the contrary is asserted. Likewise it seems to us that one cannot, following on v. 5, determine the tenor of Phil. 2:5–11 as ethical (Jesus surrendered his divine nature by a free decision, he voluntarily practised obedience "unto death"). This would result in *homoiōma* being merely the model for the obedience of faith. However, E. Käsemann has shown that the hymn is to be understood eschatologically and soteriologically (*Exegetische Versuche und Besinnungen*, I, 1960, 51 ff.). What has already been said about Rom. 8:3 applies here unequivocally. Christ has in fact taken a historically unique, unambiguously human form. He was in fact delivered to death, the curse of sinful men (cf. Gal. 3:13), although he himself was sinless (cf. Heb. 4:15). Thus at a specific point in time he broke the power of sin and death.

Here, too, the mystery of the saving significance of the incarnation must be expressed in words which cannot serve as a basis for dogmatic speculations, for this mystery can only be described in terms of paradox.

4. (a) Heb. also uses *homoioō, aphomoioō* and *homoiotēs* in connection with christological statements. Christ "had to be made like his brethren in every respect [*kata panta tois adelphois homoiōthēnai*]" (2:17). Hence he was tempted like us "in quite the same way (*kath' homoiotēta*]" (4:15; cf. Arndt, 570). "The becoming like signifies being bound to us in history and humanity, in temptation, suffering and dying" (O. Michel, *Der Brief an die Hebräer, KEK* 13, 1966¹², 163). That Christ took flesh and blood and thus was placed in the situation of man before God is seen in the light of theological reflection as a matter of → necessity ("he had to [*ōpheilen*]", 2:17). For only thus can the sentence of death, which hangs over man, be averted (cf. O. Michel, ibid).

(b) In Heb. 7 the Son of God is compared with → Melchizedek in the form of type and antitype. "God is the artist who allows a sign of the first age to correspond with the event of the last" (O. Michel, op. cit., 163). Melchizedek is said to resemble (*aphomoiōmenos*) the Son of God (7:3). His priesthood is not limited in time. No genealogy is given, and his birth and death find no mention in the OT. Hence rabbinical exegesis concluded that he possessed a special being and office (SB III 694 f.). So when, according to Heb. 7:15, Christ is installed in his priestly office "in the likeness [*kata tēn homoiotēta*] of Melchizedek", what is being said is that he has an office not limited in time and a share in the power of indestructible life (v. 16), to which he has opened the way of access (cf. 10:19 ff.) for his brothers (2:17) as their pioneer or originator (12:2; → Begin, art. *archēgos*).

5. The only other verse in which *homoiōsis* occurs (Jas. 3:9) warns against the sins of the tongue (→ Word, art. *glōssa*). The tongue is capable of contradictory opposites: → blessing God and → cursing man who, according to Gen. 1:26, is created in the image (*kath' homoiōsin*) of God. Therefore to curse man is indirectly to curse God. *E. Beyreuther, G. Finkenrath*

6. The term *homoousios* became one of the crucial terms in the history of Christian doctrine in view of its central importance in the Arian controversy. Arius and his followers denied the divinity of Christ. At the Council of Nicea (325) *homoousios* (of the same substance or stuff, of one substance, consubstantial) was inserted into the creed adopted by the council to express the faith of the church. It was reaffirmed by the Council of Constantinople (381). But in the intervening years it was questioned not only by the Arians but by many churchmen who were uneasy about making a term not contained in the Scriptures the test of orthodoxy. It was defended by Athanasius on the grounds that it contains "the sense of the Scriptures" (*Epistola de decretis Nicaenae synodi* 21; cf. Gregory Nazianzen, *Orationes* 31, 23 f.). In particular, Athanasius appealed to the fact that Christ was the offspring (*gennēma*) of the Father (→ Birth, art. *gennaō*). Among the passages he appealed to were Jn. 1:18; 6:46; 8:42; 10:30; 14:10.

Originally *homoousios* had a non-theological generic sense meaning "made of the same stuff", and was applied to physical objects which cannot be composed of identical portions of matter. It was used thus by Eusebius (*Demonstratio evangelica* 1, 10, 13) and Basil the Great (*Adversus Eunomium* 2, 19). Diodore of Tarsus

(*Commentary on Psalms* 54:4) and Chrysostom (*Homiliae* 16, 2 in 1 Tim.) used it in the sense of fellow men.

In a simple theological sense it was quite a common term among gnostic writers, as is shown by orthodox opponents such as Epiphanius (*Haer.* 33, 7, 8), Irenaeus (*Haer.* 1, 15, 1), Hippolytus (*Haer.* 7, 22, 7) and Tertullian (*Adv.Herm.* 44; Lat. *consubstantialis*). They saw it as the nature of the Good to produce or beget objects similar to itself and *homoousios* with itself. Both Clement of Alexandria (*Strom.* 2, 16; 74, 1) and Origen (*Commentarii in Joannem* 13, 25, 149) argued against those gnostics who said that some men are *homoousios* with the unbegotten nature.

Commenting on Wis. 7:25, where wisdom is said to be "a breath of the power of God, and a clear effluence of the glory of the Almighty", Origen wrote: "Both these illustrations suggest a community of substance between Father and Son. For an effluence would appear to be *homoousios*, i.e. of one substance with, that body of which it is an effluence or vapour" (*Fragmenta in Heb.*; cf. *De prin.* 4, 4, 1).

Prior to the Council of Nicea it seems that *homoousios* simply meant "of one substance" as applied to material objects. When the metaphor was applied to the divine persons, its limitations were clearly recognized. The emperor Constantine who urged the term upon the Council of Nicea emphasized that it was not being used as it would be of physical objects, "nor as if the Son subsisted out of the Father by way of division or any sort of severance" (Eusebius, *Epistula ad Caesarienses* 4). One of the reasons for the term being rejected by Arius and his followers was that they understood it in the material sense only (Arius, *Epistula ad Alexandrum Alexandrinum*). The Creed of Nicea declared that: "We believe . . . in one Lord Jesus Christ . . . begotten, not made, of one substance with the Father [*homoousion tō patri*]." It was intended to be anti-Arian, suggesting, it would seem, nothing more nor less than that the Son shares the same divine nature as the Father.

A. Robertson saw the formula of Nicea as "the work of two concurrent influences, that of the anti-Origenists of the East, especially Marcellus of Ancyra, Eustathius of Antioch, supported by Macarius of 'Aelia', Hellanicus of Tripolis, and Asclepas of Gaza, and that of the Western bishops, especially Hosius of Cordova" (*St. Athanasius: Select Works and Letters*, IV, *A Select Library of Nicene and Post-Nicene Fathers*, 1892, xvii). He further agreed with Harnack that Constantine was "prompted" by Hosius to insert the phrase *homoousion tō patri* (op. cit., xviii; cf. A. Harnack, *History of Dogma*, IV, reprint 1961, 56). It seems clear that Athanasius was not the author of the term. As F. Loofs observed, Athanasius was moulded by the Creed of Nicea, but did not mould the creed himself (*Leitfaden zum Studium der Dogmengeschichte*, 1906[4], 237–43). The minority party at Nicea, led by Hosius, in all probability saw the term as implying a great deal more than that the Son is God in the same sense as the Father. "For to the Westerns the word implied *identity* (*tautotēs*) as well as equality or unity with the Godhead" (T. H. Bindley and F. W. Green, *The Oecumenical Documents of the Faith*, 1950[4], 24).

The Eastern opponents (the Arians, semi-Arians and Origenists) of the Nicene formula seized upon the rejection of *homoousios* by the Council of Antioch in 268. It was the reasoning of Paul of Samosata (fl. 260–72) which led to this step. Paul had argued that his adoptionist view was the only one possible, on the grounds that "unless Christ has of man become God, it follows that He is *homoousios* with the Father; and if so, of necessity there are three *ousiai*, one the previous *ousia*, and the other two from it" (Athanasius, *De Synodis* 45). On this material interpretation of the term the Council of Antioch could do nothing but reject it. However, as Athanasius points out, the Council of Nicea "understanding Paul's craft, and reflecting that the word *homoousios* has not this meaning when used of things immaterial, and especially of God" (ibid.), rightly chose to use it.

The opponents of Nicea saw the term as an open door for Sabellianism. The Sabellians of Libyan Pentapolis in their dispute with Dionysius of Alexandria (*c.* 260) had accused the latter of failing to describe the Son as *homoousios* with the Father (Athanasius, *De Sententia Dionysii* 18). When the pro-Nicene Marcellus of Ancyra and his deacon Photinus moved towards Sabellianism, the Arians saw this as confirmation of their contention that the supporters of *homoousios* were implicitly Sabellian and did not believe in the separate identity of the Son. However, Basil the Great (*c.* 370) supported Athanasius in his use of the term, and added that in fact it was a safeguard against Sabellianism, "since a unitary object cannot be *homoousios* with itself; the term implies plurality of *hypostasis*" (*Epistula* 52, 3). The point was also made in 374 by Epiphanius (*Ancoratus* 6, 4).

In the years after Nicea the Arian party gradually gained the upper hand in the East to such an extent that the more moderate Origenists, under Basil of Ancyra, felt compelled to rally (358) around the compromise formula *homoiousios* (of like substance). The statesmanship of Athanasius and Hilary then gradually won them over to *homoousios* (*De Synodis* 41). In 381 at the Council of Constantinople the phrase *homoousion tō patri* was once more accepted into the creed as the orthodox view of the church, and Arianism was rejected. Summing up the dispute, the historian Socrates was to write in the 5th century: "The situation was exactly like a battle by night, for both parties seemed to be in the dark about the grounds on which they were hurling abuse at each other. Those who objected to the word *homoousios* imagined that its adherents were bringing in the doctrine of Sabellius and Montanus. So they called them blasphemers on the ground that they were undermining the personal subsistence of the Son of God. On the other hand, the protagonists of *homoousios* concluded that their opponents were introducing polytheism, and steered clear of them as importers of paganism. . . . Thus, while both affirmed the personality and subsistence of the Son of God, and confessed that there was one God and three hypostases, they were somehow incapable of reaching agreement, and for this reason could not bear to lay down arms" (*Historia Ecclesiastica*, 1, 23).

The question whether the Holy Spirit is *homoousios* with the other two divine persons was considered by Athanasius (*c.* 359). He held that although the Spirit is not directly called God, he is shown as belonging to the Word and the Father, and as sharing one and the same substance (*homoousios*) with them (*Epistulae ad Serapionem*, 1, 27). In 362 at the Council of Alexandria this proposition was accepted (*Tomus ad Antiochenses* 3; 5 f.). Epiphanius writes that the Holy Spirit is "not begotten, not created, not fellow-brother nor brother to the Father, nor forefather nor offspring, but out of the same substance [*homoousios*] of the Father and Son" (*Ancoratus* 7, 7 f.).

"The single Deity of the Father, the Son, and the Holy Spirit, under the concept

507

of equal majesty and of the Holy Trinity" (*Codex Theodosianus* 16, 1, 2, A.D. 380) became the norm of orthodoxy. It was professed by Damasus of Rome in 372 and was accepted by the Council of Antioch in 379. Its acceptance at Constantinople in 381 is seen in the Fifth Canon of the Council and in the Council's Creed.

M. Farmery

→ God, → Image, → Man, → Melchizedek, → Type

On *isos* and *homoios*:

(a). Arndt, 381 f., 570 f.; R. Bultmann, *The Gospel of John*, 1971; J. Jeremias, *The Parables of Jesus*, 1963[2]; I. H. Marshall, "The Christ-Hymn in Philippians 2:5–11;" *TB* 19, 1968, 104–27; R. P. Martin, *An Early Christian Confession: Philippians II. 5–11 in Recent Interpretation*, 1960; and *Carmen Christi: Philippians ii. 5–11 in Recent Interpretation and in the Setting of Early Christian Worship*, 1967; C. F. D. Moule, "Further Reflections on Philippians 2:5–11", in W. W. Gasque and R. P. Martin, eds., *Apostolic History and the Gospel, Biblical and Historical Essays presented to F. F. Bruce*, 1970, 264–76; G. von Rad, *Old Testament Theology*, I, 1962; J. Schneider, *homoios* etc., *TDNT* V 186–99; G. Stählin, *isos* etc., *TDNT* III 343–55.

On Athanasius and the Arian controversy see B. Altaner, *Patrology*, 1960; Athanasius, *Select Works and Letters*, IV, ed. A. Robertson, *A Select Library of Nicene and Post-Nicene Fathers*, 1892; and *Contra Gentiles and De Incarnatione*, ed. and tr. by R. W. Thomson, 1971; T. H. Bindley and F. W. Green, *The Oecumenical Documents of the Faith*, 1950[4]; A. Grillmeier, *Christ in Christian Tradition: From the Apostolic Age to Chalcedon (451)*, 1975[2]; A. Harnack, *History of Dogma*, IV, reprint 1961; J. N. D. Kelly, *Early Christian Creeds*, 1972[3]; and *Early Christian Doctrines*, 1968[4]; G. L. Prestige, *God in Patristic Thought*, 1936; J. Quasten, *Patrology*, III, 1960; G. C. Stead, "The Platonism of Arius", *JTS* New Series 15, 1964, 16–31; J. Stevenson, *A New Eusebius: Documents Illustrative of the History of the Church to A.D. 337*, 1957; and *Creeds Councils and Controversies: Documents Illustrative of the History of the Church A.D. 337–461*, 1966; M. Wiles, "In Defence of Arius", *JTS* New Series 13, 1962, 339–47; and "HOMOOUSIOS HĒMIN", *JTS* New Series 16, 1965, 454–61.

(b). D. Georgi, "Der vorpaulinische Hymnus Phil. 2, 6–11", in E. Dinkler, ed., *Zeit und Geschichte, Dankesgabe an Rudolf Bultmann zum 80. Geburtstag*, 1964, 263 ff.; F. Hauck, *Die Kirchenbriefe*, *NTD* 10, 1953[6]; E. Käsemann, "Kritische Analyse von Phil. 2, 5–11", *Exegetische Versuche und Besinnungen*, I, 1960, 51 ff.; E. Lohmeyer, *Kyrios Jesus. Eine Untersuchung zu Phil. 2, 5–11*, *Sitzungsberichte der Heidelberger Akademie der Wissenschaften, Philosophisch-historische Klasse*, 1927–28, 4. Abhandlung, 1928, 1961[2]; O. Michel, *Der Brief an die Römer*, KEK 4, 1966[13]; and *Der Brief an die Hebräer*, KEK 13, 1966[12].

Lord, Master

One of the basic facts of human existence is the power and authority that some people have over others. Gk. has two principal words for lord and master. *despotēs* denotes the lord as owner and master in the spheres of family and public life, where lordship sometimes entails harshness and caprice. *kyrios* which occurs more often means lord, and carries with it overtones of the legality and acknowledged authority of lordship. When a god is called lord, the predominant term is *kyrios*; *despotēs* is used very seldom in this connection. In classical antiquity the lord stood over against the → slave, the servant (*doulos*).

δεσπότης

δεσπότης (*despotēs*), lord, master (of a house), owner; οἰκοδεσπότης (*oikodespotēs*), the master of a house; οἰκοδεσποτέω (*oikodespoteō*), be master of a house, rule one's household.

CL *despotēs* (formed from *domos*, house and **potis* [whence *posis*], lord) means:
(a) the master of a house (who usually had absolute authority over his household); (b) master, as opposed to slave; (c) owner; (d) (transferred in the course of political developments from the sphere of the household to that of politics) the ruler, who is characterized by the scope of his power and by his high-handedness, particularly towards subject peoples. Starting from the idea of unlimited possession, *despotēs* often involves harshness and caprice, whereas *kyrios* emphasizes more strongly the idea of the legality with which someone acts.

oikodespotēs, master of a house, a pleonastic compound etymologically speaking, became an astrological technical term in secular Gk.: the planets were *oikodespotai* in particular signs of the Zodiac. In this context *oikodespotēsis* meant the predominance of a planet.

OT *despotēs* occurs only about 60 times in the LXX. Where there is a Heb. original it mostly translates *'ādôn*, lord, master. The word is used less than *kyrios*. This was no doubt because *despotēs* expresses the arbitrary, unlimited exercise of power without any real conditions, which must have been foreign to Israel's concept of God. For Israel had experienced the Lordship of God in his gracious, saving actions in history. Where it is used (especially in later writings) it particularly emphasizes God's omnipotence (cf. Isa. 1:24; 3:1; 10:33; Jer. 4:10; 15:11; Jon. 4:3; Dan. 9:8, 15 ff., 19; Wis. 6:7; 8:3; Sir. 23:1; 31[34]:24; 33[36]:1). The retreat of the term *despotēs* in the face of *kyrios* is theologically significant. *oikodespotēs* does not occur in the LXX.

NT 1. In the NT the word occurs 10 times.
(a) God is addressed in prayer 3 times as *despotēs* (Lk. 2:29 in contrast to *doulos*, slave; Acts 4:24; Rev. 6:10 quoting Zech. 1:12 and Ps. 79:5 [LXX 78:5, where the LXX translates *kyrie*]).

(b) *despotēs* is twice used with reference to Christ: 2 Pet. 2:1 (Christ the Master bought us; the background is the metaphor of the redemption of slaves); and Jude 4 which uses the same underlying idea (*despotēs* alongside *kyrios*). In both passages the term is used in opposition to heretical statements. The false teachers deny that Jesus is *despotēs*. K. H. Rengstorf suggests that "*despotēs* is here used rather than *kyrios* to suggest the function of Jesus as the One who commands and exercises influence and power." The false teachers "do not acknowledge Jesus in practice as the One whose will they must take as their guide" (*TDNT* II 49). This interpretation, in the light of the context and of 2 Pet. 2:1, seems more likely than that which sees Jesus here deliberately placed beside God as Almighty.

(c) Used of earthly lords in the sense of owner *despotēs* occurs in 1 Tim. 6:1; Tit. 2:9 (*douloi*, slaves, and *despotai* are contrasted; cf. *douloi* and *kyrioi* in Eph. 6:5; Col. 3:22); and 1 Pet. 2:18 (*oiketai*, servants, and *despotai*). Slaves are exhorted to be obedient to their masters in order that the faith may not be brought into disrepute by their disobedience. It has an essentially metaphorical sense in 2 Tim. 2:21 as master of the house. Anyone who purifies himself from false teaching is a vessel for noble use, consecrated and useful to the *despotēs*. Here Christ is to be understood as the *despotēs*.

2. *oikodespotēs* occurs 12 times in the NT, particularly in Matt. (10:25; 13:52; 24:43; in parables *oikodespotēs* illustrates God's actions by means of the activities

of the master of the house; 13:27; 20:1, 11; 21:33; cf. Lk. 14:21), where it corresponds to Heb. *ba'al habayit*, the owner of a house or land. It is frequently found in connection with *anthrōpos*, man, the master who rules over his household. In Mk. 14:14 the owner of the ass, on which Jesus intends to ride into the city, is called *oikodespotēs*. *oikodespotēs* is used pleonastically in Lk. 22:11. If the *oikodespotēs* had known when the thief was coming, he would have watched (Matt. 24:43). In the parable of Lk. 13:25 ff. Jesus is the *oikodespotēs* who will shut the door on those who come late. Through the metaphor of the *oikodespotēs* Jesus is depicted as the Lord of the → kingdom. In a further word-picture Jesus spoke of himself as the *oikodespotēs* (Matt. 10:24). His opponents have abused him and called him Beelzebul (Matt. 12:24; cf. 9:34; → Satan); how much more will the members of his household (i.e. his → disciples and followers) be exposed to abuse. Here *oikodespotēs* is used in parallel with *didaskalos* and *kyrios* (v. 24 f.) and characterizes the relationship between Jesus and the disciples as imitation of suffering.

oikodespoteō, rule over house and family, occurs only in 1 Tim. 5:14 in directions to younger women to marry and rule their households. *H. Bietenhard*

| κύριος |

κύριος (*kyrios*), lord, master, owner, Lord; κυρία (*kyria*), lady, mistress; κυριακός (*kyriakos*), belonging to the Lord, the Lord's; κυριότης (*kyriotēs*), lordship, dominion; κυριεύω (*kyrieuō*), be lord, master, rule; κατακυριεύω (*katakyrieuō*), rule over, subjugate, conquer, be master of, lord it over.

CL *kyrios* (attested from Pindar on) adj. having power, authoritative, from *to kyros*, power, might; as a noun, lord, ruler, one who has control (over people things, himself). *kyrios* always contains the idea of legality and authority. *kyrios* is often used beside *despotēs* which means especially an owner (with overtones of high-handedness). Later anyone occupying a superior position was referred to quite generally as *kyrios* and addressed as *kyrie* (fem. *kyria*). From here it penetrated as a loan-word into the Heb. of the Talmud and Midrash, and also into Aram. (cf. e.g. Tg. Job 5:2; Tg. Ps. 53:1) to denote God.

1. In classical Gk. of the early period *kyrios* was not used as a divine title. Although the term was applied to the gods (e.g. Pindar, *Isth.* 5, 53; Plato, *Leg.* 12, 13), there was no general belief in a personal creator god. The gods were not creators and lords of fate, but were like men subject to fate. In effect, gods and men belonged to the same sphere of reality (cf. the beginning of Pindar's *Ode to Alcimidas*). The Gk. of this period did not understand his position as that of a → slave (*doulos*), dependent on a god. Nor did he feel himself in any way personally responsible to the gods. Only in so far as the gods ruled over particular individual spheres in the world could they be called *kyrioi*.

2. In this respect the situation was different in the East. "For the Orientals the gods are the lords of reality. Destiny is in their hands" (W. Foerster, *TDNT* III 1048). The gods created man who, moreover, was personally answerable to them. They could intervene in the life of men to save, punish or judge. They also established justice and law, which they communicated to men, e.g. through the king. Therefore they were called lords.

3. Instances of the use of the title *kyrios* in Hellenistic times with reference to

gods or rulers do not occur until the 1st cent. B.C. (cf. W. Foerster, *TDNT* III 1049). *kyrios basileus*, Lord and King, is found frequently between 64 and 50 B.C. In 12 B.C. the emperor Augustus was called *theos kai kyrios*, God and Lord, in Egypt (*BGU*, 1197, I, 15); in Upper Egypt Queen Candace (cf. Acts 8:27) was called *hē kyria basilissa*, Mistress and Queen. The title *kyrios* was also used of Herod the Great (*c.* 73–4 B.C.), Agrippa I (*c.* 10 B.C.–A.D. 44) and Agrippa II (A.D. 27–*c.* 100). Apart from rulers, high officials could also receive this title, e.g. a Ptolemaic governor. The same was probably true in Syria as in Egypt; not until the 1st cent. B.C. were eastern lords called *kyrios*. Thus we find titles like *kyrios theos*, Lord and Governor. *kyrios* was used of the gods where, in contemporary popular thought and speech, they were referred to as lords. In this case *kyrios* translated the underlying Semitic equivalents (e.g. '*ādôn*, *mārā*', fem. *rabbat*). These terms always bore a personal suffix (my, our, etc.) and were placed in front of the name of a god. Where *kyrios* was used of a god, the servant (→ Slave, art. *doulos*) who thus used it stood in a personal relationship of responsibility towards the god, who on his part exercised personal authority. When, e.g. Heb. '*ādôn* denoted the lord of power, *kyrios* was the natural Gk. equivalent. Individual gods were worshipped as lords of their cultic communities and of the separate members of the fellowship. The worship of other lords was not excluded, for none of them was visualized or worshipped as universal lord. (See further W. Foerster, *TDNT* II 1049–54.)

4. The Roman emperors Augustus (31 B.C.–A.D. 14) and Tiberius (A.D. 14–37), in accordance with Roman feeling for justice, rejected the eastern form of monarchy and with it all that was bound up in the title *kyrios*. But Caligula (A.D. 37–41) found the title of *kyrios* attractive. From Nero (A.D. 54–68) on, who was described in an inscription as *ho tou pantos kosmou kyrios*, Lord of all the World (*SIG* 814, 31), the title *kyrios* occurs more and more frequently. One of the oldest instances is Acts 25:26. The title *kyrios* was brought into disrepute again by Domitian (A.D. 81–96), who had himself called in official letters *dominus et deus noster*, Our Lord and God (Suetonius, *De Vita Caesarum*, 13, 2). After Domitian's death this title was detested along with his memory (*damnatio memoriae*). Nevertheless, it prevailed again later. In and of itself the title *kyrios* does not call the emperor god; but when he is worshipped as divine, the title Lord also counts as a divine predicate. It was against such a religious claim, which demanded so much of the burdened conscience, that the Christians turned and rejected the totalitarian attitudes of the state. (On the early church and the Roman empire see W. H. C. Frend, *Martyrdom and Persecution in the Early Church: A Study of a Conflict from the Maccabees to Donatus*, 1965; R. M. Grant, *Augustus to Constantine: The Thrust of the Christian Movement into the Roman World*, 1970.)

OT 1. In the LXX *kyrios* occurs over 9,000 times. It is used to translate '*ādôn*, lord, and as such refers 190 times to men. It is used only 15 times for *ba'al*, lord. While *ba'al*, in marriage and property law, denotes the owner of a wife or piece of land (e.g. Hos. 2:18; Jdg. 19:22, 23), '*ādôn* is determined by social factors and means the one who commands, the responsible head of a group (e.g. 1 Sam. 25). Yahweh is rarely called owner (Hos. 2:16 [MT 18]), but more frequently Lord of the community belonging to him (cf. Ps. 123:22).

In addition *kyrios* can stand also for *gᵉbîr*, commander, or (Aram.) *mārā*', lord,

511

or *šallîṭ*, ruler. In the overwhelming majority of cases (some 6156), however, *kyrios* replaces the Heb. proper name of God, the tetragrammaton *YHWH*. The LXX thus strengthened the tendency to avoid the utterance of the name of God, and finally to avoid its use altogether. The substitution of the title *'ᵃḏōnay* for the proper name Yahweh was a result of Israel's development from a national religion in the pre-exilic period to an international one in the period of Alexander (356–323 B.C.). Where originally the exodus was the theological focal point, after the exile the emphasis fell on the creation of the world. Where *kyrios* stands for *'āḏōn* or *'ᵃḏōnay* there has been genuine translation, but where, on the other hand, it stands for Yahweh it is an interpretative circumlocution for all that the Heb. text implied by the use of the divine name: Yahweh is Creator and Lord of the whole universe, of men, Lord of life and death. Above all he is the God of → Israel, his → covenant → people. By choosing *kyrios* for Yahweh the LXX Gk. text also emphasized the idea of legal authority. Because Yahweh saved his people from → Egypt and chose them as his possession, he is the legitimate Lord of Israel. As → Creator of the world he is also its legitimate Lord with unlimited control over it. (For further discussion of the use of the title Lord instead of the name Yahweh → God, art. *theos* OT 2.)

2. Recent textual discoveries cast doubt on the idea that the compilers of the LXX translated the tetragrammaton *YHWH* by *kyrios*. The oldest LXX MSS (fragments) now available to us have the tetragrammaton written in Heb. characters in the Gk. text. This custom was retained by later Jewish translators of the OT in the first centuries A.D. One LXX MS from Qumran even represents the tetragrammaton by *IAŌ*. These instances have given support to the theory that the thorough-going use of *kyrios* for the tetragrammaton in the text of the LXX was primarily the work of Christian scribes (P. E. Kahle, *The Cairo Geniza*, 1959², 222; cf. S. Jellicoe, *The Septuagint and Modern Study*, 1968, 185 f., 271 f.). On the other hand, the Jews would already have replaced the tetragrammaton by *kyrios* in the oral transmission of the Gk. OT text.

3. In post-OT Jewish literature *kyrios* first appears as a term for God in Wis. (27 times, e.g. 1:1, 7, 9; 2:13), then particularly frequently in Philo and Josephus. Philo seems not to have been aware that *kyrios* stood for the tetragrammaton, for he used *theos*, God, to indicate the gracious power of God, while *kyrios*, on the other hand, for him describes God's kingly power (e.g. *Som.* 1, 163). Since the earliest Egyptian and Syrian instances of gods being called *kyrioi*, lords, come from the 1st cent. B.C. the substitution of *kyrios* for the tetragrammaton is no doubt connected with these non-Jewish ascriptions. At about the same time the members of the Qumran sect, in Heb. biblical MSS, were writing *'ᵃḏōnay*, Lord, instead of the tetragrammaton. A few fragments from the caves pick out the tetragrammaton in ancient Heb. script while the rest of the text is written in square characters (on this see J. A. Sanders in D. N. Freedman and J. C. Greenfield, eds., *New Directions in Biblical Archaeology*, 1969, 101–16; and "The Dead Sea Scrolls – A Quarter Century of Study", *BA* 36, 1973, 140; J. P. Siegel, *Hebrew Union College Annual* 42, 1971, 159–72). The non-biblical texts from Qumran make it clear that *'ᵃḏōnay* was used particularly as an invocation in prayers, and therefore predominantly in liturgical contexts (1QM 12:8, 18; 1QH passim; 1QSb; 1Q34; 4Q *Diḇrê Hamᵉʾōrôṭ* [Words of the Luminaries]).

4. In the Aram. scroll of the so-called Genesis Apocryphon (1QGenAp) God is addressed as *māri*, my Lord. Apart from this one instance, this form of address is not found in Aram. In the same text *māri* is used once by a woman addressing her husband. Otherwise Aram. uses *mār*, lord (with personal suffixes) only to address people who have particular authority, especially in the fields of law or education. ([F. F. Bruce]. In 11Q Targum Job *mārē'* is used as the Aram. rendering of Heb. *šadday*, Almighty [Job 34:10, 12]; and in the Aram. Enoch fragments from Cave 4 *mārē'* or *māran* is found as a designation of God [M. Black, "The Christological use of the Old Testament in the New Testament", *NTS* 18, 1971–2, 10].)

NT Of the 717 passages in which *kyrios* occurs in the NT, the majority are to be found in the Lucan writings (210) and in Paul's letters (275). This one-sidedness can be explained by the fact that Luke wrote for, and Paul to, people who lived in areas dominated by Gk. culture and language. On the other hand, the Gospel of Mk., more firmly based in Jewish Christian tradition, uses the *kyrios*-title only 18 times, and these mostly in quotations. The remaining occurrences of *kyrios* are spread over the other NT books: Matt. 80; Jn. 52; Heb. 16; Jas. 14; 1 Pet. 8; 2 Pet. 14; Jude 7; and Rev. 23. The fact that *kyrios* is one of the most frequently used words in the NT is in accordance with its varied use in the LXX.

1. *The secular use of kyrios*. The *kyrios* stands over against the → slave (Matt. 10:24 f.; 18:25, 27; 25:19; Lk. 12:36 f., 46; Eph. 6:5, 9; Col. 3:22). *kyrios* means owner (Mk. 12:9; Lk. 19:33; Matt. 15:27; Gal. 4:1), or employer (Lk. 16:3, 5). The husband faces his wife as *kyrios*, i.e. as superior (1 Pet. 3:6; cf. Gen. 18:12 LXX). A gen. qualifying *kyrios* betrays the influence of Sem. (Palestinian) usage (e.g. Mk. 12:9; Lk. 10:2). *kyrios* used as a form of address can emphasize the power of a superior over an inferior, but it can also be simply politeness (Matt. 18:21 f.; 25:20 ff.; 27:63; Lk. 13:8; Jn. 12:21; 20:15; Acts 16:30). It is also used to address angels (Acts 10:4; Rev. 7:14) and the unknown in the heavenly vision outside Damascus (Acts 9:5; 22:8, 10; 26:15). A twice repeated *kyrios* corresponds to Palestinian usage (Matt. 7:12 f.; 25:11; Lk. 6:46). The use of the nom. with the art. instead of the voc. (Jn. 20:28; Rev. 4:11) is also Sem., as is the addition of a noun in the gen. in place of an adj. (1 Cor. 2:8; 2 Thess. 3:16).

2. *God as the kyrios*. In accordance with the usage of the Hellenistic synagogues God is frequently called *kyrios*, especially in the numerous quotations from the OT in which *kyrios* stands for Yahweh, corresponding to the custom of pronouncing the title *kyrios* instead of the tetragrammaton in public reading (e.g. Rom. 4:8 = Ps. 32:2; 9:28 f. = Isa. 10:22 f.; 10:16 = Isa. 53:1; 11:3 = Lk. 19:10; 11:34 = Isa. 40:13; 14:11 = Isa. 45:23; 15:11 = Ps. 117:1; 1 Cor. 3:20 = Ps. 94:11; 14:21 = Isa. 28:11 f.). *kyrios* frequently denotes God in the Lucan birth narratives (e.g. Lk. 1:32; 2:9). *kyrios* in the gen. accompanying another word corresponds to OT usage: the → hand of the *kyrios* (Lk. 1:66; Acts 11:21); the → angel of the *kyrios* (Matt. 1:20; 2:13; 28:2; Lk. 1:11; 2:9; Acts 5:19; 8:26; 12:7); the → name of the *kyrios* (Jas. 5:10, 14); the → Spirit of the *kyrios* (Acts 5:9; 8:39); the → word of the *kyrios* (Acts 8:25; 12:24; 13:48 f.; 15:35 f.). The formula "says the *kyrios*" (Rom. 12:19 = Deut. 32:35; 2 Cor. 6:17 = Isa. 52:11; Rev. 1:8 cf. Exod. 3:14) also comes from OT. To the OT phrase *kyrios ho theos* the author of Rev. sometimes adds an emphatic, solemn *pantokratōr*, All-Sovereign

513

(Rev. 1:8; 4:8; 11:17; 16:7; 19:6; 21:22; cf. Arndt, 613 f.). The formula *ho kyrios kai ho theos hēmōn* (Rev. 4:11, cf. Jn. 20:28), our Lord and our God, is reminiscent of the title adopted by Domitian (cf. CL 4). The liturgical formulae of Rev. 11:15; 22:6 are remarkable. Jesus was adopting Jewish forms of speech (*ribbōnô šel 'ôlām*; Aram. *mārē' 'ᵃlᵉmā'*, Lord of the world) when he addressed God the Father as "*kyrios* of heaven and earth" (Matt. 11:25; Lk. 10:21; cf. Heb. 1:2; Sir. 51:1; Tob. 7:18; SB I 607; II 176; III 671 f.). God is the *kyrios* of the (eschatological) harvest (Matt. 9:38; → Seed, Harvest). God is the only ruler, the → King of kings and the *kyrios* of lords (cf. Dan. 2:47), who will cause our *kyrios* Jesus Christ to appear (1 Tim. 6:15). God is the → Creator and as such the Lord of all (Acts 17:24). By addressing and acknowledging God as *kyrios*, the NT expresses particularly his creatorship, his power revealed in history and his just dominion over the universe, and at the same time confesses the continuity of its belief with that of the OT.

3. *Jesus as the kyrios.* (a) The earthly Jesus as *kyrios*. *kyrios* applied to the earthly Jesus is in the first instance a polite form of address, as it is with other people. This no doubt goes back to the title Rabbi (perhaps also to *māri, mārā'*); cf. Mk. 9:5 (*rhabbi*) with Lk. 9:33 (*epistata*, Lord) and Matt. 17:4 (*kyrie*); cf. Jn. 4:14 f.; 5:7; 6:34; 13:6. This form of address also implies recognition of Jesus as a leader, and willingness to obey him (Matt. 7:21; 21:29 ff.; Lk. 6:46). As Son of man (→ Son of God, art. *hyios tou anthrōpou*), Jesus is also *kyrios* of the → Sabbath. He has control over the holy day of God's people (Mk. 2:28 f.). Even after his death and → resurrection the words of the earthly Jesus have unrestricted authority for the Christian community. Paul appealed to words of the *kyrios* which finally decide a question (1 Cor. 7:10; 12:25; 1 Thess. 4:15; cf. Acts 11:16; 20:35).

(b) The exalted Jesus as *kyrios*. The confessional cry used in worship, *kyrios Iēsous*, Jesus (is) Lord, no doubt originated in the pre-Pauline Hellenistic Christian community. This → confession is one of the oldest Christian creeds, if not the oldest. With this call the NT community submitted itself to its Lord, but at the same time it also confessed him as ruler of the world (Rom. 10:9a; 1 Cor. 12:3; Phil. 2:11; cf. the title *kosmokratōr* in Eph. 6:12 used of "the world rulers of this darkness" [cf. Arndt, 446]). God has raised Jesus from the dead and exalted him to the position of universal *kyrios*. Moreover, he has "bestowed on him the name which is above every name" (Phil. 2:9 ff.; cf. Isa. 45:23 f.), i.e. his own → name of Lord and with it the position corresponding to the name. (On Phil. 2:5–11 → Empty, art. *kenoō* NT.) The exalted *kyrios*, Christ, rules over mankind (Rom. 14:9). All → powers and beings in the universe must bow the knee before him. When that happens, God the Father will be worshipped (cf. Eph. 1:20 f.; 1 Pet. 3:22). This is further implied in the fact that Christ is called the ruler over all the kings of the earth, Lord of lords and → King of kings (Rev. 1:5; 17:14; 19:15 f.). In this way Jesus Christ received the same titles of honour as God himself (1 Tim. 6:15; cf. Dan. 2:47). According to contemporary Jewish thought, the different spheres of the world in nature and history were ruled by angelic powers. Since Christ has now been raised to the position of *kyrios*, all powers have been subjected to him and must serve him (Col. 2:6, 10; Eph. 1:20 f.). When Christ has overcome every power (1 Cor. 15:25), he will submit himself to God the Father. Thus Jesus' lordship will have achieved its goal and God will be all in all (1 Cor. 15:28). The one God and the one *kyrios* Jesus stand in opposition to the many gods and lords of the pagan world (1 Cor. 8:5 f., Eph. 4:5 f.).

Scriptural evidence for the exaltation of Jesus and for his installation as Lord was found in Ps. 110:1 (cf. Matt. 22:44; 26:64; Mk. 12:36; 14:62; 16:19; Lk. 20:42 f.; 22:69; Acts 2:34; 1 Cor. 15:25; Eph. 1:20; Col. 3:1; Heb. 1:3, 13; 10:12 f.; 12:2; cf. B. Lindars, *New Testament Apologetic*, 1961, 45–51, 252 ff.; R. T. France, *Jesus and the Old Testament*, 1971, 100 ff.). The Jewish interpretation of this passage from the Pss. looked forward to the messianic future – the messianic interpretation was for a long time suppressed among the Jews out of opposition to the church – but in the faith of the Christians this hope was transferred to the present. The Lordship of the messiah, Jesus, is a present reality. He is exercising in a hidden way God's authority and Lordship over the world and will bring it to completion in the eschatological future. This faith was articulated in Thomas's confession (Jn. 20:28): *ho kyrios mou kai ho theos mou*, "my Lord and my God". Primitive Christianity saw no infringement of monotheism in the installation of Jesus as Lord, but rather its confirmation (1 Cor. 8:6; Eph. 4:5; Phil. 2:11). It is God who has exalted the Lord Jesus (Acts 2:36) and made him Lord of all things.

([Ed.] Wilhelm Bousset, a leading exponent of the history of religions school, argued that the application of the title *kyrios* to Christ originated with the Gentile church which appropriated it from the surrounding world of syncretistic religion. "It was in this atmosphere that Antiochene Christianity and that of the other primitive Christian Hellenistic communities came into being and had their growth. In this milieu the young Christian religion was shaped as a Christ cultus, and out of this environment then people also appropriated the comprehensive formula *kyrios* for the dominant position of Jesus in worship. No one thought this out, and no theologian created it; people did not read it out of the sacred book of the Old Testament. They would hardly have dared without further ado to make such a direct transferal of this holy name of the almighty God – actually almost a deification of Jesus. Such proceedings take place in the unconscious, in the uncontrollable depths of the group psyche of a community; this is self-evident, it lay as it were in the air, that the first Hellenistic Christian communities gave the title *kyrios* to their cult-hero" [*Kyrios Christos*, 1913, ET 1970, 146 f.] A similar position was adopted by R. Bultmann [*Theology of the New Testament*, I, 1952, 123 ff.; cf. also Bultmann's introduction to *Kyrios Christos*, 7 ff.]. The arguments for and against it are discussed more fully in the works by W. Foerster, G. Dalman, O. Cullmann, E. Schweizer, F. Hahn, R. Longenecker and R. H. Fuller listed in the bibliography below. A telling fact against a purely Hellenistic origin and in favour of a Palestinian is the Aramaic formula *maranatha* [1 Cor. 16:22] which means "Lord come", "Our Lord has come", or as a prophetic perfect "The Lord will come" [→ Present, art. *maranatha*]. The ascription of lordship to Christ in this Aramaic formula indicates that Jesus was already called Lord in Palestinian Christianity at an early date. The synoptic accounts of the discussion of the lordship of David's son imply that this use of the title went back to Jesus himself [Matt. 22:41–46; Mk. 12:35–37; Lk. 20:41:44; cf. Ps. 110[109]:1]. How can David speak of another as Lord if he is his son? The question is presented as a dilemma to the Jewish teachers, without however Jesus being explicitly identified with this "Lord". The contexts of Matt. and Mk. intensify this dilemma by recording it immediately after the question of the great commandment [Matt. 22:23–40; Mk. 12:28–34; → Command; → Law]. Here the great commandment is defined as loving "the Lord your God [*kyrion ton theon sou*]" with the whole of one's being. Thus in reply to the Jewish teachers' question about the great commandment Jesus declares that this *kyrios* is to be given complete and undivided attention. But then Jesus puts to them the question of this other *kyrios* with its implied claims: "David himself calls him Lord; so how is he his son?" [Mk. 12:37 par. Matt. 22:45, Lk. 20:44]. This challenge marks the climax of Jesus' encounters with the Jewish religious teachers and leaders. Their failure to respond positively to this challenge marked the point of no return.)

As far as we can establish, the NT church did not reflect on the relationship of the exalted Christ to God the Father as did later church doctrinal teaching. One may perhaps say that there is indeed no developed doctrine of the Trinity in the NT, but that the writers, particularly in the later strata, thought in trinitarian forms. (On this → God, art. *theos* NT 8; and → Like, art. *homoios* NT 6 on the term *homoousios*.)

(c) *kyrios* and the Lord's Supper. *kyrios* figures frequently in expressions connected with the → Lord's Supper. There are the phrases which are partly pre-Pauline: "table of the *kyrios*" (1 Cor. 10:21); "the death of the *kyrios*" (1 Cor. 11:26); "the cup of the *kyrios*" (1 Cor. 10:21; 11:27); "provoke the *kyrios* to jealousy" (1 Cor. 10:22); "not to love the *kyrios*" (1 Cor. 16:22); "the Lord's supper" (1 Cor. 11:20), "to be judged by the *kyrios*" (1 Cor. 11:32), "to be guilty of the body and blood of the *kyrios*" (1 Cor. 11:27). These different expressions indicate that the Lord's Supper is the place where the Christian community submits itself in a special way to the saving work of the *kyrios* and receives a share in his body and in his power.

(d) *kyrios* and Spirit. Paul taught the Christian community to distinguish between the man who is speaking in the Holy → Spirit and the one who is not (1 Cor. 12:3). A man can only say "Jesus is Lord" if he is filled with the Holy Spirit (on the background of this → Curse, art. *anathema*; → Confess). Anyone who, by acknowledging his allegiance to Jesus as *kyrios*, belongs to the new → covenant belongs to the sphere of the → Spirit and no longer to that of the old covenant and of the letter. He stands in → freedom: "Where the Spirit of the Lord is, there is freedom" (2 Cor. 3:17).

(e) *kyrios* in epistolary greetings. In the opening (but not the concluding) greetings of Paul's letters "the [or "our"] Lord Jesus Christ" is frequently mentioned beside God the Father (Rom. 1:7; 1 Cor. 1:3; 2 Cor. 1:3; Gal. 1:3; Phil. 1:2; 2 Thess. 1:2; 1 Tim. 1:2; 2 Tim. 1:2; Phlm. 3). The concluding greeting, with the phrase "the grace of our [or "the"] *kyrios* Jesus Christ be with you [or "with your spirit; with you all"]", continued the pre-Pauline tradition which probably had its ultimate origin in the Lord's Supper (cf. 1 Cor. 16:23; 2 Cor. 13:13; Phlm. 25, and Rev. 22:17–21). The description of God as the Father of Jesus Christ must go back to the Gentile-Christian Hellenistic community (Rom. 15:6; 2 Cor. 1:3; 11:31; cf. 1 Pet. 1:3; Eph. 1:3, 17; Col. 1:3). The formula was introduced into an originally Jewish context (the praise of God). The one *kyrios* Jesus Christ who is contrasted with the many *kyrioi* of the pagan world and who is acknowledged as the agent of creation (1 Cor. 8:6), corresponds to the one God, confessed by Judaism and preached in the Jewish mission to the Gentiles. Hence, Christian missionaries did not just call men to faith in God the Father but also to faith in the *kyrios* Jesus (Acts 5:14; 18:8; cf. → One, art. *heis*).

4. *The Lordship of the kyrios.* (a) The activity of the Christian community (→ Church) before the *kyrios* Jesus. In every expression of its life the Christian community stands before the *kyrios* who has authority and exercises it over the community (1 Cor. 4:19; 14:36; 16:7). He causes the community to grow (1 Thess. 3:12 f.), bestows authority on the → apostles (2 Cor. 10:8; 13:10) and different ministries on the members of his → body (1 Cor. 3:5; 7:17; 12:5). The *kyrios* gives visions and revelations (2 Cor. 12:1). The whole life of the Christian community is determined by its relationship to the *kyrios* (Rom. 14:8). The body, i.e. the complete earthly existence of the Christian, belongs to the *kyrios* (1 Cor. 6:13). This precludes dealings with prostitutes. The *kyrios* gives to each one the measure of → faith (1 Cor. 3:5; 7:17; Eph. 4:7). He is the *kyrios* of → peace and gives peace (2 Thess. 3:16), → mercy (2 Tim. 1:16) and insight (2 Tim. 2:7). On the basis of faith in the *kyrios* Christ, even the earthly relationships between masters and slaves take on a new aspect. Faithful service of earthly *kyrioi* is service of the *kyrios* of the church (Col. 3:22 ff.; cf. 1 Pet. 2:13).

(b) The formulae "through" (*dia*) and "in" (*en*) the *kyrios*. The formula "through the ["our"] Lord Jesus ["Christ"]", which is probably pre-Pauline, occurs in the most varied contexts: thanksgiving (Rom. 7:25; 1 Cor. 15:57); praise (Rom. 5:11); exhortation (Rom. 15:30; 1 Thess. 4:2). In all these phrases the word *kyrios* is used in order to claim the power of the exalted Lord for the life of the church and of the individual.

The phrase "in the Lord" occurs frequently, particularly in Paul, and means the same as *en Iēsou Christō*: a door was opened for mission (2 Cor. 2:12); Paul affirms and exhorts (Eph. 4:17; 1 Thess. 4:1); is convinced (Rom. 14:14); people are received (Rom. 16:2; Phil. 2:29); the church is to rejoice (Phil. 3:1); it is to stand firm (Phil. 4:1); to work (Rom. 16:21); to greet one another (Rom. 16:22; 1 Cor. 16:19). Christians are to marry in the *kyrios*, i.e. to enter upon a Christian → marriage (1 Cor. 7:39); to be strong (Eph. 6:10); to walk (Col. 2:6); to undertake service (Col. 4:17). Paul was a prisoner "in the Lord" (Eph. 4:1); people are chosen (Rom. 16:13); beloved (Rom. 16:8; 1 Cor. 4:17); their work is not in vain (1 Cor. 15:58); the Christian has eternal life (Rom. 6:23); the church is a light (Eph. 5:8). The whole of life, both in the present and the future, is determined by the fact of Christ which is expressed by this formula: Paul and his churches stand in the presence and under the power of the *kyrios*. (On this question in general see T. Preiss, *Life in Christ, SBT* 13, 1954; J. K. S. Reid, *Our Life in Christ*, 1963.)

(c) Statements about the parousia. In his present existence the Christian is separated from the *kyrios* and longs to be with him (2 Cor. 5:6, 8). Christians who are alive at the second coming will, according to Pauline eschatology, be caught up to meet the *kyrios* (1 Thess. 4:17). Just as the present life of the church and of the individual Christian is already determined by the hidden power of the *kyrios*, the NT church looks forward to the future, visible return of Christ and to a final union with the Lord of life and death. For the church believed not only in a present Lord but in a coming Lord. We read of "the day of the *kyrios*" (1 Cor. 1:8; 5:5; 2 Cor. 1:14; 1 Thess. 5:2; 2 Thess. 2:2); of "the revealing [*apokalypsis*] of the *kyrios*" (1 Cor. 1:7); "the coming [*parousia*]" of our *kyrios*" (2 Thess. 2:1); of the "appearing [*epiphaneia*] of the *kyrios*" (1 Tim. 6:14). Other passages speak of the coming of the *kyrios*, of meeting him, of his nearness and of his heavenly revelation (1 Cor. 4:5; Phil. 4:5; 1 Thess. 6:16 f.; Jas. 5:7 f.). Such statements about the *kyrios* belong with the eschatological prayer of the Aram.-speaking church *maranatha* → Present). When he comes, the exalted One is judge (2 Thess. 1:9; 2:8) and saviour (Phil. 3:20).

5. *Derivatives of kyrios.* (a) *kyria* (fem. of *kyrios*), lady, mistress, owner, mistress of the house. In the NT it occurs only in 2 Jn. 1, 5, where it refers to the church (cf. the change from the 3rd person sing. to the 2nd person plur. in v. 6; according to v. 13 the churches are sisters and their members children, cf. vv. 4, 13). In addressing the church as lady the author is expressing his respect for it and honours it as a work of the *kyrios*.

(b) *kyriakos* (adj. derived from *kyrios*), belonging to the Lord. In secular Gk.: *pros ton kyriakon logon* means at the owner's expense; in the language of administration it means imperial.

In the NT *kyriakē hēmera* means the Lord's day, the day on which the *kyrios* rose from the dead (cf. Matt. 28:1; Acts 20:7; 1 Cor. 16:2), which the church honoured by assembling on it (→ Sabbath). John received his revelation on the Lord's day (Rev. 1:10). The *kyriakon deipnon* (1 Cor. 11:20) is the meal of the *kyrios*, the → Lord's Supper. The expression stands in parallel with *trapeza kyriou*, the Lord's table (1 Cor. 10:21); cf. Isa. 65:11; Philo, *Spec.Leg.* 1, 221. To sit down at the table of the *kyrios* is to receive food from him and through it enter into communion with him. Correspondingly, anyone who takes part in pagan sacrificial meals enters into communion with demons (cf. H.-J. Schoeps, *Theologie und Geschichte des Judenchristentums*, 1949, 192; C. K. Barrett, *A Commentary on the First Epistle to the Corinthians*, 1968, 237 f.; → Lord's Supper). The two activities are utterly incompatible.

(c) *kyriotēs*, lordly power or position, dominion. In the NT the word occurs in the plur. with reference to → angelic powers (Col. 1:16; Eph. 1:20 f.). The expression recalls Eth.En. 61:10: "And He will summon all the host of the heavens, and all the holy ones above, and the host of God, the Cherubin, Seraphin and Ophannin, and all the angels of power, and all the angels of principalities, and the Elect One, and the other powers on the earth (and) over the water" (cf. also 1 Cor. 15:24; Rom. 8:38; Eph. 6:12; Arndt, 461 f.; E. Lohse, *Colossians and Philemon*, 1971, 51; G. H. C. Macgregor, "Principalities and Powers: the Cosmic Background of Paul's Thought", *NTS* 1, 1954–55, 17–28). The NT epistles stress that the exalted Christ rules over these dominions. *kyriotēs* occurs in the sing. in Jude 8 and 2 Pet. 2:10, where the thought is not of angels but of God's dominion. False teachers disregard it in the lust of their defiling passions.

(d) *kyrieuō*, be a *kyrios*, act as master; be authorized. In the LXX it occurs more than 50 times, mostly to translate *māšal*, rule. In the NT it occurs 7 times (6 in Paul and one in Luke). The rule of kings over their people is characterized by ambition (Lk. 22:25, *kyrieuousin*), because they misuse their power for selfish ends. Paul uses *kyrieuō* to describe relationships of power. But the disciples are not to seek to be the greatest, but rather to serve like Jesus himself (Lk. 22:26 f.). Because Christ has risen, → death no longer reigns over him, i.e. no longer has any power over him (Rom. 6:9). Christ died and rose in order that he might reign over the living and the dead (Rom. 14:9). God is the ruler of those who rule (1 Tim. 6:15). Since Christians have been baptized into Jesus' death and have risen with him (Rom. 6:3 f.), sin should not and must not reign over them any longer (Rom. 6:14). For they no longer stand under → law (art. *nomos*), but under → grace, i.e. under the *kyrios* (Christ (Rom. 7:1, 6). Paul does not want to lord it over the faith of the Corinthians but to work with them for their → joy (2 Cor. 1:24). Now that Christ has demonstrated his Lordship over sin and death, Christians should, indeed must, no longer let themselves be dominated by these powers.

(e) *katakyrieuō*, rule over, conquer. The LXX uses the word principally to describe domination by foreigners; it is used of God's dominion only in Jer. 3:14. In the NT the word occurs 4 times. It is a characteristic of Gentile rulers to lord it over the people. The prefix *kata-* clearly has a negative force and implies that the princes exercise their rule to their own advantage and contrary to the interests and well-being of the people (Matt. 20:25; Mk. 10:42). The vb. is also used of the man with an evil spirit who leaped on the seven sons of Sceva and *mastered* them (Acts 19:16) as they attempted to imitate Christian exorcism. The elders are exhorted, on the other hand, not to exercise their office as lording it over the congregation, but as examples to the flock (1 Pet. 5:2 f.). *H. Bietenhard*
→ Confess, → Curse, → God, → Jesus Christ, → Son of God, → Present, → Sabbath, → Spirit

(a). G. Bornkamm, "Christ and the World in the Early Christian Message", *Early Christian Experience*, 1969, 14–28; W. Bousset, *Kyrios Christos: A History of the Belief in Christ from the Beginnings of Christianity to Irenaeus*, 1970; F. F. Bruce, "Jesus is Lord", in J. McD. Richards, ed., *Soli Deo Gloria: New Testament Studies in Honor of W. C. Robinson*, 1968, 23 ff.; R. Bultmann, *Theology of the New Testament*, I, 1952, 123 ff.; L. M. Canfield, *The Early Persecutions, Studies in History* 55, 1913; H. Conzelmann, *An Outline Theology of the New Testament*, 1969, 82 ff., 199 ff.; O. Cullmann, *The Earliest Christian Confessions*, 1949; *Christ and Time: The Primitive Christian Conception of Time and History*, 1951; "The Kingship of Christ and the Church in the New Testament", *The Early Church*, 1956, 105–40; *The State in the New Testament*, 1963²; *The Christology of the New Testament*, 1963², 195–237; and *Salvation in History*, 1967; A. Czégledy, "The Modern Pattern of Christ's Lordship", *SJT* 12, 1959, 361–72; G. Dalman, *The Words of Jesus Considered in the Light of Post-Biblical Jewish Writings and the Aramaic Language*, 1902, 324–31; and *Jesus-Jeshua: Studies in the Gospels*, 1929; A. Deissmann, *Light from the Ancient East: The New Testament Illustrated by Recently Discovered Texts of the Graeco-Roman World*, 1927⁴; E. E. Ellis, "Saith the Lord", *EQ* 29, 1957, 23–28; W. Foerster and G. Quell, *kyrios* etc., *TDNT* III 1039–98; W. H. C. Frend, *Martyrdom and Persecution in the Early Church: A Study of a Conflict from the Maccabees to Donatus*, 1965; R. H. Fuller, *The Foundations of New Testament Christology*, 1965; F. C. Grant, *Roman Hellenism and the New Testament*, 1962; R. M. Grant, *Augustine to Constantine: The Thrust of the Christian Movement into the Roman World*, 1970; F. Hahn, *The Titles of Jesus in Christology: Their History in Early Christianity*, 1969, 68–135; J. N. D. Kelly, *Early Christian Creeds*, 1972³, 1–29; J. D. Kingsbury, "The Title 'Kyrios' in Matthew's Gospel", *JBL* 94, 1975, 246–55; W. Kramer, *Christ, Lord, Son of God*, 1966; W. G. Kümmel, *Promise and Fulfilment: The Eschatological Message of Jesus*, 1961² *SBT* 24; and *The Theology of the New Testament*, 1974; R. Leivestad, *Christ the Conqueror: Ideas of Conflict in the New Testament*, 1954; E. Lohmeyer, *The Lord of the Temple: A Study of the Relation between Cult and Gospel*, 1961; R. N. Longenecker, *The Christology of Early Jewish Christianity*, 1970, *SBT* Second Series 17, 120–47; R. P. Martin, *Carmen Christi. Philippians ii. 5–11 in Recent Interpretation and in the Setting of Early Christian Worship*, 1967; V. F. Neufeld, *The Earliest Christian Confessions*, New Testament Tools and Studies 5, 1963; A. Oepke, *en*, *TDNT* II 537–43; J. C. O'Neill, "The Use of KYRIOS in the Book of Acts", *SJT* 8, 1955, 155–74; O. Plöger, *Theocracy and Eschatology*, 1967;

W. M. Ramsay, *The Church in the Roman Empire before 170*, 1906; A. Richardson, *An Introduction to the Theology of the New Testament*, 1958, 148, 153 f., 305; and *The Political Christ*, 1973; E. Schweizer, *Lordship and Discipleship*, 1960; E. Stauffer, *Christ and the Caesars: Historical Sketches* 1955; L. R. Taylor, *The Divinity of the Roman Emperor*, 1931; W. C. van Unnik, "Jesus: Anathema or Kyrios (I Cor. 12:3)", in B. Lindars and S. S. Smalley, eds., *Christ and the Spirit in the New Testament. In Honour of Charles Francis Digby Moule*, 1973, 113–26.

(b). D. Barthélemy, *Les Devanciers d'Aquila. Première Publication intégrale du Texte des Fragments du Dodécaprophéton*, 1963; H. Bietenhard, *Das tausendjährige Reich*, 1955²; L. Goppelt, "Die Herrschaft Christi und die Welt nach dem Neuen Testament", *Lutherische Rundschau*, 1967, 21 ff.; J. Herrmann, *Kyrios und Pneuma. Studien zur Christologie der paulinischen Hauptbriefe*, 1961; N. Hofer, "Das Bekenntnis 'Herr ist Jesus' und das 'Taufen auf den Namen Jesu' " *ThQ* 145, 1965, 1 ff.; E. Lohmeyer, *Kyrios Jesus. Eine Untersuchung zu Phil. 2, 5–11, Sitzungsberichte der Heidelberger Akademie der Wissenschaften, Philosophisch-historische Klasse*, 1927–28, 4. *Abhandlung*, 1928; and *Christuskult und Kaiserkult*, 1919; U. Luck, "Historische Fragen zum Verhältnis von *kyrios* und *pneuma* bei Paulus", *TLZ*, 1960, 845 ff.; R. Rendtorff, "El, Baal und Jahwe", *ZAW* Neue Folge 37, 1966, 277 ff.; E. Schweizer, "Der Glaube an Jesus, den 'Herrn' in seiner Entwicklung von den ersten Nachfolgern biz zur hellenistischen Gemeinde", *EvTh* 17, 1957, 7 ff.; S. Schulz, "Maranatha und Kyrios Jesus", *ZNW* 53, 1962, 125 ff.; P. Vielhauer, "Ein Weg zur neutestamentlichen Christologie?", *Aufsätze zum Neuen Testament, ThB* 31, 1965, 141 ff.

Lord's Supper

δεῖπνον

δεῖπνον (*deipnon*), a main meal, dinner, supper, banquet; κυριακὸν δεῖπνον (*kyriakon deipnon*), Lord's supper; τράπεζα (*trapeza*), table; κλάσις τοῦ ἄρτου (*klasis tou artou*), breaking of bread.

CL 1. In the ancient religions eating and drinking were mostly formal meals, i.e. acts of public or private fellowship linked with the sacred (*RGG*³ IV 605). Families, clans and religious fellowships received a share in divine power through the common meal, which represented their union with the deity. The origin of the sacred character of the meal is connected with magic concepts, according to which the divine is embodied in material things (animism; similar ideas also in cannibalism, cf. *RGG*³ III 1116). The thought that deity was contained in every plant (Demeter-Kore) led on to the idea that the deity possessed a → life-giving power, which was received directly by those who shared the meal. In short, there was nothing which unites man and man, and man and God, more than eating and drinking (cf. E. O. James, *The Beginnings of Religion*, [1948] 1958, 83–100; F. Bammel, *Das heilige Mahl im Glauben der Völker*, 1950).

2. *deipnon* (from Homer on), in the sense of a cultic meal, was part of the living vocabulary of Hellenistic religion, in which it played an important rôle. The participant believed that he was sitting at the *trapeza tou theou*, the god's table (cf. 1 Cor. 10:21, *trapeza daimoniōn*, "table of demons") and that through the meal he entered into fellowship with the deity. He thus became a partner or sharer *koinōnos* (cf. 1 Cor. 10:20). The Oxyrhynchus Papyri in the 2nd cent. A.D. contain the invitation: "Chairemon invites you to eat [*deipnēsai*] at the table of the Lord Sarapis [*kyriou Sarapidos*]" (*P.Oxy.* 1, 110). Sarapis is here represented as the host and the participants in the cultic meal as his table companions (for further instances of such invitations see *P.Oxy.* 14, 1755; 3, 523; cf. W. Bousset, *Kyrios Christos*, 1970, 143 ff.; H. Lietzmann, *An die Korinther I, II, HNT* 9, 1949⁴, 49 f.). Josephus

tells of an invitation to the *deipnon* of Anubis in the temple of Isis at Rome (*Ant.* 18, 3, 4). "The underlying thought is that of *communio*, of the union of those who eat with the divinity" (J. Behm, *TDNT* II 35).

ot 1. The meal in the OT. The term *deipnon* does not play a significant rôle in the LXX. Until 4 Macc. 3:9 it occurs only in Dan. and translates Heb. *paṭbaḡ*, delicacies (1:8, 13, 15, 16) and *leḥem*, bread (5:1). The vb. *deipneō* occurs only in Prov. 23:1; Dan. 11:27 and Tob. 7:8; 8:1.

Festivals and sacrifices in the OT are often connected with cultic meals and can be described as eating before the Lord and rejoicing (Deut. 12:7) (→ Feast; → Hunger, art. *esthiō*; → Joy; → Sacrifice). Table-fellowship binds a man to → God and before God (Exod. 18:12; 24:11). A meal often played a part in the conclusion of a secular → covenant (Gen. 26:30; Jos. 9:14 f.), at which Yahweh was present as an unseen guest. It was with a meal that Jacob and Laban sealed their peace treaty (Gen. 31:46, 54), Moses, his father-in-law and the elders their association (Exod. 18:12), Gaal and the Shechemites their conspiracy (Jdg. 9:26–41), and the people their agreement with their elected king (1 Sam. 11:15; 1 Ki. 1:25, 41 ff.; cf. 1 Sam. 9:22 ff.). The covenant between Yahweh and Israel on Sinai was concluded with a cultic meal for the elders with Yahweh (cf. G. Fohrer, *RGG*[3] IV 607). Such a fellowship-meal not only made the participants brothers one of another, but also of Yahweh (cf. the name Ahijah [Heb. *'aḥîyâh*, *'aḥîyāhû*], "Yahweh is my brother"). Table fellowship meant the granting of → forgiveness (2 Sam. 9:7; 2 Ki. 25:27–30; Josephus, *Ant.* 19, 7:1), protection (Jdg. 19:15 ff.) and → peace (Gen. 43:25 ff.). The breaking of table-fellowship was the most detestable of crimes (Jer. 41:1 f.; Ps. 41:9 [MT 10]; cf. 1QH 5:23 f.; Mk. 14:18).

2. The Passover meal (→ Feast, art. *pascha*) originated in Israel's nomadic period. A one year old lamb or kid (Exod. 12:5) was killed by the head of the household on 14 Nisan at sundown (Exod. 12:6), "between dusk and dark" (NEB). Its blood was smeared on the doorposts, its flesh roasted and eaten by the family during the night of 14–15 Nisan (Exod. 12:8 f.). After Josiah's reform (621 B.C.) the killing of the Passover lambs and the Passover meal took place in Jerusalem (Deut. 16:5–7; 2 Ki. 23:21–23). The Jewish Passover meal in the time of Jesus recalled the sparing of the houses marked with the blood of the Passover lambs and the redemption out of slavery in Egypt. At the same time the Passover meal looked forward to redemption in the future, of which the redemption from Egypt was the pattern (J. Jeremias, *The Eucharistic Words of Jesus*, 1966[2], 42 f., 56–62). The messiah comes on Passover night. "On this night they were redeemed and they will be redeemed," says an old proverb (Mekilta Exod. 12:42).

3. (a) Table-fellowship. Joining in table-fellowship meant sharing in Yahweh's → blessing. This was signified by the prayer at the beginning and the thanksgiving at the end of the meal. The head of the household took the bread and spoke over it the benediction on behalf of all those present (Ber. 6:1). Then he broke the bread that had been blessed and gave each at the table a piece. In this way every participant in the meal received a share of the benediction. A benediction followed after the meal. The head of the household took a cup of wine, the "cup of blessing" (cf. 1 Cor. 10:16), and pronounced the prayer of thanksgiving on behalf of all present (Ber. 7:3; 46a ff.; 50a) Then everyone drank from the cup of blessing, in

521

order to receive a part of the benediction pronounced over the wine. The use of wine at an ordinary meal was not obligatory, but a closing benediction was.

(b) The Passover liturgy. Even before the time of Christ the outlines of the liturgy to be followed during the Passover meal had been laid down (Pes. 10:2–7; cf. J. Jeremias, op. cit., 85 f.).

(i) Preliminary course. The head of the household pronounced the prayer of sanctification (*qiddûš*), comprising the benediction for the festival and the first cup (the *qiddûš* cup). The preliminary course (*karpas*), consisting of green herbs, bitter herbs and a sauce of fruit juice was eaten without bread. The meal was brought in but not yet eaten, the second cup was mixed with water and placed on the table, but not yet drunk.

(ii) The Passover liturgy. The Passover service, in which the head of the household explained the special features of the Passover meal (Exod. 12:26) and proclaimed the outline of the story, the *haggāḏâh*; the first part of the Passover Hallel (Pss. 113 f.) was sung and the second cup (*haggāḏâh* cup) was drunk.

(iii) The main meal. The head of the household pronounced a benediction over the unleavened bread, which was distributed and the meal eaten which consisted of the Passover lamb, mazzoth, bitter herbs (Exod. 12:8) and wine (optional). After grace the third cup (cup of blessing) was drunk.

(iv) Conclusion. The second part of the Hallel (Pss. 115–118) was sung and a benediction pronounced over the fourth cup (Hallel cup).

The interpreting of the special features of the Passover meal was a firmly-established part of the Passover ritual. In the Passover service which preceded the meal the Passover lamb, the unleavened bread and the bitter herbs (cf. Exod. 12:8) were explained. Thus an old Aram. formula explaining the mazzoth runs: "Behold, this is the bread of affliction" (G. Dalman, *Jesus-Jeshua*, 1929, 139; cf. Deut. 16:3).

4. The eschatological meal. Isa. 25:6–8 (cf. 65:13) refers to a bountiful feast which Yahweh will provide "for all peoples", when sorrow and death are things of the past. This feast, with the attendant removal of "the veil that is spread over all nations", has been linked closely with the Lord's Supper, especially in its Lucan setting, by P. E. Leonard (*Luke's Account of the Lord's Supper*, dissertation, Manchester, 1976).

5. The common meal at Qumran. The cultic meal at Qumran was the daily main meal of the community. A priest presided and pronounced the benediction over the bread and the wine at the beginning of the meal (1QS 6:4–6). There is a reference in 1QSa 2:17–21 to an eschatological meal with the messiah in which bread is eaten and new wine drunk. There is an analogy here with the Christian celebration of a meal, even if dependence of the one on the other cannot be proved and indeed is improbable. (On the Essene meal see K. G. Kuhn, "The Lord's Supper and the Communal Meal at Qumran", in K. Stendahl, ed., *The Scrolls and the New Testament*, 1958, 65–93; J. Jeremias, op. cit., 31–6.)

NT 1. *The NT sources.* The expression, the Lord's Supper (*kyriakon deipnon*) occurs only in 1 Cor. 11:20. In meaning it is closely related to the phrase the "table of the Lord [*trapeza kyriou*]" (1 Cor. 10:21). Both passages indicate that the term → Lord (art. *kyrios*) is firmly established in the tradition and terminology of the Lord's Supper (1 Cor. 10:22; 11:27, 31 f.). The institution of the Lord's Supper has been handed down to us in four forms (Mk. 14:22–25; Matt. 26:26–29; Lk. 22:15–20; 1 Cor. 11:23–25). Many scholars are of the opinion that the differing versions of the words of institution represent in each case the liturgical text entrusted to the writer by his own community (cf. J. Jeremias, op. cit., 106–37). The words of institution, in the form in which we have them, therefore, belong to the realm of liturgy and "behind each form is as it were a celebrating congregation for whom it is intended" (G. Bornkamm, *Early Christian Experience*, 1969, 134).

(a) 1 Cor. 11:23–25 is, from the literary point of view, the oldest version, reproducing the form of words current in the Christian community in Antioch, which Paul found there in the mid-forties (Acts 11:26) ([F. F. Bruce] or more probably at Damascus, where he first experienced Christian fellowship in the mid-thirties [Acts 9:19; Gal. 1:17]) and which he traces back to Jesus, as a tradition handed down by the church (1 Cor. 11:23). Matt.'s version is widely considered to be an expanded form of that in Mk., and therefore has no independent value as a source in a discussion of the original form. A number of MSS of Lk. omit vv. 19b, 20 (D, some Old Lat., Old Syr.; on the text see Metzger, 173–77; J. Jeremias, op. cit., 139–59). The majority of scholars regard the so-called "short text" of Lk. (without vv. 19b, 20) as secondary, holding that it arose either on the grounds of discipline (to protect the Lord's Supper from profanation, J. Jeremias, ibid.), or to avoid mentioning the second cup (v. 17, 20; cf. H. Schürmann, *Der Einsetzungsbericht, Lk. 22, 19–20, NTAbh* 20, 4, 1955, 35 ff.). A comparison with Paul and Mk. reveals that the original longer text (Lk. 22:15–20) agrees essentially in vv. 19b, 20 with 1 Cor. 11:24 f., and in v. 19a (as far as *to sōma mou*, "my body") and in the concluding formula of v. 20c (*to hyper hymōn ekchynnomenon*, "which is shed for you") with Mk. 14:22, 24. The text of Lk., therefore, on one hand betrays the influence of the Marcan version, and on the other of a text very closely related to, but older than, that of 1 Cor. 11:23–25. So we are left with Mk. 14:22–25 and 1 Cor. 11:23–25 as the oldest forms of the tradition.

(b) In addition to the four-fold record of the Lord's Supper we must take into consideration: (i) 1 Cor. 10:16, a pre-Pauline commentary on the Lord's Supper; (ii) 1 Cor. 11:26, an explanatory comment by Paul; (iii) 1 Cor. 11:27 f.; 16:20, 22; Rev. 22:17–21, parts (or references to parts) of the introductory liturgy to the primitive Christian celebration of the Lord's Supper; (iv) Acts 2:42, 46; 20:7, 11, accounts of the daily celebration of the Lord's Supper (breaking of bread) in the primitive church; (v) Jn. 6:51–58 with the Johannine version of the saying about the bread: "and the bread which I shall give for the life of the world is my flesh" (6:51c).

2. *The historical roots.* (a) The Lord's Supper in the primitive church was certainly not just the continuation of the disciples' daily table-fellowship with the earthly Jesus. But it is related to the accounts of Jesus' table-fellowship with his disciples, with tax-collectors and sinners (Matt. 9:9–13; Mk. 2:13–17; Lk. 5:27–32), and to the accounts of the feeding of the five thousand (Matt. 14:13–21; Mk. 6:30–44; Lk. 9:10–17; Jn. 6:1–13) and the four thousand (Matt. 15:32–39; Mk. 8:1–10; → Hunger, art. *esthiō*). "By coming to them and eating and drinking with them, Jesus brought them the merciful presence of God, the forgiveness of sins. This fellowship with the friend of tax collectors and sinners keeps the Christian community firm, by . . . renewing for it the consolation of forgiveness" (E. Lohse,

Geschichte des Leidens und Sterbens Jesu Christi, 1964, 57). These meals with tax-collectors and the granting of table-fellowship to the despised (Lk. 15:1 f.; 19:5 f.) are kerygmatic parabolic actions, Jesus' word of forgiveness coming to life in events (J. Jeremias, *The Parables of Jesus*, 1963², 227 ff.).

(b) The Lord's Supper in the primitive church, with its eschatological joy at present table-fellowship with the exalted Jesus, is, however, equally related to the table-fellowship of the risen Jesus with his disciples after Easter. According to O. Cullmann, the church's celebration of eschatological meals has real roots in the meals that took place on the occasion of Jesus' appearances after Easter (Acts 10:41; Lk. 24:30 f., 35, 43; Jn. 21:13; cf. *Early Christian Worship*, 1953, 14 ff.; *The Christology of the New Testament*, 1963², 212). Though the connection cannot be denied, it seems that Cullmann has ascribed to the breaking of bread at the Easter appearances too great an influence upon the emergence of the Lord's Supper in the primitive church. For the expression, to break bread (*klaō ton arton* or *klasis tou artou*), occurs only in Lk. 24:30, 35 (cf. also Jn. 21:13), and the appearances of the risen Jesus were, as the NT itself recognizes, unique occurrences and as such were limited to the original witnesses (1 Cor. 15:5 ff.). When the risen Jesus ate and drank with his disciples at his appearances after Easter, he was doing something extraordinary, which could not be repeated in the same manner nor in any way continued.

The table-fellowship of the earthly Jesus and of the risen Christ with his disciples (→ Hunger, art. *pinō*) are accordingly factors which are related to the basic motives behind Jesus' last meal. The regular celebration of the Lord's Supper by the primitive church arose from all these taken together. The Lord's Supper in the church after Easter has a strong eschatological element (cf. Mk. 14:25). Nevertheless, the retrospective look at Jesus' saving death (Mk. 14:22–25) was an essential constituent of the Lord's Supper from the first (P. Vielhauer, *Aufsätze zum Neuen Testament*, 1965, 159 f.).

3. *The original form of the words of institution.* (a) There is a general consensus of agreement on the following points:

(i) Mk. 14:22–25 and 1 Cor. 11:23–25 are the two oldest forms of the words of institution. (ii) One must assume an original Aram. (or Heb.) form, which has not been preserved and which lies behind both of the oldest forms of the text.

In Mk. the saying about the bread runs, "Take; this is my body [*labete, touto estin to sōma mou*]" (14:22); the saying about the cup, "This is my blood of the covenant, which is poured out for many [*touto estin to haima mou tēs diathēkēs to ekchynnomenon hyper pollōn*]" (14:24). In Paul the saying about the bread runs, "This is my body for you [*touto mou estin to sōma to hyper hymōn*]" (1 Cor. 11:24), and the saying about the cup, "This cup is the new covenant by my blood [*touto to potērion hē kainē diathēkē estin en tō emō haimati*]" (1 Cor. 11:25).

(b) One can deduce from Mk., an original form, "This is my body, this is my shed blood (i.e. my dying) for [the] many" (Mk. 14:22c, 24). K. G. Kuhn ("Über den ursprünglichen Sinn des Abendmahls", *EvTh* 11/12, 1950–51, 513 ff.), E. Lohse (*Märtyrer und Gottesknecht*, 1955², 122 ff.; and op. cit., 54 ff.) and others have rightly decided for this possibility. On the other side, G. Bornkamm (op. cit., 134 ff.), E. Schweizer (see bibliography), and others defend the originality of the Pauline-Lucan words of institution. They maintain that this form has in its narrative framework the older comment that the cup was not shared until after they had eaten; in Mk. body and blood are complementary terms; the original asymmetry of the Pauline-Lucan version of the sayings about the bread and the cup has been harmonized in the Marcan form on liturgical grounds, and even on grounds of content, for the parallelism of body and blood reveals the questionable idea of the body and blood of Christ as the two parts of the crucified Lord, an idea arising from the elements which represent the body and the blood.

The following 6 objections to this argument have been raised:

(i) Even in the original pre-Marcan form "body" and "blood" (*sōma* and *haima*) do not represent a commonly linked pair of terms (E. Lohse, *Märtyrer und Gottes-knecht*, 125). Flesh and blood (*sarx* and *haima*; cf. Heb. 2:14) appear more often as complementary terms. In the pre-Marcan explanatory saying, therefore, we have a pair of terms which are not complementary, either anthropologically or cultically.

(ii) The term → "blood" (14:24) in the pre-Marcan formula must not be isolated and simply made a parallel to → "body" (14:22), because in Mk. 14:24 "my blood shed [*to haima mou to ekchynnomenon*]" taken in the context of the OT and Jewish forms of expression, denoted violent death (E. Lohse, J. Behm, F. Hahn; → Blood).

(iii) In the pre-Marcan form, therefore, it is not body and blood that are related to one another, but the non-parallel phrases, "my body" (the saying about the bread) and "my dying for [the] many" (the saying about the cup). In other words, each part of the pre-Marcan saying is self-contained and can be explained without reference to the parallel phrase.

(iv) It was only due to the inclusion of the words "of the covenant", alluding to Exod. 24:8, that "blood" in Mk. became cultically complementary to "body", and even the participle "shed" only received cultic significance (a combined allusion to the atonement and to the covenant) at this point; whereupon the possibility of misunderstanding in the Marcan saying about the cup was removed in the Pauline-Lucan form by associating the allusion to the atonement with the saying about the bread, so that the idea of the covenant here only qualifies the saying about the cup.

(v) The phrase "shed for [the] many" (Mk. 14:24b) does not represent any expansion of or addition to the Hellenistic phrase "my blood of the covenant" (Mk. 14:24a; cf. W. Marxsen, "Der Ursprung des Abendmahls", *EvTh* 12, 1952–53, 299). For on linguistic grounds Mk. 14:24b is an Aramaism (J. Jeremias, op. cit., 178 ff.; K. G. Kuhn, op. cit., 513 ff.). Moreover, the expression *haima ekchynnesthai* (to shed blood) is analogous to other turns of phrase like "to pour out one's soul" (Isa. 53:12), "to give one's soul" (Mk. 10:45b), which are paraphrases of the idea of dying, sacrifice or violent death (cf. Gen. 4:10 f.; 9:6; Deut. 19:10; 2 Ki. 21:16; Ps. 106:38; Jer. 7:6; Matt. 23:35).

(vi) Therefore the Pauline-Lucan form assumes the Marcan version of the explanatory words and can only be understood as a development of them. Since the phrase in Paul's account "by my blood" (1 Cor. 11:25) does not appear in Jer. 31:31 ff., the formula is not to be understood primarily in terms of Jer.; it receives its significance which speaks of "the blood of the covenant" from Exod. 24:8. In other words, the Pauline form of the words of institution can only be explained on the basis of the older Marcan form of the words of institution, based on Exod.

24:8, and on a process of theological reflection moving from Exod. 24:8 to Jer. 31:31 ff. This is comparable with the development from the Marcan form [14:24] which is orientated towards Exod. 24:8 to that in Matt. [26:29] which reflects Jer. 31:34b.

(c) The originality of the pre-Marcan form follows then from: (i) a wealth of Semitisms (Aramaisms) of which only few recur in Paul; (ii) the considerable asymmetry which results from the pre-Marcan formulations saying about the bread not having any theological interpretation and the reference to the atonement's being attached only to the saying about the cup; (iii) the imbalance of "my body"/"my dying for [the] many"; (iv) the fact that the Pauline-Lucan form can be derived, according to the principles governing the handing down of tradition, from the Marcan, but the reverse process is unthinkable; and finally (v) the fact that the sayings about the bread and the cup, in the pre-Marcan original form, each constitute a complete saying which does not first require the parallel saying in order to be understood. This presupposes, therefore, that the sayings about the bread and the cup were originally separated by a whole meal. One must conclude, therefore, "that in the oral tradition of the earliest times there was a shorter version" (E. Lohse, *Märtyrer und Gottesknecht*, 124) which may be stated: "This is my body, this is my dying for [the] many."

4. *The setting of the words of institution.* The account of the institution, which stems from liturgical tradition, appears in the NT in the setting of the oldest account of the passion, the Passover meal and the liturgy of the primitive church. Therefore, we must investigate the significance of this setting for the understanding of the words of institution.

(a) The Lord's Supper in the setting of the oldest account of the passion.

(i) The striking fact that the Gospel of Jn. does not coincide with the Synoptics until the account of the Passion demonstrates that the passion narrative was a self-contained and very old traditional compilation. Systematic comparison of the Johannine and Synoptic passion narratives reveals that, from Judas's betrayal onwards, Jn. agrees with the Synoptics even in the order of his material, viz. betrayal (Mk. 14:10 f.; Jn. 13:2), prophecy of the betrayal and the meal (Mk. 14:18–25; Jn. 13:1–30). Jn. does not give an account of the Last Supper but has sayings about eating Jesus' flesh and drinking his blood in 6:51 ff., and also describes the arrest (Mk. 14:32 ff.; Jn. 18:2–11). The underlying oldest passion narrative, therefore, began with Judas's betrayal, then recounted the prophecy of the betrayal and the institution of the Lord's Supper and finally depicted the arrest, the trial before the Sanhedrin, the judgment by Pilate, the crucifixion and resurrection (empty tomb). If, at a very early stage, the passion narrative began with the betrayal, the oldest summaries of the passion agree with this (Mk. 9:31; 8:31; 10:33 f.), for they never mention any event of the passion earlier than Judas's betrayal (J. Jeremias op. cit., 89–105; E. Lohse, *Geschichte des Leidens und Sterbens Jesu Christi*, 1964, 23 f.). The oldest account of the passion embraces, therefore, the oldest summary of the passion (Mk. 9:31).

(ii) The theme of the passion summaries (cf. especially Mk. 9:31) and of the passion narrative that embraces them (Mk. 14:10 f., 18, 21, 44; 15:1, 10, 15) which represents the setting of the original form of the Lord's Supper sayings, is, accordingly, the representative delivering up of the Son of man by God. It is accomplished

526

through Judas's betrayal, Jesus' arrest and his violent death (Mk. 9:31; 14:21; cf. 14:41). In so far as the passion summaries and the oldest passion narrative go back to the primitive Palestinian church, this favours the conclusion that the pre-Marcan original form of the words of institution (and not first the Marcan version) also stood within this oldest passion narrative.

If that is so, the theme of the setting of the pre-Marcan words of institution casts light on their meaning. It is not the two elements representing body and blood that stand at the heart of the pre-Marcan original of the old passion summaries (Mk. 9:31, etc.), and of the oldest passion narrative which embraces them (14:21, cf. 14:41), but the violent death ("my blood shed") of the One given up by God vicariously for the many.

(iii) This conclusion is supported by the agreement of the contents of the Marcan setting and the Pauline introductory formula: "the Lord Jesus [*ho kyrios Iēsous*] on the night when he was delivered up" (1 Cor. 11:23). Comparison with the liturgical introduction to the Pauline outline of the Lord's Supper establishes not only that the nocturnal betrayal by Judas belonged to the passion narrative at an early date (J. Jeremias, op. cit., 94 ff.) and that the Son of man title (Mk. 14:21) corresponds to the Pauline "*kyrios* Jesus" (the call *maranatha* refers to the coming of the Son of man; cf. W. Kramer, *Christ, Lord, Son of God*, 1966, 99–107, 175). It also shows that *paradidomai* (to be delivered up) in the passion narrative is to be understood in the context of the salvation history of God, who "gave up his Son for us all (Rom. 8:32; cf. 4:25). . . . Thus it was not as an expression of a police measure or a villainous deed of men" (G. Bornkamm, op. cit., 132). (On the call → Present, art. *maranatha*.)

This means, however, that the setting of the pre-Marcan words of institution in the Lord's Supper, with its theme of the substitutionary delivering up by God of the Son of man, accomplished through the ungodly actions of men, corresponds exactly to the liturgical introduction to the words of institution in Paul's account of the Lord's Supper and their theme of God's delivering up for us in salvation history of the *kyrios* Jesus.

(b) The Lord's Supper in the setting of the Passover meal. (i) The Synoptic narratives agree that Jesus' Last Supper was a Passover meal (Matt. 26:17 ff.; Mk. 14:12, 14, 16; Lk. 22:7, 11, 12, 15). According to them, Jesus was crucified on the Day of Passover (15 Nisan). Execution on the day of such a high festival was not impossible historically, for in cases of very serious crime execution was to be carried out "at the feast" (Deut. 17:13; 21:21) in the sight of all the people, i.e. on 15 Nisan (H. Conzelmann, *RGG*³ III 626; J. Jeremias, op. cit., 53). According to Jn., when Jesus was accused before Pilate, the Passover lambs had not yet been eaten (Jn. 18:28). Jesus' crucifixion took place on 14 Nisan, the Preparation for the Passover (Jn. 19:14). Nevertheless, the balance of probability seems to lie with the Synoptic presentation (W. Marxsen *EKL* I 4), for Jn. fixes the moment of Jesus' death as the time when the Passover lambs were being slaughtered in the Temple and clearly wants to make his chronology a comment on the meaning of Jesus' death, i.e. Jesus died as the true Passover lamb (Jn. 1:29; 19:36; cf. Exod. 12:46, Num. 9:12; 1 Cor. 5:7). ([Ed.] For discussions of the complex question of the chronological schemes employed by the evangelists see especially the works by Jaubert, Ogg, and Ruckstuhl listed in the bibliography.) Since the Lord's Supper, celebrated daily or weekly from the beginning, had no reference to the Passover as an annual feast, an original connection of the Passover meal and the Lord's Supper is more likely than a development in the opposite direction (K. G. Kuhn, op. cit., 513 ff.; W. Marxsen, ibid.).

([F. F. Bruce] The chronological question is best solved if the combined Synoptic and Johannine evidence be interpreted as indicating that the official Passover meal was indeed eaten on the Friday evening, as John implies [Jn. 18:28; 19:14], but that Jesus, for his own good reasons, kept the Passover with his disciples the preceding evening, "before the [official] feast of the Passover" [Jn. 13:1]. The official feast was regulated by the temple calendar, but there were groups in Israel which did not accept this calendar. One of these was the Qumran community, which followed the solar calendar of the book of Jubilees, but the view of A. Jaubert [*The Date of the Last Supper*, 1965], that Jesus kept the Passover according to this calendar, has not been adequately established. More probably Jesus did not regulate his observance on this occasion by any current calendar, but since he knew that he would not be alive on the Friday evening, and "earnestly desired to eat this passover" with his disciples before he suffered [Lk. 22:15], he resolved to eat it with them twenty-four hours earlier. Provision was made in the OT for the observance of the Passover on another day than the normal one, in a case of necessity [cf. Num. 9:10 f.; 2 Chr. 30:2 f., 13, 15]; and the Lord of the sabbath was also Lord of the Passover. If the meal was eaten a day earlier than the official date, it must have been eaten without a lamb, since in post-exilic times paschal lambs were slaughtered only by the priests in the temple at the appointed time. But wherever the Passover was commemorated beyond the environs of Jerusalem before A.D. 70, and throughout the whole world since A.D. 70, it has had to be commemorated without the paschal lamb. It is unnecessary to suppose with M. Black [*The Scrolls and Christian Origins*, 1961, 201] that Judas took the "morsel" [Jn. 13:26, 30] to the chief priests as "evidence . . . that an illegal feast had been celebrated".)

(ii) Not merely the setting of the oldest passion narrative suggests that Jesus' last meal took place within the framework of a Passover meal, but also the liturgical words of institution themselves.

The setting in which Jesus held his last Supper was Jerusalem and not Bethany to which he normally went each night (Matt. 21:17 par. Mk. 11:11; Mk. 11:19; Matt. 26:6 par. Mk. 14:3). He did not, therefore, leave the Holy City. It was a rule that the Passover lamb had to be eaten within the city limits of Jerusalem.

Jesus' Last Supper closed with a hymn of praise (Matt. 26:30 par. Mk. 14:26), i.e. with the second half of the Hallel (Pss. 115–118), which was sung at the close of the Passover meal.

The liturgical account of the institution states that Jesus' Last Supper was held during the night (1 Cor. 11:23; Matt. 26:20; Mk. 14:17; cf. Lk. 22:14), whereas the normal main meal took place in the late afternoon. The Passover meal, however, was from the beginning eaten at night, and its celebration was only permitted then. Since the indication of time in 1 Cor. 11:23 (in contrast to the setting in Mk. 14:17, 26) belongs to the old liturgical formula (G. Bornkamm, op. cit., 137 ff.; J. Jeremias, op. cit., 44 ff., 95, n. 5), the liturgical tradition itself supports the idea that Jesus' Last Supper took place within the setting of a Passover meal.

Finally, the words of institution within the supper support the idea that a Passover meal was the setting for Jesus' Last Supper. "The most likely way of understanding the fact that the words of institution were spoken is evidence that Jesus' words were said within the setting of a Passover meal. But the explanation of the elements is part of the Passover service, not of the benediction before or after the meal. Jesus, however, pronounced the words of institution at the distribution of the bread and wine" (E. Lohse, *Märtyrer und Gottesknecht*, 123). But here it must be noted that the analogy between the explanatory words of the Jewish Passover meal and those of Jesus is only formal, and not a material one. The setting of the Jewish Passover gave rise to Jesus' explanatory words but it does not explain them.

(iii) The novel element is the fact that Jesus is not said to have explained the special features of the Passover (the lamb, the unleavened bread and the bitter herbs), but that he *is* said to have explained → bread and → wine as such, i.e. those elements which appeared at every other meal. To this must be added the fact that Jesus' explanatory words were connected with the benediction before and after the meal. The distribution of the blessed bread and wine after the blessing meant giving a share in the blessing pronounced over the bread and the cup. On this basis one can explain, on the one hand, the linking of the words of institution with the blessing before and after the main meal and, on the other hand, the connection of the explanation with the distribution (J. Jeremias, op. cit., 84–88).

(c) The words of institution and parabolic actions. Jesus' explanation of the elements of bread and wine in the Lord's Supper differed finally from the explanation of the special features of the Jewish Passover meal in that the distribution of the bread and wine by Jesus represents a (prophetic) parabolic action (J. Jeremias, op. cit., 204 ff.; 212; W. Marxsen, *EKL* I 5), through which the disciples participated in Jesus' death. Two things are, however, essential to parabolic actions: that they become real events and that their constituent parts are described. The explanation is an established part of OT parabolic actions (cf. Ezek. 5:5 "this is Jerusalem"; Ezek. 12:11 "I am a sign for you"; cf. H. W. Wolff, *Hosea, Hermeneia*, 1974; W. Zimmerli, *Ezekiel*, I, *Hermeneia*, 1976).

(d) The Lord's Supper and the Passover meal. Jesus' Last Supper, therefore, was in all probability a Passover meal. He spoke the words of institution in the setting of his last celebration of the Passover and "clearly referred to many features of the feast, assimilating some and changing others. . . . When, as head of the household, he passed round the bread before the main meal, he accompanied it with a word of explanation, and likewise, later, the cup" (W. Marxsen, *EKL* I 4). The cup referred to was the third cup "after supper" (Lk. 22:20; 1 Cor. 11:25), the "cup of blessing" (1 Cor. 10:16) of the Passover feast. That this is above all explanation, not of actions but of the food, is made clear only by the setting of the Jewish Passover ritual. So if the Synoptic gospels are historically correct in placing the words of institution in the setting of the Passover, this conclusion in no way determines the sense of the words of institution and the significance of the Lord's Supper (K. G. Kuhn).

5. *The Lord's Supper and the liturgy of the primitive church.* The practical setting of the words of institution in the Lord's Supper is the celebration of the meal in the Palestinian and Hellenistic primitive church.

(a) Effects of the liturgical use. The liturgical use of the words of institution

529

becomes apparent in the explicit command to repeat the act (Lk. 22:19), and its doubling for the sake of liturgical parallelism (1 Cor. 11:24, 25), in the adding of imperatives like "eat", "drink" (Matt. 26:26 f.), in the replacement of the third person "for the many" (Mk. 14:24) by the second person "for you" (Lk. 22:20), which narrows down the universal reference of the saying about the cup (Jesus' substitutionary death for the many) to a formula of distribution, in the avoidance of Aramaisms and Semitisms, which were incomprehensible to Gentile Christians, and not least in the disappearance of the historical features of the Passover meal, which were incompatible with the liturgy of the primitive church and the regular celebration of the Lord's Supper (cf. J. Jeremias, *TDNT* VI 543; → All, Many, art. *polloi*).

(i) In Acts 2:42 a liturgy of primitive Christian worship is described (J. Jeremias, *The Eucharistic Words of Jesus*, 118 ff.). After teaching, in place of which a letter could be read, and a common meal (*koinōnia*), there followed closely the Lord's Supper (*klasis tou artou*, "breaking of bread"), which was concluded with psalms and prayers (*proseuchai*). The liturgical development is visible in the fact that the sayings over the bread and the cup are no longer, as in the Pauline version (1 Cor. 11:25 "after supper"; cf. Lk. 22:20), separated by a whole meal, but that the meal proper precedes the Lord's Supper which is therefore self-contained (cf. the absence of the phrase "after supper" in Mk. and Matt.). The separation of the meal from the Lord's Supper is also assumed in 1 Cor. 11. It is here that the direct cause of the Corinthian abuses lies.

(ii) Parts of the introductory liturgy to the celebration of the primitive Christian meal are to be found in 1 Cor. 11:26 ff.; 16:20–22; and Rev. 22:17–21. Paul concludes 1 Cor. with a series of liturgical phrases – the invitation to the holy kiss, the anathema against those who do not love the Lord, and the Maranatha (1 Cor. 16:20–22) – which originate in the introductory liturgy to the Lord's Supper which will have followed closely on the reading of the apostle's letter to the assembled congregation and on the holy kiss (1 Cor. 16:20; Rom. 16:16; cf. G. Bornkamm, op. cit., 147 ff.). The anathema at the beginning of the celebration of the meal excluded the unworthy from the Lord's Supper (1 Cor. 16:22a). To strengthen this there followed the Maranatha (1 Cor. 16:22b), which called upon the *kyrios* to be present ("Our Lord, come!"; cf. Rev. 22:20). Even if the church with this call, "Our Lord, come!" was praying for the Lord's eschatological coming, this did not exclude the presence of the exalted Lord at the Lord's Supper, but rather assumed it (P. Vielhauer, *Aufsätze zum Neuen Testament*, 159 f., 175; K. G. Kuhn, *maranatha*, *TDNT* IV 466–73). The *achri hou elthē* ("until he comes") of 1 Cor. 11:26 clearly reflects the Maranatha of the Lord's Supper liturgy (J. Schniewind, *TDNT* I 72 n. 25; G. Bornkamm, op. cit., 148), and probably represents a re-modelling of this cry. Similar phrases from the introductory liturgy occur in Rev. 22:17–21 (E. Lohmeyer, *Die Offenbarung des Johannes*, HNT 16, 1970[3], ad loc.) and in Did. 10:6, where the use in a Hellenistic tradition of the Aramaic invocation Maranatha confirms its primary eucharistic setting. The holy kiss, the formulae of threat and exclusion and the invocations of the coming and present *kyrios* are thus the essential elements of the introductory liturgy of the Lord's Supper.

(b) Pre-liturgical elements in the tradition of the Lord's Supper. The tradition of the words of institution is not, as it stands, simply a historical account but a

530

liturgical text, which mentions only the points which are essential for the celebration of the Lord's Supper in the church. Nevertheless, the tradition of the institution of the Lord's Supper implies a pre-liturgical stage in the tradition which could not be fully assimilated into the liturgy itself.

(i) The historically probable information given by the Synoptics, which describes Jesus' Last Supper as a Passover meal, diverges from the rite of the primitive church, for there is not the slightest evidence that the Lord's Supper was ever celebrated as a Passover, only once a year (J. Jeremias, op. cit., 66; W. Marxsen, *EKL* I 4). Rather, the original Passover motifs were removed in the light of the regular celebration of the Lord's Supper. In primitive Christian usage, therefore, there is no ground for a subsequent interpretation of the Lord's Supper as a Passover meal (K. G. Kuhn, *EvTh* 11/12, 1950–51, 522).

(ii) While in Mk. the eschatological perspective is included in the words of institution (14:25), in Lk. it occurs before them (Lk. 22:18) and in Paul an echo of it is heard in his own explanatory phrase, *achri hou elthē* "until he comes" (1 Cor. 11:26), which may also imply an assurance of the fulfilment of this hope (cf. O. Hofius, "Bis dass er kommt," *NTS* 14, 1967–68, 439 ff.). It is no accident that the eschatological perspective (Mk. 14:25) should no longer appear in direct association with the words of institution, either in Lk. or Paul. Since it had moved, as 1 Cor. 16:22; Rev. 22:20; and Did. 10:6 attest, into the introductory liturgy, its continuing position after the words of institution (Mk. 14:25) did not fit very well into the liturgical formulation of the Lord's Supper (G. Bornkamm, op. cit., 151; F. Hahn, *EvTh* 27, 1967, 340). In Did. 10:5 the congregation celebrating the meal prays that God will perfect the church and gather it into the → kingdom; in Did. 10:6 there follow invocations referring to the parousia, and the Maranatha (→ Present, art. *maranatha*). The placing of the eschatological perspective in the Marcan tradition after the words of institution indicates a stage which does not correspond to the liturgy of the Lord's Supper in the primitive church. It should therefore be accepted as original.

(iii) While Mk. and Matt. associate the identification of the traitor with the preliminary course (Matt. 26:20–25; Mk. 14:17–21) in Lk. the prophecy of the betrayal (Lk. 22:21–23) follows on the celebration of the Lord's Supper (Lk. 22:15–20). Here the Lucan order is probably older and indicates a preliturgical stage; placing the identification of the traitor first not only shows theological reflection (the traitor must not participate in the Lord's Supper), but also liturgical influence, i.e. the order in Mk. corresponds to the formulae of threat and exclusion at the beginning of the primitive Christian Lord's Supper (cf. 1 Cor. 11:27; 16:20a; Did. 10:6).

The tradition of the words of institution, therefore, certainly reflects the Lord's Supper liturgy of the primitive church, but it equally points back to a pre-liturgical stage in the tradition.

6. *The principal theological ideas of the Lord's Supper.* A theological interpretation must begin with the original form of the words of institution. From there follows the process of development in the history of the tradition. Finally we must consider the main theological ideas which arise in connection with it.

(a) The original form. (i) To understand the saying about the bread it is important to establish the Aram. equivalent of *sōma* (→ body). J. Jeremias posits behind

531

the Gk. *sōma*/*haima* (body/blood) the Aram. *biśrā'*/*d^emā'* (flesh/blood). His translation is determined by the consideration that "flesh" and "blood" are frequently used as a complementary pair in sacrificial language. Hence, he concludes that, when Jesus spoke of body and blood, he was referring to the flesh and blood of the Passover → lamb and thereby described himself as the true Passover lamb. But since "body and blood" was not a current pair of complementary terms (E. Lohse, *Märtyrer und Gottesknecht*, 124 f.), the original form of the words of institution did not connect "body" and "blood", but "my body" and "my dying for [the] many". Since there is in fact no record that Jesus ever referred to himself as the Passover lamb, the Aram. equivalent for *sōma* should probably be *gupā'* ("body", "self", "I"; cf. J. Behm, *TDNT* III 736; G. Dalman, *Jesus-Jeshua*, 1929, 142; E. Schweizer, *TDNT* VIII 1059). The words spoken at the distribution of the bread, "this is my body" (Mk. 14:22c), mean therefore: This is myself; with this bread I am giving myself. If Jesus, then, explained the distribution of the broken bread with the words "this is myself" (a parabolic action), it means that as the disciples received the bread they received a share in Jesus' surrender of himself.

(ii) This self-surrender of Jesus, already expressed in the words over the bread, was included in the words over the cup, "this is my blood shed for [the] many" (Mk. 14:24b). There are frequent references to the shedding of → blood in the OT (cf. Gen. 9:6 etc.), in Rabbinic Judaism (examples in Dalman, op. cit., 159 f.) and in the NT (cf. Matt. 23:25 etc.), whenever the subject is violent death or the surrender of life. The oldest version of the saying about the cup therefore means that Jesus' blood is shed, i.e. his life is surrendered. "This is my dying for [the] many", therefore, like Mk. 10:45 and 1 Cor. 15:3, interprets the death of Jesus in the context of Isa. 53:11 f. as a substitutionary, atoning death, which includes the universal "[the] many". Jesus' self-surrender (the saying over the bread) is his substitutionary death for the many (the saying over the cup). The fact that the Lord's Supper was a (prophetic) parabolic action has the following consequence. In the distribution of the broken bread and the red wine the reality which they represent occurs and is repeated. The disciples received a share in Jesus' vicarious self-surrender for the many which was accomplished in the surrender of his life.

(iii) The eschatological perspective (Mk. 14:25) gave the Lord's Supper a future reference. As Jesus, by the distribution of the bread and wine, took his disciples into communion with himself and into participation in the universal atoning power of his death, he thereby placed them already within the sphere of the coming of the reign of God (→ Kingdom). In a solemn declaration of his will, in the form of an oath, Jesus promised the consummation of salvation and assured his disciples that this would be his last meal with them before the meal at the consummation. His substitutionary atoning death for the universal "many", in which the disciples participated in the Lord's Supper, also made them participants in the sovereignty of God breaking in among men. When this had been fully realized, Jesus would once again, as head of the household, break the blessed bread for his people and pass round the cup of blessing (J. Jeremias, op. cit., 233 ff.; for the eschatological meal cf. e.g. Isa. 25:6; 65:13; Eth.Enoch 62:14).

(b) The development in the history of the tradition. When we turn to the form the tradition takes in the successive strata of the NT, we get the following picture.

(i) Mark. Since the phrase "my blood of the covenant" (14:24) is supposed to be impossible in Aram., the Marcan version of these words, "this is my blood of the covenant, which is poured out for [the] many" (14:24), has been thought to belong in the realm of Hellenistic Jewish Christianity. But, since the → covenant is mentioned in all the versions of the tradition of the Lord's Supper (Mk., Matt., Paul, Lk.), it must be very early. The words of institution in the Lord's Supper were linked with the concept of the covenant. The self-surrender of Jesus (explicit in the original form) as a substitutionary death for the many now underwent closer definition through the covenant concept. The phrase "blood of the covenant" echoes the words of Exod. 24:8 LXX (cf. Zech. 9:11; Heb. 9:20; 10:29; 13:20), and makes a typological reference to the blood of the covenant sprinkled at Sinai. As the covenant on Sinai was then confirmed with the blood of sacrificial animals, the conclusion of the new covenant is now made effective through the blood of Jesus. Not only was a correspondence intended, however, but also a development. The sacrifice that was offered on Sinai to confirm the covenant long ago had no ultimate, atoning, sin-erasing power (Exod. 24:3–8). The substitutionary death of Christ, on the contrary, is superior to all the sacrifices of the old covenant. His death inaugurates the eschatological order or covenant of salvation (E. Lohse, *Geschichte des Leidens und Sterbens Jesu Christi*, 1964, 56).

(ii) The additions in the version handed down in Matt. may be explained by liturgical practice. They are the invitation "eat" (Matt. 26:26), the re-writing of the Marcan statement, "and they all drank of it" (Mk. 14:23); which comes, remarkably, before the words of institution over the cup, as an imperative (Matt. 26:27b) and the expansion of the conclusion of the words over the cup to "for the forgiveness of sins" (Matt. 26:28b), a formula perhaps originating in the baptismal liturgy (Mk. 1:4; cf. Matt. 3:6; Acts 2:38; J. Jeremias, op. cit., 173; cf. E. Schweizer, *RGG*[3] I 13). Moreover, the Matthaean form, with the epexegetic addition *eis aphesin hamartiōn*, "for the forgiveness of sins", is also evidence of a theological interpretation developing from Exod. 24:8 to Jer. 31:31–34. The covenant which is brought into effect, like the Sinai covenant, by the blood of Jesus, but which at the same time is superior to the Sinai covenant because of the substitutionary death of Christ (Mk.), is a covenant of the → forgiveness of → sins (Matt.). The fellowship with God established by Jesus' death, in which the coming rule of God dawns, is identical with the forgiveness of sins (Jer. 31:34b). Matt., therefore, gives an interpretation of the order of salvation established in Jesus' death as the gift of the forgiveness of sins. The Lord's Supper is a present expression of that forgiveness.

(iii) The Pauline version reveals a stage of advancing Gk. influence in the avoidance of Semitisms and of liturgical formulation (the command to repeat is doubled; for *anamnēsis* → Remember, art. *mimnēskomai*). In it the statement about atonement was associated with the words over the bread ("this is my body for you"), while the covenant idea qualified only the words over the cup. This covenant is described as the "new" covenant, and is thus understood as the fulfilment of the prophetic promise of the new covenant (Jer. 31:31 ff.). It may be paraphrased: This cup is the new covenant on the basis of my blood (1 Cor. 11:25). When they drink from the cup, those who celebrate the Lord's Supper participate in the new order of salvation, founded by God in Christ's death. The church thus experiences the present validity of the new covenant (Jer. 31:31 ff.), established in the death of the *kyrios* (Exod. 24:8). And when the assembled congregation eats the broken bread, they receive a share in the Lord who was delivered up to death for them. But here *sōma* (→ Body) is not thought of as substance but means the very person (cf. G. Bornkamm, op. cit., 145).

Paul's own view is most clearly expressed in 1 Cor. 10:17, "Because there is one loaf" (which gives us a share in Christ, who was delivered up to death as our substitute), "we who are many are one body," i.e. the body of Christ as a community. For Paul, Christ delivered up for us, whom we receive in the bread, automatically includes the church as the body of Christ, the church in which we are included through the Lord's Supper. Paul's particular concern, therefore, is the relationship between the Lord's Supper and the church; for him the christological concept of the body implies the ecclesiastical one as well (G. Bornkamm, op. cit., 144).

It is possible that the Corinthian abuses arose, because the Lord's Supper was conceived as granting the individual participant the food of immortality. Hence, its meaning as the basis of the body of Christ, uniting those sharing in it together as its members, was missed. Church-members from the slave class were apt to arrive too late and could therefore no longer take part in the table-fellowship of the meal proper (1 Cor. 11:21); only the sacrament itself remained for them. But if in the celebration of the Lord's Supper the one body of Christ is actualized, any Lord's Supper which does not achieve real table-fellowship (11:20) is exposed as an abuse (G. Bornkamm, op. cit., 122–30, 154 ff.; cf. E. Schweizer, *RGG*³ I 11).

(iv) In comparison with the Marcan form and even with Paul, Lk. reveals clear signs of a developing liturgical influence. In the interests of liturgical parallelism the eschatological perspective was attached to the words over the bread too (note the twofold eschatological utterances, Lk. 22:16, 18), which results in a parallelism between the twofold eschatological utterances (vv. 16, 18) and the words of institution (vv. 19, 20). Its appearance before the words of institution was no doubt determined by the fact that the eschatological theme stood at the centre of the Jewish-Christian Passover Haggadah. This comment is based on the view held by a number of scholars (e.g. B. Lohse, *Das Passahfest der Quartadezimaner*, 1953, 62 f.; J. Jeremias, *TDNT* V 896–904; and op. cit., 122 ff.; F. Hahn, *EvTh* 27, 1967, 352 ff.), that Lk. 22:15–20 mirrors the liturgy of a Jewish-Christian Passover celebration. The latter included vicarious fasting at night for → Israel, the expectation of the Parousia on Passover night and the celebration of the Lord's Supper about 3 a.m. at the end of the period of fasting. It is here also, probably, that we find the setting for the interpretation of Christ as the eschatological Passover lamb (1 Cor. 5:7), which is typologically contrasted with the Passover lambs of the exodus and is the theological reason for the renunciation of the eating of the Passover lamb in the primitive church (cf. Jesus' explanations of his renunciation according to Lk. 22:16, 18).

(v) Jn. is the only Gospel which does not give an account of the Lord's Supper in the context of Jesus' last meal (13:1–30). Jn. 6 refers to eating Christ's flesh and drinking his blood after telling of the feeding of the five thousand (6:51–58). R. Bultmann (*The Gospel of John*, 1971, 209 f., 234–7) and G. Bornkamm (*ZNW* 47, 1956, 161 ff.) consider that vv. 51c–58 are editorial additions by the church to John's Gospel. But E. Ruckstuhl (*Die literarische Einheit des Johannesevangeliums*, 1951, 149, 164, 266), J. Jeremias (*ZNW* 44, 1952–53, 256 f.), E. Schweizer (*Neotestamentica*, 1963, 371 ff.), and L. Goppelt (*TDNT* VIII 236 f.) support the literary unity of the discourse on the bread and feeding on Christ. However, Jn. 6:51c may be a late version of Jesus' words of institution of the bread: This (bread) is my flesh (*sarx*), (which I give) for the life of the world. If the introduction of the idea of the covenant in Hellenistic Jewish Christianity (Mk. 14:24) resulted in the Church's seeing Jesus' death as an atoning and a covenant sacrifice, in Jn. (6:51 ff.) we now have the first appearance of the pair of terms, *sarx/haima* (flesh/blood), as the logical conclusion of the use of the language of sacrifice. It is thought that Jn. also betrays a later stage of development by speaking of eating (lit. chewing) the flesh and drinking the blood (*ho trōgōn mou tēn sarka kai pinōn mou to haima*, "He who eats my flesh and drinks my blood"). It thus made a close connection between the elements in the meal and the component parts of the person of Christ. However, eating the flesh and drinking the blood must not, according to Jn., be misunderstood in a literal and sacramental sense, for v. 63 clearly shows that Jn. is thinking of the personal presence of Christ spiritually through his word, and his self-offering in word and sacrament through faith (6:35, 47, 54). But then the reference to eating the flesh, etc., is in an anti-docetic setting and is intended to emphasize the "scandal of the full incarnation." "Thus in Jn., so to speak, the Lord's Supper holds fast to Jesus' fleshly form and prevents it . . . evaporating to become a mere idea of Christ" (E. Schweizer, *RGG*[3] I 12). For John "eating the flesh" and "drinking the blood" of the Son of man is the continuing sign of participation in his life by faith and to share in it is to continue to acknowledge the full reality of the incarnation of the divine Logos.

([Ed.] It is commonly assumed that Jn. 6 is about the Lord's Supper, even though there is no hint in the text itself to any form of meal, liturgical or otherwise. Notwithstanding, it is repeatedly called a eucharistic discourse, even though there is no reference to the eucharist or to the Last Supper. Yet there is at least a *prima facie* case for saying the reverse. Jn. 6 is not about the Lord's Supper; rather, the Lord's Supper is about what is described in Jn. 6. It concerns that eating and drinking which is belief in Christ (6:35), which is eternal life (6:54), and which in other words is described as abiding in him (6:56). The discourse in Jn. 6 represents these activities as central to faith and to men's relationship with Jesus. They are not confined to a sacramental meal. They belong to the very essence of day-to-day relationships. In presenting this discourse and omitting an account of the institution of the Lord's Supper, Jn. is, in effect, saying that the whole of the Christian life should be characterized by this kind of feeding on Christ and that this is what the sacramental meal of the church is really about. In his account of Jesus' last meal with his disciples Jn. gives prominence to the feet-washing with the reminder, "If I then, your Lord and Teacher, have washed your feet, you also ought to wash one another's feet. . . . Truly, truly, I say to you, he who receives any one whom I send receives me; and he who receives me receives him who sent me" [Jn. 13; 14, 20].)

(c) The principal theological ideas in the words of institution. While the original form of the words of institution in Aram. contained the idea of Jesus' self-offering (Mk. 14:22), his substitutionary death for the many (Mk. 14:24), and the eschatological reference to the coming of the → kingdom of God (14:25) at its centre, in Hellenistic Jewish Christianity (Mk.) the reference to the covenant was added to the words over the cup (Mk. 14:24). Jesus' death is an atoning covenant sacrifice which inaugurates the eschatological era of salvation. Matt. (26:28) interpreted the fellowship with God set up by the covenant sacrifice as the forgiveness of sins (Jer. 31:34b). In Paul (and Lk.), for the sake of balance, the reference to atonement was transferred from the Marcan words over the cup to those over the bread (1 Cor. 11:24; Lk. 22:19), so that the words over the cup are now qualified by the reference to the covenant based on Jer. 31:31 ff. (1 Cor. 11:25; Lk. 22:20). Paul for his part, in opposition to Corinthian sacramentalism, laid his emphasis on the indissoluble link between the Lord's Supper and the church (Christ delivered up for us constitutes the church as the → body of Christ; 1 Cor. 10:16), while Jn., in an anti-gnostic confrontation, stressed the connection between eating Christ's flesh and drinking his blood and the incarnation.

([F. F. Bruce] That the covenant idea first entered into the transmitted words of institution in the Greek-speaking phase of primitive Christianity is highly improbable. The covenant idea is thoroughly Hebraic, and in any case one should treat with profound scepticism the suggestion that it was impossible to formulate in Aramaic certain expressions, such as "This is my covenant blood" or "This blood of mine is the blood of the covenant".)

The references to the covenant (Mk.) and to forgiveness (Matt.), as well as the ecclesiastical (Paul) and the anti-docetic (Jn.) emphases, embrace and actualize by a process of continuous reinterpretation the essential significance of the event of Jesus' self-offering and of his universal substitutionary death (Mk. 14:24). They underline the following aspects of the Lord's Supper: (i) The proclamation of the substitutionary self-offering of Jesus and the guarantee of the final eschatological banquet (original form). (ii) Participation in God's order of salvation, set up by Jesus' death as a covenant sacrifice (Mk.). (iii) An assurance of the forgiveness of sins (Matt.). (iv) Incorporation into the new covenant and the founding of the Church as the body of Christ (Paul). (v) The proclamation of the incarnation of the Logos, in which the Son's self-offering is accomplished (Jn.). All this is actualized and given in the Lord's Supper only because the risen Christ is present there. And in so far as the crucified and risen *kyrios* offers himself in the meal, the grace conveyed by the Lord's Supper is Jesus Christ. He himself makes his presence real as the Supper is celebrated and thus makes it the *Lord's* Supper. *B. Klappert*
→ Blood, → Body, → Bread, → Feast, → Hunger, → Present

(a). J. J. von Allmen, *Worship: Its Theology and Practice*, 1965; G. Aulén, *Eucharist and Sacrifice*, 1958; W. Barclay, *The Lord's Supper*, 1967; N. A. Beck, "The Last Supper as an Efficacious Symbolic Act", *JBL* 89, 1970, 192–98; J. Behm, *haima, haimatekchysia*, *TDNT* I 172–77; *deipnon, deipneō, TDNT* II 34 f.; and "Vom urchristlichen Abendmahl", *ThR* Neue Folge 9, 1937, 168 ff., 273 ff.; 10, 1938, 81 ff.; M. Black, *The Scrolls and Christian Origins*, 1961, 91 ff., 199 ff.; G. Bornkamm, "The Anathema in the Early Christian Lord's Supper Liturgy", *Early Christian Experience*, 1969, 169–76; and "Lord's Supper and Church in Paul", ibid., 123–60; R. E. Brown, "The Eucharist and Baptism in John", *New Testament Essays*, 1965, 77–95; O. Cullmann, *Early Christian Worship*, 1953; *The Christology of the New Testament*, 1963²; O. Cullmann and F. J. Leenhardt, *Essays on the Lord's Supper*, 1958; J. D. G. Dunn, "John vi – A Eucharistic Discourse?", *NTS* 17, 1970–71, 328–38; W. Elert, *Eucharist and Church Fellowship in the First Four Centuries*, 1966; A. Farrer, "The Eucharist in I Corinthians", in *Eucharistic Theology Then and Now*, SPCK Theological Collections, 1968, 15–33; R. H. Fuller, "The Double Origin of the Eucharist", *Biblical Research*, 7, 1963, 60 ff.; B. Gärtner, *John 6 and the Jewish Passover*, Coniectanea Neotestamentica 7, 1959; A. Gilmore, "The Date and Significance of the Last Supper", *SJT* 14, 1961, 256 ff.; L. Goppelt, *potērion, TDNT* VI 148–59; and *trōgō, TDNT* VIII 236 ff.; F. Hahn, *The Titles of Jesus in Christology: Their History in Early Christianity*, 1969; A. J. B. Higgins, *The Lord's Supper in the*

New Testament, SBT 6, 1952; N. Hook, The Eucharist in the New Testament, 1964; J. K. Howard, "Passover and Eucharist in the Fourth Gospel", SJT 20, 1967, 329–37; J. C. Hurd, Jr., The Origin of I Corinthians, 1965; A. Jaubert, The Date of the Last Supper, 1965; J. Jeremias, pascha, TDNT V 896–904; polloi, TDNT VI 536–45; and The Eucharistic Words of Jesus, 1966²; E. Käsemann, "The Pauline Doctrine of the Lord's Supper", Essays on New Testament Themes, 1964, 108–35; J. F. Keating, The Agape and the Eucharist in the Early Church, (1901) 1969; E. J. Kilmartin, The Eucharist in the Primitive Church, 1965; W. Kramer, Christ, Lord, Son of God, 1966; K. G. Kuhn, maranatha, TDNT IV 466–72; and "The Lord's Supper and the Communal Meal at Qumran", in K. Stendahl, ed., The Scrolls and the New Testament, 1958, 65–93; N. Lash, His Presence in the World: A Study of Eucharistic Worship and Theology, 1968; P. E. Leonard, Luke's Account of the Lord's Supper against the Background of Meals in the Ancient Semitic World and more particularly Meals in the Gospel of Luke, Dissertation, Manchester, 1976; H. Lietzmann, Mass and the Lord's Supper: A Study in the History of the Liturgy, with introduction and supplementary essay by R. D. Richardson, to be published in 11 fascicles, 1953–; E. Lohmeyer, The Lord of the Temple: A Study of the Relation between Cult and Temple, 1961; R. P. Martin, Worship in the Early Church, 1975²; W. Marxsen, The Lord's Supper as a Christological Problem, 1970; and "The Lord's Supper: Concepts and Developments", in H. J. Schultz, ed., Jesus in His Time, 1971; C. F. D. Moule, Worship in the New Testament, 1961; G. Ogg, "The Chronology of the Last Supper", in Historicity and Chronology in the New Testament, SPCK Theological Collections 6, 1965, 75–96; E. Ruckstuhl, Chronology of the Last Days of Jesus, 1965; E. Schweizer, sōma etc., TDNT VII 1024–94; and The Lord's Supper according to the New Testament, 1967; A. Shaw, "The Breakfast by the Shore and the Mary Magdalene Encounter as Eucharistic Narratives", JTS New Series 25, 1974, 12–26; A. Stöger, "Eucharist", EBT I 227–41; V. Taylor, Jesus and his Sacrifice, 1965⁶, 114 ff., 175 ff., 201 ff., 236 ff.; and "The New Testament Origins of Holy Communion", in New Testament Essays, 1970, 48–59; J. Wilkinson, The Supper and the Eucharist, 1965; R. Williamson, "The Eucharist and the Epistle to the Hebrews", NTS 21, 1974–75, 300–12.

(b). L. Aalen, "Der Kampf um das Evangelium im Abendmahl", TLZ 91, 1966, 81 ff.; A. Adam, "Ein vergessener Aspekt des frühchristlichen Herrenmahls", TLZ 88, 1963, 9 ff.; J.-P. Audet, "Esquisse historique du genre littéraire de la 'bénédiction' juive et de 'l'eucharistie' Chrétienne", RB 65, 1958, 371–99; F. Bammel, Das heilige Mahl im Glauben der Völker, 1950; F. Bammel and G. Fohrer, "Mahlzeiten", RGG³ IV 605 ff.; M. Barth, Das Abendmahl, Passamahl, Bundesmahl und Messiasmahl, TheolStud 18, 1945; J. Betz, Die Eucharistie in der Zeit der griechischen Väter, I, 1, 1955; and LTK III 1159–62; E. Bizer and W. Kreck, Die Abendmahlslehre in den reformatorischen Bekenntnissen, ThEH Neue Folge, 47 1957; G. Bornkamm, "Die eucharistische Rede im Johannesevangelium", ZNW 47, 1956, 161 ff.; M. Brändle, Jesu letztes Mahl im Lichte von Qumran, 1957, 111 ff., 121 ff.; G. Delling, "Das Abendmahlsgeschehen nach Paulus", KuD 10, 1964, 61 ff.; E. Gaugler, Das Abendmahl im Neuen Testament, Gegenwartsfragen Biblischer Theologie, 2, 1943; H. Gollwitzer, Coena Domini, 1937, L. Goppelt, Typos, 1967², 131 ff., 173 ff.; F. Hahn, "Die alttestamentlichen Motive in der urchristlichen Abendmahlsüberlieferung", EvTh 27, 1967, 337–74; O. Hofius, "Bis das er kommt", NTS 14, 1967–68, 439 ff.; B. van Iersel, "Die wunderbare Speisung und das Abendmahl in der synoptischen Tradition", NovT 7, 1964, 167 ff.; A. Jaubert, "Jésus et le calendrier de Qumran", NTS 7, 1960–61, 1–30; O. Koch, Gegenwart oder Vergegenwärtigung Christi im Abendmahl, 1965; H. Kosmala, "Das tut zu meinem Gedächtnis", NovT 4, 1960, 81 ff.; K. G. Kuhn, "Die Abendmahlsworte", TLZ 75, 1950, 399 ff.; and "Über den ursprünglichen Sinn des Abendmahls", EvTh 11/12, 1950–51, 508 ff.; F. J. Leenhardt, "L'Eucharistie dans le Nouveau Testament", Lumière et Vie 31, 1957; H. Lietzmann, An die Korinther, I, II, HNT 9, 1949⁴; E. Lohmeyer, "Das Abendmahl in der Urgemeinde", JBL 56, 1937, 246 ff.; and "Vom urchristlichen Abendmahl", ThR Neue Folge 9, 1937, 168 ff., 273 ff.; 10, 1938, 81 ff.; E. Lohse, Märtyrer und Gottesknecht, 1963²; "Wort und Sakrament im Johannesevangelium", NTS 7, 1960–61, 110 ff.; and Geschichte des Leidens und Sterbens Jesu Christi, 1964; W. Marxsen, "Der Ursprung des Abendmahls", EvTh 12, 1952–53, 293 ff.; and "Abendmahl", EKL I 4 ff.; J. M. Nielen, "Die Eucharistiefeier der ältesten Christenheit nach den Aussagen des Neuen Testaments", BuK 15, 1960, 43 ff.; P. Neuenzeit, Das Herrenmahl, Studien zur paulinischen Eucharistieauffasung, 1960; P. Philippi, Abendmahlsfeier und Wirklichkeit der Gemeinde, 1960; M. Rese, "Zur Problematik von Kurz- und Langtext in Luk. xxii 17 ff.", NTS 22, 1975–76, 15–31; F. Reitschel, "Der Sinn des Abendmahls nach Paulus", EcTh 18, 1958, 269 ff.; E. Ruckstuhl, "Wesen und Kraft der Eucharistie in der Sicht des Johannesevangeliums", Opfer der Kirche, 1954,

47–90; H. Schürmann, *Der Paschamahlbericht Lk. 22, (7–14) 15–18*, 1953; *Der Einzetsungsbericht Lk. 22, 19–20, NTAbh* 20, 4, 1955; "Die Gestalt der urchristlichen Eucharistiefeier", *Münchener Theologische Zeitschrift* 6, 1955, 107–31; *Jesu Abschiedsrede Lk. 22, 21–38*, 1957; *Die Abendmahlsbericht Lk. 22, 7–38*, 1957; and "Die Eucharistie als Repräsentation und Applikation nach Joh. 6, 53–58", *Trierer Theologische Zeitschrift* 68, 1959, 30–45, 108–18; R. Schnackenburg, "Die Sakramente im Johannesevangelium", *Sacra Pagina* 2, 1959, 239–43; E. Schweizer, "Das Herrenmahl, eine Vergenwärtigung des Todes Jesu oder ein eschatologisches Freudenmahl?", *ThZ* 2, 1946, 81 ff.; "Das johanneische Zeugnis vom Herrenmahl", *EvTh* 12, 1952–53, 341 ff. (reprinted in *Neotestamentica: Deutsche und englische Aufsätze, 1951–1963*, 1963, 371–96); "Das Herrenmahl im Neuen Testament, ein Forschungsbericht", *TLZ* 79, 1954, 577 ff. (*Neotestamentica*, 1963, 344–70); and "Abendmahl", *RGG*³ I 10 ff.; E. M. Skibbe, "Das Proprium des Abendmahls", *KuD* 10, 1964, 78 ff.; A. Stöger, *Brot des Lebens*, 1955; and "Die Eucharistiefeier des Neuen Testaments", *Eucharistiefeiern der Christenheit*, 1960, 10–19; P. Vielhauer, "Ein Weg zur neutestamentlichen Christologie? Prüfung der Thesen Ferdinand Hahns", *Aufsätze zum Neuen Testament*, 1965, 141–98; G. Walther, *Jesus das Passalamm des neuen Bundes*, 1950; W. Wilkens, "Das Abendmahlszeugnis im 4. Evangelium", *EvTh* 18, 1958, 354 ff.

Love

What we describe as love is differentiated in Gk. by various expressions (for details → *agapaō* CL). *phileō* is the most commonly used word, indicating a general attraction towards a person or thing. In the foreground stands the meaning of love for one's relatives and friends (cf. the typical formation of *philadelphia*, love for a brother; → Brother, art. *adelphos*), but the whole area of fondness is also included with gods, men and things as possible objects. *philia* accordingly, denotes love, friendship, devotion, favour; and *philos* is a relative or friend. By contrast *erōs* is love which desires to have or take possession. *agapaō*, originally meaning to honour or welcome, is in classical Gk. the least specifically defined word; it is frequently used synonymously with *phileō* without any necessarily strict distinction in meaning. In the NT, however, *agapaō* and the noun *agapē* have taken on a particular significance in that they are used to speak of the love of God or the way of life based on it.

ἀγαπάω

ἀγαπάω (*agapaō*), love; ἀγάπη (*agapē*), love; ἀγαπητός (*agapētos*), loved, beloved; ἐράω (*eraō*), love passionately, desire, yearn; ἔρως (*erōs*), passionate love; φιλόστοργος (*philostorgos*), tenderly loving, affectionate; ἄστοργος (*astorgos*), without natural affection.

CL In contradistinction to Eng., extra-biblical Gk. has quite a number of words for love and to love; the most important being → *phileō, stergō, eraō* and *agapaō*.

1. *phileō* is the most general word for love or regard with affection. The many derivative words show this clearly: e.g., *philos*, a friend; *philēma*, a kiss; and compound words such as *philosophia*, love of knowledge, philosophy (→ wisdom); *philoxenia*, hospitality (→ Foreign, art. *xenos*); and proper names like *Philippos* (lit. lover of horses, horse-lover). *phileō* mainly denotes the attraction of people to one another who are close together both inside and outside the family; it includes concern, care and hospitality, also love for things in the sense of being fond of. Ideas related to *phileo* do not have a clear religious emphasis.

2. The less frequent vb. *stergō* means to love, feel affection, especially of the mutual love of parents and children. It can also be used of the love of a people for their ruler, the love of a tutelary god for the people, and even of dogs for their master. It is less common for the love of husband and wife, and does not occur at all in the NT, apart from the compounds *astorgos* (Rom. 1:31; 2 Tim. 3:3) and *philostorgos* (Rom. 12:10). It is, however, found in some early Christian writings (e.g. 1 Clem. 1:3; Polycarp 4:2).

3. The vb. *eraō* and the noun *erōs*, on the other hand, denote the love between man and woman which embraces longing, craving and desire. The Greeks' delight in bodily beauty and sensual desires found expression here in the Dionysiac approach to, and feeling for, life. Sensual ecstasy leaves moderation and proportion far behind, and the Gk. tragedians (e.g. Soph., *Ant.* 781 ff.) knew the irresistible power of Eros – the god of love bore the same name – which forgot all reason, will and discretion on the way to ecstasy.

There was also a more mystical understanding of *erōs*, whereby the Greeks sought to reach and go beyond normal human limitations in order to attain perfection. As well as the fertility cults with their oriental influences, and their glorification of the generating Eros in nature, there were the mystery religions, whose rites were intended to unite the participant with the godhead. Here spiritual and psychical unity with the god came into the foreground more and more, however much erotic pictures and symbols were used. Plato sought to raise spiritual love above the physical. *erōs* for him was the striving for righteousness, self-possession and wisdom; it is the embodiment of the good, the way to attain immortality (*Symp.* 200, 206; *Phaedr.* 237 ff., 242 ff.). In Aristotle (*Met.* 12, 7p, 1072a, 27 f.) the concept was further developed in this direction, and in Plotinus (A.D. 205–c. 269) the mystical aspiration towards spiritual union with the transcendental dominates (*Enneads* 5, 5, 8; 6, 8, 15). In the early Christian era *gnōsis* (→ Knowledge) found its place in this approach, giving its own particular slant to the human desire for self-transcendence.

4. The etymology of *agapaō* and *agapē* is not clear. The vb. *agapaō* appears frequently from Homer onwards in Gk. literature, but the noun *agapē* is only a late Gk. construction. Only one reference has been found outside the Bible, where the goddess Isis is given the title *agapē* (*P.Oxy.* 1380, 109; 2nd cent. A.D.).

agapaō in Gk. is often quite colourless as a word, appearing frequently as an alternative to, or a synonym with, *eraō* and *phileō*, meaning to be fond of, treat respectfully, be pleased with, welcome. When, on rare occasions, it refers to someone favoured by a god (cf. Dio. Chrys., *Orationes* 33, 21), it is clear that, unlike *eraō*, it is not the man's own longing for possessions or worth that is meant, but a generous move by one for the sake of the other. This is expressed above all in the way *agapētos* is used, mostly of a child, but particularly of an only child to whom all the love of his parents is given.

ot In the LXX *agapaō* is used by preference to translate the Heb. vb. *'āhēḇ*. The noun *agapē* finds its origin here, in standing for Heb. *'ah\u1eb3ḇâh*. The vb. occurs far more frequently than the noun. *'āhēḇ* can refer to both persons and things, and denotes first men's relationships with each other, and secondly God's relationship with man.

1. (a) Love and hate represent for the Eastern sensibility two of the basic polarized attitudes to life. The phenomenon of love in the OT is experienced as a spontaneous force which drives one to something or someone over against itself. Love means the vital urge of the sexes for one another. The prophets Hosea (3:1; 4:18), Jeremiah (2:25) and Ezekiel (16:37) were not at all ashamed to speak of the sexual side of love. The powerful perception of the differentiation of the sexes and of marital love as an enriching gift does not only derive from the creation stories (Gen. 2:18 ff.), but even more from Cant., which celebrates the strength of passionate love. "Love is strong as death, jealousy is as cruel as the grave. Its flashes are flashes of fire, a most vehement flame" (Cant. 8:6).

(b) But as well as the relationship between the sexes, the blood relationship with father and mother and the spiritual bond between friends can also be love. (It is not possible in Heb. to distinguish between *eraō* and *agapaō*.) Thus, when the love of Jonathan and David for one another is spoken of (1 Sam. 18:1, 3; 20:17), this is expressed in terms of a communal fellowship deeper than love for a woman: "your love for me was wonderful, passing the love of women" (2 Sam. 1:26).

(c) In a further sense, love is understood as lying at the root of social community life: "you shall love your neighbour as yourself" (Lev. 19:18; → Brother, art. *plēsion*; → Command; → Law, art. *nomos*). Love in this context means devotion towards one's neighbour for his sake, accepting him as a brother and letting him come into his own. This aspect is illustrated by the social legislation, which is particularly concerned with the rights of aliens (Lev. 19:34; → Foreign), the → poor (Lev. 25:35) and → orphans.

2. The word love is used less commonly and with greater caution for describing the relationship between God and man. In this respect the OT contrasts with Gk. literature in being far removed from any mystical thinking. In the OT man can never ascend to God; in the Gk. understanding of *erōs* he can. It is because all human thought, feeling, action and worship are a response to a previous movement by God, that the LXX prefers the simpler word *agapē* to the more loaded *erōs*. The completely different direction of thought makes this quite understandable.

(a) At the beginning of the OT stands not only the God who loves, but also the God who elects, and the God who creates facts through direct action in nature and with men – in particular, with his people, with whom he has made a → covenant (Exod. 24). The great deeds of Yahweh are the deeds of his history with his people, such as the Exodus, the gift of the land and the Torah. Righteousness, faithfulness, love and grace are some of the concepts embodied in such actions. The people, in turn, reply with jubilation, praise and obedience.

God's judgment and → grace (*ḥeseḏ*) permeate the whole of the OT. It is not a characteristic of God that is being described; it is always the total activity which is based on his sovereign will. God holds to his covenant, despite → Israel's frequent relapses which draw God's wrath on them. The only ground for this is to be found in his electing grace and love (e.g. Hos. 11:1). Statements concerning this devotion of God to his people reach the level of suffering love, as Isa. 53 predicates of the Servant of God.

(b) It was the → prophets who first ventured to elaborate on the theme of the love of God as the main motif of his electing work. It was an enormity of unique proportions for Hosea, surrounded by the Canaanite world of sexual fertility-cults and love-feasts, to represent the relationship between Yahweh and his people as that of a deceived husband and a prostitute (→ Marriage). Yet, despite the fact that Israel had broken the covenant, and thus become a whore and an adulteress, Yahweh still wooed back his faithless wife, the godless covenant people, with an inconceivable love (2:19 f.). Israel is not his people (1:9), but will become his people again through Yahweh's patient and winsome wooing (2:23). But, besides using the picture of marriage, Hosea also used the picture of a → father to describe Yahweh's unfathomable love for Israel, whom he loved in → Egypt and drew to himself with bonds of love (11:1 ff.). Israel, however, turned away. So Hosea pictured the struggle, which he saw as going on inside Yahweh himself, as that between the jealous wrath of a deceived father and his glowing love: "How can I give you up, O Ephraim! How can I hand you over, O Israel?... My heart recoils within me, my compassion grows warm and tender. I will not execute my fierce anger, I will not again destroy Ephraim; for I am God and not man, the Holy One in your midst, and I will not come to destroy" (11:8 f.). This description by Hosea of the passionate and zealous love of God is unprecedented in its boldness. For, according to Hosea, the God-ness of God does not express itself in destructive power, but in tender and compassionate love, which precedes any responsive human love, and which suffers through the faithlessness of his people (6:4) and does not hand them over to ultimate ruin.

The later prophets took over from Hosea the picture of love and the theme of the beloved, with modifications. Jeremiah spoke of Israel's first love in the wilderness, and its growing cold in Canaan (Jer. 2:1 ff.). But Yahweh's love is everlasting (31:3), and he will help up the degenerate people again (3:6–10; 31:4). In Isa. 54:4–8 it is not the wife who has left her husband, but Yahweh who left his young bride, to whom he now again turns in compassion. "For the Lord has called you like a wife forsaken and grieved in spirit, like a wife of youth when she is cast off, says your God. For a brief moment I forsook you, but with great compassion I will gather you" (54:6 f.). One can even speak of Yahweh's political love which is to be recognized in the return of the exiles from Babylon: "Because you are precious in my eyes, and honoured, and I love you, I give men in return for you, peoples in exchange for your life" (43:4).

(c) Deut., also expresses similar ideas. But whereas in the prophets Yahweh's love is the sole and incredible basis for his future actions in saving his lost people, the allusions to Yahweh's electing love in Deut. always provide the ground for exhorting Israel on its side to love God and to follow his directing. (7:6–11). "You shall love the LORD your God with all your heart, and with all your soul, and with all your might" (6:5; → Command; → Law, art. *nomos*). This love for God is realized in obedience to his will as expressed in the covenant, in keeping the law (Exod. 20:6; Deut. 10:12 f.), and in devotion to one's neighbour (Lev. 19:18). There is a nice example of the way human social love is to be founded on the acts of God in the law concerning aliens: "The stranger who sojourns with you shall be to you as the native among you, and you shall love him as yourself; for you were strangers in the land of Egypt: I am the LORD, your God" (Lev. 19:34). Love, here, means dealing with a friend as a friend. Of course, the command to love one's neighbour is not, in the OT, something capable of comprehending the whole

541

law: love for Yahweh is represented in a whole gamut of instructions and directives.

3. (a) In Hellenistic and Rabbinic Judaism *agapē* became the central concept for describing God's relationship with man and *vice versa*. Despite mystical nuances derived from Greece and the Orient, the word still maintained its basic OT implications. God loves his people through every distress they meet. Proof of his love is the Torah: the believer reciprocates God's love as he obeys the commandments, emulates God's zealous compassion, and remains true to God, even to the point of martyrdom (4 Macc. 13:24; 15:3). Loving one's neighbour is the chief → commandment to the pious Jew. There are even individual examples of commands to help one's enemy, if need be, whether a member of the chosen people or not. There is also the occasional observation that God allows his forgiving love to hold sway well beyond the requirements of justice (SB I 905; 917 f.; III 451, 485; 766, 778).

(b) Essential for an understanding of the NT is the quite different structure of Qumran piety. The community believed that it had been chosen in God's love, but that this only had reference to the children of light. God loves the angel of light and hates all who belong to the company of Belial. There is an often repeated command: "Love everyone whom God elects, hate everyone he hates" (1QS 1:3 f.; contrast Matt. 5:43 ff.). The command to love does indeed play an important rôle, but since God's love is not conceived as having universal application, even love for one's neighbour only has a restricted reference to members of the community. (Cf. E. F. Sutcliffe, "Hatred at Qumran", *Revue de Qumran* 2, 1959–60, 345–55.)

NT 1. (a) In the NT love is one of the central ideas which express the whole content of the Christian faith (cf. Jn. 3:16). God's activity is love, which looks for men's reciprocal love (1 Jn. 4:8, 16).

(b) It is significant that *stergō* only occurs in the NT in Rom. 12:10 in the compound *philostorgos*, loving dearly, in an expression in which Paul emphasizes the need for love in the church by piling up words for love *tē philadelphia eis allēlous philostorgoi*, "devoted to one another in brotherly love" [Arndt, 869], and in Rom. 1:31; 2 Tim. 3:3 in the compound *astorgos*, heartless, inhuman, without natural affection. As an illustration of such lack of natural, family affection, C. E. B. Cranfield cites the practice of exposing unwanted babies and Seneca's justification for drowning weakly or deformed infants (*The Epistle to the Romans, ICC*, I, 1975, 132 f.; cf. Seneca, *De Ira* 1, 15). Moreover, *erōs* and *eraō* do not occur at all. As A. Nygren has shown, the reason for this is that the anthropocentric way of thinking which is inevitably bound up with these words does not correspond with the NT approach (*Agape and Eros*, 1953[2]). *phileō*, on the other hand, does appear commonly, though it also features in compound words. However, it remains in every case a more limited and colourless word. A typical example would be *philadelphia*, love for a friend or brother (2 Pet. 1:7). The main emphasis of *phileō* is on love for people who are closely connected, either by blood or by faith. Jn. 15:19; 11:36; 16:27 use it in the context of the father-child relationship. *agapaō* and *phileō* are used synonymously in Jn. 3:35 and 5:20 (cf. 16:27) of the Father's love for the Son, and in Jn. 21:15 ff., when Jesus asked Peter whether he loved him and in Peter's reply. ([F. F. Bruce] The attempts of B. F. Westcott and others to find significance in the variation between the two verbs in Jn. 21:15 ff. have now generally been abandoned – the more so because opposite and mutually inconsistent conclusions have been drawn from the variation [as by Westcott on the one hand, and R. C. Trench on the other]. The variation is a feature of Johannine style: in the same three verses two different words are also used for "know", two for "feed" [or "tend"] and two for "sheep" [or "lambs"].) In 1 Cor. 16:22 *phileō* is clearly used of love for the Lord Jesus: "If anyone has no love for the Lord, let him be accursed. Our Lord, come!'" (→ Present, art. *maranatha*).

(c) By contrast, *agapē* and *agapaō* are used in nearly every case in the NT to speak of God's relationship with man – not unexpectedly, in view of the OT usage. Where *agapē* is obviously directed towards things (Lk. 11:43), the very use of the vb. *agapaō* is intended to make it plain that here love is directed to the wrong ends, i.e. not towards God. Thus the vb. is used of misdirected love in Jn. 3:19 (love of *skotos*, darkness), Jn. 12:43 (love of *doxa tōn anthrōpōn*, the glory of men), and 2 Tim. 4:10 (love of the *nyn aiōn*, the present age). But in the case of the noun *agapē* there is no corresponding negative usage in the NT. It is always in the sense of *hē agapē tou theou*, the love of God, either subjective gen. (i.e. God's love of men) or the objective gen. (i.e. men's love of God), or referring to the divine love for other men which the presence of God evokes. This brings *agapē* very close to concepts like *pistis*, → faith, *dikaiosynē*, → righteousness and, *charis* → grace, which all have a single point of origin in God alone.

2. (a) In the Synoptic tradition the main emphasis falls on the preaching of the → kingdom of God and of the new way of life which breaks in with Jesus himself. God sends his beloved Son (in Matt. and Mk. *ho agapētos*), to whom to listen is to be saved (Mk. 1:11 par. Matt. 3:17; cf. Lk. 3:22; Mk. 9:7 par., Matt. 17:5; cf. Lk. 9:35; cf. Ps. 2:7; Isa. 42:1; Gen. 22:1 ff.). Lk. has *agapētos* as *v.l.* and in the parable in Lk. 20:13 as does Mk. 12:6 (but not Matt. 21:38). *agapētos* also figures in the christological interpretation of Isa. 42:1 in Matt. 12:18. However, *agapē* is scarcely ever used to express the motive behind this. Instead other words, pictures and parables take its place (e.g. *oiktirmōn*, merciful, compassionate, Lk. 6:36; *eleos*, mercy, compassion, pity, Lk. 1:50 ff.; *eleeō*, have mercy or pity, Matt. 18:33). Jesus' activity among men thus reveals the mercy and love of God: Jesus himself is the one who truly loves, and takes to himself the poor, the sick and sinners.

The word *agapē* is not found in the passion narrative either. But the underlying thought of mercy and love as the way God intends to redeem lies clearly in the background. It may be seen in the *hyper pollōn* ("for many") in the account of the → Last Supper (Mk. 14:24; Matt. 26:28; cf. also Mk. 10:45) and the *paradidonai* ("betray", "hand over") of Jesus to death (Matt. 26:45; Mk. 14:41).

The Sermon on the Mount is best understood when the Beatitudes are seen in the first instance as statements by Jesus about himself (Matt. 5:3–11; cf. Lk. 6:20 ff.; → Blessing art. *makarios*). Jesus is the first to keep the radical demands of discipleship and so fulfil the law. The command to love one's enemies (Matt. 5:44; cf. Lk. 6:27), the word of forgiveness from the → cross (Lk. 23:34), and the promise to the robber (Lk. 23:43) all fit into the same pattern.

(b) In the Synoptics love for God is based on the two → commandments (Matt. 22:34–40 par. Mk. 12:28–34; cf. Lk. 10:25–28). Here too, through God's mercy, grows the new reality of love which is revealed in Jesus' ministry. His followers enter and share this, and so fulfil the demands of the Sermon on the Mount. Discipleship (→ Disciple), however, also involves → suffering: and when a disciple does suffer he is recognized by God (Matt. 10:37 ff.; 25:31 ff.; Lk. 6:22 ff.). This demand indicates the hardship love has to face; it can only succeed in this world by way of suffering. If love cost God what was most dear to him, the same will certainly apply to a disciple.

(c) This approach provides a different interpretation for loving one's neighbour or one's brother, one unknown either to rabbis or Greeks. It is God's love, creating the new realities amongst mankind, which is itself the basis and motivation for love between people. The commands to love can again be cited here. The combination of Deut. 6:5 and Lev. 19:18 appears only in Mk. 12:28 par. (on this → Command; → Brother; art. *plēsion*; → Law, art. *nomos*). The second half, love for one's neighbour, is also quoted in Rom. 13:9; Gal. 5:14; Jas. 2:8. The two commands were also stressed by the rabbis: Rabbi Akiba calls the command to love one's neighbour a basic principle of the Torah, embracing all others (cf. SB I 900–8 on Matt. 22:36 ff.). But the summation and substantiation of the command in the love of God is a peculiarly NT insight. Further, Jesus decisively stepped over the boundaries of Jewish tradition in the radical command to love one's enemies (Matt. 5:43–48 par. Lk. 6:27 f., 32–36). It is true that a general love for people, even for all creatures, had already been accepted as axiomatic. But the radical and laconic nature of the sentence – enemies are to be loved – is quite foreign to Rabbinic teaching (cf. SB I 553–68). Jesus, the Son of God, loves those who crucify him; in fact he died for them. Jesus' interpretation of this command in the parable of the Good Samaritan implicitly extends love to include everybody (Lk. 10:37; cf. 7:47).

3. (a) Paul stands entirely in the line of OT tradition when he speaks of the love of God. *agapē* is for him electing love, as is indicated by his use of *agapētos*, "the chosen one". This adjective is commonly used by Paul, but is entirely lacking in Jn., as is also the vb. *kaleō* (→ call). Rom. 9:13 ff. and 11:28 show in particular how Paul's thought links up with the Israelite election-tradition. The *klētoi* ("called") are the *agapētoi* ("beloved") (Rom. 1:7; Col. 3:12). As in the OT the motive for the election is God's love, which can also be rendered by *eleos* or *eleeō* (→ Mercy). (The LXX translates the root *rḥm* sometimes by *eleeō*, sometimes by *agapaō*.) This love becomes a revealing activity in Jesus Christ's saving work (Rom. 5:8; 8:35 ff.). The circle of → guilt, wrath (→ Anger) and → judgment is broken through, for in Jesus Christ God appears as love. Indeed this love comes to be predicated of Jesus Christ himself (e.g. Gal. 2:20; 2 Thess. 2:13; Eph. 5:2). The contrasting concept in Paul is *orgē*, wrath (→ Anger). Men under the law find themselves on a direct road leading to the wrathful judgment of God; from this destiny God in his electing love rescues those who believe (1 Thess. 1:10). Now if God's action can be defined as love (in 2 Cor. 13:11, 13 God and his love are used synonymously), then the great love song of 1 Cor. 13 can be understood not merely as a chapter of ethics, but as a description of all God's activity. In place of the word "love" we can put the name of Jesus Christ (cf. K. Barth, *CD* I 2, 379). This does not mean that God becomes the "good Lord" who lets anything pass; for there is still the possibility of disbelief and there is still the judgment to come. But God's righteousness is realized in the fact that the beloved Son stands in the place of the unrighteous (cf. 2 Cor. 5:18 ff.).

The electing love of God is also in the background of Eph. 5:22 ff., where the relationship between man and wife is compared with the love of Christ for the church. There are two points of contact here. On the one hand, there is the election of → Israel (cf. Rom. 9); the church is the called-out body, the new Israel which has come to faith in Christ. On the other hand, there is the OT picture of marriage dating from the time of Hosea with the implication of a relationship of fidelity and covenant love. What is true for the Christian community is true also for the individual, and is also true for marriage. God's love is able to overcome every kind of difficulty and infidelity. Electing love is at the same time compassionate and forgiving love.

Certainty of salvation consists in knowing that God's loving activity, of which the resurrection is the final seal, is stronger than any other power including even → death (Rom. 8:37 ff.; 1 Cor. 15:55 ff.). The → resurrection is the crowning act of God's love. In it is displayed the victory over these forces (cf. 2 Cor. 5:19 ff.; on *katallagē* → Reconciliation).

(b) A believer is a sinner who is loved by God. When he realizes this, he enters the sphere of God's love. He himself becomes loving. Hence, also in Paul love for God and love for one's neighbour derive from God's own love.

It is this love of God, poured into our hearts by the Spirit, that moves believers (Rom. 5:5; 15:30). Man's response to God's saving act is described by Paul mostly as *pistis* (→ faith) or *gnōsis* (→ knowledge), but also frequently as *agapē* (cf. Eph. 3:19; 1 Cor. 8:3). Through the Spirit, knowing God and being known by him become the same thing. The same applies to being loved by, and loving, God (Gal. 4:9). Those who are known by God know him. Similarly, with *agapē*, the faith which knows that it is loved (Rom. 8:37) is active in love (Gal. 5:6; 1 Thess. 3:6). Thus love can be said to be the fruit of the Spirit (Gal. 5:22); faith and love in fact are often mentioned side by side (e.g. 1 Thess. 1:3; 3:6; 5:8; Eph. 6:23; 1 Tim. 1:14).

The formula *en Christō*, "in Christ", speaks of the existence of the believer in the sphere of the love of God. When I am "in Christ" or Christ is "in me", this love has taken hold of me and is making me, a believing person, into a loving person (cf. Gal. 2:20; 1 Tim. 1:14). As someone who loves, a believer is a new → creation (*kainē ktisis*, 2 Cor. 5:17) who finds his origin in the love of Christ (cf. 2 Cor. 5:14 with v. 17).

(c) Paul, therefore, characterizes love for one's neighbour as love for one's → brother in the faith (Gal. 5:6). 1 Cor. 13 summarizes everything to be said here. There *agapē* is always both God's love and man's love. Love stands over every power and authority introducing and encircling the whole. ([Ed.] In a study of the phrase *ta tria tauta*, "these three things", and *meizōn de toutōn hē agapē*, "but [the] greatest of these [is] love", R. P. Martin asks: "May it not be, then, that this tremendous chapter ends on the note of an unexpected climax, as though Paul were saying, Excellent as are the features of this well-known triad, with love the still outstanding trait, there is something greater still, the love of God expressed in Jesus Christ our Lord?" ["A suggested Exegesis of 1 Corinthians 13:13", *ExpT* 82, 1970–71, 120].) *prophēteia*, prophecy, and *pistis*, faith (v. 2), *elpis*, hope (v. 7), and *gnōsis*, knowledge (v. 8), are subordinated to it not, however, as gradations of lessening importance, but as component parts of that one powerful force which permeates and animates everything. In the context of 1 Cor. love is the greatest of the gifts of the Spirit, however readily Paul puts *pneuma* → Spirit and *agapē* side by side elsewhere (Gal. 5:13–22; 1 Cor. 14:1). 1 Cor. also makes it clear that love is the force which holds a Christian community together and builds it up. Without love, no → fellowship or shared life is possible (1 Cor. 14:1; 16:14; Eph. 1:15; 3:17 ff.). The *sōma Christou*, body of Christ, is built up by love (1 Cor. 8:1; 2 Thess. 1:3; Phil. 2:1 f.; Eph. 4:16; Col. 2:2). When Paul offers the church the example of his own love he is calling them back again to their fellowship in the love of God (2 Cor. 2:4; 8:7).

Paul also takes up the command of the OT and of Jesus to love (Rom. 13:8 ff.; Gal. 5:14), thus setting *agapē* alongside *pistis*, and over against the *nomos* (→ Law). The law has been fulfilled, because Jesus is love, and has died for sinners Insofar, therefore, as Christians love one another they too fulfil the law, not in the sense that they attain any perfection, but that they are now living in God's new reality through the strengthening power of → forgiveness. *agapē* is a reflection of what is still to come (1 Cor. 13:9, 12, 13).

4. (a) In John, God's nature and activity are illustrated with particular clarity by his use of *agapē*. That partly arises from the fact that *agapē* is used here more frequently than in Paul in its absolute form – i.e. as a noun with no gen., or as a vb. with no object. Parallel ideas such as *dikaiosynē* (righteousness), *charis* (grace) and *eleos* (mercy) recede somewhat in favour of *agapē*. John can thus speak of pre-existent love in the same way that he speaks in Jn. 1:1 ff. of the pre-existent *logos* (→ Word; cf. Jn. 3:35; 10:17; 15:9; 17:23 ff.). God is essentially love (1 Jn. 4:8), and his purpose right from the beginning has been one of love. The love of the Father for the Son is therefore the archetype of all love. This fact is made visible in the sending and self-sacrifice of the Son (Jn. 3:16; 1 Jn. 3:1, 16). For men to "see" and "know" this love is to be saved. God's primary purpose for the world is his compassionate and forgiving love which asserts itself despite the world's inimical rejection of it. In God's *agapē* his → glory (*doxa*) is simultaneously revealed. Love's triumph is seen in the *doxasthēnai* of Jesus, i.e. his glorification: his death which here includes his return to the Father (Jn. 12:16, 23 ff.). The believer, taken up into this victory, receives *zōē*, life (cf. 1 Jn. 4:9; Jn. 3:36; 11:25 ff.).

(b) If Paul's word for describing the way men turn to God is *pistis*, John's is *agapē*. The relationship between Father and Son is one of love (Jn. 14:31). In this relationship of love believers are included (Jn. 14:21 ff.; 17:26; 15:9 f.). They are to love Father and Son with an equal love (Jn. 8:42; 14:21 ff.; 1 Jn. 4:16, 20). The continual oscillation between the subject and object of love in John shows that the Father, the Son, and the believers are all united in the one reality of divine love: the alternative to which is death (1 Jn. 3:14 ff.; 4:7 f.). The typical Johannine phrase *menein en*, remain in, can refer equally to Jesus or to love (Jn. 15:4 ff.; 1 Jn. 4:12 ff.).

(c) In John, mutual love is grounded even more clearly than in Paul in the love of God (Jn. 13:34; 1 Jn. 4:21). Love is a sign and a proof of faith (1 Jn. 3:10; 4:7 ff.). Love of one's brother derives from God's love; and without love for one's brother, there can be no relationship with God.

John, in turn, takes up the command to love (Jn. 13:34; 15:12, 17; 2 Jn. 5). To love is to keep the law (Jn. 14:23 f.).

5. (a) Finally, love found expression for itself in early Christian circles by way of the kiss of fellowship, which was a regular part of the worship of the congregation (e.g. Rom. 16:16 "with a holy kiss [*en philēmati hagiō*]"). In 1 Pet. 5:14 it is called the "kiss of love [*en philēmati agapēs*]"; but practically no details of this rite are known (→ *phileō* NT 3).

(b) *agapē* is also the word used for one of the early Christian ceremonies which we only know about by way of allusion. 1 Cor. 11 shows that the actual celebration of the Lord's Supper was linked with a normal meal. Later the "love feast" (*agapē*) became separated from the → Lord's Supper itself, and celebrated in its own right (cf. Jude 12; perhaps also 2 Pet. 2:13; Ign., *Smy.* 8:2; Clem.Alex., *Paedogogus* 2, 1; cf. Lampe, 8). The difference seems to be that whereas the centre both of a service of preaching and of the Lord's Supper was the joyous declaration of faith, the common meal had its central significance in celebrating and displaying the especial → fellowship which they shared in their *agapē*. It also seems certain that this service provided an opportunity for congregations to give practical expression to their love in generous social action (cf. Acts 6:1 ff.).

(c) Evidence that the new community based on *agapē* understood itself as the family of God is provided by the variety of names used for brothers and sisters in the early church (→ Brother, art. *adelphos*).   *W. Günther, H.-G. Link*

| φιλέω |

φιλέω (*phileō*), be fond of, love; φίλος (*philos*), a relative, friend; φιλία (*philia*), friendship, love; καταφιλέω (*kataphileō*), to kiss; φίλημα (*philēma*), a kiss; φιλαδελφία (*philadelphia*), brotherly love; φιλανθρωπία (*philanthrōpia*), love for mankind, hospitality.

CL *phileō* is the regular word from Homer onwards for to show affection, love, hospitality, etc. It can also be used with less precision and colour to mean: be accustomed to, be in the habit of; and then, when joined with other vbs. to do something gladly, customarily, generally. It is also commonly used with more specific meanings. There is a very large number of words compounded from *phil*-e.g. *philoxenia*, hospitality (cf. Liddell-Scott, 1935–42). *philos*, attested in Mycenaean Gk., and originally meaning dear, expensive, valuable, became the ordinary expression for a friend or relative; *philē* similarly means a female friend. *philia* is a later abstraction meaning friendship, love, devotion, favour; *philēma* is a love token, a kiss.

OT In the LXX we are presented with a completely different picture. *phileō* occurs rarely, whereas the vb. *agapaō*, and the noun *agapē* (otherwise almost entirely unknown in Gk.) are everywhere to be found. It is not possible to say whether they are used according to set rules, for *phileō* (30 times), like *agapaō* (c. 263 times), generally translates Heb. *'āhēḇ* (e.g. Gen. 27:4 ff.; 37:4[cf. 37:3]; Isa. 56:10, Prov. 8:17[cf. 8:21]). Whereas Heb. has a whole range of different words to express the contrary concept of the hate (but the LXX has only the one word *miseō* (→ Enemy, art. *miseō*), it has virtually only the one root form *'āhēḇ* at its disposal for the range of feelings associated with love. Gk., on the other hand, has several roots and derived words to express the various nuances of love. *philia* (38 times), generally translating *'ahēḇ*, *'aháḇâh*, is comparatively rare, though *philos* (c. 181

547

times), generally translating *rēa'*, though often without Heb. equivalent, is more common in the LXX. As an alternative *plēsion*, neighbour, mainly used to indicate relatives or friends (*c.* 221 times, often for *rēa'*), and occasionally *hetairos*, friend (*c.* 27 times), are used (→ Brother arts. *ho plēsion* and *hetairos*).

NT In the NT the vb. *phileō* occurs in Matt. (5 times) and Jn. (13 times); elsewhere there are only individual instances (7 in all). The distinction from → *agapaō* is not strictly adhered to. The nouns *philos* or *philē* are used for friends, and also for people bound together in → faith; as an adjective *philos* is not found at all. *philēma* is a kiss, and in the Epistles a Christian form of greeting, the "holy kiss". The noun *philia* only appears in the NT in Jas. 4:4.

1. (a) A typical example for the original meaning of *phileō* can be seen in Matt. 6:5: the hypocrites love to pray at street corners. Matt. 23:6 and Lk. 20:46 are similar cases. The use of *agapaō* in Lk. 11:43, and Lk. 20:46 in a similar context, is an exception, showing how the difference in meaning is not always maintained. Matt. 10:37 is another typical example, love here deriving from family connections: "He who loves [*ho philōn*] father or mother more than me is not worthy of me; and he who loves [*ho philōn*] son or daughter more than me is not worthy of me." We have here, incidentally, a statement which has a theological importance in indicating the transition to a theological meaning of the word; for the phraseology, introducing the comparison, points implicitly to a love for Jesus, which is elsewhere described as *agapē*, the gift of God's rule. The starting-point of the statement, however, remains the natural love shared between relatives. But, clearly, when the → kingdom of God breaks in, even the usual family ties and links of friendship may be dissolved for the benefit of the new fellowship of the family of God (→ Brother, art. *adelphos*).

(b) Jn. characterizes love according to whether the → world is viewed as God's creation, or as the sphere of enmity towards God. Where the world is viewed as God's creation, natural creaturely love has its legitimate place. Thus Jn. 11:3, 36 speak of Jesus' bond of friendship with Lazarus. But Jn. also sees the *kosmos* as the sphere of darkness which opposes God. Viewed thus, love in or for the *kosmos* is the same as hatred for God's revelation (15:19; cf. Jas. 4:4). 1 Jn. 2:15 is directed against such people: "do not love the world, or anything in it," i.e. "do not love God-lessness." But since God loves the creation which hates him, in order to save it (3:16), the other imperative also holds: "He gave us this command: whoever loves God must love his brother too." Love for one's brothers as God's creations makes concrete one's love for the world, which is also the creation of God.

The scene with Peter in Jn. 21:15 ff. makes it clear that *phileō* and *agapaō* cannot always be neatly distinguished. Verses 15, 16 distinguish the *agapaō* in Jesus' mouth from the *phileō* in Peter's, but in v. 17 this distinction ceases. Nor is it possible to draw any particular exegetical consequences from this scene. Jn. 5:20 and 16:27 are the only places where *phileō* is predicated of God. Both times it is God the Father who is spoken of, since relationships between people become pictures of relationships within the divine being.

(c) There is a single, yet important, Pauline example of the use of *phileō*, in 1 Cor. 16:22. Love for the *kyrios*, → Lord, is the condition of salvation. The whole history of the word would have led one to expect *agapaō*. Again the impossibility of rigid distinctions is clear. As to content, clearly the meaning is that of *agapē* elsewhere. Tit. 3:15, too, can only be correctly understood when it is born in mind that through God's love in the revelation of the Son, human love understood as love in faith requires a new interpretation (cf. on this the varying translation of Prov. 3:11 in Heb. 12:6 [*agapaō*] and Rev. 3:19 [*phileō*]). For *phileō*, meaning to kiss (Mk. 14:14), see below 3, on *philēma*.

2. *philos* is also in the NT a friend to whom one is under a basic obligation (cf. Lk. 7:6; 11:5 f.; 14:10, 12; 15:6, 9, 29; 23:12; Jn. 11:11; Acts 10:24; 19:31; 27:3). Relatives (*syngeneis*) and friends are often mentioned alongside each other. But neither in Gk. nor in Jewish tradition can any firm distinction be upheld; and when *philoi*, friends, are sometimes mentioned, relatives are clearly often to be included. *philos* is also used, as in Lk. 16:9, for people linked by some inclination or relationship; Jesus here advises people to win friends for themselves by giving away their worldly wealth (→ Possessions, art. *mamōnas*). The same point is made when Pilate is threatened in Jn. 19:12 with losing his honorary title of "friend of Caesar" (*philos tou kaisaros*; Lat. *amicus Caesaris*). By way of contrast, *philos* can be used to express God's love for the godless. In Matt. 11:19 and Lk. 7:34 Jesus is called the "friend of sinners and tax-collectors." He loves them, though they are enemies, just as God loves the world which hates him. That is also what is meant when Jesus addressed his disciples as "friends" (Lk. 12:4; Jn. 15:14 f.). They come to him as sinners, and become his friends through his sacrificial love. (Jn. 15:13). So now, instead of the love and friendship they enjoyed while belonging to the world (Jas. 4:4), they belong to the new fellowship of the kingdom of God, or the family of God, in which they are brothers and friends of Jesus and children of the Father (Lk. 21:16; cf. also Jas. 2:23, where → Abraham because of his faith is called a *philos theou*). Brothers and sisters in faith can therefore be greeted as *philoi* (3 Jn. 15). For Jn. 3:29 *philos tou nymphiou*, "friend of the bridegroom", → Marriage, art. *nymphē*.

3. *philēma* is a kiss. For the vb. *phileō* and *kataphileō* are both used in the NT. The kiss was a common courtesy greeting amongst the Rabbis; and Judas' kiss was of this nature (Matt. 26:48 f.; Mk. 14:44 f.; Lk. 22:47). He addresses Jesus honorifically as Rabbi. Again, in the story of the woman who was a sinner (Lk. 7:36 ff.), the kiss was a sign of respect for Jesus. Whether at the same time there is a hint or reference to the Jewish kiss of farewell depends on the decisions one reaches in comparing this scene with the anointing in Bethany (Matt. 26:6 ff.; Mk. 14:3 ff.).

The kiss in the ancient world was both a friendly sign of greeting and an emotional token of farewell (cf. Lk. 15:20; Acts 20:37 where *kataphileō* is used). In the early Christian congregations it became a *philēma hagion*, a holy kiss. Those who have been incorporated into the fellowship of the love of God are *hagioi* (→ Holy, art. *hagios*) in being children of God, and can greet one another as such (Rom. 16:16; 1 Cor. 16:20; 2 Cor. 13:12; 1 Thess. 5:26; 1 Pet. 5:14 *philēma agapēs*, kiss of love).   *W. Günther*

4. The following compounds occur in the NT: *philagathos*, loving what is good (1 Tim. 1:8); *philadelphia*, brotherly love, love of a brother or sister (Rom. 12:10; 1 Thess. 4:9; Heb. 13:1; 1 Pet. 1:22; 2 Pet. 1:7); *philadelphos*, loving one's brother or sister (1 Pet. 3:8); *philandros*, loving one's husband (Tit. 2:4); *philanthrōpia*,

love for mankind (Tit. 3:4), hospitality (Acts 28:2); *philanthrōpōs*, benevolently, kindly (Acts 27:3); *philargyria*, love of money, avarice (1 Tim. 6:10); *philargyros*, fond of money, avaricious (Lk. 16:14; 2 Tim. 3:2); *philautos*, loving oneself, selfish (2 Tim. 3:2); *philēdonos*, loving pleasure (2 Tim. 3:4); *philotheos*, loving God, devout, in a play on words with *philēdonos* (2 Tim. 3:4); *philon(e)ikia*, dispute (Lk. 22:24); *philon(e)ikos*, quarrelsome (1 Cor. 11:16); *philoxenia*, hospitality (Rom. 12:13; Heb. 13:2); *philoxenos*, hospitable (1 Tim. 3:2; Tit. 1:8; 1 Pet. 4:9); *philoprōteuō*, wish to be the first (3 Jn. 9); *philosophia*, philosophy (Col. 2:8); *philosophos*, philosopher (Acts 17:18); *philostorgos*, loving dearly (Rom. 12:10); *philoteknos*, loving one's children (Tit. 2:4); *philotimeomai*, consider as an honour, aspire (Rom. 15:20; 2 Cor. 5:9; 1 Thess. 4:11); *philophronōs*, in a friendly manner (Acts 28:7); *philophrōn*, well-disposed, friendly (1 Pet. 3:8 TR).

In addition there are the following names: *Philadelph(e)ia*, Philadelphia, the city in Lydia in Asia Minor mentioned in the sixth letter of Rev. (1:11; 3:7) and in the letter of Ignatius to the Philadelphians, founded by Attalus II Philadelphus (159–138 B.C.); *Philēmon*, Philemon, a Christian probably at Colossae whose runaway slave, Onesimus, was won for Christianity by Paul and was sent back to Philemon with the letter that bears his name urging clemency; *Philētos*, Philetus, who is mentioned with Hymenaeus (2 Tim. 2:17) as teaching that the resurrection is already past (v. 18); *Philippēsios*, Philippian (Phil. 4:15); *Philippoi*, Philippi, city of Macedonia, founded on the site of Crenides by Philip II of Macedon in 356, the first European city to hear Christian missionaries, Paul and Silas (Acts 16:12); it is also mentioned in Acts 20:6; Phil. 1:1; 1 Thess. 2:2; *Philippos*, Philip (lit. fond of horses, horse-lover); (i) Philip Herod I, son of Herod the Great and the younger Mariamne (Matt. 14:33; Mk. 6:17) whose wife left him for his half-brother, Herod Antipas, who beheaded John the Baptist; (ii) Philip Herod II, son of Herod the Great and Cleopatra of Jerusalem, the Tetrarch (Matt. 16:13; Mk. 8:27; Lk. 3:1); (iii) Philip the disciple and apostle (Matt. 10:3; Mk. 3:18; Lk. 6:14; Jn. 1:44–47, 49; 6:5, 7; 12:21 f.; 14:8 f.; Acts 1:13); (iv) Philip, one of the Seven and later the evangelist (Acts 6:5; 8:5–40; 21:8); *Philologos*, Philologus (lit. lover of learning), a recipient of greetings in Rom. 16:15, possibly the leader of a house church (cf. vv. 5, 10 f.).

C. Brown

→ Anger, → Brother, → Command, → Gift, → Grace, → Hope, → Law, → Mercy, → Samaritan

(a). A. Barr, "Love in the Church: A Study of First Corinthians, Chapter 13", *SJT* 3, 1950, 416–25; K. Barth, "The Love of God", *CD* I, 2, 371–401; and "The Holy Spirit and Christian Love", *CD* IV, 2, 727–840; G. Bornkamm, *Jesus of Nazareth*, 1960, 109–17; and "The More Excellent Way (I Corinthians 13)", *Early Christian Experience*, 1969, 180–90; C. L. Bowen, "Love in the Fourth Gospel", *JR* 13, 1933, 39–49; R. Bultmann, *Theology of the New Testament*, I, 1952; II, 1955 (see index); and "To Love Your Neighbour", *Scottish Periodical* 1, 1947, 41–56; T. G. Bunch, *Love: A Comprehensive Exposition of I Corinthians 13*, 1952; W. G. Cole, *Sex and Love in the Bible*, 1960; M. C. D'Arcy, *The Mind and Heart of Love*, 1947⁴; J. D. M. Derrett, "The Parable of the Good Samaritan", *Law in the New Testament*, 1970, 208–27; J. Ferguson, *Moral Values in the Ancient World*, 1958; V. P. Furnish, *The Love Command in the New Testament*, 1969; J. Gaer, *Love in the New Testament*, 1952; A. E. Goodman, "*ḥsd* and *twdh* in the Linguistic Tradition of the Psalter", in P. R. Ackroyd and B. Lindars, eds., *Words and Meaning: Essays Presented to David Winton Thomas*, 1968, 105–16; W. Harrelson, "The Idea of Agape in the New Testament", *Journal of Religion*, 31 1951, 169–82; J. Jeremias, *The Parables of Jesus*, 1963², 202 ff.; C. S. Lewis,

The Four Loves, 1960; W. Lillie, "The Christian Conception of Love", SJT 12, 1959, 226–42 (reprinted in Studies in New Testament Ethics, 1961, 163–81); U. Luck, philanthrōpia etc., TDNT IX 107–12; R. P. Martin, "A Suggested Exegesis of 1 Corinthians 13:13", ExpT 82, 1970–71, 119 f.; J. Moffatt, Love in the New Testament, 1929; H. Montefiore, "Thou Shalt Love Thy Neighbour as Thyself", NovT 5, 1962, 157–70; A. Nygren, Agape and Eros: Part I A Study of the Christian Idea of Love: Part II The History of the Christian Idea of Love, 1953²; G. Outka, Agape: An Ethical Analysis, Yale Publications in Religion 17, 1972; G. Quell and E. Stauffer, agapaō, etc., TDNT I 21–55; C. E. Raven, Jesus and the Gospel of Love, 1942²; C. H. Roberts, "AGAPE in the Invocation of Isis (P. Oxy xi 1380)", Journal of Egyptian Archaeology, 39, 1953, 114; and "The Use of AGAPE in P. Oxy 1380. A Reply", JTS New Series 19, 1968, 209 ff.; J. T. Sanders, "First Corinthians 13: Its Interpretation Since the First World War", Interpretation 20, 1966, 159–87; O. J. F. Seitz, "Love your Enemies", NTS 16, 1969–70, 39–54; N. H. Snaith, The Distinctive Ideas of the Old Testament, 1944, 94–142; C. Spicq, Agape in the New Testament, I–III, 1963–66; G. Stählin, phileō etc., TDNT IX 113–71; K. Stendahl, "Hate, Retaliation, and Love", HTR 55, 1962, 343–55; E. F. Sutcliffe, "Hatred at Qumran", Revue de Qumran 2, 1969–60, 345–55; B. B. Warfield, "The Terminology of Love in the New Testament", Princeton Theological Review 16, 1918, 1–45 and 153–203; V. Warnach, "Love", EBT II 518–42; D. D. Williams, The Spirit and Forms of Love, 1968. (b). G. Bornkamm, "Das Doppelgebot der Liebe", Neutestamentliche Studien für Rudolf Bultmann BZNW 21, 1954, 85–93; H. Braun, Spätjüdisch-häretischer und frühchristlicher Radikalismus, I–II, BHTh 24, 1957; F. Buck, Die Liebe Gottes beim Propheten Osee, 1953; J. Coppens, "La doctrine biblique sur l'amour de Dieu et du prochain", Ephemerides Theologicae Lovanienses 11, 1964, 252–99; F. X. Durwell, La charité selon les Synoptiques et les Épîtres de S. Paul, 1955; F. Frerichs, "Liebe", EKL II 1096 ff.; E. Fuchs, "Was heisst: 'Du sollst deinen Nächsten lieben wie dich selbst'?", Zur Frage nach dem historischen Jesus: Gesammelte Aufsätze, II, 1965², 1 ff.; H. Gollwitzer, Das Gleichnis vom barmherzigen Samariter, BSt 34, 1062; H. Greeven, plēsion, TDNT VI 316 ff.; G. Harbsmeier, Das Hohelied der Liebe 1952; E. Jenni, 'ahaḇ THAT I 60–73; R. Joly, Le Vocabulaire chretien de l'Amour, est-il Originel? Philein et Agapan dans le Grec Antique, 1968; R. Kiefer, " 'Afin que je sois brulé' ou bien 'Afin que j'en tire orgueil'? (I Cor. xiii 3)", NTS 22, 1975–76, 95 ff.; N. Lohfink, "Auslegung deuteronomistischer Texte II. Ein Kommentar zum Hauptgebot des Dekalogs (Dtn. 6, 4–25)", Bibel und Leben 5, 1964, 84 ff.; O. Loretz, "Zum Problem des Eros im Hohenlied", BZ 8, 1964, 191–216; W. Lütgert, Die Liebe im Neuen Testament, 1905; and Ethik der Liebe 1938; O. Michel, "Das Gebot der Nächstenliebe in der Verkündigung Jesu", Die soziale, Entscheidung, 1947, 53–101; L. Malevez, "Amour païen, amour chrétien", Nouvelle Revue Théologique 69, 1937, 944–68; E. Neuhäusler, Anspruch und Gegenwart Gottes, 1962, 114 ff.; A. Nissen, Gott und der Nächste im antiken Judentum: Untersuchungen zum Doppelgebot der Liebe, WUNT 15, 1974; T. Ohm, W. Zimmerli, N. A. Dahl and R. Mehl, "Liebe", RGG³ IV 361 ff.; M. Paeslack, "Zur Bedeutungsgeschichte der Wörter philein, philia, philos in der LXX und im Neuen Testament unter Berücksichtigung ihrer Beziehungen zu agapan, agapē, agapētos", ThV 5, 1953–54, 51–142; W. Pesch, "Das Liebesgebot in der Verkündigung Jesu", BuK 9, 1964, 129 ff.; H. Preisker, Die urchristliche Botschaft von der Liebe Gottes im Lichte der vergleichenden Religionsgeschichte, 1930; B. Reicke, "Neuzeitliche und neutestamentliche Auffassung von Liebe und Ehe", NovT 1, 1956, 21–34; H. Riesenfeld, "Étude bibliographique sur la Notion biblique d'Agape", Coniectanea Neotestamentica 5, 1941, 1–27; "Note bibliographique sur I Cor. XIII", Nuntius 6, 1952, 47 f.; and "La Voie de Charité. Note sur I Cor. 12. 31" StTh 1, 1947, 146–57; K. Romaniuk, L'Amour du Père et du Fils dans la Sotériologie de Saint Paul, 1961; R. Sanders, Furcht und Liebe im palästinischen Judentum, BWANT IV, 16, 1935; O. Schilling, "Die alttestamentliche Auffassung von Gerechtigkeit und Liebe", Wort des Lebens (Festschrift M. Meinertz), 1951, 9–27; H. Schlier, "Uber die Liebe: 1 Kor. 13", Die Zeit der Kirche, 1956, 186–92; and "Glauben, Erknnen, Lieben nach dem Johannesevangelium", Besinnung auf das Neue Testament, 1964, 279–93; H. Scholz, Eros und Caritas, 1929; H. Schürmann, "Eschatologie und Liebesdienst in der Verkündigung Jesu", in K. Schubert, ed., Vom Messias zum Christus, 1964, 203 ff.; W. C. van Unnik, "Die Motivierung der Feindesliebe in Lk. 6, 32–35", NovT 8, 1966, 284 ff.; E. Walter, Glaube, Hoffnung und Liebe im Neuen Testament, 1940; and Wesen und Macht der Liebe, 1955; V. Warnach, Agape. Die Liebe als Grundmotiv der neutestamentlichen Theologie, 1951.

M

Magic, Sorcery, Magi

μαγεία

περίεργος (*periergos*), meddlesome, curious, belonging to magic; μαγεία (*mageia*), magic; μαγεύω (*mageuō*), practise magic; μάγος (*magos*), magus, magician; φαρμακεία (*pharmakeia*), magic, sorcery; φαρμακεύς (*pharmakeus*), mixer of potions, magician; φάρμακον (*pharmakon*), poison, magic potion, charm, medicine, remedy, drug; φάρμακος (*pharmakos*), poisoner, magician; γόης (*goēs*), sorcerer, juggler; πύθων (*pythōn*), the Python, spirit of divination; βασκαίνω (*baskainō*), bewitch; φάντασμα (*phantasma*), apparition, ghost.

CL 1. Evidence of magic dating from palaeolithic culture has been found in cave art depicting animals stuck with darts with a view to causing the same thing to happen in a future hunt, and in the covering of corpses with red pigment (suggesting blood, the life-substance) in order to restore them to life. The dividing line between magic and religion is often indistinct. Sir James Frazer suggested that religion was characterized by conciliation of superhuman powers, whereas magic is concerned with the control by man of the forces of nature (*The Golden Bough*, abridged edition 1957, I, 67 ff.). Even where magic deals with spirits as personal agents, it treats them as inanimate in the sense that they can be constrained and forced in an impersonal way rather than conciliating or propitiating them as in a religion. The distinction is often drawn between white and black magic. The former is held to be benevolent in intention (e.g. rain making), whereas the latter is malevolent causing loss of health, property, destruction and death. Magic may co-exist alongside a primitive knowledge of the laws of the natural world; it is invoked to deal with what cannot be controlled by known natural means.

2. Common features of magic are: (i) the spell, the utterance of words according to a set formula, without which control over the desired power is impossible; (ii) the rite, or set of actions designed to convey the spell to the object concerned, involving imitation of the desired action or the use of similar substances; and (iii) the condition of the performer who must not breach any of the relevant taboos and must be in the requisite emotional state to perform the prescribed actions.

3. Magic is known in Homer, but is doubtless much older. In *Od.* 19, 457 an incantation can stop the flow of blood from the wounded Odysseus. Circe has potions, salves and a magic wand, and is able to teach Odysseus to summon the shades from the nether world. Magic abounds in Gk. mythology. Among those accredited with supernatural powers were the Telchines, smiths who lived on the island of Rhodes who had the evil eye and who bear a resemblance to the dwarfs and gnomes of north European mythology, the Curetes of Crete who protected the

infant Zeus, and the Idaean Dactyls who were likewise dwarfs and who were masters of medicine and music. The most renowned enchantress of antiquity was Medea who also had the evil eye and was the prototype of the jilted witch of later literature (*OCD*, 637). Both Gk. and Lat. poets and dramatists give pictures of magic and witchcraft. The growth in knowledge and progress of Gk. civilization led to the suppression of magic. Nevertheless, as secularization increased in the higher social levels during the fourth cent. B.C., there was a renewed outburst of interest in magic in the lower levels.

4. Numerous forms of magic are attested in the Graeco-Roman world. To bring about the death of a person, one could make an image of that person and destroy it or pierce it. Plato believed that men could not be prevented from believing in such homoeopathic magic, or incantations and magic knots, and therefore urged punishment by law including the death penalty (*Leg.* 933b; cf. also Theocritus 2; Virgil, *Eclogues* 8; Ovid, *Heroides* 6, 91 for such practices). Contagious magic, destroying something belonging to the victim, is exemplified in Theocritus 2, 53 ff. and Virgil, *Aeneid* 4, 494 ff. The attempt to transfer by magic a disease from a person to an animal is described by the Elder Pliny in his account of whispering into the ear of an ass, "A scorpion has stung me" (*Naturalis Historia* 28, 155). Belief in the apotropaic efficacy of rings, crowns and amulets and numerous medical charms was widespread. Evocation of the spirits of the dead occurs as early as Homer, *Od.* 11, and necromancers were a recognized class of magician.

OT 1. The employment of magic not only by men but also by gods is well attested in Sumero-Akkadian and Canaanite religious literature. Behind it lies the belief that no single power has ultimate control over the universe. In order to secure the desired stability and well-being of the world, the gods must also resort to the powers which they themselves do not possess. In the Babylonian Creation Epic (*Enûma Eliš*) the hero of the younger gods, Ea-Enki is called the Lord of Incantation and is regarded as the god of magic par excellence. In his struggle against the primeval gods Tiamat and Apsu, Ea-Enki killed the latter with the aid of a spell (Tablet I, 60–70; *ANET* 61; A. Heidel, *The Babylonian Genesis*, [1951²] 1963, 20; cf. H. Ringgren, *Religions of the Ancient Near East*, 1973, 69 ff.). Ea's son, Marduk, employed magic in his fight against the monsters created by Tiamat to avenge Apsu, holding a red talisman between his lips (Tablet IV, 61; *ANET*, 66; A. Heidel, op. cit., 39). Tiamat also recited a charm and kept casting a spell (Tables IV, 91; *ANET*, 67; A. Heidel, op. cit., 40). But Marduk, the better magician, proved victorious. Compared with this account of creation, the absence of magic in the Genesis creation narratives is all the more striking.

In the Akkadian Myth of Zu the vitality of the gods appears to depend on a talisman carried by their chief (*ANET*, 111 ff.). The bird-god Zu stole the Tablets of Destinies and usurped the authority of the gods until vanquished by one of the benign deities. The gods themselves wear amulets to protect themselves and ensure victory. Similarly, in the *Descent of Ishtar to the Nether World* (*ANET*, 106–9) Ishtar wore charms.

2. In the case of Canaanite religion the use of magic in healing is illustrated by the Legend of King Keret who is healed by the magic of El (*ANET*, 148), and in fertility by the story of how the goddess Anath avenged the death of her brother

553

at the hands of Mot by slaying Mot, the god of sterility, and scattering his ashes (*ANET* 140). However, human beings also were regarded as being endowed with magical powers and the capacity to tell omens (*ANET*, 153).

3. For evidence of magic in Egypt see *ANET*, 325 ff.; K. Preisendanz, ed., *Papyri Graecae Magicae*, I-III, 1928–42; A. H. Gardiner, *ERE* VIII 262-69. Magic was under the protection of the leading god, Thoth and Isis, and was learned in the temple schools. It was a particular province of the priests. The charms included charms against snakes.

4. The reality of occult powers is recognized in the OT, but the Israelites were consistently forbidden to become embroiled in any form of magic. The law of Deut. 18:10–14 observes the various practices of the surrounding peoples, but prohibits them categorically: "There shall not be found among you any one who burns his son or his daughter as an offering, any one who practises divination, a soothsayer, or an augur, or a sorcerer, or a charmer, or a medium, or a wizard, or a necromancer. For whoever does these things is an abomination to the Lord; and because of these abominable practices the Lord your God is driving them out before you. You shall be blameless before the Lord your God. For these nations, which you are about to dispossess, give heed to soothsayers and to diviners; but as for you, the Lord your God has not allowed you to do so." The key terms here are: *qōsēm qᵉsāmîm* (Heb.), *manteuomenos manteian* (Gk.), one who practises divination (cf. Num. 22:7; 23:23; Jos. 13:22; 1 Sam. 6:2; 15:23; 28:8; 2 Ki. 17:17; Isa. 3:2; 44:25; Jer. 14:14; Ezek. 13:6, 9, 23; 21:26 ff.; Mic. 3:6 f., 11; Zech. 10:2); *mᵉ'ônēn* (Heb.), *klēdonizomenos* (Gk.), soothsayer (the Heb. means one who causes to appear, raises spirits, practises soothsaying; cf. Lev. 19:26; Jdg. 9:37; 2 Ki. 21:6; Isa. 2:6; 57:3; Jer. 27:9; Mic. 5:11; 2 Chron. 33:6); *mᵉnaḥēš* (Heb.), *oiōnizomenos* (Gk.), an augur, one who looks for an omen (cf. Gen. 44:5, 15; Lev. 19:26; 2 Ki. 17:17; 21:6; 2 Chron. 33:6; with Gen. 30:27; Num. 23:23; 24:1; 1 Ki. 20:33); *mᵉkaššēp* (Heb.), *pharmakos* (Gk.), sorcerer (cf. Exod. 7:11; 22:17; Mal. 3:5; Dan. 2:2; 2 Chron. 33:6; with 2 Ki. 9:22; Isa. 47:9, 12; Mic. 5:11; Nah. 3:4); *ḥōbēr ḥāḇēr* (Heb.), *epaeidōn epaidēn* (Gk.), a charmer, one who binds spells (cf. Ps. 58:6; Isa. 47:9, 12); *šō'ēl 'ôḇ* (Heb.), *engastrimythos* (Gk.), a medium (cf. Lev. 19:31; 20:6, 27; 1 Sam. 28:3, 7 f., 9; 2 Ki. 21:6; 23:24; 1 Chron. 10:13; 2 Chron. 33:6; Isa. 8:19; 19:3; 29:4); *yiddᵉ'ônî* (Heb.), *teratoskopos* (Gk.), wizard, familiar spirit, soothsayer (Lev. 19:31; 20:6, 27; 1 Sam. 28:3, 9; 2 Ki. 21:6; 23:24; Isa. 8:19; 19:3; 2 Chron. 33:6); *dōrēš 'el hammēṭîm* (Heb.), *eperōtōn tous nekrous* (Gk.), necromancer, lit. one who enquires of the dead (*dāraš* is the normal Heb. vb. for enquire; it is used in connection with spirits and deities in Isa. 8:19; 11:10; 19:3; an instance of necromancy is given in the story of Saul's visit to the medium [Heb. *'ēšeṭ ba'ᵃlaṭ-'ôḇ*; Gk. *gynē engastrimythos*, 1 Sam. 28:7] at Endor). The story of the raising of the spirit of Samuel by the medium at Endor casts no doubt on the reality of what happened, but clearly condemns the venture.

A number of other terms are found elsewhere in the OT. The Heb. vb. *lāḥaš* means to whisper and is used in connection with charms (cf. the piel participle form *mᵉlaḥᵃšîm* in Ps. 58:6 with 2 Sam. 12:19; Ps. 41:8). The noun *laḥaš* means whispering, serpent-charming, "charms" (RSV, Isa. 3:3; cf. Jer. 8:17; Eccl. 10:11). The Gk. word in Isa. 3:3 is *akroatēs*. The expert in charms figures among those who were currently held in esteem in Israel and who held sway over the people in

Isaiah's day; in the name of the Lord the prophet announced their removal. The same applies to the *ḥᵃkam ḥᵃrāšîm*, "the skilful magician" which is only found in Isa. 3:3. The LXX removes the magical element from both these terms by rendering them *sophon architektona kai syneton akroatēn* ("skilful architect and intelligent scholar"). But the magical element in *ḥereš* can be seen in Aramaic and Syriac parallels, and may be traced back to Ugaritic as an old West Semitic word (cf. I. Mendelsohn, "Magic", *IDB* III 225). Isa. 47:13 mentions *hōbrê šāmayim* (LXX *astrologoi tou ouranou*) "those who divide the heavens" and *haḥozîm bakkôkābîm* (LXX *hoi horōntes tous asteras*) "those who gaze at the stars", a scornful reference to the influence of Babylonian astrology. Astrology was also practised in Egypt, but there are relatively few references to it in the OT (cf. Jer. 10:2 with Dan. 2:27; 4:7 [4:4]; 5:7, 11). The *ḥarṭōm* (plur. *ḥarṭummîm*) were soothsayer priests. Egyptian ones are mentioned in Gen. 41:8, 24 (LXX *exēgētēs*; → Explain, art. *exēgeomai*); Exod. 7:11, 22; 8:3, 14f.; 9:11 (the LXX uses *pharmakos* for *ḥarṭōm*, though it also uses the word for other Heb. words). Babylonian ones are mentioned in Dan. 1:20; 2:2. Dan. 1:20 and 2:20 also mention *'aššāpîm*, conjurors, enchanters who were likewise summoned to retell and interpret the → dreams of Nebuchadnezzar. But the task proved beyond them, and it was Daniel who was able to declare the king's dreams. Isa. 19:3 contains the unique word *'iṭṭîm*, in the plur., for the shades or ghosts of a dead person. I. Mendelsohn maintains that the various forms of magic not mentioned in the law of Deut. 18:10f. represent Egyptian and Babylonian practice and that *ḥᵃrāšîm* and *kiššēp* and its cognates (Exod. 7:11; 22:17; Deut. 18:10; Mal. 5:5; Dan. 2:2; 2 Chron. 33:6) were the Heb. generic names for magic in all its aspects (*IDB* III 224f.; cf. Exod. 22:18; 2 Ki. 9:22; Nah. 3:4).

The practice of sorcery is mentioned in the Code of Hammurabi who belonged to the Old Babylonian Amorite Dynasty and who ruled from 1728 to 1686 B.C., though the copy of the Code preserved on a stele is sometime later. Paragraph 2 of the Code specified the death penalty for those guilty of sorcery and equally those who make false accusations of sorcery (*ANET*, 166). The test in both cases was to cast the person accused into the Euphrates. If he survived it was to be taken as a divine vindication of innocence. The Middle Assyrian laws preserved on clay tablets also laid down the death penalty for those guilty of making magical preparations (§47; cf. *ANET*, 184). The king himself was to investigate cases and false accusations. The OT saw magic as a potential rival to the worship of Yahweh and a threat to the well-being of the people. It was forbidden by law and those who practised it were to be put to death (Exod. 22:18 [MT 22:17]; Lev. 19:26, 31; 20:6, 27; cf. Mic. 5:12). As the passage already quoted from Deut. 18:10–14 shows, magical practices were ranked with human sacrifice as evil and an abomination to the Lord (cf. also 2 Ki. 17:17; 2 Chron. 33:6). It was denounced by the prophets as lies and deception (Isa. 44:25; 57:3; Jer. 27:9f.; Ezek. 22:28; Zech. 10:2; Mal. 3:5). Jezebel was condemned as a sorceress (2 Ki. 9:22), and Manasseh's apostate practices included various forms of magic, soothsaying and human sacrifice (2 Ki. 21:3–6). His grandson Josiah, however, "put away the mediums and the wizards and the teraphim and the idols and all the abominations that were seen in the land of Judah and Jerusalem, that he might establish the words of the law which were written in the book that Hilkiah the priest found in the house of the Lord" (2 Ki. 23:24).

6. The most significant evidence of magic in the Hellenistic world is to be found in the papyri from Egypt which date from the 3rd and 4th cents. A.D. The most important of these have been edited by Karl Preisendanz (see bibliography; see also table of abbreviations for other papyri). Early important references to magic include the *Apology* of Apuleius, written in the middle of the 2nd cent. A.D., *De Mysteriis* by Iamblichus (early 4th cent. A.D.), the Elder Pliny (died A.D. 79), *Naturalis Historia*, which contains numerous magical recipes and exorcisms, and the writings of Lucian of Samosata (born *c.* A.D. 120). In addition numerous cursing tablets, inscriptions often on thin sheets of lead known as *tabellae defixionum*, amulets, and ostraca have been found, The papyri often refer to laurel wreaths, earthen altars, white garments, all of which have naturally perished, and also to tables, discs, dishes, lamps and stands some of which have survived. For a survey of data, literature and practices see J. M. Hull, *Hellenistic Magic and the Synoptic Tradition*, *SBT* Second Series 28, 1974, 5–44. Magic in the Hellenistic world was a fusion of the Gk. spirit with Egyptian influences. Among them were the belief that magic words gained additional power if written on a gem; belief in monstrous beings, half animal and half human; the belief that whilst magic allows man to control the gods, it is at the same time a gift and revelation of the gods to men; and such figures as Seth, Thoth and Osiris. On the other hand, there was also a Persian influence which included the idea of magic as a defence against evil spirits rather than as a means of manipulating the high gods. Magical practices were also rife in Judaism. Justin Martyr testifies to the use of the → name of God in exorcism (*Dial.* 85, 3), and the use of *Ia*, *Iaō* (and numerous variants), Sabaoth, Adonai and Yahweh is common in the magical papyri. Apart from the divine names, that of → Moses appears alongside that of Thoth and Zoroaster, and → Solomon was highly important. The Heb. language itself, as a sacred language, had a special use. Angels and demons figured particularly in Jewish magic.

The normal magical ceremony consisted of two parts: the invocation (*klēsis* or *epiklēsis*) and the ritual (*praxis*). Hull (op. cit., 42 f.) lists six features of the invocation: (i) The invocation proper beginning "I call upon you, I summon you, come to me, help me . . . "; (ii) The utterance of the name of the god (though this is often omitted from the papyri to guard the secret or allow the magician to insert the name of his choice); (iii) Epithets describing the god; (iv) Descriptions of the god to increase his benevolence; (v) Remembrances of similar acts performed by the god, sometimes using substances associated with the act; (vi) The request itself. The subsequent ritual could take various forms involving the use of amulets, sacrifices, the mixing of special substances and potions, libations, and secret writing. Elaborate ceremonies could take several days. *C. Brown*

NT Magic is the technique of manipulating supernatural or supernormal forces to attain one's own ends. It may be a means of bending spirits of various grades to carry out one's wishes, or of developing psychic powers so that one can project an inner force on to some person or situation. There have always been fake magicians, or conjurers in the modern sense of the word, but even the English word "conjurer" up to the time of Shakespeare had the magical sense of one who bound spirits or people by invocation. In the light of Acts 19:18, 19 we may assume that in NT times this was the only sort of magic that interested people. The books that were burnt were books of *perierga*. The word has the root idea of being concerned with other people's business, and is translated → "busybodies" in 1 Tim. 5:13, but in Acts 19:18, 19 it has the specific sense of interfering with other people through magical arts. Thus, while magicians may well have helped out their claims by trickery, they were primarily concerned with the realm of the psychic and the occult.

1. The following magicians are named in the NT: (a) Simon, commonly referred to as Simon Magus (Acts 8:19–24). He practised spectacular magic in Samaria, but professed conversion in response to Philip's preaching. He was astounded by the manifestations of the Holy Spirit that followed the laying on of hands by Peter and John, and, being still under the influence of his old ideas, he assumed that the apostles had some secret technique that he might use as a Christian magician. For this he was roundly rebuked by Peter.

Early Christian writers speak of him as a heretic of gnostic type, and founder of the Simonians (e.g. Justin, *Apol.* I, 26; Irenaeus, *Haer.* 1, 16). The Acts of Peter 4, 6, 9, 11–18, 23, 31 describe among other things his levitation in flight over Rome, and his being brought down through the prayers of Peter (cf. Henn. Schn. II 282 ff., 286, 292, 293–301, 306, 314 f.; cf. also the Acts of Paul, Henn.Schn. II 374).

(b) Bar-Jesus, or Elymas (Acts 13:4–12). A magician on Cyprus in the employ of Sergius Paulus, the proconsul. He resisted Paul and Barnabas, but was struck down with temporary blindness. In Acts 13:8 the name Elymas is not intended as a translation of Bar-Jesus, but as an equivalent of magician (cf. RSV), probably connected with the Arabic *'alîm*, wise, magician. (On his name see Arndt, 253, 758 f.; F. F. Bruce, *The Acts of the Apostles*, 1952², 256 f.; E. Haenchen, *The Acts of the Apostles*, 1971, 398 f.)

(c) Jannes and Jambres are named in 2 Tim. 3:8 as two of the Egyptian magicians who opposed Moses. They are not named in Exodus, but in one form of another they occur in Jewish writings (cf. Schürer III 402 ff.; Arndt, 368). Thus the Babylonian Talmud writes of Yohane and Mamre (Menahoth 85a). Some Lat. and Gk. MSS have Mambres in 2 Tim. 3:8. Pliny speaks of Jannes and → Moses as magicians in Pharaoh's court (*Nat.Hist.* 30, 1 11).

2. The following descriptive words are found in the NT.

(a) *perierga*, "magic arts" (Acts 19:19 RSV). Here the reference is to the voluntary burning of books by those who had previously practised magic arts at Ephesus. The act is seen as testimony to the growth and power of the word of the Lord (19:20) especially as the value of the books was put at fifty thousand pieces of silver. On this word in other contexts → Busybody.

(b) *magos*, magus, magician; *mageia*, magic; *mageuō*, practise magic. According to Herodotus (1, 101; cf. 1, 132), the Magians were originally Medians who became priests under the Persian empire. Like the Chaldeans of Dan. 1:4 and 2:2 ff., they merged their racial identity in their profession, and their name was applied to any practitioner such as Bar-Jesus (Acts 13:6, 8; see above 1 (b)). They are referred to in Josephus, *Ant.* 10, 216; 20, 142. The term is used of the Magi who came from the East at the birth of Jesus (Matt. 2:1–16).

D. Hill regards the account of the visit of the Magi as a piece of haggadic poetry (*The Gospel of Matthew*, 1972, 82 f.). He takes the star not as a literal star, but as a messianic interpretation of Num. 24:17: "a star shall come forth [*anatelei astron*]

557

out of Jacob, and a sceptre shall rise out of Israel." In the OT this passage forms part of an oracle of Balaam to Balak, king of Moab, who attempted to bar the way of the people of Israel as they journeyed from Egypt. The messianic interpretation is attested in the Qumran literature (CD 7:19 f.; 1QM 11:6; 1QSb 5:27; 4Qtest 12 f.) and in the Pseudepigrapha (Test.Lev. 18:3 f.; Test. Jud. 24:1). It was also applied to Bar Kokhba whose name means "Son of a Star" (→ Israel OT 2 (c); → Jesus Christ, art. *christos* OT 5), and the text appears to underlie a Christian testimonium (cf. Rev. 22:16; 2 Pet. 1:19; Justin, *Dial.* 106, 4; 126, 1; Irenaeus, *Haer.* 3, 9, 2). The LXX version of Num. 24:7 already bears traces of messianic interpretation. The difficult Heb. text ("Water shall flow from his buckets") is replaced by "A man shall come forth from his seed." This makes it possible to refer the next verse ("God brings him out of Egypt") to the messiah rather than to Israel. A midrashic interpretation of the visit of the magi is also offered by M. D. Goulder who sees various other motifs such as the coming of the Gentiles, the gifts and the name of Joseph as contributing to the story (*Midrash and Lection in Matthew*, 1974, 236 ff.).

On the other hand, the story has usually been taken to refer to an actual celestial phenomenon. Kepler suggested that the star was a conjunction of Jupiter and Saturn in the constellation Pisces in 7 B.C. For a discussion of views concerning the star see B. Ramm, *The Christian View of Science and Scripture*, 1955, 112–18; H. Montefiore, *Josephus and the New Testament*, 1962, 8–14; → also Sun, Moon, Stars for the theological significance of heavenly bodies. The magi were clearly not crude practitioners of the occult arts, nor were they ordinary astrologers. They believed that God showed signs in heaven and that a certain heavenly body, whether planet, star, comet, or supernova, indicated from its appearance and position that God had fulfilled the royal promise, of which they had doubtless heard from Jews in the East (cf. E. Stauffer, *Jesus and His Story*, 1960, 36 ff.).

The noun *mageia* and the vb. *mageuō* are found in Acts 8:11 and 9 respectively of the magic of Simon Magus (see above 1 (a)).

(c) *pharmakos*, magician (Rev. 22:15); *pharmakeus*, mixer of potions, magician (Rev. 21:8); *pharmakeia*, magic, sorcery (Gal. 5:20; Rev. 9:21; 18:23). The basic word *pharmakon* does not occur in the NT, but its meaning of medicine, magic potion, poison gives the underlying idea of the words. Potions include poisons, but there has always been a magical tradition of herbs gathered and prepared for spells, and also for encouraging the presence of spirits at magical ceremonies (cf. possibly the final sentence of Ezek. 8:17: "They put the branch to their nose"). Sorcery is classed among the works of the → flesh in Gal. 5:20.

(d) *goēs*, sorcerer, juggler, occurs only in 2 Tim. 3:13. In cl. Gk. it may mean a magician, probably from the root seen in *goaō*, wail. A wizard might chant his spells. In 2 Tim. 3:13 magicians may be the correct translation in view of Jannes and Jambres in v. 8 (see above 1 (c)). Cl. Gk. also knows the meaning of imposter, since spellbinders could make false claims for their powers, and RSV prefers this translation in 2 Tim. 3:13 in the light of the closing words of the verse.

(e) The word *pythōn* is connected with the Delphic oracle, Delphi being the place where Apollo slew the mighty serpent Python that guarded the oracle (Strabo, 9, 3, 12). Later on *pythōn* came to designate a spirit of divination and also a ventriloquist who was thought to have such a spirit inside his or her belly. In Acts 16:16 a girl at

Philippi had a Python spirit (*pneuma pythōna*), the two words being in apposition. She probably had second sight fostered by a possessing spirit. Such second sight was characteristic of the priestesses of the Delphic oracle. The spirit in the girl was forced to admit the truth of the gospel, just as other spirits confessed Jesus Christ during his earthly ministry (e.g. Mk. 1:24; Lk. 4:34; Matt. 8:29), but neither Jesus nor Paul accepted testimony from this source, and they cast out the spirits. (On the term *pythōn* see further Arndt, 736; F. F. Bruce, op. cit., 315; E. Haenchen, op. cit., 495; W. Foerster, *pythōn*, *TDNT* VI 917–20.)

(f) *baskainō* is possibly related to Eng. fascinate via the Latin (cf. *fascino*, bewitch, charm). The meaning is to cast a spell by what is called the evil eye. Paul uses the word of the deceived Galatians in Gal. 3:1 ("Who has bewitched you . . . ?"). The effect of the spell, if the evil eye is detected at the time, could be averted by spitting, and some hold that this was in Paul's mind in his use of *ekptyō* in Gal. 4:14 (lit., spit out; RSV "despise").

3. The heresy in Col. 2. Whatever heresy Paul has in mind in this chapter, much of what he says is applicable to practitioners of the occult. Paul's theme is the absolute supremacy and sufficiency of Christ. If the Christian is linked to him, he shares in his supremacy over the spirit world, good and bad, and, to say the least, he is foolish to think he can gain more power through intermediate spirit beings. Thus vv. 8 and 20 speak of the Christian's deliverance from the elemental spirits of the universe, according to the probable translation of *ta stoicheia tou kosmou*. In v. 15 there is the conquest of principalities and powers (cf. Eph. 6:12) and in v. 18 the worship (service) of angels, and also induced visions. Finally the strange vs. 21–23 could describe the rigorous ritual of the magician to produce and safeguard his contacts with the spirits (cf. self-abasement, v. 18).

4. Mediumship and spiritualism. Mediumship is of a different order from manipulative magic and sorcery, but, inasmuch as it is an attempt to communicate with the departed, there is no relaxation in the NT of the OT ban (e.g. Lev. 19:31; Deut. 18:10, 11; 1 Chr. 10:13, 14; Isa. 8:19, 20). The argument is not simply from silence but from significant silence. Thus, when Paul speaks of the departed, he assures the Christians that they will meet their loved ones again, inasmuch as they are both "in Christ". He does not suggest that Christian mediums can put the bereaved in touch with those who have passed on, and thus give assurance that they have not perished (1 Thess. 4:13–18; 1 Cor. 15:17–19), whereas many spiritualists assert that NT → prophets were mediums.

The NT shows that God may allow a departed spirit to return for purposes of his own. → Moses and → Elijah returned on the Mount of Transfiguration to reassert the testimony of the law and the prophets to the sacrifice of Christ on the cross (Matt. 17:3; Mk. 9:4; Lk. 9:30 f.). There are two other references to spirits or ghosts. When Jesus walked on the water, the disciples thought they were seeing a *phantasma* (Matt. 14:26; Mk. 6:49). The word is a general one to describe an apparition. The more important reference is Lk. 24:37–41, where Jesus appeared to his disciples after his → resurrection. Some thought he was a *pneuma*, a → spirit or ghost. Jesus did not deny the existence of ghosts, but showed that his resurrection body was of a different order altogether from a spirit form. This is further testimony to the difference between his resurrection and his spiritual survival.

J. Stafford Wright

5. In *Hellenistic Magic and the Synoptic Tradition, SBT* Second Series 28, 1974, J. M. Hull provides a survey of magical ideas and practices in the Hellenistic world. He then examines the question whether Jesus had anything in common with this background in the light of traditions in the early centuries that Jesus was a magician (cf. the third-century gnostic *Pistis Sophia* ch. 102, §§ 255, 258; ch. 130, §§ 332–35; Acts of Pilate 2:1; *Clementine Recognitions* 1, 42; Act.Thom. 20; Act. Paul 15; *Pseudo-Clementines,* Homily 7, 9; Origen, *Contra Celsum* 1, 38 and 60; Tertullian, *On Idolatry* 9; the Koran 5, 113). The author sees some affinities between Mk.'s presentation of Jesus' healing work and the magical beliefs of the surrounding world. This was a decisive factor in the way Jesus appears in Mk. as a liberator from the powers of evil. Similarly in Lk. and Acts the greater power of Christ is stressed. Matthew, on the other hand, sought to avoid giving the impression of any connection between Jesus and magic. However, Hull does not think that Jesus thought of himself as a magician. A difficulty attending the thesis that Mk. and other NT writers thought of Jesus as a "Master-Magician" is the presumption that the → miracles of Jesus were works of magic. The evidence for magical practices in the gospels is slim. Jesus used saliva in healing the deaf-mute in Mk. 7:32 ff. and the blind man in Mk. 8:23. The word *ephphatha* which represents *'etpattah* or the contracted *'eppattah* is not a meaningless word like *abracadabra,* and Mk. himself provides a translation which is contrary to magical practice. It is derived from the vb. *p*e*tah* and means "be opened" or "be released" (cf. SB II 17 f. for its use in connection with blindness). The idea is that of the whole person being opened. V. Taylor compares it to "verbal encouragement" as in modern psychotherapy (*The Gospel according to St. Mark,* 1952, 354; cf. E. R. Micklem, *Miracles and the New Psychology,* 1922, 119). But C. E. B. Cranfield prefers to see it as "the command that shatters the fetters by which Satan has held his victim bound" (*The Gospel according to Saint Mark,* 1959, 252). The accounts of the healing of the woman with the issue of blood (Matt. 9:20 ff.; Mk. 5:25–34; Lk. 9:34–8) do not significantly differ in any way which demonstrates that any one of the evangelists is more interested in magic than the others. The woman herself has a faith which might seem to border upon superstition, in that she believed that she would be healed if only she could touch the clothes of Jesus. But this must be seen against the background that her unclean condition prevented her from coming openly to him. All three evangelists avoid any support for connecting the healing with magic in giving Jesus' reply, "Your faith has saved you [*hē pistis sou sesōken se*]." Whereas magicians used names in connection with spells, the way that the → name of Jesus is used in healing and casting out evil spirits stands out in marked contrast. Neither Jesus nor the apostles used secret rituals or esoteric signs to gain control over supernatural powers. Still less is there any trace of trying to coerce a reluctant God to further one's own ends. Although the imputation was made that Jesus cast out demons in the name of Beelzebul, the self-contradictory nature of the charge is at once evident in the light of the exorcisms that Jesus performed (Matt. 12:25–37; Mk. 3:23–30; Lk. 11:17–23; → Satan). For Jesus the control over evil spirits was not an end in itself. He told his followers: "Nevertheless, do not rejoice in this, that the spirits are subject to you; but rejoice that your names are written in heaven" (Lk. 10:20). (The unauthentic longer ending of Mk. gives rather greater prominence to such powers than the authentic gospel texts, cf. Mk. 16:17 f. Even so, the

emphasis is one of implied contrast between the power of Jesus and other powers.) Finally, the Lord's Prayer and other prayers of Jesus have a completely different orientation from magic. The latter is concerned with the control of the supernatural by techniques to further one's own ends. Jesus' concern was to do the will of the Father and to teach men to submit their whole lives to that will (Matt. 6:9–15 par. Lk. 11:2–4; cf. Matt. 26:36–46 par. Mk. 14:32–42, Lk. 22:40–46; Jn. 4:34; 5:30).

C. Brown

→ Angel, → Bless, → Curse, → Demon, → Dream, → Heal, → Miracle, → Satan, → Spirit

The following bibliography contains references to a number of works dealing with magic outside the Bible and the ancient world. This is for the purpose of comparing magical practices.
(a). C. Bailey, *Phases in the Religion of Ancient Rome*, 1932; J. Beattie and J. Middleton, eds., *Spirit Mediumship and Society in Africa*, 1969; H. Birkeland, *The Evildoers in the Book of Psalms*, *Avhandlinger utgitt av Det Norske Videnskaps-Akademi i Oslo* 2, 1955; E. A. W. Budge, *Egyptian Magic*, 1899; R. Bultmann and D. Lührmann, *phantasma*, *TDNT* IX 6; E. D. van Buren, "Amulets in Ancient Babylonia", *Orientalia* 14, 1945, 21 ff.; R. P. Casey, "Simon Magus", in F. J. Foakes Jackson and K. Lake, eds., *The Beginnings of Christianity*, V, 1933, 151–63; T. W. Davies, *Magic, Divination, and Demonology Among the Hebrews and Their Neighbours*, 1898; G. Delling, *baskainō*, *TDNT* I 594 f.; *goēs*, *TDNT* I 737 f.; and *magos* etc., *TDNT* IV 356–9; E. R. Dodds, *The Greeks and the Irrational*, 1951; E. Ehnmark, "Religion and Magic: Frazer, Söderblom and Hägerström", *Ethnos* 21, 1956, 1–10; S. Eitrem, *The Greek Magical Papyri in the British Museum*, 1923; *Some Notes on the Demonology of the New Testament*, *Symbolae Osloenses Supplement* 1966²; S. Eitrem, ed., *Papyri Osloenses*, I, *Magical Papyri*, 1925; S. E. Eitrem and J. H. Croon, "Magic", *OCD* 637 f.; E. E. Evans-Pritchard, *Witchcraft, Oracles and Magic among the Azande*, 1937; W. Foerster, *pythōn*, *TDNT* VI 917–20; J. G. Frazer, *The Golden Bough: A Study in Magic and Religion*, I–XII, 1911–27³; abridged edition I–II, 1957; and *The Magic Art*, I–II, 1936³; A. H. Gardiner, "Magic (Egyptian)", *ERE* VIII 262–9; M. Gaster, "Magic (Jewish)", *ERE* VIII 300–5; W. Goode, "Magic and Religion, A Continuum", *Ethnos* 14, 1949, 172–82; A. Guillaume, *Prophecy and Divination*, 1938; J. M. Hull, *Hellenistic Magic and the Synoptic Tradition*, *SBT* Second Series 28, 1974; L. W. King, "Magic (Babylon)", *ERE* VIII 253 ff.; and *Babylonian Magic and Sorcery*, 1896; C. Kluckhorn, *Navaho Witchcraft*, *Peabody Museum Papers*, 22, 1944; H. van der Leeuw, *Religion in its Essence and Manifestation*, 1964²; J. E. Lowe, *Magic in Greek and Latin Literature*, 1929; D. S. Margoliouth, "Magic (Arabian and Muslim)", *ERE* VIII 252 f.; L. Mair, *Witchcraft*, 1969; B. Malinowski, *Magic, Science and Religion and Other Essays*, (1948) 1974; M. Mauss, *A General Theory of Magic*, 1972; I. Mendelsohn, "Magic", *IDB* III 223 ff.; R. R. Marett, "Magic (Introductory)", *ERE* VIII 245–52; A. D. Nock, "Greek Magical Papyri", *Journal of Egyptian Archaeology* 15, 1929, 219–35; and "Paul and the Magus", in F. J. Foakes Jackson and K. Lake, eds., *The Beginnings of Christianity*, V, 1933, 164–88; W. M. F. Petrie, *Amulets*, 1914; J. B. Pritchard, ed., *Ancient Near Eastern Texts*, 1955²; E. Reiner, *Surpu, A Collection of Sumerian and Akkadian Incantations*, 1958; H. Ringgren, *Religions of the Near East*, 1973; E. Rohde, *Psyche*, 1925; K. F. Smith, "Magic (Greek and Roman)", *ERE* I 269–89; R. C. Thompson, *The Reports of the Magicians and Astrologers of Nineveh in the British Museum*, I–II, 1900; *The Devils and Evil Spirits of Babylonia*, I–II, 1903–4; *Semitic Magic, its Origins and Development*, 1908; L. Thorndike, *A History of Magic and Experimental Science during the first Thirteen Centuries of our Era*, 1923; J. Trachtenberg, *Jewish Magic and Superstition: A Study in Folk Religion*, 1939; V. W. Turner, *Ndembu Divination: Its Symbolism and Techniques*, 1961; M. Unger, *Biblical Demonology*, 1952; D. P. Walker, *Spiritual and Demonic Magic from Ficino to Campanella*, 1958; H. Webster, *Magic: A Sociological Study*, 1948; G. B. Wetter, *Magic and Religion*, 1958; R. C. Zaehner, *The Teachings of the Magi: A Compendium of Zoroastrian Beliefs*, 1956.
(b). E. Benveniste, *Les Mages dans l'ancien Iran*, 1938; A. Bertholet, *Das Dynamistische im Alten Testament*, 1926; A. Bertholet, C.-M. Edsman, K. Galling and W. Eilers, "Magie", *RGG³* IV 595–602; K. Beth, *Religion und Magie bei den Naturvölkern*, 1928²; J. Bidez and F. Cumont, *Les Mages Hellénisés*, I–II, 1938; L. Bieler, *Theios anēr. Das Bild des "göttlichen Menschen" in Spätantike und Frühchristentum*, I–II, 1935–36; and *"dynamis und exousia"*, *Wiener Studien* 55, 182–90; H. Birkeland, *Die Feinde des Individuums in der israelitischen Psalmenliteratur*, 1933; L.

Blau, *Das altjüdische Zauberwesen*, 1898; A. Carnoy, "Le nom des Mages", *Muséon* New Series 9, 1908; 121–58; G. Conteneau, *La Magie chez les Assyriens et les Babyloniens*, 1947; S. Eitrem, "Magische Papyri", *Münchener Beiträge zur Papyrusforschung* 19, 1933, 243 ff.; and "Kronos in der Magie", *Annuaire de l'Institut de Philologie et d'Histoire Orientales (Mélanges Bidez)* 2, 1934, 351–60; G. Fohrer, "Prophetie und Magie", *ZAW* 78, 1966, 25–47; A. E. Jensen, *Mythos und Kult bei Naturvölkern*, 1959²; F. Lexa, *La Magie dans l'Égypte antique*, I–III, 1925; H. Kaupel, *Die Dämonen im Alten Testament*, 1930; G. Messina, *Der Ursprung der Magie und der zarathustraischen Religion*, 1930; and *I magi a Betlemme e una predizione di Zoroastro*, 1933; K. Preisendanz, *Papyri Graecae Magicae: Die griechischen Zauberpapyri*, I–III, 1928–42; *Papyrusfunde und Papyrusforschung*, 1933; "Die griechischen und lateinischen Zaubertafeln", *Archiv für Papyrusforschung* 11, 1935, 153–64; "Zur Überlieferung der spätantiken Magie", *Zentralblatt für Bibliothekswesen* Beiheft 75, Georg Leyh Festgabe, 1950, 223–40; "Neue griechische Zauberpapyri", *Chronique d'Égypte* 26, 1951, 405–9; C. H. Ratschow, *Magie und Religion*, 1955; L. Röhrich, "Zauberbücher" and "Zaubersprüche", *RGG³* VI 1869 ff., 1873 ff.; E. Spranger, *Die Magie der Seele*, 1947; E. Stiglmayr, "Zauberer", *RGG³* VI 1971 ff.

Man

The basic concept behind the Gk. word *anthrōpos* is that of generic man (as opposed to gods or animals), the human race, mankind (cf. the derived word, *anthropology*, the theory or science of man). In this general sense men and women, old men and children can all be subsumed under the one overall heading (cf. Ger. *man*, Eng. "one"). *anthrōpos*, within the genus man, also refers some specifically to men, occasionally also to attendants or → slaves, as distinct from their → Lord (*kyrios*). When *anthrōpos* refers to a particular man, its meaning impinges on that of the word *anēr*, denoting a man as opposed to a → woman, whether he be husband, bridegroom, warrior, hero (similarly *arsēn*, male). The fact that *anēr* can take on the more general meaning of mankind, whereas no such similar usage is attested for woman (*gynē*) is linked up with the ancient identification of man and mankind.

| ἀνήρ | ἀνήρ (*anēr*), a man; ἀνδρίζομαι (*andrizomai*), behave in a manly way. |

CL *anēr*, attested from Mycenaean Gk. onwards, is found in secular Gk. from Homer in all the meanings which are also known in the LXX and the NT: (a) a man, as contrasted with → woman (Plato, *Gorgias* 514e; (b) husband (Homer, *Od.* 6, 182 ff.); also bridegroom (cf. SB II 393 ff.); (c) adult (Xen., *Cyr.* 8, 7, 6) and warrior; (d) manliness (Aristoph., *Achilles* 77 ff.); also gentleman, hero; (e) man, as genus (Homer, *Il.* 1, 544; → *anthrōpos*).

OT There are several Heb. words used in the OT which approximate to these various meanings which the LXX often simply translates by *anēr*. The main ones are *'îš*, man; *'enôš*, men, people; *ba'al*, lord, husband, head of a household; *gibbôr*, hero, warrior; *zāqēn*, elder; *nāśî'*, prince; *'āḏôn*, lord. The man is lord of the wife (Gen. 3:16; 18:12). He alone is competent in legal and cultic proceedings (Exod. 23:17; 34:23; 1 Sam. 1:3 f.). But alongside this typically oriental and patriarchal way of life, one can find allusions to men's responsibilities to women, above all in writings such as Deut. 20:7; 21:14; 22:13 ff.; 24:5, and occasionally also in later Judaism (cf. e.g., B. Yeb. 62b; cf. SB III 610a; → Woman, art. *gynē* OT).

NT 1. *anēr* occurs in the NT, with meanings mentioned as under CL, as follows: (a) Matt. 14:21; 1 Cor. 11:13 ff. (→ *arsēn* is sometimes used instead of *anēr*, linking up with the OT; cf. Matt. 19:4 par. Mk. 10:6 and Rom. 1:26 ff. with Gen. 1:27). *anēr* is used without emphasis in Acts 3:14; 10:28, and as a typical form of address in Acts 15:7, 13 and passim; (b) Mk. 10:2, 12; cf. Matt. 19:3, 9; Rom. 7:2 f.; Eph. 5:22 ff.; Tit. 1:6; of a betrothed person (cf. Matt. 1:19; 2 Cor. 11:2; Rev. 21:2 with Deut. 22:23); (c) 1 Cor. 13:11; cf. Jas. 3:2; (d) including maturity and dignity (Lk. 23:59; Acts 6:3, 5); (e) Lk. 5:8; Jas. 1:20 (modelled on Gk. and also OT usage).

anēr occurs most frequently in Lk. and Paul. Paul often uses *anēr* to distinguish man from *gynē* (e.g. in 1 Cor. 7:1–16). Lk. uses *anēr* usually in the more general meaning of → *anthrōpos* (as in Lk. 11:31; 19:7; Acts 2:5 and passim).

2. The organization and leadership of the Christian community in the NT (→ Church) was largely male-orientated, just as Jesus' circle of the Twelve comprised only men (but cf. → Woman, art. *gynē* NT). But the man did not receive his special position because of his natural fitness for the cult. This much came rather from Christ, by whom he was honoured and whom he was called upon to reflect (1 Cor. 11:7). In the sequence God–Christ–man–woman (1 Cor. 11:3 ff.), each one is the → "head" of the following, and, conversely, each member is the reflected splendour (*doxa* → glory) of the preceding one. This qualification of the man, however, no longer indicates preferential status but man's special task and responsibility, just as the woman has hers. For before God, according to Gal. 3:28 (cf. 1 Pet. 4:7), man and woman are, in the last analysis, on the same level. This establishment of the equality of the sexes before God which does not imply any levelling-out of their human differences – is something new and worthy of note in Christianity. It throws into sharp relief the distinction between the Christian view and the otherwise widespread contempt for women in the ancient world.

When Christ and man are put in parallel in Eph. 5:25 and 28 (cf. also Col. 3:19; 1 Pet. 3:7), the point of comparison is the responsibility of the man to love his wife in the same way as Christ loves his church, i.e. with a life of total, selfless, self-sacrificial devotion, comparable with that of Christ for the church. The exhortation *andrizesthe*, lit. "be men" (RSV "be courageous") is a summons like that to "be alert [*grēgoreite*]" and to "stand firm in faith [*stēkete en tē pistei*]" (1 Cor. 16:13; cf. 2 Sam. 10:12 LXX; Pss. 26[27]:14; 30:25 [31:24]; Josephus, *War* 6, 50). It is a powerful form of demand aimed at the whole community: their ultimate goal should be to become "a perfect man [*andra teleion*]" (Eph. 4:13 AV).

H. Vorländer

3. *anēr* is used in the sense of husband in the phrase "husband of one wife [*mias gynaikos anēr*]" which occurs in the Pastoral Epistles as one of the qualifications stipulated for bishops (1 Tim. 3:2), deacons (1 Tim. 3:12) and elders (Tit. 1:6). The latter were evidently the same as bishops (→ Bishop, Presbyter, Elder). Roman Catholic exegesis tends to take the phrase to mean that the office holder may be married, but anyone who has remarried after the death of his first wife or who has remarried after divorce (in the case of a pagan convert) is automatically excluded (cf. C. Spicq, *Les Épîtres Pastorales*, 1947, 78f. who quotes extensively from patristic sources). A similar view is evidently adopted by the RSV which

translates the phrase "married only once." Whilst such an interpretation may be consonant with later developments in the church, the literal interpretation of the text, i.e. that the man should not have more than one wife who is alive, seems to fit the first-century situation better. On the one hand, it would exclude polygamy which did occur in the first century (→ Marriage, art. *gameō* OT 7) and in this respect would meet the OT norms for marriage. On the other hand, it would also exclude divorcees who had remarried, since the first wife is still regarded as the wife despite the divorce (cf. Mk. 10:11; Lk. 16:18b; → Divorce). The converse of this phrase occurs in 1 Tim. 5:9 in the case of the enrolment of widows who must be "the wife of one man [*henos andros gynē*]." To exclude widows who had been "married more than once" (RSV) would seem unjust, especially in cases of levirate marriage (→ Marriage, art. *gameō* OT 4, 7). But the ruling is understandable, if the woman has not been involved in divorce or a polygamous marriage. It should be remembered that the passage is not concerned about welfare in general and the Christian's attitude to anyone in need, but with those *within* the church who have a claim on church resources. Elsewhere Paul advised remarriage in case of need (1 Cor. 7:8 f., 39 f.).   *C. Brown*

ἄνθρωπος	ἄνθρωπος (*anthrōpos*), man; ἀνθρώπινος (*anthrōpinos*), human.

CL *anthrōpos*, attested from Mycenaean times, means a human being, and also a man. The fem. equivalent is → woman, often in a contemptuous sense. The etymology is disputed, though it may be a compound of *anēr* and *ōps*, i.e. man's face. The adj. *anthrōpinos* is a derivative word meaning human, belonging to humanity. It is used from pre-Socratic writers and Hdt. onwards.

In secular Gk. *anthrōpos* means man, as opposed to beasts, or also to gods (in Homer). In a contemptuous sense, it means a slave (used also as fem. by Hdt. and others). There is also a voc. usage, originally employed for slaves (Hdt.), with undertones of reproachfulness: "Man!" (Plato). *anthrōpos*, as a general designation, is often rendered by "one".

OT 1. The Heb. words corresponding to *anthrōpos* are '*āḏām*, '*îš* or '*ᵉnôš*. '*āḏām* is used to designate his nature, as contrasted with God in 1 Sam. 15:29, and with animals in Gen. 1:26. In its generic use it includes both man and woman (cf. Gen. 2:7 ff., 18 ff.; → *anēr*; → Woman, art. *gynē*). It is also the word for → Adam. '*îš* occurs, e.g., in Gen. 2:24. '*ᵉnôš* often signifies the aspect of weakness, mortality (cf. Ps. 8:5).

In both accounts of creation (Gen. 1:1 ff.; 2:4b ff.) the creation of man is the high-point. In Gen. 1 he is the crowning culmination; in Gen. 2 he is the mid-point of the creation. His humanity resides in the life he has been given (2:7b) in his correspondence to God (1:27a). He is deemed worthy to be spoken to by God and to be given a task (2:16 f.; 1:28). Through disobedience he falls victim to death. '*āḏām*, a word connected with '*ᵃḏāmâ*, earth, now no longer simply alludes to his creatureliness (2:7) but also to his transitoriness (3:19).

2. The OT is not acquainted with anything corresponding to the Gk. division of man into two or three parts, consisting of *nous*, *psychē*, and *sōma* (mind, soul,

and body). The following concepts indicate, in rough outline comparison, different aspects of man, always seen as a whole. They do not represent different parts.

(a) → Flesh (Heb. *bāśār*) often indicating man's transitoriness (Ps. 78:39). (b) → Spirit (Heb. *rûah*) man as a living being (Ps. 146:4), as a person (Ezek. 11:19; spirit and heart are mentioned in reference to man in relation to God). (c) → Soul (Heb. *nepeš*) man as life bound up with his body (1 Sam. 19:11b), as an individual (Deut. 24:7a; Ezek. 13:18 f.). The soul is neither pre-existent nor immortal, for it is the whole man (Gen. 2:7). (d) → Heart (Heb. *lēb*, *lēbāb*) the essential, inner man, as opposed to his outward appearance (Job 12:3; 1 Sam. 16:7b). Due to the translation of the LXX, Gk. currents of thought became bound up with these concepts, and gained ground in Judaism, as the NT picture shows.

3. A pessimistic conception of man is found in a section of the wisdom literature (e.g. Eccl. and Job 14) which is radicalized in the Qumran texts. The utter vanity, transitoriness and sinfulness of man is presented in a wide variety of formulations. According to the Catechism of the Community Rule (1QS 3:13–4:26), men fall into two groups: the "Sons of Light" who are ruled by the spirit of truth (→ Light) and the "Sons of Darkness", who are both fighting simultaneously for the domination of man's heart. This accounts for the sins even of the pious.

Another branch of Judaism reveals the development to a body-soul dualism (4 Macc. 2:21 f.), which in Hellenistic Judaism led to an attitude of loathing for the body (2 Esd. 7:88, 100). According to Josephus, there was widespread belief that → redemption is the liberation of the → soul from the → body (*War* 2, 8; 7, 8; *Ant.* 18, 1; → Soul, art. *psychē* OT 2). The → image of God in man is restricted to the *nous*, his → mind and → reason.

4. This dualistic view of man in the Hellenistic world is found above all in gnosticism (cf. Corp.Herm. 1, 15, 18, 21), which certain sections of the NT endeavour to combat (e.g. John). The thought of man's being related to God derives from the Stoics, and this is taken up in Acts 17:28 f. (→ God, art. *theos* NT 4 (b)).

NT In the NT, as in the OT, the question about man is essentially that concerning his → sin and → redemption. Abstract definitions find no place here. Man differs from → animals and plants (Matt. 4:19; 12:12; 1 Cor. 15:39; Rev. 9:4), from → angels (1 Cor. 4:9; 13:1), from Christ (Gal. 1:12; Eph. 6:7), and from God (Matt. 7:11; 10:32 f.; Mk. 10:9; Jn. 10:33; Acts 5:29; Phil. 2:7). *anthrōpos* is used in order to belittle in Jas. 1:7; with reference to Jesus in Matt. 26:74 par. Mk. 14:71 and Jn. 19:5. Jesus is called *anthrōpos* in respect of his true humanity in Phil. 2:7 and 1 Tim. 2:5. Jesus' own self-designation was *ho hyios tou anthrōpou*, (→ Son of God; → Child). *kata anthrōpous* and *kata anthrōpon*, lit. according to men, in a human fashion, are used as common synonymous phrases for *anthrōpinos*, human (cf. Rom. 3:5; 1 Cor. 3:3; 15:32; 1 Pet. 4:6; and Rom. 6:19; 1 Cor. 10:13). If *anthrōpos* is defined as to sex, it can be used, as in secular Gk., synonymously with → *anēr*, a man (see Matt. 11:8; 19:5; 1 Cor. 7:1).

The NT is not interested in an isolated self-contained anthropology any more than the OT. Statements about man are always partly theological pronouncements. He always appears as man vis-à-vis God: in his creatureliness (as distinct from other creatures and from God), in being addressed and chosen by God, in his transitoriness and disobedience, and as subject to the wrath and grace of God.

The unity and equality of mankind are not postulates of abstract ideas: they are realized in the Christian community (Gal. 3:28; Rom. 10:12; cf. 3:22, 29; Jas. 2:1 ff.). Through Christ the "one new man [*hena kainon anthrōpon*]" (Eph. 2:15 AV) comes into being. At the same time new differentiations come to light through God's electing activity in Christ (Matt. 20:16) and through the variety of the → gifts of the Spirit in the church (1 Cor. 12).

1. *The Synoptics*. Man as a creature owes God obedience and service without any prior claim to reward (Lk. 17:17 ff.). Jesus' universal call to repentance assumes that all are sinners (Mk. 1:15; Matt. 6:12; cf. 5:45; 9:13; Lk. 15:7; → Sin, art. *hamartia*). At the same time, there are the statements concerning the great value God puts on a man (Matt. 6:26b; 10:29 f.), even as a sinner (Lk. 15). His vocation is to be a son of the → Father and to be perfect like him (Matt. 5:45, 48). Lk. 2:14 speaks in Semitic fashion of *anthrōpoi eudokias*. This does not mean, as the Vulg. translates, men of good will (Lat. *hominibus bonae voluntatis*). Rather, the gen. expresses a possessional relationship: men as the possession of the divine favour (cf. Lk. 3:22; 1QH 4:32 f.; 11:9). What is thus meant is "the elect Messianic community of salvation" (Jeremias, *TDNT* 1 365; cf. J. Jeremias, "*Anthrōpoi eudokias*", *ZNW* 28, 1929, 13–20; E. Vogt, " 'Peace Among Men of God's Good Pleasure' Lk. 2:14", in K. Stendahl, ed., *The Scrolls and the New Testament*, 1958, 114–17).

2. *Paul*. The old man without Christ (*palaios anthrōpos*), the unconverted man, is either devoted to the law (Rom. 2:17 ff.) or in rebellion against it (Rom. 1:18 ff.); he perverts his knowledge of God, and in so doing becomes himself perverted (Rom. 1:21 ff.). In either case he is unfree and culpable. Alongside statements about man's responsibility stand those about his incapability (cf. his inexcusability in Rom. 2:1 with his inability to do good in 7:18 f.). This is a tension which Paul sees removed only in God and overcome in Christ (Phil. 2:12b, 13). Through Christ, the new man (*kainos anthrōpos*) and the last → Adam (Rom. 5:9 ff.; 1 Cor. 15:21 f., 45 ff.), man becomes free. He himself becomes a new creation (2 Cor. 5:17; cf. Eph. 4:22 ff.; Col. 3:1–4:6). Baptism signifies the death of the old man with Christ (Rom. 6:6). Through incorporation into the → body of Christ man is born as a new man (→ Birth, art. *palingenesia*). To the new man is directed the imperative to be what Christ has made him (Eph. 4:22 ff.; Rom. 6:6 ff.; Col. 3:9 ff.). It is not in man's natural capacities to become this; it comes about through being renewed in Christ and in living out this new life. Rom. 8:1–17 depicts this in terms of being led by the Spirit. Rom. 7:14 ff. sees man as what the Reformers called *simul iustus et peccator* (at once just and a sinner). Paul distinguishes further between the inner and outer man, *esō kai exō anthrōpos* (2 Cor. 4:16), that is, between his essential being, often expressed in terms of the *kardia* (→ heart), and his outward appearance.

In addition, these are the most important anthropological concepts found in Paul (cf. with this OT 2). (a) *sōma*, → body, not only the physical body but the whole person, the self, "I" (see Phil. 1:20; and, for the double significance, cf. 1 Cor. 15:44 with Phil. 3:21). The body is not despised (1 Cor. 15:35 ff.; 6:19). (b) *sarx*, → flesh occasionally synonymous with *sōma*, speaks of the transience of man (2 Cor. 4:10 f.). It furthermore signifies his sinfulness (Rom. 8:1 ff.; 1 Cor. 15:50), but in the realm, not so much of nature as of history (→ Adam) and →

guilt. (c) *psychē*, → soul, man as a living being, a person (2 Cor. 12:15). 1 Cor. 15:44 relates its existence to this life as contrasted with the next: "It is sown a physical body [*sōma psychikon*], it is raised a spiritual body [*sōma pneumatikon*]" (RSV). (d) *pneuma*, → spirit. In certain passages its meaning overlaps with that of *sōma* and *psychē* and refers to the inner self. It bears a certain resemblance to the modern concept of self-consciousness (cf. Rom. 8:16 where the Spirit is said to bear witness with our spirit that we are children of God, in that we cry to him as Father). (e) From Gk. thought, and found primarily in Paul, are: *nous*, → mind (→ Reason) which focusses attention on man as a conscious, rational being; and *syneidēsis*, → conscience. Rom. 2:15 refers to the conscience of the Gentiles and its rôle in their knowledge of God.

3. *John*. Johannine statements view man as prey to the *kosmos*, the world in opposition to God, and therefore missing his real self (→ Lie, art. *pseudomai* on Jn. 8:41–7; 1 Jn. 1:10; 2:22; 5:10; Rev. 2:2). The coming of Jesus confronts man with a decision. In contrast with gnostic dualism Jn. presents a dualism of decision which in Jn. 3:3 ff. is linked with being born again (→ Birth). This decision demonstrates "whence" the man comes – whether he is "of the world" or "from God" (cf. Jn. 8:47 and 1 Jn. 4:5 with e.g. Jn. 5:24 alongside the call to decision of Jn. 6:44, 65, 12:32). But, equally, there is no depreciation of matter here (Jn. 1:14). On the contrary, the whole man is made free through Jesus (Jn. 8:31 ff.), and thus gains life (5:24; 11:25 f.). *H. Vorländer*

4. *The NT and Modern Psychology*. Biblical psychology is practical rather than scientific, but is understandable in its context. Thus, since strong emotion frequently affects the lower parts of the body from the solar plexus downwards, the bowels (→ Mercy, art. *splanchna*) is the term used where we today, in equally popular terms, would speak of the heart (e.g. 2 Cor. 6:12; 7:15; Phil. 1:8; Phlm. 7, 12). At the opposite extreme *nous* is the mind, intellect, or understanding (e.g. Rom. 12:2; 1 Cor. 14:19; → Reason, art. *nous*). *kardia* (heart) stands somewhere between the two, being sometimes emotional, though less warm than *splanchna* (e.g. Rom. 1:24; Jas. 3:14), and sometimes representing the inner set of the life-pattern, including volition (e.g. 2 Cor. 4:6; 9:7; Eph. 4:18).

Thus the NT seizes on commonsense descriptive terms to describe centres of emotion, feeling, volition, life-pattern, and comprehension. One may class these aspects of the personal *psychē* (variously → soul, animal life, person), but the Bible is concerned, not with theory, but with bringing every single part of the person into an effective whole through the Holy Spirit giving continuous life to the human *pneuma*, → spirit. (e.g. Jn. 3:6; 1 Cor. 2:10–16). The usage of all these words is discussed in detail under separate entries.

Man is seen as a whole being, and whatever touches one part affects the whole. The NT would agree with the modern term psychosomatic, but would want to turn the word into pneumatopsychosomatic.

To write in detail about modern schools of psychology lies outside the scope of this lexicon, but one can distinguish certain general aspects of psychological thinking that are likely to continue in one form or another, regardless of the prevailing fashions in psychology. The NT would have no quarrel with the investigations of academic and laboratory psychology, which explore the functions of the brain, nervous system, glands, and the animal responses of the human body. It is worth noting that the function of the brain as the organ of thought was an occasional hypothesis and not an accepted fact in the ancient world. Thus, while Plato in the *Timaeus* 69–72 made it the centre of the rational soul, Aristotle treated it as a cooler of the blood (*Part.An.* 2, 7). It is interesting that Ephesians makes Christ the head and ruler of the body (4:15, 16).

The Bible would, however, cross swords with some modern conclusions that the bodily responses that psychology can investigate are a total explanation of man, i.e. that man is wholly body, and consequently cannot survive death. One need not postulate what has been called "the ghost in the machine" (cf. G. Ryle, *The Concept of Mind*, 1949) if one sees man as a personality who responds to the world of time and sense through the body and brain, and at the same time responds to mental, aesthetic, and spiritual concepts, which are real, even though they are beyond the reach of the physical sciences. The death of the body temporarily shuts off one dimension until the resurrection, but does not destroy the whole person (cf. 1 Thess. 5:23).

Psychologists of the behaviourist schools interpret man as no more than a complicated build-up of conditioned reflexes. As has often been pointed out, if this theory is true, it cannot be true, since truth would have no meaning. One psychologist would be conditioned to certain conclusions, another to other conclusions. Obviously the NT does not deny the build-up of patterns of life through conditioning. Conditioning may produce hardness of heart (e.g. Mk. 3:5; Heb. 3:13) or reactions of self-interest (e.g. Acts 19:25–27). The renewal of the personal responses through the Holy Spirit is a form of conditioning, so that one intelligently and gladly reacts to the will of God (e.g. Rom. 12:1, 2). In other words, God has made man capable of building up a pattern of life which becomes, as we say, second nature to him.

Where the NT differs from behaviourist psychology is over the actual reality of the work of the Spirit, and the God-given ability of man to respond deliberately to the call of Jesus Christ. A psychologist takes a Christian conversion, and accounts for it after it has happened in terms of natural responses arising from such states as fear and inner stress. The NT would not deny such stresses, including guilt, but gives primacy to the Holy Spirit breaking in and supplying the dynamics of new life. The ensuing knowledge of God in and through Jesus Christ is objectively real. Certainly conditioning techniques, as at a highly emotional meeting, may produce a temporary conversion or an outburst of strange manifestations, but a truly Christian experience leads the person on afterwards in a proper walk with Christ after the NT pattern.

Other forms of psychology pay more regard to an inner world of man, postulating a realm of the unconscious, which stores up early memories and experiences, and often real or imagined occasions of guilt. These under repression may break out in disguise, and produce abnormal feelings, attitudes, and reactions. Jungian psychologists see the unconscious also as the sphere of positive dynamic drives.

This reminds us of the NT teaching of the fallenness of man, with the heart as the storage place of the host of evils that emerge in the life (e.g. Matt. 15:18, 19). A non-Christian psychologist may uncover the originating cause of some trouble, such as rivalry with one's father in infancy, and thus bring the patient to terms with himself and society. But full adjustment, as the NT sees it, involves cleansing from all sin, known and unknown, and a new relationship to God in and through Jesus Christ, and this is not given by a psychologist as psychologist.

One further school emphasizes the need for life to make sense, with purposelessness as a cause of breakdown. The NT entirely agrees, as witness Paul's words about the goal of his life in Phil. 3:12–16, and the wisdom of the gospel in 1 Cor. 2:6–13.

There is nothing in NT teaching which runs counter to sound psychological practice, but the NT has the necessary overplus of God-relationship as needed for full maturity of man in himself and in relation to his fellows in the church and in society.   *J. Stafford Wright*

ἄρσην	ἄρσην (*arsēn*), male; θῆλυς (*thēlys*), female; ἀρσενοκοίτης (*arsenokoitēs*), male homosexual, pederast, sodomite.

CL *arsēn* occurs in cl. Gk. from Homer onwards, sometimes in the Attic form *arrēn* (often in papyri, and also Philo, Josephus and Rom. 1:27 *v.l.*). (On the form see Funk § 34 (2); Moulton, *Grammar*, II, 103.) It means male as opposed to female, *thēlys* (cf. Plato, *Leg.* 2, 9 p. 665c; K. Preisendanz, *Papyri Graecae Magicae*, I, 1928, 15, 18). *thēlys* is also found from Homer onwards as an adj. meaning female, but also with the art. meaning woman (e.g. Hdt. 3, 109; Xen., *Mem.* 2, 1, 4). On the phrase *arsēn kai thēlys*, male and female, cf. Plato, *Rep.* 454d; Aristot., *Met.* 988a 5.

OT *arsēn* occurs some 54 times in the LXX canonical and uncanonical writings, chiefly for the Heb. *zākār*. It appears in the phrase *arsen kai thēly*, male and female, in Gen. 1:27 (Heb. *zākār ûnᵉqēḇâh*) of the creation of male and female in the → image of God (cf. also Gen. 5:2; 6:19 f.; 7:2 f., 9, 15 f.; Lev. 3:1, 6; 12:7, referring not only to man and woman but to the male and female of animal species in the flood story and in sacrifice). The male is referred to on his own in Gen. 17:14, 23 (the institution of male → circumcision as the → covenant sign); Exod. 1:16 ff., 22; 2:2 (Pharaoh's attempt to exterminate the Israelites by destroying male infants); Exod. 12:5 (the Passover → lamb had to be a male without blemish); and Lev. 1:3, 10; 4:23; 22:19; Mal. 1:14 (in connection with sacrifice); Lev. 6:12(29), 37(7:6) (of priests); Lev. 18:22; 20:13 (in condemnation of homosexual practices); Lev. 27:3, 5 ff. (in the valuation of the people); Num. 1:3(2); 3:40 (in the census of the people); Num. 31:17 f.; Jos. 17:2; Jdg. 21:11 f. (in historical narratives); Job 3:3; Isa. 26:14; 66:7; Jer. 20:15; 37(30):6; Sir. 33:26 (23); 2 Macc. 7:21; 4 Macc. 15:30 (of males generally). The references to the male and female correspond to those to man and woman generally in the OT. On the one hand, there is the recognition in Gen. of the divinely instituted parity in that man and woman together constitute the image of God, and their complementary roles in the transmission of life in both the human and the animal realm. On the other hand, there are certain rôles (e.g. in receiving the covenant sign, in the priesthood, and in certain → sacrifices) that only the male may fill.

569

NT 1. The creative act in Gen. 1:27 is referred to in Matt. 19:4 par. Mk. 10:6 in connection with → divorce. Jesus' reply to the Pharisees takes it as the major premise for his teaching on → marriage: "from the beginning he created them male and female." This leads to the minor premise quoted from Gen. 2:24: "for this reason a man shall leave his father and mother [Matt. also gives "and shall cleave to his wife"] and the two shall be one flesh" (Matt. 19:5; Mk. 10:7 f.). The conclusion is drawn: "So they are no longer two but one flesh. What therefore God put together, let not man put asunder" (Matt. 19:6; Mk. 10:8 f.). Gen. 1:27 is also referred to in 1 Clem. 33:5 and 2 Clem. 14:2.

2. Lk. 2:23 tells how Jesus' parents offered the sacrifice prescribed for males by Exod. 13:2, 12 at his birth (→ Bird).

3. Paul's use of *arsēn* is interesting in that it exhibits a tension between the creation ordinances and their abolition in the gospel age. By contrast the ungodly have abolished the creation ordinances for sexual relations in a way which can only bring judgment.

(a) In Rom. 1:27 *arsēn* (*v.l. arrēn*) is used 3 times which RSV translates by "men": "and the men likewise gave up natural relations with women and were consumed with passion for one another, men committing shameless acts with men and receiving in their own persons the due penalty for their error." In this passage sexual perversion is seen as a result of (and to that extent as a judgment on) man's sin in worshipping the creature rather than the creator. Because he has put something else in the place which can only properly belong to God, man's natural relationships have become perverted. Josephus also pointed out that unnatural relations between males was punishable by death (*Ap.* 1, 199; cf. Lev. 20:13; 18:22, 29). On Rom. 1 generally, see G. Bornkamm, "The Revelation of God's Wrath (Romans 1–3)", *Early Christian Experience*, 1969, 47–70. Paul uses the noun *arsenokoitēs*, a male homosexual, pederast, sodomite (→ Marriage, art. *koitē*), as one who is excluded from the kingdom (1 Cor. 6:9) and condemned by the law (1 Tim. 1:10; cf. Gen. 19; Lev. 18:22, 29; 20:13; Deut. 23:17; → Punishment).

(b) On the other hand, Gal. 3:28 asserts that "There is neither Jew nor Greek, there is neither slave nor free, there is neither male nor female; for you are all one in Christ Jesus." This, however, is not a call to abolish all earthly relationships. Rather, it puts these relationships in the perspective of salvation history. As Paul goes on to say, "And if you are Christ's then you are Abraham's offspring, heirs according to promise" (Gal. 3:29; cf. also Rom. 10:2). All who are in Christ have the same status before God; but they do not necessarily have the same function. In the context of the → circumcision question in Gal., the assertion is doubly relevant. For women could not be recipients of the sign which Judaizers were insisting as a prerequisite for full salvation. There may also be an underlying Adam-typology in the passage. Some rabbis asserted that Adam was originally androgynous (cf. J. Bligh, *Galatians: A Discussion of St Paul's Epistle*, 1969, 326).

4. Rev. 12:5, 13 takes up the imagery of Isa. 66:7 and Ps. 2:9 in the vision of the → dragon's attack on the woman with the male child: "she brought forth a male child, one who is to rule all the nations with a rod of iron, but her child was caught up to God and to his throne. . . . And when the dragon saw that he had been thrown down to the earth, he pursued the woman who had borne the male child." Whereas the child is here clearly Christ, the woman, in the light of the following

verses, represents the mother of Jesus and also the church whose other "offspring"
are now pursued by the dragon. *C. Brown*

→ Adam, → Blood, → Body, → Brother, → Child, → Earth, → Father, → Flesh,
→ Hand, → Head, → Heart, → Image, → Life, → Marriage, → Son, → Soul,
→ Spirit, → Woman

(a). J. Barr, *The Semantics of Biblical Language*, 1961; and "Man and Nature – the Ecological
Controversy and the Old Testament", *BJRL* 55, 1972–73, 9 ff.; C. K. Barrett, *From First Adam to
Last*, 1962; K. Barth, *Christ and Adam: Man and Humanity in Romans 5*, SJT Occasional Papers 5,
1962; and *CD* III, 2 *The Doctrine of Creation* (volume dealing with man); G. C. Berkouwer, *Man:
The Image of God*, 1962; T. Boman, *Hebrew Thought Compared with Greek*, 1960; N. P. Bratsiotis,
'îš, TDOT I 222–35; E. Brunner, *Man in Revolt: A Christian Anthropology*, 1939; and *The Christian
Doctrine of Creation and Redemption*, Dogmatics II, 1952; R. Bultmann, "Romans 7 and the
Anthropology of Paul", and "Man between the Times according to the New Testament", *Existence
and Faith*, (1961) 1964, 173–85, and 293–315; "The Understanding of Man and the World in the
New Testament and in the Greek World", and "Adam where art Thou?" *Essays Philosophical
and Theological*, 1955, 67–89, and 119–32; D. Burkhard, ed., *Man before God: Toward a Theology
of Man*, 1966; E. de Witt Burton, *Spirit, Soul and Flesh*, 1918; S. Cave, *The Christian Estimate of
Man*, 1944; W. Eichrodt, *Man in the Old Testament*, SBT 4, 1951; and *Theology of the Old Testa-
ment*, II, 1967, 118–50, 231–495; J. de Fraine, *Adam and the Family of Man*, 1965; R. H. Gundry,
Sōma in Biblical Theology with Emphasis on Pauline Anthropology, Society for New Testament
Studies Monograph Series 29, 1976; D. Jenkins, *The Glory of Man*, Bampton Lectures for 1966,
1967; J. Jeremias, *Adam, TDNT* I 141 ff.; *anthrōpos, TDNT* I 364–67; P. K. Jewett, *Man as Male and
Female*, 1975; R. Jewett, *Paul's Anthropological Terms: A Study of the Use in Conflict Settings*,
Arbeiten zur Geschichte des antiken Judentums und des Urchristentums, 10, 1971; A. R. Johnson, *The
Vitality of the Individual in the Thought of Ancient Israel*, 1964[2]; R. Koch and A. Deissler, "Man",
EBT 542–51; L. Köhler, *Hebrew Man*, (1956) 1973; W. G. Kümmel, *Man in the New Testament*, 1963;
J. Laidlaw, *The Bible Doctrine of Man*, 1895; R. Laurin, "The Concept of Man as a Soul", *ExpT* 72,
1960–61, 131–134; A. R. C. Leaney, "The Doctrine of Man in 1 Corinthians", *SJT* 15, 1962, 394–99;
F. Maas, *'ādām, TDOT* I 75–87; S. V. McCasland, " 'The Image of God' according to St. Paul",
JBL 69, 1950, 85–100; H. D. McDonald, *I and He*, 1966; E. L. Mascall, *The Importance of Being
Human: Some Aspects of the Christian Doctrine of Man*, 1959; J. Moltmann, *Man: Christian Anthro-
pology in the Conflicts of rhe present*, 1974; D. W. Mork, *The Biblical Meaning of Man*, 1967; C. F.
D. Moule, *Man and his Nature in the New Testament: Some Reflections on Biblical Ecology*, (1964)
1967; R. Niebuhr, *The Nature and Destiny of Man: A Christian Interpretation*, I–II, 1941–43;
A. Oepke, *anēr, andrizomai, TDNT* I 360–63; W. Pannenberg, *What is Man? Contemporary
Anthropology in Theological Perspective*, 1970; H. W. Robinson, *The Christian Doctrine of
Man*, (1911) 1926[3]; H. H. Rowley, "The Nature and Need of Man", *The Faith of Israel: Aspects
of Old Testament Thought*, 1956, 74–98; E. C. Rust, *Nature and Man in Biblical Thought*, 1953;
R. P. Shedd, *Man in Community*, 1958; R. L. Shinn, *Man: The New Humanism*, New Direc-
tions in Theology Today, 6, 1968; C. R. Smith, *The Bible Doctrine of Man*, 1951; W. D. Stacey,
The Pauline View of Man, 1958; G. E. Whitlock, "The Structure of Personality in Hebrew
Psychology: The Implication of the Hebrew View of Man for Psychology", *Interpretation*,
14, 1960, 3–13; H. W. Wolff, *Anthropology of the Old Testament*, 1974; G. E. Wright, *The Biblical
Doctrine of Man in Society*, Ecumenical Biblical Studies 2, 1954; J. S. Wright, *What is Man?
A Christian Assessment of the Powers and Functions of Human Personality*, 1955, revised edition
re-issued under the title *Mind, Man and the Spirits*, 1967; W. Zimmerli, *Man and his Hope in
the Old Testament*, SBT Second Series 20, 1971.
(b). L. Adler, *Der Mensch in der Sicht der Bibel*, 1965; P. Althaus, *Paulus und Luther über den Menschen*, 1963[4]; E. Brandenburger, *Adam und Christus*, WMANT 7, 1962; N. P. Bratsiotis, *bāśār*,
TWAT I 850–67; F. Delitzsch, *System der biblischen Psychologie*, 1861[2]; A.-M. Dubarle, "La
condition humaine dans l'Ancien Testament", *RB* 63, 1956, 321 ff.; A. Flitner, ed., *Wege zur
pädagogischen Anthropologie*, 1963; K. Galling, *Das Bild vom Menschen in biblischer Sicht*, 1947;
G. Gerlemann, *bāśār, THAT* I 376–79; W. Gutbrod, *Die paulinische Anthropologie*, 1934; M.
Hengel, "Was ist der Mensch?" in H. W. Wolff, ed., *Probleme biblischer Theologie. Gerhard von
Rad zum 70. Geburtstag*, 1971, 116–35; E. Jüngel, "Grenzen des Menschseins", in H. W. Wolff,
ed., op. cit., 199–205; E. Käsemann, *Leib und Leib Christi*, 1933; J. Kühlewein, *'îš, THAT* I 130–38;

J. Jervell, *Imago Dei, FRLANT* 58, 1960; W. D. Marsch, "Christliche Anthropologie und biologische Zukunft des Menschen", *Past. Theologie* 58, 1969, 91 ff.; H. Mehl-Koehnlein, *L'Homme selon l'Apôtre Paul*, 1951; H. Mynarek, *Der Mensch, das Wesen der Zukunft*, 1968; E. Otto, "Der Mensch als Geschöpf und Bild Gottes in Ägypten", in H. W. Wolff, ed., op. cit., 335–48; H. van Oyen, "Verantwortung und Norm in Hinblick auf die Situationsethik", *ThZ* 25, 1969, 91 ff.; G. Pidoux, *L'Homme dans l'Ancien Testament*, 1953; G. von Rad, H. Schlier, E. Wolf, *Der alte und der neue Mensch. Aufsätze zur theologischen Anthropologie, BEvTh* 8, 1942; C. H. Ratschow, A. S. Kapelrud, N. A. Dahl, "Mensch", *RGG*³ IV 860 ff.; L. Scheffczyk, ed., *Der Mensch als Bild Gottes, Wege der Forschung* 124, 1969; K. H. Schelkle, *Theologie des Neuen Testaments*, I, 1968, 91 ff.; J. N. Sevenster, "Die Anthropologie des Neuen Testaments", *Anthropologie Religieuse, Numen* Supplements 2, 1955, 166–77; F. J. Stendebach, *Der Mensch, wie ihn Israel vor 3000 Jahren sah*, 1972; H. J. Stoebe, H. J. Wachs, W. Trillhaas, H. Plessner, "Anthropologie", *EKL* I 131 ff.; W. Zimmerli, *Das Menschenbild des Alten Testaments, ThEH* Neue Folge 14, 1949.

Mark, Brand

στίγμα

στίγμα (*stigma*), mark, brand.

CL *stigma* is related to the vb. *stizō*, to prick, to mark with a pointed instrument, and when applied to the flesh of men and animals, to brand, to tattoo.

Several well-defined areas of application are seen, as *stigmata* were used to mark cattle and other animals as a protection against theft. Horses were so branded as a mark of ownership (Aristophanes, *Knights* 602; *Clouds* 122, 1298: all referring to sigma-brand). When *stigmata* were applied to the human body, this denoted a sign of disgrace, suitable for deserters (Herodotus, 7, 233, 2: "branded with the king's marks"). Criminals were marked as a punishment (Plato, *Laws* 9, 854d) and especially slaves suffered this penalty if they ran away and were caught (Aristophanes, *Birds* 760; *Lysistrata* 331) or broke the law in some other way (Diogenes Laertius, 4, 7, 46). The slave was called *stigmatias*, branded desperado, if he received this penalty (Xenophon, *Hellenica* 5, 3, 24) and it is suggested that the letters used as a brand on his hands or face were F(UG) for *fugitivus* or FUR for thief. In the imperial period the branding of slaves as a mark of ownership was practised. The mark was usually placed on the forehead, whereas soldiers who enlisted in the Roman army received a tattoo mark, in the shape of the abbreviated name of the emperor, on their hand (Aetius Amidenus, *Libri Medicinales* 8, 12).

Stigmata were also applied as sign of religious devotion to the gods (Herodotus 2, 113, *stigmata hiera*, sacred marks; Lucian, *Syr. Dea* 59 "bearing stigmata" in honour of the goddess).

OT The LXX has *stigmata* (used in the plur.) only once in the non-significant passage of Cant. 1:11, "ornaments [pointed pieces of jewelry] of gold." Nonetheless, the idea behind the word is present in the OT in the several instances where slaves were marked as a badge of ownership (Exod. 21:6; Deut. 15:16 f.); where Cain is given a sign of Yahweh's preservation of his life by a mark (Gen. 4:15); where the remnant of Israelite faithful are marked with the Heb. letter Tau as a pledge of their safety against the day of judgment (Ezek. 9:4; the letter Tau in ancient script was a cross, a feature giving rise to later Christian speculation); and especially where Yahweh's people are bidden to inscribe his name on their hands as a promise of fidelity (Isa. 44:5).

Real stigmata were expressly forbidden in Israel according to the rubric of Lev. 19:28. Only in her apostate days did Israel borrow this practice from the Gentile nations (Jer. 16:6; 41:5; cf. Jer. 47:5; 48:37). True Yahwism is thus differentiated from the fertility-cult practices of the nations in Canaan (1 Ki. 18:28). But 1 Ki. 20:41 may be an exception if the prophet had Yahweh's "mark" on his forehead.

In the inter-testamental period Jews were branded by their captors (Ps.Sol. 2:6) and slaves were branded to prevent their escape (T.Mak. 4:15). The Hellenistic persecution of the Jews took the form of the forcible imposition of pagan symbols, and Philo, *Spec.Leg.* 1, 58, regards the willing acceptance of a brand "with a red-hot iron" as a hallmark of apostasy. Circumcision was commonly regarded as the effective antidote to the desire to be tattooed, since the loyal Jew had this badge of his membership of the elect race and needed no other religious marking. Marks on bodies (in a figurative sense) and on grave sites in a literal fashion suggest a protective claim to belong to Yahweh (see the use made of Ezek. 9:4 in the Damascus Rule 9:10–12 of those who seek relief from the eschatological terror by the possession of this sign, and in Ps.Sol. 15:6–9). The sign of the cross on Jewish tombs and ossuaries is a development of Ezek. 9:4.

NT The single occurrence of the noun is in Gal. 6:17. Various possibilities of meaning are: that Paul asserts by this reference his claim to ownership by the Lord Jesus whose slave (*doulos*) he is; that he carries a badge of protection that none of his enemies in Galatia can ignore with impunity. The Galatians would be familiar with this idea of a religious teacher being under the care of the gods and so immune from attack; that the *stigmata* are the Christian counterpart to Jewish circumcision and are a sign of eschatological fulfilment marking out the new Israel (Gal. 6:16) as the true circumcision as in Phil. 3:3. On this verse Dibelius comments: "The thought is not that of a bodily mark but of the church's consciousness of being the new people of God". See too Rom. 2:25–29 and Col. 2:11–13.

The stigmata are not to be seen as symbols however (such as Paul's having tattooed the sign of the cross or the name of Jesus on his flesh). Rather they are scars and wounds received in his missionary service on behalf of the Gentile churches as the eschatological apostle (Col. 1:24; Eph. 3:1, 13).

Marking of God's people in Rev. 7:2 f.; 9:4; 14:1; 22:4 with seals is a metaphorical usage (→ *charagma*). R. P. Martin

| χάραγμα | χάραγμα (charagma), mark, stamp, graven object. |

CL The underlying vb. *charassō*, to cut to a point, then to inscribe, which is the meaning in Sir. 50:27 and in one version of Ezek. 4:1 (LXX) where it translates the MT ḥqq. The noun means a mark, a sign caused by engraving, etching, or branding.

The vb. *charassō* means to cut to a point, to sharpen, in Hesiod, *Works and Days* 387, 573 ("whet the sickle"). The later technical sense of inscribing on wood, stone, brass is attested. Then, in a specialized meaning, it describes the casting of a die, and so the minting of coins. In the Hellenistic papyri anything written down on writing material is *dia charagmatōn*. This phrase in *P. Lond.* 5, 1658, 8 seems to mean "I pray for your health in this letter" (so Ghedini, referred to in Moulton-Milligan). Ownership of property is secured by the brand-mark (*charagma*). Documents are validated as true by the imposition of a stamp or seal (*charagma*). Imperial decrees are shown to be genuine by the same token. Currency carries the impress (*charagma*) as a sign of its genuineness, so Plutarch, *Agesilaus*, 15:6; *De Lysandro* 16:2; and *P.Oxy.* 1, 144, 6: "gold in stamped money", i.e. in coins (*chrysou en obryzō charagmati*).

OT *charagma* does not appear in LXX but the vb. *charassō* occurs in the texts noted above. In 3 Macc. 2:29 *charagma* is used for Jewish markings with pagan cult symbols. Cf. Ps.Sol. 15:8-10 where the righteous who are loyal to Israel's heritage are "marked" for God.

NT In Rev. 13:11-18 there is an apparent reference to the imperial priesthood under the figure of the second beast. It requires that universal recognition and homage be given to the "first beast" (the imperial line). The image of the emperor is made to speak (v. 15). The counterpart to this claim to divinity is that all trading is possible only as men have the "mark" (*charagma*) of the first beast on their right hand or forehead. That "mark" is identified with the beast's → name or → number (v. 18). Contrast Rev. 7:3 ff. where a similar "mark" denotes divine protection. In 13:16 ff. it signifies the "protection" of Satan.

This stigmatization was common in the ancient world (→ *stigma*), denoting ownership and preservation. Repeatedly in the Apocalypse the *charagma tou thēriou*, mark of the beast, denotes subservience to anti-Christian powers (14:9; 20:4; cf. 13:17; 14:11; 16:2; 19:20). This situation is matched by a "sign" from God (7:1-8) and wrath is threatened to all who bear the first mark (14:9, 11). Those who do not wear the satanic mark are promised the right to judge the evil powers (20:4).

In Acts 17:19 *charagma* is used in the sense of handiwork, creation, produced by the artist or craftsman. *R. P. Martin*

καυστηριάζω

καυστηριάζω (*kaustēriazō*), mark by a branding iron, brand.

CL Cognate nouns are *kaustērion* (*P.Lond.* 2, 391, 7 ff.) meaning kiln and *kautērion*, branding iron. The vb. means to burn with hot iron, to brand.

Branding iron (*kautērion*) is possibly attested in Euripides, *Fr.* 815 (conj.), while the vb. is found in Strabo, *Geog.* 5, 1, 9: "a great herd of unbranded [*akautēriastōn*] horses", and in a possible reading in *BGU*, III, 952, 4 (Wilcken's reconstructed text is: [*kaustēria*]*zousi tēn gypson*).

OT The LXX does not have the vb., but 4 Macc. 15:22 has *kautērion* in the sense of branding iron.

NT The sole NT occurrence is 1 Tim. 4:2. False teachers have their conscience "branded [*kekaustēriasmenōn*]". The brand mark is the sign of ownership (→ *stigma*), and the condition of these heretics is probably that of men who are

possessed by Satan and demonic forces. Alternatively it means that their conscience is "cauterized", or "seared" (RSV), i.e. made insensible to moral distinctions.
→ Cross, → Image   *R. P. Martin*

On *stigma*:
(a). Arndt, 776; O. Betz, *stigma*, *TDNT* VII 657–64; M. Black, "The Chi-Rho Sign – Christogram and/or Staurogram?" in W. W. Gasque and R. P. Martin, eds., *Apostolic History and the Gospel, Biblical and Historical Essays Presented to F. F. Bruce*, 1970, 319–27; T. W. Crafer, "The Stoning of St. Paul", *The Expositor*, 8th Series 6, 1913, 375–84; A. Deissmann, *Bible Studies*, 1909, 349 ff.; E. Dinkler, "Comments on the History of the Symbol of the Cross", *Journal for Theology and the Church* 1, 1965, 124–45; J. H. Moulton, "The Marks of Jesus", *ExpT* 21, 1909–10, 283 f.; Moulton-Milligan, 590; W. M. Ramsay, *A Historical Commentary on St. Paul's Epistle to the Galatians*, 1900, 472 ff.
(b). F.-J. Dölger, *Sphragis*, 1911, 39 ff.; and "Beiträge zur Geschichte des Kreuzzeichens", *Jahrbuch für Antike und Christentum* 1958–61; A. Oepke, *Der Brief des Paulus an die Galater, Theologischer Handkommentar zum Neuen Testament*, 1964², 163–66; O. Schmitz, *Die Christus-Gemeinschaft des Paulus im Lichte seines Genitivusgebrauchs*, 1924, 185–94.

On *charagma*:
(a). A. Deissmann, *Light from the Ancient East*, 1927, 341; and *Bible Studies*, 1909, 240–47; Moulton-Milligan, 683; U. Wilckens, *charagma*, *TDNT* IX, 416 f. Commentaries on *Revelation* by R. H. Charles, I–II, *ICC*, 1920; and G. R. Beasley-Murray, *New Century Bible*, 1974.
(b). E. Lohmeyer, *Die Offenbarung des Johannes*, *HNT* 16, 1926, 1970³; and E. Lohse, *Die Offenbarung des Johannes*, *NTD* 11, 1960, on Rev. 13:8; E. Stauffer, "666", in *Coniectanea Neotestamentica* 11, 1947, 237 ff.

On *kaustēriazō*:
(a). Moulton-Milligan, 339; J. Schneider, *kaustēriazomai*, *TDNT* III 644 f. Commentaries on the Pastoral Epistles by M. Dibelius and H. Conzelmann, *Hermeneia*, 1973; B. S. Easton, 1947; E. K. Simpson, 1954; J. N. D. Kelly, *Harper-BNTC*, 1963.
(b). SB III 579; C. Spicq, *Les Épîtres Pastorales*, 1969⁴.

Marriage, Adultery, Bride, Bridegroom

γαμέω

γαμέω (*gameō*), marry; γάμος (*gamos*), wedding; γαμίζω (*gamizō*), give in marriage; γαμίσκω (*gamiskō*), give in marriage.

CL *gameō* is derived from the root *gam-* or *gem-*, to fit together, pair. The root is possibly related to *gennaō*, beget, bring forth. The noun *gamos* means wedding, marriage, consummation of marriage, whether regarded as temporary or permanent, the wedding feast. The vb. *gameō* means to marry, celebrate a wedding, have sexual relations. *gamizō* and *gamiskō* are later forms meaning give in marriage, i.e. a daughter.

Even though we may find numerous traces of polygamy and polyandry in the Gk. myths, monogamy predominated in the Gk. world in the historical period. Morality within marriage was strict. The Homeric hero had one wife, who was faithful and inviolable, a good manager of the home and mother. Gk. marriage was monogamous. On the other hand, the man had great freedom. He could have concubines or have relations with harlots (→ Discipline, art. *porneuō* CL). Adultery in the Gk. states and under Roman law was severely punished, especially in the case of the woman (cf. *OCD* 10 f., 649 f.).

In the Hellenistic period marriage morals had become generally looser. There

575

was much prostitution in the towns, especially in the ports, above all in Corinth. The oriental cults had introduced sacred prostitution. Sexual relationships with the priestesses became part of the cultus and granted a sharing in the divine, and were referred to by the term *hieros gamos*, sacred marriage.

OT 1. The terms *gameō* and *gamos* are only seldom found in the LXX. *gamos* (Heb. *mišteh*) occurs in the canonical books only at Gen. 29:22; Est. 2:18; 9:22. The OT law contains no prescribed form of marriage ceremony. In spite of this, marriage is in fact of great importance. Both in primeval history and in that of the patriarchs the history of tribes and people is narrated as family histories. In the genealogies (e.g. Gen. 5) marriage and the begetting of children (especially males) are the most important features of the lives mentioned. Even though from → Abraham down to the kings there is evidence for polygamy (e.g. Gen. 16:1 ff.; 25:6; 29:21–30; 1 Sam. 18:27; 25:42 f.; 2 Sam. 3:2–5), monogamy occupies the central position, especially in those passages that are important for our understanding of marriage. It is presupposed in Gen. 1:26 ff. and 2:18–24. The royal law in Deut. also demands of the king that "he shall not multiply wives for himself, lest his heart turn away" (Deut. 17:17; cf. 1 Ki. 11:1–11).

In the OT marriage is clearly regarded from the husband's standpoint and serves above all for the begetting of offspring (cf. Gen. 1:28). In order to achieve this end a man might take another wife (cf. Gen. 16:1 ff., → Abraham; levirate marriage, Deut. 25:5–10, but note Lev. 20:21; → 5 below). At the same time the wife is loved and taken seriously as a partner (Gen. 2:23 f.). She is a partner in a sexual and personal sense (Gen. 1:27 f.) and in the second creation narrative she is described as a "helper" (Heb. *'ēzer*; LXX *boēthos*) (Gen. 2:18b). The partnership continues in the fall and in the problems of sexuality created by it (Gen. 3).

2. Adultery was severely punished in the OT (Deut. 22:22–27; Exod. 20:14; Lev. 18:20; 20:10; Deut. 5:18). Even adultery committed unwittingly is hateful to God (Gen. 20:3–7). Adultery was also understood as a feature of paganism; God's people were to be fundamentally different in sexual practices and marriage (cf. 1 Cor. 6:12–20; 5:9–12). This prepares us for the prophetic picture of marriage for man's relationship to God (see below 3).

Originally → divorce depended solely on the man (cf. Deut. 24:1–4; Jer. 3:8), but later it became possible also for the woman (Elephantine). The many laws about the various sexual offences show how the elemental power of sexuality, which threatens the family and society, should be restrained and directed into the channels willed by God. Especially in the later period concern was felt with the problem of mixed marriages with foreigners which were forbidden (Deut. 7:3 f.; 20:16 ff.; 21:10 ff.; Ezr. 9 f.), though earlier cases of such marriages are exemplified (Gen. 41:45, Joseph; Exod. 2:21; Num. 12:1, Moses; Jdg. 14:1; 2 Sam. 11:3). Heathen marriages undermined allegiance to Yahweh especially in the case of Solomon (1 Ki. 11:1–11).

3. If adultery was a violation of the divine law and so also an offence against the → covenant, participation in the Canaanite fertility rites was an offence against both marriage and God. Hosea was the first to express the people's apostasy as harlotry and a breach of the marriage bond between God and Israel, and he did it more clearly than any other (Hos. 1 ff.; cf. Jer. 2:2, 10, 25; 3:1–25; Ezek. 16, 23; Isa.

576

50:1). His own act in marrying a harlot at the divine behest (Hos. 1:2) was symbolic of Yahweh's relationship with Israel. It is mercy, stretching far beyond all law, which causes God not to annihilate or cast off his people, as the law of marriage demanded, but to turn to them again in spite of all their disloyalty and even to promise them a new covenant.   *W. Günther*

4. The law contained certain forbidden degrees of marriage and sexual intercourse (Lev. 18:6–18). The Israelite was forbidden "to uncover the nakedness" of his mother, stepmother, sister or half-sister, grand-daughter, daughter of a stepmother, aunt, daughter-in-law, brother's wife (unless she died childless, see levirate marriage, below 5), a woman and her daughter, a woman and her grand-daughter, two sisters at the same time, or mother-in-law. Intercourse during menstruation was forbidden, as was adultery generally, homosexual practices and defilement with animals (Lev. 18:19–33). Certain of these offences were punishable by death (Deut. 27:20–23), whereas in other instances there is the warning that the offending parties shall bear their iniquity and die childless (Lev. 12:12–18; 20:19 ff.; but cf. also the story of Tamar, the daughter-in-law of Judah, who bore twins to him, Gen. 38).

In addition, certain prohibitions were attached to the priesthood. The high-priest was permitted to marry only a virgin selected from his own people (Lev. 21:13 f.), and priests were forbidden to marry prostitutes and divorced women (21:7). Num. 36:5–9 contains a prohibition against an heiress marrying outside her own tribe (cf. Tob. 7:10).

A man who falsely accused his bride of not being a virgin could be fined a hundred shekels, whipped, and compelled to take her as his wife (Deut. 22:13–19). But if his accusation proved true, the woman was to be stoned to death (Deut. 22:20 f.). A man who raped a virgin who was already betrothed (in open country where she could not summon help) was liable to the death penalty (Deut. 22:25 ff.). But in the case of a woman who was not betrothed, the man was to take her as his wife and pay the girl's father the sum of fifty shekels (Deut. 22:28 f.).

5. The so-called levirate marriage (from the Lat. *levir*, brother-in-law) refers to the marriage of a man with his deceased brother's widow in the event of his dying childless. The widow was not to remarry outside the family and the unmarried brother was to perform the duties of a husband to her to raise up children to the deceased, in order to perpetuate his name in Israel. If the man refused, the woman was entitled to subject him to public disgrace before the elders (Deut. 25:5–10). The practice was not peculiar to the Jews in their early history. It has been found among numerous Eastern peoples, particularly in Arabia and the Caucasus. The OT contains two instances of the practice. In the patriarchal period Onan deliberately spilled his semen on the ground, lest the offspring should be counted as his brother's. His own subsequent death was pronounced a divine judgment on him (Gen. 38:8 ff.). The book of Ruth tells the story of Ruth offering herself to Boaz, believing him to be the nearest kinsman to her deceased husband. However, Boaz at first declined on the grounds that there was a nearer kinsman. Only when the latter refused did Boaz take Ruth to wife (Ruth. 4:1–13). (On Ruth see further H. H. Rowley, "The Marriage of Ruth", in *The Servant of the Lord and Other Essays on the Old Testament*, 1965[2], 169–94; D. A. Leggett, *The Levirate and*

Goel Institutions in the Old Testament with Special Attention to the Book of Ruth, 1974; S. B. Parker, "The Marriage Blessing in Israelite and Ugaritic Literature", *JBL* 95, 1976, 23–30).

The practice of levirate marriage seems to be presupposed in the question of the Sadducees concerning the marital status in the resurrection of a woman who had married seven brothers each dying childless (Matt. 22:22–33; Mk. 12:18–27; Lk. 20:27–38). Jesus' reply rebuked the Sadducees for not knowing the scriptures or the power of God. For in the resurrection the present marital relationships with their physical ties are transcended and the dead raised are like the angels (*hōs angeloi*, Matt. 22:30, Mk. 12:25; *isangeloi†*, Lk. 20:36). Nevertheless, they live because God is the God of the living (Matt. 22:32; Mk. 12:27; Lk. 20:38; cf. Exod. 3:6).

6. No restrictions on the age of marriage are given in the OT, though early marriage is sometimes spoken of with approval (Prov. 2:17; 5:18; Isa. 62:5). In the patriarchal age it was considered the duty of the bridegroom's father to secure a bride for his son (Gen. 24:3; 38:6; Exod. 2:21; but cf. Gen. 21:21 when this fell to the mother). The selection of the bride was followed by formal betrothal, confirmed by oaths and a dowry (Heb. *mōhar*, Gen. 34:12; Exod. 22:16; 1 Sam. 18:25). The OT law contained no formal marriage ceremony. Gen. 29:22, 27 suggests that the custom at the time of Jacob was for a feast to be given by the bride's father at which the bride was given to the groom. The union was then consummated. The feast could last as long as seven and even fourteen days (cf. Jdg. 14:12; Tob. 8:19). The fact that Jacob was permitted after seven days to take Laban's other daughter, Rachel, in addition to Leah, suggests that polygamy was openly countenanced. Certain passages suggest a ratification by oath (Prov. 2:17; Ezek. 16:8; Mal. 2:14) and that a blessing was pronounced (Gen. 24:60; Ruth. 4:11 f.). The OT expression "to take a wife" seems to express the literal truth of what happened (Num. 12:1; 1 Chron. 2:21; cf. the action of Ruth in approaching Boaz, Ruth 3:6 ff.). The action was normally expressed in the ceremonial taking of the bride from her father's house to that of the bridegroom or his father. The practice of companions attending the groom (Jdg. 14:11) seems to have continued in the NT period (Matt. 19:15). He was preceded by singers or musicians (Gen. 31:27; Jer. 7:34; 16:9; 1 Macc. 9:39) and accompanied by torch-bearers or lamp-bearers (2 Esd. 10:2; Jer. 25:10; Matt. 25:7; Rev. 18:23). The bride awaited the groom with her maidens who conducted the whole party back to his own home (Matt. 25:6; Cant. 3:11). In NT times and no doubt earlier friends and neighbours participated in the feast that then took place (Matt. 22:1–10; Lk. 14:8; Jn. 2:2). A newly betrothed man was exempt from military service for a year lest he be killed in battle (Deut. 20:7). Similarly, the newly married man was exempt from military service and any public business that might take him away from his wife for a whole year (Deut. 24:5).

7. There is evidence of the practice of polygamy in Palestinian Judaism in NT times (cf. J. Jeremias, *Jerusalem in the Time of Jesus: An Investigation into Economic and Social Conditions during the New Testament Period*, 1969, 90, 93, 369f.). Herod the Great (37–4 B.C.) had ten wives (Josephus, *Ant.* 17, 19f.; *War* 1,562) and a considerable harem (*War* 1,511). Polygamy and concubinage among the aristocracy is attested by Josephus, *Ant.* 12, 186ff.; 13, 380; *War* 1, 97. The continued

practice of levirate marriage (Yeb. 15b) evidently led to polygamy, which was countenanced by the school of Shammai but not by that of Hillel. For detailed evidence of polygamy see J. Leipold, *Jesus und die Frauen*, 1921, 44–49. The practice of taking a second wife, if there was dissension with the first, was evidently often due to the high price fixed in the marriage contract which made divorce prohibitive (Yeb. 63b). According to the investigations of H. Grandqvist, in the village of Aretas near Bethlehem twelve out of 112 married men had more than one wife (*Marriage Conditions in a Palestinian Village*, II, 1935, 205).

8. According to Philo, the Essenes condemned marriage (*Hypothetica* 11, 14). Josephus reported that they disdained marriage, although one order of Essenes allowed it so as to propagate the race (*War* 2, 8, 2 and 13). The Community Rule (1 QS) is curiously silent on the subject, but the Messianic Rule permits sexual relations, i.e. marriage, on reaching maturity, i.e. the age of twenty (1QSa 1:6–11). M. Black sees in the Essene attitude an underlying tendency to regard all sexual functions and relations as unclean (*The Scrolls and Christian Origins: Studies in the Jewish Background of the New Testament*, 1961, 29). Total renunciation meant complete holiness, especially in a priestly sect. It may also be connected with the idea of the consecration of the warrior in the holy war (cf. The War Scroll, 1QM), the protest against the corrupt temple priesthood (cf. CD 8:8–18) and the Pharisaic permission of divorce (op. cit., 29–32; cf. also A. R. C. Leaney, *The Rule of Qumran and its Meaning*, 1966, 31ff., 170f., 211).   C. Brown

NT 1. The use of this word-group in the NT can hardly be distinguished from that in secular Gk. On principle the words are not used in the NT for extra-marital relationships. In Matt. 22:11 f. the gen. *gamou* is used for the adj. in the expression *endyma gamou*, wedding garment.

For the OT, Palestinian rabbinism and for Gk. Hellenistic civilization marriage and married life are self-evident institutions, and so they are taken for granted in the NT. Hence, the verb (e.g. Mk. 6:17; Lk. 14:20), and the noun (Jn. 2:1 f.) are used without any theological connotation.

The NT deals with questions concerning the relationship of men and woman far more frequently than the use of this word-group might suggest (→ Woman; → Divorce; → Discipline, art. *porneuō*; → Join, Cleave to; and below → art. *nymphē*). Sexual offences are fundamental offences against marriage. The fact that they are repeatedly mentioned in lists of sins shows that they are especially signs that sin is dependence on the *sarx* (→ Flesh).

2. Marriage as an institution is clearly presupposed in the NT. It is not based on human regulations but on God's commandment. This is shown by the frequent references to the creation story (Gen. 1:27; 2:24; cf. Mk. 10:6 f.; Matt. 19:4 f.; 1 Cor. 6:16; Eph. 5:31). It always refers to the shared life of a man with a woman. Though the NT also essentially looks on marriage from the man's standpoint (as the *kephalē*, head, 1 Cor. 11:3; Eph. 5:23), the Gk. and the OT traditions are so transcended that the man's special rights fall away, and throughout the NT the shared life of husband and wife stands in the foreground (cf. 1 Cor. 7:3; Eph. 5:21–33; Col. 3:18 f.). The NT attacks both → divorce and sexual impurity (→ Discipline). In one place there is also an attack on false teachers who in fanatical exaggeration forbade marriage (1 Tim. 4:3). An unbroken marriage is assumed

as something self-evident for the Christian (Matt. 5:27-31; 19:9; Mk. 10:11 f.; Lk. 16:18; 1 Cor. 7:10-16; 1 Thess. 4:4; 1 Tim. 3:2, 12; Heb. 13:4).

3. In the Sermon on the Mount Jesus speaks about the seventh commandment (Matt. 5:27 f.; cf. Exod. 20:14; Deut. 5:18). In the dawning kingdom of God adultery is a sin which shows that one's heart is attached to man, not to God. In God's sight the lustful eye and the desiring thought are reckoned as the completed act. The pericope concerning the woman taken in adultery is not in the oldest manuscripts of Jn. (Jn. 7:53-8:11), but nevertheless belongs to an early tradition. It shows Jesus, the Judge, as the Saviour who is prepared to forgive this sin also. Thereby he showed himself to be the sovereign Lord of Creation, of its order and of the Law. On this passage see also J. D. M. Derrett, "The Woman Taken in Adultery", *Law in the New Testament*, 1970, 156-88.

In the same context (Matt. 5:31 f.) Jesus speaks also of → divorce. In the law Deut. 24:1 in principle permits divorce, but there was controversy among the rabbis as to the grounds which justified it (Matt. 19:3; cf. SB I 303 ff.; II 23 f.). Jesus, however, met this permission in principle with a radical prohibition (Mk. 10:2-2). Only in Matt. 5:32 and 19:9 is divorce permitted on the grounds of *porneia*, unchastity (→ Discipline, art. *porneuō*). The question of divorce occupies a relatively important place in the NT (Mk. 10:2-12; Matt. 19:3-9; Lk. 16:18; 1 Cor. 7:10 f.). The fundamental rejection of divorce is based on God's command and order (Matt. 19:5 f.). (For further discussion → Divorce.)

4. Facing the question of the Sadducees concerning the status in the resurrection of a wife who had had more than one husband (Matt. 22:23-33; Mk. 12:18-27, Lk. 20:27-38) Jesus pointed to God and the dawning kingdom, where the problem raised by the scribes would lose all relevance, for marriage as an institution would then no longer exist. Jesus' statements are always to be understood in the light of the fact that the new age was dawning in his person (cf. Matt. 24:38; Lk. 17:26). In other words, passages like Matt. 19:9-12 do not simply proclaim the end of the OT marriage law. It is rather a question of the correct interpretation of this law and grasping God's will for this eschatological age. Jesus was in the perspective of Matthew, as it were, the second Moses, the law-giver of the eschatological era. The question concerning → eunuchs (Matt. 19:12) is also to be understood eschatologically. The exigencies of the times call for celibacy from those who have the gift. Those who had received it could voluntarily renounce marriage, for such a step was seen as necessary for the service of God (*dia tēn basileian*, for the sake of the kingdom of heaven). John the Baptist, and later Paul, remained unmarried. They show symbolically that marriage is only something provisional in the light of the coming kingdom (cf. 1 Cor. 7:1-9, 26-29).

5. Both in the OT and among Jesus' contemporaries a wedding was the occasion for a festive meal. Hence *gamos* can also mean the wedding feast; such a feast is described in Jn. 2:1-11. In Matt. 22:1-14 Jesus uses a royal wedding feast as a parable. As background for it we have the parallelism of God and the king, the concept of the eschatological feast (cf. Isa. 25:6), the Rab. picture of the marriage feast of the messiah with his people (SB I 517), the exposition of Cant. as expressing the love between Yahweh and his people, and the prophetic picture of marriage to represent the relationship between Yahweh and Israel given from Hosea on. Earthly marriage is to be superseded by the eschatological union of God with his

people. As the messiah Jesus is the true bridegroom (→ art. *nymphē*). The decisive factor is sharing his feast (Matt. 25:1–13; cf. Lk. 12:36–40). The record of the institution of the → Lord's Supper (especially Matt. 26:29; Lk. 22:30) links the messianic meal with the explanation of the death of Jesus. The marriage feast of the → Lamb (Rev. 19:7 ff.) means the final union of the triumphant Christ with his own.

6. (a) Arising out of certain happenings in the Corinthian church Paul deals in 1 Cor. 5 ff. with various questions concerning marriage. He starts with a warning against all kinds of unchastity, and then deals with marriage itself. He appeals to the word of Jesus and rejects divorce (1 Cor. 7:10; cf. Mk. 10:9 ff. par. Matt. 19:6–9; Lk. 16:18). Paul looks on marriage as secondary when compared to faith. He goes so far as to recommend celibacy as a special gift in the light of the near end (7:1, 7; cf. Matt. 19:12). Marriage, like all worldly activity, stands under the *hōs mē*, as if not (7:29 ff.); those who have should live as if they had not. This is the standpoint from which the question of mixed marriages with unbelievers is handled (7:12–16). The unbelieving partner is to decide whether it is to continue. The Christian partner, on the other hand, should be prepared to let it continue, i.e. only the heathen partner has freedom of choice. The consecration of such a mixed marriage by the believing partner is to be understood as a very real power, for here grace is stronger than the unbelief of the heathen partner. It is the means of bringing the children within the covenant relationship, for otherwise they would be unclean. It may also result in the salvation of the unbelieving partner.

The meaning of 1 Cor. 7:36 ff. is not absolutely clear. We do not know whether it refers to a couple living together ascetically in so-called spiritual marriage, to whom Paul is giving permission later to enter into full physical union, or to a father (or a guardian or master) who did not wish to offend against custom or Rab. command by not marrying off his daughter (ward, slave-girl) at the usual age (cf. A. Robertson and A. Plummer, *The First Epistle of St. Paul to the Corinthians*, *ICC*, 1911, 159; SB III 376 f.). The use of the verb *gamizō*, give in marriage, in v. 38 makes the second interpretation more probable. *gamizō*, a synonym of *gamiskō*, is found in the NT only in Matt. 22:30; 24:38; Mk. 12:25; Lk. 17:27; 20:20:34 f.; 1 Cor. 7:38. Except in the last passage it clearly means to give in marriage. It is a term that is normally applied only to the father, guardian or owner who gives a girl under his control in marriage to another man. The interpretation that we are here dealing with a spiritual marriage can be held only if one assumes that *gamizō* here is equivalent to *gameō* (cf. Arndt). AV, RV, Weymouth, Knox, JB, NEB mg all take *gamizō* as give in marriage; Moffatt, Phillips, RSV, NEB tx take it as equivalent to *gameo*. → *hyperakmos* below. On the interpretation of 1 Tim. 3:2, 12 and Tit. 1:6 → Man, art. *anēr* NT 3.

(b) Paul also saw marriage as a picture of man's relationship to God. In Rom. 9:25 f. he quotes Hos. 2:23 alluding to the names of Hosea's children *lō' ruḥāmâh* (Not Pitied) and *lō' 'ammî* (Not my People) (cf. Hos. 1:6 ff.). For despite these names Yahweh will nevertheless have pity on his people and restore them. Paul sees in this promise grounds for the inclusion of Gentiles in the people of God. He uses the picture of marriage in 2 Cor. 11:2 to warn against apostasy. It is reversed in Eph. 5:22 ff. Because Christ is the bridegroom of the church, marriage should be held holy. In Eph. 5:32 the marriage relationship is described as a *mystērion*, which is symbolic of the relationship of Christ to the church. It is all the more reason why husbands and wives should love one another. The picture of marriage lies also behind the expression "adulterous generation" (Matt. 12:39; 16:4; Mk. 8:38). It is possible that these passages are referring to the factual moral conditions among the people, but the context and OT linguistic usage suggest that Jesus was alluding to the people's attitude to God (→ Generation). "The woman Jezebel" (Rev. 2:20 ff.) and "the great harlot" (Rev. 17:1) are pictures of the great apostasy from God, the great Husband and Lord. The former alludes to the wife of King Ahab who served Baal and sought the life of → Elijah (1 Ki. 16:31; 18:4, 13; 19:1 f.; 21:5–25; 2 Ki. 9:7–37). The church at Thyatira is warned against tolerating the woman Jezebel (i.e. those who practice and teach things characterized by her name). The great harlot is identified as → Babylon (17:5) who typifies the world.   *W. Günther*

| μοιχεύω |

μοιχεύω (*moicheuō*), commit adultery; μοιχεία (*moicheia*), adultery; μοιχός (*moichos*), adulterer; μοιχαλίς (*moichalis*), adulteress, prostitute.

CL *moicheuō* and its Doric counterpart *moichaō* mean to commit adultery (with acc.). Sometimes they are used more generally, seduce a woman, violate; hence in mid. let oneself be seduced, in pass. be seduced to adultery. The derivatives include *moicheia*, adultery, harlotry (cf. *porneia* → Discipline); *moichos*, Adulterer; *moichalis*, first an adj. meaning adulterous, and, secondly, a noun meaning adulteress, harlot.

Adultery was punishable already in the old law codes going back to the second millennium B.C., e.g. the Lipit-Ishtar Code, the Code of Hammurabi, the old Ass. laws (cf. *ANET*, 159 ff., 163–88). Every form of sexual relationship outside marriage was forbidden to the wife, for she was the real guarantor of the integrity of the family and clan, and by adultery she broke her own marriage and she destroyed the integrity of the whole clan. A man on the contrary committed adultery only by sexual relationships with a married woman, i.e. when breaking into another's arrangement. At the same time traces of older concepts behind these legal views from different cultures may be detected: (a) adultery with a married woman involves an offence against property, i.e. the invasion of the area of another's possessions, and (b) the woman committing adultery opens the clan to the influence of evil powers. The punishment of adultery by death, ill-treatment or the payment of an expiatory fine was normally left to the private initiative of the wronged husband or of his clan.

OT 1. The LXX uses the Gk. word-group for Heb. *nā'ap* and its derivatives. There adultery, as in other societies, covered (i) every extra-marital sexual relationship by a married woman; (ii) the extra-marital sexual relationship of a man with a married or engaged woman (Gen. 16:1–4; 30:1–4; 38:15 f.; Lev. 19:20 ff.; Deut. 22:28 f. are examples of extra-marital sexual relationships by a man). Adultery was punishable by death, normally by stoning (but cf. Gen. 38:24), of both parties (Lev. 20:10; Deut. 22:22 ff.; Ezek. 16:40; cf. Jn. 8:5). In contrast to usage outside Israel (see above CL) adultery was a matter of public concern, since it offended not only against the foundations and personal rights of marriage and family but also against the law of God (Exod. 20:14) and so threatened the basis of the people's existence (Deut. 22:22b). Hence, the punishment had to be inflicted by the community. If a woman was suspected of adultery a test of guilt or innocence was prescribed (Num. 5:11-31) to be carried out by the priests who required her to take an oath of innocence and drink the water containing the ashes of a cereal offering.

2. In Hosea's life and message marriage and adultery are used allegorically for the relationship between Yahweh and his people (→ *gameō* OT 2, NT 6 (b)). The actual reason for the use of this picture may well have been the introduction of Canaanite wedding and fertility rites into Israel's life (4:12 ff.; 9:1 ff.). When Israel separated from Yahweh and sacrificed to strange gods, the nation acted as an adulteress who leaves her husband and plays the harlot with other men (2:2 ff. [MT 2:4 ff.]). God would severely punish this adultery (5:7 ff.), but this would not have as its purpose the complete destruction of the adulteress but her repentance (3:5). This picture was later taken up by Jeremiah (cf. Jer. 2:2; 3:1-10; 5:7; 13:22, 26) and by Ezekiel during the exile (cf. Ezek. 16:1-63; 23:37-45).

3. The very serious warnings against adultery in the wisdom literature (cf. Prov. 6:20-35; cf. Sir. 25:2) show a weakening of strict marriage morality in the course of Israel's history (cf. especially Prov. 6:35, which suggests compensation by money payment, and Mal. 2:14 ff.). It is the mark of the fool to be led astray by the harlot. His action will bring not only disgrace but also ruin and judgment (cf. also Prov. 2:16 ff.; 7:5-27; 30:20). The serious social consequences of adultery were also a cause for concern.

4. There are also stern warnings in Test. XII (Test.Jos. 4:6 ff.; 5:1), Philo (*Decal.* 121 f., 124, 126, 129, 131), the Mishnah (especially the Tractate Sotah' [The Adulteress]), and the Talmud (see further *TDNT* IV 731 f.). In Roman times the death penalty was no longer exacted (cf. A. N. Sherwin-White, *Roman Society and Roman Law in the New Testament*, 1965², 40 f.; *TDNT* IV 732 f.).

NT The word-group is used in the NT with the same meaning, both direct and metaphorical, as in secular Gk. sometimes quoting Exod. 20:14 (Deut. 5:18), e.g. Matt. 19:18 f.; Mk. 10:19; Lk. 18:20; Jas. 2:11; Rom. 13:9.

1. At the same time the NT's understanding of marriage and hence of adultery is carried forward to a position known neither to secular Gk. nor the OT. (a) Adultery in the man is unreservedly measured by the same standards as in the woman (Matt. 5:32; Mk. 10:11 f.; Lk. 16:18). (b) The desire, i.e. the willingness to commit the act, is equivalent to adultery itself (Matt. 5:27 f.). (c) Since the NT considers marriage by its nature to be indissoluble (Mk. 10:8), remarriage following divorce permitted by the OT on the grounds of the hardness of men's hearts enters the realm of adultery (Matt. 5:31 f.; 19:9). Admittedly, marriage in Matt. 5 is considered from the standpoint of the wife and its breach is judged accordingly (cf. Rom. 7:3 with CL and OT 1 above). In Matt. 19:9, however, Jesus applies the statement also to the man who divorces his wife, marries again, and so commits adultery. In both passages, in contrast to Mk. 10:11 f., Lk. 16:18, Matt. recognizes an exception on the grounds of *porneia* that permits divorce (→ Discipline, art. *porneuō*; → Divorce). (d) Adultery is incompatible with the hope of life in the kingdom of God (1 Cor. 6:9 f), and is under God's judgment (Heb. 13:4). It is therefore

characteristic that a destructive libertinism (2 Pet. 2:14) goes hand in hand with doubts about the return of Christ and the judgment to follow (2 Pet. 3:3–7).

2. Jesus' severe condemnation of adultery does not exclude God's mercy to the repentant sinner, whose conversion he desires (Matt. 21:13 f.; Lk. 18:9–14; cf. 1 Cor. 6:9 ff.). The adulteress, who had earned the death-penalty, had her guilt forgiven while the apparently guiltless multitude had a mirror held up to their hypocritical self-righteousness (Jn. 8:3–11). At the same time the impenitent perverts are excluded from the kingdom (1 Tim. 1:10; Heb. 13:4; Rev. 21:8; 22:15).

3. The theme of adultery is used in the NT in a metaphorical sense as in OT prophecy (cf. Jas. 4:4), where adulterers (*moichalides*; RSV "unfaithful creatures!") are lovers of the world. Similarly Israel is called "an evil and adulterous generation [*genea ponēra kai moichalis*]" as it is typified by its religious representatives; → Pharisees and scribes (Matt. 12:39), → Sadducees (Matt. 16:4). Although some expositors see in the phrase a judgment on the factual, moral situation, a metaphorical explanation is probable. This contemporary → generation, a people shown to be disloyal to God by its rejection of Jesus (cf. Mk. 8:38), is characterized by its desire for a → sign when there is already proof enough of God's love present in Jesus. *H. Reisser*

| νύμφη | νύμφη (*nymphē*), bride; νυμφίος (*nymphios*), bridegroom; νυμφών (*nymphōn*), wedding hall, bride chamber. |

CL *nymphē* is found already in Mycenaean Gk. (linear B) and is linked with Lat. *nurus*. It means the bride or betrothed. The use of the term is not restricted to the context of the wedding ceremony. It can be equally applied to a virgin, a young woman and a young wife. Similarly *nymphios* means both the bridegroom, the betrothed and the young husband. *nymphē* is also a term used for feminine deities of lower rank (→ Woman).

In Hellenism, especially in the gnostic systems, the picture of bridegroom and bride is used for the relationship of the *sōtēr*, saviour, to men, and is taken into the concept of *hieros gamos*, sacred marriage. This prepared the way for religious eroticism, which even today prefers to use the allegory of engagement and marriage to express the mystical relationship of the individual soul to the deity (→ art. *gameō*).

OT The later NT linguistic usage is primarily determined by the earlier Jewish customs and ideas. In the OT there are incidental references to the customs that preceded the wedding (e.g. Gen. 24:59 ff.; Jos. 15:18 f.; Jdg. 14; Isa. 61:10; Cant.). A girl was capable of marriage at twelve, a young man at fifteen. While their personal choice probably played a part, an agreement made between their families was essential. Because Heb. *kallâh* covers both, the LXX uses *nymphē* also for daughter-in-law (cf. Gen. 11:31; 38:11; Ruth 1:6).

In the foreground of the OT passages mentioning bride and bridegroom stands the joy that they have in one another. This finds its finest expression in Cant. (cf. also Ps. 45; Isa. 61:10; 62:5; Jer. 7:34; 16:9). This joy is applied metaphorically to the relationship between Yahweh and Israel, and especially to the worship in which the congregation rejoiced in Yahweh as the eternal king and founder of the kingdom of peace in Zion (Ps. 45; Isa. 60:1 ff.). This picture corresponds to the title of Israel as bride of Yahweh (Jer. 2:2; Isa. 49:18; 62:5).

Late Jud. continued this fig. usage. Cant. was recognized as canonical, because it was interpreted as an allegory of the relationship of Yahweh to Israel. The expected salvation was described as a marriage, i.e. as the final and complete union of God with his people (SB I 517).

NT *nymphē* is used almost exclusively as a metaphor in the NT. In Matt. 10:35 and Lk. 12:53 it means, conformably with Jewish usage, daughter-in-law. The bride can also be called *gynē* (→ Woman), because by Jewish laws of marriage the engaged woman was already regarded as wife. This usage is found in Matt. 1:20, 24; Rev. 19:7; 21:9 (cf. SB II 393 ff.). *nymphios* in the NT is bridegroom, literally and metaphorically (Jn. 2:9; 3:29; Matt. 25:1, 6; Rev. 18:23). The *hyioi tou nymphōnos*, the "children of the bride chamber" (AV) were the relations and friends; "the bridegroom's friends" (NEB) is preferable to "the wedding guests" (RSV). They were indispensable for the carrying through of the festive ceremonial (Matt. 9:15; Mk. 2:19 f.; Lk. 5:34; cf. Jn. 3:29; cf. SB I 500–18; F. W. Lewis, "Who were the Sons of the Bride-Chamber? (Mark ii. 18–22)", *ExpT* 24, 1912–13, 285).

1. The wedding period is, as in the OT, a time of joy, especially of anticipation of joy. These ideas in the NT are part of the eschatological imagery (→ *gameō*). In Matt. 9:15 par. Mk. 2:19 f. and Lk. 5:35 Jesus → rejects the need to → fast at the present time. The time of the messiah's presence was commonly compared to a wedding (Isa. 62:5). The implication is that with Jesus the messianic age has dawned. The disciples were filled with joy because Jesus was with them. The parable of the ten virgins (Matt. 25:1–13) belongs also in this setting, though it is also a parable of judgment, stressing the need for being awake and waiting. The OT parallelism bride and bridegroom, symbolizing Israel and Yahweh, is here applied to the church and Jesus (cf. SB I 501–18; 898; IV 432 f.).

2. In Jn. 3:29 f. the relationship of the Baptist to Jesus is described as that of the bridegroom's "friend", *ho philos tou nymphiou*, whose part was that of the best man. The final age first begins with Jesus, but the "friend" prepared the way for him and has no greater joy than in seeing the wedding come to pass, i.e. the dawn of reconciliation and of the kingdom in Christ. On *philos* → love, art. *phileō* NT 2.

3. The picture of the bridegroom and bride applies to Christ and the church in 2 Cor. 11:2. Paul describes himself as the one who presented them to Christ "as a pure bride to her one husband" (here *parthenos* means virgin, i.e. bride; → Woman). But he fears lest they be led astray from pure devotion, just as Eve was led astray (11:3). The picture of marriage is applied to Christ and the church in Eph. 5:22–32 (→ *gameō*).

4. In the last chs. of Rev., which describe the final consummation, we find the picture of the church-bride waiting for her heavenly bridegroom, here called the → Lamb of God. Joy once again stands in the foreground (19:7, 9). The church rejoices and adorns herself so as to welcome Christ as her Lord (21:2, 9 ff.). She is the heavenly → Jerusalem, the eschatological church, who in longing like that of a bride looks for the final fulfilment of her existence and calls out "Come, Lord Jesus!" (22:17, 20).   *W. Günther*

| κοίτη | κοίτη (koitē), bed, marriage bed, intercourse.

CL In secular Gk. *koitē*, besides its common meaning bed, connotes the marriage bed (Aeschylus, Sophocles). It was used also of the den of an animal or the nest of a bird as well as of a box or basket.

OT In Wis. 3:13 the word is used in the phrase *hētis ouk egnō koitēn en paraptōmati* ("who has not known intercourse in transgression") to describe an illicit union. In Wis. 3:16 *koitē* occurs in combination with *sperma* in a sense similar to the use of *šiḵbaṭ-zeraʿ* (lit. discharge of seed) in Heb. where the connotation is that of coitus (Lev. 15:18; 18:20; 19:20; Num. 5:13; cf. Lev. 15:16 f., 32; 22:4; see further below). The Greek expression is modified by *paranomou* (unlawful) to connote the concept of illicit sexual congress. In Sir. 23:18 *v.l.* the word *koitē* occurs in the phrase *pornos parabainōn apo tēs koitēs autou* to describe "a fornicator who strays from his marriage bed."

In the LXX *koitē* stands for a number of Heb. words, most frequently forms of the verb *šāḵaḇ*, lie down. It represents the noun *miškāḇ* on numerous occasions with the basic meaning of bed, as the place of sleep or rest (e.g. 2 Sam. 11:13; 1 Ki. 1:47; Mic. 2:1). In Exod. 10:23 *koitē* represents the Heb. *taḥaṭ*, place, in the context of the plague of darkness on Egypt. The expression is probably used more generally in the Heb. than the LXX allows, for the word *taḥaṭ* may denote a place of sitting as well as lying. In Daniel the word *miškāḇ* is represented by *koitē* in the LXX and, in each instance, refers to the bed as a place of rest. In Isa. 56:10 *koitē* is used in the sense of rest in the phrase *enypniazomenoi koitēn*, dreaming of rest.

The word *koitē* stands for several Heb. words that connote the home of an animal such as the Heb. *rēḇeṣ* (Jer. 50:6) which means sheepfold. The word also represents the verbal form *rāḇaṣ* in the phrase *koitēn poimniōn*, fold of flocks, in Isa. 17:2. In Isa. 11:8 *koitē* stands for the Heb. *meʿûrâh* which connotes the den of a snake, and in Mic. 2:12 it represents the Heb. *dōḇer*, pasture. The noun *māʿôn*, lair, is represented by *koitē* in Jer. 10:22. And the noun *meʿōnâh*, dwelling, lair, is represented by *koitē* in Job 37:8; 38:40. The word *koitē* is used of the sick bed in the LXX as in Ex. 21:18 where it represents the Heb. *miškāḇ*. See also Job 33:19; Psa. 40(41):3.

In the LXX *koitē* also stands for the Heb. *šeḵāḇâh*. The Heb. word can connote the idea of layer or deposit as in a layer of dew (Exod. 16:13, 14) as well as the act of lying. The word occurs in the latter sense in the phrase *šiḵbaṭ-zeraʿ* (lit. "a laying of seed"), a technical term in the Levitical legislation used to refer to the emission of semen. In Lev. 15:18 the expression *šiḵbaṭ-zeraʿ* occurs as the cognate accusative of *šāḵaḇ*, lie, in a section describing the means of cleansing in the case of sexual defilement. Literally the statement says "If a man should lie with a woman 'a laying of semen,'" and thus describes the act of "laying" in the sense of completion of coition. A similar usage of the expression occurs in Lev. 19:20; Num. 5:13. The word *šeḵāḇâh* seems to have another connotation in the same expression, however, for it is used in Lev. 15:16, 17 of emission of semen apart from coitus in which instance the word seems to be used in the sense of "deposit," hence emission. The concluding statement to this legislative section (Lev. 15:32) uses the phrase *šiḵbaṭ-zeraʿ* to cover both instances of emission. The expression is used similarly in Lev. 22:4.

The word *miškab* is represented by *koitē* in the LXX in a number of instances where the connotation is that of bed in the sense of a place of rest but with associative sexual implications deriving from Levitical regulations relating to various forms of sexual impurity (Lev. 15:21, 23, 24, 26). In Prov. 7:17 the word is used of the harlot's bed thus connoting in an implicit sense sexual intercourse. It is used similarly in Isa. 57:7 where the prophet berates the people for setting their beds on the mountains. The reference is to idolatry and hence is used also here in the sense of spiritual fornication.

Frequently the word *koitē* reflects a distinctly metaphorical use of the Heb. *miškāb* as a surrogate for sexual congress as in Lev. 18:22; 20:13, where the word occurs in the plural construct state with *'iššâh*, woman. In Num. 31:17, 18, 35 and Jdg. 21:11, 12 *koitē* is used in a similar fashion in the expression *yāda' miškab zākār*, to know the bed of a male. The Heb. *šekōbet* is translated by *koitē* and also connotes the concept of copulation. It always occurs in construction with *nātan*, give. This expression occurs in Lev. 18:20, 23; Num. 5:20. In each instance the term connotes illicit sexual relationships.

The word *koitē* also represents Heb. words connoting the marriage bed as Gen. 49:4 where *miškāb* is used, and 1 Chron. 5:1 where the Heb. word is *yāṣûa'*, a poetic word for bed.

NT In the NT *koitē* occurs on 4 occasions. In Lk. 11:7 it is used in the sense of bed as a place of rest. In this context, an individual in Jesus' parable protests that he cannot help someone who has solicited aid because he is in bed.

In Rom. 9:10 the word occurs in the expression *koitēn echousa*, and is a euphemism for coitus, and, by expansion, conception and pregnancy. In this sense it is similar to the use of *miškāb* as a surrogate for coition, but no clear instance exists in Heb. where the word may connote the result of coition, i.e., conception. The theological point of the passage is that Rebekah conceived children "by one man, our forefather Isaac." Yet before either of these male twins had done anything good or bad God in his divine sovereignty had decreed that "the elder shall serve the younger" (Rom. 9:12; cf. Gen. 25:23). The argument forms an important part of Paul's case demonstrating to Jewish readers the consistency of divine sovereignty in the inclusion of the Gentiles in the people of God.

The word *koitē* is used in the plur. in Rom. 13:13 in the sense of illicit sexual union. In this context the word is accompanied by such terms as revelling (*kōmos*), → drunkenness (*methē*), and licentiousness (*aselgeia*), all of which are also in the plur. Believers are warned to avoid them, together with quarreling (*eris*) and jealousy (*zēlos*), "but to put on the Lord Jesus Christ, and make no provision for the flesh to gratify its desires" (Rom. 13:14).

In Heb. 13:4 the word occurs in the sense of "marriage bed" as it does in the OT. In this context the writer affirms that the marriage relationship is an honourable one, and at the same time it is to be kept honourable.   *T. McComiskey*

ὑπέρακμος

ὑπέρακμος (*hyperakmos*), past the peak, overripe, begin to fade; or, overwhelmingly strong, overpassionate.

CL & OT The word is formed from the prep. *hyper*, for, beyond, and the noun *akmē*, peak, which is used in the sense of the peak or high point in human development in Plato, *Rep.* 5 p. 640e and Philo, *Leg.All.* 1, 10. Diod.S. 32, 11, 1 speaks of the *akmē tēs hēlikias* of a woman (on *hēlikia* → Age, Stature) and also uses it of a virgin (Frag. 34, 35, 2, 39). Diog.L. 5, 65 tells of the pity felt for a father of a virgin who because of the smallness of her dowry goes beyond the prime of her age (*ektrechousa ton akmaion tēs hēlikias kairon*). J. M. Ford links the word with the Mishnaic Heb. *bôḡereṭ*, lit. "wrinkled", but in this kind of context "past her girl-hood" or "at the age when levirate marriage is incumbent on her" ("The Rabbinic Background of St. Paul's Use of *hyperakmos*", *Journal of Jewish Studies* 18, 1966, 89 ff.). On the other hand, cognate words have been found in relation to human desires: *akmaia epithymia* (*Pseudo-Clementines*, Homily p. 8, 17 Lag.; *akmazō*, Syntipas p. 10, 14).

NT The word occurs only at 1 Cor. 7:36. Two opposing lines of interpretation have been put forward. On the one hand, the subject of the verse has tradi-tionally been taken to refer to the father of a virgin daughter. In this case, the interpretation would be: "If anyone [i.e. any father] thinks that he is not behaving properly to his virgin [*parthenon*; sc. daughter], and if she be beyond age [*ean ē hyperakmos*], and it has to be, let him do as he wishes; he does not sin – let them marry [*gameitōsan*]." This is further supported by the use of *gamizō* twice in v. 38 which normally means to give in marriage. Thus: "So that he who gives in marriage [*ho gamizōn*] his virgin does well; and he who does not give in marriage [*ho mē gamizōn*] does better." On *parthenos* in these verses → Woman, art. *parthenos*.

On the other hand, there is the interpretation which takes the subject of these verse to be the man who has some kind of liaison with the *parthenos*. This is not explicitly defined. It may imply a betrothal where marriage has been put off on the grounds of the spiritual considerations that Paul is urging in this passage. Some interpreters take this to refer to a spiritual marriage which has not been consum-mated physically. But evidence for such marriages is considerably later than the NT period, and the use of *gamizō* in v. 38 would hardly seem appropriate, if this were the case. In this case the interpretation of the verse would be: "If anyone thinks that he is not behaving properly to his virgin, and he be overpassionate [*hyperakmos*], and it has to be, let him do as he wishes, he does not sin – let them marry. But he who is firmly established in his heart, having no necessity, has power over his own will, and has judged this in his heart to keep her as his virgin, he will do well. So that he who marries his own virgin does well, and he who does not marry does better" (vv. 36 ff.). This interpretation involves no change of subject in v. 36, and offers a thoroughly realistic assessment of the situation. Moreover, there are exceptions to the general rule that *gamizō* means to give in marriage (cf. Moulton-Milligan, 121).

In view of this last point, it would also be possible to take the subject of this verse to be the man and still refer *hyperakmos* to the virgin, i.e. the man should go ahead and marry her on the grounds of her age.

In the last analysis, one cannot rule out any of these interpretations as impossible. However, the general tenor of Paul's recommendations remains clear. It is not a sin to marry; out of personal humanitarian considerations it may be right to do so. On the other hand, times make celibacy preferable.   *C. Brown*

→ Child, → Discipline, → Divorce, → Father, → Son, → Woman

(a). J. J. von Allmen, *Pauline Teaching on Marriage, Studies in Christian Faith and Practice* 6, 1963; O. J. Baab, "Marriage", *IDB* III 278–87; K. Barth, *CD* III, 4, 116–240; S. R. Brav, *Marriage and the Jewish Tradition*, 1951; J. B. Bauer, "Marriage", *EBT* II 551–56; R. Batey, "The *mia sarx* Union of Christ and the Church", *NTS* 13, 1966–67, 270–81; and *New Testament Nuptial Imagery*, 1971; E. Brunner, *The Divine Imperative*, 1937, 340–83; M. Burrows, *The Basis of Israelite Marriage*, 1938; D. R. Catchpole, *The Synoptic Divorce Material as a Traditio-Historical Problem*, 1976; J. D. M. Derrett, "The Woman Taken in Adultery" and "The Teaching of Jesus on Marriage and Divorce", in *Law in the New Testament*, 1970, 156–88 and 363–88; R. J. Ehrlich, "The Indissolubility of Marriage as a Theological Problem", *SJT* 23, 1970, 291–311; J. H. Elliott, "Paul's Teaching on Marriage in I Corinthians: Some Problems Reconsidered", *NTS* 19 1972–73, 219–25; L. M. Epstein, *Marriage Laws in the Bible and the Talmud*, 1942; J. M. Ford, "Levirate Marriage in St Paul", *NTS* 10, 1963–64, 361–65; "St Paul, the philogamist (1 Cor. vii in Early Patristic Exegesis)", *NTS* 11, 1964–65, 326–48; and "The Rabbinic Background of St Paul's Use of *hyperakmos*", *Journal of Jewish Studies*, 18, 1966, 89 ff.; W. J. Harrington, *The Bible on Matrimony*, 1963; F. Hauck, *moicheuō* etc., *TDNT* IV 729–35; A. Isaksson, *Marriage and Ministry in the New Temple: A Study with Special Reference to Mt. 19,3–12 and 1 Cor. 11,3–16*, 1965; J. Jeremias, *nymphē, nymphios*, *TDNT* IV 1099–1106; P. K. Jewett, *Man as Male and Female*, 1975; L. Köhler, *Hebrew Man*, 1956; K. Kahana, *The Theory of Marriage in Jewish Law*, 1966; D. A. Leggett, *The Levirate and Goel Institutions in the Old Testament with Special Reference to the Book of Ruth*, 1974; W. Lillie, *Studies in New Testament Ethics* 1961, 118–28; A. Mahoney, "A New Look at the Divorce Clauses in Mt. 5, 32 and 19, 9", *Catholic Biblical Quarterly* 30, 1968, 29–38; M. Mielziner, *The Jewish Law: Marriage and Divorce*, 1901; R. C. Mortimer, chairman, *Putting Assunder: A Divorce Law for Contemporary Society. The Report of a Group Appointed by the Archbishop of Canterbury in January 1964*, 1966; I. A. Muirhead, "The Bride of Christ", *SJT* 5, 1952, 175–87; E. Neufeld, *Ancient Hebrew Marriage Laws*, 1944; J. Pedersen, *Israel: Its Life and Culture*, I-II 1926, 60–81; H. Riesenfeld, "The Pericope *de adultera* in the Early Christian Tradition", *The Gospel Tradition*, 1970, 95–110; H. Root, chairman, *Marriage, Divorce and the Church, The Report of a Commission appointed by the Archbishop of Canterbury to prepare a staement on the Christian Doctrine of Marriage*, 1971; H. H. Rowley, "The Marriage of Ruth", *HTR* 40, 1947. 77–99 (reprinted in *The Servant of the Lord and Other Essays on the Old Testament*, 1965², 169–94); J. P. Sampley, *"And the Two Shall Become One Flesh": A Study of Traditions in Ephesians 5:21–33*, Society for New Testament Studies Monograph Series 16, 1971; E. Schillebeeckx, *Marriage: Secular Reality and Saving Mystery*, I *Marriage in the Old Testament and the New Testament*, II *Marriage in the History of Church*, 1965; R. Schnackenburg, *The Moral Teaching of the New Testament*, 1965, 132–43, 144–57; A. van Selms, *Marriage and Family Life in Ugaritic Literature*, 1954; J. van Seters, "The Problem of Childlessness in Near Eastern Law and the Patriarchs of Israel", *JBL* 87, 1968, 401–8; E. Stauffer, *gameō, gamos*, *TDNT* I 648–57; H. Thielicke, *The Ethics of Sex*, 1964; M. Thurian, *Marriage and Celibacy*, 1959; R. de Vaux, *Ancient Israel: Its Life and Institutions*, 1961, 19–40; G. N. Vollebregt, *The Bible on Marriage*, 1965; E. Westermarck, *History of Human Marriage*, I–III, 1922⁵; J. W. C. Wand, chairman, *The Church and the Law of Nullity of Marriage. The Report of a Commission appointed by the Archbishops of Canterbury and York in 1949 at the request of the Convocations*, 1955; H. W. Wolff, *Anthropology of the Old Testament*, 1974, 166–76; R. Yaron, "The Restoration of Marriage", *Journal of Jewish Studies* 17, 1966, 1–11.

(b). H. Baltensweiler, *Die Ehe im Neuen Testament. Exegetische Untersuchungen über Ehe, Ehelosigkeit und Ehescheidung*, AThANT 32, 1967; A. Bardtke and H. Thimme, "Ehe", *EKL* I 994 ff.; U. Becker, *Jesus und die Ehebrecherin*, BZNW 28, 1963; J. Blinzler, "Die Strafe für Ehebruch in Bibel und Halacha", *NTS* 4, 1957–58, 32–47; J. Cambier, "Le grand mystère concernant le Christ et son Église, Éph. 5, 22–13", *Biblica* 47, 1966, 43–90; H. Crouzel, "Séparation ou remariage selon les Pères anciens", *Gregorianum* 47, 1966, 472–94; G. Delling, "Ehe", *RAC* IV 666 ff.; J. Gnilka, "'Bräutigam', spätjüdisches Messiasprädikat?", *Trierer Theologische Zeitschrift*, 1960, 298 ff.; R. Goeden, *Zur Stellung von Mann und Frau, Ehe und Sexualität im Hinblick auf Bibel und alte Kirche*, Dissertation Göttingen, 1969; H. Greeven, "Zu den Aussagen des Neuen Testaments über die Ehe", *Zeitschrift für evangelische Ethik* 1, 1957, 109 ff.; and "Ehe nach dem Neuen Testament", *NTS* 15, 1968–69, 365–88; U. Holzmeister, "Die Streitfrage über die Ehescheidungstexte bei Mt. 5, 32 und 19, 9", *Biblica* 26, 1945, 133–46; F. Horst and H. Greeven, "Ehe", *RGG*³ II 361 ff.; H. Hübner, "Zölibat in Qumran?", *NTS* 17, 1970–71, 153–67; J. Jeremias,

"Die missionarische Aufgabe in der Mischehe", in W. Eltester, ed., *Neutestamentliche Studien für Rudolf Bultmann*, BZNW 21, 1954, 255–60; W. G. Kümmel, "Verlobung und Heirat bei Paulus (1 Kor. 7, 36–38)", *BZNW* 21, 1954, 275–95 (reprinted in *Heilsgeschehen und Geschichte. Gesammelte Aufsätze 1933–1964*, 1965, 310–27; J. Leipoldt, *Die Frau in der antiken Welt und im Urchristentum*, 1955³; E. Linnemann, "Die Hochzeit zu Kana und Dionysos", *NTS* 20, 1973–74, 408–18; E. Lövestam, "Ehe", *BHHW* 1 369 f.; R. Patai, *L'Amour et le Couple aux Temps Bibliques*, 1967; W. Palutz, "Monogamie und Polygamie im Alten Testament", *ZAW* 75, 1963, 3–27; H. Preisker, *Christentum und Ehe in den ersten drei Jahrhunderten*, 1927; B. Reicke, "Neuzeitliche und neutestamentliche Auffassung von Liebe und Ehe", *NovT* 1, 1956, 21–34; K. H. Rengstorf, *Mann und Frau im Urchristentum*, 1954; K. H. Schelkle, "Ehe und Ehelosigkeit im Neuen Testament", *Wissenschaft und Weisheit* 29, 1966, 1–15; H. Schlier, *Christus und die Kirche im Epheserbrief*, 1930.

Melchizedek, Salem

| Μελχσεδέκ | *Μελχσεδέκ* (*Melchisedek*), Melchizedek, ancient Canaanite king of Salem (→ *Salēm*). |

OT Melchizedek (Heb. *malkî-ṣeḏeq*, "king of righteousness", "my king is righteous") is a proper name of Canaanite origin closely akin to Adonizedek (Jos. 10:1). Melchizedek emerges without warning in the primitive history (Gen. 14:18–20) following Abram's rout of the forces of Chedorlaomer. Melchizedek is introduced as "king of Salem" (→ *Salēm*), presumably monarch of Jerusalem, which is situated not far from the Valley of Shaveh, or the King's Valley (cf. 2 Sam. 18:18). As an expression of Near Eastern hospitality, Melchizedek supplies bread and wine for the physical refreshment of Abram and his victorious warriors. The Genesis narrative concludes with the remarkable observation that the Canaanite blessed Abram and received a tenth of the spoils of battle from him, Abram thereby acknowledging the prominence of Melchizedek's priesthood.

The only other mention of Melchizedek in the OT occurs in Ps. 110:4, where the Lord (*Yahweh*) addresses David's Lord (*'āḏôn*) with the acclamation: "You are a priest for ever after the order of Melchizedek." Ps. 110:4 thus intimates that the priest-king of messianic expectation would be installed in a new non-Aaronic sacerdotal order patterned after that of Melchizedek of old. In both the pre-Christian and early Christian eras the Psalm-text was interpreted by the Jews in a messianic sense. Strack-Billerbeck argues that the disappearance of the messianic interpretation of the Psalm between *c*. A.D. 50 and 250 was due to heightened tensions between the expanding church and the Synagogue (SB IV 452 f.). By substituting a non-messianic interpretation for Ps. 110, the Rabbinate sought to undermine the church's appeal to this text in its teaching and preaching.

Philo clothes the OT figure of Melchizedek in the garb of Platonic philosophy. Here Melchizedek is presented as an incarnation of the Logos (→ *word*), the ideal form (*idea*) of the creation, which spans the chasm between God and nature. The "righteous king" and the "king of peace" (*Leg.All.* 3, 79) learned the traditions of his priesthood from none save himself (*De Congr.* 99). Philo's extreme allegorization of Gen. 14:18–20 reduces the historical features of the OT text to timeless philosophical principles. Melchizedek is royal Mind (*nous*) who, unlike despotic kings, decrees pleasing laws and who "offers to the soul food of joy and gladness" (*Leg.All.* 3, 81). He is priestly Reason (*logos*) who with the gift of wine releases the soul from earthly contemplation and intoxicates it with esoteric heavenly virtues. Thus through his offering of bread and wine Melchizedek mediates the soul's direct access to God. Abraham's presentation of the tithe is similarly spiritualized: "he gave him a tenth of all [Gen. 14:20]; from the things of sense [aisthēsis], right use of sense; from the things of speech [logos], good speaking; from the things of thought [nous], good thinking" (Congr. 99).

In pre-Christian Samaritan tradition Melchizedek figured prominently in the establishment of the sanctuary of the sect, apparently as its first priest. Not only is Salem (→ Salēm) identified with Shechem, but Mt. Gerizim (Gk. oros hypsistou, "mountain of the highest God") is named after Melchizedek, the "priest of God most high."

Josephus accepts the historicity of the Gen. 14:18–20 pericope and characterizes Melchizedek as "a potent man among the Canaanites . . . the first priest of God" (War 6, 10, 1).

Melchizedek occupies a prominent place in the 11Q Melchizedek Qumran scroll, which quotes Ps. 82:1, 2 and transfers its meaning to Melchizedek: "as it is written concerning him in the hymns of David who says: 'the heavenly one [ʾelōhîm, sing.] standeth in the congregation of God; among the heavenly ones [ʾelōhîm, plur.] he judgeth.'" Melchizedek is thus depicted in the scroll as a paramount heavenly angel standing in the tribunal of God, who preserves the faithful and executes eschatological judgment upon the perverse spirits.

Rabbinic Judaism traditionally identified Melchizedek with Shem, the most pious of Noah's sons. According to R. Ishmael, the priesthood was taken from Melchizedek and transferred to Abraham because the Salemite addressed the patriarch before God (Ned. 32b; Sanh. 108b). Elsewhere in late Jewish literature Melchizedek was variously interpreted as an incarnate angel who performed priestly functions, as the archangel Michael, or as an idealized high priest of the messianic age (kōhēn-ṣedeq) who emerges alongside the messiah.

NT Only the author of Hebrews in the NT took interest in the enigmatic figure of Melchizedek. The idea of the Melchizedekian priesthood of Christ is introduced in Heb. 5:6, 10, but full explication of the concept is interrupted by a paraenetic digression (5:11–6:19) necessitated by the dullness and immaturity of the readers. Ch. 7 is devoted to a detailed development of the novel concept of priesthood "after the order of Melchizedek" (7:1–10), and its application to the high priest of the new covenant (7:11–28).

In 7:1, 2a the writer presents a selective recitation of Gen. 14:18–20 (conspicuously omitting reference to the bread and wine, which Roman Catholic theology regards as a type of the Eucharist), followed in 7:2b, 3 by a skilful reinterpretation of the Genesis text in the light of Ps. 110:4. Via a subtle typological exegesis the writer establishes Melchizedek as a fitting model of the radical non-legal priesthood embodied by Jesus (7:1–3). (a) 7:1 – The Salemite priest-king as a harbinger of the one who would unite in his person the dual honours of royalty and priesthood. (b) 7:2b – Etymological exegesis of Melchizedek's name ("king of righteousness") and title ("king of peace") points to the messiah whose person and ministry is characterized by righteousness (Isa. 32:1; Jer. 23:5, 6; 33:15 f.; Mal. 4:2; 1 Cor. 1:30) and peace (1 Chron. 22:9; Zech. 9:10; Eph. 2:14 f.). "Both graces perfectly meet in Christ" (B. F. Westcott, The Epistle to the Hebrews, 1892, 172). (c) 7:3a – Melchizedek exercised a priesthood entirely independent of priestly pedigree.

"The parents, ancestors, children, and posterity of Melchizedec are not descended from Levi, as it had to be in the case of the Levites (ver. 6), and they are not even mentioned by Moses" (J. A. Bengel, *Gnomon of the New Testament*, IV, 1857, 403). Herewith the priesthood of Melchizedek violated the conditions of Aaronic order, which stipulated paternal descent from Aaron (Exod. 28:1; Num. 3:10; 18:1) and maternal descent from a pure Israelite (Lev. 21:7, 13 f.; Ezek. 44:22). Melchizedek thus adumbrates the messianic high priest who was descended from the non-sacerdotal tribe of Judah. (d) 7:3b – The OT figure of Melchizedek was symbolically what Christ is in reality: a ministrant who suddenly emerged from the distant reaches of eternity and who later vanished into its depths equally as mysteriously. The notion of eternity, deduced from absence of recorded birth and decease, is understood in the light of the Jewish axiom: "quod non in Thora non in mundo [What is not in the Torah is not in the world]" (SB III 694). (e) 7:3c – Melchizedek exercises a priesthood of uninterrupted duration, since he neither succeeded another nor was he himself succeeded in office.

Having sketched Melchizedek's similarity to Christ, the writer argues his dissimilarity to → Abraham (and hence to the → Levites), thereby demonstrating Christ's superiority to the antiquated legal order (7:4–10): (a) 7:5, 6a – Melchizedek received the tithes from Abraham; (b) 7:6b, 7 – The Gentile bestowed the blessing upon the patriarch; and (c) 7:8 – Melchizedek "lives on" in Scripture unlike the Levitical priests who succumbed to death.

The remainder of the chapter (7:11–28) delineates the merits of Christ as Melchizedekian priest and high priest. Expounding the implications of the Davidic Psalm-text, the writer demonstrates that the high priest of the new covenant is vastly superior to the ministrants of the old annulled order. As high priest *for ever* "after the order of Melchizedek", Christ's priesthood is indissoluble (7:16), inviolable (7:24), efficacious (7:25) and perfect (7:28). The one foreshadowed in the distant past by the fleeting figure of Melchizedek is the great high priest *par excellence*.   *B. A. Demarest*

| Σαλήμ | Σαλήμ (*Salēm*), Salem, seat of Melchizedek's rule. |

OT 1. Salem, Greek form of an ancient Palestinian city, is associated by most authorities from earliest times with Jerusalem. A less convincing proposal identifies Salem with Salim (Gk. *Saleim*), a town eight miles south of Scythopolis in the region where John baptized (Jn. 3:23). Philo, working an etymological exegesis similar to the writer of Hebrews, hails the monarch of Salem as "king of peace" (*Leg.All.* 3, 79).

2. *Proper noun.* As a place name *šālēm* occurs only twice in the OT: (a) in Gen. 14:18; and (b) in Ps. 76:3 where it is most likely a poetic abbreviation of → Jerusalem (Heb. *yᵉrûšālayim*, "possession of peace" or "foundation of peace"). In the mind of the Psalmist Salem, the dwelling place of God, is pre-eminently a place of peace. Josephus reflects the Jewish tradition that the ancient Canaanite settlement known as Salem was later renamed Jerusalem by the priest-king Melchizedek.

3. *Adjectival form.* *šālēm,* a common OT cognate of *šālôm* ("wholeness", "peace") bears the meaning peaceful in the MT in the sense of a → covenant of peace between men (Gen. 34:21). More frequently, it signifies perfect, blameless (i.e. at peace with) as a description of man's spiritual relation to God (1 Ki. 8:61; 11:4; 15:3; 2 Chron. 16:9).

NT In the NT *Salēm* occurs only in the Epistle to Hebrews (7:1, 2). After identifying Melchizedek as "king of Salem" on the strength of Gen. 14:18 the writer, in similar manner to Philo, hastens to unfold the deeper spiritual meaning implicit in Melchizedek's royal title. To the eyes of faith the "king of Salem" is "king of peace" (→ Peace, art. *eirēnē*). Hebrews reflects little interest in the geographical location of Salem. The paramount interest is to deduce from the etymology of Salem a principal characteristic (i.e. peace) of the reign of the end-time priest-king. → Abraham, → Jerusalem, → Priest, → Sacrifice   *B. A. Demarest*

(a). B. A. Barrois, "Salem", *IDB* IV 1966; B. Demarest, *A History of the Interpretation of Hebrews 7, from the Reformation to the Present, Beiträge zur Geschichte der biblischen Exegese* 19, 1976); J. A. Fitzmyer, "Further Light on Melchizedek from Qumran Cave 11", *JBL* 86, 1967, 25–41 (reprinted in *Essays on the Semitic Background of the New Testament,* 1971, 245–67); and " 'Now this Melchizedek . . .' (Heb. 7:1)", op. cit., 221–44; J. G. Gammie, "Loci of the Melchizedek Tradition of Genesis 14:18–20", *JBL* 90, 1971, 385–96; F. L. Horton, *The Melchizedek Tradition: A Critical Examination of the Sources to the Fifth Century A.D. and in the Epistle to the Hebrews, Society for New Testament Studies Monograph Series* 30, 1976; O. Michel, *Melchisedek, TDNT* IV 568–71; J. J. Petuchowski, "The Controversial Figure of Melchizedek", *Hebrew Union College Annual* 28, 1957, 127–36; H. H. Rowley, "Melchizedek and Zadok", in W. Baumgartner ed., *Festschrift für A. Bartholet,* 1950, 461 ff.; R. Williamson, *Philo and the Epistle to the Hebrews,* 1970; A. S. van der Woude and M. de Jonge, "11Q Melchizedek and the New Testament", *NTS* 12, 1965–66, 310–26; Y. Yadin, "The Dead Sea Scrolls and the Epistle to the Hebrews", *Scripta Hierosolymitana* 4, 1958, 36–55.
(b). G. Bardy, "Melchisédech dans la tradition patristique", *RB* 35, 1926, 496–509, and 36, 1927, 24–45; J. Calvin, "Trois sermons sur l'histoire de Melchisédec", *Corpus Reformatorum,* LI, 641–82; M. Friedländer, "Melchisédec et l'Épître aux Hébreux", *Revue des Études Juives* 5, 1882, 188 ff.; F. J. Jerome, *Das geschichtliche Melchisedek-Bild und seine Bedeutung im Hebräerbrief,* 1920; H. E. del Medico, "Melchisedek", *ZAW* 69, 1957, 160–70; G. Schille, "Erwägungen zur Hohepriesterlehre des Hebräerbriefs", *ZNW* 46, 1955, 81–109; C. Spicq, "L'Origine Johannique de la Conception du Christ-Prêtre, dans l'Épître aux Hébreux", *Festschrift* M. Goguel, 1950, 258–69; and *L'Épître aux Hébreux,* I–II, 1952–53; H. Stork, *Die Sogenannten Melchisedekianer, Forschungen zur Geschichte des Neutestamentlichen Kanons* 8/2, 1928; G. Wuttke, *Melchisedech der Priesterkönig von Salem. Eine Studie zur Geschichte der Exegese, BZNW* 5, 1927.

Mercy, Compassion

This article brings together three different Gk. words, *eleos, oiktirmos* and *splanchna*. In their original use *eleos* refers to the feeling of pity, *oiktirmos,* and especially its root *oiktos,* to the exclamation of pity at the sight of another's ill-fortune, and *splanchna* to the seat of the emotions, the inward parts or what today would be called the heart. The corresponding verbs in the active express these feelings shown in the sense of to help, feel pity, show mercy; where they are used in the passive, they express the experience of these emotions.

ἔλεος

ἔλεος (*eleos*), compassion, mercy, pity; ἐλεέω (*eleeō*), feel compassion, show mercy or pity; ἐλεήμων (*eleēmōn*), merciful, compassionate; ἐλεεινός (*eleeinos*), pitiful; ἐλεημοσύνη (*eleēmosynē*), charity, alms; ἀνέλεος (*aneleos*), without pity; ἀνελεήμων (*aneleēmōn*), merciless.

CL *eleos* (masc. but normally neut. in the LXX and the NT) is found from Homer onwards. It is "the emotion roused by contact with an affliction which comes undeservedly on someone else" (R. Bultmann, *TDNT* II 477), viz. compassion, pity, mercy. These feelings are the reverse of envy at another's good fortune. There is also an element of fear that one might have to suffer in the same way. Aristotle in his *Poetics* stated that tragedy aroused pity and terror and these caused *katharsis*, purging. From Plutarch onwards we find the expressions *eleon echō*, to find mercy, and *kat' eleon*, out of compassion. *eleos* was used as a technical term for the end of the speech for the defence, in which the accused tried to awaken the compassion of the judges. In Plato's *Apology* Socrates refused to conform to the pattern (23 f., 34b–35d).

aneleos, an attributive compound showing mutation (Funk § 120:2), meaning unmerciful, without compassion, is found only in the NT, and replaces the Homeric *nēlees*, and Att. *anēlees* (found in the LXX but not the NT). *aneleēmōn* has the same adjectival meaning; it is found from Antiphon (480–411 B.C.) onwards as an adv. It is the privative form of *eleēmōn* (Homer onwards), compassionate, merciful. *eleeinos* (Homer onwards, but not in the LXX) is mainly used of a person's passive condition as causing compassion, hence pitiable, distressing.

The vb. *eleeō* (Homer onwards) means to have compassion, be sorry for, show compassion, be merciful. The Koine form *eleaō* is found twice in the LXX, 3 times in the NT. The cry *eleēson*, have mercy, was addressed to the gods. With or without *logois* (with words) the vb. also means deplore, sympathize with. In the pass. it means to find mercy (in the NT also *eleos lambanō*). The derived noun *eleēmosynē* (Callimachus of Alexandria, *c.* 250 B.C., onwards) was originally the same as *eleos* but was then applied to the act of kindness following compassion. It then obtained the specialized meaning of a contribution for or gift to the poor (cf. our alms); it finds its earliest use in the LXX (Dan. 4:27) and in profane writings in Diog. Laert. (3rd cent. A.D.).

OT 1. *eleos* and its derivatives are found nearly 400 times in the LXX. It normally represents *ḥeseḏ*; only 6 times *raḥamîm*. The vb. normally represents *ḥānan* (→ Grace), but also *rāḥam*; *eleēmosynē* renders *ṣeḏāqâh*.

2. These Heb. concepts betray a completely different background of thought from the predominantly psychological one in Gk. They are based on legal concepts. Hence, we have to interpret the LXX translation from the standpoint of the Heb. original, and not the other way round. Philo is the first Jewish writer in whom a penetration of the Gk. concepts is observable in our word-group.

(a) *ḥeseḏ* means proper covenant behaviour, the solidarity which the partners in the covenant owe one another (→ Covenant). The covenant may be between equals, or it may be made by one who is stronger than his partner in it. In either case it may result in one giving help to the other in his need. So the connotations of *eleos* meaning *ḥeseḏ* may stretch from loyalty to a covenant to kindliness, mercy, pity. This is especially the case when it is linked with *oiktirmos* meaning *raḥamîm* (e.g. Isa. 63:7b; Hos. 2:21[MT 2:19]; Zech. 7:9; Pss. 25:6[LXX 24:6]; 40:11 [MT 40:12; LXX 39:12]; 51:1[MT 51:3; LXX 50:3]; 69:16[MT 69:17; LXX 68:17]). Because of Yahweh's superiority as the partner in the covenant who remains faithful, his *eleos* was understood for the most part as a gracious gift. He promised it at the making of the covenant, and he constantly renewed it. Hence Israel might request *eleos* from him including the mercy of forgiveness, when it had broken the covenant (e.g. Exod. 34:9; Num. 14:19; Jer. 3:12). When God acts like this and also when man acts similarly the stress is not on the basic attitude in *eleos* but on its manifestation in acts.

(b) *ṣᵉdāqâh* is normally rendered by *dikaiosynē* (→ Righteousness). But "since the judgment in which God's *ṣᵉdāqâh* is active will be in favour of His people . . . we can understand the rendering *eleēmosynē*" (R. Bultmann, *TDNT* II 486; cf. e.g. Isa. 1:27). Just as Yahweh enforces his covenant law mercifully, so *eleēmosynē* may also be used for human kindness, charity and even alms (though this last is found only in late Jud.) when these conform to the pattern of this law.

3. The linguistic usage of late Palestinian Judaism is that of the OT. *ḥeseḏ* is very common in the Qumran texts: the Essene community used it to praise the loyalty of God to the covenant which they had experienced in the establishment of the new, eschatological covenant. See 1QS 1:8, 22; 2:1, 4, 24; 4:4 f.; 5:4, 25; 8:2; 10:4, 16, 26; 11:12 f.; 1QM 12:3; 14:4, 8 f.; 18:11; 1QH 1:32; 2:23, 25; 4:37; 5:22; 6:9; 7:18, 20, 27, 35; 9:7, 10, 14; 10:14, 16; 11:5, 17 f., 28, 30 f.; 12:14, 21; 13:5; 16:9, 12, 16; CD 13:18; 19:1; 20:21.

NT 1. *eleos* and its derivatives are found 78 times in the NT, mainly in the Pauline writings (26 times) and Luke-Acts (20 times with preference for *eleos* itself). It is found 15 times in Matt. Only in Jn., Phil., 1–2 Thess. is the group completely absent.

2. *Synoptic Gospels.* In the Synoptics *eleeō* is found mainly in the narratives. Exceptions are Matt. 5:7; 18:33; Lk. 10:37; 16:24. The opposite is true of *eleos*, which, with the exception of Lk. 1:58, is used only in reports of speech.

(a) The vb. marks that breaking in of the divine mercy into the reality of human misery which took place in the person of Jesus of Nazareth with his work of freeing and healing which demonstrated his authority. Jesus answered the cry for help "Have mercy on me" (Mk. 10:47, 48 par. Matt. 9:27; 15:22; 17:15; Lk. 17:13) from the sick or the relatives of the demon-possessed (Matt. 15:22; 17:15) by healing. On one occasion (Mk. 5:19) he commanded a man from whom he had driven out demons to tell those at home how the Lord (here in the OT sense of "God") had had mercy on him. Normally on these occasions Jesus was addressed by the messianic title → "Son of David" (→ Son); once we find *epistata* (Lk. 17:13), Master (lit. "foreman"). (*epistata* also occurs in Lk. 5:5; 8:24, 45; 9:33, 49; see Arndt, 300.) Matt. adds the post-resurrection title of *kyrios* (→ Lord), or uses it to replace the presumably historical address of "Teacher" (*didaskale*, cf. Matt. 17:15 with Mk. 9:17, Lk. 9:38). This makes the cry, "Lord, have mercy", a confession of faith in the divine authority of Jesus.

(b) Mercy from man to man is expressed by *eleeō* or *eleēmōn* only twice in the teaching in Matt. (5:7; 18:33), and once in the material peculiar to Lk. (16:24), but in each case the motivation is clearly God's mercy. In Matt. 5:7 the merciful (*eleēmōn*) are promised God's mercy – the vb. is pass. to avoid using the name of God. In the parable of the unforgiving servant (Matt. 18:23–35) the demand for mercy (v. 33) is based on the limitless compassion of his lord (vv. 35, 27; → *splanchna*). The rich man, who had been merciless during his life, calls in his suffering on → Abraham, exalted to fellowship with God, with the same words for mercy as are otherwise used only in calling on God (Lk. 16:24).

(c) In the rest of the teaching in Matt. and Lk. we find only *eleos*. A reference, often direct, to the OT is noticeable. In his controversies with the → Pharisees Jesus bore witness to the sovereign mercy of God, which seeks a response not in ritual detail but in solidarity through action with the lowly (→ Poor) and hungry (→ Hunger) (Matt. 9:13; 12:7; cf. 1 Sam. 15:22; Hos. 6:6). In his "woes" he also levelled against them the charge that in their interpretation of the → law they had shifted the main stress from "justice and mercy and faithfulness" to a more casuistic formalism (Matt. 23:23; cf. also Lk. 10:37 where the showing of mercy is demanded as the moral of the parable of the good → Samaritan). In the prologue to his Gospel Lk. announced its main theme in the two great psalms of praise (Lk. 1:46–55, 68–79); that the covenant loyalty of God, promised in the OT and shown in action in the history of Israel, would reach its climax in the gracious self-humiliation of God to the humble (→ Poor) in the event of Christ (1:50, 54, 72, 78); v. 78 speaks of the → *splanchna eleous*, the "merciful heart", of our God. Note the many OT quotations in these psalms (cf. Lk. 1:46 with 1 Sam. 2:1–10; Lk. 1:48 with Pss. 113:5 ff.; 11:4; Lk. 1:50 with Ps. 103:13, 17; Lk. 1:51 with 2 Sam. 22:28; Lk. 1:52 with Ps. 147:6; Job 12:19; 5:11; 1 Sam. 2:7; Ezek. 21:31; Lk. 1:53 with Pss. 34:11; 107:9; 2 Sam. 2:5; Lk. 1:54 with Isa. 41:8; Ps. 98:3; Lk. 1:55 with Mic. 7:20; Gen. 17:17; 18:18; 22:17; Lk. 1:68 with Pss. 41:14; 72:18; 89:53; 106:48; Lk. 1:69 with 1 Sam. 2:10; Pss. 18:3; 132:17; Lk. 1:71 with Ps. 106:10; Lk. 1:72 with Pss. 105:8; 106:45; Lev. 26:42; Gen. 17:7; 22:16; Mic. 7:20; Lk. 1:74 with Ps. 97:10; Lk. 1:76 with Mal. 3:1; 4:5; Lk. 1:77 with Jer. 31:34; Num. 24:17; Isa. 60:1 f.; Lk. 1:79 with Isa 9:1 f.; 42:7). The thought of these two psalms in Lk. is saturated with OT ideas of judgment and mercy. (On the first two chapters of Lk. see further R. Laurentin, *Structure et Théologie de Luc I–II*, 1964.)

3. *eleēmosynē*, *as alms charity*. Matt. reports only Jesus' criticism of the attempt to obtain public praise and acknowledgment in the giving of alms (→ Poor NT) (Matt. 6:1–4), but Lk. has the definite teaching: alms instead of ritual purity (Lk. 11:41, in an argument with the Pharisees), and lays down as a rule for the disciples and the church the giving away of one's possessions to the poor (Lk. 12:33). In Acts Tabitha (9:36) and Cornelius (10:2) are singled out for their charity and as recipients of singular blessing. The former was perhaps a Hellenistic Jewess (her name is explained as Dorcas or Gazelle) and was a resident of Joppa. She fell sick and died (Acts 9:37), but was restored through Peter. Cornelius was a centurion of the Italian Cohort at Caesarea and was "a devout man who feared God *eusebēs kai phoboumenos ton theon*" (on the significance of these terms → Conversion). God honoured him by receiving his prayers and accepting his alms (10:4, 31), and bestowing on him the Holy Spirit (10:44 ff.). Whereupon he was the first Gentile to be received into the church (10:47 f.). This also took place at Joppa. In his defence before Felix in Acts Paul mentioned the bringing of alms for his

people as the purpose of his last journey to Jerusalem (24:17). By using the term "doing alms" (*eleēmosynas poieō*, Heb. *'āśâh ṣᵉḏāqâh*), a Semitic expression, he stressed his active responsibility. In Acts 3:1–8 Peter by his healing of the lame man symbolically ended the time of begging and imperfect mercy by the full mercy brought in the name of Jesus Christ (3:6).

4. *Paul.* Paul wished to be regarded as one who had received mercy (*ēleēthēn*) that he might become an → apostle (1 Tim. 1:13, 16), and who by the Lord's mercy (*ēleēmenos*) had been made trustworthy (1 Cor. 7:25). In view of the wide-scale rejection of the gospel by → Israel, he strove in Rom. to make clear that God's free mercy did not contradict his covenant loyalty (Rom. 9:15, 16, 18; v. 15 is a quotation of Exod. 33:19). God's plan of salvation, now for the Gentiles (Rom. 9:23 f.; 11:30; 15:9), then for the Jews (11:31), and so both for Jews and Gentiles (Rom. 11:32) is based on his mercy. The salvation of those made alive for faith and renewal in the Holy Spirit is based on this mercy, not on good works (Eph. 2:4–9; Tit. 3:5). Hence they are admonished to pass on the mercy they have experienced (2 Cor. 4:1; Rom. 12:1, *oktirmos*, plur.) cheerfully (Rom. 12:8), so that mercy becomes one of the signs by which a disciple can be known; cf. "full of mercy [*mestē eleous*]" in the list of virtues in Jas. 3:17, while "unmerciful [*aneleēmonas*]" (RV, RSV "ruthless"; NEB "without pity") is the lowest rung in the downward ladder of Rom. 1:29–32 and so the completest negation of the knowledge of God.

Paul and other NT writers (2 Jn. 3; Jude 2), in their confidence in God's gracious giving can greet their readers at the beginning (1 Tim. 1:2; 2 Tim. 1:2; Tit. 1:4, some MSS) or end (Gal. 6:16) of their letters with a prayer for the mercy of God and of Jesus Christ – mostly combined with → "grace" and → "peace". In so doing they took over Jewish greeting forms and expanded them. The mercy of God can heal, e.g., Epaphras (Phil. 2:27); it is a present gift for the "household" (2 Tim. 1:16); and the final, future gift ensuring salvation (2 Tim. 1:18). Paul proclaimed the Christian hope of a future resurrection of an imperishable body by contradicting the sectarian group in Corinth which affirmed that the bodily resurrection was already past; he describes those who confine this hope to this life as "most to be pitied [*eleeinoteroi*]" (1 Cor. 15:19).

5. *Other NT Writings.* (a) 1 Pet. begins by praising the mercy of God (1:3), by which Christians "have been born anew to a living hope by the resurrection of Jesus Christ from the dead" (cf. Eph. 2:4; 1 Cor. 15:19; see above). Just like Paul in Rom. 9:25 f., he praises the enlargement of God's mercy to take in the Gentiles (2:10) by using Hosea's words (Hos. 2:23[MT 2:25]).

(b) James impressed on an indolent church that mercy shown here on earth has its bearing on the final → judgment, and that "judgment without mercy" (*aneleos*, only here in the NT) awaits the one who has shown no mercy (2:13; cf. Lk. 16:24 f.; Matt. 18:33 f.; 25:40, 45).

(c) Jude, after mentioning the love of God which they have experienced and their expectation of a final merciful judgment by Jesus Christ, urges his readers to exercise a discriminating mercy to those around them (vv. 21–23; the force of v. 23a is uncertain).

(d) Rev. 3:17, just like 1 Cor. 15:19, convicts a church, that of Laodicea, of its pitiable (*eleeinos*) condition in spite of its earthly riches, and places it under the judgment of Christ, which alone is valid. (On the church at Laodicea → Cold, art. *chliaros*.)

(e) Heb. uses the type of the high priest in the OT and his functions on the great Day of Atonement (Lev. 16) to show the solidarity of Christ, who is greater than any high priest, with his brethren, which guarantees a merciful and boundless understanding (2:17; cf. 4:15), and so gives the despairing church confidence to draw near the throne of grace to find mercy (4:16).   *H.-H. Esser*

οἰκτιρμός

οἰκτιρμός (*oiktirmos*), compassion, pity; οἰκτίρω (*oiktirō*), have compassion, show pity or mercy; οἰκτίρμων (*oiktirmōn*), compassionate.

CL The root word *ho oiktos* (Aesch. and Soph. onwards) means the lamenting or regretting of a person's misfortune or death, then metaphorically sympathy, pity. *ho oiktirmos* (Pindar onwards) was originally a poetic form of *oiktos*. The derivative *oiktirmōn*, compassionate (Gorgias, 5th cent. B.C., onwards), is seldom found; *oiktros*, lamenting, and lamentable, is commoner. The vb. *oiktirō*, also *oiktizō*, (Homer onwards) means to have compassion, to pity, in the sense both of mere feeling and of active merciful action; it is often a synonym of *eleeō* (→ *eleos*).

OT The words of this group are found about 80 times in the LXX, both the noun and the vb. appearing *c.* 30 times each; they are used with the same meaning as in secular Gk. The Heb. equivalents are mostly derivatives of the root *rḥm*, have compassion, but also of the root *ḥnn*, be gracious, all of which could have equally well been translated by → *eleos* and its derivatives. They are found most frequently in the Pss. Because of the Heb. plur. form *raḥᵃmîm*, *oiktirmos* occurs always in the plur. (2 Sam. 24:14; Isa. 63:15; Pss. 25:6 [LXX 24:6]; 40:11[MT 40:12; LXX 39:12]; 51:1 [MT 51:3; LXX 50:3]; cf. Funk § 142).

NT 1. In the NT the noun occurs 4 times in Paul, once in Heb.; the vb. twice in Paul, the adj. twice in Lk. and once in Jas.
2. Since God is "the Father of mercies" (for the use of plur. see OT above) and as such shows mercy to men (2 Cor. 1:3), Paul can use "the mercies of God" (Rom. 12:1) as the bridge between doctrine and exhortation in Rom. Just as the phrase sums up God's saving acts and plan of salvation previously outlined in Rom. 11, so also God's mercies are the presupposition – the grounds of the "therefore" (12:1) – for the Christian life. Because of them heartfelt sympathy (Phil. 2:1, *splanchna kai oiktirmoi*) which creates unity of spirit must be expected from Christians; they are to put on heartfelt sympathy (Col. 3:12, *splanchna oiktirmōn*). Heb. 10:28 f. points out that the punishment of the man who has "outraged the Spirit of grace" and "has spurned the Son of God" will be even less merciful than that meted out to the violater of the law of Moses.
3. The vb. is found only in Rom. 9:15, a quotation of Exod. 33:19, where it is in parallelism to *eleeō* (→ *eleos* NT 4), with the sense of have compassion.
4. The adj. is found in Jas. 5:11, quoting Pss. 103:8 (LXX 102:8); 111:4 (LXX 110:4) together with *polysplanchnos*, merciful (→ *splanchna* NT); it expresses a quality of God. In the Sermon on the Plain (Lk. 6:20–49) Jesus calls for merciful behaviour (v. 36), putting God's merciful attitude as the measure of human action.
                                                                                         H.-H. Esser

| σπλάγχνα | σπλάγχνα (splanchna), inward parts, entrails, hence as the seat of emotion, the heart, love; σπλαγχνίζομαι |

(splanchnizomai), have pity, show mercy, feel sympathy; πολύσπλαγχνος (poly-splanchnos), sympathetic, compassionate; εὔσπλαγχνος (eusplanchnos), tender-hearted, compassionate.

CL to splanchnon (Homer onwards), used almost entirely in the plur., originally meant the inward parts, or entrails (of the sacrificial animal), especially the more valuable parts, the heart, lungs, liver, but also the spleen and the kidneys. Since immediately after the killing of the animal they were removed, roasted and eaten as the first part of the sacrificial meal, the word came to mean the sacrificial meal itself. From Aesch. (5th cent. B.C.) onwards we find splanchna used also for the human entrails, especially for the male sexual organs and the womb, as the site of the powers of conception and birth; hence children were sometimes called splanchna, and ek splanchnōn means from one's own flesh and blood. Since the intestines were regarded as the site of the natural passions, e.g. anger, fretful desires, love, the word came to have the fig. meaning of heart (as the organ of feelings and emotions), or the sense of premonition; finally it meant even affection and love. Hence in the sing. (Soph. – 5th cent. B.C. – onwards) it means pity, compassion, love. The oldest form of the vb. is splanchneuō, eat the entrails, prophesy from the entrails. The later form splanchnizomai is found only once in secular Gk., in a 4th cent. B.C. inscription from Cos, with the same meaning. The metaphorical meaning have mercy on, feel pity, is found only in the writings of Judaism and the NT.

OT The LXX has the noun 15 times, the vb. twice. Only twice does the noun translate Heb. words. In Prov. 12:10 it represents raḥᵃmîm (→ eleos OT and oiktirmos OT) mercy, and in Prov. 26:22 beṭen, inner parts, belly. The remaining cases are in books like 2 Macc. and 4 Macc. with no Heb. original. We find the meanings intestines (2 Macc. 9:5; 4 Macc. 5:30; 10:8), mother-love (4 Macc. 15:22, 29), heart (2 Macc. 9:6).

Test. XII is the first book to contain the predominant meaning merciful, show mercy, in the frequent use of both noun and vb. They represent raḥᵃmîm and rḥm and form the preparation for the NT use (cf. Test.Zeb. 7:3; 8:2, 6 with 1QS 1:21; 2:1; cf. H. Köster, TDNT VII 552).

NT 1. Apart from its use with → eleos (NT 2 (c)) in Lk. 1:78 splanchna and its adjectival derivatives are not found in the Synoptics, but the vb. is found only in them.

2. There the vb. splanchnizomai is used (a) of the attitude of Jesus, (b) of the actions of key persons at the turning points of three parables.

(a) The meaning goes beyond the lit. one of "his heart contracted convulsively" at the sight of crying human need and characterizes the messianic compassion of Jesus (cf. H. Köster, TDNT VII 554); the cases are a → leper with his petition (Mk. 1:41), the people like sheep without a shepherd (Mk. 6:34; Matt. 14:14; cf. also Mk. 8:2; Matt. 15:32: "I have compassion" in direct speech), the sight of the harassed and exhausted crowd shortly before the sending out of the Twelve (Matt. 9:36), two blind men who besought him (Matt. 20:34), and the widow at

Nain mourning her only son (Lk. 7:13). In Mk. 9:22 it is used in the petition for
the driving out of a demon (→ *eleos* NT 2 (a) on Matt. 17:15).

(b) In the two parables, Matt. 18:23–35, the unforgiving servant (→ *eleos* NT
2 (b)), and Lk. 15:11–32, the prodigal son, *splanchnizomai* expresses the strongest
feeling of a merciful (Matt. 18:27) or loving (Lk. 15:20) reaction which forms the
turning point of the story. In contrast to both these cases we have the strongest
expression of righteous rejection (→ Anger) in Matt. 18:34 and Lk. 15:28 (cf.
TDNT VII 554). In both parables *splanchnizomai* makes the unbounded mercy of
God visible; in the former we see also his deadly and decisive anger against the
one who having experienced mercy denies the fact by being unmerciful himself.
In the parable of the good Samaritan (Lk. 10:30–37) *splanchnizomai* in v. 33
expresses the attitude of complete willingness to use all means, time, strength, and
life, for saving at the crucial moment. It contrasts with the passing by on the other
side (vv. 31, 32). Since seeing and being prepared to help are one, it sets in motion
as with Jesus himself, a whole chain of events which together are called *eleos*
(v. 37a). Humanity and neighbourliness are not qualities but action (v. 37 f.).

3. In Paul the noun refers to the whole man, viz. in his capacity to love or as
one who loves (cf. Köster, *TDNT* VII 555 f.). Hence, it could be replaced by his
name or the corresponding personal pron. The frequent translation "heart" is
suitable, if we understand heart as the centre of loving action. In 2 Cor. 6:12 Paul
accuses his readers of giving their ability to love him only limited space, while in
7:15 he says of Titus that his heart goes out to them. In Phil. 1:8 the use of the
qualifying "Christ" indicates that Christ is the source of the love that embraces
and lays claim to the apostle's whole personality. In Phlm. 7 and 20 the refreshing
of *ta splanchna* of the saints and of Paul (RSV heart), means the refreshing of the
whole person; there would be no change in meaning if it were either omitted (cf.
NEB), or rendered "altogether", except that it draws attention to the conscious joy
that Philemon has given. In v. 12 it could be rendered "as a piece of me" (cf. NEB,
Phillips), or as "as though I myself were coming." That the word is used three
times in this short letter shows Paul's inner participation, his personal concern in
this matter. For Phil. 2:1, Col. 3:12 → *oiktirmos* NT 2.

4. In Acts 1:18 the bowels in the physical sense are meant. 1 Jn. 3:17 means the
heart as the source of action that helps and relieves need.

5. For *polysplanchnos* (Jas. 5:11) → *oiktirmos* NT 4. *eusplanchnos*, tenderhearted,
is found in lists of Christian virtues in Eph. 4:32 and 1 Pet. 3:8.

→ Brother, → Heart, → Love, → Man, → Righteousness   *H.-H. Esser*

(a). R. Bultmann, *eleos* etc., *TDNT* II 477–87; and *oiktirō* etc., *TDNT* V 159 ff.; J. D. M. Derrett,
"The Parable of the Good Samaritan", in *Law in the New Testament*, 1970, 208–27; R. Jewett,
Paul's Anthropological Terms: A Study of their Use in Conflict Settings, 1971; A. R. Johnson,
"*ḥeseḏ* and *ḥāsîḏ*", in N. A. Dahl and A. S. Kapelrud, eds., *Interpretationes ad Vetus Testamentum
pertinentes Sigmundo Mowinckel Septuagenario missae*, 1955, 100 ff.; E. Käsemann, "Worship and
Everyday Life: A Note on Romans 12", in *New Testament Questions of Today*, 1969, 188–95; H.
Köster, *splanchnon* etc., *TDNT* VII 548–59; W. F. Lofthouse, "*ḥēn* and *ḥesed* in the Old Testament", *ZAW* Neue Folge 10, 1933, 29–35; N. H. Snaith, *The Distinctive Ideas of the Old Testament*,
1944, 94–130; H. W. Wolff, *Anthropology of the Old Testament*, 1974, 63–66.
(b). F. Asensio, *Misericordia et Veritas*, 1949; J. Begrich, "*bᵉrît*. Ein Beitrag zur Erfassung einer
alttestamentlichen Denkform", *ZAW* 60, 1944, 1–11 (*Gesammelte Studien zum Alten Testament*,
ed. W. Zimmerli, 1964, 55–66); G. Braumann, "Jesu Erbarmen nach Matthäus", *ThZ* 19, 1963,
305.ff.; G. Delling, "Das Gleichnis vom gottlosen Richter", *ZNW* 51, 1962, 1 ff.; G. Eichholz,

Jesus Christus und der Nächste, BSt 9, 1951; and *Einführung in die Gleichnisse, BSt* 37, 1963, 78 ff.; N.
Glueck, *Das Wort ḥeseḏ im alttestamentlichen Sprachgebrauch, BZAW* 47, 1927; L. Gulkowitsch,
Die Entwicklung des Begriffes ḥāsîḏ im Alten Testament, 1934; H. Gollwitzer, *Das Gleichnis vom
barmherzigen Samariter, BSt* 34, 1962; G. Harder, *Paulus und das Gebet*, 1936, 88 f.; E. Kamlah,
Die Form der katalogischen Paränese im Neuen Testament, WUNT 7, 1964; W. Monselewski, *Der
Barmherzige Samariter*, 1967; L. Schmidt, *Die Ethik der alten Griechen*, II, 1882, 290–94; E.
Sjöberg, *Gott und die Sünder im palästinensischen Judentum, BWANT* 4, 1939; H. J. Stoebe, "Die
Bedeutung des Wortes ḥeseḏ im Alten Testament", *VT* 2, 1952, 244 ff.; S. Wibbing, *Die Tugend-
und Lasterkataloge im Neuen Testament, BZNW* 25, 1959.

Might, Authority, Throne

The word *dynamis* suggests the inherent capacity of someone or something to carry
something out, whether it be physical, spiritual, military or political. It also denotes
the largely spontaneous expression of such *dynamis. exousia*, on the other hand, is
used only with reference to people. It indicates the power to act which given as of
right to anyone by virtue of the position he holds. Such authority exists, quite
independently of whether it can be exercised in given circumstances. *thronos*,
throne, is also relevant in this context. Originally it meant the seat of government,
and then, equally, someone who was in such a position of authority or strength.
The words *bia, ischys, keras* and *kratos* are discussed under → Strength.

δύναμις

δύναμις *(dynamis)*, power, might, strength, force, ability,
capability, deed of power, resources; δύναμαι *(dynamai)*,
to be strong enough to, be able to; δυνάστης *(dynastēs)*, a ruler, sovereign; δυναμόω
(dynamoō), strengthen; ἐνδυναμόω *(endynamoō)*, strengthen; δυνατός *(dynatos)*,
powerful, strong, mighty, able; δυνατέω *(dynateō)*, be strong, able, strong enough;
ἀδύνατος *(adynatos)*, powerless, impotent.

CL 1. *dynamis*, from the stem *dyna-*, means power, strength, might; cf. also the
vb. *dynamai*, be able, have the strength to, and the noun *dynastēs*, a ruler (since
Soph.); further, the later vbs. *dynamoō* and *endynamoō*, strengthen, and finally the
adj. *dynatos*, strong, mighty, and the vb. derived from it which is only attested in
the NT, *dynateō*, be strong, have the strength to.
2. *dynamis*, frequently found from Homer onwards, means ability to achieve,
physical strength; and then troops, fighting forces, and political power. Where
Gk. philosophy and medicine reflect on the nature of man, the concept appears in
its original sense of the strength or ability to live and to act which is dependent on
physical strength and spiritual faculties.
dynamis figures in the realm of nature, e.g. in the power of heat and cold, and
the healing power of plants and elements. In Hellenistic times the word took on
metaphysical connotations. Posidonius saw the principle of being in an elementary
force (cf. K. Reinhardt, *Poseidonius*, 1921; *Kosmos und Sympathie*, 1926). The Stoics
equated the all-pervading creative-force with God (Alexander of Aphrodisiensis,
2, 308, 35 ff.; cf. J. von Arnim, *Stoicorum Veterum Fragmenta*, I–IV, 1921–4). The
gnostics honoured God as the Almighty, and hoped for men's redemption through
their incorporation into the heavenly powers (*Corp.Herm., Poimandres*, I, 26).
Men tried, above all through → magic, to obtain a share in the supranatural powers

(Iamblichus, *De Mysteriis* 2, 1); sick people looked for healing through a demonstration of the power of the god Asclepius (*P.Oxy.* XI, 1381, 206 ff.).

 OT 1. In the LXX *dynamis*, as a rule, is used to translate the Heb. *ḥayil* (138 times) or *ṣābā'* (113 times), and generally means military forces. It can also stand for *geḇûrâh* (power e.g. of a ruler), as in Jdg. 5:31;5:21, or for *'ôz* (e.g. Ps. 68 [67]:28). The plur. *ṣeḇā'ôt* often refers to the heavenly hosts (Ps. 102[103]:21); God is "Yahweh Sabaoth", i.e. the Lord of the heavenly hosts (Ps. 45[46]:7, 11; 47[48]:8; → God, art. *theos* OT 2). The personal God now becomes the subject of the transcendent powers; autonomous powers of nature and magic are pushed into the background. God's might is primarily revealed on the level of history, and to a particular people. The proof of God's power, so fundamental for Israel, was the miraculous deliverance at the Red Sea (Exod. 15:6, 13; Deut. 3:24; 9:26, 29). The subsequent theological struggle with Canaanite religion led to the introduction of → nature into the field of God's activity and power; the most comprehensive demonstration of God's power is then seen to be the creation of the world (Jer. 34[27]:5; 39[32]:17). On the basis of the nation's experience, individuals can also praise God as their refuge and strength (Ps. 45[46]:1; Sam. 22:32 ff.). God's power, at work in the believer, is the → Spirit (Mic. 3:8). God is Spirit, not flesh: he far transcends the whole creation (Isa. 31:3 f.). It is not, however, *dynamis*, but *ischys* (→ Strength) that is mostly used as a translation for Heb. *kôaḥ* and *'ôz* in the LXX: Israel did not only potentially, but actually experience the manifestation of God's power.

2. Jewish apocalyptic lived in the expectation of the judgment of the world in the near future by God, hoping to see a display of the might of which Israel, as a nation, currently experienced so little. *kôaḥ* and *'ôz* are used less, and *geḇûrâh* comes into the foreground: this represents the power of God at work in the last days. The writings from Qumran foresee the triumph of God's might in the war of the Children of Light against the Children of Darkness. The end of the age brings the conclusive and world-embracing demonstration of God's mighty deeds (*geḇûrôt*), previously experienced by Israel alone (1QM 11:1–12:5). In this, God's power is expressed through the action both of human fighters and of the "mighty ones" (*gibbôrîm*), i.e. the angels. But God himself can also engage in battle as a mighty hero (*gibbôr*), and give the cosmic struggle its decisive turn (1QM 12:9; 1QH 6:30). The world war thus becomes a world-judgment, above all ending the rule of the devil (cf. Ass.Mos. 10:1; Test.Dan., 5:13–6:4). According to popular expectation, the messiah, too, will be a victorious warrior, and will be the instrument of God's final demonstration of power (Pss. Sol. 17:24, 42 f., 51). The Teacher of the Qumran community already knows the experience of God's might (1QH 4:23), through the Holy Spirit, who dwells in him as the gift of God, and as a promise of the eschatological fulfilment (1QH 7:6 f.; cf. 1QS 3:20–22). The Teacher sees his task as that of making known God's mighty deeds to all the living (1QH 4:28 f.).

The strong feeling that it was God's might that was his essential characteristic also illuminates the fact that, in Rabbinic writings, *geḇûrâh* serves as a circumlocution for the name of God; but it is never used of the forces of the devil and his demons who oppose God. In the apocalyptic writings, the natural phenomena between heaven and earth are called powers or powers of heaven (Eth.Enoch

40:9; 61:10; 82:8; 91:16). These were placed by God under the rule of → angels (Jub. 2:2 f.). Wisdom can be described as a mirror of the power of God (Wis. 7:25 f.); and even the Torah is called "my power" by God (Mek.Exod. 3:1 on 15:2), doubtless because it is the instrument of creation and the power or order in the cosmos (cf. Ab.R.N. 3:14).

NT In the NT *dynamis* is found 118 times, and relatively frequently in the Pauline writings except in 1 Tim., Tit., Philemon; there is no use of the noun in any of the Johannine writings, nor in Jas. or Jude. *dynamoō* and *dynateō* only occur rarely in Paul, but the vb. *dynamai*, to be able (expressing possibility or capability), occurs as well in all those writings where the noun is not found, except for Tit. and Phil.

1. *The Synoptic Gospels and Acts*. Here *dynamis* denotes the power of God, the heavenly powers (in the plur.), miraculous power (in the plur., mighty deeds, miracles) and the power which brings salvation to completion.

(a) God is the Mighty One (Lk. 1:48); and, according to Mk. 14:62, Jesus himself used the reverential circumlocution of "the power" for the name of God. All his work is supported by the knowledge of the almighty power of God: with God all things are possible (Matt. 19:26 par. Mk. 10:27, Lk. 18:27; Mk. 14:35). At the end, his power is declared pre-eminently in the resurrection of the dead (Mk. 12:24).

(b) The NT also speaks of "powers", i.e. cosmic powers between heaven and earth that can appear in person (Mk. 13:25; cf. Rom. 8:38; Eph. 1:21; 1 Pet. 3:22). Significantly, superhuman representatives of evil are also credited with having power, but it is always pointed out, either that their power has already been broken, or that it will shortly be abolished (cf. Matt. 12:29 par. Mk. 3:27, Lk. 11:22; Lk. 10:19; 1 Cor. 15:24; 2 Thess. 2:9; Rev. 13:2; 17:13 f.; → Angel). It is characteristic for the NT and fundamental for its proclamation of "good news", that through and in Christ, those things have taken place to which both the OT and Judaism looked forward, God's demonstration of power in the last days, and his triumph over the climactic rise of evil.

(c) Christ was powerful in speech and action (Lk. 24:19). His → miracles are called *dynameis* (cf. Heb. geḇûrôṯ; i.e. "mighty deeds"), because in them God's rule on earth begins to have a powerful effect, and the fight against the devil is carried out on the level of human existence (Matt. 12:22–30; Mk. 6:2, 5; Lk. 19:37; Acts 10:58). Jesus is the "mightier one", who, as God's representative, subdues the strong man, i.e. the devil (cf. Mk. 1:8 with 3:22–30). Jesus' miracles are worked by a power within himself (Mk. 5:30 par. Lk. 5:17; Mk. 6:14). Lk. links this God-given power with the Holy → Spirit in Lk. 1:35; 4:14; Acts 1:8; 10:38. The miracles, therefore, are regarded as evidence from God that Jesus is the messiah, the One anointed with the Spirit (Acts 2:22; 10:38). The exaltation of the messiah further makes him the mediator of God's saving might. For it is by the power of the Spirit, bestowed on them by Jesus, that his servants perform mighty acts (Acts 4:7; 6:8; 8:13; 19:11). The apostles' authoritative preaching (Acts 4:33; cf. 6:8–10) is seen as proof of a supernatural power.

(d) All these proofs of the Spirit and of power, of course, are only recognized as such where there is → faith. They cannot take place in an area of unbelief

603

(Mk. 6:5). But the final demonstration of Christ's power will be both public and irresistible. This will be at the time of his return (Matt. 24:32 par. Mk. 13:28, Lk. 21:29), when the → kingdom of God will be consummated "in power [*en dynamei*]" (Mk. 9:1), or "with power [*meta dynameōs*]" (Matt. 24:30 par. Mk. 13:26, Lk. 21:27). In this "latter-day" demonstration of God's power the believer already now has a share, which is why no limits are put to his actions, since all things are possible for him (Mk. 9:23).

2. *John's Gospel and Revelation.* (a) In the Gospel of Jn. the word *dynamis* does not occur, because here the messianic activity of Jesus is based on the sending of the Son, and on the unity of will of both Father and Son. The Son can do nothing without the Father (5:19, 30, *dynatai*); his miracles are signs which reveal the divine power of Jesus (see 3:2; 9:16; 10:21 – always *dynatai*). Conversely, the inability of men to believe in Jesus and to enter the sphere of God's reality is due to their being imprisoned in the world of darkness (3:3; 8:43; 14:17, *ou dynatai*). Only → election (6:44) and rebirth (3:5) secure their release.

(b) Rev. sees the saints in a vision praising Christ who, by his enthronement in heaven, has crowned his redeeming work on earth. Admittedly it is God who is worshipped in the hymn of praise, for his honour and might (*dynamis*) and power (Rev. 4:11; 7:12; 19:1), but the exalted Christ is also worthy to receive such sovereign power, and that on the grounds of his sacrificial death (5:13; 12:10). For it was through Christ that God broke the power of evil rulers of the world (13:2); Christ made possible the victorious culmination of God's sovereign rule (11:17; 12:10; → Kingdom). In John's vision, the night-visions of the Son of Man are given a christological interpretation (cf. Rev. 13:1–14 with Dan. 7), and polemically contrasted with Roman world-domination and the Caesar-cult.

3. *Paul.* Paul lays a greater emphasis on the present experience of the revelation of God's might, which he understands primarily in terms of the power which raises the dead in the last days, and the new creativity of the Holy Spirit. This power of God which is at work in the last days was perceptible in Christ, the Risen One; and now Christ, the Exalted One, is the bearer and mediator of this same power. Admittedly God's invisible power can be deduced from the works of → creation (cf. Rom. 1:20). But it is the raising of Jesus from the dead that represents the central eschatological proof of God's might (cf. Rom. 1:4; 1 Cor. 5:14; 2 Cor. 13:4; Phil. 3:10; also Heb. 11:19). With the resurrection goes the exaltation (Eph. 1:20 f.), whereby Christ becomes the "power of God" (1 Cor. 1:24), i.e. the constantly available source of the power of God for his church. Paul in fact uses the vb. *endynamoō*, to strengthen, to describe this work of the exalted Christ in the lives of individual believers in Phil. 4:13 (also Eph. 6:10; 1 Tim. 1:12; 2 Tim. 4:17; and 2:1). In Christ's mediating work there is a double revelation of God's eschatological power: the → Word which brings salvation and the Holy → Spirit who creates and makes new.

(a) The gospel is effective as the power of God which brings salvation, partly because the preacher speaks in the power of Christ (2 Tim. 1:8 f.; 4:17), but above all because, as the Word of God, it grants salvation to all men (Rom. 1:16; 1 Cor. 1:18). It announces the → love of the God whom men fear as the condemning judge of the world, which was visibly proved on the → cross, where Christ died for us, while we were still sinners (Rom. 5:8). As the good news of reconciliation, the gospel itself becomes the power which creates freedom and salvation, when it is recognized and accepted as such in → faith (see Rom. 1:16). The believer sees, through the gospel, that the promises which were given in the OT have now come into force; and he discovers the previously-announced gospel of God in OT prophecy (Rom. 1:2).

(b) The natural man does not have the power to please God or to fulfil the → law. (cf. Rom. 8:7 f.; Gal. 3:21). In his weakness he even experiences the law to be a power which misleads him into → sin (cf. 1 Cor. 15:56). The believer, on the other hand, like his Risen Lord, lives in the power of God and of Christ (2 Cor. 6:7; 13:3 f.; also Eph. 1:19). It is not obedience to the law (contrast CD 16:4 f.), but the love of Christ, manifest in power, which protects him from all the cosmic powers (Rom. 8:38 f.). The kingdom of God is experienced in power, in sharp contrast to mere words (1 Cor. 4:19 f.) and merely exterior piety (2 Tim. 3:4). Because it is intended for the glorification of Christians, there is a close link between the power of God and → glory (*doxa*; cf. Rom. 1:4 with 6:4). Paul also connects the power of God with the Holy Spirit. He is the power of the → resurrection and of the life in the new aeon, and the power which works signs and wonders (Rom. 15:19; 1 Cor. 12:10; 28; Gal. 3:5), which also vindicate Paul's apostleship (2 Cor. 12:12). *dynamis* therefore denotes here the → Spirit insofar as he is revealed in the mighty works of those gifted with the Spirit (*pneumatikos*, cf. 1 Cor. 2:13, 15; 3:1; 14:37; Gal. 6:1).

(c) It is the Spirit, who, as the power of Christ, realizes the authority of the heavenly Lord in the earthly community. It is he who, to use E. Käsemann's phrase, is *Christus praesens*. ([Ed.] This is shown, for example, in the way that Paul describes the Christian life sometimes in terms of a relationship with Christ [e.g. Rom. 5:1; 1 Cor. 1:30; 2 Cor. 5:19 ff.; Gal. 2:20 f.; 4:6 ff.; Phil. 2:21; 3:8 ff.] and sometimes as a relationship with the Spirit [e.g. Rom. 8:11, 14 ff.; 1 Cor. 2:4, 12 f.; 2 Cor. 3:6; 5:5; Gal. 4:6]. Paul is describing the same basic experience, but in the one case he is approaching it from the standpoint of Christ and in the other case from that of the Spirit through whom Christ is made present to the believer. The two thoughts are brought together in, e.g., Eph. 2:18; Phil. 1:19, cf. 26.) The Spirit has power to purify and judge the church (1 Cor. 5:4). He strengthens it and trains it in patience, so that its members are kept in faith till the day of judgment (1 Pet. 1:5; cf. Col. 1:11; Eph. 3:16 f.; 2 Thess. 1:11 f.). Since the Spirit is the representative of the exalted Lord, he cannot be manipulated like the power of → magic in the hands of a magician (cf. Acts 8:18–20). Nor is he simply an extra addition to men's physical and spiritual powers. On the contrary, his supernatural origin and his characteristic as the power of God is proved by the fact that it is in weak men that he is powerful (2 Cor. 12:9 f.; cf. 1 Cor. 1:26–29; 2 Cor. 4:7; 6:4–10). For Paul, God is truly revealed as God where from a human standpoint there is nothing to hope for. God gives life to the dead, and calls into existence non-existent things (Rom. 4:17). That is why, from the human point of view, God chose weak and unworthy things to be the objects of his demonstrations of might (1 Cor. 1:27): the insignificant Israelites; Paul, the persecutor of Christians; and the social nonentities of Corinth.

However, the greatest proof of this law of divine action and the justification of the despised Christian way of life is to be found in the → cross. Christ died on the cross in weakness having renounced all personal claims to power, and now he lives by the power of God (2 Cor. 13:4). Exactly the same is true of the Christian: he is weak, but that is the very reason why God's power equips him for life with Christ. Accordingly, God's work in the life of a Christian is always contrary to human expectations. Paul, in prison, is able to say that he can do all things through the one who makes him strong (Phil. 4:13). The strong in Christ, for their part, are to regard themselves as under obligation to serve their weaker brothers. Thus they will avoid the danger of forgetting that the strength they have is not their own, but given them by Christ, and of misusing it for their own ends (Rom. 15:1). It is questionable whether Paul's opponents in 2 Cor. thought of Jesus and themselves analogously with the Hellenistic "divine man [*theios anēr*]", and so performed all kinds of powerful deeds by virtue of the *dynamis* of Christ always in them, as Dieter Georgi and others have suggested (cf. D. Georgi, *Die Gegner des Paulus im 2 Korintherbrief*, 1964, with the discussion of C. K. Barrett, *A Commentary on the Second Epistle to the Corinthians*, 1973, 102 ff.).

(d) By the power of God, the Christian is assured of future perfection. The present inner transformation, which has already begun, will be followed by the visible and total transformation of the body for eternal life. This will take place when the Christian is himself raised from the dead by the same power of God which raised his Lord (1 Cor. 6:14; cf. 2 Cor. 4:14). Christ will then change him, by his power, and so transfigure his lowly earthly body that it will be like his own glorified body (Phil. 3:21). On this account, the Christian hope is based on the resurrection, and is concerned to know the power which was made visible when Christ was raised from the dead (Phil. 3:10; cf. 1 Cor. 4:19 f.).

4. The adj. *adynatos*, powerless, impotent, is used of the lame man at Lystra, crippled from birth (Acts 14:6) who was healed in response to Paul's command to stand on his feet. It denotes what is impossible with men (Matt. 19:26; Mk. 10:27; Lk. 18:27), but which is not with God. In Rom. 15:1 it is used as a noun in the contrast: "We who are strong [*hēmeis hoi dynatoi*] ought to bear with the failings of the weak [*tōn adynatōn*], and not to please ourselves." In Heb. 6:4 *adynatos* denotes the impossibility of restoring those who commit apostasy, which stands in contrast to the impossibility of God proving false (6:18). In Heb. 10:4 it occurs in the assertion that it is impossible that the blood of bulls and goats should take away sin. This too stands in contrast with the fact that without faith it is impossible to please God (11:6).   *O. Betz*

| ἐξουσία |

ἐξουσία (*exousia*), freedom of choice, right, power, authority, ruling power, a bearer of authority; ἐξουσιάζω (*exousiazō*), have the right or power, exercise authority; κατεξουσιάζω (*katexousiazo*), exercise authority over, misuse official authority, tyrannize; ἔξεστι (*exesti*), 3rd person sing. of the unused vb. ἔξειμι (*exeimi*) which is used impersonally in the sense: it is permitted, it is possible, proper, or even lawful.

CL *exousia* (derived from *exesti*, it is possible, permitted, allowed) denotes unrestricted possibility or freedom of action; and then power, authority, right of action. From the noun comes *exousiazō*, to exercise one's rights, have full power of authority; and *katexousiazō*, a word scarcely attested in secular Gk., meaning exercise, or misuse, of the authority of one's office.

1. By contrast with → *dynamis*, where any potential strength is based on inherent physical, spiritual or natural powers, and is exhibited in spontaneous actions, powerful deeds and natural phenomena, *exousia* denotes the power which may be displayed in the areas of legal, political, social or moral affairs (Plato, *Definitiones* 415b). For instance, it is always linked with a particular position or mandate; so that it refers to the right of a king, a father or a tenant to dispose as he wishes (*P.Oxy.* II, 237); or the authorization of officials or messengers (Diod.Sic. 13, 36, 2; 14, 81, 6); but also the moral freedom of people to allow or to do something (Plato, *Definitiones* 412d). The word is thus used only of people; it cannot be applied to natural forces.

2. *exousia* is often (a) official power (cf. Lat. *potestas*) which does not necessarily require enforcement; it can simply rest, or just stand in contradiction to the existing power-structures. *exousia* can be delegated. Hence, where it is illegally seized or unsurped, it can mean (b) despotic rule. These legal applications of the word *exousia* explain the further derived meanings, (c) the office appropriate for the authority; and in the plur. (d) office-holders and "the authorities".

OT 1. In the LXX *exousia* occurs much less commonly than *dynamis* (50 as against *c.* 400 times), and the vb. is also rare. *exousia* only rarely translates a Heb. word, such as *memšālâh*, dominion, kingdom (2 Ki. 20:13; Isa. 39:2). It is found more commonly in the Gk. books of the Apocrypha, already used with its (for the Rabbis) significant reference to the law, and with the meaning of permission to do something (Tob. 2:13 S). The book of Daniel is important as background material for the NT use of the word, where *exousia*, both in the LXX and in the translation of Theodotion, is used as the Gk. equivalent for Aram. *šoltānā'*, dominion, power, with reference even to the whole world. The authority of the human world-rulers originates from the supernatural realm; it is delegated by God, the Lord of history. He whose rule is eternal (Dan. 4:31) installs and removes kings (2:21), and can take their dominion away from them all (7:12). The unsatisfactory and provisional nature of human government is grounded, in Dan. 7, in the origin of the world-powers in the dominion of Chaos, opposed to God, and in their denial of their divine commission. Therefore, at the end of the times, and when human rule has reached its lowest point, the "Son of Man" (i.e. man) is enthroned to symbolize the rule of God's mercies, and for that very reason, of true humanity. He is invested with might, glory and sovereign authority to rule all nations. His dominion is an everlasting dominion, which never passes away (7:14). The "Son of Man", according to Dan. 7:27, means "the people of the saints of the Most High", the true Israel of the last days. They shall receive kingly power, and all sovereignties must obey them. In the Similitudes of Eth.Enoch and in 2 Esd., the night-vision of Dan. 7 undergoes further exegetical development and the "Son of Man" is equated with the final judge of the world or with the messiah (→ Son of God, art. *hyios tou anthrōpou*).

2. *Josephus and Philo.* Both these writers follow the general Gk. usage, but stress the aspect of authoritative, ruling power. Thus, in Josephus *exousia* means the governmental power of kings (*Life* 112; *Ant.* 14, 302); in *Life* 72 the delegated

power of a ruler or officials (*Life* 72), or permission (*Ant.* 20, 193). It is also a basic premise for Josephus that the power of the world's governments is not gained without God (*War* 2, 140), and that no-one can escape from the power of God (*Ant.* 5, 109). *exousia*, used concretely in the plur., means the authorities (*War* 2, 350). Freedom of action, in the area of obedience to the Torah, can also be described as *exousia* (*Ant.* 4, 24). Philo follows secular Gk. usage. *exousia* denotes the absolute power of the king (*Leg.Gai.* 26, 54, 190), governor (*Op.Mund.* 17), people (*Jos.* 67), and God (*De Cherubim* 27; *Leg.All.* 1, 95; *Sacr.* 60).

3. *Rabbinic Usage.* The range of meaning of *exousia* in the NT is particularly influenced by the use of a word, not found in the OT, but of importance in the teaching in the Rab. schools, the Heb. *rāšûṭ*, ruling power, government; and *rᵉšûṭ* (Aram. *rᵉšûṭā'*), power of attorney, power to act, freedom to do something.

(a) *rāšûṭ* denotes worldly government as a whole, especially the Roman empire, which was regarded with distant suspicion (Aboth 1: 10; 2: 3). Worldly rule, here below, was distinguished from the heavenly rule above (T. J. San. 6, 23d), but God's own authority was not directly designated as *rāšûṭ*, probably because it is underived. In addition, the Rabbis were fighting the doctrine of the two powers to which dualistic and gnostic thinkers and exegetes attributed the creation of the world (Gen.R. 1:10; cf. B. San. 38a and B. Hag. 15a). Such views were rightly condemned as heretical, for they endangered Jewish monotheism.

(b) *rāšûṭ* denotes (i) authoritative power of action, competency within particular social groupings, e.g. among members of a family (Ned. 10:2–4), the rights of a house-owner (Bab.K. 5:3), and then the power of attorney linked with a particular commission, such as that of an ambassador (Kidd. 4:9). (ii) In a juridical sense, the word is used for the right to teach (B.San. 5a), to inherit (Ket. 9:5), to marry (Yeb. 4:11). All power is delegated by God. He even gives the destroying angels authority to carry out their pernicious work (B.Pes. 112b; cf. Mek. Exod. 4 on 19:21. (iii) *rāšûṭ* means, finally, freedom of action, in the God-given order of the Torah: it refers to what is allowed, as opposed to the commandments and the halachic duties (Baba Kamma 3:5; B.Hull. 106a; B.Ber. 27b). R. Akiba taught the paradoxically juxtaposed doctrines of the divine foreknowledge of all events and freedom of human action (Aboth 3:15 f.).

4. *Qumran.* The idea of *rāšûṭ* does not appear in these writings, but it is important to see in them the appointed presence of the dominion of the devil and of the power of darkness (1QS 1:18, 23 f.; 2:19; 3:23; 1QM 13:5 f.; 14:9; 17:5 f.). These will be destroyed at the end by the kingdom of the Archangel Michael (→ Angel, art. *Michaēl*), and by the Israel he represents (1QM 18:7 f.). The word *memšālâh*, used in these references for kingdom or dominion, corresponds with the Gk. *exousia*, which itself translates *memšālâh* in the LXX from time to time. In Test.Lev. 3:8 the heavenly powers are called *exousiai* (cf. Eth.Enoch 61:10). This plur. usage has the same meaning as *dynameis*. As with the similarly used *archai*, powers (→ Beginning), this word will have been influenced by Heb. *rᵉšûyôṭ* powers.

NT In the NT *exousia* appears 108 times, most frequently in Rev., Lk., and 1 Cor.

It is used in a secular sense, meaning the power to give orders (Matt. 8:9 par. Lk. 7:8; Lk. 19:17; 20:20); in a concrete sense, meaning jurisdiction (Lk. 23:7); and in the plur., meaning officials, authorities (Lk. 12:11; Tit. 3:1). In Rom. 13:1, the "powers that be [*exousiais hyperechousais*]", as the "authorities [*archontes*]" in v. 3, should be understood as state officials, not (as some suggest) as angelic powers. See further M. Black, *Romans, New Century Bible*, 1973, 158 ff., who notes the following recent studies on the question: O. Cullmann, "Zur neuesten Diskussion über die *Exousiai* in Röm. 13, 1", *ThZ* 10, 1954, 321 ff.; and *The State in the New Testament*, 1957; C. D. Morrison, *The Powers that Be: Earthly Rulers and Demonic Powers in Romans 13.1-7*, SBT 29, 1960; E. Wolf, "Politischer Gottesdienst", *Festschrift K. O. Schmidt*, 1961, 51–63; V. Zsifkovits, *Der Staatsgedanke nach Paulus in Rom. 13*, 1964; H. von Campenhausen, "Zur Auslegung von Röm. 13. Die dämonistische Deutung des Exousia-Begriffs", *Aus der Frühzeit des Christentums*, 1963, 81 ff.; E. Käsemann, "Principles of the Interpretation of Romans 13", in *New Testament Questions of Today*, 1969, 196–216; C. E. B. Cranfield, "Some Observations on Rom. 13:1-7", *NTS* 6, 1959–60, 241–49; A. Strobel, "Zum Verständnis von Röm. 13", *ZNW* 47, 1956, 67–93; O. Michel, "Das Problem des Staates in neutestamentlicher Sicht", *TLZ* 83, 1958, 161–66; E. Bammel, "Ein Beitrag zur paulinischen Staatsanschauung", *TLZ* 85, 1960, 837–40; G. Delling, *Röm. 13.1-7 innerhalb der Briefe des Neuen Testaments*, 1962.

It is characteristic for the NT that *exousia* and *dynamis* are both related to the work of Christ, the consequent new ordering of cosmic power-structures and the empowering of believers. Both words are brought together in Lk. 9:1. *exousia* is not attributed to the gift of the Spirit; whereas Jesus' *dynamis* has its foundation in his being anointed, his *exousia* is founded on his being sent. *exousia* is that power, authority and freedom of action which belongs: (1) to God himself; (2) to a commission in the last days; and (3) to a Christian in his eschatological existence.

1. *God's exousia.* (a) God's eschatological authority is linked with his rôle as disposer of world history, and as → judge of the world. By his own authority, he has fixed the dates and times of the end, and has the termination of history in his control (Acts 1:7). He has the power to consign men to eternal ruin (Lk. 12:5). Existential consciousness of the absolute freedom of God finds its expression in his predestination: Paul compares God with a potter, who can do what he likes with the clay (Rom. 9:21; cf. Isa. 29:16; 45:9; Jer. 18:6; Wis. 15:7; Sir. 36[33]:12 f.; → Determine; → Election).

(b) God can delegate eschatological authority, for instance, to the angel who punishes at the judgment (Rev. 6:8); and other creatures can be involved (Rev. 9:3, 10, 19). By way of contrast, the heavenly powers (*exousiai*) are scarcely taken into consideration in this eschatological event. They are generally mentioned along with the *archai*, and have the same significance as the *dynameis* (Eph. 1:21; 3:10; Col. 1:16; 2:10 → Beginning). Christ's exaltation means that they have been subjected to him (Eph. 1:21; 1 Pet. 3:22). But the opposition has not yet all been broken: this means that the messiah's rule must continue for the time being (1 Cor. 15:24). The natural man, as the Qumran writings also saw, stands under the domination of → darkness and the lordship of the devil (Col. 1:13; Acts 16:18). In opposition to that stands the realm of → light, the kingdom of the Son, and God himself (ibid.). In comparison with the Qumran writings, the devil (→ Satan) appears, in fact, to have increased power: he is called the "prince [or ruler] of this world [*ho archōn tou kosmou toutou*]" (Jn. 12:31; 14:30; 16:11), even "the god of this world [*ho theos tou aiōnos toutou*]" (2 Cor. 4:4; → Time, art. *aiōn*). The devil, like God, can delegate his rule over the world to others, e.g., the → Antichrist (cf. Rev. 13:2, 4, 12). He even tempted Jesus with such an offer (Lk. 4:6). But dualism is avoided, because even the devil's power is allotted him by God (ibid.); his activity fits into God's plan and is therefore limited (Lk. 22:53). Statements about the power of the devil are not to be assigned a place in a pessimistic view of the world, but in the Good News of the redemptive work of Christ. It is precisely where Jesus speaks of the devil as the "prince of this world" that he announces his downfall.

2. *The exousia of Jesus*. (a) The work of the earthly Jesus announces that the devil (→ Satan) and the → demons have been deprived of their power: the One who is sent by God has the authority to destroy the works of the devil and to snatch men from his rule. Exorcism is therefore attributed to the authority of Jesus (Lk. 4:36), which he can also pass on to the disciples he sends out (Matt. 10:1 par. Mk. 3:15, Lk. 9:1; Mk. 6:7; Lk. 10:19). Jesus acted with God's authority when he forgave a man his sins and confirmed the power of his word by a healing miracle (Matt. 9:2–8 par. Mk. 2:3–12, Lk. 5:18–26; cf. Ps. 103:3). Jesus' eschatological commission, his purpose of saving God's children, brought him into collision with the → law as the → Pharisees understood it. Jesus rejected the literalistic understanding of the letter of the law according to Rab. Halachah which stood in the way of God's saving will (Matt. 12:10, 12; Mk. 3:4; Lk. 14:3; Jn. 5:10). Jesus' authority could be seen in this → teaching, which provoked astonishment (Mk. 1:22, 27; Matt. 7:29; Lk. 4:32), because he did not teach like the scribes. The latter were guided by their teaching tradition (Matt. 7:29), whereas Jesus, the anointed One, not only received his words from the mouth of God, like Moses and the prophets, but spoke with the unique authority of the → Son who alone knows the → Father and who alone can reveal him (Matt. 11:27; Lk. 10:22; cf. also Matt. 28:18; Jn. 3:35; 13:3; 10:15; 17:25). The cleansing of the → Temple (Matt. 21:12 f.; Mk. 11:11–17; Lk. 19:45 f.; Jn. 2:13–17; Exod. 30:13; Lev. 1:14; Isa. 56:7; Jer. 7:11) also presupposes a consciousness of messianic authority.

(b) In John's Gospel Jesus' plenitentiary authority is based on the fact that he is the Son and that he is sent (cf. e.g. Jn. 17:2); he has also been given the authority of the judge at the end of time (Jn. 5:27). But in the Johannine writings, as the Synoptics, Jesus seeks to save men rather than judge them. His power is not forcible domination, but absolute freedom to be a servant to the world. He has the *exousia* to give his life and to take it again (Jn. 10:18). Jesus' sacrifice opens the way for believers to the Father (Jn. 3:16; 14:6). Those who receive him and believe in his name are given *exousia* to become → children of God (Jn. 1:12).

(c) This representation of Jesus' authority in the Fourth Gospel anticipates the resurrection. For with his exaltation, which followed on from Easter (→ Height), Jesus received from God all power in heaven and on earth (Matt. 28:18). This fulfilled Daniel's vision of the enthronement and granting of power to the Son of Man (cf. Dan. 7:14). But now in place of the collective "saints of the Most High", stands Christ. Further, God's power is not realized by violently subjugating the nations, but by the spread of the → gospel, winning the world to faith in Christ. Hence it is the church, not the sovereign rule of → Israel, which outwardly expresses the reign of the messiah on earth (Acts 1:6–8). For the cross and the exaltation of Christ signify the disarming of the evil one, the judgment and the turning-point of the ages. This must be preached as Good News to all the world. The exalted Lord therefore sends out his messengers and empowers them for their service in the gospel (Matt. 28:18–20). Analogous with Jesus' earthly ministry, and in accord with the contents of the Easter message, the → apostles of Christ received power to confer the Holy Spirit (Acts 8:19; 19:6; but cf. 2:38; 10:44–48), and to build up rather than to destroy (2 Cor. 10:8; 13:10). Because of his spiritual ministry as a servant in the church, an apostle has the right to have his physical needs looked after by the church (1 Cor. 9:4–6; 2 Thess. 3:9). *exousia* in these passages means a right or prerogative.

3. *The exousia of believers.* The authority of a Christian believer is founded on the rule of Christ and on the disarming of all powers. It implies both → freedom and service. As Luther put it in *The Freedom of a Christian* (1520): "A Christian is a perfectly free lord of all, subject to none. A Christian is a perfectly dutiful servant of all, subject to all" (*Luther's Works*, ed. H. T. Lehmann, XXXI, 1957, 344). He is free to do anything (1 Cor. 6:12; 10:23; *exestin*); this assertion which was made initially by the sectarian enthusiasts at Corinth, was taken up by Paul who acknowledged it to be correct. The believer has full freedom of action, because the law, as a prohibitive barrier, has been broken down through Christ's redeeming and saving act, and because he has received the gift of the Spirit of freedom. He has the freedom and the power to dispose everything as he will, because, now that Christ has been exalted, nothing is any longer under the rule of the powers. In practice, however, this theoretically unrestricted freedom is governed by consideration of what is helpful to other individual Christians and the congregation as a whole, in view of the fact that the complete redemption is still to come (1 Cor. 6:12; 10:13). Since God's eschatological work has not yet been consummated either in individual Christians or in the structures of the world, it is important that people should be sensible, and take into account both their own Christian lives, still bound to "the flesh of the old Adam", and also the → conscience of weaker brothers (1 Cor. 10:28, 31 ff.), and not plunge into unbridled freedom, as if the resurrection of believers had already taken place! It is just such an unrestrained use of one's freedom which could precipitate a Christian into a new servitude. Hence he is not to let anything be his master. " 'All things are lawful [*exestin*] for me', but not all things are helpful. 'All things are lawful [*exestin*] for me', but I will not be enslaved [*exousiasthēsomai*] by anything" (1 Cor. 6:12). " 'All things are lawful [*exestin*]', but not all things are helpful. 'All things are lawful [*exestin*]', but not all things build up. Let no one seek his own good, but the good of his neighbour" (1 Cor. 10:23 f.). The quotations within these quotations are probably the slogans of the libertines at Corinth. Paul counters them by admitting their truth, but by showing that it is not the whole truth.   *O. Betz*

| θρόνος | θρόνος (*thronos*), throne, seat. |

CL 1. *thronos* comes from the Indo-Germanic root **dhere-*, to hold, and is related to the Lat. *firmus* (firm, steadfast, powerful) and Ger. *dingen* (to secure). In Homer, it means a chair with an attached foot-stool (*thrēnos*; cf. Homer *Od.* 19,

57); later mainly with a high back-rest and arm-rests. The word, used originally without any particular symbolic force, was very widely used, by contrast with the Lat. *thronos*, first used by Suetonius and referring only to the seat of a god (cf. *Octavius Augustus Caesar* 70). The Gk. word only took on this meaning later in its history. It could also be used metaphorically, as in the plur. *thronoi*, for power (cf. Aesch., *Prometheus* 228; and cf. Col. 1:16 of angelic powers). To be seated on the throne (*kathēmai*, set oneself, sit) is a sign of regal or divine majesty (cf. Homer, *Il.* 4, 1; *Od.* 13, 264; → Sit).

2. In the Gk. world, from Mycenaean times, the seat of the master of the house was a seat of honour – a conception taken over via Crete from the Orient. But it is also offered to guests and bards: it does not indicate a superior position in the oriental sense. In bas-reliefs the dead are given such a chair; in epic poetry the gods (Aesch., *Eumenides* 229), and especially Zeus (Homer, *Il.* 8, 436–442), are so honoured, and represented in sculpture. This can hardly be called a throne-cult. Representations of an empty divine throne are rare and late.

ot 1. The royal throne, in the strict sense, derives from the Orient. Sitting on the throne denotes the unique exaltation of the absolute ruler, his total superiority over against those who are subject to him. It is the sole right of the ruler to sit (*kathēmai*) on the throne; the suppliant or servant stands before him – (cf. the Hammurabi Stele; see illustration in L. H. Grollenberg, *Atlas of the Bible*, 1957, plates 79–81 on p. 31). Only when the king sits on the throne does he finally take his power. The magnificent ornamentation indicates his divine dignity; at the side of the throne, to right and left, stand attendant heavenly beings, → cherubim, winged creatures with human heads or lions, as pictorial symbols of ruling power (cf. 1 Ki. 10:18 ff.). Characteristic for oriental thought is the mutual interplay of ideas of regal and divine power, something which was foreign to Greece until the time of Alexander the Great (356–323 b.c.). The earthly ruler was honoured as the "Son", or even (as in Egypt) as the incarnation of the divine. The nature of their kingship was similarly represented.

2. In the first instance the OT reflects, as one would expect, the world of oriental throne symbolism. Since the institution of the monarchy the throne (Heb. *kissē'*) was the sole prerogative of the ruler (Gen. 41:40), his relatives (1 Ki. 2:19) or representatives (Neh. 3:7). Since the → king was originally also the → judge, the throne was both a visible symbol of regal power (2 Sam. 3:9; 14:9) and of justice (Ps. 122:5). The throne was thus a constant factor, over against the changing bearers of power. In this way, Nathan's promise of the permanence of the Davidic rule (2 Sam. 7:13) was linked with the throne (cf. also 1 Chr. 28:5; 29:23). This formed the primary link with the later hope of the everlasting throne of the messiah. But, in Judaism it was not identical with the throne of God (see below ot 5).

3. Naturally in the OT the throne represents God's power and righteousness. This can never be simply identified with the king's power, however much the oriental court style was taken over. The Israelite king stood in an adoptive relationship with Yahweh (Ps. 2:7). Yahweh's throne is variously described and located in the OT. Jeremiah specified Jerusalem, on the one hand (3:17), and Israel, on the other (14:21, *thronos doxēs* "throne of glory" is more a metaphorical sense). Ezekiel, in his great vision of the future, saw the new → temple as the abode of

the divine throne (43:7); while in Isa. 66:1 heaven is said to be Yahweh's throne (cf. Isa. 6:1; 14:13).

The special nature of the divine kingship is seen in the awesome throne-vision of Isaiah (6:1–13; cf. also 1 Ki. 22:19), but most clearly in Ezekiel (1:4–28). Here Yahweh's kingly power is seen under the symbolism of transcendent creatures, representing the world-rule of their Lord. They each have four faces, representing God's omnipresence, and face the world, while above their out-spread wings "glittering like an awe-inspiring crystal" (1:22) stands the vault of heaven which, according to the account of creation in Gen. 1:6 f., keeps the destroying floods away from the creation. It is above this world, that is to say, entirely and inaccessibly out of men's reach, that God's throne is seen, surrounded by an unearthly brightness. Here is a pictorial, rather than a conceptual description, both of the sheer transcendence of God, and of his omnipresence in the world.

The throne of the "Ancient of days" in Dan. 7:9 probably has a similar significance (cf. Ps. 97:2; Eth.En. 14:18 f.) The other thrones mentioned, which have given rise to much debate, are probably for the assessors or the jury in the court proceedings. It is not certain who these would originally be. Later interpretation makes them the elect saints (cf. Matt. 19:28; 1 Cor. 6:2; Rev. 20:4). See further H. H. Rowley, *Darius the Mede and the Four World Empires in the Book of Daniel*, 1935; J. A. Emerton. "The Origin of the Son of Man Imagery", *JTS* New Series 9, 1958, 225–42; N. W. Porteous, *Daniel: A Commentary*, 1965, 107 ff.

4. The hidden dynamic of this throne-theology is revealed by the rite of Yahweh's ceremonial enthronement, which is reflected in the evidence, e.g., of Pss. 24; 93; 96–99. Yahweh's kingship is not an inactive representation, but a fight that has just been won. This is particularly clear in Ps. 93; but the fight-motif comes again in Pss. 46 and 89:7 ff. According to S. Mowinckel, "The [enthronement] festival celebrates Yahweh as the creator of the world, as king and ruler of the world, in his victory over the dragon, the flood and all his enemies" (*Religion und Kultus*, 1953, 76). In this ritual, which was part of the New Year Festival, the Ark of the Covenant is thought to have represented the unoccupied throne of God: Yahweh is pictured as present, though invisible, "enthroned on the cherubim" (Ps. 99:1), which were on both sides of the flat surface of the ark. The Ark was "the earthly counterpart of the heavenly throne" (W. Eichrodt, *Theology of the Old Testament* II, 1967, 193). For further discussion of kingship and the enthronement Psalms → Myth, art. *mythos* OT; → King, Kingdom, art. *basileia* OT; and the following literature: G. Fohrer, *History of Israelite Religion*, 1973, 139–50; J. de Fraine, *L'Aspect religieux de la Royauté Israelite*, 1954; H. Ringgren, *The Messiah in the Old Testament*, 1956; and *Israelite Religion*, 1966, 220–38; I. Engnell, *Studies in Divine Kingship*, 1943; G. Widengren, *Sakrales Königtum*, 1955; A. R. Johnson, *Sacral Kingship in Ancient Israel*, 1955; G. W. Ahlström, *Psalm 89*, 1959; S. H. Hooke, ed., *Myth, Ritual and Kingship*, 1958; S. Mowinckel, *The Psalms in Israel's Worship*, I–II 1962; and *He That Cometh* 1954; A. A. Anderson, *The Book of Psalms*, I–II, 1972; and literature in the bibliography under → King.

5. Late Judaism, in connection with Ps. 93, counted the throne of Yahweh as one of the "pre-cosmic works of God" (O. Schmitz, *TDNT* III 163). Yahweh's throne is described in detail in Eth.Enoch 14:18 ff. and Sl.Enoch 2–20; but a messiah sitting on this throne is only mentioned in Eth.Enoch 51:3; 55:4; 62:2, 3,

5 ff. This would have been a profanation for Judaism, which regarded the messiah as a man. In Eth.Enoch, the messiah, who is here a heavenly figure, administers justice before the throne of God (45:3).

6. 11QMelchizedek refers to → Melchizedek taking his seat on high as head of the heavenly court in response to Ps. 7:7b (cf. RSV). There are also references to the throne of the coming son of David in 4Q161 (pesher on Isa. 11:1 ff.) and 4Q174 (pesher on 2 Sam. 7:14).

NT 1. The NT adds little to these OT conceptions. It takes them over quite naturally and without emphasis, except for Rev., where the throne plays a dominant role. The word occurs there 41 times, over against 14 instances in the rest of the NT. In Matt. 5:34, Jesus speaks of → heaven as God's throne and for that reason forbids men to swear by it. The promise to Nathan is alluded to in Lk. 1:32, with extended reference to the messianic throne (2 Sam. 7:12, 16; cf. also Acts 3:20 f.). Genitive phrases, modelled on LXX usage, are found, such as "throne of glory" (Matt. 19:28; 25:31; cf. 1 Sam. 2:8) and "throne of grace" (Heb. 4:16). The latter is the antitype to the "mercy seat [*hilastērion*]" in the earthly sanctuary (Heb. 9:5; cf. F. F. Bruce, *Commentary on the Epistle to the Hebrews, NLC*, 1964, 86; → Reconciliation, art. *hilaskomai*).

2. A striking point in the NT is that the → Son of man sits on the divine throne of judgment. It is not the conception as such that is new (see above OT 5) but the claim of a historical man to be this eschatological judge. Matt. 19:28 even promises such ruling authority to the twelve apostles, as co-judges over Israel (→ Disciple, art. *akoloutheō*). In Matt. 25:31 ff. the Son of man judges the world from his throne of glory entirely on his own. That is the provocative claim of Jesus. There is a pictorial tension between these statements and those (following Ps. 110:1) which view the messiah "sitting at the right hand of God" (→ Hand, art. *dexios*); but there is no material contradiction.

3. (a) In Heb. the phrase "the throne of grace [*thronos tēs charitos*]" (4:16) appears, in implicit antithesis to the usual Rab. concept of two divine thrones – that of justice, and that of grace. In exhortation to stand fast to our confession, Heb. 4:15 f. declares: "For we have not a high priest who is unable to sympathize with our weaknesses, but one who in every respect has been tempted as we are, yet without sinning. Let us then with confidence draw near to the throne of grace, that we may receive mercy and find grace to help in time of need."

(b) In what is widely considered to be a baptismal hymn, Col. 1:15–20, *thronoi* are mentioned along with sovereignties (*kyriotētes*), powers (*archai*) and authorities (*exousiai*). This list, dependent on Sl.Enoch 20 and Test.Lev. 3, is dealing with the various groups of angels, who belong to the council of the heavenly throne (cf. 1 Ki. 22:19). The designation *thronoi* could derive from the fact that thrones stand at the disposal of this group of angels (cf. Rev. 4:4; and *TDNT* III 16 f.). Within the compass of the hymn, this enumeration declares that Christ's creative power does not only embrace what is visible, the earth, but also what is invisible – the world of angels. See further E. Lohse, *Colossians and Philemon, Hermeneia*, 1971, 51 ff.

4. (a) The picture of the throne in Rev. is based particularly on Ezek., and is further developed especially in ch. 4. The throne signifies again the transcendent

majesty of God. The "crystal sea" of v. 6 is not the sea of nations, but the vault of heaven, as it is in Ezek. 1. The twenty-four elders on their thrones are new (v. 4); they are the heads of the heavenly court-council. They represent the old and new Israel, consisting of the heads of the twelve tribes together with the twelve apostles. Their function is like that of the heavenly beings. They constantly adore "him who is seated on the throne" (v. 10) before whom they fall down and cry: "Worthy art thou, our Lord and God, to receive glory and honour and power, for thou didst create all things, and by thy will they existed and were created" (4:11).

(b) A new factor appears for the first time in Rev. 5:6 ff. "In the middle of the throne [*en mesō tou thronou*]" (not "between", as RSV and some translations render it), that is, right in the centre, as the divine judgment of the world begins, appears the One who is to carry it out, "the Lamb that was slain". Christ, in highest glory, is here pictured in terms of complete defencelessness. Nowhere is the paradox of the NT revelation of Christ shown so clearly as here. God's power is, from the human point of view, total powerlessness. Christ carries out the judgment in, and as, a self-sacrifice. The One who sits on the throne was man. He turned power into service and brotherhood. To him, at the end of time, the whole creation pays its homage (Rev. 5:13).

(c) Alongside this Christian conception of the throne as seen by faith, appears in Rev. (and similarly in 2 Thess. 3:4) the opposing throne of the → Antichrist, who, on his side, proclaims his power and demands submission (13:4 ff.). This throne, too, speaks of dominion – not of the → Lamb, but of the → Dragon (12:2). But his dominion succumbs to the wrathful judgment of the Lamb (16:10). Contrary to all appearances, it cannot last. The throne of the Lamb is ultimately triumphant. From it flows the river of the water of life in the new → Jerusalem (22:1).

C. Blendinger

→ Angel (see especially the bibliography for further literature), → Beginning, → Caesar, → Demon, → King, → Spirit, → Strength

(a). W. Beilner, "Authority", *EBT* I 52–55; M. Bouttier, *Christianity according to Paul, SBT* 49, 1966, 66 ff.; G. B. Caird, *Principalities and Powers*, 1956; H. von Campenhausen, "The Problem of Order in Early Christianity and the Ancient Church", in *Tradition and Life in the Church*, 1968, 123–40; and *Ecclesiastical Authority and Spiritual Power in the Church of the First Three Centuries*, 1969; O. Cullmann, *The State in the New Testament*, 1957; D. Daube, "*exousia* in Mark 1, 22 and 27", *JTS* 39, 1938, 45–59; W. Foerster, *exousia* etc., *TDNT* II 562–75; B. Gerhardsson, *Memory and Manuscript: Oral Tradition and Written Transmission in Rabbinic Judaism and Early Christianity, Acta Seminarii Neotestamentici Upsaliensis* 22, 1961; W. Grundmann, *dynamai* etc., *TDNT* II 284–317; A. T. Hanson, "The Conquest of the Powers", in *Studies in Paul's Technique and Theology*, 1974, 1–12; J. Jervell, "The Twelve on Israel's Thrones: Luke's Understanding of the Apostolate", in *Luke and the People of God*, 1972, 75–112; E. Käsemann, "Principles of the Interpretation of Romans 13", in *New Testament Questions of Today*, 1969, 196–216; H. Kleinknecht, G. von Rad, K. G. Kuhn, K. L. Schmidt, *basileus* etc., *TDNT* I 564–93; J. Michl, "Principalities and Powers", *EBT* II 712–16; C. D. Morrison, *The Powers that Be: Earthly Rulers and Demonic Powers in Romans 13.1–7, SBT* 29, 1960; R. Murray, "Authority and the Spirit in the New Testament", in J. Dalrymple *et al., Authority in a Changing Church*, 1968; C. H. Powell, *The Biblical Concept of Power*, 1963; O. Schmitz, *thronos, TDNT* III 160–67; H. Schlier, *Principalities and Powers in the New Tesaltment*, 1961; C. Schneider, *kathēmai* etc. *TDNT* I 440–54; W. Zimmerli, *Ezekiel*, I, *Hermeneia*, 1976.
(b). E. Bammel, "Ein Beitrag zur paulinischen Staatsanschauung", *TLZ* 85, 1960, 837–40; H. Bardtke and H. D. Wendland, "Macht", *EKL* II 1205 ff.; L. Bieler, *Theios anēr. Das Bild des "göttlichen Menschen" in Spätantike und Frühchristentum*, I–II, 1935–36; and "*dynamis* und

exousia", *Wiener Studien* 55, 1935, 182–90; H. von Campenhausen, "Zur Auslegung von Röm. 13. Die dämonistische Deutung des Exousia-Begriffs", in *Aus der Frühzeit des Christentums*, 1963, 81 ff. (reprinted from memorial volume for A. Bertholet, 1950, 97 ff.); O. Cullmann, "Zur neuesten Diskussion über die *Exousiai* in Röm. 13.1", *ThZ* 10, 1954, 321 ff.; G. Delling, *Röm. 13, 1–7 innerhalb der Briefe des Neuen Testaments*, 1962; M. Dibelius, *Die Geisterwelt im Glauben des Paulus*, 1909; W. Eichrodt, *Der Prophet Hesekiel, ATD* 22, 1965²; L. Goppelt, "Der Staat in der Sicht des Neuen Testaments", *Christologie und Ethik*, 1968, 190 ff.; W. Grundmann, *Der Begriff der Kraft in der neutestamentlichen Gedankenwelt*, 1932; K. Hartenstein, *Der wiederkommende Herr*, 1954³, 82 ff.; O. Michel, "Das Problem des Staates in neutestamentlicher Sicht", *TLZ* 83, 1958, 161–66; F. Neugebauer, "Zur Auslegung von Röm. 13, 1–7", *KuD* 8, 1962, 151 ff.; E. Schweizer, *Die Herrschaft Christi und der Staat im Neuen Testament*, *BEvTh* 11, 1949; O. Schmitz, "Der Begriff *dynamis* bei Paulus", *Festschrift für A. Deissmann*, 1927, 139 ff.; J. Schniewind, "Die Archonten dieses Aeons, 1 Kor. 2.6–8", in *Nachgelassene Reden und Aufsätze*, ed. E. Kähler, 1952, 104–9; N. Söderblom, D. Georgi, K. E. Løgstrup, R. Dahrendorf, "Macht", *RGG*³ IV 564 ff.; A. Strobel, "Zum Verständnis von Röm. 13", *ZNW* 47, 1956, 67 ff.; R. Walker, *Studie zu Röm. 13, 1–7, ThEH* Neue Folge 132, 1966; V. Zsifkovitis, *Der Staatsgedanke nach Paulus in Röm. 13, 1–7*, 1964.

Mind

| φρόνησις |

φρονέω (*phroneō*), think, judge, give one's mind to, set one's mind on, be minded; φρόνημα (*phronēma*), way of thinking, mentality; φρόνησις (*phronēsis*), way of thinking, frame of mind, intelligence, good sense; φρόνιμος (*phronimos*), intelligent, discerning, sensible, thoughtful, prudent.

CL Words derived from the stem *phren-* occur frequently in classical Gk. literature, the vb. *phroneō* from Homer onwards, the nouns *phronēma* and *phronēsis* from Aeschylus and Sophocles respectively, and the adj. *phronimos* likewise from Sophocles. The words are found most often in their ordinary meanings as above, although *phronēsis* frequently has the fuller sense of discernment, judicious insight, particularly in Plato and Aristotle. Similarly *phronimos* means intelligent, discerning, judicious.

OT All the words appear in the Gk. translations of the OT. The Heb. equivalents are *ḥāḵam* and *bîn* with their respective derivatives, the second occurring slightly more often than the first. Various meanings are possible, e.g., in Job 5:13 *phronēsis* stands for cunning, craftiness, *phronimos* having the corresponding adj. sense in Gen. 3:1. In one place *phronēsis* means a peasant's knowledge of his job (*da'aṭ*) (Prov. 24:5), and on two occasions in Theodotion's translation of Dan. it means intellectual acuteness, either in the interpretation of dreams (5:12) or as a qualification for training in the palace of the Persian king (1:4). The words occur predominantly, however, (especially as nouns and adjs.) in the OT Wisdom Literature, where the prevailing meaning is that of discernment. Both noun and adj. are regularly used with reference to men, though *phronēsis* occasionally denotes the creative understanding of God (e.g. Isa. 40:28; Jer. 10:12; Prov. 3:19, in these last two passages the word being used in parallel with *sophia*, wisdom). In the LXX, therefore, one can detect a tendency to fill out the meaning of these words in accordance with the OT doctrine of → wisdom (art. *sophia* OT).

NT 1. The tendency found in the LXX hardly continues into the NT, one possible reason being the NT's predominant use of the vb. as opposed to the nouns and adj. *phroneō* occurs 26 times, of which no less than 23 are in Paul, while *phronēma* is found only 4 times (all in Rom. 8), *phronēsis* twice and *phronimos* or the adv. *phronimōs* 15 times altogether. The point is that, unlike *phronēma* and *phronēsis*, the vb. tends to retain its ordinary meaning; it is, so to speak, more neutral and requires a context to indicate its true sense. This can be seen in passages where *phroneō* means to think, judge (e.g. Acts 28:22; 1 Cor. 13:11; Phil. 1:7; 4:10), where the reference is not so much to the process of thinking in itself, but rather to the content of what is thought.

This is even clearer in those places where *phroneō*, for the most part used absolutely, acquires its proper meaning only from its immediate grammatical context, e.g. from its use with the prefix *hyper-*, think more highly (Rom. 12:3), or with some characteristic word like *sōs* (as in *sōphronein* also in Rom. 12:13, "to think with sober judgment), *tapeinos* (cf. the compound *tapeinophrosynē*, Phil 2:3; → humility, art. *tapeinos*), or the object *ta hypsēla* lit. "do not think high things", i.e. "do not become proud" (Rom. 11:20 RSV; cf. 12:16). These words, some of which form compounds with *phroneō* (e.g. *hyperphroneō*, *sōphroneō*, Rom. 12:3), all indicate direction ("upwards" or "downwards") and impart to *phroneō* its specific meaning in a given context. Paul's whole use of language in Rom. 12:3 indicates how deeply a person's thoughts are affected by their object and their direction.

2. It follows that, although the vb. as such has no particular content, there can nevertheless be no such thing as neutral thinking. Man is always aiming at something. Striving and endeavour are part of his nature. He must seek to possess, and he must be committed. This is the idea behind *phronēma*, which occurs only in Rom. 8 and which is well translated by "setting the mind on" (cf. RSV). In the context of this chapter, which describes the new life in Christ as a life in the Spirit of God, Paul testifies that a man's mind is set on certain things, and that what these are depends on whether he is in → "the flesh" or in → "the Spirit". Thus, those who live according to the flesh (*hoi kata sarka ontes*, Rom. 8:5) set their minds on the things of the flesh, i.e. their thinking and striving are directed, as is the whole of their life, towards those things which are "merely human, the earthly-transitory" (R. Bultmann, *Theology of the New Testament*, I, 1952, 238). On the other hand, those who are living in the → Spirit of God (*hoi de kata pneuma ontes*) (Rom. 8:5) endeavour to live in the light of the promised gift of the Holy Spirit and under his control. To them that are thus minded there is a promise of "life and peace" (Rom. 8:6). But to set one's mind on the flesh means death, not only because there is an inevitable connection between the two (cf. Rom. 5:21; 6:23), but also because fleshly-mindedness is rebellion against God, and must be, since it cannot submit to his → law (Rom. 8:7). This passage makes it abundantly clear that the way one thinks is intimately related to the way one lives, whether in Christ, in the Spirit and by faith, or alternatively in the flesh, in sin and in spiritual death. A man's thinking and striving cannot be seen in isolation from the overall direction of his life; the latter will be reflected in the aims which he sets himself.

This close inter-relationship between life and thought is echoed by the wide range of meanings attaching to *phroneō*. It expresses not merely an activity of the intellect, but also a movement of the will; it is both interest and decision at the same time. Hence the meaning can actually extend to the idea of "taking sides" with someone or something. There is just a hint of this in Rom. 8:5, while the idea is uppermost in Mk. 8:33 (par. Matt. 16:23). Peter is reproved by Jesus because his thought and will are taking the side not of the things of God but of the things of man (which are opposed to God). It is God's will that Jesus should be offered as a sacrifice, and by opposing the divine will Peter is furthering the cause of God's enemies, indeed he is on the side of the adversary himself (hence the sharp rebuke "Get behind me, Satan!").

3. But what should a Christian strive towards? What should be his aim? What kind of thinking is fitting for him (cf. Rom. 12:3)? The answer which seems most obvious to the natural man, namely that a man should strive for high ideals, is at first sight attractive to the Christian too. After all, God has given him gifts which, as a Christian, he could seek to perfect and use for exalted purposes. But this striving after "high things" can lead to jealousy, disappointment and schisms in the church, as is shown by the example of Corinth. Hence the apostle exhorts his readers to think with sober judgment according to the "measure of faith [*metron pisteōs*]" (Rom. 12:3), for "whatever does not proceed from faith is sin" (Rom. 14:23), and faith, i.e. their new life in Christ, will direct their thinking aright, keep it within proper limits and save it from pride.

The warning that a man who sets his mind on "high things" runs the risk of becoming arrogant is also found in Rom. 11:20, where *hypsēla phronein* clearly means to cherish proud thoughts, to be haughty. In Rom. 12:16 Paul warns: "Do not be haughty, but give yourselves to humble tasks" (or "associate with the lowly", as RSV, depending on whether *tois tapeinois* is taken as neut. or masc.). For those who consider themselves clever (*phronimoi par' heautois*, Rom. 12:16b, adapting Prov. 3:7) are under God's judgment: "God opposes the proud, but gives grace to the humble" (1 Pet. 5:5, quoting Prov. 3:34; see below 6 (b)). Whether Paul is warning "charismatic" believers to beware of spiritual pride (as presumably he is in Rom. 12:16), or censuring Gentile Christians for arrogance towards the Jews (as in Rom. 11:20), the message to Christians is clear: they are to aim not higher but lower, in order to identify with the lowly and the humble, and are to strive towards the unity of the church, which is endangered by the arrogance of individuals or of whole groups.

4. Moreover, as so often in Paul, a Christian's aims are closely intertwined with the motives underlying them. The apostle frequently issues exhortations along these lines; e.g. at least 6 times his readers are commanded to "be of the same mind" (*to auto phronein*, think the same, Rom. 12:16; 15:5; 2 Cor. 13:11; Phil. 2:2; 4:2; *to hen phronein*, lit. "think the one", i.e. be "of one mind", Phil. 2:2 RSV; similarly *ouden allo phronein*, lit. "think no other", cf. RSV "take no other view", Gal. 5:10; cf. Phil. 3:15). Such exhortations, which are frequently linked with warnings against arrogance (e.g. Rom. 12:16; 15:5; implicitly in Rom. 11:20; Phil. 3:15), do not spring simply from a pragmatic outlook which on purely practical grounds puts church unity above all else. Paul argues back to the fact of Christ, since he it is upon whom the church is built and by whom it is sustained. A very good example of this occurs in the introductory verses to the "Christ-hymn" of Phil. 2:6–11. There is a lavish use of language in v. 2 to impress upon church members the need for being "of one mind", then the motivation given in v. 5 ff. is that Christians are in Christ, and are so by virtue of his life of self-abasement.

The translation and hence the interpretation of Phil. 2:5 is disputed; at first sight the AV may appear convincing: "Let this mind be in you, which was also in Christ Jesus." In that case, Christ's self-abasement would be the model for a similar attitude on the part of church members. The question is, however, whether *en Christō Iēsou* ought not to be regarded as a formula, as so often in Paul, for the individual believer's relationship to Christ: "Have the same thoughts among yourselves as you have in your communion with Christ Jesus" (Arndt, 874; cf. C. H. Dodd, *The Apostolic Preaching and its Developments*, 1944[2], 64). If this is so, then the call to unity would be based upon the fact that the → church possesses new life under the → lordship of Christ (cf. vv. 10 f.), new life which springs from his life of self-abasement. This interpretation is supported by Phil. 4:2, where church members are required to be "of the same mind in the Lord [*to auto phronein en kyriō*]". Here the phrase "in the Lord" is presumably a formula for the believer's new life in Christ (cf. Arndt, 259; → Body). Among other passages where the apostle calls for a harmonious attitude of mind, his prayer in Rom. 15:5 is noteworthy for the grounds on which he bases it: he prays that God may grant to the church *to auto phronein kata Christon Iēsoun*, lit. "to think the same according to Christ Jesus." This means both "according to the pattern of Jesus Christ" ("for Christ did not please himself") (v. 3), and also "according to the Spirit of Christ." In other words, God has given to men the opportunity of achieving unity and harmony in Christ. This would then be one of those passages supporting the statement that in the NT, and particularly in Paul, attitude of mind is closely connected with spiritual status: the believer's new standing in Christ both creates and demands a new mentality, which comes to concrete expression in the unity of the church.

5. Similar considerations underlie Paul's injunction in Col. 3:2: "Set your minds on things that are above, not on things that are on earth". Here *ta anō* (→ heaven) refers not to anything humanly exalted but to that heavenly sphere where the exalted Christ exercises his lordship (cf. Col. 3:1). He frees his people from all that would hold them down; contrast Phil. 3:19, where Paul accuses his opponents of having their "minds set on earthly things [*ta epigeia phronountes*]" and of making a god out of their → "belly".

6. The adj. *phronimos* occurs 9 times in the Gospels and 5 times in Paul. The adv. *phronimōs* occurs only at Lk. 16:8.

(a) In the Gospels the words are confined to parables or figurative language, and refer to that wise, judicious behaviour which should characterize those in the kingdom of God. The examples are taken from everyday life, though occasionally they are significantly exaggerated: the wise man builds his house on the rock (Matt. 7:24); the five wise virgins have a supply of oil (Matt. 25:1 ff.); a wise and faithful steward watches and is ready at the coming of his master (Matt. 24:45; par. Lk. 12:42); the unrighteous steward acts wisely, for "the sons of this world are wiser in their own generation than the sons of light" (Lk. 16:8; on this parable see J. D. M. Derrett, "The Parable of the Unjust Steward", *Law in the New Testament*, 1970, 48–77; → Possessions); and in Matt. 10:16 the wisdom of serpents is held up as an example to Christ's disciples. It has to be said, however, that the wisdom which is presented to the disciples as being in keeping with the kingdom of God is not just ordinary human common sense. Rather, the fact that *phronimos* is contrasted with *mōros*, foolish (→ Wisdom, Folly, art. *mōria*), in the first two parables mentioned above (Matt. 7:26; 25:2 f., 8), shows that here the OT idea of wisdom is involved: the wise man is he who does the will of the Lord (Matt. 7:24); the foolish man is he who refuses obedience. Hence the idea behind *phronimos* in the Gospels may be summarized thus: the believer's wisdom lies in his obedience.

(b) The Pauline passages clearly arise from the slogan which seems to have been in circulation among the "charismatic" Corinthians: *hēmeis de phronimoi*, "But we are intelligent [or discerning]", a claim which Paul controverts in 1 Cor. 4:10; cf.10:15; 2 Cor. 11:19. The wisdom claimed by such people was a purely human wisdom, which because of their arrogance jeopardized the unity of the church (see above NT 3, 4). Therefore, Paul counters it both with a reference to his own suffering as an apostle (not without a touch of irony, e.g. 1 Cor. 4:10; 2 Cor. 11:19) and with the warning, supported by the OT, that the man who regards himself as wise falls under the judgment of God (Rom. 11:25; 12:16). → Cross; → Wisdom, Folly.

7. Of all the words under discussion, *phronēsis* comes nearest to the OT concept of wisdom (see above OT; → Wisdom, art. *sophia*). In Eph. 1:9, where it stands beside *sophia*, it means discernment, insight. In Lk. 1:17 it could mean simply mental attitude, mentality, but the fact that it occurs in the combination *phronēsis dikaiōn* and in a context strongly reminiscent of the OT, suggests that the correct translation is "the wisdom of the just". Such wisdom, however, is not merely rational discernment, but is the result of God's people being turned to the obedience of faith, in accordance with OT prophecy.   *J. Goetzmann*

→ Empty (for discussion and literature on Phil. 2), → Head, → Heart, → Humility, → Knowledge, → Reason, → Think, → Wisdom

(a). G. Bertram, *mōros* etc. *TDNT* IV 832–47 and *phrēn* etc., *TDNT* IX 220–35; G. Bornkamm, "Faith and Reason in Paul", and "On Understanding the Christ-hymn (Philippians 2.6–11)", in *Early Christian Experience*, 1969, 29–46, 112–22; R. Bultmann, *Theology of the New Testament*, I, 1952, 214; G. Fohrer and H. Wilckens, *sophia* etc., *TDNT* VII 465–528; W. Grundmann, *tapeinos* etc., *TDNT* VIII 1–26; R. P. Martin, *Carmen Christi: Philippians ii.5–11 in Recent Interpretation and in the Setting of Early Christian Worship, Society for New Testament Study Monograph Series*, 4, 1967; C. F. D. Moule, "Further Reflections on Philippians 2:5–11; in W. W. Gasque and R. P. Martin, eds., *Apostolic History and the Gospel, Biblical and Historical Essays presented to F. F. Bruce*, 1970, 264–76; J. T. Sanders, *The New Testament Christological Hymns, Society for New Testament Studies Monograph Series* 15, 1971, 58–74; E. Schweizer, *Lordship and Discipleship, SBT* 28, 1960.
(b). G. Braumann, *Vorpaulinische christliche Taufverkündigung bei Paulus*, 1962, 56 ff.; A. Feuillet, "L'hymne christologique de l'épître aux Philippiens", *RB* 72, 1965, 352 ff., 481 ff.; E. Fuchs, *Die Freiheit des Glaubens*, 1949; D. Georgi, "Der vorpaulinische Hymnus Phil. 2,6–11", in E. Dinkler and H. Thyen, eds., *Zeit und Geschichte. Dankesgabe an Rudolf Bultmann zum 80. Geburtstag*, 1964, 263 ff.; J. Jeremias, "Zur Gedankenführung in den paulinischen Briefen", in *Studia Paulina in Honorem J. de Zwaan*, 1953, 146 ff. (reprinted in *Abba*, 1966, 269 ff.); E. Käsemann "Kritische Analyse von Phil. 2, 5–11", in *Exegetische Versuche und Besinnungen*, I, 1960, 51 ff.; E. Lohmeyer, *Kyrios Jesus. Eine Untersuchung zu Phil. 2, 5–11*, (1928) 1961; *Das Evangelium des Markus, KEK* 1/2, 1967[17]; and *Der Brief an die Philipper, KEK* 9/1 (1930) revised by W. Schmauch, 1953[9]; K. H. Rengstorf, *Das Evangelium nach Lukas, NTD* 3, 1952[6]; J. Schniewind, *Das Evangelium nach Markus, NTD* 1, 1949[5]; and *Das Evangelium nach Matthäus, NTD* 2, 1968[12]; G. Strecker, "Redaktion und Tradition im Christus-Hymnus Phil. 2, 6–11", *ZNW* 55, 1964, 63–78.

Miracle, Wonder, Sign

Etymologically the words miracle and wonder refer to the astonishment and amazement, created by an unusual or inexplicable event. In a religious context such an event is traced back to transcendent divine influence, but the unusual need not necessarily contradict the normal laws of nature. However, Christian faith has from the first attempted to understand and to interpret the happenings which have been experienced. The astonishment and amazement felt when confronted by such a spectacle or such an impression is rendered by the word-group *thaumazo*. *teras* is a specifically religious concept stemming perhaps from mantology and → magic, and throwing into relief the aspect of the extraordinary, and originally also the aspect of terror in a miraculous sign. By contrast, the originally non-religious word *sēmeion* stresses more the functional aspect of an event as a sign which draws attention (in the first instance visually) to the significance of an event. Only when this condition is fulfilled can we properly speak of miracles. This aspect is one which is frequently stressed when *sēmeion* is combined with *teras*. The investigation of the historicity of miracles lies outside the scope of this work, but details of studies dealing with this aspect of the subject are given in the bibliography.

θαῦμα

θαυμάζω (*thaumazo*), be astonished, wonder at, be surprised; θαῦμα (*thauma*), object of wonder, wonder, marvel, miracle; θαυμάσιος (*thaumasios*), wonderful, remarkable; θαυμαστός (*thaumastos*), wonderful, marvellous, astonishing; ἐκθαυμάζω (*ekthaumazo*), be greatly amazed; θαμβέω (*thambeo*), be astounded, amazed; ἐκθαμβέω (*ekthambeo*), be amazed, alarmed; ἔκθαμβος (*ekthambos*), utterly astonished; θάμβος (*thambos*), astonishment, fear; θορυβέω (*thorybeo*), throw into disorder, pass. be troubled, distressed; θόρυβος (*thorybos*), commotion, uproar, turmoil; θορυβάζω (*thorybazo*), cause trouble, pass. be troubled, distressed.

CL 1. The word-group associated with *thauma* and *thaumazo* is found in Gk. from the 8th and 7th cents., to designate that which by its appearance arouses astonishment and amazement. The root is cognate with *theaomai*, to look at. The reason for the amazement is expressed by the acc. in the trans. use of *thaumazo*, and with prepositions (*dia*, *en*, *peri*) in the intrans. use.

apothaumazo (Sir. 11:13) and *ekthaumazo* (Sir. 27:23), to be greatly amazed, are intensive compounds. The adjs. *thaumastos* and *thaumasios* take on particular nuances in Biblical usage.

2. Synonymous with these is the word-group associated with *thambos* (Hom. onwards), astonishment, dread (the latter meaning especially in LXX usage, cf. Ezek. 7:18); and *thambeo*, frighten, be frightened (trans., 2 Sam. 22:5; intrans. and pass., Wis. 17:13). The compound *ekthambeo*, terrify (Sir. 30:9), and the adj. *ekthambos*, terrifying, terrified (Dan. 7:7 Theodotion) are also intensive. Synonymous, too, is the group *thorybos*, commotion, uproar (Prov. 1:27); *thorybeo*, to throw into disorder (Wis. 18:19), is used from the 6th and 5th cents. B.C. onwards. Both word-groups are rare in biblical Gk. → Ecstasy; → Godliness; → Fear.

Examples of *thaumazo* as the human reaction to the working of a deity in the revelation of its divine power can be seen extensively in the history of Gk. religion, and are already to be found in the Homeric epics (e.g. *Od*. 1, 323; *Il*. 3, 398). From Hellenistic times mention may be made of Aelius Aristides (2nd cent. A.D.), the orator and devout worshipper of Asclepius, who in his writings alludes

621

to the marvellous (*thaumastas*) and powerful deeds of the god (G. Bertram, *TDNT* III 28). These examples, of course, only give us a very slight idea of the significance which *thaumazō* came to have in biblical writings.

OT In the LXX *thauma* appears only 4 times; 3 times in the phrase *thauma echein* (= *thaumazō*), Job 17:8; 18:20; 21:5 (*v.l. thaumasate*); and also Job 20:8 as *v.l.* for *phasma*, vision (Heb. *ḥezyôn*). The vb. *thaumazō* occurs chiefly in Job, Isa., and Sir. *thaumazō* is often combined with *prosōpon*, face; it means (like the Heb. *nāśā' pānîm*) to lift up the countenance, show favour towards, be partial towards (Prov. 18:5; Job 13:10); in Deut. 10:17 and 2 Chr. 19:7 it is expressly denied that God as judge is partisan. In a more general sense it denotes a friendly disposition which readily grants requests (e.g. Gen. 19:21, of God), a taking into consideration (Deut. 28:50) and a being highly favoured (2 Ki. 5:1, pass.). In this kind of usage, for which examples could be multiplied, the essential point is that the element of fear is not included in *thaumazō*. It is different where *thaumazō* comes to stand for the Heb. equivalent *šāmam*, be petrified with fear (Lev. 26:32; Job 17:8; 21:5; Dan. 8:27 Theodotion, or *tāmâh*, be astounded, horror-stricken (Ps. 48:6; Jer. 4:9; Heb. 1:5). The latter passages, in particular, show how the idea of astonishment passes over to that of horror. The human reaction to God's activity, which is here depicted for us, is an astonishment mingled with fear and horror. One can see the range of the word *thaumazō* in a comparison of Job 21:5 and 42:11 in the LXX text; the sight of Job suffering and stricken by God arouses a terrified astonishment (21:5), but astonishment is also caused by the marvellous help which he receives from God (42:11).

The adjs. *thaumastos* and *thaumasios* are found chiefly in the Pss. and Sir. The Heb. equivalent for *thaumastos* is often *nôrā'*, terrible: Daniel prays to the great and marvellous, i.e. fear-inspiring, God (Dan. 9:4 Theodotion). Many similar examples are found in the Pss.: God is marvellous, i.e. awe-inspiring amongst his holy ones (Ps. 68[67]:36); he is marvellous in the execution of his decrees (Ps. 45[44]:5). *thaumastos* stands chiefly for words formed from Heb. *niplā'ôt* (cf. the vb. *pālā'*, to be extra-ordinary, or marvellous): in Ps. 106[105]:22 where the marvellous and terrible acts of God (in "the land of Ham" and at the Red Sea) are compared; and in Ps. 118[117]:23 where that event is described as marvellous which in the NT is applied to Christ: the stone which the builders rejected has become the cornerstone (cf. Matt. 21:42; Mk. 12:10 f.; Lk. 20:17; Acts 4:11; 1 Pet. 2:7). With the adj. *thaumasios* the Heb. equivalents are again words formed from *pālā'* (occasionally occurring with *thaumastos*). *thaumasia* is the regular designation for the marvellous acts of God, which it is one of the Psalmists' basic concerns to proclaim and praise. These marvellous acts embrace all God's activity in creation and history (cf. Pss. 9:2; 26[25]:7; 71[70]:17; 86[85]:10). The praise of the Psalmists is continued in the book of Jesus Sirach, Ecclesiasticus (cf. Sir. 18:6; 38:6; 42:17; 48:14). Even the stars, the sun and the moon are included in this paean of praise (Sir. 43:2, 8).

In later Judaism the hymn-roll, or Hodayot, of the Dead Sea Scrolls took up the praise of the marvellous acts of God (cf. 1QH 1:30, 33; 3:23; 4:28, 29; 6:11).

NT 1. In the NT the noun *thauma* is found only twice; once in the phrase *ou thauma*, "it is no wonder" (2 Cor. 11:14), which is borrowed from Hellenistic diatribe (H. Windisch, *KEK* 9, 1924, ad loc.); then in the formulation in Rev. 17:6 *ethaumasa . . . thauma mega*, "I was greatly astonished". *thaumasios* is found only in Matt. 21:15 for the miraculous deeds of Jesus. The adj. *thaumastos* occurs 7 times: twice (Matt. 21:42; Mk. 12:11) in the quotation of Ps. 118:23 concerning the corner stone which the builders rejected, which is applied to Jesus (cf. above OT; → Rock, Stone, Corner Stone). In 1 Pet. 2:9 the light to which God has called Christians is called *thaumaston*, and its relationship to the divine sphere thus stated (Ps. 68:36, see above OT). In Jn. 9:30 the man healed by Jesus describes as "astonishing", "a marvel" (RSV), the attitude of the Jews who refuse to acknowledge where Jesus has come from. For Rev. 15:1, 3 see below, 6.

thaumazō is the word that occurs most frequently (42 times). In the Synoptic Gospels 25 certain examples are found (including the variant *exethaumazon* in Mk. 12:17), of which 13 are in Lk. Jn. offers 6 instances. The word comes 5 times in Acts, 4 times in the NT letters, and the same number of times in Rev.

The word-group containing *thambos* (astonishment, fear, Lk. 4:36; 5:9; Acts 3:10), *thambeō* (be astounded, Mk. 1:27; 10:24, 32; Acts 3:11 D; 9:6 TR), *ekthambos* (utterly astonished, Acts 3:11), and *ekthambeō* (be amazed, alarmed, Mk. 9:15; 14:33; 16:5 f.) is comparatively rare in the NT. There is a similar number of instances of *thorybos*, noise, clamour, turmoil (Matt. 26:5; 27:24; Mk. 5:38; 14:2; Acts 20:1; 21:34; 24:18), and *thorybeō*, throw into disorder (Acts 17:5; 21:13 D), pass. be troubled, distressed, in disorder (Matt. 9:23; Mk. 5:39). Matt. 26:5; 27:24 and Mk. 14:2 are concerned with disturbances in the nation which could arise from action taken against Jesus, and of which the chief priests and Pilate are afraid. Matt. 9:23 and Mk. 5:38 f. report of the din in the house of Jairus which followed the death of his little girl. According to Acts 17:5, the Jews in Thessalonica threw the town into an uproar in order to disrupt Paul's missionary work. In Acts 20:1 *thorybos* denoted the silversmiths' riot in Ephesus (Acts 19:23 ff.), and in 21:34 the riot amongst the people of Jerusalem (Acts 21:30 ff.) which led to Paul's imprisonment. The vb. and noun are also used in a similar sense in Acts 20:10 and 24:18.

2. In the Synoptic accounts *thaumazō* describes the impression which men get of Jesus' healing activity and miraculous power, such as in the case of the healing of the Gerasene demoniac (Mk. 5:20), the cursing of the fig-tree (Matt. 26:20; → Fruit, art. *sykē*), and the healing of a dumb demoniac (Matt. 9:33; Lk. 11:14). In Matt. the impression is put into words: "such a thing has never before been seen in Israel!" In the transmission of the story of the storm on the sea it is noticeable how closely astonishment and → fear belong together: Matt. speaks of astonishment (8:27), Mk. of being afraid (4:41), and Lk. combines both (8:25). Terror and astonishment are similarly juxtaposed in Lk. 9:43. The reaction of astonishment to Jesus' miraculous deeds is mentioned in a summarizing account in Matt. 15:31; the Marcan par. 7:37 speaks of terror.

If *thaumazō* includes an element of fear, Lk. 11:38 perhaps constitutes an exception. This speaks of the → Pharisees' amazement at Jesus' disregard for the Jewish purificatory prescriptions. Otherwise, however, *thaumazō* and *thambeō* or *ekplēssesthai* are closely related in the Gospels. *ekplēssesthai* is also related to the word of Jesus: "They took fright at his teaching" (Matt. 7:29 par. Mk. 1:22, Lk. 4:32; Matt. 19:25, par. Mk. 10:26; Mk. 11:18; Matt. 22:33), rendering impossible

623

any clear division between his acts and teaching (cf. Mk. 1:27). Jesus speaks as one who abolishes all otherwise valid criteria. Both Mk. and Lk. use *thambeisthai* or *thambos* (Mk. 1:27; Lk. 4:36; cf. *thambos* in Lk. 5:9, the account of the miraculous catch of fish).

Jesus' appearance in Nazareth seems to be depicted rather differently by Lk.: "All spoke well of him and wondered at the gracious words which proceeded out of his mouth" (Lk. 4:22a). But this did not stop the same people from trying to kill Jesus (4:29). Mk. reports only briefly the astonished alarm (6:2), which is the effect of Jesus' sovereign majesty. According to Mk. 9:15, even the sight of Jesus was enough to produce *ekthambeisthai*. On the way to Jerusalem Jesus' followers were filled with fear and astonishment (10:32). Hence, it must be asked whether the amazement to which Jesus' discussion with the → Pharisees gave rise, when they questioned him concerning the tax for the emperor, may not have contained an element of fear (Matt. 22:22 par. Mk. 12:17, Lk. 20:26). Such amazement, of course, in no way presupposes faith, though it may well presuppose an inkling of the presence of divine authority. Do the evangelists also postulate such a premonition on the part of Pilate, of whom they record that he was amazed that Jesus did not defend himself against his accusers (Matt. 27:14; Mk. 15:5), or that he was astounded by Jesus' speedy death (Mk. 15:44)?

There are two reports of Jesus' being surprised: at the faith of the centurion at Capernaum (Matt. 8:10; Lk. 7:9) and at the unbelief of the people in Nazareth (Mk. 6:6). A case of Jesus' *ekthambeisthai*, being frightened, is transmitted to us in the scene in Gethsemane (Mk. 14:33).

In Luke's infancy narrative (chs. 1 and 2) a *thaumazein* is spoken of 4 times. Zechariah's long delay in the temple, together with his loss of speech, caused the people surprise (1:21 f.); they took it as an indication that something extraordinary had happened, and that he had seen a vision. The same is true of the → name given to John the Baptist which his father could not utter and which evoked astonishment from the people (1:63). The Christmas message of the shepherds aroused amazement (2:18), as did the encounter of Jesus' parents with Simeon, and his words in the temple (2:33). The whole event has an air about it which caused men to marvel. The Lucan Easter narrative uses the word in two places. In Lk. 24:12 Peter ran to Jesus' grave in response to the message of the women and found it empty. Whereupon he returned home, amazed at what had happened. (The verse is absent from important textual witnesses, and its originality is admittedly not guaranteed. It is, however, supported by Metzger, 184.) Lk. depicts in 24:41 how the disciples were unable to believe for joy and astonishment, when Jesus appeared to them. The fact that the sight of the risen Lord aroused fear has already been stated in v. 37 (cf. the hint in Jn. 21:12). But the Easter joy was not mitigated by it (Matt. 28:8; Lk. 24:41; Jn. 20:20). The appearance of the → angels at the grave was also frightening (*ekthambeisthai* twice in Mk. 16:5, 6; cf. also Matt. 28:3, 5).

3. In the Fourth Gospel *thaumazein* is rarely used to denote human reaction to Jesus' attitudes and behaviour. In reply to the expressed amazement that Jesus possesses knowledge of scripture without having received instruction in it (7:15), he replied (7:16) by pointing out that his teaching comes from the Father who has sent him. In 7:21 Jesus drew the attention of the Jews to the fact that they are surprised (*thaumazete*) and annoyed by a work which he has performed on the

624

→ Sabbath (7:23), whereas for the sake of circumcision they would regularly break the Sabbath. Jesus' → works will inevitably provoke astonishment, "For the Father loves the Son, and shows him all that he himself is doing; and greater works than these will he show him, that you may marvel" (5:20). To Nicodemus Jesus directed the challenge *mē thaumasēs*: "do not be surprised!" (3:7 JB; cf. Eccl. 5:7). Nicodemus is not to take offence at the initially unintelligible language concerning the new → birth (art. *palingenesia*), about which he can only ask: "How can that be possible?" (v. 9 JB): he is to open his heart to it in faith. The formula *mē thaumasēs* is also found in 5:28 f. (the listeners are not to be surprised at Jesus' language about the → resurrection of the dead to → life and to → judgment, with which they must come to terms), and 1 Jn. 3:13 (here it is the hatred of the world, which Christians are not to be surprised at when they meet it, because it is the offence with which they will have to be able to cope).

4. According to Acts 2:7, when the Spirit was poured out, the assembled crowd of Jews were bewildered with astonishment. Terrified astonishment is the reaction of the people to the healing of the lame man (*thambos kai ekstasis*, "wonder and amazement", 3:10; cf. v. 12 *ti thaumazete*, "why do you wonder?"). For the high priests the object of astonishment is the boldness of Peter and John and the fact that they were "uneducated, common men" (4:13). Elsewhere the term occurs in Acts when OT stories are related (7:31; cf. Dan. 8:27) or quoted (13:41; cf. Hab. 1:5). The question may be asked whether the relative frequency of the word *thaumazō* in the Lucan writings is connected with the proximity of his style to the language of the LXX.

5. From among the NT epistles (apart from 2 Cor. 11:14, cf. above 1) two Pauline passages require mention. In Gal. 1:6 the apostle expresses his amazement that the Galatians have so quickly allowed themselves to be won over to another → gospel; this leads into Paul's debate concerning the Galatian teachers of false doctrine. 2 Thess. 1:10 uses *thaumazō* in an eschatological context: the Lord will come in order to be glorified among his saints (Ps. 68[67]:36) and to be marvelled at among those who believe in him (the pass. *thaumasthēnai* is not rare in the LXX [cf. 2 Ki. 5:1; Isa. 61:6]). In Jude 16 the language is Jewish-Christian, expressing in the manner of the LXX the partiality shown to people (*thaumazontes prosōpa*). On 1 Jn. 3:13 cf. NT 3, above.

6. In Rev. *thaumazō* occurs 4 times in 13:3 and 17:6 ff. Rev. 13:1 ff. reports that at the emergence of the beast (→ Animal, art. *thērion*) from the sea, the embodiment of the anti-Christian power, "the whole earth had followed the beast with astonishment" (v. 3). This astonishment leads to adoration of the beast and of the power behind him, the → dragon. The astonishment in 17:8 also refers to this adoration. The model for the apocalyptic picture was the cult of the Roman Caesars. The astonishment of the seer in 17:7 is different; this concerns the mystery of → "Babylon the great", which is → drunk with the → blood of the saints and of the witnesses of Jesus (vv. 5, 6). Further, Rev. 15:1 speaks of a great and marvellous (*thaumaston*) sign (→ *sēmeion*). The seer sees seven angels bringing the seven final plagues in which the divine judgment of wrath is consummated. But before this event of terror comes to pass, the seer catches a glimpse of the multitude who have conquered and who sing the song of → Moses and the → Lamb (15:2). In this song there resounds the song of praise of the great and

marvellous (*thaumasta*) works of God (→ Work; → Earth), which the devout men of the old covenant praised (15:3). *W. Mundle*

| σημεῖον | σημεῖον (*sēmeion*), sign, wonder, miracle. |

CL *sēmeion*, attested from Aesch. and Hdt. onwards, is a derivation from *sēma*, sign, a word common in early Gk. epic and synonymous with *sēmeion*, but one whose etymology has not yet been satisfactorily clarified. The word does not originally come from the sphere of religion, but it takes on theological colouring in appropriate contexts.

1. The basic meaning of *sēmeion* is a sign (as a rule, visually perceived, but occasionally also heard) by which one recognizes a particular person or thing, a confirmatory, corroborative, authenticating mark or token. Of the variety of nuances in meaning (see K. H. Rengstorf, *TDNT* VII 204–7) mention may be made of the foretoken or omen, which announced coming events. As distinct from → *teras*, *sēmeion* and its older form *sēma* do not necessarily have the character of the miraculous. Also – and again differently from *teras* – "its reference is to disclosure as the indispensable presupposition of all knowledge" (*TDNT* VII 204), without requiring explanation or interpretation.

2. When a *sēmeion* does have the character of the marvellous, the word acquires the meaning of "miraculous sign". It can then denote in general a miracle worked by the divinity or a miracle-worker which contradicts the natural course of things. This meaning is also found in the phrase *sēmeia kai terata*, "signs and wonders", first attested in Polyb. 3, 112, 18 in the 2nd cent. B.C.

OT 1. In the LXX *sēmeion* is predominantly a translation of the Heb. word '*ôt*, and, like it, means: (a) sign, mark, token; (b) miraculous sign, miracle.

(a) Whether directly or by authorized men, whether unrequested (e.g. 1 Sam. 10:1 ff.) or in answer to prayer (e.g. Jdg. 6:17, 36 f.), Yahweh grants and works signs, which accompany his word and vouch for its validity and reliability. Thus the sign of Cain (Gen. 4:15) vouches for the promise of divine protection, the blood on the houses of the Israelites (Exod. 12:13) vouches for the promised exemption. As the rainbow guarantees God's → covenant promise (Gen. 9:8 ff.), so → circumcision (Gen. 17:11) and → Sabbath (Exod. 31:13, 17) are also "signs of the covenant", which express and seal the particular relationship between Yahweh and Israel. Signs which reinforce the promise of the saving presence of Yahweh are spoken of in Exod. 3:12; Jdg. 6:16 ff., 36 ff.; 1 Sam. 10:1 ff.; and Isa. 7:10 ff. Yahweh's messengers can authenticate their mission and message by signs performed (Exod. 4:1 ff.) or predicted (1 Sam. 10:1 ff.; 1 Ki. 13:1 ff.; 2 Ki. 19:29). The symbolic actions of the prophets are a way of making visible the word of God (1 Ki. 11:29 ff.; Isa. 8:1 ff.; 20:1 ff.; Jer. 19:1 ff.; 27:1 ff.; 32:6 ff.; Ezek. 4–5; 24:15 ff.; Hos. 1–3). They are not simply pictorial illustrations of the oral proclamation, but, like the prophetic word itself (cf. Isa. 55:10 f.), tokens of the power which shapes history. The prior representation of that which is coming sets the realization of the thing designated creatively in motion. "The prophetic symbolic act is simply an intensified form of prophetic speech" (G. von Rad,

Old Testament Theology, II, 1965, 96). Even the prophet, as a witness of the message, can himself become a "sign" (Isa. 8:18; Ezek. 12:3 ff., 17 ff.; 21:11 f.; 24:24, 27).

(b) Alongside such signs, which are either quite ordinary incidents or ones where the aspect of the marvellous does not lie in the sign itself but in the prophetic prediction (e.g. 1 Sam. 10:1 ff.; and the announcement in Isa. 7:14 ff. that the child will be a son, → God, art. *Emmanouēl*), there are others which possess a thoroughly miraculous character. In this category belong the signs worked by Moses, for example (Exod. 4; 7–12; 14; 17; Deut. 34:11) and those granted to Gideon (Jdg. 6) and Hezekiah (2 Ki. 20:8 ff.; cf. Isa. 38:7 ff.). In the sense of a miraculous sign *'ôṯ* and *sēmeion* are closely linked with *môpēṯ* and *teras*. The phrase *'ōṯôṯ ûmôpᵉṯîm = sēmeia kai terata*, signs and wonders (where the original distinction between the two terms can no longer be felt), is found primarily in those texts which describe the time of Moses as a time of Yahweh's marvellous action in history (Exod. 7:3; cf. Deut. 4:34; 6:22; 7:19; 29:2; Jer. 32:20 f.; Ps. 78[77]:43; 105[104]:27; 135[134]:9; Neh. 9:10; also Bar. 2:11; Wis. 10:16). Moreover, there are numerous miracles witnessed to in the OT, which God works directly or through charismatic figures (e.g. Gen. 17:17; 18:11; Jos. 3; 6; 10; 1 Ki. 17 f.; 2 Ki. 6 f.). Such signs are considered to be extraordinary occurrences, but not unnatural, since the OT does not know of a natural law as an independent entity on a level with Yahweh. Every event goes back to God, nothing is impossible for him (Gen. 18:14). All signs are pointers to Yahweh himself, a revelation of his → might, and → glory. In them → Israel – indeed, all the nations of the world – are to encounter Yahweh and to recognize that he alone is God (cf. Deut. 4:35; 1 Ki. 18:36 ff.; Ps. 86[85]:10). Since the ultimate goal of signs is the universal glorification of the divine → name (Ps. 72[71]:18 f.), unbelief and disobedience in the face of the demonstrative experience of signs are regarded as the expression of an utterly incomprehensible hardness of heart (Num. 14:11, 22; Ps. 78[77]; 95[94]:8 ff.).   *O. Hofius*

(c) In point of fact, miraculous signs are not uniformly distributed throughout the OT. They are largely grouped in three main periods, each of which was marked by a life-and-death struggle for the people of God and which put Yahweh's saving power and will to the proof. These periods were: (i) The redemption of the people of God from → Egypt and their establishment in Canaan; (ii) the conflict with pagan religion under → Elijah and Elisha; (iii) the time of Daniel during the exile when the supremacy of Yahweh and the faithfulness of Daniel and his companions were vindicated. The common feature of these periods is the extremity of the people of God which is answered by Yahweh's action in abnormal events which are in themselves saving acts and at the same time pointers to an even greater salvation. The same could be said for the fourth period of miraculous signs, the coming of Jesus and the gospel age.

Outside these periods miracles are rare. Possible instances are the so-called translation of Enoch (Gen. 5:24; cf. Heb. 11:5) and the birth of Isaac to → Abraham and Sarah despite their advanced age (Gen. 21:1 ff.). With regard to Enoch, the Bible itself does not engage in the speculations of Wis. 4:10 ff. and various books of Enoch. The text need imply no more than that he was taken to the direct presence of God at the end of his life. (On Enoch in intertestamental literature see

F. F. Bruce, *The Epistle to the Hebrews*, NLC 1964, 286–89; *ODCC*, 459 f.) The prolonged childlessness of Abraham and Sarah may have been due to the fact that Sarah was Abraham's step-sister (Gen. 20:12). The birth of Isaac was miraculous in the sense that it was deemed beyond the normal course of nature.

Many of the other miraculous events in the OT did not involve suspension of natural causes. The locusts which plagued Egypt were blown there by a strong east wind and were blown away by a strong west wind (Exod. 10:13, 19). The arrival of the quails coincided with the spring migration (Exod. 16:13). On the manna which may have attracted the quails → Bread, art. *manna*. The parting of the Red Sea was caused by "a strong east wind" blowing all night (Exod. 14:21). In such instances the event is a providential ordering of natural causes for the benefit of the people of God. Similarly, the fire falling on the sacrifice of Elijah on Mount Carmel (1 Ki. 18:38) was probably a thunderbolt. In the cases of the healing of Naaman (2 Ki. 5) and the restoration to life of children (1 Ki. 17:17–24; 2 Ki. 4:18–37) we have instances of paranormal healings beyond normal medical explanation. The long day in Joshua 10 may well be a poetic description of the invigoration of Joshua's soldiers. Alternatively it has been explained as an abnormal refraction of the rays of the sun and moon and as a supernaturally induced thunderstorm giving the men relief from the burning heat (cf. B. Ramm, *The Christian View of Science and Scripture*, 1955, 107–10). The sun dial of Ahaz (Isa. 38; 2 Ki. 20) was probably a series of steps (cf. Josephus, *Ant.* 10, 2, 1). The return of the shadow ten degrees may have been due to the Shekinah Glory which lighted up the steps (A. S. D. Maunder, "The Shadow Returning on the Dial of Ahaz", *Journal of the Transactions of the Victoria Institute* 64, 1932, 83–92; for further discussion see B. Ramm, op. cit., 110 ff.). In the case of 2 Ki. 6:5 ff., John Gray comments, "The factual basis of the 'miracle' of the floating axe-head may be that Elisha with a long pole or stick probed about the spot indicated (an important point in the text) until he succeeded either in inserting the stick into the socket, or, having located the hard object on the muddy bottom, moved it until the man was able to recover it" (*I & II Kings*, 1964, 460). It may be noted that the text itself does not call the event a miracle or even a sign. Nevertheless, the event was evidently remembered as indicative of Yahweh's providential help.

The view that one takes of Daniel in the fiery furnace and the lions' den (Dn. 3 and 6) will depend on the view that one takes of the Book of Daniel as a whole. Many scholars place the book in the Maccabean period and see it as a work written to encourage pious Jews to withstand the attacks on their religion by Antiochus Epiphanes. The stories then might have a didactic value, but little basis in historical reality. Alternatively, they might be a figurative, stylized way of describing some historical event. On the other hand, the book itself is set in the exilic period. The furnace may be thought of as the kilns of the period used for baking bricks or smelting metals (cf. K. A. Kitchen, "Brick-Kiln", *NBD*, 168; T. C. Mitchell, "Furnace", *NBD*, 443; J. B. Alexander, "New Light on the Fiery Furnace", *JBL* 69, 1950, 375 f.). A sudden gust of flame or explosion killed the men who brought Shadrach, Meshach and Abednego down to where the kilns were (Dn. 3:22), but the latter survived their ordeal possibly protected by their clothing mentioned in the narrative. In the case of the lions, a spiritual presence inhibited the lions from attacking Daniel (Dn. 6:22). For various interpretations of the Book of Daniel see J. A. Montgomery, *The Book of Daniel, ICC*, 1927; E. W. Heaton, *The Book of Daniel*, 1956; N. Porteous, *Daniel: A Commentary*, 1965; E. J. Young, *The Prophecy of Daniel: A Commentary*, 1949; and the specialist literature referred to in these books.   *C. Brown*

2. According to Exod. 7 f., the Egyptian magicians had the power to perform miracles by secret magical arts, but they are inferior to the miracles of Yahweh (→ Magic). In Deut. 13:2 ff. the false prophet who wishes to seduce Israel to apostasy from Yahweh is attributed the power to perform signs and wonders. These are recognized to be opposed to God in that the word that they are intended to authenticate brings separation from him instead of binding one to him. Hence even though a prophet may perform such signs, he is to be tested by his teaching. If his teaching would lead to other gods, he is to be rejected.

3. The meaning of the apocalyptic sign of the end, portent, which → *teras* has in Joel 2:30 (LXX 3:3), is not attested for *sēmeion* in the LXX, but it is found in 2 Esd. 4:51 f.; 6:11 f.; 8:63, where the Lat. *signum* goes back to the Gk. *sēmeion*. In Sib. 3:796 ff. the older *sēma* is used. The signs of the end are partly concerned with horrible and frightening portents, which indicate that the last days are dawning. In so far as these portents are convulsions of a cosmic nature, they announce the transformation of the world – the dissolution of the old → creation and the reconstitution of the whole of → nature. On the interpretation of the cosmic language of Joel in the NT and the cosmic language of prophecy → Generation, art. *genea* NT 4; → Pentecost; → Fullness, art. *plēroō* NT 1.

4. In Rabbinic literature, where *'ôṯ* (and more rarely *sîmān = sēmeion*) has the meaning, amongst others, of miraculous sign or miracle, God's miracles, the miraculous working of great men of God and of the Rabbis, and also miracles of the messianic age are frequently spoken of (see the index in SB IV 1277). According to the Rabbinic conception, a prophet has to prove his identity by means of signs and wonders (cf. SB I 726 ff.; II 480; cf. Matt. 16:1; Jn. 6:30; and also Jn. 3:2). Miracles are equally regarded as divine confirmatory signs for the proclamation of a Rabbi (SB I 127; IV 318 f.).

NT *sēmeion* is found 77 times in the NT, predominantly in the Gospels (48 times) and Acts (13 times), but also in Paul (8 times), Heb. (once) and Rev. (7 times). In the other literature the term is entirely lacking. The linguistic usage of the LXX is adopted: *sēmeion* means: (1) sign, mark (Matt. 26:48; 2 Thess. 3:17), token (Lk. 2:12); (2) miraculous sign, miracle (Jn. 2:11; 18, 23 *et passim*; Acts 4:16, 22; 8:6; 1 Cor. 1:22). The phrase *sēmeia kai terata*, signs and wonders, occurs many times (Matt. 24:24 par. Mk. 13:22; Jn. 4:48; Acts 2:19 [Joel 2:30], 22, 43 [cf. 5:12; 14:3]; 4:30; 6:8; 7:36; 15:12; Rom. 15:19; 2 Cor. 12:12; 2 Thess. 2:9; Heb. 2:4). The apocalyptic meaning of sign of the end (see above OT 3) is found, e.g., in Mk. 13:4; Matt. 24:3; Lk. 21:11, 15 f.

1. It is the OT conception of the → prophet as Yahweh's sign that underlies Jesus' being the God-given sign (Lk. 2:34), by which the rise or fall, the salvation or ruin of every man is decided. In this connection we also have Jesus' rejection of the demand for signs (Matt. 16:1 par. Mk. 8:11, Lk. 11:16), which is linked in Matt. 12:38 ff.; 16:1 ff., Lk. 11:16, 29 ff. with the mention – although its interpretation is disputed (cf. *TDNT* III 406–10) – of the sign of → Jonah. Jesus unmasks

the demand for signs as a subterfuge concealing a refusal to repent. Anyone who does not believe the final word of God going forth in him will not be brought to repentance even by miracles (cf. Lk. 16:27 ff.). The only sign which God will give to the unrepentant → generation is God's representative who will be shown to be such by his deliverance from death. As once Jonah came back from the dead, so at his parousia (→ Present, art. *parousia*) the Son of man will come in → judgment (cf. Matt. 24:30; → Son, art. *hyios tou anthrōpou*). The parabolic actions of Jesus which betoken the dawn of the age of salvation (e.g. Mk. 2:18 ff.; 3:13 ff.; Matt. 2:1 ff., 12 ff.) are to be compared with the prophetic symbolic actions of the OT. Thus, Jesus' table-fellowship with sinners (Lk. 5:29 f.; Matt. 9:9–13; Mk. 2:13–17; 15:1 ff., 19:7) is a prophetic sign, a valid anticipation of the acquittal of the final judgment, and a practical illustration in advance of the messianic meal in the age of salvation.

2. Alongside the miracles performed by God himself (e.g. Acts 5:19; 12:3 ff.; 16:25 ff.) one can also distinguish in the NT: (a) the miracles of Jesus; (b) the miracles of his witnesses; and (c) the miraculous power of elements hostile to God.

(a) The Gospels record numerous healing miracles of Jesus (e.g. the healing of those possessed by evil spirits, → lepers, → blind → lame, → deaf-mutes (→ Demon; → Heal), three instances of people being raised from the dead (Jairus' daughter, Matt. 9:18–26; Mk. 5:21–43; Lk. 8:40–56; the widow of Nain's son, Lk. 7:11–17; and Lazarus, Jn. 11; cf. the raisings in 1 Ki. 17:17–24; 2 Ki. 4:32–37), and eight so-called nature miracles (the stilling of the storm, Matt. 8:18, 23–37, Mk. 4:35–41, Lk. 8:22–25; the feeding of the five thousand, Matt. 14:13–21, Mk. 6:32–14; Lk. 9:11–17; Jn. 6:5–13; the feeding of the four thousand, Matt. 15:32–39, Mk. 8:1–10; the walking on the water, Matt. 14:22–33, Mk. 6:45–52, Jn. 6:15–21; the cursing of the fig tree, Matt. 21:18 f., Mk. 8:12 ff., cf. Lk. 13:6–9 (→ Fruit, art. *sykē*); the coin in the fish's mouth, Matt. 17:24–27; the draught of fishes, Lk. 5:1–11; cf. Jn. 21:1–19; and the water into wine, Jn. 2:1 ff.). Critical sifting of this material has led some scholars to conclude that some of these narratives contain reduplication (e.g. the feeding of the four and five thousand, cf. J. Jeremias, *New Testament Theology*, I, 1971, 86 ff.). But it also confirms the presentation of the Synoptic Gospels, where the essential characteristic of the effective work of Jesus is seen in the combination of proclamation and healing work (cf. Mk. 1:38 f.; Matt. 4:23; 9:35; Lk. 9:11; cf. also Jesus' testimony to himself in Lk. 13:32, and the juxtaposition of seeing and hearing in the *logion* Matt. 13:16 f. par. Lk. 10:23 f. [cf. Jn. 8:56; Heb. 11:13; 1 Pet. 1:10 ff.; Isa. 6:9 f.]).

There also exist accounts of miracles of Jewish and pagan miracle-workers of antiquity (on this see C. F. D. Moule, ed., *Miracles: Cambridge Studies in their Philosophy and History*, 1965; H. van der Loos, *The Miracles of Jesus*, 1965, 139–50). A comparison of these accounts with those of the Gospels shows that the NT miracle traditions have adopted certain narrative forms and motifs from their *milieu*, but also draws attention to the particularities of the Gospel witness. With Jesus → magic, conjuration, cursing of people and spells are all absent. He performed miracles by his authoritative → word, to which can be added a gesture (e.g. Mk. 1:31, 41; 5:41; Matt. 9:29). Jesus carried out no miracles of punishment (cf. Lk. 9:51 ff. with 2 Ki. 1:10 ff.). He declined to perform miracles in order to rescue himself (Matt. 4:1 ff. par. Lk. 4:1–4; 26:51 ff.; 27:39 ff. par. Mk. 15:29 ff.; Lk.

23:35), and rejected demonstrations of power designed to prove his divine sending (Matt. 4:5 ff. par. Lk. 4:9–12; Matt. 16:1–4 par. Mk. 8:11 f.; Lk. 11:29). Jesus forbade those whom he had healed to relate his miracles to others (e.g. Matt. 8:30; Mk. 5:43; 7:36; Lk. 8:56); in the case of the healed lepers the man was to show himself "to the priest, and offer what Moses commanded, for a proof to the people" (Mk. 1:44; cf. Lev. 13:49; 14:2–22; Matt. 8:2–4; Lk. 5:12–16; this suggests that Jesus was not only fulfilling the law but directing his work in the first instance to the priests). It is not personal gain but thanks to God that Jesus looked for in men who have known his miraculous help (Lk. 17:11 ff.). By and large the accounts pay little attention to the miraculous process as such; they concentrate on the encounter of Jesus with the whole man in his physical and spiritual needs. The case of the Gadarene swine (Matt. 8:28–34; Mk. 5:1–17; Lk. 8:26–37) illustrates not only something of the nature of demon possession but also the preference of the people of those parts for their swine (in any case unclean → animals) to the healing presence of Jesus. In Matt. 9:2–8 par. Mk. 2:3–12, Lk. 5:18–26 → forgiveness of sins is linked with the healing. Healing becomes a turning point in the life of the healed person (cf. Matt. 9:32; 20:34; Mk. 5:18 ff.; 10:52; Lk. 18:43). Anyone who experiences a miracle of Jesus is thereby placed on the road of → discipleship, in the same way that miracles in general are related to → faith. Only faith, i.e. trust in the power of Jesus which transcends all human possibilities, can receive miracles (Mk. 2:5; 5:34; 7:29; 9:23 f.; Matt. 8:10; 9:28 f.; cf. Jn. 4:50; 11:40); unbelief is denied miracles (Matt. 13:53–58; Mk. 6:1–6; cf. Lk. 4:16–30). It is noteworthy that Jesus' miracles presuppose → faith, they do not first create it. Miracles are not proofs which silence all opposition: if the believer sees God at work, the verdict of his opponents is that Jesus is in league with → Satan (Matt. 12:24; Mk. 3:22; Lk. 11:15).

What finally and radically distinguishes Jesus' miracles from those of Jewish and Hellenistic narratives is their eschatological reference. As Matt. 11:2 ff. par. Lk. 7:18 ff. and Lk. 11:20 clearly show, they are signs of God's kingly rule, the dawn of which Jesus announced in his → proclamation (Matt. 4:23; 9:35; Mk. 1:39; 6:6; Lk. 4:14 f., 44). Jesus' words and works are the beginning of the age of salvation, and the miracles are a foreshadowing and a promise of the coming universal redemption. Ultimately, it is in this eschatological context that the accounts of Jesus' miracles are to be read. Thus, the casting out of demons signals God's invasion into the realm of Satan and its final annihilation (Matt. 12:29 par. Mk. 3:27, Lk. 11:21 f., cf. Isa. 49:24 f.; Lk. 10:18; Jn. 12:31; Rev. 20:1 ff., 10); the raising of the dead announces that death will be forever done away with (1 Cor. 15:26; Rev. 21:4; cf. Isa. 25:8); the healing of the sick bears witness to the cessation of all suffering (Rev. 21:4); the miraculous provisions of food are foretokens of the end of all physical need (Rev. 7:16 f.); the stilling of the storm points forward to complete victory over the powers of chaos which threaten the earth (Rev. 21:1). "When the biblical miracle stories excite serious and relevant wonderment, they intend to do this as *signals* of something fundamentally new, not as a violation of the natural order which is generally known and acknowledged. . . . Though these changes were isolated and temporary, they were nevertheless radically *helpful* and saving. What took place were promises and intimations, anticipations of a redeemed nature, of a state of freedom, of a kind of life in which there

631

will be no more sorrow, tears, and crying, and where death as the last enemy will be no more" (Karl Barth, *Evangelical Theology: An Introduction*, 1963, 68 f.).

The eschatological reference of Jesus' miracles is also expressed in its particular way by John's Gospel. For a redaction-critical approach see R. T. Fortna, *The Gospel of Signs: A Reconstruction of the Narrative Source Underlying the Fourth Gospel*, 1970. The Gospel itself stresses the historical reality of the events. At the same time the miracles are understood as signs pointing beyond themselves to the One who performs them. They prove Jesus' identity as the Christ of God (20:30), who brings the fullness of eschatological salvation (2:1 ff.; wine is already a symbol of the age of salvation in the OT, cf. Isa. 25:6; → Vine), and offers the → bread of life (6:1 ff.), grants resurrection and eternal life (11:1 ff.; cf. also 4:47 ff.; 5:1 ff.) and drives out darkness (9:1 ff.). In the miracles Jesus reveals his → glory (2:11; 11:4), which is the glory of God himself (1:14). Admittedly, the miracles have this power of statement only for those whose eyes God himself opens (12:37 ff.; cf. Isa. 6:1, 10; 53:1), so that in faith they become aware of the glory of Jesus (2:11; 11:40). Unenlightened men, by contrast, react to Jesus' miracles with sham faith (2:23 ff.) or unbelief (12:37–43; cf. Isa. 53:1; 6:1, 10).

The NT witnesses agree that the uniqueness of Jesus is also expressed in the miracles – his compassionate love as well as his divine authority (cf. also Acts 10:38). "He has done all things well" (Mk. 7:37). In him God himself "has visited his people" (Lk. 7:16). This is the pledge and promise of the consummation of salvation described in Rev. 21:1 ff.

(b) According to the witness of the Synoptic Gospels, Jesus sent out his disciples to preach and to perform miracles (Matt. 10:7 f.; Mk. 3:14 f.; Lk. 9:1 f.; 10:9; cf. Mk. 6:7 ff.; Lk. 9:6). The same is reported in the longer ending of Mk. (16:9–20) concerning the sending-out of the disciples by the Risen Christ (v. 15 ff.; on the various versions of the ending of Mk. see Metzger, 122–26; W. R. Farmer, *The Last Twelve Verses of Mark*, 1974).

Similarly, Acts mentions many times the correlation of apostolic proclamation and apostolic miracle-working (2:2 f.; 4:29 f.; cf. 3:1 ff.; 4:16, 22; 5:12; 6:8; 8:6 ff.; 9:32 ff.; 15:12; 20:7 ff.). The miracles are co-ordinated with the preaching – they are "accompanying signs", by which Christ confirms the word of the witnesses (Acts 14:3; cf. Mk. 16:20). As in the authoritative word (Acts 6:10) so in the signs is manifested the power of the Holy Spirit promised to the disciples (Acts 1:8).

For Paul, too, "word and deed", preaching and signs belong together; in both Christ is at work in the power of the Spirit (Rom. 15:18 f.). Signs and wonders accompany the proclamation which takes place "in demonstration of the Spirit and power" (1 Cor. 2:4; cf. 1 Thess. 1:5). They are marks of the divine legitimation and authority of the apostolic office and work (2 Cor. 12:12; cf. Rom. 15:18 f.). To the hearers of the preaching also the Holy Spirit mediates miraculous powers (Gal. 3:5). That is why alongside the gifts of proclamation the charisma of healing and the power to perform miracles belong to the living gifts of the Spirit in the church (1 Cor. 12:8 ff., 28; cf. Jas. 5:14 f.).

Finally, Hebrews also bears witness that God confirms the preaching of salvation, which proclaims the dawn of the age of salvation, by signs and wonders (2:3 ff.), which, as "powers of the world to come" (6:5), foreshadow the completion of salvation. Kerygma and charisma, preaching and miracles thus belong essentially together, according to the NT. In both Jesus Christ proves himself to be the living Lord, present in his church in the Holy Spirit.

(c) As the OT, so also the NT reckons with signs and wonders worked by false prophets and pseudo-messianic figures (Mk. 13:22; Matt. 24:24; Rev. 13:11 ff.; 16:14; 19:20) by whom men will be seduced into apostasy from God. The →
Antichrist is also expected to perform signs and wonders "in the power of Satan" (2 Thess. 2:3 ff.). *O. Hofius*

τέρας

τέρας (*teras*), miraculous sign, prodigy, portent, omen, wonder.

CL *teras* is attested in literature from Hom. onwards, though its etymology is obscure.

It denotes terrible appearances which elicit fright and horror, and which contradict the ordered unity of nature. This gave rise to the meaning of *teras* as a miraculous sign, or portent. The word already has the meaning of a sign from the gods in Hom., especially in the sense of some uncanny foretoken or omen requiring interpretation by a seer; this could reveal links with earlier ideas of popular religion. See further K. H. Rengstorf, *TDNT* VIII 113–17.

OT In the LXX *teras* is chiefly the rendering of Heb. *mōpēṯ*, token, sign, miracle.

Its meaning is determined by this, and is thus essentially different from the secular Gk. usage. It is true that the character of the unusual also belongs to the word in the OT, but this is "based on the biblical concept of God as the Creator and Lord of all events and thus transferred from the sphere of the marvellous and unnatural", and also "demarcated from the world of myth" (K. H. Rengstorf, *TDNT* VIII 119). Essential for *mōpēṯ* and *teras* is always the reference to the self-revelation of Yahweh. The word thus designates a → prophet who is made a sign (Isa. 8:18; 20:3; Ezek. 12:6, 11; 24:24, 27), and further, a man who becomes a manifestation of the wrath of God and a sign of horror (Ps. 71:7; cf. 31:12; cf. also 1QH 13:16; 15:20). An event which announces future judgment can also be called a sign of horror (1 Ki. 13:3, 5). In apocalyptic contexts *teras* in Joel 3:3 (LXX 2:30) is a baneful "sign of the end" (→ *sēmeion*, OT 3). Finally, the word can denote miracles in general (Exod. 7:9; 11:9; 2 Chr. 32:31, especially when linked with → *sēmeion*; cf. 2 Chr. 32:24).

NT In the NT *teras* occurs 16 times (9 in Acts), exclusively in the plur. and only in combination with → *sēmeion* (q.v. for individual details). *O. Hofius*
→ Blind, → Bread, → Deaf, → Heal, → Hunger, → Lame, → Leprosy, → Resurrection, → See, → Wine

(a). P. J. Achtemeier, "Toward the Isolation of Pre-Markan Miracle Catenae", *JBL* 89, 1970, 265–91; and "The Origin and Function of the Pre-Marcan Miracle Catenae", *JBL* 91, 1972, 198–221; G. Bertram, *thambos* etc., *TDNT* III 4–7; and *thauma* etc., *TDNT* III 27–42; G. H. Boobyer, "The Miracles of the Loaves and the Gentiles in St. Mark's Gospel", *SJT* 6, 1953, 77–87; and "The Eucharistic Interpretation of the Miracles and the Loaves in St. Mark's Gospel", *JTS* New Series 3, 1952, 161–171; C. Brown, "History and the Believer", in C. Brown, ed., *History, Criticism and Faith*, 1976; R. E. Brown, "Signs and Works", *The Gospel according to John* ,1, 1967, 525–32; "The Gospel Miracles", *New Testament Essays*, 1965, 168–91; and *The Virginal Conception*

& *Bodily Resurrection of Jesus*, 1973; A. B. Bruce, *The Miraculous Elements in the Gospels*, 1886; R. Bultmann, *The History of the Synoptic Tradition*, 1968[2]; and "The Question of Wonder", *Faith and Understanding*, 1, 1969, 247–61; J. M. Court, "The Philosophy of the Synoptic Miracles", *JTS* New Series 23, 1972, 1–15; J. D. M. Derrett, "Water into Wine" and "Peter's Penny", *Law in the New Testament*, 1970, 228–46 and 247–65; R. T. Fortna, *The Gospel of Signs: A Reconstruction of the Narrative Source Underlying the Fourth Gospel, Society for New Testament Studies Monograph Series* 11, 1970; R. H. Fuller, *Interpreting the Miracles*, 1963; A. de Groot, *The Bible on Miracles*, St Norbert Abbey Series 19, 1966; R. M. Grant, *Miracle and Natural Law in Graeco-Roman and Early Christian Thought* 1952; H. J. Held, "Matthew as Interpreter of the Miracle Stories", in G. Bornkamm, G. Barth and H. J. Held, *Tradition and Interpretation in Matthew*, 1963, 165–299; H. J. Helfmeyer, *'ôt, TDOT* I 167–88; R. F. Holland, "The Miraculous", *American Philosophical Quarterly*, 2, 1965 (reprinted in D. Z. Phillips, ed., *Religion and Understanding*, 1967, 155–70; E. Hoskyns and F. N. Davey, *The Riddle of the New Testament*, 1936[2], 145–57; D. Hume, "Of Miracles", Section X of Hume's *Philosophical Essays Concerning the Human Understanding*, 1748 (see the edition of *Hume's Enquiries: Concerning Human Understanding and Concerning the Principles of Morals*, edited by L. A. Selby-Bigge, revised by P. H. Nidditch, 1975); M. Inch, "Apologetic Use of 'Sign' in the Fourth Gospel", *EQ* 42, 1970, 35–43; J. Jeremias, *The Parables of Jesus*, 1963[2]; and *New Testament Theology*, I, 1971; J. Kallas, *The Significance of the Synoptic Miracles*, 1961; E. and M.-L. Keller, *Miracles in Dispute: A Continuing Debate*, 1969; H. Knight, "The Old Testament Concept of Miracle", *SJT* 5, 1952, 355–61; M. J. Langford, "The Problem of the 'Meaning' of Miracle", *Religious Studies* 7, 1971, 43–52; J. S. Lawton, *Miracles and Revelation*, 1959; C. S. Lewis, *Miracles*, 1947; H. van der Loos, *The Miracles of Jesus, Supplements to NovT* 8, 1965; S. V. McCasland, "Signs and Wonders", *JBL* 76, 1957, 149–52; and "Miracle", *IDB* III 392–402; J. F. Miller, "Is 'Miracle' an Intelligible Notion?", *SJT* 20, 1967, 25–36; L. Monden, *Signs and Wonders – A Study of the Miraculous Element in Religion*, 1966; L. Morris, "Miracles", *The Gospel according to John*, 1971, 684–91; C. F. D. Moule, ed., *Miracles: Cambridge Studies in their Philosophy and History*, 1965; J. B. Mozley, *Eight Lectures on Miracles*, Bampton Lectures for 1865, 1865; F. Mussner, *The Miracles of Jesus: An Introduction*, 1970; J. H. Newman, *Two Essays on Biblical and on Ecclesiastical Miracles*, (1870) 1892[10]; W. Nicol, *The Sēmeia in the Fourth Gospel: Tradition and Redaction, Supplements to NovT* 32, 1972; A. Oepke, *iaomai* etc., *TDNT* III 194–215; E. Pax, "Miracle", *EBT* II 584–89; F. S. Parham, "The Miracle at Cana", *EQ* 62, 1970, 107 ff.; I. T. Ramsey, G. H. Boobyer, M. C. Perry, H. J. Cadbury, *The Miracles and the Resurrection, SPCK Theological Collections*, 3, 1964; K. H. Rengstorf, *sēmeion* etc., *TDNT* VII 200–69; and *teras, TDNT* VIII 11326; A. Richardson, *The Miracle-Stories of the Gospels*, 1941; and *History: Sacred and Profane*, Bampton Lectures for 1962, 1964; P. Riga, "Signs of Glory. The Use of '*Sēmeion*' in St. John's Gospel", *Interpretation* 17, 1963, 402–24; R. Schnackenburg, "The Johannine Signs", in *The Gospel according to St John*, I, 1968, 515–28; and "Miracles in the New Testament and Modern Science", in *Present and Future: Modern Aspects of New Testament Theology*, 1966, 44–63; S. S. Smalley, "The Sign in John xxi", *NTS* 20, 1973–74, 275–88; R. D. Smith, *Comparative Miracles*, 1965; J. P. M. Sweet, "A Sign for Unbelievers: Paul's Attitude to Glossolalia", *NTS* 13, 1966–67, 240–57; R. Swinburne, *The Concept of Miracle*, 1970; F. R. Tennant, *Miracle & its Philosophical Presuppositions*, 1925; B. B. Warfield, *Counterfeit Miracles*, 1918 (reprinted as *Miracles: Yesterday and Today, True and False*, 1954).

(b). H. Baltensweiler, "Wunder und Glaube im Neuen Testament", *ThZ* 23, 1967, 241–56; J. Becker, "Wunder und Christologie", *NTS* 16, 1969–70, 130–48; L. Bieler, *Theios anēr. Das Bild des "göttlichen Menschen" in Spätantike und Frühchristentum*, I–II, 1935–36; D. Connolly, "Ad miracula sanationum apud Mt.", *Verbum Domini* 45, 1967, 306–25; G. Delling, "Das Verständnis des Wunders im Neuen Testament", *ZSTh* 24, 1955, 265–80; E. Fascher, *Kritik am Wunder*, 1960; P. Fiebig, *Jüdische Wundergeschichten des neutestamentlichen Zeitalters*, 1911; *Rabbinische Wundergeschichten*, (1911) 1933[2]; and *Antike Wundergeschichten*, (1911) 1921[2]; G. Fohrer, *Die symbolischen Handlungen der Propheten*, AThANT 54, 1953; A. Fridrichsen, *Le Problème du Miracle dans le Christianisme Primitif*, 1925; K. Gutbrod, *Die Wundergeschichten des Neuen Testaments*, 1967; J. Haspecker, "Wunder im Alten Testament", *Theologische Akademie* 2, 1965, 29–56; A. Heising, *Multiplicatio Panum: Die Botschaft der Brotvermehrung*, 1966; J. Hempel, *Heilung als Symbol und Wirklichkeit im biblischen Schrifttum, Nachrichten der Gesellschaft der Wissenschaften zu Göttingen, Philosophisch-historische Klasse* 3, 1958; C. A. Keller, *Das Wort* 'ôṯ als "Offenbarungszeichen Gottes". Ein philologisch-theologische Begriffsuntersuchung zum Alten Testament, 1946; B. Klappert, "Die Wunder Jesu im Neuen Testament", in Das Ungewöhnliche, Aussaat-Bücherei 45, 1969, 25 ff.; E. Linnemann, "Die Hochzeit zu Kana", NTS 20, 1973–74, 408–18; G. Mensching, Das Wunder im Glauben und Aberglauben der Völker, 1957; G. Mensching, W. Vollborn, E. Lohse, E. Käsemann, "Wunder", RGG³ VI 1831 ff.; R. Pesch, Jesu ureigene Taten? Ein Beitrag zur Wunderfrage, Questiones Disputatae 52, 1970; G. Quell, "Das Phänomen des Wunders im Alten Testament", in Verbannung und Heimkehr. Festschrift W. Rudolph, 1961, 253–300; R. Reitzenstein, Hellenistischen Wundererzählungen, 1906; R. Renner, Die Wunder Jesu in Theologie und Unterricht, 1966; J. Scharbert, "Was versteht das Alte Testament unter Wunder?" BuK 22, 1967, 37–46; G. Schille, Die urchristliche Wundertradition Ein Beitrag zur Frage nach dem irdischen Jesus, 1966; A. Schlatter, Das Wunder in der Synagoge, 1912; W. Schmithals, Wunder und Glaube. Eine Auslegung von Mk. 4, 35–6, 6a, BSt 59, 1970; J. P. Seierstad, W. Phillipp, K. Nitzschke, "Wunder", EKL III 1860 ff.; G. Siegmund, "Theologie des Wunders", Theologische Revue, 58, 1962, 289 ff.; A. Smitmans, Das Weinwunder von Kana. Die Auslegung von Joh. ii. 1–11 bei den Vätern und Heute, 1966; G. Stählin, "Die Gleichnishandlungen Jesu", in Kosmos und Ekklesia, Festschrift W. Stählin, 1953, 9 ff.; F. Stolz, 'ôṯ, THAT I 91–95; A. Suhl, Die Wunder Jesu, 1968; O. Weinreich, Antike Heilungswunder, 1909.

Moses

| $M\omega\ddot{\upsilon}\sigma\tilde{\eta}\varsigma$ | $M\omega\ddot{\upsilon}\sigma\tilde{\eta}\varsigma$ (Mōÿsēs), Moses.

OT 1. The Gk. form of the name (from the LXX on) probably originates from Egyptian sources. The first syllable (Mōÿ-) renders a Coptic, not a Heb. ō-sound (Pauly-Wissowa, XVI, 1, 360). The Heb. mōšeh is prob. to be derived from old Egyptian ms(y), with the meaning "son" (cf. Thutmosis, Son of Thoth). Moses is a short form of the name without the element of the name of the god (cf. S. Herrmann, "Mose", EvTh 28, 1968, 303 f.).

2. The following reconstruction represents a cross-section of scholarly opinion. The older OT tradition characterizes Moses as the charismatic leader of a nomadic group of people which had been thrown together from various elements, and which had been condemned to forced labour in the towns of Pithom and Ra'amses (Exod. 1:11). Through Moses' contacts with the nomadic Midianites (2:15 f.; 3:1–4:20), this group of Hebrews eventually fled from → Egypt (14:5). The destruction in the sea of a troop of Egyptian war-chariots which had been sent out to pursue them led to the call of this group of nomads by the God Yahweh, whose action the prophetess Miriam had seen in the event (15:20 f.). For the duration of a generation this group appears to have continued to live in the desert, before it decided to emigrate into another cultural territory. During this period of time it had its central shrine at Sinai; but, in addition, visited the shrines of the Mountain of God and of Massah-Meribah (Kadesh). Moses stands here on a level with the patriarchs, even though he had to lead a presumably numerically stronger group.

Before the exile, Mosaic tradition appears to have played a rôle only in the northern kingdom; it gained its fundamental significance through the association of Moses with the giving of the religious legislation in the Book of the Covenant (Exod. 20:22–23:20), linking on with the ancient note in Exod. 32:16. With the increasing significance of divine justice went a growth in the significance of Moses. He appears in the Deuteronomic law-code as the great law-giver, who shows

635

Israel the way of life and death. These traditions became important in the post-exilic restoration under Ezra, where the law was expounded as the essential basis of Judah's existence. Thus Moses was revered as the central Revealer of Israel. The Prophets, who mention Moses only rarely and in insignificant contexts (such as Jer. 15:1; Mic. 6:4; Isa. 65:1; Hos. 12:14), now become messengers of God's demand for obedience, as the Deuteronomistic history shows.   *H. Seebass*

3. Although the above account represents a marked advance upon the position once held that Moses could not be regarded as a historical figure, the Bible itself represents the life of Moses in much greater detail. In Stephen's speech in Acts his life was divided into three periods of forty years spent respectively in Egypt, Arabia and finally in leading Israel through the wilderness (Acts 7:23, 30, 36).

The Book of Exodus sets the birth of Moses in the context of the history of the descendants of Joseph who remained in Egypt after his death. Whereas they had once been favoured on his account, there arose "a new king over Egypt, who did not know Joseph" (Exod. 1:8), and fearing the growth of the Israelites subjected them to slavery, setting them to work on the store cities of Pithom and Ra'amses (Exod. 1:11). At the time of his birth there was a decree commanding the slaying of all male Israelites at birth (Exod. 1:16, 22). However, Moses who was born into a Levite family (Exod. 2:1) was saved by being hidden in a basket among the reeds along the bank of the Nile, being adopted by Pharaoh's daughter (Exod. 2:1–10). His name is explained in v. 10 from the vb. *māšâh*, draw out (cf. Jos. 8:6; 2 Sam. 22:17), "for she said 'Because I drew him out of the water.'" His own mother served as his nurse.

As a young man, he killed an Egyptian who was beating a fellow Israelite, and was forced to flee for his life (Exod. 2:11–15). He fled to the land of Midian in the Arabian Peninsula, where he adopted the nomadic way of life, marrying Zipporah, the daughter of Reuel or Jethro (cf. Exod. 2:18 with 3:1), a priest of Midian, who bore him a son, Gershom (Exod. 2:16–22). The latter's name is explained from the noun *gēr*, sojourner, "for he said, 'I have been a sojourner in a foreign land'" (2:22). Moses was summoned from his nomadic existence by Yahweh who had heard the groaning of his people in → Egypt (Exod. 2:23 ff.). He revealed himself to Moses in the theophany of the burning bush at Horeb, "the mountain of God", declaring his name (→ God, art. *theos*, OT 2) and commissioning him to lead his people out of Egypt to the land of the Canaanites, Hittites, Amorites, Perizzites, Hivites and Jebusites, "a land flowing with milk and honey" (Exod. 3:1–22). Initially Moses was to ask Pharaoh to let the people go three days' journey into the wilderness to sacrifice to Yahweh. When Moses hesitated to assume this daunting task, he was given signs (Exod. 4:1–9) and permitted to let Aaron, his brother, be his spokesman (Exod. 4:10–17). Moses then took his wife and son whom he had omitted to → circumcise, though this was rectified by his wife (Exod. 2:18–26), and joined Aaron. Together they delivered Yahweh's call to the people of Israel who responded in faith (Exod. 2:27–31).

Together Moses and Aaron confronted Pharaoh with the request to let the people go three days' journey into the wilderness to sacrifice to Yahweh. In response Pharaoh redoubled the burdens of the Israelites (Exod. 5:1–23). In despair Moses reproached Yahweh for this impossible task but received the renewed promise of

636

Yahweh's help (Exod. 6:1–7:7). At the time Moses was eighty and Aaron eighty-three years old (Exod. 7:7). Then followed the contest between Moses and Pharaoh in which the ten great plagues were sent on Egypt: the Nile was turned to "blood" (Exod. 7:19–25), i.e. blood colour caused by some chemical pollution which doubtless led to other plagues; the plague of frogs (Exod. 8:1–14); that of lice (Exod. 8:16–19; RSV "gnats"); that of flies (Exod. 8:20–32); that of the cattle (Exod. 9:1–7); that of boils (Exod. 9:8–12); that of hail (Exod. 9:13–35); that of the locusts (Exod. 10:1–20); that of darkness (Exod. 10:21–29); and the slaying of the firstborn (Exod. 11:1–12:30); though Israelite families were spared as they celebrated the Passover for the first time (Exod. 12:1–28). (On the plagues see K. A. Kitchen, "Plagues of Egypt", *NBD*, 1001 ff.; W. White, "Plagues of Egypt", *ZPEB* IV 804–7.) At this point Pharaoh relented and the exodus commenced (Exod. 12:31 ff.).

According to Exod. 13:17 f., the route taken avoided a possible clash with the Philistines lest the Israelites should be daunted and turn back. God "led the people round by the way of the wilderness of the Red Sea", carrying the bones of Joseph with them (v. 19). They were guided by a pillar of cloud by day and a pillar of fire by night. (On the route of the exodus see K. A. Kitchen, "Exodus", *NBD* 402 ff.; C. De Wit, *The Date and Route of the Exodus*, 1960; and G. I. Davies, "The Wilderness Itineraries", *TB* 25, 1974, 48–81. On the NT interpretation see R. E. Nixon, *The Exodus in the New Testament*, 1963.) Places mentioned along the route are: Marah, where the bitter waters were sweetened (Exod. 15:23); Elim, where there were twelve wells of water and seventy palm trees (Exod. 15:27); the wilderness of Sin, where the people grumbled for want of food and were supplied with quails (→ Bird) and manna (→ Bread) (Exod. 16); and Rephidim, where the smitten rock of Horeb gave water (Exod. 17:1–7). At Rephidim they were attacked by the Amalekites and defeated them through the intercession of Moses whose arms were upheld by Aaron and Hur (Exod. 17:8–16). Thereafter Moses was joined by Jethro who brought with him Zipporah, Gershom and his other son, Eliezer (from *'elî*, my God, and *'ēzer*, help, "for he said, 'The God of my father was my help, and delivered me from the sword of Pharaoh' ", 18:4). At Jethro's suggestion Moses appointed rulers of thousands, hundreds, fifties and tens to assist in judging the people (Exod. 18:24 ff.).

After Rephidim Israel encamped before Mount Sinai where Moses and the people prepared to receive a fresh revelation (Exod. 19:1–13). Here he received the Ten Commandments (Exod. 19:14–20:17; → Command). After reading to the people the laws of the community (Exod. 21:1–23:33), Moses renewed the → covenant between Yahweh and Israel (Exod. 24). Details of the tabernacle and its contents were given to Moses by God (Exod. 25–31; → Tent). While Moses was with Yahweh on Mount Sinai the people turned back to the worship of the gods, symbolized in the golden calf made by Aaron which Moses destroyed on his return (Exod. 32). Moses' indignation led him to break the tables of the law which he had made (Exod. 32:19). The → glory of Yahweh was revealed to Moses, although he was not allowed to see Yahweh's face directly (Exod. 33:12–23). The tables of the law were renewed (Exod. 34:1–4), and the covenant further renewed (Exod. 34:10–27). After this forty day sojourn on the Mount Moses returned with the tables, his shining face covered by a veil (Exod. 34:28–35). The remainder of the book of Exodus tells how Moses superintended the erection of the tabernacle (chs. 35–40).

Leviticus (1:1) names Moses as the one to whom Yahweh gave the numerous statutes for cultic → sacrifice (chs. 1–7), and for the consecration of Aaron and his sons for the priesthood (chs. 8–9). Judgment fell on Nadab and Abihu for offering unholy → fire before Yahweh (Lev. 10). Lev. 11–27 contains numerous regulations governing religious and daily life. Each chapter begins: "And the LORD said to Moses", some adding "and Aaron", especially those concerning cultic matters.

The Book of Numbers represents Yahweh's continuing dealings with Israel through Moses. In ch. 1 Moses is charged with numbering the people. Ch. 2 gives their camping and marching order. Through Moses the → Levites are assigned their particular tasks (chs. 3 and 4). Through Moses directions are given concerning unclean persons, trespass, Nazirites etc. (chs. 5 and 6). Num. 7 describes how Moses received dedicatory gifts from the leaders of the tribes. It was Moses who consecrated the Levites (Num. 8). Num. 9:1–10:10 describes the preparations for the onward journey which recommences with Num. 10:11. Features of the journey narrative in Num. are: the fire at Taberah which was quenched at Moses' intercession (Num. 11:1–3); the appointment of seventy elders to assist Moses (Num. 11:10–30); the sedition of Miriam and Aaron on account of Moses' Cushite wife (Num. 12:1–16); the mission of the spies (Num. 13–14); the rebellion of Korah, Dathan and Abiram (Num. 16); the sprouting of Aaron's rod (Num. 17); the smiting of the rock at Meribah which yielded water at a time of drought (Num. 20:1–14); the deaths of Miriam (Num. 20:1) and Aaron (Num. 20:22–29); the plague of the serpents (Num. 21; → Dragon, art. *ophis*); the abortive attempt of Balak to make Balaam → curse Israel (Num. 22–24); the worship of the Baal of Peor and the sexual relations of the people with the Midianites (Num. 25); the census (Num. 26); the appointment of Joshua as Moses' successor (Num. 27); the command to make war on the Midianites (Num. 31); the assignment of the inheritance to the Reubenites and Gadites (Num. 32); the description of the stages of the journey and arrangements for the allocation of the promised land (Num. 33–36). Interspersed with this narrative are further cultic regulations.

Deuteronomy contains a resumé of the journey and various statutes from the perspective of Moses (Deut. 1:1; cf. 31:24). It is presented as Moses' farewell address and concludes with his blessing (Deut. 33). Moses was permitted to see the promised land from Mount Pisgah, but not to enter it (Deut. 34) on account of his sin at Meribah (Num. 20:12). Deut. 18:15 contains the promise: "The Lord your God will raise up for you a prophet like me from among you, from your brethren – him you shall heed." In the NT this was given a christological interpretation (Acts 3:22 f.; 7:37; on the subsequent Jewish interpretation of Deut. 18:15 in both a messianic and a non-messianic sense see J. Jeremias, *Mōÿsēs*, *TDNT* IV 857 ff.). Deut. itself concludes with the declaration: "And there has not arisen a prophet since in Israel like Moses, whom the Lord knew face to face, none like him for the signs and the wonders which the Lord sent him to do. . . ." (Deut. 34:10 f.).

The authorship of the Pentateuch was traditionally ascribed to Moses, except of course the account of his death. The following passages are explicitly ascribed to him: the historical and legal narrative of Deut. 1:1–31:23; the song of Moses

(Deut. 32:1–43); the blessing of Moses (Deut. 33:1–29); and Ps. 90. After the defeat of the Amalekites Moses was commanded to write a memorial in a book that God would blot out all remembrance of them under heaven (Exod. 17:14). Exod. 24:4 reports that "Moses wrote all the words of the Lord." He delivered the Ten Commandments (Exod. 20:1–17; cf. Deut. 5:5–21). Exod. 24:7 refers to the "Book of the Covenant" which Moses read to the people. According to Num. 33:2, Moses wrote down all the camp sites by divine command. According to Deut. 31:9, "Moses wrote this law, and gave it to the priests the sons of Levi, who carried the ark of the covenant of the Lord, and to all the elders of Israel" (cf. 31:24 ff.). It was to be read to all Israel every seven years (Deut. 31:11). In addition, Moses commanded the law to be written on stones to be set up on Mount Ebal by the Israelites when they had passed over the Jordan (Deut. 27:2–8; cf. Jos. 8:30–35). Various warnings are given against not keeping "all the words of the law written in this book" (Deut. 28:58; cf. 28:61; 29:19 f., 26; 30:10). Genesis, however, contains no reference to Moses as its author.

The remaining reference to Moses in the OT occur chiefly in Jos. (1:1–17; 3:7; 4:10 ff.; 8:31–35; 9:24; 11:12–23; 12:6; 13:8–33; 14:2–11; 17:4; 18:7; 20:2; 21:2, 8; 22:2–9; 23:6; 24:5). He figures occasionally in other historical books (Jdg. 1:16, 20; 3:4; 4:11; 1 Sam. 12:6, 8; 1 Ki. 2:3; 8:9, 53, 56; 2 Ki. 14:6; 18:4, 6, 12; 21:8; 23:25; 1 Chron. 6:3, 49; 15:15; 21:29; 22:13; 23:13 ff.; 2 Chron. 1:3; 5:10; 8:13; 23:18; 24:6, 9; 25:4; 30:16; 33:8; 34:14; 35:6, 12; Ezra. 3:2; 6:18; 7:6; Neh. 1:7 f.; 8:1, 14; 9:14; 10:29; 13:1. Outside the historical books the name of Moses is mentioned in Pss. 77:20; 90 (title); 99:6; 103:7; 105:26; 106:16, 23, 32; Isa. 63:11 f.; Jer. 15:1; Dan. 9:11, 13; Mic. 6:4; and Mal. 4:4. Many of these passages, especially in the historical books, refer to what Yahweh has said or commanded through Moses.   *C. Brown*

4. In the Hellenistic world, information about Moses is found almost without exception in anti-Jewish utterances. As the Jews in general, so Moses was reckoned as an Egyptian (a priest from Heliopolis). He was regarded as law-giver, organizer of the nation (the twelve tribes), and founder of the Jewish state, its capital and temple. Since, in Judaism outside Jerusalem, there was no longer any sacrificial cult, Jews were regarded now as *atheoi*, those who did not give the gods their due respect, and as demon-worshippers. Moses was viewed as the scorner of every cult, or as a magician and a deceiver – his name was often used in magical formulas. Hecataeus and Posidonius alone spoke of Moses in terms of admiration. Hecataeus praised Moses for having venerated heaven as God without any images; and Posidonius relates that, though Moses had been an Egyptian priest, he left Egypt voluntarily, because their anthropomorphic and theriomorphic concepts of divinity did not correspond with his. He founded a society originally free from law (the Jewish Law provided a major stumbling-block for the whole Hellenistic world) and worshipped "what we collectively call heaven, the universe and nature" (I. Heinemann, "Moses", Pauly-Wissowa, XVI, 1, 361 ff.). See further W. A. Meeks, *The Prophet-King: Moses Traditions and the Johannine Christology, Supplements to NovT* 14, 1967.

5. Hellenistic Judaism produced its apologies in reply. Following the Gk. scientific method, they concluded that agreement implied original borrowing; and

so, since the Hellenistic world regarded Egyptian culture as the most ancient, the apologists attributed this to the patriarchs, and also extolled Moses as the discoverer of writing (cf. Eusebius, *Praep.Ev.* 9, 27). The rise and growth of the so-called Moses-romance is important. According to this, Egyptian magicians prophesied to Pharaoh the birth of a man who would save the Jews and defeat the Egyptians. For this reason he ordered all the children to be killed. But a childless daughter of Pharaoh rescued Moses and gave him an Egyptian name (Pauly-Wissowa XVI, 1, 367 ff.).

6. Throughout Palestinian Judaism Moses was the revealer without equal. For the Rabbis, the prophets were simply the bearers of the oral tradition which Moses received at Sinai. Their successors were the scribes (*TDNT* VI 817 ff.; cf. Matt. 23:2). Moses and his age were counted as the pattern of the messianic age, in accordance with the conception of the second exodus as marking the inauguration of salvation. As Moses suffered, so also the redeemer will suffer. According to R. Akiba, the messiah would hunger and thirst forty years in the wilderness. Before manifesting himself he would sojourn in Rome, the city of the enemies, as Moses sojourned in Egypt, and return from there like Moses' wife and sons (Exod. 4:20) (cf. *TDNT* IV 860 f.; SB III 824 ff.). In Qumran Moses is also often named and celebrated as a law-giver of Israel (e.g. 1QS 1:3; 5:8; 8:15, 22; 1QM 10:6; 1QH 17:12; 1Q22 1:1, 11; 2:5, 11; 4:3; 4Qflor 2:3; 4Qtest 1; 6QD 3:4; CD 5:8, 18, 21; 8:14; 15:2, 9, 12; 16:2, 5; 19:26; cf. W. A. Meeks, op. cit.).

NT In the NT Moses is the most frequently-mentioned OT figure. Jesus shook the foundations of contemporary Judaism by coming forward as a revealer like Moses, not as his interpreter, as the OT prophets had been, but distinct from him, preaching and living in the name of the final arrival of the → kingdom of God. The NT tradition presents the relationship between Moses and Christ in differing ways.

1. *Mark*. Moses is recognized as law-giver (1:44). His law establishes the resurrection of the dead, as against the Sadducees (12:19, 26); and establishes the commandment of Exod. 20:12, as against scribal tradition (Mk. 7:10 f.; in v. 14 f. Jesus reveals his new authority). At the transfiguration, → Elijah and Moses appear; they both suffered (as Jesus does now) under the hatred of their own people (9:4 f.), on account of their commission. Peter misunderstands the heavenly appearance, thinking that it is an earthly one, and that the new period in the wilderness has begun, since the three eschatological figures of Moses, Elijah and the messiah are here united (see Jn. 1:21, 25; cf. CD 9:11; 4Qtest. 5 ff.).

2. *Matthew* sees a close correspondence between Jesus and Moses. On the birth narrative (2:1–23) cf. the details and the shape of the Moses-tradition (see above OT 2), and the reference to → Egypt as the place to which they fled (cf. Matt. 2:20 with Exod. 4:19; and 1:15 with Hos. 11:1; → Fullness, art. *plēroō*). Jesus stayed in the wilderness for forty days without food and drink, as did Moses on Sinai (4:1 f.; cf. Exod. 34:28). Above all, Jesus is the new law-giver (cf. 5:1 with law given from Sinai, Exod. 19 and 20), who, like Moses, dispenses → blessing (5:3 ff.) and → curse (23:13 ff.). The Mosaic teaching-office of the scribes is recognized (23:2 f.), but at the same time superseded in that, under the guidance of Jesus, one is to display a better righteousness than the → Pharisees (5:17–20). (See further

the discussion of Jesus in relation to the Pentateuch, the exodus and Moses in W. D. Davies, *The Setting of the Sermon on the Mount*, 1964, 14–108.)

3. *Luke* sees Jesus' connection with Moses as given in the function of the prophet. Acts 3:22 and 7:37 quote Deut. 18:15 cf. 18: "a prophet like me [Moses]". As Moses was mighty both in word and deed (7:22), so Jesus was a mighty → prophet before God and the people (Lk. 24:19; cf. 7:16; 4:24; 13:33). Like Moses, Jesus gives chosen men a share in his power and Spirit (10:1, 17 ff.), the seventy (or seventy-two; on the *v.l.* see Metzger, 150 f.), and later, above and beyond Moses, to the whole church. As Moses suffered (Acts 7:25 ff.), and as the people disowned him, even though God had sent him as a ruler and redeemer (7:35), so Jesus had to be consigned to death, according to Moses and the prophets, by the chief priests and scribes, and be raised by God to be ruler (Lk. 24:27, 44; cf. Acts 26:22; 28:23). Whoever, therefore, does not listen to Moses and the prophets will also not believe the resurrected One (Lk. 16:29–31). It is not true that Stephen (Acts 6:11 ff.) and Paul (21:20 ff.; cf. also 18:18; 21:24 ff.) preached a regression from the "customs" of Moses: freedom from the requirement of circumcision was demanded by Paul, with Peter's concurrence, only for the non-Jews (15:1–21; cf. 16:3). But the righteousness of faith, which Jesus gives as a gift, Moses' law could not bring (13:38).

4. *Paul* places Moses and Christ in antithesis to one another. As law-giver (Rom. 5:14; 1 Cor. 9:9), Moses gives only the letter (*gramma*) – the man who fulfills the righteousness of the law will live (Rom. 10:5). It is in this way that Paul expresses Moses' "dispensation of death"; it possesses only a fading glory (2 Cor. 3:7; cf. Gal. 3:17 ff.). By way of contrast, the "dispensation of the righteousness which leads to faith" (2 Cor. 2:9) possesses the → Spirit (*pneuma*) and a permanent glory (eisegesis of Exod. 34:29 ff.). The "dispensations" represent synagogue and → church. To this day the Jews have a "veil over the heart" when "Moses" is read (v. 15). But the new Israel beholds the glory of the Lord "with unveiled face" and is transformed from one degree of glory to another. All this comes from the Lord who is the Spirit (3:17 f.). If Israel would open his heart to the Lord, the veil would disappear (v. 16), and Moses would be recognized as a witness to the righteousness of God. God chooses solely on the basis of his promise, not on the basis of human zeal (Rom. 9:15 f.); the calling of the Gentiles shows that Israel's law creates no privilege in God's sight (10:19). Baptism into Moses (a formation built on the analogy of "baptism into Jesus") was a promise, not a natural law. Those baptized did indeed receive the gifts of the Spirit, but since they did not remain within the promise, they perished (1 Cor. 10:2–5).

5. *John* stands starkly opposed to Judaism. The teaching of Jesus which interprets the Scriptures comes directly from God, not from their own study (7:15 f.). Anyone who wants to do God's will – the first commandment, not the individual commandments! – will know whether the teaching is from God (v. 17). But none of the Jews keep the law, for they base their lives on its letter and not, as the law itself demands, on God and his revealer (v. 19). Moses' law, as such, is surpassed by Jesus (1:17). Nevertheless, it accuses the Jews before God, because it witnesses (5:39, 45 ff.) to the revealer who will be like Moses (Deut. 18:15, 18). The people rightly recognize that Jesus is the promised prophet (6:14), but in trying to make him king they fail to understand that his kingdom is not of this world (18:36). The

leaders of the people call themselves Moses' disciples (9:28), but in untruth. For the new revealer has come (1:17), and he is the true bread of life; those who ate the bread Moses gave them died (6:32–35, 48–51). Moses lifted up the serpent in the wilderness to preserve people's earthly lives; but when Jesus is "lifted up", everyone who believes in him will have eternal life (3:14 ff.; → Dragon, art. *ophis*).

6. *Hebrews* stresses that the pattern given by Moses has been surpassed and fulfilled in Christ. Jesus' faithfulness is greater than Moses', because he, as the Son, came from God's high heaven, and is not only, like Moses, a servant in God's house (3:2 ff.). Jesus is the High Priest in the heavenly sanctuary, which Moses once saw and of which he tried to build the earthly copy (8:5). The church of Christ is not led to Sinai which terrified Moses with its fire and smoke, lightning and thunder (12:18 f.): it can approach with confidence. Even it must not refuse him who is speaking (12:25) for judgment awaits those who spurn God. Moses is pictured in 11:23 ff. as a pattern for faith, even in suffering. In 3:16 he is recalled as the leader out of Egypt; and in 7:14 and the law-giver.

7. There are three further isolated references in the NT. In Rev. 15:3 the passing through the sea is a pattern for the deliverance of the saints from suffering in the last days. The fragment of Jude 9 is based on later traditions preserved in the apocryphal Assumption of Moses and various fathers which said that Satan fought with Michael when over the body of Moses (cf. E. M. B. Green, *The Second Epistle General of Peter and the General Epistle of Jude* , 1968, 169 f.; J. N. D. Kelly, *A Commentary on the Epistles of Peter and Jude*, 1969, 264 f.; cf. also *TDNT* IV 854 f.). In 2 Tim. 3:8, Jannes and Jambres were the Egyptian magicians, according to the Moses-romance, who imitated the miracle of turning a staff into a serpent (see SB I 660 ff.). Their names are not mentioned in the account of Exod. 7:11 (cf. C. Spicq, *Les Epîtres Pastorales*, 1947, 370 ff.).   *H. Seebass*

→ Command, → Egypt, → Israel, → Law, → People, → Wilderness

(a). E. Arden, "How Moses Failed God", *JBL* 76, 1957, 50 ff.; E. Auerbach, *Moses*, 1953; B. W. Bacon, *Studies in Matthew*, 1930; D. Beegle, *Moses, the Servant of Yahweh*, 1972; J. Bright, *A History of Israel*, (1960) 1972; M. Buber, *Moses*, 1947; G. I. Davies, "The Wilderness Itineraries", *TB* 25, 1974, 46–81; W. D. Davies, *The Setting of the Sermon on the Mount*, 1964, 25–108; D. Daube, *The New Testament and Rabbinic Judaism*, 1956, 5–12; and *The Exodus Pattern in the Bible*, 1963; W. Eichrodt, *Theology of the Old Testament*, 1, 1961, 189–96; G. Fohrer, *History of Israelite Religion*, 1973, 66–86; S. Freud, *Moses and Monotheism*, 1939; J. G. Gager, *Moses in Greco-Roman Paganism*, 1972; T. F. Glasson, *Moses in the Fourth Gospel*, SBT 40, 1963; J. Jeremias, *Mōÿsēs*, *TDNT* IV 848–73; R. F. Johnson, "Moses", *IDB* III 440–50; T. Keneally, *Moses the Law-giver*, 1976; G. D. Kilpatrick, *The Origins of the Gospel according to St. Matthew*, 1946; K. A. Kitchen, "Moses", *NBD* 843–50; M. G. Kyle, *Moses and the Monuments*, 1920; J. MacDonald, "The Samaritan Doctrine of Moses", *SJT* 13, 1960, 149–62; W. A. Meeks, *The Prophet-King: Moses Traditions and the Johannine Christology*, Supplements to NovT 14, 1967; A. Neher, *Moses and the Vocation of the Jewish People*, 1959; R. E. Nixon, *The Exodus in the New Testament*, 1963; M. Noth, *A History of the Pentateuch Traditions*, 1972; G. von Rad, *Old Testament Theology*, I, 1962, 289 ff.; and *The Problems of the Hexateuch and Other Essays*, 1965; M. Rist, "Moses, Assumption of", *IDB* III 450 f.; H. H. Rowley, *From Joseph to Joshua*, 1950; "Moses and the Decalogue", in *Men of God*, 1963, 1–36; and *From Moses to Qumran: Studies in the Old Testament*, 1963; O. Schilling, "Moses", *EBT* II 593–96; H. M. Teeple, *The Mosaic Eschatological Prophet*, JBL Monograph Series, 1957; I. H. Weisfeld, *This Man Moses*, 1966; G. Widengren, "What do we know about Moses?", in J. I. Durham and J. R. Porter, eds., *Proclamation and Presence: Old Testament Essays in Honour of Gwynne Henton Davies*, 1970, 21–47; F. V. Winnett, *The Mosaic Tradition*, 1949; C. De Wit, *The Date and Route of the Exodus*, 1960.
(b). C. Barth, "Mose, Knecht Gottes", in *Parrhesia. Karl Barth zum achtzigsten Geburtstag*, 1966,

68–81; H. Cazelles *et al.*, *Moïse, L'Homme de l'Alliance*, 1955; H. Gressmann, *Mose und seine Zeit*, 1913; A. H. J. Gunneweg, "Mose in Midian", *ZTK* 61, 1964, 1 ff.; I. Heinemann, "Moses", Pauly-Wissowa, XVI, 1, 359–75; S. Hermann, "Mose", *EvTh* 28, 1968; 301 ff.; K. Kastner, *Moses im Neuen Testament*, dissertation, 1967; C. A. Keller, "Vom Stand und Aufgabe der Moseforschung", *ThZ* 13, 1957; H. Kremers, "Mose", *EKL* II 1458 ff.; E. Osswald, "Moses", *RGG*³ IV 1151 ff.; and *Das Bild Mose*, 1962; H. Schmid, *Mose. Überlieferung und Geschichte*, *BZAW* 110, 1968; H. Seebass, *Mose und Aaron, Sinai und Gottesberg*, 1962; E. Sellin, *Mose und seine Bedeutung für die israelitisch-jüdische Religionsgeschichte*, 1922; R. Smend, *Das Mosebild von Heinrich Ewald bis Martin Noth*, 1959; F. Stier and E. Beck, *Moses in Schrift und Überlieferung*, 1963; P. Volz, *Mose und sein Werk*, 1932².

Myth

μῦθος

μῦθος (*mythos*), myth, story.

CL In Homer *mythos* is used of any kind of speech (e.g. *mythoisi kekasthai, Od.* 7, 157, means to be skilled in speech) and sometimes even of unspoken thought, a plan conceived in the mind (e.g. *echet' en phresi mython, Od.* 15, 445, "you have a plan in your mind"). More particularly it is used of a story, whether true or false (*all' age moi tou paidos agauou mython enispes, Od.* 11, 92, "come, tell me the news of that noble son of mine"). In this usage there is no distinction between *mythos* and *logos* (→ Word); cf. Aeschylus, *Persae* 713, *akousei mython en brachei logō*, "you will hear a story in brief utterance [in few words]." But as early as Pindar a distinction appears between *mythos*, fiction, and *logos*, factual narrative: "popular report which exceeds the true account [*logos*]" tends to consist of "tales [*mythoi*] decked out with variegated lies" which "lead people astray" (*Ol.* 1, 28 f.), and even Homer's lore "deceives people, leading them astray with tales [*mythoi*]" (*Nem.* 7, 23).

Thucydides mentions the story-telling propensity (*to mythōdes*) of the chroniclers (*logographoi*) who preceded him, whose aim was "to please the ear rather than to speak the truth"; by contrast, he allowed that readers might be put off by the lack of this feature (*to mē mythōdes*) in his own work, but claimed that his aim was to provide an everlasting possession rather than a passing pleasure (*History* 1, 21 f.). Among those predecessors he may have had in mind Herodotus, who believed that a good story was worth recording, whether it was credible or incredible, like the "silly fable [*euēthēs mythos*]" which, he says, the Greeks tell about Heracles's adventures in Egypt (*Hist.* 2, 45).

The *mythos* plays a special part in Plato's exposition of truth. When philosophical debate leads him so far on his quest but cannot proceed further, the poet in Plato takes over and expresses in the form of an imaginative story or parable the insight which is the goal of his quest. His mythopoeic workmanship is indebted to the myths of epic poetry and to those of Orphism and the Eleusinian mysteries, but the Platonic myth has a quality of its own. Examples are the two myths of Eros (*Symp.* 189c–193d; 202d–212a), and those of creation (*Tim.* 29d–92b), of the world to come (*Gorgias* 523a–524a) and of the judgment of the dead (*Rep.* 10, 614a–621d).

The word *mythos* was a technical term in classical Greek for the plot of a tragedy or comedy (Aristotle, *Poetics* 1449 b 5; 1450 a 4; 1451 a 16). This usage probably goes back to the time when these art-forms were wholly religious: the *mythos* or

643

hieros logos was a sacred story involving the gods, and the *drama* (from *draō*, do, act) was the ritual enactment of the story, each being necessary to the other and to the whole production.

OT This last use of *mythos* in classical Greek has been thought to be applicable to the world of the OT. The vocabulary of Greek dramatic tradition has been taken over in the 20th century by the "myth and ritual" school of Near Eastern religious history ("school" being used here in a very imprecise sense). T. H. Gaster, for example, has explained the religious texts from Ugarit as the *mythoi* of seasonal rites of "emptying" and "filling" which he tries to reconstruct (*Thespis*, 1950). Some scholars have postulated a ritual pattern over a great area of the ancient Near East, exemplified in the *Akitu* or New Year festival in Babylon and in a reconstructed festival of the enthronement of Yahweh at the autumnal Feast of Tabernacles in Israel. In this pattern the myth of the dying and rising god (representing originally such phenomena as the annual withering and revival of vegetation) figured prominently; in the ritual his place was supposedly taken by the king, worsted in ritual combat, dethroned and humiliated, but subsequently restored to life and power. The king might be regarded as the embodiment of the god (divine kingship) or as his mediatorial representative among the people (sacral kingship). References to the king in the Psalms have been freely interpreted in terms of this hypothesis (e.g. in Ps. 89:38–45 he is ritually vanquished and banished to the underworld; in Ps. 18 he returns thanks for his deliverance from the power of death; in Pss. 2 and 110 he is reinstated on his throne). That the *kingship* of Yahweh was festally celebrated in Israel is certain: "God has gone up with a shout; Yahweh with the sound of a trumpet" (Ps. 47:5) points to some action suitable to the words. But it is much more likely that in such a celebration the sacred ark, not the king, represented the divine presence.

In a more general way, the narrative of Exod. 1–15 has been viewed as the "story" accompanying and explaining the annual passover meal (cf. J. Pedersen, *Israel* III–IV, 1940, 726); but if so, the story is not a seasonal myth but the record of a deliverance accomplished once in Israel's national history and annually commemorated thereafter, so that successive generations might "re-live" the event. (We may compare the reading or recitation of part of the passion narrative in the course of the holy communion; that is the story which explains the commemorative action.)

In LXX *mythos* appears very seldom, and never in books translated from the Hebrew Bible. In Sir. 20:19 (in a section for which no Heb. text is extant) an ungracious man is compared to "a story told at the wrong time [*mythos akairos*], which is continually on the lips of the ignorant." In Bar. 3:23 "the story-tellers [*mythologoi*] and the seekers for understanding have not learned the way to wisdom". In both these places the word has its most general sense of "story". In Wis. 17:4(A) *mythos* appears as a meaningless scribal error for *mychos*, inner chamber ("not even the inner chamber that held them protected them from fear").

NT In NT *mythos* is found only in the Pastoral Epistles and 2 Peter, and always in a disparaging sense. Timothy is told to forbid "certain persons" at Ephesus to "occupy themselves with myths and endless genealogies which promote speculations" (1 Tim. 1:4). Irenaeus (*Haer.* 1, praef.), followed by Tertullian (*De praescr.*

644

7; 33; *Adv.Val.* 3) supposed this to be a reference to the cosmological genealogies of Valentinianism. The context of the Pastorals, however, suggests a Jewish element in these myths; cf. the injunction to "avoid stupid controversies, genealogies, dissensions, and quarrels over the law" (Tit. 3:9). Perhaps a mixture of Jewish and incipient gnostic speculation is indicated, as in the mythical Ophite genealogies mentioned by Irenaeus (*Haer.* 1, 30, 9). The "profane and old wives' fables" (*mythoi*) of 1 Tim. 4:7 (so AV; RSV has the less colourful "godless and silly myths") are probably of the same sort (cf. Plato, *Rep.* 1, 350c, *tais grausi tais tous mythous legousais*, "the old women who tell fables"), as are the "myths" into which hearers with "itching ears" are led astray by false teachers (2 Tim. 4:4) or the "Jewish myths" to which the Cretan Christians must be admonished to turn a deaf ear (Tit. 3:14). These myths are set in contrast to "the truth"; they are subversive of sound faith. The gospel belongs to quite a different category: it is a record of fact, for "we did not follow cleverly devised myths when we made known to you the power and coming of our Lord Jesus Christ, but we were eyewitnesses . . ." (2 Pet. 1:16).

A new aspect of myth in relation to NT story was opened up with the launching in 1941 of the "demythologizing programme" specially associated with the name of R. Bultmann (see bibliography). Bultmann's thesis, in brief, is that if the gospel is to make its proper impact today, it must be freed from those features which belong to the world-view of the culture in which it was first preached and presented in terms which will expose the hearers immediately to its challenge and its "offence". These dispensable features include not only the three-decker universe but the concept of our world as open to invasion by transcendent powers – including such credal elements as the pre-existent Christ, his being sent into this world by the Father, his historical resurrection, and the personal activity of the Holy Spirit. Such demythologizing, Bultmann believes, is a necessary continuation of the work of the Reformers: security based on good works and security based on objectifying knowledge are alike inimical to the gospel of justification by faith alone. Demythologizing is naturally a negative process, and to list the negative features of Bultmann's programme may give a distorted impression of his intention, which must be seen from the perspective of his theology as a whole.

One form of demythologizing was practised by the NT writers themselves. When Paul demoted the "principalities and powers" which dominated the lives of men and women without Christ to the status of "weak and beggarly elemental spirits" (Gal. 4:9), conquered and bound by Christ who liberates their former captives (Col. 2:15), he was in effect demythologizing them; we may compare the reinterpretation of the traditional Antichrist in 1 John 2:18 in terms of the false teachers of John's day.

Many of the NT elements designated mythological by the demythologizing school are related by it to a redeemer-myth held to have originated in Iranian religion (in which the part of the redeemer was taken by Gayomart, the primal man) and to have been taken over by gnosticism. In its developed form, this gnostic myth portrays a heavenly essence which falls from the upper realm of light into the lower world of material darkness where it is imprisoned in a multitude of earthly bodies. To liberate it from its imprisonment a saviour comes from the realm of light, who accomplishes his mission by the impartation of true → knowledge (*gnōsis*). By the acceptance of this true knowledge from one who is both redeemer and revealer, the pure essence attains release from the bonds of matter and re-ascends to its proper abode.

This gnostic myth appears in its most lucid form in the Mandaean literature, which, however, is several centuries later than the NT documents. Even the Iranian redeemer-myth presumed to lie behind it is not attested until the 7th century A.D. and later. It is doubtful, indeed, if the primal man of the Iranian tradition and the concept of the redeemer-revealer were ever brought together in the characteristic gnostic myth except under the influence of the gospel. It is certainly very difficult to find evidence of the gnostic myth in the apostolic age, let alone in pre-Christian times. The most that can be said of the doctrinal devia-tions attacked in Colossians and 1 John is that they reflect incipient forms of gnos-ticism.

But forms of the gnostic myth have been recognized not only in deviations attacked in the NT but even more plainly in positive expositions of the gospel. R. Bultmann, who already accepted R. Reitzenstein's case for the pre-Christian dating of the Iranian redeemer-myth, published in 1925 an epoch-making article "Die Bedeutung der neuerschlossenen mandäischen und manichäischen Quellen für das Verständnis des Johannesevangeliums", *ZNW* 24, 100–146, in which he argued for an affinity between the discourses of the Gospel of John and the Man-daean redeemer-myth – an affinity which could be explained only if the Mandaean texts were primary and the Johannine discourses derivative. This thesis was later elaborated in Bultmann's magisterial commentary on *The Gospel of John* (1st edition, 1941; E. T. 1971).

Again, H. Schlier, formerly a disciple of Bultmann, maintained in *Christus und die Kirche im Epheserbrief* (1930) that the Letter to the Ephesians derived some of its dominant motifs from the world of gnostic thought, such as the redeemer's ascent to heaven, the heavenly wall (Eph. 2:14), the heavenly man, the church as the → body of Christ, the body of Christ as a heavenly building, and the heavenly bridal union. (It is a measure of Schlier's departure from the school in which he was brought up that by 1965, in the 5th edition of his commentary, *Der Brief an die Epheser*, he was able to combine this position with an acceptance of Pauline authorship.) But, as has been said, until more positive evidence of the pre-Christian date of this elaborate myth is forthcoming than hypothetical reconstructions from late Mandaean texts can supply, theses like Bultmann's and Schlier's cannot be regarded as having adequate foundation.

Quite different is the approach of C. Williams, C. S. Lewis and others, who have maintained that in Christianity the ancient myths have come true, that when God became Man, as Lewis put it, "Myth became Fact", so that the aspirations and insights of the human soul which have from ancient times found mythological expression have been given a satisfying answer in the historical events of the gospel.

F. F. Bruce

(a). I. G. Barbour, *Myths, Models and Paradigms*, 1974; H. W. Bartsch, ed., *Kerygma and Myth*, E. T., I, 1953; II, 1962; U. Bianchi, ed., *Le Origini dello Gnosticismo*, 1967; F. F. Bruce, "Myth and History", in C. Brown, ed., *History, Criticism and Faith*, 1976, 79–100; R. Bultmann, "New Testament and Mythology" (1941) in Bartsch, op. cit., I, 1–44; *Jesus Christ and Mythology*, 1960; D. Cairns, *A Gospel without Myth*, 1960; B. S. Childs, *Myth and Reality in the Old Testament*, *SBT* 27, 1962²; F. L. Cross, ed., *The Jung Codex*, 1955; A. Cunningham, *The Theory of Myth*, 1974; F. W.

Dillistone, ed., *Myth and Symbol*, SPCK Theological Collections 7, 1966; J. S. Dunne, *The City of the Gods*, 1974; I. Engnell, *Studies in Divine Kingship in the Ancient Near East*, 1967²; T. Fawcett, *Hebrew Myth and Christian Gospel*, 1973; H. Frankfort, *Kingship and the Gods*, 1948; H. Frankfort and others, *Before Philosophy*, 1946; T. H. Gaster, *Thespis*, 1950; F. Gogarten, *Demythologizing and History*, 1955; H. Harris, *David Friedrich Strauss and his Theology*, 1973; and *The Tübingen School*, 1975; I. Henderson, *Myth in the New Testament*, 1952; S. H. Hooke, *The Origins of Early Semitic Ritual*, 1935; *Middle Eastern Mythology*, 1963; S. H. Hooke, ed., *Myth and Ritual*, 1933; *The Labyrinth*, 1935; *Myth, Ritual and Kingship*, 1958; A. R. Johnson, *Sacral Kingship in Ancient Israel*, 1967²; R. A. Johnson, *The Origins of Demythologizing: Philosophy and Historiography in the Theology of Rudolf Bultmann*, Studies in the History of Religions, Supplements to *Numen*, 28, 1974; W. Johnstone, "The Mythologizing of History in the Old Testament", *SJT* 24, 1971, 201–17; H. Jonas, *The Gnostic Religion*, 1958; G. V. Jones, *Christology and Myth in the New Testament*, 1956; C. W. Kegley, ed., *The Theology of Rudolf Bultmann*, 1966; M. T. Kelsey, *Myth, History and Faith*, 1974; C. S. Lewis, *Till we have Faces*, 1956; "Is Theology Poetry?" in *Screwtape Proposes a Toast and Other Pieces*, 1965, 41–58; J. Macquarrie, *The Scope of Demythologizing*, 1960; A. Malet, *The Thought of Rudolf Bultmann*, 1969; L. Malevez, *The Christian Message and Myth*, 1958; G. Miegge, *Gospel and Myth in the Thought of Rudolf Bultmann*, 1960; S. M. Ogden, *Christ Without Myth*, 1962 (cf. D. L. Deegan, "Article Review: Christ Without Myth", *SJT* 17, 1964, 83–9); W. Pannenberg, "The Later Dimensions of Myth in Biblical and Christian Tradition", *Basic Questions in Theology*, III, 1972, 1–79; A. S. Peake, *Faded Myths*, 1908; G. Quispel, "From Mythos to Logos", *Eranos Jahrbuch* 39, 1970, 323–340; H. Riesenfeld, "The mythological background of New Testament Christology", in W. D. Davies and D. Daube, eds., *The Background of the New Testament and its Eschatology*, In Honour of Charles Harold Dodd, 1954, 81–95; J. W. Rogerson, *Myth in Old Testament Interpretation*, BZAW 134, 1974; W. Schmithals, *An Introduction to the Theology of Rudolf Bultmann*, 1968; G. Stählin, *Mythos*, TDNT IV, 762–795; J. A. Stewart, *The Myths of Plato*, 1905; D. F. Strauss, *The Life of Jesus Critically Examined*, (ET 1846) ed. P. C. Hodgson, 1973; B. H. Throckmorton, *The New Testament and Mythology*, 1960; P. Tillich, "Myth and Mythology", in *Twentieth Century Theology in the Making*, ed. J. Pelikan, II, 1970, 342–354; G. Wagner, *Pauline Baptism and the Pagan Mysteries*, 1967; K. Ward, "Myth and Fact in Christianity", *SJT* 20, 1967, 385–96; R. McL. Wilson, *The Gnostic Problem*, 1958; *Gnosis and the New Testament*, 1968; E. Yamauchi, *Pre-Christian Gnosticism*, 1973; varii, *La Regalità Sacrà/The Sacral Kingship*, 1959.

(b). G. Backhaus, *Kerygma und Mythos bei David Friedrich Strauss und Rudolf Bultmann*, 1956; P. Barthel, *Interprétation du Langage Mythique et Théologie Biblique: Étude de Quelques Étapes de l'Evolution du Problème de l'Interprétation des Représentations d'Origine et de Structure Mythiques de la Foi Chrétienne*, 1967; G. Bornkamm, *Mythus und Legende in den apokryphen Thomasakten*, 1933; R. Bultmann, "Die Bedeutung der neuerschlossenen mandäischen und manichäischen Quellen für das Verständnis des Johannesevangeliums", *ZNW* 24, 1925, 100–146; C. Colpe, *Die religionsgeschichtliche Schule*, 1961; C. Hartlich and W. Sachs, *Der Ursprung des Mythosbegriffes in der modernen Bibelwissenschaft*, Schriften der Studiengemeinschaft der evangelischen Akademien 2, 1952; H. W. Hässig, *Wörterbuch der Mythologie*, I–II, 1973; K. Reinhardt, *Platons Mythen*, 1927; R. Reitzenstein, *Die hellenistischen Mysterienreligionen*, 1910; *Das iranische Erlösungsmysterium*, 1921; H. Schlier, *Christus und die Kirche im Epheserbrief*, 1930; J. Sløk, J. Haekel, S. Mowinckel, R. Bultmann, E. Fuchs and H. Meyer, "Mythos und Mythologie", *RGG³* III, 1263–1283; G. Widengren, *Sakrales Königtum im Alten Testament und im Judentum*, 1955.

N

Name

$\H{o}νομα$

$\H{o}νομα$ (*onoma*), name; $ὀνομάζω$ (*onomazō*), to call, name; $ἐπονομάζω$ (*eponomazō*), call by a name, give a surname; $ψευδώνυμος$ (*pseudōnymos*), bearing a false name.

CL *onoma*, from the Indo-Germanic **(e)nomn-* (cf. Lat. *nomen*), means name.

Derived from the noun are two vbs.: (1) *onomazō*, name, specify, designate, tell, express, indicate, assent, promise; and (2) *eponomazō*, apply a word as a name, denominate, give a second name or surname, nickname. *pseudōnymos*, formed from the addition of *pseud-*, false, means bearing a false name; or falsely, incorrectly, inappropriately named.

1. In the faith and thought of virtually every nation the name is inextricably bound up with the person, whether of a man, a god, or a demon. Anyone who knows the name of a being can exert power over it. In → magic the potential energy which resides in the name can be translated into effective power if the name is mentioned or used in an oath (details in K. Preisendanz, *Papyri Graecae Magicae*, I–III, 1928–42; see also *TDNT* V 250 ff.).

In the Gk. thought of the 5th and 6th cents. B.C. the question arose of the relationship between the name and the thing or being so named. Among the Sophists, the prevalent opinion was that the name did not belong to things by nature. In the *Cratylus* Plato was concerned with problems of linguistic philosophy: in what relationship do words and things, concepts and thought stand to one another? For Plato, words are phonetic symbols, which receive their meaning through custom, general agreement and thought, and are thus of little relevance for true knowledge. The Stoics declared that speech originated by physical necessity (*physei*) in the → soul of man, and that words represented things in accordance with their nature; as regarded content, the spoken word, the concept and the object itself were all alike (*TDNT* V 248). This opinion was very widely held later on.

The discussions of the names of the gods were important for the relationship between language and its object. Hesiod had already tried to find the key to the nature of the gods from the etymology of their names. The names of the gods were viewed as "verbal cult-pictures" (Democritus, Frag. 142, in Diels-Kranz[5] I, 170, 9). The aspect of the terrible and unapproachable was thus appropriate for them (Plato, *Philebus* 12c; *Cratylus* 403a). Others, such as Menander and Aristides, represent the view-point that the higher a god stood, the more names he had. Alternatively, the Stoics attempted to overcome polytheism by transferring all the many names to one god, Zeus: here, the plurality of names expressed fullness of being. But the many names of the god of the universe can be transmuted into namelessness, in that no name does justice to the fullness of the godhead. This line of thought has continued right up to modern times (cf. Goethe's *Faust*, "Who may name him?"). The magical phrases and formulae found on the papyri of late antiquity reveal the belief in the power and effectiveness of the names of gods and demons.

OT The Heb. *šēm* appears some 770 times in the OT, the Gk. *onoma* in over 1000 references in the LXX.

1. The Israelites were also well aware of the significance of personal and proper names. The best-known example is that of Nabal, who is a fool, as his name suggests (1 Sam. 25:25). In this context belong also the numerous (national) etymological interpretations which are offered where people and places are given names: Eve, "the mother of all living" (Gen. 3:20; → Adam, art. *Heua*); Cain, "I have gotten a man with the help of the Lord", cf. *qānâh*, get (Gen. 4:1); Babel, "because the Lord confused the language of all the earth", cf. *bālal*, confuse (Gen. 11:9; → Babylon). The name Isaac is a reminder of his parents' laughter (Gen. 17:17; 18:12; → Abraham, art. *Isaak*); Jacob holds the heel (Gen. 29:31 ff. → Israel, art. *Iakōb*). To give a name is, in addition, to exercise lordship and dominion: cf. that of Adam over the animals in Gen. 2:19 f.; over a town in 2 Sam. 12:28; and over a land in Ps. 49:11. Women long to take the name of a man, and so to become his possession and enjoy his protection (Isa. 4:1). As the one who gives names to the stars, Yahweh is their Creator and Lord (Ps. 147:4); in the same way he calls → Israel by name and makes him his possession (Isa. 43:1; 63:19). Absalom, who has no son to perpetuate his name, erects a monument as a memorial to his name (2 Sam. 18:18).

Changes of name also testify to their significance (Gen. 41:45; 2 Ki. 23:34). Even Yahweh can undertake to change someone's name, when he gives his chosen ones a new importance in their own situation or for the future. Thus Abram becomes → Abraham, the father of many nations (Gen. 17:5); Jacob becomes → Israel, because he has fought with God (Gen. 32:28). Abraham's name, and also the names of Ephraim and Manasseh, have an importance over and above the actual bearers of the name (Gen. 48:20). Jerusalem receives a new name in the last days (Isa. 62:2); Isaiah gives his children symbolic names (Isa. 7:3; 8:3); and the names of the bearers of salvation are a guarantee of Yahweh's grace (Isa. 7:14; Zech. 6:12).

2. Of primary significance is the name of Yahweh, which he himself made known in his revelation (Gen. 17:1; Exod. 3:14; 6:2; → God, art. *theos* OT 2). One of the most fundamental and essential features of the biblical revelation is the fact that God is not without a name: he has a personal name, by which he can, and is to be, invoked. When appeal is made to Yahweh, he comes near and makes his promise true: "in every place where I cause my name to be remembered I will come to you and bless you" (Exod. 20:24; cf. Num. 6:24 ff.; → Remember). Priests and Levites, and even the king, → bless in the name of Yahweh (Num. 6:27; Deut. 10:8; 2 Sam. 6:18). The name of Yahweh, indeed, is such a powerful expression of his personal rule and activity that it can be used as an alternative way of speaking of Yahweh himself (Lev. 18:21; Ps. 7:17; Amos 2:7; Mic. 5:4). It is the side of Yahweh which is turned towards men, in which Yahweh reveals

himself. His historical dealings with men in the past (Exod. 3:6, 13, 15), present (Exod. 20:7) and future (Ezek. 25:17; 34:50 *et al.*) are inextricably bound up with his name. Misuse of this name in → magic or in false oaths (for oaths were accompanied by mention of Yahweh's name; → Swear) is forbidden (Exod. 20:7), for the name of Yahweh is a gift of the revelation which is not at man's disposal (Gen. 17:1; Exod. 3:14; 6:2). The name of Yahweh is committed in trust to Israel: the heathen do not know it (Ps. 79:6). Israel has the task of hallowing it. This takes place in the cult, at sacrifice, in prayer, in blessing and cursing, and also in the holy → war (Ps. 29:8), in other words, in serving Yahweh, and him alone, and in obeying his commands. To take part in the cult-worship of another god therefore involves profanation of the name of Yahweh (Lev. 19:21). The invocation of his name over → Jerusalem (Jer. 25:29), over the → temple (Jer. 7:10) and over the ark (2 Sam. 6:2), consecrating them and associating them with him, is the sole basis of that sanctity (→ Holy).

3. Deut. gives the following answer to the question as to how Israel can have dealings with Yahweh: Yahweh himself dwells in heaven, but he chooses on earth a place where he causes his "name" to dwell (Deut. 12:11; 14:23; cf. 2 Sam. 7:13; 1 Ki. 3:2; 5:17). In that his name dwells in the → temple, Yahweh's presence is itself guaranteed; but only in such a way that even if the temple is profaned, Yahweh's transcendence remains preserved (cf. 1 Ki. 8:13, where Yahweh dwells in thick darkness with 1 Ki. 8:14 ff., where Yahweh's name dwells in the temple). Yahweh's name, like Yahweh himself, remains sovereign.

4. As a result of this, Yahweh's name assumes a powerful and independent existence of its own, although it is naturally still very closely linked with Yahweh himself. Through its mighty sway, the godly experience Yahweh's protection and help (cf. Prov. 18:10; Mal. 1:11; Ps. 54:6). His name almost becomes a hypostasis of Yahweh himself (cf. Pss. 54:1; 89:24; 118:10 ff.). It occupies the place taken in other religions by the cultic image (cf. G. von Rad, *Old Testament Theology*, I, 1962, 183 f.).

5. In later times Yahweh's name is frequently used in the sense of the "praise" or "glory" of Yahweh (Isa. 26:8; 55:13; Ps. 41:10). Turns of expression, such as "for the sake of Yahweh's name" or "Yahweh is his name" (Exod. 15:3; Isa. 51:15; Jer. 10:16; Amos 4:13; Ps. 23:3), point in the same direction, indicating Yahweh's claim to sovereign authority and glory in the world and amongst those nations to whom Israel makes it known (Isa. 12:4; Ps. 105:1-3). "Indeed in the end Jahweh is to be revealed to the world in such a way that all worship of idols vanishes away, and every knee will bow to his name alone (Zech. xiv. 9; Isa. xlv. 23)" (von Rad, *Old Testament Theology*, I, 185).

6. (a) The expression "in the name" (Heb. $b^e\check{s}\bar{e}m$) occurs very frequently in the OT. Linked with the names of places or people it can mean by name (Jos. 21:9), after the name of (Jdg. 18:29), in the name (1 Ki. 21:8; Est. 3:12), on behalf of (1 Sam. 25:9).

(b) But the phrase appears most often in association with the name of Yahweh, with the primary meaning of calling upon, invoking Yahweh by his name, that is, worshipping him in the cult (cf. Gen. 4:26, 12:8). The formula is also used in order to → swear, to bless (→ Blessing) and to → curse, since by the use of the expression, Yahweh's might is called upon to interpose (Deut. 5:13; 10:8; 2 Sam.

6:18; 2 Ki. 2:24). It means further "on behalf of" Yahweh (Ex. 5:22 f.; Deut. 18:18 ff.). The appeal of false prophets to Yahweh is illegitimate, for they have received neither their commission nor their words from him (Deut. 18:20; Jer. 14:14 f.; 23:25; 29:9),

7. Philo, speaking in connection with Exod. 3:14 (LXX), and influenced by Stoic philosophy, says that God is the Existent One; being belongs to him alone as of right. But this cannot be uttered, and so God's real name never reaches men. God says to Moses, "For me, to whom alone belongs Being as of right, there is absolutely no name which fits my nature" (*Vit.Mos.* 1, 75). To men came only the name *kyrios ho theos*, the Lord God (*Mut.Nom.* 11 f.). Men can invoke God only with the relative name of "the God of Abraham, Isaac and Jacob" (*Abr.* 51). For Philo, in total opposition to the OT, God has no personal name. The words *theos* God, and *kyrios*, Lord, according to Philo merely indicate powers in God: "Lord" the power of lordship and "God" the power of grace. Philo's opinion that the power of Being has many names is also Stoic (*Som.* 2, 354). But one must still hallow even the purely relative names of God, which do not designate his essential Being; one must beware of misusing, of blaspheming these names, and of using awful and terrible names (*Spec.Leg.* 4, 40; 2, 8; *Decal.* 93 f.).

8. It is possible that Josephus, who was a priest, could have known the Heb. name Yahweh, but he never uses it. He does not even use the Gk. *kyrios*, Lord, which was used in Hellenistic Judaism to translate Yahweh. This shows the extent to which, already in Josephus, fear of uttering the name of God had gone. Instead, he uses *onoma*, and has a predilection for *prosēgoria*, address, appellation, title, even where Yahweh's name is under consideration. Thus he writes that on the headband of the High Priest the *prosēgoria*, address, appellation, of God is engraved (*Ant.* 3, 7, 6; cf. Exod. 38:36 f.). In another place he speaks in the same context of the *onoma* of God, to which Alexander the Great rendered worship (*Ant.* 11, 8, 5). This oscillation between the two words can also be seen in his rendering of Exod. 3, where he adds that he is not allowed to say anything at all about the name (*Ant.* 2, 12, 4 f.). According to Josephus, the name of God does not dwell in the temple either, but only a portion of God's spirit (*Ant.* 8, 4, 3). Israel's temple is the *epōnymon* of God, i.e. it bears God's name, like coins which are thus shown to belong to him, and like heathen temples which bear the names of their gods (*Ant.* 16, 2, 3; 4, 8, 10). It does not necessarily mean that it was the name of Yahweh when it says that they called on "the awful name of God" (*War* 5, 10, 3).

9. The Qumran writings follow exactly the same paths as the OT, as far as the use of the name of God is concerned. Names figure largely in the War Scroll (cf. 1QM 2:6; 3:4, 13 ff.; 4:1–13; 5:1 ff.; 11:2 f., 12:2; 13:7; 14:4, 8, 12; 18:6, 8) and the Hymns (cf. 1QH 1:30; 2:30; 3:23; 9:38; 11:6, 25; 12:3; 17:20; 18:8). According to Josephus (*War* 2, 8, 7), the Essenes had to swear, amongst other things, to keep the names of the angels secret.

10. Apocrypha and Pseudepigrapha. The account in Gen. 6 of the fall of the angels occupied people's imagination. In Eth.Enoch 6:7 it took the form that the names of the "leaders of tens" (i.e. → angels) were given names. Heb. Enoch is largely an angelology, a tract in which the names of innumerable angels are communicated. In 2 Esd. 7:132–139 seven names of God are mentioned: he is the

651

Compassionate, the Gracious, the Forbearing, the Generous, the Merciful, the Noble, the Forgiving. The remarkable thought appears in Eth.Enoch 69:13–21 that the name of God, by which men swear, is itself the oath, and that that is how the creation was called into being. The name of the Son of man (and thus his person?) is pre-existent (Eth.Enoch 46:7 f.).

11. (a) Among the Rabbis the name is important in the teaching of tradition. One may only pass on a doctrine or tradition if one names ($b^e\check{s}\bar{e}m$, in the name) the authority from whom one has received it (Aboth 6:6). With reference to the NT, the expression $l^e\check{s}\bar{e}m$, "into" the name, is also significant. On the one hand, it is used in a final sense, with the intention that something shall happen. A man may make an offering $l^e\check{s}\bar{e}m$ $ha\check{s}\check{s}\bar{e}m$, "for the name of the name" (i.e. for Yahweh), i.e. one offers a sacrifice to Yahweh. A freed slave takes a ritual dip in the bath "to the name of the free man", in order to become a free man. A proselyte is circumcised "to the name of the proselyte" to become a Jew. On the other hand, the expression is used in a causal sense: e.g. $l^e\check{s}\bar{e}m$ $\check{s}\bar{a}mayim$, "on account of the name of heaven", i.e. for God's sake (cf. Matt. 10:41; Mk. 9:42).

(b) The name of Yahweh is avoided if at all possible (cf. Josephus), to avoid infringing the third commandment (Exod. 20:7; → Lord, art. *kyrios*). According to one old story, after the death of Simon the Just (*c.* 200 B.C.) the priests discontinued uttering Yahweh's name in blessings (T.Sot. 13, 8). In the temple cult Yahweh's name was still used in the High Priest's blessing on the Day of Atonement; but in scriptural quotations the word Yahweh came to be replaced by $\check{s}\bar{e}m$, name, in the teaching schools. So the tetragrammaton YHWH ceased to be used and its pronunciation was forgotten. The consequence was that the name of God became a secret name which was used as a means of magical power, particularly in the piety of the lower strata of society. In addition to the existent name of God composed of four letters, other such names were known, consisting of 13, 43 or even 72 letters.

NT In the NT *onoma* occurs 228 times, most commonly relatively in Lk. (34 times in the Gospel; 60 times in Acts) and Rev. (37 times). *eponomazō*, commonly used in ancient writings, is found only once in the NT (Rom. 2:17), *pseudōnymos* only in 1 Tim. 6:20. *onoma* in the NT also means reputation (Mk. 6:14; Rev. 3:1) and person (Acts 1:15; Rev. 3:4; 11:13).

1. *Names of men and other beings.* The names of the Twelve Apostles on the foundation-stones of the new → Jerusalem (Rev. 21:14), and the names of the twelve tribes of Israel on its gates (Rev. 21:12) proclaim the final unity of the old and the new people of God. Jesus proves himself to be the Good → Shepherd by calling his sheep by name and knowing them personally (Jn. 10:3). In giving his → disciples new names, he draws them in a special way into his service (Matt. 10:2 ff.; Mk. 3:16 ff.; Lk. 6:14 ff.). On the name of Peter → Rock, art. *petros*. Mk. 3:17 mentions "James the son of Zebedee and John the brother of James, whom he surnamed Boanerges [*Boanērges*], that is, sons of thunder." Some MSS apply the name Boanerges to all the twelve, but this is too weakly attested to be likely. The word is probably an attempt to transliterate an Aramaic or Heb. phrase. *Boanē-* evidently represents $b^en\hat{e}$ (sons of). The ending *-rges* is not the ordinary word for thunder, but it may represent Heb. $r\bar{o}\bar{g}ez$ (agitation, excitement, raging;

cf. Job 37:2 of thunder); Aram. *reḡaz* (anger); or Heb. *reḡeš* (throng; cf. Ps. 55:14[15]; in later Heb. commotion, vibration; cf. Aram. *riḡšā'*, noise). The Arabic word related to *reḡeš* means thunder. Although J. Rendel Harris suggested that the reference was to their being twins (*Expositor* 7, Series 3, 1907, 146 ff.; *ExpT* 36, 1934–25, 139), the more likely explanation is to be found in the outbursts that are related in Mk. 9:38 and Lk. 9:54. As Peter's name means rock and thus contains a promise, perhaps there is also the implied promise that their witness will be as mighty as thunder (C. E. B. Cranfield, *The Gospel according to Saint Mark*, 1959, 131). The fact that the names of the disciples are written in heaven (Lk. 10:21) means that they belong to God and to his kingdom (Rev. 3:5). The new name which the victor receives expresses his inalienable fellowship with Christ himself (Rev. 2:17).

Evil spirits have names, too, which predicate something of their nature or power (Mk. 5:9). Thus, the "beast" in Rev. 13:1 (→ Animal, art. *thērion*; → Antichrist) bears blasphemous names, i.e. he is given names and honorific titles which belong to God or Christ alone. His name is contained in a → number (Rev. 13:17 ff.), and his adherents also bear it (Rev. 13:17; 15:2). The name of the "great harlot" (Rev. 17:1, cf. v. 3), "Babylon the great, mother of harlots and of earth's abominations" (Rev. 17:5), stands in contrast to the woman of Rev. 12 who bears the male child and who is the mother of all the faithful (cf. 12:4 f. with v. 17).

2. *The name of God.* God's name belongs with his → revelation: God as person turns to the person of man. God reveals himself as the loving Father, in glorifying his name in Jesus' saving work (Jn. 17:12, 26). It accords with this that Jesus, and he alone, reveals the name of God as the name of the Father to men (Jn. 17:6). In Jn. 12:28→ "Father", "glorify" (→ Glory) and "name" are closely bound together. That the disciples are "kept in the name of God" indicates that they live in the sphere of an effective power, which protects them from ruin and unites them with each other (Jn. 17:11 f.). The goal of the proclamation of the name of God as Father is that the love of the Father for the Son is also to be found in believers (Jn. 17:26). In these affirmations of John's Gospel, and above all in those of the High Priestly Prayer of Jesus (ch. 17), we have the christological interpretation of the OT affirmations concerning the name of Yahweh. The Fourth Gospel thus picks up and follows through the lines of the ancient biblical tradition, that God's revelation is bound to a personal name – to → Jesus Christ (cf. on this Matt. 11:27 and 28:18 with Jn. 3:35; 5:20; 13:3; 7:29; 10:15; 17:25).

Jesus thus acts in the name of, and on behalf of, God in fulfilment of his will and as proof of his sonship (Mk. 11:19 f.; Jn. 10:24 f.). At his parousia he will come "in the name of the Lord" (Matt. 23:39). When the name of God is conjoined with that of the Son and of the Holy Spirit it assumes the character of completeness and fullness (Matt. 28:19); this is trinitarian thought, even if a precise trinitarian formula is lacking (on this → God, art. *theos* NT 8). The first request of the Lord's Prayer concerns the hallowing of God's name (Matt. 6:9; cf. Isa. 29:23; Ezek. 36:23; → Holy, art. *hagios* NT 1 (c)). In the → kingdom of God, God's name is no longer profaned through sin. God is asked in prayer to further the hallowing of his name himself, and to bring in his kingdom. A man who despises God's will and commands, or a Christian slave who is disobedient to his master is, in effect, slandering God's name (Rom. 2:24; 1 Tim. 6:1). The beast in

Rev. 13:6 also reviles the name of God and his dwelling, as do those who suffer under the plagues of the last days (Rev. 16:9).

3. *The name of Jesus.* (a) The significance of Jesus' life and activity is evident in his name (Matt. 1:21; → Jesus art. *Iēsous*; on Emmanuel in Matt. 1:23 → God, art. *Emmanouēl*). He bears the sublime name of → Son (Heb. 1:4 f.). His name is "the Word of God" (Rev. 19:13; cf. Jn. 1:1). God's name of → Lord also becomes his name (Phil. 2:9 f.; Rev. 19:16). Above and beyond this, he bears a name which he alone knows (Rev. 19:12), "and the name by which he is called is The Word of God" (Rev. 19:13). The name "Jesus" can be replaced simply by "the name" (Acts 5:41; 3 Jn. 7; cf. the Jewish replacement of Yahweh by *šēm*). The whole content of the saving truth revealed in Jesus is comprised in his name (Acts 4:12; 1 Cor. 6:11). Belief in the name of the Son, i.e. belief in Jesus' messianic mission (Jn. 3:18), is God's command (1 Jn. 3:23; 5:13). Anyone who believes in his name receives → forgiveness of sins (Acts 10:43; 1 Jn. 2:12), has eternal → life (Jn. 20:21; 1 Jn. 5:13) and escapes the judgment (Jn. 3:18). A Christian's whole life is dominated by the name of Jesus (Col. 3:17), whose glorification is the goal of faith (2 Thess. 1:12).

The name of Jesus is the basis of the → proclamation to all nations (Acts 8:12; 9:16; Rom. 1:5). Because of the preaching of Jesus and his work, the authorities at Jerusalem forbad the apostles to preach "on the basis of this name [*epi tō onomati toutō*]" (Acts 5:17 f.; 5:28, 40). Faith and proclamation include confession of the name (Rev. 2:13; 3:8) and readiness to suffer for his name's sake (Matt. 10:22; 24:9). Faith and faithfulness to Jesus is the same as holding fast to his name (Rev. 2:13; 3:8). The name of Christ contains the implication of glory, and 1 Pet. 4:14 declares: "If you are reproached for the name of Christ you are blessed, because the spirit of glory and of God rests upon you" (cf. Isa. 11:2). Whoever calls on the name of the Lord belongs to the church (Acts 9:14; 1 Cor. 1:2) and is saved (Acts 2:17–21; Rom. 10:13; cf. Joel 2:32). Christians were so called because of this name (Acts 11:26; cf. 26:18; 1 Pet. 4:16). It is the "honourable name" which is given to the followers of Christ (Jas. 2:7). One of the gifts of final perfection is that the victors will bear the name of the → Lamb (Rev. 3:12; 14:1; 22:4).

(b) The formula "in the name of Jesus". God gives the Holy Spirit in the name of Jesus (Jn. 14:26). Thanks are given in that name (Eph. 5:20). The nations place their hope in it (Matt. 12:21; cf. Isa. 42:4). And in his name the congregation prays (Jn. 14:13 f.; 15:16) – that is, according to his will and instruction, in order that the commission may be fulfilled, which Jesus gave to his own. This is the reason why their prayers are heard. Since the disciples are sent out by Jesus they are able to act on behalf of him and in his power, performing miracles and acts of compassion (Lk. 10:17; Mk. 8:38 f.). After Easter, the name of Jesus continues to maintain its power (Acts 3:6; 14:10). Name and "power" (→ Might, art. *dynamis*) are used parallel to one another (Acts 4:7; 16:18). Jesus himself gives help and is present in his name (Acts 9:34), but not when unbelievers attempt to misuse it in magical exorcisms (Acts 19:13–16; → Magic). Such statements show that the OT manner of speaking of the name of Yahweh has been transferred to Jesus and his name. Because he was called by Jesus, Paul was able to admonish (2 Thess. 3:6; *dia*, by or through him, 1 Cor. 1:10), and give judgment "in the name of Jesus", as one commissioned and authorized by him (1 Cor. 5:4; 2 Thess. 3:6).

(c) Baptism "in the name of Jesus". The baptismal formula *eis to onoma*, "in [to] the name", corresponds with the final sense of the expression from the Rab. schools *l^ešēm* (see above OT 6). The literal meaning is that, → baptism symbolically assigns the person baptized to Christ for forgiveness of sins (Acts 8:16; 19:15; 1 Cor. 1:13, 15; cf. Matt. 28:19). The same meaning can be intended where baptism *epi*, to, or *en*, in the name, is spoken of (cf. Acts 2:38; 10:48 with LXX Jos. 9:9; 2 Sam. 22:50; Sir. 47:13; where the original Heb. text has *l^ešēm*, which would normally be translated *eis*, to: but LXX renders *en* or *epi*). The fullness of Christ's saving work is contained in his name (as Yahweh's saving work was in his) and is present in the church. This is symbolized by the individual's baptism, since he has been caught up into Jesus' death and resurrection (Rom. 6:1–11; Col. 2:12; cf. 2 Cor. 4:10).

4. The vb. *onomazō*, derived from the noun, occurs in the NT only 9 times. The name and service of an → apostle are traced back to Jesus (Lk. 6:13). A man who bears the name of brother, but lives unworthily of it, is to be denied fellowship (1 Cor. 5:11). The congregation is so detached from sin that it is not even to be named in it, i.e. it is not even to be spoken about (Eph. 5:3; cf. 2 Tim. 2:19). God names every family in heaven and on earth and so is the Father of all (Eph. 3:15; on this passage see 6 below). *eponomazō*, name after, give a nickname, give a second name, occurs in the NT only at Rom. 2:17: "If you call yourself [*eponomazē*] a Jew". Here Jew is a title of honour, the heir to the legacy described in vv. 17–20. Paul attacks the inconsistency of claiming to be a Jew and at the same time countenancing sin. The Jews stand under the divine judgment like the Gentiles. The vb. is also found in the *v.l.* of Lk. 6:14D.

5. *pseudōnymos* is attested from Aesch. and means bearing a false name. In the NT it occurs only at 1 Tim. 6:20: "Avoid godless chatter and contradictions of what is falsely called knowledge [*tēs pseudōnymou gnōseōs*]." Paul here warns against a movement which gives the lie to its name and leads from faith into error (cf. v. 21). *H. Bietenhard*

6. Eph. 3:14 f. probably means that God is "the Father [*patēr*] from whom every fatherhood [*patria*] in heaven and on earth is named", the paronomasia being deliberate: "every *patria* is so named after the *patēr*" (G. Schrenk, *patria, TDNT* V 1017). God is the archetypal Father; all other fatherhood is a more or less imperfect copy of his perfect fatherhood. M. Barth, in a full comment on this passage, mentions this among four possible interpretations, but concludes that, because of the lack of evidence for *patria* in the sense of an "abstract 'fatherhood' " as early as this, "this beautiful exposition can at best be considered a homiletical corollary to 3:15" (*Ephesians 1–3, Anchor Bible*, 1974, 379–384). But this "unique sense" (Arndt, 642) of *patria* is not abstract; it is not far removed from its classical sense of "lineage" (cf. Moulton-Milligan, 498). According to Clem.Alex., in what seems to be a reference to this passage, *epi ton poiētēn ton theon pasa anatrechei patria*, "every lineage [or fatherhood] runs back to God the maker" (*Strom.* 6, 7). See the excellent treatment by H. Schlier, who argues that God is here called the Father of all fatherhood, as he is called the creator of all things in v. 9, in order to emphasize, against gnostic misrepresentations, that he is Father not only as redeemer but also as creator – creator of angelic *patriai* in heaven (cf. Eth.En.

69:2 f.) as well as of human *patriai* on earth (*Der Brief an die Epheser*, 1957, 167 f.). He mentions the earlier statement of this interpretation by G. Estius, *In omnes D. Pauli epistolas . . . commentarii*, 1858–59, *ad loc.*   F. F. Bruce

→ God, → Jesus Christ, → Magic

(a). R. Abba, "Name", *IDB* III 500–8; J. Barr, "The Symbolism of Names in the Old Testament", *BJRL* 52, 1969–70, 11–29; J. B. Bauer, "Name", *EBT* II 611 ff.; H. Bietenhard, *onoma* etc., *TDNT* V 242–83; B. S. Childs, *Memory and Tradition in Israel*, *SBT* 37, 9–30; O. Eissfeldt, "Renaming in the Old Testament", in P. R. Ackroyd and B. Lindars, eds., *Words and Meanings: Essays Presented to David Winton Thomas*, 1968, 69–80; G. B. Gray, *Studies in Hebrew Proper Names*, 1896; and "Name", *HDB* III 478–85; G. Foucart, D. S. Margoliouth, A. T. Clay, J. D. Ball, J. Moffatt, G. B. Gray, L. H. Gray, T. Harada, I. Abrahams, C. J. Billson, S. H. Langdon, E. W. Brooks, "Names", *ERE* IX 130–78; L. Hartman, "Into the Name of Jesus", *NTS* 20, 1973–74, 432–40; W. C. Kaiser, Jr., "Name", and "Names, Proper", *ZPEB* IV 360–70; A. F. Key, "The Giving of Proper Names in the Old Testament", *JBL* 83, 1964, 55–9; H. Kosmala, "In My Name", *Annual of the Swedish Theological Institute*, 5, 1966–67, 87 ff.; G. van der Leeuw, *Religion in its Essence and Manifestation*, 1964² (see index); J. A. MacCulloch, "Nameless Gods", *ERE* IX 178–81; J. A. Motyer, *The Revelation of the Divine Name*, 1959; J. Pedersen, *Israel: Its Life and Culture*, I–II, 1926, 245–59; G. von Rad, "Deuteronomy's 'Name' Theology and the Priestly Document's 'Kabod' Theology", *Studies in Deuteronomy*, *SBT* 9, 1953, 37–44; and *Old Testament Theology*, I, 1962, 197–87; H. H. Rowley, *Dictionary of Bible Personal Names*, 1968.
(b). A. M. Besnard, *Le Mystère du Nom*, 1962; H. Bietenhard, "Der Name Gottes in der Bibel", in *Das Wort Sie Sollen Stehen Lassen*, Schädelin Festschrift, 1950; H. A. Brongers, "Die Wendung *bᵉsem* YHWH im Alten Testament", *ZAW* 77, 1965, 1 ff.; G. Delling, *Die Zueignung des Heils in der Taufe. Eine Untersuchung zum neutestamentlichen "Taufen auf den Namen"*, 1961; F. Dumermuth, "Zur deuteronomistischen Kulttheologie und ihren Voraussetzungen", *ZAW* 70, 1958, 59–98; O. Eissfeldt, "Jahwename und Zauberwesen", *Kleine Schriften*, II, 1963; J. Fichtner, "Name", *EKL* II 1499 ff.; O. Grether, *Name und Wort Gottes im Alten Testament*, *BZAW* 64, 1934; M. von Grünwald, *Die Eigennamen im Alten Testament*, 1895; W. Heitmüller, *Im Namen Jesu*, 1903; S. Herrmann, "Der altestamentliche Gottesname", *EvTh* 26, 1966, 281 ff.; B. Jacob, *Im Namen Gottes*, 1903; Mandelkern, II, 1349–1539 (for list of OT proper names); E. Nestle, *Die israelitischen Eigennamen nach ihrer religionsgeschichtlichen Bedeutung*, 1976; M. Noth, *Die israelitischen Personnamen*, 1928; W. Philipp, "Name Gottes", *RGG³* IV 1298 ff.; C. A. Schmitz, K. Baltzer, B. Reicke, "Namenglaube", *RGG³* IV 1301 ff.; J. J. Stamm, "Namengebung im Alten Testament", *RGG³* IV 1300 f.; R. de Vaux, "Le lieu que Yahvé a choisi pour y etablir son nom", in *Das ferne und nahe Wort*, Festschrift L. Rost, *BZAW* 105, 1967, 219–29.

Nature

$\phi \acute{v} \sigma \iota \varsigma$

$\phi \acute{v} \sigma \iota \varsigma$ (*physis*), nature, condition, kind, $\phi v \sigma \iota \kappa \acute{o} \varsigma$ (*physikos*), natural.

CL *physis* is a word from the Gk. world of ideas. Attested since Homer, it became a key concept among the Pre-Socratic philosophers in considering the nature of the world, and similarly the Sophists in the question of the foundation and basis of law.

The noun *physis* comes from the vb. *phyō*, to grow (trans. and intrans.), which is attested as early as Mycenaean Gk. Its root is connected with Lat. *fu-* and with Ger. *bauen* (build). The root *phy-* indicated being or presence.

1. *physis* denotes source, commencement, origin, descent (e.g. Hdt. 7, 134), and also the lineage of adults or of children (Aristot., *Met.* 1014ᵇ16; e.g. *kata physin hyion*, "his son in the line of descent", Polyb., 3, 12, 3). Aristotle (*Met.*

1014^b 22) regards it as the primal substance compounded from the elements. (On Aristotle see J. C. Owens, "Matter and Predication in Aristotle", in J. M. E. Moravcik, ed., *Aristotle: A Collection of Critical Essays*, 1968, 191–214.)

2. From the basic understanding of presence and existence due to growth, *physis* denotes the natural condition, quality or state (e.g. of the air, of blood, or the physical features of a land, Hdt. 2, 7); outward form and appearance (Hdt. 8:38); and stamp or character, e.g. of Solon who was *philodēmos tēn physin*, "patriotically minded" (Aristoph., *Nubes* 1187). The sexes (Diod.Sic., 16, 26, 6; Plato, *Leg.* 944d, 770d), the sex organs and characteristics (Diod.Sic., 32, 10, 7; Hippocrates, *Gynaikeia* 2, 143) can also be designated by *physis*. When set alongside *ethos*, custom, and *logos*, reason, it means (human) nature (Aristot., *Pol.* 1332^a 40) or the imperishable – and perishable – nature of existence of the gods (Diod.Sic., 3, 9, 1). *ta prōta kata physin*, " the first according to nature", is Zeno's description of the mental and spiritual endowment of man. One can read of the *koinē physis*, the common moral nature of all human beings (Chrysippus in Plut., *De Stoicorum Repugnantiis* 9, p. 1035c). The famous quotation from Aristot. accords with this: Man is, by virtue of his natural make-up, "a political creature [*politikon zōon*]" (Aristot., *Pol.* 1253^a 3). *physis* can be used both for the bodily physique of individuals, and for the institutions and constitutions of states (Isoc. 12, 134).

3. *physis* can further denote the → creation, the world of nature, e.g. the creatures who live in the sea (Soph., *Antigone* 345), and also the individual genera and species within nature (Plato, *Rep.* 429d).

4. *physis* is also the efficacious generative power, the charm which causes plants to appear and (e.g.) hair to grow (Hippocrates, *Peri physios paidiou* 20). *physis*, as power, and *hexis*, as bodily constitution, are thus placed alongside each other (Hippocrates, *Peri diaitēs oxeōn* [*notha*] 43). This nature is endowed with reason and determined by its end; it produces nothing without purpose or in vain (Aristot, *Cael.* 291^a33). Aristotle mentions nature and God in the same breath (ibid., 271^b33), distinguishing nature (*physis*) both from *tychē*, fate, *to automaton*, that which takes place of its own accord, and *technē*, skill (*Met.* 1070^a8). Aristotle, in fact, developed a complete theory of natural things, of the *physeion*. For Ionic philosophy, nature is the growth of plants and animals, both as phenomenon in itself, and as the power of growth.

5. *physis* also stands for the regular order of nature. The unity formulated in the law is contrasted with what has come about or grown in nature. (Antiphon Sophista, 44, A, I, 32). In the natural order of things, all men have come to be in a similar way, despite all the differences between Gks. and barbarians (Antiphon Sophista, 44, B, II, 10). By means of hair, nature distinguishes in its own way between the sexes (Epict., *Dissertationes* 1, 16, 10). Nature has powers and elements (*Corp.Herm.* 1, 8). Nature is self-sufficient and strong, as compared with *tychē*, fate, which is unstable (Democritus, 176). Men's lives are determined by the twin forces of nature and laws (Dem., 25, 15). This order fixes the natural end of life (Plut., *Vit.*, *Comparatio Demosthenis et Ciceronis*). Nature, fate and necessity are thus in control of one's existence (Philodemus, *De Pietate* 12).

Among the Stoics, *physis* became a god of the universe, as in the famous quotation from Marcus Aurelius, *ō physis, ek sou panta, en soi panta, eis se panta*, "O Nature, from you comes everything, in you is everything, to you goes everything"

657

(4, 23). Of importance for the Stoic ethos is the assertion of Chrysippus (*SVF* III, 5) that one should *akolouthōs tē physei zēn* "live by following [by keeping close to] nature." The distinction between nature and law as two different entities by which one's life is determined was sharply perceived at an early date in Gk. thought. Reference may be made to the Archelaus-fragment (Diels-Kranz, II, 45, 6): *kai to dikaion einai kai to aischron ou physei, alla nomō*, "Justice and disgrace exist not by nature but by law," i.e. it falls into the sphere of law, not of nature. Nature is here conceived of as that which is in harmony, good in itself and resting, and thus distinguished from the field of morals and ethics.

ot 1. There is no Heb. equivalent in the OT for *physis*. The Hebrews lacked the Greek conception of nature. This is connected both with the fact that all existing things are referred to the → creation or to the Creator God, and also with the stronger historical thought of the OT. In the LXX *physis* occurs only in Wis. (three times) and in 3 and 4 Macc.

(a) It is used in the sense of endowment and character (alongside virtue and communal living, 4 Macc. 13:27); it can indicate a quality, such as the power of love for one's children (4 Macc. 16:3), and also for instance (with reference to material objects) the fire-extinguishing property of water (Wis. 19:20b). *physei*, by nature, fundamentally, all men are foolish (Wis. 13:1).

(b) 4 Macc. 5:25 speaks of the law being adapted to our nature: "for believing our Law to be given by God, we know also that the Creator of the world, as a Lawgiver, feels for us according to our nature. He has commanded us to eat the things that will be convenient for our souls, and he has forbidden us to eat meats that would be contrary."

(c) In 4 Macc. 15:25, where *physis* stands alongside *genesis*, creation, and *philoteknia*, filial love, it denotes the regular order of nature. In 3 Macc. 3:29 it means created beings, the whole world of creation, including man. In 4 Macc. 1:20, linked with *physeis pathōn*, growths of instinct, human characteristics are in mind. But in Wis. 7:20 it refers to species of living beings. Nature is also spoken of as seen as a dispenser of good things: "Truly it is folly not to enjoy innocent pleasures, and it is wrong to reject Nature's favours" (4 Macc. 5:8).

2. Philo was probably the first to take over the word consciously. But at the same time he modified it, in order to utilize it to expound the Jewish faith in its strength and breadth.

(a) It goes without saying that for Philo God stands in the foreground. *physis* is now no longer itself the origin or the creative power; it is an agent of the divine activity. God has bound bodies into a context, that of nature (in this case, vital energy), and that of the → soul and man's rational soul (*Deus Imm.* 35). This vital energy consists of powers which vary and increase (ibid. 37). The soul is a vital energy which has assumed to itself conceptional potential and motion (*Leg. All.*, 2, 23).

(b) This *physis* which belongs to God is that which brings forth, e.g. all men (*Decal.* 41). It is immortal (*Sacr.* 100). It teaches the division of time into day and night, waking and sleeping, and it creates space, which remains confined to three dimensions (*Decal.* 25). It reveals man to be the one who disposes over plants and animals; it has given man speech (*Spec.Leg.* 2, 6; *Rer.Div.Her.* 302) and sexual relations (*Abr.* 248).

Philo, in fact, ascribes to *physis* much of what, from the OT point of view, is the → work of God. Nature, like wisdom, according to Philo, is a power which participates in God's work of creation. For Philo, nature is God, *tris makaria physis*, "thrice-blessed nature" (*Spec.Leg.* 4, 123; cf. *Abr.* 87), but the converse is not true. God himself stands outside material nature (*Migr.Abr.* 192) in so far as nature is understood as the totality of natural phenomena and forces.

(c) Philo interprets the regular order of nature in the same way. He can describe the *nomos*, the → law, as the *orthos physeōs logos*, "the true word of nature" (*Omn.Prob.Lib.* 62), because the law follows nature (*Virt.* 18), and because the prescriptions of the law are in agreement with nature (*Virt.* 5). They are themselves sealed with nature's own seals (*Vit.Mos.* 2, 14). That is why one must follow nature and its developments (*Spec.Leg.* 2, 42; similarly *Omn.Prob.Lib.* 160). Nature ratifies the law: this is the sole foundation on which the world is built.

(d) *physis* is used to designate the being and natural condition of things, e.g. of the elements (*Som.* 1, 33). It can also refer to the being of God (*Plant.* 91), or the (twofold) properties of light (*Abr.* 157).

(e) *physis* in either the masc. or the fem. (*Spec.Leg.* 2, 27) can denote the nature of man, which is compounded from mortal and immortal elements (*Praem.* 13). Philo regards nature as capable of receiving virtue (*Post.C.* 150); conscience makes use of it, because it hates evil and loves good (*Decal.* 87). To nature belong godliness and love of mankind (*Abr.* 208). Philo thus likes to link *physis* with *askēsis* and *mathēsis*, practice and learning (*Som.* 1, 1967; *Praem.* 65).

(f) The formula "by nature", "contrary to nature", "according to nature" is found very frequently. The body is by nature (*physei*, or *ek physeōs*) firm (*Op. Mund.* 36). A regulation can be in accordance with nature (*kata physin*, *Aet. Mund.* 34). Things can be compelled to come together contrary to nature (*para physin*, *Aet.Mund.* 28).

(g) Finally, *physis* denotes the world of creation, including the high and pure (*Leg.All.* 3, 162), the mortal and the immortal (*Decal.* 101), the earthly and the perishable (*Leg.All.* 2, 89), the divine and the human (*Spec.Leg.* 2, 225), the rational and the irrational (*Fug.* 72).

3. Josephus has similarly taken over and adopted in large measure this Gk. concept to his Jewish outlook. *physis* in Josephus stands for:

(a) The condition and characteristics of animals and humans (*War* 2, 8, 1), and of natural self-love (*Ant*, 5, 5, 4; 5, 6, 3). It is almost synonymous with character. Josephus can speak of *physis* which is *chrēstē*, *dikaia*, *eusebēs*, a nature which is good, righteous and religious (*Ant.* 9, 13, 1). The opposite is an unjust, evil disposition (*Ant.* 10, 5, 2). It can also denote the being of God (*Ant.* cf. Preface with 4, 8, 26; 8, 13, 5; 10, 8, 3; *Ap.* 1, 224) or of all things, *tōn holōn physis* (*Ant.* Preface; 3, 6, 4), or of the elements (*Ant.* 3, 7, 7).

(b) Natural qualities. Thus suicide is foreign to the common nature of all living beings (*War* 3, 8, 5). It can also mean the natural situation of a place (e.g. of the citadel of Alexander Janneus, *War* 7, 6, 2), and bodily physique (*Ant.* 6, 9, 1).

(c) The regular order of nature and its laws (*War* 3, 8, 5), juxtaposition of divine and natural law (*Ant.* 4, 8, 48).

(d) Nature as a whole (*Ant.* 1, 3, 2), the whole created world (*War* 7, 5, 5), natural instincts (*Ant.* 7, 7, 1). Thus a person can be active by nature (*War* 1, 10, 5), or naturally freedom-loving (*War* 4, 4, 3). A place can lack a natural harbour (*War* 3, 9, 3). On the other hand, sexual deviations are *para physin*, contrary to nature (*Ap.* 273, 275).

NT The majority of instances of *physis* in the NT is to be found in Paul or more precisely in Romans (7 times; also 2 instances of the adj. *physikos*); the word occurs otherwise only in isolated passages: in 1 Cor., Gal., Eph., Jas. and 2 Pet. It is found with the following shades of meaning which correspond to the previous usage of the word.

1. The use of the word in Gal. 2:15, *physei Ioudaioi*, "Jews by birth", is like that of Philo and Josephus, meaning descent, extraction. Rom. 2:27 corresponds with this: *hē ek physeōs akrobystia*, lit. "the uncircumcision by nature", i.e. those who remain physically uncircumcised from birth: the line of descent is the reason why someone has not received circumcision. But Paul also says that such a man fulfils the law and so performs God's will (by nature?) without belonging to → Israel. (On the interpretation of this passage → see further 2 below.)

God will not spare the wild olive shoot (the Gentile Christians) if he did not spare the branches which belonged to the rich → olive tree *kata physin*, by nature, in the natural way (Rom. 11:21). This use of *physis* is found once more in the same parable: the wild olive shoot is cut from the wild olive tree to which it belongs *kata physin*, by nature, and grafted *para physin*, contrary to nature, into the cultivated olive tree. Paul's argument *a minore ad maius* concludes: how much more can the olive branches which belong to the rich olive tree by nature be grafted back (again) into their own olive tree (Rom. 11:24). Paul is here following Hellenistic linguistic usage, such as we met in Philo and Josephus, with reference to the distinction between Jews and non-Jews. The heathen are, as sinners and as transgressors of the first commandment by nature, by descent (*physei*) children of wrath (Eph. 2:3; cf. Wis. 13:1). But this situation is ended by the → grace of Christ in the lives of those whom God has made alive (Eph. 2:5-10).

2. *physis* stands further for the regular order of nature, which determines the distinction between the sexes. God has given up the idolaters, so that they have exchanged natural (*physikēn*) sexual intercourse between man and woman for unnatural (*para physin*, Rom. 1:26). But there are heathen who do not have the Torah but who do what the law demands *physei*, by nature, in so far as they live in accordance with their own nature. It is not as if they read off the law from the natural order – rather this reveals itself in them to be a power which brings its own realization, as their lives and actions show; their deeds prove the law of morality to be at work in their lives. As those who fulfil the law, they become a law to themselves (Rom. 2:27), they fulfil the law which they themselves are by nature under the protection of the natural order. We are dealing here (see above OT 2 (c)) with the typically Stoic thought of the moral law founded in nature, which was taken over by Judaism and applied to the Torah. In this way the Mosaic law becomes the universal perfect expression of the moral law founded in nature (H. Lietzmann, *HNT* 8, excursus on Rom. 2:14-16). Law and universe are in common agreement and harmony (cf. Philo, *Op.Mund.* 3, *Abr.* 5). ([Ed.] For an alternative

interpretation of this passage which sees it as a description of what actually has come to pass among Gentile believers in fulfilment of the promise of the new covenant [Jer. 31:31 ff.] → God, art. *theos*, NT 4 (b).)

Paul's prescription concerning coiffure is thus not based only on the scriptures, nor solely on Haggadah, but also on Stoic thought: nature teaches that it is degrading for a man, but a source of pride for a woman, to have long hair (1 Cor. 11:14; → Head).

3. The word occurs in 2 Pet. which can even speak of believers as partakers of the divine nature: "by which he has granted to us his precious and very great promises, that through these you may escape from the corruption that is in the world because of passion, and become partakers of the divine nature [*theias koinōnoi physeōs*]" (2 Pet. 1:4). This is seen as a result of the → "knowledge of our Lord Jesus Christ" (1:8; cf. v. 3) and → "election" (1:10). The thought is evidently not that of a metamorphosis into quasi-deity, for the results of this participation are expressed in positive human qualities. It is rather that to be truly human one needs an enabling which comes from God himself. The teaching is comparable with Paul's teaching on the → new → creation and the teaching in John on being born again (→ Birth, art. *gennaō*). As with being born again in Jn. 3:3, 5, participation in the divine nature and its outworking in life are prerequisite for "entrance into the eternal kingdom of our Lord and Saviour Jesus Christ" (2 Pet. 1:11). In contrast to the divine nature stands the use of the adj. *physikos* which is applied to man in his natural state. The result is the diametrical opposite in both quality of life and outcome: "But these, like irrational animals, creatures of instinct, born to be caught and killed [*aloga zōa gegennēmena physika eis halōsin kai phthoran*], reviling in matters of which they are ignorant, will be destroyed in the same destruction with them" (2 Pet. 2:12). The corresponding adv. occurs only once in the NT in a passage which may be dependent on the latter passage: "But these men revile whatever they do not understand, and by those things that they know by instinct [*physikōs*] as irrational animals do, they are destroyed" (Jude 10). The thought of 2 Pet. 1:4 may be compared with the formulation of Athanasius: "For he became man that we might become divine [*autos gar enēnthrōpēsen, hina hēmeis theopoiēthōmen*]" (*De Incarnatione* 54, which was written some time before A.D. 323). Here the thought is not that man is transformed into the deity, but that man is enabled to share in immortality through the incarnation of the Word of God.

4. Jas. 3:7 twice uses *physis* in the correct Gk. sense of "kind": "for every kind of beast [*pasa gar physis thēriōn*] and bird, of reptile and sea creature, can be tamed and has been tamed by humankind [*tē physei tē anthrōpinē*]." The thought again corresponds with the conception of a regular order of nature. The point of the allusion is to emphasize by contrast the fact that "no human being can tame the tongue – a restless evil, full of deadly poison" (v. 8).

5. *physis*, then, is a typically Gk. and, in particular, a Stoic, concept. It was taken up by Hellenistic Judaism and thus also found a place in Christian thought. It was used mainly by Paul, though it never became a major theological concept. His use of it points in two apparently opposing directions. On the one hand, it emphasizes the gap between Jews and non-Jews. On the other hand, it indicates what they have in common, and in this sense the Stoic usage is particularly marked.   *G. Harder*

→ Adam, → Animal, → Bird, → Creation, → Fish, → Fruit, → Man, → Seed, Harvest

(a). A. J. L. Adams, "The Law of Nature in Greco-Roman Thought", *Journal of Religion* 25, 1945, 97–118; H. H. Barnette, "Towards an Ecological Ethic", *Review and Expositor* 69, 1972, 23–35; J. Barr, "Man and Nature – The Ecological Controversy and the Old Testament", *BJRL* 55, 1972, 9–32; J. W. Beardslee, *The Use of PHYSIS in Fifth-Century Greek Literature*, Dissertation, Chicago, 1918; G. Bornkamm, "The Revelation of God's Wrath (Romans 1–3)", *Early Christian Experience*, 1969, 47–70; R. G. Collingwood, *The Idea of Nature*, 1945; C. H. Dodd, "Natural Law in the New Testament", *New Testament Studies*, 1953, 129–42; P. Evdokimov, "Nature", *SJT* 18, 1965, 1–22; B. Gärtner, *The Areopagus Speech and Natural Revelation*, Acta Seminarii Neotestamentici Upsaliensis 21, 1955, 73–116; E. R. Goodenough, *By Light Light*, 1935; R. M. Grant, *Miracle and Natural Law in Graeco-Roman and Early Christian Thought*, 1952; W. A. Heidel, *"Peri physeōs. A Study of the Conception of Nature among the Pre-Socratics"*, *Proceedings of the American Academy of Arts and Sciences* 45, 1910, 77–133; R. W. Hepburn, "Nature, Philosophical Ideas, of", in P. Edwards, ed., *The Encyclopedia of Philosophy*, 1967, V, 454–58; H. Köster, "NOMOS PHYSEOS. The Concept of Natural Law in Greek Thought", in Festschrift for E. R. Goodenough, 1968, 521–41; and *physis* etc., *TDNT* IX 251–77; A. Lovejoy, "The Meaning of *Physis* in the Greek Physiologers", *The Philosophical Review*, 18, 1909, 369–83; and *The Great Chain of Being*, 1936; H. E. W. Montefiore, ed., *Man and Nature*, 1975; C. F. D. Moule, *Man and his Nature in the New Testament*, 1964; E. C. Rust, *Nature and Man in Biblical Thought*, 1953; and "Nature and Man in Theological Perspective", *Review and Expositor* 69, 1972, 11–22; S. Sambursky, *Physics of the Stoics*, 1959; N. B. Stonehouse, *The Areopagus Address*, 1949 (reprinted in *Paul before the Areopagus and Other New Testament Studies*, 1957, 1–40).

(b). G. Bornkamm, "Gesetz und Natur. Röm. 2, 14–16", *Studien zu Antike und Urchristentum*, 1963², 93–118; H. Diller, "Der griechische Naturbegriff", *Neue Jahrbücher für Antike und deutsche Bildung* 2, 1939, 241–57; F. Heinimann, *Nomis und Physis. Herkunft und Bedeutung einer Antithese im griechischen Denken des 5. Jahrhunderts*, Schweizerische Beiträge zur Altertumswissenschaft 1, 1945; H. Leisegang, "Physis", Pauly-Wissowa XX 1130–64; and "Physis" in *Lexikon der Alten Welt*, 1965; S. Lyonnet, "Lex naturalis et iustificatio Gentilium", *Verbum Domini* 41, 1963, 238–42; R. Muth, "Zum Physis-Begriff bei Platon", *Wiener Studien* 64, 1950, 53–70; H. Patzer, *Physis. Grundlegung zu einer Geschichte des Wortes*, 1940; W. Philipp, "Naturphilosophie", *EKL* II 1516 ff.; M. Pohlenz, *Der hellenische Mensch*, 1947; "Paulus und die Stoa", *ZNW* 42, 1949, 69–104; "Nomos und Physis", *Hermes* 81, 1953, 418–38; and *Die Stoa*, I, 1959², II 1964³; B. Reicke, "Natürliche Theologie nach Paulus", *Svensk Exegetisk Årsbok* 22–23, 1957–58, 154–67; K. H. Schelkle, *Theologie des Neuen Testaments*, I, 1968; O. Thimme, PHYSIS, TROPOS, ETHOS, Dissertation, Göttingen, 1935; W. Trillhaas, "Im welchem Sinn sprechen wir beim Menschen von Natur?" *ZTK* 52, 1955, 272 ff.; and "Natur und Christentum", *RGG³* IV 1326 ff.; R. Walker, "Die Heiden und das Gericht", *EvTh* 20, 1960, 302–14; W. Wieland, *Die aristotelische Physik*, 1962, 231 ff.

Necessity, Must, Obligation

The Gk. approach to life was largely shaped by the consciousness of a necessity in existence and events which is subject to the laws and norms of fate. The impersonal verb-form *dei* (it is necessary) is the most comprehensive expression for this life. It reflects the sense of a determining constraint, no matter whether it was exerted by magic or laws, by men or by gods. The general concept which expresses this feeling of having been consigned to fate (a situation which not only embraces human existence, but, in personifying a universal principle, also dominates the lives of the gods themselves) is *anankē*. By contrast with the words which are associated with fate and nature the vb. *opheilō* originally belonged to the legal sphere; it expressed initially one's legal and economic, and then later one's moral, duties and responsibilities to the gods and to men, or to their sacrosanct regulations. Whereas *opheilō* also expresses human and ethical responsibility in the NT, the typically Gk. concepts of *dei* and *anankē* could only be taken over with some modification which personalized and re-interpreted them so that they express the will of God.

ἀνάγκη

ἀνάγκη (*anankē*), compulsion; ἀναγκαῖος (*anankaios*), necessary; ἀναγκάζω (*anankazō*), compel, force; ἀναγκαστῶς (*anankastōs*), by compulsion.

CL All words based on the word-stem *anank-* (from *an* [*ank*] with reduplication) denote in varying gradations every form of outward or inward pressure which is exerted on men.

For the Greeks *anankē* was the power which determined all reality, the principle which dominated the universe. At various times men ascribed a divine character to it; Plato (*Leg.* 818c) in fact ranked it higher than the gods. Man is under a constraint because of his natural being; the final limitation of his existence by death is also part of this compulsion (cf. W. Grundmann, *TDNT* I 344 f.).

OT In the OT the naturalist outlook of the Gk. world is replaced by a historical one. *anankē* translates several Heb. words which denote the afflictions and distresses of illness, persecution, enmity etc. which were often taken by Israelites to indicate God's alienation from them. They include ṣar (Job 7:11; 15:24; 36:19) and ṣārâh (Job 5:19; 27:9; 31[30]:7; Prov. 17:17) both meaning distress; māṣôq (1 Ki. 22:2; Ps. 119[118]:143) and meṣûqâh (Pss. 25[24]:17; 107[106]:6, 13, 19, 28; Zeph. 1:15), meaning stress, distress. In the last resort, it is Yahweh alone who can save men from *anankē* (Ps. 25[24]:17), and even lead a person into it (Job 20:22; cf. Jer. 9:[15]14, la'ᵃnâh; 15:4 zewā'âh or za'ᵃwâh). He will raise up the great *anankē* on the day of his wrath (Zeph. 1:15), a conception which had powerful effect on the thought of post-exilic Judaism. *anankē* occurs without Heb. equivalent in Tob. 3:6; 4:9; Ep.Jer. 37; 2 Macc. 6:7; 15:2; 3 Macc. 1:16; 4:9; 5:6; 4 Macc. 3:17; 5:13, 16, 37; 6:9, 24; 8:14; 22, 24; 9:6.

NT In the NT the noun *anankē* occurs 17 times, the adj. *anankaios* 8 times and the vb. *anankazō* 9 times. All are predominantly part of the Pauline vocabulary. The vb. *anankazō* in the NT serves in both act. and pass. to describe a compulsion or a being compelled which does not rest on the use of outward force (Matt. 14:22; Acts 28:19; Gal. 2:3). Lk. 14:23 is undoubtedly not thinking of the use of force. The adj. *anankaios* refers once to close friends in the sense of those to whom one is bound (*anankaious philous*, "close friends", Acts 10:24 RSV), but is otherwise used predicatively meaning necessary. In Acts 13:46 this necessity is to be understood analogously to the Lucan *dei* (Lk. 24:7, 26; Acts 1:16; 21; → *dei* NT 2) as an exposition of the concept of salvation-history which is sustained by a belief in the providence of God governing the processes and events of history. The noun *anankē* can be used in everyday language in place of the vb. to denote compulsion: *kai echō anankēn exelthōn idein*, "and I must go out and see it" (Lk. 14:18; cf. 1 Cor. 7:37). In Phlm. 14 and 2 Cor. 9:7 constraint is contrasted with free will. The law involves all kinds of legal necessities (Heb. 7:12; 9:16, 23), of which one (the daily sacrifice which the High Priest offers for himself and the people) is no longer necessary for Christ on account of his one unique sacrifice (Heb. 9:25 f.).

The thought of providence in the history of salvation (→ *dei*) is found in passages such as Matt. 18:7 ("it is necessary that temptations come [*ananke gar elthein ta skandala*]"); Rom. 13:5 ("one must be subject [*dio ananke hypotassesthai*]"); and 1 Cor. 9:16 ("necessity [*ananke*] is laid on me"). Without being confined to any particular phase of salvation-history, *ananke* is used finally almost as an alternative to *thlipsis* (→ Persecution art. *thlipsis*) and to describe the tribulations which continually recur and break in upon believers from outside (1 Cor. 7:26; 2 Cor. 6:4; 12:10; 1 Thess. 3:7). It is against this background that Lk. 21:23 is to be understood: "For great distress [*ananke*] shall be upon the earth." Lk. omits the relative clause of Mk. 13:19 which in fact uses *thlipsis*. *ananke* here does not mark the end of the aeon, only that of → Jerusalem (Lk. 21:20), and with this the times of salvation for the Gentiles begin (Lk. 21:24). *R. Morgenthaler*

| δεῖ | δεῖ (*dei*), it is necessary, one must; μοῖρα (*moira*), fate. |

CL *dei* (attested since Homer) and *deon estin*, it is necessary, one must, both denote a compulsion of some undefined sort. Since the impersonal verb-form does not name the originator of the compulsion, the precise meaning is dependent on the context and on whatever force the necessity evokes. In Gk. thought the coercive power can be someone's will (Polyb., 7, 5, 2), the state laws (Xen., *Mem.* 1, 2, 42) or a spell (K. Preisendanz, *Papyri Graecae Magicae*, I, 4, 2255 ff.). But by far the most powerful and comprehensive force is Fate (*moira*) which determines the necessities of human, historical and cosmic life (Appian, *Libyke* 122, 578: Carthage just had to be conquered; cf. *Corp.Herm.*, 11, 6a: everything always has to happen in every place; → *ananke*). Even the gods are subject to *moira*. This led, notably in the later stages of Hellenism, to an anxiety-filled and fatalistic approach to life.

OT The Heb. OT does not have any word corresponding to the Gk. *dei*. The reason for this is that the Gk. conception of a necessity which works in the manner of fate is foreign to Israel. The OT picture of God is a complete contrast, conceiving him as a personal will powerfully active in history, who claims for himself the lives of individual men. Through the introduction of the notion of *dei* into the LXX the OT understanding of God was influenced by Hellenism, but on the other hand, *dei* was itself transformed by the underlying OT idea of the necessity of the divine will. Alongside its non-theological usage (e.g. 2 Ki. 4:13 f.) the word is found particularly in the context of the law and of apocalyptic expectation. In Lev. 5:17 LXX the cultic prohibitions are called *entolai kyriou, hōn ou dei poiein*, "commands of the Lord concerning those things which one must not do." The impersonal formulation makes it possible for the personal claims of Yahweh's will – the Heb. text uses the 2nd person form – to retreat into the background (cf. Prov. 22:14a). *dei* in the LXX most commonly renders the Heb. infin. (construct) and prep., "in order to". In this way originally final or future statements receive a slightly deterministic re-interpretation. This happens, for example, in the apocalyptic texts of

Dan. (e.g. 2:28: God has revealed what must take place [LXX:*dei*]), whereas the Aram. text reads "what will take place" (cf. 2:29). Another good example is 2:45 where the LXX rightly translates *ta esomena*, "the things that shall be", whereas Theodotion writes *ha dei genesthai*, "the things that must happen."

NT In the NT the Hel. Gk. *dei* and *deon estin* are used with surprising frequency (102 times), in the main in the Gospels, and especially in Lk. (44 times). But the words are freed from their traditional Gk. associations even more decisively than in the LXX. By being connected with God's saving work they are charged with new meaning. The concept of *dei* plays a distinct rôle in three contextual areas: (1) eschatological – apocalyptic expectation; (2) the salvation history interpretation of the way of Jesus; and (3) the context of the Christian life.

1. *Apocalyptic contexts. dei* as an apocalyptic term refers to the future cosmic drama which will inevitably break in upon the world. But it is not a matter of some unalterable fate. Rather, it is a necessity determined by the divine will. In the so-called eschatological discourses war, hunger and a time of great distress are announced: this must all take place (*dei genesthai*) (Mk. 13:7 par. Matt. 24:6, Lk. 21:9; cf. the *dei genesthai* of Dan. 2:28) as must the universal preaching of the → gospel (Matt. 24:14 par. Mk. 13:10) before the end comes (→ Goal).

The beginning of Rev. (1:1) is also based on Dan. 2:28: "The revelation of Jesus Christ which God gave him to show to his servants what must soon take place" (cf. 4:1; 22:6). With this "must" of → judgment and salvation belong the individual acts of the final apocalyptic drama: the enemies of God's witnesses must be killed (11:5), the monster of the last days (the seventh emperor) must remain a little while (17:10), and → Satan must be loosed for a little while (20:3), before the ultimate victory of the → Lamb (22:3).

Paul too is aware of eschatological necessity, such as the final judgment (2 Cor. 5:10), the transformation at the general → resurrection of the dead (1 Cor. 15:52 f.) and the reign of Christ "until he [God] has put all his enemies under his feet" (1 Cor. 15:25; cf. Ps. 110:1 and the whole eschatological context vv. 23–28).

2. *Jesus' life and way as salvation history.* Through his use of *dei* Lk. expresses in numerous ways the fact that Jesus' way was not the result of chance or accident, but that the saving will of God has made history in the life of Jesus into salvation history. A divine necessity expressed by *dei* requires that the twelve years old Jesus must be in his Father's house (Lk. 2:49). In his interpretation of the law Jesus' *dei* conflicts with the *dei* of the Rabbis (Lk. 13:14, 16, the healing on the → Sabbath day). Justice and love are the divine *dei* of the Torah (11:42). Jesus' preaching is directed by the divine will (4:43; 13:33). So too his road to suffering is expressly designated as a divine "must" (9:22; 17:25). It is Lk.'s underlying concern not to depict Jesus' death as the tragic failure of a prophet but to present the death and resurrection of Jesus as necessary saving acts of God; "Was it not necessary that the Christ should suffer these things and enter into his glory?" (24:26; cf. 24:7; Acts 3:21). The Scriptures must be fulfilled (24:44). The will of God manifested and recorded in the OT attained in Christ its complete fulfilment and exposition; this is what Lk. intends to say through his use of the divine *dei* of the way of Jesus.

In the other Gospels *dei* refers primarily the death of Jesus as a divine necessity (Mk. 8:31; Matt. 16:21; Jn. 3:14). Matt. and Jn., like Lk., understand it as a

665

necessary fulfilment of the Scriptures (Matt. 26:54; Jn. 20:9). "The whole will of God for Christ and for man is comprehended in this *dei* as Luke conceives it" (W. Grundmann, *TDNT* II 23).

3. *dei* in the life of the Christian. The divine *dei* covers not only the past history of Jesus and future eschatological events; it also embraces the present life of Christians. Especially in Acts are men implicated in God's saving activity. Paul is not the only one to be led in the plan of God from the days of his conversion to his journey to Rome (Acts 9:6, 16; 19:21; 23:11; 27:24). God's saving will applies to all men. "There is no other name under heaven given among men by which we must be saved" (Acts 4:12).

Jn. 3:7 designates regeneration as a divine "must" for men (→ Birth). Not only the way to salvation, but the Christian life itself is subordinated to the will of God *dei* is found, finally, in the paraenetical material of the NT: in the exhortation to persistent prayer (Lk. 18:1; Jn. 4:24; Rom. 8:26), to conduct that is pleasing to God (1 Thess. 4:1), to discipleship (2 Thess. 3:7) and to peaceableness (2 Tim. 2:24).   *E. Tiedtke, H.-G. Link*

ὀφείλω

ὀφείλω (*opheilō*), owe, be indebted to; ὀφείλημα (*opheilēma*), what is owed, a debt; ὀφειλέτης (*opheiletēs*), debtor; ὄφελον (*ophelon*), O that, would that, if only; ὀφειλή (*opheilē*), obligation.

CL 1. The word-group formed from the stem *opheil-* belongs originally to the sphere of law. *opheilō*, attested since Mycenaean Gk., means: (a) when linked with an obj., to owe someone something, e.g. money, a loan (cf. Egyptian sources in *BGU* III, 846, 16; IV, 1149, 35); and (b) with an infin., to owe in the sense of being indebted (Plato, *Leg.* 4, 717b). An *opheiletēs* is (a) a debtor (Plato, *Leg.* 5, 736d); (b) someone who is under an obligation to achieve something (not found in this sense in the LXX). *opheilē* (rare, and not in the LXX) and the more common *opheilēma* (in the LXX only in Deut. 24:10; 1 Macc. 15:8) denote a debt, particularly of a financial nature, *ophelon*, originally an aorist participle of *opheilō* with the addition of *estin* (is), became the set expression for the optative "O, that", "would that", "if only" (cf. Epict., *Dissertationes* 2, 22, 12).

2. Alongside financial there are also moral obligations in respect of people or of state laws. Thus a culprit is often punished by being required to pay compensation to the injured party (Plato, *Cra.* 400c: until he has made the necessary payments). Infringement of divine regulations and thanks which must be rendered in return for benefactions of the gods also make men debtors, in requiring from them some cultic penance or act. Thus in Plato, *Phaedo* 118, the dying Socrates says: "We owe Asclepius [the god of healing] a cock." Correlates and formations from *opheilō* thus contain both the negative component of debt and the positive one of obligation.

OT 1. In the LXX *opheilō* occurs with striking rarity (12 times in the OT; 10 in the Apocrypha). It is used either in the optative formula *ophelon*, which commonly renders the Heb. particle *lû* or *lū'* (Num. 14:2; 20:3), or in connection with the law of debt, as the equivalent of Heb. *nāšā'*, lend (what is lent becomes what is owed, Isa. 24:2) and *ḥôb*, a debt (Ezek. 18:7). In Deut. 15:2 loans are regulated in such a way that it was characteristic for sacral law in Israel, as distinct from other nations of the ancient world, that monetary debts were not permanently enforced for life. Every seven years they were to be remitted by the creditor (Heb. *šᵉmiṭṭâh*, Deut. 15:1 f., 9; 31:10; LXX *aphesis*, remission of debt). The stipulation concerning pledges in Deut. 24:10 (*opheilēma*) has a pronounced humanitarian character (cf. 1 Macc. 10:43; 13:39, remission of state taxes).

2. The OT does not make use of the concept of legal debt in order to depict obligation to Yahweh. This was due to the fact that man's relationship with God in the OT was not yet conceived as a business agreement between business partners, but as obedience to the will of Yahweh (→ *dei*).

The situation is different in later Judaism, where *opheilō* renders the late Heb. word *ḥôḇ*, which means: (a) to come off badly (from what is demanded of one), i.e. to be guilty, liable to punishment; and (b) (positively) to be indebted. *opheilēma* translates *ḥôḇ* or *ḥôḇâh*, which now comes to refer to arrears in payment, a debt, obligation, and to sin. Sin is plainly no longer now conceived of as intrinsic disobedience, but as an outstanding debt, for which one can compensate by appropriate accomplishments (cf. SB I 421, 800; IV 11, 14). The Qumran texts, significantly, do not reveal a knowledge of this kind of language.

NT In the NT *opheilō* is found linked with the dat. of persons and objects in the acc.

(commonly in Matt. and Lk.), and still more often with the infin. (chiefly in Paul and in other epistles). The word-group is lacking in Mk., the Catholic Epistles (except 1 and 3 Jn.) and Rev. *opheilō* is used in the main in two particular sets of contexts: (1) to designate men's relationship with God (in the Gospels, especially in Matt.); (2) as a paraenetical concept (in the epistles, especially in Paul).

1. From a formal point of view Jesus spoke of men as debtors to God, just as Judaism did. The difference lies in the fact that, unlike Judaism, Jesus took the business relationship to be not the reality, but a parable of men's relationship to God. Consequently the concept of debt (*opheilēma*) is linked by Jesus not with achievements or demands concerning payments of arrears, but with → forgiveness (*aphesis*).

(a) Both these differences are made clear in the parable of the unmerciful servant (Matt. 18:23–35). The picture of the creditor (*daneistēs*) and the debtor (*opheiletēs*) reveals men's dependence on and responsibility to God, who (as Matt. emphasizes again and again) will settle accounts with his servants (Matt. 18:23). The fantastically high sum of money that is stated to be owed (10,000 talents, i.e. about $10,000,000 expresses the nature of the debt: it cannot be paid. Every attempt to repay the debt, even at the expense of the lives of the debtor and of his family, is from the outset an illusion. Only through the compassion of the creditor can the debt be remitted (cf. the context with Deut. 15:2). On the other hand, the parable reveals men's responsibility ("should not [*ouk edei*] you have had mercy" v. 33; → *dei*). By virtue of the great debt that has been remitted by God, men ought to forgive one another the laughably small debts which by comparison their "fellow–servants" owe them, instead of insisting on their legal rights. In v. 28 the 100 denarii is 0.00001% of the 10,000 talents! (On this parable see J. D. M. Derrett, "The Parable of the Unmerciful Servant", *Law in the New Testament*, 1970, 32–47.)

(b) A certain parallel is offered in the parable of the two debtors, which Lk. has woven into the narrative of the sinful woman (Lk. 7:41–43), in order to point out the connection between the greater or lesser degree of love and the greater or lesser degree of debt forgiven. Compare also the falsification of debts in the parable of the unjust steward (Lk. 16:5–7). (See further J. D. M. Derrett, op. cit., 48–77.)

(c) Only in Matt. 6:12 does *opheilēma* correspond to the Rab. *ḥôḇ*, meaning debt (elsewhere in the NT replaced by *hamartia;* → Sin). The fifth request of the Lord's Prayer stresses the correspondence between divine forgiveness of debts and human readiness to → forgive. Human forgiveness is neither a pre-condition for God's forgiveness, nor can it make any claim to it; rather, it is an echo and a command of the forgiveness received (cf. the paraenetic expansion in 6:14 ff.). "The aorist of Mt. (*aphēkamen*) expresses the seriousness of the desire for reconciliation by the completed act, whereas the present of Lk. (*aphiomen*) expresses it by the constant readiness to forgive" (F. Hauck, *TDNT* V 563; cf. Matt. 6:12 with Lk. 11:4).

2. If *opheilō* in the Gospels has the primarily negative meaning of being in debt, in the Epistles it predominantly denotes the positive sense of responsibility which arises out of one's belonging to Christ. In Rom. 13:8 Paul uses the double meaning of *opheilō* to exhort his readers to the → love which is at the same time a task and a debt to one's neighbour which can never be paid. In Rom. 15:1 ff. the connection between ethical obligation and the foundation work of Christ becomes particularly clear: "We who are strong ought [*opheilomen*] to bear with the failings of the weak, and not to please ourselves. . . . For Christ did not please himself." 1 Cor. 11:7 and 10 speak of the duty of discipline in the congregation (→ Head); 2 Thess. 1:3 and 2:13 of the duty of gratitude for the spiritual growth of the congregations; 2 Cor. 12:14 of responsible parenthood; 1 Jn. 3:16 of the sacrifice of one's life; and 2 Cor. 4:11 of mutual brotherly love. 1 Jn. 2:6 summarizes the individual exhortations, "He who says he abides in him ought [*opheilei*] to walk in the same way in which he walked." Heb. uses *opheilō* (2:17; 5:3) in parallel to *dei* and → *prepei*, in order to underline the divine purpose in what befell Christ in the divine work of salvation.

3. The optative particle *ophelon* is found only in Paul (1 Cor. 4:8; 2 Cor. 11:1; Gal. 5:12) and in Rev. (3:15). *opheilē* denotes monetary debt in Matt. 18:32, civil dues in Rom. 13:7, and the command to marital sexual intercourse in 1 Cor. 7:3. *opheiletēs* is a debtor (Matt. 6:12), and one who is under obligation (e.g. Paul in Rom. 1:14) to world mission. In Gal. 5:3 it expresses the obligation to keep the whole law if one practises → circumcision. By contrast, Rom. 8:12 speaks of believers who "are debtors, not to the flesh, to live according to the flesh," and Rom. 15:27 of the debt in Christian giving.   *E. Tiedtke, H.-G. Link*

| πρέπω | *πρέπω* (*prepō*), be fitting, seemly or suitable. |

CL & OT *prepō* is found in cl. Gk. from Homer onwards most frequently in the impersonal forms *eprepen*, it was fitting, and *prepei*, it is fitting. Whereas *dei* and *opheilō* express necessity and obligation, *prepō* expresses that which is proper and appropriate. It is found in the LXX in Pss. 33(32):1 (for *nā'weh*); 65(64):1 (for *dûmiyyâh*); and 93(92):5 (for *nā'âh* in the piel). In post-canonical literature it is found without Heb. equivalent in Sir. 33:28 (30:27); 32(35):3; 1 Macc. 12:11; 3 Macc. 3:20, 25; 7:13, 19. It occurs also in several variant translations of Aquila, Symmachus and Theodotion.

NT In the Gospels it occurs only in Matt. 3:15 in Jesus' reply to the protestations of John the Baptist at Jesus' desire to be baptized: "Let it be so now; for thus it is fitting [*prepon estin*] to fulfil all righteousness" (→ Baptism; → Fullness, art. *plēroō*; → Righteousness). In discussing the question of the veiling of women in worship, Paul asks: "Judge for yourselves, is it proper [*prepon estin*] for a woman to pray to God with her head uncovered?" (1 Cor. 11:13; → Head). In the paraenetical passage Eph. 4:3 asserts: "But immorality and all impurity or covetousness must not even be named among you, as is fitting among saints [*kathōs prepei hagiois*]." The Pastoral Epistles give direction for appropriate conduct for women and the Christian teacher. The women should adorn themselves "by good deeds, as befits [*ho prepei*] women who profess religion" (1 Tim. 2:10). Titus is urged to "teach what befits [*ha prepei*] sound doctrine" (Tit. 2:1). Finally, Heb. makes two observations on the appropriateness of the way Jesus acted. "For it was fitting [*eprepen*] that he, for whom and by whom all things exist, in bringing many sons to glory, should make the pioneer of their salvation perfect through suffering" (Heb. 2:10). "For it was fitting [*eprepen*] that we should have such a high priest. holy, blameless, unstained, separated from sinners, exalted above the heavens" (Heb. 7:26). The former passage is concerned to show the identity of Christ with men; the latter with the difference between him and sinful men. The common factor of all these instances of the word is the absence of external constraint and absolute necessity. In each case the person concerned could have acted otherwise. On the other hand, righteousness and the exigencies of the situation make the conduct specified not only appropriate but imperative. *C. Brown*

(a). W. Grundmann, *anankazō* etc., *TDNT* I 344–47; and *dei* etc., *TDNT* II 21–25; F. Hauck, *opheilō* etc., *TDNT* V 559–66; E. Käsemann, "A Pauline Version of the 'Amor Fati'", in *New Testament Questions of Today*, 1969, 217–35.
(b). E. Fascher, "Theologische Beobachtungen zu *dei*", in *Neutestamentliche Studien für Rudolf Bultmann*, *BZNW* 21, 1954, 228 ff.; M. Pohlenz, *To prepon, Nachrichten der Gesellschaft der Wissenschaften zu Göttingen*, 1933, 53–92; H. Preisker, "Mensch und Schicksal in der römischen Stoa und im Neuen Testament", *Forschungen und Fortschritte* 25, 1949, 274 ff.

New

New and old are correlative and contrary ideas. In temporal terms that which is *neos*, new, young and previously non-existent stands over against that which was at the → beginning (*archē*). *palaios* (→ Old, art. *palai*), old (with the negative overtone of obsolete, worthless, and unserviceable), is materially distinguished from *kainos*, new in the qualitative sense of something previously unknown, unprecedented, marvellous. In the course of time the differences of meaning between *neos* and *kainos* became blurred, even to the point of occasional synonymity. But the NT has significantly used *kainos* with its more qualitative sense in order to give expression to the fundamentally new character of the advent of Christ. The qualitative difference between old and new comes to light most clearly in the NT contrast between the old (→ Old, art. *palai*, NT 2 (b)) and the new man (→ art. *kainos* NT 2 (c)).

καινός

καινός (*kainos*), new; καινότης (*kainotēs*), newness; καινίζω (*kainizō*), renew; καινόω (*kainoō*), make new; ἐγκαινίζω (*enkainizō*), make new, consecrate; ἀνακαινόω (*anakainoō*), renew; ἀνακαίνωσις (*anakainōsis*), renewal.

CL *kainos* is derived from the root *qen*, turn out fresh (cf. Lat. *recens*), and denotes that which is new in its own way. Derivations include: *kainotēs*, newness; *anakainōsis*, renewal (first used in Koine Gk.); *kainizō* (also *enkainizō* and *anakainizō*), renew; and *kainoō* (also *anakainoō*), use for the first time, to make new.

In secular usage *kainos* denotes that which is qualitatively new as compared with what has existed until now, that which is better than the old, whereas → *neos* is used temporally for that which has not yet been, that which has just made its appearance. But the longer these words were used, the less strictly was the conceptual differentiation maintained.

OT 1. The LXX usually translates Heb. *ḥāḏāš* by *kainos*, indicating in daily secular usage something new, something previously not there (e.g. Exod. 1:8, a new king; Deut. 20:5, a new house; Jos. 9:13, new wine-skins; 1 Ki. 11:29, a new cloak).

2. *kainos* finds its theological place chiefly in the eschatological message of the prophets, who bring into question Israel's previous experience of salvation in history and announce a new and saving divine activity in the future. This new move of Yahweh's consists, according to Jeremiah, in the establishment of a new → covenant (Jer. 31 [LXX 38]: 31 ff.: *diathēkē kainē*), in contrast to the covenant at Sinai, in which Yahweh will put his will in Israel's heart, in order to bring about a new obedience among his people. Ezekiel makes a very similar promise of a new → Spirit and a new → heart, which Yahweh will create within man himself (Ezek. 11:19; 18:31; 36:26). Isa. 43:18 f. (NEB) presents the programmatic and antithetical formulation of "Cease to dwell on days gone by and to brood over past history. Here and now I will do a new thing" (cf. Isa. 42:9; 48:6). He understands Yahweh's new activity in leading Israel back out of the Babylonian exile as new → creation which will embrace the nation and the whole created order (Isa. 43:16–21). Isa. 65:17 f. proclaims the creation of a new → heaven and a new → earth (Isa. 65:17 f.). The "new thing" which is awaited and promised in the eschatological proclamation of the prophets as Yahweh's future act reaches from the inner parts of man himself right to the universal dimensions of a new world. The Israelite covenant community responds to both the experienced and expected saving deeds of Yahweh in the new song which is sung aloud in the Psalms (33:3; 40:3; 144:9; 149:1 ff.).

NT 1. (a) The NT also follows the secular usage of *kainos*. It occurs in the sense of unused (Matt. 9:17; 27:60; Mk. 2:21; Lk. 5:36; Jn. 19:41), unfamiliar, interesting (Mk. 1:27; Acts 17:19, 21) and novel (Matt. 13:52; 2 Jn. 5).

(b) But everything in the NT which is connected with Jesus' saving work is also characterized as new; a new → covenant (Matt. 26:28; Lk. 22:20; 1 Cor. 11:25; 2 Cor. 3:6; Heb. 8:8, 13; 9:15), a new → commandment (Jn. 13:34; 1 Jn. 2:7, 8), a new → creation (2 Cor. 5:17; Gal. 6:15), the new existence of → life in the → Spirit (*kainotēs*, newness, Rom. 6:4; 7:6), the new → man (Eph. 2:15; 4:24; cf. *anakainoō*, renew, 2 Cor. 4:16; Col. 3:10), a new → heaven and a new → earth (2 Pet. 3:13; Rev. 21:1), a new → name (Rev. 2:17; 3:12), the new → Jerusalem (Rev. 3:12; 21:2), a new → song (Rev. 5:9; 14:3).

2. Leaving secular usage aside, the following features emerge from an investigation of theological usage.

(a) Most important is the use of *kainos* with *diathēkē* (→ covenant), in both the Synoptic and Pauline traditions of the Last Supper, in the words spoken over the cup: "This cup is the new covenant [*kainē diathēkē*] in my blood" (1 Cor. 11:25; cf. Lk. 22:20). In Mk. 14:24 and Matt. 26:28 only the Koine-texts have added *kainē* to *diathēkē* (→ Lord's Supper). The words signify that the → blood, or the → death, of Jesus is the basis of the new covenant. This is an evident link with the promise of Jer. 31:31 ff. Heb. develops the theme of the new covenant further, contrasting the imperfect old covenant of Sinai with the perfect new one (Heb. 8:6, 7). The quotation from Jeremiah 31:31–34 is explained thus: "In speaking of a new [*kainēn*] covenant he treats the first as obsolete [*pepalaiōken tēn prōtēn*]" (Heb. 8:13). Again and again the statements of Heb. circle around the newness of this covenant (9:15), which can also be called the second (8:7), a better (8:6) or an eternal covenant (13:20). Through Jesus' death and mediating work "those who are called" are in him to "receive the promised eternal inheritance" (9:15).

Paul interprets the new covenant as a covenant of the Spirit in opposition to the old covenant with its written code (2 Cor. 3:6). "We serve in the newness [*kainotēti*] of the Spirit and not in the oldness [*palaiotēti*] of the letter" (Rom. 7:6).

(b) The Synoptics use *kainos* from time to time with the same meaning as *neos* in order to distinguish the new which is an integral part of the appearance of Jesus from the old already in existence, as, for instance, in the parables of new wine in old wine-skins and new patches on an old garment, where *neos* and *kainos* are used synonymously (Mk. 2:21 f.). It is the same when Mk. 1:27 depicts the alarming impression which Jesus' teaching created with the words "a new teaching full of authority [*didachē kainē kat' exousian*]." The nature of the newness is characterized by its contrast with the casuistic Rabbinic method of teaching (Mk. 1:22), by its authoritativeness, and by its power to effect what it says (as the context of the healing of the spirit-possessed man shows).

(c) Paul, in Gal. 6:15, designates God's saving act in the cross of Christ as a new creation (*kainē ktisis*; cf. v. 14), and sets it in opposition to the legalistic way of salvation advocated by those who said that God must be honoured by fulfilling his law which meant that → circumcision was obligatory for all male believers. For Paul God's saving act is something fundamentally new. The new creation of God embraces not only humanity (1 Cor. 8:6) but the whole creation (Rom. 8:18 ff.; cf. Isa. 43:18 ff.).

In 2 Corinthians 5:17 Paul declares: "Therefore, if anyone is in Christ, he is a new creation. The old has passed away, behold the new has come [*hōste ei tis en Christō, kainē ktisis. ta archaia parēlthen, idou gegonen kaina*]" (RSV). Although

671

the word *ktisis* here can mean creature (cf. RSV mg), it more frequently means → creation. It may also be noted that the words "he is" are absent from the Gk. which has no vb. at this point. C. K. Barrett translates the verse: "A further consequence is that if anyone is in Christ, there is a new act of creation: all old things have gone, behold new things have come into being" (*The Second Epistle to the Corinthians*, BNTC, 1973, 162). Barrett links the verse with vv. 14 f. and sees vv. 16 and 17 as parallel, being negative and positive statements of the same truth (op. cit., 173). He regards the phrase "in Christ" not as mystical but as eschatological, "a transference by faith in Christ, who experienced the messianic affliction and was raised from the dead as the firstfruits of the resurrection, from the present age into the age to come." As such it is "a new act of creation", analogous to the original creative act by which the world came into being. *ktisis*, therefore, refers not to the believer in the first instance, but to the creative act of God. Its meaning is essentially the same as that in Gal. 6:15, and it takes up Paul's earlier thought of God's new creative act in Christ in 2 Cor. 4:6: "For it is the God who said, 'Let light shine out of darkness,' who has shone in our hearts to give the light of the knowledge of the glory of God in the face of Christ" (cf. Gen. 1:3).

Barrett points out that the idea of parallels between God's original creation and final act of redemption was familiar in Judaism (ibid.). These parallels go back at least as far as Isa. 51:9 ff. and 54:9 f., and the same book contrasts the old and the new as Paul does here (Isa. 42:9; 43:18 f.). On the rabbinic discussion of new creation (*beriyyâh hadāšâh*) see further W. D. Davies, *Paul and Rabbinic Judaism*, 1955², 119 f.; SB II 421 ff.; III 519; E. Sjöberg, "Wiedergeburt und Neuschöpfung in palästinischen Judentum", *StTh* 4, 1950, 44–85; → Baptism, art. *baptizō* OT 3. Thus Rabbi Simon (fl. A.D. 280) said that not everyone who wishes to say a Psalm may do so; rather it is certain of anyone to whom a miracle has occurred and said a Psalm, that his sins have been forgiven and he has become as a new creature (Midrash Ps. 18 §6 (69ª). Barrett sees a basic difference between Paul and rabbinic thought on the new creation. For the rabbis the emphasis falls on the new creature, whereas Paul is concerned with the new act of creation. He thinks it unlikely that Paul was borrowing a rabbinic expression, and in any case it cannot be demonstrated that the expression was current in Paul's day. He also finds unconvincing the attempts to relate Paul's thought to that at Qumran. Nor is there any concrete evidence for thinking that Paul is drawing on a baptismal tradition here.

In Gal. 4:5 Paul expresses this new reality in terms of adoption. This is not a matter of gaining some new psychological or ethical quality, or of making a new resolution. It entails a daily process of renewal: "Though our outer nature [*ho exō hēmōn anthrōpos*, lit. our outer man] is wasting away, our inner nature is being renewed [*anakainoutai*] day by day." This takes place through the creative and re-creative power of the Spirit given by Christ "in the newness of the Spirit [*en kainotēti pneumatos*]" (Rom. 7:6; cf. Tit. 3:5).

The existence of the new creature involves a new way of life. Since the new life does not exist on or derive from the natural plane, it is hidden with Christ in God (Col. 3:3). Those who enter upon it need the apostolic exhortation to hold fast to their new life and to put on the new man: "Now that you have discarded the old nature with its deeds and have put on the new nature, which is being constantly renewed [*anakainoumenon*] in the image of its Creator and brought to know God ... put on the garments that suit God's chosen people" (Col. 3:9, 10, 12 NEB; cf. Eph. 4:23 f.; Rom. 12:2). The imperative does not invalidate the indicative; rather, the concealment of the existence of the new creation is itself the basis for the energetic imperative to the new way of life (cf. Gal. 5:25). It is in the dialectic of indicative and imperative, gospel and law, gift and task, that, according to Paul, the new life of the Christian moves. It is lived in the unavoidable tension between dedication to the existence of the new creation and appropriation of the new man (cf. G. Bornkamm, "Baptism and New Life in Paul (Romans 6)", *Early Christian Experience*, 1969, 71–86).

The vb. *anakainoō*, renew, occurs in the NT only in Paul in the two passages already noted (2 Cor. 4:16; Col. 3:10). In both cases it is in the passive. The corresponding noun *anakainōsis*, renewal, is not known outside Christian literature and is found only twice in the NT. In Rom. 12:2 believers are exhorted to let this renewal affect their social attitudes: "Do not be conformed [*syschēmatizesthe*] to this world but be transformed by the renewal [*metamorphousthe tē anakainōsei*] of your mind, that you may prove what is the will of God, what is good and acceptable and perfect" (→ Form, arts. *schēma* and *morphē*). Tit. 3:5 sees salvation grounded in renewal: "he saved us, not because of deeds done by us in righteousness, but in virtue of his own mercy, by the washing of regeneration and renewal in the Holy Spirit [*anakainōseōs pneumatos hagiou*]" (→ Birth, art. *palingenesia*).

(d) John's Gospel speaks of the new → commandment, *kainē entolē*, of brotherly love. "I give you a new commandment: love one another; as I have loved you, so you are to love one another" (13:34 NEB). The commandment is new for the reason Jesus was the first to reveal fully what → love means (cf. 15:13; 1:17). Here, too, the imperative to love is grounded in the indicative of the love of Jesus. Because the Christian community has experienced the reality of the self-sacrificial love of Jesus it is freed and summoned at the same time, to transform concern for self into concern for others (cf. R. Bultmann, *The Gospel of John*, 1971, 525). It is not a question of an ethical principle, but of becoming new in love by virtue of the new love of Christ.

In 1 John the point at issue is also that of brotherly love (2:7ff.). The commandment is called, strikingly, old and new at once (2:7 f.; cf. 2 Jn. 5). The exposition is obviously directed against the schismatic desire for innovation. By "old" one should understand the beginning of the Christian life: "the old commandment is the word which you have heard" (2:7). As to content, it is simply the new love for one's brothers that is meant though the christological foundation of Jn's Gospel is not explicitly expounded (2:8–11).

(e) The vb. *enkainizō* occurs only in Heb. Arndt (214) suggests that its meaning in Heb. 10:20 is "open a way" (cf. 1 Sam. 11:14; 1 Clem. 18:10; Ps. 51:10 [50:12]). Thus believers have confidence to enter the sanctuary "by the new and living way which he opened for us [*enekainisen*] through the curtain, that is, through his flesh" (RSV). On the other hand, the meaning of inaugurate, dedicate is suggested for Heb. 9:18. RSV has "ratified": "Hence even the first covenant was not ratified [*enkekainistai*] without blood" (RSV; cf. Deut. 20:5; 1 Ki. 8:63; 2 Chr. 7:5; *IG* XII 5, 712, 58).

(f) *kainos* plays an important role in the visions of Revelation. Those who are victorious over their earthly temptations will receive a white stone with a new name

(2:17; cf. 13:12). The white stone (*psēphon leukēn*) may have been the white stone used by jurors to signify acquittal (Ovid, *Metamorphoses* 15, 41); a token entitling one to free entertainment at royal assemblies (Xiphilin., *Epit.Dion.*, p. 228), hence that which admitted one to the heavenly feast; the precious stones which in rabbinic tradition fell with the manna (Yoma 8); the precious stones on the breastplate of the high priest (Exod. 35:27; 39; cf. 28:28 f.); the white stone regarded as a mark of felicity (cf. Pliny, *Ep.* 6, 11, 3); or a combination of several of these images (cf. R. H. Charles, *The Revelation of St. John, ICC*, I, 1920, 66). The new name would not be that of the bearer, but the one giving authority to the bearer. The context of the vision of Rev. 1 suggests that the new name is that of Christ as Lord (cf. 1:8, 10, 12–20; with Phil. 2:11). For he is the one who has conquered and has assumed Lordship (cf. 2:17a with 5:5 ff.; 22:13, 20). It is he that makes the new reality possible. The heavenly community of the redeemed will strike up a new song in honour of the Lamb who was slain (5:9; 14:3). When the great and final apocalyptic battle has been fought out against Satan, and all the enemies of the Lamb have been defeated, the new → Jerusalem will arise (21:2), and a new heaven and a new earth will be created (21:1; cf. 2 Pet. 3:13). Then there will be no tears, suffering, pain or → death (21:4). In accordance with the expectations of the new in the OT the new element which entered the world with Jesus Christ stretches from the realization of the new man right to the universal hope of a new heaven and a new earth. The One who sits on the throne of the new Jerusalem says: "Behold, I make all things new" (Rev. 21:5).

H. Haarbeck, H.-G. Link, C. Brown

| νέος |

νέος (*neos*), new, young, fresh; νεότης (*neotēs*), youth; νεώτερος (*neōteros*), younger, a younger person; νεόφυτος (*neophytos*), newly planted; ἀνανεόω (*ananeoō*), renew.

CL *neos*, from the Indo-Germanic **neuos*, derived from the adv. *nu*, now, has the temporal sense of belonging to the present moment, and so new, not previously existent, just now appearing, in short: new, young.

1. Secular Gk. uses *neos* as an adj. (attested since Mycenaean Gk.) for things, generally in a temporal sense, new, fresh (cf. Hdt. 5, 19, 2, *neōtera prēgmata*, revolution); and in a fig. sense, occasionally of persons with some recently gained honour or position (cf. Aesch., *PV* 955, 960, *hoi neoi theoi*, the new gods). *neos* is most commonly used, chiefly in the comparative, to designate the age-range of youths from 20 to 30 years old as distinct from the *presbyteroi* or *gerontes*, but also now and again as a noun to denote an inexperienced person, a novice. There is no strict differentiation between *neos* and the generally synonymously used adjs. → *kainos* and *prosphatos* (originally a sacrificial term; *pros* and *phatos* [a verbal adj. cognate with *phonos*, slaughter], just slaughtered, and therefore fresh).

2. The Hellenistic and Roman world was fond of linking *neos* with the name of some god such as Asclepius or Dionysus in their emperor-cults. The ruler, revered as God, was to be celebrated as the visible representation of the divinity. In gnostic and Manichaean religious language one could also speak of the new,

i.e. the redeemed man. But this betrays a dependence on early Christianity (cf. Hippol., *Haer.* 6, 35, 4; J. Behm, *TDNT* IV 897).

ot 1. The LXX uses *neos* chiefly in the comparative form *neōteros* with the meaning of younger, a younger person. *neōteros* is so used for the following Heb. words: *ṣā'îr*, young(er), small(er) (e.g. Gen. 19:31, 34 f., 39); *qāṭān* and *qāṭōn*, small, young(er), youngest (36 times altogether; e.g. Gen. 9:24; 42:13, 15, 20, 34; Gen. 43 and 44 passim); *na'ar*, young man (e.g. Jdg. 8:20; 2 Chr. 13:7; Job 24:5); *yeleḏ*, child (2 Chr. 10:14). In Num. 28:16 the LXX renders *bikkûrîm*, first-fruits, by *ta nea* (the new things) and translates Abib (*'āḇîḇ*), the month of the ripening of the corn, as the month of the first-fruits (*mēn tōn neōn*; Exod. 13:4; 23:15; 34:18; Lev. 2:14; Deut. 16:1). *neos* is used to translate *ḥāḏāš*, new, only 4 times (Lev. 23:16; 26:10; Num. 28:26; Cant. 7:13[14]); otherwise the regular equivalent is *kainos*.

2. In the Apocrypha and inter-testamental literature *neos* comes increasingly to denote youthful inexperience, immaturity and susceptibility (cf. Tob. 1:4; Sir. 9:10; 42:8; 1 Macc. 6:17; 11:54, 57; 13:31; 4 Macc. 2:3; 6:19).

nt 1. The instances of *neos* in the NT, though not so frequent as those of → *kainos*, are scattered in numerous writings. *neos* occurs 7 times in Lk., twice each in Matt. and Mk., once in Jn., 8 times in Paul (6 of them in the Pastorals), and once each in Heb. Jas. and Acts. With *neos* the temporal aspect is dominant, marking out the present moment as compared with a former: new dough (1 Cor. 5:7), freshly prepared and not yet blended with → leaven; new wine, fresh wine, still fermenting (Matt. 9:17, par. Mk. 2:22, Lk. 5:38); a new man, God's new creation (Col. 3:9 f.) the new covenant, God's new design as contrasted with the old covenant broken by men (Heb. 12:24). *neos*, when meaning young (Tit. 2:4), is mainly used in the comparative in the NT (Lk. 15:12; Acts 5:6; Jn. 21:18; 1 Tim. 5:1 f.; Tit. 2:6; 1 Pet. 5:5); *neotēs* accordingly means youth (Mk. 10:20; Lk. 18:21; Acts 26:4; 1 Tim. 4:12). In Lk. 22:26 *ho neōteros* means the youngest. The vb. *ananeoomai* occurs only in Eph. 4:23 where it signifies the "being renewed" of the inner nature, as does *anakainoomai* in Col. 3:10 (see below 5, and *kainos* NT 2 (c)). Heb. 10:20 speaks of the new (*prosphatos*, newly consecrated) way to the sanctuary of God which Christ has first already travelled through his suffering, death and resurrection and which he has thus inaugurated (*enekainisen*) and made accessible to us (→ *kainos*, NT 2 (e)).

2. *neos* in the NT thus characterizes the new thing which Jesus has brought to men both as gift and as task, the new salvation and life which commences at his coming and is completed at his return. *neos* therefore stands in necessary opposition to that which was *palai*, earlier on, of old (Heb. 1:1), that which is *palaios* (→ Old). The *palaios anthrōpos*, the old man, is the autonomous man under sin (Rom. 7:6) which is laid aside (Eph. 4:22) and must be purified from the *palaia zymē*, the old → leaven of unregenerate ways. God himself has declared that the earlier worship which had become so superficial is obsolete. He has abrogated it (*palaioō*, Heb. 8:13), and his will is that believers serve him, not *en palaiotēti grammatos* (Rom. 7:6), in the old and worthless worship of the letter, the written code, but *en kainotēti pneumatos*, in the renewal, in the newness of the Spirit.

675

3. By contrast with *palaios*, old, both *neos* and → *kainos* denote the new salvation which Christ has brought, and the new life of faith in him. The picture of new wine and old wine-skins (Matt. 9:17; Mk. 2:22; Lk. 5:38) makes a sharp distinction between the new (the person and preaching of Jesus) and the old (Judaism and John the Baptist's followers). Jesus calls for a clean break between old and new, since both could only be linked together with resultant mutual disadvantages. The parable is to be understood against the background of the incompatible opposition in which Jesus stands to everything that has gone before. The new wine at the wedding feast at Cana also shows that the new is better than the old (Jn. 2:1–11), even though the words new and old are not used in the account.

4. The picture of the congregation as new dough (*neon phyrama*) which is separated from the → leaven of "malice and evil" takes the thought a step further (1 Cor. 5:7). Just as the old leaven has to be cleansed out annually at the Passover (Deut. 16:3 f.) and a fresh start made, so nothing of the old life should be allowed to corrupt the new. In context Paul is talking about → boasting which ill befits the Corinthians in view of their recent case of gross immorality (1 Cor. 5:1–6). He goes on to urge the Corinthians to celebrate the festival "with the unleavened bread of sincerity and truth" (5:8). For the church has entered a new era, a new Passover time, "For Christ, our paschal lamb, has been sacrificed" (5:7).

5. The vb. *ananeoō* occurs in the NT only at Eph. 4:23, where it is best taken as a passive: "and be renewed [*ananeousthai*] in the spirit of your minds." The following v. adds: "and put on the new nature [*ton kainon anthrōpon*], created after the likeness of God in true righteousness and holiness" (→ *kainos*).

6. Even though the word-groups *neos* and *kainos* are largely used synonymously, the observation may still be made that *neos* tends to stress the reality of salvation in the present, whereas *kainos* emphasizes more strongly the character of eschatological fulfilment. *H. Haarbeck*

→ Old

(a). J. Behm, *kainos* etc., *TDNT* III 447–54; and *neos* etc., *TDNT* IV 896–901; G. Bornkamm, "Baptism and New Life in Paul (Romans 6)", *Early Christian Experience*, 1969, 71–86; R. Bultmann, *The Gospel of John*, 1971, 526 f.; R. A. Harrisville, "The Concept of Newness in the New Testament", *JBL* 74, 1955, 69–79.
(b). G. Harbsmeier, " 'Alt' und 'Neu' in der Verkündigung", *EvTh* 27, 1967, 286 ff.; F. Hahn, "Die Bildworte vom neuen Flicken und vom alten Wein", *EvTh* 31, 1971, 357 ff.; A. von Harnack, "Die Terminologie der Wiedergeburt und verwandter Erlebnisse in der ältesten Kirche", *TU* 42, 1918, 101 ff., 135 ff.; W. Nagel, "Neuer Wein in alten Schläuchen (Mt. 9, 17)", *Vigiliae Christianae* 14, 1960, 1 ff.; P. Stuhlmacher, *Gerechtigkeit Gottes bei Paulus*, *FRLANT* 87, 1966², 213 ff.

Nicolaitan

| Νικολαΐτης | Νικολαΐτης (*Nikolaitēs*), Nicolaitan; cf. Νικόλαος (*Nikolaos*), Nicolas. |

1. Member of a sect of primitive Christian times, apparently formed from the personal name Nicolas or Nicolaus. The term occurs in the NT only at Rev. 2:6 and 2:15, in the epistles to the churches in Ephesus and in Pergamum. The first

passage commends the church's rejection of them without specifying the nature of their teaching. It is an open question whether they are to be identified with the "false apostles" of v. 2. The more explicit context of Rev. 2:15 must be the basis for any interpretation of the tenets of the group. There they are equated in some sense with Balaam, who taught Israel "to eat things sacrificed to idols, and to commit fornication" (cf. Num. 25:1–3; 31:16). The same sins are also ascribed to the teaching of "Jezebel" at Thyatira (Rev. 2:20), but she is never called a Nicolaitan, though the trend of her influence is represented as similar. Both passages, as far as we may judge from them, seem to concern errors of practice rather than of speculative doctrine, though the phrase "they have not known the depths of Satan" (2:24) suggests the possibility of some kind of gnostic background for the Jezebel teaching.

2. The value of the later references to Nicolaitans is debatable. Irenaeus (*Haer*. 1, 26, 3) makes them the followers of Nicolas the deacon of Acts 6:5, but adds nothing which might not possibly be explained as inference from Rev. In *Haer*., 3, 11, 7, he treats them as the earliest exponents of the error of Cerinthus and ascribes to them a gnostic cosmology. This might however be an inference from a tradition connecting John's opponents with the *"gnōsis* falsely so-called" (1 Tim. 6:20), to which Irenaeus here appears to refer. These tenets *might* then merely have been read back from subsequent developments.

Others condemn the Nicolaitans as teaching hedonism and immorality (Clem. Alex., *Strom*. 2, 20; *Apost.Const*. 6, 8, 2; Ignatius (long recension) *Trall*. 11; *Philad*. 6; Tertullian, *Adv.Marc*. 1, 29; *De Pudic*. 19), following Rev. without otherwise specifying their doctrines. In Tertullian, *Praescr.Haer*. 33, and Hippolytus, *Haer*., 736, they are associated or compared with gnostic groups, but neither passage is explicit.

3. It is sufficiently clear from the primary references that Nicolaitanism was a libertarian or antinomian movement, whatever else it may have been or become also. The most promising key to a more precise interpretation is the parallel with Balaam in Rev. 2:14–15. Balaam's evil counsel is never explicitly recorded in the OT, but the inference from comparison of Num. 31:16 with Num. 25:1–2 is that he was responsible for contriving the sin of Israel with the daughters of Moab, an incident which became much elaborated in Jewish tradition by the first century A.D. (cf. Philo, *Vit. Mos*., 1, 54, 295 ff.; Joephus, *Ant*., 4, 6; 6, 126 ff.).

C. A. Heumann in 1712 first proposed that an etymological play was intended on the names "Balaam" and "Nicolas", both being taken to mean "lord" (Heb. *ba'al*) or "destroyer" (Heb. *bāla'*) "of the people". The artificiality of this etymology is not necessarily decisive against it: the question is whether it was current in antiquity. It is very probably no more than a modern fancy. Yet Balaam is unexpectedly prominent in Jewish tradition. He was a type of lawless wickedness, the antagonist of → Moses the law-giver. And in the NT Jude 11 and 2 Pet. 2:15 refer to controversies involving his name. There is some reason to think that a polemical use of the name was already current in the milieu of the Asian churches (cf. the messianic use of Balaam's prophecy in Num. 24:17, echoed in Rev. 2:26–28). Jewish sources sometimes associated Balaam with Jesus as a representative opponent of the Torah (R. T. Herford, *Christianity in Talmud and Midrash*, [1903] 1972, 63 ff.). The point of the objection may have been that the followers of

677

Jesus opposed faith to law and therefore appeared to sanction an antinomianism which gave licence to immorality. Paul was ever conscious that his gospel was open to this perversion, but refused to countenance it (cf. e.g. Rom. 6:1).

Balaam's advocacy of eating idol-offerings and of fornication brings us also to the terms of the Apostolic Decree of Acts 15:20, 29, which echo Num. 25:1–2. The Acts represents Paul, to whom antinomians might appeal, as having assented to these terms.

In Rev. John rejects the application of the term "Balaam" to Christians as such, while turning the word against a perversion to which the gospel of faith apart from works was open.

4. It is not clear whether the Nicolaitans are necessarily to be seen as gnostics, as Harnack formerly argued. But changing conditions might bring new arguments to the fore, and those who once appealed to Pauline teaching might later use such new fashions of thought as suited their end. Nor can we judge the vexed question whether the Nicolaitans are to be connected with the antinomians of Jude and 2 Pet.

The churches of Asia were, I suggest, under severe pressures under Domitian and could secure their position only by accommodation either to Judaism or to the dictates of pagan society. The Nicolaitans (and Jezebel) are mentioned in connection with those three cities where we have reason to think the pagan compromise was most insistent. The temptation to idolatry at Thyatira may plausibly be connected with the strength of the pagan trade-guilds in that city: the Christian who valued his livelihood was under pressure to participate in the idolatrous feasts of his guild. At Ephesus there was the power of the Artemis cult. Pergamum was the provincial centre of the imperial cult, and a new rigour of enforcement of that cult by Domitian faced the church with an acute dilemma. Safety might be assured only by what John saw as amounting to apostasy. The Nicolaitans and their kind were plausible advocates of the pagan compromise (cf. further C. J. Hemer in *PEQ*. 105, 1973, 6–12, and literature there cited). *C. J. Hemer*

(a). G. R. Beasley-Murray, *The Book of Revelation, New Century Bible*, 1974, 85–91; H. Cowan, "Nicolaitans", *HDB* III 547 f.; E. S. Fiorenza, "Apocalyptic and Gnosis in the Book of Revelation and Paul", *JBL* 92, 1973, 565–81; A. von Harnack, "The Sect of the Nicolaitans and Nicolaus, the Deacon of Jerusalem", *Journal of Religion* 3, 1923, 413–22; C. J. Hemer, *A Study of the Letters to the Seven Churches with Special Reference to their Social Background*, Dissertation, Manchester, 1969, 191–206; R. W. Moss, "Nicolaitans", *ERE* IX 363–66; W. M. Ramsay, *The Letters to the Seven Churches*, 1904, 299–302, and 335–53.
(b). N. Brox, "Nikolaos und Nikolaiten", *Vigiliae Christianae* 19, 1965, 23–30; M. Goguel, "Les Nicolaïtes", *Revue de l'Histoire des Religions* 115, 1937, 5–36.

Nineveh

Νινευή

Νινευή (*Nineuē*), less common: Νινευί (*Nineui*), Nineveh; Νινευίτης (*Nineuitēs*), Ninevite.

CL Nineveh (Gk. *Ninos, Ninus*) is cited copiously in the classical Gk. historians.

Xenophon refers to the city of Mespila (*Anab.* 3, 4, 10) observing that it was once inhabited by the Medes. Mespila is modern Mosul, the city opposite Nineveh on the west bank of the Tigris. Nineveh is cited by Herodotus on a number of occasions and Dio (*Roman History*) cites it in a description of the Roman incursion into Assyria. Diodorus and Strabo make mention of the city as well. Josephus makes numerous references to the city (e.g. *Ant.* 9, 10, 21; 9, 11, 3) attributing its founding to Assyras.

OT The references to Nineveh in the LXX (cf. Gen. 10:11 f.; Isa. 37:37; Jon. 1:2; Zeph. 2:13) are similar to the references in the Heb. OT. The Heb. form *nîneweh* denotes both the district (Ass. *ninua[ki]*) and the metropolis (*[āl]-ninua*).

Nineveh is mentioned 17 times in the OT. According to Gen. 10:11, 12, the city was founded by Nimrod and, in 2 Ki. 19:36, Sennacherib is described as returning to his royal residence at Nineveh after his failure to conquer Jerusalem (cf. also 2 Ki. 18:15). A parallel reference occurs in Isa. 37:37.

The city figures prominently in the prophecy of → Jonah (1:2; 3:2, 3,4, 5, 6, 7; 4:11) where its wickedness is described as the cause for its threatened destruction. The three days' journey required to cross it (Jon. 3:3) possibly refers to the administrative district of Nineveh (Hatra-Khorsabad-Nimrud). The preaching of the prophet Jonah led to repentance on the part of the citizens of that city which averted the impending catastrophe (Jon. 3:10).

The city of Nineveh also figures prominently in the prophecy of Nahum. The book of Nahum is a prophetic oracle dealing solely with the destruction of Nineveh (cf. Nah. 1:1; 3:7). The reference to the opening of the river gates (Nah. 2:6) may picture the inundation of part of the city effected by a coalition of Medes, Babylonians and Scythians who conquered Nineveh.

Nineveh is cited in the prophecy of Zephaniah (2:13) where its destruction is mentioned along with the destruction of other peoples in an oracle depicting God's → judgment on Israel's enemies and Israel's eventual vindication.

Nineveh is mentioned in cuneiform sources from the reigns of Gudea (2200 B.C.) and Hammurabi (*c.* 1750 B.C.). Extensive archaeological excavation at the site of ancient Nineveh has revealed occupation from prehistoric times. In the reigns of Shamshi-Adad I (*c.* 1800 B.C.) and Hammurabi the city's importance as the site of the temple of Ishtar was maintained in the restoration and beautification of the temple. With the restoration of Assyria's fortunes under Shalmaneser I (*c.* 1260 B.C.) Nineveh gained in importance and became one of the royal residences.

Perhaps the Assyrian king who made the greatest contribution to the greatness of Nineveh was Sennacherib who rebuilt the defences of the city and constructed a system of dams and canals. A number of buildings and parks were constructed during his reign as well (704–681 B.C.).

Several important cultural contributions were made by Ashurbanipal (669–627 B.C.). Bas-reliefs from this time witness to the high degree of skill achieved by the artists who were encouraged by Ashurbanipal's love for the arts.

With the death of Ashurbanipal there began the events which led to the decline of the Assyrian empire and the demise of Nineveh. The alliance of Babylonians, Medes and Scythians was able to effect the fall of Nineveh in 612 B.C. after a siege of several months. Thereafter Nineveh became a symbol of Assyria's utter collapse.

Archaeological excavations have been carried on extensively at the site of ancient Nineveh beginning with the work of Austen Layard in 1847. The present site of Nineveh is marked by two mounds, Tell Quyunjiq ("hill of many sheep"), a name reminiscent of Zephaniah's prophecy concerning Nineveh (Zeph. 2:14), and Tell Nebi Yunus ("hill of the prophet Jonah") which is still covered by a village.

As the chief city of Assyria Nineveh was the crystallization of the culture and power of that kingdom. As such, it represented to the OT prophets the seat of the cruelty and oppression that the Assyrian empire had brought to bear on Israel.

T. McComiskey

NT Nineveh is referred to in the Matthaean and Lucan versions of the saying concerning the sign of the prophet → Jonah. "The men of Nineveh will arise at the judgment with this generation to condemn it; for they repented at the preaching of Jonah, and behold, something greater than Jonah is here" (Matt. 12:41 par. Lk. 11:32). The wording is identical, but whereas Matt. 12:42 goes on to cite a similar instance of the pagan "queen of the South" (the queen of Sheba, 1 Ki. 10:1–13) coming from the ends of the earth to hear the wisdom of Solomon, Lk. inverts the two illustrations. The point of both stories is to contrast the responsiveness of outsiders with the chosen people which Jesus calls "this generation". For not content with what Jesus has already said and done, they still sought a sign (cf. also Matt. 16:1; 1 Cor. 1:22). Jesus replies that "An evil and adulterous generation seeks for a sign; but no sign shall be given to it except the sign of the prophet Jonah. For as Jonah was three days and three nights in the belly of the whale, so will the Son of man be three days and three nights in the heart of the earth" (Matt. 12:39 f.; cf. Lk. 11:29). The reply was enigmatic, for it was, as one might expect, not the → generation that was judged but the prophet. In the first instance the sign indicates the rejection of the prophet (cf. Jon. 1:4, 10, 12, 15). But it also indicates that death will not be the end of the Son of man, and that his vindication will soon come. Then follows the reference to the citizens of Nineveh who responded to the preaching of Jonah when the prophet proclaimed that the Lord intended to overthrow the city because of its wickedness (cf. Jon. 3:1–10). The allusion invites a similar response, so that judgment may be averted. This is underlined by the implicit contrast between the hearers of Jesus who were not pagans (like the people of Nineveh) but members of the people of God, and by the explicit contrast between Jonah and Jesus. The expression "and behold, something greater than Jonah is here" invites the hearers to think for themselves as to who Jesus is and what was his relation to the kingdom of God which he proclaimed (cf. Matt. 16:13 ff.; Mk. 8:27 ff.; Lk. 9:18 ff.).

Lk.'s account omits the reference to the three days and nights. It focuses entirely on the response of the Ninevites: "For as Jonah became a sign to the men of Nineveh, so will the Son of man be to this generation" (Lk. 11:30). The implication is that Jonah preached to the Ninevites as one who had come from the dead.

M. Black suggests that the vb. *anastēnai . . . meta* (arise with) represents a well-attested Semitism meaning dispute, and that the words *en tē krisei* were added in the Gk. to make the Aramaic idiom intelligible (*An Aramaic Approach to the Gospels and Acts*, 1967², 134). *C. Brown*

→ Jonah, → Judgment, → Resurrection

A. H. Layard, *Nineveh and its Remains*, I–II, 1849; and *Discoveries in the Ruins of Nineveh and Babylon*, 1853; A. Parrot, *Nineveh and the Old Testament*, 1955; G. Smith, *Assyrian Discoveries*, 1875; E. A. Speiser, "Nineveh", *IDB* III 551 ff.; R. C. Thompson and R. W. Hutchinson, *A*

Century of Exploration at Nineveh, 1929; R. C. Thompson, "The Buildings on Quyunjiq, the larger mound of Nineveh", *Iraq* 1, 1934, 95–104; R. C. Thompson and R. W. Hutchinson, "The site of the palace of Ashurnasirpal at Nineveh", *Liverpool Annals of Archaeology and Anthropology* 18, 1931, 79; "The British Museum Excavations on the Temple of Ishtar at Nineveh", ibid. 19, 1932, 55–116; R. C. Thompson and M. E. L. Mallowan, "The British Museum Excavations at Nineveh, 1931, 1932", *Liverpool Annals of Archaeology and Anthropology* 20, 1933, 71–120; D. J. Wiseman, "Nineveh", *NBD* 888 ff.; and "Nineveh", *ZPEB* IV 440–44.

Noah

| $N\omega\acute{\varepsilon}$ | $N\omega\acute{\varepsilon}$ (*Nōe*), Heb. *nōaḥ*, Noah.

OT 1. Noah (Heb. *nōaḥ*, probably cognate with *nûaḥ*, "rest") was the tenth in line of descent from Adam (Gen. 5:28 f.) and figures as the hero of the flood narrative (Gen. 6:11–9:19), as an outstandingly righteous man (Gen. 6:9, 7:1; Ezek. 14:14, 20) who "found favour in Yahweh's eyes" (Gen. 6:8), and as the first man to plant a vineyard (Gen. 9:20) – which was apparently the fulfilment of his father Lamech's prophecy at his birth: "Out of the ground which Yahweh has cursed this one shall bring us relief [*yᵉnaḥᵃmēnû*] from our work and from the toil of our hands" (Gen. 5:29). With his wife, his three sons and their wives, he survived the flood in the ark which he constructed at God's command, and became the ancestor of the new, post-diluvial world.

He is mentioned in Ezek. 14:14, 20, where God affirms that, if Noah lived in Jerusalem in the period preceding its destruction by the Babylonians, his righteousness would avail to deliver himself alone (not even, presumably, the seven members of his family who were delivered with him at the time of the flood). On a more cheerful note, on the eve of the return from the Babylonian exile Jerusalem is assured that Yahweh's steadfast love to her will be as irrevocable as his covenant with the human race in "the days of Noah" (Isa. 54:9 f.; cf. Gen. 9:8–17).

2. The Jewish wisdom writers found in Noah an example of true wisdom. Because he "was found perfect and righteous", says Ben Sira, "a remnant was left to the earth when the flood came" (Sir. 44:17 f.). "When the earth was flooded", says the author of Wisdom, "wisdom saved it again, steering the righteous man in a cheap structure of wood" (Wis. 10:4). Philo notes that Noah is "the first man recorded as righteous in the sacred scriptures" (*Congr.* 90) and gives "righteousness" alongside "rest" as the meaning of his name (*Abr.* 27). He praises him as a victorious athlete, who won his citation because "he had been well-pleasing to God" (*Abr.* 35; cf. Gen. 6:9 LXX).

3. The Ethiopic Enoch incorporates parts of one or more Noah apocalypses (6–11; 54:7–55:2; 60; 65:1–69:25; 106; 107). Most of these are concerned with the fall of the angels, the ensuing → judgment of the flood and the age of blessing to follow. One of them, however (106:1–19), describes the new-born Noah as a wonder-child: Lamech suspects that he may be the son of an intrusive angel, and consults his father Methuselah, who in turn goes to "the ends of the earth" to consult *his* father Enoch. Enoch confirms that Noah is indeed Lamech's son, and that God will do "a new thing on the earth" in his day. Essentially the same story

681

appears in the Genesis apocryphon from Qumran (1Q GenApoc. 2) and in fragments from Cave 4, one of which even gives the baby's weight (J. T. Milik, *Ten Years of Discovery in the Wilderness of Judaea*, 1959, *SBT* 26, 35).

NT 1. In the teaching of Jesus the flood of Noah's day is recalled, like the destruction of Sodom and the neighbouring cities, as a pattern of the judgment that will overtake the world at the coming of the Son of man, especially in its swiftness and suddenness (Lk. 17:26 f.; cf. Matt. 24:37–39).

2. In Heb. 11:7 Noah's faith is emphasized; the quality of his faith was manifested by his prompt obedience to the divine admonition (cf. Gen. 6:22). Thus he "condemned the world" (i.e. exposed the perversity of those who refused to believe God) and (like Abraham at a later date) was justified by faith.

3. In 1 Pet. 3:19 ff. there is a reference to the spirits imprisoned because of their disobedience "when God's patience waited in the days of Noah, during the building of the ark, in which a few, that is, eight persons were saved through water." To these spirits Christ is said to have made proclamation – proclamation, it may be inferred, of his triumph which finally sealed their doom. The relevance of the flood narrative to the life-setting of 1 Peter lies in its providing an OT counterpart to Christian → baptism which the readers of the letter were "now" receiving (v. 21).

4. In 2 Pet. 2:4 f. the preservation of Noah, "with seven other persons", is set in antithesis to the imprisonment in Tartarus of the rebel angels until the last judgment (cf. Jude 6) – a guarantee of God's power to preserve the godly and punish the wicked. Noah is here called "a herald [*kēryx*] of righteousness"; cf. Jos., *Ant.* 1, 74; Sib.Or. 1:125 ff.; 1 Clem. 7:6; 9:4, and Gen. R. 30:7 (on Gen. 6:9) which says that "God had a herald [*kārōz*] in the generation of the flood." In 2 Pet. 3:5–7 the destruction by water of "the world that then existed" is viewed as a harbinger of the destruction of the present world by fire.

5. The absence of any mention of Noah in the Pauline letters is noteworthy. Although he was the second father of the human race, he is not treated as a typical figure like Adam (Rom. 5:12 ff.). Neither does Paul make any reference to the "Noachian decrees" – the injunctions of Gen. 9:1–7 which were held in rabbinical teaching to be binding on all Noah's descendants, Gentiles as well as Jews. According to the oldest forms of this teaching, six of the seven "Noachian decrees" had already been enjoined on Adam; only the seventh (the prohibition of eating flesh with the blood in it) was given for the first time to Noah (SB III 36). Paul regarded the ungodliness of the pagan world (Rom. 1:18 ff.) as disobedience to God's *creation* ordinances.

The "Noachian decrees" may be reflected in the apostolic ruling of Acts 15:20, 29; 21:25, especially in the Western text, where the original wording, with its emphasis on food restrictions, has been given the form of a mainly ethical requirement that Gentile converts to Christianity should abstain from idolatry, fornication and → "blood" (it being left uncertain whether this means eating with the blood or shedding human blood).   F. F. Bruce

(a). C. K. Barrett, *From First Adam to Last*, 1962, 23–26, 30; A. Heidel, *The Gilgamesh Epic and Old Testament Parallels*, 1946; W. G. Lambert and A. R. Millard, *Atrahasis: The Babylonian Story of the Flood*, 1969; B. Reicke, *The Disobedient Spirits and Christian Baptism*, 1946; E. Schürer, *A History of the Jewish People in the Time of Jesus Christ* II, ii, 318 f.; S. S. Schwarzschild and S.

Berman, "Noachide Laws", *Encyclopaedia Judaica*, 1972, II, 1189–1191; D. Young, E. Hallevy, *et al.*, "Noah", *Encyclopaedia Judaica*, 1972, XII, 1191–1198.
(b). G. Fohrer, "Noah", *RGG*³ III 1501 f.; G. Strecker, "Noachidische Gebote", *RGG*³ III, 1500 f.

Number

| ἀριθμός | ἀριθμός (*arithmos*), number. |

CL *arithmos*, is derived from a root **ar*, to fit; cf. *ara*, fitting; *harmonia*, construction; *arthmos*, connection, friendship; Lat. *ars*, art.

1. *arithmos* denotes in general Gk. usage (a) that which has been brought together, a quantity, total, number, extent, amount (e.g. *chrysiou*, of gold, Xen., *Cyr.* 8, 2, 16). But it can also mean (b) the assessment of numbers, i.e. count, muster (Hdt., 8, 7), and then a troop, a military unit (*CIG*, V, 187). Anyone who (c) is included in the count is a man of distinction or reputation (Homer, *Od.* 11,449; Eur., *Frag.* 519). Conversely *en oudeni arithmō einai* (to be in no number) is to be ignored, disregarded. Where *arithmos* is understood as quantity as opposed to quality it can be (d) the virtual embodiment of that which is worthless, futile, empty (cf. *arithmos logōn*, empty words, Soph., *OC* 382). Occasionally (e) *arithmos* has the sense of code, cipher.

2. In the popular and religious and philosophical thought of Hellenism *gematria* (the process of encoding a word by adding together the numerical value of its component letters) gained great significance. The decoding of a gematrical number was only possible for the initiated, since the sum itself is ambiguous. The scribbling found on a wall in Pompeii (before A.D. 79) which runs: "I love her whose number is 545" might be called a kind of gematrical frivolity. The combination of three words with the numerical value 284 (*Gaios – hagios – agathos*, found by adding together the value of the individual letters) in a Roman inscription is even more odd. *Gaios* (numerical value: 3 + 1 + 10 + 70 + 200) is at the same time to be called a *hagios* (pure; numerical value: 1 + 3 + 10 + 70 + 200) and an *agathos* (good, fine; numerical value: 1 + 3 + 1 + 9 + 70 + 200) man. The words are interchangeable from the point of view of gematria, because they are of equal value. The "number of the year" *Abrasax*, 365, mentioned in the Leiden magical papyrus, betrays the stamp of a speculative gematria, which arbitrarily replaces the number of days in a year by a meaningless – but therefore all the more mysterious – word; the word *Abrasax* retains its mysterious character in later gnostic texts.

OT 1. The LXX renders several Heb. and Aram. terms by *arithmos*, most commonly *mispār*, number, corresponding as a rule with the general Gk. meaning (a) (above CL) e.g. Gen. 34:30; Exod. 16:16. *arithmos* has the same sense when translating *middâh*, measure (Ps. 38[39]:5); *rō'š*, (lit. head) sum, total (Num. 1:49); *miksâh*, number, amount (Exod.12:4; cf. Lev. 27:23); and Aram. *minyān*, number (Ezr. 6:17); and when rendering *bimᵉṭē mᵉ'âṭ*, with few people, in small numbers (Deut. 26:5); *'ēn mispār* or *'ēn qēṣeh*, without end, i.e. innumerable (Gen. 41:49; Isa. 2:7); and *'aṣᵉmû missappēr*, to be exceedingly numerous (Ps. 40:5 [39:6]). The meaning CL 1 (b) occurs (*inter alia*) in 1 Chr. 7:5 (*yāḥaś* in hithp.), enroll by genealogy (in the family register); Isa. 34:2 (*ṣābā'*, host); 2 Chr. 17:14 (*pᵉquddâh*, muster, enumeration). Meanings CL 1 (c)–(e) are not attested in the OT.

2. In Rabbinic and Jewish Hellenistic literature, however, as well as the meanings 1 (a) and 1 (b) (e.g. 2 Macc. 8:16; 3 Macc. 5:2), gematria is also found as an exegetical method and for coding, without *arithmos* always occurring specifically or the gematrical process being identified as such. Tg.O., for example, replaces the information in Num. 12:1 that → Moses took a "Cushite" (heathen) wife by the information that the woman was "lovely to look at"; both produce the numerical value 736. (For a further succession of gematriae cf. Sib. 5:12 ff.)

NT 1. The NT links up with the LXX linguistic usage in that it generally only has the meanings CL 1 (a) 1 (b) for the word *arithmos*, which in any case only occurs 18 times (including 10 passages in Rev., and 4 in Acts). Meaning 1 (a) without concrete numerical details is found in Rom. 9:27; Rev. 20:8 (quotation of Isa. 10:22, though not the LXX); and with numerical details in (e.g.) Jn. 6:10; Acts 4:4, Rev. 5:11; 7:4. Meaning 1 (b), in the writer's opinion, appears in Lk. 22:3 (company). No usage of CL 1(c) and 1 (d) can be detected, although in Rev. 13:17 f. there is found the formulation "the name of the beast or the number of his name", an express summons to calculate "the number of the beast" which is "the number of a man". The number itself is given as 666, or according to other less significant MSS 616 (probably not original). This is thus an instance of 1 (e) (cf. also 15:2).

2. Rev. 13:17 f. is the sole place where the word *arithmos* assumes exegetical importance in the NT. Doubtless the matter in hand here is a functional gematria, which on obvious grounds puts into code the name of the person intended. The context speaks pictorially of a "beast" (→ Animal, art. *thērion*), which in church and exegetical tradition has been customarily and probably pertinently interpreted of the → Antichrist. "The number of the beast", which is stated to be "the number of a man", shows that behind the beast and the number there is concealed a human figure known to the hearers and readers of the text of that time. This excludes all attempts to decode the number which do not relate to a human figure. (In passing it may be noted that the text does not make it explicit whether one is to employ the Gk. or Heb. alphabet for the interpretation of the number 666, though the text itself is in Gk.)

Of the many attempts at interpretation the consonantal Heb. script for "Caesar Nero" (*qsr nrwn* = 100 + 60 + 200 + 50 + 200 + 6 + 50 = 666), for example, has some probability. This solution is all the more attractive in that, combined with 17:11 ("the beast which was and is not"), it could refer to the legend of *Nero redivivus*, so that the Antichrist would thus be painted in the colours of the hated Nero. The fact that the story of *Nero redivivus* is also known from Judaic apocalyptic literature (cf. e.g. Sib. 5:138 ff.) would support this. But no definite interpretation of Rev. 13:17 f. can be given; E. Stauffer interprets it of Domitian in "666", *Coniectanea Neotestamentica* 11, 1947, p. 237 ff. The same applies to the number of 153 fish in Jn. 21:11 which may also be regarded as a cipher. (See further W. Bousset, *Die Offenbarung Johannis*, KEK 16, [1906] 1966, 368–79; J. Behm, *Die Offenbarung Johannis* 1920, I, 364–68; *NTD* 11, 1949, 79 ff.; R. H. Charles, *The Revelation of St. John, ICC*, II, 70 f., 76–87; G. B. Caird, *The Revelation of St John the Divine, BNTC*, 1966, 174 ff., 216 ff.)

As the process of gematria has already shown, numbers in the ancient world do not merely indicate quantities but also qualities. Some numbers, in addition to their quantitive meaning, also possess an almost fixed inner symbolic meaning. This is especially true of the numbers four, seven and twelve, which are found in the NT with a striking cumulative frequency. *E. D. Schmitz*

Care must be taken not to attribute theological significance to the use of particular numbers where it is arguable that no such significance was intended. Many cases are better treated as literal or rhetorical or as round-number approximations where these explanations seem natural and sufficient. Thus the particular frequency of multiples of five and ten is in part a natural consequence of the use of decimal reckoning. So too the prevalence of reference to the third, sixth and ninth hours stems from the duodecimal pattern of the day.

Some cases are less obvious. In Matt. 1 the genealogy of Jesus is schematized into sequences of fourteen, which is double seven. The enumeration here is selective and cannot be treated as being exhaustive. It is therefore reasonable to suppose that the generations listed have been chosen with a purpose. The question remains how far that purpose was theologically significant rather than merely rhetorical or mnemonic.

The total of 153 fish in Jn. 21:11 is another debatable instance. There is ancient precedent for symbolic interpretation here (Jerome, *Comm.Ezek.* 14 *ad* Ezek. 47:6 ff. [*MPL* XXV, 474C]; Augustine, *Tract. in Ioh.* 122, 8). Modern scholars have explained the figure by gematria (J. A. Emerton and P. R. Ackroyd), or as a "triangular" number, following Augustine (F. H. Colson and R. M. Grant; see bibliography). The present writer prefers to follow J. H. Bernard (*The Gospel according to St. John*, ICC, I, 1928, lxxxvii, 699 f. *ad loc.*) and L. Morris (*The Gospel according to John*, NLC 1971, 867 *ad loc.*) in taking the number literally. For the practice of counting a catch for sharing among the participating fisherman see E. F. F. Bishop, " 'A fire of coals with fish laid thereon, and Bread' ", *ExpT* 50, 1938-9, 265). John elsewhere gives precise numbers where it would be superfluous to look for a symbolical meaning (46 in 2:20; 38 in 5:5), and his constant emphasis is on witness, not on esoteric *gnōsis*. See further Bernard's careful consideration of "allegorical method" in the interpretation of John (op. cit., I, lxxxiii-xc). This prompts caution, and his conclusions inform and control his treatment of numerical details. It is indeed noteworthy that the number seven, so often symbolic elsewhere, never appears in the Fourth Gospel.

There is however no doubt that numbers are often used symbolically in the Rev. Yet even here it is sometimes needful to ask whether the symbolic explanation is sufficient, or excludes the literal. It is surely significant in the context of this book that there were *seven* churches of Asia. Yet the enumeration is of a named group, whose choice seems to have been dictated by geographical particularities, and which may indeed have functioned regularly as the most efficient centres of communication for the churches of the province (W. M. Ramsay, *Letters to the Seven Churches*, 1904, 171-196).

There is then, I submit, need for discriminating appraisal of complex possibilities in the study of particular numerical usages. OT, apocalyptic, Philonic and other parallels may need consideration, but are not necessarily determinative. There are notably diverse backgrounds of thought within the NT writings themselves. And their earliest surviving interpreters were not necessarily in line with the writers' own meaning.

The following notes on some additional numbers must be highly selective. They will inevitably focus on symbolic or otherwise significant numerals, but some cases are exegetically important for other reasons.   *C. J. Hemer*

δύο

δύο (*dyo*), two.

1. The word *dyo* occurs some 135 times in the NT, but there are few of real importance. Two is the smallest expression of plurality, and naturally points to alternatives or contrasts (cf. Matt. 6:24; 21:28; 24:40–41). Emissaries are often represented as acting and travelling in pairs (cf. Mk. 6:7; Matt. 11:2; 21:1). "Two or three" is a frequent approximation for a very few. None of these obvious usages need delay us.

2. In Jn. 8:17 we read that "the testimony of two men is true": Jesus himself and the Father are the two who bear witness to him. There is evident reference here to the Jewish law of evidence deriving from Num. 35:30; Deut. 17:6; 19:15. False witnesses are suborned in pairs (1 Ki. 21:10; Matt. 26:60). There are several NT references to the need for two or three witnesses (Matt. 18:16; 2 Cor. 13:1; 1 Tim. 5:19; Heb. 10:28). Perhaps the motif may reasonably be traced elsewhere in the gospel events (Matt. 17:1 par. Mk. 9:2, Lk. 9:28; Matt. 26:37 par. Mk. 14:33; Lk. 24:13; Jn. 1:35 ff.).

3. The only significant usage of the simple numeral two in Rev. seems to be at 11:4–11. Again the theme is witness. The imagery goes back to that of Zech. 4:2–3, 11–14. Here, however, the two witnesses have powers corresponding to those of → Moses and → Elijah (Rev. 11:6), who are not named, but represent the testimony respectively of the Law and the Prophets (cf. again the Transfiguration narratives. → also on "three and a half" below).

4. In Rev. 1:16 a sharp, two-edged sword (*rhomphaia distomos*) proceeds from the mouth of the risen Christ. The elements of the concept are repeated in the letter to Pergamum in 2:12 and 16. Again the language recalls the OT (Isa. 11:4; 49:2), but is applied to the need of the Pergamene Christian who faced judicial execution by the Roman authority. *rhomphaia* was typically the foreigner's sword. Its double edge describes the Roman weapon, and the Roman proconsul wielded the "power of the sword" (*ius gladii*). But here it is Christ who holds the ultimate executive and judicial authority. The sword is associated with the "word of God" (Rev. 19:13; 15; Heb. 4:12; Eph. 6:17).   *C. J. Hemer*

τρεῖς

τρεῖς, τρία (*treis, tria*), three; τρίς (*tris*), three times.

1. This number and its derivatives are very common throughout the biblical literature, but great caution is called for in evaluating significant usages. Three is a very common and natural rhetorical number, and threefold repetition or grouping

686

occurs often where the number itself is not mentioned. Many repetitive narratives and parables have three elements. Many basic concepts are readily formalized on a tripartite pattern: beginning, middle, end; past, present, future; body, soul, spirit. Diverse examples are numerous: there are three enduring gifts in 1 Cor. 13:13, three witnesses in 1 Jn. 5:8, threefold titles of Christ and of God in Rev. 1:4 and 4:8.

2. A period of three days is very commonly mentioned in the OT. It is often the length of a journey or of an interlude before a crisis (cf. Gen. 30:36; 40:12 ff.; Exod. 3:18). Note the easy transition to the phrase "the third day" (e.g. 40:20; → tritos below), and to the fuller expression "three days and three nights" (1 Sam. 30:12; Jon. 1:17). As the ancients reckoned inclusively, this might denote a period considerably shorter than seventy-two hours.

We should not attach too much importance to these phrases in their OT context, but some of them are taken up significantly in the NT with reference to the death and resurrection of Jesus. This is particularly striking in the allusion to Jonah (Matt. 12:40), a figure elsewhere prominent in the Gospels (Matt. 16:4; Lk. 11:29–32). See also Matt. 26:61; 27:40, 63; Mk. 8:31; 14:58; 15:29; Jn. 2:19–20.

3. Although three has widely been thought a sacred number, specifically religious uses of it in the Bible seem to be relatively few. In the OT it is frequent in cultic contexts (e.g. Exod. 23:14, 17). In the Rev. it is not so noteworthy as might have been expected. In the structural pattern the characteristic seven sometimes divides into four and three (Rev. 8:13 and implicitly elsewhere), and the twelve is composed of four threes (Rev. 21:13). There is, however, no reason to think that religious symbolism there attaches to three itself.

Yet the number three assumes peculiar importance indirectly in connection with the concept of the Trinity. There are threefold formulae listing the Persons in such passages as Matt. 28:19; Jn. 14:26; 15:26; 2 Cor. 13:13; 1 Pet. 1:2 (→ God, art. theos NT 8). There seems to be no precursor of this idea in any significant usage of the numerical concept in the OT, nor may it reasonably be connected with the occurrence of triads of deities in ancient Near Eastern paganism.

C. J. Hemer

τρίτος

τρίτος (tritos), third.

1. The ordinal tritos occurs 72 times in the Rev., more often than any other ordinal, and much more than the cardinal treis. In 14 of these cases it represents the fraction $\frac{1}{3}$, referring to disasters in which a "third" part is destroyed. This idea in Rev. 8 and elsewhere may be compared with Ezek. 5:2, 12. Rev. 12:4 is problematic: see Dan. 8:10, where however the fraction is not mentioned. For discussion of suggested parallels see R. H. Charles, Revelation, ICC, I, 1920, 310–314, 319. Cf. also Baba Metzia 59^{b}.

2. The characteristic uses of tritos in the Gospels and elsewhere are quite different. Of 53 occurrences outside the Rev., 13 refer to the resurrection of Christ "on the third day". This was evidently a characteristic motif of primitive Christian preaching (Acts 10:40; 1 Cor. 15:4). The scripture to which the latter passage refers is evidently Hos. 6:2, which speaks in context of the restoration of the

apostate kingdom of Israel. Compare the parallel usages of "three days" above, and also the enigmatic expression in Lk. 13:32.

3. 2 Cor. 12:2 speaks of "the third heaven". Some have seen allusion here to a Jewish conception of seven heavens (Test. Lev. 2, 3; Sl. Enoch 3–21). This explanation is questionable: Paul would seem to imply that he was carried to the highest heaven, not to a lower place in a hierarchy of heavens. Nor is it clear that the largely Gentile Corinthians would have understood this kind of Jewish speculation. "Paradise", however, mentioned in 2 Cor. 12:4, was linked with the "third heaven" of the series (→ Heaven; → Paradise).

C. J. Hemer

$\dot{\varepsilon}\nu\iota\alpha\upsilon\tauo\dot{\upsilon}\varsigma \ \tau\rho\varepsilon\tilde{\iota}\varsigma \ \kappa\alpha\dot{\iota} \ \mu\tilde{\eta}\nu\alpha\varsigma \ \ddot{\varepsilon}\xi$

$\dot{\varepsilon}\nu\iota\alpha\upsilon\tauo\dot{\upsilon}\varsigma \ \tau\rho\varepsilon\tilde{\iota}\varsigma \ \kappa\alpha\dot{\iota} \ \mu\tilde{\eta}\nu\alpha\varsigma \ \ddot{\varepsilon}\xi$ (eniautous treis kai mēnas hex), three years and six months, three and a half years.

This number is curiously prominent under various guises both in Dan. and in Rev., and seems to denote an interval of calamity and suffering pending God's deliverance. It is the half of seven. It is also "a time and times and the dividing of time", or $1 + 2 + \frac{1}{2}$ (Dan. 7:25; Rev. 12:7). Historically the three-and-a-half-year period may have been associated with the length of Antiochus Epiphanes' possession of Jerusalem, which Josephus reckons thus (*War* 1, 7, 19). Lk. 4:25 and Jas. 5:17 treat the drought and famine of 1 Kings 17:1 as lasting three and a half years, a detail absent from the OT text (cf. however "the third year" in 1 Ki. 18:1). It seems clear that the three-and-a-half-year period was significant in apocalyptic tradition (cf. G. H. Box on 4 Ezra 5:4 in Charles, *Pseudepigrapha*, 569). In Rev. the forty-two months of Gentile or bestial domination (Rev. 11:2; 13:5) and the 1260 days of God's providing (11:3; 12:6; cf. 1 Kings 17:4) are equivalents of it (cf. again the different and varying resolutions of the $3\frac{1}{2}$ years in Dan. 8:14; 12:11, 12). At Rev. 11:9, 11 the interval shifts to three-and-a-half days before the rising of the witnesses. Note the fluidity of the use of OT allusion and of symbolism here, as in the successive links of different symbols with the Elijah motif (→ *dyo* above). See further for "$3\frac{1}{2}$" H. Burgmann in *Revue de Qumran* 8, 1972, 65–73.

C. J. Hemer

$\tau\dot{\varepsilon}\sigma\sigma\alpha\rho\varepsilon\varsigma$

$\tau\dot{\varepsilon}\sigma\sigma\alpha\rho\varepsilon\varsigma$ (tessares), four.

CL The symbolic significance of the number four (*tessares*) is derived from the four points of the compass and the four directions of the wind (whereby the earth is pictured as a four-cornered disc), and also from the four seasons and the corresponding constellations. In Babylonian mythology the four signs of the Zodiac, Taurus, Leo, Scorpio and Aquarius, appear as powerful figures which support the firmament of heaven by its four corners, or as the four beasts of burden of the four-wheeled heavenly chariot. The number four thus symbolizes the totality of earth and universe.

OT The OT makes use of the number four in this traditional sense, but without taking over the mythical connotations (Ezek. 1:4 ff.; 15 ff.). Thus, in accord with ancient geography, four streams of Paradise encircle the four quarters of the globe (Gen. 2:10 ff.). In Zech. 1:18 ff. the four horns represent four empires, the four smiths Yahweh's omnipotence which stands ranged against them; in Zech. 6:5 the "four chariots driving out from 'the Lord of the whole earth' . . . [express] Yahweh's omnipotence, effective in all directions" (W. Zimmerli, *Ezechiel, BKAT* 13, 53). The four winds or corners of the earth are mentioned (e.g.) in Isa. 11:12 and Jer. 49:36. In Judaism, and particularly in apocalyptic, the mythology of the number four is again powerful (e.g. Eth.Enoch 18:2; 77:1 ff.; 82:11 ff.; but also R. Johanan ben Zakkai and his school). A multiple of four also occurs as a round figure for a limited totality, such as a generation, a man's age; e.g. 40 (*tessarakonta*) years (Gen. 25:20 etc.); 400 years, i.e. 10 generations (Gen. 15:13); 40 days (Gen. 7:4 ff.; Ezek. 24:18 etc.), where the rough period of a month possibly played a rôle.

NT In the NT the number four occurs in the purely numerical sense, e.g. Mk. 2:3; Jn. 11:17; 19:23 where the division of Jesus' clothes into four presupposes four watches or squads of soldiers (*tetradion*, cf. Philo, *Flacc.* 111; Acts 12:4); Acts 21:9, 23; 27:29. In Peter's vision of the great sheet with four corners containing clean and unclean → animals denoting God's acceptance of the Gentiles the imagery may suggest the four corners (Acts 10:11; 11:5) of the vault of heaven. The four horns of the altar are mentioned in Rev. 9:13 (cf. Exod. 30:1–3; → Sacrifice, art. *thyō*). But in addition, especially in apocalyptic texts, the number four occurs with a symbolic meaning. All these passages reflect the imagery of their original background, but the latter is no longer literally decisive for the meaning of the text: thus the idea of gathering the elect from the four winds (Matt. 24:31 par. Mk. 13:27) is comparable with saying from all quarters. In Rev. 4:6, 7, 8, 9; 5:6, 8, 11, 14; 6:1, 3, 5, 6, 7; 7:11; 14:3; 15:7; 19:4; cf. Ezek. 1:5–22, the imagery of the ancient world is formally adopted but with a transformed significance. The four beings (*tessara zōa*), originally figures of the Zodiac supporting the vault of heaven, become (by analogy with Isa. 6:2 f.) beings who praise God's holiness by day and by night (→ Cherub). The four angels at the "four corners of the earth" who hold the winds (Rev. 7:1) and later let them go (Rev. 9:14 f.) are creatures who serve God. Rev. 20:8 makes use of the ancient geographical idea of the four-cornered disc of the earth, in the middle of which lies the holy city. In this context the expression means no more than that the nations approach the holy city for the final → war at the end "from all sides" or "from every quarter".

In addition, the number 40 (*tessarakonta*) e.g. Matt. 4:2 par. occurs in Lk. 4:2; Mk. 1:13; Acts 1:3; 23:12, 21 in OT quotations and allusions, as does 400 (*tetrakosioi*) (Acts 5:36; 7:6; 13:20; Gal. 3:17) more frequently as round figures, but also in connection with specific numbers. *E. D. Schmitz*

πέντε

πέντε (*pente*), five.

Five is common and natural as a round number wherever the decimal system is in use. Such usages as in Matt. 25:20; Lk. 12:52; 14:19; 16:28 call for no further comment. There is no clear evidence that this number should be given any symbolic meaning in the NT. The "five months" of Rev. 9:5, 10 are just a limited period of chastisement. It is an attractive conjecture that the figure is reminiscent of the actual life cycle of the locust (R. H. Charles, *Revelation*, I, *ICC*, 243). This concrete touch has no precedent in Joel. *C. J. Hemer*

ἑπτά

ἑπτά (*hepta*), seven; ἑπτάκις (heptakis), seven times.

CL The qualitative significance attaching to the number seven (*hepta*) throughout the whole history of religions can be explained from the original amazement felt at the regularity of the passage of time in seven-day periods consonant with the four phases of the moon, and secondarily from other astronomical observations. Since for primitive man there is no linear time-sequence, and he could only apprehend time as a period, seven became the symbol of the fulfilled and perfectly completed period. In Babylonian the number seven (*kissatu*) is synonymous with fullness, totality; correspondingly Heb. šᵉba', seven, denotes fullness (Prov. 3:10, where "with plenty" RSV translates the Heb. for "seven"). Seven is the symbol of perfection. Philosophical speculations concerning the meaning of the number seven are known from Greece (Solon, Pseudo-Hippocrates), which Philo took up (e.g. *Op.Mund.* 90 ff.). In other respects Judaism up till the time of the NT followed OT usage.

OT The OT adopted the symbolic imagery content of the number seven in numerous ways: the completion of → creation in seven days (Gen. 1:1 ff.); seven-day feasts are fulfilled times (Lev. 23:6, 34); sprinkling of blood, seven times repeated (*heptakis*), brought Israel complete purification (Lev. 16:14, 19); Yahweh promised Cain sevenfold, i.e. comprehensive, vengeance (Gen. 4:15); Yahweh sees everything with seven eyes (Zech. 4:10); one of the marks of the fulfilment of the age of salvation is a sevenfold increase in the sun's illuminating power (Isa. 30:26); a man's full life-span is 10×7 years (Ps. 90:10; Isa. 23:15); a multiple of seven chiefly stands for a round figure, comprising the whole (Gen. 46:27; Jdg. 20:16; cf. also the seven Jewish brothers in 4 Macc. 8 ff. – their mother is called "mother of the nation" in 15:29); in proverbs seven can virtually signify all (Prov. 26:16). According to Jewish conceptions, a total of seventy nations live on the earth (Eth. Enoch 89:59 f.), an idea which is based on the table of the nations in Gen. 10, where 70 (LXX:72) nations are enumerated, and which was also determinative of the name "Septuagint", the translation of the OT into Gk. for the "70" nations of the world (cf. Aristeas with the legend of the origin of the LXX). Lk. 10:1 ff. should also be understood against the background of the idea of the 70 nations of the earth: the sending of the 70 disciples is aimed at the nations of the world.

The number seven is also encountered as a stylistic principle of arrangement, both in Rab. and in apocalyptic literature. (On the significance of seven in ancient thought see K. H. Rengstorf, *TDNT* II 627 ff.) For discussion of the cosmic week and the millennium → *chilias*.

NT 1. In the NT epistles the number seven occurs only with background reference to the OT: Rom. 11:4 (cf. 1 Ki. 19:18); Heb. 4:4 (cf. Gen. 2:2); 11:30 (cf.

Jos. 6:1 ff.). In Rom. 11:4 Paul adduces from 1 Ki. 19:18 that in his time there is already a Christian remnant of Israel, which represents the full total of Israel as dawn heralds the day (Rom. 11:16). In Mk. 12:18 ff. the → Sadducees imagine a case where a woman contracts a levirate marriage (Deut. 25:5 ff.) six times over. They wish to indicate by taking this example of a marriage, seven times repeated, that every case of levirate marriage, which was an institution by divine commandment, reduces the resurrection to an absurdity (→ Marriage, OT 5).

2. Someone possessed by seven *pneumata*, spirits (Matt. 12:43 ff. par. Lk. 11:26), or by seven *daimonia*, demons (Lk. 8:2), is totally possessed. In Matt. 18:21 Peter inquires concerning the limits of forgiveness: "As many as seven times?" There the seven has numerical significance. But Jesus replies that forgiveness has to take place "seventy times seven times", i.e. totally and without limit (cf. Lk. 17:4). For Lk. 10:1 ff., where the number suggests a mission to the nations, see above OT and below → *hebdomēkonta*.

3. Despite all the individual differences, the genealogical trees of Jesus in Matt. and Lk. are both orientated around the number seven. Matt. 1:17 f. has three groups of fourteen → generations: from → Abraham to → David, from David to the deportation to Babylon, and from then to Christ ($3 \times 14 = 3 \times 2 \times 7$). Lk. 3:23 ff. cites seventy-seven ancestors of Jesus: from Adam to Abraham (3×7), from Isaac to David (2×7), from Nathan to Shealtiel, i.e. the end of the Exile (3×7), from Zerubbabel to Jesus (3×7). Both evangelists are obviously interested in the fulfilment of history in the person of Jesus Christ; of salvation-history (Matt.) and world-history (Lk.). In other respects Matt. shows a particular predilection for the number seven as a scheme for the arrangement of his gospel (e.g. ch. 13; 23:13 ff.). It is the stylistic expression of his theology of fulfilment.

4. Rev. uses the number seven most frequently of all the NT writings. It is directed to seven churches of proconsular Asia, i.e. all churches (1:4, 11; 2 f.). Then there are seven spirits (1:4; 4:5; 5:6), seven seals (5:1), the → Lamb with seven horns and eyes (5:6), seven angels with seven trumpets (8:2–40:1), seven thunders (10:4 ff.). The number seven here denotes in general the final eschatological appearance of God, encompassing everything and setting everything in motion, on behalf of his church. Correspondingly, on the side opposed to God, there is a final action which is well-nigh able to withstand the power of God (e.g. the Dragon with seven crowned heads 12:3 etc.).

([Ed.] The number seven plays an important part in the structure of Rev. The book consists of seven series of visions, each in turn consisting of seven items. Moreover, the seven visions appear to correspond to the seven days of the creation story in Gen. 1. Whereas the Gen. story deals with the physical creation, Rev. deals with physical world in the light of the new creation from a christological standpoint. The broad outline is as follows: Day 1, the theme of light: Christ as the light amid the seven churches as lampstands in a dark world [Rev. 1–3]; Day 2, the firmament: world history from the perspective of heaven, the seven seals revealing what will come to pass [Rev. 4:1–8:2]; Day 3, the land, sea and vegetation: the future of the physical world revealed through the vision of the seven trumpets [Rev. 8:3–11:18]; Day 4, the sun, moon and stars: the seven things seen [Rev. 11:19–16:1]; Day 5, life and death from the waters: the seven bowls [Rev. 15:2–18:24]; Day 6, man: the seven last things seen taking up the theme of Adam and Eve in

691

terms of the corruption of man by the great harlot and the judgment on Satan and death leading to a vision of a new heaven and earth, the restoration of what was lost through the fall [Rev. 19:1–21:8]; Day 7, the eternal sabbath: depicted in terms of the new Jerusalem [Rev. 21:9–22:21]. The seven series of visions appear not to be consecutive series of events, each one starting where the last leaves off, but a series of visions of world history from the ascension of Christ to the consummation, looking at the world from different standpoints and gradually building up to the end of history and the new creation.)

5. Seven appears as a round summary number in Acts 20:6; 21:4; 28:14 and possibly also in Matt. 15:34, 36, 37; 16:10; Mk. 8:5, 8, 20 (cf. A. Farrer, *St Matthew and St Mark*, 1954, 57–80). *E. D. Schmitz*

| ὀκτώ | ὀκτώ (*oktō*), eight. |

"Eight", like "six" in Lk. 13:14 and even "five" in Rev. 17:10, is occasionally involved in the significance attached to "seven", but is rarely important in itself. Thus "eight days" is just inclusive reckoning for a "week" (Lk. 9:28; Jn. 20:26). The Jewish male child was circumcised on the eighth day (cf. Gen. 17:12; Lev. 12:3; Lk. 1:59; 2:21; Phil. 3:5).

A difficulty is raised by two much debated passages, 1 Pet. 3:20 and 2 Pet. 2:5. In the latter case "Noah the eighth" is to be explained from the Greek idiom *ogdoos autos*, to give the sense "Noah and seven others". The parallel is then with 1 Pet. 3:20, not with Jude 14, and the two passages may be considered as having a similar reference. The emphasis is upon the fewness of those saved, an enumeration of → Noah's family. The concepts of 1 Pet. 3:20 were already the subject of allegoric interpretation in Justin, *Dial*, 138, 1, where the eight persons stand for the eighth day of resurrection and salvation. See further J. N. D. Kelly, *The Epistles of Jude and of Peter*, BNTC, 1969, 158 ff. It may, however, be doubted whether this was the original writer's intention or whether it represents a later and rather artificial elaboration of his typology. There is no parallel for later uses of the "eighth day" idea within the NT writings. Cf., however, Ep.Barn. 15:8–9.

C. J. Hemer

| δέκα | δέκα (*deka*), ten; δέκατος (*dekatos*), tenth; ἡ δεκάτη (*hē dekatē*), [the] tithe; δεκατόω (*dekatoō*), to tithe. |

1. Ten, as the decimal base, is naturally very common, especially in round numbers and approximations, and in its large multiples (1 Cor. 4:15; 14:19; Rev. 5:11; etc.). The most noteworthy usages are contained in Rev.

2. The "ten days" of Rev. 2:10 are usually said to denote a typically short, or alternatively a typically prolonged but limited, period of tribulation. The phrase is commonly referred back to Dan. 1:12 ff. But it is not clear whether this allusion would have been readily perceived in Smyrna unless mediated through some more specific tradition, for the imagery of the letters is often concrete and pointed. No firm solution, however, can be offered on these lines. An interesting apocalyptic parallel might be seen in the ten generations of Sib. 4:45–87, which is probably

close to Rev. in time and place. The phrase is differently paralleled in the reference to "five days" (*hēmerōn pente*) in an inscription of Smyrna, published by L. Robert (*Hellenica* V, 81–82), where the context is explained as gladiatorial. The present writer plans to discuss the problem further elsewhere.

3. Rev. refers to a dragon and a beast with seven heads and ten horns (Rev. 12:3; 13:1; 17:3, 7, 12, 16; → Animal, art. *thērion*). The beast has ten royal diadems on its horns (13:1), and the horns represent kings (17:12). The image is evidently derived from Dan. 7:24, where the horns stand for ten kings of the fourth world kingdom. But here it is differently used and the application is debated. The emperors are linked with the seven heads: the horns are eschatological beings rather than identifiable rulers. The number here may fairly be regarded as standing for the universal extension of their ephemeral power.

4. A special usage is the "tenth part" or "tithe". The substantival form *dekatē* is found in the secular papyri (e.g. *P.Hibeh* I, 115, 1): the verb *(apo)dekatoō* alludes to the specifically Jewish practice. The OT law enjoined the payment of one tenth for the support of the Levite (Num. 18:21 ff.). On tithing in the OT see further Gen. 28:22; 1 Sam. 8:15, 17; Lev. 27:30–33; Num. 18:20–32; Deut. 12:6–19; 14:22–27; 26:1–15; Neh. 10:37 f.; 12:44; 13:5, 12; 2 Chr. 31:5–12; Amos 4:4; Mal. 3:8, 10; → First; → Gift; → Sacrifice. The → Pharisees had made of this a legalistic burden (Luke 11:42; 18:12; → Herb).

The idea of the tithe is taken up in the argument of Heb. 7, which refers to Gen. 14:20. The → Levites who received the tithe prescribed by the law were the descendants of → Abraham: yet Abraham himself had given a tenth to → Melchizedek, as the lesser to the greater. How much greater then was the priesthood to which Abraham yielded place than that which his descendants exercised towards others under the law.   *C. J. Hemer*

| δεκάτη |

δεκάτη (*dekatē*), a tenth part, tithe; δεκατόω (*dekatoō*), receive tithes, (pass.) pay tithes; ἀποδεκατόω (*apodekatoō*), give a tenth part, collect a tithe; ἀποδεκατεύω (*apodekateuō*), give one tenth, pay a tithe.

CL Instances of the vb. *dekatoō* appear to be lacking in secular Gk. and the papyri. It was probably coined to match the technical religious term *dekatē*, "tithe" (Moulton-Milligan, 140) that outside Jewish circles denoted (in particular) the tenth part of the spoils of battle that the Greeks regularly dedicated to some god (e.g. Xen., *Anab.* 5, 3, 4). *apodekatoō* and *apodekateuō* also seem to be terms found only in biblical Greek.

OT The verbs *apodekatoō* (6 uses in the LXX) and *dekatoō* (only in Neh. 10:37, LXX) both render Heb. '*āśar* (piel, hiph., "pay tithes", "receive tithes"), while *dekatē* renders *ma'ăśēr* ("tithe") 9 times. The Hebrews were obligated to tithe their cereal and fruit crops and their livestock (Lev. 27:30–33), paying their tithes to the → Levites (Num. 18:20–24) or later to the descendants of Levi who served as priests (cf. Heb. 7:5). Payment was made in → Jerusalem (Deut. 12:5–6, 11, 17–18) or each third year in their home communities (Deut. 14:28–29; 26:12). Moreover, the Levites themselves were required to give one tenth of this tithe to the priests (Num. 18:26, 28; Neh. 10:38–39).

NT 1. *Gospels.* It is in connection with the → Pharisees that the 3 NT uses of the compound verbs occur. The self-righteous Pharisee of Jesus' parable (Lk. 18:9–14) seems to be claiming that by tithing all types of income (*apodekateuō panta*) he had gone beyond the law and so had put God in his debt. Perhaps the classic example of Pharisaic zeal and fastidiousness about tithing – to the neglect of "the weightier demands of the law" such as justice, mercy and fidelity – was their care to tithe (*apodekatoute*) even common garden plants that were used as condiments or as medicinal → herbs (Matt. 23:23; Lk. 11:42) although this may not have been required by the law (Deut. 14:22–23; Lev. 27:30–32).

2. *Hebrews.* Seven of the NT uses of *dekatē* and its verbal equivalents are found in Heb. 7:1–10. First (in vv. 1–2a) the author repeats the OT account (Gen. 14:17–20) of the priest-king → Melchizedek who met → Abraham returning from the slaughter of the Elamite king Chedorlaomer and three other rulers, blessed him and then received from him a tenth part (*dekatēn*, v. 2) of everything (= "the spoils of war", v. 4). Then follows (v. 2b) an explanation of the etymological meaning of Melchizedek's name and his title ("king of Salem"), and the observation that since scripture contains no record of his parentage, genealogy, birth or death, he resembles the → Son of God in remaining a → priest "for ever" (v. 3).

In vv. 4–10 the author establishes the superiority of the priesthood of Melchizedek to the levitical priesthood on three grounds. (1) Although not a Levite, Melchizedek received tithes (*dedekatōken*, v. 6) from Abraham, the ancestor of the Levites, and himself blessed Abraham who had already received the promises (vv. 4–7). (2) In Israelite law mortal men belonging to the levitical priesthood received tithes (*dekatas*). However, in the scriptural record, Melchizedek, to whom Abraham gave tithes, is never said to have forfeited his priesthood by death (v. 8; cf. v. 3). (3) Through the act of his ancester Abraham, Levi himself can in one sense be said to have paid tithes (*dedekatōtai*) to Melchizedek (vv. 9–10).

3. *The NT and tithing.* Is tithing an obligation under the new covenant? The NT writers maintain an eloquent silence on the matter (note especially 1 Cor. 9:13), choosing rather to emphasize: (1) the need for spontaneous generosity (Lk. 21:4; Acts 11:28–30; 2 Cor. 8:1–3, 7; 9:5–10; Eph. 4:28; 1 Tim. 6:18; Heb. 13:16; Jas. 2:15–16) in response to God's limitless giving (2 Cor. 8:8–9; 9:15; 1 Jn. 3:17); (2) the need for individual decision (1 Cor. 16:2; 2 Cor. 9:7; cf. Acts 11:29) apart from external pressure (2 Cor. 8:8; 9:5, 7); (3) the blessedness of giving (Acts 20:35); and (4) the consequence of giving as being the glory of God or Christ (2 Cor. 8:19; 9:12–13).

See further F. F. Bruce, *Commentary on the Epistle to the Hebrews, NLC*, 1964, 133 ff.; J. A. MacCulloch, "Tithes", *ERE*, XII 347 ff.; O. Michel, *Melchisedek, TDNT* IV 568 ff.; M. E. Tate, "Tithing: Legalism or Benchmark?", *Review and Expositor* 70, 1973, 153 ff.; L. Vischer, *Tithing in the Early Church*, 1966.

M. J. Harris

δώδεκα

δώδεκα (*dōdeka*), twelve.

CL The number twelve (*dōdeka*) gets its symbolic meaning from the twelve months; it is thus also originally an astronomical number.

OT "In the Bible one can no longer trace any memory of this. Rather, the use of the number twelve is founded almost exclusively on the number of the tribes of Israel" (*RE³* XXI 606). The number twelve (e.g. Num. 1:4–49; 10:15–27; 13:2–15; 26:4–63; 34:13–28) again most probably goes back to the ancient Israelite amphictyony. M. Noth holds that care of the cult was shared by the twelve tribes, the responsibility for the upkeep of the common sanctuary alternating monthly between the tribes (M. Noth, *The History of Israel*, 1958, 87 ff.). Even after the dissolution of this institution the OT people of God continued to understand itself as the twelve tribes of the people of → Israel (cf. Gen. 49; Jos. 19:1–22:21; 2 Chron. 6:60–80; cf. Acts 7:8). The number twelve in Holy Scripture primarily denotes the people of God in its totality. It is only in Jewish apocalyptic that an occasional astral-theological usage of the number twelve turns up (cf. e.g. Eth.Enoch 76:1 ff.; 82:11), without the concept of the twelve tribes of the people of God being lost, however.

NT The thought of the twelve tribes as the people of God is still alive in the NT, not only as historical reminiscence (Acts 7:8), but also when Paul, before Agrippa, counts himself as a member of the twelve tribes (*dōdekaphylon*), and appeals to the promises made to them, which apply to him (Acts 26:7; cf. also Phil. 3:5). The circle of "the twelve" (Matt. 10:1 par. Mk. 6:7, Lk. 9:1; Matt. 10:2 par. Mk. 3:14, 16, Lk. 6:13, Jn. 6:70; Matt. 10:5; 11:1; 19:28 par. Lk. 22:30; Matt. 20:17, par. Mk. 10:32, cf. 9:35; Lk. 18:31; Matt. 26:14 par. Mk. 14:10, 20, 43, Lk. 22:3, 47, Jn. 6:71; Matt. 26:20 par. Mk. 14:17; Mk. 4:10; 11:11; Lk. 8:1; 9:12; Jn. 6:67; 20:24; Acts 6:2; 1 Cor. 15:5) is to be seen against this background of the twelve tribes, since it owes its existence to a particular calling by the earthly Jesus. On the Twelve and other followers of Jesus → Disciple (art. *mathētēs*); → Apostle (art. *apostolos*). "The number twelve symbolizes the tribes of Israel (Mt. xix 28; Lk. xxii. 30)" (G. Bornkamm, *Jesus of Nazareth*, 1960, 150). "The twelve do not only point back to the historical twelve tribes of the people of Israel, but also forwards to the eschatological" (N. A. Dahl, *Das Volk Gottes*, 1941, 158). In view of the fact the → kingdom of God has just come upon them, their commission (Mk. 3:14 f.) points them primarily to the lost sheep of the old twelve tribes of the → house of Israel (Matt. 10:6; 15:24), although they also have a representative function in the post-Easter church. The NT people of God can be addressed in Jas. 1:1 as "the twelve tribes in the diaspora" of the world (cf. 1 Pet. 1:1), whereby not only is a dignified title of the OT people of God taken over, but a continuity of salvation–history is also maintained.

There is an echo of the astral–religious significance of the number twelve in Rev. 12:1 in the vision of a woman clothed with the sun, wearing a crown with twelve stars on her head. But the → woman is here only the symbol of the daughter of Zion, and the twelve stars of the crown signify the twelve tribes, the OT people of God, from whom the messiah comes and to whom also belong those who confess the name of Jesus (v. 17). Correspondingly the NT people of God, composed of Jews and Gentiles, is described in 7:4 ff. in the $12 \times 12,000 = 144,000$ who are sealed (→ Seal, NT 3 (c)) from the tribes of Israel; cf. also 14:3. Thus the number 144,000 does not denote a numerical limitation of those who are sealed; it symbolizes the final perfection of the people of God (cf. also 7:9). In this respect when John sees them, as opposed to hearing the number of the sealed, they are "a great

695

multitude which no man can number, from all tribes, peoples and tongues" (cf. Rev. 7:9 with 7:4).

The number twelve in the description of the new Jerusalem (21:12 ff.) is used as an expression of its glory, which is sufficient for the eschatological people of God – "the one people of God in the city of God" (*TDNT* II 323). In other respects twelve is also used in its numerical sense and as a round figure (Matt. 9:20 par. Mk. 5:25, Lk. 8:43; Mk. 5:42 par. Lk. 8:42; Mk. 8:19; Lk. 2:42; Acts 19:7; 24:11). *E. D. Schmitz*

| τεσσεράκοντα | τεσσεράκοντα (*tesserakonta*), forty.

Periods of forty days occur repeatedly in the OT (Gen. 7:4; 8:6; Exod. 24:18; etc.). Forty years was the duration of Israel's wanderings in the wilderness (Exod. 16:35; etc.). There seems to be no explicit biblical evidence for the frequent suggestion that forty years was the regular round number reckoning of a generation, though the idea is very plausible (cf. G. F. Moore, *Judges*, ICC, 1898², xxxviii). The figure is constantly associated with long periods of human endurance and with the duration of successive developments of God's redemptive acts. So Jesus was forty days in the wilderness (Matt. 4:2; Mk. 1:13; Lk. 4:2), and remained with his disciples forty days after the resurrection (Acts 1:3). There is a partial parallel in apocalyptic, where forty days is the proper period for a term of instruction (2 Bar. 76:4; cf. 4 Ezra 14:23). Again, at Qumran, the war of the Sons of Light and the Sons of Darkness was to last forty years in all (1QM 2:6; etc.), and in Sanhedrin 99a Eliezer ben Hyrcanus infers from Ps. 95:10 that the times of the messiah should last forty years.

There are several references in Acts and Hebrews to the forty-year period of Israel in the wilderness, and it seems to have been a theme of early Christian preaching (Acts 7:36, 42; 13:18; Heb. 3:9, 17; cf. Acts 7:23, 30; 13:21). The significance of the parallel is not spelled out, but it has been suggested that Heb. envisages another forty-year period of probation for Israel between the death of Jesus and the disaster he foretold (F. F. Bruce, *Hebrews*, NLC, 1964, xliv, 65 n.).

The uncompounded numeral forty does not appear in the Johannine literature or in Rev.

For the Jewish scrupulosity in not exceeding the maximum of forty stripes (Deut. 25:3; 2 Cor. 11:24) see Makkoth 22a-b, and for first-century practice cf. Josephus, *Ant.* 4, 8, 21 (238); 4, 8 23 (248). *C. J. Hemer*

| ἑβδομήκοντα | ἑβδομήκοντα (*hebdomēkonta*), seventy.

This number is often significant in the OT. The captivity of Judah in Babylon was to last seventy years (Jer. 25:11), and in Dan. seventy weeks are appointed as the period in which messianic redemption would be accomplished (Dan. 9:24). Seventy elders were appointed to assist Moses (Num. 11:16). And in apocalyptic there are the seventy (? angelic) shepherds of Eth.En. 89:59 ff.

Only two NT passages call for brief comment. Jesus commends forgiveness until "seventy times seven" (or ? "seventy-seven times"), that is, without limit. Contrast Gen. 4:24: unlimited vengeance has given place to unlimited forgiveness.

In Lk. 10:1 Jesus sends out seventy (or seventy-two) disciples. The textual evidence for or against *dyo* is finely balanced. In either case symbolic meaning has been attached to the figure. It is pointed out that the nations enumerated in Gen. 10 total seventy in the Hebrew, but seventy-two in the LXX. Again Josephus (*Ant.* 12, 2, 5) follows the tradition in the Letter of Aristeas which lists the LXX translators as seventy-two in number (*Aristeas* 47–50; 6 times 12 tribes), but goes on to call them "seventy" (*Ant.* 12, 2, 7). (See further B. M. Metzger, "Seventy or Seventy-Two Disciples?" *Historical and Literary Studies, Pagan, Jewish and Christian, New Testament Tools and Studies* VIII 1968, 67–76.)

Other large numbers. The NT does not present here the special difficulties of the OT. Some large numbers just express indefinite multitude (1 Cor. 4:15; Rev. 5:11). Those which are plainly symbolic are mostly large multiples of four, seven or twelve.

For the "thousand years" of Rev. 20:1–7 → *chilias*. The Epistle of Barnabas 15:4–5 expounds Gen. 2:2 with Ps. 90:4 in terms of a "cosmic week", a 6000-year scheme of history being followed by a millennial "cosmic sabbath" (see E. Lohse, *TDNT* IX 470 f.).

The 1600 furlongs of Rev. 14:20 are problematic. The figure may be explained as 400 times 4, or, indeed, as forty squared, but it is not clear why this amount is chosen. There is no force in the suggestion that this was the length of Palestine, and A. M. Farrer (*Revelation*, 168) is excessively over-subtle.

The array of examples considered in the above articles will serve to point the caution offered at the outset. The exegetical significance of numbers is very diverse. They may be approximate, rhetorical, schematic, proverbial or symbolic, and such explanations may or may not exclude the literal. Each case needs to be taken individually on its merits in its total context, with reference to the genre to which the passage belongs. Straightforward principles of exegesis often, I think, oblige us to take literally what has been too readily spiritualized, especially where ancient allegorical interests have offered precedent. But the world of the NT itself was complex in its intellectual heritage. There is a real danger of over-interpretation. And some numbers are a subordinate element in a complex concept: we should not look for a special numerical symbolism in a cat's "nine lives" or in a "nine days' wonder". The choice of "nine" in these phrases may be explicable, but is virtually arbitrary.

The ancients, it is true, sometimes endowed numbers with a conceptual vitality which seems forced and foreign to us. But often they did not. If the Fourth Evangelist never uses seven or forty, we may well hesitate to seek mathematical properties in his other, ostensibly precise and irregularly factual, numbers.

C. J. Hemer

χιλιάς

χιλιάς (*chilias*), a thousand; χίλιοι (*chilioi*), a thousand.

CL & OT 1. The noun *chilias* is found from Hdt. and Aesch. onwards and the adj. *chilioi* from Homer. Both forms are found in the LXX, though *chilias* (which occurs some 250 times) is much more frequent and is particularly common in Num. and the historical books. It represents the Heb. *'elep̄*.

2. *'elep̄* occurs in the numbers giving the sizes of the tribes (e.g. Num. 1:23–46; 2:4–32; 1 Chr. 7:2–40), but it also refers to the numerical part of a tribe (1 Sam. 10:19; Jdg. 6:15), alternating with *mišpāḥâh* (1 Sam. 10:21). The *'al^e p̄ê yiśrā'ēl*, the clans or tribes of Israel, are mentioned in Num. 1:16; 10:4, 36; Jos. 22:21, 30; cf. Ps. 68:18; 1 Sam. 23:23; Isa. 60:22; Zech. 9:7; 12:5 f. The historical books display an interest in the thousands involved in battles (e.g. Jdg. 1:4; 3:29; 4:6–14; 20:2–46; 1 Sam. 4:2, 10; 6:19; 2 Sam. 10:6, 18; 24:9, 15; 1 Chr. 12:20–37; but cf. Amos 5:3 which asserts Yahweh's power to decimate the mighty). There is also an interest in the numbers involved in building the temple (1 Ki. 5:11–16 [25–30]; 2 Chr. 2:2–18 [1–17]). There is, however, a strong case for thinking that in many contexts *'elep̄* does not literally mean a thousand but is a term for a considerably smaller unit or perhaps meant *'allûp̄*, captain of a band; this would make feasible the apparently large numbers in OT records (cf. J. W. Wenham, "Large Numbers in the Old Testament", *TB* 18, 1967, 19–53). Ezek. is concerned with the measurement and proportions of the land, representing the perfect ordering of the people of God (Ezek. 45:1–6; 48:8–35).

3. The plur. *chiliades* is often used for very large numbers which cannot be reckoned. Yahweh shows steadfast love to thousands of those who love him and keep his commandments (Exod. 20:6; cf. 34:7; Deut. 5:10; 7:9; Jer. 39[32]:18). His power is described in terms of "mighty chariotry, twice ten thousand, thousands upon thousands" (Ps. 68[67]:18). "A day in thy courts is better than a thousand elsewhere. I would rather be a doorkeeper in the house of my God than dwell in the tents of wickedness" (Ps. 84[83]:10). The hosts of God's servants cannot be counted (Dan. 7:10). The greatness of Yahweh is also expressed in Ps. 90[89]:4: "For a thousand years in thy sight are but as yesterday when it is past, or as a watch in the night." What to man seems a great age is as a moment to Yahweh. To someone asleep the four-hour night watch is as nothing. To Yahweh such a span of time (to which even Methuselah and the other ancestral figures mentioned in Gen. 5 did not attain; cf. also Jub. 4:20) is as nothing. A similar thought is expressed in Sir. 18:10, and it is taken up by 2 Pet. 3:8 in arguing that God's time-scale is not to be judged by man's, and hence that man should not presume upon the apparent delay in judgment.

4. Various multiples of a thousand occur in Gen. 24:60; Exod. 12:37; 32:28; 38:26; Num. 3:43; Jdg. 8:10; 12:6.

5. In the inter-testamental literature innumerable hosts figure in the apocalyptic writings of Eth.En. 14:22; 40:1. The notion of thousands features in eschatological expectation: the thousands of children of the righteous (Eth.En. 10:17); superabundance of wine (Eth.En. 10:19; Syr.Bar. 29:5). The number features in speculations about the duration of the world and the new aeon. These included the idea of a cosmic week of seven millennia followed in some instances by a new era, an eighth millennium (Test.Abr. 7 [2nd cent. A.D.]; Pseudo-Philo, *Antiquitates* 28, 2; Sl.Enoch 33:1; 33:4; cf. E. Lohse, *TDNT* IX 468). Other writings saw the seventh epoch as the final one (Sanh. 97 a–b Bar.; cf. E. Lohse, ibid., who notes that Samaritan eschatology taught that the world would last 6,000 years). The length of the messianic age varied from 1,000 years to 7,000 years. Although the idea of a

thousand-year messianic age is found only from the 1st cent. A.D., Lohse thinks it likely to derive from an older tradition (ibid.; cf. SB III 827; Test.Isaac 8:20).

6. The number 1,000 features in the military structure of the Qumran community (1QS 2:21 f.; CD 13:1 f. [15:4]; cf. 1QM 12:4). Each thousand had its commander to lead it into battle (1QM 4:2; 1QSa 1:14, 29). (See further Y. Yadin, *The Scroll of the War of the Sons of Light against the Sons of Darkness*, 1962, 49–53, 59 ff.) The community believed that those who kept God's commandments would live for a thousand generations (CD 7:6 [8:21]; 19:1 f. [8:21 f.]; 20:22 [9:45]; cf. Deut. 7:9).

NT 1. Various multiples of a thousand occur in the NT. *dischilioi*, two thousand, was the approximate number of the Gerasene swine (Mk. 5:13). About three thousand (*trischilioi*) souls were added to the church at → Pentecost (Acts 2:41). About five thousand men (*hōs chiliades pente*) heard and believed the word (Acts 4:4). The same number were fed by Jesus (*pentakischilioi andres*) were fed by Jesus (Matt. 14:21; Mk. 6:44; 8:19; Lk. 9:14; Jn. 16:10). (On the possible symbolism in these narratives see G. H. Boobyer, "The Miracles of the Loaves and the Gentiles in St. Mark's Gospel", *SJT* 6, 1953, 77–87; A. Farrer, *St Matthew and St Mark*, 1954, 57–80.) In Matt. 15:38 and Mk. 8:9, 20 four thousand (*tetrakischilioi*) were fed. Acts 21:38 mentions the revolt of the Egyptian who led *tetrakischilious*, four thousand, men. In dealing with the question whether God has rejected Israel for good, Paul recalls the remnant of seven thousand men who did not bow the knee to Baal (Rom. 11:4; 1 Ki. 19:18). But the instance is at the same time a reminder that it is God who preserves the remnant, and therefore those who are saved are "chosen by grace" (Rom. 11:5). The alternative would be salvation by works (Rom. 11:6). In 1 Cor. 10:8 Paul recalls how twenty-three thousand of the wilderness generation fell in a single day through idolatry (cf. Num. 25:1–18). The military sense of a thousand is perhaps present in Jesus' question whether a king does not first take counsel whether he is able to meet with ten thousand (*deka chiliasin*) his adversary who comes against him with twenty thousand (*meta eikosi chiliadōn*) (Lk. 14:31). The question culminates a series of illustrations on counting the cost of discipleship. Confronted by overwhelming odds, the king with only ten thousand sends an embassy and asks for peace. The illustration implies not only the need to count the cost but also the impossibility of finding an alternative way out (cf. the instructions to the Israelites in making war in Deut. 20:10–20).

2. *chiliarchos* is found in cl. Gk. from Aesch. onwards for a leader of a thousand soldiers. It became a loanword in rabbinic writings, and was used in Roman times of the *tribunus militum*, the military tribune, the commander of a cohort which consisted of about 600 men (cf. Polyb. 1, 23, 1; 6, 19, 1; Josephus, *Ant.* 17, 9, 3). In this sense it is found in Jn. 18:12; Acts 21:31 ff., 37; 22:24, 26–29; 23:10, 15, 17 ff., 22; 24:7 *v.l.*, 22; 25:23. It is used of a high ranking officer generally in Mk. 6:21; Rev. 6:15; 19:18 (in the last two passages as objects of judgment).

3. *chilioi* occurs twice in 2 Pet. 3:8 with reference to Ps. 90:4 (see above OT 3) where the readers are urged: "But do not ignore this one fact, beloved, that with the Lord one day is as a thousand years, and a thousand years as one day." The context is concerned with man's indifference and sin in the light of the apparent postponement of the day of the Lord. The Psalmist had declared that "a thousand

years in thy sight are but as yesterday when it is past." 2 Pet. takes the thought a step further and draws the corollary that "with the Lord one day is as a thousand years." This may represent a combination of Gk. and Heb. thinking, asserting that God is not bound by the time-scale of the physical world. The reason for the delay of the day of the Lord is God's forbearance "not wishing that any should perish, but that all should reach repentance" (2 Pet. 2:9).

4. The remaining 9 instances of *chilioi* are all found in Rev. (11:3; 12:6; 14:20; 20:2–7). In addition *chilias* is found in Rev. 19 times (5:11; 7:4–8; 11:13; 14:1, 3; 21:16). These instances represent an apocalyptic interpretation of OT themes. Rev. 5:11 takes up the picture in Dan. 7:10 of the heavenly hosts "numbering myriads of myriads and thousands of thousands" praising God. But the picture is given a christological interpretation, for the object of their praise is the → Lamb (Rev. 5:12 ff.). Rev. 7:4 gives the number of the sealed as "a hundred and forty-four thousand sealed, out of every tribe of the sons of Israel" (→ Seal). Verses 5–8 enumerate the tribes by name, specifying twelve thousand out of each tribe. The number symbolizes the final perfection of the people of God, based on the concept of the twelve tribes of Israel (→ *dōdeka*) and asserting the historical continuity with Israel. It is worth noting that when John hears the number he hears these round numbers which consist of members of the twelve tribes. But when he looks, the numbers are replaced by a countless host consisting of all peoples: "After this I looked, and behold, a great multitude which no man could number, from every nation, from all tribes and peoples and tongues, standing before the throne and before the Lamb, clothed in white robes, with palm branches in their hands" (Rev. 7:9). The hundred and forty-four thousand are mentioned again in Rev. 14:1, 3.

Rev. 11:3 and 12:6 mention a period of "one thousand two hundred and sixty days". This corresponds to the forty-two months of Rev. 11:2; 13:5 and the time, times and half a time of Rev. 12:14. In Rev. 11:3 it is the period of prophecy and in Rev. 12:6 it is the period of persecution. Both passages refer to the same period, the age of the church which is one of prophetic witness and at the same time one of persecution. In the light of eternity it is a comparatively short period, although when expressed in terms of days it may seem lengthy. In the background stands Dan. 7:25; 12:7 (→ *eniatous treis kai mēnas hex*), a period which is half of seven, the perfect number, comprising of severe affliction which continues until God accomplishes the end of all things. This affliction is described in Rev. 11:7 ff.; cf. 12:2–6. It will culminate in the judgment of civilization (Rev. 11:3). The seven thousand who perish in the earthquake represent the complete judgment on godless, secular society; the rest who were terrified and give glory to God represent those who respond to the witness and God's judgments.

Rev. 14:20 depicts judgment on the civilized world in terms of the sack of a city: "and the wine press was trodden outside the city, and blood flowed from the wine press, as high as a horse's bridle, for one thousand six hundred stadia." The distance is approximately two hundred miles. The number is a square number, comparable with the hundred and forty-four thousand and the dimensions of the → Jerusalem (cf. Rev. 7:4; 14:1; 21:16). It suggests the area of the four parts of the earth, i.e. the whole earth; the passage refers to the last judgment (cf. Rev. 19:11–21). By contrast, the area of the holy city, the new Jerusalem, is also square, again indicating completeness: "The city lies foursquare, its length the same as its breadth; and he measured the city with his rod, twelve thousand stadia; its length and breadth and height are equal" (Rev. 12:16). The number twelve goes back in this case to the twelve tribes and the twelve thousand from each tribe. The completeness of the new Jerusalem corresponds to the completeness of the people of God.

Rev. 20:2–7 contains 6 references to a period of a thousand years: "Then I saw an angel coming down from heaven, holding in his hand the key of the bottomless pit and a great chain. And he seized the dragon, that ancient serpent, who is the Devil and Satan, and bound him for a thousand years, and threw him into the pit, and shut it and sealed it over him, that he should deceive the nations no more, till the thousand years were ended. After that he must be loosed for a little while. Then I saw thrones, and seated on them were those to whom judgment was committed. Also I saw the souls of those who had been beheaded for their testimony to Jesus and for the word of God, and who had not worshiped the beast or its image and had not received its mark on their foreheads or their hands. They came to life again, and reigned with Christ a thousand years. The rest of the dead did not come to life again until the thousand years were ended. This is the first resurrection. Blessed and holy is he who shares in the first resurrection! Over such the second death has no power, but they shall be priests of God and of Christ, and they shall reign with him a thousand years. And when the thousand years are ended, Satan will be loosed from his prison." After this follows the final conflict, the casting of the devil, the beast and the false prophet into the lake of fire and brimstone, together with Death and Hades after the last judgment (Rev. 20:8–15).

The passage has given rise to the concept of the millennium (from Lat. *mille*, a thousand, and *annus*, year), a thousand year age of restoration in which evil is banished, and to chiliasm (deriving from the Gk. word for a thousand). The idea of a messianic kingdom, preceding the end and the coming reign of God is attested in Eth.En. 91:12 f.; 93:1–14; Sib. 3, 652–660; 2 Esd. 7:28 f.; Syr.Bar. 29:3; 30:1–5; 40:3 (cf. above OT 5). It extends the older idea of a Davidic king restoring the monarchy by combining it with that of universal judgment, resurrection and the new aeon. According to 2 Esd. 7:28 f., the messiah would reign for four hundred years before dying and the last judgment. The number 1000 is probably connected with the idea of the cosmic week and Ps. 90:4 (see above OT 3, 5). In the early church belief in some form of a literal millennium is attested by Barn. 15:3–9; Papias (cf. Irenaeus, *Haer.* 5, 33, 4); Irenaeus, *Haer.* 5, 32–36; Justin, *Dial.* 81; the Christian additions to the *Testament of Isaac* (8:11 and 19 f.; 10:11 f.); Tertullian, *Adv.Marc.* 3, 24; 4, 31; the gnostic Cerinthus (cf. Eusebius, *Hist.Eccl.* 3, 28). It was attacked by Origen (*De prin.* 2, 11, 2) and rejected by Augustine (*De civ.* 20, 7). (For a discussion of these and other views in the early centuries see H. Bietenhard, "The Millennial Hope in the Early Church", *SJT* 6, 1953, 12–30.) In addition to apocalyptic ideas, Rev. 20 draws on Ezek. 36–48 with its visions of the resurrection of Israel, the conflict with Gog and Magog and the promise of a new Jerusalem.

In modern times three main schools of thought have emerged concerning the interpretation of Rev. 20. The Premillenarians treat the passage as future prophecy in which the second coming of Christ will precede the millennium. Satan will be bound for a thousand years, the martyred dead will be raised, and Christ will reign as King of kings and Lord of lords from Jerusalem. The millennium will end with the final rebellion of Satan, but this will itself be soon put down. The resurrection and judgment of the wicked dead will precede the creation of the new heaven and earth. (For statements of this position see N. West, ed., *Premillennial Essays of the Prophetic Conference Held in the Church of Holy Trinity*, 1879; N. West, *The Thousand Years in Both Testaments*, 1880; W. E. Blackstone, *Jesus is Coming*, 1917; D. H. Kromminga, *The Millennium in the Church*, 1945 and *The Millennium: Its Nature Function and Relation to the Consummation of the World*, 1948; C. L. Feinberg, *Premillennialism or Amillennialism?*, 1954².) Postmillenarians see the second coming of Christ and the events of Rev. 20 as coming in the last thousand years of the present age (cf. D. Brown, *Christ's Second Coming: Will it be Premillennial?*, 1919; J. H. Snowden, *The Coming of the Lord: Will it be Premillennial?*, 1919; L. Boettner, *The Millennium*, 1957). Amillennialists, on the other hand, see the whole passage as an essentially symbolic description of the present age in which Satan is already bound and the dead in Christ are already reigning with him (cf. F. E. Hamilton, *The Basis of Millennial Faith*, 1942; G. L. Murray, *Millennial Studies: A Search for Truth*, 1948; W. J. Grier, *The Momentous Event*, 1945; W. Hendriksen, *More than Conquerors*, 1947, 221 ff.).

The interpretation of Rev. 20 depends partly on how this particular vision is seen in relation to the general structure of the book. Those who see the different visions in Rev. as visions of successive events will be inclined to see this vision as the last of a series, referring to a unique event immediately prior to the creation of a new heaven and a new earth. On the other hand, there is a very strong case for seeing the whole book as structured into seven series of visions, corresponding to the seven days of the creation story in Gen. 1, each of which looks at the church in the gospel age. The visions are thus seven sets of parallel visions of the church and its tribulations between the two advents of Christ (→ *hepta* NT 4). On this view the period of a thousand years refers to the present era culminating in a final outburst of Satanic activity prior to the final destruction of all the evils that afflict man.

According to this interpretation, the vision of the binding of Satan has its roots in the saying of Jesus about the binding of the strong man who first has to be bound before his goods may be plundered (Matt. 12:29 par. Mk. 3:27; cf. Augustine, *De civ.* 20, 7). The activity of Jesus is itself evidence of the binding of Satan. It is further defined in Rev. 20:3: "that he should deceive the nations no more, till the thousand years were ended." This would then refer to the spread of the gospel among the Gentile nations which previously had been deceived by Satan. There is a sense in which Satan has fallen in power already, and this is evidenced by the power of the disciples over demons (Lk. 10:17 f.; cf. Col. 2:15). The event of Rev. 20:1–3 has already been described from another standpoint in Rev. 12:9 ff., and may also reflect the saying in Jn. 12:31. The first resurrection refers to the reign of the saints with Christ now (cf. 4:2–10; 5:6–13; 7:9–17; 8:3; 12:5; 14:3, 5; 19:4 f.; 22:1, 3). The thought may reflect Jn. 5:24 (cf. Jn. 3:18; Col. 3:1). Such a scheme of interpretation is in harmony with that of Jesus and Paul, neither of whom speak of a period of a thousand years and into whose teaching such a period could not easily be inserted (Matt. 24:4–36 par. Mk. 13:5–37, Lk. 21:8–36; cf. 1 Cor. 15:20–28; 1 Thess. 5:1 ff.; 2 Thess. 2:1–12). Moreover, neither Jesus nor Paul (nor, for that matter, John in Rev.) speaks of two second comings of Christ: one before the millennium and one subsequent to it. It would, therefore, seem best to recognize

the symbolic character of the apocalyptic language of Rev. 20 and see in the passage an eschatology which is already in process of realization. *C. Brown*
→ First, Firstborn, → Goal, → King, Kingdom, → One, Once, Only, → Pentecost, → Present, → Time

On numbers in general:
(a). G. A. Barton, "Number", *Encyclopaedia Biblica* III, 1902, 3434–39; I. T. Beckwith, *The Apocalypse of John*, 1919, 250–54; R. E. D. Clark, "The Large Numbers of the Old Testament – Especially in Connection with the Exodus", *Journal of the Transactions of the Victoria Institute* 87, 1955, 82–90 (see also the discussion, ibid., 145–52); J. J. Davis, *Biblical Numerology*, 1968; G. R. Driver, "Sacred Numbers and Round Figures", in F. F. Bruce, ed., *Promise and Fulfilment Essays Presented to S. H. Hooke*, 1963, 62–90; A. M. Farrer, *A Rebirth of Images: The Making of St John's Apocalypse*, 1949, 245–60; S. Gandz, "Complementary Fractions in Bible and Talmud", *Louis Ginsberg Memorial Volume*, 1945, 143–57; R. A. H. Gunner, "Number", *NBD*, 895–98; T. Heath, *A History of Greek Mathematics*, I–II, 1921; E. König, "Number", *HDB* III 560–67; L. A. Muirhead, "Number", *DAC* II 92–96; O. Neugebauer and A. Sachs, *Mathematical Cuneiform Texts*, 1945; O. Neugebauer, *The Exact Sciences in Antiquity*, 1957; M. H. Pope, "Number", *IDB* III 561–67; O. Rühle, *arithmeō, arithmos, TDNT* I 461–64; E. R. Thiele, *The Mysterious Numbers of the Hebrew Kings*, 1966; J. W. Wenham, "Large Numbers in the Old Testament", *TB* 18, 1967, 19–53 (reprinted as a separate monograph, no date); W. White, Jr., "Number", *ZPEB* IV 452–61.
(b). H. Bardtke, "Zahl", *EKL* III 1883; A. Bea, "Der Zahlenspruch im Hebräischen und Ugaritischen", *Biblica* 21, 1940, 196 ff.; O. Becker, *Das mathematische Denken der Antike*, 1957; W. Foerster, "Bemerkungen zur Bildsprache der Offenbarung Johannis", in O. Böcher and K. Haacker, eds., *Verborum Veritas. Festschrift für Gustav Stählin*, 1970, 225–36 (especially 227–31); P. Friesenhahn, *Hellenistische Wortzahlmystik im Neuen Testament*, 1935; A. Heller, *Biblische Zahlensymbolik*, 1936; E. Kautzsch, "Zahlen", *RE* XXI 598 f.; K. Menninger, *Zahlwort und Ziffer*, I, 1957, 127 ff.; O. Neugebauer, *Vorgriechische Mathematik*, 1934; A. Schimmel and W. Funk, "Zahlensymbolik", *RGG³* VI 1861 ff.; K. Sethe, *Von Zahlen und Zahlworten bei den alten Ägypten*, 1916.

On particular numbers:
(a). P. R. Ackroyd, "The 153 Fishes in John xxi. 11 – A Further Note", *JTS* New Series 10, 1959, 94; H. Balz, *tessares* etc., *TDNT* VIII 127–39; F. H. Colson, "Triangular Numbers in the New Testament", *JTS* 16, 1914–15, 67–76; G. Delling, *treis, tris, tritos, TDNT* VIII 216–25; J. A. Emerton, "The Hundred and Fifty-three Fishes in John xxi. 11", *JTS* New Series 9, 1958, 86–89; C. L. Feinberg, "Tithe", *ZPEB* V 756 ff.; R. M. Grant, " 'One Hundred and Fifty-three Large Fish' (John 21:11)", *HTR* 42, 1949, 273 ff.; H. H. Guthrie, Jr., "Tithe", *IDB* IV 654 f.; F. Hauck, *deka* etc., *TDNT* II 36 f.; E. Lohse, *chilias, chilioi, TDNT* IX 466–71; F. McCurley, " 'After Six Days' (Mark 9:2); A Semitic Literary Device", *JBL* 93, 1974, 67–81; B. M. Metzger, "Seventy or Seventy-two Disciples?" *Historical and Literary Studies, Pagan, Jewish and Christian, New Testament Tools and Studies* VIII, 1968, 67–76; C. L. Mitton, "Threefoldness in the Teaching of Jesus", *ExpT* 75, 1963–64, 228 ff.; K. H. Rengstorf, *hepta* etc., *TDNT* II 627–35; and *dōdeka* etc., *TDNT* II 321–28; H. F. D. Sparks, "The Partiality of Luke for Three", *JTS* 37, 1936, 141–45.
(b). E. von Dobschütz, "Zwei- und dreigliedrige Formeln", *JBL* 50, 1931, 117–47; O. Eissfeldt, *Erstlinge und Zehnten im Alten Testament*, 1917.

On the millennium:
(a). J. W. Bailey, "The Temporary Messianic Reign in the Literature of Early Judaism", *JBL* 53, 1934, 170–87; G. R. Beasley-Murray, *The Book of Revelation*, New Century Bible, 1974, 287–92; I. T. Beckwith, *The Apocalypse of John*, 1919; H. Bietenhard, "The Millennial Hope in the Early Church", *SJT* 6, 1953, 12–30; L. Boettner, *The Millennium*, 1957; S. J. Case, *The Millennial Hope*, 1917; R. H. Charles, *A Critical History of the Doctrine of a Future Life*, 1913²; R. D. Culver, *Daniel and the Latter Days*, 1957²; J. Daniélou, "Millenarianism', *EBT* II 582 ff.; and *A History of Early Christian Doctrine before the Council of Nicea*, I, *The Theology of Jewish Christianity*, 1964, 377–404; G. E. Ladd, *A Commentary on the Revelation of John*, 1972; E. Lohse, *chilias,*

chilioi, *TDNT* IX 466–71; J. A. MacCulloch, "Eschatology", *ERE* V 373 ff.; M. Rist, "Millennium", *IDB* III 381 f.; J. F. Walvoord, "Amillennialism in the Ancient Church", *Bibliotheca Sacra* 106, 1949, 291–302; and *The Rapture Question*, 1957; "Millennium", *ZPEB* IV 228; B. B. Warfield, "The Millennium and the Apocalypse", *The Princeton Theological Review*, 5, 1904, 599–617 (reprinted in *Biblical Doctrines*, 1929, 643–64).

(b). W. Bauer, "Chiliasmus", *RAC* II 1073–78; H. Bietenhard, *Das tausendjährige Reich*, 1955²; J. Daniélou, "La Typologie Millénariste de la Semaine dans le Christianisme Primitif", *Vigiliae Christianae* 2, 1948, 1–16; B. Gatz, *Weltalter, goldene Zeit und sinnverwandte Vorstellungen*, 1967; A. Gelin, "Millénarisme", *Dictionnaire de la Bible*, Supplement 5, 1957, 1289–94; L. Gry, *Le Millénarisme dans ses Origines et son Développement*, 1904; H. Kraft, "Chiliasmus", *RGG*³ I, 1651 ff.; E. Lohse, *Die Offenbarung des Johannes*, NTD 11, 1960, 20 ff., 74 f.; A. Luneau, *L'Histoire du Salut chez les Pères de l'Église*, 1964; W. Nigg, *Das ewige Reich, Geschichte einer Sehnsucht und einer Entäuschung*, 1934; SB III 824 ff.; R. Schmidt, "Aetates Mundi", *Zeitschrift für Kirchengeschichte* 67, 1956, 288–317; H. Schuhmacher, *Das tausendjährige Königreich Christi auf Erden. Eine biblische Untersuchung im Lichte des Fortschreitens der göttlichen Heilsoffenbarung und Heilsgeschichte*, 1964; J. Sickenberger, "Das tausendjährige Reich in der Apokalypse", *Festschrift S. Merkle*, 1922, 300–15; G. Siedenschnur, "Chiliasmus", *EKL* I 683 ff.; A. Wikenhauser, "Das Problem des tausenjährigenden Reiches in der Apokalypse", *Römische Quartalschrift* 40, 1932, 13–27; "Die Herkunft der Idee des tausendjährigen Reiches in der Apokalypse", *Römische Quartalschrift* 45, 1937, 1–24; and "Weltwoche und tausendjähriges Reich", *Theologische Quartalschrift* 127, 1947, 399–417.

O

Offence, Scandal, Stumbling Block

Two groups of words are here linked: the key nouns are *proskomma* and *skandalon*. Originally their meanings were different. Already in the LXX, however, each had taken on the special force of the other. It was in the LXX that both groups first became closely related to human life; both in denotation and connotation the Gk. words were modified by the OT and Judaism.

πρόσκομμα

πρόσκομμα (*proskomma*), stumbling, offence, obstacle; προσκοπή (*proskopē*), an occasion for taking offence or making a false step; προσκόπτω (*proskoptō*), strike, beat against, stumble, be offended; ἀπρόσκοπος (*aproskopos*), without offence, giving no offence, blameless.

CL The vb. *proskoptō* (from Aristoph. onwards), derived from *koptō*, smite, strike, beat, knock (from Homer onwards), means trans. to strike or knock against; intrans. to knock oneself against, trip, or fall. Metaphorically it means both to give and to take offence. *proskomma* (not found earlier than the LXX) means the cause, the process and the results of the offence, and so an obstacle, offence, fall, damage, destruction. *proskopē* (from Polyb. onwards) – in the NT only in 2 Cor. 6:3 – means the offence, the dislike which causes one to take offence, the cause and reason for taking offence. The verbal adj. *aproskopos*, without offence, is seldom found in secular literature; it means both giving no offence, unobjectionable, blameless, and taking no offence, unhurt.

OT 1. Though this group of words is found in secular Gk., it first obtained a theologically relevant meaning in biblical usage. In the LXX it is used predominantly for the Heb. words *môqēš*, a trap or snare, *kāšal*, to fall or cause to fall, and also for *nāḡap*, to hit, push; but these are also frequently rendered by → *skandalon, skandalizō*.

Sin causes a fall. Though the God of Israel guards a man from tripping and falling (Ps. 91:11 f.) and bears the title of the Rock of Israel's strength and salvation (Isa. 17:10; Deut. 32:15), he can become "a stone of offence" (Isa. 8:14) for the apostate, godless man who does not fear him, so that he falls and perishes (→ Rock). The God of Israel is faithful, but he humbles those who do not reverence him as the Holy One and fear him (cf. Ps. 18[17]:26). The cause of the → falling is to be found in the sin and apostasy of the godless. Hence the people are warned against the worship of heathen gods and fellowship with the heathen inhabitants of the land, which would be a snare to them (Exod. 23:33; 34:12).

2. The OT usage lived on in late Judaism. *kāšal* and the noun *miḵšôl* are found

705

very frequently in the Qumran texts (cf. 1QS 2:12, 17; *TDNT* VI 749, 751; →
skandalon).

NT In the NT *proskomma* occurs 4 times in Rom. and once each in 1 Cor. and 1
Pet.; *proskoptō* twice each in Matt., Jn. and Rom., and once each in Lk. and
1 Pet.; *proskopē* only in 2 Cor.; and *aproskopos* once each in Acts, 1 Cor. and Phil.
Usage follows the OT and has in the background the picture of tripping over a
stone and falling. The following 4 uses may be distinguished.

1. Christ remains obedient to God and true to his task. Hence neither Satan,
who alluding to Ps. 91:11 f. says that Jesus as God's Son will not strike (*proskopsēs*)
his foot against a stone (Matt. 4:6; Lk. 4:11), nor the threat of death by the Jews
in Jerusalem (Jn. 11:7–10: the only example of the root in the Johannine writings)
could cause him to fall and make his messianic mission vain. In the temptation
narratives the sense of *proskoptō* is the lit. one of strike. In Jn. 11:9 f. the vb. is
used in the sense of stumble in the contrast: "Are there not twelve hours in the day?
If any one walks in the day, he does not stumble [*proskoptei*], because he sees the
light of this world. But if any one walks in the night, he stumbles [*proskoptei*],
because the light is not in him." The reply is given in response to the warning that
the Jews were planning to stone him, and that Jesus therefore should not visit the
sick Lazarus. "It is a parable of crisis, in which Jesus seeks to impress on his hearers
the necessity of taking prompt action before the judgment falls. It is possible, but by
no means certain, that *stumble* is an allusion to the 'rock of stumbling' in Isa. 8:14,
alluded to several times in early Christian literature (cf. Rom. 9:32; 1 Cor. 1:23;
1 Pet. 2:6–8)" (B. Lindars, *The Gospel of John, New Century Bible*, 1972, 390). The
parable is similar to that in Matt. 6:22 f. par. Lk. 11:34 ff.; cf. also Gos.Thom. 24.

2. Christ is both the stone which serves as a foundation (→ Firm, art. *themelios*)
for the church and the stone over which one can fall, the stumbling stone (Rom.
9:33; 1 Pet. 2:8; referring to Isa. 8:14; 28:16; Ps. 118:22; → Rock). This explains
why men, e.g. many Jews, do not come to salvation. Where Jesus and his message
are refused, man finds his eternal destruction (cf. also Lk. 2:34). Lk.'s version of
the saying about the corner stone presses the picture even further: "Every one who
falls on that stone will be broken to pieces; but when it falls on any one it will
crush him" (Lk. 20:18). This combines the saying about the corner stone (Ps.
118:20; Isa. 28:16; cf. Lk. 20:17; Matt. 21:42; Mk. 12:10; Acts 4:11; 1 Pet. 2:7)
with Isa. 8:14 f. which declares: "And he [Yahweh] will become a sanctuary,
and a stone of offence, and a rock of stumbling to both houses of Israel, a trap
and a snare to the inhabitants of Jerusalem. And many shall stumble thereon;
they shall fall and be broken; they shall be snared and be taken." But what was
said of Yahweh by Isaiah is said of Jesus in Lk. (cf. Rom. 9:33; 10:11; 1 Pet.
2:4 ff.). According to Lk. 20:18, man will be broken by Christ in any case. He will
be either broken on him now, as Christ shatters his preconceived plans for his life,
or he will be broken by him in judgment.

3. Whether the disciple of Christ may cause offence to others is another matter.
Paul expressly forbids the strong to cause the weak to stumble and to hurt their →
conscience (Rom. 14:13, 21; 1 Cor. 8:9). Their freedom, though justified in itself,
must not cause others to → fall. This is the law of love. He who hurts the →
conscience of another creates an obstacle for the gospel (cf. 1 Cor. 9:12 f., 19 f.).

Paul enlarges the circle still further, when he says "Give no offence [*aproskopoi* . . . *ginesthe*] to Jews or to Greeks or to the church of God" (1 Cor. 10:32).

([Ed.] The ET "stumbling-block" was first introduced by William Tyndale in his translation of Rom. 14:13: "That no man putt a stomblinge blocke or an occasion to faule [*proskomma ē skandalon*]" (1526). Later translators preferred to use it for *skandalon*. The phrase "to stumble at a block", i.e. a tree stump, is exemplified in Capgrave's *Life of St. Gilbert* 43, 123: "Sche stombeled at a blok which was hid with straw and thus fel sodeynly." After Tyndale the expression was used in the senses of an occasion for moral stumbling, an occasion for falling into calamity, an obstacle to belief, understanding, progress, and more rarely and late lit. of a kind of threshold or object sticking up in a road.)

4. The day of Christ makes it particularly imperative that the Christian should be without offence. Paul prays for the Christians in Philippi that they "may be pure and blameless [*aproskopoi*] for the day of Christ" (Phil. 1:10). Paul is not referring only to external and ethical behaviour but also to the nature of a man's relationship to Christ (v. 9). His prayer is also a warning to the church. In his defence before Felix Paul rebutted the accusations of Tertullus, declaring that "I always take pains to have a clear conscience [*aproskopon syneidēsin*] toward God and toward men" (Acts 24:16), i.e. a conscience which has remained undefiled by sin.

J. Guhrt

| σκάνδαλον |

σκάνδαλον (*skandalon*), offence; σκανδαλίζω (*skandalizō*), give offence, lead astray.

CL The noun *skandalon*, from a root meaning jump up, snap shut, was originally the piece of wood that kept open a trap for animals. Outside the Bible it is not used metaphorically, though its derivative *skandalēthron* (e.g. a trap set through questions) is so used. No non-biblical example of *skandalizō* has been found. The Eng. word scandal is derived from the noun via the Lat. *scandalum*.

OT 1. Both words have been shaped by biblical language; the secular Gk. usage is alien to biblical usage. The LXX uses them mainly to translate Heb. *môqēš*, bait or lure (cf. Amos 3:5), fig. a snare to destroy a person (cf. Ps. 141:9[140:8]; 1 Sam. 18:21) or to cause him to sin (cf. Jos. 23:13; Jdg. 2:3; 8:27; Ps. 106[105]:36) and *miksôl*, obstacle in the way of the blind (Lev. 19:14), fig. a cause of misfortune (Ps. 119[118]:165) or of troubled conscience (1 Sam. 25:31). *skandalizō* occurs in Dan. 11:41 LXX for niph. of *kāšal* and without Heb. equivalent in Sir. 9:5; 23:8; 35(32):15.

2. *skandalon* and *skandalizō* are not found in Philo, Josephus, Aristeas or Hellenistic Jewish literature (*TDNT* VII 343), but they occur in the OT translations of Aquila, and to a lesser extent Symmachus and Theodotion (*skandalon* only). However, the metaphorical meanings were clearly understood in the NT period, and they feature in the Qumran community with its conscious separation of the righteous and godless and its more legalistic religion. The words *kāšal* (to stumble; hiph. to cause to stumble; e.g. 1QS 3:24; 11:12; 1QM 14:5; 1QH 5:28, 36; 8:36; 16:5; 17:23) and *miksôl* (offence; e.g. 1QS 2:12, 17; 4:15; 8:35; 9:21, 27; 10:18; 16:15; 17:4) occur frequently in the Qumran literature. All the spirits allotted

to the Angel of Darkness "seek the overthrow of the sons of light" (1QS 3:24). On the other hand, there is no cause for offence in God's words. Hence, the word-group becomes a metaphorical expression for sinning, leading to sin, and sin.

NT The NT usage has been fixed essentially by the OT. It is often based directly on OT passages (e.g. Matt. 13:41 on Zeph. 1:3; Matt. 24:10 on Dan. 11:41 [cf. RV and Heb.]; Rom. 9:33 and 1 Pet. 2:8 on Isa. 8:14). Both the noun and the vb. are used frequently in Matt.; they are not so common in Lk. with its less Jewish background. However, the same thought is often expressed in other words (e.g. cf. Lk. 8:13 with Matt. 13:21). Though the word *skandalon* is not used, the thought is found in Lk. 2:34: "Behold, this child is set for the fall and rising of many in Israel, and for a sign that is spoken against." *skandalizō* occurs 14 times in Matt., 8 times in Mk., twice in Lk., Jn. and 1 Cor., and once in 2 Cor. *skandalon* occurs 5 times in Rom., once in Lk., 4 times in Rom. and once each in 1 Cor. and Gal.

The original conception of a bait or trap is found only in Rom. 11:9 ("pitfall", RSV; quoting Ps. 69:22 [68:23]). Otherwise *skandalon* is used rather with the thought of a stone or obstacle in the way, over which one can trip and fall. It occurs as a synonym of → *proskomma* (cf. Rom. 9:33; 1 Pet. 2:3). When the sense is to cause people to sin, the connotation of "trap" is still present (cf. Rev. 2:14).

1. If we omit Rom. 11:9, the following meanings are to be found.

(a) The noun means a temptation to sin, an enticement to apostasy and unbelief (e.g. Matt. 18:7; Rev. 2:14; Rom. 14:13; 16:17 ["difficulties" RSV]; of persons, Matt. 13:41; 16:23; Rom. 9:33; 1 Pet. 2:8). It is then used as that which causes offence or scandal, or divisions, or hinders faith (e.g. 1 Jn. 2:10; 1 Cor. 1:23; Gal. 5:11; Matt. 13:41).

(b) Correspondingly the vb. means to lead into sin, to give offence (e.g. Matt. 5:29 f.; 18:6; 1 Cor. 8:13 [in each case cf. RV with RSV]) In the passive it means to take offence, fall away, be misled (e.g. Matt. 13:21; 24:10; Jn. 16:1; 2 Cor. 11:29), to take offence at Jesus (e.g. Matt. 11:6; 13:57; 26:31, 33). It can further mean to offend, provoke, allow to go astray, raise dissensions (e.g. Matt. 17:27; Jn. 6:61; passively in Matt. 15:12 and perhaps 2 Cor. 11:29).

2. (a) The NT stresses that Jesus constantly becomes an offence. The expression *skandalizesthai en tini*, be repelled by, take offence at, is always used of him. The disciples took offence (RSV "fall away") at his → sufferings (Matt. 26:31), because such suffering was incompatible with their preconceptions. Other instances of this expression occur at Matt. 11:6; 13:57; 26:31, 33; Mk. 6:3; Lk. 7:23. When Peter took offence in Matt. 16:22, his protestation was rejected by Jesus as a Satanic suggestion. Jesus became an offence for John the Baptist (Matt. 11:6; Lk. 7:23), because John had expected him to reveal himself as messiah in a different way. The → Pharisees took offence at Jesus' teaching (Matt. 15:12), because it contradicted their concept of the law, and of man's co-operation with God's grace. How deep-rooted their offence was may be seen from Jesus' comparison of them with weeds to be rooted up (Matt. 15:13; cf. 13:24–30).

(b) The basis of the offence caused by Jesus is the → cross (1 Cor. 1:23), which nullifies all human wisdom, and excludes all human co-operation in salvation (cf. Gal. 5:11 with reference to circumcision). For the preaching of Christ crucified is a *skandalon* to the Jews (in view of their rejection of him, his death on a tree which

SB III 291). Where Paul does, quite consciously, go beyond nature is in the belief that after branches have been cut off, "God has the power to graft them in again." This is the miracle of God's grace. (See further M. M. Bourke, *A Study of the Metaphor of the Olive Tree in Romans 11*, 1947.)

5. The Mount of Olives (or Olivet, from Lat. *olivetum*, olive-orchard) is the ridge on the east side of Jerusalem, across the Kidron valley, on which olive-orchards still grow. It must be crossed by a traveller entering Jerusalem from the east, and so is mentioned in the accounts of Jesus' triumphal entry into Jerusalem (Matt. 21:1 par. Mk. 11:1, Lk. 19:28). Its commanding view of the temple area accounts for Jesus' lament there over Jerusalem's impenitence (Lk. 19:29–44), and his teaching there on the approaching ruin of the temple (Matt. 24:1–3 par. Mk. 13:1–4, Lk. 21:5–7). Somewhere on this ridge Jesus and his disciples spent the nights of his last week (Lk. 21:37), probably in the estate known as *Gethsemane* ("oil-press", so presumably an olive-orchard) to which they went after the last supper (Mk. 14:26, 32), and which was their regular rendezvous (Jn. 18:1–2). Gethsemane was the scene of Jesus' final commitment to his redemptive suffering, and of his arrest. It was also on the Mount of Olives that Jesus' ascension to heaven took place (Lk. 24:50–51; Acts 1:12); Acts 1:11, taken with Zech. 14:4, has led to the conclusion that it will also be the scene of his return.

→ Anoint, → Incense, → Light, → Sacrifice, → Temple   *R. T. France*

(a). G. A. Barrois, "Olives, Mount of", *IDB* III 596–99; M. M. Bourke, *A Study of the Metaphor of the Olive Tree in Romans 11*, 1947; R. J. Forbes, *Studies in Ancient Technology*, III, 1955, 101–4; A. T. Hanson, "Christ the First Fruits, Christ the Tree", *Studies in Paul's Technique and Theology*, 1974, 104–25; F. B. Huey, Jr., "Oil", *ZPEB* IV 513 ff.; J. Jeremias, *Jerusalem in the Time of Jesus* 1969, 6 f., 55; C. Kopp, *The Holy Places of the Gospels*, 1963, 335–50; H. N. and A. L. Moldenke, *Plants of the Bible*, 1952, 97 ff., 157–60; W. M. Ramsay, *Pauline and Other Studies*, 1906, 219–50; J. F. Ross, "Oil", *IDB* III 592 f.; W. E. Shewell-Cooper, "Oil Tree", *ZPEB* III 515; and "Olive, Olive Tree", *ZPEB* III 528; H. Schlier, *aleiphō* etc., *TDNT* I 229–32; and *elaion* etc., *TDNT* II 470–73; J. C. Trever, "Oil Tree", *IDB* III 593; and "Olive Tree", *IDB* III 596.

(b). G. Dalman, *Arbeit und Sitte in Palästina*, IV, 1935, 153–290; I. Löw, *Die Flora der Juden*, II, 1924, 286–95.

Old

πάλαι

πάλαι (*palai*), formerly, earlier; παλαιός (*palaios*), old; παλαιότης (*palaiotēs*), age, obsoleteness; παλαιόω (*palaioō*), grow old, make or treat as old.

CL *palai* (from Homer onwards), Aeolic *pēlyi*, belongs etymologically to the word-group associated with *tēle*. The original meaning of distant, far away, focuses on the earlier or past in contrast with the present (cf. *telos*, the end). *palaios* (also from Homer onwards) is commonly used in secular Gk. meaning old: (a) positively as existing for a long time and hence venerable; (b) negatively as obsolete, worn out, and hence worthless, unusable (cf. Soph., *Oedipus Rex* 290, etc.). Often *archaios*, original, venerable, is used in the same sense, but almost always positively. *palaioō* (from Plato onwards) is found only in the pass. in secular Gk.

OT In the LXX *palaios* has mostly the meaning of old, last year's, antiquated (cf. Lev. 25:22). It formally translates the Heb. *yāšān*, old, last year's. *palaioō* translates in the LXX (a) *'āṭēq* (trans.) cause to pass away (cf. Job. 9:5), and (intrans.) pass away, fall into decay (cf. Job 14:18), reach old age (cf. Job. 21:7); and (b) *balâh* be worn out (cf. Deut. 8:4; 29:5; Jos. 9:5, 13; Neh. 9:21). In this latter sense *palaioō* is used metaphorically in the exilic and post-exilic writings of the OT for the growing old and transience of man's life and work, and also of heaven and earth (cf. Ps. 32:3; Isa. 50:9; Job 13:28). By giving mankind and the whole creation over to decay and corruption God passes judgment on the sin and fall of mankind (Isa. 51:6; Ps. 102[101]:26).

NT 1. In the NT *palai* points to something which lies in the recent or remote past:
e.g., God spoke "of old" (Heb. 1:1); they would have repented "long ago" (Matt. 11:21 par. Lk. 10:13; Jude 4); "old" sins (2 Pet. 1:9); if he were "already" dead (Mk. 15:44); "all along" (2 Cor. 12:19).

2. In *palaios* and *palaiotēs* the old, obsolete past stands in contrast with the completely new (→ New, arts. *kainos, neos*). The salvation of God in Jesus Christ has already broken into this age and made it obsolete together with its institutions and practices (2 Cor. 5:17; cf. Mk. 2:21 f. on fasting; Rom. 7:6 on the law; 1 Cor. 5:7 on sin). The final fulfilment is still awaited. With the coming again of the Lord this age will be brought to an end and world-history completed (2 Pet. 3:13; → Present).

(a) The parabolic words of Matt. 9:16 f. par. Mk. 2:21 f., Lk. 5:56 f. are probably to be understood in this context, though we cannot be completely sure. Probably they were originally independent, everyday sayings which Jesus used to show that the age of the old world had passed and that the age of salvation had begun. The old, obsolete, world-age is compared with an old garment (v. 21) and with old wine (v. 22). A garment (→ Clothe, art. *himation*) and → wine were traditional symbols of the cosmos or the age of salvation. In the synoptic context the passage could also mean that the new excludes the old; the new age of salvation demands a new manner of life which cannot be inserted in the old customs, such as fasting and mourning. The old is fulfilled in the new (cf. Matt. 5:17) or, in the case of the natural man, conquered.

The proverb of Lk. 5:39 in this context is evidently ironical: "And no one after drinking old wine desires new; for he says, 'The old is good' " (some MSS read "better"; on the word there → Good, art. *chrēstos*). It implies that men (in the context those who cling to the Jewish traditions) are incorrigibly attached to the old familiar ways.

In Matt. 13:52 Jesus says: "Therefore every scribe who has been trained for the kingdom of heaven [*pas grammateus mathēteutheis tē basileia tōn ouranōn*] is like a householder [*oikodespotē*] who brings out of his treasure what is old and new [*kaina kai palaia*]." Here the scribe is seen as a steward (→ House, art. *oikonomia*) who knows both the old, the message of the OT scriptures, and also their fulfilment in the radically new, the message and person of Jesus. The saying stands at the conclusion of Matt.'s account of the parables of the sower, the mustard → seed, the → leaven, the tares, the treasure hidden in a field, the pearl of great price and the fish net. The mention of the householder and the kingdom links up with previous themes. The picture of the → disciple as a scribe is a particularly Matthaean perspective (cf. 23:34; → Scripture). Some scholars see in this an element of Matt.'s

Jewishness. At any rate, the disciple in Matt. does what the scribe should be doing, i.e. expound the scriptures as they are fulfilled by Jesus (Matt. 5:17 f.). This is, moreover, what Matt.'s Gospel itself seeks to do (e.g. Matt. 1:22 f., cf. Isa. 7:14; Matt. 2:5 f., cf. Mic. 5:2; Matt. 2:15, cf. Hos. 11:1, Exod. 4:22; Matt. 2:17 f., cf. Jer. 31:15; Matt. 2:23, cf. Isa. 11:1; Matt. 3:3, cf. Isa. 40:3; Matt. 3:15; →
Fullness, art. *plēroō*; cf. also R. H. Gundry, *The Use of the Old Testament in St. Matthew, Supplements to NovT* 18, 1967; R. T. France, *Jesus and the Old Testament*, 1971; K. Stendahl, *The School of St. Matthew*, 1968²). There may be a play on words between the name of Matthew (*Matthaios*) and the words "who has been trained" (lit. "become a disciple", *mathēteutheis*) which would further support the view that Matt.'s Gospel exemplifies the dictum here. The scribe was not simply the copyist of the scriptures in post-exilic Judaism; he was the authorized teacher and theologian who interpreted the law (cf. D. Hill, *The Gospel of Matthew, New Century Bible*, 1972, 240). But it should be noted in this saying that the "scribe" in question is not in the first instance trained in the law. He is trained in the → kingdom and thus is able to bring out old and new from his treasure. In this respect he stands in contrast with those scribes who were trained in "the tradition of the elders" (Matt. 15:1–20 par. Mk. 7:1–23) who for the sake of human tradition make void the word of God (Matt. 15:6; cf. also Matt. 23:1–39). Like Jesus himself, the scribe trained in the kingdom of heaven is able to bring out the true treasure from the law and the prophets.

(b) In Paul and Hebrews the opposition between old and new is to be understood in the same way as in the Synoptics. Baptism represents the death of the old man and the birth of the new. In the picture of the old and new man we have no doubt part of the primitive Christian baptismal exhortation (Rom. 6:6; Col. 3:9; Eph. 4:22 → Baptism; → Body; → Clothe; → Destroy; → Man). The "old" means everything connected with the fall of man and with his subjection to the distress and death of a transitory life, separated from God. In this concept we can hear deep undertones of God's wrath and the wages of sin. At the same time we are pointed to the completely new, to that healing and salvation which are given to man when he is crucified with Christ and raised with him (Rom. 6:3 ff.).

palaiotēs, age, obsoleteness, what is outdated, occurs only at Rom. 7:6, where Paul emphasizes the incompatibility of the old and the new as ways of salvation and life: we serve in the newness of Spirit and not in the oldness of letter (*en kainotēti pneumatos kai ou palaiotēti grammatos*). Paul has been appealing to the analogy of divorce: a woman is bound to her husband by the law as long as he lives. She is only free to marry someone else if the husband dies. The law is powerless to do anything else. Paul then modifies the picture. By dying to the law "through the body of Christ" (Rom. 7:4), the believer is "discharged from the law, dead to that which held us captive" (7:6a). But if we are dead to the law, we are free to serve in the Spirit. The law is thus dead in that it cannot give life but can only condemn (cf. 7:10 ff.). Life comes as something → new apart from the law and thus makes the letter of the law old (in that it came first) and obsolete (in that it is superseded by the Spirit of Christ) (cf. Rom. 7:6 with 8:5–11; and 2 Cor. 3:6). (On the place of the law in Paul's thought → Law art. *nomos* NT 2; → Goal, art. *telos* NT 1; → I Am, art. *egō eimi* NT 2 (c).)

Because Jesus is the new man, and he who believes in him is also born again to a new → life, the old life, alienated from God, is dead. It is without power or rights, and so it must daily be given over to → death. In 1 Cor. 5:7 f. Paul alludes to an OT commandment (cf. Exod. 12:19; 13:7; Deut. 16:3 f.). Just as the last remnants of the → old leaven must be eliminated before the Passover (→ Feast, art. *pascha*) so the evil and crookedness of the old life, the old leaven of sin and disobedience, must be cleared out to make room for the new life of sincerity and obedience (1 Cor. 5:6–8). Jesus' message and work bring the new which is promised in the OT and fulfils the old, or deprives it of power. The old life of legality cannot, therefore, be reconciled with faith in Jesus Christ (Rom. 7:6).

Heb. 8:13 takes up the promise of the new → covenant of Jer. 31:31–35: "In speaking of a new covenant he treats the first as obsolete [*pepalaiōken*]. And what is becoming obsolete [*palaioumenon*] and growing old [*gēraskon*] is ready to vanish away." This is entirely God's work. Seeing that God in Christ makes a new covenant, the old covenant of the law has become obsolete. In Christ the first can be regarded only as old and fulfilled (2 Cor. 3:14). Indeed, it may be said that the NT speaks of the old only from the standpoint of the new and for the sake of the new.

3. *palaios* is used in quite another sense only in 1 Jn. 2:7. The writer of the letter is not communicating a new commandment to his readers, but the old commandment which they had known from their conversion, "from the beginning". In the context of 2:1–6 "*old* refers to the primitive Christian tradition and not to Lev. 19:18" (H. Windisch, *Die katholischen Briefe*, HNT 15, 1951³, *ad loc.*).

→ Age, → Covenant, → Law, → New *H. Haarbeck*

(a). H. Seesemann, *palai* etc., *TDNT* V 717–20.
(b). R. Bultmann, *Der alte und neue Mensch in der Theologie des Paulus* (reprint of three older articles), 1964; F. Hahn, "Die Bildworte vom neuen Flicken und vom alten Wein", *EvTh* 31, 1971, 357 ff.

One, Once, Only

The NT uses three different sets of terms to express that someone or something is unique or occurs only once. Their theological interest lies in the passages where they are used in connection with God or Christ. In general terms *monos* thus has a polemical connotation, in the contrast with other gods, saviours and religions. *heis* is used to confess the oneness and uniqueness of God. *hapax* and *ephapax* stress the once-and-for-all nature of God's actions in history, especially in Jesus.

ἅπαξ

ἅπαξ (*hapax*), once; ἐφάπαξ (*ephapax*), once for all.

CL *hapax* is compounded of *ha-* (= *heis* in compounds) and *pax* (from *pēgnymi*, make firm, bring together; cf. *pagos* for anything that is firmly and surely brought together). Its fundamental meaning therefore includes numerical singularity and completeness which needs no additions.

OT In the LXX *hapax* renders Heb. *'eḥāḏ* (masc.), *'aḥaṭ* (fem.), one (e.g. Exod. 30:10; Ps. 62[61]:11; and *pa'am*, a beat, footfall, time (e.g. Neh. 13:20; Ezr. 23:20 LXX). The two Heb. words come together at Jos. 6:3, 14, meaning once, and

Isa. 66:8, meaning at once. The rabbis interpreted '*aḥaṭ* in Hag. 2:6 ("For thus says the Lord of hosts: Once again, in a little while, I will shake the heavens and the earth and the sea and the dry land") as only once more, implying the need for special readiness and watching in view of the coming of messianic kingdom (SB III 750).

NT 1. *hapax* is found only 14 times in the NT: 3 times in Paul and 8 in Heb., once in 1 Pet., and twice in Jude. It means once in contrast to twice, thrice, etc. (2 Cor. 11:25; Phil. 4:16; Heb. 9:7), and once in the sense of an event that cannot be repeated. It is so used of the sacrificial death of Christ (Heb. 9:26 ff.; 1 Pet. 3:18) and negatively of OT sacrifice (Heb. 10:2), of God's saving activity (Jude 3 and 5) and judgment (Heb. 12:26 = Hag. 2:6). With the once-for-all-ness and finality of Jesus' saving work the NT writers contrast the once-for-all-ness and finality of human reaction, either in faith or in unbelief. Those who have once found mercy cannot be restored to repentance if they → fall away (*parapesontas*) (Heb. 6:4 ff.), just as those whom God brought out of Egypt were destroyed because of their unbelief (Jude 5).

The derivative *ephapax* is not found in pre-Christian writings. In 1 Cor. 15:6 it means "at one time", i.e. together, as opposed to separately. In the other 4 cases where it is used (Rom. 6:10; Heb. 7:27; 9:12; 10:10) it means once for all and is used of the sacrificial death of Christ.

2. The theological importance of both terms lies in the fact that they stress the historical nature of God's revelation. Just as God revealed himself to Israel in history, when he brought him out of → Egypt, so he revealed himself to his covenant people, once, unrepeatably and finally in Christ. This is of decisive importance in confrontation with those religions where salvation is an ideal concept based on the mere idea of deity and divorced from history (as in gnosticism).

In contrast to the situation of the OT covenant people Heb. argues that, since the sacrificial death of Jesus once for all, we are now in the end time (*ephapax*, Heb. 10:10; *heis*, Heb. 10:12, 14). The contrast is drawn between the single, complete act of Christ and the repeated sacrifices of the old covenant which are seen to have been temporary and imperfect from the very fact that they had to be repeated every year. Otherwise those that brought these sacrifices and worshipped God through them would have ceased to bring them. They would have been once purified and would have had no more consciousness of sin (Heb. 10:2) As mere → shadows (*skia*) of the future and perfect sacrifice, of Christ, they served merely to bring sins to mind (Heb. 10:3, *anamnēsis hamartiōn*) and so to point to the One to come.

This indicates that the very nature and purpose of the OT sacrificial system were not to purify finally and once for all but to point to the final sacrifice and purification and hence to require repetition (Heb. 10:2 f.). The one true and finally valid sacrifice is Jesus, who is both the sacrifice and high priest in one. Just as man finally dies and faces the judgment, so Jesus' giving himself in death to put away sins is once for all and final (Heb. 9:26 ff.). It is this that distinguishes the activity of the Son made perfect for ever (Heb. 7:27 f.) from that of the earthly high priest with his temporal sacrifice, with its limited validity, offered daily for himself and the people.

The author of Heb. sees the death of Christ as the once-and-for-all sacrifice and

717

the resurrection and ascension of Christ in terms of the high priest entering the Holy Place on the day of atonement (Heb. 9:12; 10:12; cf. Lev. 16). Only the high priest was permitted to do this, which he did only once a year. Having offered sacrifice, he entered the Holy Place taking with him the blood of the sacrifice on behalf of the entire people of God. Christ has entered the immediate presence of God through his heavenly exaltation by his own blood to represent his people before God and obtain for them eternal salvation (cf. Heb. 9:14 with 10:19-25). This is the basis of the Christian faith and Christian way of life.

In Rom. 6:10 Paul writes: "The death he died he died to sin, once for all [*ephapax*], but the life he lives he lives to God." The statement comes at the climax of a discussion of the problem of antinomianism. If men are saved by "the free gift in the grace of that one man Jesus Christ" (Rom. 5:15) which abounds for many and not because of anything that they do to deserve it, then why not go on sinning that grace may abound (Rom. 6:1)? Paul replies that baptism implies baptism into Christ's death (Rom. 6:3), and that just as he was raised by the glory of the Father, we too should walk in the newness of life (Rom. 6:4). The whole purpose of his death was to free men from the enslavement of sin (Rom. 6:5-9). This he has done once for all; and now he lives to God (Rom. 6:10). "So you also must consider yourselves dead to sin and alive to God in Christ Jesus" (Rom. 6:11). Since the crucified Christ is eternally exalted, "the act of Golgotha is the decisive turning point in history" (G. Schrenk, "Die Geschichtsauffassung des Paulus auf dem Hintergrund seines Zeitalters", *Jahrbücher der Theologischen Schule Bethel*, 3, 1932, 68).

The finality and unrepeatability of the historic act of salvation is paralleled by the finality of personal salvation. If it is frittered away, it is also unrepeatable. "For it is impossible to restore again to repentance those who have once [*hapax*] been enlightened, who have tasted the heavenly gift, and have become partakers of the Holy Spirit, and have tasted the goodness of the word of God and the powers of the age to come, if they then commit apostasy, since they crucify the Son of God on their own account and hold him up to contempt" (Heb. 6:4 ff.). The theme of apostasy is a recurring one in Heb. which issues repeated warnings against it (cf. Heb. 3:1-4:16; 6:1-20; 10:26-39; 12:1-29; 13:1 ff., 20 ff.). On the four things mentioned here (been enlightened, tasted the heavenly gift, partaken of the Holy Spirit, tasted the goodness of the word of God and the mighty works of the age to come) see F. F. Bruce, *Epistle to the Hebrews*, NLC, 1964, 118-24; I. H. Marshall, *Kept by the Power of God: A Study of Perseverance and Falling Away*, 1969, 136 ff.

Jude 3 urges its readers "to contend for the faith which was once for all [*hapax*] delivered to the saints." "Clearly *the faith* is not the believing man's response to Christ (the *fides qua creditur*), but is to be concretely understood as the *fides quae creditur*, i.e. the message or body of saving beliefs accepted as orthodox in the Church" (J. N. D. Kelly, *The Epistles of Peter and Jude*, BNTC 1969, 247; cf. also v. 20). The source of this teaching is ultimately God himself, but it is mediated by the apostles and other human agents (cf. Jude 17 with Lk. 1:2; Acts 16:4; Rom. 6:17; 1 Cor. 11:2; 2 Thess. 2:15; 3:6; 2 Tim. 2:1 f.). The emphasis on a body of truth in opposition to heretical doctrines is more pronounced in later NT writings such as the Pastoral Epistles (cf. 1 Tim. 1:3; 4:6; 2 Tim. 2:2; 4:3 f.; Tit. 1:9). But as Kelly points out, "the idea of tradition, of the gospel as an authoritative message committed to and handed down in the Church, was integral to Christianity from the start" (op. cit., 248; cf. Rom. 10:8; 16:17; 1 Cor. 11:2, 23; 15:1–3; Gal. 1:23; 6:10; → Teach, art. *paradidōmi*). Jude 5 goes on to remind the readers that they "were once fully informed [*eidotas hapax panta*]" of the fact that "he who saved a people out of the land of Egypt, afterward destroyed those who did not believe." "Here as in 3b, we have a sharper insistence that the apostolic faith is a complete whole which has been definitely given to men and cannot be altered" (Kelly, op. cit., 254). The warning against apostasy has the same point as that in Heb. The repeated illustration in Heb. 3 and 4 and its use in 1 Cor. 10:1–5 together with the way that it is introduced here suggests that it formed part of common Christian instruction. (On the exodus theme in Christian thought see B. S. Childs, *Exodus: A Commentary*, 1974, 230–39; A. T. Hanson, *Jesus Christ in the Old Testament*, 1965, 10–25, 48–65; and *Studies in Paul's Technique and Theology*, 1974; R. E. Nixon, *The Exodus in the New Testament*, 1963.)   *K.-H. Bartels*

εἷς

εἷς (*heis*), one; ἑνότης (*henotēs*), unity.

CL The masc. form *heis* derives from Indo-European *sem-s (cf. *homos*, → Like); the fem. form *mia* from *sm-ia; and the neut. *hen* from *sem (cf. Liddell-Scott, 492).

In pre-Socratic nature philosophy *to hen*, the one, refers to the ultimate unity of being, eternity, that which has not become, the non-transient, underived, simple being (the Eleatic school). Parmenides described being as a sphere, perfect in itself and uniform, and this unique, uniform world-body is at the same time the world-concept, simple and excluding all peculiarities. (On Pre-Socratic thought see W. K. C. Guthrie, *A History of Greek Philosophy*, I, *The Earlier Presocratics and Pythogoreans*, 1962; II, *The Presocratic Tradition from Parmenides to Democritus*, 1965; and more briefly "Pre-Socratic Philosophy" in P. Edwards, ed., *The Encyclopedia of Philosophy*, VI, 1967, 441–46.)

The Sophists applied these fundamental concepts to ethics. Since all being is absolutely identical, every value judgment becomes impossible. Socrates opposed these doctrines, and posited an abiding unity which would be recognized by all over against the change and multplicity of opinions. The basis for such universally recognized demands is universally valid concepts (cf. W. K. C. Guthrie, *Socrates*, 1971; I. G. Kidd, "Socrates", *The Encyclopedia of Philosophy*, VII, 480–86). Plato taught a world of ideas in which reality increases until it reaches its peak on the highest incorporeal idea of the One as the good, divine, world-intellect. The many, the physical, and the lower are clearly differentiated from it (on Plato see A. E. Taylor, *Plato*, 1926; and G. Ryle, "Plato", *The Encyclopedia of Philosophy*, VII, 314–33). For the Stoics, however, all existence is ultimately a unity. The divine penetrates everything and manifests itself in diversity, creating order and furnishing a unitary law. All that happens is necessary by the nature of things. The rational is that which is in unison with nature as a whole regarded as divine. The soul of man is by its nature one with the world-soul (on Stoicism see P. P. Hallie, "Stoicism", *The Encyclopedia of Philosophy*, VIII, 19–22).

In gnosticism the divine world of life, light, spirit is originally and remains by nature one. In a pre-cosmic catastrophe pieces of it were broken off and handed over to the evil, the dark, and the many (creation of the world). The goal of the cosmic drama is the collecting and returning of all the scattered fragments of the spiritual and divine into the unity of God. The marks of the divine, true and good are unity, calm, peace; those of the evil, worldly and physical are manifoldness, scattering, lack of peace. (For literature on gnosticism → Knowledge.)

OT 1. The OT terms are *'eḥāḏ* (masc.) and *'aḥaṯ* (fem.) meaning: (a) one (Gen. 1:9); (b) the first (Gen. 8:5), especially in summaries (e.g. Gen. 2:11); (c) the one . . . the other (Exod. 18:3); (d) one after the other (Isa. 27:12); (e) one with another (Ezek. 33:30); (f) one to another (Job 41:16[8]); (g) any one (Gen. 26:10); (h) one and the same (Gen. 27:45); (i) one alone, the only one (Isa. 51:2) (→ *monos*). The plur. is *'ᵃḥāḏîm*, some, a few (Gen. 27:44).

The unity of God is particularly stressed in Deut. 6:4. The MT has "Hear O Israel: *YHWH 'ᵉlōhēnû YHWH 'eḥāḏ* [lit. Yahweh our God Yahweh one]." This has been variously translated: "The LORD is our God is one LORD" (RSV), "the LORD our God, the LORD is one", "the LORD is our God, the LORD is one", "the LORD is our God, the LORD alone" (all RSV mg.), "the LORD is our God, one LORD" (NEB). LXX has "[The] LORD our God is one LORD [*Kyrios ho theos hēmōn heis estin*]." Thus the RSV follows the LXX rendering of the Heb. (For discussion of the declaration see G. Quell, *TDNT* III 1079 ff.; and for the passage in general → Command; → God, art. *theos* OT; → Hear; → Love.)

In the older strata of the OT Israel still spoke of the existence of other gods (e.g. 1 Sam. 26:19 [ironic]; Exod. 15:11). Explicit monotheism became increasingly dominant from the 7th cent. B.C. (e.g. 1 Ki. 8:60; Jer. 2:11; and especially in Isa. 41:29; 43:10; 44:8). But the unique reality of God was firmly anchored in the faith of Israel from the first. This forms the basis for the call to unity among the people (Mal. 2:10). The words of Deut. 6:4 f. form the *šᵉma'*, i.e. the daily confessions by Jews of the unity of God, the basic creed of Jud., by which its separates itself from all paganism and idolatry (cf. the martyrdom of R. Akiba who died with a long drawn out *'eḥāḏ* on his lips; Ber. 61b; T. J. Ber. 2:4a: 61; cf. SB I 224).

2. The unambiguous monotheistic character of later Judaism may be seen in the fact that "the One" became a surrogate for God (cf. SB II 28 on Mk. 12:29).

NT 1. *Survey of the use of heis in the NT*. (a) As a simple numeral. (i) One (Matt. 5:41; Jn. 9:25). We find the same stress on one as in Judaism (e.g. Matt. 26:14; 5:18; Jas. 2:10; cf. also Matt. 23:15). One thing can be decisive (Mk. 10:21; cf. Matt. 19:21; Lk. 18:22); the plagues of judgment come on one day (Rev. 18:8); there is one sacrifice of Christ (Heb. 10:12, 14; → *hapax*). This means that *heis* comes to stand parallel to *monos* (e.g. Mk. 2:7 [*heis*]; Lk. 5:21 [*monos*]). The one, only, last son has a particularly high rank (Matt. 21:37; Mk. 12:6; Lk. 20:13). The one who repents is more valuable than the ninety-nine who do not need to repent (Lk. 15:7). God's will finds its climax in one decisive word and command (Gal. 5:14). (ii) The one . . . the other (Matt. 24:40 f.; 6:24). (iii) Each (Matt. 26:22 [RSV and NEB do not distinguish this usage from that in Mk. 14:19, see (iv)]; 1 Cor. 12:18 f.). (iv) One after the other (Mk. 14:19). (v) The first (Matt. 28:1); → First, art. *prōtos*. (vi) One and only (Mk. 2:7; cf. Lk. 5:21; → *monos*); this can be explained by Heb. usage.

(b) The one God and Father. The Shema (Deut. 6:4; see OT 1 above) is quoted in Mk. 12:29, cf. v. 32. Jas. 4:12 declares that "there is one lawgiver and judge." In warning against the temptation to exalt oneself to positions which only God can occupy Matt. records the words: "But you are not to be called rabbi, for you have one teacher, and you are all brethren. And call no man your father on earth, for you have one Father, who is in heaven. Neither be called masters, for you have one master, the Christ" (Matt. 23:8 ff.). The uniqueness of God is asserted over against idols in the controversy over eating meat offered to idols (1 Cor. 8:4 ff.). This means that there is but "one God, the Father, from whom are all things and for whom we exist, and one Lord, Jesus Christ, through whom are all things and through whom we exist" (v. 6). Therefore, idols have "no real existence" (v. 4). Nevertheless, on grounds of love and expediency Paul urges the Corinthians not to eat meat that has been first offered to idols. Eph. 4:3 urges unity and peace in the church on the grounds of the unity of God: "There is one body and one Spirit, just as you were called in one hope that belongs to your call, one Lord, one faith, one baptism, one God and Father of us all, who is above all and through all and in all" (Eph. 4:4 ff.). 1 Tim. 2:5 is a parenthetical reminder that all men have to do with the same God: "For there is one God, and one mediator between God and men, the man Christ Jesus." He it is "who desires all men to be saved and to come to the knowledge of the truth" (v. 4). Therefore, it is appropriate to pray for all men, including kings and those in positions of authority. There is a unity of mankind which derives from man's common origin at the hands of "the God who made the world and everything in it" (Acts 17:24): "And he made from one every nation of men to live on all the face of the earth, having determined allotted periods and the boundaries of their habitation" (v. 26). There is one abiding will of God (Matt. 5:17 f.), and in conformity with the will of this one God there is one church composed of Jews and Gentiles. One of the main themes of the Epistle to the Romans is to demonstrate the continuity of the divine purposes revealed in the OT in the light of the work of Christ and the inclusion of the Gentiles: "Or is God the God of Jews only? Is he not the God of Gentiles also? Yes, of Gentiles also, since God is one, and he will justify the circumcised on the ground of their faith and the uncircumcised because of their faith" (Rom. 3:29 f.).

(c) The one God in the one Lord Jesus Christ. Jesus is the one exclusive teacher, Lord and mediator (Matt. 28:8, 10; 1 Cor. 8:6; Eph. 4:5; 1 Tim. 2:5). He is the One who stands before the Father on behalf of all (Jn. 11:50; 2 Cor. 5:14). Adam, the disobedient one, brought death; Jesus, the obedient One, brought life (Rom. 5:12 ff.; cf. 1 Cor. 15:22; → Adam). He is one with God the → Father (Jn. 10:30; 17:11, 21 ff.). He is the one Lord, with one → faith and → baptism (Eph. 4:5), the one → shepherd with one flock (Jn. 10:14 ff.).

(d) The One God in the one Spirit of Christ. Paul bases his teaching on the multiplicity of gifts in the church and the necessity of order and harmony in their use on the unity of the Spirit who is the giver of the gifts (1 Cor. 12:9, 11, 13). Jews and Gentiles are no longer alien in Christ, "for through him we both have access in one Spirit to the Father" (Eph. 2:18). There should be unity in the church because "there is one body and one Spirit, just as you were called to the one hope that belongs to your call" (Eph. 4:4). The word *henotēs*, unity, occurs only in Eph. expressing the unity of the church in maturity which is based on the divine unity: "eager to maintain the unity of the Spirit in the bond of peace" (4:3); "until we all attain to the unity of the faith and of the knowledge of the Son of God, to mature manhood, to the measure of the stature of the fullness of Christ" (4:13).

(e) The one church of the one Lord. (i) There is a unity of believers with their Lord. There is also a unity of man and woman which comes about through sexual intercourse. For this reason the believer should not join himself to a prostitute (1 Cor. 6:16; cf. Gen. 2:24; Matt. 19:5; Mk. 10:8; Eph. 5:31; → Discipline, art. *porneuō*; → Flesh; → Marriage). The believer's union with Christ is not a physical one but a spiritual one: "But he who is united with the Lord becomes one spirit with him" (1 Cor. 6:17; cf. the marriage analogy of Christ and the church in Eph. 5:28–33; Rev. 21:2; and the images of the → body and → head).

(ii) In Heb. 2:11 "out of one" (*ex henos*; RSV "one origin"; NEB "of one stock") points to the closest possible unity of believers with Jesus, which is here uniquely expressed in terms of "brothers" in the quotation in v. 12 from Ps. 22:22. There is also a unity of believers in the body of Christ (1 Cor. 12:12 f.; Gal. 2:28; Col. 3:15) through and in the Holy Spirit (Eph. 4:4). The unity of the Lord and his lordship causes the wall of partition between Jews and Gentiles, which was broken down at the cross, to be abolished for good and all, for now there exists only the one, new people of God in Christ (Eph. 2:13–16; Jn. 11:52; 17:23; 17:11, 21). This is a particular emphasis in Jn. Those who are made one have a common life (1 Cor. 12:26; Gal. 6:2; Acts 4:32; Phil. 2:2; Rom. 15:6). Conversely those who are in rebellion against God are one (Rev. 17:13).

2. *The Theological meaning of heis in the NT.* Unity in the NT is always seen from the standpoint of Christ: "there is salvation in no one else, for there is no other name under heaven given among men by which we must be saved" (Acts 4:12). In Gk. and Roman philosophy the unity of God and the world is demanded by educated reason. In the OT the unity of God is a confession derived from experience of God's unique reality. The decisive advance in the NT, caused by God himself, is the basing of the unity and uniqueness of God on the unique revelation through and in the one man Jesus Christ, the Revealer and Lord (Matt. 23:8 ff.; 1 Cor. 8:4 ff.; Eph. 4:1–16; 1 Tim. 2:5 f.).

That is why Paul, after saying in 1 Cor. 8:4 that there are no real idols in the world and that there is no God but One, can recognize in the following sentence that there are in fact many gods and lords. But (and this is the justification for the original statement) these gods have no reality and are therefore only "so-called gods". They have no claim to lordship over us. If we ask why Paul used the term God in this dialectic way, the answer seems to be: the true unity and uniqueness, and hence the reality, of the one God comes from the fact that for us, i.e. for our gain, there is one Lord Jesus Christ (v. 6). We should not take v. 6 as consisting of two parallel statements simply joined by *kai* (and). Rather we must interpret *kai* as meaning: just in the way and with the reality in which we have one Lord Jesus Christ.

This is expressed particularly clearly in Jn. Jn. 10:30 should not be interpreted to mean that the oneness of Jesus with the Father consists of the joining of two persons or beings who were formerly separated. We must understand it in the light of Jn. 14:9: "He who has seen me has seen the Father." In a Christian sense no one can speak of God unless he is speaking concretely of Jesus. Statements like Jas. 4:12

obtain a living meaning only in the light of Jesus. Indeed, the unity of the Spirit is based on Jesus (1 Cor. 13; Eph. 4), not on a unity of outlook based on human enthusiasm.

The "one man Jesus Christ" (Rom. 5:15) is decisive for the salvation of "the many." He died for all the one decisive death (Jn. 11:50, 52; 2 Cor. 5:14; → *hapax* NT). The obedient death of the one is interpreted by the "much more" of Rom. 5:17. The one man Adam became a curse for humanity, "because all men sinned" (Rom. 5:12); in contrast the one man Jesus Christ brought righteousness and life for all (Rom. 5:17).

Rom. 5:12–20 contrasts the rôles of Christ and → Adam as the respective heads of saved and fallen humanity. Sin came into the world "through one man and death through sin, and so death spread to all men because all men sinned" (Rom. 5:12). "But the free gift is not like the trespass. For if many died through one man's trespass, much more have the grace of God and the free gift in the grace of that one man Jesus Christ abounded for the many. And the free gift is not like the effect of that one man's sin. For the judgment following one trespass brought condemnation, but the free gift following many trespasses brings justification. If, because of one man's trespass, death reigned through that one man, much more will those who receive the abundance of grace and the free gift of righteousness reign in life through the one man Jesus Christ" (Rom. 5:15 ff.; cf. also Jn. 11:50, 52; 2 Cor. 5:14).

The foundation and continuity of the church's unity are grounded in him as the one shepherd of the one flock (Jn. 10:14 ff.). Paul expresses this fact through his picture of the one → body, in which the members are linked and are mutually dependent, a picture used also by the Stoics. The several members cannot live in diversity without the one → head (1 Cor. 12). The counterpart to this in the high priestly prayer in Jn. 17 is the concept of mutual indwelling: Jesus prayed "that they may all be one; even as thou, Father, art in me, and I in thee, that they also may be in us, so that the world may believe that thou hast sent me" (Jn. 17:21).

K.-H. Bartels

μόνος

μόνος (*monos*), alone, only; μονογενής (*monogenēs*), only (preferable to "only begotten").

CL *monos*, Ionic *mounos*, Doric *mōnos* from Homer on, means only, lonely, alone; *sou monos*, without you; *monos pantōn anthrōpōn*, (he had) no other of all men. In an extended sense it means unique. The adv. *monōs* or *monon* (neut.) means only, solely. The LXX and the NT do not preserve the variety of usage which existed in cultured Gk. The use of the adj. and adv. run into one another, and the adv. *monōs* is not found, nor the use with the gen. On the other hand, the form *kata monas*, alone, does occur. All this shows that *monos* is used in the NT as in Koine Gk.

OT The LXX uses *monos* mostly for *leḇaḏ* or (*le*) *bāḏāḏ* (78 times as against 14 for the other Heb. terms), derived from *baḏ*, that which has been separated. Its basic meaning is in separation from, or in solitude from. Thus in Exod. 30:34 *baḏ beḇaḏ yihyeh* (RSV "of each shall there be an equal part") means that the various spices must be taken separately without contact with each other, and only then be mixed to form → incense (v. 35). To be alone does not imply peace but a troubled

723

mind and restlessness. The bad connotation cannot be missed and comes out clearly in a passage like Isa. 49:21 and Jer. 15:17, where the prophet, bent down by God's hand, and cut off from human contact with the other members of his people, sits alone. This sense is also found in Gen. 2:18. God says that it is not good for the man to be alone; "I will make a helper fit for him."

monos is frequently used for God's uniqueness; e.g. Deut. 32:12 (as leader of the people); Job 9:8 (as Creator). It occurs in the confessional statements in 2 Ki. 19:15, 19; Isa. 37:16. It is frequently found in Pss. (4:8; 33[32]:15; 51[50]:4; 71[70]:16; 72[71]:18; 77[76]:14; 83[82]:18; 86[85]:10; 136[135]:4, 7; 141[140]:10; 148:13). Hence it is often used in statements about the exclusive worship of the one God: e.g. Exod. 22:20(19); Deut. 6:13 (*v.l.* in LXX); Ps. 71(70):16. Ezek. 14:16 shows that the righteous alone will be delivered. Exod. 24:2 uses *monos* to stress → Moses' uniqueness. Occasionally, as in secular Gk., *monos* is intensified. Thus in 1 Ki. 19:10, 14, where → Elijah, persecuted by Jezebel, says in his despondency that he has survived *monōtatos*, utterly alone, as prophet of the Lord. The despair of this extreme solitude stands in contrast to the superior strength and numbers of the worshippers of Baal which had remained intact in spite of God's judgment in 1 Ki. 18.

NT 1. *monos* is found 46 times in the NT and *monon* 66 times. They are found most frequently in Paul (13 and 36 times) and John (9 and 5 times), while neither is found in 2 Pet., Tit. or Phlm. The adj. is used in connection with vbs. like *eimi* (be), *heuriskō* (find), *kataleipō* (leave), and absolutely with nouns and prons. The neut. *monon* is used as an adv. It means: (a) only, alone (Matt. 9:21; 1 Cor. 15:19; Lk. 24:12; Matt. 5:47); not only but also (Matt. 21:21); not only but much more (Phil. 2:12); and in the limiting sense of not yet but only (Acts 8:16); (b) alone, without others, unaccompanied (Matt. 17:8 par. Mk. 9:8; Jn. 8:16; Rom. 11:3); *kata monas*, alone by oneself (Mk. 4:10; Lk. 9:18); single (Jn. 12:24); alone without help (Lk. 10:40), alone with, face to face (Matt. 18:15); (e) with noun or pron. it means only in the sense of exclusively (e.g. Matt. 12:4; Lk. 5:21 → *heis*, NT 1; Rom. 16:27; 1 Tim. 1:17; 6:15 f.; Heb. 9:7; Gal. 6:4; Rev. 15:4); (d) one and only (Jn. 5:44; 17:3; Jude 4, 25).

2. *monos* becomes theologically significant when it is used in the confession of the one and only God, especially in doxologies (Rom. 16:27; 1 Tim. 1:17; 6:15 f.; Jn. 5:44). Rom. 16:25 ff. refers to God's command "to bring about the obedience of faith" among the nations, and 1 Tim. 6:12–16 calls on Timothy to keep the confession – the context shows the polemical background of the confession – of the one God. It is significant that the confession of the one holy God in Rev. 15:4 is found in the song of praise of the martyrs who "had conquered the beast." Similarly in Jn. 17:3, *monos* is linked with *alēthinos*, true, in contrast to the deceptive appearance (*pseudos*) of all alleged gods and revealers, and in Jn. 5:44 it stands in contrast to the false *doxa* (→ glory) of the world, which does not seek the true *doxa* of the one and only God (cf. R. Bultmann, *The Gospel of John*, 1971, 271, n. 3; E. Norden, *Agnostos Theos*, 1913, 245 n. 1).

monos is sometimes used to stress the uniqueness of God in polemical contexts. Thus Jesus, the Revealer and Son of God, is declared to be *monogenēs* (see 4 below). There is a dialectic use of *monos* in relation to Jesus. On the one hand, already the

724

earthly Jesus in not "alone" in human terms even if all forsake him, for the Father is with him (Jn. 8:16, 29; 16:32). On the other hand, in Jude 4 the uniqueness of God can be applied without qualification to Jesus (cf. Rom. 9:5 (RSV mg., NEB mg.); Jn. 20:28; Tit. 2:13). On Rom. 9:5 → God, art. *theos* NT 6(a).

4. *monogenēs*, the only begotten, or only, is found as a christological title only in Jn. Matt. and Mk. use *agapētos*, beloved (Matt. 3:17 par. Mk. 1:11; Matt. 17:5 par. Mk. 9:7). Paul has *ho heautou hyios* (Rom. 8:3), *ho idios hyios* (Rom. 8:32), his own Son, or *ho prōtotokos*, the first-born (Rom. 8:29). *monogenēs* is used to mark out Jesus uniquely above all earthly and heavenly beings; in its use the present soteriological meaning is more strongly stressed than that of origin (Jn. 1:14, 18; 3:16, 18; 1 Jn. 4:9). RSV and NEB render *monogenēs* as "only". This meaning is supported by R. E. Brown, *The Gospel according to John*, Anchor Bible, I, 1966, 13 f., and D. Moody, "God's Only Son: The Translation of John 3:16 in the Revised Standard Version", *JBL* 72, 1953, 213–19. Lit. it means "of a single kind", and could even be used in this sense of the Phoenix (1 Clem. 25:2). It is only distantly related to *gennaō*, beget. The idea of "only begotten" goes back to Jerome who used *unigenitus* in the Vulg. to counter the Arian claim that Jesus was not begotten but made. *monogenēs* reflects the Heb. *yāḥîḏ* of Isaac (Gen. 22:2, 12, 16) of whom it is used in Heb. 11:16. The meaning of *monogenēs* "is centred in the Personal existence of the Son, and not in the Generation of the Son" (B. F. Westcott, *The Epistles of St John*, [1883] 1966, 170). Jesus as *monogenēs* is the One who can say "I and the Father are one [*hen esmen*]" (Jn. 10:30). Included in the uniqueness of God, Jesus does not disappear in history and the historical, but stands over them as Lord.   *K.-H. Bartels*

→ First, → God, → Number

(a). E. Best, *One Body in Christ*, 1955; F. Büchsel, *monogenēs*, *TDNT* IV 737–41; S. Hanson, *The Unity of the Church in the New Testament: Colossians and Ephesians*, Acta Seminarii Neotestamentici Upsaliensis 14, 1946; H. Jonas, *The Gnostic Religion* 1963; E. Käsemann, *The Testament of Jesus: A Study of the Gospel of John in the Light of Chapter 17*, 1968; G. A. F. Knight, "The Lord is One", *ExpT* 79, 1967–68, 8 ff.; D. Moody, "God's Only Son: The Translation of John 3:16 in the Revised Standard Version", *JBL* 72, 1953, 213–19; C. A. Labuschagne, *The Incomparability of Yahweh in the Old Testament*, 1966; N. Lohfink and J. Bergman, 'ehād, *TDOT* 1 193–201; T. E. Pollard, " 'That They All May Be One' (John xvii, 21) – and the Unity of the Church", *ExpT* 70, 1958–59, 149 f.; J. F. Randall, *The Theme of Unity in John XVII: 20–23*, Dissertation Louvain, 1962; H. H. Rowley, "Moses and Monotheism", *ZAW* 28, 1957, –21 (reprinted in *From Moses to Qumran:Studies in the Old Testament*, 1963, 35–63); W. Stählin, *hapax, ephapax*, *TDNT* I 381–84; E. Stauffer, *heis*, *TDNT* II 434–42; and 'The Creeds of the Primitive Church", *New Testament Theology*, 1955, 235–57, see especially "Monotheistic Formulae", 242 ff.; E. L. Wenger, "That They All May Be One", *ExpT* 70, 1958–59, 333; B. F. Westcott, *The Epistles of St. John*, (1883) revised edition with introduction by F. F. Bruce, 1966, 169–72.

(b). J.-L. d'Aragon, "La Notion Johannique de l'Unité", *Sciences Ecclésiastiques* II, 1959, 111–19; G. Delling, "Monos Theos", *TLZ*, 1952, 469 ff.; E. L. Dietrich, "Gott", *RGG³* II 1713 ff.; E. Fascher, "Gott und die Götter", *TLZ*, 1956, 279 ff.; H. Jonas, *Gnosis und spätantiker Geist*, I, 1934; II, 1, 1954; O. Kern, *Orphicorum Fragmenta*, 1922; E. Käsemann, *Das wandernde Gottesvolk*, FRLANT Neue Folge 37, 1959³; F. Klinke, *Der Monismus*, 1911; E. Peterson, *Heis Theos*, 1926; G. Sauer, 'ehād, *THAT* I 104–7; K. Schelkle, "Das Gottesbild des Neuen Testaments: Gott der Eine", *BuK* 15, 1960, 12 ff.; H. Schlier, *Der Brief an die Epheser*, 1965⁵; G. Schrenk, "Die Geschichtsanschauung des Paulus auf dem Hintergrund seines Zeitalters", *Jahrbücher der Theologischen Schule Bethel* 3, 1932, 59 ff.; W. Stählin, *Allein. Recht und Gefahr einer polemischen Formel*, 1950; W. Thüsing, *Herrlichkeit und Einheit. Eine Auslegung des hohepriesterlichen Gebets Jesu (Joh. 17)*, 1962.

Open, Close, Key

ἀνοίγω

ἀνοίγω (anoigō), open; ἄνοιξις (anoixis), opening; διανοίγω (dianoigō), open, explain.

CL Since Homer (*Il.* 14, 169; 24, 455) *anoignymi* occurs together with *anoigō* meaning to open, remove that which obstructs, though not at first in the pres. tense. The pres. of *anoigō* is first found in Pindar, and of *anoignymi* in Lysias. The -*mi*-forms are the more original ones. Figuratively it can mean to reach the high seas; *thalattan* is to be supplied. In the NT the original form is replaced by the adjunct form without exception. This is in line with the decline of vbs. in -*mi* in Koine (Funk §§ 92, 101). The vb. can be used trans. (to open a door, a place, an object, a part of the body) and intrans. (to open; partly in the pass. sense of to be opened).

OT In the LXX *anoigō* is used predominantly (106 times) as the equivalent for the Heb. vb. *pāṭaḥ*; 10 times for *pāqaḥ*, both meaning open; 6 times for *pāṣâh*, unlock, open up; and in isolated passages for further Heb. vbs. *pāṣâh*, as a rule followed by *peh* as obj., means to open the mouth (in order to swallow, Ezek. 2:8). *pāqaḥ* is used exclusively for opening one's eyes and ears (e.g. Gen. 21:19; Isa. 35:5; 37:17). With *pāṭaḥ* the object can be a container (a bag, a box, a vessel, a grave; e.g. Exod. 21:33; Jdg. 4:19; Ps. 5:9), a window or a door (1 Sam. 3:15; 2 Ki. 13:17; Isa. 22:22; 26:2), or a book (Neh. 8:5). If the act of opening is related to men, it is usually God who is the subject; objects include the womb (Gen. 29:31); the mouth (Exod. 4:12, 15; Num. 22:28; cf. Ps. 81:10); the eye (Gen. 21:19; Isa. 35:5; 42:7); the ear (Isa. 50:5); the hand (Ps. 145:16). It is a striking fact that *pāṭaḥ* is not found in passages attributed to the Priestly Code. Gen. 7:11a is widely regarded as P; but 7:11b "and windows of heaven were opened" is thought not to be P. Num. 19:15 is thought to be a quotation taken over by P. The absence of the word has been explained on the basis of the theology of the Priestly Code, which saw God as so transcendent that access to him was possible only through the priest and the cult. To use *pāṭaḥ* would contradict such a transcendent view of God; for *pāṭaḥ* presupposes a view of God in which God intervenes, not indirectly, but directly in, e.g., opening a man's mouth.

NT In the NT the vb. *anoigō* is found 78 times, particularly often in the Johannine literature (27 times in Rev.; 11 times in the Gospel). It is less frequently found in Matt. (11 times) and Lk. (16 times in Acts; 7 times in the Gospel). It occurs only 5 times in Paul (Rom. 3:13; 1 Cor. 16:9; 2 Cor. 2:12; 6:11; Col. 4:3) and in Mk. only at 7:35. Following the LXX pattern the vb. is chiefly trans., and only rarely intrans. (Jn. 1:51; 1 Cor. 16:9; 2 Cor. 6:11). The sole occurrence of *anoixis* (Eph. 6:19) has a trans. meaning in Paul's request for prayer "that utterance may be given me in opening my mouth [*en anoixei tou stomatos mou*] boldly to proclaim the mystery of the gospel."

Objects include (as in the LXX) the mouth (Matt. 5:2; 6:8 D; Lk. 1:64; Acts 8:35; 10:34; 18:14), the eye (Matt. 9:30; 20:33; Lk. 24:31; Jn. 9:10, 14, 17, 21, 26, 30, 32; 10:21; Acts 9:8, 40; 26:18), the ear (Mk. 7:35), a door (Acts 5:19; 12:10, 14; 14:27; 1 Cor. 16:9; 2 Cor. 2:12; Rev. 3:20), a place (Matt. 3:16) or an object like a scroll (Rev. 5:2 ff.). If we leave aside consideration of those passages where "to open the mouth" means to begin to speak (e.g. Matt. 5:2; 13:35; Acts 8:35; 10:34), which make use of a Semitic idiom (cf. Job 3:1; 33:2; Dan. 10:16), the vb. is used with a predominantly theological sense: It is God himself who opens.

1. In the writings of Paul *anoigō* occurs in the quotation from Ps. 5:9 in Rom. 3:13a in the catena of quotations demonstrating the fact that the Jews are guilty sinners, even though they have the law: "Their throat is an open grave [*taphos aneōgmenos*], they use their tongues to deceive." In 2 Cor. 6:11 Paul writes: "Our mouth is open to you [*to stoma hēmōn aneōgen pros hymas*], Corinthians; our heart is wide." C. K. Barrett paraphrases this as "I have let my tongue run away with me", i.e. "I have spoken to you in complete freedom" (cf. 7:4; *A Commentary on the Second Epistle to the Corinthians, BNTC*, 1973, 191). Barrett sees here a Gk. idiom (cf. Aesch., *PV* 609 ff. with Ezek. 16:63; 29:21; Eph. 6:19). The following clause means that Paul has kept no secrets back from the Corinthians. There not only is room for them in his heart; he positively yearns for them. Apart from these instances, it is God himself who opens. The picture of God opening a door for Paul refers to the possibility of fruitful and effective missionary work. Form-criticism has shown that the expression is a technical term in the vocabulary of mission (1 Cor. 16:9; 2 Cor. 2:12; Col. 4:3; Acts 14:27; Rev. 3:8; cf. J. Jeremias, *TDNT* III 174). But it is characteristic of Paul that he never uses *anoigō* with Jesus Christ as subject.

2. Rev. 3:20 speaks of man opening the door to Christ: "Behold, I stand at the door and knock; if any one hears my voice and opens the door, I will come in to him and eat with him, and he with me." The underlying idea is the kingdom of God seen as a feast (Isa. 25:6 ff.; Matt. 8:11; 22:1-14; Mk. 13:29; 14:25; Lk. 12:34 ff.; 22:28 ff.; but cf. the idea of the judge standing at the doors in Jas. 5:9). There are also the promises of feeding on Christ himself (Jn. 6:35 ff., 53 ff.) and dwelling with him (Jn. 14:2 f., 23). The context of Rev. 3:20 is the letter addressed to the lukewarm church at Laodicea (→ Cold, Hot, Lukewarm). As such it is addressed to the church, but the singular subject of the verse invites an individual response.

Elsewhere in the Johannine writings God is the one who opens. It is God who opens → heaven (Jn. 1:51; Rev. 19:11), the → temple (Rev. 11:19), and the holy → tent of heaven (Rev. 15:5). It is on his authority that an angel opens the abyss of the underworld (Rev. 9:2). But the exalted Lord has the authority which belongs to God to open the way of access to God. The letter to the church at Philadelphia begins: "And to the angel of the church in Philadelphia write: 'The words of the holy one, the true one, who has the key of David, who opens and no one shall shut, who shuts and no one opens. "I know your works. Behold, I have set before you an open door, which no one is able to shut...."'" (Rev. 3:7 f.). The metaphor of the open door is not the technical term of the language of mission (see 1 above). The key of David (→ *kleis*) recalls the promise to Eliakim (Isa. 22:22) who was given authority to open and none shall shut and to shut and none shall open. Here it is construed as access to God and eternal life, as in Rev. 1:18: "I died, and behold I am alive for evermore, and I have the keys of Death and Hades" (cf. also Matt. 16:19). It is the exalted Lord, the Lamb that had been slain and who has ascended to the throne, who alone is worthy to open the scroll with the seven seals which contains the record of God's plan in history in the last days with all the profusion of eschatological events (Rev. 5:2-9). The earthly Jesus is here seen as equal with God. The Fourth Gospel contains a counterpart to this in the fact that Jesus opens the eyes of the blind which is something which God alone can do (Jn. 9:10, 14, 17, 21, 26, 30, 32; 10:21). He is also the → shepherd to whom "the gatekeeper opens; the sheep hear his voice, and he calls his own sheep by name and leads them out" (Jn. 10:3).

3. Matt. 2:11 speaks of the magi opening their treasures (→ Magic; → Gold; → Incense). Matt. also records Jesus opening the eyes of the blind (Matt. 9:3; 20:33; cf. Mk. 7:35). As in Jn., opening in Matt. is implicitly or explicitly the act of God. It is God who opens the heavens at the baptism of Jesus (Matt. 3:16) symbolizing the favour and openness of God to him and confirming the action (cf. Jn. 1:51 noted above). To those who knock the kingdom of heaven will be opened (Matt. 7:7; cf. 7:13 f.). But to those who do not come at the hour of opportunity it will not be opened (Matt. 25:11). Here it is the eschatological Lord who is speaking and who thus has the authority of God himself to open and shut. Matt. 27:52 refers to the opening of the tombs and the raising of the dead at the moment of the death of Jesus (→ Resurrection). On the coin in the fish's mouth (Matt. 17:27) → Tax.

4. In the writings of Lk. *anoigō* is particularly associated with Lk.'s concept of time (on the subject of time in Lk. → Present, art. *The Parousia and Eschatology in the NT*, 2(b).) There is an appropriate time for the devil (Lk. 4:13). But there is also an appropriate time for the opening of Zechariah's mouth (Lk. 1:64) and the opening of heaven after the baptism of Jesus (Lk. 3:21; cf. Matt. 3:16 above). The public ministry of Jesus, and with it the centre of time, begins when Jesus enters the synagogue at Nazareth and opens (Lk. 4:17) the book of the prophet Isaiah and reads from Isa. 61:1 f. thus identifying himself with the one on whom the Spirit of the Lord rests. As befitting the one on whom the Spirit rests, he is the one who opens (Lk. 13:25) and the one to whom the servants must be ready to open (Lk. 12:36). The sayings about asking, knocking and opening (Lk. 11:9 f.) are rounded off in Lk. by the promise of the Spirit: "If you then, who are evil, know how to give good gifts to your children, how much more will the heavenly Father give the Holy Spirit to those who ask him?" (Lk. 11:13). This suggests that Luke understood the sayings as having particular reference to the gift of the Spirit. He follows it with the account of the Beelzebul controversy concerning the power and authority by which Jesus acted (Lk. 11:14–26). The references in Lk. suggest that the time to open and the authority to open ultimately rest with God.

Acts 8:35; 10:34 and 18:14 use the idiom of opening the mouth. Acts 8:32 quotes Isa. 53:7: "As a sheep led to the slaughter or a lamb before its shearer is dumb, so he opens not his mouth." This is interpreted christologically by Philip to the Ethiopian eunuch. Acts 9:8, 40 refer to the opening of the eyes physically (in each case after an affliction). But Acts 26:18 uses the metaphor spiritually in its account of Paul's commission to the Gentiles: "to open their eyes, that, they may turn from darkness to light and from the power of Satan to God, that they may receive forgiveness of sins and a place amongst those who are sanctified by faith in me." The words recall the mission of the servant (Isa. 42:6, 17), and in the light of Lk. 4:17 constitute an extension of Jesus' own mission. Peter's vision of the great sheet containing both clean and unclean animals signifying God's inclusion of the Gentiles in his people descends from heaven. The fact that heaven is opened in order to let down the sheet (Acts 10:11) signifies the divine origin and authority of the vision. Several passages refer to the opening of doors. In Acts 5:19; 12:10 and 16:26 f. the doors are prison doors which are opened by divine agency. This contrasts with the doors closed by men, either to imprison the apostles (Acts 5:23) or which are kept closed by the church in incredulity (Acts 12:14, 16). Just as God opens prison doors, he also opens "the door of faith". Paul summed up his first missionary journey by telling the church at Antioch "all that God had done with them, and how he had opened a door of faith to the Gentiles" (Acts 14:27; on this expression see 1 above).

5. The vb. *dianoigō* occurs in the expression "every male that opens the womb [i.e. every first-born male] shall be called holy to the Lord" (Lk. 2:23; cf. Exod. 13:2, 12). The passage refers to the presentation of the infant Jesus in the temple and the sacrifices that were offered for him (→ Bird art. *peteinon* OT; → First, art. *prōtotokos* CL & OT 1). It is used again in the vision of Stephen just before his martyrdom when he saw "the heavens opened, and the Son of man standing at the right hand of God" (Acts 7:56). As with the other references to the opening of heaven, it signifies God's acceptance and blessing of the one who sees the heaven opened, and is a divine confirmation of the rightness of his actions.

dianoichthēti, "Be opened", is given as a translation of *ephphatha* (Mk. 7:34; cf. v. 35) in the healing of the deaf and dumb man. This Aram. word represents *'etpattaḥ*, or the contracted *'eppattaḥ*, from the vb. *pᵉṭaḥ* (cf. C. E. B. Cranfield, *The Gospel according to Saint Mark*, 1959, 252; SB II 17 f. for examples in connection with the curing of blindness). It is not a meaningless magical formula like abracadabra but an intelligible performative utterance (→ Magic, art. *mageia* NT 5).

In Lk. 24:31 f. it is used of the eyes in the sense of the understanding (cf. Gen. 3:5, 7; 2 Ki. 6:17) in the self-disclosure of the Risen Christ to the disciples at Emmaus. In v. 31 the reference is to recognizing the stranger as Christ. Upon recognition he vanishes from physical sight. In v. 32 the same word refers to the understanding of the significance of the scriptures in relation to Jesus as the Christ. It is also used of Paul's missionary work among the Jews at Thessalonica: "explaining [*dianoigōn*] and proving that it was necessary for the Christ to suffer and to rise from the dead, and saying, 'This Jesus, whom I proclaim to you, is the Christ'" (Acts 17:3). In each of these three instances of Lk.'s use of the word men require help in order to see Christ. Both the understanding and the scriptures require opening. (→ Explain, art. *hermēneuō* NT 2.)   *C. H. Peisker, C. Brown*

κλείς

κλείς (*kleis*), a key; κλείω (*kleiō*), to close, shut.

CL The noun *kleis*, which is cognate with Lat. *clavis* (key), is used since Homer for a key. *kleiō*, similarly used since Homer, means to close, or shut. In addition to lit. usage, *kleis* was used as early as the seventh cent. B.C. in connection with → heaven and the underworld depicted as a house. Certain powers, demi-gods or divinities, had control over the keys to heaven (e.g. Dike) or to the underworld (e.g. Pluto, Persephone). The imagery of the key extended also into everyday life. Thus Pindar (*Pyth.* 8, 4) could speak of rest as the most important key to deliberation and to wars, i.e. rest is the chief prerequisite for reaching the right decision.

OT In the LXX *kleis* occurs only 5 times (3 times as equivalent for Heb. *maptēah*). This was the key to the great wooden doors, which possibly consisted of one long piece of wood with various long iron spikes fixed on to it, and which as a rule was so big that it could not fit in the pocket, but had to be carried on the belt or even on the shoulder (Isa. 22:22). With this key one could turn backwards and forwards the bolt of the door from the outside. One of the particular offices of the Levites was to administer the keys to the rooms and store-rooms of the temple (1 Chr. 9:27). The announcement in Isa. 22:22 of the installation into office of Eliakim, giving him the power of the keys to the house of David, had originally no messianic reference. In later rabbinic thought it was interpreted as conferring teaching authority (Sanhedrin 38a; Gittin 88a; see further SB I 741). In Rev. 3:7 it was interpreted typologically and christologically (→ *anoigō* NT 2; see also below 4). *kleis* also occurs in Jdg. 3:25, in Job 31:22 (for *šikmāh*), and without Heb. equivalent in Ad.Dan. Bel 12.

The vb. *kleiō* occurs in Gen. 7:16; Jos. 2:5, 7; Jdg. 9:51; 1 Sam. 23:20; 2 Chr. 28:24; Neh. 6:10; 13:19; Job 12:14; Eccl. 12:4; Isa. 22:22; 24:10; 60:11; Ezek. 44:1 f.; 46:1 f. (for *sāḡar*, shut, close); in Neh. 7:3 (for *gûp*, shut); in Cant. 4:12 (for *nā'al*, bar, of a garden gate); and without Heb. equivalent in Jdg. 20:42; Sir. 30:18; 42:6; Ad.Dan. Bel 12; and several variant translations of various passages.

NT The words occur comparatively rarely in the NT. *kleis* occurs 6 times (once each in Matt. and Lk.; and 4 times in Rev.), and is used only figuratively. *kleiō* occurs 16 times (3 times in Matt.; twice each in Lk., Jn. and Acts; once in 1 Jn., and 6 times in Rev.). It is used lit. of closed, shut or locked doors in Matt. 6:6; 25:10; Lk. 11:7; Jn. 20:19, 26; Acts 5:23; 21:30, although Matt. 25:10 and Lk. 11:7 figure in parables (in the former instance illustrating that the time of opportunity is past, and in the latter illustrating the importance of importunity in prayer). Elsewhere the use of both the noun and the vb. is fig.

1. Lk. 4:25 refers to the time of → Elijah, "when the heaven was shut up three years and six months, when there came a great famine over all the land" (cf. 1 Ki. 17:1–18:1; Jas. 5:17 f.). The point alludes to the fact that Elijah was sent not to all the widows in Israel at the time of Elijah, but only to the widow of Zarephath. The implication is that Jesus of Nazareth will pass over a rebellious Israel in favour of the Gentiles.

2. Lk. 11:52 records the accusation: "Woe to you lawyers! for you have taken away the key of knowledge; you did not enter yourselves, and you hindered those who were entering." Whereas the saying in Lk. refers specifically to knowledge, the saying in Matt. 23:13 refers to the kingdom: "But woe to you, scribes and Pharisees, hypocrites! because you shut the kingdom of heaven against men; for you neither enter yourselves, nor allow those who would enter to go in." J. Jeremias cites Rabbah bar Huna (*c.* A.D. 300): "He who has knowledge of the Torah but no fear of God is like the treasurer to whom one gave the key of the inner rooms without giving him the outer. How can he enter?" (Shabbath 31ab; cf. *TDNT* III 747). In Lk. the saying comes at the conclusion of Jesus' denunciation of the religious for their hypocrisy, their misguided and perverse legalism, and their persecution of the prophets sent by God. The same points occur in Matt. only in considerably greater detail, and the saying introduces the specific accusations. The

difference in the presentation of the saying has been put down to oral tradition (cf. D. Hill, *The Gospel of Matthew, New Century Bible*, 1972, 311), and the possibility that Jesus made the denunciation more than once and in different forms (Lk. speaks of the key, whereas Matt. uses the vb.) in the course of his condemnation of the religious teachers of his day. Alternatively, the two versions may be interpretative translations: Lk.'s version with its reference to knowledge being addressed to a Gentile readership; whereas Matt.'s is more specifically Jewish in his concern for the kingdom and for the details of the condemnation of contemporary Jewish practices.

3. Matt.'s account of Peter's confession culminates in the promise: "And I tell you, you are Peter, and on this rock I will build my church, and the gates of Hades shall not prevail against it. I will give you the keys of the kingdom of heaven, and whatever you bind on earth shall be bound in heaven, and whatever you loose on earth shall be loosed in heaven" (RSV mg.). The authenticity of this passage has been questioned by many scholars. G. Bornkamm sums up their attitude to these words when he observes: "This is not only because they have no parallel in the other Gospels, and because this is the only place in the whole synoptic tradition where the word *'ekklesia'* appears in the sense of the church as a whole. (Only in Mt. xviii. 17 do we come across the word *'ekklesia'* again, in connection with Church regulations, but used here in the sense of an assembly of the Church.) But the authenticity of the passage in Matthew xvi is questioned chiefly because it is not easily compatible with Jesus' proclamation of the imminent coming of the kingdom of God" (*Jesus of Nazareth*, 1960, 187). For further discussion questioning the authenticity of the passage see the writings of H. Braun, R. Bultmann, H. Conzelmann, W. G. Kümmel listed below in the bibliography.

Among the writers who have defended the authenticity of the passage are O. Betz, O. Cullmann, J. Jeremias and A. Oepke (see also the bibliography). Cullmann gives a history of the interpretation of the saying (*Peter: Disciple – Apostle – Martyr. A Historical and Theological Study*, 1962², 164–76). He himself locates it in the passion period in a setting similar to Lk. 22:31 ff., but stresses that his interpretation does not stand or fall with his view of the setting (op. cit., 176–91). Cullmann argues that the comparative infrequency of the word *ekklēsia* is indecisive, *"for it does not designate anything like a Christian creation*, but belongs to the Jewish sphere. . . . We must start with the meaning 'people of God' when we ask the question whether or not Jesus can have spoken of the Church" (op. cit., 194 f.; → Church, art. *ekklēsia* for the OT concept supporting Cullmann's claim). Moreover, Jewish messianic expectation is inconceivable without a messianic community (op. cit., 195; cf. Eth.Enoch 38:1; 53:6; 62:8; 83:8; 84:5; Dan. 7:9–28). "If he considered himself to be the Danielic Son of Man (Mark. 14:62 and parallels), he also knew that according to Daniel 7:18 the Son of Man represents the 'people of the saints' " (op. cit., 196). The new element in the situation is the reconstitution of the people of God in view of his special messianic deed, the suffering of the servant of God. As Cullmann observes, the argument is bound up with Jesus' messianic consciousness, and it is not surprising that Bultmann who denies this also denies the authenticity of the passage. A further factor is the fact that Jesus now no longer views the messianic community as identical with the Jewish nation. The fact that he speaks of *his ekklēsia* does not contradict the fact that its building is the work of God.

731

With regard to the question of whether Jesus could have envisaged a future church in view of his teaching on the imminence of the kingdom, Cullmann points out that the alternative of a present or future messianic community presents a false perspective (op. cit., 199 f.). The Jewish idea of the people of God cannot be forced into this alternative. It is not a case of the early church developing the promised kingdom into an institutional church. "Rather, the fulfilment in the person of Jesus leads directly to the fulfilment in the Church, and the fulfilment in the Church points back in turn to the fulfilment in the person of Jesus. Therefore it is not merely possible that Jesus also sees the people of God already beginning to be constituted in his day; we would almost have to postulate this even if we had no clear texts to prove it. A direct contradiction between the future Kingdom of God and the already realized people of God is only a construction built on the basis of modern thinking" (op. cit., 201). The choice of the twelve disciples reflecting the twelve tribes of Israel is closely bound up with the reconstitution of the people of God. The band of disciples anticipates the messianic community which is constituted by the death of the Christ. But even though the Christ dies the → gates of death will not prevail against it.

Cullmann sees this concept of the church as the messianic community further supported by the saying about raising up the temple which also refers to the time after the death of Jesus (Matt. 26:61; Mk. 14:58; cf. Jn. 2:19) which involves the messianic community (cf. 1 Pet. 2:5 ff.; op. cit., 204 f.). A future community is also implied by the → Lord's Supper, and such passages as Mk. 2:18 ff.; 14:28, 62 imply that Jesus envisaged a time when his followers would continue after his death (op. cit., 206 f.).

For discussion of the significance of the name Peter (*petros*) and the meaning of the rock (*petra*) → Rock. The metaphor of building on the rock implies a → house (comparable with the house of Israel) or a → temple. "In Matthew 16:19 it is presupposed that Christ is the master of the house, who has the keys to the Kingdom of Heaven, with which to open to those who come in. Just as in Isaiah 22:22 the Lord lays the keys of the house of David on the shoulders of the servant Eliakim, so Jesus commits to Peter the keys of his house, the Kingdom of Heaven, and thereby installs him as administrator of the house" (op. cit., 209 f.; cf. the illustration of the steward in Mk. 13:34; Lk. 12:42; 16:1 ff.; 1 Cor. 4:1; 1 Pet. 4:10). Peter is given the task of leading the people of God into the resurrection kingdom. In this he stands in contrast with the Pharisees who purportedly had the key to the kingdom but who did not use it to enter and even prevented others from entering (cf. Matt. 23:13; see 2 above). Whereas they compassed land and sea to make proselytes (Matt. 23:15), Peter also has a mission to carry out by his preaching to give men access to the kingdom. His rôle in this capacity is described in Acts, particularly in opening the kingdom to Jewish believers at → Pentecost (Acts 2) and to Gentile believers at Caesarea (Acts 10).

The words bind (*deō*) and loose (*lyō*) represent the Aram. '*asar* and *š*e*rā*' (Heb. '*āsar* and *hittîr*). They have been interpreted as meaning prohibit and permit, i.e. establish rules (G. Dalman, *The Words of Jesus*, 1909, 214), and put under the ban and acquit (A. Schlatter, *Der Evangelist Matthäus*, 1963⁶, 511 f.; J. Schniewind, *Das Evangelium nach Matthäus*, NTD 2, 1968¹², ad loc.). Cullmann favours the latter interpretation in view of the connection with the forgiveness of sins and entry into the kingdom, though he would not exclude the other interpretation which is equally well attested in rabbinic texts (op. cit., 211; cf. SB I 738). The power to teach and discipline cannot be sharply separated (→ Bind). As the disciples had already shared in the work of Christ in his earthly ministry (cf. Matt. 9:35–10:42; Mk. 6:7–13; Lk. 9:1–6; 10:1–24), so now they are to share in the highest office of the forgiveness of sins. However, the idea of binding may also refer back to the picture of the binding of the strong man (i.e. Satan) who must first be bound (the same vb. *deō*) before his goods (i.e. those enthralled by him) may be plundered (Matt. 12:29 par. Mk. 3:27; cf. Lk. 8:21 which does not use the word). Thus Peter would be promised the power that Christ had to bind the powers of evil and to liberate men, and this would hold good not only on earth but also in heaven. Not even death, the power of Hades (→ Gate; → Hell) can thwart it. In the first instance the reference to Hades may be to the death of Christ, i.e. not even the impending death will thwart the messianic community, the church (cf. vv. 21 ff.). Likewise, the power of death will not prevail over the messianic community itself (cf. vv. 24–27).

The passages may be linked with similar promises in Matt. and Jn. which, however, are not specifically related to Peter: "Truly, I say to you, whatever you bind on earth shall be bound in heaven, and whatever you loose on earth shall be loosed in heaven" (Matt. 18:18); "If you forgive the sins of any, they are forgiven; if you retain the sins of any, they are retained" (Jn. 20:23). The passage in Matt. is set in the context of procedure in the church in dealing with problems of discipline caused by one brother sinning against another. The passage in Jn. constitutes the climax of the post-resurrection appearances, and is tantamount to Christ's commission to the church (cf. v. 21). E. Käsemann (see bibliography) has suggested that the mention of Peter in Matt. 16 represents the tendency of a Petrine faction, whereas the omission of his name in the other two passages shows that he did not enjoy special pre-eminence. It might also be argued that Matt. was simply making use of the paraenetical material at his disposal. Cullmann, however, sees the mention of Peter in Matt. 16:17 ff. and his omission from the other passages as fully compatible with what is known of him elsewhere as spokesman and leader in his foundational rôle in the church but as sharing in the binding and loosing with the other disciples (op. cit., 211 f.). (→ Rock for discussion of Peter's rôle in the early church.)

4. 1 Jn. 3:17 uses the vb. metaphorically: "But if any one has the world's goods and sees his brother in need, yet closes his heart against him, how does God's love abide in him?" The phrase *kleisē ta splanchna* appears to be unique; but cf. Ps. 77:9 (76:10): Has God "in his anger shut up his compassion [*synexei tous oiktirmous autou*]?"

5. Access to the eschatological Kingdom of God is also the concern of those apocalyptic passages where the key of David is spoken of (Rev. 3:7 f.). The apocalyptic writer interprets Isa. 22:22 messianically of Christ (such an interpretation is lacking in Judaism): As Eliakim received the key to the house of David, and was given the authority to decide over admission to the house of David, so Christ, as the promised descendant of David, holds the perfect key in his hand to decide over admission and exclusion to the future regal city of God. As the crucified and Risen One, he has the keys to the world of the dead (Rev. 1:18), so that → death has lost

733

its final terror for the believer. Possessing the keys to the abyss (Rev. 20:1), he is the Lord who governs the spirits of the underworld (20:3). (On this passage → Number, art. *chilias*.) *D. Müller, C. Brown*

→ Apostle, → Bind, → Church, → Gate, → Heaven, → Hell, → Kingdom, → Rock

(a). J. B. Bauer, "Binding and Loosing", *EBT* I 67; G. R. Beasley-Murray, *The Book of Revelation, New Century Bible*, 1974; G. Bornkamm, *Jesus of Nazareth*, 1960; R. E. Brown, K. P. Donfried and J. Reumann, eds., *Peter in the New Testament*, 1973; F. Büchsel, *deō* etc., *TDNT* II 60 f.; H. von Campenhausen, *Ecclesiastical Authority and Spiritual Power in the First Three Centuries of the Church*, 1969; R. H. Charles, *Commentary on the Revelation of St. John, ICC*, I–II, 1920; O. Cullmann, *Peter: Disciple – Apostle – Martyr. A Historical and Theological Study*, 1962²; G. Dalman, *The Words of Jesus*, 1909; D. Hill, *The Gospel of Matthew, New Century Bible*, 1972, 258–64; J. Jeremias, *kleis, TDNT* III 744–53; and *thyra, TDNT* III 173–80; O. Karrer, *Peter and the Church: An Examination of Cullmann's Thesis*, 1963; E. Käsemann, "Ministry and Community in the New Testament", *Essays on New Testament Themes, SBT* 41, 1964, 63–94; "Sentences of Holy Law in the New Testament", and "The Beginnings of Christian Theology", *New Testament Questions of Today*, 1969, 66–81, and 82–107; K. L. Schmidt, *ekklēsia, TDNT* III 518–26.

(b). R. Baumann, *Fels der Welt*, 1956; O. Betz, "Felsenmann und Felsengemeinde", *ZNW* 48, 1957, 49 ff.; H. Braun, *Qumran und das Neue Testament*, I, 1966, 30 ff.; and *Spätjüdisch-häretischer und frühchristlicher Radikalismus*, I–II, *BHTh* 24, 1928²; R. Bultmann, "Die Frage nach der Echtheit von Mt. 16, 17–19", *ThBl* 20, 1941, 265 ff. (reprinted in *Exegetica*, 1967, 255 ff.); G. Dalman, *Arbeit und Sitte in Palästina*, VII, 53 ff.; F. Kattenbusch, "Der Quellort der Kirchenidee", *Festgabe für Adolf von Harnack*, 1921, 160 ff.; and "Der Spruch über Petrus und die Kirche bei Mt.", *ThSt Kr* 94, 1922, 96 ff.; W. G. Kümmel, *Kirchenbegriff und Geschichtsbewusstsein in der Urgemeinde und bei Jesus*, 1968², 20 ff.; and "Jesus und die Anfänge der Kirche", *StTh* 7, 1953, 1–27 (reprinted in *Heilsgeschehen und Geschichte*, 1965, 289–309); G. Lambert, "Lier – Délier", *Vivre et Penser* 3, 1943–44, 91–103; H. Lehmann, "Du bist Petrus", *EvTh* 13, 1953–54, 44 ff.; O. Linton, *Das Problem der Urkirche in der neueren Forschung*, 1932, 157 ff.; O. Michel, *RAC* II 374–80; F. Obrist, *Echtheitsfragen und Deutungen der Primatstelle Mt. 16, 18 f. in der deutschen protestantischen Theologie der letzten 30 Jahre, NTAbh* 16, 3/4, 1961; A. Oepke, "Der Herrenspruch über die Kirche Mt. 16, 17–19 in der neuesten Forschung", *StTh* 2, 1948–50, 110 ff.; SB I 738 ff.; A. Schlatter, *Der Evangelist Matthäus*, 1963⁶; K. L. Schmidt, "Die Kirche des Urchristentums", *Festgabe für A. Deissmann*, 1927, 258 ff.; A. Schönherr,' 'Schlüsselgewalt" *EKL* III 813 ff.; H. Thyen, "Schlüsselgewalt", *RGG*³ V 1449 ff.; A. Vögtle, "Messiasbekenntniss und Petrusverheissung", *BZ* Neue Folge 1, 1957, 252 ff.; 2, 1958, 85 ff.; and "Jesus und die Kirche", in *Begegnung der Kirche, Festschrift für O. Karrer*, 1959, 54 ff.; "Der Einzelne und die Gemeinschaft in der Stufenfolge der Christusoffenbarung", in *Sentire Ecclesiam, Festschrift für H. Rahner*, 1961, 53 ff.; H. Windisch, "Urchristentum", *ThR* 5, 1933, 251 ff.

Openness, Frankness, Boldness

| παρρησία | παρρησία (*parrhēsia*), openness, confidence, boldness, frankness; παρρησιάζομαι (*parrhēsiazomai*), speak out, |

speak openly, speak boldly.

CL 1. The meaning of *parrhēsia* corresponds to its etymology (*pan*, all, *rhēsis*, speech, word, and *erō*, say, speak, from the root *wer-*; cf. Lat. *verbum*, the Ger. *Wort* and the Eng. *word*): freedom to say all. Since in practice this freedom of speech encountered opposition from time to time, *parrhēsia* acquired the further meaning of fearlessness, frankness. A negative overtone is also perceptible in some instances where freedom of speech has been misused to the point of bluntness and shamelessness. In an extended sense *parrhēsia* can mean confidence and joyfulness. The corresponding vb. *parrhēsiazomai* means to speak openly or boldly, and to have confidence.

2. The word group which is first found in Euripides and Aristophanes belonged originally to the sphere of politics. It signifies the democratic right of a full citizen of a Greek city-state (but not that of a → slave or foreigner; → Foreign): in the public assembly of the people one may speak out freely one's opinion (cf. Polyb., 2, 38, 6). This right is the characteristic of a democracy, but there is the danger of misuse, as Plato shows (*Rep.* 8, 557b). *parrhēsia* played an important rôle in private affairs, where in the context of teaching on *philia* (love) it denoted the openness with which one met a friend (cf. Aristot., *Eth.Nic.* 9, 2). In the course of history a more moral concept evolved out of the originally political one which was of central importance in Cynic philosophy as the correlative to *eleutheria*, → freedom (H. Schlier, *TDNT* V 874). Here *parrhēsia* is no longer a civil right but the mark of someone who is morally free and who does not shun public attention.

OT 1. In the LXX the word-group occurs only rarely (the noun 12 times; the vb. 6 times). In contrast with secular Gk. the concept is used both of God and man who stands over against God. It is used of God in Ps. 94:1 (LXX 93:1) where *eparrhēsiasato* (lit. "spoke freely") translates the Heb. *hôpia'*, "thou God of vengeance shine forth" (RSV; from the Heb. vb. *yāpa'*, shine forth). (The Heb. word is used in connection with theophanies [Deut. 33:2; Pss. 50:2; 80:2; Job 10:3, 22; cf. H. Schlier, *TDNT* V 877].) In Ps. 94 God is called upon to come forth as the avenger and requite the ungodly of their wickedness. A link between such a manifestation of God (cf. Ps. 11:6 LXX) and divine utterance is given in Prov. 1:20 f., where "Wisdom cries aloud in the street; in the markets she raises her voice; on the top of the walls she cries out; at the entrance of the gates she speaks." The LXX renders the second clause *en de plateiais parrhēsian agei*, "and in the broad places of a city she acts with confidence" (1:20).

parrhēsia occurs in Job 27:10: "Or when trouble comes upon him, has he any confidence before him [*mē echei tina parrhēsian enanti autou*]?" The vb. features in Job 22:26: "Then you shall have confidence before the Lord, and look upon to heaven with cheerfulness [*eita parrhēsiasthēsē enanti kyriou anablepsas eis ton ouranon hilarōs*]". In Job 27:10 there is no Heb. equivalent noun. In Job 22:26 the Heb. vb. is *'ānag*, to take delight in, which is used to describe the happy relationship of man with God that the righteous will have even in judgment (Wis. 5:1). For other uses of *'ānag* see Deut. 28:56; Ps. 34:4, 11; Isa. 55:2; 57:4; 58:14; 66:11.

The remaining instances of *parrhēsia* occur at Lev. 26:13 (for the unique word *qôm^emiyyût*, adv. upright); Est. 8:13; Prov. 10:10; 13:5; Wis. 5:1; Sir. 25:25; 1 Macc. 4:18; 3 Macc. 4:1; 7:12; 4 Macc. 10:5 (all without Heb. equivalent). The remaining instances of *parrhēsiazomai* occur at Ps. 12(11):5; Prov. 20:9; Cant. 8:10; Sir. 6:11 (all without Heb. equivalent).

2. The Gk. understanding of *parrhēsia* was taken over in the literature of Hellenistic Judaism (cf. *TDNT* V 875–79). But there are traces of OT influence, when, for instance, a good → conscience which no godless person can have is mentioned as a prerequisite for *parrhēsia*. The word is used to describe a man's attitude in prayer

735

(cf. Philo, *Rev.Div.Her.* 5–29) and the confidence of the righteous in the end-time (cf. 2 Esd. 7:98 ff.).

NT *parrhēsia* occurs 31 times in the NT (13 times in the Johannine writings; 8 times in Paul; 5 times in Acts; and 4 times in Heb.; and once in Mk.). The vb. *parrhēsiazomai* is found 9 times (7 times in Acts; and twice in Paul). The two words vary in meaning from virtually the equivalent of *eleutheria*, freedom, to *elpis*, hope.

1. In Jn. *parrhēsia* is used in the dat. in the unique sense of openly, in public: "And here he is, speaking openly, and they say nothing to him!" (Jn. 7:26; cf. 11:54; 18:20; cf. also Mk. 8:32). In each of these passages in Jn. it refers to Jesus' boldness in teaching in public. It is a rather different sense from that of his brothers who urged Jesus to do something in public in order to convince them (Jn. 7:4). In the case of Jesus *parrhēsia* does not mean, "as it originally did in Greek, the right or courage to appear in public, freedom of speech, openness . . . but as is common later, it refers to actions performed in public" (R. Bultmann, *The Gospel of John*, 1971, 291). By contrast Jn. 7:13 reports that no one spoke of Jesus openly for fear of the Jews. In Jn. 10:24; 11:14; 16:25, 29 it has the rather different sense of "plainly".

When Jesus spoke openly in public, this can also mean that he spoke unambiguously and plainly; not only in allusions (Jn. 11:14; cf. 10:24 f.) or in veiled parables (cf. Jn. 16:29). But Jesus spoke so freely only for believers (Jn. 16:25, 29). To the world he spoke in → parables (art. *paroimia*), which could not be understood without faith. Hence, there is a tension between *parrhēsia* and *paroimia* which corresponds to the Johannine dualism of life and death, truth and the lie etc. which demands a decision and which can only be resolved in faith.

2. Corresponding to the *parrhēsia* of Jesus, there is the open and authoritative testimony of the apostles. Again and again Acts reports how fearlessly Peter, Paul and others stood before the Jews or the Gentiles and proclaimed the works of God. The noun is used in Acts 2:29; 4:13; 29, 31; 28:31; and the vb. in Acts 9:27 f.; 13:46; 14:3; 18:26; 19:8; 26:26. This boldness which provokes astonishment (4:13), division (14:3 f.) and persecution (9:27) is not something that man has under his own control. It is the fruit of the Holy Spirit (4:31) that has to be sought again and again (4:29).

3. This is the view of the *parrhēsia* of the witness taken by Paul and John. It characterizes effective preaching of the mysteries of God (Eph. 6:19), and the honouring of Christ in life and death (Phil. 1:20). Since perseverence, perhaps in prison, is demanded of the disciple (cf. Eph. 6:20), *parrhēsia* has here also the sense of boldness and courage (1 Thess. 2:2). Such courage is not a human quality; it comes from God (1 Thess. 2:2) and Christ (Phlm. 8).

We should approach the future not in fear of judgment but in full confidence, openness to God and in the hope of the fullness of the glory of God (cf. 2 Cor. 3:11 f.). Therefore, we should abide in Christ (1 Jn. 2:28; Heb. 3:6; 10:35), who has already triumphed over the principalities and powers in public (*en parrhēsia*, Col. 2:15), and made possible access into the holiest (Heb. 10:18; cf. 4:16). He who perseveres in faith, holds to Christ in love (cf. 1 Jn. 4:17; cf. also the emphasis laid on *parrhēsia* gained through faithful service, 1 Tim. 3:13), and who is not condemned by his own heart (1 Jn. 3:21) will have confidence in prayer (1 Jn.

5:14). He will also "have confidence and not shrink from him in shame at his coming" (1 Jn. 2:28). Thus *parrhēsia* contains the ideas of "trust in God, certainty of salvation, the conquest of the consciousness of sin, sanction and power to pray, and expectation of the future" (O. Michel, *Der Brief an die Hebräer, KEK* 13, 1966[12], 98).   *H.-C. Hahn*

(a). Arndt, 635 f.; Liddell-Scott, 1344; M. Radin, "Freedom of Speech in Ancient Athens", *The American Journal of Philosophy* 4, 1927, 215–220; H. Schlier, *parrhēsia, parrhēsiazomai, TDNT* V 871–86; W. C. van Unnik, "The Christian's Freedom of Speech", *BJRL* 44, 1961–62, 466 ff.
(b). E. Busch, J. Fangmeier, M. Geiger, eds., *Parrhēsia. Karl Barth zum achtzigsten Geburtstag am 10. Mai 1966*, 1966 (It should be noted that this is not a study of the concept as such, but essays on a wide variety of themes concerning Christian attitudes to contemporary theological and other questions.); P. Joüon, "Divers sens de *parrhēsia* dans le Nouveau Testament", *Recherches de Science Religieuse* 30, 1940, 239 ff.; E. Peterson, "Zur Bedeutungsgeschichte von *parrhēsia*", *Festschrift für R. Seeberg*, I, 1929, 283–97; W. C. van Unnik, *De semitische Achtergrond van parrhēsia in het Nieuwe Testament*, 1962.

Orphan

| ὀρφανός | ὀρφανός (*orphanos*), orphan. |

CL In secular Gk. *orphanos* is used from Homer onwards as an adj. meaning without parents, fatherless or more generally, bereaved, bereft of; and as a noun, orphan. Careful provision was made in ancient Greece for orphan children. A guardian, usually a near relative, was appointed who was responsible for the orphan's maintenance and education. Any assets the child inherited were strictly protected until he came of age. Orphans were exempted from the regular taxes. The state undertook the maintenance of the children of soldiers killed in war (Demosthenes). *orphanos* is used figuratively of disciples left without a master (e.g. Plato, *Phaedo* 116a).

OT In the LXX *orphanos* translates *yāṭôm*. In the OT the plight of the orphan, whether or not his mother has died (cf. Job 24:9), is that he has lost his father. Without the father "the father's house", the primary unit of family life, ceases to be and the remaining members of the household become vulnerable individuals whose existence is both anomalous and tragic. Thus in many texts the reference is to orphans and widows together (e.g. Deut. 10:18; Ps. 146:9). Because the orphans are so helpless – all they can do is to "wander about and beg" (Ps. 109:9, 10) – there can be nothing more wicked than to exploit or ill-use them (Deut. 27:19; Job 6:27; 22:9; 24:3, 9; Ps. 1:23; 10:2; Jer. 5:28; Ezek. 22:7). The law codes of the OT demand that the rights of orphans be upheld and their needs met. Orphans are to have a share in the special tithe (Deut. 14:28, 29; 26:12–15) and are to be included in the annual feasts (Deut. 16:11, 14). The sheaves, the olives, and the grapes which remain after the harvest are to be left for "the sojourner, the orphan, and the widow" (Deut. 24:17–22). The repentance and moral renewal called for by the prophets must include care for orphans (Isa. 1:17; Jer. 7:6; 22:3; Zech. 7:10).

Behind this insistence on provision for orphans lies the conviction that it is ultimately Yahweh himself who "executes justice for the fatherless" (Deut. 10:18;

cf. Exod. 22:22–24; Prov. 23:10–11; Ps. 146:9; Hos. 14:3). Yahweh himself is "father of the fatherless" (Ps. 68:5; cf. Ps. 10:14).

Concern for orphans is urged upon the group to which the Zadokite Documents are addressed (CD 6:17; 14:14). One of the non-biblical psalms of the Qumran community gives praise to the Lord who has not "forsaken the orphan" (1QH 5:20). *yāṭôm* is here used figuratively to designate the member of the community, persecuted by the ungodly but under the care of God. The image of the orphan as a collective symbol of the people of God is used by Philo. "The whole Jewish race is in the position of an orphan. . . . Nevertheless the orphan-like desolate state of his people is always an object of pity and compassion to the Ruler of the Universe" (*Spec.Leg.* 4, 176–179).

Later Judaism continued to safeguard the rights of orphans, to legislate for their welfare, and to regard the care of them as meritorious. Until an orphan boy or girl marries he or she is to be maintained from the charity funds (Ket. 67a, b). Deserving of special praise and reward is the one who cares for the orphan in his home; "Whoever brings up an orphan in his own home, scripture ascribes it to him as though he had begotten him" (San. 19b; cf. Ket. 50a). A late Midrash can speak of the care of orphans as one of the "gates of the Lord" through which the righteous enter the future world (Midrash Ps. 118:19).

NT *orphanos* occurs twice in the NT. (A few MSS at Mk. 12:40 add "and orphans" to "the houses of widows", but this reading must be taken as secondary.)

1. Jas. 1:27. James enjoins practical concern for those least able to help themselves, "orphans and widows". He follows the OT in mentioning the two groups together, more fundamentally in insisting that claims to be religious are futile unless the one who makes them exercises justice and compassion (cf. especially Jer. 7).

2. Jn. 14:18. "I will not leave you orphaned" (or "[as] orphans"). This is the one instance in the Bible of the figurative use of *orphanos*. It recalls the use of the term in secular Gk. to describe the feelings of disciples bereft of their teacher. But the image draws its force from the OT estimate of the family as primarily "the father's house", a household living a single corporate life whose centre and source is the father. With the father's death his house is no more and thus the desolation of the orphan is the loss of all by which he lives. The relationship of Jesus to his disciples is presented here as that of a father to his children (cf. Jn. 13:3). His death will make them "orphans". There can be no more powerful symbol of the measure of their loss. But they will not be left in this pitiable situation. He will come to them. The metaphor of *orphanos* implies that this promise is to be fulfilled at the resurrection (rather than at the coming of the Spirit or the Parousia) for "orphans", unless intervention is swift, have small hope of survival. Easter ends the disciples' bereavement. "The very word which describes their sorrow confirms their sonship" (B. F. Westcott, *The Gospel according to St. John*, 1881, 206).   *J. Pridmore*

(a). H. Kirschenbaum, "Orphan", in C. Roth and G. Wigoder, eds., *Encyclopaedia Judaica* XII 1478 f.; H. Seesemann, *orphanos*, *TDNT* V 486 ff.
(b). M. Cohn, "Jüdisches Waisenrecht", *Zeitschrift für vergleichende Rechtswissenschaft* 37, 1920, 417–45; M. Grünwald, "Jüdische Waisenfürsorge in alter und neuer Zeit", *Mitteilungen zur jüdischen Volkskunde* 23, 1922, 3–29; F. Windberg, *orphanos*, Pauly-Wissowa XVIII, 1, 1197–1200.

Other

ἄλλος, ἕτερος

ἄλλος (*allos*), other; ἄλλος (*allōs*), otherwise; ἀλλότριος (*allotrios*), belonging to another, strange, alien, hostile; ἀλλογενής (*allogenēs*), foreign; ἀλλόφυλος (*allophylos*), foreign; ἕτερος (*heteros*), other; ἑτέρως (*heterōs*), differently; ἑτερόγλωσσος (*heteroglōssos*), speaking another tongue; ἑτεροζυγέω (*heterozygeō*), be unequally yoked, be mismated.

CL In secular Gk. *heteros* and *allos* have essentially the same meaning, other. When they are used as noun or adj., they introduce a new person, thing or group. Originally *heteros* was a dual pron. and presupposed pairs of individuals or groups. Hence *hoi heteroi* can mean the other group. It is entirely lacking in modern Gk.

OT In the LXX *allos* refers to that already mentioned in contrast to others and can even render a demonstrative pron., e.g. the Heb. '*ēlleh*, that. *heteros* had a personal connotation and was used to translate words like '*iš*, *rēa*', '*āḥ* (man, neighbour, brother). *allos* is used about 100 times; *heteros* about 150.

NT This distinction is found relatively seldom in the NT, where it is striking that the use of *heteros* (98 times in all) relative to *allos* (155 times in all) decreases in the later books. In Jn. (except 16:12), 1 and 2 Cor., Tit., 1 and 2 Pet., 1, 2, 3 Jn. and Rev., but also in 1 and 2 Thess. and Mk. (except 16:12, see below) *heteros* is lacking. Luke (both Gospel and Acts) prefers *heteros*. The polemic factor is one of the reasons why *allos* is found so frequently in 1 and 2 Cor.

1. The following details of usage may be noted.

(a) Both words are used to denote another person, thing or group; e.g. *allos* (Matt. 5:39; 12:13; Jn. 5:32); *heteros* (Lk. 5:7; 23:40). Hence *tē hetera* can mean the next day (Acts 20:15; 27:3).

(b) The same use is found in the plur. (e.g. Matt. 20:3, 6; Lk. 10:1; Jn. 7:12; 9:16; Acts 2:13).

(c) In enumerations (Matt. 13:5, 7 f.: Lk. 8:6 ff.) and in contrasts (Heb. 11:35 f.) *heteros* and *allos* are often used alternately. In enumerations *heteros* can become a definite numeral, e.g. in Lk. 19:16, 18, 20 it has the force of "the third" (RSV "another").

(d) Used as a noun *ho heteros* has the force of the neighbour that God has put in my way (1 Cor. 10:24; Rom. 2:1; 13:8; Gal. 6:4).

2. These words become important theologically when they express a more or less qualitative difference, external or internal (Mk. 12:32; 2 Cor. 1:12; 1 Cor. 3:11).

Jesus appeared to his disciples after his resurrection in another → form (Mk. 16:12), so that they did not recognize him (cf. Lk. 24:16; Jn. 20:15). At the transfiguration Jesus' appearance was similarly changed (Lk. 9:29); in this manifestation Jesus was revealed as the Son of man. The new can only be compared to the resurrection body in 1 Cor. 15:39 ff. in an argument against the denial of the → resurrection. Matt. 11:3 implies a question whether the messiah must be of another kind than Jesus.

The interpretation of Acts 2:4 ("And they were all filled with the Holy Spirit and began to speak in other tongues, as the Spirit gave them utterance") raises the question of whether the gift of tongues at → Pentecost was a form of ecstatic utterance or whether the disciples on whom the Spirit came were in fact speaking

739

other languages which they presumably did not know before. The mistaken presumption of some of the onlookers that they were "filled with new wine" (v. 13) suggests that this was ecstatic speaking in tongues as in Acts 10:46; 19:6; 1 Cor. 12:10, 30; 14:1–4. On the other hand, others among the crowd who were Jews and proselytes visiting Jerusalem from various parts of the Roman empire asked in amazement: "Are not all these who are speaking Galileans? And how is it that we hear, each of us in his own native language?... we hear them telling in our own tongues the mighty works of God" (Acts 2:7 f., 11). The story of Pentecost is a preparation for the apostles' missionary preaching and pictures the outpouring of the Spirit in a twofold manner: the speaking in tongues as a sign of the outpouring of the Spirit as prophesied by Joel 2:25–28 (cf. Acts 2:17–21) showing the last days spoken of by the prophet had now come; and the proclamation of the word of God. At Pentecost it was proclaimed to Jews and proselytes in Jerusalem. The event marks the beginning of the fulfilment of Acts 1:8 ("But you shall receive power when the Holy Spirit has come upon you; and you shall be my witnesses in Jerusalem and in all Judea and Samaria and to the end of the earth"), and forms the transition to Peter's missionary preaching.

([Ed.] For further discussion of the phenomenon → Pentecost; → Word. It may well have been that among the hundred and twenty or so followers [Acts 1:15] there were those who already knew something of the languages mentioned, and for whom therefore the gift was primarily an enabling to proclaim "the mighty works of God" [2:13]. The assumption that all the followers of Jesus were Galileans [2:7] was made by the onlookers. Whilst it may have been true that the core of Jesus' following came from Galilee, the followers may have included others like Simon of Cyrene [Matt. 27:32; Mk. 15:21; Lk. 23:26] and possibly Lucius of Cyrene [Acts 13:1] who may have been among those who spoke to those who came from "the parts of Libya belonging to Cyrene" [Acts 2:10]. Similarly Acts 11:20 mentions "men of Cyprus and Cyrene" who preached the Lord Jesus and who might have belonged to the original band at Jerusalem. There were various synagogues in the city which catered for the needs of those who came from the dispersion [cf. Acts 6:9], and the population of Jerusalem evidently included a large number of Hellenists [Acts 6:1 ff.]. It is not beyond the bounds of possibility that some of these already belonged to the followers of Jesus before Pentecost.)

1 Cor. 14:21 uses the compound *heteroglōssos*, speaking another tongue, speaking a foreign language. The word is found in Polyb., 23, 13, 2; Strabo, 8, 1, 2; Philo, *Conf.Ling.* 8; and Aquila's translation of Ps. 113:1; Isa. 33:19. In dealing with the question of speaking in tongues, Paul argued: "Brethren, do not be children in your thinking; be babes in evil, but in thinking be mature. In the law it is written, 'By men of strange tongues and by the lips of foreigners [*en heteroglōssois kai en cheilesin heterōn*] I will speak to this people, and even then they will not listen to me, says the Lord.' Thus, tongues are a sign not for believers but for unbelievers, while prophecy is not for unbelievers but for believers." Paul is here quoting Isa. 28:11 f. perhaps in a version known also to Aquila (Origen, *Philocalia* 9, 2; cf. C. K. Barrett, *The First Epistle to the Corinthians*, BNTC, 1968, 322). In the prophecy Yahweh is threatening his people, who have failed to respond to his word delivered to them in their own language by Isaiah, with the foreign speech of the Assyrian invader. It is thus a judgment on the people of God to have such a

thing inflicted on them. This is underlined by the unintelligibility of the other tongue. To be thus addressed is a sign that God is treating one as an unbeliever (cf. 1 Cor. 14:22). Such a sign may be compared with the sign of the naked prophet in Isa. 20:3 which signified the impending catastrophe and servitude of the people. In 1 Cor. 14 Paul draws an analogy between the event of Isaiah's day and the enthusiasm for glossolalia in the Corinthian church. To speak in another tongue is ineffective for building up the church and promoting faith. Indeed, it might even be regarded as a judgment on the community. Whereas prophecy can edify the believing congregation, since it is intelligible, speaking in tongues cannot. For only what is intelligible can edify others; at best only the one who speaks in tongues is edified in the case of glossolalia (cf. vv. 2–19). An utterance in another tongue can only serve to harden the unbeliever, because it communicates nothing to him, and does not show him how to be reconciled with God. The unbeliever may even conclude that the practitioners of glossolalia are mad; but if he hears prophecy he may well be convicted (vv. 23 f.).

In 2 Cor. 11:4 and Gal. 1:6 ff. Paul stresses the uniqueness of the salvation offered by his gospel. Another → gospel would not be the gospel, any more than another spirit can be the Holy Spirit (cf. J. B. Lightfoot, *St. Paul's Epistle to the Galatians*, 1870,[10] 1876, 76; W. M. Ramsay, *A Historical Commentary on St. Paul's Epistle to the Galatians*, 1899, 260 ff.). The other gospel referred to in Gal. which is in fact no gospel is the teaching of the Judaizers which insisted on → circumcision for Gentile converts, so that they would meet the requirements of the old → covenant. Paul sees that such a demand involves a matter of principle concerning the ground of salvation. To attempt to fulfil the demands of the law in this way would be to put forward a righteous act by man as a basis for salvation. The whole theme of Gal. treats the issues involved which confront men with the choice of the free grace of God in Christ or salvation by human endeavour. The "gospel" of this latter alternative is anathema to Paul (Gal. 1:8; → Curse, art. *anathema*).

In Rom. 7:23 the other → law, i.e. the carnal egoistic urge, as a tool of the law of sin fights against the good law of God, which the mind agrees with (cf. v. 25). (On this passage → I Am, art. *egō eimi* NT 2 (c).)

Phil. 3:15 contains the sole NT instance of the adv. *heterōs*, differently, otherwise. In all probability Paul is arguing against enthusiasts who claimed perfection for themselves and special revelations. Paul takes up the slogan of perfection and applies it to Christians. The perfect (*teleioi*; RSV "mature"; → Goal, art. *telos*) are, in fact, those who know that they are imperfect and are aware of the need to press on to what lies ahead, forgetting what lies behind (vv. 12 f.). They know that they have not yet reached their goal and do not yet possess "the prize of the upward call of God in Christ Jesus" (v. 14). They will await transformation (v. 21). The practical conclusion is given in v. 15; "Let those of us who are mature be thus minded; and if in anything you are otherwise minded, God will reveal that to you." The last point is evidently directed at the claim to special revelations. Paul is confident that by being realistic and patient, they will grow in insight. (See further J. B. Lightfoot, *St. Paul's Epistle to the Philippians*, 1868, 153.)

3. In addition to *heteroglōssos* there is the compound *heterozygeō*, be unevenly yoked, and several compounds with *allos* in the NT. 2 Cor. 6:14 refers to the practice of yoking together animals of different species, e.g. an ox and a donkey,

in order to draw burdens. Such practices were forbidden by the law which banned the use of oxen and asses ploughing together (Deut. 22:10; cf. also the practices mentioned in Lev. 19:19; Philo, *Spec.Leg.* 4, 203; Josephus, *Ant.* 4, 228). In 2 Cor. 6:14 Paul applies the idea to relationship of believers with unbelievers: "Do not be unevenly yoked together with unbelievers. For what partnership have righteousness and iniquity? Or what fellowship has light with darkness?" The argument goes on to refer specifically to idol worship, and compares the people of God with the → temple and therefore urges moral purity and separation from the corrupt practices of paganism. The RSV translation "Do not be mismated" reflects the injunction of Lev. 19:19 not to let cattle breed with a different kind, where the LXX uses the corresponding adj.

allotrios means what belongs to another, therefore strange, alien, unsuitable, hostile (→ Foreign, art. *allotrios*). It normally renders the Heb. *nokrî*, but also sometimes *zār*. It is found in Matt. 17:25; Lk. 16:12; Jn. 10:5; Acts 7:6; Rom. 14:4; 15:20; 2 Cor. 10:15 f.; 1 Tim. 5:22; Heb. 9:25; 11:34. Only in the latter passage does it mean hostile, and it is never used in the sense of alien to God. The vb. *apallotrioō*, estrange, alienate, occurs only in the prison epistles (Col. 1:21; Eph. 2:12; 4:18) in the perf. pass. part., where men are said to be alienated from God. It is the state that they are in prior to reconciliation, and is parallel to being an → enemy (*echthros*) of God and a stranger (*xenos*; → Foreign).

allogenēs, foreign, is found only in Jewish and Christian literature. It is used for *zār* (e.g.. Exod. 29:33; Num. 16:40 [17:5]; Lev. 22:10) and for various other words. It is found only in the NT of the grateful → Samaritan (Lk. 17:18). *allophylos*, foreign, Gentile, heathen, is found in Isa. 61:5; 2:6; 1 Sam. 13:3; Ps. 108:10 for various Heb. terms, but in the overwhelming majority of its LXX occurrences it renders "Philistines". In Acts 10:28 it denotes the Gentiles from the Jewish standpoint. The obscure word *allotriepiskopos* (1 Pet. 4:15) has been variously interpreted as a concealer of stolen goods, a spy or informer, one who meddles in things that do not concern him, a revolutionist (details in Arndt, 39 f.).

→ Foreign   *F. Selter, C. Brown*

Arndt, 39 f., 314 f.; H. W. Beyer, *heteros*, *TDNT* II 702 ff.; F. Büchsel, *allos* etc., *TDNT* I 264–67; Moulton-Milligan, 23, 257.

P

Parable, Allegory, Proverb

It has been estimated that roughly one third of the recorded teaching of Jesus consists of parables and parabolic statements, and that there are some forty of the former and twenty of the latter (A. M. Hunter, *Interpreting the Parables*, 1960, 10 ff.; for a list see below, NT 5). In its broadest sense a parable is a form of speech used to illustrate and persuade by the help of a picture. In ancient writing, including the Bible, the use of figurative speech was widespread in giving concrete, pictorial and challenging expression to religious ideas for which there were no corresponding abstract concepts. Figurative speech is still part and parcel of every day life. On a philosophical and theoretical level religious language is interpreted in terms of abstractions and concepts relative to a contemporary world view. But this is merely to translate one set of thought forms from one conceptual scheme into those of another. In so doing care must be taken to avoid losing the original content of the picture and also the challenge which was an essential feature of the language. In discussing the character of the parable, scholars distinguish the parable proper from figurative language in general, metaphors, similes and similitudes, parabolic stories, illustrative stories, and allegories. These seven categories are all linked to *parabolē*. The proverb (*paroimia*) also has a didactic religious function and is therefore treated in this article.

| παραβολή |

παραβολή (*parabolē*), type, figure, parable; παραβάλλω (*paraballō*), throw alongside, compare; αἴνιγμα (*ainigma*), riddle, indistinct image; ἀλληγορέω (*allēgoreo*), speak allegorically.

CL *parabolē*, from Plato and Isocrates on, is to be derived from *paraballō* (*para*, alongside; *ballō*, throw, bring, place) to place alongside, hold beside, throw to, compare (Plato, *Gorgias* 475e; Isocrates, 9, 34). It means: (a) holding beside, comparison (Plato, *Philebus* 33b; Isocrates, 12, 227); (b) placing beside, meeting, conjunction (as a technical term in astronomy); (c) venture; (d) parabola in conic section (as a technical term in mathematics).

1. In rhetoric the word, on the basis of its first meaning, became the technical term for a specific form of speech, which is distinguished from others. Classical rhetoric made us of the following figures of speech: (a) the image (*eikōn*); (b) the metaphor (*metaphora*); (c) the comparison (*homoiōsis*); (d) the parable (*parabolē*); (e) the illustrative story (*paradeigma*); and (f) the allegory (*allēgoria*).

According to Aristotle, the similitude and the pure parable serve as an introductory means of proof (*Rhet.* 2, 20). Through the comparison of the known with

743

the unknown, in which the listener himself has to find the similarity (the *tertium comparationis* is not in general named, in order to set in motion the listener's thought processes of grasping, comparing and considering), the point of the analogy is reached (cf. also Plato, *Leg.* 6, 758a; *Phaed*, 82e; 85e; 87b; *Apol.* 30e; and the Stoic-Cynic diatribes, e.g. Epict., *Dissertationes* 1, 24, 19 f.; 2, 14, 21 f.; 4, 7, 22 f.). The Homeric parables, on the other hand, often aim merely to illustrate or have a purely poetic function (189 pure parables occur in the *Iliad*.; 39 in the *Odyssey*). What characterizes all these comparisons and pure parables is the fact that their imagery is drawn mostly from life, the reality which is accessible to everyone.

2. In rhetoric allegory is clearly distinguished from these forms, although Quintilian (*Oratoria* 8, 6, 48) comes near to recommending mixed forms. The noun *allēgoria* (*alla agoreuō*, say something different) is found in Cicero (*Orationes* 27, 94), but the vb. not until Philo (*De Cherubim* 25; *Som.* 2, 31; *Vit.Cont.* 28), Josephus (*Ant.* Preface 24) and later in Athenaeus (2, 69c). This relatively late occurrence makes it probable that it originated in Hellenistic times, possibly in the Stoic-Cynic diatribe. The vb. means: (a) to speak allegorically; (b) to allegorize. Allegorizing has always played an important rôle where sacred writings are concerned. When they became antiquated, a new, contemporary content was injected into them by means of allegorical explanations and their canonical authority was preserved. Thus allegorization is "a late, almost decadent, literary form. It presupposes a stage of development which has already, essentially, had its day. But, although it has been left behind, people try to salvage something from it" (C. H. Peisker, "Das Alte Testament – Gabe und Aufgabe" in *Kleine Predigttypologie*, II, 1965, 17). (On allegory in Hellenistic and early Christian thought see R. P. C. Hanson, *Allegory and Event: A Study of the Sources and Significance of Origen's Interpretation of Scripture*, 1959.)

3. The riddle has nothing to do with literary forms in general or with allegory in particular, although to an uninitiated listener allegory remains enigmatic. The *ainigma*, dark saying, puzzling saying, riddle, is found from Pindar and Aeschylus (*PV* 613) on. It is the opposite of *haplous logos*, a plain, straightforward or simple word, and is related in origin (as in Eng. and Heb.) with the vb. read (Old Eng. *rede*, to take counsel, advise, commend; cf. *paraineō*, exhort, recommend, advise; *aineō*, praise, approve, recommend). The riddle likes to use the literary form of metaphor, but it is to be understood rather as a wise saying. The riddle was considered, therefore, as a touchstone of wisdom. The riddle really belongs to oracular and prophetic speech (→ Prophet CL). Thus the sayings of the Sibyl, for example, could be enigmatic (Sib. 3, 811 f.; cf. Sophocles, OT 1525; Euripides, *Phoen.* 1688, etc.).

OT In the LXX *parabolē* is always the equivalent of the noun *māšāl* or the vb.

māšāl (*paraphora* or *periphora* should be read in Eccl. 2:12). *māšāl* means: (a) a saying containing a comparison or taunt; (b) a wise saying, the instruction by wisdom; (c) the parabolic form (see NT 1 (a)–(g)). The vb. correspondingly means to speak or tell a *māšāl*.

The vb. meant originally to be similar, like. Therefore, the noun would originally have had the meaning of comparison, making like. In its long history, which passed from (1) popular speech to (2) the language of wisdom and later (3) to prophetic speech, it acquired a very broad semantic field. This was taken over, with its sharply differentiated contents, by the LXX, the Rabbis and, subsequently, the NT. It is always used, however, unambiguously as a technical term for one or other particular types or forms but not as a "general concept in which the individual genera (i.e. types and forms) are comprehended" (O. Eissfeldt, *Der Maschal im Alten Testament, BZAW* 24, 1913, 33).

1. Thus *māšāl* in popular speech first means a proverb (→ *paroimia*), which may often contain a comparison (Ezek. 18:2; 1 Sam. 10:12; 24:14). If the saying or comparison is about a person and makes fun of or disparages him as a bad example, *māšāl* means a taunt (Hab. 2:6; Isa. 14:4).

2. Later *māšāl* became a technical term among the wise and means a wise saying, rich in comparisons (→ *paroimia* OT; cf. Prov. 26:7, 9) and the instruction of the wise. Prov. and the collections contained in it carry this superscription *paroimia*, 1:1; *paideia*, 10:1; 25:1 which RSV translates as "proverbs". Like the oriental, the wise man in the OT loves the enigmatic, dark saying. Hence, in this context *māšāl* approaches *ḥîdâh*, riddle, in meaning for which it can even be used as a synonym (Prov. 1:6).

The LXX translates *ḥîdâh* appropriately and correctly by *ainigma*, i.e. (a) riddle; (b) dark saying. The former (1 Ki. 10:1; 2 Chr. 9:1; Ps. 49:4 [48:5, Aquila]) is part of the cult of wisdom at Solomon's court and has its place in the Wisdom Literature (Prov. 1:6; 30:7-30). The only OT riddle given word for word is in Jdg. 14:12-20 (*ḥîdâh* translated in the LXX by *problēma*), the solution of which is another riddle (14:18). The key-word is "love". The dark saying requires explanatory interpretation. It occurs in oracular speech (e.g. Balaam, Num. 23:7-18; 24:3, 15, 20-23), and in prophecy. God speaks to men – but not to → Moses – in dark speech (Num. 12:8), and prophetic speech also is enigmatic (Ezek. 17:2, Symmachus).

3. In the realm of prophecy (→ Prophet) *māšāl* has its place. On the one hand, it occurs as proverb and taunt (see above 1). On the other hand, it enters through the fact that, although the word is not present, the object it designates is, and most of the parabolic forms occur (see below NT 1 (a)–(g)). The later we come, the more the developed forms (see below NT 1 (d)–(g)) come into the foreground to clarify, strengthen and lend more urgency to the prophetic message. Allegory, too, aims at urgency, but goes about it another way, i.e. through a certain veiling of the truth it seeks to attract the attention of the listener (cf. Ezek.). Later, allegorical visions occur (→ Prophet OT; Zech.; Dan. 2; 4; 7; 8; Eth.Enoch 85–90; 2 Esd. 9:26–13:56). The symbolic actions of the prophets, whose meaning is called *māšāl*, stand in close relationship to the prophetic parables (→ Prophet OT). In Rab. writings *māšāl* and *maṭlā'* (parable, riddle, comparison) include the whole breadth of meaning which had grown up in the course of time. Although pure parables predominate ("Let me tell you a parable: with what is the thing to be compared?"), the later one comes, the more allegories are found (cf. F. Hauck, *TDNT* V 750 f.). In Hellenistic Judaism they become an affectation. Against the background of many Rab. parables, those of Jesus display "a definite personal character, a unique clarity and simplicity, a matchless mastery of construction" (J. Jeremias, *The Parables of Jesus*, 1963², 12).

In striking contrast with this, *māšāl* is to be found nowhere in the Qumran literature (the vb. only as a different root, to rule), although in the hymns (1QH) many more or less developed series of metaphors and similes occur.

NT In the NT *parabolē* occurs only in the Synoptic Gospels (48 times) and in Heb. (twice); *ainigma* only in 1 Cor. 13:12 (indistinct, enigmatic image); and *allēgoreō* only in Gal. 4:24 (to speak allegorically). The noun *allēgoria* does not occur in the NT. *parabolē* in the NT has the following meanings.

1. In Heb. the ritual of the tabernacle is seen as a *parabolē* (RSV "symbolic") of the time of salvation (9:9), and the restoration of Isaac as a picture of the resurrection ("hence, figuratively speaking [*kai en parabolē*] he did receive him back", 11:19). In Matt. 15:15 par. Mk. 7:17 it means a saying, and in Lk. 4:23 a proverb. In all other occurrences in the NT it has the meaning of parable in one or other of its various senses:

(a) In *figurative sayings* image and reality are placed together without a comparative adv. (as), in order that the image (the known) may elucidate the reality (the unknown), e.g. "You are the light of the world" (Matt. 5:14; cf. 25:14; Mk. 2:17, 19; and in the OT Amos 3:8; 6:12; Isa. 40:7; Jer. 12:5; Prov. 6:27–29). In such figurative sayings it often happened that the image was separated from the reality it referred to (though from time to time the latter was often expressed in the context), and was handed on in isolation. In isolation it became detached from its original context, and thus its original point became lost from view. Thus Mk. 9:49 ("For every one will be salted with fire") does not become more intelligible with the secondary addition in the TR ("and every sacrifice will be salted with salt" RSV mg.). The words appear to have been added at an early stage by a scribe who detected a clue to its meaning in Lev. 2:13 (cf. Ezek. 43:24; Exod. 30:5), and other variants were variants of this (cf. Metzger, 102 f.; C. E. B. Cranfield, *The Gospel according to Saint Mark*, 1959, 314 ff.). (On this passage → Fire, art. *pyr*; → Salt.) Similarly Matt. 7:6; 24:28 par. Lk. 17:37 do not indicate the original point of comparison. (On these sayings → Animal; → Bird.) In such instances the saying takes on the character of a metaphor (see below).

(b) The *metaphor* is a figurative expression in which a name or descriptive term is applied to some object to which it is not literally and properly applicable. It often involves the transference of the concrete to the abstract: e.g. "He is the head of the family", or "the spring of life" (cf. further Matt. 7:13 f.; 9:37 f.; 15:13; 1 Cor. 9:9; cf. Isa. 5:1–7, which pictures Israel as a bride and a vineyard, with Matt. 21:33–46; Mk. 12:1–12; and Lk. 20:9–19).

Metaphor places the image not beside the reality, as in the figurative saying, but instead of the reality. One has to know beforehand what reality lies behind the metaphor, or it remains unintelligible. Thus all metaphorical speech rests on convention.

(c) The *simile* is a sentence in which reality and image are placed beside one another by means of a comparative adv. In this case there is only one principal point of comparison: e.g. "Her hair [the reality] is as fair as straw [the image]" (cf. further Matt. 10:16; Lk. 11:44; cf. Prov. 11:22; 25:11–13; 26:1 ff.; Isa. 16:2; Hos. 2:1–5; 6:9; Ps. 127:4).

Similes occur only rarely. For the most part it will have already passed over into a figurative saying and then become metaphorically coloured in the tradition. The image in a simile is taken from the reality which is accessible to everyone.

(d) The pure *parable* is a story which has developed out of a simile or a figurative saying. Two things, events or situations (image and reality), which are similar, are compared, so that the known may elucidate the unknown. The image depicts a typical event or circumstance. It "is taken from the reality which is accessible to everyone, and points to things which happen every day, to situations, the existence of which the least willing must acknowledge" (A. Jülicher, *Die Gleichnisreden Jesu*, I, 1899[2], 93). There is only one principal point of comparison. For example: "The kingdom of heaven is like leaven . . . " (Matt. 13:33; cf. Lk. 13:20; → Leaven; cf. Matt. 13:31 f.; Lk. 14:28–33; 15:4–10; 17:7–10; Isa. 28:23–25; Jer. 18:1–6).

"The parable anticipates all opposition, in that it speaks only of what is undoubted . . . [It] operates with 'no one', 'none,' 'everyone', 'whenever', 'as often as', etc., and seeks to overwhelm the hearer by the weight of its 'at all' " (A. Jülicher, op. cit., I, 97).

(e) *The parabolic story* differs from the pure parable only in that its picture, which is a fictional story, is recounted as if it had once happened. "It places before us not what everyone does, what cannot be otherwise, but what someone once did, without asking whether others would act in the same way" (A. Jülicher, op. cit., I, 93). Thus, the parabolic story of the unjust judge begins: "In a certain city there was a judge . . ." (Lk. 18:2 ff.; cf. Lk. 11:5–8; 14:16–24; 2 Sam. 12:1–4. "The parabolic story replaces by its vividness the advantage that the parable has through the authority of the generally known and acknowledged. Indeed, the parabolic story stands higher, being more subtle and revealing is point less. . . . The parabolic story . . . requests, 'Hearer, let me tell you just one story, if it does not convince you, I will be quiet' " (A. Jülicher, op. cit., I, 97 f.).

(f) The *illustrative story* is a freely invented story which gives an example, a model case, which has to be generalized by the hearer. Thus the story of the good → Samaritan ends with Jesus saying: "Go and do likewise!" (Lk. 10:37). Conversely, the illustrative story of the Pharisee and the tax collector in the temple ends with a warning about those who are like the Pharisee (Lk. 18:10–14; cf. Lk. 10:30–37; 12:16–21; 16:19–31; 2 Sam. 14:5–7). It is noteworthy that the NT illustrative stories only occur in Lk.

(g) *Allegory* is a freely invented story, which says something other than it appears to say on the surface by heaping metaphor on metaphor. It is a continuous metaphor, e.g. "The kingdom of heaven may be compared to a king who gave a marriage feast for his son . . ." (Matt. 22:2–10; cf. Jn. 10:15; Rom. 11:17–24; 1 Cor. 3:10–13; Ezek. 16; 17; 19; 23; 31; 34; Ps. 80:8–19).

"Allegory seeks to present truth to our minds in a more expressive form by painting it in a series of pictures, which indicate but at the same time conceal the intended truth" (H. Weinel, *Die Gleichnisse Jesu*, 1929[5], 2). Like metaphor, allegory rests on convention. It is only intelligible when the metaphors are known, for they have to be translated step by step, and when the matter that they depict is known. It is a literary form intelligible only to the initiated, the function of which is not to make facts known but to appraise known facts. Ezek. 17:12–21 offers a model exposition. Allegories of this kind occur in the NT but they are designated as *parabolē* and not as *allēgoria* (Matt. 22:1). (For further discussion of allegory and its possible use in the NT see 9 below.)

2. In section 1 an attempt was made to distinguish various forms. But it must be remembered that parables spring from living speech, and therefore most often appear in mixed forms. At the same time the following further laws or rules may be noted.

(a) The parable as drama. In pure parable and the related forms a distinction may be drawn between the image and the reality. Understanding comes at the point where the two halves intersect, the point of comparison. In the developed forms the picture part of the parable is not static but presents a drama to the hearer which can be divided into scenes. In view of this one may speak of the dramatic half of the parable (cf. G. Eichholz, *Einführung in die Gleichnisse*, BSt 37, 1963).

(b) The law of conciseness requires that the dramatic half be told concisely and simply. Irrelevant emotions and motives are not disclosed. There never appear more than three characters or groups of characters (the law of three), and there are never more than two actors in one scene (the law of two on the stage). If the conclusion is unimportant or self-evident, it may be omitted.

(c) The law of unity of action demands that only one plot should be developed in the drama, never two or more on parallel lines. To this end the drama is recounted from only one point of view. ([Ed.] This point was stressed by Jülicher and those who followed him, but many scholars feel that this rule can no longer be adhered to pedantically.)

(d) For the expositor the law that the stress comes at the end is important.

(e) The law of listener-relatedness states that the material for the drama is taken from the world of the hearer and reflects his experiences and thoughts. The parables are also spoken directly to the hearer. Thus the question-parables are one single, big question, which compels the listener to reply. To this end he is drawn into the parable, in so far as he finds himself portrayed in the main character and thereby not only moved but caught (cf. H. Greeven, "Wer unter euch . . . ?", *Wort und Dienst*, Neue Folge 3, 1952, 86–101; G. V. Jones, *The Art and Truth of the Parables: A Study in their Literary Form and Modern Interpretation*, 1964; and A. C. Thiselton, "The Parables as Language-Event: Some Comments on Fuchs's Hermeneutics in the Light of Linguistic Philosophy", *SJT* 23, 1970, 437–68).

3. Besides the formal laws there is the question of the effects of tradition. In *The Parables of Jesus*, 1963[2], J. Jeremias discusses in detail the transmission of the parables. He considers that many of them acquired new addressees in the course of being handed on, and that sometimes parables directed to outsiders came to be seen as applicable to disciples (op. cit., 96–114). In the case of the parable of the sower (Matt. 13:1–9 par. Mk. 4:1–9, Lk. 8:4–8) there is considerable debate whether the explanation (Matt. 13:18–23 par. Mk. 4:13–20, Lk. 8:11–15) was a later addition by the early church. J. Jeremias argues for this (op. cit., 77 ff.), but against this see C. F. D. Moule, *The Birth of the New Testament*, 1962, 149 ff. (On this parable see also D. Wenham, "The Synoptic Problem Revisited: Some New Suggestions about the Composition of Mark 4:1–34", *TB* 23, 1972, 3–38.) Jeremias argues that the tendency to allegorization is due to the influence of tradition (op. cit., 66–89), and G. Eichholz argues that the evangelists' freedom in handling the tradition "is paradoxically to be understood as an attempt at obedience; it springs

from the very fact that they are bound to the word handed down" (op. cit., 40). On the other hand, I. H. Marshall observes that "the admission of freedom in handling the sayings of Jesus does not of itself permit us to postulate that the early Church felt free to attribute later sayings to Jesus Himself. There is clearly a difference between handing down sayings with alterations and enlarging the corpus with new sayings" (*Eschatology and the Parables*, 1963, 14). Jeremias himself maintains that "in dealing with the parables we are dealing with a particularly trustworthy tradition, and are brought into immediate relation with Jesus" (op. cit., 12).

4. The message of the parables cannot be reduced to a single theme; each one must be examined individually. In general one can say that the parables are "shot through with the same Christological significance as the miracle narratives" (E. Hoskyns and F. N. Davey, *The Riddle of the New Testament*, 1947³, 134). They are primarily eschatological (cf. C. H. Dodd, op. cit.; I. H. Marshall, op. cit.) and contain two groups of themes, the → kingdom of God and repentance (→ Conversion). (On the question of eschatology → Kingdom; → Present; → Time.) The parables of growth belong to the first group (Matt. 13; Mk. 4; Lk. 8; 13:18–21) as do the parables which speak of God and his activity (Matt. 20:1–16; 25:14–30; Lk. 15:11–32). The second group enjoins the urgency of repentance (Lk. 12:16–20; 13:6–9) which demands decisive (Lk. 16:1–8), radical (Matt. 13:44–46) and watchful action (Matt. 24:42–25:13), because the kingdom is near. The parables which speak of action towards one's neighbour (→ Brother; → Samaritan) also belong to this group (Matt. 18:23–35; Lk. 10:30–37). Much light on the meaning of particular parables has been shed by J. D. M. Derrett in his studies of their teaching against the background of rabbinic law *Law and the New Testament*, 1971. For further discussion of individual parables see the articles relative to key words in them and the literature noted in the bibliographies below.   *C. H. Peisker*

5. The following is a table of parables and parabolic sayings, set out according to the general context given in the Gospels. It should be borne in mind that there is a measure of scholarly disagreement as to what properly constitutes a parable or parabolic saying. It should also be noted that some parables and sayings are set in different contexts by different Gospels, and that there are variations and similar themes. This should be taken into account in any detailed study.

The Sermon on the Mount (Matt.)
The salt of the earth (Matt. 5:13; Mk. 9:49 f.; Lk. 14:34 f.)
The light of the world (Matt. 5:14 ff.; Mk. 4:21; Lk. 8:16; cf. 11:33; Jn. 8:12)
On treasures (Matt. 6:19 ff.; Lk. 12:33 f.; cf. 16:9)
The sound eye (Matt. 6:22 f.; Lk. 11:34 ff.)
The birds of the air and the lilies of the field (Matt. 6:26 ff.; Lk. 12:24–28)
On serving two masters (Matt. 6:24; Lk. 16:13)
The speck in the eye (Matt. 7:3, 5; Lk. 6:41 f.)
On profaning the holy (Matt. 7:6)
The two ways (Matt. 7:13 f.; Lk. 13:23 f.)
The wolves in sheep's clothing and "By their fruits . . ." (Matt. 7:15–20; cf. 3:10; 12:33 ff.; Lk. 6:43 ff.; 3:9)
The house built on the rock (Matt. 7:24–27; Lk. 6:47 ff.)

Galilaean Ministry
The harvest is great (Matt. 9:35–38; cf. 4:23; 14:14; Mk. 6:6, 34; Lk. 8:1; 10:2; Jn. 4:35)
The two debtors (Lk. 7:41 ff.)
The sign of Jonah (Matt. 12:38–42; 16:1–4; Mk. 8:11 f.; Lk. 11:16, 19–32; Jn. 6:30)
The parable of the sower (Matt. 13:1–9; Mk. 4:1–9; Lk. 8:4–8; cf. 5:1–3)
The reason for speaking in parables (Matt. 13:10–17; Mk. 4:10 ff., 25; Lk. 8:9 f., 18; Jn. 9:39)
The interpretation of the parable of the sower (Matt. 13:18–23; Mk. 4:13–20; Lk. 8:11–15)
He who has ears to hear, let him hear (Matt. 11:15; 13:9, 43; Mk. 4:9, 23; Lk. 8:8; 14:35)
The seed growing secretly (Mk. 4:26–29)
The wheat and the tares (Matt. 13:24–30)
The mustard seed (Matt. 13:31 f.; Mk. 4:30 ff.; Lk. 13:18 f.)
The leaven (Matt. 13:33; Lk. 13:20 f.)
Jesus' use of parables (Matt. 13:34 f.; Mk. 4:33 f.)
The interpretation of the parable of the tares (Matt. 13:36–43)
The hidden treasure and the pearl of great price (Matt. 13:44 ff.)
The fish net (Matt. 13:47–50)
Treasures old and new (Matt. 13:51 f.)
Jesus' true kindred (Matt. 12:46–50; cf. 7:21; Mk. 3:20 f., 31–35; Lk. 8:19 ff.; Jn. 15:14)
The unforgiving servant (Matt. 18:23–35)

On the Way to Jerusalem (*Lk.*)
The Good Samaritan (Lk. 10:29–37)
The friend at midnight (Lk. 11:5–8)
Light (Lk. 11:33; cf. 8:16; Matt. 5:15; Mk. 4:21)
The sound eye (Lk. 11:34 ff.; Matt. 6:22 f.)
The rich fool (Lk. 12:16–21)
On treasures (Lk. 12:33 f.; cf. above under *The Sermon on the Mount*)
The barren fig tree (Lk. 13:1–9; cf. Matt. 21:18 f.; Mk. 11:12 ff.)
The mustard seed (Lk. 13:18 f.; Matt. 13:31 f.; Mk. 4:30 ff.)
The leaven (Lk. 13:20 f.; Matt. 13:33)
The great supper (Lk. 14:15–24; Matt. 22:1–14)
Counting the cost of building a tower and going to war (Lk. 14:28–33)
Salt (Lk. 14:34 f.; Matt. 5:13; Mk. 9:49 f.)
The lost sheep (Lk. 15:1–7)
The lost coin (Lk. 15:8 ff.)
The lost (prodigal) son (Lk. 15:11–32)
The unjust steward (Lk. 16:1–9)
On serving two masters (Lk. 16:13; Matt. 6:24)
The rich man and Lazarus (Lk. 16:19–31)
On being unprofitable servants (Lk. 17:7–10)
The unjust judge (Lk. 18:1–8)
The Pharisee and the publican (Lk. 18:9–14)

Ministry in Judea
On riches (Matt. 19:23–30; Mk. 10:23–31; Lk. 18:24–30)

750

The labourers in the vineyard (Matt. 20:1–16)
The pounds (Lk. 19:11–27; cf. Matt. 25:14–40; Mk. 13:34)

Final Ministry in Jerusalem
The two sons (Matt. 21:28–32)
The wicked husbandmen (Matt. 21:33–46; Mk. 12:1–12; Lk. 20:9–19)
The great supper (Matt. 22:1–14)
The widow's mite (Mk. 12:41–44; Lk. 21:1–4)
The fig tree (Matt. 24:32–36; Mk. 13:28–32; Lk. 21:29–33)
The exhortation to watch (Mk. 13:33–37; cf. Matt. 25:13 ff.; Lk. 19:19 f.; 21:34 ff.)
The flood, watching and the thief in the night (Matt. 24:37–44; Lk. 17:26–36; 12:39 f.; cf. Mk. 13:35)
The good and wicked servants (Matt. 24:45–51; cf. 25:21; Lk. 12:41–46; cf. 19:17)
The ten virgins (Matt. 25:1–13; cf. Mk. 13:33–37; Lk. 12:35–38; 13:25–28)
The talents (Matt. 25:14–30; cf. Mk. 13:34; Lk. 19:11–27)
The sheep and the goats (Matt. 25:31–46)

The Discourses in Jn.
The teaching of Jesus in the Fourth Gospel is contained in discourses and dialogues which nevertheless use parabolic imagery.
The new birth (Jn. 3:1–36)
The water of life (Jn. 4:1–42)
The son (Jn. 5:19–47)
The bread of life (Jn. 6:22–66)
The life-giving Spirit (Jn. 7:1–52)
The light of the world (Jn. 8:12–59)
The good shepherd (Jn. 10:1–42)
The farewell discourses (Jn. 13:1–17:26), including the sayings about the father's house (14:2 ff.), the way (14:6), the vine (15:1–16), and the pains of childbirth (16:2 ff.)
(C. H. Dodd has noted various parabolic forms in Jn. which he believes go back to an early tradition and which preserve valuable elements which the Synoptic evangelists omitted: the grain of wheat [12:24]; the pains of childbirth [16:21]; the benighted traveller [11:9 f.]; the slave and the son [8:35]; the shepherd, the thief and the doorkeeper [10:1–5]; the bridegroom and the bridegroom's friend [3:29] [*Historical Tradition in the Fourth Gospel*, 1963, 366–87].)

6. A number of parables are contained in the Gospel of Thomas, a 4th-century Coptic MS found at Nag Hammadi in Egypt around 1945. The work is not a Gospel in the canonical sense, but a collection of 114 sayings attributed to Jesus. In its present form the work appears to date from the 4th century, containing a translation of a 2nd century Gk. MS. Some of the parables are substantially the same as those contained in the canonical Gospels: the sower (No. 8), the mustard seed (No. 20), the speck in the eye (No. 27), the rich fool (No. 64), the vineyard (No. 66), and the great supper (No. 65). There is a parable of a fish net which seems to make a point similar to the parables of the hidden treasure and the pearl of great price. "And he said: Man is like a wise fisherman, who cast his net in the sea and drew it out of the sea when it was full of little fishes. Among

them the wise fisherman found a large good fish. He cast all the little fishes into the sea. He selected the large fish without difficulty. He who has ears to hear, let him hear" (No. 7; quoted from the translation by W. R. Schoedel in R. M. Grant and D. N. Freedman, *The Secret Sayings of Jesus*, 1960, 120 f.).

Some of the sayings appear to have a gnostic thrust, e.g. the latter part of No. 25: "He who has ears, let him hear! There is a light within a light-man and it illuminates the whole world; if it does not illuminate it, [it is] darkness" (op. cit., 138). The gnostic is the one who has the illumination. Similarly, the parable of the lost sheep is changed to make the sheep (i.e. the gnostic who is more important than the rest) the motive: "Jesus said: The kingdom is like a shepherd who had a hundred sheep. One of them, the largest, lost his way. He left the ninety-nine and sought the one until he found it. After he had toiled, he said to the sheep, I love you more than the ninety-nine" (No. 104, op. cit., 181).

Some of the sayings are not found in the canonical Gospels but are found in the early fathers. "Jesus said: He who is near me is near the fire, and he who is far from me is far from the kingdom" (No. 82, op. cit., 170; cf. Origen, *MPG* 13, 531 D-32A; Didymus of Alexandria, *MPG* 39, 1488D). But other sayings are hitherto unknown. "Jesus said: The kingdom of the Father is like a woman who carries a vessel full of meal and goes a long way. The handle of the vessel broke; the meal flowed out behind her on the way. She did not notice it, she did not know how to work. When she reached the house, she set the vessel down and found it empty" (No. 94, op. cit. 176). Here the point seems to be the error of imagining that one has saving knowledge, when one has lost it. "Jesus said: The kingdom of the Father is like a man who wanted to kill a great man. He drew the sword in his house and ran it through the wall, in order to know whether his hand was strong enough. Then he killed the great man" (No. 95, op. cit., 177). This parable which appears to reflect Zealot aspirations may be compared with the canonical parables which urge the need to count the cost (cf. Lk. 14:28–32).

For further discussion of Gos.Thom. see F. F. Bruce, *ZPEB* IV 595 f.; and *Jesus and Christian Origins Outside the New Testament*, 1974, 82–158; B. Gärtner, *The Theology of the Gospel of Thomas*, 1961; E. Haenchen, *Die Botschaft des Thomas-Evangliums*, 1965; A. J. B. Higgins, "Non-Gnostic Sayings in the Gospel of Thomas", *NovT* 4, 1960, 292–306; H. W. Montefiore, "A Comparison of the Parables of the Gospel according to Thomas and the Synoptic Evangelists", *NTS* 7, 1960–61, 220–48 (reprinted in H. W. Montefiore and H. E. W. Turner, *Thomas and the Evangelists*, 1962); H.-G. Puech, in Henn. Schn., I, 278–307; R. McL. Wilson, *Studies in the Gospel of Thomas*, 1960; and "Thomas, Gospel of", *ZPEB* V 735 f.

7. It is sometimes suggested that Jesus intended his parables to be clearly understood by all, but that Mk.'s conception of the messianic secret led Mk. to present them as deliberately concealing the truth from outsiders and the uninitiated. Thus Mk. 4:10 ff. declares: "And when he was alone, those who were about him with the twelve asked him concerning the parables. And he said to them, 'To you has been given the secret of the kingdom of God, but for those outside everything is in parables; so that they may indeed see but not perceive, and may indeed hear but not understand; lest they should turn again, and be forgiven.'" The same thought is substantially repeated in the parallel passages in Matt. 13:10–15 which quotes from

Isaiah's commission (Isa. 6:9 f.) and Lk. 8:9 f. There is a similar explanation of the unbelief of the Jews in Jn. 12:40 (quoting Isa. 6:10), and Isa. is also quoted in Acts 28:26 f. Whereas Matt. quotes the LXX, Mk. agrees with the Targum of Isa. and the Peshitta. Similarly Mk. concludes his account of the growth parables with the words: "With many such parables he spoke the word to them, as they were able to hear it; he did not speak to them without a parable, but privately to his own disciples he explained everything" (Mk. 4:33 f.; cf. Matt. 13:34 f. which cites Ps. 78:2 seeing in Jesus' teaching fulfilment of the saying: "I will open my mouth in parables, I will utter what has been hidden since the foundation of the world").

The idea that Mk. invented the messianic secret was argued by W. Wrede in *Das Messiasgeheimnis in den Evangelien*, 1901 (ET *The Messianic Secret*, 1971), and has exerted considerable influence on German scholarship. It has, however, been contested on the grounds that the theme of secrecy and the avoidance of publicity was intrinsic to the whole mission of Jesus (cf. J. D. G. Dunn, "The Messianic Secret in Mark", *TB* 21, 1970, 92–117; → Secret). Moreover, Jesus' teaching never handed out truth as it were on a plate. For the truth about God and man cannot be learnt directly as if it were a series of mere facts which involved no personal commitment. The parables are language-events which challenge a personal response. They constitute disclosure situations in which the listener becomes aware of his relationship with God through identifying himself with the people in the parable. In this sense the parabolic method is integral to Jesus' entire mission.

Jeremias agrees with T. W. Manson in seeing that the use in Mk. 4:12 of the Targum of Isa. 6:10 which was commonly used in the synagogue "creates a strong presumption in favour of its authenticity" (op. cit., 15; cf. T. W. Manson, *The Teaching of Jesus*, 1935², 77). He further holds that the word parable in this context means a riddle (op. cit., 16), and thus Mk. 4:11b must be translated: " 'But to those who are without all things are imparted in riddles,' i.e. they remain obscure for them" (op. cit., 16 f.). The conjunction *hina* (so that) reflects not only the purpose of Jesus but that of God, "in fact it almost amounts to an abbreviation of *hina plerōthē*, and is therefore to be translated 'in order that'; 'in the case of divine decisions purpose and fulfilment are identical' " (op. cit., 17; cf. Arndt, 378). The conjunction *mēpote* (lest) is taken by Jeremias to mean "unless", reflecting the Targum and contemporary rabbinic exegesis. The statement thus would mean: "To you has God given the secret of the Kingdom of God; but to those who are without everything is obscure, in order that they (as it is written) may 'see and yet not see, may hear and yet not understand, unless they turn and God will forgive them' " (ibid.). In view of this general statement about the way God works, Jeremias maintains that the logion is not concerned with the parables of Jesus but with his preaching in general. (For further discussion see C. E. B. Cranfield, op. cit., 152–58; and G. V. Jones, op. cit., 225–30, who gives a review of interpretations of this passage.)

8. Apart from the use of the word *parabolē* and the numerous instances of verbal parables in the Gospels, one may also speak of the parabolic actions of Jesus. Just as OT prophets sometimes performed symbolic acts which were in themselves a message from Yahweh to those with eyes to see it, so Jesus' actions may be construed as unspoken parables. Instances of such actions by the OT prophets include

Hosea's marriage with the harlot Gomer (Hos. 1:2 ff.), Isaiah's nakedness (Isa. 20:2 ff.), Jeremiah's hiding of the waistcloth by the Euphrates (Jer. 13:1–11), his breaking of the earthen flask (Jer. 19), and purchase of a field (Jer. 32:7 ff.). Likewise, false prophets could perform symbolic acts, like the iron horns made by Zedekiah to persuade Jehoshaphat to fight at Ramoth-gilead (1 Ki. 22:11; 2 Chr. 18:10). In performing parabolic acts Jesus stood in the tradition of the OT prophets. But the acts which he performed "show that Jesus not only proclaimed the message of the parables, but that he lived it and embodied it in his own person. 'Jesus not only utters the message of the Kingdom of God, he himself is the message' " (J. Jeremias, op. cit., 229, quoting C. Maurer, *Judaica*, 4, 1948, 147).

Jesus' parabolic actions include his reception of outcasts (Lk. 15:1 f.; 19:5 f.) which corresponds to the parable of the great supper. He included them in his circle of disciples as the new Israel of God (Matt. 9:9 par. Mk. 2:14, Lk. 5:27). The Last Supper was itself a symbolic act (→ Lord's Supper), as were the healings (→ Heal; → Blind), the rejection of → fasting (Matt. 9:14–17 par. Mk. 2:18–22; Lk. 5:33–39), and the plucking of grain on the → sabbath (Matt. 12:1–8 par. Mk. 2:23–28; Lk. 6:1–5). The new age and the new Israel were signified by the bestowal of a → new → name on Peter, linking the → rock with the building of the eschatological → temple. The → number of the twelve disciples, recalling that of the twelve tribes of Israel, also signifies the new Israel, while the seventy disciples recalls the seventy elders of Israel (Lk. 10:1–12; cf. Exod. 24:1; Num. 11:16; and perhaps Exod. 15:27). Jesus' entry into Jerusalem (Matt. 21:1–9 par. Mk. 11:1–10, Lk. 19:28–40) and the cleansing of the temple (Matt. 21:12 f. par. Mk. 11:15ff., Lk. 19:45 f.; cf. Jn. 2:13–17) belong together, signifying Jesus' claims to lordship over Jerusalem, the temple and Israel. His mode of entry symbolized both kingship and humility (cf. Zech. 9:9; → Animal). His washing of the disciples' feet (Jn. 13:1 ff.) enacts the loving humility of the one who alone can make clean. Perhaps the weeping over Jerusalem has also a prophetic dimension (Matt. 23:37 ff. par. Lk. 13:34 f.). Jeremias sees a link between Jesus' action in writing in the sand in the *pericope* on the woman taken in adultery (Jn. 7:53 ff.) and Jer. 17:13 (op. cit., 228). The cursing of the fig tree (Matt. 21:18 f. par. Mk. 11:12 ff.; → Fruit, art. *sykē*) is a parabolic act of judgment on a nation which has failed to bear fruit.

9. The concept of allegory discussed above in 1 (g) differs somewhat from the allegorical method of interpreting Scripture, as it is often understood. According to the latter, Scripture should be interpreted to find hidden, spiritual meanings which are often quite different from the apparently intended or historical ones. This technique is found in pre-Christian literature, and was practised by Philo (*c.* 20 B.C. – *c.* A.D. 50) to interpret the Jewish law in terms of the Hellenistic philosophy of his day. It was taken over by the Christian Platonist theologians of Alexandria, Clement and Origen. The latter sought to follow a threefold method of interpretation, seeing in most passages a literal, moral and a spiritual meaning. Thus the story of the blind men at Jericho is not only literally true. According to the moral meaning, our eyes must be likewise opened by the Word of God and we must come out of our Jericho. According to the spiritual meaning, the two beggars represent Israel and Judah, whilst Jericho is the world (Matt. 20:29–34; cf. Origen, *De prin.* 4, 2. 45; *Commentary on Matthew* 16:9–11; 16:23; cf. R. P. C. Hanson, op.

cit., 235 f.). Similarly, Augustine saw a hidden significance in every aspect of the parable of the Good Samaritan: the man was Adam; Jerusalem, the heavenly city from whose blessedness Adam fell; Jericho, man's mortality; the thieves, the devil and his angels; the stripping of the clothes, man's former immortality; the priest and Levite, the priesthood and ministry of the OT which are ineffective to bring salvation; the Samaritan, the Lord Jesus Christ; the oil, the comfort of good hope; the wine, the exhortation to work with a fervent spirit; the beast, the flesh; the inn, the church; the morrow, the period after the resurrection; the innkeeper, the apostle Paul; the supererogatory payment, either the council of celibacy or Paul's desire not to burden the church with the cost of his upkeep (*Quaestiones Evangeliorum*, 2, 19; cf. C. H. Dodd, *The Parables of the Kingdom*, 1936³, 11 f.).

In these instances of allegorical interpretation it is clear that these spiritual meanings are read into a story in a way alien to the original intention of the story. It is also apparent that allegory in this sense is used in a sense different from that in 1 (g) above, where the original story is itself a continuous metaphor which already includes in itself the intention of having more than one point. The question arises, however, whether allegory in the sense of Origen and Augustine occurs in the NT. In 1 Cor. 9:9 Paul appeals to Deut. 25:4 in support of his contention that apostles have the right to be kept by the church: "For it is written in the law of Moses, 'You shall not muzzle an ox when it is treading out the grain.' Is it for oxen that God is concerned? Does he not speak entirely for our sake? It was written for our sake, because the plowman should plow in hope and the thresher should thresh in hope of a share in the flock" (cf. also 1 Tim. 5:18). It would seem that in his handling of the OT Paul follows a method of interpretation exemplified at Qumran of "quotation exposition, a *midrash pesher* which drew from the text the meaning originally planted there by the Holy Spirit and expressed that meaning in the most appropriate words and phrases known to him" (E. E. Ellis, "A Note on Pauline Hermeneutics", *NTS* 2, 1955–56, 131 f.). But it should be noted that in this instance there is a common principle underlying the original OT pronouncement and the application which Paul draws, and which can be formulated in terms of principle: those who labour on anything (whether man or beast) have the right to sustenance in view of the fruits of their labour. This applies to the quotation from Deut. 25:4 and to all the other illustrations that Paul adduces in support of the point.

This method of interpretation applies to other instances of alleged allegorical exegesis in Paul: 1 Cor. 5:6 ff. (→ Leaven; → Feast); 1 Cor. 10:4 (→ Eat, art. *pinō*; → Rock); Gal. 3:16 (→ Abraham); Gal. 4:21–31 (→ Abraham, art. *Hagar*; → Jerusalem). The vb. *allēgoreō* occurs only at Gal. 4:24 in a participial form which is perhaps best rendered: "which things are allegorical [*hatina estin allēgoroumena*]: for these women are two covenants. One is from Mount Sinai, bearing [children] for slavery; she is Hagar." Paul goes on to compare Mount Sinai with the present Jerusalem, symbolizing bondage to the law, which contrasts with the Jerusalem which is above which is free and is "our mother" (Gal. 4:26). In discussing whether this passage should be regarded as an allegory or a type, A. T. Hanson draws the following distinction: "An allegory is an explanation of the text that replaces the literal sense and has a purely arbitrary connection with it. In an allegory each detail corresponds to some idea or person in the complex which

755

it expresses. A type is a pattern or set of circumstances which reproduces beforehand that set of circumstances of which it is a type" (*Studies in Paul's Technique and Theology*, 1974, 94). He goes on to restate Paul's contrast in the following basic terms:

"Hagar the slave bears a son who persecutes the son of Sarah, the free woman. She and her son are cast out by divine command."	"The unbelieving Jews, enslaved to the Torah, persecute believing Christians, who are free in Christ. The unbelieving Jews are rejected by God."

Hanson concludes that the "allegory" is "really an elaborate piece of typology" (op. cit., 95). It may be added that Paul's use of the vb. *allēgoreō* should in any case not be interpreted in the light of later usage which was bound up with philosophical ideas alien to Paul. (On Paul's exegesis see further E. E. Ellis, *Paul's Use of the Old Testament*, 1955; A. T. Hanson, *Jesus Christ in the Old Testament*, 1965; and "Paul's Interpretation of Scripture", "Paul's Technique of Interpretation", and "Paul as Exegete and Theologian", in *Studies in Paul's Technique and Theology*, 1974, 136–68, 169–200, 201–224.)

10. The riddle or dark saying (*ainigma*) is not a NT literary form. The word occurs in Philo, Josephus (*Ap.* 1, 114 f.), and Sib. 3, 812, but only at 1 Cor. 13:12 in the NT. In the context Paul is contrasting → knowledge with faith, hope and love (v. 13), and points out that *blepomen gar arti di' esoptrou en ainigmati* (lit. "For now we look through a glass in a riddle"). Looking glasses were made at Corinth, and the fact that they do not give a direct vision of reality underlines Paul's point about the limitations of knowledge. The preposition *dia* (through) is to be explained by the fact that the image in the mirror appears to lie on the further side (C. K. Barrett, *A Commentary on the First Epistle to the Corinthians*, BNTC, 1968, 307), and perhaps also by the fact that it is through the medium of phenomena that we apprehend reality. Barrett also points out that the image of the mirror was used by Philo to suggest that man can have a clear and full knowledge of God (*Abr.*, 153), and that the number seven provides a mirror reflecting the way that God orders the universe (*Decal.* 105). 2 Cor. 3:18 uses the ptc. *katoptrizontes*, "beholding as in a mirror". With regard to the phrase *en ainigmati*, Barrett thinks that it reflects Num. 12:8, where God says that he will speak to Moses face to face (v. 12) and not *di' ainigmatōn*, "through riddles", i.e. obscurely. But the expression would be understandable to members of the Corinthian church not versed in the OT. Apollo was known for delivering obscure riddles (cf. the complaint of the chorus of Cassandra that she spoke in riddles [*ex ainigmatōn*], Aesch., *Ag.* 1112). For Paul what we apprehend in the present life is like a riddle. It is obscure and enigmatic. It contrasts with knowledge in the future state, when we shall see face to face and know even as we are already known (cf. Matt. 5:8).   *C. Brown*

παροιμία	παροιμία (*paroimia*), proverb, wise saying; dark saying, riddle.

CL The noun *paroimia* occurs from Aeschylus, *Ag.* 264 on; cf. Sophocles, *Aj.* 664; Plato, *Rep.* 1, 329). Etymologically it is derived from *para*, along, and *oimē* path, way, the plot of a story or song, saga, song. The *paroimia* "states an experienced truth of popular wisdom in a short and pointed form" (F. Hauck, *TDNT* V 854). As such, it expresses general timeless truth. Its popular and traditional form distinguish it from the aphorism and the maxim (*gnōmē*; → Knowledge, art. *ginōskō*). But in Aristotle, *Rhet.* 2, 21, 1395, 17, the borderline is fluid. The lack of framework distinguishes it from the apophthegm (a saying set in a particular setting). Aristotle counted it with metaphor because of its vivid imagery (Rhet. 2, 11, 1413, 14). Others, because of the frequent references to animals and plants, with fable (Quintilian, *Institutio Oratoria*, 5, 11, 21). Collections of proverbs were made by Aristotle, Clearchus, Zenobius and Diogenian.

OT In the LXX *paroimia* only occurs 7 times, including the title of the Book of Proverbs (1:1; 25:1 cf. also 26:7) and in Sir. (6:35; 8:8; 18:29; 39:3; 47:17). In Prov. 1:1; 25:1 it translates Heb. *māšāl*; elsewhere it occurs in the non-canonical Sir. and occasionally translates *māšāl*. It is also found in variant translations in other books. In Prov. and Sir. it is virtually a technical term for instruction by the wise (→ *parabolē* OT 2). In Philo (*Abr.* 235; *Vit. Mos.* 1, 156; 2, 29) it occurs with the meaning proverb. Proverbs were very popular among the Rabbis. They were introduced by such clauses as, "Thus people say ..." and "It is said in the proverb. . . ."

NT 1. The logia of Jesus are often designated in their entirety as sayings. The Gospel of Thomas, P. Oxy. 1, 654 f., 840, and the hypothetical collection of logia (Q) thought to be behind Matt. and Lk. are collections of sayings. Sayings in the sense of the instruction of the wise are to be found among the logia of Jesus (e.g. Mk. 9:50 par. Lk. 14:34; cf. Matt. 5:13; Matt. 5:15 par. Lk. 11:33; 6:19 par. Lk. 12:33; Matt. 6:22 f. par. Lk. 11:34 f.). But they also occur in the epistles (e.g. Rom. 12:20 quoting Prov. 25:21 f.; Heb. 12:5 f. quoting Prov. 3:11 f.; Jas. 4:6 quoting Prov. 3:34; 2 Pet. 2:22 quoting Prov. 26:11; 1 Cor. 15:33 with a quotation from Menander's lost comedy *Thais*, "Bad company ruins good morals" [cf. C. K. Barrett, *A Commentary on the First Epistle to the Corinthians*, BNTC, 1968, 367]). In the logia of Jesus we find also proverbs which may be taken from Rab. teaching (e.g. Matt. 9:13 par. Mk. 2:17, Lk. 5:31; 4:22 par. Lk. 18:17; Matt. 13:57 par. Mk. 6:4; Matt. 6:21 par. Lk. 13:34; Matt. 6:34; Matt. 7:4 par. Lk. 6:42; Matt. 7:18 par. Lk. 6:43; Matt. 15:14 par. Lk. 6:39; Matt. 24:28 par. Lk. 17:37; Lk. 4:23). It may be that these are sometimes new creations by Jesus, which later became proverbs. In the epistles proverbs occur (e.g. Jas. 3:5, 12). In 2 Pet. 2:22 there is a wise saying and a proverb. Both are intended to demonstrate the contemptible conduct of false teachers.

It is striking that, although sayings that can be classified as proverbs occur in many places in the NT, only in few places (Jn. 10:6; 16:25, 29; 2 Pet. 2:22) are proverbs and sayings designated by the word *paroimia*. The instances in Jn. occupy an exceptional position.

2. It is only in Jn., in fact, that *paroimia* occurs (10:6; 16:25, 29) in the sense of dark saying, or riddle. This meaning comes about because of the Heb. equivalent *māšāl* and the consequent approximation to → *parabolē*. In retrospect Jesus' discourse on the → shepherd (10:6) and, indeed, his discourses in general (16:25)

are characterized as dark sayings. The dark saying is contrasted with the later, clear revelatory saying (16:25, 29). This can be understood chronologically; the earthly Jesus spoke in riddles, the exalted Jesus speaks openly. But this interpretation contains some difficulties. One cannot really characterize Jesus' words in Jn. as intellectually difficult to understand, nor can one distinguish between dark and clear sayings. Dark here probably does not mean intellectually difficult. The darkness of the words does not reside in the words but in the hearer. Therefore the words are dark and clear simultaneously. The words remain dark so long as the hearer tries to understand them intellectually. "It is possible to understand the words of Jesus only in the reality of the believing existence. Before that they are incomprehensible – not in the sense of being difficult to grasp intellectually, but because intellectual comprehension is not enough. It is precisely this that the disciples must realize, namely that the commitment of one's whole existence is required to understand these words. They will be comprehensible in the new (i.e. eschatological) existence: *erchetai hōra hote ktl.* ['the hour comes when etc.']: only then will Jesus speak to them *parrhēsia* [openly]" (R. Bultmann, *The Gospel of John*, 1971, 587).

C. H. Peisker

→ Kingdom, → Secret, → Teach, → Wisdom, → Word

On parable:
(a). J. A. Baird, "A Pragmatic Approach to Parable Exegesis", *JBL* 76, 1957, 201–7; M. Black, "The Parables as Allegory", *BJRL* 42, 1959–60, 273–87; E. C. Blackman, "New Methods of Parable Interpretation", *Canadian Journal of Theology* 15, 1969, 3–13; G. Bornkamm, G. Barth, H.-J. Held, *Tradition and Interpretation in Matthew*, 1963; F. H. Borsch, *God's Parable*, 1975; R. E. Brown, "Parable and Allegory Reconsidered", in *New Testament Essays*, 1965, 254–64; F. F. Bruce, "Parable", *ZPEB* IV 590–97; and " 'Unwritten' Sayings and Apocryphal Gospels", and "The Gospel of Thomas", in *Jesus and Christian Origins Outside the New Testament*, 1974, 82–109, 110–58; R. Bultmann, *The History of the Synoptic Tradition*, 1968²; T. A. Burkill, "The Injunctions to Silence in St. Mark's Gospel", *TZ* 12, 1956, 585–604; "Concerning St. Mark's Conception of Secrecy", *Hibbert Journal* 55, 1956–57, 150–58; and *Mysterious Revelation – An Examination of the Philosophy of St. Mark's Gospel*, 1963; F. C. Burkitt, "The Parable of the Ten Virgins", *JTS* 30, 1929, 267–70; C. J. Cadoux, *The Parables of Jesus: Their Art and Use*, 1931; C. H. Cave, "The Parables and the Scriptures", *NTS* 11, 1964–65, 374–87; J. D. Crossan, *In Parables: The Challenge of the Historical Jesus*, 1973; "The Servant Parables of Jesus" and "Parable and Example in the Teaching of Jesus", *Semeia* 1, 1974, 17–104; "Parables as Religious and Poetic Experience", *JR* 53, 1973, 330–58; and "A Basic Bibliography for Parables Research", *Semeia* 1, 1974, 236–74; N. A. Dahl, "The Parables of Growth", *StTh* 5, 1951, 132–65; J. D. M. Derrett, *Law in the New Testament*, 1970; C. H. Dodd, *The Parables of the Kingdom*, 1936³; and *Historical Tradition in the Fourth Gospel*, 1963, 366–88; A. Feldmann, *The Parables and Similes of the Rabbis*, 1927²; J. A. Findlay, *Jesus and his Parables*, 1950; E. Fuchs, *Studies of the Historical Jesus*, SBT 42, 1964; and "The New Testament and the Hermeneutical Problem" in J. M. Robinson and J. B. Cobb, eds., *New Frontiers in Theology*, II, *The New Hermeneutic*, 1964, 111–45, 232–43; R. W. Funk, *Language, Hermeneutic and Word of God*, 1966, 133–62; B. Gerhardsson, *The Good Samaritan – The Good Shepherd?*, *Coniectanea Neotestamentica*, 16, 1958; H. L. Goudge, "The Parable of the Ten Virgins", *JTS* 30, 1928–29, 399–401; M. D. Goulder, "Characteristics of the Parables in the Several Gospels", *JTS* New Series 19, 1968, 51–69; and *Midrash and Lection in Matthew*, 1974; R. M. Grant and D. N. Freedman, *The Secret Sayings of Jesus*, 1960; W. J. Harrington, "The Parables in Recent Study (1960–1971)", *Biblical Theology Bulletin* 2, 1972, 219–41; F. Hauck, *parabolē*, *TDNT* V 744–61; A. S. Herbert, "The 'Parable' (*māšāl*) in the Old Testament", *SJT* 7, 1954, 180–196; A. M. Hunter, *Interpreting the Parables*, 1960; J. Jeremias, *The Parables of Jesus*, 1963²; A. R. Johnson, *māšāl*, *VT Supplement* 3, 1955, 162 ff.; G. V. Jones, *The Art and Truth of the Parables*, 1964; J. D. Kingsbury, *The Parables of Jesus in Matthew 13*, 1969; "Major Trends in Parable Interpretation", *Concordia Theological Monthly* 42, 1971, 579–96; "The Parables of Jesus in Current Research", *Dialog* 11, 1972, 101–7; and "Ernst Fuchs' Interpretation of the Parables",

Lutheran Quarterly 22, 1970, 380–95; E. M. Kredel, "Parable", *EBT* II 625–29; J. Krengel, "Marshal", *The Jewish Universal Encyclopedia*, 1939 ff., VII, 394 ff.; E. Linnemann, *Parables of Jesus: Introduction and Exposition*, 1966; C. E. Macartney, *The Parables of the Old Testament*, 1955[2]; T. W. Manson, *The Teaching of Jesus: Studies of its Form and Content*, 1935[2]; I. H. Marshall, *Eschatology and the Parables*, 1963; B. M. Metzger, ed. *Index to Periodical Literature on Christ and the Gospels*, 1966, 165–70 (for journal articles on the parables up to 1961); H. W. Montefiore, "A Comparison of the Parables of the Gospel according to Thomas and of the Synoptic Gospels", *NTS* 7, 1960–61, 220–48 (reprinted in H. W. Montefiore and H. E. W. Turner, *Thomas and the Evangelists*, 1962, 40–78; L. Mowry, "Parable", *IDB* III 649–54; W. O. E. Oesterley, *The Gospel Parables in the Light of their Jewish Background*, 1936; R. Otto, *The Kingdom of God and the Son of Man*, 1943[2]; N. Perrin, "The Parables of Jesus as Parables, as Metaphors, and as Aesthetic Objects: A Review Article", *JR* 47, 1967, 340–47; "The Modern Interpretation of the Parables of Jesus and the Problem of Hermeneutics", *Interpretation* 25, 1971, 131–48; "Historical Criticism, Literary Criticism and Hermeneutics in the Interpretation of the Parables of Jesus and the Gospel of Mark Today", *JR* 52, 1972, 361–75; and *Jesus and the Language of the Kingdom: Symbol and Metaphor in New Testament Interpretation*, 1976; H. Riesenfeld, "The Parables in the Synoptic and Johannine Traditions", in *The Gospel Tradition*, 1970, 139–70; D. W. B. Robinson, "The Use of *Parabolē* in the Synoptic Gospels", *EQ* 21, 1949, 93–108; J. A. T. Robinson, "The Parable of the Shepherd (John 10.1–5)", and "The 'Parable' of the Sheep and the Goats", *Twelve New Testament Studies*, SBT 34, 1962, 67–75 and 76–93; J. M. Robinson, "Jesus' Parables as God Happening", in F. T. Trotter, ed., *Jesus and the Historian: Written in Honor of Ernest Cadman Colwell*, 1968, 134–50; B. T. D. Smith, *The Parables of the Synoptic Gospels*, 1937; C. W. F. Smith, *The Jesus of the Parables*, 1948; R. A. Stewart, "The Parable Form in the Old Testament and the Rabbinic Literature", *EQ* 36, 1964, 133–47; T. Stoneburner, ed., *Parable, Myth and Language*, 1968; S. Teselle, *Speaking in Parables: A Study in Metaphor and Theology*, 1975; H. Thielicke, *The Waiting Father: Sermons on the Parables of Jesus*, 1960; A. C. Thiselton, "The Parables as Language-Event: Some Comments on Fuchs's Hermeneutics in the Light of Linguistic Philosophy" *SJT* 23, 1970, 437–68; D. O. Via, Jr., *The Parables: Their Literary and Existential Dimension*, 1967; and "Parable and Example Story: A Literary-Existentialist Approach", *Semeia* 1, 1974, 105–33; and *Kerygma and Comedy in the New Testament*, 1974; J. J. Vincent, "The Parables of Jesus as Self-Revelation", *StudEv* (*TU* 73), 79–99; R. S. Wallace, *Many Things in Parables*, 1955; D. Wenham, "The Synoptic Problem Revisited: Some New Suggestions about the Composition of Mark 4:1–34;" *TB* 23, 1972, 3–38; A. N. Wilder, "Eschatology and the Speech-Modes of the Gospel", in E. Dinkler, ed., *Zeit und Geschichte. Dankesgabe an Rudolf Bultmann zum 80. Geburtstag*, 1964, 19–30; M. F. Wiles, "Early Exegesis of the Parables", *SJT* 11, 1958, 287–301.

(b). D. Buzy, *Les Paraboles*, 1948[10]; G. H. Dalman, "Viererlei Acker", *Palästina-Jahrbuch* 22, 1926, 120–32; G. Delling, "Das Gleichnis vom gottlosen Richter", *ZNW* 53, 1962, 1–25; J. Dupont, "Le Chapitre des Paraboles", *Nouvelle Revue Théologique* 89, 1967, 800–20; G. Eichholz, "Das Gleichnis als Spiel", *EvTh* 21, 1961, 309–26 (reprinted in *Tradition und Interpretation*, ThB 29, 1965, 57 ff.); *Jesus Christus und der Nächste*, BSt 9, no date; and *Einführung in die Gleichnisse*, BSt 37, 1963; O. Eissfeldt, *Der Maschal im Alten Testament*, BZAW 24, 1913; P. Fiebig, *Die Gleichnisreden Jesu im Lichte der rabbinischen Gleichnisse des neutestamentlichen Zeitalters*, 1912; *Der Erzählungsstil der Evangelien, Untersuchungen zum Neuen Testament* 11, 1925; G. Fohrer, E. L. Dietrich, N. A. Dahl, "Gleichnis und Parabel II", *RGG*[3] II 1615 ff. W. Förster, "Das Gleichnis von der anvertrauten Pfunden", in *Verbum Dei Manet in Aeternum, Festschrift für O. Schmitz*, 1953, 37–56; K. Frör, *Biblische Hermeneutik*, 1961; *Zum hermeneutischen Problem in der Theologie*, 1959; *Hermeneutik*, 1970[4]; O. Glombitza, "Der Perlenkaufmann", *NTS* 7, 1960–61, 153–61; "Das grosse Abendmahl. Lukas 14:12–24; *NovT* 5, 1962, 10–16; M. de Goedt, "L'Explication de la Parabole de l'Ivraie", *RB* 66, 1959, 32–54; H. Gollwitzer, *Das Gleichnis vom barmherzigen Samariter*, BSt 34, 1962; H. Greeven, "Wer unter euch . . . ?", *Wort und Dienst*, Neue Folge, 3, 1952, 86–101; H. Gressmann, *Vom reichen Mann und armen Lazarus, Abhandlungen der Preussischen Akademie der Wissenschaften, philosophisch-historische Klasse* 7, 1918; T. Guttmann, *Das Maschal-Gleichnis in tannaitischer Zeit*, Dissertation Frankfurt, 1929; V. Hasler, "Die königliche Hochzeit. Matt. 22:1–14", *ThZ* 18, 1962, 25–35; M. Harmaniuk, *Les Paraboles Évangéliques*, 1947; L. Hick, "Zum Verständnis des neutestamentlichen Parabelbegriffes", *BuK* 1, 1954, 4–17; A. Jolles, *Einfache Formen*, 1956[2]; A. Jülicher, *Die Gleichnisreden Jesu*, I–II, 1910[2]; H. Kahlefeld, *Gleichnisse und Lehrstücke im Evangelium*, 1963; W. G. Kümmel, "Das Gleichnis

von den bösen Weingärtnern (Mk. 12, 1–9)", *Aux Sources de la Tradition Chrétienne, Mélanges offerts à M. Goguel* 1950, 120–131 (reprinted in *Heilsgeschehen und Geschichte*, 1965, 207–17); E. Linnemann, "Uberlegungen zur Parabel vom grossen Abendmahl (Lukas 14, 15–24/Matt. 22, 2–14)", *ZNW* 51, 1970, 246–55; H. Ljungvik, "Zur Erklärung einer Lukasstelle. Lukas XVIII, 7", *NTS* 10, 1963–64, 289–94; E. Lohse, "Die Gottesherrschaft in den Gleichnissen Jesu", *EvTh* 18, 1958, 145–57; I. K. Madsen, *Die Parabeln der Evangelien und die heutige Psychologie*, 1936; W. Marxsen, "Redaktionsgeschichtliche Erklärung der sogenannten Parabeltheorie des Markus", *ZTK* 52, 1955, 255–71; M. Meinertz, *Die Gleichnisse Jesu*, 1948⁴; "Die Tragweite des Gleichnisses von den zehn Jungfrauen", *Synoptische Studien* (presented to A. Wikenhauser), 1954, 94–106; and "Zum Verständnis der Gleichnisse Jesu", *Das Heilige Land* 86, 1954, 41–47; W. Michaelis, *Das hochzeitliche Kleid*, 1939; and *Die Gleichnisse Jesu*, 1956³; W. Monselewski, *Der barmherzige Samariter, Beiträge zur Geschichte der biblischen Exegese* 5, 1967; R. Morgenthaler, "Formgeschichte und Gleichnisauslegung", *ThZ* 6, 1950, 1–16; and *Kommendes Reich*, 1952 (cf. H. Conzelmann, "R. Morgenthaler, Kommendes Reich", *ThZ* 9, 1953, 306 f.); F. Mussner, "Gleichnisauslegung und Heilsgeschichte. Dargetan am Gleichnis von der selbstwachsenden Saat (Mk. 4, 26–29)", *Trierer Theologische Zeitschrift* 64, 1955, 257–66; and *Die Botschaft der Gleichnisse Jesu*, 1961; C. H. Peisker, "Das Alte Testament – Gabe und Aufgabe", in *Kleine Predigttypologie*, II, 1965; "Das Gleichnis vom verlorenen Schaf und vom verlorenen Groschen", *Evangelischer Erzieher*, 1967, 58 ff.; and "Konsekutives *hina* in Mark. 4, 12", *ZNW* 59, 1, 1968; E. Percy, *Die Botschaft Jesu. Eine traditionskritische und exegetische Untersuchung, Lunds Universitets Årsskrift* Neue Folge, Avd. I, 49, 5, 1953; J. Piort, *Paraboles et Allégories Évangéliques*, 1949; G. Schille, "Gleichnis", *BHHW* I 577 ff.; J. Schniewind, "Das Gleichnis vom verlorenen Sohn", *Die Freunde der Busse*, 1956, 34–87; H. Schürmann, "Das Thomasevangelium und das lukanische Sondergut", *BZ* Neue Folge⁷, 1963, 236–60; G. Stählin, "Die Gleichnishandlungen Jesu", in *Kosmos und Ekklesia, Festschrift für W. Stählin*, 1953, 9–22; W. Stählin, *Symbolen. Vom gleichnishaften Denken*, 1958; H. Weinel, *Die Gleichnisse Jesu*, 1929⁵; H. Zimmermann, "Die Botschaft der Gleichnisse Jesu", *Bild und Leben* 2, 1961, 92 ff.
See also under *paroimia* for further literature on the Gospel of Thomas.

On allegory, typology and *ainigma*:
(a). F. Büchsel, *allēgoreō*, *TDNT* I 260–63; C. H. Dodd, *According to the Scriptures*, 1952; A. T. Hanson, *Jesus Christ in the Old Testament*, 1965; and *Studies in Paul's Technique and Theology*, 1974; R. P. C. Hanson, *Allegory and Event: A Study of the Sources and Significance of Origen's Interpretation of Scripture*, 1959; G. Kittel, *ainigma*, *TDNT* I 178 ff.; G. W. H. Lampe and K. Woollcombe, *Essays on Typology*, 1957; H. E. W. Turner, *The Pattern of Christian Truth*, 1954.
(b). L. Goppelt, *Typos*, 1939; and "Allegorie", *RGG*³ I 239 f.
On *paroimia*, proverbs, and sayings:
(a). J. Doresse, *Secret Books of the Egyptian Gnostics*, 1959; A. Guillaumont, H.-C. Puech, G. Quispel, W. Till and Yassah 'Abd al Masîh *The Gospel according to Thomas, Coptic Text Established and Translated*, 1959; F. Hauck, *paroimia*, *TDNT* V 854 f.; A. J. B. Higgins, "Non-Gnostic Sayings in the Gospel of Thomas", *NovT* 4, 1960, 292–306; D. Kidner, *The Proverbs: An Introduction and Commentary, TC*, 1964; T. W. Manson, *The Sayings of Jesus, As Recorded in the Gospels according to St. Matthew and St. Luke arranged with Introduction and Commentary*, 1949; R. B. Y. Scott, *Proverbs. Ecclesiastes, Anchor Bible*, 1965; R. N. Whybray, *Wisdom in Proverbs, SBT* 45, 1965; R. McL. Wilson, *Studies in the Gospel of Thomas*, 1960.
(b). F. Baumgartner, *Israelitische und altorientalische Weisheit*, 1933; E. Haenchen, *Die Botschaft des Thomas-Evangeliums*, 1961; C. A. Keller, "Sprichwort, Spruch", *BHHW* IIII 1837 f.; U. Skladny, *Die ältesten Spruchsammlungen*, 1962; C. Westermann, "Rätsel", *BHHW* III 1552 f.

Paradise

| παράδεισος |

παράδεισος (*paradeisos*), garden, park, paradise.

CL 1. *paradeisos* is a loan-word from the Middle Iranian *pardez* (Avestan *pairidaêza*, an encircling wall, circular enclosure, garden), and means a garden, park or paradise. Xen. uses the word of the public gardens of the Persian kings and nobles (*Anab.* 1, 2, 7; 2, 4, 14; *Cyr.* 1, 3, 14; *Hell.* 4, 1, 15).

2. Myths from many nations speak of a land or a place of blessedness in primeval times or (in the present) on the edge of the known world, where gods live and whither heroes or particularly distinguished mortals were carried away or went after death. Within the world of the OT there were the paradise myths of the Mesopotamian or Iranian culture, and also the conceptions of the Phoenicians (cf. Ezek. 28:13 ff.). In Greece people were aquainted with the picture of the Elysian fields and the Isles of the Blessed.

OT In the LXX the word is found 47 times, predominantly as trans. of Heb. *gan* or *gannâh*, a garden. Of these passages 13 belong to Gen. 2 and 3, 4 to Ezek., and 3 to Isa. In each case the reference is to the garden of God, either as the Yahwistic narrative describes it or as it is expected to be again. In Neh. 2:8; Eccl. 2:5; Cant. 4:13 *paradeisos* is a translation of the loan-word *pardēs* deriving from the Iranian, meaning orchard, forest. In Isa. 51:3 it renders Heb. *ʿēḏen*.

1. A continuous or coherent paradise-myth cannot be established in the OT. At least, as far as anything of the sort was also known in Israel, it was excluded under the influence of Yahwistic faith, except for a few individual motifs which appear sporadically here and there – the tree of life, the tree of knowledge, the water of life (Gen. 2 and 3; 13:10; Ezek. 28:13 ff.; 31:8 f.; Job 15:7 f.). It is significant that there is no unified answer to the question of place. According to Gen. 2:8, paradise, at the beginning of the creation, lay in the East; according to Gen. 2:10–14, it was possibly in the North. It is conceived of as a lovely orchard in which the tree of → life and the tree of → knowledge stood. Here God walked, and has handed over the garden to men for cultivation. In consequence of the first → sin the first humans were driven out of it. Return to it is impossible since the → cherub stands in front of it guarding all access.

2. In later Judaism there were many varied speculations about the paradise of Gen. 2 and 3. It was assumed that it was created before time, or on the third day of creation, and that in consequence of Adam's sin it was removed and hidden either at the extreme edges of the earth, on a high mountain or in heaven. It is located in the third → heaven (Ap. Mos. 37:5 and Sl.Enoch 8:1).

With the infiltration of the Gk. doctrine of the immortality of the soul paradise becomes the dwelling-place of the righteous during the intermediate state. In time, pious imagination increasingly embellished the conception of paradise. It had walls and gates and angels to watch over it. Light shone on the righteous. The tree of life was there, and fragrant streams flowed through it.

In the renewed creation paradise will again emerge from its concealment. God or the messiah will bring it, as the dwelling-place of the righteous and blessed, to the renewed earth, to Palestine, in the neighbourhood of Jerusalem. Taught by God himself, the righteous will study the Torah in paradise, and God will prepare for them the messianic meal. Above all, they may then enjoy the → fruit of the tree of life.

NT 1. In the NT the word only occurs in 3 places.

(a) In Lk. 23:43 it is no doubt dependent on contemporary Jewish conceptions, and refers to the at present hidden and intermediate abode of the righteous. Jesus promises the robber fellowship with him already "today" in paradise, and thus allows him to share in forgiveness and blessedness. The intermediate state thus becomes essentially fellowship with Christ (cf. Acts. 7:58; 2 Cor. 5:8; Phil. 1:23). It may be noted, however, that E. E. Ellis offers a somewhat different interpretation. According to the late Jewish writing Test.Lev. 18:10, the messiah was expected to "open the gates of paradise". "Luke declares that in his death and resurrection Jesus opened the gates of Paradise and was exalted there with his 'body' " (*The Gospel of Luke*, New Century Bible, 1966, 269; cf. the same author's "Present and Future Eschatology in Luke", *NTS* 12, 1965–66, 27–41).

(b) In 2 Cor. 12:4 Paul speaks of an experience of the → Spirit in which he was caught up into paradise (at present hidden), and there heard words "which man may not utter." The statement is parallel to what he says in v. 2; "I know a man in Christ who fourteen years ago was caught up to the third heaven – whether in the body or out of the body I do not know, God knows." The context concerns the → boasts of the Corinthians. Paul counters this by saying: "If I must boast, I will boast of the things that show my weakness" (2 Cor. 11:30). He then relates (in the third person) this experience and declares: "On behalf of this man I will boast, but on my own behalf I will not boast, except of my weaknesses" (12:5). He concludes the argument by telling of his thorn in the flesh which God gave him to prevent him from being too elated (→ Fruit, art. *skolops*). Despite his persistent prayer for its removal, God did not remove it, but said to him: "My grace is sufficient for you, for my power is made perfect in weakness." From this Paul draws the conclusion: "I will all the more gladly boast of my weaknesses, that the power of Christ may rest upon me. For the sake of Christ, then, I am content with weaknesses, insults, hardships, persecutions, and calamities; for when I am weak, then I am strong" (12:9 f.).

For a full discussion of what Paul meant by "the third heaven" and paradise see C. K. Barrett, *A Commentary on the Second Epistle to the Corinthians*, BNTC, 1973, 308 ff. The reference to the experience fourteen years previously underlines the fact that Paul had such an experience long before the foundation of the Corinthian church. Barrett does not think that it refers to the Damascus road experience, for Paul did not regard this as a vision. To Philo contact with heaven meant being out of the body, and he held that Moses had such an experience (*Som.* 1, 36; cf. Josephus, *War* 7, 349). Paul's insistence that he does not know whether it was in or out of the body contrasts with current and gnostic views of spirituality. "The experience described in our passage may be thought of as an anticipation of the final transference of believers to heaven, or Paradise" (op. cit., 309). Barrett sees here affinities between mysticism and apocalyptic, for apocalyptists describe the future on the basis of insight granted them in the present into what is already in heaven (ibid.; cf. C. K. Barrett, "New Testament Eschatology", *SJT* 6, 1953, 138 f.). He notes parallels in various fields. Eth.Enoch 39:3 f.; 52:1; Sl.Enoch 7; 8, 11; 18; 3 Bar. 2:2 describe visits to numerous heavens. In rabbinic writing Hagigah 14b mentions four men who entered paradise. But already in Plato's *Republic* the Myth of Er tell show the soul of Er who had been slain in battle visits the place of judgment and returns with a report to the rest of mankind (10, 614–21). Philo speaks of ecstatic experiences both as the descent of a divine influence coming upon him (*Migr.Abr.* 34 f.) and as a heavenly ascent (*Spec.Leg.* 3, 1 f.).

Ancient cosmology pictured three, five, seven, ten and various numbers of heavens, though three was a commonly accepted number (SB III 531 ff.). Paul's use of either this term or that of paradise gives no clear indication of his cosmological views. He may be doing no more than using a commonly accepted image to suggest what by his own account is ineffable (cf. v. 4), though possibly the number three may imply perfection (→ Number, art. *treis*). Sl.Enoch 8 placed the third heaven in paradise, and Apc.Mos. 37:5 pictures God commanding Michael to lift Adam up into paradise, the third heaven, and leave him there until the day of judgment.

The idea of hearing unutterable (*arrhēta*) words is found in the mystery religions (cf. Apuleius, *Metamorphoses* 11, 23). But Barrett thinks that Paul was not dependent on them here (op. cit., 311). Such language is found in Philo (*Leg.All.* 2, 57; *Det.Pot.Ins.* 175), and the notion of secret revelation was also current in rabbinic Judaism (J. Jeremias, *Jerusalem in the Time of Jesus*, 1969, 237–41). The idea of a sealed revelation is found already in the OT (Isa. 8:16; Dan. 12:4; cf. Sl.Enoch 17; Rev. 14:3). In all this Paul is using contemporary images of the transcendent world to describe an ecstatic experience which he himself has had and which was evidently far more impressive than anything of which his opponents could boast. But this was something for his own private, personal edification, which would not have come out but for the boasting at Corinth. What the Christian should boast of is his weaknesses, that God may be glorified.

(c) In Rev. 2:7 the Spirit promises to the church of Ephesus: "To him who conquers I will grant to eat of the tree of life, which is in the paradise of God." The passage may be compared with Test.Lev. 18:11; Eth.Enoch 24:4; 25:4 f. which suggests that as early as the 2nd century B.C. the tree of life was thought of in connection with the temple at Jerusalem (cf. R. H. Charles, *The Revelation of St. John*, *ICC*, I, 1920, 54 f.). The thought takes up that of Gen. 3, where after eating of the tree of the knowledge of good and evil, man is barred from the tree of life. Those who overcome the trials and temptations of this world (in particular the opposition of the → Nicolaitans) are promised not only restoration of what → Adam lost but access to life in a way which Adam never had. Rev. 22:1 f., 14 gives a final vision of the tree of life in its final vision of paradise (though it does not use the word) in terms of the new → Jerusalem: "Then he showed me the river of the water of life, bright as crystal, flowing from the throne of God and of the Lamb through the middle of the street of the city; also on either side of the river, the tree of life with its twelve kinds of fruit, yielding its fruit each month; and the leaves of the tree were for the healing of the nations. . . . Blessed are those who wash their robes, that they may have the right to the tree of life and that they may enter the city by the gates."

2. In the further course of church history many extra-biblical motifs, pictures and ideas were absorbed into the conception of paradise, in order to paint the state of the blessed after death in bright colours. The point of contrast, on the one hand, was Jesus' word to the robber (Lk. 23:42), which was generalized and referred to every believer, although beyond the promised fellowship with Christ (see above 1) there is virtually no biblical motivation, least of all in the detailed descriptions of paradise. The speculations in the church concerning paradise and the conceptions of popular piety are also linked with the fact that the doctrine of the immortality

763

of the soul came in to take the place of NT eschatology with its hope of the →
resurrection of the dead and the new creation (Rev. 21 f.), so that the soul receives
judgment after death and attains to paradise now thought of as other-worldly,
whereas sinners go to → hell. In this, the statements of Rev. 21 f. are also used to
describe → heaven and paradise. H. Bietenhard, C. Brown

→ Adam, → Ecstasy, → Fall, → Heaven, → Hell

(a). C. K. Barrett, *A Commentary on the Second Epistle to the Corinthians*, BNTC, 1973, 308 ff.;
E. E. Ellis, *The Gospel of Luke*, New Century Bible, 1966, 268 f.; and "Present and Future Eschatology in Luke", *NTS* 12, 1965–66, 27–41; L. F. Hartmann, "Sin in Paradise", *CBQ* 20, 1958,
26–40; F. Hvidberg, "The Canaanite Background of Genesis I–III", *VT* 10, 1960, 285–94; J.
Jeremias, *paradeisos*, *TDNT* V 765–73; I. Lewy, "The Two Strata in the Eden Story", *Hebrew
Union College Annual* 27, 1956, 93–99; H. K. McArthur, "Paradise", *IDB* III 655 f.; J. Scharbert
and J. Michl, "Paradise", *EBT* II 629–33.
(b). J. B. Bauer, *Die biblische Urgeschichte*, 1964²; J. Begrich, "Die Paradieserzählung", *ZAW* 50,
1932, 33–116; H. Bietenhard, *Die himmlische Welt im Urchristentum und Spätjudentum*, 1951,
161 ff.; F. M. T. de Liagre Böhl, A. Jepsen, F. Hesse, "Paradies", *RGG*³ V 95 ff.; J. Dus, "Zwei
Schichten der biblischen Paradiesgeschichte", *ZAW* 71, 1959, 97–113; G. Fohrer, "Die Struktur
der alttestamentlichen Eschatologie", *TLZ* 85, 1960, 401–20; J. B. Frey, "La Vie de l'au-delà dans
les Conceptions Juives au Temps de Jésus-Christ", *Biblica* 13, 1932, 129–68; W. Fuss, *Die soge-
nannte Paradieserzählung*, 1968; K. Galling, *Paradeisos*, Pauly-Wissowa, 18, 2, 1131 ff.; H. Gross,
Die Idee des ewigen und allgemeinen Weltfriedens im Alten Orient und im Alten Testament, 1956;
J. Jeremias, "Zwischen Karfreitag und Ostern", *ZNW* 42, 1949, 194 ff. (reprinted in *Abba*, 1966,
323 ff.); G. Lambert, "Le Drame du Jardin d'Éden", *Nouvelle Revue Théologique* 76, 1954, 917–48;
H.-G. Leder, *Die Auslegung der zentralen theologischen Aussagen der Paradieserzählung (Gen. 2,
4b–3,24)*, I, *Im Alten Testament, im Judentum und im Neuen Testament*, Dissertation, Greifswald,
1960; L. Ligier, *Péché d'Adam et Péché du Monde*, 1960, 152–231; M. Metzger, *Die Paradieser-
zählung*, 1959; H. Renckens, *Urgeschichte und Heilsgeschichte*, 1959; J. Ringborn, *Paradisus
Terrestris*, 1958; SB IV, 2, 1119–65; T. Schwegler, *Die biblische Urgeschichte im Lichte der For-
schung*, 1960; J. J. Stamm and H. J. Bietenhard, *Der Weltfriede im Lichte der Bibel*, 1959; P.
Volz, *Die Eschatologie der jüdischen Gemeinde im neutestamentlichen Zeitalter*, 1934²; A. Weiser,
"Die biblische Geschichte von Paradies und Sündenfall", *Deutsche Theologie* 4, 1937, 9–37; H.
Windisch, *Der Zweite Korintherbrief*, KEK, 1924.

Patience, Steadfastness, Endurance

All the words dealt with under this heading refer to man's endurance when faced
with the adversities of life, whether his reaction be one of passive submission or of
courageous resistance. *makrothymia* almost always expresses the idea of passivity,
while *kartereō* rarely does so. Being strictly military terms, the various words are
readily used as metaphors in connection with the battles of life. The word with the
widest range of meaning is *anechomai*, which originally meant to hold up, lift up,
then, intrans., to cease, and mid., to hold oneself erect, to endure. *kartereō* means to
be strong, steadfast, also to do something persistently in the face of opposition; in
Gk. ethics it is a technical term for the upright bearing of the wise man. On the
other hand, *makrothymia*, which is rare in Gk., denotes resigned submission to a
situation which is to all intents and purposes irremediable. In theology, however,
the word acquires a more positive meaning: the *makrothymia* of God is his longsuffering or forbearance, standing between the extremes of wrath and grace.
hypomenō means in the first instance to remain behind, to await. It acquired then
the more active sense of overcoming difficulties: to persevere, stand firm, stand
one's ground.

| ἀνέχομαι | ἀνέχομαι (anechomai), bear, endure; ἀνοχή (anochē), delay, limited period, restraint, forbearance; ἀνεκτός (anektos), bearable, tolerable, endurable.

CL The vb. *anechomai* is also used in the act. in profane Gk., the prefix *ana-* giving it a wide range of meanings: with an object to hold up, to honour, to hold back; without an object, to stand out, but also to cease, to persevere, endure. It governs both the acc. and the gen. In the NT the vb. occurs only in the mid., meaning to hold out, endure. This is the form which also predominates in other literature. The Stoics had the motto *anechou kai apechou*, "Bear with and bear without" (Aulus Gellius 17, 19).

OT In the LXX the vb. translates several Heb. roots, all of which express the idea of restraining some action or emotion. But often the pressure building up behind it eventually causes it to burst forth with dire results. Such statements can refer to men (Gen. 45:1; Job 6:10), or to God (Isa. 1:13; 42:14). There is a tendency, however, to portray God as exercising the restraint, and man as giving way to the vehement reaction: man cries out in anguish at the silence and inaction of God (Isa. 63:15; 64:12). The remaining instances of the vb. occur at 1 Ki. 12:24; Job 6:26; Amos 4:7; Hag. 1:10; Isa. 46:4; Sir. 48:3; 2 Macc. 9:12; 3 Macc. 1:22; 4 Macc. 1:35; 13:27. The noun *anochē* occurs in the LXX only once (1 Macc. 12:25), and then in the purely temporal sense of "delay".

NT 1. In the NT *anechomai* occurs 15 times, mainly in Paul (10 times), but with little consistency of usage. Its meaning is difficult to determine because of its frequent occurrence in passages from an earlier tradition and also in formal phrases. In Col. 3:13 its proximity to the catalogue of five virtues is significant, but the pres. part is intended to qualify the final item in the list just enumerated, namely → *makrothymia* (E. Lohmeyer, *KEK* 9, ad loc.). "Put on then, as God's chosen ones, holy and beloved, compassion, kindness, lowliness, meekness and patience, forbearing one another [*makrothymian, anechomenoi allēlōn*]. . . ." The personal object, however, indicates a characteristic aspect of NT usage. When forbearance is exercised, virtue is no longer self-centred; an essential part of the Christian calling is the service of others. Another important point arising from the use of *allēlōn* (one another) is the reciprocal nature of forbearance, explicitly stated in the verse though clearly implied elsewhere. Eph. 4:2 makes a similar point: as the prisoner of the Lord, Paul urges his readers to walk worthily of their calling "with all lowliness and meekness, with patience, forbearing one another in love [*anechomenoi allēlōn en agapē*]".

In love there is mutual forbearance, hence Paul's plea to the Corinthians: "Do bear with me [*alla kai anechesthe mou*]!" (2 Cor. 11:1b, cf. 1a). He comes to them as weak, and insignificant in presence without any of the outward marks of apostolic authority borne by the "super-apostles" (11:5). But he *is* an → apostle and, as such, a bearer of the truth of Christ; Christ bears the Corinthians in his love, therefore they should bear with him. The strong theological content of mutual forbearance becomes apparent here. In suffering the one sent to them, the bearers "suffer" or receive the one who has sent him. When they are admonished or instructed, they accept the message as from its divine source, from the God who is

765

full of longsuffering towards them (cf. Job 13:22; 2 Tim. 4:3). There is a play on the vb. throughout the chapter in the contrast drawn with the way that they bear false teachers: "For if some one comes and preaches another Jesus than the one we preached, or if you receive a different spirit from the one you received, or if you accept a different gospel from the one you accepted, you submit to it readily enough [kalōs anechesthe]" (11:4). "For you gladly bear with fools [hēdeōs gar anechesthe tōn aphronōn], being wise yourselves! For you bear it [anechesthe] if a man makes slaves of you, or preys upon you, or takes advantage of you, or puts on airs, or strikes you in the face" (11:19 f.). (For further discussion see C. K. Barrett, *A Commentary on the Second Epistle to the Corinthians*, BNTC, 1973, 270–92.)

anechometha in 1 Cor. 4:12 should be construed as having a personal object, by analogy with the surrounding vbs. ("we bless" and "we speak peace"). In other words, Paul does not simply "endure" when persecuted: he is longsuffering towards his persecutors. There may be no clear evidence of a reference here to Matt. 25:35, but certainly Paul's words are very reminiscent of this parable.

In Acts 18:14 the vb. is used as a technical term for receiving an accusation in the pronouncement of Gallio, the proconsul of Achaia: "If it had been a question of crime or grave misdemeanour, I should, of course, have given you Jews a patient hearing [kata logon an aneschomēn hymōn]" (NEB).

The only occurrence of the vb. in the Synoptic Gospels is in the question of Jesus: "O faithless and perverse generation, how long am I to be with you? How long am I to bear with you [anexomai hymōn]?" (Matt. 17:17 par. Mk. 9:19, Lk. 9:41). The occasion, as Mk. brings it out, is the disciples' failure to cast out the dumb spirit which was afflicting an epileptic boy. "These words express, not disgust with the people, but the prophetic exasperation of Jesus at the blindness of those who refuse to accept the presence and power of God. A similar idea finds expression in Jn. 14:9" (D. Hill, *The Gospel of Matthew*, New Century Bible, 1972, 270; → Generation; cf. Deut. 32:5 LXX).

In 2 Thess. 1:4 the reference is to enduring afflictions: "Therefore we ourselves boast of you in the churches of God for your steadfastness and faith in all your persecutions and in the afflictions which you are enduring [tais thlipsesin hais anechesthe]". On the other hand, in Heb. and 2 Tim. the reference is to Christian teaching and exhortation. In the former case the appeal is to the bearing with the word of exhortation contained in the letter (anechesthe tou logou tēs paraklēseōs, Heb. 13:22). In the latter case the allusion is to the fickleness of those who cannot bear sound teaching: "For the time is coming when people will not endure sound teaching [hote tēs hygiainousēs didaskalias ouk anexontai], but having itching ears they will accumulate for themselves teachers to suit their own likings" (2 Tim. 4:3).

2. The noun *anochē* occurs only in Rom. 2:4 and 3:25, where in both cases it refers to the forbearance of God. The religious Jew is reminded that he is not exempt from judgment just because he is a member of God's chosen people (Rom. 2:3). "Or do you presume upon the riches of his kindness and forbearance and patience [tēs chrēstotētos autou kai tēs anochēs kai tēs makrothymias]? Do you not know that God's kindness is meant to lead you to repentance?" (Rom. 2:4). Later on Paul explains how the age of forbearance is related to the cross of Christ, "whom God put forth as an expiation [or propitiation, hilastērion] by his blood to be received by faith. This was to show God's righteousness, because in his divine

766

forbearance [*en tē anochē tou theou*] he had passed over former sins [*dia tēn paresin tōn progegonotōn hamartēmatōn*]" (Rom. 3:25). "God had passed over (the original word means 'connived at', 'ignored') past sins, not forgiven them, but this he had done only in his long-suffering forbearance. In the long run, a righteous God could not 'connive at' iniquity; and the full weight of his righteous anger bore down upon Christ" (M. Black, *Romans, New Century Bible*, 1973, 70). God restrained his wrath until he openly displayed his righteousness in Christ and brought to an end the period of the law.

Apart from the fact that in the NT *anochē* is used only of God, there is no clear-cut distinction between *anochē* and *makrothymia*, However, certain nuances may be detected. *makrothymia* is undoubtedly less active and vigorous, and may be equally well translated as patience. Furthermore, it has stronger eschatological overtones, looking forward to God's final judgment, whereas *anochē* denotes the period of God's gracious forbearance with particular reference in Rom. to Israel and the period up to the cross of Christ.

3. The adj. *anektos*, bearable, tolerable, occurs in the comparative form in Jesus' pronouncement on the Jewish cities which had rejected him. It will be more tolerable (*anektoteron*) for Tyre and Sidon (Matt. 11:22; Lk. 10:14) and Sodom and Gomorrah (Matt. 10:15; 11:24; cf. Mk. 6:11 TR; Lk. 10:12) in the day of judgment. The examples are instances of heathen cities on which judgment had fallen (Sodom and Gomorrah, Gen. 19; cf. Isa. 1:9; Jub. 36:10; Lk. 17:29; Rom. 9:29; 2 Pet. 2:6; Jude 7), or on which it had been pronounced (Tyre and Sidon, Isa. 23; Ezek. 26:28; Joel 3:4; Amos 1:9 f.; Zech. 9:2 ff.). There is a certain deliberate paradox in these pronouncements in that these places were notorious centres of wickedness in the OT, whereas the places in Galilee on which Jesus pronounces judgment were relatively insignificant. Moreover, there is the implicit claim that Jesus' appearance is more crucial than any of the prophetic pronouncements and therefore that the guilt of rejection is all the greater.

U. Falkenroth, C. Brown

| καρτερέω | καρτερέω (*kartereō*), be strong, steadfast, persevere; προσκαρτερέω (*proskartereō*), persevere with, persist in; |

προσκαρτέρησις (*proskarterēsis*), persistence, steadfastness, perseverance.

CL & OT *kartereō*, from *kratos*, → strength, meaning to remain strong, steadfast, to endure, is found in profane Gk. from the 4th century B.C. and has the same sense in the LXX (cf. Job 2:9 translating Heb. *ḥāzaq*, hiph., to persist in; Sir. 2:2; 12:15). In Isa. 42:14 it translates *pā'âh*, groan. Elsewhere it is without equivalent. The word is used in 4 Macc. 9:9, 28 and passim of the patient endurance of Jewish martyrs (cf. 10:1 f.; 13:11; 14:9). The compound *proskartereō* (with *en* or the dat.) has the same basic meaning, but gives greater emphasis to the time element: to hold out, to persist, persevere with a person, persist in an opinion or activity. In Num. 13:20(21) the vb. means to persevere; in Tob. 5:8 (Symmachus) to expect; while in Sus. 6 (Theodotion) it refers to a prolonged stay. Outside the NT the noun *proskarterēsis* is found once in Philodemus (1st cent. B.C.) and twice in inscriptions of the Jewish diaspora (Panticapaeum on the Black Sea).

NT 1. In the NT *kartereō* is found only in Heb. 11:27, describing the faith of
→ Moses. According to Heb. 11:1, 3, → faith is a persuasion wrought by God
(F. Büchsel, *TDNT* II 476) of invisible things. Thus Moses is said to have endured
as seeing him who is invisible [*ton gar aoraton hōs horōn ekarterēsen*]. The kind of
endurance, which clings tenaciously and expectantly to the invisible God, makes
possible that attitude of faith exemplified by Moses, whom Christian readers are
to emulate (v. 24–28). (→ Faith, art. *pistis*; → Form, art. *hypostasis*; → Guilt,
Cause, Convict, art. *elenchō*). G. H. Whitaker offers an alternative interpretation
in view of the meaning that the vb. sometimes has in Plutarch (1, 99; 2, 681; 1,
996), i.e. maintain a fixed unmoved gaze. Thus the verse would mean that Moses
kept his eyes on the invisible as one who saw ("Hebrews xi. 27", *ExpT* 27, 1915–16,
186).

2. The vb. *proskartereō* is found more frequently (10 times) and especially in
Acts. (a) It is sometimes used in a non-religious sense to indicate duration. Thus in
Mk. 3:9 Jesus tells his disciples to keep a boat constantly ready for him. Acts 8:13
and 10:7 refer to a prolonged or continuous stay with a person: after his baptism
Simon Magus resided with Philip; and soldiers are on the permanent staff of the
centurion Cornelius. In Rom. 13:6 Paul says that, as servants of God, rulers are
constantly engaged in their duties.

(b) Constancy and perseverance are particularly important in the Christian life.
Enduring faith as described in Heb. 11:27 has to be complemented by constancy in
→ prayer, hence the apostle's earnest exhortations to Christians in Rom. 12:12;
Col. 4:2, echoing Christ's teaching in Lk. 11:1–13; 18:1–8. Acts also uses the word
proskartereō to denote the spiritual attitude of the early church. The small flock
of disciples offered continuous prayer with one accord before → Pentecost, in
preparation for the promised filling of the Spirit (Acts 1:14). Similarly after Pentecost "they devoted themselves to the apostles' teaching and fellowship, to the
breaking of bread and the prayers" (Acts 2:42). In the early church the experience
of Pentecost produced Christians of great constancy and purpose. Immediately
after Pentecost they continued with one accord in the temple (Acts 2:46). The →
apostles saw it as their function to devote themselves (*proskarterēsomen*) to the
ministry of the word and to prayer (Acts 6:4).

3. In the NT the noun *proskarterēsis* is found only in Eph. 6:18. Here too Christians are encouraged to persevere in prayer and supplication; this supplication is
to be made in the Holy Spirit and is to include the apostle (see also Col. 4:2 f.).
"To that end keep alert with all perseverance [*en pasē proskarterēsei*], making
supplication with all the saints, and also for me" (vv. 18 f.). With these solemn
words the apostolic injunction receives the emphasis which its importance demands.

W. Mundle

μακροθυμία	μακροθυμία (*makrothymia*), patience, longsuffering;

μακρόθυμος (*makrothymos*), longsuffering; μακροθυμέω
(*makrothymeō*), be patient, longsuffering.

CL The word *makrothymia*, unlike other compounds of *thymos* (→ anger, wrath),
appears late in Gk. (from Menander onwards), but is extremely rare. It denotes

a purely and typically human virtue: the prolonged restraint of *thymos,* of anger or agitation, i.e. patience, longsuffering (contrast *oxythymia,* sudden anger). For whereas the gods know nothing of affliction, man has to bear his lot in patience. There is always an element of resignation in the word, even when it describes the kind of desperate endurance which one can only admire. Positively it expresses persistence, or an unswerving willingness to await events rather than trying to force them. Although perseverance and persistence were familiar to the Stoics, and were, in fact, highly valued by them, *makrothymia* does not figure in their vocabulary. This was possibly because of the widespread though erroneous belief that its basic idea was one of passive resignation. It must be said that in ancient Greece *makrothymia* is concerned primarily with the moulding of a man's own character; it is not a virtue exercised towards one's fellows.

OT Although in profane Gk. *makrothymia* is used in a psychological sense, this usage in the LXX is confined to the wisdom literature. On the other hand, the adj. *makrothymos* frequently denotes an attribute of Yahweh. The anthropomorphic Heb. phrase *'erek̲ 'appayim* (slow to anger) is often rendered by *makrothymia* or *makrothymos* (e.g. in Num. 14:18; Ps. 86:15; 103:8; Joel 2:13; Nah. 1:3). These words are, therefore, inseparably linked with the idea of restrained wrath, forbearance being exercised for a limited period only. The Israelites made frequent reference to God's forbearance (e.g. Exod. 34:6) and even appealed to it when conscious of guilt (Wis. 15:1 ff.). They knew that, being a God of forbearance, Yahweh was ready to bestow grace upon his people. But at the same time the godly Israelite was aware of the tension between grace and wrath: it is possible to exhaust God's patience and cause his anger to burst forth (Ps. 7:12 ff.). Even the obedient man sometimes found it hard to acquiesce in God's forbearance (Jer. 15:15; Jon. 4:2), but patience increasingly became a virtue required of the wise (Prov. 19:11; Sir. 29:1 ff.), and was given prominence in the wisdom literature over against other human qualities (Prov. 14:29; 16:32; 25:15). The meaning of *makrothymia* tended to degenerate into mere leniency, a tendency opposed by the rabbis in their discussions of the word. They considered that God's purpose in exercising forbearance was to lead men to amendment and repentance (J. Horst, *TDNT* IV 379).

NT In the NT forbearance is a characteristic both of God and of the man who is united with Jesus Christ. The noun is used only in the epistles; none of the words occurs in the writings of John. The subject is treated thematically in Heb. 6:9–15; Jas. 5:7–11; and to some extent in 2 Pet. 3:4 ff. *makrothymia* usually takes the prep. *epi,* but *pros, eis* and *dia* are also found.

1. The connection between divine and human patience is made clear in the parable of the unforgiving servant in Matt. 18:21–35 (note the use of the vb., *makrothymeō,* have patience, vv. 26, 29, not the noun). This parable may almost be said to sum up the whole NT teaching on the matter. The parable immediately follows instructions on what to do if a brother sins against one (Matt. 18:15–20) and Jesus' injunction to Peter to be willing to forgive not only seven times (which exceeded the common rabbinic maximum of four times and the three occasions just mentioned in the instructions of Jesus). The follower of Jesus should be willing to forgive seventy times seven, i.e. a virtually unlimited number of times. The

769

number recalls the words of Gen. 4:24 concerning vengeance: "If Cain is avenged sevenfold, truly Lamech seventy-sevenfold". The parable of the unforgiving servant illustrates the divine attitude to forgiveness and to our dealings with our fellow men. The first servant owed the king ten thousand talents (18:24), or something like a billion pounds, a sum which he could not possibly repay. He asks the king to have patience (*makrothymēson*) and he will repay everything (18:26). But the king does actually more; he remits the whole amount. But the servant then demands the repayment of a hundred denarii (perhaps four or five pounds; a denarius is a labourer's daily wage in Matt. 20:2 ff.) from a fellow servant. He even puts him in prison until he should repay the debt, despite the man's pleas to have patience (again *makrothymēson*, v. 29). On learning the true facts of the case, the king has the first servant put in prison "till he should pay all his debt" (v. 34). The parable concludes with the pronouncement. "So also my heavenly Father will do to every one of you, if you do not forgive your brother from your heart" (v. 35). It recalls the Lord's Prayer: Forgive us our debts just as we forgive our debtors (Matt. 6:14 f.). "The duty of the servant to forgive is not dependent on ordinary human feelings, but is linked directly to the attitude shown to him: 'as (or because) I had mercy . . . so must you.' This, in a sense, is the real point of the story and the key to the obvious allegorization: the unforgiving will be excluded from God's mercy (verse 35); and those who receive God's pardon must show the same forgiving attitude to others" (D. Hill, *The Gospel of Matthew, New Century Bible*, 1972, 278). (For detailed discussion of the parable in the light of its legal content and rabbinic parables about debts see J. D. M. Derrett, "The Parable of the Unmerciful Servant", in *Law in the New Testament*, 1970, 32–47.)

2. A contrast is drawn between a debt so enormous as to defy repayment, and one which could easily be met out of normal income. This is a vivid way of expressing the incomparable greatness of God's longsuffering. At the same time longsuffering makes possible our entry into newness of life. Similarly in Rom. 2:4 Paul reminds us that God's forbearance leads us to *metanoia*, repentance, by which he means the obedience of the man who has been delivered from the power of sin. In Rom. 2:4, as elsewhere, the background is that of God's righteous anger, but his patience, being linked with kindness (*chrēstotēs*), asumes the character of benevolence (→ Good). If this longsuffering were to be regarded merely as an opportunity given to men for self-improvement and amendment of life, then his wrath would be rendered innocuous. Paul puts the matter clearly in Rom. 9:22: in his patience God suffers those who are appointed to wrath, in order to display his power and mercy in the salvation of the elect (cf. 1 Pet. 3:20). 1 Tim. 1:16 speaks of the patience of Christ (cf. 2 Pet. 3:15), but likewise stresses its revelatory character: "But I received mercy, for this reason, that in me, as the foremost, Jesus Christ might display his perfect patience [*hapasan makrothymian*] for an example to those who were to believe in him for eternal life." Paul is a living example of divine patience, a proof of God's mercy to sinners, and thus Timothy should follow his example of patience (2 Tim. 3:10; 4:2).

3. In the parable of Matt. 18 human patience is shown to be related to (and dependent on) divine patience. God in his longsuffering holds open the door to newness of life, but such new life in the believer is proved genuine by the fact that he practises → forgiveness. Thus *makrothymia* comes into its own in the NT list

of virtues. Paul incorporates these lists in his practical exhortations: the virtues referred to are "the fruit of the Spirit" (Gal. 5:22; cf. Col. 1:11; 1 Thess. 5:14; 2 Tim. 3:10) or our "walk in the Spirit" (Eph. 4:2; Col. 3:12). In the light of Matt. 18, however, one cannot regard these as special "charismatic virtues" (cf. H. Schlier, *Der Brief an die Galater, KEK* 7, 1962[12], ad loc.). They are charismatic in the sense that they are gifts of the Spirit, but they are not in any sense abnormal for the Christian. Rather, they express the way a man behaves who through the forbearance of God has received grace and forgiveness (2 Cor. 6:1 ff.). The fact that *chrēstotēs* and *praÿtēs* (→ Humility, art. *praÿs*) are regularly found in the context indicates that *makrothymia* in the NT is not what Gk. humanism held it to be, namely a virtuous attitude cultivated exclusively in one's own interests. Rather, it is something active which makes a man always prepared to meet his neighbour halfway and to share his life with him. In other words, human patience or forbearance in this sense is not a character trait but a way of life. Indeed, it is the primary expression of → love, for "love is patient [*makrothymei*] and kind; love is not jealous or boastful" (1 Cor. 13:4).

4. There is, however, another aspect of patience which is required of believers as they await "the coming of the Lord" (Jas. 5:7). Jas. 5:7–11 links together the two aspects, namely that extended to our fellow-men and that which is needed to cope with all the trials and tribulations of this world until the parousia. Therefore, James exhorts his readers to be patient (Jas. 5:7 f., 10). They are to establish their hearts, for the coming of the Lord is at hand (5:8). They are not to grumble at each other, for the judge is standing at the doors (5:9). They are to follow the example of the suffering and patience of the prophets (5:10) and be steadfast like Job (5:11; cf. Job 1:21 f.; 2:10), remembering that the Lord is compassionate and merciful (5:11; cf. Pss. 10:38; 111:4).

5. Patience is an aspect of faith and hope which was exhibited by Abraham and which will likewise enable the believer to inherit the promises of God. This aspect of patience is developed by Heb.: "And we desire each one of you to show the same earnestness in realizing the full assurance of hope until the end, so that you may not be sluggish, but imitators of those who through faith and patience inherit the promises" (Heb. 6:11 f.). "And thus Abraham, having patiently endured, obtained the promise" (Heb. 6:15; cf. Gen. 22:16 f.).

6. 2 Pet. 3 discusses the apparent delay in the parousia. This is not to be taken as indefinite postponement but as a sign of God's patience to give men full opportunity to repent. "The Lord is not slow about his promise as some count slowness, but is forbearing towards you [*makrothymei eis hymas*], not wishing that any should perish, but that all should reach repentance" (2 Pet. 3:9). The remark is directed specifically at the readers ("you"). 2 Pet. 3:15 relates this to Paul's teaching: "And count the forbearance [*makrothymian*] of our Lord as salvation. So also our beloved brother Paul wrote to you according to the wisdom given him" (cf. above 2; → *anochē* NT 2).

7. The interpretation of Lk. 18:7 has been the subject of considerable discussion. The verse follows the parable of the unjust judge (Lk. 18:1–6), which was told to teach the disciples "that they ought always to pray and not lose heart" (18:1). In the parable the widow finally gets the judge to vindicate her because of her constant petitioning. Similarly, Jesus asks: "And will not God vindicate his elect, who cry to

him day and night? *kai makrothymei ep' autois*?" The RSV translates this as "Will he delay long over them?" This, however, does not bring out the meaning of the vb. E. E. Ellis notes four possible alternative interpretations (*The Gospel of Luke, New Century Bible*, 1966, 214). (i) "Will not God . . . be patient with their complaint?" Ellis himself favours this, seeing a parallel use in Matt. 18:26. It may be added that the same preposition *epi* is used in both cases. Thus, whereas the unjust judge vindicated the woman lest "she will wear me out by her continual coming" (18:5), *a fortiori* God who is both loving and good will be patient with his people and their cries. This fits the context of the parable and seems preferable to the remaining alternatives. (ii) ". . . and be patient with the wicked" (cf. W. Grundmann, *Das Evangelium nach Lukas, Theologischer Handkommentar zum Neuen Testament*, 1, 1959, ad loc.; cf. 2 Pet. 3:9 f.). (iii) ". . . and he is longsuffering over them" (RV; cf. Rev. 6:11). (iv) ". . . or can he just endure their plight" (cf. H. Ljungvik, "Zur Erklärung einer Lukas-Stelle (Luk. xviii. 7)", *NTS* 10, 1964–65, 293).
U. Falkenroth, C. Brown

ὑπομένω

ὑπομένω (*hypomenō*), be patient, persevere, endure, be steadfast; ὑπομονή (*hypomonē*), patience, steadfastness, endurance.

CL The vb. *hypomenō*, found since the time of Homer, is formed from the prep. *hypo* and *menō*, remain, stay. It means to remain behind, stand one's ground, survive, remain steadfast, persevere and also to wait, and (trans.) await. It is used frequently in military contexts and at first is ethically neutral. From the time of Plato the noun *hypomonē* also came into use, and from then on both words imply value judgments in both a positive and a negative sense. Positively, steadfastness, constancy and perseverance are among the noblest of manly virtues, equally esteemed in the ethical systems of Plato and Aristotle. A proud Greek freeman endures burdens, difficulties or dangers, without any thought of tangible or moral reward but solely for the sake of his honour. But negatively, there is the dishonourable attitude of mere passive resignation in the face of degradation, abuse, ostracism, slavery or tyranny, whether from fear, weakness or indolence (cf. F. Hauck, *TDNT*, IV 581 ff.).

OT The LXX uses the vb. predominantly in the sense of wait and await, as a rendering of the Heb. vb. *qāwâh*, await, and also hope; *yāḥal*, wait; *ḥakâh*, wait patiently; and other vbs. but which are less theologically significant. This personal expectation seems to be grounded in the → covenant relationship for often it is Israel as a nation that is called to wait upon God, while God himself, who rules over all nations, is called specifically "the Hope of Israel" (Jer. 14:8; 17:13; Ps. 52:9; 130:5 ff.). Ultimately Israel's hopes and longings were directed towards the fulfilment of the covenant promise (Ps. 36:10; 34). Israel's endurance has none of the resigned attitude of a slave but reaches out towards God and draws his strength from him as the object of all his hopes (Isa. 40:13). Thus *hypomonē* expresses the attitude of the man living in the light of "the last days" (→ Goal, art. *eschatos*) (Hab. 2:3; Zeph. 3:18; Dan. 12:12), and is later used in this sense in the Synoptic Gospels.

Job and some other later biblical writers also use the word in its Gk. sense of being steadfast, holding one's ground, persevering in distress (Job 6:10; Sir. 22:18), or with some definite object in view. This usage runs through the literature of later Judaism (especially 4 Macc.) and is eventually taken upon in the NT by Paul.

hypomenō is used for *qāwâh* at Job 3:9; 17:13; Pss. 25(24):3, 5, 21; 27(26):14; 37(36):9, 34; 40(39):1; 52(51):9; 56(55):6; 69(68):6, 20; 119(118):95; 130(129):5; Prov. 20:22; Isa. 25:9; 40:31; 49:23; 51:5; 60:9; Jer. 14:19, 22; Lam. 3:25. The corresponding noun *hypomonē* stands for nouns formed from the same root: *miqweh*, hope (1 Chr. 29:15; 2 Esd. 10:2; Jer. 14:8; 17:13); *tiqwâh* expectation, hope (Job 14:19; Pss. 9:18; 62(61):5; 71(70):5); for *qāwâh* (Ps. 39(38):7); and without Heb. equivalent at Sir. 2:14; 16:13; 17:24; 38:27; 41:2; 4 Macc. 1:11; 7:9; 9:8, 30; 15:30; 17:4, 12, 17, 23. *hypomenō* stands for *yāḥal* at Jdg. 3:25; 2 Ki. 6:33; Job 6:11; 14:14; 32:16; Mic. 7:7; Lam. 3:21, 24; for *ḥākâh* at Job 32:4; Pss. 33(32):20; 106(105):13; Hab. 2:3; Zeph. 3:8; Isa. 64:3(4); Lam. 3:26; Dan. 12:12; for *ṭāman*, hide, at Job 20:26; for *yāšaḇ*, tarry, at Num. 22:19; for *kûl*, contain, endure, at Mal. 3:2; for *māhaḥ* linger, tarry, at Exod. 12:39; and *qûm* stand up, endure, at Job 8:15. It is without Heb. equivalent at Jos. 19:47; Ez. 2:19; Tob. 5:7; Job 7:3; 9:4; 15:31; 22:21; 33:5; 41:3(2); Pss. 142(141):7; 145(144):9; Wis. 16:22; 17:5; Sir. 16:22; 22:18; 36:18(21); 51:8; Zech. 6:14; Isa. 64:4(5); 2 Macc. 6:20; 4 Macc. 5:23; 6:9; 7:22; 9:6, 22; 13:12; 15:31 f.; 16:1, 8, 17, 19, 21; 17:7, 10.

NT 1. In the Synoptic Gospels the vb. occurs in the lit. sense of staying (of the boy Jesus remaining in Jerusalem, Lk. 2:43), and in Jesus' teaching where endurance is a prerequisite of salvation. "But he who endures to the end will be saved [*ho de hypomeinas eis telos houtos sōthēsetai*]" (Matt. 24:13 par. Mk. 13:13). The parallel in Lk. is worded differently, using the vb. instead of the noun: "By your endurance you will gain your lives [or souls] [*en tē hypomonē hymōn ktēsesthe tas psychas hymōn*]" (Lk. 21:19). The context is the eschatological discourse of Jesus, where the disciples have just been warned of numerous trials including being hated by all for the name of Jesus (Matt. 24:9; Mk. 13:13a; Lk. 21:17). The severity of the situation calls for endurance. Matt. 24:10 ff. mentions that many will fall away, and betray and hate one another. Many will be led astray by false prophets, and because of the proliferation of wickedness, "most men's love will grow cold." D. Hill suggests that the phrase *eis telos* means "finally", "without breaking down", rather than "to the end" (op. cit., 321). The use of the noun in Lk. recalls the parable of the sower: "And as for that in the good soil, they are those who, hearing the word, hold it fast in an honest and good heart, and bring forth fruit with patience [*en hypomonē*]" (Lk. 8:15; cf. Matt. 13:23; Mk. 4:20). But only Lk.'s version of the parable mentions *hypomonē*, whereas Matt. and Mk. mention the superabundance of the yield which Lk. omits. This may be due to the Gentile orientation of his Gospel. Whereas the parable mentions cares, riches and pleasure which may prevent fruit from growing, the eschatological discourse has in mind trials and tribulations. But in both cases patient endurance is the prerequisite: in the one case for salvation, in the other case for bearing the fruit of the word.

The warning about endurance is also given in identical words in Matt. 10:22 in the context of the mission charge to the twelve. Here too there is the warning about

773

being hated by all, and there are eschatological overtones. The blessedness of those who endure recalls Dan. 12:12: "Blessed is he who waits and comes to the thousand three hundred and thirty-five days."

2. Paul. (a) Both the noun and the vb. figure in the argument of Rom. *hypomonē* is a quality required of men if their lives are to be pleasing to God: "to those who by patience [*kath' hypomonēn*] in well-doing seek for glory and honour and immortality, he will give eternal life" (Rom. 2:7). Both the active sense of "steady persistence in well-doing" (NEB) and the passive sense of patient endurance under difficulties are possible here (cf. M. Black, *Romans, New Century Bible*, 1973, 55 f.). In Rom. 5 Paul shows how the justified believer can turn even suffering to good account. He not only rejoices in the "hope of sharing the glory of God" (5:2). "More than that, we rejoice in our sufferings [*thlipsesin*], knowing that suffering [*thlipsis*] produces endurance [*hypomonēn*], and endurance [*hypomonē*] produces character, and character produces hope, and hope does not disappoint us, because God's love has been poured into our hearts through the Holy Spirit which has been given to us" (5:3 ff.; → Persecution, art. *thlipsis*). In Rom. 8:25 hope is characterized as waiting for what we do not see with patience (cf. the use of the vb. in v. 24 *v.l.*). The context here is the travail of the created order "as we wait for adoption as sons, the redemption of our bodies" (8:23). "For in this hope we were saved. Now hope that is seen is not hope. For who hopes for what he sees? But if we hope for what we do not see, we wait for it with patience [*di' hypomonēs apekdechometha*]" (8:25). Finally, the concept occurs again in the practical exhortations at the end of Rom. "Rejoice in our hope, be patient in tribulation [*en thlipsei hypomenontes*], be constant in prayer" (Rom. 12:12 f.; cf. the connection between *hypomonē* and *thlipsis* here with 5:3; → Persecution). The purpose of the scriptures is to promote *hypomonē* which moreover reflects the very character of God. "For whatever was written in former days was written for our instruction, that by steadfastness and encouragement of the scriptures [*dia tēs hypomonēs kai dia tēs paraklēseōs tōn graphōn*] we might have hope. May the God of steadfastness and encouragement [*ho de theos tēs hypomonēs kai tēs paraklēseōs*] grant you to live in such harmony with one another, in accord with Christ Jesus, that together you may with one voice glorify the God and Father of our Lord Jesus Christ" (15:3–6; note the reiteration of the themes of Rom. 2:7 and 5:3 ff.).

(b) Whereas *hypomonē* is a characteristic of hope in Rom. it is seen as a characteristic of love in 1 Cor.: "Love bears all things believes all things, hopes all things, endures all things [*panta hypomenei*]" (1 Cor. 13:7). In 2 Cor. Paul develops the theme of endurance, especially in the service of Christ for the church. "If we are afflicted, it is for your comfort and salvation; and if we are comforted, it is for your comfort, which you experience, when you patiently endure the same sufferings that we suffer" (2 Cor. 1:6). 2 Cor. 6:4 and 12:12 allude to Paul's own apostolic endurance.

(c) Endurance and patience are qualities for which Paul prays particularly in the Colossian Christians: "May you be strengthened with all power, according to his glorious might, for all endurance and patience [*eis pasan hypomonēn kai makrothymian*] with joy" (Col. 1:11). In 1 Thess. 1:3 the "steadfastness of hope [*hypomonēs tēs elpidos*]" of the Thessalonians is a cause for particular thanksgiving, and and in 2 Thess. 1:4 Paul writes of how he boasts of their steadfastness and hope in the churches of God. In 2 Thess. 3:5 Paul prays: "May the Lord direct your hearts to the love of God and to the steadfastness of Christ [*eis tēn hypomonēn tou Christou*]" (cf. Heb. 12:2 f.). "The Thessalonians are being reminded of the constancy exhibited by their Master, which forms the pattern on which they should model themselves" (L. Morris, *The First and Second Epistles to the Thessalonians, NLC*, 1959, 250).

(d) In the Pastoral Epistles steadfastness is mentioned as a quality required of Christian workers (1 Tim. 6:11; 2 Tim. 3:10) and older men (Tit. 2:2). It is necessary to endure all things for the sake of the elect (2 Tim. 2:10). Moreover, endurance is a precondition of reigning (2 Tim. 2:12) as in the saying quoted possibly from a liturgical or baptismal hymn: "The saying is sure: If we have died with him, we shall also live with him; if we endure, we shall also reign with him; if we deny him, he also will deny us; if we are faithless, he remains faithful – for he cannot deny himself" (2 Tim. 2:11 ff.).

3. The theme of perseverance and falling away is one of the central themes of Heb. (cf. the quotation of Ps. 95:7–11 in Heb. 3:7–11, 15 and 4:3–11; and the argument of ch. 12). Both the vb. (Heb. 10:32; 12:2 f., 7) and the noun (Heb. 10:36; 12:1) figure in the exhortations to perseverance. It stands in contrast with *hypostolē*, shrinking back (Heb. 10:39). Continued endurance is urged in the light of past endurance which included the loss of earthly goods (Heb. 10:32, cf. 34), the need of endurance to "do the will of God and receive what is promised" (Heb. 10:36), the fact that discipline is evidence of sonship (Heb. 12:7), and the example of Jesus himself "who for the joy that was set before him endured the cross, despising the shame, and is seated at the right hand of the throne of God" (Heb. 12:2; cf. v. 1; and 2 Thess. 3:5). "Consider him who endured from sinners such hostility against himself that you may not grow weary or faint-hearted" (Heb. 12:3).

4. The noun (Jas. 1:3 f.; 5:11) and the vb. (Jas. 1:12; 5:11) both feature in the Epistle of James. The rôle of steadfastness in producing Christian character in Jas. 1:3 f. may be compared with Paul's argument in Rom. 5:3 ff. and 2 Pet. 1:6. Endurance is necessary to receive the crown of life (Jas. 1:12; cf. Rom. 2:7; 8:25). Jas. 5:11 holds up the example of Job (cf. Job 1:21 f.; 2:10).

5. 1 Pet. 2:20 contrasts suffering for the sake of Christ with endurance of punishment rightly inflicted for a crime. There is no credit in the latter kind of enduring, and believers are warned not to render themselves liable for such punishment. In particular, the context suggests that some Christians thought themselves exempt from obedience to the state (1 Pet. 2:13–18), whilst some Christian slaves believed that they were no longer under obligation to their earthly masters. The argument of the second half of 1 Pet. 2 is that such earthly obligations still hold good, as they are appointed by God. Moreover, in submitting without reviling believers have the example of Christ before them (2:21–25). In 2 Pet. 1:6 *hypomonē* is twice mentioned in a list of virtues in a way which recalls Rom. 5:3 ff. and Jas. 1:3 f.

6. In Rev. patient endurance is the lot of John himself in his exile on Patmos "on account of the word of God and the testimony of Jesus" (Rev. 1:9). The churches of Ephesus and Thyatira were commended by the Spirit for their patient endurance (Rev. 2:2 f., 19). Similarly, the church at Philadelphia is encouraged: "Because you have kept my word of patient endurance, I will keep you from the hour of trial which is coming on the whole world, to try those who dwell upon the

earth" (Rev. 3:10). The conflict with the beast (→ Animal, art. *thērion*) gives rise to the exhortations: "Here is a call for the endurance and faith of the saints" (Rev. 13:10); "Here is a call for the endurance of the saints, those who keep the commandments of God and the faith of Jesus" (Rev. 14:12).

U. Falkenroth, C. Brown

→ Faith, → Hope, → Persecution, → Suffer, → Tempt

(a). G. Bornkamm, "The Revelation of God's Wrath (Romans 1–3)", in *Early Christian Experience*, 1969, 47–70; F. Büchsel, *elenchō* etc., *TDNT* II 473–76; A. Carr, "The Patience of Job", *The Expositor*, Eighth Series, 6, 1913, 511–17; W. Grundmann, *kartereō* etc., *TDNT* III 617–20; F. Hauck, *hypomenō, hypomonē, TDNT* IV 581–88; J. Horst, *makrothymia* etc., *TDNT* IV 374–87; J. Jeremias, *The Parables of Jesus*, 1963²; I. H. Marshall, *Kept by the Power of God: A Study of Perseverance and Falling Away*, 1969; W. Meikle, "The Vocabulary of Patience in the Old Testament", *The Expositor*, Eighth Series, 19, 1920, 219–25; and "The Vocabulary of Patience in the New Testament", ibid., 304–13; H. Schlier, *anechō* etc., *TDNT* I 359 f.; W. Zimmerli, *Man and his Hope in the Old Testament*, *SBT* Second Series 20, 1971.
(b). A. M. Festugière, "*hypomonē* dans la Tradition Grecque", *Recherches de Science Religieuse* 30, 1931, 477–86; E. Käsemann, "Zum Verständnis von Rom. 3, 24–26", *ZNW* 43, 1950–51, 150 ff. (reprinted in *Exegetische Versuche und Besinnungen*, I, 1960, 96 ff.); and *Das wandernde Gottesvolk. Eine Untersuchung zum Hebräerbrief*, 1957², 19 ff.; H. Riesenfeld, "Zu *makrothymein* (Lk. 18, 7)", in *Neutestamentliche Aufsätze, Festschrift für J. Schmid*, 1963, 214 ff.; C. Spicq, "Patientia", *Revue des Sciences Philosophiques et Théologiques* 19, 1930, 95–106; K. Wennemer, "Die Geduld in neutestamentlicher Sicht", *Geist und Leben* 36, 1963, 36 ff.; S. Wibbing, *Die Tugend- und Lasterkataloge im Neuen Testament und ihre Traditionsgeschichte unter besonderer Berücksichtigung der Qumran-Texte*, *BZNW* 25, 1959.

Peace

εἰρήνη

εἰρήνη (*eirēnē*), peace; εἰρηνεύω (*eirēneuō*), live in peace, have peace, keep peace; εἰρηνικός (*eirēnikos*), peaceable, peaceful; εἰρηνοποιός (*eirēnopoios*), peacemaker; εἰρηνοποιέω (*eirēnopoieō*), make peace.

CL 1. *eirēnē*, peace (from Homer onwards, also in inscriptions and papyri, etymology uncertain), denotes in profane Gk. the antithesis to war, or the condition resulting from a cessation of war. Peace is the state of law and order which gives rise to the blessings of prosperity.

2. In Plato and Epictetus *eirēnē* can also denote peaceful conduct, though peaceableness towards others is generally rendered by *philia* (→ love, friendship) or *homonoia* (unity, concord); and a peaceful frame of mind by *galēnē* (calm). Not until the Stoics (Epictetus and Marcus Aurelius) does peace occur in the sense of spiritual peace. But even so, the word is not common in their writings, and *galēnē* is more frequent in Marcus Aurelius (W. Foerster, *TDNT* II 401). *eirēneuō* (since Plato, used also in mid.), means to live in peace, to have peace, though in late writers it can occasionally mean to bring about peace (LXX 1 Macc. 6:60; Josephus *War* 2, 367; Dio Cass. 77, 12, 1; Did. 4, 3; Barn. 19, 12). *eirēnikos*, peaceful, embraces everything relating to peace (cf. *polemikos*, bellicose, warlike). The compounds *eirēnopoieō*, to make peace, establish peace (from the LXX onwards) and *eirēnopoios*, peacemaker, when found in profane Gk., can very infrequently

bear the sense of political pacification by force of arms (e.g. by the Roman emperor) (cf. Lat. *pacare*, pacify, subdue).

OT 1. (a) In the LXX *eirēnē* is almost invariably used to translate the Heb. *šālôm* which occurs more than 250 times in the OT. (Exceptions to this are largely phrases connected with coming and going, and with greetings, e.g. Gen. 26:31; 43:23; but also Jer. 20:10; Isa. 48:22; 57:21; where *sōtēria, chairein*, etc. are used.) The well-being that comes from God is, however, regularly expressed by *eirēnē* (G. von Rad, *TDNT* II 402 f.). In some 15 passages *eirēnē* corresponds to various other Heb. words which embrace the general area of meaning of rest, safety, freedom from care and trustfulness: *šāqaṭ*, have rest from (1 Chr. 4:40); *beṭaḥ*, trust, security (Job 11:18; Prov. 3:23; Isa. 14:30; Ezek. 34:27; 38:8, 11, 14; 39:6, 26); *hālak*, walk (2 Sam. 3:24); *leqaḥ*, understanding (Isa. 29:24); *ṣaḥ*, clear (Isa. 32:4); *šalwâh*, ease (Prov. 17:1). It is clear that some of these passages use *eirēnē* to give an interpretative gloss on the original Heb.

Unlike the Gk. *eirēnē*, the Heb. *šālôm* is the opposite not so much of war as of any disturbance in the communal well-being of the nation, a disturbance which, of course, may in certain circumstances make it necessary to go to war (cf. 2 Sam. 11:7). Hence in the LXX *eirēnē* too acquires the sense of general well-being, the source and giver of which is Yahweh alone. Indeed, the Heb. text of Jdg. 6:24 which gives the name of the place of Gideon's altar means: Yahweh is peace (cf. RV "Jehovah-shalom"). *šālôm* includes everything given by God in all areas of life (*TDNT* II 402). *eirēnē*, therefore, coming as it does from God, approximates closely to the idea of salvation (*sōtēria*; → Redemption; cf. Ps. 84:11). When God withdraws his peace, mourning must inevitably take its place (Jer. 16:5).

(b) Throughout the Heb. OT, *šālôm* covers well-being in the widest sense of the word (Jdg. 19:20); prosperity (Ps. 73:3), even in reference to the godless; bodily health (Isa. 57:18; Ps. 38:3); contentedness, on departure (Gen. 26:29), on going to sleep (Ps. 4:8), and at death (Gen. 15:15 etc.); good relations between nations and men (1 Ki. 5:26; Jdg. 4:17; 1 Chr. 12:17, 18); salvation (Isa. 43:7; Jer. 29:11; cf. Jer. 14:13). Participation in this peace means sharing in the gifts of salvation which are involved, while expulsion from it means the end of prosperity (Lam. 3:17). *šālôm* has a social dimension, being bound up with the political aspirations of Israel, and has a public significance far beyond the purely personal. Evidence of this is found in the close association of *šālôm* with *ṣedāqâh* (→ Righteousness; cf. Isa. 48:18; Ps. 85:10); with the concrete ideas of → law and → judgment (*mišpāṭ*; Zech. 8:16); and even with public officials (Heb. *pequddâh*, oversight, care; LXX *archontas* and *episkopous*, rulers and overseers; Isa. 60:17; → Beginning; → Bishop).

(c) The concept of peace is found at the climax of the blessing in Num. 6:24 ff., where it sums up all the other blessings and where it is closely associated with the presence of Yahweh. The blessing is attributed to Moses who is commanded by Yahweh to transmit this blessing to Aaron and his sons as the form of blessing with which they are to bless Israel (Num. 6:22 f.). "The LORD bless you and keep you: The LORD make his face to shine upon you, and be gracious to you: The LORD lift up his countenance upon you and give you peace" (Num. 6:24 ff.). The following verse adds: "So shall they put my name upon the people of Israel, and I will bless them" (6:27). J. I. Durham comments: "šālôm is the gift of God, and can be received only in his PRESENCE. But the use of šālôm in the blessing also lends credence to the view that šālôm serves as a cultic term and possesses a meaning far more comprehensive than the one usually given to it in the translations and by many commentators. For šālôm in Num. 6:24–26 is intended as a description of the man who is blessed (bāraḵ), guarded (šāmar) and treated graciously (ḥānan) by God; the man who is doubly in God's PRESENCE; the man who is 'fulfilled', and so 'complete'. Indeed has such a man answered the New Testament commandment which is attributed to our Lord: *esesthe oun hymeis teleioi hōs ho pater hymōn ho ouranios teleios estin* ['You, therefore, must be perfect, as your heavenly Father is perfect', Matt. 5:48]" ("*šālôm* and the Presence of God", in J. I. Durham and J. R. Porter, eds., *Proclamation and Presence: Old Testament Essays in Honour of Gwynne Henton Davies*, 1970, 292 f.).

Durham also draws attention to the fact that the LXX uses the adj. *teleios*, perfect, to render the adjs. from stems *šlm* and *tmm*, complete (1 Ki. 8:61; 11:4; 15:3, 14; 1 Chr. 28:9; Deut. 18:13; Jer. 13:19; Exod. 12:5; cf. G. Barth in G. Bornkamm, G. Barth and H. J. Held, *Tradition and Interpretation in Matthew*, 1963, 98; and Hatch-Redpath, 1342 f. for other cognates of both the Gk. and the Heb. words). Thus *teleios* renders one aspect of *šālôm* not immediately apparent in *eirēnē*.

Durham contends that "*šālôm* is often indicative, in Old Testament usage, of a comprehensive kind of fulfilment or completion, indeed of a perfection in life and spirit which quite transcends any success which man alone, even under the best of circumstances, is able to attain" (op. cit., 280; cf. e.g. Gen. 15:15; 29:6; 37:14; 43:27 f.; Exod. 18:7, 23; Num. 25:12; Deut. 23:6[7]; Jdg. 18:15; 1 Sam. 17:18; 22; 20:7; 25:6; 2 Sam. 11:7; 18:28 f.; 1 Ki. 22:27 f.; 2 Ki. 22:20; Isa. 45:7; 48:18; 53:5; 54:10, 13; 57:2, 19; 59:8; 60:17; 66:12; Mal. 2:5 f.). In particular, this is illustrated by the promise of Yahweh that Josiah will be gathered to his fathers not "in peace" (so RSV) which was manifestly not the case, but "in success", i.e. having achieved his calling (2 Ki. 22:20; cf. op. cit., 279).

šālôm is ultimately the gift of Yahweh (Gen. 28:21; 41:16; Lev. 26:6; Jdg. 18:6; 1 Chr. 22:9; cf. 12:19; 23:25). This is a particular theme of the prophets who are concerned with the proclamation of peace (Isa. 9:5 f.; 26:6, 12; 45:7; 48:18, 22; 52:7; 54:10, 13; 53:5; 55:12; 57:2, 19, 22; 60:17; 66:12; Jer. 14:13; Jer. 6:13; 8:11, 15; 14:13; 23:17; 28:9; 29:11; 33:6, 9; Ezek. 34:25; 37:26; Mic. 5:5[4]; Nah. 2:1[1:15]; Hag. 2:9; Zech. 6:13; 8:10 ff.; 9:10; Mal. 2:5 f.). Jeremiah, in particular, proclaimed that Yahweh also withdraws his *šālôm* in judgment (Jer. 12:12; 14:19; 16:5; 25:37). The theme of Yahweh as the giver of peace figures prominently in the Psalms (Pss. 4:8; 29[28]:10 f.; 34:15[33:14]; 35[34]:27; 37 [36]:11; 55[54]:18; 73[72]:3; 85[84]:8; 119[118]:165; 122[121]:6 ff.; 125[124]:5; 147:14). It also occurs in Prov. 3:2, 17, 23 and Job 5:24; 15:21; 25:2. Whereas all the passages which see *šālôm* as a gift of Yahweh imply a presence of Yahweh, a number of passages relate Yahweh's presence to the cult (Gen. 28:10–22; Num. 6:23 f.; Jdg. 18:6; Pss. 4:8 29[28]:10 ff.; 2 Sam. 15:24 ff.).

(d) After the conquest and fall of Jerusalem (597 and 587 B.C.) the promise of peace became central to the message of the prophets, especially Deutero-Isaiah. With the destruction of Jerusalem the false prophets of salvation (Jer. 6:14; 8:11;

Ezek. 13:10, 16) were utterly discredited. In Deutero-Isaiah the divine covenant of peace (Isa. 54:10) comes to be viewed eschatologically: righteousness, splendour, salvation and glory (Isa. 62:1, 2) are all expected to be manifest at the end. The created world, which at present is under God's righteous judgment for its sin, and is in conflict with itself, will again be made whole (Isa. 11:6–9; 29:17–24; 62:1–9), when God creates new heavens and a new earth (Isa. 65:17–19; cf. Rev. 21:1–4). The message concerning the renewal of the covenant of peace blossoms into the promise of the universal and everlasting peace, and the coming of the day of salvation is frequently linked with the Prince of peace (Isa. 9:5, 6), who as God's anointed (Isa. 61:1, 2) is the bringer and founder of the kingdom of peace.

2. (a) In Rab. literature it is the *šālôm* of Yahweh which underlies the whole concept of peace (see above 1 (b)), but it undergoes an enlargement both in the God-man relationship and on the purely human plane. The phrase for "to greet", *šā'al b*e*šālôm*, meaning to ask after (someone's) peace, i.e. to wish it for someone, turns the act of greeting into something approaching an act of blessing. *šālôm* and *b*e*rāḵâh* (blessing) begin to correspond (*TDNT* II 409). *šālôm* becomes the very essence of that salvation expected by the Jews. It is necessary to pursue such peace (Rabbi Hillel, Aboth 1:12; cf. SB I 217), and to establish peace among men. Among the rabbis the rôle of the peacemaker is similar to that in the NT, and at this point Rab. Judaism approaches the "new commandment" of the NT (→ Command, art. *entolē*). The motive-force, however, is not so much positive love for one's neighbour, as the desire to get rid of all that would hinder *šālôm*. What holds good on the purely human level also applies to the relationship between man and God. Peace thus gains a new dimension, with greater importance being attached both to what man does and to what he leaves undone.

(b) Similarly in the Pseudepigrapha, *eirēnē* implies salvation, which certainly includes the cessation of war, but goes beyond this. In the Test. XII peace means the withholding of judgment, i.e. sparing the offender out of compassion, or at least deferring his punishment. While Josephus follows the OT Rab. line completely (*Ant.* 1, 179; 11, 216; 8, 405; *War* 2, 135), in Philo the concept of peace becomes introverted and signifies peace of mind (*Som.* 2, 253; *Ebr.* 97), though this is not divorced from the external and objectively verifiable state of peace. Under the influence of Gk. philosophy, Philo also regards inward peace as being victory over temptation and lust (Jos. 57). Eth.Enoch 52:11 declares: "Blessed is he who brings peace and love."

(c) In its separation from apostate Israel (1QS 8:4–9; CD 1:4 and passim) the Qumran community considered itself to be the eschatological community of the saved; its members have already entered into the enjoyment of eschatological peace. There are references to eternal peace (1QS 2:4), the superabundance of peace (1QS 4:7), peace without end (1QH 7:15), lasting peace (1QH 15:16) and peace without limit (1QH 18:30). Yet the community is still in the midst of conflict (Belial against Israel and Michael, CD 4:13 and passim; the sons of light, 1QM 1:11, against the sons of darkness, 1QM 1:9 f.). The coming of peace is bound up with visitation (1QH 1:17); salvation is confirmed only after its recipients have been tried in the furnace of fire (1QM 17:1). God has already engraved the covenant of peace (= salvation) for all eternity with the stylus of life (1QM 12:3). Such peace no longer meets with rejection (1QH 9:11), being a present refuge replete with the blessings of salvation (1QH 9:33); peace is identical with salvation (→ Redemption, art. *sōzō*) and with happiness. "The peace of God" (1QM 3:5; 4:14) and "the joy of God" (→ Joy, art. *agalliaomai*) are the watchwords of God's people upon their safe arrival home (1QM 3:11).

NT *eirēnē* is found 91 times in the NT, 24 of which are in the Gospels. The 4 occurrences in Matt. are confined to the discourse in ch. 10, where Jesus sends out his twelve disciples (vv. 13, 34); Mk. uses it once (as a valedictory formula, 5:34), and Lk. 13 times. Christ's farewell discourses in Jn. (chs. 14–16; also ch. 20) contain the word 5 times, in each case denoting Christ's gift to his disciples (Jn. 14:27; 16:33; 20:19, 21, 26). Occurrences in the rest of the NT are as follows: 7 in Acts; 43 in the Pauline epistles (including 10 in Rom. and 8 in Eph.); 11 in the Pastoral Epistles, 4 in Heb. and 2 in Rev. On 12 occasions → grace (*charis*) and peace are mentioned together as coming from God the Father (*apo theou patros*). The vb. *eirēneuō* appears 3 times in Paul; *eirēnopoios* once in Matt. 5:9; and *eirēnikos* only in Heb. 12:11 and Jas. 3:17. The form predominating in the NT, therefore, is *eirēnē* itself, always rendered in the Vulg. by *pax*, except for 1 Pet. 5:14, where *gratia* is used.

1. It is not possible to trace any development of the idea of *eirēnē* within the NT. Both in form and content it stands firmly in the LXX and Heb. OT tradition, though in addition the meanings set out under CL continue to make their influence felt. Thus, as in CL 1, peace is the opposite of war (Lk. 14:32, an Aramaism; Acts 12:20). In Lk. 11:21 and Acts 24:2 it denotes external security. OT influence is more apparent in 1 Cor. 14:33, where peace is the opposite of disorder in the church. Similarly it is used for harmony among men (Acts 7:26; Gal. 5:22; Eph. 4:3; Jas. 3:18; negatively in Matt. 10:34), and for messianic salvation (Lk. 1:79; 2:14; 19:42). Hence the word can describe both the content and the goal of all Christian preaching, the message itself being called "the gospel of peace" (Eph. 6:15; cf. Acts 10:36; Eph. 2:17). In other words, the biblical concept of peace (from *šālôm*) is primarily that of wholeness. This divinely-wrought reality exercises a mighty influence in the present world, though it still awaits final fulfilment. Soteriologically, peace is grounded in God's work of → redemption. Eschatologically it is a sign of God's new creation which has already begun. Teleologically it will be fully realized when the work of new creation is complete. Only in a secondary sense does peace describe human and divine-human relationships, in which case it refers to a psychological state consequent upon sharing in the all-embracing peace of God. On Lk. 2:14 → Please, art. *eudokeō* NT 3(c).

2. (a) As opposed to *akatastasia*, disorder, peace is an order established by God as the God of peace (1 Cor. 14:33; cf. also Rom. 15:33; 16:20; Phil. 4:9; 1 Thess. 5:23; Heb. 13:20). The wide-ranging scope of salvation is shown by the fact that peace is linked with → love (*agapē*) in 2 Cor. 13:11; with → grace (*charis*) especially in the introductions to the epistles (Rom. 1:7; 1 Cor. 1:3; 2 Cor. 1:2; Gal. 1:3; Eph. 1:2; Phil. 1:2; Col. 1:2; 1 Thess. 1:1; 2 Thess. 1:2; 1 Tim. 1:2; 2 Tim. 1:2; Tit. 1:4; Phlm. 3; 1 Pet. 1:2; 2 Pet. 1:2; 2 Jn. 3; Jude 2; Rev. 1:4). It also features in closing salutations (Rom. 15:33; 16:20; 1 Cor. 16:11; 2 Cor. 13:11; Gal. 6:16; Eph. 6:23, cf. 15; Phil. 4:7, 9; 1 Thess. 5:23; 2 Thess. 3:16; Heb. 13:20; 1 Pet. 5:14; 2 Pet. 3:14; 3 Jn. 15). It is linked with → life (*zōē*) in

Rom. 8:6, where it is contrasted with → death (*thanatos*). Similarly in Jn. 16:33 there is an antithesis between peace and tribulation (*thlipsis*; → Persecution). Peace comes from him who is, who was, and who is to come (Rev. 1:4; cf. Heb. 7:2, a reference to → Melchizedek as a type of the king of peace, *basileus eirēnēs*). The Gospel of Jn. insists that this peace differs not only quantitatively but also qualitatively from that of the world (Jn. 16:33) in that it is given by Christ himself. Peace in heaven and → glory (*doxa*) in the highest (Lk. 19:38) also form part of the expected salvation. Peace, if it is to exist at all, must be all-embracing.

(b) Christ is the mediator of peace. He brings in the kingdom of God and is the bearer of reconciliation (Rom. 5:1; Col. 1:20; Lk. 2:14 and 1:79, referring to the birth of Jesus and John respectively). (On Lk. 2:14 → Man, art. *anthrōpos* NT 1; → Please, art. *eudokeō* NT 3 (c).) Indeed, he himself is peace (Eph. 2:14–18), as is Yahweh in the OT. While the Gospel of Jn. stresses Christ's gift of peace to his disciples (Jn. 14:27), Christ's missionary discourses make the point that his commissioned followers are to pass it on to others. If it is refused by those to whom it is offered, then it returns to the disciples (Lk. 10:5 f.; Matt. 10:13). The salutation in profane Gk. *chairein kai eirēnē* (much used at the beginning of letters) is deepened in the greetings of the Pauline epistles (→ Book, art. *epistolē* NT).

Thus in the NT *eirēnē* is described as the peace of Christ (Col. 3:15) and as the gift of the Father and the Son (Rom. 1:7; 1 Cor. 1:3 and passim). It is both obtained and maintained through communion with Christ (Jn. 16:33; Phil. 4:7; 1 Pet. 5:14). The whole process of believers' sanctification, preservation and perfecting (1 Thess. 5:23; Heb. 13:20) serves to deepen their participation in the peace of God, and → Satan, who is constantly trying to hinder this work, will be crushed by God himself (Rom. 16:20). Peace may, however, go unrecognized (Lk. 19:42); it may be forgotten and obscured (Rom. 3:12, 17), or refused (Lk. 10:5 f.; Matt. 10:13). In Heb. 13:20, the phrase *en panti agathō* may be translated "in every good work", or "in all that is good". Therefore, it can have either a moral and ethical meaning, or it can refer to believers' well-being in the broadest sense of the term. Similarly, in 2 Thess. 3:16 the phrase *dia pantos en panti tropō*, everywhere and in all ways, may include all the benefits of peace (well-being, health, happiness, harmony). But if there is a conflict between these benefits and the peace of God itself, then they must be surrendered, or else there will be disharmony instead of peace (Lk. 12:51 ff.). There is no room for false peace. By its very nature peace is grounded in the righteousness and wholeness which God gives to man for the sake of Christ and his merits (*LTK* IV 367).

3. Peace, in the sense of wholeness both for men and the world (2 Cor. 5:17; Gal. 6:15), brings a newness to human relationships. Hence the injunction: Be at peace with one another (Mk. 9:50; cf. 2 Cor. 13:11, in association with *to auto phroneite*, be of one → mind) and with all men wherever possible (see above NT 2 (b)) and so far as it depends upon you (Rom. 12:18). The kingdom of God is righteousness and peace (Rom. 14:17) in the sense of establishing righteous harmony among men. The church is upbuilt in peace, and in the → joy of the Holy Spirit (Rom. 14:17, 19). The peace to which the church is called (1 Cor. 7:15) is the gift of God (see above 2 (b); 1 Pet. 1:2; Jude 2), who fills men with it (Rom. 15:13). It is God who causes it to rule in the heart of men and so reign in the Christian community (Col. 3:15), and manifest itself as the → fruit of the Spirit

(Gal. 5:22). God in Christ has come preaching peace (*euangelizomenos eirēnēn*, Acts 10:36, quoting Isa. 52:7; cf. also Eph. 2:17; → Gospel).

2 Tim. 2:22 and Heb. 12:14 emphasize that peace in the sense of concord and harmony is to be pursued not only in the church but among men generally, so far as is possible (*TDNT* II 416 f.; cf. Eph. 4:3; 1 Pet. 3:11 quoting Ps. 34:15; Jas. 3:18). Matt. 5:9 states the beatitude: "Blessed are the peacemakers [*eirēnopoioi*], for they shall be called sons of God." The word *eirēnopoios* is an adj. meaning making peace, used only here in the NT as a noun, peacemaker. It is rare in secular Gk. (e.g. Xen., 6, 3, 4; Cornutus 16 p. 23, 2; Dio Cass., 44, 49, 2; 72, 15, 5; Plut., *Mor.* 279b; Pollux, 152; Philo, *Spec.Leg.* 2, 192), where it is applied in particular to emperors. But in the context of Matt. it is more likely to have a Heb. background, suggesting what to the Jewish hearer would be implied by *šālôm*. It may also be related to the saying in Matt. 5:48: "You, therefore, must be perfect [*teleioi*], as your heavenly Father is perfect." With regard to this concept, G. Barth comments: "Matthew does not use *teleios* in the Greek sense of the perfect ethical personality, but in the Old Testament sense of the wholeness of consecration to God, as the close relationship with the use of *tāmîm* in 1QS shows. That discipleship itself is 'perfection' and not merely the way to it follows above all from the fact that the necessity of imitation in suffering is not grounded primarily on a goal envisaged in the future but on belonging to the suffering Son of man" (op. cit., 101; cf. 1 QS 1:8 f.; 2:3; 4:22; 5:24; 8:1, 9, 18, 20; 9:2, 5 f., 8 f., 19; 11:11, 17; see above OT 1 (c)). The disciple who is perfect in the sense of bringing the wholeness which comes from God alone and which is intimately bound up with his presence is one who brings peace in the fullest sense of the term *šālôm*. As such, he is a son of God fulfilling the destiny and title of Israel (cf. Deut. 14:1; Hos. 1:10; Ps.Sol. 17:30; Wis. 2:13, 18). "The peacemakers are the true Israel and acknowledged by God as his children" (T. W. Manson, *The Sayings of Jesus*, 1947, 151).

4. The adj. *eirēnikos* occurs only at Heb. 12:11 and Jas. 3:17. In Heb. "the peaceful fruit of righteousness" is said to spring from → discipline (→ also Patience, art. *hypomonē*). This leads on to the exhortation to "Strive for peace with all men, and for the holiness without which no one will see the Lord" (Heb. 12:14), which is followed by the example of the "immoral and irreligious" Esau (Heb. 12:16; cf. Gen. 25:29–34). Esau's action in trading his birthright shows a failure to seek peace and holiness, by allowing a "root of bitterness" to spring up (Heb. 12:15; cf. Deut. 29:18 LXX). In Jas. 3:17 *eirēnikos* is also associated with fruit, but here in particular with wisdom. "But the wisdom from above is first pure, then peaceable, gentle, open to reason, full of mercy and good fruits, without uncertainty or insincerity."

5. The vb. *eirēnopoieō* is found only at Col. 1:20 where it refers to the cosmic scope of the reconciling death of Christ: "For in him all the fullness of God was pleased to dwell, and through him to reconcile to himself all things, whether on earth or in heaven, making peace [*eirēnopoiēsas*] by the blood of the cross." The verse is possibly part of a quotation from an early Christian hymn (cf. E. Lohse, *Colossians and Philemon, Hermeneia*, 1971, 59). The vb. occurs in Prov. 10:10 and Isa. 27:5. On the idea of cosmic reconciliation see Asc.Isa. 11:23 and Lohse, op. cit., 60 f.; also → Blood; → Reconciliation; → Fullness. The aor. of the Gk.

here is better translated as "having made peace", since it refers to the historic event of the → cross (cf. Col. 2:13 ff.).

6. In at least one passage (Rom. 15:13) peace is to be understood as a power which, together with → joy, can pervade the whole person: "May the God of hope fill you with all joy and peace in believing, so that by the power of the Holy Spirit you may abound in hope" (Rom. 15:13; → Hope; → Fullness, art. *plēroō*). This peace is neither the Stoic's withdrawal from the world nor a pious flight into spirituality and mystical contemplation. It is the joyful assurance of sharing already the peace of God as one goes through life and looks to eternity.

H. Beck, C. Brown

(a). J. I. Durham, "*šālôm* and the Presence of God", in J. I. Durham and J. R. Porter, eds., *Proclamation and Presence: Old Testament Essays in Honour of Gwynne Henton Davies*, 1970, 272–92; W. Foerster and G. von Rad, *eirēnē* etc., *TDNT* II 400–20; H. Gross, "Peace", *EBT* II 648–51; J. Pedersen, *Israel: Its Life and Culture*, I–II, 1926, 263–335; E. Stauffer, *New Testament Theology*, 1955, 143–46.

(b). K. Bernhardt, ed., *Schalom. Studien zum Glaube und Geschichte Israels. A. Jepsen Zum 70. Geburtstag*, *AzTh* 46, 1971; E. Biser, *Wege des Friedens*, 1961; H. Braun, *Qumran und des Neue Testament*, 1966; W. Caspari, *Vorstellung und Wort "Friede" im Alten Testament*, 1910; J. Comblin, *Theologie des Friedens*, 1963; W. Eichrodt, *Die Hoffnung des ewigen Friedens im Alten Israel*, 1920; H. Gross, *Die Idee des ewigen und allgemeinen Friedens im Alten Orient und im Alten Testament*, 1956; W. S. Leeuwen, *Eirenē in het NT*, 1940; W. Nestle, *Der Friedensgedanke in der antiken Welt*, *Philologus* Supplement 31, 1938; N. Peters, *Weltfriede und Propheten*, 1917; A. Pujol, "De Salutione Apostolorum 'Gratia vobis et pax' ", *Verbum Domini* 12, 1932, 38–42, 76–82; F. Sauer, *Die Friedensbotschaft der Bibel*, 1954; E. Schlick and E. Biser, "Friede I", *LTK* IV 266 ff.; J. J. Stamm and H. Bietenhard, *Der Weltfriede im Alten und Neuen Testament*, 1959; O. H. Steck, *Friedensvorstellungen im Alten Jerusalem, Psalmen, Jesaja, Deuterojesaja*, 1972; E. Vogt, "Pax hominibus bonae voluntatis", *Biblica* 34, 1953, 427 ff.; H. W. Wolff, *Friede ohne Ende. Eine Auslegung von Jes. 7, 1–7 und 9, 1–6*, *BSt* 35, 1962; J. Zingerle," Die Weissagungen des Propheten Jesaias (11, 6–8) vom messianischen Friedensreich", *ZKT* 4, 1880, 651–61.

Pentecost, Feast of

| πεντηκοστή |

πεντηκοστή (*pentēkostē*), Pentecost.

OT 1. *pentēcostē* is a fem. noun formed from the numeral *pentēkostos*, fiftieth, which is found in cl. Gk. from Plato onwards. In inscriptions and ostraca *hē pentēkostē* (*meris*) is a technical term meaning "the fiftieth (part)", i.e. 2%. But in Jewish and Christian literature the word stands for *hē pentēkostē hēmera*, the fiftieth day, referring to the festival celebrated on the fiftieth day after Passover (Tob. 2:1; 2 Macc. 12:32; Philo, *Decal.* 160; *Spec.Leg.* 2, 176; Josephus, *Ant.* 3, 252; 13, 252; 14, 337; 17, 254; *War* 1, 253; 2, 42; 6, 299; → Feast, art. *pascha*). In Deut. 16:10 it is the *ḥag šābu'ôṯ*, the feast of weeks (in rabbinic writings the *ḥag ḥᵃmîššîm yôm*, the feast of fifty days).

Pentecost was the second great feast of the Jewish year, a harvest festival, when the first-fruits of the wheat harvest were presented to Yahweh. It was celebrated seven weeks after the beginning of the barley harvest (hence "Feast of Weeks"), 50 days after the Passover (hence "Pentecost"). For accounts see Exod. 23:16; 34:22; Lev. 23:15–21; Num. 28:26–31; Deut. 16:9–12; Philo, *Spec.Leg.* 2, 176–88; Josephus, *Ant.* 3, 252 ff.

2. Jewish thinking about Pentecost developed during the period before and after Jesus.

(a) Pentecost has become the feast of covenant renewal in Jub. 6:17–21 (*c.* 100 B.C.) and probably also in the Qumran community (J. T. Milik, *Ten Years of Discovery in the Wilderness of Judaea*, SBT 26, 1959, 117; cf. 1QS 1:16–2:18), an association already implied in 2 Chr. 15:10–12 (cf. G. Kretschmar, "Himmelfahrt und Pfingsten", *Zeitschrift für Kirchengeschichte* 66, 1954–55, 226 ff.). This almost certainly meant a link between Pentecost and the covenant of Sinai in particular: both Ex. 19:1 and 2 Chr. 15:10 specify "the third month" (the month during which Pentecost was celebrated), and the same link was made by the Samaritans (J. T. Milik, ibid.).

(b) In Philo the Sinai traditions are themselves developed. The heavenly voice at Sinai (Exod. 19:16–19) "sounded forth like the breath [*pneuma*] through a trumpet"; "the flame became articulate speech in the language familiar to the audience" (*Decal.* 33, 46). However, Philo did not associate the Sinai revelation with Pentecost.

(c) In rabbinic Judaism these two developments eventually came together. The association of Pentecost with the giving of the law becomes explicit (*Pes.* 68b) and the words of R. Johanan are frequently quoted (in various forms), that the (one) voice (at Sinai) divided into (seven voices and these into) seventy languages (so that all the nations heard in their own language) (cf. SB II 604 f.). The link between Pentecost and Sinai is not documented before the second century A.D. (SB II 601) and R. Johanan (died in A.D. 279).

NT 1. *The Authenticity of the Pentecost Narrative.* In Acts 2:1 Luke dates the giving of the → Spirit at Pentecost. Has Luke's account of the first Christian Pentecost been influenced by these Jewish traditions? Some scholars believe that such traditions play a primary rôle in shaping the narrative of Acts 2:1–13 (cf. E. Zeller, *The Contents and Origin of the Acts of the Apostles Critically Examined*, 1875, 202 ff.; A. Loisy, *Les Actes des Apôtres*, 1920, 184–95; E. Haenchen, *The Acts of the Apostles*, 1971, 166–89). However, the thesis cannot be sustained.

(a) Only one of the developments outlined above was already well established in pre-Christian Judaism – that is, Pentecost as the feast of covenant renewal (see above 2 (a)). But had Pentecost also become specifically the feast which celebrated the law-giving at Sinai? The answer is probably, Yes. The association was inevitable from the time that festivals became also celebrations of Israel's history (Passover, cf. Exod. 12:12 f., 17, 23–7, 39; Tabernacles, Lev. 23:43). The dating of the Sinai revelation to the third month (six to ten weeks after the Passover) must clearly have suggested the association. The giving of the law at Sinai was the most important of the covenants. And the custom of reading Exod. 19 at the Feast of Pentecost was probably already established in the century before Christ (cf. A. R. C. Leaney, *The Rule of Qumran and its Meaning*, 1966, 97 f.; J. C. Kirby, *Ephesians, Baptism and Pentecost*, 1968, 90–93).

(b) The Acts 2 tradition is significantly different from the rabbinic legends of Sinai (one heavenly voice from the mountain, proclaiming the law, in seventy languages; many human voices, inspired by the Spirit to praise God, in many languages). The earlier the legend the greater the differences from Acts 2. Philo's treatment of Exod. 19 appears to be nothing more than his own (typical) exposition of a biblical narrative (contrast Heb. 12:19), and the possible point of contact with Acts 2 are minimal.

(c) The rabbis' failure or refusal to recognize a link between Pentecost and Sinai (prior to 2nd century A.D.) is not decisive against the view that the link was already established before Christ. Their silence may simply reflect their low regard for Pentecost (it is the only feast to which no tractate is devoted in the Mishnah and Talmud), which in turn may be due to a reaction on their part against the high esteem accorded to Pentecost in the "heterodox Judaism" of the Essenes and Samaritans (see above 2 (a)). Similarly the Therapeutae regarded Pentecost as the chief feast of the year (Philo, *Vit.Cont.* 65 f.), a view Philo may well have shared (*Spec.Leg.* 2, 176 ff.). The Pharisees were also in dispute with the Sadducees on the dating of Pentecost (Menahoth 10:3).

We may conclude therefore that while Luke was probably aware of an already established association between Pentecost and the law giving at Sinai, there is no evidence that this or the more developed Sinai legends present in later rabbinic writings influenced his narrative in Acts 2. Consequently there is no evidence that the dating of the outpouring of the Spirit to Pentecost is due to Lucan redaction. On the contrary, the excitement of the next pilgrim feast day would be a very likely occasion for the first communal experience of Spirit following Jesus' resurrection. It is quite likely then that the Pentecost dating belongs to the original tradition underlying Acts 2 (cf. J. D. G. Dunn, *Jesus and the Spirit*, 1975, 139–42).

2. *Significance of Pentecost for the earliest Christians.* (a) Pentecost means first and foremost the outpouring of the Spirit promised by God for the end-time. Charismatic and ecstatic manifestations attributed to God's Spirit were as distinctive and significant a feature of earliest Palestinian Christianity as of later Hellenistic Christianity (cf. e.g. Matt. 3:11 par. Mk. 1:8, Lk. 3:16; Jn. 7:38 f.; Acts 2:38; 6:3 ff.; 8:14–7; 10:44–8; 18–25; 19:1–7; Rom. 8:9, 14 f.; 1 Cor. 12:13; Eph. 4:8; Heb. 2:4; 6:5). In particular, Pentecost was seen as the fulfilment of Joel 2:28; "in the last days" (Acts 2:17) is hardly typical of Lucan eschatology and is therefore probably primitive; and the language of Joel 2:28 ("pour out") has stamped itself on early Christian talk of the Spirit (Acts 2:17 f., 33; 10:45; Rom. 5:5; Tit. 3:6). Acts 20:16 may even indicate that the Jerusalem church observed Pentecost as the anniversary of the Spirit's outpouring (cf. 1 Cor. 16:18; G. Kretschmar, op. cit., 247–53), though the thesis that Eph. is constructed on the basis of a Pentecostal renewal of the covenant baptismal liturgy (cf. J. C. Kirby, op. cit.) is built on too flimsy a foundation. That the first Christian Pentecost was an ecstatic experience involving vision (sound like wind, tongues as of fire) and glossolalia is clearly indicated by the tradition in Acts 2:1–13. In addition, the impression that the glossolalia included recognizable languages may well stem from those whose conversion to the new sect dated from that occasion (cf. similar claims in modern Pentecostalism; J. D. G. Dunn, op. cit., 146–52; → Other, art. *allos, heteros* NT 2; → Word, art. *glōssa*).

(b) This first Pentecost resulted in an enthusiastic community, bound together by common loyalty to the risen and soon coming Jesus and by their common experience of Spirit (Acts 3:19 f.) – the resurrection of Jesus and the gift of Spirit both constituting the beginning of the end-time harvest of final resurrection (Rom.

8:23; 1 Cor. 15:20, 23). Otherwise hardly distinct from the rest of Judaism, they doubtless regarded themselves as constituting eschatological Israel (cf. Matt. 16:18 f.; 19:28; Acts 1:6, 21 f.; J. D. G. Dunn, op. cit., 158–63). The Spirit was experienced primarily as the prophetic Spirit, in accordance with Jewish expectation (thus explicitly, Joel 2:28). This was seen as the privilege of all and not the prerogative of a few (Acts 2:17 f., 38 f.). The already established link between Pentecost, covenant renewal and the giving of the law probably prompted the first believers to interpret their experience of Spirit as the fulfilment of the promise of a new → covenant, as the → law written in their hearts (Deut. 30:6; Jer. 31:31–4; Ezek. 36:26 f.; 37:14; cf. Acts 2:38 f.; 3:25; 1 Cor. 11:25; Heb. 10:15 f., 29). But the implications of this insight for continuing faith and conduct were not recognized and elaborated until Paul (Rom. 2:28 f.; 7:6; 2 Cor. 3; Gal. 3:1–4:7; Phil. 3:3; Col. 2:11; 1 Thess. 4:8).

(c) The outpouring of the Spirit was probably attributed to the exalted Jesus from early on, as is implied by the tradition of the Baptist's predictions (Matt. 3:11 par. Lk. 3:16; cf. Acts 1:5; 11:16) and by Acts 2:33 (cf. 16:6 f.), perhaps also by Rom. 8:15 f.; Gal. 4:6; and the "faithful saying" of Tit. 3:5–7. But the relation between the exalted Jesus and the Spirit does not appear to have been the subject of much reflection prior to Paul and John. The suggestion that the Acts 2 narrative stems from a variant tradition of the resurrection appearance to "more than five hundred brethren" (E. von Dobschütz, *Ostern und Pfingsten*, 1903, 31–43) can hardly be sustained; the two traditions have no real point of contact. On the other hand, it is probable that most of the resurrection appearances listed by Paul in 1 Cor. 15:5–8 took place *after* Pentecost (J. D. G. Dunn, op. cit., 142–6).

3. *Significance of Pentecost for Luke.* (a) In his narrative Luke emphasizes some of the above points. It is important for Luke that Pentecost is the fulfilment of the divine promise (Lk. 24:49; Acts 1:4; 2:33, 38 f.; cf. 2:1; see E. Lohse "Die Bedeutung des Pfingstberichtes im Rahmen des lukanischen Geschichtswerkes," *EvTh* 13, 1953, 422–36). Thus it is also the fulfilment of covenant promise (2:39; 3:25; 13:23, 32; 26:6), emphasizing the rôle of Pentecost as the institution of the new → covenant. So too his description of events before and after Pentecost underlines that for Luke Pentecost is the birthday of the church (2:38, 41, 42, 43–7). And for Luke the Spirit of Pentecost is pre-eminently the prophetic Spirit, the inspirer of speech (Acts 2:4, 18 – note the addition of "and they shall prophesy"; 4:8, 31; 6:10; 10:46; 13:9; 19:6; → Prophet).

(b) Luke presents Pentecost as the beginning of world mission. The implementation of the programme of Acts 1:8 awaits Pentecost. Those who bear witness to the effects of the Spirit's outpouring and hear the gospel proclaimed by Peter represent "every nation under heaven" (2:5), while the appended list of nationalities embraces a wide sweep of the eastern Mediterranean, though with some odd omissions (2:9–11). The glossolalia is explicitly identified as the languages spoken by these foreign Jews (2:4, 6, 8, 11; cf. 1 Cor. 13:1; but contrast 1 Cor. 14:2; → Other, art. *allos, heteros* NT 2; → Word, art. *glōssa*). Finally, Peter's sermon ends with an open invitation and offer of the promised Spirit to "all that are far off" (2:39).

(c) Luke plays down the eschatological dimension of Pentecost-engendered enthusiasm. Whereas for the earliest Christians Pentecost was seen as the precursor of the end (see above 2 (b)), Luke strives to present Pentecost as the beginning of a

786

whole new epoch of salvation-history. This motif is already implicit in the fact that Pentecost begins a second volume rather than rounding off the first (cf. Acts 1:1 ff. with Luke 1:1–4). But it becomes most explicit in the sharp distinction that Luke draws between the epoch of Jesus, ended by resurrection appearances and ascension, and Pentecost, the beginning of the epoch of the Spirit. The two are clearly separated by the ten day "interregnum" when neither risen Jesus nor inspiring Spirit are in evidence and the election of Matthias has to revert to the old epoch's use of lots (Acts 1:26). The "last days" of the Spirit (Acts 2:17) seem to stretch over Luke's horizon (see J. D. G. Dunn, *Baptism in the Holy Spirit*, *SBT* Second Series 15, 1970, 44 ff.).

4. *Significance of Pentecost for the Fourth Gospel.* Jn. 20:22 may properly be called "the Johannine Pentecost", though not because John is contesting the Lucan dating of the outpouring of the Spirit, but rather because he wishes to bring out other aspects of theological significance (J. D. G. Dunn, *Baptism in the Holy Spirit*, 173–82).

(a) In particular John wishes to emphasize that the gift of the Spirit is not to be separated from the event of Jesus' death, resurrection and ascension; it is the immediate and direct result and consequence of Jesus' "glorification" and "ascending" (6:62 f.; 19:30; cf. 3:3 with 3:13, and 19:34 with 7:38 f.).

(b) So too John wishes to affirm the immediate *continuity* between Jesus and the Spirit (contrast Luke, see above 3 (c)). The Spirit is the *other* Paraclete (14:16 f.) whose coming fulfils Jesus' promise to return and dwell in his disciples (14:18–24; → Advocate). The Spirit given by the ascended Jesus constitutes the body and blood of Jesus, that is, gives the believer share in the life of the risen, glorified Christ (6:62 f.; 4:14).

(c) John brings out the epochal significance of the Pentecostal Spirit even more clearly than Luke by his use of the word *enephysēsen* ("breathed") in 20:22. Clearly echoing the use of the same word in Gen. 2:7, Ezek. 37:9 and Wisd. 15:11, John thereby presents the act of Jesus as a new creation.

(d) Finally, the earlier emphasis on mission is retained by bracketing 20:22 with vv. 21 and 23; → forgiveness or retention of sins is a charismatic authority and part of Pentecostal mission; "the disciples" thereby commissioned are not "the twelve" or "the apostles" (never in John) but those gathered round Jesus during his passion (including women) who represent all who believe in Jesus (7:37 ff.). → Feast, → Gift, → Pour, → Spirit   *J. D. G. Dunn*

(a). H. R. Boer, *Pentecost and Missions*, 1961; J. D. G. Dunn, *Baptism in the Holy Spirit: A Re-examination of the New Testament Teaching on the Gift of the Spirit in relation to Pentecostalism today*, *SBT* Second Series 15, 1970, 38–54, 173–82; and *Jesus and the Spirit: A Study of the Religious Charismatic Experience of Jesus and the First Christians as Reflected in the New Testament*, 1975, 135–56 (see also the bibliography, 457–75); S. M. Gilmour, "Easter and Pentecost", *JBL* 81, 1962, 62–6; J. H. E. Hull, *The Holy Spirit in the Acts of the Apostles*, 1967, 49–86; J. C. Kirby, *Ephesians, Baptism and Pentecost: An Inquiry into the Structure and Purpose of the Epistle to the Ephesians*, 1968; K. Lake, "The Gift of the Spirit on the Day of Pentecost", in F. J. Foakes Jackson and K. Lake, eds., *The Beginnings of Christianity: The Acts of the Apostles*, V, 1933, 111–21; C. S. Mann, "Pentecost in Acts" in J. Munck, *The Acts of the Apostles*, Anchor Bible, 1967, 271–75; B. M. Metzger, "Ancient Astrological Geography and Acts 2:9–11", in W. W. Gasque and R. P. Martin, eds., *Apostolic History and the Gospel: Biblical and Historical Essays Presented to F. F. Bruce*, 1970, 123–33; C. A. A. Scott. "What Happened at Pentecost", in B. H.

Streeter, ed., *The Spirit*, 1919, 117–57; C. F. Sleeper, "Pentecost and Resurrection", *JBL* 84, 1965, 189–99; H. J. Wotherspoon, *What Happened at Pentecost?*, 1937.
(b). N. Adler, *Das erste christliche Pfingstfest*, 1938; A. Cassien, *La Pentecôte Johannique*, 1939; E. von Dobschütz, *Ostern und Pfingsten*, 1903; J. Dupont, "La première Pentecôte chrétienne (Act. 2.1–11)", *Études sur les Actes des Apôtres*, 1967, 481–502; K. Haacker, "Das Pfingstwunder als exegetisches Problem", in O. Böcher und K. Haacker, eds., *Verborum Veritas. Festschrift für Gustav Stählin*, 1970, 125–32; J. Kremer, *Pfingstbericht und Pfingstgeschehen*, Stuttgarter Bibelstudien 63–64, 1973; G. Kretschmar, "Himmelfahrt und Pfingsten", *Zeitschrift für Kirchengeschichte* 66, 1954–55, 209–53; E. Lohse, "Die Bedeutung des Pfingstberichtes im Rahmen des lukanischen Geschichtswerkes", *EvTh* 13, 1953, 422–36; and *pentēkostē*, *TDNT* VI 44–53; K. L. Schmidt, *Die Pfingsterzählung und das Pfingstereignis*, 1919.

People, Nation, Gentiles, Crowd, City

The term people signifies a group of human beings who belong closely together because of a common history and a common country. In Gk. this concept is expressed most comprehensively and most frequently by the word *ethnos*. *laos*, on the other hand, is a term originating in the military sphere, and retains an archaic, political connotation. *dēmos* connotes the public nature of the people's assembly, while *ochlos* is the word for the crowd, the mass, the populace. *polis* has a definitely political character, signifying a community which lives together under a legal constitution, the city state.

The LXX and the NT have reserved for the old or new people of God the rarely used and not so precisely defined term *laos*, while other (pagan) peoples are generally called *ethnikoi* or *ethnē* (plur.). It may well be significant that the chief concept of Gk. political understanding, the *polis*, has only a peripheral place in the NT.

| δῆμος |

δῆμος (*dēmos*), people, populace, crowd, popular assembly; ἐκδημέω (*ekdēmeō*), leave one's country, emigrate, take a long journey; ἐνδημέω (*endēmeō*), be at home; παρεπίδημος (*parepidēmos*), foreigner, sojourner, stranger; δημόσιος (*dēmosios*), public.

CL 1. *dēmos* is derived from the root *dai-*, divide, and means originally, divided land, then district, province, subdivision of a people. But chiefly it means the people, popular assembly, commons, population. The word is used to refer to the people in contrast to the king, the nobility, or the men of power and landowners. In this kind of context it can have a derogatory sense. "But it can also have a proud ring, as in Athens, where it is used for the free, self-governing citizens" (W. Grundmann, *TDNT* II 63). In the Hellenistic period the term appears to have diminished in importance. This is connected with the general cultural development. Against the imperialism and expansionism of the Hellenistic and Roman empires, *dēmos*, like → *polis*, fell into the background.

2. Derived from *dēmos* are the vbs. *endēmeō*, to be in the homeland, at home, in the country, and *ekdēmeō* (from *ekdēmos*), to go abroad, go out of the country, travel. The latter is attested in Plato (*Leg.* 9, 864e; 12, 952d) and Hdt. (1, 30). *endēmeo* is not common until later (Plutarch, *De Genio Socratis* 6). A late form is *parepidēmos* (Polybius, 32, 6, 4), signifying a person who lives with another people in their lands. (For further examples see *TDNT* II 63 f.)

OT In the LXX the word *dēmos* is found about 100 times, chiefly to translate
mišpāḥâh, family, clan, i.e. a smaller grouping within the whole people or tribe.
dēmos is used about 50 times in Num. 3–4 and 26, and frequently also in Jos.
(especially chapter 21). Other places where it is found are Jdg., Dan., 1 and 2
Macc. The word is not used in the prophets. In Jdg. 13:2 the tribe of Dan is called
a *mišpāḥâh*, and the LXX consistently translates this by *dēmos*. In Dan. 8:24;
9:16 *dēmos* translates '*am*, people. In 1 and 2 Macc. there are a number of references
to the *dēmos tōn Ioudaiōn*, people of the Jews (1 Macc. 8:29; 12:6; 14:20–25;
15:17; 2 Macc. 11:34), a manner of description which in these writings can also
be used of other peoples. The compounds are not found in the LXX, except for
parepidēmos in Gen. 23:4 and Ps. 39:12 for Heb. *tôšāḇ*, sojourner.

NT 1. In the NT *dēmos* appears just 4 times in Acts. In Acts 12:22 it refers to the
pagan people who were present at the audience which Agrippa I gave to the
representatives of Tyre and Sidon, and who flattered him in a blasphemous fashion.
In Acts 17:5 it is uncertain whether the popular assembly is meant (W. M. Ramsay,
St. Paul the Traveller and the Roman Citizen, 1903[7], 228), before which the apostles
are to be brought in Thessalonica, or simply the throng of people who are present
(E. Haenchen, *The Acts of the Apostles*, 1971, 507). In Acts 19:30, 33, it is clearly
the crowd that is meant, and not an assembly called according to the legal provisions, as v. 39 demonstrates; *dēmos* is parallel to → *ochlos* (v. 33).

2. *ekdēmeō*, to be out of the country, abroad, and *endēmeō*, to be in the homeland, at home, in the land, are found in the NT only in 2 Cor. 5:6–9, where each
is used three times.

Paul longs for the fulfilment of Christ's work and his parousia (2 Cor. 4:18;
5:10), when according to 1 Cor. 15:43 f., 48–53 he will receive a new → body.
Now he contrasts here two realms of existence, or kinds of life, with one another:
the this-worldly, present, earthly life, and the other-worldly, future, heavenly.
In the present time he, like all men, has an earthly body: *endēmountes en tō sōmati*,
"we are at home in the body." That means, however, at the same time that he is
not living with Christ, in the other-worldly, heavenly sphere of existence. He is thus
"away from the Lord [*ekdēmountes apo tou kyriou*]"; he is as it were abroad, not
among his own *dēmos* to which he belongs. The clear and visible evidence of this
is the earthly body in which he lives. Only in faith, which is a gift of God, a guarantee (2 Cor. 5:5) of the world to come, can the gap between this world and that – or
the present and the future – be bridged, and even then not visibly (v. 7). For this
reason there grows out of faith the desire and longing to be with Christ and to
enjoy full fellowship with him. This is possible only when one leaves this body,
when one goes away from the body (*ekdēmēsai ek tou sōmatos*) and comes to
Christ, to be at home with the Lord (*endēmēsai pros ton kyrion*, v. 8). Then the
Christian will live in full fellowship with the Lord. The present is therefore marked
by the combination of "not yet" and "but already": the Christian is not yet perfect,
not yet with Christ, but he lives by faith in the certain hope that the consummation
will come, when he will be united with Christ. Always, however, whether in the
future when at home with the Lord (*eite endēmountes*) or in the present earthly life,
away from home (*eite ekdēmountes*), Paul strives to be pleasing to Christ (v. 9).
From a stylistic point of view it is interesting to note how Paul plays throughout

this passage on the vbs. *endēmeō* and *ekdēmeō* and their reference to the present and future.

3. *apodēmeō*, to go out of the country, to travel, is found 6 times in the NT, all in synoptic parables. Matt. 21:33 par. Mk. 12:1, Lk. 20:9 tell of a man (Matt. calls him a householder, *oikodespotēs*) who let out his vineyard to tenants and went out of the country (on this parable see J. D. M. Derrett, *Law in the New Testament*, 1970, 286–312). In the parable of the talents the man who is about to go out of the country (*apodēmōn*) gives his property to his servants to manage (Matt. 25:14), and goes away (*apedēmēsen*, v. 15) (on the parable see J. D. M. Derrett, op. cit., 17–31). In the parable of the prodigal son the younger son took his share of the inheritance and made a journey (*apedēmēsen*, Lk. 15:13) into a far country. In the parables of the wicked husbandmen and the talents *apodēmeō* represents God's absence and the fact that he has given his people an autonomy and responsibility of which they shall have to give account. In the parable of the prodigal son it represents the action of the son is going away from God. In the context of Lk. 15:1 it characterizes the kind of life led by the "tax collectors and sinners" who "were all drawing near to hear him."

4. The word *parepidēmos*, foreigner, sojourner, which is derived from *parepidēmeō*, to stay for a short time in a strange place, occurs 3 times in the NT (1 Pet. 1:1; 2:11, Heb. 11:13; → Foreign, art. *parepidēmos*).

5. *dēmosios* means public, i.e. belonging to the state (Acts 5:18). In the dat. form *dēmosia* it is used as an adv., publicly (Acts 16:37; 18:28; 20:20).

H. Bietenhard

ἔθνος

ἔθνος (*ethnos*), nation, people, heathen, pagans, Gentiles; ἐθνικός (*ethnikos*), heathen, Gentile; ἐθνικῶς (*ethnikōs*), like the Gentiles.

CL *ethnos*, derived from *ethos*, custom, habit, means a group which is held together by customs, a clan; then, crowd, company, people. The word came to be used in the derogatory sense of common people. *ethnos* is especially used to mean foreigners, in contrast to the → Greek who is a Hellene (Aristotle, *Pol.* 1324b, 10). This gives *ethnos* a derogatory undertone, which approaches *barbaros*, non-Greek, barbarian. Later *ethnos* was used to describe subject peoples.

OT 1. *ethnos* appears in the LXX about 1000 timcs (mostly in plur.), and in the overwhelming majority of cases it stands for the Heb. *góy* and the plur. *góyim*, though in something over 130 cases for '*am* (→ *laos*). The various other Heb. words which are translated *ethnos* are by comparison unimportant. Where mention is made of many peoples, particularly when they are non-Israelite, the plur. '*ammîm* is also translated *ethnē*, not *laoi* (Exod. 19:5 f.). There is thus a contrast between '*am* or → *laos*, i.e. Israel as the chosen people, and *góyim* or *ethnē*, the Gentiles. The Eng. Gentile derives from the Lat. *gens*, nation, which was used in the Vulg., and means of or pertaining to any or all the nations other than the Jewish nation. *ethnē* appears relatively seldom in Exod., Lev., Num., Jos., and Chr., and much more frequently in Gen., Deut., Pss., and the prophets.

790

2. Israel is the people for God's own possession (Exod. 19:5), while the rest of mankind outside → Israel are called the *ethnē*, the nations (Deut. 4:27; 18:9). A typical passage is Exod. 33:13, where *ethnos* is the multitude which by Yahweh's grace becomes his people (→ *laos*). The contrast is just as stark in Deut. 7:6. Yahweh has separated the *ethnē* over the earth and fixed their bounds according to the number of the angels of God (*angelōn theou*, LXX, followed in RSV and confirmed by a Hebrew fragment of Deut. 32 from Qumran; but the MT has *benê yiśrā'ēl*, sons of Israel). But Jacob as Yahweh's portion has become the *laos* of God (Deut. 32:8 f. LXX). On the other hand, Yahweh is certainly seen as King over the nations (Jer. 10:7). This is the point behind Gen. 10, where the thought is not of a uniform humanity sprung from the earliest patriarchs, but of "a group of nations divided according to clans and differing in language, custom and situation" (G. Bertram, *TDNT* II 367).

The Gentiles are first Israel's neighbours, some of whom live in Palestine itself (Jdg. 3:1). They entice Israel into idolatry, and so to → fall away from Yahweh. Thus we often read of the "abominations of the Gentiles" (e.g. 1 Ki. 14:24; 2 Ki. 16:3). In the face of Israel's sin, the nations can often become the means and instruments of God's wrath and judgment (Hos. 8:10; Amos 9:9). But if they over-reach themselves and go beyond the commission given them by Yahweh, they incur judgment themselves (Isa. 8:9; 10:5). The break-up of the state is a punishment for the falling away of the people into heathen practices (1 Ki. 11:1 ff.; 2 Ki. 17:7–23). On the other hand, the Gentile Cyrus can be called God's anointed and become the saviour of Israel (Isa. 45:1 ff.). A universalizing tendency in the LXX may be detected in the fact that in Dan. 9:6 LXX the prophets are said to have reached to every people on earth. Over against the world empires there stands the kingdom of God (Dan. 4:34). In the end time the nations will come to Mount Zion and there share in salvation (cf. Isa. 2:2–4; 25:6–8; Mic. 4:1–3; Zech. 8:20–23). The nations await the messiah (Gen. 49:10 LXX). Thus the negative evaluation of the Gentile world is, in the last analysis, not lasting and permanent. Even in the present the name of Yahweh is to be glorified among all the Gentiles (Ps. 18:49; 46:10). Dan., Est. and Macc. tell of the troubles of the righteous under the domination of the Gentiles.

3. (a) Judaism. In Jub. 10:22 the origin of the nations is traced to human sin (cf. Gen. 11), whereas in 2 Esd. 3:7, 12 they are said to have arisen naturally (though after the fall), because God gave man the blessing of fertility.

(b) In the view of Rabbinic Judaism, the non-Israelite *gôy* is a stranger to God and far from him, counting for nothing. The Gentiles are themselves to blame for this state of affairs: they too were offered the Torah, but rejected God's instruction. They are, therefore, condemned to the judgment of → hell, without hope of salvation, and have no part in the world to come. Only in very exceptional cases is a share in the perfect world to come promised to pious Gentiles. The basic conception is formulated in this way: "Rabbi Simeon ben Yochai said: God spake to the Israelites: I am God over all men who come into the world, but my name I have joined only to you; I am called not the God of the nations of the world, but the God of Israel" (Exod. R. 29, 88d; cf. SB III 185). In the other words, God is the creator of all, but he loves Israel alone.

As individuals, Gentiles have been given up to every possible vice (idolatry, immorality). In Jewish eyes the Gentiles were unclean: they themselves, their wives and children, their houses and lands (SB I 540, 571; II 838; IV 374 f.). If in an exceptional instance they do something good, God rewards them at once, in in order to avoid having to reward them in the world to come. The punishment for their sins is delayed by God until the measure is full; then judgment falls upon them. In contrast to Israel, the Gentile world has no eternal existence. The great turning-point will be the messianic age: then the nations who have made Israel their subjects (especially Rome!) will be destroyed by the messiah and finish up in hell. Other nations who have had no contact with Israel will be subjected to the messiah who will thus become ruler of the world. As far as religion is concerned, in the view of one universalistic school of thought, the Gentiles will then be given access to the blessings of Israel's salvation. The messiah is the → light of the Gentiles, who will flock around him; he will save all Gentiles who call on God, and many of them will join themselves to Israel as proselytes.

The political catastrophes of the years A.D. 66–70 and 132–135 created great bitterness among the Jews. The view arose that in the messianic age there would be no more proselytes. Only a person who joins himself to Israel during the time of his sufferings can be a proselyte. Nevertheless, the messiah will lay upon the nations thirty commandments, in order that they may become as much like Israel as possible. But they remain Gentiles, and in the final onslaught of the nations (Gog and Magog) they will join in the attack upon Israel (SB III 120 f., 139–42, 144–55).

(c) Jewish missionary activity and proselytism. In the pre-Christian era and up to A.D. 70 the Jews, particularly the Hellenistic Jews, carried out a strong propaganda and missionary activity or, to be more precise, proselytism (cf. Philo, *Vit.Mos.* 2, 4, 7). Matt. 23:15 indicates that this was also true of the Palestinian Jews. Josephus (cf. *Ap.* 2, 10, 36), Seneca, Dio Cassius and others bear witness to the great success of this propaganda (cf. also the many half or full proselytes whom Paul met, according to Acts, in the Jewish Diaspora; → Conversion, art. *prosēlytos*). A spectacular conversion was that of the royal house of Adiabene (in northern Iraq) to Judaism around A.D. 44 (Josephus, *Ant.* 20, 2, 4), which was won over by a Palestinian Jew by the name of Eleazar. The number of Jews in the Roman Empire was as a result of this propaganda disproportionately high, viz. some 6–8% of the population.

The position changed after A.D. 70 and A.D. 135, and from then onwards the making of proselytes declined greatly. Those who wanted to become proselytes had to come of their own initiative, though they were received in a friendly manner. An added difficulty arose in A.D. 135, when the emperor Hadrian forbade people to become Jews. It was at this point that the Christians got their great opportunity, for their Jewish rivals were disqualified. Even so, the church was not always clearly distinguished from Judaism (cf. W. H. C. Frend, *Martyrdom and Persecution in the Early Church*, 1965, 225–8).

(d) Qumran. The linguistic usage of the Qumran writings is not completely consistent. Usually the nations are called *gôy* or *gôyim*, but occasionally also *'am*, *'ammîm*. In each case the context in which the word is used must be studied with care. The attitude to Gentiles is completely negative. The Gentile nations are idol-worshippers, without God (1QpHab 12:13; 13:3 f.) and enemies of God (1QM 12:11). God commits the judgment of all nations into the hands of his chosen ones

(1QpHab 5:4). The War Scroll depicts a great forty-years war in the end time which is directed against all Gentile nations, and in which they will be destroyed (1QM 1:1–7; 2:10–15 and passim). In this way the nations will reap the reward of their wickedness (1QM 6:6). Emphasis is given to the fact that it will be the Qumran people themselves, the "sons of light", who will carry out this work of punishment and destruction (1QM 11:8f.; 14:7). No foreigner or stranger will enter the eschatological temple (1Qflor 1:4); but the riches of the nations will be brought in through the gates of Jerusalem (1QM 12:14; 19:6; cf. Isa. 60:3, 5 and in the NT Rev. 21:24).

For the present comfort may be taken from the knowledge that God will not allow his people (*'am*) to be destroyed by the hand of the nations (*gôyim*, 1QpHab 5:3). A somewhat different note is struck in 1QH 6:12 f.: "All the nations [*gôyim*] shall acknowledge Thy Truth, and all the peoples [*le'ummîm*] Thy glory. For Thou wilt bring Thy glorious [salvation] to all the men of Thy Council, to those who share a common lot with the Angels of the Face."

NT In the NT *ethnos* occurs 162 times, including 43 in Acts and 54 in the Pauline letters. It is used about 40 times in quotations from the OT. The *ethnē* mean all peoples, as is often made clear by the epithet *panta*, all (cf. Matt. 24:9; 28:19; Mk. 11:17; Lk. 21:24; Rom. 15:11).

1. (a) Even the Jewish people can be called *ethnos* (in 14 places, e.g. Lk. 7:5; 23:2; Acts 10:22). In the NT it no longer has as matter of course the meaning which overwhelmingly predominates in the OT, i.e. → *laos*. The context or qualifying phrases makes it clear in each of these cases that the reference is to Jews. In other places, however, (e.g. Acts 26:23) a clear distinction is drawn between → *laos*, the people of → Israel, and the *ethnē* or Gentiles. John's Gospel in particular calls Israel *ethnos*, because he sets himself against faith in Jesus Christ (Jn. 11:48, 50 ff.; 18:35).

(b) *ethnē* clearly refers to Gentiles in Matt. 4:15 (cf. Isa. 8:23); 20:25; Lk. 21:24; Acts 4:25 (cf. Ps. 2:1 f.); 7:7; 13:19; Rom. 1:5; Gal. 3:8 (the reference to Abraham makes it clear that Gentile nations are meant); Rev. 10:11; 14:8; 15:3 f.

2. In about 100 instances *ethnos* is used in contrast to Jews and Christians. The disciples of Jesus are told to pray differently from the *ethnē* (Matt. 6:32), and not to be anxious like them (Lk. 12:30). Gentiles are mentioned alongside → Samaritans (Matt. 10:5). Jesus teaches the future salvation of the Gentiles, although he was sent only to the Jews (Matt. 8:10 f.; 15:24). In the judgment which will come upon → Jerusalem the Gentiles will tread it down until the times of the Gentiles are fulfilled (Lk. 21:24). One of the horrors of the end-time will be the rising of nation against nation (Matt. 24:7 par. Mk. 13:8, Lk. 21:10).

3. The distinction between Jews and Gentiles is spoken of chiefly in Acts and the epistles, i.e. in the missionary documents of the NT. God is not the God of the Jews only, but also of the Gentiles (Rom. 3:29; Rev. 15:3), but the Gentiles do not know God (1 Thess. 4:5) and are led astray to idols (1 Cor. 12:2). They do not know the → law of God and do not keep it (Gal. 2:15); they live in the futility of their minds (Acts 14:16; Eph. 4:17). Although the word *ethnos* is not used, the Gentiles are meant in Rom. 1:18–32, where Paul speaks of men who do not know

God, have fallen into idolatry, and have therefore been given up by God to all kinds of evil. Nevertheless, there are *ethnē* who fulfil the requirements of the law (Rom. 2:14 f.; → God, art. *theos* NT 4 (b)). The Gentiles begin life outside the → call of God and outside the salvation of God's people (Eph. 2:11 f.). Jews and Gentiles are alike in rejecting the cross (1 Cor. 1:23).

4. Occasionally Paul can call Gentile Christians simply *ethnē* (Rom. 11:13; Gal. 2:12; cf. also Eph. 3:1), although the *ethnē* usually stand in contrast to the Christians (1 Cor. 5:1; 12:2; 1 Pet. 2:12).

5. (a) There is a soteriological distinction and contrast between Jews and Gentiles: Israel is the people whom God has appointed for his own → possession and his service. The Gentiles are outside this unique relationship. By God's own act, however, the difference has been overcome: the messiah has come in the person of Jesus, and now even those born Gentiles have a share in God's → covenant and salvation. (This is in keeping with universalistic thinking in contemporary Judaism.) Thus Peter discovers that the God-fearing Gentile is acceptable to God, so that the Holy → Spirit can come upon him, and Gentiles accept the gospel (Acts 10:35, 45; 11:1, 18; cf. Eph. 2:11 f., 17–22). In 1 Thess. 4:13; 5:6; Eph. 2:3 (cf. Rev. 9:20) *hoi loipoi*, "the rest", is practically a synonym for *ta ethnē*, "the Gentiles" (cf. F. M. Chase, *The Syro-Latin Text of the Gospels*, 1895, 93; M. Black, *An Aramaic Approach to the Gospels and Acts*, 1967³, 176).

(b) Paul is in a special way the apostle of the Gentiles, in the face of opposition from the Jews (1 Thess. 2:16). To him has been entrusted the mystery (→ Secret) that the Gentiles are called to Jesus Christ apart from the law (Gal. 1:16; 2:7–9; Rom. 1:5; cf. Eph. 3:1–13). This is not to say that Paul in any way denies the prior claim of the Jews. Rather, he strongly emphasizes it. Israel is and remains God's people, and therefore is in possession of all the gifts and titles which mark it out as different (Rom. 9:4 f.). The relationship of Jews to Gentiles is given fundamental treatment in Rom. 9–11 (cf. also Eph. 2 f.). The Gentiles who have come to faith in Jesus Christ have been grafted into the rich olive tree (Rom. 11:17; → Oil, art. *elaion*), and are supported by it. Hence, there can be no division between Christians and Gentiles. The Pauline churches consist both of born Jews and born Gentiles, and both belong to the people of God by faith in Jesus Christ. They are children of of Abraham by virtue of their faith (Rom. 4:16 f., cf. Gen. 17:5; Gal. 3:7, cf. Gen. 12:3; Gal. 3:13 f., 26–29). Gentiles, who have not pursued righteousness, have become recipients of the righteousness which comes by faith (Rom. 9:30). Salvation has come to them through the fall and unbelief of Israel (Rom. 11:11), and the failure of the Jews has meant riches for the Gentiles (Rom. 11:12). As the apostle to the Gentiles, Paul is seeking to save as many of the Gentiles as possible, in order ultimately to win the Jews for the gospel (Rom. 11:13 f.; cf. 10:19 where Deut. 32:21 is cited). When the full number of the Gentiles has come in, Israel too will turn to Christ (Rom. 11:11 f., 25). The Gentiles are no longer strangers (→ Foreign, art. *xenos*) and sojourners (→ Foreign, art. *parepidēmos*), but fellow citizens (*sympolitai*) and members (*oikeioi*) of the household of God (Eph. 2:19).

(c) Evidence of the priority of the Jews is apparent in the record of Acts, where Paul preaches to the Gentiles only after the Jews have rejected the gospel (Acts 13:46; 18:6; 19:9). The question of the mission to the Gentiles, as carried out by

Paul, is discussed and settled at the so-called Council of Jerusalem (Acts 15). The Jews accuse Paul of teaching the Jews of the Diaspora (those who live among the *ethnē*) to forsake Moses (Acts 21:21).

6. According to Revelation, Christ has ransomed a church for himself out of every nation, and has made them his → kingdom and → priests (Rev. 5:9 f., following Exod. 19:6). Along with the chosen of Israel is an innumerable multitude from the Gentiles (Rev. 7:9). The exalted Christ will rule the nations with a rod of iron (Rev. 12:5; → Crown, art. *rhabdos*; → Gold, art. *sidēros*), and also gives authority to "him who conquers" to do so (Rev. 2:26 f.). He will smite them with the sword in his mouth (Rev. 19:15). In the time of the two witnesses, the temple court is given over to the Gentiles (Rev. 11:2). All nations will see the dead bodies of the two witnesses (Rev. 11:9). The beast has authority over all nations and peoples, whose name is not written in the book of life (Rev. 13:7 f.; → Animal). The eternal gospel will be preached to all nations (Rev. 14:6). As for the harlot → Babylon, all nations have drunk "the wine of her impure passion" and have been deceived by her sorcery (Rev. 14:8; 18:3, 23). In the judgments of God, the cities of the Gentiles will fall (Rev. 16:19). During the millennium Satan is unable to deceive the nations (Rev. 20:3; → Number, art. *chilias*), but does so again as soon as he is freed (Rev. 20:8). In God's new world the *ethnē* walk in the light of the new → Jerusalem, and bring their treasures into the new city (Rev. 21:24, 26).

7. *ethnikos* (adv. *ethnikōs*) means national, foreign, like a Gentile; and as a noun, Gentile. The word does not occur in the LXX; the adj. appears only 5 times times in the NT, and the adv. once. The Gentile salutes only his brothers; if any of Jesus' disciples behave in the same way, he makes himself like an *ethnikos* (Matt. 5:47). In prayer the disciple is not to heap up empty phrases (*battalogeō*) like the Gentiles (Matt. 6:7). M. Black suggests Gentiles here might represent an Aramaic phrase meaning "the rest of men", i.e. those who were not Jesus' disciples (cf. the Bezan text of Lk. 11:2; M. Black, *An Aramaic Approach to the Gospels and Acts*, 1967³, 176 ff.). He who refuses to listen to a rebuke by the church thereby cuts himself off and joins the Gentiles and unrepentant tax-collectors (Matt. 18:17; → Bind; → Open). In Antioch Peter had eaten with Gentile Christians and so transgressed the Jewish ritual regulations, thus living *ethnikōs*, like the Gentiles; Paul argues that he therefore can no longer force the Gentile Christians to observe the law (Gal. 2:14). For membership of the Jewish people, determined by the law, has now been superseded by the fellowship of faith in Christ, which unites Jewish and Gentile Christians.   *H. Bietenhard*

λαός	λαός (*laos*), people.

CL *laos* (etymology of *laos* is uncertain; perhaps a foreign word) is a Doric and Aeolic form (Ionic *lēos*; Attic *leōs*). In Homer it means a number of men, a crowd (e.g. *Il*. 18, 497 ff.; 24, 665), and more specifically an army, a military company, men at arms, troops (e.g. *Il*. 1, 226; 9, 424; 10, 14). At a later period this meaning disappeared, and the word meant the common people, folk, population; in the plur., the multitude of individuals out of whom the people is made up (cf.

→ Church, art. *ekklēsia*; *qāhāl* in the OT). In addition to epic poetry (e.g. *Od.* 3, 214), the word is found in Hdt. (e.g. 8, 136), Pindar (e.g. *Pythian Odes* 9, 54 f.), the tragedians (e.g. Aesch. *Persae* 770) and Aristophanes (e.g. *Ranae* 676). But it is almost entirely lacking in Attic prose. It retains an archaic and solemn, poetic tone (even in Josephus, *Ant.* 4, 114).

OT 1. In the LXX the word occurs about 2,000 times, with a new meaning which brought it renewed life. The plur. (not quite 140 times) always means nations, and so is synonymous with → *ethnē* (cf. Ezek. 23:24, → *ochlos laōn*, a host of peoples, with Ezek. 31:12; *laoi tōn ethnōn*, the individual nations of the Gentile world, Ez. 9:11 LXX). In this expression *laos* could be interpreted as a group deliberately formed, and *ethnos* as a natural grouping bound by clan ties and a common descent.

laos often means the people, in contrast to the ruler or ruling class (cf. Gen. 41:40; 47:21; Exod. 1:22; Jer. 23:34), such as the inhabitants of a city (Gen. 19:4), the members of a tribe (Gen. 49:16), the people who accompanied Esau and the servants of Jacob (Gen. 33:15; 32:8; 35:6). Even the dead belong to it (Gen. 25:8; 49:33). These passages are not, however, typical for the LXX usage of the word.

2. To the translators of the LXX the term *laos*, derived from the language of high style and ceremony, and infrequently used in the Gk. of their time, seemed ideally suited for expressing the special relationship of → Israel to Yahweh. *laos* serves in the overwhelming majority of cases as a translation of the Heb. *'am* and means Israel as the chosen people of God, just as, on the other hand, the Heb. *gôy* is used particularly for the Gentiles (*ethnē*).

About 10 times Israel is called the "people of Yahweh". In another 300 cases we find forms with a pronominal suffix (e.g. *'ammî*, "my people"), where the suffix refers to Yahweh. On about 200 occasions Yahweh is called the "God of Israel"; again we must add more than 600 examples with a suffix referring to Israel. In the oldest passage we know in the OT where the expression *'am YHWH*, "people of Yahweh", occurs it means the army, the levy of the people, as they march down to battle (Jdg. 5:11, 13). This meaning of the word is still found at a later period (2 Sam. 1:12). Corresponding to it – even before the Song of Deborah – is the expression "Yahweh, God of Israel" (Gen. 33:20; Jos. 8:30; 24:23; cf. Jdg. 5:3, 5; and likewise in the mouth of the people, "Yahweh our God", or in the mouth of Yahweh, "I am Yahweh your God").

3. (a) The tribes which came into Palestine from Egypt brought to Shechem, where the so-called "Leah tribes" had already settled, not only the worship of the God Yahweh, but also the phrase "people of Yahweh". When the two groups of tribes joined one another, the covenant formula was adopted: "Yahweh the God of Israel – Israel his people". Jos. 24:17 f. contains the statement, "Yahweh is our God" (cf. Exod. 24:9 f.); yet the specific pronouncement that Israel is Yahweh's people is still lacking. Admittedly, in the story of the call of → Moses, Yahweh says of Israel, "My people" (Exod. 3:7), "My people Israel" (Exod. 3:10; cf. the word to Pharaoh, Exod. 5:1; 7:16). Moses also speaks in the same way to Yahweh, calling Israel "Thy people" (Exod. 5:23). It is now, however, until the formation of the state that the identification of Israel with the people of Yahweh is clearly made

(1 Sam. 9:16 f.; 10:1). Yahweh's people is now no longer an army brought together by the call to battle, but all Israel, and that permanently. To be "prince" or "king" over Yahweh's people" is the honorific title of the kings (cf. 1 Sam. 13:14; 15:1; 2 Sam. 5:2; 1 Ki. 14:7).

The phrase "Yahweh, God of Israel" is of great importance, and is used particularly in formal speech: in swearing an oath (Jos. 9:18 f.), in prayer (Jdg. 21:3; 1 Sam. 23:10 f.; Ps. 69:6), in praising God (1 Ki. 1:48), or to introduce divine utterances (cf. Jos. 7:13; 1 Sam. 2:30; 1 Ki. 11:31; and often).

(b) In the prophetic crisis, when the relationship between Yahweh and the people has been broken (Isa. 1:3; 5:25), Yahweh turned in words of judgment and threats "against my people Israel" (Amos 7:8, 15; 8:2). To fall away and follow Baal is all the more serious to Yahweh, because for him Israel is "my people" (Hos. 4:6 ff.). The exhortation addressed to them is, therefore, "Return to your God" (Hos. 12:6). Hosea's third child is called *lō'-'ammî*, "not my people", and the reason given by Yahweh is "You are not my people, and I am not your God" (Hos. 1:9). For Israel has behaved as if she were not Yahweh's people. In contrast to this comes the eschatological promise, "You are my people" (Hos. 2:23); i.e. when Yahweh again turns to Israel, he will again become "My people".

(c) The important mutual declaration between Yahweh and Israel in Deut. 26:16–19, which was possibly pronounced at the → covenant ceremony which took place under king Josiah (cf. 2 Ki. 23:1–3), and which was traced back to → Moses (Exod. 24:7 f.; cf. 20:2; 6:7; Lev. 26:12), became, as the covenant formula, the gateway into the history of Israel. It thus acquired permanent authority and relevance. In the style of an adoption ceremony Yahweh declares both that Israel is to be his people, and that he will be Israel's God. Thus originated the formula which was traced back into the time of Moses: "I will be their God, and they shall be my people" (Jer. 7:23; 11:4). A similar formula is found in the post-exilic writings, as a prophecy for the future: "I will be your God, and you shall be my people" (cf. Jer. 24:7; 30:22; 32:38; Ezek. 11:20; 14:11; Zech. 8:8). The priestly literature also knows the statement that Yahweh will be Israel's God (cf. Gen. 17:7 f.; Exod. 29:45; Lev. 11:45). The *Sitz im Leben* of the covenant formula may have been priestly instruction or prophetic proclamation.

(d) It is regarded among the people as an established fact that Yahweh is Israel's God. Thus there often appears with the divine name the additional phrase "your God". In the same way *'am*, people, is further defined as "people of his possession" (e.g. Deut. 4:20; 7:6), "holy people" (e.g. Deut. 7:6; 14:2). The theme of Deuteronomy is the people of God; the covenant formula is embedded in instruction for the keeping of the law (cf. Deut. 26:12–19). God's gracious approach to the people remains, however, the starting point (cf. Jer. 11:3 ff.). It appears again projected into the future in the promise of the "new covenant" (Jer. 31:31–33; cf. 24:7; 32:38–40; Ezek. 36:26 ff.). The promise of the prophets can also go out beyond the borders of Israel and embrace the Gentile world (Zech. 2:11 f.; 14:16).

4. What makes Israel the *laos* is Yahweh's → election and → grace, and not mere national, natural and historical factors. This grace must be repeatedly confirmed by faithfulness and obedience. From an earthly, human point of view, unfaithfulness on the part of the people makes him lose everything that makes him the people. He then becomes a people like all the others, and indeed worse off than

they (Deut. 28:58–64). But because Yahweh keeps faith with his people despite all its apostasy and all unfaithfulness, Israel remains the people of God. He lives as such not through any achievement of his own, but because of Yahweh's faithfulness towards him. The character of Israel is thus determined not by himself, his origin or history, but solely by the fact that Yahweh keeps faith with him.

5. Judaism. (a) Philo used *laos* and *leōs*, especially in his writings on the Pentateuch, but the specific, historical meaning of the word is lost amid his speculations (cf. *Sacr.* 6 f.). He interprets the "chosen people" (Deut. 7:7) as individual wise men also constitute the head of humanity (*Praem.* 123, 125). In Josephus' *Antiquities* the influence of LXX usage may be seen in his use of the word *laos* for Israel, though occasionally he also uses it for other nations, e.g. Egypt (*Ant.* 2, 301). In *War* and *Ap.* Josephus also uses → *ethnos* and → *dēmos* indiscriminately.

(b) In the Rabbinic literature and the Pseudepigrapha it is part of the foundation of all faith that Israel is God's chosen people. Israel is God's possession, his portion, and his lot.

Israel's special relationship to his God is expressed in metaphors taken from family life: Israel is Yahweh's → firstborn son (2 Esd. 6:58), the Israelites are God's brothers and kinsmen (SB III 263 f., 682), royal children (Shabbath 14:4). Even the poorest among them are children of Abraham (SB IV 714). As a special token of Yahweh's love it has been revealed to them that they are children of God (Aboth 3:14), and only they are called God's children (2 Esd. 6:58). Israel is also called the bride, the betrothed, the spouse of God (SB III 822 f.). What is expressed in this terminology is not an ethical relationship but an inborn one.

Alongside these ideas there is that of friendship between Yahweh and Israel (Tanh. 20). As in the OT, Israel is the "holy people", because he has the Torah and does not worship idols (Sifra Lev. 20:7). The world was created for Israel's sake, and without Israel it cannot continue in existence (2 Esd. 6:55 ff.; SB I 833; III 140, 248). Israel is the "righteous one" whom the rest of the world has to thank for its life: were it not for Israel, God would have destroyed the world long since. The present time with its gifts is of little importance in comparison with the coming messianic time. Then the people will receive all God's gifts in their fullness, and dominion over the world, and the people of the world – in so far as they still exist at all – will be his servants. The thought finds expression in the saying in the Mishnah, "All Israelites have a share in the world to come" (Sanhedrin 10:1). The only exceptions are serious sinners and the evil generations mentioned in the scriptures (SB III 293).

(c) In the writings of the Qumran community *'am* often means Israel. He is the people chosen from all peoples (1QM 10:9), with whom God has made an eternal covenant (1QM 13:7), and whom he has redeemed to be a people for ever (1QM 13:9). He is the people of God's redemption (1QM 14:5) whom he will not allow to be destroyed by other nations (1QpHab 5:3). The wicked among God's people he will destroy (1QpHab 5:5). Among the people there is, however, a "remnant" (1QH 6:8), the "saints of his people" (1QM 6:6).

The Qumran community thus described itself as the *'am*, the people (1QM 1:12), the "people of the saints of the covenant" (1QM 10:10), as the "elect of the holy people" (1QM 12:1). They called themselves the "assembly of the people" (CD 19:35). The "people" is the army in the final conflict (1QM 9:1; 10:2), or a particular company within this army (1QM 8:9; 16:7). In the hierarchy of the Qumran community the "people" has the third place following the priests and Levites (1QS 2:21; 6:9).

In numerous other places '*am* and '*ammîm* mean the nations, the Gentiles. God is praised as the creator who has brought about the division of the nations (1QM 10:14). A sword is coming over all nations (1QM 16:1), so that they will be shattered (1QH 4:26). Their heroes will be brought low by God (1QM 11:13), and their princes will be thrust down (1QSb 3:28; 5:27).

NT 1. *laos* occurs 141 times in the NT, 84 being in Luke alone (Gospel and Acts) and 14 in Matt., 12 in Paul, 13 in Heb., 9 in Rev. It is probable that the language and concepts of the LXX are here exerting an influence, though *laos* often follows a previous reference to → *ochlos* and carries the same meaning (e.g. Lk. 7:24, 29; 8:42, 47; cf. also Matt. 27:25 f.; Mk. 14:2), or stands instead of *ochlos* in a parallel passage (e.g. Lk. 19:48, cf. Mk. 11:18; Lk. 20:45, cf. Matt. 23:1). When used on its own, *laos* can mean also crowd, the common people (e.g. Lk. 1:10; 7:1; 20:1, 9; Acts 2:47). Many of these passages, however, refer to the activity of John the Baptist, Jesus or the apostles, whose ministry was practically restricted to Israel (cf. Matt. 4:23; 26:5; 27:64), and Israel is after all the *laos* and not an → *ethnos* (an exception being Jn. 11:50, where both words are used).

The plur. *laoi* is parallel to *ethnē* in Lk. 2:31 f. (cf. Isa. 40:5 f.; 42:6); Rom. 15:11 (cf. Ps. 117:1); Rev. 10:11 (cf. Dan. 3:4). The great multitude (→ *ochlos*) standing before the → Lamb comes from every → *ethnos* and *laos* (Rev. 7:9; 11:9; 17:15), and is intended to mean the whole of humanity.

A hyperbolic *pas*, → all, often precedes *laos* (e.g. Lk. 3:21; 7:29; Acts. 3:9; 5:34). We also read of the *plēthos tou laou*, lit. fullness of the people (Lk. 1:10; 6:17; Acts 21:36), which may be variously translated as the great multitude, the whole crowd. As in the LXX, *laos* can mean the people in contrast to the ruling classes (Lk. 22:2; 23:5; Acts 6:12), or in a cultic setting the broad mass of the people as opposed to the priest (Heb. 5:3; 7:27), or again, the ordinary people as opposed to the few witnesses of the resurrection (Acts. 10:41; 13:31).

2. In keeping with the LXX, → Israel is described as the *laos* (the *laos Israēl*, "people of Israel", e.g. Acts 4:10; 13:17; *houtos ho laos*, "this people", in OT quotations at Matt. 13:15 [cf. Isa. 6:10]; 15:8 [cf. Isa. 29:13]; Acts 28:26 f. [cf. Isa. 6:9 f.]). The idea is also alluded to when the high priests, scribes and elders or leaders of the *laos* are spoken of (e.g. Matt. 2:4; 21:23; Lk. 19:47; Acts 4:9); when it is said that Jesus will save his people from their sins (Matt. 1:21; → God, art. *Emmanouēl*; cf. Lk. 1:68, 77; 2:10, 32), or that God has visited his *laos* by sending his prophet Jesus (Lk. 7:16; 24:19), or that he will not reject his *laos*, Israel (Rom. 11:1 f.; cf. Ps. 94:14). Even an individual synagogue can be called *laos* (Acts 13:15); it is God's people in a particular place (→ Church, Synagogue). The same line of thought is present when Israel as the *laos* is set over against the Gentiles as *ethnē* (Acts 4:25 ff.; cf. LXX Deut. 32:43; Ps. 2:1; cf. also 26:23; Rom. 15:10). Pilate is here identified with the *ethnē*, and Herod and Israel with the *laoi*. Frequently qualifying phrases or the context show that *laos* means Israel, e.g. in the use of the word as parallel for "Jews" in Acts 12:4; in a list along with "law" and "temple" in Acts 21:28, or "customs of the fathers" in Acts 28:17;

in the comment that the God-fearing Gentile Cornelius had done much good to the *laos* (Acts 10:2).

3. Finally the honoured title of Israel, that of being God's *laos*, is transferred to the Christian → church. God has taken from the *ethnē* a *laos* for his → name (Acts 15:14). He has called a church from the Jews and the Gentiles (Rom. 9:24; Hos. 1:10). This church (even as a local church, cf. Acts 18:10) is the → temple and *laos* of God (2 Cor. 6:14 ff.; the quotations from Lev. 26:12 and Ezek. 37:27 refer in the original setting to Israel, but are here applied to the Christian church). The description of Israel as the *laos periousios*, people of his possession (Exod. 19:5 f.; 23:22; Deut. 7:6; 14:2; → Possessions), is likewise claimed for the Christian church (Tit. 2:14; cf. 1 Pet. 2:9).

In Heb., especially, the statements of the OT cultus, seen as types of Christ, are transferred to the church. The Son of God became man to atone for the sins of the *laos* (Heb. 2:17), which he sanctified with his blood (Heb. 13:12). The church is the *laos* for whom a → Sabbath rest remains (Heb. 4:9), and it is to the church that the warning of Ps. 135:14 applies (Heb. 10:30). Similarly in Rev. 18:4 (cf. Jer. 51:45) and 21:3 (cf. Zech. 2:10; Ezek. 37:27) OT passages are applied to the church as the new people of God. This means that by faith in Jesus Christ as the *kyrios*, → Lord, the church becomes the *laos theou*, people of God, irrespective of the national background of its members (Gal. 3:26 ff.; 1 Cor. 12:13; Col. 3:11). That is not, of course, to say that in the NT the church has simply taken the place of Israel as the people of God, as if Israel had lost the priority given to her by God. This is perhaps the major problem that Paul wrestles with in Rom. His conclusion is that Israel is and remains God's people, and has not been rejected by God (cf. Rom. 9–11, especially, Rom. 9:4 f.; 11:1 f.). "A hardening has come upon part of Israel, until the full number of the Gentiles come in, and so all Israel will be saved. . . . For God has consigned all men to disobedience, that he may have mercy upon all" (Rom. 11:25 f., 32; cf. also chs. 1–4). *H. Bietenhard*

| ὄχλος | ὄχλος (*ochlos*), (throng of) people, crowd, mob. |

CL *ochlos* (derivation uncertain, attested since Pindar), means a crowd, throng; the public, in contrast to individual people, and particularly in contrast to the nobility or people of rank, "*ochlos* is often the 'leaderless and rudderless mob,' the 'politically and culturally insignificant mass' " (R. Meyer, *TDNT* V 583; cf. Plato, *Leg.* 2, 670b). In the military world the word means a company, troop, army. But it can also mean people. When the thought of size is uppermost it can mean a great crowd.

OT In the LXX *ochlos* occurs about 60 times, chiefly in later books as a translation of several words including *hāmôn*, crowd (1 Ki. 20[21]:13; 2 Chr. 20:15; Dan. 11:11 LXX; 10:6; 11:10–13 Theodotion); *ḥayil*, army; *'am*, people (Num. 20:20; Jer. 48[31]:42; 38[45]:1); *qāhāl*, assembly (Jer. 31[38]:8; Ezek. 16:40; 17:17; 23:24, 46 f.); *rabbîm*, many (2 Esd. 3:12). In Dan. 3:4 it means people; in Dan. 10:6 (Theodotion) an unruly crowd; in Jer. 31:8 an assembled company of the people. The congregation of the people (*qāhāl*) which is to stone the adulteress becomes the *ochlos* in Gk. (Lev. 24:16). In other passages it means the camp-followers (Jud. 7:18; 1 Macc. 9:35), those unable to march; or, the army, mercenaries (1 Macc. 1:17; 20, 29; 2 Macc. 14:23, 43, 45 f.; 3 Macc. 2:7). In Ezek. 23:24 it is used as a term of quantity: *ochlos laōn*, a host of peoples; cf. the *ochloi ethnōn*, hosts of nations, in Wis. 6:2. In Bel 30 *ochlos* means the population of the land in contrast to the Jews.

The term was carried over as a loan-word into the Middle Heb. of the Rab. writings. There it can mean a crowd either of Jews or of Gentiles, or also military bodies of men (in the sense of troop, retinue, bands).

NT In the NT *ochlos* occurs 174 times. Of these 4 are in Rev., and all the others in the Gospels and Acts. In Mk. 14:43 the word means the armed crowd at the arrest of Jesus, but usually an unorganized crowd of people not formed or characterized by any particular background or custom. There are the people who come to hear John the Baptist (Lk. 3:7, 10) or Jesus, or who expect to be healed by him (e.g. Matt. 4:25; 5:1). It is especially to these people, who have nothing particular to offer, that Jesus directs his teaching and his compassion (Matt. 9:33), and his provision of food (Matt. 14:19; Lk. 9:16; Jn. 6:5). The contrast to these is provided by the ruling classes, the → Pharisees and scribes, who despised the *ochlos* as the ignorant masses who did not keep the law. To them the masses were accursed (Jn. 7:31, 48 f.; cf. → *ethnos*, *'am-hā'āreṣ*). In Jn. 7:49 *ochlos* doubtless refers to the term *'am hā'āreṣ*, people of the land. In the pre-exilic age the people of the land denoted full citizens who were liable to military service. But in the post-exilic age it denoted the foreign or mixed population, as distinct from the returned exiles. It became a term of abuse, connoting ignorance of and lax attitude towards the law (cf. R. Bultmann, *The Gospel of John*, 1971, 310 f.). Hence, the religious leaders with their strict attitude to the law regarded them as accursed. Jesus and later Paul were accused of leading the *ochlos* astray (Jn. 7:12; Acts 19:26). The *ochlos* was divided, however, in its opinion of Jesus (Jn. 7:43).

Herod Antipas hesitated to kill John the Baptist because he feared the *ochlos* (Matt. 14:5). The ruling class similarly fear the *ochlos* and do not dare to lay hands on Jesus (Matt. 21:26, 46); but they stir up the *ochlos* against Jesus (Matt. 27:20). Pilate acted under pressure from the populace (Mk. 15:15). Jesus told parables to the *ochlos* (Matt. 13:34). He had a whole *ochlos* of disciples (Lk. 6:17; cf. Acts 1:15). A great *ochlos* went to Bethany to see Jesus and Lazarus (Jn. 12:9). Before the throne of God and of the Lamb there stands an innumerable *ochlos* (Rev. 7:9); and in Rev. 17:15 nations are meant.   *H. Bietenhard*

πόλις

πόλις (*polis*), city, city-state; πολίτης (*politēs*), citizen; πολιτεύομαι (*politeuomai*), be a citizen, take part in government, live, conduct one's life; πολιτεία (*politeia*), rights of a citizen, commonwealth, state; πολίτευμα (*politeuma*), commonwealth, state, colony, citizenship; πολιτάρχης (*politarchēs*), politarch, civic magistrate.

CL 1. The word *polis*, attested probably from Mycenaean Gk., is perhaps derived from an Indo-Germanic root meaning to fill. This may suggest the *polis* as a filled-in wall which served as a fortress and refuge. As early as Homer *ptolis* and its lengthened form *ptoliethron* meant a city, state, and *politēs* a citizen. *politeuomai* means to be a citizen, live as a citizen, to administer the state, and conduct public affairs. The abstract noun *politeia* means citizen's rights, life of a citizen, his part in the life of the state, the condition or way of life of citizenship, and also civil policy, constitution, the state. The closely related noun *politeuma* had originally the same meaning. It was then used for individual political acts, measures or intrigues; in Aristotle for government, constitution, and also acts or branches of public administration. Later still the word meant political commonwealth, the state generally, and less frequently, citizens' rights. In the Hellenistic period colonies abroad with established political constitutions are also so described.

2. The development of the city-state in Greece is an historically logical and yet typically Gk. phenomenon. The rule of warrior kings which had been carried over from the period of the great migrations held the people together in only a very loose fashion, since it became effective only in times of war. Hence, there arose an increasing desire for concentration of the political will, not indeed to cover the Greeks as a whole, but individual, overseeable territories or districts. In the 8th and 7th centuries B.C. a large number of settlements came into being, mostly in dependence upon those already in existence. The concentration of political life and the multiplication of tasks within the new framework enabled the nobility, as the assistants of the king, to strengthen their own power and finally to supplant the monarchy. In the period which followed the city-state or *polis* became the most typical expression of Gk. culture and was regarded as the most important thing in life, to which the free citizen gave his total allegiance, and in the administration and government of which he had a part. The citizen embodied the state; citizenship was identified in terms of the city-state. The political order, defined by laws, was upheld by religious consecration. Religion was an essential part of the *polis*. The formation of city-states as an independent expression of political will, subject to no one, certainly hindered the unification of larger areas of the Gk. mainland. But even in its perversion, when rule was handed over to the mob in the Athens of the Peloponnesian War, one can see clearly how fruitful the idea of the unification of an overseeable number of free citizens had been. With the rise of the Macedonians and the spread of their blanket super-state (and later that of the Roman empire), the ancient *polis* came to an end.

OT 1. In the LXX *polis* occurs about 1,600 times, chiefly to translate *'îr*, city (e.g. Gen. 4:17; 10:11 f.; 11:4 f., 8), in Deut. also *š^e'ārîm*, gates (e.g. 12:15–21; 20:10 ff.), occasionally *qiryâh*, city (e.g. Jos. 14:15; 15:9, 13, 15 f.). In Israel the city has a different function from that of the *polis* in Greece. Israel's constitution is fundamentally a tribal one (→ Tribe). This distinguishes him also from the Canaanite city-states with their monarchy. In the OT, therefore, every fortified height can be called a "city". A memory of the impression which the fortified cities of Canaan made on the immigrating Israelites is probably retained in Num. 13:29 Moreover, it must have taken a long while following the conquest before the established cities could be overcome and occupied (cf. Jdg. 1:27 ff.; 3:1–5). Jerusalem was not conquered until David's time (2 Sam. 5:6 ff.). The city afforded its inhabitants protection against enemies and enabled them to withstand attackers. Very often cities are spoken of, when it is their inhabitants that are meant. Thus the city was to a considerable extent, as in Greece, a community of persons (cf. 1 Sam. 4:13; 2 Sam. 15:14; Est. 3:15; Isa. 40:9).

2. Of particular importance as a city is → Jerusalem. It is referred to simply as the city (Ezek. 7:23). Yahweh has chosen it (2 Chr. 6:38), to make his → name dwell there (cf. Deut. 12:5; 14:23), and that prayers and sacrifices may be offered there. Jerusalem is the "city of God" (cf. Pss. 46:4; 48:1, 8; 87:3), the "city of the great king" (Ps. 48:2; cf. Matt. 5:35), the "holy city" (cf. Isa. 48:2; 52:1). When its citizens did not live up to the character with which God had thus invested it, the prophet called them to repentance (Ezek. 22:2–4). In latter days a new Jerusalem, more in keeping with its original calling, was expected (Isa. 1:26; 32:28; Jer. 31:38; Joel 3:17).

These hopes of the renewal of Jerusalem were kept alive in Judaism (Sir. 36:12 f.; cf. the 14th of the Eighteen Benedictions, for text → Prayer, art. *proseuchomai*, OT 6). The future Jerusalem is expected to come down from heaven, where it has been kept from the beginning (cf. 2 Esd. 7:26; 8:52).

3. The derived nouns are found almost exclusively in the Books of Maccabees. (a) *politēs* occurs 10 times in 2 and 3 Macc., and 7 times in the OT besides, where it mostly translates the Heb. *rēa'*, one's neighbour of one's own people (Prov. 11:9, 12; 24:28[43]; Jer. 29[36]:23; 31[38]:34; → Brother, Neighbour). In the sense of citizen, the word is found only at 2 Macc. 9:19 and 3 Macc. 1:22. Other instances are Gen. 23:11; Num. 4:18; Zech. 13:7; 2 Macc. 4:5, 50; 5:6, 8, 23; 14:8; 15:30.

(b) *politeia* (9 times in 2–4 Macc.) usually means devout way of life (2 Macc. 8:17; 4 Macc. 17:19); in 3 Macc. 3:21, 23, citizens' rights. Other instances are 2 Macc. 4:11; 6:23; 13:14; 4 Macc. 3:20; 8:7.

(c) *politeuomai* always means to walk (Est. 8:12; 2 Macc. 6:1; 11:25; 3 Macc. 3:4; 4 Macc. 2:8, 23; 4:23; 5:16). *politeuma* occurs only at 2 Macc. 12:7, where it means community.

NT In the NT *polis* is found 161 times, being especially frequent in Luke (39 times), Acts (42 times), Matt. (26 times), and Rev. (27 times); rarely in Paul (4 times), and only 8 times each in Mk. and Jn. It never means state, but always city, in the sense of an enclosed settlement or its inhabitants (Matt. 8:34; 21:10; Mk. 1:33). The distinction between it and *kōmē*, village, often disappears (cf. Matt. 11:20 with Mk. 8:23; Lk. 2:4 with Jn. 7:42).

It is in keeping with OT and Jewish usage when Jerusalem is called the "holy city" (Matt. 4:5; 27:53; Rev. 11:2). This city kills the → prophets (Matt. 23:37) and also kills Jesus (Rev. 11:8; cf. Lk. 13:33). Her downfall is certain (Matt. 24:2 ff. par. Mk. 13:2 ff.; Lk. 21:6 ff.).

1. Over against the present Jerusalem there stands the Jerusalem above, the free Jerusalem, the mother of Christians (Gal. 4:25 f.; → Parable, art. *parabolē* NT for discussion of allegory and typology here). Heb. in particular contrasts the present and the future Jerusalem. Even the patriarchs knew of this new city and set their hope upon it. Compared with it all earthly cities are mere temporary tent-camps. For the sake of this coming city the patriarchs regarded themselves as strangers (→ Foreign, art. *xenos*) and sojourners (→ Foreign, art. *parepidēmos*). This city is Mount Zion and "the city of the living God" (Heb. 11:10, 16; 12:22 ff.).

It awaits the Christians who have here no continuing city (Heb. 13:14; cf. Rev. 3:12; 22:4). The earthly Jerusalem is only a copy and a shadow (Heb. 8:5; 10:1) or a symbol (Heb. 9:9) of the city which is to come, and which is already present in heaven. In this new city those who conquer in times of persecution have citizens' rights (Rev. 3:12). The new Jerusalem will come down upon the new earth (Rev. 21:2, 10 ff.).

2. *politēs*, citizen, occurs only 4 times in the NT, and has no political emphasis except in Acts 21:39, where Paul says that he is a citizen of Tarsus. Jerome claims that Paul came to Tarsus with his parents as prisoners of war from Gischala in Galilee (*De viris illustribus*, 5). Alternatively his parents may have come from Gischala, and Paul himself may have been born at Tarsus, where his father, liberated, may have become a Roman citizen (cf. E. Haenchen, *The Acts of the Apostles*, 1971, 620; → also Jerusalem NT 5 (b)). The other instances of *politēs* occur at Lk. 15:15; 19:14; Heb. 8:11 quoting Jer. 31:34.

3. *sympolitēs*, fellow citizen, occurs at Eph. 2:19 and indicates that Gentile Christians share through Christ in the calling of Israel, the people of God, as fellow-citizens.

4. *politeia* in Acts 22:28 means the Roman citizenship of Paul. In Eph. 2:12 it means the privileged position of Israel in salvation history, to which Gentile Christians now have access by faith in Jesus Christ.

5. *politeuma* occurs only at Phil. 3:20 where Paul contrasts the Christian life-style with that of the "enemies of the cross of Christ" (3:18): "But our common-wealth [*politeuma*] is in heaven, and from it we await a Saviour, the Lord Jesus Christ" (RSV). The older translation "citizenship" (RV) stresses the status of the believers, whereas "conversation" (AV), i.e. way of life, has affinities with the vb. *politeuomai* (see 6). M. Dibelius suggests "colony" (*An die Thessalonicher, I, II; An die Philipper, HNT*, 1937, ad. loc.) But the meaning is more likely to be that of "capital or native city, which keeps the citizens on its registers" (cf. E. Stauffer, *New Testament Theology*, 1955, 296 f.). The second half of the verse requires a place to be meant here, in order to make sense of the remark "and from it we await". Moreover, "the background of the word, in this context, is the situation of the readers who live in a city which was a Roman military colony directly related to the capital city of Rome" (R. P. Martin, *The Epistle of Paul to the Philippians, TC*, 1959, 160 f.). As Roman subjects, the Philippian Christians owed an allegiance to the far off capital city of Rome. At the same time, they had "another king, one Jesus" (Acts 17:7). Hence, on earth they are resident aliens who dwell temporarily in a foreign country but who have their capital and homeland elsewhere (cf. 1 Pet. 1:1; 2:11; Jas. 1:1; Heb. 11:13; Ep.Diog. 5).

6. *politeuomai* is found only at Acts 23:1 and Phil. 1:27, where (as in the usage of Hellenistic Judaism) it means to walk, in a way in keeping with the faith.

7. *politarchēs* means a civic magistrate, a politarch. In Macedonian cities and occasionally elsewhere a number of politarchs formed the city council. There were five or six in Thessalonica before whom the Jews dragged Jason (Acts 17:6, 8), accusing him of harbouring "these men who have turned the world upside down" and "acting against the decrees of Caesar". The politarchs dismissed the charge thereby putting the Jews in a bad light and the Christians and authorities in a good one (cf. Arndt, 692; E. D. Burton, "The Politarchs in Macedonia and Elsewhere",

American Journal of Theology, 2, 1898, 598–632).   H. *Bietenhard*
→ Brother, → Church, → Foreign, → Greek, → Israel, → Samaritan, → Tribe

(a). G. Bertram and K. L. Schmidt, *ethnos* etc., *TDNT* II 364–72; R. Bultmann, "Polis and Hades in Sophocles' Antigone", in *Essays: Theological and Philosophical*, 1955, 22–35; A. Cody, "When is the Chosen People Called a *gôy*?" *VT* 14, 1964, 1–6; O. Cullmann, *The State in the New Testament*, 1957; W. D. Davies, *The Gospel and the Land: Early Christianity and Jewish Territorial Doctrine*, 1974; J. D. M. Derrett, *Jesus' Audience: The Social and Psychological Environment in which He Worked*, 1973; V. E. Ehrenberg, "Polis", *OCD*, 851 f.; and *The Greek State*, 1960; J. H. Elliott, *The Elect and the Holy, Supplements to NovT* 12, 1966; W. G. Forrest, *The Emergence of Greek Democracy*, 1966; G. Glotz, *The Greek City*, 1929; W. Grundmann, *dēmos* etc., *TDNT* II 63 ff.; J. Jeremias, *Jesus' Promise to the Nations, SBT* 24, 1958; J. Jervell, *Luke and the People of God*, 1972; A. H. M. Jones, *The Greek City from Alexander to Justinian*, 1940; G. D. Kilpatrick, "The Gentiles and the Strata of Luke", in O. Böcher and K. Haacker, eds., *Verborum Veritas. Festschrift für Gustav Stählin*, 1970, 83–88; R. Martin-Achard, *A Light to the Nations*, 1962; R. Meyer and P. Katz, *ochlos, TDNT* V 582–90; M. Noth, "God King, and Nation in the Old Testament", in *The Laws in the Pentateuch and Other Studies*, 1966, 145–78; S. Pancaro, " 'People of God' in St John's Gospel?", *NTS* 16, 1969–70, 114–29; J. Scharbert, "People (of God)", *EBT* II 651–58; E. A. Speiser, " 'People' and 'Nation' of Israel", *JBL* 79, 1960, 157–63; H. Strathmann, *polis* etc., *TDNT* VI 516–35; H. Strathmann and R. Meyer, *laos, TDNT* IV 29–57; S. von Tilborg, "*hoi ochloi*", in *The Jewish Leaders in Matthew*, 1972, 142–65; J. D. W. Watts, "The People of God", *ExpT* 67, 1955–56, 232–37.

(b). N. A. Dahl, *Das Volk Gottes, Skrifter utgitt av Det Norske Videnskap-Akademi i Oslo*, 1941; C. Dietzfelbinger, *Heilsgeschichte bei Paulus?*, *ThEH* Neue Folge 126, 1965; J. Dupont, "LAOS EX ETHNŌN (Act. xv. 14)", *NTS* 3, 1956–57, 47–50; G. Eichholz, "Der Begriff 'Volk' im Neuen Testament", in *Tradition und Interpretation, ThB* 29, 1965, 78 ff.; H.-H. Esser, *Volk und Nation in der evangelischen Ethik, Das Gespräch Heute* 72, 1968; A. Feuillet, "La Demeure céleste et la Destinée des Chrétiens: Exégèse de II Cor. v. 1–10 et Contribution a l'Étude des Fondements de l'Eschatologie Paulinienne", *Recherches de Science Religieuse* 44, 1956, 161–92, 360–402; R. Klöbert, "*qhl – laos – ekklēsia*", *Biblica* 46, 1965, 464 ff.; R. Meyer, "Der *'am-hā'āreṣ*", *Judaica* 3, 1947, 166–99; C. Müller, *Gottes Gerechtigkeit und Gottes Volk. Eine Untersuchung zu Röm. 9–11*, *FRLANT* 86, 1969; F. Mussner, " 'Volk Gottes' im Neuen Testament", *Trierer Theologische Zeitschrift* 72, 1963, 169 ff.; and "Das Volk Gottes nach Eph. 1, 3–14", *Concilium* 1, 1965, 842 ff.; A. Oepke, *Das neue Gottesvolk in Schrifttum, Schauspiel, bildender Kunst und Weltgestaltung*, 1950; G. Rau, "Das Volk in der lukanischen Passionsgeschichte. Eine Konjektur zu Lk. 23, 13", *ZNW* 56, 1965, 41 ff.; W. Ruppel, "*Politeuma*", *Philologus* 82, 1927, 268–312, 433–52; K. L. Schmidt, *Die Polis in Kirche und Welt*, 1940; W. Schweitzer, *Der entmythologisierte Staat. Studie zur Revision der evangelischen Ethik des Politischen*, 1968; F. Thiess, *Das Reich der Dämonen* 1960; R. Walker, *Studie zu Röm. 13, 1–7, ThEH* Neue Folge 132, 1966; H. D. Wendland and J. Blau, "Volk", *EKL* III 1672 ff.; H. Wildberger, *Jahwes Eigentumsvolk*, 1960; E. Würthwein, *Der 'am-hā'āreṣ im Alten Testament*, 1936.

Persecution, Tribulation, Affliction

| διώκω |

διώκω (*diōkō*), run after, pursue, persecute; ἐκδιώκω (*ekdiōkō*), drive away, persecute severely; καταδιώκω (*katadiōkō*), search for, hunt for; διωγμός (*diōgmos*), persecution.

CL *diōkō* is perhaps connected with the Homeric *diemai*, flee. It means lit. to chase, pursue, run after, drive away, and fig. to pursue something zealously, try to achieve something, try to obtain, prosecute.

OT 1. In the LXX *diōkō*, along with *ekdiōkō* and *katadiōkō*, is used primarily of pursuit by hostile soldiers (Exod. 15:9), or by anyone whose intentions are hostile (Gen. 31:23). It translates a number of Heb. vbs., but chiefly *rāḏap̄*, pursue;

805

the other vbs. occur only in isolated instances. This gives rise to the usage which is characteristic of the Pss. of individual lamentation (e.g. Pss. 7:1, 5[2, 6]; 31[30]:15 35[34]:3; cf. also Jer. 15:15; 20:11), where persecution and persecutors refer to the circumstances and persons that cause the psalmist to suffer, without there necessarily being active persecution in the narrower specific sense.

2. The OT also contains exhortations to strive for a goal. In normal Gk. settings it will be the good, the beautiful, or virtue that is to be pursued. In the LXX it is relationships, e.g. social righteousness (Deut. 16:20; cf. also Josephus, *Ant.* 6, 12, 7), peace (Ps. 34[33]:14), and righteousness in the sense of true honouring of God (Prov. 15:9), that are to be followed. The corresponding NT usage has its roots here.

NT Summary of NT use. (a) The commonest meaning is to persecute, or be persecuted (some 30 times, especially in the Gospels, Acts, Paul, Rev.). The noun *diōgmos* refers only to persecution. In 1 Thess. 2:15 the compound *ekdiōkō* also means to persecute (RSV, NEB drive out). (b) The fig. use is found only in the Epistles, always with a positive meaning; the use in Phil. 3:12, 14 belongs here (cf. also *zēteō*, → Seek, and *zēloō*, → Zeal). (c) *diōkō* (Lk. 17:23) and *katadiōkō* (Mk. 1:36) mean to run after, follow, in the passages referred to.

1. Persecution: (a) God's messengers in particular meet persecution. This was already the experience of the → prophets (Matt. 5:12; Acts 7:52), and will equally be that of Jesus' → disciples (Matt. 5:11 f., 44; 10:23), the more so as they are followers of the Lord, who had to suffer persecution himself (Jn. 5:16). This connection is clearly expressed in Jn. 15:20: "If they persecuted me, they will persecute you." Paul, once the persecutor of the church (1 Cor. 15:9; Gal. 1:13; 23; Phil. 3:6; 1 Tim. 1:13), experienced persecution himself, once the glorified Lord had made him his messenger (Gal. 5:11; 2 Tim. 3:11). In 2 Tim. 3:12 he expresses the view that being a Christian will always be linked with persecution (→ Suffer).

(b) The message is persecuted in the Christian (Acts 22:4, the "way", the course steered by faith), or Christ himself (Acts 9:4 f.; 22:7 f;. 26:14 f.). According to Jn. 15:18 ff., persecution is caused by the world's hatred of God and his revelation in Christ (cf. also Matt. 10:22; Mk. 13:13; Lk. 21:17; Rev. 12:13). Paul sees behind it the contrast between → flesh and → spirit; the hostility of the natural man against God and so also against the man led by God's Spirit (Gal. 4:29).

(c) Hence persecution may be a sign that one is on God's side. Thus Jesus calls those blessed "who are persecuted for righteous's sake" (Matt. 5:10 ff.; → Blessing).

(d) There is the danger of corrupting the message in order to avoid persecution (Gal. 6:12). Christians are specially challenged to maintain their faith during persecution. They are to meet the hatred of their persecutors by a word of blessing (Rom. 12:14; cf. especially Matt. 5:44).

(e) But it is especially in persecution that Christians experience the help, strength and saving power of Christ (2 Cor. 4:7 ff.; 12:10; Rom. 8:35–39). In persecution Paul set an apostolic example by enduring it patiently (1 Cor. 4:12). It is a special reason for giving God thanks, when persecution is endured with faith (2 Thess. 1:3 f.).

2. Pursuit of Christian objectives. The metaphorical meaning of the word shows more strongly than *zēteō*, seek, that there are certain things which the

Christian must strive after, such as hospitality (Rom. 12:13), mutual peace (Rom. 14:19; 1 Pet. 3:11; Heb. 12:14), holiness, love (1 Cor. 14:1), doing good (1 Thess. 5:15), and righteousness (1 Tim. 6:11; 2 Tim. 2:22). These are lasting objectives in the life of faith, which has as its goal the attaining of the → resurrection from the dead. Paul sees the Christian life as ultimately directed to this goal. He presses on to it like the runner set on winning the victor's prize (Phil. 3:12 ff.), although he knows that "it depends not upon man's will or exertion, but upon God's mercy" (Rom. 9:16; cf. v. 30 f.). *G. Ebel*

$\theta\lambda\tilde{\iota}\psi\iota\varsigma$

$\theta\lambda\tilde{\iota}\psi\iota\varsigma$ (*thlipsis*), oppression, affliction, tribulation; $\theta\lambda\acute{\iota}\beta\omega$ (*thlibō*), press upon, oppress, afflict; $\sigma\tau\epsilon\nu o\chi\omega\rho\acute{\iota}\alpha$ (*stenochōria*), straits, distress, affliction, difficulty; $\sigma\tau\epsilon\nu o\chi\omega\rho\acute{\epsilon}\omega$ (*stenochōreō*), crowd, cramp, confine, oppress.

CL The verb *thlibō* (Aristophanes onwards; from the root *thlaō*, crush, squash) means press, squeeze, crush, This lit. meaning is found in Mk. 3:9; "lest they should crush him." The perf. part. pass. has the meaning of narrow, strait (cf. Matt. 7:13, of the way to life; → Gate). The fig. use is very common, both in the sense of oppress (external) and of grieve, vex (internal). Epictetus speaks of the pressures of life (*ta thlibonta*) which the true Stoic must and can overcome (*Dissertationes*, 4, 1, 45; cf. 1, 25, 17 and 28; 2, 27, 2 f.; 3, 13, 8).

The noun *thlipsis*, oppression, distress, affliction, is linked with the vb. It is occasionally found coupled with *stenochōria* (derived from *stenos*, or *steinos*, narrow, and *chōria*, space, place), which from Thucydides onwards is used to express a narrow place, and hence being pressed by inner and outer difficulties. The corresponding vb. *stenochōreō* is found in its semi-lit. sense in 2 Cor. 6:12: "you are not restricted [*stenochōreisthe*] by us."

OT In the LXX *thlipsis* is used to render a number of Heb. terms, especially *ṣārar*, *ṣar*, *lāḥaṣ*, *laḥaṣ*. These Heb. words denote need, distress, and various afflictions depending on the context, e.g. war, exile and personal hostility. Here too it is found a number of times linked with *stenochōria* (e.g. Deut. 28:53, 55, 57; Isa. 8:22; 30:6; Est. 1:1 [LXX, but not MT]), as well as with other terms expressive of fear and pain, in many cases the meaning being almost synonymous. The *thlipsis* of the LXX is often the oppression which belongs of necessity to the history of Israel and which was regarded by the faithful as part of salvation history. There is a connection between oppression (Exod. 3:9) and deliverance (Exod. 3:10). Even when the oppression is a punishment, its purpose is deliverance (Neh. 9:27; Hos. 5:14–6:2). The eschatological nature of the oppression is often stressed (cf. Zech. 1:15; Hab. 3:16). Dan 12:1 even speaks of "a time of trouble, such as never has been since there was a nation" until the writer's own time. But here also deliverance from trouble is mentioned, and this expresses the faith and hope of the faithful in Israel. "Many are the afflictions of the righteous; but the Lord delivers him out of them all" (Ps. 34:19; cf. Ps. 37:39). This was the unshakeable conviction of the faithful, who were able to pray, "Thou who has made me see many sore troubles wilt revive me again" (Ps. 71:20).

807

Judaism also knew of the troubles of the people which it expected in the end-time and described in detail in the apocalypses (Eth.Enoch., 2 Esd., Syr.Bar.). The Qumran texts accommodate themselves to this picture. They speak of the last great tribulation (1QM 1:12; 15:1) and of the personal trials of the writer of the Hymns (1QH 5:12; 9:28; 15:16).

NT *thlipsis* is used 45 times in the NT, *thlibō* 10 times, always fig. apart from Mk. 3:9 and Matt. 7:13 (see above CL). The RV and RSV translate *thlipsis* about equally by affliction and tribulation, though the RSV especially also uses other renderings. *stenochōria* is found 4 times (Rom. 2:9; 8:35; 2 Cor. 6:4; 12:10), and *stenochōreō* twice (2 Cor. 4:8; 6:12). The usage in the NT is clearly the same as in the OT. The following cases are of importance.

1. *thlipsis* has an eschatological significance for the church. This may be seen by the quotation in Matt. 24:21 and Mk. 13:19 of Dan. 12:1 (see above OT). The tribulation stands in the closest connection with the → Son of man (Matt. 24:30) of Dan. 7:13 and the birth-pangs of the messiah (Matt. 24:8; → Jesus Christ, art. *Christos*; cf. SB I 950). This tribulation belongs to the period of catastrophes before the final salvation, and it is characterized by leading astray, hate, political strife and catastrophes of nature. It is all necessary, "for this must take place" (Matt. 24:6; → Necessity). The background of this "must" may be found in Dan. 2:28 f., 45. The same thought is to be found in Rev., not merely in Rev. 2:22 and 7:14 (cf. 3:10), where the great tribulation is referred to, but also in 1:9, where tribulation is once again linked with Dan. 7:13 (cf. v. 7), and Dan. 2:28 (cf. v. 1, "what must soon take place").

2. A second element is expressed by the phrase *thlipseis tou Christou*, the afflictions of Christ. The OT statement, "Many are the afflictions of the righteous" (Ps. 34:19), is particularly applicable to the truly righteous One (Acts 3:14 f.), and so it is possible to speak of "the afflictions of Christ" (Col. 1:24, only here). It is not only a question of the afflictions left over for the church, but also of the afflictions which the Lord suffered in his unique → suffering (Col. 1:20, 22), with which the church knows itself to be linked in its own affliction. Passages like 2 Cor. 1:5 (cf. vv. 4, 6); 4:10 (cf. v. 8) allow us to infer that the thought of such afflictions was implicit in the proclamation of the passion of Christ. Both they and the whole of Christ's passion are under the divine "must" (*dei*; cf. W. Grundmann, *TDNT* II 22 ff.).

3. Only in the light of the two preceding concepts can we properly understand the third concept which is contained in statements about the afflictions of believers.

(a) Believers are implicitly included in the eschatological *thlipsis*. They are exposed to the tribulations (Matt. 24:9), especially hatred, betrayal and death. It is above all the time of leading astray (cf. Matt. 24:4 f., 11, 24; → Lead Astray), the time of testing (cf. *peirasmos* in Lk. 8:13, where the par. Matt. 13:21, Mk. 4:17 have *thlipsis* and *diōgmos*; → Tempt).

(b) Col. 1:24 (see above 2) makes it clear that Christians experience these afflictions in solidarity with Christ's passion. This is a familiar thought, especially in Paul. All distress and affliction suffered by Christians, which are caused by the pressure of the world on them, must always be understood in the light of this solidarity. Only so can they be rightly explained and endured (cf. 2 Cor. 1:5 with 1:4, 6; cf. 4:10 f. with 4:8; cf. Phil. 3:10; 1 Pet. 4:13). Precisely for this reason tribulation and all other distress cannot separate us from Christ (Rom. 8:35). Because we are suffering with him in these distresses we shall be glorified together with him (Rom. 8:17; cf. 8:37; cf. 1 Thess. 1:6, following Christ in affliction).

(c) The *thlipsis* does not come unexpectedly to the believer. Its connection with the eschatological and christological tribulation discussed above, both of which depend on the divine "must", makes it *a priori* probable that the tribulations of Christians are also conditioned by this "must". Moreover, this is stated several times in the NT. Jn. 16:33 says, "in the world you have tribulation". "Through many tribulations we must enter the kingdom of God" (Acts 14:22) was the reason why Paul and Barnabas exhorted the disciples to continue in the faith. It is perhaps most clearly expressed in 1 Thess. 3:3, where Paul writes that he had sent Timothy to exhort the church, "that no one be moved by these afflictions; you yourselves know that this is to be our lot [*eis touto keimetha*]" (cf. the *eis touto keimetha* with *eis touto gar eklēthēte*, "for to this you were called", 1 Pet. 2:21). The apostle Paul had expected nothing else for his own life (1 Thess. 3:4; cf. Acts 20:23), and had experienced it in full measure in his missionary work (2 Cor. 1:4, 6, 8; 2:4; 4:8, 17; 6:4–10; 7:4 f.; 11:16–12:10; Eph. 3:13; Phil. 1:17; 4:14; 1 Thess. 3:4, 7). But it caused him → joy, not grief: "We rejoice in our sufferings, knowing that suffering produces endurance" (Rom. 5:3; cf. Jas. 1:2 f.; → Patience, art. *hypomonē*).

(d) As a result the tribulation is already a reality in the NT situation. The church in Jerusalem had experienced it (Acts 11:19), and it became a reality for other churches, in Corinth (2 Cor. 1:4), Thessalonica (1 Thess. 1:6; 3:3) and Macedonia generally (2 Cor. 8:2). But these afflictions are determined, so far as believers are concerned, by their goal in God's plan of salvation. They are therefore never purposeless, but produce → hope (Rom. 5:3 ff.). Just as a woman, who has given birth to a child, no longer remembers the anguish in her joy (Jn. 16:21), so believers have sorrow (Jn. 16:22) and tribulation (Jn. 16:33). But Jesus' "be of good cheer" is no empty phrase, because he knows the righteousness of God which repays with affliction those who cause affliction, and grants → rest to the afflicted as compensation (2 Thess. 1:6 f.).   *R. Schippers*

→ Abomination of Desolation, → Animal, art. *thērion*, → Antichrist, → Fruit, art. *skolops*, → Judgment, → Number, art. *chilias* (on the idea of a millennium), → Patience, → Present, → Satan, → Serve, → Suffer, → Time, → War, → Weakness, → Witness

(a). G. R. Beasley-Murray, *Jesus and the Future: An Examination of the Eschatological Discourse, Mark 13, with Special Reference to the Little Apocalypse Theory*, 1954; and *A Commentary on Mark Thirteen*, 1957; W. Beilner, "Persecution", *EBT* II 667 ff.; S. G. F. Brandon, *The Fall of Jerusalem and the Christian Church*, 1951; S. Brown *Apostasy and Perseverence in the Gospel of Luke*, 1959; W. H. C. Frend, *Martyrdom and Persecution in the Early Church: A Study of Conflict from the Maccabees to Donatus*, 1965; L. Gaston, *No Stone on Another: Studies in the Significance of the Fall of Jerusalem in the Synoptic Gospels*, Supplements to NovT 23, 1970; D. R. A. Hare, *The Theme of Jewish Persecution of Christians in the Gospel according to St Mathew*, 1967; I. H. Marshall, *Kept by the Power of God: A Study of Perseverance and Falling Away*, 1969; A. Oepke, *diōkō, TDNT* II 229 f.; H. Schlier, *thlibō* etc., *TDNT* III 139–48.
(b). N. Brox, *Zeuge und Märtyrer*, 1961; E. Güttgemanns, *Der leidende Apostel und sein Herr*, 1966; E. Lohse, *Märtyrer und Gottesknecht*, FRLANT 64, 1955; and *Geschichte des Leidens und Sterbens Jesu Christi*, 1964; W. Nauck, "Freude im Leiden. Zum Problem einer urchristlichen Verfolgungstradition", *ZNW* 46, 1955, 68–80; J. Schneider, *Die Passionsmystik des Paulus*, 1929; A. Steubing, *Der paulinischer Begriff Christusleiden*, 1905; W. Wichmann, *Die Leidenstheologie*, 1930.

Pharisee

| $\Phi\alpha\rho\iota\sigma\alpha\tilde{\iota}o\varsigma$ | (*Pharisaios*), Pharisee.

ΟΤ *Pharisaioi* is the Hellenized form of the Aram. word *p^erîšayyā'* (Heb. *pārûš*; from *pāraš*, to divide, separate), and means "the separated ones". It denotes the representatives of an influential religious group in Judaism. The designation is only attested in Hellenistic Judaism up till the time of the NT, but not at all in the LXX. Rabbinic literature provides the first attestation of the word in the Aramaic-speaking world, although it is frequently found in a negative sense. The word was used in the Gk. form by Josephus and in the NT. The date of the appearance of the designation can no longer be precisely fixed. The first occurrences are from the time of Hyrcanus I (*c.* 135 B.C.). From the 1st cent. B.C. (under the reign of Alexandra [76–67 B.C.]) onwards, however, the Pharisees were in the public esteem, the most respected and thus the leading group of Judaism.

1. Josephus, himself a Pharisee, came to speak of the movement in differing ways in his writings. Perhaps in order to please his Hellenistic readers he called them one of the many Jewish "philosophies", alongside the Essenes, → Sadducees and the "fourth philosophy" (cf. *War* 2, 8, 2–14; *Ant.* 18, 1, 3–6). But much remains unclarified for us in Josephus' writings, including the meaning of the name. Since the representatives of this group never called themselves by this name but spoke of themselves rather as the *h^abērîm*, the comrades of a *h^abûrâh*, a society, the question arises as to whether the designation *Pharisaioi* is not perhaps a nick-name which the opponents gave to the exponents of that piety. The name implies separation, but it is not clear from what they were separated. Basically, three positions are held.

(a) One view is that it is a group of the *Hasidaioi* Hasidim (Heb. *h^asîdîm*), the pious, separated from Judas Maccabaeus (cf. 1 Macc. 2:42; 7:13; 2 Macc. 14:6). Although they originally fought alongside the Maccabees against the Seleucids, they later brought about the separation which this name gave them, as a protest against the Hasmonaeans' claims to political domination.

(b) The Pharisees originated out of the group of the *h^abērîm* ("confederates"), which separated itself *c.* 135 B.C. from the rest of the people who did not keep the → law, in order to follow exactly the individual prescriptions of the law. The name thus goes back to the separation of a group of pious people true to the law from a lawless – and thus godless – people.

(c) The name is a pun on the "separation", i.e. the distinction between the individual prescriptions of the law. "The law was the centre of their thought and practical life and, in continually renewed applications and metaphors, was lauded as Israel's most precious and sacred garment" (H. Lietzmann, *The Beginnings of the Christian Church*, 1953³, 30).

There is much to be said for the view that the group received their name through understanding themselves as the fellowship which embodied the true → Israel and distancing themselves from the rest of the nation (position (b)).

2. Essential to Pharisaism was the fact that it tried "by obedience to the Law ... to represent the pure community, the true people of God preparing itself

810

for the coming of the messiah" (E. Lohse, *EKL* III 181). Their views were sketched by Josephus (*War* 2, 8; cf. also Pss.Sol. *c.* 60 B.C. which is Pharisaic in outlook). Characteristic of their outlook are the following points.

(a) The legal prescriptions of Scripture were observed with minute attention to detail (e.g. tithing all goods, attending to all the purificatory regulations, all the sacred times laid down by God and the cultic actions). It is significant that the Halachah, the body of legal decisions which interpreted the law, was reckoned to be equally as binding as the biblical tradition. This is illustrated by Shammai's reply to the question, "How many Toroth do you have?": "Two; the written Torah and the oral Torah" (Shabbath 31a). Josephus reports "that the Pharisees have delivered to the people a great many observances by succession from their fathers, which are not written in the laws of Moses; and for that reason the Sadducees reject them, and say, that we are to esteem those observances to be obligatory which are in the written word, but are not to observe what are derived from the tradition of our forefathers. And concerning these things it is that great disputes and differences have risen among them, while the Sadducees are able to persuade none but the rich, and have not the populace obsequious to them, but the Pharisees have the multitude on their side" (*Ant.* 13, 10, 6). The Pharisaic experts in the Scripture, the "Scribes", gave a binding interpretation to the laws by way of casuistic exegesis. This casuistry led in part to highly rarified controversial debates and decisions between individual scholars. Thus food could not be cooked on the → Sabbath. But whereas the School of Shammai permitted water to be set on a stove which had been previously heated, the School of Hillel permitted both hot water and cooked food to be placed on it (Sabbath 3:1). Whereas fish might not be caught from a vivarium on a festival day or have food given to them, wild animals and birds could be so treated. "This is the general rule: What must still be hunted is forbidden, but what needs not to be hunted is permitted" (Yom Tob 3:1). Practically every area of human life came to be included and regulated by an abundance of individual prescriptions. The Pharisees, however, did not wish to destroy the law. Rather, they "sought by their interpretations to make the law fit the new environs, believing as they did that God had provided for every circumstance that could arise. In this they had no idea that they were introducing new notes, although of course they were; they were simply discovering old truth" (M. S. Enslin, *Christian Beginnings*, 1938, 115). The Pharisees set the people a good example in keeping the law, in that they themselves in addition adhered to the strict purificatory rites which were otherwise only binding for priests.

(b) By contrast with the Essenes, who emphasized the complete helplessness of the human will over against God, and the Sadducees, who stressed the unlimited freedom of the will, the Pharisees held firm to a conditional freedom of human will. Man may well not be able to frustrate the will of God, but within the frame of the divine plan he is able to do good or evil (cf. Josephus, *Ant.* 18, 1, 3; cf. Pss. Sol. 5:6).

(c) The Pharisees took over the partly Persian and Hellenistic conceptions of the → resurrection (cf. Sanhedrin 10:1; Sotah 9:15), of a → judgment after death and of supramundane beings (all of which had made large inroads into Judaism), including very pronounced conceptions of → angels, the Devil (→ Satan) and intermediary beings. Whereas the Pharisees believed that they could read these doctrines out of the sacred writings, the Sadducees rejected the ideas as being irreconcileable with the Holy Scriptures (cf. Acts 23:8).

(d) From the downfall of the Hasmonaeans the Pharisees, by contrast with the Zealots, strictly renounced all use of force. God himself, through his intervention, will give the decisive turn and liberate his people.

(e) The Pharisees awaited the messiah (→ Jesus Christ, art. *Christos*), whereas the Sadducees did not (cf. Pss.Sol. 17:23–18:9).

In that Pharisaism was sufficiently flexible to adjust itself to the conditions of a changed way of life, it had become the most spiritually formative power in Judaism at the time of Jesus. But with its preoccupation with the fulfilment of the laws, Pharisaism was in fact an intensely narrow and rigid formalism.

NT In the NT the Pharisees are only named in the four Gospels (Matt. 27 times; Mk. 12 times; Lk. 27 times; Jn. 19 times), Acts (9 times), and once in Paul (Phil. 3:5), where Paul himself admits to having been "as to the law a Pharisee".

In Pharisaism Jesus met → Israel as it strove for true → faith and obedience (→ Hear, art. *akouō*) to God, but which had become totally hardened in formalism and thus barred itself from precisely that for which it was searching – to please God. Jesus and the Pharisees are consequently depicted in Matt., Mk. and Jn. (with the exception of Nicodemus) as embittered opponents (cf. Mk. 3:6; 12:13; Matt. 12:14; the woes of Jesus in Matt. 23; Jn. 3:1, 4, 9; 7:50; 11:46 f., 57; 19:39).

1. It is a striking fact that Lk. does not generally represent the Pharisees as inimical to Jesus. According to Lk., Jesus was a guest of distinguished Pharisees and ate food at table with them (Lk. 7:36 f.; 11:37; 14:1). Lk. 13:31 even reports that Pharisees warned Jesus of Herod's attempts on his life. Pharisees were members of the Christian community (Acts 15:5). It may be that the strained relationship with Jesus subsequently became milder towards the church (cf. Acts 5:34; 15:5; 23:9). It is quite conceivable that Lk. slightly corrects the picture of the Pharisees in his Gospel on the basis of the experiences of the first churches. The particular Lucan material where Jesus is a guest of Pharisees, however, leads up to confrontation in which Jesus makes certain pronouncements. The historicity of Lk.'s account has been questioned on the grounds that the Pharisees would scarcely have invited a wandering preacher to a meal when he violated their purificatory regulations so blatantly (Lk. 11:38). It has also been asked why a man who is deemed worthy of being invited to table should be denied all the customary courtesies of the kiss, the anointing, and the foot-washing (Lk. 7:44 f). To this the answer may be that individual Pharisees (like Nicodemus in Jn. 3) were attracted to Jesus, but that their background prevented them from extending the formal rites of fellowship and acceptance to one who stood outside their number and was so critical of their understanding of righteousness.

2. (a) The equation of oral tradition with the OT law led to serious divergences. The nature of the difference is made clear only in the light of the two opposing understandings of God. For the Pharisees, God is primarily one who makes demands; for Jesus he is gracious and compassionate. The Pharisee does not, of course, deny God's goodness and love, but for him these were expressed in the gift of the Torah and in the possibility of fulfilling what is there demanded (cf. Aboth 3:14 ff.). Adherence to the oral tradition, with its rules for interpreting the

law, was seen by the Pharisee as the way to the fulfilment of the Torah (cf. Mk. 7:3, 5; Matt. 12:2 ff.; 15:1 ff.). The individual prescriptions are here on a par with one another. By contrast, in Matt. 12:7 Jesus cites Hos. 6:6 ("I desire mercy and not sacrifice"), and thereby grounds the entire interpretation of the law in the → command of → love (cf. Matt. 22:34–40; Mk. 12:28–34; Lk. 10:25–28). Since God himself is the Loving One, all other commands are fulfilled in loving one's neighbour (cf. Jn. 8:3–11). Jesus' elevation of the double command of love (Matt. 22:34–40) to the level of a norm of interpretation and his rejection of the binding nature of the oral tradition (cf. Lk. 11:38–42) led him into conflict with Pharisaic casuistry (Matt. 15:1–20 par. Mk. 7:1–23; cf. Isa. 29:13; Lk. 6:7; 13:3–6; → Hand; → Gift, art. *korban*).

(b) Jesus repudiated the exclusion by the Pharisees of the uneducated and notorious sinners (cf. Matt. 9:11; Mk. 2:16; Lk. 5:30) as lack of love. The Pharisees were ostensibly concerned about the judgment of God, forgiveness, and about the holy nation of Israel, but their attitude was the negative one of separation and concern for the minutiae of the law. But Jesus sought to heal the injuries of his people by bringing God's love to the helpless and sick (cf. Matt. 9:12 ff.; Mk. 2:17). The Pharisees ostensibly took God's commands seriously, but their preoccupation with fulfilling the commands exactly became an end in itself which prevented them from entering the kingdom of God themselves and also from letting others enter it (Matt. 23:1–36; → Open).

(c) This segregation essentially led the Pharisees into a conflict between what the Torah demanded and what they actually performed (see the Woes in Matt. 23). The casuistic exegesis of the law with the consequent dissociation from everything impure led them to a distinctly merit-based system of thought in which lay a disastrous self-deception (→ Reward, art. *misthos*). The Pharisees drew on themselves the accusation of hypocrisy with regard to men (→ Lie, art. *hypokrinō*) and → pride in relation to God (cf. Matt. 6:5, 16; 23:13, 15, 23, 25, 27 ff.; Lk. 19:10 ff.).

Their understanding of God and their resultant understanding of the law made the Pharisees blind to the true offer and claim of God meeting them in Jesus (cf. Matt. 23:26; Mk. 9:40). The tragedy was that the Pharisees earnestly sought God, but, because a particular picture of God had hardened in their tradition, they decided against Jesus (cf. Matt. 12:14 par. Mk. 3:6; cf. Lk. 6:11) and thus against God (cf. Matt. 12:24–32; Lk. 11:43–54). Thus the Pharisee became in the NT the type of an attitude which is by no means confined to Judaism.   *D. Müller*
→ Command, → Gift, art. *korban*, → Hand, → Herb, → Law, → Levite, → Lie, Hypocrite, → Open, → Priest, → Sadducee, → Tax, → Tithe

(a). I. Abrahams, *Studies in Pharisaism and the Gospels*, I, 1917, II, 1924; B. W. Bacon, "Pharisees and Herodians", *JBL* 39, 1920, 102–112; L. Baeck, *The Pharisees*, 1957; M. Black, "Pharisees", *IDB* III 774–81; J. Bowker, *Jesus and the Pharisees*, 1973; F. C. Burkitt, "Jesus and the Pharisees", *JTS* 28, 1927, 392–97; R. H. Charles, *Religious Developments between the Old and New Testaments*, 1914; W. D. Davies, *Introduction to Pharisaism*, 1967; J. D. M. Derrett, *Law in the New Testament*, 1970; and *Jesus' Audience*, 1973; H. L. Ellison, "Jesus and the Pharisees", *Journal of the Transactions of the Victoria Institute* 85, 1953, 33–46; M. S. Enslin, *Christian Beginnings*, 1938; W. R. Farmer, *Maccabees, Zealots and Josephus*, 1961; J. Finkelstein, "The Pharisees: Their Origin and their Philosophy", *HTR* 22, 1929, 185–261; *The Pharisees: The Sociological Background of their Faith*, I–II, 1962³; *The Pharisees and the Men of the Great Synagogue, Texts and Studies of the Jewish Theological Seminary of America* 15, 1950; and "The Ethics of Anonymity among the

Pharisees", *Conservative Judaism* 12, 1958, 1–12; W. Förster, *Palestinian Judaism in New Testament Times*, 1964; T. F. Glasson, "Anti-Pharisaism in St. Matthew", *JQR* 51, 1960–61, 316–20; F. C. Grant, *Ancient Judaism and the New Testament*, 1960²; and *Roman Hellenism and the New Testament*, 1962, 132–47; M. Hengel, *Judaism and Hellenism, Studies in their Encounter in Palestine during the Early Hellenistic Period*, I–II, 1974; R. T. Herford, *The Pharisees*, 1929; M. D. Hussey, "The Origin of the Name Pharisee", *JBL* 39, 1920, 66–69; J. Jeremias, *Jerusalem in the Time of Jesus*, 1969, 246–67; A. F. J. Klijn, "Scribes, Pharisees, Highpriests and Elders in the New Testament", *NovT* 3, 1959, 259–67; J. Z. Lauterbach, "The Pharisees and their Teachings", *Hebrew Union College Annual* 6, 1929, 69–139; T. W. Manson, "Sadducee and Pharisee: The Origin and Significance of the Names", *BJRL* 22, 1938, 144–59; and *The Servant-Messiah*, 1953; R. Marcus, "Pharisaism in the Light of Modern Scholarship", *JR* 32, 1952, 154–64; and "Pharisees, Essenes and Gnostics", *JBL* 73, 1954, 155–61; R. Meyer and H. F. Weiss, *Pharisaios*, *TDNT* IX 11–48; G. F. Moore, "The Rise of Normative Judaism", *HTR* 17, 1924, 307–73, and 18, 1925, 1–38; and *Judaism* (see index); J. Neusner, "The Fellowship (*ḥbwrh*) and the Second Jewish Commonwealth", *HTR* 53, 1960, 125–42; H. Odeberg, *Pharisaism and Christianity*, 1964; W. O. E. Oesterley, *The Jews and Judaism during the Greek Period: The Background of Christianity*, 1941; C. Rabin, *Qumran Studies*, 1955, 53–70; and "Alexander Jannaeus and the Pharisees", *Journal of Jewish Studies* 7, 1956, 3–11; D. W. Riddle, *Jesus and the Pharisees*, 1928; A. T. Robertson, *The Pharisees and Jesus*, 1920; T. H. Robinson, "Jesus and the Pharisees", *ExpT* 28, 1916–17, 550–54; C. Roth, "The Pharisees in the Jewish Revolution of 66–73", *JSS* 7, 1962, 63–80; S. Safrai, M. Stern, D. Flusser and W. C. van Unnik, eds., *The Jewish People in the First Century, Historical Geography, Political History, Social, Cultural and Religious Life and Institutions*, I, 1974; Schürer (see index); R. A. Stewart, *Rabbinic Theology: An Introductory Study*, 1961; S. van Tilborg, *The Jewish Leaders in Matthew*, 1972; S. Umer, *Pharisaism and Jesus*, 1962; S. Zeitlin, "The Pharisees and the Gospels", *Essays and Studies in Memory of L. R. Miller*, 1938, 235–86.

(b). S. Abir, "Der Weg der Pharisäer", *Freiburger Rundschau* 11, 1958–59, 29–34; L. Baeck, *Paulus, die Pharisäer und das Neue Testament*, 1961; W. Beilner, "Der Ursprung des Pharisäismus", *BZ* Neue Folge 3, 1959, 235–51; and *Christus und die Pharisäer. Exegetische Untersuchung über Grund und Verlauf der Auseinandersetzung*, 1959; E. L. Dietrich, "Pharisäer", *RGG³* V 326 ff.; W. Foerster, "Der Ursprung des Pharisäismus", *ZNW* 34, 1935, 35–51; W. Grundmann, "Die Pharisäer", in J. Leipoldt and W. Grundmann, eds., *Umwelt des Urchristentums*, I, 1967², 269 ff.; F. Heinrichs, *Die Komposition der antipharisäischen und antirabbinischen Wehe-Reden bei den Synoptikern*, Dissertation, Munich, 1957; W. G. Kümmel, "Jesus und die Rabbinen", in *Heilsgeschehen und Geschichte*, 1965, 1 ff.; E. Lohse, "Pharisäer", *EKL* III 181 f.; J. C. Margot, "Les Pharisiens d'après quelques ouvrages récents", *Revue de Théologie et de Philosophie*, 3, 1956, 294–302; F. Merkel, "Jesus und die Pharisäer", *NTS* 14, 1967–68, 194–208; R. Meyer, "Die Bedeutung des Pharisäismus für Geschichte und Theologie des Judentums", *TLZ* 77, 1952, 677–84; and *Tradition und Neuschöpfung im antiken Judentum. Dargestellt an der Geschichte des Pharisäismus, Mit einen Beitrag von H. F. Weiss, "Der Pharisäismus im Lichte der Überlieferung des Neuen Testaments", Sitzungsgsberichte der Sächsischen Akademie der Wissenschaften zu Leipzig, philosophisch-historische Klasse*, 110, 2, 1965; J. van der Ploeg, "Jésus et les Pharisiens", *Mémorial Lagrange*, 1950, 279–93; H. Rasp, "Flavius Josephus und die jüdischen Religionsparteien", *ZNW* 23, 1924, 27–47; J. Schmid, "Die Pharisäer", *BuL* 3, 1962, 270 ff.; K. Schubert, "Die jüdischen Religionsparteien im Zeitalter Jesu", in K. Schubert, ed., *Der historische Jesus und der Christus unseres Glaubens*, 1962, 15 ff.; F. Sieffert, "Pharisäer und Sadduzäer", *RE* XV 264–92; M. Simon, *Les Sectes Juives au Temps de Jésus*, 1960; M. Weber, "Die Pharisäer", *Gesammelte Aufsätze zur Religionssoziologie*, III, 1921, 401–42; J. Wellhausen, *Die Pharisäer und Sadduzäer*, 1924².

Please

ἀρέσκω

ἀρέσκω (*areskō*), strive to please, accommodate, please; ἀρεστός (*arestos*), pleasing; ἀρεσκεία (*areskeia*), the desire to please; εὐάρεστος (*euarestos*), acceptable, pleasing; εὐαρεστέω (*euaresteō*),

814

please (someone), take pleasure in; ἀνθρωπάρεσκος *(anthrōpareskos)*, one who tries to please men, a man-pleaser.

CL *areskō* comes from a root *ar-*, to fit (from which also comes *aretē*, virtue), and is originally cognate with Lat. *arma*, weapons, and *ars*, art. Attested from Homer onwards, it denotes the pleasure which men or the gods derive from something. From it are derived the adjs. *arestos*, pleasant, and *euarestos*, pleasing, content (often attested in inscriptions). The noun *areskeia*, pleasure, grace, is attested from Aristotle onwards. Formations peculiar to the LXX are *euaresteō*, find pleasure, be content, and *anthrōpareskos*, someone who seeks to please men (only in LXX Ps. 53:5[52:6] as a mistranslation of *ḥōnāḵ*, "he who encamps against you", perhaps through confusion with *ḥēn*, grace). It is later found in Pss.Sol. 4:7, 8, 19.

OT 1. In the LXX the vb. occurs some 60 times, the adj. *arestos* 33 times, as a translation of good, be good; right, be right, often with "in the eyes of" added, following the underlying Heb. text. In Dan. (e.g. 3:22) it translates *šᵉp̄ar*, be beautiful, please (well). It occurs in the expressions "It pleases God ..." (Num. 23:27), and "the offering of Judah and Jerusalem will be pleasing to God" (Mal. 3:4). A word may be said to please someone, i.e. it meets with his approval, e.g. the king and the assembly (2 Chr. 30:4), the king and his commanders (1 Macc. 6:60).

areskeia is only found in Prov. 31:30 as a translation of *ḥēn*, grace, favour; *euarestos* only in Wis. 4:10; 9:10. The vb. *euaresteō*, to please, to take pleasure in, however, occurs 14 times, generally as translation of Heb. *hālak* (in the hith.) to walk (with God) (Gen. 5:22, 24; 6:9; 17:1; 24:40; 39:4; 48:15; Exod. 21:8; Jdg. 10:16; Pss. 26[25]:3; 35[34]:14; 56[55]:13; 116[114]:9; Sir. 44:16). Gen. 5:24 is noteworthy here. In the Heb. text attention is directed to the deed of man, expressed by a vb. of action ("Enoch walked with God"), whereas the LXX stresses God's judgment ("Enoch pleased God").

2. In Josephus *areskō* is found equally of God (it pleased God to make David king, *Ant*. 6, 8, 1) as of men (King Hyrcanus will do everything that pleases God, *Ant*. 13, 10, 5).

NT 1. In the NT *areskō* is found 17 times, of which 14 instances are in Paul and the remaining three are in Matt., Mk. and Acts. The sole instance of *areskeia* is also in Paul. In general *areskō* denotes a definite attitude.

1. Paul's use of the vb. three times in Rom. 15:1–3 is noteworthy. Paul charges the self-styled "strong" Christian with being concerned to please himself, i.e. in the last analysis being self-centred (v. 1). The phrase *heautois areskein* "denotes the inversion of human existence and evasion of God" (O. Michel, *Der Brief an die Römer, KEK* 4, 1966[13], 354, n. 4). This attitude of unrestrained self-trust is met by Paul with the rejoinder that each person should please his neighbour for his good, to build him up (v. 2). This does not mean seeking to please men in the sense of an attitude which looks for approbation and recognition from others (cf. Eph. 6:6), but enacting the will of God in the form of love for one's neighbour, in the case of the weak → brother. The basic direction of Christian conduct, which Paul appeals to by *areskō*, is grounded in the attitude of Christ himself (v. 3), who did not live to

815

please himself, *ouch heautō ēresen*. Rather, he assumed the attitude of the OT servant of God (Ps. 69:9) who submitted himself in obedience towards God.

areskō in Paul is, therefore, a term which characterizes man in both a false or a valid attitude to life. The apostle knows this from his own experience. Through his conversion he has been freed from concern for the favour of men, for he stands under the command of the Lord. He, therefore, wishes to live to please God and Christ. Paul does not preach in order to please men, but God (1 Thess. 2:4). Aligning himself with Christ and the goal set by Christ of saving all, Paul seeks to live with the intention of pleasing Jews and Greeks alike; i.e. he lives for the benefit of the many, that they may be saved (1 Cor. 10:33). The same thought lies behind other passages where the vb. is not used, e.g. Rom. 12:17 f. and 1 Cor. 9:22 (on this see H. L. Ellison, "Paul and the Law – 'All Things to All Men' ", in W. W. Gasque and R. P. Martin, eds., *Apostolic History and the Gospel*, 1970, 195–202). The Christian congregation must also see how they can please God (1 Thess. 4:1).

2 Tim. 2:4 adopts the picture of the soldier used elsewhere in Hellenistic moral teaching (cf. 1 Cor. 9:7; Phil. 2:25; Phlm. 2). The soldier on active service does not get himself involved in civilian life, but aims to please his commanding officer. It is thus impressed upon the reader that he is not to let himself be diverted from his work for Christ by concern about his earthly welfare. Similarly, the unmarried man who is not tied by marital considerations can direct all his energy to gaining Christ's approbation and recognition (1 Cor. 7:32). On the other hand, "those that are in the flesh [*hoi de en sarki ontes*] cannot please God" (Rom. 8:8). Here → flesh signifies a self-centred existence guided by human considerations. It is the antithesis of being led by the → Spirit (cf. Rom. 8:4 f., 9, 11, 13, 16). It is defined in terms of having the mind set on the flesh, being hostile to God, and not submitting to God's law (Rom. 8:7). Its end is death (Rom. 8:6, 13). The Jews who put Jesus and the prophets to death "displease God and oppose all men" (1 Thess. 2:15).

2. The adj. *arestos*, pleasing, occurs 4 times in the NT. In Acts 12:3 the execution of James is said to have been pleasing to the Jews. Elsewhere it is God who is the object of the pleasing. The expression *ouk areston estin*, it is not right (i.e. before God) (Acts 6:2) reflects LXX-Gk. usage. According to Jn. 8:29, Jesus always did what was pleasing to God, i.e. what was consonant with God's will. *arestos* underlines once more the unity between the sent and the sender. Because Christians keep God's commandments and do what pleases him, they receive from him in → prayer whatever they ask (1 Jn. 3:22).

3. The vb. *euaresteō*, please (3 times in Heb.), and the adj. *euarestos*, pleasing, (8 times in Paul and once in Heb.) also have God or Christ as their object, apart from one exception (Tit. 2:9). Indirectly, even Tit. 2:9 does not deviate from this: slaves are exhorted to be *euarestoi* to their masters, and so live to their satisfaction, in order, as members of the church community, to give God glory by their conduct and to please him (cf. Eph. 6:6). Children are exhorted to be obedient to their parents, because that is pleasing to the Lord (Col. 3:20). Paul thanks the Philippians for their gift, which is a → sacrifice pleasing to God (Phil. 4:18). The Christians in Rome are exhorted to offer their "living bodies as a holy sacrifice, truly pleasing to God" (Rom. 12:1 f. JB; cf. Eph. 5:10). The Christian's whole existence is offered to God (cf. 2 Cor. 5:9). Anyone who serves (→ Serve; → Slave, art.

douleuō) Christ in righteousness, peace and joy in the Holy → Spirit pleases God and is acknowledged by him (Rom. 14:18). Therefore, we must pray that God may work in us through Christ that which is pleasing in his sight (Heb. 13:21).

Heb. 11:5 f. takes up Gen. 5:24 LXX. It is inferred from the fact that Enoch pleased God (*euarestēkenai*) that he was a believer; for without → faith one cannot please God. (On Enoch see Jude 14 f.; Eth.Enoch 1:9; 71:14; Sir. 44:16; Jub. 4:17; 10:17; Wis. 4:10 ff. [cf. F. F. Bruce, *The Epistle to the Hebrews*, NLC 1964, 286-90). In the Christian life charity and acts of love are a "sacrifice" in which God takes pleasure (Heb. 13:16).

4. *areskeia* only occurs in Col. 1:10. Paul prays that the Colossians may be filled with the knowledge of God's will, so that they may walk worthily of the Lord and always please him.

5. *anthrōpareskos* is encountered only in the rule to → slaves (Eph. 6:6; Col. 3:22; cf. also 2 Clem. 13:1). Slaves are to obey their masters not in an adulatory fashion, to please men, but in the fear of the Lord.

6. The words of this group are predominantly used in the NT to denote pleasure in the sight of God or Christ which derives from a definite attitude. Even where recognition from the side of men is meant, the gaze generally goes beyond men to God whose pleasure should be sought.   *H. Bietenhard*

| εὐδοκέω | εὐδοκέω (*eudokeō*), be well pleased, regard favourably, take delight in; εὐδοκία (*eudokia*), good will, good |

pleasure, favour, wish, desire.

CL The vb. *eudokeō* is a colloquial term from Hellenistic times (attested from the 3rd cent. B.C.). It is thought to be derived from the hypothetical *eudokos*, formed from *eu*, good, and *dechomai*, to accept. In cl. Gk. it means to be well pleased or content, to consent, approve; in the pass. to be favoured, i.e. prosper; to find favour with. From the vb. the LXX has also formed the noun *eudokia*, whereas cl. Gk. uses the noun *eudokēsis*, satisfaction, approval, consent. The goal of the Epicurean philosophy of life is the *eudokoumenē zōē*, the life with which one is content (Philodemus Philosophus, *De Morte* 30, 42; cf. G. Schrenk, *TDNT* II 740).

OT 1. (a) In the LXX *eudokeō* occurs some 60 times. Where there is an underlying Heb. text, it generally trans. *rāṣâh*, to take pleasure in, like, enjoy, decide upon, elect, and denotes a passionate and positive volition. The godly man rejoices over the sanctuary (1 Chr. 29:3; Ps. 102[101]:15), and in the works of truth (1 Esd. 4:39). One decides for Alexander Balas (1 Macc. 10:47), elects Simon as leader (1 Macc. 14:41). One is lenient and indulgent (2 Chr. 10:7; Sir. 18:31). With a negative it means to spurn (Hab. 2:4).

Yahweh takes pleasure in his people (Ps. 44[43]:4; 149:4), in a pious man (2 Sam. 22:20), in those who fear him (Ps. 147[146]:11). A man prays that it may please Yahweh to deliver him (Ps. 40[39]:13). On the other hand, Yahweh has no pleasure in the calf (i.e. the strength) of a man's leg (Ps. 147[146]:10), nor in anyone who does evil (Mal. 2:17). A penitent mind is more pleasing to Yahweh than a → sacrifice (Ps. 51:16 ff.[50:18 ff.]; Jer. 14:12).

(b) The noun *eudokia* occurs 25 times (only in Pss., Cant., 1 Chr., Sir.). In 8 places it is a translation of Heb. *rāṣôn* (56 times in MT), good-pleasure, grace, the will of God (40 times in MT). *eudokia* can denote the will or pleasure of man (cf. Ps. 141[140]:5; Sir. 8:14; 9:12), but also the divine good-pleasure, God's grace and blessing (Ps. 5:13; 51:19[50:21]; 89[88]:17; Ps.Sol. 8:22). Sir., in particular, displays the tendency to use *eudokia* to render Heb. *rāṣôn*, in order to describe God's good pleasure, his gracious will, activity and election (e.g. Sir. 1:27; 11:17; 15:15 *et al.*). *eudokia* denotes the divine purpose or determination in, e.g. Sir. 33:13; 36:13; 39:18.

2. The linguistic usage of Judaism corresponds with that of the OT. In the formula "to do God's good pleasure" which occurs frequently among the Rabbis, the Heb. *rāṣôn* denotes God's will. The expression "well-pleasing in God's sight", stemming from courtly language, is also common. In prayer the formula "May it be pleasing in thy sight", i.e. may it be thy will, is used. This corresponds exactly with the expression used by Jesus in Matt. 11:26: *eudokia egeneto emprosthen sou*, "it was well-pleasing in your sight" (cf. Matt. 18:14; Lk. 10:21; 12:32; Ber. 7d; Targ. Cant. 7:14; Tg.O.Gen. 28:17; Num. 14:8; G. Dalman, *The Words of Jesus*, 1902, 211). But the expression can also denote human good pleasure.

3. The Dead Sea Scrolls speak of "all the sons of his [or your, i.e. God's] good pleasure" (1QH 4:33; 11:9), or of "the elect of [the divine] good pleasure" (1QS 8:6). *rāṣôn* in the sense of will likewise occurs frequently (1QH 10:2, 6, 9; 14:13; 16:10; 4QpPs 37:2, 5). Parallel expressions are "the elect of heaven" (1QM 12:5), and "the elect of righteousness" (1QH 2:13). "Good-pleasure is a term of electing and predestinarian thought" (J. Maier, *Die Texte vom Toten Meer*, II, 1960, 105). It is thus not a matter of the good will of men, but of the men whom God has elected – specifically, the members of the Qumran community.

NT 1. *eudokeō* is found 21 times in the NT, including 11 times in Paul and 3 times each in Matt. and Heb., but never in the Johannine writings. *eudokia* occurs 9 times, including 6 times in Paul, twice in Lk. The vb. is used of human beings in 7 places, the noun in two.

2. In a number of passages it is man who is the subject. Thus, the congregations of Macedonia decided to make a collection for the parent community of Jerusalem (Rom. 15:26 ff.). Paul considered it preferable to be away from the body and be at home with the Lord (2 Cor. 5:8; → Flesh; → Body, art. *sōma*). He took pleasure in his → weakness for the sake of Christ (2 Cor. 12:10). He was ready to share not only the gospel with the church at Thessalonica but his own self (1 Thess. 2:8). He decided to stay behind in Athens alone (1 Thess. 3:1). All those who have found pleasure in unrighteousness will be judged (2 Thess. 2:12). In Rom. 10:1 Paul says that it is his heart's wish and his prayer that the Jews may be saved, i.e. that they may come to faith in Jesus. During Paul's time in prison, some people preached Christ out of jealousy and rivalry, but others because they were well-disposed towards Paul (Phil. 1:15).

3. (a) In all other passages it is God's purpose, resolve and choice that is spoken of. God has no pleasure in (*ouk eudokēsas*) sacrifice (Heb. 10:6, 8; cf. Ps. 40:6 ff.), and those who shrink back (Heb. 10:38; cf. Hab. 2:4). But Christ does the will of God as the One who offers himself as a sacrifice and so gains God's good pleasure.

818

It is God's purpose to give the kingdom to the little flock (Lk. 12:32). God decided to reveal Jesus Christ to Paul (Gal. 1:15), and to save believers by the folly of the preaching of the → cross (1 Cor. 1:21; → Redemption, art. *sōzō*). God had no pleasure in the majority of the Israelites in the → wilderness period, and he repudiated them (1 Cor. 10:5). God has decided that all the → fullness of the Godhead should dwell in Christ (Col. 1:19).

(b) At the baptism of Jesus God's voice sounded out from heaven: "This is my beloved Son, with whom I am well pleased" (Matt. 3:17 par. Mk. 1:11; but cf. Lk. 3:22; cf. Ps. 2:7; Isa. 42:1; Gen. 22:2; 2 Pet. 1:17). According to Matt. 17:5, this voice resounded with the same words at Jesus' transfiguration (cf. Matt. 12:18). Here, too, it is a case of God's choice and determination, by which he has installed Jesus as messiah. *eudokia* in Matt. 11:26 describes the transcendent purpose of God (see above OT 2).

(c) The best-known place in the NT where *eudokia* occurs is Lk. 2:14. One should here retain the reading *en anthrōpois eudokias* as the original. The expression corresponds with the phrases adduced above from the Dead Sea Scrolls (see above OT 3). The phrase refers to the men of God's good pleasure whom God has elected in order to bring them his salvation, Christ. The song of the angels proclaims a divine event and activity: God has sent the Christ to earth. For this he is glorified in heaven; the effect on earth is peace. In the birth of the Christ → peace, i.e. eschatological fulfilment, the kingdom of God, begins on earth. We are not, therefore, dealing here with the good will of men, as if they somehow approved of or contributed to this event. However much men are affected as recipients of salvation, the angels' announcement was not directed at those who were at the time well-intentioned. The "men of good will" ought to disappear entirely from Bible translations and Christmas meditations! Rather, we are dealing with God's sovereign and gracious will, which elects for itself a people for salvation and sanctification (→ Man, art. *anthrōpos* NT 1; cf. E. Vogt, " 'Peace Among Men of God's good Pleasure' Lk. 2:14", in K. Stendahl, ed., *The Scrolls and the New Testament*, 1958, 114–7). J. C. O'Neill wishes to support the translation "Glory be to God on high, and in earth peace, good will towards men", but his case involves an emendation of the text which treats "peace" as an early gloss on *eudokia* ("Glory to God in the Highest, And on Earth?", in J. R. McKay and J. F. Miller, eds., *Biblical Studies: Essays in Honour of William Barclay*, 1976, 172–77).

(d) In the hortatory passage Phil. 2:13 f. Paul summons the congregation to work out their salvation in fear and trembling, because God is at work in them, "inspiring both the will and the deed, for his own chosen purpose [*hyper tēs eudokias*]." This is probably the best translation, for God has chosen the believers and continues to work in them, so that his elective purpose also reaches its goal. The passage brings together the sovereignty of God and the responsibility of man. In Eph. 1:5, 9, 11 *eudokia* is synonymous with *thelēma* or *boulē*, → will, and *prothesis*, design, plan, purpose (→ Foreknowledge). Believers have a place in God's eternal will and election which have salvation as their goal. God's free grace is the central point of the statements. The concise formulation in the prayer of 2 Thess. 1:11 *plērōsē pasan eudokian agathōsynēs* (lit. "fulfil all good will for goodness") probably also means God's elective purpose directed towards the conduct of Christians. Paul therefore prays at the same time that God's will may be done and reach its goal. But it is also possible to understand it as referring to the will of men: "may fulfil every good resolve" (RSV).   *H. Bietenhard*

(a). W. Foerster, *areskō* etc., *TDNT* I 455 ff.; G. Schrenk, *eudokeō* etc., *TDNT* II 738–51; E. Vogt, " 'Peace Among Men of God's Good Pleasure' Lk. 2:14", in K. Stendahl, ed., *The Scrolls and the New Testament*, 1958, 114–17.
(b). C. H. Hunzinger, "Neues Licht auf Lk. 2, 14 *anthrōpoi eudokias*", *ZNW* 44, 1952–53, 85 ff.; J. Jeremias, "*Anthrōpoi eudokias*", *ZNW* 28, 1929, 13–20; H. Schürmann, *Das Lukasevangelium*, *Theologischer Kommentar zum Neuen Testament*, 3, 1, 1970, 113 ff.

Poor

πένης

πένης (*penēs*), poor; πενιχρός (*penichros*), poor.

CL Through its root *penēs* is linked with *ponos*, → burden, trouble. From Xen. onwards it refers to the man who cannot live from his property, but has to work with his hands. Hence the *penēs* is not like the → *ptōchos*, who is poor enough to be a beggar and needs help. He is only relatively poor; the opposite of *penēs* is *plousios*, wealthy (→ Possessions). The term includes the handworker and small peasant, who, subsequent to Solon's legislation, were the main supporters of the Athenian democracy.

For a long time security through property was considered to be the best guarantee of a virtuous life, while *penia*, poverty, was considered to be the root of moral offences, a view found as late as Plato (*Laws*, 11, 919b). Not later than the time of Socrates this concept was realized to be inadequate, for experience shows that it may in fact be *penia* that creates the will for culture (cf. Diogenes quoted by Stob. *Ecl.* 5, 783), and so may lead to virtue, which is the true ideal in life. By the art of self-sufficiency (*autarkeia*; cf. Epict., *Dissertationes* 4, 6, 3 ff.; → Suffice) a life in poverty can be rich and free (Plut., *De Vitando Aere Alieno* 3; 6; *De Virtute et Vitio* 4). No religious value was attributed to poverty.

OT 1. In the LXX *penēs* is used some 50 times, and its synonym *penichros* 3 times. It is used only 6 times for *rāš* (2 Sam. 12:1, 3, 4; Eccl. 4:14; 5:7; Ps. 82[81]:3), which is nearest to the basic meaning of the Gk., although *rāš* is found 21 times in all. Normally *penēs* is used for the economically and legally oppressed. It is used 29 times for '*eḇyôn*: 15 times in the Pss. (e.g. 72:4, 13; 86:1; 109:31), and even more clearly in Amos 2:6; 4:1; 5:12; 8:4, 6; Ezek. 18: 12. It is used 12 times for '*ānî* (e.g. Ps. 9:12, 18; 72:12; Deut. 24:14 f.), and 9 times for *dal* (e.g. 1 Sam. 2:8). Since these words are also rendered by → *ptōchos*, which is preferred for '*anî* and *dal* and which is also used 11 times for '*eḇyôn*, it is clear that the definite difference that existed in Gk. life between the one who needs alms (*ptōchos*) and the one who is forced into manual work or who has limited means (*penēs*) has been obscured. Even if this development may in part be due to the relative similarity of meaning in the Heb. equivalents, its deeper reason will have to be sought in the Israelite concept of property and social order. In the long run poverty could be created almost only by unrighteousness, i.e. the failure of the community and disobedience to God. *penichros* occurs at Exod. 22:24 ('*ānî*); Prov. 28:15; 29:7 (*dal*).

2. There follow two lines of semantic development. Hellenized Judaism clearly tends to follow the normal Gk. meaning of *penēs*: e.g. *ptōchos* is not to be found in Philo, who in contrast to the LXX even translates '*ānî* in Lev. 19:10 and 23:22 by *penēs* instead of *ptōchos* (*Virt.* 90). By so doing he employs the less offensive, politer term for poor, and thus makes the Bible more suitable for Gk. ears, but in so doing deprives it of an important stress.

NT In contrast, the NT, following OT thought but not the LXX's choice of words, has clearly decided on → *ptōchos*, so as to show not merely a man's standing in society but especially his standing before God, for he has nothing to bring him. *penēs* occurs only in 2 Cor. 9:9 in a quotation from Ps. 112:9 ("He scatters abroad, he gives to the poor; his righteousness endures for ever"), even though the reference shows that the Heb. '*ebyôn* must refer to those needing help. *penichros* is found only in Lk. 21:2, of the widow at the temple treasury, who was visibly poor. The par. in Mk. 12:42 uses *ptōchos*.   *L. Coenen*

| πτωχός | πτωχός (*ptōchos*), poor; πτωχεύω (*ptōcheuō*), be poor, beg; πτωχεία (*ptōcheia*), poverty. |

CL 1. *ptōchos* (Homer onwards) belongs to the root *ptē*, crouched together (cf. *ptēssō*, be afraid; *ptōssō*, duck in fear; *ptōx*, timid). It signifies utter dependence on society. As an adj. it means begging, dependent on the help of strangers, poor as a beggar, poor. Commoner still is its use as a noun meaning beggar. It stands in contrast to *plousios*, rich, owning property. Secular Gk. has the metaphorical meanings of meagre, inadequate, scanty, unable, conceding something (first attested in Dionysius of Halicarnassus, flourished 30–10 B.C.). Its most important derivatives are: *ptōcheuō*, beg, live the life of a beggar, be destitute; *ptōcheia*, activity of a beggar, begging, destitution, poverty.

2. In early Gk. thought poverty was not considered to have religious value. It did not give a man any special standing before the gods, nor did it place him under their special protection. Charity, especially to those impoverished by the blows of fate, was considered a virtue when exercised by the propertied classes, because it was useful to society, but it was not regarded as a religious or ethical act. There was no public care for the poor. In later Gk. philosophy poverty was regarded by some as a favourable precondition for virtue. The highest goal of life was to live virtuously in all material conditions including poverty.

OT 1. In the LXX *ptōchos* (some 100 times) is used for the following five Heb. words. In the first four it is virtually synonymous with → *penēs*.

(a) '*ānî* (37 times), oppressed, poor, humble, lowly (e.g. Lev. 19:10; 2 Sam. 22:28; Job 29:12; Pss. 10:9[9:30]; 12[11]:5; Isa. 3:14 f.). Koehler-Baumgartner connect it with '*ānâh*, afflict, oppress, humble (719 ff.). Where economic dependence is implied, the terms under (b) and (c) may be linked with it. Where there is no specific mention of an oppressor, the word becomes generally synonymous with the socially poor, with those without land. That such poverty had been caused by disinheritance or unlawful injury and not by the person's own fault is shown by its being contrasted with violence, not riches. It is, therefore, understandable that

821

Yahweh, the Judge of Israel, protects these poor (see below 2 and 3) and they place their sole trust and hope in this (→ Humility, art. *praÿs* OT).

(b) *dal*, low, weak, poor, thin (22 times), especially in Amos (2:7; 4:1; 5:11; 8:4, 6), Pss. (e.g. 72[71]:13; 82[81]:3; 113[112]:1) and Prov. (e.g. 19:4[1], 17; 28:3, 8, 15). *dal* means physically weak, and is then used of the position of the lowest social classes, of the peasants as poor, needy, unimportant.

(c) *'ebyôn*, in want, needy, poor (11 times). This is nearest to the conventional meaning of *ptōchos* and means one seeking alms, a beggar. It is then used generally for the very poor and homeless. The linked *'ānî wǝ'ebyôn*, poor and needy, especially in the Pss., connotes the attitude of one praying to God (7 times, e.g. Ps. 35[34]:10; 86[85]:1; LXX *ptōchos kai penēs*). The one who prays belongs to God and so comes before him in entreaty.

(d) *rāš*, in want, poor (11 times). This is used purely in a social and economic sense, poor, needy, in want. It is sometimes translated by → *penēs* (cf. 2 Sam. 12:3). It is a favourite word in the wisdom literature; in Prov. it is used especially as a contrast to rich (e.g. 13:8; 14:20; cf. also 17:5; 19:7, 22; 22:2, 7; 28:6, 27).

(e) In the latest OT writings *miskēn*, a term still used by the Oriental beggars for themselves, is used in Eccl. 4:13, 9:15 f. for the dependent, the socially lower (cf. Exod. 1:11: lit. "the cities of base service"); it takes the place of *'ānî* after it had received its weakened meaning of poor. Only in Sir. 30:14 is it translated by *ptōchos*. Its derivative *miskēnuṭ* (Deut. 8:9) is rendered by *ptōcheia*, poverty.

In the light of the Heb. terms it translates, *ptōchos* in the LXX has widened its meaning, especially in the social, economic and religious spheres.

2. Because Israel's land is Yahweh's land, there may be no continuing poverty among his people. Hence the Book of the Covenant (Exod. 20:22–23:19) lays down the following programme, which in principle was always valid in Israel, even if it was seldom carried out:

(a) The Israelite who as a result of economic need had to sell himself in payment of debt was to be freed in the sabbatical year (Exod. 21:2).

(b) In the sabbatical year, when the ground was allowed to lie fallow, its produce belonged to the poor (Exod. 23:10 f.).

(c) It was forbidden to exploit or oppress the poor (Exod. 22:22–27).

(d) The law may not be perverted against the poor (Exod. 23:6 ff.). Yahweh himself proclaimed himself the protector of the poor (Exod. 22:27b), and reminded Israel of how he freed from Egypt, thus ending his position of dependence there (Exod. 22:21; 23:9).

3. Under the monarchy the economy changed from one of barter to one using money, and many of the farmers became financially dependent on townsmen. This impoverishment of a wide stratum of the population was felt not merely as a major social problem but also as a religious one, for it involved a breach of the divine law. The eighth-century prophets especially attacked this social injustice in the name of Yahweh, and in particular the oppression of the farmers and the poor, threatening with the judgment of God the rich who were responsible (e.g. Amos 2:7; 4:1; 5:11; 8:4; Isa. 3:14 f.; 5:8 f.; 10:2; Mic. 2:2; 3:2 ff.).

Only in the setting of this historical situation can we understand the meaning in the Psalms of "poor", "needy". The poor man is the one who suffers injustice; he is poor because others have despised God's law. He therefore turns, helpless and humble, to God in prayer, not only for his own need, but also in the consciousness that ultimately it is a question of God's glory. Through the self-identification, generation after generation, of those who prayed with the poor in psalms of individual lamentation and thanksgiving (e.g. Pss. 25:16; 40:17(MT 40:18); 69:29(MT 69:30); 86:1; 109:22) there gradually developed the specific connotation of "poor" as meaning all those who turn to God in great need and seek his help. God is praised as the protector of the poor (e.g. Pss. 72:2, 4, 12 ff.; 132:15), who procures justice for them against their oppressors (Pss. 9; 10; 35; 74; 140).

Deuteronomy offers a plan of social reformation, based on legislation of the wilderness period. It has its own rules for the protection of the poor (e.g. Deut. 15:1–18; 24:14–22). However, the word *ptōchos* does not appear, for → "brother" is used as a technical term for one's impoverished fellow-citizen.

Ezekiel in exile saw the coming destruction of the rump-kingdom of Judah as Yahweh's punishment for their oppression of the poor and needy (Ezek. 22:29).

The misery of the exile led temporarily to the use of "poor" and "needy" as collective terms for the people. They are found in a number of hopeful eschatological promises about the future of the people (e.g. Isa. 29:19; 41:17; 49:13; 51:21 ff.; 54:11 ff.; 61:1–4).

The many reflections and varying pronouncements of the wisdom literature on the poor are much less religious in tone. They vary from explanations of poverty as the fault of those who suffer it (e.g. Prov. 6:6–11; 23:21), and warnings against it (Sir. 40:28), to the praise of the poor and a call to improve their lot (Sir. 10:30; Prov. 14:31).

4. All the main lines of OT thought occur again in Rabbinic Judaism, both concerning material poverty and its alleviation and its spiritualization and religious classification. The following points should be noted:

(a) The ritual practice of great voluntary acts of charity throughout Palestine and the Diaspora. The groups of the Pharisees, Essenes and the Hellenistic Jews of Jerusalem had their special forms of charitable work, e.g. feeding the poor, clothing the naked (cf. SB IV 536–558 on private charity in early Judaism).

(b) There was an excellent organization of care for the poor in the synagogue communities which went as far as founding hospices. This was the more remarkable as there is no trace of a programme of social equality in it. It was rooted in the ethical commandments of the OT and was made possible by the temple → tax, and after the destruction of Jerusalem by the weekly public alms (→ Serve, art. *diakoneō* OT 2; cf. Taanith 24a). In fact, fairly clear norms were laid down for the contributions expected from synagogue members; they can be traced back with certainty to the period before the destruction of the temple. The poor were expected to contribute (Shekalim 1:7; 2:5) to demonstrate their religious equality (SB II 46), though they were the first to profit from individual and synagogue care for the poor. Priests and Levites without estates, foreigners, widows and orphans could expect to receive the tithes for the poor to be paid at the end of every third year (cf. Deut. 14:29; 26:12). These continued to be collected and gained greater importance after the destruction of Jerusalem.

5. Considerable variations of opinion are to be found in the spiritual judgments on poverty.

(a) Especially the Psalms of Solomon among the pseudepigraphic writings reserve the term "poor" for those who have experienced divine acts of deliverance and are hence identical with the righteous (cf. Pss.Sol. 5:2, 11; 10:6; 15:1; 18:2). Heavy material burdens and martyrdom are generally included.

(b) The community of the "poor" in Qumran made renunciation of private property a rule of the order, and built up a well-organized community life in expectation of eschatological salvation. 1QpHab. 12:3, 6, 10; 4QpPs. 37; 2:10 show that they had chosen the term "poor" for themselves. The Hymns (1QM) frequently use the phrase "poor and needy". In their writings they attacked the priests who exploited the poor. (See further E. Bammel, *TDNT* VI 896–99; → Possessions, art. *ploutos* OT 3.)

(c) The dominant Rabbinic theology ultimately denied that poverty had any theological value. Occasionally it even saw the cause of poverty in lack of knowledge of the Torah, the one real poverty (cf. Nedarim 41a; and in contrast the first beatitude in Matt., see below NT 2 (b)). This led to a feeling of moral superiority over the poor. In striking contrast to this a form of popular eschatology clung to the belief "that the poor . . . are the primary objects of the divine mercy" (*TDNT* VI 902; cf. Exod.R. 31, 13 on 22:24). Such belief fostered the danger of idealizing poverty.

NT 1. *ptōchos* occurs 34 times in the NT, mostly in the Gospels (24 times; of these 10 times in Lk., 6 times in material peculiar to him); *ptōcheia*, poverty, 3 times; *ptōcheuō*, be poor, only in 2 Cor. 8:9.

1. The Gospels. (a) *ptōchos* occurs in its lit. sense in the Synoptic Gospels. Jesus told the rich man who wanted to inherit eternal life, "Sell what you have, and give to the poor" (Mk. 10:21; cf. Lk. 18:22). Matt. 19:21 qualifies the saying by inserting the condition, "If you will be perfect." In Mk. 12:41–44 par. Lk. 21:1–4 Jesus says that the apparently negligible gift of the poor woman, entitled to support, is far greater than those of the rich. Only in the events leading up to the Passion does Jesus in Mk. 14:7, Matt. 26:11, Jn. 12:8 say that almsgiving has to take second place, when it is a question of a last opportunity for an extravagant act of love to one destined to death (Matt. 26:11; Mk. 14:7; Jn. 12:8).

(b) Jesus speaks of the poor in Matt. 11:5 and in the first beatitude (Matt. 5:3; Lk. 6:20). The question of the original form is disputed, as is the question whether the saying was taken from Jewish tradition. There is much to be said for the view that the shorter Lucan form ("Blessed are you poor, for yours is the kingdom of God") is original, though not the use of the second person (cf. Matt. 5:3: "Blessed are the poor in spirit, for theirs is the kingdom of heaven"). Matt. gives an interpretative paraphrase which brings out the Heb. meaning.

Neither passage uses "poor" in the general social meaning. The enlarged form in Matt., "the poor in spirit [*hoi ptōchoi tō pneumati*]", brings out the OT and Jewish background of those who in affliction have confidence only in God (cf. Pss. 69[68]: 28 f., 32 f.; 37[36]:14; 40[39]:18; Isa. 61:1; Pss.Sol. 10:7; 1QM 14:7; 1QS 4:3; cf. D. Hill, *The Gospel of Matthew*, 1972, 110 f.; and *Greek Words and Hebrew Meanings*, 1967, 234, 251). In Lk. the beatitudes are essentially confined to poverty, the poor, those who weep, the hungry, the hated, and are followed by woes over the rich (Lk. 6:24 ff.). By using the 2nd person plur., Lk. indicates that the poverty of the beatitudes is that caused by → discipleship. For he who believes in the Son finds all the → promises of God for the poor and suffering, miserable and humble (e.g. Isa. 57:15; 61:1), for those who weep (Ps. 126:5 f.) and are hungry (Isa. 49:10; Ezek. 34:29) fulfilled in him. In the same way Jesus is proclaimed in Matt. 11:5 par. Lk. 7:22 (a quotation from Isa. 61:1) as the fulfiller of the longing of the OT for salvation. His acts find their culmination in the proclamation of the gospel to the poor. (→ Blessing, art. *makarios*.)

(c) Luke records this quotation from Isa. 61:1 at the beginning of Jesus' ministry as a programme (Lk. 4:18). It occurs in the words that Jesus read in the synagogue at Nazareth. In Lk. this dominant theme of poverty is linked with a sharp attack on the rich (Lk. 6:24 ff.; → Possessions). According to Lk., Jesus told the man who had invited him to a meal (Lk. 14:12 ff.) to invite the poor and others from whom no repayment could be expected, and promised him an eschatological reward for so doing. Similarly the poor are the first substitute guests at the great banquet (Lk. 14:21).

Lazarus (lit. "God helps") is the type of the poor whom God receives (Lk. 16:20, 22), and the anonymous rich man who failed in his duty to him is the type of those condemned by God (cf. Lk. 12:13–21; see further J. D. M. Derrett, "Dives and Lazarus and the Preceding Sayings", in *Law in the New Testament*, 1970, 78–99). When Zacchaeus gave the half of his goods to the poor after his conversion (Lk. 19:8) his gratitude showed itself in concern for the poor (cf. Derrett, "The Anointing at Bethany and the Story of Zacchaeus", op. cit., 266–85).

H.-H. Esser

(d) The Synoptic Gospels, in particular, depict Jesus' way of life as one of self-chosen poverty. This is highlighted by the reply that he gave to a would-be disciple: "Foxes have holes, and birds of the air have nests; but the Son of man has nowhere to lay his head" (Matt. 8:20 par. Lk. 9:58). The → disciples left all in order to follow him (Matt. 4:18–22 par. Mk. 1:16–20, Lk. 5:1–11; Jn. 1:35–51; cf. also Lk. 13:33). The sale of his → possessions and a life of discipleship in poverty were demanded of the rich young ruler as the precondition of eternal life (Matt. 19:16–22; Lk. 18:18–24). On the missions on which the disciples were sent they were to go without possessions or provisions (Matt. 10:1–16; Lk. 9:1–6; 10:1–12; → Bag, art. *pēra*). In this way of life there was in fact a double separation: from possessions and from family ties (Matt. 10:37 ff.; Lk. 14:25–33). The life-style which Jesus adopted for himself and called his disciples to adopt was one which exemplified the Sermon on the Mount, especially the Beatitudes. But the particular emphasis on poverty characterized by lack of possessions and cutting loose from family ties suggests that Jesus identified himself with the poor in the Beatitude. His whole way of life was thus a conscious identification with the poor and the OT concept of poverty. In itself this was an act of loving compassion. At the same time it was a life which deliberately chose to cast itself on the care of the Father. But in doing so, Jesus was also putting to the test the people of Israel. By being confronted by Jesus in this way the responsiveness of Israel faced its supreme test. (→ Possessions and the various sayings and parables of Jesus examined under the various key words.)

C. Brown

2. James strongly attacks the attitude of the rich both in public and in church services (2:2 f., 6 f.) and demands equal esteem for the poor. He bases his position

on the facts that God "has chosen those who are poor in the world" (2:5), and that mercy towards men on earth will be the criterion in the final judgment (2:13; cf. Matt. 25:31–46).

3. In the letters to the churches of Smyrna in Rev. 2:9 and Laodicea in Rev. 3:17 (→ Cold, art. *psychros* NT) the contrast between poor and rich shows the difference between men's estimate and that of the glorified Lord (1:9 ff.). Rev. 13:16 describes how all social and economic classes, rich and poor alike, are captured by the hypnotic power of the beast from the abyss (→ Animal, art. *thērion*).   *H.-H. Esser*

4. Paul made only occasional use of the concept, although he was deeply concerned for the poor.

(a) The poor are mentioned in the lit. sense in connection with the collection for the church in Jerusalem. "The poor of Jerusalem" was perhaps a name which they had acquired (cf. Rom. 15:26, where "of the saints" is added; cf. also Gal. 2:10). In Rom. 15:26 Paul speaks of the "some contribution" (RSV, lit. → "some fellowship", *koinōnian tina*) which the churches of Macedonia and Achaia were making. "They were pleased to do it, and indeed they are in debt to them, for if the Gentiles have come to share in their spiritual blessings, they ought also to be of service to them in material blessings" (Rom. 15:27). Paul himself was going to Jerusalem with it *diakonōn tois hagiois* (lit. "serving the saints"), prior to going to Spain (Rom. 15:25; cf. vv. 24, 28; 1:10 ff.; Acts 19:21), although he was aware of the personal risk because of Jewish antagonism in Judea (v. 31). In 1 Cor. 16:1–4 Paul gives various recommendations about the collection, suggesting (as he did to the churches of Galatia, v. 1), that they put something aside on the first day of the week (v. 2), and proposing on his arrival "to send those whom you accredit by letter to carry your gift to Jerusalem" (v. 3), and, if it seems advisable, to go himself as well (v. 4).

It would seem that the Corinthians did not follow these instructions, for Paul returns to the question in 2 Cor. 8 and 9, which some scholars hold to be separate letters which were subsequently incorporated into 2 Cor. Evidently a year had elapsed and the collection was not much further advanced (2 Cor. 8:10). Paul, therefore, sent Titus to complete the work (vv. 6, 15 f., 23; cf. 9:5) together with two men perhaps appointed by the Jerusalem church (vv. 18 f., 22 f.; cf. 9:5). Possibly the men referred to here were the same as those appointed by the council at Jerusalem to communicate its decisions (Acts 15:20). Paul writes "not as a command, but to prove by the earnestness of others that your love also is genuine" (v. 8). Moreover, he sets before them the example of Christ: "For you know the grace of our Lord Jesus Christ, that though he was rich, yet for your sake be became poor, so that by his poverty you might become rich [*hoti di' hymas eptō-cheusen plousios ōn, hina hymeis tē ekeinou ptōcheia ploutēsēte*]" (v. 9; on this verse see below (c)).

In 2 Cor. 9:1–4 Paul expresses the hope that his boasting about the Corinthians to the churches of Macedonia and Achaia will not prove vain in view of the possibility of a meagre response. He has sent on the brethren "to arrange in advance this gift you have promised, so that it may be ready not as an exaction but as a willing gift" (v. 5). He reminds them that "he who sows sparingly will also reap sparingly, and he who sows bountifully will also reap bountifully. Each one must do as he has made up his mind, not reluctantly or under compulsion, for God loves a cheerful giver" (vv. 6 f.; cf. Prov. 22:8 LXX). This is further reinforced by a quotation from Ps. 112:9 (v. 9). Paul sees the response to the needs of the poor as a free expression of obedience and gratitude: "Under the test of this service, you [*v.l.* they] will glorify God by your obedience in acknowledging the gospel of Christ, and by the generosity of your contribution for them and for all others; while they long for you and pray for you, because of the surpassing grace of God in you. Thanks be to God for his inexpressible gift!" (vv. 13 ff.).

Elsewhere, the poor are mentioned in Gal. 2:10, where Paul recalls his meeting with the "pillars" of the Jerusalem church, at which he was given the right hand of fellowship to go to the Gentiles, whilst they would go to the circumcision, i.e. the Jews, "only they would have us remember the poor, which very thing I was eager to do." The need of material relief at Jerusalem is evident from the story of the appointment of the seven to serve in the daily distribution (Acts 6:1 ff.). The situation was no doubt aggravated for the church by Jewish hostility (cf. Acts 4:1 ff.; 5:17 ff.; 6:12 ff.; 7:54 ff.; 9:1 f.; 12:1 ff.). Acts 11:27 ff. reports how the Christian prophet Agabus came from Jerusalem to Antioch and foretold the great famine which took place under the emperor Claudius. Several famines are known from other sources to have taken place about this time (Josephus, *Ant.* 3, 15, 3; 20, 2, 5; 20, 5, 2; Dio Cassius, 60, 11; Eusebius, *Chron.Canon*; Tacitus, *Ann.* 12, 43; Orosius, 7, 6, 17; cf. F. F. Bruce, *The Acts of the Apostles*, 1952², 239 f.). Acts 11:29 f. records the response of the church at Antioch: "And the disciples determined, every one according to his ability, to send relief to the brethren who lived in Judea; and they did so, sending it to the elders by the hand of Barnabas and Saul" (cf. 12:25).

For a reconstruction of the events and an interpretation of their significance see K. F. Nickle, *The Collection: A Study in Paul's Strategy, SBT* 48, 1966. Nickle holds that the prototype of Paul's collection was the famine relief sent from Antioch. Paul's collection began as an act of charity, instigated at the Jerusalem meeting described in Gal. But as the tensions increased between the Gentile mission led by Paul with its more liberal attitude to the law and those at Jerusalem who clung to Jewish practices, the collection took on a theological significance for Paul. It was a means of reconciliation which bore fruit in the decisions of the Jerusalem council. Although there were Jewish analogies in the temple → tax, the collection took on a christological and soteriological significance. It was not only an act of charity among fellow believers, motivated by the love of Christ; it was also an expression of the solidarity of the Christian fellowship, showing that God had also called the Gentiles to faith. It was, moreover, "an eschatological pilgrimage of the Gentile Christians to Jerusalem by which the Jews were to be confronted with the undeniable reality of the divine gift of saving grace to the Gentiles and thereby be themselves moved through jealousy to finally accept the gospel" (op. cit., 142). This latter point helps to explain the seriousness with which Paul regarded the collection, and lends credence to the account of the trip in Acts 19:21–21:16 which Paul insisted on completing despite the dangers (Acts 20:3, 23; 21:4, 10 ff.). Acts rightly depicts the visit to Jerusalem "as the culmination and embodiment of Paul's entire apostleship" (op. cit., 143; cf. Acts 20:24). As an act of charity and means of promoting unity between the two wings of the church, the collection produced tangible results. But it failed to provoke the unbelieving Jews to turn to Christ. Indeed, "the project not only supplied the *coup de grâce* to the faltering mission to the Jews, but also resulted in the frustration of Paul's plans for his future missionary activity and required him to reorient his apostleship to that field of limited labour available to him as a Roman prisoner" (op. cit., 155 f.). Although in the providence of God the collection was not instrumental in bringing about a widespread conversion of the Jews, it was nevertheless immensely fruitful in uniting the church and in formulating principles of Christian giving.

(b) The theme of poverty is further developed in relation to the apostles who among other things are described by Paul "as poor, yet making many rich" (2 Cor. 6:10). The paradoxical nature of the apostolic ministry follows the pattern set by Christ (see below (c)) who is himself the ground and pattern for all Christian life and giving.

(c) Paul uses the vb. only in 2 Cor. 8:9 where he applies it to Christ (see above (a)). *eptōcheusen*, "he became poor" is the ingressive aor. (Funk § 331). The passage implies the pre-existence of Christ, though it does not define the manner of Christ's becoming poor in the way that Phil. 2:6 ff. speaks of the self-emptying of Christ (→ Empty, art. *kenos* NT 3). For other descriptions of the incarnation cf. Rom. 15:3 (where Paul grounds Christian conduct on the pattern of Christ who "did not please himself"; cf. Ps. 69:9) and Gal. 4:4 f. (where Paul describes Christ as "born of woman, born under the law, to redeem those who were under the law, so that we might receive adoption as sons"). In each case the description of the manner of Christ's coming brings out the practical application that Paul wishes to make to his readers. Here Christ's becoming poor is the paradoxical ground of the true riches of the believer. It is also the ground and example for Christian giving. The richness of the Corinthians in terms of spiritual gifts is alluded to at the beginning of 1 Cor. (1:5). But Paul can also speak ironically of their being rich (1 Cor. 4:8) in view of their spiritual conceit.

(d) The cosmic spirits (*stoicheia*) worshipped by the heathen, including formerly the Galatian believers, are called "weak and beggarly [*asthenē kai ptōcha*]" (Gal. 4:9; cf. 4:3). The word translated "beggarly" here is in fact the same word which was used at Gal. 2:10 for the poor. In other words, the *stoicheia* have nothing at all to offer – but enslavement. But by listening to the Judaizers with their insistence upon the necessity of → circumcision for salvation and the observance of "months, and seasons, and years" (4:10), the Galatian Christians are themselves in danger of returning to their former enslavement, when through Christ and the Spirit they could live as sons and heirs of God himself (4:1–7). On the *stoicheia* (cf. Col. 2:8, 20) → Law, art. *stoicheia*.   C. Brown

→ Gift, → Humility, → Possessions, → Slave

(a). H. von Campenhausen, "Early Christian Asceticism", in *Tradition and Life in the Church* 1968, 90–122; A. Cronbach, "The Social Ideas of the Apocrypha and Pseudepigrapha", *Hebrew Union College Annual* 18, 1944, 119–56; J. D. M. Derrett, *Law in the New Testament*, 1970; A. Gelin, *The Poor of Yahweh*, 1964; F. Hauck, *penēs* etc., *TDNT* VI 37–40; F. Hauck and E. Bammel, *ptōchos*, etc., *TDNT* VI 885–915; M. Hengel, *Property and Riches in the Early Church : Aspects of a Social History of Early Christianity*, 1974; and *Judaism and Hellenism: Studies in their Encounter in Palestine in the Early Hellenistic Period*, I–II, 1974; J. Jeremias, *Jerusalem in the Time of Jesus: An Investigation into Economic and Social Conditions during the New Testament Period*, 1969,

109–119; M. Katz, "Protection of the Weak in the Talmud", *Columbia University Oriental Studies*, 24, 1925, 72–82; L. E. Keck, "The Poor among the Saints in the New Testament", *ZNW* 56, 1965, 100–29; and "The Poor and the Saints in Jewish Christianity and Qumran", *ZNW* 57, 1966, 54 ff.; K. F. Nickle, *The Collection: A Study in Paul's Strategy*, SBT 48, 1966; M. Rostovtzeff, *The Social and Economic History of the Hellenistic World*, I–III, 1941; and *The Social and Economic History of the Roman Empire*, ed. P. M. Fraser, 1957²; M. Stenzel, "Poverty", *EBT* II 671 f.; R. de Vaux, *Ancient Israel: Its Life and Institutions*, 1961; H. W. Wolff, *Anthropology of the Old Testament*, 1974.

(b). W. W. Graf Baudissin, "Die alttestamentliche Religion und die Armen", *Preussische Jahrbücher* 149, 1912, 193–231; H. Birkeland, *'Ānî und 'Ānāw in den Psalmen*, 1933; and *Die Feinde des Individuums in der israelitischen Psalmenliteratur*, 1933; H. Bolkestein, *Wohltätigkeit und Armenpflege im vorchristlichen Altertum*, 1939; K. Bornhäuser, *Der Christ und seine Habe nach dem Neuen Testament*, 1936; H. Bruppacher, *Die Beurteilung der Armut im Alten Testament*, 1924; A. Causse, *Les "Pauvres" d'Israel*, 1922; H.-J. Degenhardt, *Lukas, Evangelist der Armen. Besitz und Besitzverzicht in der lukanischen Schriften*, 1965; M. Dibelius, "Die soziale Motiv im Neuen Testament", in *Botschaft und Geschichte*, I, 1953, 178–203; M. von Dmitrewski, *Die christliche freiwillige Armut vom Ursprung der Kirche bis 12. Jahrhundert*, 1913; H. Donner, "Die soziale Botschaft der Propheten im Lichte der Gesellschaftsordnung in Israel", *Oriens Antiquus* 2, 1963, 229–45; J. Dupont, *Les Béatitudes*, 1954, 184–244; M. Fendler, "Zur Sozialkritik des Amos", *EvTh* 33, 1973, 32–53; P. Gauthier, *Die Armen, Jesus und die Kirche*, 1965; D. Georgi, *Die Geschichte der Kollekte des Paulus für Jerusalem*, ThF 38, 1965; H. Greeven, *Die Hauptprobleme der Sozialethik in der neuren Stoa und im Urchristentum*, 1935; F. Hauck, *Die Stellung des Urchristentums zu Arbeit und Geld*, 1921; P. Humbert, "Le Mot biblique ' 'eḇyôn' ", *Revue d'Histoire et de Philosophie Religieuses* 32, 1952, 1–6; R. Kittel, "Armengesetzgebung bei den Hebräern", *RE* 2, 60–63; R. Koch, "Die Wertung des Reichtums im Lukasevangelium", *Biblica*, 38, 1957, 151–69; H. Kreissig, *Die sozialen Zusammenhänge des judäischen Krieges, Schriften zur Geschichte und Kultur der Antike* 1, 1970; W. G. Kümmel, "Der Begriff des Eigentums im Neuen Testament", in *Heilsgeschehen und Geschichte*, 1965, 271–77; A. Kuschke, "Arm und Reich im Alten Testament, mit besonderer Berücksichtigung der nachexilischen Zeit", *ZAW* 57, 1939, 31–57; E. Kutsch, L. Hardick and F. Lau, "Armut", *RGG*³ I 622–28; J. Leipoldt, "Jesus und die Armen", *Neue kirchliche Zeitschrift* 28, 1917, 784–810; and *Der soziale Gedanke der urchristlichen Kirche*, 1952; I. Loeb, *La Littérature des Pauvres dans la Bible*, 1892; E. Lohmeyer *Soziale Fragen im Urchristentum*, 1921; N. Peters, *Die soziale Fürsorge im Alten Testament*, 1936; P. A. Munch, "Einige Bemerkungen zu '*niyyîm* und den *reʿšāʿîm* in den Psalmen", *Le Monde Orientale* 30, 1936, 13–26; W. Nowack, *Die sozialen Probleme Israel und deren Bedeutung für die religiöse Entwicklung dieses Volkes*, 1982; A. Rahlfs, *'ānî und 'ānāw in den Psalmen*, 1892; SB I 818–26; II 643–47; IV 741, 503, 524 ff.; P. Régamez, *La Pauvreté*, 1941; M. Vansteenkiste, "L'ani et l'anaw dans l'Ancien Testament", *Divus Thomas* 59, 1956, 3–19.

Possessions, Treasure, Mammon, Wealth, Money

Possessions in some form or other are necessary to life. Gk. uses *chrēma*, *ktēma* and *hyparxis* as general words for property and possessions. In the NT at least *peripoiēsis*, that which is one's own, has to be distinguished from them, because it is used in non-material contexts. Accumulated wealth may be denoted by *ploutos*, riches, and *thēsauros*, treasure. Material wealth can also be personified as a demonic power, Mammon (*mamōnas*).

θησαυρός

θησαυρός (*thēsauros*), place where something is kept, treasure box, chest, storehouse, storeroom, treasure; θησαυρίζω (*thēsaurizō*), store up, gather, save up, reserve.

CL *thēsauros* is found from Hesiod onwards. Its etymology is uncertain, and it is probably a technical loan-word. It means: (a) a treasure chamber, a storage room, granary, strong-box; (b) treasure. Even at a very early period temples were built with treasure chambers, where gifts and taxes in kind and money could be stored. The practice appears to have spread from Egypt to Greece. Collecting boxes were also known (cf. 2 Ki. 12:10). *thēsaurizō* is used similarly in the sense of storing up treasure, or putting it in safe keeping.

Mandaean gnostic literature made use of the concepts of the treasure-house and the treasure of life and light from which the soul takes its rise, and to which it may return after it has experienced salvation (cf. W. Foerster, *Gnosis: A Selection of Gnostic Texts*, II, 1974, 190, 201 f., 210, 216, 223, 225, 233, 235, 239, 263, 287).

OT 1. The corresponding OT term is '*ôṣār*. It occurs lit. in Amos 8:5. The "treasury of [the house of] Yahweh" is mentioned in Jos. 6:19, 24 in connection with the holy war and the ban (cf. 1 Ki. 7:5; 14:26); in 1 Ki. 14:26 and 15:18 "the treasures of the king's house" are also mentioned. Later, besides the common usage (Prov. 10:2), we find the concept of heavenly treasuries (Jer. 50:25 [27:25], RSV "armoury"; 15:16; Job 38:22, RSV "storehouses") in which are stored up God's weapons of wrath, and also wind, snow and hail (cf. Eth.Enoch 17:3; Philo, *Rer. Div.Her.* 76; *Fug.* 79; *Leg.All.* 3, 105). The → fear of Yahweh is Zion's treasure (Isa. 33:6). The thought, which sounds like a maxim from wisdom teaching, may be compared with Ps. 74:12; Prov. 1:4; 15:6; Eccl. 1:16; 2:21; Isa. 47:10. The verse "gives an assurance that God will not only annihilate the destroyer in the end but will also henceforth grant his people a blessed future sustained by their fear of God. The dramatic expectation of spoil is surpassed by that of a life in righteousness and the fear of Yahweh in the new Jerusalem. The intrinsic connection between the two can be seen from a study of 11:1 ff." (O. Kaiser, *Isaiah 13–39*, 1974, 344). In Isa. 45:3 "the treasures of darkness" (i.e. treasures that are hidden away) which God will give Cyrus will give him a true knowledge of Yahweh, the God of Israel. The mention of treasure may be an allusion to the fabulous wealth of Sardis which was captured by Cyrus in 546 B.C. (cf. R. N. Whybray, *Isaiah 40–66, New Century Bible*, 1975, 105 f.). This would then be a contrast between earthly treasure for which men labour and fight and the treasure which Yahweh alone gives. Men should search for the fear of the Lord and the → knowledge of God as they do for buried treasures (Prov. 2:4 f.).

2. In later Judaism good works, e.g. alms giving, are a treasure which is stored up as a reward in the world to come, while the interest is enjoyed in this world as well (cf. Tob. 4:8 ff.; 2 Esd. 6:5 ff.; 7:77; Tosefta Peah 4:18; SB I 430). "All that Israel lays up in the form of fulfilments of the Law and good works, it lays up for its Father in heaven" (Deut. R. 1 on Deut. 1:1; cf. F. Hauck, *TDNT* III 137; SB I 431). The rabbis sometimes spoke of the treasure from which the scribe draws and of the treasure house of eternal life, i.e. the place where the souls of the dead are stored up, or the "bundle" in which they are "bound" (cf. 1 Sam. 15:29; F. Hauck, ibid.; SB II 268; III 803).

NT The NT continues both the ancient meaning of *thēsauros* and its usage in OT and Rabbinic literature. It occurs twice in Paul (2 Cor. 4:7; Col. 2:3), once in Heb. 11:26 and 16 times in the Synoptic Gospels, mainly in the words of Jesus. The vb. *thēsaurizō* occurs 8 times (twice in Matt.; once in Lk.; 3 times in Paul; and once each in Jas. and 2 Pet.). The concept frequently involves the paradoxical transformation of earthly values. What is treasured by men is of no enduring worth in God's sight, and real treasure involves earthly poverty.

1. (a) In Matt. 2:11 the *thēsaurous* which the Magi opened in bringing their gifts to the infant Jesus were their treasure chests (→ Magic, art. *mageia* NT 2 (b); → Gold; → Incense). In Matt. 12:35 par. Lk. 6:45 the → heart is compared with a "good treasure" out of which a good man brings forth good. Here the picture is either that of a storehouse or a treasure chest. In either case the point is that → good can only come out of a good heart. As such, the words constitute a warning against the hypocrisy of appearing to speak good, whereas in fact one intends evil (→ Lie). In Matt. the illustration follows the warning against blasphemy against the → Spirit and precedes the sayings about the sign of → Jonah and the men of → Nineveh. In Lk. it is included in the sayings of the Sermon on the Plain.

(b) In Matt.'s account of the Sermon on the Mount Jesus says to his disciples: "Do not lay up [*thēsaurizete*] for yourselves treasures [*thēsaurous*] on earth, where moth and rust consume and where thieves break in and steal, but lay up [*thēsaurizete*] for yourselves treasures [*thēsaurous*] in heaven, where neither moth nor rust consumes and where thieves do not break in and steal. For where your treasure [*thēsauros*] is, there will your heart be also" (Matt. 6:19 ff.). Lk. gives the saying in a different context together with other sayings which in Matt. occur in the Sermon on the Mount which are prefaced by the general formula: "And he said to the disciples . . ." (Lk. 12:22). In Lk.'s version it reads: "Sell your possessions, and give alms; provide yourselves with purses that do not grow old, with treasure in the heavens that does not fail, where no thief approaches and no moth destroys. For where your treasure is, there will your heart be also" (Lk. 12:33 f.). "The parallelism and tautology of Mt. are Hebraic, and probably nearer to the original. He gives a genuine picture of Oriental wealth, garments etc. stored in barbaric abundance, too numerous for use" (A. H. McNeile, *The Gospel according to St. Matthew*, 1915, 83). On the alliteration and paronomasia of the Heb. poetic form here see M. Black, *An Aramaic Approach to the Gospels and Acts*, 1967[3], 160. The word translated here as "rust" is *brōsis* which generally means eating (cf. 1 Cor. 8:4; 2 Cor. 9:10). It is used in cl. Gk. for the decay of teeth (Galen 6, 422; cf. Arndt, 147). In Matt. it is widely assumed to denote some form of corrosion or rust, although the latter is more commonly denoted by *ios* (→ Gall). It might also refer to an insect parallel to the moth (*sēs*); in Mal. 3:11 LXX it appears to refer to the grasshopper or locust. McNeile thinks that the term refers to the devouring by mice and other vermin of wealth stored in barns (op. cit., 84). The vb. *aphanizō* which the RSV here translates by "consume" means lit. to render invisible or unrecognizable. It occurs in Matt. 6:16 in the sense of "disfigure". But it can also mean to destroy and in the passive to perish. The vb. *dioryssō* which describes the action of the thieves means to dig through, i.e. the sun-dried brick walls of the house. It is used again in the passive in Matt. 24:43 and Lk. 12:39.

"The idea of 'treasures in heaven' (i.e. what wins divine approval and reward in the coming Kingdom) is thoroughly Jewish; cf. M. Peah i. 1; Test.Levi 13.5; Ps.Sol. 9.9" (D. Hill, *The Gospel of Matthew*, New Century Bible, 1972, 142). The nature of this treasure is not more precisely defined, although the following sayings in Matt. warn against double-mindedness, trying to serve God and mammon (→ *mamōnas*), anxiety about food and clothing, culminating in the injunction:

831

"But seek first his kingdom and his righteousness, and all these things shall be yours as well" (Matt. 6:33). To this is added the warning against anxiety: "Therefore do not be anxious about tomorrow, for tomorrow will be anxious for itself. Let the day's own trouble be sufficient for the day" (Matt. 6:34; → Care). But perhaps the saying, at least in the case of Lk., may be related to the parable of the unjust steward and the succeeding sayings (Lk. 16:1–14) which also contain references to mammon. (On the interpretation of the parable → House, art. *oikonomia*, NT 1 (a).) The point of the parable and the sayings is to teach wise stewardship of worldly goods so that, when their use is past, there will nevertheless be an enduring benefit both for those who have benefited from such wise stewardship and for those who have exercised it. In particular, Lk. 16:9 states: "And I tell you, make friends for yourselves by means of unrighteous mammon, so that when it fails they may receive you into the eternal habitations." In this verse "they" may refer to those who have benefited from the wise and generous use of "mammon", or it may be a Hebraism referring to God without actually mentioning his name, or it may refer to God and his angels (cf. E. E. Ellis, *The Gospel of Luke*, *New Century Bible*, 1966, 201 f.). In any case, what is worth possessing is not material things which perish but personal acceptance by God and by those who have benefited from one's use of material things (cf. Lk. 16:9a). Lk. 12:33 with its injunction to sell one's possessions and give alms appears to be making a similar point. Matt. does not give the parable of the unjust steward or relate the saying about treasure to the injunction to sell one's possessions, but the saying is followed shortly by the warning that one cannot serve God and mammon (Matt. 6:24). Clearly the paradox involves a contrast between worldly possessions and spiritual good. But in view of its proximity to the Lord's Prayer (Matt. 6:9–13) and the saying about the kingdom in Matt. 6:33, Matt. understood the treasure primarily in terms of the → kingdom of heaven (cf. Matt. 13:44). On man's side this is understood in terms of doing the will of God; on God's side it is God's reign and gracious provision for his children. But here again the treasure is not some form of accumulated spiritual capital, it is the realization of a gracious personal relationship with the Father and with one's fellow men in the kingdom of God. For the kingdom of God is not concerned simply with one's private personal relationship with God but with man's relationship to God as it is embodied in his relationships with his fellow men.

Justin Martyr has a saying comparable with Matt. 6:21 and Lk. 12:34: "Where his treasure is, there also is the mind of man" (*Apol. I*, 15). "Each individual sets his heart on what he counts important, and this allegiance determines the direction and content of his life" (D. Hill, op. cit., 142). In the context of the Sermon on the Mount and in particular of Matt. 6, the treasure in Matt. is to be understood in terms of the kingdom of heaven, and how it affects the disciples' attitude to material possessions. Lk. 12 specifically contrasts the treasure with material possessions, but it too sets the saying in the context of the kingdom which is God's gift: "Fear not, little flock, for it is your Father's good pleasure to give you the kingdom" (Lk. 12:32).

(c) The teaching about treasure is further exemplified by the story of the rich young ruler who was told by Jesus: "If you would be perfect, go, sell what you possess and give to the poor, and you will have treasure in heaven; and come, follow me" (Matt. 19:21 par. Mk. 10:21, Lk. 18:22). But this saying makes explicit a point which is implicit in the background of the earlier sayings. Not only is the treasure, as in Judaism, seen in the light of the coming end-time; it is also connected with following Jesus.

(d) In Matt. 13:44 the kingdom is compared with a treasure: "The kingdom of heaven is like treasure hidden in a field, which a man found and covered up; then in his joy he goes and sells all that he has and buys that field." J. Jeremias draws attention to the joy that the kingdom brings and the demands that it makes. "The effect of the joyful news is overpowering; it fills the heart with gladness; it makes life's whole aim the consummation of the divine community and produces the most whole-hearted self-sacrifice" (*The Parables of Jesus*, 1963², 201). For a detailed examination of the parable against the background of rabbinic concepts of ownership in such cases see J. D. M. Derrett, "The Treasure in the Field", in *Law in the New Testament*, 1970, 1–16. According to rabbinic teaching, if a workman lifted a treasure in the course of his work, the find would belong to the master. But in the parable the man does not actually lift it until he is the actual owner of the field. It may be pointed out that the man gets the treasure free, though the field costs all that he has. Moreover, he is prepared to go to any lengths permitted by the law to obtain it. Derrett compares the parable with that of the pearl of great price which immediately follows it (Matt. 13:45 f.). The man who found the treasure came upon it without seeking it, although his purchase of the field meant a complete reorientation of his life. The merchant, however, was one who devoted his life to the search for pearls. Derrett sees a parallel in the rabbinical saying: "One wins eternal life after a struggle of years, another *finds* it in one hour" (Abodah Zarah 17a; cf. also Philo, *Deus Imm.* 20, 91; op. cit., 15). But Derrett also sees in the parable a further twist. He sees the whole of Matt. 13:36–51 as "an elaborate little sermon based on Mal iii. 16–iv. 3" (ibid.; → *peripoieomai*). "Just as a man treasures a chance find or something he is looking for for years, so God will treasure his servants. If an ordinary man will take such pains over a find of bullion or a pearl, how much the more will God gloat, as it were, over those who have served him faithfully" (ibid.). There may well be the further idea that this treasure had to be purchased at a great price – in fact, all he had and held dear.

(e) The parable of the rich fool (Lk. 12:16–21) presents the converse of Jesus' positive teaching about treasure. It paints a picture of a man who did, in fact, store up earthly possessions. "But God said to him, 'Fool! This night your soul is required of you; and the things you have prepared, whose will they be?' So is he who lays up treasure for himself [*ho thēsaurizōn heautō*], and is not rich towards God" (Lk. 12:20 f.). Lk. presents the parable in conjunction with Jesus' refusal to intervene in a family feud over possessions. In response to a request to insist upon a brother dividing his inheritance Jesus replied: " 'Man, who made me a judge or divider over you?' And he said to them, 'Take heed, and beware of all covetousness; for a man's life does not consist in the abundance of his possessions [*hyparchontōn*]' " (Lk. 12:14 f.). Lk. then takes the opportunity to present Jesus' teaching on anxiety about food and clothing, and on treasure, as discussed above.

(f) The theme of treasure is a recurrent one in Matt. and Lk. Although numerically speaking the incidence of occurrences is not great (the noun 9 times in Matt. and 4 times in Lk.; the vb. twice in Matt. and once in Lk.; cf. the noun once in

833

Mk.), the concept occurs at significant points in connection with man's fundamental relationship with God and his fellow men. *thēsauros* in the sense of treasure
chest occurs in Matt. 13:52 at the conclusion of Matt.'s account of the parables of
the sower, the wheat and the tares, the mustard seed, the leaven, the treasure, the
pearl of great price and the fish net. In response to the disciples' affirmation that
they have understood, Jesus said: "Therefore every scribe who has been trained for
the kingdom of heaven is like a householder who brings out of his treasure what is
new and what is old." The contents of the treasure chest is not simply the teaching
as such but the teaching as the occasion for appropriating the kingdom. On this
verse → Old, art. *palai* NT 2 (a); → Scribe, art. *grammateus*.

2. (a) Paul uses the vb. *thēsaurizō* in the sense of store up in his instructions to
the Corinthians about the collection for the poor of Jerusalem (1 Cor. 16:2; →
Poor, art. *ptōchos* NT 4 (a)). Similarly he uses it again in 2 Cor. 12:14 where he
declares that "children ought not to lay up [*thēsaurizein*] for their parents, but
parents for their children." In this context Paul is speaking of his forthcoming visit
and his determination not to be a burden to them. For he regards himself as their
father (cf. 1 Cor. 4:15), and hence he is under obligation to support them and not
vice versa.

(b) In Rom. 2:5 the vb. is used figuratively in addressing the Jew who "by your
hard and impenitent heart are storing up [*thēsaurizeis*] wrath for yourself on the
day of wrath when God's righteous judgment will be revealed." There is an ironic
contrast here, on the one hand, with "the riches [*ploutou*]" of God's kindness,
forbearance and patience (v. 4) on which the Jew is in fact presuming, and, on the
other hand, with the Jewish conception of treasure stored up in the world to come
as a reward for good works (see above, OT 2). (→ Anger, art. *orgē*, NT 2.)

(c) By contrast the noun is twice used in the Pauline letters, each time with a
christological connotation. In 2 Cor. 4:7 Paul compares the treasure of God's
gift in Christ to the believer with the bodily existence of those who receive it: "But
we have this treasure in earthen vessels, to show that the transcendent power
belongs to God and not to us." The treasure has been previously defined in the
preceding verse in a manner recalling the creation of light: "For it is the God who
said, 'Let light shine out of darkness,' who has shone in our hearts to give the light
of the knowledge of the glory of God in the face of Christ" (2 Cor. 4:6; cf. Gen.
1:3; Ps. 112:4; on this passage see C. K. Barrett, *The Second Epistle to the Corinthians*, BNTC, 1973, 134 ff.). The treasure is thus revealed, but at the same time
there is a sense in which it is hidden. It is hidden by the vessel that contains it and
the outward circumstances of the believer's life which presents a paradox with the
inner reality.

Col. 2:3 also speaks of treasure christologically: "in whom are hid all the
treasures of wisdom and knowledge." As in 2 Cor. 4, the treasure is linked with
revelation and knowledge (cf. Col. 2:2). But the hiddenness refers to Christ who,
though it might not appear so to earthly sight, is nevertheless "the image of the
invisible God" in whom all things were created, and in whom "all the fullness
of God was pleased to dwell" (Col. 1:15, 19). Moreover, he is now with God with
whom the life of believers is also hidden (Col. 3:3). The image in Col. 2:3 "is that
of a hidden treasure for which there are hints which entice the searcher to wager
everything on finding it. Thus this sentence implies challenge to search out the
834

only place where the treasures of wisdom and knowledge are to be found. Jewish apocalyptic often speaks of a hidden treasure in order to create interest in its invitations to right knowledge, since under the guise of the mystery lies the gift which God through revelation has allotted to the elect" (E. Lohse, *Colossians and Philemon, Hermeneia,* 1971, 82: cf. Eth.Enoch 46:3 "This is the Son of Man who has righteousness, with whom dwells righteousness, and who reveals all the treasures of that which is hidden"). Despite certain similarities, Lohse rejects the suggestion that the verse contains allusions to Isa. 45:3; Sir. 1:25; Prov. 2:3 f. (→ Hide, art. *kryptō*; → Secret, art. *mystērion.*)

3. The precise meaning of Heb. 11:26 is the subject of considerable discussion (cf. C. Spicq, *L'Épître aux Hébreux,* II, 1953³, 358 f.; F. F. Bruce, *The Epistle to the Hebrews, NLC,* 1964, 320 f.). It is commonly given a christological interpretation, as if Moses had a vision or experience of Christ comparable with that of Paul in Phil. 3:7 which caused him to prefer Christ to the treasures of Egypt. Thus RSV translates the verse: "He considered abuse suffered for the Christ greater wealth than the treasures of Egypt, for he looked to the reward [*meizona plouton hēgēsamenos tōn Aigyptou thēsaurōn ton oneidismon tou Christou, apeblepen gar eis tēn misthapodosian*]." However, F. F. Bruce questions whether there is a veiled reference here to the belief that Jesus, long before the incarnation, accompanied the Israelites through the wilderness. Certainly the OT narratives of → Moses and the exodus from → Egypt give no hint of such a belief. The NEB offers an alternative rendering which does perhaps more justice to the Gk. and the OT background: "He considered the stigma that rests on God's Anointed." For here *tou Christou* suggests a title which, in fact, means "the Anointed" (→ Jesus Christ, art. *Christos*). Moreover, the verse appears to take up the thought and phraseology of Ps. 89:50 f. (88:51 f.): "Remember, O Lord, the reproach [*oneidismou*] of thy servants . . . wherewith thy enemies have reproached [*ōneidisan*], O Lord, wherewith they have reproached thy Anointed by way of recompense [*hou ōneidisan to antallagma tou christou sou*]." Cf. also Ps. 69:9 (68:10) which Paul applies to Christ in Rom. 15:3: "The reproaches of those who reproached thee fell on me [*hoi oneidismoi tōn oneidizontōn se epepesan ep' eme*]"; and Ps. 105:15: "Touch not my anointed ones." In the first instance it is the people of God that is God's anointed. What Moses preferred to the treasures of Egypt was the lot of the people of God, as God's anointed, for he believed God's promises to them (cf. Heb. 11:27). Thus here → Israel is God's son, as God through Moses reminded Pharaoh when he demanded their release: "Israel is my son, my firstborn" (Exod. 4:22). And it was with the lot of Israel that Moses identified himself. This interpretation has the further advantage of being compatible with all the other instances of faith in Heb. 11 drawn from OT history. For none of these are given a specific christological interpretation. They are all related to the OT and Jewish background. The reproach, abuse, or stigma which was the lot of the people of Israel thus anticipates the reproach which is the lot of those who follow Christ. The same act of faith is required to prefer suffering in the light of the promises of God to material gain. As such the one is a type of the other. If we are to read *tou Christou* as a reference to Jesus as "the Christ", it is as a kind of shorthand in which the type and the antitype coalesce.

Spicq suggests that the *thēsaurōn* in Heb. 11:26 may refer to granaries (cf.

Catalogue of the Greek Papyri in the John Rylands Library, II, 1915, 231, 8, dated *c*. A.D. 40) or to stores of wine (cf. G. Vitelli and D. Comparetti, *Papiri Fiorentini*, 1906–15, I, 194, 6; *P.Oxy*. I, 101, 20; *P.Teb*. I, 6, 27; P. Mitteis and U. Wilcken, *Grundzüge und Chrestomathie der Papyruskunde*, I, 1912, 1, 376; A. Calderini, THĒSAUROI. *Ricerche di Topografia e di Storia della Publica Amministrazione nell' Egitto Greco-Romano*, 1924, IV, 3). Spicq further suggests that the use of the word in Heb. in this sense may provide a novel attestation of the Alexandrian background of the author of Heb., underlining the contrast between the abundance of agricultural products in Egypt and the chronic famines in Palestine. It would certainly lend point to the complaints of the Israelites about the lack of food and drink during the exodus wanderings (cf. Exod. 15:24; 16:2 f.; Num. 11:4 ff.).

4. Jas. 5:3 appears to take up the thought about treasure expressed in the teaching of Jesus: "Your gold and silver have rusted, and their rust will be evidence against you and will eat your flesh like fire. You have laid up treasure [*ethēsaurisate*] for the last days" (see above, 1; → Gall; → Gold). It spells out the judgment which awaits those who are preoccupied with earthly treasure. There is an irony here. For while the people concerned thought that they were storing up treasure, they were, in fact, storing up judgment (cf. Rom. 2:5).

5. 2 Pet. 3:5 takes further the idea of storing up judgment. Whereas Jesus and Paul speak of individuals storing up treasure or wrath in the age to come, 2 Pet. applies the idea to the whole world order: "But by the same word the heavens and earth that now exist have been stored up for fire [*tethēsaurismenoi eisin pyri*], being kept until the day of judgment and destruction of ungodly men." J. N. D. Kelly observes that, "The idea that the world will be finally annihilated by fire appears only in 2 Peter in the NT, and is indeed in its fully developed form not Biblical at all: in the OT passages sometimes cited to prove the contrary (e.g. Is. xxx. 30; lxvi. 15 f.; Nah. i. 6; Zeph. i. 18; iii. 8) fire is rather the instrument of God's wrath to destroy His enemies (e.g. Ps. xcvii. 4)" (*The Epistles of Peter and of Jude*, BNTC 1969, 360). There are, however, the biblical ideas of → judgment, the new → creation, regeneration (→ Birth, art. *palingenesia*), and the new → heaven and → earth. Kelly sees the idea of the annihilation of the world by fire taking shape in Jewish apocalyptic (e.g. Sib. 2:187–213; 3:83–92; 4:171–182; 5:155–161; Eth.Enoch 1:6–9; 52:6; 2 Esd. 13:10 f.). It was held at Qumran (1QH 3:29–36). It is found occasionally in early Christian literature (e.g. Eth.Apc.Pet. 5; Hermas, *Vis*. 4, 3, 3; Origen, *Contra Cels*. 4, 11–13). Kelly further observes that "There are obvious similarities, but equally marked differences (cf. esp. the alternate destruction and renewals of the world presupposed by the latter), between this teaching and the Stoic doctrine of *ekpurōsis* (e.g. Justin, *I Apol*. xx; Seneca, *Quaest.nat*. iii. 29; Diogenes Laertius, *Vit.phil*. vii. 134; Plutarch, *Mor*. 1067a), i.e. that the universe is periodically consumed by fire, and both were deeply influenced far back by Iranian conceptions and imagery" (op. cit., 361; cf. F. Lang, *pyr* etc., *TDNT* VI 928–52; → Fire). *J. Eichler, C. Brown*

| μαμωνᾶς | *μαμωνᾶς* (*mamōnas*), Mammon, wealth, property.

The Gk. word *mamōnas* is first found in the NT. It renders the emphatic state *māmōnā'* of the Aram. *māmôn*. A number of etymologies have been suggested (cf. E. Nestle, "Mammon", *Encyclopaedia Biblica*, 2914 f.; F. Hauck, *mamōnas*, *TDNT* IV 388; SB I 434; A. M. Honeyman, "The Etymology of Mammon", *Archivum Linguisticum* 4, 1952, 60–65). Hauck prefers to link it with the vb. *'āman* as "that in which one trusts", but Nestle suggests that it might also mean what is entrusted to man, or that which supports and nourishes men. The Syriac lexicographers favoured the latter view. In Lk. 16:11 there is an apparent play on words with this root: "If then you have not been faithful [*pistoi*] in the unrighteous mammon, who will entrust [*pisteusei*] to you the true [*alēthinon*] riches?" The three Gk. words *pistoi, pisteusei* and *alēthinon* all appear to translate words from the same root *'mn* from which mammon appears to be formed. This root is also found in → Amen.

The word is found in the Mishnah (Aboth 2:12) and the Damascus document (cf. Arndt, 491). In the Babylonian Talmud it is found with the sense of profit or money (Berakoth 61b; cf. M. Black, *An Aramaic Approach to the Gospels and Acts*, 1967³, 139). Black also draws attention to its use in the Palestinian Pentateuch Targum to Gen. 34:23 (C) to render Heb. *miqneh*, cattle, which constituted the wealth of the Hebrew farmer, and to its frequent occurrence in the Palestinian Talmud (e.g. Nazir 5:4:54b:12; Sanhedrin 8:8:26c:20 f.). In rabbinic writing it means not merely money in the strict sense but a man's possessions, everything that has value equivalent to money, and even all that he possesses apart from his body and life. In itself the word may be neutral, but it acquired in negative contexts the connotation of possessions dishonestly gained and wealth dishonestly used, as in bribery.

The word occurs three times in the sayings appended to the parable of the unjust steward (Lk. 16:1–8). At the end of the parable "the master [*ho kyrios*]" (the master in the parable, or perhaps Jesus or God) commended the dishonest steward for his prudence, for the sons of this world are wiser towards their generation than the sons of light (Lk. 16:8). The parable is addressed to the disciples teaching them prudence in handling this world's goods (on the exegesis of the parable → House, art. *oikonomia*, NT 1 (a); cf. J. D. M. Derrett, "The Parable of the Unjust Steward", in *Law in the New Testament*, 1970, 48–77). In particular, they are to use the goods of this world in a way which is righteous and which will benefit others. For the steward's action in remitting various debts owed to his master achieved a double object. On the one hand, the master had been charging exorbitant interest which was forbidden by the law and the steward was actually putting his master right in the eyes of the law. On the other hand, he was doing himself a favour by ingratiating himself with his master's debtors. Lk. 16:9 adds: "And I tell you, make friends for yourselves by means of unrighteous mammon, so that when it fails they may receive you into the eternal habitations." The injunction is not to befriend mammon but to use mammon for the benefit of others. In this verse "they" may refer to those who have benefited from such use of mammon, or it may be a Hebraism referring to God without actually mentioning his name, or it may refer to God and his angels. The point is that mammon itself does not endure, but it may be used to achieve something which is enduring. Mammon itself is material, but its use has personal dimensions. The pun in Lk. 16:11 has already been noted. The verse contrasts the relatively minor value of material things with the true riches which exist on a higher and personal plain: "If then you have not been faithful in the unrighteous mammon, who will entrust to you the true riches?" Stewardship of material possessions is thus a probationary test for further stewardship (cf. the parables of the pounds [Lk. 19:11–27] and the talents [Matt. 25:14–30]). The following verse implies that mammon is not something which one actually possesses but is, in fact, "another's". The disciple has to prove his faithful and wise stewardship of this before he may be entrusted with what is his own. The disciple as a steward is not yet his own master (cf. Lk. 17:7–10). But neither should he be the servant of mammon. For mammon, now personified in v. 13, inevitably becomes the master if a man tries to make himself its master by acquiring it for its own sake. Men are confronted by the stark choice: "No servant can serve two masters; for either he will hate the one and love the other, or he will be devoted to the one and despise the other. You cannot serve God and mammon."

The only other passage in which mammon is mentioned is Matt. 6:24 which is verbally identical with Lk. 16:13 but which lacks the accompanying sayings. The saying about the two masters is found in Gos.Thom. 47 but without reference to mammon. Mammon is mentioned in 2 Clem. 6:1.   *C. Brown*

| περιποιέομαι |

περιποιέομαι (*peripoieomai*), save or preserve for oneself, acquire, get something for oneself, get possession of; πεπιποίησις (*peripoiēsis*), gaining, obtaining, acquisition, a possession, property; περιούσιος (*periousios*), chosen, especial; τὰ ἴδια (*ta idia*), one's own, possessions, property.

CL *peripoieomai*, the mid. of the less frequent *peripoieō*, used from Hdt. onwards, means to cause to remain over and above, to save up, lay by, procure, keep, save for oneself. The cognate noun *peripoiēsis* means keeping safe, preservation, gaining possession of, acquisition, procuring. *periousios* means having more than enough, rich, wealthy.

OT The Heb. *sᵉgullâh*, property, treasure, is used of David's treasure (1 Chr. 29:3), the treasure of kings (Eccl. 2:8), and Israel as God's special possession (Exod. 19:5; Deut. 7:6; Ps. 134:4; Mal. 3:17). It is rendered by *peripoiēsis* only at Mal. 3:17. *periousios* is used of God's chosen people at Exod. 19:5; Deut. 7:6; 14:2; 26:18; and Exod. 23:22 (a free translation). *periousiasmos*, private possession, is used in the LXX translation in Ps. 135(134):4. The idea behind *periousios* is not just that of Israel as God's property but that of his "rich possession" (H. Preisker, *TDNT* IV 57). On the idea of Israel as God's *sᵉgullâh* see J. D. M. Derrett, *Law in the New Testament*, 1970, 15 f. Derrett sees Mal. 3:16–4:3 reflected in Matt. 13:36–51 (→ *thēsauros*, NT 1 (d)).

NT 1. In the NT *peripoieomai* (3 times) and *peripoiēsis* (5 times) are preferred to *periousios* which occurs only once. The idea of salvation stands in the background. The vb. occurs at Lk. 17:33 ("Whoever seeks to gain [*peripoiēsasthai*] his life will lose it, but whoever loses his life will preserve it"; → Soul, art. *psychē*); Acts 20:28 ("Take heed to yourselves and to all the flock, in which the Holy Spirit has made you guardians, to feed the church of the Lord which he obtained [*periepoiēsato*] with his own blood"); 1 Tim. 3:13 ("for those who serve well as deacons gain [*peripoiountai*] good standing for themselves and also great confidence in the faith which is in Christ Jesus"). The noun occurs in the following passages. In Eph. 1:14 the → Spirit is said to be "the guarantee of our inheritance until we acquire possession of it [*eis apolytrōsin tēs peripoiēseōs*]." In 1 Thess. 5:9 Paul assures his readers: "For God has not destined us for wrath, but to obtain salvation [*eis peripoiēsin sōtērias*] through our Lord Jesus Christ." In 2 Thess. 2:14 this is described in terms of → glory: "To this he called you through our gospel, so that you may obtain the glory [*eis peripoiēsin doxēs*] of our Lord Jesus Christ." Heb. 10:39 may reflect something of the thought of Lk. 17:33: "But we are not of those who shrink back and are destroyed, but of those who have faith and keep their souls [*eis peripoiēsin psychēs*]." Finally, 1 Pet. 2:9 takes up the thought of Exod. 19:5, cf. Deut. 14:2: "But you are a chosen race, a royal priesthood, a holy nation, a people for his possession [*ethnos hagion laos, eis peripoiēsin*], that you may declare the wonderful deeds of him who called you out of darkness into his marvellous light."

2. *periousios* is found only in Tit. 2:14 in a verse which summarizes the work of Christ "who gave himself for us to redeem us from all iniquity and to purify for himself a people of his own [*laon periousion*] who are zealous for good deeds." The idea of God's treasured people again takes up the Heb. idea of the '*am s*ᵉ*ḡullâh* (cf. Exod. 19:5; Deut. 14:2), but, as in 1 Pet. 2:9, it is not → Israel which is so described but the → church. Whereas 1 Pet. focuses on the priestly rôle of the people in declaring God's wonderful deeds, Tit. 2:14 draws attention to the kind of deeds which the people of God should be zealous to perform. The verse comes, in fact, at the climax of a survey of how the gospel should affect different people in their different situations.

3. The adj. *idios* means own and is widely used in a variety of contexts in various senses (cf. Arndt, 370), e.g. according to his own capability (Matt. 25:15); each one will receive his own wages according to his own labour (1 Cor. 3:8); one's own (private) interpretation (2 Pet. 1:20); his (own) sheep (Jn. 10:3 f.); each in his own turn (1 Cor. 15:23); with our own hands (1 Cor. 4:12); and as an adv. *idia* meaning by oneself, privately (1 Cor. 12:11; Matt. 14:13, 23). *idios* occurs some 113 times in the NT.

The neut. plur. *ta idia* meaning one's home is attested in secular Gk. (e.g. Polyb., 2, 57, 5; 3, 99, 4; P.Oxy. 4; further examples in Arndt 370) and the LXX (Est. 5:10; 6:12; 1 Esd. 6:31 [= 2 Esd. 6:11]; 3 Macc. 6:27, 37; 7:8; cf. also Josephus, *War*, 1,666; 4, 528). In the NT it appears to mean home in Jn. 16:32 (on this verse see E. Fascher, "Johannes 16, 32", *ZNW* 39, 1940, 171–230); 19:27; Acts 5:18D; 14:18 *v.l.*; 21:6. The RSV takes it in this sense in its rendering of Jn. 1:11: "He came to his own home, and his own people received him not [*eis ta idia ēlthen, kai hoi idioi auton ou parelabon*]" (cf. E. J. Goodspeed, *Problems of New Testament Translation*, 1945, 87 f., 94 ff.; and F. Field, *Notes on the Translation of the New Testament*, 1899, 84). It may be noted in the RSV that "home" and "people" are interpretations which try to bring out the significance of the neut. plur. in the former case and the masc., plur. in the latter. R. Bultmann disputes this interpretation (*The Gospel of John: A Commentary*, 1971, 56). He claims that *ta idia* here must mean property or possession (as e.g. *P.Oxy.* 489, 4; 490, 3; 491; 3; 492, 4). The *idioi* are "his own", those who belong to him as their creator (cf. Od.Sol. 7:12; and

Bultmann, op. cit., 44). He also sees here a background of gnostic dualism, according to which *idion* means that which shares in a common nature (cf. 8:44; 10:3 f.; 13:1; 15:19; Corp.Herm. 1, 31; Iren., *Haer.* 1, 21, 5; Hippol., *Haer.* 5, 6, 7 etc.; Act.Thom. 124, p. 233, 14; Od.Sol. 26:1). Bultmann rejects the suggestion that *ta idia* might mean the Jewish people or Israel as God's own people (cf. Exod. 19:5; Deut. 7:6; 14:2; 26:18; Ps. 135:4). For the context of the Prologue of Jn. is that of the *kosmos*, the world, and *anthrōpoi*, men. It is thus a claim that he possessed the whole universe from the beginning (cf. 1:1 ff.). Moreover, the normal expression for the '*am sᵉḡullâh* is not *idios* but *periousios*. Bultmann sees parallels with → wisdom which possesses the earth and sea (Ecclus. 24:6; cf. Prov. 1:24–31; Bar. 3:12 f.; Eth.Enoch 42:1 f. where there is a parallel to *ou parelabon*). The distinction between the neut. plur. and the masc. plur. belongs to the Gk.; in Aram. both would have been *dîlêh*.

Lk. 18:28 also may be translated as homes or possessions: "And Peter said, 'Lo, we have left our homes [*ta idia*] and followed you' " (RSV). The par. in Matt. 19:27 and Mk. 10:28 have *panta*, all. To this Jesus gives the reply: "Truly, I say to you, there is no man who has left house or wife or brothers or parents or children, for the sake of the kingdom of God, who will not receive manifold more in this time, and in the age to come eternal life" (Lk. 18:29 f.; cf. the further details including persecutions in Mk. 10:30). The saying follows the story of the rich young ruler who declined to sell all that he had to give to the poor and follow Jesus.

4. The use of three different concepts in the NT for property, quite apart from concrete possessions, mirrors the riches of that which has been revealed through the redemptive act of Jesus. He came into that which had been his own from the beginning. He won his right to his people by his suffering and death, and this people has been requisitioned by him, that it may → serve him in complete surrender and bear witness to him until his return. *E. Beyreuther*

πλοῦτος

πλοῦτος (*ploutos*), wealth, riches; πλούσιος (*plousios*), rich, a rich man; πλουσίως (*plousiōs*), richly; πλουτέω (*plouteō*), be rich, become rich; πλουτίζω (*ploutizō*), make rich.

CL 1. The word-group associated with *ploutos* is related to *polys*, much, and means initially abundance of earthly possessions of every kind. Later its meaning divided in two directions. In the one it meant riches in a technical and material sense. In the other it was more general, and occurs with a qualifying word, generally in the gen., e.g. riches of wisdom, honour, mercy, etc. All the words in this group can bear this double meaning: *plouteō*, be or become rich; *ploutizō*, make rich; *ploutos*, possession of many goods, super-abundance of something, riches; and *plousios*, as an adj, wealthy, rich and as a noun a rich man.

2. In Homer external wealth and virtue are not separated (cf. *Il.* 1, 171; 16, 596; 24, 536, 546; *Od.* 24, 486). Rich is a comprehensive term for a fortunate life blessed by the gods. Plato and Aristotle in particular judge riches by their effect on society. If they do not serve the community (*polis*), they are to be rejected. In Aristotle wealth is always material and is something that can be used wrongly or rightly (*Pol.* 1, 9, p. 1256b–1258a, 8; 2, 9, p. 1269a, 34 f.). But Plato distinguishes

material riches from true riches which consist of wisdom, virtue and culture (*Rep.* 7, 521a; 8, 547b; *Phdr.* 279c; cf. F. Hauck and W. Kasch, *TDNT* VI 322). The Cynics completely despised material possessions because they brought commitments and anxieties with them (cf. Stob., *Ecl.* 5, 782, 18; 5, 785, 15 ff.; 5, 766, 12; 5, 806, 17 ff.; see further *TDNT* VI 322). The Stoics considered that the chief danger of riches lay in their creation of a feeling of false security, but they also recognized their value because of the opportunities of developing the personality which they offered (Seneca, *De Vita Beata* 22, 1; cf. *TDNT* VI 323). Basically riches were not to be rejected, for (a) in Gk. culture riches did not have the sociologically divisive influence that they have had in other cultures, and (b) the idea never appeared that they could be given up for the benefit of the poor.

OT 1. Riches in the older parts of OT are seen as having positive value. They consisted mainly of flocks and herds, children and slaves (e.g. Gen. 13:2; 30:43) and were a gift of God. In the nomadic or semi-nomadic period riches presented no problem, for there were no blatant differences between rich and poor. At the conquest of Canaan Yahweh gave everyone his share. Since the land belonged to God, God extended his protection to the individual's property (cf. the laws in the Book of the Covenant, Exod. 20:22–23:19, which were later expanded in those of Deut.).

Under the monarchy there was the development of royal cities and courts. With the growth of commerce and trade a major social differentiation developed. There was a small upper class of the rich and influential, who, as may be seen from the prophets (Amos 2:6 ff.; 5:10 ff.; Isa. 5:8 ff.; Mic. 2:1 f.; Jer. 5:26 ff.; 34:8–11), destroyed the people of God by injustice and violence and so brought deserved judgment on the whole people.

In the wisdom literature, where our word-group is most frequent, we often find unaffected praise of riches (e.g. Prov. 10:4, 15). But there are references to their relative value (e.g. Ps. 49:16; Prov. 22:1), and their power to lead men astray (e.g. Ps. 49:6; 52:7). At the same time we find in Job and the Pss. the problem of vindicating the divine rule (especially Job 21; Pss. 37; 49; 73).

2. *plousios* normally translates the Heb. '*āšîr*, wealthy, rich (Ruth 3:10; 2 Sam. 12:1 f., 4; Job 27:19; Pss. 45[44]:12; 49[48]:2; Prov. 10:15; 14:20; 18:11; 22:2, 7, 16; cf. 23:4; 28:6, 11; Eccl. 10:6, 20; Isa. 53:9; Jer. 9:22[23]). It translates a variety of other words in Gen. 13:2; Ps. 34[33]:10; Isa. 32:9, 13; 33:20; and is without Heb. equivalent in 1 Sam. 2:10; Ezra 3:19, 21; Est. 1:20; Ps. 10:8[9:29]; Prov. 12:22; Wis. 8:5; Sir. 8:2; 10:22, 30; 13:2 f., 18–23; 25:2; 26:4; 30:14; 31[34]:3, 8; 44:6; Jer. 24:1; Ad.Dan. 4; 1 Macc. 6:2. Similarly the corresponding vbs. normally translate formations from the root '*šr*: *plouteō* (Exod. 30:15; Ps. 49[48]:16; Eccl. 5:11; Hos. 12:9[8]; Zech. 11:5; Jer. 5:27; Ezek. 27:33; Dan. 11:2; but not Gen. 30:43; Prov. 28:22; 31:28; Sir. 11:18, 21); and *ploutizō* (Gen. 14:23; 1 Sam. 2:7; 17:25; Job 15:29; Ps. 65[64]:9; Prov. 10:4, 22; 13:7; Ezek. 27:33; but there is no Heb. equivalent for Wis. 10:11; Sir. 11:21; 19:1; 2 Macc. 7:24). The noun *ploutos* mostly translates the Heb. '*ōšer*, riches (Gen. 31:16; 1 Sam. 17:25; 1 Ki. 3:11, 13; 10:23; 1 Chr. 29:12, 28; 2 Chr. 1:11 f.; 9:22; 17:5; 18:1; 32:37; Est. 1:4; 5:11; Pss. 49[48]:6; 112[111]:3; Prov. 3:16; 8:18; 11:16, 28; 13:8; 22:1, 4; 30:8[24:31]; Eccl. 4:8; 5:12, 18; 6:2; 9:11; Jer. 6:22[23]; 17:11;

Dan. 11:2). Cognate Heb. words occur in Prov. 21:17 and Mic. 6:12. Some eight other Heb. words occur in other passages, the most common of these being *ḥayil*, capacity, power, wealth (Job 20:15, 18[?]; 21:7; 31:25; Pss. 49[48]:10; 52[51]:7; 62[61]:10; 73[75]:12; 76[75]:5; Prov. 13:22; 31:3[24:71]; 31:29; Isa. 60:5). The Book of Isa. prefers *hāmôn*, which can mean commotion, crowd as well as abundance, wealth (Isa. 16:14; 29:5, 7 f.; 32:14; 60:5; but with other words in 30:6; 61:6; and no Heb. equivalent in 24:8; 29:2; 32:18; 60:16). Other words occur in Deut. 33:19 (*šepa'*, abundance); Est. 1:4; 5:11; Ps. 119(118):14; Prov. 13:7; 19:4(1); 24:4; 28:8; 29:3; Ezek. 26:12. There is no Heb. equivalent in 1 Sam. 2:10; Est. 10:10; Job 27:18; Ps. 37(36):3; Prov. 31:14; Wis. 5:8; 6:14; 7:8, 11, 13; 8:5, 18; Sir. 18:25; 21:4; 24:17; 28:10; 1 Macc. 4:23; 6:1.

3. At the end of the Inter-Testamental period these concepts are again to be found. The members of the Qumran community adopted → "the poor" as a title of honour. They practised community of possessions (cf. Josephus, *War* 2, 8, 3; 1QS 1:12; 5:2; 6:17, 19; 7:6). For discussion see M. Black, *The Scrolls and Christian Origins*, 1961, 32–39. Black describes the community as "organized as a kind of welfare state", adding that "It was also a hierocratic community: all its affairs, affecting the disposition of property no less than its purely 'spiritual' concerns, came within the jurisdiction of the priests" (op. cit., 37; cf. 1QS 5:2, 22). For Enoch the end will in any case bring with it a complete reversal of all earthly possession and fortune (Eth.Enoch 96:4; 100:6; 103:4 f.; cf. Syr.Bar. 29:6; 51:12–52; 2 Esd. 7). When the Qumran texts speak of God's → grace or → mercy they may also add in parallelism "multitude" (*rōḇ*) and "riches" (*hāmôn*) (cf. 1QM 4:32; 6:9; 7:27; 9:34; 10:24). Among the Pharisees only the righteousness derived from keeping the law had real value, but riches enabled one to do good works, carrying with them corresponding obligations (*TDNT* VI 325 f.; SB I 818, 822, 826 ff.; III 655 ff.; IV 490–500, 536–610). On the other hand, all circles where eschatological hopes were earthly or nationalistic had a high opinion of riches.

NT 1. The word-group does not appear in Jn., Acts, 1 and 2 Thess., Tit., Phlm., 1–3 Jn., Jude. *ploutos* is found in the Gospels only in Matt. 13:22 par. Mk. 4:19, Lk. 8:14, where it means, as in 1 Tim. 6:17, Jas. 5:2, Rev. 18:17, wealth in terms of earthly goods. The word is linked with God (Rom. 9:23), Christ (Eph. 3:8) and churches (2 Cor. 8:2). *plousios*, as adj. or noun, in sing. or plur., is used to describe persons rich in this world's goods (Matt. 19:23 f., par. Mk. 10:25, Lk. 18:25; Matt. 27:57; Mk. 12:41; Lk. 6:24; 12:16; 14:12; 16:1, 19, 21 f.; 18:23; 19:2; 21:1; 1 Tim. 6:17; Jas. 1:10 f.; 2:6; Rev. 3:17; 13:16). Followed by the dat., it expresses the riches of God (Eph. 2:4) or of the Christian (Jas. 2:5). In 2 Cor. 8:9 and Rev. 2:9 it means those rich in spiritual possessions. The vb. *plouteō* is used absolutely in Lk. 1:53; 1 Tim. 6:9; Rev. 18:15 in the reference to earthly possessions; and in 1 Cor. 4:8; 2 Cor. 8:9; Rev. 3:17 f. of spiritual possessions. Lk. 12:21 and 1 Tim. 6:17 refer to those works which have value with God. Rom. 10:12 indicates that God's riches are available for all. *ploutizō* means make rich, enrich. God makes the church rich in all things (1 Cor. 1:5); the Christian passes on those riches given by God so as to make others rich as well (2 Cor. 6:10; 9:11). The adv. *plousiōs* occurs only at Col. 3:16 ("let the word of Christ dwell in you richly"); 1 Tim. 6:17 (of "God who richly furnishes us with everything to enjoy;" contrasted with "the rich in this world"); Tit. 3:6 (of the Holy Spirit poured out richly); and 2 Pet. 1:11 (of the entrance to the kingdom richly provided). It thus occurs only in the epistles and always in a spiritual sense of God's rich grace.

2. Theological significance. (a) Matt. stresses throughout the dangers inherent in riches that may hinder the → kingdom of God, but it does not regard them as basically Satanic (cf. Matt. 27:57). In other words, Matt. exhibits no ascetic rejection of possessions and riches. If Jesus attacks mercilessly attachment to earthly possessions (Matt. 13:22; 19:23 f.), his denunciation applies to riches in exactly the same way as it does to every human self-contrived security and obsession which make it impossible for men to see the kingdom of God. The seed is choked by care and "the false glamour" (NEB) of riches (*he apatē tou ploutou*, Matt. 13:22; cf. Mk. 4:19; Lk. 8:14). → Care is a characteristic of this age (Matt. 6:25–32), and every kind of riches is deceitful when it so appeals to men that they are hindered from hearing the message of the kingdom of heaven. In contrast poverty in the Beatitudes means being open for the kingdom of God (→ Poor, art. *ptōchos* NT 1 (b)). We find the same in Matt. 19:23 f., where "hard" is explained by Jesus' answer in v. 26. The very reaction of the disciples in v. 25 shows that more is meant by "rich" than economic standing; they realized that they were being included among them. In other words riches are a characteristic of the man of this world. Hence we must not weaken the force of "the eye of a needle" (19:24; → Animal, *Animals in the NT*). In all this teaching Jesus entertains no possibility of man attaining the kingdom of God, i.e. life, as he stands. The new righteousness, which carries life within it, comes alone from the power and might of God. Man must receive it in repentance and faith. In other words, Jesus' view of riches cannot be separated from the crucial hour of decision which had come through him for the people of Israel.

(b) In Mark the judgment on riches is perhaps expressed somewhat more mildly. By speaking of "awakening desires" (cf. "delight", Mk. 4:19) the danger is seen in terms of a subjective threat to the individual psyche (E. Lohmeyer, *Das Evangelium nach Markus*, KEK 1/2, 1967[17], ad loc.). Riches encourage confidence in themselves and so become a great obstacle on the way to the kingdom of God (Mk. 10:23 ff.).

(c) Lk. mentions riches only in Lk. 8:14; otherwise he speaks of the rich and being rich. The rich landowner (12:16–20; → *thēsauros*, NT 1 (e)) is a type of rich men in general, if they have forgotten that God is the giver of what they have and therefore put their confidence in it, or who give themselves up to unrestrained enjoyment of it and so miss God's purpose for their life (16:19–31). The → Pharisees scoffed at Jesus' warning against mammon (Lk. 16:14; → *mamōnas*), because they were lovers of money (*philargyroi*; cf. 1 Tim. 6:10; 2 Tim. 3:2; → *thēsauros*, NT 1 (b)). The general verdict and the context of the passages in which Lk. deals with the rich suggest the possibility that the term is used for the enemies of Jesus, or that they are collectively identified by that name. Hence, there is a complete rejection of the rich. The kingdom of God brings with it the reversal of all earthly relationships (Lk. 1:53; 16:25; 6:24 ff.). Those who rejected Jesus and his message, because they were enslaved by the present age and its deceitful riches, and allowed their thoughts and imagination to be completely governed by what appeared to be the case at that moment, lost the future in their attempt to secure the present. Being delivered up to the deceptive power of possessions means destruction. Salvation comes to those who are liberated by the → gospel, and know that their riches lie in the future which is even now dawning. The reversal of all earthly values, which will become evident at the end of the age, will prove that only those riches that have been stored up with God have lasting value and bring salvation to man (16:9). Zacchaeus's behaviour (19:8) and the admonition of 14:12 ff. are models for this.

(d) The selfish rich are completely rejected in Jas. The judgment of the OT prophets is echoed and the rich are depicted as the unrighteous (2:6; 5:1–6) who can only expect calamity in the coming transformation of the world (5:1–6; 1:10 f.; cf. Isa. 40:6 ff.). In contrast it is the → poor, the rich in faith, that have been chosen (2:5).

(e) Paul is not interested in the material understanding of the term riches. He gives it a deeper and new meaning by applying it to God, Christ and the church. Fullness marks out God, the only truly rich One, e.g. in → glory (Rom. 9:23; Eph. 3:16) and → grace (Eph. 2:7; 1:7). The church shares in these riches (1 Cor. 1:5; Eph. 1:7, 18). To be rich is an eschatological gift unconnected with material possessions. Though the apostle is himself → poor, he makes many rich by his preaching (2 Cor. 6:10). Seeing that Christ could make us rich only by emptying himself (2 Cor. 8:9; cf. Phil. 2:5–11; → Empty, art. *kenos*, NT 3; → Poor, art. *ptōchos*, NT 4), the Christian's pathway through the world is one of self-emptying and helping the brethren (2 Cor. 8:2; 9:10 ff.). Israel's rejection of Christ means riches for the Gentiles, for the message of salvation is now directed to them (Rom. 11:12). (On the soteriological significance of the collection for the Jerusalem church → Poor, art. *ptōchos*, NT 4 (a).) The eschatological nature of these riches is missed, if they are used as the justification for self-praise (→ Boast) and for self-confidence within the church (1 Cor. 4:8).

(f) In 1 Tim. earthly riches are not rejected, but the rich are warned against putting their confidence in that which is transient, and are called on instead to become rich in good works by a right use of their possessions (1 Tim. 6:17 ff.). Heb. 11:26 has a Pauline flavour: transient abuse became riches for Moses as he looked to the future reward, and his sufferings for the people became a typical anticipation of the sufferings of Christ (→ *thēsauros*, NT 3). Rev. contains a double message: (1) The rich cannot stand before the wrath of the → Lamb (6:15 f.), and those who have been enriched by → Babylon fall together with it (18:3, 15, 17, 19). (2) The church in Smyrna, though, or just because, it is persecuted for the sake of the faith, is truly rich (2:9). Laodicea, on the other hand, is poor, because it thinks itself spiritually rich (→ Cold, Hot, Lukewarm). It is called on to become rich by turning to the Lord (3:17 f.). Riches are mentioned in 5:12 in the praise offered to the Lamb.

3. In the story of the rich young ruler (Matt. 19:16–22 par. Mk. 10:17–22, Lk. 18:18–23) *plousios* and → *chrēma*, or *ktēma*, are used as synonymous concepts. *chrēma*, *ktēma* and *hyparxis* mean only money, or goods and chattels which can be turned into money.

There is a close connection between → *mamōnas tēs adikias*, unrighteous mammon (Lk. 16:9, 11), and *hē apatē tou ploutou*, the deceitfulness of (RSV "delight in") riches (Matt. 13:22; Mk. 4:19), but *mamōnas* suggests wealth and property which constitute a man's capital, and we must remain free of its enticements.

pleonekteō, pleonektēs and *pleonexia* all express a drive to gain at the expense of others. The use of *plouteō* and *philargyria*, avarice, love of money, in 1 Tim. 6:9 f. reminds us of the mention of *pleonexia* in the lists of vices (→ Avarice).

F. Selter

| χρῆμα |

χρῆμα (*chrēma*), property, wealth, means, money; κτῆμα (*ktēma*), property, possessions, especially in later usage landed property; ὕπαρξις (*hyparxis*), property; τὰ ὑπάρχοντα (*ta hyparchonta*), what belongs to someone, property, goods, possessions; βίος (*bios*), life, means of subsistence, property; οὐσία (*ousia*), substance, property.

CL *chrēma*, derived from *chrē*, it is necessary, stands for what is necessary, a thing, or event, then goods and chattels, riches. It is found from Homer onwards, mostly in the plur. When it is found in the sing. it normally means quantity of, also money. *ktēma*, derived from *ktaomai*, means that which has been gained. It is used (also Homer onwards) for possessions of every kind, but from the 4th cent. B.C. it is confined to landed property. From Aristotle onwards *hyparxis* is found with the meaning of existence and generally of property, riches.

OT In the LXX the words are used to render a wide range of Heb. terms. *chrēma* in Job 27:17 and 2 Chr. 1:11 f. is used to mean money (in the latter together with *ploutos*). In Dan. 11:24, 28 it is the rich booty taken in war, and in 11:13 baggage train of an army. *ktēma* in Job 20:29 has the general meaning of possessions, heritage (RSV), lot (NEB). In Prov. 8:18; 12:27 it is riches as a reward for → wisdom and hard work. *ta hyparchonta* is found in Prov. 6:31; Gen. 13:6; 31:18; 36:6 f.; 45:20; 47:18; Eccles. 5:19; 6:2, with the general meaning of what one has, riches, possessions. Both words interchange frequently with → *ploutos* or *argyros*, (silver, money; → Gold art. *argyrion*). In general no hesitation is shown in regarding the riches mentioned as good and a blessing from God (Prov. 8:21; Eccles. 5:19; 6:2; 2 Chr. 1:12). With *hyparxis*, however, as with → *ploutos*, there is found, especially in Prov., a critical outlook on wealth, or the dangers bound up with it (cf. Job). Possessions are not the highest good. They are trivial compared with honour (Prov. 6:35), but they deceive a man into seeking protection and security in them (Prov. 18:10 f.; cf. also 11:28; 28:6, 11; Sir. 11:18 f.; 27:1 ff.; 31:3, 5 f.).

NT With the exception of Mk. 10:23 and Lk. 18:24 (par. Matt. 19:23 has *plousios*), *chrēma* is found only in Acts 8:18, 20 and 24:26 and should be translated money. The sing. is found only in Acts 4:37. The sing. of *ktēma* is found only in Acts 5:1, where it is used interchangeably with *chōrion* (vv. 3, 8), and means a piece of land. *ktēmata* (plur.) are the estates (Mk. 10:22 and par. Matt. 19:22; Lk. 18:23 has *plousios*) which in Acts 2:45 are distinguished from other possessions ("property and possessions" NEB); cf. also Acts 5:1. In the NT the plur. part. *hyparchonta* is commoner that the noun *hyparxis* (used only in Acts 2:45 and Heb. 10:34, par. to *hyparchonta*). It is found in Matt. 19:21; 24:17; 25:14; 1 Cor. 13:3; Heb. 10:34 and in the Lucan writings (Lk. 8:3; 11:21; 12:15, 33, 44; 14:33; 16:1; 19:8; Acts 4:32). It means lit. the things that belong (to someone), and thus possessions in general.

Occasionally other terms which have their primary reference elsewhere are also used to denote possessions. Thus *bios*, which otherwise means life (e.g. Lk. 8:14; 1 Tim. 2:2; 2 Tim. 2:4) and even conduct (e.g. Wis. 4:9; 5:4; 4 Macc. 1:15; 7:7; 8:8), can also mean one's means of subsistence and thus property, one's worldly goods (Mk. 12:44 par. Lk. 21:4; Lk. 8:43; 15:12, 30; 1 Jn. 2:16; 3:17). These meanings are also borne out in secular Gk. *ousia*, substance, which is connected with the vb. to be, has the sense of property, wealth in its sole NT occurrence (Lk. 15:12 f.; cf. Tob. 14:13; 3 Macc. 3:28). Again this meaning is attested in secular Gk. Various circumlocutions are also found in the NT: *hosa echeis*, what you have (Mk. 10:21 par. Lk. 18:22; Mk. 12:44; Matt. 13:44, 46; 18:25); *ta idia*, one's own (Lk. 18:28; cf. also Jn. 1:11); *idion einai*, to be one's own, in the description of the communal sharing in the Jerusalem church ("Now the company of those who believed were of one heart and soul, and no one said that any of the things which he possessed was his own, but they had everything in common," Acts 4:32); *to emon*, mine, *to son*, yours, *to hēmeteron*, ours (Matt. 25:27; Lk. 15:31; Matt. 20:14; 25:25; Lk. 6:30; 16:12); *ta par' autēs panta*, all she had (which the woman with the issue of blood had vainly spent on physicians, Mk. 5:26); *ek tou echein*, out of what you have (2 Cor. 8:11; → Poor, art. *ptōchos*, NT 4 (a), (c)); *echeis polla agatha keimena*, you have many good things laid up (Lk. 12:19); *tous mē echontas*, those who do not have (anything) (1 Cor. 11:22).

2. A number of passages are of particular theological importance. Jesus demanded from the rich young ruler a complete renunciation of his possessions for the sake of the kingdom of God (→ *ploutos*). He was told: "sell what you possess [*pōlēson sou ta hyparchonta*]" (Matt. 19:21; "sell whatever you have [*hosa echeis pōlēson*]" Mk. 10:21; Lk. 18:22 adds "all [*panta*]") "and give to the → poor". His riches, however, prevented him from following Jesus' call, for he had *ktēmata polla*, many estates (Matt. 19:22; Mk. 10:22; Lk. 18:23 says that he was "very rich [*plousios sphodra*]"). The fetters of possessions are so strong (→ *mamōnas*) that a rich man can only with difficulty enter the kingdom of God. But when they are rightly used, goods and chattels can be employed for good works, as in the cases of the women who "provided for" Jesus and his disciples (Lk. 8:3), and Zacchaeus (Lk. 19:8; cf. also Lk. 12:33). Luke's extremely critical attitude towards wealth is shown by his being the only evangelist to give the parable of the rich land owner (12:16–21; → *thēsauros*, NT 1 (e)) and that on the rich man and Lazarus (16:19–31). Covetousness (12:15) seeks security in life from material possessions and so leads a man to destruction (*pleonexia*; → Avarice). The NT judges it to be one of the worst vices in a man freed by God. On the links between the rich man and Lazarus and the unjust steward see J. D. M. Derrett, "Dives and Lazarus and the Preceding Sayings" (op. cit., 78–99). "Failure to deal righteously with *mammon* leads to 'Hell' " (op. cit., 90), even though the man was merely passive in his wrongdoing, neglecting the poor.

Probably partially motivated by Jesus' extreme demand (Lk. 12:33), but above all by the expectation of the imminent parousia (→ Present), individual members of the primitive church in Jerusalem renounced their right to private property (Acts 4:32, *hyparchonta;* 2:45, *ktēmata kai hyparxeis*), sold it when there was need (Acts 2:45), and gave the money to the apostles to be distributed (Acts 4:36 f.; 5:1 f.). Ananias and Sapphira were judged not because they had kept back the proceeds of the property that they had sold, but because they had lied to the Holy Spirit in pretending to give all to the church (Acts 5:3). What the sin of Achan (Jos. 7) was in the OT, theirs was in the NT. On the distribution to the → poor (Acts 6:1–7) → Serve, art. *diakoneō*. Mary, the mother of John Mark, allowed her house to be used as a meeting place (Acts 12:12), but seems to have retained possession of it. Elsewhere other churches do not seem to have adopted the community of goods of the Jerusalem church. (See further M. Hengel, *Property and Riches in the Early Church*, 1974, 31–34.)

Simon Magus' idea that he could buy the wonder-working power of the Holy Spirit was completely mistaken (Acts 8:18, 29; → Magic, art. *mageia*, NT 1 (a)).

In 1 Cor. 13:3 Paul uses love as the only valid criterion for evaluating good actions for our fellow men involving possessions. If one's willingness to give away one's possessions to the poor is not an expression of love, the giver has no gain from the action.

In the course of an exhortation to perseverance Heb. 10:34 reminds its readers that "you joyfully accepted the plundering of your property [*tēn harpagēn tōn hyparchontōn hymōn*], since you knew that you yourselves had a better possession and an abiding one [*kreittona hyparxin kai menousan*]." This is perhaps a reference to the expulsion of Jews from Rome by the emperor Claudius in A.D. 49. Among them were Priscilla and Aquila (cf. Acts 18:2) and doubtless other Christian Jews who would have suffered eviction and looting (cf. F. F. Bruce, "Christianity under Claudius", *BJRL* 44, 1961–62, 309 ff.; and *The Epistle to the Hebrews*, *NLC*, 1964, 268 f.). The allusion to possessions is further illustrated in the following chapter by the example of those like → Abraham who "desire a better country, that is, a heavenly one" (Heb. 11:16) and → Moses who preferred reproach suffered for the sake of the Anointed to the treasures of Egypt (→ *thēsauros*, NT 3). It contrasts with the attitude of Esau who forfeited his birthright for immediate material well-being (Heb. 12:15 ff.; cf. Gen. 25:29–34; 27:30–40; Deut. 29:18 LXX).

F. Selter

Coins in the Bible and Theological Issues

OT Although the earlier narratives of the OT contain occasional references to the use of "money" in commercial transactions (as when Abraham purchased the cave of Machpelah for the burial of Sarah, Gen. 23), the invention of coined money was deferred until the 7th cent. B.C. It was evidently in Lydia (Asia Minor) that the first coins were struck, at first in electrum, then later in gold and silver (bearing on the obverse the forepart of a lion facing the forepart of a bull, apparently in combat with each other). Very soon thereafter the Greek island of Aegina began the first minting of silver coinage, somewhat ovoid in shape, and bearing on the obverse the figure of a sea-tortoise. During the 6th cent. the coinage of the Athenians (with the head of Athena in profile, looking to the right, on the obverse) became current in the coastal regions of the Near East, including Phoenicia and Palestine; it was also the first coinage to contain a reverse type (in this case an owl, facing, with a sprig of olive in the upper left, and the three Greek letters, alpha, theta, and long epsilon, on the right – an abbreviation for *Athēnaiōn*). Yet it was not until the reign of Darius I of the Persian Empire that any government in control of Judah began to issue coins which were current in the land of Israel. The Persian (Achaemenid) imperial coins displayed but one type throughout the course of the empire: a robed king, wearing a tiara, kneeling on his right knee facing to the right, holding a bow in his left hand and a lance or arrow in his right hand. The reverse was stamped with a shapeless punch and contained no device. The gold coins of this type were known as "darics" and weighed about 8.4 grams; they are referred to in Ezr. 2:69 and Neh. 7:70 as *dark^emônîm*. In 1 Chron. 29:7 the related word *'^adarkōnîm* is used as a unit of weight for the various golden vessels offered in the time of King David for the service of God in the future temple to be built by Solomon. Since there were no minted coins whatever back in the 10th cent. B.C., it is evident that the Chronicler (perhaps Ezra himself) had calculated the weight of these vessels in terms of weight-standards familiar to his own contemporaries.

It was apparently during the late 5th century and the century following that local coinages sprang up within the Persian Empire, consisting especially of silver pieces, some of which were minted under the authority of local satraps like Mazaeus (and his predecessors, Datames and Pharnabazus) of Tarsus. These all portrayed Baal-Tars, enthroned, facing left, with sceptre in hand; the reverse types varied considerably, sometimes featuring a helmeted male head, or else a lion killing a bull, or even two standing figures flanking an altar of incense. Or else there were types minted by the rich commercial cities like Tyre and Sidon. Tyre featured the bearded, crowned figure of Baal riding the waves upon a winged hippocamp; the reverse displayed an Egyptian type of owl superimposed upon the shepherd's staff (*ḥeḳa*) and flail of the pharaonic insignia. Sidon showed a war-galley riding the waves, and on the reverse the Persian king riding in his chariot.

Interestingly enough there were even some issues that bore pagan types such as these and yet were inscribed with the name *Yehud* (Y-H-D), the Aramaic form of "Judah". Since the Torah strictly forbad the fashioning of human likenesses, or indeed of any cult animal associated with worship, it is inconceivable that such coins could have been minted with the sanction of the approval or sanction of the Jewish provincial government (except possibly by the Persian governor in charge of Jewish affairs). One type has a bearded head facing right, and on the reverse an Athenian type of owl and olive sprig, but with the "Phoenician" letters Y-H-D to the right. Another type (possibly minted in Gaza) shows a bearded Baal sitting on a two-wheeled chariot, holding a plump bird on his left hand, and facing a squat little dwarflike worshipper in the lower right corner. Across the top are the letters Y-H-D. From the preceding description of coin-types it is apparent that they fell into three general categories: (1) the symbol of the nation or city-state – often represented by some animal or bird – whether lion, bull, tortoise, owl or eagle; (2) a portrait of the patron god of the city or nation – whether Athena or Baal or the semi-divine Persian king; (3) some symbol of national power or wealth – such as the war-galley or chariot or sprig of olive. Almost always there was some clear reference to local religion or civic pride. Partly because of their lowly status as a relatively small, poor province of the Persian Empire, the post-Exilic Jews were in no position to mint coins of their own, even if they could have hit upon non-cultic types which would involve no violation of the Second Commandment.

The same was true during the ensuing period of Greek domination, after the conquest of the Near and Middle East by Alexander the Great in 330 B.C. There was undoubtedly extensive use of coined money in Palestine, but all of it was of a pagan type. The imperial coinage of Alexander himself featured the head of Heracles in his lion headdress, and on the reverse the enthroned figure of Zeus holding a sceptre in his left hand and an eagle of victory on his right. The gold coins featured Athena's head wearing the Corinthian war-helmet, and on the other side a standing figure of the winged Nike (goddess of victory). The coinages of King Lysimachus of Thrace and of Ptolemy of Egypt were the first to portray the head of Alexander himself, wearing either a ram's-horn headdress or else an elephant-type, complete with trunk and tusks, suggestive of godlike powers and prestige. But soon thereafter (probably in the 290's) Ptolemy I began to issue coins with his own portrait upon them, and before long the Seleucid emperors at Antioch began to do the same. Since the Greek custom had been to portray none but gods or demi-gods upon their coins, it is fair to conclude that the Hellenistic rulers achieved the honour of portraiture upon their national currency only because they themselves claimed divine status. (Interestingly enough, it was not until the Roman senate voted divine honours for Julius Caesar that a Roman ruler ever had his visage presented on the coinage of his time. But once the precedent had been set, it became the invariable practice, and even the members of the Second Triumvirate, such as Antony and Octavian, issued money with their own portraits upon it.)

Not until the 2nd century and the assertion of Jewish independence did the Jews ever mint coins of their own, and even then it was not until sixty years after Judas Maccabaeus had expelled the forces of Antiochus Epiphanes from Jerusalem. Perhaps around 110 B.C. John Hyrcanus produced a very modest bronze coinage, hardly the size of an American dime, and bearing the simple device of two cornucopiae bound together at the horn-tips and flanking a poppy head in the centre. The reverse of this lepton contained a Hebrew legend in epigraphic characters reading: "Jonathan the High Priest, and the community of the Jews". His successor, Jonathan (Alexander Jannaeus), followed this example, but he also minted another type featuring a half-opened flower and the inscription, "Jonathan the King"; the reverse contained a compound anchor and a Greek inscription: "King Alexander". Other types used were a war-galley or a seven-rayed star. The complete absence of pagan symbols was thus maintained throughout the period of the Hasmonean Dynasty.

NT Even after the Roman conquest the small bronze coinage was kept largely free of pagan religious symbolism by the Herods who reigned as vassal kings under Roman authority. Herod the Great continued to make use of the anchor and the double cornucopiae (although his inscriptions were always in Greek). But he also introduced the crested helmet, the tripod bearing a bowl, and an incense burner between two palm branches. His successor, Herod Archelaus (4 B.C.–A.D. 6), introduced the grape-cluster and the tall, double-crested helmet. Subsequent to his dismissal from power by the Roman government, the rule of Palestine was partially entrusted to Herod the Tetrarch (Galilee, Samaria and Peraea only) and partially to a Roman procurator, such as Coponius, Valerius Gratus, or Pontius Pilate. Symbols inoffensive to Jewish sensibilities were employed by these Roman governors (who minted their bronze lepta with wheat ears or barley, or else with palm branches or even palm trees or cornucopiae). But Pilate aroused considerable resentment when he ventured to employ such cultic implements as an augur's wand (resembling a shepherd's crook) or a simpulum – a type of ladle used in connection with Roman sacrifice. But after Pilate was recalled and sent into exile by Caligula, Herod Agrippa I was installed as king for seven years (A.D. 37–44) first over part and then over all of Israel. As a nominal Jew, Agrippa reverted to inoffensive types, such as triple ears of wheat, or a fringed umbrella (perhaps suggesting that the king was a protective shade to his people).

It will be noted that all of these bronze coins supplied only the small change required in simple commercial transactions. No issues in silver were ever minted by a Jewish government until the time of the First Revolt (A.D. 67–70). This meant that from Persian times and onward, the Jews were obliged to handle silver coins (and gold, too, for that matter) which were issued by the Persian, Greek or Roman government which was in control of the Near East. It is safe to say that such pagan coins were never accepted for use in worship at the Jerusalem temple. The only currency allowable consisted in Hasmonean or Herodian bronze lepta or dilepta, and offerings in silver or gold had to take the form of bullion or manufactured implements and vessels. Yet in daily life and in their business transactions, pagan coins were in constant and familiar use.

The most notable example of bronze coinage presented in the temple treasury was of course the contribution of two *lepta* (or "mites") placed in the offering box by the indigent widow whom Christ commended (Mk. 12:42 par. Lk. 21:2). Conceivably these consisted of the Pontius Pilate type described above, or else of the less offensive coinage of the earlier procurators. But very possibly they were of the John Hyrcanus II or Alexander Jannaeus types which are still very commonly discovered in Jewish burial sites throughout Israel even to this day. The *lepton* is also mentioned at Lk. 12:59, where the par. Matt. 5:26 has *kodrantēn*, the Roman quadrans.

The most celebrated discussion of the types or inscriptions of any coin referred to in Scripture occurred during Holy Week. Jesus was accosted by some crafty agents of the Sanhedrin who sought to entrap him in the matter of paying taxes to the Roman government. "Is it lawful to give a poll-tax to Caesar, or not?" They had him on the horns of a dilemma, for if he answered that it was perfectly all right to pay tribute to Rome, this would offend the religionists who opposed any support to a pagan power. If on the other hand he declared himself opposed to the payment of such taxes, he would incur the charge of fomenting rebellion and sedition, and he would immediately be turned over to the Roman authorities. In answer to their craftiness, Jesus simply asked them to produce a silver denarius from their own pockets. Holding it up before them he then pointed out that the portrait on the obverse was that of the Roman emperor (in all probability it was a mintage of Tiberius, who had been reigning since A.D. 14), and the inscription bore the name of Caesar. (Denarii of Tiberius read on the obverse: TI. CAESAR DIVI AVG. F. AVGVSTVS "Tiberius Caesar Augustus, son of the divine Augustus".) Quite obviously they had no compunctions about using the money which Caesar had minted for them, with all of the advantages of protection for law-abiding citizens and the safeguarding of their financial security. They had no scruples about accepting the Roman law and order and military defence against marauding invaders from the East.

Therefore, their pious question concerning the legitimacy of paying taxes to the government who guaranteed them safety and peace and order was nothing more than arrant hypocrisy. "Render therefore to Caesar that which is Caesar's" – that is, the money and support necessary for a strong, efficient government – "and to God the things that are God's" (not only their tithes and temple taxes, but also the worship of their hearts and the faithful obedience to his revealed will).

An interesting reference to the temple poll tax is found in the episode of Matt. 17:24–27. The tax-collectors approached Peter, as a representative disciple of Jesus and asked him whether his leader ever paid the standard contribution to the support of the temple, as required in Exod. 30:11–16. Since Jesus and his followers were constantly itinerating from one preach-point to another, it was difficult for tax agents to make contact with them. But now that they were back in Capernaum once more, it was time for the matter to be dealt with. After making the point that as the Son of God it was not really appropriate for him to pay a tax to his own Father, Jesus directed Peter nevertheless to secure the money for payment. He was to go down to the lake and cast in his fish-line, and pull up the first fish to strike his bait. In it he would find a "stater", in this case the same as a tetradrachma (Matt. 17:27) – although in classical times the stater was a mere two-drachma piece, or else in Corinth and its colonies the stater was a three-drachma coin. But already in Ptolemaic times the term *statēr* was applied to the four-drachma piece, and so quite generally in the Greco-Roman period, since the tax amounted to a didrachmon (two-drachma piece) per person, and the coin recovered in Peter's fish was large enough to pay for them both, it must have been a tetradrachma – quite possibly a Tyrian shekel. The silver coins of Tyre during the Greco-Roman period featured a wreathed head of Baal-Melqart on their obverse, and a leftward striding eagle on the reverse (with the inscription TYROU HIERAS KAI ASYLOU, "Tyre the holy city of refuge"). It was very likely this same coin which predominated in the payment of thirty "pieces of silver" (*argyria*) recorded in Matt. 26:15 as the price paid to Judas for his betrayal of Jesus at Gethsemane. Because of its high silver content and standardized weight, the Tyrian shekel was generally preferred in Palestine, despite the paganism of its symbols. The well-known hoard of silver coins found in 1954 at the Khirbet Qumran headquarters must have been secreted there around A.D. 1; it consists entirely of Tyrian shekels and half-shekels of this type.

In his parables Jesus told the story of the housewife who was greatly distressed to find that she had lost one of her collection of ten drachmas (Lk. 15:8 f.). She seized her broom and began to sweep up every particle on the floor until she finally came across the missing coin, much to her joy and satisfaction. The drachma was about equivalent to the Roman denarius in size and value, and it was roughly equivalent to an entire day's wages for a day-labourer (such as the vineyard workers of Matt. 20:2). To a woman in humble circumstances, even the loss of a single day's wage was a severe blow. (It is unnecessary to suppose that these coins were perforated and strung together in a sort of headpiece or necklace, as some writers have suggested. It was very unusual for the ancients to bore holes through the thick type of coin which was in vogue all during Classical and Greco-Roman times; it would result in the loss of too much silver, and greatly deface the appearance of the coin itself.)

851

It has already been mentioned that during the First Revolt (A.D. 67–70) the revolutionary Jewish government minted silver coins for the first time in history. The shekel or four-drachma piece bore a libation chalice on the obverse (with the inscription "Shekel of Israel"), and on the reverse a tripleheaded pomegranate (and the legend, "Jerusalem the holy"). But neither these nor the First Revolt bronze lepta (featuring the amphora and the vine-leaf) find any mention in the NT itself, for only the late Epistles of John and the book of Revelation postdate that tragic episode in Hebrew history. *G. L. Archer, Jr.*

→ Avarice, → Gift, → Gold, → Parable, → Poor, → Tax, → Tithe

(a). G. L. Archer, "Coins", *ZPEB* I 902–11 (with photographs and colour illustrations); B. J. Bamberger, "Money-Changer", *IDB* III 435 f.; F. Banks, *Coins of Bible Days*, 1955; H. von Campenhausen, "Early Christian Asceticism", in *Tradition and Life in the Church: Essays and Lectures in Church History*, 1968, 90–122; M. Black, *The Scrolls and the New Testament*, 1961, 32–39; C. E. B. Cranfield, "Riches and the Kingdom of God: St. Mark 10.17–31", *SJT* 4, 1951, 302–13; J. D. M. Derrett, "The Treasure in the Field", *Law in the New Testament*, 1970, 1–16; "The Parable of the Talents and Two Logia", ibid., 17–31; "The Parable of the Unmerciful Servant", ibid., 32–47; "The parable of the Unjust Steward", ibid., 48–77; "Dives and Lazarus and the Preceding Sayings", ibid., 78–99; "Peter's Penny", ibid., 247–65; "Render to Caesar . . .", ibid., 313–38; E. Haenchen, *The Acts of the Apostles*, 1971; H. Hamburger, "Money", *IDB* III 423–35 (with photograph and line illustrations); A. R. Hands, *Charities and Social Aid in Greece and Rome*, 1968; A. von Harnack, *The Mission and Expansion of Christianity*, (1908) 1961; F. Hauck, *thēsauros* etc., *TDNT* III 136 ff.; *mamōnas*, *TDNT* IV 388 ff.; F. Hauck and E. Bammel, *ptōchos* etc., *TDNT* VI 885–915; F. Hauck and W. Kasch, *ploutos* etc., *TDNT* VI 318–32; M. Hengel, *Was Jesus a Revolutionist?*, 1971; *Judaism and Hellenism: Studies in their Encounter in Palestine in the Early Palestinian Period*, I–II, 1974; and *Property and Riches in the Early Church*, 1974; A. M. Honeyman, "The Etymology of Mammon", *Archivum Linguisticum* 4, 1952, 60–65; J. Jeremias, *The Parables of Jesus*, 1963²; and *Jerusalem in the Time of Jesus: An Investigation into Economic and Social Conditions during the New Testament Period*, 1969; E. A. Judge, *The Social Pattern of Christian Groups in the First Century*, 1960; L. Kadman et al., *The Dating and Meaning of Ancient Jewish Coins*, 1958; R. Koch, "Riches", *EBT* II 775–80; K. Lake, "The Communism of Acts II and IV–VI", in F. J. Foakes Jackson and K. Lake, eds., *The Beginnings of Christianity*, V, 1932, 140–51; I. H. Marshall, *Luke: Historian and Theologian*, 1970, 141–44, 206–9; F. W. Madden, *Coins of the Jews*, 1881; H. Montefiore, "Jesus and the Temple Tax", *NTS* 11, 1964–65, 60–71; K. F. Nickle, *The Collection: A Study in Paul's Strategy*, SBT 48, 1966; H. Preisker, *periousios*, *TDNT* VI 57 f.; B. Reicke, *chrēma* etc., *TDNT* IX 480 ff.; A. Reifenberg, *Ancient Jewish Coins*, 1947²; and *Israel's History in Coins from the Maccabees to the Roman Conquest*, 1953; E. Rogers, *A Handy Guide to Jewish Coins*, 1914; P. Romanoff, *Jewish Symbols on Ancient Jewish Coins*, 1944; M. Rostovtzeff, *The Social and Economic History of the Hellenistic World*, I–III, 1941; and *The Social and Economic History of the Roman Empire*, ed., P. M. Fraser, 1957²; J. Z. Smith, "The Social Description of Early Christianity", in *Religious Studies Review* 1, 1975; E. Stauffer, *Christ and the Caesars: Historical Sketches*, 1955; E. Troeltsch, *The Social Teaching of the Christian Churches*, I–II (1931) 1960; R. de Vaux, *Ancient Israel: Its Life and Institutions*, 1961 (see especially "Finance and Public Works", 139–42; "Economic Life", 164–77; and "Weights and Measures", 195–209; and the corresponding bibliographies, 529–34); H. W. Wolff, *Anthropology of the Old Testament*, 1974, 128–33.

(b). J. Babelon, "Monnaie", *Supplément au Dictionnaire de la Bible*, V, 1957, 1346–75; L. Bergson, "Zum periphrastischen *chrēma*", *Eranos* 65, 1967, 79–117; K. Beyschlag, "Christentum und Veränderung in der alten Kirche", *KuD* 18, 1972, 26–55; K. Bornhäuser, *Der Christ und seine Habe nach dem Neuen Testament*, BFChTh 38, 3 1936; H. Braunert, *Utopia. Antworten griechischen Denkens auf die Herausforderung durch soziale Verhältnisse*, Veröffentlichungen der schles.holst. Universitätsgesellschaft, Neue Folge, 51, 1969; G. Breidenstein, *Das Eigentum und seine Verteilung*, 1968; N. Brockmeyer, *Sozialgeschichte der Antike*, Urban-Taschenbücher 153, 1972; H. Bückers, *Die biblische Lehre vom Eigentum*, 1947; P. Christophe, *L'Usage Chrétien du Droit de Propriété dans l'Écriture et la Tradition Patristique*, 1963; H.-J. Degenhardt, *Lukas, Evangelist der Armen. Besitz und Besitzverzicht in der lukanischen Schriften*, 1965; H. Donner, "Die soziale Botschaft der

Propheten im Lichte der Gesellschaftsordnung in Israel", *Oriens Antiquus* 2, 1963, 229–45; S. Ejger, *Das Geld im Talmud*, 1930; K. Farner, *Christentum und Eigentum bis Thomas von Aquin*, 1947 (reprinted in *Theologie des Kommunismus*, 1969, 9–90, but without the detailed notes); M. Fendler, "Zur Sozialkritik des Amos", *EvTh* 33, 1973, 32–53; A. Feuillet, "Les riches intendants du Christ", *RSR* 34, 1947, 30–54; J. Gagé, *Les Classes Sociales dans l'Empire*, 1964; B. Gatz, *Weltalter, goldene Zeit und sinnverwarndte Vorstellungen*, 1967; F. Geiger, *Philon von Alexandria als sozialer Denker, Tübinger Beiträge zur Altertumswissenschaft* 14, 1932; D. Georgi, *Die Geschichte der Kollekte des Paulus für Jerusalem, ThF* 38, 1965; H. Greeven, *Die Hauptprobleme der Sozialethik in der neueren Stoa und im Urchristentum*, 1935; W. Haller, "Das Eigentum im Glauben und Leben der nachapostolischen Kirche", *ThStKr* 64, 1891, 478–563; F. Hauck, *Die Stellung der Urkirche zu Arbeit und Geld, BFChTh* 2, 3, 1921; W.-D. Hauschild, "Christentum und Eigentum. Zum Problem eines altkirchlichen 'Sozialismus' ", *ZEE* 16, 1972, 34–49; J. Hemelrijk, *Penia en Ploutos*, Dissertation Utrecht, 1925; F. Horst, "Das Eigentum nach dem Alten Testament", *Kirche im Volk* 2, 1949, 87–102 (reprinted in *Gottes Recht. Gesammelte Studien zum Recht im Alten Testament, ThB* 12, 1961); and "Eigentum", *RGG³* II 363 ff.; J. Jervell, "Er kam in sein Eigentum", *TheolStud* 10, 1957, 14 ff.; E. Kamlah, "Eigentum", BHHW I 377 f.; R. Koch, "Die Wertung des Besitzes im Lukasevangelium", *Biblica* 38, 1951, 151–69; H.-J. Kraus, "Die Bedeutung des Eigentums im Deuteronomium", *Kirche im Volk*, 2, 1949, 103–11; G. Kretschmar, "Ein Beitrag zur Frage nach dem Ursprung der frühchristlichen Askese", *ZTK* 61, 1964, 27–67; H. Kreissig, *Die sozialen Zussammenhänge des jüdischen Krieges, Schriften zur Geschichte und Kultur der Antike* 1, 1970; W. G. Kümmel, "Der Begriff des Eigentums im Neuen Testament", in *Heilsgeschehen und Geschichte*, 1965, 271–77; A. Kuschke, "Arm und Reich im Alten Testament mit besonderer Berücksichtigung der nachexilischen Zeit", *ZAW* Neue Folge 16, 1939, 31–57; J. Leipoldt, *Der soziale Gedanke in der alten Kirche*, (1950) 1972; E. Lohmeyer, *Soziale Fragen im Urchristentum*, 1921; M. Lurje, *Studien zur Geschichte der wirtschaftlichen und sozialen Verhältnisse im israelitisch-jüdischen Reich, BZAW* 45, 1927; J. J. van Manen, *Penia en Ploutos in de Periode na Alexander*, Dissertation Utrecht, 1931; P. H. Menoud, "La Mort d'Ananias et de Saphire", *Mélanges Goguel*, 1950, 146–54; P. A. Munch. "Das Problem des Reichtums in den Psalmen 37, 49, 73", *ZAW* Neue Folge 14, 1937, 33–46; N. Peters, *Die soziale Fürsorge im Alten Testament*, 1935; R. von Pöhlmann, *Geschichte der sozialen Frage und des Sozialismus in der antiken Welt*, revised by F. Oertel, I–II, 1925³; H. Preisker, "Lukas 16, 1–17", *TLZ* 74, 1949, 86–92; G. Redard, "Recherches sur *chrē, chrēsthai*", *Bibliothèque de l'École des Hautes Études, Sciences Historiques et Philologiques* 303, 1953, 82–91; H. Riesenfeld, "Vom Schatzsammeln und Sorgen – ein Thema urchristlicher Paränese. Zu Mt. vi 19–34", in *Neotestamentica et Patristica. Eine Freundesgabe, Herrn Professor Dr. Oscar Cullmann zu seinem 60. Geburtstag überreicht*, 1962, 47–58; E. Salin, *Platon und die griechische Utopie*, 1921; SB I 817–28; IV 536–610; A. Schalit, *König Herodes, Studia Judaica* 4, 1969; O. Schilling, *Reichtum und Eigentum in der altchristlichen Literatur*, 1908; and "Der Kollektivismus der Kirchenväter", *ThQ* 114, 1933, 481–92; C. Schneider, *Geistesgeschichte des antiken Christentums*, I, 1954; W. Schrage, *Die konkreten Einzelgebote in der paulinischen Paränese. Ein Beitrag zur neutestamentlichen Ethik*, 1962; and "Die Stellung zur Welt bei Paulus, Epiktet und in der Apokalyptik. Ein Beitrag zu I Kor. 7.29–31", *ZTK* 61, 1964, 125–54; G. Uhlhorn, *Die christliche Liebestätigkeit in der alten Kirche*, 1882; and *Die christliche Liebestätigkeit*, (1895²) 1959; H. E. Weber, "Das Eigentum nach dem Neuen Testament", *Kirche im Volk* 2, 1949, 112–16.

Pour

ἐκχέω

ἐκχέω (*ekcheō*) and ἐκχύννω (*ekchynnō*), pour out; σπένδω (*spendō*), pour out (a drink offering); πρόσχυσις (*proschysis*), pouring or sprinkling (of blood); αἱματεκχυσία (*haimatekchysia*), shedding of blood.

CL In cl. Gk. the uncompounded form *cheō*, pour, is still in use, but the compounds, especially *ekcheō*, pour out, gradually displace it. *ekcheō* is used in secular

Greek of pouring liquids, sometimes with the idea of draining, pouring away. A Jewish inscription uses it of shedding the blood of an innocent martyr. It can also be used for scattering solid objects, and, metaphorically, for squandering money. *ekchyn(n)ō* is a Hel. Gk. form which exists alongside it.

OT In the LXX *ekcheō* normally represents Heb. *šāpak̲*, an equally general word for pour, but used in purificatory rites (Num. 19:17; Exod. 30:18) and particularly frequently of the pouring or shedding of blood, either as a part of the sacrificial ritual, or, most frequently, as a synonym for murder (cf. Gen. 9:6; 37:22; Deut. 19:10; 1 Sam. 59:7; Ps. 13:3). It is also used in the OT, as in secular Gk., of pouring out offerings, usually of water, to Yahweh (e.g. Num. 28 f.; Jdg. 6:20; 1 Sam. 7:6; 2 Sam. 23:16), and to other gods (e.g. Isa. 57:6; Jer. 7:18; 19:13); the technical term for offering libations (of wine) is *spendō* (translating Heb. *nāsak̲*).

Among non-literal uses, the most common is the expression to pour out anger, fury on someone, used of God's acts of → judgment (e.g. Ps. 79:6; Ezek. 7:8). Men also pour out their soul, or their complaint, before God (1 Sam. 1:15; Ps. 142:2). One special use is the promise that God will pour out his → Spirit on men (Joel 2:28–29 [MT 3:1–2]; Ezek. 39:29; Zech. 12:10; cf. Isa. 32:15, using a different word, *'ārâh*, which normally means to be naked, bare, but here pour out.

NT 1. In the NT, *ekcheō* is used in the literal sense, without special theological significance, in Matt. 9:17 par. Lk. 5:37 (of wine being "spilled"); Jn. 2:15 (of money "scattered"); Acts 1:18 (of Judas's bowels being "poured out"; → Akeldama).

2. The use of "to shed blood" as a synonym for murder or martyrdom is taken over from the OT in Matt. 23:35 par. Lk. 11:50; Acts 22:20; Rom. 3:15; Rev. 16:6. The shedding or pouring of blood in the OT sacrificial ritual is referred to in Heb. by the cognate nouns *proschysis* (11:28; cf. Exod. 12:22) and *haimatek-chysia* (9:22). The latter is found only in Christian writings, but cf. *ekchysis haimatos*, pouring out of blood (1 Ki. 18:28; Sir. 27:15).

3. These two OT senses of shedding blood, murder or martyrdom and sacrifice, come together in the crucial words of Jesus in the institution of the → Lord's Supper, "This is my blood of the covenant, which is poured out [*ekchynnomenon*] for many" (Mk. 14:24 par. Matt. 26:28; Lk. 22:20 reads "This cup which is poured out for you is the new covenant in my blood"). Jesus is both a martyr, an innocent victim of murder, and a sacrifice "for many". Several OT passages may be alluded to in these words, but two are particularly important. "This is my blood of the covenant" echoes Exod. 24:8, the sacrificial offering which instituted the old covenant of Sinai, now to be replaced (as Jer. 31:31–34 predicted) with a new → covenant, sealed by Jesus' sacrificial death. "For many" points to Isa. 53:11, 12, the "many" who were to be made righteous by the death of God's Servant bearing their sin; he is said in Isa. 53:12 to have "poured out" his soul to death, and while the verbs in both Heb. (*he'rāh*) and LXX (*paredothē*) are different from *šāpak̲* and *ekcheō*, an allusion to this phrase is surely intended (→ Empty, art. *kenos*, NT 3). The pouring out of Jesus' blood, then, was the sacrifice which removed the sin of "many", and introduced them to a new covenant relationship with God. It is this pouring out that is symbolized in the cup at the Lord's Supper.

4. Paul takes up the pouring of libations as a metaphor for his approaching martyrdom, in his use of *spendō* in Phil. 2:17 and 2 Tim. 4:6. The libation is not, like the blood sacrifices, an atoning offering, but an expression of dedication to God.

5. The more metaphorical uses of pour in the OT are also echoed in the NT. The pouring out of God's fury provides the imagery of the seven bowls of the wrath of God poured out in Rev. 16, where *ekcheō* occurs 8 times in this sense. But more characteristically, God's love is "poured out" in the hearts of believers (Rom. 5:5), and this has been done by the bestowal of the Holy Spirit, who is several times said, following Joel 2:28–29, to have been "poured" upon those who receive Christ (Acts 2:17–18, 33; 10:45; Tit. 3:6). (Note also the use of being "filled" with the Spirit, → Fullness, NT 4.) The use of such an apparently impersonal term, in contrast with the very personal language used about the Spirit elsewhere in the NT, is accounted for by the influence of the OT usage mentioned above.

→ Blood, → Fullness, → Pentecost, → Spirit   *R. T. France*

J. Behm, *ekcheō*, *TDNT* II, 467–469.

Prayer, Ask, Kneel, Beg, Worship, Knock

In the NT the most comprehensive term for "to pray" is *proseuchomai*. It denotes prayer in general, and may be used without further qualification. On the other hand, *deomai* and *deēsis*, like *aiteō* and *aitēma*, involve spoken supplication. Their content is usually indicated, as is the person to whom the request is made. These terms are also confined to definite acts of praying. Occasionally, in the case of *aiteō* and *aitēma*, the basic meaning of wanting something is still present, so that it has a rather more forceful and sometimes demanding tone, whereas *erōtaō*, when it means to request, is more intimate. Prayer to God may also be expressed by *boaō boē* and *krazō*, both vbs. meaning to cry, shout (→ Cry). They are generally used when prayer to God or to Jesus Christ arises from great human need or distress and is therefore a cry for help (e.g. in the case of sickness or fear). *gonypeteō* also expresses urgency in prayer or in making a request, whereas *proskyneō* tends to imply worship, adoration and obeisance. The prayer of praise and thanksgiving is expressed by *aineō* and *eucharisteō* (→ Thank). The vb. *krouō*, knock, is used metaphorically of seeking access to God.

αἰτέω

αἰτέω (*aiteō*), ask, ask for, demand; αἴτημα (*aitēma*), request, demand; ἀπαιτέω (*apaiteō*), demand back; ἐξαιτέομαι (*exaiteomai*), ask for, demand; παραιτέομαι (*paraiteomai*), ask for, request, excuse, refuse, decline.

CL The basic meaning of *aiteō* is to want something, to demand something as one's share. Hence in profane Gk. *aiteō* means both to ask and to demand. The mid. form is best translated by to ask for oneself, or occasionally by to desire for oneself. The noun *aitēma*, therefore, means the thing asked for, both in the sense of a request or desire, and of a demand (e.g. *aitēma tyrannikon*, the demand of a tyrant, Plutarch, *Demetr.* 3). *apaiteō* intensifies the basic idea of demanding (e.g.

to call to account, Plato, *Rep.* 10, 599b), usually in the sense of demanding back, such being the force of the prefix *ap-*. The derivative *exaiteomai* means to ask for oneself, while *paraiteomai*, because of the sense attaching to the prefix *par-*, means basically to ask to be released from an obligation, to present one's apologies.

OT The Heb. equivalent is *šā'al*, meaning to ask, require, wish, desire, request for oneself (Deut. 10:12; Jdg. 5:25; 1 Sam. 12:13; Job 31:30 and passim). Used with reference to God it approximates closely to the idea of prayer and is often associated with thanksgiving for answered prayer (e.g. 1 Sam. 1:20; Pss. 105[104]: 40; 21[20]:4). It also means to ask, inquire (Gen. 24:57, LXX *erōtaō*); in legal language to examine (Deut. 13:15, LXX *ereunaō*); to consult, seek counsel (Jdg. 18:5, LXX *eperōtaō*). *šā'al* is rendered by *aiteō* only when the desire is for something quite specific (Exod. 3:22; Jos. 14:12; Jdg. 5:25; 1 Sam. 12:17); e.g. Hannah asks for herself a son from Yahweh and Eli promises her "what you have asked from him" (1 Sam. 1:17). Similarly in the Pss., whenever this verb expresses a promise of answered prayer, this must always be seen against the background of a specific request (Pss. 2:8; 21[20]:4; 27[26]:4; 40[39]:6; 78[77]:18; 105[104]:40; cf. Isa. 7:11 f.; 58:2; Prov. 30:7 [24:30]).

NT 1. In the NT *aiteō, aiteomai* (occurring 70 times) generally means to request, ask (for oneself). It occurs with more or less the same degree of frequency in all four Gospels (Matt. 14 times; Mk. 9; Lk. 11; Jn. 11) and Acts (10 times) rarely in Paul (once each in 1 Cor. and Col., and twice in Eph.). It is found 5 times each in Jas. and Jude and once in 1 Pet. but not at all in the Pastorals, Heb. and Rev.

(a) On a human level the mid. form of the vb. (*aiteomai* etc.) is used almost always in addressing superiors (Matt. 14:7; 27:20; Lk. 23:23; Acts 9:2 and passim) and therefore has a somewhat official flavour. Generally speaking, the act. form of the verb (*aiteō* etc.) has no special nuances. Only in Matt. 5:42 is it clear from the context that *aiteō* has a trace of unpleasantness about it: to demand something unpleasant, or at least to ask in a way which the other person feels to be unpleasant (hence *aiteō* could virtually be translated here by "to approach" or "to accost"). D. Hill suggests that the two clauses in this verse are parallel and that *aiteō* here means to ask for a loan (cf. Exod. 22:25; *The Gospel of Matthew, New Century Bible*, 1972, 128). Jesus emphasizes that the disciple should respond even to requests such as this (cf. Matt. 7:7, 8). The ethical implications of this should be noted: I am to overcome my reluctance and open both heart and hand to the person making the request, for the request is nothing less than God calling me to open my heart to him and be obedient.

(b) In the religious sphere, i.e. in those passages when a request is made to God, no difference in meaning is discernible between the act. and mid. forms of the vb. In the nature of the case, such requests enter the realm of supplicatory prayer (cf. Matt. 21:22, to ask in prayer), though in the NT several other words are used, sometimes paired with *aiteō*, to express the idea of making supplication; e.g. → *proseuchomai* (Mk. 11:24; Col. 1:9), which usually remains unqualified and indicates prayer generally; or → *gonypeteō*, to bend the knee (cf. Eph. 3:13 f.), which particularly stresses the suppliant's humble posture before God. *erōtaō*, too, occurs in parallel with *aiteō* (1 Jn. 5:16), though as a rule it is used where there is a close relationship between the parties concerned, e.g. between the disciples and

Jesus, and between Jesus and God; when the disciples address requests to God, however, *aiteō* is generally used. *erōtaō* originally meant to ask a question (in a dialogue) and has retained its intimate conversational character. Another word for to ask in the NT is → *deomai*, generally used where the request springs from a concrete situation (hence frequently for intercession).

It is striking that *aiteō* is never used of Jesus' own requests and prayers, but always *erōtaō* or *deomai* (e.g. Jn. 14:16; 16:23-26; Lk. 22:32). This may be connected with the peculiarity of *erōtaō* mentioned above.

(c) It is significant that, wherever the NT speaks of requests made to God, it emphasizes that such requests are heard (cf. Matt. 6:8; 7:7-11; 18:19; 21:22; Jn. 14:13 f.; 15:7, 16; 16:23 f., 26; 1 Jn. 3:22; 5:14 f.; Jas. 1:5). It is as if the NT witnesses wished particularly to encourage men to pray, by assuring the suppliant that his requests are heard by God. The NT is aware that this certainty keeps all prayer alive; let such certainty become weakened or diminished through doubt, and prayer dies.

What basis does the NT give for this certainty? In Matt. 7:8 the fact that requests are heard is stated as a basic principle of the → kingdom of God: "Everyone who asks receives." This principle is here the foundation for the injunction and its accompanying promise: "Ask and it will be given to you." But the ultimate foundation is given in such passages as Matt. 6:8; Jn. 15:16; 16:23, 26 f.; Col. 1:9-12 and especially Matt. 7:9-11. God is the Father who loves his own more than an earthly father loves his son, and who therefore cannot permit their requests to be unavailing, but gives them what they need. Ultimately, therefore, the reason why a person who asks is certain of being heard, is the certainty, given by Jesus to his own, of God's fatherly goodness and love. Implicit in these passages is a further certainty which runs through the whole Bible and undergirds everything it says: the certainty that God is a living God who hears and sees, and who has a heart full of compassion.

As God deals with us, so should we deal with our neighbour and respond to his requests (Matt. 5:42). We are to give to him because we experience afresh every day the generosity and fatherly goodness of God.

(d) The NT repeatedly makes the point, however, that the prayer which God hears must be the right kind of prayer. This is alluded to in Matt. 7:7 f., where the vbs. to → seek and to knock (→ *krouō*) are used in parallel with to ask. Frequently in the Bible, seeking has God as its object; it denotes a God-orientated attitude on the part of man. This gives a clue as to what constitutes true prayer. It must be in keeping with the nature of him to whom it is addressed, in which case our requests will be well-pleasing to God and in accordance with his will (cf. 1 Jn. 5:14: to ask something "according to his will"). To ask from God means to ask from him something right and good (Matt. 7:11). Lk. interprets this specifically as asking for the Holy → Spirit (Lk. 11:13). In other places true prayer is described as asking in → faith (Matt. 21:22; Jas. 1:5 f.; note the affinity between Jas. and Matt.). In prayer we are never to forget whom we are addressing: the living God, the almighty One with whom nothing is impossible, and from whom therefore all things may be expected. To doubt God is to do him an injustice, for it belittles his deity, misjudges his character, and therefore receives nothing from him (Jas. 1:7). But true prayer is bound up with faith, i.e. with the certainty of being heard. The

857

NT encourages such a degree of certainty that the suppliant can believe he has actually received his request at the very moment of asking (Mk. 11:24; 1 Jn. 5:15). The corresponding passages in the Johannine writings expand the idea of asking in faith: it is said to arise from "his words remaining in us" (Jn. 15:7), i.e. from our being in such close union with Jesus and his word that our asking is sure to be in accordance with his will. 1 Jn. 3:22 moves rather more into the sphere of ethics: "we receive from him whatever we ask, because we keep his commandments and do what pleases him", i.e. because our asking springs from a right attitude to God. This verse presents in brief summary the implications of being united with Christ in our prayers. Elsewhere Jn. describes true prayer as "asking in the name of Jesus" (Jn. 14:13 f.; 15:16; 16:24, 26; → Name). Since such prayer is heard, and since I can be certain of the fact, the result is → joy (Jn. 16:24). Matt. 18:19 may be relevant here: united prayer by several disciples indicates that all selfish desires have been renounced, for selfish prayer is false and receives nothing from God (Jas. 4:3; Mk. 10:35).

2. When the object of *aiteō* is a subordinate person, it easily assumes the meaning to require, demand (Lk. 1:63; Acts 16:29); similarly when a creditor demands back from a debtor goods given on loan or trust, or requires an account of them (predicated of God in Lk. 12:48). In 1 Pet. 3:15 "to require an account" (of the Christian's hope) means to demand proof of its truth and credibility, or simply to demand information.

This meaning throws light on the implications lying behind the Jews' demand for "signs" (1 Cor. 1:22; → Miracle, art. *sēmeion*). When man takes this attitude, he is in fact setting himself above God and calling him to account; he is demanding that God should justify himself in relation to what he had done in Christ.

3. (a) The word *aitēma* occurs in its non-religious sense in Lk. 23:24. In its religious sense, i.e. when addressed to God, it likewise means a request and especially any individual request viewed in relation to its content (e.g. Phil. 4:6; 1 Jn. 5:15).

(b) The compound vb. *apaiteō* often carries the intensified meaning to demand, but is used particularly in the sense of reclaiming either stolen goods (Lk. 6:30b, where the command "Give to every one who begs from you" is expanded and at the same time brought into sharper focus), or goods loaned out for a limited period (Lk. 12:20, where God requires back man's life, the vb. itself indicating where the true ownership lies; cf. *aitēsousin* in Lk. 12:48b: "and of him to whom men commit much they will demand the more").

exaiteomai occurs only in Lk. 22:31 in the sense of to demand that someone (in this case Peter) be handed over. This demand has been made by → Satan to Peter's master, namely to God himself, with the alleged purpose of testing the genuineness and steadfastness of Peter's faith, but with the ulterior motive of bringing about his downfall.

(c) In Mk. 15:6 *paraiteomai* means to ask for someone's release, while in Lk. 14:18 f. it means to ask for one's own release, in this case from the obligation of accepting an invitation, i.e. to present one's apologies. Should the obligation be considered intolerable, then the vb. can mean to refuse, decline (e.g. Acts 25:11, with reference to the Roman death penalty; Heb. 12:19, 25, with reference to God and his word); or to reject (e.g. 1 Tim. 4:7, "godless and silly myths"; 5:11, the enrolment of younger women in the church's list of widows); 2 Tim. 2:23; Tit.

3:10. In the last-mentioned passages, disciplinary measures are in view both in regard to doctrine and in regard to church government, as befitted the situation being experienced by the recipients of the Pastoral Epistles. Hence, these acts of refusal or rejection begin to acquire an official character, though whether Tit. 3:10 refers to excommunication or merely to the breaking off of → fellowship (as in 1 Tim. 6:5, cf. AV) must remain an open question.   *H. Schönweiss*

| γονυπετέω |

γόνυ (*gony*), knee; γονυπετέω (*gonypeteō*), fall on one's knees, kneel down before.

CL In the Gk. world, which adopted this custom from the Orient, kneeling was practised by a slave before his master and by a suppliant before the gods, but the practice was usually expressed not by *gonypeteō* but by *proskynēsis* and *hiketeia* even though the basic idea is different (→ *proskyneō*, lit. to kiss, and thus to worship).

OT The oriental·ceremony of kneeling appeared in Israel only when its kings adopted the style of the great oriental monarchs and demanded similar tokens of servility (1 Chr. 29:20). At the same time, however, there is evidence that the widespread oriental custom of kneeling before the gods was also adopted, so that in the OT falling prostrate is a sign of submission and homage, of humility and awe before Almighty God (Ps. 95:6). In addition, the OT characteristically looks forward to the practice being continued in the messianic age of salvation (Isa. 45: 23).

NT 1. Apart from Heb. 12:12 (cf. Isa. 35:3), *gony*, knee, occurs in the NT only in association with verbs in phrases meaning to bend the knee, kneel before. In the NT the plur. *ta gonata* is combined with *tithenai* (Mk. 15:19; Lk. 5:8; 22:41; Acts 7:60; 9:40; 20:36; 21:5) or *kamptein* (Rom. 11:4 quoting 1 Ki. 19:18; 14:11 quoting Isa. 45:23; Eph. 3:14; Phil. 2:10) to give the phrase to bow the knees. It expresses:

(a) Awe before a superior or homage before a king, i.e. recognition of his might and sovereignty (as in Mk. 15:19, where the phrase occurs in parallel with → *proskyneō*, with no real difference in meaning); the adoration and veneration which is due to God alone and not to any idol (Rom. 11:4); the recognition of God as the supreme judge (Rom. 14:11) or the acknowledgment that Jesus, in his universal majesty and cosmic significance, is Lord of all (Phil. 2:10).

(b) The phrase is particularly meaningful in Lk. 5:8, where it expresses the humble attitude of a man who, having received of Christ's abundant grace, recognizes both his sinful and lost condition and the wholly unmerited nature of the gift. His falling down before Jesus is here a sign of repentance, that change of direction which marks the beginnings of faith. Similarly in Jn. 9:38 *proskyneō* is a sign of faith in Jesus.

(c) In other passages falling on one's knees is simply the gesture associated with prayer (cf. → *proseuchomai*, → *deomai*, → *aiteō*), emphasizing its earnestness and urgency (e.g. Lk. 22:41; Acts 7:60; 9:40).

2. The simple vb. *gonypeteō* is also used (e.g. Matt. 27:29), especially to intensify

the urgency of a request or question (to ask on bended knee), e.g. Matt. 17:14; Mk. 1:40 (cf. the parallel use of → *proskyneō* in Matt. 8:2); 10:17.

H. Schönweiss

δέομαι

δέομαι (*deomai*), ask, request, beseech, beg; δέησις (*deēsis*), a request, entreaty; προσδέομαι (*prosdeomai*), need (in addition or further); ἱκετηρία (*hiketēria*), supplication; ἔντευξις (*enteuxis*), petition, prayer.

CL The basic meaning of *deomai* is to lack, be in need of (cf. *prosdeomai*), from which developed the meaning to request, beseech; similarly in the case of the noun *deēsis*.

OT 1. In the LXX *deomai* is used with the meaning to beseech, quite often representing the Heb. *ḥānan* (hith.), to beg for favour. Thus Esther besought the king (Est. 8:3), and Jacob likewise the angel (Hos. 12:4). Job, ostracized and in misery, had to beseech his own servant (Job 19:16). The suppliant pleads with God for mercy (1 Ki. 8:33–47; Ps. 30:8; 14:1). But *deomai* can also translate *ḥālâh* (piel), to appease, placate. The person praying attempts to placate God's anger by his entreaties (Exod. 32:11; 1 Ki. 13:6; Zech. 8:21; Jer. 26:19). The prayer can be accompanied by an offering (1 Sam. 13:12; → Sacrifice) or associated with renunciation of sin (Dan. 9:13). Sometimes *deomai* stands for the particle *bî* or *nā'* (Gen. 43:20; 44:18; Exod. 4:10; Num. 12:13) in the sense of "if it please you . . .", "by your leave . . .", used when addressing a superior.

2. The noun *deēsis* is used in the LXX to translate several Heb. words including *tᵉḥinnâh*, supplication (e.g. 1 Ki. 8:28, 30, 38, 45, 49, 52, 54; 9:3; Pss. 6:9; 55[54]:1); the related *taḥᵃnûn* (e.g. Pss. 28[27]:2, 6; 31[30]:22; 86[85]:6; 116[114]:1; 130 [129]:2; 140[139]:6; 143[142]:1); *rinnâh*, a cry of lamentation, a prayer of lament (e.g. Pss. 17[16]:1; 61[60]:1; 88[87]:2; 106[105]:44), and *šaw'âh*, a cry for help (e.g. in Ps. 34[33]:17; 39[38]:12; 40[39]:1; 145[144]:19). It is used only for supplication and calling upon God in prayer, often standing alongside *proseuchē*, prayer (e.g. in 1 Ki. 8:38, 45; Ps. 6:9; 17:1; 39:12; Jer. 11:14). It is thus largely synonymous with the latter (→ *proseuchomai*).

NT In the NT *deomai* occurs only with the meaning to ask request, beseech, beg.

1. It is used in a general sense as a courtesy formula, without any particular object or object clause (cf. the English phrase "I beg you"), followed by direct speech (Acts 8:24; 21:39) or by an infinitive (Acts 26:3).

2. In some passages *deomai* is used in its full sense of making earnest entreaty, even imploring. There is a warmth, an attractiveness, a winsomeness about it, as in 2 Cor. 5:20 (cf. Acts 2:40); 8:4; 10:2; Gal. 4:12.

3. In all other cases *deomai* has the religious sense of beseeching Jesus or God. The requests made are quite specific, arising out of real need and expecting definite help of an external or a spiritual nature. Help in a situation of external need is sought from Jesus in Lk. 5:12; 9:38. Passages such as Lk. 8:28; 9:38 indicate that with *deomai* the reason for the request is generally given (cf. also the following passages, but cf. Lk. 1:13). 1 Thess. 3:10 shows how even an apparently external

request may be directed to a spiritual end, so that here the distinction between external and internal is no longer operative.

Prayer should be made to God for forgiveness (Acts 8:22); for labourers to bring in God's harvest (Matt. 9:38; → Seed, Harvest); and for ability to stand on the last day (Lk. 21:36). In the latter verse, as in many other passages including some already mentioned, to ask is used absolutely, i.e. without God specifically mentioned as direct object. In such cases, of course, the direct object has to be supplied.

4. If the request is made not in one's own interest but on behalf of someone else, then *deomai* means to intercede (e.g. Acts 8:24; Rom. 10:1; 2 Cor. 1:11). When, as frequently happens, the content of the intercession is not stated, the vb. indicates that brotherliness which constrains one Christian to plead with God on behalf of another (e.g. Phil. 1:4; Eph. 6:18). Thus intercession is often the visible and practical expression of that heartfelt affection and fellowship which exist among Christians (e.g. 2 Cor. 9:14; 2 Tim. 1:3), an idea implicit, probably, in other passages also. That Paul highly valued such intercession and expected great things from it, is seen from such passages as 2 Cor. 1:11; Phil. 1:19. Jas. 5:16 speaks in precisely the same vein. Its point is further sharpened by the phrase "the supplication of a righteous man" (i.e. of a believer, cf. v. 15, whose life bears out his faith) and the adj. qualifying *deēsis*, namely *energoumenē*, energetic, active, effective. This comes about when the supplication involves living, dynamic fellowship and genuine conversation with God – which in itself is a gift from God himself. This is exemplified by → Elijah (v. 17; cf. 1 Ki. 17:1; 18:1). Similarly 1 Pet. 3:12 (quoting Ps. 34:16) says that the prayer of the "righteous" is heard by God (on prayer being heard → *aiteō*).

5. Whenever the request is addressed to God, *deomai* quite naturally assumes the meaning of to pray, and can often be so translated (likewise the noun *deēsis*, prayer). This is frequently the case when no content is stated (e.g. Acts 10:2; Heb. 5:7, where the noun stands alongside *hiketēria*, entreaty, supplication, originally that of a person seeking protection). Hence, as in the OT, *deēsis* often occurs with *proseuchē*, in which case the latter has the more general meaning of the two (→ *proseuchomai*); e.g. Rom. 1:10; Eph. 6:18; Phil. 4:6, where both are used with the further addition of *aitēma*, an individual request or petition (→ *aiteō*); 1 Tim. 2:1, where the two are complemented by *enteuxis*, intercession, petition, appeal, prayer.

Prayer is the most important evidence of true Christian faith (1 Tim. 2:1). It is the very mark of a Christian (1 Tim. 5:5; cf. Acts 9:11). Even Jesus prayed (Heb. 5:7; cf. Lk. 22:44) and made intercession (Lk. 22:32).

prosdeomai occurs only in Acts 17:25 in the sense of to need, be in need of. In this word the original sense of *deomai* reappears, and Lk. uses it here to underscore the self-sufficiency and complete independence of God who is highly exalted above all that is merely human.   *H. Schönweiss*

προσεύχομαι

προσεύχομαι (*proseuchomai*), to pray, entreat; εὔχομαι (*euchomai*), request, vow; εὐχή (*euchē*), prayer, oath, vow; προσευχή (*proseuchē*), prayer.

CL *euchomai* is a technical term for invoking a deity and so covers every aspect of such invocation: to request, entreat, vow, consecrate etc. (similarly the noun: request, entreaty, vow); in a word: to pray; prayer. Since the vb.'s basic meaning is "to make confident statements about oneself", it can also mean to boast, brag and assert.

In profane Gk. prayer is often accompanied by an offering, the object of which is to make the gods favourably disposed. Here prayer mostly takes the form of supplication. Though used originally, as early as Mycenean Gk., almost exclusively with reference to tangible benefits, at a later period (e.g. in the Tragic Poets), the words have in view spiritual and ethical values (e.g. Aesch., *Cho.* 140 f.; Eur., *Medea* 635 ff.) or denote prayer for preservation from spiritual or moral harm. Characteristically, the assurance of being heard is lacking, belief in an omnipresent divine principle excluding all possibility of an epiphany. In the piety associated with the Hellenistic mysteries the worshipper at prayer experiences the nearness of the deity, especially at those rare moments of climax when he is granted a sight of the god concerned. At such times all prayer is extinguished, and is replaced by silent rapture. Intercession, and supplication for earthly things, are totally absent from this kind of prayer.

OT 1. In the OT prayer is all-important because of that which both characterizes and constitutes the nation of Israel, his relation to his God. The whole history of Israel is therefore permeated and borne along by prayer. At all its important points man is found in converse with God. This is true even when no use is made of those specific Heb. terms for to pray, such as *'āṭar* or *pālal*, both meaning to pray, request, and the noun *tepillāh*, prayer. Expressions like to speak, to call or to → cry are frequently used instead. To indicate intense emotional involvement, the Hebrew used vbs. such as to groan, to sigh or to weep (→ Lament). But however urgently he prayed, the OT suppliant never forgot that he was addressing the holy, almighty God (an utter impossibility apart from God's condescending kindness and grace). This is shown by the frequent use of the vb. *hištaḥawâh* which really means to prostrate oneself (before superior) (→ *proskyneō*), and which may therefore indicate man's customary posture in prayer, though there is also evidence of prayer being offered from a standing position. The parallel expression, to fall down on one's knees, is also used occasionally. Such phrases are intended to indicate the → humility of mind which must always characterize a man as he prays. In addition the OT contains many expressions for the prayer of praise and thanksgiving, e.g. the familiar vb. *hālal*, to praise, glorify, extol (*halelû-yâh*, praise the Lord; *yâh* = Yahweh; → Amen, art. *hallēlouia*), and a whole range of words intensifying the idea of praise: to shout with joy, to exult, to sing (often to instrumental accompaniment; → Thank).

In the LXX *proseuchomai* normally translates *pālal* in the hithpael form which is the standard Heb. vb. meaning to pray: Gen. 20:7, 17; 1 Sam. 1:10, 12, 26 f.; 2:1; 7:5; 8:6; 12:19, 23; 2 Sam. 7:27; 1 Ki. 8:28 ff., 33, 35, 42, 44, 48, 54; 13:6; 2 Ki. 4:33; 6:17 f.; 19:15, 20; 1 Chr. 17:25; 2 Chr. 6:19 ff., 24, 26, 32, 34, 38; 7:1, 14; 30:18; 32:20, 24; 33:13; Ezr. 10:1; Neh. 1:4, 6; 2:4; 4:9(3); Pss. 5:2; 32(31):6; 72(71):15; Jon. 2:2; 4:2; Isa. 16:12; 37:15, 21; 38:2; 44:17; 45:14, 20; Jer. 7:6; 11:14; 14:11; 29(36):12; 32(39):16; 37(44):3; 42(49):2, 4, 20; Dan. 9:4, 20: It translates *pālal* in the piel in 1 Sam. 2:25 and the noun *t*ᵉ*pillâh*, prayer, in Ps. 109 (108):4. It translates the vb. *'āṯar*, entreat, in Exod. 10:17 and Jdg. 13:8; *nāpal*, fall, in the hithpael in 2 Esd. 10:1; the Aram. *ṣᵉla'*, pray, in Dan. 6:11(10) and 2 Esd. 6:10. It is without Heb. equivalent in 1 Sam. 14:45; Tob. 3:1; 6:17; 8:4 f.; 12:12; Jud. 11:17; Est. 5:1; Wis. 13:17; Bar. 1:11, 13; Dan. 3:24 f. LXX; Dan.Th. 9:21; 1 Macc. 3:44; 4:30; 7:40; 11:71; 2 Macc. 1:6; 20:10; 12:44; 15:14; 3 Macc. 6:1; 4 Macc. 4:11.

The noun *proseuchē* normally translates the corresponding Heb. noun *t*ᵉ*pillâh*, prayer: 2 Sam. 7:27; 1 Ki. 8:28 f., 38, 45, 49, 54; 9:3; 2 Ki. 19:4; 20:5; 2 Chr. 6:19 f., 29, 39; 7:12, 15; 30:27; 33:18 f.; Neh. 1:6, 11; 11:17; Pss. 4:1; 6:9; 17(16):1; 35(34):13; 39(38):12; 42(41):8; 54(53):2; 55(54):1; 61(60):1; 64(63):1; 65(64):2; 66(65):19 f.; 69(68):13; 80(79):4; 84(83):8; 86(85):6; 88(87):2, 13; 102(101):1, 17; 109(108):7; 141(140):2, 5; 143(142):1; Prov. 28:9; Jon. 2:8; Hab. 3:1; Isa. 38:5; 56:7; Jer. 11:14; Lam. 3:8, 44; Dan. 9:3, 17, 21. In addition it occurs in the titles of various Pss. (17[16]; 86[85]; 90[89]; 102[101]; 142[141]). It translates *qôl*, voice, in Pss. 64(63):1; 130(129):2; *t*ᵉ*ḥinnâh*, supplication for favour, 1 Ki. 8:45; 2 Chr. 6:35; and Dan. 9:20; and *taḥᵃnûn*, supplication (for favour) in Dan. 9:18. It is without Heb. equivalent in 1 Ki. 9:3; Tob. 3:16; 12:8, 12, 15; 13:1; Jud. 12:6; 13:3, 10; Pss. 61(60):5; 88(87):14; Wis. 18:21; Sir. 3:5; 34(31):26; 35(32):17; 39:5, 7; 51:1, 13; Hab. 3:16; Isa. 38:9; 60:7; 1 Macc. 3:46; 5:33; 7:37; 12:11; 2 Macc. 1:23 f.; 3 Macc. 6:16; 7:20.

2. Prayer in the OT is characterized by being directed to the one God, who is both the God of Israel and at the same time the Lord of the nations and of the whole earth, having revealed himself as such to his people (1 Ki. 8:22 ff.; 2 Ki. 19:15). Accordingly the Israelite always prays first as a member of his people, not as an individual (Pss. 35:18; 111:1), and he knows what to expect of God. He knows too that God hears his prayer, and answers it if it is in agreement with his will (Pss. 3:4; 18:6; 65:2; Jer. 29:12). He prays therefore with firm confidence in God (Ps. 17:6 f.); he experiences temptation and doubt, to be sure, but these are possible only against the background of such confidence. He knows too that in the eyes of a holy God there is no question of his prayers counting as a work of piety which God then has to honour with his blessing. (Contrast the prayer of → Elijah, the prophet of Yahweh, with that of the priests of Baal, for whom it is nothing more than a technique, aimed at prevailing on their god by means of a torrent of words, 1 Ki. 18:26, 29.) He also knows that God is a person. Therefore, he prays in a thoroughly personal and specific fashion, aware that he is actually speaking to God, not merely invoking some dumb deity (Gen. 28:22–33; 1 Sam. 1:10 f.; Ps. 77:1–11). Such speaking to God can become a veritable wrestling with God, especially in the case of intercession (Exod. 32:11–14; Num. 14:13–22; Deut. 9:26–29; Neh. 1:4–11). Typical are the weapons with which the suppliant fights: he appeals to God's → promises, reminds him of his deeds of salvation in the past, particularly of his election of Israel and their deliverance from Egypt; he appeals to God's honour and → glory and to his very nature, which is one of forbearance, → grace and → mercy (cf. the last mentioned passages).

In addition, the suppliant thanks God for the miracles he has wrought in the history of his people (Pss. 105; 106) and asks for further guidance and continued deliverance from all possible distresses. Prayer and thanksgiving can cover practically all the material and spiritual needs both of the individual and of the community, their whole life acquiring through prayer a lasting and intensive Godward orientation.

As an aid to prayer mention is sometimes made of → fasting (Neh. 1:4; Ezr. 8:23; Joel 1:14; 2:12, 15–17; Jer. 14:12), probably as an expression of that humble penitence before God which should lie at the root of all prayer.

3. Prayer is not restricted to any special place of worship but can take place anywhere (Gen. 24:26 f., 63), though of course it is specially fostered in the early sanctuaries and later in the → temple at Jerusalem.

4. The OT distinguishes between true and false prayer in the following manner. True prayer is of the → heart, i.e. it involves the whole person and means that a man comes before God with his whole being and in an attitude of humble submission (Jer. 29:12 ff.). False prayer, by contrast, is offered merely "with the lips", i.e. a man merely utters (or simply repeats) words and phrases with no self-surrender or offering of his "heart" and life to God, except perhaps as a pure formality, with no real intention of fulfilling the will of God as revealed, e.g. in his commandments (Isa. 1:15 f.; 29:13; Amos 5:23 f.).

In this same context, the OT also speaks of hindrances to prayer, which make an answer difficult or even impossible to obtain, e.g. disobedience (Isa. 1:15–17; 59:1 f.; Deut. 1:43–45), lovelessness towards one's fellowmen (Isa.58:3–10), injustice (Mic. 3:1–4). These characteristics of OT prayer are all exemplified with especial clarity in the Book of Psalms, a unique collection of prayers for use in public worship and by the individual.

5. Prayer also played a large part in the piety of Rabbinic Judaism. Of all devout exercises, fasting and praying were the most prominent, but although the texts of prayers found at Qumran indicate the great variety of prayers, both as regards forms and content (see especially the hymns, 1QH; → Song), which were still in use at the time of Christ, → Pharisaic orthodoxy had been extending its systematization, from the closing years of the first cent. B.C. onwards to include the piety of prayer. This applied not merely to the public prayers offered in the synagogue, which included the ancient Shema (šᵉma'; Deut. 6:4 ff.; → Hear, art. akouō, NT 3) and the Eighteen Benedictions (šᵉmōneh 'eśrēh; 18 petitions, referring particularly to the salvation of the individual and of the community) but also to private prayer, e.g. on the left arm and the forehead there were to be prayer straps, to which were attached small cylinders containing papyrus scrolls with Bible texts on them – an erroneously literal compliance with Exod. 13:9, 16; Deut. 6:8; 11:18; cf. Matt. 23:5; → Guard, art. phylassō, NT 4. The prayers handed down from individual rabbis prove to be remarkably uniform. The idea of achieving righteousness dominated the whole of their piety and left its imprint upon prayer.

H. Schönweiss

6. The major element in the daily rabbinic liturgy was the Shema which consisted of three OT passages (Deut. 6:4–9; 11:13–21; Num. 15:37–41). It was said both morning and evening with set benedictions (two preceding and one following in the morning; two preceding and two following in the evening; cf. Berakoth 1:4; text in R. A. Stewart, *Rabbinic Theology*, 1961, 178–83). In addition, the Tephillah

or Eighteen Benedictions was said thrice daily. Much of this material was incorporated in the Hebrew Prayer Book and is still used in the Synagogue (Hebrew texts in D. W. Staerk, *Altjüdische liturgische Gebete*, 1910; cf. S. Singer, ed., *Authorised Daily Prayer Book of the United Congregations of the British Empire*, 1935 and numerous editions).

The Eighteen Benedictions have been preserved in the form which the Pharisees gave them after the fall of Jerusalem in A.D. 70 (cf. petition 14), but they are considerably older, and W. Förster holds that they give "a picture of the things that were precious to all Jews in Jesus' day" (*Palestinian Judaism in New Testament Times*, 1964, 156). The following translation is that given by R. A. Stewart, op. cit., 183–86, based on the text given by O. Holtzmann in G. Beer and O. Holtzmann, eds, *Die Mischna, Text, Übersetzung und Erklärung*, 1912, which he holds to be more accurate than that of Staerk.

O Lord, open thou my lips, and my mouth shall show forth thy praise (Ps. 51:17).

1. Blessed art thou, O Lord our God, the God of our fathers, the God of Abraham, the God of Isaac, and the God of Jacob, the great, mighty and revered God, the Most High God, owner of heaven and earth, our Shield and the Shield of our fathers, our confidence from generation to generation. Blessed art thou, O Lord, the Shield of Abraham.

2. Thou art mighty, bringing low the proud, strong, and the judge of the ruthless, living for evermore and raising the dead; making the wind to return and the dew to fall; nourishing the living and making alive the dead; bringing forth salvation for us in the blinking of an eyelid. Blessed art thou O Lord, who makest alive the dead.

3. Holy art thou, and revered is thy name. There is none other God beside thee. Blessed art thou, O Lord, the holy God.

4. Favour us, O our Father, with knowledge of thee, and with understanding and sagacity from thy Torah. Blessed art thou, O Lord, who favourest with knowledge.

5. Bring us back, O Lord, unto thee, and may we return. Renew our days as aforetime. Blessed art thou, who takest delight in repentance.

6. Pardon us, our Father, for we have sinned against thee. Wipe out and remove our transgressions from before thine eyes, for great are thy mercies. Blessed art thou, O Lord, who aboundest in forgiving.

7. Look on our afflictions and defend our cause, and redeem us for thy Name's sake. Blessed art thou, O Lord, the Redeemer of Israel.

8. Heal us, O Lord our God, from the affliction of our hearts and remove sorrow and sighing from us, and bring healing for our stripes. Blessed art thou, the healer of the sick of thy people Israel.

9. Bless this year to us for good, O Lord our God, in every kind of its increase, and bring speedily near the year of the fulfilment of our redemption. Grant the dew and the rain on the face of the earth, and make full the world from the storehouse of thy goodness. Grant blessing on the works of our hands. Blessed art thou, O Lord, who blessest the years.

10. Blow on a great trumpet for our liberty, and raise a standard for the gathering together of our exiles. Blessed art thou, O Lord, who gatherest together the banished ones of thy people Israel.

11. Restore our judges as at the first, and our counsellors as in the beginning, and mayest thou alone reign over us. Blessed art thou, O Lord, who lovest judgment.

12. For apostates let there be no hope, and the kingship of presumption mayest thou speedily destroy in our days. May Christians and heretics perish in a moment, may they be blotted out from the book of the living, and not be written down with the righteous. Blessed art thou, O Lord, that humblest the proud.

13. On righteous proselytes may thy compassions be moved, and grant us a good reward with them that do thy will. Blessed art thou, O Lord, a confidence for the righteous.

14. Have compassion, O Lord our God, in thine abounding compassion on Israel thy people, and on Jerusalem, and on Zion the tabernacle of thy glory, on thy Holy Place and on thy Temple, and on thy kingdom of the House of David. Blessed art thou, O Lord, the builder of Jerusalem. [Note: The wording offers clear presumption of a date prior to A.D. 70. The form used today is expressed a little differently.]

15. Hearken, O Lord our God, to the voice of our prayer, and have compassion on us, for thou art a gracious and compassionate God. Blessed art thou, O Lord, who hearest prayer.

16. Be pleased, O Lord our God, to dwell in Zion, and thy servants will serve thee in Jerusalem. Blessed art thou, O Lord, whom we will serve in fear.

17. We give thee thanks. Thou art the Lord our God and the God of our fathers. For all good things, for grace and compassion which thou has dealt out unto us, and unto our fathers before us – and if we say, Our foot has slipped, the Lord will sustain us – blessed be thou, O Lord, to thee be the praise.

18. Give thy peace to Israel thy people, and unto thy city and thy possession. Bless us, each and every one. Blessed be thou, O Lord, who makest peace.

The first three petitions give praise to Israel's God. The reference to the → resurrection in the second petition indicates Pharisaic influence. The prayers indicate a strong desire to know God and to do his will. There is repeated petition for redemption which, however, is conceived in terms of an alteration of the present world-situation in restoring the fortunes of Israel and the restoration of Jerusalem

(14th, 16th, 18th). But there is no mention of a new covenant, a new heart, a new heaven and earth or the last judgment. This suggests that the ideas which had been developed in Judaism through the Hasidic movement are lacking (cf. W. Förster, op. cit., 157). There is no prayer for the repentance of the apostates or mention of the Gentiles turning to the God of Israel. The twelfth petition which appears to have been inserted after A.D. 70 shows the deep-rooted hostility to Christians (or Nazarenes, as the text calls them). However, this reference was subsequently removed. Förster notes a similar tendency in the Psalms of Solomon, a Pharisaic work consisting of eighteen psalms dated in the post Maccabean period c. 70–40 B.C. (ibid.). Here the pious and the ungodly have both sinned. But the former has done so without intent; he cleaves to God, accepts his discipline and remains righteous; whereas the latter does not (see especially Pss.Sol. 9:6 f.; 12:6; 16:5–13; 17:21–42; cf. ibid., 157–61; H. Braun, "Vom Erbarmen Gottes über den Gerechten. Zur Theologie der Psalmen Salomos", *ZNW* 43, 1950–51, 1–50). The Eighteen Benedictions clearly regard God as the sole redeemer. He alone pardons and removes transgression in his mercy (6th petition, cf. 8th, 15th), but alongside of this there is the same emphasis on the righteous that appears in Pss.Sol. (12th, 13th) and the implication that the righteous who do God's will deserve to be rewarded (13th). On rabbinic instructions regarding the use of the Shema and the Eighteen Benedictions see the Mishnah and Talmud Tractates Berakoth.

C. Brown

NT In the NT *proseuchomai* occurs 85 times and *proseuchē* 37 times, both being particularly frequent in Acts but entirely absent from the Gospel of Jn. and the Johannine Epistles. The simple vb. *euchomai* is found only 6 times in the NT (Acts 26:29; 27:29; Rom. 9:3; 2 Cor. 13:7, 9; Jas. 5:16; 3 Jn. 2), *euchē* only 3 times (Acts 18:18; 21:23; Jas. 5:15).

1. *The nature and scope of prayer.* (a) In the NT prayer is in all respects as it had developed in the OT. It is modelled, however, upon the praying of Jesus, to which there are repeated references (cf. 2 below), and which in its turn draws upon OT prayers and ideas. NT prayer is addressed to God or to Jesus, now called → Lord (*Kyrios*), those passages containing the vb. → *proskyneō*, to worship, being particularly significant in this connection. But *proseuchesthai* can also relate to Jesus (e.g. Rev. 5:8; Acts 9:34 f.; similarly in Acts 9:11, where attention is being drawn to the entirely new factor in Paul's situation). In this way the early church bears witness to the fact that it regards Jesus Christ as its Lord and its living head, who, having conquered death, is alive for evermore (→ Resurrection). Consequently one can enter into living, personal contact with him, talking with him just as one did when he was on earth (cf. Acts 9:10–16; 2 Cor. 12:8 f.). It follows that genuine prayer is not monologue but dialogue, in which the person praying is often silent in order to listen to Jesus' word and command. As in the OT, therefore, prayer is something very personal and specific, a genuine conversation with God or Jesus Christ. And since the NT believer knows God as his Father, with even greater clarity than anything his OT counterpart could have enjoyed, his praying proceeds from a childlike trust, as expressed in the typical NT form of address "Father", which Jesus taught his disciples to use (Matt. 6:6–9; Lk. 11:2; Eph. 3:14 f.; also 'abbā', the Aramaic word for Father, Rom. 8:15; Gal. 4:6). It is precisely at this

point that NT prayer contrasts most sharply with that of Rabbinic Judaism. (On the significance of these passages and the contrast with Judaism → Father, arts. *abba* and *patēr*.)

(b) The suppliant's assurance that his prayers are heard (→ *aiteō*) is even stronger in the NT than in the OT, being grounded in an experience of God's fatherly love in Jesus Christ. Jesus explicitly strengthens this assurance, which comes from faith, by promising that the prayer will be heard (e.g. Mk. 11:24: "Believe that you have already received it"). Experiences to the contrary, i.e. that God appears not to answer prayers, must not tempt us to doubt his fatherly love or the power of prayer (cf. Jesus in Gethsemane, Matt. 26:36–46 par. Mk. 14:32–42, Lk. 22:40–46, where Jesus' passion is the Father's will).

(c) True prayer has great power. It expresses that → faith whereby the sinner is justified (Lk. 18:10, 14). It is answered with the gift of the Holy Spirit (Lk. 11:13). It clarifies the way ahead (Mk. 1:35–39). It enables the suppliant to receive and put on the whole armour of God (cf. Eph. 6:18). Paul encouraged the believer to desire spiritual → gifts (1 Cor. 14:1). It is necessary to surround all activities with prayer, especially for the perseverance of the saints and for bold and faithful witness (Eph. 6:17–20). True prayer overcomes anxieties (Phil. 4:6). But at the same time it is a fight with the powers of evil and of darkness (Rom. 15:30; Col. 4:12; cf. Matt. 6:13).

On the other hand, the NT, like the OT, warns of hindrances which can make prayer ineffectual: licentiousness and lovelessness (1 Pet. 3:7; Jas. 4:3); unbelief and doubt (Jas. 1:5–7); and an unforgiving spirit (Matt. 5:23 f.; Mk. 11:25).

(d) NT prayer can be about anything, from the smallest matter to the greatest, from the affairs of today to those of eternity. The best example of this is the Lord's Prayer (Matt. 6:9 ff. and Lk. 11:2 ff.). Here the prayer for daily bread (→ Bread, art. *epiousios*), which includes all our other daily needs, is flanked on the one side by prayer for the coming of God's → kingdom and for his will to be done on earth, and on the other by prayer for the forgiveness of sin, for preservation in → temptation and for deliverance from all → evil (also from the evil one; → *ponēros*, NT 2 (b)). It is, however, not without significance that the prayers which refer to God, his will, his kingdom and his → name stand first (→ Holy, art. *hagios*). In Matt. 6 as in Lk. 11 the Lord's Prayer is embedded in longer discourses concerning true prayer (Matt. 6:5–15; Lk. 11:1–13); it must be marked by simplicity, concentration, discipline, patient confidence – and obedience. (On the Lord's Prayer see especially J. Jeremias, *The Prayers of Jesus*, SBT Second Series 6, 1967; J. Lowe, *The Lord's Prayer*, 1962; and E. Lohmeyer, *The Lord's Prayer*, 1965.)

(e) In addition to supplication, there are, as in the OT, the following types of prayer: intercession, the efficacy of which is emphasized especially by Paul and James (Rom. 15:30; 1 Thess. 5:25; 2 Thess. 3:1; Jas. 5:14–18) and which ought to embrace all men, even enemies (Matt. 5:44); the prayer of praise and thanksgiving (→ Thank, arts. *aineō* and *eucharisteō*) and adoration, which is addressed exclusively to God himself, quite apart from his gifts whether earthly or spiritual (cf. especially Rev. 4:8–11; 5:8–14; 7:9–17; 11:15–18; 15:2 ff.; 16:5 ff.; 19:1–8; 22:3, 9). The NT frequently insists that prayer should be constant (e.g. its use of *ektenōs*, eagerly, fervently, constantly Acts 12:5; 1 Pet. 1:22; → Patience, art. *kartereō*). This amounts to saying that the Christian ought always to live in the presence of his Lord and in converse with him, and constantly to be looking to him (Col. 4:2 and passim).

The posture in prayer was either kneeling (Acts 21:5; Eph. 3:14), in which case the forehead might touch the ground (Matt. 26:39), or standing (Mk. 11:15; Lk. 18:11, 13), sometimes with uplifted hands (1 Tim. 2:8).

Communal prayer seems to have been customary in the early church, both in public worship (1 Cor. 11:4 f.; 14:13–16:26) and in smaller gatherings (Matt. 18:19, where Jesus attaches a special promise to communal prayer; Acts 2:46 f.; 12:12), though private prayer is the fountain-head of prayer in general (Matt. 6:6; Jesus frequently prayed alone: Matt. 14:23; Mk. 1:35; Lk. 5:16; 6:12; 9:18).

H. Schönweiss

2. *The form of the Lord's Prayer.* Set prayers certainly existed, but even here there was no rigidity, as can be seen from the fact that the Lord's Prayer is handed down in two variant forms (Matt. 6:9–13; Lk. 11:2 ff.; on this see J. Jeremias, op. cit., 87–94).

The RSV text reads:

Matt. 6:9–13	*Lk. 11:2 ff.*
Our Father who art in heaven, Hallowed be thy name. Thy kingdom come, Thy will be done, On earth as it is in heaven. Give us this day our daily bread; And forgive us our debts, As we also have forgiven our debtors; And lead us not into temptation, But deliver us from evil.	Father, hallowed be thy name. Thy kingdom come. Give us each day our daily bread; and forgive us our sins, for we ourselves forgive everyone who is indebted to us; and lead us not into temptation.

Certain manuscripts add to the text of Matt. various additions such as: "For thine is the kingdom and the power and the glory, forever. Amen" (RSV mg.). But these are all relatively late and not original. They do not appear in the early and important representatives of the Alexandrian, Western and pre-Caesarean types of text or the early commentaries on the Lord's Prayer by Tertullian, Origen and Cyprian. The ascription in its threefold form was probably composed to adapt the prayer for liturgical use in the early church (perhaps on the model of 1 Chr. 29:11 ff.) (cf. Metzger, 16 f.) The differences of punctuation in the above texts and the use of capitals reflect, of course, the translators' understanding, and not the original manuscripts. But certain differences are at once apparent. Lk. gives "Father" reflecting the Gk. *pater* and the Aram. *'abbā'* which may be construed as "Dear Father", whereas Matt. gives the pious and reverent form of Palestinian invocation. Whereas Matt. and Lk. agree in giving the first two "thou-petitions", Matt. gives a third. In Matt. the third of the "we-petitions" has an antithesis ("But deliver us from evil").

Jeremias points out that the shorter form of Lk. is completely contained in the longer form of Matt. He, therefore, regards it as probable that the Matthaean form is an expanded one in view of the general tendency of liturgical texts to grow by expansion (op. cit., 89 f.). Moreover, no one would have dared to shorten a sacred text like the Lord's Prayer and leave out two petitions if they had formed part of the original tradition. Jeremias also points out that "in Matthew the stylistic structure is more consistently carried through" (op. cit., 90). This is reflected in the way the RSV sets out the text of Matt. in verses, whereas it gives the text of Lk. in continuous prose. In Matt. there is a parallelism in which three "thou-petitions" are followed by three "we-petitions". But in Matt. and Lk. there is the same basic order which puts God first and man second. This, in fact, reflects the order of the two great commandments and the Shema (cf. Matt. 22:34-40; Mk. 12:28-34; Lk. 10:25-28). A further point which Jeremias regards as favouring the originality of Lk.'s version is its reflection of the word *abba*, Father, which was characteristic of Jesus.

Jeremias concludes that Lk.'s form represents that of the Gentile church and Matt.'s that of the Jewish-Christian church, and that "The Gentile-Christian church has handed down the Lord's Prayer without change, whereas the Jewish-Christian church, which lived in a world of rich liturgical tradition and used a variety of prayer forms, has enriched the Lord's Prayer liturgically" (op. cit., 91). A similar form to Matt.'s with insignificant variations is given in the Didache 8:2. At the same time Jeremias observes that, "when one attempts to put back the Lord's Prayer into Aramaic, Jesus' mother tongue, the conclusion begins to emerge that, like the Psalter, it is couched in liturgical language" (op. cit., 93; cf. C. C. Torrey, "The Translations made from the Original Aramaic Gospels", in *Studies in the History of Religions presented to Crawford Howell Toy*, 1912, 309–17; and *The Four Gospels*, 1933, 292; E. Littmann, "Torreys Buch über die vier Evangelien", *ZNW* 34, 1935, 20–34; C. F. Burney, *The Poetry of our Lord*, 1925, 112 f.; G. Dalman, *Die Worte Jesu*, I, 1930², 283–365, appendix on "Das Vaterunser" which is not in ET; K. G. Kuhn, *Achtzehngebet und Vaterunser und der Reim*, *WUNT* 1, 1950, 32 f.). "We should note three features especially: parallelism, the two-beat rhythm, and the rhyme in lines two and four, which is scarcely accidental" (ibid.). This suggests, however, that it is not only Matt.'s version which had an original liturgical form, but that Lk.'s had one as well.

A position diametrically opposed to that of Jeremias is argued by M. D. Goulder in *Midrash and Lection in Matthew*, 1974, 296–301, which modifies his earlier article "The Composition of the Lord's Prayer", *JTS* New Series 14, 1963, 32–45. He instances cases of liturgical shortening from church history and claims that Lk. often shortens the Marcan teaching that he takes over and is regularly shorter than Matt. in Q-passages. Goulder claims that "what we have in Matthew is a prayer composed by the evangelist from the traditions of prayers of Jesus in Mark and the teaching on prayer in Mark, amplified from the Exodus context of the Sermon, and couched in Matthaean language. What we have in Luke is a version pruned of the rounded Matthaean periods and slightly obvious antitheses, and couched in Lucan language" (op. cit., 298).

Clearly Goulder is right in seeing parallels with Mk. There is an obvious reiteration of the petition for forgiveness. The only teaching on prayer in Mk. follows the saying about the mountain being cast into the sea: "Therefore I tell you, whatever you ask in prayer, believe that you receive it, and you will. And whenever you stand praying, forgive, if you have anything against anyone; so that your Father also who is in heaven may forgive you your trespasses" (Mk. 11:25 f.). The saying about the mountain occurs in Matt. 21:21 in connection, as it is in Mk., with the withering of the fig tree (→ Fruit, art. *sykē*). In both cases it illustrates what God can do in response to → faith, and is occasioned by what happened to the fig tree. But the saying about forgiveness is omitted by Matt., evidently because it was already contained in the Lord's Prayer.

Goulder suggests parallels with Jesus' prayer in Gethsemane inferring that Mk.'s account supplied the source materials for the address of God as *abba*, Father (Mk. 14:36; cf. Matt. 26:39; Lk. 22:42), a term which had passed into the Pauline churches and was used ecstatically in prayer (Gal. 4:6; Rom. 8:15). Matt. renders this as *pater mou*, my Father, and Lk. simply as *pater*, Father, which is the way that he normally records Jesus' address to God (cf. Lk. 15:12; 18:21; 23:34, 46). This, Goulder suggests, explains why God is addressed simply as "Father" in Lk.'s version of the Lord's Prayer (op. cit., 299). A further parallel with the Lord's Prayer is the Gethsemane prayer: "yet not what I will, but what thou wilt" (Mk. 14:36; cf. Matt. 26:39; Lk. 22:42). Moreover, Jesus not only prayed for himself, but he also told the disciples to pray that they enter not into → temptation (Mk. 14:38; cf. Matt. 26:41; Lk. 22:46).

In Matt.'s version the Lord's Prayer consists of two halves each consisting of three petitions: three for the honour of God and three for our needs. It is widely held that Matt. sees the prayer in the context of a new Sinai, since he records it in the Sermon on the Mount with Jesus as the new lawgiver. Each half of the Lord's Prayer opens with a petition recalling Exod. The first petition is a Christian restatement of the Third Commandment (Matt. 6:9 par. Lk. 11:2; cf. Exod. 20:7; Deut. 5:11). It states positively what the Third Commandment states negatively. But in so doing it not only precludes taking the name of God in vain; it also secures what is implied in the First and Second Commandments concerning other gods and graven images (Exod. 20:3–6; Deut. 5:7–10). The fourth petition also recalls the coming to Sinai in God's provision of the manna (Matt. 6:11; Lk. 11:3; cf. Exod. 16:15; Num. 11:4–9; Deut. 8:3; Ps. 78:24 f.). On the significance of "daily" → Bread, art. *epiousios*. It may well imply provision for one's immediate needs, as in the exodus wanderings, and also provision in the coming kingdom symbolized by the messianic banquet. But apart from the first and fourth petitions, it may well be that the remaining petitions are a restatement of the Ten Commandments and the exodus wilderness themes. The petitions for the coming of God's kingdom and for the doing of God's will extend and supersede what the Fourth Commandment says about the → sabbath (Exod. 20:8–11; Deut. 5:12–15) – which, in a sense, anticipates the kingdom as the reign of God – and the remaining Commandments specifically directed at personal relationships (honouring one's parents, killing, adultery, stealing, bearing false witness and coveting, Exod. 20:12–17; Deut. 5:16–21). Similarly the fifth and sixth petitions for forgiveness and avoidance of temptation have retrospective and prospective bearing on the whole range of the Ten Commandments. These are themes which are interwoven with the history of Israel in general and the wilderness wanderings in particular. Thus Deut. 8:2 f. declares: "And you shall remember all the way which the LORD your God has led you these forty years in the wilderness, that he might humble you, testing you to know what was in your heart, whether you would keep his commandments or not. And he humbled you and let you hunger and fed you with manna, which you did not know, nor did your fathers know; that he might make you know that man does not live by bread alone, but that man lives by everything that proceeds out of the mouth of the LORD" (cf. Matt. 4:4; Lk. 4:4). What the Lord's Prayer does is to apply the themes by which ancient Israel lived to the life of the new Israel. It is thus a fulfilment of the Ten Commandments and the exodus themes (cf. Matt. 5:17 f.). At the same time it transforms the themes from external commandments into petitions with which the one who prays personally identifies himself. And thus the law may be said to be written in his heart (cf. Jer. 31:33) as in the new covenant.

Goulder's thesis is that "Matthew has thus composed a prayer that may properly be called the Lord's Prayer, since the greater part of it is his own prayers, and teaching on prayer" (op. cit., 300). But if Matt. composed it, how did substantially the same prayer find its way into Lk.? Few scholars would subscribe to the view that Lk. was dependent on Matt., and in any case Goulder seems to invoke the Q-hypothesis of a source common to Matt. and Lk. at certain points. If the Lord's Prayer was in Q (and thus presumably ascribed to Jesus by a historically earlier source), it could not have been the free composition of Matt. (although this would not in itself preclude the possibility of its being the earlier composition of someone else). Clearly Goulder has shown that the argument about the length of the respective versions is in itself inconclusive. Jeremias admits that "we must be cautious with our conclusions. The possibility remains that Jesus himself spoke the 'Our Father' on different occasions in a slightly differing form, a shorter one and a longer one" (op. cit., 91). This point is, of course, supported by the fact that Matt. and Lk. present the prayer in quite different contexts (Matt. in the Sermon on the Mount; and Lk. as Jesus' response to the disciples' request to be taught to pray after they had seen him praying).

The most positive aspect of Goulder's treatment is the way in which he draws attention to the way in which phrases and similar thoughts in the Lord's Prayer are to be found elsewhere and to the way in which the Lord's Prayer takes up themes associated with Sinai and the wilderness wanderings. In the above discussion we have gone further than Goulder in suggesting that it is not only the first and fourth petitions which recall this, but that the entire prayer is a restatement of the Ten Commandments in the form of a prayer and that the affinities with the wilderness wanderings are by no means confined to the petition for daily bread. Goulder allows that the various elements of the prayer are to be found elsewhere in the words of Jesus. What this suggests is not that the prayer was the work of the creative imagination of Matt. (which entails the difficulties already noted), but that the Lord's Prayer is not to be thought of in isolation from the practice and teachings that Jesus lived and died by. Not only is it possible to conceive (as Jeremias allows) of two forms of the prayer given by Jesus on separate occasions. It is also possible to conceive of how different themes found in the prayer recur in different situations. Thus the petition regarding temptation was not only relevant to the disciples in Gethsemane; it was also the guiding principle in Jesus' own wilderness temptation where it coincides with the thought of the provision of bread, as in the wilderness wanderings. In the way in which the Lord's Prayer takes up the

872

Ten Commandments and the life of the pilgrim people of God which Jesus also took up and taught, the prayer is integral to the life and teaching of Jesus.

C. Brown

3. *Prayer in individual NT writers.* (a) The frequent use of *proseuchomai* in the Lucan writings is striking. For Luke prayer is a basic expression of Christian faith and life, and Jesus is the very model of how to pray aright (Lk. 11:1). All the important points in the lives of Jesus, his apostles and the members of his church are marked by prayer to God; all important decisions are made with prayer (Lk. 3:21 f.; 6:12 f.; 9:18, 28 ff.; 22:44; 23:34; Acts 1:14, 24 f.; 6:6; 9:11; 10:9; 13:3). That prayer was experienced as genuine conversation with God is clear from the fact that those concerned often receive quite definite instructions from God (e.g. Acts 10:9 ff., 30 ff.; 13:2).

(b) In Jn. the *euchomai* word-group is entirely absent. In referring to Christ's prayers, Jn. uses the ordinary words for speaking and talking, qualifying them only with the statement that Jesus lifted up his eyes to heaven (Jn. 11:14; 17:1). Moreover, it is noticeable that Jesus almost always speaks to his heavenly Father in the immediate situation, i.e. in full view of others and without retiring expressly for prayer (this is especially clear in Jn. 12:27 f.). In this way Jn. indicates Jesus' continual fellowship with God; in his case praying did not require a special act, since his whole life was one of prayer. His unique relationship to God is emphasized by the fact that he never prays in company with his disciples.

(c) Paul attaches special importance to the fact that true prayer is wrought by the → Spirit (Rom. 8:15, 26; Gal. 4:6). In both passages apart from Rom. 8:26 where the vb. is *proseuchomai*, Paul uses *krazō*, to → cry, in order to express that freedom, joy and confidence in prayer which spring from our awareness of being God's sons. In other words, such prayer does not originate in any power possessed by man and can never be considered as a meritorious work. Like faith itself, from which it stems and with which in fact it is practically identical, it is a gift from above (cf. Eph. 6:18, praying in the Spirit). To Paul, prayer is ultimately the indwelling, energizing → Spirit speaking with God himself, who "is the Spirit" (2 Cor. 3:17; cf. Jn. 4:23 f.; Rom. 8:14). Thus prayer is not dependent for its efficacy on human eloquence or on any particular frame of mind. The apostle emphasizes rather that assurance of salvation is both evidenced and increased by Spirit-wrought prayer (Rom. 8:15, 16). A similar idea is expressed elsewhere, when he speaks of his thanksgiving being offered "through Christ" (Rom. 1:8; 7:25).

Paul also refers to a kind of Spirit-filled prayer which transcends the limitations of human speech and understanding: the so-called speaking in tongues or praying in the Spirit (1 Cor. 14:14–16). But he very definitely considers prayer which is intelligible to the hearers to have greater value than prayer offered in tongues (1 Cor. 14:19), because only when others can give assent is the → church edified as a body (→ House, art. → *oikos*). The fact that Jn. too regards Spirit-wrought prayer as the new departure in Christian praying, is shown by Jn. 4:23 f. (to worship "in spirit and in truth"; → *proskyneō* NT 4).

A detailed study of Paul's prayers has been made by G. P. Wiles in *Paul's Intercessory Prayers: The Significance of the Intercessory Prayer Passages in the Letters of St Paul, Society for New Testament Studies Monograph Series* 24, 1974.

Wiles notes the following prayer passages in the Pauline epistle: (i) Doxology (using *doxazō*, glorify) Rom. 1:21, 23; 4:20; 11:36; 15:6, 9; 16:25 ff.; 1 Cor. 6:20; 10:31; 2 Cor. 1:20; 4:15; 9:13; Gal. 1:5, 24; Eph. 3:20 f.; Phil. 1:11; 2:11; 4:20; (ii) Praise (using *exomologeomai*, confess; *epainos*, praise) Rom. 14:11; 15:9 ff.; Eph. 1:6, 12, 14; Phil. 1:11; 2:11); (iii) Blessing (*eulogeomai*, bless) Rom. 1:25; 9:5; 1 Cor. 14:16; 2 Cor. 1:3 ff.; 11:31; Eph. 1:3); (iv) Worship (*proskyneō*, worship) 1 Cor. 14:25; (v) Hymns, community singing, psalms, etc. (*psalmos*, hymn, psalm; *psallō*, sing; *hymnos*, hymn, song; *ōdē*, song) 1 Cor. 15, 26; Eph. 5:19; Col. 3:16; (vi) Thanksgiving (*eucharistia*, thankfulness, gratitude; *eucharistos*, thankful; *eucharisteō*, give thanks) Rom. 1:8 ff., 21; 6:17 f.; 7:25; 14:6; 1 Cor. 1:4 ff., 14; 10:30; 11:24; 14:6 f., 18; 15:57; 2 Cor. 2:14; 4:15; 8:16 f.; 9:11 f.; Eph. 1:15 ff.; 5:4, 20; Phil. 1:3 ff.; 4:6; Col. 1:3 ff.; 2:5, 7; 3:15 ff.; 4:2; 1 Thess. 1:2 ff.; 2:13 ff.; 3:9; 5:18; 2 Thess. 1:3 ff.; 2:13; Phlm. 4 ff.; (vii) Boasting in Christ or before God (*kauchaomai*, boast, and cognates) Rom. 5:2 f., 11; 15:17 ff.; 1 Cor. 1:29 ff.; 2 Cor. 1:12 ff.; 7:4; and frequently in chs. 10–12; Phil. 1:26; 2:16; 3:3; 1 Thess. 2:19; (viii) Petition for self (*deomai*, ask, request, beg; *proseuchomai*, pray) Rom. 1:10; 7:24; 9:3; 1 Cor. 14:13; 2 Cor. 12:8; 1 Thess. 3:10, though apart from 2 Cor. 12:8, these passages are problematical; (ix) Intercessory prayer for others, including blessings and curses (*hyperentynchanō*, intercede, Rom. 8:26) Rom. 1:7b; 9 f.; 8:15 f., 23, 26 f., 34; 9:1–3; 10:1; 11:2–5, 12:12c, 14; 15:5 f.; 13:30–33; 16:20a, 20b; 1 Cor. 1:3, 8; 2:9–16; 5:3 ff.; 11:10; 15:29; 16:22a, 23; 2 Cor. 1:2, 7, 11, 14; 13:7, 9b, 11b, 14; Gal. 1:3, 8 f.; 4:6; 6:16, 18; Eph. 1:2, 16–23; 3:14–19; 6:18 ff., 23 f.; Phil. 1:2, 4, 9 ff., 19 f.; 4:6 f., 9b, 23; Col. 1:2b, 3b, 9–14, 29; 2:1–3, 5; 4:2 ff., 12, 18b, 18c; 1 Thess. 1:1b, 2 f.; 3:10–13; 5:17 f., 23, 24b, 25, 28; 2 Thess. 1:2, 11 f.; 2:16 f.; 3:1–3, 5, 16, 18; Phlm. 3, 4, 6; (x) General prayer – type not specified (*proseuchomai*, pray; *laleō tō theō*, speak to God) 1 Cor. 11:4 f., 13; 14:14 f., 28; (*epikaleō*, call upon) Rom. 10:12 ff.; 1 Cor. 1:2; 2 Cor. 1:23.

Intercessory prayer is referred to in the following passages: Rom. 1:7b, 9 f.; 8:15 f., 23, 26 f., 34; 9:3; 10:1; 11:2–5; 12:12c, 14; 15:5 f., 13, 30 ff., 33; 16:20; 1 Cor. 1:3, 8 f.; 2:9–16; 5:3 ff.; 11:10; 15:29; 16:22 f.; 2 Cor. 1:2, 7, 11; 9:14; 13:7, 9, 11, 14; Gal. 1:3, 8 f.; 4:6; 6:16, 18; Phil. 1:2, 4, 9 ff., 19 f.; 4:6 f., 9, 19; 1 Thess. 1:1 ff.; 3:10–13; 5:17 f., 23; 5:24 f., 28; Phlm. 3, 4, 6, 22, 25; Eph. 1:2, 16–23; 3:14–19; 6:18 ff.; 6:23 f.; Col. 1:2 f., 9–14; 1:29–2:3; 2:5; 4:2 ff., 12, 18; 2 Thess. 1:2, 11 f.; 2:16 f.; 3:1–3, 5, 16, 18. In addition to this, Wiles draws attention to the liturgically oriented patterns of the endings of the Pauline epistles. (For full classified tables of the various kinds of prayer, see op. cit., 297–302.)

Whilst recognizing that no hard and fast line can be drawn between thanksgivings, intercessions and representative corporate supplications, Wiles nevertheless insists that intercessory prayer forms a significant feature of Paul's writings in which the one who prays "is concerned as mediator and intercessor before God, principally for the needs of others" (op. cit., 293). An important feature here is the wish-prayer which may be described as "the expression of a desire that God take action regarding the person(s) mentioned in the wish" (op. cit., 22). Thus in Rom. 15:13 Paul writes: "May the God of hope fill you with all joy and peace in believing, so that by the power of the Holy Spirit you may abound in hope" (cf. also Rom. 15:5 f.; 1 Thess. 3:11 ff.; 5:23 f.; 2 Thess. 2:16 f.; 3:5, 16; 2 Tim. 16, 18; 2:25;

4:16; Heb. 13:20 f.; for a full list see op. cit., 299 f.; for discussion of their form, background and function, op. cit., 22–107). Also significant are the prayer reports, where at the beginning of most of his letters Paul assures his readers "not only of his continual thanksgivings for them, but also of his constant intercessions on their behalf, and he indicates briefly some of the contents of his prayers" (op. cit., 156). Thus in Phlm. 4 ff. he writes: "I thank my God always when I remember you in my prayers, . . . and I pray that the sharing of your faith may promote the knowledge of all the good that is ours in Christ" (cf. Rom. 1:9 f.; Phil. 1:4, 9 ff.; 1 Thess. 1:2 f.; 3:10; 2 Cor. 1:7; Eph. 1:16–23; Cor. 1:3, 9–14; 2 Thess. 1:1 ff.; for discussion, op. cit., 156–258). Such prayer reports may also occur in the body of letters (Rom. 9:3; 1 Cor. 5:3; 2 Cor. 9:14; 13:7, 9; Col. 1:29–2:3, 5; 4:12). As far as the wish-prayers and prayer reports are concerned each in its own way epitomizes "the dominant message of the letter", underlines its central concerns, and stands at a strategic location in the letter (op. cit., 293).

While immediate concerns shape the prayers, they are "grounded in and directed by the gospel of Christ" (op. cit., 294). At the same time they are infused by warm personal feeling and "unbounded expectation". Paul's eschatological perspectives add increased urgency. "In his prayers he was always conscious of living 'before God', already in the last days with parousia and judgment close ahead, dominated by the belief that his readers and he would stand shortly at the judgment seat of Christ" (ibid.). But the prayers also indicate Paul's concern for mutual intercession, reconciliation and unity throughout the church. "Prayer buttressed all his mission work – in advance of his visits, during them, and after he had departed. All his plans were conceived under the constant sense of the guidance and will of God" (op. cit., 296). Sometimes the prayers are characterized by a tension between confident thanksgiving and anxious supplication, but invariably they lead back to thanksgiving in view of mercies already given.

(d) Jas. 5:13 ff. merits special mention. On the one hand, it is laid down that a Christian's whole life, the good times as well as the bad, should be lived in an atmosphere of prayer, i.e. that the Christian should lay before God everything that happens to him, so that each new experience is suffused with prayer. On the other hand, in cases of sickness, prayer is to be accompanied by the laying on of hands, anointing and confession of sins. Here the laying on of → hands (implicit in the phrase "let them pray over him") and the → anointing with → oil, being outward actions, are considered to be tangible, readily intelligible expressions of prayer for the benefit of the sick individual, while confession of sins is made in order to remove any hindrances to prayer (→ Heal).

4. Lastly, in one passage only (Acts 16:13, 16) *proseuchē* means a place of prayer.

H. Schönweiss, C. Brown

προσκυνέω

προσκυνέω (*proskyneō*), worship, do obeisance to, prostrate oneself, do reverence to; *προσκυνητής* (*proskynētēs*), a worshipper.

CL The basic meaning of *proskyneō*, in the opinion of most scholars, is to kiss. The prefix indicates a connection with cultic practices going back beyond Gk.

history. On Egyptian reliefs worshippers are represented with outstretched hand throwing a kiss to (*pros-*) the deity. Among the Greeks the vb. is a technical term for the adoration of the gods, meaning to fall down, prostrate oneself, adore on one's knees. Probably it came to have this meaning because in order to kiss the earth (i.e. the earth deity) or the image of a god, one had to cast oneself on the ground. Later *proskyneō* was also used in connection with the deification of rulers and the Roman emperor cult. In addition to the external act of prostrating oneself in worship, *proskyneō* can denote the corresponding inward attitude of reverence and humility.

ot In the overwhelming majority of cases in the LXX *proskyneō* translates the Heb. *šāḥâh* in the hithpael, meaning to bow down, and is used both of bowing down before men and of worship: Gen. 18:2; 19:1; 22:5; 23:7, 12; 24:16, 48, 52; 27:29; 33:3, 6 f., 9 f.; 42:6; 43:28; 47:31; 48:12; 49:8; Exod. 4:31; 11:8; 12:27; 18:7; 20:5; 23:24; 24:1; 32:8; 33:10; 34:8, 14; Lev. 26:1; Num. 22:31; 25:2; Deut. 4:19; 5:9; 8:19; 11:16; 17:3; 26:10; 29:25(26); 30:17; Jos. 23:7, 16; Jdg. 2:12, 17, 19; 7:15; Ruth 2:10; 1 Sam. 1:3, 19; 2:36; 15:25, 30 f.; 20:41; 24:9; 25:23, 41; 28:14; 2 Sam. 1:2; 9:6, 8; 12:20; 14:4, 22, 33; 15:5, 32; 16:4; 18:21, 28; 24:20; 1 Ki. 1:16, 23, 31, 47, 53; 9:6, 9; 16:31; 22:54; 2 Ki. 2:15; 4:37; 5:18; 17:16, 35 f.; 18:22; 19:37; 21:3, 21; 1 Chr. 16:29; 21:21; 29:20; 2 Chr. 7:3, 19, 22; 20:18; 24:17; 25:14; 29:28 ff.; 32:12; 33:3; Ezr. 9:47; Neh. 8:6; 9:3, 6; Job 1:20; Pss. 5:7; 22(21):27, 29; 29(28):3; 45(44):12; 66(65):4; 72(71):11; 81(80):9; 86(85):9; 95(94):6; 96(95):9; 99(98):5, 9; 106(105):19; 132(131):7; 138(137):2; Mic. 5:13; Zeph. 1:5; 2:11; Zech. 14:16; Isa. 2:8, 20; 27:13; 37:38; 44:15, 17; 45:14; 46:6; 49:7, 23; 66:23; Jer. 1:16; 8:2; 13:10; 16:11; 22:9; 25:6; 26(33):2; Ezek. 8:16; 46:2 f., 9. In the Aram. portion of Dan. it translates *sᵉg̱îḏ*, pay homage to (Dan. 2:46; 3:5 ff., 10 ff., 14, 18, 28[95]; cf. also Isa. 44:15, 17, 19). In Dan. 6:27(26) it translates *zûā'*, tremble. It is used for *kāra'*, kneel down, in Est. 3:2, 5 in conjunction with *šāḥâh*; for *nāšaq*, kiss, in 1 Ki. 19:18; and *'āḇaḏ*, serve, in Ps. 97(96):7. It occurs without Heb. equivalent in the apocryphal books and occasionally in canonical writings: Deut. 6:13; 10:20; 32:43; Jdg. 2:2; 6:19; 1 Ki. 2:13; Tob. 5:13; Jud. 5:8; 6:18; 8:18; 10:8, 23; 13:17; 14:7; 16:18; Est. 4:17; 8:13; Ep.Jer. 5 f.; Dan. 6:28(27); Bel 3, 23; 1 Macc. 4:55; 4 Macc. 5:12. The noun *proskynēsis*, worship, which is absent from the NT occurs only in the apocrypha (Sir. 50:21; 3 Macc. 3:7).

In the LXX *proskyneō* translates *hištaḥᵃwâh* and (almost exclusively in Dan.) *sᵉg̱îḏ*, both with the basic meaning to bend down, stoop, bow. Although in profane Gk. *proskyneō* is generally used trans., it hardly ever takes an acc. in the LXX, being followed instead by a prepositional phrase as a translation of *lᵉ*: *epi. . .*, to the earth (e.g. Gen. 18:2); *enantion. . .*, before the people (e.g. Gen. 23:12 and passim); *enōpion. . .*, before God (Ps. 22:27); *pros. . .*, towards thy holy temple (Ps. 5:7); alternatively there may be a dat. construction (e.g. Gen. 24:26). This Hebraism marks off the adoration of Yahweh from heathen worship, in which the the worshipper has no sense of having to keep his distance from the deity. The God of Israel is worshipped without → images and therefore is not within the grasp of the worshipper. *proskyneō* retains its physical sense of bending, however, except that this is understood as bowing to the will of the exalted One (cf. Exod. 12:27 f.).

As folding or crossing the hands and arms denotes the suppliant's mental concentration, and as the lifting up of outstretched hands expresses the fact that he is making a request, in the same way the physical act of bending indicates his readiness to bow to the will of the One whom he approaches in this manner. When *proskyneō* refers to men, it always indicates reverence shown to a person superior in position or power (cf. 2 Sam. 18:21). However, the fact that certain limits were always observed in this matter is shown by Est. 3:2, 5, where a Jew, on peril of his life, refuses to prostrate himself before a heathen prince.

NT 1. In the NT the verb occurs 59 times, of which 24 are in Rev., 11 in the Gospels of Jn. and 9 in Matt. ("the Gospel of the King"), and takes either acc. or dat. without any difference of meaning. The OT sense is taken up and further developed, except that now it denotes exclusively worship addressed (or which should be addressed) to God or to Jesus Christ (even in Matt. 18:26 the king is a symbolic figure for God). In Acts 10:25 f.; Rev. 19:10; 22:8 f. it is expressly stated that worship is to be offered to God alone, not to an apostle (even such a prominent apostle as Peter!), or even to an angelic being. Hence, whenever obeisance is made before Jesus, the thought is either explicit or implicit that he is king (Matt. 2:2), Lord (Matt. 8:12), the Son of God (Matt. 14:33), One who can act with divine omnipotence (e.g. Matt. 14:33; Mk. 5:6; 15:19). For that reason obeisance is often linked with a request for help in sore need. On the one hand, it intensifies the request, while, on the other hand, it is a sign of faith in the divine helper and redeemer, a faith certain of being heard (e.g. Matt. 8:2; 9:18; 15:25). In Jn. 9:38 obeisance is nothing less than the outward reflex action of faith: to believe means to adore Jesus, to recognize him as Lord, to render him homage as king. Thus obeisance is especially appropriate before the risen and exalted Lord (Matt. 28:9, 17; Lk. 24:52).

When Satan, reversing the true order of things, requires obeisance from Jesus (Matt. 4:9; Lk. 4:7), he proves himself by this very act to be God's great adversary, who would usurp that which is due to God alone (Matt. 4:10; Lk. 4:8) and so overthrow all the good purposes and ordinances of God.

2. In this context obeisance is a sign of man's fundamentally religious nature: his worship shows who his god is, whether it be the true God, or idols, demons, even Satan himself (cf. Rev. 9:20; 13:4, 8, 12). For man's relation to God is expressed principally in worship, and above all in prayer. The call to conversion can therefore be put in the form: "Worship God!" i.e. recognize him in all his power and glory as creator and judge, acknowledge his exclusive sovereign rights and claim upon you (Rev. 14:7).

3. Where *proskyneō* is used absolutely it means to share in public worship, to offer prayers (e.g. Jn. 12:20; Acts 8:27; 24:11), whence, in Rev., *proskyneō* comes to denote a particular kind of prayer, namely adoration. Its characteristic features find expression in the various hymns of adoration found throughout Rev. (4:8–11; 5:8–10, 12–14; 7:10–12; 11:15–18; 12:10 f.; 15:3 f.; 16:5–7; 19:1–7): it is addressed to God himself (or to Jesus Christ), is concerned with his being (i.e. not with his gifts as in thanksgiving) and with his works in a world-wide context (creation, Rev. 4:8–11; rule, 15:3 f.; 16:5–7; redemption, 5:8–10; consummation, 11:15–18). The hymns make use of ever-varied language and ideas, constantly

finding new titles of dignity with which to praise God, and ascribing to him the most exalted merits and attributes (eternity, omnipotence, honour, wisdom, holiness, power etc.), in a faltering attempt to confess his name. Frequently this takes the form of royal acclamation: "Worthy art thou!" (Rev. 4:11; 5:9, 12), "Salvation!" (7:10), interspersed with ejaculatory prayers: ("Hallelujah!" "Amen!" 7:12; 19:1, 3, 4; → Amen). Through all these hymns there runs a gloriously universal strain, and in the face of adoration such as this, human petitions and thanksgivings merely fade away into silence (cf. Matt. 6:13b).

4. The noun *proskynētēs*, worshipper, occurs only in Jn. 4:23 in the context of Jesus' reply to the woman of Samaria: "You worship what you do not know; we worship what we know, for salvation is from the Jews. But the hour is coming and now is, when the true worshippers [*hoi alēthinoi proskynētai*] will worship the Father in spirit and truth [*proskynēsousin tō Patri en pneumati kai alētheia*], for such the Father seeks to worship him. God is spirit, and those who worship him must worship in spirit and truth [*pneuma ho theos, kai tous proskynountas en pneumati kai alētheia dei proskynein*]" (Jn. 4:22 ff.). Earlier the woman had declared that her ancestors had worshipped on "this mountain", i.e. Mt. Gerizim (v.20). The allusion is to the rôle Gerizim played in Samaritan worship. In the Samaritan Pentateuch Joshua is instructed to build a shrine there (Deut. 27:4). The → Samaritans made worship on Gerizim part of the Decalogue (cf. however 2 Chr. 6:6). (On Samaritan thought and practice see J. Macdonald, *The Theology of the Samaritans*, 1964.) Jesus had countered the woman's assertion of her Samaritan faith by declaring that "the hour is coming when neither on this mountain nor in Jerusalem will you worship the Father" (v. 21).

Jesus' words are widely taken to be a reference to man's spirit and the need to take up a right personal attitude in worship as the continuance of mere custom and ritual (cf. L. Morris, *The Gospel according to John*, NLC, 1971, 270 f.). Such a meaning might be supported by the Hellenistic spiritualizing of Philo (*Quod Det. Pot. Ins.* 21; *Vit.Mos.* 2, 108; *Spec.Leg.* 1, 271; *Plant.* 108). On the other hand, R. E. Brown urges that it is the → Spirit of God that is meant here, and that one can regard "spirit and truth" almost as a hendiadys equivalent to "Spirit of truth" (*The Gospel according to John*, Anchor Bible, I, 1966, 180). This would, moreover, fit better the train of thought. For in the context both "this mountain" and "Jerusalem" have come to stand for ways in which men have seen fit to worship God in ways which were not real worship acceptable to God. But in the coming age men will worship God in the true way which he himself has chosen and provided, i.e. in and through himself (cf. also the Johannine teaching on the Spirit, Jn. 1:32 f.; 3:5–8, 34; 6:63; 7:39; 11:33; 13:21; 14:17, 26; 15:26; 16:13; 20:22; and the paraclete, Jn. 14:16, 26; 15:26; 16:7; → Advocate, art. *paraklētos*). "In true worship there is an encounter with God for which God must make man capable by his grace" (R. Schnackenburg, *The Gospel according to St. John*, I, 1968, 437). Schnackenburg sees confirmation of this interpretation by similar usage at Qumran: "Then God will purify all the deeds of man by his truth and he will cleanse the frame of man. He will eradicate the perverse spirit from within his flesh, and cleanse him by holy spirit from all his wicked deeds. He will pour out on him the spirit of truth like purifying water . . ." (1QS 4:20 f.; cf. 3:6 ff.; 8:5 f.; 9:3–6; 1QH 7:6 f.; 12:11 f.; 13:18 f.; 14:25; 16:6 f., 11 f.; 17:26; cf. also R. Schnackenburg, "Die

Anbetung in Geist und Wahrheit (Joh 4, 23) im Lichte von Qumran-Texten", *BZ* 3, 1959, 88–94; B. Gärtner, *The Temple and the Community in Qumran and the New Testament, Society for New Testament Studies Monograph Series*, 1, 1965, 44 ff., 119 f.). *H. Schönweiss, C. Brown*

| ἐρωτάω |

ἐρωτάω (*erōtaō*), ask, ask a question, request; ἐπερωτάω (*eperōtaō*), ask; ἐπερώτημα (*eperōtēma*), question, request, appeal.

CL *erōtaō* is found in cl. Gk. from Homer onwards in the sense of ask, ask a question (in Homer and the best codices of Hdt. as *eirōtaō*). *eperōtaō* occurs in secular Gk. from Hdt., meaning to consult a person or to put a question. Later Gk. used it technically for putting a formal question at a meeting or in the process of making a contract. It may even mean to accept the terms of a treaty. In religious contexts both vbs. can mean to put a question to an oracle or to a god (Hdt., 1, 53, 1 and often; *Inscriptions of Magnesia on the Meander*, ed. O. Kern, 1900, 17, 12 f., 26, 36; *SIG* III³ 1160, 1163, 1165). The noun *eperōtēma* can mean a question put to another person, to someone in authority for a formal, binding answer (*SIG* 856, 6, 2nd cent. A.D.). In the papyri (2nd cent. A.D.) the noun and the vb. are used of an agreement pledged in a contract (Moulton-Milligan, 231 f.).

OT In the LXX *erōtaō* is commonly used for *šā'al*, ask (e.g. Gen. 24:47, 57; Exod. 3:13; Ps. 35[34]:11; Isa. 41:28). *eperōtaō* is likewise used for the same vb. (e.g. Gen. 24:23; 26:27; Isa. 19:3). It is most frequent in the historical books (e.g. Jdg. 1:1; 18:5; 1 Sam. 9:9). It can be used of inquiry of God (e.g. Isa. 65:1, where some versions have *zēteō*, seek). Both vbs. are used by Josephus in this sense (*Ant*. 6, 123, 328; 9, 34; 12, 99; *War* 1, 540). *eperōtēma* occurs only in Dan. 4:14 (Theodotion, for *š⁰'ēlâh*) and Sir. 33(36):3 without equivalent.

NT 1. *erōtaō* occurs 62 times (especially in Jn., 27 times; cf. Matt., 4 times; Mk. 3 times; Lk. 15 times; Paul, 4 times; Acts, 7 times; 1 and 2 Jn., once each). It commonly means to ask, inquire. Jesus' asking and counter-questions were part of his teaching method, designed to expose the person concerned to the implications of his own questions or make him reflect on his attitudes (e.g. Matt. 16:13; 19:17; 21:24; Mk. 8:5; Lk. 20:3). But it is also used of the theological questions put by the disciples (Mk. 4:10; Lk. 9:45; Acts 1:6). Jn. 16:23 implies that in the future salvation there will be no need to ask Jesus further questions. Asking implies imperfect knowledge which will be overcome by perfect fellowship with Jesus (cf. Jn. 16:30; cf. vv. 5, 19). Conversely Jesus does not need to ask questions, for he knows already what is in man (Jn. 2:25). Apart from Jn. 9:2 and the final discourses, the disciples are never said to ask Jesus. In Jn. asking is characteristic of the doubting, contentious questions of the Jews (Jn. 1:19, 21, 25; 4:31, 40, 47; 5:12; 8:7; 9:15, 19, 21, 23; 18:19, 21; 19:31, 38). But it may be compared with the question of the → Greeks (12:21) and those of Jesus (14:16; 17:9, 15, 20; of the intercession of Jesus, where Jesus asks things for his disciples of the Father). The vb. is used of the efficacy of intercession in 1 Jn. 5:16: "If any one sees his brother committing what is not a mortal sin, he will ask, and he [i.e. God] will give him life for those whose sin is not mortal. There is a sin which is mortal; I do not say that one is to pray for that" (RSV mg.). The use here of the vb. of the praying believer extends to him a sense of the vb. which in Jn. is only applied to Jesus. H. Greeven thinks that the use of *erōtaō* in the sense of to pray may be a Semitism (*TDNT* II 686 f.). In 2 Jn. 5 it describes the action of the author in begging his readers to follow love (cf. v. 6). In Acts 1:6 it means to ask (a question). Elsewhere it generally means to request: of the disciples to Jesus (Matt. 15:23; Lk. 4:38); of the Jews to Pilate (Jn. 19:31); and in the Lucan writings of invitations (Lk. 7:36; 11:37; Acts 10:48; 18:20). In Lk. 14:18 f. it has the polite, weakened sense of "I pray you".

2. *eperōtaō* is nearly as common (56 times), and is most frequent in the Gospels. However, it is most characteristic of Mk. and somewhat less so of Lk. (Mk., 25 times; Lk., 17 times; cf. Matt., 8 times; twice each in Jn., Acts and Paul). The basic sense is to ask, and here it is synonymous with *erōtaō*, as can be seen from synoptic parallels and MS variant readings. Instances of its use in the sense of ask are Matt. 16:1; Mk. 9:32; Lk. 2:46; 1 Cor. 14:35 (the latter in Paul's instructions about the rôle of → women in public worship, who are to remain silent and ask their husbands at home). However, particular nuances of meaning may be detected in certain passages.

(a) Seeking. The → Pharisees and → Sadducees, traditionally enemies, joined together as representatives of Judaism (D. Hill, *The Gospel of Matthew, New Century Bible*, 1972, 257) or of unbelief (J. C. Fenton, *Saint Matthew*, 1963, 260) in asking for a sign which might accredit Jesus with popular authority (Matt. 16:1). A similar sense is found at Rom. 10:20, where those who do not ask for God means those who did not seek him: "Then Isaiah is so bold as to say, 'I have been found by those who did not seek me; I have shown myself to those who did not ask for me.' " This adaptation of Isa. 65:1 stands in a catena of citations from the OT which also includes Deut. 32:21. It is followed by the ensuing verse in Isa.: "But of Israel he says, 'All day long I have held out my hands to a disobedient and contrary people' " (Rom. 10:21; cf. Isa. 65:2). In the first instance Isa. 65:1 applies to Yahweh's readiness to be found by disobedient Israel, even though Israel did not seek him. Paul adapts it to apply *a fortiori* to the Gentiles who in times past did not seek Yahweh but now have found him through faith in Christ, whereas Israel remains disobedient and estranged. To them Isa. 65:2 still applies.

(b) Probing. In debate the opponents of Jesus asked probing questions to which an answer had to be given, and Jesus put counter-questions (Matt. 22:46; Mk. 11:29; Lk. 6:9).

(c) Questioning an authority. Several passages imply that the questioner is approaching an authority higher than himself. On feast days and sabbaths the temple Sanhedrin informally received questions and stated their traditions (Sanhedrin 88b), and on such an occasion the youth Jesus put questions to the temple elders (Lk. 2:46). In a similar sense the disciples dared not question Jesus about a passion prediction (Mk. 9:32 par. Lk. 9:45), and the Corinthian wives were to put questions to their husbands at home, not in the assembly for worship (1 Cor. 14:35).

3. The noun *eperōtēma* is found in the NT only at 1 Pet. 3:21 in respect of → baptism: "Baptism, which corresponds to this [i.e. the saving of → Noah in the

ark 'through water', v. 20], now saves you, not as a removal of dirt from the body but as an appeal [*eperōtēma*] to God for a clear conscience" (RSV). E. Best, following E. G. Selwyn and others, translates this as "pledge", i.e. a statement of faith given by the baptizand in answer to a formal question, like the *stipulatio* or answer given in a formal contract (E. Best, *1 Peter, New Century Bible*, 1971, 148; G. C. Richards, "1 Peter iii 21", *JTS* 32, 1931, 77; E. G. Selwyn, *The First Epistle of St. Peter*, 1947², 205; Moulton-Milligan, 231 f.; cf. P. Cairo Preiss 1, 16, of the 2nd cent. A.D.). Best prefers to regard it as "a pledge made to God to maintain a clear conscience" (cf. W. J. Dalton, *Christ's Proclamation to the Spirits, Analecta Biblica* 23, 1965, 224–28), or "a pledge made to God proceeding from a clear conscience" (cf. v. 20). Selwyn also suggests that it could mean "an enquiry of a good conscience after God", i.e. the convert's seeking after God as contrasted with the pagan's address to his favourite oracle (op. cit., 206). But he does not think that this sense is specially applicable to baptism. H. Greeven suggests that, in view of the sense of the vb. meaning to request (cf. Matt. 16:1), the meaning here could be that baptism is a "prayer to God for a good conscience" (*TDNT* II 688). However, it might also mean the answer by God to a such a question (cf. *SIG* 856, 6), i.e. the granting of a clear → conscience towards God. For a similar idea, cf. Heb. 10:19–25.

G. T. D. Angel

| κρούω |

κρούω (*krouō*), knock.

CL & OT *krouō* is used in secular Gk. from Sophocles onwards and in the LXX (e.g. Cant. 5:2) for striking something, especially knocking on a door.

NT This is the strict meaning in all 9 NT instances (Matt. 7:7 f. par. Lk. 11:9 f.; Lk. 12:36; 13:25; Acts 12:13, 16; Rev. 3:20). But apart from the passages in Acts, the context is in each case metaphorical. The saying "Knock and it shall be opened to you" (Matt. 7:7 par. Lk. 11:9) is probably a proverb since it is found in Judaism (Pesikta 176a with reference to studying the Mishnah, "If a man knocks, it will be opened to him"). But Jer. 29:13 (LXX 36:13) contains Yahweh's promise: "You will seek me and find me; when you seek me with your whole heart" (cf. the previous verses). According to D. Hill, the knocking does not mean seeking to enter the → kingdom (cf. 7:13 f.); the situation presupposed is that described in Lk. 11:5–8 of the friend at midnight (*The Gospel of Matthew*, 1972, 148). Here the lesson is drawn: "I tell you, though he will not get up and give him anything because he is his friend, yet because of his importunity he will rise and give him whatever he needs" (Lk. 11:8). Lk., however, refers this ultimately to the gift of the Holy → Spirit (Lk. 11:13). G. Bertram, however, relates it to salvation (*TDNT* III 955 f.). Knocking in Lk. 12:36 and Lk. 13:25 is a detail of the parables of the returning master and of the excluded postulants. It has a dramatic rather than a special theological meaning.

Rev. 3:20 pictures the Risen Lord standing at a door knocking, and inviting those inside to open and receive him. The Lord is addressing the spiritually luke-warm church at Laodicea (→ Cold, Hot, Lukewarm), and the anticipated offer of his return means victory and a place in the presence of his Father. This prediction of his confrontation with idle churchmen is both a disturbing warning that apathy will not go unheeded and a gracious encouragement that the Lord will not allow his people to remain ineffective, but will rather appeal insistently to establish the believer in victorious living. Although the picture has been interpreted as an initial confrontation with the Risen Lord, there is no doubt that an existing Christian community is being addressed. The background to the image could be the Lord's Supper (cf. G. B. Caird, *The Revelation of St. John the Divine*, BNTC, 1966, 58). However, G. R. Beasley-Murray comments: "The similarity of thought and language to that which is used in connection with the Lord's Supper (cf. Jn. 6:35 ff., 53 ff.) is due less to direct reminiscence of the Supper than to the event to which the Supper itself looks forward (Mk. 14:25; Lk. 22:28 ff.)" (*The Book of Revelation, New Century Bible*, 1974, 107).   *G. T. D. Angel*

ἐντυγχάνω

ἐντυγχάνω (*entynchanō*), meet, turn to, approach, petition, pray, intercede; ὑπερεντυγχάνω (*hyperentynchanō*), plead, intercede.

CL & OT *entynchanō* occurs in cl. Gk. from Soph. and Hdt. onwards and is found in inscriptions, the papyri, the LXX, Philo and Josephus. It means to approach or appeal to someone (e.g. Polyb., 4, 30, 1; Dan. 6:13[12] LXX; Josephus, *Ant.* 16, 170; 12, 18). It is found in the papyri in the sense of appealing to someone against a third person (cf. Arndt, 269). In view of the fact that petitions may be addressed to God, it has also the sense of to pray (e.g. *BGU* 246, 12; Wis. 8:21; 16:28; Eth.Enoch 9:3). *hyperentynchanō* is first found in the NT. Apart from the reading in Dan., neither vb. occurs in the canonical books of the OT.

NT *entynchanō* is used of Paul's appeal to the emperor in Acts 25:24. In Rom. 11:2 it denotes → Elijah's pleading with God against Israel (cf. 1 Ki. 19:10). It is twice used of Christ's continuing intercession: "Who is to condemn? Is it Christ Jesus, who died, yes, who was raised from the dead, who is at the right hand of God, who indeed intercedes for us [*hos kai entynchanei hyper hēmōn*]?" (Rom. 8:33); "he is able for all time to save those who draw near to God through him, since he always lives to make intercession for them [*pantote zōn eis to entynchanein hyper autōn*]" (Heb. 7:25). In both cases the intercession is grounded in the death and resurrection of Christ. However, the two vbs. are also used of the Spirit's intercession: "Likewise the Spirit helps us in our weakness; for we do not know how to pray [lit. "what"; Gk. *ti proseuxōmetha*] as we ought, but the Spirit himself intercedes for us with sighs too deep for words [*hyperentynchanei stenagmois alalētois*]. And he who searches the hearts of men knows what is the mind of the Spirit, because [or "that" RSV mg.; Gk. *hoti*] the Spirit intercedes for the saints according to the will of God [*kata theon entynchanei hyper hagiōn*] (Rom. 8:26 f.)."

This verse is commonly taken to refer to Christian prayer generally. "We take Paul's meaning to be that all praying of Christian men, in so far as it is *their* praying, remains under the sign of this not-knowing, of real ignorance, weakness and poverty and that even in their prayers they live only by God's justification of sinners . . . The Spirit Himself helps our weakness by interceding for us" (C. E. B. Cranfield, *The Epistle to the Romans*, I, ICC, 1975, 422 f.). He dismisses the idea that the *stenagmoi* refers to glossolalia on the grounds that the latter is usually associated with praise rather than intercession. He also thinks it unlikely that such utterances could be interpreted as the Spirit's own *stenagmoi*. On the other hand, E. Käsemann has set out a persuasive case for seeing this whole passage in the context of ecstatic worship in the Christian community.

As a background to this passage Käsemann sees Paul's doctrine of the → Spirit as teaching designed to counter the excess of charismatic enthusiasm in the early church ("The Cry for Liberty in the Worship of the Church", in *Perspectives on Paul*, 1971, 122–37; see especially 123 f.). Paul developed a positive doctrine of the Spirit which he related to the church and to Christ. He was well aware of a possible clash between "in the Spirit" and "in Christ" and established three safeguards: "(1) He so interpreted the spirit as the power of the risen Christ that it had to be proved daily in the individual Christian's life as the power of the *nova oboedientia*. (2) Starting from the identity of the risen and the crucified Christ, he allowed the Spirit to be the power of standing fast in temptations and suffering. (3) Like the Jewish Christians, he understood the spirit as an 'earnest' and hence placed pneumatology as well as Christology and anthropology under the eschatological proviso" (op. cit., 124; cf. Rom. 8:1–11 and chs. 12–16). Thus Paul opposed the "realized eschatology" of the Hellenists, who were proud of their possession of the Spirit as the sign of present power, with the doctrine of the future redemption of which the Spirit is the present pledge: "We know that the whole creation has been groaning in travail together until now; and not only the creation, but we ourselves, who have the first fruits [*aparchēn*] of the Spirit, groan inwardly [*en heautois stenazomen*] as we wait for adoption as sons, the redemption of our bodies [*hyiothesian apekdechomenoi, tēn apolytrōsin tou sōmatos hēmōn*]" (Rom. 8:22 f.).

Käsemann claims that it is not simply that we do not know *how* to pray but *what* we should pray, as the Gk. indicates. "Only the spirit knows and comprehends God's will. It must therefore, like the Paraclete of the Fourth Gospel, support our weakness. It does this by offering vicarious intercession for the saints" (op. cit., 128; → Advocate; cf. also 1 Cor. 2:11 ff.). Since prayer is never wordless in Paul, Käsemann takes the groans or sighs referred to here as ecstatic acclamations and cries of prayer which accompanied the acclamatory cry of "Abba! Father!" (op. cit., 130; cf. Rom. 8:15; Gal. 4:6). He claims the thought of "praying in the spirit" is presupposed in the Qumran hymns and is elsewhere attested in the NT (1 Cor. 14:13 ff.; Eph. 6:18; Jude 20; Rev. 22:17), always in the sense of the Spirit putting into man's mouth what he should pray for. Whereas the Palestinian tradition did not permit reason to be dispensed with, there is recognition here of the tradition represented in Philo, according to which inspiration uses a man as an instrument (op. cit., 131; cf. 1 Cor. 14:7 f., 13 ff.). What in 1 Cor. 14:7–12, 22 (cf. 11:5, 13) is the gift of tongues, which had a place in public worship, is here described in terms of "sighs too deep for words". In other words, they are "glossolalic utterances" (ibid.), which are the joint possession of the whole congregation. The earthly occurrence is linked with a heavenly one, for intercession can only take place at the right → hand of God (Rom. 8:34). In reply to Cranfield it may be said that to speak of glossolalia here is a kind of shorthand covering ecstatic utterance generally, and that the purported content of glossolalia in one place must not be allowed to prejudge its purported content elsewhere. Moreover, Paul clearly uses the *stenagmois alalētois* of the Spirit as a counterpart to the *stenagmois* of men. Käsemann observes: "Since the spirit itself is acting here and the glosso- lalia in the prayer of believers is the medium through which it cries to God, the earthly phenomenon is the expression and reflection of a hidden heavenly one" (ibid., 133).

Paul does not develop this in a pietistic sense of raising us above our own strength in order to bring us near to God. The Spirit does not free us from earthly things, but as our proxy brings our needs to God in ways which we cannot express ourselves. The utterances are not "the tongues of angels", indicating full possession of the presence of God, as the Corinthians falsely supposed (1 Cor. 13:1), but a sign of the church's solidarity with the rest of the creation which likewise sighs or groans (cf. *synstenazei*, groan together, v. 20, with the vb. *stenazomen*, we groan, v. 23, and the noun *stenagmois*, with groans, v. 26). For the presence of the Spirit is only the first fruits (→ Sacrifice, art. *aparchē*) of the full reality of our adoption as sons, the redemption of the body (v. 23). The reference to our body, which in the Gk. is sing., could refer to the corporate body of the church (cf. Rom. 12:4 f.), or it may refer to the physical body in view of the previous reference to the crea- tion's bondage to decay (v. 21). But perhaps the two ideas may coalesce here.

Käsemann detects a difference of attitude in Paul to glossolalia here and in 1 Cor. 14 and 2 Cor. 12:5–10. He suggests that in Corinth Paul tried to repress the phenomenon together with other ecstatic experiences and to make them a private matter as far as possible (op. cit., 134; cf. his essay, "Die Legitimität des Apostels", *ZNW* 41, 1942, 67 ff.), whereas here he allows congregational worship to be deeply influenced by these things. But to say this is to go beyond the actual evidence. What he does is to take account of the phenomenon as it occurs in the church and give it an interpretation which is positive, but which cuts across that of the charis- matics at Corinth and possibly also that of the charismatics at Rome. Moreover, it may be said that, just as those who spoke in tongues at Corinth require an interpreter to make their utterances intelligible to men (1 Cor. 14:13, 26 ff.), so in Rom. those who sigh in prayer need the Spirit as an intercessor in order to make their utterances intelligible to God (Rom. 8:26 f.).

Käsemann endorses Schniewind's suggestion that "Prayer is described in Rom. 8.26 f. as it is formed from the *dikaiosynē theou*" (ibid.; cf. J. Schniewind, "Das Seufzen des Geistes, Röm. 8, 26, 27", *Nachgelassene Reden und Aufsätze*, 1952, 81 f.). It is set in the context of justification and the → righteousness of God (cf. 8:1). Just as in justification there is the paradox of the sinner justified by faith, so here there is the paradox of the sons of God being at one with the creation. The weaknesses are not just spiritual failings but descriptions of the human condition. Moreover, the glossolalia is not a sign that the church has arrived, as it were, and of its advanced spirituality; rather it is for Paul "nothing other than the cry of the tempted for liberty" (op. cit., 135). One may go beyond Käsemann and point out that Paul is not saying here that the sighing is an adequate form of worship. In fact, he says the contrary. It is inadequate, in that it shows that we do not know what to pray for as we ought, and that these utterances do not convey what is in the mind of God. But this is more than made up for by the intercession of the Spirit who intercedes for us with sighs too deep for words, lit. unspoken sighs (v. 26). This is acceptable to God, because God knows the mind of the Spirit and the

884

Spirit intercedes according to the will of God (v. 27). Later on Paul defines spiritual or *rational* worship (*logikēn latreian*, Rom. 12:1) in terms of presenting the body "as a living sacrifice, holy and acceptable to God." He then goes on to explain what this means in terms of not being conformed to the world, of the renewal of the mind, proving the will of God, the exercise of gifts in the body of Christ and daily living in a world ruled by pagan authorities (chs. 12 and 13). These references indicate how the worship described in ch. 8 is to be complemented. It involves the dedication of the whole person to God in a way which is rational, embracing the whole mind, and practical, reaching out into the practicalities of daily living in the church and the world (→ Serve, art. *latreuō*).   *C. Brown*

→ Advocate, → Baptism, → Blessing, → Church, → Confess, → Curse, → Fast, → Father, → Feast, → Lord's Supper, → Sacrifice, → Serve, → Song, → Temple, → Tent, → Thank

(a). A. A. Anderson, *The Book of Psalms*, I–II, New Century Bible, 1972; D. R. Ap-Thomas, "Notes on Some Themes Relating to Prayer", *VT* 6, 1956, 225–41; P. R Baelz, *Prayer and Providence*, 1968; G. J. Bahr, "The Use of the Lord's Prayer in the Primitive Church", *JBL* 84, 1965, 153–59; and "The Subscriptions in the Pauline Letters", *JBL* 87, 1968, 27–41; J. A. Bain, *The Prayers of the Apostle Paul*, no date (1937?); J. B. Bauer and H. Zimmermann, "Prayer", *EBT* II 679–86; G. Bertram, *krouō, TDNT* III 954–57; G. Bornkamm, "On the Understanding of Worship", in *Early Christian Experience*, 1969, 161–79; R. E. Brown, "The Pater Noster as an Eschatological Prayer", in *New Testament Essays*, 1965, 217–53; F. Büchsel, *hiketēria, TDNT* III 296 f.; F. H. Chase, *The Lord's Prayer in the Early Church*, 1891; F. D. Coggan, *The Prayers of the New Testament*, 1967; R. M. Cooper, "*Leitourgos Christou Iēsou.* Toward a Theology of Christian Prayer", *Anglican Theological Review* 47, 1965, 263–75; O. Cullmann, *Early Christian Worship*, *SBT* 10, 1953; G. Delling, *Worship in the New Testament*, 1962; C. W. Dugmore, *The Influence of the Synagogue upon the Divine Office*, 1944; G. Ebeling, *The Lord's Prayer in Today's World*, 1966; B. Van Elderen, "The Verb in the Epistolary Invocation", *Calvin Theological Journal* 2, 1967, 46 ff.; W. Förster, *Palestinian Judaism in New Testament Times*, 1964; G. Fohrer, *History of Israelite Religion*, 1973; A. R. George, *Communion with God in the New Testament*, 1953; M. D. Goulder, "The Composition of the Lord's Prayer", *JTS* New Series 14, 1963, 32–45; and *Midrash and Lection in Matthew*, 1974, 296–301; F. C. Grant, *Ancient Judaism and the New Testament*, 1960, 39–57; H. Greeven, *deomai* etc., *TDNT* II 40 ff.; *erōtaō* etc., *TDNT* II 685–89; and *proskyneō* etc., *TDNT* VI 758–66; F. Hahn, *The Worship of the Early Church*, 1973; O. Hallesby, *Prayer*, 1936; F. Heiler, *Prayer: A Study in the History and Psychology of Religion*, 1932; J. Heinemann, *Prayer in the Period of the Tanna'im and the Amora'im: Its Nature and its Patterns*, 1964; J. Hermann and H. Greeven, *euchomai* etc., *TDNT* II 775–808; W. Herrmann, *The Communion of the Christian with God*, (1895) 1972; J. Jeremias, *The Prayers of Jesus*, *SBT* Second Series 6, 1967; R. Jewett, "The Epistolary Thanksgiving and the Integrity of Philippians", *NovT* 12, 1970, 40–53; N. B. Johnson, *Prayer in Apocrypha and Pseudepigrapha*, *JBL* Monograph Series 2, 1928; M. Kadushin, *Worship and Ethics: A Study in Rabbinic Judaism*, 1963; E. Käsemann, "The Cry for Liberty in the Worship of the Church", in *Perspectives on Paul*, 1971, 122–37; E. Lohmeyer, *The Lord's Prayer*, 1965; J. Lowe, *The Lord's Prayer*, 1962; W. Lüthi, *The Lord's Prayer: An Exposition*, 1962; B. Martin, *Prayer in Judaism*, 1968; *ML* 342–81; Moore, *Judaism*, II, 212–38; T. Y. Mullins, "Greeting as a New Testament Form", *JBL* 87, 1968, 418–26; and "Petition as a Literary Form", *NovT* 5, 1964, 46–54; P. T. O'Brien, "Prayer in Luke-Acts", *TB* 24, 1973, 111–27; W. O. E. Oesterley, *The Jewish Background of the Christian Liturgy*, 1925; W. O. E. Oesterley and G. H. Box, *The Religion and Worship of the Synagogue: An Introduction to the Study of Judaism from the New Testament Period*, 1907, D. Z. Phillips, *The Concept of Prayer*, 1965 (philosophical study); H. Ringgren, *Israelite Religion*, 1966; G. Schlier, *gony* etc., *TDNT* I 378 ff.; H. Schürmann, *Praying with Christ*, 1964; P.-O. Sjörgren, *The Jesus Prayer*, 1975; C. W. F. Smith, "Lord's Prayer", *IOB* III 154–58; G. Stählin, *aiteō* etc., *TDNT* I 191–95; R. A. Stewart, *Rabbinic Theology: An Introductory Study*, 1961; H. Thielicke, *The Prayer that Spans the World: Sermons on the Lord's Prayer*, 1965; J. G. S. S. Thomson, *The Praying Christ: A Study of Jesus' Doctrine and Practice of Prayer*, 1959; C. Westermann, *The Praise of God in the Psalms*, 1965; W. White, Jr., "Lord's Prayer", *ZPEB* III 972–78;

885

G. P. Wiles, *Paul's Intercessory Prayers: The Significance of the Intercessory Prayer Passages in the Letters of St. Paul, Society for New Testament Studies Monograph Series* 24, 1974. (b). G. Beer and O. Holtzmann, eds., *Die Mischna. Text, Übersetzung und Erklärung*, 1912; W. Bieder, "Gebetswirklichkeit und Gebetsmöglichkeit bei Paulus: Das Beten des Geistes und das Beten im Geist", *ThZ* 4, 1948, 22–40; K. Berger, "Zu den sogenannten Sätzen Heiligen Rechts", *NTS* 17, 1970–71, 10–40; T. Boman, "Der Gebetskampf Jesu", *NTS* 10, 1963–64, 261–73; H. van den Bussche, *Le Notre Père*, 1959; F. Cabrol, *La Prière des Premiers Chrétiens*, 1929; J. Carmignac, *Recherches sur le "Notre Père"*, 1969; E. Delay, "A qui s'adresse la prière chrétienne?", *Revue d'Histoire et de Philosophie Religieuses* 37, 1949, 189–201; A. Deitzel, "Beten im Geist. Eine religionsgeschichtliche Parallele aus den Hodajot zum paulinischen Beten im Geist", *ThZ* 13, 1957, 12–32; F. J. Dölger, *Sol Salutis: Gebet und Gesang im christlichen Altertum*, 1925²; J. Döller, *Das Gebet im Alten Testament in religionsgeschichtlicher Beleuchtung*, 1914; G. Eichholz, *Auslegung der Bergpredigt, BSt* 37, 1963, especially 109 ff.; I. Elbogen, *Der jüdische Gottesdienst in seiner geschichtlichen Entwicklung*, 1931³; and *Die messianische Idee in den alten jüdischen Gebeten*, 1912; J.-A. Eschlimann, *La Prière dans S. Paul*, 1934; A. Grövig, "Die Anbetung Christi im Neuen Testament", *Tidsskrift for Teologi og Kirke*, 1, 1930, 26–44; E. Gaugler, "Der Geist und das Gebet der Schwachen Gemeinde", *Internationale kirchliche Zeitschrift* 51, 1961, 67–94; E. F. von der Goltz, *Das Gebet in der ältesten Christenheit. Eine geschichtliche Untersuchung*, 1902; J. Gnilka, "Jesus und das Gebet", *BuL* 6, 1965, 79–91; H. Greeven, *Gebet und Eschatologie im Neuen Testament*, 1931; A. Grieff, *Das Gebet im Alten Testament*, 1915; A. Hamman, *La Prière*, I, *Le Nouveau Testament*, 1959; G. Harder, *Paulus und das Gebet*, 1936; J. Hempel, *Gebet und Frömmigkeit im Alten Testament*, 1922; F. Hesse, *Die Fürbitte im Alten Testament*, Inaugural Dissertation, Erlangen, 1949; O. Holtzmann, "Die tägliche Gebetstunden im Judentum und Urchristentum", *ZNW* 12, 1911, 90–107; J. Horst, *Proskynein*, 1933; J. Jeremias, "Das Gebetsleben Jesu", *ZNW* 25, 1926, 123–40; A. Juncker, *Das Gebet bei Paulus*, 1905; R. Kerkhoff, *Das Unablässige Gebet. Beiträge zur Lehre vom immerwährenden Beten im Neuen Testament*, 1954; P. Ketter, "Vom Gebetsleben des Apostels Paulus", *Theologisch-praktische Quartalschrift* 91, 1938, 23–40; A. Lawek, *Das Gebet zu Jesus*, 1921; A. Köberle, *Schule des Gebets*, 1959; K. G. Kuhn, *Achtzehngebet und Vaterunser und der Reim, WUNT* 1, 1950; J. Marty, "La Prière dans le Nouveau Testament", *Revue d'Histoire et de Philosophie Religieuses* 10, 1930, 90–98; H. Miskotte, *Der Weg des Gebets*, 1964; K. Niederwimmer, "Das Gebet des Geistes, Röm. 8, 26 f.", *ThZ* 20, 1964, 252–65; J. M. Nielen, *Gebet und Gottesdienst im Neuen Testament*, 1937; E. Orphal, *Das Paulusgebet. Psychologisch-exegetische Untersuchung des Paulus-Geisteslebens auf Grund seiner Selbstzeugnisse*, 1933; W. Ott, *Gebet und Heil. Die Bedeutung der Gebetsparänese in der lukanischen Theologie, Studien zum Alten und Neuen Testament* 12, 1965; J. M. Robinson, "Die Hodajot-Formel in Gebet und Hymnus des Frühchristentums", in W. Eltester, ed., *Apophoreta. Festschrift für Ernst Haenchen*, 1964, 194–235; I. Rohr, *Das Gebet im Neuen Testament*, 1924; *SB* I 396–404; J. Scharbert, "Die Fürbitte im Alten Testament", *ThG* 50, 1960, 321 ff.; R. Schnackenburg, "Die Anbetung in Geist und Wahrheit (Joh. 4, 23) im Lichte von Qumran-Texten", *BZ* 3, 1959, 88–94; J. Schniewind, "Das Seufzen des Geistes, Röm. 8. 26, 27", in *Nachgelassene Reden und Aufsätze*, 1952, 81–103; H. Schönweiss, *Beten? Ja, aber wie?*, 1962; W. Staerk, *Altjüdische liturgische Gebete*, 1910; R. Storr, *Die Frömmigkeit im Alten Testament*, 1927, 175–91; A. Wendel, *Das freie Laiengebet im vorexilischen Israel*, 1932; R. Zorn, *Die Fürbitte im Spätjudentum und im Neuen Testament*, 1957; L. Zunz, *Die gottesdienstlichen Vorträge der Juden historisch entwickelt*, 1892².

Present, Day, Maranatha, Parousia

The subject-matter of this article is closely associated with ideas dealt with under → goal, → come and → time. Throughout this whole area there occurs the same tension, inherent in Christian eschatology, between that which is already present and that which is still future. This tension can be shown by careful investigation not to lie between the various words used but rather to extend right to the heart of practically each individual word. However, the three concepts treated below, "the

Day", Maranatha and Parousia, are all generally considered to have a future reference and are therefore dealt with separately from the rest.

parousia, presence, coming, advent, a political and religious term in the Hellenistic world, refers in the NT mainly to the return of Jesus at the end of this age (→ Time, art. *aiōn*) and to this extent is closely related with the *hēmera*, day (cf. 2 Pet. 3:12). The latter term has OT associations and, apart from its purely technical use as a measure of time, likewise means the last day or the day of the return of Christ. The Aramaic ejaculation *maranatha* is an expression of certainty or confident hope; it can be translated either: "Our Lord has come", or: "Our Lord, come".

| ἡμέρα | ἡμέρα (*hēmera*), day.

CL A day can either denote the period of 24 hours, in which case it includes the night (Xen., *Anab.* 4, 7, 28: they remained three days; cf. Mk. 6:21) or it may exclude the night (Xen., *Anab.* 2, 2, 13: but when it was day; cf. Matt. 4:2). But *hēmera* can also mean a much longer period of time (Soph., *Aj.* 623 f., the mother, who had been brought up in an earlier day); it can cover a lifetime (Soph., *OC* 1216 f., for many have left behind sundry days, i.e. their lifetime), or time generally (Soph., *El.* 266 f., what [fateful] days are mine, think you, when I see Aegisthus sitting upon the throne; cf. Eph. 6:13; 1 Pet. 3:10).

OT 1. Like years and months (e.g. 2 Ki. 17:1; Exod. 2:2), days serve as a division of time (Gen. 1:5–2:2; Jos. 6:3), the Heb. word being almost invariably *yôm*, which often occurs within a fixed phrase. The day can include the night, in which case it begins with the evening (Gen. 1:5), or be distinguished from the night (Isa. 10:10). The word may indicate a particular day (Gen. 4:14, today; Job 3:1, birthday) or (in the plur.) a period of time (Gen. 6:3, lifetime; Gen. 8:22, so long as the earth remains; Ps. 90[89]:4, a thousand years in thy sight are but as yesterday when it is past [→ Number art. *chilias*, OT 3]; Isa. 60:22, days of mourning; Jdg. 17:10, a year). Certain days have a special character: while six days of the week are days of work, the seventh day is the → Sabbath (Exod. 20:9 f.; Lk. 4:16). There are → feast days (Hos. 2:15; Neh. 8:9; Gal. 4:10). A day in the temple courts is better than a thousand elsewhere (Ps. 84[83]:10). Man has no power over the day of his death (Eccl. 8:8).

2. Those passages which speak of the day of Yahweh (*yôm YHWH*) are of particular theological importance. But the phrase has various meanings. Originally the day of Yahweh was a day of joy (this is assumed in Amos 5:18, 20; cf. Zech. 14:7). The prophets, however, re-interpreted this popular idea of a day of salvation and proclaimed it instead as a day of unrelieved judgment (cf. Amos 5:18, 20; Joel 1:15; 2:2). The event in view may be a political (Ezek. 34:12) or a cultic one (cf. S. Mowinckel's thesis of Yahweh's coronation day in *The Psalms in Israel's Worship*, I, 1962, 116; "Jahwes dag", *Norsk Teologisk Tidsskrift* 59, 1958, 1–56, 209–29) or it may be *the* great eschatological event (e.g. Amos 8:9; Isa. 2:11 f., 17), the latter often described in cosmological language (Zeph. 1:15; Joel 3:14). H. Gressmann suggested that the day of the Lord was a foreign importation (*Der Ursprung der israelitisch-jüdischen Eschatologie*, FRLANT 6, 1905). But G. von Rad and

others see its origin within the traditions of Israel's holy war (*Der heilige Krieg im alten Israel*, 1949; "The Origin of the Concept of the Day of Yahweh", *JSS* 4, 1959, 97–108; *Old Testament Theology*, II, 1965, 119–25; cf. also K.-D. Schunk, "Strukturlinien der Vorstellung vom Tag Yahwes" *VT* 14, 1964, 319 ff.; H. W. Robinson, *Inspiration and Revelation in the Old Testament*, 1946, 135–47, who gives a critique of Mowinckel).

In many cases it is difficult to distinguish the one from the other. The day of Yahweh can mean the fall of → Jerusalem and so belong to the past (Lam. 1:21) or, as in the eschatological passages mentioned above, be still future. It can be imminent (Ezek. 7:7), so that the hearers give heed to the prophetic message (Mic. 1:2). But no time-scale may be indicated (Isa. 24:21). The day may even be regarded (by the sinner at least) as a long way off (Amos 6:3; 9:10). This shows that the prophets' preaching of the day of Yahweh cannot be isolated from concrete situations but can always be seen to have taken place in a particular historical context. However, H. H. Rowley contended that, while in some passages the day of the Lord was conceived of as nigh at hand (Isa. 13:6; Ezek. 30:3; Joel 1:15; 2:1; 3:14 [MT 4:4]; Obad. 15; Zeph. 1:14; in Lam. 1:12; 2:1, 21 f. it is already past), all OT writers thought of it as breaking into history in a spectacular fashion ("The Day of the Lord", in *The Faith of Israel*, 1956, 179). Moreover, while judgment may be nigh, there is also the thought of a golden age beyond it which may be presented as being near or far. But nowhere is it brought about by human achievement or the policies contrived by men. The golden age in which prophecy merges into apocalyptic has a universal character (cf. Isa. 11:6; 65:17, 21; Mic. 4:4). Sometimes the nations are depicted as serving Israel (Isa. 60:10 ff.; 61:5; Dan. 2:44; 7:27), or Israel's king as holding universal sway (Zech. 9:9 f.; Pss. 2:8 f.; 72:8, 10 f.; Mic. 5:2, 4 [MT 5:1, 3]). Jer. 3:17 declares that only universal submission to God can eliminate that which militates against well-being. The thought of the Gentiles sharing the faith of Israel also comes into the prophetic vision (Pss. 22:27; 96:1 ff., 9 f.; 102:15 f., 21 f.; Jer. 16:19 ff.; Zeph. 3:10; Zech. 2:11; 8:22 f.). Rowley points out that passages like Isa. 42:1, 3, 6; 43:10; 45:22; 49:6; 66:19 f. did not proclaim universalism for the first time. Rather they related it to the mission of Israel. The Gentiles are also envisaged in the books of Ruth and Jonah which are widely regarded as tracts on the theme of the Gentiles sharing in Israel's salvation and polemics against a narrow, exclusive Jewish outlook. Rowley further argues that the figures of the Son of man, suffering servant and messiah, and the idea of the kingdom of God all converge on the day of the Lord (op. cit., 194–201).

G. Braumann

3. The Hebrews had no word for time in the abstract, and similarly had no corresponding expressions for past, present and future. For fuller discussion → Time; cf. also T. Boman, *Hebrew Thought Compared with Greek*, 1960; J. Barr, *The Semantics of Bibical Language*, 1961; and *Biblical Words for Time*, SBT 33, 1962; and S. J. DeVries, *Yesterday, Today and Tommorrow: Time and History in the Old Testament*, 1975. Of the various words used to express aspects of time by far the most frequent in Heb. is *yôm* (cf. DeVries, op. cit., 42). Often it is qualified by a genitival phrase, an infinitive, or a relative clause introduced by *'ašer* (that or when).

Thus there could be a *yôm* of salvation experienced in a variety of past events: the day of Israel's election (Deut. 9:24; Ezek. 16:4 f.); the day of the plague on → Egypt and other days connected with the saving events of the exodus (Exod. 10:13; 12:17; Num. 11:32); the day of the dedication of the tabernacle (Num. 9:15); of the giving of the law (Deut. 4:10); of the victory over the Amorites (Jos. 10:12). Out of this arose a variety of stock expressions like "On the day when I brought them out of Egypt ..." (Jdg. 19:30; 1 Sam. 8:8; 2 Sam. 7:6; Isa. 11:16; Jer. 7:22; 11:4, 7; 31:32; 34:13: Hos. 2:17; Ps. 78:42). De Vries suggests that this provided the model for speaking of another past day of salvation experienced in the return from exile (Hag. 2:15, 18 f.; Zech. 4:10; 8:9) and that what was true corporately for Israel could similarly be applied to the individual (Pss. 18:18; 20:2; 59:17; 77:3; 138:3; 140:8; Lam. 3:57; cf. op. cit., 43). But the days could also be remembered as a day of judgment (Num. 32:10; 2 Chr. 28:6; Pss. 78[77]:9; 95[94]: 8; 137[136]:7; Isa. 9:3, 13; Lam. 1:12; 2:1, 21 f.; Ezek. 31:15; 34:12; Hos. 10:14; Obad. 11, 14; Zech. 14:3). Whereas in some of these instances *yôm* is a literal day, in others it appears to denote a concrete time which may have extended for more than twenty-four hours, but which was nevertheless characterized by a specific event. The plur. *yāmîm*, however, "is used not so much to memorialize a unique event as to identify and specify the duration of a period of time, whether this be limited or unlimited, definite or indefinite" (DeVries, op. cit., 43).

In connection with day thought of in the past sense it may be observed that the two Gen. creation narratives both use *yôm* and the corresponding Gk. *hēmera*: the seven-day narrative (Gen. 1:5, 8, 13 f., 16, 18 f., 23, 31; 2:2–4a, attributed to P) and the one-day creation and fall narrative (Gen. 2:4b–3:24, attributed to J). The word day occurs again in Gen. 2:17: "but of the tree of the knowledge of good and evil you shall not eat, for in the day that you eat of it you shall die." This was evidently not understood in a strictly literal sense of physical death within twenty-four hours. Rather, it brought a change in the human condition which affects man all the *days* of his life (Gen. 3:17; cf. also v. 14). Various attempts have been made to harmonize the narratives with a modern scientific view of the world involving some form of concordism, such as the view that the days correspond to geological eras. But these place a considerable strain on both scientific theory and the biblical text, e.g. the creation of light and plants before the sun and moon (for discussion see B. Ramm, *The Christian View of Science and Scripture*, 1955, 120–56). Moreover, if the six creation-days of Gen. 1 correspond to geological eras, it does not help to harmonize Gen. 2:4b, which locates the creation of man on the day that the earth and the heavens were made, apparently prior to the planting of the garden of Eden. It would, therefore, seem best to recognize both creation narratives as pre-scientific schematizations symbolically representing the origin of the world from God in its order and relative autonomy (cf. N. H. Ridderbos, *Is there a Conflict between Genesis 1 and Natural Science?*, 1957; C. Westermann, *Creation*, 1974). The type of discourse here may be compared with the → parable in the teaching of Jesus and the cosmic visions in Rev. dealing with the end-time, only here we are dealing with primeval pre-history. The six creation days followed by a rest day in Gen. 1 are seen in Exod. 20:11 to be a divine pattern for human activity in explaining the Fourth Commandment concerning the → sabbath. The par. in Deut. 5:12–15 omits the reference to creation but supplies a soteriological reason. Just as

Yahweh brought Israel out of forced labour in Egypt and gave him rest, so the servant and beast (like their master) are to be set free from toil on the sabbath day.

The present day may be characterized by laments and distress (Pss. 20[19]:9; 49[48]:5; 86:7; 102:3 f.; 2 Ki. 19:3; Isa. 37:3; 61:2; 63:4; Jer. 17:16 ff.; Lam. 1:7; Hos. 9:7), but also by salvation (Isa. 49:8). However, DeVries draws a basic distinction in the present use of *yôm* between the day that is historically present and the day in gnomic discourse (i.e. teaching that has to do with popular wisdom, especially in the form of proverbs and aphorisms) and in cultic regulations. In these latter it refers to a "today" that is continually repeated and hence continuously present. Examples of the gnomic present are Job 18:20; 20:28; 38:20; Pss. 20(19): 9; 37(36):19; 102(101):3; Prov. 11:4; and in the plur. Job 14:14; 30:16, 27; Pss. 37(36):19; 94(93):13; Prov. 15:15; Eccl. 7:15; 9:9; 11:19; 12:1. Instances of the cultic present include Exod. 20:8; 31:15; 35:3; 40:2; Lev. 15:25; 19:6; 23:15, 27 f.; 24:8; 25:9; Num. 10:10; 15:32; 28:9; Deut. 5:15; Isa. 58:13; Jer. 17:22, 24, 27; Ezek. 46:1, 4, 12 (for further details see DeVries, op. cit., 45 ff.).

The future may be described in terms of a coming (eschatological) day (Isa. 13:9; Jer. 47:4; Ezek. 38:18; cf. 39:8; Mic. 7:4; Mal. 4:1). The day of the Lord and similar expressions containing the word *yôm* figures prominently in oracles of judgment against foreign nations (Isa. 13:6; Ezek. 30:3; Joel 4:14; Obad. 15). But Israel may also be the object of judgment (Isa. 2:12; Ezek. 13:5; Joel 1:15; 2:1, 11; 3:4; Amos 5:18, 20; Zeph. 1:7; Mal. 4:5). However, "it is important to observe that there is no set technical expression for the so-called 'day of Yahweh' " (DeVries, op. cit., 48; see pp. 48–51 for details of the various expressions used). It may be referred to as "their day of calamity" (Jer. 46:21), "a day of distress" (Hab. 3:16), a "day of downfall" (Ezek. 26:18; 27:27; 32:10), "a bitter day" (Amos 8:10), "an evil day" (Amos 6:3) etc. But it can also be a day of salvation: "the day when Yahweh binds up" (Isa. 30:26), "the day when I cleanse" (Ezek. 36:33), "the day when Yahweh gives rest" (Isa. 14:3), "the day when I pay attention" (Jer. 27:22), "the day when I honour myself" (Ezek. 39:13), "the day when he fights" (Zech. 14:3). Similarly, the prophets can use the plur. and say "Behold, the days are coming, when . . ." in both oracles of judgment (Isa. 39:6; Jer. 7:32; 9:24; 19:6; 48:12; 49:2; 51:47, 52) and of salvation (Jer. 16:11; 23:5, 7; 30:3; 31:27, 31, 38; 33:14; Amos 9:13).

In addition to this, the OT contains adverbial expressions of time such as *bayyôm hahû'*, on that day, which is used of the past some 89 times and of the future 112 times, and *hayyôm* which is used of the present, today, 217 times. The central part of DeVries's work constitutes a detailed examination and classification of these various passages, showing the function of words connected with time in respect of the literary form of their respective passages. Of theological significance is his conclusion that the function of the references to Yahweh's day, whether in the past or the future, is to illuminate the present "today". "Historiography provides the model for parenesis, employing the image of revelatory event in the past to illuminate the revelatory significance of the present. Eschatology is, then, an analogical projection of the past and the present into the future, positing Yahweh's coming action on his action already experienced. . . . In the early passages, at any rate, 'the day of Yahweh' is not to be understood as the termination of history. It is analogous to *bayyôm hahû'*, used absolutely in a futuristic sense, as in

I Kings 22:25, Isa. 52:6, and Amos 8:3. The interpretative framework is not chronological, placing this day within or at the end of a sequence of days, but qualifying, characterizing it as a day of Yahweh's decisive action in which all the complexities and ambiguities of the present situation are brought to a complete – and in this sense final – resolution. But, as Yahweh has often acted decisively in the past, so there may need to be recurring days of Yahweh in the future. In fact, 'today' – this very day – may be a 'day of Yahweh' " (op. cit., 341). Any day may become Yahweh's day, but only those days actively become his day when he manifests himself in judgment and salvation (cf. Ps. 95[94]:7; Jer. 28:9; Ezek. 33:33; Mal. 3:1, 3, 19–21).

The prophets frequently spoke of the day of the Lord as imminent (cf. Isa. 10:27; 27:1; 29:19; Hag. 2:23; Zech. 6:10). DeVries comments: "In agreement with the majority of modern interpreters, we affirm that Israel's prophets were predicting the future only as a proximate projection of the present. They were immediately deducing the future out of the present, less by way of political astuteness than out of faith in the being and nature of Israel's covenant God" (op. cit., 342). In the apocalyptic writings the idea is transformed. The future is increasingly abstracted from the present and has an epoch of its own. Thus Zech. 14:21 depicts the future more in terms of a state of being than a decisive event (cf. Isa. 61:3; Dan. 7).

DeVries considers that many of the distinctions employed by scholars to characterize the Hebrew conception of time (e.g. between "outer" and "inner" history; between "linear" and "cyclical" history; between "man's time" and "God's time"; and between "secular time" and "sacred time") fall wide of the mark. "The only ready-to-hand polarity that seems really applicable is a contrast between what we would call two different approaches to the identical temporal phenomena: the quantitative approach and the qualitative approach" (op. cit., 343). The quantitative approach sees time as a succession of commensurate entities – a given number of days, months or years. These can be measured mathematically. The qualitative approach sees time as a succession of essentially unique, incommensurate experiences. Thus the day takes its determination from the event which gives it its character. Because God acts in it, it has an eschatological dimension and thus becomes the decisive day of divine action. This Hebraic view of time stands in contrast with that of the Egyptians for whom time was an endless, meaningless continuum, caught in a perpetual seasonal pattern of alteration (op. cit., 344; cf. E. Otto, "Altägyptische Zeitvorstellungen und Zeitbegriffe", Die Welt als Geschichte 14, 1954, 135–48). The early Mesopotamian writings indicate a greater awareness of the distinction between different times, but did not see any underlying purpose, significance or interrelation between different times (cf. H. Gese, "Geschichtliches Denken im alten Orient und im Alten Testament", ZTK 55, 1958, 127 ff.). But in Israel Yahweh was Lord of past, present and future. "History therefore was filled with positive potentiality. It has a goal and a meaning" (De Vries, op. cit., 344 f.). In the OT the quantitative approach provides the framework of continuity, allowing for the interconnectedness of specific events. But it is the qualitative approach which gives the historical event its theological significance. It would be inaccurate to say that the same conceptions and emphases are found uniformly throughout the OT. In the historical writings (especially after the division of the kingdom), in those concerned with the cult and apocalyptic literature the quantitative approach predominates, whereas in the prophetic writings the qualitative is dominant. But the differences between the cultic/gnomic conception of time and the historical/prophetic conception may be overstated. For while the practice of the cult could lead to a cyclical attitude to life characterized by the performance of daily rites and annual feasts, there are many passages in the OT which seek to invest the present with an awareness of the acts of God in time and of man's relationship with him in time. "For Deuteronomy the present generation is addressed as the generation that heard Yahweh speak from Horeb, being called not only to a new remembrance but to a new obedience" (DeVries, op. cit., 347). The Passover ordinance prescribed an annual rite, but the whole purpose of the rite is to summon the Israelite to reflect on the day in which his people were brought out of Egypt (Exod. 13:3–10). Similarly, Ps. 95:7 confronts the worshipper with the reflection that his "today" is the day of crisis in which the opportunities and the judgment which befell the wilderness generation are realized in his life.

C. Brown

4. Apocalyptic and later Judaism carried still further the idea of the future day, with eschatology now becoming part of the doctrine of the last things and developing strong apocalyptic features. The questions are asked: How long will this age last? When can we expect the new age? (2 Esd. 4:33, 35; cf. Mk. 13:4). The messianic age will be preceded by a time of tribulation, sub-divided into twelve shorter periods (Syr.Bar. 27) and marked, among other things, by unrighteousness and licentiousness (2 Esd. 5:2 ff.; cf. Matt. 24:12). The new age will be heralded by signs (Syr.Bar. 25:4; cf. Mk. 13:24), and "the end" (Syr.Bar. 29:7 f.; cf. Mk. 13:7) will be the transition to the days of messiah when judgment will give way to wisdom, sinlessness, life (Eth.Enoch 5:8 f.). The future eschatological world was originally thought to be identical with the age of messiah, but later these were separated into two consecutive periods (SB II 552). For further discussion see S. Mowinckel, *He That Cometh*, 1956, 261–79; D. S. Russell, *The Method and Message of Jewish Apocalyptic, 200 B.C.–A.D. 100*, 1964, 263–303; R. A. Stewart, *Rabbinic Theology*, 1961, 47–53; W. Förster, *Palestinian Judaism in New Testament Times*, 1964, 192–201; and L. Hartman, "The Functions of Some so-Called Apocalyptic Time-tables", *NTS* 22, 1975–76, 1–14. It is sometimes said that in answer to the prophets' question "How long, O Lord, how long?", the apocalyptists give the year, the day and the hour (cf. D. S. Russell, op. cit., 1). But L. Hartman questions this, suggesting that the supporting evidence is less strong than is sometimes supposed (Dan. 9 being the most clear-cut example; → Number). From his examination of Ass.Mos. 10:12, Apc.Abr. 28–31, and Eth.Enoch 91–94 in the light of modern semantics, he concludes that the time-tables have different functions. In Dan. they have a certain informative-theoretical function concerning the date of the end, but even so they are coupled with practical functions. But elsewhere they have predominantly a practical function such as exhortation. "When the literary convention of different kinds of apocalyptic timetables was developed in Jewish apocalyptical literature, it had not primarily a theoretical, informative, and calculating function, but rather some practical one. To put it another way: the time-tables were aimed less at the brain than at the heart and hands" (op. cit., 14).

The days of → messiah were expected to bring in renewal, a righting of wrongs, and the → restoration of all that had been lost through Adam's transgression. So, e.g., the nations which had oppressed Israel will be destroyed, while Israel's boundaries will be fully restored in the new → temple (though on this point there was not absolute unanimity). Israel will be rich to a degree hitherto unknown. Both man and nature will increase in fruitfulness. Sinful desires, and the devil himself, will be destroyed. The Holy Spirit will be poured out. Sickness and death will be removed and the dead will arise (see *SB* IV, 2, 799–976).

5. The Qumran texts regard the date of the eschatological day as being already fixed (1QM 13:14). It will bring the annihilation of those who do not keep the commandments (CD 8:1); it will be the day of God's visitation (ibid.), the end of days (1QpHab 2:6; 9:6), the day of vengeance (1QS 10:19), the day of slaughter (1QH 15:17), when evil-doers will be destroyed (ibid.), including all carvers of idols for the nations (1QpHab 12:13 f.; 13:1 ff.). There will be a battle with fearful carnage (1QM 1:9) as the sons of light war against the sons of darkness (1QM 1:11). In the day of catastrophe all men fit for war are to be ready for the day of vengeance (1QM 7:5; 15:2 f.). God will then be praised (1QM 18:5), and on the day of judgment those who are willing to be added to the elect will be saved (1Q 14:7 ff.). However, the Qumran texts do not appear to mention explicitly "the day of Yahweh". (On Qumran eschatology see M. Burrows, *More Light on the Dead Sea Scrolls*, 1958, 342–52; and, more fully, Y. Yadin, *The Scroll of the War of the Sons of Light against the Sons of Darkness*, 1962.)

NT 1. In the short → resurrection narratives there are striking expressions of time: on the third day (1 Cor. 15:4; Matt. 16:21; Lk. 9:22; → Number, art. *tritos*) or after three days (Mk. 8:31; 9:31; 10:34; → Number, art. *treis*). G. Delling suggests that the early Christian accounts were influenced by the eschatological expectation of Hos. 6:2 which also influenced rabbinic expectation: "After two days he will revive us [i.e. the nation]; on the third day he will raise us up, that we may live before him" (cf. *TDNT* II 949). According to Pirqe R. Eliezer 51, the passage was proof of the resurrection of the dead on the third day after the end of the world (*SB* I 747; cf. 647, 649). But in 2 Esd. 7:29 ff. it occurs after seven days. → Number, art. *hepta*.

The situation is similar with regard to the space of 40 days, which already has OT significance, both → Moses and → Elijah being said to fast 40 days and nights (Exod. 34:38; 1 Ki. 19:8; → Number, art. *tessarakonta*). The question may be asked whether the length of Jesus' fast (Matt. 4:2 par. Mk. 1:13, Lk 4:2) was merely coincidental, or whether there is a link with other OT passages (cf. Deut. 8:2 f., 15 f.). Clearly there is an allusion to the wilderness → temptation of Israel in the quotations from Deut. 8:3 (Matt. 4:4; Lk. 4:7), Deut. 6:16 (Matt. 4:7; Lk. 4:12) and Deut. 6:13 (Matt. 4:10; Lk. 4:8). There is the further parallelism between Jesus and Moses (Deut. 9:19; cf. also the giving of the Sermon on the Mount afterwards) and with Deut. 34:1–4 and Ps. 91. In the temptation stories Jesus recapitulates the experiences of Israel, particularly the wilderness generation. (On the temptation see E. Best, *The Temptation and the Passion: The Markan Soteriology*, Society for New Testament Studies Monograph Series 2, 1965, B. Gerhardsson, *The Testing of God's Son (Matt. 4:1–11 & Par): An Analysis of an Early Christian Midrash*, Coniectanea Biblica: New Testament Series 2:1, 1966.)

2. (a) The expectation of the last day is to be found in almost all the literary strata of the NT: pre-Pauline (Rom. 13:12); Paul (Rom. 2:5); Q (Matt. 10:15; Lk. 10:12); Mark and his tradition (Mk. 13:32); Matthew and his tradition (Matt. 12:36); Luke (Acts 17:31); one stratum of the Gospel of Jn., often assumed to be a later one which received prominence in the final redaction (Jn. 6:39; cf. also 1 Jn. 4:17); Jude 6; 2 Pet. 3:12; Eph. 4:30; 2 Tim. 1:12; Rev. 9:6 etc. Other portions of the Gospel of Jn. (the more primitive ones, according to modern conjecture) contain the idea that the last day is not still to come, but has already arrived with the coming of Jesus and the exercise of faith in him (Jn. 3:18 f.; see also Jn. 7:37). (On Johannine eschatology see below the note on *The Parousia and Eschatology in the NT*, 2 (d).)

The phraseology varies, reference being made to that day (2 Tim. 4:8), the last day (Jn. 6:30), the day of wrath (Rev. 6:17), the day of judgment (2 Pet. 2:9), the day of the Lord (1 Thess. 5:2), the day of the Son of man (Lk. 17:24), the day of Christ (Phil. 2:16), the great day of God (Rev. 16:14) or simply the day (1 Cor. 3:13). The plur. is also common (e.g. 2 Tim. 3:1; 2 Pet. 3:3; Rev. 9:6; 10:7).

(b) There are differing statements as to when the last day takes place. Paul teaches the received doctrine of an apocalyptic day still to come (Rom. 2:5; 2 Cor. 1:14), yet at the same time he regards himself as already involved in the eschatological event. Not only does he take over the existing tradition of the nearness of the last day (Rom. 13:12), but in addition calls upon his readers to walk "as in the day" (v. 13), "now" being the day of salvation (2 Cor. 6:2). In other words, the ages are intertwined. With the *parousia* being long delayed, the imminent day of Rom. 13:12 comes to be separated out from the remote "Last Day" (e.g. 2 Pet. 3:8). The suddenness of the last day, which has nothing to do with its imminence or otherwise, is taught in various strata of the NT: e.g. 1 Thess. 5:2, 4; Lk. 21:34 f.; 2 Pet. 3:10. The date is unknown (Mk. 13:32; Matt. 24:42; 25:13). As in apocalyptic, a period of tribulation and catastrophe will precede the last day (cf. Mk. 13; 2 Tim. 3:1; Rev. 2:10), or is inseparable from it (so apparently 2 Cor. 6:2 ff.).

(c) The events associated with the last day are as follows: God (Acts 17:31) or Christ (1 Cor. 1:8; Phil. 1:6, 10; 2 Cor. 5:10) is to be the judge of the world, and will reward each one according to his deeds (Rom. 2:5; → Judgment). Only then, according to Matt., will the separation take place between those who are to enter into the kingdom and those who are to be cast out (i.e. in this present age the church is still a mixed body, containing both groups as yet undifferentiated; Matt. 25:34, 41). The → resurrection of the dead, too, is associated with the judgment (1 Cor. 15:52; Jn. 11:24). Thus the last day becomes a day both of → fear (Matt. 10:15) and of → joy (Lk. 6:23; 21:28; 2 Tim. 4:8).

The message of the last day is not confined to the future, however, but has a definite application to the present. Paul regards the church now in existence as being his glory on the last day (Phil. 2:16; 2 Cor. 1:14). Its members are to conduct themselves even now as "on that day" (Rom. 13:13) and as answerable to God when that day comes (Matt. 25:31 ff.). They must be watchful since its date is unknown (Matt. 24:42), and because it will come suddenly (1 Thess. 5:6). There is also an eschatological aspect to the observance of the → Lord's Supper (Matt. 26:29 par. Mk. 14:25; Lk. 22:16; 1 Cor. 11:26).

3. The futurity of the last day (Matt. 25:13) does not alter the fact that the

exalted Lord is even now with his church "all the days" (Matt. 28:20; 18:20). In Jn. the *paraklētos* is the representative of Christ (cf. Jn. 16:5–15 with 16:16 ff.; → Advocate). A certain duration of time is indicated by phrases such as *kath' hēmeran*, daily (Matt. 26:55; Mk. 14:49 [though A. W. Argyle thinks that the meaning here is "by day", *ExpT* 63, 1951–52, 354]; Lk. 16:19; 22:53; Acts 2:46 f.; 3:2; 16:5; 19:9; 1 Cor. 15:31; 2 Cor. 11:28; Heb. 7:27; 10:11), *hēmera kai hēmera*, day after day, which is probably a Hebraism (2 Cor. 4:16; cf. Est. 3:4; Ps. 68[67]:20). (For these and other expressions see Arndt, 346 f.) This present → time, although it merges even now with the age to come (1 Cor. 15:20 ff.; 2 Cor. 4:16), is still characterized by tribulation (1 Cor. 15:31 f., I die daily; Rom. 8:38; 2 Cor. 11:28). It is sometimes suggested that the importance of this present time increases as the last day becomes more distant: the believer is to take up his cross daily (Lk. 9:23), and to pray for his *daily* bread (Lk. 11:3 par. Matt. 6:11; → Bread, art. *epiousios*); the early church assembles *daily* in the temple and *daily* grows in members (Acts 2:46, 47). On this question → *parousia*, NT.

4. The apostles' visits to cities and churches are generally short, lasting no more than a few days: Paul remains in Jerusalem 15 days (Gal. 1:18); according to Acts 10:48 Peter is asked to remain for some days in the household of Cornelius; Paul spends some days in Philippi (Acts 16:12). Paul's stay in Corinth (Acts 18:11, 18) is an exception to this general rule.   *G. Braumann*

μαραναθά

μαραναθά (*maranatha*), maranatha, "Our Lord has come!", "Our Lord is coming!", or "Our Lord, come!"

1. *maranatha* is an Aram. word found in the NT only in 1 Cor. 16:22: "If anyone has no love for the Lord, let him be accursed. *Maranatha* [or *Marana tha*]." Its precise meaning is disputed, though it is certainly a combination of the Aram. *māran* or *māranā'*, our Lord, and the verb *'atā'*, to come. Either we take it as a perfect (*māran 'atā'*), i.e. our Lord has come, or as an imperative (*māranā' tā*), i.e. our Lord, come! Other meanings are unlikely.

Apart from 1 Cor. 16:22, the word is found in the prayers associated with the Lord's Supper in the Didache (Did. 10:6; c. A.D. 100), but all subsequent references are based on 1 Cor. 16:22. Where the phrase originated is a matter of dispute. W. Heitmüller (*ZNW* 13, 1912, 333 f.) and W. Bousset (*Kyrios Christos*, [1921²] ET 1970, 129) assume it to have come from the bi-lingual Gk. and Aram. speaking churches of Antioch and Damascus, or even Tarsus. In Hellenistic syncretistic religion the gods were widely referred to as "lords" (*kyrioi*; cf. 1 Cor. 8:5), and the view of Heitmüller and Bousset is that *maranatha* indicates the transference of this heathen term to the Lord Jesus Christ. Our knowledge of the above-mentioned churches is too slight for this thesis to be finally disproved. On the other hand, the theory lacks confirmation. The ascription of lordship to Jesus in Aram. and its presence in this formula suggest that it goes back to the very earliest Christian church with its centre in Jerusalem which acknowledged the risen Christ as its Lord. Hence, most expositors still regard the Jerusalem church as the most likely source of the phrase. Moreover, if this is so, it suggests that the term → Lord is to be understood against a Jewish rather than a syncretistic background.

2. (a) Both translations of the phrase are tenable, i.e. it can be construed either as a perfect or as an imperative. The church fathers as a rule understood it as being perfect, though this interpretation may also include the present: "Our Lord has come and is now here". In this case, Phil. 4:5 ("the Lord is at hand") may be a reference to the phrase *maranatha*. The statement of 1 Cor. 16:22 is then a warning: the preceding words, "If any one has no love for the Lord, let him be accursed" (RSV), are further stressed by this reference to the nearness of the Lord. The same may be true of the call to repentance in Did. 10, 6.

(b) The imperative, however, is the more likely interpretation. Appeal may be made to Rev. 22:20, where the words "Amen. Come, Lord Jesus!" may be a free rendering of the original Aram. ejaculatory prayer. Then there is the fact that the word *'abbā'*, → Father (Mk. 14:36; Rom. 8:15; Gal. 4:6), is similarly handed down from Aram., the mother tongue of Jesus, and is likewise an ejaculatory prayer. It is quite understandable that these brief prayers should be passed on in their original form. No immediate connection with the context is essential.

3. Since in Did. 10:6 the word *maranatha* occurs in prayers associated with the Lord's Supper, it may be assumed to have been used in the liturgy of the Supper, perhaps even from the very beginning (cf. F. Hahn, *The Titles of Jesus in Christology: Their History in Early Christianity*, 1969, 96), though this cannot be conclusively demonstrated. 1 Cor. 11:26 shows that from the outset the Lord's Supper looked forward in hope to the coming of the Lord; also the words of institution in Matt. 26:29 par. Mk. 14:25 point forward to this final accomplishment. The prayers associated with the Lord's Supper in the Didache (chs. 9 and 10) show how very much alive this hope remained even at a later period. Thus *maranatha* is to be understood, in the light of Rev. 22:20, as a prayer for the coming of the Lord in the sense of the last advent. This need not be the only thought, however, for as Jn. 14:18 speaks of the risen Lord coming to his own, *maranatha* may also include this idea within its scope, and such a prayer was in fact partially answered whenever the church celebrated the Lord's Supper. Furthermore, if the prayer did stem from the earliest church, the latter must inevitably have been familiar with prayer to Jesus, even at such an early date. *W. Mundle*

4. Several writers have seen the possibility of an alternative or complementary setting to that of the Lord's Supper (cf. E. Peterson, HEIS THEOS, 1926; C. F. D. Moule, "A Reconsideration of the Context of *Maranatha*", *NTS* 6, 1959–60, 307–10; W. Dunphy, "Maranatha: Development in Early Christianity", *Irish Theological Quarterly* 37, 1970, 294 ff.; M. Black, "The Maranatha Invocation and Jude 14, 15 (I Enoch 1:9)", in B. Lindars and S. S. Smalley, eds., *Christ and Spirit in the New Testament: In Honour of Charles Francis Digby Moule*, 1973, 189–96). It is suggested that in the first instance at least *maranatha* in 1 Cor. 16:22, Did. 10:6 and Rev. 22:20 was used to reinforce or sanction the curse or ban (→ Curse, art. *anathema*). The NT contexts in question are not that of the Lord's Supper but that of cursing, and the idea of invoking the Lord's Presence in the Lord's Supper belongs more to later church history than the NT period. Formal parallels with ancient pagan cursing formulae have been noted (cf. R. Wünsch, *Antike Fluchtafeln*, *Kleine Texte* 20, 1907, 13, 25; K. Preisendanz, *Papyri Graecae Magicae*, I, 1928, 89–90; A. Deissmann, *Light from the Ancient East*, 1927, 413 ff.; *CIG*, IV, 9303). The

Constitutiones Apostolorum 6, 26, 5 relates *maranatha* to the historical coming of Christ. But *maranatha* occurs in connection with the anathema in early church texts (*MPL*, LXXXVII, 1274; Tert., *De Pudicitia* 14, 13; Canon 75 of the Fourth Council of Toledo, A.D. 633). This would suggest that the original idea was an invocation that the Lord would soon come in judgment to redress wrong and establish right (cf. Moule, op. cit.).

In addition to these points Black draws attention to parallels with Jude 14 f.: "It was of these also that Enoch in the seventh generation from Adam prophesied saying, 'Behold, the Lord came with his holy myriads, to execute judgment on all, and to convict all the ungodly of all their deeds of ungodliness which they have committed in such an ungodly way, and of all the harsh things which ungodly sinners have spoken against him.'" This is a quotation from Enoch 1:9 and is exemplified not only in Gr.Enoch 1:9 and Eth.Enoch 1:3–9 but also in the Aram. fragments of 4QEn 1:4–9 found at Qumran (text in Black, op. cit., 193 f.; cf. also M. Black, "The Christological Use of the Old Testament in the New Testament", *NTS* 18, 1971–72, 10). Jude is giving a christological interpretation of Enoch. Unfortunately the opening words of the Aram. of v. 9 are lost in the Qumran text, but Black suggests that they would be verbally identical with the *maranatha* formula, i.e. *Mara' 'aṭa'* or *'aṭe'*. Although it could be argued that the similarity is purely coincidental, Black thinks that it is too great to be accidental. "If the possibility is conceded, then the original setting of the *maranatha* formula at 1 En. 1:9, where it refers to a divine judgment on the wicked, not only supports the Parousia reference in the New Testament but can also account for its use as a reinforcement of the *anathema*: no formula would lend itself more to the purpose of an imprecation or a ban. At the same time, it would be equally appropriate within a eucharistic setting, since the eucharist contains, as an integral element in its structure, the proclamation of the Lord's death 'until He come'" (op. cit., 195). Black himself prefers to take the original form of the words as a future perfect, the equivalent of a prophetic perfect: "'The Lord *will* (soon, surely) come' (i.e. at the *Parousia*)" (op. cit., 196). But the Gk. could be construed as an imperative or as a perfect. Black concludes: "perhaps the popularity of the formula was its ambiguity and hence flexibility: it could be fitted into different contexts, in the eucharist, as an imprecation, or as a confession ('The Lord has come')" (op. cit., 196).

Without wishing to question this general conclusion, attention may be drawn to one further passage. A. M. Hunter suggests that far from being a piece of imprecatory mumbo-jumbo, *maranatha* was probably the first Christian prayer looking back to Matt. 18:20: "For where two or three are gathered in my name, there am I in the midst of them." Hunter relates this to the Lord's Supper, looking back to the first Easter day, invoking the presence of the Lord (cf. Lk. 24:35; Acts 10:41) and beseeching the Lord to come in glory (*Exploring the New Testament*, 98; cf. Black, op. cit., 192). But the context in Matt. is patently not eucharistic, and is read into the verse rather than read out of it. On the other hand, it does explicitly mention discipline and disputes within the community (Matt. 18:15 ff.), binding and loosing (Matt. 18:18; → Bind; → Open, art. *kleis*, NT 3), and the promise: "if two of you agree on earth about anything they ask, it will be done for them by my Father in heaven" (Matt. 18:19). The *maranatha* might conceivably be used in such a situation to confirm such an agreement, especially in view of the presence promised in v. 20. The fact that *maranatha* is not mentioned in Matt. may itself be an indication of its origin in the early church, whereas Matt. 18:15–20 is presented as having its location in the ministry of Jesus. In any case, if there is an affinity here, it confirms the suggestion that the original context of *maranatha* concerns the coming of the Lord in judgment to redress wrong and establish right. It may be noted that the following verses in Matt. concern Jesus' answer to the question on forgiving up to seven times, followed by the parable of the two debtors (Matt. 18:21–35).

C. Brown

παρουσία

παρουσία (*parousia*), presence, appearing, coming, advent; πάρειμι (*pareimi*), be present, have come.

CL *pareimi* covers both the present tense idea of "being there" and the perfect idea of "having come". *parousia* means, on the one hand, presence (with certain effects following) or (in a more neutral sense) property, fortune, income, military strength; and, on the other hand, it means arrival, someone's coming in order to be present. Technically the noun is used for the arrival of a ruler a king, emperor, ruler, or even troops from the Ptolemaic period to the 2nd century A.D. Special payments in kind and taxes were exacted to defray the costs. In Greece a new era was reckoned from the *parousia* of Hadrian, and special advent coins were struck in various places to commemorate the *parousia* of an emperor. The corresponding Lat. term is *adventus*. The cities of Corinth and Patras struck advent coins com-, memorating the visit of Nero in whose reign Paul wrote to Corinth. They bear the inscriptions *Adventus Aug(usti) Cor(inthi)* and *Adventus Augusti* (cf. A. Deissmann *Light from the Ancient East*, 1911[2], 372 ff.). From this it is an easy step to speak of an appearing of the gods on men's behalf (cf. *Corp. Herm.* 1, 22: "my *parousia* will prove a help to them"; this being in keeping with the ideas of the Hellenistic mystery religions). Such a *parousia* is not thought of merely as future, but is experienced as a reality in the present. An inscription at Tegea combines the term with the deification of the emperor: "in the year 69 of the first *parousia* of the god Hadrian in Hellas" (*c.* A.D. 193; cf. Deissmann, op. cit., 377). This was approximately at the time when Christians were beginning to speak explicitly of the first *parousia* of Christ, as distinct from the second (cf. Justin, *Dial.* 14 and 52). For further instances see A. Oepke, *TDNT* V 859 ff.

OT The Greek translations of the OT use the vb. *pareimi* for seven different Heb. words, all of which mean to come, including *bô'*, the most common word for come (Num. 22:20; 1 Sam. 9:6; 2 Sam. 5:23; 13:35;1 Chr. 14:14; Joel 2:1; Isa. 30:13; Lam. 4:18). The noun *parousia* occurs in Neh. 2:6 *v.l.* (without Heb. equivalent); Jud. 10:18; 2 Macc. 8:12; 15:21; 3 Macc. 3:17. "The absence of the word from the LXX in the books originally written in Heb. may be explained by the fact that the Semite speaks more concretely" (A. Oepke, *TDNT* V 859). Nevertheless, the idea is there, for from the earliest times the OT speaks of the coming of God: God manifests himself in victory (Jdg. 5:4); he comes as king of the world (Exod. 15:18; Ps. 24:7 ff.; 95:3 f.), in dreams (Gen. 20:3), in his Spirit (Num. 24:2), with his hand (1 Ki. 18:46), in his word (2 Sam. 7:4) and at the end of the days

(Isa. 2:2 and passim; → *hēmera*). There are references to the coming of the anointed (Gen. 49:10?; Zech. 9:9 f.). In the Qumran texts, the appearance of various messiahs is predicted (1QS 9:10 f.). Important for the NT's view is the expectation of God in the Jewish apocalyptic texts (which, however, may have been worked over by Christian hands): "A king shall arise out of Judah and shall establish a new priesthood for all the Gentiles after the fashion of the Gentiles. And his appearing is greatly desired as a prophet of the Most High, of the seed of Abraham our father" (Test.Lev. 8:14 f.); "And by men of another race shall my kingdom be brought to an end, until the salvation of Israel shall come, [until the appearing of the God of righteousness] that Jacob may rest in peace" (Test.Jud. 22:2). There are also references to the coming of messiah: "when the Righteous One shall appear before the eyes of the righteous" (Eth.Enoch 38:2); "He will judge the secret things" (Eth.Enoch 49:4). By *parousia* Josephus means the presence of God in the Shekinah (*Ant.* 3, 8 and 202; 9, 55; 18, 284) which is revealed to his people and even to the pagan governor, Petronius. Oepke suggests that Josephus's rejection of apocalyptic was rabbinic and politically opportunist (*TDNT* V 864 f.). The prophecies of Dan. were applied by him in ways which avoided giving offence to the Romans (cf. *Ant.* 10, 209 f., 267 and 276; 12, 322; *War* 6, 313). Philo used *pareimi* frequently in a non-eschatological sense but not *parousia*. Hellenistic influences have all but obliterated a coming of Yahweh or the messiah. Only in *Praem.* 16, 91–97 does he refer to the coming man (cf. Num. 24:7) who will bring universal peace, and tame man and beast (*TDNT* V 864).

NT 1. (a) Paul uses the vb. *pareimi* with the meaning of to be present, though in 1 and 2 Cor. the vb. occurs only in the part. form *parōn*. The apostle distinguishes his personal, bodily absence (*apōn tō sōmati*) from his presence in spirit (*parōn de tō pneumati*) (1 Cor. 5:3); the word also refers to his presence in Corinth (2 Cor. 10:2, 11; 11:9; 13:2, 10) and among the Galatians (Gal. 4:18, 20). The same meaning is found in Jn. 11:28; Rev. 17:8. Lk. uses the vb. in the perfect sense (to have come), so a similar interpretation is conceivable also in the case of Acts 10:33; 24:19. In Col. 1:6 *parestin* is used without a personal subject: the gospel which has come to you. Similarly in Jn. 7:6 the time has not yet come (→ Time, art. *kairos*). The phrase *pros to paron* (Heb. 12:11) means for the moment, for the present (cf. Arndt, 629), and the vb. also occurs in its sense of to be available, to be at hand (Heb. 13:5; 2 Pet. 1:9, 12).

(b) The noun *parousia* denotes generally presence and arrival. Paul, however, is the only NT writer to use it in this way: he rejoices over the presence of Stephanas (1 Cor. 16:17); he is comforted by God through the arrival of Titus (2 Cor. 7:6 f.); he speaks of his coming to Philippi (Phil. 1:26; 2:12) and has to suffer the reproach of being weighty and strong in his letters, but weak and insignificant in his personal presence and speech (2 Cor. 10:10). (See on this R. W. Funk, "The Apostolic *Parousia*: Form and Significance", in W. R. Farmer, C. F. D. Moule and R. R. Niebuhr, eds., *Christian History and Interpretation: Studies Presented to John Knox*, 1967, 249–68; cf. also (a) above.)

2. In its special NT sense, *parousia* is intimately bound up with the development of NT eschatology. Jesus proclaimed the → kingdom of God as imminent and the *parousia* as having a decisive effect upon the present in that men are to live now in

the light of this coming event (cf. e.g. Mk. 3:27; Lk. 17:23 f.). Although the present and the future are viewed as a chronological succession, the future affects the present, not in the sense of being already realized and anticipated in the present, but in the sense that man makes his decisions as one who must give account at the imminent appearing of the kingdom of God. With Jesus' → death and → resurrection (or exaltation) the eschatological perspective is modified. The idea of the *parousia* now becomes bound up with the church's expectation of Christ's appearing at the end of the age (→ Son of God, art. *hyios tou anthrōpou*). Many scholars hold that at first the coming events were still regarded as imminent (cf. Paul), but later, as time went by without the *parousia* taking place it moved further and further into the future as far as the church was concerned, and eventually ran the risk of being abandoned altogether as an article of faith. Where the presence of Christ and the present experience of salvation are stressed (e.g. Gal. 2:20), the *parousia* may be relativized to some degree: its blessings are already being experienced here and now (cf. e.g. Jn. 6:39 ff.; 11:24, 26). Certainly, therefore, the delay of the *parousia* led to difficulties, but they were not so grave as to split the church asunder, simply because her confidence in Christ was even greater than her longing for his *parousia*, which, all were agreed, would come suddenly (cf. 1 Thess. 5:1 ff.; Lk. 17:23 f.). (For a survey of critical views see below.)

In the NT the term *parousia* is not frequent. It occurs 24 times, of which 14 are in Paul: Matt. 24:3, 27, 37, 39; 1 Cor. 15:23; 16:17; 2 Cor. 7:6 f.; 10:10; Phil. 1:26; 2:12; 1 Thess. 2:19; 3:13; 4:15; 5:23; 2 Thess. 2:1, 8 f.; Jas. 5:7 f.; 2 Pet. 1:16; 3:4, 12; 1 Jn. 2:28. Clearly some of these references refer to the apostle's *parousia* (see above 1 (a), (b)). Moreover, other terms are used to describe the *parousia* of Christ (→ *hēmera*; → Revelation, art. *epiphaneia*). "The term is Hellenistic. In essential content, however, it derives from the OT, Judaism, and primitive Christian thinking" (A. Oepke, *TDNT* V 866). It thus presupposes the Hellenizing of Jewish Christianity. Although from a religio-historical point of view the NT's *parousia* doctrine belongs to the general realm of apocalyptic, the NT is singularly lacking in the usual apocalyptic embellishments. This is because its emphasis falls upon the expected coming of Christ himself. Only Rev. belongs to the genre of apocalyptic books, though apocalyptic imagery was used by Jesus and Paul. The earliest NT passage which speaks of the *parousia* is the word of the Lord quoted by Paul in 1 Thess. 4:15: "For this we declare to you by the word of the Lord, that we who are alive, who are left until the coming of the Lord [*eis tēn parousian tou kyriou*], shall not precede those who have fallen asleep". The reference to "the word of the Lord" may be (i) an allusion to Matt. 24:30 f.; (ii) a quotation from an unknown saying now lost; (iii) a reference to a private revelation (cf. 2 Cor. 12:1 ff.; Gal. 1:12; Eph. 3:3; Acts 21:10 ff.); or (iv) a statement of what Paul believes to be in accord with the mind of Christ (cf. 1 Cor. 2:16; 7:10, 12) (A. L. Moore, *1 and 2 Thessalonians*, New Century Bible, 1969, 69). Here → resurrection and *parousia* are closely intertwined, for when the latter occurs no disadvantage will be suffered by those who have fallen asleep, and no advantage enjoyed by the living. 1 Cor. 15:23 takes up the same thought, emphasizing the fact that at that decisive moment Christ is Lord over all: "But each in his own order: Christ the first fruits, then at his coming [*en tē parousia autou*] those who belong to Christ." Paul regularly uses the prep. *en* before *parousia* when the noun occurs in its strictly theological sense; *eis* is found

900

only in 1 Thess. 4:15. The *parousia* will certainly involve different categories of people, but it does not follow that the apostle has in mind a double resurrection, an intervening millennial kingdom, or a systematic chronological sequence of eschatological events (cf. W. G. Kümmel, *Promise and Fulfilment, The Eschatological Message of Jesus, SBT* 23, 1961², 88–94; → Number, art. *chilias*). Paul breaks with traditional apocalyptic ideas by insisting that eschatology is already being worked out: believers are to live not in sadness but in hope (1 Thess. 4:13; 5:23). And although separated from the Thessalonian church through the efforts of → Satan, Paul can still describe this church as his "hope", "joy" and crown of boasting "before our Lord Jesus at his coming" (1 Thess. 2:18, 19). 2 Thess. clearly has another situation in view. There is patent tension between the presence of Christ experienced here and now and the (Jewish-apocalyptic) *parousia* at some future date (2 Thess. 2:2). Evidently some claimed that "the day of the Lord has come", purporting to have relations or communications from Paul to this effect (2 Thess. 2:2). Some made it an excuse for idleness to which Paul replied: "For even when we were with you, we gave you this command: If anyone will not work, let him not eat" (2 Thess. 3:10). The epistle attacks those who claimed present experience of events which in reality were still future. This leads Paul to give a vehement warning of Satan and the *parousia* of the lawless one which will take place before the *parousia* of Christ. "For the mystery of lawlessness is already at work; only he who now restrains it will do so until he is out of the way. And then the lawless one will be revealed, and the Lord Jesus will slay him with the breath of his mouth and destroy him by his appearing and his coming [*tē epiphaneia tēs parousias autou*] The coming [*parousia*] of the lawless one by the activity of Satan will be with all power and with pretended signs and wonders" (2 Thess. 2:7 ff.; → Antichrist; → Satan; → Miracle, Sign).

3. The delay in Christ's appearing led men to question whether that day would in fact ever come. In this situation Jas. 5:7 f. calls for patience: "Be patient [*makrothymēsate*], therefore, brethren, until the coming of the Lord (*heōs tēs parousias tou kyriou*]. Behold, the farmer waits for the precious fruit of the earth, being patient over it until it receives the early and the late rain. You also be patient [*makrothymēsate*]. Establish your hearts, for the coming of the Lord is at hand [*hoti hē parousia tou kyriou ēngiken*]" (→ Patience, art. *makrothymia*). In 2 Pet. 1:16 and 3:4 ff. believers are urged to go on especting the *parousia* despite the fact that so far nothing has happened. Matt. presents a dialectical tension. On the one hand, Jesus is present whenever his church assembles (Matt. 18:20), and with his people to the end of the age as they spread the gospel (28:20). On the other hand, the coming of the → Son of man is still future (24:39), its date being unknown to any man (v. 36); it will occur suddenly and at a time when men are living entirely for the present (vv. 27, 37 f.). These two elements are so starkly juxtaposed in 1 Jn. 2:28 that some have attempted to solve the difficulty in literary-critical fashion, by assigning the present and the future elements to two different strata.

G. Braumann

The Parousia and Eschatology in the NT

The purpose of this note is to draw attention to various areas of discussion in view of the eschatological programmes set out in certain NT passages and the place of the parousia in them, whether or not the Gk. word *parousia* is actually used.

1. *Trends in NT Criticism.* (a) Consistent Eschatology. The term consistent eschatology is applied to the idea that Jesus expected the establishment of the kingdom of God in his own lifetime, brought about by his own ministry. The corollary of this thesis is that the idea of a second coming is the invention of the primitive church. In *The Quest of the Historical Jesus: A Critical Study of its Progress from Reimarus to Wrede*, (1910) 1954[3], Albert Schweitzer credited H. S. Reimarus (1694–1768) with being the initiator of the modern quest of the historical Jesus. (This latter point was inaccurate, as many of Reimarus's ideas were indebted to the English Deists, but this lies outside our present concern.) In a series of articles published anonymously and posthumously by G. E. Lessing as *Fragments of an Unknown Author* Reimarus had argued that Jesus expected that his own preaching would bring about the kingdom of God as a quasi-political reality. But Jesus' hopes failed to find the appropriate response and he was executed. The disciples, however, after having overcome their original shock, put out the story that Jesus had risen from the dead and that his teaching actually referred to a second coming, when the kingdom would be finally established. Their preaching won acceptance, and in the meantime no one has noticed that the parousia has failed to materialize. Nevertheless, Christianity is built upon a gigantic fraud (cf. H. S. Reimarus, *The Goal of Jesus and his Disciples*, tr. G. W. Buchanan, 1970; and *Fragments*, ed. C. H. Talbert and tr. R. S. Fraser, 1971). Schweitzer himself hailed Reimarus's work as "perhaps the most splendid achievement in the whole course of the historical investigation of the life of Jesus, for he was the first to grasp the fact that the world of thought in which Jesus moved was essentially eschatological" (op. cit., 23). Indeed, in view of its neglect of eschatology the whole movement of theology down to Johannes Weiss's *Jesus' Proclamation of the Kingdom of God* (1892; ET ed. R. H. Hiers and D. L. Holland, 1971) appeared to Schweitzer to be retrograde. For in the meantime the main emphasis of liberal Protestant theology had been on Jesus as a teacher of timeless moral truths, divorced from their historical background.

Schweitzer's own position was not dissimilar to that of Reimarus (in addition to the final chapter of *The Quest of the Historical Jesus* see also *The Mystery of the Kingdom of God* [1910] ET 1914; *Paul and his Interpreters: A Critical History*, 1912; *The Mysticism of Paul the Apostle*, 1931; and *The Kingdom of God and Primitive Christianity*, 1968). Jesus believed himself to be the messiah-designate and regarded John the Baptist as Elijah preparing men for him and the kingdom. The mission of the twelve was a last effort to bring about the kingdom. When this failed to materialize Jesus saw that only through his own affliction would the kingdom dawn. The entry into Jerusalem was a "funeral march to victory", and Jesus died expecting the dawning of the kingdom and his own coming as messiah. But here Jesus proved to be wrong, though this did not prevent the rise of false expectations. Paul took over the idea, transforming it into a doctrine of overlapping aeons in which the present world order would continue, though its relevance would be lost to those who are "in Christ". NT ethics are interim ethics. As even the second parousia failed to materialize the eschatological aspect of Christianity was Hellenized and receded into the background. It may be noted in all this that, for all Schweitzer's stress on the importance of eschatology for understanding the NT, it does not play any significant part in in his own beliefs and teaching, at any rate in the NT sense. For Schweitzer himself reverence for life became the dominant theme.

Schweitzer's thesis has been taken up by F. Buri in *Die Bedeutung der neutesta-mentlichen Eschatologie für die neuere protestantische Theologie*, 1934, who sought to interpret eschatology existentially. For us the ultimate concern must not be the programme of future world events but the will for life fulfilment in the present. In *The Formation of Christian Dogma*, 1957, Martin Werner also built upon the foundations laid by Schweitzer. Whereas Jesus' outlook was essentially that of late Jewish apocalyptic, which in turn affected that of Paul and the other apostles, the delay of the parousia created a great crisis for the church. This led to the falling away of many and the rise of heretics, and ultimately to the abandonment of the old eschatological understanding of the gospel. The vacuum was filled in Christian belief by its restatement in terms of Jesus' person and work which were understood in non-eschatological categories.

Schweitzer's position has been sharply criticized on the grounds of defective methodology and interpretation (cf. A. L. Moore, *The Parousia in the New Testament, Supplements to NovT* 13, 1966, 38–48). From the standpoint of methodology it raises the questions (i) whether the criterion Schweitzer used to ascertain the teaching of Jesus is necessary; (ii) whether his particular understanding of eschatology is justified in view of the complexity of thought in contemporary Judaism; and (iii) whether such a criterion can allow the possibility of any *sui generis* elements in the life and work of Jesus. Although Schweitzer was right in pointing out that eschatology had been a neglected factor in much previous study of the Gospels, his own interpretation of the eschatology of Jesus was not free from the charge of arbitrariness. As a matter of fact, the work of the messiah is never represented in apocalyptic writings as forcing in the kingdom. Moreover, the idea of a secret life of humiliation prior to exaltation is generally lacking (cf. Moore, op. cit., 41). The various elements in the life of Jesus, as depicted in the Gospels, cannot be subsumed under the category of apocalyptic eschatology as the single key to the whole.

Schweitzer and Werner claim that Paul understood Jesus' death and resurrection as the initiation of the end of the world, and even that he saw Jesus' resurrection as the literal beginning of the general resurrection. Moore counters this by suggesting that, while Paul regarded the speedy return of Christ a real possibility, he nowhere maintained it as certain or necessary either in his early or later epistles (op. cit., 46; cf. 108 ff. where he discusses 1 Thess. 4:13–18; 2 Thess. 1:5–12; 2:1–15; 1 Cor. 7; and 15; 2 Cor. 5:1–10; Rom. 13; and 15:19, 23; Phil. 3:20; 4:5). Consistent eschatology posits that Christianity is founded upon a mistaken idea which was not about some minor detail but about the central issue of the primitive church's witness. But the mistaken expectation of apocalyptic as Schweitzer understood it "cannot do justice to the soteriological understanding of Jesus' life and death which we find throughout the New Testament" (Moore, op. cit., 48).

(b) The Little Apocalypse Theory. A view which is diametrically opposed to that of Schweitzer is that propounded by T. Colani in *Jésus-Christ et les Croyances Messianiques de son Temps*, 1864, which is known as the Little Apocalypse theory. Colani argued that there was no connection at all between the teaching of Jesus and Jewish messianism. The Jewish messiah had always been a purely temporal figure and Jewish hopes had always been temporal and political. Jesus did not

903

proclaim either an eschatological kingdom or himself as the awaited messiah. He was a simple, humble teacher for whom the kingdom was a present reality identical with his teaching and life-style. Mk. 13:5–31 is a Jewish Christian interpolation representing views which were remote from Jesus' own position. The real answer to the disciples' question about the destruction of the temple (v. 4) is actually given in v. 32 ("But of that day or that hour no one knows, not even the angels in heaven, nor the Son, but only the Father"). The intervening material, the Little Apocalypse, is a tract written at a time of persecution before the fall of Jerusalem in A.D. 70. It is this teaching which underlies the parallels in Matt. 24 and Lk. 17 and 21. For discussion of Colani and his influence see G. R. Beasley-Murray, *Jesus and the Future: An Examination of the Criticism of the Eschatological Discourse, Mark 13, with Special Reference to the Little Apocalypse Theory*, 1954; cf. also the same writer's *A Commentary on Mark 13*, 1957. For surveys of the history of interpretation of the kingdom see G. Lundström, *The Kingdom of God in the Teaching of Jesus: A History of Interpretation from the Last Decades of the Nineteenth Century to the Present Day*, 1963; and N. Perrin, *The Kingdom of God in the Teaching of Jesus*, 1963.

Colani's successors included C. Weizsäcker, W. Weiffenbach, G. C. B. Pünjer, H. H. Wendt, W. Baldensperger and E. Wending. The type of approach which Colani represented was shared by many who were not directly indebted to him. Whereas Colani saw a single document behind the Little Apocalypse others thought of it more in terms of a tradition. The essential feature was alien eschatological teaching incorporated into that of Jesus and in this sense the position was adopted in some form or other by B. H. Streeter, R. H. Charles, E. Meyer, F. Hauck, R. Bultmann and G. Hölscher. Colani himself divided the Apocalypse into three sections: the beginning of the birth pangs in the form of false prophets, wars and persecutions (Mk. 13:5–13); the terrible distress that will precede the end (Mk. 13:14–23); and the end (*telos*) of events (Mk. 13:24–31). Whilst Colani attributed the whole discourse to extraneous sources, others have seen some elements of Christian exhortation (e.g. vv. 9–13, 21 ff., 28 ff.) which could go back to Jesus.

(c) Realized Eschatology. The leading exponent of realized eschatology is C. H. Dodd who argued his position in a number of works including *The Parables of the Kingdom*, 1936[2]; *The Apostolic Preaching and its Developments*, 1936; *History and the Gospel*, 1938; *The Coming of Christ*, 1952; *The Interpretation of the Fourth Gospel*, 1953; *Historical Tradition in the Fourth Gospel*, 1963; *The Founder of Christianity*, 1970; and various articles reprinted in *New Testament Studies*, 1953, and *More New Testament Studies*, 1968. (For discussion see F. F. Bruce, "C. H. Dodd", in P. E. Hughes, ed., *Creative Minds in Contemporary Theology*, 1966, 1969[2], 239–69; N. Q. Hamilton, "C. H. Dodd's Realised Eschatology" in *The Holy Spirit and Eschatology in Paul, SJT Occasional Papers* 6, 1957, 53–70; J. A. T. Robinson, "Theologians of our Time: XII. C. H. Dodd", *ExpT* 75, 1963–64, 100 ff., reprinted in A. W. and E. Hastings, eds., *Theologians of Our Time*, 1966, 40–46; and A. L. Moore, op. cit., 49–66.) Dodd used the phrase "realized eschatology" to denote the fact that the burden of Jesus' preaching especially in the parables was that the kingdom of God had come (*The Parables of the Kingdom*, 198, cf. 44). This demands a response. The traditional Jewish eschatological scheme is dislocated by the advent of Jesus: "The *eschaton* has moved from the

904

future to the present, from the sphere of expectation into that of realized experience" (op. cit., 50). Eschatology means no longer the last point in time; it refers rather to "the absolute order" (op. cit., 107). The eschatological elements in the teaching of Jesus are thus to be interpreted in this sense. However, the early church misinterpreted a good deal along the lines of Jewish literalism (*The Apostolic Preaching*, 80 ff., 92; cf. 64 ff.). Thus, whereas Jesus spoke of the one single event of the coming of the Son of man, "they made a distinction between two events, one past, His resurrection from the dead, and one future, His coming on the clouds" (op. cit., 101). Paul himself, however, underwent a considerable spiritual and psychological development in which the initial apocalyptic dualism of 1 and 2 Thess. and 1 Cor. 15 was transcended. Thereafter there was a growing emphasis on eternal life here and now in communion with Christ, and the earlier world-denial gave place to a more positive evaluation of political institutions (Rom. 13), the goodness of man (Rom. 2:14 f.) and the family (Col. 3:18 f.; Eph. 5:21–33) (*New Testament Studies*, 80 ff., 109–118). The Fourth Gospel represents the ultimate stage of this development, in which popular apocalyptic eschatology is replaced and thus we come back to the original intentions of Jesus (*The Interpretation of the Fourth Gospel*, 395, 406).

Another writer who finds the idea of a parousia inimical to the original teaching of Jesus is T. F. Glasson in *The Second Advent: The Origin of the New Testament Doctrine*, (1945) 1947[2]. He claims that the idea is absent from the OT which was the most important source of Jesus' teaching and from apocalyptic which is largely concerned with an earthly king. But the idea arose because of unfulfilled prophecies and the Antichrist legend was imported into Christianity giving rise to imminent expectation and millenarianism. Another viewpoint is that of J. A. T. Robinson in *In the End God . . .*, (1950) 1968[2]; "The Most Primitive Christology of All?", *JTS* New Series 7, 1956, 177–89; reprinted in *Twelve New Testament Studies*, SBT 34, 1962, 139–53; and *Jesus and His Coming: The Emergence of a Doctrine*, 1957. Jesus himself did not expect to return in glory. Rather he taught that God was performing a decisive act which was stated in terms of vindication and visitation, neither of which involve a parousia. The temporal chronological element was introduced through a confusion of two types of christological teaching, one of which affirmed that Christ has come and the other that he will come. These were never fully reconciled. However, the Fourth Gospel does achieve a synthesis which gives the parousia its proper meaning as the "mutual indwelling of Jesus and the disciples in love" (*Jesus and His Coming*, 178).

Dodd's method has been criticized in respect of his handling of the parables, in that he selects those passages which stress the decisive moment in the present as representing the true meaning of the parables and the authentic teaching of Jesus, and discounts other teaching as secondary additions. Similarly he posits a *Sitz im Leben* for the parables in the light of what he conceives to be their clear meaning (cf. especially op. cit., 111–53), a procedure which requires their respective life settings to have been rapidly forgotten in their transmission and commitment to writing. Glasson's claim that Jesus made no use of apocalyptic (op. cit., 63 ff.) cannot be sustained, and few scholars would deny that terms like the Son of man are derived at least in part from Dan. or Enoch. The more moderate representatives of realized eschatology admit the presence of apocalyptic elements in the teaching of Jesus, but are obliged to say that it applies only to the form and not to the meaning. Moore sees in realized eschatology an implicit form of demythologizing which has a built-in apologetic motif (op. cit., 56 ff.). It presents the eschatological expectations of the NT as resting upon a mistake, but shifts the onus for this from Jesus to the early church in the interests of rescuing Jesus from the charge of being a misguided, apocalyptic enthusiast.

Moore concludes his review of realized eschatology by pointing out that this school of thought "rightly recognizes that the New Testament emphatically declares that the Kingdom of God has come and is not 'wholly futurist'. However, this 'realization' is connected in the New Testament directly with the person and work of Christ and therefore with the lowliness and hiddenness characteristic of his ministry. It therefore carries the promise of future fulfilment, indeed demands future fulfilment" (op. cit., 63). It is perhaps not without some significance that Dodd himself somewhat modified his position by agreeing that, instead of speaking about "realized eschatology", it would be more appropriate to speak of "an eschatology that is in process of realization" (cf. the Ger. of J. Jeremias, "eine sich realisierende Eschatologie", noted in *The Interpretation of the Fourth Gospel*, 447; and J. Jeremias *The Parables of Jesus*, 1963², 230; cf. also G. Florovsky's phrase "inaugurated eschatology" noted by Dodd, ad loc.).

(d) Bultmann and Demythologizing. Rudolf Bultmann's programme of demythologizing the NT kerygma and restating it in existential terms, coupled with his radical form criticism, also entails a form of realized eschatology. In his epoch-making essay of 1941 on "New Testament and Mythology" Bultmann claimed that the NT not only contained myths, but that its thought-forms were essentially mythological, and therefore it should be demythologized in order to let the gospel speak to man today (for text and discussions see H.-W. Bartsch, ed., *Kerygma and and Myth: A Theological Debate*, I–II combined volume containing an enlarged bibliography, 1972; cf. also R. Bultmann, *Jesus Christ and Mythology*, 1960; A. L. Moore, op. cit., 67–79; N. Q. Hamilton, op. cit., 71–82; and C. Brown, ed., *History, Criticism and Faith*, 1976; → Myth). The myths, which derive from Jewish apocalyptic and gnosticism and belong to an obsolete pre-scientific world view, must be demythologized, not indeed to remove all offence but to allow the true offence of the gospel to confront men today. This alone will give men the possibility of understanding themselves and freeing them from the cares of material existence. In place of an apocalyptic programme of future external events, Bultmann prefers to say that every instant is eschatological, or rather that "every instant has the possibility of being an eschatological instant and in Christian faith this possibility is realised" (*History and Eschatology: The Presence of Eternity*, Gifford Lectures for 1955, 1957, 154). This is the meaning of eternity breaking into time, and of God breaking into history. "*The meaning of history always lies in the present*, and when the present is conceived as the eschatological present by Christian faith the meaning of history is realised. . . . In every moment slumbers the possibility of being the eschatological moment. You must awaken it" (ibid., 155). Alongside this we may put the statement: "The New Testament understanding of the history of Jesus as eschatological event is not rightly conceived either in the conception of Jesus as the centre of history, or in sacramentalism. Both are solutions of the embarrassment into which the Christian community was brought by the non-appearance of the

906

Parousia. The true solution of the problem lies in the thought of Paul and John, namely, as the idea that Christ is the ever present, or ever-becoming event (i.e. the eschatological event): the 'now' gets its eschatological character by the encounter with Christ or with the Word which proclaims Him, because in this encounter with Him the world and its history comes to its end and the believer becomes free from the world in becoming a new creature" ("History and Eschatology in the New Testament", *NTS* 1, 1954–55, 15).

An adequate critique of Bultmann's position would take us far beyond the scope of the present survey and would involve an appraisal of the complex questions of → myth, language and hermeneutics (→ Explain). It would also require a philosophical discussion of the nature of objectivity in relation to the concept of God, and an examination of the methods and sceptical results of Bultmann's *History of the Synoptic Tradition*, 1968[2] which gives his critical evaluation of the picture of Jesus presented by the Gospels. It must suffice here to pose the questions: What did Jesus himself say? How are we to interpret the apocalyptic language of the NT? How did the early church understand → time?

(e) Cullmann and Salvation History. Oscar Cullmann is a NT scholar whose views often stand in direct contradiction to Bultmann's. Of direct bearing on the question of the parousia are his *Christ and Time: The Primitive Christian Conception of Time and History*, 1951; "The Return of Christ", in *The Early Church*, 1956, 141–62; *The Christology of the New Testament*, 1959; and *Salvation in History*, 1967 (for further discussion and bibliography see D. H. Wallace, "Oscar Cullmann", in P. E. Hughes, ed., op. cit., 163–202; and J. J. Vincent, "Oscar Cullmann", in A. W. Hastings and E. Hastings, op. cit., 112–22). For Cullmann the "Christ event" is the mid-point (qualitatively speaking) in the ages of history. Eschatology embraces all the saving events beginning with the incarnation and concluding with the parousia. He illustrates this with the D-Day and V-Day terminology of the Second World War: "the decisive battle has already been won. But the war continues until a certain, though not as yet definite, Victory Day when the weapons will at last be still. The decisive battle would be Christ's death and resurrection, and Victory Day his *parousia*" (*Salvation in History*, 44). The church exists in the tension between these two historical events.

For his restatement of what is essentially a traditional understanding of the NT Cullmann has been attacked by members of the Bultmann school. Thus E. Fuchs adopted an existential approach to time in his *Studies of the Historical Jesus*, SBT 42, 1964, and P. Vielhauer has made the author of Acts responsible for the origin of the "early Catholic" idea of salvation history ("Zum 'Paulinismus' der Apostelgechichte", *EvT* 10, 1950–51, 1–15; ET "On the 'Paulinism' of Acts", in L. E. Keck and J. L. Martyn, eds., *Studies in Luke-Acts*, 1968, 33–50). What Cullmann regarded as the essence of the NT Hans Conzelmann claimed to be the special creation of Luke in *The Theology of St Luke*, 1960 (the original German title *Die Mitte der Zeit*, the mid-point of time, draws attention to the emphasis on Lk.'s conception of time). Conzelmann claimed that with his salvation history Lk. effectively abandoned the offence of the unfulfilled parousia. He achieved this by a scheme of periods which shifts the emphasis into the past and present, and substitutes the activity of the Holy Spirit for the kingdom to come. Whereas Cullmann himself sees Conzelmann's work as to some extent complementing his own (ibid., 46),

Conzelmann sees it as the antithesis. For it involves the abandonment of Jesus' eschatology in favour of an existential one, comparable with that of Bultmann. In *Das Problem der Parusieverzögerung in den synoptischen Evangelien und in der Apostelgeschichte, BZNW* 22, (1957) 1960², E. Grässer took this even further, arguing that Lk. was not as original in this as might appear. For the same process can be detected not only in the Synoptic Gospels but also in the sources that they used.

To all this Cullmann replies that the concept of salvation history begins with Jesus himself. He maintains that it is arbitrary to classify as genuine only those sayings which have to do with present salvation, and reject those which have to do with future salvation (*Salvation in History*, 191). His detailed examination of teaching in the Gospels leads to the statement: "We conclude that in Jesus' preaching the present which extends beyond his death is *already the end*. But this does not in any way justify asserting that Jesus is the end of salvation history. *The end time is, on the contrary, understood as belonging completely to salvation history, since each of its periods, short as they may be, has its own significance and is distinguished from others*" (op. cit., 230). Cullmann allows that there are differences among the various books of the NT on the subject of the *nearness of the end*, but none over the *tensions* between the "already" and the "not yet". "*The inmost essence of the New Testament messages is lost, not with the abandonment of the idea of a near end, but with the abandonment of salvation history*" (op. cit., 247).

(f) The Parousia in Recent Systematic Theology. A detailed examination of the parousia in systematic theology lies outside the scope of this volume. But attention may be drawn to the writings of Wolfhart Pannenberg and Jürgen Moltmann. To some extent Pannenberg represents a reaction to the theologies of the Word (whether that of Barth or of Bultmann) and to the idea of salvation history (cf. *Jesus – God and Man*, 1968; *Basic Questions in Theology*, I–III, 1970–73; W. Pannenberg, ed., *Revelation as History*, 1969; J. M. Robinson and J. B. Cobb, eds., *Theology as History, New Frontiers in Theology* III, 1967, including Pannenberg's "Focal Essay: The Revelation of God in Jesus of Nazareth", 101–33; cf. also A. D. Galloway, *Wolfhart Pannenberg*, 1973; and E. F. Tupper, *The Theology of Wolfhart Pannenberg*, 1974). Whereas Barth stresses revelation through the Word of God, Jesus Christ, through the Scriptures and Bultmann stresses existential illumination through demythologized kerygma, Pannenberg sees history as the revelation of God. But it is not the narrow ribbon of salvation history that is the sole revelation; rather it is universal history to which the event of Jesus Christ provides the key. "The historical event of revelation cannot be thought of in an outward way as revealing the essence of God. It is not so much the course of history as it is the end of history that is at one with the essence of God. But insofar as the end presupposes the course of history, because it is the perfection of it, then also the course of history belongs in essence to the revelation of God, for history receives its unity from its goal" (*Revelation as History*, 133). The resurrection of Jesus has the character of a proleptic revelation of this final goal. "Now the history of the whole is only visible when one stands at its end. Until then, the future always remains as something beyond calculation. And, only in the sense that the perfection of history has already been inaugurated in Jesus Christ is God finally and fully revealed in the fate of Jesus. With the resurrection of Jesus, the end of history has already occurred, although it does not strike us in this way. It is through the resurrection that the God of Israel has substantiated his deity in an ultimate way and is now manifest as the God of all men" (op. cit., 142). The resurrection, therefore, posits the parousia. "The ultimate divine confirmation of Jesus will take place only in the occurrence of his return. Only then will the revelation of God in Jesus become manifest in its ultimate, irresistible glory. When we speak today of God's revelation in Jesus and of his exaltation accomplished in the resurrection from the dead, our statements always contain a proleptic element. The fulfilment, which had begun for the disciples, which was almost in their grasp, in the appearances of the resurrected Lord, has become promise once again for us" (*Jesus – God and Man*, 108).

Jürgen Moltmann has also sought to redress the inadequate eschatological perspectives of twentieth-century theology (cf. *Theology of Hope: On the Ground and Implications of a Christian Theology*, 1967; *Hope and Planning*, 1971; *Theology and Joy*, 1973; *The Crucified God: The Cross of Christ as the Foundation and Criticism of Christian Theology*, 1974; see also E. H. Cousins, ed., *Hope and the Future of Man*, 1973; M. D. Meeks, *Origins of the Theology of Hope*, 1974; and E. F. Tupper, op. cit., 257–61 for a brief comparison with Pannenberg). Moltmann claims that *parousia* does not mean the return of someone but "imminent arrival". It can also mean presence, in the sense of an awaited presence. "The parousia of Christ is a different thing from a reality that is experienced now and given now. As compared with what can now be experienced, it brings something new. Yet it is not for that reason totally separate from the reality which we can now experience and have now to live in, but, as the future that is really outstanding, it works upon the present by waking hopes and establishing resistance. The *eschaton* of the parousia of Christ, as a result of its eschatological promise, causes the present that can be experienced at any given moment to become historic by breaking away from the past and breaking out towards the things that are to come. . . . The Christian hope expects from the future of Christ not only unveiling, but also final fulfilment. The latter is to bring the redeeming of the promise which the cross and resurrection of Christ contains for his own and for the world" (*Theology of Hope*, 227 f.). Thus for Pannenberg and for Moltmann, however they understand its particularities, the parousia is not the misconceived application of apocalyptic ideas to a non-eschatological Jesus. It is implicit in Christ and in the structure of Christian hope for the world.

2. *The Parousia in the Theology of the New Testament Writings.* (a) Mk. 13 and the Synoptic Gospels. G. R. Beasley-Murray's *Jesus and the Future* reviews the debate on Mk. 13 to the time of publication in 1954. For discussion since then see K. Grayston, "The Study of Mark XIII", *BJRL* 56, 1973–74, 371–87; and D. Wenham, "Recent Study of Mark 13", *TSF Bulletin* 71, 1975, 8–15, and 72, 1975, 1–9.

Beasley-Murray reviews six types of approach to the vindication of the discourse in Mk. 13. (i) One way of doing this is to take the prophecy concerning Jerusalem as a prefiguration of the end (op. cit., 114 f.). This view was taken by J. Neander in *The Life of Jesus Christ in its Historical Connection and Historical Development*, (1837; ET from 4th ed. 1853). Similarly A. Plummer saw the day of judgment symbolized in the judgment on the guilty city (*Commentary on the Gospel according to St. Matthew*, 1909, 328; cf. N. Geldenhuys, *Commentary on the Gospel of*

Luke, NLC, 1950, 523, 533). Beasley-Murray comments: "This view proceeds from an act of faith; it can neither be demonstrated nor denied from other statements in the Gospels. Its major defect is the presupposition that the discourse was intended to cater for two events separated by a long stretch of time" (op. cit., 115). (ii) A second view is that the discourse combines two prophecies of Jesus into one (op. cit., 115–27; cf. F. Godet, *A Commentary on the Gospel of Luke*, ET from 2nd French edition of 1870; W. Beyschlag, *New Testament Theology*, 1891; B. Weiss, *Die Evangelien des Markus und Lukas, KEK*, 1878; J. Weiss, *Jesus' Proclamation of the Kingdom of God*, [1892] ET 1971). In the one Jesus looked forward to the impending fall of Jerusalem; in the other to the end at a time unknown. (ii) A third view sees the discourse as a continuous description of the Christian era (op. cit., 127–31; cf. T. Zahn, *Introduction to the New Testament*, II, 1909). Mk. 13:30 declares: "Truly, I say to you, this generation will not pass away before all these things [*tauta panta*] take place." On this interpretation *tauta panta* were only the beginning, and the end would not come until the gospel had been preached throughout the world. Against this Beasley-Murray adduces Mk. 9:1 and Matt. 10:23 which refer to the imminent coming of the Son of man. This he finds irreconcilable with the apparently prolonged ongoing events of much of Mk. 13. (iv) A fourth view is the application of "Prophetic Perspective" which brings together events which in fact may be widely separated, as in a view of a mountain range in which the peaks appear to be close together (op. cit., 131–141; cf. J. A. Bengel, *Gnomon*, I, ET 1857, 417, 426; C. A. Briggs, *Messianic Prophecy*, 1886; *The Messiah of the Gospels*, 1984; *The Messiah of the Apostles*, 1895; P. Schwarzkopf, *Die Weissagungen Jesu Christi, von seinem Tode, seiner Auferstehung und Wiederkunft und ihre Erfüllung* 1895; C. H. Turner in C. Gore, H. L. Goudge and A. Guillaume, eds., *A New Commentary on Holy Scripture*, 1928, 102). Turner took the ignorance which Jesus attributed to himself (v. 32) to imply that Jesus was mistaken about the time-scale of events. (v) A fifth view suggests that the discourse is a composition of isolated fragments (op. cit., 141–46; cf. D. E. Haupt, *Die eschatologischen Aussagen Jesu in den synoptischen Evangelien*, 1895; F. C. Burkitt, *Jesus Christ: An Historical Outline*, 49 ff. (vi) Finally Beasley-Murray reviews works since about 1930 which move towards a synthesis (op. cit., 146–67). The works include G. Gloege, *Gottes Reich und Kirche im Neuen Testament*, 1929; H. D. Wendland, *Die Eschatologie des Reiches Gottes bei Jesu*, 1931; F. Busch, *Zum Verständnis der synoptischen Eschatologie. Markus 13 neu untersucht*, 1938; C. C. Torrey, *Documents of the Primitive Church*, 1941; C. J. Cadoux, *The Historic Mission of Jesus*, 1941; H. H. Rowley, *The Relevance of Apocalyptic*, 1944; P. Althaus, *Die letzten Dinge*, 1949[5]; J. Schniewind, *Das Evangelium nach Markus, NTD*, 1949[5], and *Das Evangelium nach Matthäus, NTD*, 1950[5]; and A. Farrer, *A Study of St. Mark*, 1951. The consensus of opinion is that Jesus did expect a near end and that Mk. 13 is to some extent composite. But the main thrust of the teaching is to bring home to people the significance of the present.

Beasley-Murray himself sees no contradiction between the need for watchfulness and the suddenness of the end. But he insists that *genea* (v. 30) must mean → generation (op. cit., 260 f.). Jesus was thus mistaken in his prophetic time-scale, though this is mitigated by v. 32, and it does not undermine Jesus' authority as a teacher. Although some sayings may have been added (e.g. vv. 15 f.), Beasley-Murray does not think that the discourse as a whole is a composite work. Although it shares a common OT background with Jewish writings, the apocalyptic in the discourse omits a great deal of typical Jewish apocalyptic (op. cit., 220–26). The parousia is in fact integral not only to the teaching of Jesus but to his life and death. "If it is true, as William Manson wrote, 'We do not approach the parousia prediction rightly unless we come to it by way of Gethsemane and Calvary', the reverse is also true: it requires the vindication of the parousia to set Gethsemane and Calvary in their right context" (op. cit., 220; cf. W. Manson, *Christ's View of the Kingdom of God*, 1918, 163).

Beasley-Murray inclines to the view that Matt. (cf. ch. 24) and Lk. (cf. ch. 21) had independent access to the teaching that occurs in Mk. 13 (op. cit., 226–30). He also suggests that Paul was also familiar with it (op. cit., 232 ff.; cf. 1 Thess. 4:15 ff. = Mk. 13:26 f., Matt. 24:31; 1 Thess. 5:1–5 = Mk. 13:32 f., Lk. 21:24–35; 1 Thess. 5:6 ff. = Mk. 13:35 f., cf. 33, 37; 1 Thess. 5:4–10 = Mk. 13:22; 2 Thess. 1:3 ff. = Mk. 13:9–13; 2 Thess. 1:6–10 = Mk. 13:16 f.; 2 Thess. 1:11 f. = Lk. 21:36; 2 Thess. 2:1 f. = Mk. 13:26 f.; 2 Thess. 2:3 = Mk. 13:5, Matt. 24:12; 2 Thess. 2:4 ff. = Mk. 13:14; 2 Thess. 2:7 = Matt. 24:12; 2 Thess. 2:8–12 = Mk. 13:22, cf. Lk. 24:11, Mk. 1:36; 2 Thess. 2:13 = Mk. 13:27, cf. Lk. 21:8; 2 Thess. 2:15 = Mk. 13:23, cf. 31). There are also affinities with Jn. in the shape of "the thought of the disciples witnessing to a hostile world by the aid of the Holy Spirit amidst acute suffering, in the period between the death and resurrection of Jesus and the parousia. If the keynote of Jn. 13–17 is 'In the world you have tribulation, but be of good cheer, *I have overcome the world*' (16.33), in Mk. 13 the stress is on the *future* victory. Both these characteristic emphases of the gospels are needed" (op. cit., 238). Similarly the theme of wars, international strife, famine, pestilence, persecutions, earthquakes and heavenly portents which are found in Rev. 6 all occur in Mk. 13, Matt. 24 and Lk. 21, though not necessarily in that order (op. cit., 238 ff.).

In view of its independent use by Paul and various other factors, Beasley-Murray suggests that if the material existed in documentary form it might even be "the most ancient document of Christianity" (op. cit., 246). He rejects the case that the discourse contains traces of the LXX, and holds that there are positive indications that the discourse was Aramaic in origin, having a quasi-poetic structure. Although this does not automatically authenticate the discourse, it would be consonant with tracing it back to Jesus himself. If the unity of these sayings with other known sayings of Jesus has been shown, "the Aramaic background of the discourse will confirm our belief that the discourse is authentic" (op. cit., 250).

W. G. Kümmel is among those who think that Mk. 13:30 (par. Matt. 24:34, Lk. 21:32) was understood by Mk. to refer to the events leading up to the end which will occur within the lifetime of this generation (*Promise and Fulfilment: The Eschatological Message of Jesus*, SBT 23, 1961², 60). However, he suggests that "these things" in v. 29 are not necessarily the same as "all these things" in v. 30. Moreover, he believes that "it is wrong to attempt to derive the exegesis of the saying from the *immediate* context given by Mark, which the original independence of the saying does not justify." To Kümmel Matt. 10:23 confirms the conclusion "that Jesus reckoned on the coming of the Kingdom of God and of the Son of Man in glory within the lifetime of the generation of his hearers" (op. cit., 64).

A. L. Moore gives an alternative interpretation of Mk. 13:30: it refers not "to specific events but rather to the entire complex of events which may be termed 'signs of the end' and which are to be experienced, though not necessarily exhausted by, the contemporary generation" (*The Parousia in the New Testament, Supplements to NovT*, 13, 1966, 133). The answer to the question "when?" (v. 4) is not given here but in vv. 32 ff. (with Jesus' professed ignorance and the parable of the doorkeeper). Mk. 13:30 answers the question of the "signs" (v. 4). "But whereas the signs will occur within the immediate future (though not necessarily exhausted by that immediate future), the End itself is not so delimited" (op. cit., 134 f.). In both cases there is a parable attached. In the case of the signs it is the parable of the fig tree (vv. 28 f.; → Fruit, art. *sykē*). The question remains whether the versions of Matt. and Lk. support this interpretation. In Matt. G. Barth claims that expectation of the imminent end recedes, and exhortation comes to the fore (in G. Bornkamm, G. Barth and H. J. Held, *Tradition and Interpretation in Matthew*, 1963, 61). If this is so, it is indeed surprising that Matt. 24:34 is included in the discourse, if it were understood by him to express a delimited parousia expectation. It would be insufficient, as Moore points out (ibid.) to say that this is counterbalanced by the parables of Matt. 25 envisaging some delay. It would have been simpler for Matt. to omit the verse entirely. In the case of Lk., H. Conzelmann thinks that Lk. altered the meaning of Mk. 13:30. Whereas in Mk. *genea* means generation, in Lk. 21:32 it means "humanity in general" (*The Theology of St Luke*, 1960, 131). Lk. also omits *tauta*, so that his version reads: "Truly, I say to you, this generation will not pass away until all has taken place." Thus the verse refers to "the whole of the Divine plan" (ibid.). However, Moore rightly questions whether there is a significant shift of understanding (ibid.). For even in Lk. *genea* is best understood as generation. And the omission of *tauta* is probably a stylistic alteration. Moreover, the saying is preceded by a reference to the coming of the Son of man, the impending redemption and the parable of the fig tree (vv. 27–30). This would seem to delimit the end for the contemporary generation also in Lk., in view of the rejection of Conzelmann's understanding of generation. Thus there is no essential difference between the Synoptic Evangelists, for all three are concerned with the signs which the contemporary generation will see which inaugurate the end, but do not necessarily contain the end. With this view we may compare Cullmann's view noted above that we are already in the end time, though the end has not yet come (see above 1 (e)).

In *Prophecy Interpreted: The Function of Some Jewish Apocalyptic Texts and of the Eschatological Discourse, Mark 13 Par., Coniectanea Biblica, New Testament Series* 1, 1966 L. Hartman argues that Mk. 13 is a midrash on various passages from the book of Daniel. Among the parallels that he sees are the following: *dei genesthai*, "this must take place" (Mk. 13:7 = Dan. 2:28; → Necessity, art. *dei*); *to bdelygma tēs erēmōseōs*, → "the abomination of desolation" (Mk. 13:14 = Dan. 9:27; 12:11); *thlipsis hoia ou gegonen toiautē ap' archēs ktiseōs hēn ektisen ho theos heōs tou nyn*, "such tribulation as has not been from the beginning of the creation which God created until now" (Mk. 13:19 = Dan. 12:1; → Persecution, art. *thlipsis*); and *ton hyion tou anthrōpou erchomenon en nephelais*, → "the Son of man coming in clouds" (Mk. 13:26 = Dan. 7:13 f.). The whole passage is seen as an exposition or meditation on the texts in Dan. for the end time. Both the hortatory and the apocalyptic material in Mk. 13 are derived from Dan., apart from the conclusion (Mk. 13:33 f.) which was added. The presence of the same themes in 1 and 2 Thess. (noted above by Beasley-Murray) suggests that Paul also knew the pre-Marcan midrash. For discussion of Hartman's speculative reconstruction of how the discourse came into being see D. Wenham, *TSF Bulletin* 71, 10 f., who concludes that while there are firm links between Mk. 13 and Dan., the case has not been established that it is a midrash of the kind posited by Hartman, involving no less than nine stages of development and adaptation before it reached its Marcan form.

A considerable degree of redaction in Mk. 13 is claimed by J. Lambrecht in *Die Redaktion der Markus-Apokalypse: Literarische Analyse und Strukturunter-suchung, Analecta Biblica* 28, 1967. Mark was not just a collector of stories but a careful theological editor. (For a review of his verse-by-verse treatment of the chapter see D. Wenham, op. cit., 11–15.) Lambrecht sees the discourse as Jesus' last revelation and warning following his final break with the Jewish authorities. Much of it goes back to pre-Marcan traditions, including Q, and has close connections with the LXX. But a considerable amount is due to Mark himself who has imposed on it his own structure. The description of Jesus' coming (vv. 24–27) is the central element, but the thrust of the chapter as a whole is more towards warning and encouraging than giving apocalyptic information. Whilst recognizing many acute observations, Wenham concludes that Lambrecht's suggestion about the origins of the material are highly speculative, often exaggerating difficulties and apt to equate sayings in the Gospel tradition that are similar but far from identical. Moreover, his argument is cumulative, often taking certain verses to be secondary Marcan compilations on the ground that they make sense in the Marcan context (which he has earlier concluded to be secondary) and not elsewhere.

Another work which adopts a redaction-critical approach is R. Pesch's *Nah-erwartungen: Tradition und Redaktion in Markus 13*, 1968. His review of previous students of the passage includes Beasley-Murray, Hartman (who, he thinks, has proved the opposite of what he claims, i.e. that Mk. 13 is *not* a Danielic midrash) and Lambrecht. His chief complaint is that most scholars have tended to jump from the exegetical question to that of the historical Jesus without paying adequate (redaction-critical) attention to the chapter within its Marcan context. He agrees with Lambrecht in dividing the discourse into three sections: vv. 5b–23, 24–27, 28–37. According to Pesch, the pre-Marcan tradition included: (1) a group of persecution logia which were the work of Christian prophets (vv. 9, 13a, 11), since they do not reflect Jesus' earthly ministry; (2) two parables which may go back to Jesus (vv. 28b, 34); (3) two logia which could go back to Jesus in their original form (vv. 31, 32, the latter especially with its confession of Jesus' ignorance); (4) an apocalyptic tract whose contents are typical of the apocalyptic tradition, but whose vocabulary is not typical of the Gospel (vv. 6, 22, 7b, 8, 13b–17, ?18, 19 and 20a, 24–27). In direct contrast to Beasley-Murray, Pesch argues that there is here an unusually close dependence on the LXX which suggests that it was not part of Jesus' teaching. He thinks that it arose in Gk.-speaking circles. The tract was originally purely Jewish, but was taken over by Christians some time before A.D. 70 and applied to the Jewish War. Mk.'s intention is to warn against those

913

who were deceiving people by their calculations about the end-time, and also maintain a hope for a near end in the interests of attitudes to the present. D. Wenham sees in the work a propensity to unwarranted speculation (though not so great as Lambrecht's) and to lean on questionable assumptions (*TSF Bulletin* 72, 3). He regularly explains the tension between the second and third persons in the chapter as a reflection of Mk.'s use of sources, when it need not be. He is apt to assume that a saying which describes a church situation (e.g. v. 9b) must derive from that situation, and that a phrase reflecting Marcan vocabulary must derive from Mark himself. The work is characterized by an apparent unwillingness to try to make sense of the chapter not only in terms of Mk.'s theology but also in terms of Mk.'s apparent intention, i.e. to record what Jesus said.

In *No Stone on Another: Studies in the Significance of the Fall of Jerusalem in the Synoptic Gospels, Supplements to NovT* 23, 1970, Lloyd Gaston urges the need for a form-critical approach to Mk. 13. On the ground that the discourse is a farewell discourse in form, but that there is no reference to Jesus' coming death in it, he suggests that it may go back to a synoptic apocalypse that was originally regarded as part of Jesus' post-Easter teaching. To look for an apocalyptic source to which paraenetic elements have been added is to approach the question from the wrong end. "The framework of the discourse is provided by the parenetic, to which apocalyptic elements have been 'added' " (op. cit., 52). The characteristic words are *blepete*, "see" (vv. 5, 9, 23, 33) and *grēgoreite*, "watch"(vv. 34, 35, 37). The hortatory elements (vv. 5b, 7a, 8b, 9a, 13b, 21, 23, 28 f., 33–37) can readily be separated from the apocalyptic elements (vv. 6, 7b, 8a, 14–20, 22, 24–27), a division which very nearly corresponds to the formal distinction between the second and third persons. But, "It should be clear that this separation of different 'elements' has nothing to do with literary criticism in the sense of looking for 'sources', for neither series is capable of standing alone. We are only trying to isolate special characteristics of the chapter in order to determine the original function" (op. cit., 52). Gaston thinks that the discourse was originally the work of Christian → prophets which went through various stages of adaptation (op. cit., 61 ff.). The core was an unfulfilled oracle (vv. 14–19) which had its origin between the winter of A.D. 39–40 and the following winter. The original oracle referred to a situation similar to that of the time of Dan. It was then reapplied to the fall of Jerusalem. Jesus had spoken of a decisive event that would happen during the lifetime of those who witnessed his death. Because he had also predicted the fall of Jerusalem the two events were combined, and coupled with the winter oracle. Various other features were added in the course of time. Mk.'s own contribution (which was in fact to "mislead interpreters down to the present" [op. cit., 63]) was to set the whole discourse in answer to a question concerning the destruction of the temple. D. Wenham rightly draws attention to exegetical weaknesses in the build-up of the case here: "The author explains with confidence the history of the traditions contained in the chapter, but like others he builds too much on too little" (*TSF Bulletin* 72, 5). Moreover, he tends to deal with the chapter verse by verse without analyzing carefully the direction and purpose of the whole. If Jesus could predict separately the decisive event after his death and the fall of Jerusalem, it is difficult to see why he could not have predicted them together or foreseen some relationship between the two himself, especially in view of Jewish attitudes. Finally, considerable weight here is placed on the creative rôle of Christian prophets who were evidently at least as influential as Jesus himself in their eschatological teaching and whose word was equally authoritative. But the evidence for them is very slight (for discussion → Prophet, art. *prophētēs* NT).

A redaction critical approach is adopted by Willi Marxsen in his study of Mark 13 in *Mark the Evangelist: Studies on the Redaction History of the Gospel*, 1969, 151–206. Despite what he considers to be the divergent material and inner contradictions, he maintains that Mk. intended the chapter as a unity (op. cit., 166). But "here as elsewhere, Mark does not give thought to utterances of the historical Jesus. It is rather the Risen Lord who speaks – through the evangelist. That is, for Mark the gospel is the proclamation of the Risen Lord to the present" (op. cit., 170). The destruction of the temple has already taken place. "The end time has begun its course. Men stand right at the beginning of the end. And he who is with the community is the same who was and is to come" (op. cit., 188). The whole discourse is thus presented by Mk. with many of the events described already in the past, but preparing the church for the imminent final end. Marxsen goes on to argue that Matt. has somewhat modified the material to adapt it to the situation of the missionary church, having surrendered the imminent expectation of Mk. Similarly, Lk. writes from the standpoint of his own experience and composes the first "church history", beginning with Jesus. In the evaluation of Marxsen's thesis much depends upon the evaluation of his use of redaction critical techniques. But a pivotal point is clearly the dating of the NT books. It is frequently assumed that the Gospels were composed sometime after A.D. 70 which in turn is partly based on the assumption that the prophecies in Mk. 13 are *vaticinia ex eventu*, i.e. not really prophecies at all but history written to look like prophecy. But a recent challenge to the widely accepted dating has come from J. A. T. Robinson in *Redating the New Testament*, 1976, who maintains that the whole of the NT together with the Didache was written before the fall of Jerusalem in A.D. 70. Whilst we may agree that the chapter is essentially a discourse for the present, it may be thought that Marxsen, like so many of his predecessors, has too readily assumed the imminence of the parousia in the sense of the end of the world through not paying sufficient attention to the linguistic background of the concepts used.

With regard to the chronology of events in Mk. 13, D. Wenham adopts what is perhaps the most common conservative verdict: "Unless it is to be concluded that the Jesus of Mark is mistaken in his understanding of timing, we have then to assume that the time-scale is very compressed, so that what seem like near events are so only theologically; chronologically they are widely separated" (op. cit., 8). But in conclusion attention may be drawn to the somewhat different approach shared by two conservative scholars, J. M. Kik, *Matthew Twenty-Four: An Exposition*, 1948 (reprinted in *An Eschatology of Victory*, 1971, 53–173), and R. T. France, *Jesus and the Old Testament: His Application of Old Testament Passages to Himself and his Mission*, 1971. France argues that the whole context and argument of Mk. 13:4–23 could and does apply to events leading up to the judgment on Jerusalem (op. cit., 232). Kik similarly argues that Matt. 24:4–35 refers to the destruction of Jerusalem and the excision of the Jewish nation from the kingdom, whereas Matt. 24:36–25:46 refers to the second coming of Christ (*An Eschatology of Victory*, 73). There is warning of false Christs and persecution (Mk. 13:5–13 par.),

915

together with that of the → abomination of desolation (vv. 14 f. par.) which is a sign of the intensification of persecution, the greatest tribulation yet experienced and more false Christs. But all this can be read as applicable to the events leading up to the fall of Jerusalem. Then come the crucial verses Mk. 13:24–27 par. Matt. 24:29 ff., Lk. 21:25–28 which traditionally have been taken to refer to cosmic events and the second coming in view of the reference to the sun and moon not giving their light, the stars falling, the powers of heaven being shaken: "And then they will see the Son of man coming in clouds with great power and glory. And then he will send out the angels, and gather his elect from the four winds, from the ends of the earth to the ends of heaven." This is followed by the parable of the fig tree, the promise that "this generation will not pass away before all these things take place" (Mk. 13:30 par. Matt. 24:34, Lk. 21:32) which in turn is followed by Jesus' profession of ignorance of the time (Mk. 13:32 par. Matt. 24:36), and the parable teaching watchfulness (Mk. 13:33–37; cf. Matt. 25:14 f., Lk. 19:12 f.).

In context the theme of the discourse is the destruction of the → temple which symbolizes the judgment on Israel in view of its rejection of Jesus and his preaching. But the discourse is not simply concerned with Israel; it is also concerned with the disciples and the new Israel. For paradoxically the judgment which will fall on ancient Israel will bring them great trial and tribulation (Matt. 24:21; Mk. 13:19; cf. Dan. 12:1). Indeed, it is for the sake of the elect that the Lord has cut short (*ekolobōsen*) those days (Mk. 13:20, cf. Matt. 24:22). All this leads up to Mk. 13:24–27 par. which we might expect to deal with the judgment on Israel. Whereas other scholars assume that there is a jump in Jesus' thought here to the second coming, Kik and France say that these verses are actually a description of the judgment on Israel which did indeed occur within the lifetime of that generation and which in fact is also supported by the parable of the fig tree (→ Fruit, art. *sykē*). The language is, in fact, that of OT prophecy and apocalyptic which in the context of the OT is used to describe *this-worldly* events, in particular, judgments. The phrases in Mk. 13:24 f. par. are drawn from Isa. 13:10 and 34:4 (the former predicting the doom of Babylon; the latter that of "all the nations", but with special reference to Edom). Similar examples may be seen in Ezek. 32:7 (concerning Egypt), Amos 8:9 (concerning the northern kingdom), Joel 2:10 (concerning Judah), and constantly in Joel 3–4 concerning God's judgment on Judah and other nations (France, op. cit., 233; Kik, op. cit., 129 ff.). Similarly, Peter uses the cosmological language of Joel 2:28–32 in his Pentecost sermon (Acts 2:17–21) to interpret the outpouring of the Spirit, when there were no patent celestial phenomena. Thus Jesus is not predicting abnormal astronomical events; he is predicting the judgment of God on the Jewish nation in the OT language of judgment. We might add that the cosmic symbolism has the double function of drawing attention to the fact that this judgment is in the main stream of prophetic judgment and of emphasizing the divine dimension of something that is happening in history using imagery associated with the day of the Lord. But it may also have the further function of disclosing the significance of events in the same way that the → parables function. For those who have ears to hear and eyes to see, the utterance has significance, otherwise it remains veiled. It is on a par with the messianic secret, and indeed belongs to it.

916

Mk. 13:26 par. takes up Dan. 7:13. France writes: "Jesus is using Daniel 7:13 as a prediction of that authority which he exercised when in A.D. 70 the Jewish nation and its leaders, who had condemned him, were overthrown, and Jesus was vindicated as the recipient of all power from the Ancient of Days" (op. cit., 236). The coming in clouds referred to here is thus not a visible return in judgment but an allusion to Jesus' ascent to the Father and accession of authority. The visible events of the fall of Jerusalem are in fact the vindication of Jesus. A similar sense is present in Mk. 14:62. The seeing means that they will see for themselves that their time of power is finished, and that God has given all power in heaven and earth to Jesus. The parallelism of "coming" and "sitting" in Mk. 14:62 is itself a warning against taking the "coming" too literally. Clouds are a common piece of OT symbolism, denoting the power of God especially in judgment (cf. Isa. 19:1; Pss. 97:2 f.; 104:3). Matt. 24:30 takes up the language of Zech. 12:10 ff., which in context refers to the mourning of the Jews, and is appropriate in this context. Mk. 13:27 par. Matt. 24:31 uses the language of Deut. 30:4 and Zech. 2:6[10] (also Isa. 27:13 in the case of Matt.), none of which passages demand an eschatological sense in context. Here they are typologically applied to the gathering of the Christian church, the new Israel, from all the nations, as distinct from the old Israel descended from Abraham (France, op. cit., 238).

The parable of the fig tree is a parabolic warning that these things are beginning to happen, and Mk. 13:30 par. emphasizes that they will all happen within a generation. But Mk. 13:32 par. looks ahead to "that day" and "hour" which is known only to the Father. Two lines of interpretation may be considered. One is that it refers to the events in history that Jesus has been talking about, and thus the whole discourse does not look beyond the fall of Jerusalem, the consequent rejection of the Jewish nation and the vindication of the Son. This would not preclude a further parousia of the Son of man or a culmination of history (e.g. Matt. 13:40 f.; 25:1–46); it would merely state that this is not the theme of the present discourse. The other would be to say, with France and Kik, that the final part of the discourse looks ahead to the second coming of Christ. In the meantime the disciples are like servants put in charge of property whilst the master is away on a journey. They are to watch, lest when he comes, he should find them asleep. France's examination of the language rejects the view that the alleged Septuagintalisms in the text show that it could not have had a Semitic origin. From the standpoint of both language and thought, the discourse is entirely conceivable as the teaching of Jesus in the context set by the evangelists. It provides teaching for the disciples that is relevent to their situation as followers of the historical Jesus. He foresaw his own death which was paradoxically the final culminating act of Israel's rejection of him and thus also of God, and at the same time it was the decisive act in God's rejection of Israel. From that point onwards the temple (and with it Jerusalem and Israel) had no more future in salvation history. The disciples will live to see Jesus vindicated and Israel judged. But in the meantime they must expect persecution and watch.

(b) The eschatology of Luke. We have already had occasion to note Hans Conzelmann's argument in *The Theology of St Luke*, 1960, that the traditional Christian time-scheme which divides history into three periods, the age of Israel, the time when Jesus was on earth, and the age of the church, was the creation of

Luke (see above 1 (e); cf. also Conzelmann's *An Outline Theology of the New Testament*, 1969). Luke, he argues, developed this ostensibly because the expected parousia failed to materialize. Conzelmann himself further subdivides the middle period of Jesus into three parts: Jesus in Galilee, on the way to Jerusalem, and the time in Jerusalem. Similarly, Acts can be subdivided into three parts: Jerusalem, Samaria and the neighbouring regions, and the world (Asia Minor, Greece and Rome). Since Lk.'s Gospel is more of a biography than Mk., and his Acts is the first history of the church, Luke is often credited by contemporary NT scholars as the creator of early catholicism, though it is not often made clear whether the term is positive or pejorative or indeed what precisely it means. Conzelmann argues that the ministry of Jesus and the age of the church are separated by a holy time, consisting of the resurrection appearances at Jerusalem over a period of forty days. The Holy Spirit, given at Pentecost, is no longer the eschatological gift "but the substitute in the meantime for the possession of ultimate salvation" (op. cit. 95). Lk. does not expect the parousia soon. Apocalyptic signs may occur, but "the end will not be at once" (Lk. 21:9; cf. Mk. 13:7; Matt. 24:6). Lk. is concerned with the period of the church in Acts which reaches from Jesus' ascension to the future parousia. He is interested in relations with the Roman empire and the Jewish people (op. cit., 148). The church is the new people of God continuing salvation history and existing under persecution. Thus Luke replaces the imminent parousia with a scheme in which the institution of the church occupies a more prominent place.

A somewhat different approach is that put forward by H. Flender in *St Luke: Theologian of Redemptive History*, 1965. From his analysis of the dialectical structure of Luke-Acts Flender concludes that Luke had an overriding theological concern. He places side by side what belongs to the old world and to the new world of God, showing the gulf between the sinful world under judgment and God (op. cit., 34 f.). The time-scheme of salvation in Lk.-Acts is like that in Rev. 12: first victory in heaven, and then victory on earth (op. cit., 102 f.). As a historian and theologian of redemptive history, Luke had a threefold task: "First, he had to preserve the unique character of the Christ event in on-going history. Secondly, there was the problem of historical continuity between Israel and the Church. Thirdly, there was the problem of how to describe the presence of salvation in the Christian community as it passes through time" (op. cit., 91). Christ's exaltation is seen as "the consummation of salvation in heaven" (ibid.). Christ's occupation of the temple "is a kind of symbolic anticipation of his enthronement in heaven" (op. cit., 93). The ascension story "contains unmistakable echoes of the parousia terminology" (ibid.; cf. Acts 1:9 ff.; Dan. 7:13). In his handling of Lk. 17:22 ff., and the above material, Luke is not simply postponing the parousia: "He transfers theological statements previously associated with the parousia to the exaltation" (op. cit., 98). "The ascension, as Luke sees it, is a kind of anticipation of the parousia in heaven" (op. cit., 94). The apocalyptic sayings in Lk. 17 have an individual application in Lk.: "in that day one shall be taken and the other left" (Lk. 17:34; cf. 12:20) is similar to the words addressed to the dying thief (Lk. 23:43). Both refer to the individual's death by which he either loses or gains life. "The cross is not now the absolute end of the world. It is the preliminary end for the individual Christian who hears its message in the word of preaching" (op. cit.,

918

19; cf. 15). Flender holds that there is a continuity and a discontinuity between this age and the age to come. History goes on, as it were, on a horizontal plane. But there is also the vertical dimension of the divine realm. Flender concludes that Luke solves the problem of their relationship by discovering "a *via media* between the gnostic denial and the early catholic canonization of history. His solution is to give simultaneous expression to the supernatural mystery and the earthly visibility of Christ and his history" (op. cit., 167). For in his humility Jesus "belongs to the new period.... In his divinity he stands outside of any chronological scheme, sharing God's contemporaneity with all human time" (op. cit., 125). The corollary for Flender is that "Luke has no notion of any redemptive history extending in time" (op. cit., 162).

E. E. Ellis replies to this by drawing attention to two premises of Lucan thought (*Eschatology in Luke, Facet Books*, Biblical Series 30, 1972, 8 ff.). On the one hand, man is understood as a unified totality who may indeed be viewed from different perspectives but who is not a dualism consisting of body and soul. This understanding of man is taken over from the OT and was shared by Jesus and Paul. It may be seen in Lk.'s sources. Thus *psychē* usually means "life" or "self" which is lost at death (Lk. 9:24; 12:19 f.; Acts 2:27 = Ps. 16:10; 20:10; 27:22). In the midrash at Acts 2:31 the parallelism of self and *sarx* (flesh) follows the parallelism of *psychē* and self in the preceding quotation (Acts 2:27; cf. 13:37). There is a parallelism of *psychē* and *pneuma* (spirit) at Lk. 1:46 f., of *psychē* and *sōma* at Lk. 12:22 f., and the equivalent use of *pneuma* and *psychē* for life-principle at Lk. 8:55 and Acts 20:10. Lk. 12:20 ("your soul is required of you") and 23:46 (cf. Acts 2:27, 31) reinforce the impression that no anthropological dualism affects Luke's handling of his traditions. Even in the Areopagus address, Ellis claims that Luke understands Acts 17:28 differently from the traditional Stoic-pantheistic concept or is using it as an *argumentum ad hominem*. On the other hand, the Platonic contrast of time and eternity is equally absent from Luke's eschatology, as it is from the NT generally. The contrast between heaven and earth is not an occasion for cosmological speculation. It is a contrast of the "seen" and the "unseen" which, like his anthropology, has antecedents in Paul and the OT (cf. Acts 7:56; 12:6–11; 2 Ki. 6:17; and W. C. van Unnik, "Die geöffneten Himmel" in W. Schneemelcher, ed., *Apophoreta. Festschrift für Ernst Haenchen, BZNW* 30, 1964, 269–80). "Luke's conception of 'heaven' and 'earth' may be compared to two television channels showing different segments of the same auto race. The action is contemporaneous with and related to the other. But viewers of Channel 1 do not see the action of Channel 2" (op. cit., 10). In this connection Ellis agrees with Cullmann that the resurrection hope is not a compromise between Judaism and Platonism. A theology that includes the departure of the soul to a timeless realm or sees death as the anticipation of the parousia contradicts the NT concept of the temporal redemption of the whole man (ibid.; cf. O Cullmann, *Immortality of the Soul or Resurrection of the Dead? The Witness of the New Testament*, 1958).

In view of this, Luke's eschatology should be seen "within the framework of a two-stage eschatology and a monistic anthropology, a temporal redemption of the whole man from death. It is characterized by a concern to show the exclusive mediation of the eschatological fulfilment through Jesus and, thereby, to show the relationship of this age to the age to come" (op. cit., 11). In the mission of the earthly Jesus the new age of the kingdom of God becomes present in his creative word and acts (Lk. 11:20; cf. 10:9, 11, 18; 19:11; 21:8 f.; E. E. Ellis, "Present and Future Eschatology in Luke", *NTS* 12, 1965–66, 27–41). This is not simply a Lucan perspective, but goes back to Jesus himself (cf. W. G. Kümmel, *Promise and Fulfilment: The Eschatological Message of Jesus, SBT* 23, 1957, 106–24, 138 ff.). The mission of the seventy (Lk. 10) presupposes the identification of Jesus' followers with his own person (Lk. 10:16; cf. Matt. 10:40; Jn. 13:20) and is thus a means of making the kingdom present. Similarly the dying thief will be "with me" in his exaltation (Lk. 24:43). In the Last Supper the participants are invited to "see the eschatological consummation in the present through union with the departing Jesus" (Kümmel, op. cit., 121; quoted by Ellis, op. cit., 12). The Semitic idea of corporate solidarity of the group with its leader underlies Acts 9:4 and probably the temple motif (Lk. 20:17 f.; Acts 6:14; 7:48; 15:16; 17:24; cf. B. Gärtner, *The Temple and the Community in Qumran and the New Testament, Society for New Testament Studies Monograph Series* 1, 103, 122, 123–42).

From all this Ellis concludes that "The identification of the eschatological fulfilment exclusively with Jesus provides the rationale by which the relationship of this age and the age to come is to be understood" (op. cit., 13). The twofold eschatology of apocalyptic Judaism of blessing and judgment becomes a *two-stage eschatology*. "The Spirit's activity in and through Jesus brings eschatological blessings of the coming age now, but the judgment and the consummation of the kingdom are deferred" (ibid.). Whereas Flender sees the vertical dimension in Luke's eschatology as a consummation in heaven that is manifested on earth, Ellis sees a consummation on earth in the resurrection and exaltation of Jesus that is presently manifested in heaven. Salvation history on earth incorporates in it a heavenly dimension. "For Jesus' followers the vertical dimension is not a road map of their individual pilgrimage but rather a relationship with the One who is in heaven 'until the times of universal *apokatastasis*' " (op. cit., 14; cf. Acts 3:21; Lk. 17:34 f.; 21:27; Acts 1:11; 17:31).

Moreover, the person and mission of Jesus define for Luke the nature of the *continuity and discontinuity* the age to come (ibid.). The healings (cf. Lk. 5:23 f.; 13:16; Acts 26:18), the nature miracles and Jesus' own resurrection point to the new age as a fulfilment and deliverance of the created order from the death-powers of the present age (cf. the references to → paradise [Lk. 23:43], → Adam [Lk. 3:38], restoration [Acts 1:6; 3:21]; and the parallel between "sons of the resurrection" and those who "live in God" [Lk. 20:38; Acts 17:28]). Yet the kingdom of God is also something radically new whose discontinuity with the present age is as radical as that between death and resurrection. "The fate of Jesus is the fate of the disciple, who also must go 'through many tribulations' and 'lose his life' if he, like Jesus, is to become 'a son of the resurrection' " (ibid.; cf. Acts 14:22; Lk. 17:33; 20:36; 22:28 ff.; and the parallels in Paul in Rom. 6:4, 10–13; Col. 3:1–5, 12).

Whilst issuing a timely warning against the tendency to see an opponent behind every bush in the NT theological garden, Ellis does allow that Luke's eschatology may contain certain correctives. Thus the prologue (Lk. 1:4) suggests that Lk. may be correcting heretical misinformation. The strong emphasis on the physical nature of Jesus' resurrection and the careful distinction between the resurrection and the ascension are intended to safeguard the resurrection against a heavenly

920

or spiritual interpretation. The discontinuity between the present age and the kingdom is a warning against political messianism. And the emphasis on the presence of the Spirit and the unity of the disciple with the exalted Lord (Lk. 23:43; Acts 7:56) corrects an improper anticipation of the coming end of the age (op. cit., 15).

In Ellis's view, to suggest that Luke's eschatological framework arose out of embarrassment over the delay in the parousia is to misconceive the nature of the problem. In any case, there is a basic tension between "Thy kingdom come" and "If I by the Spirit of God cast out demons, the kingdom of God has come upon you" which goes back to Jesus himself (Matt. 6:10; 12:28; cf. W. G. Kümmel, op. cit.; and "Futuristic and Realized Eschatology in the Earliest Stages of Christianity", *JR* 43, 1963, 303–14). In point of fact, the delay-motif in Lk. "appears before there was time to get embarrassed" (op. cit., 18). In Luke's traditions there was already the twin motif of "imminence and delay". But Luke's problem is not the delay of the parousia, "but a false apocalyptic speculation that has misapplied the teachings of Jesus and threatens to pervert the church's mission" (op. cit., 19).

The presence of apocalyptic fever in the second half of the 1st century is documented in both Christian sources and other writings (cf. Josephus, *War* 6, 5, 4; Tacitus, *History* 5, 13; Suetonius, *Lives of the Caesars, Vespasian* 4; 2 Thess. 2:2). It is against this background that Luke records: "Being asked by the Pharisees when the kingdom of God was coming, he answered them, 'The kingdom of God is not coming with signs to be observed; nor indeed will they say, "Lo, here it is!" or "There!" for behold, the kingdom of God is in the midst of you' " (Lk. 17:20 f.). Similarly Acts 1:6 ff. records the question of the disciples: " 'Lord, will you at this time restore the kingdom to Israel?' He said to them, 'It is not for you to know the times or seasons which the Father has fixed by his own authority. But you shall receive power when the Holy Spirit has come upon you; and you shall be my witnesses in Jerusalem and in all Judea and Samaria and to the end of the earth.' " The theme of Acts is the church's task as mission which is not served by preoccupation with chronological speculation. "Because the eschatological reality is present the length of the interval until the consummation of is no crucial significance" (op. cit., 19). The Lucan eschatology is set within the context of a two-stage manifestation of the kingdom of God as present and future. Whereas Matt. couples eschatology with the church, Luke combines eschatology and the → Spirit (Lk. 3:16 f.; 11:31 f.; 17:21 ff.; Acts 1:2–16; 2:4–38; 4:8, 25, 31; 5:3, 9, 16, 32; 6:3, 5, 10; 7:51, 55, 59; 8:7–29; 9:17, 31; 10:19–47; 11:12–28; 13:2, 4, 9, 52; 15:8, 28 f.; 16:6–18; 17:26; 18:25; 19:1–21; 20:22 f., 28; 21:4, 11; 28:25) and Jesus (Lk. 22:28 ff.; 23:43). However, it must also be said that these references show the activity of the Spirit in relation to the church and Jesus. It is Jesus who gives the Spirit (Lk. 3:16; Acts 2:33) and who represents in his resurrection an individual fulfilment of the age to come. "His followers not only manifest the same *eschatological powers of the Spirit* as he does, but they also have a *corporate identification with the (risen) Lord*. In both ways Luke sets forth the new age as a present reality" (op. cit., 20). But it is a present reality that requires future consummation.

(c) Paul. It is a common presupposition of much NT interpretation that Paul expected the parousia within his own lifetime. A more sophisticated version of this belief is that argued by C. H. Dodd that Paul's eschatology underwent a development in the course of time (cf. "The Mind of Paul" I and II, in *New Testament Studies*, 1953, 67–128; and the discussions of D. E. H. Whiteley, *The Theology of St. Paul*, 1974², 241–48; J. Lowe, "An Examination of Attempts to Detect Developments in St. Paul's Theology", *JTS* 42, 1941, 129–42; and J. C. Hurd, Jr., *The Origin of I Corinthians*, 1965, 8 ff.; see above 1(c)). This draws a distinction between the earlier epistles of Paul (1 and 2 Thess.; 1 Cor.; 2 Cor. 6:14–7:1 which was originally part of a separate letter; 2 Cor. 10:1–13:10 which was also separate) which envisaged an imminent parousia and the later ones (Rom.; 2 Cor. 1–9; and the Captivity Epistles) where the parousia has receded giving way to concerns which imply an ongoing view of history. The change of mind came about through the tensions with the Corinthian church involving a harsh, puritanical letter (2 Cor. 6:14–7:1 cf. 1 Cor. 5:9) and a further letter which included 2 Cor. 10:1–13:10. Following the capitulation of the dissident attitude, Paul wrote 2 Cor. 1–9 in which Paul himself mellowed somewhat and is more inclined to accept the world than to deny it, as in his allegedly earlier attitude.

In support of the specific eschatological contentions Dodd argues that 1 Thess. 4:15 ff. imply that Paul himself expected to experience the parousia: "For we declare to you by the word of the Lord, that we who are alive, who are left until the coming of the Lord, shall not precede those who have fallen asleep. For the Lord himself will descend from heaven with a cry of command, with the archangel's call, and with the sound of the trumpet of God. And the dead in Christ will rise first; then we who are alive, who are left, shall be caught up together with them in the clouds to meet the Lord in the air; and so we shall always be with the Lord" (cf. 5:1; and Dodd, op. cit., 110). But in 2 Cor. 4:12 and 5:4 Paul faces the possibility that he will die. The Thess. passage may be paralleled by the following: "Lo! I tell you a mystery. We shall not all sleep, but we shall all be changed" (1 Cor. 15:51); "the night is far gone, the day is at hand" (Rom. 13:12); "The Lord is at hand" (Phil. 4:5); and "the appointed time has grown very short; from now on, let those who have wives live as though they had none" (1 Cor. 7:29). Apart from Rom. 13:11–14 among the later Pauline writings, there is a lack of emphasis on the second coming. But here it must be noted that the same kind of language is present in 2 Tim. 1:12, 18. Moreover, Phil. 4:5 also belongs to a later Pauline epistle. Admittedly, the earlier references to the Day of Christ (Phil. 1:6, 10; 2:16) do not specifically mention its proximity, but Phil. 4:5 implies no fundamental shift of emphasis. Phil. 3:20 refers to heaven from which "we await a Saviour, the Lord Jesus Christ." To this Whiteley suggests that Paul may have reverted to his earlier doctrine of the Thessalonian Epistles and 1 Cor., or even that Phil. may have been an early epistle (op. cit., 247)!

Support for Dodd's hypothesis is further seen in Paul's allegedly changed attitude to human institutions. In 1 Cor. 6:1–11 he is said to take a low view of Roman law courts, whereas in Rom. 13:1–11 he takes a more positive attitude towards the Roman state. But here it may be objected that the point in 1 Cor. is not to disparage civil law courts, but to draw attention to the incongruity of believers reverting to them to settle their internal disputes. In 2 Cor. 6:14–7:1 Paul urges the Corinthians to have nothing to do with unbelievers, whereas in Rom. 2:14 he envisages a Gentile knowledge of God. But here too it may be said that the two passages deal with quite different things. The passage in 2 Cor. is concerned with sexual relations with pagans in the context of the cult at Corinth, whereas Rom. 2:14 may well refer to the fulfilment of the covenant promise of Jer. 31:33 among Gentile believers (→ God, art. *theos*, NT 4 (b)). In 1 Cor. 7 → marriage appears to be a second best whereas in Col. 3:18 f. and Eph. 5:21-33 marriage is highly esteemed. However, a high estimate of marriage can be combined with imminent expectation (1 Pet. 3:1-7; 4:7; cf. J. Lowe, op. cit., 139; see also E. G. Selwyn, "Eschatology in 1 Peter", in W. D. Davies and D. Daube, eds., *The Background of the New Testament and its Eschatology: In Honour of Charles Harold Dodd*, 1954, 394-401). Moreover, the difference of emphasis is not so sharp as might appear at first sight. For in 1 Cor. 7 Paul does not condemn marriage as such. His positive point with regard to marriage and everything else is that believers should deal with the world "as though they had no dealings with it. For the form of this world is passing away" (1 Cor. 7:2). In 1 Cor. 7 this point is applied specifically to marriage, but it remained for Paul a fixed point on which he never went back.

D. E. H. Whiteley admits that subsequent criticism has weakened Dodd's case, but he does not think that it has destroyed it (op. cit., 248). Clearly it would be absurd to posit that Paul's thought was insusceptible to any development in the light of his missionary experience and further reflection. The crucial question is not whether Paul grew in understanding but whether he shifted his position from an expectation of the parousia in his lifetime to an indefinite postponement of it. Part of Dodd's case turns on the chronological order of Paul's epistles. In general scholarly opinion favours the broad outline which he accepts. However, there is no general endorsement of attempts to divide 2 Cor. in Dodd's way, and C. K. Barrett concludes his review of the various theories by suggesting that the epistle is basically a unity, though chs. 10-13 were written at a later stage than chs. 1-9 (*The Second Epistle to the Corinthians*, BNTC, 1973, 21). There are, however, other ways of explaining the differing emphases in Paul's writing. J. A. T. Robinson sees in Paul a change which "is to be described as a shift from an apocalyptic to a non-apocalyptic form of eschatology" (*Jesus and His Coming*, 1957, 161; on this see the discussion of W. Baird below). C. F. D. Moule sees the shift in thought from 1 Cor. 15 to 2 Cor. 5 as involving the acknowledgement that the new clothing cannot be simply put over the old, but rather the old must be given up in exchange ("St Paul and Dualism: The Pauline Conception of Resurrection", *NTS* 12, 1965-66, 106-23). But even in 1 Cor. there is the recognition of the process of mortality (cf. 1 Cor. 6:14; 15:53 f. with vv. 36 ff.). Moreover, the case for assuming that Paul expected the parousia soon in 1 Thess. is far from water-tight. As early as 1 Thess. 5:10 Paul reckoned with the possibility that he might die. The possibility cannot be dismissed that in speaking of "we" in 1 Thess. 4:15 and 17 Paul was identifying himself with the last generation without necessarily supposing that he himself belonged to it (cf. J. Bonsirven, *L'Évangile de Paul*, 1948, 338 ff.; L. Morris, *The First and Second Epistles to the Thessalonians*, NLC, 1959, 141 f.). On the other hand, M. J. Harris believes that 2 Cor. 5 "marks a decisive turning-point in the apostle's estimate of his own relation to the Parousia. No longer is his pre-Advent decease a possibility more hypothetical than real. For the first time – to judge by the extant Pauline Epistles – he has begun to reckon with the implications of that possibility, a possibility that has ceased to be a distant reality by becoming a probability"

("2 Corinthians 5:1–10: Watershed in Paul's Eschatology", *TB* 22, 1971, 39). This was due to his confrontation with death in Asia (2 Cor. 1:8–11). There is also the possibility that the varying emphases of Paul's eschatology were affected by the different polemical situations in which Paul found himself. Thus 1 Thess. 4:13–18 and 5:10 is addressed to those who need assurance that both the living and dead believers will be with the Lord, whereas 2 Thess. 2:3 implies the teaching of some that the day of the Lord is already past and 1 Cor. 15:12 ff. the denial of the resurrection. Harris suggests that Paul further modified his own views in 2 Cor. Whereas he had previously regarded the resurrection of deceased Christians as transpiring at the Parousia, in 2 Cor. 5 he envisages his own receipt of a spiritual body, comparable to Christ's, as occurring at the time of his death (op. cit., 39–45). And by the time of 2 Cor. he no longer viewed the Christian dead as resting in "sleep" in the grave or Sheol until the Parousia; he now anticipates conscious personal communion with Christ in heaven immediately after death (op. cit., 45–57). Harris believes Paul's thinking was influenced by the tribulation of 2 Cor. 1:8 and the illness of 2 Cor. 2:12 f.; cf. 7:5.

W. Baird suggests a somewhat different line of approach in "Pauline Eschatology in Hermeneutical Perspective", *NTS* 17, 1970–71, 312–27. He points out that eschatological statements are found throughout most of Paul's epistles, though references to a future eschaton are lacking in 2 Cor. 10–13 and are scarce in Gal. (cf. 5:5, 21; 6:8). The absence of such key eschatological terms as *parousia* (presence), *orgē* (wrath), *anastasis* (resurrection) and *aphtharsia* (incorruption) from these passages suggests that in epistles (or sections of epistles) of sharpest polemic futurist eschatology plays no major rôle (op. cit., 321). But in fact, no clear pattern emerges from the contexts of the major eschatological passages in Paul. Rom. 13 and 1 Thess. 4–5 are set in paraenetic sections, the latter being concerned with care for the departed (4:18) and edification (5:1). 1 Cor. 15 answers Corinthian questions concerning the denial of the resurrection (15:12) and its mode (15:34). But it is also related to ethical concerns (vv. 34 and 58). In 2 Cor. 4:7 ff. and 5:6 ff. apostolic suffering and exhortation provide the context for discussion about the body and death. In Phil. 1:25 eschatology is bound up with the fulfilment of Paul's mission. There is a polemical note in Phil. 3:2 ff., 19 ff., and exhortation in Phil. 4:1.

Baird argues that just as the contexts of Paul's eschatological statements display a variety of interest embracing the paraenetic, the polemical, the pastoral, and the personal, so does the structure of his eschatological language. Whilst there is a broad parallelism between 1 Thess. 4:16 ff. and 1 Cor. 15:23 ff., the sequence of events is not identical (op. cit., 322). 1 Thess. lists the descent of the Lord (accompanied by shout, archangel's voice and trumpet), the resurrection of the dead and the catching of those who are alive for meeting the Lord in the air. 1 Cor. lists the raising of Christ (a past event), the resurrection of those who belong to Christ, and the end when Christ delivers the kingdom to God. 1 Thess. distinguishes between the raising of the dead and the elevation of the living, whereas 1 Cor. 15:51 speaks of transformation. 1 Cor. 15:23 and 1 Thess. 4:16 link the resurrection of Christians with the parousia, but the lifting up appears to be slightly later (1 Thess. 4:15, 17), whereas the whole occurs in a flash in 1 Cor. 15:52. Similarly, parallels with differences can be found in Phil. 1 and 2 Cor. 5 (op. cit., 323). Baird suggests that a shift of eschatological language may be observed between 1 Thess. 4 and 1 Cor. 15, on the one hand, and 2 Cor. 5 and Phil. 1, on the other. The terms *koimaomai* (sleep), *salpinx* (trumpet) and *parousia* (presence) in an eschatological sense appear in Paul only in 1 Thess. and 1 Cor. Phil. 1:22 speaks of "living in the flesh" and 2 Cor. 5:2 refers to the heavenly dwelling, and both speak of being with Christ or the Lord (Phil. 1:23; cf. 2 Cor. 5:8), and of desire (Phil. 1:23) and groaning (2 Cor. 5:2, 4) for the new life.

However, the thesis that Paul completely changed his eschatological language and ideas is confounded by a comparison of 1 Thess. 5 (as an example of Paul's earliest writing) with Rom. 13 (as an example of later thought). For both passages share a view of the imminent eschaton, using the word *kairos* (time; Rom. 13:11; 1 Thess. 5:2), the contrast between night and day (1 Thess. 5:4; Rom. 13:12), that between sleeping and waking (1 Thess. 5:6; Rom. 13:11), and that between drunkenness and sobriety (1 Thess. 5:7; Rom. 13:13). The vb. *endyō* (put on) is also a common factor: the Thessalonians are to put on the breastplate of faith and love and the helmet of the hope of salvation (5:8); the Romans are to put on the armour of light (13:12; cf. also Eph. 6:11–17).

Just as there are also linguistic shifts between epistles, there are also different types of language within the same letter. 1 Thess.4 is one of the most apocalyptic passages, but it also contains the idea of being with the Lord always (4:17; 5:10), an idea paralleled in the more "Hellenistic" texts of 2 Cor. 5:8 and Phil. 1:23. 1 Cor. 15:51 f. preserves the apocalyptic idea of a trumpet and provides the only NT instances of *atomos* (that which cannot be cut in two; *en atomō*, in a moment) and *rhipē ophthalmou* (in the twinkling of an eye). It also expresses the hope of putting on immortality, a concept parallel to that of being clothed with the heavenly habitation (2 Cor. 5:2 f.). On the other hand, 2 Cor. 5 which describes the house eternal in the heavens (5:1) also depicts the apocalyptic judgment seat of Christ (5:10; cf. Rom. 14:10). Rom. 14:11 cites the prophecy of Isa. 45:23 that every knee shall bow to Yahweh and every tongue praise him, which Phil. 2:10 applies christologically and eschatologically.

In addition to these shifts of language, Baird draws attention to the fact that similar concepts are also expressed in different words (op. cit., 324). The word *parousia* is used in an eschatological sense only in 1 Thess. and 1 Cor., though Paul uses it elsewhere of human presence and the idea of the triumphal coming of the Lord is depicted in other language in 2 Cor. 4:14 and Phil. 3:20. The vb. *koimaō* (sleep) is used as a euphemism for → death in 1 Thess. 4:13 ff. and 1 Cor. 15:6, 18, 20, 51, but is replaced by *analyō* (unloose, depart) in Phil. 1:23. The noun *thanatos* (death) does not occur in 1 Thess., but is frequent in the later epistles. *anhistēmi* (rise) is the distinctive vb. for the resurrection of believers in 1 Thess. 4:14, 16, but is not used elsewhere by Paul to denote future resurrection. *egeirō* (raise) is used 15 times in 1 Cor. 15, but is found only once in 1 Thess. (1:10) with reference to the resurrection of Christ.

Corresponding to this varied use of eschatological language is the wide variety of contexts in which similar language is found. Baird draws attention to the following (op. cit., 324 f.). 1 Thess. 4:16 ff. has parallels in Jewish apocalyptic: the descent of the Lord (Mic. 1:3); the archangel (2 Esd. 4:36); the trumpet (2 Esd. 6:23); the clouds (Sl.Enoch 3:1). The image of the sons of light (1 Thess. 5:5; cf. Rom.

13:13) recalls the Qumran War Scroll (1QM). The day of the Lord (1 Thess. 5:2; Rom. 2:5; Phil. 1:6, 10) is found in the OT in passages like Amos 5:18; Zech. 14:1; → *hēmera*, OT). The judgment seat of Christ (2 Cor. 5:10; Rom. 14:10) recalls Eth.Enoch 62:3, 5. Such terms belong to the predominantly Jewish thought-world. But other ideas have Hellenistic affinities. Putting on the heavenly habitation is similar to the post-biblical Hymn of the Pearl 82 ff. which speaks of the "bright embroidered robe" which "was made ready in its home on high" (cf. R. M. Grant, *Gnosticism: An Anthology*, 1961, 121). Although the fear of nakedness is a Jewish concept (Isa. 30:4; Mic. 1:8; Ezek. 23:29), the idea of the naked bodiless soul is found in Plato (*Cratylus* 403) and Philo (*Virt.* 76), and the departure of the soul from the body under the cloud of nakedness is found in the Nag Hammadi gnostic texts (Gos.Phil. 23 f.; Gos.Thom. 20, 37).

It is not necessary to maintain that Paul was making explicit conscious reference to all or any of these passages. What they show is not so much literary dependence as the common currency of ideas in a variety of cultures. In addition to this, however, Paul may having been drawing on Christian tradition prior to himself. Thus 1 Thess. 4:15 ff. is presented as a "word of the Lord" (→ *parousia*, NT 2). Phil. 3:20 f. may express a pre-Pauline hymn. The illustration of the thief in the night (1 Thess. 5:1) occurs in Matt. 24:43 and Rev. 3:3. Death is personified in 1 Cor. 15:26; Rev. 6:8; 20:13 f.

Baird suggests that the distinctive feature of Paul's understanding of eschatology is its variety (op. cit., 325). He does not give a clear, simple apocalyptic picture of the end. His language is drawn from external sources and is not used with uniform emphasis. For in the last analysis Paul is using pictorial language to describe an indescribable future. He does not have a distinctive "Hellenistic" doctrine of life after death. There is no clear-cut pattern of development. However, Baird notes the following constant factors (op. cit., 325 ff.). (i) The death and resurrection of Christ as the decisive eschatological event has already occurred, and is the basis of the believer's own hope and faith (1 Thess. 4:14; 1 Cor. 15:3, 12–24; 2 Cor. 4:14; cf. Phil. 2:8–11; 3:18, 20 f.; Rom. 8:17). (ii) There will be a future consummation in which God's purposes will be fulfilled. This is described in a variety of ways: the parousia of Christ (1 Thess. 4:15; 1 Cor. 15:23); the judgment seat of Christ (1 Cor. 5:10) or God (Rom. 14:10); the subjecting of all things to Christ (1 Cor. 15:24 ff.; Phil. 3:21); the universal acknowledgment of Christ (Phil. 2:10 f.); and subjection of all to God (1 Cor. 15:28). Since the future remains hidden (Rom. 11:33–36), precise description is impossible (cf. Rom. 8:23). (iii) The future can be faced with confidence because of oneness with Christ. Again the precise images differ (Rom. 13:14; 1 Cor. 15:23; 2 Cor. 5:8; Phil. 1:23; 3:21; 1 Thess. 4:17; 5:10). (iv) The present is conditioned by the past eschatological occurrence and the hope of future consummation. The realized aspect is apparent only to the eyes of faith. It is also the ground of exhortation and argument.

The use of particular concepts does not present a uniform development capable of being traced in a linear trajectory. The course is zig-zag. However, Baird concedes that there is an overall reduction in the use of apocalyptic language in the later Pauline writings. But it does not amount to the disappearance of apocalyptic (op. cit., 327). Corresponding to this, there is an increase in the concern for the past and the present – a concern which is apparent even in Gal. (cf. 5:1–12;

926

6:7–10) and 2 Cor. 10–13 (cf. 10:3 f.; 11:12–15). At the same time Paul's thought becomes increasingly personal and realistic. Euphemisms like "sleep" (only in 1 Thess. and 1 Cor.) are reduced, while realistic terms like "death" (not in 1 Thess., but more than 20 times in Rom.) and "die" (twice in 1 Thess.; 19 times in Rom.; 7 times in 1 Cor.) are increased (→ Death, arts. *thanatos* and *katheudō*). Perhaps the underlying explanation is that death is a present reality which can be described concretely. As Paul grew older he reflected even more on death in relation to himself and believers, on the one hand, and Christ's death, on the other. But whereas death can be described both literally and metaphorically, the parousia is a reality to which we have no direct access. It cannot, therefore, be described in literal language; it can only be discussed in terms of picture and metaphor. In Paul's treatment of it he did not make a simple shift from apocalyptic to non-apocalyptic language. He was using the language and concepts that were available to him as the common property of himself and his readers. Whilst Paul's precise choice of terminology may well have been determined by the way in which the readers in any given community conceived the eschaton, we cannot rule out a growing understanding in the mind of Paul. What remains throughout is an awareness of accountability for what we do in this life and the possibility that at any time the end may come to us, either through death or with the parousia of Christ, and for this we must be constantly ready.

(d) John. John's eschatology involves two lines of thought. On the one hand, there is what R. E. Brown calls the "vertical" and "horizontal" views of God's saving action; and on the other hand, there is the interrelation of realized and future eschatology (*The Gospel According to John, I, Anchor Bible*, 1966, cxv–cxxi). The "horizontal" line traces God's acts in and through the sequence of history. Thus the Prologue sees the incarnation of the Word in relation to God's existence even before creation (1:1 ff.). In his dialogue with the → Samaritan woman Jesus sees the whole of history as leading up to the eschatological hour when both Samaritan worship on Mt. Gerizim and Jewish worship in the temple at Jerusalem will be superseded (Jn. 4:20 ff.). Moreover, that hour has arrived. "But the hour is coming, and now is, when true worshippers will worship the Father in spirit and truth, for such the Father seeks to worship him. God is spirit, and those who worship him must worship him in spirit and truth" (Jn. 4:23 f.; → Prayer, art. *proskyneō* NT 4). When the woman replies "I know that Messiah is coming (he who is called Christ); when he comes, he will show us all things", Jesus declares: "I who speak to you am he" (Jn. 4:25 f.). Similarly the → feasts find their fulfilment in him (cf. 1:29; 2:13, 23; 4:45; 5:1; 6:4; 7:2, 8, 10 f., 14, 37; 11:55 f.; 12:12, 20; 13:1, 29; 18:28, 39; 19:14). Not only the historic traditions of worship but the scriptures find their fulfilment in Jesus: "You search the scriptures, because you think that in them you have eternal life; and it is they that bear witness to me" (Jn. 5:39). To John everything is leading up to the "hour" which culminates the history of God's dealing with his people (cf. Jn. 2:4; 4:21; 8:20; 12:23, 27; 17:1; → Time, art. *hōra*). This has led some critics to suppose that Jn. is only interested in the "hour" of the ministry of Jesus. But R. E. Brown replies that Jn.'s "problem is not whether there will be a 'time of the Church,' but how this is related to Jesus" (op. cit., cxvi). He presupposes Christian missionary activity (Jn. 4:35–38; 20:21), a conflict of Christianity with the world (16:8), an influx of those who have come to believe through the proclamation of the word (17:20), and the gathering of a flock to be shepherded (11:52; 10:16; 21:15 ff.).

But the acts of God do not operate only on the "horizontal" plane of history. The crucial events are seen as a "vertical" breaking into history. The Son of man has come down from heaven (3:13). The word has become flesh and dwelt among us. The culmination of the activity of Jesus will occur when he is lifted up to heaven in death and resurrection to draw all men to himself (12:32). There is a constant contrast between the above and the below, the divine realm and the world of men (3:3, 31; 8:23). There is a sphere that belongs to Spirit and a sphere that belongs to the flesh (3:6; 6:63). Jesus brings eternal life to a world which in its natural state is given over to death and judgment (3:16–21; cf. 1:12 f.). Death has no power over this life (11:25). The life-sustaining gifts which he gives from above are contrasted with earthly sustenance which has no enduring power: he gives the real water of life which never fails to satisfy (4:10–14); he is the bread of life, as contrasted with the manna in the wilderness that perished (6:27); he is the real light of the world (3:19).

R. E. Brown thinks that the Johannine integration of the "horizontal" and "vertical" elements argues against a gnostic interpretation of the Gospel (op. cit., cvi). Indeed, it represents a blending of the Hellenistic and Hebrew approaches to salvation. C. H. Dodd points out that the concept of "eternal life" (*zōē aiōnios*) is not found in pagan religious and philosophical writers until long after the NT period (*The Interpretation of the Fourth Gospel*, 1953, 146). But the concept has Jewish roots long before this. Life may be thought of as prolonged (Eth.Enoch 10:10) or prolonged after the grave (Dan. 12:2; Test.Ash. 5:2; Pss.Sol. 3:16; 14:6; Eth.Enoch 37:4; 40:9; 2 Macc. 7:9, 14). There is also the doctrine of the two ages, the present age and the age to come, which is fully developed in 2 Esd. *c.* A.D. 100 (7:12 f.; 8:52 ff.; cf. also Eth.Enoch 48:7 with 71:15; Tosefta Peah. 4, 18, p. 24 [*c.* A.D. 50]; → Life, art. *zōē*; → Time, art. *aiōn*). Such references indicate that Jn.'s eschatological concepts were not a novelty. Rather, his presentation of Christ in terms of the "vertical" breaking into the "horizontal" made use of concepts current within Judaism. The novelty lies not in the concepts themselves but in the fact that Christ fulfils them.

At this point we may consider the other line of thought to which R. E. Brown, in common with many other NT scholars, draws attention: the relationship between realized and future eschatology in Jn. At first sight it might appear that Jn. teaches a thoroughly realized eschatology. The coming of the → glory of God is something that is represented as having already come with the incarnation: "And the Word became flesh and dwelt among us, full of grace and truth; we have beheld his glory, glory as of the only Son from the Father" (1:14). The → judgment is decisively brought forward to the present time: "He who believes in him is not condemned; he who does not believe is condemned already, because he has not believed in the name of the only Son of God. And this is the judgment, that the light has come into the world, and men loved darkness rather than light, because their deeds were evil" (3:18 f.). Whereas Matt. 25:31 ff. represents a future judgment scene, Jn. is not concerned with the scene itself. He is concerned with the act on which the judgment turns. Whatever else may follow is ratification of the choices that man makes here and now. In the Synoptics "eternal life" is something that one receives at the last

928

judgment or in a future age. In Jn. it is something that a man enters into here and now: "Truly, truly I say to you, he who hears my word and believes him who sent me, has eternal life; he does not come into judgment, but has passed from death to life" (5:24). For Lk. sonship is something that one has conferred as a future reward (Lk. 6:35; 20:36). In Jn. it is entered into here and now: "But to all who received him, who believed in his name, he gave power to become children of God" (Jn. 1:12).

But these passages must not be taken in isolation. Even in themselves they are not a repudiation of futuristic eschatology. Rather, they draw attention to the eschatological dimension of the present. The whole work, as Brown reminds us (op. cit., cxviii) was written in a post-resurrection situation. The readers would read about the new birth and entry into the kingdom (3:5), feeding on the living bread (6:27, 54, 57), and the life-giving Spirit (6:63; 7:38 f.; 16:7; 19:30; 20:22) in the light of a belief which extended beyond the plane of the continuously horizontal present. However, there are a number of passages which contain explicitly futuristic elements. Jesus' reply to Martha in respect of her affirmation of belief in the raising of her dead brother Lazarus in the resurrection relates it to himself in the present in a way which admits a future aspect: "I am the resurrection and the life; he who believes in me, though he die, yet shall he live" (11:25). The saying about Jesus' going away to prepare dwelling places in his Father's → house implies a future beyond the present (14:2 f.). At the climax of the high priestly prayer Jesus intercedes for the future state of the disciples: "Father, I desire that they also, whom thou hast given me, may be with me where I am, to behold my glory which thou hast given me in thy love for me before the foundation of the world" (17:24).

From what has been said so far it might be concluded that, while Jn. lays great emphasis on the eschatological dimension of the present but also hints at its future dimension, he does so in ways which avoid as far as possible apocalyptic language and concepts. But there are passages which refer to a second coming, a resurrection at the end time and the last judgment. Thus in the discourse in Jn. 5 Jesus declares: "Truly, truly, I say to you, the hour is coming, and now is, when the dead will hear the voice of the Son of God, and those who hear will live. For as the Father has life in himself, so he has granted the Son also to have life in himself, and has given him authority to execute judgment, because he is the Son of man. Do not marvel at this; for the hour is coming when all who are in the tombs will hear his voice and come forth, those who have done good, to the resurrection of life, and those who have done evil, to the resurrection of judgment" (5:25–28). In the middle of the discourse on the bread of life Jesus declares that he has come to do the will of him that sent him: "and this is the will of him who sent me, that I should lose nothing of all that he has given me, but raise it up at the last day. For this is the will of my Father, that every one who sees the Son and believes in him should have eternal life; and I will raise him up at the last day" (6:39 f.). This theme is further underlined in the same discourse: "No one can come to me unless the Father who sent me draws him; and I will raise him up at the last day. . . . He who eats my flesh and drinks my blood has eternal life, and I will raise him up at the last day" (6:44, 54). Similarly, the public ministry of Jesus reaches its climax with the declaration: "He who rejects me and does not receive my sayings has a judge; the word that I have spoken will be his judge at the last day" (12:48). This is endorsed by the affirmation

929

that what Jesus has said has been uttered on the authority of the Father and that his commandment is eternal life" (12:49 f.).

R. Bultmann deals with these passages by claiming that they are the work of the evangelist-redactor who inserted them to adapt the theology to the original Johannine church at large (*The Gospel of John*, 1971, 219 ff., 229, 233, 260 f., 345). Brown rejects this on purely literary grounds (op. cit., cxviii; cf. D. M. Smith, *The Composition and Order of the Fourth Gospel*, 1965, 230 ff.). Moreover, he suggests that if we take Rev. into account to form an overall picture of Johannine theology, the excision from Jn. of apocalyptic passages is unwarranted. E. Stauffer explains the emphasis in Jn. on realized eschatology and the hidden messiah as the work of the evangelist who sought to counter the vulgar apocalyptic elements that had become current in Christianity since the death of Jesus ("Agnostos Christos: Joh. ii. 24 und die Eschatologie des vierten Evangeliums", in W. D. Davies and D. Daube, eds., *The Background of the New Testament and Its Eschatology*, 1954, 281–99). Thus with Dodd, Stauffer believes that Jesus himself taught an eschatology with a strongly realized emphasis. M.-E. Boismard, however, thinks that the apocalyptic passages in Jn. were the earlier and the ones emphasizing the realized element reflect a later insight ("L'Évolution du Thème eschatologique dans les Traditions Johanniques", *RB* 68, 1961, 507–24). R. E. Brown believes that the tension between the realized and apocalyptic elements reflects the tension within the teaching of Jesus himself which is reflected in the Synoptic Gospels (cf. Matt. 10:23; 26:64; Mk. 9:1; 13:30; with Mk. 13:32 f.; Lk. 17:22). "It is a dubious procedure to excise one or the other group of statements in order to reconstruct a consistent eschatological view held by Jesus. The recognition that there were both realized and final elements in Jesus' own eschatology means that in the subsequent developments . . . the NT writers were not creating *ex nihilo* theories of realized or of final eschatology, but were applying to a particular situation one or the other strain already present in Jesus' thought" (op. cit., cxix). In fact, both strains were already present in Judaism. The War Scroll from Qumran (1QM) shows expectation of a final intervention, but other teaching at Qumran suggests that the community believed that they already shared in the heavenly gifts, that they were saved from judgment and enjoyed the companionship of the angels. Brown thinks that Jn. 21:22 f. (with its attempt to clarify that Jesus did not say that the disciple in question would not die but rather "If it is my will that he remain until I come, what is that to you?") was included to counter belief that Jesus would return within the lifetime of the disciples (op. cit., cxx; cf. 2 Pet. 3:4 and the discussion of Mk. 13:30 above). He also allows for the possibility of redaction.

Perhaps the best explanation of the eschatological emphases of Jn. is to recognize that it contains in tension the same elements as the Synoptic Gospels, but that stress on the eschatological dimension of the present is laid in view of the current apocalyptic beliefs canvassed in Judaism at a time when the existence of Judaism is under threat and the fall of Jerusalem is imminent. Jn.'s equivalent of the warnings in the apocalyptic discourse in the Synoptics about false Christs and wars is to stress the "now" of the Christ-event. His equivalent to the warnings of judgment on Jerusalem in the Synoptics is to speak about judgment here and now and depict the conduct of the Jews. It falls outside the scope of this note to discuss the relationship between Jn. and Rev. But if they were the work of the same author or even reflected a basic underlying Johannine theological standpoint, it could be that the eschatology of Jn. and Rev. is to be understood as being complementary. The fourth Gospel stresses especially the eschatological dimension of the present in the light of the advent of Christ; Rev. stresses the eschatological dimension of history in the light of the advent of Christ. But in neither case can the present be divorced from the future, and in both cases the decisive factor is Christ. (For discussion of the eschatology of Rev. → Number, arts. *hepta* and *chilias*. Here it is argued that the number "seven" provides the key to the structure of the book in terms of seven parallel but cumulative visions of history culminating in the vision of the new → Jerusalem, corresponding to the seven days of creation of Gen. 1. The question of the millennium is also discussed.) *C. Brown*

→ Abomination of Desolation, → Antichrist, → Heaven, → Hell, → Judgment, → King, Kingdom, → Number, → Sabbath, → Time

On *hēmera* and eschatology in the OT:
(a). L. Černy, *The Day of Yahweh and Some Relevant Problems*, 1948; A. J. Everson, "The Days of Yahweh", *JBL* 93, 1974, 329–37; F. C. Fensham, "A Possible Origin of the Concept of the Day of the Lord", *Biblical Essays*, 1966, 90–97; F. V. Filson, "*Yesterday": A Study of Hebrews in the Light of Chapter 13*, *SBT* Second Series 4, 1967; H. Gross, "Day of Yahweh", *EBT* 1 179 ff.; L. Hartman, "The Functions of Some So-Called Apocalyptic Timetables", *NTS*, 22 1975–76, 1–14; J. Lindblom, *Prophecy in Ancient Israel*, 1962, 316 ff.; F. R. McCurley, " 'And after Six Days' (Mark 9:2): A Semitic Literary Device", *JBL* 93, 1974, 67–81; S. Mowinckel, *He That Cometh*, 1956; and *The Psalms in Israel's Worship*, I–II, 1962; G. von Rad, "The Origin of the Day of Yahweh", *JSS* 4, 1959, 97–108; and *Old Testament Theology*, II, 1965, 119–25; G. von Rad, and G. Delling, *hēmera*, *TDNT* II 943–53; H. W. Robinson, *Inspiration and Revelation in the Old Testament*, 1946, 135–47; W. Rordorf, *Sunday: The History of the Day of Rest and Worship in the Earliest Centuries of the Christian Church*, 1968; H. H. Rowley, "The Day of the Lord", in *The Faith of Israel; Aspects of Old Testament Thought*, 1956, 177–201; D. S. Russell, *The Method and Message of Jewish Apocalyptic*, 200 B.C.–A.D. *100*, 1964; N. H. Snaith, "Time in the Old Testament", in F. F. Bruce, ed., *Promise and Fulfilment: Essays Presented to Professor S. H. Hooke*, 1963, 175–86; S. J. DeVries, *Yesterday, Today and Tomorrow: Time and History in the Old Testament*, 1975; T. C. Vriezen, *Prophecy and Eschatology*, Supplements to *VT* 1, 1953; 199–229, M. Weiss, "The Origin of the 'Day of the Lord' Reconsidered", *Hebrew Union College Annual* 37, 1966, 29–60.

(b). J. Bourke, "Le Jour de Yahvé dans Joël", *RB* 66, 1959, 5–31 and 191–212; W. Bousset, *Die Religion des Judentums im späthellenistischen Zeitalter*, 1926², 202 ff.; H. Gressmann, *Der Ursprung der israelitisch-jüdischen Eschatologie*, *FRLANT* 6, 1905; and *Der Messias*, *FRLANT* 43, 1929; S. Herrmann, *Die prophetischen Heilserwartungen im Alten Testament*, 1965; G. Hölscher, *Die Ursprünge der jüdischen Eschatologie*, 1925; E. Jenni, "Das Wort '*ōlām* in Alten Testament", *ZAW* 64, 1952, 197–248; 65, 1953, 1–35; and *yôm*, *THAT* 1 707–26; R. Largement and H. Lemaître, "Le Jour de Yahvé dans le Contexte Oriental", *Bibliotheca Ephemeridum Lovaniensium*, XII, 1959. *Sacra Pagina, Miscellanea Biblica Congressus Internationalis Catholici de Re Biblica*, 1, 159–66; H.-M. Lutz, *Jahwe, Jerusalem und die Völker*, 1968, 130–46; S. Mowinckel, "Jahves Dag", *Norsk Teologisk Tidsskrift* 59, 1958, 1–56, 209–29; H.-P. Müller, *Ursprünge und Strukturen alttestamentlicher Eschatologie*, *BZAW* 109, 1969; G. von Rad, *Der heilige Krieg im alten Israel*, 1949; SB I 953; II 812 ff.; K.-D. Schunck, "Strukturlinien in der Entwicklung der Vorstellung vom Tag Jahwes", *VT* 14, 1964, 319 ff.; C. Steuernagel, "Die Strukturlinien der Entwicklung der jüdischen Eschatologie", *Bertholet Festschrift*, 1950, 479 ff.; P. Volz, *Jüdische Eschatologie von Daniel bis Akiba*, 1903; and *Die Eschatologie der jüdischen Gemeinde im neutestamentlichen Zeitalter*, 1934.

On *maranatha*:
(a). W. F. Albright and C. S. Mann, "Two Texts in I Corinthians", *NTS* 16, 1969–70, 271–76; M. Black, "The Maranatha Invocation and Jude 14, 15 (I Enoch 1:9)", in B. Lindars and S. S.

Smalley, eds., *Christ and Spirit in the New Testament: In Honour of Charles Francis Digby Moule*, 1973, 189–96; G. Bornkamm, "The Anathema in the Early Christian Lord's Supper Liturgy". *Early Christian Experience*, 1969, 169–79; W. Bousset, *Kyrios Christos*, 1970; R. Bultmann, *Theology of the New Testament*, I, 1952, 52; O. Cullmann, *The Christology of the New Testament*, 1959, 210 ff.; W. Dunphy, "Maranatha: Development in Early Christianity", *Irish Theological Quarterly* 37, 1970, 294 ff.; J. A. Emerton, "MARANATHA and EPHPHATHA", *JTS* New Series 18, 1967, 427–31; W. Kramer, *Christ, Lord, Son of God*, *SBT* 50, 99–107; K. G. Kuhn, *maranatha*, *TDNT* IV 466–72; R. Longenecker, *The Christology of Early Jewish Christianity*, *SBT* Second Series 17, 1970, 121–24; C. F. D. Moule, "A Reconsideration of the Context of *Maranatha*", *NTS* 6, 1959–60, 307–10.
(b). J. Betz, "Die Eucharistie in der Didache", *Archiv für Liturgiewissenschaft* 9, 1969, 26 ff., 34 ff.; B. Botte, *Noël-Épiphanie, Retour du Christ*, 1967, 25–42; E. Peterson, HEIS THEOS, 1926; S. Schultz, "Maranatha und Kyrios Jesus", *ZNW* 53, 1962, 125–44.

On *parousia* and eschatology in the NT:
(a). A. W. Argyle, "Does 'Realized Eschatology' Make Sense?", *Hibbert Journal* 51, 1952–53, 385 f.; J. W. Bailey, "The Temporary Messianic Reign in the Literature of Early Judaism", *JBL* 52, 1934, 170 ff.; W. Baird, "Pauline Eschatology in Hermeneutical Perspective", *NTS* 17, 1970–71, 314–27; R. F. Barkey, "*engizein, phthanein* and Realized Eschatology", *JBL* 82, 1963, 177 ff.; C. K. Barrett, "New Testament Eschatology", *SJT* 6, 1953, 136–55 and 235–43; "The Holy Spirit in the Fourth Gospel", *JTS* New Series 1, 1950, 1–15; "The Place of Eschatology in the Fourth Gospel", *ExpT* 59, 1947–48, 302–5; *The Holy Spirit and the Gospel Tradition*, 1947; *The Gospel according to St. John*, 1955; *Luke the Historian in Recent Research*, (1963) 1970; *The First Epistle to the Corinthians*, *BNTC*, 1968; *The Second Epistle to the Corinthians*, *BNTC*, 1973; H.-W. Bartsch, ed., *Kerygma and Myth*, I and II in combined volume, 1972; W. A. Beardslee, "Was Jesus More Optimistic than Paul?" *Journal of Biblical Religion* 24, 1956, 264–68; G. R. Beasley-Murray, *Jesus and the Future: An Examination of the Criticism of the Eschatological Discourse, Mark 13, with Special Reference to the Little Apocalypse Theory*, 1954; *A Commentary on Mark 13*, 1957; "A Century of Eschatological Discussion", *ExpT* 64, 1952–53, 312–16; and *The Book of Revelation*, New Century Bible, 1974; G. C. Berkouwer, *The Return of Christ*, 1972; E. Best, *The First and Second Epistles to the Thessalonians*, *BNTC*, 1972; O. Betz, "The Kerygma of Luke", *Interpretation* 22, 1968, 131–46; H. Bietenhard, "The Millennial Hope in the Early Church", *SJT* 6, 1953, 12–30; G. Bornkamm, *Jesus of Nazareth*, 1960; *Paul*, 1971; G. Bornkamm, G. Barth and H. J. Held, *Tradition and Interpretation in Matthew*, 1963; W. Bousset, *Kyrios Christos*, 1970; J. W. Bowman, *The Intention of Jesus*, 1945; and "From Schweitzer to Bultmann", *Theology Today* 11, 1954, 160–78; R. E. Brown, *The Gospel according to John*, I, 1966; II, 1971; J. E. Bruns, "The Use of Time in the Fourth Gospel", *NTS* 13, 1966–67, 285–90; R. Bultmann, *Jesus Christ and Mythology*, 1960; *History and Eschatology: The Presence of Eternity*, 1957; "History and Eschatology in the New Testament", *NTS* 1, 1954–55, 5 ff.; *The Gospel of John: A Commentary*, 1971; G. B. Caird, "Eschatology and Politics: Some Misconceptions", in J. R. McKay and J. F. Miller, eds., *Biblical Studies: Essays in Honour of William Barclay*, 1976, 72–86; R. H. Charles, *A Critical History of the Doctrine of a Future Life in Israel, in Judaism and in Christianity* 1913²; and *Religious Development between the Testaments*, 1914; K. W. Clarke, "Realized Eschatology", *JBL* 59, 1940, 367 ff.; W. K. Lowther Clarke, "The Clouds of Heaven: An Eschatological Study", *Theology* 31, 1935, 63 ff. and 128 ff.; H. Conzelmann, *The Theology of St Luke*, 1960; and "Luke's Place in the Development of Early Christianity", in L. E. Keck and J. L. Martyn, eds., op. cit., 298–316; A. Correll, *Consumatum Est: Eschatology and Church in the Gospel of St. John*, 1958; C. T. Craig, "Realized Eschatology", *JBL* 56, 1937, 17 ff.; O. Cullmann, *Christ and Time: The Primitive Christian Conception of Time and History*, 1951; *Immortality of the Soul or Resurrection of the Dead? The Witness of the New Testament*, 1958; *The Christology of the New Testament*, 1959; "The Return of Christ", in *The Early Church*, 1956, 141–62; *Salvation in History*, 1967; W. D. Davies and D. Daube, eds., *The Background of the New Testament and its Eschatology: In Honour of Charles Harold Dodd*, 1954; A. Deissmann, *Light from the Ancient East*, 1911², 372 ff.; G. Delling, *koloboō*, *TDNT* III 823 ff.; C. H. Dodd, *The Parables of the Kingdom*, 1936²; *The Apostolic Preaching and its Developments*, 1936; *History and the Gospel*, 1938; *The Coming of Christ*, 1952; *The Interpretation of the Fourth Gospel*, 1953; *Historical Tradition and the Fourth Gospel*, 1963; *The Founder of Christianity*, 1970; *New Testament Studies*.

932

1953; *More New Testament Studies*, 1968; J. W. Drane, "Eschatology, Ecclesiology and Catholicity in the New Testament", *ExpT* 83, 1971–72, 180–84; G. Ebeling, "Time and Word", in J. M. Robinson, ed., *The Future of Our Religious Past: Essays in Honour of Rudolf Bultmann*, 1971, 247–66; E. E. Ellis, *The Gospel of Luke*, New Century Bible, 1966; "II Corinthians v. 1–10 in Pauline Eschatology", *NTS* 6, 1959–60, 211–24; "Present and Future Eschatology in Luke: For W. G. Kümmel on his Sixtieth Birthday", *NTS* 12, 1965–66, 27–41; and *Eschatology in Luke*, Facet Books, Biblical Series 30, 1972; H. Flender, *St Luke: Theologian of Redemptive History*, 1967; R. T. France, *Jesus and the Old Testament: His Application of Old Testament Passages to Himself and His Mission*, 1971; F. O. Francis, "Eschatology and History in Luke-Acts", *Journal of the American Academy of Religion* 37, 1969, 49–63; E. Franklin, "The Ascension and the Eschatology of Luke-Acts", *SJT* 23, 1970, 191–200; and *Christ the Lord: A Study in the Purpose and Theology of Luke-Acts*, 1975; E. Fuchs, "Jesus' Understanding of Time", in *Studies of the Historical Jesus*, SBT 42, 1964, 104–66; R. W. Funk, "The Apostolic *Parousia:* Form and Significance", in W. R. Farmer, C. F. D. Moule and R. R. Niebuhr, eds., *Christian History and Interpretation: Studies Presented to John Knox*, 1967, 249–68; W. W. Gasque, "The Historical Value of the Book of Acts: An Essay in the History of New Testament Criticism", *EQ* 41, 1969, 68–88; L. Gaston, *No Stone on Another: Studies in the Significance of the Fall of Jerusalem in the Synoptic Gospels*, Supplements to NovT 23, 1970; T. F. Glasson, *The Second Advent: The Origin of the New Testament Doctrine*, 1947²; *His Appearing and His Kingdom: The Christian Hope in the Light of its History*, 1953; G. Gloege, *The Day of His Coming: The Man in the Gospels*, 1963; K. Grayston, "The Study of Mark XIII", *BJRL* 56, 1973–74, 371–78; N. Q. Hamilton, *The Holy Spirit and Eschatology in Paul*, SJT Occasional Papers 6, 1957; M. J. Harris, "2 Corinthians 5:1–10; Watershed in Paul's Eschatology?" *TB* 22, 1971, 32–57; and "Resurrection and Immortality: Eight Theses", *Themelios* 1, 1976, 50–55; L. Hartman, *Prophecy Interpreted: The Function of Some Jewish Apocalyptic Texts and of the Eschatological Discourse, Mark 13 par.*, Coniectanea Biblica, New Testament Series 1, 1966; R. H. Hiers, "The Problem of the Delay of the Parousia in Luke-Acts", *NTS* 20, 1973–74, 145–55; W. F. Howard, *Christianity according to St John*, 1943, 106–28; and *The Fourth Gospel in Recent Criticism and Interpretation*, revised by C. K. Barrett, 1955; E. Käsemann, "An Apologia for Primitive Christian Eschatology", in *Essays on New Testament Themes*, SBT 41, 1964, 169–95; and "On the Subject of Primitive Christian Apocalyptic," in *New Testament Questions of Today*, 1969, 108–37; L. E. Keck and J. L. Martyn, eds., *Studies in Luke-Acts*, 1968; J. M. Kik, *Matthew Twenty-Four*, 1948 (reprinted in *An Eschatology of Victory*, 1971); W. G. Kümmel, *Promise and Fulfilment: The Eschatological Message of Jesus*, SBT 23, 1961²; "Eschatological Expectation in the Proclamation of Jesus", in J. M. Robinson, ed., op. cit., 29–48; *The New Testament: The History of the Investigation of its Problems*, 1973; and "Futuristic and Realized Eschatology in the Earliest Stages of Christianity", *JR* 43, 1963, 303–14; G. E. Ladd, *Jesus and the Kingdom*, 1966; and "Apocalyptic and the New Testament Theology", in R. Banks, ed., *Reconciliation and Hope: New Testament Essays . . . Presented to L. L. Morris*, 1974, 285–96; J. Lowe, "An Examination of Attempts to Detect Developments in St. Paul's Theology", *JTS* 42, 1941, 129–42; G. Lundström, *The Kingdom of God in the Teaching of Jesus: A History of Interpretation*, 1963; G. T. Manley, *The Return of Christ*, 1960; T. W. Manson, "Realized Eschatology and the Messianic Secret", in D. E. Nineham, ed., *Studies in the Gospels: Essays in Memory of R. H. Lightfoot*, 1955, 209–22; W. Manson, G. W. Lampe, T. F. Torrance and W. A. Whitehouse, *Eschatology*, SJT Occasional Papers 2, 1953; J. Marsh, *The Fulness of Time*, 1952; I. H. Marshall, *Eschatology and the Parables*, 1963; *Luke: Historian and Theologian*, 1970; and "Martyrdom and the Parousia", *StudEv* IV, 1, 1968, 333–39; W. Marxsen, *Mark the Evangelist: Studies on the Redaction History of the Gospel*, 1969, 151–206; P. S. Minear, "The Time of Hope in the New Testament", *SJT* 6, 1953, 337–61; J. Moltmann, *Theology of Hope: On the Ground and Implications of a Christian Theology*, 1967; *Hope and Planning*, 1971; *Theology and Joy*, 1973; and *The Crucified God: The Cross of Christ as the Foundation and Criticism of Christian Theology*, 1974; A. L. Moore, *The Parousia in the New Testament*, Supplements to NovT 13, 1966; and *1 and 2 Thessalonians*, New Century Bible, 1969; L. Morris, *The First and Second Epistle to the Thessalonians*, NLC, 1969; C. F. D. Moule, "The Influence of Circumstances on Eschatological Terms", *JTS* New Series 15, 1964, 1–15, R. H. Mounce, "Pauline Eschatology and the Apocalypse", *EQ* 46, 1974, 164 ff.; A. Oepke, *parousia* etc., *TDNT* V 858–71; J. J. O'Rourke, "The Historical Present in the Gospel of John", *JBL* 93, 1974, 585–90; R. Otto, *The Kingdom of God and the Son of Man*, 1938; H. P. Owen, "The

Parousia in the Synoptic Gospels", *SJT* 12, 1959, 171–92; E. Pax, "Parousia", *EBT* II 633–38; W. Pannenberg, *Jesus – God and Man*, 1968; *Basic Questions in Theology*, I–III, 1970–73; "Focal Essay: The Revelation of God in Jesus of Nazareth", in J. M. Robinson and J. B. Cobb, eds., *Theology as History, New Frontiers in Theology*, III, 1967, 101–33; W. Pannenberg, ed., *Revelation as History*, 1969; N. Perrin, *The Kingdom of God in the Teaching of Jesus: A History of Interpretation from the Last Decades of the Nineteenth Century to the Present Day*, 1963; *Rediscovering the Teaching of Jesus*, 1967; "Eschatology and Hemeneutics: Reflections on Method in the Interpretation of the New Testament", *JBL* 93, 1974, 3–14; and *Jesus and the Language of the Kingdom: Symbol and Metaphor in New Testament Interpretation*, 1976; H. S. Reimarus, *The Goal of Jesus and his Disciples*, tr. G. W. Buchanan, 1970; and *Fragments*, ed. C. H. Talbert and R. S. Fraser, 1971; J. A. T. Robinson, *In the End God . . .*, (1950) 1968²; and *Jesus and His Coming: The Emergence of a Doctrine*, 1957; J. Rohde, *Rediscovering the Teaching of the Evangelists*, 1968; E. C. Rust, "Time and Eternity in Biblical Thought", *Theology Today*, 10, 1953, 327–56; and *Towards a Theological Understanding of History*, 1963; R. Schnackenburg, *God's Rule and Kingdom*, 1963; *The Church in the New Testament*, 1965; *Present and Future*, 1966; A. Schweitzer, *The Quest of the Historical Jesus: A Critical Study of its Progress from Reimarus to Wrede*, (1910) 1954³; *Paul and his Interpreters: A Critical History*, 1912; *The Mystery of the Kingdom of God*, 1914; *The Psychiatric Study of Jesus*, 1968; *The Kingdom of God and Primitive Christianity*, 1968; R. B. Y. Scott, "Behold he Cometh with the Clouds", *NTS* 5, 1958–59, 127–32; S. S. Smalley, "The Theatre of Parousia", *SJT* 17, 1964, 406–13; R. H. Smith, "The Eschatology of Acts and Contemporary Exegesis", *Concordia Theological Monthly* 29, 1958, 641–63; and "History and Eschatology in Luke-Acts", ibid., 881–901; W. Stott, "A Note on the Word ΚΥΡΙΑΚΕ in Rev. i. 10", *NTS* 12, 1965–66, 70–75; K. A. Strand, "Another Look at 'Lord's Day' in the Early Church and in Rev. i.10", *NTS* 13, 1966–1967, 174–81; W. Strawson, *Jesus and the Future Life*, 1959; T. F. Torrance, *When Christ Comes and Comes Again*, 1957; G. Vos, *The Pauline Eschatology*, 1952; J. Weiss, *Jesus' Proclamation of the Kingdom of God*, 1971; D. Wenham, "Recent Study of Mark 13: Part 1", *TSF Bulletin* 71, 1975, 6–15; "Recent Study of Mark 13: Part 2", ibid. 72, 1975, 1–9; M. Werner, *The Formation of Christian Dogma*, 1957; D. E. H. Whiteley, *The Theology of St. Paul*, 1974²; A. N. Wilder, *Eschatology and Ethics in the Teaching of Jesus*, revised edition 1950; *Kerygma, Eschatology, and Social Ethics*, Facet Books, Social Ethics Series 12, 1966 (reprinted from W. D. Davies and D. Daube, eds., op. cit., 509–36); and "Eschatology and the Speech-Modes of the Gospel", in E. Dinkler, ed., *Zeit und Geschichte Dankesgabe an Rudolf Bultmann zum 80. Geburtstag*, 1964, 19–30; S. G. Wilson, "Lukan Eschatology", *NTS* 16, 1969–70, 330–47.

(b). P. Althaus, *Die letzten Dinge*, 1949⁵; J. Blank, *Untersuchungen zur johanneischen Christologie und Eschatologie*, 1964; M.-E. Boismard, "L'Évolution du Thème eschatologique dans les Traditions Johanniques", *RB* 68, 1961, 507–24; H.-W. Bartsch, "Zum Problem der Parusieverzögerung bei den Synoptikern", *EvTh* 19, 1959, 116 ff.; G. Bornkamm, "Die Verzögerung der Parusie", in W. Schmauch, ed., *In Memoriam E. Lohmeyer*, 1951, 116 ff.; and "Enderwartung und Kirche im Matthäusevangelium", in W. D. Davies and D. Daube, eds., op. cit., 222–60; W. Bousset, *Die Religion des Judentums im späthellenistischen Zeitalter*, ed. H. Gressmann 1926³; H. Braun, "Der Sinn der neutestamentlichen Christologie", *ZTK* 54, 341 ff.; R. Bultmann, "Geschichte und Eschatologie im Neuen Testament", *Glauben und Verstehen*, III, 1960, 91 ff.; F. Buri, *Die Bedeutung der neutestamentlichen Eschatologie für die neuere protestantische Theologie*, 1935; F. Busch, *Zum Verständnis der synoptischen Eschatologie. Markus 13 neu untersucht*, 1938; T. Colani, *Jésus Christ et les Croyances Messianiques de son Temps*, 1864²; H. Conzelmann, "Eschatologie, IV", *RGG³* II 665 ff.; and "Parusie", *RGG³* V 130 ff.; O. Cullmann, "Das wahre durch die ausgebliebene Parusie gestellte neutestamentliche Problem", *ThZ* 3, 1947, 177 ff. (reprinted in *Vorträge und Aufsätze*, 1967, 414 ff.); "Parusieverzögerung und Christentum – der gegenwärtige Stand der Diskussion", *TLZ* 83, 1958, 21 ff. (reprinted in op. cit., 427 ff.); and "L'Évangile Johannique et l'Histoire du Salut", *NTS* 11, 1964–65, 111–22; G. Delling, *Das Zeitverständnis des Neuen Testaments*, 1940; M. Dibelius, *An die Thessalonicher*, 1937³ (excursus on 1 Thess. 2:19); J. Dupont, *Syn Christō*, 1952, 55 ff.; E. E. Ellis, "Die Funktion der Eschatologie im Lukasevangelium", *ZTK* 66, 1969, 387–402 (English version revised in *Facet Book* noted above); G. Gloege, *Reich Gottes und Kirche im Neuen Testament*, 1929; E. Grässer, *Das Problem der Parusieverzögerung in den synoptischen Evangelien und in der Apostelgeschichte*, *BZNW* 22, 1957; H. Greeven, "Kirche und Parusie Christi", *KuD* 10, 1964, 113 ff.; L. van Hartingveld, *Die Eschatologie des Johannesevangeliums*, 1962; J. Körner, "Endgeschichtliche Parusieerwartung im

Neuen Testament und ihrer Bedeutung für eine christliche Theologie", *EvTh* 14, 1954, 177 ff.; H. W. Kuhn,·*Enderwartung und gegenwärtiges Heil, Studien zur Umwelt des Neuen Testaments* 4, 1966; W. G. Kümmel, "Luc en Accusation dans la Théologie Contemporaine", *Ephemerides Theologicae Lovanienses* 46, 1970, 265–81; *Kirchenbegriff und Geschichtsbewusstsein in der Urgemeinde und bei Jesus*, 1943; and "Futuristische und präsentische Eschatologie im ältesten Urchristentum", *NTS* 5, 1958–59, 113–26; J. Lambrecht, *Die Redaktion der Markus-Apokalypse. Literarische Analyse und Strukturuntersuchung, Analecta Biblica* 28, 1967; E. Lohmeyer, *Das Evangelium des Markus, KEK* 1/2, 1967[17]; E. Lohse, "Lukas als Theologe der Heilsgeschichte", *EvTh* 14, 1954, 256 ff.; and "Zur neutestamentlichen Eschatologie", *Verkündigung und Forschung*, 1956, 184 ff.; W. Michaelis, *Der Herr verzieht nicht die Verheissung*, 1942; and "Kennen die Synoptiker eine Verzögerung der Parusie?", *Synoptische Studien für A. Wikenhauser*, 1953, 107 ff.; R. Morgenthaler, *Die lukanische Geschichtsschreibung als Zeugnis. Gestalt und Gehalt der Kunst Lukas*, I–II, *AThANT* 14–15, 1949; E. Pax, *Epiphaneia*, 1955, 208–44; R. Pesch, *Naherwartungen Tradition und Redaktion in Markus 13*, 1968; P. Ricca, *Die Eschatologie des vierten Evangeliums*, 1966; F. J. Schierse "Himmelssehnsucht und Reich-Gottes-Erwartung", *Geist und Leben* 26, 1953, 189–201; E. Schweizer, "Der Menschensohn", *ZNW* 50, 1959, 185 ff. (reprinted in *Neotestamentica*, 1963, 56 ff.); J. A. Sint, "Parusie-Erwartung und Parusie-Verzögerung im paulinischen Briefkorpus", *Zeitschrift für katholische Theologie* 86, 1964, 47 ff.; B. Stählin, "Zum Problem der johanneischen Eschatologie", *ZNW* 33, 1934, 225–59; E. Stauffer, "Agnostos Christos: Joh. ii. 24 und die Eschatologie des vierten Evangeliums", in W. D. Davies and D. Daube, eds., op. cit., 281–99; A. Strobel, *Untersuchungen zum eschatologischen Verzögerungsproblem*, 1961; P. Vielhauer, "Gottesreich und Menschensohn", *Festschrift für G. Dehn*, 1957, 51 ff. (reprinted in *Aufsätze zum Neuen Testament, ThB* 31, 1965, 55 ff.); G. Voss, *Die Christologie der lukanischen Schriften in Grundzügen, Studia Neotestamentica* 2, 1965; H. E. Weber, *"Eschatologie" und "Mystik" im Neuen Testament*, 1930; H.-D. Wendland, *Die Eschatologie des Reichs Gottes bei Jesus*, 1931.

Addenda

S INCE THE PUBLICATION OF THE FIRST EDITION OF *The New International Dictionary of New Testament Theology* the following general books have been published, which supplement those listed previously in the bibliographies: R. Banks, *Paul's Idea of Community: The Early House Churches in their Historical Setting*, 1980; C. Bekker, *The Apostle Paul*, 1980; H. Boers, *What is New Testament Theology?*, 1979; F. F. Bruce, *Men and Movements in the Primitive Church: Studies in Early Non-Pauline Christianity*, 1980; R. A. Guelich, ed., *Unity and Diversity in New Testament Theology: Essays in Honor of G. E. Ladd*, 1978; R. A. Edwards, *A Concordance to Q*, 1975; R. A. Edwards, *A Theology of Q: Eschatology, Prophecy, Wisdom*, 1976; E. Ellis and E. Grässer, eds., *Jesus und Paulus: Festschrift für Werner Georg Kümmel zum 70. Geburtstag*, 1975; F. O. Francis and J. P. Sampley, *Pauline Parallels*, 1975; L. Gaston, *Horae Synopticae Electronicae: Word Statistics of the Synoptic Gospels*, 1975; D. A. Hagner and M. J. Harris, eds., *Pauline Studies: Essays Presented to Professor F. F. Bruce on his Seventieth Birthday*, 1980; G. F. Hasel, *Old Testament Theology: Basic Issues in the Current Debate*, 1975; G. F. Hasel, *New Testament Theology: Basic Issues in the Current Debate*, 1978; P. Henry, *New Directions in New Testament Studies*, 1979; M. D. Hooker, *A Preface to Paul*, 1980; G. Howard, *Paul: Crisis in Galatia, A Study in Early Christian Theology*, *Society for New Testament Studies Monograph Series* 35, 1979; G. Hughes, *Hebrews and Hermeneutics: The Epistle to the Hebrews as a New Testament Example of Biblical Interpretation*, *Society for New Testament Studies Monograph Series* 36, 1979; E. Käsemann, *Commentary on Romans*, 1980; R. P. Martin, *Reconciliation: A Study of Paul's Theology*, 1980; R. P. Martin, *The Family and the Fellowship: New Testament Images of the Church*, 1980; R. P. Martin, "New Testament Theology: Impasse and Exit", *ExpT* 91, 1980 (in two parts); R. Morgenthaler, *Statische Synopse*, 1971.

The following works supplement the bibliographies under their respective titles.

Generation
R. R. Wilson, *Genealogy and History in the Biblical World*, Yale Near Eastern Researches 7, 1977.

Goal
G. McConville, "God's 'Name' and God's 'Glory' ", *TB* 30, 1979.

J. Bogart, *Orthodox and Heretical Perfectionism in the Johannine Community as Evident in the First Epistle of John*, Society for Biblical Literature Dissertation

Series 33, 1977; L. Dey, *The Intermediary World and Patterns of Perfection in Philo and Hebrews*, 1975.

God, Gods, Emmanuel

M. Delcor, "Les diverses manières d'écrire le tetragramme sacré dans les anciens documents hébraïques", *RHR* 147, 1955, 145 ff.; D. Flusser, "Paganism in Palestine", in S. Safrai, M. Stern *et al.*, eds., *The Jewish People in the First Century: Historical Geography, Political History, Social, Cultural and Religious Life and Institutions*, II, 1976, 1065–1100; C. E. L'Heureux, *Rank among the Canaanite Gods: El, Baal, and the Rephaim*, Harvard Semitic Monographs 21, 1979; C. H. Holladay, *Theios Aner in Hellenistic-Judaism: A Critique of the Use of this Category in New Testament Christology*, Society for Biblical Literature Dissertation Series 40, 1977; G. W. H. Lampe, *God as Spirit*, The Bampton Lectures 1976, 1977; B. A. Mastin, "The Imperial Cult and the Ascription of the Title *Theos* to Jesus (John xx.28)", *StudEv, TU* 112, 1973, 352 ff.; S. A. Matzcak, ed., *God in Contemporary Thought*, Philosophical Questions Series 10, 1977; E. T. Mullen, *The Assembly of the Gods: The Divine Council in Canaanite and Hebrew Literature*, Harvard Semitic Monographs 24, 1980; K. Rahner, *The Trinity*, 1974; C. Stead, *Divine Substance*, 1977.

Gospel

D. P. Fuller, *Gospel and Law: Contrast or Continuum?*, 1980; R. H. Gundry, "Recent Investigations into the Literary Genre 'Gospel' ", in R. N. Longenecker and M. C. Tenney, eds., *New Dimensions in New Testament Study*, 1974, 97–114; C. H. Talbert, *What is a Gospel? The Genre of the Canonical Gospels*, 1977.

Grace

C. H. Pinnock, ed., *Grace Unlimited*, 1975; D. L. Tiede, *The Charismatic Figure as Miracle Worker*, Society for Biblical Literature Dissertation Series 1, 1972.

Greek

G. Mussies, "Greek in Palestine and the Diaspora", in S. Safrai and M. Stern *et al.*, eds., *The Jewish People in the First Century: Historical Geography, Political History, Social, Cultural and Religious Life and Institutions*, II, 1976, 1040–64.

Hand, Right Hand, Left Hand, Laying on of Hands

M. Gorgues, *A la Droite de Dieu. Résurrection de Jésus et Actualisation de Psaume 110:1 dans le Nouveau Testament*, 1978; W. R. G. Loader, "Christ at the Right Hand—Ps. cx.1 in the New Testament", *NTS* 24, 1977–78, 199–217.

Heal

M. T. Kelsey, *Healing and Christianity in Ancient Thought and Modern Times*, 1973; F. McNutt, *Healing*, 1974.

Hear

"The Shema and the Shemoneh 'Esreh", in Schürer, II², 1979, 454–63.

Height, Depth, Exalt
J. T. Witney, " 'Bamoth' in the Old Testament", *TB* 30, 1979.

House, Build, Manage, Steward
S. Safrai, "Home and Family", in S. Safrai and M. Stern *et al.*, eds., *The Jewish People in the First Century: Historical Geography, Political History, Social, Cultural and Religious Life and Institutions*, II, 1976, 728–92.

I Am
L. McGaughy, *Toward a Descriptive Analysis of Einai as Linking Verb in the New Testament, Society for Biblical Literature Dissertation Series* 6, 1972.

Image, Idol, Imprint, Example
G. D. Fee, "II Corinthians vi. 14–vii. 1 and Food Offered to Idols", *NTS* 23, 1976–1977, 140–61; D. Flusser, "Paganism in Palestine", in S. Safrai, M. Stern *et al.*, eds., *The Jewish People in the First Century: Historical Geography, Political History, Social, Cultural and Religious Life and Institutions*, II, 1976, 1065–1100; D. De Lacey, "Image and Incarnation in Pauline Christology: A Search for Origins", Tyndale New Testament Lecture 1976, *TB* 30, 1979.

Israel, Jew, Hebrew, Jacob, Judah
M. Avi-Yonah, *The Holy Land from the Persians to the Arab Conquest (536 B.C.–A.D. 640): A Historical Geography*, 1977²; M. Avi-Yonah, ed., *A History of the Holy Land*, 1969; S. J. D. Cohen, *Josephus in Galilee and Rome: His Vita and Development as a Historian, Columbia Studies in the Classical Tradition* 9, 1979; S. Freyne, *Galilee from Alexander the Great to Hadrian, 323 B.C.E. to 135 C.E.: A Study of Second Temple Judaism, University of Notre Dame Center for the Study of Judaism and Christianity in Antiquity* 5, 1980; J. H. Hayes and J. M. Miller, eds., *Israelite and Judaean History, Old Testament Library*, 1977; A. Negev, ed., *Archaeological Encyclopedia of the Holy Land*, 1980; J. Neusner, *A History of the Jews in Babylonia*, I-V, *Studia Post-Biblica*, 1965–70; S. Safrai and M. Stern, eds. in co-operation with D. Flusser and W. C. van Unnik, *The Jewish People in the First Century: Historical Geography, Political History, Social, Cultural and Religious Life and Institutions, Compendia Rerum Iudaicarum ad Novum Testamentum*, II, 1976; E. Schürer, *The History of the Jewish People in the Age of Jesus Christ*, II, revised by G. Vermes, F. Millar, M. Black, literary editor P. Vermes, 1979; E. M. Smallwood, *The Jews under Roman Rule, From Pompey to Diocletian, Studies in Judaism in Late Antiquity*, 1976; R. De Vaux, *The Early History of Israel*, 1978.

Jerusalem
R. L. Cohn, *The Shape of Sacred Space: Four Biblical Studies*, 1980; J. Wilkinson, *Jerusalem as Jesus Knew It: Archaeology as Evidence*, 1978.

Jesus Christ, Nazarene, Christian
G. Aulen, *Jesus in Contemporary Historical Research*, 1976; J. Becker, *Messianic Expectation in the Old Testament*, 1980; F. J. van Beeck, *Christ Proclaimed:*

Christology as Rhetoric, 1979: L. Boff, *Jesus Christ Liberator: A Critical Christology for Our Time*, 1978; J. B. Cobb, Jr., *Christ in a Pluralistic Age*, 1975; J. Donahue, *Are You the Christ? The Trial Narratives in the Gospel of Mark, Society for Biblical Literature Dissertation Series* 10, 1973; J. G. D. Dunn, *Christology in the Making*, 1980; M. D. Goulder, ed., *Incarnation and Myth: The Debate Continued*, 1979; E. M. B. Green, ed., *The Truth of God Incarnate*, 1977; D. R. Griffin, *A Process Christology*, 1973; J. Hick, ed., *The Myth of God Incarnate*, 1977; C. H. Holladay, *Theios Aner in Hellenistic-Judaism: A Critique of the Use of this Category in New Testament Christology, Society for Biblical Literature Dissertation Series* 40, 1977; A. J. Hultgren, *Jesus and His Adversaries: The Form and Structure of the Conflict Stories in the Synoptic Gospels*, 1979; H. Johnson, *The Humanity of the Saviour*, 1962; M. De Jonge, *Jesus: Stranger from Heaven and Son of God, Society for Biblical Literature Sources for Biblical Study* 11, 1980; D. Juel, *Messiah and Temple: The Trial of Jesus in the Gospel of Mark, Society for Biblical Literature Dissertation Series* 31, 1977; W. Kasper, *Jesus the Christ*, 1976; W. H. Kelber, ed., *The Passion in Mark: Studies on Mark 14–16*, 1976; L. Landman, ed., *Messianism in the Talmudic Era*, 1979; I. H. Marshall, *I Believe in the Historical Jesus*, 1977; E. L. Mascall, *Theology and the Gospel of Christ; An Essay in Reorientation*, 1977; B. A. Mastin, "The Imperial Cult and the Ascription of the Title *Theos* to Jesus (John xx.28)", *StudEv, TU* 112, 1973, 352 ff.; J. P. Meier, *The Vision of Matthew: Christ, Church and Morality in the First Gospel*, 1978; B. F. Meyer, *The Aims of Jesus*, 1979; C. F. D. Moule, *The Origin of Christology*, 1977; G. O'Collins, *What are they Saying about Jesus?*, 1977; J. O'Neill, "The Source of Christology in Colossians", *NTS* 26, 1979–80, 87–100; E. Schillebeeckx, *Jesus: An Experiment in Christology*, 1979; E. Schillebeeckx, *Christ: The Experience of Jesus as Lord*, 1980; Schürer, II², 488–554; M. Smith, *Jesus the Magician*, 1978; J. Sobrino, *Christology at the Crossroads*, 1978; G. Strecker, ed., *Jesus Christus in Historie und Theologie: Neutestamentliche Festschrift für Hans Conzelmann zum 60. Geburtstag*, 1975; D. L. Tiede, *The Charismatic Figure as Miracle Worker, Society for Biblical Literature Dissertation Series* 1, 1972.

Jonah
D. J. Wiseman, "Jonah's Nineveh", Tyndale Biblical Archaeology Lectures 1977, *TB* 30, 1979.

King, Kingdom
B. Birch, *The Rise of the Israelite Monarchy: The Growth and Development of 1 Samuel 7–15, Society for Biblical Literature Monograph Series* 27, 1976; J. H. Hayes and J. M. Miller, eds., *Israelite and Judaean History, Old Testament Library*, 285–488; C. L. Mitton, *Your Kingdom Come*, 1978; I. C. Rottenberg, *The Promise and the Presence: Toward a Theology of the Kingdom of God*, 1980.

Knowledge, Experience, Ignorance
E. H. Pagels, *The Gnostic Gospels*, 1979; J. M. Robinson, ed., *The Nag Hammadi Library in English*, 1977.

Lord, Master
W. W. Graf von Baudissin, *Kyrios als Gottesname in Judentum und seine Stelle in der Religionsgeschichte*, ed. O. Eissfeldt, I–IV, 1929; J. A. Fitzmyer, *The Genesis Apocryphon of Qumran Cave 1, A Commentary*, 1971[2]; C. F. D. Moule, *The Origin of Christology*, 1977, 35–46; M. J. Suggs, *Wisdom, Christology and Law in Matthew's Gospel*, 1970.

Lord's Supper
J. A. Emerton, "The Aramaic Underlying *to haima mou tēs diathēkēs* in Mk. xiv. 24", *JTS* New Series 6, 1955, 238–40; J. A. Emerton, "*to haima mou tēs diathēkēs:* The Evidence of the Syria Versions", *JTS* New Series 13, 1962, 111–117; J. A. Emerton, "Mark xiv. 24 and the Targum of the Psalter", *JTS* New Series 15, 1964, 1958; H. Lietzmann, *Mass and Lord's Supper*, 1979.

Love
J. Piper, "*Love Your Enemies*": *Jesus' Love Command in the Synoptic Gospels and the Early Christian Paraenesis; A History of the Tradition and Interpretation of its Uses, Society for New Testament Studies Monograph Series* 38, 1979; K. Sakenfeld, *The Meaning of* Hesed *in the Hebrew Bible, Harvard Semitic Monographs* 17, 1978; L. Schottroff, C. Burchard, R. H. Fuller and M. J. Suggs, *Essays on the Love Commandment*, 1978.

Magic, Sorcery, Magi
R. E. Brown, *The Birth of the Messiah: A Commentary on the Infancy Narratives in Matthew and Luke*, 1977; B. Malinowski, *Magic, Science and Religion and Other Essays*, 1948; J. W. Montgomery, *Principalities and Powers: The World of the Occult*, revised and enlarged edition 1975; M. Smith, *Jesus the Magician*, 1978.

Man
G. Carey, *I Believe in Man*, 1977.

Marriage, Adultery, Bride, Bridegroom
C. M. Carmichael, "Marriage and the Samaritan Woman", *NTS* 26, 1979–80, 332–46; G. Parrinder, *Sex in the World's Religions*, 1980.

Lamb, Sheep
J. D. M. Derrett, "Fresh Light on the Lost Sheep and the Lost Coin", *NTS* 26, 1979–80, 36–60.

Law, Custom, Elements
D. P. Fuller, *Gospel and Law: Contrast or Continuum?*, 1980; H. Gilmer, *The If-You Form in Israelite Law, Society for Biblical Literature Dissertation Series* 15, 1975; S. Pancaro, *The Law in the Fourth Gospel: The Torah and the Gospel, Moses and Jesus, Judaism and Christianity according to John, Supplements to NovT* 42, 1975; H. Raïsänen, "Das 'Gesetz des Glaubens' (Rom. 3.27) und das 'Gesetz des Geistes' (Rom. 8.2)", *NTS* 26, 1979–80, 101–17; Schürer, II[2], 464–87; C. Wright, "The Israelite Household and the Decalogue", *TB* 30, 1979.

Miracle, Wonder, Sign

P. J. Achtemeier, "The Lukan Perspective on the Miracles of Jesus: A Preliminary Sketch", *JBL* 94, 1975, 547–62, reprinted in C. H. Talbert, ed., *Perspectives on Luke-Acts*, 1978, 153–67; O. Betz and W. Grimm, *Wesen und Wirklichkeit der Wunder Jesu: Heilungen, Rettungen, Zeichen, Aufleuchtungen, Arbeiten zum Neuen Testament und Judentum* 2, 1977; C. Brown, *I Believe in the Miracles of Jesus*, 1981; U. Forell, *Wunderbegriffe und logische Analyse: Logisch-philosophische Analyse von Begriffen und Begriffsbildungen aus der deutschen protestantischen Theologie des 20. Jahrhunderts, Forschungen zur systematischen und ökumenischen Theologie* 17, 1967; A Fridrichsen, *The Problem of Miracle in Primitive Christianity*, 1972; R. W. Funk, ed., *Early Christian Miracle Stories, Semeia* 11, 1978; R. W. Funk, "The Form of the New Testament Healing Miracle Story", *Semeia* 12, 1978, 57–96; C. H. Holladay, *Theios Aner in Hellenistic-Judaism: A Critique of the Use of this Category in New Testament Christology, Society for Biblical Literature Dissertation Series* 40, 1977; B. M. F. van Iersel and A. J. M. Linmans, "The Storm on the Lake, Mk iv. 35–41 and Mt. viii 18–27 in the Light of Form-Criticism, "Redaktionsgeschichte" and Structural Analysis", in T. Baarda, A. F. J. Klijn and W. C. van Unnik, eds., *Miscellanea Neotestamentica*, II, *Supplements to NovT* 48, 1978, 17–48; M. De Jonge, "Signs and Works in the Fourth Gospel", in *ibid.*, 107–26; D.-A. Koch, *Die Bedeutung der Wundererzählungen für die Christologie des Markusevangeliums, BZNW* 42, 1975; W. L. Lane, "Theios Anēr Christology and the Gospel of Mark", in R. N. Longenecker and M. C. Tenney, eds., *New Dimensions in New Testament Study*, 1974, 144–61; X. Leon-Dufour, ed., *Les Miracles de Jesus selon le Nouveau Testament*, 1977; G. Petzke, *Die Traditionen über Apollonius von Tyana und das Neue Testament, Studia ad Corpus Hellenisticum Novi Testamenti* 1, 1970; L. Sabourin, *The Divine Miracles Discussed and Defended*, 1977; M. Smith, *Jesus the Magician*, 1978; G. Theissen, *Urchristliche Wundergeschichten: Ein Beitrag zur formgeschichtlichen Erforschung der synoptischen Evangelien*, 1974; D. L. Tiede, *The Charismatic Figure as Miracle Worker, Society for Biblical Literature Dissertation Series* 1, 1972.

Moses

M. R. D'Angelo, *Moses in the Letter to the Hebrews, Society for Biblical Literature Dissertation Series* 42, 1976.

Myth

J. M. Court, *Myth and History in the Book of Revelation*, 1977; M. D. Goulder, ed., *Incarnation and Myth: The Debate Continued*, 1979; J. Hick, ed., *The Myth of God Incarnate*, 1977; G. S. Kirk, *Myth: Its Meaning and Function in Ancient and Other Cultures*, 1970; B. Otzen, H. Gottlieb, K. Jeppesen, *Myths in the Old Testament*, 1980.

Name

C. T. R. Hayward, "The Holy Name of the God of Moses and the Prologue of St. John's Gospel", *NTS* 25, 1978–79, 16–32; G. McConville, "God's 'Name' and God's 'Glory' ", *TB* 30, 1979.

942